EARLY WEST TENNESSEE MARRIAGES

VOLUME II

BRIDES

BY

BYRON SISTLER and BARBARA SISTLER

JANAWAY PUBLISHING, INC.
Santa Maria, California
2011

Early West Tennessee Marriages, Two Volumes

Copyright © 1989 by Byron Sistler and Barbara Sistler
All rights reserved.

Originally published, Nashville, 1989
by Byron Sistler and Associates, Inc.

by

Janaway Publishing, Inc.
732 Kelsey Ct.
Santa Maria, California 93454
(805) 925-1038
www.JanawayPublishing.com

2007, 2011

Two Volume Set, ISBN: 978-1-59641-039-8
Volume I, ISBN: 978-1-59641-226-2
Volume II, ISBN: 978-1-59641-227-9

Made in the United States of America

INTRODUCTION

We have attempted in these two books to set forth the essential data on all early West Tennessee marriages for which records have survived. The area included is outlined on the map on the next page; records published here are for 15 shaded counties. Official ante-bellum marriage records do not exist for the rest of them.

All pre-1861 marriages are set forth here. When feasible and convenient (primarily because of cutoff dates of the original books) we have also included later records as well.

The information in the brides book is a duplication of that in the grooms, the difference being in the order in which they appear. Each book is a single area-wide alphabetical listing of the records.

Where two dates appear on an entry, the first one is the date license was issued, the second (in parentheses) the date marriage was solemnized. If only one date, it usually means that the date of execution was the same as the date of license issuance.

It should be remembered that the entries are, in most cases, far from complete. They show names of the celebrants, county and dates, and no more. The original books and the books from which this information was extracted usually contained additional data, much of which can be of inestimable importance to the genealogist. Such data as names of bondsmen, ministers, justices of the peace, churches, etc. is omitted. In some cases age, names of parents, occupations and similar information are to be found with the source material cited in the Bibliography (at the end of each volume), or in the original marriage books.

At the end of each entry is a county symbol in brackets. Key to the county symbols is on the following page. Immediately before the county symbol may be a B or an *, or both. The B is for black or colored; the * means that the source material included additional information of sufficient importance that we urge the researcher to obtain a copy of the source books or microfilm if possible.

Almost all of the original marriage books are available on microfilm at the Tennessee State Library and Archives in Nashville. This, of course, is the nearest we can come to "truth" in the records. Keep in mind that the clerks who entered the data were fallible; glaring errors appear frequently. As in all genealogical searching, certainty or something near it requires corroborating records.

Byron Sistler
Barbara Sistler

Nashville, Tennessee
May, 1989

COUNTY SYMBOLS, COUNTIES, YEARS REPRESENTED

Be	Benton	1832-1869	Hn	Henry	1838-1867
Cr	Carroll	1838-1873	L	Lauderdale	1838-1867
Dy	Dyer	1860-1879	Ma	Madison	1823-1871
F	Fayette	1838-1871	Mn	McNairy	1861-1865
G	Gibson	1824-1870	O	Obion	1824-1877
Hr	Hardeman	1823-1861	Sh	Shelby	1819-1865
Hy	Haywood	1859-1878	T	Tipton	1840-1874
		We	Weakley	1843-1863	

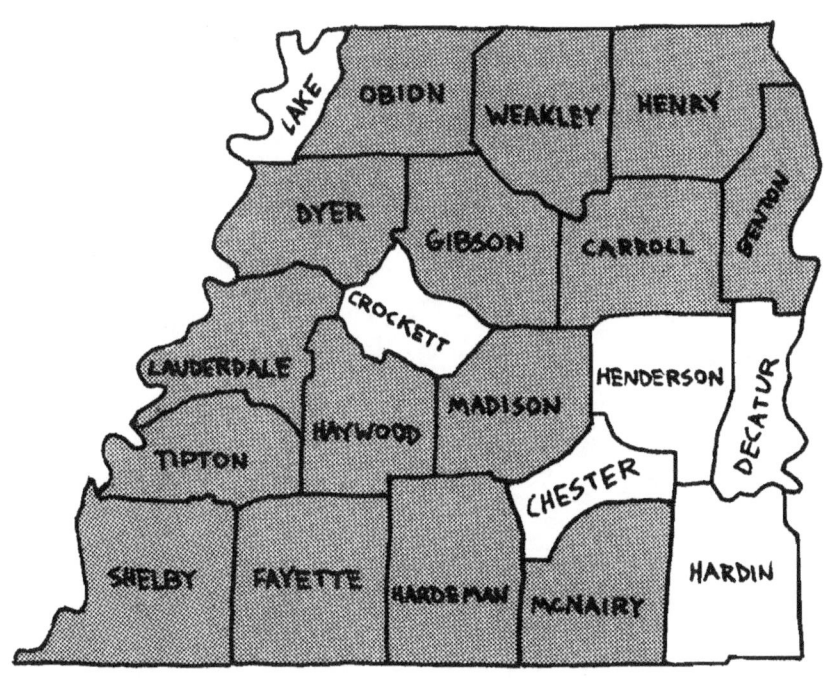

Brides — Page 1

Aaron, Ann E. to E. M. Dunn 2-7-1849 (no return) F
Aaron, Malissa W. to C. C. Reynolds 8-5-1857 Hn
Aaron, Sarah to William A. Seawright 12-24-1857 Hn
Abanathy, Jane to John E. McAnally 4-18-1833 Sh
Abbernathy, Mary L. to James M. Straughn 7-11-1846 F
Abbett (Albert), Nancy to Illa G. B. Brown (Broom?) 12-26-1837 Sh
Abbett, Julina Jane to R. A. Adams 7-3-1853 Be
Abbett, Sarah to J. W. Sanders 8-16-1857 Be
Abbington, Frances E. to Henry H. Dean 5-18-1846 (5-22-1846) F
Abbington, Sally Ann to Wm. D. Whittaker 5-18-1846 (5-22-1846) F
Abbot, V. E. to J. P. Harrison 5-30-1870 G
Abbott, Clara to James Simmonds 5-7-1870 (5-8-1870) Cr
Abbott, E. C. to A. L. Lett 1-28-1850 (1-31-1850) G
Abbott, Frances to Willis Beckman 2-23-1847 Cr
Abbott, Isabella to J. R. Hicks 10-24-1866 Be
Abbott, J. A. to A. B. Bryant 1-18-1858 Cr
Abbott, Lucinda to Alfred Gooch 9-20-1869 (9-21-1869) Cr
Abbott, Mary E. to Timothy H. Word 12-21-1843 G
Abbott, Mary J. to A. H. Johnson 11-15-1858 G
Abbott, Roeana P. to William C. Barton 7-18-1844 G
Abbott, S. E. to J. L. Willeford 5-6-1863 Be
Abbott, Tabitha to Daniel Harrison 6-14-1838 Sh
Abels, Martha to Francis C. Kizer 2-1-1842 F
Abernatha, Mary R. to Hiram G. Devinport? 11-23-1846 (11-26-1846) Hr
Abernatha, Mary to Joseph Backloop 9-19-1865 (no return) Hy
Abernatha, Sina to J. V. Riggans 12-7-1855 (in question) We
Abernathy, Ann to Uriah M. Alexander 1-30-1871 (2-1-1871) F
Abernathy, Belsia to J. J. Brown 1-2-1871 (no return) F
Abernathy, Didema to B. M. Williams 10-13-1862 (no return) Cr
Abernathy, Elizabeth to Hezekiah Moore 10-10-1861 Cr
Abernathy, Harriett A. to Wm. M. Brewer 2-21-1866 (2-22-1866) Cr
Abernathy, Lucy A. to G. W. Trotter 7-21-1851 (7-22-1851) F
Abernathy, Madora L. to W. A. Clark 12-13-1882 (12-14-1882) L
Abernathy, Martha A. V. to Samuel Swetland (Sweetland) 4-20-1847 Sh
Abernathy, Martha A. to Thomas B. Daly 12-12-1844 Sh
Abernathy, Martha to Franklin Carver 8-30-1855 Cr
Abernathy, Martha to James M. Roach 1-18-1843 We
Abernathy, Mary E. to Samuel B. Williamson 10-26-1869 (10-31-1869) Cr
Abernathy, Mary J. to Thomas E. Sauls 2-22-1851 Cr
Abernathy, Mary Jane to Samuel Sweetland 5-15-1854 (5-17-1854) Sh
Abernathy, Nancy H. to Richard H. Crouch 11-30-1837 Sh
Abernathy, Sarah C. to Robert H. Swindell 3-14-1864 (no return) Cr
Abernathy, Sarah C. to Robt. H. Swindell 3-14-1864 (3-20-1864) Cr
Abernathy, Sarahann to John P. Phillips 10-28-1841 (no return) F
Abernathy, Virginia J. to William H. Watson 10-29-1845 Sh
Abington, C. M. to A. J. Bowers 12-18-1843 O
Abington, Elinora to Wm. Lowry 3-25-1839 (4-3-1839) F
Abington, Mary C. to Wm. L. Moore 12-7-1846 (12-9-1846) F
Abington, Matilda to Charles Crittendon 1-22-1855 (1-23-1855) O
Abington, Melissa to James R. Gardner 10-24-1854 O
Abington, Narcissey J. to S. T. Crittendon 3-18-1852 O
Abington, Rosa B. to Starke Duprey 2-15-1838 F
Abington, Rose to Solomon Burris 12-22-1868 (12-23-1868) F B
Abington, Sarah to W. G. Boyett 9-20-1848 O
Abington, William (Miss) to William S. Roscoe 10-19-1846 (10-21-1846) F
Able, Adeline to James A. Sheahan 10-20-1858 (10-21-1858) Ma
Able, Charlotte to Elijah Isham 4-8-1847 (4-9-1847) F
Able, Lucy to Wm. Hammons 7-3-1838 F
Able, M. F. to D. R. Bull 9-2-1867 (9-5-1867) F
Able, Mary to J. Z. Gibson 10-6-1847 Sh
Ables, Mary A. to Jacob Davis 2-21-1859 (2-23-1859) Hr
Ables, Sarah to Hillary Coats 2-26-1858 (no return) L
Ablett, Elvira J. to Wiley J. Aaron 5-3-1866 Hn
Abney, Callie to John W. Robinson 12-19-1867 G
Abraham, Rhoda to Robert Park 3-13-1843 (4-2-1843) Hr
Absent, Martha W. to Robt. R. Rogers 11-9-1859 Hr
Abston, A. M. to W. T. Baker 10-2-1866 Hy
Abston, Emily to Bowling Green 2-6-1873 (no return) Hy
Acabe (Aecker), Denah to Nicholas Frick 2-12-1847 Sh
Ackers (Akers), Lidia Ann to C. McPherson 10-30-1862 Be
Acklin, Hannah to David Cole 12-22-1871 (no return) Hy
Acklin, Martha S. to John W. Ballentine 9-17-1858 (9-18-1858) G
Aclin, Kitty to George Shelton 12-28-1868 Hy
Acock, Amanda to Thomas A. (J.) Cloar 1-31-1846 Sh
Acock, Emaly to George Walton 8-19-1872 (8-20-1872) T
Acock, M. W. to Geo. W. Smith 10-10-1863 (10-12-1863) Sh
Acock, Margaret to C. Hunley 12-10-1854 We
Acock, Marina Jane to James Henry Bowers 3-12-1846 Sh
Acock, Martha V. to Saml. J. Marsh 12-22-1874 (12-23-1874) T
Acock, Sarah E. to J. B. Fletcher 8-4-1873 (8-7-1873) T
Acre, Martha Jane to Marion Alexander Snider 5-18-1866 (no return) Hn
Acre, Mary Ann to John Cofer 6-29-1839 (7-2-1839) Ma
Acree, D. to M. L. J. McGuire 6-30-1861 We
Acree, Elizabeth to John M. Love 10-12-1869 (10-14-1869) Ma
Acree, Sarah to Doger Brauner 1-14-1855 We
Acres, Artelia Y. to Ephraine L. Grey 3-29-1854 (3-30-1854) Ma
Action, Margarett Ann to Joseph C. Sharp 6-19-1839 Ma

Action, Sarah L. to John Brooks 12-7-1848 Ma
Acuff, Elizabeth to Robert Miller 6-26-1875 (6-27-1875) L
Acuff, Lucinda Jane to Ezra Cheaney 10-29-1859 L
Acuff, Malinda A. to Christopher Cheek 5-30-1874 (5-31-1874) L
Acuff, Martha to William Gates 4-24-1878 (4-26-1878) L
Acuff, Mary A. E. to James M. Edwards 3-18-1872 (3-21-1872) L
Acuff, Mary J. to William J. Allen 10-12-1885 (10-24-1885) L
Acuff, Nancy C. to Wm. R. Ledbetter 12-8-1855 (12-11-1855) L
Acuff, Sarah J. to Robert D. Freeland 10-6-1859 Hn
Adair, H. B. (Miss) to J. Patton Anderson 4-28-1853 (4-30-1853) Sh
Adair, Jennie F. to J. N. Hairsten 2-27-1861 Sh
Adair, Martha P. to William M. Iams 2-18-1859 (2-24-1859) Sh
Adair, Mary R. to Wm. E. Wilkins 11-27-1854 (11-29-1854) Hr
Adair, Polly to Allen L. Wood 8-8-1839 G
Adair, Polly to Allen L. Woods 8-8-1838 G
Adair, Susan to J. N. Baker 3-3-1859 Sh
Adaline, Sutton to Richd. Powell 6-17-1876 Hy
Adam, Ann to John Waters 1-9-1830 Ma
Adams, A. C. to W. J. Campbell 5-21-1866 (no return) Hy
Adams, Adaline to James L. Kee 9-4-1865 (9-6-1865) F
Adams, Adaline to Richard C. Hite 12-24-1849 Sh
Adams, Adaline to Theopholus Bland 4-27-1834 Sh
Adams, Agasy Caroline to William Malichi Allison 11-18-1857 Ma
Adams, Alleline to James Harrison 5-7-1846 (5-10-1846) G
Adams, Allice to L. W. Williams 11-6-1881 L
Adams, Ann V. to Jno. Morrill 7-25-1846 Sh
Adams, Ann to Wm. H. Jones 10-26-1842 (11-3-1842) Hr
Adams, Aurena to Kindid C. Rose 11-13-1843 Hn
Adams, Bettie J. to J. A. Lucas 2-8-1872 (2-13-1872) Dy
Adams, C. J. to G. W. Mills 12-14-1871 (no return) Cr
Adams, Callie to Sam Jones 9-13-1870 (9-15-1870) Cr B
Adams, Catharine to Edgmere? Umpstead 1-24-1868 (no return) Cr
Adams, Chaney to Anthony Collier 12-25-1868 (no return) Hy
Adams, Chaney to Jasper Jones 8-19-1872 Hy
Adams, Christiana E. to James E. Stewart 5-9-1854 Hr
Adams, Cornelia B. to James A. Wright 9-29-1860 Hr
Adams, Crecy to Henders. Williams 9-6-1866 Hy
Adams, Delaney C. to Jefferson P. Workman 5-6-1858 Be
Adams, Delany C. to Jefferson J. Workman 5-6-1858 Be CC
Adams, Delia to Silas Boyd 11-18-1871 Hy
Adams, Dora to R. P. Young 12-24-1877 (12-30-1877) L
Adams, E. H. (Mrs.) to J. C. Taylor 11-30-1865 G
Adams, Easter to Hugh Gerred? 3-15-1853 T
Adams, Eliza Ann to William Cup 10-21-1869 (10-22-1869) T
Adams, Eliza to John Pewett 7-25-1846 (9-26-1846) L
Adams, Eliza to Madison Williams 2-18-1872 Hy
Adams, Eliza to Sam Storks 1-30-1869 Hy
Adams, Elizabeth E. to David Sherman 4-17-1859 Hn
Adams, Elizabeth J. to Allen D. Adams 9-9-1858 We
Adams, Elizabeth J. to R. F. Chambers 1-14-1867 (1-15-1867) L
Adams, Elizabeth to Benjamin F. Lamb 2-21-1848 (2-22-1848) L
Adams, Elizabeth to Benjamin Harper 11-1-1842 O
Adams, Elizabeth to George E. Grave 10-25-1829 (11-5-1829) Hr
Adams, Elizabeth to H. T. Bridges 11-21-1856 We
Adams, Elizabeth to Hiram Horton 9-12-1871 Cr
Adams, Elizabeth to James R. Webb 7-27-1846 (7-30-1846) F
Adams, Elizabeth to Jason Cloud 1-2-1830 Hr
Adams, Elizabeth to Josiah Glass 11-1-1841 (11-2-1841) L
Adams, Elizabeth to Nathl. D. Ellis 12-3-1833 (12-5-1833) Hr
Adams, Elling to Haywood Cannon 1-1-1854 (no return) F
Adams, Emeline to George Bruce 10-3-1840 (10-4-1840) F
Adams, Emma P. to James B. Bright 10-29-1873 (10-30-1873) T
Adams, Fanney to John Trice 3-19-1874 Hy
Adams, Fannie (Mrs.) to J. Coleman Ross 1-24-1867 (1-27-1867) Ma
Adams, Fanny to Isaac Adams 4-10-1867 (no return) Hy
Adams, Frances W. to James G. Hanley 5-24-1842 (5-25-1842) T
Adams, Frances to T. J. Sanders 1-1-1862 Mn
Adams, Georgiana to Berryman Lax 12-27-1852 Hr
Adams, Gerusha to John Hurly 11-26-1839 (11-28-1839) F
Adams, Hanora to John Crowley 12-14-1858 (12-16-1858) Sh
Adams, Harrett to George W. Browning 10-16-1840 (11-17-1840) Hr
Adams, Harriet to Robert Peat 10-19-1866 (no return) Hy
Adams, Henrietta Emaline to William Cooper 4-1-1857 O
Adams, Isabella D. to John McNama 2-17-1841 (2-18-1841) F
Adams, Isabella to James H. Harriss 10-28-1847 Hr
Adams, Isabella to James W. Black 9-3-1847 Hr
Adams, Isabella to Washington Smith 7-26-1869 (7-27-1869) F B
Adams, Jane to John Becksterling 8-18-1863 (8-20-1863) T
Adams, Jane to John Cashes 5-21-1856 Cr
Adams, Julia to Nathaniel Moore 5-17-1831 Sh
Adams, Kessiah to William L. Fowler 9-15-1837 Sh
Adams, Lany to F. M. Forest 12-5-1853 Be
Adams, Lavina to William D. Weatherred 12-20-1870 (12-22-1870) T
Adams, Leanna to Sanco Adams 12-24-1866 (no return) Hy
Adams, Louisa to James M. Reese 1-11-1847 Hn
Adams, Lucinda to Archer Allen 2?-17-1867 (3-26-1867) T
Adams, Lucy A. to Jim Thomas 10-8-1870 Hy

Adams, M. A. to W. J. Lankford 1-24-1883 L
Adams, M. J. to B. J. Blescot(Hescot?) 12-2-1874 T
Adams, M. J. to T. C. Spain 2-25-1873 (2-27-1873) Cr
Adams, Malinda C. to Charles M. Templeton 1-14-1861 (no return) We
Adams, Mandana to Ormond Knot 3-24-1842 Sh
Adams, Margaret M. to Joel G. Lemmons 1-5-1842 G
Adams, Margaret V. to W. W. Osborne 1-26-1865 (1-31-1865) F
Adams, Margaret to A. B. Wilson 3-23-1840 (3-29-1840) F
Adams, Margaret to John Dinney (Denney) 11-27-1850 Sh
Adams, Margaret to Norman Crowell 9-14-1853 (9-15-1853) Ma
Adams, Martha F. to Richard M. Firth 2-18-1841 F
Adams, Martha J. S. to John W. Heckiman 10-27-1856 Cr
Adams, Martha to James Benton 7-31-1845 Hn
Adams, Martha to John Worrell 10-31-1878 Hy
Adams, Mary A. to S. A. Pugh 5-22-1869 (5-29-1869) L
Adams, Mary A. to Thos. C. Anthony 4-11-1866 T
Adams, Mary A. to Wm. W. McDugal 4-6-1868 (4-8-1868) Cr
Adams, Mary Ann T. to Joseph Caldwell 3-4-1830 Sh
Adams, Mary B. to Geor. Paulson 4-17-1845 F
Adams, Mary B. to Wm. A. Duncan 9-27-1867 (10-1-1867) Ma
Adams, Mary C. to John S. Williams 2-9-1870 (no return) Dy
Adams, Mary D. to J. H. Blakeman 11-15-1854 We
Adams, Mary D. to John M. Harris 2-26-1862 Mn
Adams, Mary E. to Robert Smith 3-17-1863 Sh
Adams, Mary Elizabeth to William Henry Massey 2-16-1859 (2-17-1859) Ma
Adams, Mary H. to Jonathan Higgs 7-25-1844 We
Adams, Mary J. to William H. Palmer 9-15-1856 Hn
Adams, Mary J. to Wm. Alexander 10-18-1853 Sh
Adams, Mary Jane to Gilbert Mowhorn 6-5-1869 (6?-1-1869) F B
Adams, Mary L. to Henry Johnson 12-13-1876 (no return) Hy
Adams, Mary L. to Jas. O. Harris 1-3-1853 T
Adams, Mary M. to Edward T. Rooker 4-3-1858 (4-4-1858) Ma
Adams, Mary Morgan to William Williams 12-18-1848 (12-19-1848) Ma
Adams, Mary S. to James A. McDugal 1-8-1861 (1-10-1861) Cr
Adams, Mary to George Wallace 6-12-1874 T
Adams, Mary to J. R. A. D. Oliver 11-24-1842 Cr
Adams, Mary to Lawson Parsons 8-9-1865 Mn
Adams, Mary to Peter R. Crews 8-30-1854 Hr
Adams, Mary to Samuel M. Pierce 4-2-1846 Cr
Adams, Mattie G. to Dr. T. A. Kyle 7-2-1860 (7-3-1860) T
Adams, Millie to Henry Taylor 2-26-1870 Hy
Adams, Mollie E. to S. H. Lockhart 6-30-1862 (not endorsed) F
Adams, Mollie to T. J. Mitchell 12-21-1875 (12-22-1875) L
Adams, N. A. to W. M. Merrick 4-29-1866 G
Adams, N. J. to R. M. Gilliam 10-20-1857 Be
Adams, Nancy Ann to Henry H. Worrell 10-3-1842 O
Adams, Nancy E. to J. C. G. Townsend 9-13-1860 Dy
Adams, Nancy J. to Ander J. Jones 12-16-1852 Cr
Adams, Nancy J. to A. I. Harvey 12-25-1844 Cr
Adams, Nancy to E. Emmons 1-28-1863 Mn
Adams, Nancy to Frank Edwards 12-24-1869 (12-30-1869) Cr
Adams, Nancy to John L. Webb 8-29-1846 (8-31-1846) F
Adams, Olive to Kinchen Cox 12-22-1867 Be
Adams, Priscilla S. (Mrs.) to Sidney Y. Watson 10-1-1860 (10-2-1860) Sh
Adams, Rebecca to William Murphy 5-9-1838 G
Adams, Rebecca to William Yancey 12-23-1882 (12-26-1883?) L
Adams, Rodah to George Hufner 11-19-1830 Ma
Adams, S. C. (Mrs.) to Benj. F. Vantreece 1-15-1867 (1-17-1867) Ma
Adams, S. F. to J. W. Moore 12-1-1874 (12-2-1874) T
Adams, S. J. to Wm. H. Taylor 12-24-1851 Cr
Adams, Sabrina E. to Neil Alexander Holt 8-8-1848 (8-10-1848) G
Adams, Sallie Ann to George Battle 1-27-1867 Hy
Adams, Sallie F. to James J. Fletcher 1-31-1878 Hy
Adams, Sallie to Ben Sanders 1-16-1873 Hy
Adams, Sallie to G. W. Pate 1-12-1876 Dy
Adams, Sally to John Givin 12-5-1864 (no return) Cr
Adams, Sarah A. to John B. Corgett 11-8-1860 (no return) Hn
Adams, Sarah Ann to A. W. Williams 3-23-1845 Be
Adams, Sarah Ann to A. W. Williams 3-23-1845 Be CC
Adams, Sarah E. to Eleazar Gaugh 6-25-1861 Hr
Adams, Sarah E. to James M. Black 12-29-1858 (12-30-1858) T
Adams, Sarah Eliza to John J. Guy 5-7-1856 (5-22-1856) O
Adams, Sarah P. to C. M. Brown 2-12-1872 (2-13-1872) T
Adams, Sarah R. to Cris R. Harrison 4-22-1845 Hr
Adams, Sarah to James Tolliver 11-22-1871 (11-23-1871) T
Adams, Sarah to William H. Cole 11-4-1861 Hr
Adams, Sharlott to James Whitney 8-29-1848 (no return) F
Adams, Sidney E. to Turner Delviney 3-8-1860 Sh
Adams, Slatyra J. to J. T. Osborn 12-12-1865 (12-13-1865) L
Adams, Sophronia to A. Stevens 10-23-1862 Be
Adams, Sue E. to A. M. Wilson 12-8-1871 Hy
Adams, Susan A. to Wilson Oliver 2-16-1843 Cr
Adams, Susan Ann to Edmund L. Gardiner 5-20-1844 Sh
Adams, Susan E. to Martin T. Johnson 8-14-1865 (8-15-1865) T
Adams, Susan E. to William P. Stewart 11-9-1842 G
Adams, Susan F. to F. J. G. Eddlemon 3-3-1856 (3-6-1856) Hr
Adams, Susan to W. E. Thompson 5-12-1873 (5-13-1873) Cr
Adams, Susannah U. to J. H. Jeter 7-21-1865 (no return) Hy
Adams, T. to Benjamin Palmer 9-24-1852 Hn
Adams, Unaty to William A. Adams 2-15-1861 We
Adams, _____ to _____ Fitzgerald 9-5-1838 (no return) F
Adamson, Anna to J. Thomas McCutchen 11-4-1867 (11-5-1867) Ma
Adamson, Hannah to John Cherry 9-10-1853 (9-11-1853) O
Adamson, M. E. to W. H. Price 1-8-1868 G
Adamson, Rebecca to Holloway Swindle 7-17-1838 Hr
Adcock, Charlana to Ezra Gitchell 7-9-1870 (7-10-1870) L
Adcock, Edney J. to Joseph A. Covington 8-11-1866 (8-12-1866) Ma
Adcock, Mary S. to R. J. Poindexter 6-5-1867 G
Adcock, Nancy to Luny McDaniel 3-6-1830 (3-11-1830) G
Adcock, Sarah J. to James B. Kilzer 2-1-1855 G
Adcock, Susan F. to Eugene York 7-24-1875 (no return) Dy
Adcock, Teracey (Mrs.) to Laban Benthel 3-31-1846 G
Adcocks, Elizabeth to J. W. Baker 2-18-1882 (2-20-1882) L
Addams, Eliza to David Ford 7-22-1846 (no return) L
Addams, Jane to Abraham Humble 12-13-1838 L
Adden, Adaline to Levi S. Brinkly 1-2-1859 Cr
Adderton, Mary Jane to Jesse T. Parham 1-17-1857 (1-19-1857) Ma
Addfield, Jane to E. S. Wilson 3-29-1861 Sh
Addington, Elvira E. to James H. Lakey 9-8-1860 Hr
Addison, Frances E. to J. E. Styers 2-21-1885 (2-24-1885) L
Addison, Hanna to W. T. Sexton 11-23-1872 (11-26-1872) L
Addison, Margret A. to Velarious J. Paschal 12-10-1869 (12-12-1869) L
Addyman, Anna S. to Taylor Wilson 1-12-1860 Hy
Aden, Elizabeth to P. G. Williamson 12-31-1865 Be
Aden, Jane to Thomas Elam 4-23-1863 G
Aden, Lauretta E. to William M. Martin 11-6-1857 Hn
Aden, Lydia A. to John H. Winsett 12-27-1841 Sh
Aden, Mattie to James R. Hughes 12-13-1866 Hn
Aden, Melvina to G. C. Spellings 6-8-1858 Be
Adison, Emily to Henry Thomas 2-4-1867 (2-6-1867) L B
Adison, Sarah to James Weatherall 1-16-1869 Hy
Adkerson, Louise to Granvell Gouch 10-24-1861 (10-27-1861) O
Adkerson, Rachel to Lemuel Stover 8-3-1854 (8-6-1854) O
Adkin, Nancy P. to George H. Gee 3-14-1844 Cr
Adkins, Bettie J. to W. D. Hawze 6-18-1874 (6-25-1874) T
Adkins, Charlott to James Faulk 1-2-1872 T
Adkins, Charlotte to Adam Calaway 6-15-1873 T
Adkins, Darcas to Mathew Nichols 10-24-1854 (no return) F
Adkins, Elizabeth to H. L. Whitsitt 4-1-1843 Sh
Adkins, Elizabeth to Hudson Jarrett 4-11-1856 Ma
Adkins, Elizabeth to Ratliff Booth 10-13-1846 G
Adkins, Elizabeth to Wiley Payne 2-4-1841 T
Adkins, Emer H. to Daniel McLennen 12-23-1865 (12-26-1865) T
Adkins, Georgetter to Granderson Downing 5-14-1874 (4?-15-1874) T
Adkins, Hannah to Birch Page 4-1-1874 (4-2-1874) O
Adkins, Josephine to Gilbert Payne 12-24-1868 (12-26-1868) T
Adkins, Louisa C. to James L. Benthel 4-22-1857 T
Adkins, Lucinda to James W. Bowen 9-13-1843 (9-14-1843) F
Adkins, Margaret to James Kirts 3-20-1865 T
Adkins, Nacy (Nancy?) to R. A. Paschal 11-15-1838 F
Adkins, Rebecca to John H. Tallent 5-16-1842 F
Adkins, Silvia to Mike Hill 10-13-1874 (10-14-1874) T
Adkins, Susanna M. C. to John McLennon 1-24-1850 T
Adkinson, Jane to James Patterson 5-11-1857 (5-18-1857) O
Adkison, Harriett to Richard Jones 9-21-1867 (no return) Cr
Adkisson, Bettie to Louis Wiliamson 12-26-1871 (12-28-1871) Cr B
Adkisson, Louisa to David J. Bushins? 8-5-1846 (8-6-1846) T
Adler, Helena to Herman Auger 10-3-1854 L
Adlerbaum, P. to Henry Poss 1-26-1864 Sh
Admon, Mary to Jesse R. McCaslin 10-28-1857 Cr
Adones, Susan to John Charlton 3-12-1828 L
Aery, Malica to W. M. Cabe 9-25-1850 (not endorsed) We
Aff, Mary to Frank Rickenbacker 5-11-1848 Sh
Agee, E. F. to J. B. Burrow 12-20-1865 G
Agee, Frances to Wm. R. McMullin 3-19-1840 F
Agee, Jane E. to Absolom F. Hays 1-24-1855 G
Agee, Lucy A. P. to Thomas B. Davis 12-29-1857 G
Agee, M. M. to W. A. H. Coop 1-7-1871 (1-10-1871) Dy
Agee, S. C. M. to J. F. Pyland 9-30-1867 (no return) Dy
Ager, Mary C. to Augustus Larrantree 4-22-1856 Sh
Agnew, Sarah M. to David Hooper 2-28-1854 (3-11-1854) O
Aiden, Henryetta to James M. Cole 8-24-1865 G
Aiken, Minerva to Willis Hume 7-11-1857 (7-12-1857) Sh
Aiken, Nancy to Robert F. Finley 11-16-1835 (11-18-1835) G
Aiken, Parthena to Craig N. Shaw 9-22-1869 Dy
Aiken, Sarah E. to A. C. Harmon 8-30-1870 (8-31-1870) Dy
Aiken, Susan J. to James T. Hester 9-5-1860 Dy
Aiken, Susanah to James W. Palmere 8-31-1868 (9-1-1868) Dy
Aikens, Jemina to John H. Hodges 9-5-1835 Sh
Aikens, Martha to Abner Perkins 4-30-1874 Dy
Aikin, Aceneth E. to W. S. Bays 4-10-1861 (4-17-1861) T
Aikin, Dolly to Ambrose Hodge 10-1-1835 Sh
Aikin, H. H. to W. A. Hardy 12-13-1873 Hy
Aikin, Lizie to M. S. Wills (Wells) 1-3-1876 Hy

Brides — Page 3

Aikin, P. J. to J. A. Thitford 1-8-1867 (1-9-1867) Dy
Aikins, Caroline to Alex Williams 11-26-1872 Hy
Aikins, Julia Ann to John Coleman 2-17-1830 Sh
Aikins, M. L. to W. J. Littleton 9-29-1879 (9-30-1879) L
Ailsey, McClish to Edman Polk 12-29-1874 Hy
Airolo, Theresa to J. A. Signaigo 8-5-1858 (8-8-1858) Sh
Airs, Sarah And. to A. B. Forbess 9-4-1848 (9-27-1848) F
Airy, Edy to Samuel W. Rucker 4-12-1843 Cr
Airy?, Savannah A. to L. A. Styles 2-21-1850 Hn
Aitkin, Mary A. L. to Ezekiel E. Low 9-3-1847 (9-5-1847) Hr
Aker, R. M. to G. T. Brownlow 4-3-1866 O
Akers, Lucinda A. to W. H. Lindsey 12-7-1860 Be
Akers, Lucy to J. W. Adams 12-9-1882 (12-10-1882) L
Akers, Malvina to B. F. Lawless 2-26-1867 G
Akers, Q. L. A. to J. F. Edwards 1-7-1871 (1-8-1871) Cr
Akers, Susan to A. J. Wynn 7-7-1857 Be CC
Akers, Susan to A. J. Wynn 7-9-1857 Be
Akin, Amanda to John Johnson 12-26-1855 Sh
Akin, Caifa? Frances to W. A. Hall 2-25-1869 (no return) Dy
Akin, Caroline J. to Charles R. Pipkins 9-10-1879 L
Akin, Elizabeth to Foster B. Harris 6-8-1836 Sh
Akin, Ellen to James Thos. Burton 11-5-1867 (11-6-1867) T
Akin, Emily to Cartwright Price 9-7-1848 Cr
Akin, Fanny to Charles Sawyer 12-26-1868 (12-28-1868) Dy
Akin, Julia Ann to S. D. Carroll 11-28-1870 (11-30-1870) Dy
Akin, Margaret to John Newsom 5-24-1842 Hy
Akin, Margaret to Nicholas Sanguinetti 2-19-1855 (2-20-1855) Sh
Akin, Mary Catharine to Tho. J. Barnes 3-12-1856 (3-13-1856) T
Akin, Mary E. to Allen Adcock 12-10-1862 We
Akin, Minerva to Samuel Nunery 3-10-1840 Cr
Akin, S. A. to R. F. Templeton 1-21-1868 (1-22-1868) Dy
Akin, Sarah T. to Joseph H. Updegraff 9-18-1848 Sh
Akin, Susan to Benj. F. Dowdy 2-2-1839 (no return) F
Akins, A. J. to B. F. Duvall 12-27-1874 Hy
Akins, Louisa J. to Daniel H. Barns 11-29-1838 (12-6-1838) G
Akins, M. to W. T. Wright 6-3-1842 Be
Akins, M. to W. T. Wright 6-3-1842 Be CC
Akins, Martha to Wm. Purvis 1-16-1856 Cr
Akmaugh, Nancy to Edward F. Watson 11-14-1855 Cr
Alberson, Matilda to George Kelling 11-28-1849 Hn
Albert, Louisa to Adolph Bauman 1-16-1855 Sh
Albert, Louisa to John C. Hauck 10-24-1860 (10-25-1860) Sh
Albert, Matilda to A. Beer 12-30-1862 Sh
Albright, Dilla to A. J. Pauf 3-12-1873 Hy
Albright, E. M. to E. M. Gaylaaor 12-29-1875 (no return) Hy
Albright, Elimly J. to Assa Harper 1-20-1848 Cr
Albright, Eliza to Isaac McCustin 1-19-1872 Hy
Albright, Ellen to J. J. Gorman 8-20-1861 (8-21-1861) Cr
Albright, Lethie to Samuel J Cooker 1-20-1870 (no return) Hy
Albright, Mary E. to John M. Parker 12-22-1846 We
Albright, Mary T. to N. B. Crenshaw 5-24-1864 (5-26-1864) Sh
Albright, Mary to John Stires 1-2-1845 Be
Albright, P_less to Pleasant G. Kemp 5-12-1857 Cr
Albritten, Mary Jane to Eli McClure 1-13-1867 Hn
Albritton, Florence to G. W. Cherry 1-5-1872 (1-7-1872) Dy
Albritton, Martha E. to R. A. Wade 3-18-1862 Hn
Albritton, May J. to Eli McClain 1-12-1867 (no return) Hn
Alderson, Lou A. to E. A. Shryack 3-2-1859 (3-8-1859) F
Aldridge, Amanda E. to W. P. Mangrum 1-27-1857 (1-29-1857) Hr
Aldridge, Clarisa to John Fell Fowler 9-14-1868 T
Aldridge, Eliza to John Ray 9-13-1879 (9-14-1879) L
Aldridge, Kiziah to John E. Davis 11-29-1862 Mn
Aldridge, L. C. to G. W. Daniel 12-26-1864 (1-2-1864?) T
Aldridge, L. E. to W. G. Atkins 10-17-1864 Mn
Aldridge, Mancy (Mary) to Reuben Mayfield 4-6-1842 Sh
Aldridge, Martha L. to William I. Allen 12-31-1865 Mn
Aldridge, Nannie to Thomas Russell 1-15-1856 Cr
Aldridge, S. V. to S. G. Patterson 3-16-1863 Mn
Aldridge, Sally A. M. to Lewis De. C. Hays 1-25-1853 (1-27-1853) Sh
Aldridge, Sarah W. to A. Tully 4-15-1843 Ma
Alen, Mary M. to Spiner Wood 3-20-1848 (no return) F
Alender?, Salina A. to H. B. McKinley 11-26-1850 (12-3-1850) F
Alexader, Mary A. to Riley F. Nix 10-17-1838 Hn
Alexander, A. E. to Robt. H. Underwood 12-8-1875 (12-16-1875) O
Alexander, A. E. to S. R. D. Brown 12-15-1853 G
Alexander, Amanda C. to David Underwood 1-17-1850 Hn
Alexander, Amanda C. to W. O. Campbell 2-12-1878 (2-13-1878) L
Alexander, Amanda to L. V. Corbitt 5-7-1861 (5-9-1861) Sh
Alexander, Angeline R. to John B. Hutchens 1-19-1858 Hn
Alexander, Anna to John D. Tarrant 7-24-1879 L
Alexander, B. A. to Peter Lacewell? 7-1-1852 (no return) Hn
Alexander, Bess to Lewis Pemberton 7-1-1840 Hn
Alexander, Betsy to Ephraim Whitehead 1-31-1867 Hn B
Alexander, Bettie to Guss Chambers 12-13-1873 (12-15-1873) T
Alexander, Caroline C. to Elijah Cass 12-29-1846 Hn
Alexander, Caroline C. to Elijah Cup 12-29-1846 Ma
Alexander, Caroline M. to Barrum R. Ray 8-26-1841 Hn

Alexander, Caroline to Henry Taylor 8-3-1870 (8-4-1870) Dy
Alexander, Charlotte A. to L. Y. Beadles 10-1-1866 (no return) Hn
Alexander, Cintha A. to Joseph M. Wade 10-19-1839 Hn
Alexander, Cresia to Jim Pearce 3-21-1868 F B
Alexander, Cynthia to Moses Taylor 1-9-1843 (1-12-1843) Ma
Alexander, D. M. to Seth M. Moore 8-30-1865 (no return) Hy
Alexander, Davy Theresa to John W. Heasenburg 6-13-1854 (6-15-1854) Ma
Alexander, Dosia to Prince Ervins 11-12-1868 (no return) Hy
Alexander, E. E. to B. F. C. Brooks 2-13-1855 (2-14-1855) Sh
Alexander, Elenor L. to C. W. Rich 8-22-1854 (no return) F
Alexander, Eliza R. to John W. Matthews 1-23-1839 Hr
Alexander, Eliza to Jefferson Alexander 3-9-1846 Hn
Alexander, Eliza to John Green 11-17-1875 (no return) Hy
Alexander, Eliza to John Lea 9-7-1846 (no return) We
Alexander, Eliza to William S. Shell 3-19-1847 Hn
Alexander, Elizabeth A. to A. D.? Hunter 1-4-1866 T
Alexander, Elizabeth C. to Benjamin F. Parish 10-6-1859 (no return) Hn
Alexander, Elizabeth E. to Thomas Thompson 8-18-1846 (8-19-1846) Ma
Alexander, Elizabeth to Jack Alexander 10-8-1873 (10-20-18730 T
Alexander, Elizabeth to John Swor 9-24-1857 Hn
Alexander, Elizabeth to Robert Lowry 8-22-1859 Hn
Alexander, Ella M. to Saml. T. Avant 1-13-1860 Hr
Alexander, Elmyra to J. Mathis 12-14-1843 Hn
Alexander, Emily to John Hurt 6-10-1859 Cr
Alexander, F. A. to A. J. Vaughn 8-5-1855 We
Alexander, F. A. to J. B. Cunningham 1-25-1882 (1-26-1882) L
Alexander, F. M. to I. J. Crockett 7-14-1866 O
Alexander, Fany C. to William L. Bodkin 1-21-1847 G
Alexander, Flora M. to Elias Tomlinson 11-14-1848 (no return) Hn
Alexander, Frances C. to William S. Crafton 12-18-1852 (12-19-1852) O
Alexander, Frances O. to Pinkney R. Penn 8-30-1851 (8-29?-1851) G
Alexander, Frances to E. Arbuckle 2-8-1861 (no return) Hn
Alexander, Frances to James Freeman 3-15-1838 Hn
Alexander, G. A. to John M. Smyth 10-27-1854 We
Alexander, Hanabell M. to James M. Dial no date G
Alexander, Hanna to Parriss? Harper 3-13-1869 (3-14-1869) T
Alexander, Harriet A. to Henry F. Molton 11-27-1855 Hn
Alexander, Harriet C. to Bibb Wills 6-29-1838 F
Alexander, Harriet C. to John H. McCure 11-16-1845 We
Alexander, Harriet M. to Allen C. Williams 8-4-1852 (8-5-1852) G
Alexander, Harriet to Kit Roach 12-7-1866 (12-8-1866) F B
Alexander, Henrietta (Mrs.) to John S. Townsley 6-11-1863 Sh
Alexander, Henrietta to O. C. Alexander 5-31-1866 (no return) Hn
Alexander, Isabella M. to Fredk. Davis 8-26-1842 (8-31-1842) F
Alexander, Isabellar to Isaac J. Rude 6-15-1854 G
Alexander, Izabellar to John Phaling 9-20-1836 (9-?-1836) G
Alexander, J. L. (Mrs.) to J. B. Braden 1-23-1878 L
Alexander, Jane C. to Joseph Morton 11-10-1847 (11-11-1847) F
Alexander, Jane E. to John D. Carne 1-5-1864 G
Alexander, Jane E. to Richd. Sandford 5-17-1851 (no return) F
Alexander, Jane Elizabeth to Richard Sanford 5-17-1851 Hr
Alexander, Jane to Elijah Davis 11-29-1824 G
Alexander, Jane to George L. Brotherton 1-2-1830 Hr
Alexander, Julia to George Wright 8-27-1883 (8-28-1883) L
Alexander, L. A. to D. A. Moore 1-10-1869 Hy
Alexander, Laura H. to Joseph E. Lake 11-7-1860 (11-8-1860) Hr
Alexander, Laura M. to William Ray 12-14-1846 (12-22-1846) F
Alexander, Laura to John H. Wyly 3-15-1871 L
Alexander, Lemmende E. to German U. Windgo 1-20-1865 Hn
Alexander, Livinda to Westley Overton 4-6-1839 Hn
Alexander, Louisa J. to John F. Hunt 6-1-1868 (6-3-1868) Ma
Alexander, Louiza A. to Lewis Stunson 1-9-1845 We
Alexander, Louvina to Evan Maynard 1-1-1855 We
Alexander, Luentia to Green Manley 1-2-1856 (no return) Hn
Alexander, M. A. C. to T. A. Roberts 12-29-1860 G
Alexander, M. A. to G. B. Milner 9-8-1874 (9-9-1874) O
Alexander, M. J. to J. M. Tines 7-11-1868 (7-11-1870?) G
Alexander, M. M. to James M. Mathis 3-25-1839 Hn
Alexander, M. R. to Wm. Gallimore 12-5-1846 (no return) Cr
Alexander, Malinda to B. R. Emerson 1-16-1862 Hn
Alexander, Malvina to Jim Arrington 9-1-1870 G B
Alexander, Margaret A. to J. C. F. Chamberlin 12-24-1861 (12-25-1861) Sh
Alexander, Margaret A. to J. L. G. Matheny 6-2-1844 Hn
Alexander, Margaret A. to Joseph E. Whiteside 11-21-1855 (11-22-1855) Ma
Alexander, Margaret E. to T. J. Nix 2-23-1853 Hn
Alexander, Margaret L. to George D. Odancer? 11-14-1850 Hn
Alexander, Margaret M. to Nicholas P. Stone 8-7-1832 Sh
Alexander, Margaret to Ezekiel Richmond 2-16-1832 Hr
Alexander, Margaret to P. J. Diggs 8-20-1863 Hn
Alexander, Margaret to W. J. Robards 5-20-1848 Sh
Alexander, Margarett C. to James W. Anderson 1-17-1842 (1-23-1842) F
Alexander, Martha L. to Thomas J. Cody 2-25-1856 (2-28-1856) Sh
Alexander, Martha to James Alexander 1-18-1841 (1-21-1841) F
Alexander, Martha to Joseph Warner 9-24-1857 Ma
Alexander, Mary A. to J. Solomon 10-8-1866 Hn
Alexander, Mary A. to John Coppedge 8-29-1855 (9-4-1855) Ma
Alexander, Mary A. to John H. Weeks 1-27-1852 Hn

Brides

Alexander, Mary A. to W. B. Paschell 2-11-1856 We
Alexander, Mary A. to Wilson E. Stewart 8-5-1878 (8-10-1868?) Ma
Alexander, Mary Ann to Andrew Jackson 12-23-1867 (12-25-1867) T
Alexander, Mary Ann to D. F. Bobo 11-16-1854 Hn
Alexander, Mary Ann to Samuel W. Mathis 10-28-1841 Hn
Alexander, Mary C. to Abner S. Matthews 5-10-1842 (5-19-1842) Hr
Alexander, Mary C. to N. S. Moore 11-28-1866 (no return) L
Alexander, Mary C. to Rob. S. Alexander? 11-15-1846 F
Alexander, Mary E. to J. H. Thomas 12-17-1860 Hy
Alexander, Mary E. to James B. Milam 5-15-1867 Hn
Alexander, Mary F. to Isaac T. Johnson 10-12-1869 (10-13-1869) Ma
Alexander, Mary G. to William L. Smith 10-19-1859 Hn
Alexander, Mary J. to Charles R. Hendrickson 1-3-1855 Sh
Alexander, Mary J. to J. R. Kerr 11-10-1847 F
Alexander, Mary Jane to Alfred Jackson 6-14-1854 (3-23-1854?) Ma
Alexander, Mary Jane to Berry P. Alexander 1-27-1850 Hn
Alexander, Mary Jane to Martin D. Alexander 5-14-1853 Ma
Alexander, Mary Jane to Samuel Roark 9-18-1841 Sh
Alexander, Mary M. to Robert W. Barnett 12-4-1827 (12-6-1827) Hr
Alexander, Mary P. to John N. Ward 11-11-1858 We
Alexander, Mary W. to Alexr. C. Caldwell 11-7-1860 Ma
Alexander, Mary to Daniel Jackson 12-26-1872 T
Alexander, Mary to John J. Taylor 7-20-1846 Ma
Alexander, Mary to John Philpot 3-14-1831 (3-15-1831) Hr
Alexander, Mary to Stephen Calhoon 12-12-1872 Hy
Alexander, Melissa to J. H. Solomon 12-26-1860 G
Alexander, Mollie B. to J. P. Smith 3-25-1865 (3-29-1865) F
Alexander, Mollie C. to Thos. S. Tate 2-9-1865 (no return) Cr
Alexander, N. A. to G. W. Burnett 5-29-1860 (not endorsed) F
Alexander, N. T. to N. H. Hart 1-23-1859 Hn
Alexander, Nancy Ann to Robert Whiteside 3-24-1855 Ma
Alexander, Nancy D. to W. T. M. Davis 1-5-1849 Sh
Alexander, Nancy E. to D. B. Emerson 12-13-1866 (no return) Hn
Alexander, Nancy J. to Hugh A. Cullum 11-17-1854 (no return) F
Alexander, Nancy to Andrew Taylor 6-1-1877 Hy
Alexander, Nancy to William Irwin 3-30-1841 (4-1-1841) F
Alexander, Nannie to W. H. Chance 8-24-1870 (8-25-1870) Cr
Alexander, O. J. to W. C. Champion 10-22-1868 F
Alexander, Olie to S. M. Turnley 2-8-1877 Hy
Alexander, Ouida C. to Moses A. Dawson 4-30-1847 Hn
Alexander, P. Q. to James G. Boyd 3-17-1851 Cr
Alexander, P. to William C. Mooney 9-11-1844 Hn
Alexander, Paulina F. to Alonza Killgore 4-19-1867 Hn
Alexander, Peggie to Jerry Walker 8-23-1875 (8-24-1875) O
Alexander, R. A. to W. C. Dickerson 2-9-1865 F
Alexander, Rachel to N. F. Plummer 8-12-1834 Sh
Alexander, Roberta D. to Thomas Henry 3-3-1859 Hr
Alexander, Rody to Peter Small 8-13-1867 T
Alexander, Rosa to Jim Tarry 12-21-1873 T
Alexander, Rosanna to Edward Blyne 10-11-1859 (no return) Hn
Alexander, S. H. to E. H. Ranale 12-14-186? Hn
Alexander, Sadie E. to Calvin V. Hart 2-20-1871 (2-22-1871) Ma
Alexander, Sarah A. to John Mathis 10-13-1839 Hn
Alexander, Sarah A. to John T. Gains 10-23-1865 (10-24-1865) L
Alexander, Sarah A. to Samuel B. Hill 11-21-1839 Hn
Alexander, Sarah Amanda to Andrew Jackson Sellars 1-18-1871 (1-19-1871) Ma
Alexander, Sarah Ann to Robt. Moseley 5-26-1869 G
Alexander, Sarah C. to Lewis Lefever 1-9-1844 Hn
Alexander, Sarah D. to Isaac B. Mercer 8-13-1849 (no return) F
Alexander, Sarah E. to John R. Gardner 3-30-1861 Ma
Alexander, Sarah E. to Joseph A. Betty 2-2-1852 (2-10-1852) Ma
Alexander, Sarah M. to Francis Elliott 1-2-1843 (1-5-1843) G
Alexander, Sarah to Charles Myrick 4-14-1850 Hn
Alexander, Sarah to Isaac D. Gore 6-14-1838 Hn
Alexander, Sarah to Jasper N. Butler 2-17-1857 (2-26-1857) Ma
Alexander, Sarah to Robert Collier 12-16-1868 (no return) Hy
Alexander, Sidney to Jacob Cummings 5-19-1866 (8-11-1866) F B
Alexander, Sophia to Josephus Vaughn 11-6-1858 We
Alexander, Susan A. to Wm. Johnson 2-15-1847 (2-16-1847) F
Alexander, Susan B. to Ashvill Garrett 11-25-1857 We
Alexander, Susan C. to M. L. Tood? 1-?-1866 (1-17-1866) Cr
Alexander, Susan C. to Panes T. Utley 2-8-1841 Hn
Alexander, Susan D. to James B. McClurere? 3-24-1848 (4-16-1848) F
Alexander, Susan H. to B. Roberts 1-8-1850 Sh
Alexander, Susan H. to J. O'Daniel 3-16-1864 Hn
Alexander, Susan J. to John K. Orr 1-7-1836 Sh
Alexander, Susan R. to R. W. Davis 1-15-1859 (1-20-1859) G
Alexander, Susan to Arvell Garrett 4-4-1838 (4-5-1838) Ma
Alexander, Susan to Henry Fletcher 10-25-1842 Sh
Alexander, Tennessee to Lewis Edwards 3-18-1873 Hy
Alexander, Ursala M. to Elias Pharr 10-14-1847 Sh
Alexander?, M. H. to J. W. Swanson 12-21-1837 Sh
Alford, Amanda to A. R. Jones 11-3-1864 G
Alford, Elizabeth S. to Henry R. Dickson 10-22-1867 G
Alford, Elizabeth to Jesse Turner 6-15-1835 (6-16-1835) G
Alford, Gingeanna to James T. Dement 3-17-1852 G
Alford, Judith to Adam Trent 9-2-1866 F

Alford, Louisa to John H. Stone 2-17-1874 (2-15-1874) L
Alford, Martha to Riley Tolliver 11-19-1878 (11-20-1878) L
Alford, Mary E. to B. F. Langley 5-30-1871 L
Alford, Mary L. Mede to Manian Patrick 6-21-1838 (6-26-1838) Hr
Alford, Nancy to Isaac Futrel 3-23-1843 (3-30-1843) Hr
Alford, S. L. to J. F. Winburn 4-22-1882 (4-24-1882) L
Alford, Sarah Ann to William M. Glass 8-13-1863 L
Alford, Sarah E. to A. G. Jones 12-5-1869 G
Alfred, Margaret? to Jonathan Budgett? 12-29-1862 T
Algea, Charlotte to John D. Martin 12-27-1854 Cr
Algea, E. P. to Lewis A. Williams 1-21-1843 Cr
Algea, Emily to Peter Bray 12-24-1868 G B
Algea, Margery to Wm. J. Edwards 2-2-1843 Cr
Algee, A. G. to H. Wood 10-1-1869 (10-3-1869) Cr
Algee, Emma to Richard McDonald 2-1-1872 Cr B
Algee, J. C. to W. K.? Baxter 1-1-1861 (1-2-1861) Cr
Algee, Jane to James Rhodes 1-19-1843 Cr
Algee, M. J. to J. L. Sales 1-19-1861 (1-21-1861) Cr
Algee, Martha A. to A. S. J.? Neely 5-23-1860 (no return) Cr
Algee, Mollie to Boyd Bryant 7-31-1873 (7-27?-1873) Cr
Algee, Virginia to A. F. Estes 9-29-1868 (10-1-1868) Cr
Algen, E. (Mrs.) to W. B. Dickinson 3-24-1870 G
Alger, Mary E. to R. D. Shofner 4-4-1848 Cr
Alguire, Frances to Thomas? B. Douglass 9-3-1855 (9-4-1855) O
Alice E., McCool to M. E. Ragland 11-25-1862 Hy
Alice, Newby to Daniel T. Pope 1-4-1866 Hy
Alison, Alsa Ann to Thomas N. Stephenson 4-25-1843 Ma
Alison, Cornelius to Burgis Dickie 12-28-1876 Hy
Alison, Elizabeth to Thos. N. Stephens 10-10-1843 (10-12-1843) Ma
Alison, L. I. to Edward D. Williams 1-12-1870 Hy
Alison, Nellie to Dave Williams 12-2-1871 Hy
Alison, Sindy to Sandy Cerron 10-16-1869 Hy
Alison, Tennessee to Jerry Dickey 10-16-1873 Hy
Alkins, Louisa Jane to James M. Cook 5-11-1856 We
Alkire, Lelia to Isaac Bevlin 2-13-1868 F
Allbright, Eliza Ann to John Harper 5-30-1844 Cr
Allbright, Mary J. E. to Robert S. Gordon 10-9-1854 G
Allcock, Mollie to S. J. Rogers 9-18-1867 O
Allen, A. C. to J. M. Taylor 6-22-1865 O
Allen, A. E. to W. P. Walker 1-15-1867 O
Allen, Allie to Flemming S. Allen 8-19-1847 Hn
Allen, Amanda F to J. M. Whitworth 7-2-1863 Hn
Allen, Amanda J. to Alfred Stuart 3-12-1844 G
Allen, Amanda to Edward Glenn 9-28-1867 (9-29-1867) T
Allen, Amanda to James Alexander 9-4-1860 Cr
Allen, Amanda to Louis Julius 10-25-1881 (10-25-1882?) L B
Allen, Amanda to T. S. Alvis 12-3-1867 G
Allen, Ann B. to Andrew A. Allen 12-22-1845 (12-23-1845) F
Allen, Ann C. to Joseph S. Thompson 3-9-1847 (3-10-1847) Hr
Allen, Ann C. to S. C. Chambers 7-8-1858 O
Allen, Ann Eliza to Ezekiel Sanderlin 1-13-1848 Sh
Allen, Ann R. to N. L. Owen 5-7-1855 (no return) F
Allen, Annice to Granville Nixon 1-17-1853 (2-8-1853) Hr
Allen, Annie E. to Lewis Drennan 6-7-1869 (no return) Hy
Allen, Annisy to Wm. J. Fortenberry 8-10-1842 (8-11-1842) Hr
Allen, B. (Miss) to R. J. Allison 9-12-1863 (9-16-1863) Sh
Allen, Babe to David Halliburton 12-28-1882 L
Allen, Betty to Melville Giles 12-23-1879 (12-24-1879) L B
Allen, Caroline to Wm. W. Kilpatrick 2-20-1864 Sh
Allen, Cassandra C. to James M. Harrell 1-17-1853 Sh
Allen, Catharin to Wm. Hughes 8-26-1850 (9-1-1850) F
Allen, Catharine to James Medlin 4-22-1865 (4-23-1865) Cr
Allen, Catharine to Jessie Whittier 9-1-1833 Sh
Allen, Catherine to Reddiee Berry 12-12-1843 (12-13-1843) G
Allen, Charity to Jerry Harris 5-13-1871 Hy
Allen, Cynthia A. to Frederick W. Smith 4-11-1849 Sh
Allen, Cynthia Ann to Egbert H. Gates 5-31-1838 Hn
Allen, D. A. to Thomas B. Nayns? 5-24-1862 Hy
Allen, Darcus E. to Howell Adams 2-19-1848 G
Allen, Delia to Sandy Campbell 3-4-1871 (no return) Hy
Allen, Dilsy to Wm. White 7-9-1866 (6?-10-1866) Dy
Allen, E. J. to James P. Shaw 10-16-1866 G
Allen, E. J. to S. _. Milam 12-13-1852 Hn
Allen, E. to Loid Ozier 1-12-1846 Be
Allen, Eizabeth to J. H. Bell 12-14-1870 Hy
Allen, Elender to George Holowell 1-1-1851 Be
Allen, Elisabeth to Robert Snipes 7-13-1877 Hy
Allen, Eliza Ann to John S. Edwards 1-30-1860 Sh
Allen, Eliza Ann to Thos. J. Halstead 9-2-1855 Hn
Allen, Eliza to Benj. Gilbert 10-28-1857 G
Allen, Eliza to Joseph T. Ranka 9-16-1849 Sh
Allen, Elizabeth F. to Thos. H. Price 1-12-1859 Cr
Allen, Elizabeth Frances to Robert Gill 1-21-1867 (1-22-1867) Ma
Allen, Elizabeth J. to B. G. Ezzell 5-12-1847 Hn
Allen, Elizabeth J. to Pinckney A. Casteel 12-23-1866 Be
Allen, Elizabeth L. to Minor Steel 3-26-1850 Be
Allen, Elizabeth P. to David H. Johnson 8-?-1842 (not endorsed) F

Brides

Allen, Elizabeth Temple to Augustus B. Simmons 3-13-1866 (3-18-1866) Ma
Allen, Elizabeth to Elmer Rowland 1-10-1839 Cr
Allen, Elizabeth to George W. Haislip 7-21-1834 O
Allen, Elizabeth to M. C. Peel 6-10-1845 Sh
Allen, Elizabeth to Stephen Childress 2-29-1840 (3-3-1840) Hr
Allen, Elizabeth to T. J. Kee 3-2-1863 Be
Allen, Elizabeth to W. H. Jackson 3-10-1864 Sh
Allen, Elizabeth to Wiley Powell 5-28-1823 Sh
Allen, Ellen C. to C. (Dr.) Harris 12-15-1842 Ma
Allen, Ellen E. to James Warpole 2-11-1870 G B
Allen, Emily to Henry B. Walters 7-18-1850 Hn
Allen, Emily to James Brown 12-28-1866 (12-30-1866) F B
Allen, Emma to A. J. Crittendon 10-14-1875 L B
Allen, Evelin to James T. Medlin 6-15-1872 (no return) Cr
Allen, F. J. to Jeremiah J. Jones 2-11-1863 (2-12-1863) O
Allen, Fannie E. to David A. Jones 3-26-1868 Ma
Allen, Fanny to William Johnson 8-17-1869 F B
Allen, Frances R. to John P. Morgan 4-24-1866 T
Allen, Frances to Benj. Brewer 2-22-1844 Cr
Allen, Francis L. to Thomas Jones 1-30-1860 (1-31-1860) O
Allen, Francis to William M. Duncan 9-3-1839 (10-3-1839) O
Allen, Harriett to Thomas Lee 10-6-1877 (no return) Hy
Allen, Hattie W. to John P. Gause 5-22-1867 L
Allen, Helen L. to W. N. Brown 12-7-1859 Sh
Allen, History to Joe Shepherd 5-19-1870 (5-21-1870) F B
Allen, I. to R. Allen 6-5-1865 O
Allen, Jane O. K. to Allen Bowers 7-20-1858 (7-21-1858) G
Allen, Jane W. to Henry G. Hunt 8-24-1846 (8-25-1846) G
Allen, Jane W. to Wm. McQuistin 2-24-1845 (2-25-1845) F
Allen, Jane to Andrew Jackson 7-6-1850 (7-10-1850) Hr
Allen, Jane to James A. Hart 4-29-1845 Cr
Allen, Jane to James C. Davis 1-16-1855 (no return) F
Allen, Jane to John Littleton 12-7-1852 (1-30-1853) O
Allen, Jane to WilliamB. Fullerton 12-21-1851 Be
Allen, Josephine to Tecumseh Cockran 1-19-1870 F B
Allen, Josephine to William A. Reddin 1-16-1866 (1-18-1866) Cr
Allen, Julia Ann to Samuel D. Jones 1-5-1843 Hr
Allen, Julia E. to Samuel A. Craig 3-4-1853 Hn
Allen, Louisa A. to John W. Campbell 4-27-1852 O
Allen, Louisa J. to Green B. Curtis 8-23-1841 Hr
Allen, Louisa Malinda to Matthew B. Barnett 3-19-1870 (3-22-1870) Ma
Allen, Louisa to Matthew Bray 3-23-1858 Sh
Allen, Louisa to William Fletcher 1-19-1871 (1-22-1871) T
Allen, Lowella to Allen Fumbanks 7-5-1879 (7-6-1879) Dy
Allen, Lucinda to Crawford Bradford 11-16-1852 Hn
Allen, Lucy A. to John D. Nordon 10-3-1853 Cr
Allen, Lucy to Wm. H. Balus 2-14-1847 Be
Allen, Lydia to James Hansard 6-23-1849 (6-24-1849) Hr
Allen, M. A. (Mrs.) to Jacob N. (M?) Williams 7-10-1864 (7-11-1864) Sh
Allen, M. A. to William G. Glass 3-27-1851 Hn
Allen, M. B. to L. H. C. Branch 12-18-1865 (12-20-1865) F
Allen, M. C. to J. M. Hitt 12-19-1865 (no return) Hn
Allen, M. E. to David Heckle 3-22-1854 (3-23-1854) Sh
Allen, M. L. to G. W. Bird 10-15-1870 (10-17-1870) O
Allen, M. to W. Steele 3-21-1842 Be
Allen, Maggie to Peter Conley 12-22-1863 Sh
Allen, Mahaly A. to Thomas Holder 3-28-1861 G
Allen, Mahaly to John B. Stuart 1-2-1837 (1-5-1837) G
Allen, Manerva to J. W. Gilbert 6-27-1867 Hn
Allen, Margaret B. to Mahlon R. Morton 2-14-1848 Sh
Allen, Margaret C. to H. T. Perry 6-18-1866 (no return) Hn
Allen, Margaret C. to Wm. F. Forest 9-23-1871 (9-24-1871) Cr
Allen, Margaret D. to T. C. Willson 8-21-1866 (8-23-1866) Cr
Allen, Margaret J. to Jacob Bowers 6-26-1850 Sh
Allen, Margaret to Isrial Mayfield 10-20-1835 (10-22-1835) Hr
Allen, Margaret to J. E. Crabtree 1-19-1858 (no return) We
Allen, Margaret to Loyd W. Deloach 6-16-1846 Sh
Allen, Margaret to Moses B. Alexander 10-26-1837 Sh
Allen, Margaret to Thomas Collins 1-24-1849 Sh
Allen, Margarett G. to John McCaughan 10-21-1854 (no return) F
Allen, Margarett J. to Robt. M. Gabbie (Gallbie?) 1-27-1845 (1-28-1845) F
Allen, Martha A. to James T. White 7-8-1846 Sh
Allen, Martha C. to Sumners D. Bowden 1-12-1860 Hn
Allen, Martha F. Ellenor to T. B. Morgan 10-28-1839 Cr
Allen, Martha J. to A. C. Walker 11-30-1853 Hn
Allen, Martha J. to E. H. Bennett 11-29-1870 (11-30-1870) F
Allen, Martha J. to Thomas W. Colew? 11-13-1849 Hn
Allen, Martha R. to George W. Minter 11-28-1853 Hr
Allen, Martha T. to Isaac R. Hutchins 1-15-1872 (no return) Cr
Allen, Martha to G. W. Freeman 10-15-1854 (no return) F
Allen, Martha to J. W. Brown 1-11-1862 (no return) Cr
Allen, Martha to John Howard 4-11-1871 Cr B
Allen, Martha to Richard A. Nash 12-29-1859 Hn
Allen, Martha to Richard Vaughan 4-23-1870 Hy
Allen, Marthann to M. L. Turner 10-13-1847 (10-19-1847) F
Allen, Mary A. to E. F. Bracchus 11-22-1858 Sh
Allen, Mary A. to G. L. Carmack 10-22-1856 Cr
Allen, Mary A. to John B. Cravins 4-14-1859 We
Allen, Mary A. to John H. Bowers 2-16-1848 (2-17-1848) Hr
Allen, Mary Adaline to John C. McLister 11-21-1855 (11-22-1855) T
Allen, Mary C. to Josephus Loving 4-5-1854 Sh
Allen, Mary E. to E. M. Lindsey 12-24-1863 Hn
Allen, Mary E. to J. H. Taylor 7-8-1871 (7-9-1871) Cr
Allen, Mary E. to Mecajah Buchanan 10-29-1865 (10-31-1865) O
Allen, Mary F. to William Halliburton 11-19-1856 G
Allen, Mary G. A. to Charles H. Leech 11-28-1867 T
Allen, Mary J. to Isaac Dodds 4-29-1845 (no return) F
Allen, Mary J. to J. S. Brinkley 5-1-1861 (5-2-1861) Dy
Allen, Mary J. to James B. Williams 9-24-1840 (no return) F
Allen, Mary J. to James F. Palmer 2-24-1866 (2-26-1866) Cr
Allen, Mary M. to Newton M. Thomas 1-30-1855 (1-31-1855) Sh
Allen, Mary Susan to Asher Stone 12-26-1849 Sh
Allen, Mary T. to Benjamin Hollad 12-1-1831 Hr
Allen, Mary W. to Jacob D. Bledsoe 11-19-1863 (no return) Cr
Allen, Mary to Alstin Bond 7-28-1869 (no return) Hy
Allen, Mary to Austin Cook 3-16-1861 Sh
Allen, Mary to C. Short 6-29-1863 Sh
Allen, Mary to Caswell Coates 12-27-1841 (12-30-1841) Hr
Allen, Mary to Colbert Blankenship 12-26-1863 (1-21-1864) Dy
Allen, Mary to Edmund S. Rodgers 4-18-1840 Cr
Allen, Mary to Harvey Bacon 7-28-1831 Sh
Allen, Mary to Joel Massey 8-13-1840 Sh
Allen, Mary to John Johnson 12-12-1841 Cr
Allen, Mary to John Perryman 1-20-1846 Ma
Allen, Mary to Joseph Gordon 6-12-1839 Sh
Allen, Mary to R. H. McClelian 11-20-1873 (11-26-1873) O
Allen, Matilda to William H. Busby 10-27-1858 Sh
Allen, Mattie to William A. Osborn 11-13-1867 Hn
Allen, Mildred to Alfred Yancey 4-27-1842 (5-28-1842) F
Allen, Mollie to Phil Day 12-25-1871 Hy
Allen, Myra T. to Wm. H. Bledsoe 12-8-1864 (no return) Cr
Allen, Nancy A. to W. E. Moss 8-12-1864 (no return) Cr
Allen, Nancy C. to W. M. Cunningham 2-2-1848 Cr
Allen, Nancy E. to Calvin Lemons 11-27-1858 Hn
Allen, Nancy to Calvin Dodson 6-27-1855 (no return) Hn
Allen, Nancy to James Ralls 6-28-1846 Hn
Allen, Nancy to John Farris 12-12-1850 Hn
Allen, Nancy to Perry Brown 12-31-1869 Hy
Allen, Nancy to William D. McCloud 5-31-1846 Sh
Allen, Nannie C. to C. A. W. Jetton 12-19-1878 Hy
Allen, O. E. to J. T. Lowry 5-26-1846 Sh
Allen, Obedience to Marquis L. Glover 11-20-1838 (no return) Hn
Allen, Orelia Ann to James Hunter 5-20-1870 (5-21-1870) F B
Allen, Phebe Turner to Zachariah Bledsoe 10-22-1849 (10-21?-1849) G
Allen, Piecia to Jas. P. Churchwell 5-10-1873 (5-11-1873) Cr
Allen, Polly to John A. Saunders 11-2-1841 O
Allen, Portia J. to James E. Freeman 4-7-1858 Hn
Allen, R. Jane to Henry Franklin 1-22-1870 (1-27-1870) F B
Allen, R. Y. to G. H. Hunter 2-15-1872 T
Allen, Rebeca to William Gillespie 8-7-1845 (8-8-1845) T
Allen, Rebecca A. to John E. Alexander 1-11-1859 Hn
Allen, Roberta to Sam Phillips 2-28-1866 (3-10-1866) F B
Allen, Rose to Henry Talley 1-19-1871 T
Allen, Sabella to Benjn. R. Lewis 7-19-1852 Sh
Allen, Salina E. to John Moore 10-7-1853 (10-13-1853) G
Allen, Sarah A. B. to John H. Mathews 3-21-1839 F
Allen, Sarah A. to Pryor H. Smith 10-18-1860 (no return) Hn
Allen, Sarah E. to Jno. C. Jones 1-7-1869 Be
Allen, Sarah Eliza to James G. Smith 1-2-1854 T
Allen, Sarah H. to Elijah Brooks 1-26-1848 Sh
Allen, Sarah I. to Cyrus F. Shelby 12-25-1838 Sh
Allen, Sarah J. to John J. Boswell 10-29-1856 Be
Allen, Sarah Jane to Thomas E. Miller 7-5-1855 Hn
Allen, Sarah M. to Sidney F. Campbell 2-16-1859 (2-17-1859) G
Allen, Sarah R. to Robert H. Davis 10-22-1837 O
Allen, Sarah to Hiram Canaday 11-10-1855 O
Allen, Sarah to Thomas Lurry 12-17-1844 Sh
Allen, Sarah to Thos. Craig 3-17-1843 Be
Allen, Sarah to William Scott 12-12-1859 (12-15-1859) Hr
Allen, Setta to James Allen 10-29-1870 (11-2-1870) T
Allen, Siller to Willis Bond 3-17-1875 (no return) Hy
Allen, Susan (Mrs.) to Samuel R. Anderson 2-13-1856 Sh
Allen, Susan Ann to Stitts M. Nelson 2-26-1835 Sh
Allen, Susan F. to Sireneus W. Boyer 10-27-1851 (10-28-1851) Sh
Allen, Susan T. to Henry Baker 1-10-1865 G
Allen, Susan to John R. Stalcup 1-3-1850 Cr
Allen, Sylvia to John Glover 8-22-1848 Ma
Allen, Tabitha to William Haislip 2-29-1832 (4-7-1832) O
Allen, Tempie to Joe Peete 2-9-1871 Hy
Allen, Tennessee to John Allen 10-22-1859 Hn
Allen, Venia to Melvin Jarrell 12-30-1875 (no return) L B
Allen, Virginia to J. M. Ashley 1-15-1867 G
Allen, Virginia to John C. Cooper 8-10-1852 Hn
Allen, W. M. to Joel Cooper 8-13-1865 G

Allen, Williametta to Isaac Sheppard 2-22-1868 (no return) F B
Allen?, Elizabeth P. to R. L. Evans 10-13-1847 (11-12-1847) F
Alleson, Sarah C. to Nathaniel P. Norman 12-22-1851 G
Alley, Harriett A. to Samuel J. Rigsby 11-21-1867 Hn
Alley, Kittie to Spencer Johnson 4-12-1868 (no return) F B
Alley, M. E. to W. W. Briant 11-15-1865 Hn
Allford, Lucinda to J. T. Mitchell 7-1-1862 (7-3-1862) L
Allgiar, Margaret to Ivy S. Chandler 12-6-1854 (12-7-1854) O
Allguiar, Martha Ann to William M. Carter 8-9-1853 (8-10-1853) O
Allin, Alice to Beverly Taylor 4-7-1872 Hy
Allison, Ada to Henry Griggs 12-15-1884 (12-?-1884) L
Allison, Amanda to Thomas Black 12-2-1846 (12-3-1846) Ma
Allison, Ann Caroline to W. D. Thompson 3-10-1867 Hn
Allison, Arriemita to J. W. B. Abraham 11-16-1885 (11-17-1885) L
Allison, Christina to Mathias Hartz 12-23-1854 (12-25-1854) Sh
Allison, Delilah to Jacob Williams 1-12-1854 Ma
Allison, E. A. to D. C. Dickey 3-16-1860 G
Allison, Elizabeth A. to Green W. Parker 5-5-1845 O
Allison, Elizabeth P. to Samuel Kellough 4-16-1840 G
Allison, Ella to George Jeffres 3-8-1875 (no return) Hy
Allison, Elvira to Thomas H. Maxey 5-26-1845 O
Allison, Fannie to Thos. Bonner 2-28-1868 Hy
Allison, Francis J. to Ambrose Bramlett 6-7-1838 O
Allison, Hannah to William Whitehead 7-1-1849 Be
Allison, Harriett to John Wilborn 10-4-1851 (10-28-1851) O
Allison, Jane to Amos Morison 6-8-1848 Sh
Allison, Julia to Gustaf Johnson 7-28-1858 Sh
Allison, Laurie J. to Robert W. Nicholson 6-9-1861 Hn
Allison, Lizzie D. to Beverly A. Rodgers 8-9-1868 (no return) F
Allison, Lou to William Goodman 8-3-1872? (7-28-1872?) L B
Allison, Lucy to Washington Wood 1-17-1869 Hy
Allison, M. A. to N. B. Rezins 10-28-1875 L
Allison, M. V. to Lee A. Cannon 11-11-1869 G
Allison, Margaret J. to Samuel Hodge 12-18-1838 G
Allison, Margaret to John B. Alexander 7-14-1866 (7-15-1866) Ma
Allison, Martha A. to Samuel H. Davis 9-19-1840 (9-24-1840) O
Allison, Martha to James Riley 7-23-1844 Sh
Allison, Mary D. to C. B. Alexander 3-13-1849 Sh
Allison, Mary E. to Benjamin Landrum 6-25-1846 O
Allison, Mary J. to Abner Teague 3-16-1866 Ma
Allison, Mary J. to Robert F. Henderson 5-2-1870 (5-4-1870) Ma
Allison, Mary Jane to David P. Barnett 8-15-1853 (8-16-1853) G
Allison, Mary Jane to John S. Strickland 12-20-1841 (12-29-1841) Hr
Allison, Mary to James Douglass 12-15-1877 (12-16-1877) L B
Allison, Matilda to Robert C. Wright 6-13-1846 Sh
Allison, Melissa to William Henry 1-17-1848 Be
Allison, Milly to William W. Nichols 5-16-1849 (5-17-1849) Ma
Allison, Mollie S. to J. B. Hillis 2-1-1858 (2-2-1858) L
Allison, Nancy F. to Jonathan B. Dryden 5-12-1836 (5-13-1836) G
Allison, Rebecca E. to William M. Dunlap 12-2-1844 (12-3-1844) G
Allison, Sarah E. to John L. Booth 8-6-1861 O
Allman, Elizabeth to Thomas P. Jackson 3-5-1856 Hn
Allman, Keziah to John M. Rombly 6-23-1839 Hn
Allman, Lucinda to William R. Lee 6-25-1846 Hn
Allman, Sarah E. to John Pinkley 12-26-1858 Cr
Allman, Sarah to Thomas P. Jackson 1-16-1846 Hn
Allmon, America to Seth Brinkley 8-27-1860 (8-28-1860) Cr
Allmond, Mary A. to Jas. J. Deason 3-8-1863 Hn
Allmond, Sarah to George Chatham 9-15-1849 Hn
Alls (Able), Sarah A. to Jno. B. Dewitt 11-15-1848 Sh
Allsup, Alsey to Barnet Clifft 1-23-1828 (1-24-1828) Hr
Alltop, Susan to Pat Carney 4-4-1871 (no return) Hy
Alman, Mary Polly to Stephen Smith 11-1-1830 Ma
Almon, Jane to James (John) Stroud 10-2-1849 O
Almon, Tennessee to Henry Bruce 2-11-1866 Hn
Almond, Geraldine to Samuel H. Rall 3-19-1863 Hn
Almond, Jane to William A. Morphis 8-31-1843 Hn
Almond, Jane to Wm. C. Collins 12-29-1856 Cr
Almond, Nancy to Sampson Woods 1-16-1848 Hn
Almund, Mary to John W. Harris 1-8-1854 Hn
Alphan, Ruth H. to Richard Adams 2-14-1854 O
Alphin, Mary to P. A. Bottoms 2-24-1865 G
Alphin, Venus to Henry Taylor 10-12-1867 Hy
Alread, Elizabeth to Thomas Milsap 3-31-1839 L
Alrich?, Louisa F. to Thomas J. Foster 12-18-1866 (12-19-1866) Cr
Alsabrooks, Charlott H. to Harvey M. Latta 10-16-1834 G
Alsabrooks, Rebecca J. to Parson M. Sherman 12-18-1838 G
Alsabrooks, Sarah A. to Edwin H. Hintom 12-20-1843 G
Alsbrook, P. F. to S. L. Gains 11-14-1865 (no return) L
Alsbrook, Visena to Edwin Mize 10-3-1837 Sh
Alsobrook (Ashbrook), Mary to John Onley 8-29-1847 Sh
Alsobrook, Louisa to James Clarke 3-12-1840 Sh
Alsobrook, Mary E. to Cincinnatus Jackson 5-27-1841 Sh
Alsobrooks, Allie D. to Charles H. Love 12-17-1880 (12-21-1880) L
Alsobrooks, Caldonia to W. H. Cherry 7-25-1877 (8-2-1877) L
Alsobrooks, Henrietta to Henry Wright 7-8-1881 (7-10-1881) L B
Alsop, Cary to George W. Hazlegrove 12-18-1847 (12-23-1847) Hr

Alsop, Martha to Wm. J. Price 10-25-1850 Be
Alsop, Matilda to John Easom 8-20-1851 (8-24-1851) Hr
Alsten, Josephine to James Patterson 6-18-1869 G
Alston, Aggie to Tom lawson 11-20-1871 (11-23-18710 T
Alston, Agnes to Thos. Alston 12-30-1867 (12-2-1868?) T
Alston, Ann Eliza to Oliver H. Pegues 1-9-1829 Ma
Alston, Aquilla to Ned Lake 3-11-1868 (3-13-1868) L B
Alston, Betty to John Randolph 7-28-1871 (7-18?-1871) T
Alston, Caroline to John C. Crawford 10-8-1839 Sh
Alston, Edwanna? to Josephus Loving 1-21-1840 (1-22-1840) F
Alston, Eliza Jane to Sabert Wood 10-28-1856 (10-29-1856) L
Alston, Elizabeth P. to John Brown 5-25-1840 (5-26-1840) F
Alston, Elizabeth to Henry Brown 2-24-1872 (no return) L B
Alston, Elizabeth to Jessee Riche 4-29-1868 (5-21-1868) T
Alston, Ellen to Amus Sherrill 9-23-1869 (9-26-1869) T
Alston, Eva M. to W. H. Richardson 8-31-1868 (9-2-1868) T
Alston, Evelina to R. S. Green 2-16-1885 (2-18-1885) L
Alston, Fanny to Abe Armstrong 11-20-1871 911-23-1871 T
Alston, Godey A. to Anthony Parker 1-25-1868 L B
Alston, Henrietta to Jessee Sherrill 10-14-1874 T
Alston, Katie to Wylie Alston 9-28-1872 (9-29-1872) T
Alston, Livia? to Fenton Smith 10-5-1874 T
Alston, Lucy to Tob? Brooks 7-10-1868 (7-11-1868) T
Alston, Luisa to S. Nichols 3-21-1862 Be
Alston, Lusina to John Hill 11-9-1866 (11-10-1866) T
Alston, Margt. J. to William L. McGaughey 9-21-1869 (no return) L
Alston, Martha A. to Wm. T. Lucas 7-23-1851 Sh
Alston, Mary Ann to Handy Wood 12-11-1860 (12-12-1860) L
Alston, Mary Hardy to Nathaniel Green Wormley 6-22-1850 (6-23-1850) T
Alston, Mary M. to Johnson B. Tyson 6-27-1849 (6-28-1849) Ma
Alston, Mary to George Ramsey 6-10-1867 (6-11-1867) Ma
Alston, Mary to Richard Alston 12-27-1867 (12-2-1868?) T
Alston, Mary to Thomas E. Adams 10-8-1839 Sh
Alston, Matilda to James Barnell 1-28-1870 T
Alston, Missouri to Geo. Dickens 12-23-1872 (12-25-1872) T
Alston, Nancy C. to James W. Black 5-8-1848 F
Alston, Nancy to Henry Payne 7-5-1873 (7-6-1873) T
Alston, Sallie A. to T. P. Wood 12-24-1873 L
Alston, Sallie D. to Lackfield Maclin 12-30-1871 (1-3-1875?) T
Alston, Sallie J. to John Henry Skillern 11-19-1870 (11-23-1870) Ma
Alston, Sarah to William Bell 4-25-1872 (4-27-1872) L
Alston, Susana F. to J. S. Wood 12-8-1866 (12-12-1866) L
Alston, Temperance S. to John Johnston 8-31-1831 Ma
Alsup, Almeda to Wm. Caraway 8-13-1861 Be
Alsup, Elizabeth to Isaac P. Russell 8-22-1828 (9-24-1828) Hr
Alsup, Lydia J. to Joseph L. Mannon 5-2-1862 Be
Alsup, Mahala Jane to John L. McRae 4-24-1860 Be
Alsup, Mary A. to Lewis T. McDaniel 11-14-1867 Be
Alsup, Mary M. to William A. J. Finley 7-31-1861 (8-1-1861) Sh
Alsup, Mary to J. M. Brewer 12-19-1867 Be
Alsup, Minerva to Thomas J. Middleton 1-17-1846 Sh
Alsup, Nancey to Moses Bolton 9-21-1848 Sh
Alsup, Susan Ann to Andrew Alsup 7-26-1856 Be
Alsup, Susan to H. Forest 12-5-1856 Be
Alsup, Urcilla to Even S. Alexander 9-17-1844 Sh
Alt, Catharine to Henry Berg 11-13-1860 Hn
Altman, Mary E. to Josiah F. Cook 1-22-1868 G
Altman, Mary Jane to William J. Maddox 10-27-1856 (10-19?-1856) Ma
Altom?, Martha J. to Charles W. Burton 10-9-1859 Hn
Altome?, L. E. to R. B. Warren 2-2-1865 Hn
Alton, Mary S. to William H. Hite 12-23-1841 Sh
Altum, M. E. to G. L. Russell 6-29-1865 Hn
Alvianson?, Sarah to Theophilis Ellis 2-21-1840 Hn
Alvis, Anna L. to N. A. Coleman 4-14-1867 G
Alvis, Caroline to Samuel Craige 2-16-1839 G
Alvis, Elizabeth to L. M. Stallings 1-14-1867 (2-14-1867) G
Alvis, Julia to James Johnson 9-15-1869 G B
Alvis, Martha P. to William H. Tuggle 10-4-1854 G
Alvis, Mary A. to Joseph Tarkington 3-21-1848 Sh
Alvis, Mary Jane to Robert Adkins 4-4-1844 Sh
Alvis, Tabitha to Bryant B. Stallings 10-18-1865 G
Alvorde, Harriet to J.(P?) kD. Nietschke(Dietrike?) 2-4-1851 Hr
Alytt?, Feliciana to Andrew J. Price 3-23-1843 Hn
Amanda, Carney to Walley Polk 2-2-1873 Hy
Ames, Casa to Benjamin Cooper 4-26-1855 G
Ames, Ellen to Henry Harder 6-30-1853 Sh
Ames, Mary Jane to William S. Leggett 11-27-1845 Hr
Amis, Berlin to W. H. McCully 11-10-1866 (11-11-1866) F
Amis, Clara to Samuel S. Amis 12-10-1866 F
Ammen, Mary (Miss) to J. M. Alexander 7-25-1863 Sh
Ammonet, Charlotte to James B. Turnage 10-20-1852 Sh
Ammons, Clarissa Ann to Henry M. Roberts 5-16-1846 (5-17-1846) Hr
Ammons, Clarissa Ann to Julius M. Tucker 12-8-1851 G
Ammons, Clarissa to W. W. Thompson 12-23-1873 Hn
Ammons, Dovey L. M. to Elijah Stephenson 10-25-1842 F
Ammons, Eleanor to Wm. Williams 5-6-1847 (5-9-1847) F
Ammons, Elizabeth Ann to Wm. H. Ammons 2-21-1837 (2-26-1837) Hr

Ammons, Elizabeth to David Stephenson 9-12-1843 (9-14-1843) Hr
Ammons, Mary to Green Bennett 8-20-1845 (8-21-1845) F
Ammons, Telitha to Solomon Forehana 11-29-1837 We
Ammons, Winney E. to Jonathan Hodges 1-4-1851 (1-16-1851) Hr
Amonett, Mary E. to James B. Taylor 12-20-1848 Sh
Amonett, Nancy J. to James A. Creath 2-1-1843 Sh
Amons, E. A. to D. A. McCorkle 8-29-1864 O
Amos, Mary to James H. McGee 5-16-1869 G B
Amos, Sallie to George Wilson 2-1-1883 (no return) L
Amouse, Emaline to William Stallings 1-8-1862 (1-9-1862) F
Amyett, Mary C. to William H. Beard 1-17-1856 We
Anden, Margaret to James Kennedy 7-17-1862 (7-27-1862) Sh
Anders, Billie to John M. Williamson 3-27-1872 (3-28-1872) Cr
Anders, Miss to Thos. Gardner 1-17-1850 We
Anders, N. A. to J. C. Bowls 4-25-1869 Hy
Anders, Sarah to Samuel Martin McKinie 9-4-1855 (9-6-1855) Hr
Anders, Wynne to Samuel Sewell 10-25-1830 (10-27-1830) G
Anderson, A. A. to Alfus C. Harrell 1-9-1854 Cr
Anderson, A. H. to A. L. Rainey 10-12-1871 Hy
Anderson, A. L. to J. W. Amis 8-12-1867 (8-13-1867) F
Anderson, Adaline to James T. Dinwiddie 12-30-1845 Hn
Anderson, Adline M. to Andrew Moore 3-9-1846 (3-10-1846) Hr
Anderson, Agnes P. A. to M. M. Deaton 10-1-1851 Hr
Anderson, Agness to Johnathan Polk 8-4-1851 Hr
Anderson, Alice G. to James L. Stewart 3-30-1830 Sh
Anderson, Allis to Charles Freeman 11-15-1845 (11-18-1845) Hr
Anderson, Amanda to ____ Mench? 2-12-1849 (no return) F
Anderson, Amelia to Joseph White 1-21-1871 Hy
Anderson, America T. to Ralph W. Daniel 11-25-1854 (12-10-1854) Ma
Anderson, Anna F. to H. M. Clark, jr. 9-11-1872 Hy
Anderson, Annie to W. R. G. Myett 2-17-1872 (2-18-1872) Dy
Anderson, Ardela to J. R. Notgrass no dates (not executed) Hy
Anderson, Aurelia to Andw. James Bond 3-14-1878 Hy
Anderson, Betsy to Younger Wilson 9-11-1876 (9-15-1876) L B
Anderson, Bettie to William C. Marshall 5-3-1870 Ma
Anderson, Burtie to Isaac Nelson 12-10-1868 Hy
Anderson, Catharine to Wash Hall 3-2-1874 T
Anderson, Charlett to Wm. Wedgestaff 10-17-1872 Hy
Anderson, Charlott to Henry Candis 10-17-1868 (no return) Hy
Anderson, Cinthia to Anderson Carter 9-30-1885 L
Anderson, Cylvia to Charly Ales 10-13-1871 T
Anderson, Cynthia to Robert G. Babcock 10-29-1863 O
Anderson, Diner to Edward Bledsoe 10-21-1870 (10-23-1870) Cr
Anderson, Dycy? to Turner J. Martin 12-31-1839 Hr
Anderson, E. G. to Wm. B. G. Sneed no dates (with Sep 1844) F
Anderson, E. K. to N. J. Stubbs 11-26-1870 (12-1-1870) Cr
Anderson, Easter to John Renshaw 5-21-1842 (5-24-1842) Ma
Anderson, Eleanor F. to Charles W. Alman 11-10-1862 (no return) Hy
Anderson, Eliza A. to James F. Franklin 4-26-1858 (4-27-1858) Ma
Anderson, Eliza C. to Alison Linton 3-17-1842 (no return) Hn
Anderson, Eliza Jane to J. C. Armstrong 12-20-1847 Hr
Anderson, Eliza Jane to William L. Winford 12-1-1846 Sh
Anderson, Eliza to Chas. Anderson 11-18-1873 Hy
Anderson, Eliza to Johnson Stuart 10-30-1871 (11-4-1871) T
Anderson, Eliza to Tho. J. Bailey 3-18-1835 (3-24-1835) Hr
Anderson, Elizabeth to G. C. Swindle 10-25-1840 Be
Anderson, Elizabeth to George Phillips 2-21-1839 Sh
Anderson, Elizabeth to Greenville Chitwood 9-19-1843 Sh
Anderson, Elizabeth to J. A. C. Calhoon 12-22-1846 Sh
Anderson, Elizabeth to J. C. Stewart 3-2-1853 (3-8-1853) O
Anderson, Elizabeth to John H. Hundley 11-26-1860 (11-27-1860) Ma
Anderson, Elizabeth to John M. Lester 7-2-1838 (7-19-1838) Ma
Anderson, Elizabeth to John S. Brown 10-29-1828 Ma
Anderson, Elizabeth to Jonathan T. Farrington 8-24-1847 Sh
Anderson, Elizabeth to Noah Sawyer 12-23-1867 (12-24-1867) L
Anderson, Elizabeth to Robert Henry 4-13-1848 Sh
Anderson, Elizabeth to Saml. Kindrick 5-18-1872 (5-19-1872) T
Anderson, Elizabeth to Samuel S. Berry 3-7-1854 Be
Anderson, Elizabeth to Thomas White 3-6-1834 Sh
Anderson, Elizabeth to Wesley Ely 11-1-1836 (11-2-1836) G
Anderson, Elmira J. to A. L. Henly 4-18-1867 Hy
Anderson, Elmira J. to Thos. H. Hancock 2-24-1859 Hr
Anderson, Emily E. to Robert P. Alexander 7-31-1837 Hr
Anderson, Emma C. to R. T. Duke 2-20-1861 Sh
Anderson, Emma Eliza to Joseph N. Wesson 12-23-1858 Ma
Anderson, Esther E. to William R. Norvell 10-17-1844 Ma
Anderson, Fannie R. to Henry S. Maddox 1-10-1860 Sh
Anderson, Fannie to Alfred Stevens 9-30-1863 (10-1-1863) L
Anderson, Ferdelia to R. Pender 10-23-1859 Hy
Anderson, Frances E. to Isaac C. Jones 2-26-1851 (2-27-1851) Sh
Anderson, Francis to Sam Nelson 3-13-1869 Hy
Anderson, Fredericka to James D. Bush 3-10-1874 Dy
Anderson, Gatson Ann S. to George W. Price 12-17-1849 (12-20-1849) G
Anderson, Georgia to Marshall Currie 12-31-1867 Hy
Anderson, Harriet T. to Robert J. Jennings 5-17-1843 Sh
Anderson, Harriet to Thomas J. Shepherd 1-10-1833 Hr
Anderson, Henrietta F. to Benjamin Irby 10-15-1853 (10-18-1853) Sh

Anderson, Isabella L. to Nathan Reaves 8-6-1850 Sh
Anderson, Issie to Henry King 2-16-1873 Hy
Anderson, J. A. M. to William M. Baker 3-17-1877 (3-18-1877) L
Anderson, J. E. to Wm. M. Mayo 12-23-1844 (12-24-1844) F
Anderson, J. to Balder D. Bowden 9-5-1850 Hn
Anderson, Jane C. to Thomas J. Stubbs 1-3-1870 (1-20-1870) Cr
Anderson, Jane to A. M. Chamberlin 4-13-1837 O
Anderson, Jane to Henry Lewis 11-28-1870 Hy
Anderson, Jane to Lewis Moore 8-5-1839 (8-7-1839) Hr
Anderson, Josephine to R. W. Algee 4-6-1863 (no return) Cr
Anderson, Judah to Robert H. Hester 9-30-1846 Hr
Anderson, Julia A. to W. F. Jones 3-2-1864 F
Anderson, Julia Ann to Isaac Booe 1-13-1842 Hr
Anderson, Julia M. to Wm. P. Grant 11-7-1871 (11-8-1871) T
Anderson, Julia to John W. Wadlingford 1-31-1878 (2-3-1878) Dy
Anderson, K. L. to C. Blanton 6-1-1858 We
Anderson, Kittie to John Riley 9-5-1869 Hy
Anderson, L. A. to J. H. Dulin 3-14-1866 (3-15-1866) F
Anderson, L. A. to J. W. Erwood 5-25-1869 (no return) Hy
Anderson, Levina to Samuel Chambers 11-20-1862 Mn
Anderson, Lois to J. G. Crockett 3-3-1885 (3-4-1885) L
Anderson, Louisa to Jacob Robison 5-23-1867 (no return) Cr
Anderson, Louisa to James Jackson 11-21-1861 Mn
Anderson, Louisa to John Cowgill 5-31-1842 Sh
Anderson, Louisanna I. to A. B. Jones 2-22-1839 Sh
Anderson, Lovie E. N. to Abner F. Pyland 10-6-1869 L
Anderson, Lucina T. to Wm. J. Hendrick 12-31-1849 (1-1-1850) F
Anderson, Lucinda to Bennette Henderson 4-14-1847 (4-15-1847) O
Anderson, Lucrita A. to William H. Cooper 12-14-1838 Ma
Anderson, Lucy F. to J. F. Ivie 2-2-1865 Hy
Anderson, M. C. to F. G. Whitly 3-14-1849 (no return) F
Anderson, M. F. to W. A. Martin 11-21-1874 Hy
Anderson, Mahala to Hugh Sweeney 8-30-1862 (8-31-1862) Ma
Anderson, Malinda to Riley Williams 3-29-1870 Hy
Anderson, Manda to Lewis Ware 8-27-1870 Hy
Anderson, Margaret A. to William Yearout 3-2-1840 Ma
Anderson, Margaret L. to Charles L. Sullivan 5-14-1860 (5-15-1860) Sh
Anderson, Margaret to Samuel A. Calhoun 11-27-1855 (11-28-1855) O
Anderson, Margaret to Wm. Smith 3-23-1875 (3-25-1875) Dy
Anderson, Margrett to Miles Wilson 2-25-1847 Hr
Anderson, Mariah J. to Jackson Walker 12-11-1871 Hy
Anderson, Marry to A. H. Neely 3-25-1847 Cr
Anderson, Martha A. to John M. Justice 5-18-1852 Ma
Anderson, Martha Ann to Saml. Bradford 1-8-1873 (1-11-1873) L B
Anderson, Martha E. C. to R. D. Hill 12-28-1865 G
Anderson, Martha S. to James A. Haley 12-30-1868 Be
Anderson, Martha to Benjamin Read 9-6-1842 (9-8-1842) Ma
Anderson, Martha to James M. Jacobs 12-13-1843 (12-14-1843) Hr
Anderson, Martha to Theophalus W. Allen 11-2-1859 Sh
Anderson, Mary A. M. to William V. Vasser 8-10-1846 Sh
Anderson, Mary A. to G. W. Rone 10-22-1857 Sh
Anderson, Mary A. to George W. Brown 4-23-1860 (4-25-1860) Ma
Anderson, Mary Ann to Abner Moore 6-21-1842 (6-22-1842) Hr
Anderson, Mary Ann to William W. Dew 1-5-1859 Ma
Anderson, Mary Anne to Andrew J. Dunn 6-16-1846 Sh
Anderson, Mary C. to James J. Edwards 10-17-1844 Ma
Anderson, Mary D. to Hasen W. Sherill 11-24-1854 (11-25-1858) We
Anderson, Mary E. to Powell Ford 3-10-1854 (3-13-1854) L
Anderson, Mary E. to Robt. A. Landers 12-17-1869 Ma
Anderson, Mary E. to William C. Oglesby 11-7-1859 (11-9-1859) Sh
Anderson, Mary Elizabeth to Josiah A. Evans 3-26-1854 Be
Anderson, Mary Ella to Emannuel Ashton 3-15-1873 (3-18-1873) L B
Anderson, Mary J. to Christopher Whitson 8-29-1849 (8-30-1849) L
Anderson, Mary Jane to John Nash 7-23-1858 G
Anderson, Mary L. to Elijah Isham 12-6-1841 Sh
Anderson, Mary M. to E. T. Yancy 11-9-1839 F
Anderson, Mary Salaake? to Jacob Perkins 10-11-1831 (10-12-1831) Ma
Anderson, Mary T. to John B. Ruffin 3-12-1856 (3-13-1856) Ma
Anderson, Mary T. to N. R. Yarbrough 12-20-1865 (12-2-1865) Cr
Anderson, Mary to Archibald Hogge 12-18-1833 O
Anderson, Mary to Augustus Tucker 11-23-1867 Hy
Anderson, Mary to Elijah Whitney 2-17-1842 (2-22-1842) F
Anderson, Mary to George Turner 6-28-1839 Sh
Anderson, Mary to T. P. Wiley 8-24-1848 Sh
Anderson, Mary to W. B. Lewellen 1-30-1871 (2-1-1871) Ma
Anderson, Matilda A. to Edward Barnes 5-1-1849 (5-3-1849) Ma
Anderson, Matilda to Henry D. Collins 7-7-1823 7-15-1823 Ma
Anderson, Matilda to Jesse King 12-6-1827 Ma
Anderson, Mattie to James McGarrity 11-2-1874 (11-3-1874) L
Anderson, Melinda A. to Thomas B. Brooks 3-8-1855 Cr
Anderson, Minerva to Robert D. McMillan 10-13-1836 Hr
Anderson, Minirva to John N. Neely 1-28-1833 Hr
Anderson, Miram S. to Samuel Glover 9-8-1858 (9-9-1858) Ma
Anderson, Miriam L. to James Blackman 1-4-1843 (1-5-1843) Ma
Anderson, Mollie J. to Francis W. Watlington 4-26-1867 (4-27-1867) Ma
Anderson, N. C. to G. B. Renalds 2-27-1873 Hy
Anderson, N. J. to G. W. Wood 10-6-1875 O

Brides

Anderson, Nancy C. to John E. Coker 1-2-1866 G
Anderson, Nancy G. to Henry T. Jones 3-6-1855 (3-8-1855) Sh
Anderson, Nancy G. to William J. Crawford 12-9-1860 Hn
Anderson, Nancy to Henry Curran 10-13-1866 Hy
Anderson, Nancy to Solomon Glenn 4-19-1852 (4-25-1852) Ma
Anderson, Narcissa to J.? P. Butler 11-16-1867 (11-17-1867) Cr
Anderson, Narcissa to Thomas Watson 9-20-1859 Ma
Anderson, Octavia D. to Hugh Moore 8-11-1859 (8-14-1859) Hr
Anderson, Parolee to A. Williams 6-5-1849 Sh
Anderson, Permelia J. to Wm. R. Henderson 7-13-1853 (7-14-1853) O
Anderson, Rebecca B. to F. M. Tarkington 10-2-1854 (10-10-1854) Sh
Anderson, Rebecca Jane to Wm. E. Campbell 6-2-1863 (6-4-1863) L
Anderson, Salina to John A. Compton 3-19-1861 (no return) Cr
Anderson, Saluda to Nathaniel L. Jones 12-17-1850 (12-19-1850) Ma
Anderson, Sarah A. to John A. Vincent 1-9-1850 Ma
Anderson, Sarah A. to R. M. Townsend 11-23-1869 T
Anderson, Sarah A. to Samuel Ragsdale 12-23-1873 (12-24-1873) O
Anderson, Sarah B. to P. C. Straylin 5-26-1853 Cr
Anderson, Sarah C. to John H. Carr 1-18-1849 Sh
Anderson, Sarah E. to Archibald Overton 8-16-1859 (8-17-1859) Hr
Anderson, Sarah E. to G. W. Stricklin 5-21-1861 Mn
Anderson, Sarah E. to William W. Lockard 11-7-1853 (11-10-1853) Ma
Anderson, Sarah M. to J. C. Harris 8-10-1865 O
Anderson, Sarah to Alfred King 8-10-1871 Cr
Anderson, Sarah to Calvert Laney 1-19-1846 Ma
Anderson, Sasander to D. M. Simmons 5-16?-1853 Hn
Anderson, Serena to Dutton M. Sweeton 7-19-1836 Hr
Anderson, Sophia to Richard Pain 7-1-1872 (7-4-1872) L B
Anderson, Sophrona to Ed Taliaferro 2-9-1871
Anderson, Sophronia to Franklin Brock 7-12-1853 (7-14-1853) Ma
Anderson, Suck to Rhodes Montague 2-3-1868 (2-9-1868) F B
Anderson, Sue to Wiley P. Sugg 2-8-1868 (2-12-1868) L
Anderson, Susan to Brice L. Garner 12-16-1840 Hr
Anderson, Susan to Jones Williams 1-25-1853 Ma
Anderson, T. A. to J. J. Staton 5-31-1865 Hn
Anderson, Tempence A. to William Rosser 9-7-1854 Ma
Anderson, Temperance Y. to William P. Walker 8-11-1858 Hn
Anderson, Tennessee to Charles Spence 8-23-1866 (8-24-1866) Dy
Anderson, V. M. to Trenton Wells 11-24-1866 (11-28-1866) F
Anderson, V. S. to S. G. Bradford 2-17-1869 (no return) Hy
Anderson, Virginia A. to William H. Croom 2-26-1856 (2-27-1856) Ma
Anderson, Willie B. to W. L. Sangster 11-30-1876 L
Anderton, Mary A. to Wm. J. Tucker 1-9-1861 Sh
Andonon, Mary to Joseph Duncan 11-7-1839 Ma
Andrew, H. A. to B. B. Stone 12-12-1867 G
Andrew, Nancy Jane to Sittlelen Blaylock 1-11-1857 (1-13-1857) We
Andrew, Sarah J. to William Gallimore 10-25-1851 Hn
Andrew, Sarah T. to D. W. S. McGuire 9-14-1858 We
Andrews, Abby to Grasty Mansfield 9-19-1832 (9-25-1832) O
Andrews, Ann to William J. Holoman 11-27-1869 (no return) L
Andrews, C. to D. W. Thompson 3-3-1847 Hr
Andrews, Catharine to James Walker 3-27-1828 Sh
Andrews, Drucilla to Gilbert Hopkins 3-9-1859 (3-10-1859) Ma
Andrews, Elizabeth to B. S. Boyett 9-10-1853 (9-15-1853) G
Andrews, Elizabeth to Daniel Evans 9-28-1852 (9-30-1852) G
Andrews, Elizabeth to Thomas W. Elliot 4-5-1871 Ma
Andrews, Elizabeth to Wm. A. Langley 3-16-1865 (no return) L
Andrews, Georgia to J. A. Lay 11-30-1859 (12-2-1859) Hr
Andrews, Isabella to A. F. Gibbs 5-21-1844 Sh
Andrews, Lenora to Alson G. Winslow 1-28-1853 (1-3-1853?) Ma
Andrews, Lucy A. D. to William G. Bryant 10-4-1859 (10-6-1859) G
Andrews, Lundy to Thomas W. Ewell 10-12-1853 (10-18-1853) Ma
Andrews, M. E. to F. M. Morrison 10-24-1857 (no return) We
Andrews, M. to James McCall 7-27-1866 (no return) F
Andrews, Margaret to David E. Roberts 8-15-1861 Ma
Andrews, Martha E. to John W. Hicks 2-26-1868 (2-27-1868) F
Andrews, Mary Ann to Charles Rittenberry 2-11-1868 G
Andrews, Mary E. to Samuel P. Ming 1-17-1843 Sh
Andrews, Mary G. to John W. Brown 2-22-1871 (2-23-1871) Dy
Andrews, Mary Jane to John Y. Cribbs 8-27-1855 (9-4-1855) G
Andrews, Mary to Miles H. Follis 7-23-1853 G
Andrews, Nancy Jane to Thos. E. Fisher 5-17-1862 (5-18-1862) L
Andrews, Rosa L. to R. B. Hicks 12-19-1866 (no return) F
Andrews, Sallie to C. A. Duncan 12-14-1870 F
Andrews, Sarah C. to William W. Williams 7-10-1864 Mn
Andrews, Susan A. to G. W. Kelley 12-10-1856 We
Andrews, Susan to Daniel Luron 3-18-1840 (3-19-1840) Ma
Anesworth, Elizabeth A. to John R. Williams 12-14-1847 (12-15-1847) F
Angus, Ariadna to Wm. Granville Yarbro 6-23-1851 (6-24-1851) T
Angus, Bettie to Jerry Moten 5-6-1867 (5-7-1867) T
Angus, Caroline E. to Harrison McClamrock 12-16-1844 (12-17-1844) Ma
Angus, Caroline to William Waggener 3-24-1866 T
Angus, Eliza J. P. to Hesekiah Cobb 11-2-1857 (11-3-1857) T
Angus, Elizabeth to George Mann 1-4-1869 (1-10-1869) T
Angus, Jane to H. L. Woodard 1-13-1857 (1-14-1857) T
Angus, Maria to Phil Alston 3-8-1867 (3-10-1867) T
Angus, Ramola N. to Thomas Traylor 1-5-1841 Ma

Anlada, Martha C. to Wm. D. Abbey 10-20-1859 (no return) Cr
Ann M., Grizzard to Wm. H. Poindexter 9-8-1872 Hy
Anna, Clark to Silas Price 5-7-1878 Hy
Anna, Sherron to William Price 9-7-1877 Hy
Anthony, Adeline to John Moorer 1-7-1885 L
Anthony, Alice E. to W. H. Fitzpatrick 7-18-1876 (7-19-1876) L
Anthony, Amelia R. to Archie A. Young 12-18-1878 L
Anthony, Caroline to Daniel Cuningham 12-23-1875 (no return) Hy
Anthony, Cincinnati to T. L. Hamton 8-25-1869 Dy
Anthony, Elizabeth to James A. Rainey 5-19-1858 L
Anthony, Elizabeth to Thomas Walker 1-21-1869 Hy
Anthony, Elizabeth to W. L. Jones 12-22-1869 (12-23-1869) Dy
Anthony, Ellen to James Walker 3-4-1868 Hy
Anthony, Fannie to B. G. Gregory 12-19-1861 L
Anthony, Fannie to Dick Cuningham 1-2-1879 Hy
Anthony, Felicia to Robert S. Porter 10-9-1861 (10-10-1861) L
Anthony, Francis to Claborn Demoss 2-4-1871 (2-5-1871) L
Anthony, Josephine L. to Wm. Linn Anthony 9-11-1872 Hy
Anthony, Julia Ann to Saml. Thompson 7-25-1841 Hr
Anthony, L. N. to A. S. Anthony 11-26-1884 (11-27-1884) L
Anthony, Linnie E. to C. W. Baird 2-18-1878 (no return) Hy
Anthony, Louise to L. C. Moorer 9-22-1874 (9-23-1874) L
Anthony, Lucy to James A. Barbee 1-7-1866 G
Anthony, M. A. to J. A. Anthony 7-11-1877 Dy
Anthony, Malinda to Robert Buck 1-23-1877 Hy
Anthony, Mariah E. to George W. Young, jr. 6-28-1871 L
Anthony, Martha Elizabeth to George W. Fortner 12-22-1852 (12-23-1852) Hr
Anthony, Mary E. to Kenneth Quick 9-16-1867 G
Anthony, Mary Jane to William C. Duncan 12-17-1849 Hr
Anthony, Mattie to Henry Bond 11-17-1874 Hy
Anthony, Patsy to Jordan Jones 5-27-1871 (no return) Hy
Anthony, Rebecca to Asa A. Brown 2-15-1868 Hy
Anthony, S. E. to C. S. Ball 1-17-1868 Hy
Anthony, Sallie M. to John M. Shaw 8-8-1878 Hy
Anthony, Sarah L. to Hugh Brady 9-7-1857 (9-30-1857) Hr
Anthony, Sue M. to H. W. Sanford 2-1-1881 (2-2-1881) L
Anthony, Sue to N. A. Currie 12-11-1866 Hy
Anthony, Susan to Rowland Greer 1-19-1849 (2-6-1849) G
Anthony, Tilda to Jessee Wise 1-12-1877 Hy
Anthony, Topsie to James Robinson 1-23-1877 Hy
Antridge, Eliza Ann to Thomas Edwards 1-2-1863 (12-19-1863?) Sh
Antwine, Lear M. to D. H. Powel 12-6-1860 Sh
Antwine, Sarah E. to James W. Nichols 1-9-1868 (1-12-1868) Dy
Anyon, Jane to Abraham Norman 10-29-1857 Sh
Apleton, Martha A. to Nathaniel M. Hutchins 12-16-1847 (12-18-1847) F
App, Cecilia to Philip Meiler (Wiler) 12-23-1862 Sh
Apperson, C. J. to Henry Dean 12-24-1863 (12-30-1863) Sh
Apperson, Jennie to G. R. Wade 11-23-1863 Sh
Apperson, S. R. to B. Franklin Burford 10-31-1863 Sh
Apperson, Susan A. to G. V. Rambout, jr. 3-5-1860 (3-6-1860) Sh
Appleberry, Elizabeth to James W. Roberts 2-22-1869 (2-24-1869) T
Appleberry, Jane to William F. Newton 11-18-1847 Sh
Appleberry, Martha Ann to P. P. Luckada 1-21-1851 (2-5-1851) Sh
Appleberry, Nancy to Thomas D. Johnson 7-1-1854 (7-20-1854) Sh
Appleberry, P. E. to W. C. Isom 7-20-1864 (7-24-1864) F
Appleberry, Permelia to W. A. Appleberry 12-18-1845 Sh
Appleberry, Sallie to J. P. Royall 9-27-1869 (9-30-1869) F
Appleberry, Tabitha to W. B. Newton 3-18-1856 Sh
Applebury, Nancy to Dorsey Miles 12-14-1839 Sh
Appleby, Martha to T. Walker Allen 5-20-1869 (5-23-1869) Ma
Applegate, Charlotte Ann to Thomas Prather 1-17-1848 (1-18-1848) O
Applegate, Elenor to William Stansbury 8-16-1843 (8-17-1843) O
Applegate, Henrietta C. to Samuel C. Debow 1-19-1859 O
Appleton, R. S. to Burrell Branch 12-18-1847 (no return) F
Appleton, Sally to Joseph Sample 10-7-1850 (no return) F
Applewhite, Jennie to L. J. Clements 5-29-1878 Dy
Applewhite, M. L. to E. R. Garrett 2-1-1873 Dy
Applewhite, Martha W. to T. J. Nettles 8-5-1869 Dy
Applewhite, Mary E. to Alexander Caraway 8-9-1853 (8-12-1853) O
Applewhite, Mazana to Zelman Reed 3-30-1857 (3-31-1857) Sh
Applewhite, Missie to David Scott 12-17-1872 (12-18-1872) Dy
Applewhite, Rebecca to James Blankenship 1-14-1839 O
Applewhite, Sallie to E. J. V. Jones 1-23-1878 Dy
Applewhite, Sarah Jane to Elisha Ogelsbie 12-2-1838 O
Arant, Malinda to Charles Littlejohn 3-31-1840 Hn
Arata, Cecilia to Joseph Reborri 2-13-1858 (2-15-1858) Sh
Arbrough, Jane to William Ward 3-11-1851 (3-13-1851) G
Arbuckle, C. C. to Lewis Graves 12-6-1849 (no return) F
Arbuckle, Catharine to Alexander Smith 11-9-1843 G
Arbuckle, Lucy F. to Robert L. McNees 11-6-1854 (no return) F
Arbuckle, N. J. to W. L. Ship 8-4-1859 (8-10-1859) F
Arbuckle, Sarah A. to Green B. Y. McEwen 11-25-1845 G
Archer, Ann to F. G. N. Motin 5-31-1858 T
Archer, Annie? to Saml. Smith 4-5-1871 T
Archer, Eliz. Mary Isabella to Thomas C. Campbell 12-5-1849 (12-6-1849) T
Archer, Elizabeth to Charles M. Spesard 12-29-1866 (12-30-1866) T
Archer, Ellen to Robert T. Walker 11-27-1859 Hn

Archer, Julia A. to A. S. White 9-6-1875 (9-8-1875) Dy
Archer, Mariah to E. P. Williams 3-29-1838 Sh
Archer, Mary Elam? to E. J. Maxwell 2-11-1856 (2-14-1856) T
Archer, Milley to Manuel Smith 8-30-1866 (8-31-1866) T
Archer, Sarah E. to P. H. Whitt 10-23-1865 Mn
Archey, Annie to James Harvey 1-4-1860 O
Archey, Catharine to B. Smith 2-24-1850 O
Archey, Hannah Jane to David Payne 9-4-1854 O
Archibald, M. H. to J. F. Dickey 12-8-1869 (12-9-1869) Dy
Archibald, Mattie to Harry Truelove 2-9-1876 Hy
Archibald, T. A. to John D. Smith 2-24-1865 (2-28-1865) Dy
Archie?, Mary E. to Henry W. Walker 11-10-1850 Hn
Arelia, Fields to William Plummer 12-26-1877 Hy
Argo, C. S. to R. D. Johns 12-17-1872 (12-19-1872) Cr
Argo, Cary to Joseph Quinn 6-17-1847 Cr
Argo, Kizia M. to Samuel S. Stone 2-10-1848 Cr
Argo, Mary L. to Newton F. Cloid 1-17-1870 Cr
Arington, Martha L. to Coleman J. French 11-15-1860 (11-20-1860) Cr
Arington, Mary to Wesley M. Haise 10-2-1856 Cr
Armer, J. A. to C. W. M. Park 1-3-1861 (1-11-1861) O
Armer, Mary to Wm. Watson 10-26-1839 Be
Armer, Sophia Catherine to G. W. Thacker 9-19-1869 G
Armes, Mary Ann to Alphard Moore 6-29-1865 G
Armfield, Margarett to Ezechal Armstrong 4-19-1839 (4-21-1839) G
Armor, Margaret to Alexander Rhodes 7-17-1835 Hr
Armor, Mary J. to John W. Allison 9-20-1858 O
Armour, Alice to Jno. A. Martin 11-20-1855 (11-21-1855) Sh
Armour, Emily to Tom Stewart 11-18-1865 F B
Armour, Frances to William Laurence 11-4-1847 Sh
Armour, Isabella to J. S. Haden 1-4-1844 (no return) F
Armour, J. H. (Mrs.?) to Argile McVey 12-19-1859 Sh
Armour, Jannitte to Edwin A. Spotswood 5-21-1862 Sh
Armour, Lizzie to John P. Perkins 6-29-1858 (6-30-1858) Sh
Armour, Lydia M. to George Jenkins 2-7-1839 (2-14-1839) Ma
Armour, Margaret to Joseph R. Neal 10-31-1854 (11-9-1854) O
Armour, Mary An to Calvin Beacham 8-?-1842 (no return) F
Armour, Mary C. to John H. Bowen 4-30-1845 S
Armour, Mary J. to William Person 11-6-1860 (11-7-1860) Sh
Armour, Mary W. to E. G. Davidson 11-19-1856 (11-20-1856) Sh
Armstead, Julia V. to Richard G. Day 12-19-1856 Hr
Armstrong, Adaline to Alfred Ray 6-9-1841 O
Armstrong, Ann P. to Edmund Fleming 9-11-1848 (no return) Hn
Armstrong, Arabella to John J. Foreman 9-14-1855 (9-17-1855) Sh
Armstrong, Caroline to William Curtis 3-6-1861 Dy
Armstrong, Clara to Samuel B. Fry 12-31-1853 (no return) Cr
Armstrong, Eliza Ann to Jarvis Emory 6-26-1841 Hn
Armstrong, Eliza to Gilliam Jones 12-30-1867 (12-31-1867) F B
Armstrong, Emely V. to Elisha Rains 12-9-1852 G
Armstrong, Eveline to John Holliday 3-12-1848 (no return) F
Armstrong, Frances J. to Hiram C. Moorman 1-27-1870 F
Armstrong, Jane to Edward H. Bartlett 12-15-1856 Sh
Armstrong, Julia A. to William R. White 3-11-1846 (3-12-1846) G
Armstrong, Julia to John Casson 12-2-1833 Hr
Armstrong, Julia to John Jarel 3-17-1845 Cr
Armstrong, Lila to Bob Turner 5-2-1868 (no return) F B
Armstrong, Louisa (Mrs.) to Peter Gross 12-24-1862 Sh
Armstrong, Louisa to Joseph M. Jolly 1-5-1842 Cr
Armstrong, M. H. to A. J. Lambert 3-29-1879 (4-1-1879) Dy
Armstrong, M. I. to W. F. Drummond 12-26-1851 Cr
Armstrong, Malinda to Zeek Maclin 12-23-1871 (no return) Hy
Armstrong, Malvina to James Carter 12-22-1846 (12-24-1846) Ma
Armstrong, Martha C. to Paul S. Jones 12-23-1847 Hn
Armstrong, Martha to Elijah Rains 11-30-1850 (12-3-1850) G
Armstrong, Mary A. to William L. Coppedge 9-21-1844 (9-?-1844) T
Armstrong, Mary to J. H. Tombs 12-30-1864 Mn
Armstrong, Mary to Martin Dagan 6-6-1860 Sh
Armstrong, Minerva to J. H. McNeill 7-20-1859 (7-21-1859) Sh
Armstrong, Nancy to Tom Wilkerson 7-5-1867 (no return) F B
Armstrong, Parmela to John Williams 11-10-1841 (11-11-1841) G
Armstrong, Polly to John Barbee 12-9-1846 (no return) Hn
Armstrong, Rebecca to S. B. Wise 8-3-1865 Mn
Armstrong, Safronia to John Taber 8-28-1832 Hr
Armstrong, Sallie to A. F. Todd 9-6-1866 Dy
Armstrong, Tennessee to T. J. Carter 12-29-1869 (12-30-1869) Dy
Armstrong, Tibitha to William N. McCain 11-9-1846 (11-11-1846) G
Arn, Margaret J. to James J. Dunlap 9-19-1851 Hn
Arnal, Elizabeth to Richard F. Butler 4-27-1854 (no return) We
Arndt, Cornelia to James H. Pearson 5-7-1861 Sh
Arnett, Jane A. to P. R. McAdoo 12-17-1857 Hn
Arnett, Lucinda to Hugh Morrison 12-22-1869 (12-23-1869) T
Arnett, M. S. to H. H. Dozier 2-5-1873 (2-6-1873) Dy
Arnett, Nancy A. to James T. Russell 1-27-1861 Hn
Arnett, S. M. to J. H. Hudson 2-14-1867 Be
Arnis, Elizabeth S. to George J. Buckingham 12-18-1866 (12-19-1866) Ma
Arnn, Fanney V. to James F. Parker 2-2-1865 Hn
Arnol, Jane to James Alford 1-30-1850 (2-5-1850) G
Arnold, A. E. to F. M. Wilkinson 9-14-1865 G

Arnold, Agnes to Thos. H. Smith 4-27-1841 Cr
Arnold, Amanda to R. M. Brown 1-7-1875 (1-10-1875) Dy
Arnold, Ann I. to Samuel A. Roberts 4-22-1854 G
Arnold, Belle to J. G. McBain 12-15-1864 Sh
Arnold, Caroline Matilda to John T. Bowie 10-28-1874 L
Arnold, Caroline to Joseph Bogin 4-19-1862 G
Arnold, Catherine to Thomas A. Upchurch 10-8-1865 Hn
Arnold, Cyntha C. to Alga Ellis 11-19-1873 L
Arnold, Elizabeth A. to W. G. Clement 10-28-1868 G
Arnold, Elizabeth to R. F. Buttler 4-27-1854 (no return) We
Arnold, Elizabeth to William H. Hall 8-4-1861 G
Arnold, Elizabeth to William McElroy 10-29-1866 Be
Arnold, Ellen M. to John D. Mitchell 3-15-1854 Sh
Arnold, Ellen to J. A. Green 2-20-1873 (2-23-1873) L
Arnold, Emaline to Marion Holland 9-19-1867 Be
Arnold, Emarilla to Calib Cherry 6-17-1876 (6-18-1876) O
Arnold, Emiline to George Fondren 9-29-1870 Hy
Arnold, F. W. to J. W. Hodges 11-2-1865 G
Arnold, Felecana to H. H. Hubbard 10-5-1857 We
Arnold, Frances C. to Benjamin Warmack 9-4-1846 (9-6-1846) G
Arnold, Frances E. to C. B. Forester 4-7-1870 G
Arnold, Francis to James Pafford 11-16-1865 Be
Arnold, Hdy? to S. A. Thomas 11-12-1865 G
Arnold, Jane to G. H. Keaton 11-2-1857 G
Arnold, Lavenia (Mrs.) to Green H. Ramsey 11-1-1869 Ma
Arnold, Lavina to Felix G. Newman 1-7-1842 (no return) L
Arnold, Louisa to John Pafford 10-22-1851 Be
Arnold, Louisa to Joseph Lambert 10-10-1863 Sh
Arnold, Lucendia to George C. Hellard 11-4-1850 G
Arnold, Lucy to James Middlehook 3-5-1867 F
Arnold, M. J. to W. K. Wynn 10-15-1863 Be CC
Arnold, M. J. to W. R. Wynn 10-16-1863 Be
Arnold, M. L. to Wm. A. Cole 1-14-1874 O
Arnold, M. W. to W. W. Whitehead 8-15-1854 (no return) F
Arnold, Mahaly C. to Wm. Boswell 1-9-1850 Be
Arnold, Malinda to Burriss Knight 12-30-1844 We
Arnold, Margaret to Frank Turner 12-21-1870 Dy
Arnold, Margaret to J. J> Durden 7-29-1855 Be
Arnold, Margaret to John Callison 12-10-1860 (no return) We
Arnold, Mariah to Thomas Hollinsworth 11-1-1855 Be
Arnold, Martha A. E. to George W. Arnold 9-27-1873 (9-29-1873) L
Arnold, Martha A. T. to George Shane 11-16-1841 (12-6-1841) G
Arnold, Martha E. to Joseph J. Chaney 10-16-1866 (10-17-1866) F
Arnold, Martha J. to James B. Harris 9-29-1852 Sh
Arnold, Martha to James B. Hains 9-29-1852 Sh
Arnold, Martha to John Williams 1-9-1855 G
Arnold, Martha to N. R. Newell 1-31-1867 G
Arnold, Martha to W. H. Hollomon 11-14-1867 Be
Arnold, Mary A. to R. D. Wade 3-5-1868 Be
Arnold, Mary C. to John W. Thomas 3-20-1864 G
Arnold, Mary E. to N. S. Pierce 8-4-1855 (8-7-1855) G
Arnold, Mary M. to Allen D. Ranken 11-6-1854 (no return) We
Arnold, Mary M. to Allen D. Ranken 11-7-1855 We
Arnold, Mary M. to Robert A. Porter 10-5-1853 (10-6-1853) G
Arnold, Mary N. to William H. Witt 7-2-1845 G
Arnold, Mary to Robert E. Burgess 12-25-1850 (12-31-1850) G
Arnold, Mary to Wm. D. G. Eaves 12-30-1852 Hn
Arnold, Milly to N. B. Hiett 10-20-1869 L
Arnold, N. C. to J. M. Arnold 11-25-1880 L
Arnold, N. C. to W. T. Dunnigan 8-23-1865 G
Arnold, Nancy A. to Mc Rayburn 8-29-1849 O
Arnold, Nancy J. to William Henderson 2-25-1852 G
Arnold, Nancy to Frank Holland 10-9-1869 G
Arnold, Nancy to Herbert A. Ragsdale 7-29-1837 (8-1-1837) G
Arnold, Narcissa to James Bowen 11-2-1870 (no return) Dy B
Arnold, Rebecca to Amos L. Gaskins 6-18-1860 We
Arnold, S. J. to S.D. Ballentine 2-20-1865 G
Arnold, Sarah Ann to Robert Morris 7-10-1850 Be
Arnold, Sarah Ann to William Howard 12-24-1840 Sh
Arnold, Sarah J. to James W. Eastman 9-24-1856 (9-25-1856) Sh
Arnold, Sarah Jane to J. R. Wiggin 4-12-1871 (4-13-1871) Dy
Arnold, Sarah to William Williams 7-2-1853 (7-3-1853) G
Arnold, Sardinia E. to William M. Lourance 5-26-1855 (5-27-1855) G
Arnold, Susan to George Johnson 3-30-1850 Hn
Arnold, Susan to Preston Brackin 2-6-1840 Cr
Arnold, T. to Francis M. Kimbrel 1-15-1860 We
Arnold, William J. to William C. Ree 1-19-1853 G
Aronhart, Rachael to George W. Tatam 5-25-1865 Dy
Aronhart, Rachel to W. F. Lamarr 8-18-1866 Dy
Arrata, Maria to Sebastian Morelli 4-12-1856 (4-13-1856) Sh
Arrington, Ellen to Thos. Russell 6-8-1863 (6-11-1863) Cr
Arrington, Sarah to John F. Fuzzell 12-3-1857 Cr
Artis, Ann Eliza to Henry Clement 12-24-1868 G B
Arun, Judith to William M. Frazier 10-10-1839 (could be 1849) Hn
Arun, Lucy Ann to William B. Berkley 9-5-1855 (no return) Hn
Arun, M. E. to Abram Hudgens 10-16-1855 (no return) Hn
Arun, Sarah E. to William Hudgens 10-11-1858 Hn

Brides

Arun?, Martha to P. M. Huddleston 8-25-1842 Hn
Arwood, Hettie C. to L. M. Vaughan 9-24-1879 L
Arwood, M. S. to Thomas Dennie 3-5-1873 L
Arwood, Mahala Jane to J. W. Childress 2-10-1873 L
Arwood, Mary C. to John Rice 9-22-1869 (no return) L
Asberry, Lucy M. to Simpson Matlock? 8-18-1858 (8-19-1858) O
Asberry, Martha Ann to William Henry 12-13-1853 (12-15-1853) O
Asberry, Nancy C. to Alfred H. Short 3-13-1864 (3-27-1864) O
Asburn, Kitty Ann to Henry C. Hicks 12-10-1855 (12-11-1855) G
Asbury, Carson E. to Smith Kerby 12-17-1866 (12-18-18??) O
Asbury, Emeline to James Dunn 2-28-1848 (no return) L
Ash, Jane to Squire Kilberth 12-12-1837 Be
Ash, Mary to Robt. England 5-29-1867 (no return) Hy
Ash, Sally to Wm. E. Wooten 11-13-1867 Hy
Ash_ow, Mariah to James Johnson 12-30-1870 L
Ashbey, Elizabeth to Hezekiah Pool 4-9-1864 (no return) Hn
Ashbrooks, Elizabeth to Elijah Reaves 5-13-1830 (5-19-1830) O
Ashburn, Malinda to Lewis Thomas 11-27-1843 T
Ashby, Amanda to James R. Mason 9-8-1858 Hn
Ashby, Angelin R. to Alex G. Campbell 9-14-1852 (9-15-1852) Hr
Ashby, Mary Virginia to Levin D. Grant 12-19-1861 Sh
Ashby, Tennie L. to William A. Highfield 12-25-1867 Hn
Ashcraft, Mary to R. J. Mathews 4-4-1864 (4-6-1864) Sh
Ashe, Charity to London DeGraffenried 1-8-1866 (1-13-1866) F B
Ashe, Lucy S. to Weems Wooton 1-9-1871 Hy
Asher, Mary E. C. to Young Kirksey 8-27-1832 G
Ashford, Ann to F. F. Wall 4-23-1857 T
Ashford, Juda C. to W. A. Cook 7-18-1883 (7-19-1883) L
Ashland, Sarah M. to E. G. Seaton 1-1-1867 (no return) Hn
Ashley, Ann to James C. Allcock 12-25-1851 O
Ashley, Elizabeth to James A. Foster 4-21-1861 Hn
Ashley, Luizer to B. B. Watson 12-6-1865 G
Ashley, Mary A. to Wm. H. Dodson 1-23-1860 G
Ashley, Mary to W. P. Wilson 2-11-1866 G
Ashley, Miram to Peter Wyatt 11-2-1869 G B
Ashley, Naomi A. to Richard Ingram 2-28-1856 Sh
Ashley, Sarah J. to John C. Carlton 9-8-1859 G
Ashlock, June to George P. Blane 3-1-1848 Hn
Ashlock, Martha A. to John W. Brannon 1-26-1860 Hn
Ashlock, Mary E. to Hilyard M. Thompson 1-10-1861 Hn
Ashmire, Jennie to Fredrick (Franch) Clemontine 1-21-1873 (1-22-1873) L
Ashmore, Ella to Robert E. Doyle 8-1-1873 (8-3-1873) L
Ashmore, Ida to Eligia Best 7-16-1877 (7-17-1877) L
Ashworth, Sarah to Jas. C. W. Causler 1-4-1869 (1-7-1869) Ma
Asken, Sarah H. to Caswell P. Dill 3-27-1874 Cr
Askew, Celia A. to David C. Tyler 3-1-1869 F
Askew, Elizabeth to William Robertson 4-2-1857 (4-5-1857) O
Askew, Henrietta to James N. Greer 9-13-1858 Ma
Askew, Jane to Charley Murrell 12-31-1869 (no return) F B
Askew, Jane to Joseph Harris 5-15-1869 (no return) F B
Askew, La to George Newsom 6-8-1867 F B
Askew, Lackey Ann to James H. Cunningham 9-26-1853 G
Askew, Lucim to Eli Brown 3-13-1866 W
Askew, Manervey to John A. Doherty 7-4-1854 Be
Askew, Margaret E. to Burkett L. Houghton 1-17-1853 (1-18-1853) Ma
Askew, Margrett E. to R. C. Pierce 2-26-1847 Cr
Askew, Mary J. to David E. Tonage 11-25-1851 (no return) F
Askew, Mattie E. to Jesse A. Darnall 12-15-1868 Ma
Askew, Nancy E. to J. R. Young 11-4-1867 Be
Askew, Rachel to James M. Tomlinson 3-9-1848 Ma
Askew, Virginia A. to Ezekial R. Johnson 10-26-1869 (10-28-1869) Ma
Askew?, Sarah to James Coats 2-26-1858 (no return) L
Aslin, Charity to Presley Waldrop 1-23-1856 G
Asper, Rebecca to Ed Simmons 8-9-1873 (no return) Dy
Asprog, Sarah J. to John S. Eason 12-24-1861 G
Aspy, Mary Ann to Thomas Scott 3-12-1846 Cr
Astin, Josie M. to Samuel B. Kyle 12-12-1868 (12-17-1868) F
Astin, Sallie E. to George F. Dupree 12-12-1868 (12-17-1868) F
Aston, Ann H. to Nathaniel Gordon 4-22-1838 F
Aston, C. H. to Wm. B. Neville 2-3-1851 (2-11-1851) F
Atcherson, Eliza to Jesse Bugg 12-13-1843 Hn
Atcheson, Nancy to James Yarbrough 4-24-1840 Hn
Atcheston, E. H. to Wayne Rye 3-30-1856 Be
Atchison, Harriet to James Murphy 12-23-1869 G B
Atchison, Margaret Ann to Barnabas Gross 7-17-1860 Be
Atchison, Martha Jane to Wm. S. Barger 6-19-1860 Hn
Atchison, Mary Jane to Walker Johnson 10-13-1867 G B
Atchison, Parthenia J. to W. H. Linton 12-2-1860 G
Atchison, Virginia R. to Bolen A. Totty 9-1-1867 Hn
Athens, Christianer to Luke Bowers 4-22-1871 (4-23-1871) F B
Athony, Harriet to Jonas Ellis 7-26-1867 (8-8-1867) L B
Atkenson, Sarah to Walter E. Daniel 7-6-1838 G
Atkerson, Harriett to Wm. M. Morris 1-30-1859 He
Atkins, Amanda E. to Matthew T. Bowden 11-13-1850 Hn
Atkins, Artimesia (Miss) to V. A. Sanders 1-4-1864 Sh
Atkins, D. C. to B. R. Stafford 4-26-1854 (no return) F
Atkins, E. J. to Charley Hill 8-25-1873 (no return) Dy

Atkins, Elizabeth Ann to James Leslie 8-18-1832 (8-19-1832) Hr
Atkins, Frances to Lemuel Boggess 10-24-1848 Hn
Atkins, Francis to Miles Wood 10-20-1845 We
Atkins, H. A. to F. G. Mason 12-13-1865 (12-14-1865) Dy
Atkins, Hollandberry to Pleasant P. Saunders 8-26-1846 (8-27-1846) F
Atkins, J. P. to W. H. Hinson 9-27-1867 G
Atkins, Jane to Tazwell Travis 5-20-1866 W
Atkins, Juby Ann to Joseph Witt 9-8-1842 (no return) Hn
Atkins, Julia to Tobe Porter 4-17-1867 (no return) Hn B
Atkins, Lean to Henry Hall 1-15-1877 (no return) Dy
Atkins, Louisa to Harvey Trotter 4-3-1844 Sh
Atkins, M. J. to J. F. Smith 11-20-1872 T
Atkins, M. to Vergil McAdoo 12-22-1855 (no return) Hn
Atkins, Margaret to Charles Bobbitt 11-23-1846 (12-1-1846) F
Atkins, Margaret to David Pettis 10-4-1871 (10-5-1871) Dy
Atkins, Mariah to Lewis Albea 12-30-1866 G
Atkins, Martha F. to Jos. H. Standley 12-26-1859 Hy
Atkins, Martha Jane to Daniel Harris 10-27-1866 (10-28-1866) Ma
Atkins, Martha to Charles Bradley 4-22-1851 He
Atkins, Mary A. to Solomon Jones 4-11-1867 (no return) Hn
Atkins, Mary E. to G. L. Brooks 12-16-1857 We
Atkins, Mary to John Wray 10-27-1859 (11-3-1859) F
Atkins, Mary to Joseph L. Rosson 6-9-1858 (6-29-1858) Hr
Atkins, Matilda to Alexander Huntsman 10-11-1849 Hn
Atkins, Nancy A. to William Simpson 3-30-1856 We
Atkins, Nancy S. to Will S. Lawso 11-30-1846 Hn
Atkins, Raines to Daniel Cobert 3-13-1875 O
Atkins, Rebecca to William Shotwell 2-7-1839 Hn
Atkins, Rosie to Joshua Teague 5-21-1866 (no return) Hn B
Atkins, Sarah B. to James E. Boon 3-11-1845 G
Atkins, Sarah E. to Levi T. Simpson 3-26-1856 We
Atkins, Susan Amanda to C. L. Chambers 7-4-1861 Mn
Atkinson, Anon to Michl. Ledwith 12-20-1852 Sh
Atkinson, Bettie to G. B. Peterson 4-28-1884 (4-30-1884) L
Atkinson, Elizabeth (Mrs.) to J. W. Dillehay 12-21-1864 (12-22-1864) Sh
Atkinson, Elizabeth to Wm. S. Daugherty 1-9-1846 (1-11-1846) Hr
Atkinson, Esther A. to David Diggs 8-6-1874 O
Atkinson, Lucinda to George Holden 12-20-1869 (12-23-1869) F B
Atkinson, Martha to Clem Pulliam 12-30-1852 Hr
Atkinson, Mary A. to John Trulove 8-5-1843 Sh
Atkinson, Mary E. to Jno. E. Mastin 10-20-1848 (10-26-1848) Hr
Atkinson, Mary to John L. James 5-19-1867 G
Atkinson, Nancy J. to A. H. Green 1-15-1855 (1-18-1855) Hr
Atkinson, S. A. to C. A. Ellis 12-15-1884 (12-24-1884) L
Atkinson, Sarah to Elias Chambers 12-22-1866 (12-23-1866) F
Atkinson, Serena to George W. Willi 1-5-1847 (1-6-1847) Hr
Atkison, Malissa to Charles Phillips 8-27-1869 Cr
Atterberry, Adelia to Archibald Reid 3-6-1855 O
Attkisson, Mary E. to Claudius L. Milan 6-24-1868 (6-25-1868) Ma
Attmson, Martha to William V. Foutch 2-12-1852 G
Atts(Alts), Celia to James R. Smith 8-18-1830 (8-19-1830) Hr
Attwood, Frances to William C. White 6-22-1838 (6-24-1838) Hr
Atty, Ann Eveline Van to Matthew M. Garrison 7-24-1849 (7-26-1849) G
Atwell, Anne Maria Bernard to James Peter Fenegan 6-5-1861 Sh
Atwell, Margaret L. to James Burke 9-7-1861 (9-8-1861) Sh
Atwell, Nancy to James D. Cook 1-8-1850 (1-9-1850) Hr
Auff, Elizabeth to John H. Alexander 3-5-1846 Hn
Aughey, V. R. to R. K. Knight 7-8-1854 Sh
Auker, Carrie to Emanuel Felsenthal 1-15-1873 Hy
Auker, Hannah to Emanuel Tamm 2-4-1874 Hy
Aulford, Phebe A. to Jesse P. Dugger 5-14-1845 (5-15-1845) Hr
Aulsup, Lucinda to Francis M. Forbes 7-2-1870 (7-4-1870) F
Aulton, Rebecca to William Baty 4-8-1843 (4-9-1843) Hr
Aurenchine, H. S. to Albert Nicler 6-26-1873 (no return) Cr
Ausbon, Mary Susan to Wm.H. Landadal 3-21-1872 T
Auslian, N. M. to C. C. Hammonds 11-3-1860 G
Austen, Ada to Henry Stewart 2-24-1882 (no return) L
Austin, Adaline to Lisbon Dudley 4-28-1878 Hy
Austin, Adeline to Ambrose Rucker 1-31-1872 Hy
Austin, Aggy to Edward Yarbrok 2-17-1858 (2-18-1858) T
Austin, Ellen to Freeman Rice 3-26-1878 L B
Austin, Eviline F. to H. L. Harris 10-24-1859 (no return) We
Austin, Isabella to Sandy Read 8-17-1878 Hy
Austin, Kate E. to J. A. McNeill 1-9-1865 (1-10-1865) F
Austin, Lizer J. to Wilson Austin 7-16-1865 G
Austin, Martha Ann to James R. Osteen 12-19-1859 L
Austin, Mary A. to Robt. A. Rice 12-17-1871 (12-19-1871) T
Austin, Mary E. to William C. Ray 11-28-1855 L
Austin, Mary L. to James Haygood 12-5-1857 (no return) We
Austin, Mary P. to Jas. N. Watt 12-6-1858 (12-12-1858) G
Austin, Nannie (Mamie?) to John T. Bibb 11-28-1883 L
Austin, Paralee to Daniel F. B. Abernathy 4-7-1861 We
Austin, Polly to Wiley King 1-18-1849 Be
Austin, Sarah E. to Richard Strouse 12-31-1867 (1-1-1868) L
Austin, Sarah S. to F. T. Bennett 1-7-1852 We
Austin, Susan to G. W. Holland 12-25-1865 (12-27-1865) Dy
Austin, Vinie to Buck Williams 2-11-1875 Hy

Austin, Winnie to William Warmic 2-10-1878 Hy
Auston, Emily to John Gillis 12-6-1843 Sh
Auten, F. L. to G. M. Boles 1-8-1863 Mn
Autney, Hannah to Govner Burdon 12-27-1870 Hy
Autney?, Fannie to Jim Bond 12-22-1867 Hy
Autrey, Sarah S. to Frederick C. Guthrie 2-27-1856 (2-28-1856) O
Autry, Eliza A. to Wm. D. Flowers 3-12-1856 Cr
Autry, Eliza to Samuel Hedge 7-20-1845 Cr
Autry, Froney to Wm. Pedigrew 2-23-1850 Cr
Autry, L. R. to J. C. Haywood 6-21-1867 (6-23-1867) Cr
Autry, Margaret to John Singleton 7-27-1854 Cr
Autry, Mary M. to Robt. P. Hall 11-7-1871 (11-8-1871) Cr
Autry, Melinda to Mark Roberts 11-2-1856 Cr
Autry, Millie to Milton Mahan 12-30-1870 Hy
Autry, Nancy E. to Philip H. West 12-17-1858 (not executed) Ma
Autry, Nancy to Thomas S. Jones 11-9-1845 (11-12-1845) O
Autry, Nancy to Thos. S. Jones (Janes) 11-9-1846 (11-12-1846) O
Autry, Rebecca Ann to Wesley King 8-1-1838 Sh
Autry, Rebecca to Everett R. Ritter 9-7-1840 Cr
Autry, S. L. to H. Langford 7-8-1867 O
Autry, Thiaza to James Grisham 5-8-1830 (5-15-1830) Hr
Avann, Rebecca to Alexander McDonald 9-8-1837 (9-14-1837) Hr
Avant, Anna D. to Wm. L. R. Johnson 8-22-1861 Hr
Avant, Jane to James Vickers 12-23-1846 (12-24-1846) Hr
Avant, Mary to N. B. Sallier 12-18-1844 (12-19-1844) Hr
Avant, Sarah J. to James H. Marshall 11-6-1854 (11-15-1854) Hr
Avenshire, Mary to John H. Allen 2-3-1848 Cr
Avent, Eliza M. C. to John H. Gates 11-23-1852 (11-25-1852) Hr
Avent, Mary to William McClend(McLeod?) 3-21-1847 Hr
Averet, George A. to Peter Booth 4-6-1869 Hy
Averett, Cynthia to B. F. Southern 5-14-1859 (5-15-1859) F
Averett, Delila to R. W. Robinson 8-22-1833 Hr
Averett, Lucy A. to John C. Portis 11-23-1855 (no return) F
Averett, Lucy A. to W. H. Largent 11-26-1860 (12-5-1860) F
Averett, Martha R. to George S. Davidson 12-30-1867 (12-31-1867) Dy
Averett, Martha to Thomas J. Martindale 7-8-1833 Hr
Averett, Mary J. to G. M. Crook 5-2-1854 (no return) F
Averett, V. E. to S. P. Glenn 1-28-1868 Hy
Averitt, Martha to B. F. Sutherland 1-24-1866 Hy
Avery, A. M. to J. A. Atertwim 12-5-1866 G
Avery, A. M. to J. A. Atutwim 12-5-1866 G
Avery, Adaline to Ben Sinclair 9-28-1871 (no return) Dy
Avery, Alace to Armstead Gray 6-28-1872 T
Avery, Amanda A. to Nathl. M. Trezevant 11-30-1848 Sh
Avery, Ann to J. P. Stott 10-3-1845 Sh
Avery, E. Jane to J. Thomas Boswell 1-7-1860 (1-8-1860) G
Avery, E. V. to W. S. Lanier 8-18-1869 Hy
Avery, Eliza to John G. Warren 3-25-1831 G
Avery, Elizabeth E. to Minor Meriwether 1-5-1852 Sh
Avery, Elizabeth to William G. Triplet 10-30-1863 Mn
Avery, Emly A. M. to Absolum H. Tatum 3-7-1855 (3-9-1855) G
Avery, Emma E. to Thomas Crooms 10-15-1859 (no return) Hy
Avery, Estella to Spencer H. Lamb 11-8-1849 Sh
Avery, F. D. to H. C. Booth 1-2-1860 (1-4-1860) G
Avery, Harriett A. T. to J. T. J. Avery 10-2-1848 G
Avery, Harriett to Henry B. Hardy 10-31-1854 Hn
Avery, Henrietta S. (Mrs.) to John H. Bowen 7-19-1864 (7-20-1864) Sh
Avery, J. R. to J. W. McDonald 6-24-1875 Hy
Avery, Jannie to Aaron Alston 7-10-1869 (7-13-1869) T
Avery, Lidda J. to A. Britt 8-17-1865 (no return) Hy
Avery, Martha A. P. to James B. Tatum 12-29-1857 (12-31-1857) G
Avery, Martha to Levi Thacker 3-23-1867 (3-24-1867) Ma
Avery, Mary N. W. to Daniel McLane 4-1-1845 (4-3-1845) G
Avery, Mary to F. M. Luscombe 3-24-1849 Sh
Avery, Mollie to Shade Bass 3-14-1874 T
Avery, Nancy J. to J. S. Lanier 7-10-1867 Hy
Avery, Nancy to Westley Christopher 3-26-1851 Hn
Avery, Patsey to Riley Cates 10-15-1867 G B
Avery, R. A. to C. A. Boswell 3-28-1865 G
Avery, Ritta to Thomas Hudson 6-6-1867 G B
Avery, Sarah A. E. to Henry Babb 11-28-1842 G
Avery, Sarah E. to Archibald C. McDougald 2-5-1845 G
Avery, Sarah E. to D. B. Hall 9-11-1858 G
Avery, Sarah to Zackriah Fleming 11-13-1860 (no return) Hy
Avery, Sary to Patrick Boyd 4-8-1863 Mn
Avery, Susan E. to S. A. Greable 10-25-1866 Hy
Avery, Susan to Spencer Wall 11-18-1850 Hn
Avery, Unia to James Pate 2-13-1843 G
Avery, Wineford to F.L. W. McEwen 8-7-1829 (8-20-1829) G
Avrett, Margaret to James H. Kizer 3-6-1864 Mn
Avry, Lucas to W. T. Coker 8-4-1874 Hy
Avry, Sally to Solomon Elrod 1-26-1860 (no return) Hy
Axly, Sophronia to R. H. McCord 11-14-1865 (11-16-1865) L
Axsom, Elizabeth to John F. Riley 8-3-1859 (8-7-1859) Sh
Aycock, A. C. to Henry M. Rose 7-15-1866 Hy
Aycock, Elizabeth to George W. Wharton 7-29-1851 Hn
Aycock, N. A. to Richard D. Collins 2-21-1861 Hn

Aycres, Lucinda to James Holmes 11-1-1841 (no return) Hn
Aydlote, Mary Eliza to James Johnson 10-29-1857 Sh
Aydlotte, Martha Ann E. to Richmond W. Yarbrough 11-6-1852 (11-7-1852) Sh
Ayeres, Jane to John B. Clack 12-9-1856 (12-10-1856) O
Ayeres, Jelpha Ann to John W. Smith 11-7-1856 (11-8-___) O
Ayers, Adaline to Jas. M. Webster 8-8-1832 (9-11-1832) Hr
Ayers, Amanda M. to William G. Fulps 2-21-1854 Hr
Ayers, Elizabeth C. to Wm. R. Holyfield 7-8-1839 Hr
Ayers, Louisa I. to Patrick F. Robinson 11-29-1850 (11-30-1850) Hr
Ayers, Lucinda E. to Charles S. Robertson 5-12-1852 (6-12-1852) Hr
Ayers, M. E. to W. F. Steele 1-10-1876 (1-12-1876) Dy
Ayers, Manna E. to Edmond Wade 7-30-1829? Hr
Ayers, Manna to Edwin Wade 7-30-1832 (8-8-1832) Hr
Ayers, Martha C. to E. G. Smothers 1-15-1859 Cr
Ayers, Mary J. to Isaac N. Thompson 3-9-1840 (3-12-1840) Hr
Ayers, Nancy E. to Henry Taylor 1-28-1874 (1-29-1874) Dy
Aynesworth, Caroline M. to John Limbarger 8-25-1841 (8-29-1841) F
Ayres, L. J. to W. L. B. Cook 2-12-1856 Sh
Ayres, Laura M. to Charles McCormick 2-15-1860 (2-16-1860) Sh
Ayres, Martha to John Y. Reed 2-18-1840 Hr
Ayres, Mary G. (Mrs.) to Thos. H. Todd 2-13-1856 Sh
Ayres, Mary Jane to James M. S. Jemerson 10-4-1838 F
Ayres, Matilda E. to Joseph C. Wheless 4-5-1853 Sh
Ayres, Sarah Green to Isaac Neal 7-9-1858 (7-11-1858) O

B____?, Nancy to Waid Mitchell 5-11-1857 Cr
Babb, Ann to David Arun 6-14-1853 Hn
Babb, Ann to William T. Cook 3-6-1864 Mn
Babb, Clarissa to William M. Frazier 1-14-1846 Hn
Babb, E. L. C. to R. T. Smith 12-7-1865 G
Babb, Elizabeth F. to Daniel F. Tipton 10-15-1860 Hn
Babb, Jane C. to F. A. Bryant 9-16-1861 Mn
Babb, M. A. L. to W. A. Powers 8-13-1884 (8-14-1884) L
Babb, Margaret E. to Andrew T. Henson 1-28-1850 (1-29-1850) Hr
Babb, Margarett to James Huff 7-7-1850 O
Babb, Martha A. L. to J. D. W. Lamar 1-14-1869 G
Babb, Mary Jane to James Carter 9-21-1847 Hn
Babb, Mary to John Fitzpatrick 9-17-1865 Mn
Babb, Mary to W. M. Sheneer 2-8-1867 G
Babb, Nancy H. to W. H. Mitchell 3-4-1864 Mn
Babb, Polly to R. T. S. Avery 10-13-1836 Hr
Babb, Roena to Kenion Williams 10-21-1870 G
Babb, Sarah to Isaac L. Shelby 11-26-1849 (11-29-1849) O
Babcox, Mary to Wiley Bridjman 8-19-1845 We
Baber, Ann (Mrs.) to William Taylor 11-21-1864 Sh
Baber, Eliza M. to W. H. Scrape 10-9-1862 Hn
Baber, Elizabeth to Eaton Roach 2-18-1849 Be
Baber, Lucy A. to Munroe B. Elder 11-2-1837 G
Baber, Sarah J. to Stephen Holowell 12-9-1852 Be
Bacchus, Henrietta to John W. Dowdy 12-20-1854 Hn
Bacigalupo, C. to John Peagio 4-22-1854 (4-24-1854) Sh
Backus, Minnie F. to A. B. Burr 1-15-1861 Sh
Bacon, Amy to Lemuel D. Simmons 9-17-1842 Ma
Bacon, Kate L. to Thomas D. Berry 12-16-1867 O
Bacon, Mattie L. to E. R. Oldham 12-5-1876 (12-6-1876) L
Bacyas?, Eliza to William S. Calhoon 4-2-1867 T
Badaw, Amanda to Cloyd Williams 12-29-1869 (no return) F B
Badgett, Mary to George A. Finch 12-31-1864 Dy
Badwell, Bell to William Burks 12-24-1866 (12-25-1866) T
Bagby, Elizabeth H. to R. E. D. Smith 1-11-1848 Hn
Bagby, Elizabeth P. to George Wahls 3-1-1871 (3-2-1871) Cr
Bagby, Martha Jane to Thomas C. Bell 1-9-1849 (no return) Hn
Bagby, Mary E. to William M. Daughtry 4-7-1877 (4-8-1877) L
Bagdale (Ragsdale?), F. to Thos. R. Seymore 1-11-1855 (1-12-1855) Sh
Bagg, Harriett C. to Jordon Soloman 10-22-1850 Cr
Baggett, Cath to James Nowell 10-12-1847 Be
Baggett, Martha H. to Wm. N. Ballowe 9-9-1850 Be
Baggett, Nancy E. to J. C. Bate__ 6-1-1856 Be
Baggett, Paralee to Hardy Hatley 1-2-1853 Be
Baggett, Polly to Wm. Crabb 8-6-1844 Be
Baggett, Sarah to William Hogg 9-9-1846 Be
Baggett, Susan M. to James H. Hogg 8-25-1853 Be
Bagley, Elizabeth to Edward C. Ford 8-30-1845 (9-25-1845) F
Bagley, Emily G. to Robt. A. Boyd 11-8-1858 (11-11-1858) Hr
Bagley, Fred E. to H. J. Forbers 8-31-1861 (9-5-1861) Hr
Bagwell, E. J. to L. H. Kesterson 6-10-1865 (6-14-1865) O
Bagwell, Martha to James F. Fisk 7-9-1863 O
Bailess, Martha E. to Pinkney B. Rowland 11-25-1865 (11-26-1865) Cr
Bailey, A. G. R. to James Clark 11-19-1847 We
Bailey, Amanda to Lewis Rice 8-26-1873 Hy
Bailey, Ann W. to John McSwine 2-19-1852 (no return) F
Bailey, Ann to Morris Tucker 2-5-1878 Hy
Bailey, Berta to Clifton J. Haynes 9-7-1878 Hy
Bailey, Catharine M. to Wm. Henry Lake 5-22-1854 (5-23-1854) Sh
Bailey, Cela Ann to William Stewart 2-12-1849 (2-17-1849) Hr
Bailey, Cornelia to Bryant Cox 10-17-1851 (10-23-1851) Hr
Bailey, Dizia Ann to Jeremiah Bailey 6-22-1857 (6-23-1857) Ma

Bailey, E. J. to J. L. Ferguson 11-29-1850 Hr
Bailey, Elenora to J. T. Dudney 11-4-1867 (11-6-1867) F
Bailey, Eliza F. to Wm. B. Booker 2-12-1862 (no return) Hy
Bailey, Eliza Jane to Daniel H. Caviness 12-23-1851 (1-1-1852) Hr
Bailey, Eliza Jane to James F. Grant 12-25-1870 (12-28-1870) Ma
Bailey, Eliza N. to Peleg Bailey 9-13-1832 G
Bailey, Elizabeth M. to John T. Shroat 9-26-1858 Hn
Bailey, Elizabeth to John D. Ussy(Ussery?) 2-8-1848 (2-17-1848) Hr
Bailey, Elizabeth to John J. Price 8-7-1858 Sh
Bailey, Elizabeth to R. K. Morrison 3-13-1866 F
Bailey, Ellen J. to Daniel H. Strook 1-5-1854 (no return) Hn
Bailey, Emily H. S. to Cyrus Black 11-20-1843 Hr
Bailey, Emily to Thos. W. Kenner 3-17-1868 (3-18-1868) Ma
Bailey, Hannah to Thomas Harrison 5-24-1842 Sh
Bailey, Harriet E. to Jeremiah Woodworth 12-26-1853 Sh
Bailey, Jane to E. J. Smith 10-2-1867 (no return) F
Bailey, Jane to Pleasant Colvard 6-28-1826 (6-29-1826) Hr
Bailey, Julia to Charley Logan 7-18-1882 (7-23-1882) L
Bailey, Lavenia to Daniel Mann 10-23-1875 (no return) Hy
Bailey, Louisa to C. H. Stephens 11-11-1844 (11-14-1844) Hr
Bailey, Louisa to George Love 12-27-1876 (no return) L B
Bailey, Louise to J. E. Carroll 12-23-1861 (12-24-1861) O
Bailey, Lucinda G. to Cladius C. Jones 9-1-1834 Hr
Bailey, Lucy to Chas. Gist 9-28-1869 (9-29-1869) T
Bailey, Luvenia to A. O. Prewett 2-16-1859 (2-17-1859) Hr
Bailey, M. A. to W. Maclin 6-10-1877 Hy
Bailey, Mahala to John T. Hodges 3-11-1836 Hr
Bailey, Malissa to John C. Cogburn 10-15-1862 G
Bailey, Margaret to Alexander Chamberlin 12-2-1863 (12-3-1863) Cr
Bailey, Maria to Elijah Howard 3-7-1867 Hn B
Bailey, Maria to Thomas Hudson 3-7-1867 Hn B
Bailey, Martha A. to William P. Walker 9-23-1852 (9-24-1852) Ma
Bailey, Martha Ann to Elijah H. Carter 6-15-1867 (6-16-1867) Ma
Bailey, Martha C. to Elijah Bailey 12-28-1866 (12-31-1866) Ma
Bailey, Martha to John James 12-14-1868 (12-17-1868) F
Bailey, Martha to Reubin Stone 4-13-1835 Hr
Bailey, Mary A. to John W. Hammonds 11-20-1850 Hn
Bailey, Mary E. to John F. Rives 5-14-1846 Ma
Bailey, Mary J. to Moses H. Grantham 5-18-1860 Hr
Bailey, Mary Jane to Samuel Henderson 5-31-1849 Hn
Bailey, Mary K. to Abner Johnson 5-23-1867 (6-3-1867) Ma
Bailey, Mary W. to James Walker 10-19-1836 (10-18?-1836) O
Bailey, Mary to John Kipp 3-8-1862 Hn
Bailey, Mary to Nelson Peete 3-29-1883 L
Bailey, Mary to Robert H. Childs 1-29-1854 (1-19?-1854) Hr
Bailey, Mary to Samuel Allen 6-4-1831 Sh
Bailey, Milley to Charlie Green 9-9-1876 (no return) L B
Bailey, Millie E. to J. H. Mead 6-10-1871 (6-11-1871) Dy
Bailey, Nancy E. to Felix Z. Johnson 5-23-1867 (6-6-1867) Ma
Bailey, Nancy to Hugh S. Todd 2-16-1864 (no return) Cr
Bailey, Roan to Willis Houston 1-17-1859 (1-19-1859) F
Bailey, Rose to Henry Graves 10-29-1849 Hy
Bailey, Sarah A. to William A. Winn 12-19-1866 (12-25-1866) Ma
Bailey, Sarah E. to Jacob E. Williams 11-8-1855 Sh
Bailey, Sarah to James Curley 7-31-1878 (8-1-1878) L
Bailey, Susan P. M. to C. C. Davidson 7-13-1834 O
Bailey, Susan to George Roberts 4-25-1844 Hn
Bailey, Tennessee to W. C. Burnham 9-21-1875 (9-22-1875) Dy
Bailgar (Bilgar?), Mary F. to Cyrus J. Bailey 8-6-1864 Sh
Baily, A. H. to John Kilzer 9-16-1866 G
Baily, Dyzer to James Taylor 2-7-1878 Hy
Baily, Eliza J. to Stanley D. Cobern 3-18-1866 Hy
Baily, Ellen to Solomon A. Baily 4-5-1854 (4-13-1854) G
Baily, Jane to William D. McDermet 4-10-1832 G
Baily, Lacy to John Oliver 6-16-1853 G
Baily, Lucy to Wm. Patterson 3-5-1873 (no return) Hy
Baily, M. M. to E. K. Pitts 8-21-1865 G
Baily, Nellie to Aaron Taylor 12-29-1869 Hy
Baily, R. E. to Harris Bailey 12-28-1859 F
Baily, Tempy A. to J. W. Jones 5-14-1868 (5-15-1868) Dy
Bain, Elizabeth to John D. Little 2-5-1829 (2-17-1829) G
Bain, Josie to J. B. Lucas 11-20-1878 Hy
Bain, M. A. to W. L. Macon 11-29-1871 Hy
Bain, Margaret Ann to William T. Land (Laird) 12-23-1847 Sh
Bain?, Mary R. to Joseph S. Harris 11-11-1850 (11-12-1850) T
Baine, Menervia to Isaac Anderson 7-22-1868 (no return) Hy
Baines (Barnes?), July Florence Cath. to Thomas J. Childress 3-19-1874 L
Baines (Barnes?), Nancy C. to Thomas E. Alston 9-15-1852 (9-16-1852) L
Baines, L. A. to J. A. Pringle 9-30-1867 O
Baines, Lila to Henry May 1-7-1828 Hr
Bainey, Sarah J. to Porter Gibson 5-8-1863 (5-17-1863) Cr
Bains, Hannah to Daniel Butler 10-29-1860 Ma
Bains, Joanna to George Smith 10-12-1878 (no return) L B
Baird (Bird), Christian to William Furlong 12-20-1849 O
Baird, Alice to J. B. Flippin 12-30-1869 G
Baird, Ann to James A. Littlefield 8-4-1846 Sh
Baird, Anne to Eli McGinnis 3-27-1868 G B

Baird, Belle to R. T. Perkins 8-8-1870 F
Baird, C. A. to T. O. Holloway 2-21-1867 Hy
Baird, C. R. to C. H. Bryant 12-21-1878 (12-22-1878) L
Baird, Drucilla A. to J. W. Smith 11-24-1860 G
Baird, Eliza Ann to William sr. McQuiston 7-23-1844 (7-25-1844) T
Baird, Eliza S. to Rufus S. Joiner 4-15-1845 Sh
Baird, Elizabeth L. to W. R. Lanhann 1-31-1855 (2-1-1855) G
Baird, Elizabeth to Charles Bland 1-30-1860 (no return) Hy
Baird, Elizabeth to J. L. McDaniel 6-6-1861 T
Baird, Elvira J. to N. Couch 1-27-1858 G
Baird, Hannah to Ben Jones 2-22-1867 (2-23-1867) F B
Baird, Isabella to Oliver Shivers 11-16-1866 (11-25-1866) F B
Baird, Julia to John Bates 2-1-1867 (2-2-1867) F B
Baird, Lamiza Ann to Joseph C. Stark 4-22-1847 F
Baird, Martha to Aron L. Hurley 10-20-1856 L
Baird, Mary A. to W. T. White 12-14-1866 G
Baird, Mary to Andy Bowers 7-6-1867 (no return) F B
Baird, Mary to William H. Morris 8-6-1840 (8-13-1840) G
Baird, N. A. to C. M. Teague 10-27-1860 (10-30-1860) F
Baird, Nancy to Gideon Goodrich 2-13-1862 G
Baird, Phoeba to Richard Spaulding 10-8-1870 F B
Baird, Rosannah L. to Woodson Rountree 6-18-1838 G
Baird, Sallie to Jno. Herron 8-5-1868 (8-6-1868) F B
Baird, Sarah J. to James M. Baird 6-21-1852 G
Baird, V. A. to W. H. Walker 7-20-1869 G
Baird, artha to Christopher Simonton 8-31-1853 T
Baisinger, Sarah M. to Josiah L. Horn 9-15-1847 G
Baison, Lizzie to Mitchell Sullivan 4-24-1878 Hy
Bake, Louise to Louis F. Eilert 7-6-1858 Sh
Baker, Adaline to B. H. Nunn 11-14-1850 Sh
Baker, Amanda to G. W. Mason 11-17-1864 Mn
Baker, Amanda to Thomas Baker 10-9-1865 Hn
Baker, Angelina to George W. Laws 9-13-1850 Ma
Baker, Ann E. to Emanuel Turnage 5-22-1848 Sh
Baker, Ann E. to Mosel C. Danniel 12-13-1867 (12-15-1867) T
Baker, Ann to Albert Willis 2-7-1850 Ma
Baker, Anne to James W. Jackson 9-23-1850 (9-25-1850) Ma
Baker, Anney to John Blanchet 2-28-1844 G
Baker, Becky Jane to George W. Piercy 5-26-1856 Ma
Baker, Betcy Ann to Calven Jones 2-16-1865 (no return) Dy
Baker, Bettie to John W. Williams 5-4-1878 (5-5-1878) L
Baker, Caroline to B. F. Henwood 12-12-1879 (12-12-1880?) L
Baker, Caroline to George W. Wheeler 9-10-1867 Be
Baker, Catharine to Reddick Jones 5-16-1861 Dy
Baker, Catherina to Frederick Bigord 1-8-1857? (1-8-1856?) Sh
Baker, Catherine to Peter K. Norton 1-9-1839 (1-10-1839) Hr
Baker, Celia to John Johnson 8-16-1869 G
Baker, Charlotte to Edwin Brooks 9-2-1840 T
Baker, Clementine to Louis C. Cooper 1-28-1861 Hn
Baker, Cynthia to William Burton 9-12-1829 Hr
Baker, Dorothy Ann (Mrs.) to Wm. H. McCook 3-18-1871 (3-19-1871) Ma
Baker, E. F. to E. W. Webb 10-18-1879 (10-19-1879) Dy
Baker, Eliza J. to Miles Wood 4-2-1840 T
Baker, Eliza Jane to James F. Edington 10-1-1866? Be
Baker, Eliza L. to Joseph Kail 1-20-1860 (1-24-1860) Sh
Baker, Elizabeth F. to Jessee Blancett 11-21-1843 G
Baker, Elizabeth J. to L. L. Barber 6-4-1869 F
Baker, Elizabeth N. to John L. Davis 8-25-1840 O
Baker, Elizabeth V. to Wilson Williams 10-1-1859 (10-2-1859) Ma
Baker, Elizabeth to Edwin McLemore 1-28-1845 Hn
Baker, Elizabeth to James L. Lusby 12-16-1841 (12-23-1841) F
Baker, Elizabeth to Jonathan Wright 1-29-1844 Hn
Baker, Elizabeth to Thomas J. Warmack 9-18-1867 Be
Baker, Elizabeth to W. T. Lockard 3-19-1863 (no return) L
Baker, Elizabeth to Warren W. Dew 2-18-1867 (3-12-1867) Ma
Baker, Elizabeth to William W. Gallion 12-22-1853 G
Baker, Emeline to W. B. Houseman 4-11-1876 (4-23-1876) L
Baker, Emily L. to James Faulk 10-31-1844 G
Baker, Emly A. to James A. Connell 1-22-1851 (1-23-1851) G
Baker, Frances to Adam Davis 9-13-1855 G
Baker, Gemima N. to Jefferson H. Legate 3-30-1842 O
Baker, Georgia to James Bigelow 2-15-1868 G
Baker, Harrel to William E. Crowder 1-8-1853 G
Baker, Irmandy S. to A. G. Crocker 2-6-1860 (2-7-1860) G
Baker, Jane M. to Josiah A. Hood 12-17-1845 (12-18-1845) O
Baker, Jane to James Hinds 1-22-1859 (1-28-1859) L
Baker, Jane to Lawson Glenn 12-27-1847 (12-30-1847) Ma
Baker, Jane to Noah Gidcomb 7-?-1857 (no return) L
Baker, Jane to Saml. Hutcherson 3-4-1850 (3-7-1850) Ma
Baker, Jennie Lee to Thomas H. Owens 4-16-1866 (4-25-1866) F
Baker, Josephine to John B. Walters 12-19-1861 (12-21-1861) Sh
Baker, Josephine to W. T. Richie 10-10-1855 (no return) F
Baker, Julia to Carr Crenshaw 9-11-1845 Sh
Baker, Juliana (Mrs.) to Rudolph Bittermann 9-27-1858 Sh
Baker, L. F. to D. C. Dozier 7-13-1866 (7-15-1866) Dy
Baker, Laura to Paul Jones 10-16-1876 (no return) Hy
Baker, Lielia to James Hammett 7-22-1862 (no return) Cr

Baker, Lorey A. to William Liggon 6-2-1848 Hn
Baker, Louisa C. to Levi W. Mason 1-1-1858 (1-5-1858) Ma
Baker, Louisa to A. D. Shell 6-12-1832 (6-?-1832) Hr
Baker, Louisa to M. Shifley 5-25-1860 Sh
Baker, Louizer to J. W. C. Davidson 12-8-1866 G
Baker, Lucinda to Wm. P. Goode 12-27-1870 F B
Baker, Lurena to James Myers 10-5-1854 We
Baker, Luvisa P. to I. N. Dozier 9-20-1859 (9-22-1859) G
Baker, M. A. to A. L. Lett 11-22-1856 G
Baker, M. F. to A. J. Kelley 9-14-1859 T
Baker, M. J. to N. A. Pennington 10-9-1865 G
Baker, M. L. to S. F. Thompson 11-5-1873 (11-6-1873) Dy
Baker, M. M. to J. R. Churchman 11-7-1865 (no return) Dy
Baker, Mahala A. to James T. George 2-12-1845 G
Baker, Malilda to John Brawder 9-8-1859 We
Baker, Malisa to William Sanford 9-15-1867 G
Baker, Malissa to Joseph Suratt 8-16-1831 G
Baker, Margaret to Robert F. F. Fortner 12-29-1846 Sh
Baker, Margarett J. to James T. Boyett 7-7-1857 (7-8-1857) G
Baker, Martha F. to John J. Glenney 5-20-1875 (5-23-1875) L
Baker, Martha J. to James M. Bailey 1-21-1867 G
Baker, Martha J. to John G. Smiler? 6-12-1859 Cr
Baker, Martha J. to Marcellus Blackburn 12-14-1848 Sh
Baker, Martha L. to Bennett G. Gordon 4-24-1850 Hn
Baker, Martha M. to James A. Danniel 12-13-1867 (12-15-1867) T
Baker, Martha to Anderson Cash 2-29-1852 Hn
Baker, Martha to Andrew McGowan 7-21-1882 (7-24-1882) L
Baker, Martha to John M. Craig 1-21-1850 O
Baker, Martha to Patrick Whevelin 8-26-1861 (no return) We
Baker, Mary A. E. to John A. Manning 1-9-1862 Sh
Baker, Mary A. to Benj. A. F. Thompson 3-10-1846 We
Baker, Mary A. to William Campbell 7-3-1860 Dy
Baker, Mary Ann to Robert H. Peacock 12-1-1868 (12-2-1868) L
Baker, Mary Ann to William A. Carter 7-14-1852 Sh
Baker, Mary E. to A. C. McNeell 7-28-1862 (7-29-1863?) Dy
Baker, Mary E. to L. G. Dawson 5-24-1871 (5-25-1871) Ma
Baker, Mary E. to Wam. A. Baker 3-28-1862 We
Baker, Mary J. to S. C. Breedlove 1-9-1866 Hn
Baker, Mary J. to Samuel Baker 12-6-1855 G
Baker, Mary J. to Thomas T. Richardson 3-7-1857 We
Baker, Mary J. to Thos. T. Richardson 2-28-1857 (no return) We
Baker, Mary J. to William H. Abbott 8-16-1847 We
Baker, Mary S. to William M. Hutchinson 12-15-1869 G
Baker, Mary T. to Henry J. Reames 1-29-1842 (2-1-1842) F
Baker, Mary to E. Cooper 11-4-1861 (11-7-1861) L
Baker, Mary to James Perry 10-24-1857 (10-25-1857) Sh
Baker, Mary to Joseph Walker 12-26-1871 (12-27-1871) L
Baker, Mary to Robert Bradford 10-22-1853 (10-23-1853) G
Baker, Mary to Saml. McConnell 5-23-1869 G
Baker, Matilda to Cornelius Barrett 10-13-1830 (10-14-1830) Hr
Baker, Melissa Catherine to Joseph A. Nevils 7-3-1861 (7-4-1861) Sh
Baker, Menton to Henry Richie 8-13-1843 We
Baker, Mexico to J. G. Glasgow 11-23-1866 Hn
Baker, Mollie C. to J. A. Oates 2-18-1871 (no return) F
Baker, Nancy Ann to Silas N. Kemp 3-28-1850 We
Baker, Nancy E. to Thomas J. Terry 3-20-1852 Hn
Baker, Nancy E. to J. N.(W?) Williams 11-17-1870 G
Baker, Nancy Jane to Francis M. Overton 8-13-1866 Ma
Baker, Nancy M. to W. C. Carpenter 10-2-1868 (10-4-1868) Dy
Baker, Nancy to Belfred C. Washbern 1-27-1847 (1-18?-1847) O
Baker, Nellie to William Walker 12-31-1868 F
Baker, P. A. to William Jackson 9-5-1846 (no return) Hn
Baker, Pamella A. to T. C. Finney 11-2-1859 (11-3-1859) Sh
Baker, Rachell E. to Jno. S. Brown 6-25-1870 We
Baker, Rebecca to Drury Deberry 11-20-1858 (11-23-1858) Ma
Baker, Rutha Jane to Y. W. Richey 7-21-1852 (no return) F
Baker, Sarah A. to James R. Cole 11-11-1866 Be
Baker, Sarah E. to Henry G. Waggoner 10-12-1856 We
Baker, Sarah E. to W. J. Combs 3-15-1869 (no return) Dy
Baker, Sarah J. to J. W. Lyon 12-25-1855 (12-27-1856?) We
Baker, Sarah M. V. to E. A. Sharp 10-26-1857 (10-27-1857) G
Baker, Sarah to Epraim D. Ford 3-22-1838 (no return) Hn
Baker, Sarah to J. G. W. Jamerson (Gimmerson) 3-14-1848 (3-21-1848) O
Baker, Sarah to James Black 2-18-1832 Ma
Baker, Sarah to Mike Libo 11-20-1876 (no return) L
Baker, Sarah to Tinsley T. Bailey 9-4-1872 (no return) L
Baker, Susan G. to L. B. Crowder 12-30-1859 G
Baker, Susan Jane to James H. Davenport 9-11-1860 (9-13-1860) Ma
Baker, Susan to James Snyder 5-19-1861 We
Baker, Susan to John H. Reaves 5-26-1856 Ma
Baker, Susan to Joseph Luckey 12-24-1845 (12-27-1845) Ma
Baker, Susannah to James V. Garrison 12-14-1846 (no return) F
Baker, Susannah to John F. Lucky 8-16-1847 (8-26-1847) Hr
Baker, Tabitha C. to William P. Rowlin 9-22-1849 (no return) Hn
Baker, Tabitha to Joseph White 8-4-1852 Ma
Baker, Tennessee J. to James R. Richey 8-11-1852 (no return) F
Bakere, Katherine to Thomas E. Williams 12-1-1853 Hn

Bakers, Mary Jane to Hezekiah Burton 11-15-1843 (11-16-1843) T
Balch, Nannie B. to James L. Penn 4-25-1848 Sh
Balcum, Penny to Thomas Birdsong 9-29-1866 (9-30-1866) F
Balderidge, Louisa E. to Joseph Brantley 5-23-1857 (no return) We
Balderson, Martha to Bryant Beasly 12-16-1884 (12-19-1884) L
Balderson, Tina to C. M. Bagbey 1-3-1872 L
Balderson, Virginia to Washington Johnson 4-20-1867 (4-21-1867) L
Baldlridgge, Josephine to J. M. Bartlett 8-30-1864 O
Baldock, Mary Helen to John Pool 12-26-1854 (12-28-1854) T
Baldock, Parthinia to John H. Draffin 10-9-1855 Sh
Baldridge, Araminta J. to Joseph J. Brogdon 6-24-1858 We
Baldridge, Bettie to John Gregory 12-15-1867 G
Baldridge, Catherine to William Ring 8-13-1836 (8-18-1836) O
Baldridge, E. to James J. Griffet 1-20-1852 We
Baldridge, Ella to A. M. Robinson 4-12-1864 (4-13-1864) O
Baldridge, Isabella F. to William Cawthon 12-30-1854 (1-1-1855) G
Baldridge, Isabella N. to John H. Lasly 12-30-1844 (1-1-1845) G
Baldridge, Martha J. to Charles W. Baldridge 5-31-1854 (no return) We
Baldridge, Martha J. to Charles W. Baldridge 6-1-1854 We
Baldridge, Mary N. to William M. Zearicor 11-18-1850 G
Baldridge, Mary to James Kinsey 12-14-1864 (12-15-1864) O
Baldridge, Nancy A. to W. H. Masfield 12-26-1860 We
Baldridge, Nancy to Joseph S. Evans 5-15-1847 (no return) F
Baldridge, Nancy to Robert H. Goodlow 12-9-1834 G
Baldridge, Orphelia A. to Thomas J. Shaw 2-17-1869 F
Baldridge, Polly Ann to Sam Thompson 10-22-1870 G
Baldridge, S. E. to R. E. Holmes 7-3-1858 (7-8-1858) G
Baldridge, Sarah J. to S. G. Taylor 2-13-1859 We
Baldrlidge, Ellen W. to Francis M. Shuck 8-3-1857 O
Baldwin, Aggie to Elbert Watkins 12-31-1871 Hy
Baldwin, Caroline M. to William Sanders 10-26-1865 Hn
Baldwin, Chany to Abraham Holmes 2-14-1878 Hy
Baldwin, Delila F. to Thomas Irion 5-6-1851 Hr
Baldwin, Elizabeth J. to Francis M. Cole 8-24-1860 Hn
Baldwin, Elizabeth to F. Samuel Groom 11-5-1855 (no return) Hn
Baldwin, Lucy to Wm. Franklin 1-1-1869 (1-2-1869) F B
Baldwin, Margaret to L. Boyer 12-6-1854 (12-7-1854) Sh
Baldwin, Martha to William W. O'Daniel 10-12-1858 Hn
Baldwin, Mary C. to Leroy T. Groom 9-27-1857 Hn
Baldwin, Mary Jane to R. H. Cartmell(Cartwell?) 3-26-1850 (3-27-1850) Hr
Baldwin, Mary to Israel Adams 3-12-1874 Hy
Baldwin, Nancy C. to James M. Stone 1-15-1861 Sh
Baldwin, Rachel to Thomas Greer 1-7-1875 Hy
Baldwin, Sarah to Stephen Holcum 11-14-1850 Hn
Balen, Mary G. to William S. Jones 10-19-1841 (no return) Hn
Balentine, Elizabeth to George M. Reaves 3-13-1858 We
Balentine, Mary K. to James Humble 8-8-1845 (8-9-1845) G
Balentine, Mary to Needham Wilber 11-7-1864 Sh
Balew, Eliza to John T. Browning 12-29-1852 G
Balew, Susan to James Sullivan 11-7-1867 G
Baley, Betsey to Jerry McGee 12-31-1828 G
Baley, Cary to Charles Porter 2-11-1832 (3-8-1832) G
Baley, Delila to William Griffin 9-12-1838 Ma
Baley, Isabella to William Lane 12-21-1840 (12-22-1840) G
Baley, Jacksy to John T. Armour 10-16-1844 (10-17-1844) G
Baley, L. to Dempsey Parker 12-16-1839 Ma
Baley, M. J. to A. J. Goatley 7-14-1860 (7-17-1860) Dy
Baley, Martha to Freeman Cross 8-24-1841 G
Baley, Obediance to thomas Bowers 3-13-1833 (3-14-1833) G
Baley, Sally to Joel Miller 3-26-1828 G
Baling, Lisetta to Geo. Bergmann 12-29-1858 (12-30-1858) Sh
Balis, Fannie to William Stevens 11-25-1871 T
Balis, Hester Ann to J. N. Walker 5-30-1855 Be
Balknight, Ellen to James Young 8-21-1873 (8-23-1874?) L B
Ball (Batt?), Telitha to Green Reed 12-31-1868 G B
Ball, Augustine to Jake Overall 12-24-1869 G B
Ball, Betty J. to Dallis Harris 1-8-1867 G
Ball, Caroline to Broady Lett 11-19-1866 G
Ball, Cordelia to James H. Bryant 3-29-1855 Sh
Ball, Effy to John F. Heiskell 9-14-1852 (9-16-1852) L
Ball, Elizabeth (Mrs.) to C. G. B. Klophel 7-8-1885 (7-12-1885) L
Ball, Elizabeth J. to Dallas Harris 1-12-1866 G
Ball, Elizabeth to George W. Trotter 1-10-1844 F
Ball, Elizabeth to Solomon Cooper 7-13-1852 G
Ball, Elizer Jane to Dodson Reynolds 12-24-1865 G
Ball, Ida A. to James P. Selph 1-25-1877 Hy
Ball, Louisa G. to D. Glasgow James 4-18-1855 Sh
Ball, Lucy Ann to Mc. Keltner 12-31-1866 (1-1-1867) L
Ball, Margaret to Stephen Dennis 6-23-1850 (no return) Hn
Ball, Mary C. to Patrick H. Sanford 1-5-1859 (1-6-1859) Ma
Ball, Mollie M. to Graves Fondville 8-4-1870 G
Ball, Nancy to T. G. Sorter 7-2-1867 G
Ball, Rhoda to George Greer 5-15-1869 G B
Ball, Sarah A. to J. R. G. Stephens 2-7-1871 Hy
Ball, Sarah J. to A. S. Hancock 1-11-1841 (1-12-1841) F
Ball, Sarah J. to N. P. Vincent 3-10-1866 (no return) Dy
Ball, Sarah J. to William A. Sanford 1-29-1855 Ma

Ball, Sarah to Jerry Thompson 12-31-1869 G B
Ballance, Charlott to John M. Reeves 1-15-1841 (1-17-1841) G
Ballance, Emely to William Davidson 12-3-1845 G
Ballaner, M. A. to W. H. Camp 9-9-1840 Be
Ballard, Avarilla to John Lefevre 1-6-1863 Hn
Ballard, Carolin to John Ballard 9-18-1865 (9-19-1865) T
Ballard, Catharine to G. W. Armor 2-2-1865 Be
Ballard, Drusilla to J. L. Hart 10-22-1863 Hn
Ballard, Elizabeth A. to James M. Ballard 11-17-1844 Hn
Ballard, Elizabeth to Wm. Rittenburgh 8-11-1859 (8-12-1859) Sh
Ballard, Elsie to Ennis Pewett 1-13-1867 Hy
Ballard, Fanny to James A. Furr 11-5-1870 (11-10-1870) F
Ballard, H. A. to C. H. Cogbill 7-21-1859 F
Ballard, Jane to James C. Graham 1-16-1841 (1-20-1841) F
Ballard, Jane to James Carroll Winters 7-28-1855 (7-29-1855) T
Ballard, Jane to Jesse Farmer 4-20-1867 Be
Ballard, Jennie to J. H. Burlison 12-21-1873 T
Ballard, Jerline to Burrell Lashlee 11-26-1847 Be
Ballard, Julian B. to Wm. H. Johnson 12-2-1852 Be
Ballard, Lucy Ann to E. C. Tull 6-1-1881 L
Ballard, Lucy E. to William H. Hudspeth 9-19-1860 Hn
Ballard, Lucy to James H. Armstrong 4-12-1877 Hy
Ballard, M. A. to C. H. Stokes 5-11-1883 (5-13-1883) L
Ballard, Margarett M to Wm. S. Temple 4-18-1843 Ma
Ballard, Martha E. A. to John D. Ballard 7-26-1858 (7-18-1858) T
Ballard, Martha J. to J. Y. Price 2-14-1878 (no return) L
Ballard, Martha J. to Malachi Jones 1-30-1851 Hn
Ballard, Martha Jane to John Allen West 2-24-1874 L
Ballard, Martha to James McCullough 7-11-1855 (no return) F
Ballard, Mary A. to John C. Tims 12-5-1877 L
Ballard, Mary to John Elliett 3-5-1866 (3-8-1866) T
Ballard, Matilda to Aaron R. Lewis 1-30-1854 (no return) Hn
Ballard, Mattie J. to R. W. Webb 12-28-1867 Hy
Ballard, Mollie E. to W. M. Butler 2-28-1857 Sh
Ballard, Nancy E. to R. K. Haley 11-26-1861 Be
Ballard, Rebecca C. to David Watson 7-22-1851 Be
Ballard, Rebecca to James V. Ruth 6-19-1843 F
Ballard, Rebecca to John Jenkins 1-12-1849 Sh
Ballard, Sarah L. A. to Benjamin F. Swor 12-30-1866 Hn
Ballard, Sarah to James R. Welb 8-26-1857 (8-31-1857) T
Ballard, Tabitha to Thomas Lewis 7-29-1841 Hn
Ballaw, Jyncy to J. R. Brobbeck 9-20-1851 (no return) F
Ballenger, M. A. to S. W. Walpole 8-23-1884 (8-26-1884) L
Ballentine, Ann E. to E. D. Screws 10-15-1859 (10-16-1859) G
Ballentine, Marzella to John Bonds 9-3-1862 (9-4-1862) Dy
Ballew, Emily J. to George W. Burton 12-30-1865 (12-31-1865) Cr
Ballew, M. W. to W. J. Leach 3-31-1865 (no return) Cr
Bailey, Margaret to Enoch Dellender 10-8-1857 We
Balling, S. E. to Thomas T. Green 9-23-1861 (9-24-1861) Sh
Ballinger, Martha J. to Joseph L. Beasely 12-30-1859 (1-1-1860) L
Ballintine, Mahetable to Jno. M. Northern 1-9-1837 (1-17-1837) G
Ballowe, Caroline to Joseph Whitly 10-26-1849 Be
Ballowe, E. H. to H. W. Baggett 9-20-1854 Be
Ballowe, Elizabeth to Nicholas Holland 1-8-1852 Be
Ballowe, Martha J. to Wm. C. Boatright 10-5-1856 Be
Balmer, Mary (Mrs.) to Jacob Hartman 8-8-1863 (8-9-1863) Sh
Baltin, Lucy to Cenica Irons 4-24-1877 Hy
Bambridge, Eleanor Valentin to Jno. Boyd Campbell 2-1-1843 (2-7-1843) T
Bambridge, Jane D. to J. W. Trobough 6-4-1872 (6-5-1872) T
Band, Jane to William Hine? 12-1-1852 T
Bandin?, Susan to Needham Branch 8-9-1837 (8-13-1837) O
Bandy, M. E. to K. B. Touchton 9-18-1878 Hy
Bandy, Mary H. to William Bull 11-16-1869 T
Bandy, Sue E. to Thomas T. Gaines 2-27-1873 T
Bane, Elizabeth to Stephen Roach 2-27-1826 G
Bane, Harriet to M. R. Bloodworth 11-10-1847 Be
Bane, Mandy to Carroll Greer 2-8-1840 Be
Bane, Mary to William Cox 3-18-1852 (3-21-1852) Sh
Bane, Sarah Ann to Wiley F. Sammons 8-5-1852 G
Bane, Sary to Johnston Cribbs 9-7-1824 (9-9-1824) G
Bane, Wine to Alexander R. McFall 1-5-1830 (1-7-1830) G
Baner, Louisa to F. H. Trudeau 5-6-1845 Sh
Bangster, Adeline to Isham Hopkins 2-27-1883 (3-1-1883) L
Banister, A. E. to T. J. Michael 9-29-1870 G
Banister, A. J. to George F. Edwards 1-5-1864 G
Bankhead, Agnis M. to George S. Howell 4-24-1841 (4-30-1841) F
Bankhead, Isabella to James Webster 3-11-1841 F
Banks, Ann to Coleman Stillwell 12-28-1868 (12-29-1868) T
Banks, Eliza J. to John J. Franklin 1-15-1868 Dy
Banks, Eliza to William Huntsman 1-19-1829 Sh
Banks, Elizabeth to Jesse Fowler 6-20-1850 Hn
Banks, Ellen to David L. Fite 10-14-1857 (10-15-1857) T
Banks, Emily Ann to Wm. S. Whitley 12-21-1854 T
Banks, Flora to Lee Martin 10-15-1869 G B
Banks, Jane M. to David McDonald 12-3-1851 (12-4-1851) T
Banks, Jennie to Washington Simmons 2-15-1867 G B
Banks, Julia A. C. to Wm. A. Huffman 11-29-1854 (12-1-1854) T

Banks, Julia to Bruce Walker 3-14-1878 Hy
Banks, Martha to John N. Robertson 9-28-1850 Hn
Banks, Mary Ann to Wm. Rowe 4-25-1843 Be
Banks, Mary E. to James R. Reeble 10-8-1856 G
Banks, Mary to William Morris 4-21-1838 (no return) Hn
Banks, Nancy to William Fodge 6-27-1844 Hn
Banks, Sarah Ann to Edmon M. Johnston 11-9-1843 Hn
Banks, Tempa to Berry Hartsfield 2-16-1867 G B
Bannon, Elizabeth to George Humphries 11-25-1851 Sh
Baptist, Caladonia to Mack Dugget 1-21-1871 T
Baptist, D. to Robert Taylor 12-23-1872 T
Baptist, Frances to John Whitley 2-12-1872 T
Baraxtin, Sarah to Abell Sawers 10-24-1858 We
Barbee, Bettie to James F. Green 2-14-1866 Hy
Barbee, Elizabeth to James J. Sweeney 6-18-1844 Hn
Barbee, Emma to George Henning 8-20-1877 L
Barbee, Fannie to John Hentz 5-26-1881 L B
Barbee, Fannie to Joseph Smith 1-12-1875 Hy
Barbee, Frances to Richard Mann 12-21-1870 Hy
Barbee, H. A. P. to John T. Thomas 11-21-1864 Sh
Barbee, Haseltine to R. R. Aycock 7-15-1850 Hn
Barbee, Jane to Bob Bond 8-21-1869 (no return) Hy
Barbee, Jane to Jacob Anderson 3-17-1866 Hy
Barbee, Jane to William Boothe 3-9-1839 Hn
Barbee, Julia to Lewis Davis 12-29-1872 Hy
Barbee, Julia to Thad Taliaferro 1-26-1877 L
Barbee, Lizzie to Charles Mann 1-2-1878 Hy
Barbee, Maria to Alex Graham 1-23-1873 Hy
Barbee, Mary Anne E. to David A. Fawcett 11-6-1844 Sh
Barbee, Nannie to Frank Stewart 12-9-1866 Hy
Barbee, Rose to Dawson Ivy 12-25-1866 (no return) Hy
Barbee, Sallie Ann to Allen Boyd 1-20-1870 Hy
Barbee, Sarah C. to Thos. W. Railford 9-26-1846 Sh
Barbee, Sarah J. to William J. Ramsay 2-21-1864 (no return) Hn
Barbee, Sarah J. to William J. Ramsay 3-8-1864 Hn
Barbee, Taylor to Phil Henning 1-19-1881 L B
Barber, Barbery B. to Wildon Foster 9-11-1838 Ma
Barber, Elizabeth to Travis L. Milner 5-24-1838 (5-27-1838) O
Barber, Emma F. to Henry T. Harrison 3-19-1855 Sh
Barber, Harriet to C. H. Adams 1-17-1856 We
Barber, Kate to George W. Kellar 12-21-1870 Ma
Barber, Lavinia to James Evans 1-15-1868 Hy
Barber, Martha E. to Henry Guthery 3-14-1865 (3-16-1865) O
Barber, Martha to James Wells 1-15-1873 Hy
Barber, Mary A. R. to James B. Beckley 12-23-1858 We
Barber, Mary Ann to William L. Bumpious 2-19-1841 (2-23-1841) O
Barber, Molley to John Campbell 4-24-1870 (no return) Cr
Barber, Nancy A. to W. R. D. Howerton 8-3-1867 (8-4-1867) L
Barber, S. F. to M. V. B. Alexander 5-14-1863 We
Barbie, Rose to Dewery Taylor 12-27-1867 Hy
Barbie, S. T. to P. T. Glass 12-18-1868 Hy
Barbieri, Eloise (Miss) to Geo. W. Scott 3-3-1863 (2?-3-1863) Sh
Barby, Fanny to Aleck Wray 7-9-1870 F B
Barclay, Emily to John Clinton 8-7-1861 (no return) Hy
Barclay, Jane to Thomas M. Oswald 7-6-1842 Sh
Barclay, Mattie to J. K. Walker 4-2-1872 Hy
Barcley, H. L. to G. L. Walker 9-6-1871 Hy
Barcroft, Ella to J. W. Shepherd 12-20-1871 Hy
Barcroft, Martha A. to L. W. Tatum 3-18-1860 Hy
Barcroft, S. C. to R. W. Haralson 12-15-1870 O
Bard, Catharine to Reuben Dalton 1-12-1857 O
Bardell, Annie to C. H. Upchurch 2-2-1860 (2-3-1860) Sh
Barden, C. (Mrs.) to J. P. Phillips 12-11-1856 (12-17-1856) Sh
Barden, Lucinda to Joseph Hughs (Hugger) 1-5-1847 Sh
Barden, Mollie E. to Joseph A. Morton 12-18-1877 Hy
Barding, Eliza to Wm. A. Brooks 10-2-1840 Sh
Bardon, E. V. to Francis N. Marion 12-9-1864 Sh
Barfield, Alice to Charles F. Lankford 2-25-1880 L
Barfield, Anna to J. H. Evans 1-4-1882 L
Barfield, Cairo A. to T. J. Kee 2-11-1878 (2-13-1878) L
Barfield, Deborah L. to John W. Adams 9-26-1865 L
Barfield, E. T. to W. S. Wilkes 2-13-1883 (2-14-1883) L
Barfield, Ella to Currie Wood 1-24-1883 L
Barfield, F. W. to G. L. Raines 1-21-1873 L
Barfield, M. V. to J. Tucker Gains 6-21-1882 L
Barfield, Mariah J. to William M. West 2-3-1874 L
Barfield, Mary E. to John Lary 9-3-1873 L
Barfield, Mary F. to William J. Lewis 9-24-1864 (9-25-1864) L
Barfield, Mary N. to William S. Wilkes 11-28-1871 L
Barfield, S. A. to D. F. Jennings 2-11-1878 L
Barfield, S. E. to O. R. Dunavant 2-10-1875 (2-11-1875) L
Barfield, Sarah Francis to John G. Thum 12-19-1870 (12-21-1870) L
Barfield, Susan P. to D. W. Bron (Broun?-Brow?) 3-3-1885 (3-5-1885) L
Barfield, Susan W. to M. P. Lankford 12-10-1851 (12-11-1851) L
Barfoot, Martha A. to James Campbell 2-3-1850 Be
Bargan (Hargan?), Ellen to Michael Kelly 3-31-1861 Sh
Bargan, S. R. to Levi Lounsford 12-24-1868 Hy

Bargantey, Madeline to Jno. Geo. Schnider 4-13-1846 Sh
Barger, Martha L. to John R. Haslewood 3-11-1859 We
Bargo, Elizabeth to Thos. H. Melton 8-23-1846 We
Bargo, Elizabeth to W. H. Scott 5-4-1846 (no return) We
Bargo, Sarah L. to William M. Berry 10-24-1844 We
Barham, Adaline to William Bolin 10-26-1871 (10-31-1871) Cr
Barham, Almedy to Terry Turner 3-11-1867 Hy
Barham, Ann to D. I. Asler 1-3-1850 (1-?-1850) G
Barham, Ardelia to Wm. D. Hallum 1-3-1851 Cr
Barham, C. O. to G. T. Barksdale 1-30-1871 (2-1-1871) Cr
Barham, Callie to W. H. Abernathy 2-5-1886 (2-7-1886) L
Barham, F. H. to Wm. McCaskill 4-27-1859 Cr
Barham, Frances Ann to Calvin Birdwell 12-20-1847 (12-21-1847) O
Barham, Louisa S. to Edward D. Matthews 4-26-1865 G
Barham, Louisa to Luke Carley 4-21-1852 (4-22-1852) Hr
Barham, Louisa to Richard Carson 8-17-1868 (8-18-1868) Cr
Barham, M. A. to W. B. May 11-9-1858 Cr
Barham, Martha J. to Thomas Bird 3-30-1843 Cr
Barham, Mary A. to Samuel Aslin 12-19-1839 G
Barham, Mary to Daniel Stovall 3-28-1867 G
Barham, Mary to Harvy McBryde 1-30-1832 (1-20?-1832) Ma
Barham, Mary to William Cate 12-4-1866 Hn
Barham, Mattie E. to A. C. (Dr.) Pearce 12-8-1866 (12-11-1866) Cr
Barham, N. C. (Mrs.) to T. J. Dill 4-9-1860 Cr
Barham, Nancy C. to J. B. Peeples 3-1-1862 Mn
Barham, Prudence to H. M. P. McGee 11-15-1853 Cr
Barham, S. B. to John Anderson 12-27-1865 Hn
Barham, Sarah E. to D. J. York 12-29-1851 Cr
Barham, Susan E. to William C. Owens 7-19-1860 (no return) Hn
Barham, Susan E. to William D. Haynes 1-23-1861 Hn
Barham, Tobitha to J. T. Johnson 11-16-1866 (11-18-1866) Cr
Barham, Vandelia R. to Wilson Y. Hale 12-11-1844 O
Barhum, Adaline to John Darnell 3-27-1848 (no return) Cr
Barken, Adeline to Isom Miller 12-22-1869 F B
Barker, Amy to Samuel Corckett? 9-10-1846 Be
Barker, Angaline to Polk Thomas 1-22-1873 (1-23-1873) Cr B
Barker, Catharine to William Black 11-3-1835 (11-5-1835) Hr
Barker, Celey to Gray Barker 9-1-1841 (9-2-1841) G
Barker, Cyntha to Pinkney Reed 5-9-1855 (no return) F
Barker, Cynthia E. to Caswell Simmons 1-29-1859 Hr
Barker, Delia to Watson Gordon 9-15-1858 (9-16-1858) G
Barker, Dicy to Starling Burrow 11-4-1837 (11-5-1837) Hr
Barker, E. W. to W. S. Crocker 12-3-1857 G
Barker, Elizabeth R. to Henry Harris 4-15-1848 (4-18-1848) Ma
Barker, Elizabeth to George Beck 8-19-1834 Hr
Barker, Elizabeth to J. M. Leath 7-7-1868 G
Barker, Frances M. to Wm. C. Johnson 10-7-1848 Sh
Barker, Frances to Henry Jefferson Fisher 11-4-1857 O
Barker, Frances to James A. Stewart 9-22-1841 Cr
Barker, Hannah F. to D. F. Goodyear 1-2-1860 (1-3-1860) Sh
Barker, Harriet J. to J. K. Todd 1-1-1867 F
Barker, Jane E. to William A. Blair 10-20-1856 G
Barker, Jane to Calin? Wm.? Bland 12-21-1860 (not executed) Sh
Barker, Kizzy to Jas. H. Slaydon 9-12-1859 (9-13-1859) G
Barker, Levisa to John L. Moultrie 4-18-1838 (4-26-1838) O
Barker, M. B. to D. W. Barker 4-10-1842 Be
Barker, M. E. to V. King 7-3-1870 G
Barker, M. to J. J. Parker 12-2-1857 G
Barker, Malisa Jane to Wm. H. Davidson 7-10-1845 Be
Barker, Manervy C. to Azilvin Howe 7-23-1848 Be
Barker, Margaret S. to Benj. F. Patten 9-30-1857 (no return) We
Barker, Martha A. M. to E. C. Ross 10-12-1849 Be
Barker, Martha A. to Wm. Cooper 10-7-1868 (10-8-1868) Dy
Barker, Martha I. to Runion Williams 9-10-1866 Hn
Barker, Mary A. to Jesstromer Defoy 10-18-1851 (no return) Cr
Barker, Mary E. to Rufus F. Reed 12-9-1857 (12-10-1857) G
Barker, Mary J. to W. H. Nivins 10-26-1869 Be
Barker, Mary to Edwin G. Barker 2-21-1869 G
Barker, Mary to Thomas Fisher 11-12-1856 (11-13-1856) G
Barker, Mary to Wm. J. Wynn 6-19-1843 O
Barker, Nancy Elmiria? to William Hall 5-7-1842 (5-8-1842) Hr
Barker, Penelope to John C. Gibb 10-1-1850 G
Barker, Rachel Talbot to Gabriel M. Anderson 1-2-1855 (1-3-1855) T
Barker, Rebecca (Mrs.) to James Downs 3-10-1883 (6-10-1883) L
Barker, Rebecca to John W. Ballentine 7-3-1845 G
Barker, Rosannah to Benjamin Roney, Jr. 1-20-1840 (1-23-1840) O
Barker, Sarah A. to Spencer Bomer 3-25-1851 Cr
Barker, Sarah to Alvin Jourdan 10-12-1850 O
Barker, Sarah to Alvin Jourdan 10-12-1850 (10-13-1850) O
Barker, Sarah to Fed Nesbett 10-18-1866 Cr B
Barker, Sarah to Henry Loving 9-8-1847 O
Barker, Sarah to James Wilson 9-27-1858 O
Barker, Sarah to Samuel G. H. Watson 6-21-1841 (6-24-1841) O
Barker, Sarah to William James 1-5-1836 Hr
Barker, Susan C. (Mrs.) to W. A. Austin 9-12-1862 (9-13-1862) Dy
Barker, Susan E. to L. Evans 10-17-1866 G
Barker, Susan to Wm. P. Buckner 1-2-1851 Cr

Barkley, Elizabeth to Wm. Stockton 1-22-1837 Hr
Barkley, Martha M. to G. M. Bradford 12-26-1864 G
Barkley, Mary Ann to Thos. J. Clift 4-4-1842 (4-7-1842) Hr
Barkley, Sarah Knox to Wilie D. Fleet 12-24-1850 (12-25-1850) Hr
Barkley?, Susan C. to M. G. Cagle 5-24-1836 Hr
Barksdale, Fannie to Austin P. Little 5-14-1863 (no return) Cr
Barksdale, Julia E. to James F. Gordan 12-31-1853 (1-1-1853) G
Barksdale, Luellen to J. D. Abbett 1-6-1864 (no return) Cr
Barksdale, Mary M. to Wade W. Richardson 6-15-1854 Cr
Barksdale, Ora to Saml. W. Harper 9-15-1867 G
Barksdale, Sarah C. to L. J. Cook 1-18-1858 G
Barlow, L. W. to E. M. Ellsberry 7-12-1864 (7-13-1864) Cr
Barlow, Lucy J. to James W. Ledbetter 11-17-1864 Mn
Barlow, Margaret to Nathan Morris 7-23-1862 Cr
Barlow, Mary to Ellis White 4-20-1872 L
Barlow, Nancy to R. M. Pierce 8-22-1855 (8-23-1855) G
Barn, Pruda A. to W. C. Jones 1-3-1860 (1-4-1860) G
Barndell, Martha M. to Joseph Hopson 1-6-1843 (no return) Hn
Barne?, Harriett A. to Edward Robertson 4-4-1839 Hr
Barner, Mary to J. K. McDaniel 4-20-1856 We
Barnes (Baines?), Martha to William Griggs 1-23-1865 (1-24-1865) L
Barnes, Ada to R. F. Miller 8-6-1879 (8-10-1879) L
Barnes, Amanda L. to James A. Hargiss 6-11-1852 (no return) F
Barnes, Amanda to Leonard Owens 9-23-1854 (10-10-1854) Ma
Barnes, America to James R. Witherspoon no date (with Aug 1838) G
Barnes, Clementine to A. G. Yergan 11-17-1869 (11-18-1869) Cr
Barnes, E. L. to N. J. Hipp 4-30-1873 (5-1-1873) G
Barnes, Edna C. to William J. Bentley 1-11-1881 (1-12-1881) L
Barnes, Eliza M. to Jno. G. Wallace 10-4-1850 Sh
Barnes, Elizabeth to Hansford Smith 9-13-1839 (9-19-1839) Ma
Barnes, Elizabeth to Henry L. Williams 7-13-1848 Hn
Barnes, Elizabeth to J. R. Beaton 12-10-1865 Be
Barnes, Frances E. to Robert F. Benton 8-31-1852 (no return) F
Barnes, Frances to John Sawyer 1-25-1869 (1-28-1869) L
Barnes, Francis to George Chipman 3-16-1861 (3-17-1861) O
Barnes, Hannah to Michael Walsh 4-14-1858 Hn
Barnes, Henrietta to Austin Hardy no date (not executed) Hy
Barnes, Jane to John Helm 1-3-1883 (1-4-1883) L
Barnes, Jennie A. to Redman Jefferson 10-8-1871 Hy
Barnes, Keziah to George Billings 5-26-1873 (5-27-1873) T
Barnes, L. C. to Thos. H. Cook 1-10-1850 Cr
Barnes, Louisa F. to Andrew J. Williams 7-8-1857 L
Barnes, Lucinda to J. W. Tyner 12-8-1847 Be
Barnes, M. J. to R. P. Tidwell 1-7-1868 O
Barnes, Malvira F. to S. R. Davidson 10-20-1855 Sh
Barnes, Martha J. to W. G. Hallmark 3-6-1872 (no return) Cr
Barnes, Martha M. to James H. Cruise 6-15-1865 G
Barnes, Mary E. to James M. Clayton 10-19-1865 Mn
Barnes, Mary E. to Lavander Jinkins 1-27-1858 (1-28-1858) Sh
Barnes, Mary Jane to Charles Dalton 1-5-1848 Be
Barnes, Mary to D. B. Jones 11-3-1851 O
Barnes, Mary to David B. Jones 11-3-1851 (12-3-1851) O
Barnes, Mary to James Sherly 1-7-1849 Be
Barnes, Mary to John Mothershed 9-23-1844 Be
Barnes, Minnie to John Adam 2-27-1864 (2-29-1864) Sh
Barnes, Msary to George W. Tycen no date (with 1862) T
Barnes, Nancy M. to F. E. Timmons 6-28-1845 (no return) L
Barnes, Nancy to Lewis Bridges 11-10-1866 (no return) Hy
Barnes, Perlina to William Johnson 12-25-1872 (12-26-1872) O
Barnes, Rachel to Lewis Bishop 4-27-1867 G
Barnes, Rebecca J. to Robert W. Lowery 1-22-1851 Hn
Barnes, Rebecca to Henry S. Roberts 4-22-1861 Hn
Barnes, Sarah A. to Thomas Jefferson Morgan 12-15-1855 (12-18-1855) Ma
Barnes, Sarah Ann to John Hallmark 9-24-1865 Be
Barnes, Sarah E. to William A. Kidd 6-19-1851 (no return) F
Barnes, Sarah Jane to Archie Morrison 12-23-1872 (12-25-1873) T
Barnes, Sarah to John M. Thompson 1-19-1836 (1-20-1836) G
Barnes, Sena Ann to Calvin Douglas 3-3-1853 Be
Barnes, Susan to William Wright 3-6-1845 Hn
Barnes, T. A. to A. J. Yarbrough 12-11-1855 Sh
Barnes?, Mary A. E. to M. W. Hall 5-27-1858 (6-10-1858) Hr
Barnet, M. D. to R. B. Love 9-18-1860 G
Barnet, M. W. to M. A. Dickey 1-30-1854 (1-31-1854) G
Barnet, Martha M. to James F. Cannon (Camron) 11-3-1827 Sh
Barnet, Mary M. to John J. Coppage 2-5-1845 Sh
Barnet, Nealy to Wm. M. McGuiver 5-21-1866 (5-22-1866) T
Barnet, S. E. to William M. Dearman 3-22-1865 Hn
Barnett, Alice M. to Wm. C. Manscoe 7-23-1853 (7-24-1853) Sh
Barnett, Alice to Stephen Wood 12-30-1874 (12-31-1874) Dy
Barnett, Annie to Jake Lea 7-27-1877 (7-29-1877) L B
Barnett, Arcenoe to G. H. Nease 7-18-1871 Cr
Barnett, Beate to Ben Marley 5-16-1877 (no return) L
Barnett, Catherine L. to Nathaniel T. Barnett 5-26-1843 Hn
Barnett, Cordela to R. W. Cherry 12-14-1874 O
Barnett, Eliza to M. L. Travis 1-18-1844 Be
Barnett, Elizabeth F. to Littleberry Arnold 12-15-1862 (12-17-1862) Ma
Barnett, Elizabeth to Dempsey Nowell 10-29-1866 (10-30-1866) Ma

Brides

Barnett, Ella to C. A. Love 8-2-1870 G
Barnett, Emily to Samuel Roach 11-12-1863 O
Barnett, J. E. to D. S. Burgie 10-13-1869 Dy
Barnett, Jane C. to William J. McAfee 3-16-1858 (3-25-1858) Ma
Barnett, Jane to William H. Woods 10-22-1847 (10-26-1847) Ma
Barnett, Loreza to Hiram Dempsey 2-21-1856
Barnett, Lou to Jery Fowlkes 3-28-1876 (no return) Dy
Barnett, Love to James Puckett 9-30-1861 Sh
Barnett, M. A. to J. W. Crawford 2-11-1866 (2-12-1866) Dy
Barnett, Margaret to A. Q. Sanders 12-24-1868 G
Barnett, Martha A. to G. P. Goodrich 7-28-1854 (8-?-1854) Ma
Barnett, Martha E. to R. F. Stroud 1-4-1866 Hn
Barnett, Martha Francess to Geeorge Luster 12-17-1846 (12-20-1846) O
Barnett, Martha J. to George W. Schabel 5-23-1844 Sh
Barnett, Martha L. to Samuel L. Bibb 5-6-1847 Hn
Barnett, Martha to Andrew Nabors 2-8-1864 Sh B
Barnett, Martha to Porter Bridges 12-15-1864 Be
Barnett, Martha to Saml. Lambert 1-11-1826 (1-12-1826) Hr
Barnett, Mary A. to Joseph Day 5-3-1845 Hn
Barnett, Mary Ann to John P. S. Nelson 5-24-1870 (5-26-1870) Ma
Barnett, Mary E. to Joseph E. Smith 8-24-1840 (8-25-1840) Ma
Barnett, Mary Eliza to Alexander Thompson 12-19-1866 (12-20-1866) Ma
Barnett, Mary M. to Sandford W. Gilliam 2-15-1861 (5-15-1861) Ma
Barnett, Mary S. to W. C. Marbury 5-11-1872 T
Barnett, Mary to John O'Mahony 5-21-1868 (5-23-1868) T
Barnett, Mary to Martin Poulson 7-2-1850 Sh
Barnett, Mary to N. G. Foulks 8-20-1865 (8-20-   ) O
Barnett, Mary to Philip Arthur 12-12-1857 (12-13-1857) L
Barnett, Melcenia V. to David W. Turner 2-16-1857 (2-19-1857) Ma
Barnett, Nancy E. to I. N. Davis 2-20-1863 (2-23-1863) Dy
Barnett, Nancy M. to William A. Graves 9-7-1867 (9-12-1867) Ma
Barnett, Nancy to M. A. Kennaday 8-14-1866 (8-16-1866) Cr
Barnett, Naoma M. to Joseph Wilkes 3-12-1829 Hr
Barnett, Rebeccah C. to James H. Cooper 3-23-1865 Dy
Barnett, Sallie to John M. McCaslin 5-10-1870 Ma
Barnett, Sarah C. to Harvey Mullins 9-11-1866 (9-12-1866) Ma
Barnett, Sarah Jane to James B. Thompson 5-2-1842 Ma
Barnett, Sarah to N. G. Foulks 7-5-1876 (7-6-1876) O
Barnett, Sidney E. to Wm. P. Moore 4-13-1858 Cr
Barnett, Susan J. to Peter B. Barnett 9-2-1859 (9-8-1859) Ma
Barnett, Victoria J. L. to John M. Brooks 11-4-1856 (11-6-1856) Sh
Barnhart, Angeline to Alexander Glawson 1-7-1847 Cr
Barnhart, Charlotte to Albert Cleaver 7-29-1856 Cr
Barnhart, E. C. to J. H. Wyatt 10-10-1859 Cr
Barnhart, E. J. to Lewis N. Phillips 1-9-1858 Cr
Barnhart, Elizabeth Jane to John Holcomb 2-27-1834 Sh
Barnhart, Elizabeth to William Rowland 12-17-1840 Cr
Barnhart, Permintia to Richardson Whitbey 9-1-1831 Sh
Barnhart, Sarah A. to Jesse C. Easters 8-6-1866 (8-7-1866) Cr
Barnhart, Sarah to Wm. Moore 2-19-1840 Cr
Barnheart, N. A. to E. H. Hutchins 8-2-1839 Sh
Barnhill, Delila to James Lawson 2-11-1868 Be
Barnhill, Elizabeth C. to Nehemiah M. Hansell 8-31-1848 Sh
Barnhill, Emily L. to Elisha E. Council 12-21-1865 Hn
Barnhill, Mahala to William Dickerson 3-5-1844 (3-7-1844) O
Barnhill, Margaret J. to E. E. Council 11-8-1863 Hn
Barnhill, Nancy to V. S. Mathis 6-8-1850 O
Barnhill, Nancy to Valentine I. Mathews 6-8-1850 (6-12-1850) O
Barnhill, Sarah E. to F. Mendenall 1-21-1858 Hn
Barnner, Cherry to Moses Brogdon 8-14-1845 Hn
Barnres, Elizabeth T. to Isaiah Jones 4-10-1855 (4-12-1855) O
Barns (Bunn-Burris?), Mary C. to James S. Hipp 8-1-1860 (8-2-1860) L
Barns, Ann to John Austin 7-16-1857 Be
Barns, Culine? to Arthur Spalding 7-22-1860 Cr
Barns, Dysy to Micajah Busby 2-15-1830 Ma
Barns, Eliza J. to Solomon Walls 8-5-1841 (8-6-1841) G
Barns, Elizabeth M. to T. J. Ralph 2-5-1839 Sh
Barns, M. E. to J. P. Smawley 8-27-1840 Be
Barns, M. to Henry T. Crossett 12-21-1841 Cr
Barns, Martha M. to John Oxford 12-25-1851 Be
Barns, Nancy to James Saunders 11-11-1857 Be
Barns, Sarah Ann Elizabeth to William c. Hudson 12-10-1850 Sh
Barns, Sarah E. to James Smothers 4-29-1857 Be
Barns, Sarah to James Smith 11-15-1830 O
Barnum, Harriet to Armstead Wilks 1-26-1884 (2-17-1884) L
Barnwell, Lucy S. to W. H. Crosby 11-4-1860 G
Barnwell, Matilda to Philip Delph 8-4-1856 Ma
Barr, Amanda J. to John W. Cravin 12-31-1844 Cr
Barr, Amanda Jane to James W. Vestal 9-17-1867 (9-18-1867) Ma
Barr, Julina to David Fullerton 6-6-1854 Be
Barr, Margaret to Parham Ezzell 3-20-1838 (no return) Hn
Barr, Martha A. to W. J. Cox 12-8-1868 Be
Barr, Nancy J. to James A. Webb 11-14-1860 We
Barr, Pattie to Chalres T. Bates 8-16-1871 (8-19-1871) Ma
Barren, Mary L. to R. L. Ivey 7-11-1865 F
Barret, Margret V. to Henry Fields 8-9-1865 T
Barret, Matilda to Wallace Clark 2-4-1870 T

Barret, Sallie A. to John W. Calhoun 1-19-1870 T
Barret, Susan E. to E. L. Tillman 5-29-1865 G
Barrett, Ann to Samuel Hooker 3-19-1867 G
Barrett, Arabella to George W. Baker 8-15-1846 (8-17-1846) Ma
Barrett, Clarissa to Hiram Bohannon 8-31-1838 Hn
Barrett, Elizabeth to B. F. Haltom 9-24-1856 Hr
Barrett, Elizabeth to Madison Johnson 2-13-1849 Ma
Barrett, Harriett to George Haughton 9-14-1840 (9-15-1840) Ma
Barrett, Henrietta S. to Christopher W. Dickson 12-7-1846 T
Barrett, Lucinda to James Watkins 11-14-1850 Hn
Barrett, Mariam to Hansell Cawbourn? 7-9-1839 (no return) F
Barrett, Martha A. to Wm. R. Brown 2-12-1875 (2-14-1875) Dy
Barrett, Martha to William Chapman 1-30-1862 G
Barrett, Mary to Dean McCarley 8-9-1838 F
Barrett, Mary to Hugh Elmore 10-23-1863 (10-25-1863) Cr
Barrett, Mary to Hugh Elmore 10-23-1864 (no return) Cr
Barrett, Mary to John Donahoe 4-28-1844 Sh
Barrett, Mexico to R. T. D. Norman 1-27-1876 (1-28-1876) Dy
Barrett, Rhoda C. to Morgan Thrailkill 6-5-1861 (6-9-1861) Hr
Barrett, Sarah to Thos. W. Williams 10-7-1858 G
Barrett, Susie to Rolly Thornton 12-15-1878 Hy
Barrier, Agnes J. to Sidney P. Jones 9-16-1859 (9-18-1859) Ma
Barrier, Catherine to William H. Edwards 7-3-1866 Ma
Barrier, Mary to Adolphus Britton 9-27-1848 (11-27-1848) Ma
Barron (Barrow?), Nancy C. to Lee Dunnegan 12-30-1863 G
Barron, C. A. to Wiley P. Russell 10-22-1856 G
Barron, Elizabeth J. to John D. Roberson 9-22-1843 (9-28-1843) Ma
Barron, F. M. to William Fewell 1-17-1848 (1-18-1848) F
Barron, Johanna to William Hyland 7-10-1858 Sh
Barron, Mary J. H. to James K. P. Oakley 6-27-1860 Ma
Barron, Mary M. to Elijah B. Russell 2-26-1852 G
Barron, Mary to Amus Worrell 1-13-1840 Hr
Barron, Mary to John Foley 8-21-1858 (8-22-1858) Sh
Barron, Mary to Sanders Barron 9-18-1869 (no return) F B
Barron, Missouri C. to William Howerton 11-23-1866 (11-25-1866) Ma
Barrott, Elizabeth A. to William G. Bowls 8-24-1860 G
Barrott, Sarah J. to John M. Barton 1-13-1847 (1-15-1847) G
Barrow, Elizabeth to J. A. Fulks 8-4-1859 (no return) Cr
Barrow, Elizabeth to William Smith 2-8-1830 (2-16-1830) O
Barry, Ann to Michael Louney 1-10-1856 Sh
Barry, Eudora R. to Marshall J. Miller 8-15-1846 Sh
Barry, Eudora to Roger Barton 5-2-1832 Hr
Barry, H. to James Callahan 6-26-1856 (6-28-1856) Sh
Barry, Margaret to Hugh Toley 5-13-1863 G
Barry?, Martha Ann Eliza to William Clark Kendel 3-11-1841 Hr
Barten, Sarah A. to John F. Walker 9-13-1843 (9-14-1843) G
Barth, Louisa to John Goethals 1-10-1861 Sh
Bartis, Elizabeth A. (Mrs.) to William J. McLean 7-3-1848 (7-4-1848) F
Bartlett, Cornelia A. to Isaac B. Smith 10-13-1856 G
Bartlett, Mary to Adli S. Morrison 10-16-1833 (10-17-1833) Hr
Bartlett, Mary to William F. Campbell 12-31-1849 (1-2-1850) T
Bartlett, Sarah to John Smith 3-20-1839 G
Bartlett, Sarah to W. D. Underhill 10-18-1854 We
Bartley, Bridgett to John Jones 5-20-1854 Sh
Barton(Baston?), Mary M. to Eli Littrell 5-29-1846 (6-2-1846) Hr
Barton, C. E. to A. J. King 11-6-1860 G
Barton, Eliza to William F. Elam 1-7-1868 G
Barton, Elizabeth to John J. Davis 9-27-1847 Ma
Barton, Ellin to John K. Seymore 9-27-1842 (9-29-1842) F
Barton, Fanny to John Russell 6-17-1852 G
Barton, Getteller to John Lamb 3-30-1875 Hy
Barton, Jane to G. K. Miller 6-29-1859 (7-1-1859) Sh
Barton, Jemima G. to William W. Brizendine 12-3-1857 Hn
Barton, Lilly A. to William J. Bryant 9-24-1854 G
Barton, M. C. to James S. Wells 8-6-1852 Hn
Barton, Martha A. to A. T. Colley 12-6-1841 Hn
Barton, Martha to John M. Speight 5-2-1856 Hn
Barton, Mary A. to Washington C. Reed 9-14-1866 Cr
Barton, Mary E. to Harden W. Bateman 7-27-1848 Sh
Barton, Mary Jane to Robert E. Beasley 2-12-1839 Sh
Barton, Mexico to William Barrett 2-15-1850 G
Barton, Minerva Ann to Joshua W. Nichols 10-6-1841 (10-7-1841) Ma
Barton, Nancy J. to Green H. Paschal 10-13-1867 Hn
Barton, Nancy to Thomas Blair 1-1-1868 (1-2-1868) Ma
Barton, Nancy to Wilson L. Davidson 10-18-1837 (10-19-1837) G
Barton, Neer to J. P. Robertson 9-8-1857 We
Barton, Rebecca E. to James T. Abbott 4-8-1846 (4-10-1846) G
Barton, Rebecca to James Parker 2-11-1851 Hn
Barton, S. M. to V. L. Payne 5-17-1873 (5-20-1873) T
Barton, Sarah C. to S. C. Wilson 10-5-1865 G
Barton, Sarah S. to John C. McWhirter 9-29-1869 G
Barton, Sarah to Jas. Kennedy 7-17-1850 Sh
Barton, Semilda A. to Jessee Needham 4-3-1854 (4-6-1854) G
Barton, Sophia W. to Asa Coxe 7-22-1852 Hn
Barton, Susan E. to William D. Walker 12-2-1853 Hn
Barville, Mary J. to J. A. Wright 11-2-1874 (11-6-1874) T
Barwell, Elizabeth to Joseph Knight 1-12-1869 (1-13-1869) T

Baryhill, M. A. to G. C. McCalister 10-20-1846 We
Bas, Elizabeth to Elijah Gibson 12-5-1839 Sh
Basemore, Mary to Phillip West 9-6-1852 (9-28-1852) Sh
Basford, Earry? to William Shoemaker 10-30-1839 Ma
Basford, Sarah L. to Hugh W. Alexander 8-5-1851 Be
Basham, Martha J. to John Davis 2-11-1860 (2-15-1860) O
Bashears, Amanda J. to James Willis Perwit? 9-6-1868 (9-7-1868) T
Bashears, Sarah T. to J. H. C. Richmond 8-7-1865 (8-8-1865) T
Basin, Dora to Gust Bolder 12-17-1870 (12-24-1870) F B
Basinger, Margaret to Eli Dickason 2-4-1836 G
Basinger, Martha C. to James J. Hosea 10-31-1860 G
Baskem, Margaret to James O. Day 12-30-1865 Mn
Baskerville, Ann to Monroe Goodman 12-29-1866 F B
Baskerville, Nancy to Isaac Jones 12-28-1866 (12-29-1866) F B
Baskin, Eliza J. to Turby Baskin 2-26-1867 (2-28-1867) T
Baskin, Frances to Pat? Lovell 12-23-1867 (12-24-1867) T
Baskin, Thursby to F. Farmer 6-25-1829 (6-27-1829) O
Baskins, Eliza Jane to Nicholas H. Boswell 6-9-1842 T
Baskins, Malinda J. to J. M. Kelly 1-21-1861 (1-23-1861) T
Baskins, Sarah Allen to John Lewis Lyons 1-2-1868 G
Baskins, Sarah Ann to Thomas Lavell 11-27-1869 (12-2-1869) T
Baskins, Sarah C. to J. W. Hill 1-12-1869 T
Baskins, Tennessee to George Evans 1-4-1870 (1-6-1870) T
Baskwell, Maria S. to Stephen F. Power 9-13-1838 (SB 1839) Hr
Baskwell, Maria S. to Stephen F. Power 9-13-1839 (9-26-1839) Hr
Baskwell, Rebecca B. to Valentine Vantrease 1-13-1851 Hr
Baskwell, Rutha Ann to John W. Randolph 3-16-1853 Hr
Baskwell, Sophronia to Irvin Q. Rogers 12-28-1854 Hr
Bason, Susan R. to J. F. Saltler 1-30-1862 Sh
Bass, Ailsy to John Fuller 12-17-1878 (no return) Hy
Bass, Amanda to T.(F?) S. Shoulders 8-27-1863 (8-31-1863) Sh
Bass, Arina to Camel Cesterson 12-12-1832 (12-23-1832) Hr
Bass, Berthena to William Brooks 7-2-1832 (7-15-1832) Hr
Bass, C. J. to Hendley Stone 9-4-1858 (9-5-1858) Hr
Bass, Eliza Jane to James F. Carter 10-8-1858 Sh
Bass, Eliza to Benjamin Bean 11-21-1836 (11-22-1836) G
Bass, Elizabeth V. to William M. Campbell 5-2-1853 G
Bass, Elizabeth to Franklin M. Hatler 12-16-1861 We
Bass, Fanny B. to Thos. T. Bowman 4-24-1867 F
Bass, Georgia Bell to John Duncan 10-13-1862 O
Bass, Harriett P. to Drury L. Bass 12-5-1838 Sh
Bass, J. E. to Jesse Estes 12-28-1869 Hy
Bass, M.F. to S. L. Prewett 9-29-1860 (10-24-1860) Hr
Bass, Margaret A. to Leonidas H. Boyce 12-31-1861 (1-5-1861) Hr
Bass, Marselia to B. F. Gay 5-21-1857 (5-24-1857) Hr
Bass, Martha E. to James L. Benthel 4-6-1848 G
Bass, Mary L. to D. M. Duke 12-20-1854 We
Bass, Mary N. to Phillip Reeder 1-13-1851 (1-14-1851) Sh
Bass, Mary T. to Caswell E. George 8-25-1846 (8-26-1846) G
Bass, Mary to B. C. Finney 1-23-1856 (1-24-1856) T
Bass, Mary to John Jesse Lappet 4-13-1871 (no return) F B
Bass, Mary to Tho. D. McFarland 10-7-1850 (10-9-1850) T
Bass, Matilda W. to Alexander M. Jones 12-18-1850 G
Bass, Matilda to John Bain 8-4-1837 Hr
Bass, Matilda to Richard Bennett 7-31-1839 Ma
Bass, Nancy E. to John H. Hunt 9-8-1867 G
Bass, Nancy to James E. Morgan 4-16-1844 (4-24-1844) F
Bass, Orphia C. to Lovit Caraway 3-23-1856 We
Bass, Sallie E. to O. L. Townsend 12-16-1868 (12-17-1868) F
Bass, Sarah J. to William C. Marsh 1-19-1860 (6?-19-1860) T
Bass, Sarah to Calvin Jackson 10-22-1832 (10-31-1832) G
Bass, Sarah to William Jacobs 8-4-1824 Hr
Bassham, A. M. to William J. Caruthers 7-27-1852 (7-26?-1852) O
Bassham, Caroline to Major J. M. White 8-24-1838 (8-25-1838) O
Bassham, L. B. to Benjamin F. Thompson 8-7-1849 O
Bassham, Sarah to George Sanders 10-10-1864 (10-25-1864) O
Bassham, Vicy to Jarret Bell 2-14-1839 O
Bassham, Winna Angeline to Ira Bell 2-25-1844 O
Bassinger, Mary S. to Henry Wells 8-1-1859 G
Batchellor, Rutha A. E. to G. H. Bradford 9-5-1883 (9-6-1883) L
Batchelor, Ada M. to James Bond 9-12-1877 Hy
Batchelor, Elvira to Austin Wharton 11-15-1877 Hy
Batchelor, Emma to Willis Randolph 5-18-1877 Hy
Batchelor, Flora to Charles Cobb 1-15-1874 Hy
Batchelor, Lizzie to Reuben Mann 12-25-1874 Hy
Batchelor, M. A. to Jack Brooks 12-27-1869 (no return) Hy
Batchelor, Malinda to Rufus Cooper 1-24-1877 Hy
Bateman, Caroline to John Haywood 1-3-1839 Cr
Bateman, Caroline to John Neale 1-14-1836 Sh
Bateman, Eliza J. to John Barton 11-30-1848 Sh
Bateman, Frances to David Henderson 9-18-1871 (9-20-1871) T
Bateman, H. F. to Thos. D. Massey 4-17-1858 Sh
Bateman, Margaret E. to C. C. Thomas 5-12-1857 (5-13-1857) Sh
Bateman, Mary R. to James L. Walt 12-5-1859 (12-8-1859) T
Bateman, Nancy M. to Thomas C. Eastham 5-1-1851 (5-8-1851) Sh
Bateman, Sarah C. to Cyrus G. McCrory 10-20-1851 T
Bateman, Virginia F. to John W. W. Crawford 8-29-1857 (8-1?-1857) Ma

Bates (Batey?), Mary E. to S. D. Jenkins 10-5-1864 (10-6-1864) L
Bates, Ann E. V. to Calvin E. McCord 3-7-1860 Hr
Bates, Ann E. V. to Turner J. Harris 4-1-1854 (4-2-1854) Hr
Bates, Callie to Bob Watson 12-29-1883 (12-30-1883) L
Bates, Elizabeth L. to Simeon T. Irvin 1-28-1851 (1-29-1851) O
Bates, Fereby to Frederick Young 12-26-1866 Hy
Bates, Harrett to Kemp Stallings 12-19-1845 (12-23-1845) Hr
Bates, Harriet E. to S. M. Gaines 5-3-1859 (5-4-1859) L
Bates, Jennie (Mrs.) to J. H. Styers 10-3-1885 (10-4-1885) L
Bates, Judia to William B. Convill 5-11-1833 G
Bates, Lucinda to John Jones 12-26-1835 Hr
Bates, Martha J. to Benj. F. Condry 12-31-1864 (1-11-1865) L
Bates, Martha J. to Benjamin Condrey 12-31-1864 (no return) L
Bates, Martha to Hiram C. Crisp 10-20-1842 Hr
Bates, Mary Ann to Robert L. D. Thompson 2-13-1850 L
Bates, Mary T. to Peter C. King 9-27-1861 (no return) We
Bates, Mary to John Connell 5-29-1837 (not executed) G
Bates, Nannie M. to William E. Dickinson 6-12-1874 (6-16-1874) L
Bates, Permelia to Richard Glenn 7-19-1853 Ma
Bates, Roseana M. to John Stewart 8-23-1837 (8-24-1837) G
Bates, Sue V. to Guilford J. Hutchinson 12-18-1866 (no return) L
Bates, Susannah to Wm. A. Moore 12-14-1842 (12-17-1842) Hr
Batewright, Ann to Henry Yount 7-24-1868 T
Bathune, Emmiline E. to C. C. Enderson 8-25-1867 Hy
Bats, Cathrine to H. H. Waldrop 1-7-1863 Mn
Batt, Elizabeth Ann to Labon Holt 5-25-1842 F
Batt, Elizabeth F. to A. G. Pickens 1-17-1842 (1-19-1842) F
Batt, Martha A. (Mrs.) to Young Montague 5-25-1848 F
Batt, Martha J. to Thomas Y. Beard 12-7-1862 We
Batt, Millie to Robert McClerrin 12-6-1870 (no return) F B
Batt, Sarah A. to William G. Sommers 11-19-1862 We
Batte, Mary to E. P. Stewart 9-11-1840 Sh
Battle, Catherine to William Sandlin 7-23-1867 (7-24-1867) L
Battle, Deborah J. to John W. Varner 3-11-1852 G
Battle, Elizabeth B. to Wm. E. Rodgers 5-25-1853 Sh
Battle, Elizabeth to James Gibson 11-22-1837 (11-23-1837) G
Battle, Flora C. to Thos. I. Turley 4-26-1843 Sh
Battle, Keziah to Harris Chaffin 2-1-1871 (no return) F B
Battle, Keziah to Thomas Sorrell 9-7-1861 (9-8-1861) Ma
Battle, Louise A. to Edmund Keely 10-12-1853 G
Battle, Lucy to George Reed 12-2-1869 (no return) F B
Battle, Mary F. to John Fuller 4-3-1873 Dy
Battle, Sanaol Fort to John C. Humphreys 2-14-1842 Sh
Battle, Sarah Ann to Richard Crihfield 11-24-1863 (11-25-1863) L
Battle, Sarah V. to William G. Malone 2-26-1836 Sh
Battle, Temperance P. to Bernard M. Patterson 10-21-1849 Sh
Batts, Jane to Frank Boon 11-18-1866 G
Batts, Jane to Frank Boren 11-18-1866 G
Batts, Martha C. to Jesse J. Smith 10-12-1846 F
Batts, Sarah Jane to John P. Tatum 11-12-1869 G
Baty (Batty, Bety?), Therace to Vincent Bernard 10-10-1863 Sh
Baty, Catherine A. to James W. Batchelor 4-17-1860 (no return) Hy
Baty, Rachel to John Webb 12-28-1867 (12-29-1867) T
Batz, Rosinna to G. A Zunkermann 3-21-1856 Sh
Bauchman, Jane to Thomas Hart 3-4-1847 Hn
Baucom, Candis to Gorton H. Banks 4-26-1838 Cr
Baucom, Charity to John Carter 1-2-1840 Cr
Baucum, A. W. to A. T. Thompson 5-1-1856 We
Baucum, Clara to James Sparks 3-8-1870 Cr
Baucum, Ellen to J. H. W. Hughes 6-12-1854 (no return) F
Baucum, Frances G. T. to C. H. Cowell 10-21-1868 Be
Baucum, Isabella J. to William Fisher 10-3-1852 Hn
Baucum, Mahilda to James Denton 8-4-1864 G
Baucum, Mary A. to J. F. Williams 1-13-1867 Hy
Baucum, Mary M. to Leonard B. Stem 8-21-1856 Hn
Baucum, Mary S. G. to Merrell W. Elkins 9-25-1859 Hn
Baucum, Nancy E. to W. A. Vaughan 4-29-1861 G
Baucum, Nancy to Andrew R. Weaks 8-7-1842 Hn
Baucum, S. F. to J. B. Pace 2-12-1873 Hy
Baucum, Sarah to Joseph Yarbrough 1-21-1845 (1-22-1845) F
Bauer, Mina to Marcus RoJoux 8-27-1855 (8-28-1855) Sh
Bauert, Kate to F. Felix 10-24-1860 Sh
Baugh, Agnes A. B. B. to Charles W. Hutcheson 2-27-1841 (3-4-1841) Hr
Baugh, Ann M. to Irvin Davis 11-15-1852 Sh
Baugh, Elizabeth J. to G. C. Summerell 9-13-1849 Sh
Baugh, Fannie to John R. Baugh 4-6-1858 T
Baugh, Harriet S. to A. T. Watson 10-4-1859 Sh
Baugh, Jennie to C. Crews 9-21-1864 (9-22-1864) Sh
Baugh, M. S. to W. J. Shillings 7-31-1866 F
Baugh, Mariah to John W. Dotson 2-13-1857 (2-14-1857) Sh
Baugh, Martha E. to M. H. Jones 2-10-1857 We
Baugh, Martha T. to Gustavus Berdon 6-11-1867 (6-18-1867) F
Baugh, Mary E. to R. F. Warren 2-17-1868 (2-20-1868) F
Baugh, Mary N. to William L. Wooten 12-31-1851 (no return) F
Baugh, Mary to U. T. Stewart 9-?-1854 (no return) F
Baugh, Sarah to Reuben Daulton 4-15-1863 Sh
Baughman, Angeline to John R. Wood 11-22-1860 (5-21-1861) O

Baughs, Mary D. to G. W. Alexander 8-24-1870 (no return) Hy
Baugus, Sarah to Howard Owen 12-25-1845 Sh
Baugus?, Mary to Albert G. Ritus (Retus) 7-6-1836 Sh
Baulkum, Matilda to James Davidson 10-18-1866 G
Baulkum, Polly to Winfrey Scott 2-4-1839 (2-6-1839) F
Baumgardner, Louisa to George Keller 4-11-1860 (4-12-1860) Sh
Baumgartner, Elizabeth to Joseph Keller 5-22-1845 Sh
Bavard, Sarah E. to Eli Tilghman 12-22-1866 O
Baw, Allice to Robt. Johnson 12-3-1867 (no return) F
Baw, Catharin to Calvin E. Stewart 12-28-1851 (no return) F
Baw, Harriet to George Robertson 8-22-1867 (no return) F B
Baw, Julia to William Farley 12-15-1854 (no return) F
Baw, L. M. to C. W. McConnell 4-23-1860 (4-26-1860) F
Baw, Winny Ann to Edward D. Stewart 12-30-1845 F
Baxler, Lizzie to Zedrick Warren 12-23-1867 (12-24-1867) F B
Baxter, Adaline to Richard Jones 7-18-1870 (8-1-1870) Dy
Baxter, Annie to J. J. Winburn 12-12-1878 Hy
Baxter, C. E. to W. M. Mays 4-2-1883 (4-3-1883) L
Baxter, Dinah to John Strain 8-20-1879 L B
Baxter, E. E. to W. H. Beal 12-12-1865 F
Baxter, Elizabeth to James M. Matheny 8-25-1859 We
Baxter, Emily A. to E. H. Blankenship 12-12-1865 F
Baxter, Henrietta to Augustus Kerr 7-6-1868 (7-18-1868) L
Baxter, Lizzie to Jo Chamberlain 6-28-1871 (no return) Dy
Baxter, Lucy C. to D. S. Nicholson 12-17-1868 F
Baxter, Malinda to Isaac Lewis 12-21-1867 (12-24-1867) F B
Baxter, Margaret A. to John Rutledge 1-22-1846 Sh
Baxter, Margaret A. to William Curry 10-26-1865 Mn
Baxter, Margaret E. to E. T. Spears 11-8-1849 Cr
Baxter, Margaret Lucinda to Tamberlin Wood 11-11-1829 (2-5-1830) O
Baxter, Margaret R.? to Rufus W. Powell 2-6-1850 F
Baxter, Martha to William Childress 3-31-1842 O
Baxter, Mary A. to William Strong 1-25-1841 Sh
Baxter, Mary C. to Cyrum Sharp 1-16-1849 Ma
Baxter, Mary to James D. Martin 12-20-1849 Cr
Baxter, Mary to James D. Mitchell 12-20-1849 Cr
Baxter, N. J. to William A. Sayle 1-23-1861 (1-24-1861) Cr
Baxter, Nora to Wm. Lazenby 11-20-1869 (11-25-1869) F
Baxter, Sallie E. to J. F. Humphreys 12-18-1860 F
Baxter, Sarah E. to John W. McNeely 3-6-1838 Sh
Baxter, Virginia C. to B. W. Barfield 1-9-1885 (1-12-1885) L
Baxter, Willie to J. W. Hawkins 12-3-1878 (12-4-1878) L
Baxter?, Martha to John Fitzpatrick 11-14-1877 (12-6-1877) L
Bay, Mary to J. H. Markum 7-14-1862 (7-15-1862) Sh
Bay, Mary to J. H. Muskum 7-14-1862 Sh
Bayby, Mary to Thos. Fitzgerald 12-11-1872 (12-12-1872) Cr B
Bayer, Gimima to Edmend Pleasant 10-20-1859 We
Bayer, Nancy C. to Daniel Mooney 9-9-1844 We
Bayers (Bayliss)?, Eliza to Wm. H. Sneed 4-28-1838 Sh
Baylep, Lucy to William Crews 12-11-1857 We
Bayles, Lucy to C. L. Holliday 3-20-1867 (3-21-1867) Cr
Bayles, Nancy P. to Isaac H. Walker 7-20-1858 Cr
Bayless, C. S. to M. A. Allen 4-17-1860 (4-18-1864) Sh
Bayless, Ellenorah E. to Anguss Greenlaw 7-13-1844 (7-14-1844) F
Bayless, Martha to Isaac Allen 1-10-1849 Cr
Bayless, Melvina to Jacob S. Guren 12-10-1862 (no return) Hn
Bayley, Elizah to W. A. Scoby 10-25-1870 (10-26-1870) Cr
Bayley, Lillie to W. C. Woodruff 2-19-1861 (2-21-1861) Sh
Baylis, Eliza Ann A. to John M. Speight 10-13-1858 (no return) Hn
Bayliss, E. J. to J. C. Davis 4-17-1860 (4-18-1860) Sh
Bayliss, M. E. A. to Theophilus Munford 12-22-1846 Sh
Bayliss, Martha F. A. to Isaac N. McCarter 9-18-1853 Hn
Bayliss, Susan E. to James Coleman 5-31-1851 Sh
Baylor, E. Ann to David Walker 11-11-1865 Hn
Bayn, Ann to Jonah Y. Dodson 8-11-1846 (8-13-1846) G
Bayne (Bain), Mary Ann to Michael Powers 2-5-1848 Sh
Bayne, Caroline to Wm. B. McSpadden 4-13-1848 Sh
Bayne, Frances to James S. Farris 2-9-1835 Sh
Bayne, Mary Ella to James I. Harris 6-7-1879 L
Bayne, Mary to John Edwards 7-25-1828 G
Bayne, Sarah to Jesse L. Harris 8-20-1856 (8-21-1856) Sh
Baynes, Caroline to Zeb Mann 1-15-1870 Hy
Baynes, Rachel to Jim Oldham 2-6-1873 Hy
Baynes, Sue O. to J. M. Smoot 10-3-1877 Hy
Bayns, Rachal to Buck Mann 1-5-1878 Hy
Bays, Frances Betcy to Thomas Wesley Roberts 9-10-1857 (9-11-1857) T
Bayse, Sarah Narcissa to Alexander Tims 3-1-1854 (3-2-1854) T
Baysinger, Elizabeth to Reuben Fletcher 9-21-1831 (9-22-1831) G
Bazdel, Penelope to Lemuel H. Flemming 2-23-1853 Sh
Bazdel, Susan A. to M. E. Pritchett 1-19-1852 Sh
Bazemore, Martha A. to Mercer McWest 7-6-1853 (7-7-1853) Sh
Bazemore, Sally to L. M. West 8-15-1853 (8-17-1853) Sh
Bazzel, Eliza to Henry Barmon 10-3-1849 (no return) F
Beabers(Biebers), Sophia F. to W. J. Beavers 11-9-1858 Hr
Beach, Eliza L. to John S. Irvin 10-4-1866 Hn
Beach, Mary J. B. to Dempsey Been? 11-29-1849 Hn
Bead, Katie to Jake Cole 1-30-1872 (no return) Hy

Beaden, Mary to James Hines 12-21-1860 (1-1-1861) Hr
Beadles, Elizabeth to Alfred T. Polsgrove 2-22-1857 O
Beadles, Mary J. to Joseph D. Thompson 12-27-1859 We
Beal, Elisabeth to James Gregory 7-5-1852 Hn
Beal, Mollie to Francis O. Browning 12-9-1867 Ma
Beall, Mattie H. (Mrs.) to John F. Duke 12-23-1867 G
Bealtin?, Jane to W. Thos. Tillman 1-30-1869 (2-4-1869) T
Bealy, Sarah E. to Henry S. Johnson 4-19-1850 (4-24-1850) Ma
Beaman, F. to John Pentecost 8-24-1853 Hn
Beaman?, Nancy A. F. to James F. Moore 2-1-1852 Hn
Bean, M. A. T. to Stephen Tucker 10-25-1870 (no return) Dy
Bean, Martha Ann to Hiram H. Banks 2-15-1837 (2-23-1837) G
Bean, Nancy to Abner D. Thomas 4-15-1840 (4-16-1840) G
Bean, Rhoda J. to Thomas A. Sanders 1-3-1848 Sh
Bean, Sarah J. to E. G. Parham 2-11-1862 Hr
Bean, Tempe to H. C. Hendricks 12-8-1873 (12-9-1873) Dy
Beard, Alice to Jackson Henley 12-14-1882 (12-15-1882) L
Beard, Amelda L. to M. D. Fly 1-16-1861 Sh
Beard, Elizabeth Ann to Robert J. McFarlin 10-21-1858 Hn
Beard, Elizabeth M. to James R. Tyson 12-18-1848 Hn
Beard, Elizabeth M. to Wm. T. Shaply 4-20-1846 (4-28-1846) Hr
Beard, Ellen to Charlie Lanier 11-28-1872 Hy
Beard, Fanny A. to Henry Windrow 11-6-1885 (11-7-1885) L
Beard, Harriet Ann to Henry Strother 7-18-1873 (no return) Dy B
Beard, Harriet to Jerry Marley 2-27-1878 (2-28-1878) L
Beard, Jamima to Joseph Jones 12-6-1841 G
Beard, Kitty to Bob Glass 8-26-1871 O B
Beard, Lucinda to F. S. Whitman 11-2-1864 Sh
Beard, Lydia to William Wilson 4-30-1873 T
Beard, M. E. to Wiley Baucum 12-21-1865 Mn
Beard, M. J. to William R. Vires 10-29-1865 Mn
Beard, Margaret to Jonas Young 8-5-1847 Ma
Beard, Margarett to William Baker 1-25-1844 F
Beard, Martha A. to John G. Hill 11-4-1862 We
Beard, Martha J. to J. M. Beard 7-5-1867 Hn
Beard, Martha R. A. to Thomas Harley 7-2-1849 (7-11-1849) Hr
Beard, Martha to Isaac Johnson 1-19-1872 (1-20-1872) Dy
Beard, Mary A. to William A. Tyson 9-22-1852 Hn
Beard, Mary Jane to Doc Tyus 2-24-1880 (2-25-1880) L
Beard, Mary Jane to Lawrence Smiley 11-14-1850 Hn
Beard, Mary to Samuel Bell 12-2-1869 (12-4-1869) Cr
Beard, Mollie to Armistead Smith 11-11-1880 Dy
Beard, Nancy to Frank Moore 12-11-1878 Dy
Beard, Rebecca J. to Nicholas B. Byars 2-26-1852 Hn
Beard, Sarena to Thomas H. Bell 5-18-1861 Mn
Beard, Susan to William Seawright 12-5-1853 (no return) Hn
Bearden, Martha Ann to Abraham Parker 1-27-1840 Sh
Bearden, Mary A. to David Williams 8-13-1849 Sh
Bearden, Nancy A. to Noah Dunning 3-1-1840 Sh
Beasley, Alice to John A. Robins 3-25-1860 Hn
Beasley, Ann E. to T. J. Pinson 12-4-1854 Hn
Beasley, E. to W. E. Guthery 2-27-1841 Be
Beasley, Eliza to James Griffin 2-8-1875 L
Beasley, Fanny to Henry Buford 2-6-1867 (2-7-1867) F B
Beasley, Florentine to Thomas W. Crawford 2-17-1847 Hn
Beasley, Frannie T. to James A. Brown 1-5-1869 L
Beasley, Jane to Joseph Kerr 3-7-1871 (3-8-1871) Dy
Beasley, L. F. to G. W. Smith 11-14-1853 (no return) F
Beasley, Louisa F. to James M. Gray 4-17-1839 (4-18-1839) F
Beasley, Mahala C. to Charles W. Harrell (Howell?) 11-17-1858 (no return) L
Beasley, Martha Ann to John R. Alston 11-8-1853 Be
Beasley, Mary A. to Wm. J. Robinson 1-16-1847 Cr
Beasley, Mary C. to John A. Grissam 8-13-1863 (no return) Hn
Beasley, Mary Jane to Hiram W. Wadkins 7-29-1846 We
Beasley, Matilda to Logan T. Cole 6-14-1873 (6-17-1873) T
Beasley, Mitta to H. Trump 11-2-1867 (11-4-1867) B
Beasley, Nancy (Mrs.) to John Hawthorne 11-16-1864 Sh
Beasley, Nancy M. to G. M. D. Haislip 9-18-1866 O
Beasley, Nancy to Dennis Bell 2-5-1855 Be
Beasley, Priscilla E. to James A. McGuire 10-5-1871 L
Beasley, Rebecca to S. A. Pinson 10-11-1854 (no return) Hn
Beasley, Sarah E. to R. C. Pinson 12-28-1858 Hn
Beasley, Sarah H. to A. J. Hudspeth 3-28-1858 We
Beasley, Sarah J. to W. D. Springer 12-21-1867 (12-22-1867) L
Beasley, Sarah to John Douglas 1-12-1853 Be
Beasley, Thersey Ann to Houston Craig 2-8-1865 L
Beasley, Virginia A. to James R. Hodge 6-13-1854 (no return) F
Beasly, Lee to S. Thompkins 2-1-1882 (2-2-1882) L
Beasly, Lucy Q. (Mrs.) to John M. Thomas 4-8-1844 (no return) F
Beasly, Mary F. to Jas. P. Kavanaugh 3-7-1863 (no return) Hy
Beasly, Nancy J. to James P. Lovelace 11-19-1885 L
Beassee, Sarah Jane to Logan Franklin 5-20-1857 O
Beatie, Lucas to Jim Porter 12-28-1870 Hy
Beaton, Adaline to James Doughty 11-15-1866 Be
Beaton, Eveline to James F. Cooper 1-6-1858 Be
Beaton, Hannah Matilda to James Hines 12-27-1848 (12-28-1848) Hr
Beaton, Margaret P. to Wm. R. Powel 5-28-1851 Be

Beaton, Mary to John West 10-10-1844 Be CC
Beaton, Mary to John West 10-12-1844 Be
Beatty, Eleanor L. to John T. Trezevant 1-31-1838 Sh
Beatty, Frances J. to Henry R. Pugh 4-20-1842 Sh
Beaty, Harriet E. to E. D. Maxwell 1-3-1856 T
Beaty, Mary A. to Thos. C. Rainey 12-20-1869 Ma
Beaty, Mary Ann to William Dickinson 12-25-1852 (12-26-1852) Ma
Beaty, Mary F. to Calier F. Sawyer 2-8-1870 Ma
Beaty, Mattie E. to John H. (Dr.) Jones 10-7-1867 Ma
Beaty, Nancy J. to Tho. H. Long 11-17-1859 (11-18-1859) Hr
Beaumont, Jane to Jo Eudaly 1-5-1867 Dy
Beaumont, Lou to Dan Parker 2-19-1869 (no return) Dy
Beaumont, Lou to Stephen Townsend 8-16-1877 Dy
Beaver, A. F. to E. J. Turnage 7-10-1872 (7-11-1872) T
Beaver, Angeline to W. H. Harrison 1-25-1878 (1-27-1878) Dy
Beaver, Anna to Abraham S. Dial 5-2-1835 G
Beaver, Cordelia to John D. Waldrop 7-27-1851 Hn
Beaver, Eliza F. to John B. Thomson 12-23-1867 (12-24-1867) F
Beaver, Elizabeth to John A. Goad 9-17-1852 (9-22-1852) Hr
Beaver, Isabella to B. F. Houk 4-20-1867 (4-21-1867) F
Beaver, J. V. to A. A. Bambridge 8-6-1870 (8-9-1870) T
Beaver, Leira to Charles Park 10-23-1858 Be
Beaver, Mary to Henry Ballard 2-1-1867 (8-15-1867) F B
Beaver, Mildred to Wm. A. jr. Turnage 2-14-1865 T
Beaver, Rebecca Ann to Mathew Barberry 9-15-1842 F
Beaver, Sarah Ann to S. Williams 7-23-1845 (8-7-1845) F
Beavers, Anna? to John Stevens 5-10-1869 (5-13-1869) T
Beavers, C. M. to A. C. Atherton 1-8-1866 (1-10-1866) F
Beavers, Cathrine E. to Joshua Huffman 5-9-1847 Cr
Beavers, E. to D. Pearce 3-4-1841 Be
Beavers, Elizabeth to Obediah March 10-29-1850 (10-30-1850) Hr
Beavers, Ellen to David Hill 7-13-1867 (7-14-1867) Cr
Beavers, Jane to Baher Ruse 5-23-1864 (5-27-1864) Cr
Beavers, Jane to Wm. McMillan 4-4-1843 Sh
Beavers, Laura L. to Virgil Long 9-1-1866 (9-6-1866) T
Beavers, Lucinda to John W. Ables 2-26-1839 F
Beavers, Mandy to Joe Oliver 12-3-1868 (12-5-1868) F B
Beavers, Martha H. to Isaac Cail no date (with Jun 1853) G
Beavers, Martha Jane to Noah R. Ussery 12-20-1852 (1-4-1853) Hr
Beavers, Mary A. to A. G. Ralph 1-2-1860 (not endorsed) F
Beavers, Mary to Phil May 1-6-1868 (no return) F B
Beavers?, Mehaly to Joseph Culpepper 5-30-1844 (no return) Hn
Beavors, Sarah E. to William J. Rains 4-8-1864 Hn
Beazley, Elizabeth S. to Henry Head 1-13-1838 (1-24-1838) G
Beazley, Liza to J. H. Gilbert 11-4-1866 Be
Beazley, Malissa J. to Thomas P. Childress 8-15-1867 Be
Beazley, Virlinda C. to James A. Harwood 7-22-1834 G
Bechtold, Caroline R. to Balthasar Decker 2-7-1860 Sh
Beck (Berk), Margaret to Samuel F. Haegan (Haagan) 11-23-1849 Sh
Beck, Alsey M. to John O. Fox 5-6-1850 (5-8-1850) G
Beck, Ann to W. H. Tisdel 3-24-1851 Sh
Beck, Annis to John Meredith 12-20-1853 Hn
Beck, Aurelia to J. Schlesinger 6-24-1864 Sh
Beck, Isabella to W. S. McClintock 12-31-1861 Mn
Beck, Josephine to G. W. Murray 3-22-1854 Sh
Beck, Lively to Tipton Horsted? 1-29-1849 Hn
Beck, Louisa to F. Koerper 12-27-1855 Sh
Beck, Louisa to Frederick Kooper 12-27-1855 Sh
Beck, Lucy J. to Salathial Ruddell (Buddell?) 9-25-1855 (9-26-1855) Sh
Beck, Margaret to Bernard Hollander 3-7-1860 (3-8-7860) Sh
Beck, Martha to William Brandon 1-7-1839 (no return) Hn
Beck, Mary A. to G. N. Gerris 9-18-1856 We
Beck, Mary to _____ 10-16-1851 Hn
Beck, Nancy to James Rice 1-11-1844 Hn
Beck, Rebecca Ann to Cornelius Hughes 6-23-1857 O
Beck, Rutha to William Davis 12-3-1868 G
Beck, Susan A. to Eli Douglass 9-20-1869 (no return) Cr
Beckam, L. A. to W. H. Cartwright 1-3-1864 G
Beckam?, Mitilda F. to J. T. Fletcher 6-13-1860 G
Beckert, Enna to Charles Willenberg 5-13-1861 Sh
Becket, Eliza to Thomas Jones 12-25-1879 (12-26-1879) Dy
Becket, Sarah to Jack Fumbanks 2-10-1869 (no return) Dy
Beckett, Frances to Joseph McKnight 1-29-1872 (1-30-1872) Dy
Beckett, Malinda to Knight? Harrell 2-23-1878 (no return) Dy
Beckett, Sarah to William Meadows 1-15-1873 (1-16-1873) Dy
Beckham, Elizabeth to Wm. Jack 6-26-1868 (7-5-1868) F
Beckham, Sarah to Smith H. Gee 12-12-1835 G
Beckley, Lucy Ann to Wm. P. McWherter 1-12-1859 We
Beckley, S. M. to H. Gatewood 5-14-1856 We
Beckner, Mary (Mrs.) to S. B. Wilcox 11-2-1857 Sh
Beckom, Henrietta to Caleb Howell 8-26-1868 G
Beckum, Mary to William Hardy 12-18-1851 O
Beckworth, L. to David L. Wright 9-12-1842 (9-15-1842) O
Becten, E. C. to William Capps 3-24-1867 G
Becton, Delitha to Benjamin May 10-28-1833 (10-29-1833) G
Becton, Elizabeth (Mrs.) to William Russel Palmer 3-1-1855 (3-4-1855) Sh
Becton, Frances E. to A. M. Grier 2-11-1852 (2-12-1852) G

Becton, Mary L. W. to Milton B. Boyd 10-26-1850 (10-27-1850) Ma
Becton, Mattie A. to H. C. Barton 2-16-1869 G
Beddo, Phoeba to John R. Pandry 9-23-1869 Ma
Bedford, Elenor to John J. Hudspeth 3-15-1840 O
Bedford, Jane to G. Edwards Fletcher 9-21-1824 O
Bedford, Jane to Robert T. Caldwell 3-15-1840 O
Bedford, Lydia M. to Lysander Adams 7-23-1826 O
Bedford, Mary A. to Thomas Atwood 11-6-1851 (11-7-1851) Sh
Bedford, Mary to John Matheney 12-17-1828 (12-18-1828) O
Bedford, Matilda to Joe Titus 10-29-1877 L
Bedford, Sarah M. to Shelby Teater 3-15-1840 O
Bedford, Susan S. to Larkin M. Mathews (Mathis?) 1-2-1873 L
Bedford, Susannah to James Bain 2-21-1829 O
Bedford, Teresa M. to George Burwell Loftin 4-29-1831 (5-4-1831) Ma
Bedlock, Mary E. to Joseph B. Ridgeway 12-25-1860 Hn
Bedtick, Mary J. to Joseph Rosson 3-3-1865 G
Bedwell, Elizabeth to John H. Brown 4-13-1845 Hn
Bedwell, Elizabeth to Lewis Hutchens 8-21-1859 Hn
Bedwell, Mary E. to John Pennington 1-23-1861 (no return) Hy
Bedwell, Nancy to William Fleming 5-25-1859 (5-29-1859) Ma
Beech, Sarah J. to Edward W. Smith 6-19-1855 Hn
Beechamp, Caroline to William Ellison 6-7-1842 (no return) Hn
Beedles, Lucinda to James Polsgrove 5-29-1856 Hn
Beedles, Martha A. to G. P. Murrell 2-10-1857 We
Beeman, Susan to John Spates 12-18-1846 Hn
Been?, Eliza A. to James C. Crawford 11-29-1849 Hn
Beer, Roselia to Joseph Hauf 1-24-1854 (no return) F
Beever, Nancy G. to Caswell Finch 10-20-1852 Cr
Beger, Christina to D. Shifley 10-3-1859 Sh
Beggs, M. E. to R. J. E. Byrn 11-16-1881 L
Behrens, Theriasia to Gotlieb Pfisterer 4-13-1859 (4-14-1859) Sh
Beirns, Wineford to Patrick Herny (Haney) 5-6-1858 (5-9-1858) Sh
Beiver, Martha to Isham Finch 10-12-1856 Cr
Belch, Elizer A. to John C. Grissom 5-5-1867 G
Belch, M. A. to Benj. F. Cooper 11-25-1856 G
Belch, Mary A. to W. H. Foster 12-27-1867 G
Belch, Mary E. to Jas. Tarpley 5-6-1869 Hy
Belch, Mary to William R. Stublefield 6-1-1858 (6-3-1858) G
Belew, Amanda to Ned Long 11-25-1877 Hy
Belew, Cornelia to Aaron Springer 10-8-1853 (10-10-1853) G
Belew, Frances C. to Stephen McPherson 3-17-1849 (3-16?-1849) G
Belew, Hanah to Thos. A. Flippin 12-20-1840 G
Belew, Jane to Aaron Belew 3-6-1841 (3-9-1841) G
Belew, L. E. F. to Harrison Simpson 10-24-1867 G
Belew, M. A. to W. A. Palmer 10-27-1868 (10-28-1868) Cr
Belew, Martha to William Walker 2-28-1842 G
Belew, Mary to F. M. Seymore 10-28-1869 G
Belew, Nancy to Ammon Coleman 7-19-1831 Sh
Belew, P. J. to H. M. Flippin 11-11-1866 G
Belew, S. C. to W. Prat 9-13-1870 Cr
Belew, Tennessee to W. H. Seymore 1-19-1864 G
Belew, Vandelia to William M. Belew 1-15-1870 G
Belford, Rena to Dan Calhoun 5-16-1870 (5-18-1870) T
Beliew, Sarah to Gordon Smith 1-8-1861 G
Bell, Abigill? to Hiram Bowlin 5-16-1869 Hy
Bell, Adelia C. to Thomas Chambliss 9-7-1853 (9-8-1853) Hr
Bell, Amanda J. to George W. Cain 9-9-1871 (9-10-1871) Ma
Bell, Amanda to Henry Adams 12-31-1869 Cr
Bell, America J. to Marshall Stiles 11-10-1855 Sh
Bell, Angeline to Isaac Jones 10-17-1885 (10-18-1885) L
Bell, Ann T. L. to William C. Ervin 7-12-1855 (7-15-1855) Hr
Bell, Ann to George W. Terrill 9-5-1839 G
Bell, Ann to Willis Grissom 6-17-1865 G
Bell, Barbary Ann to Mathew Yeates 7-24-1852 (7-25-1852) G
Bell, Caroline to Joseph Warren 4-14-1868 (no return) Dy
Bell, Charlotte E. to Marshall Stiles 3-26-1860 (3-28-1860) Sh
Bell, Charlotte to David Stone 6-18-1841 Cr
Bell, Charton to Henry Woodson 1-3-1868 G B
Bell, Claney to Wm. Bush 10-5-1843 Cr
Bell, Columbia A. to Sydney Markham 1-6-1851 (1-8-1851) Sh
Bell, Darcus E. to William McQuary 8-14-1871 (no return) Hy
Bell, E. E. to J. O. Craig 3-26-1877 (3-28-1877) Dy
Bell, E. J. to W. J. Churchman 2-2-1871 Dy
Bell, Eliza A. to James E. Winsett 5-16-1867 F
Bell, Eliza to Bristow Danner 1-19-1870 G B
Bell, Eliza to Nelson Watfort 2-3-1877 Hy
Bell, Eliza to Robert H. Reed 11-14-1848 G
Bell, Elizabeth A. to John H. Mitchell 3-9-1861 (3-10-1861) Sh
Bell, Elizabeth Ann to Henry C. Wyatt 10-5-1843 Hn
Bell, Elizabeth J. to Jacob Webb 7-12-1846 Sh
Bell, Elizabeth to Albert H. Legion 2-1-1858 G
Bell, Elizabeth to J. C. Armour 6-23-1853 Be
Bell, Elizabeth to Wm. B. Delaney 12-1-1852 Cr
Bell, Elizabeth to Wm. T. Gardner 10-9-1861 (no return) L
Bell, Ella A. to John A. Coolidge 12-23-1864 (12-28-1864) Sh
Bell, Ellen C. to Samuel H. Reed 2-22-1848 (2-24-1848) G
Bell, Ellen P. to R. H. Joyner 11-28-1865 O

Bell, Ellen to John Knox 12-4-1839 (12-5-1839) G
Bell, Emeline R. to Alexander Terry 3-6-1843 G
Bell, Emily to David Holloway 9-23-1857 O
Bell, Emma to T. C. Buchanan 4-26-1877 Dy
Bell, F. J. to Joseph Corder 6-29-1872 (6-30-1872) T
Bell, Fannie to Peter Pillow 9-12-1875 (no return) Dy
Bell, Fanny A. to Emerson Etheridge 10-17-1849 We
Bell, Francetta V. to H. B. White 1-16-1863 Sh
Bell, Harriett to John R. Hall 9-26-1845 (no return) Cr
Bell, Isabella to George Broach 10-1-1839 Cr
Bell, Isabella to Henry Hale 9-25-1878 (10-16-1879?) L B
Bell, Jane to A. G. McAuley 9-20-1872 (9-22-1872) Cr B
Bell, Jennie to Saml. Enochs 12-27-1871 (12-28-1871) Dy
Bell, Jinnie to Carroll Hawkins 4-14-1872 (no return) Cr B
Bell, Judia to James Parker 1-10-1867 Hy
Bell, Juley to John M. Wallis 12-11-1864 (no return) Hn
Bell, Ledia? Rosanna to Jobe Jackson 9-6-1850 Cr
Bell, Linda C. to Joseph A. Blythe 4-26-1844 Hn
Bell, Lively to Jno. Dudley 11-29-1840 Be
Bell, Lizzie to Henry Spence 6-30-1876 Dy
Bell, Lizzie to Thos. C. Michell 5-11-1867 (no return) Dy
Bell, Louanna to Arther Harbert 1-23-1871 Hy
Bell, Louisa E. to C. J. Wallis 5-15-1862 O
Bell, Lucinda to Lewis Hutchins 9-30-1865 (10-1-1865) F
Bell, Lucretia to Henry I. Hurt 10-24-1870 Dy B
Bell, Lucy A. to Granville Drake 3-19-1873 Cr B
Bell, Luticia to Robt. J. Bragg 11-19-1845 T
Bell, M. A. to John W. Finley 11-30-1857 Cr
Bell, M. E. to T. W. Chrisman 2-27-1877 Dy
Bell, M. J. to J. H. Dunlap 11-13-1855 Hn
Bell, M. J. to Richard Holloway 3-1-1856 O
Bell, M. M. to M. M. Bell 9-2-1858 Cr
Bell, Maggie A. to H. F. Smith 11-12-1867 Ma
Bell, Malinda to William Grantham 8-30-1849 Hr
Bell, Malvina B. to John B. Ash Duncan 10-11-1862 (no return) Hy
Bell, Margaret to Nicholas M. Darnall 8-29-1865 (no return) Cr
Bell, Margarett L. to William H. Thompson 4-4-1855 (no return) F
Bell, Mariah to James Dillon 3-23-1874 (3-24-1874) Dy
Bell, Mariah to Sam Jones 12-29-1879 (no return) Dy
Bell, Marina T. to John P. Harris 4-1-1856 (4-2-1856) O
Bell, Martha Ann to James E. Hays 8-18-1853 G
Bell, Martha Ann to Wm. W. Yarbrough 2-5-1847 Be
Bell, Martha J. to Lovick J. Griffin 7-2-1861 (no return) Hy
Bell, Martha M. to C. S. Aston 12-6-1847 F
Bell, Martha to Harvey Bell 1-3-1871 (1-10-1871) Dy
Bell, Martha to Henry Blackman 7-27-1863 G
Bell, Martha to James B. Carnahan 4-1-1831 (4-2-1831) G
Bell, Martha to Richard C. Tyler 10-28-1858 G
Bell, Mary An to Jesse H. Sullivant 12-12-1848 (12-14-1848) F
Bell, Mary Ann K. to Wm. J. Lowder 2-16-1864 (no return) Cr
Bell, Mary E. to O. B. Goodman 10-19-1860 (no return) Dy
Bell, Mary J. to W. M. Gwin 12-19-1855 Cr
Bell, Mary Jane to Richard Holloway 3-1-1851 O
Bell, Mary M. to James F. Smith 3-19-1845 (3-20-1845) G
Bell, Mary to Barnett Smith 12-20-1834 G
Bell, Mary to H. D. Hay 7-19-1871 (7-20-1871) Dy
Bell, Mary to Moses Carter 7-8-1863 Sh
Bell, Maryann K. to Wm. J. Lowder 2-16-1864 Cr
Bell, Matilda to John Tipton 12-26-1873 (12-27-1873) T
Bell, Mattia to J. L. Franklin 4-9-1863 Mn
Bell, Mattie to Alex Swift 2-28-1885 L
Bell, Michel to James Bell 5-8-1832 G
Bell, Minerva S. to Joseph Lusk 7-23-1833 (7-24-1833) Hr
Bell, Mollie E. to T. C. Price 2-17-1859 Cr
Bell, N. to J. K> Morris 8-23-1842 Be
Bell, Nancy A. to Peter Clyatt 7-10-1879 (7-16-1879) L
Bell, Nancy A. to James F. Smith 6-4-1860 (6-6-1860) Hr
Bell, Nancy P. to James J. Logan 7-3-1841 G
Bell, Nancy Rebecca to Lemuel B. Nance 5-15-1855 O
Bell, Nancy to Barnabas Nowell 3-19-1831 Ma
Bell, Nancy to John J. McCain 12-4-1856 Hn
Bell, Nancy to Peter Worrell 6-2-1856 Ma
Bell, Nancy to T. G. Sertor 7-2-1867 G
Bell, Nannie B. to Jas. W. Brooks 6-22-1865 (6-23-1865) F
Bell, Narcissa to Alexander Black 8-25-1833 (9-26-1833) G
Bell, Pauline A. to Robert R. McLeary 9-18-1849 Sh
Bell, R. A. to W. H. Hamell 1-20-1869 Hy
Bell, R. J. to Wm. R. Love 9-17-1859 (9-18-1859) F
Bell, Rada E. to H. P. Lowry 10-17-1855 (no return) Hn
Bell, Ragner to B. F. France 1-26-1858 Cr
Bell, Rebecca A. to Richard C. Dowell 7-16-1863 Sh
Bell, Rebecca to Richard D. Powell 7-16-1863 Sh
Bell, Rebecca W. to Lenard W. Morris 4-26-1849 F
Bell, Rebecca to David Kelley 9-1-1866 G
Bell, Rebecca to John Cobb 9-4-1866 (9-15-1866) T
Bell, Rebecca to William C. Rainey 9-27-1858 (9-29-1858) L
Bell, S. A. to J. T. Stamps 12-6-1865 (12-13-1865) Dy

Bell, S. C. to G. R. Owen 12-13-1865 Hn
Bell, Sallie C. to J. H. Walton 12-7-1868 (no return) Dy
Bell, Sally to James H. Smally 7-10-1850 Be
Bell, Sarah (Mrs.) to Vinson Kenedy 4-21-1841 (no return) F
Bell, Sarah A. J. (Mrs.) to S. Pitmon 5-15-1841 (no return) F
Bell, Sarah A. to T. C. (Capt.) Buchanan 6-28-1875 (6-29-1875) Dy
Bell, Sarah C. to N. H. Aycock 12-11-1861 Dy
Bell, Sarah E. to James W. Cooper 6-12-1870 G
Bell, Sarah F. to J. W. Locke 5-17-1860 (no return) Hy
Bell, Sarah J. to James B. Owen 10-10-1859 (no return) Hy
Bell, Sarah to John W. Bell 6-2-1849 (6-5-1849) G
Bell, Sarah to Joseph Brantley 1-24-1878 Hy
Bell, Sarah to Solomon Chilton 12-31-1883 (1-1-1884) L
Bell, Sintha to Eli Todd 12-29-1857 Hn
Bell, Sue to R. G. Harrell 12-19-1866 (12-20-1866) Dy
Bell, Susan J. to Bryant Johnson 1-9-1861 G
Bell, Susannah W. to Lewelyn T. Tisdale 12-16-1854 (12-17-1854) T
Bell, Unity Jane Brigget to Thomas W. Wallingford 12-17-1855 Ma
Bell, V. P. to B. F. Barnes 1-12-1870 Hy
Bell, Zelpha A. to William HSansel 11-4-1852 Be
Bell, ____ to ----- Holloway 3-1-1858 O
Bell?, Isabella H. (Miss) to Chas. L. Allen 6-25-1864 (6-26-1864) Sh
Bellamy, Eliza Jane to James Foster 1-3-1853 Sh
Belle, Rosette to Nilson Gannaway 7-6-1876 Dy
Bellew, Elizabeth to Andrew Littlefield 8-17-1837 (8-20-1837) G
Bellew, Sarah P. to John Kimbro 8-12-1837 G
Bellew, lAmanda to J. D. Melton 9-19-1861 Be
Belliew, Vandalia to W. H. Belliew 9-10-1870 Cr
Bellow, Luizer to Jesse Goodman 10-25-1869 G
Bellows, Ann (Mrs.) to M. W. Mays 11-28-1863 Sh
Bells, Eliza J. to George W. Hardin 1-26-1852 (1-29-1852) G
Beloat, Lucy J. to P. S. Ellis 10-6-1864 Sh
Beloat, Lydia Ann to Woodson L. Smith 1-23-1849 Sh
Beloat, Susan A. to Johnathan H. Mitchell 12-26-1854 Sh
Beloate, Mamie to M. T. Boswell 1-12-1880 (1-13-1880) L
Beloate, Mary E. to James W. Ridout 3-31-1841 Sh
Belote, A. S. T. to J. L. (Dr.) Neel 9-22-1855 Sh
Belote, Anvalina to Mabry D. Williams 6-30-1856 (7-3-1856) Hr
Belote, E. S. to W. M. Duese? 6-24-1857 Hr
Belote, Elizabeth to William Costler 3-26-1838 Sh
Belote, Fredonia Q. to T. J. Clancy 11-23-1857 Sh
Belote, Jane to Dorriss Ammons 7-10-1843 (no return) F
Belote, L. C. to M. D. L. Wilds 11-15-1858 Sh
Belote, Lou A. to H. B. Bickerstaff 10-19-1864 Sh
Belote, Lucy M. to John T. Vick 11-15-1851 (no return) F
Belote, Margrett C. to John Young 12-15-1846 (12-17-1846) Hr
Belote, Martha A. to George S. Oliver 1-20-1854 Sh
Belote, Mary E. to G. W. Dickson 8-3-1858 Sh
Belote, Mary to J. W. Bertram 1-10-1872 (1-11-1872) Dy
Belote, Nancy S. to G. W. Redditt 7-25-1855 (7-26-1855) Sh
Belote, Victoria to R. W. Pegram 1-2-1860 Hr
Belotte, Ariminta R. to William P. Gibson 11-29-1852 (12-16-1852) Hr
Belt?, Alethy to Wiley A. Braden 9-9-1859 (9-15-1859) L
Belton, Angelina to Henry McFarlin 7-27-1850 (7-28-1850) Ma
Belton, E. F. to N. F. Cates 4-1-1882 (4-5-1882) L
Belton, Jane to William Allen 3-12-1850 (3-14-1850) Ma
Belton, Johanna A. to William H. Cox 3-2-1885 (3-3-1885) L
Belton, L. A. to G. H. Keltner 5-12-1875 L
Belton, Louisa (Mrs.) to William R. Freeman 10-12-1861 (10-13-1861) Ma
Belton, Margaret to George Brogden 12-26-1854 (12-27-1854) Ma
Belvin, Martha to J. A. Sneede 10-7-1855 We
Beman, Sarah Hall to McDonald Lewis 9-9-1855 Hn
Bemas, Mary to Charles N. Robinson 6-11-1851 Sh
Bemis, Mima to Robert Oliver 4-8-1866 Hy
Bender, Catharine to T. H. Glidewell 11-12-1855 Sh
Bender, Christiana to Martin Gates 1-11-1860 (1-12-1860) Sh
Bender, Dorothea to Charles Muller 1-19-1858 Sh
Bender, Mary (Mrs.) to David Jones 9-12-1854 Sh
Bender, Sallie to H. Henrick 8-22-1860 Sh
Benders, Rose to Geo. Clark 4-20-1872 Hy
Bendon?, Adaline to Limerick Smith 8-3-1867 (8-4-1867) Dy
Bene, Analiza to A. I. Cattrell 8-18-1859 We
Bene, Susan to Allen Rutland 9-7-1841 Sh
Benett, Juliah to John A. Wilson 1-30-1845 Cr
Benge, Mary A. to John Gates 8-29-1840 (9-3-1840) F
Benger, W. to Augustus Klinke 7-14-1857 Sh
Benges, Maria to Charles C. Seballa 6-30-1858 Sh
Benjes, Dora to F. W. Baltzunot 4-6-1859 Sh
Bennet, Mary Ann to Martin W. Kerby 7-2-1857 Ma
Bennet, Nancy to John Hamlin 9-8-1828 (9-9-1828) Hr
Bennet?, May to Preston Elcan 11-11-1871 T
Bennett, Almarinda to William Moore 10-7-1850 Hr
Bennett, Amatha to Isaac Pritchard 10-24-1848 Cr
Bennett, Ann B. to James Prescott 2-9-1857 Be
Bennett, Annie B. to Marville Hicks 7-21-1850 Be
Bennett, Bettie to Henry Sangster 3-18-1878 Hy
Bennett, Edney to Washington Richardson 1-28-1862 Mn

Bennett, Elizabeth S. to Duncan T. Rich 9-2-1861 (9-3-1861) Hr
Bennett, Elizabeth to John T. Bennett 8-21-1845 Hn
Bennett, Elizabeth to Robert Pirtle 9-19-1833 Hr
Bennett, Emily to Samuel Webb 3-19-1857 Be
Bennett, Emmy to James Colvett 5-24-1864 (5-25-1864) Cr
Bennett, Fannie to I. N. Brock 1-8-1875 (no return) Hy
Bennett, Frances to Pinkney Cooper 4-21-1856 We
Bennett, Harrett J. to Isiah Carnell 2-?-1848 Cr
Bennett, Jane to John Cooper 4-2-1860 (4-6-1860) Cr
Bennett, Jantha to Albert Yancey 9-13-1878 Hy
Bennett, L. Ann to B. T. Forbus 10-26-1871 Cr
Bennett, Louisa J. to Robert Stoker 12-17-1846 Cr
Bennett, Louisa to Iverson Walker 12-18-1878 Hy
Bennett, Louisa to John Richy 2-3-1846 (2-5-1846) F
Bennett, M. C. to A. F. Glosson 3-7-1872 Cr
Bennett, M. D. to R. H. Scarce 10-2-1867 (10-3-1867) O
Bennett, M. F. to James T. Hazlewood 12-30-1866 G
Bennett, Mahaly to Davis C. Rushing 5-27-1846 Be
Bennett, Martha D. to Alvis Kirby 12-4-1854 (12-5-1854) Ma
Bennett, Martha to Benjamin Sellers 6-30-1848 Sh
Bennett, Martha to Eli Dudney 8-4-1840 Cr
Bennett, Martha to L. A. Burton 2-14-1865 Hn
Bennett, Mary A. E. to W. C. Isom 12-23-1851 (12-24-1851) Sh
Bennett, Mary E. to Newton C. Jordon 3-15-1854 (3-23-1854) Ma
Bennett, Mary to Benj. Whillis 2-11-1841 Cr
Bennett, Mary to Ed Thomas 12-4-1877 Hy
Bennett, Mary to George F. Cole 6-2-1857 Cr
Bennett, Mary to George W. Hood 2-23-1841 F
Bennett, Mary to Raiford Bizzel 1-23-1835 (1-29-1835) Hr
Bennett, Mollie to A. G. Haughton 3-2-1869 G
Bennett, N. E. to G. W. Vickers 10-6-1858 Cr
Bennett, Nancy M. to J. H. Rogers 8-19-1871 (8-20-1871) Cr
Bennett, Nancy M. to Jesse Kirby 2-24-1846 Ma
Bennett, Nancy to Duwery Bennett 8-28-1853 Be
Bennett, Nancy to Jacob Stacy 1-14-1840 Cr
Bennett, Nannie to Samuel Howell 5-20-1877 Hy
Bennett, Paralee E. to William W. Tally 8-20-1849 Hn
Bennett, Rebeca C. to Jon F. Williams 2-28-1867 Cr
Bennett, Rosa to Ned Jone 1-6-1867 G
Bennett, Sabina A. to W. G. Thompson 1-8-1852 Hn
Bennett, Sarah Ann to Gabriel Breaden 4-19-1853 Sh
Bennett, Sarah C. to L. P. Moody 10-28-1866 Hn
Bennett, Sarah E. to Willis M. Eitel 7-3-1855 (7-11-1855) Sh
Bennett, Sarah L. to George T. Wheeler 1-16-1867 F
Bennett, Sarah to Asa Woodward 3-22-1846 (3-24-1846) F
Bennett, Sarah to Joel Sawyers 9-20-1873 (9-21-1873) T
Bennett, Selina to Thomas Boyd 9-6-1838 Cr
Bennett, Susan to Thomas R. Lifsey 1-12-1858 Cr
Bennett, Susan to lHenry McClory 1-25-1862 Hr
Bennett, Theresse C. to J. A. Hargiss 1-3-1850 Sh
Bennett, Verdona C. to John Mitchell 2-20-1853 Cr
Bennett, W. M. to John P. Hopper 11-16-1857 Cr
Benson (Burrows?), Harriet to W. Farmer 6-1-1851 Sh
Benson, Ann to Thos. H. Evans 4-25-1822 Sh
Benson, Caroline to Elisha Farrow 1-23-1858 (1-24-1858) G
Benson, Elenor B. to Charles R. Black 9-8-1864 (9-11-1864) F
Benson, Elizabeth R. to Thomas B. Casey 10-11-1858 (10-13-1858) Ma
Benson, Ellen to William White 3-18-1867 L
Benson, L. C. to J. A. Murchison 1-27-1873 (1-29-1873) T
Benson, M. J. to M. B. Walker 3-17-1848 (3-19-1848) F
Benson, Margaret to James W. Arnold 9-21-1850 (9-25-1850) Hr
Benson, Margaret to Rowland G. Harris 11-23-1859 (11-24-1859) Ma
Benson, Martha to Jacob S. Shipman 12-13-1842 G
Benson, Mary A. to Alfred Pool 3-15-1855 Ma
Benson, Mary to Andrew Glover 5-11-1867 O
Benson, Milly to Daniel J. Riley 7-10-1847 (7-11-1847) G
Benson, Mollie A. to D. B. Elam 1-25-1873 (1-29-1873) T
Benson, P. to J. E. Cole 12-6-1859 (12-13-1859) F
Benson, Sally to Jos. B. Lacey 10-13-1866 (10-17-1866) F
Benson, Winey to R. H. Newman 11-9-1862 Mn
Benson, Zany Ann to Thos. J. Farrer 12-14-1844 (12-19-1844) F
Benthall, Catharine to Jessee Jackson 8-2-1854 (8-3-1854) Ma
Benthel, Sarah A. to James H. Bass 1-28-1845 Ma
Bentley, Allice to Sam Allen 6-14-1867 (no return) F B
Bentley, Analine to W. C. Reid no date (with Jun 1855) F
Bentley, E(ddy?) E. to John H. Griffin 9-17-1867 (9-20-1867) L
Bentley, Frances B. to Williamson Bonner 1-10-1837 F
Bentley, Harriet to H. P. Barfield 2-26-1884 L
Bentley, J. R. to T. L. Furgerson 2-23-1867 (2-24-1867) L
Bentley, Lelia E. to Edmond Gaines 3-1-1884 L
Bentley, Mary O. to William Hafford 9-17-1867 (9-20-1867) L
Bentley, Matilda R. to James H. Markham 9-19-1847 Sh
Bentley, Mollie L. to W. J. Mangrum 12-9-1873 (12-10-1873) L
Bentley, S. N. J. to C. H. Lloyd 11-7-1874 (11-11-1874) L
Bently, Jane to Peter Young 6-30-1866 (no return) F B
Bently, Louisa B. to Josiah Goforth 1-1-1873 (1-2-1873) T
Bently, Mary to Thomas Carter 12-17-1846 Sh

Benton, Ann to T. C. Gardner 10-9-1862 (not endorsed) F
Benton, C. to D. L. Norman 5-29-1842 Be
Benton, Elizabeth Ann to J. H. Vester 7-4-1844 Be
Benton, Elizabeth J. A. to James N. Carruthers 1-1-1845 Ma
Benton, Ella to David L. Bain 7-27-1866 (10-15-1866) F
Benton, Isabel to John Melton 1-17-1855 Be
Benton, Louisa to Mac Gaskins 7-22-1848 (7-23-1848) O
Benton, Louisa to Mc Gaskin 7-22-1848 O
Benton, Lucinda to Z. T. Rhodes 2-19-1869 (2-23-1869) Cr
Benton, M. L. to G. P. Williams 1-11-1873 (1-12-1873) Cr
Benton, Martha C. to Randoll Pafford 10-22-1863 Be
Benton, Mary A. to Isaac Sampson 9-19-1865 (9-20-1865) L
Benton, Mary Ann to Harmon Holomon 8-20-1852 Be
Benton, Mary Ann to Simon Nobles 3-20-1856 Be
Benton, Mary E. to W. R. Pickett 1-14-1862 Cr
Benton, Rosanna A. to C. S. Brandon 7-3-1861 (7-4-1861) Cr
Benton, S. A. to Wm. S. Miller 2-3-1867 O
Benton, Sabeany to Henry Trought 12-26-1848 Cr
Benton, Sarah to Gwinn Harper 5-16-1844 Cr
Benton, Scarlet J. to Solomon Burrow no date (not executed) Cr
Benton, Viola to John W. Coley 1-9-1843 Be
Beny, Mary J. E. to Mark Ethridge 8-9-1856 (8-14-1856) G
Berchun, N. P. to Sy Townsend 3-12-1873 (3-16-1873) Cr
Berger, Elizabeth L. to J. T. Wilson 12-18-1866 (no return) Cr
Bergert, Susan to David Cashen 8-21-1859 (no return) We
Bergman, Sallie E. to Phinias G. Baker 6-13-1874 (6-14-1874) T
Bergman, Wanda to Lehman Loeb 9-12-1864 T
Berk, Fannie to William Bledsoe 8-16-1864 G
Bernard, Hettie L. to Thomas H. Rutherford 10-18-1869 (10-19-1869) T
Bernard, Laura Elizabeth to William Oscar Pryor 1-6-1850 T
Bernard, Lauretta L. to William James Strong 11-16-1847 T
Bernard, Lucetta to Charles S. Dickson 9-1-1846 (9-2-1846) T
Bernard, Lucy to George Smith 1-4-1868 T
Bernard, Lusetta to E. McDanniel 4-22-1868 T
Bernard, Martha to Nathan Johnes 7-20-1867 T
Bernard, Mary to Isham A. Wright 1-3-1848 (1-6-1848) T
Bernard, Mary to William Booker 12-27-1870 T
Bernard, Nelly to M. F. Roney 10-26-1872 (10-27-1872) Cr
Bernard, Sarah to Thos. Calhoun 6-5-1869 (6-6-1869) T
Berry (Beary?), Susan to David Venturini 8-20-1853 Sh
Berry(Beny), Kissiah to Everet Staton 7-26-1828 (7-28-1828) Hr
Berry, A. E. to James N. Reese 8-31-1854 G
Berry, Amanda to William B. Craige 7-13-1846 (7-15-1846) G
Berry, Caroline to Ashley Olive 1-28-1841 Hn
Berry, Cary Ann to Tias Williams 7-16-1869 (7-17-1869) T
Berry, Cassandra to John McFarland 4-17-1852 (4-21-1852) G
Berry, Charity to Warner Maclin 11-11-1871 (11-12-1871) L
Berry, Chester to Nathan Bongerent 12-25-1867 (no return) Hn B
Berry, Elizabeth J. to John A. Smith 2-27-1851 Hn
Berry, Elizabeth W. to William W. McNeal 11-26-1844 Hr
Berry, Elizabeth to J. A. Winsore 4-7-1852 Cr
Berry, Elizabeth to Miles S. Allen 10-7-1848 (10-11-1848) G
Berry, Elmyra to John A. Holland 1-1-1867 Be
Berry, Elvira to Jacob McHamy 6-27-1840 (no return) Hn
Berry, Elvira to John Finley 4-1-1838 (no return) Cr
Berry, Emily A. to Robert T. Dickson 9-22-1858 G
Berry, F. A. to J. W. Hodges 4-12-1860 Sh
Berry, George A. (Miss) to Perry G. Carter 3-8-1859 (3-17-1859) Sh
Berry, Harriet M. to William Carr 6-29-1852 G
Berry, I.(D.?) A. to George F. Reasons 8-10-1870 Cr
Berry, J. T. to Alfred H. Turner 8-20-1840 Cr
Berry, Jane to Sip Hull (Hall?) 12-30-1869 F B
Berry, Josephine H. to William Collins 4-5-1861 (4-8-1861) Sh
Berry, Julia Ann to George W. Myrick 8-11-1868 (8-12-1868) Cr
Berry, Julia to David Brown 12-24-1874 T
Berry, Lucinda A. to Pleasant W. Hopper 11-26-1855 (11-28-1855) G
Berry, Lucy Ann to F. M. Bloodworth 1-29-1853 (2-2-1853) Sh
Berry, Lucy Ann to Francis Snowden 12-11-1852 (12-23-1852) Sh
Berry, Lucy to Charles Alexander 5-8-1873 Hy
Berry, M. J. M. to F. M. Davis 8-17-1864 (8-18-1864) Cr
Berry, Martha A. to John Jesse Naill 12-25-1856 Cr
Berry, Martha G. to William A. Farris 5-30-1861 (no return) Hn
Berry, Martha H. to Nathan G. Rich 10-15-1866 (10-17-1866) Cr
Berry, Martha Jane to S. K. P. Houn 7-28-1864 G
Berry, Martha to Richard Berry 9-6-1858 G
Berry, Martha to W. F. Lumpkins 2-4-1861 (2-5-1861) Dy
Berry, Mary E. to B. F. Bobbett 12-27-1854 (12-28-1854) G
Berry, Mary G. to Ricks Porter 9-9-1841 Cr
Berry, Mary Jane to J. B. Horne 8-2-1860 Sh
Berry, Mary Matilda to Marklin Edwards 1-12-1848 Sh
Berry, Mary to James W. Cowgill 9-13-1843 Sh
Berry, Mary to Wyatt Banks 12-25-1867 (no return) Hn B
Berry, Matilda C. to Benj. F. Scallion 7-10-1846 G
Berry, N. C. B. to J. W. Barnes 12-16-1850 Cr
Berry, Nancy J. to Lewis Cole 8-10-1854 Be
Berry, Nancy to Isaac W. Alexander 4-15-1831 (4-22-1831) Ma
Berry, Pathena to T. R. Biggs 11-29-1865 G

Berry, Penelope J. to Francis P. Drinkard 12-11-1855 (12-13-1855) G
Berry, Penelope Juen to Henry Shearer 1-16-1837 (1-19-1837) G
Berry, Phebe J. to John Rambo (Ramber) 9-2-1846 Sh
Berry, Piety A. to Jackson C. Oliver 10-26-1865 Hn
Berry, Purnetta A. to George Haley 3-20-1852 (3-25-1852) G
Berry, Sally to T. K. Vaught 2-21-1866 G
Berry, Sarah A. to George P. Panel 3-28-1871 O
Berry, Sarah A. to Larkin J. Gallimore 11-8-1853 Cr
Berry, Sarah E. to James A. Abernathy 3-4-1845 Cr
Berry, Sarah to William Baxter 1-7-1832 G
Berry, Susan A. to F. W. Turner 11-27-1840 Cr
Berry, Tennessee C. to James Berry 12-5-1864 Be
Berry, Winney H. to G. W. Mitchell 3-3-1864 Mn
Berry?, Easter to Edward Thorton? no date (with 1874) T
Berrycroft, Sarah A. T. to John C. Oliver 6-2-1855 Ma
Berryhill, Elizabeth Caroline to James Read 11-23-1843 We
Berryhill, Magaret A. J. to John M. Hanna 4-3-1844 We
Berryhill, Martha Ann to W. J. Black 12-11-1858 (12-1_-1858) Sh
Berryhill, Rachel A. to Miles Covington 6-19-1853 Hn
Berryman, E. to I. N. McCarver 10-23-1865 O
Berryman, Martha C. to Joseph L. Lain 8-22-1860 (9-2-1860) We
Bert, Margaret to Lee Ward 3-21-1874 T
Berton, Emily M. to John M. Hicks 1-31-1850 Hn
Berton, Sarah A. to Absalem Fields 8-26-1859 (8-29-1859) O
Berton, Trianna to Elijah Shipley 11-27-1851 Hn
Bertow, Martha W. to William L. Bertow 3-16-1848 Hn
Besheers, Ann to Herrill Shren 5-13-1846 Sh
Bess, Mary to Moses Wortham 10-19-1866 G
Bess, Nancy E. to Henry C. Winburn 11-19-1866 Hy
Bessent, Ann to J. G. Hill 12-24-1873 Dy
Bessent, Elizabeth to James M. Rucker 7-19-1869 (7-21-1869) Dy
Bessent, Kitty to J. T. Capell 10-15-1868 Dy
Bessent, Lou to Joel Blankenship 2-27-1871 (2-28-1871) Dy
Bessent?, Temperance to John A. Mills 1-1-1867 Dy
Best, Amelia to Thomas Klink 9-21-1852 Sh
Best, Caroline to Henry Someraner (Somorer) 11-3-1864 Sh
Best, Eliza Ann to R. T. Weatherly 12-15-1875 Hy
Best, Lizzie to Robt. Orr 12-2-1853 Sh
Best, M. A. to J. M. Currie 11-19-1878 (11-21-1878) L
Best, M. E. to J. R. Osteen 1-27-1880 L
Best, Mary Ann E. to Andrew J. Sanders 1-25-1858 L
Best, Perlina to C. F. Herring 9-16-1872 (not executed) L
Best, Sarah to Jessee Kinny 12-30-1873 (12-31-1873) T
Best, S. A. (Mrs.) to A. Hatchett 3-10-1863 (3-11-1863) Sh
Best, Sarah Ann to Thomas J. Lewis 5-14-1831 Sh
Bestwick, Martha A. to D. A. Brown 12-26-1837 Sh
Bethay, Elizabeth to David A. Greer 5-28-1851 Be
Bethell, Anne to Jas. F. Boren 9-9-1845 Sh
Bethell, Jane E. to Hartwell W. Bass 10-30-1844 Sh
Bethell, M. E. to J. E. Rust 10-1-1867 O
Bethell, Nancy M. to Isaac T. Osteen 4-9-1859 (4-11-1859) O
Bethell, Zelly to A. J. Norrid 3-21-1848 (3-28-1848) O
Bethory, Mary Ann to Calvin Bond 8-13-1849 Be
Bethsheares, Tabitha to Elhanon Reynolds 3-11-1868 Hy
Bethune, Fannie to J. W. Pipkin 3-26-1884 (3-27-1884) L
Bethune, Mary to William A. Ball 9-3-1873 (9-24-1873) L
Bethune, Mattie to J. H. Chambers 5-31-1876 (6-4-1876) L
Beton, Martha to John Sheppard 4-29-1845 Hr
Bets, Sarah Ann E. to J. B. George 3-30-1858 O
Betten, Ellen to George Allen 9-16-1871 (9-21-1871) T
Bettes, Ann to Daniel Harklervad 2-10-1830 Sh
Bettis, A. S. to J. T. Jaycocks 4-25-1866 (no return) Dy
Bettis, D. E. to I.J. N. Vail 8-5-1871 (no return) Dy
Bettis, Elizabeth to Raleigh W. Barber 6-11-1842 (6-12-1842) L
Bettis, Elizabeth to Seth G. Yarbrough 9-19-1849 Sh
Bettis, L. N. to G. M. Rowland 10-9-1865 (10-10-1865) Dy
Bettis, Lucy to Charles F. King 9-20-1842 Sh
Bettis, Mary J. to William Pittman 2-5-1850 Sh
Bettis, Mary Jane to W. L. Stokes 1-30-1858 (2-2-1858) Sh
Bettis, Peggy Ann to John W. McFarlane 12-13-1866 (12-26-1866) Dy
Bettis, Salena to A. G. Blakemore 8-10-1847 Sh
Bettis, Sarah C. to Simeon Horne 10-10-1848 Sh
Bettis, Virginia C. to Robert K. Craft 9-9-1856 (9-10-1856) Sh
Betts, Amanda to Christopher Clark 6-4-1854 Hy
Betts, Ann M. to G. L. Rutherford 5-11-1842 (no return) L
Betts, Arvazena to Micajah Hillman Brown 8-22-1867 G
Betts, Cottury to James Whitington 2-5-1844 Ma
Betts, E. C. to J. B. White 7-5-1876 Hy
Betts, Elizabeth to Ehu A. Stephens 7-6-1852 Hn
Betts, Jane to J. N. Wallace 9-28-1856 Hn
Betts, Luticia C. to Charles L. Wortham 1-9-1861 G
Betts, Margrett to Benj. Hue 9-8-1845 (9-10-1845) G
Betts, Mary to Andrew J. Medling 9-22-1870 G
Betts, Sarah A. to Isham Bailey 12-17-1854 G
Betts, Susan to John Sandrey 1-22-1844 Ma
Betty, Martha A. to John W. Allison 10-24-1859 Ma
Betty, Sarah (Mrs.) to Henry T. Johnson 9-6-1869 (9-7-1869) Ma

Beuhl, Alvina to Joseph Berman 4-16-1857 Sh
Bevan, Sally to Robert Hallows 12-13-1860 Sh
Bevel, Allice to Geo. W. Benson 11-25-1859 (11-27-1859) G
Bevel, Sarah to Edmond Faulks 12-4-1861 G
Bevell, A. T. to W. S. Smith 8-12-1867 (8-13-1867) Cr
Bevens, Tennessee L. to John J. McFarland 10-3-1862 G
Bever, Margaret to Leonard A. Walker 11-7-1858 Cr
Bever?, Marry Ann to C. F. Culbreth 6-26-1840 F
Beverage, Susan R. to F. W. Yancy 1-18-1844 Ma
Beverly, Mrs. Malissa to Samuel Patterson 1-13-1870 T
Bevil, Lucinda C. to Robert Throgmorton 3-9-1848 Hn
Bevill, America Catherine to F. S. Clements 8-26-1868 (8-27-1868) Ma
Bevill, E. H. to W. P. Smith 2-4-1867 (2-7-1867) Cr
Bevill, Emily to Asbury McCord 6-26-1856 Hn
Bevill, Jennie (Mrs.) to John W. Howell 11-30-1867 (12-1-1867) Ma
Bevill, Lucy A. to E. F. Jordon 3-14-861 Cr
Bevill, Luzana C. to George N. Roberts 10-16-1869 (10-17-1869) Cr
Bevill, Lydia to Richard W. Kirby 11-12-1870 (11-13-1870) Ma
Bevill, Malinda to John Rich 2-23-1842 Hn
Bevill, Martha A. to B. F. Hedge 2-10-1855 Hn
Bevill, Nancy J. to William Stofte 12-23-1838 Hn
Bevill, Nancy to John Underwood 12-26-1850 Hn
Bevill, Narissa C. to Abram Rice 3-23-1846 Hn
Bevill, Sallie G. to Jesse McCord 8-22-1857 Hn
Bevill, Sarah J. to John Mathis 12-14-1843 Hn
Bevill, Sarah M. to Granville C. Lowe 12-22-1859 Ma
Bevill, Susan J. to William F. Huff 4-14-1847 Hn
Bevill, T. H. to S. G. Leslie 11-26-1872 (11-27-1872) Cr
Bevins, Catharine to James P. Williams 12-25-1841 F
Bevins, Julia to Thomas White 9-5-1872 T
Bi_gart, L. C. to J. S. Loveless 8-16-1866 L
Bibb, Charlotte Frances to Henry Coats 2-23-1847 T
Bibb, Emmaline to Jesse R. Parker 4-6-1843 Hn
Bibb, Jane to William G. Spence 6-24-1852 L
Bibb, L. E. to W. R. Chandler 2-8-1876 (2-7?-1876) L
Bibb, Lucy A. F. to Edward F. Tally 9-6-1850 (9-12-1850) L
Bibb, Mary A. E. to Real J. Chandler 9-10-1850 (9-12-1850) L
Bibb, Mary E. to Benj. F. Forrest 11-11-1871 (11-12-1871) T
Bibb, Mary E. to Elisha McCoy 11-6-1845 L
Bibb, Melvina E. to W. P. Johnson 12-21-1869 (12-24-1869) Cr
Bibb, Sarah E. to Arval Michel 7-18-1845 Cr
Bibbs, Elizabeth Jane to Plesant K. Parsons 10-29-1845 Cr
Bibbs, L. A. E. to F. M. Dell 6-15-1859 Cr
Bibbs, Mary E. to D. L. Bohanon 3-6-1866 (3-8-1866) Cr
Bibbs, Nancy B. to W. C. White 1-19-1871 Cr
Bibbs, O. M. to N. H. McLevee 3-7-1867 Cr
Bibee, Marian to Calvin Goodman 3-4-1840 Sh
Bickel, Martha to A. B. Jenkins 3-12-1864 Sh
Bickers, Allie to James T. Perciful 12-24-1868 (1-4-1869) Ma
Bickers, Jane to Simon Powelson 9-18-1863 F
Bickers, Lucy to George Kilpatrick 3-15-1856 Ma
Bickerstaff, Frances A. to James S. Graham 9-4-1839 Sh
Bickerstaff, Mary to Alfred C. Robertson 10-12-1838 (10-16-1838) F
Biddix, Elizabeth to J. A. Riley 7-18-1863 (7-19-1863) O
Biddix, Elmira to John M. Claxton 1-21-1867 O
Biddy, Aley A. to Wm. R. Blake 11-20-1867 (no return) F
Biddy, Elizabeth to Josiah Taylor 10-19-1831 (10-20-1831) Hr
Biddy, Mary to Anderson Glidewell 4-13-1835 Hr
Biddy, Mary to James Butler 12-9-1829 (12-10-1829) Hr
Biddy, Sarah to Jesse Bryant 11-21-1866 (11-22-1866) F
Bidix, C. to J. M. Glassco 2-25-1869 G
Bidix, S. I. to J. W. Wright 2-25-1869 G
Bidwell, Hester Ann to Joseph B. Venable 8-26-1856 Hn
Bieber, Equilla to Benjn. H. W. Portis 6-20-1842 (6-?-1842) Hr
Biebers, Mary to James C. Chapman 9-5-1845 (9-?-1845) Hr
Biebers, Nancy to John Shelly 12-29-1852 (12-30-1852) Hr
Biele, Louise to G. J. Strehl 11-15-1858 Sh
Biers, Susan A. to A. O. Bayne 12-23-1861 G
Biffell, Mary L. to P. O. Porte (Parte) 7-16-1854 We
Biford, Mary to Thomas Howard 9-29-1871 L
Bigby, Minerva to John E. Bigby 11-1-1874 O
Bigelow, Amanda C. to Amos W. Jones 4-1-1857 (4-2-1857) Ma
Bigelow, Eliza to Joseph D. Mason 9-17-1844 (9-18-1844) Ma
Biggart, Margaret to M. R. Mathis 10-20-1866 (10-21-1866) Cr
Biggers, Jane A. to Richard B. Quinley 12-23-1848 (12-25-1848) Ma
Biggs, Arcena L. to R. A. Atkinson 1-14-1856 (1-21-1856) Sh
Biggs, Charlotte to Elijah Grant 2-10-1871 (2-15-1871) F B
Biggs, Elizabeth F. to Thomas A. Ray 11-10-1858 G
Biggs, Emma J. to Daniel H. Scates 10-20-1858 (10-21-1858) G
Biggs, Harriet E. to J. R. Person 2-13-1858 (2-22-1858) Sh
Biggs, Jackoleno to James Burleson 3-20-1830 Sh
Biggs, Julia to Jacob Barnett 12-22-1870 (1-1-1871) Dy
Biggs, Louisa to J. M. Tarply 6-27-1867 Be
Biggs, M. A. to R. N. Ramsey 5-30-1865 G
Biggs, M. C. to D. T. Barnes 3-9-1869 G
Biggs, Martha A. to William H. Bailey 12-20-1843 G
Biggs, Martha to Wilson Doxey 12-17-1847 G

Biggs, Mary Ann to Francis M. Chapman 11-12-1842 (11-13-1842) T
Biggs, Mary Ann to Henry Kennady 1-18-1854 (1-24-1854) G
Biggs, Mary E. to R. H. Thomas 3-24-1863 G
Biggs, Mary E. to Sterling B. Scott 11-23-1847 G
Biggs, Maryann to Hiram S. Walker 11-29-1847 F
Biggs, Matilda C. to Needham Whitley 2-22-1854 G
Biggs, Nancy to A. R. Landrum 10-5-1854 G
Biggs, Nancy to William H. Partiel 6-29-1852 (6-30-1852) G
Biggs, Rachell to George Miller 4-7-1847 Sh
Biggs, Rachell to Richard Neeley 4-14-1849 (4-15-1849) F
Biggs, Sarah M. to S. H. Strayhorn 12-8-1868 (12-9-1868) Dy
Biggs, Virginia to Wyatt Arnold 12-29-1853 Be
Bigham, Addie to C. F. Osborne 2-4-1868 (2-5-1868) Cr
Bigham, Adline to Ben Bigham 2-10-1872 Cr B
Bigham, Amanda M. to Wm. B. Kennon 5-18-1854 Cr
Bigham, Callie D. to Louis P. Meyers 6-3-1872 (6-6-1872) Cr
Bigham, Emma to John P. Johnson 7-23-1866 (no return) Cr
Bigham, Lizzie to J. R. Plummer 7-14-1869 (no return) Cr
Bigham, M. J. B. to Charles O. Hill 1-13-1842 Cr
Bigham, Mary to Samuel M. O'Neill 11-1-1869 Cr
Bigham, P. P. to W. B. W. Gray 3-5-1867 (no return) Cr
Bigham, Sarah C. to Samuel H. Bell 9-28-1865 (10-22-1865) T
Bigham, Sarah J. to T. M. McCollum 7-14-1858 Cr
Bigham, Sarah P. to W C. Mathes 12-19-1847 Cr
Bigham, Sophina A. to John W. Blair 11-2-1854 Cr
Bilbery, Alice to Thomas A. Michum 12-3-1856 Cr
Bilerly, Mary to Wm. D. Forest 6-21-1854 Cr
Biles, Caroline A. to John Marberry 11-11-1841 Hn
Biles, Caroline to William Hipp 7-7-1873 (7-9-1873) L B
Biles, Catharine F. to John Dillahunty 9-27-1842 (no return) Hn
Biles, Margaret Y. to John H. Gay 12-19-1831 Hr
Biles, Martha A. to Samuel M. Hastings 5-18-1853 Hn
Biles, Mary E. to Henry G. Hays 2-15-1847 (no return) Hn
Biles, Mary E. to Reuben B. Nance 12-18-1845 Hn
Biles, Nancy W. to John G. Taylor 6-27-1844 Hn
Biles, Nancy to John M. Caton 6-5-1849 Hn
Bill (Bell?), Amanda to S. D. Willson 10-2-1875 (10-3-1875) L
Bill, Lizzie D. to Jas. D. Butler 11-1-1855 Sh
Bill, Sarah W. to Henry Fitzgerald 7-23-1850 Sh
Billing, Elizabeth to Francis M. Max 11-26-1866 (11-27-1866) T
Billing, Sarah to Oliver Smith 12-13-1867 T
Billings, Amanda J. to G.? J. Jones 1-1-1863 T
Billings, Amanda to Marcus L. Literal 10-17-1870 (10-18-1870) L
Billings, Barbara Luticia to James Knox Polk Glass 12-8-1859 T
Billings, Barbra to William J. Parker 1-27-1850 Hn
Billings, Ellen to Dorstal Hill 9-10-1869 T
Billings, L. B. to Allen Sterling 9-7-1864 Sh
Billings, Malinda Anne to Jacob Nicholas 8-7-1845 L
Billings, Margaret Jane to Alfred B. Owen 5-22-1844 T
Billings, Margaret to John Nicholas Bringle 7-14-1846 T
Billings, Martha A. to N. T. Pugh 10-19-1867 (10-20-1867) T
Billings, Mary to Joshua Weatherington 1-8-1857 T
Billings, Pearle M. to Richard C. Moore 9-6-1860 Sh
Billings, Susan to W. H. Tinnen 2-4-1869 (1?-31-1869) T
Billingsley, Adaline E. to William Wormack 7-18-1850 (7-23-1850) G
Billingsley, Adaline to Samuel Kincey 11-27-1848 G
Billingsley, Artina to Wright H. Rutherford 11-25-1845 G
Billingsley, G. F. to James Boon 4-27-1863 G
Billingsley, Mary L. to Richard Wormack 1-9-1847 (1-12-1847) G
Billingsley, Mary to Philip R. K. Claiborne 1-18-1837 G
Billingsly, Mahaly to William C. Northcutt 2-13-1834 G
Billingsly, Sonya to John A. Argo 12-2-1848 G
Billington, Mary Ann to William A. P. Williams 5-2-1854 (5-4-1854) Ma
Billips, Dolly to Simon Reynolds 2-8-1854 G
Bills, Evilina M. to Marshall T. Polk 1-10-1856 Hr
Bills, Jane (Mrs.) to Alford Jennings 2-23-1864 (2-27-1864) Sh
Bills, Mary Carolin to Robert H. Wood 1-12-1847 Hr
Bills, Mattie L. to G. T. Rutledge 6-12-1870 L
Bills, Ophelia J. to Horace M. Polk 6-15-1843 (6-20-1843) Hr
Binam, Fannie to Anderson Bumpas 11-11-1871 (11-24-1871) T
Binford, Rebecca to George Dunnigan 10-30-1868 (no return) Dy
Bingham, Amanda to Lafayette Barrier 12-4-1859 Ma
Bingham, Anna J. M. to John M. Clement 10-1-1863 Hn
Bingham, Frances to John R. Rogers 2-1-1838 Sh
Bingham, Jennie to Fountain Murry 8-10-1867 (8-13-1867) Ma
Bingham, Mary J. to C. W. Atchison 6-20-1866 Hn
Bingham, N. A. to James M. Savage 8-10-1853 Hr
Bingham, Sarah A. to Edward Powers 9-6-1854 Sh
Binkle (Burkle?), Rosina to Jacob Beurer 5-31-1852 Sh
Binkley, Lavanda to George Gibson 4-11-1866 (no return) Dy
Binkley, Malinda to William Carley 8-10-1839 Hr
Binkley, Matilda C. to John Murdaugh 1-1-1842 (1-2-1842) Hr
Binkley, Susan R. to Elias Sperlin 1-25-1858 Hr
Binkly, Mary M. to Eldrige W. Dorris 1-21-1846 Hr
Binkly, Nancy to Jeptha Yarbrough 7-6-1846 (7-9-1846) Hr
Binkly, Rosa Ann to John C. Baily 4-11-1853 (4-12-1853) Hr
Birat, Catherine to John G. Newbill 4-18-1844 Cr

Birchett, Eliza A. to William Chandler 9-28-1865 Mn
Bird, A. V. to H. M. Timms 1-4-1871 (1-12-1871) T
Bird, Allice to William Furlong 4-29-1873 (no return) Cr
Bird, Catherine to Isaac Cain 7-17-1856 Cr
Bird, Elizabeth A. to Chesley L. Burnwant 11-16-1850 (11-21-1850) G
Bird, Elizabeth to Francis Phillips 9-2-1845 Cr
Bird, Elizabeth to James Gibson 9-20-1854 O
Bird, Elizabeth to James W. Moore 12-23-1848 Cr
Bird, H. J. to J. R. Hamilton 2-23-1869 (2-25-1869) T
Bird, J. M. to J. L. Dougherty 6-19-1865 (6-25-1865) O
Bird, Jane to Anderson Curry 9-28-1867 Hy
Bird, Jane to R. D. Suter 12-24-1850 (no return) Cr
Bird, Levina to Samuel C. Liggett 1-8-1849 G
Bird, Louisa to Benjamin Williams 6-4-1852 (6-6-1852) O
Bird, Malinda J. to William R. Guy 3-13-1851 O
Bird, Margaret A. to Edward E. Hope 2-4-1851 (2-5-1851) O
Bird, Martha Ann to John Akers 12-23-1852 Cr
Bird, Mary A. to H. A. Myers 8-18-1867 Be
Bird, Mary F. J. to R. H. Philips 12-22-1856 Hn
Bird, Minerva to Richard Best 4-12-1863 G
Bird, Nancy to Caleb Holland 3-25-1867 (4-6-1867) T
Bird, Nancy to Joseph D. Bird 1-3-1841 Cr
Bird, Nancy to Lewis Girley 6-16-1844 Cr
Bird, Nancy to Nathaniel Brewer 5-30-1867 (no return) Cr
Bird, Nancy to Robert McCullough 7-25-1853 (7-26-1853) T
Bird, Rebecca L. to John Collins 9-28-1850 Cr
Bird, S. T. to J. T. Palmer 7-30-1864 Hn
Bird, Sarah F. to Wilee Wallace 3-25-1854 (3-26-1854) G
Bird, Sarah H. to William S. Nelson 11-23-1867 (11-24-1867) Cr
Bird, Sarah J. to Sam'l. A. Doughtery 1-3-1860 (1-6-1860) O
Bird?, Martha to Bedford Riggin 3-4-1846 (maybe 1845) Hn
Birdah?, Margaret to George W. Kirkland 10-23-1839 Hn
Birdson, Winney to Benjamin Griffin 2-8-1847 F
Birdsong, Altha to Joshua Johnson 10-28-1851 (11-5-1851) Hr
Birdsong, Altha to Joshua Johnson 9-9-1847 F
Birdsong, Cavell F. to Benjamin Wilkerson 8-17-1839 (8-21-1839) Hr
Birdsong, Cinthia A. to W. C. Adkins 6-27-1851 (6-30-1851) F
Birdsong, Eliza Jane to John Mitchell 3-23-1848 Hr
Birdsong, Eliza to John W. Denney 7-15-1850 Sh
Birdsong, Elizabeth J. to Alfred M. Rainey 7-11-1855 (7-12-1855) Hr
Birdsong, Elizabeth to Samel Phillips 12-26-1839 (no return) F
Birdsong, Lemisa R. to Wm. H. McKee 9-12-1871 (9-13-1871) Ma
Birdsong, Margaret to Thomas Sanders 8-27-1859 (8-28-1859) Ma
Birdsong, Mary A. to C. H. Williams 10-29-1851 (10-31-1851) Hr
Birdsong, Mary N. to Francis M. Howard 10-9-1866 Ma
Birdwell, Jame P. to Allen Quillen 7-10-1845 Cr
Birdwell, Lidia to John Evans 2-21-1853 Cr
Birdwell, Martha to William Fellow 10-16-1841 (10-17-1841) F
Birdwell, Mary Ann to Presley Thornton 1-20-1853 Be
Birdwell, Rebecca to Jas. M. Cole 10-3-1854 Cr
Birdwell, Susan to A. W. Jacobs 12-9-1869 G
Birk, Sarah H. to George P. Ferrell 5-22-1864 G
Birmingham, Angeline to Thomas D. Jackson 12-4-1845 (12-5-1845) Ma
Birmingham, Emelina to Hasting J. Smith 2-19-1840 Ma
Birmingham, Kate to M. M. Wright 1-18-1859 Sh
Birmingham, Malvina to William T. Edwards 5-9-1844 Ma
Birmingham, Mary A. to Richard C. Jackson 6-22-1861 (6-23-1861) O
Birmingham, Nannie to B. J. King 6-12-1871 (no return) Hy
Birmingham, Sarah E. to John L. Boothe 11-13-1856 O
Birmingham, Sarah J. to G. J. Gilbert 9-16-1872 Cr
Birthwright, Gennetta to George Parsons 2-13-1861 (2-14-1861) O
Biscoe, Laura E. to Thos.(Jas?) (Maj.) H O'Connor 4-8-1863 Sh
Bishop, Amey to Alfred Bryant 12-31-1870 (1-5-1871) Cr
Bishop, Ann to John L. Vaughter 1-4-1859 Cr
Bishop, Caroline to Atlas Phillips 8-15-1848 Ma
Bishop, Carrie to T. E. Bond 7-17-1878 (no return) Hy
Bishop, E. F. to T. M. Jackson 12-16-1849 Cr
Bishop, Edny to Cader Cox 12-16-1835 (12-17-1835) Hr
Bishop, Elizabeth to Zachriah Bryant 11-19-1858 Cr
Bishop, Elizar to Benjamin Ivie 10-10-1859 We
Bishop, G. A. to J. F. King 12-3-1878 (12-4-1878) Dy
Bishop, Georgie to William H. Shaub 1-27-1862 (1-28-1862) L
Bishop, Harriet to William L. Henderson 6-1-1841 (no return) Hn
Bishop, Jane to Lewis Bailey 7-5-1869 G
Bishop, Letty to A. A. Bowles 11-2-1853 Cr
Bishop, Louisa to Richard E. Strickling 7-20-1846 Sh
Bishop, Lucy A. to Wm. J. Crates 4-29-1861 (5-1-1861) Hr
Bishop, Lucy G. to Richard H. Harrison 7-15-1852 Ma
Bishop, Lucy M. to Joe F. Jones 6-4-1846 Cr
Bishop, M. M. to John W. Smith 10-31-1869 Hy
Bishop, Maco to Alfred Word 5-25-1872 Hy
Bishop, Margaret to Joel Oldham 4-26-1853 Sh
Bishop, Martha (Mrs.) to Frank Woodard 11-10-1864 Sh
Bishop, Martha ANn to William R. Ledbetter 10-4-1864 Mn
Bishop, Martha C. to John W. Finley 8-13-1869 Mn
Bishop, Martha to Benjamin S. Connor 11-18-1869 O
Bishop, Martha to William Bunn 9-12-1866 (no return) L

Bishop, Martha to William Bunn 9-26-1867 (9-12?-1867) L
Bishop, Mary A. (Mrs.?) to John D. Wands 10-13-1863 Sh
Bishop, Mary A. to James M. Armstrong 3-26-1845 Hn
Bishop, Mary E. to Marcus Baird 7-2-1862 G
Bishop, Mary Elvina M. to George S. Harrison 4-27-1838 (5-10-1838) Ma
Bishop, Mary J. to G. J. Coppadge 1-7-1856 (1-10-1856) Hr
Bishop, Mary J. to G. W. Bryant 11-6-1856 Cr
Bishop, Mary Palmer to J. H. Burns (Bunn?) 3-15-1867 (no return) L
Bishop, Monticeli (Mrs.) to A. Dupont Lindsey 2-2-1863 Sh
Bishop, Nancy E. to Stephen E. Williams 5-2-1859 Sh
Bishop, Nancy to Elijah Crass 3-24-1844 (no return) Hn
Bishop, Nancy to William R. Wilks 1-4-1874 Hy
Bishop, Paralee to James Prewett 12-18-1869 (12-19-1869) O
Bishop, Pheobe to William Ellis 5-30-1875 Hy
Bishop, Priscilla to Robert Jones 10-17-1868 (10-18-1868) F B
Bishop, Queen V. to William Coley 5-15-1869 G
Bishop, Sallie to Hiram P. Rains 1-27-1870 G
Bishop, Sarah to Alfred Cox 9-11-1839 (9-12-1839) Hr
Bishop, Sarah to David Bryant 12-1-1842 Cr
Bishop, Sarah to Joe Adams 4-24-1872 Hy
Bishop, Sarah to William F. Tipler 1-6-1838 Hr
Bishop, Susan T. to William D. Cooper 1-19-1833 (1-20-1833) Hr
Biskirk, Mary to John B. Harris 12-30-1856 (12-31-1856) L
Biskirk, Mary to John Harris 12-30-1856 (no return) L
Bittney, Jane to Simon Doxey 11-9-1850 (11-10-1850) G
Bivens, Mollie to John Thomas 7-18-1885 (7-19-1885) L
Bivens, Sallie to James A. Collins 12-6-1866 Ma
Bivens, Sarah to Jessee Blackburn 8-21-1856 G
Bivens, Susan to Ben Brockman 4-9-1845 (4-10-1845) F
Bivins, Elender to George L. Williams 2-6-1850 Be
Bivins, Fanny to William O'Neill 10-7-1881 (10-9-1881) L B
Bivins, Margaret to James McKinney 12-29-1842 Sh
Bivins, Martha O. to Henry C. Boroughs 12-23-1846 (12-24-1846) F
Bivins, Mary A. to John Cole 10-11-1852 Cr
Bivins, Mary to David C. Presson 8-19-1856 Be
Bivins, Susan to J. D. Cunningham 10-12-1868 G
Bizzell, Martha A. to Thomas R. Grantham 12-16-1857 (12-17-1857) Hr
Bizzell, S. C. to J. F. McKee 7-11-1885 (7-12-1885) L
Bizzle, Martha A. to B. F. Edney 1-29-1866 (no return) Dy
Bkaer, Martha J. to P. B. L. Gold 7-16-1845 Hn
Black (Block), Louisa to Benjm. F. Wolfe 9-7-1848 Sh
Black, America L. to P. H. Sutton 2-16-1867 Hy
Black, Ann E. to G. L. Carr 12-28-1837 Sh
Black, C. B. to Ransom Hardenbrook 1-5-1859 (1-6-1859) Sh
Black, Caroline A. to John O. H. Buford 11-2-1846 (11-5-1846) F
Black, Caroline V. to Jas. B. Campbell 1-30-1866 F
Black, Caroline to Joseph H. Tucker 2-22-1866 (2-25-1866) Cr
Black, Caroline to Leonard Burnett 1-26-1869 (no return) F B
Black, Cena M. to George Davis 11-2-1844 (11-4-1844) Hr
Black, Chaney to Frank Jones 2-3-1871 (5-20-1871) F B
Black, Charity to James Russell 3-21-1853 (3-22-1853) O
Black, Eliza J. to Berry A. Davis 6-18-1853 (7-19-1853) Ma
Black, Elizabeth to Lenord Butler 4-8-1851 Sh
Black, Elizabeth to Walter C. Graves 1-1-1846 Cr
Black, Ellen (Mrs.) to Thomas Carswell 7-26-1863 (7-27-1863) Sh
Black, Ellen B. to John R. Robley 12-25-1852 (12-28-1852) Ma
Black, Ellen to Timany Bagby 6-3-1859 Hn
Black, Eveline to James Holt 5-10-1852 (5-14-1852) Sh
Black, Fanny to John McKay 9-5-1839 Sh
Black, Harriet to Robert R. Boyd 12-3-1861 Sh
Black, Jane B. to Thomas L. McCann 8-14-1852 (8-17-1852) Hr
Black, Jane Mildred to Wm. Henry Smith 11-13-1852 (11-16-1852) T
Black, Jane to Benjamin F. Greer 6-12-1851 Be
Black, Jane to Chauncey Shephard 9-17-1851 (9-18-1851) Sh
Black, Lucinda to M. P. Hill 2-18-1850 Sh
Black, Lucinda to W. K. Bludworth-Bloodworth 9-3-1865 Be
Black, M. E. to John W. Bellew 12-26-1871 (12-27-1871) Cr
Black, M. J. to John Thornton 12-27-1866 G
Black, Margaret E. to James B. Burns 7-10-1865 Hn
Black, Margaret K. to Hamilton J. McKnight 11-2-1847 Ma
Black, Martha C. to James H. Humphrey 4-6-1848 (no return) Cr
Black, Martha L. to Richard P. Clark 6-18-1862 (6-19-1862) L
Black, Mary Caroline to James Harris Jameson 6-30-1846 T
Black, Mary E. M. to Alexander Stuckey 1-31-1855 (2-7-1855) L
Black, Mary E. to Joseph Barton 1-10-1863 Mn
Black, Mary Eliza to Fenton Edward Hunt 12-16-1878 Hy
Black, Mary F. to John S. Martin 3-8-1870 Ma
Black, Mary Jane to Isaac M. Acuff 7-13-1870 (7-17-1870) L
Black, Mary P. to Wm. J. Bishop 3-8-1849 (3-13-1849) F
Black, Mary to Henry Williams 12-3-1838 Sh
Black, Mary to John M. Hendricks 12-20-1848 Ma
Black, Mary to Patrick Winters 5-8-1858 Hn
Black, Mary to Tom Bailey 8-26-1868 (no return) F B
Black, Melissa Jane to William Scott 11-20-1866 (11-22-1866) L
Black, Nancy Elizabeth to Saml. T. McMaster 10-4-1858 Ma
Black, Nancy J. to James M. Anderson 7-13-1840 Ma
Black, Nancy to Thomas F. Barton 12-28-1847 (12-30-1847) Ma

Black, Nannie J. to M. M. Wells 11-28-1870 Hy
Black, Narissa to Pleasant Champ 10-20-1853 (10-23-1853) L
Black, Pemelia to Shelby Alexander 12-16-1840 Sh
Black, Rebecca to Abner Moore 1-2-1854 (1-3-1854) Hr
Black, Rosah to Dennis McGinnis 4-30-1868 (no return) F B
Black, Sallie L. to M. J. Webb 10-4-1860 (10-5-1860) F
Black, Sallie to A. W. Loving 10-21-1857 (10-22-1857) Ma
Black, Sarah (Mrs.) to Francois Lelievre 12-31-1864 Sh
Black, Sarah A. to James Dillions 6-6-1870 (6-9-1870) L
Black, Sarah to Alexander Ramsey 12-?-1843 (12-22-1843) Hr
Black, Sarah to Isam Beasley 3-3-1845 (no return) F
Black, Sarah to William Jones 7-12-1872 (no return) Hy
Blackamore, Mary to Joshua Kimber 10-10-1851 (10-12-1851) Hr
Blackard, Julion to Turner Perry 8-7-1848 Ma
Blackard, Amanda C. to Wm. S. Balser 2-18-1878 Dy
Blackburn, Jermima to Jesse H. Spencer 12-28-1858 G
Blackburn, Lydia Ann to John Morton 1-13-1870 (1-18-1870) F B
Blackburn, M. E. to W. B. Phips 3-27-1872 O
Blackburn, M. J. to J. J. Fields 11-4-1871 O
Blackburn, Mary E. to James R. Moss 9-25-1844 (9-26-1844) F
Blackburn, Mary E. to James R. Moss no dates (with Feb 1844) F
Blackburn, Mary to William Kennedy 10-19-1868 G
Blackburn, Nancy E. to E. G. Roberson 12-25-1858 (12-28-1858) G
Blackburn, Sarah A. to Henry A. Archer 3-31-1865 G
Blackburn, Susan (Mrs.) to Benjamin Allen 12-2-1872 Dy
Blackley, Mary J. to W. C. Claerben 9-12-1854 We
Blackman, Alice to Josiah Loyd 6-1-1867 G B
Blackman, Betty to James D. (Joseph L?) McCutcheon 1-20-1870 G
Blackman, Evaline to John Brown 7-20-1850 Sh
Blackman, Mollie to W. S. Tolbert 2-27-1876 (2-28-1876) Dy
Blackman, Nancy C. to W. H. Hammond 10-8-1856 O
Blackman, Thiresa to Nathaniel Hammond 2-21-1854 (2-28-1854) O
Blackmon, E. I. to William A. Benson 9-22-1842 Ma
Blackmon, Elizabeth K. to James Rollins 2-21-1855 (2-25-1855) Ma
Blackmon, Jonnie L. to John T. Rone 1-3-1867 (1-6-1867) Ma
Blackmon, Sarah L. to henry Roberson 10-5-1859 (11-6-1859) G
Blackshar, Matilda C. to Lacy? Craven 12-31-1854 (1-3-1855) O
Blacksheer, Caroline to Robert H. Thomason 9-8-1842 Hn
Blacksheer, Sarah to Arnold D. Thomason 10-18-1843 Hn
Blackshire, Amanda to James A. Lawrence 11-20-1850 Hn
Blackwell, A. L. to M. J. Green 10-1-1872 (10-2-1872) T
Blackwell, Ann to Henry Dunlap 10-25-1871 T
Blackwell, Barshebn? E. to William M. Roberson 12-22-1859 G B
Blackwell, Bell to Allen Tarry 12-31-1872 T
Blackwell, Bettie to Ceasar Pickett 1-16-1875 L B
Blackwell, Dilsey to Daniel Hurt 10-27-1872 (11-2-1872) Cr B
Blackwell, Eliza to Gwin D. Myrick 9-10-1844 Hn
Blackwell, Elizabeth to Charles G. Mitchell 8-21-1838 F
Blackwell, Ella to W. S. Wilkes 12-23-1880 L
Blackwell, Fannie C. to E. D. Rhea 9-17-1885 L
Blackwell, Frances to Peter Marshal 1-13-1872 (1-21-1872) L
Blackwell, Harriett to D. P.(T) Woodside 9-27-1846 Sh
Blackwell, Lucy Ann to John Bell 1-17-1847 L
Blackwell, Mariah to A. Tucker 10-17-1840 (no return) L
Blackwell, Martha C. to Jas. W. White 11-3-1850 Sh
Blackwell, Mary E. to James B. Nixon 4-16-1861 (4-17-1861) L
Blackwell, Mary E. to W. H. Hawkins 10-7-1868 (10-9-1868) Cr
Blackwell, Mary J. to Gideon Leach 2-8-1840 Sh
Blackwell, Mary to Harrison Moppin 6-1-1868 (no return) Cr
Blackwell, Melissa to L. Knowlton 6-15-1869 (6-16-1869) Dy
Blackwell, Mollie to William Ridings 8-30-1871 (no return) Hy
Blackwell, Sarah A. to Joseph Harper 1-31-1861 Sh
Blackwell, Sarah L. to J. B. Brisdendine 1-20-1869 (1-29-1869) L
Blackwell, Virginia J. to Henry Webster 1-18-1869 (1-19-1869) L
Blackwood, Ellen to W. Conner 11-2-1875 (no return) Dy
Blackwood, Lucey to J. Madison Scott 11-12-1831 Hr
Blackwood, Martha J. to Newton J. Bevill 6-21-1860 Hn
Blackwood, Martha to Granville Lucas 12-24-1870 (12-25-1870) F B
Blackwood, Mary E. to Robert L. Raines 9-7-1865 Hn
Blackwood, P. A. C. to Alfred Smith 3-27-1853 Hn
Blackwood, Rachel to Thompson Brooks 8-10-1832 (8-14-1832) Hr
Blackwood, S. M. P. to J. D. Craig 10-21-1871 (10-25-1871) T
Blade, Rosanna to Thos. J. Read 1-1-1866 Hy
Blades, Georgeanna to Gem Taylor 7-21-1866 Hy
Blain, Adeline W. to M. B. Broyles? 11-30-1855 (no return) F
Blain, Betty to Rufus Warr 12-25-1868 (12-27-1868) F B
Blain, E. L. to W. C. Jenkins 3-3-1868 (3-5-1868) F
Blain, M. E. to A. Waller 12-20-1852 (no return) F
Blain, M. E. to James L. Jenkins 11-6-1865 (no return) F
Blain, Mariah to John P. Wiseman 12-17-1860 (12-20-1860) F
Blain, Mary C. to John W. Baker 2-13-1850 (2-14-1850) G
Blain, Sarah to Asburry Harrell 12-13-1866 (no return) F
Blaine, Easter to Jesse Heaslett 9-27-1871? (SB 1870?) F B
Blair, Anneta J. to C. C. Short 11-5-1845 Cr
Blair, Elizabeth J. to James C. Blackshear 3-10-1853 G
Blair, Elizabeth to John Scott 2-24-1861 G
Blair, Emma to B. F. Farabee 1-30-1861 (1-31-1861) Sh

Blair, Fannie to Willis Strayhorn 1-31-1872 (2-1-1872) Dy
Blair, J. S. to Elisha Lawrance 2-5-1846 Cr
Blair, Jenny to James Williams 1-15-1868 G B
Blair, Juda A. to James McClary 11-13-1846 Cr
Blair, Julia Ann to Joseph W. Hooten 12-15-1870 Hy
Blair, Kate A. to Frank C. Carter 1-25-1877 (no return) L
Blair, Lidia to Wm. A. Naylor 12-18-1855 (12-20-1855) Hr
Blair, M. A. E. to A. G. B. Harris 9-14-1866 (9-16-1866) F
Blair, Margaret C. to John W. Reynolds 12-3-1859 Hr
Blair, Margarett J. to Tilman Palmer 12-20-1866 Cr
Blair, Margaretta to Hardamon Abington 9-19-1839 (9-26-1839) F
Blair, Margarette M. to Roland Childs 8-16-1854 (8-17-1854) G
Blair, Martha Ann to David B. Hilliard 2-2-1846 (2-5-1846) F
Blair, Martha J. to George C. Harley 2-8-1844 G
Blair, Martha M. to A. Neeley 1-23-1848 Cr
Blair, Martha to W. D. Gleaves 12-16-1874 Dy
Blair, Mary A. to James A. Blair 7-24-1849 Cr
Blair, Mary C. to Benjamin A. Smith 11-10-1852 Sh
Blair, Mary E. to A. R. Adams 7-17-1853 Cr
Blair, Mary E. to Richard L. West 12-21-1849 (12-23-1849) G
Blair, Mary Jane to Nuton Coker 4-14-1870 Hy
Blair, Mary to C. C. Dunlap 3-19-1868 Hy
Blair, Mary to James Ward 2-13-1836 Hr
Blair, Mary to Noah Dane 11-1-1841 (11-10-1841) F
Blair, N. J. to J. L. Chappell 1-6-1874 Dy
Blair, Nancy to Benjamin F. Haltom 10-30-1850 (10-31-1850) Ma
Blair, Nancy to John W. Pope 4-14-1863 (4-15-1863) Cr
Blair, Nancy to John W. Pope 4-14-1864 (no return) Cr
Blair, Rebecca C. to Luke L. Williams 7-20-1846 (no return) F
Blair, Sopha to George W. Cook 12-16-1872 (12-19-1872) Cr
Blair, Susan E. to John L. Dudley 11-10-1868 Hy
Blair, Tabitha C. to Joel H. Blackshear 4-13-1854 G
Blair, Tennessee to William M. Seeton 12-9-1828 Ma
Blairs, Nancy to Benj. B. Enloe 9-27-1840 Cr
Blake, Caroline to Wily E. H. Page 8-10-1861 (no return) Cr
Blake, Eliza C. to Samuel R. Brown 12-6-1838 Sh
Blake, Elizabeth to W. M. Diggs 1-15-1866 F
Blake, Emma S. (L.?) to G. H. Ramsey 12-20-1860 G
Blake, Frances S. to Levi Killebrew 11-16-1866 Hn
Blake, Frances to Wm. A. Ross 8-13-1855 Cr
Blake, Hester Ann to John Todd 10-22-1850 Hn
Blake, Hezebeth (Hipzebeth) to Samuel Runkle 7-26-1831 Sh
Blake, Jane to Lewis McCall 3-10-1867 Hn
Blake, Julia to Henry Blake 7-4-1866 O
Blake, Louisa to Henry Jackson 5-28-1869 (5-29-1869) Cr
Blake, Mary M. to John H. Ourie? 6-5-1851 Hn
Blake, Mary to William Cobb 5-13-1834 Sh
Blake, S. E. to S. C. Debow 9-?-1863 (9-24-1863) O
Blake, Sally M. to David Walker 3-7-1831 (3-8-1831) Hr
Blake, Saphronia C. to David H. Russell 1-?-1866 (1-11-1866) Cr
Blake, Sarah ANn to William Ship 5-15-1843 (no return) Hn
Blake, Susan U. A. to Thomas Blankenship 9-15-1867 O
Blakeley, Amanda to Jimmy Coker 3-5-1886 (3-6-1886) L
Blakeley, Ellen to J. A. Click 3-18-1880 (no return) L
Blakeley, Louisa Ann to J. N. Ednsley 1-13-1863 Hn
Blakeley, Margaret to G. C. Weaver 4-3-1880 (4-4-1880) L
Blakely, Elizabeth to Duncal Neal 9-19-1862 Mn
Blakely, Lula to Charlie Hammock 1-11-1886 L
Blakely, N. J. to Joseph C. McBroom 7-30-1878 (7-31-1878) L
Blakeman, Martha F. to P. M. Rogers 1-3-1858 We
Blakemon, Annie V. to Robert H. Mahon 12-14-1865 G
Blakemore, Alcy to Lyman Jackson 5-5-1866 G
Blakemore, Edmonia to George Nettles 2-8-1877 Hy
Blakemore, Elizabeth J. to Dewitt A. Reese 9-5-1854 G
Blakemore, Harriet to William Johnson 5-10-1868 G B
Blakemore, Isadora to W. H. Ellis 1-28-1868 G
Blakemore, Jarusa A. to Wadkins D. Dodson 6-15-1847 (6-17-1847) G
Blakemore, Margaret to Isaac Taylor 7-8-1856 We
Blakemore, Margaret to Joseph M. White 3-6-1860 We
Blakemore, Mary J. to Ovid Upchurch 12-22-1867 Hn B
Blakemore, Mollie F. to J. D. Gullett 4-10-1867 G
Blakemore, Nancy S. to Samuel Zericor 1-4-1827 (1-7-1827) G
Blakemore, Sarah J. to John D. Hannah 7-6-1826 Hy
Blakemore, Sophia J. to Charles Harrill 2-20-1847 Sh
Blakemore, Susan V. to William R. Fulghum 12-14-1857 (12-16-1857) G
Blakemore, Susan to Philip Alsten 8-18-1846 We
Blalock, Elizar to John Bates 10-1-1858 (no return) We
Blalock, Emily H. to Solomon E. Cooper 12-23-1861 (12-26-1861) Hr
Blalock, Emma E. to David S. Reed 12-19-1863 (12-24-1863) F
Blalock, Harriet to William F. Neale 3-26-1855? (no return) Hn
Blalock, M. E. to Champ Swearengin 10-12-1871 G
Blalock, Nancy to Andrew Dunning 5-29-1861 We
Blan, Jane C. to Elisha Avery 9-29-1848 Hn
Blan, Jane to Thomas Alexander 2-27-1838 Hn
Blan, Martha Jane to James R. Connell 1-15-1843 Ma
Blan, Sophronia to James B. Hughes 12-27-1856 (1-1-1857) G
Blan?, Adline to Philip Smith 1-13-1872 (no return) Cr B

Blancet, Virginia to James Williams 3-24-1861 G
Blanchard, Sarah E. to Reding Whitehead 2-4-1852 (no return) F
Blanchett, Cas to J. N. Petty 1-4-1866 Hn
Blanchett, Elizabeth N. to James M. Marshall 5-8-1859 Hn
Bland, Caroline to John Henrichs 1-9-1860 Sh
Bland, Eliza to William Rodgers 8-28-1844 Sh
Bland, Elizabeth (Mrs.) to John W. Jones 11-16-1847 Sh
Bland, Ivana A. to J. F. Turner 5-6-1864 Sh
Bland, Julia (Mrs.) to Jonathan W. Weaver 3-22-1856 (4-2-1856) Sh
Bland, Keziah E. to John M. Walls 12-17-1857 Hn
Bland, Martha F. to James M. Peel 12-31-1851 (1-8-1852) Sh
Bland, Martha W. N. to William A. Taylor 4-17-1839 (4-24-1839) F
Bland, Mary E. to Luther D. McKnight 6-14-1843 Sh
Bland, Mary Jane to Nathan Gregory 1-19-1843 Sh
Bland, Mary to Wm. L. Nelson 3-5-1860 (3-7-1860) F
Bland, Rachael to J. D. Mayfield 2-16-1870 Sh
Bland, Rutha to Absolum Maxwell 1-9-1845 Cr
Bland, Sarah A. to John Delf 6-14-1869 Dy
Bland, Selina to W. S. Montgomery 4-3-1856 (4-4-1856) Sh
Bland, Thrulina to John Kennedy 3-18-1832 Sh
Blane, Elizabeth to James Morris 12-9-1856 We
Blankenship, Amanda J. to Joshua Baker 12-4-1861 G
Blankenship, Ardenia A. to J. G. Meek 10-22-1860 G
Blankenship, E. A. to T. P. Martin 12-30-1865 G
Blankenship, Elisa to John H. Wright 2-21-1856 Cr
Blankenship, Eliza Jane to Green Hall 10-30-1840 (11-4-1840) G
Blankenship, Ellen M. to H. S. Drumwright 11-30-1874 (12-2-1874) L
Blankenship, Emily A. to William K. Bryant 7-1-1854 G
Blankenship, Frances E. to J. A. Darr 10-11-1861 G
Blankenship, Lucinda to Michael Larkin (Larker?) 1-4-1869 G
Blankenship, Lucinda to Thomas Brown 4-13-1868 G
Blankenship, Manarca F. S. J. W. to Thomas C. Bogle 11-13-1855 (11-14-1855) G
Blankenship, Martha A. to Geo. W. Bowles 11-7-1861 G
Blankenship, Martha E. to Wm. N. Stewart 12-7-1868 G
Blankenship, Martha F. to James F. Knox 9-8-1858 (9-9-1858) G
Blankenship, Martha to Henry C. Duncan 8-17-1836 O
Blankenship, Mary A. to John W. Pitts 6-24-1873 (no return) Dy
Blankenship, Mary A. to William A. Hill 12-14-1863 (12-15-1863) Dy
Blankenship, Mary Adelaide to Andrew J. Pitts 9-5-1876 (9-6-1876) Dy
Blankenship, Mary J. to Rufus A. Via 1-16-1856 G
Blankenship, Mary to Edwin Warren 5-9-1840 (5-14-1840) G
Blankenship, Ollie to William D. Pennington 11-8-1871 L
Blankenship, Narcissa to John H. Crawford 3-6-1854 (3-10-1854) G
Blankenship, Pemilia A. to William Cannon 5-14-1845 (5-15-1845) G
Blankenship, S. C. to A. I. Upton 8-31-1867 G
Blankenship, S. C. to A. J. Upton 8-31-1867 O
Blankenship, S. J. to J. R. Green 11-24-1866 (11-25-1866) Dy
Blankenship, Sarah to Isaac Y. Welborne 10-22-1856 (10-25-1856) O
Blankenship, Sarah to Isaac Y. Wilbourn 10-22-1856 (10-23-1856) O
Blankenship, Susan E. to N. A. Shelton 10-7-1866 G
Blankenship, Susan to Wm. T. Moseley 8-24-1853 L
Blankenship, V. H. to W. L. Duncan 9-26-1884 L
Blankenship, Virginia J. to M. C. McCollum 8-28-1878 L
Blankinship, E. J. to James H. Holt 9-1-1859 (9-2-1859) G
Blankinship, Elizabeth A. to Jesse S. Blankinship 9-30-1853 (10-2-1853) G
Blankinship, H. L. to J. L. Lane 1-31-1866 (2-10-1866) O
Blankinship, Lucy A. to Peter Claybrook 5-9-1866 G
Blankinship, Martha A. C. to James M. Blankinship 6-25-1868 G
Blankinship, Mary P. to Joseph H. Thompson 1-15-1863 G
Blankinship, S. E. to C. E. Fisher 6-23-1870 G
Blankinship, Sarah Matilda to William B. McGuire 9-23-1874 L
Blanks, Mary Catharine to James A. Cagle 11-25-1865 Be
Blanks, Recca to John Briant 9-2-1867 (no return) Cr
Blanten, Sallie to William Robertson 10-4-1866 G
Blanton, America D. to Benjamin Wootten 9-10-1855 Sh
Blanton, Ellen to Adam Beasley 7-7-1866 Hn B
Blanton, Jane to John Williamson 9-12-1867 (no return) Hn B
Blanton, Jane to Thomas Ruffin 12-18-1854 (12-20-1854) O
Blanton, Katie to W. R. McBride 6-6-1877 Dy
Blanton, Lucy to Harvey Cowan 12-21-1867 Hn
Blanton, Martha to James P. Cooper 1-27-1864 Hn
Blanton, Mary L. to B. F. Hawkins 9-8-1862 O
Blanton, Mattie to W. A. Carroll 8-9-1879 (no return) Dy
Blanton, Nannie to A. F. Walker 1-30-1868 G
Blanton, Rebecca to John Postlethwaite 2-15-1866 Hn
Blanton, Sophia L. to Joseph W. Furgarson 6-9-1858 G
Blasengame, Margaret E. to John Holloway 1-25-1863 Mn
Blasingame, Nancy J. to Calvin Davis 1-17-1872 (1-18-1872) T
Blassingame, Mary J. to John F. Tidwell 1-9-1862 Mn
Blaw, Mozella to Taylor Broom 12-21-1868 (12-25-1868) F B
Blaydes, Lucy Ann to George E. Thomas 2-11-1862 Hy
Blaydes, M. A. to I. F. Castellow 10-5-1867 Hy
Blaydes, Margaret to Felix Read 6-20-1868 Hy
Blaydes, Mary F. to W. H. Jelks 3-10-1852 (3-11-1852) Ma
Blaydes, Nellie to W. H. Montague 12-31-1868 Hy
Blaydes, Nicie to Hanks Parker 2-4-1871 (no return) F B

Blaydes, Sarah E. to Samel D. Ware 2-22-1851 (2-27-1851) F
Blaylock, M. G. to W. C. Wood 9-7-1856 We
Blaylock, Mary to James Gilbreth 1-12-1871 Cr
Blaylock, Nancy J. to Joseph B. Kirkland 1-9-1858 (1-13-1858) Hr
Bledsoe, Adeline to Samuel Wilson 10-13-1865 (10-24-1865) Cr
Bledsoe, Amanda M. to John T. Beveridge 12-20-1854 (12-21-1854) Ma
Bledsoe, Ann to William Allen 1-25-1871 (1-26-1871) T
Bledsoe, Annie to John Adkins 8-18-1874 (8-8?-1874) T
Bledsoe, Armantha A. to Willis Grady 2-14-1856 G
Bledsoe, Asinith to WilliamD. McDummitt 12-24-1839 Ma
Bledsoe, Avolina G. to Thos. Watt 9-29-1857 (9-28-1857) G
Bledsoe, Bulah J. to Robert B. Koen 4-17-1856 Cr
Bledsoe, Catharine M. to Hosea W. Sherrill 4-1-1850 (4-3-1850) T
Bledsoe, Centhy to Wellington H. Bledsoe 4-1-1838 (4-4-1838) G
Bledsoe, Cynthia M. to Napolian Fleming 12-11-1868 T
Bledsoe, Dizey to Martin L. Baley 3-13-1846 (3-15-1846) G
Bledsoe, Dora to William Henry Feezor 10-17-1867 T
Bledsoe, Dorothy to Joel R. Smith 1-12-1841 G
Bledsoe, E. Kate to Wm. V. Allen 12-30-1857 (1-6-1858) Sh
Bledsoe, Elizabeth B. to Jessee Ballentine 8-26-1845 (8-27-1845) G
Bledsoe, Elizabeth to George A. Whittenton 2-5-1846 Ma
Bledsoe, Elizabeth to James A. Johnson 11-2-1856 Cr
Bledsoe, Elizabeth to John W. Hicks 2-18-1867 G
Bledsoe, Elizabeth to William H. Rains 8-20-1839 (8-22-1839) G
Bledsoe, Ellenor to Samuel P. Rust 11-10-1829 (11-12-1829) G
Bledsoe, Emaline to Nathan Ray 2-6-1838 (not endorsed) G
Bledsoe, Emma to Haden Miller 2-11-1871 (no return) F B
Bledsoe, Ernesta? to George Johnson 4-6-1867 (4-7-1867) T
Bledsoe, Fanny C. to George W. Hill 2-20-1867 Cr
Bledsoe, Fidelia to Raves E. Jordon 12-26-1838 Ma
Bledsoe, Hanna to Peter Hill 2-7-1867 T
Bledsoe, Hannah to Green Allen 8-31-1872 (9-1-1872) Cr
Bledsoe, Hannah to Hiram Hughes 9-29-1874 T
Bledsoe, Harrett to Jessee Childers 12-1-1848 (12-3-1848) G
Bledsoe, Harriet Jane to William Smith 4-25-1832 G
Bledsoe, Harriett to W. C. Moore 12-3-1860 (12-6-1860) Cr
Bledsoe, Hawkins to William Mobley 11-12-1840 G
Bledsoe, J. T.? to J. W. Hill 2-11-1871 (2-12-1871) Cr
Bledsoe, Julia to Brinkley Barker 9-30-1865 G
Bledsoe, Louisa to John A. Shaw 9-13-1879 (9-14-1879) Dy
Bledsoe, Louisa to John H. Pritchard 10-27-1851 Cr
Bledsoe, Louisa to Joshua Bell 10-19-1833 (10-22-1833) G
Bledsoe, Lucy to Allen Williams 7-21-1842 Ma
Bledsoe, Lucy to Levi Hawkins 11-26-1871 Cr B
Bledsoe, Lucy to Newton Putman 3-19-1868 G
Bledsoe, M. J. to David A. Gardener 1-11-1866 T
Bledsoe, Manerva B. E. to Daniel Reynold 8-23-1853 G
Bledsoe, Margarette A. to John A. Barker 1-26-1865 G
Bledsoe, Mariah to Stephen Conner 9-21-1867 G
Bledsoe, Martha Ann to Francis A. Bledsoe 7-31-1837 G
Bledsoe, Martha C. to E. T. Keel 5-14-1864 (5-16-1864) Sh
Bledsoe, Martha to Cyrus Elcan 10-10-1870 (10-29-1870) F B
Bledsoe, Martha to Dick Beadls? 1-12-1868 G
Bledsoe, Martha to Jerie Morgan 12-30-1865 T
Bledsoe, Martha to Jerre Morgan 12-30-1865 T
Bledsoe, Martha to Jerry Morgan 12-30-1867 (12-30-1866?) T
Bledsoe, Mary E. to Wilie L. Sexton 4-19-1853 G
Bledsoe, Mary L. to Gaih Holland 12-4-1854 G
Bledsoe, Mary L. to Hearvy Bledsoe 3-18-1833 (3-20-1833) G
Bledsoe, Mary N. to John Lynch 12-3-1844 (12-4-1844) G
Bledsoe, Mary T. to Williamson Houze 5-31-1853 Sh
Bledsoe, Mary V. to Benj. P. Tyson 10-27-1859 (10-26?-1859) G
Bledsoe, Mary to E. Clarke 12-13-1866 G
Bledsoe, Mary to John McMicken 12-26-1867 T
Bledsoe, P. G. to R. C. Beard 7-30-1856 Sh
Bledsoe, R. H. to M. H. McCain 10-24-1850 Cr
Bledsoe, Sallie to Frank McGregor 2-19-1873 (2-20-1873) T
Bledsoe, Sarah H. to Clinton Brigance 10-12-1852 (10-13-1852) G
Bledsoe, Sarah P. to J. C. Massey 2-14-1854 Sh
Bledsoe, Sarah to Levi Young 11-1-1867 (no return) L B
Bledsoe, Susan F. to J. F. Johnson 8-20-1866 G
Bledsoe, Susan M. to Joseph Witherspoon 3-22-1850 G
Bledsoe, Susan to Solomon Smith 1-28-1870 T
Bledsoe, Sylvia to Arden Taylor 5-7-1870 (5-8-1870) Cr
Bledsow, Nesia A. to Lewis F. Kinney 6-15-1864 (6-16-1864) O
Blessing, Elizabeth to Alexander Bowland 7-29-1841 F
Blessing, Julia to George Walls 12-3-1863 G
Blessing, Louisa to Mark M. Frazer 9-11-1845 (12-6-1845) F
Blessing, Martha to Joseph Scallions 6-8-1847 (6-9-1847) F
Blilder?, Samatha to Stephen Smith 8-24-1856 Cr
Bloar, S. L. to W. F. Rawles 1-22-1870 (1-23-1870) Dy
Block, Baslette to Zaclok Moock 11-14-1849 Sh
Block, Caroline to Lewis Kern 5-18-1848 Sh
Block, Clarice to David Hirshberg 2-28-1876 Hy
Blocker, Martha J. to Edwin A. Pagan 1-18-1848 Sh
Blockmann, Amelia to Aaron Hirsh 6-16-1852 (6-17-1852) Sh
Blood, Henrietta Thompson to Edmond Urguhart 10-7-1864 (10-12-1864) Sh
Bloodwood, M. E. to John F. Hubbs 9-26-1863 (9-27-1863) O
Bloodworth, Delila to Wallace Nixon 9-7-1869 (no return) L
Bloodworth, Elizabeth to Elisha Bloodworth 1-4-1843 Sh
Bloodworth, Harriett to Alsey B. Armour 5-7-1845 Sh
Bloodworth, Mary Jane to James R. Childs 11-28-1846 Be
Bloodworth, Narisa M. to Ira Gaines 3-25-1845 Sh
Bloodworth, S. E. to Jno. Thompson 11-3-1839 Be
Bloodworth, Sarah A. to W. M. Carter 11-6-1854 (11-9-1854) Sh
Bloodworth, Sarah L. to William Booth 2-21-1847 Sh
Bloodworth, Sarah M. to James Mitchell 7-21-1842 Sh
Bloomingdale, Eunice to George M. Tatum 11-27-1877 (11-28-1877) Dy
Blount, Elizabeth C. to Daniel Mosier 9-19-1849 (9-20-1849) O
Blount, Lucinda to Robert Smith 1-16-1878 Hy
Blount, Martha A. to Thomas D. Stevens 11-16-1856 Hn
Blount, Mary to William Hutson Chandler 8-15-1839 (8-15-1839) Hr
Blount, S. L. to M. A. Sanders 1-15-1872 (1-17-1872) Cr
Blount, Susan to Levi Pearce 5-15-1844 (5-16-1844) Hr
Blous?, Martha J. to John H. Woods 7-25-1860 T
Blow, Celina to James F. Stewart 8-28-1848 Cr
Blow, Charlotte to Thos. S. Adams 11-18-1852 Cr
Bloyce, Jane to George Riddle 10-22-1857 O
Bloyce, Margaret to David P. McCracken 1-26-1841 Cr
Bloyd, Haddy to John Allen 6-26-1848 Hn
Bloys, Caroline to E. C. Dougherty 7-19-1849 O
Bloys, Elizabeth to Abraham King 4-17-1830 (4-18-1830) G
Bloys, Mary to John W. Tylor 4-24-1849 O
Bloys, Maryt to John H. Tylor 4-24-1849 (5-14-1849) O
Bludworth, Mary S. to Samuel J. Taylor 8-4-1867 Be
Bludworth, Susan to J. R. Ragsdale 9-13-1867 O
Blue, Martha N. to Micajah Mason 9-22-1847 Sh
Bluford, Vina to Andy Hunter 1-10-1871 (no return) F B
Blume, Josephine to W. R. McLagan? 11-3-1863 (no return) L
Blumenthal, Betty to M. D. Marks 7-22-1856 Sh
Blunt, Cintha to Haywood Johnson 2-27-1873 Hy
Blunt, Eliza to Wm. C. McCord 3-28-1843 Cr
Blunt, Louisa to Armstrong Mifflin 8-30-1845 G
Blunt, Sabrinah Jane to William Morris 4-12-1858 (4-14-1858) Hr
Blunt, Sarah to William Vails 1-18-1842 (1-23-1842) Hr
Blurton, Mary to Ruffin Permenter 9-24-1866 (9-25-1866) Ma
Bly, Sophronia to Isaac Brock 11-17-1875 (no return) Hy
Blye, Lucy to Wm. B. Hay 3-23-1871 Hy
Blyler, Josephine to D. J. Garrett 2-11-1878 (2-13-1878) L
Blythe, Amanda to John W. Nance 11-14-1844 Hn
Blythe, Caroline to John A. Gibbs 1-21-1851 Hn
Blythe, Elizabeth Jane to William C. Owens 4-21-1860 (4-22-1860) Ma
Blythe, Ellen to Thomas Clark 1-29-1866 Hn
Blythe, Frances A. to John Caldwell 8-1-1854 (no return) Hn
Blythe, Lacky M. to James C. Graham 12-15-1835 Sh
Blythe, Martha Ann to Joseph Thorn 12-18-1848 (12-21-1848) Ma
Blythe, Martha P. to William Gibbs 12-5-1841 Hn
Blythe, Martha to Henry Murphey (Umphrey) 2-29-1844 Sh
Blythe, Martha to Henry Umphrey 2-29-1844 Sh
Blythe, Mary C. to Hardy Crowder 7-27-1841 Hn
Blythe, Mary J. to Hezekiah Crittenden 12-10-1846 Hn
Blythe, Sarah E. to George Coleman 2-16-1848 Hn
Blythe, T. C. to James W. Lindamond 12-13-1854 Hn
Blythe, Theodosia T. to Henry McCallen 11-19-1834 Sh
Boage, Mary to Henry A. Cooper 10-1-1854 We
Boales, Margarett A. to Joseph B. Bounds 9-21-1847 (10-10-1847) F
Boals, A. S. to Edwin H. Poor 3-21-1867 F
Boals, Emeline to James Capher 8-11-1847 (8-12-1847) Ma
Boals, Malissa to Richard T. Bolton 1-9-1849 (1-10-1849) Ma
Boals, Margaret to Gus Griffin 2-24-1869 (2-25-1869) F B
Boals, Sally to Anthony Towles 12-28-1868 (12-30-1868) F B
Boals, Susan Jane to Miles Wilson Piercy 8-2-1869 Ma
Board, Amanda to Henry Whitaker 5-22-1875 (5-30-1875) O
Board, M. E. to J. K. P. Lancaster 3-6-1872 (3-7-1872) O
Board, Mary L. to S. M. Hudson 4-28-1857 O
Boardman, Cornelia M. to L. A. Rhodes 9-21-1864 (9-27-1864) Sh
Boatman, Caroline to William Murphy 6-13-1863 Mn
Boatman?, Sarah Ann to William Cain 6-4-1852 (no return) F
Boatright, Mary to Caleb Smith 1-13-1856 Be
Boatright, Nancy G. to G. W. Rasberry 12-3-1868 (12-9-1868) Dy
Boatright, R. A. to J. E. Crisp 10-13-1869 (no return) Dy
Boatwright, Fannie E. to W. C. Todd 8-31-1870 G
Boatwright, M. F. to J. N. Lewelling 2-25-1873 (2-27-1873) Dy
Boaz, Betsy to William Moore 6-1-1867 G B
Boaz, Elizabeth J. to Joseph C. King 10-24-1861 We
Boaz, Elizabeth to A. G. Allmond 1-7-1859 We
Boaz, L. A. to James Copeland 8-24-1854 (8-25-1854) G
Boaz, Mary S. to Liberty W. Brimingham 10-18-1859 (10-20-1859) Ma
Boaze, Sarah E. to C. W. Adams 12-18-1851 We
Bobbet, Mary A. to W. E. Orr 2-12-1865 G
Bobbett, Elizabeth to Ephraim Burrow 4-2-1834 (4-5-1834) G
Bobbett, Francis M. to Jno. H. Dinwiddy 7-1-1840 G
Bobbett, M. J. to Quincy M. Grier 8-26-1848 G
Bobbett, Martha C. to John B. Williams 1-29-1851 (1-31-1851) G

Bobbett, Martha R. to Benj. Blankenship 8-29-1856 (9-1-1856) G
Bobbett, Mary E. to Uriah J. Hammonds 3-27-1864 G
Bobbett, Susan to H. L. M. Barton 9-15-1838 (9-16-1838) G
Bobbit, Moriah to Abner Jones 1-29-1830 (2-4-1830) Ma
Bobbitt, Anna E. to W. J. Pyland 8-13-1868 G
Bobbitt, Catharine to Jerome Davis 9-16-1870 (9-18-1870) F B
Bobbitt, Dorraty to Wm. J. Davidson 8-30-1838 G
Bobbitt, Electa to Josiah Prescott 10-20-1831 Sh
Bobbitt, Harriet to Washington Goodwin 12-9-1869 (12-16-1869) F B
Bobbitt, Isabella S. to James Gwin 1-10-1853 (no return) F
Bobbitt, Martha J. to Thomas B. Blankenship 7-2-1864 G
Bobbitt, Matilda to H. F. Warren 12-22-1877 Hy
Bobbitt, Nancy to George Garwood 2-28-1869 G B
Bobbitt, S. J. to James P. Snoddy 10-16-1867 G
Bobbitt, Susan to Cleiborn Culp 9-27-1869 (10-2-1869) F B
Bobby, Mary M. to Wm. Bell 10-12-1857 Cr
Bobett, Mary to Geo. W. Jamey? 4-12-1873 (4-16-1873) Dy
Bobitt, Jane to Loyd Ozier 11-7-1861 (no return) Cr
Bobo, Adaline to Marcus Jones 9-9-1846 Sh
Bobo, Elizabeth to G. W. Morgan 3-9-1847 Sh
Bobo, M. J. to William Travis 1-3-1868 (1-6-1868) Cr
Boce, Mary A. to Thos. C. Busick 10-30-1844 Ma
Bocock, Almira A. to M. S. Borthwick 4-27-1861 Sh
Boden, Sallie to G. F. Paterson 6-4-1865 Hn
Bodican?, Mary M. to Robert Smith 6-7-1843 Sh
Bodkin, Jane to Henry Lowry 10-3-1855 (10-4-1855) G
Bodkin, Mary G. to P. E. Hill 8-16-1866 G
Bodkin, Sarah E. to W. T. Allen 2-11-1868 G
Boen, B. J. to J. T. Williams 6-12-1870 G
Boen, Sarah E. to John E. Coker 9-16-1859 (9-20-1859) G
Boet, Harriet to Washington Parkin 9-15-1842 (9-16-1842) Ma
Bogal, Mary J. to Thomas G. Roachel 6-28-1865 G
Bogant, Penina to Meekins Williams 3-29-1866 (4-1-1866) Ma
Boggess, Susan to James Comrie? 6-13-1867 Dy
Boggiana, Columbia to Lazzario Rocco 8-20-1860 Sh
Boggs, Jane S. to William B. Konegay 2-25-1845 O
Boggs, M. A. to H. W. Rea 1-14-1872 Hy
Boggs, Martha to William F. Allen 6-11-1859 Hn
Boggs, R. to T. C. Mercer 2-2-1873 Hy
Bogle, Margarette Jane to A. C. McGee 5-25-1854 (5-26-1854) G
Bogle, Mary E. to Lewis J. Milligan 10-1-1860 (10-4-1860) Cr
Bogle, Mary E. to Lewis J. Mullins 10-?-1860 (10-4-1860) Cr
Bogue, Sarah S. to S. M. Harehaw 9-1-1860 Hr
Bohanan, Mary to Joseph M. Cooper 5-27-1857 We
Bohannan, Mary to John Rushing 11-3-1854 G
Bohannon, June to William L. Phelps 4-7-1850 Hn
Bohannon, Mary F. to T. G. Tomlinson 2-21-1850 Hn
Bohannon, Mary to George a. Caton 8-15-1839 Hn
Bohannon, Sarah Ann to Robert B. Reynolds 2-4-1857 Hn
Bohanon, Martha L. to Green Hatley 3-9-1848 Be
Bohanon, Martha to John McFarland 5-29-1859 Hn
Bohean, Catherine to Judson Ewing (McEwing?) 1-20-1864 (1-21-1864) Sh
Boher, Amelia W. to William A. Griffing 1-17-1855 Sh
Bointon, A. V. to H. J. Stuck 5-9-1860 Sh
Boke, Caroline to Frank Mahler 5-25-1858 Sh
Bolam, Mary to Robert A. Tate 4-4-1864 Sh
Bolan, Susan to James M. Clayton 1-3-1841 Sh
Boland, Alice to Peter Comas 1-29-1853 Sh
Boland, Cornelia O. to Lafayette Faulkner 4-3-1862 Dy
Bolden, Mary to Jno. M. Lawson 5-21-1856 (5-22-1856) Hr
Bolden, Matilda S. to John M. Workman 1-11-1859 Hn
Boldin, Eliza A. to Robert Cole 11-5-1846 Hn
Boldin, Elmyra to Jacob Bushart 10-27-1846 Hn
Bolding, Nancy J. to John C. Barber 3-13-1852 (3-17-1852) Sh
Bolding, Venie to J. W. Fitzgerald 1-1-1879 Hy
Bolen, Frances to Humphrey Redick 12-27-1864 (12-29-1864) Dy
Bolen, Mandy to John Smith 1-28-1866 G
Boles, Adeline to James Roberts 7-19-1863 We
Boles, Elizabeth A. to James K. Rooks 12-31-1868 G
Boles, Elvira T. to Jackson J. Polk 2-21-1835 (2-24-1835) Hr
Boles, Joannah to Albert T. McMullins 6-6-1859 (6-9-1859) Ma
Boles, Josephine to J. B. Neal 2-25-1871 (2-26-1871) Cr
Boles, Mary to Samuel Powers 11-26-1825 Sh
Boley, Ann E. to Thomas M. Means 10-4?-1853 (no return) F
Bolin, A. L. to Ambros House 2-9-1858 G
Bolin, Jane to William F. Harris 6-1-1849 Sh
Bolin, Mary A. to Needham H. Cook 12-4-1855 (12-9-1855) G
Bolin, Mary J. to J. D. Nearn? 6-5-1869 (6-9-1869) Dy
Bolin, Rebecca f. to Henry McCall 12-29-1845 (12-30-1845) Ma
Bolin, Susan to Robert Caldwell 10-8-1856 G
Boling, C. D. to P. E. Smith 4-27-1853 (no return) F
Boling, N. E. to J. D. Prescott 10-23-1882 L
Boling, Tericey Elender to John Hoskins 12-25-1849 Sh
Bolling, Elisabeth A. to William N. Morgan 10-24-1848 (11-1-1848) F
Bolling, Elizabeth to Jacob M. Haden (Haiden) 9-2-1846 Sh
Bolling, M. E. to J. L. Baldridge 1-29-1866 Hy
Bolling, Patience to Henry Jackson 3-17-1866 (3-21-1866) F B

Bolling, Patsy to William Cornelius 1-21-1834 Hr
Bolls, Martha to Anthony Wilson 12-24-1868 Hy
Bolt, Mary E. to Saml. F. Force 7-15-1879 (no return) L
Bolt, Mary to James Borum 12-17-1838 Sh
Bolt, Susan to Cicero Rhodes 11-25-1850 (11-28-1850) Hr
Bolten, Lucinda to S. J. Goldsby 10-1-1860 Sh
Bolton, Cairy Ann to Wm. J. Black 1-14-1847 Sh
Bolton, Cindirilla to Moses Bolton 3-16-1861 Sh
Bolton, F. L. to Moses Bolton 6-28-1860 Sh
Bolton, Lucasia to Anthony T. Bledsoe 10-6-1841 Sh
Bolton, Lucretia to Bertrande E. Elliott 5-26-1838 Sh
Bolton, Mandy to William Cox 11-9-1875 (no return) Hy
Bolton, Mary A. to John C. Bolton 8-31-1857 (9-25-1857) Sh
Bolton, Mary L. to P. G. Truce 11-1-1859 Sh
Bolton, Mary T. to A. T. Bledsoe 8-23-1849 Sh
Bolton, Sallie to J. A. Swinney 6-14-1871 (6-15-1871) Cr
Bolton, Sarah E. to S. C. Maddox 11-1-1859 Sh
Bolton, Sarah S. to James J. Sigler 6-22-1842 Sh
Bolton, Winnie to Claiborn Clements 10-4-1870 (10-8-1870) T
Boman, Martha to Benjamin J. Shirley 11-29-1855 Ma
Boman?, Ann to John Walters 5-8-1842 Hn
Bomar, Dialtha Emeline to Lorenzo D. Williams 6-5-1857 (6-7-1857) Ma
Bomar, Elizabeth to John A. French 8-6-1848 Hn
Bomar, Ferriby to James Mitchell 10-8-1865 Hn
Bomar, Harriett to Lewis Clark 1-22-1873 (1-23-1873) Cr B
Bomar, Love Ann to Hugh F. Nelson 1-12-1860 Hn
Bomar, M. B. to N. B. Porter 1-25-1866 Hn
Bomar, Martha Ann to W. B. McCullough 7-26-1865 (no return) Hn
Bomar, Prudence to M. B. Morris 1-11-1848 (no return) Hn
Bomar, Rebecca to David T. Bomar 5-13-1843 Hn
Bomar, Salina to Alexander McCullough 11-24-1859 Hn
Bomar, Sarah A. to Archibald W. Carter 7-26-1860 Hn
Bomar, Sarah E. to Calvin Bomar 10-17-1853 Cr
Bomer, E. R. to C. L. Kelly 4-11-1856 Hn
Bomer, M. P. to Jeptha Cole 3-19-1851 (no return) Hn
Bomer, Mary E. to Thos. J. Stafford 2-24-1840 (2-27-1840) F
Bond, Alice to Charles E. Evans 1-17-1878 L
Bond, Amanda to James M. Arun 12-29-1848 Hn
Bond, Ana H. to James R. Newbern 7-23-1878 (no return) Hy
Bond, Ana to Rufus Blakely 8-29-1873 Hy
Bond, Ann to Louis Vaughan 10-31-1879 (11-11-1879) L B
Bond, Anna to Thomas Brown 9-7-1877 (no return) Hy
Bond, Any to A. I. Clay 12-30-1876 Hy
Bond, Arrena to Oliver Lightfoot 12-24-1885 L
Bond, Bettie to H. H. Witherspoon 10-24-1871 (10-25-1871) Ma
Bond, Biddy (Mrs.) to William P. Ripley 11-28-1860 Ma
Bond, Brittannia to Jas. Freenson 6-1-1868 Hy
Bond, Caroline to George Turner 7-31-1879 (8-8-1879) L
Bond, Caroline to James Dolen 9-16-1852 (9-30-1852) Sh
Bond, Catharine (Mrs.) to J. W. Gillespie 10-8-1858 (10-12-1858) Sh
Bond, Catharine Whittier to Bartholomew Dunn 5-27-1834 (5-29-1834) Hr
Bond, Catharine to Irvin R. Sherrod 1-7-1862 Hy
Bond, Celia to F. M. Cogswell 9-26-1854 (9-27-1854) Sh
Bond, Celia to Frank Johnson 1-21-1877 Hy
Bond, Celia to Henry Green 2-11-1866 (no return) Hy
Bond, Chany to Alex Haley 4-11-1878 Hy
Bond, Charity to John Hastin 3-3-1841 (no return) Hn
Bond, Cinda to William Oldham 2-22-1877 Hy
Bond, Clara to Anderson Malone 8-5-1873 Hy
Bond, D. K. to James Gamble 3-3-1844 Hn
Bond, Dealy to Wm. Transon 1-11-1878 Hy
Bond, Dianah to John Mills 8-21-1832 (8-24-1832) Hr
Bond, Drusilla A. to M. C. Hooks 11-22-1858 (11-25-1858) Sh
Bond, E. R. to J. J. Hawkins 8-2-1864 (no return) Hy
Bond, Eliza A. to Jenkins Newsom 4-17-1850 Ma
Bond, Eliza to Phil Critendon 6-2-1878 Hy
Bond, Elizabeth to Enos Holland 11-13-1853 Hn
Bond, Elizabeth to Farrington B. Snipes 5-3-1854 Ma
Bond, Elizabeth to John C. Stewart 12-13-1847 Sh
Bond, Elizabeth to Thos. R. Atkinson 1-4-1849 Sh
Bond, Ella to Shedric Cotter 12-31-1878 Hy
Bond, Emaly to Sam Lea 1-4-1869 Hy
Bond, Emma to Tom King 12-28-1878 Hy
Bond, Etta to John Thomas 2-3-1885 L
Bond, Fannie to Alfred Cain 5-8-1873 (no return) Hy
Bond, Fannie to Brown Wiley 12-11-1873 Hy
Bond, Fanny to Wm. Farington 8-17-1867 (no return) Hy
Bond, Ferribee(Fenibee) G. to John A. Ross 11-3-1851 (11-13-1851) Sh
Bond, Florence to Soloman Sherrod 12-25-1866 T
Bond, George Ann to Neal Reed 6-12-1874 (no return) Hy
Bond, Georgia E. to John W. Bell 7-29-1871 (no return) Hy
Bond, H. O. to W. W. Simmons 3-16-1860 Sh
Bond, Hannah O. to Whitmell T. Bond 5-3-1852 (5-4-1852) Ma
Bond, Harriet to Henry Watford 1-9-1872 Hy
Bond, Harriet to Gabriel Davis 12-10-1871 Hy
Bond, Harriett W. to John A. Mickleberry 7-8-1824 Sh
Bond, Harriett to Jo L. Boyd 9-15-1880 (9-18-1880) L B

Bond, Jane M. to Henry Forgey 10-8-1852 Sh
Bond, Joanna to John Bowles 3-5-1866 (no return) Hn
Bond, Josey to John Cooper 12-23-1870 Hy
Bond, Julia to Clay Currie 5-5-1877 Hy
Bond, Julian to James McGill 9-27-1853 Be
Bond, Kate P. to Charles W. Jacobs 1-1-1878 Hy
Bond, Laura to John Owen 10-10-1872 (no return) Hy
Bond, Liza to Kennie Jones 11-7-1869 Hy
Bond, Lizzie to George Williams 3-16-1872 Hy
Bond, Lottle to Charley Williams 11-21-1878 Hy
Bond, Louisa J. to J. N. Jones 11-25-1852 Sh
Bond, Louisa to John Doggett 1-3-1876 (no return) Hy
Bond, Lucinda to Wily Greaves 4-1-1877 Hy
Bond, Lucy to Bob Smith 11-21-1871 Hy
Bond, Malissa to Robert Patten 12-14-1874 Hy
Bond, Margaret W. to Daniel Bond 1-9-1874 Hy
Bond, Margaret to Thomas C. Wilson 10-2-1827 Hr
Bond, Mariah P. to George W. Nelson 10-24-1866 Be
Bond, Marin D. to Alex Cotter 2-20-1872 (no return) Hy
Bond, Marina to John Bate 9-13-1872 (no return) Hy
Bond, Martha D. to Henry G. Trobaugh 8-21-1854 Sh
Bond, Martha M. to M. K. Herring 3-23-1848 Sh
Bond, Mary F. to R. F. Butts 12-3-1868 L
Bond, Mary L. to A. Beaty 5-5-1856 (5-13-1856) Sh
Bond, Mary P. to John M. Hunt 10-11-1866 G
Bond, Mary to Andy Claiborne 12-10-1870 Hy
Bond, Mary to Peter Anthony 1-20-1877 Hy
Bond, Mary to William Hargrove 3-14-1868 T
Bond, Mattie to J. A. Crews 8-8-1866 Hy
Bond, Milly to James Ingram 1-5-1876 (no return) Hy
Bond, Minnie to F. P. Bond 8-2-1877 Hy
Bond, Minnie to Nelson Henley 11-20-1871 (no return) Hy
Bond, Mollie to Stephen Harvey 10-19-1871 Hy
Bond, Nancy H. to John S. Cowan 1-9-1861 Hn
Bond, Nancy to Abram Hoy 9-16-1867 Be
Bond, Nancy to Tom Farrington 7-29-1872 (no return) Hy
Bond, Nanny W. to Wm. E. Tate 10-23-1861 Hy
Bond, Narciss to Henry Folts 4?-18-1868 (no return) L B
Bond, Narcissa H. to T. C. (Dr.) Edwards 3-2-1876 (no return) Hy
Bond, Nellie to John A. Davis 3-8-1871 Hy
Bond, Neppie R. to C. W. Harbert 12-5-1859 (no return) Hy
Bond, Paralle to Gilbert Bond 1-14-1876 (no return) Hy
Bond, Parthenia to Robt. Hess 11-14-1872 Hy
Bond, Patsy to Peter Starks 12-18-1877 Hy
Bond, Penny to Bob Rayner 3-24-1866 (no return) Hy
Bond, Phillis to John Neal 1-20-1872 Hy
Bond, Rachal to Amus Bond 3-30-1872 Hy
Bond, Rosa to Henry Newbern 4-5-1871 Hy
Bond, Rose to Jack Tyus 2-1-1872 Hy
Bond, Ruth to Michael T. Byrne 9-7-1847 Hn
Bond, S. C.(H.?) to A. Witherington 6-23-1870 G
Bond, S. M. to C. P. Winkley 2-15-1854 (2-16-1854) Sh
Bond, Sallie to J. I. Howell 11-26-1872 T
Bond, Sallie to John Henry Jones 9-14-1869 (no return) Hy
Bond, Sarah Ann to James Lashby 10-16-1849 Sh
Bond, Sarah Ann to Samuel H. Ross 4-14-1839 Sh
Bond, Sarah J. to Chas. J. Calloway 12-13-1869 (12-14-1869) Ma
Bond, Sarah L. to J. B. Waters 7-21-1853 Be
Bond, Sarah to Isaac H. Conagan 12-28-1870 (no return) Hy
Bond, Sarah to James Bailey 11-17-1877 Hy
Bond, Sarah to Wm. Pender 9-16-1869 (no return) Hy
Bond, Tennessee to Eli Craig 3-10-1870 G B
Bond, Tenny to Robert Farrington 3-16-1872 Hy
Bond, Tiller to Mame Bradford 9-28-1868 (no return) Hy
Bond, Tillie to Moses Read 4-1-1884 L
Bond, Tracey to Moses Bradford 10-15-1874 Hy
Bond, Venis to Thomas Bond 12-20-1871 Hy
Bond, Winny to Alx. King 1-27-1868 (no return) Hy
Bond, Zilpha to Henry Dorch 12-20-1873 Hy
Bond, Zilpha to Matt Johnson 11-6-1875 (no return) Hy
Bond?, Elizabeth to Wm. T. Sanders 12-30-1855 Cr
Bonds, A. B. to J. G. Lovelace 1-24-1871 (1-25-1871) Dy
Bonds, Anna to Geo. Wyatt 2-28-1877 (no return) Dy
Bonds, Elizabeth to Geo. W. Young 12-28-1859 Hr
Bonds, Frances K. to Loami Harris 11-13-1854 (11-14-1854) Hr
Bonds, Harriet to Joseph May 1-2-1854 Cr
Bonds, M. E. to W. M. Flowers 9-29-1867 G
Bonds, M. M. to W. F. Dawson 10-10-1865 G
Bonds, Mahaly to John P. House 10-20-1874 Be
Bonds, Martha Jane to T. B. Tucker 8-13-1854 Hn
Bonds, Melviny to Frank Newman 8-26-18__ (probably 1870) G B
Bonds, Mozella to William B. Greenlaw 3-14-1832 Sh
Bonds, Tempe to Joseph Hooper 12-10-1873 (12-16-1873) T
Bondurance, Susan to Walter D. Bell 9-27-1858 (9-28-1858) Sh
Bondurant, Adalaida to A. C. Brasfield 3-18-1857 We
Bondurant, Eliza W. to Robert J. Winston 11-19-1850 We
Bondurant, H. G. C. to William Greer 12-30-1845 Hn
Bondurant, Jacksey M. to John K. Jones 10-3-1843 We
Bondurant, Martha E. to John A. Gardner 11-6-1850 We
Bondurant, Mary to B. F. Murrell 6-?-1842 (no return) F
Bondurant, Sarah E. to W. C. Tines 12-28-1858 We
Bondurant, Susan J. to Wm. J. Cook 10-24-1844 (no return) We
Bone, Amanda to Henry Hellums 3-22-1873 (3-29-1873) Dy
Bone, Esther to Lewis Parks 7-20-1867 G B
Bone, Harriet B. to J. B. Park 11-22-1846 Sh
Bone, Mahala to Thomas Gay 6-25-1829 O
Bone, Margaret E. to Benjamin Holmes 11-4-1840 (11-5-1840) G
Bone, Martha to Benj. F. Bond 2-19-1861 Ma
Bone, Martha to Macca Write 7-23-1836 (7-24-1836) G
Bone, Mary to Hamilton Smith 8-21-1866 (8-23-1866) F
Bone, Rachael Ann to John Davis 8-30-1846 O
Bone, Sarah J. to Cato Clark 1-5-1870 G B
Bone, Siloa to Ed Williams 6-9-1870 (6-25-1870) F B
Bone, Susan M. to James Sampson 8-27-1840 O
Bone, Susan to Anderson Smalley 5-30-1871 (5-31-1871) Dy
Bonear, Caroline to Benis (Berni?) J. Baptiste 3-13-1852 Sh
Boner, Julia S. (Mrs.) to William A. Anthony 3-1-1858 (3-8-1858) Ma
Boner, Julia to John Dalin 5-17-1867 T
Boner, Margarett to Sam Lea 12-27-1875 (no return) Hy
Boney, Elizabeth C. to Malcom H. Greenwood 6-29-1838 (7-1-1838) Hr
Boney, Martha to Wm. Alford 1-16-1851 L
Bonigle?, Mary Ellin to Thomas P. Bowden 12-26-1866 (12-27-1866) T
Bonner, Caroline to Peter Filaboe 2-17-1851 Sh
Bonner, Eliza to William Brack 8-5-1885 (8-7-1885) L
Bonner, Elizabeth A. to W. B. Battle 12-8-1846 F
Bonner, M. F. to T. J. Marshall 9-24-1874 Hy
Bonner, Margaret Jane to Chas. Christopher Moffett 10-27-1855 (10-30-1855) T
Bonner, Sarah A. to J.R. Burdine 1-6-1855 (no return) Hn
Bonner, Sarah Drue to Jas. Thompson 12-22-1851 Sh
Bonner, Susan E. to Felix R. Hardgrave 2-28-1852 (3-2-1852) Ma
Boo, Callie to J. M. Williamson 10-21-1879 (10-23-1879) Dy
Boo, Emiline to Andrew Williams 3-1-1858 Hr
Bookart, Margarett to David Glen 9-4-1834 Hr
Booker (Barker), Mary F. to Lewis Scott 3-2-1847 Sh
Booker, Caledonia to Sam Scott 2-20-1870 G B
Booker, Cornelia R. to Joseph R. Mosly 5-26-1847 Sh
Booker, Frances to Richard Baskerville 12-22-1870 (12-28-1870) F B
Booker, Indianna P. to Thomas W. Markham 5-28-1846 T
Booker, M. M. to J. Lewis Janell 2-1-1858 G
Booker, Mariah to Hesekiah Smoot 6-13-1869 G B
Booker, Mary to Amos H. Lucey 8-10-1865 Hn
Booker, Mary to B. C. Brown 11-21-1855 Sh
Booker, Puss to Monroe Jones 10-30-1870 G
Booker, Rachel to Wm. Bernard 12-24-1867 T
Booker, Virginia A. to Dewitt C. Mosby 11-19-1841 (11-20-1841) F
Bookers(Brookran), Mary to Henry Womack 9-22-1835 Hr
Bookout, Mary J. to Hugh Agnugh 1-26-1859 We
Books, Eliza to J. F. Bailey 12-17-1868 G
Bools, Lucety to Allen Carr 1-4-1859 (1-5-1859) Ma
Boon, Ann E. to Lunsford M. R. Wallis 3-17-1846 G
Boon, Ann E. to Remon Mayo 1-10-1839 Ma
Boon, Ann to James Graves 9-21-1857 (9-22-1857) Ma
Boon, Colista E. to Samuel D. Alexander 1-27-1859 G
Boon, Cyntha I. to Richard S. Vaden 12-16-1845 G
Boon, Eady Mozelle to Ezekiel T. McCoy 10-22-1845 (10-23-1845) Ma
Boon, Elizabeth to Abraham Kirksey 6-28-1832 G
Boon, Elizabeth to Merlin Perry 9-12-1843 (9-21-1843) Ma
Boon, Elizabeth to Swain D. Phillips 11-4-1846 Cr
Boon, France R. (Mrs.) to James M. Sharp 10-27-1868 Ma
Boon, Laura A. to George W. Cocke 1-15-1856 Ma
Boon, Lecia A. to J. .W. Hollis 11-1862 O
Boon, M. A. to F. M. Price 1-17-1870 (1-19-1870) Dy
Boon, M. J. to Milton L. Deberry 1-25-1867 (1-31-1867) Ma
Boon, Malissa G. to David T. Smith 10-1-1844 (10-3-1844) F
Boon, Margaret A. M. to W. J. Hail 1-12-1870 (no return) Hy
Boon, Margaret J. to N. S.(L.?) Burrow 8-28-1866 G
Boon, Marina to John Thomas 12-20-1828 (12-23-1828) Ma
Boon, Martha A. L. to John T. Hale 9-1-1861 G
Boon, Martha to Buckner S. Sollis 11-21-1851 G
Boonear, Martha to Jeremiah McWhorter 10-1-1835 G
Boon, Mary to James M. Brown 5-3-1854 (5-4-1856) Ma
Boon, Mary to James H. Aubrey 8-23-1845 (8-25-1845) Ma
Boon, Mary to William B. Sorrels 5-14-1846 Sh
Boon, N. T. to A. P. Davidson 11-6-1862 G
Boon, Nancy to Sandford Bramblett 10-17-1843 (10-18-1843) O
Boon, Nancy to T. C. Beard 6-7-1852 (no return) F
Boon, Polly to Nicholas Newton 1-4-1845 O
Boon, S. E. to W. M. Edmonston 3-31-1868 G
Boon, Sarah Ann to Isaac W. Whitley 5-3-1851 Be
Boon, Sarah Ann to Isaac W. Whitley 5-3-1851 Be CC
Boon?, M. to A. King 11-2-1870 G
Boon?, Margarette W. to And. F. David 5-20-1844 (5-22-1844) F
Boone, Bettie to J. F. Hailey 2-1-1870 G

Boone, Emma to S. S. Zaricor 2-23-1874 (2-24-1874) O
Boone, Fanny to W. V. Busby 12-13-1861 (12-15-1861) Sh
Boone, Jane to B. L. Sollis 12-14-1867 (12-15-1867) Dy
Boone, Juliam to William H. Parker 1-5-1840 (1-7-1840) Ma
Boone, Kate to Julius A. Pollock 9-20-1864 Sh
Boone, Louisa to J. B. Maxey 10-1-1859 (no return) Hy
Boone, Lucinda to Richard W. Stone 6-2-1832 (6-6-1832) O
Boone, Malinda Caledonia to David Jones 10-24-1857 (10-25-1857) O
Boone, Margaret J. to Enoch Bryan 7-29-1840 Ma
Boone, Nettie to S. M. Hobday 10-21-1873 Dy
Boone, R. A. to T. R. Inman 8-3-1865 O
Boone, S. I. to I. H. Hill 12-27-1865 O
Boone, Susan A. to David Whitton 2-19-1856 (2-21-1856) Sh
Boos, Martina to Frederick Hellenk 12-6-1856 Sh
Booth, Dalmedia to Jacob Jost 6-22-1871 Hy
Booth, Eliz. to Green B. Cooke 1-22-1857 G
Booth, Elizabeth F. to Jos. Quarmby 8-8-1860 Sh
Booth, Eudora M. to James T. Woods 7-19-1845 (7-29-1845) G
Booth, Eveline to John Gabley 4-17-1852 (no return) F
Booth, Josephine to J. H. Doyle 12-24-1883 (12-26-1883) L
Booth, M. A. to E. A. Watson 12-18-1873 Hy
Booth, Martha A. to Thomas P. Watkins 9-18-1838 F
Booth, Martha to Philip M. Alston 3-14-1844 Sh
Booth, Mary E. to M. M. White 11-10-1868 Hy
Booth, Matilda J. to Thomas Beard 7-14-1854 Cr
Booth, N. P. to J. E. Lott 11-10-1869 Hy
Booth, Paralee to Wm. R. Terril 3-14-1873 Hy
Booth, Sarah Clementine to William McFadden 10-29-1857 Hn
Booth, Sarah E. (Mrs.) to Lewis C. Bivins 12-15-1864 (12-16-1864) Sh
Booth, Sarah E. to J. W. Chipman 5-21-1864 O
Booth, Sarah to Benj. Tims 12-17-1871 (12-19-1871) T
Booth, Silvesta A. to Simon F. Morrow 1-18-1865 Hn
Booth, Victoria to Louis E. Cliffordth? 7-4-1872 Hy
Boothe, Adeline to William Marberry 8-24-1856 (no return) Hn
Boothe, Ann to A. Pinckney Starnes 3-23-1844 T
Boothe, Charlotta J. to N. R. Latum 10-2-1860 G
Boothe, Eliza J. to Benj. F. Hagar 1-15-1855 (no return) L
Boothe, Elizabeth to David Wilson 7-21-1851 (7-22-1851) T
Boothe, Elizabeth to N. M. Crenshaw 1-20-1849 (1-24-1849) Hr
Boothe, Emeline N. to Jesse Brake 10-21-1858 Hn
Boothe, Lucretia Ann to Elijah Gibson 9-11-1848 (9-14-1848) T
Boothe, Lucy to Henderson Cane 2-3-1843 (2-2?-1843) Hr
Boothe, Martha A. to Amos R. Bird 10-4-1854 Hn
Boothe, Martha to Benjamin Council 1-2-1845 Hn
Boothe, Mary M. to Joel R. Manasco 12-20-1859 (12-21-1859) T
Boothe, Medira to James T. Tims 12-13-1877 Hy
Boothe, Milly to John W. Carley 10-1-1840 (10-4-1840) Hr
Boothe, Nancy to William T. Jenkins 6-22-1838 Hn
Boothe, Rilla to David Sinclair 10-14-1869 G B
Boothe, Rowan to John High 8-4-1859 Hn
Boothe, Sarah E. to G. W. Chipman 5-21-1864 (5-24-1864) O
Boothe, Sarah S. to John N. Mayfield 1-1-1861 G
Boram, Joella to W. P. H. Butler 11-9-1870 L
Boran, Ellen to John King 7-19-1864 Sh
Borchedt, Anna C.(S?) to John B. Miller 12-31-1863 (1-2-1864) Sh
Borden, Julia to Charles White 7-2-1859 (5?-2-1859) Sh
Borden, Mary to Joseph Herron 3-21-1876 Dy
Borden?, Sarah to John Leet 12-14-1860 (12-16-1860) L
Bordley, Jane S. to Charles Potts 9-1-1840 (9-10-1840) F
Bordman, Eliza V. to Louallen Jones 12-20-1844 (12-22-1844) Hr
Boreing, Susana to John McIntosh 11-11-1826 G
Boren, Kisey E.? to John W. Martin 2-26-1867 L
Boren, Lidia Ann to Washington Blasingham 10-26-1842 Sh
Borman (Bauman?), Louisa A. to Orlin B. Lone (Love?) 1-7-1853 (1-8-1853) Sh
Boro, Benedetta to Jno. Canepa 6-1-1860 (6-3-1860) Sh
Boro, Teresa to V. Sbarbaro 1-9-1861 Sh
Borough, Rebecca to Michael Conway 2-12-1840 (2-18-1840) L
Borran, Nancy to Turner R. Gibbs 11-30-1839 (12-1-1839) G
Borran, Sarah A. to Thomas W. Smith 5-14-1842 (5-15-1842) G
Borren, Eliza to Joseph Massey 2-4-1830 Ma
Borrin, Parzada to John Flowers 5-24-1838 G
Borum, Cornelia F. to J. H. Nixon 1-2-1878 L
Borum, E. M. to W. C. Green 11-15-1884 (11-16-1884) L
Borum, Elizabeth to D. R. Dupree 5-3-1848 (no return) L
Borum, M. L. to J. H. Moore 11-1-1877 L
Borum, Martha T. to John G. Cole 12-15-1849 (12-19-1849) L
Borum, Martha to Robert C. West 10-18-1854 (10-19-1854) L
Borum, Mollie to Edmond Pullin 11-19-1872 T
Borum, N. E. to R. J. Gullett 8-10-1874 L
Borum, Nancy A. to Edward N. Cook 10-8-1849 (no return) L
Borum, Sallie E. to T. F. Rice 8-17-1869 (8-19-1869) L
Borum, Sarah E. to H. Houpt 2-14-1863 (2-15-1863) L
Borum?, K. G. to R. B. Gaines 12-25-1879 (12-26-1879) L
Boschamp, Elizabeth (Mrs.) to Weije F. Ottmans 8-3-1863 Sh
Bose, Elizabeth to James F. Hubbert 7-11-1843 O
Bosher, Nancy to Howell Harris 6-1-1853 Sh

Bosley, Martha E. to Bernard M. Patterson 10-25-1848 Sh
Bosley, Martha E. to Wm. S. Cockrill 7-31-1850 Sh
Bost, Nannie to Abraham Porter 10-21-1876 L B
Bostic, Claricy to William Wiley 2-3-1867 Hy
Bostic, Sallie to William Lea 1-22-1872 (1-23-1872) L
Bostick, A. to Joseph Iver 11-1-1842 Ma
Bostick, Anna to James Parr 10-13-1881 (10-16-1881) L B
Bostick, Lucy to A. Curran 1-20-1883 (1-24-1883) L
Bostick, Margaret C. to W. B. Williams 7-28-1856 Ma
Bostick, Margaret C. to Wilson E. Stewart 10-17-1859 Ma
Bostick, Mariah to James Egleston 12-13-1876 (12-14-1876) L
Bostick, Martha L. to James M. Wester 11-18-1858 We
Bostick, Mary A. to John J. Matthews 9-2-1847 Ma
Bostick, Millie to Charlie H. Davis 9-15-1884 L
Bostick, Sarah to William M. McLeod 6-7-1841 (7-29-1841) Hr
Bostick, Winney C. to Willie Ozier 12-1-1843 F
Boston, C. to Bill Slaughter 12-28-1874 T
Boston, Margaret to Wm. Hicks 10-17-1857 Cr
Boston, Martha C. to Henry C. Wellons 4-12-1859 (4-14-1859) Hr
Boston, Mary A. to B. F. Bunch 3-8-1870 Cr
Boston, Sarah A. C. to M. L. Todd 3-26-1868 G
Bostrick, Sophronia to Bartlett F. Bird 12-18-1850 Ma
Bostwick, Nancy to Isaac R. Dishough 12-15-1841 (12-16-1841) Hr
Bosvell, Mary Francis to Hannibal Hays 7-4-1863 Sh
Boswell, Amanda to H. C. Whitfield 1-22-1862 T
Boswell, Anna to James Glosson 12-22-1869 (12-23-1869) Cr
Boswell, Callie B. to Charles W. Jordan 12-10-1866 (12-12-1866) F
Boswell, Caroline to Edward Elmore 1-31-1843 Be
Boswell, Cathrine to John Marchbanks 1-27-1859 Cr
Boswell, Charlotte F. to John W. McCrary 4-6-1851 Be
Boswell, Elizabeth A. to John A. Alexander 5-1-1865 F
Boswell, Elizabeth to Alan Coats 12-24-1843 (12-26-1843) T
Boswell, Elizabeth to Bluford L. Davis 2-16-1858 (2-17-1858) Sh
Boswell, Elizabeth to W. J. Pace 10-5-1857 (10-16-1857) T
Boswell, Elizabeth to William Rogers 3-24-1853 O
Boswell, Emily F. to Geo. W. Parratt 10-6-1848 (10-12-1848) F
Boswell, Frances Jane to Felty Coats 9-18-1845 F
Boswell, Gray to George Hughes 6-18-1867 (no return) F B
Boswell, Lizzie to Walter Mosely 1-11-1873 (no return) Hy
Boswell, Lucy J. to Edmund G. Underwood 1-17-1853 Ma
Boswell, Lucy to Hughlut Harris 2-16-1870 (2-22-1870) T
Boswell, Lucy to James Kelly 4-19-1849 Cr
Boswell, Lucy to James Roark 2-18-1828 Sh
Boswell, Margaret to J. W. N. Holland 11-7-1869 G
Boswell, Martha J. to Nathaniel Owen 10-4-1871 (10-5-1871) Cr
Boswell, Martha to Alfred Kelly 3-9-1847 (no return) F
Boswell, Martha to James C. Lashlee 7-6-1851 Be
Boswell, Mary A. to Wm. A. Park 10-10-1852 Cr
Boswell, Mary H. to James A. Shaw 4-28-1849 (4-29-1849) Ma
Boswell, Mary to Alphius King 12-10-1850 Cr
Boswell, Mary to M. A. Redmond 1-12-1848 F
Boswell, Nancy J. to C. K. Butler 9-13-1865 (9-15-1865) Cr
Boswell, Penina to J. A. Browning 9-20-1849 Be
Boswell, S. J. to R. B. Eubanks 3-10-1870 Cr
Boswell, S.(L.) C. to D. V. Avery 12-16-1866 G
Boswell, Salina to John Coates 4-21-1845 F
Boswell, Sallie Jane to L. C. Crenshaw 8-18-1866 (no return) F
Boswell, Sarah Ann to George Gattas 4-27-1843 Ma
Boswell, Sarah to Hiram Howard 9-28-1872 (9-29-1872) T
Boswell, T. to Wm. Milton 1-28-1858 Cr
Boswell, Virginia M. to P. A. Bonne 8-6-1857 T
Bott, Adaline to Charles Session 3-23-1867 (3-30-1867) F B
Bott, Annie to W. H. McCage 7-9-1863 Sh
Botto, Katy to John Rogers 4-30-1859 Sh
Botto, Margaret to Grismani Carlo 10-22-1863 Sh
Botto, Margaret to Joseph Botto 5-4-1860 (5-6-1860) Sh
Botto, Rosa to Thomas Reeves 4-30-1859 Sh
Bottoms, Elizabeth to D. M. Crockett 12-17-1856 (12-18-1856) G
Bottoms, Harrit S. to G. T. Boyett 1-13-1868 G
Bottoms, Nancy E. to B. H. Holland 11-5-1854 (11-6-1854) G
Botton (Bolton?), Josephine to Samuel Dickens 1-22-1856 (1-23-1856) Sh
Botton (Bolton?), Louisa to William Dickens 1-17-1859 Sh
Botton, Elizabeth to Wm. A. Webb 12-29-1868 (12-31-1868) Ma
Botts, Lucy? J. to John W. Finch 9-16-1849 F
Botts, Martha D. to Joshua Whitemore 9-2-1857 Sh
Boucher, Martha P. to John D. Kersey 9-15-1853 L
Boucher, Mary A. to N. D. Thomas 8-12-1848 Cr
Bouchier, Julia to Buford Terrill 2-15-1854 G
Boughcom(Bawcum), Martha to Albert Z. Cowell 9-20-1865 Be
Boulten, C. to R. J. Huckaby 3-12-1867 G
Boulten, Tennessee to Alvin J. Oliver 9-24-1868 G
Boulton, Ann to Edward F. Fletcher 7-14-1862 (7-16-1862) Sh B
Boulton, Louisa to Milton Estill 4-12-1833 Sh
Boulton, Mary to Alfred Ravenall 6-18-1862 (5?-19-1862) Sh
Boulton, Sanderilla to Isaac L. Bolton 12-9-1835 Sh
Boun, Pricilla to Burrell Patterson 7-9-1836 G
Bounds, Eliza to Thomas May 1-13-1870 (1-31-1870) F B

Brides

Bounds, Frances G. to Mothen? R. Price 12-17-1849 (no return) F
Bounds, L. A. to Franklin Hooper 2-8-1838 F
Bounds, Louisa to Allen Coulter 9-18-1854 (no return) F
Bounds, Martha Ann to John T. Thompson 8-10-1846 (8-13-1846) F
Bounds, Mary Ann to James S. Denniston 10-23-1844 F
Bounds, Mary E. to Chas. W. Rich 12-3-1844 (no return) F
Bounds, Sarah Ann to John W. Van Pelt 9-7-1840 (9-24-1840) F
Bounds, Stacy to William Grisham 10-31-1845 (no return) F
Bourman, Elenor E. to Willis J. Ingram 11-7-1844 (11-12-1844) G
Bourne, Caroline E. to S. D. Bond? 4-24-1854 (no return) F
Bourne, Mary to Albert Middlebrook 9-20-1875 (no return) Hy
Bowden, Adaline to James A. Coley 5-12-1850 Hn
Bowden, Adaline to William H. Conyers 2-3-1858 Hn
Bowden, Caroline B. to Robert L. Veasey 11-22-1843 Hn
Bowden, Catherine to James E. Carter 3-9-1842 Hn
Bowden, Clementine to J. W. Brown 5-4-1859 Hn
Bowden, D. F. to L. D. Poynter 12-8-1845 Hn
Bowden, Elizabeth E. to Daniel W. Janes 12-19-1844 Hn
Bowden, Elizabeth J. to Daniel Jones 4-10-1848 Hn
Bowden, Elizabeth to B. T. Milam 9-16-1848 Hn
Bowden, Elizabeth to Jonathan Duncan 1-3-1858 Hn
Bowden, Emaline to E. P. Bates 8-24-1849 Hn
Bowden, Helen to J. Y. Freeman 1-24-1866 Hn
Bowden, Julia F. to Wm. A. Butt 11-13-18__ Cr
Bowden, Juntia to Roy Sauls 1-23-1849 Cr
Bowden, Laura L. to Charles M. Ferrel 9-27-1864 (9-28-1864) Sh
Bowden, Louiza S. to J. Wade Barton 3-22-1864 Hn
Bowden, Luan F. to George Cox 10-21-1847 Hn
Bowden, M. A. to M. P. Chambers 11-26-1878 (11-27-1879) L
Bowden, Margaret A. to G. L. Roper 7-13-1848 Hn
Bowden, Marge A. to John Todd 11-16-1844 Hn
Bowden, Mary A. to W. A. Bostick 9-11-1866 Hn
Bowden, Mary C. to Gross Elbowe 9-13-1865 (9-17-1865) Cr
Bowden, Mary E. to James Adams 11-22-1866 (no return) Hn
Bowden, Mary to Samuel Harrell 7-21-1846 Sh
Bowden, Mildred C. to Robert P. Erwin 9-2-1867 (9-5-1867) T
Bowden, Nancy J. to William H. Byars 12-9-1855 (no return) Hn
Bowden, Nancy M. to John Linton 1-2-1855 Hn
Bowden, Nancy to John Fodge 11-18-1842 Hn
Bowden, R. T. to R. P. Erwin 6-8-1874 T
Bowden, Rachel to George Alexander 12-23-1865 (no return) Hn
Bowden, Rachel to George Alexander 12-30-1865 (no return) Hn
Bowden, Reamy to Samuel Linton 3-1-1848 Hn
Bowden, Sarah Ann to Brison Greer 11-8-1867 Hn
Bowden, Starry to Richard Burns 4-3-1880 (no return) L B
Bowden, Susan to Thomas J. Linton 2-20-1850 (no return) Hn
Bowden, Tilla to Jack Watson 2-28-1866 Hn
Bowden, V. C. to C. C. Speed 1-14-1867 O
Bowden, W. to A. E. Watson 3-21-1854 Cr
Bowder, Elizabeth to John G. Keathley 2-1-1851 G
Bowen (Brown), Jane to Andrew Rhoads 7-15-1838 Sh
Bowen, Amanda M. to W. P. Yearwood 4-31-1871 Hy
Bowen, Amanda to Mastion Morrow 12-29-1863 Mn
Bowen, Betsey F. to Reynold Reynolds 11-6-1828 Sh
Bowen, Helen E. to W. H. Taylor 9-17-1856 Sh
Bowen, Jane to Andrew Rhoads 7-13-1838 Sh
Bowen, Jennie to Wm. Clark 1-12-1870 (1-13-1870) Dy
Bowen, Josephine to J. M. Davis 1-1-1866 (1-4-1866) F
Bowen, Lizzie to Harry Buchanan 1-8-1872 (no return) Dy
Bowen, Lucy E. to R. W. Willard 10-17-1859 Sh
Bowen, M. A. to T. J. Rice 6-17-1876 (6-20-1876) Dy
Bowen, Martha Ellen to S. A. Yearwood 12-21-1869 Hy
Bowen, Mary B. to W. W. Harris 5-18-1870 Hy
Bowen, N. P. to T. J. Rice 4-6-1868 (4-9-1868) Dy
Bowen, Nannie to Jeremiah Dunnigan 12-22-1869 (no return) Dy
Bowen, Polley to Grengor McDaniel 1-13-1828 Sh
Bowen, R. J. to N. Echols 1-27-1877 (1-28-1877) Dy
Bowen, Rebecca A. to William King 12-17-1860 (12-18-1860) Dy
Bowen, Rebecca to Austin Hicks 12-31-1872 Dy
Bowen, S. A. to Silas L. Brooks 3-11-1869 (no return) Hy
Bowen, S. L. to J. H. Kerr 2-12-1861 (2-13-1861) Sh
Bowen, S. S. to J. Q. Craig 9-17-1859 Dy
Bowen, Tennessee to Frank Baines 4-15-1872 (4-17-1872) Dy
Bower(s), Catherina to Charles Mesmer 5-18-1863 Sh
Bower, Aulenor to E. C. Butler no date (with Jun 1864) G
Bower, Emma to Bruce Leath 1-8-1872 Hy
Bower, Mary A. to Wm. L. Porter 3-21-1861 Sh
Bowers, Ada to Hamilton Ware 4-14-1873 Hy
Bowers, Aggie J. to George W. Overall 9-24-1867 T
Bowers, Agnes A. to Zachariah Freeman 11-15-1853 G
Bowers, Ann C. to Rouland H. Galey 10-23-1845 We
Bowers, Beda A. to D. A. Freeman 11-8-1854 We
Bowers, C. P. to J. B. Chapman 11-10-1874 (11-11-1874) T
Bowers, Caroline to Leonard Brantlin Smith 10-2-1848 (10-4-1848) T
Bowers, Catharine R. to L. B. Smith 1-23-1861 (1-24-1861) T
Bowers, Catharine to P. M. Dinwiddie 10-11-1852 G
Bowers, Catherina to Charles Mesmer 5-28-1863 Sh

Bowers, Clarissa Eliza to Lemuel Rogers 9-28-1833 (10-3-1833) Hr
Bowers, D. Ellen to R. A. Dunkum 2-25-1854 (no return) F
Bowers, Drusey E. to James M. Brewer 10-24-1858 We
Bowers, E. W. G. to J. H. Johnston 10-14-1868 (10-25-1868) F
Bowers, Eliza Jane to Thomas Lowry Angus 3-22-1851 (3-25-1851) T
Bowers, Eliza to Fed Becton 1-1-1885 (no return) L
Bowers, Elizabeth N. to Benj. F. Tally 12-11-1845 G
Bowers, Elizabeth to M. D. Lain 11-29-1860 We
Bowers, Elizabeth to Robert C. West 4-29-1861 (5-2-1861) L
Bowers, Ellen V. to Albert L. Overall 4-27-1868 (4-28-1868) T
Bowers, Florrence to Robbin Bowers 1-5-1867 F B
Bowers, Frances to W. M. Towler?(Lowler?) 9-13-1850 (9-18-1850) Hr
Bowers, Henrietta T. to Jacob C. Manning 6-5-1848 Sh
Bowers, Julia R. to Roland R. Harris 10-18-1860 We
Bowers, Julia to Simon Feucht 4-18-1864 Sh
Bowers, Kate G. to Allen F. Morgan 6-10-1861 (6-12-1861) Sh
Bowers, Lou to Jacob Jeffries 2-23-1878 (2-24-1878) L
Bowers, Lucy to W. M. West 5-14-1872 L
Bowers, M. L. to G. D. French ?-6-1873 (9-7-1873) O
Bowers, Maria to Wash Wils? 9-12-1873 (9-15-1873) T
Bowers, Martha C. to W. B. Stafford 9-14-1847 (no return) F
Bowers, Mary A. W. to Wm. R. Ross 12-28-1843 We
Bowers, Mary A. to G. C. Miller 8-9-1860 O
Bowers, Mary A. to Greene B. May 1-31-1853 Cr
Bowers, Mary C. to Peterson P. Broom 11-5-1838 (11-17-1838) F
Bowers, Mary E. to G. M. D. Bowers 10-24-1868 (no return) L
Bowers, Mary to John C. Bates 8-25-1835 G
Bowers, Mary to John Smith 12-13-1877 Hy
Bowers, Mollie to Mack Hall 9-1-1877 Hy
Bowers, Olivia to Bernard Bowling 2-13-1861 (2-14-1861) Hr
Bowers, Panthia to John H. Talley 10-8-1845 We
Bowers, Parthina to Jacob Bradshaw 9-28-1867 (9-29-1867) T
Bowers, Rozanna to Jeff Northcross 11-7-1869 G B
Bowers, Ruth to Wilie J.? Riddle 7-29-1833 (8-8-1833) Hr
Bowers, S. A. to W. L. Rawls 12-19-1876 (2-21-1876) L
Bowers, Sallie to Dabna Spencer 11-9-1874 T
Bowers, Sarah Ann Rebecca to Algernon S. Bowers 9-22-1840 Hr
Bowers, Susan A. to W. A. Cox 2-22-1872 G
Bowes, Mary Jane (Mrs.) to Fondell Carpenter 5-28-1853 (no return) F
Bowie, M. C. to W. B. Arnold 8-23-1875 (8-24-1875) L
Bowland, Elizabeth J. to George W. Park 11-3-1860 (11-4-1860) Cr
Bowland, Susan to David Humphrey 8-24-1866 Cr
Bowlen, Mary to Alvadas Hill 8-13-1839 G
Bowles, A. H. to J. J. Bishop 5-18-1853 Cr
Bowles, Amy to William P. Mears 1-17-1848 (1-?-1848) T
Bowles, Angeline to James Laurie 1-20-1854 T
Bowles, Eliza Jane to Lemuel M. Campbell 12-1-1841 (12-2-1841) T
Bowles, Emma J. to James T. Cooney 1-7-1854 Hn
Bowles, Frances J. to Hyram W. Sullivan 8-2-1848 Hn
Bowles, Frances to Isaac Wilson 2-18-1846 (could be 1847) Sh
Bowles, Judy Ann to James A. Jackson 1-11-1841 Hn
Bowles, Lucinda to Jacob Shane 8-11-1825 Sh
Bowles, Margarette N. to D. H. Bottoms 3-28-1865 G
Bowles, Maria to Luck Bolton 7-15-1876 Hy
Bowles, Mary (Mrs.) to Russel Breeden 3-18-1852 Sh
Bowles, Mary E. to Eugene Latapie? 10-17-1853 Hn
Bowles, Mary to Charles Moor(e) 12-20-1827 Sh
Bowles, Sarah to James Davis 7-26-1858 (no return) Hn
Bowlin, Dorathy to John Murry 3-23-1846 Hr
Bowlin, Mary J. to G. W. L. Smithwick 12-16-1856 (no return) We
Bowling, Adelener H. to William D. Partlow 9-4-1831 (9-29-1831) Hr
Bowling, Ann to Charles Osborn 2-21-1870 (no return) Hy
Bowling, Betsy to Geo. Maline 1-20-1872 Hy
Bowling, Charlotte to Neal Penneuter 5-19-1870 Hy
Bowling, Emeline to Thomas J. McDurmit 1-17-1857 (1-18-1857) Ma
Bowling, Mandy to Wm. Readen 4-17-1869 (no return) Hy
Bowling, Martha to Wiley Morgan 9-16-1870 (9-21-1870) F B
Bowling, Mary Ann to Franklin W. Noble(s) 12-12-1853 O
Bowling, Nancy to Francis Edney 4-23-1835 G
Bowling, Sarah to Robert Gee 7-29-1835 Sh
Bowls, Catharine to John P. Morriss 11-29-1863 Be
Bowls, Hariot to Johnson Douglas 2-12-1874 Hy
Bowls, Mary Jane to Claiborne Gray 9-22-1866 (no return) F B
Bowls, Rissa to John Conly 1-12-1876 (no return) Hy
Bowls, Sarah A. to James A. Tucker 7-13-1855 We
Bowman, Abagal A. to George C. Ferris 10-24-1844 G
Bowman, Ann E. to M. A. Sanford 11-22-1865 Hn
Bowman, Ann to W. H. Powell 10-13-1863 Hn
Bowman, Cassandra to Zachariah Shaw 12-21-1840 (12-22-1840) G
Bowman, China to Henry Bowman 5-23-1866 (no return) Hy
Bowman, Cintha to Thomas A. Finch 5-24-1841 (no return) Hn
Bowman, Elizabeth to Jesse Ledbetter 5-27-1842 (6-2-1842) L
Bowman, Elizabeth to Lewis C. Pipkin 9-9-1828 Ma
Bowman, Hanah to Jackson Skeen 2-21-1872 Hn
Bowman, Lucy to Alex Bowman 5-23-1866 (no return) Hn
Bowman, Malinda to James Jose Osteen 3-5-1838 (3-8-1838) L
Bowman, Mariah S. to Roland Ledbetter 12-3-1839 L

Bowman, Martha to J. M. Steely 11-27-1867 Hn
Bowman, Mary (Mrs.) to Joshua M. Bowman 12-14-1867 (12-15-1867) Ma
Bowman, Mary E. to J. W. Dennis 3-22-1862 G
Bowman, Narcissa to Richard D. Harris 10-20-1846 G
Bowman, Rebecca M. to Joseph G. Mayfield 10-12-1850 (10-13-1850) G
Bowman, Sarah to W. P. Coleman 11-3-1870 G
Bowslon?, Lucy A. to Thomas H. Newson 12-1-1865 (12-4-1865) Cr
Box, Angelin to Wm. Gatland 8-21-1842 Cr
Box, Anna to Jackson McCowan 4-11-1835 (4-16-1835) Hr
Box, Becca A. to John J. Brewer 12-1-1857 Be
Box, Caroline to John Webb 12-4-1854 (12-6-1854) Hr
Box, Charlotte to Travis Paul 9-9-1834 (9-17-1834) Hr
Box, E. Jane to William C. Thomason 2-12-1862 Be
Box, Elizabeth A. to Hiram C. Key 10-4-1841 (10-7-1841) O
Box, Isabela to J. H. Swindle 4-23-1863 Be
Box, Jane to John Martin 1-15-1823 Sh
Box, Keziah to Simeon Bright 4-24-1828 (4-29-1828) Hr
Box, LuAnn to S. M. Shepperson 12-19-1881 (12-21-1881) L
Box, Malinda to Benjamin Roney 5-24-1845 (6-1-1845) O
Box, Maranda to Enoch Henslee 1-6-1859 (5-29-1859) Hr
Box, Mary Ann M. to John H. Christopher 1-9-1866 Be
Box, Mary Ann to James L. Stephens(on) 8-17-1853 (8-18-1853) O
Box, Mary Jane to John C. Fare 12-6-1864 (12-25-1864) O
Box, Nancy T. to Thos. H. Allison 5-6-1864 (5-8-1864) O
Box, Nancy to James W. Williams 12-22-1857 O
Box, Nancy to W. P. Holland 8-29-1864 Be
Box, Narcissa to James S. Barnett 10-22-1855 (10-24-1855) Hr
Box, Parilee to Lewis Jackson Bullington 7-4-1850 (7-11-1850) Hr
Box, Polly to Saunders Kennedy 4-14-1827 (4-19-1827) Hr
Box, Priscilla to Stephen Gatlin 10-14-1867 (10-15-1867) Cr
Box, Racheal to John Bell 5-17-1832 (5-24?-1832) Hr
Box, Ruth to Moses Harper 2-14-1843 (2-15-1843) Hr
Box, Sarah to John Newton 9-9-1839 (9-12-1839) O
Box, Sarah to Thomas Gore 1-8-1840 (1-9-1840) Hr
Box, Seeny to James F. Hogan 1-8-1845 O
Box, Susan A. to James G. Treece 8-10-1858 (8-12-1858) Hr
Box, Susan to Anderson Cates 12-8-1850 (12-15-1850) O
Boyce, C. to H. H. Shannon 6-29-1863 Sh
Boyce, Harriet E. to Alexander K. Boyce 9-3-1848 Sh
Boyce, Harriett to June Green 11-9-1870 (11-11-1870) T
Boyce, Mary Jane to Saml. W. Lyon 3-24-1857 (3-25-1857) Sh
Boyce, Mary L. to Jas. L. Boyce 9-3-1848 Sh
Boyce, Rose to Joshua Wright 12-27-1867 (12-28-1867) T
Boyce, Texie C. to William C. Penn 10-21-1862 Ma
Boyd (Becton?), Mary L. W. (Mrs.) to George W. Hurley 11-2-1858 Ma
Boyd (Bond?), Mollie to George Washington Halliburton 1-11-1873 (1-13-1873) L B
Boyd, A. P. to W. P. Gardner 9-19-1858 Cr
Boyd, Adaline to Fletcher Whitehead 7-20-1867 (8-10-1867) F B
Boyd, Amanda to George Gorden 8-23-1872 (8-20?-1872) T
Boyd, Amelia A. to John L. Gaines 3-24-1874 L
Boyd, Becky to David Cotter 12-21-1878 Hy
Boyd, Belle H. to N. Wilson Baptist 1-11-1871 (1-18-1871) T
Boyd, Catherine to George Washington Barret 12-27-1870 (12-28-1871?) T
Boyd, Dianna to E. M. Rodgers 11-25-1841 Cr
Boyd, E. F. to S. L. Saunders 1-9-1871 (no return) Dy
Boyd, E. J. to W. W. Ballard 1-16-1845 Hn
Boyd, Easter to John Akin 11-2-1868 T
Boyd, Easter to John Akin 11-7-1868 T
Boyd, Eliza E. to Joseph H. Alexander 5-25-1843 L
Boyd, Eliza to Jack Word 3-27-1869 (no return) F B
Boyd, Eliza to Tom Bracken 5-19-1868 (5-22-1868) F B
Boyd, Elizabeth D. to William C. Saunders 3-18-1869 Cr
Boyd, Ellen J. to William L. Bullock 7-12-1863 Hn
Boyd, Elliott to Wiley E. Farrow 3-23-1843 Sh
Boyd, Etta to Anderson Wilkins 10-15-1868 Hy
Boyd, Fannie to Lewis Bond 12-3-1873 (12-5-1873) T
Boyd, H. H. (Mrs.) to Matthew Rhea, jr. 9-15-1859 F
Boyd, Hadnah? to Francis A. Wilson 1-29-1850 F
Boyd, Harriet E. to John H. White 6-17-1873 (6-18-1873) L
Boyd, Harriet to Alex Porter 1-4-1872 (1-15-1872) T
Boyd, Ider C. to Marion Jones 10-22-1854 Cr
Boyd, Irene to Howel L. Read 11-18-1873 Hy
Boyd, Jane H. to William Montgomery 3-12-1852 (3-16-1852) Ma
Boyd, Jane to James Wright 10-22-1862 O
Boyd, Jane to R. H. Trobough 12-14-1865 T
Boyd, Jane to Taylor Akins 12-22-1875 (no return) Hy
Boyd, Jennie to W. R. Halliburton 2-9-1874 (2-10-1874) L
Boyd, Lottie to Giles Matney 11-30-1871 Hy
Boyd, Lou to Ike Morrow 12-8-1868 (no return) F B
Boyd, Lou to Littleton H. Perkins 3-1-1871 F
Boyd, Lydia to Henry Stoup 11-16-1864 Sh
Boyd, Lydia to Ira W. Forbes 11-19-1864 Sh
Boyd, M. E. to Stephen G. Bradsher 12-7-1869 (12-16-1869) F
Boyd, Margaret to William K. Stapleton 4-15-1841 Ma
Boyd, Mariah I. to Martin Shaw 1-14-1839 (1-15-1839) Ma
Boyd, Mariah to Charley Jackson 3-16-1875 (3-17-1875) O
Boyd, Martha G. to Jesse Strange 10-11-1849 Sh
Boyd, Martha J. to John N. P. Spence 10-27-1846 (10-28-1846) L
Boyd, Martha Jane to Henry C. Cassels 1-7-1867 Ma
Boyd, Martha to Bloom. Newburn 12-19-1872 (no return) Hy
Boyd, Martha to John Duke 12-28-1870 T
Boyd, Mary A. K. to Daniel P. Boroum 2-19-1842 (2-22-1843?) L
Boyd, Mary E. to J. R. McGinnis 12-21-1862 (1-1-1863) F
Boyd, Mary E. to William F. Hughes 8-10-1844 Hr
Boyd, Mary F. to Abner Stacy 2-23-1854 L
Boyd, Mary J. to W. H. Gilbert 1-22-1876 L
Boyd, Mary R. to William A. Trobaugh 5-18-1849 Sh
Boyd, Melinda to Robert W. Galloway 3-24-1852 O
Boyd, Mildred L. to Sam? P. Rose 4-12-1871 T
Boyd, Minerva to Sandy Johnson 8-10-1866 Hy
Boyd, Mollie E. to B. D. Taliaferro 7-19-1861 Hy
Boyd, Nancy to Lot Harvey 3-23-1866 (4-1-1866) F B
Boyd, Nancy to Orrin Guthry 1-20-1827 (1-21-1827) Hr
Boyd, Nancy to Robert Currie 10-31-1877 (no return) Hy
Boyd, Polly to Joe Pete 12-30-1874 Hy
Boyd, Rebeca to J. W. Morris 6-15-1855 (no return) F
Boyd, Rebecca to Gamaliel Parker 1-28-1829 (1-29-1829) Hr
Boyd, Rebecca to L. D. Pierce 9-3-1850 Cr
Boyd, Rebecca to Richard Massey 2-13-1841 Ma
Boyd, Rose to Henry Harris 3-23-1867 (3-30-1867) F B
Boyd, Rosetta to Albert Lane 11-21-1872 T
Boyd, S. E. to H. R. Parnell 9-20-1858 Cr
Boyd, S. E. to M. R. Gilbert 5-5-1852 We
Boyd, Sallie E. to Wm. H. Strange 10-10-1866 (10-11-1866) T
Boyd, Sallie to Saml. Sharp 5-11-1872 (5-12-1872) T
Boyd, Sallie to Wyatt Bailey 1-11-1871 F
Boyd, Sarah C. to Philip T. Butler 3-2-1864 (no return) Cr
Boyd, Sarah Jane to W. J. Denis 1-1-1864 Mn
Boyd, Sarah M. to Jacob T. Norton 3-16-1847 Cr
Boyd, Sarah to Benjamin Pope 6-15-1867 (6-23-1867) L B
Boyd, Sarah to George W. Cabe 11-22-1841 Hn
Boyd, Sarah to James Bobbitt 5-31-1856 Cr
Boyd, Susan H. to Albert W. Posey 12-21-1843 L
Boyd, Susan to John Huckabee 3-3-1834 (3-6-1834) G
Boyd, Susan to Mack Bowers 3-27-1869 (3-28-1869) F B
Boyd, Susan to Peter Mitchell 1-8-1869 (1-9-1869) F B
Boyd, Susan to William Gray 10-6-1860 (10-7-1860) Ma
Boyd, Susana to Nelson Nance 8-5-1868 (8-6-1868) F B
Boyd, Tabitha to Henry Baker 10-13-1866 T
Boyd, Tenness to Austin Branoch 11-23-1871 (11-25-1871) Cr B
Boyd, Tennessee to J. G. Raines 11-23-1868 G
Boyd, Victoria to Henry Mathews 3-3-1877 (no return) Hy
Boyd, Zuby to William Sexton 7-17-1843 (7-18-1843) G
Boyde, Mary to James G. Harris 12-26-1830 Ma
Boydston, Cintha to Williamson N. Burt 7-19-1838 Hr
Boydston, Elizabeth D. to John Monrow 4-1-1861 (4-3-1861) L
Boydston, M. C. to J. W. Moore 11-12-1884 L
Boydston, Mattie P. to J. I. Moore 2-16-1881 (no return) L
Boydston, Nellie to N. M. Stacey 9-27-1883 L
Boydston, Sally to Jacob L. Edwards 2-7-1824 (2-8-1824) Hr
Boydston, Sarah Jane to Samuel Leird 2-29-1860 L
Boydston, Tabitha A. to G. B. Jennings 8-?-1862 L
Boydston, Talitha A. to Green B. Jennings 8-5-1862 (no return) L
Boyed, Lucinda to William Wright 4-30-1850 (5-1-1850) F
Boyet, Catharine M. to A. G. Tilghman 11-24-1855 (no return) F
Boyett, Alabama to R. D. Ward 1-3-1865 O
Boyett, Easter R. to Jesse Wyatt 2-12-1849 (2-13-1849) O
Boyett, Elizabeth to J. H. McKnight 3-19-1863 O
Boyett, Esther R. to Jessie Wyatt 2-12-1849 O
Boyett, Lucenda to Calvin Flowers 3-11-1851 (3-14-1851) G
Boyett, M. A. to A. S. Clark 1-30-1861 (1-31-1861) O
Boyett, Mahulda J. to J. K. Bottoms 1-13-1868 G
Boyett, Mahulda to C. H. Watts 1-23-1866 O
Boyett, Martha to James Dowell 12-15-1851 (12-18-1851) G
Boyett, Mary A. F. to Abner N. Read 8-26-1848 O
Boyett, N. L. to R. N. Jetton 10-13-1873 (10-16-1873) O
Boyett, Poilee to John O. Clayton 4-2-1866 (4-14-1866) O
Boyett, S. M. to N. Holloman 3-17-1851 O
Boyett, Selia to George Smith 12-11-1839 (12-12-1839) O
Boyett, Susan to Andrew Massey 12-3-1844 (12-4-1844) Ma
Boyett, Wincey (Nancy) Ann to William L. Cochran 1-28-1854 (1-29-1854) O
Boykin, C. A. to Edmond Burnett 7-20-1866 (8-11-1866) F B
Boykin, Martha S. to C. C. Hutchings 8-30-1856 Ma
Boykin, Mary Ann Eliza to Robert N. McLemore 9-1-1855 (9-5-1855) Ma
Boykin, Mary E. to Samuel M. Kirk 9-5-1843 Ma
Boylan, Missouri to Ben Burt 8-31-1867 (no return) F B
Boylan, Priscilla P. (Mrs.) to Wm. F. Brown 3-14-1839 F
Boyle, Arabella to Joe Sewell 2-7-1868 (2-8-1868) F B
Boyle, Clarentine M. to Elias Alexander 2-9-1847 (2-11-1847) Hr
Boyle, Hennorah to J. W. Owen 2-3-1848 Hr
Boyles, Judah Ann to Marcus L. Marshall 9-15-1845 Sh
Boyles, Nancy to James M. Walker 12-9-1835 G
Boyls, Nancy to James V. Walker 12-9-1833 (12-12-1833) G

Boyne, Nancy Y. to J. B. Campbell 1-25-1866 G
Boyssian, Henrietta to Isham Fields 11-28-1843 (11-29-1843) F
Boyt, Charity to James Shaw 7-26-1831 (7-28-1831) Ma
Boyt, Exaline to Reuben Tyson 7-30-1831 (8-4-1831) G
Boyt, Martha to Urius Reeves 4-11-1833 (4-13-1833) O
Boyt, Nancy C. to Ashley Roades 5-30-1846 (5-31-1846) Hr
Boyt, Nancy to William Nedry 8-23-1836 (8-25-1836) G
Boyt, Rebecca J. to Hezekiah J. Davis 7-16-1842 (7-20-1842) G
Boyt, Sarah to James F. Crittenden 9-22-1860 (no return) We
Boyt, Zilpha to Jesse Cox 7-14-1832 (7-?-1832) Hr
Boyte, Abbe to Cullen Dunn 3-8-1833 G
Boyte, Ailsy E. to John Kennedy 8-21-1839 (8-29-1839) Hr
Boyte, Alsy to James B. Brint 9-13-1828 Hr
Boyte, Ann to Morris Raiford 12-12-1837 (1-4-1838) Hr
Boyte, Barbay to William Pate 10-8-1834 Hr
Boyte, Elizabeth to Elliot Stevens 2-13-1832 Hr
Boyte, Mary H. to William H. Ammons 1-6-1844 (1-11-1844) Hr
Boytt, Clorence to William Crockett 3-18-1830 (3-25-1830) G
Boytt, Martha to John P. Tucker 7-19-1842 (7-20-1842) G
Brabst, Maria W. to Haman G. Barner (Barnes) 1-25-1849 Sh
Brace, Louiza to Jno. W. Tripp 5-4-1868 (5-10-1868) F B
Brach, Susan H. to Wm. E. Waddle 2-4-1868 (2-5-1868) Cr
Bracken, Amanda J. to Richard Thomason 10-20-1859 (no return) Cr
Bracken, Bettie to James Chaffin 2-13-1869 (2-16-1869) F B
Bracken, Ella to D. A. Brigham 5-1-1878 Dy
Bracken, Rebecca to James Rhea 3-30-1867 (no return) F B
Brackett, N. E. to J. Stout 1-3-1859 (1-5-1859) Sh
Brackin, Ann to Patrick Lurgan 9-6-1861 (9-7-1861) Sh
Brackin, Julia A. to A. M. Stevens 12-19-1865 (12-21-1865) Dy
Brackin, Lucinda to S. A. Forsyth 12-28-1872 (1-7-1873) Dy
Brackins, A. to S. Pinkston 7-28-1841 Cr
Brackins, Adaline to Lewis Norwood 3-11-1845 Cr
Brackins, Amanda J. to James Allen 8-8-1861 Be
Brackins, Martha to Jacob Cooper 8-26-1866 Be
Brackins, Mary E. to H. C. Trout 4-22-1865 Be
Brackins, R. to Robert Arnold 2-10-1844 Cr
Bradberry, Almira to Stephen J. Roach 2-4-1830 (3-11-1830) G
Bradberry, Ann to Gideon Tucker 6-11-1834 G
Bradberry, Delia to Robert Clark 10-8-1870 Ma
Bradberry, Elizabeth J. to Washington B. Hargus 5-16-1844 (5-17-1844) F
Bradberry, Elizabeth R. to Joseph L. Medling 5-11-1838 (5-17-1838) Ma
Bradberry, Margaret to William M. Richards 1-14-1861 (no return) We
Bradberry, Mary A. to Andrew C. Stewart 2-16-1846 Ma
Bradberry, Piercy to William B. Moore 1-5-1828 (3-3-1828) G
Bradberry, Polly T. to Benjamin Roach 9-11-1833 (9-12-1833) G
Bradberry, Sacisa to James K. Williams 1-10-1861 (no return) We
Bradberry, Sarah S. to James B. McNeely 3-19-1586 (3-20-1856) Ma
Bradberry, Sarah to Charles McCormack 12-22-1856 (12-23-1856) Sh
Bradberry, Sarah to James Coker 6-20-1851 G
Bradberry, Sudie A. to John R. A. Bowers 12-29-1858 We
Bradberry, Tabitha to John Thompson 12-19-1848 Cr
Bradberry, Virginia to James Scott 1-26-1853 Cr
Bradbery, Martha to W. M. Richards 10-12-1854 We
Bradbery, Susan to A. J. Butler 9-30-1867 (10-1-1867) Cr
Bradbury, Epsey Ann to William A. Moore 1-15-1846 Ma
Braddy, Aneliza to James H. Lucas 8-20-1851 (8-21-1851) S
Braden, Abby E. to Andrew Trusdale 11-22-1869 (no return) F B
Braden, Bettie to J. M. Cowan 8-1-1883 (8-2-1883) L
Braden, Eliza Jane to Andrew J. Nelson 12-15-1851 (12-18-1851) L
Braden, Elizabeth to Crockett D. Webb 11-21-1849 L
Braden, Elizabeth to John D. Robertson 1-12-1848 L
Braden, Elizabeth to John Thomas 9-21-1847 (no return) L
Braden, Elmira A. to John A. Glimp, jr. 9-23-1876 (9-24-1876) L
Braden, Emily to John Foutch 6-9-1855 (6-10-1855) L
Braden, Gillee Derrinda to C. B. S. Fain 12-1-1863 (12-2-1863) L
Braden, Harriet J. to W. H. Freeman 11-4-1865 (11-5-1865) F
Braden, Harriet to Ebenezer Best 8-7-1856 L
Braden, Joella to Hillard Cunningham 11-21-1883 (11-1?-1883) L
Braden, Julia to Henry Harris 3-8-1867 (3-9-1867) F
Braden, Letitia to James Wilson 12-22-1836 Sh
Braden, Lucinda to Milton F. Lake 5-21-1843 L
Braden, Mahala to James Prescott 8-16-1843 (8-17-1843) L
Braden, Margaret J. to Samuel C. Williams 11-19-1853 (11-20-1853) Sh
Braden, Margaret O. to Harden J. Turner 8-22-1863 (8-23-1863) L
Braden, Margaret to John Stump 4-15-1861 Mn
Braden, Martha A. to William M. Brown 12-20-1870 (12-21-1870) L
Braden, Martha E. to A. G. W. Byrn ?-30-1839? (1-3-1840) L
Braden, Martha to Thomas Davenport 5-27-1843 (6-1-1843) L
Braden, Mary D. to S. D. Lewis 12-3-1877 (12-6-1877?) L
Braden, Mary L. to Jacob A. Perkins 6-7-1879 (6-8-1879) L
Braden, Mary to I. F. Huddleston 3-7-1861 Mn
Braden, Mollie to Caz Fitzpatrick 6-14-1873 (no return) L B
Braden, Nancy Caroline to W. S. Harrell 10-19-1871 (10-26-1871) L
Braden, S. A. to J. F. Steward 12-7-1875 (12-8-1875) L
Braden, Serena to John N. Crocket 7-16-1866 (7-19-1866) L
Braden, Susan E. to J. F. Cranford 11-26-1867 (12-1-1867) F
Braden, Terrison A. to James M. Love 5-31-1828 Ma

Bradey, Mary W. to N. M. Mullhollan 2-22-1848 (2-24-1848) L
Bradford, Adaline to Joe Taylor 12-28-1869 Hy
Bradford, Alice to Thad Mann 12-11-1873 Hy
Bradford, Ann to Brice E. Helm 2-13-1872 Hy
Bradford, Annie C. to L. Ketchum 4-15-1858 Sh
Bradford, Betsy Jane to Benjamin Moore 2-8-1868 (2-10-1868) Cr
Bradford, Caldonia to C. Leachman 4-3-1874 (no return) Hy
Bradford, Caldonia to Sam. Martin 10-16-1872 Hy
Bradford, Charity to Jack Harland 11-2-1868 G B
Bradford, Delia A. to Thomas Wingo 9-20-1868 G
Bradford, Delia to Price Currin 7-6-1885 (7-12-1885) L
Bradford, Eliza to Andrew Yates 12-6-1865 O
Bradford, Eliza to Stephen S. Taylor 12-21-1880 (12-22-1880) L
Bradford, Elizabeth J. to William Polk 10-24-1850 H
Bradford, Elizabeth to David Davis 12-8-1842 (12-11-1842) O
Bradford, Elizabeth to Henry Schlemmer 5-14-1862 Sh
Bradford, Ellen to J. B. Blackwell 12-6-1860 (no return) Hy
Bradford, Ellen to Sam Jones 11-5-1877 (11-9-1877) L
Bradford, Elvira to Dempsey Cox 11-14-1866 (11-15-1866) Ma
Bradford, Elvira to Peter Williams 2-3-1881 L B
Bradford, Fannie to Samuel Killebrew 2-14-1872 Hy
Bradford, Fanny to Alexander H. Vaughn 4-7-1830 G
Bradford, Fanny to John Lock (Lack?) 8-6-1867 (8-7-1869?) G
Bradford, Florence to Lucius C. Simmons 2-25-1860 (2-27-1860) L
Bradford, Ida to James Tyus 12-29-1869 Hy
Bradford, Jane (Mrs.) to J. M. Ledbetter 10-2-1872 Dy
Bradford, Jane to Bundy King 8-22-1869 Hy
Bradford, Judy to Pleasant Mann 11-10-1866 (no return) Hy
Bradford, Julia A. E. to James M. McCaleb 7-23-1850 (7-31-1850) L
Bradford, Julia G. to W. J. Jennings 8-24-1868 (8-25-1868) L
Bradford, Julia to Richard Jordan 2-8-1870 (no return) L
Bradford, L. S. to J. D. Barrett 12-4-1866 G
Bradford, Laura to Wyatt Halliburton 6-2-1877 (6-7-1877) L
Bradford, Lizzie to Granville Jones 9-8-1870 (no return) Dy
Bradford, Lizzie to John Holcomb 12-16-1882 (12-20-1882) L
Bradford, Lou to Elijah McKinney 8-16-1871 Hy
Bradford, Lucy to John Porter 12-28-1878 (12-31-1879) L B
Bradford, Lucy to John W. Waggoner 3-18-1862 Ma
Bradford, Lucy to Wesby Upchurch 12-26-1867 Hn B
Bradford, Lydia A. to John Ingram Sturdevant 11-24-1868 (11-25-1868) Ma
Bradford, M. F. to Jesse Taylor 12-26-1867 Hy
Bradford, M. J. to William Holloman 7-1-1851 (no return) Hn
Bradford, M. L. to R. R. H. Melton 9-5-1866? (9-8-1867) Cr
Bradford, Maggie to Ed Davis 1-7-1866 Hy
Bradford, Malinda to Henry Culbertson 1-29-1841 (1-31-1841) O
Bradford, Mandy to Jim Jarrett 2-1-1875 Hy
Bradford, Margaret to James L. Coburn 7-5-1855 Hr
Bradford, Mariah to Dick Kirk 1-1-1879 (1-2-1879) Dy
Bradford, Martha E. to W. Jasper Dean 10-25-1859 (11-2-1859) Hr
Bradford, Mary A. (Mrs.) to J. B. Miller 10-16-1854 Sh
Bradford, Mary Ann to James H. Williams 10-31-1843 Hn
Bradford, Mary Ann to Peyton Dyson 10-11-1872 (10-26-1872) T
Bradford, Mary C. to J. F. Knapp 7-20-1858 Sh
Bradford, Mary C. to J. W. Deming 2-3-1860 Hr
Bradford, Mary C. to Kimbro E. Hornesby 1-2-1860 Hr
Bradford, Mary G. to Jasper M. Cannon 8-29-1852 Cr
Bradford, Mary Jane to Robert F. McKnight 4-7-1859 Ma
Bradford, Mary June to G. M. Willis 7-22-1842 Hn
Bradford, Mary M. to W. R. Jeffries 11-30-1876 L
Bradford, Mary N. to John W. James 9-28-1859 G
Bradford, Mary to Bob Ellis 9-26-1877 Hy
Bradford, Mary to Chas. Sawyer 6-29-1868 Dy
Bradford, Mary to Daniel W. Crafton 11-22-1826 G
Bradford, Mary to King (Cain) Wilson 10-18-1858 Hy
Bradford, Mary to Merradett Alvis 10-1-1838 (10-3-1838) G
Bradford, Mila to Wilson Smith 3-16-1878 Hy
Bradford, Millie to Ike Jones 2-8-1878 Hy
Bradford, Mittie to Charles Wilson 4-4-1876 Hy
Bradford, Nancy C. to Jerry Morgan 12-25-1873 Hy
Bradford, Nancy to Lafayett Green 10-25-1854 G
Bradford, Narcissa to V. H. Bell 7-25-1859 G
Bradford, Rose to Charles C. Johnson 9-23-1876 Hy
Bradford, Sally to Alston Bond 7-31-1875 Hy
Bradford, Sarah (Miss) to George W. Summers 11-3-1864 (11-5-1864) O
Bradford, Sarah K. to James M. Gray 7-23-1846 Hn
Bradford, Sarah to Felix H. Clark 11-10-1869 (11-14-1869) Cr
Bradford, Sarah to H. W. Hefley 7-31-1860 G
Bradford, Silva to Anthony Newhouse 1-13-1867 G
Bradford, Sylvia to James Fuller 2-18-1877 Hy
Bradford, Teressa Ann to E. H. Dorris 11-10-1853 Hr
Bradford, Tilda to Peter Jelks 8-14-1873 (no return) Hy
Bradford, Vina to Jerry Scott 12-30-1865 Hy
Bradford, Vina to Jerry Scott 3-4-1866 Hy
Bradley, Ana to John Wood 9-21-1832 (9-23-1832) G
Bradley, Betsy to Wm. P. Reaves 6-14-1827 Sh
Bradley, Bettie to James M. Browning 10-29-1874 Hy

Bradley, C. L. to G. W. Rogers 1-27-1874 Dy
Bradley, Charlotte Coosy to Daniel L. Saunders 6-19-1831 Sh
Bradley, Charlotte L. to Henry Woodburry 1-31-1861 (1-30?-1861) Dy
Bradley, Elizabeth S. to William F. Hays 11-30-1853 O
Bradley, Elizabeth to Isaac N. Terry 9-9-1855 Hn
Bradley, Frances to Joseph Garrett 8-22-1855 Cr
Bradley, M. A. to S. C. Cooper 1-16-1855 Hn
Bradley, M. A. to W. R. Hall 12-1-1857 G
Bradley, Margaret W. to Henry J. Simons 2-5-1842 (2-23-1842) G
Bradley, Martha to David Cochran 2-28-1846 Hn
Bradley, Martha to Newt Price 4-20-1867 Hn
Bradley, Mary A. to O. C. Maxey 8-16-1865 (8-17-1865) O
Bradley, Mary E. to J. D. Bearden 12-25-1867 Hy
Bradley, Mary to Jesse Hughes 7-7-1840 (7-9-1840) F
Bradley, Mary to John Dolohry 11-28-1859 Sh
Bradley, Mary to William Cooper 3-9-1880 L
Bradley, Mollie to S. W. Augustus 3-3-1860 (3-5-1860) Hr
Bradley, N. J. to W. G. Landers 12-31-1875 (no return) Hy
Bradley, Nancy to J. W. Brandon 2-10-1863 (no return) Hn
Bradley, Nancy to James D. Sipe 3-11-1862 Cr
Bradley, Patience to James Robb 8-16-1848 Ma
Bradley, Polly to David G. Kincaid 12-26-1829 Sh
Bradley, R. J. to J. P. Dunlap 12-14-1865 Hn
Bradley, Rebecca to Thomas Bird 6-7-1863 Mn
Bradley, Sarah to Cornelas Woolard 11-19-1840 (11-22-1840) G
Bradley, Z. Z. to J. B. Altom 5-25-1843 Sh
Bradly, M. E. to James B. Adams 1-23-1860 (1-24-1860) F
Bradly, Martha J. to Hiram C. Lawrence 3-15-1859 Hn
Bradly, Sousin to James Boon 3-14-1848 Hr
Bradly, Susanah to Samuel Fitzpatrick 11-2-1840 (11-5-1840) F
Bradshaw, Adalade to James H. Hall 12-14-1864 (12-15-1864) Dy
Bradshaw, Eliza S. to Aaron Borroughs 6-22-1835 (6-23-1835) Hr
Bradshaw, Elizabeth to Joseph F. M. Jenkins 1-21-1866 Hn
Bradshaw, Ellen to Daniel Hale 2-12-1880 Dy
Bradshaw, Ellen to Geo. Shaw 12-22-1860 (12-25-1860) Sh
Bradshaw, Ellen to John Owens 12-31-1873 T
Bradshaw, Elvira to Frank Richmond 9-19-1864 (no return) Dy
Bradshaw, Emma to Harberd Gibson 12-7-1880 Dy
Bradshaw, Hannah to Richard A. Partee 11-4-1883 L
Bradshaw, Harriet to John Burnham 11-16-1854 We
Bradshaw, Henrietta B. to Solomon A. Rhodes 12-21-1846 (12-23-1846) T
Bradshaw, Joanna to James White 11-6-1855 Sh
Bradshaw, L. E. to John T. Stewart 1-13-1864 (1-14-1864) Sh
Bradshaw, Lizzie to Fernando Dunavant 2-10-1870 (no return) Dy
Bradshaw, Lucinda A. to Wm. Rutlage 7-9-1846 We
Bradshaw, Lucy to Phill Sadden? 12-24-1869 (1-9-1870) T
Bradshaw, Lucy to Phill Sodden? 12-24-1869 T
Bradshaw, Maggie to J. T. C. Hill 2-27-1867 G
Bradshaw, Malinda to Thos. J. Johnson 5-7-1846 We
Bradshaw, Margaret to James S. Leapord 10-6-1865 Mn
Bradshaw, Margaret to Lams (Larns?) Dugan 4-11-1863 Sh
Bradshaw, Martha A. to C. H. Culwell 5-3-1869 F
Bradshaw, Martha to James W. McGee 3-7-1843 Hn
Bradshaw, Mary (Mrs.) to W. T. Powell 1-8-1867 Dy
Bradshaw, Mary Ann to John Swinney 3-23-1869 (3-24-1869) F
Bradshaw, Nannie to H. F. Grimes 12-15-1877 (12-19-1877) Dy
Bradshaw, R. W. to R. P. Powell 3-16-1861 Dy
Bradshaw, Sarah to Henry Smith 9-15-1873 (9-16-1873) Dy
Bradshaw, Susan to Green Smith 3-10-1880 (3-11-1880) Dy
Bradsher, Demaris A. to James E. Yancey 5-25-1863 (5-26-1863) F
Bradway, Eliza to Zach. Beadgit 10-21-1841 We
Brady, Bridget to James Bennett 4-9-1864 (4-11-1864) Sh
Brady, Catharine to Stephen M. Brady 12-27-1844 (no return) We
Brady, Ellen to Larry Silver 4-9-1861 Sh
Brady, Emily to J. R. Ivy 11-4-1847 G
Brady, L. J. to Irvin Byford 1-9-1866 (1-10-1866) T
Brady, Levina to J. Weber 1-6-1840 Sh
Brady, Luseetta to F. M. Gardner 10-1-1866 O
Brady, Mary J. to Samuel M. Durham 1-27-1852 (no return) F
Brady, Mary to Thomas Needham 1-12-1856 (1-13-1856) Sh
Brady, Sarah E. to Thomas W. Polk 10-11-1838 (10-12-1838) Hr
Brag, Sarah E. to William H. Teague 2-24-1863 We
Bragden, Folly Ann to John Simmons 8-24-1864 (no return) Cr
Bragdon, Bevy to Hesikaik Chaney 8-16-1853 Cr
Bragdon, Nancy to Thos. Carter 12-17-1851 Cr
Bragg, Emaline to Harry Claiburne 9-9-1865 (9-14-1865) T
Bragg, Frances Ann to Saml. A. Holmes 12-17-1851 T
Bragg, Jane to Albert Green 9-1-1870 G B
Bragg, Louisa to Daniel R. Bushart 8-17-1848 Hn
Bragg, Lucy Ann to Caleb Field 12-27-1872 (1-1-1873) T
Bragg, Lucy M. to Robert B. Turner 9-27-1869 (9-28-1869) T
Bragg, Lucy to William Bush 12-2-1852 Hn
Bragg, M. J. to G. R. Green 12-12-1877 (12-13-1877) L
Bragg, Margaret E. to Henry Cobb 3-11-1844 F
Bragg, Margarett C. to James H. Bandy 1-28-1858 We
Bragg, Martha to George W. Bell 10-2-1845 T
Bragg, Mary Jane to R. P. Smith 8-7-1857 T
Bragg, Mary to James H. Cate 5-31-1841 (no return) Hn
Bragg, Nancy to P. L. Dunlop 12-2-1857 We
Bragg, Polly to Tom Simmons 12-26-1868 (1-1-1869) T
Bragg, Sarah to James F. Davis 3-30-1869 G
Bragg, Virginia L. to Thomas F. Scott 11-2-1870 (11-3-1870) T
Braiden, D. E. to James W. Finley 8-8-1859 Sh
Brake, Caroline to William Miller 10-15-1857 Hn
Brake, L. P. to M. A. Robertson 1-16-1852 Hn
Bram, Matilda N. to M. E. Johnston 8-17-1848 Be
Bram, N. to J. K. Nance 3-1-1841 Be
Bram, Sarah J. to James B. Baker 6-19-1854 (no return) F
Bramblet, Catsey to James H. Farr 9-21-1836 O
Bramblett, Francis to Enoch Ward 6-28-1845 (6-29-1845) O
Bramblett, Jane to James Honeycutt 4-18-1858 O
Bramblett, Laney to Samuel H. Davis 11-19-1838 O
Bramblett, Martha to William Carroll Norrid 6-26-1836 O
Bramblett, Rebecca to Josiah W. Crane 8-8-1845 (8-10-1845) O
Bramblett, Wincie to Storkie Purvis 12-28-1830 (1-30-1831) O
Brame, E. S. to John W. Hester 1-7-1841 F
Brame, Elizabeth I. to John A. R. Brim 6-14-1838 (no return) F
Brame, Elizabeth to W. G. Barker 1-8-1848 F
Bramlett, Annie to T. J. Blackwell 12-25-1872 Hy
Bramlett, Frances J. (Mrs.) to H. A. Polly 11-18-1867 O
Bramlett, M. (Miss) to Edwin W. Smith 6-30-1862 (6-31-1862) O
Bran, Mary to Noah Curtis 9-28-1836 (9-29-1836) G
Branan, Ann to Thomas Kelley 5-19-1862 Sh
Branans, R. to J. Lores 5-29-1842 Be
Branch, A. V. to S. W. Baxter 12-19-1850 F
Branch, Amanda to John O. Johnson 12-8-1859 G
Branch, Amy to P. A.? May 12-7-1852 (no return) F
Branch, Angelina to Geo. M. Stewart 1-7-1846 F
Branch, Ann E. to J. S. Speed 3-10-1863 Hy
Branch, Anna to John Soward 12-23-1880 (12-24-1880) L B
Branch, Chelly to Stephen Gatlin 12-16-1840 (12-17-1840) Ma
Branch, Darcus to James A. Haselet 9-21-1867 (no return) F B
Branch, Eliza to James B. Mallory 10-27-1830 Ma
Branch, Elizabeth (Mrs.) to A. Leech 10-8-1861 Cr
Branch, Elizabeth to Aliner Leech 10-1-1861 (10-8-1861) Cr
Branch, Elizabeth to Bogan Branch 9-10-1842 (9-20-1842) Ma
Branch, Frances to Tho. J. Brown 1-14-1846 (1-15-1846) F
Branch, Grizzy Ann to William Ralph 8-4-1841 T
Branch, Henrietta E. to Nicholas Vowel 2-23-1873 Hy
Branch, Hepsey (Hessy?) to Dabney Crenshaw 2-6-1845 Sh
Branch, Hepsey Ann to J. G. Keathley 12-1-1851 G
Branch, Kitty to Frankllin (Dr.) Crenshaw 12-12-1849 Sh
Branch, Laurany to William Johnson 2-26-1848 (2-29-1848) Ma
Branch, M. A. to C. Howard Onion 10-31-1871 Hy
Branch, M. L. J. to L. J. Mulligan 12-23-1872 (12-24-1872) Cr
Branch, Martha A. to William P. Butterworth 2-17-1843 (2-23-1843) F
Branch, Mary A. Elizabeth to George J. Norton 11-11-1857 (11-12-1857) Ma
Branch, Mary A. to Wm. Carroll French 9-17-1854 Cr
Branch, Mary E. to Washington Graves 12-17-1876 Hy
Branch, Mary Jane to J. K. Price 2-5-1873 O
Branch, Mary R. to Geo. R. Lipscomb 2-21-1870 (2-22-1870) F
Branch, Mary to Isaac F. Cowan 11-29-1848 G
Branch, Maryann to Jesse T. Butterworth 9-13-1847 (9-16-1847) F
Branch, Minerva to John A. Moody 6-11-1860 (6-13-1860) F
Branch, Mollie to Ned Bell 12-17-1871 Hy
Branch, Molly to Jim Read 8-20-1875 (no return) Hy
Branch, Nancy Jane to R. W. Newby 10-27-1852 (no return) F
Branch, Octavia to A. D. Hooks 10-19-1865 (10-24-1865) T
Branch, Olivid? P. to Peter N. Bond 5-8-1865 (5-10-1865) T
Branch, Phillis to Doc Shelton 7-17-1879 (no return) Dy
Branch, Polly to R. D. Grant 6-23-1849 F
Branch, S. J. to T. J. Firth 8-28-1868 (9-9-1868) F
Branch, Sallie G. to H. L. Blancett 5-5-1867 Hy
Branch, Sarah R. to Beverly L. Dyer 10-27-1852 (no return) F
Branch, Sarah to David Crenshaw 8-9-1841 Sh
Branch, Sarah to James Green 11-15-1850 O
Branch, Sarah to W. S. Weeks 9-6-1868 Be
Branch, Sarrah to Archalus Keathly 5-28-1840 (5-31-1840) G
Branch, Susan to James Cowgill 1-17-1845 Sh
Branch, Susan to Littleberry White 7-7-1830 Ma
Branch, Tennessee to W. S. Pearce 11-28-1862 (12-2-1862) F
Branch, Zilpha to Geo. G. Holloway 10-18-1851 (10-21-1851) Sh
Brand, C. A. E. to Jerry White 1-22-1863 (1-25-1863) O
Brand, Mary E. to Gerard Broens 4-30-1861 G
Brand, Reubecca to William Myric 12-27-1843 We
Branden, Nancy C. to Thomas C. Bowen 3-13-1872 Hy
Branden, Virginia to Benjamin Dougan 8-14-1868 Hy
Brandon, Cathrine to W. L. Bigham 10-24-1844 Cr
Brandon, Elizabeth to Ephraim Bradhsaw 1-19-1854 Hn
Brandon, Elizabeth to Henry N. Rourk 11-15-1854 Cr
Brandon, Elizabeth to W. A. Gauden 11-5-1873 Hy
Brandon, Emma to James Campbell 8-28-1867 (no return) Hy
Brandon, Frances to J. R. Holmes 5-28-1873 Cr
Brandon, Hilly (Mrs.) to R. R. Espy 9-23-1863 (no return) Dy

Brandon, Issabel to William Pritchard 10-14-1867 (10-15-1867) Cr
Brandon, Jane to Maxwell Dunn 4-23-184_ (no return) Hn
Brandon, Lucy C. to Thos. Springer 12-5-1872 (12-6-1872) Cr
Brandon, M. M. to J. F. Salisbury 2-25-1879 (2-26-1879) Dy
Brandon, Margaret to C. M. Young 8-30-1870 (9-1-1870) Dy
Brandon, Martha A. to Henry A.(L?) Johnson 11-4-1846 Sh
Brandon, Matilda to Amos Roach 7-31-1845 Cr
Brandon, Melissa to William N. Rayborn 5-27-1841 Hn
Brandon, Mildred F. to John M. Warren 10-15-1856 O
Brandon, Orrenia to Frank Hilliard 8-1-1872 (8-4-1872) Cr
Brandon, Rienia to W. D. Roark 7-23-1872 (no return) Cr
Brandon, Sarah J. to Peter B. Pirtle 12-22-1847 (12-23-1847) Hr
Brandon, Sarah Jane to W. C. Cartwright 4-1-1850 Ma
Brandon, Sarah to John White 3-4-1856 Sh
Branham, E. C. to Charls Land 1-14-1869 Hy
Branhama, Sally C. to George C. Isbell 11-3-1859 (11-10-1859) O
Branhart, Elizabeth to Wm. Roland 9-14-1845 Cr
Branish, Cara C. to George Crosby 12-6-1862 (12-7-1862) Sh
Brann, Delila to Joseph Lell? Cashon 9-11-1855 (no return) We
Brann, Jossiphia to William Thrulkiler 10-9-1859 We
Brann, Mary A. to J. W. Brundridge 12-4-1856 We
Brann, Mary M. to S. G. Parrish 5-23-1858 We
Brann, N. A. E. to Calven S. Brundridge 12-26-1858 We
Brannan (Brennan?), Mary to Timothy Murphy 8-4-1854 (8-6-1854) Sh
Brannans, V. C. G. to W. G. Doughitt 3-17-1864 Sh
Brannen, Vezie to Owen McCormick 9-5-1864 Sh
Brannock, Louisa to George Coleman 9-4-1869 (9-19-1869) Cr
Brannock, Nannie M. to John E. Gwin 9-10-1852 (no return) Cr
Brannom, Elizabeth to J. G. Robins 2-19-1865 (no return) Hn
Brannon, Bridget to Bartholomew Cullan 6-25-1859 (6-26-1859) Sh
Brannon, Eliza to William Fitzgerald 1-18-1864 (1-19-1864) Sh
Brannon, Jane E. to B. B. Fitzhugh 12-25-1862 Dy
Brannon, Letitia to John Haney 12-13-1841 (no return) Hn
Brannon, Mary E. to William J. Daniel 12-2-1847 (no return) Hn
Brannon, Sarah Ann E. to Evans S. Robins 2-5-1860 Hn
Branoch, Sallie to John Carson 3-28-1872 (no return) Cr B
Branscomb, Lou to Silas Ewell 2-24-1868 (2-29-1868) F B
Bransett, Sarah to J. W. Davis 12-27-1874 Hy
Bransford, M. C. to Wm. McGaugh 6-24-1865 O
Bransford, Martha J. to F. A. Wilkerson 7-24-1866 O
Bransford, Martha to Thomas J. Spradlin 12-10-1852 O
Bransford, Sarah W. to James H. G. Fields 2-16-1858 (2-18-1858) O
Branson, Louizer to Isaac Oliver 5-16-1869 G
Branson, Mary to John Glass 11-15-1853 (11-16-1853) G
Branson, Sibby to L. B. Miller 10-3-1861 G
Brant, Hannah A. to Francis A. Jean 9-16-___ (9-17-1857) L
Brant, Paralee to J. D. Jackson 2-8-1871 (2-10-1871) Dy
Brant, Susan to Henry Harston 10-13-1846 (10-14-1846) Ma
Brantley, Ann E. to J. B. Compton 1-31-1854 (2-2-1854) Ma
Brantley, Betsy to John M. Graham 5-5-1826 (5-20-1826) Hr
Brantley, Laura E. to Charles H. Nichols 6-26-1878 L
Brantley, Martha to John Vicker 12-16-1842 (12-22-1842) Hr
Brantley, N. B. to J. B. Ryan 7-25-1876 (7-28-1876) L
Brantley, Nancy to Moses Bumpass 7-14-1826 (7-16-1826) Hr
Brantley, S. A. to A. Landers 7-3-1866 O
Brantley, Sarah to Wm. B. Stovall 6-13-1840 (6-14-1840) Hr
Brantly, Frances to Perry Nabers 1-21-1826 Hr
Brantly, Mary to Mizo Casee 2-16-1839 (2-23-1839) Hr
Brantly, Sarah L. to Green Jennings 11-1-1882 (11-2-1882) L
Brasfield, Ann to Frank Avery 2-27-1868 G B
Brasfield, Nancy M. to P. M. Whitworth 11-23-1857 We
Brasfield, Nancy to John C. Park 8-26-1869 G
Brashear, Penelope A. to Wesley Kelley 5-13-1869 Cr
Brashears, Rebecca to Augustus Holmgrist 8-6-1870 (no return) Cr
Brasher, Nancy E. to Isham L. Forsythe 9-5-1873 (9-7-1873) L
Brashers, Hannah E. to Wm. M. Copher 3-5-1861 (no return) Hy
Brashers, Jane to H. M. Laurence 4-20-1867 (4-21-1867) Cr
Brashers, Josephine F. to John F. Deer 1-22-1868 (1-28-1868) Cr
Brashier, Charity Ann to W. H. Nelson 1-21-1878 (1-22-1878) Dy
Brashier, K. J. to J. D. Bradley 3-22-1873 (3-23-1873) Dy
Brass, Bernardin to Sixtus Neff 9-25-1856 Sh
Brassfield, Emeline F. to S. W. Redmon 2-2-1860 G
Brassfield, ____ (Mrs.) to Hugh D. Neilson 2-4-1830 G
Braswell, H. C. to Marcus Raines 10-8-1861 Sh
Braswell, H. C. to Marcus Rankens 10-8-1861 (10-10-1861) Sh
Braswell, Harriett to Ira Moore 1-10-1847 Sh
Braswell, Julia to Jacob Cross 1-28-1870 (no return) F B
Braswell, Lucretia A. to Wm. B. Briley 10-3-1848 Sh
Braswell, Lucy to W. G. Wickham 4-27-1847 Sh
Braswell, Lucy to Willis Ethridge 12-19-1845 Sh
Braswell, Martha to Giles Belew 2-13-1864 Cr
Braswell, Martha to Giles Belew 2-13-1864 (no return) Cr
Braswell?, Elizabeth to James Huffman 12-22-1846 Sh
Bratcher, S. E. to W. F. Yancey 9-19-1859 (9-21-1859) F
Bratton, Dorothy T. to Elijah Rodgers 5-1-1851 Cr
Bratton, Emma C. to E. P. Walker 10-25-1870 (10-30-1870) T
Bratton, Lively A. to B. E. Alexander 12-11-1852 (no return) Hn

Bratton, M. J. to John Edwards 9-22-1856 G
Bratton, Malinda to Alen King 3-4-1833 G
Bratton, Margarett Ann to Alfred Ross 10-31-1849 (11-1-1849) G
Bratton, Margarett to Daniel Delph 11-10-1831 G
Bratton, Martha J. to Robert W. Bratton 3-19-1879 (3-20-1879) L
Bratton, Mary D. to Albert Ross 1-15-1853 (1-18-1853) G
Bratton, Mary J. to William A. Ross 9-21-1844 (9-25-1844) G
Bratton, Mary to G. D. Stone 9-23-1840 (9-24-1840) G
Bratton, Rachel B. to Francis H. Read 10-20-1853 Hn
Bratton, Sarah to William Johnson 9-18-1855 Hn
Brauner, Permelia to T. M. Richardson 6-24-1863 (no return) We
Brawner, Elizabeth to L. J. Boltin 8-25-1856 (no return) We
Brawner, Everline to John Berryhill 3-13-1863 (no return) We
Brawner, M. I. to S. R. McBride 8-27-1858 We
Brawner, Mary E. to W. P. C. Jinkins 5-10-1861 We
Bray, Becky Ann to John W. Jones 10-17-1870 (10-19-1870) Ma
Bray, Elizabeth to R. Emison 2-9-1856 Hn
Bray, Ella J. to James C. Rowe 10-4-1858 Hn
Bray, Frances E. to John W. Dismukes 11-24-1866 (11-27-1866) Ma
Bray, Isabel to Benjamin T. Rhea 11-5-1854 Hn
Bray, Isabella R. to M. H. Williams 8-17-1854 We
Bray, Louisa to Nathaniel Moore 8-7-1862 G
Bray, Mary Ann to Ephraim B. Adams 10-30-1841 (10-31?-1841) Hr
Bray, Satey to Joseph WRey 7-31-1848 Hr
Brayden, Eveline to Thomas Wilson 9-9-1830 Sh
Brazier, Mary to Joab Dowdy 3-9-1849 Hn
Brazile, Sarah J. to Wm. H. Doile 10-3-1861 (no return) Hy
Breaden, Catharine C. to Clemons Ingram 3-9-1854 Sh
Breasted?, Laura to Will Sandford 12-28-1880 Dy
Breatt, Feliste to John W. Lain 2-13-1846 Sh
Brecheen, Nancy A. E. to Harvey Neighbours 11-27-1860 Cr
Brechum, Martha M. to Osaah Parnell 3-6-1855 Cr
Brechum, Mary C. to Jerimiah Carnelton 12-10-1850 Cr
Breckhouse, Elizabeth to Ashville B. Whiteherst 2-11-1854 (2-14-1854) G
Breece, Melissa J. to J. B. Leggett 2-21-1870 (2-23-1870) L
Breechum, Mary J. to Joel W. Chambers 9-15-1857 Cr
Breeden, Catharine to Nathan Phillips 8-21-1856 Hr
Breeding, Elizabeth to James Hamilton 1-2-1830 Hn
Breeding, Elizabeth to Pleasant Lusby 1-30-1829 Sh
Breeding, Elizabeth to Stephen Pruett 4-19-1827 Hr
Breedlove, Clarissa M. to J. J. Atkins 12-19-1867 Hn
Breedlove, Frances e. to George W. Walton 1-11-1848 Hn
Breedlove, M. J. to E. B. Rorie 5-11-1854 Hn
Breedlove, Sarah Ann to Samuel W. Todd 11-11-1856 Hn
Breedlove, Virginia to William Todd 1-14-1852 Hn
Breedmon, Martha R. to Wm. Martin 6-3-1868 T
Breedon, Julia A. to Wm. M. Phillips 8-20-1859 (8-21-1859) Hr
Breedon, Mary C. to W. F. Price 3-21-1861 Hr
Breen, Johanna to Patrick Nowlan 1-7-1857 Sh
Breen, Katherine to Jeremiah Galvin 4-10-1863 Sh
Breene?, S. A. to James D. Hesther 6-28-1842 (7-14-1842) F
Bregance, Mosiah to William F. Thompson 2-21-1838 Ma
Brei, Louisa to Frederick Walter 1-27-1862 Sh
Breining, Bridget to David Goldsmith 2-11-1854 (2-12-1854) Sh
Bremaker, Matilda to George Cooper 4-24-1852 (4-25-1852) Sh
Bremer, E. to W. Halay 11-19-1841 Be
Bremer, Mary to Wm. Thompson 12-9-1846 Sh
Brenakin, Mary to George McDonnell 4-14-1865 (4-17-1865) Dy
Brenard, Elizabeth to Andrew L. Murphy 12-10-1828 (12-11-1828) Hr
Brenen, Julia to Martin Ganen 6-10-1862 (7-8-1862) Sh
Brenish, Eliza A. to Geo. Reed 11-17-1863 (11-19-1863) Sh
Brennan, Mary to Thomas Foley 6-19-1860 Sh
Brenner, Magdalena to Frederick Heidelberg 5-31-1864 Sh
Brennon, Margaret to Wm. McCormick 7-16-1863 Sh
Brennon, Mary to Bartholomew Brown 2-14-1852 (2-15-1852) Sh
Brent, Ann Eliza to Charles L. Stewart 1-31-1848 Ma
Brent, Eliza J. to Rubin Wichard 11-12-1847 (11-14-1847) G
Brent, Elizabeth to Marion Davis 4-20-1865 Dy
Brent, Evaline to Ethelbert Kellett 12-25-1866 (12-27-1866) Dy
Brent, Leitha Jane to Joseph T. North 9-1-1862 (9-2-1862) Dy
Brent, Lucretia A. E. to Jefferson Marcum 7-1-1858 G
Brent, Sarah to Alfred Price 3-5-1835 (no return) Hn
Bresinhan, Bridgett to Thos. Boyle (Boyd) 10-31-1860 Sh
Bretton, Martha A. to L. M. Edwards 6-9-1870 (6-12-1870) Ma
Brevard, Amanda to Peter Bledsoe 12-30-1872 Cr
Brevard, Caledonia C. to John F. Mills 12-19-1853 (12-21-1853) O
Brevard, Cleresy H. to James C. Crenshaw 2-11-1859 (2-13-1859) O
Brevard, Josephine to R. Holaday 12-28-1870 Cr
Brevard, R. F. to Brum Henderson 8-30-1866 O
Brevard, Tabitha G. to Andrew J. Knox 10-15-1852 (10-17-1852) O
Brewer, A. E. to H. D. Chambers 3-23-1868 (3-24-1868) O
Brewer, Alice to W. E. Prichard 9-18-1878 (9-19-1878) Dy
Brewer, Ann (Mrs.) to David Mitchell 12-5-1865 Hy
Brewer, Arcada to Hosea Hamberger 4-1-1857 Be
Brewer, Caroline to Zechariah W. Price 2-7-1851 Be
Brewer, Delpha to Hosea D. Allen 11-20-1851 Be
Brewer, Drusillar to A. G. McFerson 9-4-1855 Be

Brewer, E. to John Blount 1-7-1847 Cr
Brewer, Effa to B. F. Farmer 6-5-1866 Be
Brewer, Eliza A. to William Oakley 11-25-1871 (no return) Dy
Brewer, Elizabeth A. to W. H. Brady 6-11-1865 O
Brewer, Elizabeth to Jessee Parker 2-22-1855 Be
Brewer, Elizabeth to John Brewer 1-25-1865 Be
Brewer, Emma to Bernard Hale 12-20-1867 (12-28-1867) F B
Brewer, Frances to Nathaniel Nunnery 10-31-1860 (11-10-1860) Cr
Brewer, Frances to Robt. Mason 2-7-1868 (2-9-1868) F
Brewer, Harriett to Thomas Pitt 11-5-1867 Be
Brewer, J. A. to B. R. Prichard 12-27-1877 Dy
Brewer, J. H. to T. Brewr 9-30-1840 Be
Brewer, Jantha to Booker Flippin 1-7-1870 (no return) F B
Brewer, Josephine to F. H. Todd 12-3-1866 (12-5-1866) Cr
Brewer, Julia A. to Rufus Ellis 10-24-1858 Hn
Brewer, Kissiah A. to John G. Blount 8-25-1853 Cr
Brewer, L. C. to W. H. Hall 1-29-1877 (no return) Dy
Brewer, Lucinda Jane to James W. Spraggins 11-24-1869 (11-25-1869) Ma
Brewer, Lurany J. to Jas. T. Elmore 12-20-1856 Be
Brewer, M. A. to A. J. Reddick 10-16-1869 (10-19-1869) Dy
Brewer, M. A. to H. B. Wright 1-21-1857 Be CC
Brewer, M. A. to H. B. Wright 1-21-1858 Be
Brewer, M. E. to Samuel Wilson 3-15-1843 Be
Brewer, M. E. to Samuel Wilson 3-15-1843 Be CC
Brewer, M. F. to J. L. Reddick 11-28-1866 (11-29-1866) Dy
Brewer, Mahulda to John N. Brewer 8-21-1855 Be
Brewer, Margaret E. to S. A. Reed 12-27-1865 Dy
Brewer, Margarette Ann to Bennett B. Brogden 10-23-1865 G
Brewer, Martha E. F. to Thos. G. N. Tomson 9-29-1848 (with 1858) Hr
Brewer, Martha J. to Wm. D. Willet 11-14-1867 Be
Brewer, Martha Jane to John W. Hammett 10-15-1856 (no return) Cr
Brewer, Mary Ann to John R. Price 8-25-1854 Be
Brewer, Mary E. to G. W. Lock 11-8-1865 G
Brewer, Mary to J. J. Cheatham 11-6-1862 Be
Brewer, Mary to W. H. Lowry 4-13-1864 Be
Brewer, Matilda to A. B. Herringdon 3-1-1840 Be
Brewer, Matilda to James White 8-5-1863 Be
Brewer, Nancy J. to William R. Holland 10-30-1863 Be
Brewer, Nancy to Felix Carey 5-14-1870 (5-18-1870) Cr
Brewer, Nancy to Zack Olds 12-28-1870 F B
Brewer, Pricilla B. to Thos. J. Edwards 2-6-1865 (2-7-1865) Dy
Brewer, Robina to W. A. Aikin 8-27-1870 (8-28-1870) Cr
Brewer, S. A. to S. D. Abinathey 12-11-1866 (12-16-1866) Cr
Brewer, Sarah A. to John A. Pierce 11-28-1867 Be
Brewer, Sarah to David A. Crews 8-8-1858 Cr
Brewer, Willy to James McCann 7-27-1841 (7-28-1841) Hr
Brewr, Matilda to James White 8-5-1863 Be CC
Brewster, Lavenia to Albert Gwyn 12-23-1866 (12-27-1866) F B
Briant, Angeline to Josh Jordan 8-1-1871 Cr
Briant, Elen J. to Harris Bradford 12-11-1856 (12-12-1856) G
Briant, Emily to John Mellworth 6-23-1860 O
Briant, Jinnie to John Hill 7-24-1869 (7-29-1869) Cr
Briant, L. C. to J. A. Taylor 2-28-1872 (3-1-1872) Cr
Briant, Lu? to Ephraim Burrow 2-1-1869 Cr
Briant, Martha A. to Samuel Graddy 1-31-1855 (2-1-1855) G
Briant, Mary to T. J. Harris 4-26-1867 (no return) Cr
Briant, Nancy to W. F. Carr 1-24-1855 (1-25-1855) G
Brice, Martha A. to J. S. Gann 6-19-1870 Hy
Bricheen, Cordelia P. to Robt. Drinkard 9-22-1853 Cr
Brickeem, Frances J. to Montgomery Jones 12-5-1865 Mn
Bricken, A. E. to W. H. Jackson 6-24-1861 Mn
Brickene, Ann to John Milegan 7-30-1864 O
Brickhouse, Harrett to William M. Jones 4-16-1846 (4-26-1846) G
Bridgeman, Dousilla to Harper Brown 2-5-1869 G B
Bridger, Alfreda to J. H. Bridger 10-18-1880 (10-19-1880) L
Bridger, C. A. to C. P. Pitner 12-10-1876 Hy
Bridger, Lotta to J. D. Margraves 11-2-1869 Hy
Bridger, Martha E. to Wm. M. Tyler 10-27-1859 Hy
Bridgers, Harriet A. to D. L. Herron 2-16-1859 Sh
Bridgers, Sophia A. to Edward C. Walthall 8-16-1855 Sh
Bridges, Ann P. to John W. Fuller 4-26-1833 Sh
Bridges, Cintha W. to William A. Estes 1-23-1839 (1-24-1839) G
Bridges, Eliza Ann to Joseph A. Pope 7-8-1844 Be
Bridges, Eliza to Thos. R. Cross 2-13-1856 Cr
Bridges, Emeline to A. H. Stublefield 6-2-1859 Hn
Bridges, H. E. to D. F. Howard 5-31-1871 (6-1-1871) L
Bridges, Hannah to John Eastridge 7-30-1857 O
Bridges, Josephine to J. B. Eastridge 9-23-1865 (9-24-1865) O
Bridges, Lucy J. to Malone Pary 8-31-1866 (9-2-1866) Cr
Bridges, Lucy J. to Theoplius? Heuly 7-10-1853 Cr
Bridges, M. E. to Crittendin Scott 2-7-1851 Cr
Bridges, Mandeville to C. B. Linn 10-18-1856 Hn
Bridges, Martha J. to Joseph Suggs 8-2-1848 Cr
Bridges, Martha J. to S. T. Biggs 10-26-1862 Be
Bridges, Mary A. to Joseph B. Boyd 12-16-1862 Hn
Bridges, Mary C. to Wm. A. Suggs? 8-18-1860 Cr
Bridges, Mary to Daniel McBride 11-20-1830 Sh

Bridges, Nancy A. to Robert H. Solmon 10-18-1860 Hn
Bridges, Narcissa to Protestant P. Dupriest 8-9-1850 (8-11-1850) Ma
Bridges, Nina C. to Abram C. Lowrance 2-4-1855 Cr
Bridges, Paralee to William K. Hicks 9-6-1860 Hn
Bridges, Perlina to John B. Atkins 12-16-1852 Hn
Bridges, Sarah D. to Lunsford W. Scott 1-14-1843 (1-25-1843) Hr
Bridges, Sarah J. to Josephus Gillespie 3-29-1868 G B
Bridges, Sarah to G. T. Robison 2-14-1870 (2-15-1870) Cr
Bridges, Sary to Charles B. Smith 3-3-1841 Cr
Bridgewater, A. to Eli Cavnes 12-9-1869 (12-25-1869) F B
Bridgewater, Allice to Henry Stott 2-18-1871 (3-1-1871) F B
Bridgewater, Emily M. to Jos. Anderson 2-24-1853 Sh
Bridgewater, Henrietta to James Johnston 11-15-1865 (11-16-1865) F
Bridgewater, K. S. to A. C. Dixon 10-13-1879 (10-15-1879) L
Bridgewater, Martha A. to John H. Hardin 7-26-1849 (7-31-1849) F
Bridgewater, Mary to Moses Walker 5-1-1867 (5-4-1867) F B
Bridgwater, L. A. to R. A. Crowder 1-11-1859 (not endorsed) F
Bridly, Ellen to Granville Fitzpatrick 1-26-1842 (1-27-1842) F
Brier, M. to H. F. McElwain 8-23-1842 Hy
Briers, Hannah to Josiah Culbertson 1-7-1842 (1-9-1842) O
Briford, Amanda to Allen Claybrook 10-2-1868 (no return) Hy
Brigaman, Julia A. to B. F. Harrison 12-1-1857 Cr
Brigance, C. J. to G. M. Rust 2-4-1858 We
Brigance, M. E. to C. A. Yancy 11-8-1879 (11-9-1879) L
Brigance, M. L. to C. A. Yancy 9-23-1881 (9-25-1881) L
Brigance, Malissa A. to William V. Rust 11-25-1860 We
Brigance, Martha A. to James Henderson 4-9-1861 (not executed) O
Brigance, Mary Jane to Wm. R. Sneed 2-25-1847 Cr
Brigance, Mary to H. W. Lowry 4-16-1857 Hn
Brigance, S. A. to W. M. Doss 2-4-1880 (2-5-1880) L
Brigance, Zelphia J. to Ransom H. Bell 1-24-1870 (1-25-1870) Ma
Brigens, Nancy to J. W. Evans 1-10-1871 Cr
Briggance, Henrietta to Robert N. McClellan 5-25-1860 (5-27-1860) Ma
Briggance, Tennessee R. to Sidny A. Mebene 2-12-1861 Cr
Briggers, Sarah A. to David Wilson 12-23-1844 Cr
Briggins, L. J. to C. A. Yancy 7-21-1877 (7-24-1877) L
Briggins, Martha C. to William J. Keel 4-10-1862 Sh
Briggins, P. C. to James Roark 4-4-1850 L
Briggs, Elizabeth to Wm. Leach 1-22-1856 Sh
Briggs, Mary R. to John B. D. Henley 10-9-1849 (no return) L
Brigham, Elizabeth to John M. Roberson 1-2-1850 Ha
Brigham, Frances to John A. Hampton 4-13-1850 (no return) Hn
Brigham, Susan R. to Wm. A. Wheatley 11-30-1848 Be
Bright, Annie to Alfred Draper 5-3-1871 (5-4-1871) O B
Bright, Artemesia to James T. Davis 5-16-1867 Be
Bright, Catherine to Phillip Garrison 8-6-16888 O B
Bright, Elender to Mansfield Massey 5-23-1850 Be
Bright, Emma to William T. Grigsby 5-31-1854 G
Bright, Lockey to Robert Milliner 3-19-1853 (3-23-1853) O
Bright, Malinda to Benton L. Stovall 2-11-1862 (2-10?-1862) O
Bright, Martha to Logan B. Adams 10-14-1851 Hr
Bright, Mary C. to Ro L. White 3-21-1855 (3-22-1855) Hr
Bright, Mary to Felix Daniel 3-30-1876 (no return) Hy
Bright, Matilda Ann to Thomas Swindle 12-16-1856 Be
Bright, Nancy to Evan Crawford 10-26-1825 O
Bright, S. Belle to C. A. Elder 6-2-1861 G
Bright, Verginia to J. B. Buchanan 9-4-1867 O
Brighton, Eliza to W. L. Porter 3-1-1861 Sh
Brightwell, Ann N. to John Vanhog 12-6-1852 (12-7-1852) G
Brightwell, Martha R. to Thomas J. Alford 7-5-1858 G
Brightwell, Mary L. to James T. Richardson 12-29-1845 (1-1-1846) G
Brightwell, Nancy to James P. Thompson 2-2-1852 (2-5-1852) G
Brightwell, Peggy to Terrish Turner 5-4-1853 (5-5-1853) G
Brightwell, Sarah J. to William P. Dickson 10-22-1857 G
Brigman, Rosa to James E. Scott 7-17-1873 (7-18-1873) T
Brigman, Sarah Jane to W. C. Ramsey 2-25-1861 (2-26-1861) Hr
Brigman, Tabitha to G. D. Campbell 6-23-1857 Hr
Brignadello, Theresa to Vincent Boro 1-7-1858 (1-10-1858) Sh
Brigniola, Caroline to Angelo Monteverde 1-21-1863 Sh
Brignole, Louisa to Peter Devote 3-9-1860 Sh
Brigum, Matilda to Masha? Price 9-2-1828 Ma
Briley, Callie to Wesley Garrett 12-21-1872 Hy
Briley, Desha to Lemuel B. Tison 8-9-1832 Sh
Briley, Lottie to William Hill 7-7-1872 Hy
Briley, Lucretia to Thomas Etheridge 4-21-1853 Sh
Briley, Susan to James R. Taylor 9-11-1842 Sh
Brillmayer, Mary S. to G. A. Eckerty (Eckerly?) 4-21-1862 (4-24-1862) Sh
Brily, Nancy E. to J. B. F. Shivers 12-27-1852 (12-28-1852) Sh
Brim, Amanda to Davis Patterson 12-30-1868 L
Brim, Celia to Lee Sawyer 10-6-1881 (10-7-1881) L
Brim, Eliza J. to R. Eison 8-2-1876 (8-3-1876) L
Brim, Elizabeth to J. D. Robison 2-16-1854 L
Brim, Ida to Henry Sawyer 12-23-1872 (12-26-1872) L
Brim, Louisa to Jeff Young 2-3-1881 L B
Brim, Mary Jane to Henry E. Hogan 6-25-1870 (6-26-1870) L
Brim, Rebecca L. to William A. Thomas 6-4-1867 (6-6-1867) L
Brim, Sallie to Wesley Puryear 4-16-1885 (4-18-1885) L

Brimage, Sarah J. to Joshua D. Clark 7-3-1871 (7-6-1871) Cr
Brimingham, M. S. to Rufus King 12-3-1874 Dy
Brimingham, Malvina to William D. Carnetzer 12-29-1859 Ma
Brimingham, Mary E. to Joel Walker 10-3-1853 (10-4-1853) Ma
Brimingham, Susan A. to Wm. S. Vick 11-16-1864 Dy
Brimley, Margaret A. to Isaac T. Winford 6-9-1870 (6-12-1870) T
Brimm, Fluviana to Billy Pitts 12-11-1878 L
Brimm, Margaret Ann to A. B. Lunsford 1-12-1863 (no return) L
Brimm, Margaret Ann to William J. Anthony 8-8-1859 (no return) L
Brimm, Martha to Henry Roberson 7-12-1866 (no return) Hy
Brimm, Nancy to H. T. Pitts 3-5-1877 (3-6-1877) L
Brinder, Alice to George Conner 5-8-1869 Cr
Bringle, Catharine to Alexander Wood 6-4-1846 T
Bringle, Crarisa C. to Barzilla C. McBride 2-3-1853 T
Bringle, Margaret to John Smith 1-1-1873 (1-2-1873) T
Bringle, N. J. to A. Homan 12-11-1869 (12-12-1869) T
Brinkey, Nancy to Willingham Cooper 6-18-1839 (6-20-1839) F
Brinkley, Alcy Brener Eliz. to Robert F. Hall 1-21-1868 Be
Brinkley, Angeline to Guilford W. Payne 3-26-1846 Hn
Brinkley, C. D. to Charles F. Newton 9-5-1872 (9-8-1872) T
Brinkley, Elizabeth to D. M. Ballard 1-6-1868 (1-8-1868) T
Brinkley, Elizabeth to E. S. Hampton 5-13-1852 Cr
Brinkley, Fannie to James Hampton 12-29-1842 Cr
Brinkley, Frances to George Doty 7-3-1841 (no return) F
Brinkley, Huldy to Charles Chamberlin 12-27-1841 Ma
Brinkley, Huldy to William Phillips 4-16-1842 (4-17-1842) Ma
Brinkley, Jane R. to L. D. Keywood 3-7-1855 (no return) F
Brinkley, Kitty to Fed Wilson 9-3-1870 (9-4-1870) F B
Brinkley, Lucy J. to John Matheny 12-21-1862 We
Brinkley, Martha to William Williams 5-1-1863 (5-13-1863) Sh
Brinkley, Mary Ann to P. G. Cox 11-13-1839 Ma
Brinkley, Mary to John B. Phillips 5-27-1860 Sh
Brinkley, Melvina to Alexander Johnson 7-14-1846 We
Brinkley, Nancy to S. H. Hollowell 1-8-1866 (no return) Cr
Brinkley, R. T. to J. G. Bailey 2-23-1878 (2-26-1878) Dy
Brinkley, Sarah to Jeremiah Brinkley 1-27-1849 (2-1-1849) F
Brinkley, Winnie to Seth H. Chambless 12-31-1840 Cr
Brinkly, Elizabeth to Mark Parrish 6-27-1866 (no return) Cr
Brinkly, Margaret to J. A. Brinkley 9-22-1866 (9-23-1866) Dy
Brinkly, Mary J. to A. E. Rogers 10-9-1865 (no return) Cr
Brinkly, Susan to James Sutton 10-18-1844 (10-19-1844) F
Brinkly, Winfred to Jones? R. Haywood 1-19-1861 (1-27-1861) Cr
Brinley, Harriett A.? to Wm. R. Hall 1-19-1861 (1-24-1861) Cr
Brint, Narcissa Jane to John W. Brown 12-13-1853 (12-15-1853) Hr
Briscoe, Mary Ann to John W. Martin 9-5-1864 Sh
Brisendine, E. W. to E. P. Paschall 12-29-1864 Hn
Brisendine, Sarah A. to James B. Mathis 9-15-1850 Hn
Brisolari, Mary to James O'Connor 10-5-1861 G
Brissalara, Louisa to Dominie Bringadello 2-7-1858 Sh
Brissolary, Mary to John Carroll 5-2-1852 Sh
Brister, Lutisha to J. W. Conner 2-1-1847 (2-2-1847) F
Bristoe, Sarah A. to Thomas J. Smith 10-13-1858 Hn
Brit, Sarrah Ann to Benton Witherington 10-13-1865 G
Britenham, Hannah M. to P. P. Patterson 7-30-1839 G
Briton, Frances to Thomas Britton 4-1-1850 Ma
Britt, Adaline L. to John Mason 12-9-1843 (12-?-1843) T
Britt, Amanda to Nelson Cuningham 1-7-1873 (no return) Cr B
Britt, Gracy to John Mabrey 4-13-1849 Cr
Britt, Helen to George Harris 9-26-1872 Cr B
Britt, Julia A. to T. R. Lounder 10-3-1854 Cr
Britt, L. J. to Jas. E. Dunn 12-11-1872 Hy
Britt, M. C. to H. J. Redden 7-24-1872 (no return) Cr
Britt, M. C. to P. M. Williams 8-25-1858 (9-1-1858) Sh
Britt, M. L. to J. R. McAdoo 12-22-1868 (12-23-1868) Cr
Britt, Mattie to John C. Etheridge 12-3-1873 (no return) Hy
Britt, Sophia H. to Wm. Johnson 11-18-1857 Cr
Britt, Winiford to Alford B. Thomerson 1-3-1841 We
Brittenhaus, Sarah A. to William E. Dyer 4-12-1853 Sh
Britton, Bertha H. to Fredrick Anderson 2-23-1846 (2-26-1846) Ma
Britton, Harriet to Samuel H. Kelton 9-27-1866 G
Britton, M. E. to John J. McKing 1-27-1866 (2-1-1866) Cr
Britton, Nancy P. to Daniel W. Bunten 5-12-1860 (5-?-1860) Ma
Brizalaro, Mary to Vincent Bacigalupo 4-22-1852 (4-25-1852) Sh
Brizandine, Nancy A. to Thomas Mathis 9-5-1852 Hn
Brizendine, Charlotte to Calvin B. Rodery? 2-2-1848 Hn
Brizendine, Eliza Jane to W. H. Mathis 10-25-1866 Hn
Brizendine, Julia A. to Chas.B. Matheney 9-11-1864 Hn
Brizendine, Martha J. to William T. Mathis 8-10-1856 Hn
Brizendine, Pamela Ann to James M. Mathis 10-11-1857 Hn
Brizendine, Tabitha to Cullen M. Duffin 3-19-1840 Hn
Broach, L. J. to W. H. Carter 12-4-1872 Cr
Broach, Sarah Ann to William M. Winsett 1-2-1861 Hn
Broaden, Dice to Hiram House 7-10-1867 (no return) Hy
Broadnax, Annie to William R. Hulbert 7-29-1864 Sh
Broadnax, Frances to Berry Ware 11-27-1878 Hy
Broadnax, Henrietta to Bevly Maclin 2-20-1869 (2-23-1869) F B
Broadnax, Martha to Martin Broadnax 10-16-1869 F B

Broadnax, Susan to Neverson Hacklin 12-26-1867 F B
Broadwaters, Lucinda H. to William Sprouce 12-9-1839 (12-10-1839) F
Broadway, Elizabeth to R. C. James 6-17-1857 We
Broche, Sarah Jane to K.? H. Arendale 3-26-1864 Sh
Brock, Ann to Council M. Peacock 1-14-1857 (1-15-1857) O
Brock, Caroline to Thomas Kirk 9-26-1861 O
Brock, Elizabeth to Lawrence Stephens 12-8-1840 (12-13-1840) Hr
Brock, Josephine to Logan Hopkins 11-16-1857 Ma
Brock, Lizzie to C. H. Fox 1-13-1875 Hy
Brock, Mollie A. to J. F. Armstrong 3-14-1867 (3-19-1867) Dy
Brock, Sallie P. to Jas. P. Love 12-19-1868 (1-13-1869) F
Brock, Sarah to Andrew J. Hays 9-11-1841 (10-12-1841) Hr
Brockmann, Louisa to John Geo. Stubenrauck 4-22-1854 (4-23-1854) Sh
Brockwell, Elizabeth to George W. Flagg 7-5-1858 (no return) Hn
Brockwell, Jane to William Glover 12-28-1852 Hn
Brockwell, Margaret E. to James J. Derrington 1-8-1860 Hn
Brockwell, Martha A. to Wm. Brockwell 6-2-1865 O
Brockwell, Mary A. to Granville Underwood 10-21-1867 O
Brockwell, Mary to Wm. W. Lynch 9-20-1877 O
Broddie, Dona to Pink Williams 1-7-1874 (1-8-1874) L B
Brodenax, Lucindy to Mitchell Ware 1-6-1875 Hy
Brodie (Brodice), Margaret to William Cotter (Cotton?) 8-20-1850 Sh
Brodie, Margaret to Patrick Tamplin 6-9-1849 Sh
Brodie, Mary to Henry Smith 6-24-1871 (no return) L
Brodnax, Amelia to Scipio Field 9-6-1872 (no return) Hy
Brodnax, Florence to J. N. Maclin 5-24-1869 (5-30-1869) F
Brodnax, Mary J. to J. W. Maclin 6-17-1861 (6-19-1861) F
Brodnax, Sally to Benj. Thomas 2-2-1867 (no return) F B
Brodway, Phebe Ann to Alex Malone 10-13-1865 T
Broeg, Mary to August Berdon 9-1-1859 (9-6-1859) Sh
Brogany?, Henena R. to Jno. Joseph Joeggy 2-3-1845 Sh
Brogden, Armitty to Washington McFarlin 1-8-1858 (6-23-1858) Ma
Brogden, D. A. (Mrs.) to John Cotton 12-29-1863 (12-31-1863) Dy
Brogden, Mary A. F. to Benjamin Hoofman 4-26-1843 Hn
Brogden, Mary Ellen to John R. Bazen 5-30-1859 (6-2-1859) L
Brogden, Mary Jane to William O. Taylor 12-21-1868 G
Brogden, Mary to Clement Pierce 12-30-1852 Hn
Brogden, Polley Ann to Bennet Gooch 8-5-1841 G
Brogden, Rebeca to Absalom Karnes 11-15-1869 G
Brogden, Rody (Mrs.) to James Harden 2-28-1872 (2-29-1872) L
Brogden, Aminisa M. to Lewis L. Reynolds 7-28-1858 (7-29-1858) G
Brogdon, Ann M. to A. J. Brogdon 6-1-1853 Hn
Brogdon, Ann to James C. Patterson 3-10-1859 Hn
Brogdon, Annitta to David C. Glimp 1-11-1858 (1-12-1858) G
Brogdon, Calpernia to Reuben D. Roberts 1-20-1855 Hn
Brogdon, Delia to Hugh S. Rodgers 1-1-1839 Hn
Brogdon, Delina C. to Josiah Owen? 7-15-1858 (no return) Hn
Brogdon, Edy to John R. Price 10-5-1857 G
Brogdon, Elizabeth to Young M. Dehanan 7-21-1849 (no return) Cr
Brogdon, L. E. to T. W. Glimp 10-9-1882 (10-12-1882) L
Brogdon, M. A. C. to W. H. Reynolds 9-28-1847 Hn
Brogdon, Margaret to Thomas A. Williams 9-25-1860 Hn
Brogdon, Martha J. to Jesse Hicks 2-24-1862 Hn
Brogdon, Mary A. to J. B. Kilzier (Rilzier?) 2-8-1871 (no return) L
Brogdon, Mary V. to C. S. Hooper 3-17-1874 (3-19-1874) L
Brogdon, Mary to James Baldridge 9-15-1857 Cr
Brogdon, Sarah Isabell to M. M. Mathis 1-18-1863 Hn
Brogdon, Sophronia to Benjamin F. Lamb 4-23-1853 Hn
Broger, Mary to C. M. Gardner 2-21-1851 (no return) Cr
Brogg, Catharine to Woodford Bandy 3-7-1859 (no return) We
Broggton, Nancy to F. M. Alley 1-5-1867 Cr
Broiles, Mary to Ethan A. Murphy 2-25-1828 (4-5-1828) Hr
Broils, Laura to Wesley Stray 2-27-1868 G B
Brom, Narcissa to W. N. Burch 2-7-1861 Be
Bromley, Ella to Sampson Bowls 8-28-1877 (no return) Hy
Bromley, Lidia E. to Wm. H. Garrett 9-23-1849 Be
Bromly, Frances M. to Wm. A. Perry 11-25-1852 Sh
Bromly, Sarah Ann to Warren J. Boothe 12-9-1853 Sh
Bromly, Susan J. to Thomas J. W. Dilliard 12-19-1866 F
Bronaugh, Anna L. to John S. Pondexter 2-3-1852 (2-4-1852) Sh
Broncell?, Charity to John Dallas 12-23-1873 L B
Bronn (Brown?), Sarah C. to H. C. McCauley 12-22-1874 L
Bronson, Mary F. to Neil McNair 2-16-1860 (2-22-1860) Sh
Brontly, Ella to Z. C. Nolen 8-17-1859 (no return) Hy
Brook, Marcindy to Henry Luster 3-12-1867 (3-15-1867) F B
Brook, Sarah to Andrew J. Byner 9-1-1841 Ma
Brooke, Jennie to Geo. R. Scott 1-4-1870 (1-6-1870) F
Brookens, Georganna to W. M. Wilson 7-11-1876 Hy
Brooker, Caroline to David Burkle 11-24-1860 (11-28-1860) Sh
Brookins, Martha A. to Robert L. Gill 3-2-1876 (no return) Hy
Brooks(Polk?), Betsy to Isaac Jackson 10-22-1828 (10-29-1828) Hr
Brooks, Addie V. to James H. Long 1-22-1867 Ma
Brooks, Amanda C. to Abner Leach 12-10-1850 Cr
Brooks, Amelia E. to William Rodgers 6-26-1849 Sh
Brooks, Ann C. to Joseph H. Borum 2-9-1841 T
Brooks, Beedy to Thomas Allison 1-31-1869 Hy
Brooks, C. E. to Augustus A. Templeton 12-3-1872 (12-5-1872) T

Brooks, Catharine J. to A. C. Foster 12-23-1844 We
Brooks, Catherine E. to James L. Robinson 3-4-1859 Ma
Brooks, Cherry to Travis Oldham 12-15-1866 (no return) Dy
Brooks, Cynthia to Isaac D. Cummins (Currin) 12-22-1848 Sh
Brooks, Dora to Benj. Fowlkes 4-1-1870 (4-3-1870) T
Brooks, E. M. to D. F. Talley 2-8-1871 Ma
Brooks, E. R. to John Hutcheson 2-16-1839 Hn
Brooks, Eliza T. to Wm. O'Daniel 12-23-1846 (no return) F
Brooks, Eliza to John H. Gregory 11-3-1846 (11-6-1846) Ma
Brooks, Elizabeth A. to G. H. Davis 1-4-1854 (no return) F
Brooks, Elizabeth to Jessee Whitford 5-5-1838 (5-6-1838) Hr
Brooks, Elizabeth to Robert Philips 12-23-1842 Hn
Brooks, Ellen F. to J. C. Holst 6-27-1855 (7-2-1855) Sh
Brooks, Elvira to William Cooper 10-18-1838 Hn
Brooks, Ema to William Bell 11-19-1865 G
Brooks, Eugenia A. to James M. Muse 11-13-1868 Ma
Brooks, Fannie to William Brooks 11-13-1866 Ma
Brooks, Hanah to Nepoleon Jones 11-30-1872 (no return) Hy
Brooks, Incinda to Andrew Job 2-27-1830 Ma
Brooks, Isabella to William J. Rose 12-16-1867 Ma
Brooks, Isadora to Thos. W. Lamar 5-8-1867 G
Brooks, Jane to John C. Algee 10-5-1852 Cr
Brooks, Jane to John Wyman 12-2-1844 Sh
Brooks, Jane to William Wagoner 7-20-1865 Mn
Brooks, Jinny to Henderson Allen 12-26-1866 G
Brooks, Josephine to H. W. Hall 10-2-1860 We
Brooks, Kizzie to Andrew Fonville 1-23-1872 (no return) L
Brooks, L.(S?) A. E. to J. A. Watson 3-23-1852 (3-24-1852) Sh
Brooks, Lavanda to James Murdaugh 6-2-1859 Hr
Brooks, Lila to David Dawson 12-3-1870 F B
Brooks, Lizzie H. to George K. Brooks 11-13-1866 Ma
Brooks, Lizzy to Andrew Hamons 12-30-1873 Hy
Brooks, Louisa to Isaac Payne 1-26-1867 (2-2-1867) T
Brooks, Louisa to John Morse 11-17-1852 Ma
Brooks, Louisa to Robert Smith 1-6-1868 T
Brooks, Louisa to William Brown 7-23-1867 T
Brooks, Lucy N. to Alvis Boothe 4-18-1854 (no return) Hn
Brooks, Lucy T. to H. M. Stringfellow 5-30-1860 (5-31-1860) Sh
Brooks, Lucy W. to B. W. Wheatley 12-10-1856 Be CC
Brooks, Lucy W. to B. W. Wheatly 12-10-1856 Be
Brooks, Lucy Wade to George I. Bibb 1-28-1847 Sh
Brooks, Lucy to Stephen Belan 10-5-1870 F B
Brooks, M. A. (Mrs.) to D. H. Harper 5-14-1864 Sh
Brooks, M. A. E. to W. R. Smith 1-17-1870 Hy
Brooks, Maggie to Nelson Shaw 2-21-1880 (2-22-1880) L B
Brooks, Malinda to Pleasant Rhodes 2-17-1852 (2-19-1852) Hr
Brooks, Malissa to George McDowell 9-26-1868 (9-27-1868) F B
Brooks, Manerva A. to William P. Taylor 1-6-1851 (1-7-1851) F
Brooks, Margaret (Miss) to Thornton F. Anderson 6-15-1853 Sh
Brooks, Margaret to Joseph H. Stewart 2-23-1860 We
Brooks, Margarett to Jacob L. Thompson 5-14-1841 Sh
Brooks, Martha Jane to Richard Thomas Elmore 12-9-1841 T
Brooks, Mary A. (Mrs.) to Lewis Norwood 7-20-1860 (7-22-1860) Cr
Brooks, Mary A. E. to John Kennedy 3-19-1867 G
Brooks, Mary C. to Matthew Brown 9-7-1849 Sh
Brooks, Mary C. to J. M. Singh? 12-13-1852 Hn
Brooks, Mary E. to J. R. Parker 5-13-1863 (no return) We
Brooks, Mary F. to Eli Bynum 9-13-1863 Hn
Brooks, Mary J. to Ephram G. Lewis 3-8-1863 We
Brooks, Mary L. to Richard Vaughn 10-9-1838 Hn
Brooks, Mary to Felix Walker 7-1-1866 Hy
Brooks, Mary to William Maxwell 7-15-1839 Hn
Brooks, Mary to Wm. Peck 2-6-1849 Sh
Brooks, Mollie to Lewis Connor 12-13-1872 (4-24-1873) T
Brooks, Molly T. to John H. Williamson 8-10-1857 Sh
Brooks, Nancy C. to James B. Caperton 10-15-1844 (no return) F
Brooks, Nancy C. to James F. Smith 9-4-1851 Hn
Brooks, Nancy M. to Isaac Nichols 8-20-1854 Be
Brooks, Nancy to Allen Williams 2-3-1847 Cr
Brooks, Nannie J. to James M. Hays 11-9-1868 (11-12-1868) Ma
Brooks, Narcissa L. to William Crain 1-26-1837 Sh
Brooks, Rachel to Smith Leach 12-14-1842 Cr
Brooks, Rachel to William Nellums(Nelms) 8-1-1840 (8-4-1840) Hr
Brooks, Sallie F. to G. B. Lipscomb 11-10-1856 Sh
Brooks, Sallie to Ben Adams 3-28-1872 Hy
Brooks, Sarah C. to John A. Riggin 11-2-1871 Hy
Brooks, Sarah J. to Jno. Moss 10-13-1857 (10-14-1857) Hr
Brooks, Sarah to David Whitford 9-26-1837 Hr
Brooks, Sarah to J. T. B. Andrews 11-1-1848 Sh
Brooks, Sarah to Miles W. Goolsby 6-6-1834 Sh
Brooks, Sarah to Wesly Blackburn 12-29-1846 (12-31-1846) Ma
Brooks, Susanah J. to Alexander Davis 11-26-1856 Sh
Brooks, Tabithy to W. A. Moody 6-27-1869 G
Brooks, Temperance to Alphus P. Moore 12-24-1841 (12-30-1841) Ma
Brooks, Virginia A. to Allen Parham 6-21-1858 We
Brooks, Willie to William Bains 3-6-1873 Hy
Brooksher, Ann E. to Saml. A. Moore 4-11-1855 Sh

Brookshire, Catharine M. to Jacob B. Chism 11-23-1837 Sh
Brookshire, E. to Thomas Cubbins 3-13-1848 Sh
Brookshire, Elizabeth A. to John D. Henning 12-12-1859 Ma
Brookshire, Emily L. to Ignatius Gruff (Graff) 12-14-1848 Sh
Broom, Ann Eliza to Geo. T. Hunter 11-2-1846 (11-5-1846) F
Broom, Clara to Beverly Lacy 12-28-1868 F B
Broom, Eliza to John T. Herron 3-22-1838 F
Broom, Frances to J. Lenow 1-7-1845 (1-9-1845) F
Broom, Jane to Wm. A. Verser 10-1-1841 F
Broom, Lucinda to John Walker 1-4-1868 (no return) F B
Broom, Martha to James W. Beasley 10-1-1847 (10-2-1847) F
Broom, Mary Jane to James W. Hamlet 5-8-1840 (5-14-1840) F
Brooten, Mary to Hosey Holcomb 9-4-1841 G
Brooton, Charlott to James McCollum 2-11-1840 G
Brothers, Nancy C. to William Simpson 3-16-1835 Sh
Brotherton, Margaret to John F. Duncan 10-20-1828 Hr
Brotherton, Sarah E. to Richard Johnson 7-1-1868 (7-19-1868) Dy
Brotherton, Susan to Thomas L. Duncan 6-11-1829 (6-21-1829) Hr
Broughton, Amanda to Edward Stelle 9-3-1883 (no return) L
Broun, Bridget to Samuel A. Harlen 4-22-1863 Sh
Browder, Elizabeth W. to Joseph P. Franklin 1-24-1865 Mn
Browder, Josephine to James McMack 4-27-1858 Be
Browder, Martha F. to Arthur Harris 10-26-1862 Mn
Browder, Martha to David Redding 11-24-1861 Mn
Browder, R. A. to H. C. Hamilton 10-2-1863 (10-4-1863) O
Browder, Susan to Amos Ventress 12-29-1870 (12-31-1870) O B
Browder, Uphrasia America Fr. to Aron W. Williams 12-17-1855 (12-20-1855) Ma
Brower, Mary Jane to William R. Wadley 10-15-1862 (10-19-1862) Ma
Brown, A. A. to F. T. Rooks 1-10-1872 (1-11-1872) Dy
Brown, A. M. to E. G. Cowell 10-2-1866 Be
Brown, A. M. to R. H. Norvell 4-13-1875 Hy
Brown, Abigail J. to Julon Nail 11-13-1842 O
Brown, Adelaide F. to J. R. Boswell 3-28-1861 (3-29-1861) Sh
Brown, Adeline to Leonard Lewis 7-23-1869 (7-24-1869) F B
Brown, Alcinia Catherine to Reuben Braden 1-20-1853 L
Brown, Alderana Jane to Richard Ray 5-22-1848 Sh
Brown, Alice to Charles Hilams? 3-23-1870 Hy
Brown, Alice to York Outlaw 12-20-1873 Hy
Brown, Amanda to A. J. Epley 1-6-1868 G
Brown, Amanda to Shadrich Hail 8-2-1837 (8-3-1837) Hr
Brown, Amanda to W. C. Gannon 12-6-1871 (12-7-1871) Dy
Brown, Amazon to Z. F. Childress 6-14-1856 (6-15-1856) L
Brown, Amelia Ann to John F. Walker 3-20-1855 (3-21-1855) Ma
Brown, Amerca J. to W. H. Bowers 10-2-1865 (10-3-1865) T
Brown, Amy to Tom Mahan 12-13-1873 Hy
Brown, Ann (Mrs.) to J. D. Stamps 2-15-1860 Sh
Brown, Ann Adeline to James High 9-8-1838 (9-10-1838) Hr
Brown, Ann M. to Jno. Cowan 11-2-1853 (11-3-1853) Hr
Brown, Ann to Geo. A. Lashlee 4-14-1853 Be
Brown, Ann to John Talty 5-24-1861 Sh
Brown, Ann to Jordan Jackson 1-21-1843 G
Brown, Ann to Joseph S. Graves 3-29-1852 G
Brown, Ann to Mat Reiley 1-6-1852 Sh
Brown, Ann to Silas Evans 2-10-1869 (2-11-1869) O
Brown, Anna to W. Swift 6-21-1868 G
Brown, Anne to Henry Olive 12-19-1874 (12-20-1874) T
Brown, Annie to M. Miller 11-9-1885 (11-10-1885) L
Brown, Aquilla Ann to William B. Mason 8-4-1841 Ma
Brown, Armenta to John Leach 4-8-1855 (4-14-1855) T
Brown, Aseny (Ammy) to David Huffman 8-23-1836 Sh
Brown, B. A. to Wm. F. Shelby 6-20-1865 O
Brown, Barbara to Hardy Mashburn 1-9-1836 (1-10-1836) Hr
Brown, Betsie (Mrs.) to Charles Eans (Evans) 1-18-1860 Sh
Brown, Betsy to Thos. J. Hall 1-21-1857 Cr
Brown, Bettie to Saml. Perkins 11-14-1878 Hy
Brown, Bridget to Daniel Duffy 11-10-1863 Sh
Brown, Candis to Wesley R. Gossett 7-22-1846 (7-23-1846) G
Brown, Caroline E. to B. W. Odom 12-26-1856 We
Brown, Caroline V. to George R. Hellard 6-1-1857 (6-2-1857) Ma
Brown, Caroline to John Stafford 7-10-1861 We
Brown, Caroline to Nelson Willie 1-7-1872 (1-9-1872) T
Brown, Catharine F. to L. C. Key 10-5-1865 O
Brown, Catharine to Amanuel Harris 12-10-1873 (12-11-1873) T
Brown, Catharine to James Wilman 10-22-1855 Sh
Brown, Catherine to Fre. Phillman Fisher 4-28-1863 Sh
Brown, Catherine to Isham Tuck 11-8-1844 We
Brown, Charlotte to William Murphy 11-13-1843 (11-15-1843) Hr
Brown, Christiana to John Graham 3-9-1847 (3-11-1847) O
Brown, Clara to Landon Harrison 12-12-1868 F
Brown, Clementine Josephine to J. M. Wrinkle 5-30-1865 Hn
Brown, Corella to George Fitzgerald 7-26-1880 (no return) Dy
Brown, Cornelia to R. A. Whitmore 6-30-1851 Hr
Brown, Demaris E. to A. B. McGinnis 10-11-1851 (10-12-1851) Sh
Brown, Dina to Peter Thomas 10-1-1874 (10-3-1874) T
Brown, Dony to Jacob Bradford 12-24-1868 Hy
Brown, Duicy (Drucy?) to Josiah Hast 8-24-1850 L

Brown, E. A. to J. G. Tatum 1-11-1866 (1-14-1866) F
Brown, Eady to James Webb 3-23-1874 Hy
Brown, Eda A. to Starky S. Hare 2-14-1859 (2-22-1859) F
Brown, Edny to V. Hopson 1-30-1860 (no return) L
Brown, Eleander to Curtis Winfield 12-16-1848 F
Brown, Eleanor C. to Geo. W. Martin 12-11-1849 F
Brown, Eliza J. to Alex. Field 10-15-1842 (no return) F
Brown, Eliza S. to John S. Watkins 4-7-1868 Ma
Brown, Eliza S. to William Laurence 11-22-1821 Sh
Brown, Eliza to Enoch Beale 2-22-1868 F B
Brown, Elizabeth A. V. to David Newell 11-4-1861 Sh
Brown, Elizabeth A. to George M. Turner 1-3-1843 Hn
Brown, Elizabeth A. to George W. Walton 12-25-1867 (12-29-1867) T
Brown, Elizabeth A. to Robert T. Rodgers 1-31-1856 Cr
Brown, Elizabeth C. to James O. Fleming 2-3-1851 (2-4-1851) Hr
Brown, Elizabeth C. to Nathan Moore 9-4-1848 Ma
Brown, Elizabeth F. to John Campbell 2-19-1856 (2-22-1856) O
Brown, Elizabeth Jane to Asa? Lenek? 2-19-1853 T
Brown, Elizabeth M. to James M. Key 9-4-1854 (9-12-1854) Sh
Brown, Elizabeth N. to William S. Calloway 1-22-1840 Ma
Brown, Elizabeth to A. J. Hughey 11-20-1849 Hn
Brown, Elizabeth to Abraham White no date (with Dec 1856) F
Brown, Elizabeth to Casper Schmidt 9-10-1862 We
Brown, Elizabeth to Ephram Thompson 12-4-1838 G
Brown, Elizabeth to J. T. Owen 10-10-1856 We
Brown, Elizabeth to John Shultz 12-29-1843 We
Brown, Elizabeth to John Thomas 8-8-1851 Be
Brown, Elizabeth to L. D. Moore 9-13-1867 (9-15-1867) Dy
Brown, Elizabeth to M. J. M. White 10-3-1862 (not solemn.) O
Brown, Elizabeth to Martin V. Brooks 7-29-1856 Hr
Brown, Elizabeth to Michael Price 8-17-1837 Hr
Brown, Elizabeth to Rufus R. Howell 11-19-1850 (11-24-1850) Hr
Brown, Elizabeth to Shadrack Black 9-30-1854 (10-1-1854) L
Brown, Elizabeth to Tyos Koffod 12-5-1860 Sh
Brown, Ella to George Harvey 9-22-1877 (9-28-1877) L
Brown, Ella to William Lewis 8-28-1869 (8-29-1869) F B
Brown, Ellen J. to Jessee Meacham 1-7-1861 Hy
Brown, Ellen to Jacob Bell 12-28-1867 (12-13?-1868) F B
Brown, Elmira to Charley Lowry 9-29-1876 (10-1-1876) L
Brown, Elmyra to Miles McPherson 10-11-1882 (10-29-1882) L
Brown, Emeline Z. to Thomas Rose 9-8-1856 (9-11-1856) Hr
Brown, Emily Matilda to Asa Leach 11-28-1854 T
Brown, Emily to Marcus L. Bevill 10-4-1860 Ma
Brown, Emma M. to James M. Torrence 4-26-1870 Dy
Brown, Emma to Farris Pearson 12-6-1877 (no return) Hy
Brown, Emma to Lewis Bowers 12-27-1869 (12-23?-1869) F B
Brown, Emma to Louis Rogers 12-7-1869 (no return) F B
Brown, Emma to N. K. Stevenson 1-1-1863 Dy
Brown, Evaline to William Vincent 9-26-1866 (9-27-1866) Ma
Brown, Evelina to Jonothan Jones 7-15-1825 Hr
Brown, Eveline F. to James Mobley 1-15-1856 G
Brown, Fannie C. to Ira T. Beasley 10-14-1868 (10-15-1868) L
Brown, Frances to J. R. Mitchell 2-11-1866 Hn
Brown, Frances to Napoleon Stanney 2-1-1871 (2-4-1871) F B
Brown, Frances to Wm. H. Manus (Meincus) 7-18-1843 Sh
Brown, Gilly to Isaac Pratt 10-31-1867 G B
Brown, Halma A. to Martin Thorn 11-23-1845 (11-28-1845) Ma
Brown, Hannah to John A. McFall 8-9-1828 (8-10-1828) Hr
Brown, Hannah to Patrick Spellman 10-3-1863 Sh
Brown, Harriet to George R. Carter 2-2-1863 (no return) Hy
Brown, Harriet to Perry Haneline 5-5-1841 Hn
Brown, Hattie to Charley Allen 10-21-1880 L B
Brown, Hellen T. to T. W. Steart 10-18-1871 (no return) Dy
Brown, Henrietta to Grandison Rives 12-25-1867 (12-26-1867) F B
Brown, Hester to John McNeely 1-17-1843 Hr
Brown, Ione S. to J. A. Signiago 10-23-1863 (10-25-1863) Sh
Brown, Irene to James B. Cozart 9-5-1871 Ma
Brown, Isabeler to J. W. Sanders 1-18-1866 O
Brown, Issabella J. to John W. Rawls 11-21-1842 O
Brown, J. H. P to J. S. Dawson 11-20-1850 Hn
Brown, J. L. to John D. Hunter 5-30-1870 (no return) F
Brown, Jane W. to William G. Ward 12-5-1849 (12-6-1849) G
Brown, Jane to A. J. Langham 2-7-1842 (no return) F
Brown, Jane to Andrew J. Titus 7-27-1836 Sh
Brown, Jane to Fredrick Prehit 1-18-1867 T
Brown, Jane to James Williams 11-18-1835 Sh
Brown, Jane to John Byrum 5-9-1867 L
Brown, Jane to Lewis Duncan 1-4-1853 Ma
Brown, Jane to William Finley 4-23-1870 (no return) F B
Brown, Jane to Wm. Hooker 1-3-1849 (no return) F
Brown, Jennie to Robt. Hooper 5-28-1872 Hy
Brown, Josephine to J. G. Dorris 2-3-1853 Be
Brown, Julia Ann to Alfred Moore 12-30-1847 Cr
Brown, Julia Ann to Anderson Kirk 8-20-1853 (8-25-1853) O
Brown, Julia Ann to John Tyler Anderson 10-9-1860 Ma
Brown, Julia C. to James C. Canady 3-2-1863 G
Brown, Julia to Martin B. Holbrook 9-9-1858 Sh

Brown, Julie A. to J. D. Brown 1-17-1866 Cr
Brown, Kate to Jerry Evans 12-31-1885 L
Brown, Keziah to Kemp Stallions 5-23-1829 (5-24-1829) Hr
Brown, Kezziah to Mathew T. Buffalo 5-13-1839 (5-15-1839) Hr
Brown, L. A. to Edmond M. Goza 2-11-1864 G
Brown, L. D. to W. C. Williams 5-16-1857 (5-22-1857) Sh
Brown, L. J. to J. H. Granberry 4-9-1866 (4-11-1866) F
Brown, L. M. to Irvin L. Turner 1-28-1874 L
Brown, L. P. to L. Haislip 10-14-1867 (10-15-1867) O
Brown, L. T. to James S. Neely 11-29-1871 (11-30-1871) Dy
Brown, L. to A. Lashlee 9-20-1866 G
Brown, Laura to R. M. Hawley 1-14-1869 Be
Brown, Lizzie to J. A. Brown 12-29-1881 L
Brown, Lizzie to Zack Shaw 12-25-1866 (12-27-1866) F B
Brown, Louisa to J. D. Erwin 6-29-1863 Mn
Brown, Louisa to William Miller 10-31-1837 Sh
Brown, Luan to Alexander C. McRae 1-1-1868 Be
Brown, Lucinda A. to Henry C. Jones 10-27-1869 (10-28-1869) Ma
Brown, Lucinda M. to Joseph J. Rawlings 3-10-1840 Sh
Brown, Lucinda P. to G. W. L. Marr 8-5-1841 (8-8-1841) O
Brown, Lucy to Thos. H. Moore 2-4-1839 (2-5-1839) Hr
Brown, Lula to Promise Glass 12-30-1885 L
Brown, Lurinda B. to James A. Hart 5-27-1856 Sh
Brown, Lyda to George Kinnard 2-25-1840 (2-26-1840) Hr
Brown, Lydia Ann to William Hamlin 7-10-1847 (7-18-1847) Hr
Brown, Lydia to Albert Cook 3-2-1852 We
Brown, M. A. (Mrs.) to A. J. Thomas 5-3-1868 G
Brown, M. H. to Rufus Mobley 2-24-1867 G
Brown, M. J. to C. F. Brown 6-14-1875 (6-17-1875) Dy
Brown, M. M. to W. G. Newbill 11-30-1872 (no return) Cr
Brown, M. W. to F. A. Campbell 8-9-1869 (no return) Hy
Brown, Mahala to David Walton 12-28-1870 (12-29-1870) F B
Brown, Mahala to James Allen 1-23-1849 Cr
Brown, Mahaly to Moredack Scaggs 7-15-1830 Sh
Brown, Malinda A. to George Foust 1-15-1842 Hn
Brown, Malinda C. to John P. F. Prewitt 9-20-1843 Hr
Brown, Malinda to Nat Vaughan 12-10-1868 (no return) F B
Brown, Malinda to Paul Cash 4-26-1870 (4-30-1870) F B
Brown, Malissa to Washington Alston 7-8-1873 T
Brown, Marcilla C. to Braddock Foster 2-11-1860 (2-14-1860) Hr
Brown, Marey B. to Horace Head no date (with Oct 1837) O
Brown, Margaret A. to James M. Reavis 2-13-1862 Ma
Brown, Margaret C. to P. C. Hally 5-18-1853 (5-31-1853) Sh
Brown, Margaret L. to J. Marcum 1-12-1868 G
Brown, Margaret M. to Wm. B. Ewell 4-2-1855 Ma
Brown, Margaret T. to T. J. Melton 12-18-1865 Mn
Brown, Margaret to J. N. Beaty 7-26-1863 Mn
Brown, Margaret to Michael Murphey 10-10-1859 Sh
Brown, Margaret to Travis Webb 9-17-1839 Cr
Brown, Margaret to Young Fitch 11-25-1865 F B
Brown, Margarett M. to James M. Birdwell 4-6-1853 (no return) F
Brown, Mariah to John Patten 10-17-1874 T
Brown, Mariah? M. to Elijah M. Brown 1-4-1866 (1-7-1866) L
Brown, Marie to James H. Laurence 6-9-1824 Sh
Brown, Marinda M. to Josiah Bennett 9-2-1850 (9-17-1850) Hr
Brown, Martha A. to William Johnson 9-14-1850 (9-18-1850) G
Brown, Martha A. to William W. Hindes 3-28-1868 (4-16-1868) L
Brown, Martha Ann to David W. Chapman 8-16-1849 O
Brown, Martha Ann to James Braden 12-17-1855 (12-18-1855) L
Brown, Martha Ann to S. L. Childers 3-24-1866 Hy
Brown, Martha Ann to Thomas Leonard 4-13-1848 Sh
Brown, Martha C. to Jourdan W. McVay 11-16-1843 (no return) Hn
Brown, Martha D. to Nathan G. Caldwell 8-14-1849 (8-16-1849) L
Brown, Martha E. to W. M. McGaugh 8-11-1867 O
Brown, Martha E. to William T. Pierce 9-8-1859 Hn
Brown, Martha E. to Wm. A. Lea 6-14-1852 (no return) F
Brown, Martha J. to G. H. Haislip 1-22-1877 (1-24-1877) L
Brown, Martha J. to Jno. W. Buffaloe 11-30-1869 Hy
Brown, Martha J. to Sam P. Albritton 6-1-1861 (no return) Dy
Brown, Martha Jane to Thomas H. Garrett 10-29-1856 Ma
Brown, Martha L. to William D. Frost 9-13-1854 O
Brown, Martha Louisa to James Johnson 7-3-1880 (no return) L
Brown, Martha to Francis M. Parker 8-22-1862 We
Brown, Martha to Green Parks 11-26-1873 (11-27-1873) Dy
Brown, Martha to J. W. Powell 12-16-1858 Cr
Brown, Martha to John Cubbins 12-16-1845 Sh
Brown, Martha to W. H. Adams 2-12-1873 (2-13-1873) T
Brown, Martha to W. R. Cooper 5-7-1870 (no return) Hy
Brown, Martha to Wash Hardy 3-20-1870 Hy
Brown, Martha to William D. Roberts 12-7-1843 Hn
Brown, Martha to William J. Barnes 7-18-1862 (9-4-1866?) Cr
Brown, Mary A. to Belford Brown 12-30-1858 Cr
Brown, Mary A. to George W. Griffin 6-17-1856 Sh
Brown, Mary A. to Hiram L. Bennett 11-18-1866 Hn
Brown, Mary A. to J. C. Clements 2-8-1842 (no return) F
Brown, Mary A. to J. T. Garner 7-13-1856 Cr
Brown, Mary A. to Willie J. Welch 9-27-1866 Ma

Brown, Mary Ann to David Woods 4-4-1832 (4-5-1832) O
Brown, Mary Ann to George W. Tomson 12-16-1848 (12-23-1848) Hr
Brown, Mary Ann to James M. Ross 9-8-1831 O
Brown, Mary Ann to Wm. R. Duncan 8-29-1844 Sh
Brown, Mary Belle to Robert Cecil Hoggins 8-2-1866 Hn
Brown, Mary C. to William C. Reeves 11-17-1842 (11-22-1842) O
Brown, Mary E. to Jesse T. Gaines 7-7-1869 (7-28-1869) L
Brown, Mary E. to R. W. Pegram 9-10-1847 F
Brown, Mary E. to S. Y. Owen 1-21-1869 (1-23-1869) T
Brown, Mary E. to Thomas Brown 8-27-1872 Hy
Brown, Mary E. to W. B. T. Gooch 10-22-1864 Mn
Brown, Mary E. to William F. Sanders 8-30-1854 (no return) L
Brown, Mary E. to William P. Lacy 7-15-1867 (7-18-1867) Ma
Brown, Mary F. to John J. Matthewson 11-10-1846 Hn
Brown, Mary H. to Benjamin F. Foley 12-22-1853 Sh
Brown, Mary J. to Joseph Dickery? 2-15-1858 (2-16-1858) T
Brown, Mary J. to Zach T. (D.?) Denny 11-28-1865 G
Brown, Mary Jane to J. Stell 12-20-1864 Sh
Brown, Mary Jones to Morris Moore 8-29-1853 (9-7-1853) Sh
Brown, Mary M. to Madison Johnson 12-12-1866 (12-13-1866) O
Brown, Mary V. to J. B. Moore 10-23-1867 (10-24-1867) F
Brown, Mary W. to William G. Skiles 9-26-1848 (9-27-1848) G
Brown, Mary to A. M. V. Ledbetter 9-8-1867 G
Brown, Mary to Alfred Wilkins 6-15-1869 F B
Brown, Mary to Arch Turner 10-18-1873 Hy
Brown, Mary to Brooks Carter 11-30-1878 (12-1-1878) Dy
Brown, Mary to Cairo Brown 12-24-1873 (12-25-1873) O
Brown, Mary to Duke H. Harris 10-30-1824 Sh
Brown, Mary to Enoch Rollins 12-12-1838 (12-13-1838) Ma
Brown, Mary to J. G. Jenkins 12-19-1851 Cr
Brown, Mary to John Jones 3-16-1867 (3-17-1867) F B
Brown, Mary to M. T. Robinson 11-12-1852 Sh
Brown, Mary to Michael Looby 5-29-1852 (5-30-1852) Sh
Brown, Mary to Murt Donoho 1-7-1861 Sh
Brown, Mary to Nathan Berry Eskew(Askew?) 3-6-1849 Hr
Brown, Mary to Newton Neal 10-4-1858 Ma
Brown, Mary to Roderick A. McIntosh 6-3-1828 Ma
Brown, Mary to Saml. Boggs 1-5-1867 (1-6-1867) F
Brown, Mary to William Cannon 12-31-1866 T
Brown, Matilda to Absalem Lane 7-10-1837 (7-15-1837) Hr
Brown, Matilda to Thomas Reddick 3-16-1867 (3-18-1867) F B
Brown, Matilda to William Wright 6-10-1867 G
Brown, Mattie A. to J. R. McCracken 11-19-1866 (no return) Cr
Brown, Mattie to A. R. Robertson 3-8-1867 L
Brown, Mattie to W. T. Moore 5-23-1869 Hy
Brown, Meranda to Robert W. Braden 12-17-1860 (12-19-1860) L
Brown, Mima to Henry Reynolds 3-31-1871 (4-2-1871) Cr
Brown, Mima to Matthew T. Gibson 5-27-1870 (5-28-1870) F B
Brown, Minerva to Z. H. Manees 6-2-1853 Sh
Brown, Mollie E. to William Cook 9-9-1871 (9-12-1871) Dy
Brown, Mollie J. to J. M. Lea 9-26-1868 (no return) Hy
Brown, Mollie to George Sawyer 1-25-1869 (1-20?-1869) L
Brown, Molly to S. A. Jackson 4-12-1866 (5-13-1866) O
Brown, Mrs. to John Conness 9-8-1869 (9-9-1869) Dy
Brown, N. E. to A. Hamil 3-21-1877 (3-22-1877) L
Brown, N. S. to Charles N. Gavens 2-5-1863 Sh
Brown, N. S. to Chas. N. Ables 2-3-1863 Sh
Brown, Nancy A. F. to R. F. Freeman 12-5-1876 Dy
Brown, Nancy C. to John H. Hill 9-23-1853 (no return) F
Brown, Nancy E. to John H. Hogan 9-27-1870 (9-28-1870) Ma
Brown, Nancy H. to M. B. Franklin 8-18-1850 O
Brown, Nancy J. to Thomas M. Chapman 1-22-1856 Sh
Brown, Nancy to Charles Caricker 7-28-1854 (7-30-1854) Hr
Brown, Nancy to George Hooks 1-16-1870 Hy
Brown, Nancy to Jesse Humphrey 11-24-1848 F
Brown, Nancy to John McShaw 12-5-1870 (no return) F
Brown, Nancy to John Rhodes 8-13-1851 Hr
Brown, Nancy to W. R. Howell 5-19-1842 H
Brown, Nancy to William H. Murley 7-24-1848 (7-26-1848) Hr
Brown, Nancy to William May 3-3-1829 Ma
Brown, Patra to Tip Weaver 10-14-1874 T
Brown, Pattie to J. H. W. Latham 12-13-1870 Hy
Brown, Pauline A. P. to John R. Frayser 11-22-1837 Sh
Brown, Peggy to Wash Jones 5-2-1867 (5-5-1867) F B
Brown, Penelope A. to Wm. W. Cargil 4-6-1849 (5-2-1849) F
Brown, Peninie to D. H. Brogden 4-17-1829 L
Brown, Precilla W. to Eli Cox 8-2-1848 Hr
Brown, Priscilla to Lewis Glenn 8-9-1836 Hr
Brown, R. H. to John B. Neely 3-26-1864 Cr
Brown, Rebecca F. to Benj. Batter 3-18-1846 (no return) L
Brown, Rebecca G. to J. H. Emmons 1-12-1865 Mn
Brown, Rebecca to Alexander Cooper 9-24-1827 (8-25-1827) G
Brown, Rebecca to Fed Hughlett 3-5-1873 (3-6-1873) T
Brown, Rebecca to Gabriel Ary 10-20-1842 (10-21-1842) Hr
Brown, Rebecca to John Hays 10-10-1826 Hr
Brown, Rebecca to Robt. Gray 7-21-1870 (7-22-1870) F B
Brown, Rebecca to W. T. House 3-8-1874 Hy

Brown, Rissy to Columbus Chatman 3-29-1877 Hy
Brown, Roberta to Spencer Walker 2-4-1880 (2-5-1880) L B
Brown, S. J. to L. H. Massey 6-9-1848 O
Brown, S. M. to C. C. Neely 12-28-1865 Cr
Brown, S. P. to Thomas Phoebus 4-7-1828 Sh
Brown, Sabina to Robert Ward 1-5-1859 Cr
Brown, Sallie E. to Thos. J. Gray 11-23-1867 (11-24-1867) T
Brown, Sallie to John C. Morris 2-25-1870 (no return) F B
Brown, Sally D. to Samuel Hodge 8-12-1843 (no return) F
Brown, Sally s. to James H. Orr 10-6-1857 (no return) Hn
Brown, Sarah A. E. to James Matlock 1-25-1858 (1-27-1858) O
Brown, Sarah A. to G. B. Medlin 5-15-1859 Hy
Brown, Sarah Ann to James H. McRee 5-5-1857 O
Brown, Sarah C. to John Dixon 2-1-1853 (2-2-1853) Sh
Brown, Sarah E. to P. S. Gayle 11-17-1867 Hy
Brown, Sarah E. to Zachariah P. Warren 11-3-1862 Hy
Brown, Sarah F. to John N. Cannon 12-4-1856 Hn
Brown, Sarah J. to James B. Allen 8-3-1848 Sh
Brown, Sarah J. to John Somers 2-4-1851 (2-5-1851) O
Brown, Sarah J. to Robt. J. Russell 8-24-1857 Hr
Brown, Sarah Jane to John M. Condry 7-31-1861 (8-2-1861) L
Brown, Sarah S. to B. L. Benton 9-18-1869 (9-19-1869) Cr
Brown, Sarah to Elijah Wroten 2-14-1846 (no return) F
Brown, Sarah to James C. Dawson 1-7-1839 (1-8-1839) Hr
Brown, Sarah to John Blair 1-22-1839 Ma
Brown, Sarah to John Caraway 5-30-1835 Hr
Brown, Sarah to Patrick Glesson 9-6-1843 G
Brown, Sarah to William Shipman 12-23-1846 Hn
Brown, Sarah to Wm. Enochs 11-22-1855 Cr
Brown, Sary to Williams Perkins 7-10-1827 (7-12-1827) Hr
Brown, Siller to Simon Cruse 12-29-1874 Hy
Brown, Sirtha to James Martin 7-28-1858 Cr
Brown, Sophronia A. to James T. Spain 8-9-1870 G
Brown, Sophronia A. to John T. Benton 11-22-1867 (11-23-1867) Cr
Brown, Susan A. M. to Meciagah Bullock 9-29-1841 Ma
Brown, Susan C. to Jos. H. Hawley 9-28-1843 Sh
Brown, Susan to Isaac Henson 1-15-1870 (1-16-1870) Dy
Brown, Susan to James Antwine 3-17-1849 Hr
Brown, Susan to John Whiteside 10-1-1850 Cr
Brown, Susan to Johnson Bunton 10-23-1845 F
Brown, Susan to Robert Brown 3-25-1828 Ma
Brown, Susanah C. to R. G. Morrison 9-27-1857 We
Brown, Tennessee to James E. Smith 11-3-1865 L
Brown, Tennessee to Samuel W. Pickens 8-14-1871 L
Brown, Tilpha A. to Gilbert Rhodes 5-2-1857 Hr
Brown, Vinetta to James McAbee 12-17-1850 Hn
Brown?, B. C. to J. P. Clopton 2-12-1868 (2-13-1868) Cr
Brown?, Cernelia to B. F. Allen 2-21-1863 (2-22-1863) Sh
Brown?, Mary Ann to Thoas Ralph 12-2-1843 T
Browne, Bettie to Wm. Brisentine 5-16-1868 (5-17-1868) T
Browne, Charlotte Edwards to John Gardiner Scott 3-31-1864 Sh
Browne, Cintha to Joseph Johnson 2-3-1845 (2-4-1845) F
Browne, Cordelia to Wm. M. Watt 6-2-1845 (no return) F
Browney, M. A. to Z. B. Briant 7-22-1864 (no return) Cr
Browning (Bronning), Harriet L. to James R. McGinty 6-18-8161 (7-1-1861) Sh
Browning, Adaline to Houston Crockett 12-23-1885 (12-24-1885) L
Browning, Addia to Chas. E. Bradley 12-1-1853 Hn
Browning, Adeline to Thomas M. Palmer 1-7-1863 Mn
Browning, Ann to David Quillin 2-7-1851 Be
Browning, Ann to Richard Howard 7-28-1866 Hn B
Browning, Caroline N. to Jno. S. Bradford 12-17-1855 Hr
Browning, Caroline P. to Alphus H. Fleming 12-26-1854 Hn
Browning, D. M. H. to B. B. Wells 11-13-1874 Hy
Browning, Elizabeth N. to Thades Stribbling 1-11-1850 Cr
Browning, Elizabeth to Daniel Knight 4-15-1852 We
Browning, Elizabeth to Henry Jones 6-2-1833 Sh
Browning, Elizabeth to J. M. Keating 4-27-1857 Cr
Browning, Elizabeth to Peter Baker 9-1-1841 Hn
Browning, Ellen to D. A. Bullington 11-27-1869 (12-2-1869) Cr
Browning, Eunita to William Carter 9-1-1841 Hn
Browning, Harriet to Anderson Campbell 2-5-1869 (no return) L
Browning, Julia to James E. Elliott 12-26-1877 Hy
Browning, Julia to John White 2-1-1851 Cr
Browning, Lucy to Robert Spellings 8-17-1847 (8-18-1847) G
Browning, M. E. to James M. Jones 10-7-1859 G
Browning, Martha to J. J. Durden 7-2-1849 Be
Browning, Martha to Robert Smith 5-18-1855 (5-20-1855) G
Browning, Mary E. to R. C. Taylor 7-22-1864 (no return) Cr
Browning, Mary to Thomas B. Moore 2-17-1841 Cr
Browning, Mary to Thomas Boyle 11-3-1846 Hr
Browning, Massely? to Nelson Robison 10-4-1870 (10-6-1870) Cr
Browning, Molly to Thomas Buchanan 8-26-1866 Hn B
Browning, Nancy to Mark Bullington 9-26-1837 G
Browning, P. A. to A. M. Hopper 11-25-1871 (no return) Cr
Browning, R. J. to James A. Keaton 12-29-1855 Cr
Browning, S. A. to Isaac Pearce 1-9-1871 (1-12-1871) Cr B
Browning, Sarah E. to Joseph Fulcher 3-18-1867 (3-19-1867) Ma

Browning, Sarah F. to W. M. Crawford 12-3-1867 Cr
Browning, Sarah J. to Wlilliam C. Bullington 12-2-1862 (12-5-1862) Cr
Brownlow, Edna J. to William J. Floyd 8-8-1846 (no return) F
Brownlow, Patsey to Marton McConnell 9-30-1841 (10-15-1841) F
Broyle, T. E. to Andrew J. Johnson 12-23-1875 (no return) Hy
Broyles, Mahaly to William W. Nelson 5-10-1826 (not endorsed) Hr
Broyles, Matilda to Nathaniel Tatum 11-23-1843 (11-25-1843) F
Broyls, Louisa to Stephen G. Wilkinson 12-11-1850 (12-13-1850) L
Bruce (Brown), Katie to J. B. Thomas 2-28-1872 Hy
Bruce, A. M. to J. M. Jones 10-27-1859 We
Bruce, Delaney to L. H. Tippett 8-25-1844 Be
Bruce, Eady to John Woodell 9-27-1847 (9-29-1847) Ma
Bruce, Elender K. to Samuel Presson 12-1-1853 Be
Bruce, Elizabeth to F. B. Moore 7-26-1866 (no return) Hn
Bruce, Emaline to D. B. Gully 3-12-1854 Be
Bruce, Frances M. to J. B. Geter (Jeter) 8-13-1865 Hy
Bruce, Jennie to John Thornton 4-3-1876 Hy
Bruce, Lorina to Wm. J. Cox 7-19-1846 Be
Bruce, Margaret to J. Y. Flack 5-25-1874 (5-26-1874) Dy
Bruce, Martha A. to T. N. Barr 12-18-1853 Be
Bruce, Martha J. to Abraham N. Allder 3-3-1860 Sh
Bruce, Martha to lJohn H. Carroll 2-12-1845 (2-18-1845) G
Bruce, Mary E. to Peter Looney 10-5-1865 Hn
Bruce, Mary J. to John McHenry Andrews 8-8-1854 Be
Bruce, Mary J. to Marion E. Chapman 11-3-1859 Hn
Bruce, Mary J. to Robt. T. Jackson 7-28-1845 (7-30-1845) F
Bruce, Nirva to Sidney King 1-29-1876 (no return) Hy
Bruce, Poka to Harris Wiley 4-3-1865 Hn
Bruce, Sarah A. to Wm. Scott 3-20-1843 (3-22-1843) F
Bruce, Sarah to Samuel Kinsey 1-1-1849 (1-2-1849) G
Bruce, Susan M. to John H. Carroll 11-27-1842 G
Bruce?, Aga to Moses Lomas 2-25-1845 (no return) Hn
Bruce?, P. A. C. to P. B. Capps? 4-20-1867 (4-21-1867) Cr
Bruer?, A. C. to J. F. L. Melton 8-11-1841 G
Bruff, Calista L. to James W. Jones 3-22-1865 G
Bruff, Lean to W. M. Lowery 8-23-1863 G
Bruff, Lethia to Cincematus Roach 8-25-1835 G
Bruff, Matilda to James J. Bradberry 1-6-1830 (1-7-1830) G
Brugger, Annie to Frank Menschel 12-23-1859 (12-24-1859) Sh
Bruison, Darcas to Luther N. Mitchell 8-5-1848 Ma
Bruithwick, I. J. to E. H. Swindle 2-26-1866 Dy
Brumage, Hetha to Howell F. Graves 11-9-1848 (no return) Cr
Brumager, Sarah F. to Z. Lee 11-2-1865 Be
Brumfalow, Phebe to Wm. H. Carlton 8-22-1847 Cr
Brumley, Elizabeth to Barnett M. Trainer 6-27-1839 (7-4-1839) F
Brumley, Fannie to Frank Tapp 3-4-1878 Hy
Brumley, June E. to William Couch 12-31-1859 Sh
Brumley, Mary to J. J. Holloway 10-27-1849 (10-28-1849) F
Brumley, N.E. to William H. Jones 3-5-1860 Sh
Brumley, Nancy to Isaac Shinault 2-2-1843 F
Brummer, Ernestine to Louis Kaufmann 5-21-1858 Sh
Brummet, Leah to John Duncan 10-2-1828 G
Brummett, Addie to J. A. Jenkins 12-6-1870 (no return) Hy
Brummett, Bettie to D. A. Brumitt 2-6-1872 Hy
Brummett, Eliza F. to John A. Dickinson 12-20-1865 Hy
Brummett, Julia A. to J. T. Jacocks 3-13-1875 (no return) Hy
Brummitt, Susan A. to Benjamin F. Phelps 8-30-1863 We
Brundage, Elizabeth to John Hart 10-10-1844 Hn
Brundage, Margaret to Alexander Sprowls 6-10-1858 Hn
Brundidge, Mary M. to John Smily 5-25-1854 Hn
Brundredge, E. J. to Columbus J. Collins 1-6-1853 Hn
Brundridge, Mary A. to John Royister 6-4-1860 We
Brunschwiler, Jennie to Rudolph Bertschy 2-7-1862 (2-10-1862) Sh
Brunson, Anny to Solomon Pinion 7-21-1838 G
Brunson, Martha Jane to Isaac S. Oliver 11-8-1848 G
Brunson, Sarah Ann to Robert L. P. Oliver 10-25-1848 G
Brunston, Harriet to John Malona 2-19-1845 Sh
Brunsull?, Lidda to Hugh Laddamare 1-10-1867 (1-13-1867) Cr
Brunt, Nancy P. to G. W. Burnham 10-19-1872 (10-20-1872) Dy
Brunus?, Mary to A. Carelli 5-25-1853 Sh
Brush, Kiziah to N. K. Johnson 12-15-1849 (12-16-1849) Hr
Brush, Marg to George W. Crider 2-15-1842 Hn
Brush, Mary to James Dick 9-10-1840 Hn
Brush, Polly Ann to R. S. Campbell 3-14-1876 (3-17-1876) Dy
Bruton, Nany to Elias Oldham 1-8-1831 Sh
Bruton, Sarah Ann to John B. Love 6-13-1848 (6-14-1848) Ma
Bryan, Annie M. to Thomas A. Fisher 4-10-1858 Sh
Bryan, Bridget to John Kaley 4-26-1851 (4-28-1851) Sh
Bryan, Elvira J. to Abram J. Buford 12-20-1852 (12-22-1852) Sh
Bryan, Frances to Gilbert Holland 8-15-1854 Be
Bryan, Francis T. to John Y. Strayhorn 12-4-1854 Ma
Bryan, Jane to McNeal Powel 8-25-1831 Sh
Bryan, Louisa to Southerland Bowers 12-14-1854 Hn
Bryan, M. A. to K. S. Purvis 10-4-1869 G
Bryan, Martha Ann to Ezekiel McNabb 3-16-1833 Sh
Bryan, Mintha to John W. Fitzhugh 2-2-1829 Ma
Bryan, Rachel E. to George E. Hassell 12-3-1865 G

Bryan, Sarah C. to Lyman C. Castle 12-5-1864 (12-6-1864) Sh
Bryan, Sarah E. to W. B. Garrison 3-1-1836 Sh
Bryan, Sarah W. to John Bivren 1-22-1839 F
Bryan?, Sarah E. to J. M. Turner 4-29-1869 G
Bryans, Susans to William P. Mauldin 5-14-1827 Ma
Bryant, Agness to R. J. Johnson 10-26-1861 (10-27-1861) Cr
Bryant, Amanda E. to John Balew 12-29-1858 (1-6-1859) G
Bryant, Arretta to A. W. Webber 1-11-1853 (no return) F
Bryant, Avira R. to Isaac Solomon 2-10-1852 (2-12-1852) G
Bryant, Carroline to J. M. White 11-6-1837 G
Bryant, Cathrine to Boyna Mich 5-13-1858 Cr
Bryant, Celester A. to Geo. B. Cole 10-10-1872 (10-11-1872) Cr
Bryant, Christina to Isaac A. Henley 1-28-1848 (no return) F
Bryant, Cordelia to B. F. Gill 12-25-1876 (1-4-1877) O
Bryant, Cornelia to Harvey Jackson 2-6-1844 G
Bryant, Demarious to John C. Dolton 10-3-1853 (no return) F
Bryant, Dicy J. to C. W. Hix 1-17-1865 G
Bryant, Eliz. to Chas. McNamee 6-21-1845 (no return) F
Bryant, Eliza E. to W. C. Penn 4-12-1854 G
Bryant, Elizabeth C. to Benjamin Fortner 12-15-1847 (12-21-1847) Hr
Bryant, Elizabeth J. to Thomas P. Alston 11-5-1858 (11-6-1858) L
Bryant, Elizabeth to B. M. Burress 10-24-1861 G
Bryant, Elizabeth to Franklin Hayns 9-1-1846 (8-29-1846) G
Bryant, Ella to Robt. Forrest 2-26-1873 Hy
Bryant, Elvira to William R. Smith 10-22-1856 G
Bryant, Eveline to Henry Conner 12-16-1845 (12-18-1845) Ma
Bryant, Fanney to John Attkisson 10-20-1871 (10-25-1871) Cr
Bryant, Frances L. to Thos. D. Newhouse 1-1-1857 (1-2-1857) G
Bryant, H. to Zack Smith 2-7-1867 G
Bryant, Hannah to W. T. Pratt 10-17-1860 G
Bryant, Hiley? to T. D. Leech 10-6-1861 G
Bryant, Jane F. to John A. Greer 10-24-1855 (11-4-1855) G
Bryant, Jane to Alfred Johnson 5-31-1870 G
Bryant, Jane to Joshua Wilburn 2-19-1829 G
Bryant, Jane to Joshua Wilburn 2-19-1829 (2-20-1829) G
Bryant, Jane to William Durden 11-30-1854 (12-3-1854) Hr
Bryant, Julia A. to Jacob M. Pate 2-19-1856 (2-20-1856) G
Bryant, Lavina to George Harbison 11-13-1875 (11-14-1875) Dy
Bryant, Lizzie to Selim Goodman 2-29-1868 G B
Bryant, Louisa to Elias Nordon 5-21-1850 Cr
Bryant, Louiza to Thomas J. Akin 3-17-1859 (3-18-1859) G
Bryant, Lucinda to David L. Snowden 10-7-1850 Cr
Bryant, M. A. E. to Henry Woods 3-19-1868 Be
Bryant, M. J. to W. B. Wright 3-27-1866 (3-28-1866) F
Bryant, Mahala to F. J. Conley 4-1-1858 G
Bryant, Manda to Lewis Rice 10-7-1872 (no return) Hy
Bryant, Margaret F. to James E. Stewart 8-27-1861 Mn
Bryant, Margaret to Jesse L. Shelton 1-31-1850 Sh
Bryant, Martha A. to John C. Dalton 1-9-1862 Sh
Bryant, Martha C. to Moses E. Mosley 2-22-1858 G
Bryant, Martha E. to C. F. Hames 2-27-1844 G
Bryant, Martha Jane to Elam D. Henderson 10-27-1856 (10-29-1856) Ma
Bryant, Marthy to John Kiltennor 12-26-1876 Hy
Bryant, Mary A. P. to Barnett S. Demoss 10-3-1852 Cr
Bryant, Mary A. to William Bishop 2-12-1845 (2-13-1845) G
Bryant, Mary E. to Austin Farris 6-9-1853 Sh
Bryant, Mary E. to Thomas G. Hargis 12-1-1860 (12-2-1860) O
Bryant, Mary E. to W. F. Moss 12-14-1869 (no return) Hy
Bryant?, Mary to Ralph H. Ramsey 10-14-1830 Sh
Bryant, Mattie to Oliver Drake 5-25-1873 Hy
Bryant, Mollie to Tom Mulherin 12-8-1880 (12-9-1880) Dy
Bryant, Nancy A. M. to Thos. D. Baird 12-9-1850 (12-8?-1850) G
Bryant, Nancy E. to Wm. Green McClellan 11-14-1849 T
Bryant, Nancy to John Cline 7-11-1872 O
Bryant, Nannie to J. W. Porter 8-2-1873 (no return) Cr
Bryant, Patsey to Martin Belew 11-15-1853 (11-17-1853) G
Bryant, Penelope E. to Levey Lacy 7-10-1848 (7-12-1848) Ma
Bryant, Rachael to John A. Dunnaway 7-30-1846 Ma
Bryant, Ruth Ann to Wily Cole 1-1-1877 Hy
Bryant, Sandal to William R. Gammon 1-27-1846 (1-28-1846) G
Bryant, Sarah A. to Jno. L. Flippin 2-3-1838 G
Bryant, Sarah Ann to Governor Belew 1-2-1854 (1-4-1854) G
Bryant, Sarah C. to Yancy D. Glisson 9-10-1855 (9-12-1855) G
Bryant, Sarah to Charles E. Jones 6-9-1860 O
Bryant, Sarah to Charles E. Jones 6-?-1860 (6-10-1860) O
Bryant, Sarah to John Mundin 7-15-1844 Hr
Bryant, Susan Ann to William F. Tilman 6-15-1866 (6-17-1866) T
Bryant, Susan to Norflet Jean 9-17-1856 (9-18-1856) Ma
Bryant, Tempe. S. to Francis Erickson 1-28-1851 F
Bryant, V. S. P. to G. W. Moss 2-24-1869 Hy
Bryen, Sarah F. to Samuel Graham 3-18-1855 We
Bryles, Carolin to James L. Ormann 1-9-1843 (1-16-1843) F
Bryles, Rebeca to John Holloway 1-8-1841 F
Bryson, Clarissa E. to Samuel S. Steel 5-5-1867 Hn
Buchanan, Alabama T. to Warren P. Willett 2-16-1853 (no return) Hn
Buchanan, Ann E. to Geo. W. Swink 5-14-1869 Ma
Buchanan, Ann to George Menzies 12-19-1865 (12-22-1865) Dy

Buchanan, Barbara to S. M. Curry 11-27-1867 O
Buchanan, Catharine to Wm. Alsup 7-3-1861 Be
Buchanan, E. C. to D. S. Price 12-18-1862 Mn
Buchanan, Elizabeth C. to William D. McKamy 8-29-1852 (9-2-1852) O
Buchanan, Elizabeth to John J. Forest 6-22-1863 Be
Buchanan, Emma to A. J. Hess 3-1-1870 G
Buchanan, L. F. to W. M. Simins 5-6-1855 We
Buchanan, L. I. to T. I. Culp 1-24-1867 O
Buchanan, Louisianne to William H. Fitch 2-13-1860 Hn
Buchanan, M. A. to Stephen Phillips 2-20-1872 (2-22-1872) O
Buchanan, M. E. to S. M. Porch 9-21-1867 O
Buchanan, M. I. to I. W. Ramsey 10-22-1866 O
Buchanan, Maggie A. to M. K. Cook 4-13-1864 (4-14-1864) Sh
Buchanan, Margaret to A. D. Freeland 9-3-1854 Hn
Buchanan, Margaret to Sandford Bramblett 9-15-1847 O
Buchanan, Martha to Charles Neal 11-3-1869 G B
Buchanan, Mary to J. B. Leathe 11-21-1867 O
Buchanan, Matti to A. G. Hicks 8-31-1864 G
Buchanan, Nancy to Joseph A. Ross 3-5-1848 Be
Buchanan, Rebecca to James B. Reeves 12-25-1851 O
Buchanan, S. J. to Jas. Myers 2-5-1867 O
Buchanan, Sarah M. to William L. Legate 9-21-1859 (9-22-1859) O
Buchanan, Sarah to David Childress 8-12-1841 O
Buchannan, Martha to John F. Inman 11-11-1858 O
Buchannan, Rose to Ambrose M. Swimm 11-29-1858 Sh
Buchannon, Susan G. to Abram Harper 11-10-1864 (no return) Cr
Buchanon, Nancy to Stephen Clement 9-10-1844 Be
Buchinm?, Claricy to Charley Logan 1-29-1875 (1-30-1875) L B
Buck (Burk?), Margaret to David A. Bradford 2-11-1839 (2-12-1839) L
Buck, Amanda to William Currie 12-25-1866 Hy
Buck, Ann to Lewis Claybrook 4-5-1871 (no return) Hy
Buck, Bell to Jonas Mann 10-29-1875 (no return) Hy
Buck, Eliza to Wm. Claybrook 1-3-1878 Hy
Buck, Emily to Lewis Jetton 9-18-1871 Hy
Buck, Emily to Walter D. Bayne 9-13-1842 Sh
Buck, Frances E. to John E. Bosler 12-27-1852 (12-29-1852) Sh
Buck, Harriett to James Jackson 9-3-1855 Cr
Buck, Ida to Samuel Young 12-15-1882 (12-19-1882) L
Buck, Laura to Mortimer Taylor 12-25-1866 Hy
Buck, Lizzie to Robert Grigsby 10-8-1868 (no return) Dy
Buck, Lucinda C. to Joseph S. Spence 7-10-1865 Hy
Buck, Malind J. to Nathaniel Jones 7-8-1862 Sh
Buck, Malvina to Jessee J. Turner 8-29-1855 Sh
Buck, Mariah to Jan L. Miller 7-15-1851 (no return) F
Buck, Martha to Jordon Whitelow 4-16-1868 Hy
Buck, Mary to John L. Pollard 2-6-1850 Sh
Buck, Misouri to S. H. Young 7-16-1867 Hy
Buck, Nannie C. to Robt. S. Torian 4-24-1872 Hy
Buck, Pulina to Charles A. Bosler 11-10-1854 (11-12-1854) Sh
Buck, Sallie P. to J. C. Bruce 12-10-1872 Hy
Buck, Susan M. to J. M. Young 6-5-1867 Hy
Buck, Tamasia to Austin Sutton 12-23-1869 Hy
Buckannon, Mary Ann to Anderson Skillern 12-1-1841 Ma
Buckhannon, J. A. to D. S. Willett 11-18-1852 Hn
Buckley, Bridget to George Couch 1-6-1862 Sh
Buckley, Catharine to Fabian S. Sebastian 5-1-1861 Sh *
Buckley, Catherine to Michael McNamee 12-27-1843 Sh
Buckley, Eliza M. to Franklin McKnight 11-7-1843 (11-14-1843) F
Buckley, Ellen to Patrick Ryan 5-15-1858 (5-16-1858) Sh
Buckley, Eveline to W. L. Land 2-11-1861 (2-13-1861) Sh
Buckley, Isabella to W. A. Land 11-8-1858 (11-9-1858) Sh
Buckley, Margaret to Joseph Chambers 2-6-1855 Sh
Buckley, Mary E. to John Burrough 10-4-1848 Sh
Buckley, Mary E. to Saml. Latermend? 7-7-1852 We
Buckley, Mary F. to M. G. Poe 8-6-1849 Hn
Buckley, Mary to George Hicks 5-8-1858 (5-9-1858) Sh
Buckley, Mary to John D. W. Barton 10-11-1853 Hn
Buckley, Mary to Lawrence Leonard 11-22-1856 (11-23-1856) Sh
Buckley, N. E. to G. W. Bowden 3-31-1856 Hn
Buckley, Rebecca to Hall Kersey 12-1-1863 (12-3-1863) F
Buckley, Susan to John Hall 5-16-1844 Hn
Buckley, Virginia C. to William Hilliard 5-29-1860 We
Buckly, Mary to Michael Noonan 11-3-1853 (11-6-1853) Sh
Buckmuller, Christina to Jacob Aebly 10-20-1860 Sh
Buckner, A. E. to George A. Johnson ?-?-1841 Cr
Buckner, Emma to Chas. B. Houston 9-22-1869 Ma
Buckner, Kittie C. to Jno. M. Snow 4-8-1861 Sh
Buckner, Lucy F. to M. J. Sapp 12-23-1884 L
Buckner, Ma_ L. to R. G. Jenkins 4-10-1876 (4-11-1876) L
Buckner, Mary to C. C. P. Sharpe 3-26-1857 Hr
Bucy, Elizabeth to W. H. Bucy 1-14-1866 Hn
Bucy, Lucy C. to George W. Wisehart 6-18-1859 Hn
Bucy, M. S. to E. G. Everett 12-18-1846 We
Bucy, Margaret T. to Jno. P. Sensing 9-5-1867 (9-10-1867) F
Bucy, Margaret to Jourdan Champion 3-17-1843 Hn
Bucy, Mary Ann to William C. Bailey 11-20-1846 Hn
Bucy, Mary E. to James E. Guinn 11-29-1866 Hn
Bucy, Mary E. to James T. Berry 1-22-1857 Hn
Bucy, Nancy E. to Nathaniel C. Clement 1-1-1860 Hn
Bucy, Nancy to John A. Burton 2-8-1844 Hn
Bucy, Samantha M. to J. J. S. Buckannon 7-9-1863 Hn
Bucy, Tebitha to W. C. Bailey 11-2-1848 Hn
Budget, M. Adline to William Dueast 10-12-1857 (10-16-1857) T
Buerklin, Louisa to George Fliedner 1-16-1854 Sh
Buff, Eliza to J. C. Wellsman 10-10-1868 T
Buffalo, Nancy to Robert Stobaugh 1-4-1869 (1-6-1869) Ma
Buffalo, Nancy to William H. Nelson 3-19-1866 (not executed) Ma
Buffalo, Sarah to Jas. R. Wood 12-11-1856 Hr
Buffaloe, Julia A. to A. L. Southall 4-3-1857 (4-5-1857) Hr
Buford, A. M. to Jesse B. Brown 6-19-1840 (6-24-1840) F
Buford, E. A. to F. C. Manley 12-22-1869 F
Buford, Frances to John Williams 11-2-1866 (11-3-1866) F B
Buford, Hannah to Washington Boile 12-27-1869 (12-31-1869) F B
Buford, Jane to William McPherson 2-27-1871 (3-4-1871) F B
Buford, Lemon to Rasmus Maclin 12-23-1869 (no return) F B
Buford, Malinda to Charley Jones 12-27-1869 (12-30-1869) F B
Buford, Susan J. to C. P. Lemons 5-5-1840 (5-7-1840) F
Bugg, Alice to Columbus R. Parr 8-22-1866 Dy
Bugg, Allice to John W. Graham 6-26-1867 (6-27-1867) Cr
Bugg, Elizabeth D. to John C. Waddell 8-15-1846 F
Bugg, Frances to Silas Dunlap 1-28-1841 Hn
Bugg, Jane V. to Albert L. Burrow 11-28-1842 (11-22?-1842) Ma
Bui?, S. A. to J. T. Stamp 12-6-1865 (12-13-1865) Dy
Buie, Mary Jane to Joshua Charles 2-26-1857 Hn
Buise, Caroline to William Davis 10-28-1842 T
Bull, Luzenia to D. P. Cowan 3-11-1851 F
Bull, M. H. to H. C. Able 9-2-1867 (9-5-1867) F
Bull, Mary to G. W. Robertson 1-22-1853 (no return) F
Bull, Nancy C. to Wm. C. Hunter 5-19-1847 (5-20-1847) F
Bull, Rebecca to A. F. Cowan 10-22-1845 F
Bull, Sarah Ann to H. Falkner 1-8-1868 (no return) Dy
Bullard, Juda to James Dillard 1-4-1869 Hy
Bullard, Mefrinda? to Alfred Linnell 8-30-1862 (9-11-1862) Dy
Bullard, Sarah to J. A. Jones 10-14-1869 Dy
Bullard, Sarah to James Herod 3-14-1866 O
Bullard, Sarah to Jason Landrum 7-19-1854 O
Bullard, Susan to Thomas Ferrel 3-6-1850 G
Bullen, Elizabeth V. to Madison G. John 3-16-1843 O
Bullen, Georgia Ann to William Click 7-29-1854 O
Bulleton, Rachal to Jas. M. Williamson 1-29-1845 (1-30-1845) G
Bulliner, Emeline to William Burkley 9-20-1863 Mn
Bullington, Edna K. to P. H. Jackson 2-9-1869 G
Bullington, Elizabeth to Wm. J. Green 7-28-1844 Cr
Bullington, Julia to William H. Woodson 4-9-1842 G
Bullington, Martha to Jno. Bryant, jr. 8-15-1861 G
Bullington, Mary to J. C. Bullington 12-29-1865 (12-31-1865) Cr
Bullington, Soniza to John A. Argo 12-26-1848 (12-27-1848) G
Bullock, Agnes to Jerry Rudd 6-19-1878 Hy
Bullock, Ann R. to Richard A. Sneed 12-15-1869 Ma
Bullock, Elizabeth to Charles W. Wells 6-12-1843 (no return) We
Bullock, Frances A. to G. W. Paschal 8-10-1854 We
Bullock, Francis A. to John H. Bradberry 1-15-1859 We
Bullock, Jane to Manuel Jones 1-27-1866 (no return) F B
Bullock, Julia A. to Elisha S. Seymore 10-20-1847 F
Bullock, Louisa J. to T. W. Bucy 12-24-1867 Hn
Bullock, Malinda to O. Alsup 1-17-1863 Be
Bullock, Milly F. to E. A. Pierce 12-11-1865 Be
Bullock, S. A. to J. M. Woods 11-7-1856 We
Bullock, S. M. to R. P. Russell 1-31-1866 (no return) F
Bullock, Tabitha to Warren Freeman 11-19-1854 Hn
Bulter, Minerva P. to C. P. Shipman 5-26-1858 Cr
Buly?, Mary C. to Temple C. Walker 5-6-1848 (5-7-1848) F
Bumbley, Nancy to Wilson B. Rhodes 11-10-1861 (11-17-1861) Cr
Bumpas, Cohaly? to Ben Bell 7-28-1866 (7-29-1866) T
Bumpass, A. R. to T. F. Wright 2-10-1844 Hn
Bumpass, Amanda M. F. to W. D. Poyner 4-14-1853 Hn
Bumpass, Anna to Christopher Akin 11-29-1870 (12-3-1870) Dy B
Bumpass, Elizabeth to Jonathan Crews 9-26-1827 Hr
Bumpass, Ella to Thomas Brown? 12-11-1869 T
Bumpass, Emma to James Currey 8-28-1880 (8-29-1880) Dy
Bumpass, Harriett to William Kitchen(s) 2-9-1854 O
Bumpass, Harrit A. to John A. Austin 1-5-1860 We
Bumpass, Martha Ann to Milos C. Cook 1-16-1842 Ma
Bumpass, Mary E. to Robt. Caldwell 11-3-1846 F
Bumpass, Mary to Alexander Ross 2-3-1870 Dy
Bumpass, Sarah? to E. J. Watson 3-1-1842 F
Bumpass, Sophia Arabella to Thomas W. Poyner 4-24-1866 Hn
Bumpass, Tempy Ann to Nep Thompson 10-30-1871 Hy
Bumpass, Tennie to Brandon Lane 1-14-1871 (1-15-1871) Ma
Bumpasss, Caroline to Fley O. Burton 2-25-1870 (no return) Dy
Bumphass, Loveann to Dick Cothran 12-25-1873 T
Bunce, Sarah to Peter Gross 12-31-1861 L
Bunch, Catharine E. to Jesse Boston 4-30-1870 (5-1-1870) Cr

Bunch, Ellen A. to Samuel W. Thompson 9-4-1857 Hn
Bunch, Jennie M. to Joseph B. Webb 12-5-1872 T
Bunch, Julia to John P. McCormick 6-7-1853 Hn
Bunch, Karen C. to E. J. McFarland 1-8-1846 Hn
Bunch, Louisa to Harrison Smith 7-26-1842 Sh
Bunch, Matilda to David F. Butterworth 12-27-1845 Hn
Bundage, Sarah J. to James H. Derington 12-26-1843 Hn
Bundrige, Martha to Rich D. L. Payne 1-24-1845 We
Bunds, Elizabeth to Pleasant Robertson 3-18-1842 Hn
Bundy, Francis to James H. McRee 10-28-1863 O
Bundy, Lovanna to Willialm Godwin 6-14-1862 (6-15-1862) O
Bundy, Margaret J. to M. L. Reed 8-22-1860 O
Bungle, Eve Ann to Flranklin Huffman 1-29-1846 T
Bungner, Mary to John A. F. Henniger 8-2-1862 (8-3-1862) Sh
Bunks, Hettie to J. M. Jackson 5-29-1863 (6-2-1863) Dy
Bunn, Amanda M. to James K. Polk Rich 2-18-1868 (no return) L
Bunn, Elizabeth to Adam Rooter 7-2-1854 Be
Bunn, Emaline to Tomes Nany 2-14-1842 Cr
Bunn, Emily to Jasper N. Rentfro 3-16-1853 G
Bunn, Jane to Benjamin L. Wells 11-18-1866 Be
Bunn, Mary H. to R. Turner 10-19-1870 (10-20-1870) Cr
Bunnell, Clarasa to Jim Peacock 2-13-1868 (2-19-1868) Dy
Bunnell, Elizabeth C. to Peter Ballentine 12-17-1847 (12-22-1847) G
Bunnell, Lyda Ann to Jackson Brown 5-20-1839 G
Bunnell, Marcila A. to Hugh M. McBride 10-6-1845 (10-9-1845) G
Buntin, Sarah G. to Jeremiah Cherry 11-6-1835 G
Bunting, Caroline to A. N. Prewett 11-15-1858 (11-18-1858) Hr
Bunting, Eliza A. to John H. Raines 12-22-1849 (12-23-1849) Hr
Bunting, Elizabeth C. to William Sauls 10-18-1849 (10-22-1849) Hr
Bunting, Julia A. to E. O. Humphrey 12-18-1852 (12-30-1852) Hr
Bunting, Virginia to Wm. E. Robinson 10-14-1859 (10-18-1859) Hr
Bunton, Catherine to Fredrick Mayo 3-5-1843 Ma
Bunton, Elizabeth to Thomas Hoofman 3-7-1844 We
Bunton, Lucy to Alexander Sampson 4-21-1858 We
Bunton, Maggie to Washington Smith 3-15-1871 T
Buntyn, Amanda to David A. Whitelaw 1-27-1841 Sh
Buntyn, Indiana to Robert E. Titus 5-16-1843 Sh
Buntyn, Lizzie to A. B. Haynes 12-31-1859 (1-1-1860) Sh
Buntyn, Sallie A. to R. D. Goodwyn 1-5-1854 Sh
Burbins, Amanda to J. J. Norris 5-2-1864 Sh
Burch (Bunge), Temperance to William Prewett 8-10-1837 Sh
Burch, Bettie to John Landrum 3-7-1877 (3-8-1877) Dy
Burch, Laura to Frank Lanier 1-19-1878 (1-20-1878) Dy
Burch, Lucinda to Moses McFarland 8-1-1860 G
Burch, Martha J.? to James H. Rainey 12-21-1867 (12-24-1867) Cr
Burch, Mary to John Stewart 4-8-1846 Cr
Burch, Nancie to Alford Joilet 3-30-1874 (4-2-1874) L
Burch, R. J. to E. A. Hendrix 5-30-1875 Hy
Burch, Sarah A. to John J. McFarland 8-29-1859 (8-30-1859) G
Burchet, A. to P. Burchet 7-27-1870 (9-1-1872?) T
Burchet, Mariah to Isaac Pryer 4-26-1870 T
Burchett, Ann to W. J. Dancer 12-24-1865 Mn
Burchett, Laura to Guy Bynum 11-9-1871 T
Burchit, Sally A. to Samuel Trap 1-16-1864 (1-18-1864) Cr
Burchit, Sally Ann to Samuel Trat 1-16-1864 (no return) Cr
Burdaux, Mary E. to Richard F. Cooper 2-9-1839 (2-10-1839) F
Burday, Catharine to Hugh McAnally 2-2-1856 (2-3-1856) Sh
Burden, Ann to Ben Mullen 12-28-1876 L
Burden, Jane M. to Isaac Wilson 9-28-1855 (9-30-1855) Hr
Burden, Smithy to John Clark 8-23-1853 (9-8-1853) Hr
Burdick, M. J. to Theodore Anderson 12-31-1859 (1-3-1860) Sh
Burditt, Elizabeth J. to William Gardner 10-14-1860 G
Burdon, Rebecca to W. D. Fennel 12-16-1868 (no return) Hy
Burford, Caroline to Thomas W. Harris 8-21-1843 (no return) F
Burford, Charlotte to Ephraim Pirdle 12-25-1868 (12-28-1868) F B
Burford, Elizabeth to Tho. R. Tuggle 10-1-1846 (no return) F
Burford, F. R. to John Wesley Wier 8-27-1863 Sh
Burford, Lucy to John S. Herron 10-14-1854 (no return) F
Burford, Lydia E. to Wm. D. Dickinson 11-13-1867 (no return) Hy
Burford, M. B. to D. B. Hilliard 12-14-1875 (no return) Hy
Burford, M. to W. P. Cherry 6-22-1875 (no return) Hy
Burford, Martha G. to John W. Youngs 12-21-1840 (12-23-1840) F
Burford, Mary to Benjamin Evans 12-31-1842 (1-3-1843) O
Burford, Nancy S. to John S. Normont 7-27-1847 (7-28-1847) F
Burford, Nannie M. to John D. Gullett 3-8-1861 G
Burford, P. C. to F. Shaw 10-24-1850 (no return) F
Burford, Rebeca C. to Marcus D. Harvey 4-8-1839 (4-9-1839) F
Burford, Rebecca C. to Daniel G. Marshall 4-13-1839 (4-19-1839) O
Burford, Rebecca to B. F. Southard 11-9-1873 Hy
Burgan, Canzey to William H. Holmes 12-17-1850 O
Burgan, Elizabeth J. to William Edmundson, jr. 8-20-1842 (8-21-1842) G
Burge, Martha to John Loffman 4-4-1844 We
Burgent, Mary to Talton Barnett 10-11-1871 O
Burgess, Julia A. S. to Thomas Wright 2-11-1852 (2-12-1852) Sh
Burgess, Martha A. to John N. Lowery 8-2-1842 Hn
Burgess, Sarah E. to J. R. Pierce 3-11-1866 Be
Burgett, M. A. to J. Roberts 2-6-1860 (2-7-1860) O

Burgh, Jane A. to John Tull 1-27-1842 Ma
Burgner(Burger), Ann to Allen Trousdale 9-7-1827 Hr
Burk (Buck?), Ellen to Thomas Walsh 1-3-1853 (1-29-1853) Sh
Burk, Alice to John Wilson 7-12-1856 (7-14-1856) Sh
Burk, Ann to George W. Stover 12-20-1854 Ma
Burk, Bettie A. to W. B. Drake 1-15-1873 L
Burk, Bettie E. to W. A. Cates 7-20-1870 (no return) Hy
Burk, Caledonia T. to James W. Parr 4-4-1853 (4-9-1853) L
Burk, Elizabeth J. to H. W. Moseley 10-10-1865 G
Burk, Joana to Charles Bierbrower 6-26-1860 Sh
Burk, K. A. to William Blair 3-5-1856 We
Burk, Margaret to John Young 4-7-1864 Sh
Burk, Mary J. to William J. Pitts 12-20-1848 L
Burk, Mary to James Quigley 2-19-1857 (2-22-1857) Sh
Burk, Mary to John Wells 8-13-1857 Sh
Burk, Sisly to Nathaniel Vaughn 3-18-1856 Hn
Burke, Alice to Thomas Ford 12-16-1845 Sh
Burke, Annie to Edward Riley 10-29-1864 Sh
Burke, Augusta to John Lang 5-5-1858 Sh
Burke, Bridgett to Richard W. English 12-1-1845 Sh
Burke, Catharine to John Towhey 5-13-1860 Sh
Burke, Catharine to Patrick Kennedy 11-5-1855 Sh
Burke, Eleanor A. to James H. Nunn 11-1-1851 (11-4-1851) L
Burke, Ellen to John Burke 7-18-1849 Sh
Burke, Ellen to Peter Kelly 12-26-1858 Sh
Burke, Ellen to Rody (Rodny) Quinlan 6-29-1847 Sh
Burke, Emiline O. to Noah G. Steed 1-31-1850 We
Burke, Fanny to Robert Peplow 12-15-1864 Sh
Burke, Hannora to Patrick Kelly 7-21-1864 (8-17-1864) Sh
Burke, Honora to James Downing 7-2-1860 (7-3-1860) Sh
Burke, Johanna to Charles Kuger 2-13-1863 Sh
Burke, Julia to Owen Riley 4-25-1861 Sh
Burke, Maggie to Thomas Fitzgibbon 9-5-1863 Sh
Burke, Margaret C. to Geo. A. Stalls 1-8-1861 Sh
Burke, Margaret to John Young 7-5-1864 Sh
Burke, Margaret to Michael McLaughlin 8-22-1863 Sh
Burke, Margaret to Timothy Casey 1-28-1856 Sh
Burke, Margaret to Wm. Bourk (Burke) 7-26-1856 (7-29-185_) Sh
Burke, Maria to John Malone 2-6-1855 Sh
Burke, Mary to Edwqrd Lynch 8-7-1850 Sh
Burke, Mary to Thos. Shinley 4-30-1851 (5-1-1851) Sh
Burke, Matilda L. to W. F. Tipler 3-7-1856 (3-8-1856) Hr
Burke, Winney to Barney English 8-8-1855 Sh
Burken, Elizabeth to Isaac P. Sellers 3-1-1842 Cr
Burkett, E. to John Parker 7-29-1872 (7-31-1872) Dy
Burkett, Martha M. to B. D. Lightfoot 11-14-1877 (11-15-1877) Dy
Burkett, Mary C. to Benjamin Dodd 4-25-1860 (4-26-1860) Cr
Burkett, Mary to Christopher Stevens 4-18-1840 Cr
Burkett, Sarah L. to James C. Flowers 11-9-1854 Be
Burkham, M. F. to John Massey 3-25-1847 O
Burkhart, Indiana M. to Charles G. Griffith 11-12-1866 (11-13-1866) T
Burkhart, Nancy A. to Isral C. Moore 8-1-1838 G
Burkhart, Safronia Evaline to James H. Fortner 8-27-1846 (9-3-1846) T
Burkhead, Mary Ann to Joshua D. Nailor 1-21-1857 Hr
Burkley, Susan to John Marbry 10-9-1850 Be
Burklow, M. M. to Wm. Therrell 11-6-1868 (no return) F
Burks (Burke), Alice to Dennis Quinlen 5-20-1850 Sh
Burks (Burke), Johanna to Edmond Duggan 11-20-1849 Sh
Burks, Amanda to Wash Fitzpatrick 4-2-1881 (4-4-1881) L B
Burks, Anna to John D. Lankford 2-15-1879 (2-19-1879) L
Burks, Callie to Jim Brown Wardlaw 1-5-1876 (2-6-1876) L
Burks, Callie to W. B. Lankford 12-7-1880 (12-8-1880) L
Burks, Cordelia to Enoch Hume 9-30-1869 L
Burks, Delia A. to Isaac Read 1-15-1886 (1-17-1886) L
Burks, Elizabeth to William Griffin 3-21-1864 Cr
Burks, F. M. to John P. Thompson 12-23-1879 L
Burks, Fannie E. to S. B. Burks 1-15-1884 (1-16-1884) L
Burks, Hattie C. to I. J. Barfield 12-17-1884 L
Burks, L. A. to C. M. Rucker 12-21-1881 (1-5-1882) L
Burks, M. A. to L. B. Keneley 12-21-1881 (12-22-1881) L
Burks, Mary F. to J. R. Smith 8-20-1865 Mn
Burks, Mary Jane to J. R. W. Barfield 12-17-1872 (12-18-1872) L
Burks, Mary to John Trainham 12-21-1866 (12-24-1866) L
Burks, Minnie to R. A. Carnell 11-23-1883 L
Burks, Nancy J. to F. M. Brown 8-17-1864 Mn
Burks, Nancy to W. L. Wood 2-14-1872 L
Burks, Roberta C. E. to Hiram W. Keller 12-18-1860 (12-19-1860) L
Burks, Sarah Adaline to R. L. Wood 11-28-1881 (11-29-1881) L
Burks, Sarah Ann to Z. C. Alvis 1-24-1853 (1-25-1853) Sh
Burks, Tilda to Henry Scott 12-18-1876 (12-26-1876) L
Burks, Viney to Willis Wilson 9-30-1879 (10-1-1879) L B
Burl, Pennie to Phillip Shaw 12-5-1874 T
Burlen, Ella K. to W. B. Malone 1-6-1869 Hy
Burleson, Elizabeth to Jacob Burleson 12-24-1828 (1-8-1829) Hr
Burleson, Jane to William Beachum 1-14-1833 (1-15-1833) Hr
Burleson, Lucinda to William Ervin 7-23-1835 Hr
Burleson, Rebecca to John Baker 12-15-1831 Hr

Burleson, Sarah to Lorenso D. Baker 7-10-1834 (7-15-1834) Hr
Burlesson, Mary to Henry W. Duncan 10-24-1827 (10-27-1827) Hr
Burlison, Katie to R. B. Rogers 9-22-1874 (9-23-1874) L
Burn, Bridget to Michael Cenagan 6-23-1864 (6-24-1864) Sh
Burn, R. E. to W. F. Barritt 2-16-1867 G
Burnam, Mary Ann to Alfred Bigloe 11-13-1854 (11-16-1854) Ma
Burne, Mary to Augustin Dariac (Dauriae?) 11-17-1855 (11-18-1855) Sh
Burnell, Amanda to W. B. Meyers 8-31-1848 Sh
Burnes (Burrus), Fannie to John James 3-26-1874 O
Burnes, Bridget to Edward Farren 6-3-1862 Sh
Burnes, F. E. to C. H. Hill 12-12-1861 Mn
Burnes, Fannie to Andrew Jackson 8-3-1871 (8-4-1871) T
Burnes, Jane to Bird Smith 11-27-1839 (12-1-1839) F
Burnes, Jane to Joseph Butcher 5-6-1829 Hr
Burnes, M. J. to D. C. Thompson 8-5-1859 Hr
Burnes, Manirva to Branch Keathly 5-27-1850 G
Burnes, Margaret E. to Jacob W. Mitchell 11-10-1874 (no return) L
Burnes, Mary to Edward Basset 7-8-1862 Mn
Burnes, Mary to Joseph T. Doulon 4-24-1857 (4-26-1857) Sh
Burnet, Bridget to Michael O'Donald 4-30-1864 (5-1-1864) Sh
Burnet, Hettie to Jim Wilson 11-7-1874 (11-9-1874) T
Burnett, Angeline L. to Benjamin Rutledge 10-23-1854 (10-29-1854) G
Burnett, Ann L. to Charles D. Smith 12-11-1829 Hr
Burnett, Bettie to Tom Mitchell 3-12-1870? Hy
Burnett, Callie E. to J. A. Summers 1-25-1869 (1-27-1869) F
Burnett, Chainey to Steaven Gallaspie 2-6-1878 Hy
Burnett, Charlotte to Henry Campbell 12-18-1870 G B
Burnett, Emily to Samuel Webb 3-19-1857 Be CC
Burnett, Espran to Wm. Flake 2-18-1865 (2-21-1865) Cr
Burnett, Georgianna to J. A. Carter 1-8-1862 Sh
Burnett, Harriett to W. H. Boswell 12-5-1853 (no return) F
Burnett, Ida to Nickodemus Dawson 8-13-1870 G B
Burnett, Letitia to Thos. Simons 1-1-1867 (1-3-1867) Dy
Burnett, M. T. to J. G. Garvin 9-6-1862 (9-9-1862) F
Burnett, Martha A. to William Privett 12-19-1862 (12-25-1862) Dy
Burnett, Martha Ann to C. H. Beachum 7-6-1854 Hr
Burnett, Martha to Will Goodman 9-23-1871 (no return) Hy
Burnett, Mary J. to William H. Wells 5-29-1858 (5-30-1858) L
Burnett, Mary to James W. Boden 12-30-1863 (no return) Hn
Burnett, Moriah to Nat Livingston 12-28-1871 Hy
Burnett, Nancy to M. F. H. Douglass 12-26-1865 (12-31-1865) Cr
Burnett, Rachel to Bennett Noe 9-3-1870 (9-4-1870) Dy
Burnett, Rose to James Counts 11-?-1868 (11-22-1868) Cr
Burnett, Sarah A. to William R. Cooper 10-29-1857 Hn
Burnett, Sarah A. to N. A. Rochell 8-29-1861 (no return) Hy
Burnett, Sarah to James Vaughn 4-26-1855 Hr
Burney, Lou to S. S. Scales 11-22-1876 (no return) Dy
Burney, Martha to Wm. F. Chandler 7-21-1859 Hr
Burney, Nancy A. M. to Allen A. Justice 9-28-1853 G
Burney, Nancy to James Hamilton 10-6-1856 Hr
Burnham, M. W. to T. N. Lott 2-15-1882 (no return) L
Burnham, M. W. to Z. T. Gleaves 12-24-1874 Dy
Burnham, Margaret to Edgar Troy 2-10-1869 (no return) Dy
Burnham, Mary E. to W. H. H. Murray 10-10-1865 (10-11-1865) Dy
Burnham, Nancy Ann to T. B. Ghann? 9-18-1866 (9-19-1866) Dy
Burnham, Parilee to J. P. Freeman 12-23-1873 Dy
Burns, Ann to Daniel Shevlin 10-5-1861 (10-8-1861) Sh
Burns, Ann to Thomas G. Elmore 4-28-1834 Hr
Burns, Annie to James Larkin 12-21-1860 (12-22-1860) Sh
Burns, Augusta A. to J. A. Robinson 12-10-1857 Cr
Burns, Barbary to H. H. Wesson 10-14-1847 Be
Burns, Bridget to Michael Canaghen 6-23-1864 Sh
Burns, C. T. to S. J. Veach 12-5-1853 (12-11-1853) O
Burns, Catherine to Wm. A. Crossett 3-20-1845 Cr
Burns, Civil H. to Soloman Braden 11-15-1868 Hy
Burns, Clora to Isaac Owen 3-30-1871 Hy
Burns, Delila J. to J. Strange 4-11-1842 (4-12-1842) F
Burns, E. to James Bitter 12-13-1861 (12-15-1861) Cr
Burns, Eliz. to Franklin Cox 11-13-1871 T
Burns, Elizabeth C. to Lindsy B. Brown 11-18-1852 Sh
Burns, Elizabeth S. to John Guffey 8-3-1868 (8-4-1868) Cr
Burns, Elizabeth to John A. Pierce 9-4-1849 Cr
Burns, Elizabeth to Shadrach Sl. Frye? 6-28-1834 (7-3-1834) Hr
Burns, Ellen to Wm. Ahearn 2-22-1854 Sh
Burns, Ellen to Wm. Henry 9-26-1857 Cr
Burns, Elzy to James Ritter 12-13-1861 (12-15-1861) Cr
Burns, Emily to J. M. Hiant 3-17-1853 Be
Burns, Fannie to Frank Tucker 5-6-1878 Hy
Burns, H. A. to J. F. Kelley 8-2-1879 (8-3-1879) L
Burns, Harriet to Elisha Earls 9-12-1858 Cr
Burns, J. J. to E. Johnson 8-28-1858 Ma
Burns, Keziah to Plumer Thomas 3-28-1872 Hy
Burns, L. J. to A. R. Goodman 12-27-1860 (no return) Cr
Burns, L. S. to W. P. Wilkins 10-8-1860 (10-9-1860) L
Burns, Lamira R. to James T. Gibbon 8-21-1861 (8-22-1861) Cr
Burns, Laura Anna (Mrs.) to Williamson Coleman O'Leary 11-5-1864 (11-6-1864) Sh
Burns, Lavinia (Lousiana) to David G. Campbell 8-13-1846 Sh
Burns, M. A. to J. B. Griggs 8-2-1879 (8-3-1879) L
Burns, Maggie to J. C. Saunder 2-2-1870 Dy
Burns, Martha to David D. Harris 11-20-1843 Sh
Burns, Mary E. to John A. Barnes 12-4-1851 Be
Burns, Mary L. to Wm. W. Smith 1-16-1857 (1-23-1857) Sh
Burns, Mary to Austin J. Albright 2-4-1864 (no return) Cr
Burns, Mary to Moses Garrett 4-16-1879 L
Burns, Mary to Peter Cunningham 6-28-1853 Sh
Burns, Matilda J. to John W. Jones 10-20-1859 Cr
Burns, Matilda to Johnson Sutherland 11-24-1881 L B
Burns, Nancy L. to Graves H. Walker 2-24-1870 G
Burns, Nancy to Geo. Stephenson 12-31-1851 Sh
Burns, Nancy to Hiram W. Ross 7-7-1828 Hr
Burns, Nancy to James Tedder 6-14-1846 Be
Burns, P. to James Goodlow 2-4-1869 Cr
Burns, Phildes to Hardyman Forhand 6-4-1846 Be
Burns, Rebecca to Bradford Read 12-7-1833 Hr
Burns, Sally to Joseph M. Wells 1-2-1830 (1-9-1830) Hr
Burns, Sarah A. to Thomas F. Crawford 12-24-1857 Cr
Burns, Sarah to C. H. Martin 7-22-1861 (7-24-1861) Cr
Burns, Sarah to Wm. Puryear 9-7-1848 Sh
Burns, Virginia B. to J. T. McKinney 6-20-1881 (no return) L
Burns?, Ammy to Gipson Earp 12-11-1851 Be
Burns?, Ellen to James McGowen 7-27-1854 Sh
Burnset, Charlotte E. to Mark Holman 9-10-1846 (9-17-1846) F
Burnum, Sarah to Silas S. Lynton 9-15-1840 (no return) Hn
Burnwat, D. A. to James M. Ray 5-4-1858 (5-6-1858) G
Burr, Mary to Lewis Casey 3-28-1863 Sh
Burr, Sidy to John S. Wood 10-30-1849 G
Burras, Francis Ann to Robert Z. Watson 9-8-1853 (9-7?-1853) Ma
Burrel, Catharine to Christofer Hunt 2-22-1868 T
Burrel, Katie to Charles Smith 12-17-1873 T
Burrel, Mary to Cambridge Taylor 12-28-1869 T
Burrel, Maryetta to Jacob Davis 12-17-1873 (12-20-1873) T
Burrell, Mary to Caesar Washington 1-15-1870 G B
Burres, Emily to Thomas Lewis 4-18-1843 Sh
Burres, Lucinda to Daniel Hopper 10-4-1838 Ma
Burress, Lucinda to William Markham 1-26-1840 Hn
Burress, Nancy M. to Wm. Twitty 8-19-1851 Sh
Burress, Nancy to John Elder 4-27-1842 T
Burris, Elizabeth to Daniel Cunningham 5-7-1863 Sh
Burris, M. E. to Wm. C. Brown 2-19-1865? O
Burris, Mollie W. to G. W. Dent 10-11-1869 (10-12-1869) Cr
Burris, Sally V. to J. D. Jones 11-20-1861 (11-21-1861) O
Burriss, Martha to Richard B. Wilson 10-14-1847 F
Burrough, Ellen to Henry Smith 12-4-1869 (no return) F B
Burrough, Mary C. to James M. Hafley 2-1-1870 Ma
Burroughs, Eugenia E. to Sterling M. Black 10-23-1869 (10-27-1869) F
Burrow, Addie H. to James A. L. Davie 12-15-1860 (12-16-1860) Ma
Burrow, Beverly to Wm. Robinson 9-15-1844 Cr
Burrow, Caroline to Wm. Perser 8-16-1849 (no return) F
Burrow, Catharine to Levi S. Bone 2-4-1839 (2-7-1839) O
Burrow, Catherine to James M. Medlin 12-18-1850 Ma
Burrow, Charity E. to Isaac Jones 8-15-1844 Cr
Burrow, Delila M. to Thomas W. Leach 1-31-1866 (2-1-1866) Cr
Burrow, Elender to John McWilliams 11-12-1846 Cr
Burrow, Eliza E. to Samuel L. Collins 8-19-1856 Cr
Burrow, Elizabeth R. to J. L. Burrow 3-12-1859 (3-13-1859) G
Burrow, Elizabeth to G. F. Bishop 3-27-1866 (3-29-1866) Cr
Burrow, Ellen to Estorn Parks 1-21-1867 G
Burrow, Elvira M. to J. W. Williams 12-4-1865 (12-6-1865) Cr
Burrow, Emily to Smith A. Herron 10-3-1859 (no return) Cr
Burrow, Harriett to James W. Mchelby 12-8-1854 Cr
Burrow, Jane to Daniel Ramsey 4-30-1846 Cr
Burrow, Jane to John M. Meak 10-24-1848 (no return) F
Burrow, Jula Ann to Samuel Daniel 4-30-1873 (5-1-1873) Cr B
Burrow, Letha to William Crenshaw 1-4-1870 (1-5-1870) Cr
Burrow, Lucinda O. to Miles A. Dillard 7-28-1854 (no return) F
Burrow, Lucy to Wm. G. Nipper 12-16-1848 Cr
Burrow, M. A. to S. C. Mills 1-27-1873 Cr
Burrow, M. E. C. to John S. Bryant 1-19-1860 Cr
Burrow, Margaret Ann to James Balentine 2-19-1857 Ma
Burrow, Martha E. to Warren B. Seward 7-12-1855 (7-13-1855) G
Burrow, Martha to Moses Hurley 2-10-1846 (2-12-1846) G
Burrow, Mary H. to Jubelee P. Rogers 4-15-1847 Ma
Burrow, Mary H. to Jubille P. Rodgers 4-15-1847 Cr
Burrow, Mary J. to Benj. H. Wortham 9-8-1846 (no return) F
Burrow, Mary J. to Evanda McGowen 8-16-1854 Cr
Burrow, Mary P. to Wm. Blanks 1-17-1859 Cr
Burrow, Mary to Abram Gurganes 1-31-1859 (2-2-1859) G
Burrow, Meloria S. to T. Lewis Smith 6-11-1856 (7-3-1856) Hr
Burrow, N. J. to K. K. Patterson 10-9-1861 Mn
Burrow, Nancy to William Mays 9-26-1860 Cr
Burrow, Penelope E. to Z. T. Bellows? 10-3-1860 (10-7-1860) Cr
Burrow, Rebecca A. to James A. McDougal 9-17-1853 Cr
Burrow, Rebecca to James Blanks 10-7-1850 Cr

Burrow, Sarah A. to Henry Carter 10-20-1847 Cr
Burrow, Sarah E. to Jonathan B. Agee 12-18-1850 G
Burrow, Sarah Jane to A. R. Nichols 5-26-1865 (no return) Cr
Burrow, Sarah to Henry Burrow 11-23-1847 Cr
Burrow, Sarah to T. H. McGowen 8-16-1854 Cr
Burrow, Susan to James Moten 8-5-1871 (8-13-1871) Cr
Burrow, Susan to Samuel Enloe 11-2-1868 (11-8-1868) Cr
Burrow, Tennessee A. to John D. Agee 7-4-1865 G
Burrow, Timitha E. to Wm. G. Ward 6-13-1854 G
Burrow?, Frances to George Ray 11-7-1833 Hr
Burrows, Catharine to Wm. M. Chambers 1-29-1855 (no return) F
Burrus, Martha J. to William R. Faucett 5-7-1870 (5-8-1870) Ma
Burrus, Martha to John W. Robinson 11-22-1842 (11-23-1842) Ma
Burrus, Mary to Austin J. Albright 2-4-1864 (2-7-1864) Cr
Bursbe, Mary A. to James K. Widener 5-31-1870 L
Burson, Catherine to John L. Robison 11-29-1862 Ma
Burt, H. W. to A. B. Finny 10-29-1854 (no return) F
Burt, Martha W. to Gilliad A. Sanders 8-19-1840 Hr
Burt, Mary Ann to James Harper 12-21-1838 Sh
Burt, Mary Ann to James Robinson 8-18-1832 Hr
Burtie, Harriet to Branch Currie 5-30-1874 Hy
Burtis, N. E. to J. Deloach 9-4-1882 (9-5-1882) L
Burton, A. P. to A. H. McClane 12-20-1864 Hn
Burton, Anna A. to Vincent R. Stafford 12-19-1838 (12-20-1838) F
Burton, Arky to William Roberts 12-8-1844 Be
Burton, C. C. to Thomas Kendal 11-12-1860 We
Burton, Callie to Alfonza S. Jones 12-18-1862 We
Burton, Carmelia to James Ratteree 6-16-1840 (no return) Hn
Burton, Caroline to Felix Hicks 1-19-1869 L
Burton, Catherine to Edmund Dickens 12-25-1838 Ma
Burton, E. W. to J. Lax 11-7-1865 Hn
Burton, Eliza A. H. to Jas. M. Halford 10-30-1837 (10-31-1837) G
Burton, Elizabeth E. to Henry Warren 11-1-1838 Sh
Burton, Elizabeth to A. B. Cavens 12-22-1860 (12-24-1860) Hr
Burton, Elizabeth to Cullen Phillips 3-31-1842 Hn
Burton, Elizabeth to E. L. Peters 4-18-1850 (no return) F
Burton, Elizabeth to Henry Thomas 2-20-1867 Hy
Burton, Elizabeth to John McIntosh 12-13-1838 Hr
Burton, Elizabeth to Wm. Parish 1-12-1854 Cr
Burton, Ellen to Levy Harris 1-18-1874 Hy
Burton, Frances J. to James B. Hunt 12-7-1872 (12-12-1872) T
Burton, Jane A. to Samuel Z. Watson 2-12-1857 Hn
Burton, Julia A. to T. J. Towlkes 7-16-1857 F
Burton, Kitty to James Johnston 10-30-1882 (11-17-1882) L
Burton, Laura A. to Sam N. Sidney 12-4-1876 (12-14-1876) Dy
Burton, Louisa to Mc Gaskins 7-22-1848 (7-23-1848) O
Burton, Lucy F. to J. J. Pulliam 4-24-1850 F
Burton, M. J. to Joseph Shipley 3-23-1856 Hn
Burton, Mariah to James C. Clough 8-4-1846 Hn
Burton, Marieller to James P. Mercer 5-12-1855 (no return) F
Burton, Martha A. to Edward T. Busey 1-3-1842 (no return) Hn
Burton, Martha to John Watson 2-15-1850 Hn
Burton, Martha to William Oldham 2-14-1883 L
Burton, Marthena to Cornelius Perkins 10-26-1858 O
Burton, Mary Ann to Daniel Adams Trobough 6-24-1846 (6-25-1846) T
Burton, Mary F. to David Menzies 10-31-1872 (no return) Dy
Burton, Mary T. to Samuel Carter 10-31-1843 Hn
Burton, Mary to Monroe Bucy 11-29-1865 Hn
Burton, Nancy E. to Wm. A. Murphy 11-2-1855 (11-4-1855) Sh
Burton, Nancy to Benjamin C. Rou___? 12-7-1843 Hn
Burton, Paulina to Isaiah Ford 1-22-1879 (1-23-1879) L
Burton, Pheby A. to Silas Bradford 2-22-1871 (no return) Hy
Burton, Sarah to E. D. Pryer 5-4-1848 Hn
Burton, Sarah to John Hargroves 12-28-1856 Hn
Burton, Susan to Geo. K. Stockslager 10-15-1857 Sh
Burton, Susan to Josiah Keith 2-13-1857 (2-16-1857) O
Burton, Tabitha Ann to Joseph Shipley 1-19-1862 Hn
Burton, Traney to James W. Wofford 1-16-1839 (no return) Hn
Burton, Virginia C. to Jas. C. Allbritton 12-27-1865 Hn
Burton, Winney Sidney to C. T. Lippard 8-31-1857 O
Burton?, Polly to William Winn 4-25-1846 Hn
Burtus, Sarah to William L. Cole 12-22-1847 (12-23-1847) F
Burus, Ellen B. to Calier A. Steed 1-20-1857 Ma
Burwell, Ann to Henry Avery 3-25-1863 (3-25-1863) Dy
Buryhill, Hannah to Wm. Ketchum 2-7-1846 We
Buryhill, Mary A. to G. C. McAllister 10-20-1846 We
Buryman, I. Ann to Columbus Sweat 10-27-1861 Mn
Busbee, Angeline to A. J. Hudson 12-24-1863 Hn
Busbee, Susan to John W. Thomas 10-29-1866 Hn B
Busbee?, Sucett to Valentine M. Cramnatt 5-26-1860 Hn
Busby, Dilly A. to Thomas G. Richardson 12-7-1852 Hn
Busby, E. J. to William Landrum 8-2-1871 O
Busby, Heneritta to Allen Bethune 7-31-1830 (8-2-1830) Ma
Busby, Jane to J. R. Taylor 12-28-1865 Hn
Busby, Jennie to Grant A. DeBow 8-20-1861 We
Busby, Lotta to John Rees 11-30-1856 We
Busby, Martha H. to H. Pettyjohn 5-1-1864 Hn

Busby, Mary A. to Joshua L. Jones 5-25-1847 Hn
Busby, Polly to John Measles 7-31-1830 Sh
Busby, Sarah to S. B. Allen 1-19-1858 (no return) We
Busby, Senly to Newten J. Capps 1-13-1858 (no return) We
Busey, Sarah M. to Benj. W. Jeter 4-13-1868 (4-16-1868) F
Busey, Sarah to James Russel 1-6-1872 (no return) Cr
Bush, Ann Jane to Edwin Fonville 12-12-1831 G
Bush, Elizabeth A. to John B. L. Rye 10-15-1854 Hn
Bush, Honell M. to James Jackson 9-3-1856 Cr
Bush, Isabella to William Hazell 1-8-1879 (1-9-1879) L
Bush, Jane to G. W. Greer 10-5-1854 Be
Bush, Lanny to Jacob Emmerson 1-4-1844 Hn
Bush, Lucinda M. to A. E. Mullins 6-4-1857 Sh
Bush, Maranda H. to Wm. H. Ward 4-14-1853 Be
Bush, Martha E. to H. B. French 10-17-1867 Hn
Bush, Martha L. to Benjamin Hailey 12-28-1854 Hn
Bush, Martha to John Carter 3-15-1839 Cr
Bush, Mollie to Phil Mootry 12-12-1883 (12-13-1883) L
Bush, Mollie to Thomas Lucas 12-23-1868 (no return) L
Bush, Nancy Jane to John J. Bush 12-3-1845 Be
Bush, Nancy V. to Robert S. Waters 11-2-1865 (no return) Hn
Bush, Susan Ann to Elisha Emerson 1-2-1849 Hn
Bush, Susan Elizabeth to David Cole 10-24-1845 Be
Bush, Tanizen E. to George W. Emmerson 12-29-1853 Hn
Bushard, Emeline to Benj. F. White 12-19-1866 (12-20-1866) Ma
Bushart, Amanda to William Haley 11-11-1854 Hn
Bushart, Delila A. to J. N. Hermon 11-12-1867 Hn
Bushart, Elizabeth to Charles L. Bacchus 11-2-1843 Hn
Bushart, Mariah C. to Elijah Harnesberry 2-8-1853 Hn
Bushart, Martha J. to John W. McCord 8-14-1848 Hn
Bushart, Mary Ann to John S. Puckett 9-23-1851 Hn
Bushart, Susan to David Underwood 1-27-1864 Hn
Busick, Betsy J. to George Giles 2-7-1858 Cr
Buslen, L. K. to A. M. Gladish 7-13-1862 Mn
Busse, Hulda to August Halberstadt 4-27-1861 Sh
Busseck, Nancy to Thomas Williams 8-3-1840 Cr
Bussel, Martha Ann to Hiram Watkins 12-25-1850 Be
Bussey, Ann Eliza to J. M. Tidwell 3-22-1850 (3-26?-1850) Sh
Bustard, Lucy A. to Wm. Mullins 3-12-1857 Sh
Busted, Elizabeth I. to Samuel L. Slack 9-6-1838 Sh
Buster, Frances S. to John W. Kilpatrick 11-17-1869 T
Buster, Nancy A. to L. C. Bill 10-18-1854 (no return) We
Buster, Nannie M. to Drew H. Pope 9-11-1850 (9-18-1850) Sh
Bustin, Nancy (Mary) to William S. Williams 1-22-1846 Sh
Bustle, Ellender to John M. Palmer 12-7-1855 (no return) We
Butcher, Betsy to James Campbell 12-18-1828 Sh
Butcher, Josephine to James A. Dugard 5-31-1843 Sh
Butcher, Martha L. to John D. Latham 3-18-1863 We
Butcher, Neely to George Davis 11-30-1875 (no return) Hy
Butler, A. B. to H. L. Mooring 2-27-1854 (3-2-1854) Ma
Butler, A. E. to J. A. Lorance 9-15-1865 G
Butler, Abigail (Mrs) to Albert Townsend 6-25-1862 (no return) Cr
Butler, Adaline E. to M. M. Conley 12-22-1869 Cr
Butler, Adaline to J. M. Spellings 1-20-1851 Cr
Butler, Angeline to E. R. Kyle 5-17-1866 (5-13-1866) Cr
Butler, Ann A. to John A. Boyte 1-11-1854 (1-12-1854) Hr
Butler, Ann E. to John T. Brown 11-23-1859 (11-24-1859) Ma
Butler, Ann to Edward Tighe 2-20-1860 Sh
Butler, Anna to Thos. L. Rowland 9-18-1872 Cr
Butler, Artemissa to Willis Roberts 12-8-1869 (12-9-1869) Cr
Butler, Carroline to Peter Glascock 2-12-1842 (2-15-1842) G
Butler, Clarissa C. to Henry Williamson 12-13-1856 (12-14-1856) G
Butler, Daney Ann to Albert Birdwell 4-5-1864 (4-6-1864) Cr
Butler, Deby D. to Phillip West 1-3-1849 G
Butler, Eliza to J. R. Mills 2-21-1870 G
Butler, Eliza to John W. Lawrance 4-2-1849 Cr
Butler, Elizabeth B. to John R. King 4-18-1870 (4-19-1870) Cr
Butler, Elizabeth C. to Caleb Odam 8-30-1853 (8-31-1853) Ma
Butler, Elizabeth D. to William C. Royal 8-26-1866 (8-27-1866) Cr
Butler, Elizabeth M. to Jackson G. Butler 12-4-1852 (12-8-1852) Ma
Butler, Elizabeth to Jesse Edwards 3-10-1867 G
Butler, Elizabeth to Jones Jackson 11-6-1845 Cr
Butler, Elizabeth to Thomas King 6-12-1824 Hr
Butler, Elizabeth to William N. Morgan 9-11-1828 Ma
Butler, Elmira to James Cothran 12-18-1843 (12-21-1843) T
Butler, Emanda C. to Kirby Dows 5-8-1855 Cr
Butler, Epsey M. to Jessee J. Hays 9-25-1845 G
Butler, Eugenia to William Jack 2-16-1854 Sh
Butler, Eviline to Thomas Welch 10-29-1866 G
Butler, Frances C. to Minus O. Adams 1-10-1859 (1-11-1859) Ma
Butler, Frances P. to Wm. R. Salmons 9-9-1841 Cr
Butler, Hannah to Hugh Hone 10-21-1861 Sh
Butler, Harriett to Harvey Palmer 1-13-1872 (1-14-1872) Cr
Butler, Isabella to William A. Kennedy 6-18-1840 Sh
Butler, J. A. to B. F. Cox 6-8-1867 (6-23-1867) Cr
Butler, J. P. to Wm. A. Brackin 8-28-1872 (8-29-1872) Cr
Butler, J. to W. A. Taylor 8-18-1867 G

Brides

Butler, Jane E. to David F. Smith 10-31-1864 (4-9-1864?) Dy
Butler, Jane to John Millard 9-12-1867 G B
Butler, Jenny to Henry Nash 12-25-1873 Hy
Butler, Judith O. to Wm. A. Britt 5-14-1854 Cr
Butler, Judith to Claborn Parish 2-7-1839 Cr
Butler, Judy to Jeremiah O'Donald 7-25-1857 (7-26-1857) Sh
Butler, Julia to Sam Davis 11-24-1880 (11-25-1880) L B
Butler, Julian to John P. Steller 11-17-1832 (11-18-1832) G
Butler, Katharine J. to W. W. Ritchie 8-24-1858 Sh
Butler, Kathrine to John B. McArthur 8-23-1855 Cr
Butler, L. E. to W. M. Smith 11-11-1872 (11-13-1872) Cr
Butler, L. W. to J. M. McAulay 12-29-1870 Cr
Butler, L. to Jas. T. Holt 4-10-1860 G
Butler, Lanna to Nathaniel Townsend 9-18-1871 Cr
Butler, Letty to John Griffin 9-16-1871 (9-21-1871) T
Butler, Levinia R. to Byrd Hill 10-21-1852 Ma
Butler, Lilphia to Joel M. Stone 8-23-1826 Hr
Butler, Louisa Ann to Miles W. Sedberry 2-24-1852 Cr
Butler, Louisa C. to J. Copeland 12-18-1855 Sh
Butler, Louisa C. to J. G. Smith 12-4-1868 Be
Butler, Louisa J. to Haywood F. Harris 3-2-1863 Cr
Butler, Louisa J. to Haywood F. Harris 3-2-1863 (no return) Cr
Butler, Louisa to Carroll J. Pickler 9-5-1854 Cr
Butler, Lucy to Jesse Pickler 8-2-1865 (8-3-1865) Cr
Butler, Lucy to John Mills 12-4-1852 (12-9-1852) Ma
Butler, Luentia to W. H. R. Alexander 2-28-1850 (no return) Hn
Butler, M. A. to Samuel Jack 2-16-1864 (2-17-1864) Sh
Butler, M. F. to M. Jacobs 1-1-1867 G
Butler, M. J. to Thos. A. Selmons 6-25-1864 (7-3-1864) Cr
Butler, Manerva to J. D. Pinkston 4-29-1870 (5-7-1870) Cr
Butler, Margaret A. to Tapley Adam 8-24-1853 (8-25-1853) Ma
Butler, Mariah J. to Patrick H. Soloman 1-30-1844 Cr
Butler, Marinda to Wm. R. Wynn 3-7-1849 Be
Butler, Martha E. to Charles P. Lynch 7-31-1849 Sh
Butler, Martha J. to J. W. W. Borum 1-2-1869 (1-4-1869) Dy
Butler, Martha J. to Joshua C. Boyd 3-15-1847 Cr
Butler, Martha J. to S. P. Kirtland no dates (with 1860) T
Butler, Martha L. to Elijah G. Rogers 1-21-1868 (1-22-1868) Cr
Butler, Martha T. to Ely Morris 5-1-1856 Cr
Butler, Martha to Andrew Sexton 3-7-1850 (3-8-1850) G
Butler, Martha to Robert Crawford 10-19-1869 (10-24-1869) Cr
Butler, Martha to S. P. Kirkland 1-2-1860 (1-4-1860) T
Butler, Mary A. to Jenkins Cox 12-22-1848 Sh
Butler, Mary A. to Nathan Williams 1-1-1853 Cr
Butler, Mary A. to S. E. Hawkins 6-21-1864 (6-22-1864) Sh
Butler, Mary Ann to A. J. Blane 2-15-1864 F
Butler, Mary Ann to Edmond Tho. Yarbrough 7-14-1853 T
Butler, Mary Ann to John C. Rogers 4-12-1847 Ma
Butler, Mary Ann to Wiley Bunch 2-16-1837 Sh
Butler, Mary E. to Benj. A. Saunders 9-19-1860 (9-20-1860) Cr
Butler, Mary E. to Howell Little 11-12-1840 G
Butler, Mary E. to Robert Espy 2-28-1868 Hy
Butler, Mary E. to William J. Knowles 6-12-1875 (6-13-1875) Dy
Butler, Mary H. to Joll B. Medines 10-27-1848 Cr
Butler, Mary J. to A. Barker 12-5-1857 Cr
Butler, Mary L. to Alexa Rogers 1-27-1842 Cr
Butler, Mary S. to James T. Willson 2-22-1871 Cr
Butler, Mary to James Hegarty 11-23-1864 (11-24-1864) Sh
Butler, Mary to John Reynolds 2-11-1862 G
Butler, Mary to Larkin Bibee (Jenkins?) 5-22-1839 Sh
Butler, Mary to P. C. Garrison 12-27-1840 Cr
Butler, Mary to Peola? Howard 12-22-1842 (12-?-1842) T
Butler, Mary to Thomas G. Pate 8-3-1831 Ma
Butler, Mary to William Arnold 11-16-1843 We
Butler, Matilda to George Wood 10-7-1869 T
Butler, Matilda to Henry Haynes 1-2-1828 (1-3-1828) Ma
Butler, Miss A. S. to G. W. Cherry 7-18-1861 (7-19-1861) T
Butler, Nancy A. to A. C. Andrews 1-24-1871 (no return) Dy
Butler, Nancy C. to Jarvis Starkey 10-25-1858 (10-27-1858) Ma
Butler, Nancy J. to J. D. Carrol 3-26-1861 G
Butler, Nancy to Hiram D. Bunch 11-14-1829 Sh
Butler, Nancy to Wm. Parker 12-15-1842 Cr
Butler, Narcissa E. to George E. Hassell 10-6-1855 (10-7-1855) G
Butler, Narcissa H. to Napoleon Gentry 7-1-1868 (7-2-1868) Ma
Butler, Neter T. to W. A. McArthur 5-1-1856 Cr
Butler, Ortha N. to William J. Townsend 8-27-1868 (8-28-1868) Cr
Butler, Paralee to Charles Austin 7-25-1870 (7-27-1870) Cr
Butler, Parthena A. M. to William McLain 8-9-1861 (8-10-1861) T
Butler, Parthena to R. Wilson Latham 6-1-1872 (6-2-1872) Cr
Butler, Polly J. to J. M. Elkins 10-11-1871 (10-12-1871) Cr
Butler, Polly to Wm. Hartwell Burke 6-13-1827 Sh
Butler, R. C. to W. C. Horton 3-11-1872 Cr
Butler, Rebecca S. to Joseph Wise 4-1-1877 Hy
Butler, Rebecca to Preston Hess 10-28-1859 O
Butler, S. F. to J. W. Rowe 8-10-1872 (8-12-1872) Cr
Butler, S. L. to Elias McAuley 1-1-1851 Cr
Butler, Sally to John Bunch 6-13-1827 Sh
Butler, Sally to Robert Baden 4-25-1877 Hy
Butler, Sally to W. E. Jacobs 12-22-1869 G
Butler, Sarah A. to Duncan McMillian 12-19-1850 Cr
Butler, Sarah A. to W. C. Trice 8-21-1854 Sh
Butler, Sarah C. to Phillip T. Butler 3-2-1864 (3-3-1864) Cr
Butler, Sarah F. to Wm. R. Roberson 11-27-1872 Cr
Butler, Sarah Jane to William H. Seat 8-25-1856 (8-26-1856) Ma
Butler, Sarah T. to J. W. Swearengin 1-10-1855 Cr
Butler, Sarah to Eliza Spoon 6-8-1845 Cr
Butler, Sarah to J. K. Sampson 2-10-1848 Cr
Butler, Sarah to Joshua B. Marsh 4-3-1848 Ma
Butler, Sarena to James Powers 10-28-1845 We
Butler, Sophena A. to Wm. H. Peace 1-15-1857 Cr
Butler, Sophia to J. R. Batten 11-27-1869 (11-30-1869) Cr
Butler, Susanah A. to David Hassell 12-6-1854 Cr
Butler, T. B. to J. M. Woods 2-1-1868 (2-5-1868) Cr
Butler, Tempy to Wm. G. Butler 12-21-1842 Cr
Butler, Terry to Robert G. Raney 11-18-1843 Ma
Butler, Virginia E. to Elijah M. Lowrey 2-24-1870 (2-25-1870) Cr
Butler?, Laura L. to William B. Lee 11-8-1869 (no return) L
Butram, Delila to Eli Eaton(Caton) 10-26-1839 Be
Butram, E. N. to H. A. Huff 10-2-1870 G
Butram, Louisa B. to James P. Butler 2-1860 O
Butram, M. L. to N. W. Halford 3-8-1866 G
Butram, Mary Ann D. to James M. Brown 8-11-1856 O
Butram, Metilda F. to J. F. Fletcher 6-13-1860 G
Butram, Nancy to Allen Leroy Dunlap 8-16-1848 (8-17-1848) G
Butram, Rebecca to Abraham Hancock 3-10-1858 G
Butrum, Sarah A. F. to George Box 11-3-1858 (11-4-1858) O
Butry?, M. N. to John Cloar 7-22-1866 G
Butt (Britt), Ella to John Riley 9-30-1874 Hy
Butterworth, Ann to Uel H. Farmer 10-10-1839 F
Butterworth, Ann to William Gerritt 6-1-1867 (no return) Dy
Butterworth, Isabella to Jacob McCoy 3-18-1868 (3-19-1868) Dy
Butterworth, L. J. to R. T. Butterworth 2-9-1872 (2-10-1872) Dy
Butterworth, Mary E. to Lucien W. Smith 8-14-1877 (8-15-1877) Dy
Butterworth, Mary E. to Wm. W. Spence 12-6-1847 (12-8-1847) F
Butterworth, S. E. to Richd. R. Gwyn 11-10-1859 (11-15-1859) F
Buttner?, Lucy to Daniel Mason 11-20-1872 T
Butts, Elizabeth B. to John Wood 6-27-1859 Sh
Butts, Judia H. to Joseph E. Langford 1-2-1860 (1-4-1860) Ma
Butts, Mary A. L. to Henry Worrell 11-26-1849 Ma
Butts, Mary A. to Isaac Bagnell 1-24-1849 Ma
Byars, Alabama S. to William J. Renfro 10-27-1863 Hn
Byars, Armenta to Simpson Cox 11-12-1845 Hn
Byars, Coatney to Patrick Clay 12-25-1870 Hy
Byars, Dicy M. to John R. Townsend 12-17-1872 (12-18-1872) T
Byars, E. M. to C. S. Henley 1-8-1878 Hy
Byars, Elizabeth to Franklin Clore? 5-30-1864 (no return) Hn
Byars, Emeline to Albert Bowers 12-28-1870 (no return) Hy
Byars, Emily J. to Alexander Lampkins 2-6-1850 Hn
Byars, Fannie to Pleasant Parker 12-21-1876 Hy
Byars, Febby to Clarance Tyus 3-5-1875 Hy
Byars, Isay to Isaac R. Coffman 3-4-1866 Hn
Byars, Joanna to Henry Gause 1-29-1881 (1-30-1881) L
Byars, Julia to Samuel Winstead 8-13-1856 We
Byars, Lillie to Shedrick Jones 11-18-1873 Hy
Byars, M. A. to A. H. Lampkins 9-11-1863 Hn
Byars, Mary Ann to G. W. Scott 12-7-1854 Hn
Byars, Mary to Henrique Henley 4-11-1876 Hy
Byars, Sarah H. to G. W. Scott 5-15-1863 Hn
Byars, Sarah to Plesant Thacher 12-14-1852 We
Byars, Sue to Geo. Johnson 11-29-1872 Hy
Byars, Susan P. to John H. Collins 3-2-1859 Hn
Byas, Ella to Henry Towsen 1-28-1882 (1-29-1882) L
Byas?, Paralee to I. N. Olive 10-2-1864 Hn
Byers, Rosina to Jno. G. Frick 6-30-1849 Sh
Byers, Sarah E. to Jeremiah T. Bolton 9-20-1865 (9-21-1865) Cr
Byford, Milly to John Hatfield 11-7-1870 L
Byford?, Aphra to James Hatfield 11-29-1870 (12-1-1870) L
Byler, Caro A. to Henry D. Rulkley (Bulkley?) 12-15-1853 Sh
Byler, Johanna M. to J. W. Goff 3-9-1883 L
Byler, M. F. to W. F. Keltner 6-22-1882 (6-28-1882) L
Byler, Mary to Hardy Hicks 11-3-1853 L
Byler, S. E. to J. S. Cowell 1-7-1879 (1-8-1879) L
Bylor, Fannie L. to G. W. Webb 1-24-1877 L
Bynum, Catherine C. to Rufus D. Pouncy 7-15-1860 We
Bynum, Elizabeth to Washington Eddins 5-12-1846 (5-22-1846) F
Bynum, J. A. to J. T. Rowland 4-7-1876 (3-11-1877) O
Bynum, M. A. to David S. Wagster 12-31-1850 We
Bynum, Mary to J. R. Riggans 12-7-1854 We
Bynum, N. L. to Wm. B. Boyett 4-20-1865 O
Bynum, Nancy S. to Benjamin H. Dick 1-25-1861 We
Bynum, Nancy to William Yates 8-4-1866 (8-5-1866) T
Bynum, Rosalean to W. Y. Pickens 12-18-1877 O
Bynum, Sallie J. to Rob't S. Matthews 1-3-1868 O
Bynum, Sarah J. to Bennett B. Williams 1-5-1863 We

Bynum, Susan to Jack Roberson 12-15-1876 Hy
Bynum, T. A. to B. F. Lancaster 12-14-1876 O
Byram, Ann C. to James J. Tarry 6-20-1863 Sh
Byram, Annie F. to J. D. McGrath 11-23-1874 (11-25-1874) T
Byram, Eliza Jane to David M. Snell 2-1-1851 (2-4-1851) Sh
Byram, Ellen O. to Giles Brough 8-12-1863 (8-16-1863) T
Byram, Jemima to D. T. Perkins 10-31-1872 Hy
Byram, Margaret to William Bland 5-22-1861 (5-24-1861) Sh
Byram, Mary F. to J. C. Grisham 12-20-1874 Hy
Byram, R. F. to T. E. Silvertooth 6-6-1881 (6-8-1881) L
Byrd, A. A. to Jessee C. Benson 2-14-1868 (2-20-1868) T
Byrd, Amanda to W. B. Glisson 11-6-1871 O
Byrd, Elvira M. (Mrs.) to William Pope 12-12-1859 Ma
Byrd, M. R. to L. W. Hamilton 2-15-1870 (2-20-1870) T
Byrd, Mrs. E. A. to J. F. Timmon 12-19-1867 (12-22-1867) T
Byrd, Mrs. to John C. Caughein 10-2-1869 T
Byrd, V.? F. to B. L. Matthis 2-21-1866 (2-22-1866) T
Byrn, Amanda M. to W. R. Miller 3-26-1874 L
Byrn, Amanda to Charles Barnes 11-26-1855 Be
Byrn, Bettie A. to David Dennie 11-7-1866 L
Byrn, Darthala to Felix G. Fergason 10-10-1854 (10-11-1854) L
Byrn, Darthula E. to Edward M. Stacy 2-4-1864 (2-5-1871) L
Byrn, F. E. to John A. Stewart 12-31-1878 (1-1-1879) L
Byrn, Fannie to Elbert Scott 12-29-1883 L
Byrn, Frances A. to Clabourn Herren 11-6-1865 Be
Byrn, G. A. to J. W. Thompson 12-22-1880 L
Byrn, Jane to Nelson Palmer 3-12-1869 (3-13-1869) L
Byrn, Katy to Andrew Rankin 3-18-1876 (3-19-1876) L B
Byrn, L. B. to Lafayett Wilson 11-16-1867 O
Byrn, Louisa to Alfred Gaunt 11-6-1875 L
Byrn, Lucretia to Church Partee 2-24-1877 L
Byrn, M. F. E. to William E. Lynn 7-8-1869 L
Byrn, Manirva F. to John McIver 11-9-1854 L
Byrn, Margaret to Wilson Frost 11-18-1867 Dy
Byrn, Mary Ann to William J. Moore 12-2-1857 L
Byrn, Mary E. to Saml. D. Furgerson 6-26-1860 (6-27-1860) L
Byrn, Mary H. M. to George Miller 9-7-1843 (no return) L
Byrn, Mary Jane to Samuel Tanner 12-18-1873 L B
Byrn, Mary W. to Charles P. Cloys 5-6-1850 (5-8-1850) O
Byrn, Matilda to Dempsey Copland 11-17-1828 Ma
Byrn, Moriah to Nelson Palmer 1-18-1873 L
Byrn, Parlee to Thos. D. Ruffin 6-27-1861 (6-30-1861) L
Byrn, Penelope to William H. Bryan 1-21-1843 (1-24-1843) Ma
Byrn, Sarah J. to Henry C. Russom 9-12-1866 L
Byrn, Sonora to Benj. C. Price 12-17-1866 (12-19-1866) L
Byrn, Vina to Madison Partee 12-8-1860 L B
Byrn?, Ellen to William Wilson 10-3-1870 (not executed) L
Byrne, Alice to W. E. Stone 10-6-1858 (10-7-1858) Sh
Byrne, Bridgit to Pat Fenesy 5-29-1851 Sh
Byrne, Lendora to Geo. Moore 4-12-1864 Sh
Byrns, Amelia to William Partee 11-27-1869 (11-29-1869) L B
Byrns, M. D. to M. F. Gray 10-27-1883 (10-29-1883) L
Byrns?, Susan C. to Jas. W. Coonts 10-15-1856 (10-16-1857?) T
Byron (Byrum?), Mary E. to D. L. Conder 12-27-1852 (12-28-1852) Sh
Byron, Mary A. to David Carter 8-27-1864 Sh
Byrum, Artemicia to W. L. McPherson 7-15-1878 (7-17-1878) L
Byrum, Mary A. to Robert L. Conder 1-6-1858 (1-7-1858) Sh
Byrum, Mary Ann to William Hines 10-31-1849 Ma
Byrum, Sarah to Daniel Smith 7-17-1849 Ma
Byrum, Sarah to Hugh Henley 10-26-1871 Hy
Bysinger, Susana A. to John Morgan 4-23-1835 G
Byus, America to Nash Lea 4-17-1867 (no return) Hy
Bywater, Laura D. to Oscar H. Womick 12-22-1864 Sh

C___, Sally to William T. Klee 2-3-1871 (3-5-1871) O
C___, Rocinda to James Martin 6-6-1850 Hn
Cabe, Elizabeth A. to James R. Larkin? 9-10-1846 (no return) Hn
Cabe, Millie A. to Sol Burrow 12-23-1841 Cr
Cabler, Indiana M. to A. W. Moore 8-16-1838 F
Cachman, Nancy to John McGee 11-21-1868 L
Cadwell, Cloe to John Thompson 1-28-1824 (2-5-1824) Hr
Cady?, Ellen to R. J. McConley 5-19-1870 G
Caff, Mary Ann to W. S. Adams 1-14-1859 (1-17-1859) Sh
Caffrey, Martha to J. W. Kee 9-29-1860 Cr
Caffrey, Sarah to Martin Clack 2-21-1837 Cr
Cafrey, Kissandria to Burrell Killien 7-6-1842 (7-7-1842) O
Cagbills, N. to S. W. Mathews 2-20-1868 Hy
Cage, Canna? to Hamilton Stanup? 5-8-1869 (2-19-1871?) T
Cage, Cherlie to Lewis B. McCuie 12-1-1866 (12-14-1866) L
Cage, Fannie to Richmond Burrell 5-9-1874 T
Cage, Harriet to Alx. Estes 5-26-1870 Hy
Cage, M. A. (Mrs.) to Richard Hines 8-9-1870 Ma
Cage, Matilda to George Bailey 1-8-1874 T
Cage, Nancey to Lenord Lewis 11-25-1876 L
Cage, Sadie (Sallie?) to John Douglas Smith 7-21-1874 T
Cage, Susan to Thomas G. Anderson 4-8-1838 (no return) F
Cage, Valleria Ann to W. T. Banks 10-14-1857 Sh

Cagle, Nancy D. to Geo. S. Whitmore 9-6-1850 Sh
Caigle, J. A. to J. D. Weaver 11-22-1882 (11-23-1882) L
Cail, Eliz. P. to D. S. Phelan 2-4-1858 G
Cain, Agnes to J. F. Johnson 7-6-1865 Be
Cain, Ann to George Bleckley 8-13-1864 (8-14-1864) Sh
Cain, Belviretta to Franklin H. Weare 11-16-1857 (11-19-1857) Ma
Cain, Catherine to James Carmichael 1-16-1861 Sh
Cain, Elizabeth H. to Ott Andrews 11-25-1850 Hr
Cain, Elizabeth to George A. Muse 5-25-1830 Ma
Cain, Hannah to Henry Marsh 9-17-1828 (9-18-1828) Hr
Cain, Martha to Wm. Hardridge 12-24-1831 (12-?-1831) Hr
Cain, Mary F. A. to Robt. E. Armstrong 9-22-1853 Sh
Cain, Mary to Thomas Dunn 4-24-1852 (4-25-1852) Sh
Cain, Polly to Jefferson Ford 6-31?-1828 (7-3-1828) Hr
Cain, Sene? to Madison Williams 12-13-1867 Hn
Cain, Tabitha to Wm. P. Harris 11-27-1868 (12-3-1868) Ma
Cain, Texana L. to D. G. Baird 2-17-1870 G
Cain, V. E. to T. J. Rochelle 1-6-1869 G
Cain?, Jane to Charles Dodson 3-9-1867 G
Caina, Margaret to James Ryan 6-3-1861 (6-4-1861) Sh
Calahan, Catharine to James Welsh 3-28-1864 Sh
Calahan, Margaret C. to E. B. Boyd 1-1-1864 (no return) Hn
Calahan, Margrett to Hiram Thompson 12-29-1846 Hr
Calahan, Prudence to James A. Todd 1-14-1859 Hn
Calahan, Rosina to Moses Allen 1-9-1838 Hn
Calaway, Oriann Washington to Criss Titus 12-27-1877 L B
Calbert, Eliza Jane to C. M. Williams 2-8-1858 Sh
Caldon, Bridget (Mrs.) to Patrick Martin 11-7-1864 (11-28-1864) Sh
Caldwell, A. S. to John H. McDonald 11-12-1856 Hn
Caldwell, Adaline to Ben Dickson 6-3-1871 (6-5-1871) T
Caldwell, Alice A. to James M. Ray 6-4-1861 Hn
Caldwell, Amanda M. H. to Robert Park 12-8-1857 O
Caldwell, Amanda to Cornelius Cunningham 12-16-1868 (12-17-1868) Cr
Caldwell, Angeline to James Parry 12-15-1874 Hy
Caldwell, Ann to Ham Stewart 11-27-1865 (no return) F
Caldwell, Annie to J. J. Culbreath 8-24-1878 (no return) Hy
Caldwell, Annie to Nelson Morgan 1-2-1871 Hy
Caldwell, Caroline to Daniel Humphreys 9-16-1867 Hn
Caldwell, Caroline to H. M. Tomlinson 8-5-1850 Sh
Caldwell, Caroline to John Harper 4-6-1849 O
Caldwell, Caroline to W. D. Nored 3-8-1855 Hn
Caldwell, Clara to Henry Towns 9-26-1885 L
Caldwell, E. A. to T. D. Felt 2-29-1848 Hn
Caldwell, Elenora A. to William Johnson 10-18-1869 G B
Caldwell, Eliza J. to John W. Vaulx 5-31-1869 Ma *
Caldwell, Eliza Jane to Benj. M. Flippin 7-22-1838 L
Caldwell, Elizabeth to Syrus Park 11-16-1838 Hr
Caldwell, Frances to James Eddings 11-18-1866 G
Caldwell, Hannah E. to William White 3-9-1842 (3-10-1842) O
Caldwell, Hannah R. to Durin O. Allcock 12-16-1854 (11?-17-1854) O
Caldwell, Hannah W. to James Giles 8-31-1843 Hn
Caldwell, Jane S. to David H. Whipple 3-15-1836 O
Caldwell, Jennetta W. to James G. Glover 3-14-1855 (3-15-1855) O
Caldwell, Julia to Washington Green 1-12-1877 Hy
Caldwell, Kinah to Thomas McNutt 10-5-1851 Hn
Caldwell, L. B. to A. H. Caudle 10-14-1863 O
Caldwell, Lucinda to Josiah M. Hill 3-6-1843 (3-7-1843) Hr
Caldwell, Lucy A. to John P. Johnson 7-1-1868 G
Caldwell, M. D. to G. N. Grear 1-19-1876 L
Caldwell, Maria to Peter Jordan 3-11-1885 (3-12-1885) L
Caldwell, Maria to Pleasant Marberry 11-5-1840 Hn
Caldwell, Martha A. to James F., jr. Dunavant 10-8-1853 (no return) L
Caldwell, Martha E. (Mrs.?) to William Fleschbert 10-24-1863 (11-17-1863) Sh
Caldwell, Martha E. to Thomas J. Kendall 5-2?-1853 Hn
Caldwell, Martha V. to John W. Trevathan 6-29-1858 Hn
Caldwell, Mary A. to James W. Willis 2-3-1853 Hn
Caldwell, Mary Ann to John P. Morgan 1-16-1849 O
Caldwell, Mary C. to Geo. E. Armstead 10-12-1860 (10-17-1860) Hr
Caldwell, Mary J. to J. D. Rice 7-22-1879 (7-23-1879) L
Caldwell, Mary to Thomas Webb 11-24-1866 G
Caldwell, N. D. to James A. Shaw? 11-24-1866 (11-27-1866) Cr
Caldwell, Ocie to W. H. Adams 2-27-1867 (2-28-1867) O
Caldwell, Phebe to Andrew McFarland 8-31-1854 Hn
Caldwell, Rebeca W. to L. L. Hawkins 10-2-1861 Cr
Caldwell, Rebecca (Mrs.) to Henry Norman 7-17-1858 (7-18-1858) Ma
Caldwell, Rebecca to James Cox 12-20-1867 (no return) Hy
Caldwell, Rebecca to Jas. A. Cox 12-15-1868 (12-16-1868) F
Caldwell, S. A. M. to S. P. Bennett 12-21-1843 Hn
Caldwell, Sallie H. to Van B. Allbritton 12-1-1866 (no return) Hn
Caldwell, Sarah J. to Edley P. Smith 6-2-1842 Hn
Caldwell, Sarah Jane to Samuel J. Garrett 1-14-1878 (1-16-1878) L
Caldwell, Sarah M. to James T. Williams 12-8-1859 Hn
Caldwell, Sarah to Benjamin Evans 7-2-1860 (7-8-1860) O
Caldwell, Susan A. to David Bomer 12-23-1857 Hn
Caldwell, Susan E. to John J. Ward 1-22-1858 (2-2-1858) O
Caldwell, Susan E. to Thos. A. Douglas 3-27-1844 Cr
Caldwell, Tirzah to Samuel F. Neely 11-14-1837 (11-16-1837) Hr

Caley, Mary to Edward McGrath 1-26-1861 (1-27-1861) Sh
Calhon?, Delia Elizabeth to B. L. Clark 5-25-1872 T
Calhoon, Fannie to W. H. Adams 1-4-1857 (1-6-1857) T
Calhoon, Nancy to Jonathan L. Hanes 2-13-1840 (2-16-1840) O
Calhoon, Sallie to Jacob Cheek 1-20-1866 (1-21-1866) T
Calhoun, A. W. to B. F. Crenshaw 9-10-1873 O
Calhoun, Addie L. to Jno. D. Warmack 12-15-1873 (12-16-1873) T
Calhoun, Amanda to Elyer? Tanner 1-4-1867 (1-14-1867) T
Calhoun, Bettie to E. T. Wilson 8-21-1860 (8-22-1860) T
Calhoun, C. H. to D. T. J. Kersey 3-5-1861 O
Calhoun, E. H. to J. N. Tucker 10-23-1868 O
Calhoun, Elizabeth to H. P. Blassengame 6-3-1861 O
Calhoun, Elvary J. to Wm. D. McKamy 9-28-1866 O
Calhoun, Esther A. to H. L. Dickey 4-20-1864 O
Calhoun, Feebe to George Hall 10-29-1870 T
Calhoun, Jane to Julius Clarke 12-30-1837 (12-31-1838) G
Calhoun, K. T. to James Mays 11-27-1871 (11-28-1871) T
Calhoun, Lizzie A. to James L. Travis 10-15-1860 Sh
Calhoun, M. to N. Moore 12-22-1874 (12-24-1874) T
Calhoun, Mahala H. to John N. Whitesides 2-6-1845 O
Calhoun, Margaret E. to William B. Youree 1-1-1861 O
Calhoun, Margaret J. to J. Barnett Gracy 12-9-1868 (12-10-1868) T
Calhoun, Maria to Thomas Yarbro 6-2-1870 T
Calhoun, Martha E. to Clark Brown 11-29-18?? (with 1866) O
Calhoun, Martha E. to W. O. Menefee 11-14-1860 (11-15-1860) T
Calhoun, Mary Ann to Daniel J. Young 1-14-1863 We
Calhoun, Mary Jane to Martin Vance 12-31-1844 O
Calhoun, Mary P. to Sam'l H. Wilson 1-31-1856 O
Calhoun, Mollie A. to J. R. Love 7-28-1863 Hn
Calhoun, Mollie J. to Samuel W. Stitt 1-10-1860 (1-11-1860) T
Calhoun, Nancy J. to Robert D. Wilson 2-26-1866 O
Calhoun, Ory Ann to James Dickson 3-23-1863 O
Calhoun, Phoebe to R. Green 12-15-1866 (3-30-1867) T
Calhoun, Polley to John Gore 10-28-1828 T
Calhoun, R. A. to I. D. Gillis 12-7-1866 (12-9-18??) O
Calhoun, Rebecca to Dick Still 6-20-1872 T
Calhoun, Rener to Wm. Price 4-11-1874 (4-8?-1874) T B
Calhoun, Sallie A. to J. J. Rice 12-6-1866 T
Calhoun, Sallie to Harris Lankford 3-14-1867 Hn B
Calhoun, Sallie to Jacob Cheek 1-20-1866 T
Calhoun, Sarah to John B. Osburn 5-25-1853 O
Caliway, K. J. to B. F. Brazier 1-26-1870 Dy
Call (Cole), Mary Ann to Henry Foster 3-7-1859 Sh
Call, Avarilla E. to S.? P. Atkison 1-31-1867 Hn
Call, Marry Ann to James K. Huffstutter 12-11-1863 O
Call, Nora W. to Harry Diggs 12-28-1865 Hn
Callaghan, Ellen to Thomas Duffy 4-30-1853 (5-1-1853) Sh
Callahan, Alice to Michael Kenney 5-14-1853 Sh
Callahan, Clarinda to Eli Parks 5-11-1859 (5-15-1859) Hr
Callahan, Clarinda to John J. Fitch 12-28-1854 Hr
Callahan, M. F. (Mrs.) to E. A. Henderson 8-31-1874 (no return) Dy
Callahan, Margaret to Hugh Feran 2-8-1860 (2-12-1860) Sh
Callahan, Margaret to Timothy Forley 5-1-1858 (5-2-1858) Hr
Callehan, Mary Martha to Rufus Thomas McPherson 1-10-1872 L
Callenden, Catharine to Andrew Kitsoe 10-18-1851 Sh
Callicott, Elizabeth to A. Critenden 11-16-1848 Hn
Callicott, Lenore to G. C. Killabru 10-7-1850 (no return) Hn
Callicott, Linda to Jas. M. Smith 1-13-1867 T
Callicott, Mary E. to Charley Crittenden 12-24-1839 Hn
Callicott, Sarah N. to G. C. Davis 2-24-1859 (3-1-1859) O
Callihan, Patsey G. to Green? Alford 6-18-1855 L
Callis, B. A. to George J. Petty 4-23-1853 Sh
Callis, Francis C. to I. W. Russell __-7-1865 (9-7-1865) O
Callis, Lucy C. to T. B. Shore 11-29-1865 O
Calloway, Josephine to James B. Young 10-11-1863 Hn
Calloway, Lizzie to David P. Davis 5-8-1867 Ma
Calloway, Mary to Elijah Foust 3-1-1849 Hn
Callus, Milbery to John K. Williams 6-10-1855 Be CC
Caloway, Mary C. to R. M. Williams 4-26-1866 Hn
Calvin, M. J. to J. A. Arnold 10-5-1872 (10-6-1872) Dy
Cambell, Hannah to James Jones 10-13-1866 (no return) Dy
Cambell, Mollie to Jerry Ward 11-11-1870 G
Camden, Mary to Clay Hamilton 8-15-1869 G B
Camden, Susan to Tom Williams 1-13-1870 G B
Cameron, Bell to C. C. Clark 3-17-1868 Hy
Cameron, Callie to Jessee Mahan 12-28-1877 Hy
Cameron, Catherine to Whitmill Crain 7-14-1855 (7-15-1855) Sh
Cameron, Eliza to Henry Allen 1-7-1871 Hy
Cameron, M. C. to T. J. McMahon 2-14-1878 Hy
Cameron, Mary J. to P. C. Carter 12-1-1851 Sh
Cameron, Mollie E. to J. S. Musgraves 1-20-1869 (no return) Hy
Cameron, Nancy Ann to John H. Hankins 7-15-1857 (7-16-1857) Sh
Cammerdy, Johanna to T. J. Crosby 1-20-1862 (1-22-1862) Sh
Cammond, Unity to B. A. N. Walden 10-3-1853 (no return) F
Camp, Ann Eliza to Moses Campbell 2-14-1854 Hr
Camp, Annis to H. H. Raines 8-30-1865 G
Camp, Elizabeth V. to G. W. Utley 8-29-1860 Be

Camp, F. E. to J. T. Ferguson 10-17-1861 (10-22-1861) Hr
Camp, Frances to B. L. Utley 3-23-1851 Be
Camp, Margaret to Howell R. Robards 5-9-1848 Sh
Camp, Martha Ann to Robert B. Turner 6-21-1856 O
Camp, Martha J. to Egbert McLemore 9-20-1865 G
Camp, Mary E. R. to Lanson N. Chamberlain 12-31-1855 Sh
Camp?, Elizabeth to J. R. Anderson 11-11-1864 (no return) Hn
Campbell, Alithia to John Murrill 11-5-1850 Ma
Campbell, Almarinda E. to Willis J. Heath 10-7-1860 G
Campbell, Amanda to A. J. Shinault 8-29-1850 F
Campbell, Ann H. to Samuel Milliken 6-18-1855 (no return) L
Campbell, Ann to Joseph Farrell 4-16-1856 Sh
Campbell, Anna J. to Phillip D. Jarvis 11-15-1870 G
Campbell, Anna to Wm. Burris 11-3-1874 Hy
Campbell, Anne Eliza to J. W. Penn 5-14-1868 G
Campbell, Bettie W. to Joseph A. Jackson 12-7-1868 (12-8-1868) L
Campbell, Bettie to Ben Hill 1-26-1876 (no return) Hy
Campbell, Bettie to Simeon? Hall 8-16-1881 L
Campbell, C. E. to G. P. Wright 11-19-1866 O
Campbell, Carolin E. to Alfred M. Lambeth 4-8-1835 (4-16-1835) Hr
Campbell, Catherine E. to Thomas P. Newton 4-21-1862 (4-22-1862) Sh
Campbell, Celie to George Jackson 7-5-1876 Hy
Campbell, Charlotte M. to Mines P. Wilson 3-19-1845 Hn
Campbell, Charlotte to Arch Jarrett 12-19-1875 Hy
Campbell, Clara to Joe Williams 12-29-1866 G
Campbell, Cornelia A. to Joel Mayo 12-13-1855 Ma
Campbell, Didama to James Lovel 12-7-1872 (12-8-1872) Dy
Campbell, E. J. to J. H. Barlow 12-18-1872 (12-19-1872) Cr
Campbell, Edith to Samuel G. Tatum 8-19-1859 L
Campbell, Eldendor to P. A. Vinsen 11-30-1852 Cr
Campbell, Eliza J. to Harry S. Heath 7-12-1859 L
Campbell, Eliza R. to Benj. Scott 1-25-1839 (1-31-1839) F
Campbell, Eliza to Austin Clay 11-9-1872 (11-10-1872) L
Campbell, Eliza to Mit Baxter 8-1-1870 Dy
Campbell, Eliza to Thomas P. Cooper 6-12-1853 O
Campbell, Elizabeth A. to John W. Wingo 2-7-1859 G
Campbell, Elizabeth to A. G. Foster 4-27-1853 (no return) F
Campbell, Elizabeth to Andrew Satterfield 10-13-1843 Hn
Campbell, Elizabeth to D. Platt 5-21-1861 Dy
Campbell, Elizabeth to Denis Callaghan 11-19-1864 (11-23-1864) Sh
Campbell, Elizabeth to Enons J. Grissom 7-4-1846 (7-9-1846) Hr
Campbell, Elizabeth to G. W. Perry 8-8-1874 (8-17-1874) T
Campbell, Elizabeth to George Singer (Lingner?) 1-3-1856 (1-8-1856) Sh
Campbell, Elizabeth to John Lovelady 7-15-1839 F
Campbell, Elizabeth to John R. Dunn 10-7-1847 Hn
Campbell, Ella to David Gardner 12-31-1883 (1-1-1884) L
Campbell, Ella to R. C. Patty 11-8-1869 (11-11-1869) F
Campbell, Ellen to Richard Clay 5-15-1869 (5-22-1869) L
Campbell, F. A. to W. I. Wardeau (Wardlaw) 9-6-1876 L
Campbell, Fannie A. to James Harrison 12-21-1869 (12-23-1869) Ma
Campbell, Fannie to Green Batchelor 3-4-1873 Hy
Campbell, Frances M. to Moses Smith 3-10-1845 (3-17-1845) T
Campbell, Harriet to Edmund Jones 5-21-1868 (5-23-1868) F B
Campbell, Irene H. to William Stephens 1-14-1885 (1-15-1885) L
Campbell, Jane Dean to William B. Baenbridge 11-15-1847 (11-16-1847) T
Campbell, Jane E. to Preston B. Scott 11-12-1861 (11-13-1861) Ma
Campbell, Jane to Hiram Bohannon 3-19-1841 (no return) Hn
Campbell, Jane to Joseph K. Newland 11-2-1846 (11-4-1846) Hr
Campbell, Jane to Offee Flemmen 11-19-1874 Hy
Campbell, Jane to Saml. Alexr. Thompson 2-13-1843 (2-16-1843) T
Campbell, Jennie to Andrew Coppedge 1-25-1872 Hy
Campbell, Jennie to Chas. A. Gaston 6-18-1867 (6-20-1867) F
Campbell, Josephine to S. J. House 9-9-1876 (9-10-1876) Dy
Campbell, Judat to George Olivar ?-?-1861? Mn
Campbell, L. C. to C. H. Hood 9-14-1864 O
Campbell, L. J. to J. B. Higgins 12-14-1869 G
Campbell, L. to J. Bates 4-21-1839 Be
Campbell, Lanie to Peter Tyler 10-25-1874 Hy
Campbell, Laura G. to J. N. Hamlett 1-11-1858 (1-13-1858) Sh
Campbell, Laura to Phillip Fraley 12-30-1869 (1-7-1870) T
Campbell, Letha to James Thompson 3-22-1839 G
Campbell, Lina to Shepard Crewel 1-22-1874 Hy
Campbell, Lucinda Elizabeth A. to Newton Benjamin Wilkins 12-20-1873 (12-21-1873) Dy
Campbell, Lurany Ann to James C. Harkins 12-17-1845 (12-18-1845) Ma
Campbell, M. A. B. to Samuel Croft 6-16-1864 (6-19-1864) Sh
Campbell, M. A. to James Morton 10-21-1869 (no return) Hy
Campbell, M. E. to R. M. Parker 12-22-1879 (12-23-1879) L
Campbell, M. J. to L. R. Jones 10-20-1879 (10-21-1879) Dy
Campbell, M. to E. A. Cannon 12-1-1863 Sh
Campbell, Margaret E. to William M. Shelton 2-17-1849 Ma
Campbell, Margaret to Henson G. Newland 8-21-1839 (8-22-1839) Hr
Campbell, Margaret to Robert Wood 4-27-1867 (4-28-1867) L B
Campbell, Martha Ann to William J. Burris 11-7-1844 (11-9-1844) T
Campbell, Martha J. to William Watson 2-8-1853 Ma
Campbell, Martha N. to C. T. Wilson 10-28-1848 (no return) Hn
Campbell, Martha to Jno. B. McIntosh 12-25-1868 (12-27-1868) Dy

Campbell, Mary A. to James McCracken 11-9-1840 (no return) Hn
Campbell, Mary A. to Jo. (Dr.) Hedgepeth 9-28-1872 (9-29-1872) L
Campbell, Mary A. to T.C. Park 3-24-1849 (4-5-1849) Hr
Campbell, Mary J. to Thos. L. Smith 6-20-1844 Cr
Campbell, Mary Jane to Alexr. W. Murphy 2-5-1851 T
Campbell, Mary L. to James T. Mahaffy 6-3-1849 Sh
Campbell, Mary P. to Wilie Umstead 10-3-1833 G
Campbell, Mary S. to Willis F. McCasling 11-15-1848 (11-16-1848) G
Campbell, Mary to Edward Reuther 7-6-1859 (7-7-1859) Sh
Campbell, Mary to G. J. Hubbard 2-16-1848 (no return) Hn
Campbell, Mary to Howell P. Crane 8-8-1850 Sh
Campbell, Mary to James V. Moore 9-18-1865 (9-19-1865) T
Campbell, Mary to Moses E. Cox 3-20-1849 L
Campbell, Mary to R. W. Binkley 11-5-1874 (no return) Dy
Campbell, Mary to William Sample 11-12-1850 (12-2-1850) O
Campbell, Mattie to Ambrose Barbee 9-11-1884 (10-4-1884) L
Campbell, Mattie to E. C. Strength 3-28-1878 Hy
Campbell, Melinda to Frank Holt 11-25-1880 L B
Campbell, Minervia to William J. Jones 6-8-1848 (6-11-1848) Hr
Campbell, Mollie to Harry Cardwell 1-10-1878 Hy
Campbell, Mollie to James Tyler 3-18-1879 (3-19-1879) L B
Campbell, Nancy E. to W. D. Currin 8-7-1854 (8-14-1854) Hr
Campbell, Nancy Ann to James Harris 9-22-1877 (9-23-1877) Dy B
Campbell, Nancy H. to Thos. Y. Blacknall 11-28-1855 (11-29-1855) G
Campbell, Nancy J. to A. O. McVay 1-13-1846 Hr
Campbell, Nancy to Alfred Carter 10-17-1859 (10-18-1859) L
Campbell, Nancy to James M. Lillard 10-26-1841 (10-27-1841) Hr
Campbell, Nancy to James Price 6-26-1848 G
Campbell, Nancy to John House 1-21-1867 (1-22-1867) Cr
Campbell, Olia to Gilbert Clapp 1-4-1871 (2-14-1871) F B
Campbell, Parthena to Spencer Sweet 5-7-1878 Hy
Campbell, Penelope P. to Robert Sterling 6-5-1856 Ma
Campbell, Phillis to John WEsley Topp 1-31-1868 G B
Campbell, Polly to Thomas W. Floyd 5-19-1820 Sh
Campbell, Rachael C. to John Linebarger 12-19-1860 (12-25-1860) Hr
Campbell, Rosanna to Cornelius Brown 9-5-1872 (9-14-1872) T
Campbell, S. E. to J. F.? Cousar 9-1-1870 (5-10-1871) T
Campbell, S. J. to J. M. Buchanan 3-9-1864 (3-10-1864) O
Campbell, Sallie to J. N. Smith 9-1-1860 (9-2-1860) F
Campbell, Sarah A. to A. J. Brumley 8-20-1846 F
Campbell, Sarah E. to James R. Finley 6-11-1878 Hn
Campbell, Sarah V. to John Annis 3-28-1867 Hy
Campbell, Sarah to Charles Boulton 6-6-1830 Sh
Campbell, Sarah to John A. Ayers 10-15-1850 L
Campbell, Sarah to Nathaniel B. Moore 7-25-1837 (7-31-1837) Hr
Campbell, Sarah to Robt. E. Andrews 6-13-1846 (6-14-1846) Hr
Campbell, Susan A. to Dolphin W. Cates 9-12-1853 G
Campbell, Susan A. to William H. Heath 10-3-1853 (11-17-1853) G
Campbell, Susan C. to I. P. Griffin 12-31-1866 (no return) Hy
Campbell, Susan Jane to Thomas W. Coats 8-24-1841 (8-26-1841) T
Campbell, Susan to Joe Ferguson 3-5-1868 (3-7-1868) L B
Campbell, Tennessee to William T. Sutton 8-3-1865? (9-5-1866?) L
Campbell, Unity to Richard J. Smith 7-2-1831 G
Campbell, ____ to J. W. Ayers 3-2-1878 (no return) Dy
Campell, Margarett to George Erwin 2-5-1849 (2-26-1849) O
Campfield, Ann to Patrick McGrath 1-15-1841 Sh
Canada, Elizabeth A. to W. N. Williams 10-17-1859 Sh
Canada, Harriet to James Whichard 3-19-1867 G
Canada, Julia A. F. to Chas. Ward 12-16-1867 (12-20-1867) F
Canada, Malissa H. to Joseph A. Foster 11-8-1859 G
Canada, Mary E. to J. C. Thetford 12-12-1868 (12-13-1868) Dy
Canada, Sarah to Alfred Pruett 10-5-1846 (10-7-1846) G
Canada, Susan E. to Elihu Flowers 2-6-1867 G
Canaday, Amanda J. to William D. Jones 12-20-1852 G
Canaday, Cardine to Alexander Norton 1-15-1853 (1-16-1853) G
Canaday, Charlotta to John D. Davis 7-9-1851 (7-10-1851) G
Canaday, E. C. to Z. T. Warren 1-11-1868 O
Canaday, Elizabeth M. to Nathl. A. Coulter 11-30-1853 O
Canaday, Louisa Jane to Monterville Pentecost 12-23-1856 Hn
Canaday, Mary C. A. to James W. Robinson 7-17-1851 G
Canaday, Rutha to Walter M. Thedford 7-3-1838 (7-8-1838) G
Canadey, Elizabeth to Thos. Canady 4-6-1837 G
Canady, Allia? to William Davidson 11-7-1867 G
Canady, Emoline to William W. Smith 1-30-1857 (2-3-1857) G
Canady, Rebecah E. to Arman B. McDaniel 12-12-1848 Hn
Canapa (Cassapa?), Helen to Paul B. Cicallo 5-15-1854 (5-17-1854) Sh
Candler, Ann E. to James A. Haynes 9-20-1849 Sh
Cane, Frances to Marsellis Jones 10-6-1869 Cr
Canford, Mary to Michael Wade 12-13-1851 Sh
Canida, Alice to Mack Johnson 3-20-1873 Hy
Caniday, Tabitha to Wilie Saunders 9-27-1858 Hn
Cannady, Josephine to Benj. J. Jones 1-11-1867 (1-13-1867) Ma
Cannon (Cameron), Mary Catharine to Thomas M. Ward 9-15-1845 Sh
Cannon, Amanda to Meredith Wheeler 8-4-1862 Sh
Cannon, Armenta to Edward White 11-29-1849 Cr
Cannon, Eliza J. to W. J. Carmack 4-24-1867 G
Cannon, Eliza to James Leach 6-24-1854 (6-26-1854) T

Cannon, Elizabeth to Joseph Liggett 6-2-1845 (6-4-1845) G
Cannon, Elizabeth to Joshua Bailey 1-3-1867 T
Cannon, Ellen to Edward Reiley (Riley) 9-24-1860 Sh
Cannon, Emma L. to William J. Bennett 11-2-1853 Hn
Cannon, Josafine to George Allen 9-13-1870 (no return) Dy
Cannon, Julia F. to William E. Elmore 7-18-1840 T
Cannon, Louisa to James Redford 5-9-1856 (5-10-1856) G
Cannon, Mahala A. to Benjamin Morgan 11-28-1860 Cr
Cannon, Margaret to John C. Blankinship 8-21-1845 (8-26-1845) G
Cannon, Martha to Samuel Eskew 11-7-1844 Cr
Cannon, Mary E. to Earls Crossett 1-13-1857 Cr
Cannon, Mary J. to Oliver Bridges 10-1-1842 (no return) Hn
Cannon, Mary to James Tillman 4-20-1839 (4-25-1839) Hr
Cannon, Mary to John Dempster 5-19-1852 (5-20-1852) Sh
Cannon, Mary to Sterling Vaughan 8-14-1851 Hn
Cannon, Mollie to L. P. Ray 12-18-1872 (12-19-1872) Cr
Cannon, N. H. to C. R. Ownby 10-9-1868 (10-11-1868) Cr
Cannon, Phoebe to Stephen Stull 7-21-1866 (7-22-1866) F B
Canon, Eliza J. to J. C. M. Crews 9-19-1866 (no return) Cr
Canon, Martha J. to T. R. Brassfield 10-27-1864 G
Cansen, Mary A. J. to W. W. Dudley 6-6-1854 We
Cantrel, Nancy E. to A.(W.?) A. Frazier 3-27-1865 G
Cantrell, Lucinda to Joseph G. Huskett 8-9-1846 We
Cantrell, M. to John Ivins 9-17-1845 We
Cantrell, Mahaley to Henry Forristed 1-21-1854 (1-22-1854) G
Cantrell, Malinda to Dillard Forester 5-28-1831 (6-17-1831) G
Cantrell, Martha to Robert L. Hopkins 7-28-1854 G
Cantrell, Minerva to P. H. Johnson 9-15-1846 We
Cantrell, Nancy J. to Pleasant Capps 12-17-1856 Cr
Cantrell, Parmelia to George D. Matthews 4-22-1857 (4-23-1857) O
Cantrell, Penina to Hugh Bateman 9-?-1860 (9-7-1860) Cr
Cantrell, Peronia to Hugh Bateman 9-6-1860 (9-7-1860) Cr
Cantrell, Preciller to J. M. King 1-3-1871 (1-4-1871) Cr
Cantrell, Sarah E. to David C. Carlton 3-14-1861 W
Cantrell, Sarah to William T. Thedford 9-9-1860 (9-10-1860) G
Cantrol, Charlott to Charles J. Lawrance 11-3-1842 G
Cantroll, Pollie to Rewbin King 8-5-1871 (8-6-1871) Cr
Cantwell, Mary A. to Robert B. Jones 2-25-1858 We
Cantwell?, Barbra to James A. Jackson 11-26-1845 (11-27-1845) Hr
Capehart, Mary E. to James Dunn 9-14-1857 Sh
Capelinger, Loucinda C. to R. George 4-8-1868 Be
Capell, Francis to Calvin Carter 12-28-1874 L B
Capell, Martha to Green Tyus 12-24-1867 Hy
Capell, Melissa to Vivont Bevill 5-6-1859 (no return) Hy
Capell, Mollie to M. D. Gaulden 9-29-1875 (9-30-1875) Dy
Capell, Rose to Bob Richardson 12-4-1873 Hy
Capell, Sarah C. to Sylvester Suggs 11-15-1884 L
Capell, Sarah to Isham Whitehurst 4-4-1866 Hy
Capell, Sarah to Joe Noble 2-8-1886 (2-9-1886) L
Capelle, T. P. to William L. Duckworth 12-24-1867 L
Capers, Betty to W. H. Woollen 2-223-1880 (2-24-1880) L
Capers, Ella to C. H. Rice 12-19-1870 (12-20-1870) F
Capers, Fanny to Virginius A. McElroy 10-14-1869 (10-18-1869) F
Capers, Rosa to Alfred Sherrod 12-27-1869 (12-30-1869) F B
Capes, Margaret Ann to Wm. A. Shelton 10-16-1864 G
Caple, Hepsabeth to Richard Iby 2-22-1841 (2-24-1841) F
Caple, Mary E. to Thomas Curtis 6-24-1852 G
Caples, Ann Eliza to J. G. Field 10-23-1865 (10-26-1865) F
Caples, Mary P. to Murry W. Foster 1-6-1855 (1-7-1855) G
Caplinger, Amanda J. to Duncan C. Lee 9-27-1857 Hn
Caplinger, Ann to Robert F. Rickman 5-8-1866 (5-9-1866) L
Caplinger, Araminta to Thomas Maynard 9-17-1858 Hn
Caplinger, Eliza to Samuel Ingram 2-28-1844 Hn
Caplinger, Isabella to J. F. Bratton 6-17-1861 (no return) L
Caplinger, Lucinda to Alexander Ramsey 12-16-1858 Hn
Caplinger, Mary Jane to John McLeroy 10-2-1856 Be
Caplinger, Peggy to Miles B. Griffin 8-9-1842 Hn
Caplinger, Pernita to James Hays 7-9-1863 Hn
Caplinger, Sarah to Edmond E. Rolls 12-29-1853 Be
Capp, Artis Y. to David Mendeth? 12-28-1840 (no return) F
Capps, Elizabeth to Peyton Lashlee 3-6-1846 Be
Capps, Ellen P. to Elias A. Clabrun 1-14-1857 We
Capps, Ellen P. to S. M. Stephen 7-6-1851 Cr
Capps, Ellen to Earnest Clayborn 10-1-1854 Cr
Capps, Emily C. to Nathan Lewis 8-16-1845 (no return) F
Capps, Emily to Preston Holt 8-13-1857 We
Capps, Leoma to George Webb 12-24-1857 We
Capps, Martha to John E. Jeffries 12-9-1840 (no return) F
Capps, Martha to Lewis Barnhill 8-19-1851 (8-20-1851) O
Capps, Mary Ann to James M. Wiseman 2-18-1845 Be
Capps, Mary Ann to James M. Wiseman 2-18-1845 Be CC
Capps, Mary to James N. Watson 9-18-1864 Be
Capps, N. M. A. to R. M. Webster 2-4-1857 We
Capps, Nancy to Samuel Ribsy 3-17-1859 Cr
Capps, Polly P. to M. Earls ?-?-1840 Cr
Capps, S. L. D. to James M. Belew 9-12-1867 G
Capps, S. M. to M. V. Morris 10-3-1859 Cr

Capps, Sarah A. to Leonard A. Clayborn 8-6-1858 Cr
Capps, Sarah C. to Henry J. Dilday 5-6-1861 (5-12-1861) Cr
Capps, Sarah to Kinchen Taylor 12-7-1855 Be
Capps, Sarah to William Harden 7-1-1851 Be
Capps, Susan to James Hardin 2-13-1867 (2-14-1867) L
Capps, Telitha T. to Lewis Bahanan 6-4-1860 (no return) We
Caps, Elizabeth to Charles Stout 8-26-1843 (no return) We
Caps, Jane to F. M. Johnson 4-30-1855 Sh
Caps, Martha to Wm. Byars 7-15-1846 We
Caps, Sarah A. to Granville S. Sharp 5-21-1855 (5-22-1855) G
Caraway, Adaline to John R. Jones 1-7-1856 (1-9-1856) O
Caraway, Charlotte to David S. Hannis 12-26-1849 Hr
Caraway, Clarisa? to Albert H. Lawhorn 4-5-1845 (4-24-1845) Hr
Caraway, Elizabeth to James Flowers 5-3-1868 G
Caraway, Elmira to Lucas Roane 11-6-1869 (11-7-1869) F B
Caraway, Fanny to Oney C. Wall 2-14-1867 F
Caraway, Gatsey to William Standley 12-30-1851 (1-1-1852) Hr
Caraway, Luvenia to William C. Summers 1-14-1857 We
Caraway, M. C. to G. W. Lewers 1-15-1856 Sh
Caraway, Martha J. to David J. Jernigan 9-30-1844 (no return) F
Caraway, Mary Eliza to Wm. J. Warren 8-19-1854 (8-24-1854) O
Caraway, Mary S. to J. S. McWhorter 1-2-1860 G
Caraway, Mary to Henry McGill 4-23-1862 Be
Caraway, Nancy M. to W. H. Piller 12-22-1856 (no return) F
Caraway, Narcissa to Joseph Collier 5-27-1859 (5-28-1859) T
Caraway, Rachel to B. C. Brown 1-12-1860 (1-26-1860) O
Carbery, J. to Thomas Keely 11-13-1863 Sh
Cardin, Elizabeth to Hiram Hinson 5-20-1845 (no return) Hn
Cardle, Margaret to John Green 9-26-1855 Hr
Cardozo, Adelia to Cyrus Thompson 9-25-1842 Sh
Cardwell, Agnes to Andrew Paskel 12-28-1872 (no return) Hy
Cardwell, Elenor to Richard Tanner 3-29-1863 Mn
Cardwell, Frances E. to John C. Turner 12-21-1857 Ma
Cardwell, M. J. to C. M. Cole 11-21-1858 Hn
Cardwell, Mariah to Bruce Hutchings 1-21-1861 O
Cardwell, Mary E. to W. A. Tomlinson 2-5-1863 We
Cardwell, Mary Ellen to Richard Tanner 11-25-1865 Mn
Cardwell, Sarah to J. T. Cobb 2-3-1863 Mn
Cardwell, Tennessee to Alfred M. Carroll 10-10-1862 We
Cardwell, Virginia to Thos. L. Bowden 5-4-1858 (5-6-1858) O
Cardwell?, Ann E. to Robert Davis 12-13-1858 (12-14-1858) O
Care, E. J. to Allen Griffith 10-31-1837 (11-2-1837) G
Care, Mary to Christopher Hite 2-21-1837 G
Carethers, Amanda to I. E. McMurry 12-7-1866 O
Carey, A. C. to W. H. Eaton 5-10-1860 G
Carey, Eliza A. to John Thomas 6-10-1857 (6-28-1857) G
Carey, Elizabeth to James Hearn 3-12-1856 O
Carey, Lina to Myer Carey 8-11-1866 O
Carey, Malinda to Blakers Flowers 10-19-1858 G
Carey, Margaret to Patrick Murray 4-12-1861 Sh
Carey, Martha F. to Isaac L. Flowers 8-14-1860 G
Carey, Mary E. to R. W. Craddock 7-28-1866 O
Carey, Mary J. to Marshall Goodman 4-17-1855 (4-19-1855) O
Carey, Mary to Robert Duke 9-10-1860 Sh
Carey, Permilia (Pernelia) to Thomas Landrum 11-11-1854 (11-14-1854) O
Carey, Sally to William B. Price 6-25-1846 We
Carey?, Cinnie to Lewis B. Spellman 8-3-1863 Sh
Cargell, Mary A. to Mad Plant 3-14-1853 (no return) F
Cargil, L. J. to John L. Evans 12-28-1849 (no return) F
Cargill, Lucinda to James Watkins 12-28-1866 (no return) F B
Cargill, Lucinda to Tom Cargill 8-8-1867 (12-28-1867) F B
Cargit, Martha R. to Isaac D. Evans 10-20-1849 (no return) F
Carigan, Alice to W. H. Turner 1-24-1882 (1-25-1882) L
Cariker, Elizabeth to Doke Callihan 11-29-1852 (11-30-1852) Hr
Carington, Nancy to William L. Carington 2-23-1848 Hn
Carison, Martha J. to George H. Prince 5-4-1846 (no return) Cr
Carithers, E. R. to R. F. Mackey 10-24-1864 (10-26-1864) O
Carithers, Eliza R. to Richard F. McKay 10-20-1864 O
Carithers, Mary Ann to Stephen Sandford 10-27-1853 O
Carithers, Nancy Ann to William M. Wilson 5-24-1853 O
Carithers, Susan E. to Stephen J. Hill 2-18-1858 O
Carl, Harrett to Samuel S. Greer 11-3-1853 G
Carl, Mary (Mrs.) to Benjamin R. McGenley 1-4-1864 Sh
Carlan, Jane E. to John R. Barber 12-27-1859 We
Carley, Levada to John G. Binkly 3-2-1850 (3-3-1850) Hr
Carley, Martha to Joshua Estes 6-8-1838 (6-10-1838) Hr
Carley, Mary E. to George Henson 1-24-1861 Hr
Carley, Nancy to Elvy Mills 9-11-1841 (9-12-1841) Hr
Carley, Nancy to Peter Young 10-30-1854 Hr
Carley, Rachel to James Leggett 2-15-1844 Hr
Carley, Sarah to Robert A. Cozby 12-17-1847 (12-28-1847) Hr
Carley, Sarah to William Carley 10-1-1840 (10-2-1840) Hr
Carlile, Mary Ann to C. Christie 2-19-1867 O
Carlin, Pricilla to Dan Williams 2-17-1827 (2-18-1827) Hr
Carlisle, Elizabeth J. to Ivey (Irey?) W. Sparkman 6-29-1853 Sh
Carlisle, Mary Ann to Osborn Harris 1-10-1847 Sh
Carlisle, Nancy H. L. to Levi Sparkman 12-19-1855 (12-20-1855) Sh

Carlisle, Willie to Aaron Jackson 3-14-1861 Sh
Carloss, Cornelia A. to Berry Mutemas? 2-3-1871 (2-8-1871) F B
Carlten, Ann B. to Francis E. Welch 8-12-1858 We
Carlton, Ann W. to James L. Livingston 12-12-1860 (no return) Hy
Carlton, C. L. to J. B. Ashley 1-13-1859 G
Carlton, Cassa L. to William A. Tinner 11-12-1856 G
Carlton, Catherine to Samuel C. Winn 12-10-1846 Cr
Carlton, E. C. to J. H. Joyce 12-6-1866 G
Carlton, Eviline H. to Ralph Hathaway 10-15-1856 Sh
Carlton, Iza J. to B. O. Carlton 2-1-1863 G
Carlton, Lucinda K. to Olediah Davidson 10-8-1851 Sh
Carlton, Lucy A. to Jno. T. White 12-18-1850 We
Carlton, Manda to Morris Brown 11-7-1871 Hy
Carlton, Margarett to J. D. D. R. Carter 6-24-1848 Cr
Carlton, Margrit to William Easley 2-4-1867 Hy
Carlton, Mary D. to Young McKenny 3-3-1849 Cr
Carlton, Mary M. to J. G. Cullipher 12-16-1867 G
Carlton, Melissa C. to Sol. B. Humphreys 9-24-1862 (no return) Hy
Carlton, Nancy E. to F. M. Purser 1-12-1853 (1-13-1853) Sh
Carlton, Ownnie to George Maxwell 12-24-1867 (no return) Hy
Carlton, Parolee to John A. Wagster 3-30-1862 We
Carlton, Sarah A. to F. M. Purser 12-20-1860 Sh
Carlton, Sarah C. to Joseph A. Brandon 2-12-1863 We
Carlton, Sarah E. to James T. Norman 10-14-1867 (10-15-1868?) L
Carlton, Sarah T. to Alex V. Wyatt 11-11-1845 Cr
Carlton, Susan to William Parks 1-17-1860 We
Carlton, W. E. to J. M. Groms 12-20-1852 We
Carly, Elizabeth to John A. Powell 11-17-1858 Cr
Carly, Martha C. to James D. Yarbrough 3-10-1859 Hr
Carmack, Catharine to John Barbee 10-1-1840 We
Carmack, Elizabeth to Charles Nix 7-21-1853 O
Carman, Sarah to R. H. Cobb 1-27-1863 Mn
Carmichael, Mary M. to James M. Caroway 1-22-1863 We
Carmody, Mary to John O'Brien 11-20-1858 (11-2_-1858) Sh
Carmon, Sarah D. to George R. Purdy 10-9-1845 (no return) We
Carnal, Frances E. to N. M. Cousins 7-28-1863 (7-29-1863) L
Carnal, Mary Elizabeth to William Owen 11-6-1847 (11-7-1848?) L
Carnall, Clementia to E. W. Carnall 1-9-1849 (1-11-1849) L
Carnall, Elizabeth V. to Allen Anthony 6-11-1866 (6-14-1866) L
Carnall, Hester Ann to Charley L. Sumerow 3-29-1867 (3-30-1867) L B
Carnall, Zelinda to James I. Sayles 5-7-1866 (6-28-1866) L
Carne, Mary to G. M. Hopkins 12-22-1863 L
Carneal, Mary Jane to Wm. Atkinson 3-20-1863 Sh
Carnell, Adeline to Wm. C. Carnell 1-6-1872 (1-9-1872) L
Carnell, Almeda Jane to Asa Bradshaw 5-10-1879 (5-11-1879) L
Carnell, Amanda E. to Walter E. Bentley 1-1-1884 (1-2-1884) L
Carnell, C. J. to Edward Harris 1-10-1872 (1-17-1872) L
Carnell, Doretha E. to William Adams 8-3-1857 (8-5-1857) L
Carnell, Matilda to E. P. Carnell 2-1-1865 (no return) L
Carnell, Virginia to Benjamin Owen 1-1-1850 (1-3-1850) L
Carnes, Clemintine B. to F. W. Irvine 11-16-1850 (12-18-1850) Hr
Carnes, Cornelia Ann to John F. Hamlin 6-24-1858 (6-28-1858) Sh
Carnes, Eliza B. to James M. Hall 3-16-1840 Hr
Carnes, Elizabeth to R. A. Tucker ?-?-1849 Cr
Carnes, Ellen to Gerome Gandolph 1-19-1853 Sh
Carnes, Emma to Jack Bird 2-23-1873 Hy
Carnes, Eulah A. to James G. Blandit 1-8-1860 Cr
Carnes, J. to J. Fields 8-30-1842 Be
Carnes, Mary to John Pugh 8-29-1867 (9-6-1867) F B
Carnes, Mary to Samuel Tate 4-19-1843 F
Carnes, Matilda A. to George W. Davidson 8-9-1860 Be
Carnes, Rebecca to James Lay 2-21-1832 (2-23-1832) Hr
Carney, Ann M. to James G. Bell 2-17-1852 (2-19-1852) G
Carney, Margaret to Wm. Lonnergan 10-13-1856 Sh
Carney?, America? to James H. Given 8-30-1858 (9-1-1858) L
Carns, Martha to Harbert Edwards 2-5-1844 (2-13-1844) G
Carns, Mary Katharine to Harvy Louther 12-22-1844 Be
Carns, Pharuba to Sampson Brownings 4-19-1842 Cr
Carns?, Ann to J.R. Reves 2-15-1848 Be
Caroker, Nancy' to W. H. McCommon 12-3-1851 Hr
Caroline, Emaly to William Everett 1-14-1851 (1-16-1851) O
Caroline, Spivey to Nelson Pugh 12-8-1871 Hy
Carolton, Nellie to Needham H. Herron 12-27-1870 (12-28-1870) T
Carooth, Nancy to William Reaves 12-23-1850 Hr
Carother, E. C. to W. B. Reavas 3-29-1866 (4-5-1866) T
Carothers, Frances to Willis McNary 6-13-1866 (6-15-1866) T
Carothers, H. G. to A. N. Randle 9-10-1846 Hn
Carothers, Susan to John Ross 8-8-1870 T
Carow, Catharine to Thomas Haley 8-4-1854 (8-6-1854) Sh
Carpenter, Adaline to D. W. Chapman 8-28-1875 (8-29-1875) O
Carpenter, Amy to Thos. Tappan 12-22-1870 F B
Carpenter, Ann J. to Joel C. Howell 9-13-1851 (no return) F
Carpenter, Delilah to William Everett Williamson 5-2-1878 Dy
Carpenter, Ellen to Harvy Johnson 3-17-1869 (3-19-1869) F B
Carpenter, Ellen to William Gilbert 4-16-1867 (not executed) F B
Carpenter, Frances E. to Charles C. Howell 12-21-1847 (12-23-1847) F
Carpenter, Frances to Orange Harris 11-21-1885 L

Carpenter, J.(I?) M. to B. F. Wyatt 9-16-1884 (9-17-1884) L
Carpenter, Julia to Frank Maddox 1-13-1869 (1-14-1869) F
Carpenter, L. V. to B. J. W. Cocke 9-17-1860 F
Carpenter, Lucy Jane to William A. Ealey 7-20-1852 (no return) F
Carpenter, Margaret P. to Thomas B. Trimble 6-19-1882 L B
Carpenter, Margaret T. to G. S. Carson 7-3-1855 L
Carpenter, Mary Ann to John H. Reid 2-1-1858 (2-4-1858) O
Carpenter, Rilda to Richard Henry 5-29-1869 (no return) F B
Carpenter, Sarah A. to Isaac Read 12-24-1878 Hy
Carpenter, Sarah J. to Carroll J. Miller 12-27-1869 (no return) L
Carpenter, Sarah M. to George M. Tomlin 11-27-1850 (11-28-1851?) Ma
Carpenter, Susan M. to James M. Hopper 11-16-1855 (11-20-1855) Ma
Carpenter, Susan T. to William C. Fletcher 1-20-1852 (1-21-1852) O
Carpenter, Tennessee C. to Thos. W. Kennon 9-26-18686 (9-27-1866) F
Carpenter, Violet to Sam Dickinson 5-1-1869 (5-3-1869) F B
Carper, Mary E. to M. W. Gruber 8-9-1859 (7?-14-1859) Hr
Carper, Mary H. to H. M. Goforth 6-20-1859 (6-23-1859) Hr
Carper, Sarah Ann to F. D. H. Wright 12-4-1850 (12-11-1850) Hr
Carper, Susan C. to P. M. Deraberry 9-18-1857 (10-2-1857) Hr
Carper, Susan to Malcome A. Wright 4-29-1853 (4-21?-1853) Hr
Carr, A. F. to C. D. Bostick 2-5-1851 Hn
Carr, A. P. to Laban Hall 12-21-1857 Hr
Carr, Amanda F. to Edmond Charlton 10-18-1837 Sh
Carr, Ann to Thomas D. Parran 2-29-1828 Sh
Carr, B. to J. W. Wingard 2-21-1861 Sh
Carr, C. to Jas. B. Bragg 3-5-1838 (no return) Hn
Carr, Catherine to Chas. Deck 3-20-1845 We
Carr, E. C. to Ancel Chappell 4-22-1865 (4-26-1865) O
Carr, Eliza Ann M. to James Carr 10-3-1849 (10-4-1849) G
Carr, Elizabeth C. to Solomon H. Hobgood 7-19-1853 (7-25-1853) G
Carr, Elizabeth M. to John M. Stewart 1-16-1845 Hn
Carr, Elizabeth to Michael Casey 5-19-1860 (5-21-1860) Sh
Carr, Emes to James Roberts 2-21-1868 (no return) Hy
Carr, G. M. to G. F. Blanz 10-6-1864 G
Carr, Harriet to John A. Cheek 1-8-1852 Sh
Carr, Juliann to Jam. A. Johnston 10-14-1846 Hn
Carr, M. J. to A. M. Oliver 8-9-1870 G
Carr, Magdaline to Newton Young 1-30-1840 Hn
Carr, Mahuldah to S.(L?) P. Stewart 2-19-1847 (2-21-1847) Hr
Carr, Marth J. to James Parker 3-31-1843 T
Carr, Martha A. to C. C. Hale 1-19-1861 Sh
Carr, Martha to John Cooney 8-11-1857 Sh
Carr, Mary A. to Francis W. Jeggetts 9-11-1855 Sh
Carr, Mary A. to Samuel A. McDaniel 10-10-1854 G
Carr, Mary J. to P. S. Carey 8-4-1863 G
Carr, Mary Jane to B. Garner 7-14-1863 G
Carr, Mary Jane to W. H. Rose 2-4-1835 Sh
Carr, Mary to A. W. Dew 10-26-1828 Sh
Carr, Mary to Geo. W. Richardson 6-8-1871 (6-11-1871) Ma
Carr, Mary to N. F. Stallings 4-28-1860 (4-29-1860) G
Carr, Mary to Wm. Irvine 5-11-1820 Sh
Carr, Mildred H. to Henry Alexander 1-21-1846 Sh
Carr, Nancy E. to John R. Thetford 11-10-1870 G
Carr, Nancy M. to John K. Reynolds 8-19-1869 G
Carr, Nancy to A. H. Williams 12-13-1847 Sh
Carr, Nancy to Lewis Thomas 9-13-1828 Hr
Carr, Sarah Ann to J. G. Mendenall 7-3-1850 Sh
Carr, Sarah C. to Barnett Graham 10-10-1850 Sh
Carr, Sarah L. to John M. Carter 11-27-1866 Cr
Carr, Violet L. to James H. Martin 9-11-1836 (9-13-1836) G
Carr, Virginia to William Thomas 7-16-1849 Sh
Carracle?, Nancey to A. W. Donnaway 12-19-1868 (12-20-1868) T
Carrahan, Martha to George W. Mitchell 11-22-1834 (11-23-1834) G
Carraway, Mary A. to D. G. Morris 2-3-1866 (2-8-1866) F
Carraway, N. B. to R. H. Cook 8-16-1851 (no return) F
Carraway, Narcissa to Joseph Collier 5-27-1859 (5-28-1859) T
Carraway, Sarah A. to David H. Johnson 11-26-1845 (11-27-1845) F
Carraway, Winiford S. to Wm. H. Neal 7-3-1853 (no return) F
Carrel, Evaline to Thomas M. Murray 6-30-1874 (7-1-1874) Dy
Carrell, Maggie to J. W. Griffin 7-7-1875 (no return) L
Carrell, Martha M. to William A. Sigler 9-1-1853 Sh
Carrell, Sarah Ann to Joseph Barkley 11-19-1870 L
Carrick, Margaret to Matthew Clyne 4-4-1853 Sh
Carrick, Martha E. to P. F. Bethshares 7-28-1861 G
Carricker, Caroline to D. P. Rainey 5-1-1848 (5-16-1848) Hr
Carricker, Nancy S. to James Rainey 8-23-1852 (8-26-1852) Hr
Carricker, Tabitha D. to William D. Hannis 7-15-1848 (7-20-1848) Hr
Carrigan, Amanda C. to Saml. F. Henley 3-4-1846 (3-5-1846) L
Carrigan, Fannie O. to Erastus D. Hall 7-15-1873 L
Carrigan, H. C. to E. N. Cook 2-26-1856 (2-27-1856) L
Carrigan, Julia A. E. to Richardson W. Henley 12-1-1841 (12-2-1841) L
Carrigan, M. E. (Mrs.) to W. A. Hines 10-17-1881 (10-18-1881) L
Carring, Caroline to Levi Bostick 10-15-1846 Hn
Carrington, Ann F. to Moses Moore 1-25-1840 (1-29-1840) Ma
Carrington, Caroline to William Croom 6-24-1840 (7-8-1840) Ma
Carrington, D. A. to Andrew D. Flowers 2-19-1869 (2-20-1869) T
Carrington, Elizabeth M. to Francis G. Smith 12-20-1852 Ma

Carrington, Elizabeth to James Freeland 8-2-1847 (no return) Cr
Carrington, Lou to John Cox 12-28-1880 (12-29-1880) L B
Carrington, Louisa to John W. Norton 7-23-1849 Ma
Carrington, Mary to John Bostick 12-30-1845 (12-31-1845) Ma
Carrington, Sarah J. to Charles H. Peters 9-24-1866 (9-25-1866) Ma
Carrington, Sarah to James M. Cole 12-31-1849 Cr
Carrington, Tennessee B. to E. B. Palmer 1-24-1861 Cr
Carrol, Bridget to Henry Christopher 10-5-1858 Sh
Carrol, L. M. to T. J. Flowers 3-11-1863 G
Carrol, Lucy M. to George W. Carroll 12-13-1854 G
Carroll, Adaline to William Crow 7-18-1850 Sh
Carroll, C. F. to T. W. Evans 8-24-1869 Dy
Carroll, Caroline to Joseph M. Eastlack 2-5-1844 Hr
Carroll, Charity to Paten Hare 11-16-1869 (no return) F B
Carroll, Cynthia to John N. Hill 1-21-1847 Hn
Carroll, Elizabeth V. to Lonis? Adams 4-13-1833 (4-16-1833) Hr
Carroll, Elizabeth to Robert L. Smith 9-4-1841 G
Carroll, Ellen to Bernard Riley 2-14-1862 (2-18-1862) Sh
Carroll, Elvinie to Edward J. Bunpsups? 10-1-1857 We
Carroll, Emma to John Geoghegan 12-31-1860 Sh
Carroll, Eunity to G. W. Hamner 6-19-1838 (6-24-1838) O
Carroll, Euvilinah M. to Leroy D. Webb 6-13-1846 (7-14-1846) L
Carroll, Frances W. to J. M. Martin 11-22-1873 (11-26-1873) Dy
Carroll, Harriett H. to Thos.B. Murphrey 8-4-1832 G
Carroll, Jane to Charles Thomas 7-9-1860 Sh
Carroll, Judia A. to J. W. Murrell 1-18-1869 (no return) F
Carroll, Judith to Obadiah W. Davidson 4-3-1848 O
Carroll, L. D. to R. B. Baker 11-30-1865 (12-5-1865) Cr
Carroll, Lucy to Nathan Meadows 8-8-1848 (8-10-1848) G
Carroll, M. C. to Hiram Smith 7-20-1872 (no return) Cr
Carroll, M. C. to W. F. Kendell 9-27-1854 We
Carroll, M. J. to Wylie W. McGee 12-10-1857 (1-19-1858) O
Carroll, Margaret (Mrs.) to Henry McArdle 6-26-1858 (6-27-1858) Sh
Carroll, Martha Ann to John Wesley Pope 9-11-1867 (no return) Dy
Carroll, Martha L. S. to J. R. B. Hamilton 2-11-1854 Cr
Carroll, Martha to William Burton 10-24-1838 (no return) Hn
Carroll, Martha to William Shinpeck 12-23-1826 Hr
Carroll, Mary A. to Wm. A. Crawford 12-5-1854 Cr
Carroll, Mary Ann to William C. Newton 8-14-1851 (no return) Hn
Carroll, Mary to Albert Cain 10-4-1856 Sh
Carroll, Mary to Jonas Brown 7-17-1837 G
Carroll, Mary to William Moultrie 5-17-1838 (5-27-1838) O
Carroll, N. B. to W. R. Barker 8-14-1867 (no return) Cr
Carroll, Nancy Ann to William Jones 7-6-1861 Mn
Carroll, Niecy to William J. Lyon 4-17-1861 Ma
Carroll, Priscilla N. to Wiley Perry 5-7-1860 (5-9-1860) Ma
Carroll, Rosina to Rufus Stunston 8-12-1866 Hn
Carroll, S. A. (Mrs.) to W. J. Meador 12-10-1867 Cr
Carroll, S. J. to J. H. Aiken 2-28-1871 (3-2-1871) Dy
Carroll, Sarah A. to Jim Johnson 3-12-1867 Cr
Carroll, Sarah A. to John Haley 3-2-1859 (3-3-1859) O
Carroll, Sarah to James E. Vickers 6-10-1839 L
Carroll, Sarah to W. T. Evans 12-27-1869 (12-29-1869) Dy
Carrothers, Margaret to Turley Hopper 9-22-1852 (9-23-1852) Ma
Carruth, Elizabeth to William C. Reed 7-12-1841 Ma
Carruth, Sidney Jane to Thomas A. Osborne 12-22-1858 Hr
Carruth?, Unetta? E. to Jesse Jones 8-13-1847 (8-15-1847) Hr
Carruthers, Martha B. to David C. Bates 10-9-1854 (10-10-1854) Hr
Carruthers, Mary to Hardin Jones 1-9-1845 (1-10-1845) Ma
Carry, Ann to Nathan Carry 11-26-1835 G
Carsine, Charlotte F. to James H. Moore 4-20-1846 Cr
Carso, T. E. to E. M. Colwell 1-1-1871? (1-1-1872) L
Carson, Amanda M. to John W. Houston 6-14-1880 (6-17-1880) L
Carson, Ann to Robt. Burdit 12-19-1870 (12-20-1870) Cr B
Carson, Betsy to Benjamin Sparks 7-3-1869 (7-4-1869) Cr
Carson, Bettie C. to R. E. D. Smith 1-28-1868 Cr
Carson, Dorah to James Sparks 12-31-1872 (1-2-1873) Cr B
Carson, Emaline to Anderson Bell 12-27-1870 (1-2-1871) Cr B
Carson, Julia to Ezekiel Green L. Bumpass 7-15-1838 Hn
Carson, M. E. to J. H., jr. Thompson 6-3-1880 (6-5-1880) L
Carson, Margaret to Thomas Smith 1-7-1870 (no return) L
Carson, Martha Ann to Robert B. Moore 4-17-1867 (4-18-1867) L
Carson, Mary Jane to Patrick H. Pugh 11-17-1853 (no return) L
Carson, Mary to John W. Douglas 8-22-1845 (no return) Hn
Carson, Nancy W. to Clark Martin 2-13-1858 (2-15-1858) L
Carson, Nancy to John Moore 12-7-1854 Cr
Carson, Penelope to A. J. Slater 6-17-1857 L
Carson, R. J. to Lewis J. Hutcherson 12-3-18879 (12-3-1880?) L
Carson, Rachel E. to Richard C. Jennings 7-17-1868 (7-19-1868) L
Carson, Rebecca Jane to Thomas M. Hardy 12-28-1870 (12-29-1870) L
Carson, S. E. to J. K. Adams 7-1-1880 L
Carson, S. M. to C. H. Childress 12-21-1882 L
Carson, Septempa to J. P. Woodard 9-3-1845 Cr
Carson, Theresa to Thomas J. Byrn 10-6-1866 (10-7-1866) L
Cartay, Julia to Andrew Kealey 6-20-1857 (6-21-1857) Sh
Cartege? (Cortiez?), Ellen to Cornelius Regan 2-20-1853 Sh
Carter (Sartin), Margaret to G. W. Crawford 1-1-1858 O

Brides

Carter, A. C. to R. B. Gibbs 12-7-1860 (11-9-1860) Dy
Carter, Aggie to Thornton Davis 2-16-1832 O
Carter, Alcy to Samuel Matthews 7-5-1846 (8-30-1846) O
Carter, Amanda L.? to Joseph Wilson 12-17-1867 (12-18-1867) Cr
Carter, Ann to William Chambers 1-22-1855 Sh
Carter, Anna E. J. to William Bomar 12-23-1866 Hn
Carter, Anna to L. N. Craig 3-24-1874 O
Carter, Anne E. to Samuel Stiles 3-24-1855 (3-25-1855) Sh
Carter, Anthus to Alex. Davis 6-26-1845 Cr
Carter, B. to David Harrell 3-2-1838 F
Carter, C. F. to Thomas Brooks 11-1-1859 We
Carter, Caroline to James W. Hines 2-23-1847 Hr
Carter, Catharine to Alpia G. Ray 11-4-1847 (12-1-1847) G
Carter, Catharine to Thos. O'Donnell 4-4-1861 (4-7-1861) Sh
Carter, Catherine to Alfred McKissick 2-19-1839 Hn
Carter, Charity to Burrell Oliver 2-24-1843 Cr
Carter, Ciney to L. D. Hood 10-6-1840 (10-27-1840) F
Carter, Dina to Elias Williams 6-12-1879 (6-18-1879) L
Carter, Dolly to Heck Shaw 12-23-1870 Hy
Carter, E. E. to Jo. M. Leskey 6-29-1858 We
Carter, E. E. to Wm. D. Jenkins 2-6-1845 Cr
Carter, Eliza B. to Levi S. Smith 12-3-1855 O
Carter, Eliza J. to O. W. Davis 10-29-1842 (no return) Hn
Carter, Eliza to Zedekiah Stone 9-9-1840 Sh
Carter, Elizabeth H. to Franklin Shole 4-5-1848 Cr
Carter, Elizabeth to Allen J. Wheatley 4-19-1857 Be
Carter, Elizabeth to Allen J. Wheatley 4-19-1857 Be CC
Carter, Elizabeth to James H. Chapel 10-16-1837 O
Carter, Elizabeth to James M. Dunlap 12-11-1848 (12-14-1848) Ma
Carter, Elizabeth to Jessie Hickman 11-22-1842 Cr
Carter, Elizabeth to Joseph Deman Fayette 2-10-1844 Hn
Carter, Ellen to John FitzPatrick 7-13-1860 (7-15-1860) Sh
Carter, Ellin to Henry Benson 9-2-1839 (no return) F
Carter, Elzada to J. H. Bowden 2-23-1851 Hn
Carter, Emily to Henry Moore 8-3-1872 (no return) Hy
Carter, Emily to Wm. (Esq.) Morris 5-12-1857 Cr
Carter, Ester M. to James J. McAlexander 2-11-1851 Cr
Carter, Ester W. to Edwards G. Hatchett 7-12-1839 Cr
Carter, Evaline to Joseph Nicholson 6-24-1871 (no return) Hy
Carter, F. E. to Lewin? Williamson 7-21-1873 (7-22-1873) Cr
Carter, Fanny to V. H. Bell 1-23-1839 (1-24-1839) G
Carter, Frances to Henry Shepherd 11-3-1877 Hy
Carter, G. Caroline to Michael Kemph 7-10-1854 (7-11-1854) Sh
Carter, Georga to R. M. Nelson 5-7-1872 (5-8-1872) T
Carter, H. M. E. to D. L. McCarter 3-10-1873 (no return) Cr
Carter, Hannah E. to Elisha C. Williams 11-22-1854 O
Carter, Hannah E. to L. R. Walker 1-15-1849 (1-18-1849) O
Carter, Harriet to Live (Levi?) Vales (Voles?) 5-15-1854 Sh
Carter, Harriet to Pompey Con? 8-22-1871 Sh
Carter, Harritt A. to John Kennon 12-20-1870 (12-21-1870) Cr
Carter, Hester to Henry Maclin 1-11-1877 Hy
Carter, Heurin C. to Junius H. Elcan 3-2-1865 T
Carter, Heurin? C. to Junius H. Elcan 3-2-1865 (3-7-1865) T
Carter, Iren? M. to John T. McCrory 4-17-1876 (4-18-1876) L
Carter, Jane to William H. Jones 2-7-1843 Hn
Carter, Jennie to Andrew J. Dearth 8-26-1862 (8-27-1862) Sh
Carter, Julia A. to Wm. A. M. Carter 3-1-1859 Cr
Carter, Julia to Green Levy 10-19-1867 (10-20-1867) F B
Carter, Julia to Luke Loving 4-10-1877 Hy
Carter, Julia to Patrick Vaughan 2-22-1852 (2-23-1852) Sh
Carter, L. J. to R. T. Brown 9-11-1868 Hy
Carter, Lizzie to Wiley Pearce 3-6-1885 L
Carter, Louisa to Reynard Clack 6-9-1847 O
Carter, Louiza to Henry Brewder 6-21-1871 (6-22-1871) Cr B
Carter, Love to Henry Allen 1-13-1867 (1-19-1867) F B
Carter, Lucinda to Henry Rice 6-19-1869 G B
Carter, Lucy to Sam Carter 1-7-1867 (1-12-1867) F B
Carter, M. A. to T. J. Godsey 10-9-1865 O
Carter, M. C. to H. W. Lankford 1-17-1854 Hn
Carter, M. E. to George W. Montgomery 1-3-1870 (1-5-1870) Cr
Carter, M. E. to P. Wilson, jr. 7-25-1863 (7-29-1863) F
Carter, Mahina to Burton Bailey 6-1-1843 Hr
Carter, Malinda E. to David P. Jones 3-28-1839 Hn
Carter, Mandy to Isaiah Harland 2-12-1866 G
Carter, Margaret to H. A. Gibson 8-9-1865 Mn
Carter, Marian to W(illiam) W. Wheatley 4-25-1850 Sh
Carter, Martha A. to A. B. Kemp 12-27-1854 Cr
Carter, Martha C. to Samuel Mabson 10-26-1859 Hn
Carter, Martha E. T. to Joseph S. Biggart 3-5-1868 (no return) Cr
Carter, Martha J. to Benjamin L. Blake 10-24-1838 O
Carter, Martha to Carl Bimmer? (Beimer?) 12-14-1864 Sh
Carter, Martha to James D. Vaughan 12-4-1869 (12-5-1869) T
Carter, Martha to John Pankey 10-17-1832 O
Carter, Martha to Manuel Pender 6-5-1871 (no return) Hy
Carter, Martha to W. H. McNair 2-25-1860 Hn
Carter, Martha to Z. H. McNar 2-25-1860 T
Carter, Mary A. to James S. Young 8-24-1854 Hn
Carter, Mary A. to William F. Ethridge 7-18-1863 (no return) Hn
Carter, Mary Ann to Alvin Grantham 12-25-1849 Hr
Carter, Mary Ann to George W. Reeves 9-15-1856 (9-23-1856) Ma
Carter, Mary Ann to James A. Edwards 11-28-1860 Hn
Carter, Mary Ann to Thomas L. Carter 6-2-1869 Ma
Carter, Mary E. to David C. Blankinship 12-27-1859 (12-28-1859) G
Carter, Mary Ellen to Monroe Lawrence 10-4-1877 (no return) L B
Carter, Mary F. to Henry M. Taylor 2-15-1869 (2-9?-1869) L
Carter, Mary J. to D. L. Jones 12-28-1859 (12-29-1859) T
Carter, Mary J. to Thos. J. Cunningham 2-23-1863 (2-26-1863) Cr
Carter, Mary J. to Thos. J. Cunningham 2-25-1863 Cr
Carter, Mary M. to Charles B. Wilcox 3-14-1859 Cr
Carter, Mary S. to J. N. Cole 12-19-1867 Hn
Carter, Mary to C. L. Bullock 9-25-1854 (no return) F
Carter, Mary to Mooreman T. Coleman 1-22-1831 Sh
Carter, Mary to N. D. Logan 1-20-1846 O
Carter, Mary to Nathan Smith 7-17-1838 Cr
Carter, Mary to Thomas Buding? 1-9-1838 Hr
Carter, Mary to Thomas L. Duncan 8-6-1853 Sh
Carter, Mary to Thomas O'Hallan 2-13-1858 (2-15-1858) Sh
Carter, Mary to Thos. Fisher 10-17-1868 (10-24-1868) L B
Carter, Mary to Thos. S. Hill 12-3-1856 O
Carter, Matilda Jane to John H. Mitchell 4-19-1869 (no return) L
Carter, Milija C. to Sterling W. Allen 12-10-1850 Cr
Carter, Milly to L. N. French 10-7-1867 Cr
Carter, Moriah to Geo. Williams 5-24-1868 Hy
Carter, Nancy E. to Ruben F. Carter 2-24-1848 Cr
Carter, Nancy V. to Thomas A. Cothran 12-16-1868 (12-17-1868) L
Carter, Nancy to Hubbard P. Scott 6-16-1842 Hr
Carter, Nancy to Wm. Phillips 7-18-1844 Cr
Carter, Narcissa to John A. Chapman 2-24-1869 T
Carter, Paulina to Abram Stull 7-4-1855 Sh
Carter, Polly to Samuel L. Owens 3-18-1829 (3-22-1829) Hr
Carter, Rebecca V. to Abram B. Langford 5-16-1860 (5-17-1860) Ma
Carter, Rebecca to Everett H. Verhine 4-9-1839 O
Carter, Rocinda to Joseph T. Kerby 12-19-1868 (12-23-1868) Cr
Carter, Ruth A. to D. W. Kirby 12-11-1869 (12-12-1869) Cr
Carter, Ruth E. to A. J. Bell 1-6-1848 Cr
Carter, S. A. to C. W. Todd 10-1-1879 Dy
Carter, S. E. to T. M. Reeser 12-23-1861 (12-27-1861) Hr
Carter, S. J. to W. R. Caton 2-16-1843 (no return) Hy
Carter, Sarah A. L. to Daniel W. Mann 11-3-1874 (11-4-1874) L
Carter, Sarah A. to Allen Tucker 6-20-1850 Sh
Carter, Sarah A. to Edward L. Jones 3-4-1843 (no return) Hn
Carter, Sarah A. to R. D. Phillips 12-16-1862 (no return) Cr
Carter, Sarah A. to R. W. Reams 7-12-1849 F
Carter, Sarah Ann to Atkins Stevens 12-8-1835 Hr
Carter, Sarah C. to Robert W. Moore 1-13-1854 Cr
Carter, Sarah E. to J. T. Hicks 9-21-1848 Sh
Carter, Sarah I. J. to John W. Williams 9-24-1858 Cr
Carter, Sarah M. to Lacy B. Walker 4-5-1858 (4-8-1858) O
Carter, Sarah Porter to Saml. Thomas 12-19-1873 (12-20-1873) T
Carter, Sarah a. to Alfred Trout 4-6-1852 Cr
Carter, Sarah to A. A. Acock 2-10-1848 Sh
Carter, Sarah to John R. Jones 1-2-1851 Sh
Carter, Sarah to Martin Talley 1-12-1848 (1-13-1848) O
Carter, Sarah to R. M. Hawley 12-12-1857 Be
Carter, Sophia B. to W. H. Barham 10-8-1848 Hn
Carter, Sophia to John T. W. Milam 6-27-1844 Hn
Carter, Susan E. to Francis M. Dillahunty 3-16-1843 (no return) Hn
Carter, Susan to Henry Hodge 6-23-1845 Hn
Carter, Syrena to Eppy Crews 2-9-1837 Hr
Carter, Tabitha to B. E. Warren 1-4-1853 (1-5-1853) O
Carter, Tabitha to William Sutton 12-6-1852 O
Carter, Urany (Mercury) to Richard Ballew 2-10-1834 Sh
Carter, V. A. to S. W. Speight 1-11-1866 Hn
Carter, Virginia C. to Joseph G. Cooke 10-26-1870 Hy
Carter, Virginia C. to L. L. Williams 4-27-1854 G
Carter, Virginia G. to Samuel L. Williamson 11-24-1858 Cr
Carter, Virginia to Fred Dressell 5-14-1878 Hy
Carter, Virginia to J. C. Sisco 12-1-1868 (12-2-1868) F
Carter, Z. A. to B. F. Neal 12-15-1870 Dy
Carthal, Sarah C. to M. T. McCulloch 12-23-1841 G
Carthel, Almira to William E. Elder 12-24-1851 G
Carthel, Easter to Alfred Fitzgerald 4-21-1866 G
Carthel, Emily L. to William T. Byers 10-12-1858 (10-13-1858) G
Carthel, Jinsey to J. Carthel 5-6-1866 G
Carthel, R. M. to E. N. Elder 9-5-1866 G
Cartmell, Ann Jane to John A. Tyson 2-1-1843 (2-2-1843) Ma
Cartmell, Margaret to J. D. Nicholson 7-2-1864 Sh
Cartwell, C. to Alfred Bridges 3-31-1852 We
Cartwright, A. V. to J. T. Murrell 9-27-1852 (no return) F
Cartwright, Adeline to P. H. Duggins 10-28-1848 (not executed) Sh
Cartwright, Alsey to Jehocakin Griffin 5-28-1862 (no return) Hy
Cartwright, Anna J. to J. A. Clay 11-18-1867 (11-20-1867) F
Cartwright, E. to C. R. Love 1-3-1850 We
Cartwright, Eliza Ann to Haywood Miller 6-3-1869 (no return) F B

Brides

Cartwright, Eliza to Benjamin F. Gilliland 1-15-1872 (no return) L
Cartwright, Eliza to Henry Clay 12-20-1867 (no return) F B
Cartwright, Elizabeth J. to James T. Wood 11-12-1844 (11-14-1844) G
Cartwright, Jane to Thomas Harvey 5-20-1859 (5-22-1859) Hr
Cartwright, Marinett to Thadios Wilson 9-8-1849 (10-3-1849) F
Cartwright, Sarah Ann J. to Henry C. Brewer 7-24-1845 Sh
Cartwright, Sarah to Needham Skipper 3-14-1832 (3-?-1832) Hr
Carune, Catharine to James O'Donnell 4-19-1852 Sh
Caruth, Elizabeth to Jacob Gingry 3-23-1861 (3-26-1861) L
Caruth, Emaline to W. J. Sewell 4-15-1865 Mn
Caruth, Hannah E. to S. F. Huggins 2-11-1855 (2-13-1855) L
Caruth, Jane C. to Thomas Wilcox 8-16-1842 (8-24-1842) L
Caruth, Margaret A. to William B. Burney 8-21-1844 (8-22-1844) L
Caruth, Melinda to Thomas Wilcox 12-22-1851 L
Caruthers, Charlotte D. to James Z. Gilbert 12-11-1845 Cr
Caruthers, Churney to Thomas Johnson 9-11-1873 T
Caruthers, Elizabeth to John A. Wilson 11-5-1838 (11-6-1838) Ma
Caruthers, Elmeranda M. to Charles Wright 7-27-1858 (11-21-1858) O
Caruthers, Francis N. to Richard L. McKey 10-18-1860 O
Caruthers, Harriet B. to William J. Wooddell 2-21-1853 (2-22-1853) Ma
Caruthers, Laura E. to A. S. McClanahan 12-18-1860 Ma
Caruthers, Leeva? to Nathan Sanford 10-2-1873 T
Caruthers, Margaret E. (Mrs.) to John M. Meals 1-19-1867 (1-22-1867) Ma
Caruthers, Margaretta A. T. to William H. Harper 11-19-1847 T
Caruthers, Mariah Olivia to William W. Chisum 3-11-1867 Ma
Caruthers, Martha M. to William Agnew 12-1-1840 O
Caruthers, Mary M. to William S. Rogers 12-31-1840 (no return) Hn
Caruthers, Mary to William D. Branch 12-23-1830 Ma
Caruthers, Nancy to Alpha Fulbright 12-31-1840 Ma
Caruthers, Sallie P. to Middleton Hays 12-16-1868 Ma
Caruthers, Sarah F. to Joseph F. Miller 4-13-1857 (4-16-1857) O
Caruthers, Susan to John H. Randle 11-6-1845 (no return) Hn
Caruthers, Tyre Elizabeth to Robert H. Sanford 1-10-1856 O
Caruthers, Virginia to Jose. B. Freeman 10-25-1849 Ma
Carven, Mary to Wm. Goforth 12-2-1865 (12-3-1865) O
Carver, Amanda P. to James E. Vancleave 7-24-1868 (7-26-1868) Cr
Carver, Anna M. to Daniel Prescott 5-18-1828 Hr
Carver, Caratt to Wm. Cross 1-13-1857 Cr
Carver, Elender to Wm. M. Rodgers 12-28-1854 Cr
Carver, Emaline to James Carver 2-18-1842 O
Carver, Emeline to John Rodgers 5-29-1843 O
Carver, Jane to James F. Blasengame 1-25-1863 Mn
Carver, Margaret M. to Abner Akins 12-12-1849 Cr
Carver, Martha to William L. Mann 1-12-1870 Cr
Carver, Mary E. to J. C. Abernathy 8-21-1853 Cr
Carver, Mary J. to Wm. H. Vancleave 4-1-1869 Cr
Carver, Mary T. to E. B. Birmingham 6-17-1871 (6-18-1871) Cr
Carver, Mitilda to Johnson Perritt 10-5-1854 Cr
Carver, Nancy A. to James H. Smith 12-17-1854 Cr
Carver, Sarah to Andrew Liles 4-13-1858 Cr
Carver?, Nancy to Wm. Marshall 12-24-1850 Cr
Carver?, Sarah to John Crouse 5-17-1849 Hr
Carwell, Parthenia J. to James M. Shaw 8-21-1869 (8-22-1869) Ma
Carwile, Louisa E. to John H. Odam 12-25-1842 Sh
Cary, Ann (Miss) to James McAlister 3-5-1863 O
Cary, Ann to Jordan A. Moore 4-16-1868 (4-23-1868) L
Cary, E. C. to J. R. Halford 2-21-1861 G
Cary, Mary Jane to Henry D. Small 12-31-1845 Sh
Cary, Mary to John Griffin 8-9-1862 (8-10-1862) Sh
Cary, N L. to William Davis 6-7-1865 G
Cary, Nancy to James Jackson 4-26-1848 (4-27-1848) O
Case, A. M. to W. J. Smith 1-6-1864 O
Case, Elvine to J. T. Cox 2-24-1858 We
Case, Frances to W. Henry Murdoch 9-22-1863 Sh
Case, Mary Virginia to James J. Stevens 1-14-1862 Sh
Case, Olive to I. P. Neely 12-6-1866 O
Case, P. S. to G. W. Pratt 3-8-1860 Sh
Casen, Mary to Frederick Leap 11-21-1854 (11-23-1854) O
Casey, Anney (Mrs.) to Phillip Holland 2-8-1844 (2-13-1844) G
Casey, Catharine B. to M. H. Paul 10-21-1850 (10-22-1850) Hr
Casey, Darthula to James Sloane 7-18-1848 (no return) F
Casey, Elizabeth to Spier Rogers 10-27-1836 Hr
Casey, Epsey J. to Joel S. Sasser 11-24-1857 (11-26-1857) Hr
Casey, Mahala to Joseph Pullian 12-13-1877 (12-30-1877) O B
Casey, Martha Jane to John G. Gearing 2-6-1856 Be
Casey, Mary to James Marler 8-1-1838 Hr
Casey, Mollie E. to Cullen P. Hopkins 6-7-1867 (6-12-1867) Ma
Casey, Nancy to James Gee 12-18-1847 (12-19-1847) Hr
Casey, Nancy to John T. Jones 4-22-1828 Hr
Casey, Rebecca Jane to Thos. J. Hicks 12-22-1856 (12-23-1856) Hr
Casey, Rebecca to E. P. Latham 8-14-1860 We
Casey, Rebecca to James M. Jones 3-18-1835 Hr
Casey, Ruth G. to Thos. D. Hankins 1-7-1860 (1-8-1860) Hr
Casey, Ruth to John H. Russell 1-7-1829 (1-9-1829) Hr
Casey, Sarah to Jesse Webster 12-12-1835 (12-17-1835) Hr
Casey, Susan C. to Jas. M. Carraway 11-23-1858 (11-25-1858) Hr
Casey, Tabitha to Lomax Brasher 6-6-1853 (6-7-1853) T

Casey, Tennessee to James C. Casey 8-15-1870 (8-17-1870) Ma
Casey, Violet to Fred Fitzpatrick 5-24-1876 L B
Cash, Del to John McGuiver 3-15-1870 T
Cash, Elizabeth J. to J. F. Davidson 1-3-1871 (1-5-1871) Ma
Cash, Evelina W. to Thomas R. F. Simpson 1-6-1842 F
Cash, Frances to William Watkins 11-12-1857 Hn
Cash, Louisa to William R. Jarrell 12-22-1857 Hn
Cash, Margrette E. to Willis B. Grissom 10-3-1854 G
Cash, Nancy N. to Walter L. Thedford 1-16-1869 (1-20-1869) Ma
Cash, Sarah to Thomas Askew 6-22-1857 Ma
Cashar, Sarah J. to James W. Edward 2-6-1851 G
Cashen, Elizabeth to Samuel B. Sneed 8-1-1859 We
Cashen, Martha to George McDough 2-1-1855 We
Cashen, Sarah E. to Adam Milten 7-30-1859 We
Cashian, Mary to M. E. Odle 9-19-1859 We
Cashion, Cynthia I. to James Newton 3-26-1845 We
Cashion, Nancy to John L. Moultrie 4-16-1853 (4-19-1853) O
Cashow, Nancy E. to John Haggard 3-7-1865 Mn
Casin, Elizabeth to Ben Johnson 6-6-1878 (6-8-1878) L
Casinger, Cynthia to William Hamilton 11-12-1838 Hn
Caskey, Joanna to P. B. McWilliams 1-20-1869 (1-21-1869) T
Caskey, M. W. to C. A. Johnson 12-31-1870 (1-5-1871) T
Caskey, Margaret W. to James O. Lynn 12-31-1870 (1-2-1871) T
Caslin, Elizabeth to Patrick Hughes 5-5-1858 (6-6-1858) Sh
Cason, Annie to Lewis Scott 2-15-1886 L
Cason, Francis to Isaiah Thomas 12-24-1877 L
Cason, Martha to George Leap 10-25-1857 O
Cason, Mary to Thomas I. Heath 5-28-1838 (5-21?-1838) Ma
Cason, Pattie H. to J. S. Hendricks 10-23-1866 Hn
Cason, U. C. to W. A. Murchison 11-16-1847 Ma
Cassa, Elizabeth to Robert C. Calhoun 6-12-1861 (6-18-1861) Sh
Cassady, Catharine to John Higgins 5-21-1857 Sh
Cassel, Harriet V. to Joseph M. Figgins 2-16-1867 (2-22-1867) F
Cassell, Elizabeth Jane to Andrew J. Allen 6-27-1853 (6-30-1853) O
Cassell, Lucenda J. to Joyner W. Bady 9-8-1851 (9-10-1851) G
Cassell, Lydia T. to Thomas J. Pardew 12-3-1866 (12-4-1866) F
Cassell, Martha M. to John B. Butler 8-1-1855 G
Cassells, Carline to John Crage 11-20-1847 (11-21-1847) G
Cassells, Mahaly C. to L. H. Canady 9-3-1857 G
Cassels, Mary to Andrew J. Lemons 12-7-1862 G
Cassels, Susan M. to William R. Hazlewood 9-13-1848 (9-14-1848) G
Cassett, Anna A. to W. J. Montgomery 2-25-1860 (5-2-1860) F
Cassett?, Mary C. to R. H. Malone 10-2-1849 (10-3-1849) F
Cassilman, Jane C. to Isaac C. Reavis 11-3-1861 We
Cassles, Elizabeth to Robert Boyd 2-11-1852 G
Cassles, Mary Ann to Joshua Bullock 4-3-1866 Hn
Cassody, Catharine to Cornelius Dunn 10-5-1851 Sh
Castalaw, Z. E. to W. H. Wateridge 12-24-1868 Hy
Castaloe, Josephine to A. A. Terrell 12-28-1876 Hy
Casteel, Jenny (Mrs.) to Hiram Green 11-23-1864 Sh
Casteel, Mary to John Smoot 11-1-1857 Hn
Casteel, Sophia C. to John W. McRee 3-11-1863 Sh
Castelaw, Elizabeth to William Singleton 3-3-1856 (3-4-1856) L
Castelaw, Mary to John F. Manley 4-1-1865 (no return) L
Castell, Jane to Wm. A. Chamlind-Chamberland 3-12-1860 (3-15-1860) Sh
Castell, Sophia C. to John W. McKee 3-11-1863 Sh
Castellaw, Amanda to Matthew Johnson 12-29-1866 (no return) Hy
Castellaw, Jane E. to James W. Braden 9-17-1857 L
Castellaw, Mary A. to Henry B. Pope 1-31-1856 L
Castellow, Violet to Pompy White 3-16-1871 Hy
Castilaw, Luisa S. to John R. Austin 8-1-1863 (8-9-1863) L
Castill, Vicy to James Davis 8-25-1856 (no return) Hn
Castle, M. A. to G. W. Moore 3-23-1865 (3-27-1865) O
Castle, Martha to Wm. C. Butts 12-31-1845 We
Castleman, Juliet V. to John W. Watson 7-25-1854 Sh
Castles, Charity to Edmund D. Screws 3-26-1846 (4-2-1846) Ma
Castles, Eliza to Jack Peterbock 1-15-1869 (1-16-1869) F B
Castles, Susan to Joshua S. Vick 1-22-1845 Ma
Casy, Hannah to Needham Jackson 1-25-1834 (1-26-1834) Hr
Casy, M. to John Oliver 9-10-1831 Hr
Cate, Ann D. W. to Daniel F. Birmingham 5-19-1846 Ma
Cate, Caroline to Samuel W. Cochran 7-16-1860 Hn
Cate, Elizabeth D. to Bryant Peel 11-17-1847 (no return) Hn
Cate, Elizabeth to Eli McCarroll 5-29-1873 Dy
Cate, Ella to J. H. Wyman 10-24-1874 D
Cate, Jane to Wilie Ayrens? 8-7-1871 Dy
Cate, Kiddy A. to Bryan D. Deets 9-17-1867 Hn
Cate, Lucinda Caroline to James Madison Palmer 4-19-1865 Hn
Cate, Mary A. to Robert T. Osburn 3-20-1860 We
Cate, Mary Catherine to Samuel H. Medlin 8-1-1865 Hn
Cate, Mary E. to Wm. G. Nordon 1-9-1853 Cr
Cate, Mary F. to Thomas Patterson 5-14-1857 Hn
Cate, Sarah to Creed T. Greer 7-15-1843 (no return) Hn
Cate, Sarah to Martin Reeder 4-18-1855 Hn
Caten, . J. to W. E. Lusk 12-28-1860 G
Cater, Eliza W. to E. H. Smith 5-5-1863 (5-6-1863) F
Cates, Adie to Wm. Walker 2-2-1872 Hy

Cates, Arabella to Albert M. Estes 10-19-1869 Ma
Cates, Eliza Jane to William Henry Driskell 6-11-1863 Sh
Cates, Elizabeth to E. W. Hall 10-25-1851 (no return) Cr
Cates, Ellen to William R. Cunningham 3-4-1867 (no return) L
Cates, Lewellen E. to Willes N. Campbell 2-21-1853 (2-22-1853) G
Cates, M. J. to J. C. Norvil 3-25-1866 Hy
Cates, Maday W. to Calvin H. Ward 2-19-1852 We
Cates, Margaret C. to John W. Perkins 4-5-1862 (4-9-1862) L
Cates, Margaret F. to M. L. Pool 6-2-1857 We
Cates, Margaret to J. D. Neely 9-5-1865 O
Cates, Martha Ellen to John Estes 1-6-1882 (1-10-1882) L
Cates, Mary M. to John F. Butler 2-25-1869 G
Cates, Mary to S. R. Stribling 5-6-1863 Mn
Cates, Nancy to William Anderson 11-26-1854 We
Cates, Samanthia Octavia to George William Spence 2-24-1879 (2-25-1879) L
Cates, Sarah E. to J. M. Moore 10-1-1870 (no return) Hy
Cates, Susan E. to Charles H. Haynes 1-26-1870 (1-27-1870) Cr
Catha, Araminta to William Thos. Clifton 1-24-1847 Sh
Cathcart, Eliza A. to E. L. Morrow 11-18-1867 G
Cathen, Eliza to G. R. Watson 3-14-1878 Hy
Cathery, Parile to John T. James 9-3-1857 We
Cathey, Elva to J. F. Edmondson 10-23-1870 G
Cathey, Louisa to Thomas J. Flowers 9-12-1860 G
Cathey, M. A. to Jas. F. Thomas 1-12-1875 (1-14-1875) O
Cathey, Mahala to George C. Moore 10-21-1852 G
Cathey, Nancy M. to Henry Abbington 11-28-1853 O
Cathey, Narcissa to John T. Jones 11-9-1848 (no return) F
Cathey, Susan to Henry S. Myer 4-22-1861 Cr
Caton, L. H. to W. J. Bowden 10-1-1865 Hn
Caton, Mary to William C. Manley 10-29-1857 Hn
Caton, Rutha to Daniel Feeley 5-28-1850 G
Caton, S. F. to G. M. Foster 6-29-1865 (no return) Hn
Catron, E. J. to L. Palmer 1-28-1868 (1-29-1868) O
Catron, H. E. to T. L. Bransford 2-1-1872 (2-21-1872) O
Catron, Lou to Tom Seymour 1-16-1866 F B
Catron, Rebecca to William Catron 7-23-1870 (no return) F B
Catron, Susan E. to Robert Wade 11-3-1857 (11-5-1857) O
Cats, Delia to Danel Ward 12-26-1854 (12-28-1855) We
Catten, Lida to William Boykin 11-26-1868 T
Catten, Mary to Frank Hall 6?-15-1867 (6-16-1867) T
Caudle, Francis to John W. Cummings 11-11-1863 (11-12-1863) O
Caudle, M. A. to F. M. McFarlin 1-29-1863 O
Caudle, M. A. to T. M. McFarlin 1-29-1863 (1-31-1863) O
Caudle, Mary E. to Edwin Williams 9-25-1865 Cr
Caudle, Nancy C. to Damman Tillman 4-18-1861 We
Cauley, Rebecca Ann to Samuel J. Bell 7-20-1846 (7-22-1846) L
Caurdel, Sarah Ann to Elbert Rollins 4-27-1857 Ma
Causey, Araminta to D. O. Winns 7-20-1840 (no return) Hn
Causey, Susan to William T. Smithey 1-20-1856 Hn
Causly (Causby?), Jane A. to Josiah King 12-7-1849 (no return) L
Cauthern, S. C. to P. R. Owen? 1-13-1868 (1-16-1868) Cr
Cauthorn, Mollie to J. M. Pate 9-29-1875 (9-30-1875) Dy
Cauthran?, Martha J. to James S. Rankins 9-17-1861 We
Caven?, Elizabeth to Asa Mason 1-16-1840 Hn
Cavenaugh, Mary E. to James S. Wyatt 2-14-1871 Hy
Cavenaugh, Susan to Jim Williams 8-24-1869 Hy
Cavenor, Nannie M. to George A. Walker 12-26-1870 (12-29-1870) T
Cavinar, Mary E. to William Jones 7-12-1850 (7-14-1850) Hr
Caviness, Arimetta B. to Jasper G. Cannon 6-3-1861 Hn
Caviness, Cornelia A. to Stephen Cup 8-30-1850 (9-1-1850) Hr
Caviness, Delila A. to Thomas A. Robertson 11-11-1854 (11-12-1854) Hr
Caviness, Delilah M. to William K. Smith 12-26-1853 Hr
Caviness, Mary C. to John Moffitt 2-21-1853 (2-22-1853) Hr
Cavitt, Emely A. to Brice H. Beadles 3-4-1861 We
Cavitt, M. E. to D. L. Brooks 1-4-1860 (no return) We
Cavitt, M. E. to S. H. King 9-3-1878 (9-4-1878) Dy
Cavitt, Minerva E. J. to Benjamin W. Hall 10-4-1841 (no return) Hn
Cavitt, Rosean C. to W. J. Harrion 9-10-1854 We
Cavitt, Sarah A. to Charlie M. Powell 2-10-1859 We
Cavnar, Emma to W. T. Leggett 2-27-1875 Hy
Cavnar, Sarah to J. P. Lumley 1-31-1859 Hr
Cavnaugh, Nanna to T. M. Pugh 8-1-1872 (8-4-1872) T
Cawhon, Rebecca J. to A. C. McFarlan 7-14-1865 (7-16-1865) Dy
Cawthan, H. E. to W. H. Woods 1-27-1868 (1-29-1868) Cr
Cawthan, L. A. to W. C. Christian 12-1-1866 (no return) Cr
Cawthan, Martha A. to John M. Worel? 1-9-1863 (no return) Cr
Cawthen, Susan A. to James McClesky 7-14-1866 Cr
Cawthon, Ann to A. J. Dickey 4-12-1870 G
Cawthon, F. A. to Samuel A. Owens 4-23-1866 (4-26-1866) Cr
Cawthon, S. E. to J. R. Owen 10-19-1870 (10-20-1870) Cr
Cayce, Allice J. to A. C. Walker 10-13-1858 (10-15-1858) Sh
Cayton, Cass Ann to Nathan Nicholls 2-25-1846 (2-26-1846) G
Cazort, Mary I. to Thomas Moore 1-22-1873 Hy
Cearce, M. R. to William S. Liggett 2-19-1872 (2-21-1872) Dy
Cearley, Martha A. A. to James Young 11-23-1854 Hr
Cearley, Martha to John Ward 8-12-1867 Dy
Cearley, Mary J. to J. L. Eaton 2-8-1862 Hr

Cearly, Elizabeth to John Richardson 9-26-1869 (9-27-1869) Dy
Cearly, Hannah to Samuel Murdaugh(Mordough) 11-30-1848 Hr
Cearly, Mary Ann to Jacob A. Cozby 2-17-1847 Hr
Cenuse, Elizabeth E. to Wm. B. Johnson 12-23-1858 We
Cerley, Harriett L. B. to William A. Davidson 2-2-1860 Hn
Cerly, Nelly to Jno. C. Davis 11-28-1849 Hr
Cerry, Rena to Ephraim Bush 12-24-1870 (no return) Dy
Chadwick, Jennie S. to A. J. Wheeler 12-22-1859 Sh
Chadwick, Lizzie to Dan T. Wilson 6-6-1869 (no return) Dy
Chadwick, Louiza to John Sale 3-9-1849 (3-11-1849) G
Chadwick, Martha to Edward Johnston 8-9-1860 (8-12-1860) Cr
Chafero, Martha to Lions C. Scott 2-22-1838 G
Chaffee, Annie to Wm. C. Ashkettle 4-6-1864 (4-10-1864) Sh
Chaffin, Adney to Thad Moore 2-28-1868 (no return) F B
Chaffin, Charlott to Wm. Lenard 7-20-1867 (7-27-1867) F B
Chaffin, Ella E. to A. A. Prichard 9-23-1868 F
Chaffin, Eveline to James Blaydes 7-3-1867 F B
Chaffin, Mollie A. to P. D. Ewell 8-5-1867 F
Chaffin, Sue to Beverly Isbell 9-26-1867 F B
Chaffin, Viola L. to William S. Green 12-20-1870 (no return) F
Chairs, Mary to Joseph Williams 2-17-1855 Sh
Chalk, Allis to Anton Rodrin 11-21-1870 (12-4-1870) L
Chalk, M. B. to J. D. Lanier 12-24-1874 Hy
Chalk, S. E. to J. A. McKinnon 7-30-1862 (no return) Hy
Chamber, Louisa to Henry Coward 11-17-1865 (11-18-1865) T
Chamber, Lucinda C. to James T. Ward 8-31-1869 (9-1-1869) L
Chamber, Martha to Dock Talley 2-25-1873 (2-26-1873) T
Chamber, Nancy J. to John Gray 1-15-1844 We
Chamberlain, Caroline to Oney Sheldon 12-28-1848 Ma
Chamberlain, Etta to William A. Boatwright 4-13-1876 Dy
Chamberlain, Frances J. to Green T. Chamberlain 10-11-1858 Cr
Chamberlain, Henrietta Jane to Geo. Wyatt 1-14-1880 (1-17-1880) Dy
Chamberlain, Louiza S. to William Key 1-31-1861 Dy
Chamberlain, M. E. to C. M. Boatwright 9-1-1870 Dy
Chamberlain, Martha Ann to Alexander Munns 5-28-1828 Ma
Chamberlain, Martha to Matthew Horne 3-19-8150 (3-21-1850) Ma
Chamberlain, Mary E. to Asa S. Stratton 7-10-1849 Sh
Chamberlain, Mattie C. to S. E. Beardsley 1-13-1863 Sh
Chamberlaine, Martha A. to W. H. Stricklin 1-5-1856 Sh
Chamberlin, Elizabeth to Sherwood Folks 4-11-1858 Cr
Chamberlin, Frances J. to James Scott 11-4-1870 Cr
Chamberlin, Margaret L. to Andrew Irwin 8-31-1840 Sh
Chamberlin, Nancy to Wm. J. Thompson 1-27-1857 Cr
Chamberlin, Sallie L. (Mrs.) to Thomas P. Davidson 11-7-1855 (11-9-1855) Sh
Chamberlin, Susan to Charles W. Chamberlin 1-13-1841 (1-14-1841) Ma
Chambers, Ann H. to John D. Harberson 10-8-1839 Sh
Chambers, Ann R. to Benjm. F. Wever 1-9-1854 (1-10-1854) Sh
Chambers, Catherine Ann to Robert B. Sanford 12-23-1839 (12-24-1839) Ma
Chambers, Eliza Jane to Philander D. W. Conger 12-14-1842 (12-15-1842) Ma
Chambers, Eliza P. to John, sr. Moore 12-21-1864 (12-22-1864) L
Chambers, Elizabeth D. to W. A.? Hilliard 2-1-1847 (2-4-1847) F
Chambers, Elizabeth to Wm. C. Uptegrove 4-16-1845 Cr
Chambers, Elizabeth to Wm. P. Blow 10-12-1843 Cr
Chambers, Emily R. to Wm. R. Jones 5-19-1864 O
Chambers, Emma C. to J. F. Cox 4-19-1870 (4-21-1870) F
Chambers, Eveline T. to Creed T. McDearman 10-28-1867 (10-30-1867) L
Chambers, Frances M. to John A. Hamil 12-18-1867 (no return) Hy
Chambers, Hannah to Freeman Holt 11-6-1869 (12-4-1869) F B
Chambers, Jane to Wm. Crockett 1-12-1867 (1-13-1867) O
Chambers, L. A. to H. T. Burks 2-23-1881 (2-24-1881) L
Chambers, Louisa A. to G. W. McDearmon 8-25-1884 (8-27-1884) L
Chambers, Louisa to George Williams 11-16-1867 Hy
Chambers, M. A. to S. N. Burks 12-10-1878 (12-11-1879?) L
Chambers, M. E. to H. P. Rowland 7-7-1873 (7-4?-1873) L
Chambers, M. E. to J. M. Reed 2-11-1874 (2-25-1874) O
Chambers, M. J. to H. C. Chambers 1-18-1843 Cr
Chambers, M. J. to John Pruett 2-7-1871 Cr
Chambers, M. R. to W. S. Teague 1-31-1864 (2-2-1864) F
Chambers, Margaret A. to Orren B. Vincent 7-11-1861 We
Chambers, Margaret to Giles Smith 4-25-1873 (4-26-1873) T
Chambers, Mariah to George Henderson 11-24-1871 O
Chambers, Martha (Mrs.) to William D. Turner 12-5-1847 Sh
Chambers, Martha H. to H. L. Harris 1-1-1867 O
Chambers, Martha H. to W. L. Ayers 9-23-1872 (9-26-1872) O
Chambers, Martha H.? to William P. Pillow 5-22-1843 (5-23-1843) L
Chambers, Martha J. to Charles Overton 5-2-1873 (no return) Hy
Chambers, Martha J. to Zacheriah Quinn 1-7-1873 (1-8-1873) L
Chambers, Martha Jane to T. E. Salisbury 4-9-1870 (4-12-1870) L
Chambers, Martha to J. F. Taylor 12-29-1866 (12-30-1866) F
Chambers, Mary A. to George W. Johnson 11-30-1870 Cr
Chambers, Mary A. to J. W. T. Hilliard 12-6-1854 (no return) F
Chambers, Mary A. to R. S. Wyatt 9-13-1870 (9-14-1870) Cr
Chambers, Mary Ann to A. H. Price 10-9-1848 (10-23-1848) F
Chambers, Mary Jane to Geo. W. Rodgers 2-16-1863 L
Chambers, Mary W. to D. R. Nowlin 6-14-1853 Hn
Chambers, Mary to Henry Chambers 6-19-1869 G B
Chambers, Mary to Isaac Miller 11-4-1841 Cr

Chambers, Mary to William Terrett 8-19-1846 (8-23-1846) O
Chambers, Mollie F. to James M. Thompson 12-17-1869 (12-19-1869) L
Chambers, Nancy J. to A. Burkhart 1-24-1855 (no return) F
Chambers, Palina to Gloster Chambers 11-6-1869 (12-4-1869) F B
Chambers, Parthenia to John M. Overton 7-27-1867 (no return) Hy
Chambers, Rebecca to Owen Gillis 3-27-1842 Cr
Chambers, Roxan to George Boty 2-26-1872 O
Chambers, S. E. to E. Keller 5-19-1880 L
Chambers, Sarah A. E. to Wesley Whitaker 12-24-1865 Mn
Chambers, Sarah A. to Z. T. Grantham 3-5-1862 Mn
Chambers, Sarah Ann to William H. Smith 2-25-1861 (2-27-1861) L
Chambers, Sarah C(aroline) to Orvill L. Thurmond 1-11-1848 (1-13-1848) L
Chambers, Sarah J. to John E. Watson 12-25-1860 (12-26-1860) L
Chambers, Sarah to Thomas C. Bondurant 1-7-1858 O
Chambers, Tusa to Richard Drewery 3-29-1869 (3-31-1869) O
Chambless, Jane Ann to William Y. McBride 7-25-1852 (7-29-1852) Hr
Chamblin, Belle to George D. Southall 9-5-1855 Sh
Chamblin, Jennie to W. H. Simpson 8-14-1867 (no return) Dy
Chamblin, Louella to W. R. (Dr.) Hays 12-9-1874 Dy
Chambliss, Clara Adela to John Pope 1-5-1857 (1-8-1857) Sh
Chamness, Lusetta to Chesley Rummen 10-12-1862 Mn
Champ, Drucilla V. to Geo. J. Hunter 10-16-1850 Hr
Champ, Louisa J. to Joel Mayfield 11-17-1854 (11-19-1854) Hr
Champain, Martha to H. D. Baldwin 6-11-1865 Hn
Champain, Rossan to John Pruitt 8-8-1829 (8-9-1829) G
Champin, Rachel E. to B. F. Foy 6-28-1848 Hn
Champion(Anderson), Parthena H. to James Champion 10-2-1833 Hr
Champion, Elizabeth H. to Washington C. Fraser 1-16-1836 Sh
Champion, Elizabeth to Enoch S. Galling(Gatling?) 9-2-1845 Hr
Champion, Fannie to J. J. Wall 1-10-1867 F
Champion, Malinda M. to T. M. Shepard 9-28-1867 F
Champion, Mary B. to John A. Pirtle 8-19-1831 (8-24-1831) Hr
Champion, Mary C. D. to Joseph Rudisill 12-6-1832 Hr
Champion, Matilda to Henry Deakins 8-27-1866 (8-28-1866) T
Champion, Mildred N. to Josiah A. Morrow 9-3-1849 (9-6-1849) T
Champion, Nancy J. to James A. Bucy 10-4-1855 (no return) Hn
Chance, Eliza to James S. Jones 1-12-1857 (no return) Hn
Chance, Emily R. to Wm. T. Jones 2-20-1860 Cr
Chance, Margaret E. to Meredith W. Luten 10-12-1858 Hn
Chance, Mary A. to Thomas C. Phillips 12-31-1860 (or 1859?) We
Chance, Sarah A. to George W. Barrett 11-7-1858 Hn
Chance, Susan B. to Miles F. Tyler 12-14-1852 Hn
Chancelor, Victoria to James Grandee 2-16-1882 (2-19-1882) L
Chandelor, Anna B. to F. M. Phelps 3-29-1863 We
Chandler, Annie to Thos. Crews 5-2-1844 Cr
Chandler, Christiana to James A. Davis 7-6-1867 (7-7-1867) Dy
Chandler, Christianna to D. R. Inman 1-7-1864 Mn
Chandler, Elizabeth S. to James L. Groom 7-5-1862 (7-11-1862) Cr
Chandler, Elizabeth to T. P. Alexander 2-12-1863 Mn
Chandler, Elizabeth to William L. Paris 4-5-1858 (4-8-1858) G
Chandler, Ellener to Allen I. Wilson 12-7-1843 Ma
Chandler, Elvira to Isham Burrow 2-14-1838 Ma
Chandler, Hannah to Duncan L. Alexander 1-31-1854 Ma
Chandler, Harriett to Moses D. Francis 8-20-1845 Hn
Chandler, Ida to J. G. Owenby 12-17-1872 (12-18-1872) Cr
Chandler, Jane to John Young 10-29-1846 Ma
Chandler, Juda to John McCormack 4-24-1873 Hy
Chandler, Judy to Uriah Pierce 4-26-1833 (4-30-1833) Hr
Chandler, July Ann to David A. Liles 8-7-1866 (8-8-1866) Cr
Chandler, Margaret to E. A. Cowley 6-24-1862 O
Chandler, Martha A. to J. K. Jones 12-24-1873 Hy
Chandler, Martha V. to Benjamin J. Williams 6-20-1853 Hr
Chandler, Mary A. to Alexander E. Calhoun 11-11-1857 O
Chandler, Mary J. to Burel H. Sparks 12-9-1857 Hn
Chandler, Mary M. to Allen J. Wilson 9-10-1855 Ma
Chandler, Mary to James N.? Burd 9-2-1866 Hn
Chandler, Matilda A. to John B. Dedjamatt 5-25-1858 (no return) L
Chandler, Nancy M. to Henry P. Stephens 1-22-1854 Hn
Chandler, Nancy to Hamilton Foster 12-27-1847 (12-28-1847) G
Chandler, Nancy to James L. Groom? 3-20-1868 Cr
Chandler, Rebecca R. to Green B. Hancock 2-16-1859 L
Chandler, Rhoda to John Brown 3-13-1828 Ma
Chandler, Rosa Lee to M. H. Campbell 9-24-1872 (no return) L
Chandler, S. F. to Eli W. Arington 8-23-1866 Cr
Chandler, Sarah J. to John B. White 3-10-1868 Ma
Chandler, Sarah to Wilie Futrell 7-7-1855 Hr
Chandler, Susan to Abner C. McGehee 11-11-1849 Hn
Chandler, Susan to Joseph P. Hale 4-24-1850 G
Chandley, Sarah to David Crews 7-24-1844 Cr
Chaney, Ada to George Love 12-24-1884 (12-25-1884) L
Chaney, Belinda to Thomas Caffrey 12-10-1850 Ma
Chaney, Emily M. to Mordica Powell 7-29-1836 Sh
Chaney, Lutitia E. to John S. Moore 12-19-1866 Hy
Chaney, M. C. to J. G. Williams 9-8-1865 Hy
Chaney, Manerva A. to Jesse A. Hughes 9-2-1868 (9-6-1868) Cr
Chaney, Mariah A. to William Carriston? 3-4-1871 T
Chaney, Martha to Henry Seals 1-9-1869 G B

Chaney, ____ to Andrew Barron 10-10-1867 Hy
Chapel, Frances to Matthew Howe 9-26-1867 O
Chapell, Emaline E. to Kirksey W. Russell 8-27-1839 Cr
Chaplin, Seley to John C. Bates 11-15-1849 O
Chapman, Amanda E. to N. H. Adams 11-26-1860 Hn
Chapman, Angeline to John C. Oliver 4-2-1832 (4-3-1832) Ma
Chapman, Ann to Andrew Blair 11-13-1868 (no return) Hy
Chapman, C. T. to W. D. Simpkins 2-6-1866 (2-8-1866) F
Chapman, Charity to W. F. Perry 5-17-1858 (5-18-1858) Hr
Chapman, Charlotte to Bill Jones 1-3-1870 G B
Chapman, D. J. to J. E. Cooper 3-9-1868 (3-12-1868) Dy
Chapman, Delia to J. B. D. Henley 12-16-1869 Hy
Chapman, E. T. to Harvey Landen 1-27-1847 Sh
Chapman, Elisabeth to Geo. Sharps 3-22-1862 (3-27-1862) Sh
Chapman, Eliza to William L. Bond 12-2-1844 (12-4-1844) Ma
Chapman, Elizabeth J. to W. J. K. Rucker 11-23-1841 Hr
Chapman, Elizabeth to Albert Phillips 12-7-1863 G
Chapman, Elizabeth to Henderson Peach 1-2-1844 (1-4-1844) Ma
Chapman, Fannie to T. P. Owen 1-4-1868 (no return) Hy
Chapman, J. F. to S. T. Bowers 3-19-1874 (3-20-1874) T
Chapman, Josie R. to Reuben Graves 5-4-1876 (no return) Hy
Chapman, Louisa to John B. Gehen 12-13-1859 (12-15-1859) T
Chapman, Louisa to Robert Lamkin 4-14-1874 T
Chapman, Louisiana to John B. Gehen 12-13-1859 (12-15-1859) T
Chapman, Maria to William Chapman 1-4-1847 Sh
Chapman, Martha A. to J. C. Slover 3-9-1855 (3-11-1855) Sh
Chapman, Martha E. to Thomas P. Owen 11-18-1877 Hy
Chapman, Mary Ann to Sherrod Hines 9-9-1844 (9-?-1844) Hr
Chapman, Mary M. W. to Peyton L. Robison 12-22-1858 L
Chapman, Mary to William A. Johnson 10-23-1860 Hy
Chapman, Mattie to W. E. Parker 5-7-1867 F
Chapman, Molie B. to Solomon P. Lea 3-23-1861 (3-28-1861) L
Chapman, Nancy E. to Theodore Burtis 6-15-1866 (6-19-1866) T
Chapman, Nancy to Andrew Conner 6-21-1845 (6-24-1845) Ma
Chapman, Sallie to John J. Akin 4-18-1865 (4-20-1865) T
Chapman, Sallie J. to Samuel J. Ackin? 4-18-1865 T
Chapman, Susan to Able Hodges 7-12-1836 Hr
Chapman, Teresy? to William Dallas 3-21-1869 G B
Chapmana, Martha A. to Vanburen Harris 4-12-1859 O
Chappel, Pruda to Wm. B. Oliver 9-17-1839 (9-19-1839) F
Chappel, Sarah A. to Heran Glover 10-12-1857 We
Chappell, A. E. to J. H. Dillehunt 11-13-1862 O
Chappell, Catherine to R. C. Curbey 10-22-1860 (10-29-1860) O
Chappell, Elizabeth F. to John High 3-22-1855 We
Chappell, H. C. to Avery Parham 1-28-1852 We
Chappell, Lavina to Wm. H. Case 5-16-1863 We
Chappell, Living A. to S. W. Chapell 1-25-1859 We
Chappell, Louisa to Noah Huie 8-24-1856 Hn
Chappell, Lucy to S. F. Scarbrough 7-23-1844 Cr
Chappell, Sarah E. to John R. Hurt 6-20-1860 (6-21-1860) Ma
Chapple, Elizabeth to James Newhouse 4-12-1873 (4-13-1873) O
Chapple, Martha J. to A. G. Little 7-4-1857 Cr
Charles, M. to James Parker 7-23-1849 Hn
Charles, Sarina J. to John F. Buie 12-23-1860 Hn
Charles, Zilpha to Alexander McClure 2-6-1863 Hn
Charley, Reyna to James Yarbrough 4-27-1841 Cr
Chasum, Caroline to Lawrence P. Williams 9-9-1847 (9-10-1847) Ma
Chatman, Lou to W. H. Payne 11-23-1876 Dy
Chavers, Sarah to Richard Madison 9-30-1841 G
Cheairs, Martha K. to John M. Rook 1-17-1859 (1-18-1859) F
Cheairs, Mary F. to Atlas Jones 3-7-1853 (3-10-1853) Hr
Cheairs, SophiaH. to Jos. T. Knight 12-11-1860 Hr
Cheany, Susan to N. H. Chaney 8-26-1865 (no return) Hy
Chears, A. H. to A. H. Hughey 12-24-1855 (no return) Hn
Chears, Margaret B. to Theophelus Higgs 1-24-1856 (1-31-1856) Hr
Cheatam, Meriah to James McDaniel 10-15-1844 Be
Cheatham, Eliza to Martin Wirt 4-25-1857 O
Cheatham, Frances to Aaron Walker 4-6-1885 (no return) L
Cheatham, Jane to Elijah Toy 12-13-1846 Be
Cheatham, Lula to J. W. Witt 4-9-1863 Sh
Cheatham, Martha C. to Henry W. Campbell 2-14-1844 We
Cheatham, Mary A. to Thomas Othello Smith 11-24-1857 Sh
Cheatham, S. L. to J. W. Williamson 7-8-1868 O
Cheek, Amelia to William Powers 9-2-1854 Sh
Cheek, Caroline I.(J) to Jno. Wildbenga 5-17-1849 Sh
Cheek, Hannah to Calvin Swinny 3-2-1863 Hn
Cheek, Irene to W. S. Hughes 7-24-1855 (7-25-1855) Sh
Cheek, Jane to James W. Almond 10-16-1856 Hn
Cheek, Louisa to George Malone 10-18-1859 Sh
Cheek, M. Adella to Robert L. Fowler 3-4-1879 L
Cheek, M. J. to F. L. Smith 9-5-1871 (9-6-1871) T
Cheek, V. E. to C. M. Olds 3-5-1884 (3-6-1884) L
Cheeke, Sallie A. to John H. Waggener 10-22-1851 Sh
Cheers, Louiza to James Mott 10-12-1858 Hy
Cheisher, Louisa to Wilson N. Pankey 12-16-1844 (12-17-1844) Hr
Chenault, Elvira to William Archer Dubois 4-14-1863 (4-15-1863) Sh
Cheney, Almina to Isaac Miller 2-6-1877 (2-8-1877) L

Brides

Cheney, Elzira to John Perry 2-15-1882 (3-15-1882) L
Cheney, Sarah C. to Wm. B. Newton 12-28-1844 (1-3-1845) L
Cheny, Elizabeth to Joel Jones 2-23-1864 (no return) Dy
Cherry, A. C. to J. K. Lowrance 5-28-1860 G
Cherry, Adalaid V. to Jessee L. Tolen 4-8-1854 G
Cherry, Allis to Henry A. Davis 1-22-1868 L B
Cherry, Almira A. to Herrod C. Anderson 4-11-1849 (4-24-1849) G
Cherry, Analiza to E. T. Walton 2-25-1864 Hr
Cherry, Anna to Ross Lane 8-18-1879 (no return) L B
Cherry, Augustie to J. A. Hodges 1-18-1870 (no return) Hy
Cherry, E. O. to S. A. Jennings 6-7-1855 G
Cherry, E. W. to Calvin Hall 5-21-1840 Be
Cherry, Eliza K. to Richard S. Templeton 12-18-1860 (12-20-1860) T
Cherry, Elizabeth to James J. Alsup 9-3-1857 Be
Cherry, Irabella C. to George W. Patrick 3-19-1849 Ma
Cherry, Jane to Burton Hall 11-30-1844 G
Cherry, Jinnette C. to Kinchen L. Rose 10-20-1853 (10-27-1853) Hr
Cherry, Julia W. to J. V. Rison 6-26-1856 Hn
Cherry, Lillie to Chatman Price 11-25-1885 (11-29-1885) L
Cherry, Loda? to John Blackwell 8-28-1872 (no return) L B
Cherry, Lucinda to Moses Bond 8-17-1876 (no return) Hy
Cherry, Lucinda to Wash Smith 8-28-1868 (8-30-1868) L B
Cherry, M. to J. T. Elledge 5-26-1861 (4?-26-1860?) O
Cherry, Mahala C. to James L. Armour 5-28-1856 (6-2-1856) O
Cherry, Mandy to J. T. Elledge 4-26-1860 O
Cherry, Margaret to Elijah Griffin 2-1-1858 (2-2-1858) Sh
Cherry, Martha to G. T. Roberts 11-8-1865 (11-9-1865) O
Cherry, Mary E. to J. L. Smith 1-2-1856 (1-3-1856) Sh
Cherry, Mary E. to J. S. Jones 2-2-1875 (no return) Hy
Cherry, Mary to William Ballowe 9-30-1864 Be
Cherry, Mary to William Sumerow 10-18-1880 (10-20-1880) L
Cherry, Milly B. to Joel A. Harris 11-8-1848 Be
Cherry, Nancy to James E. Johnson 9-16-1854 (9-19-1854) O
Cherry, Nercissa L. to Francis M. Williamson 8-1-1871 L
Cherry, R. A. to D. D. Mays 2-5-1867 (no return) Hy
Cherry, Rebecca to James Autry 8-7-1865 (8-10-1865) O
Cherry, S. C. to J. B. Burrus 6-26-1868 (6-30-1868) O
Cherry, Sallie to John Sutherland 1-16-1861 L
Cherry, Sarah Ann to John R. P. Whitehorne 9-9-1857 O
Cherry, Sarah N. to C. B. Howel 7-2-1866 O
Cherry, Sarah to John H. Bowen 9-18-1865 Hn
Cherry, Zilphy to C. P. Jourdan 10-26-1847 (10-28-1847) Hr
Chesher, Nancy to Benjamin R. Hainline 7-27-1847 (7-29-1847) Hr
Cheshier, Alvira to James Hutson Harrison 4-1-1844 (4-2-1844) Hr
Cheshier, Lucinda to Thomas Harris 10-17-1838 (10-18-1838) Hr
Cheshier, Mahala to William S. Beaton 1-1-1850 Hr
Cheshier, Mary to Clinton Crisp 9-28-1854 Hr
Chesolm, Margaret H. to Willie J. Littlejohn 1-18-1843 F
Chesser, Kisiah to James Durrum 3-8-1858 Sh
Chessher, Emeline to Marshall Raines 4-8-1847 Hr
Chester, A. J. to B. F. Blakeman 1-14-1858 We
Chester, Ann Elizabeth to Peter Simmons 9-7-1857 (9-10-1857) Ma
Chester, Ann to Jo Brown 1-1-1873 (1-2-1873) L
Chester, Cynthia to Robert Oliphant 8-14-1845 Sh
Chester, Fanny to J. H. Blakemore 11-27-1867 G
Chester, Julia S. (Mrs.) to John Trigg 12-10-1855 Sh
Chester, M. B. to W. M. Patterson 1-6-1858 Sh
Chester, Mary J. to George W. Bond 10-6-1845 (10-7-1845) Ma
Chester, S. M. to W. N. Thompson 1-28-1857 We
Chester, Unie to Thomas H. Boswell 7-29-1859 We
Chilcut, Emily to John W. Scarborough 12-30-1841 Hn
Chilcut, Malinda to James T. Lee 4-19-1842 Hn
Chilcut, Polly Ann to Joel Cotner 10-14-1838 Hn
Chilcutt, Celia to George Ross 3-4-1858 Hn
Chilcutt, Elizabeth to Franklin Ross 3-1-1855 Hn
Chilcutt, Maria to William C. Lax 8-3-1865 Hn
Chilcutt, Martha Jane to Richard Bradhsaw 1-13-1853 Hn
Chilcutt, Mary A. to Benjamin K. Wisehart 11-17-1867 Hn
Chilcutt, Mary Ann to Jesse Bradshaw 3-4-1849 Hn
Chilcutt, Nancy E. P. to William W. Weldon 2-3-1846 Hn
Chilcutt, Nancy to James English 7-28-1844 Hn
Chilcutt, Rebecca to Elijah W. Moody 11-4-1857 Hn
Chilcutt, Sarah E. to John W. Oliver 12-5-1860 Hn
Childers, Eliza to Lewis Griffith 7-25-1859 Sh
Childers, Elizabeth A. D. to Thomas Jones 1-4-1855 Sh
Childers, Elizabeth to Robert? C. Baley 4-23-1861 (4-25-1861) Dy
Childers, Elizabeth to Young Jenkins 9-2-1861 Hn
Childers, Harriet to Thomas C. McCraw 1-28-1860 T
Childers, Louiz to James Yarbrough 4-27-1845 Be
Childers, M. J. to L. B. Davis 4-22-1863 (4-23-1863) O
Childers, Margrate to S. J. Voss 3-11-1876 (3-12-1876) L
Childers, Martha to Jonah Bowen 11-9-1864 (11-10-1864) Dy
Childers, Mary E. to Marion A. Lemons 12-30-1867 Dy
Childers, Mary to Jno. M. Childers 12-28-1867 (no return) Dy
Childers, Rosella to John A. Scott 10-29-1877 (10-30-1877) O
Childers, Virginia to William Overton 5-16-1861 We
Childes, Cinetia M. to Mathew M. Cullum 1-26-1848 (no return) F

Childress, Ann to William Johnson 3-29-1841 (4-1-1841) Hr
Childress, Anna to G. W. Davis 7-16-1870 (7-17-1870) F
Childress, Anne to Etheldred Jones 10-7-1862 (10-8-1862) Dy
Childress, Catharine to D. W. Hall(Hale) 6-19-1837 (6-20-1837) Hr
Childress, Cynthia J. to Thomas J. Feely 10-3-1868 (10-25-1868) L
Childress, Eliza C. to C. H. Brown 11-2-1869 (no return) L
Childress, Eliza to Henderson Kirby 4-26-1848 (4-27-1848) Ma
Childress, Eliza to John W. Rogers 2-23-1858 (2-25-1858) O
Childress, Elizabeth to Andrew Sissom 7-5-1846 (7-6-1846) Hr
Childress, Elizabeth to John Dilliard 1-13-1829 (1-15-1829) Ma
Childress, Elmira to John Hudson 4-10-1850 Hn
Childress, Frances to Joseph Tilmon 9-29-1838 Hr
Childress, Francess to Jesse Stroud 12-20-1842 (no return) Hn
Childress, Francis to B. T. Akers 1-8-1862 Be
Childress, Fredonia to Lewis (Lt.) Hurst 8-11-1863 (8-13-1863) Sh
Childress, Hollie J. to Ben R. Butler 11-17-1869 G
Childress, Jane to Daniel Reynolds 2-5-1846 L
Childress, Julia L. to Charles D. (Capt.) Fee 9-26-1863 (9-27-1863) Sh
Childress, Julian to John Forbis 12-5-1832 Hr
Childress, L. P. to A. J. Lewelling 2-25-1873 (2-27-1873) Dy
Childress, Louisa V. to Newton D. Jacobs 11-23-1870 G
Childress, Louiza to James Yarbrough 4-27-1845 Be CC
Childress, Lucinda to Braetin Nelson 8-28-1834 (9-3-1834) Hr
Childress, M. C. to S. R. Bibb 4-19-1882 (4-20-1882) L
Childress, M. E. to A. E. Bell 5-20-1867 (5-21-1867) L
Childress, M. R. (Mrs.) to G. W. Showin 1-22-1877 (1-25-1877) L
Childress, Mahala J. to Isaac N. Johnson 3-9-1876 L
Childress, Mahala to W. M. Alston 12-19-1859 Be
Childress, Malvina H. to Richard McGowan 8-7-1841 (8-8-1841) Ma
Childress, Martha to B. N. King 8-17-1857 (8-18-1857) O
Childress, Martha to Edwin Clark 8-17-1852 Ma
Childress, Martha to William Blanton 1-20-1847 (2-16-1847) O
Childress, Martha to William Blanton 1-20-1848 (2-16-1848) O
Childress, Mary Jane (Mrs.) to Henry Blake 12-8-1862 (12-10-1862) Sh
Childress, Mary to Hugh Jackson 4-17-1828 Ma
Childress, Mildred M. to John A. S. Parrish 2-8-1841 (2-11-1841) Ma
Childress, Minerva to G. Glasgow 11-30-1830 Hr
Childress, Miss Minerva to L. W. Clark 11-4-1874 (11-8-1874) T
Childress, Mollie O. to W. G. Jacobs 10-4-1866 G
Childress, Nancy L. to William I. Moore 6-10-1874 (no return) L
Childress, Nancy W. to John D. Edney 11-2-1861 L
Childress, Nannie L. to W. M. Webb 1-21-1880 L
Childress, Peggy to Jacob Harbour 5-8-1827 (5-10-1827) G
Childress, Polly S. to Alfred James Thomas 12-23-1845 G
Childress, Sarah A. to Henry Webb 11-18-1852 Hn
Childress, Sarah B. to W. C. Jones 7-27-1854 We
Childress, Sarah S. to Edward Covington 2-22-1868 (2-24-1868) L
Childress, Sarah V. to W. H. Hicks 12-30-1862 (12-31-1862) L
Childress, Susan B. to James S. Hutcherson 7-3-1858 (no return) L
Childress, Susan M. to James M. Brown 3-17-1860 (no return) Hy
Childs, L. F. to J. W. Bethune 7-12-1876 (7-13-1876) L
Childs, Leve to Matt. Campbell 12-31-1866 O
Childs, Mary G. to Littleton I. Joyner 1-2-1844 Ma
Chiles, Josephina to James Shelton 7-2-1857 Sh
Chilton, Caroline to Bob Flag 12-23-1871 (no return) Hy
Chilton, Eliza A. to Stephen D. Chandler 3-17-1869 (3-18-1869) Cr
Chilton, Martha to Robert Duke 9-27-1877 Hy
Chilton, Mary E. to G. C. Townley 9-13-1866 Hn
Chilton, Susan to James S. Graves 10-17-1859 (no return) Cr
Chilton, Susan to Joe Brantly 7-29-1867 Hy
Chilton, Susie to William Pearson 3-27-1884 L
Chipman, Ann to Prince Glass 1-4-1873 (1-5-1873) L B
Chipman, Ann to Taylor Smith 2-16-1869 L B
Chipman, Annie to Isaac Wheatley 11-11-1876 (11-12-1876) L
Chipman, C. J. to Thomas M. Garrott 11-13-1875 (11-14-1875) L
Chipman, Cynthia to Jessee Woodard 1-1-1878 L
Chipman, Delila to William H. Davis 12-7-1840 Ma
Chipman, Eliz. J. to Wiley Suser 5-13-1853 Ma
Chipman, Elizabeth to John J. Jones 8-8-1846 (8-11-1846) Ma
Chipman, M. D. to R. M. Byrn 12-17-1878 L
Chipman, Malvina E. to Asberry Chapel 12-17-1838 (12-19-1838) O
Chipman, Margaret to Chesley P. Pipkins 5-18-1854 Ma
Chipman, Mary Ann to William E. Miller 9-4-1867 (10-6-1867) L
Chipman, Nancy to James Kenner 4-1-1852 (4-3-1852) Ma
Chipman, Perlina to James H. Davis 4-9-1853 Ma
Chipman, Sarah E. to Uriah M. Ezell 6-28-1865 (6-29-1865) O
Chipman, Sarah to Edmond Ruffin 12-2-1874 L B
Chipman, Tennessee to R. B. Furgason 2-14-1877 L
Chisenhall, L. to E. I. Warren 9-22-1867 O
Chisham, Levina to Andrew Turner 4-23-1827 Hr
Chisholm, Alice to B. F. Robertson 12-27-1885 (12-30-1885) L
Chism, Amanda J. to William Sawyer 2-24-1842 L
Chism, Amanda to Marion Richmond 12-30-1873 Hy
Chism, Ann to John Dennie 10-14-1882 (10-15-1882) L
Chism, Caroline to Pleasant H. Lunsford 5-14-1857 L
Chism, Catherine to Thomas B. Mercer 12-4-1838 Ma
Chism, Francis H. to John W. Meadows 5-18-1842 (5-19-1842) L

Chism, Jemima E. to E. B. Reynolds 9-29-1840 L
Chism, Juntly to N. A. Fields 5-29-1861 (5-30-1861) L
Chism, Louisa to Elisha Robins 3-2-1872 L
Chism, Mary Jane to Ashley Anderson 2-26-1849 (2-28-1849) L
Chism, Minerva to Samuel Deason 7-9-1853 L
Chism, Mollie C. to W. J. Drake 8-8-1883 (8-9-1883) L
Chism, Peggy to Elijah Brown 5-16-1833 Hr
Chism, Syrena Ann to James V. Smith 8-6-1862 (8-7-1862) L
Chism, Syrina Ann to James V. Smith 8-6-1862 (no return)
Chisolm, Eliza Ann to William Littlejohn 9-10-1833 (9-11-1833) Hr
Chisolm, Matilda to James M. Vinson 2-5-1842 (2-10-1842) Ma
Chisum, A. P. to Elisha Sawyer 10-5-1864 L
Chisum, Barbara to Elisha Robinson 1-5-1830 (1-7-1830) Hr
Chisum, Belinda to Thomas G. Chisum 11-19-1829 Hr
Chisum, Elizabeth to Jonas Robertson 8-6-1828 (8-7-1828) Hr
Chisum, Ellen to Harris Wiggins 7-1-1851 Ma
Chisum, Mary Ann to John Sasser 6-10-1834 (6-20-1834) Hr
Chisum, Mary Ann to William Chisum 2-24-1828 Hr
Chisum, Mary C. to G. P. Harris 5-16-1860 (5-23-1860) Hr
Chisum, Mary to James Jacob 11-22-1827 Ma
Chisum, Rachael to John F. Rhodes 7-19-1839 (7-29-1839) Hr
Chisum, Sarah to John Miller 11-3-1827 Ma
Chisum, Tabitha to William Dickson 9-20-1827 Ma
Chitman, Mary E. (Mrs.) to John R. Woodard 2-25-1867 (2-26-1867) Ma
Chitman, Susan E. to Wm. W. Jones 8-7-1857 (8-16-1857) G
Chitmun, Mary to Burton (Dr.) Pipkin 5-16-1855 Ma
Chitts, Fannie V. to J. H. Perkins 10-3-1867 F
Chitwood, Amarilla to Henry Hamlet 4-14-1866 (no return) Dy
Chitwood, Angeline to G. W. Waggoner 1-20-1869 (1-21-1869) Dy
Chitwood, Blanchie to Arnett Pursley 11-24-1874 (11-25-1874) Dy
Chitwood, Dona to S. A. Wood 5-11-1875 Dy
Chitwood, H. B. to J. C. Skipweth 10-30-1867 (no return) Dy
Chitwood, Judy to Matt Fowlkes 12-22-1866 (12-24-1866) Dy
Chitwood, Louisa to R. W. Barker 1-16-1866 (1-17-1866) Dy
Chitwood, Malinda to Richard Callehen 1-3-1859 (1-6-1859) Sh
Chitwood, Martha A. to Stephen V.? Bizzel 11-27-1860 Dy
Chitwood, Mary E. to J. R. Webb 9-30-1865 (no return) Dy
Chitwood, Nancy to Robert Woods 12-16-1879 (no return) Dy
Chitwood, Nannie to R. M. Rainey 10-16-1873 Dy
Chitwood, Sarah to Charles Ratzall 11-7-1861 Sh
Chives?, Martha (Mrs.) to Jno. L. Richardson 10-14-1844 (10-17-1844) F
Chivvis, Annie M. to Joseph Werne 11-28-1860 Sh
Choate, Eliza to Thomas W. Cole 9-30-1846 Sh
Choate, Laurine to John W. Williams 5-15-1831 Sh
Choate, Lavinie to Robert Gift 8-13-1833 Sh
Choate, Lucretia to Joseph Willett 9-27-1831 Sh
Choate, Lucy to William Hillis 5-12-1831 Sh
Choate, Margaret A. to W. E. King 11-2-1865 (11-5-1865) Cr
Choate, Margaret to Chas. K. Nell 12-7-1864 Sh
Choate, Mary to Thomas R. F. Hewett 11-11-1859 Sh
Choate, Nancy to Joel Pierce 12-28-1854 Sh
Choate, Nancy to Solomon P. Wheeler 10-6-1828 Hr
Choate, Phoebe F. to J. J. Meinrath 12-1-1853 Sh
Choate, Susan E. to A. T. Littleton 3-6-1845 Sh
Cholwell, Darcus to Eli Park 2-26-1840 (3-10-1840) Hr
Chounce (Chance?), Oma to James Mo(o)re 4-6-1876 L
Chrisenberry, Sarah S. to Aaron Hart 5-8-1860 Hn
Chrisman, Betsy to Lewis Hooks 3-4-1867 Dy
Chrisman, Louisa J. to James R. Baley 1-13-1862 G
Chrisman, S. A. to R. G. Simmons 2-19-1868 G
Chrisman, Sallie to J. C. Grace 2-8-1877 Dy
Chrismon, Mary C. to Quincy A. Tipton 9-1-1841 F
Chrismus, Sarah Jane to Joseph Voss 4-15-1862 (4-17-1862) L
Chrisp, Anna (Mrs.) to Lee Jones 9-8-1867 G B
Chrisp, F. W. to Cannon H. Lain 10-3-1854 G
Chrisp, Martha to Samuel C. Lane 12-22-1852 (12-23-1852) G
Chrisp, N. E. P. (Mrs.) to Creed T. Woodson 2-19-1868 G
Chrisp, Nancy F. to Alex M. Denwiddle 7-17-1847 (7-20-1847) G
Christ, Belle to Henry C. Hill 2-4-1867 Ma
Christain, Mary C. to Edward J. Killingsworth 3-25-1855 Cr
Christenberry, Sarah E. (Mrs.) to Wm. H. Harriman 7-17-1868 Ma
Christenbury, Mary Maria to Pinckney Carter 3-21-1866 (no return) Hn
Christian, Ann to William Simpson 2-24-1869 Be
Christian, Eliza Jane to John C. Mooring 3-9-1850 (3-12-1850) Ma
Christian, June to I. H. Barham 2-14-1840 (2-16-1840) Ma
Christian, Lucinda to Joseph F. Hathaway 5-18-1848 Sh
Christian, M. E. to J. H. Lanear 12-18-1866 (12-20-1866) Cr
Christian, Margaret McDowell to Anderson Skillern 5-3-1830 Ma
Christian, Martha E. to Wm. E. Love 12-8-1853 Cr
Christian, Mary C. to Jno. B. Weld 7-20-1846 Sh
Christian, Mary to W. B. Milan 3-23-1844 Cr
Christian, S. J. to C. C. Palmore 9-11-1876 Dy
Christian, Sallie A. to David T. Johnson 10-22-1849 Sh
Christian, Sarah to Gordius F. Etheridge 4-27-1847 Sh
Christie, Charlotte A. to H. W. Johnson 1-30-1869 (no return) Dy
Christie, Louisa to C. Whittington 5-3-1849 Sh
Christie, Mary S. to Wiley J. Marcum 10-22-1867 Dy

Christie, R. J. to Enoch McPherson 8-16-1866 Dy
Christie, S. A. to T. I. Wilson 1-12-1878 Hy
Christman, Bettie to William Price 10-15-1868 Ma
Christman, Elizabeth to William Currhey 1-27-1849 Sh
Christman, Lucinda H. to Isaac Lacy 2-7-1843 (2-9-1843) F
Christman, Rutha E. to W. H. Taylor 2-12-1853 (no return) F
Christmas, Mollie E. to John Woods Harris 6-29-1858 Sh
Christopher, Fancy to William F. Hampton 2-1-1863 Hn
Christopher, Margret A. E. to Berry A. Russell 2-18-1869 Be
Christopher, Mary A. to B. D. Blunt 11-17-1863 Be
Christopher, Mary C. to James L. Mizell 7-1-1861 We
Christopher, Susan to J. F. Williams 3-10-1867 Be
Chronister, Annis L. to R. S. Fulkerson 9-11-1884 L
Chronister, Eugene E. to J. C. (or C. C.) Chism 1-22-1876 (1-24-1876) L
Chronister, Tempy to William J. Ferguson 1-18-1833 (1-20-1833) G
Chumbly, Isabelle to John Garner 7-25-1846 (no return) Hn
Chumney, Ann to Wm. S. Forrest 9-23-1864 (9-25-1864) O
Chumney, L. M. to I. H. P. Holoway 8-1-1865 (8-2-1865) O
Chumney, Rebecca A. to George Williams 10-24-1866 O
Chunn, Chrischania to Thomas Jones 9-15-1842 Hn
Chunn, Eliza to Archie Sellers 3-11-1870 (3-12-1870) F B
Chunn, Lydia to Sylvester Slaughter 6-1-1847 Hn
Chunn, Mary to A. G. Colly 11-27-1843 We
Chunn, Sarah L. to Rev. R. V. Taylor 7-21-1853 Hr
Chunn, Sarah P. to William Black 10-29-1848 Hn
Chunnia, Madalina to Gunbatista Costta 7-12-1860 Sh
Chups, Harriet to Daniel Yancy 1-27-1870 Hy
Church, Maggie to L. M. Sanders 7-19-1869 (7-20-1869) Dy
Church, Mary to William Still 7-3-1857 (7-5-1857) G
Church, Nancy to A. D. Mangrum 9-12-1862 G
Churchhill, Harrett J. to J. M. Pickins 10-11-1852 (no return) F
Churchhill, M. M. V. to W. H. Walden 11-7-1865 (11-9-1865) F
Churchill, Rachel to B. F. Nelson 1-30-1849 F
Churchman, M. E. to A. H. Carpenter 10-27-1874 (10-28-1874) Dy
Churchman, Mary to Marcus Wright 2-2-1840 Sh
Churchwell, Caroline to John Garrett 12-1-1854 Sh
Churchwell, Cyntha Ann to Marshal Livingston 11-28-1860 (no return) L
Churchwell, Maggie to Marshall Stearns 9-2-1884 (9-3-1884) L
Churchwell, Margarett to Robert Vickers 12-23-1852 Cr
Churchwell, Mary E. to William L. Rust 12-16-1871 (no return) Cr
Churchwell, Nancy to Joseph P. Lacey 6-24-1840 Cr
Churchwell, V. P. to W. F. Williams 10-24-1871 Cr
Cillett, Tabitha A. R. to J. B. Campbell 8-6-1878 Dy
Cirk, Nancy to Wm. Wallace 1-20-1855 Cr
Cisco, Ada to James T. Carter 12-30-1867 (1-14-1868) F
Cisco, Mollie to J. E. Alexander 1-27-1869 (1-28-1869) F
Cisco, Nancy to John Bennett 10-26-1851 Be
Clabrooks, Becky to Robert Miller 9-18-1877 Hy
Clack, Dorcas to Wesley Tibbs 10-10-1871 Hy
Clack, Jane to Saml. Banks 4-28-1866 Hy
Clack, Lucinda C. to John W. Cumings 7-20-1861 (7-21-1861) O
Clack, Mary Jane to Calvin Knight 7-3-1868 (7-5-1868) O
Clack, Mary to James Hudspeth 4-11-1839 W
Clack, Sarah to Joshua Sneathan 8-24-1839 (8-25-1839) O
Clack, Scyntha to Benjamin B. Logan 5-31-1838 (6-7-1838) O
Clacks, G. A. to Henry Sain 12-10-1851 (no return) F
Clackston, Ellen to William B. Hill 6-18-1833 O
Claeber?, Sarah A. to J. F. Hopkins 1-9-1855 We
Clag, N. A. to J. B. Terrell 8-23-1860 Sh
Claibon, Hatty to Charles F. Hooks 2-24-1867 Hy
Claiborne, Cora to Green Estes 12-17-1867 Hy
Claiborne, Elmirah to Simon Taliaferro 12-31-1870 Hy
Claiborne, Lucy T. to J. R. Blair 6-24-1874 Dy
Claiborne, Martha to Jesse Maxwell 7-24-1827 G
Claiborne, Martha to Jessee Maxwell 7-24-1828 G
Claiborne, Mary to Joseph R. Taylor 2-27-1843 G
Claiborne, Mildred E. to Eli T. Hooper 2-10-1877 Hy
Claibourne, Maria to Weddle Taylor 3-6-1871 T
Claibourne, O. E. to P. E. White 12-26-1878 Hy
Claibun?, Rose to John Johnson 1-28-1867 (1-30-1867) T
Claiburn, Adeline to Buckham Martin 1-6-1868 (1-11-1868) T
Claiburn, Sarah to Mat Winford 10-17-1869 (1-3-1869?) T
Claiburn, Sarah to Mat. Winfrow? 10-17-1868 T
Claiburne, Betsy to Michael Hicks 3-6-1869 T
Claiburne, Emily to William Fletcher 1-15-1868 T
Claiburne, Louisa to Thos. Markham 2-1-1866 (2-7-1866) T
Claiss, Florence to William Welch 7-29-1874 Dy
Clampit, E. J. to James Hood 1-3-1842 (1-13-1842) F
Clampitt, Nancy to Jonthan Thompson 3-30-1844 Ma
Clancey, Lititia to B. Carter 2-7-1865 F
Clancy, C. F. to J. H. Wray 10-17-1866 Hy
Clancy, Emma to Barons Carter 1-1-1866 (no return) Hy
Clancy, L. G. to S. N. Coppedge 4-19-1869 (no return) Hy
Clancy, Mary A. to Jacob S. Stoat 7-29-1846 Hy
Clancy, Mary A. to R. M. Campbell 7-1-1869 Hy
Clandolt (Claudett), Matilda to Thomas Heiss 2-27-1850 Sh
Clanton, Elizabeth to John Hart 12-20-1869 (12-22-1869) Ma

Clanton, Patsey A. to John E. Sullinger 9-5-1868 T
Clanton, Patsey to John E. Sullinger 9-5-1868 (9-7-1868) T
Clanton, Susannah to John A. Harding 2-26-1867 (2-28-1867) Ma
Clara, Julia to Daniel Tracey 7-28-1856 Sh
Clare, Mary to George Owens 7-6-1864 Mn
Clark, A. L. to T. M. Blackburn 5-20-1867 G
Clark, A. M. to J. C. Pybas 5-2-1870 (5-3-1870) Ma
Clark, A. W. to J. G. Williams 12-9-1850 (12-11-1850) Hr
Clark, Adaline to Wm. T. Miller 1-13-1859 T
Clark, Agnes W. to Citizen Burns 7-20-1838 Sh
Clark, Allice to Willis Currin 12-3-1870 (12-12-1870) L
Clark, Amanda Malvina to Jacob Hillman Miller 12-21-1853 (12-22-1853) T
Clark, Amanda to Dock Howard 1-10-1870 (no return) Dy
Clark, Amanda to Frank Beaumont 1-1-1866 Dy
Clark, Amanda to J. M. Thomas 12-6-1865? (12-9-1862) F
Clark, Amanda to Mike Jordan 12-27-1870 (12-29-1870) Cr B
Clark, Ann (Mrs.) to L. G. B. Seat 7-11-1865 G
Clark, Ann A. to P. M. Shelton 5-1-1855 We
Clark, Ann to George Parker 3-2-1860 Sh
Clark, Anna to Francis M. Oneal 2-28-1871 (3-1-1871) Ma
Clark, Bell to Noah Briant 12-9-1871 (no return) Cr
Clark, Bettie L. to W. M. Crutcher 11-18-1882 L
Clark, Biddie to John R. Stricklin 9-2-1869 Hy
Clark, C. A. to Wm. H. Evans 11-9-1871 Hy
Clark, C. C. to W. s. Baxter 1-28-1874 Hy
Clark, Catherine to James McFadden 2-4-1869 (2-9-1869) Ma
Clark, Chrisriana to Eli M. Andrews 6-28-1843 Hr
Clark, E. A. to Benj. A. Bailey 11-27-1855 (no return) F
Clark, E. E. to J. B. Booth 12-17-1878 Hy
Clark, E. J. to R. S. Pate 9-7-1856 We
Clark, E. T. to D. S. Milliner 11-13-1871 (11-15-1871) O
Clark, Eliza F. to M. M. Tillman 1-17-1861 G
Clark, Eliza to Elias D. Tarbrok 2-11-1857 Hn
Clark, Eliza to William J. Jernagun 12-20-1847 G
Clark, Elizabeth J. to E. Clark Palmer 4-9-1861 (4-10-1861) Dy
Clark, Elizabeth W. to W. K. Waddy 9-5-1860 G
Clark, Elizabeth to Jessee Parker 8-27-1859 We
Clark, Elizabeth to Joshua Linton 2-25-1846 (no return) Hn
Clark, Elizabeth to M. B. (Dr.) Harris 11-16-1861 (11-19-1861) Cr
Clark, Elizabeth to Morris Killingsworth 1-31-1844 (1-?-1844) T
Clark, Ellen C. to William V. Goodman 9-26-1865 T
Clark, Ellen to F. W. Jacobs 6-8-1864 (6-9-1864) Sh
Clark, Ellena J. to W. M. Holcomb 6-28-1868 G
Clark, Emily to Wm. O. Lofland 10-29-1846 Sh
Clark, Fannie to Tobe Jones 1-9-1878 (1-10-1878) Dy
Clark, Fanny to Nash Jones no date (1-1-1867) Dy
Clark, Frances to A. H. Walker 9-4-1877 (9-9-1877) O
Clark, G.? A. to Benjamin H. Terrell 12-19-1868 (12-22-1868) T
Clark, Hannah to Daniel? Smith 11-24-1869 (11-25-1869) T
Clark, Hannah to _____ 10-19-1848 Hn
Clark, Henrietta T. to Samuel J. Ray 9-22-1857 Hn
Clark, Jane to John Stricklin 12-24-1849 G
Clark, Josephine to Ben M. Night 12-30-1866 (no return) Dy
Clark, Judith D. to Josiah Porter 10-15-1846 Hn
Clark, Julia A. to John A. Hurt 9-12-1850 G
Clark, Julia to Alfred Bradford 12-27-1866 Hy
Clark, Julia to W. G. Upchurch ?-21-1861 (1-20-1861) T
Clark, Juliann Minerva to James Harvey Armstrong 1-29-1842 (2-?-1842) T
Clark, Juliet M. to H. M. McKay 3-10-1856 Sh
Clark, K. E. to N. E. Redden 3-3-1842 Be
Clark, L. A. E. to George Huffman 12-23-1858 Cr
Clark, Laura Ann to Thomas Claiborne 9-24-1849 (10-4-1849) T
Clark, Laura C. to Lorenza Goodell 8-24-1847 Ma
Clark, Laura N. to Rufus Bass 2-5-1868 (2-6-1868) F
Clark, Leathie to Fredrick Young 2-9-1871 Hy
Clark, Letitia to Ben Pierce 12-27-1877 Dy
Clark, Lizzie to Solomon Haynes 12-9-1874 T
Clark, Lonezar to Larance Elison 9-26-1870 (10-9-1870) Cr
Clark, Lony to John Young 2-20-1868 G
Clark, Lou to Sandy Read 10-28-1875 (no return) Hy
Clark, Louis to Zachariah Elliott 4-3-1838 Hn
Clark, Louisa to James M. Brown 8-27-1857 (8-30-1857) L
Clark, Louiza E. to Lycurgus Boyett 12-27-1858 (12-29-1858) G
Clark, Louiza J. (Mrs.) to Wm. T. Cleveland 2-27-1864 (3-3-1864) Sh
Clark, Louiza to Thos. J. Watson 9-18-1850 Hn
Clark, Lucinda to James Robards 10-18-1884 (10-19-1884) L
Clark, Lucy M. to Charles Bowers 10-3-1867 G
Clark, Lucy to Albert G. Newton 7-18-1858 We
Clark, Lueser to Nathan Lake 3-4-1867? Hy
Clark, Lutetia to Bob Poindexter 9-16-1867 (9-21-1867) F B
Clark, M. E. to Samuel Howell 7-18-1874 (7-19-1874) O
Clark, M. E. to W. H. Jones 11-13-1865 (no return) Hy
Clark, Maggie to Joseph Coleman 3-20-1872 (no return) Cr B?
Clark, Maggie to Syd M. Demmond (McDemmond?) 10-28-1864 Sh
Clark, Mahaly to James Howard 12-27-1870 (no return) Cr B
Clark, Mam to George Williamson 12-24-1871 Hy
Clark, Margaret A. to Conner Riley 9-1-1864 (9-4-1864) O
Clark, Margaret A. to Thos. Harris 8-17-1854 Cr
Clark, Margaret E. to Francis M. Braden 11-15-1855 (no return) L
Clark, Margaret to Anderson Blaydes 2-24-1872 (no return) Hy
Clark, Mariah L. to A. C. Hall 5-8-1866 T
Clark, Marsha to G. W. McKnight 1-15-1859 Cr
Clark, Martha A. to John T. Mann 1-2-1854 (no return) Hn
Clark, Martha Ann to William T. Dement 12-8-1853 (12-9-1853) O
Clark, Martha J. (Mrs.) to William Hamlin 12-21-1858 Sh
Clark, Martha J. to E. T. Hopkins 8-31-1847 Cr
Clark, Martha J. to John T. Jones 6-9-1873 (no return) Cr
Clark, Martha J. to Robert McCollum 2-28-1848 Cr
Clark, Martha Louisa to James Milton Brown 8-23-1873 (8-24-1873) L
Clark, Martha to George Fumbank 3-1-1867 (3-2-1867) Dy
Clark, Martha to Isaac Smith 3-1-1870 (3-2-1870) T
Clark, Martha to James A. Fuzzell 4-24-1858 We
Clark, Martha to Steven Tucker 10-2-1866 G
Clark, Martha to Thos. W. Jourdon 4-21-1845 Cr
Clark, Mary (Mrs.) to Samuel Ewing 3-24-1855 (3-25-1855) Sh
Clark, Mary A. to Benj. F. Bond 11-11-1862 G
Clark, Mary A. to Benjamin G. Johnson 8-7-1847 (9-12-1847) Hr
Clark, Mary A. to William E. Bledsoe 1-10-1860 G
Clark, Mary A. to William W. Allen 3-17-1841 Hn
Clark, Mary Ann to Lewis Atkins 3-26-1867 Hn B
Clark, Mary Ann to Robert B. Wadley 9-12-1839 Cr
Clark, Mary E. (Miss) to Sherwood Allen 2-15-1864 Sh
Clark, Mary E. to James Ellis 3-17-1851 L
Clark, Mary E. to Robt. Black 11-18-1858 Sh
Clark, Mary Elizabeth to Otho S. Feezor 12-21-1854 T
Clark, Mary F. to George R. Thomas 10-1-1867 Hy
Clark, Mary I. to Willis Overton 11-28-1842 Ma
Clark, Mary Jane to J. J. Carruth 5-27-1858 (8-10-1858) Hr
Clark, Mary Jane to John C. Robertson 4-23-1868 G
Clark, Mary Jane to John W. Suddith 1-5-1853 Hn
Clark, Mary Jane to Wm. Henry Clay Weatherley 6-18-1866 (no return) Hn
Clark, Mary to Allen White 1-10-1862 Hy
Clark, Mary to Andrew J. Elliott 1-30-1847 (2-3-1847) G
Clark, Mary to Edmond Tate 3-4-1869 T
Clark, Mary to Geo. W. Kerby 12-27-1850 Hn
Clark, Mary to Hezekiah Dyson 2-14-1860 (3-18-1860) Hr
Clark, Mary to J. L. Kirk 9-7-1875 (not executed?) Dy
Clark, Mary to R. B. Hutchinson 2-10-1845 (no return) Cr
Clark, Mary to Robert Edmonson 1-5-1833 (1-8-1833) G
Clark, Mary to W. F. Thomas 12-17-1866 Hy
Clark, Matilda J. to David Fuller 4-21-1866 (no return) F
Clark, Metilda J. to W. P. Mayfield 10-6-1856 (10-9-1856) G
Clark, Mildred Ann to Eli R. Compton 8-13-1840 F
Clark, Mollie to James E. Caldwell 2-24-1868 (2-27-1868) O
Clark, Mollie to R. B. Vanallstine 3-5-1878 (3-6-1878) L
Clark, Molly to Henry Clark 12-18-1869 (12-23-1869) Cr
Clark, Nancy Ann to John Moore 1-20-1885 L
Clark, Nancy J. to Barker Smith 9-9-1863 (9-10-1863) L
Clark, Nancy J. to Parker Smith 9-9-1863 (no return) L
Clark, Nancy to Alfred Boren 7-24-1827 Sh
Clark, Nancy to C. R. Bostic 11-20-1865 Hn
Clark, Nancy to John Drake 2-23-1867 (no return) Hy
Clark, Nancy to Joseph Lacewell 12-31-1843 (no return) We
Clark, Nancy to Richard Harkus 7-2-1867 (no return) Hn B
Clark, Nannie to James Dewalt 11-13-1880 (11-19-1880) L
Clark, Narcissa to Lewis Yarbrough 3-11-1839 (3-26-1839) Hr
Clark, Permelia W. to J. H. Palmer 11-23-1863 (no return) Cr
Clark, Phoebe Jane to Alfred H. Jones 2-25-1846 (2-26-1846) Ma
Clark, Priscilla to Charles Curtis 7-29-1866 Hn B
Clark, Provie to Alex Works 9-8-1877 Dy
Clark, Prudence to George Wyatt 9-25-1871 (10-2-1871) Cr B
Clark, Prudy to Nixon Powell 3-10-1868 G B
Clark, Rachiel to John Rainey 3-23-1843 Be
Clark, Rebecca to John J. Dickinson 12-10-1860 (no return) Hy
Clark, Rhody Ann to H. A. Taylor 3-23-1864 Sh
Clark, Rodena to Nathan Parker 3-6-1863 Mn
Clark, Ruth D. (Mrs.) to S. W. Cochran 9-12-1861 O
Clark, S. E. to A. F. Hudson 12-24-1853 (no return) F
Clark, S. J. to Stephen Youree 11-16-1874 O B
Clark, S.? M. to E. F. Parish 3-14-1872 Cr
Clark, Sallie A. to Oliver C. Woodward 12-6-1852 (12-7-1852) Sh
Clark, Sallie to E. R. (Dr.) Vernon 12-25-1867 Dy
Clark, Sally to Davy Cole 7-27-1875 (no return) Hy
Clark, Sarah A. to John N. Cannon 11-15-1848 G
Clark, Sarah Ann to John Smith 1-26-1843 (1-?-1843) T
Clark, Sarah C. to S. L. Gaines 7-5-1860 (7-8-1860) L
Clark, Sarah Eliza to John Dearing 1-7-18557 G
Clark, Sarah F. to Benj. F. Cunningham 7-19-1855 Cr
Clark, Sarah J. to James Porter Cribbs 10-11-1867 (or 10-16) G
Clark, Sarah Jane to Wm. Wilson Morris 1-31-1866 T
Clark, Sarah to Jacob J. T. Brogdon 9-14-1854 Hn
Clark, Sarah to James Barcroft 2-2-1864 (no return) Hy
Clark, Sarah to James Lycurgus Givin 11-11-1843 (11-?-1843) T
Clark, Sarah to Washington Bond 12-2-1866 Hy

Clark, Susan Ann to Joseph A. Donley 6-1-1864 (6-2-1864) Sh
Clark, Susan W. to M. A. May 1-20-1847 F
Clark, Susan to J. J. Taylor 2-24-1846 We
Clark, Susan to Thomas E. Hall 3-22-1848 Hn
Clark, Temperance Lucintha to Peter Juchoore? Hicks 6-20-1850 (7-3-1850) T
Clark, Tempy to Robert Taylor 5-16-1872 L B
Clark, Willy to David Little 8-7-1868 (8-12-1868) Cr
Clark, Zaoda Alice to James H. Ingram 1-12-1867 (no return) Hn
Clarke, America C. to Gilbert E. Herrin 11-12-1844 (no return) Hn
Clarke, B. M. to John W. Floyd 7-19-1859 (7-24-1859) O
Clarke, Dianna to John Wilson 3-30-1837 Sh
Clarke, Jane to D. J. Shofner 5-15-1861 Cr
Clarke, Lou to W. M. Peeks 12-15-1878 Hy
Clarke, Luvinia P. to Joel Lax 3-31-1841 (no return) Hn
Clarke, Mollie R. to Marcus V. Crump 4-16-1873 Hy
Clarke, Nancy to Riley Diggs 12-10-1846 Hn
Clarke, Sarah to Riley Diggs 7-27-1852 Hn
Clarke, Sophronia to John M. Warren 11-15-1834 Hr
Clarkson, Sarah to John W. Smith 3-23-1861 (3-26-1861) Sh
Clary, Arabella E. to Randolph H. Brown 10-13-1854 Hn
Clary, Harriet to Iveson Huggins 2-16-1841 (no return) Hn
Clary, Jane to J. A. J. Parker 10-7-1858 Hn
Clary, Marthantha to Andrew Harper 1-30-1856 We
Clary, Mary E. to J. B. Brown 7-19-1853 Hn
Clary, Sarah A. to J. P. Bond 1-21-1867 (1-24-1867) F
Claton, Manerva to Joseph Stagner 9-28-1856 Be
Claton, Martha to John Merell 3-31-1865 Hn
Claxton, Jane E. to J. T. Tucker 9-19-1860 G
Claxton, S. C. to L. Lashlee 4-29-1842 Be
Claxton, Susan A. to W. R. Pearce 10-24-1860 G
Clay, A. P. to S. C. Harris 10-30-1867 T
Clay, Ala Jane to Henry Bond 6-19-1870 Hy
Clay, Anna to Geo. Tyler 10-13-1864 Sh
Clay, Annie to L. A. Hurt 6-28-1870 (6-30-1870) Cr
Clay, Betetie to George Parker 6-5-1875 L B
Clay, Bettie to George Utley 8-29-1872 Cr
Clay, Betty to Joe Isbell 8-22-1876 L
Clay, Caroline M. to George C. Sawyer 12-14-1859 Hy
Clay, Caroline M. to James W. Gardner 3-31-1862 (4-1-1862) Ma
Clay, Christina to John J. A. Bradley 10-9-1864 G
Clay, Cinda to Callus Woods 2-16-1876 Hy
Clay, E. M. to W. L. Collins 2-15-1860 Cr
Clay, Emily to John A. Hagar 1-29-1848 (1-30-1848) L
Clay, Evelina L. to James A. Richardson 10-9-1837 (10-19-1837) G
Clay, Fanny Jane to Allen Taylor 2-8-1854 G
Clay, Hannah to Grand Fuqua 12-13-1868 G B
Clay, Iola to James I. Jones 11-15-1869 (11-17-1869) F
Clay, Jane to Adam Hurt 5-14-1870 (5-15-1870) Cr
Clay, Jane to B. Bradley 4-11-1863 G
Clay, Jenny to Wm. Clay 7-28-1866 Hy
Clay, Jinny to Willis Clay 12-30-1865 (no return) Hy
Clay, Judy to John Jones 10-4-1869 (10-9-1869) Cr
Clay, Laura Green to J. L. Stokes 9-1-1885 L
Clay, Lew A. W. to Thadeous N. Terril 3-15-1853 (3-16-1853) G
Clay, Louisa to Henry Fields 1-10-1866 (1-13-1866) Dy
Clay, Lue to Robt. Bell 10-5-1870 (10-6-1870) Cr
Clay, M. A. to S. Shaw 4-28-1837 (5-2-1837) G
Clay, M. P. to W. F. Landreth 4-8-1863 (4-30-1863) F
Clay, Margaret to Smith Carson 9-2-1874 L B
Clay, Martha H. to George Trafford 6-19-1868 Ma
Clay, Martha Jane to Enzkial W. Polk 6-22-1840 (6-23-1840) Ma
Clay, Mary A. to John R. Moore 2-26-1867 (2-28-1867) Dy
Clay, Mary E. to M. Marckmolter 3-14-1859 Sh
Clay, Mary P. to Thos. G. Tate 8-10-1869 Hy
Clay, Matilda to Thos. McIntyre 7-3-1872 (7-4-1872) T
Clay, Mattie to Lea Bowden 7-2-1874 (7-3-1874) L B
Clay, Nancy to Robert Partee 12-30-1865 (no return) Hy
Clay, Nancy to Robert Partee 2-10-1866 Hy
Clay, Narcissa H. to Josiah C. Marley 10-17-1870 L
Clay, Polly to Alex Norval 1-2-1866 Hy
Clay, Sarah to William Halfacre 10-27-1870 L
Claybern, Amanda J. to John B. Reacouik 2-15-1859 We
Clayborn, M. A. to Wm. C. Cantrell 7-6-1850 Cr
Clayborn, Rebecca to Calvin Forest 5-3-1845 Cr
Claybourn, Nancy to Guss Devine 7-18-1867 Hy
Claybrook, Fannie to Ples Buck 8-3-1870 (no return) Hy
Claybrook, Mary to Henry Winburn 11-23-1857 (11-26-1857) Sh
Claybrook, Sallie to Anderson Buck 8-27-1869 Hy
Claybrook, Sallie to Ed Jetten 2-18-1871 (no return) Hy
Claybrooks, Isabella to J. F. Robertson 8-6-1868 Hy
Clayburn, Harrit to Thomas Clayburn 12-28-1868 Hy
Clayton, Eliza Jane to John D. Garrett 5-23-1863 (5-31-1863) Sh
Clayton, Elizabeth F. to J. M. Markham 6-5-1860 Be
Clayton, Elizabeth to S. B. Kelly 2-3-1846 Sh
Clayton, Elizabeth to William H. McCollister 7-31-1848 Hn
Clayton, Elizabeth to William Measles 2-8-1835 Sh
Clayton, Emma to Elisah Pippin 3-16-1869 (3-18-1869) F

Clayton, Frances to Russell Shipley 5-21-1846 (no return) Hn
Clayton, Julia Ann to Mansfield Ham 9-24-1836 Sh
Clayton, L. A. to Thomas McNutt 1-1-1856 (no return) Hn
Clayton, Lockey to B. Seward 9-26-1869 G
Clayton, Lucy J. to J. P. Maness 9-3-1862 Mn
Clayton, Mary A. to J. G. Ridgeway 1-27-1857 We
Clayton, Mary A. to Thomas Cowan 9-25-1853 Hn
Clayton, Mary C. to Josiah Bryant 12-20-1864 Mn
Clayton, Mary L. to G. M. Pool 5-14-1866 (5-16-1866) F
Clayton, Mary N. to Abram Montcries 2-21-1860 (2-23-1860) Sh
Clayton, Nancy to George W. Wimberley 1-20-1850 Hn
Clayton, Parlee to E. R. Collins 4-28-1863 (4-30-1863) F
Clayton, Ruth to John McWherter 3-5-1829 (3-6-1829) O
Clayton, S. J. to J. W. Hughes 11-29-1866 (11-30-1865?) F
Clayton, Susan to Lewis Roberts 2-21-1842 Sh
Clayton, Susannah to Joseph J. Brantley 7-19-1835 Hr
Clear, Lucy to J. S. Luck 11-5-1869 (11-9-1869) F
Cleary, Margaret to Patrick Carney 4-24-1855 Sh
Cleary, Mary to Martin Shelee 2-22-1862 (2-23-1862) Sh
Cleary, Mary to Michael Grady 7-23-1855 Sh
Cleave, Indiana to Frank Hubbard 8-27-1870 (no return) F B
Cleaver, Emily to Jasper Henley 1-8-1870 (no return) Cr
Cleaver, Mary Jane to James A. Williamson 8-11-1852 G
Cleaver, Nancy S. to Henry Joiner 7-18-1854 (no return) Hn
Cleaves, Caroline to Ephraim Chaney 2-20-1869 (2-27-1869) F B
Cleaves, Julia D. to H. W. Yarborough 9-10-1860 (9-13-1860) F
Cleaves, Laura A. to Benj. F. Reddick 1-27-1840 F
Cleaves, Mary H. to John T. Garrison 5-7-1863 F
Cleaves, Sarah to John P. Smith 3-10-1843 (no return) F
Cleavis, Elizabeth to Thos. R. Holmes 1-30-1844 L
Cleek, Mary E. to J. A. Jones 2-20-1871 (2-26-1873) Dy
Cleek?, Charlotte to Benjamin Byrn 12-25-1868 (12-26-1868) L B
Cleere, Mary E. to Wm. F. Jones 9-2-1845 (9-4-1845) F
Clehorn, Ellen S. to C. G. Stephens 5-3-1857 We
Clemace, P. B. to W. G. Green 5-12-1858 Cr
Clemant, Lavina E. to John W. Williams 6-6-1854 (6-7-1854) T
Clement, A. S. to R. H. Warmoth 3-26-1867 G
Clement, Bettie to West Peete 12-25-1873 T
Clement, C. A. to Jesse Brown 2-7-1861 (2-12-1861) T
Clement, C. to J. H. Mannon 6-19-1856
Clement, Caroline H. to W. D. Beaton 11-23-1865 Be
Clement, E. J. to W. N. Hamilton 1-3-1865 G
Clement, E. O. to J. S. McCorkle 8-14-1862 (no return) We
Clement, Effy W. to John Andrews 10-31-1867 Be
Clement, Esper Ann to Zachariah Wainright 1-3-1852 (7-8-1852) G
Clement, Frances A. to Henry H. Warmath 6-12-1855 Ma
Clement, Jane to Matthew Mannon 12-2-1860 Be
Clement, M. A. T. (Mrs.) to B. T. Porter 1-18-1872 Dy
Clement, Mary C. to John C. McCollum 10-20-1850 Cr
Clement, Mary J. to Lewis J. Metheny 1-5-1854 Be
Clement, Minerva to Grandison Calhoun 12-29-1865 (12-30-1865) T
Clement, Mollie to J. W. Pinson 9-23-1872 T
Clement, R. to William Taylor 3-23-1866 (4-1-1866) T
Clement, Rachel to William B. Allen 11-25-1841 Hn
Clement, Samantha C. to Euphrates Moore 3-3-1860 Hn
Clement, Susan S. to G. S. Allen 1-16-1850 (1-17-1850) G
Clement, U. L. to Wm. R. Nelms 2-9-1860 Hr
Clements, A. F. to John W. Freeman 1-23-1855 We
Clements, Ann E. to Johnathan Cheshier 2-15-1860 (2-16-1860) Hr
Clements, B. A. to Peter Wells 1-5-1869 Hy
Clements, Candis to John Tipton 3-12-1870 T
Clements, Caroline to James O. Densford 4-2-1862 (4-3-1862) T
Clements, E. R. to C. T. Booker 11-16-1874 (11-18-1874) T
Clements, Eliza to Isaac Young 4-12-1870 G B
Clements, Emily to Lumon Sherrod 1-5-1867 (1-6-1867) T
Clements, F. to Isaac Dyson 12-5-1871 T
Clements, F. to Isaac Dyson 12-5-1871 (1-6-1872) T
Clements, Fannie to M. Roberts 8-17-1867 (8-18-1867) T
Clements, Frances C. to Hiram C. Trout 7-15-1845 F
Clements, Isabella C. to James G. Howard 1-23-1861 We
Clements, Jenny to Owen Thomas 11-23-1866 (11-24-1866) T
Clements, Lenord to M. A. Lassiter 12-17-1872 (12-19-1872) T
Clements, Margaret to David Moore 9-19-1849 Cr
Clements, Martha to Moses Robinson 10-17-1871 T
Clements, Mary A. M. to Levi Wright 10-5-1846 G
Clements, Mary A. to Thomas M. Williams 10-9-1848 (10-11-1848) T
Clements, Mary A. to W. J> Roberts 11-6-1865 (12-5-1865) T
Clements, Mary D. to M. T. Parish 12-2-1856 G
Clements, Mary E. to L. V. Taliaferro 12-20-1868 Hy
Clements, Mary S. to W. C. Scott 4-19-1854 (6-19-1854) We
Clements, Mary to Blunt Cockrill 1-10-1869 G
Clements, Melvinie to Simon W. Green 6-23-1862 F
Clements, Phillis to John Wooten 1-13-1866 (1-14-1866) T
Clements, Polly to Stanley Griffin 4-28-1834 (5-1-1834) G
Clements, Rosa to Isaac? Clark 9-7-1872 (9-8-1872) T
Clements, S. A. to G. H. C.(G.?) Penn 10-10-1866 G
Clements, Sarah E. to Wm. E. Mathis 5-26-1862 G

Clements, Susan to Julius Stubbs 12-27-1866 T
Clements, Udora J. to George D. Buffalow 2-20-1871 (2-21-1871) Ma
Clements, Violet to Alfred Gibbs 3-23-1872 (3-31-1872) T
Clements, Virginia E. to N. H. Elcan 7-4-1859 (7-6-1859) T
Clemer, Elizabeth H. to William Baldridge 3-13-1855 We
Clemins, Nannie to E. H. Thompson 10-14-1856 Cr
Clemm, Nancy to Rush Phillips 1-3-1866 (1-10-1867) Dy
Clemments, Millie to Henry Yancy 11-21-1876 Hy
Clemmit, Malina to John Richardson 11-27-1874 T
Clemmons, Jane to John Deaton 1-23-1863 Mn
Clemmons, Maggie to E. L. Burks 12-24-1875 (12-26-1875) Dy
Clemmons, Mattie J. to Judge Shaw 12-12-1874 (12-17-1874) Dy B
Clemms, Maggie to Jack Patrick 11-24-1880 (11-25-1880) L
Clemons, Keziah to N. Darnell 3-25-1860 Cr
Clemons, Millie to Monro Patton 9-5-1870 (no return) Cr
Clemons, Nancy to William P. Wilson 1-26-1835 (2-9-1835) G
Clemons, Patient to Albert Gilbert 5-18-1875 O
Clemons, Sallie J. (Mrs.) to Thomas H. Earle 6-3-1873 Dy
Clendenen, Lydia A. to Robert C. Black 8-15-1840 (8-21-1840) F
Clendenin, Aratanna to Peter W. Buchanan 11-23-1859 Hn
Clendenin, Ava to Stanstill Moore 3-21-1838 Hn
Clendenin, June to James Fitch 5-3-1838 Hn
Clenton, Annie to John J. Flinn 12-5-1867 Hy
Clevies, Frances A. to J. V. B. Rogers 2-24-1869 (2-25-1869) T
Cliatt, Mollie to W. D. Ashmore 6-2-1879 (6-8-1879) L
Click, Amanda E. to John Force 4-12-1879 (4-13-1879) L
Cliff, Martha M. to W. B. Park 10-25-1878 (10-27-1878) Dy
Clifford, Catherine to James Haragan 10-1-1864 (10-4-1864) Sh
Clifford, Cathey to James N. Capps 7-2-1839 Cr
Clifford, Ellen to James Curry 7-18-1857 Sh
Clifford, Margaret (Mrs.) to Patrick Donehue 5-9-1863 Sh
Clifft, Martha A. to Mathew Dickens 10-31-1857 (11-3-1857) Hr
Clifft, Polly Ann to John J. Thompson 3-14-1846 (3-24(14?)-1846 Hr
Clifft, Susannah to Thomas Morrow 11-29-1830 (11-30-1830) Hr
Clift, Lucinda to Joseph Warren 11-7-1840 (11-26-1840) Hr
Clift, Sarah Ann to Radford F. Blackard 7-30-1836 Hr
Clift, Sarah to Edwin Pennington 12-16-1844 (12-19-1844) F
Clifton, Amanda E. to J. W. Cavenar 12-26-1870 (12-27-1870) T
Clifton, Harriet to Curtis B. New 9-25-1854 (9-28-1854) O
Clifton, Lancy to W. R. Hicks 11-30-1862 Mn
Clifton, Letha to Jackson Williams 6-16-1866 (no return) F B
Clifton, Martha A. to Isaac Johnson 4-22-1841 Sh
Clifton, Mary P. to John G. Tatum 1-18-1841 (1-21-1841) F
Clifton, Sarah A. to J. E. Puckett 12-23-1858 Hr
Clifton, Sarah E. to Louis H. Poindexter 1-23-1871 (1-25-1871) F
Clifton, Virginia to C. C. Poindexter 1-24-1870 (1-25-1870) F
Climer, Margarett C. to Fordham Blackmon 2-26-1856 G
Climer, Margret to J. D. Brice 8-18-1870 Hy
Climer, Nancy to J. Y. Brice 8-11-1870 Hy
Cline, Catherine to William R. Jackson 8-7-1854 (8-15-1854) Ma
Cline, Dorcas J. to William F. Walker 8-5-1860 Hn
Cline, Sarah to Jacob Daniel Cline 3-30-1841 Ma
Cline, Susan Frances to Y. W. J. Allen 12-31-1868 G
Clines, Nancy t. to John Shofer 8-16-1859 (8-17-1859) Hr
Clinton, E. J. to West Harriss 10-29-1857 Hr
Clinton, Eliza to John B. Hall 9-27-1828 Ma
Clipper, Alethia to W. B. Adair 7-17-1850 Sh
Cloar, Elizabeth to William L. Crawford 4-23-1851 Hn
Cloar, M. to David P. Davis 3-6-1861 (3-7-1861) O
Cloar, Martha to J. R. Moser 4-15-1861 (4-18-1861) O
Cloar, Mary A. E. to L. M. Shults 11-19-1867 O
Cloar, Mary E. to Moses S. Marshall 1-17-1853 (1-20-1853) O
Cloar, Nancy Caroline to Saml. L. Chandler 9-23-1857 O
Cloar, Patsey to Joseph Davis 5-26-1842 O
Cloar, Pricilla to Joseph B. Crawford 1-31-1851 Hn
Cloch, Johanna to Leopold Greenwald 5-25-1861 (no return) Hy
Cloe, Angeline to Riley Kimbell 2-10-1852 (2-12-1852) Sh
Cloid, Amanda J. to J. J. Rochell 1-15-1873 (no return) Cr
Clonch, Harriet A. to E. D. Kemp 7-13-1862 Mn
Clopton, Mariah T. to W. A. Thompson 8-6-1859 Cr
Clopton, Nancy to John Buchannon 9-27-1848 L
Clore, A. J. to Edward Kemmitt 11-3-1875 G
Clouch, M. C. to S. W. Hair 10-11-1861 Mn
Cloucher, N. J. to Grandison A. Campbell 4-2-1884 L
Cloud, Amanda L. to Wm. P. Freed 9-22-1871 (9-28-1871) O
Cloud, Artemesia to Pleasant Oliver 11-5-1836 M
Cloud, Josephine to William T. Brandon 10-10-1871 (10-12-1871) O
Cloud, Nancy M. to James Weddington 11-29-1859 We
Cloud, S. S. to Sam C. Pain 4-29-1861 Sh
Cloude, Elizabeth to Alphine (Alpheus?) Thompkins 12-24-1868 G
Clouse (Clove), Wealthy to Jas. T. Wade 12-26-1850 Sh
Clouse, Creesy to James W. Scoggins 8-20-1836 Hr
Clowe, Elizabeth to Robert Staples 11-1-1842 Sh
Clowe, Susan to William F. Thompson 11-15-1843 Sh
Cloyd, Cynthia to Albert Johnson 7-23-1870 (7-29-1870) F B
Cloyd, Margaret Milissa to Stephen Henry Rainey 8-26-1848 (8-29-1848) Hr
Cloyd, Mary Jane to James A. Kerly 8-9-1860 (8-12-1860) Cr

Cloyd, Rose to Moses Finney 3-14-1870 (no return) F B
Cloyed, Eliza A. to D. T. Boyed 12-6-1854 (no return) F
Cloyed, Martha C. to Joseph A. F. Sharpe 9-24-1838 (10-2-1838) F
Cloyed, Sarah Jane to Joseph H. Trotter 9-22-1852 (no return) F
Cloyeds, Pernalia S. to J. N. Caffey 7-6-1841 F
Cloys, Harriett E. to B. Drinker 1-4-1866 Hn
Cloys, Martha to Albert C. Harpole 3-24-1849 (4-11-1849) O
Cloys, Mary to David N. Mayes 3-7-1855 (3-11-1855) O
Cloys, Ruth to Freeman Mitchell 3-21-1849 (3-22-1849) O
Clug (Clay?), Francis to John W. Williams 5-28-1850 (5-31-1850) L
Clure, Martha to Dennis Wilson 12-15-1870 (no return) F B
Clusen, Elizabeth to Ole Indseth 8-11-1862 Sh
Clutch, M. C. to W. G. Stevenson 6-25-1863 (6-28-1863) F
Clutts, Martha Ann to F. L. Betts 1-6-1867 Hn
Clyatt, E. J. to G. J. Doby 10-11-1880 (10-17-1880) L
Clyatt, Susie to G. B. Crain 3-4-1884 (3-5-1884) L
Clymor, Mary F. to George W. Upton 5-26-1860 (5-27-1860) O
Cnanon, Lillian A. to Richard W. Randle 11-23-1841 (no return) Hn
Coachman, Eliza E. to Alexander Fry 8-27-1867 (8-?-1867) L B
Coachman, Harriet to Dock Lea 12-31-1872 Hy
Coachman, Nancy to Buck Mann 1-25-1879 L B
Coachman, Phoebe to Joe Eaton 1-5-1880 L
Coates, Ann E. to John T. Hodges 1-9-1850 (1-11-1850) Hr
Coates, Elizabeth to John C. Davenport 3-26-1833 Sh
Coates, Mary Ann to Henry Johnson 1-3-1857 (1-4-1857) Hr
Coates, Sarah Ann to William S. Clinton 1-22-1850 Hr
Coats, Atlanta E. to James M. Price 2-3-1851 (2-2?-1851) G
Coats, Bettie to Franklin Wiseman 2-18-1871 (2-19-1871) T
Coats, Delitha to Benjamin Franklin Smith 12-22-1873 (12-23-1873) T
Coats, Elizabeth C. to Asa Humphreys 1-11-1853 Hn
Coats, Elizabeth to Lawrence Raynor 9-4-1861 (9-5-1861) T
Coats, Elizabeth to Wm. Smith 3-30-1872 (4-14-1872) T
Coats, Gilly Eglentine to Berry Coats 11-1-1850 (11-3-1850) T
Coats, Josephin T. to J. L. West 1-13-1872 (1-16-1872) L
Coats, Martha to Henry Coats 10-4-1845 (10-15-1845) T
Coats, Martha to L. W. Wiseman 12-1-1874 (12-2-1874) T
Coats, May Y. to William C. Wilson 12-21-1855 (no return) Hn
Coats, Minerva to Francis U. Humphrey 1-10-1855 Hn
Coats, Polly J. to John W. McKelvey 12-20-1851 (12-22-1851) G
Coats, Rosa Ann to John E. Murphey 2-7-1872 (2-8-1872) T
Coats, Sarah Ann to H. Humphreys 11-7-1848 Hn
Coats, Sarah to Lewis Grattum 3-3-1842 T
Coats, Susan E. (Mrs.) to Franklin E. Collins 6-26-1869 (6-27-1869) Ma
Cobb, Amanda J. to J. F. Clayton 5-2-1861 Mn
Cobb, Amanda to Samuel M. Roy 1-14-1868 L
Cobb, Catharine to A. Young 11-27-1867 (11-28-1867) Cr
Cobb, Charity to Marshall Anthony 1-27-1876 (no return) Hy
Cobb, Delia to Therm B. Cobb 9-22-1825 Sh
Cobb, Elizabeth K. to Thos. Z. Huddleson 12-29-1865 (12-30-1865) O
Cobb, Elizabeth S. to S. J. Neely 12-1-1866 (12-4-1866) Dy
Cobb, Elizabeth to John R. Volentine 5-24-1869 Ma
Cobb, Elizabeth to Thomas Grooms 11-14-1855 Hn
Cobb, Ella to R. D. Barfield 2-13-1878 (2-14-1878) L
Cobb, Ellen E. to Charles M. Ross 6-10-1863 Cr
Cobb, Ellen E. to Charles M. Ross 6-10-1863 (6-14-1863) Cr
Cobb, Ellen E. to Charles M. Ross 6-10-1863 (no return) Cr
Cobb, Ellen to Wesley Garrett 10-31-1878 Hy
Cobb, Emma F. to Jeptha V. Harris 12-28-1869 Ma
Cobb, Emma to Wm. Cotter 2-5-1871 Hy
Cobb, Fannie (Mrs.) to Lorenzo (Rev.) Lea 3-29-1858 (3-30-1858) Ma
Cobb, Fannie S. to J. D. Powell 12-20-1882 L
Cobb, Georgian to Tabner Dison 1-4-1872 Hy
Cobb, H. A. J. to Jas. L. White 7-2-1872 Hy
Cobb, Harriet to Naum Powell 5-18-1857 (5-19-1857) Ma
Cobb, Henrita to J. M. Pinson 1-13-1859 Cr
Cobb, Isabell C. to David Karr 12-6-1838 Sh
Cobb, Isabella to Albert Chambers 8-10-1871 O
Cobb, Issabella T. to Solomon R. B. Walton 4-25-1839 F
Cobb, Jennie to John Anderson 4-7-1868 (no return) Hy
Cobb, Leonora to E. B. Lauderdale 12-30-1871 (1-1-1872) Dy
Cobb, Lidy to Aron Forrest 12-26-1877 Hy
Cobb, Lou to John Smith 10-13-1875 Dy
Cobb, Louisa to Joseph C. Brooks 11-14-1861 T
Cobb, Lucinda S. to Henry A. Gooch 1-30-1861 (1-31-1861) Dy
Cobb, Margt. E. to Joseph Samples 11-9-1850 (11-10-1850) F
Cobb, Martha A. to Benjamin B. Buckley 4-17-1857 (4-19-1857) O
Cobb, Martha S. to William F. Bennett 1-28-1869 Cr
Cobb, Martha to Anderson Mungel 6-22-1878 (no return) Hy
Cobb, Mary A. to Harvey S. Crittendon 1-26-1853 Ma
Cobb, Mary F. to E. B. Eddings 1-24-1870 O
Cobb, Mary Jane to James M. Alexander 11-17-1871 Ma
Cobb, Mary R. to Benjamin Duncan 6-15-1838 Sh
Cobb, Mildred M. to E. B. Hotchkiss 12-16-1858 Sh
Cobb, Nannie to Charley Taylor 3-24-1875 (no return) L B
Cobb, Newty L. to J. Z. Nash 1-30-1869 (1-31-1869) Cr
Cobb, S. E. to David Waggoner 10-22-1879 (10-23-1879) Dy
Cobb, Sarah J. to Charles K. Fleming 12-12-1865 Hy

Cobb, Sarah to Telemicus H. Collier 10-10-1849 (10-11-1849) Hr
Cobb, Violi (Mrs.) to James Stephenson 5-4-1864 Sh
Cobbs, Amy to Henry Boyd 2-6-1869 F B
Cobbs, Bettie to Ham Gaither 2-1-1870 F B
Cobell, Sarah O. to F. S. Burrow 10-27-1858 Cr
Cobins, Marthy to James Chambers 10-20-1867 Hy
Coble (Colte), Margaret to Nathaniel Kendrick 7-26-1840 Sh
Coble, Lucinda to L. M. Frost 11-6-1855 (no return) Hn
Coble, M. C. to D. M. Lankford 4-9-1867 (4-10-1867) Cr
Coble, Margaret to Wyatt Bettis 11-14-1839 L
Coble, Martha E. to Thos. Chism 5-15-1861 L
Coble, Martha F. (Mrs.) to Frederick Wilhelm 1-26-1864 Sh
Coble, Mary Ann to R. D. Dickson 10-5-1861 (10-6-1861) Cr
Coble, Mary Ann to Richard D. Dickson 10-?-1861 (10-6-1861) Sh
Coble, Mary L. to James Briley 12-5-1875 Dy
Coble, Maunda to Samuel C. Osier 8-19-1851 (no return) F
Coble, Nancy A. to J. T. Cockram 1-7-1864 Mn
Coble, Nancy A. to Joseph Pinson 11-11-1840 O
Coburn, Elvira E. to John G. Freeman 2-7-1842 (2-8-1842) Hr
Coburn, Lucinda E. to John C. Graham 1-18-1851 (1-27-1851) Hr
Coby, Marey E. F. to William Hamrick 12-14-1859 F
Cochrain, Louise E. to Eli Edwards 5-3-1831 (5-5-1831) O
Cochram, Harriet J. to W. A. Cochrum 4-12-1866 Hn
Cochram, Marsha L. to Hyram Nimmo 10-28-1845 Hn
Cochran, A. to William Capps 12-1-1856 (no return) We
Cochran, Caroline to Edward Turner 6-28-1847 (no return) L
Cochran, Eliza to Thomas Meers 5-11-1861 (5-12-1861) Sh
Cochran, Ellen to Joseph R. Hawkins 9-19-1860 We
Cochran, Huldah M. to John M. Wood 3-26-1850 Sh
Cochran, Jane to Thomas B. Stone 4-23-1833 O
Cochran, Kathleen to William G. Murphey 12-9-1861 We
Cochran, Margaret M. to John M. Latta 2-8-1848 Sh
Cochran, Mary J. to Thomas J. Turnbow 7-25-1861 Hn
Cochran, Matilda to J. P Wilson 12-8-1855 Hn
Cochran, Permelia W. to R. L. Turnbow 1-4-1855 Hn
Cochran, Sarah to Robert W. Orton 8-9-1838 F
Cochrane, E. T. to W. R. Spoon 12-1-1876 (12-3-1876) Dy
Cochrane, Mattie W. to Lewis W. Hall 3-5-1868 Ma
Cochrin, Sarah A. to Robert R. Capps 9-9-1841 Cr
Cochrow, M. C. to R. N. P. Fields 8-29-1852 We
Cochrum, America to Francis M. Freeman 9-26-1849 Hn
Cochrun, Amanda M. to William W. W. B. Langley 8-4-1861 We
Cochrun, Margaret to James Shadwick 4-2-1856 (no return) We
Cock, Christenia R. to Othneil Whitenton 1-13-1858 Ma
Cock, Louisa F. to Green L. Hill 6-19-1861 (6-27-1861) Ma
Cock, Lucy to Willis S. O'Kelly 12-17-1850 (no return) F
Cock, M. A. to A. H. Kimbrell 12-3-1867 Ma
Cock, Perlina to Ezekial B. W. Hobbs 4-14-1862 (4-17-1862) Ma
Cocke, Bettie A. to Wm. F. Mitchell 8-22-1860 (8-28-1860) F
Cocke, Dolly to Ransom H. Byrne 11-18-1828 G
Cocke, Eliza J. to Richd. E. Moody 1-20-1849 (1-24-1849) F
Cocke, Eliza to A. H. Hearn 11-5-1862 G
Cocke, Elizabeth to Joseph Henderson 6-11-1839 Sh
Cocke, Frances to Henry Nickols 1-3-1867 (no return) F B
Cocke, Hattie to R. C. Smith 6-12-1867 T
Cocke, L. V. to J. M. Scott 12-20-1869 (no return) F
Cocke, Laura to F. A. Mayo 2-23-1869 (2-25-1869) F
Cocke, Lucy N. to Tho. R. Polk 6-11-1846 (6-24-1846) F
Cocke, Lucy W. to James W. Burton 7-12-1865 F
Cocke, Mary A. to Daniel Freeman 4-23-1870 (4-28-1870) F B
Cocke, Mary P. to James H. Cocke 5-4-1870 (5-5-1870) F
Cocke, Mary R. to James B. Adair 1-20-1849 F
Cocke, Nancy E. to H. S. Haley 12-16-1867 (no return) F
Cocke, Nancy to John C. Hudspeth 8-30-1834 Hr
Cocke, Patsy to Jessey Winfrey 2-24-1870 F B
Cocke, Rebecca to William Park 10-18-1838 Sh
Cocke, Sallie A. to D. R. Town 2-4-1864 Sh
Cocke, V. Carolin to Owen Turnage 10-30-1867 (10-31-1867) T
Cockeburn, Polly to Daniel Royer 8-7-1825 Sh
Cockeram, Mary to Joshua Wright 2-13-1824 Hr
Cockerham, Sarah to John Chandler 5-21-1829 Sh
Cockerill, Martha E. to Christian Spiegel 3-26-1856 (3-27-1856) Sh *
Cocklen, Mary to Jeremiah Donohoe 6-6-1864 (6-8-1864) Sh
Cockraham, Nancy to Shadrock Hargis 12-17-1829 Sh
Cockram, Eliza Jane to Jos. Calls 12-2-1851 (12-16-1851) Sh
Cockram, Jenny A. to T. H. Wiley 1-23-1862 Mn
Cockram, Phoebe to Anderson Willis 10-5-1838 Hn
Cockram, Sarah to Joel J. Reynolds 11-27-1834 Hr
Cockran, Martha C. to G. D. Blane 8-26-1863 Hn
Cockran, Nancy to James Choate 1-2-1838 Sh
Cockream, Ellen to Benjamin Francis Cowell 9-27-1861 (9-30-1861) Sh
Cockrill, Josephin to Alexander Dennis 1-14-1869 (1-18-1869) T
Cockrill, Maria to Rihd. Sadler? 10-7-1867 (10-13-1867) T
Cockrill, Martha J. to Constantine S. Hamner 8-18-1857 (8-19-1857) Ma
Cockrill, Sarah J. to J. C. Caulbreath 4-11-1868 (4-12-1868) T
Cockrill, Sarah Y. to Charles H. Hill 10-28-1840 (10-29-1840) T
Cocks, Jane (Mrs.) to J. H. C. Burk 9-21-1870 G

Cocks, Lizzie to J. F. Peck 7-11-1860 (no return) Hy
Cocks, Martha A. to G. H. Bryant 1-8-1866 G
Codry, Anna to Spencer Howell 6-10-1875 Hy
Cody, Criddie to John Burdet 8-31-1872 (no return) Cr B
Cody, E. F. to William Travis 3-16-1840 (no return) Hn
Cody, Elizabeth W. to Doctor Henry Wright 9-1-1827 (9-6-1827) Hr
Cody, Ellen to Martin Costello 3-7-1860 Sh
Cody, Frances to Henry Coleman 3-15-1871 (1-?-1872) F B
Cody, Harriet A. to Jos. L. Cody 1-2-1868 (no return) F
Cody, Jeroline to Madison Covington 1-26-1870 Cr
Cody, Martha L. J. to Abner J. Hallum 12-23-1851 Hn
Cody, Nancy E. to Joseph A. Barham 9-10-1843 Cr
Cody, Nancy to Andrew Ross 6-6-1826 (6-7-1826) Hr
Coe, Alice E. to Jesse Coe 2-16-1859 Hr
Coe, Barthenia to Jack Williamson 12-23-1865 (12-26-1865) F B
Coe, Eliza to George Anderson 1-21-1874 T
Coe, Eliza to Jesse Merriwether 12-28-1865 (12-29-1865) F B
Coe, Ella M. to Charles J. Philips 1-25-1860 Sh
Coe, Isadore to Granison Brown 2-26-1869 (no return) F B
Coe, Lovy to Julian Bumpbass 4-23-1870 T
Coe, Mary Frances to Harcus Coe 5-31-1869 (6-13-1869) F B
Coe, Sallie to Samuel J. Bunch 12-1-1855 Hr
Coffee, Elizabeth to James A. Bentley 12-15-1845 (12-18-1845) F
Coffee, Johanna to Dennis Kelly 1-22-1861 (1-23-1861) Sh
Coffey, Adaline to John Coates 10-31-1846 (11-11-1846) Hr
Coffey, Ann E. to Joshua H. Powell 11-13-1866 L
Coffey, Isabella to John Griffin 5-2-1840 (5-3-1840) F
Coffield, Elizabeth to Anthony Grieshaber 3-22-1849 Sh
Coffin, Amy to Senson Taylor 8-21-1869 (8-22-1869) F B
Coffman, Allice to Willis Cook 3-19-1870 F B
Coffman, Amanda M. to Samuel Reed 12-24-1851 Hn
Coffman, Bell F. to William Roberts 11-19-1873 (no return) Hy
Coffman, Carusa to Lewis Payton? 12-31-1873 T
Coffman, Elizabeth to J. W. Baley 6-15-1864 Mn
Coffman, Margrette S. J. to William Thomas 8-30-1855 (9-9-1855) G
Coffman, Mariah to Pleasant Murry 1-3-1870 (no return) F B
Coffman, Mary E. to David W. Martin 12-20-1865 (no return) Hy
Coffman, Nancy E. to T. D. Vawter 12-24-1870 (12-25-1870) Cr
Coffy, Margaret to Thomas Kennedy 5-28-1862 Sh
Coffy, Sarah to Henry Rhodes 1-12-1867 (not executed) F B
Cofield, T. A. to John M. Lowry 7-11-1844 Hn
Cogan, Catharine to Cornelius Donohue 9-14-1860 (10-14-1860) Sh
Cogan, M. A. to James Healey 1-8-1864 Sh
Cogan, Mary Ann to James Haley 1-8-1864 (1-10-1864) Sh
Cogbell, Elvira to Jack Hooper 6-15-1870 (no return) F B
Cogbell, Josephine to William E. Loveless 9-20-1848 (9-27-1848) F
Cogbill, F. M. to James H. Johnson 12-15-1852 (no return) F
Cogbill, Harriet to Bennit Wilson 2-15-1869 (2-16-1869) F B
Cogbill, Lucy B. (Mrs.) to John Priest 12-22-1863 Hn
Cogbill, Martha J. to Thos. F. Moore 12-19-1870 (12-21-1870) F
Cogbill, Mollie to James Walkup 8-17-1867 (8-18-1867) F
Cogbill, Patsy to William Britton 12-22-1870 (12-27-1870) F B
Cogburn, Charlotte to John Brown 6-5-1870 G
Cogburn, Henrietta (Mrs.?) to Charles (Dr.) Shackleford 1-1-1872 (1-2-1872) Dy
Coggchall, Sallie to James Givens 3-26-1883 (3-29-1883) L
Coggen, Bridget to Hugh Kelly 4-16-1860 Sh
Coggins, M. A. to W. G. Fondille 12-14-1867 Ma
Coggins, Mary L. to Edward Buckner 8-14-1860 (8-15-1860) Ma
Coggshall, Ella to Dick Auterbridge 12-26-1876 Hy
Cogial, Treasy to Kinion Pipkin 10-24-1828 (10-27-1828) Ma
Cohen, Jennetta to S. Dreyfus 11-26-1861 Sh
Coil, Nancy W. to S. H. Smith 2-28-1861 G
Coin, Margaret to Thos. Morrisy 9-19-1856 Sh
Cokely, Sue M. to F. N. Cathcart 7-26-1870 G
Coker, Beckey to Jeff Ballard 6-11-1883 (6-17-1883) L
Coker, Charity to B. Dickson 4-10-1838 Ma
Coker, Fannie to Rily Pierce 1-1-1873 (12-2-1873) Dy
Coker, Mary E. to S. A. Wood 10-16-1879 Dy
Coker, Mary F. to J. H. Walls 4-24-1876 Hy
Coker, Nancy E. to James Blair 4-13-1876 Hy
Coker, Nancy to Loyd Wilson 10-22-1839 (11-9-1839) F
Coker, Rebecca to Joseph Stephens 7-30-1879 L
Coker, Sai to W. H. Jefferson 7-8-1877 Hy
Coker, Sarah Ann to Oscar O. Forwell 7-30-1859 Ma
Coker, Sarah to Jackson Loyd 3-26-1846 F
Coker, Susan to Redmond Jefferson 10-13-1874 Hy
Colbert, Elizabeth to Alexander Ross 1-3-1826 (1-5-1826) Hr
Colbert, Elizabeth to Charles F. Eastman 7-28-1834 (7-29-1834) Hr
Colbert, Janie to James Cody 4-19-1826 (4-20-1826) Hr
Colbert, R. E. to A. C. Glaze 12-16-1872 (12-19-1872) L
Colbert, Rebecca to John H. Ricks(Riggs) 5-2-1829 (5-7-1829) Hr
Colburn, Mary Jane to Troy Frazier 9-2-1852 G
Coldwell, Frances to John Wilson 9-27-1882 L
Coldwell, Mary C. to Henry C. Bradley 8-26-1876 L
Coldwell, Mary E. to A. G. Harris 7-16-1867 G
Coldwell, Mary E. to G. W. Lucy 8-19-1873 L
Coldwell, Polly to John W. Gillem 5-29-1868 (no return) Hy

Coldwell, Puss to Gib. Tally 12-10-1870 Hy
Coldwell, Rachel M. to Thos. A. McNeill 8-11-1862 (no return) Cr
Coldwell, Rebecca E. to Riley C. Ledbetter 5-25-1871 L
Coldwell, Silvy to Frank Harris 12-31-1868 Hy
Coldwell, V. to James Johnson 2-14-1885 L
Cole, A. B. to W. R. King 11-23-1872 (11-24-1872) Dy
Cole, A. L. to T. C. Thomas 7-19-1864 G
Cole, A. P. to John Presson 6-10-1863 Be
Cole, Adline to Loyd Stokes 10-26-1870 (10-27-1870) Cr
Cole, Alvina to R. W. McFadden 8-8-1849 Hn
Cole, Amanda to William Moore 9-1-1862 (no return) Hy
Cole, Ann E. to Thomal C. Poindexter 9-20-1847 F
Cole, Anna to J. W. Walters 2-22-1872 Cr
Cole, Ary C. to Edward C. Slator 11-27-1854 (11-28-1854) Ma *
Cole, Benthie? L. to John A. Gillespie 2-5-1861 G
Cole, Betsy R. to Henry Harris, jr. 12-26-1868 (no return) Hy
Cole, C. D. to H. Leigh Priddy 10-29-1866 (10-31-1866) F
Cole, Candice to Emsley Howe 12-30-1839 Be
Cole, Caroline to Burril Jones 1-11-1867 Dy
Cole, Celea A. to David S. Phelan 7-26-1853 G
Cole, E. F. to Robert J. Dodson 11-8-1858 (11-18-1858) G
Cole, Eady Ann to Pleasant B. McBride 9-14-1857 (9-15-1857) Hr
Cole, Edy Ann to Thomas Grantham 6-23-1841 Hr
Cole, Elen B. to F. M. Elmore 1-15-1856 Be
Cole, Eliza to George Armstrong 7-18-1849 Sh
Cole, Elizabeth A. to B. F. Presson 12-10-1863 Be
Cole, Elizabeth C. to H. Alexander Stewart 3-17-1853 (3-23-1853) Hr
Cole, Elizabeth Minerva to Allen Jones 2-15-1836 (2-23-1836) O
Cole, Elizabeth W. to John C. McCasburn 3-24-1846 Ma
Cole, Elizabeth to Beverly Herron 7-29-1854 Be
Cole, Elizabeth to David Radford 3-5-1866 (no return) Hn
Cole, Elizabeth to E. R. McBride 12-15-1849 (12-26-1849) Hr
Cole, Elizabeth to James Rackly 5-5-1832 G
Cole, Elizabeth to John M. Buckley 11-13-1861 We
Cole, Elizabeth to Joseph E. Caldwell 3-31-1858 (4-1-1858) O
Cole, Elizabeth to Richard Heath 12-20-1834 G
Cole, Elizabeth to William H. Turner 2-5-1844 (2-13-1844) Ma
Cole, Elizabeth to William Leeton 12-18-1832 (12-23-1832) G
Cole, Emline to James H. Johnson 9-18-1839 Be
Cole, Eva Ann to Jo? Wright 3-11-1871 (3-12-1871) Dy
Cole, Florence to J. H. Jones 6-25-1867 (6-30-1867) T
Cole, Frances Jane to James Daniel 7-14-1850 Hn
Cole, Frances to Levi C. Simmons 1-21-1857 (1-23-1857) O
Cole, H. L. to James E. Rigsbee 11-13-1856 G
Cole, Hester Ann to William Hasty 8-27-1855 O
Cole, Hester Ann to William Master 8-27-1855 (8-30-1855) O
Cole, Isabella to Thos. P. Neuton 7-20-1864 Sh
Cole, Jane to F. Williams 5-15-1867 O
Cole, Jane to James W. Edwards 8-9-1849 G
Cole, Jennie to Nora (Nord?) Gogchell 4-17-1877 (4-18-1877) L
Cole, Joe Ann to Camillus Hawkins 11-9-1868 (11-12-1868) Cr
Cole, Julia C. C. to Geo. D. McAllister 7-8-1862 Ma
Cole, L. to Henry McCorry 12-16-1868 Hy
Cole, Lacy to Malachiah B. Bush 1-11-1852 Be
Cole, Latalia B. to R. M. Swift 10-13-1853 Cr
Cole, Laura S. to Guilford James 8-28-1850 (9-2-1850) Ma
Cole, Lucy F. S. to S. W. Dent 1-3-1860 We
Cole, Lucy J. to Robert J. Green 6-7-1853 (6-8-1853) Sh
Cole, Lusetta to Andrew Weaks 7-8-1867 Hn
Cole, M. P. to L. V. Shelton 5-10-1859 (5-11-1859) F
Cole, Mahala to William Yearwood 12-14-1860 Hy
Cole, Malissa to John Reynolds 6-15-1853 (6-16-1853) G
Cole, Manerva to Sam Byars 4-13-1867 Hn B
Cole, Margaret to Ben DeGraffenreid 10-2-1838 F B
Cole, Margaret to James C. Harrison 8-13-1852 (9-19-1852) Hr
Cole, Margaret to Thomas J. King 2-26-1861 Sh
Cole, Maria L. to John F. Whitelaw 11-5-1849 (11-8-1849) Ma
Cole, Martha A. to John C. Foster 8-30-1843 (8-31-1843) G
Cole, Martha C. to Isaac N. Presson 1-29-1867 Be
Cole, Martha C. to Thomas E. Marchbanks 7-2-1858 Be
Cole, Martha Ellen to Berry Cowell 12-5-1844 Be
Cole, Martha Jane to James C. Abbott 3-2-1854 Be
Cole, Martha Jane to W. J. Thompson 12-17-1860 (12-19-1860) T
Cole, Martha R. to Thomas J. Williams 11-8-1852 (11-11-1852) G
Cole, Martha to James Alsup 9-14-1854 Be
Cole, Martha to Joseph O'Daniel 9-11-1863 Hn
Cole, Martha to Wade Busby 3-7-1849 Be
Cole, Mary Ann to Francis M. Harrison 8-13-1852 (8-14-1852) Hr
Cole, Mary Ann to George Holmark 3-20-1863 Be
Cole, Mary Ann to J. M. Thompson 2-19-1866 (no return) Hn
Cole, Mary Ann to Stephen Smith 2-3-1844 (2-8-1844) T
Cole, Mary E. to S. R. Wood 10-10-1876 Hy
Cole, Mary J. to James M. Castele (Castile) 9-23-1867 Be
Cole, Mary J. to Wm. R. Granade 12-11-1865 (12-14-1865) Cr
Cole, Mary Jane to Thomas F. Evetts 10-19-1834 Sh
Cole, Mary P. to John E. Elmore 11-1-1861 Be
Cole, Mary W. to Wm. D. Bardon 3-29-1863 Be

Cole, Mary to James Greer 4-25-1839 Be
Cole, Mary to Theophilus Presson 4-16-1868]
Cole, Mary to Thomas Hamilton 8-19-1869 Hy
Cole, Maryan to William Ferguson 8-26-1829 G
Cole, Mazy Jane to Wm. W. Greer 12-24-1866 Be
Cole, McUla to Allen Ferguson 11-14-1831 G
Cole, Minervy to John Coley 2-8-1845 Be
Cole, Minevery J. to John H. Raspbury 3-28-1843 Be
Cole, Mulindy to Julius M. Hall 3-28-1838 G
Cole, Nancy Ann to W. F. Prewitt 11-25-1846 Be
Cole, Nannie D. to John H. Thomas 10-29-1859 (11-1-1859) Ma
Cole, Pamelia R. to Jeremiah Baugh 11-30-1848 Sh
Cole, Paralee to Wm. Thomas Chappell 4-11-1870 (4-5?-1870) Ma
Cole, Parolle to J. M. Davis 1-10-1856? (1-10-1857) G
Cole, Rachel to Jno. B. Ingram 11-14-1869 Hy
Cole, Rebecca E. to James W. Wilson 6-19-1856 Hn
Cole, Rebecca to Henry Jordon 4-11-1847 Be
Cole, Rebecca to Milton J. Allison 3-10-1862 (3-22-1862) O
Cole, S. A. to J. S. Ray 12-29-1875 Dy
Cole, S. F. to G. S. Jordan 10-29-1860 Sh
Cole, S. J. to W. E. Benton 2-20-1866 (2-21-1866) O
Cole, S. M. to J. M. McClure 4-4-1864 (no return) Hn
Cole, S. P. to W. P. Maning 8-4-1842 Sh
Cole, Sallie to Willie Ridley 1-11-1871 (1-12-1871) Cr
Cole, Sarah A. to John H. Forest 2-2-1865 Be
Cole, Sarah A. to Preston Holland 10-1-1838 (10-2-1838) G
Cole, Sarah J. to John W. Arun? 11-20-1866 Hn
Cole, Sarah to Booker Hays 5-11-1871 (5-27-1871) F B
Cole, Sarah to J. C. Taylor 3-5-1874 Hy
Cole, Stacy to Samuel Booker 5-14-1854 Be
Cole, Susan E. to B. H. Eddins 10-12-1842 Sh
Cole, Susan M. to James F. Kelly 2-20-1855 Ma
Cole, Susan O. to N. P. Richardson 9-8-1855 (9-9-1855) G
Cole, Susan to T. P. Tully 1-19-1865 Mn
Cole, Susan to Turner Barfoot 11-10-1850 Be
Cole, T. J. to J. G. Davis 11-5-1870 G
Cole, Tebitha C. to Seth Brownlee McCommon 1-6-1841 (1-7-1841) Hr
Cole, Tennessee to Allen Orr 12-28-1868 (1-3-1869) F B
Cole, Unity to Thomas Veach 1-7-1848 Be
Coleman, A. A. to James Cohorn 3-18-1863 G
Coleman, A. E. M. to F. G. Rich 8-4-1859 G
Coleman, Ann to Richmund Facen 7-8-1875 L
Coleman, Asa A. to Jas. A. Childress 1-3-1856 (SB 1857?) G
Coleman, Charlotte to Ross Montgoery 8-23-1866 (8-26-1866) T
Coleman, Clara M. to John Brown 1-14-1832 Hr
Coleman, Dafney to Spencer Jones 8-23-1866 (8-26-1866) T
Coleman, Drue A. to Sterling H. Pettus 6-20-1866 (6-21-1866) L
Coleman, Ednie J. to A. M. Gaines 10-28-1865 (10-31-1865) L
Coleman, Eliza A. to R. B. Sangster 1-4-1861 Hy
Coleman, Elizabeth A. to Ashley R. Wilson 6-7-1853 G
Coleman, Elizabeth to Franklin Walker 4-15-1858 We
Coleman, Elizabeth to John Dudley 4-11-1871 (4-15-1871) Cr
Coleman, Elizabeth to John M____ 3-18-1856 Hn
Coleman, Elizabeth to W. A. Young 1-22-1867 Hy
Coleman, Elizabeth to W. J. Rose 2-28-1882 (3-1-1882) L
Coleman, Elizabeth to William T. Yopp 8-30-1844 Hr
Coleman, Emily Permelia to William r. Parks 8-7-1863 Hn
Coleman, Frances to William Watson 9-12-1857 (9-18-1857) G
Coleman, Hanah to Geor. Gardner 6-10-1871 Cr
Coleman, Hariat to Hiram McCrary 6-20-1850 Hn
Coleman, Julia A. to J. B. Pate 10-7-1872 (10-8-1872) O
Coleman, Julia to C. W. Ellis 1-27-1875 (1-28-1875) Dy
Coleman, Kate to William Jones 10-11-1877 Hy
Coleman, Lotta to Wash King 7-10-1875 (7-4?-1875) Dy
Coleman, Lucy to T. T. Taylor 9-10-1860 (9-11-1860) Sh
Coleman, M. Fanny to R. W. Stubblefield 11-16-1866 Hn
Coleman, M. L. to G. H. Morgan 12-29-1866 (12-20-1866) Cr
Coleman, M. L. to J. M. McKenzie 3-5-1842 Cr
Coleman, M. L. to J. W. Fuqua 3-2-1868 (3-4-1868) Cr
Coleman, Maney to Thos. Pearson 9-25-1874 Hy
Coleman, Margaret A. to John H., jr. Day 8-29-1850 Ma
Coleman, Margaret to Dan Donaldson 1-4-1869 G
Coleman, Margaret to Jas. M. Love 12-15-1867 Hy
Coleman, Martha J. to Charles T. Latta 12-28-1859 G
Coleman, Martha T. to Joseph A. Sandeford 4-10-1835 Sh
Coleman, Martha to Richard Richardson 12-27-1877 Hy
Coleman, Mary A. to William Bailey 2-4-1846 (no return) Hn
Coleman, Mary B. to John M. Ruffin 9-27-1846 Sh
Coleman, Mary F. to John W. Rawlins 6-26-1860 G
Coleman, Mary J. to G. H. Bradford 1-18-1866 Hy
Coleman, Mary to Christopher Pidgeon 1-6-1862 Sh
Coleman, Mary to George W. Boswell 10-30-1848 Cr
Coleman, Mary to Nicholas Jones 11-13-1871 T
Coleman, Mary to Wm. D. Ballinger 9-12-1860 Sh
Coleman, Mattie to J. E. Castellow 10-25-1870 Hy
Coleman, Mattie to William Cox 7-22-1871 Hy
Coleman, Mollie to ____ Edmunds 3-7-1867 Hn

Coleman, Nancy A. to Arthur Lowrey 2-28-1848 (no return) Hn
Coleman, Nancy J. to James M. Coffman 2-4-1846 Hn
Coleman, Nannie B. to Elvis R. Traywick 12-26-1872 Cr
Coleman, Narcissa T. to J. J. McFarlen 12-27-1854 G
Coleman, Paralee to Moses Bell 4-25-1867 (no return) F B
Coleman, Patsy to Cook Ruffin 1-28-1872 Hy
Coleman, R. F. to J. J. P.(B.?) Parrish 1-11-1870 G
Coleman, Rosetta to James Jones 3-1-1869 (no return) L B
Coleman, S. A. to J. N. McMinn 2-26-1866 (3-1-1864?) G
Coleman, S. J. to M. F. Blackman 8-11-1872 O
Coleman, Sallie to M. D. L. Stewart 10-18-1854 Sh
Coleman, Santefee B. to J. G. Sayles 7-9-1862 (no return) Cr
Coleman, Sarah A. to Henry Lancaster 12-26-1844 (12-29-1844) O
Coleman, Sarah Ann to Andrew Caps 12-1-1855 (12-6-1855) Hr
Coleman, Sarah E. to John C. Gleen (Glenn?) 10-19-1870 G
Coleman, Sarah J. to Joseph L. Park 12-7-1863 Be
Coleman, Sarah M. to Thomas J. Etheridge 6-6-1859 Hn
Coleman, Sellah to Samuel Hoesey 4-13-1867 G
Coleman, Sue H. to J. E. Graves 3-8-1875 Hy
Coleman, Sue to Reps Goode 3-3-1872 Hy
Coleman, Susan C. to A. R. Wilson 11-29-1859 G
Coleman, Susan E. to J. F. Williamson 8-31-1860 Dy
Coleman, Susan to Thos. D. Jackson 1-15-1867 O
Coleman, Susan to U. R. Haylon 12-24-1867 O
Coleman, Sylla to Hilliary Roberts 1-3-1878 Hy
Coles, Nancy G. to J. G. Chapman 11-2-1854 Hn
Colevitt, Sarah to W. A. Peery 3-16-1875 Dy
Coley, Caroline to James S. Scott 11-8-1860 Hn
Coley, J. A. to W. S. Curtis 3-13-1857 (no return) We
Coley, Jane to Rufus Todd 11-17-1853 Hn
Coley, M. E. to R. N. Pearce 2-15-1866 G
Coley, M. to J. M. Speight 12-10-1865 Hn
Coley, Margarett to Babe Baird 8-26-1869 G
Coley, Polly to Joab Tue 6-18-1843 Be
Coley, Prissa to George Smith 12-2-1843 (12-4-1843) G
Coley, Sarah to William Curtis 12-16-1868 Hn
Colhoun, Jennie E. to Daniel G. Shelby 10-12-1876 Hy
Colie, Miller to Lewis Pinson 12-3-1867 (no return) Hy
Colier, Elizabeth to Henry Mabery 3-11-1850 Be
Colier, Nancy to Hambleton Gossett 4-20-1847 Be
Collam, Hetty to Tim Collam 5-11-1852 Be
Collens, Eliza Emiline to John Croose 5-10-1870 (5-11-1870) L
Collens, Martha Caroline to Walter Conner 4-13-1870 (4-15-1870) L
Coller?, Mary H. to Thomas C. Gale 1-31-1861 Hn
Colleth, Sarah A. to Abell Pittman 7-13-1860 (no return) Dy
Colley, Ann to Thomas McCampbell 9-11-1866 Hn B
Collier, Eliza W. to William J. Hall 7-9-1850 (7-10-1850) T
Collier, Eliza to William Williams 3-30-1854 Sh
Collier, Eliza to Winston Elkin 2-13-1867 (no return) Hy
Collier, Elizabeth C. to Thomas C. Muse 9-5-1855 (9-12-1855) Ma
Collier, Emily J. to James C. Hudson 12-9-1850 Ma
Collier, Frances to Wm. Taylor 6-6-1868 F B
Collier, Kesiah P. to Hilman Walker 1-1-1846 We
Collier, Martha to Robert Weatherington 9-11-1869 (9-12-1869) T
Collier, Mary E. to Wm. W. Brown 12-15-1878 Hy
Collier, Mary J. to Peyton Skipwith 3-23-1859 (3-24-1859) Sh
Collier, Mary to W. W. Holland 1-27-1856 Be
Collier, Mattie to Preston Alexander 3-13-1872 Hy
Collier, Milberry to John K. Williams 6-10-1855 Be
Collier, Moriah to Monroe Williamson 12-28-1867 Hy
Collier, Pheaby to William Wood 1-5-1855 Be CC
Collier, Pheraby to William Wood 1-5-1855 Be
Collier, Rose E. to J. N. Swayne 10-25-1871 Hy
Collier, Rosella to Nathan Johnson 2-8-1878 Hy
Collier, Rosetta to Randal Collier 6-29-1866 (no return) Hy
Collier, Ruth to Felix Elcan 1-26-1876 (no return) Hy
Collier, Sarah to Anderson McGill 12-24-1845 Cr
Collier, Sarah to J. H. Gracey 11-16-1864 (11-21-1864) Sh
Collier, Susan Elizabeth to Ephraim Hall Smith 10-16-1851 T
Colligan, Mary to John Flinn 11-24-1863 Sh
Collin, Mary to J. Neehan Branch 6-24-1877 Hy
Collin, Olive L. to Anthony O. Johnson 1-16-1850 Cr
Collingsworth, Margaret W. to Jas. A. Cox 12-16-1850 (12-19-1850) G
Collins, Ann E. to Wm. H. Crittenden 1-3-1843 Hr
Collins, Ann Jane to Philip Teaffe 7-28-1858 Sh
Collins, Anna A. to Thomas Nunn 10-9-1866 Hn
Collins, Annie to John Sanford 2-28-1870 (3-17-1870) L
Collins, Asena to Thomas Ferguson 8-22-1839 Hn
Collins, Bethenea C. to Louisa Humphrey 7-20-1853 Cr
Collins, C. E. to E. E. Collins 12-24-1868 (maybe 12-29) G
Collins, Catherine to Ezekiel T. Whitworth 3-5-1856 Ma
Collins, Catherine to F. M. C. Hughes 4-9-1867 (4-11-1867) F
Collins, Crecy to Houston Nance 5-21-1866 Hn B
Collins, Drusilla Jane to James L. Brundige 8-6-1857 Hn
Collins, Eliza J. to Wm. J. Shaw 8-13-1853 Cr
Collins, Elizabeth T. to Joseph F. Williams 11-21-1843 Sh
Collins, Elizabeth to George W. Lett 11-5-1849 Cr

Collins, Elizabeth to Miles Lacewell 8-24-1867 O
Collins, Elizabeth to Wm. T. Letsinger 11-5-1849 Cr
Collins, Ellender J. to Isham Clayton 7-18-1848 Hn
Collins, Emily P. to Wm. M. Dunn 1-11-1848 Sh
Collins, Evaline F. to John Grant 6-7-1848 Hn
Collins, Haner L. to Lecusgal Stoder 10-4-1849 Cr
Collins, Janie to Alfred Willis 12-6-1852 (no return) L
Collins, Judith A. to Gideon Carr 4-12-1856 (4-13-1856) Sh
Collins, L. M. to W. H. Swan 6-22-1864 Sh
Collins, Lively to David Switzer 2-24-1833 Sh
Collins, Louisa J. to Thomas B. Madden 9-23-1851 Be
Collins, M. A. to B. M. Holland 7-8-1842 Be
Collins, M. A. to Benj. G. Garrett 12-25-1856 Sh
Collins, M. E. to Thomas Eskew 12-6-1858 (no return) Cr
Collins, M. I. to W. H. Hood 3-13-1865 O
Collins, M. J. to W. H. Hood 3-13-1865 O
Collins, Mahaley K. to C. J. Byrs 1-11-1858 We
Collins, Margaret to Patrick H. Kernes (Korns) 11-3-1845 Sh
Collins, Maria to Harrison N. Hancock 11-1-1855 O
Collins, Martha to S. F. Johnson 1-3-1873 (1-5-1873) Dy
Collins, Mary A. to Francis M. Pylant 7-11-1849 (7-12-1849) Hr
Collins, Mary E. to Jordan Y. Cummings 2-24-1845 Sh
Collins, Mary L. to J. H. Nale 6-15-1864 (6-16-1864) Sh
Collins, Mary to James Cically 1-6-1857 (1-7-1857) Sh
Collins, Mary to John Switzer 3-26-1833 Sh
Collins, Mary to Michael Mullany 4-28-1862 Sh
Collins, Mary to Nicholas Leip 2-12-1850 O
Collins, Nancy A. to W. S. Brewer 3-20-1867 Be
Collins, Nancy Jane to Joseph L. Stewart 10-9-1845 We
Collins, Perlina to B. H. Thompson 1-15-1859 (1-16-1859) Sh
Collins, Priscilla W. to Bryce A. Collins 9-26-1848 Sh
Collins, Randy to Daniel Tate 8-25-1848 Cr
Collins, Sally to Henry Kimbrough 12-29-1876 Hy
Collins, Salma to George Driggs 1-5-1845 Cr
Collins, Sopha to Berry Hurt 10-12-1867 Cr
Collins, Tennessee V. to Wyatt A. Taylor 7-29-1858 Ma
Collins, Tennessee to Wilson Y. Hale 10-22-1855 (10-23-1855) O
Collinsworth, Elizabeth to Stephen Crain 11-18-1828 Ma
Collinsworth, Martha (Mrs.) to Laburn Perry 11-10-1869 (11-11-1869) Ma
Collinsworth, Martha P. to Samuel H. Denaway 12-15-1861 G
Collinsworth, Susan T. to Thos. J. Craddock 2-14-1852 (2-17-1852) G
Collman, Nancy to Morris Bond 1-28-1872 Hy
Collum, Jane to H. T. Day 11-1-1855 Sh
Colly, Frances P. to John V. Moore 12-10-1856 We
Colly, Martha M. to J. H. Watson 3-4-1861 Hy
Colly, Sarah J. to Gilbert W. Hendrix 8-21-1861 (no return) We
Colly, Sarah to A. E. Tucker 3-13-1856 We
Colman, Bell to Joe L. Boyd 2-12-1880 (no return) L
Colman, Elizabeth to Moses Fyker 1-31-1870 (no return) Dy
Colman, Livina to Wm. Cornell 11-26-1850 We
Colman, Martha A. to Solman D. Hicks 8-5-1858 We
Colmer, Tommy to James C. Jackson 12-11-1869 (12-14-1869) T
Colsharp, Louisa M. to John T. Damron 12-21-1858 We
Colt, Mary Ann to Matthew Bayne 2-24-1840 Sh
Coltart, Amana to John Rickter 3-1-1869 (3-5-1869) L B
Coltart, Angeline to Frank Farmer 5-22-1874 Hy
Coltart, Anna to Jefferson Byars 1-27-1872 Hy
Coltart, C. O. to Shelby S. Currie 11-28-1873 Hy
Coltart, Ella to George Young 12-2-1880 L B
Coltart, Emily to Nathan Young 4-25-1874 Hy
Coltart, Harriett to Epps Haliburton 2-24-1868 Hy
Coltart, Mary to B. W. Alison 11-9-1865 Hy
Coltart, Milly Ann to Arthur Currie 7-16-1881 L B
Coltart, Paralee to Ed Sanders 2-16-1873 Hy
Coltart, Sarah to Moses Young 11-4-1865 Hy
Coltart, Susan to Joe Nelson 12-30-1865 Hy
Colter, Hannah L. to M. H. Burton 2-7-1870 (no return) Hy
Colter, Maria to Alex Whitehead 9-14-1874 Hy
Coltharp, C. A. to William R. Raney 9-6-1839 (9-9-1839) F
Colverd, Sarah to John Dunaway 7-14-1828 (7-17-1828) Hr
Colvet, Ellen C. to Columbus J.? Wilds 10-15-1872 (10-6?-1872) Cr
Colvett, Mary J. to John Key 12-26-1866 (12-27-1866) Cr
Colvin, Anne to J. H. Vaughan 9-7-1878 (9-8-1878) Dy
Colvin, Ida to J. A. Webb 9-11-1877 (9-12-1878?) L
Colvin, Jennie to James Suttlemore 12-29-1875 (1-2-1876) Dy
Colvin, Julia to G. W. Walker 4-13-1876 Dy
Colvin, Louisa to William Eudaily 2-10-1868 (no return) Dy
Colvin, M. J. to J. P. Boyd 10-14-1882 (10-18-1882) L
Colvin, S. E. to G. D. Mays 2-24-1870 Dy
Colwell, Mary T. to Andrew J. Elzey 9-4-1867 (9-5-1867) L
Colwell, Mealey to Jackson Vaulx 12-13-1874 Hy
Colyer, Martha to William Downey 2-24-1834 G
Comb, Eliza J. to A. Hawley 12-19-1865 Be
Comb, Martha to Tony Anthony 7-20-1866 U
Comboy, Ann to James Quinn 6-7-1860 Sh
Combs, A. to Neil McMillan 2-27-1868 G
Combs, Eliza Jane to John H. Legate 6-2-1855 (6-3-1855) O

Combs, Emily C. to J. W. Smith 1-7-1866 G
Combs, Frances E. to John Dancer 7-25-1844 Be
Combs, Frances R. to Felix G. Hudson 11-14-1867 Be
Combs, Jane C. to A. C. Wiseman 5-8-1856 Be
Combs, Jane E. to A. C. Wiseman 5-8-1856 Be CC
Combs, Lamira to W. D. Jarrell 3-6-1860 Be
Combs, Martha E. to W. H. Watson 12-24-1860 Be
Combs, Martha to John Bradbury 2-19-1846 G
Combs, Martha to John Madison Simpson 11-22-1853 (11-24-1853) Ma
Combs, Mary Caroline to Berry Dolton 8-5-1845 Be
Combs, Mary E. to A. K. Hopper 8-27-1857 G
Combs, Nancy to John Prince 9-15-1853 Be
Combs, Susan H. to Robt. N. Mathis 2-18-1867 (2-20-1867) Ma
Comer, E. J. to S. R. Shaw 12-1-1861 (12-2-1865?) Cr
Comer, E. J. to S. R. Shaw 12-?-1861 (12-2-1861) Cr
Comer, Elizabeth to Joseph B. Teague 1-1-1844 Hr
Comer, Harret? to Braxton W. Kiernan 11-20-1845 Hr
Comer, Louisa to Wilson S. Sanderlin 8-29-1842 (9-1-1842) Hr
Comer, Lucy Ann W. to George W. Wood 5-24-1867 (no return) Hn
Comer, Lucy R. to W. S. Fryer 10-25-1859 Hn
Comer, Margaret S. to John A. Campbell 9-7-1867 Hn
Comer, Martha A. to William H. Gillespie 3-22-1854 Hn
Comer, Sarah F. to James S. Roseberry 3-5-1857 Hn
Comer, Sarah to Wm. T. Jones 12-5-1855 Hr
Comer, Susan F. to Andrew Pinckley 12-18-1869 (12-19-1869) Cr
Comes, Margarette E. to George Cook 10-12-1859 (10-13-1859) G
Comes, Martha E. to William Cook 3-26-1862 G
Compton, Amanda to Joseph Smith 11-14-1868 (no return) L
Compton, Caroline to John T. Fletcher 1-7-1840 (1-16-1840) Ma
Compton, E. J. to William G. Erwin 11-11-1846 Hn
Compton, Eliza to J. H. Still 12-1-1854 (no return) F
Compton, Emma A. to Richard G. Herring 12-5-1877 Hy
Compton, Lucinda to Columbus Rice 12-18-1872 (no return) L B
Compton, M. J. to J. C. Modlin 3-4-1865 (3-5-1865) G
Compton, Malvina to William Hinson 11-10-1838 (11-11-1838) F
Compton, Margaret to Jacob Jones 12-17-1872 (12-22-1872) T
Compton, Mary J. to William English 7-8-1857 Sh
Compton, Mildred A. to Henry D. Roberts 6-3-1853 (no return) F
Compton, Mildred N. to Jno. Henry Hooks 12-12-1867 (no return) F
Compton, Nancy A. to Ashley Askew 4-3-1850 Hn
Compton, Nancy to Samuel Hankins 10-28-1846 (no return) Hn
Compton, Narcessus to John G. Hinson 8-15-1838 F
Compton, Nellie to Isaac Moorer 6-4-1883 (no return) L
Compton, P. C. to N. G. Muzzall 1-2-1871 (1-5-1871) Cr
Compton, S. E. to W. C. Bomar 9-7-1869 Cr
Compton, Sarah E. to J. W. Poston 10-20-1863 (10-21-1863) F
Compton, Sarah P. to John Simmons 11-13-1849 Cr
Comsay?, M. A. to C. F. Potts? 5-30-1865 Hn
Comton, M. A. to G. H. Wadkins 6-1-1868 (6-4-1868) Cr
Comwell?, Rhoda N. to Edward J. Mathews 12-6-1859 Hr
Conally, Mary to John Thomas Owens 11-12-1853 Sh
Condelly, Caroline to John Rolins 11-29-1858 Cr
Conder, Mandy Jane to Oliver Stanfield 2-28-1871 (3-1-1871) Ma
Condon, Bridget to Dennis Kerney 10-18-1859 (10-23-1859) Sh
Condon, Martha to William Dillon 6-19-1862 Sh
Condor, Margaret A. E. to John B. Flowers 1-13-1863 (no return) Dy
Condra, Matilda to Asa McKinza 2-17-1828 Hr
Condray, Louisa to James Crocker 1-25-1865 (2-26-1865) L
Condrey, M. E. to A. J. Parker 12-22-1879 (12-24-1879) L
Condry, Cyntha T. to J. A. Bylor 12-19-1876 (12-20-1877?) L
Condry, Mary to Stephen Bates 12-22-1865 (12-24-1865) L
Condry, Nancy J. to William Leird 4-8-1858 L
Condry, Subra Ann to James M. Crocker 1-27-1853 L
Conel, Drucilla M. to John Word 11-16-1842 G
Conell, Elizabeth to William Banister 12-18-1834 (12-23-1834) G
Conell, Margaret to Arthur A. Williams 8-8-1846 G
Conelly, Mary to Nelson H. Heany 10-18-1838 Sh
Conerly, Elizabeth to Wm. Flargan? 4-29-1851 (4-?-1851) L
Conery, Mary to James Galagher 4-29-1858 (5-13-1858) Sh
Conger, A. W. to Joel R. Chappell 9-23-1839 (9-24-1839) Ma
Conger, Cora C. to Andrew B. Langford 8-14-1866 (8-15-1866) Ma
Conger, Emma to E. E. Flippin 7-1-1871 (7-3-1871) Ma *
Conger, Roena P. to George D. King 9-11-1860 Ma
Conger, Winney Ann to William N. Winston 9-28-1848 Ma
Conghley, Susan D. to J. S. Strickland 7-29-1866 G
Conkey, M. A. to R. H. Whitehead 12-13-1868 (12-20-1859) F
Conklin, D. F. to J. N. Chambers 9-20-1879 (9-22-1879) Dy
Conklin, M. J. to W. T. Moore 12-12-1876 (no return) L
Conlee, Luemma S. to Daniel T. Agee 3-13-1855 G
Conlee, Mahaly to Absolom Smith 12-22-1834 (12-25-1834) G
Conlee, Tabitha C. to John W. Featherston 12-6-1855 G
Conley (Corley?), E. L. to S. L. Wagster 10-17-1869 G
Conley (Corley?), Edney V. to A. L. Thompson 7-24-1862 G
Conley, Agnes to Joseph Conley 7-30-1868 C B
Conley, Gemima to John C. Barham 3-13-1839 (3-20-1839) O
Conley, Henrietta to John Carter 2-22-1878 L
Conley, Martha C. to R. L. Davidson 1-22-1863 G

Conley, Martha E. to Robert Sanford 8-30-1852 (9-2-1852) G
Conley, Martha S. to R. S. Dickson 12-22-1862 (12-23-1862?) G
Conley, Martha to Mathias Nichols 12-4-1862 Be
Conley, Mary A. to David Kinghin 5-8-1851 Sh
Conley, Nancy to Andrew Johnson 9-20-1883 (9-24-1883) L
Conley, Nancy to Thomas H. Dyer 3-12-1855 Be
Conley, Sarah E. to M. S. Wallice 1-16-1856 G
Conley, Susan A. to Jack Norville 3-6-1870 Hy
Conley, Susan J. to John W. Pierce 12-5-1848 G
Conlin, Catharine to Edward Mullen 5-3-1859 Sh
Conly, Mary to John H. Tipler 1-9-1851 (1-15-1851) Hr
Conn, Amelia Ann to James Alexander 1-24-1829 Ma
Connally, Rebecca F. to John Oliver 9-17-1850 (9-18-1850) Ma
Connally, Susan R. to Edwin R. Lancaster 9-2-1850 Ma
Connell, Arie F. to John Knott 1-17-1854 G
Connell, Bettie to John F. Thomas 12-25-1865 G
Connell, Catherine to C. M. Padgett 6-26-1862 Sh
Connell, Charlotte Mary to John A. Mooring 12-20-1860 (12-21-1860) Ma
Connell, Clarrasy Ann to James H. Davis 10-26-1853 (10-27-1853) G
Connell, Eliz J. to Thomas L. Pounds 2-29-1848 G
Connell, Ellen to Charles Snelling 10-23-1861 (10-27-1861) Sh
Connell, Emiline to Hiram Findle 11-19-1869 (no return) Dy
Connell, Fannie to Ben Shallow 6-19-1876 Dy
Connell, Fannie to Wm. Mulherin 10-22-1868 Dy
Connell, Julia to Magor Norment 4-29-1880 Dy
Connell, Lizzie to Church Burklen? 5-1-1876 Dy
Connell, Manirvy to Charles J. Little 3-21-1867 G
Connell, Margaret to C. G. Jameson 11-4-1861 Hn
Connell, Margaret to William H. Hunt 1-14-1860 (no return) We
Connell, Martha M. to Jas. Pearce 5-31-1858 G
Connell, Mary A. to W. P. Lane 1-5-1871 Dy
Connell, Mary to Carroll Holt 5-13-1837 (5-25-1837) G
Connell, Mary to Jerry Fowlkes 11-28-1867 Dy
Connell, Mary to Martin Flanigan 2-8-1864 Sh
Connell, Millie to Nelson Shaw 9-12-1872 Dy
Connell, Minerva to S. M. Smith 1-22-1852 We
Connell, Mollie to Thomas Howard 6-3-1871 (6-4-1871) Dy
Connell, Nancy to Clark Reed 1-25-1863 G
Connell, Peggy to Hiram McCullough 2-22-1872 Dy
Connell, S. L. to C. C. Agee 3-29-1865 G
Connell, Sarah E. to William P. Fowlkes, jr. 6-15-1863 Dy
Connell, Susan J. to Robert Mann 9-15-1871 (9-20-1871) Cr
Connell, Susan to J. C. Reasons 10-18-1879 (10-19-1879) Dy
Connell, Susan to John William Giles 10-27-1866 (10-28-1866) Ma
Connell, Tibitha to Franklin Williams 1-27-1858 G
Connelly, Caroline H. to Thomas McGill 2-2-1862 Ma *
Connelly, Honera to Stephen Jones 4-20-1861 Sh
Connelly, Mary Ann to James O'Conner 8-25-1860 (8-26-1860) Sh
Conner, Ann to William Devitt 1-29-1852 Sh
Conner, Annie M. to Calvin C. Verser 11-10-1885 L
Conner, Catheran to James Laird 12-19-1866 T
Conner, Docia to York Lawrison 5-25-1871 L
Conner, Eliza Ellen to George S. Penn 2-15-1854 G
Conner, Elizabeth L. to Edward J. Read 5-17-1859 L
Conner, Eloise C. to L. C. Gillespie 12-2-1868 Hy
Conner, Emily V. to John L. Alston 1-11-1870 L
Conner, Hannah to Owen Mangum 2-27-1871 (2-28-1871) F B
Conner, Jane to George L. Priddy 3-1-1870 (3-3-1870) Ma
Conner, Juanna to Woolsey Thompson 1-31-1863 Sh
Conner, Kittie Ann to John Green 2-2-1884 (no return) L
Conner, Lilly to Starling Crowder 12-30-1868 G B
Conner, Lizzie to Albert Scott 6-12-1875 L B
Conner, Lizzie to William H. White 12-19-1882 (12-23-1882) L
Conner, Margaret to John L. Smith 4-15-1869 Ma
Conner, Martha to William H. Miller 7-11-1837 Hr
Conner, Mary Agnes to Wm. Naylor 1-2-1864 Sh
Conner, Mary Jane to Michael Joyce 1-19-1861 (1-22-1861) Sh
Conner, Mary to J. N. Johnakin 11-8-1858 (11-9-1858) O
Conner, Mary to Robert West 10-8-1861 G
Conner, Mary to Wilson George 6-30-1864 (7-1-1864) Sh
Conner, Melvina to Henry J. Trotter 1-26-1848 F
Conner, Polly to Spencer Birdin 8-23-1830 Hr
Conner, Rebecca to Harvey Holt 7-28-1846 (7-30-1846) Ma
Conner, Sarah L. to Nelson Wiley 2-4-1842 (2-6-1842) Hr
Conner, Susan to William A. Partee 12-18-1856 L
Conner, Susan to Zach Walker 12-13-1868 Hy
Conner, Theresa to Henry Rocco 6-29-1859 Sh
Connerey, Mary to Richard Culigan 8-22-1861 Sh
Conners, Ann to John Powers 5-18-1861 (5-20-1861) Sh
Conners, Catherine to Thos. H. Conway 1-13-1863 Sh
Conners, Ellen to Thomas E. Mulvehill 2-15-1867 (no return) Hn
Conners, Mary to Peter Flanarey 7-25-1857 (8-2-1857) Sh
Connor, Harriet A. to Duncan M. Spencer 12-29-1859 (1-1-1860) Ma
Connors, Johanna to Michael Cunningham 7-9-1859 (7-17-1859) Sh
Conrad, Catharine to Conrad Schmidt 12-18-1852 Sh
Conrad, Delila (Delile F.) to Joseph Clark 1-12-1847 Sh
Conrad, Margaret S. to William Burchard 8-2-1848 Sh

Conray, Ann to John Dennegan 1-9-1864 Sh
Conray, Ann to John Dunnagin 1-9-1864 (1-10-1864) Sh
Considine, Jane to Anderson Davidson 12-25-1866 G
Considine, M. A. to M. K. Considine 6-3-1864 G
Considine, M. A. to T. A. Bryan 11-29-1866 G
Conway, Catharine to D. H. Ray 4-22-1855 Sh
Conway, Catharine to James Monaghan 5-31-1858 Sh
Conway, Johanna to Jeremiah D. Lynch 1-26-1858 (1-27-1858) Sh
Conway, Mary to David R. Wilson 12-27-1849 F
Conway, Mary to John Williams 8-2-1854 Sh
Conway, Priscilla (Mrs.) to James Step 2-10-1845 G
Conwell (Cornwell?), Martha T. to Francis Kently (Kietley?) 6-12-1851 Sh
Conwell, Matilda to Thomas Runolds 2-24-1827 G
Conwell, N. (Mrs.) to H. L. W. Tunely? 8-3-1868 (8-4-1868) Dy
Conyers, Frances J. to George W. Dean 12-20-1860 (no return) Hy
Conyers, Jane to John K. Graham 12-20-1847 (no return) Hn
Conyers, Tabitha N. to James W. Aycock 2-1-1843 (no return) Hn
Conyers, Verginia to James Fugate 1-21-1865 (1-22-1865) Dy
Conyors, Lavitha E. to Gilbert Harding 10-28-1865 Hn
Coody(Cody), Eliza to John Little 10-9-1834 Hr
Cook (Kisk), Barbara to H. C. Evans 4-9-1848 Sh
Cook, Ada E. to B. R. McGinley 10-6-1857 Hy
Cook, Alice W. to Samuel H. Edwards 12-3-1867 Ma
Cook, Alice to R. W. Allen 1-22-1868 G
Cook, Amanda A. to Armenious McCarty 2-4-1867 G
Cook, Aneliza to H. H. Hargett 11-26-1871 Hy
Cook, Ann to Denis Ryan 5-27-1859 (6-2-1859) Sh
Cook, Annie to Saml. M. Ozier 9-26-1866 Ma
Cook, Annie to Willis Alford 9-22-1877 (no return) L
Cook, Avy to Burwell Warmack 5-9-1840 (5-12-1840) G
Cook, C. M. to Z. Wainwright 11-28-1861 Hy
Cook, Cassa to J. H. Puckett 5-26-1874 (5-27-1874) L
Cook, Catherine E. to J. F. W. Oberst 5-3-1858 Sh
Cook, Cathie to J. S. Moore 11-29-1877 Dy
Cook, Catie to F. M. Doyle 2-9-1875 Hy
Cook, Delina to Thos. Notgrass 5-10-1845 (5-13-1845) F
Cook, Didama to William Vaughan 1-22-1828 (1-24-1828) Hr
Cook, Eliza to J. L. Lax 12-7-1859 Hr
Cook, Eliza to Josiah Harmon 7-26-1856 We
Cook, Elizabeth A. to George W. S. Coss 3-25-1858 We
Cook, Elizabeth L. to Samuel W. Ayers 1-2-1850 Sh
Cook, Elizabeth W. to Joel Lax 6-8-1838 Hn
Cook, Elizabeth to B. F. Hunt 10-29-1831 (11-3-1831) Hr
Cook, Elizabeth to David Patton 7-28-1830 (7-29-1830) G
Cook, Elizabeth to Garland Adams 8-11-1838 (8-16-1838) G
Cook, Elizabeth to J. P. Pritchard 10-13-1855 Cr
Cook, Elizabeth to Thomas Baker 3-4-1839 (3-5-1839) Ma
Cook, Elizabeth to Whitson Cooper 9-13-1856 (9-14-1856) G
Cook, Elsey to Isaac Rogers 3-22-1841 G
Cook, Emma to James A. Johnson 8-26-1863 (8-27-1863) Cr
Cook, Evelina to Alexander T. Cole 10-26-1850 (10-28-1850) Ma
Cook, Frances I. to T. E. Salisbury 8-8-1875 Hy
Cook, Frances to William Yarbroh 12-8-1857 (12-9-1857) T
Cook, Francis to J. R. Bradberry 5-16-1859 We
Cook, H. H. to J. F. Dixon 4-28-1861 We
Cook, Hannah Josephine to Wm. N. Fussell 7-23-1868 G
Cook, Harrett to John Lee 8-21-1856 Cr
Cook, Harriet to Charles Glass 12-25-1869 (12-28-1869) T
Cook, J. L. to S. J. Morris 1-16-1860 Cr
Cook, Jane L. (Mrs.) to Jacob L. Russell 12-26-1864 Sh
Cook, Jane to Calvin L. Lee 12-13-1852 Cr
Cook, Johanna to Philip Barron 11-25-1858 Sh
Cook, Judie B. to William Brown 7-18-1855 (7-19-1855) Ma
Cook, L. C. to A. M. Burns 9-9-1874 Dy
Cook, Lizzie to J. M. Jones ?-19-1878 (with Nov 1878) Dy
Cook, Lucinda C. to Moses E. Jones 1-25-1856 Cr
Cook, M. A. F. to W. T. Lamb 11-22-1851 (no return) F
Cook, M. E. to J. H. Dublen 5-2-1856 (no return) We
Cook, M. E. to Thomas Cook 10-28-1866 Hy
Cook, M. J. to John D. Dudley 4-30-1878 Dy
Cook, Mahuldah to John Marberry 12-2-1855 Be
Cook, Margaret E. to John W. Nichols 1-22-1850 (1-23-1850) G
Cook, Margaret E. to Albert J. Hartley 12-11-1856 (12-10?-1856) Sh
Cook, Margaret to Richard Cushing 4-14-1863 G
Cook, Margaret to William Dunn 2-14-1851 (2-16-1851) Hr
Cook, Margarett to Jeremiah Smith 10-4-1853 G
Cook, Margarett to Phillip McGrath 7-29-1851 Sh
Cook, Maria to W. F. Young 4-22-1850 Sh
Cook, Martha E. to James H. Dubb 5-6-1856 We
Cook, Martha G. to William A. Finch 7-13-1857 We
Cook, Martha J. to Alfred A. White 12-18-1862 We
Cook, Martha to Alfred Nunn 12-28-1868 G B
Cook, Martha to John W. Shinault 3-7-1856 (3-9-1856) Hr
Cook, Martha to Thomas Collins 9-6-1858 We
Cook, Martha to Wm. Roberson 1-16-1845 Cr
Cook, Mary A. to J. A. Right 11-5-1846 We
Cook, Mary A. to Jacob A. Wright 11-5-1846 We

Cook, Mary A. to M. R. Parrish 12-10-1856 Sh
Cook, Mary E. to Robert W. Aclin 3-26-1861 We
Cook, Mary Jane to Allen Cannady 11-16-1870 (11-17-1870) Ma
Cook, Mary to Henderson Burrow 11-15-1871 (no return) Cr
Cook, Mary to John C. Pigg 10-6-1838 Hn
Cook, Mary to Lion Hill 9-9-1831 (9-13-1831) O
Cook, May Ann to Ransom H. Bryan 12-17-1838 (12-18-1838) Ma
Cook, Mollie to Wiley Pope 10-27-1874 Dy
Cook, Nancy M. J. to Samuel Cole 2-17-1843 (2-21-1843) O
Cook, Nancy to Adam Sevier 12-5-1838 Ma
Cook, Nancy to John S. Harmon 1-20-1858 We
Cook, Pheba E. to Thomas C. Saddler 12-2-1857 We
Cook, Rebecca to Stephen Pearce 7-18-1853 G
Cook, Rebeccah to W. C. Pace 4-26-1865 Dy
Cook, Roberta to Dave Wilson 7-2-1878 (12-13-1878) L
Cook, Rodia to Jesse Jones 11-18-1831 Sh
Cook, S. E. to Harry Oliver 7-13-1863 (7-19-1863) O
Cook, Sabra Ann to William B. Waldran 2-13-1840 Sh
Cook, Salina Jane to Stephen A. Rushing 2-18-1867 Be
Cook, Sally to Watson Pridy 7-5-1831 (7-6-1831) G
Cook, Sarah A. to Gideon Smith 1-4-1869 Ma
Cook, Sarah J. to L. F. Henley 11-14-1871 (11-16-1871) L
Cook, Sarah Jane to William L. Ward 6-14-1847 F
Cook, Sarah L. to C. B. Mays 7-11-1866 (7-19-1866) Cr
Cook, Sarah S. to Henry D. Atkinson 11-20-1856 We
Cook, Sarah to Francis Trowell 8-12-1846 F
Cook, Sarah to James Cannon 9-17-1850 (9-18-1850) G
Cook, Sarah to Jasen W. Fussell 3-5-1867 (3-7-1867) Ma
Cook, Sarah to Jesse Cockrell 8-14-1861 O
Cook, Sophronia J. to Thomas Jennings 4-20-1881 L
Cook, Susannah to George Russell 7-11-1830 Ma
Cook, Tennessee Bell to Alfred Hughes 12-27-1877 (12-30-1877) L B
Cookburn?, Tabitha to William Reynolds 11-4-1830 Hr
Cooke, A. S. to John B. McFarland 3-4-1845 G
Cooke, American P. to John R. McCall 2-6-1843 Hn
Cooke, Louisa V. to Robert J. Hamby 3-5-1838 Hn
Cooke, Mariah to John Scott 2-27-1871 (3-2-1871) T
Cooke, Mela to Joshua P. Williams 11-21-1844 Hn
Cooke, Rebecca to Wesley Holland 12-10-1846 Hn
Cooke, S. J. to G. B. Lewis 2-19-1867 Hy
Cooke, Tennessee to James Blowers 8-29-1842 Sh
Cooker, Mary to Peter Ammen 10-17-1843 (no return) F
Cooksey, Elizabeth to Hiram Terry 11-3-1843 (11-5-1843) Hr
Cooksey, Jane to John Vaughan 3-2-1844 Hr
Cooksey, Mary to William Green 1-14-1847 Hn
Cooksey, Melissa to Archibald Pennington 11-16-1833 (11-17-1833) Hr
Cooksey, Rebecca to William Henly 11-19-1834 (11-20-1834) Hr
Cooley, Lydia A. to Joseph Lasswell 7-22-1860 We
Coolidge, Hannah to Clarence P. Ashbrook 12-10-1861 Sh
Cooly, A. M. to D. G. Campbell 3-4-1846 (no return) We
Cooly, Phebee to John Phifer 7-27-1855 Be
Cooly, Rebecca to Tedrick Ball 8-8-1844 Hn
Coon, Jane to Jerry Chambers 12-18-1874 Hy
Cooney, Ann to James Humphreys 12-30-1854 Sh
Coonrod, Sarah to Robert Clinton 3-8-1826 (3-9-1826) Hr
Coop, Annie L. to J. W. Hudson 11-13-1868 G
Coop, Jane to William L. Goodman 6-30-1831 G
Coop, Margaret E. to John B. Hay 1-7-1846 G
Coop, Mary M. to Aaron Sanders 12-27-1859 G
Coop, Sarah E. to Thomas Storer 12-23-1863 G
Coop, Sarah E. to Thomas Straer 12-23-1863 G
Coop, Sarah R. to William R. Nail 11-25-1850 (12-4-1850) G
Coope, Rachael to William Hendrick 11-7-1835 (11-12-1835) G
Coopender, Sarah to Hugh Blevins 1-18-1840 (1-19-1840) Ma
Cooper, A. E. to J. G. Dubois 10-9-1845 (10-10-1845) Hr
Cooper, Abgret to Simon Butler 4-6-1844 Cr
Cooper, Amanda J. to Richard Wagster 12-31-1857 We
Cooper, Amanda to Dave Smith 2-23-1870 Hy
Cooper, Amanda to J. W. Scrape 9-1-1870 G
Cooper, Angeline to W. S. Robins 10-23-1871 L
Cooper, Ann Eliza to John T. Postlethwaite 1-15-1857 Hn
Cooper, Ann to Elias Rogers 1-5-1851 (1-7-1851) O
Cooper, Arrotta to William Rowten 8-8-1867 Be
Cooper, Barbary A. to John M. Williams 11-18-1860 Hn
Cooper, Bell to Richard Morton 11-18-1873 Hy
Cooper, Bell to Wm. Estes 3-8-1870 (no return) Hy
Cooper, Bettie B. to Stephen G. Carnes 3-30-1869 F
Cooper, Caladonia to W. T. Harris 2-7-1874 T
Cooper, Catharine M. to Hiram B. Willoughby 2-3-1830 Hr
Cooper, Cealey to Henry Cooper 3-25-1846 F
Cooper, Charlotte to Isaac Adkisson 3-6-1843 (3-9-1843) T
Cooper, Charrity to Joshua Sanders 12-28-1846 (12-31-1846) G
Cooper, Corilla to William B. Chandler 5-21-1869 Cr
Cooper, Delana A. to Allen Moore 1-2-1861 G
Cooper, Dicy to N. J. Keating 2-2-1846 (no return) Cr
Cooper, Drucilla to John R. Bomar 9-19-1849 Hn
Cooper, Eliza E. to William Wade 11-29-1866 Be

Cooper, Eliza to George W. Tate 3-11-1835 Hr
Cooper, Elizabeth C. to E. A. Feezor 11-27-1867 (11-28-1867) T
Cooper, Elizabeth C. to Robert E. Myers 2-11-1863 Cr
Cooper, Elizabeth to James M. Ross? 9-29-1845 Be
Cooper, Elizabeth to Robert E. Myers 2-11-1863 Cr
Cooper, Elizabeth to Thomas M. Harrington 12-17-1863 Sh
Cooper, Elizer to John Stallings 1-24-1867 G
Cooper, Fannie H. to Samuel H. Broun 1-10-1860 (1-11-1860) Sh
Cooper, Frances J. to Gilbert Hamilton 9-17-1868 G B
Cooper, Francis E. to Charles Carter 8-25-1859 We
Cooper, Gelina to Charles Strickland 9-9-1849 Be
Cooper, Georgia to James Pettit 10-27-1857 Sh
Cooper, Harriet to Andrew Olds 12-24-1867 (12-31-1867) F B
Cooper, Isabella to George Bishop 3-3-1857 (3-4-1857) Ma
Cooper, J. M. to S. G. McCluney 9-5-1870 (9-13-1870) T
Cooper, Jane to J. J. Owenby 9-7-1857 Cr
Cooper, Jane to William M. Jack 11-15-1852 G
Cooper, Josephine C. to Orlando Brown 3-17-1859 Sh
Cooper, Julia Ann to John H. Robertson 9-15-1853 (9-17-1853) G
Cooper, L. to W. J. Fuqua 9-10-1864 (9-12-1864) Cr
Cooper, Laura A. to Thomas B. Reed 11-30-1858 Sh
Cooper, Lavina(Lavivian) to Levi Spurling 6-22-1827 (6-23-1827) Hr
Cooper, Lucinda to Baswell Billingsby 1-29-1850 We
Cooper, Lucy to Greene Young 1-3-1856 Cr
Cooper, Lucy to Wm. Bossie 8-10-1840 Cr
Cooper, Lula to W. A. Dinwiddie 6-18-1872 (no return) Cr
Cooper, Lydia to Thos. J. Williams 8-9-1864 (8-14-1864) O
Cooper, M. A. to J. B. Wren 10-22-1868 Cr
Cooper, M. A. to N. L. Lewis 11-11-1853 Hn
Cooper, M. A. to T. M. Simmons 6-20-1854 Be
Cooper, M. C. to William H. Gibson 5-23-1872 (no return) Dy
Cooper, M. E. to James Bessent 3-17-1879 (3-18-1879) Dy
Cooper, M. M. to E. Campbell 11-15-1844 Hn
Cooper, M. S. to James W. Pritchett 9-6-1862 (no return) Hn
Cooper, Malinda to Michael B. Martin 10-20-1849 (10-21-1849) T
Cooper, Margaret to S. A. Jackson 11-7-1857 Cr
Cooper, Margarett to James D. Harrison 12-5-1843 (12-12-1843) G
Cooper, Martha A. to James Ward 6-15-1844 (6-18-1844) G
Cooper, Martha A. to Wm. C. Robertson 10-28-1840 (10-29-1840) G
Cooper, Martha to Claborn Hicks 12-10-1843 Be
Cooper, Martha to David Dowling 5-7-1853 (5-19-1853) Ma
Cooper, Martha to John Fullerton 7-10-1866 (7-12-1866) Ma
Cooper, Martha to Milford Gage 1-27-1842 G
Cooper, Martha to Robert M. Webb 11-7-1848 (11-9-1848) G
Cooper, Martha to ____ Nelson 11-16-1858 Cr
Cooper, Mary A. to A. J. Caudle 8-1-1860 O
Cooper, Mary A. to John J. Wingo 5-8-1864 Cr
Cooper, Mary C. to E. Henry Sheldton 10-3-1843 (no return) F
Cooper, Mary E. to Bensom Needham 10-4-1860 G
Cooper, Mary E. to G. W. Whitson 5-6-1871 Dy
Cooper, Mary E. to Ichabud Moore 10-1-1845 G
Cooper, Mary E. to James M. Mathena 3-28-1863 (4-1-1863) O
Cooper, Mary E. to Timothy W. Ward 1-10-1849 G
Cooper, Mary F. to Americus F. Buckly 1-13-1860 We
Cooper, Mary F. to David N. Wilson 12-25-1869 (12-26-1869) Cr
Cooper, Mary F. to Thomas T. Trusty 8-21-1872 Dy
Cooper, Mary J. to Lazarus Williams 7-19-1858 Hn
Cooper, Mary J. to Moses R. Allen 12-23-1862 Cr
Cooper, Mary Jane to John Horton 12-18-1848 Ma
Cooper, Mary M. to Wm. F. Babb 3-26-1860 (4-3-1860) Hr
Cooper, Mary R. to Azariah Smotherman 5-3-1849 Hn
Cooper, Mary W. to John R. Pearson 9-14-1854 (no return) F
Cooper, Mary to Anderson Hunt 11-21-1860 (11-22-1868) T
Cooper, Mary to I. H. D. Webb 11-15-1848 G
Cooper, Mary to James K. P. Bond 11-17-1867 Be
Cooper, Mary to James McIntyre 3-20-1843 (3-23-1843) T
Cooper, Mary to Jerman W. Lea 6-29-1843 (7-4-1843) G
Cooper, Mary to John Lee 2-21-1879 (2-23-1879) L
Cooper, Mary to William Pierce 1-4-1865 Be
Cooper, Mima to Wm. Cooper 9-10-1843 We
Cooper, Missouria A. to Moses Myers 12-12-1864 (12-13-1864) Cr
Cooper, Nancy E. to Symon Baker 4-3-1860 G
Cooper, Nancy M. to A. A. Fergerson 3-9-1865 G
Cooper, Nancy S. to Nasthaniel H. Corley 10-27-1846 (11-28-1846) G
Cooper, Nancy to H. O. Sykes 7-3-1861 (7-4-1861) Hr
Cooper, Nancy to Isham Cooper 4-21-1847 (no return) Hn
Cooper, P. A. to J. B. Finch 11-30-1851 Cr
Cooper, Philadelphia F. to A. V. Ivey 5-1-1847 (5-2-1847) F
Cooper, Rebecca to Isaac Fowler 10-21-1843 (10-24-1843) G
Cooper, Rose to Scott Wilson 10-12-1864 Sh
Cooper, S. J. to F. C. Hogger 1-7-1869 Hy
Cooper, Sabra to Isaac Fowler 3-17-1840 G
Cooper, Sarah J. to John Foren 1-1-1866 Be
Cooper, Sarah Jane to John H. Perkins 12-28-1848 Be
Cooper, Sarah M. to William Bechtol 12-27-1867 (no return) L
Cooper, Sarah to H. B. Barnes 2-28-1863 Be
Cooper, Susan E. to Edwin J. Barham 11-8-1849 Hr

Cooper, Susan E. to William E. T. Atkins 4-20-1863 Hn
Cooper, Susan to William H. Ticer 11-4-1858 (1-28-1859) T
Cooper, Terissa S.? to Richard A. Barham 3-28-1848 (3-30-1848) Hr
Coopwood, E. J. E. to John Bowen 4-22-1851 Sh
Coopwood, Maggie Q. to Wm. J. Polk 4-28-1860 Sh
Coopwood, Mary Caroline to John P. McAlexander 12-12-1844 Sh
Coor(Coon), Caroline to Miles Elkins 7-31-1838 (8-2-1838) Hr
Coor, Nancy to Raiford Crawford 7-1-1839 (7-15-1839) Hr
Coor?, Zilphia to Benjamin Rose 7-20-1833 Hr
Cope, Elizabeth to R. W. Covington 3-29-1857 Hn
Cope, Elmina to J. W. Reynolds 9-19-1863 (9-28-1863) Dy
Cope, M. J. to D. A. Shaw 8-3-1866 (8-12-1866) Dy
Cope, N. A. to G. T. Bullock 2-27-1866 Hn
Cope, Sarah H. to James M. Bowden 12-18-1856 (no return) Hn
Cope, Susan to Thomas F. Petty 1-3-1861 (no return) Hn
Cope, W. M. to W. T. Cathcart 3-5-1879 (3-9-1879) Dy
Copeland, Bettie to Geo. Travis 1-28-1874 (1-29-1874) Dy
Copeland, Catherine C. to Newton J. Harris 1-7-1861 Ma
Copeland, Delia J. to James R. Fletcher 8-9-1856 (8-14-1856) G
Copeland, Deliah to Henry J. Grove 12-27-1864 (12-29-1864) Sh
Copeland, Eliza to Wilson Kendall 4-30-1843 Hn
Copeland, Ellen to Norflet F. Parrot 5-12-1856 Ma
Copeland, Julia Ann to Isaac Doak 9-27-1877 Dy
Copeland, Laura to John Fowlkes 12-29-1880 (12-30-1880) Dy
Copeland, Mary A. to William B. Harper 4-3-1851 (no return) Hn
Copeland, Mary E. to Wm. H. Massey 1-13-1855 (1-16-1855) Ma
Copeland, Minerva to Silas Lassiter 1-12-1855 (1-16-1855) Ma
Copeland, Mollie to John Copeland 5-8-1877 Dy
Copeland, Racal (Mrs.) to Hugh Webb 3-19-1846 G
Copeland, Rebecca H. to Edward W. Tatem 2-10-1849 F
Copher, Susan to Michie Acre 7-1-1843 Ma
Cophir, Lizzie to G. A. Rice 11-24-1867 Hy
Copin, Mary A. J. to W. W. Dudley 6-3-1854 We
Copland, M. to Blewford Gore 10-21-183_ (with 1837) O
Coplend, Susanna to Thomas N. Bottoms 11?-6-1871 (9?-6-1871) L
Coppadge, Caroline to Jack Moore 12-25-1868 Hy
Coppage, Alice to W. S. Curry 2-11-1868 (no return) Hy
Coppedge, Mary A. to L. A. Jones 2-7-1877 Hy
Coppedge, S. I. to L. C. Cherry 1-11-1875 (no return) Hy
Coppedge, Sallie J. to W. F. Black 4-16-1872 (no return) Hy
Coppedge, Silva to Ben Richmond 6-18-1869 (6-20-1869) F B
Copperthwaite, Julie to Charles H. Hammersly 7-18-1864 (7-24-1864) Sh
Cops, Catherine to M. R. Head 3-12-1856 (3-13-1856) G
Corbet, Hity to William Dowd 8-28-1854 We
Corbet, L. E. to James D. Roberson 11-24-1869 (11-25-1869) T
Corbet, Mary E. to Jesse G. Brown 9-23-1868 (9-24-1868) T
Corbett, Keziah to John Howell 6-23-1857 (6-30-1857) O
Corbett, Mahaly to John A. Shelton 8-30-1843 Sh
Corbett, Mary A. to Jesse B. Blackshere 12-3-1860 (12-6-1860) O
Corbett, Mary A. to John B. Owens 12-30-1847 Hn
Corbett, Nad to W. H. Spence 1-7-1862 Be
Corbett, V. L. to Edward V. Clifto 6-30-1868 (7-2-1868) O
Corbit, Lucy aNN to James Norrey 12-1-1846 Sh
Corbitt, Cynthia A. to Stephen McDuffie 12-6-1858 (12-8-1858) Sh
Corbitt, Elizabeth to James A. Evans 1-23-1851 Be
Corbitt, Elizabeth to Saml. T. Scott 7-16-1849 Be
Corbitt, Jane to Jesey Waldran 12-14-1852 (12-16-1852) Sh
Corbitt, Louisa C. to Alexander Bell 9-26-1858 Be
Corbitt, Mary to Charles Evans 11-13-1856 Be
Corbitt, Pollie (Mrs.) to Robert Hood 11-29-1856 (11-30-1856) Sh
Corburn, Winefred C. to Andrew C. Webb 5-25-1847 Hr
Corburn?, Elizabeth to John Mason 12-1-1834 (12-2-1834) Hr
Corcoran, Ellen to John Hayes 3-18-1863 Sh
Corden, Clara to Thomas C. Warren 7-16-1857 Cr
Corder, Margaret J. to W. H. Archer 11-27-1861 (11-28-1861) T
Corder, Susan to S. J. McCullough 12-3-1872 (12-5-1872) Cr
Cordes, Clara to H. A. Cordes 12-7-1864 Sh
Cordle, Jane to William Lakey 3-9-1856 Hy
Cordoza, Adelene to David Woodward 2-14-1844 Sh
Core, Avy to John D. Holley 4-20-1833 Hr
Core, Harriet to Clark Freeman 5-2-1843 (5-5-1843) Hr
Core, Lucinda to Reubin Core 7-21-1872 Hy
Core, Margaret to Wm. Mourning 1-7-1875 (no return) Hy
Core, Mary A. to John J. Mann 2-4-1863 (no return) Hy
Core, Sarah to Joseph Fleming 9-16-1854 (9-21-1854) Hr
Corella, Mary to James Bringanello 1-27-1855 (1-28-1855) Sh
Corely, Martha to H. C. Wherten 2-1-1844 Cr
Corgell, Aby A. to W. P. Smart 8-10-1854 We
Corisar?, Eliz. Ann to Thomas L. Angus 10-12-1846 (10-13-1846) T
Coritt, Mary to John Wilkes 10-31-1855 Cr
Corlern, Mary to John M. Garrett 9-10-1863 Mn
Corlern, Sarah M. to Thomas J. Goode 9-10-1863 Mn
Corles, Anny to Pietro Pulmigino 7-5-1861 (7-7-1861) Sh
Corley, Jane to Geo. Fowlkes 1-6-1876 (1-13-1876) Dy
Corley, Martha J. to John A. Williams 3-3-1845 (3-6-1845) L
Corley, Mary E. to A. S. Hart 1-3-1855 (3-30-1855) G
Corley, Mary Jane to William Hornbuckle 2-5-1864 (5-30-1864) Cr

Corley, Mary Jane to Wm. Hornbuckle 2-5-1864 (no return) Cr
Corley, Patsy A. to W. A. Turner 12-27-1858 (1-22-1859) G
Corley, R. A. to J. H. Blakemore 7-27-1878 (7-28-1878) Dy
Corley, S. E. to R. A. Wagster 2-28-1867 Dy
Corley, Sarah E. to Joseph M. Terrell 8-3-1863 G
Corley, Sarah J. to Lycurgus Thompson 2-9-1860 G
Corley, Sarah J. to William H. Thompson 12-27-1858 G
Corley, Willy to William J. Featherston 1-8-1845 (1-9-1845) G
Cormick, Eliza to Thomas Grady 1-8-1857 Sh
Cornegys, Katie to John Conner 12-18-1878 Hy
Cornelia, T. to Thomas Blackburn 6-18-1858 Sh
Cornelius, Bella to Thomas B. Taylor 11-11-1863 Hy
Cornelius, Cornelia to T. M. Dupree 2-8-1854 Sh
Cornelius, Isabella to J. H. Hendren 1-13-1874 (no return) Hy
Cornelius, Matilda to Win Adams 7-2-1827 (7-4-1827) Hr
Cornelius, Nancy to Hugh Shaw 9-26-1827 (9-28-1827) Hr
Cornelius, Sally Ann to Jessee Fletcher 11-17-1838 (11-18-1838) Hr
Cornelius, Vina to John H. Robertson 11-4-1832 (11-6-1832) Hr
Cornell, Mollie to Jake Pierson 12-27-1872 (1-11-1873) L B
Cornell, Nelly E. to Jesse K. Williams 6-29-1854 We
Corner, Matilda C. to W. R. Ring 3-25-1861 (3-29-1861) O
Cornnell, Frances M. to James J. Robinson 3-15-1853 Sh
Cornton, Priscilla to Edward Shuffey 12-26-1867 L B
Cornwell, Emma J. to J. L. Williamson 6-22-1858 Sh
Cornwell, M. F. to John N. Harbin 4-7-1862 (4-8-1862) Sh
Correll, Alice to J. A. Rose 11-9-1881 (11-14-1881) L
Correll, F. to Fredrick Hock 10-1-1858 (9?-4-1858) Sh
Correthers, Laura A. to James Tucker 12-5-1857 (12-8-1857) T
Corsort, Sally to Weight Price 1-11-1830 (1-17-1830) Ma
Corss, Henrettia to John Burrell 2-15-1873 (2-16-1873) T
Corum, Angeline to Benjamin T. Pulliam 3-26-1842 (3-27-1842) O
Corum, Elizabeth D. to M. H. Huddleston 8-27-1863 (8-28-1863) O
Corum, H. to J. H. Douglas 1-11-1868 O
Corum, Isabella to James R. Hale 11-16-1845 (11-18-1845) O
Corum, M. D. to Almus Domingus 9-4-1875 (9-6-1875) O
Corum, Margaret to John Routon 1-17-1859 (1-19-1859) O
Corum, Mary to John B. Hale 11-11-1851 (11-12-1851) O
Corum, S. E. to J. N. Hudson 2-20-1871 O
Corvin, Lizzie to James McCarroll 3-7-1873 Dy
Cosby, Elizabeth to Columbus West 4-30-1854 Hn
Cosby, Jane Ann to James C. Lanier 5-16-1854 (5-17-1854) T
Cosby, Margarett to Messer Norton 1-6-1829 Hr
Cosby, Mary to M. D. Pate 1-10-1867 Hr
Cosby, Sarah T. to Geo. W. Doyle 9-29-1860 (9-30-1860) Hr
Cose, Alsey to Beverly Fields 11-5-1870 (no return) Hy
Cossett, M. E. to Sam'l Kurkendall 5-24-1864 Sh
Cossett, Mary A. to John W. Base? 8-21?-1843 (9-5-1843) F
Cossett, Mary E. to G. S. Russell 12-3-1856 Hn
Costello, Anne to Robt. Sculley 3-5-1862 Sh
Costello, Bridget to James Lyncg 12-2-1862 Sh
Costello, Johanna to Michael Lonalgan 9-30-1856 Sh
Costello, Margaret to Edward Lester 9-28-1848 Sh
Costen, H. A. to Slarter Vaughn 5-25-1856 We
Coster, Motherlinda (Mrs.) to Jerome Rogers 2-5-1865 (2-7-1864) Sh
Costi, Mary to Simone Pierone 9-19-1864 Sh
Costillo, Elizabeth to Wm. B. Bellfield 12-26-1861 Sh
Costilo, Margaret to Patrick Dugin 10-18-1862 Hn
Coten, Elizabeth (Mrs.) to A. W. Malone 12-20-1866 Hy
Cothan, Mary M. to Albert Long 2-3-1868 (no return) Dy
Cotheran, A. L. to S. M. Bell 2-17-1874 (2-18-1874) T
Cotheran, Elizabeth to Richard H. Abbott 10-16-1855 Sh
Cotheran, Mary Jane to Lewis Harris 3-6-1872 (3-7-1872) T
Cotherin, Ann to Frank Smith 12-2-1869 (12-3-1869) T
Cothern, Sallie to Robert Freeman 9-5-1870 (9-7-1870) Dy
Cotherun, Eldora to Saml. Polk 1-5-1870 T
Cothram, Mary to J. S. Mickleberry 11-30-1841 (12-2-1841) F
Cothran, Ann E. to V. J. Smith 2-20-1863 (2-24-1863) Dy
Cothran, Jane to D. T. Holloway 7-16-1866 (7-18-1866) F
Cothran, Louisa to Jonathan Fawlk 1-17-1848 (1-20-1848) F
Cothran, Mary to Isaac Crawley 2-8-1873 (2-9-1873) T
Cothran, Mollie to Sam Strange 6-18-1874 T
Cothran, Rebecca B. to Edmond S. Jackson 11-30-1866 (12-4-1866) F
Cothran, S. to Tobert Elbertson 2-8-1838 F
Cothran, Sarah J. to Curtis Harris 5-27-1854 (no return) F
Cothrel?, Jane to Lewis Anderson 9-20-1883 (9-24-1883) L
Cotner, Emily J. to Miles Graves 9-27-1853 Hr
Cotner, Mary (Mrs.) to Harris Bailey 5-5-1852 (no return) F
Cotner, S. E. to R. M. Koonce 1-12-1871 F
Cotner, Sarah to John Upshaw 5-5-1845 Hn
Cottam, Amanda M. B. Moorney 1-28-1864 (1-29-1864) Dy
Cotten, Ann to Walter Turner 12-30-1874 T
Cotten, Celia to Jacob Wilson 3-13-1866 (8-27-1866) T
Cotten, Fannie to Jason Cotten 12-26-1868 T
Cotten, Sarah Carolin to Joseph Henry Dunham 12-12-1848 T
Cotter, Harriet to Thomas Pender 4-13-1874 Hy
Cotter, Kisza to Sam Weddle 12-23-1877 Hy
Cotter, Silvy to Hanibell Evans 11-20-1868 Hy

Cotter, Sophia to Joyner Harris 3-9-1873 Hy
Cotter, Tobitha J. to Thos. N. Cotter 1-11-1848 (1-12-1848) F
Cottingham, E. to R. C. Parker 12-12-1847 Be
Cottingham, Maryann to John M. Elmore 3-9-1843 Be
Cottingham, Polly Ann to John T. Taylor 3-9-1845 Be
Cottingham, Sally to W. H. Taylor 10-12-1842 Be
Cottingham, Susan to Michael Click 2-22-1853 Be
Cotton, E. to D. W. Benton 4-24-1842 Be
Cotton, Frances S. to Jessee Dewberry 6-2-1860 (6-3-1860) G
Cotton, Margaret E. to Wm. J. Kents 12-18-1852 (12-21-1852) T
Cotton, Martha to Britton Hines 1-27-1855 Sh
Cotton, Mary Ann to William D. Mays 12-11-1837 Sh
Cotton, Mary E. to F. M. Wright 10-26-1844 (10-29-1844) F
Cotton, Mary E. to John S. Butram 11-18-1873 O
Cotton, Mary J. to Thomas Parker 7-28-1853 Be
Cotton, Mary to Robt. Dickerson 6-22-1867 (6-23-1867) T
Cotton, Nancy to Saml. P. Bernard 2-13-1854 T
Cotton, Rachel to Geo. Elam 7-2-1870 T
Cotton, Sallie to Daniel Hill 6-8-1872 (6-9-1872) T
Cotton, Sally A. to William C. Smith 6-3-1847 (6-10-1847) F
Cotton, Sarah Jane to M. D. L. F. Caswell 5-13-1842 Sh
Cottrell, Susan E. to Luther N. Pankey 3-9-1864 Hy
Couch, Caroline M. to Washington G. Pass 9-17-1843 Sh
Couch, Caroline to W. J. Green 6-18-1854 Cr
Couch, Evalina Pantillie? to Harvey Hughes 5-15-1843 T
Couch, Jennie to C. W. Peach 3-17-1863 Sh
Couch, Martha to John D. Davis 10-3-1849 (no return) Cr
Couch, Nancy F. to J. W. Thomas 6-22-1861 (6-25-1861) Sh
Couch, Rebecca to Tilman A. Crisp 4-8-1848 (4-9-1848) Hr
Couch, Sarah A. to McDonald Graves 7-11-1859 Cr
Coulter, Bettie to J. P. Harris 10-3-1869 G
Coulter, Cornelia H. to Geo. W. Rowlett 3-21-1861 (3-22-1861) Sh
Coulter, E. F. to S. F. Coulter 11-22-1859 (11-23-1859) Sh
Coulter, Julia F. to Wm. L. Montgomery 1-9-1855 (1-11-1855) Sh
Coulter, Martha to Moses Hudgens 4-13-1867 (no return) Hn B
Coulter, Mary S. to William Abel 8-9-1853 (no return) F
Council, Araminta to L. C. Ross 12-3-1847 Hn
Council, Temperance to Ephraim Burkitt 3-7-1840 Be
Council, Zoda to John Perry 5-7-1867 Hn
Council?, Mollie to William Yarwood 1-8-1883 (1-9-1883) L
Counsal, Alta to Leon Adams 5-21-1846 (6-1-1846) G
Counts, Elizabeth to Samuel (James?) Cox 7-1-1836 Sh
Counts, Mary to Stephen Speer 2-25-1834 Sh
Counts, Sarah A. to Robert R. Crawford 1-12-1859 Hn
Countz, Louia to F. Strohwig 4-20-1858 Sh
Coursey, Auvenia Tennessee to John O. Ellis 5-7-1856 (5-8-1856) O
Coursey, Julia Ann to John J. Wilkerson 9-14-1860 Hn
Courtley, Martha J. to Seth Hall 5-18-1864 Dy
Courtney, Jane to John S. Moore 12-10-1841 Hn
Courtney, Susan L. to G. R. Edwards 2-1-1864 (2-3-1864) Dy
Courts, Amanda to James Boden 8-24-1843 Hn
Courts, Ann E. to William A. Morgan 6-23-1839 Hn
Courts, Anna to Walter B. Grizzurd? 9-7-1858 Hn
Courts, Frances M. to William Parker 3-12-1839 (no return) Hn
Courts, Mary Alice to James A. Grizzard 10-24-1866 Hn
Courts, Susan M. to Hiram F. Cummins 8-7-1858 Hn
Cousar?, Sarah Ann to James Chalmers Moore 11-5-1842 (11-8-1842) T
Cousins, M. J. to R. A. Carnell 11-11-1876 (11-12-1876) L
Couster, Annie to Ernst Wise 4-15-1851 Sh
Couts?, Cynthia to Bradford Smith 3-24-1842 T
Cove, Nancy to Jordan White 1-29-1867 (2-5-1867) F B
Covington, Ann to Alfred Henderson 12-8-1869 (12-9-1869) Cr
Covington, Ann to Wilson Moon 9-19-1842 Ma
Covington, Betty to Luther Grenade 12-25-1865 (no return) Hn
Covington, Callie to J. H. Goodwin 11-18-1867 Hn
Covington, Catherine D. to Alonza C. Biglowe 12-17-1862 (no return) We
Covington, Clementine T. to Samuel T. Jackson 1-13-1859 We
Covington, Elizabeth H. to Nathan W. McNeal 12-15-1858 Cr
Covington, Jane to G. S. McKensie 10-8-1856 Hn
Covington, Jennie to Thos. W. Brinkley 10-18-1870 (10-20-1870) F
Covington, Julia A. to F. H. Henderson 12-11-1844 (no return) Cr
Covington, Julia to William Price 10-24-1883 (10-30-1883) L
Covington, Louisa to M. W. Shepherd 9-30-1869 Hy
Covington, Lovis to Ransom W. Owen 10-10-1843 (no return) Hn
Covington, Lucinday Ann to John S. Clark 11-2-1838 (11-4-1838) Hr
Covington, M. L. to D. Barcroft 10-1-1873 Hy
Covington, Malinda to Terrell White 4-14-1868 (4-16-1868) L
Covington, Martha J. to Hugh W. Swayne 10-8-1858 Cr
Covington, Mary E. to Luke Thomas 11-19-1870 (11-24-1870) Cr
Covington, Mary E. to S. C. Caudele 11-27-1855 We
Covington, Mary M. to Rufus Elmore 12-23-1875 L
Covington, Mary to William Price 6-28-1882 (no return) L
Covington, Nancy P. to Benjamin M. Huggins 2-12-1857 Hn
Covington, Nannie to A. F. Shepherd 4-1-1874 Hy
Covington, Patty to York? Maxwell 12-25-1865 (no return) Hn
Covington, Polly to Jonathan Steepleton 4-2-1844 Ma
Covington, Sarah J. to James F. Spears 12-30-1843 (1-4-1844) Hr

Covington, Sophia L. to James Travis 1-12-1852 Hn
Covington, Susan Jane to Kincheon L. Rose 6-5-1841 (6-10-1841) Hr
Covinton, T. H. to Jeremiah T. Rodgers 9-22-1841 Cr
Covinton, Dicy A. to Andrew Davis Flower 2-19-1869 T
Cowan, A. C. to L. M. Caldwell 1-10-1849 Hn
Cowan, Ann M. to Simeon Horne 4-27-1841 T
Cowan, Frances J. to S. W. Sharp 9-3-1851 Hn
Cowan, Letta to Henry Caldwell 12-27-1867 Hn
Cowan, Lizzie to J. W. Davis 7-26-1884 (7-28-1884) L
Cowan, Lucinda to James L. McDougal 3-22-1838 (no return) Hn
Cowan, Margaret J. to James G. English 2-11-1850 (2-12-1850) G
Cowan, Margarett A. to Hiram R. A. McCorkle 11-14-1849 (11-?-1849) G
Cowan, Mariah to William H. Henley 9-9-1840 F
Cowan, Mary F. to J. M. Abel 12-24-1867 (12-26-1867) F
Cowan, Mollie A. to G. W. Brannon 12-11-1862 (12-16-1862) F
Cowan, N. E. to C. C. Thomas 7-15-1867 G
Cowan, Sarah R. to Leander B. Venable 5-25-1843 Hn
Cowan?, Ann G. to A. H. Smiley 5-13-1846 Hn
Cowans, Mary M. to James W. Hays 6-2-1844 Hn
Coward, E. J. L. to James P. McFarland 2-3-1859 Hn
Coward, Elizabeth to Samuel Pettijohn 12-13-1837 Sh
Coward, Frances Eliza to Jno. Mesina Harding 12-22-1855 (1-2-1856) T
Coward, Harriet to Henry Colman 12-23-1867 (12-27-1867) T
Coward, Louisa to Nathan Adkins 10-22-1874 (10-23-1874) T
Coward, Mary to Charles A. Weaver 12-28-1869 T
Coward, Susan to Joseph Fransiolo 6-16-1863 Sh
Cowardin, Mary E. to Thomas C. Bayliss 9-15-1853 We
Cowden, Annie to H. H. Higbee 11-30-1863 Sh
Cowel, Mary E. (Mrs.) to Joseph Woodard 2-11-1867 L
Cowel, Matilda R. B. to Richard R. Woodard 4-26-1878 (no return) L
Cowell, Elizabeth to A. C. Olds 4-4-1853 (no return) L
Cowell, Mary C. to Alfred Goforth 9-27-1860 Dy
Cowell, Mary E. to Eugene E. Gookin 1-7-1874 Hy
Cowell, Nancy H. to Charles T. Stokes 8-15-1868 (no return) L
Cowell, Naoma to George W. Devinport 11-28-1843 Be
Cowell, Rachel A. to Gideon Olds 1-2-1861 L
Cowell, Sarah A. to Gideon Olds 1-25-1857 (no return) L
Cowell, Sarah Jane to R. B. Travis 2-10-1861 Be
Cowell, Susan E. to C. A. Cole 2-3-1856 Be
Cowgil, Caroline (Mrs.) to Wm. Rails 12-30-1863 Sh
Cowgill, Caroline (Mrs.) to William Wales 12-30-1863 (1-7-1864) Sh
Cowherd, Julian to Edward Jones 4-12-1836 W
Cowrie?, Elizabeth to W. W. Whitson 4-13-1881 L
Cowry (or Conry), Catharine to Thomas Ryan 2-25-1851 (2-27-1851) Sh
Cowsert, V. A. to S. H. Bruff 5-24-1866 (5-27-1866) O
Cowthen, Martha A. to O. B. Corthan 10-8-1854 Cr
Cox, A. C. to James F. Taylor 9-21-1869 (9-23-1869) Cr
Cox, Amanda E. to Ellis Scales 1-23-1863 (1-29-1863) Cr
Cox, Amanda to B. J. Sherron 1-7-1859 Hr
Cox, Amanda to B. S. Shearon 7-11-1860 (7-15-1860) Hr
Cox, Bettie to Brittan Spence 2-24-1868 (2-26-1868) Ma
Cox, Bridget to Thomas Henry 5-27-1861 Sh
Cox, Capy to Salmon Call 5-5-1857 Hn
Cox, Catharine to Joseph Correll 8-28-1857 We
Cox, Catharine to Monrow Frogan 8-15-1857 Be
Cox, Catherine to Pat Maginty 5-8-1863 Sh
Cox, Celia to John T. Ford 4-28-1845 Cr
Cox, Diannah to Thomas Whitesides 9-20-1866 Ma
Cox, Dolly to Benton Wofford 3-28=1848 Hn
Cox, E. C. to J. M. C. Coffman 9-18-1866 (no return) Hn
Cox, Eddie C. to Jesse H. Lowry 10-30-1851 Cr
Cox, Edin to Dudly Pritchard 2-6-1841 Cr
Cox, Eldiss to Isaiah Macon 3-1-1844 Hr
Cox, Eliza A. to Alvay J. Mitchell 1-15-1855 (no return) F
Cox, Eliza Ann to James W. Weatherford 6-16-1836 Sh
Cox, Eliza E. to James M. Boykin 12-6-1861 (12-8-1861) Ma
Cox, Eliza Jane to John J. Martin 4-1-1844 T
Cox, Eliza to James A. Barr 7-21-1841 Cr
Cox, Eliza to John jr. Rogers 10-28-1835 (10-29-1835) Hr
Cox, Eliza to Joseph Roper 12-30-1840 Cr
Cox, Elizabeth to Christian Krauss 10-29-1855 Sh
Cox, Elizabeth to F. F. Eason 12-20-1853 Cr
Cox, Elizabeth to J. M. Huff 12-9-1850 We
Cox, Elizabeth to John F. Jackson 12-23-1840 Hn
Cox, Elizabeth to Young Bradford 11-24-1846 (11-25-1846) Ma
Cox, Emily to John Whorton 12-4-1879 Hy
Cox, Fannie E. to James Lamb 1-14-1863 Sh
Cox, Fannie to John Newburn 12-29-1871 Hy
Cox, Frances to N. S. Lockard 12-10-1884 L
Cox, Frances to Wm. P. Anderson 1-15-1870 (1-16-1870) Ma
Cox, Granville M. L. to John F. Canada 9-13-1859 (no return) Hy
Cox, H. E. to H. D. Street 12-26-1844 Hn
Cox, J. A. J. to R. M. Midgett 2-12-1880 L
Cox, Jane to Shepherd Hunter 1-30-1873 (no return) Hy
Cox, Jemima to Philip Brantly 7-9-1833 (7-11-1833) Hr
Cox, Jimmie Ann to Haywood C. Stoker 4-18-1870 (4-19-1870) Cr
Cox, Julia to Wm. Glosson 6-30-1846 Cr

Cox, L. A. to C. F. Greenfield 9-26-1870 (9-27-1870) Cr
Cox, Latitica A. to John W. French 7-21-1866 (7-22-1866) Cr
Cox, Laura E. to John A. Laney 9-12-1871 (9-14-1871) Ma
Cox, Lavina to John Ludwick 7-17-1865 T
Cox, Lucinda Mary to W. B. Thornton 1-29-1857 Be
Cox, M. C. to W. L. White 2-15-1886 (2-16-1886) L
Cox, M. E. to G. A. Young 7-15-1880 L
Cox, Margaret C. to Edwin E. Rennolds 1-11-1866 Hn
Cox, Margaret C. to John Huber 6-22-1859 Sh
Cox, Margaret H. to David H. James 2-12-1849 (2-13-1849) G
Cox, Margaret H. to Samuel Reed 11-3-1853 G
Cox, Margaret to David Allison 5-16-1828 (5-22-1828) Hr
Cox, Margaret to Lemmon B. Gay 12-22-1852 (12-29-1852) Hr
Cox, Margaret to Richard Hawkins 12-20-1874 Hy
Cox, Maria to W. J. Clements 4-8-1858 (4-15-1858) Sh
Cox, Marion B. to T. B. Johnson 6-15-1856 (6-16-1856) Sh
Cox, Martha to John Stafford 6-19-1850 Cr
Cox, Martha to Ruben Persey 9-26-1856 Cr
Cox, Marthene to James Nowell 11-1-1849 Be
Cox, Mary A. E. to Isaac H. Mason 9-21-1846 (9-24-1846) Ma
Cox, Mary Ann to John B. Scudder 6-23-1857 (6-24-1857) Sh
Cox, Mary E. to James B. Thornton 4-21-1870 F
Cox, Mary E. to John B. Stokes 11-28-1841 Cr
Cox, Mary J. to Charles Kee 4-14-1849 Cr
Cox, Mary Jane to Alvin Bishop 10-15-1841 (10-21-1841) Hr
Cox, Mary Jane to John J. Lambert 7-12-1858 (7-14-1858) Hr
Cox, Mary Jane to Perry Dawson 10-14-1872 (10-16-1872) T
Cox, Mary Jane to Wm. King 1-21-1853 Cr
Cox, Mary S. to James M. Martin 8-14-1861 (8-15-1861) Cr
Cox, Mary to Colemon Brewer 6-30-1843 Be
Cox, Mary to Daniel H. Trout 10-15-1870 (10-16-1870) Dy
Cox, Mary to James H. Rhodes 3-12-1832 Hr
Cox, Mary to James M. Horton? 8-?-1861 (8-15-1861) Cr
Cox, Mary to John Drake 1-15-1861 Sh
Cox, Mary to T. W. Scott 11-7-1865 Mn
Cox, Mary to William Hicks 3-14-1828 (3-18-1828) Hr
Cox, Matilda to Nineviah Glidwell 7-21-1847 (7-22-1847) Ma
Cox, Mattie to J. D. Newman 12-5-1878 L
Cox, Minerva to J. F. Briggance 12-24-1867 G
Cox, Minnie to Richard Key 11-25-1856 Cr
Cox, Nan to Henry Winfield 6-26-1869 (6-25?-1869) F B
Cox, Nancy C. to Kinchen Taylor 1-27-1850 Be
Cox, Nancy C. to Robert A. Tucker 3-22-1875 L
Cox, Nancy to Allen F. Cunningham 2-14-1848 G
Cox, Nancy to H. H. Wesser 8-12-1841 Be
Cox, Nancy to James M. Bradberry 12-20-1843 Cr
Cox, Nancy to Wm. Russell 11-29-1857 Cr
Cox, Nelly(Ellen) to William Hughes 9-28-1829 (10-2-1829) Hr
Cox, Parthenia Ann Melisa to James Norfleet Martin 7-8-1844 T
Cox, Pheriby to Mark Cole 9-4-1853 Be
Cox, Rachel to Ludson Palmer 12-20-1866 Hn B
Cox, Rebecca to J. H. Swindle 1-15-1863 Hn
Cox, Rebecca to William Galloway 12-20-1837 (12-21-1837) Hr
Cox, Sapponia to Needham Moore 7-29-1843 (7-31-1843) G
Cox, Sarah Ann to John M. Faucett 3-26-1853 (3-29-1853) Hr
Cox, Sarah C. to Richard Hendrix 12-12-1864 Mn
Cox, Sarah Frances to William D. Walton 2-12-1844 (2-13-1844) T
Cox, Sarah J. to B. Farmer 5-13-1861 Hn
Cox, Sarah to John A. Lanier 12-15-1856 (12-18-1856) Hr
Cox, Sarah to William Brown 7-22-1834 (7-24-1834) Hr
Cox, Sarah to William Peck 2-19-1861 G
Cox, Sidney to A. H. Bowers 2-2-1856 (2-4-1856) Sh
Cox, Sillah?(Lillah?) to George Tipler 3-24-1841 (3-25-1841) Hr
Cox, Sophia to J. L. Key 11-21-1865 Hn
Cox, Sophronia A. to William F. Bowden 6-9-1859 Hn
Cox, Susan A. to R. M. Callahan 1-28-1860 (1-29-1860) Hr
Cox, Susan E. to William W. Barns 11-28-1868 (11-29-1868) Cr
Cox, Susan to G. W. Hudson 12-17-1859 (12-15?-1859) Hr
Cox, Susan to John McDonald 2-8-1836 Hr
Cox, Susan to Shareons Taylor 1-27-1846 Cr
Cox, Susie A. to R. C. Wilson 5-31-1879 (6-1-1879) L
Cox, Tabitha J. to Franklin Haley 9-4-1858 (9-5-1858) Hr
Cox, Tersey E. to Thos. Chromate 10-27-1864 Cr
Cox, Thena Jane to George L. Ousler 8-13-1850 (8-14-1850) G
Cox, Tiercy Lizzie to J. W. Mason 1-19-1870 G
Cox, Unicy to M. V. Creed 6-27-1859 O
Cox, Vashti to Moses J. Mashburn 4-7-1828 (4-10-1828) Hr
Cox, Virginia to Josiah Franklin 4-2-1860 (no return) Hy
Coyle, Mary A. to John Cannovan 2-1-1858 Sh
Coyne, Anna to James W. Smith 8-7-1863 Sh
Coyne, Bridget to John Connally 6-28-1861 (7-1-1861) Sh
Coyne, Margaret to Patrick Kyle 9-12-1857 (9-13-1857) Sh
Coyne, Mary Ann to P. M. Bachman 12-8-1862 Sh
Cozart, Elizabeth to Benjamin West 4-18-1831 Ma
Cozart, Elizabeth to Priestley Gooch 8-13-1870 (8-14-1870) Cr
Cozart, Fannie to I. N. Jetton 1-12-1870 (no return) Hy
Cozart, Helen S. to James B. Pittman 3-24-1869 (3-25-1869) Ma *

Cozart, Julia A. to Joseph T. Williamson 4-8-1856 (4-9-1856) Ma
Cozart, Maggie J. to Ephraim McIlwain 12-4-1866 (12-5-1866) Ma
Cozart, Mahulda to William H. Marlow 12-25-1852 (12-26-1852) Ma
Cozart, Mollie to Anthony Furgeon 6-21-1868 Hy
Cozart, Nancy Ann to Sidney Gray 2-10-1842 Ma
Cozart, Susan to Kinchen Hathaway 12-5-1859 (12-8-1859) Ma
Cozby, Elizabeth J. to H. Scruggs Hays 6-4-1856 (6-5-1856) Hr
Cozby, Frances to Asa Robinson 12-29-1833 Hr
Cozby, Jane to Buckner Jones 2-28-1829 Hr
Cozby, Jane to William W. Glidewell 9-10-1851 (9-28-1851) Hr
Cozby, Lotty to Samuel Henson 9-21-1849 (9-23-1849) Hr
Cozby, Mary J. to Edwin Fish 8-13-1855 Hr
Cozby, Mary to Mathew Gillaspie 8-29-1835 Hr
Cozby, Semon to Jonathan McKennie 3-31-1836 Hr
Crabb, Martha E. to J. J. Allen 10-24-1871 (no return) Cr
Crabb, Martha to James Henry 8-29-1844 Be
Crabb, Susan P. to Moses C. Graves 8-22-1852 Be
Crabtree, E. J. to Thos. J. Patten 1-19-1858 (no return) We
Crabtree, Emily to William P. Wilson 12-28-1858 Hn
Crabtree, Mary Ann to William A. McCuiston 12-28-1858 Hn
Crabtree, Mary to James Kindrick 4-13-1838 F
Crabtree, Misanies to Alexander Ridgeway 7-22-1829 (7-23-1829) O
Crabtree, S. E. to S. P. Wirt 5-4-1868 (5-5-1868) F
Craddac, Melinda to George Stafford 4-12-1856 (4-13-1856) G
Craddick, Frances to James Wales 10-1-1859 (10-2-1859) Sh
Craddoc, E. D. to J. H. Clay 5-21-1873 (5-22-1873) Cr
Craddock, Elizabeth Jane to William L. Morrow 11-21-1867 G
Craddock, Mary to Prier W. Nobles 7-18-1849 G
Craddock, Sarah J. to James Porter 10-14-1833 (12-16-1833) G
Craddock, Susanna Jane to John Irvin Wales 9-26-1859 (9-27-1859) Sh
Cradle, Susan M. to William M. Gray 12-13-1838 Hn
Crafford, Nancy S. to Green R. Manley 12-23-1841 G
Craft, Eliza J. to Abnur Blair 10-21-1853 (no return) F
Craft, Elizabeth to Andrew J. Nevill 2-9-1846 (2-11?-1846) Hr
Craft, Jessie Marie to James Sands 1-13-1853 Sh
Craft, Judith L. to James W. Matheny 2-23-1870 (no return) Cr
Craft, Julianna E. to W. L. C. Williams 12-9-1850 (12-12-1850) Hr
Craft, Marina to Henry C. Terrell 7-2-1855 Sh
Craft, Martha to C. H. Primm? 8-16-1863 (10-4-1863) Sh
Craft, Mary Ann to Thomas Williams 1-30-1860 (2-1-1860) Hr
Craft, Sally Ann to William New 9-21-1846 (9-22-1846) Hr
Crafter, Sarah L. to James T. Gilkey 1-11-1870 (1-13-1870) Cr
Crafton, Elizabeth to Joe Rogers 4-10-1869 G B
Crafton, L. A. to John H. Parker 3-13-1865 G
Crafton, Lucy to Thos. Cunningham 7-24-1850 (7-25-1850) G
Crafton, Margarett J. to J. T. Thompson 12-23-1858 G
Crafton, Martha M. to Benjamin W. Murphy 8-25-1835 (8-27-1835) G
Crafton, Mary W. to W. R. Thomas 10-19-1865 G
Crafton, Mary to James Ham 10-18-1851 (10-21-1851) G
Crafton, N. L. to L. J. Law 2-21-1869 G
Crafton, Sarah P. to Harris J. Furgerson 8-18-1855 (8-19-1855) G
Crafton, Sarah T. to J. C. Coleman 12-8-1868 (12-10-1868) O
Crafton, Sarah W. to Henry King 3-19-1842 (3-24-1842) G
Crafton, Sarah to Watson Forest 11-?-1834 G
Crafton, Texana to James Hill 11-4-1867 G B
Crague, Elizabeth to Henry Terry 2-7-1867 O
Craig, Amanda to Elisha A. Webb 7-7-1858 (7-27?-1858) L
Craig, Anna F. to Thomas J. Stroud 5-19-1864 Hn
Craig, Caroline to John Z. Hurt 12-4-1865 (12-6-1865) T
Craig, E. L. to David Dotsen 10-1-1867 (10-2-1867) Dy
Craig, Easter D. to William Bowen 2-4-1833 (2-7-1833) G
Craig, Eliza Jane to James Turner 1-28-1864 (no return) Dy
Craig, Elizabeth to James Babb 3-6-1831 G
Craig, Elizabeth to John L. Guy 1-9-1862 O
Craig, Elizabeth to Michell G. Hilliard 6-7-1838 F
Craig, Elvira to William G. Adams 11-7-1842 G
Craig, Frances C. to R. S. Hill 9-13-1862 (9-14-1862) F
Craig, Georgiana to A. W. Wright 2-22-1870 F
Craig, Isabella C. to James M. Winsett 1-24-1860 Hn
Craig, Julian to Silas Brown? 7-22-1869 (7-25-1869) Dy
Craig, Lou to J. H. Randolph 8-9-1871 (no return) Dy
Craig, Maggie to Ben E. Norment 9-7-1868 (no return) Dy
Craig, Malinda to Geo. C. Webb 6-17-1864 (6-19-1864) L
Craig, Margaret S. to John Draffin 2-24-1855 T
Craig, Margaret W. to Silas M. McKnight 9-21-1828 (9-25-1828) G
Craig, Margaret to J. T. Alford 3-12-1885 L
Craig, Margarett E. J. to Henry Hutson 1-8-1848 O
Craig, Martha F. to Abner Harwell 5-28-1867 Dy
Craig, Martha P. to John Hundley 5-13-1844 Hr
Craig, Martha to Alexander Patterson 7-28-1858 Ma
Craig, Mary A. to Joseph R. Robertson 6-26-1840 (7-7-1840) Hr
Craig, Mary Ann to Wm. W. Brown 1-6-1859 L
Craig, Mary E. to Henry T. Starnes 2-24-1872 (no return) L
Craig, Mary L. to John Druffin 11-19-1851 T
Craig, Mary M. to Squire F. Park 10-15-1854 (10-23-1855) O
Craig, Matilda C. to Thomas A. Horton 12-6-1868 Be
Craig, Nancy A. to Wright Bonds 5-15-1861 Be

Craig, Nancy E. to A. J. Witham 8-3-1869 L
Craig, R. T. to W. C. Howell 10-1-1867 (10-2-1867) Dy
Craig, Sally M. to John B. Hays 2-5-1827 (2-8-1827) G
Craig, Sarah J. to J. P. Simmons 8-24-1854 (no return) F
Craig, Sarah Jane to L. M. Harrison 10-15-1857 (10-18-1857) Hr
Craig, Sarah Rhoda F. to James A. Hutson 12-24-1848 O
Craig, Sophronia to Marshall Green 3-18-1876 (no return) Hy
Craig, Susan to Raiford Fulghum 11-26-1836 (11-27-1836) Hr
Craig, Virginia F. to John Camel? 4-10-1871 (4-11-1871) T
Craige, Eliza to Joshua Bledsoe 2-24-1841 G
Craige, Jane to Jessee Cassells 7-13-1846 (7-15-1846) G
Craige, Juliana to Wm. A. Lemmons 12-24-1838 G
Craige, Polly Ann to Willis Person 4-30-1864 (5-4-1864) F
Craigg, Elizabeth A. to Wm. H. Brakefield 1-22-1846 F
Craighead, Ann to Edward Thomas 9-10-1872 T
Craighead, Callie to Jeff Bond 2-21-1871 Hy
Craighead, Mariah to David Jones 4-14-1874 Hy
Craighead, Sallie to Thomas Henderson 12-21-1876 Hy
Craighead, Tilda to Monrow Garison 9-16-1876 (9-17-1876) L B
Craigue(Craig), Elizabeth to Thomas A. Watson 6-27-1863 Be
Crain, Bitsy to William Sample 11-26-1842 (12-1-1842) F
Crain, Dorothy to Benjamin Alsup 1-20-1830 W
Crain, Frances to E. G. Thompson 11-16-1833 (11-?-1833) Hr
Crain, Harriet H. D. to Alfred Worrell 10-16-1837 (10-22-1837) O
Crain, M. L. to W. B. Oakley 12-12-1874 (12-14-1874) O
Crain, Martha E. to Julius Laymare 9-10-1857 Sh
Crain, Mary J. to James L. Cash 6-24-1873 (6-26-1873) T
Crain, Nancy to Eli Tilghman 7-20-1839 (7-23-1839) G
Crain, Rosetta E. to James F. Hayes 3-22-1876 (3-26-1876) L
Craine, Harriet to Surgeon S. J. Bell 8-25-1864 Sh
Craine, Jane to P. H. Nokes 9-10-1862 (9-14-1862) Sh
Cramer, Jane to George Huffstutter 4-2-1849 (4-5-1849) O
Crammer?, Frances to James W. Fish 4-22-1873 (4-27-1873) Dy
Crandle, Mollie G. to Geo. T. Glenn 2-18-1873 Hy
Crane, Elizabeth to Alfred Ware 3-9-1848 Sh
Crane, Laura Ann to Thomas Demmons 5-25-1861 Sh
Crane, Margaret J. to Ephraim McGlothlin 3-12-1857 Hr
Crane, Mary J. to Edward Mayer 11-27-1856 Sh
Crane, Missourie to William Manley 9-11-1877 (9-12-1877) L
Crane, Sarah A. to Ira Stanbrough 2-26-1856 (2-27-1856) Sh
Crane, Selina (Selma) to Drury Hodges 11-19-1837 Sh
Crane, Susan to Elijah Boyt 4-25-1830 G
Crane, Susan to Elijah Boyt 4-25-1831 G
Cranford, Eliza to Edwin Stevens 6-26-1832 Hr
Cranford, Mary A. to A. J. Polly 7-9-1864 (7-11-1864) O
Crank, Lucinda W. to William J. Corbitt 10-1-1852 (10-2-1852) G
Crank, Lucy M. to Robert L. Foster 5-6-1852 (no return) F
Crank, Matilda to Francis W. Shelton 3-16-1854 G
Crank, Rebecca to Samuel Harris 1-9-1870 G B
Crank, S. D. to A. C. Trousdale 12-2-1866 Hn
Crass, Flavis to Obadiah Waldrop 10-9-1838 Hn
Craton, Polly to Buckner Candell 2-18-1828 Hr
Craton?, Margaret to John H. Parker 5-28-1833 (6-9?-1833) Hr
Crausby, M. to M. Steward 11-4-1850 (no return) L
Crausby, Martha to Martin Stewart 11-4-1850 (no return) L
Crause, Manirva A. to Thompson A. Parker 11-28-1848 (11-30-1848) Ma
Cravans, Elizabeth to D. S. Lowry 9-4-1844 We
Crave (Crans), Catherine to J. P. Lewis 10-31-1837 Sh
Craven, Eliza Caroline to John Wesley Little 9-2-1854 (9-3-1854) Hr
Craven, Lavina J. to William J. Foster 12-27-1854 (12-28-1854) Hr
Craven, Samira C. to John C. Foster 12-22-1854 (12-24-1854) Hr
Cravens, Andromacha to Russell B. Shelby 11-15-1848 Sh
Cravens, B. F. to Henry Bridges 6-2-1849 Cr
Cravens, Carrie A. to James T. Griffin 2-21-1865 Hn
Cravens, Darthula to Westly Williams 11-21-1865 Cr
Cravens, Tennessee to E. Y. Bumpass 2-25-1862 Hn
Cravins, Elizabeth to John Brauner 9-25-1858 We
Cravins, Mary J. to William C. Patterson 10-3-1855 We
Crawford (Carthel?), Martha to Winny Shields 10-20-1867 G B
Crawford, A. C. to Alex W. Raines 11-17-1868 G
Crawford, A. E. to R. C. Sellers 1-29-1867 G
Crawford, Abbie to York Bridges 11-11-1870 (11-20-1870) F B
Crawford, Ada to W. D. Kendall 1-1-1868 Hn
Crawford, Adelia to Alfred Myrick 5-18-1844 (5-19-1844) Hr
Crawford, Amanda to John Ewell 1-2-1854 (1-7-1854) Hr
Crawford, Ann to Abraham Abernathy 9-3-1869 (11-25-1869) F B
Crawford, C. C. to S. M. Edwards 10-23-1865 (10-24-1865) F
Crawford, C. E. to B. F. Allen 8-10-1865 G
Crawford, C. L. to E. A. Levy 7-17-1858 (7-19-1858) G
Crawford, Caroline to H. F. Underwood 1-2-1861 We
Crawford, Caroline to Hickman F. Underwood 1-1-1861 (no return) We
Crawford, Cela M. to Charles M. Wellons 11-28-1850 Hr
Crawford, Charlotte to John F. Greathouse 1-28-1868 (1-30-1868) Ma
Crawford, Cholley to Abraham Baker 11-16-1858 (11-18-1858) Hr
Crawford, Cynthia A. (Mrs.) to Mark P. Pulliam 11-19-1864 (11-24-1864) Sh
Crawford, Eliza C. to William K. Dowdy 10-31-1855 (11-1-1855) Hr
Crawford, Eliza E. to Elias Carter 10-17-1860 (no return) We

Brides

Crawford, Eliza J. to W. G. Jones 6-18-1866 Hn
Crawford, Elizabeth A. to George M. Porter 1-4-1839 Hn
Crawford, Elizabeth Ann to Willouby L. Thompson 10-23-1837 Hr
Crawford, Elizabeth J. to Lary A. Sanders 1-16-1849 (1-18-1849) Hr
Crawford, Elizabeth to Simeon B. Hartsfield 11-15-1856 (no return) Hn
Crawford, Elizabeth to Thos. Laham 2-14-1848 Cr
Crawford, Elizabeth to William Farris 7-3-1848 G
Crawford, Fannie C. to J. S. Lambert 2-24-1879 (2-25-1879) Dy
Crawford, Helen to B. G. Bledsoe 5-17-1857 Cr
Crawford, Isabella T. to John Hall Dantrell 8-12-1852 Cr
Crawford, J. C. to A. B. Avery 3-12-1865 G
Crawford, Jenny to Levi Harrell 10-6-1866 (10-8-1866) F B
Crawford, L. S. to Jas. A. G. McEwen 6-19-1855 (6-20-1855) G
Crawford, Lou to Cornelius Russell 8-8-1868 (no return) F B
Crawford, Lucinda J. to John B. Stanley 8-26-1846 (no return) F
Crawford, M. F. to James A. Park 1-3-1856 Hr
Crawford, M. J. to James H. (W.?) Weatherly 2-7-1871 F
Crawford, M. J. to W. T. Swaringin 12-3-1864 (12-5-1864) Cr
Crawford, M. T. to R. C. Wallace 3-5-1850 (no return) F
Crawford, Malinda to Simeon B. Hartsfield 12-21-1841 (no return) Hn
Crawford, Margaret to Anderson Neal 1-9-1869 (1-10-1869) F B
Crawford, Margaret to George W. Hensley 6-7-1843 (6-13-1843) Hr
Crawford, Martha Ellen to Calvin Lamb 8-20-1870 G
Crawford, Martha J. to John C. Jones 12-28-1858 (12-29-1858) G
Crawford, Mary A. to F. J. Braun 6-15-1859 (6-16-1859) Sh
Crawford, Mary A. to F. N. Kelso 3-5-1873 (3-6-1873) Dy
Crawford, Mary A. to James T. Land 8-8-1852 (no return) F
Crawford, Mary A. to Saml. B. Hawkins 7-23-1846 Sh
Crawford, Mary Angeline to John W. Carter 8-16-1855 Hn
Crawford, Mary J. to C. Woodfin 4-27-1843 Hr
Crawford, Mary J. to W. C. Old 2-4-1863 F
Crawford, Mary Jane to David K. Edwards 4-30-1853 (5-1-1853) Hr
Crawford, Mary to G. H. Wyatts 5-17-1856 (5-20-1856) Hr
Crawford, Mary to Henry Whitton 11-27-1869 F B
Crawford, Mary to James Harder 10-11-1838 Hn
Crawford, Merinda to Benjamin R. Fulghum 6-22-1840 (6-25-1840) Hr
Crawford, N. A. to J. Y. Britt 9-8-1869 (9-9-1869) Cr
Crawford, N. E. to G. T. Johnson 11-27-1865 (11-30-1865) F
Crawford, Nancy A. to Newton A. Willis 10-4-1849 Hn
Crawford, Nancy to Harvey House 3-20-1872 Hy
Crawford, Nannie S. to F. J. Allson 1-15-1868 Hy
Crawford, Olive to Solomon Jacobs 1-30-1838 (2-1-1838) Hr
Crawford, Polly to Oliver Hanin 2-6-1845 Sh
Crawford, Rachel J. to William S. McCall 6-3-1861 (no return) Cr
Crawford, Rachel to William Crane 3-19-1846 Sh
Crawford, Rebecca E. to J. M. McQuire 1-14-1859 Cr
Crawford, Salina to D. T. Levisay 1-11-1842 (no return) F
Crawford, Sarah Ann to Alvin Williams 9-3-1837 Hr
Crawford, Sarah Ann to Enoch Eskew? 4-22-1847 (4-18?-1847) Hr
Crawford, Sarah Ann to Peter Cathey 9-17-1864 Sh
Crawford, Sarah F. to Wm. P. McKinnie 12-1-1832 (12-5-1832) Hr
Crawford, Sarah to Doctor Ammons 12-13-1854 (1-14-1854) Hr
Crawford, Susan F. to John R. McKinnie 2-11-1830 (2-16-1830) Hr
Crawford, Susan to Israel Vanpelt 11-29-1870 (12-20-1870) F B
Crawford, Temperance to Wm. Faison 2-2-1846 (2-5-1846) Hr
Crawford, Texana to W. C. Fay 5-19-1864 Be
Crawford, Viney to James Gwynn 3-21-1870 (3-31-1870) F B
Crawley, Cripia N. to Wm. H. Rodgers 6-8-1859 Sh
Crawley, Elizabeth J. to Isaac J. Newberry 9-4-1863 (no return) We
Crawley, Harriet to Reps Good 3-14-1876 (no return) Hy
Crawley, Jane to James (Jonas) Long 11-18-1845 Sh
Crawley, Mary E. W. to Allen Mobley 11-29-1852 (12-7-1852) G
Crawley, Milley E. to Josiah H. Moore 1-29-1863 We
Crawley, Rebecah to Absolem Broom 6-15-1847 (no return) F
Crawley, Susan to Madison H. Chambers 9-1-1831 Sh
Creamer, Mary W. to John J. T. Heinrich 1-15-1861 (1-22-1861) Sh
Creasin, G. to Killian Shaffer 2-29?-1847 Sh
Creasy, Margaret to Wm. Cantrell 12-17-1864 Be
Creasy, Trusiana C. to Elisha Kelly 2-7-1864 Be
Creed, Lucinda to James Alexander 10-8-1825 O
Creg, M. J. to Lee Gray 12-17-1872 O
Creighton, Catharine to Timothy Hickey 5-23-1856 (5-24-1856) Sh
Creighton, Mary E. to Michael H. Riley 5-30-1857 Sh
Creighton, Matilda J. to Geo. W. James 5-12-1851 (5-14-1851) Sh
Crenshaw, Amanda to Yeatman Crenshaw 2-24-1870 T
Crenshaw, America Ann to Joel W. Reeves 1-14-1850 (1-15-1850) Ma
Crenshaw, Arena to Edward Curd 9-11-1838 Hn
Crenshaw, B. S. to J. W. Shipp 4-30-1855 (no return) F
Crenshaw, Clarinda to Charles Williams 1-21-1874 T
Crenshaw, Eliz. J. to Geo. C. Howard 10-28-1851 (10-29-1851) T
Crenshaw, Elizabeth A. to William Thompson 12-6-1842 (12-8-1842) G
Crenshaw, Indiana to Allen Debow Lake 11-15-1848 (11-16-1848) T
Crenshaw, Jane to William Williams 2-7-1833 Sh
Crenshaw, Julia C. to Thomas L. Garland 2-23-1865 T
Crenshaw, Julia to Jessee Faulk 12-20-1865 T
Crenshaw, Louisa to Stephen C. Treadwell 10-10-1835 Sh
Crenshaw, Lucy H. (Mrs.) to E. W. Caldwell 1-19-1859 (1-20-1859) Sh

Page 69

Crenshaw, Lucy H. to Wm. A. Crenshaw 12-17-1844 Sh
Crenshaw, Margaret to Joseph McDaniel 8-11-1826 Sh
Crenshaw, Martha F. to Isaac H. Flowers 8-21-1866 G
Crenshaw, Martha to B. S. Wynne 12-27-1854 (1-2-1855) Sh
Crenshaw, Mary Ann to William E. Griffin 9-11-1846 (9-18-1846) F
Crenshaw, Mary E. to B. F. Boydston 7-26-1838 Hn
Crenshaw, Mary to E. H. Person 7-7-1836 Sh
Crenshaw, Mary to Lafayette Robertson 12-28-1868 T
Crenshaw, Mildred to William Neal 10-28-1830 Sh
Crenshaw, Mollie E. to S. J. Taylor 10-13-1873 (10-15-1873) Dy
Crenshaw, Viola S. to J. S.? Winford 4-13-1857 T
Crenshaw, Viola S. to John S. Winford 4-13-1857 (4-16-1857) T
Crenshaw, Virginia E. to F. M. Crenshaw 3-21-1864 (3-28-1864) Sh
Cresap, J. H. to Alvis Baker 10-16-1858 (10-21-1858) G
Cress, Elizabeth to John E. David 10-10-1855 G
Cress, Sarah C. to James A. Barber 3-4-1855 We
Cress, Sarah E. to G. W. Newten 9-7-1854 We
Cress, Suretta to Thomas C. Carson 7-12-1867 (no return) Hn
Cresswell, Angeline to Sidney R. Neil 3-12-1879 Dy
Cresswell, Octavia C. to Rob't A. Posey 11-8-1872 O
Creswell, F. A. to A. A. Sharp 3-19-1861 G
Creswell, F. A. to A. A. Short 3-19-1861 G
Crewdson, Anna R. to Wm. F. Talley 6-1-1858 (6-2-1858) Sh
Crewer, Rosanna to Davy Hardy 12-21-1867 F B
Crewes, Perina to John Harper 5-7-1849 (no return) Cr
Crews, Charrinda to D. G. Boyett 8-17-1838 (8-20-1838) G
Crews, E. F. to A. E. Lewis 7-16-1856 Hr
Crews, Eliza T. to James A. Rose 3-10-1852 (3-11-1852) Hr
Crews, Elizabeth A. to Corneleus J. Crews 3-4-1860 We
Crews, Elizabeth to Bolivar Leek 6-4-1860 (6-5-1860) Cr
Crews, Emily to James A. Crews 12-20-1859 We
Crews, Fannie N. to John W. Holford 3-14-1859 (3-15-1859) Hr
Crews, Harriet V. to Allen G. McColum 1-6-1868 (1-7-1868) Cr
Crews, Judy to William Scales 11-17-1868 G B
Crews, Margaret to Jackson King 11-19-1856 Hn
Crews, Mariah to Wm. Tolston 5-8-1844 Cr
Crews, Martha C. to Saml. H. Lambert 4-14-1858 (4-15-1858) Hr
Crews, Mary Ann to Richard C. Hill 11-27-1849 (11-29-1849) Hr
Crews, Mary H. to Timothy Lax 12-17-1852 (12-19-1852) Hr
Crews, Mary Jane to Jonathan Joyner 4-14-1858 (4-20-1858) Hr
Crews, Mary to Wm. Brock 9-20-1846 Cr
Crews, Milly to Jack Tines 9-30-1868 G B
Crews, Milly to Willson B. McElroy 10-15-1838 Hr
Crews, Minervia J. to Geo. W. Spurling 3-1-1858 Hr
Crews, Nancy Ann to Green B. Carter 1-3-1839 H
Crews, Nancy Elizabeth to John M. Stewart 10-12-1870 (10-13-1870) Dy
Crews, Nancy to B. W. Rogers 2-7-1866 G
Crews, Olivia C. to Isaiah Watkins 12-24-1849 Hr
Crews, Ophelia J. to Wm. Dodson 3-19-1857 (3-17?-1857) Hr
Crews, Parilee J. to Joseph H. Watkins 12-5-1870 (12-6-1870) Cr
Crews, Pernecia L. to Alfred Banks 10-2-1859 We
Crews, Prudy M. (Mrs.) to Thomas B. Kerin 7-1-1868 G
Crews, Sarah A. to Will H. Berry 1-25-1845 Hr
Crews, Sharlatta V. to James A. Barker 12-13-1860 We
Crews, Susan C. to Calvin Flowers 5-17-1845 (5-22-1845) G
Crews, Virginia G. to Andrew Anderson 1-27-1869 (2-4-1869) F
Crews?, Martha R.(P?) to Thomas Oliver 1-14-1840 Hr
Crewsdon, Lucy E. to Foster D. Talley 7-6-1858 (7-7-1858) Sh
Cribbs, Amanda C. to Joseph D. Leach 10-19-1859 (10-20-1859) G
Cribbs, Clarinda E.? to James C.? Elzan 7-28-1860 (7-31-1860) Cr
Cribbs, Elizabeth to Samuel M. Stone 11-23-1852 G
Cribbs, H. E. C. to George P. Pierce 1-23-1868 (no return) Dy
Cribbs, M. J. to Noah Green 12-1-1874 Dy
Cribbs, M. M. to G. W. Flippin 4-11-1867 G
Cribbs, Margaret Jane to John L. Thedford 1-30-1850 G
Cribbs, Martha to Madison Hale 9-25-1855 (9-27-1855) G
Cribbs, Mary C. to Wm. W. Harris 12-23-1848 (no return) Cr
Cribbs, Nancy to Allen White 12-19-1827 G
Cribbs, Sarah E. to W. D. Argo 9-8-1866 (no return) Cr
Cribbs, Sarah J. to Wm. M. Stone 10-31-1846 G
Crichfield, Effi to Arthur Olds 12-23-1840 (12-24-1840) L
Crichfield, Sarah A. to Thomas Groom 1-19-1878 (1-23-1878) Dy
Crichloe, Margaret to Harry Claybrook 12-11-1868 (no return) Hy
Crichlow, Harriet to Lee Johnson 11-25-1880 (11-26-1880) L B
Crichlow, Jullia A. to John E. Grigby 2-25-1869 Hy
Crickmure, Martha A. to H. B. Jones 11-13-1878 Hy
Crider, A. E. to David Wilson 8-18-1841 Cr
Crider, Amanda to Martin Nix 1-8-1853 (1-9-1853) O
Crider, Beanthur to Eli D. Brown 11-8-1862 (11-9-1862) Cr
Crider, Betty to Richard Tucker 4-2-1872 (4-3-1872) Cr B
Crider, Catharine to Daniel H. Dalton 12-23-1867 (12-24-1867) Cr
Crider, E. B. to J. C. Hall 12-17-1872 (12-18-1872) Cr
Crider, Emaline to Steven C. Holladay 1-16-1844 (no return) Cr
Crider, Emma E. J. to O P. Wright 2-19-1860 We
Crider, Frances M. to Allen Reed 8-8-1839 G
Crider, Fronnie E. to Lea Palmer 12-15-1853 Cr
Crider, M. A. to W. M. Smith 9-22-1870 G

Crider, Martha to Samuel J. Alston 10-17-1867 Hn
Crider, Mary E. to Joseph S. Brown 12-20-1866 Cr
Crider, Mary L. to Charles Nix 5-28-1846 G
Crider, Narcissa (Mrs.) to W. R. Stubblefield 12-7-1865 G
Crider, Rosanna to Thomas Word 9-25-1834 (9-25-1834) G
Crider, Sarah to W. J. Jones 8-4-1857 Hn
Crider, Sophronia J. to W. W. Thorn 1-26-1870 G
Crihfield, C. D. to J. H. Underwood 3-31-1880 L
Crihfield, Elizabeth J. to Moses W. Cunningham 11-23-1868 (11-25-1868) L
Crihfield, Elizabeth to Nedrick Curtis 3-15-1855 (3-17-1855) L
Crihfield, Emily A. to Wm. S. Duggan 10-13-1857 (10-15-1857) L
Crihfield, Jane to Thomas C. Olds 6-22-1842 (6-23-1842) L
Crihfield, Mahala to Elhanon W. Latham 5-30-1852 L
Crihfield, Martha A. E. to Jonathan McKinney 8-16-1859 (8-17-1859) L
Crihfield, Martha to A. P. Smith 11-18-1876 (11-22-1876) L
Crihfield, Martha to Reding T. Coaker 7-15-1865 (7-16-1865) L
Crihfield, Mary M. to James H. Heiskell 7-22-1851 (7-23-1851) L
Crihfield, S. M. to T. A. Brice 7-4-1885 (7-5-1885) L
Crihfield, Sarah E. V. to R. H. Pennington 12-25-1872 L
Crim, L. E. to Wiley Payne 10-25-1871 Hy
Crime, Annie to Peter Soger 7-15-1863 Sh
Crimen, Bridget to Michael Kelly 6-16-1856 (6-17-1856) Sh
Crimmans, Margaret to Michael Foley 4-24-1861 (4-28-1861) Sh
Crimmin, Honora to Plumpton Siddall 5-21-1859 Sh
Crimmins, Catherine to W. Sullivan 2-10-1862 Sh
Crippin, Rachel A. to John Jones 5-12-1860 (5-13-1860) F
Crisenberry, Caroline to Aaron Hart 3-16-1843 Hn
Crisenberry, Louisa to Benjamin Spinson 3-16-1854 Hn
Crisp, Bettie to E. H. Osborne 7-20-1870 Hy
Crisp, Cynthia to E. H. Osborne 6-24-1850 Hr
Crisp, Dora to Edward J. Martin 1-14-1869 (1-19-1869) Ma *
Crisp, Eliza G. to Wm. Bowman 12-21-1837 G
Crisp, Elizabeth J. to Shelton Oliver 6-26-1850 (6-25?-1850) Hr
Crisp, Elizabeth to Greenberry Bright 1-28-1830 Hr
Crisp, Eva A. to T. O. Hendren 12-18-1880 (12-20-1880) L
Crisp, Fannie to Thomas Fithugh 11-26-1871 Hy
Crisp, Lucy J. to Thos. J> Gardner 6-14-1843 Hr
Crisp, Lydia to Wm. Reaves 5-14-1844 Hr
Crisp, Mary F. to Albert G. Sullivan 5-4-1843 Hr
Crisp, Mary J. to James E. Weathers 2-28-1844 G
Crisp, Melvina to James Johnson 8-22-1829 (8-23-1829) Hr
Crisp, Nancy to Charles A. Crisp 4-7-1842 Hr
Crisp, S. A. to J. W. Fuller 9-7-1868 (9-8-1868) Dy
Crisp, Sarah Jane to Thomas S. Slaughter 5-26-1850 Hr
Crissman, Jane to Isaac Nixon 5-27-1847 Sh
Crist, Mary E. K. to Wm. D. Anthony 8-7-1867 (8-8-1867) Ma
Cristenberry, Jane to J.R. Hall 4-16-1868 (no return) Hy
Criswell, Emer J. to Elija Coker 9-10-1856 (9-11-1856) G
Critchlow, Kate M. to W. W. Whitaker 1-6-1862 Hy
Crittenden, Celia J. to Stephen K. Oats 5-11-1867 (5-16-1867) F
Crittenden, Elizabeth to William Wagster 1-6-1843 Hn
Crittenden, Lucy to Leonard H. Blake 12-18-1842 Hn
Crittenden, Martha S. to Leonard K. Howard 7-29-1858 Hn
Crittenden, Mary to William F. Callicott 10-8-1841 Hn
Crittenden, ____ to R. G. Kyle 2-18-1858 We
Crittendon, Agnes to E. D. Toliver 1-10-1876 O B
Crittendon, E. L. to Thomas Wagginer 2-2-1852 (2-12-1852) O
Crittendon, Jane to James D. Jones 8-22-1850 (no return) Hn
Crittendon, Mary M. to James H. Denning 5-6-1860 We
Crittendon, Sarah J. to T. B. M. Dunlop 11-16-1852 We
Crittenton, Mary C. to Allen F. Oliver 1-2-1856 (1-3-1856) Ma
Crocker, Ada to Isaiah Flewellen 12-24-1874 L B
Crocker, Cynthia J. to Green Berry Smith 12-20-1868 G
Crocker, Deborah to James Rosson 1-23-1841 (1-26-1841) Hr
Crocker, Fannie E. L. to William L. Byler 1-20-1875 G
Crocker, Hanley to LaFayette Thompson 3-24-1834 (3-30-1834) Hr
Crocker, Irena M. to E. H. Hancock 6-27-1846 (7-2-1846) G
Crocker, Jane to John Raborn 5-21-1861 Mn
Crocker, Mahaly A. to Henry Woolard 2-18-1864 G
Crocker, Rutha to W. M. Cantrell 4-15-1866 G
Crocker, Sarah S. to Joseph K. Newland 10-28-1858 (11-10-1858) Hr
Crocker, Sarah to Christopher Miller 11-21-1869 G
Crocker, Urshula to James Wright 11-8-1847 (11-10-1847) Hr
Crocket, Kate D. to Samuel B. Allen 2-20-1861 (2-21-1861) Sh
Crocket, Louisa J. to James H. Berry 7-1-1858 We
Crocket, Sarah Jane to William R. Jordon 12-?-1871 (12-11-1871) L
Crockett, Alice A. to W. A. Tharpe 8-1-1854 O
Crockett, Alice C. to Henry C. Townes 12-17-1868 Cr
Crockett, Anna to Robert S. Parker 11-5-1842 (11-6-1842) O
Crockett, Anne Marie to Jas. McKibben 6-10-1844 Sh
Crockett, B. E. to T. H. Barham 11-9-1867 O
Crockett, Barthena to Norman Anderson 12-14-1869 (12-16-1869) L
Crockett, Delilah A. to William Wells 6-2-1858 (6-14-1858) L
Crockett, E. to H. H. Brown 5-29-1867 (5-30-1867) G
Crockett, Elizabeth J. to John W. Caldwell 1-23-1854 (1-29-1854) O
Crockett, Elizabeth J. to Moses F. Whitehurst 12-7-1844 (12-8-1844) G
Crockett, Elizabeth S. to Sean Dawtry 11-20-1849 G

Crockett, Elizabeth to William Thedford 11-3-1829 G
Crockett, Ellin to William Cole 2-26-1861 O
Crockett, Elvira to Benj. A. Cooper 8-20-1850 (8-22-1850) G
Crockett, Fannie to Reuben Anderson 2-14-1867 O
Crockett, Fannie to Ruben Anderson 2-14-1867 O
Crockett, Gracey to John Crockett 12-20-1843 O
Crockett, Hester to William C. Webb 1-7-1836 G
Crockett, Jane to Robert Clark 12-26-1840 (12-29-1840) G
Crockett, Julia to John Cleare 12-28-1870 (no return) F B
Crockett, Laura A. to George W. Brown 5-23-1843 O
Crockett, Lida to William P. Dunivant 12-29-1883 (1-1-1884) L
Crockett, Lucinda to John Wheeler 12-5-1854 (12-9-1854) O
Crockett, Malinda to William P. Robinson 11-24-1847 O
Crockett, Malissa to William Plyland 3-21-1853 G
Crockett, Margaret A. to Benjamin F. Taylor 12-26-1862 (no return) We
Crockett, Margaret to Wile Flowers 3-22-1830 (3-25-1830) G
Crockett, Martha J. to Wm. H. H. Martin 8-14-1862 O
Crockett, Martha Jane to William H. Webb 9-6-1847 G
Crockett, Mary Ann to Nathana Kelley 10-16-1842 O
Crockett, Mary E. to Charles B. Grizzard 12-17-1861 (12-18-1861) Cr
Crockett, Mary E. to Charles B. Grizzard 12-19-1861 Cr
Crockett, Mary E. to William T. Crockett 1-22-1862 We
Crockett, Mary L. to John B. Hudson 1-29-1861 O
Crockett, Mary to David Simons 5-24-1842 G
Crockett, Mary to Jackson Mathis 10-15-1834 (10-16-1834) G
Crockett, Mary to Luco M. Tharpe 10-10-1845 Ha
Crockett, Mary to William Crouch 2-1-1853 (2-3-1853) O
Crockett, Mattie to Robert Hale 1-15-1876 (2-17-1876) L
Crockett, Melinda to George W. Davis 8-17-1855 O
Crockett, Minnie to F. M. McRee 11-13-1867 O
Crockett, Nancy C. to William Ware 8-5-1848 (8-6-1848) O
Crockett, Nancy J. to David Smith 12-4-1862 We
Crockett, Nancy to Ruffin Yates 3-12-1833 (3-14-1833) G
Crockett, Nancy to Whitfield Taylor 6-24-1844 We
Crockett, Nancy to Wilban Webb 6-11-1835 G
Crockett, Nancy to William Ware 8-5-1848 O
Crockett, Pheby to Benjamin Garrison 8-31-1864 (9-1-1864) O
Crockett, R. A. to A. M. Smith 7-12-1875 (7-13-1875) O
Crockett, R. A. to J. A. Glisson 8-19-1867 L
Crockett, Rebeca to Calvin Byrns 9-9-1882 (9-10-1882) L
Crockett, Rebecca E. to Christopher G. Simpson 11-29-1843 (11-30-1843) O
Crockett, Rebecca M. to Wm. D. Jones 2-13-1866 (2-14-1866) O
Crockett, Rebecca to Joe Taylor 8-27-1880 L B
Crockett, Rebecka E. to George Himbrough 2-25-1839 (2-26-1839) G
Crockett, Rebecka to Edmond Woods 11-22-1826 G
Crockett, Rutha to Samuel C. Foster 10-14-1845 We
Crockett, Rutha to Stephen W. Eaves 10-21-1844 (no return) We
Crockett, S. E. to Z. T. Smothers 4-25-1872 (no return) Cr
Crockett, Sallie to H. Pate 4-12-1871 Dy
Crockett, Samantha A. to William Hill 6-13-1863 (no return) We
Croff, Amanda R. to George F. Stein 9-1-1881 (9-4-1881) L
Crofford, Josephin to Plesant Manasco 6-19-1867 (6-18?-1867) T
Crofford, Lanah to Steward Cody 10-27-1870 (10-28-1870) Cr B
Crofford, Louisa to John L. Minton 2-6-1855 Sh
Crofford, S. A. to Plesant Manasco 5-6-1870 (5-8-1870) T
Croger, Dinah to W. Buscamp 6-1-1852 Sh
Croghan, Margaret to Patrick Collins 12-12-1854 Sh
Cromes, Frances C. to William A. Harbor 6-4-1853 G
Cromwell, Ann to David Armour 5-26-1828 Ma
Cromwell, Ellen to Felix Walker 10-4-1838 (10-4-1838) Ma
Cronk?, Rachel to Adam T. Llewelling 1-13-1856 T
Crook, Alice to D. C. Haller 4-11-1857 Sh
Crook, Berchie to Jeff Wynn 10-18-1880 (10-19-1880) Dy
Crook, Elmira A. to John J. (I?) Braden 12-14-1869 (no return) L
Crook, Emma to Alfred Turpin 12-6-1884 (12-11-1884) L
Crook, Jane to William Tate 12-24-1869 (no return) F B
Crook, Mary A. to A. H. Walker 12-30-1856 We
Crook, Mary L. to James Ascue 11-14-1855 (11-16-1855) L
Crook, Mary to Abraham Perry 11-19-1844 F
Crook, Sarah J. to Thomas P. Alston 10-2-1860 (10-3-1860) L
Crook, Sarah P. to James Coates 2-22-1845 (2-26-1845) L
Crook, Susie to W. J. Ross 9-29-1884 (10-5-1884) L
Croom, Amanda F. to R. H. Davis 12-17-1863 (11?-17-1862?) Ma
Croom, Catharine to Sterling M. Watlington 5-14-1866 Ma
Croom, Elizabeth W. to Chas. E. Bellamy 5-11-1858 (5-12-1858) Sh
Croom, Ema E. to Z. T. Fleming 12-28-1873 Hy
Croom, Jane to Samuel Bobbit 12-8-1841 (12-9-1841) Ma
Croom, Laura to John G. Haynes 2-16-1870 (2-17-1870) Ma
Croom, Lucy J. to A. J. Payne 1-11-1866 Hy
Croom, Mollie F. to E. W. Cawthon 1-9-1866 (1-11-1866) Dy
Croom, Rachell W. to John Umphlett 6-4-1853 (no return) F
Croom, Susan to Major Langston 1-10-1843 Ma
Croomes, Frances M. to S. L. Paine 1-28-1868 (no return) Hy
Crooms, Emma to J. McClish 3-13-1873 (no return) Hy
Crooms, Nancy E. to J. P. Epps 1-25-1866 Hy
Crooms, S. E. to G. M. Crook 3-5-1868 Hy
Croose, Sarah to John Polk 1-16-1830 (1-17-1830) Hr

Crop (Cross), Lidda to Rufus Wiley 1-2-1872 Hy
Crop, Elizabeth C. to Jefferson Burton 11-17-1840 Ma
Crosby, Elizabeth to Abner W. Mason 3-7-1853 (3-8-1853) G
Crosby, Louisa to Thomas Nanse 9-17-1850 (no return) L
Crosby, Lucy A. to James A. Edwards 2-10-1863 G
Crosby, Mary Ann to A. B. B. Bone 11-13-1855 Sh
Crosby, Mary to Felix Boyd 1-6-1871 (no return) F
Crosby, Sarah to James Rene, jr. 6-7-1845 (6-9-1845) Ma
Crose, Nancy Jane to Moses West 7-6-1849 Be
Croslin, Elizabeth to William Hamblin 7-23-1824 Hr
Crosno, Lucinda to Henry Nisler 7-25-1839 Be
Cross, Aminta J. to R. W. Black 10-22-1867 (10-23-1867) F
Cross, Angeline to David McBride 9-11-1830 (9-12-1830) G
Cross, Caroline to John Boone 1-5-1876 Dy
Cross, Eliza J. to James McCarver 2-15-1849 Cr
Cross, Elizabeth S.? to Jason A. Bridges 6-23-1860 (6-25-1860) Cr
Cross, Elizabeth to James Harris 3-3-1855 Ma
Cross, Emma to Henry Miller 1-4-1870 (no return) F B
Cross, Frances C. to Madison Parker 12-27-1847 (12-30-1847) F
Cross, Frances J. to James M. Fortner 2-5-1850 (2-10-1850) Hr
Cross, Harriet to Benjamin Stone 5-26-1855 (5-28?-1855) Hr
Cross, Harriet to M. D. Pankey 2-20-1860 Hr
Cross, Jane to James P. Stewart 9-7-1837 (9-8-1837) G
Cross, Lettie to Charlie Houston 12-27-1870 (12-29-1870) F B
Cross, Louisa E. to John W. Ross 10-8-1859 (10-12-1859) Hr
Cross, Louisa to M. D. L. Anderson 7-25-1856 (8-5-1856) Hr
Cross, Lucy Ann to John A. Gatlin 9-26-1849 (9-27-1849) Hr
Cross, Mandy to James Greer 4-3-1853 Be
Cross, Margaret to James W. Morgan 12-5-1843 Hn
Cross, Maria to Abraham Cobern 12-21-1868 (no return) F B
Cross, Maria to James Hamilton 7-29-1882 (7-30-1881) L
Cross, Martha A. to J. M. Shelton 8-7-1849 (8-21-1849) F
Cross, Martha A. to J. S. Lalusan? 7-7-1849 (not endorsed) F
Cross, Martha A. to Robert H. Black 2-19-1867 (2-20-1867) F
Cross, Martha A. to Thos. C. Lowder 6-24-1847 Cr
Cross, Martha to Alexr. Boon 10-13-1877 (10-14-1877) Dy
Cross, Martha to James Rushing 9-16-1849 Be
Cross, Mary E. to Robert L. Ellis 1-6-1849 Sh
Cross, Mary J. to J. S. Farmer 10-16-1858 We
Cross, Mary J. to John J. Slaughter 3-8-1866 (3-11-1866) F
Cross, Mary to James W. Quinn 11-1-1858 (11-2-1858) Sh
Cross, Parthenia to Harrison Bevill 12-19-1843 Hn
Cross, Phredonia to Robert H. Cato 12-23-1854 (12-24-1854) Sh
Cross, Polly to John Thompson 2-16-1828 (2-17-1828) Hr
Cross, Rebecca B. to Littleberry Stainback 3-6-1844 (3-7-1844) Hr
Cross, Rebecca to G. M. Bartlett 1-4-1854 (no return) F
Cross, Rhody to William Willbanks 8-12-1866 Hy
Cross, Susan C. to G. W. Richie 1-9-1867 (1-11-1867) Dy
Cross, Verona May to John E. Coleman 2-26-1879 (3-9-1879) L
Cross, Vic to William Anderson 1-23-1867 Dy
Cross, Viney to Bob Frasier 9-6-1867 Hy
Cross, Virginia A. to G. C. Evans 2-7-1857 (2-12-1857) Hr
Crossby, Mary R. to Absolum B. Laymon 5-27-1848 (5-31-1848) G
Crossett, Elizabeth to Merite Huchins 11-4-1850 (11-7-1850) F
Crossett, G. A. to J. W. Newby 11-13-1867 (11-14-1867) F
Crossett, Sarah M. to Robert Vawter 1-11-1870 (no return) Cr
Crosslin, Angaline to James Day 11-14-1850 We
Crossno, Elizabeth to John G. Brewer 2-11-1863 Be
Crossno, Mary to John McGill 12-30-1865 Be
Crossno, Sarah A. to Malcom Brewer 8-22-1861 Be
Crossno, Susan E. to Stephen J. Trice 3-25-1852 Be
Crossnoe, Charlotte to P. Kenedy 6-27-1869 Be
Crossnoe, Elizabeth Ann to John N. Niceler 10-5-1852 Be
Crosswell, Julia to S. P. Leflore 10-20-1869 (10-21-1869) Cr
Crosthwaite, M. A. to J. F. Herring 11-24-1879 (11-25-1879) L
Crouch, Emily to William Woodson 8-26-1841 Sh
Crouch, Lucy A. to Richard Walsh 2-3-1838 Sh
Crouch, Martha E. to Thomas T. Ellis 3-9-1842 Sh
Crouch, Mary P. to Robert Wooldridge 9-3-1839 Sh
Crouch, Mary R. to Jerome Dorsey 5-10-1855 (6-12-1853?) T
Crouch, Nancy C. to Harder Scott 2-21-1838 Sh
Crouch, Sarah A. to Milton Harrell 11-20-1838 Sh
Crouch, Sarah E. to George W. Pennel 1-14-1846 (1-15-1846?) T
Crouch, Sarah to John Alvis 5-10-1838 Sh
Crouch, Susannah to Henry T. Robinson 6-17-1845 Sh
Croupe, Catharine to Henrick Rinn 6-10-1851 (6-10-1850?) Sh
Crouse, Elizabeth to W. A. Davidson 6-13-1861 Mn
Crouse, Lioty(Sioty?) to Vinson King 7-5-1847 Hr
Crouse, Sarah to Giles Taylor 11-17-1842 Hr
Croutch, S. E. to Robert Jackson 2-4-1866 Hn
Crow, Acinnath to J. H. Butler 10-9-1860 Be
Crow, Adaline to Ricahrd Maddrey 12-18-1866 (12-25-1866) Dy
Crow, America to Marcellus A. Cross 1-15-1868 Dy
Crow, Caroline to Daniel Fowlkes 10-11-1877 Dy
Crow, Elizabeth to George House 6-24-1845 (6-26-1845) O
Crow, Elizabeth to Tobe Powell 10-22-1879 (10-23-1879) Dy
Crow, Emma to Anderson Jones 1-2-1879 Dy
Crow, Hannah to Michael Fitzpatrick 7-22-1862 Sh
Crow, Louisa Jane to Richard Nelms 6-20-1836 (7-21-1836) O
Crow, Louisa to Andrew J. McIntosh 6-28-1852 (7-1-1852) O
Crow, Louisa to J. W. Price 5-21-1857 We
Crow, Lucy to James Farrow 12-28-1870 (12-29-1870) Dy
Crow, M. A. to F. A. Troy 12-11-1872 Dy
Crow, Mary W. to George Yousman 11-15-1843 O
Crow, Mary to Edmund Gilstrap 4-4-1844 Sh
Crow, Mary to Henry Taylor 11-21-1874 (11-24-1874) Dy B
Crow, P. A. to J. A. Luntsford 12-24-1875 (no return) Dy
Crow, Paralee to J. W. Burtin 10-14-1872 (10-17-1872) Dy
Crow, Rachel to J. W. H. Burton 10-15-1863 Be
Crow, Rebeca to Jess Montgomery 7-1-1867 Cr
Crow, Rebecca Ann to W. Carson 7-8-1857 (7-9-1857) Sh
Crow, Rebecca F. to N.(A.?) W. Johnson 7-22-1860 Be
Crow, S. A. to Zach T. Troy 12-28-1867 (12-29-1867) Dy
Crow, Susan to Wm. J. Butler 3-16-1850 Cr
Crow, Zilla L. to Henry P. Brawner 7-19-1844 We
Crowder, Ama to John Haskell 11-26-1871 Hy
Crowder, Amanda to Edward Williams 12-23-1873 Hy
Crowder, Amelia to Elias James 1-14-1869 (1-16-1869) F B
Crowder, Angeline to P. B. Edmunds 8-5-1855 Hn
Crowder, Ann M. to R. H. Drewry 4-5-1858 We
Crowder, Ann M. to R. H. Henry 4-5-1858 We
Crowder, Bettie to Thurman Holcomb 12-23-1874 Hy
Crowder, Caroline to Obediah Johnson 1-31-1870 (2-1-1870) Ma
Crowder, Cena to Joe Outlaw 11-17-1871 Hy
Crowder, Cenia to Asa Read 1-30-1867 (no return) Hy
Crowder, Cyntha W. to William J. Pillow 10-22-1854 Hn
Crowder, Emiline G. to William Thomas Warren 11-19-1840 (12-2-1850) Hr
Crowder, F. J. to H. R. Smith 9-5-1871 Hy
Crowder, Frances to Ephraim L. McAdoo 1-8-1859 (1-11-1859) Ma
Crowder, Harriet to John Crowder 10-31-1868 (11-14-1868) F B
Crowder, Julia Ann to Samuel Stratton 1-4-1868 G B
Crowder, Louisa E. to Joseph F. Collins 11-22-1855 (no return) Hn
Crowder, Maria to Benjamin Perry 1-1-1866 (1-7-1866) F B
Crowder, Marinda T. to James Poyner 12-2-1847 Hn
Crowder, Martha A. to William R. Johnson 3-15-1870 Ma
Crowder, Martha to William A. Carroll 12-1-1865 (no return) Hn
Crowder, Marthy A. to Willis Ball 12-29-1877 Hy
Crowder, Mary Ann to William B. Veazey 11-17-1844 (no return) Hn
Crowder, Mary M. to James McLode 8-22-1865 Hy
Crowder, Mary V. to J. R. Johnson 12-1-1869 (12-8-1869) F
Crowder, Mary to Peter Walker 3-28-1871 Hy
Crowder, Mollie to W. A. Ellis 9-13-1869 (9-15-1869) F
Crowder, Nancy to Lemuel Newsom 2-25-1832 (2-28-1832) Ma
Crowder, Sallie J. to William E. Kirley 10-14-1860 Hn
Crowder, Sarah A. to Wm. T. Cross 9-15-1855 Hr
Crowder, Sarah B. to Joseph Carter 5-11-1848 Hn
Crowder, Sarah to John Litton 1-15-1856 (1-17-1856) O
Crowder, Susan F. to Samuel T. Poyner 6-23-1853 Hn
Crowder, Susan H. to W. T. Jackson 10-7-1867 (10-10-1867) Cr
Crowder, Virginia A. to Wm. A. Tanner 9-13-1851 (9-17-1851) Hr
Crowder, ____ J. (Mrs.) to D. L. McAdoo 10-20-1867 G
Crowel, Nancy Jane to James B. Leech 12-12-1868 (12-15-1868) Cr
Crowel, ____ to Eli Wallace 1-21-1840 Hn
Crowell, Rosanna to James Ivy 2-5-1840 Hn
Crowell, Susan to Reubin Clenahan 3-16-1873 Hy
Crowley, Mary Ann to J. N. Wallace 10-11-1838 (no return) Hn
Crowson, Saryan to William C. Franklin 9-22-1847 O
Cruce, E. J. to A. J. Netherly 6-8-1875 (6-9-1875) O
Crudup, M. R. to J. E. Wade 8-20-1878 (8-21-1878) Dy
Crudup, Mary to Wm. Parnell 1-7-1867 (1-10-1867) Dy
Cruis, Ann to Martin Rhodes 12-21-1867 (12-22-1867) F B
Cruise, Mary to Presly Night 10-5-1870 (10-6-1870) Cr
Crump, Eliza J. to Joseph Travis 11-24-1842 Hn
Crump, Elizabeth J. to John F. Goodman 8-9-1854 (no return) F
Crump, Mildred T. (Mrs.) to Alfred Eldridge 4-13-1844 Sh
Crump, Sophia A. to L. M. Travis 8-6-1851 Hn
Crumply, Sarah to Thomas D. Moore 2-9-1852 (2-10-1852) Hr
Crumpton, Caroline (Mrs.) to James Coble 11-26-1862 (11-27-1862) Sh
Crumpton, Caroline to Alexander Reed 8-3-1861 Sh
Crums(Crews?), Nancy C. to Milton Smith 3-27-1845 Hr
Crunk (Crank?), M. L. to Thomas I. Thompson 9-9-1865 G
Cruse, Eliza Ann to Jethro S. Radford 10-23-1856 Hn
Cruse, Eliza to John P. Williams 10-27-1831 Hn
Cruse, Jane to James McCollum 7-12-1852 We
Cruse, Jane to William Forrest 4-7-1858 Hn
Cruse, Martha to W. C. Moxley 11-17-1863 O
Cruse, Sopha Ann to James H. Stacy 9-4-1852 (no return) F
Crutcher, Henrietta to German Baker 11-20-1854 (11-21-1854) Sh
Crutcher, Jane to Samuel Brandon 6-3-1839 Hn
Crutcher, Lavinia to Spencer Teague 9-20-1866 (9-21-1866) F B
Crutcher, Sallie E. to John Kennedy 12-5-1866 (12-10-1866) F
Crutcher, Sarah to Sterling H. Briggs 10-13-1842 Hn
Crutchfiel, Mary J. to P. A. Gibbs 2-14-1855 We
Crutchfield, America to Samuel C. Dobbins 12-30-1851 Hn

Crutchfield, B. B. to J. W. Palmer 2-11-1863 (no return) Hn
Crutchfield, D. to Samuel C. Love 11-18-1852 Hn
Crutchfield, E. A. to John W. Campbell 2-24-1850 Hn
Crutchfield, Elizabeth C. to William H. Fields 12-21-1864 (12-22-1864) Cr
Crutchfield, Elizabeth F. to Madison Farrer 8-3--1853 Be
Crutchfield, Elizabeth to C. W. (C. F.) McDonald 11-24-1869 Hy
Crutchfield, Harriet to Cane Baucom 4-19-1871 (4-20-1871) Cr B
Crutchfield, Lavina P. to John E. Walden 1-30-1845 (no return) We
Crutchfield, Lucy M. to R. W. Acuff 10-11-1866 Hy
Crutchfield, Maria L. to Charles Overton 10-25-1866 Hy
Crutchfield, Mary A. to Geo. W. Moore 1-2-1839 Hn
Crutchfield, Mary to John Youre 4-13-1871 O
Crutchfield, Nancy to John W. Rhoads 8-16-1838 (no return) Hn
Crutchfield, Sarah J. to James M. Hayes 10-24-1844 Cr
Crutchin-McCrutchin, Minereva M. to William Merrill 12-16-1834 Sh
Cryant?, Martha to Morrison Griffin 12-4-1858 Cr
Cuff, Elmina J. to Robert C. Pafford 9-24-1865 Be
Cuff, Hester Ann to Allen R. Sykes 2-23-1845 Be
Cuff, Mary E. to T. W. Pafford 5-13-1868 Be
Culbeath?, Carnea to Wm. Marshall 11-15-1865 (11-16-1865) T
Culberhouse, Lucy to Joseph Fields 8-26-1855 Hn
Culberson, Amy to W. L. Norid 3-5-1860 O
Culbertson, Catherine to Carney Barbouor 6-18-1836 (6-20-1836) O
Culbertson, R. R. to Jonathan Haislip 9-3-1846 O
Culbreath, Annie to John D. Hopkins 10-2-1871 (10-5-1871) T
Culbreath, Dicy to J. A. Ballard 2-23-1860 T
Culbreath, Dicy to R. M. Knox 7-1-1868 (7-2-1868) T
Culbreath, Elizabeth F. to James Colwell 5-4-1860 (5-5-1860) T
Culbreath, Elizabeth to James Buckley? 12-4-1843 (12-?-1843) T
Culbreath, Elizabeth to William T. J. Burton 6-6-1855 Hn
Culbreath, Lucy to Colemon Cooper 6-18-1870 T
Culbreath, Lucy to Ebenezer T. Walker 1-3-1842 (1-4-1842) T
Culbreath, Martha to Joseph W. McCetcham 1-12-1869 (1-13-1869) T
Culbreath, Mary E. to Saml. Winfree 2-26-1868 T
Culbreath, Mary to Archibald Pinson 1-11-1841 (1-?-1841) T
Culbreath, Mollie E. to W. F. Prewett, 12-15-1874 T
Culbreath, S. T. to M. T. Richardson 7-16-1872 (7-20-1872) T
Culbreath, Tomsella to John W. Robins 5-30-1855 Hn
Culbreath, Virginia to Daniel T. Lake 1-11-1855 T
Culbreth, E. C. to James N. Turner 2-19-1868 (no return) F
Culbreth, Mary A. L. to Macon McClain 12-27-1860 Hn
Culbreth, Mary Frances to Joseph S. Waller 11-14-1857 (3-20-1858) T
Culbreth, T. C. to L. P. Marshall 9-28-1870 T
Cull, Ann to Michael Lawler 7-23-1855 Sh
Culla, Almyra to William Puryer? 5-2-1842 Hn
Cullen, Ann to John T. Faucett 7-4-1842 (no return) L
Cullen, Catharine to Timothy Maroney 6-9-1860 (6-10-1860) Sh
Cullen, Louisa St. C. to R. W. Flannery 12-10-1858 Sh
Cullepher, Mary A. to J. P. Harper 9-30-1868 L
Culley, Sarah F. to Lucilius A. Holloman 6-13-1869 G
Cullin, Harriet to Anderson Williams 1-1-1844 (1-4-1844) L
Cullom, J. M. to J. J. Matty 12-17-1859 (12-20-1859) F
Cullum, A. C. to J. J. Jones 1-4-1871 (1-5-1871) T
Cullum, Eliz. Caroline Rebec to William Gillom Grace 1-13-1846 T
Cullum, Elizabeth to Jeremiah Swaggard 6-7-1847 O
Cullum, Nancy to John D. Verhine 1-5-1846 (1-25-1846) O
Culnan, Ellen to Joseph Nolan 4-4-1863 Sh
Culp, Albenia T. to John A. Garvin 12-11-1866 (12-13-1866) F
Culp, Drucilla to Robert J. Gilchrist 7-10-1832 G
Culp, E. A. to S. L. Barrow 12-20-1864 (12-24-1864) F
Culp, Elizabeth to Andrew Blankenship 12-3-1850 Cr
Culp, Elizabeth to Edward White 8-11-1869 (8-12-1869) Cr
Culp, Esther to Wm. P. Norman 7-14-1849 F
Culp, Fanny to Linsey Dowdy 12-15-1870 (12-28-1870) F B
Culp, Jennie to Jesse Waller 1-29-1870 (3-6-1870) F B
Culp, Martha J. to Thos. Blackstock 1-4-1851 Cr
Culp, Mary A. to Moses Parks 12-2-1850 (12-3-1850) F
Culp, Mary Jane to Micajah Reeder 10-29-1847 Hn
Culp, Mary M. to Wm. P. Leach 12-2-1846 Cr
Culp, Mollie E. to W. J. Barron 12-11-1866 (12-13-1866) F
Culp, Sarah J. to Francis Hill 12-2-1850 (12-3-1850) F
Culp, Sarah to Jonathan Bell 10-27-1871 (no return) Cr
Culp, Susannah J. to John J. Lytlee 9-11-1851 (no return) Cr
Culpeper, Mary to John Kaplinger 1-12-1860 Be
Culpeper, Sabina E. to Amos F. Lewis 6-17-1845 Be
Culpepper, Bathsheba to Charles P. Graham 12-12-1846 (no return) Hn
Culpepper, Laura to S. S. Hollowell 2-16-1869 (2-18-1869) F
Culpepper, Lucy A. to Zerubbable Scott 7-17-1858 Hn
Culpepper, Martha A. to David S. Dortch 3-9-1843 Hn
Culpepper, Sely to Ellis Evans 7-30-1863 Be
Culpepper, Susan to John Caplinger 4-6-1867 (no return) Hn
Cultin, Sarah E. to Thomas D. Pennel 12-16-1858 (12-23-1858) T
Culwell, Emily to Emanuel Frosh 2-17-1872 (2-18-1872) Dy
Cumings, Eliza to Overton Harris 2-23-1867 (3-2-1867) F B
Cumins, L. Jane to Wm. Taylor 1-10-1870 T
Cummings, Eliza A. to Calvin E. Shore 10-17-1861 O
Cummings, Emily to Hampton C. Misenheimer 3-4-1848 (3-9-1848) Hr

Cummings, Frances to I. W. Robertson 12-19-1866 (12-20-1866) O
Cummings, Lou to Gipson S. Fitz 12-30-1873 Hy
Cummings, M. E. to C. T. Wallis 11-9-1865 O
Cummings, M. E. to W. G. Hartzfield 3-18-1861 Sh
Cummings, M. F. to Wm. H. Malone 7-3-1861 (7-4-1861) Sh
Cummings, Maggie to W. A. McClain 4-29-1862 Sh
Cummings, Martha A. to Elias D. Cummings 9-22-1873 (9-23-1873) Dy
Cummins, C. A. to A. J. Sargent 11-2-1856 Be
Cummins, C. to William Martin 8-3-1865 Be
Cummins, Dora to William Brooks 3-30-1870 (4-2-1870) F B
Cummins, Mary E. to W. P. Flowers 5-8-1871 F
Cumpton, Della to Sam Rowland 7-29-1868 (7-30-1868) Cr
Cunagham, Mary to Marshall Bridgeman 7-13-1871 Cr
Cunif, Annie to Maximilian Noger 1-13-1862 Sh
Cuningham, M. to S. S. Long 8-21-1872 (no return) Cr B
Cuningham, Mary to Daniel O'Neal 10-20-1862 Sh
Cunliffe, Susan H. to B. Bowers 10-31-1859 (11-1-1859) F
Cunning, Jane to James Broach 3-26-1844 Cr
Cunningham, Adaline to W. D. Blankenship 11-8-1880 (no return) L
Cunningham, Adiline to W. L. Easterwood 12-16-1868 G
Cunningham, Alice to John Lambert 3-11-1870 (3-13-1870) Cr
Cunningham, Alice to Ned Woodson 1-22-1869 (1-23-1869) Cr
Cunningham, Amanda to Henry H. Miller 7-30-1864 Sh
Cunningham, America to James W. Webb 6-5-1854 G
Cunningham, Ann E. to Isaac C. Haynes 12-17-1853 (12-20-1853) G
Cunningham, Betty to Doctor Woodson 6-28-1871 (6-29-1871) Cr B
Cunningham, Caroline to William Carmack 11-8-1825 G
Cunningham, Catharine S. to Thomas F. Reeves 12-24-1839 (12-25-1839) O
Cunningham, Elen to W. L. Cunningham 9-6-1858 G
Cunningham, Elizabeth J. to Shadrick Webster 4-19-1857 Hn
Cunningham, Emily to John M. Brewer 10-22-1860 (no return) Dy
Cunningham, Emily to S. H. Hale 8-6-1865 G
Cunningham, Esther to James F. Nall 9-17-1856 (10-2-1856) O
Cunningham, Eunisa to Isaac Pirtle 12-13-1828 Hr
Cunningham, Fannie to John W. Moore 3-4-1876 (3-5-1876) L
Cunningham, Frances to L. S. Smith 2-7-1859 (2-8-1859) O
Cunningham, Frances to William Ekle 8-28-1862 Mn
Cunningham, H. E. to John W. Rodgers 7-28-1858 Cr
Cunningham, H. to P. Gatens 4-26-1864 Sh
Cunningham, Hannah C. to Thomas W. Dickerson 5-23-1837 (5-24-1837) O
Cunningham, Irena to Daniel Smith 12-21-1843 O
Cunningham, Jane (Mrs.) to Tim McNamara 12-31-1864 Sh
Cunningham, Jane to James Bedford 5-19-1854 (5-21-1854) Sh
Cunningham, Jane to Michael Myers 2-10-1855 (2-11-1855) Sh
Cunningham, Kitsey Swan to Ephraim Dorherty 10-9-1863 (10-11-1863) Dy
Cunningham, L. E. to W. A. C. Bridges 12-16-1867 (12-18-1867) Cr
Cunningham, Laura to Robert Johnson 12-23-1868 (no return) Hy
Cunningham, Louiza to Patrick J. Welch 5-28-1873 Cr
Cunningham, Lucinda to Clinton Galey 12-19-1842 G
Cunningham, M. M. to D. C. Caldwell 3-2-1857 G
Cunningham, Macilda E. to Wallis Pollard 4-22-1870 (4-24-1870) Cr
Cunningham, Malissa Jane to W. L. Cunningham 5-7-1870 G
Cunningham, Martha J. to M. J. Williams 10-12-1869 Dy
Cunningham, Mary A. to Pinkney Baker 8-25-1877 (8-29-1877) L
Cunningham, Mary C. to John Cloar 9-11-1865 (9-13-1865) O
Cunningham, Mary E. to Alexander G. Goodloe 12-21-1863 (no return) Cr
Cunningham, Mary E. to J. W. Bunton 1-15-1860 Hn
Cunningham, Mary E. to L. M. Huffman 2-3-1870 Cr
Cunningham, Mary F. to Thomas J. Gambill 1-16-1868 G
Cunningham, Mary H. to Reuben S. Turney 9-17-1850 Hn
Cunningham, Mary J. to James F. Turner 3-23-1868 (3-24-1868) Cr
Cunningham, Mary J. to Philemon Hurt 3-8-1852 (3-10-1852) G
Cunningham, Mary W. to A. H. Goodloe 9-27-1871 Dy
Cunningham, Mary to Calvin Crow 4-7-1851 (4-10-1851) O
Cunningham, Mattie A. to W. E. Mitchum 6-5-1869 G
Cunningham, Mattie to J. R. Cook 3-2-1876 Dy
Cunningham, Mollie to Mitchell Clark 12-5-1868 (12-6-1868) Cr
Cunningham, Nancy M. to G. W. Crocker 5-17-1866 G
Cunningham, Nancy S. to Thomas E. Jones 12-15-1850 Hn
Cunningham, Nannie to W. H. Arnett 1-22-1874 Dy
Cunningham, Norra to Robert Childress 5-14-1863 Sh
Cunningham, Ruth R. to William C. Cobb 5-21-1866 (5-23-1866) L
Cunningham, Sarah A. to A. G. Propst 11-3-1867 G
Cunningham, Sarah E. to Lafayette Ridgeway 2-17-1859 Hn
Cunningham, Sarah J. to James McClain 5-17-1857 O
Cunningham, Sarah J. to James T. Archer 9-21-1854 Hn
Cunningham, Sarah J. to Richard R. Watson 1-4-1859 G
Cunningham, Sarah J. to Thomas Little 3-11-1863 Cr
Cunningham, Sarah J. to Thomas Little 3-11-1863 (no return) Cr
Cunningham, Sarah to Joshua D. Young 10-16-1851 Hn
Cunningham, Sarah to Thos. Hooker 1-13-1866 (1-21-1866) Cr
Cunningham, Susan B. to William T. Lowry? 1-16-1846 Hn
Cunningham, Susan to Thomas Goodin 5-2-1870 (no return) Cr
Cunningham, T. F.? to William Thompson 8-4-1883 (8-5-1883) L
Cunningham, Winny to William Bennett 11-11-1846
Cup, Mary Ann Elizabeth to James Brim 7-27-183 (7-28-1833) Hr
Cup, Mary Ann to Taylor Adams 10-21-1869 (10-22-1869) T

Cupp, Adaline to Thomas B. Clifton 1-1-1855 (1-5-1855) Hr
Cupp, Elizabeth to John Garner 1-19-1843 Be
Cupp, Mary E. to Alfred F. Cannon 3-7-1844 Cr
Cupp, Sarah C. to Charles D. Chamberlain 10-9-1855 Ma
Cupples, Rebecca to Goodman Richardson 7-14-1849 Ma
Cupps, Mary to Wm. C. Benton 7-10-1838 Cr
Curd, Annah to James C. Love 8-14-1856 Sh
Curd, E. E. to E. R. Atchison 9-16-1853 Hn
Curd, Josie to Pleasant M. Hope 10-4-1859 Hn
Curd, M. A. to John L. Utterback 9-17-1851 Hn
Curd, Sarah to J. H. Russell 10-30-1845 Hn
Curl, M. S. to Z. H. Patrick 6-20-1842 (no return) F
Curlee, Martha to Thos. J. Honea 1-28-1855 Cr
Curlee, Sarah F. to W. N. McClure 1-27-1858 Cr
Curley(Carley?), Elizabeth to Jacob N. Norton 12-22-1838 (12-25-1838) Hr
Curley, Nancy Ann to Francis W. Brooks 1-15-1842 Sh
Curley, Virginia W. to Marion Twitty 9-16-1847 Sh
Curley?, Elizabeth to John McLain 12-13-1837 Hr
Curley?, Sidney to Tom Boyd 12-17-1870 Hy
Curlin, Callie to W. G. Cook 5-25-1880 L
Curlin, Charlotte to William H. Hubbs 12-19-1848 O
Curlin, D. E. to J. P. Taylor 12-23-1885 L
Curlin, Lucy A. to S. J. Boyers 8-26-1871 O
Curlin, Nancy J. to Joseph R. Edwards 6-21-1855 (6-22-1855) O
Curlin, Nancy to Wylie A. Johnson 10-13-1856 O
Curlin, Sarah E. to Lycurgus Hall 11-1-1872 (11-27-1872) O
Curlins, Sarah to Edward E. Angus 5-1-1860 Sh
Curren, Alice to Willis Gray 12-24-1875 L B
Curren, Elizabeth to Peter Bradford 1-12-1878 L
Curren, Millie to Anderson Bostic 12-8-1877 (12-16-1877) L
Curren, Rachel to Joe Cotter 3-13-1873 (no return) Hy
Curren, Tennessee to John Helm 1-7-1875 L B
Curren, V. R. to J. W. Brasher 10-22-1870 (10-23-1870) Cr
Currey, Cofie to E. J. Buchanan 11-7-1867 G
Currey, Emmer to Moses Read 11-10-1867 Hy
Currey, Mary Ida to James Grayer Wells 12-23-1868 G
Currie, Alice to J. B. Currie 2-6-1882 L
Currie, Allie to H. H. Dickinson 11-17-1875 (no return) Hy
Currie, Amanda to Henry Clay 12-25-1865 Hy
Currie, Ann to Peter Night 12-26-1868 Hy
Currie, Beller to James Neuborn 4-18-1868 Hy
Currie, Bettie to J. F. Modlin 7-18-1867 Hy
Currie, Cora to George Taliaferro 12-27-1876 Hy
Currie, Dilcy to Jim Birks 12-26-1871 Hy
Currie, Dilly to Green Thomas 10-30-1878 Hy
Currie, E. to Howell Jordan 2-24-1886 (2-25-1886) L
Currie, Eliza to Glenn Hicks 10-14-1873 Hy
Currie, Eliza to Josiah Sumroe 12-25-1866 Hy
Currie, Elizabeth A. to Louis R. Martin 5-6-1869 L
Currie, Elizabeth Caroline to William M. Ewing 4-29-1857 Ma
Currie, Ella to Harry Currie 12-12-1870 (no return) Hy
Currie, Ellen to Caesar Wheatly 6-9-1866 Hy
Currie, Ellen to Charles Greer 7-5-1869 (7-17-1869) F B
Currie, Ellen to Frank Hooker 1-31-1883 (1-29?-1883) L
Currie, Ellen to Steven Taylor 5-5-1867 Hy
Currie, Em to Mat McFarland 1-3-1868 Hy
Currie, Emma to Alonza Miron? 1-11-1872 Hy
Currie, Emma to George Wells 6-14-1876 Hy
Currie, Emma to Washington Estes 5-11-1871 Hy
Currie, Frances to Danl. Wells 10-12-1872 Hy
Currie, Frances to Jackson Young 9-13-1882 L
Currie, Francis to Jacob Estes 6-29-1878 (no return) Hy
Currie, Henrietta to Wm. King 12-11-1878 Hy
Currie, Ida to Richard Graves 1-4-1876 Hy
Currie, J. N. to J. Human 12-18-1878 L
Currie, Joanah C. to Soloman G. Alston 12-11-1865 (12-12-1865) L
Currie, Julia to Taylor Sangster 3-17-1870 Hy
Currie, Laura J. to Alfred Cannon 2-20-1874 (no return) Hy
Currie, Lizzie to John Jones 12-12-1876 Hy
Currie, Lucinda to John Henry Currie 1-21-1866 Hy
Currie, M. F. to W. H. Crawford 11-28-1866 Hy
Currie, Manda to William Johnson 12-29-1875 (no return) Hy
Currie, Margaret to Wm. Johnson 1-23-1873 Hy
Currie, Maria to Henry Newborne 3-26-1869 Hy
Currie, Mary A. to Alex. Smith 12-29-1869 Hy
Currie, Mary Ann to Wm. D. Winchester 2-6-1858 Ma
Currie, Mary Emma to Willis Green Maclin 10-20-1878 Hy
Currie, Mary to David P. Steele 12-16-1858 L
Currie, Mary to George Roberts 10-15-1874 Hy
Currie, Mary to Jerry Maclin 3-21-1869 Hy
Currie, Maurina to James Day 2-10-1870 (no return) Hy
Currie, Nancy to Armstead Hains 12-23-1870 Hy
Currie, Puss to Fed Bevens 5-16-1872 Hy
Currie, Roena J. to John R. Dodd 2-12-1867 Ma
Currie, Sadie to R. A. (Rev.) Neely 4-16-1868 Hy
Currie, Sallie to George Burks 2-28-1877 Hy
Currie, Sarah B. to Joseph B. McLish 11-14-1859 (no return) Hy
Currie, Sarah J. to Rezin S. Wood 1-2-1850 L
Currie, Sarah to John Williams 12-31-1865 Hy
Currier, Marianna to J. P. Mathewson 11-20-1866 Hn
Currin, Ann E. to Alfred J. Walton 3-20-1843 (no return) F
Currin, Cassy to James Henning 12-9-1885 L
Currin, Cherry to Beverly Oldham 1-18-1883 (1-19-1883) L
Currin, Ellen to Buck Kinney 5-13-1881 (5-15-1881) L B
Currin, Laura A. to George Chapman 11-29-1856 Sh
Currin, Low to Handy Soward 8-30-1871 (8-31-1871) L
Currin, Margie to John McColler 2-24-1868 (7?-29-1868) L B
Currin, Margt. to Alfred Redman 12-18-1867 (12-22-1867) L B
Currin, Mary Jane to J. c. Smith 10-31-1885 (11-2-1885) L
Currin, Sallie to Nelson Pitts 1-19-1880 (1-20-1880) L
Currin, Sarah J. to John McKairy Currin 1-17-1876 (1-19-1876) L
Currin, Selinia to Auther Halliburton 10-13-1871 Hy
Curry, Elvira to Phillip Shedrick 12-30-1877 Hy
Curry, Estell to Kent H. WWhitten 9-25-1871 T
Curry, Jessie E. to James A. Smith 12-31-1870 (1-2-1871) T
Curry, Laura to Elijah Bond 7-4-1874 (no return) Hy
Curry, Mary to Stephen Taylor 9-14-1867 Hy
Curry, Sarah to Eli Wilkinson 1-12-1862 Mn
Curry, Sophia to Reeves Turner 12-17-1862 We
Cursey, Sarah to W. T. Crawford 11-22-1862 (12-4-1862) F
Cursie, Bridget to Anthony Powers 6-12-1861 Sh
Curtice, Fredonia to Robt. D. Moore 2-18-1863 (2-29-1863) L
Curtis, Benny to J. W. Carmack 1-1-1868 (no return) Dy
Curtis, Betsy to Harry Milam 2-10-1866 Hn
Curtis, C. L. to John A. Maddox 7-26-1867 (no return) Hy
Curtis, E. M. to Ephraim Elington 10-25-1871 (no return) Hy
Curtis, E. P. C. to M. V. White 5-22-1867 (5-23-1867) Dy
Curtis, Eliza Ann to James W. Saxton 11-21-1844 T
Curtis, Eliza to James Swift 8-2-1871 (8-19-1871) Dy
Curtis, Elizabeth to John P. Freeman 6-3-1844 T
Curtis, Emma to J. H. Johnson 12-20-1879 (12-23-1879) L B
Curtis, Frances Elizabeth to W. H. Mathis 9-22-1877 (9-23-1877) L
Curtis, H. R. to A. L. Shekle 10-3-1870 (no return) Dy
Curtis, H. R. to A. L. Shikle 10-3-1870 (12-5-1870) Dy
Curtis, Harritt to Delfras Brooks 1-18-1877 (no return) L
Curtis, Janusy to J. W. Boals 3-4-1869 (no return) Dy
Curtis, Jemima L. to John M. Swindell 4-7-1861 (4-8-1861) G
Curtis, Julia Virginia to Jo Dangerfield 7-2-1880 (7-12-1880) L B
Curtis, K. to J.(T?) W. Crabb 2-4-1842 Be
Curtis, L. M. to S. A. Pugh 12-21-1865 (12-22-1865) L
Curtis, Laura E. to W. B. Richardet 6-9-1863 Sh
Curtis, Lizzie to Freeman Hayes 3-3-1877 Hy
Curtis, Lou to J. T. Gibson 10-24-1883 (10-25-1883) L
Curtis, Lucinda Jane to W. D. Tinslay 2-28-1873 (3-20-1873) L
Curtis, M. E. to T. M. Pate 1-2-1878 Dy
Curtis, Mahalia to John Clark 1-23-1850 Sh
Curtis, Martha Ann to William F. Hooper 7-14-1852 (no return) L
Curtis, Martha P. to James B. Dinwiddie 8-6-1867 Hn
Curtis, Martha to Charles R. Brown 6-22-1860 (6-25-1860) L
Curtis, Martha to James C. Gill 3-24-1856 Sh
Curtis, Mary Ann to James W. Milam 10-9-1849 (no return) Hn
Curtis, Mary C. to Joseph E. White 1-31-1883 (2-1-1883) L
Curtis, Mary E. to Green B. Jennings 8-7-1852 (8-8-1852) L
Curtis, Mary E. to Thomas M. Lemons 1-30-1861 G
Curtis, Mary Lavina to James W. Braden 7-7-1871 (7-8-1871) L
Curtis, Mary to John A. Gilliam 1-22-1853 (no return) F
Curtis, Matilda J. to J. W. Hall 12-15-1873 (12-18-1873) Dy
Curtis, Mattie B. to Sam W. Lyle 11-21-1871 (no return) Hy
Curtis, Mollie L. to James C. Freeman 11-16-1870 Hy
Curtis, Nancy Louisa to Thomas Bryant 11-4-1866 Be
Curtis, Parlee to Ephram Hart Freedman 2-9-1866 (no return) Dy
Curtis, Peletha to Marcus Holeman 3-30-1838 G
Curtis, Rebecca A. to Edmond Chitwood 6-3-1868 (no return) Dy
Curtis, Rebecca to Melford Hall 4-29-1832 Ma
Curtis, S. J. to R. A. James 7-10-1878 L
Curtis, Sallie A. to J. R. McCullers 10-20-1859 Sh
Curtis, Sallie E. to D. R. Weakley 3-8-1872 Dy
Curtis, Sarah to Albert Powell 1-1-1851 L
Curtis, Sue M. to George L. Holmes 6-28-1860 (6-29-1860) Sh
Curtis, Susan B. to W. T. Mays 4-17-1867 Dy
Curtis, Susan to Elisha Thorgmorton 11-30-1844 We
Curtiss, M. J. to A. A. Denton 1-1-1884 L
Curtner, Malinda to Harrison Boon 9-9-1850 O
Curtus?, Elizabeth (Mrs.) to S. B. Piles 1-7-1873 (1-9-1873) L
Cusick, Bridget to Michael Whalen 4-2-1864 (4-3-1864) Sh
Cusick, M. P. to F. M. Utley 2-17-1881 (2-28-1881) L
Cusick, Mary to G. W. Tripp 10-30-1880 (11-5-1880) L
Custan, Catherine to Stefano Denegri 4-1-1850 Sh
Custard, Ellen to John Robert Mitchell 12-11-1867 Hn
Custer, Mary E. to Daniel C. Jenkins 12-20-1859 (no return) We
Cutberth, Eliza to Jesse G. Tudor 6-20-1833 (7-19-1833) Hr
Cutler, Victoria A. to Jesse A. Gibbs 12-13-1859 We
Cutz, Rosina to Louis Walter 7-28-1856 Sh
Cyle, Agness to Eli Vinston 8-23-1866 (8-26-1866) T

D_wns?, Elizabeth Jane to Reuben West 5-1-1853 Hn
Dabbs, Mary to Joseph Hilliard 1-31-1855 O
Dacus, Amanda to John D. Boswell 9-3-1859 T
Dacus, Elizabeth Jane to John Boswell 2-11-1847 T
Dacus, Frances to Daniel Buford Boswell 9-27-1848 (9-28-1848) T
Dacus, Hester Ann to Franklin Huffman 10-3-1859 (10-4-1859) T
Dacus, Martha L. to John Davis Boswell 12-28-1854 T
Dacus, Mary B. to J. G. Sherill 8-8-1860 T
Dacus, Parthana to James M. Olive 8-11-1857 We
Dacus, Rebeca A. to F. M. Knight 11-22-1860 T
Dacus, Viney to Peter M. Wilson 1-12-1869 T
Dagling, Elizabeth to William Ralph 11-7-1866 (11-8-1867?) T
Dailey, Julia A. to John J. Perry 12-29-1860 F
Dailey, Mary F. to John Seavers 8-21-1858 Cr
Daily (Danby?), Mary Ann to Silvester Umphries 6-17-1854 (7-12-1854) Sh
Dairden, Anna E. to John R. Devenport 10-24-1867 F
Dale, Catharan E. to John A. Haines 10-15-1870 (10-16-1870) T
Dale, Frances A. to John A. Shirley 12-29-1862 Hn
Dale, Marilda M. to Samuel R. Tucker 6-7-1848 G
Dale, Martha C. to Granville Lemonds 10-22-1861 (no return) Hn
Dale, Nancy J. to Thomas S. Morgan 1-12-1858 Hn
Daley, Anan to Jas. Appleton 7-20-1852 Be
Daley, Letitia to Charles C. Johnson 5-5-1860 (5-6-1860) Sh
Daley, Margaret to P. Bannon 5-5-1853 Sh
Dallas, Anna to John H. Welch 10-24-1849 O
Dallas, Elizabeth Jane to A. W. Duncan 7-3-1854 Sh
Dallas, Katie to Isaac Morgan 7-3-1871 L
Dallas, Martha A. to A. R. Stewart 2-16-1858 Sh
Dallas, Martha Caroline to Claiburne Gunter 10-26-1850 Sh
Dallas, Mary to Marshall Goodman 5-18-1864 (5-26-1864) O
Dallas, Sarah Ann to Andrew Goss 1-29-1850 Sh
Dalle?, Willie Helen to Robert H. White 3-23-1871 T
Dallis, Mattie to Nathan Napper 2-28-1876 (3-2-1876) L
Dallohite, Lora M. to A. J. Swaim 3-22-1857 Sh
Dalning, Sarah M. to Richard Waggoner 3-13-1846 (no return) We
Dalson, Caroline to Beverly D. Hagar 12-5-1857 Sh
Dalson, Caroline to John W. Madden 6-27-1859 (7-4-1859) Sh
Dalsy (Daley), Ellen to James Welsh 11-18-1849 Sh
Dalsy, Mary to Daniel Foley 9-25-1847 Sh
Dalton, Annie B. to Josiah Davis 11-13-1855 Cr
Dalton, Catharine to Jessee Tharp 4-2-1846 G
Dalton, Eliza J. to E. J. Lipsey 3-29-1864 Sh
Dalton, Elizabeth A. to James Hendricks 5-27-1851 Hn
Dalton, Elizabeth to E. G. Richardson 5-2-1856 Cr
Dalton, Frances A. to John M. Dalton 3-6-1849 Hn
Dalton, Frances to John Marberry 7-27-1850 Hn
Dalton, L. A. to R. Madison 2-17-1862 (2-18-1862) Sh
Dalton, Lizzie to Z. Haas 4-8-1869 Ma
Dalton, Mary Ann to George Simpson 1-9-1854 (1-12-1854) T
Dalton, Mary C. to J. R. H. Mitchell 6-11-1846 Cr
Dalton, Mary C. to Thomas Janes 9-4-1855 Hn
Dalton, Mary E. to John J. Boyed 5-25-1848 F
Dalton, Rebecca to James Davis 3-13-1839 M
Dalton, Sarah to James R. Powell 3-10-1845 O
Daly, Bridget to Owen Kiernam 5-23-1858 Sh
Daly, Ellen to F. W. Reinhardt 1-24-1856 Sh
Daly, Mary to Jeremiah Sullivan 3-14-1863 Sh
Daly, Mary to John McNamara 3-17-1860 Sh
Daly, Mary to John Walsh 10-11-1854 Sh
Daly, Mary to Michael Moylan 1-18-1854 (1-19-1854) Sh
Daly, Nancy to Owen Winters 9-8-1858 Sh
Daly, Sarah N. to Robt. T. Patterson 4-24-1870 G
Daly, Sarah to John Shehan 5-17-1862 (5-20-1862) Sh
Damron, Emily to Jno. D. Cook 9-2-1850 We
Damson-Damron-Dawson, Nancy Jane to Travis P. Vail 12-11-1848 (12-26-1848) Hr
Danbury, Emma L. to Jerome B. Gilmore 5-6-1854 Sh
Dance, Martha to Edmond Skinner 12-28-1846 G
Dance, Mollie E. to C. H. Tyree (Tyne?) 12-19-1866 G
Dance, Virginia E. to Richard A. Campbell 12-19-1872 Hy
Dancer, Elizabeth to Joseph Woods 8-21-1829 Sh
Dancey, Nancey to Thomas J. Scott 7-3-1861 Hy
Dancy, Emiline to Allen Thompson 1-8-1874 Hy
Dancy, Jane to Henry Carney 1-4-1873 Hy
Dancy, M. E. to J. B. Wright 2-24-1870 G
Dandridge, Agnes Neilson to Joseph Brooks 2-22-1847 (2-25-1847) Hr
Dandridge, Martha F. to Calloway B. Moore 3-11-1846 Sh
Dandridge, Sarah to Washington Boulton 1-15-1833 Sh
Dandrige, Mildred S. to Benjamin Cash 7-23-1838 (8-1-1838) Hr
Dangerfield, Felicia to William Mills 6-22-1843 G
Dangerfield, Jane to Moses Smith 12-1-1877 (12-2-1877) L B
Dangerfield, Julia to Wesley Halliburton 5-15-1884 L
Dangerfield, Willie to Corbin Lewis 5-27-1874 (no return) L
Daniel, Alice to Henry Searcy 10-21-1885 (10-27-1885) L
Daniel, Ariminta to Thomas J. Rawlings 2-12-1837 Sh
Daniel, Delila Ann to James C. Parker 9-24-1855 (10-1-1855) Sh
Daniel, Dollie to Wm. Smith 12-1-1877 (12-2-1877) Dy

Daniel, Elisabeth L. to Benjamin F. Furgason 12-6-1848 (no return) F
Daniel, Eliza to Peter White 8-26-1872 Hy
Daniel, Elizabeth F. to David W. Settle 12-28-1859 (no return) Hn
Daniel, Elizabeth to Samuel Roberts 2-25-1848 Be
Daniel, Ella to A. Coleman 2-5-1874 Hy
Daniel, Emily O. to C. Carrol 7-25-1856 (9-10-1856) G
Daniel, Frances to Henry M. Teague 1-27-1851 Hr
Daniel, H. A. O. to F. M. James 7-2-1858 G
Daniel, Harriet to Aleck Whitmore 8-6-1868 Hy
Daniel, Harriet to Thos. Parker 8-1-1868 (8-3-1868) T
Daniel, Josephine to A. Campbell 2-7-1866 Hn
Daniel, Judy to Harbert Ferrell 2-22-1841 (3-2-1841) Ma
Daniel, Lucy E. to Henry M. Comer 10-25-1842 Hr
Daniel, Manerva to Zachariah Harrison 1-31-1857 (2-5-1857) T
Daniel, Margaret A. to James R. Randle 9-27-1854 Hn
Daniel, Martha A. to William R. Mayo 12-26-1848 Sh
Daniel, Martha to Surs Scott 2-16-1886 (no return) L
Daniel, Mary A. to Robert A. Walker 5-8-1873 (5-3?-18730 T
Daniel, Mary F. to Henry M. Fletcher 9-22-1848 Hn
Daniel, Mary Jane to George Donnell 2-24-1851 Hr
Daniel, Mary O. to Booker Bomar 12-17-1854 (no return) F
Daniel, Mary to Joseph Bush 12-5-1850 Be
Daniel, Millie to George Saunders 3-5-1883 L
Daniel, Nancy A. E. W. to John Pentecost 3-17-1860 Hn
Daniel, Nancy A. to Wm. Bizzle 12-22-1856 (12-23-1856) Hr
Daniel, Nancy to Elisha J. Bush 2-20-1848 Be
Daniel, Penina to John Cloe 2-6-1844 Sh
Daniel, Polly to Rice B. Yates 3-24-1835 Hr
Daniel, Rebecca to Thomas Brandon 4-18-1849 Hn
Daniel, Roxanna M. to Thomas Morton 8-1-1865 Mn
Daniel, Sarah to Aaron Joplin 3-27-1880 (3-29-1880) L
Daniel, Sarepta J. to Ivey Kail 4-26-1871 (no return) Hy
Daniel, Tillie A. E. to William J. Prince 4-6-1867 (4-9-1867) T
Daniels, Louisa C. to Jesse G. Brown 2-27-1871 (2-22?-1871) T
Daniels, Martha M. to Aurelius L. Goff 8-2-1849 Sh
Daniels, Sobrina to Michael Archard 12-25-1850 Sh
Danks, Julia to Benjamin Gilbert 5-2-1846 Sh
Danly, Margaret F. to Noah Rushing 7-16-1865 Hn
Danner, Elizabeth to William C. Robertson 12-17-1853 (12-22-1853) G
Danner, P. G. to W. H. Reeves 3-1-1859 G
Darby, Cecilia Beverly to William A. Old 1-30-1847 (2-?-1847) T
Darby, Martha S. to J. P. Clark 11-3-1866 (11-5-1866) Cr
Darby, Mary Elizabeth to Norman Reynolds 6-26-1850 T
Darby, Mary Jane to Wilson C. Jones 12-29-1845 (1-1-1845?) Ma
Darby, Mary to Clement McDearmon 5-14-1854 Hn
Darby, Matilda A. to Thomas V. Burns 4-28-1868 Ma
Darby, Melia F. A.? to James R. Powell 10-8-1850 O
Darby, Sibella A. to Elias Cook 5-22-1843 (5-24-1843) Ma
Darby, ____ Vanhook to John Wesley Clark 11-24-1842 (12-?-1842) T
Darden, Katherine to L. J. Smith 12-18-1868 (12-20-1868) F
Darden, Lizzie to Robt. Barker 1-31-1876 (2-1-1876) Dy
Darden, Mary to D. B. Massey 12-16-1850 (no return) F
Darden, S. A. to H. F. Freeman 12-15-1862 (12-17-1862) F
Darden, Sarah F. to J. S. Allen 6-4-1879 (no return) Dy
Dargan, Sarah to Wyatt Bailey 2-15-1838 (no return) Hn
Dark, Alice to Abe Wardlaw 12-18-1878 (12-20-1878) L B
Dark, Belden to Bird Graves 10-30-1884 L
Dark, Nancey to Rankin Shover 7-22-1876 (7-23-1876) L
Darley, Elizabeth Ann to Thomas Sullivan 6-11-1855 (no return) F
Darlin, Lillie F. to John Goss 12-30-1868 (no return) F
Darlin, Nancy to P. G. Clement 1-30-1855 We
Darmon, Jane to John Wilson 9-22-1842 (9-?-1842) Ma
Darnald, Hannah H. to William B. Dyall 8-12-1847 G
Darnall, Amand to Stephen Mayes 9-2-1872 (no return) Cr B
Darnall, Ann E. to Saml. N. Abraham 2-27-1860 (3-15-1860) Hr
Darnall, Emeline to William M. Stevenson 6-23-1841 O
Darnall, M. V. to George M. Edwards 11-26-1859 (11-29-1859) O
Darnall, Mariah to William Spear 8-16-1849 Hn
Darnall, Mary A. to David C. Vickers 3-4-1863 Cr
Darnall, Mary A. to David C. Vickers 3-4-1863 (no return) Cr
Darnall, Mary E. to J. B. Fuller 11-16-1867 (11-17-1867) Cr
Darnall, Mary E. to Robert D. Watson 7-29-1853 (8-2-1853) O
Darnall, Mary J. to J. W. Smith 12-7-1865 O
Darnall, N. L. to J. A. McKenzie 6-16-1864 (6-19-1864) O
Darnall, Salina to John Pigg 1-20-1834 O
Darnall, Sally J. to John H. Yancey 9-16-1847 Hn
Darnall, Sophia to J. D. Malady 12-2-1862 (12-3-1862) O
Darnel, Amanda D. to John Hays 1-10-1867 O
Darnell, Caladonia J. to J. H. McKiney 9-17-1861 (9-23-1861) Cr
Darnell, Elizabeth to JohnH. New 3-8-1848 Cr
Darnell, Harriet A. to A. J. McClure 3-5-1856 We
Darnell, Jane to J. C. H. Fowler 11-1-1850 Hr
Darnell, Jane to J. C. H. Fowler 7-14-1853 Hr
Darnell, Mary Elvira to James M. Cook 10-12-1841 (10-13-1841) Ma
Darnell, Nancy C. H. to N. M. Darnell 4-3-1855 Cr
Darnell, Salina to James T. Pugh 9-28-1853 (9-29-1853) Hr
Darnell, Sallie to W. B. Cherry 1-20-1875 (1-21-1875) O

Brides

Darnell, Sarah A. to Gilbert Arey 8-20-1851 Hn
Darnell, Sarah to Joseph Rumley 12-8-1841 Cr
Darnell, Sophia to James L. Miller 3-2-1854 Hr
Darnell, Susan A. to Jacob S. Shipman 9-9-1851 G
Darnell, Tempy M. to Nathaniel M. Young 3-1-1850 (3-3-1850) Hr
Darnell?, Sarah G. to John E. Hopkins 9-7-1847 (9-9-1847) Hr
Darnold, Mary G. to Thomas A. McCluer 4-30-1844 (no return) We
Darough, Nancy A. E. to T. A. Watson 9-26-1867 Hy
Darr, Lucy to Peter Long 12-9-1840 T
Darrett (Dennett?), Elizabeth to Fidelis (Felix) Benderbis(Bardelis?) 8-22-1853 (9-4-1853) Sh
Daryberry, Cynthia to A. D. Lucas 9-29-1864 Sh
Dashiell, Ellen O. to Charles W. Dunning 1-3-1863 Sh
Daugherty, Almanda J. to Jessee Hughsand 2-20-1863 Mn
Daugherty, Catherine to Michael Spilman 6-3-1848 Sh
Daugherty, Charity A. to John D. Bishop 12-30-1868 (1-6-1869) F
Daugherty, Clary to Stephen Rains 5-15-1830 (5-20-1830) G
Daugherty, Eliza to Alex Haskins 3-15-1877 (no return) Dy
Daugherty, Emma E. to R. W. Dunlap 12-18-1876 (12-24-1876) Dy
Daugherty, M. C. to W. P. Hays 6-25-1879 (6-27-1879) Dy
Daugherty, Susan C. to J. R. Breeze 5-6-1863 Mn
Daughry, Margaret A. to John Neagle 3-7-1873 Hn
Daughtry, Mary to Sterling Strother 8-30-1842 (9-1-1842) G
Daughty, Nancy to A. M. Vaught 11-10-1856 G
Davenport, Amanda E. to William M. Currie 11-6-1856 (no return) L
Davenport, Bettie to W. H. Fisher 7-22-1871 F
Davenport, Emiline to Eli Whitaker 4-9-1835 Hr
Davenport, Louisa to James M. McClelland 10-4-1843 (10-5-1843) L
Davenport, M. A. to Lemuel White 5-5-1883 (5-7-1883) L
Davenport, Margaret to J. J. Langdon 10-19-1866 (10-28-1866) F
Davenport, Martha J. to Manly Durham 2-11-1858 F
Davenport, Mary E. to Joseph Seligman 11-25-1858 Sh
Davenport, Mary G. to J. M. Smith 11-19-1856 (no return) L
Davenport, Naomi C. to John H. Phillips 4-24-1854 (no return) L
Davenport, Sarah Ann to Ennis Hooper 6-8-1853 (7-29-1853) O
Davenport, Sarah to Joseph Watson 12-23-1835 Hr
Davenport, T. O. to S. D. Morrow 11-8-1882 L
Davenport, Zilla Ann to John Perry 8-27-1844 We
Daverson, Emily to John D. Woods 4-30-1839 Cr
Daves, Ann to Henry Hayes 3-19-1862 O
Davese, S. M. to John J. Reeves 1-5-1859 G
Davey, Ellen to James W. Heath 12-16-1857 (12-17-1857) Sh
David, Ann to James Capella 3-12-1860 Sh
David, Anna L. to P. B. Jones 1-10-1872 Hy
David, Arelia to John McKenzie 5-10-1861 (7-8-1861) T
David, E. J. to Wm. M. Hope 4-19-1854 (no return) F
David, Ellen to James Coleman 1-4-1853 (1-5-1853) Hr
David, J. A. to John W. Webb 6-17-1871 (6-19-1871) T
David, Louisa C. to John Sadler 7-1-1844 (7-10-1844) F
David, Luvica W. to James W. Ray 8-6-1860 (8-8-1860) Cr
David, Margaret R. to Prestly H. Roberts 9-14-1853 Hr
David, Mary A. to G. M. Dugan 2-2-1857 Hr
David, Milly to Joseph Hughes 12-18-1849 (no return) F
David, Miriah to Elisha Tate 5-15-1858 Cr
David, Sarah to J. M. Bradshaw 1-21-1860 (1-22-1860) G
David, V. C. to W. F. Jones 12-17-1868 (12-3-1869?) T
David, Violet to Henry Chilton 10-8-1873 Hy
Davidson, A. M. to N. W. Clement 8-25-1853 (no return) Hn
Davidson, Adaline to William Rogers 10-17-1869 G B
Davidson, Alice to L. H. Brogdon 1-20-1885 (1-21-1885) L
Davidson, Amanda to Joseph Bowers 11-18-1871 (12-20-1871) L
Davidson, Catharine R. to James J. McCollum 4-16-1840 O
Davidson, Cordelia to R. L. Ball 11-10-1852 Sh
Davidson, D. Ann to James Starnes 3-13-1866 (3-14-1866) T
Davidson, Edy to Anderson Mackling 10-17-1868 G B
Davidson, Eliza A. to Eliphlet G. Fulton 7-21-1845 Hr
Davidson, Eliza Ann to James P. Churchwell 5-17-1859 (5-19-1859) L
Davidson, Eliza F. to Atlas J. Cate 8-7-1866 (8-9-1866) Ma
Davidson, Elizabeth Ann to William Counts 7-12-1836 (7-13-1836) G
Davidson, Elizabeth Wade to James Timbs 12-21-1853 (12-22-1853) T
Davidson, Elizabeth to John H. Harmon 12-17-1867 (12-18-1867) Dy
Davidson, Elizabeth to John W. Summers 1-8-1851 (no return) Hn
Davidson, Elizabeth to Noah Strickland 3-3-1861 Be
Davidson, Elizabeth to W. T. Tinkle 8-26-1866 G
Davidson, Ellen C. to Jabus Timms 12-28-1859 (12-29-1859) T
Davidson, Emeline to Ned Jones 10-29-1869 G B
Davidson, H. A. to L. F. Becton 12-2-1866 G
Davidson, Harratt E. to Robert W. Barton 12-5-1839 G
Davidson, Harriet to Elihu W. Dano 10-4-1864 G
Davidson, Harriet to Elihu W. Davis 10-4-1864 G
Davidson, Harriett to Eli McMullin 12-22-1832 (12-27-1832) G
Davidson, J. to W. H. Baker 2-1-1865 G
Davidson, Jemima to John Deboard 11-5-1859 Sh
Davidson, Judith J. to Humphrey Donaldson 11-5-1835 G
Davidson, Julia A. E. to Wm. H. Talley 1-17-1867 G
Davidson, Julia C. to Z. C. Cullen 8-27-1860 (8-28-1860) T
Davidson, Julia L. to John D. Cabler 3-15-1835 (3-17-1835) G

Davidson, Lucy Jane to Reason Rutledge 2-24-1859 G
Davidson, Lucy M. to Wm. G. Gordon 6-26-1862 Be
Davidson, M. to J. Farmer 3-11-1842 Be
Davidson, Malissa to Hosea D. Browning 5-16-1867 Be
Davidson, Margaret to T. L. Clark, jr. 11-1-1873 (11-2-1873) L
Davidson, Mariah E. to John S. Hill 1-26-1843 G
Davidson, Martha J. to W. J. Thompson 6-14-1859 Sh
Davidson, Martha M. to Joel B. Lewis 11-19-1846 G
Davidson, Martha to H. W. Swinney 9-6-1849 Hn
Davidson, Martha to Henry Staggs 12-24-1864 (1-2-1865) Dy
Davidson, Mary A. to James Williams 12-4-1856 Ma
Davidson, Mary A. to Reason A. Rutledge 12-2-1867 G
Davidson, Mary Ann to James Williams 12-6-1856 Be CC
Davidson, Mary Ann to Lewis P. Collins 9-17-1856 Be
Davidson, Mary Ann to Mathias Neighbors 8-13-1847 Be
Davidson, Mary C. to James P. Throgmorton 1-20-1864 Hn
Davidson, Mary E. to Thomas H. Meek 8-19-1852 G
Davidson, Mary F. to William Falker 5-1-1880 (5-2-1880) L
Davidson, Mary Jane to William Godsey 1-18-1854 (1-19-1854) Sh
Davidson, Mary Valentia to Wm. Carroll Marsh 12-21-1853 (12-22-1853) T
Davidson, Mary to G. A. Camp 7-11-1856 Be
Davidson, Mary to John Moore 2-27-1884 L
Davidson, Mary to Martin V. Nance 9-6-1858 (9-9-1858) G
Davidson, Mary to William Bunn 2-25-1868 (2-26?-1868) L
Davidson, Menurva F. to Juleus A. Skiles 12-24-1857 G
Davidson, Mildred to Chas. Delashmet 11-18-1867 (11-21-1867) T
Davidson, N. J. to A. P. Mays 6-7-1884 (6-11-1884) L
Davidson, Nancy A. to James D. Nevill 12-22-1866 (12-23-1866) Ma
Davidson, Nancy C. to Henry C. Davidson 3-17-1867 G
Davidson, Nancy W. to Edmond W. Caldwell 3-20-1845 O
Davidson, Paralee to Harrison Thurman 12-25-1862 Mn
Davidson, Pelina to Daniel H. Burnett 2-4-1860 (no return) Hy
Davidson, R. F. to M. P. Norton 1-27-1869 (1-28-1869) F
Davidson, Rebecca C. to A. B. DeBruce 12-22-1853 Hn
Davidson, Ruth P. to James C. Brown 8-11-1843 (8-15-1843) O
Davidson, S. E. to John D. Moore 8-2-1872 (8-6-1872) T
Davidson, Sally to John Dunagan 11-11-1830 G
Davidson, Sarah W. to J. B. McAdams 12-15-1868 G
Davidson, Sarah to William R. Nunn 9-6-1858 (9-9-1858) G
Davidson, Sophia to Hugh McVay 9-13-1827 Sh
Davidson, Susan E. to Reuben W. Williams 10-19-1859 (10-20-1859) L
Davidson, Susan J. to Bennett W. McDade 2-13-1858 (2-17-1858) Ma
Davidson, Susie to M. B. Fortner 9-16-1884 (no return) L
Davidsson, Sabry to Thomas Williams 10-18-1828 G
Davie, Adaline to Thos. Clement 2-11-1873 O
Davie, Anias to Jim Williams 3-16-1867 Hy
Davie, Cornelia J. to James B. Davie 7-21-1853 Ma
Davie, Elizabeth J. to Lacy L. Brown 12-4-1857 (12-6-1857) Ma
Davie, Elizabeth to Calvin C. Sloan 12-8-1869 Hy
Davie, Emily H. to James White 9-19-1855 Ma
Davie, Louisa to Benjamin F. Elder 12-6-1858 Ma
Davie, Martha to R. W. Peacock 4-21-1860 (no return) Hy
Davie, Mary R. to Edward Telfair 10-28-1850 Ma
Davie, Millie to Joseph A. Austin 12-14-1871 Hy
Davie, Mollie J. to John A. Reid 10-30-1878 Hy
Davie, Prisie to Turner Spivey 12-28-1871 Hy
Davie, Rachael to Green Smith 2-17-1866 Hy
Davie, Sarah A. to John L. Fly 12-19-1853 (12-21-1853) Ma
Davie, Sarah J. to Alexander Bowling 11-29-1850 Ma
Davie, Sarah to Jeptha Mathews 4-20-1830 Hr
Davis, A. E. to J. R. Covington 6-7-1857 We
Davis, A. J. to J. R. Prichard 8-9-1867 (8-10-1869) Dy
Davis, A. L. to W. E. Lunsford 2-14-1877 Dy
Davis, Abigal to Jessee J. McCloud 10-15-1836 G
Davis, Adaline to Martin Russell 12-5-1843 O
Davis, Aga to Sherwood Bone 8-27-1839 (8-30-1839) O
Davis, Allice to William Searcy 12-22-1873 (12-24-1873) L B
Davis, Allis to J. N. Branch 10-26-1875 (no return) L
Davis, Amanda A. to Samuel Frey 11-1-1852 (11-2-1852) Sh
Davis, Amanda Harris to George Carson Gattis 6-11-1853 Ma
Davis, Amanda J. to Elijah H. Williams 12-23-1867 (12-27-1867) Ma
Davis, Amanda to W. H. George 8-10-1850 Cr
Davis, Amelia Ann to Thomas Douglass 7-4-1855 Sh
Davis, Amelia to Saml. Kindrick 10-17-1846 (no return) F
Davis, Angaline E. to Michal McNutty 12-23-1839 (12-24-1839) G
Davis, Ann E. to Richd. M. Manley 8-5-1846 F
Davis, Ann F. to James M. Bottoms 1-10-1855 G
Davis, Ann M. to John Ervel 7-1-1865 (7-2-1865) O
Davis, Ann Salina to Willis A. Hogue 10-1-1855 (10-2-1855) O
Davis, Ann W. to Joseph Yates 11-15-1840 Hn
Davis, Ann to Wiley Read 12-26-1867 Hy
Davis, Anna E. to C. C. Drumwright 10-21-1873 (10-22-1873) L
Davis, Anna J. to M. H. Coover 7-4-1862 Sh
Davis, Anna to Bryant Nash 5-27-1867 Hy
Davis, Annie to Andrew Foley 10-14-1874 (10-15-1874) T
Davis, Annie to F. A. Newton 12-16-1878 (12-17-1878) Dy
Davis, Aramenta to Richard Davis 11-20-1855 O

Davis, Araminta S. to Abraham C. Romaine 1-15-1862 (1-16-1862) Sh
Davis, Artela F. to Joshua M. Reams 12-2-1868 (12-4-1868) Ma
Davis, Artilla to William C. Fleming 7-26-1847 (7-26-1847) O
Davis, B. I.? to G. W. Smith 1-10-1869 G
Davis, Bazilla Jane to Elam Richardson 1-11-1853 Ma
Davis, Bethi to David Bradford 5-20-1877 Hy
Davis, Bettie to James Womble 1-29-1873 Hy
Davis, Bettie to Joseph Kunckel 4-23-1863 Sh
Davis, C. A. to A. C. Taylor 1-31-1867 G
Davis, Callie to S. A. Taylor 9-18-1873 Hy
Davis, Caroline to John Soward 10-27-1856 (12?-4-1856) L
Davis, Caroline to W. H. Emberson 9-6-1847 (9-9-1847) F
Davis, Carrie to John E. Mitchell 10-14-1877 Hy
Davis, Catharine to William H. Yarbrough 7-24-1854 (7-27-1854) Hr
Davis, Catherine to John A. Gladney 3-27-1869 (4-1-1869) Ma
Davis, Catherine to W. D. Humphreys 9-1-1862 (no return) Hn
Davis, Charlotte A. to James Rankin 1-6-1868 (1-7-1868) Dy
Davis, Charlotte to R. T. D. Norman 10-28-1869 Dy
Davis, Charlotte to Robt. Lewellen 12-24-1878 Hy
Davis, Clara J. to Gabriel Cannon 2-24-1853 (no return) F
Davis, Clarinda to Wm. T. Newton 12-1-1845 (no return) We
Davis, Clary to Jessee Hutchison 8-6-1855 Be
Davis, Cordelia to Isaac Canada 1-20-1877 (1-21-1877) Dy
Davis, Cornelia Ann to P. G. Voss 8-12-1879 (8-13-1879) L
Davis, Cornelia E. to W. A. H. Graham 2-14-1861 Sh
Davis, D. E. to W. F. Jones 12-17-1868 (1-7-1869) T
Davis, Darcus C. to John Rutledge 9-3-1855 (9-4-1855) Sh
Davis, Delelah to James P. Panky 11-29-1845 (11-30-1845) Hr
Davis, Delina to Samuel Wiles 9-23-1833 (9-26-1833) O
Davis, Dicey (Mrs.) to Solomon Godfrey 12-18-1860 Ma
Davis, Dinah to Isaac Spicer 12-23-1871 Hy
Davis, E. J. to Robert Thompson 11-23-1857 (11-24-1857) O
Davis, E. to William Booth 6-12-1857 Sh
Davis, Edy to Miles Nichelson 12-25-1868 Hy
Davis, Eleanor B. to Adam Dean Campbell 12-3-1855 (12-4-1855) T
Davis, Eleanor C. to William C. Hart 1-28-1850 T
Davis, Eliza Angeline to Thos. E. Dent 11-3-1857 We
Davis, Eliza Ann to Wm. McKinstry 12-16-1858 T
Davis, Eliza Jane to John Davis, jr. 12-18-1856 (no return) F
Davis, Eliza to Allen McCuiston 6-13-1852 Hn
Davis, Eliza to Elijah May 5-3-1840 O
Davis, Eliza to Ephraim Cooper 5-3-1849 (5-4-1849) G
Davis, Eliza to John N. Cooper 3-3-1848 (3-5-1848) G
Davis, Eliza to Manson Fowlkes 7-11-1878 Dy
Davis, Eliza to Orin Guthrie 1-23-1829 Hr
Davis, Elizabeth A. to Silas Doren 12-14-1848 Hn
Davis, Elizabeth B. to Benjamin J. Powell 2-2-1848 Ma
Davis, Elizabeth C. to William E. Wade 2-9-1832 G
Davis, Elizabeth F. to Martin F. Careley 2-11-1868 Dy
Davis, Elizabeth Jane to Abraham K. Rea 3-18-1841 Sh
Davis, Elizabeth Jane to Arthur Deloach 11-3-1846 Ma
Davis, Elizabeth Jane to Marcus H. Cullum 1-27-1845 T
Davis, Elizabeth T. (Mrs.) to William J. McKinney 8-9-1858 (8-10-1858) Ma
Davis, Elizabeth to G. W. Britt 7-28-1873 (no return) Hy
Davis, Elizabeth to Gaston L. Jones 3-14-1855 (2?-14-1855) O
Davis, Elizabeth to J. P. Cheatham 4-30-1866 O
Davis, Elizabeth to James Carter 4-9-1833 O
Davis, Elizabeth to Job Hamliln 2-13-1840 O
Davis, Elizabeth to John Carley 1-27-1849 (2-4-1849) Hr
Davis, Elizabeth to John Hailey 1-19-1847 Hr
Davis, Elizabeth to Lemuel B. Hammond 11-2-1862 Mn
Davis, Elizabeth to Sterling Howell 6-9-1842 (6-11-1842) O
Davis, Elizabeth to T. R. Parker 7-2-1846 Cr
Davis, Elizabeth to William Vaughn 8-19-1858 G
Davis, Ellen (Mrs.) to Nicholas Cummins 10-14-1864 Sh
Davis, Ellen to Albert Cox 1-30-1869 (no return) Hy
Davis, Ellen to John Reans 3-21-1869 Hy
Davis, Ellen to John Taylor 8-18-1867 Hy
Davis, Ellen to Lemuel Wade 11-22-1867 Hy
Davis, Emeline to Daniel Moody 10-20-1872 Hy
Davis, Emilina to John Rodenhizer 8-21-1858 (8-22-1858) Ma
Davis, Emily M. (Mrs.) to James Moffatt 9-28-1864 Sh
Davis, Emily to Kenny L. Tudor 7-7-1833 (8-8-1833) Hr
Davis, Emily to Thomas S. Babb 5-13-1845 (5-14-1845) O
Davis, Emma E. to Joseph F. Ellis 3-16-1852 (no return) F
Davis, F. B. (Mrs.) to Geo. P. Logue 8-26-1858 Sh
Davis, Fanny E. to H. P. Keller 12-16-1879 L
Davis, Frances C. to George W. Davidson 4-13-1867 (4-14-1867) L
Davis, Frances C. to William A. McDonald 3-10-1847 (3-11-1847) Hr
Davis, Frances E. to R. T. Chambers 9-26-1866 (9-30-1866) Dy
Davis, Frances E. to Robert T. O'Daniel 12-22-1858 (12-28-1858) G
Davis, Frances L. to Peter P. Wilson 9-24-1856 We
Davis, Frances to A. J. Wilson 1-15-1867 L
Davis, Frances to James B. Williams 5-3-1857 Cr
Davis, Francisia to A. J. Smith 12-18-1858 (12-22-1858) Hr
Davis, Frankie to J. H. Bills 12-23-1878 (no return) Dy
Davis, Fredonia to J. Nunnery 9-6-1860 Be

Davis, Gabriella to James C. Miller 1-24-1861 Dy
Davis, Gracey to Thomas Jordan 11-25-1869 (no return) L
Davis, Hannah to Harry Jordan 7-26-1877 (7-27-1877) O
Davis, Harriet D. to Cornelius Youree 8-7-1874 (8-9-1874) O
Davis, Harriet M. to J. S. Jimason 10-16-1856 Sh
Davis, Harriet to Hiram (of Illinois) Crow 9-19-1862 Ma
Davis, Harriet to Hiram J. Crow 9-23-1862 Mn
Davis, Harriett E. to Fields H. Johnson 3-6-1861 (3-7-1861) O
Davis, Huldah to Thos. Wheelus 10-8-1846 We
Davis, J. C. to William Hollinsworth 2-2-1854 Be
Davis, Jane (Mrs.) to R. R. Johnston 1-10-1863 Sh
Davis, Jane B. to William A. Davie 11-8-1841 Ma
Davis, Jane E. to James G. Houston 8-10-1848 Sh
Davis, Jane F. C. to John N. Pullion 9-3-1860 Hy
Davis, Jane N. to Samuel Kendall 12-9-1838 Hn
Davis, Jane R. to B. F. West 10-12-1857 Sh
Davis, Jane to Crockett Currie 5-16-1878 (no return) Hy
Davis, Jane to Granderson Taylor 7-21-1872 Hy
Davis, Jane to John B. Murrell 11-27-1845 Hn
Davis, Jane to John Reagan 9-19-1833 Hr
Davis, Jane to John Soward 7-14-1856 L
Davis, Jane to Stephen L. Brook 8-6-1829 Hr
Davis, Jena (Tena?) to Hugh Branch 1-6-1874 (1-8-1874) L
Davis, Jennie to John Bond, jr. 8-13-1872 (no return) Hy
Davis, Jennie to Louis Bond 4-16-1872 Hy
Davis, Joanna to David Breaderick 9-2-1838 Hn
Davis, Josephine to Chas. P. Brewton 4-2-1857 Hr
Davis, Judith to William E. Marlow 6-26-1833 Sh
Davis, Julia A. to Lucius P. Howard 12-18-1853 Hn
Davis, Julia A. to William Phelps 11-9-1852 Hn
Davis, Julia to Dodson Hoskins 7-24-1856 G
Davis, Julia to Nick Willis 5-18-1868 G
Davis, Kate to John M. McDonald 9-28-1864 Sh
Davis, Laura A. to A. L. Cornelius 6-30-1862 Sh
Davis, Laura to Jerry Wright 1-10-1874 (1-12-1874) L B
Davis, Leitia to Wm. Moor 3-2-1856 Be
Davis, Lizzie to B. H. Harmon 11-5-1867 (11-7-1867) Dy
Davis, Lizzie to Danl. Brooks 1-4-1874 Hy
Davis, Lou Jane to Felix G. Sherrod 5-4-1868 (5-18-1868) Ma
Davis, Louisa A. to R. B. Leewright 5-11-1859 (5-12-1859) Sh
Davis, Louisa O. to A. W. Bryant 10-13-1847 (10-14-1847) Hr
Davis, Louiza C. to Robert Norman 8-20-1851 (8-21-1851) G
Davis, Loula to Isaac Green 12-8-1876 (no return) Hy
Davis, Lucy A. to Hamilton J. Green 11-19-1850 (11-21-1850) F
Davis, Lucy Ann to Wm. B. Chambers 2-20-1841 (2-25-1841) L
Davis, Lucy to Dutton Sweeton 10-4-1841 (10-10-1841) Hr
Davis, Lucy to James L. Davis 6-26-1848 (6-29-1848) Ma
Davis, Lucy to John Dickie 11-1-1851 (11-2-1851) Ma
Davis, Lucy to Tandy P. Duncan 4-19-1839 O
Davis, Lucy to William Sparks 4-16-1855 (4-10?-1855) Ma
Davis, M. C. to Thomas Carson 10-11-1865 T
Davis, M. E. to Franklin Hertsfield 2-12-1872 (2-13-1872) T
Davis, M. E. to J. W. Seward 9-11-1871 (no return) Dy
Davis, M. E. to W. E. Lunsford 1-22-1879 (1-23-1879) Dy
Davis, M. F. to William Payne 9-6-1865 (9-7-1865) T
Davis, M. to D. Spures 11-30-1841 Be
Davis, Maggie to Wm. A. Dismukes 8-20-1870 (8-21-1870) Ma
Davis, Mahala I. I. to Patrick H. Old 2-27-1845 We
Davis, Mahaly to Abraham Deeson? 12-18-1826 Hr
Davis, Malinda to John Moser 2-20-1843 (2-26-1843) O
Davis, Manerva A. E. to Saml. M. Williams 2-11-1857 (2-12-1857) T
Davis, Manirva to Henry McGee 9-3-1868 G B
Davis, Mantora F. to Albert L. Rains 10-13-1870 G
Davis, Margaret A. to Austin McAdoo 9-?-1862 (9-14-1866?) Cr
Davis, Margaret A. to James A. Dodd 1-7-1853 (1-11-1853) Ma
Davis, Margaret Ann to Danl. B. Hood 9-8-1857 (9-10-1857) Hr
Davis, Margaret C. to J. W. Johnson 11-15-1855 (no return) Hn
Davis, Margaret E. to James D. Jenkins 12-18-1856 Hn
Davis, Margaret E. to Joseph N. Haynes 6-15-1831 Ma
Davis, Margaret F. to Peter Miner 10-5-1861 (10-9-1861) Sh
Davis, Margaret J. to Thomas Branch 12-19-1846 (no return) F
Davis, Margaret R. to John S. Dearmond 12-30-1852 Sh
Davis, Margaret S. to Benjamin R. Sappington 2-13-1841 Sh
Davis, Margarett A. to Paul C. Grafton 6-22-1854 (6-23-1854) G
Davis, Margret to William Pounds 9-24-1860 O
Davis, Maria Jane to Nathaniel Bates 11-29-1871 (no return) L
Davis, Maria L. to James Brookes 6-21-1842 (6-22-1842) F
Davis, Maria to Joseph Newell 2-12-1846 G
Davis, Mariah to Austin Coldwell 4-10-1870 F
Davis, Mariah to Haywood Caldwell 1-3-1872 Hy
Davis, Mariah to Rolling H. Johnson 12-15-1851 (no return) F
Davis, Marth E. to J. C. Clayton 10-21-1865 (10-25-1865) T
Davis, Martha A. E. to Wm. G. Grace 5-1-1855 T
Davis, Martha A. to Robert Gammill 2-1-1864 Sh
Davis, Martha Ann to James S. Jester 1-20-1854 (1-26-1854) Ma
Davis, Martha Ann to William H. Henning 10-15-1839 Ma
Davis, Martha C. to James M. Thompson 5-9-1854 (5-11-1854) O

Davis, Martha E. to John Wesley Davis 3-9-1870 (3-10-1870) F
Davis, Martha Helen to Rufus T. Basheres 7-24-1843 T
Davis, Martha J. to Jas. M. Benton 9-25-1866 (9-27-1866) Cr
Davis, Martha J. to William Henry 8-20-1872 (8-21-1872) L
Davis, Martha L. to Jos. C. Tarkinton 2-12-1852 Sh
Davis, Martha L. to Wm. G. Honey 10-10-1838 Cr
Davis, Martha T. to P. H. Nance 10-5-1864 (10-9-1864) Cr
Davis, Martha to Alex Bullock 1-13-1878 Hy
Davis, Martha to Charles G. Redden 6-6-1848 Hn
Davis, Martha to Charles Powell 9-23-1842 O
Davis, Martha to Jesse Cerly 1-18-1849 Hr
Davis, Martha to John Cannon 3-24-1865 (3-28-1865) F
Davis, Martha to John H. Morgan 4-23-1868 Hy
Davis, Martha to Joseph Peete 4-19-1871 (no return) Hy
Davis, Martha to Thomas Taylor 11-18-1850 (11-19-1850) Ma
Davis, Martha to Thos. M. Carter 10-31-1844 Cr
Davis, Martha to W. T. Wells 7-11-1859 (7-14-1859) Hr
Davis, Martha(Maletha?) J. to Caleb jr. Cope 7-1-1856 (7-2-1856) Hr
Davis, Mary A. to Henry D. Smith 3-8-1866 (3-10-1866) O
Davis, Mary A. to James W. Jackson 9-2-1861 O
Davis, Mary A. to William L. Gattis 12-21-1847 (12-22-1847) Ma
Davis, Mary Ann to Jacob Reeden 4-11-1842 Hy
Davis, Mary Ann to Robert A. Campbell 8-11-1847 (8-12-1847) Ma
Davis, Mary C. to Thomas C. Durham 11-10-1864 (no return) L
Davis, Mary Daniel to Samuel Clark Davis 10-7-1850 Ma
Davis, Mary E. to Abner Alexander 5-26-1853 (no return) F
Davis, Mary E. to Charles W. Sullivant 7-23-1850 (no return) F
Davis, Mary E. to James P. Martin 3-20-1861 Hn
Davis, Mary E. to James Wood? 8-15-1867 (8-16-1867) Dy
Davis, Mary E. to John F. Davis 12-22-1865 L
Davis, Mary E. to Reubin Buntin 12-16-1850 (1-1-1851) Ma
Davis, Mary E. to S. G. McClanahan 2-20-1867 (no return) Dy
Davis, Mary Ellen to J. A. McAllister 12-6-1861 (12-8-1861) Sh
Davis, Mary G. to Lewis Dorch 8-29-1849 (no return) Hn
Davis, Mary J. to Benjamin F. Terrell 10-31-1839 G
Davis, Mary J. to Hiram K. Alexander 1-28-1858 O
Davis, Mary J. to John D. Simmons 10-12-1862 Mn
Davis, Mary J. to John T. McGehee 9-4-1871 O
Davis, Mary J. to Wm. Snowden 12-16-1841 Cr
Davis, Mary Jane to John M. Spickenagle 2-18-1832 Sh
Davis, Mary K. to Tinsly W. Halliburton 2-23-1843 Ma
Davis, Mary Nolan to Jesse McIntosh 10-16-1850 O
Davis, Mary R. to John D. Chisum 12-24-1860 (12-27-1860) Hr
Davis, Mary S. to Robert M. Seay 6-7-1856 (6-8-1856) O
Davis, Mary Susan to Joseph L. Roberts 12-8-1852 (12-9-1852) T
Davis, Mary to Arthur Olds 4-24-1849 (4-26-1849) L
Davis, Mary to Isaiah Cheatham 7-5-1858 Hn
Davis, Mary to James F. Guinn 6-21-1862 (6-22-1862) Ma
Davis, Mary to James H. Kirkland 1-21-1857 Sh
Davis, Mary to Jeremiah Parnel 12-23-1873 O
Davis, Mary to John G. Wilson 12-7-1843 Hr
Davis, Mary to Matthew A. Poterfieth 10-4-1838 Hr
Davis, Mary to Norflet T. Young 1-11-1869 (1-14-1869) F
Davis, Mary to Oscar F. Prescott 2-14-1855 Sh
Davis, Mary to Pinckney S. Pierce 1-26-1853 Hn
Davis, Mary to Samuel Jackson 5-22-1839 (5-25-1839) Ma
Davis, Mary to T. H. Fitzhugh 8-12-1868 Dy
Davis, Mary to Thomas M. Jones 2-29-1840 (3-1-1840) O
Davis, Mary to Wm. H. Evans 10-4-1859 (10-6-1859) Hr
Davis, Mary to _____ Childres 4-7-1863 Hn
Davis, Maryan to Thomas D. Rachel 1-8-1848 F
Davis, Matilda E. to W. L. Johnson 3-9-1858 Cr
Davis, Matilda to B. H. Ruvers (Reevers?) 11-11-1856 Sh
Davis, May to Alfred Mashburn 4-19-1847 H
Davis, Melissa V. to C. A. Chamberlain 2-7-1859 Sh
Davis, Melvina to John A. M. Covington 6-11-1857 T
Davis, Milley to E. L. Peal 1-24-1849 Hn
Davis, Minerva to John F. Patterso 11-11-1856 G
Davis, Minta E. to Silas Hughes 7-11-1863 (7-22-1863) F
Davis, Mollie E. to W. A. Lee 8-5-1868 (8-5-1870?) G
Davis, Mollie to C. L. Wagner 12-21-1869 G
Davis, Mollie to Duke Branch 12-8-1871 Hy
Davis, Mollie to Stephen Walton 3-5-1873 (3-6-1873) Dy
Davis, Mollie to Willis Chambers 11-12-1871 O
Davis, Molly E. to Thomas R. Meux 6-3-1874 Hy
Davis, Myra A. to Seth B. Davis 3-2-1870 (3-3-1870) L
Davis, N. J. to J. N. Evans 3-10-1863 (3-12-1863) Dy
Davis, Nancy C. to James M. Tillman 7-31-1869 (8-3-1869) F
Davis, Nancy E. to W. H. Macon 12-26-1864 (no return) L
Davis, Nancy J. to J. O. Cheatham 3-24-1867 Hn
Davis, Nancy J. to Thomas H. Faris 2-12-1863 (no return) Cr
Davis, Nancy J. to Thos. H. Farris 2-12-1863 Cr
Davis, Nancy Jane to John Tinnen 2-7-1859 T
Davis, Nancy L. to Joel S. Brooks 7-4-1857 (7-7-1857) Sh
Davis, Nancy L.(S.) to James H. Glass 1-18-1858 (1-21-1858) Hr
Davis, Nancy P. to Nathan F. Rutledge 2-23-1858 (2-24-1858) Sh
Davis, Nancy R. to John W. Finch 11-15-1846 O

Davis, Nancy Susan to Pitt C. Browder 12-9-1867 (12-10-1868?) Ma
Davis, Nancy to Arthur Macon 4-21-1865 (4-22-1865) L
Davis, Nancy to Bevily Towns 11-1-1871 (11-15-1871) Cr
Davis, Nancy to Daniel M. Prewett 6-6-1838 (6-12-1838) Hr
Davis, Nancy to David Cowan 11-7-1846 (11-8-1846) Hr
Davis, Nancy to Dickson Bradford 7-21-1867 Hy
Davis, Nancy to E. S. Little 10-9-1858 (10-12-1858) Hr
Davis, Nancy to Gilford Brown 6-3-1877 Hy
Davis, Nancy to Jack Turner 12-27-1866 G
Davis, Nancy to John Davidson 12-17-1863 G
Davis, Nancy to Joseph Mosier 11-24-1836 G
Davis, Nancy to Leander Alford 1-30-1844 Ma
Davis, Nancy to Matthew Walker 1-28-1868 (2-1-1868) F B
Davis, Nannie to J. H. Mitchell 10-10-1881 L
Davis, Nannie to J. T. Davis 12-27-1879 (12-28-1879) L
Davis, O. C. to J. G. McCain 1-26-1862 (1-29-1862) T
Davis, Ofilia to Jerry Omara 1-8-1867 T
Davis, Parmelia Lewis to Richard Stanley 4-2-1858 (4-4-1858) O
Davis, Parmelia Louisa to Richard Stanley 4-2-1838 (4-4-1838) O
Davis, Patsy to John P. Chappell 12-14-1839 (12-15-1839) Hr
Davis, Patsy to Kelly Taylor 8-23-1868 Hy
Davis, Phereby (Mrs.) to Robert Wallace 8-17-1867 G B
Davis, Pochahontas to H. M. Bauen (Baren?) 2-2-1860 (2-4-1860) Sh
Davis, Pochahontas to James B. Powell 1-21-1854 (1-22-1854) O
Davis, Polly to D. D. Vaden 3-11-1854 G
Davis, Polly to James Rodgers 4-14-1842 F
Davis, Polly to John Mosier 7-2-1831 O
Davis, Polly to Thos. Riggs 12-13-1853 (no return) F
Davis, Pricilla to James G. Hampton 2-25-1845 Cr
Davis, Priscilla to Elijah Adams 7-10-1838 Cr
Davis, Priscilla to Henry Jackson 10-16-1867 (no return) L
Davis, Prudence A. to W. T. Marlar 12-7-1848 Sh
Davis, R. E. to J. B. McConnell 2-16-1863 (2-18-1863) Sh
Davis, R. E. to John Cook 4-14-1869 G
Davis, R. E. to N. J. Caldwell 10-12-1856 Hn
Davis, R. J. to H. N. Simpson 4-4-1871 Hy
Davis, R. L. to C. D. Strickland 7-3-1876 (7-4-1876) L
Davis, Rachael to Louis Elkins 7-1-1840 (7-2-1840) Ma
Davis, Racheal to John C. Gullender? 1-18-1835 Hr
Davis, Rachel to Albard H. Hubbard 12-29-1874 Hy
Davis, Rebecca Jane to Drury B. Williams 10-20-1857 (10-22-1857) Ma
Davis, Rebecca to H. Bear 1-3-1845 Hn
Davis, Rena Caroline to James Parr 11-4-1833 (11-5-1833) Hr
Davis, Rhoena Jane to Jessie Smith 7-14-1877 (7-16-1877) L
Davis, Rosa to J. A. Green 12-6-1881 (12-7-1881) L
Davis, Roxana O. to Wm. H. Stanfield 11-4-1868 (no return) Dy
Davis, Rusia to B. W. Hubert 12-28-1851 O
Davis, Ruth to William F. Ray 5-18-1850 O
Davis, S. F. to H. F. V. Branch 12-5-1883 L
Davis, S. J. to J. L. Hall 5-9-1878 (5-12-1878) Dy
Davis, S. J. to J. T. Boatwright 10-28-1873 (10-29-1873) Dy
Davis, S. M. A. to J.R. Culbreath 6-20-1874 T
Davis, S. M. to T. E. Fletcher 8-30-1871 O
Davis, Salina M. to James M> Hill 12-27-1859 (12-28-1859) T
Davis, Sallie to John Henry Adkins 11-8-1870 G
Davis, Sallie to Richard Hagerty 8-3-1877 (no return) Hy
Davis, Sallie to Richard Jones 3-6-1871 F B
Davis, Sally to Terry Odell 10-25-1831 G
Davis, Salvina? M. to James McHale 12-27-1859 T
Davis, Sarah A. to William A. Thomas 10-27-1852 (10-28-1852) G
Davis, Sarah A. to A. W. Hopper 12-24-1867 G
Davis, Sarah A. to James A. Johnson 10-30-1860 Cr
Davis, Sarah A. to Martin Skinner 12-23-1859 (12-25-1859) F
Davis, Sarah Adiline to Wm. Carroll Davis 9-4-1854 (9-6-1854) T
Davis, Sarah Ann to Joseph Moser 3-2-1854 (3-3-1854) O
Davis, Sarah C. to James W. Hamel 11-27-1872 Cr
Davis, Sarah D. to J. D. Montgomery 3-7-1860 (3-8-1860) Sh
Davis, Sarah E. to Dempney Ellington 5-28-1861 (5-30-1861) Ma
Davis, Sarah E. to James H. Pollock 1-4-1849 F
Davis, Sarah Elizabeth to Robert H. Morris 6-10-1852 Hr
Davis, Sarah F. to G. W. Patrick 12-14-1867 (12-23-1867) Dy
Davis, Sarah F. to William Latham 7-21-1856 (7-24-1856) Ma
Davis, Sarah Francis to Edmund Haltom 12-17-1856 (12-18-1856) Ma
Davis, Sarah J. to James C. Gooch 8-28-1848 (no return) Cr
Davis, Sarah J. to Noah Skipper 5-1-1856 G
Davis, Sarah Jane to J. L. Carnall 11-11-1873 (11-13-1873) L
Davis, Sarah Jane to Thomas? James Wiley 8-10-1854 T
Davis, Sarah M. to Cyrus T. Davis 10-24-1850 Sh
Davis, Sarah S. to Nathan Barksdale 7-25-1827 G
Davis, Sarah T. to Washington R. Browder 10-17-1857 (10-18-1857) Ma
Davis, Sarah to Edward Buck 7-28-1848 (7-30-1848) F
Davis, Sarah to Elias Lawrence 12-3-1840 (12-8-1840) Ma
Davis, Sarah to J. B. Parnell 11-13-1867 (11-14-1867) Dy
Davis, Sarah to Jeptha Mathews 4-20-1831 (4-21-1831) Hr
Davis, Sarah to John C. Baker 2-18-1874 (2-19-1874) L
Davis, Sarah to Joseph Barton 2-21-1839 Hn
Davis, Sarah to Levy Holmes 12-27-1869 (1-1-1870) F B

Davis, Sarah to Samuel Mosier 4-6-1831 O
Davis, Sarah to William M. Layne 12-14-1859 (no return) Hy
Davis, Sarah to Willis Vincent 10-4-1855 O
Davis, Siller to Rubin Davis 11-5-1874 (11-8-1874) T
Davis, Sophia to John Houston 3-10-1885 (3-15-1885) L
Davis, Sophie to Daniel Newborn 1-31-1869 Hy
Davis, Sophronia to Melvin Howell 1-17-1873 (no return) Hy
Davis, Susan A. to Carroll J. Key 10-27-1859 Hn
Davis, Susan Ann to J. Lambkins 8-8-1873 (8-9-1873) T
Davis, Susan Ann to Osburn Taylor 5-29-1867 Hy
Davis, Susan Maria to Samuel H. Fielders 8-5-1848 O
Davis, Susan T. to Council Buntin 1-28-1867 Ma
Davis, Susan to Benjamin F. Croom 12-12-1862 (12-13-1862) Ma
Davis, Susan to Robert G. Adams 3-17-1862 Ma
Davis, Susan to William J. Ragsdale 8-14-1847 (8-17-1847) Ma
Davis, Susanah to John Baswell 8-2-1848 (no return) F
Davis, Synthey D. to Milton J. Allison 9-22-1840 (9-24-1840) O
Davis, Tennessee to James M. Spencer 8-26-1858 (8-29-1858) Hr
Davis, Theodocia to Green L. White 9-9-1845 (9-11-1845) O
Davis, Violett to Reuben Stafford 1-6-1876 Hy
Davis, Virginia C. to Thomas Jones 5-17-1849 Hn
Davis, Virginia E. to Thomas J. Yates 3-28-1865 (no return) Hn
Davis, Visa Ann to John B. Daniel 1-24-1852 (1-26-1852) Hr
Davis, Williammetta to Miles N. Lockard 11-20-1860 Hr
Davison, Ann M. to Elija Foust 11-17-1857 Hn
Davison, Elizabeth E. to Armstead G. Morris 1-15-1839 Cr
Davison, Julia (Mrs.) to H. P. Miller 6-17-1861 Sh
Davison, Mary to Charles Taylor 12-30-1856 Hn
Davy, Threasy L. to William Atchison 8-20-1831 Ma
Daw, Martha Jane to Eli A. Summers 11-12-1856 G
Dawkins, Martha to Calvin Langston 2-2-1839 Ma
Daws, Nancy to Z. T. Douglas 9-10-1863 Mn
Dawson, Ann Elizabeth to Peter Holt 10-20-1856 (10-21-1856) Sh
Dawson, Caroline to William Williams 11-28-1854 G
Dawson, Charlottie to Richard Hudsons 8-18-1875 O
Dawson, Eliza Janie to Absolam Hendricks Evans 10-8-1853 (10-9-1853) T
Dawson, Elizabeth Jane to W. L. Baskins 8-1-1866 (8-10-1866) T
Dawson, Emma Bet. to Harris L. Baker 12-25-1872 Dy
Dawson, H. J. to James D., sr. Porter 12-18-1850 Hn
Dawson, Hester Anne to George Bailey 5-24-1869 (SB 1868?) G B
Dawson, Lena H. to E. H. Baker 12-24-1874 Dy
Dawson, Lottie to A. F. Hughes 7-12-1876 Hy
Dawson, Lucinda B. to Thomas J. Cogbill 8-21-1842 Sh
Dawson, Lucinda to Major Harrolson 3-31-1832 Sh
Dawson, Martha J. to Wm. C. Quinly 9-3-1842 (9-4-1842) Ma
Dawson, Martha to J. W. Johnson 1-16-1846 Cr
Dawson, Mary E. to Robert R. McCall 9-16-1846 (9-20-1846) Hr
Dawson, Mary to Barnabas Nelson 12-15-1834 (12-18-1834) Hr
Dawson, Minerva C. to Wm. H. Fogarty 9-10-1866 (9-11-1866) Ma
Dawson, Sarah to Elijah F. Warren 6-20-1845 (6-22-1845) Hr
Dawson, V. E. to R. A. Barcroft 3-24-1870 Hy
Dawtry, Susan C. to Christopher C. Strother 1-27-1851 (1-28-1851) G
Dawyer, Ellen to John Gorman 5-14-1863 En
Day, Cathran to Napolion Pete 3-26-1866 (3-31-1866) T
Day, Clara to John Shane 9-4-1866 Ma
Day, Elizabeth J. to John W. Grant 9-25-1850 Ma
Day, Evalina to William Scott 3-20-1861 (3-21-1861) Hr
Day, Felicia to Tom Mamier? 5-19-1866 (8-11-1866) F B
Day, Frances L. to W. W. Penny 12-11-1861 G
Day, Harriett R. to John J. Oliver 6-2-1853 (6-3-1853) Ma
Day, I. Virginia to John s. Fenner 2-27-1867 Ma
Day, Jane to Jeremiah Desmond 3-24-1859 G
Day, Janetta J. to Francis J. Baber 10-6-1859 Ma
Day, Luvina M. to Flavius Fly 11-9-1852 (11-12-1852) Ma
Day, Malvina H. to Henry C. Watkins 11-5-1845 Ma
Day, Marinda M. to John W. Estress 11-29-1866 Hn
Day, Martha A. to Robert P. Ford 1-23-1850 (1-25-1850) Ma
Day, Martha E. to Francis E. Woodide 12-6-1853 G
Day, Mary E. to Calvin C. Vesser 9-30-1867 Ma
Day, Mary E. to James T. Willett 11-15-1862 (11-19-1862) Ma
Day, Mary Elizabeth to Henry L. Bray 3-15-1859 (not executed) Ma
Day, Mary T. to Tobeas Klutts 10-12-1857 (no return) We
Day, Miss Emma C. to Dr. A. Perry 11-12-1860 (11-13-1860) T
Day, Nancy J. to Isaac Parlow 2-8-1868 (2-13-1868) Ma
Day, Nannie to W. M. Balser 3-15-1879 (3-20-1879) Dy
Day, Olivia to James McRoe 10-10-1842 Ma
Day, S. P. to M. Perry 2-6-1866 T
Day, Sallie Cornelia to Albert Talmedge Lovallette 10-6-1855 (10-9-1855) Ma
Dayley, Mary Ann E. to E. A. Burns 12-25-1848 (12-26-1848) F
Dayton, R. E. to N. J. Hess 12-10-1870 (12-13-1870) F
Ddupree, Bettie E. to J. A. Flippin 4-11-1864 (4-16-1864) F
De Armond, Sarah Jane to James Marlon Foster 8-27-1857 Sh
De Moore (Morse?), Ellen to Tom Lucas 3-19-1873 (3-20-1873) L B
De'lieu, Mina to William Fayers 12-14-1859 Hy
DeBruce, Louisa M. to Thomas Dortch 8-30-1853 Hn
DeGraffenreid, Fillis to Robt. Henderson 10-3-1868 (10-4-1868) F B
DeKine, Lizzie to Andrew J. Ferguson 3-26-1879 L B

DeLagorio, Catharine to Antonio Bora 4-18-1855 (4-22-1855) Sh
DeLaroque, Kate to Richard Booth 11-1-1864 (11-3-1864) Sh
DeLoach, Callie Virginia to Benjamin J. Porter 1-15-1867 (1-16-1867) L
DeMent, Mary Jane to J. C. Hall 4-14-1862 Sh
DeWitt, Mary L. to William T. Yancy 12-31-1856 (1-1-1857) Sh
Deaderick, Eliza G. to David Armour 11-20-1839 Sh
Deadrick, Mary E. to Jno. H. Speed 4-18-1849 Sh
Deak, Harriet Ann to Henry Wilkins 4-14-1880 (4-15-1880) Dy
Deakin, Harriet V. to Jas. H. Cook 11-14-1856 (11-19-1856) T
Deakins, Ann Eliza to David H. Woods 12-8-1847 (12-?-1847) T
Deakins, Indiana to Josiah A. Monroe 3-23-1852 (3-25-1852) T
Deakins, Mary E. to David H. Wood 12-17-1850 (12-19-1850) T
Deakins, Sarah Ann to David M. Parish 2-12-1853 (2-16-1853) T
Deal, Avy to Henry D. Moore 4-13-1842 (no return) Hn
Dean, Catharine A. to Joshua M. Teague 1-16-1856 Hr
Dean, Eliza to George A. Harbour 4-28-1851 (4-29-1851) G
Dean, Eliza to Hol. Kee 11-16-1840 Be
Dean, Elizabeth to Franklin M. Farmer 9-15-1860 (no return) Hy
Dean, Elizabeth to J. S. Moss 11-30-1868 G
Dean, Gilly to Randolph Casey 5-25-1828 (5-26-1828) Hr
Dean, Laura to Netanial Rhoades 11-13-1864 (11-15-1864) Sh
Dean, Linda to Tom Bradford 12-31-1875 (no return) Hy
Dean, Louisa (Miss) to Dan Seigers 8-6-1864 Sh
Dean, Lucy to Jefferson C. Savage 1-10-1843 (1-13-1843) Hr
Dean, M. A. to B. F. Webb 10-31-1866 (11-5-1865?) F
Dean, M. J. to T. N. Skelton 10-13-1870 Hy
Dean, Malinda to John B. Hardage 11-6-1837 Hr
Dean, Martha E. to William Fuqua 12-29-1840 (12-31-1840) G
Dean, Martha to James Boulton 3-16-1825 Sh
Dean, Matilda to Williamson B. Rainey 11-5-1841 (11-7-1841) Hr
Dean, Mattie C. to Wm. T. Teague 3-9-1870 (3-10-1870) Ma
Dean, Milly F. to Francis Chambers 12-26-1860 (no return) Hy
Dean, Minnie to William Holdsworth 11-21-1870 Ma
Dean, Rebecca to James E. Cole 12-17-1846 (12-18-1846) G
Dean, Rebecca to William Pare 12-12-1837 Hr
Dean, Salina to James Carter 4-27-1836 Hr
Dean, Sarah to John S. Hawkins 1-17-1846 Sh
Dean, Susan A. to James M. Jimmerson 11-26-1873 (12-3-1873) T
Deane, Martha to A. J. Elliott 5-7-1857 Sh
Deaner, Martha A. to William A. Old 9-30-1845 (no return) F
Dearen, S. D. to W. N. Rast 7-24-1862 Mn
Dearman, Martha M. to David Rutlige 12-28-1853 Sh
Dearmond, M. J. to C. C. Rice 11-3-1859 Sh
Dearmond, Margaret J. to B. F. West 11-8-1855 Sh
Dearmore, Ann to Zachariah Holliday 3-21-1846 (4-2-1846) Ma
Dearmore, Mary Jane to Powhattan B. Littlepage 4-20-1841 Ma
Dearmore, Perlina W. to Enoch Gaskins 9-17-1849 Ma
Dearmore, Susan P. to Lea H. Johnson 1-24-1853 (1-30-1853) Ma
Dearmore, Susan to Stafford Luster 6-19-1860 Dy
Dearren, M. J. to R. H. Best 11-6-1865 (11-14-1865) F
Deason, Ann to John Langley 11-27-1839 (11-28-1839) L
Deason, Caroline to Moses Thomas 12-7-1869 (no return) L
Deason, Eliza Ann to James Nichols 7-19-1846 T
Deason, Elizabeth to William Johnston 9-9-1849 Sh
Deason, Jane to Milton Sawyer 1-3-1849 (1-4-1849) L
Deason, Synthia to W. Henderson Rackly 10-31-1847 L
Deason?, Mary to Henry Evans 12-4-1839 Hr
Deaton, Amanda C. to James F. Baker 7-26-1869 (7-28-1869) Ma
Deaton, Cena D. to Andrew W. Cole 5-1-1872 Hy
Deaton, Fanny to Harrison Beazll 8-11-1863 Be
Deaton, Lidia A. to Wesley Estes 7-24-1865 Mn
Deaton, Senna A. (Mrs.) to Peter F. Crowel 7-1-1867 Ma
Deats, Eliza Jane to Abraham Briley 3-17-1842 Hn
Deauran, Margaret to Samuel H. Williams 4-17-1867 G
Deberry, Anna M. to W. T. Nelson 12-20-1870 (12-21-1870) Ma
Deberry, Elizabeth F. (Mrs.) to Wm. R. Cunningham 6-30-1859 Ma
Deberry, Lizzie to James G. Meriwether 1-24-1871 (1-25-1871) Ma
Deberry, Lou E. to Emmett J. Lewis 11-26-1864 (11-27-1864) O
Deberry, Rebecca to William H. Meriwether 12-15-1838 Hn
Deberry, Susan A. to Robert H. Hurt 6-1-1843 (6-3-1843) Ma
Debnam, Susan F. to Thomas F. Gowan 10-3-1867 G
Debow, Rozetta to Ben Thompson 12-22-1873 (12-25-1873) O
Debruce, Caroline E. to M. A. Beaton 9-24-1857 Be
Debruce, Lucinda J. to T. D. Cooper 1-6-1858 Be
Deburgan, Adelia T. to Frederick A. Wilmans 10-15-1864 Sh
Deck, Rebeca to Michael Ward 8-12-1845 We
Deck, Susan to James H. Parham 7-16-1845 We
Deck, Weney to James M. Graham 10-8-1857 We
Decker, Helen M. to H. M. Keller 12-14-1859 (12-15-1859) Sh
Decker, Margaret M. to John W. Applebee 10-3-1859 (10-12-1859) Sh
Deen, Avena B. to John C. Lee 5-30-1866 O
Deen, Delilah to Theopilus Thornton 11-17-1827 (12-3-1827) Hr
Deen, Polly to John Palmer 12-11-1843 Cr
Deener, Ann to George Green 9-14-1868 (11-15-1868) F B
Deener, Anna to Abraham Heaslet 12-3-1869 (no return) F B
Deener, Mary to Robert Heaslet 11-29-1869 (no return) F B
Deener, Omy to Anderson Pitt 8-31-1867 F B

Brides

Deener, Zoa Ann to Taylor Woods 12-26-1867 (no return) F B
Deener?, Priscilla to Bill Williamson 4-22-1871 (no return) F B
Dees, Nancy to A. Shotwell 10-22-1843 Hn
Dees, Sarah to Jonathan Cress 9-2-1854 (no return) We
Deeson, Rebeca to R. F. Trantham 5-10-1855 We
Defeli, Rosina to Jacob Brotsepe 8-1-1854 Sh
Degraffenreid, Evaline H. to E. L. Evans 10-6-1841 (no return) F
Degraffenreid, Sarah B. to Solomon Green 10-30-1848 (no return) F
Degraftenreid, Elizabeth to Blunt Springfield 12-4-1843 (no return) F
Dehart, Mary Bryant to William B. Densford 10-13-1849 (10-14-1849) T
Deight, Eliza J. to James H. Day 1-22-1849 O
Delancey, S. L. to R. S. Ford 2-23-1874 (2-26-1874) T
Delancey, Sarah E. to Joseph W. Earwood 9-18-1867 (9-22-1867) T
Delaney, Bridget to Patrick Flaherty 9-2-1858 Sh
Delaney, Mary J. to W. W. McKinny 8-3-1872 (8-4-1872) T
Delaney, Mary L. to Green Broach 3-12-1863 (no return) Cr
Delaney, Mary to John Ryan 7-15-1850 Sh
Delaney, Sally to Isaac Elsberry 1-31-1843 Cr
Delaney, Sarah A. to Richmond R. Wren 2-23-1858 Cr
Delany (Delary?), Mary to John Bell 11-13-1852 Sh
Delany, Araminta to M. D. Braswell 7-18-1860 (no return) Cr
Delany, Eliza J. to Simon Berry 1-13-1848 Cr
Delany, Mary L. to Green Brach 3-12-1863 (no return) Cr
Delany, P. to J. M. McClusky 1-5-1866 (1-6-1866) Cr
Delapp, Jane to James M. Wilie 4-11-1853 (4-12-1853) Ma
Delapp, Lucy to William l. Trask 6-19-1858 (6-21-1858) Ma
Delashmeit, Mariah W. to John L. Turnage 7-1-1865 T
Delashment, Lavina to P. C. Alexander 11-11-1862 (11-13-1862) T
Delashment, Mary F. to Wm. M. Eldridge 1-23-1865 T
Delashment, Mary to Green Martin 1-8-1850 (1-10-1850) O
Delashmet, Adaline G. to Andrew J. Loyd 1-16-1872 (1-17-1872) T
Delashmet, Elzabeth to William Mears 11-21-1848 (11-22-1848) T
Delashmet, Marth J. to Saml. R. Timberlick 5-6-1867 (5-14-1867) T
Delashmet, Martha A. to George W. Haynie 5-29-1852 (5-30-1852) T
Delashmet, Sarah Margaret to John Craig 8-2-1871 (8-3-1871) T
Delashmet, Susan D. to Wm. J. Cullam 12-13-1869 (12-14-1869) T
Delashmit, Nancy E. to Robert H. Ralph 8-8-1871 (8-10-1871) T
Delbeck, Manerva to George W. Yandle 1-1-1846 O
Delda, Susan to Thomas Archa 11-15-1838 Ma
Dell, Margaret T. to Peter P. Puckett 10-8-1849 (10-9-1849) Ma
Deliny?, Sarah A. to R. D. Wren 12-22-1858 Cr
Delk, Louisa l.? to Reubin M. Riggs 12-18-1850 (12-24-1850) Hr
Delk, Matilda to James M. Ray 3-12-1859 (3-13-1859) Hr
Delk, Nancy E. to James T. Little 6-16-1857 (6-18-1857) Hr
Delkie, Rosa to Augustus Lander 7-28-1858 Sh
Dell, Martha A. to J. H. Thomson 5-5-1861 Mn
Dellahunty, L. A. to Joseph B. Harrell 11-17-1868 (11-18-1868) T
Delnice, Harrett C. to James Huston 7-7-1850 Be
Deloach, A. D. to T. O. Chapman 1-31-1882 (2-?-1882) L
Deloach, Ann R. to Gideon Hicks 12-19-1860 (12-20-1860) Ma
Deloach, Anna E. to Richard Prichard 11-21-1854 (11-22-1854) Sh
Deloach, Emma to R. N. J. Wilson 9-11-1861 (9-12-1861) Sh
Deloach, Lou to George L. Harding 12-12-1866 (12-20-1866) Ma
Deloach, Martha Jane to Earl Wilson 2-10-1856 Be CC
Deloach, Martha to Josiah F. Clanton 9-6-1847 (9-9-1847) Ma
Deloach, R. E. to G. W. Walter 4-1-1869 (4-6-1869) L
Deloach, Rose Ann to G. G. Looney 8-26-1838 (no return) F
Deloach, Susan A. to Eugene R. Willoughby 12-3-1866 (12-6-1866) Ma
Deloach, Viola L. to Thomas Low (Law) 3-28-1848 Sh
Delony, Lucy J. to J. B. Bouchell 9-30-1857 Sh
Delph, Annariah to Bryant Fitzhugh 3-26-1879 Dy
Delph, Elizabeth A. to Calvin Gardner 2-26-1856 (2-27-1856) Ma
Delph, Mary to Joseph Blackwell 12-2-1856 (12-7-1856) Ma
Delph, Matilda A. to William Shane 1-24-1859 (1-27-1859) G
Delph, Sally to George Pate 10-3-1864 (no return) Dy
Delph, Sarah Eveline to Hartwell M. Stone 3-31-1856 Ma
Delphina, Pipkin to Francis M. Pipkin 1-27-1863 (no return) Hy
Delshmen, Mary to Green Martin 1-8-1850 (1-10-1850) O
Demall, G. E. to John H. Carlton 11-22-1856 G
Demara, Permelia to Waimon Jones 9-4-1874 (9-5-1874) L
Dement, Eliza A. to F. M. Vermillon 12-28-1858 We
Dement, Elizabeth C. to Wesley W. Wood 9-24-1858 We
Dement, Elizabeth C. to William J. Cherry 12-4-1852 G
Dement, Elizabeth to Levi Webb 12-9-1844 (12-10-1844) G
Dement, Jane to Johnson Hicks 12-27-1866 G
Dement, Louisa to Simpson Weaver 10-2-1857 (10-4-1857) O
Dement, Martha E. to J. J. A. Lee 3-20-1851 G
Dement, Martha L. E. to J. W. Alford 1-12-1863 G
Dement, Marting S. to John J. J. Lee 8-3-1846 G
Dement, Mary F. to James Ward 5-12-1853 G
Dement, Sarah A. E. to Malichi C. Bright 8-30-1851 (9-2-1851) Sh
Deming, Ive Ann to George M. Nevils 2-11-1871 (2-12-1871) T
Demming, Lucinda J. to Wm. C. Harris 1-21-1850 (1-22-1850) F
Demoss, Amanda to Harey Todd 8-16-1865 (no return) Cr
Demoss, Eliza D. to R. G. Null 1-7-1847 Cr
Demoss, Ferroby to Thomas Mullens 8-31-1853 G
Demoss, Francis J. to M. D. Null 1-12-1846 Cr

Demoss, Matilda C. to James P. Gee 8-6-1861 (8-7-1861) Cr
Demoss, Parlee to James M. Goodman 4-18-1849 (no return) Cr
Demow, Catherine to Wright Fitzpatrick 9-23-1880 L
Demril?, Lucinda to George Sparrow 4-17-1869 (no return) F B
Dencan (Duncan?), Ellen to William Coghlan 12-27-1854 Sh
Denham, Nancy to Thomas J. Agnew 1-2-1854 (1-4-1854) O
Denie (Dennis), Mary to Asa Wallace 7-7-1847 Sh
Denie?, Harriet to Artha F. Crihfield 11-28-1860 (11-28-1861?) L
Denington, S. J. to G. A. Romine 3-9-1874 O
Deninney, Rhoda to Hartwell Walker 7-26-1841 Sh
Denmark, Catherine to Edmund J. Eddington 8-24-1852 (8-25-1852) Ma
Dennegan, Bridget to Henry Hanna 5-26-1862 (5-27-1862) Sh
Denney, H. L. to Eli Tilghman 10-3-1860 (10-4-1860) O
Denney, Margaret M. to John S. Nobles 4-28-1856 O
Denney, Mary Jane to George M. Ba(y)singer 12-27-1853 (1-3-1854) O
Denney, Susan R. to James A. Tuley 8-22-1859 (8-23-1859) O
Denngtin?, Mary to Thos. J. Long 3-14-1844 We
Dennie, Amanda to A. J. Norris 8-19-1869 (no return) L
Dennie, Julia M. to W. Y. Pennington 4-30-1874 L
Dennie, Martha to W. B. Vaughn 12-24-1877 (12-25-1877) L
Dennie, Mary F. to W. R. Childress 4-7-1883 (4-11-1883) L
Dennie, Sallie to Elbridge Estes 12-18-1885 (12-20-1885) L
Denning (Dunning), Sarah E. to W. N. Capps 1-13-1858 (no return) We
Denning, Harriet to T. S. Perry 11-18-1843 We
Denning, Mary J. to Alfred H. Anderson 9-7-1860 We
Denning, Mary J. to J. H. Ezell 6-24-1865 (no return) Hn
Denning, Mollie M. to E. D. Farris 9-4-1867 (9-5-1867) O
Denning, S. E. to J. M. Todd 9-10-1869 (9-12-1869) Cr
Dennington, Sarah J. to Elija Hamlin 11-30-1859 (12-1-1859) O
Dennis, Carolina I. to John B. Canada 10-17-1850 Sh
Dennis, Charlotte to Josiah Bone 8-14-1852 (8-15-1852) O
Dennis, Ellen (Mrs.) to Isaac F. Basford 7-25-1854 (7-26-1854) Sh
Dennis, Florence D. to Wm. N. Howell 12-20-1879 (12-21-1879) L
Dennis, Haskey to John W. Pope 4-30-1837 G
Dennis, J. M. to W. A. Allen 1-5-1868 G
Dennis, Judy to James Winberry 1-26-1852 Be CC
Dennis, Judy to James Winbury 1-26-1852 Be
Dennis, Margaret Ann to John J. Lovin 10-23-1854 Sh
Dennis, Martha O. to John J. Givens 11-29-1854 (11-29-1854) Hr
Dennis, Sarah A. to Benj. K. Simmons 2-17-1868 (2-18-1868) T
Denny (Dennis), Mary to John Able 12-10-1845 Sh
Denny, Elizabeth to Carison Bailey 6-15-1850 Sh
Denny, Liley to Kingsberry German 4-1-1856 (4-11-1856) Ma
Denny, Louisa to Archibald Joyce 1-1-1838 Hr
Denny, Mary J. to Miles P. Chandler 10-18-1842 Ma
Denny, Sarah A. to W. J. Glasgo 8-13-1862 (8-14-1862) O
Densford, Amanda to John Adams 4-6-1866 (4-7-1866) T
Densford, Julia to Wm. D. Erwin 6-4-1866 (6-12-1866) T
Densford, Sallie to Mat McElmore 12-12-1872 T
Densmore, Julia to John Alexander 4-15-1857 Sh
Dent, Caroline to Philip M. May 5-25-1830 (5-26-1830) Ma
Dent, F. A. to N. B. Waterfield 4-13-1855 We
Dent, Frances to James Caradine 12-27-1843 (12-28-1843) Ma
Dent, Laura to Gilford Strederick? 3-30-1874 (5-31-1874) O
Dent, Martha E. to John Nash 10-31-1847 (11-1-1847) Ma
Dent, Mary S. to Will M. Jones 3-6-1854 Hn
Dent, Mary to Steven Calhoon 2-4-1867 (no return) Hy
Dent, Nartecea F. to William Campbell 12-17-1856 We
Dent, Vianna E. to S. W. Ezell 6-29-1859 We
Dentenac, Manda to Thomas Lewis 8-15-1867 T
Denton, A. E. to R. M. Hooker 1-28-1865 (1-29-1865) Cr
Denton, Catharine to W. B. Cox 1-2-1860 Hr
Denton, Catherine B. to George Fodge 1-4-1865 (no return) Hn
Denton, Ellen W. to Abe White 11-10-1869 (11-11-1869) Cr
Denton, Martha A. to T. H. Tines 3-28-1858 We
Denton, Mollie to Briant Nowlin 11-27-1871 (no return) Cr
Denton, Mollie to Samuel McPherson 9-26-1881 (9-23?-1881) L
Denton, Nancy (Mrs.) to Arnold Winston 11-9-1857 (11-10-1857) Ma
Denton, Patricia to Janier? L. Smith 7-31?-1859 (maybe 7-21) Cr
Denton, Virginia to William Trainam 2-9-1859 (2-10-1859) L
Denttinger-Dutlinger, C. to Frederick Beurer 11-28-1855 Sh
Derden, Milly to Green McNeill 12-31-1866 (1-6-1867) F B
Derrah, Ann Caroline to George C. Rogers 12-17-1840 Ma
Derriberry, Emily to John D. Rhine 3-26-1860 (no return) We
Derribery, Emily M. to Lee Thompson 3-21-1853 Hr
Derriggon, Nancy Caroline to A. V. Lesner 4-15-1858 Cr
Derryberry, Louisa to David Gibson 12-6-1865 Mn
Desberry, Fannie to Robt. Jeffries 11-23-1876 Hy
Deshazer, Margaret to H. W. Saddler 10-22-1857 We
Deshong, Mollie G. to P. C. Loveless 12-27-1865 (12-28-1865) Cr
Desmond, Julia M. L. to Samuel B. Hurt 7-2-1842 (7-16-1842) T
Detherage, Eliza to Chapman Williams 11-28-1838 Ma
Detta, Nancy Tennessee to James W. McGee 9-10-1862 (no return) Hy
Deuser, Barbara to Dedrick Negel 2-18-1858 Sh
Devalt, Nancy to Andrew Wise 4-24-1874 Hy
Devaughn, Mary J. to L. B. Smith 11-5-1862 G
Devault, Celia Ann to J. R. Caruthers 9-11-1861 Mn

Develin, Annie to Wm. H. Smith 6-1-1863 Sh
Devenport, James to Joel Johnson 3-13-1846 Be
Devenport, Jane E. to Levi Park 12-7-1846 (12-8-1846) Hr
Devenport, R. E. to John H. Dixon 2-5-1870 (2-10-1870) F
Devenport, Sarah F. to Andrew J. Watson 11-11-1867 (11-13-1867) L
Devenport, Sarah to Thomas J. Marler 8-12-1838 F
Devine, May to F. Hack 2-15-1859 Sh
Deving (Deviney), Julia to Michael O'Lery 1-25-1864 (1-28-1864) Sh
Devitt, Penny to Austin Deberry 11-11-1876 Hy
Devlin, Margaret to John Lough (Laugh) 4-17-1844 Sh
Devlin, Mary to Bartholomew Scanlin 4-22-1861 (4-23-1861) Sh
Devney, Bridget to Thomas Southwell 1-11-1860 Sh
Devota, Rosa to Joseph Mereto 11-20-1858 (11-28-1858) Sh
Dew, Joanna to William J. Sturdevant 1-15-1861 (1-16-1861) Ma
Dew, Joannah to William G. Cardwell 5-4-1860 Ma
Dew, Narcissa to Jefferson Anderson 5-11-1855 Ma
Dewalt, Ida to Stephen Gildon 7-11-1884 (7-13-1884) L
Dewalt, Jamima to A. J. Baker 5-14-1861 L
Dewalt, Rebecca A. G. to Richard F. Gains 9-18-1866 (9-20-1866) L
Dewalt, Tama to Presley Dewalt 10-15-1883 L
Deware, Bridget to Michael Silliman 2-27-1859 Sh
Dewberry, Martha (Mrs.) to Jacob H. Mattern 11-5-1864 (11-7-1864) Sh
Dewease, Maggie to J. N. Leach 12-18-1874 (12-22-1874) T
Dewhit, Mary B. to E. G. H. Bennett 1-7-1866 Cr
Dewitt, Eliza Ann to George M. Harris 6-19-1838 Hn
Dewitt, Mary S. to D. W. McRee 12-27-1860 O
Dewoody, Mary Jane to Robert L. Smith 7-11-1849 Sh
Deyson (Dyson), Isobel to Isaac Crouch 1-27-1825 Sh
Dial, A. C. to Theophulis S. Robertson 5-24-1847 (5-30-1847) Hr
Dial, Artimissa to William T. Myers 9-25-1850 Hr
Dial, Candis to William Jackson 2-15-1866 G
Dial, Hester Ann to William Crafton 3-27-1830 (4-1-1830) G
Dial, Jane C. to Wm. R. Robertson 12-26-1844 (12-28-1844) Hr
Dial, Jane to W. K. Dowdy 3-19-1856 Hr
Dial, Manervia Ann to John W. Harrison 7-23-1844 (7-24-1844) Hr
Dial, Marcilla E. to W. K. Dowdy 9-3-1860 (9-4-1860) Hr
Dial, Martha A. to Robert Dowdy 1-1-1857 (1-8[18]-1857 Hr
Dial, Mary Ann to E. Donaho 2-8-1842 (no return) L
Dial, Mary to J. J. Patric 12-28-1864 G
Dial, Matilda to Joseph M. Lowry 4-18-1845 (4-19-1845) L
Dial, Milly to James Lammons 4-2-1828 (4-3-1828) G
Dial, Rebecca E. to Norris M. Lindsey 9-11-1852 (9-14-1852) L
Dial, S. J. to T. W. Jackson 8-24-1865 G
Dial, Sarah J. to W. T. Williford 6-15-1869 G
Dial, Sarah to Joseph D. Rentfro 6-24-1835 G
Dial, Unissa J. to Landy Watson 9-7-1846 (9-10-1846) L
Dibrell, Sarah E. to Henry Valentine 3-4-1850 (3-6-1850) G
Dibrill, Lean G. to Abner C. Beacham 9-4-1834 G
Dick, Anna to James N. Nimrod 2-2-1839 Cr
Dick, Elizabeth to Benjamin W. Perry 12-22-1854 Ma
Dick, Elizabeth to Culbert M. Laney 5-5-1828 Ma
Dick, Martha C. to Iverson Burton 10-16-1850 (10-17-1850) Ma
Dick, Martha M. to Wade Byrum 5-9-1861 Ma
Dick, Mary A. to Green Nance 12-30-1858 Hn
Dick, Mary E. J. to William L. Copeland 3-19-1853 Ma
Dick, Susan Jane to William D. Marr 6-13-1857 Hn
Dickason, F. A. to D. Brock, jr. 8-13-1872 (8-14-1872) Dy
Dickason, Fannie to Benj. Elder 3-17-1862 F
Dickason, Josephine J. to Simon W. Caldwell 1-23-1867 (1-30-1867) F
Dickason, Louisa M. to Wm. B. Washington 5-1-1850 F
Dickason, Mary A. to John L. Verser 11-23-1846 (11-24-1846) F
Dickason, Mollie L. to Geor. B. Garrett 6-3-1872 (6-5-1872) Cr
Dickason, S. A. to J. M. Elder 1-15-1861 F
Dickason, Virginia to Wm. B. Washington 8-7-1860 (8-8-1860) F
Dickason, arion to Ned Graham 11-26-1869 (11-27-1869) T
Dickens, Betsey to Alexander Moss 1-6-1831 Sh
Dickens, Dicey Ann to W. A. Moore 1-11-1860 (1-12-1860) Hr
Dickens, Elizabeth F. to William H. Hunt 8-2-1830 Ma
Dickens, Emaline to Louis Fisher 3-20-1866 (3-24-1866) T
Dickens, Emely K. to Pleasant H. Simmons 3-5-1849 (3-7-1849) G
Dickens, Hasty to Isaac Bobbett 12-14-1846 (12-17-1846) G
Dickens, Henrietta to Wm. Shackleford 12-16-1868 (12-25-1868) T
Dickens, Juda to James S. Witt 12-2-1845 G
Dickens, Lucresha? to Edwin A. Hicks 9-8-1831 Ma
Dickens, M. I. S. S. to Albert L. Bobbett 9-1-1854 (9-5-1854) G
Dickens, Mary E. to James T. Arnett 9-11-1872 (9-12-1872) Dy
Dickens, Mary Frances to W. H. Williams 2-2-1868 G
Dickens, Nancy to Thomas Mills 2-4-1830 Sh
Dickens, Sarah C. to Avery Hunt 12-18-1841 (12-23-1841) Ma
Dickens, Sarah to John D. Martin 1-10-1830 Ma
Dickens?, Emeline to J. C. Gann 1-17-1866 (no return) Hn
Dickenson, Evelina to William Rives 1-3-1839 F
Dickenson, Nancy J. to A. T. Butler 1-26-1866 (1-28-1866) Cr
Dickenson, Sarah to Lewis Taylor 5-29-1863 (5-30-1863) O
Dickenson, Sarah to Sam Ealy 12-29-1868 (12-30-1868) F B
Dickerson, Amanda to Watt Dancey 1-30-1877 (no return) Hy
Dickerson, Belle to J. S. Yates 12-13-1877 (12-18-1877) Dy

Dickerson, E. A. to G. W. Hichcock 2-22-1850 We
Dickerson, E. F. to S. C. Burford 1-10-1871 (no return) Hy
Dickerson, Eliza to Booker Scott 12-8-1871 Hy
Dickerson, Elizabeth to John Baker 1-13-1858 Sh
Dickerson, Franky to Green Doyle 12-28-1866 Dy
Dickerson, Ibby to James Denny 2-13-1839 O
Dickerson, Jane to John J. Walker 3-31-1849 O
Dickerson, Jane to John T. Gaines 4-7-1859 (4-13-1859) L
Dickerson, M. F. to D. T. Whittick 7-17-1864 G
Dickerson, M. J. to J. W. Curlin 4-12-1871 (no return) Hy
Dickerson, Martha E. to John A. Russell 6-18-1863 G
Dickerson, Martha to Francis Riley 4-25-1860 (4-29-1860) Sh
Dickerson, Martha to James M. Baysinger 8-24-1844 (8-25-1844) G
Dickerson, Mary A. to Benjamin W. Walker 8-16-1861 We
Dickerson, Mary E. to John Rowland 8-22-1850 L
Dickerson, Mary E. to Robert B. Batte 10-17-1866 (10-25-1866) T
Dickerson, Mary Janice to Albert Martain 7-12-1871 (7-21?-1872?) T
Dickerson, Mary L. to David May 10-22-1850 Cr
Dickerson, Mary M. to Alvin R. Williams 12-14-1859 (12-15-1859) Ma
Dickerson, Mildron to Major Conner 1-9-1869 (no return) Hy
Dickerson, Mollie to John Anthony 10-18-1881 (10-19-1881) L B
Dickerson, N. A. to J. F. Robertson 7-14-1868 Hy
Dickerson, Nancy J. to Columbus F. Gay 6-22-1867 T
Dickerson, R. C. to Levi Jones (Janes) 10-17-1863 O
Dickerson, Rachel C. to Levi Jones 10-17-1864 O
Dickey, Amy E. to Stephen Duncan 3-3-1856 (3-4-1856) G
Dickey, Ann to William B. Conwell 2-26-1844 G
Dickey, Caroline T. to Ebenezer D. Tucker 9-4-1855 (9-5-1855) G
Dickey, E. J. to S. S. Calhoun 3-14-1848 O
Dickey, Elizabeth to William Pope 2-8-1841 Ma
Dickey, Emma to G. R. Fuller 12-22-1873 (12-23-1873) Dy
Dickey, M. E. to J. W. Barrette 11-8-1875 (11-10-1875) Dy
Dickey, M. E. to W. H. Lawson 4-9-1865 G
Dickey, M. P. to O. T. Brown 4-29-1847 O
Dickey, Margaret E. to T. W. Hall 1-22-1868 (no return) Dy
Dickey, Martha C. to Edward D. Farris 6-10-1852 O
Dickey, Martha E. to Valentine Trail 4-23-1864 (4-26-1864) Dy
Dickey, Mary Ann (Mrs.) to William Starr 2-27-1861 Sh
Dickey, Mary Ann to John S. Toler 5-5-1849 (5-7-1849) G
Dickey, Mary to Robert Dickins 9-16-1846 (10-10-1846) G
Dickey, Nancy R. to Francis M. Youree 8-26-1858 O
Dickey, Nancy to L. B. Smith 5-11-1874 (5-13-1874) T
Dickey, P. A. to J. D. Wesson 2-3-1875 (2-4-1875) Dy
Dickey, Permelia T. to Samuel B. Lusk 2-4-1840 Sh
Dickey, Polly to Richardson Arnold 7-3-1843 (7-27-1843) G
Dickey, Rachel R. to J. J. Dozier 10-23-1862 G
Dickey, Rebecca Jane to Absolum H. O'Neal 12-12-1848 G
Dickey, Sary to William Leonard 2-5-1831 (2-10-1831) G
Dickey, T. E. to Stephen Duncan 9-6-1859 G
Dickie, Katie E. to John Deloach 3-14-1871 Ma
Dickie, Margaret to J. H. Chambers 1-4-1868 (1-9-1868) L
Dickin, Louisa to James A. Gray 3-27-1863 O
Dickins, Louisa to John D. Pepkins 9-23-1851 G
Dickins, Manassa to S. M. Carrington 9-19-1856 (9-20-1856) G
Dickins, Marsha A. to S. W. Edwards 3-5-1856 Cr
Dickins, Teressa H. to Peyton J. Smith 12-16-1848 (12-17-1848) G
Dickinson, Adaline to Wm. Richardson 5-26-1866 F B
Dickinson, Anna E. to O. T. Edwards 1-30-1867 F
Dickinson, Berlin to Silo Fraser 1-3-1868 (no return) F B
Dickinson, Dinah to Sam Dickinson 12-25-1866 (no return) F B
Dickinson, Eliz. R. to Joseph A. Fogg 10-9-1860 M
Dickinson, Elizabeth to Herod Kirby 12-27-1853 Ma
Dickinson, Hannah F. to H. P. Hudson 11-8-1878 (no return) Hy
Dickinson, Hannah to Robt. Leavy 10-17-1868 (10-18-1868) F B
Dickinson, L. A. to Sampson Deaton 2-22-1854 (2-23-1854) Ma
Dickinson, Laura to Wiley Jones 5-4-1870 (5-7-1870) F B
Dickinson, M. Caroline to Wm. J. Anderson 1-29-1867 (1-31-1867) Ma
Dickinson, M. D. to William P. Ripley 9-18-1849 (9-20-1849) Ma
Dickinson, Manerva to Shed Cole 12-9-1870 F B
Dickinson, Margaret to Dennis Hall 9-7-1867 (9-8-1867) F B
Dickinson, Martha to Louis Justice 8-28-1869 (10-17-1869) F B
Dickinson, Mary C. to R. R. Gwyn 11-1-1854 (11-9-1854) Hr
Dickinson, Mary to William F. Jackson 6-8-1863 G
Dickinson, Mattie A. to S. H. Dunaway 11-5-1866 G
Dickinson, Rachel to Evans Rives 2-20-1869 F B
Dickinson, Rose to Henry Butler 12-22-1867 G B
Dickinson, Rosena to Peter Walton 12-25-1866 (12-27-1866) F B
Dickinson, Rutha Jane to Rufus A. Weatherly 12-12-1859 Ma
Dickinson, Sallie N. to C. A. S. Shaw 4-25-1866 (4-26-1866) F
Dickinson, Sally G. to Hugh A. Gwyn 6-7-1852 (6-9-1852) Hr
Dickinson, Sarah A. to James B. Thompson 3-5-1859 (3-7-1859) G
Dickinson, Sarah Ann to John West 1-13-1853 Ma
Dickinson, Sarah to George T. Cathey 10-30-1856 O
Dickison (Dickerson), Emily to James Denino 3-16-1842 Sh
Dickison, Rachel L. to John H. Harber 9-26-1859 Ma
Dickson, Ann Eliza to William R. Howlett 10-7-1843 (10-12-1843) Ma
Dickson, Ann to Thomas Davis 11-17-1868 G

Dickson, Caroline H. to Jesse A. Toon 12-11-1844 Sh
Dickson, Celia to Calvin Goforth 2-4-1854 (2-5-1854) Ma
Dickson, Chloe to David Taliaferro 1-10-1872? Hy
Dickson, Cora to Daniel Wiley Payne 11-12-1867 (11-14-1867) T
Dickson, D. M. to Elijah Bramlet 2-15-1873 (2-14?-1873) O
Dickson, E. A. to W. P. Bourland 1-22-1870 G
Dickson, E. A. to William Moore 7-5-1848 O
Dickson, Eliza to James Evans 2-7-1872 (2-8-1872) O
Dickson, Eliza to K. L. A. Burrough 8-17-1848 Cr
Dickson, Elizabeth to Franklin Fields 12-25-1855 Cr
Dickson, Emily to C. P. H. Wright 9-17-1843 Cr
Dickson, Fannie to John Randolph 5-15-1867 (5-18-1867) T
Dickson, Harriet to J. W. McBride 1-14-1847 Sh
Dickson, Isabella M. to John D. Smith 12-19-1840 Ma
Dickson, J. M. to James A. Canon 1-3-1861 (1-6-1861) Cr
Dickson, Julia A. E. to Samuel J. S. Berry 10-20-1855 (10-24-1855) G
Dickson, Letha to Spivy Fuller 3-12-1832 G
Dickson, Levina I. to Thomas H. McAvery 10-3-1831 (10-4-1831) G
Dickson, Louisa J. to W. T. McGee 12-6-1875 (no return) Hy
Dickson, Lue to Isaac Ellis 1-1-1873 O
Dickson, M. M. to J. J. Yarbrough 3-29-1863 Mn
Dickson, Manda to James N. Lankford 2-12-1856 Cr
Dickson, Margarett to Gary Tyler 6-2-1865 G
Dickson, Martha Ann to Charles Strong 1-21-1857 (1-22-1857) T
Dickson, Martha E. to Daniel H. Staton 6-27-1856 (6-28-1856) G
Dickson, Martha F. to H. C. Alford 9-11-1846 G
Dickson, Martha to Gideon Wallace 4-22-1830 Sh
Dickson, Mary A. to Isaac S. Patton 9-13-1848 F
Dickson, Mary E. to Edwin J. McAdams 1-21-1870 (1-30-1870) Ma
Dickson, Mary E. to Gabriel Hardin 6-5-1858 (6-6-1858) Ma
Dickson, Mary E. to J. H. Alexander 10-29-1839 G
Dickson, Mary E. to Wm. W. Owenby 11-4-1846 Cr
Dickson, Mary Eliza to Stephen King 11-14-1848 G
Dickson, Mary Jane to William Goforth 1-28-1854 (1-31-1854) Ma
Dickson, Mary R. to Ira Spight 1-24-1832 (1-31-1832) G
Dickson, Mildred Jane to Jesse A. Strange 3-15-1855 Sh
Dickson, Mollie to R. C. Thompson 12-28-1869 (12-30-1869) T
Dickson, Nancy to Philip D. Carly 10-27-1840 (10-29-1840) Ma
Dickson, Pegy to Singleton Cock 7-11-1827 (7-17-1827) G
Dickson, Rebecca to William Booth 10-23-1839 (10-31-1839) F
Dickson, Sallie to Thos. A. Caton 2-17-1873 G
Dickson, Sarah A. G. to Claudius Herring 2-7-1842 (2-9-1842) O
Dickson, Sarah J. to Joshua Nobles 4-10-1848 G
Dickson, Sarah to James M. Terrell 10-8-1856 Cr
Dickson, Susan E. to J. H. Dickinson 7-24-1869 (8-4-1869) Cr
Dickson, Susan E. to Wm. B. Scates 3-21-1844 Cr
Dickson, Susan R. to John Paschal 8-17-1865 Mn
Dickson, Susan to Thomas N. Payne 7-25-1866 Hn
Dickson, Vandalia to Levi Shad 1-24-1870 (1-27-1870) Cr
Dickson, Z. L. to J. L. Hubbard 6-28-1865 (6-29-1865) O
Dickson, Zelpha to Jesse Pugh 5-26-1842 (5-27-1842) Ma
Didman, Frances to H. H. Dobbs 8-17-1852 F
Didny?, Mary to G. H. Siscoe 12-23-1848 (no return) F
Dieta, M. A. to G. M. Turner 9-16-1846 Hn
Diew (Dieu), Mary to William Glenn 1-18-1871 Hy
Diffy, Anne to John Shuffield 10-1-1842 F
Diffy, Sarah to Stephen Moore 3-6-1840 Ma
Digg, Malinda D. to Randolph Hazlewood 8-12-1839 (8-13-1839) Ma
Diggins, Nancy to Mark Gosey 12-28-1834 (12-30-1834) G
Diggins, Sally to John Nobles 10-14-1831 G
Diggs, A. Jane to James R. Allen 8-31-1847 Hn
Diggs, Amanda E. to John W. Cardwell 2-3-1859 Hn
Diggs, Cilia to Samuel Cox 9-26-1839 Cr
Diggs, Edna to S. N.? Jackson 11-29-1865 Hn
Diggs, Elizabeth to James R. Vinson 1-31-1872 Cr
Diggs, Elizabeth to R. G. L. Garner 2-7-1842 Hn
Diggs, Harriet A. to Thomas K. P. Wright 9-13-1866 Hn
Diggs, Harriett L. to J. J. Blake 12-27-1864 Hn
Diggs, Lidia J. to John M. Barnett 1-13-1860 Hn
Diggs, Lucretia to J. W. Diggs 8-27-1867 Hn
Diggs, M. J. to W. M. Davis 4-13-1867 (no return) Hn
Diggs, M. L. to W. R. Collins 11-8-1855 Hn
Diggs, Manta to Thomas Barnett 7-16-1874 O
Diggs, Margaret E. to John M. McCorkle 11-18-1840 (no return) Hn
Diggs, Margaret N. to Edward H. Palmer 5-4-1858 Hn
Diggs, Martha to William H. Darnall 5-18-1858 Hn
Diggs, Mary A. to W. W. Dorris 2-26-1867 Hn
Diggs, Mary Ann to James C. Hill 12-29-1842 (no return) Hn
Diggs, Mary to William F. Hill 5-9-1850 Hn
Diggs, Matilda to John Manly 1-20-1842 Hn
Diggs, Mintee to William Garner 11-4-1860 (not endorsed) Cr
Diggs, N. E. to James Snider 2-3-1863 Hn
Diggs, Nancy E. to John M. Rushing 3-28-1861 Hn
Diggs, S. E. to James R. Carter 12-4-1851 Hn
Diggs, Winney to Charles Dilday 8-5-1869 Cr
Dilday, Frances M. to James R. Page 1-20-1853 Cr
Dilday, Lucinda to Henry O. Honey 11-7-1839 Cr
Dilday, Nancy to James W. Pruett 8-9-1865 (8-10-1865) Cr
Dilday, Sarah to William S. May 2-10-1863 Cr
Dildy, A. J. to J. M. Eskew 11-1-1870 Cr
Dildy, Elizabeth to John Walker 1-30-1867 (no return) Cr
Dilelay?, Ann to Wyley P. Gibson 3-12-1861 Cr
Dilion, Thursey to A. Massengill 12-3-1865 Be
Dill, Eliza J. to James H. Noell 12-20-1865 Cr
Dill, Lucy to James Huffman 11-7-1866 (11-8-1866) Cr
Dill, Lydia B. to Benager Stewart 4-4-1868 (4-5-1868) Cr
Dill, Martha E. to Alphonzo Freeland 11-15-1865 (11-16-1865) Cr
Dill, Mary to Theophila W. Odum 12-7-1857 (no return) We
Dill, Mary to Wm. Kee 6-7-1855 Cr
Dill, N. C. to John C. Laycook 12-31-1868 Cr
Dill, Nancy to Benjamin Malone 4-25-1845 Cr
Dill, Nancy to Samuel Glidwell 2-6-1835 (2-8-1835) G
Dill, R. to Albert Prewett 12-31-1846 Cr
Dill, Sallie to J. J. Christerbery 2-7-1867 Cr
Dill, Samantha E. to Amos G. King 12-19-1857 Cr
Dillahenty, Laura to Saml. Helm 2-24-1872 T
Dillahunt, Ann (Mrs.) to James A. Henley 12-19-1877 Dy
Dillahunty, Charlotte M. to Newton A. Dinwiddie 12-26-1839 Hn
Dillahunty, E. to R. N. Harrel 11-6-1865 (11-15-1865) T
Dillahunty, Fanny A. to Reuben H. Dodson 8-10-1852 Sh
Dillahunty, H. R. to William Dinwiddie 2-20-1845 Hn
Dillahunty, Lucinda to R. C. Young 3-19-1874 T
Dillahunty, M. L. to John D. Love 9-7-1848 (no return) Hn
Dillahunty, Martha to A. R. Wylie 9-12-1870 (9-13-1870) T
Dillahunty, S. J. to John T. Greer 3-5-1867 Hn
Dillahunty, Sallie to J. L. Jamison 12-15-1874 T
Dillard, Eliza (Mrs.) to John A. Hickman 9-10?-1864 (9-9-1864) Sh
Dillard, Elizabeth to Poleman Martin 8-16-1836 (8-17-1836) Hr
Dillard, Holland P. to Samuel Luckey 10-15-1838 (10-16-1838) Ma
Dillard, Jane to Henry Jacobs 5-14-1826 (5-15-1826) Hr
Dillard, Jane to Theophilus Ervin 1-22-1861 Hr
Dillard, Julia A. to William Lott 12-29-1855 (1-1-1856) Sh
Dillard, Lavinia to C. H. Austin 12-5-1878 Hy
Dillard, Lucretia to William O'Steen 2-11-1829 Ma
Dillard, Martha L. to Willis Dillard 9-3-1834 Hr
Dillard, Mary to John Toony 2-13-1858 Sh
Dillard, Nancy to Jessie Childress 1-15-1829 Ma
Dillard, Rebecca to John T. Garner 8-29-1832 (8-30-1832) Hr
Dillard, Rebecca to Solomon Needham 12-3-1834 (12-4-1834) Hr
Dillard, Rosannah to Martin Prichard 9-1-1869 (no return) Dy
Dillard, Sarah to Linnear Dixon 9-10-1836 Hr
Dillard, Sarah to Owen Dillard 7-13-1833 (7-14-1833) Hr
Dillard, Susan to Leonard Moore 5-25-1827 Ma
Dillenham, Permelia to Richard D. Hutson 10-10-1828 Hr
Dillian, Elizabeth Cora to James M. D. Tyner 3-23-1858 Be
Dillian, Phebey J. to Kinchen Nunnery 5-15-1858 Be
Dilliard, A.a C. to Geo. Honley 3-15-1866 F
Dilliard, Sarah A. to Julias Johnson 9-25-1865 (9-26-1865) F
Dilliard, Sarah to Elias Walker 10-1-1830 Ma
Dillihunty, Susan to Robert Gee 6-15-1859 (6-?-1859) T
Dilling, Mary A. to Pinkney Bird 10-24-1855 We
Dillinger, Mary to Henry Engelhercher 9-18-1855 Sh
Dillingham, Amanda to Monroe Hicks 10-10-1878 (no return) Dy
Dillingham, Elizabeth Ann to Vann R. Chism 6-18-1836 Hr
Dillingham, Jane to James Webster 9-8-1827 Hr
Dillingham, Louretta E. to Seth L. Andrews 11-26-1861 Be
Dillion, Amarantha to Elijah D. Thompson 3-26-1863 Be
Dillion, C. to J. R. Morgan no date (with 1861) Be
Dillion, Katy to Mark Thomason 9-15-1861 Be
Dillion?, Catharine to Wiley Smothers 6-30-1869 Cr
Dillon, Celia A. to R. T. Green 2-5-1874 Dy
Dillon, F. C. to J. H. Richardson 12-20-1862 (12-25-1862) O
Dillon, Joanna to John Tilmartin 8-4-1853 Sh
Dillon, Manerva A. to J. W. N. Miller 4-23-1867 Be
Dillon, Mary to Charles Shiers 6-9-1858 Sh
Dinkins, Caroline to James M. Pemberton 12-1-1857 Hn
Dinkins, Lucy Eliza to Horace Wilson 2-6-1850 Sh
Dinkins, Sarah J. to Wm. H. Largent 2-12-1855 (no return) F
Dinkins, Zylpha to John M. Ward 9-27-1838 Sh
Dinkins, _____ to S. H. Hawkins 5-6-1868 T
Dinwiddie, Alice to Thomas Covington 1-27-1866 Hn
Dinwiddie, B. J. to J. B. Stewart 3-13-1859 Cr
Dinwiddie, Caroline to Larkin Breedlove 2-25-1868 Hn
Dinwiddie, Jane C. to Henry Bobbitt 9-13-1838 Hn
Dinwiddie, Jane to Grundy Manly 2-21-1866 Hn
Dinwiddie, Jane to Henry Haynes 1-27-1867 Hn B
Dinwiddie, Martha A. to Benjamin F. Bobbett 2-13-1850 Hn
Dinwiddie, Martha J. to M. Gordon 8-26-1840 Cr
Dinwiddie, Mary A. S. to David Bell 12-23-1850 (no return) Hn
Dinwiddie, Mary S. to James F. Dinwiddie 3-28-1860 Hn
Dinwiddie, Mary to Thos. Blackman 9-24-1856 Cr
Dinwiddie, Rebecca J. to John Kirkpatrick 9-17-1842 (9-21-1842) G
Dinwiddie, T. H. to Calvin McDougal 4-5-1866 G
Dinwoody, Dilly to Malica C. Bright 1-24-1848 T

Dinwoody, Marget to Albert Williams 9-19-1859 T
Dippel, Mary to P. J. Mahon 5-26-1862 (7-4-1862) Sh
Dirk, Drusilla to Walker Henry 10-22-1881 (10-23-1881) L
Dis?, Eliza to Frnaklin J. Parker 6-17-1871 (6-18-1871) Ma
Disek (Disch), Mary to William Viers 9-28-1848 Sh
Dishough, M. E. to N. J. Cox 11-12-1860 Hr
Disley, Mary to John Todd 3-3-1848 Sh
Dismuke, Mary I. to I. A. Wetherford 1-1-1861 Hn
Dismuke, Sarah A. to Joseph B. Jones 8-4-1849 Ma
Dismukes, Elisabeth to Richd. C. Bridger 5-11-1870 (no return) Hy
Dismukes, Mary J. to Benjamin W. Travis 12-29-1840 Hn
Dison, Elizabeth A. to John A. Moore 1-8-1852 Hr
Dison, Ester to Geo. W. Clarke 4-1-1871 (no return) Hy
Dison, Jennie to Stephen Anthony 3-23-1872 Hy
Dison, Sallie to George Washington 8-21-1873 T
Ditto, Mary to Hardin Jackson 2-29-1866 Hy
Ditto, Nancy T. to James McGee 12-23-1861 (no return) Hy
Ditto, Sarah to William Chisem 9-21-1870 Hy
Divine, Mary to Louis Foster 8-24-1864 Sh
Dix, Edie to Samuel Rainey 8-12-1865 F
Dixon, A. E. to T. J. Ferguson 9-12-1861 (10-21-1861) Hr
Dixon, Albertie to Howell Read 3-2-1871 F
Dixon, Amanda to Covey Moore 12-1-1873 (12-3-1873) T
Dixon, E. O. to T. S. Cole 3-29-1859 (3-31-1859) Sh
Dixon, Elizabeth A. to Thomas E. McClendon 6-5-1856 Hr
Dixon, Fannie to George Gaskins 8-15-1878 (no return) Hy
Dixon, Fannie to William H. Ursery 9-13-1867 (9-15-1867) Ma
Dixon, Hariet to Wash P. Mitchell 10-2-1844 Cr
Dixon, Harriet J. to J. K. Andrews 12-17-1861 Mn
Dixon, Lidia to Henry Colyear 1-5-1828 (1-6-1828) G
Dixon, M. E. to Wm. S. Mason 8-11-1873 (no return) Hy
Dixon, M. Pryor to James P. Holloway 8-24-1861 Hr
Dixon, Malissa A. to John C. Naron 12-18-1838 Hn
Dixon, Martha A. to Stephen A. Burk 10-19-1850 Cr
Dixon, Mary Ann to J. F. Crawford 11-13-1867 Hy
Dixon, Nancy E. to Jefferson Harden 2-1-1862 (no return) L
Dixon, Sarah E. to G. W> Bearden 11-13-1867 Hy
Dixon, Susan J. to Joel T. Justice 8-14-1849 Ma
Dixon, Susan to Leolen Jones 12-10-1857 Hr
Dizen, Lucretia to Willis E. Lewis 3-12-1829 Hr
Doak, Amanda M. to Christopher C. Fly 3-6-1841 (3-7-1841) Ma
Doak, Bette to Allen Mahan 1-4-1871 (no return) Dy
Doak, Eliza Jane to Scott Pillow 2-8-1877 Dy
Doak, Elizabeth to James D. Pope 8-20-1873 (no return) Dy
Doak, Harriet to Harry Copeland 1-7-1874 (no return) Dy
Doak, Lucinda to Felix Pinion 9-27-1879 (9-29-1879) Dy
Doak, Lucy A. to W. H. Hendrix 4-16-1879 (4-17-1879) Dy
Doak, Margarett H. to George H. Wright 11-26-1839 Ma
Doak, Martha Ann to John R. Jones 7-5-1839 Cr
Doak, Mary Jane to John W. Lile 5-27-1843 Ma
Doak, Sarah to John Smith 1-20-1871 (1-22-1871) Dy B
Doake, Eunica A. to Rufus M. Mason 10-5-1850 Ma
Doake, Mary Jane to John E. Clark 1-25-1849 (1-30-1849) Ma
Dobbin, Sarah to Axum Porter 12-27-1867 F B
Dobbins, Cornelius to Mack Vaysor? 4-16-1868 (no return) F B
Dobbins, Mary E. to Samuel M. Blake 1-7-1855 Hn
Dobbs, Blanch Ann to Fielding Heaslet 12-2-1869 (no return) F B
Dobbs, Kitty to Joseph T. Rankin 11-10-1854 (11-12-1854) Ma
Dobkins, Mary M. to Moses Pearson 1-31-1855 Sh
Dobson, C. C. to James Morgan 12-20-1870 (12-22-1870) T
Dobson, Frances M. to Dewitt Easley 9-28-18857 Hn
Dobson, Lucy to George Harper 12-13-1868 G B
Dobson, Martha Jane to Robert Smith 12-11-1867 T
Dobyn, C.L. to Aldred Wilson 12-23-1845 Sh
Dobyns, M. M. to R. P. Archer 12-27-1849 Sh
Dock, Sarah A. to Alex Bugg 5-3-1869 (no return) Dy
Dockens, Sarah to S. C. Collins 10-30-1872 Dy
Dockings, Sarah to Hardy Fowler 3-15-1839 (3-20-1839) G
Dockins, Celia to Jose Davis 9-3-1847 O
Dockins, Cynthia to David G. Mason 7-3-1849 Ma
Dockins, Elizabeth to Joseph H. Maxey 4-12-1844 (4-16-1844) O
Dockins, Jane to William Vincent 7-23-1841 (7-28-1841) O
Dockins, M. E. to Luke Matheny 3-9-1867 O
Dockins, Martha A. E. to James W. Jones 2-17-1859 O
Dockins, Milly Ann to John Dockins 6-17-18514 O
Dockins, R. A. to J. W. Foster 8-29-1866 G
Dockins, Susan C. to Jonas S. Pipkin 10-10-1850 (10-13-1850) G
Dockins, Susan to William Fussell 3-31-1830 Ma
Dodd, Allice J. to Thomas L. Stringer 1-12-1875 (1-14-1875) L
Dodd, Amanda J. to R. K. Jackson 4-16-1857 We
Dodd, Caroline to John Reynolds 6-15-1863 Dy
Dodd, Eliza A. to George D. Harpole 8-4-1868 (8-6-1868) Dy
Dodd, Eliza J. to G. W. D. White 7-13-1868 (7-15-1868) L
Dodd, Eliza Jane to Stephen Campbell 2-23-1846 (2-244-1846) O
Dodd, Eliza to J. A. McCarroll 12-12-1867 G
Dodd, Elizabeth C. to James M. Tosh 1-9-1871 (1-10-1871) Cr
Dodd, Elizabeth to Alexander Nordin 2-16-1828 (2-17-1828) Hr

Dodd, Elizabeth to J. J. Lane 5-1-1867 G
Dodd, Elizabeth to M. W. Neeley 6-5-1873 Dy
Dodd, Ellen to Calvin Curtner 9-17-1855 (9-20-1855) O
Dodd, Elvira S. J. to W. P. Knight 9-10-1866 (9-11-1866) Dy
Dodd, F. L. to J. M. White 9-10-1865 (9-11-1865) Dy
Dodd, Fannie S. to J. P. James 8-18-1863 G
Dodd, M. E. to J. F. Haskill 12-20-1869 (no return) L
Dodd, M. L. to J. T. Castle 11-15-1862 (11-20-1862) O
Dodd, M. M. to J. W. Wesson 5-24-1869 (5-27-1869) Dy
Dodd, Manerva? C. to Harbird Williams 8-11-1859 O
Dodd, Martha to Benjamin F. Bertram 1-14-1849 Hn
Dodd, Mary Ann to John Davis 2-10-1857 (2-11-1857) L
Dodd, Mary E. to John N. Moore 1-25-1860 (1-29-1860) Sh
Dodd, Mary W. to Lemuel M. Pledge 12-23-1826 (12-24-1826) Hr
Dodd, Mary to J. G. Giles 8-31-1857 We
Dodd, Mary to John A. Rhoads 12-23-1857 (12-24-1857) O
Dodd, Minerva to Smith McDearmin 12-27-1866 G
Dodd, Permelia to Joseph J. Ware 11-5-1853 Cr
Dodd, Rachel (Mrs.) to Robert H. Givens 12-13-1867 Ma
Dodd, Rebecca F. to Robert C. Hill 3-27-1866 (3-29-1866) Cr
Dodd, Sarah A. C. to Samuel S. Harris 6-11-1840 O
Dodd, Sarah E. to Benjamin Davis 12-19-1845 (12-23-1845) F
Dodd, Sarah F. to V. M. L. Taylor 10-29-1858 O
Dodd, Sarah to Allen Ganaway 1-13-1870 G
Dodd, Susan E. to William Branson 10-13-1860 G
Dodd, Tabitha to Levi D. Miller 1-22-1858 (1-27-1858) Hr
Doddridge, Frances E. to George Millirons 4-23-1838 F
Dodds, Julia A. to Edward F. Alexander 6-22-1870 Ma
Dodds, Nancy C. to Wm. B. Jeffress 11-21-1846 (no return) We
Dodds, Penniah to Solomon W. Fisk 3-6-1854 (no return) F
Dodson, Adaline to Charles Smith 9-14-1866 (9-16-1866) F B
Dodson, Emily Jane to William R. House no dates (with Dec 1845) F
Dodson, Emma to James A. Steward 4-22-1862 (4-23-1862) F
Dodson, F. P. to J. J. Swanson 1-11-1868 Hy
Dodson, J. A. to J. W. Carmack 12-17-1875 (12-19-1875) Dy
Dodson, Jane to George Carpenter 3-24-1866 F B
Dodson, Jean V. to Joseph M. Terrell 6-29-1863 G
Dodson, Joan to J. C. Spencer 12-9-1866 G
Dodson, Lucy A. to J. S. Watkins 9-13-1865 G
Dodson, Margaret Ann to J. C. Turner 11-3-1857 (11-4-1857) Sh
Dodson, Margaret Ann to Saml. D. Long 2-9-1846 (2-12-1846) F
Dodson, Maria to Alfred Payne 7-19-1858 (7-20-1858) F
Dodson, Martha (T?) to Wm. L. Eddins 11-27-1850 Sh
Dodson, Martha E. to Vincent Middleton 7-14-1855 (no return) F
Dodson, Martha to John A. Parnell 12-26-1857 Cr
Dodson, Mary A. to John A. Jackson 9?-17-1853 (no return) F
Dodson, Mary E. to John S. Herndon 1-18-1854 (no return) F
Dodson, Mary to Jack Miller 3-30-1867 Hy
Dodson, Nancy Jane to Elipha Z. Robinson 4-21-1857 (4-26-1857) Ma
Dodson, Nancy to A. S. Bills 12-22-1853 (12-25-1853) Hr
Dodson, Rachael to C. C. Crenshaw 12-14-1858 (12-15-1858) Sh
Dodson, Sallie E. to J. R. Dance 11-1-1865 G
Dodson, Sallie to J. F. Greer 12-30-1868 G
Dodson, Sally (Mrs.) to Asa W. Green 8-24-1827 Sh
Dodson, Sarah Benton to Saml. Clements 8-9-1851 (8-10-1851) T
Dodson, Sarah E. to William B. Terrell 1-7-1859 (12-10-1859) G
Dodson, Sarah Frances to Michael McNelis 3-9-1869 (3-21-1869) F
Dodson, Sarah to Wesley Chronister 1-30-1866 (1-31-1866) Dy
Doeble, Sabrina E. to Nickolas Caraline 5-11-1853 Sh
Doebler, Caroline to John Able 10-30-1855 Sh
Doebler, Sabrina to Cyrus A. Doebler 6-7-1849 Sh
Doeller, Lucretia to Robert T. O'Hanlon 9-5-1850 Sh
Doer, Lizzie to L. E. Brasfield 1-12-1886 (1-13-1886) L
Doerle, Mary (Mrs.) to Joseph Achtman(n) 5-28-1863 Sh
Dogget, Eliza to Wm. Runnels 5-5-1869 (5-9-1869) T
Doggett, Ferlea? U. to John D. Carroll 8-16-1853 (8-18-1853) Sh
Doggett, Mary B. to J. C. Mills 9-28-1863 Sh
Doherity, Nannie to James Haris 9-26-1870 (9-28-1870) Cr
Doherty, Bell to J. F. Crews 7-11-1865 Be
Doherty, E. Jane to George McGlon 5-11-1852 Be
Doherty, Elizabeth A. to Jas. T. Cannon 10-12-1858 (10-13-1858) G
Doherty, Esther to Lewis Russell 6-1-1870 (6-5-1870) Cr
Doherty, J. T. to J. M. Hogan 7-11-1867 Cr
Doherty, Margret to Meradeth Corbitt 2-23-1853 Be
Doherty, Mary A. to James A. Scoby 10-26-1854 Cr
Doherty, Mary E. to Beverly S. Allen 11-12-1856 Cr
Doherty, Rutha J. to Joseph D. Askew 12-19-1857 Ma
Doherty, Susan to William F. Overstreet 11-3-1867 Be
Dolan, Ann to James McKeon 1-7-855 Sh
Dolan, Catharine to Thomas Keane 1-21-1860 (1-22-1860) Sh
Dolan, Elizabeth to George Cleaves 4-28-1852 Sh
Dolan, Hanora to James McCabe 7-2-1861 Sh
Dolan, Jane to William Rogers 9-21-1847 (9-23-1847) G
Dolan, Lyda to Milton Thomas 3-11-1848 (3-12-1848) G
Dolan, Mary J. to Robert Dolan 12-22-1866 (12-23-1866) Cr
Dolan, Mary to Christopher Murray 9-9-1861 (9-15-1861) Sh
Doland, Elizabeth to Alfred Gage 4-5-1843 (4-9-1843) G

Brides

Doldon?, Mary C. to E. F. Walker 9-14-1859 T
Dolen, Mary jane to Thomas Raffalty 5-9-1861 Sh
Dolen, Sarah to Henry Nease 8-19-1838 Cr
Dolin, Jane to Jacob Cooper 1-1-1839 Cr
Doll, Charlotte to George Gray 5-18-1860 Sh
Dollahite, Evalyn to Drewry Burton 2-6-1838 (no return) Hn
Dollar, Angy to Daniel A. Young 4-8-1868 Ma
Dollar, Elizabeth to John Brooks 3-16-1853 (3-17-1853) Hr
Dollar, Martha A. L. to Arthur Forbis 7-19-1847 (7-20-1847) Ma
Dollar, Mary C. to Samuel Duffey 7-4-1854 Ma
Dollar, S. C. to Asher Simpson 1-3-1871 Cr
Dollar, Sarah E. to George Belue 6-7-1854 (6-8-1854) Ma
Dollern, G. C. to F. M. Handley 8-17-1867 (8-18-1867) O
Dollerson, Mary W. to Richard L. Tylor 1-22-1850 (2-5-1850) O
Dollman, Augusta (Mrs.) to Frederick Sonnemann 11-25-1863 Sh
Dollohite, Temperance to Josiah Cook 8-9-1860 (8-14-1860) Cr
Dolohite, Carline A. to Robert Mosley 1-31-1856 We
Dolron, Sarah E. to Ed Nesbett 1-25-1871 (1-26-1871) Cr
Dolton, Sarah to Henry Green 1-6-1852 Be
Donahoe, Ellen to Robert Crow 8-17-1848 Sh
Donahue, Margaret to John Conner 1-7-1863 Sh
Donald, Emily S. to Felix J. Birdwell 1-9-1848 Cr
Donald, Harrit (Mrs.) to Green Phelps 12-26-1867 G B
Donald, Jane to John Durden 12-27-1877 Dy
Donald, L. M. to Thos. I. Person 9-20-1842 (9-29-1842) Ma
Donald, Levina to Robert A. Atkison 10-30-1840 Ma
Donaldson, Ann E. to Needham Holland 12-7-1839 (12-19-1839) G
Donaldson, C. to Jacob Chrenshaw 10-12-1870 G
Donaldson, E. D. to J. W. Robinson 12-4-1860 G
Donaldson, Elizabeth A. to Obed Nicholasson 1-26-1837 (1-?-1837) G
Donaldson, Jane C. to William P. Maclin 8-5-1846 (8-6-1846) G
Donaldson, Julia to Wm. D. Bethell 10-30-1837 G
Donaldson, Lucinda to Ben Moore 12-22-1869 (12-23-1870?) G B
Donaldson, Margarett J. to Peleg Bailey 2-23-1846 (2-26-1846) G
Donaldson, Mariah to Foster Glenn 6-8-1867 G
Donaldson, Mary A. to A. D. Kingman 4-21-1849 (4-28-1849) O
Donaldson, Mary A. to Elisha Mandenall 1-2-1844 G
Donaldson, Mary E. to James C. Tarkington 7-28-1863 O
Donaldson, Mary W. to Richard L. Tyler 1-22-1850 (2-5-1850) O
Donaldson, Mary to M. C. M. Abernathy 9-9-1846 (9-10-1846) F
Donaldson, Matilda to Henry O. Etherby (Etherley?) 2-27-1851 (2-26?-1851) Sh
Donaldson, Sarah J. to William D. Merriwether 4-9-1860 (4-10-1860) O
Donaldson, Sarah J. to William J. Jennings 2-9-1845 G
Donaldson, Susan G. to William B. Foster 3-5-1849 G
Donalson, C. M. to A. W. Whittaker 2-11-1856 (2-13-1856) Sh
Donavan, Margaret to James Kennedy 5-4-1857 Sh
Donaway, S. A. to James R. McClain 12-29-1866 O
Donaway, Sarah A. to James R. McClain 12-29-1866 O
Donegan, Allis to Joseph Kelough 4-23-1867 O
Donel, Harriet to John Heathcock 1-14-1835 (1-15-1835) G
Donell, M. E. to J. R. Sanders 7-14-1864 Mn
Donelson, Ann to Andrew Jackson 8-18-1867 G B
Donelson, Jane P. to Robert J. Chester 12-22-1855 Sh
Donelson, Laura to Edmond Lewis 9-2-1868 (no return) F B
Donelson, Rachael S. to William B. Knox 11-28-1860 Sh
Donlan, Sarah to Michael Whelan 7-26-1864 Sh
Donley, Hannonah to William Stack 2-1-1860 Sh
Donly, Martha S. (Mrs.) to Andrew Cunningham 4-12-1864 Sh
Donne (Donna?), Mary to William Foster 11-23-1864 (11-24-1864) Sh
Donnell, Elizabeth to David Evans 2-6-1843 (2-9-1843) Hr
Donnell, M. E. to B. F. Burnett 4-17-1863 (4-19-1863) O
Donnell, Margaret (Mrs.) to Mauris Morrissey 9-25-1858 (9-26-1858) Sh
Donnelson, Martha to Wm. Fulgham 3-10-1831 (3-16-1831) Hr
Donner (Danner?), Melissa to Mitchell Woodson 7-29-1869 G
Donner, Luizer to Williie Woodson 2-23-1867 G
Donnevan, Hannevah to John Torpey 5-30-1864 (5-31-1864) Sh
Donnily, Mary to Henry Reddick 1-15-1869 (no return) F B
Donohoo, Margaret to John Needham 4-20-1867 T
Donovan, Ann to John J. Bourk (Burke) 8-15-1863 Sh
Donsho, Catharine to William Corr 7-27-1861 Sh
Dony, Lea to Ransom Pirkins 12-29-1870 Hy
Dooley, Catharine to John Coleman 4-3-1860 (4-15-1860) Sh
Dooley, Z. A. to David K. Bryson 3-22-1859 (no return) L
Doolinger, Mary to Peter Outhouse 11-21-1850 We
Doomas?, Frances L. to James S. Henry 11-12-1838 Hn
Dooner, Ellen to Cornelius Cannon 5-2-1861 (5-6-1861) Sh
Doorens, Caroline to T. Adams 1-16-1845 Hn
Doragh, Sarah to John McInnes 10-8-1860 Sh
Doran, Hannah to John Kelly 1-7-1857 Sh
Doran, Harriett to Travis Pickard 12-21-1867 (no return) Hn
Doren, Elizabeth Jan to Answell F. Morris 10-14-1857 Hn
Dorfeville, Amanda to Barnett Graham 2-6-1843 Sh
Dorgon, Bridget to Michael Manning 11-30-1860 Sh
Dorhorty, Elizabeth to Henry Oakley 3-21-1845 (no return) We
Dorhorty, Nancy Ann to A. E. Francis 8-1-1846 We
Dority(Daugherty?), Orphy to Alford Eskew 3-9-1846 (3-11-1846) Hr
Dority, Sarah J. to Fayette (Fate) Brigance 1-24-1880 (1-25-1880) L

Page 83

Dorough, Margaret to Edward McGrory 5-1-1860 Sh
Dorris, Caroline to Thomas Hughlet 5-18-1836 (6-2-1836) O
Dorris, Jane to Jefferson Cook 5-20-1834 O
Dors, Margaret to Carter Holt 1-6-1868 (no return) F B
Dorset, Mary A. to Daniel W. Norman 11-17-1846 G
Dorset, Mary to Willis Joslin 11-8-1838 G
Dorsett, Elizabeth E. to Hance Newsom 6-30-1862 G
Dorsey, Belinda to John Kesterson 2-1-1827 (2-?-1827) Hr
Dorsey, Eliza to Kirtley Waymon 2-8-1847 Sh
Dorsey, Julia A. to J. B. Synnott 6-9-1859 (6-13-1859) Sh
Dorsey, Mary to Timothy Ryan 2-24-1852 Sh
Dorson, Caly to Henry Petty 1-1-1877 Hy
Dortch, Amanda J. to Henry L. Sexton 8-18-1861 Hn
Dortch, Ann to William Winfrey 5-3-1869 (no return) F B
Dortch, Elizabeth E. to R. C. Webb 4-30-1851 (5-1-1851) F
Dortch, L. A. to Henry Dunlap 10-19-1866 F
Dortch, Martha E. to John S. Boothe 6-24-1852 Hn
Dortch, Martha J. to J. A. Foster 5-26-1867 Hn
Dortch, Mary E. to Simon Fletcher 1-25-1870 (1-26-1870) F B
Dortch, Mary F. to W. C. Key 1-25-1867 Hn
Dortch, Mary Jane to Abram Clement 9-14-1848 Hn
Dortch, Rebecca A. to Smith Gibson 12-27-1860 Hn
Dortch, Sarah Ann to Thomas B. Culpepper 4-16-1857 Hn
Dortch, Sarah to Gaines Johnson 1-2-1869 F B
Dortch, Susan to Elijah S. Adams 11-28-1852 Hn
Doser, Carolina to John Schurmayer 11-22-1860 Sh
Doss, Charlotte to Alexander Franklin 12-30-1866 (1-1-1866?) F B
Dosson, JSane to _____ Martin 5-26-1863 (5-28-1863) T
Dots, Holland to Edward Tarrey 12-25-1874 (12-27-1874) T
Dotson (Watson?), Mary A. J. to G. C. Jennings 2-3-1873 (2-12-1873) L
Dotson, Alcy to Nichelous Newton 10-7-1839 (10-10-1839) O
Dotson, Martha J. to William Holt 11-29-1861 We
Dotson, Mary Ann to Henry H. Brown 2-11-1835 Hr
Dotson, Matilda to Major Searcy 6-28-1867 Hy
Dotson, Rebecca to Lewis Battle 10-7-1872 (10-14-1872) Dy
Dotson, Syntha A. to Samuel S. Jentry 9-2-1861 (no return) We
Doty, Catherine L. to Robert F. Cook 8-6-1840 Sh
Doty, Drew J. to Joseph L. Smith 6-27-1848 Sh
Doty, Mary A. to Nathaniel Hazelwood 1-27-1833 Sh
Doud, Melinda to James F. Randolph 3-10-1848 G
Doudel, Ellen to Wm. Costilow 8-14-1860 Sh
Doudy, Rebecca H. to Jacob Bowers 4-2-1845 (4-9-1845) F
Dougal, Nancy M. to Kindred A. Cooper 3-10-1852 We
Dougan, Amanda to M. S. Renfroe 1-25-1860 (1-26-1860) F
Dougan, Melissa to William T. Wells 9-25-1843 (no return) G
Dougan, Nancy A. to James M. Baxter 10-2-1850 (10-3-1850) Ma
Dougan, Nancy A. to William F. Joyner 10-22-1849 Ma
Dougherty, Abigail to William Sarrett 10-22-1837 Hr
Dougherty, Annie to Rady Maro (Mary) 5-29-1863 Sh
Dougherty, Hollen to John Davis 8-13-1836 Hr
Dougherty, Irene E. to R. G.? Cook 9-10-1867 (no return) Cr
Dougherty, Jennie to Thomas Fisher 4-1-1864 (4-5-1864) Sh
Dougherty, Katie to Frank Gentry 7-20-1865 (no return) Dy
Dougherty, L. A. to J. B. Morgan 11-23-1857 (11-24-1857) Sh
Dougherty, Martha R. to J. M. Bradford 7-7-1860 O
Dougherty, Mary Ann to Patrick Quinn 10-24-1857 (10-25-1857) Sh
Dougherty, Mary Ellen to George Olmstead 3-20-1882 L
Dougherty, Mary L. to W. H. Daniel 7-15-1860 (7-17-1860) Hr
Dougherty, Mary O. (Miss) to J. M. Semmes 11-23-1857 (11-24-1857) Sh
Dougherty, Rosa to Robert W. Whitworth 8-19-1851 Sh
Dougherty, S. E. to E. C. Carroll 10-12-1867 O
Doughty, Elizabeth J. to Stephen Nash 2-23-1848 (no return) Hn
Doughty, Nancy W. J. to William C. Lowry 4-15-1857 Hn
Doughty, Sarah to Frederic L. Harris 4-29-1863 G
Doughty, Serilda to Harrison Brown 12-8-1838 (12-10-1838) Hr
Douglas, Agnes W. to Joseph S. Waller 7-27-1835 Sh
Douglas, Ann to Benjamin F. Harrol 4-10-1835 Sh
Douglas, Anna to R. R. Johnson 6-30-1866 (no return) Dy
Douglas, Anny to Harry Miller 12-25-1873 Hy
Douglas, Bettie to William Sanford 1-17-1867 T
Douglas, Dilcey to Alex Hall 2-14-1866 T
Douglas, E. T. to T. H. Park 9-10-1867 O
Douglas, Elizabeth to James Gift 5-14-1835 Sh
Douglas, Eva L. to Jno. K. Russel 5-19-1869 T
Douglas, Francis J. to Jesse Toler 11-24-1866 O
Douglas, Jane to Wm. Mabery 10-16-1869 Hy
Douglas, Josephine to Jasper Jones 3-8-1877 Hy
Douglas, Lucinda to William Smith 9-23-1835 Sh
Douglas, Lucy to Davy Qualls 2-20-1869 F B
Douglas, Margaret to George M. McQuirter 10-20-1869 (no return) F B
Douglas, Martha V. to L. B. Lamb 12-16-1865 (12-19-1865) F
Douglas, Mary E. to Norvell A. Page 11-26-1850 Hn
Douglas, Mary Jane to Reuben Alphin 8-13-1856 O
Douglas, Mary to William W. Lyon 7-20-1858 Hn
Douglas, Mattie to Wade M. Patton 11-15-1876 Hy
Douglas, Myra to Albert Jones 5-17-1867 (5-18-1867) Dy
Douglas, Nancy to Frank Wilkes 11-26-1874 Hy

Douglas, Susan J. to Thomas J. Haynie 12-31-1866 (1-1-1867) T
Douglas, Susan to Essex Mabin 1-10-1878 Hy
Douglass, Agnes to John Marcum 7-29-1851 Sh
Douglass, Amanda to Edmund Grimm 2-19-1873 (2-20-1873) Dy
Douglass, Ann (Mrs.) to F. Wm. Crossland 2-25-1858 Sh
Douglass, Ann E. to J. C. Haskins 11-12-1866 (11-13-1866) Dy
Douglass, Ann E. to Stephen A. Hodgeman 6-28-1855 (6-29-1855) Sh
Douglass, Ann to Henry Smith 12-30-1865 T
Douglass, C. R. to Norman Sheron 12-27-1868 Hy
Douglass, Caroline to Solomon H. Shaw 4-22-1846 F
Douglass, Catherine J. to Joseph W. Slater 4-4-1839 Sh
Douglass, E. to Jno. B. Robinson 3-26-1851 (no return) F
Douglass, Eliza to Cornelius Scott 9-28-1872 Dy
Douglass, Emily E. to Jesse W. Lassiter 2-6-1871 (2-7-1871) Ma
Douglass, Fannie J. to F. A. Tepe 7-20-1858 Sh
Douglass, Fannie to Turner McGallary 10-3-1878 Hy
Douglass, Frances to George Edge 1-23-1878 (no return) Dy
Douglass, Hester Ann to Isaac J. Lynch 11-1-1853 O
Douglass, Jane to Alex Smith 3-9-1871 Dy
Douglass, Jane to Jordan Harris 9-2-1876 (9-3-1876) Dy
Douglass, Jane to William Parton 1-25-1842 (1-27-1842) O
Douglass, Lucinda to Thomas Tyner 7-14-1847 Be
Douglass, Lucy to Jesse Degraffenreid 12-22-1866 (12-27-1866) F B
Douglass, M. V. to J. H. Degraffinreid 4-9-1874 (4-12-1874) O
Douglass, Martha A. to Felix McFarland 6-28-1842 F
Douglass, Mary A. E. to Wm. F. Vaughn 2-21-1866 Hy
Douglass, Mary to Dalles Mathis 12-11-1869 (no return) Hy
Douglass, Parilee to Nelson Watkins 8-12-1866 Hy
Douglass, S. A. to B. R. Parks 12-24-1872 (12-25-1872) Dy
Douglass, S. E. to H. A. Dean 10-3-1872 (no return) Dy
Douglass, Sarah J. to Lewis Stell 2-24-1855 Sh
Douglass, Vina to Geo Neddie 5-16-1874 Hy
Douherty, Catherine to Thomas Winters 9-12-1862 Sh
Doutaz, Louisa to H. Guilmord 6-11-1864 Sh
Dove, Lucinda (Mrs.) to John Chrisehall 1-30-1867 O
Dove, Martha to David Baily 11-29-1869 Dy
Dove, Mary Jane to Thomas Morrison 6-11-1863 Dy
Dove, Patsey to D. L. Carvin 11-3-1874 (11-4-1874) Dy
Dover, Ann to Barney McCoy (Coy) 7-15-1863 Sh
Dover, Julia A. to J. M. Walls 9-8-1870 F
Dow, Margaret O. to Warren Blackwell 4-15-1871 (4-17-1871) F B
Dowd, Amanda to Joseph Strange 11-1-1860 G
Dowds, Catherine to James McNamara 4-1-1864 (4-3-1864) Sh
Dowdy, Ann to David Moore 11-1-1852 (no return) F
Dowdy, Charlotte to Erasmus Darwin Edwards 8-27-1844 T
Dowdy, Elizabeth to J. H. Hutchison 6-1-1864 Be
Dowdy, Elvira to Robert Parks 12-29-1868 (12-31-1868) F B
Dowdy, Fanny to William Woods 1-31-1870 (2-10-1870) F B
Dowdy, Jane to Henry Crews 1-31-1848 Cr
Dowdy, Jennie to G. W. Allen 11-29-1870 (11-31?-1870) F
Dowdy, Louisa to Davy Branch 12-28-1865 (no return) F B
Dowdy, Lucinda to Sam Baker 12-27-1815 (no return) F B
Dowdy, M. J. to Thomas Watt 10-6-1867 G
Dowdy, Margaret A. to William C. Lowry 4-25-1861 Hn
Dowdy, Martha J. to Robert Hollinsworth 11-4-1845 Hn
Dowdy, Mary F. to Geo. H. Ledger 2-26-1851 F
Dowdy, Mary M. to George W. Doughty 12-22-1853 Hn
Dowdy, Nancy M. to S. A. Doughty 12-20-1854 Hn
Dowdy, Nancy to Samuel Myric 5-10-1867 Hy
Dowdy, Narcissa A. to R. W. Redman 9-18-1864 Hn
Dowdy, Sarah E. to Wm. Parke 2-13-1851 (no return) F
Dowdy, Sarah F. to G. W. Fletcher 3-4-1841 (no return) F
Dowel, Mildred to Warren Woodson 6-19-1842 Sh
Dowell, Charlotte to Hendleton Ingram 12-10-1831 G
Dowell, Emaline to Edmond Carter 12-4-1873 T
Dowell, F. M. to E. W. Randolph 5-2-1855 (5-3-1855) Sh
Dowell, Julia Ann to Henry Lowary 3-5-1838 (3-8-1838) F
Dowell, Julian to Lorenza B. Boyd 12-11-1852 (12-15-1852) G
Dowell, Martha A. to W. B. Shankle 1-20-1870 (no return) Dy
Dowell, Mildred A. to Edward M. Bateman 2-16-1860 (2-20-1860) Sh
Dowell, Nancy A. to J. D. Covington 1-2-1849 Cr
Dowell, Sarah A. to J. C. Hudson 2-5-1860 Be
Dowell, Susan to Hiram Landrum 4-26-1872 (5-10-1872) Dy
Dowiggin, Mary E. to John Barham 12-16-1858 Cr
Dowin, Margarett to Daniel White 8-20-1838 Ma
Dowing, Catharine to Stephen Lacy 2-?-1838 F
Dowland, Martha R. to John Thornton 9-22-1867 G
Dowland, Mary A. to John T. Mets (Mils?) 4-15-1861 G
Dowland, Metilda S. to Isaac Mathis 5-22-1860 G
Dowland, Susanah to David Cage 12-31-1855 G
Downes, Mary to John Hines 8-8-1858 Sh
Downey, Catharine to Elisha T. Johnson 12-24-1844 F
Downey, Catharine to R. Manley 12-27-1839 (3-9-1840) F
Downey, Inda to ___ Bramblett 1-26-1830 O
Downey, Margret C. to Thomas Woods? 2-3-1843 (2-5-1843) O
Downing, Elizabeth to Valentine McMillan 1-25-1843 (1-27-1843) Ma
Downing, Narcissa to John Croom 8-27-1842 (8-28-1842) Ma

Downing, Sarah L. to Richd. Vaughan 8-4-1868 T
Downing, Sealy to William Summers 2-25-1829 O
Downing, Susan A. to M. V. B. Harris 5-5-1871 T
Downs, Jennie to John A. Williams 1-22-1876 (1-28-1876) L
Downs, Mary to Daniel Leary 7-4-1857 (7-5-1857) Sh
Downs, Minerva to John Parmour 11-26-1836 (11-27-1836) Hr
Downy, S. to Wm. R. Langdon 12-29-1869 F
Dowtin, Frances H. to Daniel G. McAuley 2-14-1860 Cr
Doxey, Banina L. to George W. Cook 1-10-1852 Sh
Doxey, Lener to Philip Dozer 3-31-1841 (4-1-1841) G
Doxey, Lorenda to James H. Southern 12-24-1832 Hr
Doxey, Virginia to Wm. H. Moon(Moore?) 4-27-1846 (4-28-1846) Hr
Doyle, Ana E. to John F. Walden 10-27-1862 (10-28-1862) Sh
Doyle, Ann to Michael Kelly 8-19-1863 Sh
Doyle, Bettie to Ned Grimm 12-21-1878 (12-25-1878) Dy B
Doyle, Bridget to James Kennan 2-14-1859 Sh
Doyle, Bridget to Rody Ryan 6-15-1857 Sh
Doyle, Bridget to Thomas Morighan (Molhan) 2-20-1863 Sh
Doyle, Bridget to William Maxwell 6-9-1860 (6-10-1860) Sh
Doyle, Caroline R. to Benj. P. Lewis 4-4-1874 (4-5-1874) L
Doyle, Eliza to Jacob Foster 1-7-1868 Dy
Doyle, Ellen to M. C. Costello 2-4-1858 Sh
Doyle, Ellen to Michael O'Brien 11-22-1856 (11-23-1856) Sh
Doyle, Isabella to George Maggard 8-26-1869 (no return) Dy
Doyle, Julia L. to James R. Fleming 12-22-1860 (12-24-1860) Sh
Doyle, Laura F. to James Wilkes 8-21-1854 (8-23-1854) Hr
Doyle, Leonora to William T. Neely 1-3-1867 (1-9-1867) F
Doyle, Lucy J. to John R. Strange 5-17-1873 (5-18-1873) L
Doyle, Luella to George W. Pearce 10-1-1879 L
Doyle, M. D. to R. J. Johnson 1-6-1868 (1-7-1868) F
Doyle, M. E. to C. F. Neely 9-27-1859 (10-6-1859) F
Doyle, M. Eleanor to Jno. F. Page 3-1-1860 Sh
Doyle, Margaret A. to Wm. H. Coburn 3-20-1861 G
Doyle, Maria to James K. Polk Smith 1-30-1867 Dy
Doyle, Mary to John Keliher 8-25-1862 Sh
Doyle, Mary to Patrick Quin 4-26-1855 Sh
Doyle, Matilda to Peter Dunavan 8-15-1867 Dy
Doyle, Mollie to Thomas Wynn 9-25-1879 Dy
Doyle, Pennie to Wash Porter 11-4-1875 Dy
Doyle, Rebecca J. to Harmon Harrison 12-21-1858 (12-22-1858) Hr
Doyle, Sue to J. K. P. Harrell 6-16-1868 (no return) Dy
Dozer, Nany to wiley Taylor 7-7-1838 (7-8-1838) G
Dozier, Amanda C. to John W. Howell 9-30-1862 G
Dozier, C. to W. L. McCulloch 10-1-1866 (10-4-1866) Dy
Dozier, Ellenor to William H. Holmes 12-10-1855 (12-11-1855) G
Dozier, Emma J. to T. A. White 6-12-1871 Cr
Dozier, Jane to John Cook 7-23-1862 (7-24-1862) Dy
Dozier, Julya Ann to Gabriel Greer 8-18-1867 G B
Dozier, Lucy F. to J. A. Pope 12-23-1868 Dy
Dozier, Mary E. to W. L. Howell 10-3-1867 G
Dozier, Penny E. to Charles H. Allen 10-8-1862 G
Draffin, M. J. to W. B. McCoy 5-5-1873 T
Draffin, Margaret J. to J. W. Pinner 1-3-1874 (1-15-1874) T
Drake, Ann E. to Robert M. Barnett 10-15-1855 (10-18-1855) G
Drake, Caroline (Mrs.) to Jacob Mathis 7-13-1853 (7-16-1853) G
Drake, Catherine to Nathan Francis 1-29-1859 Ma
Drake, Earnest to Wm. Baird 5-7-1876 Hy
Drake, Eleira? to James Henderson 2-3-1868 (2-6-1868) Cr
Drake, Elizabeth H. to F. M. Case (Cash) 8-1-1850 Sh
Drake, Elizabeth T. to Martin Davis 10-3-1853 Ma
Drake, Elizabeth to Isaac Elsberry 6-28-1830 Ma
Drake, Ella to Ned Campbell 3-4-1874 Hy
Drake, Flora to Jack Medlin 9-11-1872 Hy
Drake, Hanner to Henderson Hays 2-16-1867 Hy
Drake, Harriet to Ben Shaw 12-23-1865 Hy
Drake, Isabella J. to Alex. Duckworth 3-7-1860 (no return) Hy
Drake, J. B. to J. B. Robertson 11-20-1861 (no return) Hy
Drake, Jenny to Felix Daniel 4-2-1874 Hy
Drake, Louisa to D. H. Porter 3-7-1851 (3-9-1851) Hr
Drake, Luceney E. to James Elkins 7-22-1841 (no return) Cr
Drake, M. M. to John S. Scoby 11-23-1841 Cr
Drake, Malinda J. to John W. Taylor 10-16-1866 Hn
Drake, Marcella Frances to Benjamin Hainline 6-13-1857 (6-16-1857) Hr
Drake, Margaret to William E. Parham 12-28-1859 We
Drake, Mariah to E. G. Harris 2-13-1855 (2-14-1855) Ma
Drake, Martha R. to William Sensing 5-24-1847 (no return) F
Drake, Martha to Thomas A. Shaw 11-19-1870 Hy
Drake, Mary H. to James E. Harris 11-7-1857 (11-10-1857) Ma
Drake, Mary J. to John D. Mathis 2-6-1854 (2-7-1854) G
Drake, Mary to Richard Johnson 2-27-1845 Ma
Drake, Molly to Green Drake 9-8-1866 Hy
Drake, Myra to Calvin Gilbert 11-30-1878 Hy
Drake, O. V. to J. F. Barksdale 2-20-1865 (no return) Cr
Drake, Puss to Robt. Kirby 9-25-1870 Hy
Drake, S. T. C. to W. S. Norris 1-29-1870 (no return) Hy
Drake, S. T. C. to W. T. Baker 8-6-1866 (no return) Hy
Drake, Saphronia to Leroy Croly 4-8-1855 We

Drake, Sarah Ann to Samuel R. Brown 6-19-1842 Sh
Drake, T. L. to P. A. Warren 10-9-1856 Cr
Drane, Louisa to R. B. Wilkinson 5-16-1878 (5-17-1878) Dy
Drane, Mollie J. to James H. Smith 12-1-1857 Sh
Drannon, Elizabeth to Joshua McCarver 10-25-1838 (10-26-1838) Hr
Draper, Ann E. to R. L. Gifford 7-26-1856 (7-27-1856) Sh
Draper, Louisa R. to John Dewberry 7-12-1856 (7-13-1856) G
Draper, M. J. to J. B. Haskins 8-8-1860 G
Draper, Mary to William Clifton 9-22-1828 Ma
Draper, Polly A. N. E. to William H. Cassels 8-24-1853 (8-25-1853) Ma
Draper, S. L. to R. M. Ashley 7-9-1865 G
Drave, Mittie E. to John C. Harris 10-18-1866 (no return) Dy
Draw, Ellen to Richard Oakly 1-29-1875 (1-31-1875) Dy B
Drennon, Marinda to T. J> Tull 1-5-1857 (1-9-1857) Hr
Drennon, Millie to B. F. DuRoss 12-18-1872 (no return) Hy
Drennon, Sarah C. to John R. Maxwell 1-15-1850 (1-20-1850) Hr
Drenon, H. M. to Thomas N. Allen 1-11-1870 (no return) Hy
Drew, Paralee to A. H. McCall 3-25-1858 We
Drew, Winifred B. to James M. Humphreys 12-29-1851 (12-30-1851) Sh
Drewry, Florence A. to J. K. Kearney 12-27-1869 (12-28-1869) Cr
Drewry, M. K. to Thomas A. Overton 1-15-1860 We
Drewry, Margaret to William Edwards 2-15-1870 Hn
Drewry?, Sarah E. to L. W. Simmons 7-22-1863 We
Driggers, Penelopee L. to Worelson Clements 12-21-1860 (12-25-1860) Cr
Drinkard, E. J. to G. W. Lewis 10-30-1866 G
Drinkard, Lucinda H. to A. J. Allen 3-7-1867 G
Drinkard, Sarah F. to Benjamin Todd 10-21-1865 (10-29-1865) Cr
Drinnon, C. J. to T. W. Chambliss 6-3-1848 (6-4-1848) Hr
Drisel, Leonora to James Conner 8-6-1854 Sh
Driskell, Julia A. to Samul. Cunningham 11-19-1844 (11-20-1844) G
Driskell, Nancy L. to William C. Warrin 12-25-1843 G
Driskell, S. A. to N.J. Witherspoon 2-1-1865 G
Driver (Dineve), Sarah F. to W. R. Hunt 2-12-1850 Sh
Driver, Anna to Booker Lucas 9-27-1879 L
Driver, Elizabeth to M. S. McCall 9-21-1871 T
Driver, Mary S. to Thos. H. Logwood 11-1-1855 Sh
Driver, Sarah E. to David McMackin 9-11-1859 Hn
Driver, Sarah J. to James W. McMAckin 10-14-1866 Hn
Driver, Sarahann to Patrick H. Elder 7-17-1844 (7-18-1844) F
Driver?, Mary Vanburen to Josiah Washington Bandy 8-28-1852 T
Droke, Martha Ann to Samuel Barnes 1-22-1863 Mn
Drolinger, Sarah to J. F. Philips 12-21-1845 We
Drown, Margery E. to C. M. Job 6-2-1845 (no return) We
Drown, Margery E. to C. M. Job 6-2-1846 We
Drowup, Elizabeth M. to Joseph Causbey 12-7-1847 Hn
Drum, Julia to Thomas Smith 11-12-1856 Sh
Drummond, Franca? J. to J. B. Burton 4-3-1868 (4-5-1868) T
Drummond, W. to James McKeown 2-8-1869 (2-10-1869) T
Drummond?, Virginia D. to James Stricklin 7-5-1869 (no return) Dy
Drummonds, Elizabeth to Wm. Harper 9-17-1847 (no return) Cr
Drummonds, M. F. to J. A. Self 11-11-1873 (11-15-1873) Dy
Drummons, Ann H. to H. H. Joyner 11-5-1866 (11-6-1866) T
Drummons, Drucilla D. to William E. Clements 12-19-1843 (12-21-1843) T
Drumonds, Maggie to L. C. Smith 8-16-1864 G
Drumwright, Lucy L. to T. H. Trotter 1-5-1881 L
Dryhall, S. C. to G. P. Whitehead 11-21-1867 O
Duberry, Caroline to R. Reaves 6-8-1862 G
Duberry, Frances to Rob. T. Manuel 12-6-1845 (12-7-1845) F
Duberry, Mahulda to Hardy Carr 2-29-1840 (3-1-1840) Hr
Duberry, Mary E. to Martin F. Cashar 10-21-1849 G
Duberry, Mary to Mathew Hood 10-3-1853 (no return) F
Duberry, Nancy to Hugh S. McCaleb 10-7-1846 (10-10-1846) G
Duberry, Rebecca to Williamson E. Rainey 3-21-1843 Hr
Dublin, A. C. to Willis Lipscomb 3-23-1856 We
Dubois, Catharine I. to George W. Deaton 1-7-1835 Hr
Dubois, Harriett E. to Benjamin W. Pirtle 12-29-1837 (1-4-1838) Hr
Dubois, Mary C. to John Kirkwood 3-14-1856 (no return) Hn
Dubois, Mary to Wilson Luckado 2-3-1835 Hr
Duboise, Martha Jane to Martin Pirtle 12-20-1833 (12-25-1833) Hr
Dubose, Elizabeth R. to G. W. Bayne 1-14-1856 (1-15-1856) Sh
Dubose, Sallie P. to Oswald Pope 4-30-1856 Sh
Duboyce, Nancy to Robert Harrison 3-1-1830 (3-2-1830) Hr
Duckworth, Cathrin to Arter Bright 2-6-1871 (no return) Hy
Duckworth, M. A. to A. F. Smith 8-7-1867 Hy
Duckworth, Malissa to Hugh Cannady 7-15-1828 Ma
Duckworth, Mollie J. to H. F. Russell 10-13-1870 Hy
Duckworth, Sarah E. to Ben F. Grant 12-28-1859 (no return) Hy
Duckworth?, Caroline to Hugh B. Robeson 12-28-1830 Ma
Dudley, Adaline to Elijah Pope 1-20-1846 We
Dudley, Alice Ella to A. R. (Lt.) Murdoch 4-3-1864 Sh
Dudley, Anne to Nelson T. Pratt 6-18-1879 (6-19-1879) Dy
Dudley, Betsey to Lewis Baker 4-7-1845 (no return) We
Dudley, Charlotte to Wm. Houston 4-4-1843 Cr
Dudley, Eliza J. to W. H. Clemmons 3-17-1874 Dy
Dudley, Elizabeth to Simon Garrett 10-3-1849 Cr
Dudley, Josephine to Charles White 3-4-1863 We
Dudley, Mary K. to Henry Jones 9-2-1873 Dy

Dudley, Mary to James Sutton 3-4-1877 O
Dudley, Rebecca to Isaac N. McCater 3-29-1860 We
Dudley, Sarah H. to Phillip H. Rodgers 12-20-1855 Cr
Dudley, Sarah to Tillman Gregory 9-28-1845 Cr
Dudley, Susan G. to James A. Patterson 6-12-1852 Cr
Dudling, Rosena to Ferdinand Maas 12-24-1862 Sh
Dudney, Sarah to John Huffman 9-20-1842 Cr
Dueley, Eliza C. to William P. Harrelson 10-18-1860 Cr
Duerkap, Anna to B. Wieners 11-17-1856 Sh
Duet, Rosa Ann to Henry W. Estes 7-6-1847 G
Duff, Eliza to Joseph H. Shultz 1-30-1833 (1-31-1833) Hr
Duff, Jemima to Thomas H. Bell 2-14-1833 Sh
Duff, Maria to Abner Kerkendall 12-8-1829 (9-30-1830) Hr
Duff, Nancy to Alford M. Walker 1-24-1829 (1-27-1829) Hr
Duff, Sarah A. to Frederick Carpenter 9-30-1862 (10-2-1862) O
Duff, Sarah A. to W. H. Creswell no date (1860-1870) G
Duff, Sophia to Winfrey Owens 2-14-1827 (2-18-1827) Hr
Duffee, Nancy to Andrew Grave 10-30-1840 (11-5-1840) G
Duffer, Martha to T. S. Barnett 11-1-1866 G
Duffer, Mary E. to Robert Warren 12-8-1864 G
Duffer, Susan Ann to Richard M. Price 11-13-1869 (11-14-1869) Ma
Duffery, Kedie H. (Mrs.) to Daniel A. Young 1-4-1870 (1-6-1870) Ma
Duffey, Elizabeth to William Lassiter 4-3-1852 (4-7-1852) Ma
Duffey, Malvina to David T. Phillips 4-17-1869 (4-25-1869) Ma
Duffey, Malvina to David T. Phillips 5-7-1866 (not executed) Ma
Duffey, Patsey to Patrick M. Duffey 10-27-1862 (10-28-1862) Ma
Duffy, Eliza to John H. Dollar 1-?-1847 (1-14-1847) Ma
Duffy, Elizabeth B. to William E. Stewart 3-7-1853 (3-8-1853) Ma
Duffy, Lucy J. to Lewis Dollar 4-18-1854 (4-20-1854) Ma
Duffy, Martha to James Duffy 10-17-1865 G
Dugan, Margarett to William Yancey 12-23-1841 Ma
Dugan, Mary to John L. Shelton 9-12-1870 Ma
Dugan, Susanna to F. King 3-4-1861 (3-5-1861) G
Duggel, S. C. to H. W.(M?) Wood 12-6-1865 G
Dugger, Amanda M. to James G. Hancock 3-9-1863 (no return) Hn
Dugger, Jane A. to William C. Williams 10-8-1857 Hn
Duggin, Eliza Ann to S. C. Arnold 4-29-1870 G
Duggor, Nancy to J. A. McEwen 12-4-1865 G
Duglas, Lucinda to Antina Pearson 6-14-1872 (no return) Cr B
Duglas, Martha to Robert Fuller 10-31-1867 (12-5-1867) Dy
Duglass, Ella W. to W. H. Compton 10-17-1870 Hy
Duke, Amanda B. to G. F. Bowman 5-13-1867 (5-14-1867) Dy
Duke, Caroline to Robert W. Conn 2-17-1842 (2-24-1842) F
Duke, Christiana A. to D. W. Wright 5-30-1853 (no return) F
Duke, Eliza to John Thompson 12-22-1870 (12-25-1870) F
Duke, Emily to David Smith 8-25-1872 Hy
Duke, Frances C. to Geo. M. Watson 4-26-1849 Sh
Duke, Louisianna C. (Mrs.) to Emory P. Seymour 2-16-1864 (2-17-1864) Sh
Duke, Lucinda W. to Thos. Williams 2-24-1848 F
Duke, Margaret R. A. to Richard Morris 4-15-1858 Cr
Duke, Marsha to Enos McAuley 8-8-1854 Cr
Duke, Martha A. to Jno. M. J. Moore 8-8-1867 G
Duke, Mary A. to James Teague 10-22-1866 (10-24-1866) F
Duke, Mary C. to William Carter 9-28-1869 (9-29-1869) Dy
Duke, Mary to Richard Madding 12-23-1870 (no return) Dy B
Duke, Miss _____ to D. W. Wright 5-23-1853 (no return) F
Duke, Nancy to Garldas? Batts 7-17-1844 F
Duke, Sallie to W. M. Barton 2-12-1870 (no return) Hy
Duke, Sarah to Robertson Lewis 8-20-1848 Be
Dukes, Dina to Willis Taylor 2-20-1873 Hy
Dukes, Jane to Henry W. Williams 2-21-1878 Hy
Dukes, Susan to Claiborne Edwards 12-17-1877 (no return) Hy
Dumanet, Martha W. to Benj. F. Epperson 11-13-1861 (11-17-1861) Ma
Dumas, B. J. to B. C. Bledsoe 12-27-1855 (no return) Hn
Dumas, Ludie J. to M. P. Sutherlin 1-22-1867 Hn
Dumay, Mary (Mrs.) to M. C. Allen 11-4-1864 Sh
Dumis, Sarah to Thos. Davidson 12-2-1874 T
Dun, Arenar to Squire Clay 1-5-1870 (2-1-1870) F B
Dun, Sarah to William Lucas 4-27-1855 Sh
Dunagan, Margarett to W. J. Russell 10-30-1870 G
Dunagan, Rody Ann to Robert F. Noel 10-30-1861 G
Dunagan, Sally to Zacheriah Biggs 7-10-1829 (7-16-1829) G
Dunagin, Mary C. to Wm. M. Culberson 8-5-1862 (8-6-1862) O
Dunagin, Nanny H. to James W. McGinnis 5-9-1866 O
Dunahon, Mary to Timothy O'Conner 8-17-1855 Sh
Dunavant, Cecelia B. to James L. Mitchell 2-2-1852 L
Dunavant, Ella M. to William J. Jordan 11-25-1871 (11-26-1871) L
Dunavant, Margaret T. to John G. Jones 6-1-1846 (6-9-1846) L
Dunavant, Martha to Andrew J. Suthen 3-17-1866 (3-18-1866) L
Dunavant, Mary Jane to Joseph Holloman 6-18-1844 (6-20-1844) L
Dunavant, Mary W. to T. L. Johnston 12-18-1877 (12-19-1877) L
Dunavant, Susan to Robert Coker 4-20-1880 (not executed) L
Dunavant?, Sallie M. to Thomas L. Johnston 1-28-1873 (1-29-1873) L
Dunaway, Caldonia to William Lea 7-13-1878 (no return) L
Dunaway, Ellen B. to James W. Anderson 5-8-1861 Ma
Dunaway, Lucy E. to James Tomlinson 6-25-1884 (6-26-1884) L
Dunaway, Nancy A. to William Pits 11-3-1865 O

Dunaway, Susan T. to William F. Salisbury 5-5-1863 (5-6-1863) L
Dunbar, Annie C. to David L. Gibson 12-22-1859 Sh
Dunbar, Sarah C. to William C. Allen 6-20-1846 (6-21-1846) F
Duncan (Dilbeck), Levisa to William Hall 11-4-1840 O
Duncan, A. B. to L. A. Slater 1-4-1864 (no return) Dy
Duncan, Ada to A. L. Pugh 4-12-1871 (4-13-1871) L
Duncan, Amacivil to James Gillikin 2-17-1844 Ma
Duncan, Amanda to William S. Blasingame 12-21-1857 (2-12-1858) Hr
Duncan, Ann to S. S. Rembert 2-3-1840 Sh
Duncan, C. B. to L. M. Mitchell 2-23-1860 (4-3-1860) O
Duncan, C. H. to William J. Fowler 8-25-1853 Hn
Duncan, Casander to Felix Pierce 2-6-1860 (2-21-1860) O
Duncan, Celia A. to James K. Webb 11-19-1847 (11-20-1848?) Ma
Duncan, E. A. to G. W. Inman 6-5-1855 Hn
Duncan, Elizabeth C. to F. W. Hall 8-14-1855 (8-15-1855) G
Duncan, Elizabeth Ellen to Andrew J. Miller 6-20-1866 Ma
Duncan, Elizabeth M. to Willis Davis 8-2-1845 (8-3-1845) Hr
Duncan, Ellen to Adam Little 7-30-1870 (7-31-1870) Cr
Duncan, Ellen to Thomas Franklin 9-23-1867 (9-24-1867) Cr
Duncan, Emilia to Johnson Isbell 10-15-1827 Hr
Duncan, Emily to John S. Black 3-30-1863 Sh
Duncan, Fannie T. to John R. Hicks 9-18-1866 (9-19-1866) Ma
Duncan, Frances Adeline to John Buttram 2-21-1855 (2-23-1855) Sh
Duncan, Freedonia to Henry H. Brooks 1-17-1855 Hr
Duncan, Helan M. to Alexander Sloan 5-16-1853 (5-18-1853) Hr
Duncan, Joan Harrison to J. W. Williams 4-28-1860 (4-29-1860) Hr
Duncan, Kate to Henry F. Fuller 1-24-1859 Sh
Duncan, Katharin to Crofford Taylor 5-16-1865 Dy
Duncan, L. Jane to A. W. C. Pittman 10-21-1872 (10-24-1872) T
Duncan, Lotty L. to James Gillikins 5-27-1850 Ma
Duncan, Lou to Joshua Burnam 11-15-1865 (11-16-1865) Dy
Duncan, Louisa to William H. Parrot 12-22-1841 (12-23-1841) Ma
Duncan, Louisiana to Geo. Robinson 2-18-1863 Sh
Duncan, Lucy R. to W. B. Dozier 2-7-1868 G
Duncan, M. E. to G. W. Haislip 7-4-1861 O
Duncan, M. E. to W. H. Murrphey? 1-13-1877 (1-14-1877) L
Duncan, M. O. to E. W. Walpole 8-13-1879 (8-14-1879) L
Duncan, Mahaley to William Jarrett 9-16-1830 Ma
Duncan, Malinda to John Duncan 2-17-1830 (2-18-1830) Hr
Duncan, Margaret to John C. Yandle 8-26-1842 O
Duncan, Mary E. to Robert E. Wright 12-17-1853 (12-18-1853) Sh
Duncan, Mary F. to K. K. Ward 3-31-1865 Hn
Duncan, Mary J. to John W. Little 12-17-1856 (12-18-1856) Hr
Duncan, Mary Jane to John B. Simons 3-5-1849 (3-6-1849) G
Duncan, Mary Jane to William L. Gregory 3-18-1852 Ma
Duncan, Mary to J. C. Anderson 10-19-1854 Be
Duncan, Melinda W. to W. W. Wilson 11-24-1852 Hn
Duncan, Minney(Winney) W. to Abner Harvey 2-12-1836 (1?-1??-1836) Hr
Duncan, Nancy C. to J. H. Briggs 5-24-1875 Dy
Duncan, Nancy F. to Mansel M. Taylor 7-20-1858 O
Duncan, Nancy to Silas Cooper 2-13-1840 Cr
Duncan, Neoma to Lewis Gregory 9-18-1841 Ma
Duncan, Parmelia to Abraham G. Wright 11-19-1853 (11-21-1853) Sh
Duncan, Perline to Joseph S. Utley 5-14-1849 (5-17-1849) Ma
Duncan, Rachel to Thomas H. Clark 2-26-1846 Hn
Duncan, Rebecca to Michael Curran 10-4-1853 (10-5-1853) Sh
Duncan, Ruth A. to Washington D. Shuffield 7-31-1850 (8-1-1850) Ma
Duncan, S. A. to J. A. West 9-28-1881 (9-29-1881) L
Duncan, S. C. to W. H. Howell 5-28-1873 (5-29-1873) T
Duncan, S. O. to J. F. Davis 2-9-1885 L
Duncan, Sallie J. to Henry T. Allison 10-12-1871 Ma
Duncan, Sallie J. to Wm. M. Shelton 10-4-1870 Ma
Duncan, Sally Ann to Benjamin Replogle 9-19-1854 (9-21-1854) Ma
Duncan, Sarah G. to John Warren 6-21-1842 (6-22-1842) O
Duncan, Sarah T. to Joseph H. Evans 4-21-1868 (4-23-1868) Dy
Duncan, Susan F. to H. O. Park 3-30-1861 (4-5-1861) Cr
Duncan, Winaford to James Jones 10-5-1848 (11-7-1848) Hr
Duncans, Hattie to Richard Hand 7-3-1878 (no return) Dy
Duncen, Cyntha to W. D. Harris 1-18-1868 (1-22-1868) Dy
Dunegan, Jane to Theodore Murphy 4-7-1870 G
Dunevant, A. A. to B. F. Wynne 3-5-1873 (3-6-1873) Dy
Dunevant, Frances C. to Henry L. Harrison 12-3-1878 (12-4-1878) Dy
Dunevant, Lavina to A. T. Ferguson 9-18-1879 Dy
Dunevant, Mary Ann to John Burkett 9-13-1877 Dy
Dunevant, Mary B. to L. H. Bass 2-9-1874 (2-11-1874) Dy
Dunevant, Paralee to John Prichard 12-27-1877 Dy
Dunevant, Susan to E. L. Hester 8-23-1884 (8-24-1884) L
Dunfey, Catharine to James Chaill 1-25-1860 (1-29-1860) Sh
Dungan, Mary A. E. to Julius Edwards 11-6-1852 (11-11-1852) Ma
Dungan, Mary Jane to Robert H. Burns 12-11-1862 Ma
Dungan, Parthenia A. E. to William J. McFarland 2-23-1856 (12-25-1856) Ma
Dunham, Arrency to Samuel Redden 10-28-1826 (10-29-1826) O
Dunham, Martha E. to Benjamin Kissell 5-17-1879 (5-18-1879) L
Dunheiser, Charlotte to Samuel Dreyfus 11-24-1855 Sh
Dunigan, Dolla Ann to Stephen H. Russell 10-11-1859 (10-12-1859) G
Dunigan, Emeline to John W. Young 10-11-1848 G
Dunigan, Jane to Joseph Cooper 1-30-1855 G

Duning, M. L. to A. J. Rogers 12-2-1872 (12-5-1872) Cr
Dunivant, Caldonia to Ellis Parker 12-27-1870 (12-28-1870) L
Dunivant, Martha A. to J. D. Powell 3-15-1864 (3-16-1864) Dy
Dunivant, Tenny to J. F. Keller 9-25-1873 Hy
Dunkin, Lizzy L. to Henry B. Powell 11-11-1856 Sh
Dunkin, Mary I. to Samuel B. Hawkins 6-2-1842 Sh
Dunlap, Adaline to Henry Hester 1-10-1843 Hn
Dunlap, Amanda to Thomas Dillingham 8-5-1870 Dy
Dunlap, Amantha to William A. McFarland 2-8-1838 Hn
Dunlap, Ann J. to Wm. Elison 1-27-1868 (1-30-1868) T
Dunlap, Ann to Robert Calhoun 4-29-1867 (no return) Hn
Dunlap, Bethenia Ann to T. C. Harcourt 1-15-1862 Hn
Dunlap, Caroline to Aaron Jennings 1-17-1885 (1-18-1885) L
Dunlap, Caroline to Ezekiel Jones 7-11-1882 L
Dunlap, Eliza A. to Asa M. Gainer 12-22-1842 Hn
Dunlap, Elizabeth to H. G. Roland 8-27-1869 G
Dunlap, Elizabeth to Phillip Tucker 3-1-1867 Hn
Dunlap, F. B. to A. M. Robbins 1-2-1873 Hy
Dunlap, Harriet A. to A. B. Blair 9-28-1850 (10-10-1850) G
Dunlap, I. A. to S. M. Robinson 3-27-1859 O
Dunlap, Junie to William Bragg 8-13-1840 Hn
Dunlap, Louisa J. to Joseph W. Bandy 2-29-1860 We
Dunlap, Louisa to Benjamin Dunlap 4-5-1840 Hn
Dunlap, Margaret C. to Jacob Latimer 5-15-1845 Hn
Dunlap, Margaret R. to Thomas James 7-11-1843 (7-13-1843) G
Dunlap, Margaret to Preston Dunlap 3-12-1845 Hn
Dunlap, Martha to Henry Battle 7-14-1842 Hn
Dunlap, Mary A. to E. W. Ing 12-19-1865 G
Dunlap, Mary A. to James M. Lunday 8-28-1856 Cr
Dunlap, Mary Ann to Erasmus B. Raines 12-19-1854 (12-20-1854) G
Dunlap, Mary Ann to Jacob Foust 11-15-1846 Hn
Dunlap, Mary L. to Thomas J. Powell 12-16-1864 Hn
Dunlap, Mary V. to William A. Wiles 3-6-1855 G
Dunlap, Minerva J. to J. T. Harris 4-1-1868 G
Dunlap, Nancy E. to Thomas J. Norton 8-10-1857 (no return) L
Dunlap, R. E. to B. F. Craig 1-31-1849 (2-1-1849) F
Dunlap, Rebecca to Josiah Riggs 1-23-1843 (1-24-1843) F
Dunlap, Rebecca to Thomas Griffin 11-10-1867 G
Dunlap, Sally to Charlie Myers 9-25-1867 Hn B
Dunlap, Sarah Ann to W. M. Burkley 9-3-1863 Hn
Dunlap, Sarah C. to William A. Allison 3-6-1845 G
Dunlap, Sarah to John H. Butram 8-20-1846 G
Dunlap, Sarah to Nelson Cotton 11-24-1879 (no return) L
Dunlap, Sue to Bob Read 9-25-1873 Hy
Dunlap, Susan A. to James C. Porter 6-18-1851 Hn
Dunn, A. B. to John Kennedy 12-4-1872 T
Dunn, Adeline to W. N. Russel 10-24-1864 Sh
Dunn, Amdan F. to E.? C. Joyner 8-9-1867 (no return) Hn
Dunn, Ann to David Lamb 7-21-1843 Hn
Dunn, Ann to Matthew Cummings 11-13-1858 Sh
Dunn, Anna to A. J. Lloyd 10-16-1884 L
Dunn, Camilla F. to A. B. C. Dubose 11-19-1833 Sh
Dunn, Caroline T. to William C. Brooks 2-6-1845 Hn
Dunn, D. A. to James W. Dunn 10-25-1851 (no return) Hn
Dunn, Elizabeth A. to Calvin C. Fowler 1-31-1850 Hn
Dunn, Elizabeth J. to John R. Patten 11-2-1857 T
Dunn, Elizabeth to James Boothe 1-4-1842 Hn
Dunn, Elizabeth to John Walsh 3-7-1852 Sh
Dunn, Elizabeth to W. R. Dean 2-19-1859 (2-26-1859) Hr
Dunn, Emily F. (Mrs.) to B. F. Ball 10-8-1860 Sh
Dunn, Florida to Robert Kee 8-7-1867 F B
Dunn, Frances to Isaac Leftwich 12-24-1870 T
Dunn, Harriet to Bird Marsh 12-28-1852 (no return) F
Dunn, Jacksey B. T. to J. B. Manley 11-14-1850 Hn
Dunn, Jane C. to Charles W. Ferguson 12-2-1869 Ma
Dunn, Julia Ann to Joseph M. Mooney 1-13-1850 Hn
Dunn, L. L. to Alex Brady 1-4-1845 Cr
Dunn, Lucy to Nelson Abington 2-26-1868 (2-29-1868) O B
Dunn, Luiza J. to Henry H. Jones 11-8-1849 Hn
Dunn, Margaret R. to G. M. Dunn 12-23-1855 Hn
Dunn, Margaret to Thomas Madden 1-6-1856 Sh
Dunn, Maria to Patrick McConnell 12-28-1864 Sh
Dunn, Martha A. to James H. Woods 12-21-1843 Cr
Dunn, Mary A. C. to G. W. Smith 4-18-1839 Sh
Dunn, Mary to George Holland 2-24-1874 T
Dunn, Mary to Patrick Conwary 10-13-1864 Sh
Dunn, Mary to William H. Hay 6-27-1838 (no return) Hn
Dunn, Mary to William Scaggs 10-15-1830 Hr
Dunn, Nancy to Anderson Blackwood 12-13-1857 Hn
Dunn, Perlina Jane to Martin A. Barbee 9-27-1857 Hn
Dunn, Rebecca to William Martin 12-27-1873 (12-28-1873) T
Dunn, Rety to J. M. B. Eliott 3-10-1864 Hn
Dunn, S. J. to Thomas A. Bass 4-12-1861 Hr
Dunn, Sarah A. to Hogekiah Bevill 3-27-1856 Hn
Dunn, Sarah B. to James Meriwether 2-8-1840 Sh
Dunn, Sarah to Louis Besor 7-10-1855 (7-13-1855) Sh
Dunn, Susan Ann to LaFayette Jones 3-16-1832 Sh

Dunn, Winifer to Matthew Riorden 5-24-1856 (5-25-1856) Sh
Dunnahoe, Louisa to John Watson 12-21-1846 (12-23-1846) L
Dunnavant, Laura J. to Wm. Johnson 12-16-1877 Hy
Dunnavant, Tennie to George Blakely 7-22-1877 Hy
Dunnaway, Mary A. to Richard Shelton 3-10-1854 Hn
Dunnaway, Sallie E. to Wm. R. (Dr.) Cole 11-12-1870 (11-17-1870) Ma
Dunnegan, Elizabeth to Drury Martin 11-4-1829 (11-?-1829) G
Dunnegan, Mollie to L.(D?) H. Powell 8-11-1869 G
Dunnegan, Nancy E. to Thomas T. Landrum 10-6-1864 G
Dunnegan, Septimus to Albert Treadwell 1-31-1874 (2-8-1874) Dy
Dunnegin, Elizabeth A. to Turner B. Joyner 9-24-1853 (9-25-1853) O
Dunnegin, Margaret to Carey H. Cloyd 3-30-1857 (4-2-1857) O
Dunnegin, Sarah Jane to LaFayette Reddit 1-5-1854 O
Dunnevant, M. T. to J. G. Wynne 2-6-1868 Dy
Dunning, Betsy to Jonathan T. Hampton 1-14-1847 Hn
Dunning, Martha to David Busby 5-25-1859 (5-28?-1859) We
Dunning, Martha to David R. Littleton 7-17-1860 We
Dunning, Martha to S. Newton 12-14-1848 (no return) Hn
Dunston, Rebecca to Henry Abbott 1-10-1871 (1-13-1871) Dy
Dunt, Delila to Samuel M. Thornton 7-15-1842 (7-21-1842) O
Dunvegard?, Ellen to Daniel Liggin 1-26-1867 (no return) Dy
Dunwoody, Harriet to Frank Crichlow 12-27-1869 (no return) Hy
Dunwoody, Isabella R. to John F. Sinclear 1-21-1841 G
Dunwoody, Mary to Seth Williams 2-15-1834 (2-20-1834) G
Dupew, Rebeca H. to Lemel J. W. Parker 11-21-1840 (11-25-1840) F
Dupree, A. T. to W. A. Dillard 8-10-1861 (no return) Hy
Dupree, Amy to Bob Estes 8-13-1867 (no return) Hy
Dupree, Caroline to William Mewborn 1-3-1871 (no return) F B
Dupree, Liddie to John Cleere 12-26-1867 (no return) F B
Dupree, Martha C. to B. L. Taliaferro 12-10-1861 Hy
Dupree, Massey L. to D. C. Taliaferro 7-25-1860 Hy
Duprey, Mary B. to John W. Moreland 10-10-1852 Sh
Dupriest, Francis to John Wright 1-3-1848 Ma
Dupuy, Mary Ellen to Thomas J. Truehart 12-2-1852 (12-22-1852) Sh
Dupuy, Sarah L. to V. C. Peers 10-23-1855 (no return) F
Durden, Caroline to John M. Browning 4-1-1858 Be
Durden, Celia to Stephen Boswell 4-16-1851 Be
Durden, Pocahontas to John A. Brown 3-12-1879 (3-16-1879) Dy
Durden, Sarah to Lucian Merritt 1-20-1867 Be
Durham, Amelia L. to Elias Carroll 1-29-1840 (1-30-1840) F
Durham, Ann C. to Charles Mulherron 12-12-1849 (12-13-1849) Hr
Durham, Bettie to C. T. Mulherren 1-24-1866 (no return) Hy
Durham, Cornelia B. to William A. Edwards 12-28-1868 (12-31-1868) F
Durham, Delany to James M. Hulen 10-27-1847 Sh
Durham, Elizabeth A. to William M. Helm 3-11-1872 (3-12-1872) L
Durham, Elizabeth M. to E. J. Hubbard 7-15-1844 (no return) F
Durham, Emma E. to Armsted W. Boydston 2-25-1874 L
Durham, Lucinda to Bryant Durham 12-18-1850 (12-19-1850) L
Durham, M. C. to A. J. Targart 12-18-1854 (no return) F
Durham, M. M. to J. A. Holmes 2-21-1878 L
Durham, Margaret G. to Richard Manley 9-6-1854 (no return) F
Durham, Martha J. to James H. Borum 6-29-1868 (6-30-1868) L
Durham, Martha to George Akin 2-8-1844 F
Durham, Mary E. to William M. Roberson 1-13-1874 L
Durham, Mary Jane to George W. Griffen 4-8-1862 Sh
Durham, Nancy to Ezekiel Bennett 9-7-1849 Sh
Durham, Nancy to Robert O. Shelton 7-29-1846 (7-30-1846) L
Durham, Nancy to William B. Russell 9-22-1840 (9-24-1840) F
Durham, Nannie J. to William C. Martin 1-15-1879 L
Durham, R. O. to James W. Smith 12-27-1843 (12-28-1843) F
Durham, Rebecca J. H. to O. H. P. Wood 5-7-1840 F
Durham, Sarah to A. J. Cullom 5-8-1850 (no return) F
Durham, Susan C. to William F. B. Price 1-14-1858 L
Durham, Susan F. to William Carrigan 11-14-1866 L
Durham, Tralucia L. to Joseph W. Pender 4-1-1847 F
Durham, Ula to F. P. Hart 12-5-1877 L
Durley, Eliza Ann to William Cannon 10-18-1848 G
Durley, Frances A. to William Benthill 1-12-1854 G
Durley, Huldy to Nathan Parker 7-18-1833 G
Durley, Jamima E. to Wilson D. Hunt 11-14-1838 (11-16-1838) G
Durley, Keziah A. to William H. Gant 3-22-1842 G
Durley, M. E. to J. M. Ing 11-26-1860 G
Durley, Mary P. to William Brown 4-3-1865 G
Durley, Nancy P. to James E. Talley 11-24-1858 G
Durnay, Mary F. to C. Underwood 6-27-1863 (6-28-1863) O
Durner, Nancy E. to Ralph Byram 2-6-1860 (2-9-1860) Hr
Durran, Hellen M. to Joseph H. Mulherin 5-30-1869 Hy
Durrett, Jane C. to John A. Jarrett 11-30-1842 (12-1-1842) Hr
Durrett, Martha to A. D. Neilson 3-19-1851 Hr
Dutlinger, Hellena to Lewis Wohrum 5-13-1856 Sh
Dutlinger, Theresa to F. Beurer 7-11-1859 (7-12-1859) Sh
Duttlingar, Agatha to John N. Hack 6-5-1854 Sh
Duttlinger, Louisa to Herm (Harmon) Backer 9-11-1863 (9-13-1863) Sh
Duttlinger, M. to Fr. Maender 10-3-1859 (10-4-1859) Sh
Duval, Sarah E. to Benjn. Humphries 7-15-1858 (7-18-1858) Sh
Duvall, Joella S. to Philip R. Webber 10-28-1861 (10-31-1861) Sh
Duvall, Nannie J. to William H. McAdoo 12-20-1858 (12-21-1858) Ma

Duvalt, Jane E. to Benj. Reno 8-24-1869 Hy
Duvaughn, Sarah to John Ferrell 5-21-1862 G
Duveast, Rhoda to Samuel Forbess 12-18-1854 (12-26-1854) T
Duvirage, Cordelia (Mrs.) to Richard Arnold 9-17-1864 Sh
Dwiggins, Caroline to Willis Rumley 8-29-1854 Cr
Dwyer, Ann to Thomas Morrassey 2-1-1862 (2-9-1862) Sh
Dwyer, Ellen to David Leonard 4-14-1860 (4-15-1860) Sh
Dwyer, Ellen to James Nolan 8-24-1863 Sh
Dwyer, Ellen to Thomas Eagan 5-27-1859 Sh
Dwyer, Helen to Thomas Doubleday 1-17-1856 Sh
Dwyer, Margaret to Daniel Connors 11-27-1861 Sh
Dwyer, Margaret to Philip Phigeon 1-26-1861 (1-27-1861) Sh
Dwyer, Mary to John Phelin 7-13-1857 Sh
Dyal, Lenory to John M. Alexander 11-23-1843 G
Dyal, Matilda to Noah Baker 10-21-1840 (no return) L
Dye, Elizabeth H. to Alfred R. Banner (Bonner) 10-9-1845 Sh
Dye, Mary to James W. Stewart 8-21-1845 Sh
Dyer, A. E. to S. Medaris 1-6-1855 (1-7-1855) O
Dyer, E. V. to R. T. DeAragan 6-21-1854 (no return) F
Dyer, Elizabeth to James A. Wilson 8-31-1865 O
Dyer, Eugene P. to R. Branch 5-11-1853 (no return) F
Dyer, Frances Ann to G. W. Holder 6-30-1851 O
Dyer, Frances S. to John B. Hubbard 3-7-1829 (3-8-1829) G
Dyer, Hester to John Hollowell 12-25-1869 (12-26-1869) O
Dyer, Holen E. to W. F. Johns 1859 O
Dyer, Louisa to William Niemeyer 12-3-1853 Sh
Dyer, M. E. to J. C. Lasater 7-28-1873 (7-31-1873) Dy
Dyer, M. J. to Henderson Hemp no date (with 12-1874) T
Dyer, N. E. to Edward M. Wilson 2-21-1866 O
Dyer, Rebecca J. to Henry B. Claridge 9-8-1853 Ma
Dyer, Sarah Eliza to James L. Totten 6-19-1833 (6-20-1833) G
Dyher, J. Cordelia to Oliver E. Durivage? 4-7-1853 (4-14-1853) Sh
Dyke, Jno. Cordelia L. to W. T. Byars 9-6-1847 Sh
Dyre, Sarah A. to Jefferson W. Stein 3-13-1843 F
Dyre, Susan to John Cox 3-1-1874 O
Dyre, Virginia to Wiley Griggs, jr. 6-26-1866 L
Dysen, Tabitha to Stephen E. Moris 4-25-1842 Sh
Dysen, Eliza to Gilbert Hill 10-5-1871 (10-6-1871) T
Dyson, Fannie to Watkin? Smith 11-9-1872 (11-15-1872) T
Dyson, Louisa to Sam Winn 3-26-1874 Hy
Dyson, M. E. to C. Bass 10-17-1854 G
Dyson, Mary E. to Thomas Ingram 8-16-1847 Ma
Dyson, Mary J. to William Spain 12-1-1854 (12-2-1854) Hr
Dyson, Milly to Lemuel Shelton 8-18-1866 T

Eadon, Elenor to Samel Sherrill 11-18-1840 F
Eady, Mendie to W. F. Lamar 11-12-1870 (11-15-1870) Dy
Eagan, Eliza to Wm. A. Nelson 8-11-1862 Sh
Eagan, Helen to H. L. Epps 11-1-1869 (11-2-1869) F
Eagan, Katharine to Michael Archard 1-15-1856 Sh
Eagan, Margaret to Michael Barrett 5-25-1860 (5-27-1860) Sh
Eagan, Mary to Michael Fitzgerald 11-5-1861 Sh
Eagan, Sarah Ann to Edward Holan 10-7-1856 Sh
Eagle, R. to John W. Fowler 1-6-1858 Sh
Eaker, Anna to Dew H. C. Wallace 3-30-1858 Hn
Ealey, Mary Jane to Augustine W. Wortham 2-20-1862 Sh
Eally, Nancy to Moses Cox 9-28-1841 Cr
Ealy, Harriet to George Matthews 4-8-1871 (4-3?-1871) F B
Ealy, Harriet to Russel Jones 8-7-1869 (8-9-1869) F B
Eanes, Jennie W. to Noland Fontaine 4-18-1864 (4-21-1864) Sh
Eanes, Mary E. to Samuel B. Williamson 5-1-1845 Sh
Earhart, Catherine to David Willis 11-24-1840 Cr
Earl (Carl?), Eliza to James Ford 6-24-1864 (6-23?-1864) Sh
Earl, Margaret to John H. McCully 12-6-1853 (no return) F
Earle, M. J. to A. C. Bowen 2-21-1871 (no return) Dy
Earle, Sallie L. to W. J. Allen 9-28-1864 (10-1-1864) O
Earle, Sallie to T. J. Harvey 12-30-1878 (12-31-1878) Dy
Earles, Ann to Levi Stout 6-15-1843 We
Earls, Elizabeth to S. P. Smithson 12-14-1854 (no return) We
Earls, Harriett F. to John L. Carter 1-28-1868 (1-30-1868) Cr
Earls, Mary J. to G. B. Mosely 5-20-1858 We
Earls, Rebecca to Adam Hopkirk 5-4-1847 We
Early, Martha to Alfred Shelton 2-27-1867 (3-5-1867) Dy
Earmon, Eliza to Drue Long 9-14-1875 L
Earneast, Elizabeth to David Harris 11-8-1828 Ma
Earnest, Emeline L. to B. S. Barnes 3-28-1867 G
Earnheart, J. J. to Geo. N. Stoops 7-2-1869 (7-4-1869) F
Earp, Alcy Jane to Rubin Mitchell 1-30-1867 Be
Earp, Cherry L. to John G. Prince 1-13-1850 Be
Earp, Ellen to C. C. Mitchel 4-4-1858 Be
Earp, Ellen to Simpson Smith 11-16-1856 Be
Earp, Fanny to John Smith 12-22-1844 Be
Earp, Harriet to R. Mitchell 1-4-1863 Be
Easeley, Mit to John Currie 6-23-1875 (no return) Hy
Easley, Amanda J. to W. H. (Rev.) Daniel 1-20-1876 (no return) Hy
Easley, Annice? to Terry Johnson 3-24-1873 Hy
Easley, Bettie to Hiram Johnson 6-22-1871 (no return) Hy

Easley, Eliza to Bynum Adkison 5-31-1858 (6-1-1858) T
Easley, Elizabeth J. to William W. Smith 7-29-1860 Hn
Easley, Elizabeth to Samuel P. Kendall 3-11-1855 Hn
Easley, Lucinda to Jo Battle 7-18-1878 Dy
Easley, Mary C. to John A. Moore 10-4-1842 T
Easley, Mary to James Adkison 11-20-1869 (11-23-1869) T
Easley, Mary to Michael Burk 10-30-1859 Hn
Easley, Nina to George Tucker 4-9-1876 Hy
Easley, Parthenia to Poke Alexander 3-2-1867 Hy
Easley, Rachel to Stephen Walker 7-11-1874 Hy
Easley, Sarah J. to William M. French 1-1-1874 T
Easley, Sarah to Andrew Lamar 8-1-1867 (8-2-1867) T
Easley, Susan A. M. S. to Joshua N. Brunson? 9-14-1840 (9-15-1840) T
Easly, Bety to Rogers Read 3-11-1875 Hy
Easly, Molly to Ewell Parker 7-21-1873 Hy
Easly, S. A. to A. L. Forbess 1-8-1872 T
Easly, Sarah J. to W. W. Daughtry 11-12-1855 (11-15-1855) Sh
Eason, Amanda to James P. Park 2-8-1851 Cr
Eason, Arabella to J. E. Weathers 10-16-1855 Cr
Eason, Bethany to Marcus J. Pennington 9-4-1842 (9-20-1842) F
Eason, C. J. to L. F. Butler 6-8-1867 Cr
Eason, Della to Axlanda Luter 1-24-1855 Cr
Eason, Elizabeth to A. J. Foster 7-29-1865 (8-1-1865) Dy
Eason, L. M. H. to R. R. Ruff 5-16-1851 Cr
Eason, Louisa to James G. Mays 12-16-1861 (12-18-1861) Dy
Eason, Louisa to W. E. Mebane 1-29-1867 (1-30-1867) Cr
Eason, Margaret to Richard Tatum 11-4-1845 (no return) F
Eason, Martha A. to John Ruff 8-3-1853 Cr
Eason, Mary (Mrs.) to William Griffin 12-12-1837 Sh
Eason, Mary E. to Thomas H. Benton 7-1-1847 O
Eason, Mary E. to Thos. C. Cooper 12-28-1866 Hy
Eason, Mary J. to Jesse Benson 10-17-1846 (no return) F
Eason, Mary L. A. to Redding White 5-23-1841 Ma
Eason, W. F. to William H. Ruff 11-24-1851 Cr
East, Marry A. to Sterling Bounds 8-29-1843 (9-5-1843) F
East, Mary A. to Thomas Twigg 1-30-1855 We
East, Nancy to H. H. Wesson 8-12-1841 Be CC
Easter, Sutton to Henry Plummer 5-22-1871 Hy
Easterwood, Amanda M. to Uriah M. Vincent 1-6-1858 (1-7-1858) O
Easterwood, Eliza A. to James Burris 7-27-1850 (7-29-1850) G
Easterwood, Elizabeth to James Ringgold 10-11-1842 (10-14-1842) G
Easterwood, J. to J. M. Huggard 10-22-1870 G
Easterwood, M. I. to J. W. Darnall 3-2-1863 (3-3-1863) O
Easterwood, Mary Elizabeth to James W. Webb 8-27-1867 G
Easterwood, Mary to Thomas Beard 10-27-1846 G
Easterwood, Nancy E. to Samuel Miller 4-17-1854 (4-20-1854) G
Eastham, A. A. (Mrs.) to L. M. Moore 5-5-1864 (5-9-1864) Sh
Eastham, Amelia A. W. to A. P. Graves 12-4-1852 (no return) F
Eastham, M. E. M. to D. W. Anderson 3-7-1853 (no return) F
Eastland, Annie E. to B. Patrick 8-23-1864 Sh
Eastland, Nancy J. to John Hunter 1-2-1860 Sh
Eastman, Ruby R. to George Carnahan 6-23-1854 Sh
Eastman, Sarah Ann to Stephen Lacy 9-16-1847 Sh
Eastridge, Agness to William Bassham 1-20-1855 (1-22-1855) O
Eastridge, Elizabeth to Grief G. Stone 6-14-1836 (6-16-1836) O
Eastwood, Lucy to George Using 10-16-1839 Ma
Eastwood, Martha to Pinkney Kerr 10-29-1869 (11-7-1869) L
Eathan, Ann L. to Franklin Crawford 3-2-1840 (3-5-1840) F
Eathridge, Martha A. E. to Lorenzo D. Mathis 3-15-1853 G
Eaton, Ailsy to John F. Curtis 4-28-1855 (5-1-1855) Hr
Eaton, Alsy to Jacob Harty 9-26-1845 (10-1-1845) Hr
Eaton, Catherin to Ezekal Butler 4-3-1872 (4-4-1872) T
Eaton, Elizabeth to Lawrence B. Dodson 10-9-1849 Cr
Eaton, Lidia to Joseph Smith 10-14-1852 (1-10-1854) Hr
Eaton, Lizzie M. to Peter C. Winne 12-23-1869 Ma
Eaton, Nancy to John M. Curtis 6-23-1855 (6-25-1855) Hr
Eatus, Dovist? Ann to Andrew Jackson Pugh 1-22-1852 Hr
Eaver, Elizabeth to William Y. Rook 12-23-1834 Hr
Eaves, Ellen to Andrue Roberts 12-17-1846 We
Eaves, Elmira P. to L. E. Stover 3-6-1852 (3-7-1852) O
Eaves, Margaret Ann to D. S. Rowlett 6-19-1852 Hn
Eaves, Martha Jane to George W. Murphey 4-22-1866 Hn
Eaves, Mary J. to B. R. Janes 1-3-1860 (1-4-1860) O
Eaves, Mary M. to Moses H. Keinman 9-1-1855 (9-2-1855) O
Eaves, Sarah E. to Hugh H. Crockett 1-30-1861 (1-31-1861) O
Eberts, Margaret to Phillip Sauer 5-28-1861 Sh
Echard, Margaret to Francis Cornell 6-22-1853 Sh
Echols, Altonetta to John Henderson 3-17-1866 (3-22-1866) Dy
Echols, M. J. (Mrs.) to John McAfee 5-20-1874 Dy
Echols, Margaret to Robt. Purcell 9-20-1879 Dy B
Echols, Martha A. to W. F. Stubblefield 11-1-1853 Sh
Echols, Mary J. to J. Lanier 7-24-1867 Dy
Echols, Mary to Thomas A. Bledsoe 8-31-1876 (9-1-1877?) Dy
Echols, Sallie to John W. Kellow 11-22-1877 Dy
Echols, Sarah P. to Noah Leggit 7-11-1862 (7-13-1862) Dy
Echols, Sarah W. to John R. Kent 11-26-1829 Sh
Echols, Susan C. to Thos. Moore 10-24-1863 Sh

Eckford, Mary Ann to Thomas C. Gayle 3-5-1857 Sh
Eckford, Nancy to Jas. P. Thompson 11-10-1865 (11-12-1865) T
Eckles, Alvira H. to W. J. W. Wilson 9-25-1856 (9-27-1856) G
Eckles, G. to Daniel M. Finch 9-3-1862 (9-16-1862) O
Eckley, Evelly to W. J. Watts 1-21-1873 (1-22-1873) O
Eckley, Theodocia to David W. Finch 9-3-1862 O
Ecklin, Emma A. to Rosco Feild 1-5-1861 Sh
Ecklin, Sallie to John P Thuran 9-15-1856 (9-16-1856) Sh
Eckolds, Jane to Wm. M. Fellow 10-12-1841 Sh
Eckols, Elizabeth to Levi W. Lowrance 10-28-1841 Sh
Edcock, Josephine to Wm. H. Wyatt 11-19-1868 Be
Eddie, Kate to James Browning 4-27-1872 (4-29-1872) T
Eddings, Elizabeth to John R. McCarroll 6-12-1830 Ma
Eddings, Henrietta E. to John W. Rodgers 3-15-1854 Sh
Eddings, Ida Frances to John H. Crenshaw 11-6-1866 (11-7-1866) F
Eddings, Louisa to Bird Hill 6-12-1830 (6-15-1830) Ma
Eddins, Angirary? to John C. Davy 4-18-1843 F
Eddins, Ann R. to Leonidas J. Hill 2-27-1856 Ma
Eddins, Ann T. to Marshall P. Yancy 11-20-1843 (11-23-1843) F
Eddins, Elizabeth W. to Thomas Harwell 1-17-1848 (1-20-1848) F
Eddins, Frances H. to Clayton A. Yancy 12-12-1843 F
Eddins, Margarett L. to Anthony T. Williams 3-27-1850 Ma
Eddins, Martha Jane to George W. McGuire 11-11-1856 Ma
Eddins, Martha to Simon T. Turner 5-24-1831 Sh
Eddins, Mary E. to Charles L. Burkes 3-4-1856 Sh
Eddins, Mary to W. H. Garvin 7-27-1863 (8-11-1863) F
Eddins, Rebecca M. to Burwell S. Hasbey 1-13-1840 (1-14-1840) F
Eden, Ellen to Abraham Sneedon 10-30-1850 Hn
Ederington, Sarah to Joseph Fuller (Fulton) 1-3-1832 Sh
Edgar, Henrietta to William Williams 4-17-1860 Hn
Edgar, Nancy S. to William S. Shaw 4-23-1840 Hn
Edgar, Nancy to S. W. Puckett 11-12-1865 Hn
Edgarton, Frances to John Woodfin 4-23-1841 Hr
Edge, Nancy J. to N. E. Delaney 3-4-1863 Be
Edings, Levenia C. to John A. Cole 4-6-1865 G
Edington, Polly Ann to J. D. Claton 8-17-1865 Be
Edition, Laura? to Alexander Zender 8-26-1881 (8-27-1881) L
Editt, Sarah E. (Miss) to Chas. H. Sanger 4-20-1864 Sh
Edleman, Nancy R. to T. T. W. Turner 8-15-1869 G
Edmerson, N. C. to J. W. Mann 3-23-1872 (3-24-1872) Cr
Edmindston, Sarah Ann to E. B. Webber 10-2-1855 (10-14-1855) Sh
Edmison, Margaret to Joseph Mitchell 2-8-1869 (no return) Cr
Edmond, Elizabeth to Arthur E. Hill 3-28-1834 O
Edmonds, Eleanor E. to Lewis Davis 2-16-1832 O
Edmonds, Isabella W. to Thomas J. Parr 5-3-1858 (5-4-1858) O
Edmonds, Issabella to John Morgan 8-8-1839 O
Edmonds, Margaret to Jesse Meacham 6-15-1830 (6-16-1830) O
Edmonds, Marget C. to Thomas A. Davidson 7-22-1829 O
Edmonds, Martha M. to William W. Allison 4-18-1837 (5-18-1837) O
Edmonds, Mary to Chas. Morrison 2-29-1864 Sh
Edmonds, Nancy Belle to John A. Buchanan 3-11-1856 O
Edmondson, Alley to James H. Gibson 2-17-1844 (2-18-1844) G
Edmondson, E. S. to F. L. Allen 12-15-1855 (12-25-1855) Sh
Edmondson, E. to W. R. Johnston 1-2-1866 G
Edmondson, Eliza K. to Charles H. Blacknall 11-23-1852 (11-25-1852) Ma
Edmondson, Elizabeth A. to William W. Brown 11-24-1840 O
Edmondson, Lucretia J. to Benjamin Thompson 1-17-1857 (1-20-1857) Sh
Edmondson, M. E. to E. T. Ward 9-29-1868 G
Edmondson, Mary (Mrs.) to Thomas Underwood 9-26-1849 Sh
Edmondson, Nancy to Dennis Thompson 10-10-1853 (10-13-1853) G
Edmondson, Sarline to Allen Gibson 12-22-1864 G
Edmondson?, Wilmouth O. to Thomas D. Tarver 8-22-1854 (no return) F
Edmonson, Charlotte to Rufus W. Dickinson 1-20-1845 Ma
Edmonson, Lavender D. to Will O. Furgason 10-12-1838 (10-14-1838) Hr
Edmonson, Mary to Billy Means 11-3-1858 Sh
Edmonson, Naoma R. to Daniel S. Rapelje 11-22-1859 O
Edmonson, W. A. to W. B. Edmonson 9-21-1854 Sh
Edmonston, Elvira to Thomas M. Meriwether 7-16-1845 Ma
Edmund, Frances to Moses Dyer 2-7-1850 Hn
Edmunds, Catherine to G. A. Taylor 12-5-1864 (no return) Hn
Edmunds, Mary Ann to John W. Buchanan 4-11-1861 Hn
Edmundson, Allee M. to James O. Phillips 12-20-1841 (12-21-1841) G
Edmundson, Alley M. to David W. Jarvis 7-2-1844 (7-4-1844) G
Edmundson, Elizabeth to James A. Thomas 10-28-1852 G
Edmundson, Ellen M. to John P. Reager 2-12-1853 (2-17-1853) G
Edmundson, Martha M. to J. W. Brickhouse 6-6-1861 G
Edmundson, Martha to William D. Cress 1-6-1846 Hn
Edmundson, Nancy to Robert Edmundson 1-11-1839 (1-14-1839) G
Edmundson, Sarah to William Gibson 10-20-1838 (10-21-1838) G
Edmundston, Sarrah to John Crews 8-14-1838 G
Edmunston, Adeline to William Anderson 12-27-1843 (no return) F
Edney, Amanda M. to James M. Cox 10-28-1856 (10-31-1856) Sh
Edney, Nancy to S. H. Bibb 2-9-1867 (2-10-1867) L
Edny, Mary Ann Benton to Frederick Barfield 2-6-1841 (2-9-1841) L
Edward, Elizabeth to Burrel Symes 10-6-1869 G
Edward, Elizabeth to C. I. Huntsman 2-10-1844 Ma
Edward, Frances A. to John H. McKinney 12-8-1842 Cr

Edward, Jane to David Carlile 8-8-1848 Sh
Edward, Margaret E. to James J. Giles 12-2-1850 G
Edward, Nancy to Joseph Morris 1-25-1854 (1-26-1854) G
Edward, Nancy to Thomas Stockard 10-10-1850 G
Edward, Sarah to Henry T. Baker 12-11-1867 G
Edwards (Edmonds?), Bettie to William Dumas 1-22-1866 G
Edwards, A. B. to Samuel D. Munn? 1-29-1852 Hn
Edwards, Alice to Reuben Selvidge 1-20-1870 G B
Edwards, Allavana to Richard Wortham 6-21-1848 Sh
Edwards, Allsey M. to John C. Green 11-23-1856 Cr
Edwards, Alsey to Henry S. Paris 10-14-1858 G
Edwards, Amanda to James Winters 1-2-1877 Hy
Edwards, Amanda to Wash Topp 12-28-1870 (12-29-1870) Dy
Edwards, Amanda to Wm. Brown 12-19-1867 Dy
Edwards, Amey to Bob Wilson 11-14-1874 T
Edwards, Angeline to Wm. D. Warren 12-13-1852 Sh
Edwards, Ann E. to Morgan M. Bateman 5-11-1854 Sh
Edwards, Ann to James May 1-12-1863 (no return) Cr
Edwards, Ann to Matthew Glidewell 4-6-1857 (4-8-1857) Ma
Edwards, Anna to Joseph Landrum 1-5-1861 (5-21-1861) O
Edwards, Anna to Peter Gause 12-22-1870 Hy
Edwards, Carissa R. to William Fifer 4-7-1848 G
Edwards, Caroline to Timothy Glidwell 5-27-1867 G
Edwards, Caroline to Wyatt Oates 11-24-1858 (11-25-1858) Ma
Edwards, Celly to John Roper 4-6-1847 Cr
Edwards, Chloe Ann to Jonas C. Rudisill 11-21-1838 Sh
Edwards, Dora to Edwin Degernett 2-18-1878 (2-21-1878) Dy
Edwards, Eliza F. (Mrs.) to Isaac Burrell 12-23-1872 (no return) Dy
Edwards, Elizabeth A. to Alfred T. Tune 9-17-1849 (9-19-1849) O
Edwards, Elizabeth to E. A. Walker 8-18-1857 (8-20-1857) T
Edwards, Elizabeth to Enoch W. Levy 10-11-1842 (10-13-1842) Ma
Edwards, Elizabeth to James Edwards 11-5-1849 (11-8-1849) Hr
Edwards, Elizabeth to James H. Brinkley 4-28-1859 Cr
Edwards, Elizabeth to Rhesa? R. Sullivant 1-4-1842 (1-11-1842) F
Edwards, Elmira J. to Thomas M. Palmer 1-23-1861 Hn
Edwards, Elvy Jane to James T. Ward 8-16-1854 (8-18-1854) Ma
Edwards, Emily to Beverly Scott 10-13-1880 L
Edwards, Eveline to James McIntire 7-20-1877 (7-22-1877) L
Edwards, F. Elizabeth to B. M. McAdoo 12-23-1855 Cr
Edwards, F. M. to W. J. Hemson 11-27-1865 (11-28-1865) F
Edwards, Fanny to Shadrick Davis 5-27-1866 F
Edwards, Gemima Jane to John Yarbrough 12-29-1851 (12-30-1851) Hr
Edwards, Harriet D. to John B. Stanley 9-28-1847 Hn
Edwards, Isabella to Saml. M. Turrentine 8-28-1858 (9-2-1858) Sh
Edwards, Isabella to Wm. l. Moore 8-27-1858 Cr
Edwards, J. E. to Nathaniel Mills 12-30-1873 Dy
Edwards, Jacka Ann to Charles B. English 11-22-1858 (11-24-1858) Sh
Edwards, Jane to Henry Mason 3-12-1877 Dy
Edwards, Jane to McKinney Bennett 2-22-1847 O
Edwards, Jane to RLobert B. Dukes 6-30-1847 (7-1-1847) Hr
Edwards, Jane to Reubin Mitchel 3-15-1849 Be
Edwards, Jane to Thomas Woodson 10-31-1846 (11-1-1846) G
Edwards, Jemima C. to John M. McCorkle 2-3-1858 (no return) Hn
Edwards, Juatt? to Benji. Chambers 9-22-1847 (9-16?-1847) F
Edwards, Judah to James Lacy 4-26-1848 F
Edwards, Judy Belle to Reuben Hague 12-23-1875 (no return) Hy
Edwards, Julia Ann Eliza to W. P. Williams 11-22-1860 (11-25-1860) Ma
Edwards, Julia to Richard McGehee 12-30-1866 Hn B
Edwards, Julie to N. J. Wren 11-18-1867 (11-20-1867) Cr
Edwards, Keziah C. to Henry Todd 4-6-1864 G
Edwards, Kitta A. R. to Thomas B. Swift 9-6-1853 Hn
Edwards, L. E. to J. H. Taylor 9-21-1871 Cr
Edwards, Laura Ann to Thomas Parsons 8-16-1850 (8-20-1850) T
Edwards, Lavina H. to De Demoss 11-28-1866 (11-29-1866) Cr
Edwards, Lizzie to Henry C. Gill 10-12-1863 Sh
Edwards, Louisa to Christopher Hutchings 3-16-1829 Ma
Edwards, Lucinda M. to Cannon L. Brooks 9-11-1849 Sh
Edwards, Lucretia J. to Enoch Galloway 2-2-1855 (no return) F
Edwards, Lucy A. to Joseph O. Pulliam 11-26-1855 (11-27-1855) Sh
Edwards, M. E. to W. B. Briant 2-14-1870 (2-15-1870) Cr
Edwards, Margaret to Green B. Chambers 5-26-1837 G
Edwards, Mariah L. to James A. Fitz (Fith?) 9-4-1843 (9-6-1843) Ma
Edwards, Martha A. to William Mainor 10-8-1847 G
Edwards, Martha Ann to John a. McKiney 1-16-1867 L
Edwards, Martha J. to H. J. Boren 12-26-1865 (12-28-1865) Cr
Edwards, Martha Jane to William H. Martin 4-18-1844 Hn
Edwards, Martha M. to John B. Sutherland 10-5-1868 L
Edwards, Martha to Allen Northing 8-3-1842 Cr
Edwards, Martha to Wm. Percell 5-31-1840 Cr
Edwards, Mary Ann to John Betts 8-7-1853 Hn
Edwards, Mary B. W. to Richd. G. Scott 11-2-1867 (11-5-1867) F
Edwards, Mary C. to H. C. McCutchen 5-30-1846 (no return) We
Edwards, Mary C. to T. C. Spain 12-30-1840 T
Edwards, Mary E. to Joseph Marley 9-20-1853 (9-22-1853) Ma
Edwards, Mary Love to James Henry Caraway 12-28-1844 (1-2-1845) T
Edwards, Mary W. to Hosea Bonner 12-7-1853 Cr
Edwards, Mary to H. W. Arnold 11-28-1884 (12-3-1884) L
Edwards, Mary to Jacob Beamer 12-20-1880 (12-30-1881?) L
Edwards, Mary to John House 9-7-1848 (no return) Cr
Edwards, Mary to Robert Robertson 11-26-1865 Hy
Edwards, Mary to Vincent A. Bennett 9-7-1833 (9-8-1833) O
Edwards, Mary to W. F. Spraggins 5-5-1877 Dy
Edwards, Mary to William H. Fitts 1-8-1852 (no return) F
Edwards, Mary to William Perry 2-19-1870 Ma
Edwards, Matilda A. to W. H. Barnes 11-12-1866 G
Edwards, Matty to Obadiah Roberts 1-12-1826 O
Edwards, Mima to Alfred Winbery 11-3-1869 G
Edwards, Mollie to J. W. Thompson 2-23-1876 Dy
Edwards, Mollie to Manuel Barbee 12-5-1869 Hy
Edwards, Nancy B. to Franklin Alexander 3-21-1844 Cr
Edwards, Nancy C. to Rufus D. Mathis 11-8-1856 (11-17-1856) G
Edwards, Nancy J. to William H. Cobb 3-27-1851 (4-13-1851) O
Edwards, Nancy J. to William H. Cobb 3-27-1851 (4-14-1851) O
Edwards, Nancy Jane to Aaron Joplin 10-20-1870 L
Edwards, Nancy L. to James T. Watson 1-27-1869 (1-28-1869) Ma
Edwards, Nancy V. to John M. Harte 4-3-1856 (no return) We
Edwards, Nancy to Cader Bunn 12-9-1845 Cr
Edwards, Nancy to G. W. Bennett 9-17-1846 G
Edwards, Nancy to Taylor Boshiers 7-1-1865 (7-2-1865) O
Edwards, Nancy to Thomas Akins 11-25-1843 (11-26-1843) G
Edwards, Nannie to Frank Prince 12-15-1872 Cr B
Edwards, Nannie to Henry Clay Boyd 6-28-1867 (6-29-1867) Dy
Edwards, P. E. to Jane E. Lane 3-12-1872 Dy
Edwards, Penelope C. to David H. Boyd 4-14-1840 Cr
Edwards, Polly to James Hodge 4-26-1838 Cr
Edwards, Polly to Matthew Bishop Forrest 8-8-1850 Cr
Edwards, Rachel C. to H. M. Phillips 9-24-1870 (no return) Dy
Edwards, Rebecca A. to Clem C. McDearmon 4-12-1863 Hn
Edwards, Rebecca J. to James H. Slaughter 3-31-1841 Hn
Edwards, Rebecca to James M. Wortham 9-28-1853 (10-?-1853) Sh
Edwards, Rebecca to James Stobaugh 5-24-1838 Ma
Edwards, Retha L. W. to James A. _____ 4-4-1849 Hn
Edwards, Rosa A. to G. R. Lynch 12-4-1874 (12-6-1874) O
Edwards, Rosa A. to William H. Martin 1-10-1848 (1-11-1848) F
Edwards, Rosaella to Anderson Bass 12-28-1876 Hy
Edwards, S. A. to J. H. Johnston 12-1-1866 (12-5-1866) F
Edwards, S. G. to F. M. Aker 4-10-1866 O
Edwards, S. J. (Mrs.) to Samuel J. Morrow 2-6-1868 Ma
Edwards, Sallie to Esquire Cothran 2-20-1873 (2-21-1873) T
Edwards, Sarah ANn to Joseph Graves 11-7-1844 (11-14-1844) F
Edwards, Sarah Angeline to Edward? James Cherry 6-15-1857 (6-17-1857) O
Edwards, Sarah E. to Henry W. White 12-2-1861 Dy
Edwards, Sarah F. to Obidiah Gravitt 12-22-1845 Ma
Edwards, Sarah Frances to Alexander D. Whitley 2-26-1856 (2-28-1856) O
Edwards, Sarah H. to W. H. Taler 12-6-1859 (12-22-1859) O
Edwards, Sarah Jane to James N. White 9-7-1868 Ma
Edwards, Sarah P. to N. A. Manley 12-10-1861 Hn
Edwards, Sarah R. to Richard B. Price 10-9-1855 O
Edwards, Sarah S. to John H. Edwards 12-25-1861 We
Edwards, Sarah to H. C. Tevilla 11-28-1868 (11-30-1868) Dy
Edwards, Sarah to James Gurat 2-2-1839 Hn
Edwards, Sarah to Jim Fielder 5-14-1880 (5-16-1880) Dy
Edwards, Sarah to William Trice 12-19-1868 Ma
Edwards, Sarah to Wm. H. Rynolds 1-9-1855 Cr
Edwards, Sophronia to William Thedford 10-4-1849 (1-8-1849?) Ma
Edwards, Susan E. to Holoway Kee 1-27-1867 Be
Edwards, Windsor J. to Ephram W. Williams 7-29-1850 Cr
Eeson, Rachael to Jeptha O. Sorrell 3-28-1865 Dy
Egan, Margaret to W. Welsh 8-13-1864 (8-14-1864) Sh
Egglestin, Sukey to Solomon James 12-27-1867 (12-30-1867) L B
Eggleston, Adalade E. to L. L. Brodie 7-8-1863 (7-9-1863) L
Eggleston, Candace to William Freeman 10-27-1880 L B
Eggleston, Charlotte to Benjamin Bates 5-21-1870 (no return) L
Eggleston, Eliza to Benjamin Cobb 3-10-1882 (3-12-1882) L
Eggleston, Eugenia C. to John W. Saunders 6-16-1858 L
Eggleston, Fannie to John Jones 4-7-1874 L
Eggleston, Fannie to William Dickson 12-14-1876 L
Eggleston, Fosey to Ben Wright 12-26-1868 (1-1-1865) L B
Eggleston, Frances to John Pierson 10-1-1880 (10-2-1880) L B
Egnew, Margaret to A. D. Harrel 8-5-1856 We
Ehrman, Hanna to Julius Nathan 5-21-1864 (5-24-1864) Sh
Eison, Elizabeth C. to Wm. P. Pillow 5-12-1869 (5-14-1869) L
Eison, Emma to Louis Wright 2-20-1879 L
Eison, Jans to Monroe Jones 6-10-1874 (6-11-1874) L B
Eison, Martha to Dave Jordan 1-22-1878 (1-24-1878) L
Eison, Sarah A. to Ben F. Pillow 5-12-1869 (5-14-1869) L
Eison, Susan to Henry Moore 3-30-1880 (4-1-1880) L
Eison, Susannah R. to William P. Soward 6-28-1856 (7-2-1856) L
Eison, Winnie to Henry Jones 3-18-1868 (3-22-1868) L B
Eital, Tempy to T. C. Osborne 8-16-1849 Ln
Elam, Ann to Jefferson McCain 8-9-1867 (8-10-1867) T
Elam, Ann to L. Wright 3-17-1866 (3-18-1866) T
Elam, Emily F. to A. A. Senter 8-17-1859 (8-18-1859) G
Elam, Fannie to J. W. Thomas 3-11-1863 G

Elam, Frances M. to Robert G. Ezzell 6-28-1855 We
Elam, Jennie M. to Harvey L. Raines 10-23-1867 G
Elam, Kitsy to John McGee 9-27-1872 (10-16-1872) T
Elam, L. J. to J. S. Mayes 4-1-1867 (4-2-1867) T
Elam, Lucinda A. to James Claybrook 12-12-1854 (12-15-1854) G
Elam, Margaret J. to Moses E. Senter 2-10-1840 G
Elam, Margaret to JSames A. Knight 11-13-1866 T
Elam, Martha to J. W. Oliver 3-27-1866 G
Elam, Mary to Jacob Dyson 5-21-1866 (5-22-1866) T
Elam, Mollie S. to R. F. Blair 12-12-1866 G
Elam, Rebecca to Orville Williams 9-23-1856 G
Elam, S. A. to W. R. Slate 11-13-1866 (11-14-1866) T
Elam, Sallie to John Moore 12-27-1872 Hy
Elam, Sarah J. to Benj. F. Powers 7-28-1856 Sh
Elam, Susan E. to Hamlin S. Manly 12-20-1843 (no return) We
Elander, Jane to John J. Landen 2-24-1852 We
Elb, Rosale to Samuel Kirsch (Hirsch?) 10-11-1856 Sh
Elcan, Hettie to Ike Taylor 3-10-1873 T
Elcan, Martha S. to Marcus J. Wright 11-2-1854 Sh
Elcan, Mollie to Henry Johnson 1-1-1872 Hy
Elcan, Peggie to Edward Solea 6-23-1871 Hy
Elcan, Seigniora P. to George West 10-21-1845 Sh
Elcon, Elizabeth to G. Couper Gibbs 4-9-1847 Sh
Elder, Amanda C. to John L. H. Tomlin 5-19-1846 G
Elder, Anna Bell to John H. Freeman 9-20-1866 G
Elder, Annie to Sparrel Hill 10-20-1864 G
Elder, Bassie to Guilliame Berson? 4-8-1869 G
Elder, Bassie to Guilliame Buson? 4-8-1869 G
Elder, Carolinie to Tobe Vaughan 8-7-1867 G
Elder, Eliza Jane to Ben Mitchel 3-31-1873 (4-3-1873) T
Elder, Emma to W. G. Patterson 8-22-1863 G
Elder, Fanny to Georgge Blackwell 1-3-1829 (1-8-1829) G
Elder, Frances to John S. Bivins 9-24-1867 (9-25-1867) L
Elder, I.(J?S?) E. to James A. Underwood 3-2-1885 (3-4-1885) L
Elder, Jane to Junor Burchett 9-9-1837 (9-21-1837) O
Elder, Jennie C. to J. P. McGee 2-22-1866 G
Elder, Jennie to Allen Barnes 6-30-1883 L
Elder, Justina to Joseph Barber 7-17-1847 O
Elder, Lorania C. to Wm. Franklin Elder 8-18-1851 (8-19-1851) T
Elder, Lucella to W. O. Kelley 10-1-1867 G
Elder, Lucenda to John Jackson 11-21-1831 G
Elder, Malissa to W. L. Sanders 7-14-1854 (no return) F
Elder, Margaret F. to Jeremiah Stephens 5-1-1854 (5-4-1854) O
Elder, Marietta C. to S. H. Dunscomb 11-15-1854 Sh
Elder, Martha J. to John W. Conway no date (with Dec 1847) F
Elder, Mary (Mrs.) to James B. Williams 10-9-1862 (10-12-1862) O
Elder, Mary J. to Jabize S. Anderson 12-4-1847 (12-7-1847) F
Elder, Mary to Benj. F. Burruss 6-3-1851 (no return) F
Elder, Mary to Newton Dickson 2-28-1850 T
Elder, Missouri to Mosel? Bellar 3-1-1869 (3-3-1869) T
Elder, Nancy to Asa Clements 10-4-1841 (10-6-1841) F
Elder, Ritter to Ephraim Currey 3-15-1870 G B
Elder, S. E. to Asa Oliver Hickman 7-4-1850 O
Elder, Sally to Jesse Grady 6-13-1828 G
Elder, Sarah C. to W. C. Ozier 1-2-1863 F
Elder, Sarah F. B. to C. A. Goins 3-17-1843 (no return) F
Elder, Sarah L. to Joel Nunn 4-13-1864 G
Elder, Sarah ann to John A. Walthall 6-13-1848 (6-18-1848) F
Elder, Sila (Lila) to Stephen Vaulx 8-16-1867 Hy
Elder, Tennessee to James T. Bridges 7-19-1865 (7-22-1865) O
Elder?, Elizabeth to Levy Evans 9-23-1867 L
Eldridge, Emma to J. H. Dawson 10-11-1853 Sh
Eldridge, Martha E. to A. L. Yancy 5-10-1849 Sh
Elender, Martha P. to Joel A. Tucker 3-17-1861 We
Elenor, F. M. to A. H. Miller 9-25-1872 (9-26-1872) Cr
Elerson, Jane to Murph Brantly 11-3-1868 (no return) Hy
Eleston, Martha Ann to Francis M. Rutledge 1-19-___ (12-23-1856) O
Eley, Jane to Morgan Jones 7-13-1867 (7-14-1867) F B
Elidge, Nancy Jane to J. R. Maxey 1-3-1863 Sh
Elinder, Sylvester to James R. Wilkerson 12-21-1848 Hn
Eliott, Elizabeth P. to Green B. Goodwin 7-7-1849 (7-8-1849) G
Elison, Sally to Joseph Taylor 10-14-1828 Hn
Eliz, Williams to George Powell 12-31-1867 Hy
Eliza, Bradford to Daniel Pope 5-16-1867 Hy
Eliza, Morton to Henry Fouse (Foust) 8-21-1875 (no return) Hy
Elizabeth, Ozment to J. H. Poling 7-31-1861 (no return) Hy
Elizabeth, Robertson to R. M. Pitner 11-24-1870 Hy
Elizabeth, Todd to Perry Possie 2-7-1878 Hy
Elizabeth?, Sarah to James Y. Kirk 11-9-1868 Ma
Elkin, Mary to William Jones 9-7-1868 (9-10-1868) T
Elkin, Sallie to Profeit Taylor 3-3-1869 T
Elkins, Alsey to Elias Smith 11-16-1846 (5-23-1847) Hr
Elkins, Exy(Elizabeth) S. to Samuel B. Harris 1-14-1834 (1-14-1834) Hr
Elkins, Mahala to Isaac Rogers 3-18-1834 Hr
Elkins, Martha A. to T. Baily 10-31-1865 O
Elkins, Mary Ann to David Evans 12-24-1861 (12-26-1861) Hr
Elkins, Mary E. to C. A. Rogers 1-22-1873 (1-23-1873) Cr

Elkins, Mary J. to Thomas I. Douglass 4-7-1851 (4-8-1851) O
Elkins, Mary to Allen Wethington 6-21-1853 (6-23-1853) T
Elkins, Matilda Jane to Elisha T. Boyd 12-17-1868 Be
Elkins, Sarah to Carner Barber 6-24-1839 (6-27-1839) O
Elkins, Winney to George R. Langston 5-21-1841 (5-26-1841) Hr
Ella, Polk to Shed Ragland 2-12-1874 Hy
Ellen, Susan to John C. Porter 12-6-1837 G
Ellender, Jane to Jno. W. Hurt 1-19-1850 We
Elles, M. C. F. P. to Thornton Rhodes 5-22-1861 Mn
Elleson, Nancy J. to Curtis Smith 12-12-1854 We
Elliff, Nancy 'A. to A. O. Elliff 12-17-1861 Mn
Ellige, M. M. to W. A. Johnson 11-14-1865 (11-15-1865) O
Elliner, M. J. to J. G. Rust 7-27-1863 (7-27-1866?) Cr
Elling, Julia to G. H. Rice 2-13-1878 (2-14-1878) L
Ellington, C. V. to M. W. Nelson 4-18-1854 (no return) F
Ellington, Cheney (Mrs.) to Ned McGavoc 1-28-1868 G B
Ellington, E. A. to James H. Perry 12-4-1871 (12-6-1871) Dy
Ellington, Eliza Jane to Thomas T. Thompson 5-13-1861 (5-17-1861) Ma
Ellington, Elvira C. to Madison D. Smith 1-26-1841 (2-2-1841) Hr
Ellington, Frances to Berry H. Williams 12-22-1868 (12-23-1868) Ma
Ellington, Jane Thomas to E. Elington 5-8-1848 (5-9-1848) F
Ellington, M. J. to Bethnell Garner 10-18-1864 Dy
Ellington, Martha H. to Henry M. Sheffield 2-25-1851 (2-26-1851) F
Ellington, Martha M. to Abraham Glisson 1-18-1858 G
Ellington, Mary Ann to Edward Davis 12-21-1838 (12-25-1838) Ma
Ellington, Mary D. to Willis Haughton 10-23-1867 (10-24-1867) Ma
Ellington, Nancy O. to V. C. Wright 1-20-1858 (1-21-1858) G
Ellington, Puss to Geo. Saffoon 12-15-1868 (12-17-1868) F
Ellington, S. L. to W. B. O'Daniel 10-20-1866 G
Ellington, Sarah A. T. to Wm. J. Harrison 10-4-1849 F
Ellington, Sarah Elizabeth to Wm. R. Pettigrew 9-18-1867 (9-20-1867) Ma
Ellington, Sophie to Milton Cook 7-28-1838 (7-29-1838) Ma
Ellington, Sophronia to Newton Williams 12-15-1850 (12-17-1850) Ma
Ellington, Terza Jane to Wm. J. Carroll 1-10-1852 G
Ellinor, Julian to John Guffie 4-2-1838 Hn
Ellinor, Martha J. to C. T. Rust 8-1-1867 (8-2-1867) Cr
Ellinor, Nancy to John Clendenin 2-17-1839 Hn
Ellinor, Sarah to Joseph Swor 9-9-1841 Hn
Elliot, Cynthia Ann to William R. Webb 12-22-1866 (12-26-1866) Ma
Elliot, Harriet to Griffin Ellis 1-5-1866 (1-27-1866) T
Elliot, Jane to William Harvey 11-28-1883 (12-1-1883) L
Elliot, N. H. to S. W. Olive 3-3-1859 We
Elliot, Sarah A. to J. L. Collier 1-8-1859 (1-9-1859) Sh
Elliott, Agnes A. to Joseph Johnson 1-31-1870 (2-4-1870) F
Elliott, Catharine P. to Thomas H. Parker 4-2-1846 G
Elliott, Catherine to John G. Baker 3-28-1850 Sh
Elliott, Elizabeth to James S. Alexander 12-20-1843 (12-21-1843) G
Elliott, Elizabeth to Wm. A. Williams 1-29-1845 (no return) We
Elliott, Mary A. to E. F. (Capt.) Rutts 5-9-1844 We
Elliott, Mary J. to W. A. Flemming 5-31-1859 (6-8-1859) F
Elliott, Mary N. to Augustus A. Simmons 11-25-1846 (11-26-1846) F
Elliott, Mary to James T. Linson 1-21-1857 (1-22-1857) L
Elliott, Paralee M. to Jasper Holliday 6-16-1852 Ma
Elliott, Sarah A. to Jno. Barcco 9-5-1850 Sh
Elliott, Sarah ann to Francis M. Pettey 8-26-1848 (no return) F
Ellis, Almedia C. to Nat. A. Mills 11-6-1866 (11-7-1866) Dy
Ellis, Amanda to Isaiah Crutchfield 3-11-1845 (no return) Hn
Ellis, Amandy to W. L. Glidewell 12-7-1869 (12-8-1869) Dy
Ellis, Ann to Alexander Still 12-26-1873 (12-29-1873) T
Ellis, Anna to John A. Elder 9-28-1880 (9-29-1880) L
Ellis, Burdie to J. R. Sumners 10-19-1880 (10-20-1880) L
Ellis, C. A. to W. C. Johnson 3-7-1872 (3-12-1872) L
Ellis, Catharine E. to William Maynard 4-15-1870 (4-17-1870) Cr
Ellis, Charlotta to W. N. Jones 12-15-1870 Dy
Ellis, Cherrie C. to Samuel C. Clark 8-15-1870 G
Ellis, Edy to Washington Dunome 3-21-1839 Hn
Ellis, Elizabeth to C. G. Barnett 1-15-1861 (1-24-1861) O
Ellis, Emily to Vinson Malone ?-?-1850 Cr
Ellis, Emmia L. to John F. Fortner 8-14-1876 L
Ellis, Etherline to J. D. McCorkle 1-6-1879 (1-8-1879) Dy
Ellis, Fanny E. to G. W. Chambers 7-23-1864 Sh
Ellis, Fanny to J. M. Chinesman 10-17-1866 Hn
Ellis, Frances to Henry Davis 1-2-1867 (no return) Hy
Ellis, Hanna to Alex Simonton 10-7-1873 (10-9-1873) T
Ellis, Hannah to M. T. Foy 10-22-1865 Mn
Ellis, Jane to James M. Moore 2-26-1856 (3-2-1856) O
Ellis, Josephine to G. W. Darnell 2-12-1859 Cr
Ellis, Jullia to John Holland 4-1-1859 Hr
Ellis, L. C. to Michael Cochran 4-19-1862 O
Ellis, L. C. to Michael Cochran 8-19-1862 (8-20-1862) O
Ellis, Laura to A. E. Cox 9-22-1884 (9-23-1884) L
Ellis, Laura to Marion F. Savage 4-13-1885 (4-15-1885) L
Ellis, Leacy to Booker Peak 11-21-1844 Hn
Ellis, Lucrecia? to W. G. Newman 2-16-1876 L
Ellis, Lucy D. to J. D. Crop 9-5-1859 (9-6-1859) Sh
Ellis, M. C. C. to J. R. Warren 9-13-1867 O
Ellis, M. L. to J. T. Ellis 2-2-1874 (2-3-1874) Dy

Ellis, M. P. to Wm. Harvy 8-17-1864 O
Ellis, Maggie A. to Noah S. Speers 12-25-1865 Hy
Ellis, Manerva to Redick Bass 4-27-1845 Sh
Ellis, Margaret to A. W. Fitch 4-17-1845 (no return) Hn
Ellis, Margaret to Henry Kirk 8-21-1867 (8-22-1867) Dy
Ellis, Margaret to Jacob Byler 11-25-1851 L
Ellis, Margaret to Thomas Stubblefield 10-28-1862 Hn
Ellis, Martha to William Bomar 6-25-1849 Hn
Ellis, Mary Ann to R. S. Crow 11-28-1870 (11-29-1870) Dy
Ellis, Mary E. to William R. Ford 11-1-1843 Hn
Ellis, Mary Jane to Samuel Goodman 1-31-1850 Sh
Ellis, Mary L. to Frank W. Ellis 8-5-1880 L
Ellis, Mary to John O. Keane 10-25-1860 (10-28-1860) Cr
Ellis, Mary to R. W. Freeman 9-2-1876 (8?-3-1876) O
Ellis, Mattie to R. L. Wilson 12-9-1869 (12-14-1870?) G
Ellis, Meriah E. to Isaac E. Williams 12-27-1844 Cr
Ellis, Milberry to James Sexton 8-5-1839 (no return) Hn
Ellis, N. E. to J. M. Pettigrew 7-27-1862 Mn
Ellis, N. M. to James W. Finch 10-31-1849 Hn
Ellis, Nancy H. to Z. T. Crockett 9-19-1867 Be
Ellis, Nancy to Duncan D. Taylor 10-14-1868 (10-15-1868) Dy
Ellis, Nancy to J. V. Ruth 6-5-1880 (6-6-1880) L
Ellis, Nancy to William Flora 1-26-1858 Sh
Ellis, Nancy to William Henry Robertson 9-16-1871 (9-17-1871) L
Ellis, P. to Hugh Marr 6-29-1848 Hn
Ellis, Priscilla to John F. Morris 4-22-1862 Be
Ellis, Rhoda to J. W. Kerby 2-13-1872 (2-14-1871?) L
Ellis, S. M. to J. E. Meacham 9-5-1884 (9-7-1884) L
Ellis, Salina to Nathan Kelly 9-16-1862 O
Ellis, Sarah A. to A. F. Ray 1-6-1863 (1-8-1863) Dy
Ellis, Sarah Anne to John H. Fenton 3-19-1845 Sh
Ellis, Sarah P. to J. W. Bowles 9-18-1844 Hn
Ellis, Sarah to William Peterson 2-12-1862 (2-13-1862) L
Ellis, Sibbey to John H. Parrot 8-15-1850 (8-18-1850) T
Ellis, Spicy to P. R. McDaniel 2-27-1849 Hn
Ellis, Sue E. to F. P. Griffin 12-1-1878 Hy
Ellis, Susan A. to Thomas Lambert 5-12-1863 (5-17-1863) Dy
Ellis, Tabitha G. to Zack Biggs 7-9-1861 G
Ellis, Tibitha to Isaac Bland 11-12-1834 Sh
Ellis, Victoria to R. A. Mobley 11-26-1868 (no return) L
Ellis, Virginia L. to A. J. Deloach 5-18-1880 (5-20-1880) L
Ellison, Elizabeth M. to William P. Hill 12-10-1840 Hn
Ellison, Emily to B. Malone 9-16-1847 (no return) F
Ellison, Fannie to Woodson Knight 5-16-1870 T
Ellison, Frances to Lorenza D. Strongham 7-23-1832 (7-24-1832) Hr
Ellison, Geraldine to John G. Collins 2-5-1857 Hn
Ellison, Isabella to George E. Hays 7-9-1849 Sh
Ellison, Louisa J. to John L. Webb 2-19-1850 (2-23-1850) F
Ellison, Manda C. to Isaac P. Henley 12-8-1842 F
Ellison, Margaret A. to Robert H. Carr 10-27-1845 (10-28-1845) G
Ellison, Mary to James W. Davis 2-11-1864 Hn
Ellison, Matilda to A. T. Fleming 2-12-1852 Sh
Ellison, Nancy to Perry Lyons 7-31-1865 (3-2-1865) O
Ellison, Susan A. to J. A. Watson 10-27-1874 (10-28-1874) T
Ellison, Susan to Chas. J. Plank 4-16-1861 Sh
Ellisono, Pamela to Wm. C. Smith 8-12-1847 F
Elizer, Fanny L. to John T. Shipley 6-2-1870 (7-25-1870) F B
*Elll*is, Lurann to G. J. Lucas 7-27-1861 (7-28-1861) L
Ellmor, M. J. to John Y. Rust 7-27-1862 (no return) Cr
Elmore, Ann to P. Green Upchurch 10-16-1873 G
Elmore, Eliz. Lucretia to Saml. Crawford Sanford? 11-22-1855 T
Elmore, Elizabeth F. to James H. Little 2-11-1861 (2-13-1861) L
Elmore, Emma to Newton J. Carlton 8-12-1868 G
Elmore, M. C. to J. J. Weaver 11-7-1867 (11-8-1867) T
Elmore, Margaret E. to William D. Meadows 3-14-1885 (3-15-1885) L
Elmore, Mary Ann to Wm. R. Rodgers 12-10-1846 Be
Elmore, Mary to Martin Dodson 4-19-1879 (4-20-1879) L
Elmore, Nancy J. to Wm. A. Bryant 10-22-1851 (10-23-1851) Hr
Elmore, Rebecca to Robert Brown 4-5-1847 F
Elmore, Sarah E. to Robert F. Shoemake 10-15-1884 L
Elmore, Sarah to Harvey Brown 7-29-1847 F
Elnor, Margarett E. to John W. Ray 1-16-1859 (no return) We
Elrod, Isabel to William Davis 12-31-1865 Hy
Elrod, Mary Eliza to John T. Oates 5-7-1856 (5-8-1856) Ma
Elrod, Sarah R. to Benjamin Barr 1-4-1843 Ma
Elrod, Slomy L. to G. M. Harvy 11-4-1867 (no return) Hy
Elsberry, Isabella to Theopolous McDade 4-6-1851 Cr
Elsten, Hicksey G. to William Canada 7-23-1866 G
Elston, Frances S. to Charles Cannough Duncan 5-3-1856 (5-4-1856) O
Elston, Martha Ann to Francis M. Rutledge 12-19-1850 (12-23-1850) O
Elston, Nancy P. to Burwell Wilks 3-2-1829 Ma
Elum, Mary O. to John W. Williams 12-21-1850 (12-24-1850) G
Elum, Mildred A. to David P. Jenkins 1-9-1844 (1-11-1844) G
Elum, Nancy to Alvin Senter 1-27-1851 (2-7-1851) G
Elvill, Ann to Thos. I. Tuggle 11-6-1841 (11-12-1841) Ma
Elvington, P. W. to B. F. Curlin 7-11-1868 (no return) Hy
Ely, Lou to Green Jones 12-30-1868 F B

Emaline, Davis to Alfred Phillips 2-14-1876 (no return) Hy
Emanuel, Anna to David Kaufman 7-20-1850 Sh
Emanuel, Fannie to A. S. Levy 12-21-1853 Sh
Emarson, Sarah to B. F. Watkins 2-18-1860 G
Emberson, Adeline E. to Pleasant D. Walker 11-30-1841 Hn
Embry, Jane to Lewis Parr 8-14-1880 (no return) L
Embry, Margaret to Henry Anderson 4-27-1867 (5-2-1867) L B
Emerson, Caroline to Alexander Daniel 12-29-1855 (no return) F
Emerson, Eddie to Charles R. Gess 12-7-1874 (12-8-1874) L
Emerson, Ema E. to T. L. Voss 5-11-1876 L
Emerson, Mary Ann to Archibald Boyd 9-22-1858 (9-23-1858) Ma
Emerson, Mary E. to J. H. Cate 10-15-1865 Hn
Emerson, Mary E. to Joel A. Thomas 1-27-1869 (1-28-1869) Ma
Emerson, Mary Jane to Ralph Williams 12-15-1868 (12-17-1868) Ma
Emerson, Nancy Ann to Francis M. Leggett 8-7-1867 (8-11-1867) Ma
Emerson, Permelia Ann to Richard K. Hathaway 8-23-1870 (9-11-1870) L
Emerson, Rebecca to Daniel Hershaw 3-4-1850 (3-7-1850) Ma
Emerson, Sarah A. to James H. Underwood 12-17-1860 (no return) Hn
Emerson, Sarah Jane to Dempsey Bird 7-15-1848 (7-20-1848) Ma
Emery, Drew to John Brewer 5-18-1883 (5-21-1883) L
Emery, Katharine to Thomas B. Davidson 9-14-1848 G
Emery, Lucinda P. to John Younger 9-28-1859 Hn
Emery, N. L. to J. W. Hogg 1-9-1866 Hn
Emery, Sarah A. to John W. Hogg 12-29-1852 Hn
Emery, Susan to Peter Snider 10-21-1847 Hn
Emison, Mary to W. Bush 10-18-1855 Hn
Emma F., Hathaway to Amos J. Powell 7-27-1870 (no return) Hy
Emma, Ware to Adolphus Pybus 10-26-1876 Hy
Emmerson, Sarah E. to William K. Stone 11-25-1844 Ma
Emmerson, Sarena to James Hester 11-23-1853 Hn
Emmerson, Vicey to Henry Parham 1-27-1883 (2-16-1883) L
Emmerson, Vickey to Conway Conner 12-17-1885 (12-18-1885) L
England, Laurie Ann to Wm. T. Cole 4-19-1857 Be
England, M. L. to David H. Sanders 6-28-1859 (6-30-1859) F
England, Malinda to Charles P. Cuff 3-30-1854 Be
England, Martha E. to John R. Reynolds 5-26-1852 G
England, Mary J. to Q. T. Holloway 10-12-1852 (no return) F
England, Sarah to Henry Arnold 12-19-1853 Be
England, Sarah to John Cole 9-18-1849 Be
Engle, Sophia to Arnold Neliuse 3-13-1856 Sh
English, A. J. to Francis Butler 1-9-1866 G
English, Ann E. to R. W. Ricks 12-16-1854 (12-21-1854) Sh
English, Delila F. to Solomon Reed 11-10-1841 G
English, Johanna to Edward Leonard 12-5-1859 Sh
English, Lucinda C. to Daniel L. Williams 2-29-1848 (2-30?-1848) G
English, Margaret to C. L. Barnes 1-8-1873 (1-9-1873) T
English, Margaret to David Owen 3-9-1866 T
English, Margaret to James McCormack 3-20-1865 T
English, Mariah to Allen Louisen 9-7-1866 (9-9-1866) T
English, Martha E. to Eugene W. Mallory 10-2-1851 Sh
English, Martha J. to Thos. Alston 3-3-1874 (3-26-1874) T
English, Mary A. E. to Richard F. Butler 12-14-1859 G
English, Mary to Seaborn Vines 8-29-1860 (not executed) Sh
English, Nancy A. to J. H. Harville 10-16-1867 (10-17-1867) O
English, Nancy Jane to Winfield S. Hicks 3-1-1854 (3-28-1854) G
English, Nancy K. to Joseph E. Buchannan 5-13-1859 (5-14-1859) Sh
English, Perny to Samuel C. Pearson 7-4-1841 Hn
English, S. C. to M. B. Holt 3-16-1867 G
English, Sarah E. to W. S. Willis 9-12-1852 Hn
English, Sarah to Charles C. Gordon 4-30-1831 Sh
Enhel, Madelia to Frederick Woerne 9-10-1857 Sh
Enix?, Nancy to William Jackson 5-12-1858 Hn
Enloe, Agness (Mrs.) to Jas. T. Collier (Hollier) 1-7-1860 (1-9-1860) Sh
Enloe, Mollie E. to William W. Deshong 6-8-1869 (6-10-1869) Cr
Enlow, Mary E. to Abner Nobles 4-14-1858 (no return) L
Ennis, Dovey to W. R. Etchison 10-3-1853 (10-6-1853) G
Ennis, Margarette C. to Samuel J. Webb 12-20-1860 G
Ennis, Martha Jane to Thomas Mathis 12-21-1865 G
Ennis, Martha to Joseph Jordan 1-21-1880 (1-23-1880) L
Ennis, S. A. to Samuel Doughtry 2-27-1855 (2-28-1855) G
Enoch, Eliza H. to George W. S. Graves 7-31-1867 (8-1-1867) Dy
Enoch, Jamy to James Rose 1-10-1870 (1-11-1870) Dy
Enoch, M. A. K. to John S. Taylor 12-23-1865 (12-27-1865) Dy
Enoch, M. C. to J. W. Laconier 9-14-1874 O
Enoch, Nancy Ann to Henry Pierce 9-15-1869 (no return) Dy
Enochs, Amanda M. to John W. Cravin 2-25-1849 Cr
Enochs, Carolina to Benj. Williams 7-5-1840 Cr
Enochs, F. E. to William Taylor 10-8-1872 (10-9-1872) Dy
Enochs, Lizzie to John Townsend 12-29-1873 (12-30-1873) Dy
Enochs, Lou to Pate Thomas 1-3-1878 Dy
Enochs, M. T. to Ben C. Wadlington 9-24-1877 (9-27-1877) Dy
Enochs, Malinda to George Phillips 8-23-1879 (no return) Dy
Enochs, Malinda to Thomas Willis 2-23-1872 (2-24-1872) Dy
Enochs, Martha F. to R. J. Hill 10-7-1872 (10-9-1872) Cr
Enochs, Martha to James M. Young 3-23-1844 Cr
Enochs, Mary A. to Wm. H. Traywick 10-2-1844 Cr
Enochs, Nancy J. to Robert J. Read 12-24-1846 Cr

Enochs, Sarah T. to Sam A. McKnight 10-27-1873 (10-28-1873) Dy
Enochs, Sarah to Perry Carter 5-23-1871 (5-25-1871) Dy
Enocks, Celia to John L. Cozart 12-23-1869 (12-26-1869) Cr
Epperson, Cassandra to William Hodges 8-7-1847 Sh
Epperson, Elenore to B. Alexr. Person 5-9-1866 Ma
Epperson, Elizabeth to James Hodges 8-7-1843 Sh
Epperson, Jane to James M. Stewart 8-30-1849 Sh
Epperson, Jane to Nelson Smith 7-6-1870 G B
Epperson, Mary A. to James H. Yarbro 1-20-1870 T
Epperson, Mary Ann to James Donald Stewart 6-1-1848 Sh
Epperson, Mary Ann to William H. Edwards 3-22-1854 (3-3?-1854) Ma
Epperson, Mary E. to Duke Klyce 6-8-1844 (6-12-1844) G
Epperson, Susan to John F. Newsom 5-4-1853 Ma
Eppes, Bettie W. to James R. Upshaw 5-5-1856 (5-6-1856) Sh
Eppes, Orleana T. to William H. Hunt 4-23-1860 (4-24-1860) Ma
Epprs, Margaret to Reuben Hinton 4-4-1861 (no return) Hy
Epps, Elizabeth S. to Patrick H. Cliburn 1-11-1833 (1-13-1833) Hr
Epps, Elizabeth to Jack Bivens 3-15-1871 (4-10-1871) T
Epps, Elizabeth to John T. Wilson 1-24-1844 Sh
Epps, Eugenia to B. F. Walker 2-13-1864 Hy
Epps, L. B. to James Ings? 12-12-1874 T
Epps, Mary to S. T. Elrod 6-9-1860 (no return) Hy
Epps, Nancy Ann to Archy Stallion 12-13-1869 (12-26-1869) F B
Epps, Sarah Jane to J. B. Sanders 6-30-1841 Sh
Epps, Susan E. to Isaac J. Suggs 4-7-1851 (4-9-1851) Sh
Erck, Lizzie to Robt. Banks 10-12-1864 (10-13-1864) Sh
Ermand, Mary Jane to James Givens 12-19-1881 (12-28-1881) L
Ernest, Emeline to George Bond 1-25-1863 G
Erocker, T. E. to J. R. Scott 12-14-1865 (12-21-1865) Cr
Ervin, Angie C. to John Darr 7-25-1839 Ma
Ervin, Margarett to I. H. Putman 10-16-1866 (10-17-1866) O
Ervin, Martha to A. B. Mayfield 8-20-1836 G
Ervin, Olivia to Benjamin Bell 4-24-1857 Hr
Ervine, Jane to Samuel H. Roper 7-11-1857 O
Erwin, A. E. to F. M. Robertson 1-10-1852 (no return) F
Erwin, Anna to John Wiley 11-16-1867 (11-20-1867) T
Erwin, Elizabeth C. to Joseph M. W. Alderson 1-1-1841 Hn
Erwin, Elizabeth to Martin Young 7-27-1841 (7-29-1841) Hr
Erwin, Harriet W. to Samuel Johnson 6-12-1839 F
Erwin, M. A. to J. S. Stafford 8-27-1872 (8-28-1872) O
Erwin, M. J. to F. B. Robinson 3-24-1858 (3-25-1858) Sh
Erwin, Martha to J. S. Baker 5-31-1866 O
Erwin, Mary Ann to L. H. McCollum 1-8-1863 Mn
Erwin, Mary E. to T. C. Burks 2-11-1863 Mn
Erwin, Mary J. to Thos. P. Bowder 7-1-1874 T
Erwin, Nancy to James McClemen 7-19-1852 (8-2-1852) O
Erwin, Nancy to Reuben Linn 5-13-1838 Hn
Erwin, Sally to Abraham McLemore 5-4-1823 (5-8-1827) G
Erwin, Sarah to Eli Scott 11-23-1835 L
Erwin, Susan Jane to Ralph Hawkins 9-14-1861 (9-16-1861) Hr
Erwood, Rachel Ann to Pleasant M. Long 9-20-1873 (9-21-1873) T
Eskeridge, Afphie to B. M. Jones 11-3-1866 G
Eskew, Cordelia to Daniel Bodkin 11-21-1876 (11-22-1876) Dy
Eskew, Elizabeth L. J. to Wm. S. Hampton 11-21-1852 Cr
Eskew, Elizabeth to John Eskew 11-10-1844 Cr
Eskew, M. E. to H. H. Tosh 11-30-1871 (12-15-1871) Cr
Eskew, Polly to William Eskew 4-7-1873 (8-8-1873) O
Eskew, Rebecca to Jerimiah Walton 5-3-1840 Cr
Eskew, S. J. to J. W. Adams 12-12-1872 (no return) Cr
Eskridge, Elizabeth E. to Thos. Brunderidge 9-20-1857 We
Eskridge, Louisa J. to Noah H. Posten? 3-2-1854 (no return) F
Eskridge, Lucy A. to Elam Dunn 12-24-1859 We
Eskridge, Mary E. to Ruben M. Ross 12-15-1855 We
Eskridge, Nancy B. to Lemuel C. Stow 12-2-1859 We
Eskridge, Nancy B. to Lewis B. Ragsdale 11-15-1846 We
Eskridge, P. D. A. L. to David Cohn 1-17-1853 (no return) F
Eskus (Estus?), Fann to Daniel Rice 4-5-1872 (4-10-1872) L B
Eson, Susan M. to William Marberry 3-16-1842 O
Espary, Josephine L. to Joseph Jennings 2-12-1879 L
Espey, M. E. to Wm. B. Chambers 12-23-1843 (no return) L
Espy, Mariah to William D. Turner 12-31-1828 (1-1-1829) Ma
Espy, Nancy to William R. Helen 3-20-1862 G
Espy, Narcissa C. to James W. Chambers 12-31-1839 (1-2-1840) L
Essary, Bettie J. to Jesse A. Brown 9-23-1868 Dy
Essex, Mildred M. to Lewis Herring, sr. 2-1-1851 Sh
Essig, Mary to George Wiegand 11-15-1864 Sh
Estas, Nany E. to David Dair 7-7-1845 (7-17-1845) G
Estes, Annie L. to P. H. Mann 12-6-1859 (no return) Hy
Estes, Annie to Ed Winston 12-29-1870 Hy
Estes, Caroline to Sam Marr 10-23-1869 Hy
Estes, Eliza Ann to John Holmes 1-17-1880 (1-18-1880) L
Estes, Elizabeth to L. W. Patterson 8-22-1861 Mn
Estes, Fanny to Alex Johnson 2-13-1879 L
Estes, Francis to David M. W. Hatcher 11-20-1862 We
Estes, Julia to Columbus Burns 1-17-1880 (1-18-1880) L B
Estes, Kiziah L. to W. T. Morris 1-17-1863 Mn
Estes, Louisa to Columbus C. Sharp 12-22-1857 Ma

Estes, Louisa to Henry Watson 5-28-1876 Hy
Estes, Lucy Q. to C. S. O. Rice 8-29-1865 (no return) Hy
Estes, Margaret to S. Lafayette Allen 7-9-1862 Ma
Estes, Martha to James A. Wilkins 9-1-1845 (9-4-1845) Ma
Estes, Mary Elizah to James D. Rooks 11-24-1870 Ma
Estes, Mary Jane to Benjamin Bond 11-25-1865 (no return) Hy
Estes, Matilda to Lewis Williams 9-23-1866 Hy
Estes, Minnerva A. to Wilie Jones 9-21-1849 (9-23-1849) Hr
Estes, Nancy L. to Wm. P. Howell 7-5-1858 (7-8-1858) Hr
Estes, Nancy to Henry Searcy 2-2-1881 L B
Estes, Nancy to James W. Paton 2-10-1867 Hy
Estes, Nancy to Jordan Kilzer 3-23-1863 G
Estes, Penelope to James W. Tomlin 12-14-1861 (12-15-1861) Ma
Estes, Pocahuntus to N. T. Perkins 1-29-1868 Hy
Estes, Rachel to A. S. Anderson 10-14-1879 Dy
Estes, Rachel to Jno. H. McGee 11-11-1868 Ma
Estes, Rebecca (Mrs.) to Peter Claybrooks 6-7-1841 (6-10-1841) G
Estes, Roxannah to Peter McCollum 1-28-1854 Ma
Estes, Sarah J. to T. M. Henry 5-17-1863 Mn
Estes, Sophronia to Joseph Pope 5-17-1859 (5-18-1859) Ma
Estes, Virginia to James R. Anderson 10-8-1870 (10-13-1870) Ma
Estill, Cynthia to Hiram Hardin 10-29-1838 We
Estill, Elizabeth to Jno. McKee 10-18-1837 Sh
Estis, Bettie to Robt. Claiborne 12-15-1869 Hy
Estis, Cordelia to Albert Nelson 6-6-1872 Hy
Estis, Emmer to J. P. Brooks 10-12-1878 Hy
Estis, Fannie to Anderson Burks 4-19-1885 (4-22-1885) L
Estis, Fannie to Dick Graves 1-26-1870 (no return) Hy
Estis, Hester to Amos Pennix 3-6-1872 (no return) Hy
Estis, Juda to George Taylor 6-30-1883 (7-1-1883) L
Estis, Martha B. to Jackson Compton 9-7-1867 (9-12-1867) L B
Estis, Martha to Grandonfield Lambert 9-14-1839 (9-15-1839) Ma
Estis, Mary E. to Lewis Graves 1-18-1872 (no return) Hy
Estis, Mira to Nelson Moore 3-16-1872 (no return) Hy
Estis, Rosa A. to R. S. Estis 7-21-1868 G
Estis, Sarah to Irvin Gaus (Gans) 1-27-1869 Hy
Estis, Vira to Esaw Outerbridge 4-28-1870 Hy
Eston, Ellen to Jessee T. Maddox 9-4-1852 (9-9-1852) Sh
Estridge, Sarah R. to Archibald R. Harris 2-12-1848 Ma
Estus, Agnus to Joseph Allison 6-24-1870 (no return) L
Estus, Ann to M. H. Estus 6-5-1872 L B
Estus, Sarah to Columbus Utley 12-23-1873 L
Etchison, Ester C. to Thos. A. Tucker 12-19-1853 (12-22-1853) G
Etherage, Ellenander to James Doxey 1-11-1838 (1-21-1838) G
Etherage, M. C. to W. N. Bomar 1-21-1856 (no return) Hn
Etherage, Rutha A. to Beverly G. Allbritten 4-13-1845 Hn
Etheredge, Rachael to Coburn Stone 10-5-1833 (10-6-1833) G
Etheredge, Sarah to Pleasant Fisher 11-15-1833 (11-16-1833) G
Etheridge, Ann F. to J. G. Parker 9-29-1858 We
Etheridge, Ann Tennessee to John Roan 8-30-1868 G
Etheridge, Caroline to J. G. Mosley 4-14-1879 (4-17-1879) L
Etheridge, Eliza to John Kirksey 10-12-1846 (no return) We
Etheridge, Lizzie to Theodore Merriman 6-4-1865 (no return) Hn
Etheridge, M. D. to J. C. Wilson 10-8-1874 Hy
Etheridge, Mary C. to John Turner 8-14-1854 We
Etheridge, Mary E. to C. P. Bondurant 12-18-1845 We
Etheridge, Nancy T. to Washington Williva 8-12-1862 Dy
Etheridge, Nancy to Martin Holliday 8-17-1838 Hn
Etheridge, R. A. to James W. Swor 11-5-1855 (no return) Hn
Etheridge, Sallie to Colin M. Farmer 4-14-1856 Sh
Etheridge, Sally A. to Robert Bluck 11-1-1854 Sh
Etheridge, Tempy to Andrew Jackson 11-7-1861 Mn
Ethridge, Elizabeth to James Thomas 11-30-1865 G
Ethridge, Louella to M. A. Melton 9-9-1866 Hn
Ethridge, Mary E. to James W. Robison 3-9-1840 Hn
Ethridge, Mary to D. A. McDaniel 7-3-1854 G
Ethridge, Matilda to J. Columbus Newport 12-4-1859 Hn
Ethridge, Queen E. to J. W. Jackson 8-21-1862 Hn
Ethridge, Rhoda to James T. Hall 4-18-1849 (4-19-1849) G
Ethridge, Sarah E. to Thomas E. Bradshaw 5-22-1859 Hn
Ethridge, Sarah J. to J. B. Venable 1-19-1854 Hn
Ethridge, Smiley J. to William Lowther? 12-17-1850 Hn
Eubanks, F. to Calvin King 2-12-1864 (2-14-1864) Cr
Eubanks, Mary A. to J. W. Campbell 6-21?-1855 (no return) F
Eubanks, Mary to Thomas Warburton 6-25-1848 Sh
Eudaley, Martha to Micajah W. Warmath 8-23-1850 (8-27-1850) G
Eudaly, Fannie to E. R. Johnson 12-22-1875 Dy
Eudaly, Harrit to Clement Eudaly 4-1-1844 (4-2-1844) G
Eudaly, Malessa to William F. Williams 7-22-1856 (7-29-1856) G
Eudaly, Mary to Frank Colbert 12-12-1874 Dy
Eudaly, S. J. to J. D. Carter 1-1-1873 Dy
Evalinie, Nanny to James Barchy 7-30-1830 (8-15-1830) Ma
Evan, Mahulda to Baptist Boyte 5-3-1828 (5-9-1828) O
Evans, Adalin to Mathew W. House 12-12-1848 (no return) Cr
Evans, Aden to David Darvin ?-16-1873 (12-16-1873) O
Evans, Alice to James Green 1-28-1874 (no return) Hy
Evans, Bettie A. to Frank G. Falls 2-24-1871 (3-1-1871) F

Evans, Betty to Thomas Hudson 1-5-1867 (no return) Dy
Evans, Candis A. to William A. Tharp 2-23-1846 (3-3-1846) F
Evans, Catharine to Thomas Spight 6-5-1834 (6-6-1834) G
Evans, Charity A. to H. L. Evans 7-26-1859 (7-1859) O
Evans, Charity to Nelson Walton 10-26-1885 (10-28-1885) L
Evans, Clarissa to Samuel Smith 1-17-1873 (1-18-1873) L B
Evans, D. J. to David Patrick 12-24-1867 G
Evans, Eliza J. to Jacob D. White 9-22-1843 Cr
Evans, Eliza to Nathan Naper 5-25-1882 (6-10-1882) L B
Evans, Eliza to William Buckley (Burkley) 6-7-1847 O
Evans, Elizabeth to L. W. Rust 1-9-1856 We
Evans, Elizabeth to Monroe Howard 6-21-1879 (6-25-1879) L
Evans, Elizabeth to N. S. Hilliard 12-29-1865 (1-3-1866) F
Evans, Elizabeth to Terrell Shankle 1-1-1842 T
Evans, Ellen to Elkins Cash 5-3-1845 (5-8-1845) F
Evans, Ellen to George Alston 1-4-1871 T
Evans, Ellen to Wm. Henry Harris 11-17-1866 (no return) Hy
Evans, Elzira to John Guthrie 12-7-1869 Hy
Evans, Emily to James Orr 11-1-1854 (11-2-1854) Sh
Evans, Emma L. to E. C. Lloyd 1-5-1883 (1-10-1883) L
Evans, Emma to Charley Bowman 2-25-1873 (no return) Hy
Evans, Emma to J. N. Dazey 12-3-1869 (12-8-1869) F
Evans, Fanny to John Rhodes Walker 6-22-1876 Hy
Evans, Frances to Seth Upchurch 3-24-1867 Be
Evans, Harrit to Will Young 2-15-1869 Hy
Evans, Hattie to Hillary Hardy 9-11-1880 (9-16-1880) L
Evans, Ida to Enoch Osborn 12-24-1869 (12-26-1869) Dy
Evans, J. M. to W. C. Fitzhugh 1-9-1878 (1-10-1878) Dy
Evans, Jane to William Blakemore 1-16-1860 (no return) Hy
Evans, Jerusha L. to Thomas B. Alexander 4-8-1869 (no return) L
Evans, Louisa to Marion Goodwin 12-7-1853 Ma
Evans, Lucinda to David J. Wrenn 7-5-1841 (7-6-1841) Ma
Evans, Luverny I. to John Harris 1-10-1867 O
Evans, M. A. (Mrs.) to Peter W. Evans 10-4-1860 Sh
Evans, M. A. to N. T. Lassiter 1-10-1866 Dy
Evans, Malinda to Lewis Taylor 4-3-1872 Hy
Evans, Malvina to Samuel Baker 12-19-1881 (12-21-1881) L
Evans, Margaret to Thomas Hamilton 12-30-1873 (1-1-1874) T
Evans, Maria to Danl. Neeves 5-5-1832 Sh
Evans, Martha A. to W. H. Prewett 10-19-1860 Hr
Evans, Martha E. to A. J. Wainwright 4-14-1860 Hy
Evans, Martha G. to William H. Wells 12-10-1838 (12-11-1838) F
Evans, Martha M. to James H. Lynch 7-2-1846 G
Evans, Martha to Daniel Deans 10-20-1851 (10-21-1851) Sh
Evans, Martha to E. Nokes 11-10-1864 (11-10-1865?) Sh
Evans, Mary A. to Samuel D. Killough 9-22-1845 Cr
Evans, Mary E. to A. H. Murray 12-20-1871 Hy
Evans, Mary E. to Benjamin T. Duval 4-14-1845 Sh
Evans, Mary F. to W. H. Hill 2-1-1868 (no return) F
Evans, Mary H. to John A. Rapler? 6-7-1849 Hn
Evans, Mary J. to James I. Palmer 1-8-1842 (1-11-1842) O
Evans, Mary Jane to W. C. Crossnoe 12-13-1870 (no return) Dy
Evans, Mary L. to J. H. McKiney 11-2-1865 (11-5-1865) O
Evans, Mary L. to W. M. Warren 10-10-1860 (not executed) Cr
Evans, Mary M. to T. B. Hilton 12-15-1866 (12-17-1866) O
Evans, Mary Penelope to John Griffin 2-10-1844 Sh
Evans, Mary to Joshua Thomas Mitchell 8-16-1847 (8-17-1847) T
Evans, Mary to William Hathcock 1-8-1857 Sh
Evans, Mattie O. to Edward H. Anderson 1-2-1871 (1-8-1871) F
Evans, Mila A. to Daniel Dodd 6-17-1851 Be
Evans, Morning P. to James N. Martin 9-23-1847 G
Evans, Nancy J. to J. H. Midgett 5-10-1860 Hy
Evans, Nancy to F. N. Forshee 5-13-1866 Dy
Evans, Nancy to Jessup? Grimm 11-14-1877 Dy
Evans, Nancy to Sebastian Boon 8-6-1834 O
Evans, Nancy to Wm. Flag 1-20-1871 Hy
Evans, P. T. to F. F. Summers 12-10-1868 Hy
Evans, Pathena to G. W. Stallings 2-16-1866 G
Evans, Sallie to Stephen Blackwell 1-21-1870 G B
Evans, Sally to G. Busbee 2-14-1870 (2-17-1870) Cr
Evans, Sarah Ann to Frank Taylor 9-22-1869 G
Evans, Sarah to Harason Lunsford 1-8-1870 (no return) L
Evans, Sarah to John W. Taylor 1-25-1860 Sh
Evans, Sarah to S. C. Cate 8-22-1852 Cr
Evans, Sela to Andrew Johnson 1-15-1878 Hy
Evans, Susan A. E. to W. F. Carlton 2-2-1860 Hy
Evans, Susanna to Alfred Baucom 11-3-1866 Hy
Evans, Susanna to Clem Roberts 12-13-1876 Hy
Evans, Unis T. to A. G. McKinney 10-10-1855 Cr
Evens, Susan F. to Hilary J. Flowers 10-18-1870 G
Everett, Amanda F. to E. D. Portis 1-27-1853 (no return) F
Everett, D. C. to Phillip A. Wright 10-22-1860 (10-25-1860) O
Everett, Elizabeth to Thomas Spears 3-22-1869 (3-23-1869) Cr
Everett, Julia C. to J. M. Lucas 12-22-1875 (12-23-1875) Dy
Everett, Julia F. to Isaac C. Reavis 12-27-1860 (no return) We
Everett, M. C. to J. A. Hill 9-17-1866 (9-18-1866) Cr
Everett, Margaret to Charles Small 2-7-1850 Sh

Everett, Margarett to Jas. H. Cannon 12-18-1872 (no return) Cr
Everett, Mary (Mrs.) to George Wade 12-23-1867 G
Everett, Mary M. H. to W. M. Cannon 12-19-1866 Cr
Everett, N. N. to S. W. Davidson 4-5-1873 (no return) L
Everett, Rebecca to G. L. Lutsinger 11-26-1870 (11-27-1870) Cr
Everett, S. A. to Wm. B. Everett 12-7-1860 Cr
Everett, Tempey to N. C. Tomlinson 7-17-1872 (no return) Cr
Everette, Georgianna to Luke Thomas Sweate 4-2-1878 (4-3-1878) L
Everitt, Sarah A. to William B. Everett? 12-7-1860 (12-13-1860) Cr
Evert, Elizabeth to William Lemmons 8-9-1849 O
Evert, Elizabeth to William Lemons 8-9-1849 O
Evetts, Almira to John Stocks 3-9-1837 Sh
Evetts, Margaret to Charles Dinney 7-7-1853 Sh
Evins, Mary A. to David Davenport 3-30-1861 (3-31-1861) L
Ewart, Elizabeth to Moses Smith 5-22-1858 (6-2-1858) Sh
Ewell, A. P. to Henry F. Scott 8-1-1860 (8-2-1860) F
Ewell, Bettie to W. B. Langford 7-26-1870 Ma
Ewell, Julia Ann to A. W. Murphey 12-20-1869 (12-21-1869) T
Ewell, Julia to Harry Ewell 5-12-1870 (5-15-1870) F B
Ewell, Lydia to Jack Rives 11-19-1866 (11-20-1866) F B
Ewell, Maria H. to W. D. Somers 12-25-1864 F
Ewell, Mary S. to Benj. W. Britt 8-3-1846 (no return) F
Ewell, Nancy to William Roberts 1-22-1869 (1-24-1869) F B
Ewell, Rebecca to W. A. J. Hartsfield 3-5-1857 T
Ewell, Susan E. to Edward Shankle 9-4-1855 (9-6-1855) T
Ewen, Martha Jane to Wm. A. Powell 12-24-1864 (12-25-1864) Sh
Ewill, Martha Jane to Jesse F. Blount 1-11-1851 (1-12-1851) T
Ewing, E. J. to James C. Carroll 10-20-1883 (10-21-1883) L
Ewing, Jane to James N. Steed 1-11-1859 Ma
Ewing, Medora to J. H. Catson 3-28-1861 Sh
Ewing, Rebecca to Duncan McMellon 11-21-1840 Ma
Ewing, Sarah to Owen Dillard 1-7-1828 (1-8-1828) Hr
Exum, Charlotte to Geo. W. Washington 12-21-1868 (no return) F B
Exum, E. M. to B. A. Moss (Mop?) 4-17-1860 (4-19-1860) Sh
Exum, Eliza A. to William W. Garland 1-13-1841 (1-15-1841) Ma
Exum, L. A. to Robert D. Guarrant 8-26-1847 (no return) F
Exum, Louisa to John A. Pope 12-6-1852 (no return) F
Exum, Lucata to William Sturges 12-23-1858 O
Exum, Lucy E. to James Cody 2-1-1870 (no return) F
Exum, M. J. to Wm. C. Exum 9-17-1859 (9-20-1859) F
Exum, Martha A. (Mrs.) to Dudley C. Talley 1-13-1870 Ma
Exum, Martha H. to Richd. E. Galloway 5-14-1849 (no return) F
Exum, Martha to Lytle Newton 3-20-1871 Ma
Exum, Mary A. E. to W. O. Meriwether 8-29-1854 (8-30-1854) Sh
Exum, Mary to Jas. S. Pickens 6-3-1849 F
Exum, Mildred to Richd. Miller 8-30-1867 (8-31-1867) F B
Exum, Patience F. M. P. to Frederick L. Reeves 2-3-1857 (2-4-1857) O
Exum, Rebecca A. to Robert A. Cathey 11-12-1856 Ma
Eyrich, Bertie to F. Boie 7-20-1859 Sh
Eyrick, Bertha to Jacob Fischer 6-20-1859 Sh
Eyson (Eison), Fannie S. to John H. Pillow 9-2_-1866 (9-22-1866) L
Ezale, Nancy to James G. Phillips 4-11-1855 Cr
Ezell, America to John Miller 6-14-1846 We
Ezell, Ann C. (Miss) to George W. Pool 7-23-1862 (7-27-1862) O
Ezell, Caroline to E. D. Phipps 7-17-1860 (no return) Cr
Ezell, Christian E. to Samuel C. Klutts 5-9-1858 Hn
Ezell, Eliza to W. A. Sherin 8-4-1862 (8-10-1862) O
Ezell, Emily to John H. Costin 11-20-1862 Hn
Ezell, Harriet to Harvy Gregory 2-20-1869 Cr
Ezell, Jane to Washington Scott 10-1-1852 Hn
Ezell, Louisa to W. H. Cox 3-28-1865 (3-30-1865) Cr
Ezell, Margaret A. to John Klutts 9-18-1849 Hn
Ezell, Martha (Mrs.) to Edward Partridge 7-19-1866 G
Ezell, Mary E. to James Knight 6-3-1865 Mn
Ezell, Nancy M. to Joseph N. Spear 5-6-1866 G
Ezell, Susan to Thomas Foster 5-17-1855 (no return) We
Ezzell, Lucy to Samuel Richardson 9-27-1848 Hn
Ezzell, Matilda to B. F. Womble 7-23-1857 We
Ezzell, Susan to Thomas Foster 5-17-1856 (no return) We

Faben (Fater-Faber), Barbara to Francis Gruber (Gruten) 3-18-1850 Sh
Facen, Mary to John Bradshaw 4-27-1846 We
Fadley, Emma J. to J. W. Burgett 1-11-1861 Sh
Fagan, Nancy to Albert Thompson 1-26-1870 T
Fagg, Martha Jane to Thomas D. Blanchet 11-4-1850 Ma
Fahnisihon, Frances to Heinrich Kepler 10-11-1852 Sh
Fahrigheon, Edda to Mike Otman 12-27-1855 Sh
Fain, Emerilla A. to David J. Boatwright 8-24-1847 Hn
Fain, Martha L. to Richard Green 8-10-1859 L
Fain, Mary Ann to James M. Sanderson 1-2-1867 L
Fain, Mary J. to Elisha M. White 12-21-1857 Hn
Faine, Victoria to Needham B. Bairfield 5-2-1870 Dy
Fainer, Edney to Alfred Williams 4-11-1872 Hy
Fair, Mary Jane to Edward Fair 4-16-1849 (4-17-1849) G
Faircloth, Frances to William A. Carroll 2-9-1858 Hn
Faircloth, Louisa to John Daniel 6-13-1841 Hn
Fairfax, Emma H. to James Landen 12-17-1869 T

Fairless, Celia F. to John W. Cail 4-29-1858 G
Fairless, Martha to James M. Skiles 1-12-1870 G
Fairless, Penelope to James C. Teal 3-10-1838 Ma
Faison, Sarah to Danl. J. McCalap 1-16-1839 (1-?-1839) Hr
Fakes, Patsy to Smith Woods 2-29-1868 G B
Fakes, Sallie to Will R. (Dr.) Hayes 12-18-1878 Dy
Falanigan?, Winnie L. to William Parker 6-22-1871 T
Falden, Ann Eliza to Thomas Eason 8-31-1853 Ma
Faldwell, Martha A. to Henry Bistwick 9-20-1847 (9-26-1847) F
Falkner, Civil to James H. Burns 11-2-1865 Hy
Falkner, Margaret to John Orr 10-18-1865 Cr
Fallen, Bridget to Frederick Smith 5-28-1857 Sh
Faller, Terissa to William Mayfield 10-6-1828 Hr
Fallin, Martha A. to S. J. Oliver 3-31-1853 Cr
Falls, Bella C. to P. D. Ewell 11-12-1863 (11-17-1863) F
Fallwell, Marze M. H. to James M. Williams 12-12-1858 Hn
Fanales, Lucy W. to H. C. Stark 6-12-1848 Sh
Fanan (France?), Cynthis Jane to Luther S. Burr 1-3-1848 Sh
Fance?, Nancy to Robertson G. Gilbert 7-26-1873 (no return) L
Fancher, Mollie E. to Wm. T. Morton 5-8-1871 (5-9-1871) Ma
Fanin, Amanda to Andrew Sandlin 2-1-1872 Hy
Fannassay, Nora to Thomas Crotty 2-11-1861 (2-12-1861) Sh
Fannell, Adaline to Jacob Behmer 5-30-1877 (no return) Hy
Fanner, Margaret E. to J. N. Cooper 11-16-1859 (11-17-1859) Ma
Fannessey, Margaret to William Ryan 5-21-1857 Sh
Fannie, Jeter to Dudly Puiett 1-24-1878 Hy
Fannigan, Bridget to Edward Maloney 1-18-1862 (1-19-1862) Sh
Fanning, Drucilla to John B. Kendrich 12-4-1833 Sh
Fanny, Hair to Alfred Phillips 12-30-1877 Hy
Fansioli, Josephine to L. Saino 7-24-1858 (7-25-1858) Sh
Fantom, Mary Ann to Franklin Meyer 11-30-1861 Sh
Farabee, Lew A. to W. L. Treadwell 12-21-1858 (12-22-1858) Sh
Farabough, Sarah Jane to ___ Palmer 1-31-1849 Hn
Faran, Kate to Patrick Dwyer 8-17-1859 Sh
Fararow, Matilda to James H. Pool 10-12-1848 Sh
Farce, Laura to Samuel Vastbinder 11-9-1874 Hy
Fargason, Charity? to William Morrow 1-3-1837 Hr
Fargurgson, Martha J. to Larkin H. Irwin 12-29-1853 G
Ferguson, Olive W. to Leroy Cook 1-22-1840 Hr
Farington, Theodocia E. to Thomas J. Ross 5-13-1858 T
Faris, Ann to Charles Henry Hart 1-31-1844 (2-8-1844) T
Faris, Harriet Jane Eliz. to John Allen Quimmly 9-26-1853 (9-27-1853) T
Faris, Judy Bell to J. W. McMurry 2-27-1878 Hy
Faris, Margaret to James Ellis 5-19-1852 (no return) Hn
Faris, Mary to James Grubbs 8-24-1846 Sh
Faris?, Elizabeth Ann to Saml. Woodfin Pilkington 12-3-1851 T
Fariss, Melvina to Davis N. Bell 11-21-1832 Hr
Farley, Ann E. to James H. Ramsey 9-4-1855 (9-6-1855) Sh
Farley, Ann to Walter Lynch 8-21-1848 Sh
Farley, Kassandre M. to Daniel jr. Waggoner 8-21-1842 Be
Farley, Maria to Peyton Moore 12-30-1865 (12-31-1865) F B
Farley, Martha E. to A. Baker 2-9-1846 (2-11-1846) F
Farley, Mary E. to D. K. Pulliam 2-5-1867 (no return) Hn
Farley, Mary E. to James Irwin 8-8-1857 (8-9-1857) Sh
Farley, R. C. to James M. Ham 3-9-1850 (no return) F
Farley, Sarah to Wilkins Wesson 7-10-1859 F
Farmer, Ann M. to Benj. R. Pettus 4-6-1866 (3?-7-1866) Ma
Farmer, Artemisa to Wm. J. Montgomery 7-29-1855 We
Farmer, Drucilla to Micajah Webb 1-11-1828 Ma
Farmer, Elizabeth to W. D. Snider 8-7-1868 Be
Farmer, Elizabeth to W. L. Young 10-7-1855 We
Farmer, M. J. to James Boyd 12-20-1858 (12-22-1858) T
Farmer, M. to J. Phifer 4-21-1842 Be
Farmer, Margaretta to John F. Wade 12-22-1870 (12-23-1870) F
Farmer, Marget C. to Jarrette Jones 2-21-1829 (2-22-1829) O
Farmer, Martha A. E. to M. P. G. Farmer 2-17-1872 (2-18-1872) L
Farmer, Martha A. to F. W. Zeller 12-24-1856 Sh
Farmer, Martha E. to James H. Jamison 4-23-1857 T
Farmer, Mary J. to T. T. Reddick 3-30-1864 (no return) Dy
Farmer, Mary M. to William Staret 1-10-1867 T
Farmer, Mary to John W. C. Mitchell 7-31-1844 We
Farmer, Mattie to W. R. Hall 9-23-1862 G
Farmer, Melissa Jane to Robt. Mann 2-28-1868 G B
Farmer, Mildred E. to Arthur Moore 12-28-1847 G
Farmer, Mollie F. to J. B. Sevier 5-20-1863 G
Farmer, Nancy L. to Oliver G. Tenney 8-31-1850 O
Farmer, Nancy to John W. Forest 12-31-1860 (1-1-1861) Sh
Farmer, O. C. to R. F. Eperson 10-24-1868 (10-25-1868) T
Farmer, Rebecca to William Reynolds 12-4-1858 (12-5-1858) G
Farmer, Sabra M. to L. G. Broyls 9-4-1871 (9-10-1871) L
Farmer, Sally to Nate Jones 7-1-1866 Hn B
Farmer, Sarah A. to Robert A. Cheny 9-18-1861 (9-20-1861) Dy
Farmer?, Susan A. to J. C. Pamper? 3-14-1868 (no return) Hy
Farmer?, Janie Frances to Kenneth B. Lanier 1-13-1856 (1-31-1856) T
Farmington, Nancy to Simon Wilson 6-20-1840 (could be July) Sh
Farn (Fain?), Elizabeth to Lewis Koonce 4-18-1853 (4-19-1853) L
Farned, Sophronia W. to Thomas Cox 1-18-1858 (1-19-1858) Hr

Farnsworth, Julia C. to J. B. Wasson 1-28-1864 Sh
Farr, Elizabeth to Thomas Whitehorn 7-9-1844 (7-10-1844) Hr
Farr, Emeline to Jas. S. Holder 2-1-1855 G
Farr, Martha J. to A. D. Furgerson 1-19-1865 G
Farr, Mary A. to David G. Keys 8-24-1858 (8-26-1858) G
Farr, Mary Ann to James H. Banks 11-3-1838 Cr
Farr, Mary to Joshua Evert 8-9-1849 H
Farr, Matilda Ann to Andy Sanders 6-26-1844 Hr
Farr, Polly (Patsy) to Ephraim Bradford 2-14-1850 (2-17-1850) O
Farran, Julian to Thomas H. Wells 2-12-1838 Hn
Farrar, Caroline to J. T. Mitchel 2-24-1857 Be
Farrar, Eliza to Reuben Capps 8-18-1860 Be
Farrar, Fannie to Burton L. Smith 12-19-1868 T
Farrar, Hattie V. to T. H. Poindexter 12-6-1866 (12-12-1866) F
Farrar, J. to W. K. Aden 6-5-1842 Be
Farrar, Lavina to John Thompson 10-10-1866 (10-15-1866) F B
Farrar, Louisa H. to D. W. Orton 1-30-1868 G
Farrar, Mattie M. to Thomas B. Murrell 11-2-1876 Hy
Farrar, Rosa P. to Benjamin B. Benson 8-14-1848 (8-?-1848) T
Farrar, Susan to Adam Jefferson 12-19-1866 (no return) F B
Farrar, Z. A. to R. F. Stacy 7-21-1866 (7-22-1866) F
Farrell, Alice C. to W. M. Harvey 8-1-1860 (8-2-1860) Sh
Farrell, Ellen E. to James W. Shorkey 4-30-1863 Sh
Farrell, Martha J. to James Cook 1-3-1863 Sh
Farrell, Mary to Thos. Maly 10-3-1864 (10-4-1864) Sh
Farrell, Mary to William Cain 10-25-1852 Sh
Farrell, Temperance to Fielding Huddleston 10-29-1842 Sh
Farrer, Caroline to E. D. Miller 10-3-1860 Be
Farrer, Ellen to Robert LeRoy 7-20-1857 Sh
Farrer, Martha S. to J. T. Farrer 7-21-1851 (7-24-1851) F
Farrer, N. E. to D. M. Chamberlain 3-10-1868 (no return) Dy
Farrill, Fanny P. to Wm. C. Bailey 10-8-1849 (10-11-1849) F
Farrington, A. C. to James Stone 1-2-1866 (1-3-1866) T
Farrington, Z. T. to James C. Hill 2-6-1867 F
Farris, Almeta to W. E. Parker 11-2-1875 (no return) Hy
Farris, Amanda to Wesley Harris 3-18-1854 (no return) F
Farris, Ann to John L. Davis 1-10-1860 Cr
Farris, Eliza to John Bryant 11-19-1853 (11-20-1853) Sh
Farris, Eliza to John H. Broom 4-1-1844 (no return) F
Farris, F. T. to T. B. Maloney 7-21-1859 O
Farris, Jane to ___ McWherter 4-22-1830 O
Farris, Jennie to W. M. Cruse 10-23-1874 O
Farris, L. V. to John W. Moore 11-6-1865 (11-7-1865) F
Farris, Levice to Moses Wright 1-14-1836 O
Farris, Malinda H. to John B. Hogue 1-23-1843 O
Farris, Malinda to Peter R. Nants 3-5-1844 O
Farris, Martha A. to Thos. R. Blankenship 1-5-1852 (1-6-1852) G
Farris, Martha V. to A. A. Aycock 10-22-1864 (9-26-1864) T
Farris, Mary A. E. to William Floyd 7-8-1847 Sh
Farris, Mary W. F. to J. B. Scott 8-11-1865 Mn
Farris, Mary to Henry Mathis 8-8-1871 (no return) Hy
Farris, Mary to P. M. North 4-29-1862 Mn
Farris, N. J. to Samuel Jones 9-27-1862 Mn
Farris, Nancy J. to John Lee 4-19-1863 Mn
Farris, Nancy M. to Thomas P. Hord 11-1-1841 (11-7-1841) O
Farris, Nancy to Edmund H. Hampton 7-26-1843 (7-27-1843) O
Farris, Nancy to K. P. Howell 7-25-1859 Hr
Farris, Rebecca (Mrs.) to Wyatt Mason 6-9-1866 G
Farris, Sarah Jane to D. W. M. Woolverton 1-12-1861 (1-15-1861) Hr
Farris, Sarah to Isaac Miller 6-11-1853 Ma
Farris, Sarah to N. B. Jones 1-5-1837 G
Farris, Sarah to William Reeves 4-3-1835 (4-7-1835) Hr
Farriss, Lucy M. to E.B. Stewart 1-26-1859 (1-27-1859) Hr
Farriss, Mary Ann to J. P. Lokey 9-27-1854 Hr
Farriss, Nancy to L. M. Hargrove 11-14-1857 (11-16-1857) Hr
Farriss, Sarah F. to M. A. Stewart 12-26-1854 (12-27-1854) Hr
Farriss, Sarah F. to Thos. D. Pennel 8-10-1861 (8-14-1861) T
Farror, Emaline to William H. Utley 9-21-1852 Hn
Farrow, Catherine M. to John A. Spencer 3-30-1844 (no return) Hn
Farrow, M. F. to James A. Bowling 2-11-1860 (no return) Hy
Farrow, Margarett to John Bivins 12-19-1848 Be
Farrow, Martha to J. C. England 1-25-1856 Be
Farrow, Mary Ann to W. E. Smith 7-24-1867 Be
Farrow, Mary E. to John C. Smothers 1-19-1869 G
Farrow, Mary Jane to Elias Smith 6-5-1868 T
Farrow, Mary Jane to James D. House 8-27-1850 Be
Farrow, N. J. to John K. Taylor 11-30-1858 (12-1-1858) Sh
Farrow, Sarah E. to John E. Lewis 3-17-1860 (no return) Hy
Farrow, Sarah to Thomas F. House 1-1-1852 Be
Farrow, Tricy to Calhoun Horton 7-30-1850 Be
Fartherlain, Frances to John Wain 8-12-1838 F
Farthing, Lydia to James Coneway 9-2-1858 G
Faucett, Ella? to Migugol? Adams 10-30-1869 T
Faucett, Lucinda C. to James W. Lowdermilk 5-7-1870 (5-8-1870) Ma
Faucett, Margarett E. to William A. Glass 10-29-1845 (10-30-1845) Ma
Faughton?, Louisa to Richard Gilmore 1-9-1837 (1-15-1837) Hr
Faulden, Martha to Nathanel F. Uptegrove 12-2-1847 Cr

Faulk, Alabama to Albert Jordan 12-21-1867 (12-22-1867) T
Faulk, Caroline to George Phillips 1-1-1874 (1-2-1874) T
Faulk, E. J. to James Dickey 9-25-1851 O
Faulk, Emily L. to Samuel Patterson 8-10-1847 Sh
Faulk, Jane? to John K. Robinson 10-28-1841 T
Faulk, Louisa to I. T. Reich 10-1-1863 O
Faulk, Marinda J. to James P. Baldock 10-8-1855 Sh
Faulk, Mary L. to W. F. Shropshire 9-14-1865 O
Faulkes, Elizabeth to Lemuel Watson 3-1-1856 (3-25-1856) O
Faulkner, Abagail to James Lawry 6-27-1859 (6-28-1859) Ma
Faulkner, Catherine to John W. Blurton 12-16-1870 (12-18-1870) Ma
Faulkner, Cornelia to E. M. Hall 11-28-1882 (11-29-1882) L
Faulkner, Cornelia to George Alexander 1-26-1874 (1-28-1874) Dy
Faulkner, Eliz. Agnes to Wm. Druffin Strain 4-8-1851 T
Faulkner, Margaret A. to Thos. Cowser 12-24-1866 (12-25-1866) T
Faulkner, Martha (Mrs.) to Barnabas Edwards 11-9-1872 (11-10-1872) Dy
Faulkner, Martha to Wm. H. Harrison 10-26-1870 (10-27-1870) Dy
Faulkner, Mary to Samuel G. Walthall 1-2-1866 Hy
Faulkner, Nancy to Elbert L. Phillips 12-23-1852 Cr
Faulkner, Sarah J. to W. H. Wharton 4-22-1877 Hy
Faulkner, Sarah Jane to Silas Wherry 10-11-1843 Sh
Fausett, Fidelia A. to Jessee M. Hughes 9-10-1852 (no return) F
Fausett, Frances E. to Robert Grifford 12-3-1851 (no return) F
Fausett, Sarah F. to William Yarbrough 12-17-1850 (no return) F
Faussett, Mary O. to John E. Hanna 1-10-1867 T
Faussette, E. C. to J. C. McLuster 7-10-1873 (7-11-1873) T
Faust, Alice to John J. Rice 6-11-1859 (6-12-1859) Sh
Faust, Elizabeth to James A. Guy 2-1-1832 (2-7-1832) O
Faust, Lucinda C. to William J. Alexander 8-16-1860 Hn
Faust, Martha J. to Joseph M. Palmer 6-28-1865 (no return) Hn
Faw?, Mary to Leroy D. Butts 8-25-1851 (8-28-1851) Hr
Fawbess, Soniza C. to Daniel Womack 8-20-1849 (8-27-1849) G
Fawbin?, S(e)cily to Andrew A. Edwards 7-2-1832 O
Fawcett, Eliza Jane (Mrs.) to Bartholomew C. Britton 7-27-1870 (7-28-1870) Ma
Fawcett, Margaret to Henry Whitehurst 5-10-1881 (5-11-1881) L B
Fawcett, Neely to Henry Poole 1-15-1881 L
Fawcett, Ruth to J. M. Grace 3-8-1859 Hr
Fay, Martha to James G. Jones 8-16-1862 Sh
Feagan, Sarah A. to J. A. J. Pierce 3-3-1858 Sh
Fearless, Martha to Fullington Rooks 1-30-1847 Ma
Fearse, Lucy to Frank Nicholson 12-23-1869 (no return) Hy
Featherston, Adaline to J. H. Waldren 2-12-1873 (no return) Dy
Featherston, E. J. to J. S. Robbins 10-31-1877 (no return) Dy
Featherston, E. L. to J. W. Hall 3-8-1870 (no return) Dy
Featherston, Harriett to W. G. Wynne (Wyman) 6-26-1845 Sh
Featherston, Louisa H. to Lewis J. Salyton 11-1-1854 (11-6-1854) G
Featherston, M. E. to S. E. Milam 12-4-1873 Dy
Featherston, Martha L. to William A. Jones 12-1-1842 Sh
Featherston, Martha to Charley Sawyer 1-1-1874 Dy
Featherston, Mary to A. H. Herron 2-6-1838 F
Featherston, Phebe A. to John H. Wallace 11-10-1853 G
Featherston, Susan S. to Wm. P. Bradley 6-26-1845 Sh
Featherstone, Mary L. to William E. Price 12-21-1858 (no return) We
Fedleton, Mary to Thomas Brown 9-27-1860 G
Fedrick, Mary Ann to Jas. C. Enscow 4-27-1863 Dy
Feely, Mary to John Key 5-31-1856 (6-15-1856) Sh
Feenay, Margaret to Thomas Corbett 2-15-1859 (2-20-1859) Sh
Feezor, Caroline to Smith M. Bandy 12-20-1851 (12-28-1851) T
Feezor, Christena to James C. Jones 12-24-1849 T
Feezor, E. A. to A. J. Harris 10-2-1865 (10-3-1865) T
Feezor, Margaret to Thomas A. Maxwell 8-27-1866 (8-29-1866) T
Feezor, Martha F. to Joseph F. Wiseman 11-16-1865 T
Feezor, Martha V. to Cyrus C. Rice 1-30-1859 T
Feezor, Mary A. to J. H. Stevens 1-3-1865 T
Feezor, Mary E. to Robert P. Collier 5-29-1845 T
Feezor, S. L. to F. Flemming 10-12-1870 (10-13-1870) T
Fegan, Amana (Amena) to Felix Fransiola 8-3-1850 Sh
Feibelman, Mary to J. W. Simon 5-21-1864 (5-24-1864) Sh
Feidlin, Caroline to John F. A. Petre 3-12-1853 Sh
Feild?, Sarah to Fed Bales 2-9-1867 T
Feley, Cyntha J. to J. C. Brigance 11-2-1871 L
Felica, Relien to Baptiste Mazic 5-7-1862 Sh
Fellow, Mary to James A. Sims 11-25-1840 Sh
Fellowes, Lizzie to Bernard Carolan 6-18-1861 Sh
Fellows, Ellen to James S. Boston 6-18-1859 (6-19-1859) Sh
Fellson, Bridget to John T. Bateman 8-1-1859 (8-2-1859) Sh
Felphs, Susan Malrina to Robert M. Jones 4-9-1861 Sh
Felps, Elizabeth to Benjamin D. Vincent 1-29-1868 (no return) Cr
Felsenthal, Rachael to Joseph Felsenthal 6-17-1862 (no return) Hy
Felts, Dennie to R. T. D. Arragon 6-26-1866 (7-4-1866) F
Felts, E. J. to R. C. Wade 1-22-1855 (1-23-1855) Hr
Felts, Lavinia to Lewis H. Featherston 10-15-1856 (10-16-1856) Sh
Felts, Martha to John W. McKendrick 9-7-1852 (9-9-1852) G
Felts, Mary B. to Harman J. Houser 10-9-1873 (10-10-1873) O
Felts, Mattie J. to E. Keck 1-27-1864 Sh
Felts, Susan H. to William A. Justice 1-5-1854 Hr
Felts, Susan to Wm. Christenberry 10-31-1867 Hy

Femins?, Mary to John W. Edwards 5-10-1861 T
Feney, Mary to Jerry Cronin 5-1-1863 Sh
Fenler?, Martha to James Harris 12-15-1834 Hr
Fenley, C. J. to S. A. Anthony 10-9-1883 (10-10-1883) L
Fennel, R. A. to R. W. Potts 6-2-1870 Hy
Fennell, Matilda to William Escue 2-9-1873 Hy
Fenner, Ann to Francis M. Whitlow 2-2-1857 (2-5-1857) Ma
Fenner, Ella to Frank Monroe 11-24-1869 Ma
Fenner, Eunice B. to Alexander Jackson 10-21-1850 (10-22-1850) Ma
Fenner, Lizzie V. to Henry D. (of Ala.) Smith 4-28-1869 (4-29-1869) Ma
Fenner, Lucy Ann to Isaac D. Walton 3-1-1859 (3-2-1859) Ma
Fenner, Rebecca Ann to Etheldred L. Smith 12-17-1856 Ma
Fennessey-Hennessey, Maria to Wm. McKenzie 5-24-1861 Sh
Fenster (Feuster?), Sarah to J. Ezen (Izen) 10-18-1864 Sh
Fenster, Rebecca to Benjamin Newman 2-20-1862 Sh
Fenton, Margaret to Daniel Dowd 7-29-1862 (7-31-1862) Sh
Fentress, Sarah to Aaron Norton 2-17-1857 O
Fentris, Mary Ann to Baptist Boyett 1-16-1848 O
Ferell, Willietta to P. R. B. Brown 11-30-1859 Sh
Fergason, Elizabeth to J. H. Thompson 1-20-1857 (no return) L
Fergason, Margaret to Joseph Willey 3-13-1845 Sh
Fergason, Mary to Charles Hallum 7-31-1845 Sh
Fergerson, Ann to Thomas Keirman 4-10-1869 (4-17-1869) Cr
Fergerson, E. M. to Wm. G. Butler 2-25-1851 Cr
Fergerson, Fanny to Frank Fields 2-4-1876 (no return) Hy
Fergerson, Jane to George W. Williams 2-13-1845 Sh
Fergerson, N. A. to R. B. Carter 1-15-1851 Cr
Fergerson, Susan E. to G. H. George 2-24-1855 Cr
Ferguson, A. A. to G. W. Hawkins 10-6-1868 (no return) Dy
Ferguson, Amanda to George Anderson 10-15-1873 (10-16-1873) Dy
Ferguson, America to William Fowlkes 6-29-1871 Dy
Ferguson, Ann to Henry Strother 12-24-1868 Dy
Ferguson, Anny to Tony Richardson 3-13-1880 (3-14-1880) L B
Ferguson, Elen to Charly King 2-23-1878 Hy
Ferguson, Eliza J. to Thos. R. McCommon 4-5-1859 (6-11-1859) Hr
Ferguson, Elizabeth J. to W. M. McCommon 12-21-1857 (12-22-1857) Hr
Ferguson, Ellen to James Carnatzer 12-26-1860 Ma
Ferguson, Emily J. to Griffin G. Ware 3-26-1854 Hn
Ferguson, Emma to W. A. Birch 12-22-1880 (12-23-1880) L
Ferguson, Esther A. to Robert Hood 7-31-1849 Hr
Ferguson, Harriet L. to E. E. Hawkins 2-12-1867 (2-13-1867) Dy
Ferguson, Hattie to James I. Garrett 1-26-1878 (1-29-1878) L
Ferguson, Ida M. to A. T. Harrell 12-23-1867 Dy
Ferguson, Lavanda to John M. Barnett 3-20-1860 Hr
Ferguson, Lucinda to Jerry Fowlkes 10-4-1873 Dy
Ferguson, Lucy to Arch. McLean 10-6-1839 Sh
Ferguson, M. A. to J. C. Wells 3-28-1859 (3-29-1859) Hr
Ferguson, M. N. to J. F. McAlister 10-17-1861 (10-28-1861) Hr
Ferguson, Martha A. to Alfred Reddick 2-10-1866 (no return) Dy
Ferguson, Martha M. to W. R. Bentley 12-14-1860 (12-19-1860) Dy
Ferguson, Martha to L. H. Pyron 12-22-1846 Sh
Ferguson, Martha to O. J. Smith 2-12-1868 (2-13-1868) L
Ferguson, Mary Louisa to Thomas F. Ledsinger 9-27-1865 Dy
Ferguson, Mary M. to J. M. Melton 11-23-1865 Mn
Ferguson, Mary to Isham Johnson 2-6-1833 (2-7-1833) G
Ferguson, Mary to Jack Parker 1-10-1880 (1-18-1880) Dy
Ferguson, Mary to Robert Young 3-12-1856 (3-13-1856) T
Ferguson, Matilda to John Mabin 3-15-1879 Dy
Ferguson, Matilda to Pleasant Terry 12-14-1864 Dy
Ferguson, Montie to James A. Foster 5-11-1875 Dy
Ferguson, P. I. to K. H. Bentley 2-25-1861 (no return) Dy
Ferguson, Rachel to John James 1-4-1844 Sh
Ferguson, Sallie to A. C. Minor 5-31-1855 Sh
Ferguson, Sarah A. to C. Brownlee 7-4-1860 G
Ferguson, Sarah A. to W. H. Black 12-11-1852 (12-22-1852) Hr
Ferguson, Susan E. to John R. Hood 12-24-1855 Hr
Ferguson, Tracey to Nathaniel Moody 6-14-1831 Sh
Ferless, Mary J. to Harrison J. Conley 1-17-1856 G
Fernandy, A. M. to W. L. Scott 7-26-1870 G
Ferrald, Ellen to Hugh H. Thompson 6-12-1860 We
Ferrel, Mary to John Devine 1-16-1864 Sh
Ferrel, Mattie to Samuel B. Boykin 12-12-1870 (12-14-1870) Ma
Ferrell, Amanda to Oliver Spurrell 2-18-1877 Hy
Ferrell, Docia E. to J. M. Webb 10-24-1853 (10-28-1853) Hr
Ferrell, Elizabeth to Levi Wallis 11-20-1867 O
Ferrell, Ezader to Jaret McClure 11-4-1863 Hn
Ferrell, J. A. to T. H. Folks 2-18-1874 (2-19-1874) O
Ferrell, Jane C. to David C. Bullard 2-4-1867 (2-5-1867) Dy
Ferrell, Jennie to L. C. Woodard 12-16-1874 Hy
Ferrell, M. T. P. to Wm. B. Bowles 12-3-1864 (12-4-1867) T
Ferrell, Maletta to Josiah Young 6-28-1838 Ma
Ferrell, Malissy to A. S. Sorrell 5-3-1855 (no return) F
Ferrell, Maranda to James Bullard 7-27-1843 (7-28-1843) G
Ferrell, Marmu? to Augustus Taylor 7-18-1855 Hr
Ferrell, Mary Ann to James L. Garland 8-29-1863 (9-1-1863) L
Ferrell, Nancy H. to William Wingo 1-5-1859 O
Ferrell, Sarah Jane to Andrew Cart 10-11-1870 Dy

Ferrell, Sarah Jane to Andrew Hart 10-11-1870 (10-12-1870) Dy
Ferrelll, Marnetta to John W. Pipkin 2-3-1875 (2-4-1875) L
Ferress, Lucy T. to William C. Rives 12-16-1839 (12-17-1839) F
Ferress, Mary F. to B. S. Flowers 8-25-1859 G
Ferri, Ann E. to J. G. McGowan 9-26-1866 (9-27-1866) Ma
Ferril, Josie to James A. T. Neal 10-14-1874 (10-19-1874) Dy
Ferril, Martha H. to Levi Brown 7-26-1848 (7-27-1848) G
Ferril, Nancy to Arthur Turner 12-25-1848 G
Ferrill, Eliza Jane to Alfred P. Moore 10-19-1870 (10-20-1870) Ma
Ferrill, Ellen to J. K. P. Holland 8-19-1869 Dy
Ferrill, Frances C. to Levi H. Pitt 9-30-1868 (no return) Dy
Ferrill, L. W. (Mrs.) to W. H. Sollis 3-5-1867 G
Ferrill, Lucy E. to T. B. Lane 11-18-1878 (11-20-1878) Dy
Ferrill, Lucy to Osborn Thomasson 12-27-1880 (no return) Dy
Ferrill, M. A. to Robert A. Woodard 12-21-1881 (no return) L
Ferrill, Margaret A. to Jesse Dixon 2-19-1879 (2-20-1879) Dy
Ferrill, Martha Jane to Stephen Sawyer 4-17-1873 (no return) Dy
Ferrill, Mary Elizabeth to James W. Monroe 9-14-1853 (9-16-1853) O
Ferrill, Mary W. (Mrs.) to H. W. Gill 10-30-1866 G
Ferrill, Queenie? to Henry Patterson 12-18-1879 (12-25-1879) Dy
Ferrill, Sarah Frances to William Martin 11-11-1871 (11-12-1871) L
Ferrill, Sarah to M. L. Bledsoe 5-16-1874 (5-17-1874) Dy
Ferrill, Tennie to Andrew Boose 5-18-1876 Dy
Ferris, Amanda to R. J. Dew 1-8-1868 G
Ferris, Eliza to David Winston 10-9-1866 G
Ferris, Laura to George Ward 2-23-1867 G
Ferris, Sarah A. to Daniel W. Burton 12-9-1854 (12-10-1854) Ma
Ferror, Tenie to Edmund Miller 12-17-1878 Hy
Feser, Isabella to A. P. Waterfield 4-21-1857 We
Fetherstone, Mary L. to Wm. E. Price 12-23-1858 We
Fewell, Sarah E. to William R. Burke 10-28-1868 G
Fewtrill, Agelina to William Cumings 1-26-1853 (1-27-1853) Hr
Field, Annie (Mrs.) to Jesse McHenry 11-24-1864 G
Field, Annie M. to Jos. D. Whitley 5-11-1866 (5-15-1866) F
Field, Caroline to M. Van Davelt? 1-18-1871 (1-19-1871) T
Field, Clarisa to Willis Stevens 1-14-1874 T
Field, Delila S. to John Cokeley 5-5-1849 (5-10-1849) G
Field, Elizabeth to James O. Trible 1-2-1858 Hn
Field, Fannie Ann to John McCan 4-8-1870 T
Field, Farrie Ann to John McCan 4-8-1870 T
Field, Franky Jane to Watson Webb 1-19-1847 (1-21-1847) Hr
Field, Lucey to Henry Clay Davis 9-22-1874 T
Field, Martha A. to Virginius Leake 10-2-1849 Sh
Field, Martha Ann to Cornelius Rain 4-11-1838 (4-12-1838) Hr
Field, Mary Catherine to Fras. M. Green 11-15-1853 (11-16-1853) T
Field, Mary Harriett to John Hutt 12-8-1831 Sh
Field, S. B. to L. B. Listen 12-22-1870 Cr
Field, Susan E. to Daniel G. Kelly 4-3-1843 (4-5-1843) Hr
Fielder, E. H. to Robert S. Adams 9-22-1857 G
Fielder, Elizabeth to R. B. McCabe 1-7-1880 (1-8-1880) L
Fielder, Lucenda C. to James Y. Deshong 8-30-1853 (9-15-1853) G
Fielder, M. S. to S. F. Haley 10-26-1867 (no return) Dy
Fielder, Martha to W. W. Blanton 10-3-1869 G
Fielder, Mary Ann to Thomas J. Sumner 6-29-1869 (no return) L
Fielder, Myra V. P. to Francis M. Johnson 9-8-1863 (no return) Dy
Fielder, Phebe to John R. Watson 1-6-1869 (no return) L
Fielder, Sarah A. to Josiah Roberts 12-6-1860 We
Fielder, Sarah F. to A. G. Dodd 1-2-1854 (1-3-1854) G
Fielding, Matilda J. to Thomas S. Stone 5-17-1834 (5-18-1834) G
Fields, Abagail to Simeon Young 11-12-1840 Hn
Fields, Ann to George Coleman 9-14-1869 (no return) Dy B
Fields, Belle to R. M. Foster 1-19-1881 L
Fields, Caroline to John Gray 2-17-1869 (2-18-1869) Cr
Fields, Chaney to Benj. Fields 2-11-1871 (no return) Hy
Fields, Della to Henry Word 12-25-1879 Dy
Fields, Elinora T. to S. L. Chism 9-23-1873 (9-24-1873) L
Fields, Eliza to Ed Lemons 1-6-1871 (no return) F B
Fields, Elizabeth G. to John D. Whitson 5-14-1834 (5-15-1834) G
Fields, Elizabeth J. to Michael H. Hicks 6-16-1840 G
Fields, Elizabeth W. to J. W. Browder 2-5-1857 Sh
Fields, Elizabeth to Joseph Dowson 4-27-1863 Sh
Fields, Elizabeth to Thos. Griggs 10-26-1850 (10-27-1850) L
Fields, Ellen to Bill Davis 8-19-1875 Hy
Fields, Emily to William M. Thompson 12-24-1860 O
Fields, Etta to Robert Read 7-2-1881 N
Fields, Frances to James Welch 9-29-1835 (9-30-1835) G
Fields, Julia A. to John W. H. Mays 1-30-1836 (1-31-1836) G
Fields, Kate to Phillip Buggs 8-30-1873 (8-31-1873) T
Fields, Katharine to Robert L Rider 6-30-1847 O
Fields, Linnie to Sam A. Williams 11-23-1876 Dy
Fields, Louisa to Silas Walker 6-8-1854 O
Fields, Louiza V. to J. W. Ledbetter 7-19-1862 L
Fields, Lucy C. to A. L. Russell 10-5-1861 O
Fields, Lucy M. to N. A. Fields 6-9-1843 We
Fields, Lucy to Henderson Cowan 2-14-1874 T
Fields, Lucy to Lyttleton Harrison 1-29-1878 Hy
Fields, Luzun M. to Thos. L. Woodson 12-14-1849 G

Fields, M. E. to D. J. Cope 8-1-1869 G
Fields, M. E. to J. J. Fussell 4-22-1867 Cr
Fields, M. F. to A. C. Heddin 5-27-1869 (no return) Dy
Fields, Malissa A. to H. W. Potts 11-22-1865 Hn
Fields, Margarett to Henry McCraw 1-3-1871 (no return) F B
Fields, Martha C. to James A. McAlister 4-20-1865 G
Fields, Martha C. to John M. Glasgow 10-19-1858 G
Fields, Martha J. to Harris B. Mebane 1-11-1854 Cr
Fields, Martha to Jacob Romon 4-15-1869 (no return) Hy
Fields, Martha to Jeffersn Prince 9-5-1855 Hn
Fields, Martha to Moses P. Lockard 10-4-1848 L
Fields, Mary A. F. to John G. Fields 11-2-1843 We
Fields, Mary A. to Edward E. Williams 9-3-1842 (9-6-1842) O
Fields, Mary Ann to Semion E. Buford 4-20-1840 (4-22-1840) G
Fields, Mary E. to H. W. Edwards 2-9-1867 G
Fields, Mary M. to Calvin M. Reese 9-22-1849 (10-3-1849) G
Fields, Mary M. to William B. Fields 3-26-1849 (3-27-1849) G
Fields, Mary to James E. Sevier 5-17-1871 Hy
Fields, Mary to Lee Ferguson 10-24-1876 Dy
Fields, Mary to Thomas Finley 1-25-1844 Cr
Fields, Mary to W. L. Fitzgerald 1-7-1880 (1-8-1880) L
Fields, Mollie to Richard Rideout 12-28-1867 (no return) F B
Fields, Morean to Green Douglass 4-1-1878 (4-3-1878) Dy
Fields, Nancy C. to Tho. E. Lockard 8-31-1848 L
Fields, Nancy J. to Thomas B. Riden 7-27-1847 O
Fields, Nancy J. to William A. Basinger 1-3-1842 (1-7-1842) G
Fields, Nancy to James Benton 7-11-1837 Hr
Fields, Permelia to Samuel Meux 1-4-1877 Hy
Fields, Rose to Jack Fields 12-24-1866 (12-29-1866) F B
Fields, Sallie to Guy Grimm 3-18-1873 (3-19-1873) Dy
Fields, Sallie to William Wilson 8-4-1873 (8-9-1873) T
Fields, Sarah F. to James S. Rodgers 1-16-1851 Cr
Fields, Sarah to Daniel R. Hendrick 3-29-1839 G
Fields, Sarah to Daniel R. Hendrick 3-29-1839 (4-2-1839) G
Fields, Sarah to Hamilton C. Payne 10-31-1848 Sh
Fields, Sarah to John Hunter 5-19-1850 (6-19-1850) Hr
Fields, Sealy to Green B. Rodgers 3-24-1848 G
Fields, Silva to Richmond Williams 12-24-1868 (12-25-1868) F B
Fields, Sinora to Joseph Smith 5-24-1871 T
Fields, Susan to Alexander R. Tucker 4-3-1858 (4-6-1858) L
Fields, Susan to G. B. Vaugh 10-1-1858 Cr
Fields, Susan to James T. Metheny 6-22-1853 Hn
Fields, Susan to Wm. Spence 1-15-1868 Dy
Fields, T. E. to John Gray 1-21-1871 (1-24-1871) Cr
Fields, Tempe to Aubner Tinsly 2-21-1871 T
Fife, Ann to James D. Ware 11-2-1868 Hy
Fife, Julia H. to Davis Worrell 2-9-1863 Hy
Fife, Margaret B. to James Stewart 11-4-1863 Sh
Fifer(Phifer), Elizabeth to James Shurley(Shirley) 11-26-1865 Be
Fifer, Mary P. to James H. Bratton 4-29-1846 G
Fifer, Sarah J. to Monan Woods 7-15-1859 (no return) Hn
Fight, Ellen to Daniel Shea 6-29-1860 (6-30-1860) Sh
Fika, Minna to John C. Henneger 10-14-1858 Sh
Fike, Matilda to William Hegel 9-22-1860 Sh
Filed, Martha to Jefferson Pentacost 2-11-1851 Hn
Fillingham, Sarah to D. J. James 6-24-1851 Sh
Fillmore, Jane C. to John H. A. Knight 7-26-1844 (no return) F
Finacy, Mary to James Brearton 11-21-1856 (11-23-1856) Sh
Finan, Catharine to John Gallagher 3-28-1857 (3-29-1857) Sh
Finch, Aramenta to Henry Carter 10-3-1861 Hn
Finch, B. A. to R. R. Tugwell 8-18-1867 Hy
Finch, Caroline to Richard M. Nance 8-8-1867 Hn
Finch, Elizabeth to L. A. Arnold 4-16-1863 O
Finch, Emily L. to John H. Finch 12-26-1844 We
Finch, Emily to Briant Medlin 9-1-1845 We
Finch, Emily to Charles McNamee 1-11-1849 (no return) F
Finch, Flenda to John H. Park 2-9-1861 (2-10-1861) Cr
Finch, Frances to Eli Moody 7-18-1849 Hn
Finch, Harriet to Edward McMackin 2-2-1841 Cr
Finch, Jane to A. J. Hall 8-16-1873 (8-18-1873) Dy
Finch, Juday m. to James R. Cook 8-21-1855 We
Finch, Lucy E. to Fountain E. Hughes 11-12-1863 Dy
Finch, Lucy F. to John Falls 5-13-1862 (5-14-1862) F
Finch, M. B. to John Carey 6-20-1865 O
Finch, Martha A. to Henry Eckley 6-10-1846 O
Finch, Mary N. to John W. White 1-8-1857 Cr
Finch, Mary to James Dick 1-22-1841 (1-27-1841) F
Finch, Minerva to Allen A. Cole 1-8-1850 Hn
Finch, P. B. to J. C. Montgomery 4-6-1852 We
Finch, Pinkie L. to Joseph P. Gregory 9-10-1873 Hy
Finch, Rebecca to B. Arnold 11-4-1856 G
Finch, Sallie A. to George Wilborne 1-5-1876 Dy
Finch, Sarah to Joseph Trase 8-20-1843 We
Fincher, Sarah L. to D. C. Booth 3-17-1880 (3-21-1880) L
Findley, Elisabeth to J. D. Whitman 2-14-1862 (2-16-1862) Sh
Findley, Emily to John Willoughby 11-12-1845 Hn
Findley, F. A. to G. W. Powers 7-22-1852 Hn

Findley, Louiza F. to James A. Burton 1-30-1851 Hn
Finessey, Catharine to Jno. Peters 7-15-1861 (7-16-1861) Sh
Finey, Mary Ann to James Hays 4-13-1837 (4-15-1837) G
Finger, Julianne C. to Coleman H. Tucker 7-14-1845 (7-15-1845) Ma
Finger, Rebecca A. to L. F. Melton 11-3-1865 Mn
Fink, Louisa to Charles Williams 5-7-1873 T
Fink, Louisa to Martin Mettler 2-10-1860 Sh
Fink, Mary to Frank Gruben 6-19-1855 Sh
Finler, Susan to James Butler 12-22-1860 (no return) We
Finley, Amanda to William F. Hinson 8-11-1838 (no return) Hn
Finley, Elizabeth to Caswell Welsh 3-19-1844 Sh
Finley, Elizabeth to H. P. Woodard 5-9-1845 Cr
Finley, Ellen to Thomas Ryan 2-18-1854 (2-20-1854) Sh
Finley, Ellen to William Horan (Horne) 10-10-1863 Sh
Finley, Emma to Edmund Wright 6-3-1873 (6-4-1873) O
Finley, Ida F. to S. M. Drummonds 12-21-1870 Dy
Finley, Jennie to R. M. Bledsoe 2-1-1877 Dy
Finley, M. E. to T. J. Richardson 3-6-1873 (3-5?-1873) Dy
Finley, M. J. to M. F. Roney 12-31-1862 (1-1-1863) Cr
Finley, Martha E. to C. A. Dupre 11-27-1865 Dy
Finley, Mary to William A. Willoughby 9-11-1859 Hn
Finley, Mattie E. to S. H. Webb 1-28-1869 Be
Finley, Mollie to Wm. Wright 9-1-1874 O
Finley, Nancy E. to Robert C. Phillips 6-14-1848 Cr
Finley, Nancy J. to James Jackson 12-9-1863 Hn
Finley, Nancy to Francis M. Raney 7-5-1849 (no return) Cr
Finley, S. L. to J. W. Ledbetter 3-27-1873 (no return) Dy
Finly, Mary J. to E. E. Thompson 7-23-1867 Be
Finly, Sarah A. to Joseph Sanford 11-2-1867 (11-3-1867) Dy
Finly?, Kezziah to Hadley Merritt 1-16-1861 Cr
Finn, Bettie to Henri Koch (Cook?) 12-8-1857 Sh
Finn, Bridgett to James Dolan 11-14-1859 (11-15-1859) Sh
Finn, Heding to Conrad Behrens 12-17-1855 Sh
Finnerty, Ann Eliza to Marton Reddington 8-2-1862 (8-10-1862) Sh
Finnessey, Alice to Mathew Maher 6-23-1856 Sh
Finney, Anna M. to R. D. Winsett 1-22-1868 (12-23-1868) F
Finney, Caroline to John Freemon 12-24-1846 Be
Finney, Caroline to Mack Curray 12-17-1870 F B
Finney, Ellen to Billy Day 12-31-1866 (1-5-1867) F B
Finney, Frances to Isaac Cox 6-23-1866 F B
Finney, Margaret to George Ligon 9-3-1869 F B
Finney, Martha Ann to Richd. F. Finney 1-5-1839 (1-6-1839) F
Finney, Martha J. to W. P. Finney 9-28-1849 (9-10?-1849) F
Finney, Martha to Joseph L. Edwards 10-23-1844 F
Finney, Patience to Sandy Douglas 8-27-1869 F B
Finnigan, Mary to Chas. Boulger 12-31-1847 Sh
Finnigen, Mary to Henry Hayes 5-27-1856 Sh
Finny, Martha to A. Smalley 2-26-1860 Be
Finty?, Miss Jane to Aux? W. Gravy 3-13-1869 (3-17-1869) T
Fipps (Flippo), Eliza to Nathan N. Baker 12-7-1843 Sh
Firrell, Sarah to William Hufman 6-27-1854 We
Firth, Lavinia A. (Louisa?) to Robt. P. White 10-20-1866 (10-23-1866) F
Firth, Martha to Richd. Mc. Kirtland 8-24-1863 F
Fish, America to Calvin H. Dunahoe 3-4-1856 (3-6-1856) Hr
Fish, Elizabeth to Bryant Johnson 5-9-1849 (5-17-1849) Hr
Fish, H. A. to Joseph Johnson 11-19-1859 (11-20-1859) Hr
Fish, Martha C. to Hance S. Eskew 12-?-1861 (12-22-1861) Cr
Fish, Temperance to Jesse Wilson 9-23-1851 (9-25-1851) Hr
Fisher, A. B. to J. R. Garrison 4-10-1858 Sh
Fisher, Amanda T. to Edmond T. Baldridge 2-27-1868 G
Fisher, Ann E. to J. T. Voss 8-28-1857 (no return) L
Fisher, Annie L. to James B. Hamilton 10-24-1867 T
Fisher, Bell to Andrew Green 3-13-1876 (3-16-1876) L
Fisher, C. J. to L.(C?) W. Holowell 3-21-1864 Sh
Fisher, Catherine L. to Joseph Fassett 11-10-1852 (11-12-1854?) L
Fisher, Chaney to Jim Bunch 2-6-1874 (no return) Hy
Fisher, Clara Jane to Thomas S. Damron 3-8-1851 (3-12-1851) F
Fisher, Eleanor C. to Norborne E. Sutton 10-19-1848 L
Fisher, Eley to Jasper Alexander 1-8-1872 (1-19-1872) L
Fisher, Elizabeth C. to Amos Ayres 8-10-1841 O
Fisher, Elizabeth C. to Robert N. Lewis 8-2-1844 (8-6-1844) O
Fisher, Elizabeth Glover to Gabriel J. Slaughter 3-6-1849 T
Fisher, Elizabeth to Berry F. Wilson 11-30-1854 Hn
Fisher, Elizabeth to J. G. Horn 6-3-1857 Sh
Fisher, Emma F. to George J. McBride 1-20-1869 (1-21-1869) T
Fisher, Evilina to Patrick Henry Sutton 4-30-1850 (no return) L
Fisher, Fanny to Wm. Goodrun 4-1-1869 (4-27-1869) Cr
Fisher, Frederica to Charles Bueckner 4-25-1861 (4-26-1861) Sh
Fisher, H. M. to S. N. Furguson 1-12-1876 F
Fisher, Harriet A. to William J. King 9-12-1846 (9-17-1846) F
Fisher, Harriet to Elijah Dismukes 12-22-1874 (12-31-1874) L
Fisher, Harriet to Nerv Tyler 12-27-1867 Hy
Fisher, Jane to James Phillips 12-3-1874 Cr
Fisher, Jane to M.? J. Williams 9-3-1867 (no return) Dy
Fisher, Josephine to Henry Fisher 3-10-1868 F B
Fisher, Julia A. S. to Z. R. Walker 4-21-1866 (no return) Cr
Fisher, Kate to R. W. Green 12-19-1879 (12-21-1879) L

Fisher, Lizzie to Albert Freeman 1-28-1864 Sh
Fisher, Lizzie to Monroe Lawrence 1-4-1886 (1-7-1886) L
Fisher, Louisa A. to Lewis Smith 12-10-1857 Sh
Fisher, Lucinda to William Golden 8-14-1845 Ma
Fisher, Lucy to Hut Rucker 1-21-1882 L B
Fisher, Lusten to Bill Hemp 1-5-1869 (not executed) T
Fisher, M. A. E. to John C. Johnson 6-9-1856 (6-11-1856) Sh
Fisher, Magdalaine to N. R. Williams 10-21-1858 (11-3-1858) Sh
Fisher, Mahulda to Andrew M. Davidson 11-13-1844 Ma
Fisher, Mallie to Jack Braden 4-5-1879 (4-7-1879) L B
Fisher, Margaret L. to Isaac C. Dodds 3-1-1848 (3-2-1848) F
Fisher, Margarett J. to Alexander J. McClarren 2-4-1840 (2-19-1840) F
Fisher, Martha A. to Thomas M. Wilson 1-1-1850 Hn
Fisher, Martha P. to G. W. Ham 1-4-1841 (1-7-1841) F
Fisher, Martha to Thomas I. Ham (Haines?) 2-1-1838 F
Fisher, Mary Ann to Andrew Thurmond 4-12-1867 (4-13-1867) L B
Fisher, Mary E. to George Kelly 10-25-1849 F
Fisher, Mary E. to Robert Sanford 7-1-1869 (7-4-1869) Dy
Fisher, Mary E. to Robert W. Watkins 11-24-1856 (no return) L
Fisher, Mary J. to H. T. Blythe 9-27-1842 (9-29-1842) L
Fisher, Mary Jane to J. W. McBride 12-27-1854 (no return) We
Fisher, Mary Jane to Jas. W. Glasgow 10-25-1837 (10-26-1837) G
Fisher, Mary K.(H?) to Robert M. Smith 12-23-1885 L
Fisher, Mary to J. J. Suter 10-28-1856 Sh
Fisher, Mattie F. to Carter Wright 11-30-1878 (no return) L B
Fisher, Nancy C. to Joseph H. McKnight 1-24-1859 (2-1-1859) G
Fisher, Nancy M. to Benjamin L. Rodgers 11-16-1830
Fisher, Nancy S. to W. N. Wilson 10-31-1866 Hn
Fisher, Nancy to George W. Davenport 1-?-1841 (no return) Cr
Fisher, Nancy to Henry Angel 12-17-1878 (12-18-1878) L
Fisher, Nancy to William Fletcher 7-14-1830 G
Fisher, Rachel to Robin Williamson 4-18-1866 F B
Fisher, Rosa to Gerrit DeVries 8-12-1872 (9-1-1872) T
Fisher, S. M. to S. F. Forsythe 1-29-1866 G
Fisher, Sarah J. to C. F. Johns 10-11-1860 O
Fisher, Sarah to George Carter 12-9-1846 Cr
Fisher, Selina to J. M. Tripp 1-4-1855 Sh
Fisher, Susan to Henry Golding 2-8-1876 L
Fisher, Susan to Thomas Smith 8-7-1875 (no return) L
Fisher, Willie S. to Robert D. Owen 12-1-1866 (12-2-1866) L
Fisher, Winny to Anderson Green 12-17-1881 (12-18-1881) L B
Fisher?, Lucinda A. to Hugh J. Cooper 10-5?-1853 (no return) F
Fisk, Louisa C. to Willis P. Sledge 12-3-1853 (12-6-1853) Sh
Fitch, Emma to C. K. Marshall 3-27-1856 Sh
Fitch, Frances to Benjamin Weaks 9-24-1857 Hn
Fite, E. J. to R. H. Bellew 9-17-1872 (9-18-1872) Cr
Fite, Elizabeth to George M. Wilburn 3-3-1853 (3-?-1853) G
Fite, H. E. to A. Davis 3-18-1871 (4-11-1871) Cr
Fite, Martha to Elisha Billingsly 12-14-1829 G
Fite, Mary to Alex M. Beadles 3-17-1847 G
Fite, Phebe to Lewis Levy 7-15-1835 G
Fite, Sarah J. to Zachy G. Jackson 12-16-1856 (12-18-1856) G
Fitsgerald, Willie A. to John Cowan 8-17-1867 (8-18-1867) F
Fitshugh, Jane to Miles W. Sykes 11-25-1847 (11-27-1847) F
Fitts, Jane to John Grogan 12-24-1857 Hn
Fitts, Marianna to Wm. G. (Gibson Co.) Hollowell 8-3-1870 (8-4-1870) Ma
Fitz, Caroline to Robert L. McCracken 2-2-1858 Ma
Fitz, Harriet E. to Thomas J. Jett 3-23-1846 (4-9-1846) Ma
Fitz, Minerva to William D. Gravette 12-30-1847 (12-31-1847) Ma
Fitz, Sarah A. to David Fields 12-12-1869 Hy
FitzGibbon, Judith to William Butler 11-27-1854 Sh
Fitzgerald, Adaline to Isaac B. Williams 4-27-1841 Hn
Fitzgerald, Ailsey to John Childress 1-1-1833 Sh
Fitzgerald, Ann Elizbeth to William Jarrett 12-21-1854 (12-23-1854) Ma
Fitzgerald, Anna to Bernard Gunn 6-20-1861 (6-22-1861) Sh
Fitzgerald, Arbella G. to Aquiller P. Graves 10-23-1846 Hn
Fitzgerald, Elizabeth J. to Wm. W. Freeman 7-4-1856 G
Fitzgerald, Ellen to John Leroy Lockard 5-29-1871 (5-30-1871) L
Fitzgerald, Harriet to Henry Moore 1-8-1870 G B
Fitzgerald, Laura A. to Henry Greer 5-1-1855 Hn
Fitzgerald, Margaret to Stephen jr. Jones 9-19-1832 (9-27-1832) Hr
Fitzgerald, Margarett to Wm. Bunicum 4-4-1864 Sh
Fitzgerald, Mary F. to W. W. Freeman 9-29-1859 G
Fitzgerald, Mary to Edward Murphy 2-22-1862 (2-25-1862) Sh
Fitzgerald, Mary to J. T. Kettering 12-29-1859 (1-1-1860) Sh
Fitzgerald, Mary to Joseph William Hocke 10-20-1860 (10-21-1860) Sh
Fitzgerald, Minerva to G. W. Neel 11-12-1856 (11-13-1856) Sh
Fitzgerald, Nancy to John Brimmage 8-11-1855 Cr
Fitzgerald, Sarah J. to Henry G. Philips 3-6-1860 (3-7-1860) G
Fitzgerill, Emmer to A. W. Dickerson 2-14-1872 L
Fitzgerrald, Caroline to Henry Allison 10-27-1866 G
Fitzgibbon, Catharine to Edward W. Hally 9-13-1859 Sh
Fitzhugh, Anne E. to John R. Fentress 6-15-1848 Hr
Fitzhugh, Ellen M. to Charles P. Polk 10-7-1835 Hr
Fitzhugh, Mary B. to John T. Macon 7-21-1842 Hr
Fitzhugh, Mary T. to Jestice Byrum 12-15-1852 Ma
Fitzhugh, Sophia B. to Thos. E. White 4-2-1834 (4-3-1834) Hr

Fitzhugh, Susan M. to Jarrod Harston 10-21-1871 Ma
Fitzmorris, Maria to William Delaney 2-18-1871 Ma
Fitzpatarick, Rachel to Armstead Lee 11-22-1883 L
Fitzpatrick, Ada to Milton Wall 1-2_-1882 (1-23-1882) L B
Fitzpatrick, Allen? to Allen Burks 7-7-1868 (7-8-1868) L
Fitzpatrick, B. L. to John T. Hargrove 9-29-1881 L
Fitzpatrick, Beulah to J. W. Frazier 3-1-1880 (3-2-1880) L
Fitzpatrick, Bridget to William Kelly 5-2-1859 Sh
Fitzpatrick, Catherine to Wright Alexander 9-20-1869 (9-25-1869) L B
Fitzpatrick, Charlotte to Jim Dunavant 12-9-1867 (no return) L B
Fitzpatrick, Edmonia to Daniel H. Jones 6-3-1865 (6-6-1865) L
Fitzpatrick, Eliza A. to James R. Carrigan 5-15-1860 (no return) L
Fitzpatrick, Emily to George Fitzpatrick 9-10-1868 (9-20-1868) L B
Fitzpatrick, Francis to George Nelson 2-2-1878 (no return) L
Fitzpatrick, H. to Paatrick Donahoe 9-25-1863 Sh
Fitzpatrick, Henny Ann to Ephraim Fitzpatrick 12-29-1875 L B
Fitzpatrick, Henry Ann to Ben Johnson 1-16-1883 (no return) L
Fitzpatrick, Hettie B. to Charles L. Ridley 11-6-1869 (no return) L
Fitzpatrick, J. Elizabeth to Robert Pickett 12-15-1857 (12-16-1857) L
Fitzpatrick, Jennie to Prince Glass 11-6-1879 L
Fitzpatrick, Julia to Cornelius Kelly 8-25-1860 (8-26-1860) Sh
Fitzpatrick, Lucy to George W. Davidson 10-3-1868 (10-4-1868) L
Fitzpatrick, Martha to George Washington 7-25-1876 (7-27-1876) L
Fitzpatrick, Mary Lee to Henry A. Jones 10-31-1859 (11-1-1859) L
Fitzpatrick, Mary to Lewis Campbell 2-11-1871 (2-13-1871) L
Fitzpatrick, Mary to Sam Frasier 12-22-1876 L
Fitzpatrick, Rachael to Robert Briscoe 2-18-1884 L
Fitzpatrick, Rhoda E. to Nelson Lovelace 12-29-1875 L B
Fitzpatrick, Rosella to Samuel Graves 1-7-1879 L
Fitzpatrick, Sarah to William Smith 7-6-1868 (7-10-1868) L B
Fitzpatrick, Telia to Richard Estes 12-9-1878 (12-30-1878) L
Fizer, Lizzie to Haywood Ruff 1-4-1877 (1-5-1877) Dy
Flack, F. to B. A. Carroll 3-11-1874 Dy
Flack, Mary E. to Hulon? W. Grizzard 11-20-1860 (11-21-1860) Cr
Flag, Nanie to Clay Owen 3-7-1877 Hy
Flagg, Sarah to Newton Russell 1-22-1876 Hy
Flaherty, Anne to James Wallace 10-4-1864 Sh
Flaherty, Bridget to James Hackett 5-11-1861 Sh
Flaherty, Hannora to Edward Carter 7-19-1856 (7-20-1856) Sh
Flaherty, Kate to Peter G. Bigley 9-22-1864 (9-27-1864) Sh
Flaherty, Mary to John McNally 4-21-1858 (4-22-1858) Sh
Flaherty, Mary to Joseph Broeder 7-21-1860 (7-22-1860) Sh
Flaherty, Mary to Michael Harhen 11-24-1853 Sh
Flake, Delpha A. to Henry C. Wall 10-20-1871 (10-22-1871) Cr
Flake, Elizabeth to James Olive 9-9-1865 (9-13-1866?) Cr
Flake, M. J. to L. H. Meals? 1-6-1873 Cr
Flake, Martha S. to Josiah Hall 6-28-1849 (no return) Hn
Flake, Sophia to Hoyle Holly 5-12-1835 Hr
Flanagan, Catharine to John Johnson 12-1-1858 Sh
Flanagan, Mary to Moses Simpson 10-11-1825 O
Flanakin, J. F. to A. J. Montgomery 5-7-1868 T
Flanakin, Martha to Robert E. Tycen 10-3-1857 T
Flanakin, Mary Jane to Jeremiah Manasco 7-6-1857 T
Flanakin, Nancy C. to William Griffee 1-11-1860 T
Flaniken, Sarah to Wm. Brown 7-3-1841 (10-17-1841) T
Flanikin, Mary R. to Hubbard Ferrell 5-26-1855 (5-31-1855) T
Flanikin, Mary to Michael Foley 1-6-1857 (1-7-1857) Sh
Flannagan, Sarah H. to David H. Friend 12-29-1848 (1-25-1849) L
Flannegan, Maria to T. Cash 8-8-1860 Sh
Flatt, Elizabeth E. to Samuel J. Utley 12-10-1865 Mn
Flatt, Martha J. to J. H. Utley 10-28-1862 Mn
Flatt, Nancy J. to John C. Miller 7-8-1867 O
Fleece, Jinney to Jack Scott 8-15-1868 (8-19-1868) F B
Fleedwood?, Mary to Don Fernando Sims 6-22-1836 Sh
Fleet, Nancy to Richard Anderson 3-20-1856 Hr
Fleming, A. R. to P. P. Carmack 1-23-1867 G
Fleming, Amanda F. to J. E. Smith 10-24-1874 (10-25-1874) T
Fleming, Amy to John Thomas 6-19-1873 Hy
Fleming, Ann E. to Wm. B. Douglass 8-25-1866 (8-29-1866) F
Fleming, Ann to George Russell? 12-21-1869 Hy
Fleming, Caroline M. to Francis F. Fowler 1-7-1841 Sh
Fleming, Catharine K. to John B. Low 7-19-1856 (7-20-1856) Sh
Fleming, Elizabeth A. to John C. Wright 8-20-1868 G
Fleming, Elizabeth A. to Malachi Sanderlin 6-11-1844 Sh
Fleming, Elizabeth B. to John H. Terrell 7-4-1843 We
Fleming, Elizabeth to James M. Roberts 5-21-1856 (5-24-1856) G
Fleming, Elizabeth to John McKee 9-5-1850 Sh
Fleming, Gertrude to M. Shelby 8-22-1864 Sh
Fleming, Kissire to Hiram House 8-18-1877 Hy
Fleming, Lenny to F. J. Sherrill 11-4-1868 T
Fleming, M. A. to W. H. Moten 7-16-1867 (7-18-1867) T
Fleming, M. E. to Downey Fleming 12-25-1871 T
Fleming, Maggie to Morris Henley 12-6-1876 Hy
Fleming, Margaret J. to Robert W. Campbell 9-13-1859 (9-14-1859) O
Fleming, Margaret M. to Andrew J. Phillips 10-12-1857 (10-14-1857) Sh
Fleming, Margaret to Hawood Branch 11-9-1838 Sh
Fleming, Margaret to J. C. Rhodes 1-23-1861 (1-24-1861) T

Fleming, Mariah T. to Benjamin Hayley 11-24-1846 (11-25-1846) Ma
Fleming, Martha to Henry McGee 11-21-1854 G
Fleming, Mary Ann to Artemas Shaw 4-26-1838 Sh
Fleming, Mary E. to Hillard Alphin 2-15-1867 G
Fleming, Mary T. to Henry E. Oglesby 10-13-1866 O
Fleming, Matilda C. to James Fulton 9-10-1856 (9-11-1856) Sh
Fleming, Nancy Catharin to John A. Goss 2-4-1857 T
Fleming, Nannie to Augustus Hynson 10-11-1853 Sh
Fleming, Nannie to J. B. Farley 12-7-1860 (12-18-1860) Sh
Fleming, Polly Anne to Isaac Rogers 12-26-1873 Hy
Fleming, S. J. to J. P. Ford 11-26-1867 G
Fleming, Sarah Ann to John Fullen 12-12-1844 L
Fleming, Synthia A. to O. B. Crumpley 7-10-1856 Sh
Fleming, Winona to Henry McDowell 2-8-1864 Sh
Flemings, Elizabeth to George Boyd 4-27-1867 Be
Flemming, Amanda B. to Alexander C. Maxwell ?-?-1839 Cr
Flemming, Anna P. to William C. Drury 5-26-1852 O
Flemming, Elisabeth to Daniel Gillman Rittenhouse 9-22-1864 Sh
Flemming, Elizabeth to Claiborne Gunter 8-23-1850 Sh
Flemming, Elizabeth to G. W. Grantham 6-30-1858 (7-4-1858) Hr
Flemming, Elizabeth to Louis Sanford 12-17-1865 (12-28-1865) T
Flemming, Eveline to Joseph Sanderlin 5-21-1845 Sh
Flemming, Frances F. to C. F. Slack 9-8-1866 T
Flemming, Harriet to Washington Lamb 10-27-1851 Hn
Flemming, Mattie J. to Joseph D. Ewell 1-8-1868 Ma
Flemming, Susan L. to Jno. D. Reid 1-1-1866 T
Flenn, Sarah J. to Jarman W. Davis 1-5-1858 Hr
Flenn?, Margaret to John Gorman 7-20-1849 Sh
Fleshart, Mary E. to Martin L. Fletcher 11-25-1847 Sh
Fleshart, Susan A. to Wm. C. Causey 4-10-1843 Sh
Fleshhart, Lucy L. to Thomas Maydwell 7-25-1859 (7-26-1859) Sh
Fletcher, Almira M. to James L. Robinson 11-4-1846 Cr
Fletcher, Arena to Isam Cross 1-31-1867 (1-8?-1867) F B
Fletcher, Barbary to James C. Davidson 2-2-1848 G
Fletcher, C. C. to Abner Roper 12-8-1874 O
Fletcher, Carolin to David Rogers 10-9-1845 (10-12-1845) Hr
Fletcher, Casey L. to Arch B. Barron 1-17-1859 (1-20-1859) G
Fletcher, Elizabeth N. to Benjamin F. Woods 10-6-1852 (10-12-1852) G
Fletcher, Elizabeth to Simeon Butram 2-5-1838 (2-14-1838) G
Fletcher, Elizabeth to William J. Davis 8-9-1856 (8-13-1856) G
Fletcher, Elvy to Hugh Vanhog 12-31-1840 G
Fletcher, Emily to David McClanahan 2-3-1835 Sh
Fletcher, Emma G. to F. H. Pate 5-15-1869 (5-17-1869) Cr
Fletcher, Emma to N. H. Cotton 3-12-1864 Sh
Fletcher, Frances to George Stewart 12-20-1869 F B
Fletcher, Jane A. to James D. Robinson 10-7-1850 Cr
Fletcher, Jane S.? to Frank Ferguson 5-1-1865 (5-4-1865) Dy
Fletcher, Jane to W. F. Woodard 7-24-1862 G
Fletcher, L. A. to C. T. Allen 6-7-1865 (6-8-1865) Cr
Fletcher, Lucy to Henry Hatcher 6-26-1851 G
Fletcher, M. J. to Thos. D. Ingram 11-13-1866 (11-14-1866) Cr
Fletcher, Malinda to Sidney J. Porter 3-2-1843 (3-9-1843) G
Fletcher, Margaret L. to D. F. Rice 4-3-1866 G
Fletcher, Martha A. to B. F. Allen 7-26-1848 Sh
Fletcher, Martha A. to Turner Garrett 11-26-1860 (11-27-1860) Hr
Fletcher, Martha C. to Peter Wilson 3-15-1853 (3-19-1853) G
Fletcher, Martha N.? to George W. Hall 2-14-1864 G
Fletcher, Martha to James Woodard 9-18-1862 G
Fletcher, Martha to Robert M. Jones 12-31-1861 G
Fletcher, Martha to William A. Fonville 9-7-1833 G
Fletcher, Mary Ann to George Hardy 5-18-1868 (no return) F B
Fletcher, Mary Ann to Robert W. Jones 8-9-1852 (8-10-1852) G
Fletcher, Mary E. to Hugh B. Thomas 10-19-1864 G
Fletcher, Mary J. to R. S. Rodgers 6-22-1850 G
Fletcher, Mary Josephine to James F. Carpenter 1-29-1853 (1-30-1853) O
Fletcher, Mary M. to William H. Duncan 8-20-1846 Sh
Fletcher, Matilda to John W. Foster 11-22-1841 (11-23-1841) G
Fletcher, Mollie P. to E. L. Rice 2-6-1871 (no return) Cr
Fletcher, N. A. to James W. Damren 5-12-1859 We
Fletcher, Nancy to G. W. Long 1-10-1855 G
Fletcher, Nancy to Stephen Snowden 1-25-1836 (1-?-1836) G
Fletcher, Nannie to John B. Roy 5-14-1872 (5-15-1872) O
Fletcher, Phebe to Reese R. Long 8-31-1853 G
Fletcher, Rebecca to Robert Sellers 11-16-1826 G
Fletcher, Rebecca to Robert Sellers 11-6-1826 G
Fletcher, S. J. (Mrs.) to J. W. Johnson 4-27-1870 G
Fletcher, Sarah to Matthew Hunt 1-7-1862 G
Fletcher, Susan P. to Henry M. Blanchard 12-29-1865 (12-31-1865) O
Fletcher, Virginia A. to James A. Brown 7-14-1851 Sh
Flewellen, Nancy to Henry H. Morgan 7-13-1838 Cr
Flinn, Mary to Pleasant B. Williams 2-5-1847 T
Flint, Elizabeth D. to Sterling E. Williams 2-14-1834 (2-18-1834) Hr
Flint, Sarah M. to Joel Furguson 2-6-1834 (2-11-1834) Hr
Flinter, Charity to Middleton McCortney 10-18-1833 (10-20-1833) G
Flippin, Anna to Henry Bowers 12-17-1868 (no return) F B
Flippin, Cornelia to John Henry Ferguson 2-4-1880 (no return) L
Flippin, Darcus to Ben Jones 11-3-1866 (11-4-1866) F B

Flippin, E. C. to David A. Pennington 12-7-1867 (no return) L
Flippin, F. B. to Z. C. Work 2-21-1873 (2-26-1873) L
Flippin, Frances R. to William Aston 11-18-1845 F
Flippin, Frances to Samuel Mount 9-27-1854 G
Flippin, Lizy to Julius Broom 11-26-1869 F B
Flippin, Mary to John, jr. Belew 11-1-1866 G
Flippin, Nancy Ann to Wiley P. McNair 6-21-1868 G
Flippin, Patience E. to James E. McNair 1-18-1862 G
Flippin, Patience E. to James White 10-3-1853 (10-13-1853) G
Flippin, Rody to John Bryant 1-10-1856 G
Flippin, Sarah A. to J. M. Mount 12-2-1863 G
Flippin, Sscotin to W. M. Winn 6-14-1870 G
Flippin, Tennessee to Giles Belew 7-31-1856 (8-3-1856) G
Flippin, Virginia E. to Geo. W. Farrar 11-5-1866 (11-7-1866) F
Flippins, Nancy to John Young 8-23-1863 G
Flippo, Lucinda to James M. G. Blood 6-24-1839 Sh
Flora, Charlotte to James Jones 11-29-1853 (11-30-1853) O
Florence, Ann to James West 10-25-1858 (11-7-1858) Ma
Florence, M. E. to J. L. Frasure (Frazier) 12-18-1862 Be
Florence, Malissa Jane to David S. Cuff 10-13-1868 Be
Florence, Martha A. to James Beasley 2-7-1858 Be
Flower, Casey Lee to Isaac Moore 7-12-1834 (7-17-1834) Hr
Flower, Hannah to Henry Cotheran 1-13-1866 T
Flower, Mary T. to Mike Green 12-25-1868 (12-26-1868) T
Flowers, Amanda J. to S. J. Hammond 12-14-1866 G
Flowers, Amanda L. to Elias S. Hall 8-23-1860 G
Flowers, Calista C. to W. M. Flowers 1-17-1865 G
Flowers, Celia to Jerry Smith 12-22-1884 (12-23-1885?) L
Flowers, Darancy to Major Freeman 3-21-1869 G B
Flowers, E. A. to H. C. Toombs 9-20-1869 G
Flowers, E. B. to John W. Matlock 10-18-1848 Be
Flowers, E. E. to J. M. Miller 7-29-1860 G
Flowers, E. L. to Sydney Porter 12-9-1866 G
Flowers, Edney to Martin Halliburton 10-23-1841 (10-26-1841) G
Flowers, Eliza to Isah Holland 8-27-1839 G
Flowers, Elizabeth L. to James C. Brown 1-28-1847 Be
Flowers, Elizabeth to Benjamin Trafton 12-28-1842 (12-29-1842) G
Flowers, Elizabeth to James Williams 3-24-1859 (3-27-1859) G
Flowers, Elizabeth to John W. Flowers 9-29-1835 G
Flowers, Emeline to Green Smith 12-19-1869 G B
Flowers, Eveline to David Flowers 11-8-1869 G
Flowers, Harrett to George W. Glisson 1-10-1852 G
Flowers, Harrett to James Crews 12-23-1843 (12-26-1843) G
Flowers, Jane A. to E. F. Taylor 2-11-1857 (2-12-1857) G
Flowers, Jane to Thomas H. Agee 7-28-1861 G
Flowers, Julia to William Bledsoe 12-29-1870 (12-31-1870) F B
Flowers, Ketsey to Rufus E. King 12-17-1853 (12-24-1853) G
Flowers, L. F. to John T. Gordon 12-5-1867 G
Flowers, Lillie E. to H. S. Young 10-23-1883 (10-24-1883) L
Flowers, Lizzie W. to R. Fenner Johnson 5-20-1868 (5-21-1868) T
Flowers, Louisa G. to Calvin McAuley 1-1-1845 Be
Flowers, Lucinda W. to J. A. Lain 1-9-1868 G
Flowers, Lucinda to John Johnson 10-29-1870 F B
Flowers, Lucy D. to S. D. Roach 1-18-1860 (1-19-1860) Sh
Flowers, M. A. to W. M. McDowell 12-1-1857 G
Flowers, Manurvy E. to David Rutledge 8-27-1864 (8-28-1864) O
Flowers, Mariah to John S. Russell 8-4-1846 (8-6-1846) Ma
Flowers, Martha E. to James M. Dickson 7-12-1855 G
Flowers, Martha M. to Marshall B. Glisson 11-26-1855 (11-29-1855) G
Flowers, Martha M. to Richard Turner 7-25-1859 (7-31-1859) G
Flowers, Martha to Alexander McAnelly 2-10-1846 G
Flowers, Martha to Hillory W. Moseley 1-20-1849 (1-24-1849) G
Flowers, Martha to James Travis 3-28-1863 Hy
Flowers, Mary A. E. to J. P. Armstrong 6-6-1865 G
Flowers, Mary A. to Burnell Flowers 1-21-1860 (1-22-1860) G
Flowers, Mary C. to B. A. Ring 7-19-1860 G
Flowers, Mary Eliza to Claudius B. Hall 4-11-1859 (4-13-1859) Ma
Flowers, Mary to C. N. Wright 11-27-1856 G
Flowers, Mary to Modnaca Wilks 4-7-1845 (4-10-1845) G
Flowers, Mary to Nathaniel Creel 8-7-1850 (8-8-1850) G
Flowers, Mary to Riley Hicks 4-9-1871 Hy
Flowers, Mary to Thomas Corley 12-27-1841 (1-4-1842) G
Flowers, Mary to Thomas Ray 10-9-1861 (10-12-1861) Dy
Flowers, Mattie to Harrison Jones 5-2-1884 (5-5-1884) L
Flowers, Nancy to William T. Moseley 7-1-1852 (7-6-1852) G
Flowers, Phebe Ann to Reuben Berry 8-14-1868 (8-29-1868) L *
Flowers, Rachel M. to W. R. Reasoner 3-12-1853 Sh
Flowers, Rebecca to Abraham Glisson 7-23-1863 G
Flowers, S. A. M. N. C. to William Terry 2-8-1866 G
Flowers, S. A. to D. F. Haliburton 2-25-1865 G
Flowers, S. A. to E. Whitley 1-27-1870 G
Flowers, S. J. to D. H. Cuson 10-15-1867 G
Flowers, Sallie A. to William N. J. Fields 3-4-1852 Sh
Flowers, Sarah A. to Benassa King 10-12-1847 G
Flowers, Sarah E. to Nathan Miller 11-23-1868 G B
Flowers, Sarah J. to G. B. Mosely 3-21-1841 (3-28-1841) G
Flowers, Sarah J. to J. S. Driskill 3-14-1859 We

Flowers, Sarah Jane to R. A. jr. Parker 5-24-1858 (5-25-1858) T
Flowers, Sarah to Thos. Aclin 3-31-1869 Hy
Flowers, Sarah to W. M. Thetford 10-29-1856 G
Flowers, Sophia C. to Geo. Washington Cook 12-21-1851 (not executed) T
Flowers, Sophia Cotten to William Dunham Fisher 1-19-1852 (1-20-1852) T
Flowers, Susan (Mrs.) to Isaac Spencer 9-21-1841 (9-26-1841) G
Flowers, Tempy to Robert Howell 4-21-1841 (5-13-1841) G
Floyd, Analiza to John Stanley Cherry 5-13-1858 Be
Floyd, Elizabeth A. to Zachariah Bryant 1-8-1840 (1-9-1840) G
Floyd, Elizabeth to James Watson 12-6-1836 Hr
Floyd, Elizabeth to William Clayton 12-28-1836 Hr
Floyd, Lucy J. to Reddick Arnold 10-14-1839 (10-24-1839) F
Floyd, Mary E. to Wm. D. K. Miller 1-22-1859 Sh
Floyd, Mary Jane to J. D. Ferrill 7-3-1866 (7-5-1866) Dy
Floyd, Tabitha A. to Wm. M. Farned 11-12-1857 (11-15-1857) Hr
Floyed, Margarett to Thomas Bounds 12-7-1841 (12-9-1841) F
Floyed, Nancy Emily to Wm. R. Brinkley 2-1-1841 (no return) F
Flurnoy, Gracey to Saml. Jones 12-28-1870 F B
Fly, Almira E. to William H. Higden 6-21-1858 (6-22-1858) Ma
Fly, Ann to Dell Gilliam 1-1-1874 Dy
Fly, Elizabeth A. to Wm. J. Kirk 11-2-1854 Cr
Fly, Fanny P. to Salmon Sedwick 1-22-1827 G
Fly, Frances M. to Tarlton H. Graves 1-27-1844 (1-30-1844) Ma
Fly, M. T. to W. J. D. Leigh 11-25-1868 G
Fly, Martha T. to Nicholas C. Stone 10-18-1834 (10-26-1834) G
Fly, Mary A. to Calvin C. Clements (Gibson Co) 11-10-1849 (11-13-1849) Ma
Fly, Mary Ida to W. A. Williams 10-2-1867 G
Fly, Mary to Bird B. Stone 5-21-1834 (5-27-1834) G
Fly, Mollie D. to R. L. (Dr.) Bigham 5-22-1867 (5-23-1867) Cr
Fly, Rebecca to John A. Williamson 6-30-1857 (7-1-1857) Ma
Fly, Rebeccah to David Gill 10-12-1840 Ma
Fly, Sarah E. to William Hall 12-31-1838 Ma
Fly, Sarah J. to Thomas J. Senter 11-1-1848 (11-2-1848) Ma
Fly, Sarah to Zachariah H. Roberts 8-2-1830 Ma
Fly, Virginia Ann to L. G. B Seat 1-5-1854 Ma
Fly, Winiford to Minor C. Cole 9-15-1837 G
Flynn, Alice to Thomas O. Donnell 6-15-1856 Sh
Flynn, Catharine to John Williams 5-23-1861 Sh
Flynn, Elizabeth Jane to Joseph G. Walton 10-2-1851 Hr
Flynn, Margaret to Barney McDearmon 4-11-1857 (no return) Hn
Flynn, Margaret to John Gillooly? 4-13-1857 Hn
Flynt, Caroline C. to Moses McKnight 6-12-1852 Hr
Flynt, Mary P. to Robert T. Dodson 12-31-1849 (1-8-1850) Hr
Foard, Mary to M. (Rev.) Whittle 1-3-1863 (no return) Dy
Fodge, Elizabeth to William Powers 1-28-1846 Hn
Fodge, Jane to William Marrs 10-23-1858 Hn
Fodge, Jemima to A. L. Banks 8-16-1864 (no return) Hn
Fodge, Mary Jane to B. F. Dinkuns 1-1-1863 Hn
Fodge, Mary to David M. Michael 12-31-1854 Hn
Fodge, Sarah to Pearson Miller 1-27-1846 (no return) Hn
Fogarty, Maggie to Ed Stack 11-26-1861 Sh
Fogerty, Catharine to John McGrath 8-10-1853 Sh
Fogerty, Maria to Paul Green 4-13-1850 Sh
Fogg, Archelius Ann (Mrs.) to Samuel Neely 6-29-1858 (7-1-1858) Ma
Fogg, Celia Ann to Samuel Boone 8-22-1869 G B
Fogg, Christina to W. F. Dawson 11-8-1869 G
Fogg, L. Annie to Mark Hodges 2-5-1867 Ma
Fogg, Mary L. to Samuel D. Barnett 5-25-1857 Ma
Foggerson, S. A. to J. H. Parnell 9-8-1860 (9-11-1860) Dy
Folay, Mary to Patrick Whelen 7-30-1859 We
Foley, Abby to Francis Johnson 4-29-1843 Sh
Foley, Ann to Patrick Kinseule 2-21-1862 (2-23-1862) Sh
Foley, Bridget to Patrick Burke 3-6-1843 Sh
Foley, Ellen to Patrick Baker 10-31-1864 Sh
Foley, Mary (Mrs.) to Charles Woolner 2-10-1863 Sh
Foley, Mary (Mrs.) to Eugene Sullivan 1-25-1864 (1-26-1864) Sh
Foley, Mary A. to John Travis 7-5-1862 (7-6-1862) Sh
Foley, Mary to C. A. Foley 4-4-1855 Sh
Foley, Mary to Daniel Brotly? 2-28-1843 Sh
Foley, Mollie to Samuel Winegardner 2-17-1863 Sh
Folks, Elizabeth Frances to John J. Gallege 12-23-1868 G
Folks, L. E. C. to J. F. Graddy 8-9-1858 (8-12-1858) G
Folks, Mary to Wm. G. Allen 9-29-1849 Cr
Follis, Mary J. to W. C. Fitzhugh 9-29-1869 (9-30-1869) Dy
Follis, Rebecca M. to William J. Oliver 3-12-1853 Ma
Follis, Salina E. to William C. Young 10-2-1857 (10-5-1857) Ma
Folmer, Anna to Augustus Kesfel (Kessel?) 10-1-1855 Sh
Foltz, Nancy E. to Dennis M. Lyles 7-21-1840 Hr
Folwell, Mary to Needham Horton 5-1-1840 (5-6-1840) F
Folwell, Mary to Wily Cargil 7-7-1851 (no return) F
Fonner, Mary to Vincent Garrett 2-6-1841 Ma
Fonshee, Mary H. to James Black 9-26-1867 (no return) Dy
Fonvill, Henrietta M. to J. L. McGlothin 2-26-1856 We
Fonville, Ann to G. W. Terrell 4-11-1867 G
Fonville, Julian to John Sellers 7-12-1828 (7-17-1828) G
Fonville, Martha P. to W. W. Wiggs 10-27-1869 G
Fonville, Mary A. to J. T. Tansill 11-5-1858 We

Fonville, Merica to Dickson Brown 7-30-1841 (8-2-1841) O
Fonville, Nancy to W. H. Hearn 10-24-1869 G
Foot, Susan to L. H. Bradford 2-11-1856 (2-12-1856) Hr
Footts, Alsey to Brown Cubbins 5-16-1869 G B
Forbbs, Carolin M. to Wm. H. Evans 4-28-1846 F
Forbert, Jinny to Michael Dowling 9-28-1861 (9-29-1861) Sh
Forbes, Lucy to W. B. Simons 4-27-1872 (4-28-1872) Dy
Forbess, Elizabeth to James T. Bailey 8-5-1856 (8-6-1856) Hr
Forbess, Elizabeth to James W. Ballard 8-23-1838 Hn
Forbess, Harriet to Green Palmer 8-13-1851 Cr
Forbess, Mahala to Isaac J. Lucade 12-16-1843 (12-20-1843) Hr
Forbess, Margaret C. to John C. George 12-19-1870 (12-22-1870) T
Forbess, Mary E. to Wm. Henry Joyner 2-27-1866 (3-1-1866) T
Forbess, Morgan E. to Wm. H. Smith 12-29-1857 Cr
Forbess, Sarah Ann to Washington Joyner 7-21-1868 (7-23-1868) T
Forbiss, Martha E. to Stephen H. Bibb 1-25-1856 (1-26-1856) L
Forbs, Mary Isabella to Sterling Harris 3-25-1851 (no return) F
Forbs, Mary to Washington Thompson 12-5-1839 (12-18-1839) F
Forbus, A. H. to H. C. Muse 11-2-1854 We
Forbus, Margaret to Sterling Harris Pinner 12-22-1845 T
Forbush, Annie to Holly Whitesides 12-19-1883 (12-20-1883) L
Forbuss, Martha M. to Eli Harriss 2-25-1846 (2-26-1846) Hr
Force, Amanda to Chas. O. Force 11-24-1884 (11-26-1884) L
Ford, A. M. to W. W. Joyce 1-3-1849 Sh
Ford, Ann (Mrs.) to Henry Gevert 8-16-1864 Sh
Ford, Ann Henry to Ambrose E. Green 10-3-1868 (10-8-1868) F
Ford, Ann Rebecca to Bolivar C. Wesson 11-22-1848 (11-23-1848) T
Ford, Arta M. to J. B. Cassels 2-18-1858 G
Ford, Bettie to D. W. Bynum 1-15-1857 Sh
Ford, Catharine to James McCloskey 5-20-1861 Sh
Ford, Eliza to Andrew Phillips 2-27-1870 G
Ford, Eliza to George Nettles 8-21-1872 Hy
Ford, Elizabeth J. to W. P. Ross 7-4-1852 We
Ford, Elizabeth to Donald Gawley 9-8-1860 (9-9-1860) Sh
Ford, Elizabeth to J. J. Knott 10-29-1857 G
Ford, Elizabeth to James R. Brannon 10-5-1859 Hn
Ford, Elizabeth to Patrick Fallon 4-26-1843 Sh
Ford, Elizabeth to Robert A. Rose 7-19-1869 (7-20-1869) T
Ford, Emily to Thoas Thompson 1-24-1849 T
Ford, Emmer to Thomas Dickerson 1-8-1873 T
Ford, Frances K.(R?) to J. B. Hester 3-19-1835 Sh
Ford, Francisco C.(K.) to Thomas S. Tate 3-19-1835 Sh
Ford, Harriett to Saml. F. Halloway 11-9-1847 F
Ford, J. A. to C. M. Harrison 9-9-1866 G
Ford, J. A. to P. M. Reeves 8-13-1856 G
Ford, J. M. to C. F. Aslin 11-30-1865 G
Ford, Julia F. to John S. Wells 7-15-1862 (7-16-1862) L
Ford, Louisa to Hiram Cox 3-16-1860 Cr
Ford, Lucinda to Henry Calvin 12-29-1850 Be
Ford, Lucy to A. B. Salisbury 10-9-1850 (10-18-1850) L
Ford, M. E. to J. J. Kelso 10-18-1870 (no return) Hy
Ford, M. V. to E. W. Sales 6-5-1865 Be
Ford, Marth to Z. A. Flanigan 2-13-1867 (2-15-1867) T
Ford, Martha E. to John H. Betts 6-9-1859 G
Ford, Martha J. to Ezekiel Fitzhugh 1-20-1852 (1-21-1852) Ma
Ford, Martha to Benjamin F. Arnold 3-28-1853 (3-29-1853) G
Ford, Martha to Robert Bradford 9-9-1857 Sh
Ford, Mary Ann to Isham I. Parker 12-6-1849 G
Ford, Mary Ann to Washington Sturdivant 7-21-1852 (7-23-1852) Ma
Ford, Mary E. to Rowan Bridges 10-11-1866 Ma
Ford, Mary J. to William Willoughby 11-25-1861 (no return) Hn
Ford, Mary Jane to Andrew Parker 9-4-1868 (no return) L
Ford, Mary to Joseph Bradberry 9-10-1852 We
Ford, Mary to Martin Hubner? 7-3-1841 Hn
Ford, Mary to Saml. L. Raines 1-15-1856 Sh
Ford, Meed to T. P. Simmons 2-4-1865 Be
Ford, Nancy A. to Robert C. Deeds 9-17-1850 Hn
Ford, Nancy to Patrick Hayes 3-10-1841 Sh
Ford, Nancy to Spencer Porter 1-17-1866 (1-20-1866) F B
Ford, Nelley to Due Nailing 8-19-1876 O
Ford, Pelina N. to J. W. Harrison 6-26-1857 (6-28-1857) G
Ford, Rebecca to Charles W. Almon 5-23-1859 (5-26-1859) L
Ford, Rebecca to James Morris 1-1-1829 (1-7-1829) G
Ford, Rebecca to James Morris 1-15-1830 G
Ford, S(arah) A(melia) to R. E. Stanfield 1-2-1877 (no return) L
Ford, Sallie to Isaac McNary 5-21-1868 (5-27-1868) F B
Ford, Sarah A. to J. W. Sanders 1-8-1867 G
Ford, Sarah S. to James D. Nixon 8-19-1847 Hn
Foreham, M. A. to J. H. Mullinicks 8-27-1840 Be
Forehand, Fendee to R. M> Hawley 8-4-1856 Be
Foreman, Sallie to Jessee Hunt 12-29-1866 T
Foreman, Susan L. to R. T. Chandler 1-21-1861 (1-23-1861) Hr
Foren, Lucretia to Stephen Wallace 1-27-1853 (1-28-1853) G
Foren, Martha C. to William Yarbrah 8-8-1869 G
Foren, Mary A. to James F. Ballard 3-14-1859 (3-24-1859) Sh
Foren, Mary to Cornelias Woolard 7-21-1857 G
Foreshee, Eliza I. to W. A. McClain 11-7-1866 O

Forest, Abby to Jerry Crawford 2-2-1867 F B
Forest, Delita F. to Hircutus W. Lemons 7-1-1858 Cr
Forest, E. S. S. to Samuel H. Dunlap 11-30-1857 Cr
Forest, Elizabeth to Henderson Willis 12-27-1855 Be
Forest, Elizabeth to Henderson Willis 12-27-1855 Be CC
Forest, K. J. to E. M. Vickers 11-7-1861 Mn
Forest, Kizear to Suger D. Pierce 8-21-1848 Cr
Forest, Lucy Jane to Milton Wakeland 10-29-1840 Hn
Forest, Luzia D. to Thos. J. Acres 7-25-1854 Cr
Forest, Mariah J. to David E. McSwain 9-13-1853 Cr
Forest, Mary A. E. to William W. Poyner 10-22-1850 Hn
Forest, Mary M. to William P. Miller 10-5-1858 (10-6-1858) T
Forest, Permilee S. to James D. Allen 9-12-1852 Cr
Forest, Sarah A. to T. F. Starnes 2-29-1861 Be
Forest, Sarah J. to L. A. Pierce 6-16-1858 Be
Forest, Sarah Jane to Leonard A. Claborn 3-7-1854 Be
Forest, Sissie to Henry Hickman 12-4-1868 (no return) Hy
Forest?, Martha to C. W. Hunter 7-24-1845 Hn
Forester, Cinthia to W. A. Sanders 3-14-1879 (no return) Dy
Forester, Elizabeth to W. A. Fletcher 9-4-1866 G
Forester, Lucy A. to W. N. Williams 3-19-1855 (no return) We
Forester, Mary Jane to Lewis Allen 1-13-1840 Sh
Forester, Mary to Josiah Baker 12-2-1834 G
Forester, Nancy (Mary) to Thompson C. Clarke 8-20-1841 Sh
Forgey, Elizabeth to William H. Holmes 3-26-1846 Sh
Forgey, Martha J. to W. B. Jones 5-11-1861 (5-15-1861) Sh
Forister, Caroline to David Forester 3-15-1840 Be
Forkam, Elizabeth to John Petty 3-20-1855 Sh
Forks, Mary to Patrick Maloney 6-23-1866 Hy
Forluss, Mary J. to Francis M. Laycock 7-28-1860 (7-29-1860) Cr
Forran, Harriet to Jerry Traynor 4-23-1836 (4-29-1836) G
Forrest, Amanda to Monroe Lane 4-8-1869 Cr
Forrest, Becky to Phil Lewis 10-15-1875 Hy
Forrest, Betha J. to J. H. Musgrave 11-24-1875 (no return) Hy
Forrest, Eliza J. to Richard Lewis 1-28-1868 (1-30-1868) Cr
Forrest, Georgeanna to Lewis Maxey 5-28-1868 Hy
Forrest, Jane E. to G. W. Tel 1-20-1863 (1-22-1863) Sh
Forrest, Julia Ann to John T. Iler 12-26-1852 Sh
Forrest, Kiziah J. to John Reynolds 9-19-1865 Mn
Forrest, Lizzie to Peter Shaw 2-15-1877 Hy
Forrest, Martha E. to Joseph Dane 9-17-1868 (no return) Cr
Forrest, Martha to Burges Aker 2-6-1867 (no return) Hy
Forrest, Mary Elizabeth to R. R. Moore 12-5-1874 (12-8-1874) T
Forrest, Mary to Leroy M. Blake 11-19-1844 We
Forrest, Rhody to W. Clark 11-23-1872 Hy
Forrest, Violet to George Nash 12-6-1867 (no return) Hy
Forrest, Zilpha to Hector Cameron 12-5-1878 Hy
Forrester, Anne to Samuel Baker 5-25-1828 (5-29-1828) G
Forrester, Elizabeth to Michael Carney 12-21-1854 (12-22-1854) O
Forrester, Rebecka to Joseph Fletcher 9-8-1829 (9-10-1829) G
Forsheath, Margaret to Elam Rogers 10-23-1844 (10-25-1844) Hr
Forshee, Nancy J. to R. P. Wade 11-12-1868 Dy
Forsheer, M. L. V. to Lewis K. Kee 8-6-1873 (8-7-1873) Cr
Forsyth, B. C. to J. M. Bissel 3-5-1862 Mn
Forsyth, Elizabeth to David Harrison 10-1-1840 (10-4-1840) Hr
Forsyth, Jane to Jonathan Hagans Strain 1-26-1854 T
Forsyth, L. A. to G. W. Casey 1-29-1871 Hy
Forsythe, A. J. to J. L. Devinney 1-2-1878 (1-3-1878) L
Forsythe, Elizabeth to William Armstrong 2-21-1850 Ma
Forsythe, I. M. to James A. Hughes 12-21-1862 Mn
Forsythe, Josie to W. A. Dunavant 12-7-1883 (12-10-1883) L
Forsythe, Lucretia to Miles Welch 9-24-1859 (9-25-1859) G
Forsythe, Mary E. to Francis J. Sherrill 11-15-1871 T
Forsythe, Mary I. to N. M. Hopper 9-22-1859 (9-23-1859) G
Forsythe, Milley to Wm. R. Harrison 4-29-1840 (4-30-1840) Hr
Forsythe, Sarah Ann to John Riley 4-2-1855 (4-5-1855) L
Forsythe, Sarah to John Hurley 1-4-1869 T
Fort, Eliza to Wm. Carpenter 6-19-1869 (6-20-1869) F B
Fort, Elizabeth to John Mott 3-7-1827 Hr
Fort, Frances E. to Wm. W. Wair 2-15-1841 (2-17-1841) Hr
Fort, Priscilla to Alfred Castellaw 7-8-1833 Hr
Fort, Sarah to Thos. L. Collins 6-15-1847 Hr
Forte, Sylvester to B. T. Richards 10-3-1836 (10-4-1836) Hr
Fortner, Annie to J. J. Haynes 12-13-1882 L
Fortner, Caroline to Will H. Cole 9-16-1846 (9-20-1846) Hr
Fortner, E. E. to J. T. Hasting 11-12-1874 L
Fortner, Elizabeth (Mrs.) to William A. Lewis 3-19-1870 (3-24-1870) Ma
Fortner, Elizabeth to Angish McEver 7-14-1860 (no return) Hy
Fortner, Martha L. to Lewis Grantham 10-11-1853 Hr
Fortner, Nancy Eleanor to Lovod Stevens 1-20-1858 T
Fortner, S. Evolin to Isaac W. Owen 3-24-1862 T
Fortner, Susan A. to Simpson Hastings 8-21-1844 (8-?-1844) T
Fortner, Susan F. to A. H. Mitchell 12-2-1872 (12-5-1872) L
Fortner, Susan to Wm. Tackett 3-1-1859 (3-2-1859) L
Fortson, Julia A. E. to James Smart 10-15-1861 Sh
Fortum, Mary E. to R. B. Nail 3-19-1868 Hy
Fortune, Amanda S. to James E. Bryant 9-1-1858 (9-2-1858) Hr

Fortune, Amanda to Patrick Ryan 12-25-1862 Mn
Fortune, Edmonia to A. L. Haskins 12-23-1869 Hy
Fortune, Jinnetta A. to William R. Jacobs 12-10-1855 (12-13-1855) Hr
Fortune, Laura V. to Samuel McClanahan 12-28-1858 (12-29-1858) Ma
Fortune, Martha Ann to Bailey Macon 11-25-1846 (11-26-1846) Hr
Fortune, Mary Jane to James M. Townes 4-26-1870 (4-27-1870) Ma
Fortune, Mary to Henry Jacobs 10-11-1854 (10-12-1854) Hr
Fortune, Nancy C. to John Cheshier 11-28-1849 (11-29-1849) Hr
Fortune, Sarah Marcella to Andrew J. Jones 10-5-1868 (10-6-1868) Ma
Forwerk, Mary to William Newman 1-3-1856 (1-5-1856) Sh
Foshee, Lenora to Jesse Worrel 1-1-1870 (1-2-1870) Cr
Foss, Emily to A. J. Hutcheson 1-8-1868 (1-9-1868) L
Fossett, Annie to Manuel Walker 1-6-1883 (1-8-1883) L
Fossett, Bettie to Wm. H. Long 12-25-1869 (12-20?-1869) Ma
Fossett, Mary Jane to John N. Carnell 12-18-1871 (12-20-1871) L
Foster, A. E. to Benjamin Fletcher 8-21-1863 Hn
Foster, A. M. to W. H. Yates 6-27-1860 Dy
Foster, Aletha to William Shell 2-25-1839 Hn
Foster, Almeda to Allen Morris 6-12-1868 G
Foster, Alsey to John P. Mason 12-26-1833 O
Foster, Amanda to Zadoc Casey 3-6-1841 Hr
Foster, America to Willis Clinton Thomason 9-3-1867 (no return) Hn
Foster, Ann to W. N. Dinwiddie 12-5-1854 Hn
Foster, Annie C. to J. F. Watt 11-9-1869 G
Foster, Arabella W. to James A. Riley 11-18-1866 Hn
Foster, Artilia Ann to James Jackson 6-22-1853 Cr
Foster, C. A. to D. L. Gray 1-27-1846 Sh
Foster, C. M. to E. P. Eastham 11-28-1860 Sh
Foster, Caroline to A. T. Buck 1-13-1848 Hn
Foster, Drusilla T. to T. B. Bronaugh 1-11-1883 L
Foster, E. A. to P. P. McAdoo 11-25-1865 Hn
Foster, Eliza Ann to Samuel B. Miller 2-19-1842 (2-27-1842) T
Foster, Eliza J. to C. R. Parham 12-23-1844 We
Foster, Eliza to J. N. Hughes 6-27-1853 Hn
Foster, Elizabeth H. to Martin R. Gilbert 12-1-1842 Hn
Foster, Elizabeth to James Webb 8-4-1865 (8-6-1865) Cr
Foster, Elizabeth to Jesse H. Irwin 7-20-1861 (7-22-1861) Hr
Foster, Elizabeth to Marion Lewellyn 3-4-1860 Sh
Foster, Ella to Wade Watkins 8-21-1873 Hy
Foster, Emma to H. H. Lovelace 5-1-1861 We
Foster, Fannie to Gantry Parr 10-16-1879 Dy
Foster, Francis to George Bond 5-3-1877 Hy
Foster, Hanna to Anthony Clement 12-30-1869 G B
Foster, Hannah Jane to Henry Clay VanLien 6-15-1848 (6-24-1848) T
Foster, Jane (Mrs.) to J. T. Dalton 4-27-1872 (4-28-1872) Dy
Foster, Jane to John Clayton 1-10-1874 (1-11-1874) Dy
Foster, Jane to Wm. Needham 3-23-1867 O
Foster, Katherine to William H. Daniel, jr. 1-31-1866 Hn
Foster, Louisa to J. K. Burnett 6-11-1867 O
Foster, Louisa to Jerry Maggard 7-14-1869 (no return) Dy
Foster, Louisa to John McKee 12-22-1856 (12-23-1856) Hr
Foster, Louiza to William H. Jackson 12-26-1855 (12-27-1855) G
Foster, Lucinda to Jo Fowlkes 9-22-1877 (9-25-1877) Dy
Foster, Lucy to Charles Ferrill 12-24-1873 (12-25-1873) Dy
Foster, Lucy to James Madison 11-13-1871 (no return) Cr B
Foster, M. C. to Simon Q. Murphy 9-21-1859 We
Foster, M. F. to J. T. Miller 12-23-1880 L
Foster, M. J. to Thomas Armstrong 5-9-1868 (5-10-1868) O
Foster, Malinda to Robt. Atkinson 3-1-1852 (3-2-1852) Sh
Foster, Margaret E. to Parson Brown 3-10-1869 G B
Foster, Margaret to Nelson McCauley 4-23-1874 T
Foster, Martha A. to A. W. Henry 11-22-1865 Dy
Foster, Martha J. to G. W. Johnston 10-9-1845 Hn
Foster, Martha to Henry Webb 10-17-1867 Cr
Foster, Mary A. to Robert M. Strain 7-13-1842 (7-14-1842) G
Foster, Mary Ann to Claiborn Elder 4-29-1840 (5-3-1840) O
Foster, Mary F. to James Reavis 4-10-1863 O
Foster, Mary to James Hancock 12-23-1862 (12-25-1862) O
Foster, Matilda to Henry Clay 10-8-1870 F B
Foster, Mattie to I. N. Moseley 8-15-1867 G
Foster, Mattie to L. B. Watkins 12-2-1878 (12-4-1878) L
Foster, Molly to Arch Sandige 6-19-1875 Hy
Foster, N. M. to R. F. Webb 8-15-1871 (no return) Cr
Foster, Nancy to Sterling Haley 1-27-1851 (1-30-1851) G
Foster, P. E. to George D. Webb 12-22-1885 L
Foster, Patty to William Hagler 3-29-1863 Hn
Foster, Permelia to Wm. Hunley Townsend 2-10-1855 (2-14-1855) T
Foster, Polly Ann to J. J. Hix 4-25-1863 (4-26-1863) O
Foster, Prudence to Enoch Ross(Rass-Russ) 1-14-1829 Hr
Foster, Prudence to Robert Nabers 11-21-1829 Hr
Foster, Reubicca to John F. Williford 12-27-1868 G
Foster, S. F. to H. H. Scruggs 7-15-1867 (7-18-1870) Dy
Foster, Sarah A. to John B. Parks 2-2-1856 (2-5-1856) Hr
Foster, Sarah C. to B. F. Jones 1-25-1858 G
Foster, Sarah F. to Richard Griffie 2-13-1860 (no return) We
Foster, Sarah F. to S. J. Adams 9-20-1865 G

Foster, Sarah Jane to Ewell C. Hutchinson 7-28-1855 O
Foster, Sarah L. to Henry J. Meacham 12-10-1883 (12-11-1883) L
Foster, Sarah L. to John Booker Payne 12-2-1863 (12-3-1863) T
Foster, Sarah to Albert Spenser 7-24-1869 Hy
Foster, Sarah to Henery W. Turner 1-29-1846 Cr
Foster, Sarah to S. R. Davis 1-28-1862 (1-29-1862) Hr
Foster, Sarrah F. to S. J. Odom 9-20-1865 G
Foster, Savannah to Thomas Morrow 12-16-1865 Hn
Foster, Sindey to Isham Sitton 4-24-1874 T
Foster, Sindy to Isham Litten 4-23-1874 (4-25-1874) T
Foster, Susan J. to John C. Snell 11-26-1868 G
Foster, Susan to Hansford Hank 1-7-1829 (1-11-1829) Hr
Foster, Susan to Jo Moore 1-21-1880 (1-22-1880) Dy
Foster, Susannah to Thos. A. Turner 3-13-1845 Cr
Foster, T. P. to H. P. Snowde 3-31-1866 G
Foster, Virginia to Howard Owen 1-14-1857 Sh
Foster, Winsey to Thomas Morrow 9-16-1838 (9-22-1838) Hr
Fouch, Elizabeth E. to Lazarus Sires 10-13-1857 (10-14-1857) G
Foulks, M. S. to Edward Cullem 9-22-1871 (9-23-1871) L
Fourshee, Virginia to Matthew J. Mitchell 1-11-1857 We
Foushee, Mary A. to S. Morris 3-6-1860 We
Foushee, S. M. to J. F. Batts 11-28-1877 O
Foust, Ann to Jackson Smith 12-14-1872 (12-26-1872) Dy
Foust, B. P. to W. J. Morphis 5-10-1865 Hn
Foust, Barbary to Isham Higgs 1-9-1840 (no return) F
Foust, Eliza B. to Calvin Hogg 1-3-1860 We
Foust, Elizabeth Jane to William Bogsen? 2-20-1846 (2-22-1846) F
Foust, Elva to Ben Graham 11-28-1878 Dy
Foust, Malinda to Isaac Maddrey 12-21-1868 (no return) Dy
Foust, Mary A. to Newton J. Barham 1-27-1859 Hn
Foust, Mary E. to W. W. Womble 12-22-1856 We
Foust, Mary F. to James L. Pettyjohn 10-31-1855 (no return) Hn
Foust, Melvina to Berry Simmons 4-8-1875 Dy
Foust, Milly to Matt Bradshaw 8-14-1872 Dy
Foust, Rebecca A. to Calvin Baxter 12-25-1866 (12-26-1866) Dy
Foust, Rebecca C. to L. D. Smith 3-14-1840 (3-16-1840) O
Foust, Ruth to Matt Bradshaw 12-27-1869 (no return) Dy
Foust, Sarah A. to J. R. Crosswell 10-24-1866 G
Foust, Sarah A. to James Powell 1-2-1852 (no return) Hn
Foutch, Elizabeth A. to James M. McMinn 1-30-1870 G
Foutch, Sarah Jane to William H. West 4-23-1851 (5-1-1851) G
Fowell, Louiza M. to John S. Medlock 12-31-1854 (no return) Hn
Fowler (Fonter?), Sarah C. to John a. McKennon 3-29-1871 (3-30-1871) L
Fowler, A. M. to T. R. Smith 6-15-1856 We
Fowler, Amanda Susan to George W. Holland 1-31-1858 Be
Fowler, Amanda to A. G. Settle 8-3-1869 G
Fowler, Ann H. to Peyton Powell 6-23-1835 Hr
Fowler, Catharin to James Travis 11-23-1846 (no return) We
Fowler, Catharine to Ansel W. Pierce 12-29-1853 Be
Fowler, Dicey M. to Stephen Alley 3-9-1845 Sh
Fowler, Drucilla to William Crain 5-24-1830 Hr
Fowler, Edna F. to Benjamin Molin 5-3-1858 We
Fowler, Eliza Jane to B. F. Newton 5-7-1857 We
Fowler, Eliza M. to Elijah Coffey 7-15-1834 Sh
Fowler, Elizabeth A. to Alexander Brady 4-18-1852 Hn
Fowler, Elizabeth P. to John T. Holland 8-29-1865 Be
Fowler, Elizabeth to James W. Yargon 1-8-1842 Cr
Fowler, Elizabeth to Redding Cooper 10-31-1838 Hn
Fowler, Ellender to Joseph Mathis 3-22-1841 (3-30-1841) G
Fowler, Hannah to John E. Smith 1-23-1851 (1-28-1851) G
Fowler, Jacky N. to W. R. Chappel 4-1-1855 (no return) We
Fowler, Jane to James Crook 2-15-1883 L
Fowler, Jane to Thomas Marchbanks no date (with 1861) Be
Fowler, Jane to Thos. Marchbanks 12-5-1860 Be
Fowler, Laura Ann to John Hayley 11-9-1842 Ma
Fowler, M. to Wilkerson Carter 3-12-1860 O
Fowler, Malinda C. to J. W. Cooper 12-19-1846 We
Fowler, Martha Ann M. to Wm. B. Matthis 6-3-1834 Hr
Fowler, Martha E. to H. B. Bridges 9-7-1854 Be
Fowler, Martha to F. M. C. Roberts 4-6-1847 Hn
Fowler, Martha to Moses B. Wallingsford 1-15-1835 (1-20-1835) G
Fowler, Mary A. to Henry W. Brown 7-4-1831 (7-7-1831) Hr
Fowler, Mary A. to Robert Stone 7-8-1846 (7-13-1846) F
Fowler, Mary A. to W. R. Williams 6-19-1850 We
Fowler, Mary Ann to William Walker 8-3-1833 (8-?-1833) Hr
Fowler, Mary J. to James M. Dunn 5-5-1848 Hn
Fowler, Mary to G. B. McAfee 3-24-1860 Hr
Fowler, Mary to Thomas Watt 12-21-1842 G
Fowler, Matilda to John Simmons 2-28-1843 (3-1-1843) F
Fowler, Mattie H. to J. H. Coleman 6-24-1870 (6-28-1870) Cr
Fowler, Milly B. to Wilson P. Harpole 2-23-1850 (2-26-1850) G
Fowler, Nancy to John B. Wallingford 9-16-1833 G
Fowler, S. A. to Thos. L. Taylor 5-28-1873 (no return) Cr
Fowler, Sallie to Cullin Brasfield 5-2-1873 (5-6-1873) O
Fowler, Sarah F. to Pleasant G. Turner 11-29-1854 (12-10-1854) Hr
Fowler, Sarah to G. W. Midkiff 9-7-1856 We
Fowler, Sarah to William Cole 11-13-1854 (11-16-1854) G

Fowler, Unity P. to Alexander Haven 1-6-1840 Sh
Fowler, Winney to John Oakes 2-10-1832 G
Fowler?, Elizabeth to Thomas H. Robertson 12-17-1857 Hn
Fowlkes, Agg to Jo Jones 5-8-1869 (no return) Dy
Fowlkes, Alice to Boss Ledsinger 4-26-1876 (4-27-1876) Dy B
Fowlkes, Amanda to Walter Scott 1-6-1866 (no return) Dy
Fowlkes, Amelia to Lot Brown 1-24-1879 (1-26-1879) Dy
Fowlkes, America to Dallis Smith 12-8-1873 (no return) Dy
Fowlkes, Angaline to Dick Smith 1-26-1867 (1-27-1867) Dy
Fowlkes, Ann to Pleas Smith 1-2-1871 (1-8-1871) Dy
Fowlkes, Annie to Thomas Horton 1-13-1874 (1-14-1874) Dy
Fowlkes, Belle to Miller Moore 9-15-1877 Dy
Fowlkes, Bettie to H. A. Tyler 4-1-1868 (4-2-1868) Dy
Fowlkes, Cheney to Bailey Walker 6-22-1872 (6-30-1872) Dy
Fowlkes, Cornelia A. to Charles McDonald 4-12-1854 Sh
Fowlkes, Deliah to James Oliver 12-27-1871 (12-28-1871) Dy
Fowlkes, E. E. to H. T. Pursell 12-9-1873 Dy
Fowlkes, E. F. to W. C. Ward 3-19-1864 G
Fowlkes, Eliza to Frank Moore 1-6-1872 Dy
Fowlkes, Eliza to James Barnes 3-1-1877 Dy
Fowlkes, Eliza to James Johnson 10-5-1880 Dy
Fowlkes, Embra to N. Coker 2-7-1867 Dy
Fowlkes, Emma to Daniel Woods 1-6-1872 (no return) Dy
Fowlkes, Emma to Pompey Smith 2-16-1879 Dy
Fowlkes, Fannie to Morris Louder 1-30-1879 Dy
Fowlkes, Fanny to Jerry Pitts 2-2-1867 Dy
Fowlkes, Florence to John Doak 3-3-1880 Dy
Fowlkes, Judy to Allen Fisher 5-13-1874 (5-15-1874) Dy
Fowlkes, Letheann to Archer Walker 12-25-1877 (no return) Dy
Fowlkes, Lizzie to Jerry Marchant 7-6-1867 Dy
Fowlkes, Louisa to Polk Jones 7-6-1867 (7-7-1867) Dy
Fowlkes, Louisa to Richd. Gleason 12-29-1880 (not executed) Dy
Fowlkes, Loula to Charlie Becket 9-22-1880 (9-23-1880) Dy
Fowlkes, Lucinda to Henry Cowles 7-17-1869 (no return) Dy
Fowlkes, Lucy to Scott Anderson 1-28-1880 Dy
Fowlkes, Luella to Ben Parr 3-22-1877 Dy
Fowlkes, M. F. to Robt. W. Drane 12-2-1874 (no return) Dy
Fowlkes, Malinda to Wesley Howard 5-26-1871 (5-25?-1871) Dy
Fowlkes, Mary J. (Mrs.) to Gilbert Jones 10-19-1864 Sh
Fowlkes, Mary W. to Allen Oliver 8-28-1848 (9-1-1848) O
Fowlkes, Mary to Louis Dunavant 4-28-1869 (no return) Dy
Fowlkes, Millie to Nelson Alston 8-31-1871 Dy
Fowlkes, Mollie E. to C. W. Johnston 12-5-1859 Sh
Fowlkes, Mollie to Thomas Jones 1-13-1876 Dy
Fowlkes, Parthena to Toler Cook 1-24-1874 Dy
Fowlkes, Sarah to Wm. Hudgens 5-22-1880 Dy
Fowlkes, Tabitha to F. M. Hambrick 11-15-1866 (no return) Dy
Fowlkes, Z. F. to H. A. Fowlkes 10-29-1872 Dy
Fox, Agnus S. to E. Gustan 8-8-1865 (no return) Cr
Fox, Catharine to Peter Murray 1-30-1860 Sh
Fox, Darcus to Enoch Fox 7-15-1845 G
Fox, Delila to Edward Morris 9-5-1866 G
Fox, Elizabeth to Alexander Cox 8-31-1831 (9-8-1831) G
Fox, Jane to Ed Jackson 7-28-1875 (7-29-1875) Dy
Fox, Luizer to Wesley Parsons 1-1-1867 G
Fox, M. E. to J. H. Patton 1-23-1869 (1-26-1869) Cr
Fox, Martha A. to James A. Utley 1-1-1853 Cr
Fox, Mary I. to Isaah Hogan 12-24-1866 O
Fox, Mary Jane to Joseph Parsons 1-3-1869 G
Fox, Mary L. to T. F. Fields 3-17-1864 (3-21-1864) O
Fox, Mary to Silas Mullens 9-7-1858 (9-8-1858) G
Fox, Nancy Elizabeth to C. C. Young 6-21-186_ (probably 1869) G
Fox, Nany to Wm. Thedford 11-16-1841 G
Fox, Polly to Benjamin Bell 12-5-1834 Hr
Fox, Polly to Zebulm Dill 6-14-1827 (6-25-1827) G
Fox, Sarah A. to Daniel Fox 2-21-1856 We
Fox, Susannah to P. W. Duncan 12-7-1857 (12-8-1857) O
Foxwell, Kittura to James M. Hammons 4-12-1841 Ma
Frailkill, Berthenia to Joseph E. Wilkerson 9-17-1864 Sh
Frain, Emma to Jno. D. Danbury 10-24-1846 Sh
Frain, Serilda W. to Wm. W. Brown 12-28-1843 Sh
Frain, Virginia P. to George C. Eyrich 12-30-1864 Sh
France, Mary to Louis Malick (Moelch) 1-27-1848 Sh
Frances, Susan A. to Alexander Jackson 1-24-1843 (1-28-1843) Ma
Francis, Catharine to Benjamin Eskridge 8-9-1863 We
Francis, Lovey to Andrew I. Hulsey 9-7-1842 Sh
Francis, Mary A. to Peter Brown 12-31-1846 We
Francis, Rutha A. to Joseph Newten 9-10-1859 We
Francis, Sarah D. to John C. Singler 12-24-1870 (12-25-1870) Ma
Francisco, Dinah to John C. Hasten 11-23-1854 Be
Francisco, Mahaly E. T. to William D. Hasten 3-11-1852 Be
Francisco, Mahaly to William Wadkins 11-17-1853 Be
Francisco, Martha A. to Elijah P. Crews 9-8-1866 Hn
Frank, Johnana to Charles H. Brown 6-28-1875 O
Franklin, Ann Mariah to Jonathan Gardner 1-27-1862 (no return) L
Franklin, Emeline to Robert Douglass 4-1-1867 F B
Franklin, Fannie E. to Almarine Simmons 11-12-1867 (11-14-1867) Ma

Franklin, Frances C. to Joseph G. Huie? 7-28-1868 (7-29-1868) Dy
Franklin, Jane to Green Adams 3-3-1874 T
Franklin, Jane to Louis Cardinal 8-5-1849 Sh
Franklin, Livey to Williamson Hicks 2-26-1863 (no return) Hn
Franklin, Lucy J. to T. H. Omesly? 2-12-1849 (no return) F
Franklin, Martha A. to William T. Browder 10-29-1860 (10-30-1860) Ma
Franklin, Martha Frances to John Faulkner 3-24-1854 (3-29-1854) T
Franklin, Mary E. to Jo Baird 6-5-1866 (1?-6-1866) Dy
Franklin, Mary J. to T. J. Griffin 12-28-1875 (no return) Hy
Franklin, Mary to Franklin White 12-18-1854 Cr
Franklin, Mattie to J. R. Shroyer 10-23-1863 (10-25-1863) Sh
Franklin, Nancy to John H. Moss 6-5-1839 F
Franklin, Rosea A. to J. Simmons 5-17-1871 O
Franklin, Sarah R. to James A. Pate 11-14-1868 (11-15-1868) L
Franklin, Susan E. to Logan J. Anderson 12-8-1862 (12-9-1862) Ma
Franklin, Susan to William Walker 12-20-1866 (12-23-1866) O
Fransioli, F. A. to Daniel Venturini 1-5-1855 (1-7-1855) Sh
Fransioli, Guiseppa A. to Giovanni Dado 7-6-1870 Ma
Fransioli, Josephine to Paul Migliozzo 7-26-1854 Sh
Franson, Cornelia C. to W. K. Linyard 5-20-1875 Hy
Fraser, Catherine to Harry Green 3-20-1866 (3-28-1866) F B
Fraser, Elizabeth to Washington Green 2-13-1869 (2-17-1869) F B
Fraser, Feddie to John Catron 12-9-1868 F
Fraser, Hattie E. to Wm. L. Fraser 6-8-1865 F
Fraser, Mary J. to Wm. T. Thomas 9-12-1861 F
Frasier, Eliza I. to Job Hood 9-18-1845 F
Frasier, N. C. to Walter Shinault 12-1-1866 (12-2-1866) F
Frasier, Virginia Bell to Columbus Bryant 10-21-1865 (10-22-1865) F
Frasier?, Rhody to J. C. Harriss 1-6-1845 (1-8-1845) F
Fravel, Margaret to William Long 2-26-1862 Sh
Frayer, Helana S. to Elias Miller 1-22-1846 G
Frayser, Mary F. to N. S. Trice 3-28-1860 (3-29-1860) Sh
Frazar?, A. M. F. to J. B. Kimbo 10-12-1852 Sh
Frazer, Cynthia to William H. Counsel 5-13-1830 Ma
Frazer, Delia (Mrs.?) to John N. Walker 4-13-1863 Sh
Frazer, Florence to Johns Gillespie 7-2-1872 Hy
Frazer, Melinda to Benjamin Wright 2-9-1844 Sh
Frazer, Polly to Branch Taylor 7-30-1867 Hy
Frazer, Rachel to William S. Runaldo 12-23-1831 (12-29-1831) G
Frazier, E. A. to J. R. Caldwell 1-17-1855 Hn
Frazier, Edna B. to Simon H. Walker 7-3-1849 (7-4-1849) F
Frazier, Eliza A. to William E. Henry 2-5-1846 Hn
Frazier, Elizabeth T. to Alex. A. Bumpass 9-4-1848 Ma
Frazier, Elizabeth V. to T. J. Riley 11-18-1868 Be
Frazier, Emma (Mrs.) to W. H. Fowler 7-11-1874 (7-12-1874) Dy
Frazier, F. S. to K. S. Spicer 2-8-1863 O
Frazier, Frolens to W. L. Whitelaw no date (not executed) Hy
Frazier, Jane to John Wimberley 5-13-1849 Hn
Frazier, Julia to Nelson Pitts 4-10-1873 Hy
Frazier, K. (Mrs.) to Boon Hays 11-19-1844 Sh
Frazier, Lucy to Henry Tharpe 11-28-1839 (no return) Hn
Frazier, Marcha A. to James M. Bumpus 3-15-1842 (3-17-1842) Ma
Frazier, Margarett to James Robinson 12-17-1851 (12-18-1851) O
Frazier, Martha H. to General M. Wright 1-8-1858 O
Frazier, Martha Jane to Randle Pafford 3-24-1867 Be
Frazier, Mary C. to J. S. McCorkle 8-23-1871 (8-24-1871) Dy
Frazier, Mary E. to W. W. Newhouse 12-31-1861 G
Frazier, Mary J. to Thos. J. Mays 1-4-1879 (1-5-1879) Dy
Frazier, Mary to James Robinson 12-24-1857 O
Frazier, Mary to Robt. L. Harper 11-19-1860 (11-27-1860) Dy
Frazier, Nancy E. to Allen Powell 12-28-1869 G
Frazier, Nancy to E. W. Applegate 1-24-1849 Sh
Frazier, Rhody (Mrs.) to J. W. (Dr.) Stout 3-13-1838 Sh
Frazier, Sallie J. to Daniel J. Crisp 12-13-1869 (12-15-1869) F
Frazier, Sarah J. to Elijah A. C. McGehee 10-18-1860 Sh
Frazier, Sarah to Lee Tipton 10-10-1874 (10-19-1874) Dy
Frazier, Sarah to Thomas Wadkins 2-16-1853 Sh
Frazier, Susan L. to Henry H. Trevathan 1-19-1858 Hn
Frazier, Tempy to Nelson Kennon 4-15-1871 (4-17-1871) F
Frazor, Margaret V. to George S. White 9-3-1857 O
Frederick, Caroline to Edward L. Birmingham 7-6-1859 (7-7-1859) Ma
Fredericks, Eveline V. to John H. Norwood 6-5-1860 (6-7-1860) Ma
Freding, Mary E. (Mrs.) to Wm. D. Wilkerson 8-8-1870 (8-9-1870) Ma
Freeland, Abigale to John Moore 12-31-1845 Cr
Freeland, Amanda C. to George Buchanan 10-31-1859 Hn
Freeland, Ann J. to Sidney Steel 5-20-1846 Cr
Freeland, Ardella to John Dunn 4-5-1864 (4-7-1864) Cr
Freeland, Emily R. to Samuel Housden 2-12-1858 Hn
Freeland, Mariah A. to William Walton 8-15-1864 (no return) Hn
Freeland, Mary Jane to Joseph H. Weaver 12-30-1851 Hn
Freeland, Mary M. to James E. Buchanan 1-6-1857 (no return) Hn
Freeland, Nancy J. to Henry Housden 11-23-1861 (no return) Hn
Freeland, Sarah G. to H. McMurray 6-24-1849 Hn
Freeland, Sarah J. to John M. King 12-30-1845 Cr
Freeling, Elizabeth to John V. Anderson 8-8-1831 Ma
Freeling, Sarah to Hinton Bryan 4-4-1842 (4-7-1842) Ma
Freeling, Susan G. to Phillip A. Donlin 8-3-1842 (8-4-1842) Ma

Freeling, Tennessee to Alfred D. Garrett 1-23-1849 (1-24-1849) Ma
Freels, M. E. to L. Bond 5-26-1870 (no return) Hy
Freels, Nancy J. to Wm. Eaton 9-21-1860 (9-23-1860) Hr
Freeman, A. E. to W. C. Trent 12-7-1865 Hn
Freeman, Amanda to William Walker 11-6-1872 Hy
Freeman, Ann E. to George T. Akens 1-15-1861 (no return) Hy
Freeman, Ann E. to W. H. Humphreys no date (1838-1852) Hn
Freeman, Ann to Theo. Pitts 5-10-1864 (5-12-1864) Dy
Freeman, Anna M. to Henrich Groth 5-20-1882 (no return) L
Freeman, Anne to Nick Willis 5-16-1870 G B
Freeman, Bettie to Jas. Shelton Minor 1-4-1869 (1-8-1869) F B
Freeman, Carlin to Joseph Seat 8-5-1870 G
Freeman, Caroline to Allen Snotgrass 11-3-1877 Hy
Freeman, Caroline to Henry Lain (Lion?) 10-17-1860 G
Freeman, Cary Ann to Francis M. Claxton 2-24-1857 Hr
Freeman, Cynthia W. to Thomas W. Freeman 11-18-1851 G
Freeman, Delila to Alfred Reddick 2-2-1869 (no return) Dy
Freeman, E. J. to H. P. Martin 6-19-1869 (6-20-1869) Cr
Freeman, Eliza Jane to Asberry M. Webb 10-5-1833 (10-10-1833) G
Freeman, Elizabeth J. to John L. Ruff 5-16-1843 Cr
Freeman, Elizabeth to Blount Cooper 9-5-1839 Hn
Freeman, Elizabeth to C. B. Jackson 12-13-1873 O
Freeman, Elizabeth to Seth T. Moore 8-19-1850 (8-21-1850) G
Freeman, Elizabeth to Wm. H. Rose 8-20-1860 (8-23-1860) Hr
Freeman, Elvira to James W. Hunt 3-4-1857 Hn
Freeman, Emily A. to Charles Phillips 11-13-1848 Ma
Freeman, Emma A. (Miss) to Frank M. Arnold 12-2-1863 Sh
Freeman, Fannie M. to W. F. McNamee 11-2-1866 (11-7-1866) F
Freeman, Fannie to Wm. Ezell 5-1-1862 Hy
Freeman, Fanny S. to Thomas Stewart 9-1-1842 Hn
Freeman, Fanny to Stewart Harmon 10-19-1867 Hy
Freeman, Frances to Culpepper Cooper 4-3-1848 Cr
Freeman, Frances to J. W. Hammock 11-3-1880 (11-7-1880) L
Freeman, Frances to Thos. W. Freeman 7-20-1854 G
Freeman, Fredonia Olivia to Regis Dunwood 2-16-1853 (2-17-1853) T
Freeman, Helen to Miles P. Chandler 4-6-1847 Hn
Freeman, Hester A. to A. G. Grisamore 6-15-1852 Sh
Freeman, Indiana to Jefferson Shantly 9-17-1866 (9-19-1866) T
Freeman, Jane to Daniel B. Shaw 3-20-1844 (no return) We
Freeman, Jane to Newton Larrison 2-1-1886 L
Freeman, L. A. to T. B. Swann 5-15-1860 F
Freeman, Lou to G. W. Baxter 6-10-1872 Hy
Freeman, Lou to Isham Wade 2-4-1869 G
Freeman, Louisa to Frank Ward 11-20-1866 Hy
Freeman, Louisa to Scott Carrington no date (Aug/Sep 1873) L
Freeman, Lucindy to Wm. Finley 4-6-1856 Cr
Freeman, Lucy A. to C. C. DuBose 2-16-1860 Sh
Freeman, Lucy P. to O. G. Fitzgerald 3-24-1868 G
Freeman, Mahola? to Amma? Kittell 2-22-1831 Ma
Freeman, Margaret to Hezekiah Morris 2-21-1843 Hr
Freeman, Margaret to W. L. Higgs 2-27-1855 We
Freeman, Marilyn to James White 7-5-1851 (7-?-1851) T
Freeman, Martha A. to Wm. Carson 2-2-1859 (2-3-1859) T
Freeman, Martha D. to Joshua H. Dodds 5-27-1854 (no return) We
Freeman, Martha W. to Thos. P. Wade 11-4-1853 G
Freeman, Martha to Ed Freeman 11-5-1866 G
Freeman, Martha to Joseph H. Talbot 8-16-1842 Ma
Freeman, Martha to W. H. McBroom 7-28-1874 (7-30-1874) L
Freeman, Mary A. to Morgan Snodgrass 4-13-1873 Hy
Freeman, Mary Ann to James Brush 9-11-1861 (9-12-1861) O
Freeman, Mary E. to James Kimbrough 4-6-1842 Sh
Freeman, Mary E. to Milton H. Crider 1-16-1864 (no return) Cr
Freeman, Mary E. to Milton H. Crider 1-26-1864 (no return) Cr
Freeman, Mary E. to Thomas C. McCraw 2-22-1865 (2-23-1865) T
Freeman, Mary F. to J. C. Jones 11-5-1868 G
Freeman, Mary Jane to James S. Bryant 8-7-1843 T
Freeman, Mary P. to Alexander P. Sanders 2-9-1871 L
Freeman, Mary to James E. O'Quinn 7-13-1853 (7-14-1853) Sh
Freeman, Mary to Silas Edwards 11-18-1853 (11-24-1853) G
Freeman, Mary to Thomas C. McCraw 3-14-1868 T
Freeman, Mary to Wm. Finley 4-28-1853 Cr
Freeman, Matilda to J. McLenon (McClean) 6-29-1869 (no return) Hy
Freeman, May M. to George M. Atkins 1-1-1868 Hn B
Freeman, Milly to Andrew Jackson 10-3-1867 G B
Freeman, Mollie to Milton Jett 12-24-1869 Hy
Freeman, N. A. to A. Williams 10-17-1854 We
Freeman, N. J. to J. H. Davis 10-5-1874 (10-6-1874) Dy
Freeman, Nancy to John Pinkston 2-12-1857 We
Freeman, Nanny to John C. Weisheiver 8-15-1870 (8-16-1870) T
Freeman, Neely A. M. to Terrel Thompson 9-1-1845 (9-4-1845) Ma
Freeman, P. R. to R. D. Grady 11-23-1869 C
Freeman, Parthenia to Albert Moses 3-16-1867 Hy
Freeman, Precilla H. to Aaron Word 4-21-1836 (4-21-1836) G
Freeman, R. F. to T. W. Yeates 5-3-1851 (5-7-1851) G
Freeman, Rachael to Isack Word 12-5-1836 (12-8-1836) G
Freeman, Rachel to George Watkins 6-20-1878 Hy
Freeman, Sallie to David J. Baskins 7-12-1864 (7-13-1864) T

Freeman, Sarah E. to John C. Murphy 9-30-1868 Ma
Freeman, Sarah J. to John C. Sturt 9-19-1856 We
Freeman, Sarah P. to Benjamin H. Diggs 4-12-1860 Hn
Freeman, Sarah Sopornia? to John Adams Stokes 8-6-1851 (8-7-1851) T
Freeman, Sarah W. to Joshua J. Jones 10-23-1843 F
Freeman, Sarah to John W. Cole 6-29-1857 O
Freeman, Sindy to Thos. White 1-5-1873 Hy
Freeman, Susan A. to Marcelius N. Rison 2-13-1840 Hn
Freeman, Tennessee to George McDowell 5-27-1867 O
Freeman, Unity to Abner McDaniel 5-19-1847 Hr
Freemas, Martha D. to Joshua H. Dodds 5-28-1854 We
Freleigh, Jennie L. (Mrs.) to W. D. (Capt.) Hutchens 12-5-1863 (12-6-1863) Sh
Frence, Dorcus to Elijah M. Bush 8-8-1838 (no return) Hn
Frence, Emeline to William F. Hester 10-29-1866 (no return) Hn
French, C. A. to N. W. Grimes 1-17-1861 (1-20-1861) T
French, Eliza Jane to Samuel B. Roberts 3-19-1843 Hn
French, Elizaeth C. to James G. Wilson 2-24-1870 Cr
French, Ella H. to James L. Jones 5-17-1884 (5-18-1884) L
French, Kate Louis to John C. Read 5-7-1873 Hy
French, Liza Ann to A. N. Wiseman 10-18-1866 Hn
French, Lovey A. to J. P. Medlin 11-11-1864 (11-12-1864) Cr
French, Martha A. to J. P. Lowry 10-24-1867 Hn
French, Martha to John Fry 8-7-1875 (no return) Hy
French, Mary Ann to William H. Cummings 1-17-1856 Be
French, Mary J. to Samuel C. French 12-31-1859 Hn
French, Mattie to F. L. Blum 2-13-1871 Hy
French, Nancy to James S. May 3-5-1870 Cr
French, Nancy to Jarrett Taylor 6-4-1864 Cr
French, Rebecca W. to Stokeney Patterson 9-25-1856 Hn
French, Rebecca to J. J. Lowry 2-21-1864 Hn
French, Sarah C. to Henry Carter 10-30-1869 (10-31-1869) Cr
French, Susan F. to William Frields 6-25-1857 We
French, Susanah A. to Cullen Beaton 3-25-1855 Be
French, Susannah to Samuel H. Stanley 6-24-1846 Hn
Frenk, Catherine to Herman Glindcauf 9-18-18?? Sh
Freno, Mary Ritty to Berry H. Williams 2-4-1857 (2-5-1857) Ma
Frensley, Sarah to John Todd 8-5-1841 Hn
Frest (French-Frech), Amelia to W. Ringwald 4-4-1850 Sh
Frey, Catharine to J. C. Gregg 1-21-1860 (1-22-1860) Sh
Frey, Elizabeth to John Cooper 12-18-1854 (12-21-1854) Sh
Frey, Mary Magdalina to Joseph Frey 6-3-1863 (6-6-1863) Sh
Friar, Creasy to David Grigg 2-12-1880 (no return) L
Friar, Polly to Julius Wilhight 3-2-1837 Hr
Frick, Barbara to George Duckle 10-28-1858 Sh
Frick, Mary to Daniel Fox 2-11-1843 Sh
Frick, Mary to Jacob Benken 8-24-1854 Sh
Frick, Rosina to George Heidel 7-19-1856 Sh
Fricke, Christiana to William Hamerle 4-21-1851 Sh
Fricke, Hannah to Frederick Simson 12-3-1856 (12-4-1856) Sh
Fields, Catherine to James F. Morris 10-28-1858 We
Frieles, Frances (Mrs.) to Joseph F. Alexander 12-10-1868 (12-13-1868) Ma
Friend, H. E. to D. H. Friend 7-21-1873 (7-23-1873) L
Friend, Mary E. to R. D. McLeod 7-19-1873 (7-29-1873) L
Frierson, Cordelia C. to W. B. Shapard 10-23-1849 Sh
Frierson, Louisa to Richard Wiley 12-29-1865 (12-30-1865) F B
Frierson, Margaret E. to Benjamin F. Taylor 6-8-1842 G
Frierson, Sophia R. D. to T. H. Jackson 8-11-1851 (8-12-1851) Sh
Frietag, F. to Fred Friel 1-5-1856 (1-6-1856) Sh
Frisbee, Sarah to Henry Hudson 10-22-1860 Cr
Frith, M. W. to Eli Johnson 12-23-1868 (12-24-1868) Dy
Frith, Martha to Champ Lankford 2-13-1872 (2-14-1872) Dy
Fritz, Christiana to Anderson Grider 9-7-1852 Sh
Fritz, Teresa to Federline Seitz 1-7-1856 Sh
Friz?, Amanda to Steward Ruskin 1-25-1873 (1-27-1873) L B
Frizzele, S. S. to Peter Mates 1-22-1852 Sh
Frizzell, Lavinia Ann to John T. Pistol 10-23-1855 (10-24-1855) O
Frizzell, S. C. to James Younger 1-12-1853 Hn
Frizzell, Virginia to Joseph A. Ore 11-4-1846 (no return) We
Frollie, Catharine A. to Alfred E. Gile 7-28-1864 (7-29-1864) Sh
Frost, Amy M. to Frederick B. Clapp 3-2-1863 Sh
Frost, Eliza Jane to A. P. Thurmond 2-26-1884 (2-27-1884) L
Frost, Julia to Rufus Henderson 9-7-1867 (9-12-1867) Dy
Frost, Lou to Henry McGarg 1-14-1879 (no return) Dy
Frost, Louisa to Wesley B. Davis 4-30-1840 G
Frost, Lucinda to John D. Farmer 6-26-1856 We
Frost, Sarah Frances to E. D. Thurmond 7-14-1883 (7-23-1883) L
Fruman?, Margaret to Jessa Loften 1-27-1874 (1-29-1874) L
Fry, Ann to Wm. S. Kincaid 5-23-1871 Ma
Fry, Bettie to W. H. Powers 6-21-1875 (6-22-1875) O
Fry, Catherine to John W. Rowsey 11-12-1861 (11-14-1861) Ma
Fry, Charlotte to James Jolly 3-30-1854 Cr
Fry, Elizabeth E. to Peter E. Hall 8-16-1860 T
Fry, Elizabeth to Samuel L. Cole 8-13-1845 Hn
Fry, Emma J. to Johns W. Jolly 10-1-1861 Cr
Fry, Jane to Asa P. Holtsford 8-23-1855 Ma
Fry, Lacy J. to Lawson D. Taylor 11-26-1849 (11-29-1849) Ma
Fry, Levy Ann to John C. McDaniel 3-30-1854 Be

Fry, Lucinda to John J. Cole 9-19-1844 Hn
Fry, Margaret E. to Archibald S. Rogers 7-15-1856 (7-17-1856) Ma
Fry, Mary E. to Robert N. Gillispie 11-12-1845 Ma
Fry, Minnie to Joseph Dickson 4-11-1881 (4-17-1881) L B
Fry, Mollie B. to J. L. Montgomery 10-18-1870 (10-19-1870) Cr
Fry, Permelia to Robert Lampkins 2-8-1856 (no return) Hn
Fry, Polly to Dennis Thornton 8-18-1867 Be
Fry, Sallie A. to Edmond Winston 5-21-1852 (no return) F
Fry, Zeulah to Jonathan Montgomery 10-4-1842 Cr
Fryar, Mary A. to S. W. Cates 11-5-1854 Hn
Fryers, Lydia to James Oldham 7-7-1877 (7-21-1877) L B
Fryor, Martha to Henry B. Covington 5-12-1863 Hn
Fuchs, Eliza to Ernst (Ernest) Ebeler 7-19-1862 (7-20-1862) Sh
Fuchs, Philomene to Simon Kerrman 11-27-1856 (11-29-1856) Sh
Fulas, Axie to John Bunton 10-10-1840 Sh
Fulbright, Adeliza to Lawrence T. Hudson 12-21-1846 (12-22-1846) Ma
Fulbright, Catharine to James G. Mays 2-7-1831 Ma
Fulbright, Margaret E. to James M. Davis 2-9-1858 Ma
Fulbright, Nancy J. to John G. Lea 5-17-1854 (5-?-1854) Ma
Fulerton, Margarett to George W. Dickey 1-8-1831 G
Fulgham, Charlotte N. to Robert D. Hooks 3-16-1828 (3-18-1828) Hr
Fulgham, Louisa R. to John H. Deberry 11-25-1856 Ma
Fulgham, Polly to Stephen Rogers 12-8-1829 (12-10-1829) Hr
Fulgham, Susan to John N. Jenkins 9-5-1826 Hr
Fulgham, Winefred to R. W. Howell 2-15-1835 (2-26-1835) Hr
Fulghum, A. V. to G. M. Keenan 12-15-1869 G
Fulghum, Idotha to Saml. Sharpe 6-19-1866 Ma
Fulghum, Sophronia A. to Benjamin E. Lewis 8-23-1854 (8-25-1854) Ma
Fulgum, Caroline to Giles B. Crain 2-15-1832 (2-16-1832) Hr
Fulgum, Sarah to John B. Donaldson 3-21-1833 Hr
Fulkerson, M. F. to John Wesley Cannon 2-9-1882 L
Fulkerson, Rachel B. to Wm. J. Woodard 10-8-1857 L
Fulkerson, S. E. to J. D. Cannon 1-14-1882 (1-15-1882) L
Fulkerson, Sarah Ann to W. J. Woodard 10-8-1867 (10-10-1867) L
Fulks, Ann to Milton McDonal 3-12-1872 Cr B
Fulks, E. H. to James J. Hays 10-11-1866 G
Fullbright, Barborah to Francis Weight 12-15-1828 Ma
Fullen, Ellen to Marion Philips 8-8-1872 (7?-3-1872) L
Fullen, Harriet to Anderson Craig 6-8-1854 L
Fullen, Harriett to Dennie Anderson 12-6-1881 L
Fullen, Louisa to Joel Thomas Roberson 6-25-1856 L
Fullen, Matilda to James Coon 3-1-1848 (3-2-1848) L
Fullen, Missrie to Charles Brantley 8-18-1885 (8-20-1885) L
Fullen, Sarah E. to David Taylor Webb 1-19-1871 L
Fuller, Amanda J. to Gilbert Cozart 12-2-1867 (12-3-1867) Dy
Fuller, Amanda to Marion Pitt 9-2-1867 Dy
Fuller, Ann J. to H. H. Bailey 2-4-1867 (2-5-1867) F
Fuller, Ann to William Wright 2-12-1873 (2-13-1873) L B
Fuller, Candice to Louis Fowlkes 2-6-1878 (2-7-1878) Dy
Fuller, Catherine to William E. Dale 3-9-1852 Hn
Fuller, Celinda to William Anderson 1-22-1828 Ma
Fuller, Clarisa to John White 1-17-1848 Sh
Fuller, Cornelia to Willis Mitchell 11-29-1876 L B
Fuller, Eliza A. to J. W. Enochs 2-20-1861 Dy
Fuller, Elizabeth T. to James H. Scott 8-23-1854 Hn
Fuller, Elizabeth to Jacob Shipman 10-29-1834 Sh
Fuller, Ellen C. to George W. Grainger 12-1-1859 Hn
Fuller, Fanny to Henry Caton 2-15-1853 (2-17-1853) O
Fuller, Gilla to James Hundley 10-23-1849 (10-25-1849) Ma
Fuller, Harriet to Columbus Carter 1-21-1870 Cr
Fuller, L. C. to William H. Campbell 2-4-1863 (2-5-1863) Dy
Fuller, L. J. to T. M. Jackson 12-19-1874 (12-20-1874) Dy
Fuller, L. L. to F. T. Green 1-16-1856 (no return) Hn
Fuller, Laura to Thomas M. Paine 3-19-1878 (3-29-1878) Dy
Fuller, Leathen to Thos. McKneely 11-21-1836 (12-1-1836) G
Fuller, Lena to Andrew Barham 8-23-1871 (8-24-1871) Cr B
Fuller, Levina to Wm. Richardson 4-9-1873 Cr B
Fuller, Louisa to James Mitchell 2-17-1878 Hy
Fuller, M. C. to William Jackson 2-15-1865 (2-16-1865) Dy
Fuller, Malinda to Thomas Carroll 11-17-1841 Hn
Fuller, Maria to A. B. Taylor 10-25-1864 (10-26-1864) Sh
Fuller, Martha A. to T. Dewhit 7-28-1853 Cr
Fuller, Martha E. to L. J. Beavers 9-21-1872 (9-22-1872) T
Fuller, Martha L. to Charles N. Taylor 12-29-1852 Sh
Fuller, Martha to Augustus Smith 10-12-1842 L
Fuller, Mary C. to Beverly _____ 4-8-1849 Hn
Fuller, Mary E. to Sherrod Johnson 12-29-1869 (12-30-1869) Dy
Fuller, Mary J. to Thomas Vinson 1-2-1851 Cr
Fuller, Mary to G. W. Thurman 5-26-1863 Sh
Fuller, Mary to Thomas S. E. Joiner 9-15-1837 Sh
Fuller, Matilda C. to Clinton I. White 2-18-1841 Sh
Fuller, Phebe to John G. Heathcot 4-4-1865 (4-5-1865) L
Fuller, Pricilla H. to David C. H. Gowen 10-26-1854 Cr
Fuller, Rebecca to John M. Porter 12-20-1830 Sh
Fuller, Sabre to T. J. Tytus 9-30-1877 (not executed) L
Fuller, Sabry to Alexander Mitchell 9-21-1878 (9-?-1878) L B
Fuller, Sarah E. to George W. Hill 11-13-1866 (11-15-1866) Dy

Fuller, Sarah to George Fox 2-17-1873 (no return) L
Fuller, Stacy A. R. to W. T. Gwaltney 4-28-1869 (no return) Dy
Fuller, Sue M. to J. C. Vann 10-28-1868 (11-29-1868) Dy
Fuller, Susan to U. W. Scott 11-28-1846 (11-29-1846) We
Fullerton, Adaline to Henry Parks 6-24-1852 Be
Fullerton, Latrissa to James R. Reece 2-2-1856 Sh
Fullerton, M. H. to J. N. Roberson 1-9-1867 G
Fullerton, Margaret to Elisha Jenkins 12-28-1870 (12-29-1870) Dy
Fullerton, Mary to William Wallace 1-26-1847 Be
Fullerton, Sarah E. to M. A. Simpson 3-6-1877 Dy
Fultcher, Nancy C. to W. R. Privett 4-17-1875 (4-20-1875) Dy
Fulton, Ellen to Aurelius Daniel 1-15-1856 We
Fulton, Louisa (Mrs.) to Wm. Richardson 10-15-1864 Sh
Fulton, Mary Jane to Brister Taylor 10-24-1872 O
Fulton, Sidney to T. F. Green 6-20-1861 Mn
Fults, Violet Ann to Armistead Boyd 2-2-1869 T
Fumbank, Eliza to Allen Edney 9-23-1869 (no return) Dy
Fumbank, Jane to David Fowlkes 9-8-1866 (no return) Dy
Fumbanks, Bettie to John Smith 3-11-1880 Dy
Fumbanks, Lucretia to Mose Smith 2-14-1878 Dy
Fumbanks?, Martha to Jacob Cobb 8-8-1860 (8-9-1860) Dy
Funches, Mary F. to James Mason 2-23-1875 (2-24-1875) L
Funderburk, Mary to W. James Martin 3-4-1868 (3-8-1868) Ma
Funk, A. E. (Mrs.) to John A. Henry 5-14-1861 Sh
Fuqua, Armon A. to Giles Adams 10-22-1850 Cr
Fuqua, Elizabeth to R. A. Bellew 9-14-1866 Cr
Fuqua, Elizabeth to William C. Stuart 2-13-1844 (2-14-1844) G
Fuqua, Ellen to G. W. Boswell 1-23-1871 (no return) Cr
Fuqua, Lucinda E. to James L. Cassels 9-13-1848 (9-19-1848) G
Fuqua, M. L. to Henry T. Kirk 3-19-1878 Dy
Fuqua, M. M. to Clinton Adin 5-28-1865 (6-8-1865) Cr
Fuqua, Martha E. M. to T. J. Higgs 1-22-1870 (1-27-1870) Cr
Fuqua, Sarah E. to C. L. Keaton 4-4-1868 (no return) Cr
Fuqua, Virginia E. to Samuel M. Taylor 9-29-1859 (no return) We
Fuqua, Virginia H. to J. A. Moss 1-18-1865 Cr
Furber, Ann to Walter A. Hilliard 10-25-1854 (10-30-1854) Sh *
Furgarson, Emaly to Phillip King 3-18-1846 G
Furgarson, Mary E. to Andrew J. Griffin 6-7-1851 (7-8-1851) G
Furgarson, Pheby to Milton Ray 7-26-1839 G
Furgarson, Susan E. to John S. Griffin 9-22-1853 (9-23-1853) G
Furgarson, Teletha (Mrs.) to George W. Grisham 12-31-1844 (1-1-1845) G
Furgason, Elizabeth (Mrs.) to R. C. West 1-4-1872 Hy
Furgason, Mary F. to James E. Cox 2-16-1864 G
Furgenson, Martha J. to Martin Benson 12-3-1849 (12-4-1849) G
Furgerson, Ann Eliza to Daniel Campbell 8-19-1875 L
Furgerson, Lucinda to Isom Robinson 1-17-1871 (2-4-1871) Cr B
Furgerson, Martha to George Aldridge 6-8-1870 (6-28-1870) L B
Furgerson, Mary F. to E. Oakley 3-23-1853 (3-24-1853) Sh
Furgerson, Nancy M. to James Gurganus 7-12-1854 G
Furgerson, Phebe A. to John F. Thomas 7-16-1867 (no return) L B
Furgerson, Sallie to Charles Burton 4-28-1867 Hn
Furgerson, Sarah C. to Samuel S. Waddle 12-20-1853 (12-21-1853) Sh
Furgeson, Tibitha C. to Amos Granville 9-6-1859 G
Furguson, Anna to Alex Currie 2-8-1877 Hy
Furguson, Elizabeth to Franklin Sturges 3-22-1848 Sh
Furguson, Emma P. to John T. Stratton 9-18-1851 Sh
Furguson, Nally (Hally) to Hiram Sturgis 9-17-1847 Sh
Furguson, Sarah B. to Filmore J. Whitworth 2-18-1852 (2-19-1852) Sh
Furlong, Elizabeth to Robert Wilson 10-21-1857 We
Furlong, Martha J. to Isaac Pettyjohn 10-26-1859 (no return) We
Furlong, Mary to George Pentecost 1-27-1855 (2-1-1855) O
Furnandez, Candis to Richard Wood 9-19-1867 (9-21-1867) T
Furrah, Fanny to J. L. (Dr.) Hines 7-1-1859 (7-5-1859) Sh
Fusell, Mary F. to M. S. Blackley 11-7-1857 (no return) We
Fussel, Susan to Jonas Mayo 3-8-1848 (3-9-1848) Ma
Fussell, Elizabeth to James W. Boren 12-12-1867 Ma
Fussell, J.? A. to B. F. Arington 5-23-1861 (5-18-1861) Cr
Fussell, Mary J. to W. A. Rogers 9-2-1861 (9-3-1861) Cr
Fussell, Matilda W. to John J. Anderson 9-8-1847 Ma
Fussell, Minerva to Robert Harris 8-6-1846 (8-20-1846) Ma
Fussell, N. E. to R. H. Surber 3-4-1872 (3-7-1870?) Cr
Fussell, Susan to William Smith 6-12-1860 Ma
Futhery?, Rosa to J. R. Tenny 1-27-1868 (1-29-1868) T
Futhey, Louisa to Andrew Gaither 12-20-1870 T
Futhey, Margaret to James C. Marshall 3-22-1852 Sh
Futhey, Nancy to John Hunter 2-13-1850 T
Futill, Eliz R. to Lindsey Haney 8-12-1839 (8-13-1839) Hr
Futrel, Penelope to Jefferson Sparks 9-4-1833 (9-5-1833) Hr
Futrell, Arella to James W. Warren 10-6-1847 (10-6-1847) Ma
Futrell, Elizabeth to Thomas Poyner 3-29-1853 Sh
Futrell, Martha S. to John S. James 11-29-1838 Hn
Futrell, Sarah C. to H. M. Stice? 2-11-1856 (no return) Hn
Futurell, Mary to A. J. Haslerigg 10-30-1860 (11-1-1861) We
Fuzzell, Elizabeth to Wiley J. Arrington 10-16-1856 Cr
Fye, Kate to Florentin Echerle 2-23-1864 Sh

Gabbert, Maria M. to E. D. Duncan 12-31-1856 (1-1-1857) Sh
Gabbert, Minnie to Henry Glass 8-18-1858 Sh
Gabbrough, Annie M. to Elbert Andrews 1-1-1862 G
Gable, Louisa E. to John A. Wilson 4-19-1863 (4-22-1863) Sh
Gablin, Mary A. E. to Barney Mathews 3-5-1841 (3-9-1841) F
Gabrel, Angeline to L. Deason 5-17-1870 (5-19-1870) Dy
Gabriele, Carmela to Carmelo Rando 1-10-1856 Ma
Gaccer, Eliza to John Wildberger 3-27-1855 Sh
Gadd, E. J. to R. H. Powell 1-10-1860 (1-11-1860) Hr
Gaddis, Sarah to Robert P. Manson 12-26-1877 Hy
Gaddy, Malinda to John B. Ferrell 8-28-1856 Hr
Gaddy, Sarah Ann Eliza to Francis M. Ross 9-23-1851 Sh
Gaffaney, Bridget to Michael Solan 3-10-1860 Sh
Gafford, Mary Eliza to M. F. Wilson 9-16-1861 Sh
Gafford, Mary Eliza to Mack Wilson 7-10-1861 Sh
Gage(Ross), Nancy to Robert Wright 7-4-1827 Hr
Gage, Ann A. to John S. Jack 2-10-1857 (2-11-1857) G
Gage, Caroline to Pink Davis 11-26-1870 (11-21?-1870) F
Gage, Lathey to Wade H. Colbert(Colvard) 1-30-1830 Hr
Gage, Lucinda to William Taylor 12-15-1827 Hr
Gage, Lucinda to William Taylor 12-15-1829 (12-24-1829) Hr
Gage, Mary to William Barr 2-26-1863 Mn
Gage, Sarah to Samuel Ewing 12-3-1852 (12-4-1851?) Sh
Gage, Seletha to John Wilkinson 5-8-1830 Hr
Gage, Susannah to Jacob Laraner 9-19-1831 (9-?-1831) Hr
Gahagan, Mary C. to Henderson C. Wallace 5-25-1841 Hr
Gailard, Narcissa to John D. Davidson 1-30-1836 G
Gailey, Eliza A. U. to James Robertson 12-26-1855 (no return) We
Gailey, Elizabeth A. to Alexander S. Perry 5-6-1863 We
Gailey, Manervia E. to Sevie C. Hill 6-24-1860 We
Gailor, Mary Ann to James E. Teel 10-18-1841 F
Gailor, Parthena to Elias Hinesly 2-29-1873 Hy
Gailor, Susan Jane to Charles Underwood 2-27-1878 Hy
Gain?, Nancy Ann Somerfield to Jeremiah O'Leary 10-18-1870 (10-29-1870) L
Gaine, Rebecca to Thos. M. Stroud 4-11-1854 Sh
Gainer, Martha E. to J. J. Matheney 2-7-1848 Hn
Gainer, Mary M. to James B. Morris 2-4-1847 Hn
Gainer, Sallie to Ned Richardson 5-8-1872 T
Gainer, Tennessee to James Lee 7-26-1838 Hn
Gaines, A. V. to J. A. Glenn 1-20-1874 L
Gaines, Alzira to Wm. H. Simpson 10-7-1848 Sh
Gaines, Clara C. to Samuel R. Haynes 11-28-1867 (no return) L
Gaines, E. J. (Mrs.) to A. M. Elmore 12-27-1871 Hy
Gaines, Elizabeth F. to Albert Thompson 2-25-1847 L
Gaines, Elizabeth to Lemuel White 8-11-1847 (8-12-1847) L *
Gaines, Emma to Alfred McNeill 4-20-1870 (4-21-1870) Cr
Gaines, Eugenia E. to R. W. Vaden 12-1-1868 L
Gaines, Jennie to Bryant A. Shelton 2-10-1871 L
Gaines, Laura J. to J. H. Glenn 1-5-1875 (1-6-1875) L
Gaines, Lucy Ann to James H. Smith 11-25-1841 Cr
Gaines, Lucy to George H. Raulston 9-2-1856 Cr
Gaines, M. E. to J. T. Whitson 12-7-1878 (12-8-1878) L
Gaines, M. L. to C. F.(L?) Rhodes 11-20-1876 (11-21-876) L
Gaines, Martha to Benjamin G. Stokes 10-29-1856 (11-9-1856) L
Gaines, Martha to John Bush 10-12-1859 Cr
Gaines, Maryann to James Cavenness 2-8-1840 (2-11-1840) F
Gaines, Mildred A. to George W. Barnes 12-18-1883 (12-19-1883) L
Gaines, Nancy A. to James A. McMahon 11-23-1869 (11-25-1869) L
Gaines, Nancy to Whitfield Taylor 10-16-1845 We
Gaines, S. A. to L. W. Dunivant 12-24-1872 L
Gaines, Sarah J. to Benjamin A. Sinclair 11-13-1849 L
Gaines, Sue E. to J. D. Coleman 3-11-1886 L
Gaines, Susan S. to James W. Pitts 6-10-1852 L
Gaines, Virginia to W. W. Hines 5-15-1856 Cr
Gainor, Sarah C. to John P. Gillaspie 5-19-1859 Hn
Gains, Elizabeth F. to Henry T. Pitts 1-23-1866 (1-25-1866) L
Gains, Janey F. to J. T. Sistrunk 11-26-1877 (12-2-1877) L
Gains, Mary F. to John S. Temple 12-14-1868 (12-16-1868) L
Gains, Nancy E. to James W. Borum 6-17-1868 (6-18-1868) L
Gains, Nanie L. to W. E. Dickerson 12-21-1865 L
Gains, Susanna to Joseph Ladyman 11-17-1845 (no return) We
Gains, Virginia C. to James S. Coleman 12-20-1860 (no return) L
Gair, Susan C. to Wm. H. Russell 2-24-1858 (3-2-1858) Sh
Gaiters, Josephine to J. S. Childress 7-12-1882 L
Gaither, Genett to Thos. Lovelace 11-9-1865 F
Gaither, Harriet to Jerry Williamson 12-31-1866 (no return) F B
Gaither, Harriet to Offy Shaw 6-20-1868 (no return) F B
Gaither, Mary to June Tyas 3-6-1886 (12-30-1886) L
Gaither, Tobitha A. to Jacob H. Sink 12-2-1848 (12-6-1848) T
Gaitley, Louving to A. G. Richey 11-29-1869 (11-26?-1869) F
Galard, Mary A. to John T. Head 6-22-1854 G
Galaway, Ann to Bryant Hill 9-24-1869 (9-25-1869) T
Galaway, Martha to William A. Darling 11-11-1857 We
Galberie, Catherine to James Dondare 5-7-1863 Sh
Galbreath, Caroline to Abner Clements 8-2-1858 (8-3-1858) T
Galbreath, Dicy to J. A. Ballard 2-23-1860 T
Galbreath, Sally to John E. Sullivan 9-23-1867 T

Galbreath, Susan L. to A. J. Clements 4-4-1870 (4-5-1870) T
Gale, M. A. to C. W. Sanders 12-19-1871 Hy
Galemore, Martha A. to Joseph B. Turner 2-17-1852 Hn
Galeor, Susanah M. to Thos. W. Deener 11-20-1848 (11-23-1848) F
Gales, Louisa to T. N. Kingston 11-15-1854 We
Galespie, Lucindy (Mrs.) to Allen Canady 12-18-1853 (12-28-1853) Sh
Galey, Elizabeth A. to Egbert W. Drewry 11-10-1846 We
Galihar, Eliza to William A. Tipton 10-22-1839 (11-1-1839) O
Galion, Mary J. to Silas P. Jones 10-13-1841 Cr
Gallagan (Garragan?), Mary to Michael Kennedy 10-18-1859 Sh
Gallagher, C. Martina to John Park 7-7-1852 Sh
Gallagher, Catharine C. to Joel F. Lightfoot 2-15-1846 Sh
Gallagher, Fanny to George Parker 5-4-1853 (5-9-1853) Sh
Gallagher, Mary W. (Mrs.) to Michaell Magevney 12-29-1857 Sh
Gallagher, Mary to P. C. Gallagher 12-1-1844 Sh
Gallaher, Elizabeth to J. Y. Crocker 7-7-1868 (no return) Dy
Gallaher, M. J. to H. Banks 10-31-1874 (11-3-1874) Dy
Gallant, Mollie to Jerome Herndon 12-28-1867 (1-2-1868) Ma
Galleher, Cecile L. to Evan L. Ragland 9-18-1844 (9-24-1844) O
Gallery, B. A. to Wm. H. Mann 4-4-1863 Sh
Gallery, Martha J. to August Branan 8-6-1855 (no return) F
Galleway, Martha A. to J. W. Rafe 3-18-1847 (3-26-1847) L
Gallian, S. M. to W. B. Weddington 8-11-1859 (8-14-1859) G
Gallien, Mary F. to Henry Hales 9-22-1852 G
Galligan, Mary Ann to Daniel Tooky 7-5-1856 (7-6-1856) Sh
Gallimore, Elizabeth to William C. Morton 1-7-1851 Hn
Gallimore, Frances J. to F. L. Green 9-16-1865 (9-20-1865) Cr
Gallimore, Sarah A. to James P. Throgmorton 8-3-1847 (no return) Hn
Gallion, Permelia F. to John C. Gibbs 8-2-1862 G
Gallion, S. A. to W. L. Carter 3-6-1871 (3-7-1871) Dy
Gallion, Sarah A. to Franklin S. Harvey 1-11-1855 G
Gallop, Catharine to Francis M. Wright 8-14-1852 (8-16-1852) O
Gallop, Mary to Thomas Grubbs 1-13-1845 (1-23-1845) Ma
Gallop, S. E. to D. A. Parkman 2-12-1863 O
Galloway, A. P. to J. C. Hancock 3-14-1859 (3-28-1859) F
Galloway, Adelia (Dibzorah?) to Thomas A. Tripp 3-10-1866 (3-11-1866) F
Galloway, E. to Michael Kelly 11-16-1863 Sh
Galloway, Eliza J. to Jas. H. Warford 11-27-1856 Hr
Galloway, Elizabeth to Sidney Redding 12-6-1853 (no return) F
Galloway, Ellen to R. W. Ing 12-3-1856 (no return) F
Galloway, Mary J. to Joseph Crabbe 5-16-1861 Sh
Galloway, Mary to Cunningham Cox 12-30-1834 (1-2-1835) Hr
Galloway, Nancy to Timothy Winford 6-16-1838 Sh
Galloway, Sylva to Frank Shaw 10-1-1870 (10-8-1870) F B
Galoven (Currie), M. to Owen Sullivan 9-11-1875 Hy
Galoway, Eliza E. to Young E. Gray 9-28-1846 We
Galoway, Margaret Jane to E. S. Caldwell 12-23-1857 (12-24-1857) Hr
Galvin, Julia to Daniel Downs 4-27-1864 (4-28-1864) Sh
Gambell, Fanny to John Jackson 4-18-1845 (4-25-1845) Hr
Gambell, Lucy A. to William Gray 2-7-1839 Hr
Gambell, Mary H. to Hiram C. Short 6-26-1847 (6-29-1847) Hr
Gamble, Lavina to Joshua Laster 1-8-1833 O
Gamble, Mary to Louis Laster 6-29-1830 (6-30-1830) O
Gamble, Nancy to Thomas D. Gray 12-23-1848 Hr
Gamble, S. J. to William Bledsoe 11-28-1877 (11-29-1877) Dy
Gamble, Sarah to John Bramblett 4-13-1846 (8-18-1846) O
Gamble, Susan to Alfred W. Gray 8-26-1851 (8-27-1851) Hr
Gamble, W. E. to John Bledsoe 9-8-1877 (9-9-1877) Dy
Gambles, G. A. B. to Wm. A. Dunlap 8-28-1870 G
Gambol, R. H. to George Chilcut 2-1-1844 Be
Gambrell, Susan to Jesse Gordon 2-14-1844 (no return) F
Gambriel, Lucy Ann to Martin G. Adams 8-1-1840 Hr
Gamer, Elizabeth to Jarrett Perry 1-5-1858 G
Gamewell, Jacinda? to Isham G. McNeal 9-6-1867 (9-14-1869?) T
Gamewell, Leonilla E. to Thomas S. Vincent 12-1-1869 Ma
Gamlin, Asita to William Croft 2-15-1846 Hn
Gammel, Lucinda to Harville Cole 11-7-1836 O
Gammelle, C. to Rasmus Taylor 10-13-1871 T
Gammill, Mary to Stephen Francis 10-6-1863 Sh
Gammon, Fatitia to Jas. Gammon 5-15-1863 (5-17-1863) Dy
Gammon, L. R. to R. J. Smith 2-6-1869 (no return) Dy
Gammon, Mary E(liza) to Thomas J. McGinnis 1-24-1866 (1-25-1866) Dy
Gammon, S. A. to W. S. B. Bottoms 11-3-1873 Dy
Gammons, Ann to M. R. Vire 12-21-1866 (12-27-1866) Dy
Gammons, Beckie to William Sledge 7-15-1879 (7-16-1879) Dy
Gammons, Elizabeth to H. S. Walker 12-14-1870 (12-15-1870) Dy
Gammons, Lavenia to David Fautner 8-16-1864 Dy
Gammons, Louisa to James M. Farris 4-29-1867 (no return) Dy
Gammons, Margaret A. to Presley S. Beak 3-6-1861 Dy
Gammons, Mollie to J. F. Pyles 2-17-1875 (2-18-1875) Dy
Gammons, Nancy A. to Frank E. Gammons 4-29-1867 (no return) Dy
Gammons, Sally to Peter Anthony 1-9-1869 (1-10-1869) F B
Gammons, Sarah to Robert Sledge 3-8-1879 (3-9-1879) Dy
Gamons, Martha M. E. to C. J. French 10-7-1873 (10-8-1873) O
Ganbetti, C. V. to Jos. Baknet 12-8-1864 (12-14-1864) Sh
Gandey, Sarah to William Patterson 12-30-1844 Sh
Ganionhil, Laura to Martin Geiger 11-18-1854 (11-19-1854) Sh

Brides

Gann, Matilda to Rainy Neron? 11-21-1871 T
Gannaway, Sarah E. F. to William Adkins 11-24-1866 (11-25-1866) Ma
Gannin, Margaret A. E. to Scott Dyer 9-8-1853 Sh
Gannon, Fannie to H. J. Mason 11-7-1871 (11-9-1871) Dy
Gansey, Harriet to Walter P. Steaverson 4-19-1871 L
Gant, Elizabeth L. to A. R. Love 9-9-1856 G
Gant, Jennie to Isaac Payne 10-9-1874 T
Gant, Martha J. to Britten H. Holland 10-2-1843 (12-7-1843) G
Gant, Matilda W. to James T. Hunt 7-8-1834 G
Gantert, S. to M. Duttlinger 1-23-1858 Sh
Gantlet, Lydia to Henry Morris 11-11-1854 (11-19-1854) O
Gantlett, Lidia to Henry Morris 11-11-1852 (9?-19-1852) O
Gantlett, Martha Jane to James M. Pate 3-10-1857 (3-11-1857) O
Gantlett, Sarah to John P. Bullard 5-25-1863 (5-26-1863) O
Gardiner, Susan Ann to John B. Person 6-11-1851 Sh
Gardner, Ada B. to W. P. Caldwell 9-21-1854 We
Gardner, Alabama L. to A. P. Guess 8-31-1856 We
Gardner, Alice to Guss Scott 8-28-1875 O
Gardner, America Jane to Thomas B. Winford 10-13-1841 T
Gardner, America to J. L. Carney 3-10-1874 Hy
Gardner, Ann Louiza J. to George W. Moore 2-22-1849 G
Gardner, Catharine to R. A. Woodard 3-20-1878 (3-20-1878) L
Gardner, Darcy to Burk Thomas 11-28-1872 (11-30-1872) O
Gardner, Dema to Thomas Brooks 5-23-1885 (5-24-1885) L
Gardner, E. J. to W. C. Grace 12-22-1868 G
Gardner, E. M. to W. C. Malone 7-20-1850 (8-8-1850) F
Gardner, Elizabeth to George Dunning 10-20-1824 O
Gardner, Elizabeth to Peter Scott 7-28-1858 (8-1-1858) T
Gardner, Elizabeth to W. M. Sheppard 3-6-1865 (no return) Hn
Gardner, Emily to Jo. Claxton 4-9-1880 (no return) L
Gardner, Herbenia to Edwin Daniel 12-19-1846 Sh
Gardner, Hester? B. to Samuel W. Hawkins 3-20-1867 Cr
Gardner, J. A. to W. B. Carroll 9-4-1871 Cr
Gardner, Jane Ann to Jeremiah G. Weddle 2-15-1847 G
Gardner, Jane to Frank Love 7-16-1868 G B
Gardner, Jemmina A. to Calvin Ashley 11-4-1851 (11-6-1851) G
Gardner, Julia Ann to John David Chapman 5-26-1879 (6-5-1879) L
Gardner, Laura to J. C. Taylor no date (not executed) Hy
Gardner, Laura to John Thompson 12-22-1875 Hy
Gardner, Luisa M. to David L. Shares 12-2-1851 We
Gardner, Lydia to Henry Gardner 11-11-1843 (11-16-1843) Hr
Gardner, M. L. to N. W. Shankle 2-14-1860 Cr
Gardner, Margaret S. to Elbert F. Strain 12-20-1842 (12-22-1842) L
Gardner, Margaret to Bartley Hicky 3-23-1871 (4-2-1871) L
Gardner, Martha to Geo. H. West 10-22-1859 (10-27-1859) G
Gardner, Martha J. to John G. Boyd 8-16-1858 Hr
Gardner, Martha to John Bradberry 3-21-1846 (3-25-1846) G
Gardner, Mary A. to Thos. J. Seay 3-8-1858 (3-11-1858) We
Gardner, Mary E. to G. W. Darnell 11-12-1852 We
Gardner, Mary E. to J. A. Renfro 1-4-1866 Hn
Gardner, Mary E. to Wilson Miller 12-21-1847 (12-30-1847) F
Gardner, Mary J. to George White no date (with Feb 1863) Cr
Gardner, Mary J. to Martin W. Miller 4-17-1860 Hr
Gardner, Mary L. to J. W. Mitchell 1-21-1868 (1-22-1868) Cr
Gardner, Mary to Charles Bradshaw 4-16-1843 L
Gardner, Mary to John Brassell 12-6-1861 (12-7-1861) Sh
Gardner, Mary to Jonas M. Waller 2-26-1862 (2-27-1862) Ma
Gardner, Palunie A. to John D. Shelly 10-30-1850 We
Gardner, Rose to Hill Raynor 12-24-1869 (no return) F B
Gardner, S. A. to A. C. Finch 11-17-1859 (11-18-1859) F
Gardner, S. E. C. to Reuben Harris 5-5-1851 (no return) F
Gardner, Saletha to Joseph Hester 9-11-1871 (9-12-1871) Cr
Gardner, Sarah T. to Campbell D. Gray 10-19-1856 We
Gardner, Sarah to John Rose 1-14-1856 (1-15-1856) F
Gardner, Susan E. to Wm. C. Armour 9-2-1850 (9-4-1850) F
Gardner, Susan M. to Thomas Rosebery 4-14-1866 (4-15-1866) Cr
Gardner, Susanna H. to Wm. Bogle 7-19-1842 Cr
Gardner, Temptha Ann to Jesse J. Milton 11-8-1844 We
Gardon, Mary B. to James Jones 1-24-1840 F
Garett, Mary Ann to Calvin Cole 9-27-1854 Be
Gargarius, Martha A. to William A. Davis 11-27-1860 We
Gargus, Elenor E. to John C. Workman 6-26-1844 He
Gargus, Margaret to Wm. Workman 10-10-1844 We
Garham, Margaret A. to Soleman Pery 8-3-1848 We
Garland, Eliza to John R. Rowlett 11-11-1841 Ma
Garland, Fannie to Elijah Beats 12-23-1873 T
Garland, Harriett to Stephen Miller 2-27-1838 Ma
Garland, Margaret C. to N. B. Winston 9-13-1856 (9-17-1856) Ma
Garland, Martha C. to John L. Walsh 11-18-1856 (11-30-1856) Ma
Garland, Rebecca L. to John C. Simmons 10-21-1867 (10-22-1867) Ma
Garland, Sarah M. to Ira M. McJones 8-22-1839 Ma
Garland, Virginia to Jos. O'Neil 4-12-1856 (4-13-1856) Sh
Garley, Mary a. to John A. Barham 7-11-1848 Cr
Garlin, Mary Ann to E. J. Crihfield 7-13-1875 L
Garlington, Morning Ann J.(Mrs.) to Robert Thomas 6-22-1863 Sh
Garman, Rebecca to Hiram Melton 8-28-1861 Mn
Garmany, Mary to Dick Johnson 12-27-1866 G

Garner, Charlotte A. to William S. Noblin 5-5-1858 Sh
Garner, Dionca Ann to David Poindexter 4-4-1842 (4-7-1842) Ma
Garner, Dola to Frank C. Lewis 3-26-1884 L
Garner, Elizabeth C. to Samuel Cope 1-7-1841 Hn
Garner, Elizabeth to James M. McDougle 10-22-1850 Be
Garner, Jane to Emanuel Bond 12-20-1880 (12-25-1880) L B
Garner, M. E. to C. C. Adams 12-20-1882 L
Garner, M. J. to W. T. Reynolds 6-22-1861 (8-1-1861) Cr
Garner, Martha E. to James R. Mills 3-5-1872 (3-7-1872) Dy
Garner, Martha to Martin Reddick 11-25-1860 Be
Garner, Mary Jane to Levi Pahal 1-2-1863 Be
Garner, Nancy Ann to John F. Snow 4-21-1869 G
Garner, Nancy to Franklin Denhower 5-12-1846 Sh
Garner, Nancy to Jas. Coley 4-14-1840 Be
Garner, Rebecca to F. T. Hines 9-19-1870 (9-21-1870) Dy
Garner, Recy to Cornelius Cook 11-10-1844 We
Garner, Sophronia Ellen to John Thomas Olds 1-14-1873 (1-15-1873) L
Garner, Susan to Wm. H. Yarbrough 7-22-1845 Sh
Garner, Susannah to Berry Beany(Beny) 10-23-1841 (10-24-1841) Hr
Garner?, Mary E. to Wm. Samuel Carnell 5-5-1855 (5-7-1855) L
Garnett, Cassandera to William Turner 6-23-1852 (6-29-1852) L
Garren, Anora to Timothy Marrer 12-3-1853 Sh
Garret, Margaret M. to John Harrigan 7-29-1861 (7-30-1861) Sh
Garret, Martha to George Elliot 5-26-1863 Sh
Garret, Martha to Wm. Ashley 2-13-1856 (2-14-1856) Sh
Garrett, Adeline to Albert Bond 12-28-1870 (no return) L
Garrett, Almeda F. to Benjamin Harper 12-24-1860 (12-27-1860) O
Garrett, Alra to M. D. Caufman 11-4-1884 (11-6-1884) L
Garrett, Amand to L. L. French 2-16-1871 Cr
Garrett, Amelia to D. M. Moore 12-14-1854 Sh
Garrett, Bettie to T. S. Anderson 12-28-1866 Hy
Garrett, Elizabeth V. to Thos. J. Griffin 12-20-1870 (no return) Dy
Garrett, Elizabeth to J. H. Sample 8-8-1864 Sh
Garrett, Emily H. to W. H. Low 8-13-1859 (8-14-1859) Sh
Garrett, Emma to James Hustin 10-17-1868 (no return) Hy
Garrett, Febia to G. D. Chalk 11-11-1872 (no return) L
Garrett, Grisom E. to John C. Adams 6-6-1866 (6-7-1866) Dy
Garrett, H. F. to D. F. Chrifield 5-6-1884 L
Garrett, Henrietta Y. to M. J. Turner 1-17-1854 (1-19-1854) Sh
Garrett, Hulda Ann to Elijah H. Bomer 8-28-1856 Hr
Garrett, Jane E. to J. T. Curlin 2-7-1872 L
Garrett, L. N. J. to B. L. Sutton 11-15-1880 L
Garrett, M. A. to W. L. Maxwell 5-10-1848 Ma
Garrett, M. M. to J. R. Pennington 1-28-1879 (1-29-1879) L
Garrett, Mahala V. E. to Peter B. Barnett 12-3-1860 (12-5-1860) Ma
Garrett, Malinda to Joseph Nabors 8-2-1838 Hr
Garrett, Martha J. to Elihu S. Pannell 8-24-1859 Hr
Garrett, Mary Ann A. to Thomas J. Sturdevant 9-14-1858 Ma
Garrett, Mary E. to John H. Clay 1-30-1868 Ma
Garrett, Mary E. to T. S. Anderson 12-20-1871 (12-22-1871) L
Garrett, Mary F. to Jesse L. Perkins 2-8-1858 (no return) L
Garrett, Mary T. to Asa Baker 10-29-1856 Sh
Garrett, Mary V. to G. W. Bussey 5-6-1858 Sh
Garrett, Mary to Elijah E. Bayliss 5-23-1850 Hn
Garrett, Mary to James Craig 1-8-1867 (1-13-1867) Dy
Garrett, Mary to Peter Rainey 6-10-1846 Ma
Garrett, Mary to William B. Henry? 4-7-1847 Hr
Garrett, Maryann to Benson F. Lynn 12-20-1840 F
Garrett, Nancy J. to Eli Halton 11-10-1856 (11-12-1856) Hr
Garrett, Nancy to Wiley Nat 12-31-1877 Hy
Garrett, P. E. to W. G. Hendren 8-25-1869 Hy
Garrett, Patsy to Thos. J. Hollis 11-16-1867 (11-17-1867) F
Garrett, Pemela E. to Isaac Baker 1-7-1852 Sh
Garrett, Penelope to Patrick White 12-29-1856 Sh
Garrett, Rachel to George Grilesby 10-20-1855 Cr
Garrett, S. E. to S. T. Rushing 2-20-1868 Hy
Garrett, S. J. to C. V. Childs 12-28-1881 L
Garrett, Samantha to G. T. Smith 12-12-1859 Hy
Garrett, Sarah to A. M. Robbins 1-19-1871 (no return) Hy
Garrett, Stachey to William Jarrett 2-19-1842 (2-?-1842) Ma
Garrett, Stacy J. Y. to William Harburger 8-6-1859 (8-7-1859) Sh
Garrett, Stacy Jamima Young to Jas. M. Cunningham 4-29-1858 Sh
Garrett, Susan to Anderson Butler 8-18-1831 Ma
Garrett?, C. to A. Alloway 9-7-1846 Hr
Garrison, Adlinea to Julius Anderson 3-2-1878 (3-3-1878) L
Garrison, C. A. to William D. Taylor 8-7-1878 (8-8-1878) Dy
Garrison, Cicey to Sidney Smith 3-16-1878 Hy
Garrison, Elizabeth A. to A. M. Finch 10-4-1849 O
Garrison, Elizabeth A. to William Cooper 11-12-1861 (no return) We
Garrison, Elizabeth E. to John P. Taylor 4-1-1856 (4-2-1856) O
Garrison, Elizabeth to L. Gallaher 10-25-1860 (no return) Dy
Garrison, G. M. to W. H. Farris 5-14-1866 O
Garrison, Geraldine to Sanders Williams 11-21-1870 (11-23-1870) Ma
Garrison, Grace S. to Thomas A. Buchanan 2-3-1857 O
Garrison, Harriet to William E. Troy 5-27-1862 (no return) Dy
Garrison, Isabella to J. K. Hutchison 8-20-1867 F
Garrison, Jane to James Ketcham 10-4-1848 F

Garrison, M. E. to E. J. Peacock 10-10-1867 Hy
Garrison, M. J. to S. G. Dickey 11-1-1859 (11-8-1859) O
Garrison, M. M. to W. C. McDaniel 11-13-1867 O
Garrison, Margaret to Henry Rogers 12-5-1866 (no return) Hy
Garrison, Margarett A. to John W. Holoman 11-7-1866 O
Garrison, Marinda to Benj. A. Crisp 2-16-1870 (2-17-1870) Dy
Garrison, Martha E. to James H. Irvy? 4-12-1844 (no return) F
Garrison, Martha to E. W. Brinkley 12-13-1860 Dy
Garrison, Mary E. to James D. Walker 2-?-1862 (no return) Cr
Garrison, Mary J. to A. Dolphis Wells 1-11-1847 (no return) F
Garrison, Mary J. to William L. McCutchin 10-29-1857 (11-3-1857) O
Garrison, Mary Malina to James Shivers 3-27-1843 Ma
Garrison, Melvina to Gilbert Matthews 8-10-1853 (8-11-1853) O
Garrison, Nancy A. to John D. Cunningham 9-18-1864 O
Garrison, Nancy to William J. Hogue (Hogan) 3-27-1849 O
Garrison, Rebeccca to J. D. Blaydes 2-26-1866 (3-1-1866) F
Garrison, Sina to Jack Cox 5-1-1869 (no return) Dy
Garrison, Susan J. to W. S. Morrow 3-4-1864 G
Garrison, Susan to William D. Reeves 1-6-1845 (1-7-1845) O
Garrison, Tinsey to Adam Chronister 1-5-1826 Hr
Garrison, Virginia to David King 11-29-1875 (12-2-1875) O
Garrisson, Amand to Henry T. Crassett 8-7-1860 (no return) We
Garrott, Mary Frances to Jesse L. Perkins 2-8-1858 L
Garson, Parlee to Mitchell Liles 7-30-1856 Cr
Garvey (Gancy), Jane to Wm. Lang 3-6-1849 Sh
Garvey, Catherine to Jerry Cronin 8-8-1863 Sh
Garvin, Adelia N. to Joshua E. Bennett 3-18-1864 (3-22-1864) F
Garvin, Ann to John Duffy 10-20-1848 Sh
Garvin, Bridget to Hugh Feely 5-31-1856 (6-22-1856) Sh
Garvin, Caroline to Joe Harris 5-9-1866 F B
Garvin, Elizabeth to M. B. Paxton 2-18-1862 Sh
Garvin, Martha to Charles W. Jeter 12-28-1848 Sh
Garvin, Mary Jane to R. E. Paxter 5-14-1859 (5-15-1859) Sh
Garvin, Nancy N. to F. M. Mathis 9-14-1860 Hy
Garwood, Mary A. to C. T. Harrell 7-26-1853 Cr
Garwood, Nancy to John Hicks 1-26-1870 G
Gary, Elizabeth to E. H. Burks 10-24-1865 Hn
Gary, Mrs. to John Taylor 12-1-1863 T
Gaskins, Delila to John Wilhauks 5-9-1860 (no return) We
Gaskins, Eliza J. to William H. Alexander 10-24-1859 (no return) '
Gaskins, Harriet M. to Wm. A. Stephens 11-19-1866 (11-21-1866) Ma
Gaskins, Malinda to George Tripp 6-4-1879 (6-22-1879) Dy
Gaskins, Susan to David Ranes 2-11-1858 We
Gaskins, Vicey Ann to William J. Dearmore 2-20-1850 (2-21-1850) Ma
Gastings, Drucilla to N. Roe 1-7-1840 (2-2-1840) Ma
Gaston, Nancy to John H. Billington 10-29-1866 (10-31-1866) Ma
Gate, Caroline C. to William H. Beninger 12-25-1843 (12-28-1843) F
Gateley, Nancy to William C. Childress 4-7-1856 (4-10-1856) Ma
Gateley, Phebe to Wm. F. West 8-6-1850 (8-7-1850) Ma
Gateley, Sarah P. to E. H. Roaz 1-11-1865 (1-14-1865) Cr
Gately, Jemima J. to James M. Lewis 10-25-1853 Ma
Gately, Lavinia to Gabrial Cannon 6-11-1841 (6-12-1841) Hr
Gately, Lucinda S. to Reuben M. Hutchens 5-27-1849 Hn
Gately, Martha M. to H. Allen 12-16-1849 Hn
Gately, Mary W. to Emery H. Volentine 6-30-1848 Hn
Gately, Mary to William R. Hampton 2-?-1866 (2-26-1866) Cr
Gately, Nancy to Marshall W. Cox 11-21-1840 (11-26-1840) Hr
Gately, Phebe to Jesse G. Grace 8-31-1830 (9-2-1830) Ma
Gately, S. E. to Alford Nichols 3-2-1859 Cr
Gately, Sarah E. to Nelson Evans 1-3-1870 Cr
Gates, Ann E. to J. M. Osborn 11-19-1868 (no return) L
Gates, Anna E. to R. L. Cochran 10-27-1875 (no return) Hy
Gates, Elizabeth to Nathan Nooner 8-28-1828 Hr
Gates, Elmira Elizabeth to H. B. Smith 2-26-1879 L
Gates, Emily F. to Henry C. Fox 3-17-1862 (3-20-1862) F
Gates, Eugenia to Thos. T. Butler 6-1-1870 (6-11-1870) Ma
Gates, Jane H. to Thos. F. Anderson 12-5-1834 (12-9-1834) Hr
Gates, Lucy V. to Milton W. Prewitt 12-7-1867 (12-10-1867) F
Gates, Martha to Stephen Vault 5-4-1846 (5-6-1846) Hr
Gates, Mary A. to H. M. Collins 12-25-1866 Hn
Gates, Mary Jane to W. (Wm.) Lowill (Lovel?) 1-6-1863 Sh
Gates, Mary to W. T. M. Winstead 1-5-1859 We
Gates, Nancy V. to Benjamin Lax 3-2-1846 (3-5-1846) Hr
Gates, Rhoda R. to E. B. Lodwick 1-19-1847 Sh
Gates, Susan to Drewry Avent 3-29-1845 (4-3-1845) Hr
Gatewood, Amanda J. to Geo. L. Burnet 2-6-1858 (2-7-1858) Hr
Gatewood, Caroline to William P. Burnett 12-26-1860 Hr
Gatewood, T. to William C. Lee 12-6-1858 We
Gatey, Malinda Jane to J. B. Mosley 10-15-1862 (no return) L
Gather, Elizabeth to James T. Jackson 4-18-1845 G
Gatland, Susan to E. W. Morgan 12-15-1862 (12-16-1862) Cr
Gatlin, Eveline to Elijah, jr. Jones 4-11-1850 Ma
Gatlin, Fanny to Solomon Perry 1-4-1871 (1-5-1871) F B
Gattis, Mary F. to C. B. Russell 11-8-1859 (11-9-1859) Ma
Gattis, Mattie A. to Richd. W. Fisher 12-8-1866 (12-11-1866) Ma
Gattis, Rebecca Ann to Thomas R. Warren 12-15-1848 (12-20-1848) Ma
Gatz, Mary to Antone Engele 11-4-1864 Sh

Gaul, Mary to James Murphey 1-8-1859 (1-10-1859) Sh
Gauldin, Bettie to Andrew Harris 9-30-1868 Dy
Gauldin, Maggie to Fillmore Ferguson 9-29-1875 Dy
Gauldin, Martha to Elisha Jackson 12-25-1871 (no return) Dy
Gauntlet, Mary to Jansy J. Spights 5-23-1866 O
Gauntlett, Sarah to Daniel P. Gibson 3-6-1860 O
Gause, Amanda to James W. Waddle 6-1-1861 Hy
Gause, Anica to Houston Dirwin 10-14-1869 L
Gause, Ann to Wm. Jones 1-23-1866 Hy
Gause, Bettie to Isaac Halliburton 12-18-1872 (no return) L B
Gause, Challie A. to David John Rice 1-19-1867 L
Gause, Dilly to M. T. Townsley 3-4-1882 (3-15-1882) L
Gause, Elizabeth B. to Thomas A. Jordan 11-9-1859 (11-11-1859) L
Gause, Elizabeth V. to James M. Scott 4-5-1856 (4-8-1856) L
Gause, Emma to John W. Sains 12-15-1885 (12-20-1885) L
Gause, Isabella to William Snow 12-25-1867 (12-26-1867) L B
Gause, Jennie to Nathan Williams 10-1-1873 Hy
Gause, Jenny to Cole Wood 6-6-1885 (no return) L
Gause, Laura to Richard Nichols 10-10-1885 (10-11-1885) L
Gause, Leanor to Henry Jordan 2-28-1868 (no return) Dy
Gause, Lou to David Fitzpatrick 2-2-1876 (no return) L
Gause, Lucendy to Joseph Peete 8-14-1872 Hy
Gause, Margaret A. to W. A. Hunter 4-30-1861 (no return) Hy
Gause, Martha J. to G. H. Miller 12-19-1864 (12-21-1864) L
Gause, Mary Alice to William F. Greaves 5-29-1866 (6-6-1866) L
Gause, Mollie E. to J. H. Hunter 4-29-1861 (no return) Hy
Gause, Mollie to Carter Bush 7-6-1877 (no return) L
Gause, Pat to Zach Allen 1-18-1871 (1-19-1871) L
Gause, Pattie to Cubit Walker 1-22-1868 (1-23-1868) L B
Gause, Rozillia to William A. Mabrey 3-16-1868 (3-19-1868) L
Gause, Sarah A. to George A. Green (Guin-Given?) 10-25-1853 (10-27-1853) L
Gause, Sarah to Henry Rogers 6-9-1875 Hy
Gavage?, Tallie to Sanford Runnels 1-22-1876 Hy
Gay, Drucilla to William Allen 3-12-1875 Hy
Gay, Elizabeth to Caswell E. George 5-2-1855 G
Gay, Emeline to John Davis 4-9-1870 (4-12-1870) F
Gay, Inda to Gary Scott 9-29-1867 G
Gay, Jane to William Foster 11-18-1844 We
Gay, Lydia Ann to Thomas J. Clifft 2-11-1860 (2-13-1860) Hr
Gay, Mary S. S. to F. L. Hudson 12-7-1859 G
Gay, Mary to Richard E. Powell 10-15-1836 (10-20-1836) Hr
Gay, Mary to Thomas Hester 9-30-1850 Hr
Gay, Mattie to E. A. Oquinn 7-28-1874 (7-30-1874) Dy
Gay, Mila (Milla) to Green Lea Oldham 2-17-1839 Sh
Gay, Nannie to Thos. Hays 1-4-1871 T
Gay, P. M. to B. F. Bean 8-1-1859 G
Gay, Purlee to Wm. Scruggs 11-16-1858 Cr
Gayheart, Catherine to Johonn (John) Baker 8-27-1863 (8-28-1863) Sh
Gayle, Fany J. to Samuel M. Jobe 5-2-1855 (5-3-1855) Sh
Gayle, Sarah L. to Henry G. Dent 10-30-1851 Sh
Gayle, Virginia M. to A. R. McWilliams 2-26-1856 Sh
Gayler, Joana B. to Daniel S. Cannon 1-13-1857 Hr
Gaylor?, Catherine C. to Pascall G. Traylor 11-16-1836 Hr
Gaylord, Rebecca A. to James Bowles 7-18-1860 G
Geary, Honone to Martin Mancenier 6-21-1851 (6-22-1851) Sh
Geary, Margaret to John Wherry 10-24-1832 Sh
Geary, Mary to Andrew Kitson 6-15-1851 Sh
Geary, Mary to Edward Geary 1-14-1862 Sh
Gee, A. S. to Henry Comes 1-1-1873 (1-2-1873) Cr
Gee, Aira to Mathew Brown 5-9-1833 Sh
Gee, Eliza F. to Fleming C. Todd 10-21-1861 (10-22-1861) Cr
Gee, Emily S. to F. M. Welch 10-4-1858 (10-7-1858) Hr
Gee, Frances A. to N. G. Warbriton 12-12-1864 Cr
Gee, Hannah to Samuel Pate 8-25-1870 (8-28-1870) O
Gee, M. W. to J.H. Merrett 1-17-1871 (1-20-1871) Cr
Gee, Martha A. to M. L. Boston? 12-13-1858 Cr
Gee, Mary Ann to Wm. B. Ross 12-27-1847 Cr
Gee, Mary M. to John M. Bethill 2-12-1844 Cr
Gee, Mary to Archibald Mayfield 11-1-1852 (11-2-1852) Hr
Gee, Matilda E. to Westly Brasier 1-1-1866 (1-4-1866) Cr
Gee, Nancy to John Thompson 3-10-1857? (3-10-1858) Hr
Gee, Rebecca to George W. Hadin 11-6-1844 G
Gee, Sarah to Thomas Bolling 10-23-1834 Sh
Gee, Willey to James Lambert 9-15-1859 Hr
Gehan, Cordelia to William S. Herring 10-23-1849 (10-24-1848?) T
Geiberger, Hellen to W. Weiner 9-18-1860 Sh
Genberger, Louisa to Morris Hiltz 3-9-1863 Sh
Gendren, Rebecca Ann to Andrew Stevens 8-20-1845 (8-21-1845) T
Genest, Louisa to Benjamin F. Spellings 2-20-1838 G
Gennan, Ellen E. to Rufus Daniel 1-15-1856 Sh
Geno, Mary to Zachariah Thomas 5-15-1836 Sh
Genokio, Mary to Giovanni (John) Daneri 1-3-1860 (1-8-1860) Sh
Gensberger, Sarah to Saml. Levi 12-15-1852 Sh
Gensburger, Yittel to Itzig Happek 5-3-1856 Sh
Gentry, Amelia to John Yeargen 10-19-1858 We
Gentry, Caroline to Stephen Fuqua 2-4-1834 G
Gentry, Charlotte to Calvin A. Haly 7-2-1864 Sh

Gentry, M. A. to J. M. Webster 1-10-1872 Dy
Gentry, M. E. to C. J. Patterson 9-21-1865 G
Gentry, Martha to J. G. Weddle 2-24-1863 G
Gentry, Mary C. to James T. Hains 12-14-1831 G
Gentry, S. J. to J. M. Richardson 12-21-1864 O
Gentry, Susan to Alfred Caldwell 1-13-1879 (1-15-1879) L
Gentry, Susan to W. C. Stephenson 1-12-1876 Dy
George, A. S. to J. C. McBride 11-4-1865 (11-7-1865) T
George, Elizabeth B. to William H. Fuller 12-29-1844 T
George, Ellender to John W. Bentley 3-14-1855 Sh
George, Julia C. (Mrs.) to Frank Maior 5-10-1858 Sh
George, Laney to James Featherston 9-7-1854 G
George, Louisa to John F. Holt 1-31-1853 (2-3-1853) Sh
George, Lucinda to J. R. West 10-3-1866 G
George, Lydia Ann to Bernhart Hilson 6-2-1838 Sh
George, Martha to James S. Walker 12-10-1868 (12-15-1868) T
George, Mary E. to William H. Jones 8-25-1863 O
George, Mary Jane to W. A. Woodson 9-17-1856 (9-18-1856) T
George, Matilda Carolina to George Whooten 6-9-1852 Be CC
George, Matilda Caroline to George Whooton 6-9-1852 Be
George, Melvina to A. R. Hall 12-13-1870 (12-15-1870) Cr
George, Minerva to George B. Massey 10-18-1848 Sh
George, Nancy M. to Isaiah Edwards 9-1-1856 O
George, Nancy W. to William Lawrence 4-11-1826 (4-12-1862) Hr
George, Polina C. to William H. Gurley 11-12-1840 (11-18-1840) T
George, Polly K. to W. L. McLeyea 7-3-1863 G
George, R. E. (Mrs.) to W. H. Foster 5-30-1867 G
George, Rebecca to Samuel Hicks 4-26-1857 Cr
George, Ruth to William Massey 6-14-1855 G
George, Sarah C. to J. W. Foster 12-11-1865 (12-31-1865) Cr
George, Sarah to James F. Ross 4-27-1841 Hr
George, Sarah to Pleasant K. Larimore 5-18-1847 (5-20-1847) T
George, Susan A. to Wm. J. Williams 12-14-1854 Cr
Gerlach, Mary to William Horster 4-17-1860 Sh
Gerley, Thursey to John Brogdon 5-1-1846 (no return) Hn
German, Amanda P. to Luther Ables 4-10-1858 (4-13-1858) Hr
German, Elizabeth to William E. Gartman 11-3-1829 (11-4-1829) Hr
Germany, Nancy (Mrs.) to J. G. Elrod 11-5-1867 G
Germany?, Emily C. to F. C. Stephenson 12-25-1849 Sh
Gernerson, Elizabeth S. to J. D. Darnell 7-4-1852 Cr
Gester, Charlotte to Wm. H. Eitel 4-2-1846 M
Geter, Mary to Raleigh Shells 4-7-1866 (4-22-1866) F B
Geter, Susan W. to Tapley Oldham 8-18-1857 Sh
Geyle, P. E. to Lemuel B. Haughton 5-8-1860 (5-9-1860) Ma
Gholson, Frances to John Dodd 8-16-1853 (8-?-1853) Ma
Gholson, Margarett to Samuel G. Ganaway 10-12-1843 Ma
Gholson, Mary Ann to William Carson 12-10-1839 (12-12-1839) Ma
Gholston, Nancy to Meredith Alexander 11-15-1855 (no return) Hn
Ghrum, Louisa A. to Wm. N. Caps 8-15-1843 (no return) We
Gibbins, Mary K. to James Riggs 2-6-1845 Sh
Gibbins, Melissa A. to Jno. F. Morean 4-28-1842 Sh
Gibbins, Virginia J. to Henry E. Gartman 2-14-1850 Sh
Gibbon, Elizabeth B. to Samuel P. Finley 12-1-1853 Sh
Gibbons, Elizabeth to Henry Lebdor 4-8-1850 T
Gibbons, Frances A. to J. R. Patterson 11-4-1844 Sh
Gibbons, Julia to Patrick Doyle 8-16-1854 Sh
Gibbons, Margarett L. to J. W. Mills 9-18-1865 (9-20-1865) Cr
Gibbons, Mary to Michal Grogan 9-22-1862 Sh
Gibbons, Millissa A. to John F. Moran 4-28-1842 Sh
Gibbons, Sarah A. to John Walker 2-19-1855 Cr
Gibbons, Virginia C. to Willie C. Richardson 11-29-1871 (11-30-1871) Cr
Gibbs, Bettie to David Thompson 12-25-1883 (no return) L
Gibbs, Cylvia to Charles Lemes? 5-26-1866 (5-27-1866) T
Gibbs, E. J. to N. P. Pendleton 10-30-1858 (11-3-1858) Sh
Gibbs, Eliza to John Oakley 12-7-1858 We
Gibbs, Hannah to Fred Wanniger 4-9-1857 Sh
Gibbs, Judy F. to John Y. Harrison 12-23-1845 (12-25-1845) G
Gibbs, Laury E. to William May 3-15-1868 Be
Gibbs, Margaret to R. K. Blackwood 6-15-1854 Sh
Gibbs, Martha B. to J. R. A. Blackburn 11-30-1854 G
Gibbs, Martha D. to David D. Bell 4-9-1846 Ma
Gibbs, Martha M. to Thomas A. Simmons 12-23-1858 Sh
Gibbs, Sarah E. to William F. Tilly 11-26-1860 Hn
Gibbs, Sarah to David Harrison 5-8-1873 (no return) Hy
Gibson, Amanda to Ward, jr. Taylor 2-29-1860 (3-2-1860) Sh
Gibson, America to Saml. Cooper 3-6-1869 (3-9-1869) T
Gibson, Anna F. to John Myers 3-6-1854 (3-21-1854) Sh
Gibson, Anna to W. J. Bryant 3-11-1868 (no return) Dy
Gibson, Caroline to Alfred Loomis 3-11-1844 Hn
Gibson, Conne to David Warbritton 8-10-1856 Cr
Gibson, Dora to Mose Reed 3-29-1883 (4-1-1883) L
Gibson, E. A. to John W. Riggs 12-26-1867 F
Gibson, Elizabeth J. to Joseph B. Seawright 5-3-1849 Hn
Gibson, Elizabeth Jane to William Taylor 1-6?-1847 (1-7-1847) Hr
Gibson, Elizabeth to James I. Nicholdson 7-17-1846 O
Gibson, Elizabeth to Thomas Hudgens 7-10-1849 Hn
Gibson, Elizabeth to William J. Hansel 2-16-1860 Hn

Gibson, Ellen to Burton (Birton) Butler 6-24-1866 G
Gibson, Fanny to P. D. Monroe 11-4-1868 Hy
Gibson, Frances C. to Henry F. Denton 12-29-1868 (12-31-1868) L
Gibson, Harriet E. to G. W. Sudsberry 12-31-1884 L
Gibson, Izellah J. to Samuel W. Frazier 9-8-1863 G
Gibson, Jane to Winfrey McConnel 10-23-1866 O
Gibson, Jemima to James F. Hopkins 3-25-1868 Cr
Gibson, Katherine to J. W. Demoss 11-21-1855 Cr
Gibson, Lissey to A. McGill 10-28-1869 Be
Gibson, Lizzie to W. K. Gorsuch 2-1-1870 G
Gibson, Lucenda to Berry Patterson 6-13-1837 G
Gibson, Lucinda to Isaac Lemons 3-31-1839 Hn
Gibson, Lucy to A. G. King 3-2-1863 (3-3-1863) O
Gibson, Lue to Heywood Moore 2-10-1872 G
Gibson, Maggie to W. J. Bryant 10-28-1871 (10-29-1871) Dy
Gibson, Malinda to William Richardson 12-18-1851 Be
Gibson, Margaret Jane to Sheppard B. Thompson 3-20-1858 (4-6-1858) O
Gibson, Martha A. to William R. Moore 10-6-1855 (no return) Hn
Gibson, Martha Jane to James H. Parret 10-21-1854 Sh
Gibson, Martha to Allen Kenady 6-20-1849 Hn
Gibson, Mary Ann to James M. Hall 11-26-1846 Cr
Gibson, Mary Ann to John Behns 2-5-1870 Ma
Gibson, Mary C. to William Hanks 7-30-1864 G
Gibson, Mary O. to Felix Parker 6-22-1826 G
Gibson, Mary to G. A. Wicks 1-4-1875 (1-5-1875) Dy
Gibson, Mary to James R. Black 10-1-1857 Sh
Gibson, Mary to Newton Corbitt 8-18-1842 Sh
Gibson, Mary to Wm. R. Sawyer 1-27-1840 G
Gibson, Mattie E. A. to John D. Edson 8-15-1864 Sh
Gibson, Mattie J. to W. H. Mangrum 1-16-1866 Dy
Gibson, Milissia A. to A. A. O'Kane 8-8-1873 (9-3-1873) Cr
Gibson, Mollie E. to Benjamin F. Meter 1-8-1873 (1-9-1873) L
Gibson, Nancy E. to Wm. P. Ware 4-17-1858 Hr
Gibson, Nancy S. to Henderson A. Irby 4-10-1846 Sh
Gibson, Nancy to Robert Lipsey 12-8-1824 Sh
Gibson, Nancy to Thos. Dewey 3-4-1840 Cr
Gibson, Paty (Patsy) P. to Noah W. Dill 5-29-1850 Sh
Gibson, Permelia to John S. Mathews 1-25-1858 Be
Gibson, Persnetia A. to Wm. C. Bush 3-10-1847 Cr
Gibson, Phebe to Francis M. Walker 8-20-1849 (8-23-1849) O
Gibson, Rebecca to John Hale 5-30-1839 Cr
Gibson, Ruth to Robert W. Burns 7-17-1839 (7-19-1839) Ma
Gibson, Sallie to William Shepard 6-12-1872 Hy
Gibson, Sarah A. to John H. C. Moore 10-4-1853 Hn
Gibson, Sarah Catharine to Joseph A. Black 3-17-1859 Hr
Gibson, Sarah E. to James Dodson 9-8-1846 (9-9-1846) T
Gibson, Sarah H. to Wm. R. Sawyers 6-22-1836 (6-23-1836) G
Gibson, Sarah J. to James W. Chambers 1-22-1867 (1-23-1867) Dy
Gibson, Sarah J. to John Trout 7-15-1850 (7-16-1850) G
Gibson, Sarah to James C. Perkins 2-11-1863 Mn
Gibson, Sarah to William Grainger 7-19-1838 Hn
Gibson, Satira to Wm. H. Bland 6-30-1842 Sh
Gibson, Susan M. to William H. Thompson 8-1-1863 (8-2-1863) Dy
Gibson, Susan to Therling Pingston 3-18-1847 Hn
Gidcomb, Christiana to B. F. Woodruff 9-23-1880 L
Gidcomb, Emily C. to A. J. Hinds 8-25-1874 (8-26-1874) L
Gidcomb, Martha to Harrison A. Elverton 7-16-1873 L
Gidcomb, S. A. to J. C. Lacy 4-21-1877 (4-22-1887) L
Gidcombe, Luella to John Byram 4-26-1881 (4-27-1881) L
Gidcombe, Nancy J. to Nelson D. Brown 11-7-1866 (no return) L
Gidcum, Cornelia J. to Gideon Brogden 9-9-1861 (9-11-1861) L
Gidcum, Mary Ann to James Cessel 8-25-1863 (no return) L
Gidcum, Susan to John Irvin 9-1-1863 (no return) L
Gideons, Ada to Elisha Robbins 12-6-1871 (no return) Hy
Giffrey, Zilpha to Balam Lundy 3-9-1867 (3-12-1867) T
Gift, E. R. to John A. Trigg 3-13-1854 (3-14-1854) Sh
Gift, J. Volney to R. H. Taylor 10-6-1859 Sh
Gift, Kate to Adolphus Cooper 5-14-1864 Sh
Gift, Maaria L. to M. L. Sims 6-3-1846 Sh
Gift, Mary A. to J. J. Rawlings 8-3-1848 Sh
Gilaspie, Caroline to Zachariah D. Barker 7-4-1844 O
Gilaspie, Caroline to Zachariah D. Barker 7-9-1842 O
Gilbert, A. M. to Samuel C. McClanahan 10-9-1860 We
Gilbert, C. L. to George Neuell? 11-8-1858 Hn
Gilbert, Eliza to Joseph Moore 9-25-1868 (9-27-1868) Cr
Gilbert, Elizabeth P. to Carter L. Allen 12-28-1858 We
Gilbert, Elizabeth to Doctor P. Wrays 8-6-1856 We
Gilbert, Elizabeth to Isaac Thomas 8-14-1838 Cr
Gilbert, Elizabeth to John D. Upton 5-18-1852 Hn
Gilbert, Ellen H. to J. L. Kennedy 10-1-1850 Sh
Gilbert, Ellen to Robert Gilbert 2-18-1870 (2-20-1870) Cr
Gilbert, Emeline to Joseph Gilbert 1-21-1871 (no return) Cr B
Gilbert, Esabella to George Drake 9-2-1868 (9-3-1868) Cr
Gilbert, Frances M. to W. L. Foster 10-22-1856 We
Gilbert, Harriet to Wm. A. Rhea 9-7-1861 (9-8-1861) Sh
Gilbert, Mary Ann to James R. Rogers 8-1-1861 Mn
Gilbert, Mary S. to D. M. Upton 11-15-1865 Hn

Gilbert, Mary to Charles Perkins 4-10-1874 (no return) Hy
Gilbert, Mary to N. R. Hays 2-5-1845 Sh
Gilbert, Milly N. to W. M. Pierce 4-5-1866 Be
Gilbert, N. F. to W. H. M. Brooks 4-14-1857 We
Gilbert, Penelope to I. W. Covington 10-15-1860 (no return) We
Gilbert, Rebecca to William Litton 12-20-1866 Be
Gilbert, Sarah E. to M. E. Roberts 8-7-1847 Sh
Gilbert, T. A. to W. I. Bynum 1-1-1867 O
Gilbert, Vira to Carroll Moore 12-25-1871 (no return) Cr B
Gilbins, Cornelia E. to Jacob Gartman 4-6-1856 (6-5-1856) Sh
Gilbreth, Mary E. to B. S. Ables 7-8-1844 (no return) F
Gilchrist, Amanda G. to William D. Scott 6-9-1835 G
Gilchrist, Juliana to Thomas Taylor 9-19-1831 (9-21-1831) G
Gilchrist, L. J. to H. A. Pettigrew 12-31-1865 Mn
Gilchrist, Martha E. to Robert Seat 7-7-1831 G
Gilchrist, V. M. (Mrs.) to Augustus A. Fulghum 6-6-1862 G
Gilerland, Nancy A. to Solomon H. Stanley 12-16-1839 (no return) F
Giles, Alminda N. J. to W. F. Perry 12-7-1852 (12-9-1852) G
Giles, Bettie (Mrs.) to John R. Rust 10-12-1867 (10-13-1867) Cr
Giles, Elizabeth to R. B. Saunders 10-1-1866 (10-2-1866) Dy
Giles, J. L. to R. F. Person 2-23-1858 (2-24-1858) Sh
Giles, Larue to R. H. Randolph 5-27-1863 (5-29-1863) Sh
Giles, M. C. to J. C. McCollum 12-28-1872 (12-29-1872) Cr
Giles, M. E. to J. W. Wingo 9-4-1865 G
Giles, Malvina C. to Joseph Minton 5-8-1856 Sh
Giles, Margaret A. to George Wilkerson 1-17-1850 Sh
Giles, Margaret M. to Tallassee G. Bond 3-28-1844 Sh
Giles, Mary M. to Wm. Humphrey 9-10-1851 (no return) Cr
Giles, Mary Margaret to Wade Henry 10-30-1849 (11-1-1849) T
Giles, Mary to T. R. Salmon 5-24-1843 Cr
Giles, Matilda F. to George Abbott 4-6-1842 Cr
Giles, Mollie to Charles Kunholz 11-1-1859 Sh
Giles, Puss to L. C. Harvell 3-7-1865 (3-8-1865) Dy
Giles, Rachel to Wesley Kelly 3-30-1858 Cr
Giles, Sarah F. to Alfred W. Campbell 10-13-1851 (no return) F
Giles, Sarilda F. to William P. Day 9-25-1856 (9-28-1856) Sh
Giles, Susan C. to R. E. Bogle 12-27-1868 (12-28-1868) Cr
Gilespie, America A. to A. J. Perkins 5-24-1854 Be
Gilfil, Mary to John J. Kiser 3-30-1861 (3-31-1861) Sh
Gilham, Mollie to George Dickerson 1-19-1872 T
Gilhan, Harriet to Moses Morris 1-1-1871? (1-1-1872) T
Gilhouly, Bridget to John Mahan 2-1-1856 (2-3-1856) Sh
Gilkey, E. J. to J. A. Harper 3-4-1869 (3-7-1869) Cr
Gilkey, Martha Jane to Isaac Day 10-20-1859 Sh
Gill, Albina to James Day 3-6-1873 (no return) Hy
Gill, Amanda to Thompson James 10-16-1840 (no return) F
Gill, Caroline T. to William Hazlewood 2-11-1856 Ma
Gill, Cynthia A. to Kenneth G. Hicks 9-28-1858 (9-29-1858) Ma
Gill, Elizabeth A. F. to William Fortune 1-25-1842 G
Gill, Elizabeth to Thomas S. Sellars 2-11-1861 (2-13-1861) Sh
Gill, Emily J. to Thomas T. Kelsey (Kilsey) 5-29-1850 Sh
Gill, Fannie E. to Handsel W. Burrow 10-12-1857 (10-13-1857) Ma
Gill, Feliceann to Seburn Bickerstaff 10-12-1826 (SB 10-26?) Sh
Gill, Fillis to Jacob Rayner 1-25-1870 (no return) Hy
Gill, J. E. to Charles A. Miller 1-2-1867 G
Gill, Laura E. to Henry R. Brooks 12-21-1866 (12-30-1866) F
Gill, Lina to Doctor Snipes 3-11-1869 Hy
Gill, Lucy to James R. West 5-23-1859 (5-24-1859) G
Gill, Mariah to U. W. Lester 9-16-1864 Sh
Gill, Martha C. to J. Frank Jones 12-14-1870 (12-15-1870) Ma
Gill, Mary C. to W. J. Johnson 3-12-1870 (3-13-1870) Cr
Gill, Mollie F. to William H. Bruton 12-18-1866 (12-20-1866) Ma
Gill, Nancy A. to Eli Arnold 2-19-1855 (8-9-1855) Sh
Gill, Rebecca Elender to Lafayett Varden 5-23-1854 G
Gill, Rebecca to Nathan Harris 3-28-1860 Sh
Gill, Sarah to Henry Ligen Taylor 11-9-1874 Hy
Gill, Sarah to Pat O'Huie 4-29-1861 Sh
Gill, Susan to Charles Somerville 11-11-1869 Hy
Gillaland, Lyd A. to Edward Williams 1-30-1861 (no return) Dy
Gillam, Elizabeth to Z. Scott 10-26-1851 Hn
Gillam, Francis to G. W. Rogers 7-19-1863 We
Gillam, Martha to H. J. Trent 1-25-1845 (no return) We
Gillam, Mary to Dudley Glass 4-15-1855 We
Gilland, Florence to Harrison Smith 9-5-1872 T
Gilland, Julia to Peter Connelly 5-21-1862 Sh
Gilland, Sarah to Herrod Holt 12-28-1833 (1-2-1834) G
Gilland, Susan to William James 1-6-1863 (1-7-1863) Sh
Gillaspie, Alevy C. to James W. Cathey 2-23-1859 We
Gillaspie, Faney E. to H. T. Hollis 10-25-1849 We
Gillaspie, Margaret L. to D. D. Brooks 11-27-1861 (no return) We
Gillaspie, Martha to G. G. Hudson 12-26-1860 (12-3?-1860) F
Gilleland, Elizabeth to Henry C. Cave 11-10-1852 Hn
Gilleland, Sarah A. F. to Johnathan (Norman?) Williams 10-7-1873 (10-9-1873) T
Gillen, Cathern to Mickeal Galliger 8-24-1862 Sh
Gillen, Mary E. (Miss) to W. b. Archer 1-3-1863 (1-4-1863) Sh
Gilles, Mary to Alford Gleason 2-1-1847 (2-3-1847) O

Gillespie, A. S. to B. F. Roe 6-4-1861 G
Gillespie, A. V. to James McIntosh 12-15-1869 G
Gillespie, Amanda to H. W. Bradford 5-10-1854 G
Gillespie, Cynthia to Felix Houston 6-6-1832 Hr
Gillespie, Delia to Marvin (Marion?) Sanford 7-29-1870 G
Gillespie, Elizabeth H. to James A. McGee 11-8-1854 (11-9-1854) G
Gillespie, Lucy A. to Willis C. Ward 1-1-1851 G
Gillespie, Mariah W. to Thomas Bradford 7-30-1850 G
Gillespie, Martha to John R. Lanom 12-5-1860 G
Gillespie, Mary A. to John Rodiman 5-2-1850 Sh
Gillespie, Mary Ann to William H. Stilwell 11-26-1850 (11-28-1850) G
Gillespie, Mary E. to Robert Gillespie 2-6-1864 Sh
Gillespie, Mary J. to R. B. Travis 12-10-1857 Be
Gillespie, Mary M. to John Nelson 11-20-1851 L
Gillespie, Mary V. to Patrick Cowan 1-14-1862 Sh
Gillespie, Mary to Drew Neel 10-20-1869 (10-21-1869) F B
Gillespie, Melinda C. to Saml. R. Morrow 1-24-1842 (1-27-1842) Hr
Gillespie, N. A. to John Lee 9-14-1862 G
Gillespie, Nancy Jane to James A. Hudson 2-6-1840 Sh
Gillespie, Sally to Andrew McQuiston 11-13-1856 Sh
Gillespie, Sarah E. to D. M. Witherington 12-20-1853 Sh
Gillespie, Sarah J. to Jessee L. Branch 1-16-1844 (1-18-1844) G
Gillespie, Sarah L. to James D. Driver 11-21-1860 L
Gillett, Mary to Robert Tucker 12-31-1840 Cr
Gillette, Julia Ann to John D. Norris 6-17-1843 Sh
Gillham, Sarah A. to J. Crafton 8-26-1859 Sh
Gilliam, Alline O. to F. R. Jones 12-14-1876 Hy
Gilliam, Cynthia to Andrew Derryberry 4-8-1853 Ma
Gilliam, Ednie to Jeff Frence 11-24-1878 Hy
Gilliam, Elizabeth to Beverly A. Allen 8-14-1856 (8-16-1856) O
Gilliam, Elizabeth to M. B. Fryar 5-22-1866 O
Gilliam, Hannah to W. G. Lane 12-14-1864 G
Gilliam, Lucy E. to Wm. I. Dinwiddie 9-13-1838 Cr
Gilliam, Martha Ann to John E. Gilliam 11-19-1866 (11-20-1866) Ma
Gilliam, Mary P. to T. N. Hughes 2-18-1868 (2-27-1868) F
Gilliam, Prissilla to William Smith 8-12-1841 (no return) F
Gilliam, S. P. to R. E. Boges 3-15-1866 G
Gilliland, Ann E. to A. C. Wilson 9-16-1859 Sh
Gilliland, Elen to Hugh Clay 12-10-1873 (12-11-1873) L B
Gilliland, Eliza to James Searcy 2-15-1876 (2-17-1876) L
Gilliland, Elizabeth to Wm. Smith 5-8-1838 (5-12-1838) G
Gilliland, Frances to Adam Trout 11-23-1834 G
Gilliland, Frances to Miles H. Travis 8-28-1863 G
Gilliland, Liddy to Francis M. Crocker 8-9-1837 (8-13-1837) G
Gilliland, Luanna to Samuel Dewalt 2-18-1871 (2-19-1871) L
Gilliland, Malinda to Richardson P. White 1-13-1845 (1-16-1845) G
Gilliland, Manerva to Sandford Thedford 2-6-1843 (2-9-1843) G
Gilliland, Margaret E. to Bartholomew C. Britton 4-11-1861 Ma
Gilliland, Mary to Socrates Tompkins 1-10-1872 L
Gilliland, Tericy to J. A. W. Pittman 11-29-1853 (12-1-1853) G
Gillim, Mary to Jesse Harris 9-7-1856 We
Gillis (Giles), Catharine to Jesse Hines (Hynes) 4-22-1841 O
Gillis, Christian to Andrew J. Baird 1-19-1844 (1-21-1844) O
Gillis, Flora to Carney Barber 2-14-1838 O
Gillis, M. C. to John M. Letsinger 10-7-1849 Cr
Gillis, M. J. G. to John B. Avey 12-27-1871 Dy
Gillis, Mary to Patrick Powers 6-15-1863 Sh
Gillis, Mollie to David C. James 1-16-1867 Dy
Gillis, S. E. to D. H. Stephens 3-11-1875 Dy
Gillis, S. M. C. to B. A. B. Peery 4-4-1871 (4-6-1871) Dy
Gillispie, E. to R. H. Hawthorn 12-24-1847 Be
Gillispie, Louisa Jane to Joel S. Herrin (Hening) 1-7-1840 Sh
Gillispie, Martha E. to John J. Kee 1-26-1868 Be
Gillispie, Mary L. to J. S. Stewart 8-15-1849 Sh
Gillispie, Olivia to William Gillispie 12-28-1853 Be
Gillispie, Rebecca Jane to Stephen B. Herring 1-2-1845 Sh
Gillispie, Sarah G. to J. P. B. Alexander 12-15-1842 Sh
Gillmore, Mary D. to Presley Turner 1-4-1869 (1-6-1869) F
Gills, Amanda to Joseph Nash 2-12-1873 O
Gills, Elizabeth to Edmond M. Davis 9-9-1877 O
Gills, Hellen to Nicholas Young 1-29-1867 Hy
Gills, M. J. to H. J. Farmer 10-1-1862 O
Gills, Martha E. to Robert H. Statham 4-15-1858 O
Gills, Martha Louisa to James Gills 5-12-1858 O
Gills, Nancy S. to James R. Gills 9-28-1844 (10-29-1844) O
Gills, S. W. to N. G. Nicols 1-11-1868 O
Gillum, Eliza to Samuel Scott 12-28-1855 (no return) Hn
Gillum, Ellen to James W. Pillow 9-13-1855 (no return) Hn
Gillum, Frances to Isaac N. Little 10-25-1849 Hn
Gillum, Mary A. to Andrew Dinwiddie 3-5-1844 Hn
Gillum, Mary to Benjamin W. Bond 4-24-1850 Sh
Gillum, Mary to ____ Wallace 5-25-1867 T
Gillum, Matilda to Saml. Adkins 1-11-1873 O
Gillum, Sarah E. to William A. Biddle 10-22-1866 (10-30-1866) Ma
Gillun, Harriet to Rufus Howard 5-25-1867 T
Gilmon(Gilmore?), Deborah to Po A. Williams 3-16-1847 (3-23-1847) Hr
Gilmore, Ann to James McCordell 4-19-1853 Sh

Gilmore, Eleonor to Jeremiah Hooper 12-30-1841 Hr
Gilmore, Jane C. to William M. Claunch 7-22-1844 (7-25-1844) F
Gilmore, Jane to Anderson King 1-4-1849 (1-7-1849) Hr
Gilmore, Jane to John Ferrell 2-6-1848 Sh
Gilmore, Rebecca H. to Wm. H. Potts 11-25-1848 Sh
Gilmore, Sintha to Albert G. Jeter 6-9-1847 (no return) F
Gilpin, Margarett to Joshua Cathey 8-5-1862 G
Gilstrop, Mary Ann to David L. Bishop 11-14-1842 (11-17-1842) L
Gilstrop, Nancy to Wade A. Alverson 8-20-1847 (8-26-1847) L
Giner, Martha A. to Edmund J. Hagler 8-26-1842 Hn
Gingery, Elizabeth R. to Carrol J. Bradford 8-9-1847 (8-17-1847) L
Ginn, E. H. to I. I. Kidd 5-14-1866 O
Ginn, Georgie to J. T. Carington 3-22-1871 Hy
Ginn, Melvina to Samuel Johnson 8-6-1863 Mn
Ginor (Genoe), Sarah A. to D. H. Blaylock 7-9-1838 Sh
Gire, Caroline to William S. Potter 1-26-1861 We
Gisel, V. to M. Shilling 9-6-1855 Sh
Gist, Elizabeth to John Tesh 9-26-1861 Cr
Given, America to W. W. Melton 5-25-1866 (5-27-1866) L
Given, Caroline to Washington Eddins 1-24-1857 (1-28-1857) Ma
Given, Katie L. to J. A. Hendron 7-20-1885 L
Given, M. E. to J. T. Sistruck 1-25-1882 (1-30-1882) L
Given, Mary Loulie to Francis M. Sangster 1-19-1869 (1-21-1869) L
Given, Nancy to Zinas Alexander 5-14-1844 (5-16-1844) L
Given, ____ Caras to Stephen G. Barnes (Burnes?) 9-27-1849 L
Given?, Elizabeth to Benjamin Jenkins 3-26-1873 (3-28-1873) L B
Givens, Adaline to A. G. Hall 2-24-1852 (no return) Hn
Givens, Amanda to John M. Johnson 6-14-1848 (6-15-1848) Ma
Givens, Carrie L. to Thomas E. Scales 4-28-1856 (4-30-1856) G
Givens, Delila to John B. Fields 1-9-1880 (1-11-1880) L
Givens, Elizabeth to E. F. Vernon 6-4-1884 (6-8-1884) L
Givens, Harriet to Robt. Morgan 8-20-1870 T
Givens, Lucy A. to John W. Hall 12-21-1853 Hn
Givens, M. C. (Mrs.) to Spencer Hall 8-2-1866 G
Givens, Mary to Willim A. Wright 3-25-1829 (3-26-1829) Ma
Givens, Nannie to John T. Harrison 5-6-1867 (5-16-1867) Ma
Givens, S. A. to S. R. Roach 11-26-1874 Hy
Givens, Sarah to Bob Donaldson 12-16-1866 G
Givens, Sarah to Hardy Mayo 3-31-1853 Ma
Givens, Violetta to James Cowgile (Cowgill) 8-25-1837 Sh
Givens, Winnefred H. to Harrison Johnson 9-25-1845 Ma
Givin, Bertha to Henry Cooper 8-22-1843 We
Givings, Mary A. to William Jones 10-6-1853 Sh
Givins, Bettie to Antonio Andrews 5-29-1867 G B
Givins, Elizabeth to Joel Sawyer 1-29-1846 Sh
Givins, Margaret to Patrick Manning 12-23-1854 (12-26-1854) Sh
Gizzard, Elizabeth B. to Gabriel Chandler 1-22-1855 (1-25-1855) Ma
Glaason, Mary Ann E. to William S. Brooks 10-15-1849 (10-18-1849) G
Gladding, Susan W. to Elias Edward Bruner 6-10-1850 Sh
Gladney, Ann to Joseph W. McClohm 5-10-1842 (5-12-1842) Ma
Gladney, Elizabet L. to Joseph J. Cooper 11-20-1845 Ma
Gladney, Jane R. to Jesse Currie 10-29-1860 Ma
Gladney, Louisa Jane to Stephen Miller 9-28-1849 (10-2-1849) Ma
Gladney, Margarett M. to James L. Longhorn 11-22-1842 Ma
Glancy, Julie to Patrick Johnson 9-24-1866 (9-28-1866) Cr
Glancy, Maria to Patrick Conway 11-16-1857 Sh
Glancy, Mary to John Farmer 12-26-1859 Sh
Glancy, Mary to John Joyce 11-29-1862 Sh
Glascock, A. A. to T. J. Pate 8-6-1863 G
Glascock, Martha to Leroy H. Bell 11-12-1838 G
Glascock, Nany to Spenson Glascock 10-14-1844 G
Glascoe, Eliza to David Laird 9-30-1858 Hn
Glascow, Susanah to David Denney 11-15-1864 (11-16-1864) O
Glasgow, Ann Eliza to Thomas Peters 6-15-1837 (6-22-1837) Hr
Glasgow, Eliza J. to James W. Waren 8-3-1856 G
Glasgow, Elizabeth G. to Gabriel M. Bartlet 12-3-1846 F
Glasgow, Maranda P. C. to William M. Hicks 3-20-1862 We
Glasgow, Mary A. to Wm. M. Irion 3-19-1851 (3-20-1851) Sh
Glasgow, Melissa to William G. Skiles 6-18-1855 (6-19-1855) G
Glason, Cenith C. to Horace R. Barksdale 10-27-1849 (10-28-1849) G
Glason, Sarey to William Ridgeway 4-3-1830 G
Glasper, Caroline to John Baily 8-28-1867 Hy
Glass, Ada P. to W. P. H. Butler 7-5-1876 L
Glass, Ada to John Ruffin 11-24-1880 L B
Glass, Artemisia to Isaac Terrell 1-25-1856 T
Glass, Caroline E. to William D. Nowlin 11-29-1862 We
Glass, Cele to Nicholas P. Smith 2-8-1842 (2-10-1842) L
Glass, Cora to George Burks 1-26-1877 L
Glass, Elizabeth I. to Nicholas H. Whitehorn 11-26-1849 (11-29-1849) Hr
Glass, Ellen to Robert Gardner 5-29-1877 (5-31-1877) O
Glass, Emma to L. E. Warrington 1-1-1856 Sh
Glass, Jan M. to Wm. Bryant 9-1-1845 (9-16-1845) Hr
Glass, Jones to S. A. Dewees 11-2-1874 (11-4-1874) T
Glass, Lou A. to D. L. Paty 1-15-1867 (no return) Hn
Glass, Louisa E. (A.) to T. B. Phelps 9-18-1855 (no return) We
Glass, Lousa to William Gilliland 1-25-1877 L
Glass, Lucinda to George Blackwell 1-16-1867 (1-17-1867) L B

Glass, Malissa J. to John H. Hightower 1-30-1869 (2-4-1869) T
Glass, Margaret Ann to George R. McCommon 10-1-1852 (10-3-1852) Hr
Glass, Mary A. to Daniel Gray 1-29-1848 (2-1-1848) Hr
Glass, Mary A. to Wm. A. Yarbrough 11-12-1851 (11-13-1851) T
Glass, Mary D. to Benjamin A. Tansil 12-8-1862 We
Glass, Mary Jane to Geo. E. Armstead 2-8-1870 (2-9-1870) Ma
Glass, Mary L. to Robert C. Campbell 12-12-1843 Sh
Glass, Mary to George C. Henderson 3-9-1843 Hn
Glass, Mary to Jacob Scurry 11-8-1873 T
Glass, Mary to T. F. Gregory 6-11-1885 L
Glass, Matilda to Samuel McClish 1-8-1885 L
Glass, N. A. to Z. W. Allen 1-8-1863 We
Glass, Nancy A. to William J. Brantly 12-31-1844 (1-2-1845) Hr
Glass, Nancy to John Henderson 10-18-1842 Hn
Glass, Rachel S. to Maxfield Wilson 1-25-1856 (1-30-1856) Hr
Glass, Rachel S. to George W. Belote 6-2-1838 Hr
Glass, Rebecca Ann to Mathew Thomas Prewitt 4-10-1848 (4-11-1848) Hr
Glass, Rebecca T. to John K. Neely 11-29-1858 (11-30-1858) Hr
Glass, Sarah A. to W. A. Wilson 10-20-1866 (10-21-1866) L
Glass, Sarah Ann to Henry Cannon 8-12-1858 T
Glass, Sarah to James Orr 2-24-1869 (2-25-1869) T
Glass, Silvia to Moses Harris 7-17-1869 (7-18-1869) T
Glass, T. to John Kelly 10-24-1874 (10-29-1874) T
Glasscock, Lucenda to Owen Tombs 2-28-1835 G
Glasscock, Malinda to William C. Jack 9-24-1831 (10-2-1831) G
Glasscock, Nancy J. to F. Marcum 9-6-1868 G
Glasscock, Nancy to Joseph Pate 6-22-1836 G
Glasscock, Polly to Wilson Brown 11-18-1828 G
Glasscock, Rachael to James Trosper 7-12-1834 G
Glasscock, Sarah to Wm. T. Huckby 11-22-1836 (11-23-1836) G
Glawson, E. to A. J. Bonds 12-1-1851 Cr
Glaze, Docid to Thomas Dallis 12-19-1870 (12-29-1871?) L
Glaze, Lucy to Jasper Lockheart 7-1-1875 (7-7-1875) L
Gleason, Eliza Jane to Calvin Keathley 2-21-1843 (2-?-1843) O
Gleason, Elizabeth to Sinclar Taylor 11-30-1848 O
Gleason, Emy to John Scott 1-2-1867 G
Gleason, Mary to W. R. Kimble 10-21-1852 Hn
Gleason, Nancy to Rigdon Grady 8-1-1836 (8-19-1836) G
Gleason, Nancy to Samuel Houghs 8-19-1838 G
Gleason, Sarah J. to James G. Barksdale 12-8-1860 G
Gleaves, Harriet to R. S. Crow 1-17-1872 (1-18-1872) Dy
Gleaves, Susan to Franklin Miller 6-5-1852 (6-6-1852) O
Gleen, Malinda to Lewis Moody 9-27-1869 G B
Gleeson, Margaret E. to Andrew Maloan 12-27-1846 We
Gleeson, Martha K. to George A. Smith 12-8-1847 (12-9-1847) Ma
Gleeson, Mary A. to Calvin J. Rogers 10-9-1845 (no return) We
Glen, Mary to William Lamkin 4-4-1840 Hr
Glenn, Anna to Carroll Mitchell 11-15-1871 Hy
Glenn, Annie to J. E. Smith 7-4-1872 Hy
Glenn, Bedience to Joe L. Boyd 10-1-1876 Hy
Glenn, Bettie H. to Jno. W. Fitzhugh 1-2-1869 Ma
Glenn, Daphne to John Tyus 12-18-1878 L B
Glenn, E. R. to S. A. Winston 2-4-1857 We
Glenn, Elizabeth C. to Samuel G. Anderson 2-9-1860 Hn
Glenn, Elizabeth to James H. Baker 12-27-1849 (12-29-1849) Ma
Glenn, Elizabeth to Shadrach Williams 1-26-1871 (2-9-1871) L
Glenn, Elizabeth to William Perciful 3-16-1854 Ma
Glenn, Elizabeth to Wm. Dillingham 10-10-1878 Dy
Glenn, Emily to George Smith 3-26-1868 G B
Glenn, Laura L. to R. H. Warren 12-26-1866 (12-27-1866) L
Glenn, Lourana L. to R. W. Warren 12-26-1866 (12-27-1866) L
Glenn, Lydia to John T. Byrum 11-1-1866 Ma
Glenn, Maie to Henry C. Brown 5-19-1871 (5-22-1871) Ma
Glenn, Marcilla? to Abner Warren 8-17-1846 (8-20-1846) Hr
Glenn, Margaret to Barney Burns 3-15-1862 (3-17-1862) Sh
Glenn, Martha to J. Y. St. John 12-4-1865 O
Glenn, Mary J. to H. R. Mullins 2-9-1864 (2-16-1864) O
Glenn, Mary to F. M. Davis 12-1-1856 (12-2-1856) Ma
Glenn, Mary to James Velse 4-11-1848 Sh
Glenn, Mattie T. to L. C. Carrigan 3-26-1868 Hy
Glenn, S. T. to Robert Seat 2-23-1846 We
Glenn, Sarah A. to William Morrow 11-11-1854 (12-10-1854) O
Glenn, Susannah to Green? B. Elerson 11-18-1845 (11-20-1845) Hr
Glevur?, Lizzie to Henry Taylor 11-30-1872 (12-1-1872) Dy
Glidewell, Eliza to George W. Miller 8-4-1846 (8-5-1846) Ma
Glidewell, Elizabeth J. to William Cox 8-3-1846 Ma
Glidewell, Martha to Eliazer Sullivan 9-26-1870 (9-28-1870) Ma
Glidewell, Martha to Isaac McCarver 8-6-1849 Ma
Glidewell, Mary to William Tims 8-6-1852 Ma
Glidewell, Nany to Francis Perry 7-23-1842 (7-26-1842) G
Glidwell, Catherine to Jesse Edwards 10-25-1856 Ma
Glidwell, Evalina L. to Nathaniel Miller 8-27-1856 Ma
Glidwell, Jane (Mrs.) to John T. Tims 9-7-1858 (9-9-1858) Ma
Glidwell, Mary M. to James M. Jackson 5-5-1856 (5-13-1856) Hr
Glidwell, N. to Wiseman Savage 1-26-1848 Hr
Glidwell, Sarah to Thomas Percival 11-27-1840 Ma
Glimp, D. M. to Thomas N. Wakefield 3-7-1871 (3-8-1870?) L

Glimp, Delilah to John Hunter 12-7-1880 (12-8-1880) L
Glimp, Elizabeth D. to Aruous E. Lundsford 2-14-1866 L
Glimp, Elizabeth to William M. Hunter 2-26-1867 (2-27-1867) L
Glimp, Joana A. to Absolum C. Braden 12-1-1868 (12-2-1868) L
Glimp, L. E. to C. W. Tull 1-3-1883 (1-10-1884) L
Glimp, M. J. to H. B. Braden 2-7-1882 (2-8-1882) L
Glimp, Millie to W. C. Crook 1-6-1869 (1-?-1869) L
Glimp, Nancy W. to Thomas E. Whitson 2-27-1861 L
Glimp, Winna Frances to William Hunter 11-6-1856 L
Glisson, Barbery to Stephen Jones 2-6-1852 G
Glisson, Catherine to Caswell C. Mifflin 1-21-1871 (1-22-1871) Dy
Glisson, Clarissa to John R. Pate 9-19-1850 (9-22-1850) G
Glisson, Elizabeth J. to Paul T. Barner 11-21-1853 (11-22-1853) G
Glisson, Eveline to Tobe Thompson 12-10-1867 (12-12-1867) T
Glisson, Harrett to Absolum Witherington 11-26-1851 G
Glisson, Louisa to A. C. Ridgway 12-29-1861 G
Glisson, Martha R. to Crockett Kimpel 8-29-1861 Hn
Glisson, Mary E. to Pinkney P. Phillips 12-12-1837 (12-15-1837) O
Glisson, Mary to Polk Perry 4-4-1867 Hn
Glisson, Mattie to D. H. Jackson 3-28-1874 (4-12-1874) O
Glisson, Nancy to Wiley P. Mangrum 3-9-1857 (3-10-1857) O
Glisson, Piercy to William Robbins 2-25-1843 (2-?-1843) O
Glisson, Rachal to John N. Bush 10-12-1847 G
Glisson, Sally Ann to Thomas Fleming 11-21-1854 (11-22-1854) Sh
Glisson, Sarah I. to James R. Harrell 8-9-1838 Sh
Glisson, Susan to Wm. B. Ross 1-21-1848 Sh
Glosson, Rebecca to Thos. Dickson 8-18-1854 (no return) Cr
Gloster, Martha to Edmond Dortch 4-9-1866 (4-30-1866) F B
Gloster, Mary D. to Alex P. Rose 1-22-1867 (1-24-1867) F
Gloster, Roberta to Marion Allen 4-25-1866 (6-17-1866) F B
Glover, A. C. to Wm. C. Fleming 2-22-1864 (2-24-1864) O
Glover, Adaline to William T. Gore 3-16-1852 O
Glover, Commency A. to W. F. White 10-25-1856 (10-26-1856) Sh
Glover, Delila to John Hudgens 3-17-1851 Hn
Glover, E. A. to J. F. Lewis 12-2-1871 (no return) Cr
Glover, Eliza to John Cooper 1-24-1868 (1-25-1871?) T
Glover, Elizabeth H. to Jacob Parker 9-22-1850 Ma
Glover, Elizabeth to A. D. Whitley 7-31-1867 O
Glover, Elizabeth to J. S. Williams 10-22-1864 (10-23-1864) O
Glover, Elizabeth to William H. Houston 3-17-1866 (3-18-1866) Cr
Glover, Ellen V. to Wm. D. S. Cook 9-8-1861 Sh
Glover, Judy A. to Henry S. Fleming 5-22-1854 (no return) Cr
Glover, Laura to Wesley Jones 2-24-1876 (no return) Hy
Glover, Letha E. to John G. Lamb 7-21-1841 Hn
Glover, M. J. to J. L. Mosier 3-23-1863 O
Glover, Margaret to T. S. Hickman 1-7-1856 (1-9-1856) O
Glover, Mariah to Barney Duffie 12-25-1849 O
Glover, Martha E. to William J. Boaz 2-7-1862 (no return) Cr
Glover, Martha F. to John E. Cloar 9-11-1865 (9-13-1865) O
Glover, Martha J. to T. J. Utley 8-19-1861 Mn
Glover, Martha to David Haynes 4-1-1847 Hn
Glover, Martha to David Upchurch 11-7-1851 Hn
Glover, Martha to Levi W. Lorance 2-5-1839 Cr
Glover, Mary A. to John M. Myrick 9-6-1860 Sh
Glover, Mary A. to Thos. S. Carson 4-20-1853 (no return) F
Glover, Mary D. to Jonatan Haynes 1-7-1841 (1-7-1842?) O
Glover, Mary Jame? to Jeremiah McCarter 3-14-1854 Sh
Glover, Mary M. to Robert D. Morris 12-3-1850 (12-5-1850) Ma
Glover, Melica A. to G. C. Dodds 4-12-1858 O
Glover, Melicia A. to G. C. Dodds 4-12-1850 O
Glover, Nancy Ann to J. D. Killyon 8-21-1866 Hn
Glover, O. L. to T. C. Cloar 6-22-1865 O
Glover, S. E. J. to Wm. G. Chambers 3-10-1863 (3-11-1863) O
Glover, Samantha to A. J. Forgey 10-26-1853 Sh
Glover, Susan to A. J. Wheeler 3-2-1859 (3-3-1859) Sh
Glowson, Sarah to Demsey Dickerson 1-5-1856 (no return) Cr
Glraham, E. C. to George M. Williams 12-5-1853 (12-7-1853) Hr
Goad, A. E. to D. E. Park 4-19-1865 (5-21-1865) O
Goad, Emily E. to Richd. Grantham 12-5-1844 (12-12-1844) Hr
Goad, Jane to Boyd Treese 3-7-1852 (3-18-1852) Hr
Goad, M. Mary to Manoah F. Jones 7-23-1853 (7-24-1853) Ma
Goad, Margarett to George W. Lumpkins 8-2-1848 (8-3-1848) Ma
Goad, N. J. to R. M. Orverby 9-21-1872 (9-22-1872) O
Goan, Louisa to John Timmons 1-19-1874 (no return) L B
Gobble, Mary E. to Alexander Hall 12-20-1858 (12-29-1858) O
Gober, Eliza F. to Caleb W. Richerson 7-12-1839 (7-18-1839) F
Gober, S. A. to J. J. Deener 11-12-1851 F
Gocher, Tempa to Saml. Middleton 2-8-1860 Hr
Godbey, Mary F. to John M. Beloate 1-10-1871 (1-11-1871) F
Godbey, Susan to Michael B. Martin 9-14-1864 (no return) F
Godby, Sarah to S. B. Williams 2-10-1848 (no return) Sh
Goddard, Mary (Mrs.) to W. M. Fagan 2-23-1863 Sh
Godlin, Nancy to Alexander Chapman 6-5-1846 (6-6-1846) Hr
Godsey, E. E. to G. W. Potter 9-15-1866 (9-16-1866) O
Godsey, Mary to James C. Journey 10-8-1848 O
Godsey, Nancy to Seraphim Nenningar 10-19-1853 Sh
Godwin, E. M. to G. W. McClain 10-20-1863 Hn

Godwin, Effie J. to John Trice 7-15-1848 Sh
Godwin, Mary to John S. Cole 3-1-1859 Hn
Goff, Anna G. to Frank M. Looney 9-16-1859 Sh
Goff, Anna G. to R. W. Halbert 11-17-1864 Sh
Goff, Carline M. to Felise G. Whetty 2-6-1841 (2-10-1841) G
Goff, Elizabeth to G. W. Mosley 2-8-1879 (2-12-1879) L
Goff, Fanny to William Maddox 11-2-1846 (11-4-1846) Hr
Goff, Join to Alfred Stewart 10-7-1839 G
Goff, Sophia to I. A. Williamson 12-27-1865 (12-28-1865) O
Gofford, Nelly to Samuel Killim 3-10-1853 Be
Goforth, Adaline M. to Milson? D. ___ 9-29-1842 T
Goforth, Dicey to Jackson Turner 4-13-1855 (4-14-1855) Hr
Goforth, Lucinda Jane to Starky Hogg 9-9-1846 Be
Goforth, Margaret to William Carper 2-2-1861 (2-5-1861) Hr
Goforth, Margaret to William Trantham 1-11-1845 (1-13-1845) T
Goforth, Martha to A. A. Myres 2-22-1860 T
Goforth, Mary to Erasmus Rose 12-20-1853 (12-21-1853) T
Goforth, Mary to John Lenoir Gray 8-10-1852 T
Goforth, Mattie to Harrison Phillips 12-28-1880 (12-29-1881?) L
Goforth, Sarah E. to M. B. Harrison 1-19-1870 T
Goforth, Sarah F. to Robt. J. Rankin 4-11-1859 (4-17-1859) Hr
Gofourth, Alzora to Leroy Culp 2-29-1844 F
Goganus, M. M. (Mrs.) to W. H. McLin 10-9-1866 G
Goheen, Helen to Reuben Fletcher McFarland 9-30-1850 (10-2-1850) T
Gohlson, Sarah to Wm. Dunlap 8-9-1867 (8-11-1867) F B
Goilliot, Rose to E. Trigallez 4-23-1864 Sh
Goin, Fannie to Nelson Bland 1-4-1876 Dy
Goin, Susan to Shack Oldham 3-16-1880 Dy
Goings, Nancy to Edmond Shirley 5-2-1878 Dy
Goins, Eliza to Joseph Parrish 10-24-1872 O
Goins, Rutha Jane to E. P. Ashmore 9-10-1873 L
Goins, S. C. to R. S. Warford 10-17-1870 O
Gold, Finey to A. J. Barrett 1-24-1874 (1-25-1874) Dy
Gold, Mary E. to W. E. Connell 11-11-1871 (11-12-1871) Dy
Golden, Berneta R. to John C. Dearmore 7-19-1848 (7-20-1848) Ma
Golden, Charlatta A. to James H. Golden 1-14-1861 We
Golden, Clementine F. to F. M. Arnold 8-11-1861 Hn
Golden, Elizabeth to Francis Riley 6-25-1845 G
Golden, Elizabeth to William Anderson 6-3-1830 Ma
Golden, Elizabeth to William Davidson 3-20-1852 Sh
Golden, Frances P. to F. M. Arnold 10-25-1863 Hn
Golden, Harriet to Jacob Sturdivant 7-17-1869 G B
Golden, Lethe E. to Isham James 8-24-1868 (no return) Dy
Golden, Lotty to John McMahan 7-7-1851 (7-10-1851) Hr
Golden, Lucinda to David B. Porter 8-7-1848 (8-?-1848) Ma
Golden, Lucy A. to Elias W. May 12-2-1846 (12-3-1846) Ma
Golden, Maria to Dick Sikes 1-30-1869 G B
Golden, Martha to George W. Allen 7-27-1855 (no return) Hn
Golden, Mary A. to J. H. McClain 1-31-1870 (2-1-1870) T
Golden, Susan to Henry Boon 1-16-1830 Ma
Golden, Susanna to E. Hadson 8-16-1842 (8-18-1842) Ma
Golding, Caroline to G. W. Kirkpatrick 12-7-1851 L
Golding, Eliza to Benjamin Turner 5-28-1853 (5-29-1853) L
Golding, Eliza to N. H. Tanner 10-24-1851 (no return) L
Golding, Elizabeth to Jerry Jackson 8-29-1868 (8-30-1868) L B
Golding, Elmira to January Davis 11-26-1878 L B
Golding, Lucinde to Ben Halfacre 4-4-1867 (no return) L B
Golding, Mary E. to Isaac Acuff 11-17-1854 L
Golding, Mary E. to Isaac M. Acuff 3-21-1856 (6-22-1856) L
Golding, Milly Ann to Edmond Montgomery 3-15-1871 L
Golding, Milly Ann to George Owen 5-22-1876 (5-23-1876) L
Golding, Mollie to C. M. Jolley 8-2-1877 L
Golding, Rebecca to Amos Latham 4-12-1849 (4-15-1849) L
Golding, Sarah to Marsall Starnes 12-5-1838 L
Goldsby, Elizabeth to James H. Tucker 12-15-1849 Hn
Goldsby, Gilly A. to Isaac W. Moon 10-19-1848 Sh
Goldsby, Louisa W. to Isaih S. Perry 4-5-1842 Sh
Goldsby, O. C. to R. S. Atkins 10-19-1852 We
Goldsby, Parthenia to Henry Braden 7-13-1854 We
Goldsmith, Eliza to John Power 3-25-1864 Sh
Goldzinsky, Rachel to Louis Solomon 8-17-1871 Ma
Golen, Levena to Jesse Baker 10-18-1840 F
Goling, Mary E. to W. W. Wilcox 12-8-1874 Hy
Gooch, C. to Richard Moore 4-3-1838 Cr
Gooch, Dorcus to Mordecai Newport 12-8-1842 Hn
Gooch, Elizabeth to E. F. Baker 8-5-1859 Cr
Gooch, Elizabeth to John C. LaRue 12-30-1865 Mn
Gooch, Fannie to Robert Hale 9-23-1842 Cr
Gooch, Frances to Charles W. Hays 11-4-1842 Cr
Gooch, Isabella to Geo. L. Gordon 10-11-1858 Cr
Gooch, L. J. to J. G. Mebane 2-4-1868 (2-5-1868) Cr
Gooch, M. to A. A. Montinues 3-2-1854 Cr
Gooch, Martha J. to Albert G. Hill 1-31-1839 (no return) Cr
Gooch, Martha M. to Harman M. Wilson 9-29-1862 O
Gooch, Mary A. to W. Blount 1-14-1846 Cr
Gooch, Mary Ann to Riley Taylor 11-22-1838 Cr
Gooch, Mary C. to Cannon Horn 12-23-1872 (12-24-1872) Cr

Brides

Gooch, Mary Jane to H. A. Lemons 4-20-1864 Mn
Gooch, Mollie E. to John L. McCalla 1-3-1870 (1-4-1870) T
Gooch, Pamoni? A. to G. W. Robinson 2-15-1855 Cr
Gooch, Roanne to Alfred Morgan 12-18-1850 Cr
Gooch, Sarah to Benjamin King 9-20-1871 Cr B
Gooch, Winney to Thomas Gregory 1-11-1843 G
Good, Hester A. to John F. Comer 2-9-1860 Hn
Good, Mahala to Caswell Shore 8-15-1845 (8-28-1845) O
Good, Margaret M. to Jacob Baugh 4-23-1857 Hn
Good, Martha J. to L. A. Baker 6-12-1866 G
Good, Mary W. to John W. Sexton 2-1-1860 G
Goodall, Mary Ann to William R. Hughes 10-28-1868 (10-29-1868) Ma
Gooddin, Ally to Lewis Jones 1-27-1868 (1-30-1868) T
Goode, Adeline D. to David W. Fort 12-6?-1841 (no return) F
Goode, Allice to Dennis Cline 1-5-1869 (1-6-1869) F
Goode, Eliza Ann to John T. Turner 10-28-1858 Hn
Goode, Eliza J. to Robert D. Bowden 12-29-1840 Hn
Goode, Jane to Henry Tines 6-17-1867 (6-22-1867) F B
Goode, M. E. to L. A. Waterman 9-21-1857 Sh
Goode, Marietta to Noah Potts 8-23-1867 (8-24-1867) F B
Goode, Mary A. to J. H. Jones 9-21-1857 Sh
Goode, Mary A. to J. J. H. Greer 7-9-1860 Hr
Goode, Mary to J. W. Harris, jr. 9-12-1865 (9-13-1865) F
Goode, Nancy to Henry W. Walker 12-28-1842 Hn
Goode, Sarah A. to Shelby Crittenden 11-9-1839 Hn
Goode, Sarah Lucinda to George W. Stewart 1-19-1860 Hn
Goode, Sarah to James H. Johnson 6-19-1857 Ma
Gooden, Miranda E. to William E. Allmon 5-7-1857 We
Gooden, Polly to Peyton Babb 7-13-1870 (7-14-1870) F B
Gooden, Sarah to Ladd Moore 5-12-1853 (5-14-1853) O
Goodgion, Caroline P. to R. A. Stewart 10-13-1867 Hn
Goodhart, Elizabeth to Mathias Schwartz 2-25-1850 Sh
Goodin, C. E. to J. M. Jones 12-11-1866 Hn
Goodin, Elizabeth to Wm. Parker 7-22-1846 Sh
Goodin, M. A. to P. N. Smith 7-11-1864 (no return) Hn
Goodin, Sophrona J. to Saml. B. Robinson 12-14-1848 (12-20-1848) F
Goodin, Susan V. to Thos. E. Buchannan 4-8-1856 Sh
Gooding, Betsey to Henry Bragg 2-21-1872 (2-22-1871?) L B
Gooding, J. L. to J. M. Pope 1-19-1878 (1-20-1878) Dy
Goodlett, Candis to Cato Williams 2-11-1868 (2-16-1868) F B
Goodloe, Amandy C. to Robert Hale 7-29-1856 G
Goodloe, Cat to T. B. Osborne 6-26-1867 O
Goodloe, Martha to Flanders Elliott 3-6-1871 (3-11-1871) F B
Goodloe, Mattie I. to J. J. Harper 2-20-1867 G
Goodloe, Susan to Henry A. King 10-23-1854 (10-29-1854) G
Goodloe, Susan to William T. Woods 11-28-1862 (12-?-1862) Dy
Goodlore, T. E. to I. W. Norton 10-9-1865 O
Goodlow, Mencus J. to James G. Watson 3-12-1855 (no return) F
Goodman, Ann to Isham Parker 6-19-1860 G
Goodman, B. L. to S. B. Turner 12-21-1869 T
Goodman, Bythenia A. to John H. Day 8-15-1868 G
Goodman, Eliza M. to Robert Gill 9-16-1857 G
Goodman, Eliza M. to Robert Gill 9-16-1857 (9-21-1857) G
Goodman, Elizabeth to Eno Real Madaras 7-2-1840 G
Goodman, Elizabeth to Nathan New 1-1-1838 Hr
Goodman, Elizabeth to Samuel Sullender 8-5-1834 Hr
Goodman, Elizabeth to Thos. Bell 12-17-1836 (12-22-1836) Hr
Goodman, Frances to Samuel G. Talkington 4-3-1852 G
Goodman, Harriet O. to James H. Ford 12-16-1867 (no return) Hy
Goodman, Jane to L. C. Baker 11-10-1869 G
Goodman, Josephine H. to William Turner 3-23-1871 T
Goodman, Louiza V. to Marion Holder 1-2-1860 (1-5-1860) G
Goodman, Malinda J. to Joseph Harrell 7-22-1861 (no return) Dy
Goodman, Mareny Eleonor to Thomas Young 1-11-1836 Hr
Goodman, Martha A. (Mrs.) to Samuel Jamison 10-11-1866 G
Goodman, Martha A. to W. D. Nickleson 11-15-1865 T
Goodman, Martha to Paul G. Clement 1-11-1865 (no return) Dy
Goodman, Mary A. to Jas. H. Petty 5-21-1870 T
Goodman, Mary Ann to Henry Edwards 8-28-1848 G
Goodman, Mary E. to J. T. Burnett 1-17-1871 (1-18-1871) Dy
Goodman, Mary E. to S. B. Witt 10-9-1873 Hy
Goodman, Mary Jane to William Wilson 12-8-1852 (12-9-1852) Sh
Goodman, Mary to Jas. M. Allred 3-2-1852 (3-4-1852) Sh
Goodman, Mercilla to Samuel Rankin 9-18-1832 G
Goodman, Meriah to Burrel Odom 11-25-1844 Be
Goodman, Nancy H. to Charles Mulherron 2-7-1861 (no return) Hy
Goodman, R. to Chas. Taylor 1-1-1872 T
Goodman, Rebecca to John P. Masons 5-19-1847 (5-20-1847) O
Goodman, Sallie O. to D. H. Smith 5-2-1871 (5-3-1871) T
Goodman, Sallie to Saml. Collins 12-24-1874 (12-25-1874) T
Goodman, Sarah Ann to Osborn Brown 3-29-1853 Sh
Goodman, Sue to Thos. Angus 1-23-1869 (1-26-1869) T
Goodman, Susan A. to Stephen C. Barker 6-20-1857 (6-21-1857) G
Goodner, Amanda to R. A. Sperry 10-1-1850 (10-2-1850) F
Goodnoe, Mary Elizabeth to HGenry Wisener? 2-13-1844 (2-16-1844) T
Goodpaster, Mary to Charles Fingenbeim 5-1-1838 Sh
Goodric, Amanda to John Devenport 5-14-1870 (5-17-1870) Dy
Goodrich, Caroline (Mrs.) to Wm. A. Barnhill 2-16-1871 Ma
Goodrich, Catharine to William J. Taylor 12-2-1846 (12-9-1846) G
Goodrich, Elizabeth A. to Levin Thomas 3-7-1861 Dy
Goodrich, Elizabeth M. to John Burrus 1-9-1849 Ma
Goodrich, Elizabeth to Andrew I. Bailey 2-8-1842 Ma
Goodrich, Jane to James Turner 12-23-1864 Dy
Goodrich, Jane, jr. to John Harris 4-6-1849 (4-17-1849) Ma
Goodrich, Margarett L. to John H. Lintchicum 8-19-1841 Ma
Goodrich, Mary A. to B. G. Stewart 12-19-1839 (12-23-1839) Ma
Goodrich, Mary Ann to George P. McAlelley 12-12-1850 Ma
Goodrich, Missouri to John Oaks 7-9-1873 Dy
Goodrich, Nancy to Nathan Johnson 9-7-1847 (9-14-1847) Ma
Goodrich, Phebi Jane to Gabriel Barnes 12-28-1845 G
Goodrick, Mary M. to Caswell C. Cock 11-4-1857 (11-5-1857) Ma
Goodridge, Mary to Wm. Farrow 10-11-1869 (no return) Hy
Goodwin, Anna to Everett Ritter 5-15-1828 (5-20-1828) Hr
Goodwin, Diana C. to John McKee 9-20-1832 Hr
Goodwin, Eliza to A. H. Darden 7-30-1869 (8-1-1869) F
Goodwin, Elizabeth A. to Joseph J. Crossett 12-26-1846 (1-14-1847) F
Goodwin, Elmira to Warren Gooldin 11-25-1859 Sh
Goodwin, Emeline to John A. Bogle 1-10-1870 G
Goodwin, Emma C. to John W. Harris 1-4-1870 (1-5-1870) Ma
Goodwin, Haley to Josiah Pierce 11-5-1836 (11-7-1836) Hr
Goodwin, J. to T. B. McDonald 2-16-1870 G
Goodwin, Lizzie V. to J. H. Goodwin 1-26-1869 (1-28-1869) Dy
Goodwin, Lou J. to Richard B. Moore 11-10-1870 (11-24-1870) Cr
Goodwin, Luiza J. to John C. Buchannan 10-31-1854 G
Goodwin, Mary E. to John W. Benham 12-30-1868 G
Goodwin, Mary to Charles S. Ball 7-30-1860 Ma
Goodwin, Matilda to H. B. Dilliard 7-4-1851 (7-6-1851) F
Goodwin, Meedy to Alexander M. Robertson 7-29-1852 G
Goodwin, S. F. to R. J. Fielder 12-19-1869 G
Goodwin, Winny to Benj. Dickinson 12-19-1866 (1-16-1867) F B
Goodwinn, Martha to George Ellis 2-12-1855 (2-14-1855) Sh
Gooldsby, Elizabeth to John H. Coseton 1-30-1845 (no return) We
Gooldsby, Martha to Robert L. Dunkins 2-3-1860 We
Goonley, Ellen to William Dobbin 4-2-1861 Sh
Goosby, Lizzie to J. A. Fulkerson 2-13-1877 (2-14-1877) L
Goosby, Mary J. to Alanson Nichols 3-27-1864 Be
Gopher, Jemima to George W. Johnson 3-22-1853 Ma
Gordan, Betsey to Pearse Gwinn 12-23-1871 (no return) Cr B
Gordan, Emma T. to James H. Moss 1-18-1869 (1-20-1869) Ma
Gorden, Carry to Scott Morris 12-21-1876 Hy
Gorden, Louisa to Mercer D. Wilson 9-1-1844 We
Gorden, Martha J. to George W. Moore 1-4-1870 Hy
Gorden, Mary A. to E. Walker 11-21-1862 (3-25-1862?) O
Gorden, Mary A. to Thomas S. Short 12-10-1857 Be
Gorden, Mary to Rafe Dinwiddie 1-15-18?? (1-27-1870) Cr
Gorden, Nancy A. to Enoch P. Arnold 1-12-1858 We
Gorden, Rosanah J. to Joel M. White 2-23-1854 Be
Gordon, Caroline to Jack Howard 2-27-1871 Cr
Gordon, Colann to Alexander Turner 1-10-1827 Ma
Gordon, Cordelia to G. N. Combs 11-26-1860 Be
Gordon, Eliza J. to Jas. N. Keys 3-27-1858 (3-28-1858) G
Gordon, Eliza to Robt. M. Rutherford 12-13-1866 Ma
Gordon, Elizabeth to James L. Gillespie 7-11-1842 (7-14-1842) O
Gordon, Elizabeth to Stephen O'Daniel 7-_-1863 G
Gordon, Esther to Wm. H. Williams 11-20-1844 (no return) F
Gordon, Frances to E. M. Cearnell 7-20-1862 Be
Gordon, Isabella to Joseph T. Howard 3-2-1869 (3-4-1869) Ma
Gordon, Kandis to Jackson Gordon 4-5-1869 Cr
Gordon, L. to S. A. Bridges 1-31-1859 Cr
Gordon, Lizzie to Jno. C. Spencer 2-28-1871 (3-2-1871) Ma
Gordon, Margarett A. to G. W. Brewer 11-11-1866 G
Gordon, Martha A. to James Smith 11-27-1856 Cr
Gordon, Martha E. to James D. Rowland 1-20-1855 Cr
Gordon, Mary E. to James Keys 12-10-1856 G
Gordon, Mary L. to Wm. Hughey 10-22-1857 (no return) Cr
Gordon, Mary Jane to George Pieper 5-15-1856 O
Gordon, Mary P. to John J. Johnson 12-?-1859 (no return) Hy
Gordon, Nancy to R. M. Stewart 1-10-1869 Hy
Gordon, Nanie (Mrs.) to A. G. Williamson 5-10-1864 Sh
Gordon, Naomi to Leroy Barnett 9-25-1850 (10-1-1850) Ma
Gordon, Parthena E. to John A. English 9-5-1833 Sh
Gordon, Polly to William Branch 7-13-1866 (no return) F B
Gordon, Queen A. to Thomas Spears 12-18-1856 (12-22-1856) Ma
Gordon, Sarah A. to Green G. Flowers 12-11-1866 Be
Gordon, Sarah Jane to Isham F. Davis 11-15-1848 G
Gordon, Sarah L. to J. R. D. Dinwiddie 2-22-1860 Cr
Gordon, Sarah to Andrew Burge 4-27-1838 Ma
Gordon, Sarah to Joshua Carnal 1-4-1853 Cr
Gore, Edny Jane to James B. Smith 8-25-1855 (8-28-1855) Hr
Gore, Eliza J. to James H. Turner 12-6-1850 Hn
Gore, Elizabeth F. to John Pustell 1-1-1846 Sh
Gore, Emaline to Isaac Menees 5-30-1831 O
Gore, Martha A. to John Owen 1-17-1860 (1-18-1860) O
Gore?, Margaret E. to William A. Bridges 1-13-1857 (1-14-1857) O

Goren, Frances J. to Jesse Kinney 11-23-1859 (11-24-1859) T
Gorgass, Emeline to Elihu Jones 8-9-1854 Hn
Gorhan, Anna to Danl. W. Brenn (Brown) 5-9-1864 Sh
Gorin, Frances Jane to James Payne 12-17-1850 T
Gorman, Alice Cora to G. P. Atcheson 9-11-1854 Be
Gorman, Caroline R. to Thomas M. Moore 7-1-1861 Sh
Gorman, Hannah O. to Barney Cating 1-14-1860 (1-15-1860) Sh
Gorman, Margaret to Michael Hallaran 1-18-1854 (1-19-1854) Sh
Gorman, Margaret to Michael Hickey 5-30-1847 Sh
Gorman, Margaret to William English 4-4-1853 Sh
Gorman, Martha to Wm. Shelley 2-1-1867 (7-6-1867) F B
Gornet?, Julia Ann to Henry W. Cotton 6-28-1869 T
Gosey, Catharine to James L. Boone 7-22-1879 L
Goss, Charlie to J. R. Cheatham 10-13-1875 (10-14-1875) O
Goss, Eleanor to Richmond Winkler 1-13-1841 (1-14-1841) T
Goss, Henrietta to L. M. Isbell 2-12-1859 (2-15-1859) Sh
Goss, Jane to Walter H. Reckord (Keckord?) 11-23-1864 Sh
Goss, Mary Ann to J. W. Parker 12-5-1850 O
Goss, Sarah to William Walker Hutchinson 4-12-1844 (4-15-1844) T
Gossett, Amanda to James Smith 12-24-1860 Ma
Gossett, Clemintine M. to Wm. McD. Rains 12-9-1840 (12-10-1840) Hr
Gossett, Elizabeth to William Vernon 4-12-1855 Be
Gossett, Mary Ann to James R. Gully 3-6-1853 Be
Gossett, Mary M. to Joseph F. Fenner 8-31-1852 (8-30?-1852) Hr
Gossett, Pheby to J. H. Mullinicks 3-12-1850 Be
Gossett, Polly Ann to Edward Hatley 9-21-1845 Be
Gossett, Sarah P. to M. V. Utley 9-26-1867 Be
Gossitt, E. T. to T. W. Wilkinson 5-28-1856 Sh
Goswick, Elizabeth J. A. F. to John T. Leroy 11-29-1853 (12-1-1853) Sh
Gouger, Sarah to Augustin Wood 8-11-1855 (8-12-1855) G
Gould, Harriet A. to James W. Weldon 5-27-1850 Hn
Gould, Jane W. to Samuel Craig 10-13-1839 Hn
Gouldsby, Martha A. to ____ Crawly 10-12-1841 (no return) Hn
Goure, Mary to George Owenes 7-24-1852 We
Gowan, M. J. to J. T. Turner 2-8-1873 (2-18-1873) Cr
Gowan, Malissa C. to James F. Webb 7-31-1878 (8-1-1878) Dy
Gowan, Martha E. to George H. Martin 11-14-1868 (11-12?-1868) Cr
Gowan, Martha to G. Canbrul 2-19-1852 We
Gowan, Mary Jane to Thomas Pittman 10-24-1882 L
Gowan, Mary Susan to Wm. Andrew Poteete 5-28-1870 (5-29-1870) Ma
Gowan, Mattie to B. F. Loving 1-26-1885 (1-28-1885) L
Gowan, Sophonia E. to George M. Taylor 1-17-1853 G
Gowan, Tennie C. H. to E. L. Loving 3-9-1885 (3-10-1885) L
Gowen, Mary F. to J. C. C. Thompson 12-12-1865 (12-14-1865) Cr
Gowen, Mary to Lemuel Day 7-21-1849 (7-26-1849) Ma
Gowen, Sarah Jane to E. F. Atkin 1-28-1848 (1-30-1848) F
Goyer, Rachel to Joseph T. Barker (Baker) 3-17-1858 Sh
Goza, Amada E. to John F. Ray 7-13-1863 G
Goza, S. J. (Mrs.) to John L. Baker 5-2-1866 G
Grace (Groce), Louisa C. to Ezekiel T. Keel 2-17-1842 Sh
Grace, Ardenia F. to Wm. E. Fawcett 7-26-1859 Hr
Grace, Callie to Richard Thurmond 8-28-1877 (8-29-1877) Dy
Grace, Catherine to Willie Allen 12-28-1828 Sh
Grace, Eliza Violet to Wilson Billings 5-3-1851 (5-4-1851) T
Grace, Ellen to J. R. Palmer 10-5-1876 (10-7-1876) Dy
Grace, Evaline to Rufus Wsh. Myers 1-18-1853 T
Grace, Julia A. (Miss) to Wm. H. Andrews 4-29-1858 Sh
Grace, Martha A. to E. A. F. Wesson 2-3-1857 Hr
Grace, Mary Jane to Benj. W. Davis 2-24-1847 Hr
Grace, Mary to David Carotti 1-1-1858 Sh
Grace, Mollie to W. A. Webb 8-22-1877 Dy
Grace, Nancy to James Lugoria 5-24-1858 Sh
Grace, Polina M. to John R. Rutherford 4-29-1851 (4-30-1851) Hr
Grace, Suphinia to W. J. Christian 5-30-1869 G
Grace?, Peggy to Joab (Jacob) Bean (Beard) 6-27-1820 Sh
Gracey, Maney to Daniel Webster Chamber 1-27-1866 T
Gracy, Martha A. to David Wood 4-19-1855 T
Graddy, Catherine to Thomas Flowers 11-29-1841 (11-30-1841) G
Graddy, J. A. to N. D. Page 12-25-1883 L
Graddy, Lena E. to John Wilson 9-29-1856 (10-2-1856) G
Graddy, Sarah M. to James M. Edmundson 3-4-1856 (3-5-1856) G
Graddy, Susan F. to Chapman Kinton 1-24-1857 G
Grady, C. C. to W. T. Gleason 12-25-1866 G
Grady, Catherine to Thomas Jennings 9-21-1863 Sh
Grady, Frances to A. F. Betts 4-5-1860 G
Grady, Hepsy A. to Elisha Keathly 5-23-1854 (5-25-1854) G
Grady, Hester to Bryant Carnigay 1-16-1843 G
Grady, Jane C. to James T. Smith 3-12-1846 G
Grady, Mary Jane to T. P. Lewis 4-27-1853 (4-28-1853) Sh
Grady, Mary to Michael Cunningham 11-15-1861 (11-18-1861) Sh
Grady, Nancy H. to James Skipper 7-2-1863 G
Grady, Rachel to Henry A. Stewart 12-17-1858 (12-20-1858) Sh
Grady, S. F. to A. M. Denwiddie 1-5-1869 H
Grady, Sarah A. to Lazerus Fergarson 3-9-1853 (3-10-1853) G
Gragsdon, S. E. to A. J. Walters 1-30-1866 Hn
Graham, Abigail to Abram Jones 5-28-1855 We
Graham, Alice to Stephen Barnett 1-21-1867 Hy

Graham, Angeline A. to John S. Gilmore 8-28-1860 Hr
Graham, Ann (Mrs.) to Thomas Quarmby 3-23-1852 Sh
Graham, Ann to Michael Fitzgibbons 10-18-1857 Sh
Graham, Annie (Miss) to Michael Anthony 9-1-1863 Sh
Graham, Caroline L. to David Alsop 2-9-1848 Be
Graham, Caroline to J. P. Cooper 1-22-1863 Be
Graham, Cintha J. to W. P. Woodard 1-8-1868 (1-9-1868) Cr
Graham, E. P. to J. M. Harpool 10-2-1862 (10-5-1862) O
Graham, E. R. to T. J. Simpson 3-4-1864 Mn
Graham, Elizabeth to J. M. Daniel 5-25-1851 Mn
Graham, Ellen M. to Geo. J. Campbell 6-21-1864 (6-22-1864) Sh
Graham, Emily to Erasmus Cannon 9-27-1866 (no return) Hy
Graham, Jane to Alfred Linnell 2-11-1860 (2-12-1860) Sh
Graham, Jane to Charles Butler 1-15-1853 Sh
Graham, Julia Ann to Henry Washington Cotton 6-28-1869 (7-1-1869) T
Graham, Lizzy to Billy McLeliand 12-23-1875 (no return) Hy
Graham, Louisa to Henry Polsgrove 8-9-1861 (8-11-1861) O
Graham, Lydia A. to Wm. C. Rutland 12-11-1850 F
Graham, M. J. to Wesley Vollentine 4-24-1869 O B
Graham, Margaret to Michael Manley 10-25-1856 (10-26-1856) Sh
Graham, Martha J. to Freeman H. Seeley 5-19-1866 (5-20-1866) Ma
Graham, Mary E. to C. L. Stephenson 6-26-1848 O
Graham, Mary E. to C. L. Stinson 6-26-1848 (7-2-1848) O
Graham, Mary E. to J. M. Maynard 6-28-1871 Cr
Graham, Mary to Dudley Morris 2-4-1874 (2-5-1874) O
Graham, Mollie to R. C. Fraser 9-5-1866 (9-6-1866) F
Graham, Nancy J. to Isaac J. Doughty 10-14-1860 Be
Graham, Peggy Ann to Ed Hodge 1-15-1878 Hy
Graham, Rosa T. to William C. York 12-18-1867 Ma
Graham, Rosa to John W. Herridge 10-20-1866 Ma
Graham, Sarah A. to John W. Rogers 2-16-1863 L
Graham, Susan to Scott Lee 10-16-1880 L
Graiger, Ann to James Boyd 11-10-1852 Hn
Grainger, Eliza to George C. Davis 1-21-1847 Hn
Grainger, Lively to Richard A. Grainger 1-2-1861 Hn
Grainger, Malinda to John H. Whitworth 2-18-1846 Hn
Grainger, Margaret J. to Isaac Watkins 1-29-1867 Hn
Grainger, Margaret J. to Isaac Watkins 2-6-1866 (no return) Hn
Grainger, Mary Anne to Jesse E. Markham 11-2-1854 Hn
Grainger, Mary J to Elijah W. Counsell 1-14-1857 Hn
Grainger, Tabitha to W. H. Rayburn 4-12-1853 Hn
Graitt?, M. E. to J. E. Walker 11-20-1871 L
Gramer, Mary A. to James Mayo 12-12-1854 (no return) F
Grammar, Mary Ann to D. B. O'Bannian 7-17-1852 (7-18-1852) Sh
Grammar, Menervia to Mat Graves 5-17-1871 (no return) Hy
Grammer, Ann R. to Robert W. Warren 10-21-1854 (10-25-1854) L
Grammer, Susan J. (Mrs.) to Joseph R. Blankenship 10-17-1871 (no return) L
Granberry, Adeline to Kit Roach 8-19-1870 (no return) F B
Granberry, Annie to Vig Shaw 3-30-1871 (3-31-1871) F B
Granberry, Celena to Zang Wiggins 12-23-1869 (no return) F B
Granberry, Louisa to Henry Edwards 6-1-1866 (6-3-1866) F B
Granberry, Lucy to James W. Morris 2-5-1845 (2-6-1845) F
Granberry, Luvenia to Milton Granberry 1-18-1868 (1-26-1868) F B
Granberry, Margaret to Everett Granberry 10-23-1869 (10-24-1869) F B
Granberry, Sarah E. to Richard B. Gatling 7-8-1844 (7-9-1844) F
Granberry, Winney to George Fortson 4-27-1869 (no return) F B
Granbery, H. M. to G. W. Morris 3-26-1855 (no return) F
Granbery, Louisa to Richard A. Dunaho 4-3-1848 (4-5-1848) F
Granbery, Mary Jane to Wm. A. Jones 3-2-1848 F
Granby, Louisa to William Combs 3-22-1847 (3-25-1847) Hr
Grandee, Virginia A. to A. B. Collins 4-14-1863 T
Granderson, Katy to John Blackwell 11-17-1873 T
Grant, Anne to Terrence O'Laughlin 2-7-1848 Sh
Grant, Betsey to Peter Clipas 10-8-1869 (10-9-1869) T
Grant, Bridget to Edward E. Rice 10-8-1860 (10-9-1860) Sh
Grant, Carrie to Wilson Barr 11-8-1840 Cr
Grant, Catherine to William Meritt 9-9-1848 Hn
Grant, Charlotte to William Widdis 4-12-1869 (4-13-1869) Cr
Grant, Clarky to Sion Grantham 8-31-1833 (9-1-1833) Hr
Grant, Elender to T. L. Moore 4-28-1845 Cr
Grant, Eliza to Stephen Maphey 6-6-1838 Ma
Grant, Elizabeth T. to William W. Boyet 10-6-1851 (10-9-1851) Ma
Grant, Francis M. to James B. Griffing 2-5-1851 Sh
Grant, H. L. to M. N. C. Robins 12-13-1867 (12-16-1867) Cr
Grant, Juliet M. to George C. Horbin 5-18-1853 Sh
Grant, L. Lizzie to W. A. Steffey 6-13-1860 (6-14-1860) Sh
Grant, Margaret A. to Lafayette Tosh 11-8-1858 Cr
Grant, Margaret J. to Canter B. Ralph 9-12-1855 T
Grant, Margaret J. to Johnathan B. Faulk 11-24-1874 (11-25-1874) T
Grant, Martha to Britain Tulley 2-20-1841 Cr
Grant, Mary A. to Charles A. Griswold 11-22-1858 Sh
Grant, Mary H. to Ethan H. Parrot 12-3-1855 (12-24-1855) Ma
Grant, Mary to Thomas Chatten 8-7-1853 (9-8-1853) Ma
Grant, Milly to James E. Wood 11-15-1858 (11-16-1858) Ma
Grant, Minerva to Daniel M. Gaston 12-22-1866 (12-23-1866) Ma
Grant, Mlda? B. to Elijah Bennet 7-3-1855 (7-4-1855) Ma
Grant, Nancy to Mathias Harrington 4-1-1856 Ma

Brides

Grant, Nancy to Thomas Jackson 1-15-1845 (1-16-1845) Ma
Grant, Polly to Hiram Williams 12-27-1824 (1-13-1825) Hr
Grant, Rosa to Michael Cody 2-7-1848 Sh
Grant, Sarah A. to John H. Means 4-15-1847 Sh
Grant, Sarah to Samuel S. Gettys 6-8-1857 (6-9-1857) Sh
Grant, Virtuous? C. to Eli Cox 8-2-1836 Hr
Grant, W. J. to A. H. Smallwood 7-10-1864 Mn
Grantham, Abegill to Chalkley Grantham 5-29-1841 (5-31-1841) Hr
Grantham, Caledonia to Robt. Strickland 7-10-1868 (no return) F
Grantham, Elizabeth to Robt. J. Fortner 8-6-1856 (8-7-1856) Hr
Grantham, Levisa to John Robinson 8-28-1826 (8-28-1826) Hr
Grantham, Louisa to David Bishop 10-1-1856 (10-2-1856) Hr
Grantham, Lydia M. to Wm. J. Brown 8-1-1857 (8-4-1857) Hr
Grantham, Malvira to G. B. Simpson 9-7-1835 Hr
Grantham, Mary to James M. Gray 9-5-1850 (9-8-1850) Hr
Grantham, Nancy to John Hamilton 9-24-1842 (9-25-1842) Hr
Grantham, Rachel to Anson Brown 2-12-1831 (2-14-1831) Hr
Gravault, Eliza to Robert McCall 9-2-1848 (9-3-1848) F
Graves, Adaline to Tom Lanier 8-27-1878 (no return) L B
Graves, Antoinette A. to James S. Eastham 10-11-1852 (no return) F
Graves, Cela to Charley Patterson 12-2-1872 Hy
Graves, Celier to John Edwards 10-31-1877 Hy
Graves, Delia to Thomas G. Black 1-20-1869 G
Graves, Dinah to Martin Wagner 8-24-1847 Sh
Graves, Dixie E. to M. D. Hollowell 12-21-1868 (no return) F
Graves, Eliza J. to Andrew J. Harrison 9-9-1845 (9-11-1845) Ma
Graves, Elizabeth to John Whitfield 11-4-1838 Hn
Graves, F. E. A. to G. M. D. Bowers 11-1-1875 (no return) L
Graves, Fannie to Jim Drake 1-20-1871 Hy
Graves, India D. to C. L. Turner 10-28-1867 (10-31-1867) F
Graves, Isabella to Danl. Baucum 1-7-1841 (1-10-1841) F
Graves, Josie to J. W. Koen 12-4-1878 Hy
Graves, Liza to Isaac Tyus 9-16-1869 Hy
Graves, Lue to Solomon Shirley 7-9-1868 Hy
Graves, M. C. to A. M. Green 3-7-1867 (3-11-1867) Cr
Graves, M. C. to Joseph McLemore 3-22-1883 (no return) L
Graves, M. D. to T. B. Jones 5-21-1862 Hn
Graves, Mahala to Haywood Coldwell 1-2-1873 Hy
Graves, Malinda R. to Nathan Edmonds 3-30-1844 Sh
Graves, Margaret to Manuel Lobdale 5-21-1870 (5-22-1870) L
Graves, Mariah to John M. Spears 4-28-1846 (4-29-1846) Ma
Graves, Mary Ann to Samuel Gordin 11-6-1838 (12-3-1838) Ma
Graves, Mary J. to Geo. M.(W.?) Nolen 8-3-1859 Hr
Graves, Mary M. to W. R. Glenn 12-13-1870 (12-14-1870) L
Graves, Mary to Noel Jackson 9-11-1841 (9-15-1841) Ma
Graves, Mollie to John Anderson 5-31-1877 (4?-1-1877) L
Graves, Musidora to Francis M. Harrison 8-10-1853 Ma
Graves, Naomie Jane to Jno. Frankliln King 5-23-1868 (5-26-1868) Ma
Graves, Narcissus to Gwinn Harper 8-9-1851 Cr
Graves, P. J. to J. F. Jarratt 1-16-1864 (no return) Cr
Graves, P. J. to J. T. Jarratt 1-16-1864 (1-17-1864) Cr
Graves, Patsy to Sikes Parham 4-18-1866 (6-16-1866) F B
Graves, Peggy to Isaac Harris 9-9-1869 Hy
Graves, Rachel E. S. to W. S. Enoch 7-31-1867 (8-1-1867) Dy
Graves, Rebecca A. to J. F. Meek 2-5-1862 Mn
Graves, Rebecca to Jeff Mott 8-11-1872 O
Graves, Rhoda to Edmond Robertson 4-27-1872 (no return) Hy
Graves, S. V. to M. B. Umsted 11-21-1866 G
Graves, Samantha L. to George W. Freeman 1-17-1859 Ma
Graves, Sarah A. to D. W. Rosson 3-14-1853 (3-16-1853) Hr
Graves, Sarah A. to Henry C. Baker 6-23-1866 (6-24-1866) Ma
Graves, Sarah Emeline to Cornelius Ruddle 7-23-1849 (7-12?-1849) Ma
Graves, Sarah to Hudson J. Spears 6-3-1850 (6-30-1850) Ma
Graves, Sarah to James Edwards 10-31-1877 Hy
Graves, Susan D. to Albert A. Rains 12-22-1859 Ma
Gravette, Sallie C. to W. C. Ingram 1-25-1869 G
Gravit, Sarah Jane to John Wadlington 8-15-1859 (8-16-1859) Ma
Gravitt, Adaline to J. C. Betts 7-5-1867 G
Gravitt, Ellen to Joseph McLeary 12-13-1866 G
Gravitt, Fanny to Samuel Stewart 1-3-1870 G B
Graw (McGraw?), M. A. S. to John H. Tarrant 9-24-1866 (9-25-1866) Dy
Gray, Allice to James C. Pollard 11-30-1850 Sh
Gray, Amanda to James Tweedle 9-15-1857 (9-27-1857) O
Gray, Angeline to John Riley 5-27-1862 O
Gray, Araminta to Neadham Whitfield 6-18-1848 Hn
Gray, Arrena to R. Bostick 12-20-1882 (12-21-1882) L
Gray, Bettie T. to L. L. Asburry 11-4-1858 Hr
Gray, C. D. to J. S. Kerkpatrick 12-6-1873 T
Gray, C. V. to C. A. Johnson 12-1-1874 T
Gray, Caroline to Abner Cowgill 8-3-1854 Sh
Gray, Caroline to Tobe Partee 1-5-1870 (no return) L
Gray, Casey M. to Wm.J. Long 10-18-1849 Sh
Gray, Cathanne(Catharine) to Saml. Enis 2-18-1858 Hr
Gray, Cinda to Isaac Cross 2-3-1877 Hy
Gray, Elizabeth to George M. Carricker 8-7-1852 Hr
Gray, Ellen to James Kelly 10-12-1852 Sh
Gray, Fanny to Pleasant Henderson 12-27-1877 Hy

Gray, Henrietta M. to Jasper L. Glover 1-24-1866 O
Gray, Hester H. to Denis Thedford 8-4-1829 (8-5-1829) G
Gray, Jane H. to John O. Hardeman 9-6-1853 (9-7-1853) Sh
Gray, Jennie to Sandy Alston 12-16-1873 T
Gray, Lizzie to Lewis Parr 5-18-1884 L
Gray, Lucilla to Nelson Borihus 2-12-1863 Mn
Gray, Lydia to James Herron 1-29-1839 Ma
Gray, Maggie M. to Robly H. Anderson 4-19-1876 Hy
Gray, Margaret E. to A. E. Calhoun 8-21-1863 (8-23-1863) O
Gray, Margaret E. to William N. Williams 6-25-1858 (6-27-1858) O
Gray, Margaret F. to M. J. Holmes 3-9-1858 (3-10-1858) Sh
Gray, Margarett M. to George Taylor 1-21-1864 (no return) Cr
Gray, Martha A. E. to Peter H. Manly 9-12-1860 Hn
Gray, Martha A. to J. C. Lane 12-15-1858 (12-16-1858) Sh
Gray, Martha I.? to Thomas H. Feagan 11-14-1843 (11-15-1843) Hr
Gray, Martha J. to Saml. Ray 7-16-1870 (7-17-1870) T
Gray, Martha S. H. to Wm. F. Staton 6-3-1867 (6-6-1867) T
Gray, Martha to A. W. Howard 4-1-1847 (4-5-1847) O
Gray, Martha to Jeremiah Sullivant 1-3-1842 Hr
Gray, Mary A. to Jesse W. Meley 12-24-1867 G
Gray, Mary Ann to John Springfield 7-7-1856 (7-8-1856) Hr
Gray, Mary E. to John E. Bass 10-16-1844 Sh
Gray, Mary E. to Wm. Pool 5-8-1854 (5-9-1854) T
Gray, Mary Jane to James Pettit 8-3-1852 (no return) F
Gray, Mary M. to J. Y. Williams 1-30-1873 O
Gray, Mary to James M. Stout 7-14-1848 Hr
Gray, Matilda to Albartis Chapman 11-20-1828 Hr
Gray, Nancy Ann to Charles Hicks 11-18-1856 (11-29-1856) Sh
Gray, Nancy Jane to James B. Patterson 8?-22-1859 (8-23-1859) Hr
Gray, Nancy to John Holder 1-30-1854 (2-2-1854) Hr
Gray, Permelia to Henry Graham 2-19-1874 Hy
Gray, Polly Jane to G. G. Howard 7-11-1866 (7-12-1866) O
Gray, Pricilla to Henry Baker 2-5-1863 Mn
Gray, R. M. to W. P. Stewart 2-11-1856 Sh
Gray, Rachael (Miss) to Hiram H. Honeycutt 8-19-1862 O
Gray, Rachel to Wm. Alexr. Kent 11-29-1851 (12-3-1851) T
Gray, Sarah T. to James T. Williams 1-29-1870 (2-3-1870) Cr
Gray, Sarah to Henry D. Walker 12-22-1845 (12-23-1845) L
Gray, Sophia to Jesse Kirkman 10-27-1871 (10-28-1871) T
Gray, Sophia to John Pulliam 12-20-1868 (12-28-1868) F B
Gray, Susan C. to Milton Smith 3-4-1831 Hr
Gray, Temperance to Robert Box 1-4-1841 (1-7-1841) Hr
Gray, Winaford to Ephraim B. Gamble 12-6-1853 Hr
Grayer, Sarah M. to Jessie J. Wills 1-1-1846 G
Grayham, Eliza J. to W. N. Murphey 1-19-1859 (no return) We
Grayham, Elizabeth to Thomas S. Shelby 9-29-1840 (10-1-1840) O
Grayham, Margaret to Stephen C. Clement 10-8-1862 Be
Grayham, Sarah J. to William J. Cooper 7-17-1866 Be
Grayor, Charlotte to Sampson Curtis 7-4-1831 (7-5-1835) G
Grayson, Martha A. to Wm. B. NIcholson 9-3-1849 Sh
Grayum, Lavina to William Warmack 8-17-1870 (8-29-1870) Dy
Grazum, Elizabeth to Herny? Medlin 2-16-1860 We
Grear (Green?), Margaret to Peter Leonard 3-30-1853 (3-31-1853) Sh
Grear, Betsy to Wm. Robinson 12-29-1877 Hy
Greathouse, Eliza to H. Cardy 9-19-1863 (9-20-1863) Sh
Greaves, Alice L. to W. B. Burton 10-17-1877 (no return) Hy
Greaves, Ellen to Anthony Jelts 8-18-1880 (8-20-1880) L
Greaves, M. A. to R. O. Crump 12-8-1875 L
Greaves, Margaret to Isham Jarrett 11-10-1878 Hy
Greaves, Mary Ann to Adam Trotter 1-10-1878 Hy
Greaves, Mary E. to Clifton J. Haynes 11-18-1859 (no return) Hy
Greeds, Mary Ann to John McCarrus 10-22-1838 Ma
Greem, Lucenda to Allen Claybrook 2-5-1869 Hy
Green (Gause?), Ninah V. to T. A. Rice 10-23-1871 (10-25-1871) L
Green (Greer?), Sarah to George Taylor 6-19-1869 G B
Green (Gunn?), Ann to Ornal Hale 4-4-1874 (no return) L B
Green, A. E. to T. P. Harper 12-3-1866 O
Green, A. J. to J. A. McCharen 11-9-1868 (11-11-1868) F
Green, A. V. to J. D. Singleton 12-12-1871 (12-14-1871) Cr
Green, Abby to William Thompson 4-6-1870 (4-7-1870) Dy
Green, Ada Noel to John Haml. Freeman 11-1-1871 Hy
Green, Ailsey to George Bailey 1-3-1877 Hy
Green, Ailsey to Robert Richardson 3-19-1880 (3-20-1880) L
Green, Alice to J. M. Fennell 11-27-1880 (11-28-1881?) L
Green, Alice to Jake Adams 11-15-1877 Hy
Green, Allice to Deal Taylor 11-13-1873 Hy
Green, Amy to William Stokeley 3-9-1881 (3-2?-1881) L
Green, Ann E. to John Marberry 6-6-1838 Hn
Green, Ann E. to S. E. Johnson 5-30-1859 T
Green, Ann S. to Edward T. Jordan 10-27-1846 (10-28-1846) F
Green, Ann to Christopher Chappel 12-31-1838 (1-1-1839) Hr
Green, Ann to Daniel McNamara 10-17-1858 Sh
Green, Ann to Francis Hardgraves 5-25-1830 Ma
Green, Ann to Michael McNamarer 4-27-1864 Sh
Green, Anna to H. K. Mathes 1-16-1875 (1-17-1875) O
Green, Anna to Henry Sidney 11-15-1879 (11-16-1879) L B
Green, Aubanett to A. M. Phillips 10-7-1867 (10-10-1867) T

Brides

Green, B. A. to H. H. Headen 2-19-1866 G
Green, Bridget to P. Madigan 11-5-1863 Sh
Green, C. L. to G. L. Nelson 11-3-1846 Cr
Green, C. P. to John A. Nowell 1-20-1858 G
Green, C. R. to C. Davent 12-23-1867 O
Green, Caroline to Edmond Hill 1-20-1873 Hy
Green, Caroline to Frank Parker 12-1-1877? Hy
Green, Caroline to Henry Hall 1-7-1869 T
Green, Catharine (Mrs.) to Lorenzo D. Stout 2-18-1858 (7-15-1858) Ma
Green, Catharine B. to Thomas Read 11-11-1847 Sh
Green, Catharine G. to Geo. W. Thompson 12-10-1845 F
Green, Celia to Robert Ward 7-11-1871 (7-13-1871) L
Green, Charlotte to Carter Green 6-16-1866 (no return) F B
Green, Charlotte to John Anthony 4-18-1872 L
Green, China to A. C. Ingram 8-18-1846 L
Green, Cora to Cubie Mason 8-4-1866 (no return) Hy
Green, Cora to Jack Jones 5-29-1873 Hy
Green, Cordelia J. to Tobbert F. Conley 10-9-1858 G
Green, Drucilla to Calvin Searcy 1-24-1884 L
Green, E. J. to Richard W. Barnes 8-4-1853 Hn
Green, Eliza F. to James P. Parker 1-4-1868 (1-5-1868) T
Green, Eliza I. to William Scott 10-20-1843 Ma
Green, Eliza Jane to Thomas Hickerson 12-29-1869 T
Green, Eliza to Bill Halliburton 10-9-1877 (10-10-1877) L
Green, Eliza to M. M. Boyd 7-19-1865 F
Green, Eliza to Stephen Sutton 2-5-1863 Mn
Green, Elizabeth B. to John C. Ware 1-28-1857 Cr
Green, Elizabeth S. A. to Phillip Tuggle 5-2-1842 (no return) L
Green, Elizabeth to Bart Bledsoe 2-12-1873 (2-13-1873) T
Green, Elizabeth to J. D. Abbott 9-5-1870 (9-6-1870) Cr
Green, Elizabeth to Jordan Malone 1-16-1878 (1-28-1878) L
Green, Ella to John Williford 12-27-1880 (12-28-1880) L
Green, Ellen to Jas. Gooden 12-1-1869 (12-4-1869) T
Green, Eller to John Jordan 10-9-1867 (10-12-1867) L B
Green, Emily M. to J. M. Manning 7-10-1871 (7-12-1871) Cr
Green, Emily to David L. Covington 9-18-1853 Cr
Green, Emily to Isham Dodson 12-26-1867 (12-28-1867) L B
Green, Emily to John D. Verhine 3-2-1859 (3-3-1859) O
Green, Eveline to Solomon Hannings 12-2-1868 (12-6-1868) Cr
Green, Evelyn to S. Frank Brock 2-24-1866 Dy
Green, Fannie S. to Chas. P. Noell 9-23-1873 (9-24-1873) T
Green, Fannie to Henry Dewalt 1-15-1875 (1-19-1875) L B
Green, Fannie to Howell Taylor 12-10-1878 Hy
Green, Fanny to Thomas Walker 2-13-1844 G
Green, Finie to Edmond Taylor 1-5-1875 Hy
Green, Frances to Fayett Green 4-7-1873 O
Green, G. V. to T. L. Green 9-3-1870 (9-4-1870) Cr
Green, H. E. to J. M. Palmer 2-4-1866 Hn
Green, Harrett M. to Thos. D. Warmath 9-20-1854 G
Green, Harriet A. to Peyton jr. Dyson 7-16-1870 (7-17-1870) T
Green, Henrietta to W. R. Webb 9-7-1880 (9-9-1880) L B
Green, Hollen Applewight to John N. Hall 3-5-1842 (3-8-1842) T
Green, I. J. to G. M. Holmes 12-23-1867 (1-23-1868) Cr
Green, Isadore to Robt. Middlebrooks 1-3-1868 (no return) Hy
Green, J. P. to W. H. Woods 10-2-1869 (10-6-1869) Dy
Green, Jane to James Grooms 10-14-1846 Cr
Green, Jane to Joseph Taylor 7-6-1826 (7-19-1826) Hr
Green, Jane to Sip Hull 12-29-1865 (1-30-1865) F B
Green, Janie to William Carson 6-26-1878 L
Green, Jennie to Leonard Waggoner 12-13-1878 (12-18-1878) Dy
Green, Julia to Robert Marr 5-6-1870 (no return) Hy
Green, Julina to James French 11-3-1846 Cr
Green, Katie to Robert B. Bell 10-14-1876 (10-17-1876) L
Green, Katie to Stephen Otterbridge 12-9-1875 (no return) L B
Green, Kezia to James Isham (Eison) 3-3-1884 L
Green, Kizziah Ann to Thomas Fitzpatrick 12-19-1870 (12-30-1870) L
Green, Laura to William Field 12-27-1870 T
Green, Lena to Willis Green 10-15-1875 (no return) Hy
Green, Lily to Henry Magee 10-23-1873 (12-16-1873) T
Green, Linday to Eli W. Rodgers 12-9-1841 L
Green, Lizzie to Armstead Green 2-1-1875 L
Green, Lizzie to William Taylor 1-10-1877 Hy
Green, Louisa E. to Richard Harper 9-4-1854 G
Green, Louisa to Andrew Fowler 12-8-1880 L
Green, Louise to G. C. Batten 12-10-1849 Cr
Green, Louza to James Taylor 9-4-1865 (no return) Cr
Green, Lucinda to Alonzo Caldwell 11-24-1880 (no return) L
Green, Lucinda to Frank Woods 4-2-1881 (4-5-1881) L B
Green, Lucy K. to Hamden McClanahan 1-27-1851 (2-4-1851) Hr
Green, Lucy to Henry Buchanan 10-24-1885 (10-27-1885) L
Green, Lucy to Henry Riggins 10-9-1872 L
Green, Lucy to John Crawford 1-6-1874 (no return) Hy
Green, M. A. to J. D. McLin 11-25-1866 G
Green, M. E. to John N. Green 11-11-1875 Dy
Green, M. J. to H. R. Reed 1-3-1872 Hy
Green, M. P. to David M. Butler 10-8-1870 (10-9-1870) Cr
Green, Manerva to Stephen Harvey 11-22-1876 L

Page 115

Green, Margaret A. to David Dilts 8-1-1863 (8-3-1863) Sh
Green, Margaret B. E. to Lewis Everman 3-27-1849 (no return) Cr
Green, Margaret E. to Geo. G. Garrett 11-6-1850 (no return) Cr
Green, Margaret to Benjamin Kruse 3-26-1859 (3-27-1859) Sh
Green, Maria to John Scott 5-13-1858 Sh
Green, Marier to Leroy Jones 12-28-1865 T
Green, Martha A. to Archibald Giles 10-1-1848 (no return) Cr
Green, Martha A. to John F. Bomar 3-1-1854 Cr
Green, Martha P. to Manoah B. Guinn 8-6-1857 (8-7-1857) O
Green, Martha T. to Erasmus Piper 8-9-1860 Cr
Green, Martha T. to Hardy W. Shelton 12-12-1848 (12-14-1848) G
Green, Martha to Anthony Walton 4-17-1872 T
Green, Martha to Armstead Bayley 12-27-1867 (12-25?-1867) L B
Green, Martha to Bob Butts 3-2-1872 (11-20-1872) T
Green, Mary A. to W. H. Palmer 11-1-1871 (no return) Cr
Green, Mary Ann R. to S. Horn 5-18-1870 L
Green, Mary Ann to John C. Claiborne 2-21-1843 L
Green, Mary C. to W. E. Person 2-19-1862 T
Green, Mary E. to C. C. Stockard 3-26-1859 (3-27-1859) G
Green, Mary E. to Jacob Peter John 3-30-1852 We
Green, Mary E. to Thomas Grooms 12-13-1869 (12-14-1869) Cr
Green, Mary E. to W. R. Garrett 9-23-1862 (9-25-1862) Cr
Green, Mary F. to James R. Hall 11-17-1868 (11-18-1868) Dy
Green, Mary J. to Jerry Kerr 2-19-1877 (not executed) L B
Green, Mary Jane to Jerry Carr 9-23-1878 (7?-13-1879) L B
Green, Mary Jane to Thomas Helmes 12-6-1853 Be
Green, Mary L. to Wm. Z. Rodgers 1-2-1857 L
Green, Mary Pricilla to George F. Nappier 11-29-1849 Hr
Green, Mary to Albert Bivins 9-7-1867 (9-8-1867) L B
Green, Mary to Alford Jones 10-14-1870 (no return) L
Green, Mary to Armistead Lake 7-1-1867? T
Green, Mary to J. H. Kesterson 9-6-1854 We
Green, Mary to J. U. Trout 1-7-1869 G
Green, Mary to Joe Moseley 8-26-1866 L
Green, Mary to M. J. Gibbons 4-16-1861 Sh
Green, Mary to Monroe Franklin 4-6-1867 (4-20-1867) L B
Green, Mary to Neptune Green 3-27-1878 L
Green, Mary to Reuben Beckwith 3-15-1880 (3-16-1880) L B
Green, Mary to Squire Evans 2-11-1870 G
Green, Mary to Wm. C. Johnson 12-30-1874 Hy
Green, Matilda to Edward Springfield 12-25-1866 (12-26-1866) F B
Green, Matilda to George Anderson DeWalt 3-28-1868 (4-5-1868) L
Green, Minnie to Joseph Hill 12-20-1871 (no return) Cr
Green, Mollid A. to W. T. Anderson 7-6-1869 (7-8-1869) F
Green, Mollie to G. W. Barnett 8-11-1874 (8-13-1874) T
Green, Mollie to Nathan Piger 6-26-1869 (6-27-1869) Cr
Green, Moriah to Harrison Richardson 10-4-1872 (no return) Hy
Green, Mosella to George Williams 9-15-1880 L B
Green, Nancey to Wmson. Henley 3-10-1845 F
Green, Nancy A. to N. L. Rice 3-27-1868 (3-29-1868) Cr
Green, Nancy C. to Joseph H. Smith 9-2-1858 Cr
Green, Nancy C. to Miles J. Roberts 9-6-1860 (9-19-1860) Cr
Green, Nancy J. to A. H. Holmes 10-19-1866 (10-21-1866) Cr
Green, Nancy M. to Robert Morris 10-6-1857 (10-8-1857) Sh
Green, Nancy M. to Wm. H. Grooms 11-18-1850 (no return) Cr
Green, Nancy to Ham Fitzpatrick 2-11-1880 (2-12-1880) L B
Green, Nancy to John Arnold 12-16-1868 G
Green, Nancy to Joseph Baker 7-25-1837 Hr
Green, Rachal to Rubin Snelling 12-10-1870 T
Green, Rebecca to Jonathan N. Taylor 9-5-1831 Ma
Green, Rochoanna to George Conaley 1-30-1875 (1-31-1875) L B
Green, Rose to F. A. Becton 5-29-1873 (6-1-1873) L B
Green, Rose to John Calway 4-30-1868 (no return) F B
Green, Roxana to Lewis Herron 2-1-1879 (2-2-1879) L
Green, S. F. B. to W. H. Henderson 5-25-1862 Mn
Green, Sallie Ann to John Uriah Green 3-29-1865 (3-30-1865) T
Green, Sarah Adeline to David Henry Limbarger 3-1-1865 T
Green, Sarah M. to John Gillooly 7-26-1866 Hn
Green, Sarah to Peter S. Clack 8-23-1862 (8-24-1862) O
Green, Sarah to William Powell 12-8-1868 L
Green, Serinda to Henry Doak 5-27-1869 G B
Green, Slalie to John Kirksey 12-27-1869 F B
Green, Sophia to John L. Parker 9-10-1833 Hr
Green, Sophronia to Samuel J. Simmons 9-9-1858 Cr
Green, Susan A. to Brother M. Jones 3-12-1860 (3-20-1860) T
Green, Susan E. to Benjamin B. Person 10-20-1842 Ma
Green, Susan J. to Booker Jones 3-12-1860 T
Green, Susan to Minus M. Ward 11-8-1856 (11-11-1856) Ma
Green, Susan to Thos. Jacocks 1-3-1878 (no return) Hy
Green, Susan to Wm. O. Taylor no date (with 1868) T
Green, Vannie to J. H. Fly 11-27-1866 G
Green, Venie F. to W. S. Wright 2-10-1875 Hy
Green, Victoria to Madison Matmass 12-14-1870 (12-18-1870) F B
Green, W. A. to W. P. Harness 10-23-1869 Cr
Green? (Gunn?), Ellen to Matthew Ohern (Ahern) 1-21-1859 (1-23-1859) Sh
Green? (Gwin?), Isabella to William Fisher 1-25-1873 (no return) L B
Green?, Ellen to W. H. R. Tiner 10-29-1867 Dy

Green?, Flora to George W. Campbell 11-3-1871 (11-6-1871) L
Green?, Jane to Jerry Lake 12-31-1873 (no return) L B
Green?, P. E. to Wm. P. Slaughter 5-6-1844 (5-8-1844) Hr
Green?, Smith Ann to Ezekial Williams 12-18-1872 (12-25-1872) L B
Greene, Ann Eliza F. to F. M. Upchurch 12-14-1858 Hn
Greene, Mary Ann to A. Wilson 1-20-1864 Hn
Greene, Mary E. to Richard Leigh 3-30-1859 Cr
Greene, Susan F. to Joseph W. Nance 11-1-1863 Hn
Greenfield, Bettie to Robt Linden 12-28-1874 T
Greenhaw, Mary to Tallassee Bond 3-14-1833 Sh
Greenhaw, Sarah E. to G. W. Sherman 8-1-1861 Mn
Greenlaw, Alice B. to Richard Mason 9-24-1832 Sh
Greenlaw, Donna M. to DeSoto B. McHenry 6-12-1862 (6-16-1862) Sh
Greenlaw, Lucy Ann to Jesse M. Tate 3-30-1842 Sh
Greenlaw, Mary A. to Hinson Gift 12-8-1836 Sh
Greenlaw, Nancy to Armistead Boring 9-17-1831 Sh
Greenleaf, Martha to Joseph I. Dew? 7-23-1831 (7-24-1831) Hr
Greenlee, Zilpha to Joseph S. Rainer 12-18-1851 (12-19-1851) Hr
Greenwall, Ginnett to Solomon Anker 6-21-1856 (no return) F
Greenway, M. F. to H. P. R. Wilson 10-15-1854 (no return) F
Greenwell, Martha M. to Matthew Tetterton 1-31-1849 (2-1-1849) Ma
Greenwell, Sarah A. to Thos. Martin 3-26-1860 G
Greenwood, C. B. to Jerome B. Peery 5-8-1869 (no return) Dy
Greenwood, D. A. to James T. Lingo 9-11-1860 (9-13-1860) Cr
Greenwood, D. A. to James T.? Lingo 9-11-1860 (9-13-1860) Cr
Greenwood, Judy to James W. Barns 5-28-1845 Cr
Greenwood, M. J. to S. T. Demoss 9-15-1852 Cr
Greenwood, Martha to Sampson P. Demoss 4-26-1859 Cr
Greenwood, Mary E. to Virgil R. Burk 6-12-1863 Cr
Greenwood, Mary E. to Virgil R. Burk 6-12-1863 (no return) Cr
Greenwood, Nancy Ann to James W. Hunt 4-19-1843 (4-20-1843) Hr
Greer (Green?), M. A. to F. G. Thomas 12-23-1869 G
Greer, A. T. to J. O. Penick 8-19-1865 Hn
Greer, Amanda C. to James H. Orr 9-26-1859 G
Greer, Ann H. to R. S. Fife 3-9-1860 (3-11-1860) Sh
Greer, Anna to Haskins Halliburton 2-27-1873 Hy
Greer, Annis to Z. Williams 7-6-1869 T
Greer, Beedy C. to Isaac W. Nichols 12-26-1867 Be
Greer, Caroline to Robert Spires 5-14-1846 Be
Greer, Catherine (Mrs.) to John Cogan 3-18-1863 Sh
Greer, Charlotte to William Blanchett 10-22-1851 Hn
Greer, Cintha to J. B. Flornce 10-16-1862 Be
Greer, D. M. to W. McGill 6-5-1839 Be
Greer, Dorthula to William Thornton 6-30-1859 G
Greer, Drucilla C. to Henry D. Smith 4-8-1853 Hn
Greer, Eliza to Richard Clay 4-19-1870 (4-20-1870) Cr
Greer, Elizabeth J. to Thomas McGill 3-9-1853 Be
Greer, Elizabeth to Nathaniel Simpson 1-1-1866 Hy
Greer, Elizabeth to Nathaniel Simpson 1-3?-1866 Hy
Greer, Ellen to Green Saunders 8-18-1866 G
Greer, Ellen to J. L. Cunningham 12-17-1868 (12-24-1868) Dy
Greer, Helen to W. M. Winbush 3-6-1866 Hn
Greer, Isabel P. to A. R. Black 12-23-1855 Be
Greer, Julia Ann to Isaac J. Biggs 4-1-1852 G
Greer, Laura J. P. to Wm. Doublin 2-29-1844 We
Greer, Lesa Ann to Thos. H. Presson 9-29-1868 Be
Greer, Lide A. to John Reid 10-1-1867 (10-2-1867) Ma
Greer, Louisa E. to Rufus Ellis 12-18-1852 Hn
Greer, Louisa J. to Thomas J. Presson 12-23-1851 Be
Greer, Lucinda to Isaac Watson 6-10-1846 Be
Greer, Lucy to James M. Barham 8-21-1844 Hn
Greer, Margaret S. to William J. R. Becton 9-13-1853 (9-15-1853) G
Greer, Mariah to William Wood 4-2-1874 (4-24-1874) L B
Greer, Martha Ann to W. F. T. Bloodworth 8-6-1843 Be
Greer, Martha S. to Wm. W. Presson 11-1-1866 Be
Greer, Martha to Thomas Young 12-19-1856 (12-21-1856) O
Greer, Mary C. to James T. Childress 6-30-1867 Be
Greer, Mary C. to Wesley W. Cleaver 12-27-1851 (no return) Hn
Greer, Mary Frances to Samuel M. Presson 1-13-1862 Be
Greer, Mary to Wm. Bell 9-15-1861 Be
Greer, Minerva J. to Ray Bradford 1-11-1844 (1-1?-1844) O
Greer, Nancy O. to George W. Burress 9-29-1851 G
Greer, Nancy to John T. Presson 1-2-1844 Be
Greer, O. A. to J. P. Canada 9-27-1867 G
Greer, Rebecca A. to Samuel H. Madden 12-21-1853 Be
Greer, Rebecca A. to William Cooper 1-20-1867 Be
Greer, Rebecca to A. J. B. Hudson 6-12-1858 Be
Greer, S. R. to J. B. Goodlett 10-6-1851 (no return) Cr
Greer, Susan Ann Elizabeth to Reubin F. Garland 7-25-1853 (7-26-1853) Hr
Greer, Susan C. to Robert Counts 2-16-1852 G
Greer, T. E. to Elijah Wren 10-6-1856 (10-16-1856) G
Gregg, Lucy Ann to James H. Roberts 9-3-1838 (no return) F
Gregg, Malinda Jane to James T. Jackson 12-6-1857 Sh
Gregg, Sallie M. to John G. Whitson 3-30-1872 T
Greggery, Sarah Jane to Henry McConkey 10-7-1864 (10-8-1864) Sh
Greggory, Mary to Samuel Oneal 11-4-1839 (1-1-1840) G
Greggory, Polly to Redic (Reddick) Overton 1-20-1832 Sh

Greggs, Fannie to Henry Shaw 12-25-1867 (12-28-1867) F B
Gregory, Adelia to William McKee 12-31-1844 Sh
Gregory, Agnes to O. T. Hendron 11-28-1842 F
Gregory, Agnis to Johnson J. Whitefield 11-19-1839 (no return) F
Gregory, Amanda to J. W. Jones 7-4-1844 Sh
Gregory, Catharina to James R. Porter 9-4-1851 G
Gregory, Cornelia M. to Levi P. Osborn 7-24-1848 (7-27-1848) F
Gregory, Eliza to James S. Vann 8-30-1846 (no return) F
Gregory, Elizabeth t. to John S. Appleton 3-11-1870 Ma
Gregory, Elizabeth to J. C. Davison 10-5-1850 Sh
Gregory, Elizabeth to Jesse Parker 1-30-1841 Hr
Gregory, Emma to J. J. Blaydes 9-20-1870 Hy
Gregory, Fatne-Fabney (Mrs.) to David Dodd 4-12-1833 Sh
Gregory, Frances R. to Francis J. Wood 2-7-1871 Hy
Gregory, Harriet J. to James H. Harbert 1-24-1859 (1-27-1859) Ma
Gregory, Isabella J. to John B. Collins 2-10-1862 (no return) Hy
Gregory, Jane to John P. Anderson 1-13-1842 (1-15-1842) G
Gregory, Jane to William Robinson 4-17-1830 Ma
Gregory, L. A. to G. W. Sulivan 11-25-1874 Hy
Gregory, L. E. to A. J. Grills 11-14-1871 Dy
Gregory, Livina to Wm. C. Patterson 6-8-1846 Cr
Gregory, Lou N. to John C. Moore 2-13-1860 (2-14-1860) Sh
Gregory, Louisa to John Tucker 8-9-1874 Hy
Gregory, Lucy to William Roach(Roark?) 7-17-1844 Hr
Gregory, M. A. to Sardis S. Goodner 12-22-1856 (12-23-1856) Sh
Gregory, M. J. to Willis Bobo 10-14-1851 Cr
Gregory, Margaret to John Flowers 9-1-1832 G
Gregory, Margarett to James K. Hallaway 7-31-1857 We
Gregory, Martha Ann to Richard B. Vaughter 12-4-1854 (12-7-1854) Ma
Gregory, Martha B. to P. H. Marbury 9-20-1868 Hy
Gregory, Martha to Athlin (Arthur) Simmons 2-12-1840 Sh
Gregory, Martha to Joel Booth 10-2-1851 Hr
Gregory, Mary A. to Benjamin H. Green (Guin-Given?) 10-24-1853 (10-25-1853) L
Gregory, Mary E. to Lea Yancy 12-10-1874 Hy
Gregory, Mary J. to N. (Niel) B. Holt 11-3-1836 Sh
Gregory, Mary to James M. Bond 7-7-1839 Hn
Gregory, Mary to Jos. H. Edgerly 6-23-1857 (6-24-1857) Sh
Gregory, Mary to Nathan Snowden 3-18-1841 Sh
Gregory, Mattie to Jack Culp 10-25-1870 (10-26-1870) Cr B
Gregory, Penelope to George J. Terrell 5-9-1861 G
Gregory, Ruby Elmira to Wm. Jasper Prince 9-12-1860 (9-13-1860) T
Gregory, Sarah A. to H. F. Wooten 11-14-1857 We
Gregory, Sarah A. to Wm. Travis 4-14-1845 Cr
Gregory, Sarah Jane to Thomas Gregory 10-13-1870 (10-14-1870) T
Gregory, Sina to Arch McCollum 2-3-1872 (no return) Cr B
Gregory, Sinia to Arch McCollum 1-7-1870 (not endorsed) Cr
Gregory, Susan P. to John R. Gurley 12-22-1856 (12-23-1856) Sh
Gregson, Caroline T. to William L. Hagler 2-21-1865 Hn
Gregson, Sarah C. to Isaac Akers 3-6-1845 Hn
Gregson, Sarah to Perry Osburn 2-13-1840 Sh
Gregston, Mary to Joseph M. Hastings 4-17-1850 Hn
Gren, Margarett A. to Mosses Brown 5-7-1868 G B
Gresam, Mary to John Crab 2-28-1840 Be
Gresham, Lucy A. to John A. Comer 12-26-1866 Hn
Gresham, Mary to John Mossman 1-15-1840 Hn
Gresham, Mary to Lewis W. Harper 9-2-1850 (9-4-1850) F
Gresham, Sarah K. to Jasper S. Cole 8-27-1854 Hn
Gresham, Susan to Joseph Petty 8-29-1850 Hn
Gresharber, Helena? to Jacob Schnaller 1-28-1853 Sh
Grey, Eliza V. to James Pettett 1-31-1838 F
Grey, Mollie to Turner Forrest 1-26-1867 Hy
Grey, Nancy to David W. Stanley 1-30-1860 Cr
Grey, Parthenia W. to J. L. McAlenny 9-23-1851 (9-24-1851) Sh
Gribbin, Helen to Edwin Palmer 1-1-1852 Sh
Grice, Elizabeth to Humphrey Curtis 12-26-1838 G
Grider, Barbara to Christian Hale (Hak) 12-21-1849 Sh
Grider, Elizabeth to Geor. A. Smith 12-27-1844 (1-7-1845) F
Grider, Elizabeth to Harrison Davis 6-30-1837 O
Grider, Ellen to W. S. Shuford 2-15-1851 (2-19-1851) F
Grider, Mary to Mitchell Heaslett 1-11-1870 (no return) F B
Grider, S. A. to R. C. Slaughter 12-20-1849 Sh
Grider, Sarah to Jonathan Raima 8-24-1832 O
Gridly, Annie to E. H. Kelly 11-20-1866 (no return) Hy
Grier, A. L. to James K. Snody 6-24-1863 G
Grier, Amanda to Elisha Hedgecock 1-10-1863 G
Grier, Julia A. to H. A. Longworth 4-2-1860 (4-5-1860) G
Grier, Martha Ann to J. D. Mitchell 4-5-1848 (4-6-1848) G
Grier, Martha J. E. to J. L. Berry 2-20-1861 G
Grier, Mary to Wm. C. Gregory 2-27-1865 (3-1-1865) Dy
Grier, Nancy Jane to R. W. Mitchell 7-22-1841 (7-29-1841) G
Grier, R. M. to Benjamin Phillips 2-11-1866 G
Grier, S. E. to Charles Robertson 9-20-1876 Dy
Grier, S. R. to M. E. Hearn 3-22-1868 G
Grier, Susan H. to J. W. McCartney 12-6-1868 G
Griffee, Eliza Ann to John P. Johnson 10-11-1869 (no return) Hy
Griffee, Margaret to William Fletcher 4-28-1831 (5-3-1831) G

Griffee, Penelope to James Curtis 12-27-1831 (12-27-1831) G
Griffen, Emily Ann to Marshall Herring 8-10-1848 Sh
Griffen, Martha to James B. Horn 8-18-1842 Sh
Griffen, Minerva J. to W. R. Weatherford 9-17-1863 G
Griffies, Fannie to J. M. Dill 1-22-1854 Cr
Griffin, Abbie to Charles Silver 12-27-1856 (12-28-1856) Sh
Griffin, Ada F. to W. P. Logan 2-13-1860 (2-14-1860) F
Griffin, Adline to B. C. Clark 4-2-1867 Cr
Griffin, Agness to Thos. J. Beasley 1-21-1867 (1-24-1867) F
Griffin, Alsey to Peter Craws 1-5-1878 (no return) Hy
Griffin, America to B. H. Looney 1-17-1870 (1-18-1870) Cr
Griffin, Angeline to William C. Wadkins 9-27-1867 Hn
Griffin, Ann E. to James Wilson 10-23-1860 (10-25-1860) Sh
Griffin, Arreana to William Foren 5-9-1836 (5-10-1836) G
Griffin, Bramley to Hiram Canady 10-22-1849 (10-23-1849) O
Griffin, Bridget to George Collins 4-24-1854 (4-30-1854) Sh
Griffin, Bridget to Thomas Fitzgerald 2-27-1860 Sh
Griffin, Callie V. to W. J. Harrel 9-14-1869 (no return) F
Griffin, Caroline W. to Geo. W. Queen 1-31-1859 F
Griffin, Caroline to William H. Burns 9-17-1840 Hn
Griffin, Cornelia M. to Henry Boardman 11-20-1857 Sh
Griffin, Cynthia to J. M. King 10-12-1865 Hy
Griffin, Delina to Geo. Seaton 5-13-1845 (5-16-1845) F
Griffin, Dicy to Elihu Snyder 9-27-1840 Hn
Griffin, Drusilla to Anthony Bledsoe 7-4-1842 (7-7-1842) Ma
Griffin, Eliza J. to Marshall B. Jones 12-15-1870 F
Griffin, Eliza Jane to John Glenn 10-25-1845 (10-28-1845) F
Griffin, Elizabeth C. to Cyrus D. Byars 7-17-1855 Hn
Griffin, Elizabeth H. to A. J. Neal 10-15-1852 (no return) F
Griffin, Ella to W. P. Coldwell 11-26-1872 (11-27-1873?) L
Griffin, Ema to J. F. Whitten 3-15-1869 G
Griffin, Emma to S. C. D. Bain 2-20-1878 Hy
Griffin, Fanny to Thomas McGuire 12-5-1866 G
Griffin, Harriet to Peter Mitchell 1-6-1874 (1-7-1874) Dy
Griffin, Hester to Charley Dolly 12-3-1868 Hy
Griffin, Jane to Henry McNiel 10-9-1855 Be
Griffin, Jane to William Horne 5-2-1837 Sh
Griffin, Jantha Virginia to Lewis G. Evans 5-20-1859 Sh
Griffin, Julia A. to Samuel F. Murrah 4-22-1848 Sh
Griffin, Louisa A. to Charley Darley 12-4-1876 L
Griffin, Louisa to Henry Griffin 12-27-1866 Dy
Griffin, Lucinda to John D. Hines 12-12-1850 Sh
Griffin, M. C. to William Midchiff 5-23-1850 We
Griffin, M. L. to R. T. Hill 12-21-1870 (12-22-1870) Dy
Griffin, M. R. to T. H. Thornton 1-16-1878 Dy
Griffin, Margrat G. to Crawford Prewitt 10-25-1836 (10-27-1836) G
Griffin, Mariah S. to Robert S. Allen 1-13-1844 (1-25-1844) F
Griffin, Martha Jane to Joshua S. Williams 12-30-1848 O
Griffin, Martha S. to Hiram W. Priest 1-20-1860 (no return) We
Griffin, Martha to George W. Lawrence 7-27-1852 G
Griffin, Martha to Toney Parks 12-17-1879 (12-18-1879) Dy
Griffin, Mary C. to W. C. Gibson 11-29-1853 Cr
Griffin, Mary E. to Crispin D. Arnn 1-2-1859 Hn
Griffin, Mary E. to John Bushart 5-26-1857 Hn
Griffin, Mary E. to John C. Yearwood 5-10-1862 Hy
Griffin, Mary E. to William R. Bonner 2-6-1840 Hn
Griffin, Mary J. to Henry Ervine 11-10-1859 O
Griffin, Mary J. to Turner W. Hines 7-20-1847 Sh
Griffin, Mary J. to William B. Borough 7-1-1862 (no return) Hy
Griffin, Mary Jane to Thomas J. Peel 1-6-1874 (1-7-1874) Dy
Griffin, Mary Jane to William H. White 6-25-1866 (6-26-1866) L
Griffin, Mary Jane to Wilson R. Gilbert 11-10-1871 (11-12-1871) Ma
Griffin, Mary to Bucy Jones 1-11-1876 (no return) Hy
Griffin, Mary to Dennis Ryan 1-24-1860 (1-25-1860) Sh
Griffin, Mary to J. N. Thompson 4-8-1866 Hy
Griffin, Mary to John Griffin 7-7-1857 Hn
Griffin, Minerva Jane to Andrew Stephens 8-21-1860 Ma
Griffin, Olivia L. to J. Y. Barnett 11-9-1864 (11-10-1864) Sh
Griffin, R. to John Ellis 5-7-1849 Sh
Griffin, Sarah C. to Saml. L. Pleasant 10-11-1870 (no return) Dy
Griffin, Sarah C. to Samuel L. Gleason 10-11-1870 (no return) Dy
Griffin, Sarah to Richard Robertson 11-24-1838 (11-25-1838) G
Griffin, Sarah? (Mrs.) to Benj. Mitchell 8-20-1839 (9-3?-1839) F
Griffin, Serenia E. to James L. Wooten 12-9-1850 Sh
Griffin, Sophria W. to Ezra T. Morrison 1-3-1842 (1-6-1842) F
Griffin, Teresa to Robert Vail 6-13-1845 Sh
Griffin, Virginia to G. W. Quinn 9-21-1853 (no return) F
Griffing, Teresa to James Banfield 1-11-1849 Sh
Griffini, M. E. to T. Wilson 5-8-1884 (5-9-1884) L
Griffith, Ada R. to L. D. Fortner 7-30-1883 (7-31-1883) L
Griffith, C. C. to J. M. Anderson 11-30-1866 (12-5-1866) L
Griffith, Eliza E. to Wm. J. Rice 12-21-1868 (12-22-1868) T
Griffith, Emma to W. F. Winn 11-15-1871 (11-14-1872) L
Griffith, Jane C. to Bassel Jeanes 3-6-1870 (5-9-1870) T
Griffith, M. B. to Henry Pearson 6-20-1865 (6-21-1865) O
Griffith, Mary E. to A. O. Irwin 1-15-1859 (1-20-1859) Sh
Griffith, Mary W. to William Newsome 6-18-1864 G

Griffith, Nancy to John F. Burton 10-14-1850 (10-17-1850) Hr
Griffith, Nancy to Robert J. Flanakin 9-9-1867 T
Griffith, Rebeca A. to Benj. Harrell 11-8-1854 (no return) We
Griffith, Roxanna to A. M. Winn 12-9-1875 Hy
Griffith, S. A. to O. D. Winn 4-11-1872 (4-14-1872) L
Griffith, Sarah Ann to Foster Perry 12-9-1857 (12-10-1857) Ma
Griffith, Sarah to James Rily 3-10-1858 We
Griffiths, Lizzie to J. B. Taylor 2-17-1870 G
Griffy, Elizabeth to Blaney Harper 9-3-1832 (9-12-1832) G
Griffy, Margaret E. to Nathaniel Nobles 10-5-1846 (10-6-1846) G
Griffy, Sarah A. to S. C. Bivens 9-19-1849 G
Grifin, Elzira to Moses Garrison 10-30-1865 Cr
Grigery, Emily to Samuel M. Sturges 5-9-1835 Sh
Grigg, Altha L. to Thomas M. Sheridan 11-24-1847 Hn
Grigg, Bettie to Byrd Danniel 5-3-1873 T
Grigg, Lucy to George Clark 10-7-1865 Hy
Grigg, Ora E. to C. C. Taliaferro 1-18-1872 Hy
Grigg, Sarah to Benj. Bond 4-10-1878 Hy
Griggs, Agnes to R. D. Atkinson 1-30-1869 (2-4-1869) F
Griggs, Bettie to E. J. Jones 12-22-1885 (12-23-1885) L
Griggs, Betty to Byrd Daniel 5-3-1873 (5-4-1873) T
Griggs, Caroline to Thomas Miller 2-5-1870 (no return) L
Griggs, Caroline to William Smith 8-19-1874 L
Griggs, Elizabeth to J. W. Hatch 12-16-1846 Cr
Griggs, G. A. G. to James M. Burns 5-26-1874 (5-27-1874) L
Griggs, Hester Ann to Harvey D. Standfield 3-13-1840 (3-15-1840) Hr
Griggs, Julia Ann to Jackson Conner 5-25-1867 G
Griggs, Lucretia to James Shoemake 1-30-1861 (no return) L
Griggs, Mary E. to Carroll A. Chandler 9-6-1859 (9-7-1859) L
Griggs, Mary E. to John W. Raney 6-25-1870 (6-26-1870) L
Griggs, Mary to J. P. Black 12-18-1883 (12-19-1883) L
Griggs, Millie to C. W. Rice 8-14-1875 (8-15-1875) L
Griggs, Rebecca to John T. Glimp 2-11-1885 L
Griggs, Sarah Ann to Ivy Chandler 4-10-1844 (no return) L
Griggsw, Margaret to J. A. Shoemake 2-22-1872 L
Grigory, May to John H. Fisher 1-27-1841 G
Grigsby, Harriet to Coleman Barmer? 3-12-1874 T
Grigsby, Sarah to William M. McBryde 11-16-1847 G
Grills, Dicey E. to J. F. Snow 10-31-1873 (11-4-1873) Dy
Grimbley, Sophia to J. W. Bowen 3-21-1860 (3-22-1860) Sh
Grimes, Elizabeth F. to G. W. Alexander 4-13-1848 Hn
Grimes, Elizabeth J. to A. C. Dudley 5-12-1859 We
Grimes, Henrietta to Saml. Crosby 12-28-1868 T
Grimes, Julia A. to J. W. Insco 11-4-1861 (no return) We
Grimes, Leah Elizabeth to Clarence Millard 5-25-1864 Sh
Grimes, Lear Elizabeth to Clarence B. Willard 5-25-1863 Sh
Grimes, Luizer C. to James N. Hicks 2-6-1870 G
Grimes, M. M. to J. W. Cox 2-5-1857 We
Grimes, Mary to Derry Cooper 11-23-1870 (11-27-1870) T
Grimes, Mary to Elijah Shelton 9-10-1866 (9-16-1866) T
Grimes, Nancy C. to D. Morris 9-15-1852 We
Grimes, Pattie E. to George F. Grimes 2-25-1873 (2-26-1873) T
Grimes, Tennessee to N. T.? Akin 11-10-1874 (11-11-1874) T
Grimes, Virginia to Henry Chilsen 12-26-1867 Hy
Grimm, Bettie to Elijah Grimm 1-10-1876 (1-12-1876) Dy
Grimm, Bettie to Richard Mann 2-8-1876 (no return) Dy
Grimm, Letitia to Fernando Dunevent 5-19-1875 (5-20-1875) Dy
Grimm, Mourning to Gay Grimm 9-26-1877 (no return) Dy
Grimm, Polly to Hampton Smith 12-6-1877 Dy
Grinstead, Josephine to J. D. Cox 7-14-1846 Hn
Grisham, Manerva S. to Ezra Holtzclaw 12-8-1852 (no return) F
Grisham, Mary to Merrell Elkins 1-6-1851 Hn
Grisham?, Fanny A. to William Hutson 10-28-1847 Hn
Grisharber, Elizabeth to William W. Dearmond 11-5-1856 (11-13-1856) Sh
Grishom, Candis to Solomon Gordon 9-14-1846 (9-17-1846) T
Grishum, Elizabeth to James Hogan 4-28-1854 (5-2-1854) G
Grissam, Nancy J. to John A. Ragsdale 9-15-1858 (9-16-1858) O
Grissom, Ann to William H. Ferrell 12-15-1855 (12-16-1855) L
Grissom, Cornelia to B. L. Thompson 11-15-1851 (no return) F
Grissom, Eliza Jane to Joseph Rich 12-23-1844 (12-25-1844) F
Grissom, Elizabeth D. F. to Joseph Allen 12-27-1852 (no return) F
Grissom, Elizabeth to James Martin 9-9-1865 (9-10-1865) O
Grissom, Elizabeth to Thomas Parks 6-27-1860 G
Grissom, M. V. to R. G. DeBow 12-14-1868 (12-15-1868) F
Grissom, Martha to Thomas A. Phelps 5-1-1859 We
Grissom, Mary Elizabeth to Robert Thomas Parks 6-17-1860 G
Grissom, Mary L. to A. D. Trantham 7-12-1855 We
Grissom, Mary to Anderson Herndon 10-21-1858 G
Grissom, Nancy Ann to Jones (James) Rogers 9-17-1853 (9-18-1853) O
Grissom, Nancy to Leander Fullerton 4-28-1844 Be
Grisson, Mary Jane to J. A. W. G. Rogers 7-31-1861 (8-1-1861) Cr
Grissum, Pantha to Elijah Henley, jr. 9-28-1843 F
Grist, Eliza R. to W. H. Callis 12-25-1869 G
Grist, Lucinda J. to Wm. P. Cotton 3-2-1864 (3-8-1864) Sh
Grist, Sarah to Jordan Knox 11-4-1848 (11-5-1848) G
Griswell, A. M. to P. B. Gilbert 12-16-1866 O
Grizzard, Louisa to Milton Priest 9-8-1858 Cr

Brides

Grizzard, Mary E. to Henderson M. Hardy 11-21-1872 Hy
Grizzard, Mary to Pleasant Wright 8-23-1870 (8-24-1870) Cr
Grizzard, Susan to William Walker 2-8-1867 (2-10-1867) L B
Grizzle, Nancy E. to W. H. Sanders 1-11-1868 (1-12-1868) F
Grogan, Alice to Frank E. Watson 12-29-1885 (12-30-1885) L
Grogan, Elizabeth to J. B. Brandon 11-7-1872 Cr
Grogan, Martha J. to John O. Wall 1-6-1870 (1-7-1870) Cr
Grogan, Mary A. to A. J. Chism 3-10-1886 (3-11-1886) L
Grogan, Mary Ann to Meredith Johnson 3-11-1852 Be
Grogan, Sarah to W. F. Dalton 4-6-1859 Hn
Gromes?, Johanna F. to William B. Baldin 10-4-1855 (no return) Hn
Grone (Grove?), Beth to Gustavus Bornemann 7-3-1856 Sh
Groom, M. A. to D. H. Overton 2-12-1852 We
Groom, Mary B. to Jesse P. French 1-6-1870 Cr
Groom, Mary F. to Thos. W. Groom 3-1-1871 Cr
Groom, Mary to G. W. Thomason 2-15-1866 Hn
Groom, Mary to Pinkey A. Scott 10-4-1857 Hn
Groom, S. C. to J. W. Luallen 3-12-1852 We
Groom, Sophia A. to Z. P. Byars 6-24-1863 Hn
Groome, A. F. to R. H. Davis 12-18-1862 Mn
Grooms, Elizabeth to James McMackin 8-8-1858 Cr
Grooms, Frances to John A. Brown 1-20-1855 Cr
Grooms, Harriett to Geo. McCarter 11-28-1850 Sh
Grooms, Jane to E. R. Hatch 6-28-1841 T
Grooms, Louiza to James Angle 7-11-1871 Cr
Grooms, M. A. to J. D. Redicks 6-24-1846 We
Grooms, Mary A. to James D. Redick 7-2-1846 We
Grooms, Mary A. to James Lipe 11-12-1846 Cr
Grooms, Mary to Ca_y Jones 1-4-1851 (1-5-1851) Sh
Grooms, Paulina to William Imes 7-1-1838 Sh
Grooms, Sarah to Drury Lane 1-17-1839 Sh
Grooms, Susan A. to Wm. Cobb 9-27-1870 (10-16-1870) Cr
Grooms, Susan to William Johnson 9-28-1836 Sh
Grooms, Wilmurth to Thomas Butler 10-28-1824 Hr
Groran, Sarah L. to Highim Ross 1-7-1855 Sh
Gross, Ethel Maybell to Elmer Troy 12-4-1854 Be CC
Gross, Malinda to James McDaniel 6-19-1850 Be
Gross, Mary to J. W. Balentine 4-2-1877 (4-7-1877) L
Gross, Nancy Jane to W. T. Valentine 7-21-1865 T
Grot, Verona to John Reutter 8-25-1849 Sh
Grove, Annie E. to Henry, sr. Johnson 12-20-1871 Hy
Grove, Eliza Jane to James T. Williams 9-28-1841 (9-29-1841) Hr
Grove, Sarah Ann to J. C. Parmer 9-29-1847 Hr
Groves, Ellen to Joseph Taylor 6-2-1866 (6-17-1866) F B
Groves, J. D. to Thomas Birdsong 10-22-1859 (8-12-1860) F
Groves, Mary F. to J. R. Grehan 6-25-1861 We
Groves, Minerater to B. H. Smith 10-28-1856 Cr
Grubb, Gemema G. to William Adkins 12-31-1857 We
Grubb, Mary Jane to Stephen C. Dismukes 6-2-1856 (no return) Hn
Grumbleby, Anna to Mathias Jones 11-22-1860 Sh
Grundy, Dilly to George Hardy 12-28-1867 (no return) F B
Gryson (Guyson), Mary to George W. Bell 6-16-1842 Sh
Guaranes, Belle to Thomas A. Baker 1-27-1859 We
Guardner, Decena to J. W. McBroom 1-8-1877 (1-9-1877) L
Guardner, Rebecca to Ezekil Bennett 6-4-1855 (6-7-1855) T
Guarrant, Elizth. to John A. Jelks 11-25-1844 (no return) F
Guarrant, Harrett L. to William Wash 3-30-1840 F
Gudzer, Hant to Henry Porter 9-30-1871 (10-1-1871) L B
Guesent, V. H. to William H. Powell 12-13-1859 (12-14-1859) Sh
Guess (Gross), Harriett to David B. Brown 8-25-1841 Sh
Guess, Elizabeth to John Rackley 1-3-1839 G
Guffe, Amanda C. to John W. Tucker 1-2-1869 Cr
Guffee, Margarett to R. A. Clopton 3-4-1868 (3-15-1868) Cr
Gugman, Jane to Wm. B. Campbell 11-23-1846 Hn
Guiheni? (Gresham?), C. E. to Thomas L. Hall 8-29-1877 L
Guile, Linda to James Gardner 6-8-1848 Hn
Guill, Caroline to George W. Inman 10-5-1859 Hn
Guill, E. A. to J. C. Puckett 1-24-1856 (no return) Hn
Guill, Emily M. to A. C. Rateree 9-13-1866 Hn
Guill, Lucy Ann to James Steel 12-23-1852 Hn
Guin (Green?), Elizabeth to Alexander Gay 1-25-1873 (no return) L B
Guin, Alpha to William H. Walls 7-16-1873 Hy
Guin, Emery to Benjamin R. Perron 1-2-1844 (1-9-1844) Ma
Guin, Mary A. to L. C. Covington 1-8-1856 We
Guin?, D. M. to Daniel D. Berry 4-12-1831 Hr
Guinn (Gause-Green?), Mary H. to J. L. Winfield 2-9-1860 (2-15-1860) L
Guinn, Amanda to W. C. Huffman 11-30-1873 (12-2-1874?) T
Guinn, Caroline to William Gillam 5-23-1857 (no return) We
Guinn, Christiana to John Dubois 10-14-1847 Hn
Guinn, Eliza to Shad Cunningham 12-31-1869 Cr
Guinn, Elizabeth to Benjamin F. Fields 10-31-1858 O
Guinn, Emily E. to Jno. W. Chandler 3-14-1871 Ma
Guinn, Harriet to Abraham Morrow 11-24-1857 (11-25-1857) O
Guinn, Harriet to B. R. Simpkins 10-2-1863 (10-5-1863) Dy
Guinn, Jane to Philip D. Alexander 12-22-1869 (12-23-1869) Ma
Guinn, Katie to Emmett Hobbs 1-1-1879 (1-15-1879) Dy
Guinn, Martha J. to R. S. Jones 11-17-1867 Hn

Guinn, Martha P. to E. H. Verhine 3-5-1866 (3-8-1866) O
Guinn, Nancy A. to J. S. Smith 6-7-1863 Hn
Guinn, Nancy N. to William Alexander 3-18-1868 Ma
Guinn, P. C. to John K. Graham 12-5-1864 (no return) Hn
Guinn, Polly to Richard Moore 10-31-1861 Hn
Guinn, Sarah E. to Elijah Alexander 12-22-1868 (12-23-1868) Ma
Guinn, Sarah G. to Robert F. Cox 10-8-1865 Hy
Guinn, Sarah to Berd Shert 3-17-1860 (3-22-1860) O
Guinn, Victoria to Joseph Dinwiddie 12-29-1868 (1-2-1869) Cr
Guise, Caroline to S. B. Holyfield 2-6-1861 (1?-10-1861) Hr
Guise, Elvira E. to Daniel Campbell 12-21-1857 (12-23-1857) Hr
Guise, Rachael Ann to J. C. Fowler 6-3-1864 Sh
Guise, Rebecca to Isaac Sellars 8-27-1857 (8-28-1857) Hr
Gullage, Elizabeth to Urias Springer 12-13-1870 Cr
Gullage, Martha C. to Newton C. Stanly 9-12-1860 Hn
Gullage, Rebecca to Beverly Allbritten 4-20-1842 Hn
Gullage, Sarah J. to B. G. Volentine 12-23-1851 Hn
Gullage, Zilphy to Thomas M. Wilson 9-1-1842 (no return) Hn
Gulledge, D. J. to H. C. Scott 6-22-1867 (6-23-1867) Cr
Gulledge, Zelphia to Thos. Springer 2-15-1846 Cr
Gullege, Mary to Samuel Holmes 9-1-1848 (no return) Cr
Gullet, A. E. to J. R. Hickman 1-11-1869 (1-14-1869) Cr
Gullet, Sally to Thomas S. White 10-2-1832 (10-8-1832) Hr
Gullett, Eliza to Caleb B. Crowley 4-28-1849 Cr
Gullett, Jane to C. R. Jones 8-5-1844 Cr
Gullett, Jane to C. W. Cosley, sr. 12-2-1857 G
Gullett, Martha R. to David S. Lacey 5-17-1844 O
Gully, Mary Ann to James Nowell 3-26-1865 Be
Gully, P. Jane to Robert Duncan 4-10-1854 Be
Gully, Temperance A. to Wm. R. Thomason 1-30-1851 Be
Gully, Virginia D. to James Cottingham 1-25-1866 Be
Gunlege, Parmelia E. to William H. Dunley 7-11-1844 Hn
Gunn, Ann to Hugh McAnally 1-27-1860 Sh
Gunner, Nancy C. to Jas. F. A. M. Avery 12-5-1854 (12-7-1854) G
Gunnings, Eliza to W. T. Buzbee? 6-29-1861 Sh
Gunson, F. J. to Thomas J. McElyea 3-21-1850 O
Gunter, Diana to Greenbury Worthy 9-19-1853 Sh
Gunter, Eliza G. to Geo. W. Martin 7-24-1850 Sh
Gunter, Eliza Jane to Thomas T. Kimbrough 11-25-1833 Sh
Gunter, Eliza L. to James E. Johnston 11-26-1861 Sh
Gunter, Elizabeth to Absolum Carns 10-27-1842 (12-5-1842) G
Gunter, Emaline to Carroll Callison 3-2-1863 We
Gunter, Emma to Charlie Toombs 6-16-1879 (6-29-1879) L
Gunter, Flora to Jessee Blackburn 2-29-1848 (3-2-1848) G
Gunter, Jane to John W. Bonds 7-27-1841 (no return) Hn
Gunter, M. E. to G. W. Bandy 9-?-1866 O
Gunter, Mahala to Jas. H. Brown 6-28-1832 Hr
Gunter, Martha Ann to Starkey Fleetwood 7-22-1854 Sh
Gunter, Martha to James Davidson 1-16-1842 Hn
Gunter, Martha to Robert L. Criner 12-28-1835 Hr
Gunter, Mary F. to Alexander H. Pillow 9-3-1845 Sh
Gunter, Mary Jane to John Gray 5-26-1862 Sh
Gunter, Mary to Bevely Cannon 2-10-1844 (2-15-1844) G
Gunter, Mary to John Hurley 12-28-1835 Hr
Gunter, Mary to Peter Fore 1-10-1849 Sh
Gunter, Rebecca to John H. Turner 4-13-1862 We
Gunter, Sarah D. to Thomas Vaughn 7-4-1853 Sh
Gunter, Susan A. to William Kennedy 12-24-1857 Sh
Gunter, Tennessee to James Day 3-26-1855 We
Gurat?, Elizabeth to Wyatt Hawes 2-28-1839 Hn
Gurganus, Mary A. to Thomas H. Ward 11-12-1853 G
Gurganus, Runinia to Elijah H. Shelton 9-29-1865 (10-1-1865) Dy
Gurganus, S. A. M. to J. W. Shelton 8-26-1867 Dy
Gurgarus, Margarett to James H. Workman 10-19-1858 We
Gurgett, M. A. to R. N. Dennis 10-25-1879 (10-26-1879) Dy
Gurley, Martha to A. L. Kendall 11-30-1851 Cr
Gurley, Martha to J. L. Kendall 11-30-1857 O
Gurley, Mary Jane to Thos. H. Robertson 1-28-1848 (2-2-1848) F
Gurley, N. E. to William L. Owen 5-3-1856 (5-4-1856) Sh
Gurley, Nancy A. to John Dwyer 11-30-1860 (no return) L
Gurley, Sarah to George Shelton 9-7-1867 (9-8-1867) L
Gurley, Z. C. to W. H. Steelman 8-11-1862 (9-11-1862) O
Gurly, Elizabeth to W. H. Goforth 12-8-1854 Hr
Gurly, Rachel A. to Bennett Blackman 1-15-1865 O
Gustins?, Ann Savanna? to James Irwin Carn? 1-5-1843 (1-5-1843) T
Gutherie, Nancy J. to A. B. Holbrook 11-7-1869 Hy
Guthery, Anna to William D. Hawkins 9-28-1864 (10-2-1864) Sh
Guthery, Francis to A. Rowlett 10-15-1859 (no return) We
Guthery, Lena to Mark D. Flowers 9-28-1864 (10-2-1864) Sh
Guthery, Martha R. W. to Thomas W. Miles 4-18-1855 We
Guthery, Virginia to Smith A. Boges 9-25-1860 We
Guthore, Caroline to Mordecai Cooper 2-11-1860 Hn
Guthrie, Amanda P. to R. R. Aycock 9-1-1853 Hn
Guthrie, C. W. to Soloman E. Burten 9-25-1860 We
Guthrie, Callie to L. T. Landrum 6-3-1872 (6-5-1872) Cr
Guthrie, Corar to James W. Wilder 9-24-1867 (no return) Cr
Guthrie, Fannie M. to Absolem D. Hunt 1-1-1868 (1-2-1868) Ma

Guthrie, Jane to John Hines 1-15-1872 (no return) Cr B
Guthrie, Margaret H. to Lewis Wells 10-29-1850 Hr
Guthrie, Mary A. to William F. Guthrie 11-28-1852 Hn
Guthrie, Mary Ann to John B. Cobb 5-27-1862 Ma
Guthrie, Mary C. to John W. Riggs 11-8-1856 (11-9-1856) Hr
Guthrie, Mary C. to William Worrell 10-4-1855 O
Guthrie, Mary E. to Samuel Landrum 8-3-1863 (8-6-1863) O
Guthrie, Sarah to Elias A. Claiborne 1-11-1863 (no return) We
Guthrie, Susan to Benjamin L. Thompson 3-15-1840 (3-25-1840) Ma
Guthrie, Virginia to Joseph Henderson 12-19-1848 (12-21-1848) O
Gutner, Jane to Thos. Gaskins 10-5-1857 Hr
Guy, Agnes to W. J. Morris 3-11-1867 (3-12-1867) O
Guy, Elcy Jane to Samuel M. Robinson 9-4-1839 (9-5-1839) O
Guy, Emily T. to E. Gaither 3-14-1864 (3-15-1864) F
Guy, Fanny S. to Wm. C. Oates 10-11-1859 (10-12-1859) Hr
Guy, Lenora M. F. to Henry C. Wellions 12-11-1851 Hr
Guy, Louisa C. to Gilbert D. T. Malone 10-17-1848 (10-25-1848) Hr
Guy, M. F. to G. A. Guy 3-20-1867 O
Guy, Martha to R. A. Guthrie 9-25-1860 We
Guy, Mary E. to Cornelius Sheeks 12-13-1830 O
Guy, Mary M. to John I. Shores 12-10-1867 O
Guy, Mary M. to John J. Shores 12-11-1867 O
Guy, Nancy to Allen Hood 7-18-1843 (7-20-1843) O
Guy, Pauline E. to John R. Wood 9-21-1859 Hr
Guyman, Rebecca to Henry Bradford 6-6-1844 Hn
Guyn, Elizabeth to Thomas Black 10-21-1840 (12-6-1840) F
Guynn, Cynthia G. to Jackson M. Clay 12-14-1839 (12-15-1839) Hr
Guynn, Julia A. to E. R. Larrabee 9-27-1866 O
Guynn, L. C. to F. M. Litton 12-26-1859 (12-27-1859) O
Gwaltney, Frances to S. J. Self 12-5-1860 (no return) Dy
Gwin, Elizabeth to E. Wright 1-1-1845 Cr
Gwin, Louisa E. to Benj. F. Johnson 10-12-1858 Cr
Gwin, M. J. to E. T. Burns 11-10-1851 Cr
Gwin, Margaret C. to Burrell Gossett 5-13-1839 (no return) Cr
Gwin, Mary E. to Wm. C. Gilbert 7-17-1848 (no return) Cr
Gwin, Pamelia to John Falkner 11-30-1850 F
Gwin, Sarah Ann to William Anderson 1-13-1845 (no return) Hn
Gwinn, C. C. to J. J. Berryhill 10-11-1871 (10-12-1871) Cr
Gwinn, Levina to Joshua Sneathen 1-25-1842 (1-26-1842) O
Gwinn, Mollie to William Mann 4-9-1884 (no return) L
Gwinn, Nancy to Ralph G. Alexander 7-30-1839 (no return) Hn
Gwinn, Nancy to William Gibson 8-17-1847 G
Gwinn, Rozina to Thomas G. Overton 12-17-1840 F
Gwinn, Sarah C. to J. M. Brannoch 4-6-1852 Cr
Gwyn, Georgia B. to John S. Stanton 10-19-1863 (10-21-1863) Sh
Gwyn, Julia A. to Oswell Jones 10-31-1838 (11-1-1838) F
Gwyn, Mary G. to S. J. Hooker 12-8-1866 (no return) F
Gwyn, Octavia I. to Francis W. Leggett 10-26-1848 Sh
Gwyn, Sarah A. M. to Thomas J. Massey 9-5-1866 (7?-11-1866) F
Gwyn, V. C. to Henry E. Clark 6-10-1857 Sh
Gwynn, Elizabeth J. to Neill S. Brown 2-14-1871 F
Gwynn, Judy to William Ewing 12-23-1866 (12-29-1865?) F B
Gwynn, S. M. to S. J. Gwynn 1-28-1866 (1-30-1866) F
Gwynne, Catharine to Wm. T. (Dr.) Bailey 4-9-1860 (4-10-1860) Sh
Gwynne, Charlotte to James J. McKeever 2-24-1859 (2-28-1859) Sh

H___, Martha A. to Robert J. Bomar 1-9-1853 Be
Haas, Catherine to N. Weber 8-8-1850 Sh
Haas, Eliza to Joseph Greenwalt 3-9-1864 Sh
Haase, Amelia to Anthony Snoor 8-23-1862 Sh
Hackney, Amanda to Thomas A. Morris 11-7-1862 (11-9-1862) F
Hackney, Fanny C. to John R. L. Huffman 12-20-1869 (12-23-1869) F
Hadaway, Rachel to Augustus W. Johnson 8-17-1866 Ma
Hadden, Nancy T. to M. W. Hall 4-27-1861 (4-29-1861) Hr
Haden, Bridget to Jas. L. Parsons 6-17-1854 Sh
Haden, Ellen to J. G. Dorris 11-5-1855 Be
Hadley, Cornelia to A. C. Lansdell 6-4-1860 (no return) Hy
Hadley, Helen M. to Samuel P. Stone 8-31-1865 Hn
Hadley, M. to J. B. Lancaster 7-10-1855 We
Hadly, M. to Jeff Conner 1-4-1872 T
Hadnott, Elizabeth to John L. Meazles 1-9-1830 Sh
Hadol, SaHa? to C. G. Lemoutoy 6-17-1862 Sh
Hafarman, Christiana Wlhlmena. to Matias Finn 6-18-1849 Sh
Hafercamp, Henrietta Mary to Henry H. Paynter 11-11-1841 Sh
Hafflabower, Ella V. to George C. Corbitt 11-17-1869 (11-18-1869) Ma
Hafford, Aneliza to Stephen Baird 2-16-1871 Hy
Hafford, Betsy to Hilbert Morris 7-26-1878 (7-28-1878) L
Hafford, Mary to Daniel Pierson 12-28-1869 (no return) L
Hafford, Sarah A. V. to John W. Dunavant 12-19-1859 (12-21-1859) L
Hafford, Sarah S. to Hugh W. Lee 12-8-1885 (12-9-1858) L
Haflen?, Elizabeth to Alfred Robinson 1-2-1847 Hn
Hafter, Martha E. to Charles W. Hafter 4-16-1872 T
Hagan, Ellen (Miss) to Frederick Agassiz 8-3-1863 Sh
Hagan, Lou to George Morton 3-30-1876 (no return) Hy
Hagans, Margaret A. to E. D. Wright 1-31-1853 Sh
Hagard, Emily C. to A. J. Nale 2-12-1855 (2-14-1855) G
Hagen, L. A. to James P. Ragen? 1-11-1856 (no return) Hn

Hager, Adeline to Albert Busby 7-22-1852 Sh
Hagg, Sarah E. to William T. Scates 9-17-1859 (no return) We
Haggard, Frances to Thomas Stofle 4-23-1849 Hn
Haggard, M. A. (Mrs.) to S. L. Brigance 7-25-1876 (no return) L
Haggard, Mary to Phillip Curlen 2-26-1863 (2-10?-1863) Sh
Haggart, Mary F. to John McCracken 1-21-1862 (1-23-1862) Dy
Hagler, Bell to Peter Travis 5-20-1866 Hn B
Hagler, E. J. to William H. Martin 1-16-1848 Hn
Hagler, Ellen to Roderick Bowden 2-15-1868 (no return) Hn
Hagler, Elvira A. to William G. Hastings 10-10-1852 Hn
Hagler, Frances to Diggo Travis 5-20-1866 Hn B
Hagler, Harriet to Fell White 8-15-1867 Hn B
Hagler, Isabella C. to James T. Vaughan 6-2-1863 We
Hagler, Lotty to John Hudson 9-8-1866 Hn B
Hagler, Manerva to C. M. Neese 9-30-1856 Hn
Hagler, Martha to Thomas Walters 5-13-1845 Hn
Hagler, Mary F. to John C. Looney 8-26-1860 We
Hagler, N. G. to W. E. Travis 9-10-1846 Hn
Hagler, Nancy J. to Addison Broach 11-20-1867 (no return) Hn
Hagler, Nancy to Blount Hagler 5-21-1866 Hn
Hagler, Parmelia C. R. to J. U. Hudson 4-10-1850 Hn
Hagler, Parmelia R. to Thomas A. Manley? 12-1-1859 Hn
Hagler, Sallie to Cash Hagler 5-20-1866 Hn B
Hagler, Vergency S. to Jobe Hicks 2-24-1847 Hn
Hagood, Nancy E. to William Snider 2-27-1862 (no return) Hn
Hagsetts, Sarah Ann to John P. Carson 5-5-1856 (5-6-1856) L
Hague, Mary C. to Charles C. Stell 5-13-1848 (5-17-1848) G
Hague, Roda A. to James M. Banister 10-25-1859 (10-26-1859) G
Hague, Selina A. to John R. Runalds 2-6-1847 G
Haguewood, Elizabeth to John B. Crafton 7-23-1839 (7-25-1839) G
Hail, Elizabeth to Wm. D. Fields 11-7-1842 (11-8-1842) G
Hail, Emeline J. to John Hail 2-4-1841 (2-7-1841) G
Hail, Lydia A. to William B. Peace 7-11-1849 G
Hail, Mary A. to Wm. H. Clemmont 12-26-1837 (1-17-1838) G
Hail, Mary E. to James H. Pearce 10-21-1851 (10-22-1851) G
Hail, Percilla to Levin E. Ross 12-29-1846 Sh
Hail, Sarah to William C. Maxwell 8-22-1832 Hr
Hailey, Angeline to Samuel Aslin 3-17-1861 G
Hailey, Elizabeth to Aaron Sherron 12-3-1838 (12-4-1838) G
Hailey, Emmeline J. to Elijah B. Sanders 2-2-1866 (2-6-1866) F
Hailey, Louiza J. to Henry C. Vaden 1-11-1860 G
Hailey, Margaret A. to James P. Foster 10-4-1849 G
Hailey, Margarett to Thomas P. Key 1-23-1863 G
Hailey, Mary J. E. to George M. Hall 1-11-1858 (no return) Cr
Hailey, Mary to Bevely Price 3-29-1847 (4-7-1847) G
Hailey, Matilda to Howel Stroud 2-24-1842 G
Hailey, Pheby to James Penney 7-2-1842 (7-3-1842) G
Haily, Candis to John Fuller 12-22-1853 (no return) F
Haily, Martha to Hugh A. Gray 10-26-1857 Hr
Haily, Martha to James Vaughan 3-11-1846 (no return) Hn
Haines, Elizabeth S. to James r. Jones 7-13-1853 Hn
Haines, Fannie to John D. Lush 12-11-1860 (12-13-1860) Cr
Haines, Harriett W. to D. M. Manning 3-23-1859 Cr
Haines, Mary A. B. to John Gray 3-17-1847 Sh
Hainey, Mary Ann to Henry Warren 8-10-1877 Hy
Hainie, Caroline c. to W. R. Slate 12-7-1858 (12-9-1858) T
Hainline, Sarah Ann to George A. Booe 7-4-1839 Hr
Hains, Milly to Richard Sharrod 3-4-1828 G
Hair, Isabella to Alvan Wallace 2-27-1863 Mn
Hair, Mary Jane to John W. Pennington 2-18-1863 Mn
Haislip, Ann to Hiram Elkins 3-9-1844 (3-10-1844) O
Haislip, Eleanor to Samuel C. Henry 3-14-1844 O
Haislip, Eliza Ann to Madison M. Webb 12-11-1871 L
Haislip, Lucinda L. to Franklin Orsburn 9-5-1850 O
Haislip, Lucinda to Samuel J. Patterson 11-1-1852 (11-2-1852) Ma
Haislip, Mary F. to James Elder, jr. 10-25-1853 (10-26-1853) O
Haislip, Rebecca to Andrew J. Pounds 12-7-1860 Ma
Haislip, Rebecca to Nathan C. Smith 7-31-1854 (8-1-1854) Ma
Haislip, Ruth A. to John Elder 1-10-1846 (1-11-1846) O
Haislip, Sarah E. to James W. Hampton 11-22-1860 O
Haites, Jane to Joseph Priest 12-10-1850 Cr
Halbrook, Amanda to Barthelemey Labesque 6-17-1862 Sh
Halbrooks, Mary A. to John Stephens 8-11-1863 Dy
Halbrooks, Mary to John Milligan 5-7-1856 (5-8-1856) Sh
Halbrooks, Sarah Ann to Alfred Watson 2-27-1850 Be
Halcomb, Mary to Wm. Pendergrass 5-20-1853 (no return) Cr
Halcrom, Mary Ann to Laburn W. Harris 10-31-1833 Sh
Hale (Hall?), Josie P. to D. A. McGuair (Mcguire) 2-12-1879 L
Hale, Agnes to Henry Weakley 8-1-1877 Dy
Hale, Amanda J. to T. J. Moon 2-8-1866 (2-15-1866) F
Hale, Amanda to Richardson Bass 8-16-1842 Sh
Hale, Ann to Peter Jones 12-27-1871 O
Hale, Arimencia to John C. Blackwell 8-23-1830 (9-3-1830) Hr
Hale, Bettie to Silas Beckett 1-3-1877 (1-4-1877) Dy
Hale, C. to Th. Kee 4-21-1840 Hr
Hale, Caroline to Mance Turnipseed 4-6-1867 G B
Hale, Catharine to M. W. Corum 2-17-1851 (2-18-1851) O

Hale, E. P. to R. W. McDaniel 11-12-1859 (11-13-1859) Sh
Hale, Eliza Jane to John Inman 7-14-1852 (7-16-1852) O
Hale, Eliza to John Turner 1-30-1861 Hr
Hale, Elizabeth to Joseph Ferguson 11-21-1844 Sh
Hale, Elmyra to Richard Bason 11-12-1852 Sh
Hale, Emily to W. G. Thompson 6-11-1854 Cr
Hale, Emma R. to Edward S. Todd 4-14-1846 Sh
Hale, Frances A. E. to William S. Knox 8-24-1847 (no return) F
Hale, Harriet to Jesse G. Gardner 9-9-1852 We
Hale, Harriett to John Corum 12-30-1843 (1-4-1844) O
Hale, Hettie E. to John C. Stewart 2-6-1854 (2-14-1854) Sh
Hale, Jane to Joseph Lacewell 3-4-1877 O
Hale, Joana to Anderson Dickey 10-29-1842 G
Hale, Laviny C. to Isaac M. Presson 6-10-1865 Be
Hale, Lucinda to Sam Williams 5-27-1866 Hy
Hale, Lucy to William S. Wyatt 12-22-1841 (12-23-1841) G
Hale, M. C. to C. J. Witt 8-26-1868 G
Hale, Martha E. to W. A. Fly 11-14-1860 G
Hale, Martha Elizabeth to Isaac T. Bryant 12-31-1857 Sh
Hale, Martha S. to William Adams 8-6-1850 (no return) Hn
Hale, Mary A. to R. A. Edwards 12-11-1855 (12-12-1855) Ma
Hale, Mary D. to Robert Taylor 5-12-1842 Ma
Hale, Mary F. to Sherwood Looper 9-5-1850 Be
Hale, Mary J. to A. R. Thomas 10-18-1856 G
Hale, Mary W. to J. H. Patterson 3-6-1855 Cr
Hale, Mary to Edward H. Steward 12-18-1852 (12-19-1852) Hr
Hale, Mary to John A. King 12-19-1850 G
Hale, Mary to W. B. Hester 3-20-1860 Cr
Hale, Matilda to Abraham Jones 10-4-1834 (10-7-1834) Hr
Hale, Nancy E. to Henry C. Elmore 10-9-1863 Be
Hale, Nancy E. to Samuel N. White 1-1-1855 (1-4-1855) G
Hale, Phafama Elizabeth to Richd. T.k Lyon 12-21-1854 (12-27-1854) Hr
Hale, Rachel to Lewis Hallmark 12-6-1843 Be
Hale, Rebecca M. to James E. Ruff 10-26-1847 (10-28-1847) Ma
Hale, Rebecca to David Hodges 6-28-1839 Hn
Hale, Reen Allice to William Patton 5-2-1859 (5-3-1859) G
Hale, Rhoda E. to Spencer Fly 12-26-1867 G B
Hale, Roseann to Wm. H. Welch 4-16-1863 Sh
Hale, Sarah A. to Wm. J. Thompson 11-23-1852 Cr
Hale, Sarah Ann to James Barham 1-15-1848 (1-18-1848) O
Hale, Sarah E. to William Washam 10-11-1859 O
Hale, Sarah J. to Eddie Graves 12-11-1873 L
Hale, Sarah Jane to James Grantham 4-17-1850 (4-24-1850) Hr
Hale, Sarah to James C. Williams 9-30-1851 (10-20-1851) Sh
Hale, Sarah to James C. Williams 9-5-1851 Sh
Hale, Scyntha to L. L.(S?) Davis 7-10-1836 O
Hale, Sydney M. to lHiram Casey 6-4-1861 (6-6-1861) Hr
Hale, Zelpha to William Adams 8-6-1841 O
Haley, Biddey to Austin Edwards 8-28-1846 O
Haley, Caroline to James F. Holliday 3-6-1854 (no return) Hn
Haley, E. C. to W. H. Hilliard 10-5-1866 (10-7-1866) F
Haley, Elizabeth to John A. Stadtmiller 8-9-1851 (8-11-1851) Sh
Haley, Elizabeth to Robert Erwin (Ervin) 9-23-1853 (9-25-1853) O
Haley, Lizzie M. to Wm. T. Murphey 7-25-1859 Sh
Haley, Maranda to John Vaughan 3-2-1845 Hn
Haley, Martha to Salesbury Fasthing 12-14-1830 (12-29-1830) G
Haley, Mary Jane to James H. Stroud 1-13-1848 O
Haley, Mary W. to A. B. Childress 11-20-1867 G
Haley, Nancy to George Younger 8-23-1857 Hn
Haley, Narcissa to Samuel Smith 10-10-1843 We
Haley, Rachel to John D. Hickman 8-22-1844 O
Haley, Sarah C. to James F. Holiday 10-17-1854 Hn
Haley, Susan E. to John W. Haley 12-15-1858 (12-16-1858) G
Haley, Susan E. to John W. Oliver 12-15-1858 G
Halfacre, A. E. to David Boney 12-12-1882 (12-13-1882) L
Halfacre, Bule to Jerry Barney 3-22-1876 (no return) L B
Halfacre, Lucinda S. to Wilson Miller 3-3-1886 L
Halfacre, Lucy to Price (Prince?) Hunter 12-16-1871 (12-17-1871) L
Halfacre, M. M. to J. T. Goodman 3-13-1882 (3-15-1882) L
Halfacre, Mary to David Titus 6-15-1872 (6-16-1872) L B
Halford, E. L. to J. F. Standley 6-14-1864 G
Halford, M. A. to J. C. Cathey 2-16-1865 G
Halford, Sarah L. to Allen Edmundson 4-4-1842 (4-6-1842) G
Halford, Sarah to Jessee Flowers 9-18-1845 G
Haliburton, E. L. to B. L. Flowers 1-10-1866 G
Haliburton, Eady to Scott Irvin 3-2-1875 Hy
Haliburton, Mariah to Thomas Smith 9-10-1875 (9-11-1875) L
Haliburton, Susan to Henry Thomas 7-1-1845 (7-2-1845) G
Haliburton, Tilde to Himon Harden 1-1-1877 Hy
Hall (Nall?), Margarett L. to H. W. Wright 1-30-1866 G
Hall (Stanley), Arvazena to W. O. Fisher 9-19-1869 G
Hall, A. E. to James Wilson 3-23-1852 (no return) F
Hall, A. J. to R. A. Arnold 9-5-1866 G
Hall, A. L. to C. A. G. Taylor 9-19-1867 Dy
Hall, A. to Wm. Nealey 12-18-1874 (12-19-1874) T
Hall, Adalin to Stevens Davis 1-7-1865 (6-10-1865) T
Hall, Adaline to Edward R. Rose 12-1-1869 (no return) Hy

Hall, Alice to Anthony Bernard 3-27-1869 (3-28-1869) T
Hall, Aly to William H. Williams 9-12-1840 (9-25-1840) Ma
Hall, Amanda E. to Moses H. Kinman 5-3-1866 O
Hall, Amanda J. to J. L. Burrow 11-14-1874 O
Hall, Angelina L. to Isham Hubbard 6-20-1847 Sh
Hall, Ann E. to Daniel N. Jackson 11-3-1849 Sh
Hall, Ann E. to George Fowler 2-11-1867 (2-17-1867) T
Hall, Ann Row to Luke P. Seay 9-22-1831 G
Hall, Ann to Wm. S. Smith 9-23-1857 Cr
Hall, Anna Eliza to William Edgar Peters 12-15-1864 Hn
Hall, Anne E. to Edward Sanders 7-12-1841 Sh
Hall, Annie to J. G. Young 1-15-1873 T
Hall, Candis M. to T. J. Sanders 11-19-1860 (11-20-1860) Dy
Hall, Canzada to George W. Farmer 12-26-1861 Be
Hall, Carolin W. to J. B. Danniel 12-20-1865 T
Hall, Caroline to Thomas Beck 4-16-1849 (4-18-1849) F
Hall, Caroline to W. R. Hamer 7-25-1854 Be
Hall, Catharine Clamentine to Edward Holister Green 7-17-1851 T
Hall, Catharine to William L. Bumpus 2-15-1858 O
Hall, Ceelin Ethalinda to Enos Alexander Sherrill 4-7-1845 (4-16-1845) T
Hall, Clarissa to Lewis Haywood 6-16-1867 T
Hall, Clavina to David Quillen 10-28-1841 We
Hall, Clementine to William J. Atkins 12-3-1845 Hn
Hall, Cornelia W. to J. B. Daniel 12-20-1865 T
Hall, Delia M. to James Stephenson 11-7-1868 (11-8-1868) Cr
Hall, Delia to William Sykes 1-21-1879 (1-27-1879) L
Hall, E. D. to Geo. W. Legion 3-15-1858 (3-31-1858) G
Hall, E. E. to Wm. E. Sherrill 2-8-1866 T
Hall, Eliza Ann to Benjamin Chapel 7-17-1840 (7-19-1840) O
Hall, Eliza J. to John C. McCauley 11-8-1855 (11-16-1855) T
Hall, Eliza to James Sanders 2-4-1839 Cr
Hall, Eliza to James Williams 3-27-1859 Hn
Hall, Eliza to John Walker 11-25-1821 (no return) F
Hall, Elizabeth Ann to George W. Tinkle 3-18-1840 (3-19-1840) G
Hall, Elizabeth F. to James M. Gilliam 6-3-1852 (no return) F
Hall, Elizabeth I. to Lafayett Bell 1-11-1859 We
Hall, Elizabeth R. to James Leander Stitt 8-9-1854 T
Hall, Elizabeth T. to S. S. B. McCrary (McCrory?) 10-15-1868 G
Hall, Elizabeth to Geo. W. Dibrell 4-4-1850 We
Hall, Elizabeth to George F. Tatum 5-14-1865 G
Hall, Elizabeth to Henry H. Brogdon 3-7-1842 (no return) Hn
Hall, Elizabeth to J. L. Ralls 9-5-1865 (9-7-1865) Dy
Hall, Elizabeth to Thos. Cresaso 1-7-1846 Cr
Hall, Elizabeth to Willey (Wiley) Mangum 1-12-1830 Sh
Hall, Elizabeth to William D. Eaves 2-7-1861 Hn
Hall, Elmira to Andy J. Campbell 3-3-1877 (3-4-1877) Dy
Hall, Ema C. to W. C. Kerr 6-29-1854 G
Hall, Emaline to George Ross 2-24-1866 T
Hall, Emely to William Carradine 1-21-1832 (2-23-1832) G
Hall, Emly to James King 8-23-1877 Hy
Hall, Emma A. to Chas. F. Taylor 6-20-1864 Sh
Hall, Eolino to George Baldrige 12-20-1866 (12-29-1866) Dy
Hall, Fannie W. to James A. Mann 1-2-1869 (1-6-1869) F
Hall, Fannie to Melvill Vaughn 3-9-1869 (3-11-1869) T
Hall, Fannie to Robt Winn 11-1-1873 (11-2-1873) T
Hall, Fanny to Drury Gowan 1-17-1853 (1-19-1853) G
Hall, Fanny to George Badget 12-9-1844 G
Hall, Frances M. to A. R. Montgomery 12-14-1864 (no return) Dy
Hall, Frances M. to T. F. Williams 11-26-1849 (no return) F
Hall, Frankie (Mrs.) to W. S. Hines 2-12-1873 Dy
Hall, H. (M.?)J. to J. R. Prichard 3-2-1878 (3-7-1878) Dy
Hall, H. A. to W. L. Buford 8-2-1859 (8-3-1859) T
Hall, H. I. to B. S. M. Stalcup 1-19-1871 Dy
Hall, Hannah to John Rhodes 9-25-1880 (no return) L B
Hall, Hawkins to Edmund Holland 9-17-1838 G
Hall, Henritta to James Hunt 6-17-1871 T
Hall, Jane G. to Richard H. Berge 11-27-1834 G
Hall, Jane to Alen Fox 4-11-1828 G
Hall, Jane to George Anderson Johnson 5-5-1873 T
Hall, Jane to John J. Fulford 4-6-1844 Sh
Hall, Jane to Loyd Lassater 3-14-1867 (3-17-1867) T
Hall, Jane to Orvill Carter 5-13-1840 Hn
Hall, Katie E. to W. S. Davie 9-29-1874 (9-30-1874) T
Hall, L. J. to J. A. Goodwin 11-24-1866 (11-24-18??) O
Hall, L. S. to F. W. Hill 12-12-1872 T
Hall, Laisa J. to John Perry 10-12-1865 Hn
Hall, Lany to Thomas W. Pafford 10-18-1849 Be
Hall, Levica to Robert Jackson 9-6-1853 Be
Hall, Lidia to William Hall 1-5-1829 G
Hall, Lila to William Scott 4-16-1870 (4-17-1870) F B
Hall, Lizzie T. J. to D. C. Allen 5-28-1879 (6-15-1879) L
Hall, Lucinda to Joseph Bell 10-11-1845 Cr
Hall, Lucy to Abron Kenaday 8-28-1837 (9-21-1837) G
Hall, M. A. E. to Richard Fletcher 12-20-1865 (12-24-1865) Dy
Hall, M. A. E. to W. S. Hatch 9-19-1869 G
Hall, M. A. to W. R. G. Crow 1-7-1867 (1-8-1867) Dy
Hall, M. A. to Wm. P. Wilson 12-14-1874 (12-17-1874) O

Hall, M. E. to D. C. Lively 1-8-1868 (1-9-1868) Dy
Hall, M. E. to J. C. Farmer 1-21-1866 Be
Hall, M. F. to R. H. Michell 8-5-1868 (no return) Dy
Hall, M. J. to E. T. McAuly 2-4-1868 (2-5-1868) Cr
Hall, Malinda to Arris Sorrel 12-7-1848 F
Hall, Malisa to Daniel S. Farrell 11-17-1851 (no return) F
Hall, Margaret Jane to William A. Crouch 10-18-1854 Sh
Hall, Martha A. to W. H. Flippin 6-14-1864 (6-17-1864) L
Hall, Martha C. to Fielding A. Ezell 7-28-1859 We
Hall, Martha E. to Samuel H. Ritchey 4-6-1848 Cr
Hall, Martha Elizabeth to Wm. Riley Laws 6-3-1861 Sh
Hall, Martha to Alfred Thomas 3-12-1873 (4-5-1873) T
Hall, Martha to Elijah Perry 6-17-1852 (no return) Hn
Hall, Martha to J. M. Beluw 1-9-1860 (1-10-1860) G
Hall, Martha to James C. Owen 8-13-1850 (no return) Hn
Hall, Martha to John Brown 9-6-1862 (9-8-1862) Cr
Hall, Martha to John Flasher 12-29-1860 Sh
Hall, Martha to W. W. Wheatley 12-1-1864 Be
Hall, Martha to W. W. Wheatley 12-10-1864 Be CC
Hall, Mary Ann to John F. Carlton 10-28-1861 (no return) Cr
Hall, Mary Ann to Robert Brogdon 4-4-1848 Hn
Hall, Mary E. to J. R. Hill 1-1-1873 (1-2-1873) Cr
Hall, Mary E. to James B. McCally 2-13-1870 Cr
Hall, Mary E. to James J. Hall 1-2-1866 T
Hall, Mary E. to Jas. J. Hall 1-2-1866 T
Hall, Mary E. to W. A. Phillips 11-21-1860 G
Hall, Mary E. to William Thomas 1-9-1870 G
Hall, Mary F. to Robert Bradford 7-30-1851 Cr
Hall, Mary Jane F. to James F. Alexander 11-17-1858 We
Hall, Mary N. to William S. Coward 10-10-1865 (10-11-1865) T
Hall, Mary to Amsey Flake 4-27-1848 (no return) Hn
Hall, Mary to Geo. Morrison 12-2-1865 T
Hall, Mary to James Weakly 5-22-1867 Dy
Hall, Mary to Robert W. Robinson 5-10-1831 Hr
Hall, Mary to T. H. Cleghorn 9-7-1840 Be
Hall, Mary to William Oliver 9-26-1861 (no return) We
Hall, Mattie A. to Smith Buford 2-6-1866 (2-7-1866) T
Hall, Mattie to John R. Wilbon 12-22-1869 Ma
Hall, Mattie to S. C. Brandon 9-23-1868 G
Hall, Mennie to Christopher Miller 4-7-1868 G
Hall, Minerva to L. H. Morris 12-19-1860 F
Hall, N. E. to J. L. Wood 12-12-1865 (12-15-1865) Cr
Hall, N. J. to J. H. S. Simerson 12-30-1853 Sh
Hall, Nancy Ann to George Hancock 12-19-1874 (12-20-1874) L
Hall, Nancy E. B. to Thomas Butler 10-29-1860 (10-30-1860) Cr
Hall, Nancy E. to Rylin B. Sloan 4-4-1867 G
Hall, Nancy J. to J. H. S. Simmerson 12-21-1853 (no return) F
Hall, Nancy J. to William Baker 6-1-1870 (6-2-1870) Cr
Hall, Nancy M. to John D. Bryant 8-19-1867 T
Hall, Nancy to Edward Bass 8-10-1847 (8-12-1847) G
Hall, Nancy to Stephen H. Glisson 6-22-1852 G
Hall, Obediance E. to B. Y. Trotter 10-10-1848 F
Hall, Olive to John Deason 10-30-1828 Hr
Hall, P. E. to J. T. Boon 10-5-1869 Dy
Hall, P. P. to J. Joyner 1-19-1875 Hy
Hall, Parmelia W. to Robert W. Jenning 2-21-1848 (2-22-1848) Ma
Hall, Parthana to Henrey Kirby 7-22-1848 Cr
Hall, Patsy to Thomas V. Yeates 12-8-1848 Sh
Hall, Phoebe to P. W. Yates 1-9-1866 Hn
Hall, R. C. to R. W. Johns 10-9-1866 G
Hall, Rachael Ann to John Etheridge 12-11-1848 G
Hall, Rebecca Jane to James A. Kirby 12-21-1853 (12-22-1853) Ma
Hall, Rebecca to George W. Brewer 11-16-1850 (11-17-1850) G
Hall, Rebecca to William A. Wilson 12-18-1854 Hn
Hall, Rody J. to George N. Clark 2-3-1873 (2-9-1873) L
Hall, Ruth A. to D. B. Bayn 3-9-1858 (3-10-1858) G
Hall, Rutha to William McGehe 3-13-1849 G
Hall, S. J. to Asa M. Davis 5-17-1873 (5-18-1873) Dy
Hall, S. J. to N. A. Edwards 12-21-1864 (no return) Dy
Hall, Sadie to Z. T. Reynolds 1-7-1879 (1-9-1879) Dy
Hall, Sallie E. to G. W. Smith 1-5-1866 (1-10-1866) F
Hall, Sallie A. to M. C. Humphrey 3-15-1858 (3-17-1858) Hr
Hall, Sarah (Mrs.) to Joseph Walden 1-13-1864 Sh
Hall, Sarah A. to S. J. Stephens 1-16-1861 G
Hall, Sarah A. to William Durley 2-15-1848 G
Hall, Sarah F. to R. G. Menzies 7-18-1853 Be
Hall, Sarah J. to James H. Palmer 12-20-1841 Cr
Hall, Sarah to B. F. Booth 12-21-1859 (12-24-1859) Sh
Hall, Sarah to James H. Russell 12-10-1840 Cr
Hall, Sarah to John A. Stone 3-5-1838 Hn
Hall, Sarah to John Pope 12-21-1878 (no return) Dy
Hall, Sidney S. to Pascal A. Ellington 1-29-1860 G
Hall, Sidney to Bryant D. Carraway 10-28-1843 (10-29-1843) G
Hall, Susan A. to Pleasant G. Wright 2-5-1845 Cr
Hall, Susan to Wm. Culberson 3-31-1862 (4-1-1862) O
Hall, Susanah to Joseph Melton 1-18-1850 Be
Hall, Tenny to A. J. Farmer 12-25-1867 Be

Hall, Trophenia to R. A. Ball 11-29-1864]
Hall, Vilet to John Ford 9-28-1829 (9-29-1829) G
Hall, Virginia A. to Joseph H. Smith 1-2-1869 (1-6-1869) F
Hall, Willy A. to Charles M. Sarrett 9-27-1843 Cr
Hall, Winny to Henry Stevens 12-28-1870 (12-29-1870) T
Hall, ___ane to Benj. Bernard 9-9-1865 T
Hallaburton, Martha to C. F. Moliter 3-6-1857 (3-8-1857) Hr
Hallam, Sarah F. to Thomas J. Seals 6-28-1852 (7-6-1852) O
Halleburton, Mary to Benjamin Thompson 9-20-1870 (9-22-1870) L
Halleburton, Margaret to Jeff Harvey 1-28-1871 (no return) L
Hallen, Martha L. J. to James N. Thomas 4-25-1858 Cr
Haller, Mary to Lewis Keith 12-6-1854 Sh
Hallet, N. B. to Z. N. Morris 2-19-1866 (2-20-1866) Dy
Halley, Lucy A. to Hezekiah Cobb 11-20-1849 Sh
Halley, Matilda D. to Green P. Snow 1-30-1843 Sh
Hallian, Mariah to Patrick Joyce 7-29-1869 Ma
Halliburton, Ada to Dave Williams 12-31-1885 (1-1-1886) L
Halliburton, Alice to Lewis Beard 11-28-1883 L
Halliburton, Ann to Joseph Reynolds 1-6-1875 (1-7-1875) Dy
Halliburton, Annie E. to James B. Wilkes 2-23-1885 (12-24-1885) L
Halliburton, Beccy to Norah Parker 4-4-1877 (4-5-1877) L
Halliburton, Bettie P. to Morgan Cartwright 12-12-1871 L
Halliburton, Caroline to Joseph Lloyd 12-3-1870 (12-4-1870) L B
Halliburton, Cassie to John Harper 12-24-1880 (12-31-1881?) L
Halliburton, Eliza to David C. Dewalt 1-14-1881 L
Halliburton, Eliza to Thomas Henning 12-16-1872 (no return) L
Halliburton, Ella to Harry Rucker 3-30-1878 (3-31-1878) L
Halliburton, Ella to Henderson Lee 6-14-1878 (6-15-1878) L B
Halliburton, Emma to J. H. Henning 12-6-1884 (12-10-1884) L
Halliburton, Fannie to Gratten Tucker 2-19-1873 L
Halliburton, Frances to Harry Clay 9-24-1870 (no return) L B
Halliburton, Jennie to Philip Green 7-31-1879 L
Halliburton, L. P. to James Wilkison 1-10-1861 Be
Halliburton, Lucy to Joe Watson 3-16-1871 Hy
Halliburton, M. A. R. to F. M. Wilkinson 1-10-1867 (no return) L
Halliburton, Malinda to Hugh Clay 10-8-1870 (10-9-1870) L
Halliburton, Martha to Thomas Wardlaw 8-23-1853 (8-25-1853) L
Halliburton, Mary A. to Jonathan Warren 10-24-1869 G
Halliburton, Mary Allice to Lewis Nixon 12-17-1874 L
Halliburton, Mary Jane to Matthew Wilson 7-11-1869 G
Halliburton, Mary T. to Henry Flowers 9-20-1836 G
Halliburton, Mary to Augustine Carter 9-28-1848 (10-10-1848) Ma
Halliburton, Mary to George Graham 4-18-1868 Hy
Halliburton, Mattie L. to L. V. Taliafero 1-10-1885 (1-11-1885) L
Halliburton, Mattie to Albert Parker 12-28-1874 (12-31-1874) L B
Halliburton, Mattie to Lewis Nelson 4-4-1873? (4-5-1874) L B
Halliburton, Mildred A. to Jos. A. Jenkins 12-10-1879 L
Halliburton, Mollie E. to William H. Boyd 6-17-1873 (6-18-1873) L
Halliburton, Rachel to E. H. Jennings 6-12-1873 (no return) L B
Halliburton, Ruth A. to Ervin Chapman 10-4-1867 Hy
Halliburton, Sada to J. E. Halliburton 1-31-1882 (2-2-1882) L
Halliburton, Sarah to Frank Moore 8-7-1873 L B
Halliburton, Silvy to Richard Hawkins 4-4-1874 (4-5-1874) L B
Halliburton, ___rinia to Bob Fisher 2-22-1877 L B
Hallmark, Cynthia A. to John Gann 8-14-1862 Mn
Hallmark, Mary A. to George Townsend 7-29-1871 Cr
Halloway, Mary to John M. Burton 11-4-1847 (11-5-1847) F
Hallum, Amanda to James Slate 11-24-1858 (11-25-1858) Sh
Hallum, Emarilla J. to John D. Stroud 9-20-1869 (9-22-1869) Cr
Hallum, Jane to Martin M. Berry 3-7-1863 (3-8-1863) Sh
Hally, Lucy A. E. to William F. Thomas 3-3-1841 F
Halmark, E. J. to Beverly Freels 4-5-1841 Cr
Halmark, Mahuldy to John Cooper 4-29-1846 Cr
Halmark, Nancy A. to R. G. Bonds 8-17-1852 Cr
Halser, Martha to James R. Land 12-26-1835 Sh
Halstead, Martha J. to Jesse Allen 9-2-1855 Hn
Halstead, Susan A. to Lewis E. Webb 9-16-1852 Hn
Halstead, Virginia C. to Wm. Thos. Beauchamp 5-1-1861 Sh
Halsted, Mary Ann to Thomas McCarty 9-27-1848 Sh
Haltom, Amanda to Francis M. Johnson 9-30-1847 Ma
Haltom, Ann E. to Thomas D. Harris 12-15-1860 Hr
Haltom, Deborah to John R. Blair 11-21-1855 Ma
Haltom, Frances M to Edwin R. Johnson 8-31-1842 Ma
Haltom, Helen to Jep. Johnston 4-7-1840 (4-30-1840) Ma
Haltom, Jane Elizabeth to William F. Gardner 6-4-1855 Ma
Haltom, Margaret R. to Robert F. Cain 5-18-1858 (5-19-1858) Ma
Haltom, Marinda C. to Jesse D. Tucker 12-2-1869 (12-5-1869) Ma
Haltom, Rebecca E. to Daniel B. Cooper 11-20-1866 (11-21-1866) Ma
Halton, Hannah to James T. Maroney 8-24-1854 Ma
Halton, Hester Ann to George R. Scott 2-7-1839 (2-14-1839) Ma
Halton, Mary Jane to Mathew Williamson 1-22-1868 (1-26-1868) Ma
Halton, Sarah to William Hall 2-27-1830 (3-20-1831?) Ma
Haltum, Louisa to Hansel Caleb 1-7-1829 Ma
Halum, Miley to W. T. Pace 9-18-1866 (9-20-1866) Dy
Haly, Ann to Robert Logan 3-18-1840 Sh
Ham, Caroline to Wm. C. Fleet 12-15-1842 Hr
Ham, Dicey to John J. Taylor 3-19-1850 Ma

Ham, Emblem to James C. Pruete 9-23-1839 (9-26-1839) Hr
Ham, Lucinda to Franklin Minter 1-19-1847 Hr
Ham, Mary to Nathaniel Scott 11-13-1838 (11-22-1838) Hr
Ham, Visy to John Handly 11-29-1842 Ma
Ham?, Susan S. to Andrew J. Howard 7-23-1850 (7-24-1850) Hr
Hamah, M. A. to Calvin McAlpin 3-22-1862 Mn
Hamblen, Elizabeth C. to Ephraim Dunlap 9-10-1846 Hn
Hamblen, Frances to John A. Slate 9-10-1838 Hn
Hamblet, Martha to Sanders Montcuff 8-2-1844 (8-4-1844) F
Hamblet, Sarah B. to Pli Walker 12-31-1849 (1-2-1850) F
Hamblet, Virginia to Jno. W. Hodges 12-2-1867 (12-11-1867) F
Hambleton, Susan to J. N. Freeman 10-8-1870 (10-9-1870) Cr
Hamblin, Sarah to Robert Cartwright 4-7-1828 Hr
Hamblin, Selina to John A. Haynes 7-3-1837 O
Hamby, Ann E. to George Robinson 8-2-1870 G
Hamby, Nancy to John Gunson 9-8-1853 (9-10-1853) O
Hamelton, Mary Jane to Patrick McDonough 7-23-1859 Sh
Hamelton, N. A. to Thomas B. Moffatt 2-20-1861 O
Hamer, Catherine to Austin Robinson 1-2-1868 (1-5-1868) F B
Hamer, Emma H. to Thos. H. Webb 5-27-1858 Hr
Hamer, Frances A. to Newton Wright 12-15-1851 (12-17-1851) Hr
Hamer, Junetta to Jerry Estridge 4-30-1868 (5-10-1868) F B
Hamerly, Mollie to Claudius E. Chappell 5-22-1867 Ma
Hames, G. A. to J. P. Clark 10-22-1874 Hy
Hamet, Rebecca to Shepherd Landrum 11-9-1848 O
Hamett, Mehaley to Joseph Lenord 1-29-1842 Cr
Hamette, Louisa T. to Hughes Smith 8-26-1848 Cr
Hamil, Amanda E. to G. W. D. White 10-24-1865 Hy
Hamil, Margaret E. to R. R. Anthony 7-29-1866 Hy
Hamil, Martha F. to R. N. Anthony 9-3-1861 (no return) Hy
Hamil, Mary to M. T. White 12-1-1869 Hy
Hamill, Miza to J. L. Craig 12-24-1884 L
Hamill, Nancy to Hezekiah Austin 6-8-1854 L
Hamilton, A. A. to Henry Pryer 8-2-1852 (8-3-1852) O
Hamilton, A. A. to Henry Pryor 8-2-1852 (8-3-1852) O
Hamilton, A. J. to M. T. Bird 11-20-1871 T
Hamilton, A. R. (Mrs.) to Jno. R. S. Taliaferro 10-23-1868 G
Hamilton, Adeline to John G. Williams 1-14-1864 G
Hamilton, Alabama to Pink Alston 7-8-1868 G B
Hamilton, Amanda to James R. Hurd 11-2-1869 (11-4-1869) Dy
Hamilton, Amanda to Williamson McClelland 7-12-1859 T
Hamilton, Angaline K. to Jacob W. Arnold 12-27-1847 (1-25-1848) G
Hamilton, B. J. to A. C. McCleary 10-9-1866 G
Hamilton, C. J. to H. S. Burnside 1-8-1875 (1-12-1875) Dy
Hamilton, Caroline to Joven Davisky 9-1-1859 (9-1859) O
Hamilton, Catharine to Daniel Hooper 3-10-1853 O
Hamilton, E. A. to E. M. Cannon 1-25-1849 Cr
Hamilton, E. J. to J. D. Thompson 10-17-1867 (no return) Cr
Hamilton, E. L. to W. T. Perkins 1-8-1863 Mn
Hamilton, E. T. O. to John Spelling 9-19-1867 (no return) Cr
Hamilton, Edney S. to B. F. Garner 1-15-1872 (1-16-1872) Cr
Hamilton, Elizabeth P. to Wilborn G. Graves 9-22-1858 Cr
Hamilton, Elizabeth P. to Wilborn H. Graves 9-22-1858 Cr
Hamilton, Elizabeth to Bartlett Y. Armfield 2-20-1865 Sh
Hamilton, Emily A. to Thomason Moore 11-13-1856 Cr
Hamilton, F. A. to W. P. Shofner 3-18-1873 (3-23-1873) Dy
Hamilton, Giney to Benjamin Vaughn 4-16-1831 Hr
Hamilton, Gussie to Felix Baker 2-2-1870 G B
Hamilton, I. C. J. to E. R. Fulghum 9-5-1861 G
Hamilton, J. Lou to C. B. Stewart 6-13-1871 Ma
Hamilton, Jame L. to James R. Knox 9-18-1839 Cr
Hamilton, Josie to Daniel Davis 8-16-1878 (8-21-1878) Dy
Hamilton, Louisa to Cyrus Wilson 1-21-1840 Ma
Hamilton, Lucinda to Anderson W. Fitch 11-22-1856 (no return) Hn
Hamilton, Lucinda to Jason Wilson 2-1-1833 (2-5-1833) Hr
Hamilton, Lucinda to M. C. Estes 12-24-1843 Hn
Hamilton, Lucy F. to Sydney S. Carroll 12-2-1858 Cr
Hamilton, M. A. to E. L. Williams 9-23-1864 (9-27-1864) O
Hamilton, M. C. to H. M. Hamilton 7-16-1855 (7-17-1855) G
Hamilton, M. J. to J. W. Ellis 2-15-1870 (2-16-1870) Dy
Hamilton, M. K. to H. G. Bruit? 12-23-1866 G
Hamilton, Malissa J. to Samuel Neely 2-6-1855 Cr
Hamilton, Manerva to George W. Graves 6-6-1861 Cr
Hamilton, Margaret B. to Sidney Broach 1-27-1841 Cr
Hamilton, Margaret V. to Benj. F. Elder 7-21-1853 G
Hamilton, Margaret to Alexander A. Montgomery 12-29-1856 (12-30-1856) T
Hamilton, Martha (Mrs.) to Henry J. Pearson 8-8-1867 Ma
Hamilton, Martha F. to G. S. Gardner 2-12-1863 Cr
Hamilton, Martha J. to John Morris 3-16-1868 (3-17-1868) F
Hamilton, Martha P. to James W. Allison 7-2-1853 G
Hamilton, Martha to Wm. B. Worrell 12-21-1857 (12-23-1857) Hr
Hamilton, Mary E. to Calvin C. Clemment 12-9-1839 (12-10-1839) G
Hamilton, Mary F. to Wm. J. Warbritton 8-18-1854 Cr
Hamilton, Mary J. to William L. Fox 4-21-1852 (4-27-1852) Ma
Hamilton, Mary Jane to Nicholas J. Vedder 4-16-1837 Sh
Hamilton, Mary Jane to William C. Cason 6-26-1860 (6-27-1860) Ma
Hamilton, Mary M. to Robert F. Garret 1-23-1871 (1-25-1871) T

Hamilton, Mary to Addison McFerrin 7-23-1869 (no return) F B
Hamilton, Mary to John P. Craig 12-10-1860 O
Hamilton, Mary to Williamson McClelland 11-28-1854 T
Hamilton, Milly to Benj. Sperling 9-25-1833 Hr
Hamilton, Minerva to George W. Graves 6-?-1861 (6-6-1861) Cr
Hamilton, Mirilda to Hyram Payne 3-1-1832 Sh
Hamilton, Nancy E. to Edmund A. Freeman 11-4-1847 (12-3-1847) G
Hamilton, Nancy L. to J. H. Gardner 11-27-1860 (11-28-1860) Cr
Hamilton, Nancy L. to J. H. Gardner 11-27-1863 (no return) Cr
Hamilton, Nancy to Davis M. Hubbard 12-3-1867 G
Hamilton, Nancy to Isaac Witt 12-23-1846 (no return) We
Hamilton, Nancy to Jesse Scroggins 7-17-1830 (7-20-1830) Hr
Hamilton, Nancy to Tandy Bowden 12-28-1868 G B
Hamilton, Narcissa H. to James W. Ozier 10-15-1867 (no return) Cr
Hamilton, Pelma to John W. Bartcliff 3-2-1866 (3-4-1866) O
Hamilton, Pemela S. H. to Michel Keenan 6-18-1845 (6-19-1845) G
Hamilton, Phoebe J. to W. P. Elrod 1-9-1866 G
Hamilton, Polly to Christopher Creekmore 11-3-1825 (11-4-1825) O
Hamilton, Prudence to Jephthan Duff(e)y 7-25-1864 G
Hamilton, R. L. to T. F. Parnell 11-30-1869 (12-3-1869) Dy
Hamilton, Rebecca A. to J. N. Ellis 8-26-1868 (8-27-1868) Dy
Hamilton, Rebecca E. to J. T. Leath, jr. 7-19-1855 Hn
Hamilton, S. E. to M. R. Pace 12-17-1878 (12-19-1878) Dy
Hamilton, Sarah A. to Wm. L. Stephens 9-21-1862 G
Hamilton, Sarah E. to Saml. S. Johnson 3-24-1857 Ma
Hamilton, Sarah E. to William D. Black 1-1-1857 G
Hamilton, Sibby to William W. Roberts 10-2-1851 G
Hamilton, Siby T. to H. D. Lankford 7-20-1867 G
Hamilton, Susan F. to John J. Flannagan 11-4-1868 G
Hamilton, Susan M. to Thomas D. Thomas 5-4-1847 G
Hamilton, Susan to Ephriam E. Davidson 1-28-1846 Cr
Hamilton, Susan to Jas. Tool 7-26-1874 (7-29-1874) T
Hamilton, T. N. to John S. Wadkin 12-13-1839 Ma
Hamilton, Tennessee O. to W. E. Brown 3-10-1840 Cr
Hamilton, Tennessee to D. G. Tull 2-5-1868 G
Hamlet, Frances to Joseph J. Boguss 9-24-1845 (9-27-1845) Hr
Hamlett, Elizabeth to Thomas B. Thompson 10-25-1856 (10-26-1856) Ma
Hamlett, H. H. (Mrs.) to J. B. Shackleford 1-22-1866 G
Hamlett, Mary A. to Jesse S. Harvey 8-14-1855 (8-15-1855) Hr
Hamlett, Mary to Thomas W. Brown 12-15-1838 (12-20-1838) F
Hamlett, Rose Ann to Buckner Harwell 7-8-1840 (7-9-1840) F
Hamlin, Martha A. to R. F. Scarbrough 7-5-1858 We
Hamlin, Pricilla to Henry Hess 11-10-1873 Hy
Hamlin, S. E. to T. R. Rider 5-1-1864 Hn
Hamlin, Sarah to W. C. Winscot? 5-8-1845 Hn
Hamlin?, Elizabeth to A. C. Spurlin 11-30-1849 (11-31?-1849) Hr
Hamm, Delphia E. to William H. Vicky 1-10-1864 Mn
Hamm, Elizabeth to R. H. Isbell 4-24-1841 (4-29-1841) Hr
Hamm, Susan to Alvis Warren 9-15-1862 Mn
Hamm--had, Christine to W. B. Schulz 6-20-1863 Sh
Hammel, E. S. to J. F. Murray 12-20-1870 (12-22-1870) Dy
Hammell, Martha to James Marlow 11-12-1857 (11-13-1857) O
Hammer, Cordelia to S. E. Williamson 4-1-1871 (4-4-1871) Cr
Hammer, Martha F. to George A. Little 4-28-1843 Sh
Hammers (Hanners), Mary to John Lambert 10-13-1842 Sh
Hammers, Lyda to J. C. Tims 3-2-1854 (3-3-1854) Hr
Hammet, Martha Jane to William Cobb 9-20-1852 O
Hammett, Caroline to Wm. Cary 12-10-1840 Cr
Hammett, Frances to Nelson Clark 10-26-1861 (10-30-1861) Cr
Hammett, Martha A. to W. R. Bennett 4-19-1857 Cr
Hammett, Martha to Jorden Jamison 7-6-1870 (7-10-1870) Cr
Hammett, Mary C. to John C. Antry 2-26-1861 (no return) Cr
Hammett, Mary J. to James L. Grooms 2-9-1848 Cr
Hammett, Sucky to Thos. King 2-15-1844 Cr
Hammil, Manirva to William White 2-18-1871 (2-19-1871) L
Hammon, Elizabeth A. to William Yanakay 6-24-1863 Sh
Hammon, Margaret to David Huddleston 5-4-1842 (5-5-1842) Ma
Hammon, Mary E. to Andrew J. Klyce 6-24-1841 G
Hammon, Mary to Robert A. Pool 2-10-1869 F
Hammon, Patience to Henderson Grundy 2-20-1869 (2-12?-1869) F B
Hammon, Priscilla J. to M. L. Jackson 3-11-1850 F
Hammond, Adeline to Jesse Mask 5-16-1855 Ma
Hammond, Amanda F. to George W. King 2-24-1869 (2-25-1869) Ma
Hammond, Eliza Caroline to William West 12-29-1862 Sh
Hammond, Elizabeth to William P. Howard 4-23-1856 Ma
Hammond, Marteller Ann to Sidney R. Timms 10-16-1867 (10-19-1867) T
Hammond, Martha to John Pennington 8-16-1842 (8-18-1842) Ma
Hammond, Mary A. to Francis M. Thomas 8-20-1852 (8-22-1852) Hr
Hammond, Mary K. to William P. Howard 4-24-1869 Ma
Hammond, Mary to Young W. Allen 2-1-1850 G
Hammond, Nancy A. to Wm. S. King 1-4-1870 (1-5-1870) Ma
Hammond, Sallie R. to D. Harpole 3-19-1868 G
Hammond, Sally to Freeman Johnson 12-28-1866 G
Hammond, Sarah C. L. to John Dominger 12-12-1852 O
Hammonds, A. R. to C. C. Adams 5-1-1867 G
Hammonds, Elmira to Levi Mobley 11-24-1866 G
Hammonds, Fanny to Allen Sexton 3-2-1859 (3-3-1859) Hr

Hammonds, Louisa to Alford M. Witt 11-21-1855 (11-22-1855) G
Hammonds, Mary B. to Newton S. Revel 11-23-1855 (11-25-1855) G
Hammonds, Zady F. to B. F. Thomas 8-27-1856 Hr
Hammons, Billa E. to William W. McKinnie 12-18-1855 (12-26-1855) Hr
Hammons, Emily to Alfred Peebles 9-28-1870 F B
Hammons, Emla to Jesse Lassiter 11-11-1840 F
Hammons, Frances to James Hollice 12-15-1863 (12-17-1863) F
Hammons, Lucy to Mat Rutledge 12-31-1866 (1-8-1867) F B
Hammons, Martha B. to W. R. Rutledge 4-6-1842 F
Hammons, Martha J. S. to Giles G. Hudson 7-1-1853 (7-3-1853) Hr
Hammons, Mary to Isaiah Crabb 2-23-1839 (2-26-1839) F
Hammons, Mourning to Mark Crocker 7-7-1856 (7-10-1856) G
Hammons, Priscilla to Alex Williams 8-4-1856 (8-10-1856) G
Hammons, Rosa to Stephen Bradford 8-19-1880 L B
Hammons, Sarah A. to Keeble T. Thompson 9-30-1846 (10-1-1846) Hr
Hammons, Susan J. to E. T. Thompson 11-8-1855 (11-9-1855) Hr
Hamner, C. M. to B. F. Stacy 9-25-1852 (no return) F
Hamner, E. A. to F. P. Stark 11-13-1863 Cr
Hamner, Jane to James King 11-2-1839 (11-3-1839) Ma
Hamner, Louisa M. to Harrington Owens 10-4-1855 Sh
Hamner, Mary Elizabeth to Wm. W. Little 2-23-1843 Sh
Hamonds, Narcissa J. to Jefferson P. Workman 3-27-1864 G
Hampden, M. J. to J. B. Ward 9-7-1872 (no return) Dy
Hampton, Amanda M. to John H. Crawford 8-31-1869 G
Hampton, Artell to A. I. Crider 6-16-1853 Cr
Hampton, C. A. to E. W. Dougan 11-16-1869 (11-18-1869) F
Hampton, Edy to Andrew Flake 1-8-1872 (no return) Cr B
Hampton, Elenna to Alex Kirk 12-24-1844 Cr
Hampton, Elenora H. to William P. James 10-28-1868 Ma
Hampton, Eliza B. to Bodley Johnson 11-23-1846 (11-24-1846) F
Hampton, Elizabeth A. to John Prewett 12-22-1846 Cr
Hampton, Emiline to Calvin Anderson 2-25-1870 (no return) Dy
Hampton, H. N. to J. B. Dunavant 6-25-1883 L
Hampton, Harriet Caroline to John S. Conger 5-20-1861 Ma
Hampton, Harriet to Louis Gordon 3-21-1872 (no return) Cr
Hampton, Lila to Henry Boyd 12-27-1877 Hy
Hampton, Lizzie to John Hart 3-7-1871 Cr B
Hampton, Louisa M. J. to Yoring F. Kerr 11-19-1850 Cr
Hampton, Louisa to Henry Hargus 1-27-1869 (1-29-1869) Cr
Hampton, M. J. to M. D. Alexander 6-25-1864 (6-26-1864) O
Hampton, M. J. to W. S. Davis 5-16-1874 (5-19-1874) Dy
Hampton, Marey to Hubbart Littleton 7-2-1834 O
Hampton, Mariah to Richard C. Sellars 5-18-1846 G
Hampton, Marianna to Joseph H. Sewell 5-8-1871 (5-9-1871) Ma
Hampton, Martha Ann to James Phillips 2-17-1866 Cr
Hampton, Martha E. to B. J. Sutton 9-2-1865 (9-4-1865) F
Hampton, Mary A. to Enoch V. McAdoo 8-6-1846 Cr
Hampton, Mary A. to Joseph W. Fox 2-9-1869 G
Hampton, Mary E. to Ben F. Prichard 12-21-1872 (no return) Dy
Hampton, Mary E. to Calvin Jones 11-6-1856 Cr
Hampton, Mary L. to John T. Lane 1-30-1872 Dy
Hampton, Mary to Calvin Jones 12-2-1847 Cr
Hampton, Mary to John A. Cunningham 10-27-1845 (12-28-1845) G
Hampton, Mathena C. to William Blackburn 2-14-1831 Hr
Hampton, Mollie to Edward Barnett 10-2-1869 Cr
Hampton, Nancy A. to R. B. Vannoy 12-7-1864 O
Hampton, Nancy to Richard W. Cashien 2-10-1842 O
Hampton, Rachell P. to Isham Walker 8-15-1850 Hn
Hampton, Rebecca to Warren Hall 11-10-1877 (no return) Dy
Hampton, Ridley to Presley King 11-28-1849 Cr
Hampton, Roan to Sidney Horn 4-24-1852 Cr
Hampton, S. A. J. to J. A. Brown 5-30-1864 (5-31-1864) Cr
Hampton, Sarah E. to Benjamin Taylor Phillips 12-8-1866 (12-12-1866) Cr
Hampton, Sarah L. to J. M. King 3-21-1868 (3-22-1868) Cr
Hampton, Sarah to John Williams 4-29-1839 (3-1-1839?) O
Hampton, Sarrah to Robert Mount 9-19-1867 G
Hampton, Susannah R. to John S. Emmerson 4-25-1857 O
Hampton, Virginia to E. W. Dougan 10-16-1866 (11-10-1866) F
Hamrick, Jane to John E. G. Covey 11-13-1865 (no return) F
Hamrick, Sally to J. T. Garrett 12-31-1866 (no return) F
Hams, Martha to Nathaniel Tate 1-7-1858 Cr
Hamsbury, Sarah A. to B. D. Bowden 10-?-1842 Hn
Hamwick, Malvina to Jas. M. Thompson 5-26-1851 (5-29-1851) Sh
Han, Cleopatria A. R. to John A. Clayton 10-18-1836 Sh
Hancock, Adaline O. to Enock Stewart 12-3-1851 (12-4-1851) Hr
Hancock, Agnes to William Hudspeth 7-26-1838 Hn
Hancock, Elizabeth M. to James A. Dimond (Dearwood) 6-8-1859 Sh
Hancock, Elizabeth to Ed Fouch 11-25-1867 G B
Hancock, Elizabeth to Joseph T. Flippin 2-12-1842 (2-17-1842) G
Hancock, Evalene to Wm. M. Tucker 1-27-1876 (1-28-1876) L
Hancock, Hellen M. to James W. Falkner 2-25-1861 (2-26-1861) Sh
Hancock, Jane to John H. Hill 1-22-1876 (1-28-1876) L
Hancock, M. E. to Charles Coleman 3-31-1879 (4-1-1879) Dy
Hancock, Margaret L. to Isaac B. Matheney 3-10-1858 Hn
Hancock, Martha E. to A. P. Powell 10-19-1862 G
Hancock, Martha to Elijah J. Drake 11-29-1871 L
Hancock, Mary Jane to Abram Maury 8-22-1859 Hr

Hancock, Molly to Anderson Williams 2-2-1870 G B
Hancock, Nancy to Stephen Frazier 10-25-1863 G
Hancock, Patience W. to William L. Crocker 8-31-1848 G
Hancock, Prissilla to Joshua Swindle 12-9-1845 (12-17-1845) G
Hancock, Rebecca to Alexr. J. Patton 1-1-1868 (1-2-1868) L
Hancock, Sarah to Cullen Cribbs 10-20-1852 G
Hand (Hard?), V. M. to J. W. Ramsey 1-3-1866 G
Handcock, Magdalana to Wilson Cooper 3-16-1843 G
Handcock, Nancy to John M. White 5-26-1836 (5-27-1836) G
Handiworker, Agnes to Phillip R. Bohlen 10-7-1854 Sh
Handley, Bridget to Thomas Danaher 4-12-1862 Sh
Handwerker, Ottilia to Andrew Renkert 9-24-1863 Sh
Handworker, Ida A. to Adolphus Helbing 8-8-1856 (8-12-1856) Sh
Hanegin, Sarah Ann to W. B. Robinett 5-9-1846 (5-12-1846) T
Haneline, Elizaeth to James A. Wrather 12-3-1846 Hn
Hanes, Hanah to Nathaniel Sherrod 4-5-1828 T
Hanes, M. A. to W. W. Deberry 4-11-1865 O
Hanes, Sarah Margaret to Robt. E. Newton 12-10-1867 Ma
Haney (Harvey), Eliza to William Miller 5-2-1840 Sh
Haney, Nancy C. to Wm. Terrell 2-24-1878 Hy
Haney, Nancy to John A. Hughes 2-9-1869 (2-11-1869) F B
Haney, Rebecca to A. Lee 4-26-1858 Be
Hanfred?, Frances E. to Jason Pritchard 3-24-1866? (3-25-1868) Cr
Hanie, Charlotte to Charles Davis 12-31-1840 Sh
Hanis(Harris?), Mary A. to James W. Prewett 1-21-1848 (1-25-1848) Hr
Hankins, Elenora E. to Alexander Kirsey 12-14-1858 (12-16-1858) Sh
Hankins, Martha J. to James W. Huie 2-19-1860 Hn
Hankins, N. C. to William Usher 1-17-1835 (1-22-1835) Hr
Hankley, Philadelphia Ann to Gilbert B. Boucher 12-1-1858 Hr
Hankly, Dohorty J. to Robert K. Ruddle 1-23-1849 (1-29-1849) Hr
Hanks, C. B. to Thomas Taylor 4-1-1861 Mn
Hanks, Elizabeth to Uriah Stafford 11-76-1825 (11-8-1825) Hr
Hanks, Joisey to Wm. R. Rogers 9-8-1827 Hr
Hanks, Kesiah to Wilie Caldwell 7-11-1827 Hr
Hanks, Mary Jane to Wm. Elliott 11-30-1864 (no return) Dy
Hanks, Mary to George M. D. Bullen 2-28-1865 G
Hanley, Ellen to Thomas O'Donnell 9-7-1860 Sh
Hanley, Lottie T. to W. M. Dickerson 1-26-1858 T
Hanley, Lucretia to Calvin Philley 7-18-1827 (7-22-1827) Hr
Hanley, Margaret to Isaac Pool 10-3-1835 Sh
Hanley, Marion W. to Edwin K. Austin 7-15-1845 (7-18-1845) F
Hanlin (Harlin?), Elvira to Thos. J. Simpkins 1-20-1851 (1-23-1851) Sh
Hanlin, Gracy to Wm. Hall 12-30-1871 T
Hanlin? (Harlen?), Elizabeth to John B. Williams 12-22-1862 Sh
Hanline, Nelly to Elijah Bennett 4-8-1841 Hn
Hanly, Cynthia P. to James Farris 11-8-1834 Sh
Hanly, Joana to William Gorman 6-14-1860 (6-25-1860) Sh
Hanly, Mary to Thomas Kelly 8-2-1862 Sh
Hanly, Nancey to Samuel Davis 4-5-1861 T
Hanmon, L. A. to Jas. M. Witherspoon 1-5-1861 G
Hann, Mary V. to S. G. Halliburton 12-26-1868 (no return) Hy
Hanna, E. C. to N. W. Hanna 12-22-1864 (1-1-1865) Cr
Hanna, Emalin to Chas. Kilpatrick 2-22-1872 T
Hanna, Mary J. to Garland J. Read 3-11-1851 Cr
Hanna, Meliara J. to G. W. Elder 2-17-1859 Cr
Hanna, Rosetta J. to John A. Yarbro 10-13-1866 (10-16-1866) T
Hanna, S. J. to J. A. Crow 1-16-1869 (1-20-1869) Cr
Hannah, Agness to G. W. Dismukes 12-10-1867 (12-11-1867) Cr
Hannah, Bettie to G. B. Hrris 7-25-1868 (7-27-1868) Cr
Hannah, Eliza M. to George E. Hunt 4-9-1856 (4-10-1856) Sh
Hannah, M. J.? to W. A. Loyd 12-12-1866 (12-13-1866) T
Hannah, Martha J. to Henry Moore 5-15-1855 (5-16-1855) T
Hannah, Mildred to Jonathan Starnes 7-6-1845 Sh
Hannah, Nelly to Thomas L.(Q?) Moody 3-9-1830 Sh
Hannea, Huldy C. to John H. Denny 1-25-1846 Cr
Hanner, Mary to Robert G. Cleghorn 2-11-1833 Sh
Hannery, Margaret to Jesse Richards 5-13-1863 Sh
Hanness, Charlott to Benjamin Strong 3-15-1847 (no return) F
Hannig, Julia to Louis Daum 2-4-1860 Sh
Hannigan, Ellen to James Eagan 5-5-1863 Sh
Hanning, Rebecca J. to Elisha Scates 12-6-1849 Cr
Hanning, Sarah Jane to Spencer Edwards 6-19-1850 Cr
Hannings, Ann E. to John A. Matthews 11-13-1861 (no return) We
Hannings, L. D. to J. B. Hall 10-28-1858 We
Hannis, Lucinda to James G. Wilkison 7-4-1827 (7-5-1827) Hr
Hannis, Nancy T. to Larkin M. Wellons 9-25-1841 (9-30-1841) Hr
Hannis, Rebecca E. to James W. Phillips 6-9-1849 (6-10-1849) Hr
Hannis, Sinah P. to James Duncan 7-7-1831 Hr
Hannis?, R. E. to Robert J. Marrs 3-9-1848 Hr
Hannis?, Sarah C. to John N. Timms 4-9-1867 (4-10-1867) T
Hanniss, Martha Ann to Wm. B. Ragan 11-10-1838 (11-15-1838) Hr
Hansberry, Bertha Ann to J. W. Smithson 10-4-1855 Hn
Hansboro, Sarah V. to John H. Terry 1-1-1858 Cr
Hansbro, Callie T. to W. T. Younger 1-16-1869 (no return) Cr
Hansbrough, Catherine to Simpson Ray 11-7-1838 Hn
Hansbrough, Mary L. to Robert C. Seymore 3-30-1857 Cr
Hansbrough, Rebecca to Levie Dickson 2-22-1846 (no return) Cr

Hansburrow, Susan to Calvin P. Thomas 1-18-1851 Cr
Hansel, Caroline to William H. Boothe 6-2-1853 Hn
Hansel, Eveline F. to Henry Bradford 4-4-1850 Be
Hansel, Marthan to A. M. Brooks 8-27-1847 Be
Hansel, Mary to Milford Council 12-9-1856 Hn
Hansel, Mary to Thos. Beasley 3-18-1852 Be
Hansel?, Susan R. to W. L. Hall 2-14-1852 (no return) F
Hansen, Henrietta to A. J. Norman 5-19-1852 Hr
Hansey, Minerva to James M. Greer 2-10-1846 Cr
Hansford, Deliah L. to Jno. W. Rogers 10-25-1858 (10-28-1858) Hr
Hansil, Mary S. to John R. Manning 12-23-1851 (no return) F
Hanson (Harson), Jerusha B. to Wm. A. Johnson 11-19-1846 Sh
Hanson, Jane to James Boling 7-13-1830 (7-15-1830) Hr
Hanston, Elizabeth to Albert A. Fulks 10-1-1850 (no return) Cr
Hapsens, E. H. to Marshal L. Beadles 1-12-1860 We
Haralson, E. A. to R. A. Barcroft 11-23-1871 Hy
Haralson, Eunicy to Tobias C. Henderson 12-10-1823 Ma
Haralson, Isabella to Wm. Spickenagle 12-28-1842 Sh
Haralson, Jane to Silas Buck 5-20-1841 Sh
Haralson, Mary E. to Bowler Cocke 9-1-1842 Sh
Harber, Camantha J. to Lewis S. Hutcherson 9-16-1845 G
Harber, Catherine to John Manley 9-7-1853 (9-8-1853) G
Harber, Eliza Ann to Joseph H. Partee 11-20-1869 (11-21-1869) L
Harber, Martha Ann to William Mathis 9-16-1836 (9-18-1836) G
Harbert, Adelia E. to Rufus W. Rice 4-5-1853 Ma
Harbert, Fanny to Sam Weddle 3-14-1876 Hy
Harbert, Kate to Albert Nickleson 2-28-1878 Hy
Harbert, L. S. to Wm. W. Bond 4-27-1854 (5-3-1854) Ma
Harbert, Molly to Webster Curry 3-24-1874 Hy
Harbert, Narcissa to Henry V. Berson 11-28-1877 Hy
Harbert, Neppie L. to Ed. H. Taylor 3-14-1876 Hy
Harbert, Sarah W. to John F. Hicks 12-5-1853 (12-6-1853) Ma
Harbert, Senia A. to David S. Nicholson 2-1-1859 Ma
Harbeson, Melinda to Andrew Dollins 11-1-1855 O
Harbet, Charlott to L. W. Strickland 9-18-1862 (10-30-1862) L
Harbin, Ellen V. to A. M. Davis 5-14-1861 (5-21-1861) Hr
Harbin, Ellen V. to B. A. McDaniel 4-28-1858 (5-13-1858) Hr
Harbor, Ella to Joe Crenshaw 8-8-1885 (no return) L
Harbor, Nancy to John Cribbs 1-18-1828 (2-19-1828) G
Harbor, Silvian to Thos. Woods 12-26-1854 (12-28-1854) G
Harbour, Ibby M. J. to Jeremiah Hay 3-20-1848 G
Harbour, Jane to William Cribbs 6-16-1826 G
Harbour, Lucinda to John Kinley 3-17-1831 G
Harbour, Mary L. to Ebenezar Dunlap 4-20-1829 (4-21-1829) G
Harbour, Nancy to Dr. ? Cribbs 8-11-1831 G
Harbut, Eliza to George Nicholson 4-12-1874 Hy
Harbut, L. Alice to O. E. (Dr.) Herbert 3-25-1867 G
Harcey, Susan E. to Edmond W. Goodrich 9-3-1839 G
Hardage, Eliza J. to John B. Long 12-7-1847 (12-?-1847) Ma
Hardage, Margaret A. to Wm. F. Hudson 11-17-1870 Ma
Hardage, Nancy A. to Jerome B. Tate 12-24-1859 Ma
Hardaway, Ann H. to John Kesterson 5-13-1847 Sh
Hardaway, Elizabeth R. H. to Wiley Carlisle 12-30-1847 Sh
Hardaway, Lucy R. to B. A. Whitsitt 12-18-1845 Sh
Hardaway, Sarah to Parham Adams 3-4-1853 Sh
Hardeman, Mary to John M. Hardeman 5-13-1828 Hr
Harden (Haiden), Sarah J. to W. G. Watkins 5-19-1847 Sh
Harden, Elizabeth to J. W. Benson 1-20-1862 Mn
Harden, Fannie to Rubin Beasley 3-30-1867 (4-2-1867) T
Harden, Jane to David White 5-12-1858 Sh
Harden, Julia to Joseph Roberts 10-20-1877 (10-25-1877) L B
Harden, L. J. to S. M. Smith 7-27-1862 Mn
Harden, L. N. to J. M. McClintock 3-23-1862 Mn
Harden, Margarette C. to George W. Blackwell 12-22-1858 (12-28-1858) G B
Harden, Mary Ann to W. V. Crownover 1-6-1863 Mn
Harden, Mary J. to Andrew Woods 12-1-1877 (12-2-1877) L
Harden, Rebecca to Hardy Hatley 12-28-1856 Be
Harden, Sarah Ann to Alexander Fincher 6-2-1877 (6-3-1877) L
Harder, Amanda M. to A. D. Gipson 9-13-1866 Hn
Harder, Elizabeth A. to James H. Crissman 11-26-1851 (11-27-1851) G
Harder, Lucy A. to Chas. M. Ross 4-22-1871 (4-27-1871) Cr
Hardeson, Lucinda to Benjamin Sharp 4-15-1866 G
Hardgrave, Louissanna to L. B. Mitchell 6-24-1839 (6-26-1839) Ma
Hardgraves, America E. to William M. Avery 8-26-1867 Ma
Hardgraves, Nancy B. (Mrs.) to Robert O. Lowry 1-19-1867 (1-20-1867) Ma
Hardgrove, Lavinia B. to Neil M. Gardner 6-18-1857 (6-23-1857) Ma
Hardican, E. F. to J. M. Lemons 2-8-1870 (no return) Dy
Hardican, L. C. to Roy Gaskin 3-5-1873 (3-10-1873) Dy
Hardican, Margaret H. to Thomas Lemmons 3-3-1862 (3-4-1862) Dy
Hardican, Martha to H. B. Williams 10-19-1863 Dy
Hardidge, Tabitha J. to Reuben Martin 9-7-1850 O
Hardie, Sarah L. to Allen Fenlen? 9-5-1870 (9-6-1870) Dy
Hardigan, Catharine to Michael Muirhill 2-20-1860 Sh
Hardin, Adaline to Nelson Dickens 2-8-1872 Hy
Hardin, Amanda E. to James M. Whitney 11-19-1867 (11-20-1867) F
Hardin, Amanda to Lindsey Upshaw 6-6-1868 G B
Hardin, Amelia to Bob Wright 12-27-1877 (12-28-1877) L

Hardin, Bell to Zach Robinson 1-8-1874 Hy
Hardin, Catherine to Smith Wiley 6-12-1875 L
Hardin, Eliza to Charles W. Carrington 3-12-1868 Ma
Hardin, Elizabeth C. to N. Moroney 11-15-1852 (?-2-1852) Sh
Hardin, Ella to John Harbour 2-27-1880 (2-29-1880) L
Hardin, Jane to F. Thad. Tanner 2-12-1876 Hy
Hardin, Louiza J. to Wallace Bills 1-23-1852 (1-27-1852) G
Hardin, Margaret to John Lightfoot 8-31-1841 Hn
Hardin, Maria to Peter Anderson 2-26-1883 (3-11-1883) L
Hardin, Martha T. to James H. Wimberley 11-26-1867 Hn
Hardin, Mary J. to Jno. W. Dawlton 12-19-1867 Hn
Hardin, Mary to Jack Davidson 5-29-1866 (6-30-1866) Dy
Hardin, Milly to Nelson Maclin 12-31-1867 G
Hardin, Misoura Ann to Patterson Graves 12-17-1853 Ma
Hardin, Polly Ann to Pleasant McBride 2-14-1841 Cr
Hardin, Rocky (Rody) to William Bridgewater 2-2-1871 (2-8-1871) F B
Hardin, Sarah A. to S. P. Hawkins 4-5-1870 (4-6-1870) Dy
Hardin, Sarah Ann to Henry Lea 4-17-1845 Sh
Hardin, Sarah R. to James Aston 2-14-1837 Hr
Hardin, Sarah to George Vinson 6-24-1852 Ma
Hardin, Sarah to Nathaniel Timms 1-20-1849 (1-21-1849) Ma
Hardin, Sophronia to John Drake 10-16-1848 (3-10-1850) Ma
Harding, Dilcy to George Ballard 7-18-1869 G B
Harding, Margaret A. to Robert W. Shelton 2-23-1858 Sh
Harding, Mary Jane to Henry A. Welsh 9-11-1854 (9-13-1854) Ma
Harding, Sarah P. to Benjamin F. Watkins 1-19-1857 Ma
Harding, Willie E. to David H. McGavock 5-23-1850 Sh
Hardion, Mebelda to Isian Cox 4-2-1850 Cr
Hardison, Laura J. to A. M. Hamer 11-29-1858 Hr
Hardison, Louisa to W. N. Robertson 1-15-1879 (1-16-1879) Dy
Hardison, Sallie J. to J. W. Clarke 1-26-1874 (1-27-1874) Dy
Hardison, Sarah Ann to Thomas Hanson 9-4-1856 Cr
Hardison, Sue P. to C. I. W. Albright 12-23-1868 G
Hardister, Addie T. to Joseph W. Felts 8-31-1865 (no return) Cr
Hardister, Ann to William Goodman 7-27-1831 (7-28-1831) G
Hardister, D. P. to A. P. Felts 4-16-1866 (4-25-1866) Cr
Hardister, Emma to W. T. Moore 11-23-1874 Hy
Hardister, Jans to Edward Haley 9-17-1833 (9-19-1833) G
Hardlage, Elizabeth to William Fisher 4-13-1854 (4-24-1854) Sh
Hardridge, Tabitha T. to Reuben Martin 9-7-1850 (9-9-1850) O
Hardwick, Pritena to Bryant Hunphreys 4-16-1839 (5-1-1839) Hr
Hardy, C. L. to W. T. Hatcher 10-5-1865 Hn
Hardy, Currillea J. to N. H. Belew 11-23-1870 (no return) Cr
Hardy, Eliza J. to Francis A. Merweather 3-2-1853 (no return) F
Hardy, Elizabeth to James Gilfillan 12-6-1857 (12-7-1857) Sh
Hardy, Elvira to Thomas Cheatham 8-8-1846 F
Hardy, Lucinda to Thomas Campbell 12-13-1852 Ma
Hardy, Manda to Chris Cheek 3-30-1876 (4-9-1876) L
Hardy, Marah H. to Sebastian Schoffer (Schaffer) 1-13-1874 O
Hardy, Martha E. to Johnson Perrett 10-16-1872 Cr
Hardy, Martha E. to Jos. H. Neilson 5-26-1859 Hr
Hardy, Martha E. to W. H. Rose 3-4-1861 (3-19-1861) Cr
Hardy, Mary E. to Jesse H. Lewis 12-30-1848 Ma
Hardy, Mary Elizabeth to J. W. Glasscock 3-3-1870 G
Hardy, Mary F. to Thomas H. H. Carter 12-18-1869 (12-19-1869) Cr
Hardy, Mary F. to Wm. C. Pinkley 12-29-1858 Cr
Hardy, Mary M. to Josiah Hinds 1-23-1860 Sh
Hardy, Melinda to Arnold Hall 11-15-1866 (no return) Hy
Hardy, Nancy to John N. Franklin 2-8-1852 Ma
Hardy, Sarah A. to Benj. F. Kelton 1-11-1854 (1-12-1854) Sh
Hardy, Susan E. to Jonathan Coleman 10-12-1851 (10-15-1851) O
Hardy, Susan M. to P. H. Schofer 2-10-1874 O
Hardy?, Verona A. to James R. Belew 12-22-1869 (12-23-1869) Cr
Hardy?, Elizabeth Ann to Isaac M. Daniels 4-3-1852 (4-4-1852) Hr
Hare, A. T. (Mrs.) to Jno. T. (Rev.) Baskerville 1-7-1857 (1-8-1857) Sh
Hare, Celia to Emanuel Bartlett 12-13-1869 (12-14-1869) F B
Hare, Fannie to Jim Loving 1-15-1868 F B
Hare, Hannah to Monroe Tucker 12-28-1865 (1-1-1866) F B
Hare, M. J. to A. B. Hamilton 2-6-1871 (2-7-1871) Dy
Hare, Maria to James Goode 12-24-1866 (no return) F B
Hare, Sarah S. to Eaton Bond 7-27-1840 (no return) F
Hare, Virginia A. to James F. Green 10-14-1848 (10-18-1848) F
Haren, Ann to Daniel Griffin 7-8-1863 Sh
Hargas, Sarah Ann to Riley S. Kennedy 9-17-1842 (9-21-1842) F
Hargas, Sarah to Hastings Burrow 12-9-1842 Cr
Hargate, Angelina to James A. Cooper 1-28-1858 L
Hargate, Ann to James Hodges 5-6-1858 (5-8-1858) L
Hargate, Catherine to Henry Denny 6-24-1854 (6-25-1854) L
Hargate, Ellen to A. A. Spry 1-21-1859 (1-23-1859) L
Hargate, Susan to William B. Goodman 12-18-1859 L
Hargess, J. P. to J. D. Brook 1-16-1852 (no return) F
Harget, E. A. to J. W. Curtis 4-13-1865 (no return) L
Harget, Eliza Ann to William S. Moore 6-17-1854 (6-22-1854) O
Harget, Elizabeth R. to Benjamin N. Ward 10-5-1857 (10-13-1857) O
Harget, Susan M. to Benjamin Jorden 12-28-1865 Hy
Hargett, E. A. to John W. Curtis 4-13-1865 (4-16-1865) L
Hargett, Ellen to Cornelius Young 2-23-1880 (no return) L

Hargett, Exeline to Wm. Bethsheres 3-9-1863 (no return) Hy
Hargett, M. L. to N. F. Rives (Reeves) 10-24-1866 Hy
Hargett, Mary Frances to Robert M. Patrick 4-28-1868 (4?-7-1868) L
Hargett, Mary J. to George W. Miller 2-26-1861 (no return) Hy
Hargett, Nancy E. to James H. Flowers 8-31-1876 O
Hargett, Nancy to Richard G. Reynolds 12-4-1841 (12-5-1841) O
Hargett, Rebecca M. to Daniel F. Hargett 8-3-1842 (8-4-1842) O
Hargett, Susan M. to A. G. West 2-20-1865? (2-22-1863) O
Hargett, Susan to Jonathan Nichols 6-21-1848 (6-22-1848) O
Hargis, Augustine L. to J. W. L. Hargis 12-22-1841 (12-23-1841) F
Hargis, Letha to Howard Miller 6-20-1844 Sh
Hargis, Margaret to C. R. Howal 10-24-1851 We
Hargis, Nancy S. to Robert Calewell 1-29-1844 (2-5-1844) F
Hargis, Nancy to Mathew Ervine 10-22-1830 Sh
Hargis, Phebe Emily to Andrew Herron 1-10-1833 Sh
Hargis, Priscilla J. to Ebenezer Scaggs 12-26-1850 Sh
Hargiss, Augustina to Isaac Osborne 9-16-1851 (no return) F
Hargress, Nancy to Able Whitewoth 1-10-1869 Hy
Hargrove, Amanda to George Cowan 12-16-1853 Hr
Hargrove, Elizabeth to James Barnes 9-22-1845 (9-25-1845) F
Hargrove, Harriet to Robert Kuykendall 10-5-1841 (no return) Hn
Hargrove, Mary J. to Thos. D. Baum 11-26-1849 F
Hargrove, Pamelia B. to David Fitzpatrick 11-14-1847 (11-18-1847) L
Hargus, M. to A. J. Hardin 3-24-1846 We
Hargus, Sarah Ann to Allen H. Bobo 6-3-1844 (no return) F
Harigan, Mary to M. J. Green 6-8-1861 Sh
Harington, Mary Jane to Noel E. West 2-18-1839 (2-20-1839) F
Haris, Caroline to Ervin Stephens 12-8-1847 O
Haris, Mina to John Laycook 12-6-1843 Cr
Harkey, Melinda E. to Wm. S. Nooner 10-18-1858 We
Harkins, Jane to Anthony Seals 9-27-1827 Ma
Harkleroad, Mary C. (Charlotte) to Russell Bean 5-6-1820 Sh
Harlan, Ann to Andrew Woods 12-15-1867 G B
Harlan, Charlotte C. to Levi G. Danner 6-23-1845 G
Harlan, Laura A. to R. H. Lusk 12-2-1867 G
Harlan, M. J. to J. H. Davis 6-6-1882 (6-7-1882) L
Harlan, Martha N. to John L. Jordian 8-8-1843? (9-12-1844) G
Harland, Ellen to Sim Taylor 12-12-1867 G
Harland, Harriet to John O'Neal 12-13-1866 G
Harland, Manerva Ann to James P. Kinnard 8-10-1832 (8-13-1832) Hr
Harland, Mary J. to Joseph Howard 9-9-1859 (9-11-1859) G
Harland, S. A. to D. A. Layton 8-3-1861 G
Harland, Winie C. to Julius Hale 10-7-1858 G
Harlean, Sarah B. to Phillips Holcomb 10-27-1836 (11-25-1836) G
Harlen, Frances J. to B. R. Wade 2-18-1858 We
Harley, Alice J. to Jno. C. Ellam 11-20-1871 T
Harley, Aney to Leonard Worley 3-2-1824 (3-3-1824) G
Harley, Nancy to Absolum A. White 12-1-1836 G
Harlow, N. S. to J. S. (Dr.) Hunter 10-12-1872 (10-16-1872) L
Harlow, Nancy J. to James Jenkins 4-4-1855 Hn
Harlowe, Betsy to John Christopher 3-2-1845 Hn
Harly, Margaret A. to Josiah Ward 3-26-1863 We
Harly, Martha A. R. to Benjamin Williams 10-26-1853 (3-13-1854) Hr
Harman, J. A. F. to J. H. Garrett 9-21-1871 Cr
Harman, Louisa M. to Harrington Owens 9-21-1855 Sh
Harman, Sarah F. to Thomas R. Hendricks 11-19-1858 Hn
Harman, Susan to A. S. Kieroif 5-22-1852 Sh
Harman?, Mary F. to J. M. Carter 11-13-1867 Hn
Harmen, Mariah to Sam Martin 12-21-1870 (no return) Hy
Harmes (Hannes?), Henrietta to Wm. T. White 9-10-1851 (9-13-1851) Sh
Harmon (Hannon), Fanny A. to Alexander Wheatley (Wheartly) 5-22-1856 We
Harmon(Hannon), Charlotte to Saml. Kelly 12-16-1833 Hr
Harmon, Caroline to Joseph Wray 1-20-1846 We
Harmon, Eliza Jane to James Ray 12-2-1860 Hy
Harmon, Elizabeth to Warren Bradford 2-28-1839 Hn
Harmon, Emeline to Alfred Conelly 12-26-1874 (12-27-1874) T
Harmon, Feriba A. to Willis R. Bonner 4-23-1857 Hn
Harmon, M. R. to R. D. Whitley 12-5-1867 Hy
Harmon, Martha W. to D. Reddick 3-13-1852 (no return) F
Harmon, Mary A. to Henry C. Bray 10-15-1854 Hn
Harmon, Rosanna to Josephus Barnes 12-5-1867 Hy
Harmon, Sarah T. to Thomas Woods 1-11-1862 (1-12-1862) Dy
Harn, Lucsicia to Wm. Paris 4-25-1863 Sh
Harnes, Susan J. to Marion L. Martin 7-11-1861 G
Harness, Mary A. to Wm. Hornbuckle 12-27-1858 Cr
Harns, Amanda to A. H. Fleming 5-29-1859 Hn
Harns, Elizabeth to Augustin Rollins 3-29-1843 Ma
Harnsberry, Nancy to B. J. Bush 1-4-1865 Hn
Harold, Elizabeth to W. R. Rust 5-21-1854 We
Harold, Mary N. to Richard C. Drewry 1-10-1861 We
Harp, Araminta Eveline to John Daviss 3-4-1845 F
Harp, Jackey J. to John M. Barnet 2-21-1855 (2-27-1855) Ma
Harp, Mary E. to Payton Southall 9-24-1845 O
Harp, Pernella to James M. Anderson 12-20-1867 (no return) Hn
Harp, Susan to Hiram Anderson 5-8-1828 Ma
Harp, Virginia to Green C. Howlett 9-15-1842 (9-13?-1842) Ma
Harpe, Mary to John Pollan 11-13-1827 Ma

Harper (Hanssen?), Caroline H. to Charles P. Wiley 6-8-1854 Sh
Harper, Agnes M. to Calvin H. Callicott 11-1-1849 O
Harper, Agnes to Alexander Hamure? 12-17-1850 Hn
Harper, Allice to Richard Newbill 12-28-1872 (12-24?-1872) Cr
Harper, Amanda to Henry Elder 12-27-1869 G B
Harper, Annie to Thomas Cruse 7-7-1865 (7-10-1865) Cr
Harper, Arminta H. to James W. Powell 11-15-1860 O
Harper, Bennie to Bayless D. Vaught 4-2-1866 G
Harper, Betsy to Richard Dabb 6-22-1826 Hr
Harper, Catherine A. to Joseph H. Barton 2-3-1849 Sh
Harper, E. A. to Jas. Polk 5-14-1867 O
Harper, Eliza L. to John N. Whiteside(s) 11-21-1839 O
Harper, Eliza to William Elder 3-4-1829 (3-7-1829) G
Harper, Elizabeth to Nimrod Burrow 11-15-1861 (no return) Cr
Harper, Elizabeth to Stephen Box 1-28-1835 Hr
Harper, Elizabeth to Wm. A. Freeman 3-20-1845 (no return) We
Harper, Emily to Wm. Newbill 12-4-1863 (no return) Cr
Harper, Emma to Wesley Harris 1-27-1879 (no return) L B
Harper, F. E. to F. P. Smith 7-22-1876 (7-23-1876) Dy
Harper, Frances to William Clark 3-9-1850 Sh
Harper, Frances to Wm. Simpson 8-15-1844 (8-20?-1844) Hr
Harper, Hariett E. to James H. Maupin 8-22-1850 O
Harper, Harriett to Wesley Wallis 4-7-1866 O
Harper, Isadora to William H. Cullim 12-21-1871 T
Harper, Jennie to Abraham Brown 5-26-1869 (5-29-1869) F B
Harper, Kizzy to Parker Hines 6-4-1881 (no return) L
Harper, L. A. to James M. Hooper 1-26-1861 (no return) Hy
Harper, L. E. to T. J. Pierce 1-23-1872 (1-24-1872) Dy
Harper, L. J. to W. C. Bird 6-2-1862 (no return) Hy
Harper, L. to George Wade 3-7-1867 G
Harper, Louisa C. to John R. Luton 9-5-1867 (no return) Hy
Harper, Louizer Ellen to W. S. Harper 4-17-1868 G
Harper, Luler to J. D. Cullens 10-28-1868 T
Harper, M. C. to P. W. Hester 8-6-1865 Cr
Harper, M. E. to P. H. Marbery 12-26-1867 O
Harper, M. E. to W. H. Anderson 7-4-1866 (7-4-1866) O
Harper, M. F. to C. C. Moody 2-21-1861 (no return) Hy
Harper, M. J. to A. C. Anderson 10-15-1867 (10-17-1867) O
Harper, Margaret J. to Hezekiah J. Wade 2-13-1856 O
Harper, Margaret to George Gibson 12-8-1825 O
Harper, Margarett A. to James H. Whiteside 9-20-1848 (9-21-1848) O
Harper, Martha Jane to Marion Adams 9-29-1852 (9-30-1852) O
Harper, Martha M. to William H. Whiteside 6-23-1840 (6-25-1840) O
Harper, Martha T. to Charles McAlister 2-6-1833 O
Harper, Martha T. to William A. Brown 9-1-1832 O
Harper, Martha to Edward Irby 3-12-1851 (3-13-1851) Sh
Harper, Mary A. to J. B. Rickman 1-3-1867 (no return) Hn
Harper, Mary A. to P. H. W. Grammar 12-24-1853 (no return) F
Harper, Mary Ann to Thos. P. Callicoat 5-29-1861 O
Harper, Mary D. to William H. Whiteside 1-9-1843 (1-12-1843) O
Harper, Mary E. to James Bedford 9-15-1850 (10-4-1850) O
Harper, Mary L. to James B. Hogge 10-9-1833 O
Harper, Mary to Parsons Owen 4-28-1874 Hy
Harper, Mary to Wm. Wallis 7-20-1866 O
Harper, Mattie A. to J. A. B. Batchelor 11-2-1869 (no return) Hy
Harper, Mattie H. to J. M. King 1-2-1862 G
Harper, Mattie to Ben F. Benton 12-2-1874 L
Harper, Minnie to Virgil Nevels 2-8-1871 Hy
Harper, N. H. to J. J. Carroll 2-13-1873 Cr
Harper, Nancy Adaline to Briggs Barker 8-20-1862 Be
Harper, Nancy Ann to Lindsey G. Nixon 8-22-1845 (8-28-1845) Hr
Harper, Nancy C. to Fielding W. Derrington 10-?-1849 Hn
Harper, Nancy J. to S. M. Gardner 5-30-1866 O
Harper, Nancy Jane to E. W. Cain 8-10-1848 Be
Harper, Nancy R. to John C. Johnston 12-31-1844 O
Harper, Nancy to Cyrus Turner 3-18-1868 G
Harper, Permelia to Joseph B. Anderson 1-20-1845 (no return) F
Harper, Phillis to Anderson Williams 12-28-1868 (12-30-1868) T
Harper, Pressilla to F. E. Becton 2-17-1838 (2-18-1838) Hr
Harper, Rebecca C. to Goerge W. Culipher 2-13-1866 Hy
Harper, S. J. to M. N. Frink 12-19-1866 Hy
Harper, Sallie Ann to Walker Fitzpatrick 11-30-1872 L B
Harper, Sarah A. to S. P. Jones 12-22-1845 Sh
Harper, Sarah Ann to Thomas J. Wray 12-9-1849 Hn
Harper, Sarah Jane to Denis Durham 1-31-1851 Sh
Harper, Sarah Jane to Dennis Durham 2-5-1851 (2-7-1851) Sh
Harper, Susan G. to W. R. Sparks 3-8-1873 (3-28-1873) Cr
Harper, Susan to George Chamber 10-16-1874 (10-17-1874) T
Harper, Susan to William Polk 4-3-1856 O
Harper, Tibetha C. to Nicholas W. Cabler 8-22-1838 G
Harpeth, Sarah J. to Wm. H. Beard 1-3-1862 We
Harphan, Annie to Henry Egner 11-7-1863 Sh
Harpole, Arabella E. to William G. Newgent 4-19-1853 (4-20-1853) O
Harpole, Roda to B. F. Hester 12-16-1875 O
Harpole, Sallie P. to C. B. Hodges 11-18-1873 (11-20-1873) O
Harpole, Sarah H. to John A. Harpole 1-3-1855 (1-9-1855) G
Harpole, Sarah Jane to Solomon P. Harpole 2-4-1868 G

Brides

Harpole, Sarah P. to Wm. Tinsley 8-21-1841 (8-30-1841) G
Harpole, Susannah B. to Andrew Patrick 12-7-1846 G
Harpoll, Barbary J. to William G. James 1-4-1843 (1-5-1843) G
Harpoll, Eliza A. to Cooper B. Jones 10-7-1837 (10-10-1837) G
Harpon, Laura to C. W. Goyer 7-3-1849 Sh
Harpool, Cincinnatti T. to Thomas F. Underwood 2-27-1869 (3-4-1869) O
Harpool, E. C. to O. C. Graham 6-14-1863 O
Harpool, M. H. to Jas. a. Jones 12-12-1871 (12-14-1871) O
Harpool, Permelia to James H. Chandler 7-18-1846 (7-19-1846) O
Harpool, Susan B. to Andrew J. Patrick 11-2-1846 Ma
Harral, Mary Ann to Henry Stewart 8-27-1845 Sh
Harralston, Jane to James E. Lipford 10-19-1848 Sh
Harred, Milly H. to P. J. Fullen 12-21-1867 (12-22-1867) L
Harrel, Elizabeth Jane to Jesse M. Hunt 9-8-1847 Sh
Harrel, M. C. (Mrs.) to W. B. Hines 11-4-1864 (11-10-1864) Sh
Harreld, Malinda to J. J. W. Pittenger 4-27-1867 G
Harrell (Howell?), Sarah C. to Sanders Isham 1-8-1873 (1-9-1873) L
Harrell(Howell?), Nancy to Robert Michell 8-5-1828 (4?-6-1828) Hr
Harrell, Adaline to Henry Jones 6-2-1866 (no return) F B
Harrell, Adline to T. J. Smothers 12-26-1867 Hy
Harrell, Amanda E. to Calvin W. Bland 2-7-1863 (2-8-1863) Sh
Harrell, Amanda to Henry Johnson 1-28-1868 (no return) Hy
Harrell, Bell to John Crowder 1-25-1874 Hy
Harrell, Caledonia to V. H. Swift 11-12-1859 (11-13-1859) F
Harrell, Drusilla P. to J.(I) J. McDaniel 12-8-1855 (12-13-1855) Sh
Harrell, E. T. to James S. Brown 2-14-1854 Cr
Harrell, Elizabeth Jane to Alfred McBride 8-29-1849 Sh
Harrell, Elizabeth S. to Robert J. Morris 1-30-1855 (2-1-185_) Sh
Harrell, Elvira C. to J. Milton Sanders 2-17-1854 Sh
Harrell, Emily W. to Campbell C. Coleman 1-13-1836 Sh
Harrell, F. J. to J. G. McMahan 9-26-1855 (9-27-1855) Ma
Harrell, J. C. to John Cotterill 8-28-1863 Sh
Harrell, Lucy A. to John H. Mitchell 5-13-1862 (5-21-1862) F
Harrell, Lucy A. to John H. Mitchell 5-13-1862 (not endorsed) F
Harrell, M. A. to J. N. Williams 10-29-1860 (11-1-1860) F
Harrell, M. C. to S. G. Neal 12-13-1859 O
Harrell, M. J. to Wm. H. Vawter 1-2-1866 (1-3-1866) Cr
Harrell, Martha M. to B. F. Woodall 9-16-1861 (no return) Cr
Harrell, Mary Ann to Miles Goolsby 8-15-1837 Sh
Harrell, Mary E. to Robt. A. Haley 10-17-1860 Dy
Harrell, Mary Y. to J. W. Wilson 9-26-1856 Cr
Harrell, Maurina to Wm. C. Lewis 7-27-1843 Sh
Harrell, Molly to Wm. D. Lannum 11-28-1864 (no return) Cr
Harrell, Susan A. to Wm. P. Kirkpatrick 1-29-1840 Cr
Harrell?, Malinda to Absalom Overton 1-18-1845 (1-23-1845) Hr
Harrell?, Sarah G. to Andrew Merrell 12-24-1851 Cr
Harrelle, M. E. to W. T. Maclin 9-1-1868 Hy
Harri, Mary Ann to R. J. Flanigan 5-14-1864 Sh
Harriett, McFarland to Sam Pewett 12-6-1877 Hy
Harrill, Martha A. to Robert N. Bond 2-16-1849 Sh
Harrington, Bridget to Richard Rambury (Bambury?) 4-28-1864 Sh
Harrington, Louisa to Joel Rutherford 3-19-1846 Sh
Harrington, M. to S. L. Davis 12-9-1863 Sh
Harrington, Margaret to John Hassett 6-30-1862 Sh
Harrington, Mary W. to Alfred W. Powel 10-2-1828 Ma
Harris (Haynes), Evaline to Collin H. Adams 7-4-1849 O
Harris(Hanis?), Mary R. to Benj. Owens 5-29-1839 (6-1-1839) Hr
Harris, A. E. to Pinkny Dickson 10-22-1851 (no return) F
Harris, Ada to Henry Connell 5-18-1876 (no return) Dy
Harris, Adaline to James Talley 4-29-1876 (4-30-1876) Dy B
Harris, Adaline to Ralph Davis 9-19-1869 (no return) Cr
Harris, Ailsy O. to John J. Lambert 7-19-1848 Hr
Harris, Amanda A. to George Brimm 12-25-1871 Dy
Harris, Amanda A. to Vinson Edwards 12-4-1866 (12-5-1866) Ma
Harris, Amanda to Isaac Canada 9-6-1879 (9-7-1879) Dy
Harris, Amanda to Phillip Curry 8-21-1867 G
Harris, Amanda to Robt. Boyce 10-28-1871 (11-2-1871) T
Harris, Ammarilla to Alfred Williams 8-6-1839 F
Harris, Ann C. to Duke J. Beadles 11-18-1857 Ma
Harris, Ann Eliza to Richmond Turpin 9-22-1863 (9-23-1863) Dy
Harris, Ann F. to Clark Pinkley 8-19-1852 Cr
Harris, Ann to Columbus Helm 2-9-1877 L B
Harris, Anna L. to James C. Roe 2-20-1867 (no return) Dy
Harris, Anna to Christopher C. Poindexter 4-24-1871 (5-5-1871) F
Harris, Annetta to A. M. O'Quinn 2-3-1866 (2-6-1866) F
Harris, Annis to James Bogard 7-14-1837 (7-27-1837) Hr
Harris, Annis to Steven Cannon 3-11-1863 (3-17-1863) F
Harris, Arineth to James Mickleberry 10-28-1823 Sh
Harris, Artesia to Frankling Holcomb 12-28-1875 (no return) Hy
Harris, Athena to Sam Alexandra 6-11-1870 (6-10?-1870) Dy
Harris, Aurelia to Whitman H. Hearn 1-11-1847 Hy
Harris, B. J. to A. E. Moore 12-24-1872 (12-25-1872) Dy
Harris, Bettie to Archer Rayond 10-2-1869 T
Harris, C. to R. R. Safaran(Saffamans?) 12-23-1869 G
Harris, C. I. W. to Jonathan A. Harris 9-29-1853 O
Harris, C. to Henry Eubanks 7-11-1845 Cr
Harris, Candas to Redman Bramblett 2-6-1840 O

Harris, Caroline to Thomas Rickett 1-7-1870 (1-8-1870) F B
Harris, Cassa to Friday Payne 2-5-1870 T
Harris, Catherine to Alexander Flemming 3-10-1846 Sh
Harris, Charlotte J.(C) to Dan C. Young 10-21-1840 T
Harris, Clemintine to John C. Hubbard 10-24-1837 Hr
Harris, Colorado to Robert Gutherie 11-4-1854 (11-5-1854) T
Harris, Cora E. to W. T. Watson 1-14-1861 (1-15-1861) F
Harris, Cornelia to Jas. Rodgers 6-30-1849 (7-1-1849) F
Harris, Costinza Missouri to Doctor Wesley McFarlane 12-18-1844 (12-19-1844) T
Harris, Cynthia Ann to Everett B. Fleming 6-25-1845 Sh
Harris, Damsel to Mason Clabron 1-4-1868 Hy
Harris, Delia to Isaac Smith 11-26-1869 (no return) F B
Harris, Delila to W. H. Lindsy 10-22-1839 F
Harris, Delilah to Jesse B. Lindsay 8-3-1843 T
Harris, Densi to John Scott 4-23-1870 Dy
Harris, E. F. to J. W. Smith 5-29-1866 (6-3-1866) Cr
Harris, E. M. to J. D. Carroll 1-14-1861 (1-15-1861) Dy
Harris, E. M. to James Bedford 3-14-1861 O
Harris, E. R. to W. H. Corum 9-4-1875 (9-6-1875) O
Harris, E. W. to M. C. Lane 1-25-1858 (1-27-1858) G
Harris, Eadie to Allen Campbell 1-21-1873 (1-3?-1873) Dy
Harris, Eady to Frank Walker 12-16-1867 T
Harris, Eady to Frank Walker 8-12-1867 T
Harris, Eliza A. to Joseph D. Tidwell 10-31-1866 Ma
Harris, Eliza W. to David J. Kenaday 3-8-1838 Ma
Harris, Eliza to John Barnett 6-10-1863 O
Harris, Eliza to John C. Goodrich 3-27-1844 (3-28-1844) Ma
Harris, Eliza to Reuben Rawlings 4-24-1871 (4-25-1871) F B
Harris, Elizabeth H. to William N. Butt 6-20-1856 Ma
Harris, Elizabeth P. to Jonathan McCraw 1-4-1851 (no return) F
Harris, Elizabeth to David E. Putney 9-25-1831 (9-27-1831) Hr
Harris, Elizabeth to E. D. Scates 1-11-1859 (no return) We
Harris, Elizabeth to J. C. Bowlin 1-4-1853 (1-5-1853) Sh
Harris, Elizabeth to John Coleman 8-3-1857 Cr
Harris, Elizabeth to Jonathan J. Jones 2-19-1855 (2-21-1855) Sh
Harris, Elizabeth to Joseph Hogg 3-3-1867 Be
Harris, Elizabeth to Joseph Reddeck 11-28-1869 Hy
Harris, Elizabeth to Ridley Clifton 4-11-1846 (no return) F
Harris, Elizabeth to S. Melton 10-4-1866 Hn
Harris, Elizabeth to Thomas Boyett 12-15-1839 (12-19-1839) Ma
Harris, Ella to Alex Horton 6-6-1874 (6-11-1874) Dy B
Harris, Ella to J. M. Wilkinson 9-19-1870 (9-24-1870) F
Harris, Ella to John Banks 11-3-1870 G
Harris, Ellen to Henry Eubanks 6-24-1852 Cr
Harris, Ellen to J. W. Watson 10-18-1860 L
Harris, Ellen to Marion Mills 5-25-1868 (5-26-1868) Ma
Harris, Ellen to Wm. R. Gantlett 5-20-1864 (5-26-1864) O
Harris, Emeline D. to Robert Y. Mickleberry 10-23-1823 Sh
Harris, Emeline to Hampton Liggett 11-21-1838 (11-25-1838) Ma
Harris, Emeline to James W. Scott 12-6-1848 G
Harris, Emily to Jim Jordan 1-26-1878 (1-31-1878) L B
Harris, Emma G. to William E. Tomlinson 11-19-1866 (11-21-1866) Ma
Harris, Emma to Aleck Saunders 8-22-1874 (9-22-1874) Dy
Harris, Emma to Charlie Hinton 3-15-1884 (3-16-1884) L
Harris, Emma to J. P. Walker 10-29-1873 Dy
Harris, Esther to Wesley Davis 8-21-1869 (8-13?-1869) F B
Harris, Fannie F. to J. I. Johnson 2-7-1866 (2-8-1866) F
Harris, Fanny to Dennis Parker 12-28-1868 (no return) Dy
Harris, Fanny to Jack Drake 2-24-1875 Hy
Harris, Florence M. to John G. Rives 5-10-1864 Sh
Harris, Florence to James Jones 5-13-1874 T
Harris, Frances Eviline to J. H. Crihfield 10-30-1883 (11-1-1883) L
Harris, Frances to Nathan Smith 4-19-1870 (no return) Dy
Harris, Francis J. to James L. Bell 9-27-1859 (no return) We
Harris, Georga to Willis Johnson 12-17-1873 T
Harris, Hannah to William Jarratt 11-11-1869 (no return) Hy
Harris, Harriet R. to James T. Williams 1-29-1850 (1-31-1850) Hr
Harris, Helen to William N. Butts 7-15-1852 Ma
Harris, James to J. B. Neal 4-7-1879 Dy
Harris, Jane A. to James H. Porter 7-25-1848 Sh
Harris, Jane A. to Robert Quinn 5-14-1852 F
Harris, Jane C. to Ben Calhoun 1-5-1871 T
Harris, Jane H. to James H. Grove 1-29-1850 (1-31-1850) Hr
Harris, Jane L. to John M. Phillips 6-7-1855 Ma
Harris, Jane to James G. Casey 9-30-1861 (10-6-1861) Hr
Harris, Jane to Solomon Parker 8-16-1868 G
Harris, Jane to Willis W. Slayton 11-20-1860 Dy
Harris, Jane to Zeke Heald 2-16-1860 (2-17-1860) O
Harris, Jenny to Sam Garner 12-28-1874 Hy
Harris, Jerome W. to James R. West 9-4-1841 Ma
Harris, Julia A. to Richd. Borum 1-4-1870 (no return) Hy
Harris, Julia Ann to James Greer 10-21-1849 Be
Harris, Julia to Jefferson Bolton 1-20-1836 Sh *
Harris, Julia to Reuben Bunch 1-29-1883 (not endorsed) L
Harris, Juliet to M. B. King 6-16-1846 Hn
Harris, Kate to R. W. Dorsey 4-16-1868 G

Harris, L. C. to James E. Fowler 3-1-1848 Hn
Harris, L. to P. R. Mitchel 1-30-1872 (1-31-1872) T
Harris, Laura N. to W. P. Proudfit 11-24-1852 Sh
Harris, Laura to J. A. Mason? 10-26-1871 (10-27-1871) T
Harris, Laura to Lewis Edwards 5-11-1867 (no return) Hy
Harris, Levica Ann to Franklin Reddick 3-10-1860 (no return) Hy
Harris, Livina to Francis Williams 7-30-1870 T
Harris, Lou to John W. Wilson 10-21-1867 (no return) Dy
Harris, Louanna to William P. Robertson 9-3-1867 (9-4-1867) Ma
Harris, Louisa A. to Samuel J. Jones 10-26-1869 (no return) Dy
Harris, Louisa C. to Samuel S. Watkins 12-20-1847 (12-21-1847) Ma
Harris, Louisa D. to C. E. Birthwright 4-2-1846 (no return) We
Harris, Louisa H. to Elijah Williams 5-29-1852 (5-30-1852) Sh
Harris, Louisa P. to Wm. D. Lee 5-7-1844 Cr
Harris, Louisa to James O. Manard 2-1-1847 Cr
Harris, Louiza to Isaac Marley 12-19-1868 (no return) L
Harris, Louiza to James Hibbitt 10-31-1882 (11-2-1882) L
Harris, Lucenday to Pleasant Cussip 6-9-1840 Cr
Harris, Lucinda B. to Charles M. Jackson 2-15-1859 Ma
Harris, Lucinda to Austin Cook 12-13-1851 Sh
Harris, Lucinda to Lafayette Haskin 12-30-1878 (1-18-1879) Dy
Harris, Lucretia to Edward M. Myrick 10-14-1840 (10-15-1840) Hr
Harris, Lucy to Mingo Bernard 12-27-1871 (12-28-1871) T
Harris, Lundy? to John McCoy 1-22-1878 (1-23-1878) Dy
Harris, Lydia P. to William N. Province 2-13-1840 O
Harris, Lydia to John McAnally 1-1-1832 Sh
Harris, M. Alice to James H. Clayton 3-6-1866 (3-7-1866) Ma
Harris, M. E. to Andrew S. Parks 7-8-1868 (no return) Dy
Harris, M. F. to W. J. Lowe 12-5-1867 G
Harris, Malinda to John E. Smith 4-10-1848 (4-15-1848) T
Harris, Malsey to Newit Harris 2-14-1853 (no return) F
Harris, Malvina to J. B. White 7-10-1884 (7-15-1884) L
Harris, Malviny to Alexander Rhodes 6-10-1862 We
Harris, Manerva F. to William F. Rollins 6-1-1867 (6-2-1867) T
Harris, Manerva to Lee Foster 12-24-1872 (12-26-1872) Cr B
Harris, Margaret A. to Adam S. Hope 6-28-1855 Hn
Harris, Margaret D. to General M. Francis 6-23-1866 (6-24-1866) Ma
Harris, Margaret J. to Henry Holcomb 1-2-1834 Sh
Harris, Margaret L.? to William Henry Wilson 4-16-1840 T
Harris, Margaret to Alle G. Tipton 6-30-1840 (7-9-1840) O
Harris, Margaret to Harrison Warbritton 11-18-1851 Cr
Harris, Margaret to John McNairn 11-5-1874 (11-6-1874) L
Harris, Margaret to Thomas C. Nelson 3-16-1846 Sh
Harris, Margaret to Willis Lane 4-1-1861 (4-3-1861) O
Harris, Maria to Robert Coleman 12-28-1869 Cr
Harris, Mariah to Samuel Espy 2-25-1875 (2-26-1875) L B
Harris, Mariah to Samuel Hollaway 8-25-1845 G
Harris, Martha A. to Buford Bond 2-16-1850 Cr
Harris, Martha A. to Granville C. Hurt 8-2-1839 Cr
Harris, Martha Ann to J. W. Harbson 10-1-1865 G
Harris, Martha B. to John Swor 4-1-1846 (no return) Hn
Harris, Martha F. to Jackson McClure 12-23-1852 (12-26-1852) Sh
Harris, Martha J. to Samuel Ball 12-8-1869 Hy
Harris, Martha J. to W. R. Osteen 2-22-1875 (2-23-1875) L
Harris, Martha V. to Jas. McWherter Faris 2-4-1856 T
Harris, Martha to Daniel Williams 2-25-1846 (2-26-1846) T
Harris, Martha to Harry Grimm 6-30-1876 Dy
Harris, Martha to Jacob Ross 5-13-1863 (5-16-1863) Cr
Harris, Martha to John Sumers 2-16-1857 We
Harris, Martha to Richard Haskins 8-19-1874 (8-20-1874) Dy
Harris, Martha to Wm. P. Ingram 6-4-1849 (6-5-1849) F
Harris, Marthena to Joseph T. Leverett 11-26-1870 (11-27-1870) F
Harris, Mary A. E. to Pleasant A. Gowan 7-30-1849 Ma
Harris, Mary A. to Alexder. Burkhart 12-4-1856 (no return) F
Harris, Mary A. to David A. Jones 11-10-1868 (11-11-1868) Ma
Harris, Mary A. to James Mayfield ?-?-1862? Mn
Harris, Mary A. to William Dorrin 2-14-1845 (no return) We
Harris, Mary Ann to John Caldwell 10-12-1827 Hr
Harris, Mary Ann to Joshua Monan 7-6-1831 G
Harris, Mary Ann to M. H. Dozier 5-19-1860 (5-20-1860) Sh
Harris, Mary C. to J. H. Clifton 5-15-1875 (5-16-1875) L
Harris, Mary E. to Gastin Rollins 5-27-1846 (6-4-1846) Ma
Harris, Mary E. to Henry M. Robards 5-28-1867 (5-29-1867) F
Harris, Mary E. to Jackson Hamblin 7-25-1861 We
Harris, Mary E. to T. N. Prewett 1-4-1860 (1-5-1860) Hr
Harris, Mary E. to W. H. Province 12-17-1850 Cr
Harris, Mary E. to William S. Scott 4-4-1861 O
Harris, Mary F. to R. A. Carson 10-5-1863 (no return) Hn
Harris, Mary G. to Alexander Baber 11-13-1838 (no return) Hn
Harris, Mary J. to Jno. L. Tabor 9-26-1859 (9-28-1859) Hr
Harris, Mary J. to John W. Hester 12-12-1854 (no return) F
Harris, Mary J. to W. B. Beavers 2-19-1866 (2-20-1866) F
Harris, Mary J. to W. D. Wilkerson 10-9-1854 (no return) F
Harris, Mary M. to Wm. J. Laycook 1-31-1849 Cr
Harris, Mary Matilda to Richard S. Barret 12-22-1847 T
Harris, Mary R. to Henry A. Slate 1-6-1855 (1-7-1855) Sh
Harris, Mary S. to William O. Bryan 12-16-1833 (12-18-1833) Hr

Harris, Mary T. to John W. Stanley 2-24-1842 O
Harris, Mary to Addison McMillin 5-18-1830 Hr
Harris, Mary to Albert Clay 12-28-1870 (12-29-1870) T
Harris, Mary to Amos Vincent 9-21-1835 Sh
Harris, Mary to B. F. Warbritten 12-21-1864 (12-22-1864) Cr
Harris, Mary to Christopher C. Pickings 1-31-1840 Hn
Harris, Mary to D. C. King 2-6-1869 (2-8-1869) F
Harris, Mary to Dyes Cain 12-15-1832 (12-27-1832) Hr
Harris, Mary to Ed. Jeruiza? Max 9-11-1869 (9-15-1869) T
Harris, Mary to George Rollins 3-9-1871 T
Harris, Mary to Green Jones 1-1-1874 T
Harris, Mary to Joel J. Green 8-13-1878 (8-15-1878) L
Harris, Mary to John Dickason 10-25-1851 (no return) F
Harris, Mary to Thos. S. Jackson 5-26-1845 (no return) F
Harris, Mary to William A. Thompson 1-24-1838 Hn
Harris, Mattie A. to Jas. E. Yancey 12-5-1866 F
Harris, Melvina to Thomas H. Winslow 10-5-1866 (10-7-1866) Ma
Harris, Melvina to William Holloman 1-7-1863 (1-?-1863) Ma
Harris, Milley Jane to G. W. Wilson 6-23-1863 (6-24-1863) L
Harris, Millie to Polk Howard 12-26-1872 Dy
Harris, Milly to Isham Sills 3-1-1833 Hr
Harris, Minerva to W. W. Bruce 5-25-1861 (5-30-1861) Dy
Harris, Miranda A. to Andrew Mills 12-17-1853 Ma
Harris, Mollie to Travis G. Golding 1-15-1874 L
Harris, N. E. to A. S. McFarlan 1-15-1867 G
Harris, Nancy Ann to John D. Blanton 6-13-1868 (6-14-1868) O
Harris, Nancy E. to Lemuel Newsom 1-4-1856 Ma
Harris, Nancy J. to Thomas H. Harris 3-12-1848 Hn
Harris, Nancy to A. J. Covdy? 10-15-1874 T
Harris, Nancy to Asa Cox 12-21-1835 (12-22-1835) Hr
Harris, Nancy to D. Steelman 8-19-1880 L
Harris, Nancy to Finny Wiggins 10-10-1866 (10-13-1866) F B
Harris, Nancy to T. P. Guinn 6-26-1858 O
Harris, Nancy to William Mulherin 4-22-1875 Dy
Harris, Narcissa D. to James M. Alexander 8-29-1844 Ma
Harris, Narcissus to Robert Newsom 10-15-1850 Ma
Harris, Nelly Ann to Wm. Riley 10-1-1869 (10-3-1869) F B
Harris, Octavia to Wm. C. White 11-20-1859 (11-21-1859) Hr
Harris, P. S. to W. M. Shepherd 11-5-1860 (11-6-1860) Sh
Harris, Pamelia P. to John Caraway 8-28-1854 (9-4-1854) Sh
Harris, Parmelia to James M. Jacobs 12-2-1858 (12-8-1858) Hr
Harris, Patience to Ben Hill 8-29-1868 (8-30-1868) F B
Harris, Phalba M. to William Hammon 2-28-1867 Ma
Harris, Piety to Anthony Brinkley 7-24-1848 Cr
Harris, Prudence to Solomon P. Bright 12-8-1833 O
Harris, Prudence to Solomon P. Wright 12-8-1833 O
Harris, Puss to Champ Peak 12-11-1876 (no return) Dy
Harris, R. to J. S. Farrar 1-21-1861 (1-23-1861) F
Harris, Rachel to Alonzo Outlaw 12-20-1877 Hy
Harris, Rachel to Will Woods 4-5-1879 (4-7-1879) Dy
Harris, Rebecca A. to Wm. C. Jones 9-23-1858 Cr
Harris, Rebecca to J. A. Minard 11-25-1845 Cr
Harris, Rebecca to Theophilus Shaw 5-5-1835 Hr
Harris, Ritteran to John Dougan 1-15-1845 F
Harris, Rose Ann to Wm. Mason 12-26-1867 (12-29-1867) F B
Harris, Rosetta to Henry Beacham 1-24-1869 G B
Harris, Rosetta to Peter Lark 1-18-1872 (1-20-1872) T
Harris, Ruhamy to Andrew J. Barnes 9-18-1851 Be
Harris, S. M. to Wm. N. Marshall 12-11-1854 Cr
Harris, Sallie E. to M. D. Welch 10-5-1858 Sh
Harris, Sallie to Albert Jones 10-10-1877 (no return) Dy
Harris, Sallie to Booker Howard 4-2-1873 (3?-2-1873) Dy
Harris, Sally to Nat. Cox 7-24-1855 Be
Harris, Sally to Saml. Ross 1-24-1841 Cr
Harris, Sarah A. E. to George W. Hardin 6-11-1838 (no return) F
Harris, Sarah Ann to Robert H. Adams 11-9-1843 Sh
Harris, Sarah C. to Jesse W. Gillespie 9-23-1845 Sh
Harris, Sarah E. to D. J. Herrington 1-27-1842 (2-2-1842) F
Harris, Sarah E. to L. G. Carter 2-1-1863 G
Harris, Sarah J. to James Amones 9-12-1865 (9-13-1865) F
Harris, Sarah to B. P. Braden 2-3-1849 F
Harris, Sarah to S. S. Nesbitt 12-26-1864 (12-27-1864) Cr
Harris, Sarah to Samuel L. Swinney 4-17-1868 (no return) Cr
Harris, Sela to Clark Mange 11-20-1869 (12-6-1869) L
Harris, Susan H. to N. W. Galloway 5-1-1871 (5-2-1871) F
Harris, Susan to Jasper Cozart 1-13-1876 Dy
Harris, Susan to John R. Waldrop 10-22-1845 (10-23-1845) G
Harris, Susie to W. M. Paris 11-5-1873 L
Harris, Tempie to H. Russell 4-25-1870 Hy
Harris, Thedonia to L. T. Sweat 3-14-1868 (3-16-1868) F
Harris, Thera to Charles Chamberlin 1-7-1847 (1-10-1847) Ma
Harris, Tishie to A. Bradshaw 12-28-1870 (12-29-1870) Dy
Harris, V. F. to Peter H. Woods 12-18-1850 Cr
Harris, Virginia A. to John A. Covington 2-26-1866 (2-27-1866) F
Harris?, Becky to Boyd Calhoon 12-29-1865 (1-14-1866) F
Harris?, Marry A. to Josiah Grantham 11-3-1859 Hr
Harrison(Hardison?), Frances A. to James G. Wyatt 2-12-1847 Hr

Harrison, Aggy M. to William E. Nelson 12-28-1875 L
Harrison, Alice to A. L. Love 12-12-1870 (12-15-1870) Dy
Harrison, Amanda to Robert Guthrie 11-26-1855 (11-29-1855) T
Harrison, Anna to Albert P. Erwin 12-16-1861 Sh
Harrison, Aurora to John Peterson 6-26-1866 Ma
Harrison, B. A. to A. Odom 3-6-1866 G
Harrison, Bettie P. to Robt. T. Bond 10-11-1864 (10-25-1865?) Sh
Harrison, Caroline to James Green 10-5-1867 Be
Harrison, Caroline to Luke Bond 1-12-1870 (1-13-1870) L
Harrison, Catherine to Aaron Branch 12-5-1838 (12-6-1838) G
Harrison, Charlett to Charles Claiburne 3-22-1869 T '
Harrison, E. A. to Robert P. Baker 12-8-1866 G
Harrison, Eliza Jane to Thomas Anderson 8-7-1854 Ma
Harrison, Eliza Rebecca to James M. Bandy 3-22-1879 (3-23-1879) Dy
Harrison, Elizabeth A. to W. N. Wilson 8-25-1853 Be
Harrison, Elizabeth A. to W. N. Wilson 8-25-1853 Be CC
Harrison, Elizabeth to Henry Ellerman 8-6-1864 (8-8-1864) Sh
Harrison, Elizabeth to Peter S. Moore 10-1-1846 Sh
Harrison, Ellen to Joseph Kelly 4-1-1857 Sh
Harrison, Emer to Cyrus Gibbs 2-15-1867 (2-16-1867) T
Harrison, Emma to A. H. Lott 12-24-1881 (12-25-1881) L
Harrison, Emma to James Snell 7-20-1867 G
Harrison, Frances America to Geo. Gideon Coats 9-2-1846 (9-3-1846) T
Harrison, Hannah T. to Nathan M. Burns 1-13-1840 Hr
Harrison, Hesterann to Daniel J. Stafford 8-2-1841 (8-12-1841) F
Harrison, Isabella I. to Wiley B. Jones 11-20-1867 Hy
Harrison, Isabella to John M. Jefferies 1-19-1871 Hy
Harrison, J. E. to M. F. Ward 1-3-1868 G
Harrison, Jane to Samuel Roe 6-24-1851 (6-26-1851) T
Harrison, Julia (Mrs.) to James M. Hammond 7-8-1866 G
Harrison, Julia A. to M. L. Hays 11-11-1854 (11-12-1854) G
Harrison, Julia to James Willis 1-1-1868 G
Harrison, L. C. to H. S. Walker 12-24-1862 (1-8-1863) Dy
Harrison, Louisa V. to Wm. B. Massengale 1-4-1872 O
Harrison, Louisa to James M. Thompson 10-5-1843 F
Harrison, Lucinda to John Tipler 11-7-1843 (11-9-1843) Hr
Harrison, Lucy A. to William H. Myrick 2-24-1855 (2-26-1855) Sh
Harrison, Lucy Ann to John Reeves 10-31-1855 Sh
Harrison, Lula F. to J. A. Webb 12-24-1877 (12-26-1877) L
Harrison, Lydia Wheaton to W. R. Kendall 12-27-1869 Ma
Harrison, M. E. to J. Thomas Talley 12-24-1873 Dy
Harrison, M. J. to J. A. Bishop 4-14-1880 L
Harrison, M. J. to John W. Burkett 2-2-1861 Be
Harrison, M. W. to A. D. Furguson 2-9-1869 G
Harrison, Margaret A. W. to Walter J. McDaniel 3-22-1850 (3-26-1850) O
Harrison, Marinda F. to Richard Lannum 1-10-1866 G
Harrison, Martha C. to Benj. J. Brevard 1-24-1851 Cr
Harrison, Martha J. to James Latta 12-7-1846 (12-8-1846) G
Harrison, Martha J. to William A. Hargett 5-2-1871 (5-4-1871) L
Harrison, Martha L. to J. L. McBride 3-19-1855 (3-21-1855) Hr
Harrison, Martha N. (Miss) to Robt. Sanderson 9-15-1864 Sh
Harrison, Martha to Isaac Williams 3-1-1870 (3-3-1870) F B
Harrison, Mary A. to John Sommer 5-30-1859 Sh
Harrison, Mary Ann to Maxvill Davis 4-24-1844 Sh
Harrison, Mary Ann to Reubin B. Brown 12-17-1855 (12-19-1855) Sh
Harrison, Mary E. to James A. McBride 2-28-1845 (3-6-1845) Hr
Harrison, Mary F. to P. G. Tucker 5-6-1863 (5-7-1863) O
Harrison, Mary Lucretia to William McFarland 12-6-1854 O
Harrison, Mary W. to Rufus F. King 1-12-1852 G
Harrison, Mary to Frank Lamar 8-1-1867 (8-2-1867) T
Harrison, Mary to John Ringgold 11-30-1843 (12-12-1843) G
Harrison, Mary to Lawson Parrish 5-20-1873 (5-25-1873) Dy
Harrison, Mary to T. T. Goldsby 11-29-1861 Sh
Harrison, Mary to Thomas F. Mosley 5-29-1871 Ma
Harrison, Matilda H. to Thos. A. Field 10-31-1859 (11-1-1859) G
Harrison, Matilda to John M. Tittle 11-6-1845 Be
Harrison, Miss ____ to S. F. Woodruff 9-20-1855 (no return) F
Harrison, Missouri to David L. Fulbright 11-12-1866 (11-14-1866) Ma
Harrison, Musie Dora to James Hill 12-22-1870 L
Harrison, Nancy A. C. to John W. Street 8-31-1848 (9-7-1848) Hr
Harrison, Nancy Emaline to Samuel Darby Simons 7-22-1845 (7-?-1845) T
Harrison, Nancy J. to S. B. Nance 9-5-1850 G
Harrison, Nancy J. to William Wiseman 12-17-1860 T
Harrison, Nancy to James P. Ellis 12-27-1869 (no return) L
Harrison, Nancy to John Dunagan 4-21-1863 Sh
Harrison, Nannie to John M. Rogers 4-26-1879 (4-27-1879) Dy
Harrison, Paralee to D. Foster 9-21-1867 G
Harrison, Pheoba to Allison Davis 8-5-1851 (8-7-1851) Sh
Harrison, Polly to John Sullivan 8-11-1855 (8-15-1855) Hr
Harrison, Ruth W. to Joseph H. Trotter 7-6-1846 (7-9-1846) F
Harrison, Ruth to Robert Walker 5-11-1859 (5-15-1859) O
Harrison, S. L. to H. C. West 1-29-1879 L
Harrison, Sally Ann to A. B. Williams 1-4-1866 Dy
Harrison, Sarah Becca to G. W. Sherron 11-4-1859 Hr
Harrison, Sarah C. to John A. Pemberton 6-17-1846 Ma
Harrison, Sarah E. to Geo. B. Black 12-22-1868 (12-24-1868) Ma
Harrison, Sarah Jane to James A. Sweeny 1-11-1848 Ma
Harrison, Sarah to H. C. Lawrence 2-20-1850 Hn
Harrison, Sarah to William Gibson 7-18-1853 (7-21-1853) O
Harrison, Susan C. to Benjamin F. Duncan 9-14-1857 (9-16-1857) Sh
Harrison, Susan E. to Peter S. Duncan 9-30-1847 Ma
Harrison, Susan to J. H. Bruce 4-7-1864 Be
Harrison, Tenie to Joseph W. Nailing 5-28-1868 (5-8?-1868) O
Harrison, Tex Ann to J. C. Hammond 8-9-1866 G
Harrison, Tilda to Jim Bagby 2-22-1871 Hy
Harrison, Virginia B. to Daniel McIver 1-10-1843 (1-11-1843) Ma
Harrison, Virginia D. to Lewis M. Williams 10-19-1857 Hr
Harrison, Virginia L. to Geo. A. Barbee 9-30-1851 Sh
Harrison, Zilphia to Wm. S. Robbins 11-22-1859 (no return) Hy
Harrison?, Della Ann to Richd. H. Harvey 12-19-1848 F
Harriss, Abigil P. to Robert W. Wynn 8-25-1858 (8-27-1858) Hr
Harriss, Amanda M. to Robert F. Robertson 6-11-1855 L
Harriss, Charlotte to Isaac Brewer 3-13-1843 (3-14-1843) Hr
Harriss, Eady to Binkley Freeman 4-17-1839 (4-18-1839) F
Harriss, Elizabeth S. to John P. Moore 12-23-1843 Hr
Harriss, Helen C. to Martin L. Hardin 6-22-1846 (6-25-1846) Hr
Harriss, Martha O. to Benjamin A. Simmons 1-21-1861 (1-24-1861) Hr
Harriss, Mary Jane to George Warren 10-15-1859 (10-16-1859) Hr
Harriss, Nancy to Walter M. Shinault 2-26-1853 (3-2-1853) Sh
Harriss, Olivia F. to John H. Simmons 1-13-1858 Hr
Harriss, Ruth to James jr. Toone 1-16-1861 (1-17-1861) Hr
Harriss, Sydney to Lewis R. Sutton 12-16-1850 (12-17-1850) Hr
Harrissinger, Lou to Thomas Carberry 10-18-1873 (10-19-1873) L
Harrisson, Caroline to John A. Taliaferro 6-24-1830 L
Harrisson, Dorothy to William Mobley 12-29-1851 G
Harrisson, Polly to John W. Hutson 9-17-1828 (9-30-1828) G
Harrisson, Winey to John N. Jack 9-1-1831 (9-4-1831) G
Harrold, Elizebeth to Wm. R. Rust 5-20-1854 (no return) We
Harrold, M. A. (Mrs.) to S. A. Baker 10-2-1867 O
Harrold, Malinda J. to James Parks 7-29-1867 (no return) Dy
Harrold, Matilda to James Jones 1-2-1856 Sh
Harrold, S. W. to Jeremiah Jones 2-20-1867 (no return) Dy
Harry, Mary D. C. to Samuel C. Haynes 1-18-1859 O
Harsen, Sophia to James Maydwell 12-22-1858 (12-23-1858) Sh
Harshaw, Lizzie to John W. Murray 5-4-1864 Sh
Harston, Barbara A. to Stephen R. Bryan 12-8-1856 (12-10-1856) Ma
Harston, Louisa J. to David C. Woodelle 9-5-1849 Ma
Hart, Adeline to Mat Taylor 2-5-1869 (2-9-1869) F B
Hart, Amanda to Thomas C. Davidson 3-27-1865 Hn
Hart, Angeline to C. F. McFarland 9-11-1867 Hn
Hart, Bathis to Jesse G. Grice 11-14-1827 Hr
Hart, Bulia to John Graves 12-20-1882 L
Hart, Catharine to George Hudspeth 1-25-1847 Hn
Hart, Dovie to James Miller 6-4-1876 Hy
Hart, Dovy to John Vaulx 5-13-1876 Hy
Hart, Eliza H. to Edward Coates 9-13-1852 (no return) F
Hart, Eliza Jane to William McDaniel 11-7-1857 (11-11-1857) Ma
Hart, Eliza to Robert Hays 6-4-1827 (6-7-1827) Hr
Hart, Eliza to Solen Boland 7-23-1839 Sh
Hart, Elizabeth B. to John R. Leach 12-17-1857 Cr
Hart, Elizabeth R. to Hugh Nanny 11-26-1853 (11-29-1853) Ma
Hart, Elizabeth to Anderson Sturdivant 10-12-1854 Hn
Hart, Elizabeth to David M. Craig 11-26-1860 Dy
Hart, Elizabeth to Davidson P. Sturdivant 12-27-1866 Hn
Hart, Elizabeth to Isaac Clark 12-27-1866 (12-13?-1866) T
Hart, Elizabeth to Jonathan McClure 11-14-1844 Hn
Hart, Elizabeth to Lewis F. Mitchum 2-17-1840 Cr
Hart, Elizabeth to R. K. Ray 12-25-1867 (no return) Hn
Hart, Elizabeth to S. H. Ridgeway 11-12-1854 We
Hart, Ellen to Thomas B. Jackson 8-10-1852 Hn
Hart, F. M. to J. T. Wheeler 1-14-1879 (1-15-1879) Dy
Hart, F. V. to J. G. Younger 11-22-1870 Hy
Hart, Ginny to William Kates 7-23-1868 (no return) Cr
Hart, H. M. to T. D. Peek 3-5-1873 (3-6-1873) Dy
Hart, Hannah H. to John McIntosh 3-6-1839 (3-7-1839) Ma
Hart, Harriett C. to Jas. N. Foley 1-5-1843 Hn
Hart, J. M. to Wm M. Alexander 3-28-1854 (no return) F
Hart, Jane C. to Edward Haley 1-5-1859 Hn
Hart, Jane to James Carter 7-6-1836 G
Hart, Jane to John H. Yancy 7-25-1853 Cr
Hart, Lizzie S. to H. G. Miller 12-7-1859 F
Hart, Lizzie to Isaac Clark 12-29-1866 T
Hart, Loucrecia to George Banks 11-14-1874 (no return) Hy
Hart, Louisa to Aleck Eaton 2-15-1867 T
Hart, Louisa to Joseph Hooper 8-22-1843 Hn
Hart, Louisa to Willis Taylor 4-9-1829 (5-11-1829) Hr
Hart, Louiza to Alfred Morrow 12-23-1867 (12-24-1867) F B
Hart, Lucy to Charles Hart 7-25-1882 L
Hart, Lucy to John L. Seaton 11-17-1853 (no return) F
Hart, M. A. to G. B. Alexander 10-3-1855 We
Hart, M. J. to J. E. Wheeler 2-17-1872 (2-18-1872) Dy
Hart, M. T. to James K. P. Clements 8-31-1868 (9-3-1868) Cr
Hart, Malinda to Hyman Norred 3-10-1863 Hn
Hart, Margaret J. to Thomas A. Simmons 12-21-1848 Ma

Hart, Margaret to James Wesley Williams 9-28-1868 Ma
Hart, Martha L. to J. C. Griffing 11-14-1850 Sh
Hart, Martha M. to James W. Whitehead 10-20-1846 Hn
Hart, Martha to George Mathews 8-26-1867 (8-29-1867) Ma
Hart, Martha to William T. McLain 1-5-1860 We
Hart, Mary D. to H. W. Arnold 12-25-1876 (12-26-1876) L
Hart, Mary I. to Benj. M. R. Campbell 12-22-1842 Cr
Hart, Mary M. to Robert B. Harper 9-12-1864 (9-13-1864) F
Hart, Mary to J. M. McMillon 12-15-1849 (12-18-1849) F
Hart, Mary to William Emery 2-28-1836 (no return) Hn
Hart, Mary to William R. Swor 8-27-1846 (no return) Hn
Hart, Mary to Wm. Elmore 6-3-1863 Dy
Hart, Maryann E. to William Mayo 9-22-1860 We
Hart, Mollie J. to Lemual J. Humphreys 1-10-1870 (1-12-1870) Ma
Hart, Nancy L. to Robert S. Mathews 10-29-1866 (10-30-1866) Ma
Hart, Nancy to William H. Lasater 5-31-1857 Hn
Hart, Nannie M. to Joel Buntin 1-18-1871 (1-19-1871) Ma
Hart, Nelly to Remkin M. Alexander 11-5-1839 Hn
Hart, Rachel E. to W. J. Sims 10-7-1866 (no return) Hn
Hart, Robin T. to Daniel E. Parker 11-12-1856 Cr
Hart, S. L. to James T. Wood 12-13-1876 L
Hart, Sallie to Albert Yates 2-6-1868 G
Hart, Sarah A. to D. L. Folks 6-10-1855 Hn
Hart, Sarah A. to Phillip A. Frazier 8-18-1863 (no return) We
Hart, Sarah to William T. Gholson 4-9-1831 Sh
Hart, Selay A. to David S. Phelan 10-5-1840 (10-5-1840) G
Hart, Sirena to Jonas Hoeser 10-28-1854 (11-2-1854) G
Hart, Susan P. to John Dearmore 12-14-1846 (12-15-1846) Ma
Hart, Susan to Ned Gooden 12-30-1869 (12-31-1869) F B
Harte?, Adaline to Jordan Walker 3-15-1872 T
Harter, Elizabeth to Samuel L. Forrest 2-7-1850 Hn
Harter, Elizabeth to Samuel L. Foster 2-7-1850 Hn
Hartfield, Eliza to Wm. Holmes 2-26-1869 (no return) Hy
Hartfield, Rachel M. to Silas Luttrell 9-25-1867 (9-26-1867) T
Hartgrave, Minerva to Noah G. Hearn 1-15-1839 Ma
Hartgraves, Mary to Wm. M. Moore 12-14-1852 Sh
Hartigan (Hantigan?), Bridget to William Collins 10-30-1853 Sh
Hartigan, Margaret to Michael Welch 4-9-1864 (4-10-1864) Sh
Hartizen, Joana to Michael Loughman 4-23-1852 Sh
Hartley, Mary Elizabeth to Hugh Lashlee 8-11-1869 Be
Hartman, Susan J. to William M. Baker 1-5-1859 Sh
Harton, Fannie to Charles B. Bloomingdale 7-31-1871 Dy
Harton, Julia P. to William Carrington 6-4-1842 Ma
Harton, Louanna to E. W. Smith 2-10-1874 (2-11-1874) Dy
Harton, Rebecca E. to W. N. Taylor 11-14-1870 (11-15-1870) Dy
Harton, Sarah A. E. to Claibourne Weaver 7-19-1843 (7-20-1843) Ma
Harts, Jane to James W. Carten 7-6-1837 G
Hartsfield, Elizabeth A. to Benjamin P. Martin 4-5-1860 Hn
Hartsfield, Elizabeth to Rufus King 8-21-1860 Hn
Hartsfield, Flotilla to Ewing P. Bates 10-25-1852 Hn
Hartsfield, Frances E. to Alex Murphy 2-7-1859 (2-10-1857) T
Hartsfield, Frances Malvina to Chas. David McCoy 12-22-1853 (SB 1852?) T
Hartsfield, Gilley Ann to William M. Milliken 1-2-1845 Hn
Hartsfield, Helen to Preston B. Edmunds 9-17-1840 Hn
Hartsfield, Isabella to Thomas Highfill 9-10-1850 Hn
Hartsfield, Julia Ann to Oliver P. Kelley 7-14-1847 T
Hartsfield, Juliana to Richard Anderson 5-6-1840 Hn
Hartsfield, Louisa J. to Alfred McGuire 2-12-1842 (2-15-1842) T
Hartsfield, Lula S. to J. S. Boon 12-16-1869 G
Hartsfield, M. H. to Willis Cox 1-8-1851 Hn
Hartsfield, Martha C. to sDaniel M. Myers 12-28-1843 T
Hartsfield, Martha F. to Jacob Hartsfield 1-3-1873 (1-5-1873) T
Hartsfield, Mary W. to J. H. Ragan 3-14-1855 (3-15-1855) G
Hartsfield, Mollie to T. A. Thornton 10-24-1867 G
Hartsfield, Nancy Kesiah to William T. Jones 10-24-1864 (no return) Hn
Hartsfield, Nancy to Alexander Edmunds 11-19-1839 Hn
Hartsfield, O. to R. D. Fitzgerald 3-7-1860 G
Hartsfield, Rachael A. to Jacob C. Menes 7-3-1858 T
Hartsfield, Rachael to Jessee Hill 12-5-1860 T
Hartsfield, S. C. to Edward Shankle 6-4-1860 (6-14-1860) T
Hartsfield, Sallie A. to James Yewell 1-15-1862 (1-16-1862) T
Hartsfield, Sallie F. to Charles Fox Fennel 11-22-1859 (11-23-1859) Hr
Hartsfield, Sarah Elizabeth to Peter P. Wood 7-7-1869 (7-8-1869) T
Hartsfield, Sarah L. to Marcus L. Grady 11-2-1852 (11-3-1852) G
Hartsfield, Sarah to James L. Bailey 12-20-1851 (12-21-1851) T
Hartsfield, Sophia to N. C. Alexander 11-28-1866 G
Hartsfields, Demetra E. to G. T. Mitchell 1-15-1861 G
Hartsugg, Happy to Alford Jones 6-30-1853 Cr
Hartsville, M. C. to T. M. Hicks 4-4-1874 (4-8-1874) O
Hartwell, Eliza to F. M. Williams 6-6-1857 (6-7-1857) Sh
Hartwell, Maria to Ebenezer Slocum 1-6-1842 Sh
Hartwell, Sarah to Thomas Moore 8-29-1850 Sh
Harty, Louisa Jane to Joseph Herryman 11-10-1842 Hr
Harty, Parrylee Ellen to Stephen Harriman 9-6-1858 (9-12-1858) Hr
Harvel, Sarah E. to John B. Redick 1-17-1854 Cr
Harvell, Ann to James Henderson 12-25-1866 (12-26-1866) F B
Harvell, Margaret to Robert Rives 12-25-1866 F B

Harvell, Missouri to W. M. Scallions 5-17-1869 (5-18-1869) Dy
Harvey, Ann E. to Robert E. Rogers 10-6-1869 (10-7-1869) F
Harvey, Bridgett to Michael Brady 11-24-1850 Sh
Harvey, C. M. to G. Holmes 1-2-1843 (no return) Cr
Harvey, Caroline to George Lowrey 8-18-1866 (not endorsed) F B
Harvey, Elizabeth to Augusta Fioke (Hicke?) 8-27-1851 Sh
Harvey, Elizabeth to Crawford A. Duncan 4-11-1838 Hr
Harvey, Elphidel to Mark Nix 10-24-1839 Hn
Harvey, Emaline to S. R. Quinn 11-21-1842 (no return) Cr
Harvey, Emily to Charles Murphy 12-29-1828 (1-1-1829) Hr
Harvey, Hannah to Ninian Steele 11-2-1826 Hr
Harvey, Harriet A. to James B. Walls 12-13-1836 (12-21-1836) Hr
Harvey, James L. to Achilles Barnett 7-20-1837 Sh
Harvey, Lee to Alfred Jones 2-26-1870 (12-28-1870) F B
Harvey, Louisa to Willie B. Quinn 5-10-1843 Cr
Harvey, Lucy Ann to James S. Harwell 2-15-1844 Sh
Harvey, Martha A. to Elisha Rodgers 12-11-1854 Cr
Harvey, Mary A. to Thomas D. Gray 7-13-1838 Hr
Harvey, Mary H. to Milton G. Frazer 2-11-1854 (no return) F
Harvey, Mary Jane to C. P. Braswell 10-25-1848 Hn
Harvey, Mary W. to Lewis Walter 5-15-1855 Sh
Harvey, Mary to Larkin Adkins 5-29-1851 (no return) F
Harvey, Mollie to Washington Sweet 2-1-1877 Hy
Harvey, Newoma to Smith H. Hill 1-13-1844 Hr
Harvey, R. C. to Abel Grace 10-20-1849 (10-28-1849) F
Harvey, R. E. to Henry Yarber 3-1-1868 Hy
Harvey, S. B. to W. T. McCutchen 7-28-1873 (7-31-1873) Dy
Harvey, S. P. (Mrs.) to K. R. Spence 12-16-1867 F
Harvey, Sarah C. to John Hoeg 12-28-1843 Sh
Harvill, Elizabeth to Samuel J. Cabell 6-1-1827 (6-3-1827) Hr
Harvy, Mary to Martin Runnals 4-9-1870 F
Harvy, N. C. to Henry C. Stone 8-29-1866 (no return) Cr
Harvy, Netty to Manuel Butcher 1-14-1870 (1-16-1870) F B
Harvy, Willie S. to Wm. E. Tinkle 10-1-1838 (10-2-1838) G
Harwell, Anna to Jno. Parham, jr. 12-18-1860 (12-19-1860) F
Harwell, Eliza to Robert Bragg 8-6-1868 T
Harwell, Indiana A. to John Wesley Bell 4-2-1877 (4-4-1877) Dy
Harwell, Maggie to Primus Williamson 3-25-1870 F B
Harwell, Margaret to Daniel Miller 12-30-1868 (12-31-1868) Dy
Harwell, Mary A. S. (Mrs.) to Leander Black 5-20-1844 (5-29-1844) F
Harwell, Mary E. to W. W. Winfield 6-1-1859 (6-26-1859) F
Harwell, Polly (Mrs.) to John Z. Morton 11-12-1862 (not endorsed) F
Harwell, Polly to John Z. Morton 11-12-1862 (not endorsed) F
Harwell, S. A. L. to Jesse Ross 11-8-1865 Mn
Harwell, S. E. to R. A. Sawrie 11-4-1868 (no return) Dy
Harwood, Louisa to John Allen, jr. 10-13-1857 G
Harwood, Lydia R. to R. D. Wilson 2-17-1869 G
Hasaway (Hataway?), R. A. to A. W. Johnson 8-22-1866 G
Hase?, Amanda C. to Wm. Little 10-6-1840 F
Haselett, Artemecia to Jake Johnson 1-18-1868 (no return) F B
Haselett, Harriet to Charley Van 5-15-1868 (no return) F B
Haselett, Margaret to Henry Tate 7-19-1867 (no return) F B
Haselett, Susan to John A. Nesbitt 5-18-1867 (no return) F B
Haselette, Alsey to Nuggy Parris 12-23-1867 (no return) F B
Haselette, Martha to Frank Dunkin 12-23-1867 (12-28-1867) F B
Haskeah?, Delilia to John Simerson 7-1-1841 F
Haskell, Effe Jane to William W. Nearn 7-23-1843 L
Haskell, Ellen N. to Wallace C. Claiborne 11-12-1853 Ma
Haskell, Jane M. to Robt. Searcy 6-16-1857 Sh
Haskell, Martha to John Trigg 1-14-1858 Sh
Haskell, Sally to James S. Dees 6-16-1842 Hn
Haskiel, Ada to D. H. Green 12-19-1882 (12-20-1882) L
Haskin, Louis to John Miller 11-7-1867 Dy
Haskins, Ann to George Walton 7-14-1877 (7-15-1877) Dy
Haskins, Annie E. to Jno. A. Steadman 11-8-1869 (11-11-1869) Ma
Haskins, Cloe to Dock Hendon 7-30-1870 F B
Haskins, Eddy Carter to Samuel H. Williams 12-23-1874 (12-24-1874) Dy
Haskins, Eliza to George Wood 2-13-1835 W
Haskins, Elizabeth to Joseph Williams 6-11-1879 (6-12-1879) Dy
Haskins, George R. to George Williamson 4-15-1844 Ma
Haskins, L. M. to R. D. Harris 12-21-1869 (no return) Dy
Haskins, Lucinda to James Godsey 1-19-1853 Sh
Haskins, M. to James Hawkins 12-26-1855 (no return) Hn
Haskins, Mahala to J. B. Johnson 1-9-1866 Hn
Haskins, Martha to Cash McDonald 1-5-1871 F B
Haskins, Mary E. to Wm. H. Harris 12-14-1870 Ma
Haskins, Mary to John Carter 11-5-1857 Hn
Haskins, Millie to Thomas Humphreys 2-10-1874 (2-12-1874) Dy
Haskins, Rachel to John Hatler 1-28-1856 (no return) Hn
Haskins, Rhoda to Lewis Fowlkes 7-8-1871 (no return) Dy
Haskins, S. R. to B. T. Nichols 9-26-1865 Hn
Hasler, Caroline to Nicholas Block 8-16-1847 Sh
Haslip, Mary Ann Frances to John Voss 9-12-1885 (9-13-1885) L
Haslip, Sarah to Daniel Rust 1-21-1841 Ma
Hass, Minerva to Geo. Ward 11-25-1850 (11-26-1850) F
Hassel, Elizabeth to Louis Weigel 3-21-1857 Sh
Hassell, Dinkie to Joseph F. Roberts 3-3-1875 Dy

Hassell, Louisa T. to Richmond Turpin 6-13-1864 (no return) Dy
Hassell, Margaret J. to James B. Parrish 8-20-1868 (no return) Dy
Hassell, Margaret to John H. Poll 11-18-1866 G
Hassell, Martha to Saml. Alexandner 12-22-1867 G
Hassell, Mary A. to W. H. Ball 4-1-1867 (4-3-1867) Dy
Hassell, Mary H. to Israel M. L. Barker 3-8-1852 (3-9-1852) G
Hassell, Mary to Samuel McCollum 12-14-1869 (12-16-1869) Cr
Hassler, Anne to John M. Smithson 11-7-1872 T
Hast, Judy to Thomas Thorn 1-11-1844 G
Haste, Mary E. to Joseph J. Burris 10-16-1866 G
Hasten, Frances to John Culberson 11-22-1841 Hn
Hastin, Christy to Dillion A. French 7-28-1846 Cr
Hastin, Susanah to Robert King 5-20-1840 (no return) Hn
Hasting, Sarah to Berry R. Winsett 3-1-1838 Hn
Hasting, Sarah to Robert P. Stanfield 11-27-1856 Hn
Hastings, Catherine to Henry L. Mooring 1-4-1858 Ma
Hastings, Elizabeth to John Ellis 4-1-1855 Hn
Hastings, M. J. to Robert Shaddow 11-16-1854 Hn
Hastings, Martha A. to John S. Wood 8-11-1853 Hn
Hastings, Martha H. to Orlanda E. Muzzle 11-13-1850 Hn
Hastings, Martha J. to Silas M. Hicks 3-24-1853 (no return) Hn
Hastings, Martha to William Woods 7-9-1848 Hn
Hastings, Mary A. to C. C. Gum 1-8-1848 Hn
Hastings, Mary to Benjamin W. Lewis 1-2-1851 Hn
Hastings, Nancy Elizabeth to Paulding A. Sullivan 8-4-1867 Hn
Hastings, Nancy H. to Jacob Lewis 2-2-1852 Hn
Hastings, Rebecca J. to W. D. Cate 10-10-1867 Hn
Hastings, Rebecca to William H. Boothe 10-25-1849 Hn
Hastings, Riddy? to Booker Peak 11-7-1848 Hn
Hastings, Savannah to W. S. Simmons 8-30-1879 (9-1-1879) Dy
Haston, Sarah P. to Vicent Moon 7-3-1839 (7-9-1839) Ma
Hatachett, Mahulda to Richard Stanley 11-6-1862 (11-7-1862) O
Hatch, Amanda M. to A. C. Akin 8-23-1856 (8-24-1856) O
Hatch, Cinthy to W. F. Rainey 6-9-1852 Cr
Hatch, Dillie to J. W. Evans 4-23-1872 (no return) Cr
Hatch, Elizabeth to T. C. Raney 11-21-1854 Cr
Hatch, Loucinda to N. W. Hampton 8-24-1858 Cr
Hatch, Mary S. to Thomas Whitelaw 2-4-1841 (2-11-1841) F
Hatch, Roasina to James H. Lauderdale 6-2-1841 T
Hatch, Sarah A. to John L. Dickey 10-16-1855 Cr
Hatch, Sopha A. to B. C. Smith 1-24-1872 (1-25-1872) Cr
Hatchcock, Sarah J. to William L. Morris 11-25-1862 (no return) Hy
Hatchell, Sarah F. to Thos. J. Smith 2-19-1870 (2-20-1870) T
Hatchell, Sophia to John Duidlinger 12-22-1851 (12-26-1851) Sh
Hatcher, Almeda to James J. Ward 10-14-1845 (no return) We
Hatcher, Mary Ann to Hezekiah Cobb 11-22-1845 Sh
Hatcher, Mary to Jas. Lovel 1-2-1847 Sh
Hatchett, A. R. to J. H. Willard 12-17-1863 G
Hatchett, Hardinia J. to Benj. N. D. Harper 1-8-1849 (1-9-1849) G
Hatchett, Margaret H. to Wm. H. Giles 10-19-1843 (no return) Cr
Hatchett, Mary A. to Sion Boon 6-6-1846 G
Hatchett, Mary to Joseph Stanley 10-1-1864 (not exec) O *
Hatchett, Mary to Thomas Flippen 1-4-1865 O
Hatchett, Nancy L. to Gilbert Boon 3-29-1839 (4-4-1839) G
Hatchett, Nancy to B. W. Kemp 9-27-1849 Cr
Hatchett, Pelina C. to Moses A. Hawkins 9-11-1861 G
Hatchett, Sarah R. to L. Vinson 2-18-1844 Cr
Hateley, Susan to Gabril Bumpass 9-22-1844 Hr
Hatfield, Ellen to John Ferguson 2-22-1849 Sh
Hatfield, Mary Jane to William S. Devenport 11-27-1848 (11-28-1848) Hr
Hatford, Rebecca M. to G. L. Quarles 4-7-1863 G
Hathaway, Adaline to Meyer Helfer 10-17-1848 Sh
Hathaway, Ann E. to Robert E. Armstrong 8-4-1858 Ma
Hathaway, Elisabeth to J. Talbot Nicholson 8-23-1852 Sh
Hathaway, Elizabeth F. to Elisha Rains 10-10-1862 (10-23-1862) Ma
Hathaway, Elizabeth to Thomas T. Taylor 12-21-1859 Ma
Hathaway, L. A. V. to Joseph F.(T?) Shore 2-21-1855 Sh
Hathaway, Mahulda A. to Thomas Laman 12-14-1867 (12-18-1867) Ma
Hathaway, Mary to Milton A. Brown 10-4-1866 (10-9-1866) Ma
Hathaway, Nancy J. to George W. Boals 7-19-1859 (7-21-1859) Ma
Hathaway, Sarah V. to Edward L. Smith 2-5-1852 Sh
Hathcock, Leavicy to Thos. J. Brown 4-24-1834 (no return) L
Hathcot, Darcus to George Wilson 3-7-1861 G
Hathorn, Lucy A. to Franklin King 6-28-1874 Hy
Hathorn, Sopha to Joe Thompson 10-15-1872 Hy
Hathway, Manda to Billie Williams 12-31-1874 O
Hathway, Paulina to Harrison Rutland 12-16-1847 Sh
Hatler, E. A. E. to G. W. Bass 12-29-1858 (no return) We
Hatler, Elizabeth A. to John H. Osburn 4-29-1860 We
Hatler, Emaline to Person Yates 6-29-1871 Hn
Hatler, Jane to Samuel Hatler 9-18-1860 We
Hatler, Matilda P. to Alfred W. Vowell 10-17-1862 We
Hatler, Nancy to Elijah Fletcher 4-1-1845 (no return) We
Hatler, R. C. to F. M. Speight 12-28-1865 Hn
Hatley, Frances C. to John Gossett 1-15-1840 Hr
Hatley, Izora to M. V. Wry 11-14-1867 Hn
Hatley, Mariah C. to A. C. Waller 8-4-1845 (8-5-1845) F
Hatley, Martha A. to Samuel H. Bayless 7-22-1844 F
Hatley, Martha to F. J. Smothers 8-29-1867 Be
Hatley, Martha to Irvin Gibson 1-6-1866 Be
Hatley, Mary A. to Alsey W. Hatley 2-7-1865 Be
Hatley, Mary F. to John T. Saunders 11-14-1868 Be
Hatley, Mary N.? to V. D. Gossett 3-21-1825 (3-24-1825) Hr
Hatley, Rebecca Jane to John W. Cooley 6-27-1864 Be
Hatley, Rebecca to John Hicks 5-5-1867 Be
Hatley, Sally to Clyde Lynch 1-25-1832 Be CC
Hatley, Sarah C. to Green Oatsvall 3-7-1868 Be
Hatley, Sarah to Abram Gossett 4-2-1848 Be
Hatley, Sarah to Joseph W. Matthews 1-1-1829 Hr
Hatley?, Sally to John Stafford 2-6-1837 Hr
Hatly, Maria H. to Ezekiel Wall 1-6-1834 (1-4?-1834) Hr
Hatly, Rebecca to Hillsbury Hinant 1-4-1855 Hr
Haton, Anastasia to F. P. Daniel 2-2-1856 (no return) Hn
Hatsell, Caroline E. to R. C. Hon 5-7-1860 (no return) Hy
Hatten, Martha A. to Nicholas Byars 6-18-1839 Hn
Hattom, Sarah F. to Geo. W. Richardson 12-10-1866 Ma
Hatton, M. A. to J. B. Turnage 1-12-1874 (1-14-1874) T
Hatton, Sophronia to James M. Nolin 8-16-1842 Ma
Hauger, Henrietta L. to John W. Brown 4-30-1855 (5-3-1855) G
Haughton, Emma to Alonzo F. Love 4-25-1871 Ma *
Haughton, Sally B. to Jonathan W. Crook 10-2-1855 (10-3-1855) Ma
Haun, Ellen to Friday Mockrell McConnaway 3-18-1868 G B
Haun, Martha A. to John N. Allen 1-8-1863 We
Hauser, Sallie A. to J. W. Gaylord 2-7-1869 G
Haven, Lula A. to John H. Wiley 12-2-1856 Cr
Haveway, Elizabeth to Samuel Moncreef 1-1-1839 F
Hawes, Ann E. to William H. Blalock 3-21-1866 Hn
Hawes, Sarah to R. J. Evans 2-26-1866 (no return) Hn
Hawk, Jane to A. G. Pierce 5-2-1866 (5-3-1866) Dy
Hawkens (Nankens?), Mollie J. to L. C. Woodard 1-9-1870? (1-11-1871) L
Hawkins, Alice to Ambros Carlton 1-9-1873 Hy
Hawkins, Ann M. to Hugh D. Hays 7-17-1837 (7-18-1837) G
Hawkins, Ann to B. T. Bibb 11-11-1867 Dy
Hawkins, Beluchery to David Davis 8-1-1848 (8-2-1848) O
Hawkins, C. C. to J. T. Smith 11-7-1863 (11-8-1863) O
Hawkins, Caroline to Moses Mitchell 12-19-1873 T
Hawkins, Catharine to R. H. Glisson 4-25-1854 (4-27-1854) Sh
Hawkins, Celestia to James P. Wilson 9-17-1855 (no return) We
Hawkins, Eleanor to George Basinger 6-24-1861 Mn
Hawkins, Elizabeth to William Newhouse 9-15-1861 (12-25-1861) O
Hawkins, Fannie J. to John N. Chaney 1-20-1870 Hy
Hawkins, Flora A. to J. W. McCullough 9-25-1869 (9-26-1869) Cr
Hawkins, Frances to Robert Forsythe ?-?-1862? Mn
Hawkins, Isabella to W. H. Harpole 1-30-1872 O
Hawkins, Jane to Elleson Howard 12-25-1839 G
Hawkins, Jane to Joseph C. Kindria 6-4-1834 O
Hawkins, Jane to Lemuel Taylor 9-26-1844 Cr
Hawkins, Julia to Jasper Phillips 6-22-1872 (no return) Cr B
Hawkins, L. R. to Lewis B. Bond 7-3-1860 (7-4-1860) Ma
Hawkins, Laura to Freeman Johnson 8-5-1870 (no return) Cr
Hawkins, Lillie to Thos. Brown 10-14-1868 Hy
Hawkins, Liza to W. M. Guinn 1-4-1860 Hn
Hawkins, Lucinda to Daniel W. Word 5-16-1837 (5-?-1837) G
Hawkins, Lucy A. to T. H. Hicks 1-1-1867 (no return) Hy
Hawkins, Lucy E. to J. P. G. Roulhac 12-6-1851 (12-7-1851) Sh
Hawkins, Lucy to W. R. Plaxco 10-25-1860 Sh
Hawkins, M. J. to J. Geyer 7-23-1853 (no return) Hn
Hawkins, Margaret to Samuel Prince 12-25-1868 (12-30-1868) Cr
Hawkins, Martha E. to Smith B. Sanders 3-18-1858 Cr
Hawkins, Martha to Edward Fitzgerald 8-27-1856 Hn
Hawkins, Martha to Wm. Miller 4-1-1858 Cr
Hawkins, Mary E. to Henry D. Sherman 3-2-1846 Sh
Hawkins, Mary M. C. A. to Daniel R. Morris 5-27-1856 Hn
Hawkins, Merica to William W. B. Langley 7-16-1831 (7-17-1831) G
Hawkins, Rebecca J. to John C. Brashears 9-3-1867 Dy
Hawkins, S. A. to W. F. Watson 5-23-1874 (5-24-1874) O
Hawkins, S. J. to D. F. Taylor 1-7-1879 (1-8-1879) Dy
Hawkins, Sallie D. to F. W. Chany 8-19-1863 (8-23-1863) L
Hawkins, Sarah B. to David Dunn 4-24-1834 We
Hawkins, Sarah C. to E. W. Chapman 9-13-1867 (no return) Dy
Hawkins, Sarah C. to W. L. Low 2-23-1850 (2-26-1850) Hr
Hawkins, Susan E. to Daniel C. Newton 9-5-1866 L
Hawkins, Susan M. to Wm. B. Glenn 4-9-1844 We
Hawkins, Winney to Ephraim Fitzpatrick 12-23-1867 (12-24-1867) L
Hawks, Emily E. to George W. L. Childress 10-28-1846 Hn
Hawks, Margaret E. to L. A. Childers 12-8-1845 Hn
Hawks, Mary D. to N. G. Childress 1-9-1845 Hn
Hawks, Phebe A. to Simeon T. Smith 11-1-1860 We
Hawks, Salinda K. to Edward R. Cook 10-15-1845 (no return) We
Hawley, Josephine to Aaron Arnold 8-23-1853 Be
Hawley, Julia to Archieleus Woodward 9-20-1855 Sh
Hawley, Laura E. to James M. Allen 9-14-1852 (no return) F
Hawley, Louisa to James E. Totty 9-10-1857 Be
Hawley, Margaret to Wm. Summers 5-26-1863 Sh

Hawley, Rosmond to George A. Madden 4-11-1867 Be
Hawood, Ellen to Pomp Calhoun 8-15?-1871 T
Hawse, Martha E. to George A. Sharp 12-14-1852 (12-15-1852) Ma
Hawthorn, Margaret A. to Charles B. Murray 5-5-1836 Sh
Hawthorn, Mary Ann to Francis M. Barker 6-29-1856 Be
Hawthorn, Susan F. to W. W. Jordan 12-6-1855 Be
Hawthorne, Neicie to William Henry 12-16-1863 Sh
Hawtin, M. A. to Robt. D. Norvell 12-20-1871 (no return) Hy
Hay(May), Polly to John Bosberne 9-9-1829 Hr
Hay, Arene to William Kent 12-23-1873 Hy
Hay, Eliza to Alexander Duke 8-2-1877 Hy
Hay, Hattie to Thomas Johnson 11-13-1877 Hy
Hay, Martha E. to H. H. Lanier 12-23-1869 G
Hay, Myra to Marcellus Boyd 5-19-1861 Hy
Hay, Nancy to John Lee 4-19-1873 T
Hay, Queen to Bob Loving 12-29-1869 Hy
Hay, Sarah to Wm. T. Rice 8-25-1859 (no return) Hy
Hayatte?, Susan P. to John Capps 1-9-1865 (no return) L
Hayce, Silva to Isaac Hayce 5-6-1866 G
Haye, M. E. to W. T. Dickerson 12-10-1867 T
Hayes, A. E. to John James 12-22-1870 (no return) Hy
Hayes, Ella to Mat Olds 6-11-1869 (6-12-1869) F B
Hayes, Emeline to John Phelan 2-1-1853 G
Hayes, Harriet to Henry Henning 12-14-1882 (no return) L
Hayes, Isabel to Archibald McAlister 12-23-1853 (12-25-1853) Sh
Hayes, Margaret to James Evetts 12-23-1846 Sh
Hayes, Mirth Y. to James Powell 8-27-1856 Cr
Hayes, Polly to Charles Vincent 4-12-1834 Sh
Hayes, Polly to John Chamberlin 8-18-1831 Sh
Hayes, Sarah to Archibald C. Hogue 7-21-1855 (7-26-1855) O
Hayley, Harriet (Mrs.) to George Hayley 8-15-1871 (8-17-1871) Ma
Hayley, Louisa to J. H. Drummonds 10-30-1867 Cr
Hayley, Martha I. to William Vantrice 1-10-1845 (SB 1843?) Ma
Hayley, Susan Catherine to William T. Pearce 3-9-1857 (3-10-1857) Ma
Hayley?, Eliza to Henry Hamilton 1-18-1871 T
Haymes, Bettie E. to W. L. Dunnegin 12-8-1867 Hn
Haymes, Mary C. to Stephen P. Routon 6-1-1858 Hn
Haynee, Mary E. to J. M. Pearson 12-18-1860 Rh
Haynes (Harris), Sarah E. to Thomas M. Gore 11-15-1854 O
Haynes, Alice to Ed Rutherford 12-1-1871 Hy
Haynes, Alsey to William Crawford 12-25-1867 (no return) Hn B
Haynes, Anna E. to James T. Haynes 9-22-1858 Hn
Haynes, Arabella V. to M. D. Lafayette Wiles (Wiley?) 3-17-1856 Sh
Haynes, Bettie to Sandy Wilson Downing 5-13-1874 (5-14-1874) T
Haynes, Charity to Robt. Ridley 12-22-1870 (12-29-1870) Cr B
Haynes, Easther to March Henderson 5-27-1866 Hn B
Haynes, Elender to Drury Massey 10-21-1844 L
Haynes, Eliza C. to W. W. Haynes 5-3-1870 Dy
Haynes, Elizabeth to A. L. Terry 9-25-1856 O
Haynes, Elizabeth to David Kirkland 3-31-1853 (4-7-1853) Sh
Haynes, Elizabeth to E. W. Lea 3-4-1850 (3-7-1850) Ma
Haynes, Ellen to Frank Graham 2-24-1868 (no return) Hy
Haynes, Ellen to Richard Michell 12-12-1876 (no return) L
Haynes, Emily E. to Wm. W. Perkins 1-13-1850 Cr
Haynes, H. M. to T. W. Younger 2-10-1865 (2-12-1865) Cr
Haynes, Hannah A. to John D. Seivers 12-5-1848 (12-7-1848) Hr
Haynes, Harriett to Richard Haynes 9-30-1865 (no return) Hn
Haynes, Irene M. to J. B. Crocker 5-28-1884 (5-29-1884) L
Haynes, Jane C. to Jesse B. Ward 11-24-1866 Ma
Haynes, Jane to Ed Burton 1-8-1872 Hy
Haynes, Jane to Major McLemon 7-28-1866 Hy
Haynes, Julene M. to James Bomar 12-15-1842 Hn
Haynes, Julia B. to Wm. W. Bain 12-18-1866 (12-20-1866) Ma
Haynes, Kattie to Wm. Partee 10-12-1859 Hy
Haynes, Laurena L. to J. W. Burns 1-6-1886 L
Haynes, Lucy Ann to Lewis Hill 9-25-1867 Hn
Haynes, Lucy C. to Craven A. Davis 6-15-1831 Ma
Haynes, Lucy to Jordan Wilson 6-19-1873 Hy
Haynes, Luizer to E. W. Parker 10-7-1865 G
Haynes, M. E. to J. C. Pace 12-24-1867 G
Haynes, Martha J. to John W. Stewart 2-18-1847 Hn
Haynes, Martha J. to Simpson Alexander 2-27-1847 (no return) Hn
Haynes, Martha to Allen Mathis 12-23-1866 Hn B
Haynes, Martha to W. A. Kelly 12-15-1866 (12-17-18??) O
Haynes, Mary E. to James Wooten 5-19-1846 Hn
Haynes, Mary E. to Morgan B. Cook 5-31-1850 Ma
Haynes, Mary F. to Thomas F. Diggs 10-3-1860 (no return) Cr
Haynes, Mary Q. to J. M. Riggs 12-27-1869 (12-29-1869) Cr
Haynes, Mary S. to Andrew L. Finger 12-15-1843 (12-20-1843) Ma
Haynes, Matilda to John Anderson 7-17-1838 Hn
Haynes, Matilda to Thomas B. Williams 5-21-1861 Ma
Haynes, Mollie L. to William H. Latham 11-24-1870 (12-1-1870) Ma
Haynes, Nancy C. to Thomas A. Wakefield 1-19-1858 (1-20-1858) L
Haynes, Nancy G. to Hiram S. Griffith 5-14-1848 Sh
Haynes, Nancy J. to Robert Alexander Jones 7-31-1856 Hr
Haynes, Sallie to Bob Chapman 11-25-1871 Hy
Haynes, Sally G. to Turner Mobley 2-15-1854 G
Haynes, Saluda J. to Isaac E. Dickie 9-25-1848 Ma
Haynes, Sarah A. to Franklin Greer 10-11-1862 (10-12-1862) Dy
Haynes, Sarah A. to Robert H. Perry 12-24-1849 (12-25-1849) Ma
Haynes, Sarah Jane to E. S. Brogden 1-7-1878 (1-9-1878) L
Haynes, Sarah L. to E. M. Keltner 12-17-1879 L
Haynes, Sarah to John Odonald 12-26-1860 (no return) Hy
Haynes, Sarah to P. D. Weidgwoood 5-8-1847 Sh
Haynes, Sidney to Edward Hall 10-18-1840 Cr
Haynes, Sue W. to J. William Johnson 5-14-1856 Hn
Haynes, Susan A. to William H. McAdoo 3-18-1856 Ma
Haynes, Susanah to R. J. Lawrence 3-23-1845 Be
Haynes, Tabitha E. to J. M. Oliver 5-5-1866 (5-9-1866) Cr
Haynes, Tennessee T. to John A. Glimp 7-24-1866 (?-28?-1866) L
Haynes, Tennessee V to Zachariah Gaines 9-7-1869 L
Haynes, V. B. to J. W. Glimp 12-11-1882 (12-12-1882) L
Haynes, Vester to R. J.(I?) Gaines 12-1-1885 L
Haynes, Violet to W. A. Bigham 11-5-1840 Cr
Haynes, Virginia A. to G. S. Sims 8-4-1852 Sh
Haynest, Sally to Handy W. Byrn 8-31-1831 Ma
Haynie, Elizabeth Catharine to LaFayette Hill 10-13-1847 T
Haynie, Elizabeth E. to Timmon S. Treadwell 10-1-1850 Hr
Haynie, Elizabeth H. to Robert G. Fellow 1-18-1848 Sh
Haynie, Jane to Peter Martin 10-20-1866 (10-21-1866) T
Haynie, Leonora A. to John D. Fogg 9-4-1860 Sh
Haynie, M. A. to John W. Murphy 5-11-1869 T
Haynie, Martha Ann to James Henry Cockrell 10-13-1847 T
Haynie, Mary C. to John Jarrett Peebles 2-24-1852 T
Haynie, Sarah Jane to Robert L. Rogers 1-17-1843 Ma
Haynis, Nancy M. to Andrew Vance 12-9-1850 Sh
Hayns, America to Wm. B. Howard 12-27-1839 (12-29-1839) G
Hayns, Nancy to Charles G. Baird 11-20-1843 Ma
Hays, Addie to Charles McDonald 12-3-1863 Sh
Hays, Amelia Ann to W. F. Drappin 10-7-1856 T
Hays, Ann M. to Mark Selph 12-16-1841 G
Hays, Arcenia to Howard Morton 5-10-1868 Hy
Hays, Catherine to Marcus Plummer 7-24-1839 Sh
Hays, Celia to Wm. W. Shackelford 4-8-1837 (4-9-1837) Hr
Hays, Cora to Henry Burchett 5-7-1870 T
Hays, Cora to Philip Anthony 3-21-1878 (no return) Hy
Hays, E. J. to Solomon Argo 11-7-1847 Cr
Hays, Edmonia to Miles Cherry 7-23-1868 Hy
Hays, Elizabeth A. to William H. E. Goff 1-28-1874 L
Hays, Elizabeth to P. L. Talbert 1-28-1863 We
Hays, Ellen to Thomas Culligan 1-7-1856 Sh
Hays, Emelia to Calvin M. Blankenship 9-22-1838 (9-23-1838) F
Hays, Emily to Charles D. Hoofman 11-18-1857 Hn
Hays, Emily to William Thompson 10-26-1847 Hr
Hays, Etmonia to Jessee Mabin 10-11-1877 Hy
Hays, Fannie Middleton to Walter E. Preston 3-9-1858 (3-10-1858) Ma
Hays, Frances (Mrs.) to William H. Jackson 1-20-1858 (1-21-1858) Ma
Hays, Frances A. to H. M. Skiles 12-21-1869 G
Hays, Frucy to Thomas J. McMahon 9-28-1831 Ma
Hays, H. F. N. E. to George A. Lee 10-3-1850 Hr
Hays, Hannah Melisa to Lewis Taylor 12-4-1872 Hy
Hays, Hannah to Thomas Daily 10-24-1861 Ma
Hays, J. A. to B. E. Williams 1-7-1878 L
Hays, J. M. to James M. Randle 12-24-1855 (no return) Hn
Hays, Jane D. to Burkie A. Fossett 8-23-1867 (8-25-1867) Ma
Hays, Jane to James Hill 11-3-1869 (no return) L
Hays, Jane to John Cortner 7-5-1824 (7-7-1824) Hr
Hays, Jane to William Ingram 11-8-1847 (11-11-1847) G
Hays, Johanna to Thomas Ryan 4-7-1863 Sh
Hays, Josephine C. to Jesse B. Gordon 1-9-1871 Ma
Hays, Julia to John Sheridan 11-28-1859 Sh
Hays, Kate to R. J. Stewart 11-19-1864 Sh
Hays, Lettie to James M. Jones 9-24-1872 (11-24-1872) T
Hays, Livey ann to Joseph A. Ealy 9-12-1867 Hn
Hays, Lodoriska to Asa Parker 2-14-1834 (2-15-1834) Hr
Hays, Lucinda to Gabriel Malone 1-11-1839 (1-6?-1839) Hr
Hays, M. E. to J. E. Miller 11-26-1860 Hn
Hays, M. E. to James Bulger 1-30-1862 T
Hays, M. L. to Charles Phillips 12-8-1859 O
Hays, Mahala A. J. to Robert A. Vandike 4-29-1868 Hy
Hays, Margaret to Frederick Williams 11-30-1868 Hy
Hays, Mariah to George Glass 8-14-1867 (8-15-1867) L
Hays, Martha to Allen A. Bruce 11-4-1850 Ma
Hays, Mary A. to Benjamin M. Gresham 2-17-1853 Hn
Hays, Mary C. to John H. Morgan 8-12-1865 (8-13-1865) O
Hays, Mary D. to Joshua L. Sturgis 3-14-1861 T
Hays, Mary M. to J. P. Sullivan 8-15-1857 Sh
Hays, Mattie to James G. Oliver 5-7-1868 Ma
Hays, Mexico to James T. Mitchell 11-27-1844 We
Hays, Nancy to John H. Miller 9-21-1842 (10-13-1842) O
Hays, Nancy to Zackary A.? Henly 10-13-1855 (10-14-1855) T
Hays, Pernisia to John Neil 11-26-1832 Hr
Hays, Rachel J. to William Pitt Deadrick 5-9-1855 Ma
Hays, Rachel to Abram Castell 8-2-1826 Hr

Hays, Rebecca H. to Silas Brook 1-6-1832 (1-5?-1832) Hr
Hays, Rebecca J. to Lucius J. Thomas 7-27-1859 Ma
Hays, Sarah E. to George W. Hunt 1-3-1869 G
Hays, Sarah Jane to Sam Alexander 1-15-1876 (no return) Hy
Hays, Susan T. to George H. Prince 9-19-1839 Cr
Hays, Susannah to Littleton Moore 11-12-1869 (11-13-1869) F B
Hays, Tennessee to Jonathan Looney 11-16-1864 Hn
Hayslett, T. to Phil Wall 2-12-1869 (no return) F B
Haywood, Agnes to Sidney Read 4-20-1872 Hy
Haywood, America to Calvin Burnett 11-23-1869 Hy
Haywood, Anna E. to Elija Neighbors 11-5-1855 Cr
Haywood, Belinda to Wm. Autry 10-9-1848 Cr
Haywood, Cassy to Wm. Edwards 12-17-1846 Cr
Haywood, E. C. to S. F. Wallace 2-20-1855 Cr
Haywood, Elizabeth J. to Jethro L. Byrd 2-26-1833 O
Haywood, Ella to Charley Wilson 1-23-1873 Hy
Haywood, Famia to Fred Wm. Wilson 11-9-1871 T
Haywood, Fanny to Sandy Currie 12-19-1873 Hy
Haywood, Jane to Thomas B. Boyd 12-22-1842 Cr
Haywood, Lucindy C. to Green Bateman 4-11-1847 Cr
Haywood, Luisa to Presley King 12-8-1865 (12-10-1865) Cr
Haywood, M. E. to A. G. Chamberlin 7-11-1872 (7-13-1872) Cr
Haywood, Mariah to Wesley Barnes 7-21-1867 Cr
Haywood, Martha to Joshiah? Haywood 5-26-1842 Cr
Haywood, Mary to Wm. Bateman 1-30-1840 Cr
Haywood, Pricella to Wm. P. Birdwell 2-17-1852 Cr
Haywood, Sarah C. to Wm. C. Morris 9-28-1850 Cr
Haywood, ____ to Anderson Robinson 10-21-1866 (10-23-1866) Cr
Haze?, C. A. to J. W. Rieves 5-29-1872 Cr
Hazel, Doney to Adam Estes 4-17-1883 (4-18-1883) L
Hazel, Frances to James E. Demoss 11-26-1880 (11-28-1880) L B
Hazel, Linnie to Van Turrentine 3-18-1880 (3-19-1880) L B
Hazel, Martha to Henry Shaw 8-14-1875 L
Hazelwood, Lucy Ann to John H. Jones 7-1-1847 Sh
Hazelwood, Martha to John Watson 1-16-1843 G
Hazle, Jennie to Henry Hentz 12-25-1885 (12-27-1885) L
Hazle, Jenny to Henry Hentz 10-27-1881 (10-28-1881) L
Hazle, Lucinda to Ephraim Shaw 1-2-1875 (no return) L
Hazle, Rebecca to Henry Read 2-1-1876 (2-4-1876) L B
Hazlewood, B. J. to W. T. Hazlewood 12-19-1865 (12-20-1865) F
Hazlewood, Letitia F. to David C. House? no date (with Dec 1852) F
Hazlewood, M. F. to Jas. S. Wood 1-20-1857 G
Hazlewood, Mollie E. to Lewis C. Howse 11-9-1866 (11-14-1866) F
Head, Lucy to E. S. W. Wallon 3-22-1860 O
Head, Mahala to Williamson Hicks 5-25-1859 (5-29-1859) O
Head, Mary E. to Wm. H. Spiker 12-5-1864 O
Head?, Evalina to Erasmus King 9-6-1873 (9-14-1873) L
Headden, Mary M. to W. H. Hendricks 7-24-1877 Dy
Heade, H. R. to Thomas J. Killick 12-17-1870 (12-22-1870) L
Headen, Martha M. to Wm. W. Wright 1-16-1871 (1-18-1871) Dy
Headrick, Matilda to G. T. Bond 10-15-1853 (10-16-1853) Sh
Healey, Rosetta Ann to S. J. Freel 2-5-1863 Sh
Heard, Mary to Burrell M. Thompson 6-3-1854 (6-4-1854) G
Hearn, Cassie A. to W. A. Henson 2-14-1870 G
Hearn, Elsey to William Hammond 9-13-1845 (9-14-1845) Ma
Hearn, Jane P. to Allen W. Morgan 3-18-1859 Ma
Hearn, Jearn to John W. Hearn 12-9-1854 (12-10-1854) Ma
Hearn, Letitia F. to James M. Moore 10-5-1860 (10-9-1860) Ma
Hearn, M. A. to James T. Cook 12-23-1869 G
Hearn, Mary to Jackson Walton 12-30-1841 Cr
Hearn, Rachel to Wm. C. Thacher 1-15-1846 We
Hearn, Sarah to Henry Doling 7-31-1842 Cr
Hearring, Fannie N. to William R. Neighbors 1-31-1866 (2-1-1866) L
Hearring, Hittie to A. W. Montague 11-29-1875 L
Hearring, Kate to Samuel A. Given 2-22-1871 L
Heart, Sarah Virginia to Philip D. Bowles 10-27-1846 (10-28-1846) T
Heaslet, Fanny to Daniel Alexander 12-24-1869 (no return) F B
Heaslet, Sarah to David Shackelford 4-17-1869 (no return) F B
Heaslet, Virtue to Ned Herron 3-5-1870 (3-6-1870) F
Heaslett, Abbie to Dock Scott 2-11-1871 (no return) F B
Heaslett, Adaline to Henry Cogbill 2-2-1867 (no return) F B
Heaslett, Bettie to Alexander Randal 3-27-1869 (no return) F B
Heaslett, Lila to Edmund Tate 1-22-1869 (no return) F B
Heaslett, Paralee to Spencer Williams 2-2-1867 (no return) F B
Heaslett, Texanna to Clem Mitchell 12-25-1868 (no return) F B
Heaslitt, Mary to Henry Shackleford 3-9-1867 (no return) F B
Heath, Evelina G. A. to Andrew J. Crawford 9-17-1853 (9-19-1853) G
Heath, Harett J. to Wiley B. Dowell 9-7-1842 G
Heath, Malissa to George Webb 1-8-1861 We
Heath, Mary Ann to E. R. Bower 12-6-1849 G
Heath, Mary J. to Albert Smith 3-14-1863 (no return) We
Heath, Nancy (Mrs.) to Daniel Holt 8-6-1850 (8-9-1850) O
Heath, Nancy to Daniel Holt 8-6-1850 (8-9-1850) O
Heath, Susan to J. P. Ward 8-30-1865 G
Heath?, Mary M. to Isaiah White 5-10-1860 Hn
Heathcock, Amanda J. to William A. Johnson 11-9-1870 (11-10-1870) F
Heathcock, Matilda A. to John A. Luke (Luker?) 12-30-1868 G

Heathcock, Nannie B. to Robert A. Carson 3-3-1878 Hy
Heathcock, Sarah to H. J. Right (Kight) 9-22-1869 Hy
Heathcott, Darcus A. to John J. Stanley 2-21-1867 L
Heathcott, Jessie to William Dickerson 9-3-1849 Hn
Heathcott, Roana to Christian Hoffman 3-9-1843 Sh
Heatherington, Sarah J. to Asberry Chappell 5-25-1853 O
Heathscott, Mary A. to James Jolley 9-26-1855 We
Heathscott, Phoebe to Joseph Smith 1-4-1881 (1-5-1881) L
Hechelman, Barbara to Christopher Keaner 2-3-1849 Sh
Heckle (Hooker), Eliza to Peter H. Stevens 1-16-1838 Sh
Heckle, Lydia to E. H. Wilson 12-20-1852 (12-23-1852) Sh
Hector, Martha to Thomas W. King 6-25-1831 (6-30-1831) G
Hector, Susan Caroline to James William King 7-13-1843 Sh
Hedden, S. E. to James C. Green 11-18-1862 (11-19-1862) Dy
Hedge, Emaline to Wm. Hollaway 12-11-1844 Cr
Hedge, Mary to Joseph Gullege 5-19-1857 (no return) Cr
Hedge, Sarah B. to Cuthbert B. Lawrence 1-1-1856 (no return) Hn
Hedge, Sarah to Henry Brewer 12-27-1855 Cr
Hedgecock, Malinda to W. T. Thomas 10-9-1862 (no return) Cr
Hedgecock, Mary Elizabeth to Wm. T. Mount 7-28-1870 G
Hedgecock, R. J. to D. F. McKelvy 9-11-1867 G
Hedges, Susan to Dungan Autry 10-24-1849 Cr
Hedges, Virginia A. to Micajah Stokes 7-7-1870 F
Hedigs (Hediger), Mary to Markas Miller 8-22-1846 Sh
Hedin, Lutitia Mahala to John D. Alexander 9-1-1863 (no return) Dy
Hedleburg, Eveline to William Bryant 11-4-1840 Ma
Heely, Martha J. to Wm. A. Thompson 1-6-1865 (no return) Cr
Heely (Keeley?), Mary to James Hickey 9-14-1850 Sh
Heer, Celia to Johan Gieser 9-27-1860 Sh
Heffernan, Annie to Francois Lavigne 8-14-1862 Sh
Heffman, Bettie to J. A. Lynn? 12-31-1870 T
Hefley, Julia to W. C. Reeves 11-2-1847 Cr
Hefley, Mary J. to William D. Rainey 7-18-1859 (7-20-1859) Ma
Hefley, Sarah A. to John A. Kennedy 10-28-1858 (10-30-1858) Ma
Heflin, Laura to Thomas Lammond 11-16-1869 (11-17-1869) Cr
Heflin, Mary to Edward Brady 9-12-1838 Hn
Hefron, Annis to William Lewis 7-2-1836 Sh
Heggie, Martha A. to B. W. Ayers 3-24-1858 Be
Heickmott, Mary Ann to James Curran 4-9-1861 Sh
Heidel, Frederica to Henry Neif 5-31-1852 (6-3-1852) Sh
Heidel, M. to Augustus Crone 9-26-1864 (9-27-1864) Sh
Heidel, Rosina to Philip Wenner 6-28-1860 Sh
Heidle, Catherine (Mrs.) to L. F. Muller 4-22-1862 (4-24-1862) Sh
Heidleburg, Jane to Jesse Hooten 2-13-1843 (2-14-1843) Ma
Heidleburg, Louisa to Nowes Miller 10-11-1842 (10-12-1842) Ma
Heidrieger, Ann to Henrich (Henry) Straessler 2-26-1846 Sh
Heig, Berta to Adolph Fischer 8-28-1854 Sh
Heiman, Sophia to L. Falkenburg 12-16-1856 Sh
Hein, Doragherty to Jack Roose 4-19-1858 (4-25-1859) Sh
Hein, Frances to Edward Doutaz 10-29-1863 Sh
Heiney, Eliza to John Silk 1-7-1861 Sh
Heinman, Mary N. to William A. Johnson 5-9-1857 (5-10-1857) O
Heinz (Heiney), Charlotte to John F. Benner 9-10-1842 Sh
Heistan, Eliza to Jacob D. Hadway 3-27-1849 Sh
Heistand, Fannie V. to Charles May 5-21-1856 Sh
Heistand, Susan J. to Thomas B. King 8-9-1860 Sh
Heit (Hart), Lizzie to James W. D. Henry 2-8-1867 (2-12-1867) F
Helen M., Brown to Lankford Phebus 9-25-1877 Hy
Helen, Boyd to Peter Purham 8-15-1872 Hy
Helfer, Adeline to John Ashbrook 7-14-1850 Hn
Hellard, Adaline to Thomas E. James 3-31-1868 G
Hellard, Mary C. to Burrell W. Utley 12-11-1855 (12-12-1855) Ma
Hellis, M. E. J. to James G. Hatcher 2-28-1850 We
Hellix, Margaret to James N. Garrett 12-11-1866 O
Helm, Catherine to Jordan Young 11-28-1883 (11-19-1884) L
Helm, Mattie to Alex Thomas 4-13-1882 (no return) L
Helm, Pheby Jane to John W. Forsyth 1-23-1869 (1-28-1869) L
Helms, Adaline to John Howard 1-30-1869 (1-31-1869) Cr
Helms, Catharine to Thos. Bridges 3-31-1866 O
Helms, Eady Matilda to James F. N. Presson 3-31-1867 Be
Helms, Lucind to John W. Atkins 1-30-1865 Dy
Helms, M. A. to L. T. McElyea 10-12-1863 (10-13-1863) O
Helms, Martha C. to John Tims 12-13-1871 (12-14-1871) T
Helms, Martha J. to W. J. Smith 1-11-1864 Be
Helms, Martha to Alex Bennett 8-24-1876 Hy
Helperin?, Martha to James C. Nelson 3-20-1860 T
Helton, Maryann to James Seaton 12-17-1838 (12-20-1838) F
Helum, Mattie to Albert Parker 12-24-1875 (no return) Hy
Hemphill, Catharine to Henry Burlison 2-15-1868 (2-6?-1868) T
Hemphill, Ellen to Jacob Angus 1-17-1871 (1-18-1871) T
Hemphill, Sallie to Ed Overall 1-31-1871 (2-1-1871) T
Hempstead, Elizabeth to R. C. Brinkley 12-24-1860 (12-31-1860) Cr
Henby, Mary A. to Williams Edmonds 8-3-1854 We
Hendde, Nancy to Joseph Hutchinson 1-15-1867 (1-16-1867) O
Henderson, Adna to Thomas Scarbrough 12-22-1860 Hn
Henderson, Amanda Jane to John S. Webb 12-2-1864 (12-6-1854) O
Henderson, Amanda to Dempsey N. Sewell 2-1-1849 Ma

Henderson, Amanda to Matthew Edwards 8-16-1873 (8-21-1873) L B
Henderson, Amelia to M. F. Whitelaw 12-1-1885 (12-3-1885) L
Henderson, Angeline to Thad Tanner 1-19-1868 Hy
Henderson, Anjaline to Anderson Green 8-2-1877 Hy
Henderson, Ann Eliza to David W. Jamison 12-6-1856 Ma
Henderson, Bettie to Wm. W. Durham 12-21-1869 Ma
Henderson, Caroline to James Miller 12-27-1866 (no return) Dy
Henderson, Chaney to Bob Perkins 6-12-1864 (6-14-1864) Sh *
Henderson, Clary to Prince Henderson 12-13-1870 (12-12?-1870) Cr B
Henderson, Cora to J. U. Owen 10-23-1877 Hy
Henderson, Corriana A. to Henry W. McCorry 12-11-1838 Ma
Henderson, Dena A. to Jackson Williams 11-11-1871 Hy
Henderson, Dinah to Friday Thomas 1-5-1867 F B
Henderson, E. C. to J. F. Looney 12-19-1865 Cr
Henderson, E. T. to Newton M. Ligon 12-22-1852 Sh
Henderson, Eliza A. to A. D. Gwynne 9-7-1859 Sh
Henderson, Eliza to Hugh Hone 8-1-1852 Sh
Henderson, Eliza to Wilson Mires 1-27-1838 Sh
Henderson, Elizabeth to George White 10-4-1846 (10-5-1846) O
Henderson, Elizabeth to J. M. Fletcher 10-7-1846 Sh
Henderson, Elizabeth to John A. Johns(t)on 5-9-1848 O
Henderson, Elizabeth to Memory Wooten 12-31-1868 Ma
Henderson, Elizabeth to Robert Midkeff 5-9-1856 We
Henderson, Elizabeth to Robert Wade 8-24-1847 Hn
Henderson, Ella to George Smith 3-29-1877 Hy
Henderson, Ellen to Wallace Nixon 12-27-1883 L
Henderson, Emily V. to Varnum Ozment 5-10-1847 (no return) F
Henderson, Emma to Wade H. Nowlin 10-17-1870 (10-20-1870) Cr
Henderson, Gracy to Wiley Alexander 12-23-1871 (12-29-1871) L B
Henderson, Harriet to William Lapier 12-16-1873 Hy
Henderson, Isabella to Alexander Roberson 4-5-1859 Sh
Henderson, J. E. to A. H. Tatum 11-20-1867 G
Henderson, Jane to Isham Garret 3-8-1867 (3-9-1867) T
Henderson, Janie to George Graves 8-5-1867 (8-6-1867) T
Henderson, L. to E. G. Exum 11-6-1860 O
Henderson, Laura to J. P. Bowen 10-4-1870 (10-6-1870 Dy
Henderson, Lockey Ann to William M. Perkins 5-13-1841 Sh
Henderson, Locky Mariah to Whitfield Boyed 2-25-1841 F
Henderson, Lotta to John Porter 3-18-1873 (no return) Dy
Henderson, Lucinda J. to Enos H. Barnett 8-17-1846 (8-20-1846) Ma
Henderson, Lucy to Jackson Cole 12-27-1870 (12-28-1870) Cr
Henderson, M. E. to Charles F. Boon 8-24-1869 Ma
Henderson, M. Emma to Robert A. Roe 1-23-1867 (1-24-1867) Dy
Henderson, Margaret Ann to Thomas S. Neel 6-1-1857 Sh
Henderson, Margaret to John H. George 1-24-1845 (no return) F
Henderson, Margaret to Ransom Hinton 4-28-1871 (5-1-1871) L
Henderson, Margarett A. to Alonzo M. Chamberlin 4-14-1842 Ma
Henderson, Martha Ann to Hilliary Conemer 11-25-1839 Cr
Henderson, Martha Ann to Richard Smith 12-25-1851 Hn
Henderson, Martha J. to George Duke 2-7-1865 Dy
Henderson, Martha to James Campbell 1-18-1875 Hy
Henderson, Martha to Thomas W. Martin 9-3-1849 (9-4-1849) O
Henderson, Mary A. to William A. Hudson 10-5-1841 Ma
Henderson, Mary A. to William M. Kirk 12-6-1842 Hn
Henderson, Mary Ann to James Miles Burkhart 8-15-1843 (8-18-1843) T
Henderson, Mary E. to James S. Oglesby 9-3-1851 Sh
Henderson, Mary E. to Williams H. Bradley 1-15-1850 (1-17-1850) Ma
Henderson, Mary J. to J. D. Killebrew 12-24-1844 We
Henderson, Mary Jane to Edwin M. Yerger 10-21-1857 (10-22-1857) Sh
Henderson, Mary K. to Joseph E., jr. Plummer 4-11-1853 Sh
Henderson, Mary L. to Craig N. Lasley 12-18-1850 O
Henderson, Mary to Moses Hudgens 8-11-1864 (no return) Hn
Henderson, Matilda M. to Samuel D. Wilson 12-27-1839 (SB 1838) F
Henderson, Matilda to James M. Parrish 4-25-1845 We
Henderson, Mattie to Buck Curry 9-10-1881 (9-24-1881) L
Henderson, Millie to Zach Badgett 10-15-1880 (10-24-1880) Dy
Henderson, Minerva to Haywood Clements 12-28-1866 Hy
Henderson, Minnie W. to John C. Chilton 7-22-1877 Hy
Henderson, Molly to Thomas Everett 12-24-1869 (12-25-1869) Cr
Henderson, Nancy J. to I. T. Smoot 2-20-1861 Hn
Henderson, Nancy Minerva to James W. Barclay 3-10-1857 (3-11-1857) Ma
Henderson, Narcissa J. to William D. Powell 12-3-1861 Dy
Henderson, Panthia M. to F. M. Thompson 12-19-1860 G
Henderson, Paulina to J. C. Ward (Word) 2-12-1856 Sh
Henderson, Penny to Clarence Dyer 2-12-1875 (no return) Hy
Henderson, Permelia J. to G. W. Haden 4-11-1866 O
Henderson, Rachel to Thos. M. Means 4-27-1843 Sh
Henderson, Sally to Britton Polk 12-25-1866 (12-26-1866) F B
Henderson, Sarah J. to E. Pheaton P. Knox 3-28-1838 Cr
Henderson, Sarah J. to Knox E. Pheaton 3-28-1838 Cr
Henderson, Susan A. to B. J. Brevard 12-8-1868 Cr
Henderson, Susan B. to Thomas H. Garrett 11-30-1859 (12-1-1859) Ma
Henderson, Susan to Henry Washington 3-21-1868 (3-22-1868) O
Henderson, Susan to Thos. M. Walker 6-1-1846 We
Henderson, Tarissa M. to Charles Talley 4-4-1848 O
Henderson, Tarissa M. to Charles Talley 4-4-1848 (4-6-1848) O
Henderson, Vandalia to James Penick 10-25-1865 Hn
Henderson, Vilott Amanda to Thomas W. Goff 12-26-1836 (12-29-1836) G
Henderson, Vina to James Williams 1-20-1874 Hy
Henderson, Virginia to John Eldler 1-3-1855 (1-4-1855) O
Hendley, Holly to James H. Lowrey 11-17-1850 We
Hendley, Juli Ann to Eli Culp 12-27-1842 (no return) F
Hendley, Mariah P. to George Barnwell 8-19-1847 Hn
Hendly, Jenny to Ben Parham 7-6-1868 (7-10-1868) F B
Hendly, Malissa to Gillard King 2-3-1836 Hr
Hendly, Mary Margaret to John B. Todd 11-8-1867 (11-10-1867) Cr
Hendon, Margaret E. to Thomas J. Wheatley 9-6-1856 Be CC
Hendren, Frances to Henry Thomas 5-27-1871 Hy
Hendren, Jane to James McGuire 11-22-1878 Dy
Hendren, M. E. to J. C. McCrory 1-15-1878 (1-17-1878) L
Hendren, M. F. to W. J. Pittman 10-4-1856 Hy
Hendren, Martha A. to A. B. Henry 4-25-1867 (4-26-1867) L
Hendren, S. J. to C. L. Crisp 11-30-1880 (12-1-1880) L
Hendren, Sallie to Alfred Whitmore 7-11-1878 Hy
Hendren, Sarah E. to James W. Rainey 8-16-1866 L
Hendren, Sarah J. to James Stewart 11-7-1866 T
Hendren, V. F. to G. W. Fortner 4-4-1876 (no return) Hy
Hendrick, Elizabeth to Edwin Warrin 5-8-1831 G
Hendrick, Nancy E. to J. J. Thomas 2-17-1847 Hr
Hendricks, Caroline to Samuel Gunnon 3-19-1861 Sh
Hendricks, Cassa Ann to George W. Watson 2-8-1854 Ma
Hendricks, Elizabeth J. to Bedford Thomas 1-10-1849 (1-12-1849) Hr
Hendricks, Fanny to Jno. McMahan 3-3-1848 Sh
Hendricks, H. E. to W. H. Cope 8-12-1872 (no return) Dy
Hendricks, Harriet D. to Armstrong Swor 12-10-1839 Hn
Hendricks, Harriet to W. L. Wyatt 10-3-1871 (10-4-1871) Dy
Hendricks, Margaret M. to B. W. Teater 10-30-1867 (no return) Dy
Hendricks, Martha A. to H. A. Reed 7-15-1878 (no return) Dy
Hendricks, Martha A. to James C. Newport 3-30-1849 Hn
Hendricks, Martha E. F. to Samuel J. Goforth 10-31-1853 Hr
Hendricks, Mary Teresa to Charles Rest 1-12-1863 Sh
Hendricks, Mary to Benj. Lux(Sax?) 3-13-1860 (3-14-1860) Hr
Hendricks, Mary to John A. Wood 6-9-1860 O
Hendricks, Mary to Robert B. Davidson 12-24-1838 G
Hendricks, N. L. to J. W. Trout 12-24-1876 (12-26-1876) Dy
Hendricks, Polly to Wm. H. DeBerry 6-23-1828 (6-24-1828) Hr
Hendricks, S. A. to J. H. Chitwood 11-27-1878 (11-28-1878) Dy
Hendricks, Theresa to Charles West 1-12-1863 Sh
Hendrix, E. J. to Malekiah Bledsow 5-19-1849 (5-24-1849) O
Hendrix, E. to D. C. Clark 4-5-1865 (4-9-1865) O
Hendrix, Elizabeth A. to T. F. Petty 8-29-1861 Hn
Hendrix, Lucy C. to John J. Cooley 12-31-1860 (12-30-1861) We
Hendrix, M. E. to John Boyd 1-30-1866 (1-31-1866) Dy
Hendrix, Martha J. to W. H. Haste 10-26-1865 G
Hendrix, Martha to William J. Haynes 9-20-1879 L
Hendrix, Mary A. to Andrew J. (I?) Wasborn 4-12-1860 We
Hendrix, Mary D. to Henley Humphries 8-21-1864 Hn
Hendrix, Mary J. to I. A. Armfield ?-?-1862? Mn
Hendrix, Mary Jane to James M. Provine 7-31-1864 Hn
Hendrix, N. A. to J. M. Dickson 8-11-1862 Mn
Hendrix, Nancy Jane to James B. Dalton 7-13-1851 Hn
Hendrix, Nancy to H. T. Phelan 1-3-1866 G
Hendrix, S. J. to W. L. Wilcox 12-10-1867 (no return) Dy
Hendrix, Susan E. to Robert Jacobs 1-21-1863 (1-22-1863) O
Hendrix?, Samantha to John Faulk 6-22-1850 F
Hendron, Bettie to L. T. Johnston 1-22-1884 L
Hendron, Elizabeth J. to Josephus Crenshaw 1-28-1850 T
Hendron, Martha E. to James O. Henry 9-26-1855 T
Hendron, Mary J. to Henry Read 10-31-1868 (no return) Hy
Hendson, Susan to Thos. M. Walker 7-11-1846 (no return) We
Henigar, Anna to M. Koch 4-25-1859 Sh
Heniger, Catharine to Johan Hotter 9-18-1854 Sh
Hening, Mary J. E. to George Akers 12-2-1846 (12-3-1846) G
Hening, Tallulah to Richard K. Gamble 3-14-1873 Hy
Henings, Celestia A. to Charles H. Ross 2-28-1873 G
Henkle, Catherine N. to Wm. W. Trout 4-26-1859 Sh
Henkle, Fannie to Thomas H. Pewett 2-25-1869 G
Henkle, Fannie to Thomas H. Prewett 2-25-1869 G
Henley, Bridget to Edward O'Meley 5-30-1858 Sh
Henley, Elizabeth Jane to M. C. Holloway 11-20-1845 F
Henley, Estell to John Jeffries 1-26-1875 (1-27-1875) L
Henley, F. L. to Wm. Stedham 7-12-1860 (7-12-1860) F
Henley, Fannie T. to John A. Williams 11-17-1869 (11-18-1869) L
Henley, Jane to Culbertson B. Payne 11-27-1828 Sh
Henley, Louisa to Josiah Ward 6-8-1843 T
Henley, Margarett to James B. Morris 2-16-1841 (2-18-1841) F
Henley, Marietta to A. J. Meadows 3-17-1866 (3-20-1866) L
Henley, Martha to Alfred M. Kelly 4-7-1843 Sh
Henley, Martha to Green Burrow 5-19-1840 F
Henley, Mary Ann to Leigh Worsham 12-24-1872 (1-5-1873) L
Henley, Mary to William Ford 2-10-1854 Sh
Henley, Sallie M. to William Carrigan 4-1-1879 (4-2-1879) L
Henley, Sarah E. to Wm. H. Henley 11-9-1868 (11-11-1868) F
Henley, Susan to Armsted Dowdy 3-1-1852 (no return) F

Henley, T. S. to G. M. Midlin 6-17-1870 (6-19-1870) Cr
Henley, Tennessee V. to Armstead W. Boydston 11-30-1868 (12-1-1868) L
Henly, Anne E. to D. M. Coffey 12-12-1859 (no return) Hy
Henly, Catherine to Bill Davis 11-19-1875 (no return) Hy
Henly, Florence H. to James B. Michell 10-18-1876 L
Henly, Jane to James L. Page 11-18-1866 Hn
Henly, Lucy to Fed Davis 12-24-1877 Hy
Henly, Mandy to Smith Holloway 8-21-1876 (no return) Hy
Henly, Martha to D. G. Mussy 3-14-1849 (no return) F
Henly, Phillis to George W. Cherry 12-20-1878 Hy
Henly, Toerzer to Cornelius Mann 10-12-1876 Hy
Henly, W. A. (Mrs.) to J. P. Spear 6-21-1870 G
Henndon, Mary R. to Enoch B. Childress 12-15-1873 L
Henneley, Hannah to Patrick Gallaher 11-7-1857 (11-8-1857) Sh
Hennesy, Mary to John McGowan 8-20-1850 Sh
Henning, Adelade Rachel to James Dup___ Hall 10-5-1870 L
Henning, Charity to William Wardlaw 10-10-1871 (10-12-1871) L
Henning, Cilla to Dennis Fitzpatrick 2-5-1885 (no return) L
Henning, Eliza J. to L. P. Haynie 12-7-1867 (no return) L
Henning, Eliza to Ben Halliburton 2-5-1885 (no return) L
Henning, Eliza to Robert Allison 3-21-1873 L B
Henning, Ellen to Robert Braden 5-25-1874 L B
Henning, Emma (Mrs.) to Richard Rice 1-28-1886 L
Henning, Fannie A. to William H. Moorer 11-16-1859 L
Henning, Fannie to Elijah Barnes 5-1-1885 (no return) L
Henning, Fannie to William Allison 8-25-1877 (no return) L
Henning, Frances to Philip Reader 3-13-1858 (no return) L
Henning, Frankie to Alfred Turpin 9-13-1883 L
Henning, H.(A?) E. to W. W. Felts 2-22-1870? (2-23-1871) L
Henning, Hannah to Thomas Hamilton 3-12-1864 (3-16-1864) Cr
Henning, Hannah to Thomas Hamilton 3-12-1864 (no return) Cr
Henning, J. M. Henrietta to W. H. Cole 3-29-1881 (3-30-1881) L
Henning, Judie A. to Wm. P. Merriwether 12-20-1859 (12-21-1860) Ma
Henning, Judie B. to S. R. Sadler 12-7-1867 (no return) L
Henning, Judie R. to D. W. Brandon 1-25-1870 (1-26-1870) L
Henning, Judith M. H. to H. Winrow 8-12-1850 (no return) L
Henning, Judy to Captain Pickett 3-2-1882 L
Henning, Julia A. (Mrs.) to John C. McKelsey 1-30-1861 (no return) Cr
Henning, Lizzie to William M. Butler 12-21-1870 L
Henning, Lou to Nathan Sutherland 2-20-1877 (2-23-1877) L B
Henning, Lucy to Boyd Cogshell 3-31-1873 (4-1-1873) L
Henning, Lucy to Richd. Graves 8-5-1876 (no return) Hy
Henning, Martha P. to N. G. Powers 8-30-1851 Sh
Henning, Mary E. to H. B. Moorer 12-14-1875 (12-15-1875) L
Henning, Mary E. to Thomas J. Gillispie 7-15-1851 (7-16-1851) Sh
Henning, Missouri to David Duglass 12-23-1870 (no return) L
Henning, Nancy to Bob Read 5-19-1870 Hy
Henning, Nicy to Jerry Lake 4-22-1871 L
Henning, Rachel to Alexander Lake 1-22-1868 (no return) L B
Henning, Sallie F. to Robert W. Bond 2-17-1869 Ma
Henning, Sarah J. to James O. Cage 12-15-1852 (no return) L
Henning, Sarah Thomas to John N. Arnold 1-5-1844 (1-2?-1844) Ma
Henning, Silvia to Henderson Morehead 8-18-1877 (8-19-1877) L
Henning, Sinda to Jeff McKinny 6-5-1885 (6-26-1885) L
Henning, Winnie A. to John Blackwell 10-20-1867 (no return) L
Hennings?, Amanda to James H. Brogdon 5-3-1861 (no return) L
Hennisey, Ellen to William O'Hern 6-10-1855 Sh
Henrich, Dorothea E. to J. Joseph Schneider 11-27-1858 Sh
Henry, Addie F. to William C. Dupree 12-30-1885 L
Henry, Amanda J. to Robert G. Rainey 8-24-1861 (8-25-1861) L
Henry, America to John Monger 2-26-1869 G B
Henry, Amy to Richard Parks 10-28-1867 Ma B
Henry, Ann Eliza to E. J. Crosthwait 10-2_-1859 (10-23-1859) L
Henry, Ann to Frank Brown 12-27-1866 (no return) Dy
Henry, Anna M. to George T. Huntsman 12-17-1857 Sh
Henry, Bethenia to Sample Mills 11-24-1851 (11-27-1851) Hr
Henry, Betsy to Joseph Page 11-11-1866 Hn B
Henry, Buelah B. to W. J. Parker 3-23-1885 L
Henry, Caroline to James L. Chisum 12-2-1867 Ma
Henry, Cornelia F. to Moladeous B. Carroll 3-20-1848 (3-22-1848) G
Henry, E. T. to James M. Davie 10-11-1860 O
Henry, Elizabeth H. to William T. Edwards 9-27-1860 We
Henry, Francis to C. B. Jones 10-23-1856 We
Henry, Hanah E. to Walter Caruth 12-23-1852 L
Henry, Isabel to John Crow 9-22-1829 Hr
Henry, Isabela to William Dearmon 8-18-1863 (no return) Dy
Henry, Jane to D. S. Moore 9-11-1869 Hy
Henry, Julia A. to B. F. Smith 2-22-1869 Dy
Henry, Laura E. to Francis M. Haflin 4-12-1866? (with 1862) Cr
Henry, Laura to Jerry Criddle 12-25-1869 (6-25-1871) F B
Henry, Louisa to Swinson? Gardner 4-13-1843 (4-15-1843) T
Henry, M. F. to J. Z. McAlister 2-7-1872 Dy
Henry, Ma to William L. Hickman 4-4-1837 O
Henry, Margarett M. to Alpha R. Bumpus 1-3-1843 Ma
Henry, Maria to William House 10-13-1867 Hn B
Henry, Martha A. to H. B. Wilson 11-11-1862 G
Henry, Martha to Grief George 5-17-1849 Sh

Henry, Martha to Squire Bishop 12-15-1861 Be
Henry, Mary A. to Albert Hunt 12-23-1866 G
Henry, Mary A. to Francis Marion Lee 10-9-1848 (10-12-1848) T
Henry, Mary A. to John E. Lewellyng 1-1-1868 (1-15-1868) L
Henry, Mary A. to W. K. Simpson 12-29-1869 (12-30-1869) Dy
Henry, Mary E. E. to A. L. Smothers ?-?-1850 Cr
Henry, Mary to William Hare 4-6-1853 (6-12-1853) Sh
Henry, Mira to Joseph A. McCall 4-21-1846 Sh
Henry, Nancy M. to William H. Kindrick 2-17-1853? (2-21-1855) Hr
Henry, Nancy to Ivy Cole 5-25-1854 O
Henry, Nancy to Ivy Cole 5-25-1856 O
Henry, Parthenia C. to John H. Smith 9-13-1853 (9-14-1853) G
Henry, Rachel to William Moody 12-31-1857 Hn
Henry, Sarah E. to L. Milton Whitman 7-12-1848 Sh
Henry, Sarah H. to Isaac Ellam (Elam?) 2-7-1850 Hn
Henry, Sarah T. to J. M. King 12-26-1860 (12-29-1860) O
Henry, Sarah to Samuel Bray 12-10-1861 (12-11-1861) L
Henry, Sarah to Silas Land 5-17-1849 Sh
Henry, Tabitha S. to Robert P. Maxwell 9-24-1854 We
Henry?, Elizabeth to James H. King 2-3-1848 O
Henry?, Lula to William Asberry Wilkirson 10-28-1873 L
Henry?, Sarah J. to James D. Doomas 12-13-1864 Hn
Henshaw, Margaret A. to David Kirkland 7-6-1846 (7-12-1846) F
Henshaw, Martha J. to George Howard 8-28-1854 Sh
Henslee, C. A. to R. H. Pool 7-14-1858 (no return) Hn
Hensler, Sallie E. to S. U. Howell 10-4-1857 Ma
Hensley, Callie to John T. Hooton 2-16-1876 (no return) Hy
Hensley, Elizabeth to A. M. Fleming 2-7-1868 (no return) Hy
Hensley, Gracey A. to George W. Cox 3-5-1867 (no return) Hy
Hensley, Sarah E. to Calvin White 7-21-1856 Hr
Hensly, Mary E. to L. W. Brown 12-23-1858 Hr
Henson, Charlotte to James F. Hall 4-22-1860 Sh
Henson, Charlotte to James Smith 9-21-1858 Sh
Henson, Elizabeth to James M. Mitchell 11-17-1858 (11-20-1858) Hr
Henson, Lucy to Wm. H. Bass 9-20-1859 Hr
Henson, Margaret to Hiram Elkins 12-24-1850 (12-29-1850) Hr
Henson, Martha Ann to John Newsom 4-25-1854 Sh
Henson, Martha J. to N. P. Haltom 10-10-1861 (10-13-1861) Hr
Henson, Mary to Stephen Gibson 11-1-1836 Hr
Henson, Minny E. to John Dill 3-7-1856 (3-9-1856) Hr
Henson, Nancy to George S. Gibson 1-27-1828 (1-29-1828) Hr
Henson, Nancy to Wm. G. Hays 3-7-1833 Hr
Henson, Polly to John Anderson 12-7-1843 Sh
Henson, Sally to Arma Shoefer 2-17-1830 (2-18-1830) Hr
Henson, Sarah C. to John Baker 3-1-1850 (3-7-1850) Hr
Henson, Sarah to Hiel Gibson 12-23-1846 (12-24-1846) Hr
Herald, Charity A. to Jesse C. Perkins 2-7-1853 (3-1-1853) O
Herald, Elizabeth to Thomas Canady 11-26-1877 Dy
Herald, Sarah Ann to Wm. A. Overton 11-26-1843 We
Herald, Susan to W. Woods 3-6-1878 (3-7-1878) Dy
Herall, M. A. to J. W. Neal 6-22-1865 O
Herbert, S. E. to Wm. H. Wallace 10-29-1860 Hy
Herbertson, Maggie to Geo. Sherman 12-17-1859 Sh
Herch, Leona to Moses Goldsmith 3-27-1872 Hy
Herendon, Mary Jane to J. R. Parish 3-18-1858 Hr
Hering, Mary A. to W. J. Tucker 7-8-1865 (7-9-1865) O
Herington, Candis A. to A. F. Clements 2-25-1845 (no return) We
Herington, Catharine to Wm. H. Neesbit 12-27-1843 (12-28-1843) F
Herington, Elizabeth to William Morris 12-27-1843 (12-28-1843) F
Herington, Frances to W. C. Childress 2-20-1860 G
Heriod, Mary to James Baxter 11-28-1854 G
Hermany, Catharine to Hermann Scheer 3-15-1858 (3-16-1858) Sh
Hern, Ellen to Wm. Gantlett? 5-25-1841 (no return) Cr
Hern, Jane E. to James M. Strown 12-25-1843 Cr
Hern, Mary M. to Elmer Finch 8-12-1858 Cr
Hernard, Elizabeth to Benjamin Price 2-13-1842 Cr
Hernden?, Mary A. C. to Thomas Jenkins 11-30-1851 Hn
Herndon, Arabella to Hugh B. Robinson 8-8-1868 (9-3-1868) Ma
Herndon, Elizabeth to H. W. Nordon 4-21-1847 Cr
Herndon, Julia to James Melton 9-12-1867
Herndon, Levina to J. B. Grayham 10-22-1865 Be
Herndon, Margaret E. to Thomas J. Wheatly 9-6-1856 Be
Herndon, Mary A. to M. Y. Moran 1-24-1849 (1-26-1849) F
Herndon, Mary E. to Wm. F. Duffy 10-14-1871 (10-18-1871) Ma
Herndon, Mary M. to Walter N. Thedford 10-22-1855 (10-24-1855) G
Herndon, Matilda to John Herndon 8-27-1848 Sh
Herndon, Mollie M. T. to Frank L. Moffatt 1-27-1870 F
Herndon, Virginia T. to Henry W. Merriweather 9-8-1858 Sh
Herne, E. L. to G. W. Perkins 7-13-1847 (7-15-1847) O
Herne?, Elizabeth to Jacob Cox 2-27-1834 Hr
Hernes, Mary F. to George Barnes 12-5-1867 F
Herney, Mary (Mrs.) to Louis Casey 5-3-1863? Sh
Heron, M. F. to P. J. Wright 2-14-1868 G B
Heron, Sarah to William Perkins 7-30-1856 (8-2-1856) O
Herralston, Elizabeth to A. W. Meek 8-2-1858 Sh
Herrell, Mrs. L. J. to T. D. Lane 12-17-1873 T
Herrell, Penny to Columbus Herrell 10-23-1868 Cr

Herrell?, Elizabeth to William B. Seaton 1-4-1851 (1-5-1851) Hr
Herren, Frances M. to Charles Barns 1-3-1863 Be
Herren, M. A. to G. Gerren 1-26-1837 Be
Herren, Melvina to L. J. Okelly 8-19-1862 (not endorsed) F
Herren, Sarah to John M. Madden 3-21-1865 Be
Herril, Martha to Jessee B. Baker 3-16-1876 Dy
Herrin, Elizabeth to Rufus Reed 7-4-1863 (7-5-1863) O
Herrin, Ellen to Samuel Lowe 5-10?-1868 T
Herrin, Mary E. to J. R. Ogwain 9-14-1868 Be
Herrin, Mollie to James Pierce 10-25-1871 (10-26-1871) T
Herrin, N. to P. G. Herrin 3-18-1842 Be
Herrin, Parthena to W. K. Perkins 3-26-1839 Be
Herrin, Polly to Wilson Jones 10-25-1847 (10-26-1847) O
Herrin, Priscilla C. to J. F. Edington 3-3-1861 Be
Herring (Henning?), Elizabeth J. to John W. Morrison 1-28-1851 Sh
Herring, Elizabeth to Alfred A. Whitley 12-17-1846 Sh
Herring, Emily A. to William H. Rankin 12-31-1849 (1-1-1850) O
Herring, Flora to John Dunn 12-4-1872 Hy
Herring, Ida to Mike Dunphy 7-15-1874 Hy
Herring, M. E. to Philip E. Broocke 1-19-1876 (no return) Hy
Herring, Mary to Thomas J. Wherry 4-24-1840 Sh
Herring, Nancy to Joseph Massey 5-25-1843 Sh
Herring, Pearcy to Robert Griffin 2-2-1843 Sh
Herring, S. A. to A. J. Graham 6-14-1863 O
Herring, S. A. to J. F. White 10-11-1875 Hy
Herring, Susan A. G. to Allen Oliver 9-18-1854 (9-20-1854) O
Herring, Susan to John Long 4-26-1854 (4-27-1854) Sh
Herrington, Elizabeth to Willis Langford 9-24-1850 (9-25-1850) Ma
Herrington, Rosa Ann to Levi Darr 10-27-1852 G
Herrod, Charlotte to Jordan Dickerson 5-26-1866 F B
Herrod, Tabitha to Milet Busby 3-20-1858 O
Herron, Angeline to Thomas N. Presson 10-15-1845 Be
Herron, Carena to John McCall 6-4-1862 Sh
Herron, Elender to Richard Reame 7-6-1843 Be
Herron, Ella C. to John M. Lacy 11-20-1872 (11-21-1872) Cr
Herron, Emily Jane to Thomas A. McNail 11-5-1855 (11-7-1855) Ma
Herron, Fannie A. to Henry M. Cocke 1-16-1861 F
Herron, Hilean Ann to D. P. Murchison 10-14-1868 (10-16-1868) F
Herron, Lizzy to King McLemore 4-16-1870 (4-17-1870) Cr
Herron, Malinda to William Scarborough 4-14-1841 Ma
Herron, Malvina to L. J. OKelly 8-19-1862 (8-23-1862) F
Herron, Margaret to Isaac Jackson 4-28-1860 (4-29-1860) Dy
Herron, Mariah to Francis Parmer 1-16-1844 Ma
Herron, Martha C. to Robert W. Mason 3-30-1859 (3-31-1859) Ma
Herron, Martha J. to Starkey Dawes 6-19-1869 (6-20-1869) Cr
Herron, Martha to Henry Liles 12-9-1869 Cr
Herron, Martha to John W. Smith 1-30-1850 Cr
Herron, Mary A. to G. R. Petty 9-28-1842 (no return) Hn
Herron, Mary A. to Moses Grooms 12-24-1850 Sh
Herron, Mary Ann to B. J. Holden 12-24-1848 Be
Herron, Mary Ann to George Jackson 9-20-1860 Dy
Herron, Mary M. to George B. Searingen 11-28-1866 (11-29-1866) Cr
Herron, Milly to George Holland 8-1-1868 (8-2-1868) Cr
Herron, Nancy B. to Lewis J. O'Kelly 9-5-1866 (9-9-1866) F
Herron, Nancy to Abner C. Herron 9-3-1849 Be
Herron, Priscilla C. to James F. Edington 3-3-1861 Be
Herron, Sallie F. to L. (Dr.) Holmes 12-8-1857 (12-9-1857) Sh
Herron, Sally to Abram Banister 5-21-1869 (5-22-1869) Cr
Herron, Sarah A. to Jesse Hickman 2-12-1857 Cr
Herron, Sarah to R. R. Reaves 9-12-1844 Cr
Herron, Sophia A. to M. R. Sneed 2-2-1848 Sh
Herron, Susan to W. B. Wall 1-24-1866 (1-25-1866) F
Herron, Z. H. to A. R. Snead 1-20-1849 Sh
Herron?, Martha C. to J. F. Bellew 12-11-1865 (no return) Cr
Herryman, Sarah to James C. Irvin 2-4-1836 Hr
Hersch?, Ann to E. G. Wright 10-16-1856 Be
Herse, Matilda to Asa Patterson 5-3-1852 Ma
Hersey, Alvira to Thomas Bryant 8-10-1854 G
Hert, Antonia to Conrad Ludwig 8-4-1855 Sh
Hertle, Jane to W. D. Stephens 12-23-1868 (12-25-1868) F
Hervell?, Sarah L. to David A? Gates 11-9-1850 Hr
Hervey, Ann to Willoby D. Simmons 3-29-1843 Hr
Hervey, Elizabeth to James Murphy 10-31-1843 (11-2-1843) Hr
Hervey, Lovenia to John A. Long 12-20-1848 Hr
Heskett, Mary M. F. to David Jones 12-14-1865 O
Hesler, Ann J. to H. M. Farmer 7-13-1849 (7-17-1849) F
Hess, Ann to Perry Weems 12-18-1873 Hy
Hess, Critina to Polk Taylor 12-28-1870 Hy
Hess, Elizabeth W. to W. A. Jones 2-16-1857 G
Hess, Louisana to James A. McKnight 10-31-1831 (11-3-1831) G
Hess, Margaret E. to James M. Senter 10-14-1852 G
Hess, Maria to William Price 12-31-1838 (1-2-1839) G
Hess, Marion W. to Elias Jackson 10-9-1854 (10-11-1854) G
Hess, Mary Adaline to Edwin Crossland 3-2-1847 G
Hess, Mary to John Ragan 2-21-1867 G
Hess, Molly to H. C. Taylor 12-25-1874 Hy
Hess, Parlea to David Lanom 4-7-1870 G B

Hess, Tennessee to Sandy Alexander 7-19-1867 (no return) Hy
Hesse, Jeanette to Isaac Bomberger 12-6-1858 Sh
Hessing, Louisa to August Berton 6-27-1864 Sh
Hester, Amanda A. to Benjamin Hay 5-19-1865 (5-21-1865) O
Hester, Ann Eliza to William High 8-8-1837 Hr
Hester, Fanny to John Davis 4-2-1865 (4-9-1865) Cr
Hester, Francis D. to Bennett Byrum 1-8-1878 Hy
Hester, G. A. to Thos. D. Bryan 11-21-1876 (11-23-1876) O
Hester, Judah to Edward L. Peters 6-7-1848 Hr
Hester, Lucinda to Claiborne Campbell 1-25-1836 (1?-7-1836) Hr
Hester, Lucy J. to Lacy J. Hester 4-26-1858 Cr
Hester, Mary E. to James M. Neely 10-25-1865 Cr
Hester, Mary E. to William H. Dotson 3-30-1862 (no return) Cr
Hester, Mary to Arnold B. Everson 2-22-1848 Sh
Hester, Matilda to Jno. Mitchell 3-1-1842 Sh
Hester, Nancy to Jerome Mitchel 8-1-1849 (no return) F
Hester, Sarah F. to W. P. Gills 12-30-1868 O
Hester, Sarah to Silas Whiting 6-21-1848 (6-23-1848) F
Hethcock, Rebecca to William Lindsay 8-15-1866 Hy
Hetherington, Mary to John W. Damron 12-21-1853 O
Hethpeth, Mary E. to William Dorch 10-3-1860 We
Hetirzir, Eliza to John Fisher 10-15-1862 (10-16-1862) Sh
Heuey, T. J. to Rufus L. Traywick 6-2-1858 Cr
Hewett, Delia to John W. Bell 2-13-1879 (2-16-1879) L
Hewett, Emily to William W. Sexton 8-16-1867 (8-18-1867) Ma
Hewett, Malinda C. to Phineas T. Scruggs 5-22-1861 (5-23-1861) Ma
Hewey, Frances J. to John Evans 8-29-1866 (9-2-1866) Cr
Hewitt, Bettie B. to M. W. Smith 10-24-1869 F
Hewitt, Ella M. to J. B. Hogan 12-6-1877 (no return) Hy
Hewitt, Mary E. to Asbury Pegues 1-27-1843 (2-1-1843) Ma
Hewlett, Minerva P. to James L. Cashion 4-24-1855 (4-30-1855) O
Hewlett, Sarah Ann to Wiley C. Matheney 7-9-1855 (8-7-1855) O
Hewlett, Virginia J. to Williamson Curtner 2-21-1853 (3-1-1853) O
Hezekiah, Catherine to Mathias App 2-18-1850 Sh
Hiatt, S. V. to J. R. Jones 1-3-1867 Cr
Hibbitts, Sarah J. to Patrick Y. White 2-6-1866 (2-7-1866) Dy
Hickam, Dolly Ann to J. P. Beavers 5-17-1857 Hn
Hickerson, Margaret to Allen M. C. Smith 1-6-1828 Sh
Hickerson, Martha to Thomas D. Dalby 1-8-1836 Sh
Hickerson, Mary L. to Jeremiah Massey 8-15-1849 Sh
Hickey, Bridget to James McAleer 6-21-1861 (6-23-1861) Sh
Hickey, Sally to John H. Elder 2-2-1826 G
Hickey, Sally to John H. Elder 2-2-1828 G
Hickey, Susan to Francis M. Hobbs 8-23-1865 F
Hickman, Amanda to H. L. Glover 1-19-1865 O
Hickman, E. J. to W. A. Porter 9-5-1870 (9-8-1870) Cr
Hickman, Ediah to James W. Ryder 3-6-1843 (3-12-1843) O
Hickman, Elizabeth to Elijah Lincoln 3-22-1852 (3-23-1852) Sh
Hickman, Ellender to N. W. Taylor 9-30-1847 Cr
Hickman, Julia Ann to John Hammer 3-31-1845 O
Hickman, Louisa to George W. Ryder 6-25-1839 (6-30-1839) O
Hickman, M. E. to Nelson McAlexander 3-17-1871 (3-18-1871) Cr
Hickman, Martha A. to John Cox 11-5-1857 Cr
Hickman, Martha Ann to David B. Mason 10-6-1837 (10-10-1837) G
Hickman, Mary A. to James Winn 11-18-1864 Sh
Hickman, Mary C. to William Thomas Baldridge 12-24-1853 (12-27-1853) Ma
Hickman, Mary E. to David T. Spain 2-4-1859 Cr
Hickman, Nancy J. to Milton D. Norvell 7-10-1849 Ma
Hickman, Rebecah F. to Jesse McAlexander 2-24-1868 Cr
Hickman, S. A. E. to P. M. Breeden 7-19-1865 Hn
Hicks (Kicks), Holly Ann to M. D. Cardwell 6-18-1846 (no return) We
Hicks, A. P. to J. J. Hagler 12-27-1865 Hn
Hicks, Ally to Nathaniel S. Isbell 11-4-1846 (11-9-1846) Hr
Hicks, Alvinia to Reding Hicks 7-25-1854 (7-26-1854) G
Hicks, Amie to Allen King Wilson 11-10-1829 (11-9?-1829) Hr
Hicks, Angeline to James A. Black 4-11-1850 Cr
Hicks, Ann to Jack Harlan 8-30-1867 G B
Hicks, Caroline to David Petty 4-4-1856 W
Hicks, Caroline to Frank Phillips 11-6-1869 (no return) F B
Hicks, Catherine to John McCulloch 10-25-1865 (10-26-1865) Dy
Hicks, Centhia to John Fish 9-24-1844 (9-26-1844) Hr
Hicks, Cherry A. to Turner P. Holmes 8-30-1854 Ma
Hicks, Cornelia to Turner Outlaw 11-9-1878 Hy
Hicks, E. C. to F. A. Collins 1-27-1879 Dy
Hicks, Eliza Ann to Solomon C. Casey 9-8-1856 (9-11-1856) Hr
Hicks, Eliza to John P. Bushart 9-24-1851 Hn
Hicks, Elizabeth J. to Robert Rushing 2-28-1861 Be
Hicks, Elizabeth to Caleb Cox 8-4-1832 (8-9-1832) Hr
Hicks, Elizabeth to J. E. Southerland 1-8-1857 Cr
Hicks, Elizabeth to Richard King 4-2-1867 Hn
Hicks, Ella J. to J. T. Obenchain 6-8-1868 Ma
Hicks, Elmina to William G. McCord 7-12-1853 Hn
Hicks, Elsa to Ashley Hicks 8-12-1854 (8-?-1854) G
Hicks, Emily to Jason Wilson 2-28-1848 (3-2-1848) Hr
Hicks, Fa_ba to John Carrigan 5-3-1863 G
Hicks, Frances C. to Thomas M. Hardy 11-30-1878 (12-3-1878) L
Hicks, Frances to Arch Gillis 4-18-1839 Cr

Hicks, Harriet G. to William H. Palmer 9-18-1848 Hn
Hicks, Hulda to William M. Allen 3-15-1870 (3-16-1870) Ma
Hicks, Jane M. to Silas Deloach 1-14-1857 (1-15-1857) Ma
Hicks, Jane to David L. Haley 2-17-1830 (2-12-1830) G
Hicks, L. to Wilson Killey 3-16-1848 Cr
Hicks, Lamira J. to Jesse C. Cate 12-2-1857 Hn
Hicks, Laura J. to T. A. Ballard 5-24-1874 Hy
Hicks, Levina to William F. Karnes 1-24-1867 G
Hicks, Lizzie V. to E. W. Carnall 8-22-1863 (8-23-1863) L
Hicks, Lizzie to Stacey Riley 8-13-1874 O B
Hicks, Louisa to H. H. Mitchel 12-19-1852 Be
Hicks, Lucinda to Henry C. Finch 8-31-1870 (9-1-1870) Cr
Hicks, M. C. to John Powers 10-21-1856 We
Hicks, M. C. to W. R. Hobday 11-25-1874 Dy
Hicks, M. E. to Green Mills 12-28-1857 (12-29-1857) Sh
Hicks, M. J. to E. H. Shaw 8-21-1877 Hy
Hicks, M. J. to R. M. Webb 12-29-1879 (12-30-1879) L
Hicks, Margaret to James Cook 2-8-1853 G
Hicks, Margaret to John W. Avery 1-8-1839 G
Hicks, Margarett to George Stone 11-28-1865 G
Hicks, Martha A. to Dennis Cole 10-17-1852 Be
Hicks, Martha Ann to Thos. H. Leake 7-14-1846 Ma
Hicks, Martha B. to Rufus Vickers 8-10-1854 Cr
Hicks, Martha D. to Carroll J. Pickler 8-10-1854 Cr
Hicks, Martha E. to James B. Pearcy 12-4-1849 Ma
Hicks, Martha F. to James F. Cate 12-26-1852 Hn
Hicks, Martha K. D. to Washington L. Shell 3-23-1865 Hn
Hicks, Martha to Gideon Gibson 9-9-1862 Be
Hicks, Martha to Lafayette Lawler 10-6-1867 Be
Hicks, Martha to Wm. Butler 7-15-1856 Cr
Hicks, Mary Alice to James Merriwether 12-12-1878 Hy
Hicks, Mary Ann to George W. Harrison 2-20-1866 Be
Hicks, Mary C. to J. S. Middlebrook 3-7-1872 Hy
Hicks, Mary J. to James H. Irby 3-28-1860 Be
Hicks, Mary J. to Joseph Sherron 9-25-1855 Cr
Hicks, Mary J. to Thomas C. Edwards 7-24-1841 Hn
Hicks, Mary L. to Jesse Bryant 9-30-1856 (10-2-1856) Hr
Hicks, Mary to Jame A. Dotson 9-14-1854 Cr
Hicks, Mary to R. L. Blaney (Blarney) 11-15-1849 Sh
Hicks, Mary to W. A. Harper 12-31-1844 Cr
Hicks, Milisa to G. W. Butler 12-25-1867 G
Hicks, Mollie T. to J. D. Allen 12-16-1874 (12-17-1874) L
Hicks, Nancy C. to James Batty 4-28-1859 Cr
Hicks, Nancy to H. S. Owen 3-21-1846 Hr
Hicks, Nancy to John Vantreese 10-2-1847 (10-6-1847) Ma
Hicks, Nancy to Mitchell Dengo 9-18-1852 Sh
Hicks, Nannie to John Moore 1-6-1876 (no return) Hy
Hicks, Narcissa E. to Harmon Cos 7-8-1852 Be
Hicks, Rachel to William A. Walls 1-5-1854 (1-8-1854) G
Hicks, Rhoda Ann to Samuel A. Kelsey 7-25-1848 Hn
Hicks, S. A. to A. P. Gilliam 9-9-1867 (no return) Hy
Hicks, Sallie to E. H. Hinton 6-6-1866 L
Hicks, Sallie to Thos. A. Tripp 5-26-1869 (5-27-1869) F
Hicks, Sallie to W. P. Keenan 4-18-1878 (4-19-1878) Dy
Hicks, Sally to Green B. Hicks 3-26-1844 (3-28-1844) Hr
Hicks, Sally to Rhea Wallace 3-1-1848 Be
Hicks, Sarah A. to William Harris]2-21-1869 Be
Hicks, Sarah Ann to Ansel P---? 8-29-1844 Hn
Hicks, Sarah L. to Nathaniel M. Edwards 11-21-1848 Hn
Hicks, Sarah S. to James M. Gholston 4-17-1858 (4-20-1858) O
Hicks, Sarah to Eacle McKinney 2-6-1851 Cr
Hicks, Sarah to Jesse Vincent 4-22-1855 Cr
Hicks, Savanah to Milton B. Kee 6-16-1866 (6-17-1866) Cr
Hicks, Sophronia to Campbell Price 2-9-1867 (2-10-1867) Ma
Hicks, Susan A. to Thos. P. Williams 8-4-1846 Cr
Hicks, Susan T. to John J. Clanton 5-11-1870 (5-12-1870) Ma
Hicks, Susan to Richard Walls 8-31-1854 G
Hicks, Synthan C. to Thos. A. Carrington 8-14-1856 Cr
Hicks, Tempy Jane to John Walker 3-22-1848 Cr
Hicks, Vina to Elijah Grier 3-20-1854 G
Hicox, Sarah E. to Eldridge L. Fisher 9-21-1857 Ma
Hidle, J. to Charles Kney 11-11-1862 Sh
Hielderbrand, Elmedia to James Rainy 8-3-1830 Ma
Hiflin, Elizabeth to Isaac G. Frazier 12-22-1857 We
Hifs (Hiss?), Elizabeth to John Nagel 8-30-1851 Sh
Higdon, Levina to Drewberry White 9-5-1855 Be
Higdon, Levina to Drewberry White 9-5-1855 Be CC
Higdon, Sidney C. to Samuel Crockett 2-12-1845 Be
Higenbothem, Sarah P. to Bernard G. Hendrick 2-19-1851 (no return) F
Higganbottom, Nancy to Thomas Moody 6-12-1836 Sh
Higganson, Sarrah D. to Marcus D. L. Sumner 4-18-1843 (4-25-1843) F
Higgarson, Mary S. to N. J. Cocke 9-1-1847 F
Higgason, Alice to Mat Carpenter 4-12-1871 F B
Higgason, Ann to Logan Jones 3-19-1866 (no return) F B
Higgason, Fannie M. to Edmund R. Scruggs 3-18-1868 F
Higgason, Lizzie L. to John W. Shaw 3-3-1870 F
Higgason, Mallissa to Wm. C. Burton 10-23-1860 (10-24-1860) F

Higgin, Ellen to M. Kelly 5-15-1856 Sh
Higgin, Mary to Henry Driscol 12-27-1866 (12-28-1866) Dy
Higginbottom, Pamina to John Foreman 11-23-1842 Ma
Higgins, Ann E. to Jesse D. Partee 8-15-1835 (8-16-1835) G
Higgins, Ann to Alex McMillen 1-15-1852 (1-16-1852) Sh
Higgins, Bridgett to John Glancy 5-10-1851 (5-11-1851) Sh
Higgins, Eliza A. (Mrs.) to Thos. Matthies (Mathias) 8-1-1863 Sh
Higgins, Margaret to Joseph H. Jenning 2-5-1860 We
Higgins, Mary Ann to John H. Fentern 12-28-1857 (12-29-1857) Sh
Higgins, Mary to John McPartlin (McWarlin) 1-10-1863 Sh
Higgins, Moley J. to Robert Atchison 8-18-1841 G
Higgins, Sarah Ann to Absolem Knox 4-13-1833 (4-14-1833) G
Higgins, Winney to Marion Coleman 4-1-1870 (4-2-1870) Cr
Higgs, Elizabeth C. to Mathew Lynn 6-14-1862 We
Higgs, Emily H. to Ephraim Davis 12-27-1843 We
Higgs, Louvenia to Elija Cannon 5-25-1850 (5-26-1850) Hr
Higgs, Martha J. to Cannon Smith 12-27-1857 (1-5-1858) Hr
Higgs, Mary M. to Dempsey E. Curl 12-4-1858 (12-5-1858) Hr
Higgs, Mary to Solomon Pope 12-7-1855 We
Higgs, Molly A. to W. M. Dinwiddie 9-11-1860 We
Higgs, Nancy E. to Wm. Thompson 10-24-1859 Hr
Higgs, Rebecca to W. D. Simmons 6-30-1846 Hr
High, Analiza to C. H. Brumley 5-6-1841 F
High, Celia to Evans Williams 4-18-1870 (5-1-1870) F B
High, Fannie to H. P. Taylor 12-6-1864 Hn
High, Frances M. to H.S. Wills 5-4-1845 Hr
High, Luraney to J. P. Matheney 1-27-1854 Hn
High, Mary A. to James Bagley 4-12-1836 (4-14-1836) Hr
High, Mary to Horatio S. Wells 10-26-1842 F
High, Mary to J. K. Gordon 1-22-1865 Hn
High, Nancy Jane to Freman Hubbard 9-11-1850 (9-12-1850) F
High, Penelope to Joseph Eli 3-26-1844 Hn
High, Sarah Elizabeth to William Hollerday 9-28-1862 Hn
High, Sarah Jane to John Flag (Flager) 10-15-1862 (10-16-1862) Sh
High, Sarah to Thomas P. Gilliam 12-23-1847 F
High, Theney to Richard Todd 8-27-1838 (no return) Hn
High?, Lucy to James Hall 2-11-1846 (no return) Hn
Highfield, Cela A. to Stephen Gibson 5-28-1856 (5-29-1856) Hr
Highfield, Delilah to John Threlkeld 3-28-1828 (3-30-1828) Hr
Highfield, Julia Ann to N. C. Riggs 2-7-1867 Hn
Highfield, Nancy to James W. Norton 1-26-1853 (2-2-1853) Hr
Highfill, Malenda to Henry J. Rogers 12-6-1845 Hr
Hight, Amelia Jane to Conrad Seuberth 11-22-1855 Ma
Hight, Christiana to Jesse Blount 9-7-1840 Hr
Hight, Elizabeth M. to David Jordan 1-14-1852 G
Hight, Mary E. (Mrs.) to W. M. Hendrix 7-5-1865 G
Hight, Milla to John S. York 11-20-1838 Ma
Hight, Molly to W. S. Walker 12-24-1865 Hn
Hightower, Adaline to O. E. Muzzall 11-6-1851 Hn
Hightower, Betsy Jane to Edward Owen 3-4-1871 (3-5-1871) Ma
Hightower, Crisey to Shelby Jones 11-11-1867 Hn B
Hightower, Elizabeth to John P. Good 4-21-1873 (5-1-1873) T
Hightower, Jessie to Wash Haskins 4-3-1873 Hy
Hightower, Louisa A. to James L. Holyfield 1-14-1863 Mn
Hightower, M. J. to E. G. Berges 12-15-1873 (12-16-1873) T
Hightower, N. J. to S. F. P. Glass 12-20-1871 (12-21-1871) T
Hightower, N. J. to W. C. Worley 12-12-1874 (12-27-1874) T
Hightower, Susan A. to H. B. Wolfkill 4-24-1857 (4-26-1857) Sh
Hignight, Mary to Thomas J. Hines 2-29-1836 G
Hile, Mary (Mrs.) to Josiah E. Attwood 12-12-1864 Sh
Hill, Adaline to Elias Lawrence 11-30-1851 G
Hill, Amanda to Thomas A. Jamison 4-3-1858 Cr
Hill, Ann J. to A. J. Morriss 5-2-1865 Be
Hill, Ann to John Edwards 12-13-1858 Sh
Hill, Anna to James Lacy 12-14-1850 Ma
Hill, Annie to James D. McClerkin 4-19-1877 Dy
Hill, Arvenia to Andrew J. Breaden 11-6-1854 Sh
Hill, Augusta B. to John Trice 1-11-1854 (1-12-1854) Sh
Hill, Awila D. to John Smith 1-22-1840 (1-23-1840) G
Hill, B. M. to John G. Matthews 12-18-1872 T
Hill, Betheny to John Berry 1-25-1851 (1-26-1851) G
Hill, Betsey J. to Daniel G. Frazier 2-23-1846 (2-25-1846) F
Hill, Buena Vista to F. M. Holbrook 5-6-1868 G
Hill, Catharine H. to Neilson J. Hess 7-2-1840 G
Hill, Catherine P. to James P. Renshaw 10-8-1854 Hn
Hill, Celia to Harvie Nobles 8- -1847 Be
Hill, Celia to Sommerset P. Jones 2-16-1871 Hy
Hill, Christiana to H. A. Goss 12-31-1857 Sh
Hill, Cle. to Willis Lowe 12-22-1870 T
Hill, Daisy E. to J. F. Caldwell 10-19-1885 (10-20-1885) L
Hill, E. B. to J. B. Evans 3-11-1868 G
Hill, E. C. to D. W. Woodruff 4-15-1854 (4-20-1854) G
Hill, E. F. to Sidney Martin 8-24-1872 (8-25-1872) T
Hill, E. to John N. Hawkins 11-11-1844 Hn
Hill, Eda (Edna) C. to Peter Bush 9-18-1850 Sh
Hill, Elender to Edward O'Connel 10-24-1840 (10-25-1840) O
Hill, Eliza Ann to Sidney Hill 12-27-1854 (12-27-1854) O

Hill, Eliza Ann to Thos. Lacy 10-25-1841 (10-28-1841) Ma
Hill, Eliza Ann to William Gallaher 4-26-1851 (4-29-1851) O
Hill, Eliza N. to James Tate 2-5-1852 Sh
Hill, Eliza to Austem Wright 2-27-1871 (2-28-1871) T
Hill, Eliza to James Sale 5-5-1870 (no return) F
Hill, Eliza to Samuel Carithers 6-24-1865 (6-28-1865) O
Hill, Elizabeth A. to Darius D. Newbern 3-25-1850 Ma
Hill, Elizabeth C. to Robert E. Raines 12-9-1868 G
Hill, Elizabeth H. to Samuel Epperson 11-18-1844 Ma
Hill, Elizabeth L. to Ferdinand N. Tuck 9-16-1858 We
Hill, Elizabeth L. to Wm. D. Story 5-25-1863 Sh
Hill, Elizabeth L. to Wm. P. Wise 4-20-1861 (4-21-1861) Hr
Hill, Elizabeth to Edwin P. Philips 2-14-1843 Sh
Hill, Elizabeth to F. H. Simmons 1-31-1864 Mn
Hill, Elizabeth to Jeremiah Massey, jr. 3-16-1842 Sh
Hill, Elizabeth to Roger T. Sulenger 8-25-1828 (8-27-1828) Hr
Hill, Elizabeth to William Gibson 4-28-1850 (5-3-1850) O
Hill, Elizabeth to William H. Whitfield 8-18-1854 (8-20-1854) O
Hill, Elizabeth to Wm. Thatcher 8-4-1847 Sh
Hill, Ellen Queen Ann to William Hallum 5-10-1855 Sh
Hill, Ellen to Grundy Hunter 8-22-1870 G B
Hill, Ellen to Lewis Rutherford 10-21-1869 (10-22-1869) T
Hill, Emeline to James W. Thedford 9-25-1862 G
Hill, Emily J. to Jesse Ray 11-20-1856 (no return) We
Hill, Fannie to J. S. Caruthers 11-13-1858 (11-23-1858) Sh
Hill, Frances E. to William H. Elliott 8-19-1830 Sh
Hill, Harriet H. to Zack Edmunds 11-19-1833 Sh
Hill, Harriet to Leander D. Edwards 12-8-1866 (12-9-1866) Ma
Hill, Harriett to Primos Morris 1-21-1871 Hy
Hill, Ida to R. H. Hunter 2-17-1886 (2-25-1886) L
Hill, Indiana to John F. Williams 9-19-1865 (9-20-1865) T
Hill, Indianna to John F. Williams 9-19-1865 T
Hill, Isabella C. to Ellison T. Potts 1-20-1846 Hn
Hill, Jane to Doctor Dodd 9-22-1867 G B
Hill, Jane to James L. Adkins 2-3-1847 (2-10-1847) T
Hill, Jane to John Upchurch 7-20-1867 (7-21-1867) T
Hill, Jennie to W. J. Robinson 12-14-1867 G
Hill, Josie to Edwin Berry 9-30-1863 (10-1-1863) Sh
Hill, Judah to John Phifer 4-15-1847 Be
Hill, Julia A. to W. L. Gardner 11-26-1863 G
Hill, Julia to I. N. Carroll 2-13-1867 G
Hill, Kate to Pat Mack 10-29-1870 Hy
Hill, Kattie to Newman Anderson 3-12-1871 Hy
Hill, L. J. to J. M. Armstrong 4-28-1863 Mn
Hill, Laura to Owen Lewis 1-12-1867 (1-13-1867) F B
Hill, Laura to Richard Green 3-2-1872 (3-5-1872) T
Hill, Lizzie to Jas. Neeley 3-14-1874 T
Hill, Lizzie to W. J. Brooks 4-3-1850 Sh
Hill, Louisa A. P. to Robert Thompson Foster 12-20-1847 (12-23-1847) T
Hill, Louisa C. to George W. Newbern 8-10-1852 Ma
Hill, Louisa to Abe W. McCrutchen 2-2-1869 (2-3-1869) T
Hill, Louise to Daniel Umstead 4-12-1856 T
Hill, Lucey A. to R. P. McClenny? 3-21-1868 (3-24-1868) T
Hill, Lucinda to Robert H. Givens 8-9-1831 Ma
Hill, Lucy to Milton Walker 9-12-1873 T
Hill, Lurannia to Richard G. Henning 10-11-1831 Ma
Hill, Lutisha R. to Archabald Williamson 4-15-1852 (no return) F
Hill, M. D. to F. P. Miller 12-15-1880 (no return) L
Hill, M. J. H. to W. H. White 10-15-1863 T
Hill, M. J. to John W. Martin 11-25-1873 (11-15-1873?) T
Hill, Margaret L. to Robert L. McFadden 7-24-1866 T
Hill, Margaret Leventen to Charles Strong Dickson 1-31-1849 (2-1-1849) T
Hill, Margaret to Peter Moore 3-30-1862 Mn
Hill, Marth to Adkin Hughlette 12-28-1868 (12-29-1868) T
Hill, Martha Ann to A. J. Wall 1-11-1863 Hn
Hill, Martha Ann to T. P. Munson 10-8-1855 Hn
Hill, Martha D. to Charles C. Locke 11-22-1832 Sh
Hill, Martha E. to J. H. Prewett 12-18-1858 (12-22-1858) Hr
Hill, Martha E. to Thompson Moore 10-5-1869 Cr
Hill, Martha R. to John J. Pierce 10-19-1847 Hn
Hill, Mary A. to David A. Short 6-16-1873 Hy
Hill, Mary A. to W. F. Nance 10-16-1854 Hn
Hill, Mary A. to Wesley B. Nance 2-5-1845 Hn
Hill, Mary E. to C. M. Boyd 12-23-1856 Cr
Hill, Mary J. to B. S. McAnley 12-17-1866 (12-20-1866) Cr
Hill, Mary J. to W. S. Hall 12-12-1855 We
Hill, Mary Jane to Alfred Parham 4-11-1867 (5-12-1867) F B
Hill, Mary Jane to Derastus Baldock 12-26-1853 (1-2-1854) T
Hill, Mary Jane to Isaac M. Thetford 10-10-1854 G
Hill, Mary Jane to M. L. Robertson 2-25-1842 (3-3-1842) F
Hill, Mary Jane to Samuel Williams 12-13-1842 (12-15-1842) Ma
Hill, Mary R. to Jacob S. Maus 4-28-1848 Sh
Hill, Mary S. to Durant H. Bell 3-12-1838 Sh
Hill, Mary W. J. to Robert S. Manard 12-7-1854 Hn
Hill, Mary to Arch Morgan 3-15-1867 (7-4-1867) T
Hill, Mary to Hughey Hickine 6-23-1860 T
Hill, Mary to James Wheeler 12-5-1859 (12-11-1859) F

Hill, Mary to Leander Latham 2-18-1852 (2-19-1852) G
Hill, Mary to N. B. Crook 10-2-1860 We
Hill, Mary to Nathan Ray 12-28-1850 (not endorsed) We
Hill, Mary to Overton W. Carr 5-1-1820 Sh
Hill, May E. to E. C. Mohundrow 1-13-1867 Hn
Hill, May Eller to Robert Beriam 11-28-1871 (11-29-1871) T
Hill, Merandra C. to Wm. C. Hill 12-22-1841 Cr
Hill, Miss M. E. to Heb. C. Morrison 3-28-1861 T
Hill, Miss Peggy to Hibrey? Cage 12-2-1865 T
Hill, Mollie E. to G. W. Fletcher 2-15-1873 (2-16-1873) Cr
Hill, Molly A. to C. A. J. Hitchings 6-23-1855 (6-24-1855) Sh
Hill, N. T. to Alex Rogers 9-24-1869 (9-28-1869) Dy
Hill, Nancy A. to John W. Wainscot 9-2-1856 We
Hill, Nancy C. to J. Richardson 1-7-1860 T
Hill, Nancy P. to John A. Stokes 11-28-1861 T
Hill, Nancy to John Jackson 8-11-1851 Hr
Hill, Nancy to Matthew Brown 11-28-1853 (12-1-1853) Sh
Hill, Nancy to Robt. R. Benton 12-23-1849 Be
Hill, Nannie E. to A. B. Charlton 11-8-1859 We
Hill, Nanny to James Howell 7-26-1865 G
Hill, Ollie to W. D. Cook 12-25-1884 (12-30-1884) L
Hill, R. J. to R. M. Shull 4-24-1863 Mn
Hill, Racheal to Asa Arnold 9-22-1828 Hr
Hill, Rebecca to Anthony R. Barret 8-7-1850 Sh
Hill, Rebecca to Walter Robertson 6-15-1824 (6-17-1824) Hr
Hill, Rosa to Charles Appel 1-2-1854 (1-3-1854) Sh
Hill, Sallie to Frank Denney 12-25-1871 (no return) Cr
Hill, Sallie to John C. Rutherford 12-18-1873 (12-17?-1873) T
Hill, Sallie to John W. Fallin 1-7-1874 T
Hill, Sally H. to George G. Hughes 5-8-1860 (5-9-1860) Ma
Hill, Sarah A. to Thomas Connell 2-28-1861 G
Hill, Sarah E. to Joseph C. Sharp 2-16-1857 (2-17-1857) Ma
Hill, Sarah E. to Richard Campton 5-20-1854 (no return) T
Hill, Sarah Elizabeth to John P. Townsend 3-16-1852 (3-17-1852) T
Hill, Sarah Isabella to Edward Bassett 6-18-1856 (no return?) Sh
Hill, Sarah N. to James J. Sloan 1-1-1867 G
Hill, Sarah P. to David Kay 8-10-1842 Ma
Hill, Sarah P. to Thomas Mitchel 3-30-1867 (3-31-1867) Cr
Hill, Sarah to Benjamin Dunn 2-26-1838 Hn
Hill, Sarah to John Ligon 1-5-1868 G
Hill, Silusla? H. to Peter Vaughn 4-4-1867 T
Hill, Sina to James Pippin 7-27-1851 Be
Hill, Sina to Silas Miller 6-27-1869 Hy
Hill, Sina to Willes Bowls 7-26-1869 Mn
Hill, Susan A. to John H. Winberry 7-3-1855 Sh
Hill, Susan G. to Bailey Sanford 1-6-1865 T
Hill, Susanna to Benj. Hines 3-1-1869 (no return) Hy
Hill, T. P. to D. A. Smith 12-18-1868 (12-21-1868) Dy
Hill, Tabitha to John Harmon 7-3-1860 Hn
Hill, Vina to George Boyd 8-8-1873 T
Hillard, Cloa to Philip Flinn 7-30-1840 G
Hillard, Elizabeth C. to Levi Bodkin 8-30-1855 (8-31-1855) G
Hillard, Pherraby to Frederick Becton 2-18-1847 G
Hillhouse, Martha C. to L. B. Murdaugh 12-1-1853 Hr
Hilliard, Clara A. J. to Henry Stokes 10-23-1856 Cr
Hilliard, Cynthia A. to Elkanor Williams 6-18-1855 O
Hilliard, Delia A. to John D. Crider 2-9-1865 (no return) Cr
Hilliard, E. J. to W. H. Graham 6-21-1864 Sh
Hilliard, Eliza W. to Saml. B. Jordon 1-31-1849 F
Hilliard, Eliza to James P. Johnson 1-1-1849 Cr
Hilliard, Elizabeth to G. W. Nolly 11-3-1862 (not endorsed) F
Hilliard, Ellen to Andrew Perry 1-19-1871 (1-21-1871) F B
Hilliard, Fannie to J. H. Speight 11-10-1873 (no return) Dy
Hilliard, Harriet to Nelson Boals 9-13-1867 (9-14-1867) F B
Hilliard, Jane to A. J. Mitchell 12-19-1848 T
Hilliard, Julia to Abram Greenlee 7-25-1870 F B
Hilliard, L. B. to P. M. Bondurant 4-3-1854 (no return) F
Hilliard, M. E. to L. M. Rhodgers 4-5-1869 (4-9-1869) F
Hilliard, M. J. to Elmore Bragg 3-30-1858 Cr
Hilliard, M. L. to B. C. Stewart 8-23-1860 Hy
Hilliard, Margarett J. to J. N. Fentress 10-6-1867 O
Hilliard, Mary J. to D. S. Haley 2-15-1853 (no return) F
Hilliard, Minerva E. to Joseph A. Watson 11-5-1856 Cr
Hilliard, R. F. to Albert C. White 12-22-1869 Ma
Hilliard, Ruthy to Andy Jefferson 8-17-1869 (8-18-1869) F B
Hilliard, S. J. to Thadius H. Boykin 10-10-1860 T
Hilliard, S. S. to Jesse W. Porter 7-10-1855 We
Hilliard, Susan F. to J. W. Sanders 12-11-1865 (12-12-1865) F
Hilliard, Tempy E. to B. F. Smith 6-15-1843 Cr
Hilliard, Winniford L. to Raleigh W. Poindexter 9-7-1846 (no return) F
Hillis, Nancy A. to William Baker 2-4-1857 We
Hillis, Nancy Ann (Mrs.) to John R. Morris 1-27-1836 Sh
Hillman, Amanda to Mack Thomas 1-25-1873 (1-26-1873) Cr
Hills, Jenny E. to W. F. Boyle 12-17-1861 (12-18-1861) Sh
Hills, Mary E. (Miss) to J. F. Sellers 11-2-1858 Sh
Hills, Prudence S. to Wm. McClelland 11-2-1858 Sh
Hillsman, Caroline to George Atkison 12-30-1869 (1-9-1870) Cr

Hillsman, Charlotte to John Gaska 5-3-1849 Sh
Hillsman, E. A. to A. B. Mitchum 11-30-1842 Cr
Hillsman, Eliza to Daniel Hutcheson 6-28-1870 (6-30-1870) Cr
Hillsman, Martha to M. D. L. Jordon 11-8-1858 Cr
Hillsman, Meria to Spencer Bomar 12-2-1844 Cr
Hillsman, S. J. to Thomas Hutchinson 2-23-1860 Cr
Hillsman, Sally to Norvell Hillsman 8-29-1868 (no return) Cr
Hillyard, Martha A. to J. H. Burd 11-2-1867 Hn
Hilton, Mary A. to John A. Coleman 4-22-1859 (no return) L
Hinant, Frances Ann C. to Little B. Earp 4-9-1855 Be
Hinant, Martha E. to James H. Combs 12-18-1856 Be
Hinant, Sarah Ann to Reding Lyles 12-9-1852 Be
Hinchey, Emaline to James Bevill 9-14-1851 Hn
Hinchey, Sarah C. to Francis R. McConnell 3-18-1840 Hn
Hinchey, Theresa to Francis McConnell 6-13-1838 Hn
Hindman, Hellen to James Caskey 12-8-1861 T
Hindman, Roxanne W. to James M. McCheshire 9-18-1850 T
Hindman, Sarah S. to G. N. McCormick 1-22-1861 (1-23-1861) T
Hinds, Billie to O. B. Dixon 12-11-1878 Dy
Hinds, Mary to Jacob Shankle 7-20-1853 T
Hine, Cornelia Ann to Lemuel Crane 7-8-1851 Sh
Hines, Amanda to John C. Shepperd 2-6-1849 (2-13-1849) Hr
Hines, Amanda to Lewis Olivar 12-4-1872 Hy
Hines, Anne to Jacob F. Sheets 1-20-1838 (1-23-1838) Hr
Hines, Cytha to Joseph Minton 5-19-1836 Hr
Hines, Eleanor A. to James W. Shoemaker 5-30-1848 (5-31-1848) L
Hines, Frances E. to Marcus Sewell 10-25-1875 (10-27-1875) Dy
Hines, Hester A. to Pearce Fulgham 3-3-1832 (3-6-1832) Hr
Hines, J. E. to W. R. Kelloum 10-13-1879 (no return) L
Hines, Jane to James Cissell 4-30-1883 (5-1-1883) L
Hines, Martha to George Morgan 1-2-1877 (1-4-1877) L
Hines, Mary to Charles C. Gregg 2-12-1838 Hr
Hines, Mary to Lewis Smoot 9-4-1857 Sh
Hines, Mary to Thomas McBride 2-26-1860 Sh
Hines, Mary to Wm. Beim? (Benim?) 1-31-1853 Sh
Hines, Rachael A. to Ready Durham 10-6-1873 (no return) Hy
Hines, Rachel to John Hines 8-1-1872 (no return) Hy
Hines, Sarah J. to Geo. W. Sheets 12-18-1859 Hr
Hines, Velandeo A. to William P. Smith 10-2-1860 (10-3-1860) O
Hinnant, Rebecca to Chesley Dodd 9-3-1860 Be
Hins (Hines), Elizabeth to Robert Knox 2-6-1841 Sh
Hinshaw, M. C. to W. H. Simmons 2-24-1860 Sh
Hinson, Allis to Rolan T. Cook 1-18-1858 (1-21-1858) G
Hinson, Ann to Joseph Davis 8-31-1867 Hn B
Hinson, Eliza T. to John L. Balthrop 12-20-1869 (12-22-1869) F
Hinson, Elizabeth to S. Robinson Gaddy 12-18-1848 Sh
Hinson, Lucinda M. to John A. Crutchfield 9-26-1856 Cr
Hinson, M. J. to W. T. Galliher 2-6-1872 (2-9-1872) Dy
Hinson, Martha J. to Joell W. Walters 2-1-1868 (2-5-1868) Cr
Hinson, Martha J. to Tilman P. Pulliam 12-20-1854 Hr
Hinson, Nancy J. to Martin Skinner 12-28-1850 (12-31-1850) Hr
Hinson, S. E. to C. T. Winters 11-18-1863 Hn
Hinton, Ann Eliza to John F. Bibb 3-9-1853 L
Hinton, Charlotte to Jordan Johnson 1-1-1879 (1-2-1879) L B
Hinton, Emma to Ruffin Harper 11-8-1873 L B
Hinton, Henrietta A. to John H. Lusk 6-28-1866 L
Hinton, Hester E. to John A. J. Byrn 5-23-1866 L
Hinton, Julia to Henry Currin 4-5-1879 (4-6-1879) L B
Hinton, Lucy to Robert Lea 1-6-1875 (1-7-1875) L B
Hinton, Mary E. to Alex G. Hinton 4-23-1849 (4-25-1849) L
Hinton, Matilda to Aaron Wiseman 3-3-1882 (no return) L
Hinton, Rose to Luke Johnson 11-15-1871 (11-16-1871) L B
Hinton, Sarah H. to W. E. Childs 12-16-1884 (12-17-1884) L
Hipkins, Minah to John W. Rose 9-17-1831 O
Hipp, Francis E. to W. F. Watson 12-28-1877 (12-29-1877) L
Hipp, Henrietta to William Hutchison 11-25-1872 (11-26-1872) L
Hipp, L. H. J. to John Y. Braden 7-5-1851 (7-6-1851) L
Hipp, Maggie to Martin Arl 12-22-1885 (12-31-1885) L
Hipp, Martha E. to M. M. M. Pevehouse 3-22-1855 (no return) L
Hipp, Nancy N. to James A. Shoemaker 9-5-1871 (9-6-1871) L
Hipp, Rosanna to William W.(H?) Talbot 12-4-1852 (12-5-1852) L
Hipp, Ruthy Ann to Doctor McC Stuckey 12-26-1855 (12-27-1855) L
Hipp, S. A. to J. T. Rush 11-13-1884 (11-23-1884) L
Hipps, Mary E. to John C. Enlow 9-17-1846 L
Hirsch, Schanett to August Rosensteel 1-3-1867 Hy
Hisaw, June to John Polk 12-24-1844 (12-25-1844) G
Hisaw, Martha to John Stephenson 8-8-1844 Cr
Hise, Julia Ann to Pinkney Wortham 3-26-1868 T
Hitchcock, Jennette to S. A. Thorp 5-16-1866 (5-20-1866) Dy
Hitchcock, P. to Wm. T. Cheairs 9-6-1847 Hr
Hitchcok, Parthenia to James S. Nunnelly 8-6-1852 (8-15-1852) Hr
Hite, Emma to Scot Pierson 2-16-1883 (2-17-1883) L
Hite, Frances Jane to John Campbell 3-6-1869 (3-7-1869) T
Hite, Mattie to George Davis 1-19-1880 (no return) L
Hitower, Amanda to W. H. Guthrie 6-17-1871 (6-22-1871) T
Hitower, Fannie to W. Archer 4-8-1874 (4-5?-1874) T
Hitt, Ida to Robert Ellis 12-5-1883 (12-6-1883) L

Hix, Elvina to William E. Biggs 10-22-1856 G
Hix, Jane to Rhodham Martin 9-28-1840 (9-30-1840) G *
Hix, Martha A. to Andrew Mayo 5-10-1852 (5-?-1852) G
Hix, Mary E. to Paschal Bullington 9-27-1860 G
Hix, Nancy M. to S. C. Fly 12-11-1866 G
Hix, Rebecca E. to E. C. Butler 7-11-1860 G
Hoas, Eliza to Dennis Johnson 12-29-1875 (no return) L
Hoban, Margaret to Michael McDonough 5-16-1864 Sh
Hobb, Esther to Archibald M. Nicholson 2-25-1856 (2-26-1856) Ma
Hobbs, Ann M. to Caleb Howell 6-24-1839 (6-27-1839) G
Hobbs, Any to Tas Nixon 8-9-1873 Hy
Hobbs, Caroline C. to George W. Turner 1-18-1848 (1-19-1848) Ma
Hobbs, Eliza Ann to William Cross 10-23-1837 (10-24-1837) Hr
Hobbs, Elizabeth J. to Samuel G. Hogue 2-12-1861 G
Hobbs, Isabella to Robert Whitworth 10-15-1857 (10-16-1857) Ma
Hobbs, Lucy A. to Thos. L. Harris 8-9-1852 Cr
Hobbs, Martha E. to Redden C. Thomas 1-12-1846 (1-15-1846) G
Hobbs, Martha W. to Robert M. Dickinson 12-4-1844 (12-5-1844) Ma
Hobbs, Martha to Jordan Husten 4-22-1865 (5-25-1865) O
Hobbs, Mary Ann to William Brim 4-8-1834 Hr
Hobbs, Mary to Pleasant A. Vencir 11-19-1849 (11-20-1849) G
Hobbs, Nanny to Leoma Flowers 12-27-1849 G
Hobbs, Sallie to Wm. Bolton 8-16-1873 (no return) Hy
Hobday, M. F. to A. S. Berry 8-4-1877 (no return) Dy
Hobs, M. E. C. to E. J. Weever 12-17-1874 T
Hobs, Nancy J. to R. D. Ellis 6-3-1863 Mn
Hobsen, Martha to J. H. Mitchell 9-12-1870 (9-13-1870) Dy
Hobson, Agnes to Charles Ancromb 12-11-1869 (no return) F B
Hobson, Camelia to Sam Price 1-5-1867 (1-6-1867) F B
Hobson, Lizzie to D. M. Stephens 1-14-1878 (1-16-1878) Dy
Hobson, Mary T. to B. F. Fitzgerald 3-13-1850 Sh
Hobum, Adelia (Mrs.) to John W. Knox 5-11-1863 Sh
Hockaday, E. V. C. to J. W. Sharp 10-28-1850 G
Hockaday, Mary A. to W. H. Stillwell 8-8-1845 (8-11-1845) G
Hodge, Eliza L. to L. J. Holloman 12-15-1869 G
Hodge, Lucinda to Henry Denny 5-17-1849 L
Hodge, M. S. to W. N. Murray 12-17-1873 Dy
Hodge, Martha Jane to John P. Smith 10-31-1848 Hr
Hodge, Martha to Lewis Grayham 9-22-1869 G B
Hodge, Martha to Wash. Taliaferro 12-28-1870 Hy
Hodge, Mary E. to J. W. Lipe 11-30-1872 (12-1-1872) Cr
Hodge, Mary Henry to Peter Perkins 1-20-1841 Hr
Hodge, Mary to Charley Holland 8-30-1838 Hr
Hodge, Mary to James Stephens 3-22-1839 Hr
Hodge, Minerva to Malechi Oliver 11-30-1830 (12-2-1830) Ma
Hodge, Nancy Jane to Thomas Collier 9-2-1852 Be
Hodge, Nicey to Robert Smith 8-11-1868 (no return) Dy
Hodge, Priscilla to G. W. Willi 9-6-1852 Hr
Hodge, Sarah E. to J. L. Sims 10-1-1842 Sh
Hodge, Sary to Jonas Baker 10-30-1828 Hr
Hodge, Susan to Louis Sales 12-27-1876 (or 12-28?) Dy
Hodges, A. E. to C. F. Wharton 12-9-1862 Mn
Hodges, Basney? to Edward Hodges 12-9-1863 (no return) Hn
Hodges, E. S. to William Nix 7-16-1867 (7-17-1867) O
Hodges, Elenor to John Glover 12-29-1840 O
Hodges, Elizabeth C. to Theophilus Caldwell 1-19-1846 (no return) F
Hodges, Elizabeth to John Sneed 6-8-1843 (7-?-1843) Hr
Hodges, Fanny to Peyton Black 3-9-1839 Sh
Hodges, Frances L. to Thomas A. Humphreys 6-22-1845 Sh
Hodges, Hetty to Linzy J. Rutherford 9-28-1830 (10-7-1830) Hr
Hodges, Martha to John D. Adams 3-4-1847 Hr
Hodges, Mary E. to Larkin P. Jones 8-9-1838 F
Hodges, Mary L. to John Carr 2-14-1849 Sh
Hodges, Olive to John E. Farr 10-31-1831 O
Hodges, Rebecca to Alston Grant 1-7?-1834 Hr
Hodges, Rebecca to Amasa Rice 4-23-1836 Hr
Hodges, Rebecca to Robert D. Chapman 10-6-1836 Hr
Hodges, Sarah ANn to James T. Gregory 8-5-1852 Sh
Hodges, Sarah T. to Joseph B. Edwards 11-6-1865 (11-15-1865) F
Hodges, Sarah to George Tackett 7-31-1834 (8-5-1834) Hr
Hodges, Telitha to Alfred Neding 6-15-1829 G
Hodges, Unis to J. D. Mitchell 10-1-1868 G
Hodges, Virginia A. to P. C. Thompson 12-3-1868 (no return) F
Hodgson, Amanda to William M. Allen 6-15-1839 (6-18-1839) Ma
Hoetterbar, L. to Friedrich Krocker 5-11-1863 Sh
Hoffler, Elizabeth Trotman to Charles D. Walker 2-11-1850 T
Hoffler, Martha Caroline to Spencer Thomas Hart 6-1-1844 (6-6-1844) T
Hoffman, Antonia to Conrad Gamp 12-6-1862 (12-8-1862) Sh
Hoffman, E. R. to M. H. Middaugh 8-5-1856 Sh
Hoffman, Eliza to Frederick Hochersberger 1-27-1842 Sh
Hoffman, Elizabeth to Henry Shmid 1-12-1858 Sh
Hoffman, M. A. (Mrs.) to Neal Wicker 11-2-1867 O
Hoffman, Mary Ann to William W. Givins 1-28-1861 Hn
Hoffman, Mary to Charles A. Heinzer 3-28-1863 (3-31-1863) Sh
Hoffman, Mary to Sebastian Rutshuan 11-11-1858 Sh
Hofford, Mattie H. to Elias W. Meeks 2-8-1872 (2-13-1872) L
Hogan, Amanda J. to Robert C. Starrett 2-15-1851 (2-18-1851) O

Brides

Hogan, C. A. to T. J. Crobum? 4-27-1854 Cr
Hogan, Catherine to Michael Huet 3-5-1849 Sh
Hogan, Elizabeth to William M. Bevill 6-12-1865 (no return) Hn
Hogan, Hannorah to John Renshaw 9-28-1857 Sh
Hogan, Lucinda to I. H. Martin 12-27-1865 O
Hogan, Margaret Jane to Robert Park 10-6-1841 (10-7-1841) Hr
Hogan, Martha E. to William H. Wood 11-22-1842 Hn
Hogan, Martha R. to Hugh S. Murphy 11-13-1843 (11-14-1843) O
Hogan, Mary E. to George Ervin 9-28-1848 (9-29-1848) F
Hogan, Mary J. to M. C. Webb 11-21-1856 (11-23-1856) Hr
Hogan, Mary to Patrick Manning 8-18-1855 Mn
Hogan, Mary to Thos. McCarty 6-10-1862 Sh
Hogan, Mollie to Charles Weatherford 11-29-1866 (11-2?-1866) Cr
Hogan, Nancy A. to Richd. A. Sexton 3-7-1861 (3-10-1861) Hr
Hogan, Nancy to John Brockwell 1-16-1839 (1-17-1839) O
Hogan, Rebecca H. to Franklin Travis 3-7-1855 Cr
Hogan, Sarah to John Harvey Ursery 8-22-1866 Ma
Hogden, Eleanor to John J. Hunter 1-28-1836 Sh
Hoge, Elizabeth to Andrew Hammond 1-16-1855 Sh
Hoge, Sofrona to Silas Skipper 5-2-1865 (5-3-1865) Dy
Hogg, Eliza G. to James P. H. Grundy 5-13-1828 G
Hogg, Lucy Ann to Joshua Curtis 5-15-1848 Be
Hogg, Nancy to Joshua Robertson 9-17-1845 Be
Hogg, R. E. to J. N. Cunningham 7-8-1880 (7-11-1880) L
Hogg, Sarah A. F. to William C. Fite 10-14-1841 G
Hogg, Susan E. to Wm. P. Spicer 4-18-1853 Be
Hoggard, Emily Ann to Henry Jones 7-28-1852 We
Hoggard, Rena to Green Coleman 12-9-1868 (12-10-1868) Cr
Hogge, Melisa E. to Andrew L. Brown 8-31-1861 (no return) L
Hoggis, Nancy B. to Hugh Arant 10-14-1840 Hn
Hoggsett, Mary Jane to P. T. Maynard 7-13-1864 (7-14-1864) L
Hogin (Hogue), Jane to Isaac N. Farris 6-27-1849 O
Hogin, Elizabeth to Wm. McBride 5-18-1863 (no return) We
Hogsett, Donia C. to William T. Henderson 12-2-1867 Ma
Hogsett, Jane to Wm. Lemmons 4-26-1845 (4-27-1845) L
Hogsett, M. J. to P. T. Maynard 7-13-1864 (7-14-1864) L
Hogsett, Mary Ann to James Little 6-17-1846 (6-18-1846) L
Hogsett, Mary Ann to Mark C. Henderson 2-6-1867 (2-7-1867) Ma
Hogue, Eliza Ann to J. W. Elkins 12-27-1860 Hn
Hogue, Emily E. to John J. Smith 8-12-1850 (8-13-1850) Hr
Hogue, Jane to Isaac N. Farris 6-27-1849 O
Hogue, Louisa to Caldwell Pleasant 6-2-1842 O
Hogue, Margaret Jane to William F. Calhoun 12-17-1853 (12-17-1853) O
Hogue, Martha Jane to John Somers 11-10-1853 (11-?-1853) O
Hogue, Martha M. to James W. Osbourn 9-17-1856 (10-2-1856) O
Hogue, Martha to Sam'l. A. Calhoun 11-30-1859 (12-1-1859) O
Hogue, Mary to E. T. Gantlett 3-24-1847 O
Hogue, S. D. to S. A. McCollum 7-21-1861 O
Hogue, Selina to John C. Tedrow 12-4-1816 T
Hoke, Martha to Morgan P. Norman 11-28-1842 Sh
Hoke, Mary Magdalin to Kinchin Pace 5-6-1851 T
Hoke, Rebecca to Jesse Pence 6-22-1839 (6-23-1839) Hr
Holaday, Sarah Ann to Stephen Pearce 7-19-1848 Hn
Holaman, Emma to Francis Kennedy 6-15-1876 (6-16-1876) L
Holaway, Hanah to Zachariah Bowen 9-21-1837 (9-28-1837) G
Holaway, Liza to Blunt Bond 12-26-1867 (no return) Hy
Holbut?, Lucretia to Abner Rosson 8-26-1836 (8-25?-1836) Hr
Holcomb, Lucy to Wyatt Betty 1-4-1867 G
Holcomb, Mary to Thomas Sullivan 9-20-1866 (9-3?-1866) Cr
Holcomb, Priscella P. to Charles H. Brown 3-4-1859 (3-6-1859) G
Holcomb, Rachal to Harvy Belew 8-14-1839 G
Holcombe, Laura to Isaac Walden 10-29-1857 Hr
Holden, Catherine R. to Joseph W. Phillips 1-21-1868 (1-22-1868) F
Holden, Drewhannah to J. L. Robinson 7-20-1865 Hn
Holden, Elizabeth to Washington F. Ray 12-21-1841 Hn
Holden, Louisa J. to Nathan Maddox 1-19-1858 Hn
Holden, Tennessee Bell to E. F. Vernon 12-26-1885 (12-29-1885) L
Holder, Ann Eliza to W. R. Smith 2-27-1855 (no return) We
Holder, Ann to Hinton Willis 11-15-1832 G
Holder, Ann to James S. Hayns 10-22-1842 (10-25-1842) G
Holder, E. F. to H. M. Willis 12-23-1866 G
Holder, Elizabeth to Robert Madison 10-14-1841 (12-16-1841) G
Holder, Josephine to W. B. Henry 11-15-1863 G
Holder, L. A. to Jerry Bailey 3-2-1857 G
Holder, Martha to William Gamble 3-10-1851 (3-13-1851) Hr
Holder, Matilda C. to Howel M. Mahon 12-30-1850 (12-31-1850) G
Holder, Millia to Mark Selph 11-20-1832 G
Holder, Precilla to Valentine Bell 10-12-1850 (10-13-1850) G
Holder, Susan V. to S. F. Davidson 12-12-1866 G
Holderfield, Frances J. to William Ballentine 10-23-1858 (10-28-1858) G
Holderfield, Nancy Jane to Henry N. Simpson 7-28-1868 Ma
Holderfield, Sarah M. to Hiriam Hall 7-26-1843 (7-27-1843) Ma
Holdsbrooks, Vina to Austin Hicks 7-11-1844 Hn
Holeday, Elizabeth to J. H. Petty 5-22-1861 Mn
Holeman, Clarisee I. to Suel Roberts 1-17-1872 Hy
Holeman, Mary to J. M. Wolverton 8-27-1861 Mn
Holend, Bridget to Michael Lestrange 8-19-1859 Sh

Holford, Alley E. to George W. Dickson 10-15-1850 (10-17-1850) G
Holiday, Arlamesa to Abijah Baker 5-18-1830 Hr
Holiday, Penelope to John Perry 12-23-1852 (12-24-1852) Hr
Holiday, Permelia A. to N. G. Phillips 12-20-1855 Cr
Holifield, C. G. to W. H. Moore 5-4-1861 O
Holifield, M. F. to Joseph White 2-16-1869 O
Holihan, Ann to John Flahive 8-20-1860 Sh
Holihan, Mary to Thomas Condon 12-29-1857 Sh
Holiman, Lucy Ann to William T. Valentine 7-1-1846 O
Holinsworth, Caroline to F.? M. Holland 11-1-1862 Be
Holladay, Elizabeth to James A. Warren 10-10-1840 Hn
Hollahan, Bridget to Timothy Nealen? (Nealy) 6-5-1860 Sh
Hollan, Hannah R. to John Keath 1-29-1838 (1-31-1838) G
Holland, A. F. to Westley C. Teel 3-23-1843 (3-24-1843) F
Holland, A. M. to U.(N?) A. Weaver 8-31-1865 G
Holland, Adra A. A. to Charles T. Cowell 10-5-1865 Be
Holland, Caroline to Robert C. Browning 11-18-1861 Cr
Holland, Conelia to John D. Pearson 12-15-1851 (no return) F
Holland, E. C. H. to Wm. Campbell 10-7-1845 Hr
Holland, Elizabeth S. to Lemuel J. Cook 10-8-1860 G
Holland, Elizabeth to David Melton 8-23-1849 Be
Holland, Elizabeth to G. W. Farmer 12-13-1843 Be
Holland, Elizabeth to Henry L. Ladyman 8-5-1852 We
Holland, Ellen to William R. Johnson 10-6-1864 Sh
Holland, F. J. to James Sykes 10-16-1847 Be
Holland, Fannie to A. J. Taylor 9-15-1869 G
Holland, Fanny H. to Robert J. McCombs 4-27-1867 G
Holland, Isabella to Thomas Sykes 7-2-1850 Be
Holland, Julia Ann to John B. Duckworth 1-18-1875 Dy
Holland, Julia F. to Daniel Witherington 3-1-1863 G
Holland, Katy to Bill Jordan 12-23-1869 G B
Holland, Lena to William H. Worsly 1-21-1884 (1-22-1884) L
Holland, Louisa L. to Benjamin Dilliard 5-25-1858 Be
Holland, Lucinda to Rawley Fields 11-10-1869 (not executed) F B*
Holland, Lucinda to Wiley A. Woodward 7-11-1854 Cr
Holland, Lucretia A. to William S. Martin 8-23-1855 G
Holland, Lucritia to Coonrod J. Melton 4-10-1844 Be
Holland, Lucy to J. W. Corley 10-2-1860 G
Holland, M. E. to J. B. Armstrong 1-13-1870 (1-18-1870) F
Holland, Manerva B. to William Sykes 9-9-1851 Be
Holland, Manerva to J. H. Dillon 4-7-1870 (no return) Dy
Holland, Martha A. to Martin L. Chandler 2-9-1869 (2-11-1869) Ma
Holland, Martha F. to James A. Hathway 11-2-1862 (11-30-1862) Dy
Holland, Martha P. to H. W. Davis 3-17-1864 Be
Holland, Martha to James Legate 9-30-1855 Be
Holland, Mary E. to B. Alford 1-17-1884 (1-21-1884) L
Holland, Mary P. to John G. Bell 1-6-1862 (no return) Dy
Holland, Mary to Archibald Thompson 3-9-1840 (3-12-1840) Ma
Holland, Mary to James Berry 11-9-1852 Be
Holland, Mary to Joel A. Rogers 11-11-1857 Be
Holland, Mary to Michael Grifen 9-15-1864 (9-16-1864) Sh
Holland, Mary to William Gibbson 1-17-1851 (1-20-1851) T
Holland, Mazeppa E. to L. V. Mosby 12-2-1864 Sh
Holland, Melissa J. to Stephen B. Jones 3-1-1863 Be
Holland, Nancy (Mrs.) to William Gant 12-7-1843 G
Holland, Nancy to Jerry Sherrill 3-2-1874 T
Holland, Parthena to Julius Hall 2-23-1844 G
Holland, Peggie A. to H. W. Davis 11-7-1850 Be
Holland, Phebee M. to J. W. Jones 10-28-1856 Be
Holland, Pincky to William Head 4-17-1854 (4-16?-1854) L
Holland, Rachel to William Melton 12-5-1855 Be
Holland, Rebecca to Gean Doty 8-3-1865 Be
Holland, Rhoda to Absalom Head 5-13-1854 (5-14-1854) L
Holland, Rody to John A. Strickland 8-24-1853 Be
Holland, Rody to W. N. Jerden(Jordan) 8-16-1865 Be
Holland, S. C. to J. G. W. Akin 9-4-1876 (no return) Dy
Holland, Sally to N. B. Barker 8-16-1865 Be
Holland, Sarah A. to Andrew C. Goforth 9-3-1857 Be
Holland, Sarah C. to D. M. Gwaltney 5-13-1861 (no return) Dy
Holland, Sarah M. to Daniel Earnhart 10-17-1855 (no return) F
Holland, Sarah to Anely Thompson 11-27-1860 Dy
Holland, Syntha to James F. Presson 12-21-1846 Be
Holland, Winiford J. to William Y. Newbern 9-16-1861 (no return) Hy
Hollands, Catherine to W. B. Hendrix 5-6-1863 Mn
Hollaway, Dolly J. to James Read 2-29-1872 Hy
Hollemon, Martha to Calvin D. Maddin 6-10-1847 F
Holley, Eliza to John Thos. Yancy 12-23-1867 (12-25-1867) T
Holley, Melinda J. to William A. Dill 10-2-1851 O
Holliday, Callie to John Bell 2-10-1875 (no return) Hy
Holliday, Emily to Albert Hilliard 4-18-1857 Cr
Holliday, Martha Jane to Jackson Tatum 9-11-1847 F
Holliday, Mary Ann to Louis Beauchamp 12-18-1827 Hr
Holliday, Mary E. to John Stafford Mossman 5-1-1867 Hn
Holliday, Mary J. to James High 12-19-1863 Hn
Holliday, Rosanna to William Adkins 7-9-1865 Hn
Holliday, Sarah Jane to William B. Elks 7-16-1850 (7-21-1850) Hr
Holliday, Sarah to Wilie Jones 12-26-1837 Hr

Hollin, Mary A. to W. H. F. Rusk 10-17-1850 We
Hollingshead, Mary M. to D. C. Spiller 9-3-1879 (9-4-1879) L
Hollingsworth, Elizabeth to B. F. James 10-18-1856 (10-19-1856) Sh
Hollingsworth, Frances A. to James P. Blankinship 11-12-1866 (11-13-1866) Ma
Hollingsworth, Louisa to Washington L. Saratt 2-16-1854 Hn
Hollingsworth, Sarah to Joseph McKinny 8-26-1830 Sh
Hollins, Fannie to E. L. Brassfield 1-28-1868 (1-29-1868) Dy
Hollins, Mary to John Keenon no date (with 1861) Be
Hollinsworth, Mary to A. L. Serratt 8-11-1864 Be
Hollinsworth, Sarah Ann to Wm. S. Hicks 3-31-1864 Be
Hollinsworth, Sarah to James H. Bush 9-10-1849 Hn
Hollis, E. A. to Joseph Elledge 1-5-1858 Sh
Hollis, Elender A. (Mrs.) to N. W. Willis 12-16-1854 (no return) F
Hollis, Isadora to S. D. Whitehead 3-20-1851 F
Hollis, S. A. to J. G. Hardin 5-9-1878 (5-12-1878) Dy
Holliway, Emily to Thomas Robertson 4-25-1855 (4-28-1855) Hr
Holloman, Jane to Stephen A. Boyett 2-23-1858 (2-25-1858) O
Holloman, Leona to Sanders Holladay 5-23-1869 G B
Holloman, Mary to Charles H. Weathers 12-11-1867 (12-12-1867) Ma
Holloman, Nancy to Arthur Williams 2-16-1869 (2-17-1869) Ma
Holloman, Rachael to Jefferson Kincaid 10-5-1870 G B
Holloman, Sarah E. to Thadius S. Edringtar 12-18-1858 (12-19-1858) O
Holloman, Sarah Eliza to Salathiel Medaris 2-3-1854 O
Holloman, Winny to John D. Strain 9-8-1830 Ma
Hollomon, Ann E. to Calvin Nichols 1-1-1845 (1-5-1845) O
Hollomon, Cecilia A. to Isaiah R. Wright 8-29-1842 (9-1-1842) O
Hollomon, Isabel to William Pickler 6-18-1865 Be
Hollomon, Matildy to M. L. Cole 9-28-1845 Be
Hollomon, Nancy J. to J. E. Orsburn 10-19-1849 O
Hollomon, Susan to Henry Barnes 10-10-1850 Be
Holloway, Adaline to Lewis Houser 12-21-1852 (12-22-1852) O
Holloway, Alice L. W. to James W. Rogan 4-11-1871 (4-12-1871) F
Holloway, Amanda to S. S. King 3-31-1859 Hy
Holloway, Cely to John Shanklin 6-13-1831 (6-14-1831) O
Holloway, Diana to Isham Curso? 11-1-1872 (no return) L
Holloway, Dolly to Frank Williamson 5-23-1868 (5-25-1868) F B
Holloway, Eliza J. to Thos. Barham 1-5-1848 F
Holloway, Eliza to Billy Seymour 12-17-1870 F B
Holloway, Elizabeth to Merrit D. Hix 9-14-1853 (no return) F
Holloway, Elizabeth to Samuel Moore 10-4-1862 Mn
Holloway, Emma D. to Wm. A. Gilliam 2-17-1869 F
Holloway, Helen E. to E. A., jr. Raworth 9-16-1869 Hy
Holloway, Isabella H. to B. G. Phelan 4-16-1865 G
Holloway, Judy J. to Henry Snelling 12-17-1849 (12-20-1849) F
Holloway, Lee to Joseph Rankin 2-15-1870 (2-17-1870) F
Holloway, M. J. to D. W. Nobb 2-20-1855 (no return) F
Holloway, Mahalia to Iszrell Westbrooks 10-17-1877 Hy
Holloway, Marta Jane to Curtis Mills 1-27-1848 (no return) F
Holloway, Mary A. to Michael Johnson 3-30-1857 Hr
Holloway, Mary Frances to James E. McGowan 1-19-1855 (1-30-1855) Sh
Holloway, Mary Frances to James Lewis Green 2-20-1871 (no return) Hy
Holloway, Mary to J. J. Terrell 9-26-1870 F
Holloway, Nancy to William Perry 2-25-1851 (2-27-1851) F
Holloway, Nora to Wyott Ivy 2-9-1870 (2-10-1870) F B
Holloway, Parthena B. to Benjamin B. Suggett 1-27-1846 (1-28-1845?) F
Holloway, Rebecca S. to Wm. F. Blankenship 11-7-1854 (no return) F
Holloway, Roanna to Daniel Isbell 7-9-1870 F B
Holloway, Roena to Joe Shaw 12-6-1883 L
Holloway, Rose to Buck Mann 1-23-1873 Hy
Holloway, Rose to John Grigg 12-28-1866 (no return) Hy
Holloway, S. J. to S. W. Casey 10-18-1861 Hr
Holloway, Sarah J. to William Cook 3-2-1867 (3-3-1867) Cr
Holloway, Sarah to Bradford Brewer 4-30-1853 (5-1-1853) Sh
Holloway, Sarah to John J. Wilson 1-16-1839 (no return) F
Holloway, Sarahjennett to Josiah R. Baugh 11-2-1847 F
Holloway, Violet to Jas. Dick Bragg 8-3-1871 (8-4-1871) T
Hollowell, A. J. to J. Atcherson 6-16-1842 F
Hollowell, A. J. to J. Atcheson 6-16-1842 Be
Hollowell, Bamley to G. W. Anthony 11-8-1862 (not endorsed) F
Hollowell, E. A. to A. J. Weglesworth 12-27-1856 Sh
Hollowell, Lucinda J. to Alfred Pettigrew 6-1-1864 Be
Hollowell, Mary J. to W. F. Mitchell 12-19-1853 (no return) F
Holly, Ava to John F. Smith 3-18-1844 (3-19-1844) Hr
Holly, Margaret to James W. Hudspeth 12-21-1859 Hn
Holly, Martha J. to John W. Hudspeth 4-28-1855 Hn
Holly, Sally Ann to Ephraim S. Venable 11-12-1861 Hn
Holly, Sarah J. to James L. Brown 9-11-1854 (9-12-1854) Hr
Hollyfield, Emsey to Louis Rider 7-12-1839 (7-2?-1839) Ma
Hollyman, Elizabeth to James H. Short 12-14-1847 (12-25-1847) Ma
Holm, Elizabeth to C. P. Thomas 2-5-1880 Cr
Holman, Delia A. to W. E. Penick 12-12-1870 (12-14-1870) F
Holman, Elizabeth to John Morris 9-23-1845 Hn
Holman, Frances to Benjamin Wesson 12-30-1847 Hn
Holman, Kate to H. C. McDaniel 12-29-1869 G
Holman, Marry to Hartwell Howard 5-17-1829 Hr
Holman, Mollie C. to Jas. C. Cogbill 1-6-1866 (1-11-1866) F
Holman, Rachel E. to R. A. Owings 9-9-1865 (9-12-1865) F

Holman, Rinda to Edmond Brown 9-16-1873 O
Holmes, A. E. to H. A. Walker 9-13-1866 (9-16-1866) Cr
Holmes, A. to A. J. Meadows 7-16-1883 L
Holmes, Anna W. to Thos. F. Patterson 10-25-1866 T
Holmes, Bettie A. to Burrell Jordan 1-11-1871 (1-12-1871) F
Holmes, Cary to Sam Jackson 3-18-1869 F B
Holmes, Catherine to Jasper N. Candenove 9-4-1856 Cr
Holmes, Charlott to Wm. H. Scalbrough 8-9-1860 (8-11-1860) Cr
Holmes, Cornelia to W. A. Underwood 10-20-1870 G
Holmes, E. J. to J. A. Ingle 11-20-1868 (11-22-1868) Cr
Holmes, E. to R. N. Van Eaton 12-30-1869 G
Holmes, Eliza Jane to Richard L. Shephard 1-1-1849 (1-2-1849) G
Holmes, Elizabeth A. to John Slough 11-30-1857 (12-3-1857) Sh
Holmes, Elizabeth to John Scott 9-18-1847 Cr
Holmes, Ella to Rhoden Bond 11-29-1873 Hy
Holmes, Emma to David Hays Cummins 8-14-1843 T
Holmes, Fortna to John Scott 10-2-1853 Cr
Holmes, Frances A. to Edmond Cooper 5-28-1851 (5-29-1851) Sh
Holmes, Harriet to Jefferson Carter 10-30-1866 (no return) F B
Holmes, Harriet to Phillip Adkins 4-2-1866 (4-7-1866) T
Holmes, Isabella to George Watkins 12-31-1843 Hn
Holmes, J. E. to W. C. Kelley 9-5-1867 G
Holmes, Jane to D. H. Shanon 4-12-1863 Mn
Holmes, Josie P. to Saml. T. Scott 2-13-1872 Cr
Holmes, Julia A. L. to William Thompson 9-9-1856 G
Holmes, Julia A. to John N. Hill 2-19-1866 (2-20-1866) T
Holmes, Louvina to J. A. Argo 12-31-1847 Cr
Holmes, Lucy W. to Lindsley Durham 9-17-1839 (no return) L
Holmes, M. A. to L. W. Pitman 3-31-1869 (4-1-1869) Cr
Holmes, M. C. to W. H. H. Dysart 8-23-1870 (8-24-1870) Cr
Holmes, M. J. to John F. Holmes 11-26-1872 Cr
Holmes, M. M. to W. F. Durley 1-11-1870 G
Holmes, M. T. to Pleasant W. Pritchard 2-1-1844 Cr
Holmes, Margaret to A. E. Barnett 1-5-1869 (no return) Cr
Holmes, Margaret to George Akins 7-17-1848 Cr
Holmes, Margarett to Jno. R. Sellers 1-18-1872 (1-19-1872) Cr
Holmes, Martha A. to William J. Anderson 7-5-1859 G
Holmes, Martha M. to Henry W. Davis 12-25-1844 Ma
Holmes, Mary A. to James R. Hodge 7-28-1866 (7-29-1866) Cr
Holmes, Mary A. to Jesse Mitchum 6-11-1840 Cr
Holmes, Mary A. to Louis McNeely 1-31-1854 (2-1-1854) Ma
Holmes, Mary B. to James D. Keal 8-28-1856 Cr
Holmes, Mary E. to Sammie T. Scott 5-15-1856 Cr
Holmes, Mary J. to James McCord 12-29-1854 Hn
Holmes, Mary to Green McCaslin 11-6-1835 G
Holmes, Milly J. to Ephraim Perkins 11-7-1854 Be
Holmes, Nancy A. to H. C. Ramage 2-?-1863 G
Holmes, Nancy C. to John R. Hall 4-23-1868 G
Holmes, Nancy W. to Thomas C. J. Reeves 4-14-1853 (no return) F
Holmes, Nancy to J. A. Kirby 1-30-1848 Cr
Holmes, Nora to Granville Harris 12-22-1880 (12-23-1880) Dy
Holmes, Sally to Thomas B. Blair 12-8-1829 G
Holmes, Sarah Rebecca to William Minor Hall 8-7-1849 (8-8-1849) T
Holmes, Sidny to John Bailey 10-14-1875 (10-15-1875) Dy
Holmes, Susan to Lewis Williams 9-30-1871 T
Holmes, Susan to William Cox 9-23-1842 (no return) Hn
Holms, Arytine to J. C. Merrett 4-28-1873 (4-29-1873) Cr
Holms, Casire to Bob Lyons 1-12-1869 Hy
Holms, Lucinda to J. P. Burns 11-12-1869 Hy
Holoman, Mary Ann to William Haislip 10-24-1866 L
Holson (Wolson), Francis to Daniel Huffman 10-31-1839 (11-3-1839) O
Holsouser?, Eurind to Wm. L. Burlerson 12-20-1853 T
Holsowser, Catherine to John J. Philips 8-16-1866 (8-17--1866) T
Holt (Hast?), Mag to Currie Garrison 7-24-1875 (7-25-1875) L
Holt, Ann Eliza to George W. Rooker 9-15-1856 (9-17-1856) Ma
Holt, Artilla to William G. Knott 10-10-1854 (10-11-1854) G
Holt, Barbary L. to William B. Little 5-6-1863 G
Holt, Barbary to Walter Thetford 10-4-1834 (10-9-1834) G
Holt, Callie to Nathan Mitchell 4-13-1869 (4-14-1869) Cr
Holt, Caroline J. to D. H. Echols 1-8-1861 Sh
Holt, Donie to Simon Morrow 9-27-1870 F B
Holt, Drucella to Joshua Swindle 2-18-1853 (2-19-1853) G
Holt, E. A. to J. L. Dickey 12-29-1868 G
Holt, Eliza to B. R. Fouster 2-11-1857 G
Holt, Elizabeth E. to J. W. McKelvy 2-1-1870 G
Holt, Elizabeth to Isham Thomas 7-10-1855 (7-11-1855) G
Holt, Elizabeth to John Martin 11-19-1847 (11-21-1847) G
Holt, Flora to William McCasling 11-16-1850 (11-13?-1850) G
Holt, Hannah to Ned Walker 12-24-1877 (12-26-1877) L
Holt, Jane to James W. Gardner 2-2-1841 (3-1-1841) G
Holt, Judith F. to Augustus B. Alston 3-14-1854 (3-15-1854) Ma
Holt, Julia to James W. Littlefield 2-6-1868 G
Holt, Lucinda to Lafayett Morris 12-30-1847 (12-31-1847) G
Holt, Lucy to Stephen J. Bobbett 1-13-1845 (1-16-1845) G
Holt, Luvilla to John Crowell 1-2-1862 Sh
Holt, Lydia L. to John G. William 1-22-1856 (1-24-1856) G
Holt, M. A. to H. J. Nutt 10-21-1866 G

Holt, M. J. to W. N. Nevin 7-19-1866 G
Holt, Margaret Ann to William M. Connell 10-5-1853 (10-6-1853) G
Holt, Margarett to J. G. McIntosh 8-11-1867 G
Holt, Margarett to N. J. Holt 7-28-1866 G
Holt, Martha A. to Allen Flippin 8-3-1862 G
Holt, Martha A. to W. T. Prewett 11-3-1842 Sh
Holt, Martha Ann to J. K. P. Cantrell 10-17-1860 (no return) We
Holt, Martha Ann to Robert N. Ricketts 6-25-1844 Sh
Holt, Martha J. to William T. Blackard 2-11-1850 Ma
Holt, Mary F. to J. G. McFarlin 12-1-1870 G
Holt, Mary L. to Jackson Thomas 5-23-1859 (no return) We
Holt, Mary to Edmund Parker 2-17-1880 L
Holt, Mattie L. to Geo. W. Tatum 11-13-1860 F
Holt, Nancy to James W. Baker 8-23-1866 G
Holt, Nancy to John F. Butler 10-7-1868 G
Holt, Neely to Knob Braden 4-30-1878 (5-1-1878) L
Holt, Paralee to Thomas P. Betts 12-25-1869 G
Holt, Patience A. to Jabes H. Flippin 5-19-1860 (5-21-1860) G
Holt, Sallie to W. L. Hart 10-16-1865 (10-17-1865) F
Holt, Sarah F. to Andrew J. McCaslin 1-27-1858 (1-28-1858) G
Holt, Sarah J. to W. H. Cunningham 1-20-1868 G
Holt, Sarah to John Watson 11-3-1852 (11-4-1852) Sh
Holt, Susan to Henry Sampson 10-27-1866 (no return) F B
Holt, Susan to John F. McCaslin 5-29-1854 (5-30-1854) G
Holt, Sussie T. to Wm. G. Pickett 2-8-1864 Sh
Holt, Syntha to Jordan Dent 12-28-1867 G
Holt, Viney to Wash Anderson 11-5-1881 (11-6-1881) L B
Holte (Hault), Marjiana A. to Ezekiel Anderson 2-13-1851 (2-20-1851) Sh
Holyfield, Frances E. to Thomas D. Isbell 11-10-1838 (11-13-1838) Hr
Holyfield, Frances J. to Green Castles 9-3-1846 (8?-3-1846) Ma
Holyfield, Lydia to Green B. Moore 1-26-1847 Ma
Holyfield, Susan A. to James L. Medlin 4-16-1850 Ma
Hommel, Margaret M. to Edward Willis 12-31-1860 (1-1-1861) Dy
Hon, Martha P. to T. J. McMurray 1-15-1868 Hy
Hon, R. C. H. to J. D. Cobb 7-4-1869 Hy
Hon, Susie J. to A. G. Overton 10-22-1873 Hy
Hon, Tennie to William E. Overton 9-10-1873 Hy
Honan, Ellen to Patrick Butler 4-4-1864 (4-6-1864) Sh
Hone, Catharine to Alexander Rose 11-5-1861 (11-6-1861) Sh
Honel, Margaret to James A. Casey 5-5-1829 Hr
Honey, Adah to Thomas A. Driggers 8-30-1843 (8-31-1843) F
Honey, Frenetta to J. T. Quinn 10-18-1854 (no return) Cr
Honey, Lucinda to Esau Bates 12-11-1843 (12-14-1843) F
Honey, Mary A. to Jas. H. Trulove 6-17-1846 (6-18-1846) F
Honey, Nancy to Henry Louch 12-23-1843 (12-24-1843) F
Honeycut, Nancy to John Arnold 7-24-1846 We
Honeycutt, Malissa J. to Stephen A. Burris 4-22-1862 O
Honnell, Sarah J. to Tho. B. Henderson 9-1-1846 (9-3-1846) F
Honner?, Mary to W. M. Murphy 9-23-1872 (9-26-1872) L
Hood, Amanda S. A. to George W. Hendricks 2-10-1864 (no return) Dy
Hood, Bettie E. to M. J. Reams, jr. 11-3-1870 F
Hood, Delia (Mrs.) to Thomas McCounts 1-7-1874 (1-24-1874) Dy
Hood, Eliza to Jim Durham 12-26-1866 (12-27-1866) F B
Hood, Eliza to W. H. Wing 12-17-1866 (12-20-1866) F
Hood, Elizabeth M. to Lawson W. Brown 9-19-1843 Hr
Hood, Elizabeth to William B. Harper 11-25-1847 O
Hood, Frances R. to W. D. Dalton 6-14-1879 (no return) Dy
Hood, Harriet A. to James H. Box 9-25-1865 (10-18-1865) Cr
Hood, Harriet Rebecca to James S. P. Craig 11-24-1855 (11-25-1855) O
Hood, Harriett H. to Ben W. Johnston 10-11-1855 (no return) F
Hood, Harriett N. to M. B. Todd 10-4-1860 We
Hood, Jane E. to Micado Murchison 2-4-1841 (3-15-1841) T
Hood, Jane to Andrew Jackson Sanders 4-5-1843 Sh
Hood, Lue E. to John H. Parker 10-8-1868 Hy
Hood, Mamie V. to J. C. Douglass 10-17-1877 Hy
Hood, Manda I. to Washington Honborn 11-16-1855 Cr
Hood, Martha J. to W. F. Carter 3-11-1849 (no return) F
Hood, Martha to Clabaorn Johnson 10-7-1841 Cr
Hood, Martha to James L. Buchanan 2-14-1861 O
Hood, Mary A. to A. J. Johnson 4-15-1846 Cr
Hood, Mary Ann to Moses D. Harper 4-20-1839 (4-23-1839) O
Hood, Mary E. to J. W. Wilson 7-10-1884 L
Hood, Mary E. to L. D. Collins 1-22-1855 Cr
Hood, Mary J. to L. E. Murphy 10-6-1868 (10-7-1868) F
Hood, Mary to Samuel F. Vaught 7-6-1857 (7-22-1857) O
Hood, Maryann D. to Wm. H. Stafford 2-17-1845 (2-18-1845) F
Hood, Mattie R. to Henry H. Moore 12-17-1874 Hy
Hood, Mollie E. to G. H. Reames 12-11-1867 (12-12-1867) F
Hood, Nancy Jane to Robert Nix 9-23-1857 O
Hood, Nancy R. to L. D. Johnson 7-5-1846 Cr
Hood, Ragile G. to T. W. Bennett 10-5-1848 (no return) We
Hood, S. A. to I.(J?) R. Ward 12-31-1875 Hy
Hood, S. E. to M. H. Kelley 12-26-1867 F
Hood, Salenah to Hezekiah Davis 9-2-1850 O
Hood, Sallie A. to Robert D. McLeod 1-30-1878 Hy
Hood, Sarah (Mrs.) to Geo. F. A. Spiller 11-11-1862 (11-12-1862) F

Hood, Sarah A. to A. J. Sanders 7-9-1851 (7-11-1851) Sh
Hood, Sarah M. to Etheridge Staggs 1-11-1877 Dy
Hood, Sarah to George W. White 1-16-1844 (1-18-1844) T
Hood, Sarah to James Lee 12-14-1848 Cr
Hood, Susan A. to R. R. Grizzle 10-3-1868 (10-7-1868) F
Hood, Telitha C. to James L. Ferguson 11-28-1855 (11-29-1855) Hr
Hood, Tirzah to James W. Buchanan 1-17-1854 O
Hood, Tresa Ann L. to Henry McBride 5-30-1879 (6-1-1879) Dy
Hoofman, Lucy to David C. Cabe 11-23-1851 Hn
Hoofman, Sarah C. to Samuel R. Boyd 10-25-1838 Hn
Hook, P. E. to W. R. Dodd 10-10-1868 Dy
Hooker, A. Z. to W. A. Derryberry 4-12-1863 Mn
Hooker, Caroline C. to Jas. A. Eddins 12-10-1850 (12-11-1850) F
Hooker, Elizabeth to Vincent S. Moore 5-2-1843 Hn
Hooker, Emeline (Mrs.) to William Trailor 1-1-1868 G
Hooker, Frances to C. W. Richardson 7-14-1848 Sh
Hooker, Lizzibella to Samuel Oldham 10-24-1877 (10-25-1877) L
Hooker, Lucinda to Robert P. Leach 1-11-1854 Cr
Hooker, Lucy Jane to Fielding A. Payne 7-31-1849 Sh
Hooker, M. A. V. to A. B. Hamner 8-31-1857 (9-10-1857) Sh
Hooker, Mary T. to James A. Hamner 1-19-1858 Sh
Hooker, Nancy P. to A. J. Fletcher 9-11-1863 Sh
Hooker, Nancy to Socrates Cannon 12-7-1853 Cr
Hooker, Susan to John Howel 7-4-1846 Sh
Hooker, Susannah to John W. Yow 11-6-1859 Hn
Hooker, Winney to Robert McCullough 10-15-1845 Hn
Hooks, Ann M. to John M. Siler 2-2-1848 T
Hooks, Callie to Geo. G. Wells 11-19-1867 Hy
Hooks, Caroline to Thomas Fitzgerald 10-11-1853 (10-12-1853) T
Hooks, Josephine to Wiley T. Cargil 12-13-1866 (12-24-1866) F
Hooks, M. J. A. to Jackson Woodard 10-27-1848 (no return) F
Hooks, Mary A. to James R> McCall 4-23-1846 (5-25-1846) T
Hooks, Rozeny to Richard Fletcher 6-28-1858 (6-29-1858) O
Hoolihan, Catharine to John Keegin 10-25-1859 Sh
Hooper, Alcy to Stephen Babb 6-6-1842 Hn
Hooper, Amanda M. to Wm. H. Howell 11-29-1861 Hr
Hooper, Anna to Milton N. McGehee 7-9-1846 We
Hooper, Bettie to Dick Maclin 2-3-1866 Hy
Hooper, Elizabeth to Alex Morris 2-22-1858 (2-24-1858) Hr
Hooper, Elizabeth to Stephen Marler 4-6-1839 Hr
Hooper, Eva to Brooks Eison 3-29-1879 (3-30-1879) L
Hooper, Fannie to J. E. Tooms 12-27-1878 Hy
Hooper, Frances to Henry Killman 6-20-1846 (6-21-1846) Hr
Hooper, Gennie S. to W. A. Conklin 1-15-1883 (1-17-1883) L
Hooper, Lauryan to Benj. F. Hooper 1-18-1843 (no return) F
Hooper, M. A. to G. W. Carnell 3-19-1879 (3-20-1879) L
Hooper, Martha to Rowan H. Vail 6-18-1850 (no return) L
Hooper, Mary E. to Joseph Jeffrey 9-1-1863 L
Hooper, Mary to Pete Hamilton 12-30-1872 Cr B
Hooper, Mary to Robert Hillard 5-7-1864 O M
Hooper, Mary to William Adams 12-15-1858 (12-16-1858) L
Hooper, Melissa Ann to Elijah P. Stricklin 3-13-1849 L
Hooper, Mollie E. to Geo. T. Hurt 2-20-1873 Dy
Hooper, Sally to Lewis Bobbit 11-11-1831 Ma
Hooper, Serbnny? to Jno. W. Blunt 12-25-1844 (12-26-1844) Hr
Hooper, Tennessee J. to John W. Milum 2-18-1866 Hn
Hooper, Tennie to Harrison Robertson 12-25-1872 (12-26-1872) Dy
Hooper, Virginia J. to Wm. A. Albritton 5-9-1851 Hn
Hoopert, Mary to Christian Baker 1-11-1855 (1-15-1855) Sh
Hooten, Caldonia to W. P. Newton 10-17-1877 Hy
Hooth, Fanny to James Mansfield 9-8-1864 Hn
Hooton, M. E. to C. C. Himmaugh 8-15-1871 (no return) Hy
Hooton, Malinda to Jas. H. Hughes 2-12-1863 Hy
Hooton, Sarah Jane to Julius C. Gordon 3-9-1860 (no return) Hy
Hoover, Elizabeth A. to A. R. Coleman 7-25-1860 G
Hoover, Mahaly to Anderson Brown 11-25-1870 G B
Hoover, Nancy S. to Robert Taylor 1-23-1852 G
Hoozer, Julia J. to George W. Moore 12-23-1847 (12-30-1847) G
Hope, Eliza to David P. Cloyed 4-21-1841 F
Hope, Elizabeth to John Martin 12-6-1842 Hn
Hope, Femby to David Mathews 7-29-1860 Sh
Hope, Josie (Mrs.) to James E. Totty 4-14-1873 (4-24-1873) Cr
Hope, Manerva A. to John S. Johnson 10-1-1851 (no return) F
Hopgood, Arrinda to James Mann 12-7-1876 Hy
Hopkikns, Sarah to James Coly 12-20-1834 Hr
Hopkins, Ann B. to Stephen C. Wright 12-17-1847 Cr
Hopkins, Elizabeth to Edward Crow 12-22-1842 Cr
Hopkins, Elizabeth to R. F. Tanner 11-15-1865 Mn
Hopkins, Elizabeth to Thos. Mitchell 6-14?-1851 (6-2?-1851) Sh
Hopkins, Emily to Joseph Gallaway 1-24-1855 Ma
Hopkins, H. E. to C. D. C. Wallis 2-6-1861 G
Hopkins, H. H. to F. K. Peary 2-22-1837 G
Hopkins, Harrett to Duncan H. Black 7-23-1849 (7-25-1849) G
Hopkins, Heneretta T. to William C. Hunt 1-21-1845 (1-23-1845) G
Hopkins, Julia Ann to Ruebin Heatcock 5-22-1838 Hr
Hopkins, Kesiah to Amos Bullock 10-16-1843 (no return) We
Hopkins, Logan to Josephine Brock 11-16-1857 Ma

Hopkins, Lucrety C. to Ratliff Boon 5-6-1844 G
Hopkins, Lugina to Finiss Reed 7-28-1831 (8-4-1831) Hr
Hopkins, M. A. J. to Benjamin Norred 8-24-1853 Hn
Hopkins, Margarette to J. J. Gardner 10-9-1854 G
Hopkins, Martha Ann to Samuel M. Thomas 4-11-1843 Sh
Hopkins, Martha to James Gibbs 3-27-1869 (no return) Dy
Hopkins, Mary A. J. to J. M. Whitten 3-9-1857 Hr
Hopkins, Mary E. to A. H. Crews 12-28-1858 G
Hopkins, Mary E. to James Smith 3-13-1860 Hy
Hopkins, Mary J. to James C. Childress 11-18-1849 Hn
Hopkins, Mary to William F. Shankel 9-26-1855 Hn
Hopkins, Melissa L. to James H. Banks 1-30-1859 G
Hopkins, Milly to E. P. Ross 8-18-1867 Hn
Hopkins, Nancy M. to John L. Saddler 3-29-1859 We
Hopkins, Olive to Mason Gilliam 2-27-1854 (2-28-1854) Ma
Hopkins, Rebecka to John Gambell 7-21-1829 G
Hopkins, Rutha to Richard Hall 10-21-1841 G
Hopkins, Sarah E. to J. T. Sutherland 8-17-1873 Hy
Hopkins, Sarah to Thomas Boling 11-21-1827 G
Hopkins, Talitha to Randle Mitchell 5-12-1866 O
Hoppee, Elizabeth Ann to B. F. Curtis 7-6-1868 G
Hopper, Amanda to Elvis Perry 10-6-1870 Cr
Hopper, Catharine to Franklin H. Griffin 1-24-1855 O
Hopper, Dicey to Wesley J. Johnson 3-10-1864 (no return) Cr
Hopper, Dicey to Wiley J. Johnson 3-10-1864 (3-12-1864) Cr
Hopper, E. M. to Jesse Perry 9-1-1870 Cr
Hopper, Emeline to Daniel O. March 4-6-1852 Ma
Hopper, Jamima J. to Erasmus A. Fleming 6-24-1852 G
Hopper, Jemina to Clinton Fitzgerald 3-9-1833 (3-19-1833) Hr
Hopper, Laura A. to B. F. Young 3-20-1878 (3-21-1878) Dy
Hopper, Lucinda to James M. Bumpass 8-9-1853 (8-10-1853) Ma
Hopper, Mahaly to Allen McCollum 9-28-1844 Cr
Hopper, Margaret L. to Geo. W. Price 12-24-1869 G
Hopper, Margaret to Peyton Somerville 12-26-1865 (no return) F B
Hopper, Martha Susan to James Goodram Adams 2-9-1849 (2-15-1849) T
Hopper, Martha to James W. Barrett 2-16-1870 (2-17-1870) Dy
Hopper, Mary A. to J. W. Lemond 3-3-1867 G
Hopper, Mary Ann to John R. Weakes 12-21-1869 (12-23-1869) Ma
Hopper, Mary Jane to Harvey Winford 11-1-1849 Sh
Hopper, Mary Jane to Samuel S. S. Smithwick 1-27-1862 (1-29-1862) Ma
Hopper, Mary P. to Judison L. Thompson 12-15-1858 Cr
Hopper, Mary to Wm. B. Grogan 1-9-1873 G
Hopper, Nancy A. to Edmund F. Taylor 12-17-1852 (12-25-1852) G
Hopper, Nancy to John Wesley Jacob 4-8-1850 Cr
Hopper, Olly B. to M. V. Baird 3-30-1860 G
Hopper, Prudence T. to James T. Gill 1-8-1850 (1-19-1850) Ma
Hopper, Rachel J. to Josephus Sims 12-28-1852 (12-29-1852) Ma
Hopper, S. A. to E. G. King 5-28-1866 G
Hopper, Sally to Thomas Crain 8-31-1829 Hr
Hopper, Sarah A. to O. K. Carpenter 12-10-1855 (12-11-1855) Ma
Hopper, Sarah to John P. Tatum 6-12-1851 G
Hopper, Susanna to William Parker Day 4-8-1845 Ma
Hopper, Tabitha E. to Hugh A. Montgomery 2-21-1848 (2-23-1848) Ma
Hopper, Tabitha to John Spencer 10-8-1853 (10-9-1853) G
Hopper, Ulissus to J. T. Barrett 6-26-1873 Dy
Hopper, Welthy Ann to David Ewing White 5-26-1855 (5-27-1855) T
Hoppers, Mariah Frances (Mrs) to Thos. D. Hoppers 8-26-1868 (8-27-1868) Ma
Hoppers, Rebecca to William G. Smithwick 1-5-1850 (1-9-1850) Ma
Hoppman, M. to S. Hoofman 7-19-1852 We
Hopton, Anna to J. J. Marshall 9-12-1859 Hr
Hord, Ella J. to J. D. Vinsent 4-25-1864 Sh
Hord, Margaret J. to F. M. Kerby 3-29-1862 (3-30-1863?) Cr
Horgot, Mary Emma to William Hughs 1-18-1870 Hy
Horman, Sallie E. to J. N. McLeon 3-13-1862 Sh
Horn, Alcy C. to P. B. Brewer 12-18-1865 (12-19-1865) Cr
Horn, Catharine to Thomas M. Hastings 10-16-1845 Hn
Horn, Catherine to Daniel Rouse 9-10-1865 Mn
Horn, Charlotte to Charles J. Cox 4-24-1844 (4-25-1844) Hr
Horn, Frances to Ansil Linch 7-13-1863 Cr
Horn, Fredricka to Ansel Pierucci 12-24-1860 Sh
Horn, Julia Ann to Calvin W. Sullivan 6-27-1858 Hn
Horn, Louiza to Tyson Autry 11-26-1861 (no return) Cr
Horn, Lucy to Daniel Settle 8-21-1848 Be
Horn, Martha to Valentine Tims 12-23-1846 Ma
Horn, Mary E. to A. O. Elliff 11-19-1865 Mn
Horn, Mary J. to Austin Lovin 1-24-1872 Cr
Horn, Mary Jane to Thomas Barber 1-11-1849 Ma
Horn, Mary to Alfred Wallace 2-16-1842 Cr
Horn, Merris to Thos. J. Baysinger 9-8-1838 (9-9-1838) G
Horn, Nancy to S. R. Birdwell 12-23-1851 Cr
Horn, Rachel to Benjamin Biggs 12-29-1833 Sh
Horn, Rebecca to Andrew B. Nesbitt 3-2-1840 Cr
Horn, Sarah to Anderson Horn 3-18-1846 Ma
Horn, Sarah to Thomas Floyd 9-11-1838 (9-13-1838) Hr
Horn, Susan J. to William C. Morris 10-27-1844 Hn
Horn, Wilhemina to George Schneider 2-8-1859 Sh
Horn, ____ E. to John G. Joiner 3-1-1864 (3-2-1864) T

Hornbeak, Alice to J. H. Beard 2-8-1859 We
Hornbeak, Eliza R. to Phillip W. White 6-17-1846 We
Hornbeak, Eliza R. to Phillip W. White 6-18-1846 We
Hornbeak, Margaret J. to George Price 3-27-1861 We
Hornberger, Juliana to Edward Pleitz 6-15-1857 Sh
Horne, Augusta to G. J. Scheuermann 1-25-1862 Sh
Horne, Elizabeth to Jonathan Boswell 10-30-1849 Ma
Horne, F. V. to A. F. McNear 11-12-1856 Sh
Horne, Lucinda to B. F. Gillespie 12-25-1848 Sh
Horne, Martha to John Allen Cox 12-13-1847 (12-17-1847) Hr
Horne, Mary J. to William H. Jones 12-19-1853 (12-21-1853) Sh
Horne, Rachel E. to William B. Jackson 12-18-1849 (12-20-1849) T
Horne, Susan A. to H. W. Stedman 6-3-1863 Sh
Horne, Susan E. to Isham B. Roberts 9-18-1848 (9-19-1848) T
Horner, Sarah E. to John F. Cummings 12-13-1860 O
Hornesby, Olivia Ann to Jno. M. Mitchell 2-25-1857 (2-26-1857) Hr
Hornsby, Catharine to Martin Tally 1-1-1839 O
Hornsby, Lucy Ann to Lealin Satterfield 4-27-1841 O
Hornsby, Lucy to Spencer Jones 9-7-1842 (9-8-1842) O
Hornsby, Sarah H. to William Jones 11-29-1839 (12-3-1839) O
Horskins, Elizabeth A. to Edmund V. Tucker 8-20-1838 G
Horten, Catherine to James G. Hale 12-20-1857 We
Horten, E. E. to S. W. Morris 6-5-1866 G
Horten, Elizabeth to John W. P. Lamb 3-25-1863 (no return) We
Horten, Elizabeth to Martin Shikle 4-24-1844 (no return) We
Horten, Elizabeth to Michael Dale 1-19-1863 Sh
Horten, Marandy P. to Thomas J. McGinnis 7-10-1865 G
Horton, Amada to James P. Park 3-1-1861 (no return) Cr
Horton, E. A. to John A. Wheeler 9-26-1869 G
Horton, Eliza to Geo. W. Garrett 9-16-1848 (no return) Cr
Horton, Elizabeth to Moses P. Cook 3-14-1854 O
Horton, Fannie L. to Saml. S. Spicer 11-28-1860 Sh
Horton, Fannie to C. B. Crutcher 3-30-1875 (4-7-1875) L
Horton, Harriet F. to John A. Kirkpatrick 7-29-1863 (8-2-1863) Dy
Horton, Hesiltine to Geo. C. Miller 12-14-1864 Sh
Horton, Isabella to James Halliburton 1-30-1886 (2-4-1886) L
Horton, Judy Ann to W. M. Anderson 4-3-1880 (4-4-1880) L B
Horton, Levisa to Frederick C. Brown 5-13-1845 (5-18-1845) O
Horton, M. P. to W. W. Taylor 10-5-1865 G
Horton, Malvina E. to Guilbord Jones 10-1-1861 Sh
Horton, Margaret J. to Santrel F. Leach 11-20-1858 Cr
Horton, Margaret to Elisha Bennett 1-23-1840 Cr
Horton, Martha V. to N. J. Heathcock 4-30-1867 G
Horton, Martha to Alexander Smith 9-24-1872 (9-25-1872) Dy
Horton, Mary A. to Francis M. Allen 8-28-1856 G
Horton, Mary A. to George W. Cooper 11-12-1866 (11-13-1866) Ma
Horton, Mary Ann to Irvin Finch 1-21-1841 Cr
Horton, Mary Elizabeth to J. R. Neil 9-25-1877 Dy
Horton, Mary to D. A. Covington 5-25-1841 Cr
Horton, Mary to Samuel Huntsman 10-3-1840 Ma
Horton, Millie to Chas. Springfield 12-2-1871 Hy
Horton, Millie to Peter Forrest 1-11-1878 (no return) Hy
Horton, Milly to James Crutchfield 12-16-1845 Cr
Horton, N. O. to L. P. Lucy 11-12-1875 (11-4?-1875) L
Horton, Nancy to Tom Byrum 12-8-1871 Hy
Horton, Rebecca to Pierce Moore 9-20-1873 Dy
Horton, Reddie to Peter McDonald 1-17-1878 Dy B
Horton, Retta to Henry Jones 10-14-1876 (10-15-1876) Dy
Horton, Sarah A. to S. H. Hughs 2-9-1865 G
Horton, Sarah P. to Wiley Martin 8-23-1838 Cr
Horton, Sarah to James W. Hinson 1-4-1860 G
Horton, Sophena to Wm. White 6-26-1856 Cr
Hosea, Matilda J. to Joseph Nee 1-12-1859 G
Hosey, Emily to B. P. Dyer 10-4-1879 (10-7-1879) Dy
Hosford, Clementine P. to William Taylor 12-15-1850 Hn
Hoskins, Elmira J. to Daniel Hodman 1-20-1850 (no return) F
Hoskins, Julia A. to Joseph Hutson 5-3-1856 (5-4-1856) G
Hoskins, Julia Ann to Jacob Cantlin 2-12-1875 (2-25-1875) Dy
Hoskins, L. R. to W. M. Branch 6-18-1875 (6-21-1875) Dy
Hoskins, Louisa to Ahi (Ase) Mitchell 8-31-1848 Sh
Hoskins, Mildred to George M. Harder no date (with Oct 1842) G
Hoskins, Nannie to David H. Keeling 4-16-1852 (5-4-1852) Sh
Hoskins, Sarah Ann to Richard Oliphant 9-1-1848 Sh
Hoskins, Susan F. to Coleman H. Witt 11-21-1853 (11-23-1853) G
Hosley, Elizabeth E. to Marion M. Dyer 7-26-1851 G
Hotchkiss, Jane to Jno. A. Perkins 7-12-1848 Sh
Hotchkiss, Martha to William G. Black 1-10-1850 Ma
Houck, Cornelia to W. L. Whitelaw 6-10-1878 Hy
Houe, Sarah to Henry Pryor 5-19-1859 O
Houghton, Maggie to David Mathis 2-13-1873 Hy
Houghton, Martha to Elizabeth J.? Barnett 10-20-1845 (10-21-1845) Ma
Houlehan, Catharine to Edmd. Keaton 5-8-1852 (5-9-1852) Sh
Hourbeight, Octavia (Miss) to Manuel Aragon 3-18-1857 (3-21-1857) Sh
Houry, D. C. to Sam'l. L. Haynes 1-18-1859 (1-19-1859) O
House, Adeline to Oliver Stott 12-26-1870 Hy
House, Amanda C. to E. D. Cullen 11-20-1856 Hn
House, Amanda F. to John Lendsy 11-29-1856 Cr

House, Ann M. to A. J. Hunter 1-16-1851 (1-22-1851) F
House, Annie B. to G. W. D. Jones 10-6-1872? Hy
House, Charlotte to John Myers 12-5-1848 (12-6-1848) Hr
House, Christina to Wm. N. Sauls 9-28-1854 Cr
House, Dilcey to Anthony Smith 11-23-1869 (11-28-1869) F B
House, E. I. to Robt. T. Jones 12-28-1862 G
House, Eleanor G. to James H. Nicholson 3-11-1876 (no return) Hy
House, Eliza E. to C. G. Rice 12-8-1863 (no return) Hy
House, Elizabeth A. to Elam Goodwin 9-18-1850 G
House, Elizabeth A. to Jacob C. Flowers 2-3-1852 (2-5-1852) G
House, Elizabeth A. to William Duke 9-29-1841 Hn
House, Ellen to Aaron Cooper 4-8-1875 Hy
House, Emiline to David Jones 3-30-1867 G B
House, F. A. to S. M. Jones 11-10-1860 (no return) Hy
House, Isabella to Spence Henry 12-24-1867 Hn B
House, Jane C. to Silas C. Irbey 12-15-1846 (12-22-1846) F
House, Jane to David House 12-22-1843 Hr
House, Julia E. to Richard E. Rogers 2-12-1861 G
House, L. A. to J. J. Parish 12-27-1866 G
House, L. A. to S. Shane 8-10-1865 G
House, L. A. to S. Shaw 8-10-1865 G
House, L. M. to G. L. Dickenson 12-21-1875 (12-23-1875) O
House, Lethy to Peter Bowlin? 5-15-1848 Hn
House, Lizzie to D. H. Johnson 1-15-1863 Sh
House, Loueser to Henry Macon 9-15-1867 Hy
House, Louisa to Robert Williams 1-28-1871 (2-22-1871) L
House, Louisa to William Dickerson 12-29-1870 (no return) Hy
House, Lucinia to John M. Stephens 2-3-1839 Hn
House, M. C. to John Foreshee 5-28-1867 Dy
House, M. R. to J. H. Spain 10-14-1871 (10-15-1871) Cr
House, Mannie to C. L. Williams 10-7-1851 Cr
House, Maranda F. to Asa Thomas Farrar 6-27-1852 Be
House, Martha Ann to James C. Hays 5-1-1839 Hn
House, Martha A. to Wm. N. Cole 1-12-1853 Cr
House, Mary C. to Benjamin W. Ivy 7-12-1859 We
House, Mary J. to Benjamin F. Carr 12-2-1848 Hn
House, Mary L. to P. M. Replogle 1-17-1856 (1-20-1856) G
House, Mary T. to Daniel W. Nichols 11-9-1868 (11-12-1868) Cr
House, Mary to G. G. Henderson 2-2-1868 Hy
House, Mary to James House 11-5-1869 (11-11-1869) F B
House, Mary to Major Mathis 6-8-1867 G
House, Melvina F. to William Duke 3-19-1851 Hn
House, Merseny to James M. Brazell 9-8-1838 Hr
House, Nancy to J. D. Clifton 9-1-1851 (9-4-1851) Hr
House, S. C. to J. W. Leach 12-27-1870 (12-28-1870) Cr
House, Sarah A. to Daniel M. Featherston 10-11-1860 We
House, Sarah to Colliver Williams 3-1-1853 Cr
House, Susan Ann to B. J. Cooper 7-24-1855 G
House, Teresa to A. B. Murphey 3-20-1875 Hy
Houseman, Mary to Henry Vaughan 4-1-1866 (no return) Cr
Houseman, Viola to James Purchais 7-11-1874 (7-12-1874) O
Houser, Loueza A. to William M. Miller 11-25-1863 O
Housman, Emily to Chris Cheek 6-16-1884 (7-9-1884) L
Houston, C. H. to James B. Forbiss 2-25-1859 (2-28-1859) T
Houston, Clerisa H. to James P. Forbiss 2-25-1859 (2-28-1859) T
Houston, Cynthia to P. M. Williams 2-12-1842 F
Houston, Cynthia to T. M. Williamson 2-12-1842 (no return) F
Houston, Delilia to William Williams 11-13-1872 (11-27-1872) T
Houston, Dinah to Thornton Bolling 3-29-1866 (4-1-1866) F B
Houston, Elizabeth F. to John H. Patrick 1-1-1869 (no return) F
Houston, Ella to Wm. Waddell 2-8-1868 (no return) F B
Houston, Francis to John Casey 12-7-1843 Cr
Houston, Julia L. to David C. Doyle 11-15-1849 Sh
Houston, Laura A. to S. S. Lewis 5-5-1846 Sh
Houston, Lydia A. to G. W. Rodgers 12-20-1855 Cr
Houston, Mahala to Robert Brown 10-13-1855 Hn
Houston, Malinda to Wm. Baxter 1-14-1847 Sh
Houston, Margaret A. to Benj. F. Allen 12-1-1857 Sh
Houston, Margaret to Humphrey Mills 12-29-1832 (12-30-1832) Hr
Houston, Margaret to Samuel McNeely 6-12-1841 (could be 1842) Sh
Houston, Mary E. to J. D. Wilson 11-28-1857 Sh
Houston, Mary E. to O. B. Caldwell 11-6-1850 G
Houston, Mary E. to W. L. Hughes 12-27-1852 (12-29-1852) Sh
Houston, Mary J. to Joseph Sidle 5-9-1848 Sh
Houston, Mathe to J. W. Weams 1-20-1868 (1-21-1868) Cr
Houston, Mattie J. to J. A. Adams 10-17-1871 (10-19-1871) Cr
Houston, Narcissa to David Bocks? 12-25-1867 (no return) Hn
Houston, Rebecca to John D. Fulks 9-10-1845 Cr
Houston, Roann to H. H. Taylor 7-21-1864 F
Houston, Sallie to Benj. C. Vickers 4-16-1862 Hn
Houston, Sarah to Barrett Houston 4-22-1866 G
Houston, Sarah to Johnathan Keathley 12-28-1859 (12-29-1859) T
Houston?, Mary Frances to Mussintyre? Sloane Mathews 11-10-1842 T
Houton, Mary N. to Alsman Gideon 8-1-1859 (no return) Hy
How, Elizabeth to Henry Fielding 2-16-1859 Sh
Howard(Howell?), Martha to Wrigdon Jernigan 1-28-1848 Hr
Howard, A. C. to M. Bragg 5-21-1870 (5-22-1870) T

Howard, Adeline to Abner Akers 2-28-1865 Hn
Howard, Alice C. to J. B. Gatti 5-26-1853 (6-5-1853) Sh
Howard, Alpha to Thomas J. Ragan 12-24-1863 G
Howard, Amanda to John Hogan 6-21-1854 L
Howard, Amanda to Lee Gray 2-18-1840 (2-19-1840) O
Howard, Amanda to Lee Gray 2-18-1846 O
Howard, America to Billy Byford 8-25-1877 (8-26-1877) L
Howard, Angeline to George W. Wilson 9-25-1866 Hn
Howard, Ann Eliza to Arthur J. Hedgepath 8-20-1846 Ma
Howard, Ann Eliza to Martin Breedlove 8-16-1867 Hn B
Howard, Ann Rebecca to Jesse S. Cothran 11-14-1840 (11-19-1840) T
Howard, Caroline to David F. Matthews 5-27-1835 (5-28-1835) G
Howard, Catharine to Hana? Miller Larimore 5-31-1853 T
Howard, Chainey to Thomas Jones 10-3-1874 T
Howard, Delilah to James Allison 8?-31-1829 (8-6-1829) Hr
Howard, E. J> to J. A. Williams 1-1-1882? (1-2-1883) L
Howard, Elizabeth A. to John W. Timberlake 1-6-1840 (1-7-1840) Hr
Howard, Elizabeth A. to Felix W. Lee 2-12-1839 F
Howard, Emaly to Thomas Beaver 11-8-1873 T
Howard, Frances J. to William M. McConnell 11-3-1844 Hn
Howard, Henrietta to James Rhodes 4-28-1868 (5-2-1868) T
Howard, J. E. to J. V. W. Pennington 12-6-1883 L
Howard, Jane to Joseph H. Lacey 6-25-1833 (6-26-1833) Hr
Howard, Jennie to Sam Auston 9-1-1870 (9-5-1870) L
Howard, Joanah to Columbus Hogan 9-11-1871 T
Howard, Joanah to Frank Robertson 7-31-1868 (8-1-1868) T
Howard, Joanna to Wm. Stricklun 11-10-1866 T
Howard, Josephine to George Plattenburg 9-15-1855 (no return) F
Howard, Josephine to W. G. Woodson 6-6-1869 G
Howard, Latitia to Jordan Moore 8-13-1866 (no return) Dy
Howard, Letta to Gabriel Byars 3-8-1866 Hn B
Howard, Lonesome to E. H. Troutt 1-28-1870 (1-29-1870) Dy
Howard, Louisa to J. M. Huggans 9-25-1856 We
Howard, Lucinda to Joshua Collier 9-18-1869 Hy
Howard, Lucy J. to T. F. Simpson 10-13-1873 (10-14-1873) Dy
Howard, M. F. to A. P. Parker 5-30-1871 (5-31-1871) T
Howard, Margaret A. to Henry C. Powell 12-2-1857 Hn
Howard, Margaret Ann to Walker Henry 7-28-1880 (not executed) L
Howard, Margaret to J. C. Miller 12-7-1881 L
Howard, Mariah V. to Geo. R. Bridges 11-6-1844 (11-8-1844) Hr
Howard, Martha A. to Wm. M. Herndon 12-5-1856 (no return) F
Howard, Martha D. to D. W. Owen 12-13-1859 (12-14-1859) O
Howard, Martha J. to William M. Maxwell 1-13-1848 Hn
Howard, Martha Jane (Mrs.) to Ransom Hawkins 3-18-1856 Sh
Howard, Martha M. to William Bragg 12-29-1869 (12-30-1869) T
Howard, Martha to B. H. Crocker 2-28-1861 G
Howard, Martha to H. Cowles 12-31-1874 Dy
Howard, Martha to John H. Spivy 10-31-1845 (11-2-1845) Hr
Howard, Martha to John Liston 11-12-1847 Cr
Howard, Mary A. to Dick Smith 12-24-1866 (12-29-1866) Dy
Howard, Mary A. to James Holmes 7-15-1864 Sh
Howard, Mary A. to Stephen Howard 4-21-1860 (4-24-1860) Dy
Howard, Mary E. to J.F. Hargett 9-3-1879 L
Howard, Mary E. to T. A. Brady 11-14-1867 Hn
Howard, Mary J. to John Curtis 12-24-1840 G
Howard, Mary J. to Stephen P. Childress 1-8-1840 (1-9-1840) G
Howard, Mary Jane (Mrs.) to Wm. M. McCullough 8-4-1857 Sh
Howard, Mary Louisa to Henry W. Hickman 3-5-1855 (3-8-1855) O
Howard, Mary P. to George W. Moser 1-2-1860 (1-1860) O
Howard, Mary W. to Theophass Baugh 12-11-1856 We
Howard, Mary to Clinton Gaily 7-9-1855 (7-12-1855) G
Howard, Mattie to Anthony Morgan 2-7-1882 L
Howard, Mattie to James Walker 9-26-1881 (no return) L
Howard, Minerva P. (Mrs.) to Riley Privett 10-31-1865 Dy
Howard, Mollie E. to Allen C. Hall 3-22-1864 (no return) Cr
Howard, Mollie J. to W. R. Massey 11-18-1869 G
Howard, N. A. to E. J. Mitchell 7-5-1852 We
Howard, Nancy A. to William Wattson 1-8-1862 Hn
Howard, Nancy to Andrew W. McConnell 10-21-1841 Hn
Howard, Nancy to Cavert Presley 7-4-1876 (7-5-1876) L
Howard, Nancy to Lee Gray 2-27-1848 (2-29-1848) O
Howard, Nancy to William Wilson 6-30-1830 (7-1-1830) G
Howard, Ophelia P. to Geo. W. Wynne 6-21-1871 (6-22-1871) T
Howard, Rebecca E. to T. S. McKelvy 11-22-1858 (11-25-1858) G
Howard, Rebecca J. to G. W. Winn? 6-10-1863 T
Howard, Rebecca to William Sales 12-18-1843 (12-20-1843) G
Howard, S. E. J. to T. A. Mahan 11-30-1859 G
Howard, S. E. to J. W. Pennington 1-10-1882 (1-11-1882) L
Howard, Sarah Ann to Jesse McCollom 12-21-1868 (12-22-1868) Cr
Howard, Sarah E. to F. M. Jordan 11-8-1867? Hn
Howard, Sarah J. to Charles Murphy 3-4-1852 L
Howard, Sarah M. to Woodring Ferrell 11-24-1866 (11-25-18??) O
Howard, Sarah P. to William J. Blythe 8-26-1841 Hn
Howard, Sarah to James A. Crank 1-28-1851 G
Howard, Sarah to John C. Carroll 1-2-1843 (1-5-1843) G
Howard, Savannah S. to B. S. Yates 11-27-1859 Hn
Howard, Susan A. to Robert D. McCutchen 9-20-1854 Hn

Howard, Susan C. to Asberry M. Freeman 6-26-1858 (6-30-1858) G
Howard, Susan to Richd. Archer 2-25-1869 T
Howard, Susanna to Jno. H. Fletcher 10-19-1854 Sh
Howard, Winnie to William Harrison 11-21-1870 G
Howard?, Josey to N. J. Jordan 10-4-1877 (10-5-1877) L
Howcott, MaryL. to Jno. C. Lanier 12-15-1852 Sh
Howe, Drucilla to Thomas Duglas 12-4-1863 Be
Howe, Manerva C. to Lewis M. Cowell 4-11-1860 Be
Howe, Margaret to Thomas H. Ash 7-17-1861 Sh
Howe, P. to Jessee Johnson 10-25-1855 Be
Howe, Perlenza to John Smith 1-1-1857 Be
Howel, E. H. to T. B. Crane 1-16-1867 O
Howell (Harvell), Margaret Rebecca to Joseph D. Bird 11-21-1853 (11-23-1853) O
Howell(Harrell), Mary to Benj. M. Hill 8-9-1833 (8-15-1833) Hr
Howell, Amandy J. C. P. to William H. Wilkes 2-4-1860 G
Howell, Catharine to Irwin Parker 2-8-1847 G
Howell, Charlotte to Thomas Brassfield 2-18-1868 Dy
Howell, Elizabet M. to David M. Goza 2-14-1867 G
Howell, Elizabeth (Mrs.) to Owen Pickens 4-26-1871 Ma
Howell, Ella to Bill Davis 4-1-1871 Hy
Howell, Fatis C. to Joseph J. Robertson 4-12-1845 (4-15-1845) F
Howell, Gray to Wm. F. Ayers 4-15-1858 T
Howell, Jennie O. to Samuel D. Simmons 3-16-1858 (3-?-1858) Hr
Howell, Juliann to William Lee 11-13-1846 Hn
Howell, Kittie to Henry Stokley 2-25-1869 Hy
Howell, Lizie to Lewis Bird 7-23-1874 Hy
Howell, Lizzie to Mark Bowen 4-15-1885 (no return) L
Howell, Lucinda to Franklin Simmons 9-25-1853 Hn
Howell, Lucy to John Barrott 6-9-1842 Cr
Howell, Lumisa to James M. Gately 9-22-1857 (10-1-1857) Ma
Howell, M. J. to John Garner (Gasner?) 7-26-1870 G
Howell, Mahulda to James Howard 2-25-1847 Sh
Howell, Margaret A. (Mrs.) to I.L. Reneow 9-9-1870 Ma
Howell, Margaret A. to James Jernigan 2-27-1854 (3-2-1854) Hr
Howell, Margaret to Edward Jackson 1-2-1868 Hy
Howell, Margarett A. to Thomas N. Kirkpatrick 1-9-1840 Cr
Howell, Margart A. to Thos. R. McKnight 12-12-1850 (no return) F
Howell, Marietta to Will F. Ferguson 11-27-1854 (11-29-1854) Hr
Howell, Marinda to M. Garrison 6-24-1869 (6-30-1869) F
Howell, Martha E. to A. N. Henley 8-15-1850 Hn
Howell, Martha to T. R. Turner 6-20-1838 (6-24-1838) G
Howell, Mary Ann to Henry J. Austin 9-30-1857 (10-1-1857) Ma
Howell, Mary E. to Henry Leonly? 4-20-1867 (4-22-1867) Dy
Howell, Mary E. to Wm. F. Ayres 3-1-1854 (3-2-1854) Sh
Howell, Mary J. to J. J. Farrow 2-1-1866 (no return) Hy
Howell, Mary J. to W. A. Buffaloe 12-17-1850 Sh
Howell, Mary Jane to Elisha L. King 1-25-1870 G
Howell, Mary W. to John C. Forbess 5-23-1845 (5-25-1845) T
Howell, Minney Jane to William Brown 5-14-1857 Hr
Howell, Nancy A. to J. W. Lemons 1-20-1857 (1-21-1857) G
Howell, Nancy J. to Henry Flowers 11-18-1866 G
Howell, Nancy to Solomon Dinny 7-15-1846 (7-16-1846) G
Howell, Nancy to Stephen L. Carter 2-5-1851 F
Howell, Nany to David W. Powers 2-16-1843 (2-20-1843) G
Howell, Polly to Andrew Porter 1-2-1837 (1-17-1837) G
Howell, Rachel to Martin Sewell 2-8-1867 (2-10-1867) Ma
Howell, Sallie to George Thompson 1-31-1866 (no return) L
Howell, Sallie to Joseph Deal 8-16-1866 Dy
Howell, Sallie to William Becktel 11-3-1868 Hy
Howell, Sarah E. to James L. Trevathan 3-22-1848 Hn
Howell, Susan P. to S. K. Jackson 12-14-1870 (12-15-1870) Dy
Howell, Zelpha to Lewis Dickerson 8-26-1845 Hy
Howell?, E. C. to W. T. Goodwin 1-10-1870 (1-12-1870) Dy
Howell?, Elizabeth E. to Thomas C. Harrell(Howell?) 10-13-1846 Hr
Howerton, Caroline Winiford to William Henry Wooten 12-14-1841 T
Howerton, Mary C. to Thadeus A. Alexander 1-19-1858 (1-20-1858) T
Howlett, Ellen V. to James M. Moorhead 1-30-1862 Sh
Howlett, Mary M. to Herbert Perry 11-27-1848 (11-30-1848) Ma
Howlett, Mary to Champion Terry 1-25-1855 Hn
Howlett, Virginia to Edwin L. Wingrove 1-8-1862 Ma
Howley, Mary E. to William H. Floyd 8-14-1867 (8-15-1867) L
Howse, Susan A. to Thomas N. Newsome 11-14-1866 Hy
Hrrington, Elizabeth W. to John W. Allison 12-21-1849 (12-27-1849) G
Hub, Barbery to John Dener 5-8-1856 Sh
Hubard, Elizabeth W. to Jesse W. Wallis(Wilson) 12-13-1845 (12-18-1845) Hr
Hubart, M. J. to M. V. Moore 4-20-1876 (4-23-1876) O
Hubbard, Alice to John Jay Lane 2-28-1859 (3-2-1859) Ma
Hubbard, Caroline J. E. to William Cloar 12-24-1839 Sh
Hubbard, Easter A. to Hiram G. Reeves 1-6-1852 O
Hubbard, Eliza to William Case 12-5-1833 Sh
Hubbard, Elizabeth A. to R. S. Menifee 12-1-1859 Hn
Hubbard, Elizabeth to William W. Hughes 3-14-1853 (3-17-1853) O
Hubbard, Georgia to B. Waldrop 10-14-1875 O
Hubbard, Lucinda to Elijah D. Henley 11-11-1846 F
Hubbard, M. A. to Elias J. Hostetter 3-21-1861 Mn
Hubbard, Margaret L. to Calvin Pitan 3-30-1881 L

Hubbard, Mary A. to Charles Mitchell 3-23-1837 Sh
Hubbard, Mary Jane to James D. White 8-8-1837 Hr
Hubbard, Mary L. to James Strong 11-12-1844 Sh
Hubbard, Mary M. to R. P. Moore 10-25-1831 (10-27-1831) Hr
Hubbard, Mary to William Jimmerson 7-5-1848 O
Hubbard, Nancy B. to Wm. F. Palmer 6-9-1840 Hr
Hubbard, Nannie B. to Thomas C. Salter 8-7-1866 (8-8-1866) Ma
Hubbard, Nannie to R. B. Colley 5-22-1879 L
Hubbard, Sallie G. to G. W. Wells 7-24-1869 Hy
Hubbard, Sally M. to Edmund M. Ricks 2-23-1863 (no return) Hy
Hubbard, Samantha E. to John C. Hughes 3-3-1857 Hr
Hubbard, Sarah C. to William Harron 7-24-1839 G
Hubbard, Sarah L. to B. F. Gilliland 2-4-1876 L
Hubbard, Sarah M. to Thomas Moore 12-13-1848 Hr
Hubbard, Sarah to Henry Chipman 12-25-1882 (12-26-1882) L
Hubbard, T. C. to Thomas C. Calhoun 12-11-1860 (12-13-1860) Cr
Hubbard, Virginia to J. W. Miller 9-10-1860 (no return) Hy
Hubberd (Hubert), Adaline N. to Robert D. Caldwell 3-12-1858 (3-4?-1858) O
Hubbert, Katharine to William Gilliland 12-23-1846 O
Hubbs, Ann to Thomas E. Everight 5-4-1846 (5-20-1846) O
Hubbs, Elizaeth C. to John Palmer 2-8-1845 O
Hubbs, Jane to George W. Stevenson 12-12-1862 O
Hubbs, Mary A. C. to James R. Whitley 11-3-1852 (11-4-1852) O
Hubbs, Mary J. to A. J. Barnett 8-1-1847 Be
Hubbs, Rebecca to Nathaniel Greene 2-17-1853 Hn
Hubert, Charlotte to John H. Good 9-15-1836 O
Hubert, Easther to Thomas J. Macon 2-1-1834 O
Hubert, Elizabeth to William Stephen 4-26-1825 (4-28-1825) O
Hubert, Esther to Newton Bramblett 7-4-1834 O
Hubert, Frances to Henry D. Logan 1-24-1828 (1-26-1828) O
Hubert, Francis M. to William M. Alexander 10-31-1860 O
Hubert, Linda Catharine to John B. Corum 3-22-1857 O
Hubert, Martha to George W. Cunningham 7-9-1829 O
Hubert, Matilda to John Cloar 8-13-1836 O
Hubert, Polly P. to Elij. S. Jones 1-8-1833 (2-8-1833) O
Hubert, Sarah to Anson A. R. Cunningham 6-17-1830 O
Hubert, Susan to Absolem Cloar 5-31-1834 O
Hubert, ____ to Wilson Dickerson 8-9-1828 O
Huce, Martha T. to F. (Dr.) Lucas 12-12-1849 G
Huckabe, Mary Jane to Sterling A. Hagar 1-11-1847 (1-13-1847) L
Huckabee, Frances to William Tomlinson 7-26-1860 L
Huckabee, Susan E. to Henry Glimp 5-4-1857 (no return) L
Huckaby, Martha to Joseph E. Bailey 1-6-1844 (1-8-1844) Hr
Huckaby, Mary S. to Mathew Marcum 12-28-1859 G
Huckeby, Emiline to Lewis Hutcheson 11-19-1842 (11-20-1842) L
Huddle, M. J. to S. W. Williamson 9-15-1869 (no return) Cr
Huddleseton, Martha F. to William J. Winston 6-4-1855 (6-7-1855) O
Huddleston, Amanda I. to Robert Corum 11-12-1863 (11-13-1863) O
Huddleston, Ann to W. F. Ayers 7-27-1848 O
Huddleston, Biddy to Grove Rook 7-26-1845 (7-29-1845) Hr
Huddleston, Catharine J. to Asa Hewin 5-2-1853 (no return) F
Huddleston, Catharine to David M. Huddleston 11-26-1855 Hr
Huddleston, Cytnha to Pleasant Huddleston 8-18-1844 Hn
Huddleston, Eliza to Hiram Seaton 6-24-1846 (6-25-1846) Hr
Huddleston, Elizabeth to Andrew Willoughby 3-28-1843 (no return) Hn
Huddleston, Emily to Alexander Hamilton 10-16-1852 (10-17-1852) Hr
Huddleston, Harriet E. to Harvey C. Donaho 11-23-1853 (11-25-1853) O
Huddleston, Mahala to William H. Huddleston 3-27-1850 Hr
Huddleston, Malinda to Josiah T. Faucett 5-13-1853 (5-17-1853) Hr
Huddleston, Manervia to M. F. Westbrook 7-19-1858 Hr
Huddleston, Martha to William Arms 11-14-1839 Hr
Huddleston, Mary E. to Elisha T. Stewart 7-20-1859 Hr
Huddleston, Mincy Jane to Jehu Lambert 9-15-1854 (9-18-1854) Hr
Huddleston, Orphy to Thomas Hawkins 7-28-1841 Sh
Huddleston, Tennessee to John S. Cook 8-2-1841 Sh
Huddleston, Virginia to W. E. Rhegness 7-14-1867 G
Hudgens, Arnetta T. to Thomas W. Legan 12-22-1864 Hn
Hudgens, Arrena to S. V. Rose 9-21-1856 Hn
Hudgens, Isabella to Robert Brizendine 4-1-1847 Hn
Hudgens, Julia F. to J. M. Neal 4-29-1867 (no return) Hn
Hudgens, Laura to Wm. H. Mason 6-19-1871 (6-22-1871) Ma
Hudgens, Margaret to Thomas K. Rose 9-30-1858 Hn
Hudgens, Martha J. to J. B. Stevenson 8-13-1856 Hn
Hudgens, Nancy to William Tharpe 8-31-1848 Hn
Hudgens, Sarah D. to W. C. Brizendine 1-29-1867 Hn
Hudgins, Catherine to John Bur? 1-8-1845 Hn
Hudgins, Mary T. to Charles W. Wright 2-24-1869 (2-25-1869) Ma
Hudgins, Mary to Edward Ivers 2-15-1862 Sh
Hudgins, Mary to William A. Boyd 1-11-1844 Hn
Hudgpith, R. A. to B. C. Osment 9-12-1855 We
Hudson, Allis to Louis Thomas 7-13-1871 (7-14-1871) Cr B
Hudson, Amanda E. to Benjamin F. Dickinson 3-26-1857 Ma
Hudson, Amarintha to Henry C. Jobe 2-22-1858 (2-24-1858) Hr
Hudson, Arena to Ed Bowers 3-28-1870 (3-29-1870) F B
Hudson, Caroline to Henry Gaither 12-28-1869 F B
Hudson, Caroline to S. James Rogers 3-22-1858 (3-25-1858) Hr
Hudson, Cyntha V. to John Y. Prince 5-8-1862 (5-11-1862) T

Hudson, E. P. to W. A. Combs 1-1-1863 Be
Hudson, Eleanor F. to Davidson R. Caldwell 1-6-1848 Sh
Hudson, Eliza A. to James W. Cole 11-28-1866 (11-29-1866) F
Hudson, Eliza I. to William W. Deberry 1-4-1839 Ma
Hudson, Eliza to Thomas Pettyjohn 11-22-1855 (no return) Hn
Hudson, Elizabeth to Ephraim Christmas 8-5-1853 Sh
Hudson, Elizabeth to John Corley 12-29-1834 (12-30-1834) Hr
Hudson, Elizabeth to W. N. Hearn 12-21-1846 Ma
Hudson, Elvira to Elijah V. Brown 6-12-1843 (6-13-1843) Hr
Hudson, Elvira to W. A. Loyd 12-19-1866 G
Hudson, Euginia J. to George R. Scott 10-27-1866 (10-30-1866) Ma
Hudson, Fanny G. to Robert B. Ozment 4-23-1853 (5-1-1853) G
Hudson, Frances S. to James M. Box 10-7-1846 Hr
Hudson, Jane C. to David Myers 4-24-1852 (no return) F
Hudson, Jennie to Daniel McLeod 7-26-1871 (no return) Hy
Hudson, Laura to Henry H. Dean 1-23-1854 (1-26-1854) Ma *
Hudson, Louisa to William D. Gilmore 4-16-1851 Sh
Hudson, Lucinda A. to John M. Neal 11-23-1841 (11-25-1841) Ma
Hudson, Mahaly A. to Francis M. Greer 2-14-1867 Be
Hudson, Margret to Peter P. Crawford 8-22-1845 Hr
Hudson, Martha A. to Chas. T. Newland 3-24-1860 (4-3-1860) Hr
Hudson, Martha A. to John A. Baker 8-20-1857 (8-26-1857) Hr
Hudson, Martha Ann to John N. Walker 10-26-1867 (11-7-1867) Ma
Hudson, Martha F. to Wylie Doyerl? 2-11-1840 (2-13-1840) F
Hudson, Martha to John Davis 7-17-1846 Hr
Hudson, Mary A. to William B. Worrell 9-14-1849 (9-20-1849) Hr
Hudson, Mary E. to Henry H. Hudson 1-25-1866 (1-30-1866) T
Hudson, Mary L. to Lilborn Honey 9-5-1866 (9-9-1866) O
Hudson, Mary to W. O. Heren 1-8-1864 Be
Hudson, Mattie E. to W. H. Cocke 12-18-1871 (12-19-1871) T
Hudson, Nancy J. to J. H. Wiseman 8-13-1868 Be
Hudson, Nancy to Richard Allen 2-4-1869 G B
Hudson, Nannie to Wm. Jordan 3-26-1880 Dy
Hudson, Nicy E. to J. P. Dowell 1-18-1866 Be
Hudson, Sarah F. to Thomas H. Pettyjohn 11-20-1855 Hn
Hudson, Sealia Ann to E. D. Y. Hundley 7-16-1849 (7-17-1849) G
Hudson, Susan A. to William H. Johnson 7-28-1842 F
Hudson, Susan E. to D. H. Slayton 11-17-1863 Hy
Hudson, Susan F. to James G. House 12-5-1866 (12-6-1866) Ma
Hudson, Susan to Calvin C. Edmunds 11-21-1850 Hn
Hudson, Susanna J. to John Bostick 2-22-1841 (2-24-1841) Ma
Hudson, Susannn E. J. to John A. Malin 12-3-1868 Be
Hudson, Tempy Ann to C. W. Ferrell 2-9-1846 F
Hudson, Virginia M. to Louis H. Tune 7-22-1867 G
Hudspeth, Caroline to Austin Muncrief 11-3-1845 (11-2?-1845) F
Hudspeth, Emily Margaret to Jesse P. Pride 11-24-1855 (11-26-1857) O
Hudspeth, Esther Ann to Isaac Watkins 12-3-1860 (no return) Hn
Hudspeth, Frances A. A. to Alexander Bogards 2-13-1861 (2-14-1861) Hr
Hudspeth, Lillie Ann to Allen Cox 3-11-1833 Hr
Hudspeth, Lucy A. to Tho. J. Bell 12-16-1845 (12-17-1845) F
Hudspeth, M. J. to A. F. Pate 8-24-1856 We
Hudspeth, Mary to S. C. Henderson 7-4-1848 Hn
Hudspeth, N. J. to A. D. Roberts 5-18-1856 We
Hudspeth, Rebecca to John Bolen 5-27-1837 (5-30-1837) Hr
Hudston, Amanda J. to L. D. Milliner 9-15-1871 (9-17-1871) O
Hues, Cally to John Voss 11-30-1874 (12-2-1874) L
Huett, Elizabeth (mrs.) to B. S. Stephens 8-8-1867 G
Huey (Henry), Lucretia to Jonathan King 4-14-1849 O
Huey, Halley White to J. A. Bridges 11-11-1855 Cr
Huey, Mary A. to John Horn 5-17-1843 Cr
Huff, Elizabeth to S. S. Pate 10-24-1854 We
Huff, Susan J. to Asbury F. McCord 11-14-1858 Hn
Huffine, Malinda to Alse L. Pope 11-28-1877 (11-29-1877) Dy
Huffine, Margaret Jane to B. G. M. Cole 12-14-1876 Dy
Huffine, Sarah C. to H. T. Pope 12-4-1878 (no return) Dy
Huffman, Ann to Lewis Fields 12-31-1868 (1-3-1869) Cr
Huffman, Dilla to W. D. Owenby 8-14-1867 (8-15-1867) Cr
Huffman, Elender M. to George W. Brown 4-29-1841 Sh
Huffman, Eliza to W. G. Miller 12-9-1856 (12-11-1856) T
Huffman, Elizabeth A. to Wilsons Wall 6-25-1848 Cr
Huffman, Elizabeth to Wm. Stephen 8-22-1844 Cr
Huffman, Jane to John Swayne 4-27-1872 (no return) Cr B
Huffman, Julia A. to N. R. McCormick 8-29-1855 T
Huffman, L. A. to H. C. Dacus 11-7-1874 (11-10-1874) T
Huffman, L. P. to W. A. Williams 1-24-1873 (1-30-1873) Cr
Huffman, M. C. to O. S. Feezor 2-23-1874 T
Huffman, Marsha (Martha) to Lewis Brown 12-20-1842 Sh
Huffman, Martha Ann to J. R. Morrasett 1-8-1872 (1-9-1872) T
Huffman, Martha to Jacob Braun (Brann?) 6-5-1862 Sh
Huffman, Mary A. to Alexander Lawrance 4-15-1852 Cr
Huffman, Mary A. to Richels D. Haynes 7-15-1858 Cr
Huffman, Mary to Alexander Carper 5-19-1857 (5-22-1857) Hr
Huffman, Mary to R. R. Simonton 2-8-1870 F
Huffman, Mary to William G. Harris 1-7-1867 (1-13-1867) T
Huffman, May to William Hannah 11-20-1838 Sh
Huffman, Milly to Atlas J. Butler 1-3-1847 Cr
Huffman, Nancy C. to G. H. Williams 7-14-1866 (7-15-1866) Cr

Huffman, Nancy J. to F. M. Harris 4-3-1871 (4-4-1871) T
Huffman, Rowenna to John Kaiser 1-5-1854 Sh
Huffman, Susan to B. Butler 9-20-1848 Cr
Huffman, ___ to Franklin Phillips 9-15-1857 Cr
Huffstutter, M. A. to J. W. Mitchell 12-25-1867 O
Huffstutter, Martha to J. R. P. Hutchinson 12-15-1865 O
Huffstutter, Mary E. to Jas. A. Call 9-13-1865 O
Hufstettler, F. E. to A. J. Blackmore 8-21-1875 (8-23-1875) Dy
Hufstettler, Margaretta A. to James L. McCoy 7-21-1874 (7-27-1874) Dy
Hufstettler, Mary J. to A. M. Green 6-22-1874 (6-23-1874) Dy
Hufstutte, Jane to Lewis Hutchison 4-19-1865 O
Huges, Matilda A. to L. P. Pickard 2-23-1846 We
Hugganes, Eliza D. to John E. Workman 2-27-1857 We
Huggans, Mary L. to James M. West 12-24-1857 We
Huggens, Hanah E. to John Starnes 1-12-1861 (1-13-1861) L
Huggins, Alice to Balaam Emerson 10-25-1876 (no return) Dy
Huggins, Augusta L. to Robert E. Quinan 4-7-1855 Sh
Huggins, Emaline to John Clay 7-1-1865 (no return) L
Huggins, Lura A. to Samuel A. Anthony 5-15-1879 L
Huggins, Margaret to Allen Ramsey 12-31-1845 We
Huggins, Mary to John Permenter 12-19-1844 (no return) We
Huggins, Saphronia to Benjamin George 12-25-1864 G
Huggins, Winny to Bush Bond 2-26-1874 Hy
Hugh, Eunice B. to John M. Fenner 7-25-1844 Ma
Hughes, Angelina to John G. Allen 8-9-1837 (8-24-1837) Hr
Hughes, Anna to A. J. Henry(Heniny) 9-28-1829 Hr
Hughes, Balm to William Warren 6-20-1868 G
Hughes, Catharine to John E. Meek(Merk) 5-7-1838 (5-10-1838) Hr
Hughes, Eliza E. to J. M. Elder 1-6-1871 (1-12-1871) F
Hughes, Elizabeth Caroline to William B. Turnage 6-5-1843 (6-6-1843) T
Hughes, Elizabeth to John Culbreth no date (12-28?-1838) F
Hughes, Elizabeth to John Ferrel 5-2-1846 (no return) F
Hughes, Elvira to William H. Wilson 9-12-1844 Hn
Hughes, Harriet to Elbert Randle 10-20-1847 Hr
Hughes, Harriet to James Cannell 1-30-1860 (no return) Hy
Hughes, Jane B. to William M. Neill 8-11-1831 Ma
Hughes, Jane to Geo. W. Vincent 7-14-1858 Hr
Hughes, Jane to George Reeves 1-26-1857 (1-29-1857) O
Hughes, Joan to Enoch Heath 1-13-1863 We
Hughes, Lottie to A. J. Tucker 3-3-1875 Hy
Hughes, M. A. to J. C. Whitaker 8-2-1860 Sh
Hughes, M. K. to H. H. Rogers 2-1-1870 (2-2-1870) Ma
Hughes, Margaret M. to Joseph J. Weatherley 11-10-1858 (no return) Hn
Hughes, Margaret to Samuel B. Drake 4-28-1846 Hn
Hughes, Mary Ann to Jas. Goldsmith 4-27-1843 Sh
Hughes, Mary E. to Gilfin W. Bass 8-8-1861 We
Hughes, Mary E. to Thomas Gipson 11-22-1857 Hn
Hughes, Mary S. to James Underwood 10-7-1856 Hn
Hughes, Mary to Thomas McKeon 9-24-1846 Sh
Hughes, Mary to William Flinn 6-9-1860 (6-10-1860) Sh
Hughes, Nancy E. to Saml. Thompson 1-31-1854 (2-1-1854) O
Hughes, Nancy O. to John Elgin 3-24-1839 (3-25-1839) Hr
Hughes, Penelope to Jno. C. Dunn 8-29-1850 Hn
Hughes, Sarah J. to William Laughlin 9-7-1861 Mn
Hughes, Sarah to Brown Scisson 12-21-1843 We
Hughes, Susannah to Wm. Wilson 12-13-1843 Sh
Hughes, Teresa to James Farrel (Famel?) 4-22-1851 (4-24-1851) Sh
Hughes, Virginia E. to Wm. P. Smith 11-24-1850 Sh
Hughleette, Jane to Calvin Harris 6-18-1870 T
Hughlett, Emma to Geo. Wilson 1-18-1868 (1-19-1868) T
Hughlett, Martha to Louis Kennedy 12-27-1868 T
Hughlett, Martha to Needhan Kilpatrick 9-28-1872 T
Hughlette, Emmer to Erwin? Yarbro 6-8-1867 T
Hughs, Allice to Milton Walker 12-23-1872 (12-26-1872) Cr B
Hughs, C. J. to J. A. Walding 10-13-1868 Hy
Hughs, Elizabeth to Bernard Dunn 10-25-1856 (10-26-1856) Sh
Hughs, Lou J. to Robert J. Baxter 8-1-1866 (no return) Cr
Hughs, M. S. to J. M. Edwards 12-26-1871 Hy
Hughs, Mary E. to Henry Saunders 3-19-1877 (no return) L
Hughs, Sarah E. to S. C. Coleman 1-25-1860 Cr
Hughs, Sarah to Thos. Vaulx 12-23-1867 Hy
Hughs, Sintha to John Voss 2-31-1869 Hy
Hughs, Tennie to R. E. Allen 11-21-1868 (no return) Hy
Hugueley, C. R. to D. J. Scoby 5-5-1863 (5-6-1863) Dy
Huguely, Margaret M. to W. B. Scoby 2-8-1862 (2-12-1862) Dy
Huie, M. E. to E. K. Tucker 8-13-1866 G
Huie, Mary J. to J. W. Rains 2-11-1864 Hn
Huie, Sarnisa to B. S. Vaneaton 3-13-1860 (3-14-1860) G
Huie?, Martha to W. H. Rhodes 2-11-1864 Hn
Huison?, Miss Jane to D. M. Twisdale 12-12-1865 (12-13-1865) T
Hulday, E. M. Cathy to G. W. Horten 8-8-1855 We
Hulett, Martha A. to Michael Plunk 11-26-1850 (12-2-1850) O
Huligens, Eva to Jojada S. Van Rinkel 5-14-1864 Sh
Huling, Sarah to James Laurence 12-19-1838 T
Hull (Hall?), Dolly to Andy Freeman 7-5-1870 G B
Hull, Adaline to Henry Bushart 12-26-1857 Hn
Hull, E. M. to George A. Tower 7-6-1870 Dy

Hull, M. E. to A. P. Brewer 3-27-1877 (3-29-1877) Dy
Hull, Mary to R. J. Neely 4-2-1851 Hr
Hull?, Elizaeth L. to James K. Rogers 8-8-1867 (8-9-1867) Cr
Hullum(Hull?), Louisa to Ingram Wilson 9-2-1840 (9-6-1840) Hr
Hullum, Harriet A. to Jerimiah S. Claunch? 4-24-1835 (4-27-1835) Hr
Hullum, Louisa J. to William R. Woford 3-12-1849 (3-21-1849) Hr
Hullum, Louisa T. to William H. Taber 11-25-1831 (12-1-1831) Hr
Hullum, Mary to William Brown 6-19-1829 (6-25-1829) Hr
Hullum, Miss Martha M. to Reuben W. Biggs 12-24-1845 Hr
Hullum, Zelia A. to Wm. T. Wells 9-24-1859 (9-25-1859) Hr
Hulon, Matilda to James D. Stacy 10-13-1821 Sh
Hulon, Rebecca to Lewis Reaves 10-18-1821 Sh
Hulsey, Mary Ann to Oliver Butler 8-5-1848 Ma
Hult?, M. E. to M. L. Keene 12-16-1874 T
Humble, Gillie Ann to William Cirtis 8-6-1866 (8-7-1866) L
Humble, V. A. to P. L. Scott 5-22-1879 (6-7-1879) Dy
Humbles, Mary A. to Francis Lamoine 11-12-1858 (11-17-1858) G
Hume, Alcina A. (Mrs.) to Wm. T. (Capt.) Joyce 3-30-1838 Sh
Humes, Sarah A. to Henry C. Dollis 6-5-1846 Sh
Hummil, Delia A. to Uriah Davis 8-16-1851 L
Humphrey, Annie to Thomas Neely 8-5-1862 (no return) Cr
Humphrey, Catharine to Smith Patterson 1-19-1844 (not endorsed) F
Humphrey, Frances to Wm. M. Price 2-26-1855 (no return) F
Humphrey, Gennett to James Richey 4-18-1840 (4-19-1840) F
Humphrey, Jesse to J. S. Colvin 9-25-1878 (9-26-1878) Dy
Humphrey, Julia A. to M. C. Pearce 9-29-1860 Hr
Humphrey, Julia to Jasper N. N. Scott 12-9-1850 Cr
Humphrey, Lucinda to Henry S. Hay 12-24-1863 Sh
Humphrey, Lucy E. to Wm. C. Hudson 3-31-1845 Hr
Humphrey, Martha to Jas. L. Richie 1-19-1850 (1-20-1850) F
Humphrey, Martha to Joseph M. Green 10-11-1852 Ma
Humphrey, Mary E. to Jno. H. McCleland 11-4-1858 (11-10-1858) Hr
Humphrey, Mary L. to John Williams 12-2-1858 Cr
Humphrey, Mary P. to James H. Rollins 2-10-1869 Cr
Humphrey, Mary to Doy Humphrey 12-30-1857 Cr
Humphrey, Melinda to John S. Key 4-7-1853 Cr
Humphrey, Nancy to Benj. House 1-11-1849 (no return) Cr
Humphrey, Nancy to Lem Jarrott 7-7-1841 Cr
Humphrey, Sarah to John W. Rolins 9-16-1858 Cr
Humphrey, Sarah to Nicholas Long 9-10-1844 F
Humphrey, Susan A. to C. W. Rozelle 10-7-1840 Sh
Humphrey, Susan to Lemuel Doty 6-24-1832 Sh
Humphrey, Truly to Wm. A. Jones 5-27-1852 Cr
Humphreys, A. J. to P. D. Benson 8-18-1843 (9-8-1843) F
Humphreys, Ann to Thomas McClain 11-9-1848 Hn
Humphreys, Azalee M. to Hinton J. Jelks 1-22-1845 Ma
Humphreys, Clara R. to Levin Hill Harris 11-15-1871 (11-22-1871) Ma
Humphreys, Grace to Stephen K. Watkins 12-12-1866 F
Humphreys, Jane to Richard H. Jones 11-30-1851 Hn
Humphreys, L. A. to John S. Vickers 4-9-1873 (4-10-1873) Cr
Humphreys, L. J. to I. M. Escue 12-15-1878 Hy
Humphreys, Luiza to W. H. Paschall 11-8-1866 F
Humphreys, M. J. to John Safferans 6-21-1856 (6-23-1856) Sh
Humphreys, Margaret J. to Thomas G. Arnold 9-14-1853 (9-15-1853) Ma
Humphreys, Margaret J. to Thos. G. Arnold 9-4-1853 Ma
Humphreys, Margarett to James Baxter 7-20-1849 Ma
Humphreys, Mary E. to John A. Cochrum 1-12-1858 Hn
Humphreys, Mary H. to Timothy K. David 10-14-1840 (10-22-1841?) F
Humphreys, Mary to Henry Matthews 3-22-1870 (3-18?-1870) F B
Humphreys, Mary to W. A. Milliken 2-3-1870 F
Humphreys, Mary to Wm. S. Camp 11-19-1856 Sh
Humphreys, Nancy J. to W. F.? Vinyard 12-24-1868 (no return) Dy
Humphreys, Pernelia to James Warmack 11-25-1841 Hn
Humphreys, Rhoda to Thos. Brown 4-4-1851 (1-5-1851) F
Humphreys, S. A. to J. C. Holland 10-20-1858 Sh
Humphreys, Susan to William J. Fudge 8-23-1839 L
Humphreys, Winney to Tazewell M. Jones 2-5-1852 Hn
Humphries, Curly to Jonathan Jarrett 9-14-1845 Cr
Humphries, Winnie to Thomas C. Starks 8-11-1842 Hn
Humphris, Rebecca C. to William W. Gooden 3-8-1837 (3-12-1837) G
Humphry, Catharine to William F.? Condray 3-10-1866 (3-11-1866) Cr
Hundey, Tobithia to James Bohannan 7-2-1840 L
Hundley, Elizabeth V. to H. M. Anderson 12-16-1858 (12-18-1858) Hr
Hundley, Gilly to Arthur Williams 11-4-1857 Ma
Hundley, Rebecca to Terrell Branch 9-3-1856 G
Hungerford, Amelia to W. T. Howard 7-10-1858 (7-12-1858) Sh
Hunley, Catharine to Henry C. Smith 1-1-1857 F
Hunley, Joice to John Gross 2-16-1841 (2-17-1841) T
Hunn?, Sallie B. to J. H. Balley 12-12-1868 (12-10?-1868) T
Hunnacutt, M. A. to G. Sawyers 8-24-1852 We
Hunnell, Cinderralla to Harmon O. Jackson 11-30-1833 (12-4-1833) Hr
Hunnell, Martha to Claiburn Wilson 3-28-1842 (3-29-1842) Hr
Hunnell, Polly to Henry Rogers 3-3-1831 Hr
Hunsucker, Martha E. to W. W. Lyles 1-30-1867 F
Hunsucker, Sarah Ann to Archey Burleyson 12-21-1866 (12-22-1866) F
Hunt (Hurt?), Mollie C. to W. M. P. Mitchell 8-20-1872 (8-25-1872) L
Hunt, A. J. E. to Elisha Harrison 5-13-1868 G

Hunt, Adaline to Isaiah Nash 8-26-1866 G
Hunt, Ann E. to Nathaniel Atkinson 10-27-1837 (10-29-1837) Hr
Hunt, Annie to Robt. Lewis 6-2-1876 (no return) Hy
Hunt, Bettie M. to Wm. H. Long 11-30-1868 (12-8-1868) F
Hunt, C. C. to A. C. Bond 10-11-1866 G
Hunt, C. to Abel Robinson 12-2-1867 G B
Hunt, Clarissa to Jno. M. Neely 7-9-1833 (7-23-1833) Hr
Hunt, Dora O. to W. G. Poindexter 11-16-1872 (11-20-1872) T
Hunt, E. L. to A. J. Wilson 9-9-1885 L
Hunt, Eliza A. to George W. Durley 4-9-1834 G
Hunt, Eliza to James Greer 3-20-1845 Cr
Hunt, Elizabeth A. to William R. Sellers 11-24-1856 G
Hunt, Elizabeth S. to Joseph J. Bass 5-9-1843 G
Hunt, Elizabeth T. to R. B. Sommerville 1-9-1853 (1-12-1853) T
Hunt, Emily to William W. Hudgens 1-31-1858 Hn
Hunt, Emma to William Winn 4-13-1874 T
Hunt, Emma to Wm. Winn 4-13-1874 T
Hunt, Eugenia D. V. to Beverly L. Holcomb 6-25-1829 (7-2-1829) Hr
Hunt, Fannie S. to Nat M. Kimbrough 5-20-1867 (5-22-1867) T
Hunt, Frances C. to Joseph D. Hudson 7-30-1861 G
Hunt, Frances to Henry Penn 3-23-1870 G B
Hunt, L. F. to L. O. Strayhorn 3-2-1869 G
Hunt, Laura to Robert M. Drummons 8-4-1865 (8-5-1865) T
Hunt, Louisa C. to C. W. Hix 3-9-1860 (3-11-1860) G
Hunt, Lucy Eugenie to Jas. G. Glenn 10-5-1868 (10-6-1868) Ma
Hunt, M. E. to R. M. Arnett 5-13-1873 Dy
Hunt, M. W. B. to B. F. Trousdale 6-28-1853 Hn
Hunt, Malisa B. to William Brinkley 12-2-1855 We
Hunt, Martha A. to H. H. Elcan 7-10-1865 T
Hunt, Martha Maria to Jeptha Hogue 2-24-1847 (2-25-1847) T
Hunt, Mary A. to William S. Witherington 12-16-1862 We
Hunt, Mary Ann to James F. Smith 12-4-1839 Hn
Hunt, Mary Cassa A. to R. J. Corley 10-27-1857 (10-28-1857) G
Hunt, Mary Jackson to Wm. R. Clements 9-9-1854 (9-14-1854) T
Hunt, Mary S. to Jno. R. Dickins 2-21-1842 (2-22-1842) Hr
Hunt, Mary to G. F. Basinger 11-28-1861 G
Hunt, Melvina to William Rosser 5-29-1833 Hr
Hunt, Minerva to Merideth Busby 6-19-1826 Sh
Hunt, Mollie J. to Marshall Hobson 5-7-1867 Hn
Hunt, Phebe to James Paschal 5-20-1862 (no return) Hn
Hunt, Phoebe Ann to William M. Jamison 10-5-1855 (no return) Hn
Hunt, Polly to Patrick Richerson 1-13-1866 T
Hunt, Rebecca C. to Samuel C. Pierce 1-23-1854 (1-24-1854) G
Hunt, S. C. to John Wagster 1-19-1864 G
Hunt, S. E. to W. D. Cash 3-23-1869 (3-24-1869) T
Hunt, S. S. to C. H. Dabbs 12-5-1834 Hr
Hunt, Sallie Anderson to Wm. Little Tarry 4-4-1850 (4-10-1850) T
Hunt, Sarah E. to James Williams 7-8-1870 G
Hunt, Sarah to Ira Alexander 12-8-1840 Hn
Hunt, Sarah to Isaac W. Bass 5-20-1850 (5-28-1850) G
Hunt, Sissee to Lawson Williamson 1-31-1870 T
Hunt, Susan H. to Samuel Mosby 5-31-1843 Sh
Hunt, Susan to Edmond Walls 2-16-1867 G
Hunt, Susan to Edmond Watts 2-16-1867 G
Hunt, Susannah E. to James S. Boney 6-7-1838 (6-10-1838) Hr
Hunt, Tempe to Joseph Rice 1-3-1866? (1-5-1867) T
Hunt, Unicy T. to Benjamin Boon 5-16-1838 (5-17-1838) G
Hunt, Virginia to Samuel Dickins 2-21-1842 (2-22-1842) Hr
Hunt?, Sallie B. to Thos. H. Poindexter 11-16-1872 (11-20-1872) T
Hunter, Agness E. to John W. Shaw 11-1-1838 Hr
Hunter, Allice L. to Samuel H. Wilson 1-23-1869 (1-27-1869) F
Hunter, Amanda E. to W. R. Layton 7-2-1863 Mn
Hunter, Ann Eliza to Lewis Robertson 11-5-1866 (no return) Hy
Hunter, Anna J. to G. C. Pinkston 2-8-1871 F
Hunter, Caroline to George Martin 12-29-1869 (no return) F B
Hunter, Charlett to Charles Temple 11-3-1828 Ma
Hunter, Clarinda to Thomas C. Jackson 12-11-1858 Hn
Hunter, Cyntha A. to Dewees C. Lloyed 1-15-1872 (1-17-1872) L
Hunter, Diena M. L. to Jefferson M. Fields 1-8-1851 (1-9-1851) Hr
Hunter, E. to James Evans 8-12-1871 (no return) Hy
Hunter, Elisabeth to Henry Clay Anderson 11-17-1870 L B
Hunter, Eliza A. to William Cochrum 3-2-1845 Hn
Hunter, Elizabeth M. to James R. Glenn 4-3-1854 (4-5-1854) Ma
Hunter, Elizabeth to A. W. Shelton 9-7-1848 Hn
Hunter, Emeline to Jordan Taylor 2-27-1866 (12-28-1866) F B
Hunter, Emeline to Ned Giles 12-12-1868 (12-19-1868) F B
Hunter, Emeline to William Stout 12-26-1868 (12-27-1868) F B
Hunter, Evey to Ed Ballard 12-12-1868 (12-21-1868) F B
Hunter, Frances F. to Oren A. Hearn 12-9-1859 (12-11-1859) Ma
Hunter, Gilly to Isaac Braden 10-22-1842 (10-23-1842) L
Hunter, Hannah to Middleton Smith 4-18-1878 L
Hunter, Harriet to Mark Lewis 1-1-1869 F B
Hunter, Jane to Landdon Duffiel 5-10-1873 (5-11-1873) L B
Hunter, Jenny to Blueford Paine 12-28-1868 F B
Hunter, Julia to Fred Douglass 1-6-1871 (no return) F B
Hunter, Louisa to Sam Deberry 1-24-1878 Hy
Hunter, Louise E. to Henry S. Taylor 10-16-1838 F

Hunter, Margaret A. to Wm. H. Bray 5-15-1866 Ma
Hunter, Margaret to J. W. Sangster 1-16-1860 Hy
Hunter, Martha E. to Newton A. McCoy 11-7-1855 (11-?-1855) Ma
Hunter, Martha to James Merriwether 11-4-1843 (no return) F
Hunter, Martha to Jim Beckwith 4-17-1844 We
Hunter, Mary C. to J. S. Temple 12-4-1883 L
Hunter, Mary S. to John S. Wright 2-1-1865 (2-2-1865) T
Hunter, Mary to Geo. Tackett 7-3-1860 Hr
Hunter, Mary to James W. Perry 12-22-1838 Ma
Hunter, Mary to John L. Dawson 2-2-1866 (2-4-1866) F
Hunter, Mollie to Cornelius Coleman 12-25-1872 Hy
Hunter, Nancy Ann to Marvin Hunter 4-3-1869 (4-18-1869) F B
Hunter, Nancy Lenorah to John Willoughby 1-12-1848 (1-13-1848) Hr
Hunter, Nancy to Hugh Moore 6-8-1837 Sh
Hunter, Rebecca J. to A. A. Black 7-30-1854 (no return) F
Hunter, S. E. to A. W. Shaw 1-29-1869 (1-30-1869) T
Hunter, S. E. to J. W. Martin 1-20-1860 (1-1860) O
Hunter, Sarah Ann to John A. Mashburn 3-13-1854 (3-16-1854) Hr
Hunter, Sarah F. to Allison S. Winston 2-21-1853 O
Hunter, Susan to William Ellis 12-21-1857 O
Hunter, Susan to William Ellis 3-25-1858 O
Hunter, Tennessee to David Boyd 12-21-1875 (no return) Hy
Hunter, Tennessee to Henry Campbell 12-14-1867 (no return) Hy
Hunter, Tennessee to Matt Johnson 5-25-1878 (no return) Hy
Hunter, Tiller to Rubin Walker 2-8-1877 Hy
Hunter, Virginia to J. F. Harpole 10-21-1874 (10-22-1874) O
Huntington, M. E. to Wm. F. Smith 7-27-1859 (7-28-1859) Sh
Huntsman, Ann to Timothy P. Spurlock 12-21-1840 (12-22-1840) Ma
Huntsman, Nancy to William H. Noblin 7-10-1856 (no return) We
Huntsman, Paradise to Nathiel W. Williams 5-30-1855 Ma
Huntsman, Sarah L. to Isaac D. Parker 12-27-1845 (12-28-1845) Ma
Hupley, Mattie to N. E. Duncan 11-19-1864 (11-20-1864) Sh
Hurdle, Bettie to Hampton Harden 1-?-1871 Hy
Hurdle, Fannie to D. A. Walker 2-2-1884 (2-7-1884) L
Hurdle, Maria to Henry Jayroe 5-22-1873 (no return) L B
Hurendon, Elizabeth S. to Samuel S. Allison 4-20-1852 Be
Hurley, A. J. to G. A. Scott 2-19-1878 (2-21-1878) Dy
Hurley, C. F. to Wm. F. Farmer 1-30-1871 (2-14-1871) F
Hurley, Cornelia M. to A. T. Anders 9-29-1856 (9-30-1856) L
Hurley, Elizabeth to J. G. Ruby 12-16-1845 F
Hurley, Elizabeth to Wm. James 5-18-1863 (5-20-1863) Dy
Hurley, Ellen E. to George Milo Miers 1-6-1862 Sh
Hurley, Jane to D. C. Carroll 8-14-1858 Sh
Hurley, Jane to Normon Williams 12-17-1847 (12-22-1847) F
Hurley, L. C. to B. C. James 1-23-1862 Mn
Hurley, M.E. to John C. Pate 8-3-1872 (no return) Dy
Hurley, Martha Ann to John Wesley Patrick 7-13-1854 (8-17-1854) Sh
Hurley, Martha to Thomas Walpole 9-15-1859 Sh
Hurley, Mary to Richard Young 11-17-1862 Sh
Hurley, Nancy to James Howard 2-1-1870 Dy
Hurley, Patsey to Samuel S. Rust 12-22-1825 (12-25-1825) G
Hurly, Amanda to Thomas Reynolds 6-19-1863 L
Hurst, Caroline to John Hartie 6-2-1860 Sh
Hurst, Charlotte to Andrew Johnson 4-16-1868 G B
Hurst, Orlena to Needham Holmes 10-29-1861 Mn
Hurt (Hust), Cela to John Smith 10-12-1872 Hy
Hurt, Amanda to Benjamin G. Griffy 1-25-1873 (1-26-1873) O
Hurt, C. M. to J. N. Dozier 12-7-1864 G
Hurt, C. V. to E. B. Saunders 10-10-1865 Hy
Hurt, C. to J. B. Jordan 8-18-1874 (8-23-1874) L
Hurt, Cintha to Saml. Currie 12-16-1873 Hy
Hurt, Elizabeth to John Hanagan 7-30-1857 Sh
Hurt, Ella to N. P. Barksdale 1-15-1872 (1-18-1872) Cr
Hurt, Fannie to Geo. T. Johnson 11-29-1877 Dy
Hurt, Frances to J. C. Jones 2-19-1872 Cr
Hurt, Frances to J. T. Higgason 1-13-1868 (1-15-1868) Dy
Hurt, H. F. to P. M. Patterson 10-11-1854 Cr
Hurt, Harriett C. to Archibold W. O. Toten 3-29-1843 Ma
Hurt, Jane to Charles S. Lewis 2-14-1843 (no return) Hn
Hurt, Josephine to William H. Banks 12-18-1850 (no return) Hn
Hurt, Lear to Pett Harrell 9-27-1871 (9-28-1871) Cr B
Hurt, Leona to W. W. Hurt 12-27-1884 (12-28-1884) L
Hurt, Lizzie J. to Guy Leeper 1-6-1869 Ma
Hurt, Louisa to James Jones 12-19-1871 (no return) Cr B
Hurt, Malissa A. to Thomas A. Leech no date (10-31-1865) Cr
Hurt, Martha A. to Solomon Cook 2-25-1861 Dy
Hurt, Martha E. to George T. Baker 9-27-1865 (9-28-1865) Dy
Hurt, Martha to F. M. Ray 10-4-1847 Cr
Hurt, Martha to John T. Fuqua 10-21-1867 (no return) Cr
Hurt, Mary Jane to Hinton Chambless 10-11-1869 (10-13-1869) Cr
Hurt, Mary to Abel Pennington 3-14-1841 Hr
Hurt, Mattie C. to R. E. Aikens 1-1-1866 (1-4-1866) T
Hurt, Minnie to Gilbert Bond 3-9-1876 Hy
Hurt, Mollie A. to Thos. A. Leach 10-27-1865 Cr
Hurt, Nancy to Richard W. Kirklin 1-18-1838 (no return) Hn
Hurt, Pattie to Joseph D. Neilson 4-30-1867 (5-1-1867) Ma
Hurt, Rachel to Silas Bigham 9-27-1871 (9-28-1871) Cr B

Hurt, Sarah E. to J. F. Tinnen 8-10-1861 (8-14-1861) T
Hurt, Sarah Jane to Robert Littlefield 11-8-1843 Sh
Hurt, Sarah to C. A. Collins 12-19-1860 (no return) Cr
Hurt, Susan to Albert Sutton 12-27-1865 Hy
Hurt, Virgina C. to Jessee Wright 10-11-1873 (10-13-1873) T
Hurt?, Ann Elizabeth to John Hendin? Crouch 3-7-1853 (3-8-1853) T
Husband, Lavina to T. J. Lockhart 7-1-1875 (no return) Dy
Husbands, S. T. to G. B. Pierce 9-18-1874 (9-20-1874) Dy
Huskey, Martha D. to H. C. Sanders 3-22-1868 Hy
Huskey, Martha to Isaac Stutman 7-3-1842 Sh
Huskey, Rebecca Caroline to Major Gregory 12-28-1845 Sh
Husky, Lucind to E. W. Howard 3-16-1869 (no return) L
Huss (Hemp), Miranda to J. S. Willes 4-9-1854 We
Hussah, Ann to E. G. Wright 10-16-1856 Be CC
Husted, Rachel to T. H. Fowler 10-16-1854 (no return) We
Hustigan, Johannah to Timothy Fannasey 7-29-1862 (8-3-1862) Sh
Huston, Adaline to Wm. Turner 7-15-1871 T
Huston, Jane to B. A. Mann 11-10-1866 (no return) Hy
Huston, Mary Ann to John Manard 3-8-1846 Be
Hut, Mary to Charley Rice 8-10-1877 (8-11-1877) L B
Hutchans, Mary E. to Smith K. Cocke 2-27-1856 G
Hutchens, Caroline N. to Hezekiah Womack 11-18-1849 (11-13?-1849) G
Hutchens, Catharine to Thomas Wilson 8-28-1845 Sh
Hutchens, Catherine to William Starns 7-24-1844 Sh
Hutchens, Elviry A. to Joel W. Harrison 4-4-1843 (4-13-1843) G
Hutchens, Fannie to Charles C. Swoope 7-13-1858 Sh
Hutchens, Jane to Henry Pelworth 2-19-1845 Sh
Hutchens, Nancy to J. M. Welch 7-9-1857 We
Hutchens, Sarah to John Clayton 11-11-1841 (no return) Hn
Hutchens, Sarah to John J. Scherman 7-26-1850 Hn
Hutcherson, Addie C. to Harvey N. Milligan 11-16-1870 Ma
Hutcherson, Anne to Solomon Ray 3-25-1868 G B
Hutcherson, Clementine to W. J. Overall 2-28-1860 G
Hutcherson, Eliza to Arthur Torbiss? 12-10-1842 (12-15-1842) T
Hutcherson, Elizabeth A. to W. O. Chapman 5-29-1861 G
Hutcherson, Frances to W. H. Bizzell 12-29-1868 Hy
Hutcherson, Ida to Benj. A. (of AR) Word 2-22-1870 Ma
Hutcherson, Juan G. to Thomas S. Condry 7-27-1871 L
Hutcherson, Louisa to George R. Williams 8-13-1849 (8-14-1849) L
Hutcherson, M. E. to T. B. Latour 1-15-1878 (1-16-1878) L
Hutcherson, M. J. to S. P. Goble 1-23-1882 (1-24-1882) L
Hutcherson, Nancy to Joseph Waters 1-12-1863 Mn
Hutcherson, Pasley to George Patterson 3-16-1858 L
Hutcherson, S. J. to Robert S. Palmer 12-16-1862 (no return) We
Hutcherson, Sarah to Richard H. Page 1-23-1856 G
Hutcherson, Susan F. to Joseph Rooks 5-16-1869 Hy
Hutcherson, Susas S. to John P. Laney 6-28-1871 (6-29-1871) L
Hutcheson, Julia A. to James M. Bottem 12-18-1866 (12-5?-1866) L
Hutcheson, Martha to Jackson Hutcheson 3-18-1844 L
Hutcheson, Martha to John Matthew Patterson 3-29-1844 (3-31-1844) L
Hutcheson, Mary to James H. Means 11-15-1862 Mn
Hutchings, Elizabeth to Jason H. Wilson 5-10-1828 Ma
Hutchings, Mary C. to John H. Cross 11-30-1848 Ma
Hutchings, Susan M. to Thomas P. Aydlett 6-12-1850 Sh
Hutchins, Elizabeth to Calvin Ursery 12-20-1844 (12-19?-1844) F
Hutchins, Jane to Nathaniel Hobbs 9-23-1851 Sh
Hutchins, Jane to Ruffin Willis 1-10-1844 F
Hutchins, Julia to James T. Willis 4-9-1845 F
Hutchins, Lucy to Needham Walker 2-10-1836 Sh
Hutchins, Margaret A. to William Holloman 2-12-1857 O
Hutchins, Martha to Creed Whitworth 3-5-1836 Sh
Hutchins, Martha to William Myers 11-10-1869 (11-11-1869) F B
Hutchins, Mary to Thomas M. Bates 5-6-1845 Sh
Hutchins, Permelia to Silas M. Chiles 2-28-1838 F
Hutchinson, Amanda to Tiller Shipp 12-4-1852 (12-9-1852) O
Hutchinson, E. A. to John A. Sanders 10-13-1866 Hy
Hutchinson, Eliza J. to Albert C. G. Burton 2-15-1871 (no return) F B
Hutchinson, Elizabeth B. to Wilson R. Hogue 4-12-1848 (4-20-1848) O
Hutchinson, M. A. to B. F. Davis 1-12-1867 (1-13-1867) O
Hutchinson, M. E. to Abraham B. Enloe 5-1-1856 O
Hutchinson, Martha to Eleazar Harris 4-15-1833 O
Hutchinson, Mary Carolin to Richard Trotter 9-3-1867 T
Hutchinson, N. H. to W. F. Clark 12-7-1859 (12-8-1859) O
Hutchinson, Nancy to Thomas Wade 1-29-1855 (1-30-1855) O
Hutchinson, Polly A. to J. H. Hancock 11-17-1866 O
Hutchinson, Rachael A. to Richard M. Neal 10-3-1851 (10-5-1851) O
Hutchinson, Rachel A. to Richard M. Neal 10-3-1851 (10-5-1851) O
Hutchinson, Sarah A. to William W. Goss 12-22-1847 (12-25-1847) T
Hutchions, Nancy N. to Benjamin F. Cowen 5-26-1847 G
Hutchison, Angelina to George Whitworth 5-8-1851 L
Hutchison, Caroline to Alexander Stuckey 5-15-1861 (no return) L
Hutchison, Caroline to John Pitchford 6-23-1854 (no return) L
Hutchison, Elizabeth J. to J. W. Best 8-5-1861 (no return) L
Hutchison, Elizabeth to J. W. P. Lewis 4-6-1856 Be
Hutchison, Elizabeth to John C. Nevils 4-19-1849 L
Hutchison, Frances to Mitchell Quinn 3-6-1871 (no return) Cr
Hutchison, Laura to Thomas A. Reid 11-16-1869 (11-18-1869) Ma

Hutchison, Mandy to Elihuge Moore 8-30-1860 (no return) Hy
Hutchison, Mary J. to Levi A. McCord 6-11-1874 (no return) Hy
Hutchison, Melinda to Marion Parker 3-31-1842 (4-1-1842) L
Hutchison, Nancy E. to Peleg K. Given 1-21-1861 (no return) L
Hutchison, Nancy Wilmoth to Levi B. Herron 12-29-1858 (12-30-1858) Ma
Hutchison, R. to T. J. Allen 7-25-1866 G
Hutchison, Rebeca to B. J. Stroud 10-6-1866 G
Hutchison, Rebecca to Ezekiel Wakefield 9-25-1841 (9-30-1841) L
Hutchison, S. E. to James Faircloth 1-6-1867 G
Hutchison, Sally to H. P. Gray 2-12-1868 Hy
Hutchison, Sarah to Jesse S. L. Stuckey no date (with Aug 1862) L
Hutchison, Tempee to Thomas C. Harbut 5-11-1870 Ma
Hutchson, Mary Ann to Henry Buchanan 4-22-1862 O
Hutley, Eliza L. to Addison J. Harris 8-4-1836 Sh
Hutson, Barbara A. to S. D. Bates 1-24-1877 (no return) Dy
Hutson, Elizabeth J. to John M. Alexander 3-29-1860 (3-?-1860) O
Hutson, Jane to Alex Tipton 2-20-1878 (no return) Dy
Hutson, Jane to Mathew Cozby 6-12-1833 (6-15-1833) Hr
Hutson, Louisa to King G. W. Davis 1-1-1856 (1-25-1856) G
Hutson, Lucretia to Reuben Pearce 10-23-1851 Hn
Hutson, Mary E. to John M. Alexander 12-11-1860 O
Hutson, Mary J. to R. G. Moore 10-26-1854 G
Hutstette, Alice A. to Henry Ledbetter 9-7-1850 Sh
Huttleson, Tabitha to Thomas Newsom 8-5-1839 Sh
Hutton, Mary to Aderson Laremore 2-27-1869 (3-4-1869) T
Hutton, Sarah J. to W. G. Nelson 3-11-1850 Hr
Huzza, Annabella to Marion Smith 10-5-1858 O
Huzza, Elizabeth to Theophilus Williams 5/31/1847 (6-1-1847) O
Huzza, Isabella to Mrion Smith 10-5-1853 O
Huzza, Matilda to J. J. Bane 1-23-1848 Be
Huzza, Ruth E. to Lewis L. Williams 12-13-1844 (12-19-1844) O
Huzzy, Mary E. to George Johnson 7-17-1852 O
Hyatt, Sarah to A. J. Thomason 5-24-1863 Be
Hyer, Eliza to Simon House 10-29-1842 (no return) Hn
Hyer?, Martha to Robert Klutts 12-15-1845 (no return) Hn
Hyett, Amanda to William White 1-5-1850 (1-4?-1850) G
Hyett, Mary to John Ingram 7-17-1851 (7-20-1851) Sh
Hymen, Rosa to Emanuel Hahn 4-7-1854 Sh
Hynant, Nancy to Levi Furr 4-28-1867 Be
Hynds, Caroline to Christopher R. Clark 10-15-1846 We
Hyne, Mary L. to Josiah Ogburn 2-7-1845 Be
Hyner, Elizabeth to James B. Dowell 9-17-1844 Be
Hynes, Catharine to Patrick Connally 9-17-1864 (9-18-1864) Sh
Hynes, Judah Brown to James Cook 11-14-1832 Sh
Hynes, Susan T. to Peter W. Titus 11-23-1854 Sh
Hynnell, Permelia to William Ragan 12-9-1837 Hr
Hysan, Eliza to R. L. Mitchell 1-2-1856 We
Hysinger, Mary to George W. Woodard 7-25-1878 Hy
Hyslap, Elizabeth E. to Francis M. Cunningham 5-28-1856 Sh
Hysmith, Athenia to J. L. Smith 7-24-1862 Mn
Hysmith, Marilda to John Gray 11-20-1864 Mn
Hytower, Charlotte to James Coats 1-24-1860 (1-26-1860) T

Iley, Elizabeth to A. Bevins 12-18-1847 (12-17?-1847) F
Imboone, Fredericka to Wilhelm Reinhardt 5-26-1856 (5-27-1856) Sh
Imbush (Imlish), Catherine to Harman H. Wesling 8-13-1846 Sh
Imes (Innes), Elizabeth to Lewis Grooms 6-5-1838 Sh
Imes, Jane to John W. Collins 11-22-1838 Sh
Imes, Mary to Richard Grooms 7-13-1847 Sh
Imes, Pauline to Dennis C. Whitehead (White) 7-18-1841 Sh
Ince, Aberville Jane to Hugh Shaw 7-6-1852 O
Indman?, Rachel R. to Henry P. Haney 10-12-1854 Hn
Ing, E. M. to W. H. Durley 8-16-1866 G
Ing, Kitty to David Marsh 12-14-1861 (12-15-1861) Sh
Ing, Martha L. to J. S. Thomas 1-18-1860 (1-19-1860) G
Ing, Sarah to Wm. C. McClour 9-15-1839 (9-19-1839) G
Ingling, Margaret to Wm. Kruze 10-20-1853 (10-21-1853) Sh
Ingraham, Martha A. to Samuel A. Goodman 12-1-1856 (12-4-1856) G
Ingraham, Mary E. to O. D. Young 1-5-1865 Mn
Ingram, Ann to Matthias Deberry 11-3-1847 Ma
Ingram, Caroline J. to Philemon T. Burford 5-22-1839 (5-24-1839) F
Ingram, Dicy to Jim Fly 2-1-1869 G
Ingram, Elizabeth J. to Newton J. Rice 2-19-1852 Hn
Ingram, Elizabeth N. to H. A. Tatum 9-19-1851 (no return) F
Ingram, Elizabeth to Daniel McGran 4-26-1858 (4-27-1858) G
Ingram, Elizabeth to Elisha Lay 9-16-1839 (no return) F
Ingram, Ellen to William D. Blakemore 6-30-1867 G
Ingram, Francis A. to T. J. Michaiett 10-27-1855 Cr
Ingram, H. M. to S. Jimeson 12-1-1864 G
Ingram, Jane to Billy Patterson 3-2-1870 G B
Ingram, Jane to Thomas H. Taylor 5-1-1849 Ma
Ingram, Julia Ann to Phillip Caple 9-6-1839 (no return) F
Ingram, Julia to J. H. Estes 1-18-1869 G
Ingram, Lamb to Jake Rice 9-6-1869 G B
Ingram, Louisa to James McCord 6-2-1850 Hn
Ingram, Louisa to John A. Greer 5-21-1859 (5-22-1859) Ma
Ingram, Louise H. to H. H. Mitchell 5-10-1875 Hy

Ingram, Luch sH. to C. H. Hicks 10-6-1848 Hr
Ingram, Lydia to James Johnson 12-8-1858 Ma
Ingram, Mariah to William Simpson 1-22-1831 Hr
Ingram, Martha L. to G. W. Housman 11-27-1867 (12-1-1867) Cr
Ingram, Martha S. to Samuel C. Scott 2-9-1849 (4-10-1849) Hr
Ingram, Martha to Stephen C. Durham 1-29-1842 (2-3-1842) F
Ingram, Mary to Francis Hite 4-26-1853 (no return) F
Ingram, Maryk to Bernard Riley 2-1-1855 Hn
Ingram, Matilda to Daniel Fox 10-18-1848 (10-19-1848) G
Ingram, Mattie to Peter Combs 10-10-1871 (10-14-1871) Ma
Ingram, Minerva to James Doran 5-7-1839 Hn
Ingram, Mourning to Samuel D. Stewart 4-5-1852 (4-6-1852) Hr
Ingram, Nany to Johnston Fox 6-13-1843 G
Ingram, Puss to Charles Dodd 10-1-1869 G B
Ingram, Rebecca W. to James E. Dodson 4-7-1851 (4-9-1851) Hr
Ingram, Rebecca to Wilson Ingram 12-4-1878 (no return) Hy
Ingram, Sarah E. T. to Boling Branch 7-22-1840 (7-23-1840) Hr
Ingram, Sarah E. to John F. Hays 12-22-1847 (12-23-1847) G
Ingram, Sarah to David W. Waller 9-23-1844 (9-26-1844) O
Ingram, Virginia C. to N. A. D. Bryant 5-27-1856 Hr
Ingram, Winney to Isaac Miller 9-17-1828 (9-21-1828) Ma
Inman, Arabella to Josephus Davidson 12-28-1853 O
Inman, Caroline to J. W. Moss 6-29-1862 Hn
Inman, Eliza Ann to James E. Hailey 2-17-1857 O
Inman, Frances B. to R. H. Algea 4-29-1846 Cr
Inman, M. J. to J. J. Buchanan 3-1-1866 O
Inman, Malvina (Matilda?) to Noah Baker 3-16-1848 L
Inman, Martha E. to Jno. W. Leonard 2-6-1871 Ma
Inman, Mary Ann to Matthew Doyle 12-9-1843 (12-17-1843) Hr
Inman, Mary Ann to Wm. D. Neff 12-27-1869 (12-29-1869) Ma
Inman, Mary to S. W. Smith 6-27-1863 (6-28-1863) Hn
Inman, R. B. to E. S. Williams 6-30-1872 (7-1-1872) O
Inman, S. H. to J. R. Drake 11-27-1857 (11-28-1857) Sh
Inman, Testimony Free Love to Brice T. McElroy 7-29-1844 (no return) L
Innes?, Martha Ann to Reuben Starks 10-19-1854 Hn
Innis, Elizabeth to Norman Norton 9-19-1853 (9-21-1853) G
Innis, Nancy J. to Thomas Gross 4-7-1870 T
Inns, Mollie to Andrew Baker 12-17-1870 Hy
Iohe, Clara to A. Castelbery 5-5-1863 Sh
Irabella, Sarah to Robert C. Cowan 8-5-1862 (no return) Hy
Irby, Ann E. to W. J. Duval 2-23-1861 (3-7-1861) Sh
Irby, B. V. to J. F. Wylie 10-22-1864 (10-29-1864) F
Irby, Belle to J. A. Neely 12-18-1868 (12-23-1868) F
Irby, Eliza to James S. Wimberley 12-24-1861 Hr
Irby, Elizabeth to John Heathcot 7-28-1846 (no return) Hn
Irby, Fannie to John L. Moore 1-24-1862 (1-30-1862) Sh
Irby, Jane W. to Edward P. Luckado 6-23-1845 F
Irby, Julia S. to J. D. Hazlewood 12-8-1866 F
Irby, Nancy M. to Silas R. Irby 3-12-1847 (no return) F
Irby, R. J. to C. R. Black 12-12-1866 (12-20-1866) T
Irby?, Delinda to Randolph H. Brown 2-14-1842 Hn
Iringlas, Bregreta to I. I. Jenny 3-9-1844 Sh
Irion, Dora A. to W. S. Bomar 11-11-1866 Hn
Irion, Mary E. to Reuben Bomar 11-11-1866 Hn
Irions, Ann Eliza to James M. McCalla 1-29-1842 (2-1-1842) Hr
Irions, Sarah Jane to Thomas Peters 10-28-1841 Hr
Irons, Ann A. to M. M. Moody 5-26-1866 (no return) Hn B
Irons, Mary C. to Thomas C. Jones 5-17-1837 Hr
Irvens, Fanny to Clark Williamson 5-2-1871 (5-13-1871) F B
Irvin, Adriadna to T. G. Osburn 1-10-1870 (1-11-1870) Ma
Irvin, Ann to George Crawford 9-14-1867 (9-15-1867) F B
Irvin, Jinnetta to William Pate 6-23-1836 Hr
Irvin, Julian to Newton Butes 7-5-1841 Ma
Irvin, M. J. to A. H. Irvin? 2-11-1860 T
Irvin, Malvina to Nathan W. Whittington 9-6-1842 Ma
Irvin, Mary S. to E. V. Hurst 9-24-1861 Mn
Irvin, Mary to Jas. M. Blankenship 2-17-1851 (2-15?-1851) G
Irvin, Mollie R. to Wm. A. Rhea 2-11-1869 F
Irvin, Nancy to William McCartney 5-24-1852 (5-27-1852) G
Irvin, Polly to Wm. Harrison 2-18-1830 Hr
Irvin, Sarah M. to Joshua L. Pemberter 11-12-1850 (11-13-1850) G
Irvin, Suzy Ann to William A. Alexander 3-21-1843 (3-23-1843) Ma
Irvine, Hannah to Eli C. Chandler 6-5-1850 Ma
Irvine, Mary to James Hunt 1-31-1830 Sh
Irwin, Annie (Mrs.) to Alexander Dunn 8-8-1864 Sh
Irwin, Dollie to Augustus Harding 11-8-1869 (no return) F B
Irwin, Harriett J. to T. J. Duvall 3-17-1851 (no return) F
Irwin, Leanorah to J. W. Northcross 11-16-1865 G
Irwin, M. W. to W. W. Pierce 11-25-1862 (11-26-1862) F
Irwin, Margaret to James H. Hailey 3-11-1869 F
Irwin, Martha E. to Elijah W. Cross 11-9-1842 (11-10-1842) Hr
Irwin, Martha to C. F. Turner 8-6-1853 Sh
Irwin, Mary Elizabeth to George King 4-8-1869 F
Irwin, Mary to John C. Brown 3-18-1841 Sh
Irwin, Nancy to Foster B. Harris 11-30-1837 Sh
Irwin, Ruth to Henry D. Harper 1-22-1851 G
Irwin, Tempy M. to Josiah F. Rainey 9-9-1839 (9-10-1839) F

Isaacs, Harnett N. to Hiram Andlerson 3-14-1842 Hr
Isalm?, Johnita to Thomas Sellas 12-30-1847 F
Isam, Elizabeth to Giles Parker 10-29-1828 Hr
Isam, Tempie to Benjamin Parker 1-6-1827 (1-7-1827) Hr
Isbel, Lucinda to Hesekiah L. Palmer 1-13-1850 Sh
Isbell, A. G. to A. V. Ware 2-6-1860 (2-8-1860) F
Isbell, A. M. to J. E. Flack 12-27-1867 (12-28-1867) O
Isbell, Ann P. to John N. Cox 10-5-1865 Mn
Isbell, Bell to Taylor McDonald 1-3-1868 (1-7-1868) F B
Isbell, Bettie to John Nixon 3-19-1879 L B
Isbell, E. J. to J. N. Underwood 6-30-1863 (7-2-1863) O
Isbell, Eliz. H. to John A. Goss 12-30-1859 (1-1-1860) Sh
Isbell, Emma to Collin Humphreys 4-18-1867 F B
Isbell, Fanny to Mose Williams 1-18-1868 (no return) F B
Isbell, Mary E. to Wm. A. Page 12-16-1865 (12-19-1865) O
Isbell, Mattie to Scott Warr 3-1-1869 (3-3-1869) F
Isbell, Mollie to George Hamilton 6-11-1868 (6-13-1868) O B
Isbell, Priscilla to Joe Morgan 12-15-1883 (12-18-1883) L
Isbell, Sarah E. to J. S. Palmore 6-20-1849 (6-29-1849) F
Isele, Catharine to Henry Henniker 3-3-1851 Sh
Isham, Alsie to King Ferguson 8-4-1883 (8-5-1883) L
Isham, Charlotta to Jno. Butler 11-6-1828 Sh
Isham, Mollie to John F. Manley 11-14-1874 (11-15-1874) L
Isham, Zillie to John T. Clayton 1-19-1857 Sh
Isler, Mary H. to Richard G. Clark 7-1-1845 Sh
Isler, Salina to Theophile Gourgues 5-10-1860 Sh
Isler, Sally Ann to Joel B. Burnett 8-20-1849 Sh
Isler, Sally Ann to Joseph P. (Joel B.) Barnette 8-30-1849 Sh
Isom, Alsa to W. F. Appleberry 7-27-1839 Sh
Isom, Caroline to G. G. Howell 8-8-1863 (8-9-1863) T
Isom, Harriott to John M. Marsh 6-27-1839 Ma
Isom, Martha Jane to Jesse Clayton 7-18-1860 Sh
Israel, Mary A. to Franklin Simmons 7-22-1862 We
Israel, Nancy to Joseph D. Hardin 10-22-1850 (10-23-1850) G
Israil, Mary to William Saunders 12-30-1830 Hr
Isrial, Amanda F. to William R. Edmondson 3-14-1846 (3-17-1846) G
Isum, Annie to Isaac Parker 10-25-1827 (11-18-1827) Hr
Ivans, Lucinda to W. C. Cantrell 9-6-1845 (no return) We
Iverson, Martha to Washington Hoover 4-25-1876 Hy
Ivey, E. H. to B. H. Rains 3-20-1863 G
Ivey, Elizabeth A. to Daniel T. Lake 4-4-1861 T
Ivey, Harriet to W. Harrison Jackson 9-22-1867 Hy
Ivey, Julea to Louis Turnipseed 5-18-1870 G B
Ivey, Louisa to J. B. Culpeper 10-8-1849 (10-10-1849) F
Ivey, Lucy Ann to James L. Garrison 8-31-1847 (no return) F
Ivey, Mary to C. R. Dunn 4-6-1878 (4-7-1878) Dy
Ivey, Mary to D. H. Wateridge 10-11-1866 Hy
Ivey, Nancy E. to Thos. E. Abernathy 11-6-1867 Hy
Ivey, S. T. to M. Fletcher 12-14-1864 (12-18-1864) T
Ivey, Sarah A. to Aaron J. Yarnell 11-11-1868 Hy
Ivey, Venie to George Hyte 8-19-1866 Hy
Ivey?, Jenny to Peter Blakemore 7-18-1868 G B
Ivie, America C. to Robert Z. Taylor 10-6-1869 G
Ivie, Araminta H. to W. T. Currie 12-18-1860 (12-20-1860) F
Ivie, Bettie (Mrs.) to H. H. Wilson 7-2-1867 G
Ivie, Eliza to James Powell 12-11-1866 (12-13-1866) F
Ivie, Frances to Henry Bone 11-12-1866 (12-1-1866) F B
Ivie, Martha A. to John H. Mitchell 12-13-1854 (no return) F
Ivins, Louisa R. to Alfred A. Caolman 8-23-1846 We
Ivory, Lucy to George White 4-17-1882 (4-18-1882) L
Ivory, Mahala to Alex Moore 3-11-1882 (3-12-1882) L
Ivy, M. F. to Albert Webber 10-24-1866 (11-11-1866) F
Ivy, Margaret Ann to W. M. Scallions 11-13-1871 (11-14-1871) L
Ivy, N. M. to A. A. Porter 10-25-1865 (1-6-1865) T
Ivy, Sallie to Jeff Johnson 2-15-1868 (2-16-1868) F B
Ivy, Susanna D. to John Crowel 2-5-1840 Hn
Jabasford?, _____ to Moses Harden 12-15-1842 Ma
Jack, Mary C. to James A. Wallace 11-11-1862 (11-13-1862) Dy
Jack, Mary to Stephen Wallis 12-30-1856 Cr
Jack, Winney to Samuel Blackley 1-16-1850 (1-17-1850) G
Jacksn, Emela to Joshua Donaldson 12-19-1838 (12-20-1838) G
Jackson, A. C. to James M. Drewry 6-1-1858 Hn
Jackson, A. J. to J. G. Capps 1-12-1867 G
Jackson, A. M. to J. T. Avants 1-23-1872 (1-28-1872) Dy
Jackson, A. to James R. Miller 1-11-1865 (1-12-1865) T
Jackson, Ace Catherine to James Webber 2-28-1869 G
Jackson, Adaline to Calvin Upchurch 2-24-1873 (2-26-1873) T
Jackson, Adeline to John Winn 2-2-1871 T
Jackson, Agnes to Dick Bradford 12-7-1870 G
Jackson, Alice to J. M. Woodsides 8-23-1875 (8-25-1875) Dy
Jackson, Alice to James Herring 8-31-1872 (9-1-1872) O
Jackson, Almedia L. to W. P. Williams 10-19-1870 (10-20-1870) Ma
Jackson, Amarylla to John J. Hudspeth 5-5-1847 Hn
Jackson, Amelia F. to John H. Scott 6-14-1831 (6-16-1831) O
Jackson, Amelia M. to Charles Morrison 2-9-1855 (2-11-1855) Sh
Jackson, Ana H. to W. J. Watts 10-7-1871 (10-8-1871) O
Jackson, Angelina to Hugh S. King 3-26-1850 Ma

Jackson, Anjanet to Calvin J. Curtis 8-20-1842 (8-21-1842) G
Jackson, Ann C. to Thomas W. Felts 11-30-1864 Hn
Jackson, Anna E. to M. A. Melson 10-14-1864 (11-10-1864) Sh
Jackson, Anna to John Jackson 12-13-1838 (12-20-1838) Ma
Jackson, Annie to Marion Norman 5-5-1871 (no return) Hy
Jackson, B. A. to H. M. Wilson 1-1-1866 O
Jackson, B. F. to L. Carter 10-2-1844 Hn
Jackson, B. Z. to M. C. McCormack 9-23-1879 (9-24-1879) Dy
Jackson, Barbry to Martin Case 1-2-1845 Hr
Jackson, Butie to Andrew Hall 10-31-1842 Hy
Jackson, Callie to John J. Shepard 7-1-1878 Hy
Jackson, Caroline (Mrs.) to John Davis 4-29-1871 (4-20?-1871) Ma
Jackson, Caroline to M. B. Sherman 9-22-1856 Ma
Jackson, Catharine to Charles Bland 12-6-1854 (12-7-1854) Sh
Jackson, Catharine to J. E. Spence 11-12-1860 (11-13-1860) Sh
Jackson, Catharine to Robert Terrill 12-25-1852 O
Jackson, Charlotte L. to R. P. Wade 12-20-1867 (12-28-1867) Dy
Jackson, Charlotte to George W. Norman 4-30-1860 Dy
Jackson, Clara A. to David K. Crenshaw 10-19-1853 (10-20-1853) T
Jackson, Clara to Austin Buford 1-8-1867 F B
Jackson, Clara to John Bozzle 4-29-1851 (5-4-1851) Hr
Jackson, Clementine to Reuben Upchurch 7-17-1852 O
Jackson, Cornelia to M. P. Mitchell 8-22-1861 Hr
Jackson, Cressy to Robert Maxey 12-21-1876 Hy
Jackson, Dicey to Harmon Gamble 12-13-1846 Hn
Jackson, Didama to Jefferson W.? Mallard 2-10-1841 F
Jackson, Dora to Henry Conney (Cowrey?) 8-18-1881 L
Jackson, Dorcas to Bryant Andrews 2-4-1834 G
Jackson, E. P. to W. L. Palmer 4-21-1863 Hn
Jackson, Ebby to John L. Ash 8-4-1835 Hr
Jackson, Ebediance to John Thompson 12-6-1849 O
Jackson, Eddie to Joe Watson 1-22-1876 Hy
Jackson, Eddy to Henry Dancey 2-24-1873 (no return) Hy
Jackson, Ednay to John Parrish 7-14-1856 (no return) We
Jackson, Edy to William Merlin 2-13-1827 Hr
Jackson, Eliza Ann to Thomas J. McGill 7-23-1866 Be
Jackson, Eliza Jane to Tho. B. Trobough 3-16-1850 (3-19-1850) T
Jackson, Eliza to Gabriel Taylor 6-10-1857 O
Jackson, Eliza to Henderson Bailey 8-14-1845 (8-22-1845) G
Jackson, Eliza to Hezekiah Watkins 12-23-1854 Sh
Jackson, Eliza to Jonas Dyson 12-27-1870 (12-28-1870) T
Jackson, Elizabeth A. to Caswell H. Martin 1-29-1857 O
Jackson, Elizabeth F. (Mrs.) to Thomas J. Fite 9-2-1856 Cr
Jackson, Elizabeth J. to Hyman Nored 1-1-1857 Hn
Jackson, Elizabeth to Alexander Polk 6-17-1829 Hr
Jackson, Elizabeth to Ebeneze Oldham 12-11-1827 Ma
Jackson, Elizabeth to George Shepherd 8-11-1866 O
Jackson, Elizabeth to Harrison Kirkland 12-3-1862 (no return) Hn
Jackson, Elizabeth to J. P. Spencer 9-19-1878 (9-20-1878) Dy
Jackson, Elizabeth to Micajah Heflin 9-12-1838 Hn
Jackson, Elizabeth to Samuel Irvey 5-23-1857 Ma
Jackson, Elizabeth to Tillmon P. Walker 12-25-1848 O
Jackson, Elizabeth to W. D. Clemomson 1-21-1858 Cr
Jackson, Elvina A. to George W. Arnold 10-20-1853 Be
Jackson, Elviry to John A. Harpole 6-23-1841 (6-29-1841) G
Jackson, Emila T. to P. H. Willis 7-6-1847 (7-7-1847) F
Jackson, Emiline to F.(T.?) W. Seymore 9-18-1870 G
Jackson, Emily to W. R. McFarland 9-24-1865 Hn
Jackson, Emily to William King 7-2-1861 (7-3-1861) Ma
Jackson, Emmer to George Mann 10-28-1877 Hy
Jackson, Eugenia Lafayette to William H. Hunt 12-22-1846 Ma
Jackson, Eugenia to P. H. Jackson 2-7-1870 (2-9-1870) L
Jackson, F. A. to C. A. Muse 10-17-1862 Mn
Jackson, Florenc to Wm. Taylor 9-17-1868 (9-18-1868) T
Jackson, Frances (Mrs.) to A. M. Brown 1-10-1866 G
Jackson, Frances C. to John A. Tomlinson 4-25-1848 Ma
Jackson, Frances J. to Isaac N. Swift 5-22-1859 Hn
Jackson, Frances J. to James H. Nowell 2-8-1854 (2-9-1854) G
Jackson, Frances to Hamilton Murley 12-9-1857 Hr
Jackson, Francis to L. M. Clark 11-25-1858 We
Jackson, H. E. to J. R. Bruce 7-24-1848 (no return) F
Jackson, Hannah to Elijah Spencer 2-27-1836 (2-28-1836) G
Jackson, Hannah to Jim Gorman 10-8-1870 (no return) Hy
Jackson, Harriet M. to Joseph Bailey 12-18-1847 (12-20-1847) Ma
Jackson, Harriet to George Williams 10-15-1870 (10-18-1870) L
Jackson, Harriet to Sidney Baucum 8-18-1852 (no return) Hn
Jackson, Harriett to John Broady 1-14-1870 (1-16-1870) O
Jackson, Hollis to Sampson Rogers 12-8-1830 (12-9-1830) Hr
Jackson, I. E. to J. T. Prewett 9-20-1870 O
Jackson, Isabella to R. S. Strong 4-12-1870 (4-13-1870) T
Jackson, J. L. to J. E. White 3-15-1877 Dy
Jackson, J. L. to J. E. White ?-?-1877 (no return) Dy
Jackson, Jane A. R. to William J. Walker 10-3-1846 (10-6-1846) G
Jackson, Jane to Jesse Guinn 1-1-1879 (1-2-1879) Dy
Jackson, Jane to Joshua Little 9-15-1834 (9-18-1834) G
Jackson, Jennie to J. G. Swanner 10-26-1871 Dy
Jackson, Julia Ann to S. M. Beard (Baird) 1-26-1859 (1-27-1859) L

Jackson, Julia C. to Richard Morning Epperson 5-27-1843 (5-30-1843) T
Jackson, Julia E. to Robert H. Draper 3-3-1855 (no return) F
Jackson, July to Henry Strausberg 12-6-1869 G
Jackson, L. A. to E. B. Lowrance 12-21-1869 G
Jackson, Laura to J. B. Jennings 10-23-1868 (no return) Dy
Jackson, Leaner to Joseph Willie 2-1-1847 (2-2?-1847) Hr
Jackson, Leanna to Samuel C. Weas 2-4-1861 O
Jackson, Lou E. (Miss) to A. M. Scarbrough 9-30-1863 Sh
Jackson, Lou to Robt. Jones 4-24-1877 (no return) Dy
Jackson, Louisa E. to Solomon Smith 7-16-1856 (7-17-1856) Ma
Jackson, Louisa to J. H. Redick 1-10-1869 Be
Jackson, Louisa to W. L. Hampton 7-1-1867 (7-2-1867) Dy
Jackson, Louisa to William H. Morris 1-25-1859 Ma
Jackson, Louisa to William Tomlinson 10-1-1839 (10-2-1839) Ma
Jackson, Louise to Albert Bragg 1-11-1871? (2-11-1872) T
Jackson, Lovina to John Scallorn 12-20-1830 G
Jackson, Lucinda C. to Wm. T. Dial 1-19-1857 (1-20-1857) Hr
Jackson, Lucinda P. to J. M. Arnett 1-1-1869 (1-14-1869) Cr
Jackson, Lucy A. to William Upchurch 2-26-1845 Hn
Jackson, Lucy C. to Peter H. Collins 9-30-1852 Cr
Jackson, Lucy to Boyd Smith 2-3-1868 G B
Jackson, Lucy to Jas. P. White 12-31-1870 Hy
Jackson, Lucy to Washington Carter 12-28-1867 (12-29-1867) F B
Jackson, Lydia Candace to James M. Jackson 8-12-1870 G
Jackson, M. A. to J. M. C. Barrett 12-16-1857 (12-17-1857) Hr
Jackson, M. A. to Wm. G. David 12-27-1868 (12-28-1868) Cr
Jackson, M. E. A. to John W. Love 12-4-1867 (11?-20-1867) G
Jackson, M. E. to W. R. Calloway 2-18-1866 Hn
Jackson, M. E. to Wm. L. Harmen 1-10-1861 G
Jackson, M. F. to J. A. Prast? 7-12-1847 Hr
Jackson, M. M. to T. H. Lewis 11-2-1865 G
Jackson, M. O. to M. J. Butler 4-3-1877 (4-4-1877) Dy
Jackson, Macia to Nelson Speller 12-22-1873 Hy
Jackson, Malissa to Allen Jones 5-10-1873 T B
Jackson, Malissa to Mack Cleere 2-12-1867 (2-14-1867) F B
Jackson, Malissa to Phillip Ferbury 10-12-1867 (10-13-1867) T
Jackson, Margaret C. to J. K. P. McLemore 10-11-1870 G
Jackson, Margaret to Asa McAfee 12-6-1866 Ma
Jackson, Margaret to Benj. Camp 3-11-1852 Sh
Jackson, Margaret to Isaac J. Suggs 5-4-1848 Sh
Jackson, Margaret to John Upchurch 1-2-1869 O
Jackson, Margarett to Lewis Hill 12-16-1848 (12-17-1848) Hr
Jackson, Maria to Isaac Rhodes 12-16-1874 T
Jackson, Mariah to Henry Vaughn 12-26-1867 T
Jackson, Marietta to N. B. Cannon 1-26-1874 (1-27-1874) O
Jackson, Martha A. to Geo. W. Blankenship 3-15-1847 (3-16-1847) G
Jackson, Martha C. to Elisha Baly 1-14-1852 (1-15-1852) Ma
Jackson, Martha E. to William S. Lee 2-23-1867 (2-27-1867) Cr
Jackson, Martha E. to Wm. W. Slaydon 6-12-1856 G
Jackson, Martha G. to William H. Trent 3-14-1846 (3-17-1846) F
Jackson, Martha J. to Francis Gamewell 5-17-1849 Ma
Jackson, Martha J. to L. J. Worrel 10-17-1871 (10-19-1871) O
Jackson, Martha Jane to James N. Jackson 10-14-1868 (10-14-1868) Ma
Jackson, Martha M. to Wm. H. Akin 9-23-1841 Sh
Jackson, Martha W. to Wilson T. Beaver 7-19-1841 (7-22-1842?) F
Jackson, Martha to J. W. King 9-28-1842 Hn
Jackson, Martha to James Highfill 4-22-1833 (4-25-1833) Hr
Jackson, Martha to Joseph Scott 9-1-1829 (9-2-1829) O
Jackson, Martha to William P. Quinn 2-24-1864 (no return) Cr
Jackson, Martha to Wm. P. Quinn 2-24-1864 (2-26-1864) Cr
Jackson, Mary A. to Joseph C. C. Tucker 7-3-1843 (7-6-1843) F
Jackson, Mary A. to Robert H. Taylor 7-20-1847 (7-21-1847) G
Jackson, Mary A. to W. H. Evans 3-20-1856 Sh
Jackson, Mary Ann to Hiram Terry 6-9-1850 Hn
Jackson, Mary B. to Jonathan H. McCraw 10-16-1843 F
Jackson, Mary C. to Wm. B. Hays 11-9-1868 (11-12-1868) Ma
Jackson, Mary E. (Mrs.) to T. J. Manly 2-23-1867 F
Jackson, Mary E. to Isaac M. Daniel 12-10-1857 (12-13-1857) Hr
Jackson, Mary E. to J. T. Cannon 9-11-1857 G
Jackson, Mary E. to Joseph H. Yarbrough 6-7-1854 (6-8-1854) Hr
Jackson, Mary E. to William Crawford 4-26-1862 (no return) Hn
Jackson, Mary F. to Joseph Taylor 3-17-1851 O
Jackson, Mary F. to Joseph Taylor 3-17-1857 O
Jackson, Mary Jane to William W. Dowlen 10-8-1853 (10-18-1853) Sh
Jackson, Mary L. A. to Benj. F. Priest 1-31-1855 (2-1-1855) Hr
Jackson, Mary M. to Washington Gardner 7-14-1852 Hn
Jackson, Mary S. to George W. Wood 11-4-1852 Hn
Jackson, Mary S. to Henry W. Smith 7-4-1841 Sh
Jackson, Mary to Berry H. Davis 11-2-1853 Cr
Jackson, Mary to David Fortner 10-10-1859 (9-11-1859) Hr
Jackson, Mary to David Holms 9-8-1874 T
Jackson, Mary to George B. Moore 1-30-1839 Ma
Jackson, Mary to James C. Nutt? 1-23-1851 (no return) Hn
Jackson, Mary to Michael Beavers 11-30-1839 (12-5-1839) F
Jackson, Mary to Thomas Case 6-24-1840 Hr
Jackson, Mary to Wm. Davis 12-17-1846 We
Jackson, Matilda to John Briant 1-12-1830 G

Jackson, Mattie Ann to J. W. Olive 10-31-1878 Dy
Jackson, Melissa Ann to Joseph Atkins 1-17-1861 Hn
Jackson, Mellvan P. to William Mitchell 12-12-1853 (1-4-1854) O
Jackson, Mollie to Ras Nelson 6-6-1874 (no return) Hy
Jackson, Mollie to Wm. Hutchison 6-5-1865 (6-8-1865) O
Jackson, N. W. to W. G. Fuzzell 8-5-1865 (8-6-1865) O
Jackson, Nancy C. to James Kelly 6-28-1828 Ma
Jackson, Nancy C. to Joseph M. Winn 12-9-1855 Hn
Jackson, Nancy F. to John J. Evans 12-31-1867 Ma
Jackson, Nancy J. to John W. Washburn 8-4-1867 Hn
Jackson, Nancy Jane to Alexander Davis 2-3-1845 We
Jackson, Nancy M. to John H. Yancey 4-23-1843 G
Jackson, Nancy to James Howard McMillan 3-22-1842 Hr
Jackson, Nancy to James W. Lewis 11-14-1878 (11-17-1878) Dy
Jackson, Nancy to John Jinkins 5-15-1847 Be
Jackson, Nellie to Willie Maclin 11-11-1874 T
Jackson, Olivia F. to W. C. Penn 8-22-1872 L
Jackson, Oma to Jurdon Neel 1-4-1871 (no return) F B
Jackson, Pamelia A. to John Y.(Z?) Scarbrough 1-11-1854 (1-12-1854) Hr
Jackson, Peneler to C. D. Vinson 3-7-1866 O
Jackson, Prissy to John M. Saunders 5-5-1834 (5-8-1834) G
Jackson, Prudence to George F. Keiser 1-1-1831 O
Jackson, Rachael to Ben Taylor 9-23-1874 Hy
Jackson, Rachael to T. J. Barret 1-2-1860 (1-5-1860) Hr
Jackson, Rachel to Lemuel Williams 10-9-1852 (10-12-1852) T
Jackson, Rada to Henry Scales 10-11-1868 O
Jackson, Rebecca to Ira N. Green 10-7-1840 (10-13-1840) F
Jackson, Rebecca to Jacob Baker 11-4-1850 Ma
Jackson, Rhoda to Nelson Riley 4-6-1866 G
Jackson, Rose to Alx Taylor 4-18-1868 Hy
Jackson, S. A. (Mrs.) to Henry Davis 11-24-1843 Sh
Jackson, S. A. to F. M. Watson 2-6-1878 (no return) L
Jackson, S. A. to W. L. Wilder 12-6-1859 (12-8-1859) F
Jackson, S. J. to F. A. McCorkle 12-19-1867 O
Jackson, S. V. to W. C. Oliver 12-12-1865 G
Jackson, S. to Aleck Smith 12-13-1866 (12-16-1866) F
Jackson, Sallie A to Anderson R. Selph 12-24-1867 (12-29-1867) Ma
Jackson, Sallie to Dallas Tipton 8-13-1868 T
Jackson, Sally to Patrick Harper 1-5-1841 (1-10-1841) Ma
Jackson, Sarah A. to Bennet M. Ruff 2-22-1853 (2-23-1853) Sh
Jackson, Sarah A. to Charles A. Bowls 2-1-1855 (2-3-1855) G
Jackson, Sarah A. to James A. Lackie 2-29-1868 G
Jackson, Sarah Ann to Franklin Elder 3-28-1857 (3-31-1857) L
Jackson, Sarah J. to James Stanley 12-13-1859 (12-15-1859) O
Jackson, Sarah L. to Andrew J. King 1-27-1868 (1-30-1868) Ma
Jackson, Sarah to Asa Rasbury 7-18-1849 Be
Jackson, Sarah to James H. Beakley 2-19-1876 (2-20-1876) Dy
Jackson, Sarah to James Hays 10-13-1880 (10-14-1880) L
Jackson, Siny E. to Charles Godfreyson 10-12-1854 Sh
Jackson, Sopronia J. to C. D. White 8-14-1856 We
Jackson, Susan F. to John M. Hicks 3-12-1863 G
Jackson, Susan J. to John G. Robinson 4-9-1849 Cr
Jackson, Susan L. to Joseph A. Pardue 6-6-1859 (6-10-1859) O
Jackson, Susan to R. W. Vancleave 10-4-1855 Hn
Jackson, Susanna to Samuel Henry 10-28-1828 (11-19-1828) O
Jackson, Susannah? to Lewis Pirtle 10-8-1846 (10-13-1846) Hr
Jackson, Tabitha to Alfred Kelly 6-2-1842 Hn
Jackson, Tabitha to Joshua S. Yeates 8-16-1849 Be
Jackson, Tempey to Lewis Medders 12-13-1831 Ma
Jackson, Tennessee to Wade Robinson 7-27-1867 O
Jackson, V. H. to J. Terrell 1-29-1867 G
Jackson, Viola to Peter Williams 12-14-1849 (12-19-1849) Ma
Jacob, Elizabeth to William Rossen 12-22-1824 Hr
Jacob, Mary to William O'Conner 8-13-1859 Sh
Jacob, Maud Hunter to Henry Smith 4-18-1873 T
Jacobbs, Nancy C. to J. V. Robb 9-4-1869 T
Jacobs, Adeline M. to Eli Moore 7-16-1839 (7-18-1839) Hr
Jacobs, America R. to Robert J. Mays 12-14-1866 (12-18-1866) Cr
Jacobs, E. C. to W. S. Moore 1-16-1863 Mn
Jacobs, Eliza to Payton L. Parker 8-12-1840 (8-13-1840) Hr
Jacobs, Elizabeth to Benjamin J. Boydston 11-12-1825 (11-15-1825) Hr
Jacobs, Elizabeth to David Macon 11-20-1848 (11-23-1848) Hr
Jacobs, Elizabeth to John Manning 7-20-1843 Hn
Jacobs, Ellen S. to C. T. Jenkins 2-12-1879 L
Jacobs, Elmina to Edward Bass 7-15-1828 (not executed) Hr
Jacobs, Elmina to Ethelana Pitman 9-27-1829 Hr
Jacobs, Gertie to Edward J. Griffin 4-18-1868 (4-20-1868) Ma
Jacobs, Louiza M. to Andrew M. Bugg 10-13-1866 Cr
Jacobs, Lucinda to William McFarland 9-18-1838 G
Jacobs, M. S. to H. P. Reynolds 12-13-1870 (no return) Cr
Jacobs, Malissa A. to James C. Fly 9-25-1865 (10-3-1865) Cr
Jacobs, Martha M. to A. J. White 9-18-1854 (9-20-1854) G
Jacobs, Mary A. to W. P. Malone 5-21-1870 (5-22-1870) T
Jacobs, Mary L. to D. F. McFarland 8-3-1854 G
Jacobs, Mary to John W. Barnett 6-7-1834 (6-12-1834) Hr
Jacobs, Nancy McK. to lPerry Sain 1-6-1845 (1-7-1845) Hr
Jacobs, Nancy to Hugh Robinson 10-31-1858 Cr

Jacobs, Sarah to J. P. Armstrong 6-7-1869 Cr
Jacock, Margaret C. to J. N. Nunn 1-30-1867 (1-31-1867) Dy
Jacocks, Ann to John Henry Currie 10-23-1878 Hy
Jacocks, Cinda to Alison Taylor 7-6-1876 Hy
Jacocks, Delia to Wm. Thompson 5-26-1869 Hy
Jacocks, Patient to James Gill 2-18-1871 Hy
Jacocks, Sarah to Gus Drake 7-7-1877 Hy
Jakubs, Mary to Valentine Newhiski 9-7-1852 Sh
Jaler (Jaben), Harriet to John Smith (Smidt) 11-23-1849 Sh
Jamerson, Frances to John Cawthon 11-22-1866 Cr
Jamerson, Victoria to John Burton 1-23-1861 (1-27-1861) Cr
James, Adaline to William Wiley 5-17-1848 Sh
James, Amanda to John Hughes 3-6-1869 G B
James, Aminda to William Bradley 3-13-1858 (3-14-1858) G
James, Ann to Elijah Peel 12-?-1843 (no return) Hn
James, Annie to Thomas James 12-31-1860 (1-1-1861) Sh
James, Caroline M. to John Hutchins 4-7-1833 (5-12-1833) G
James, Caroline M. to John Hutchins 5-7-1833 G
James, Cate S. to J. J. Stephenson 4-9-1860 (4-10-1860) O
James, Cate to Ed Chapman 2-29-1868 G B
James, Eliza D. to James C. Bird 1-31-1847 Hn
James, Eliza E. to George Harber 11-7-1863 (no return) L
James, Eliza E. to Wm. Robinson 2-17-1860 F
James, Eliza J. to Jas. W. Allen 12-28-1857 Hr
James, Eliza W. to Alonzo C. Mallory 4-23-1851 (4-24-1851) Sh
James, Eliza to Henry W. Helfley 2-5-1847 G
James, Elizabeth D. to George Mellersh 11-24-1858 Sh
James, Elizabeth R. to William Epps 11-25-1848 Sh
James, Elizabeth to Harris Bradford 5-12-1845 (5-15-1845) G
James, Elizabeth to John W. White 9-20-1848 O
James, Elizabeth to John W. White 9-20-1848 (9-21-1848) O
James, Elizabeth to Jonathan Woodard 10-30-1828 G
James, Elizabeth to Sam Williams 4-6-1859 (4-7-1859) Sh B
James, Elizabeth to William H. Edmunds 12-14-1842 Hn
James, Elizabeth to William J. Guthra 1-24-1842 (5-16-1842) F
James, Ellen to C. C. Mifflin 1-8-1870 (1-9-1870) Dy
James, Emely F. to James Organ 2-22-1853 (3-1-1853) G
James, Emley to James McClary 2-3-1838 (2-8-1838) G
James, Emma to John W. Curby 7-23-1874 Dy
James, Evaline to Charles Jackson 11-23-1877 (11-24-1877) Dy
James, Fannie E. to John E. Waddill 10-6-1869 (10-7-1869) Cr
James, Fidelia to Thomas Washington Dinwoody 5-19-1842 T
James, Frances to Joe Sweet 9-24-1881 (9-29-1881) L
James, G. W. to S. D. Parnell 12-19-1870 (12-21-1870) Cr
James, Harriet L. to Norris Kendall 11-17-1862 Sh
James, J. B. to Wm. E. Jones 11-27-1871 (no return) Cr
James, Jane A. to Nathan J. Hopson 4-7-1846 Hn
James, Jane to David Ellis 6-13-1854 Sh
James, Jane to James M. Jones 12-16-1841 Hr
James, Kate J. to W. W. Davidson 3-29-1855 (4-18-1855) Sh
James, Katharine to James M. Fields 9-18-1848 (9-27-1848) O
James, Katie C. to W. H. Jones 12-22-1874 (12-23-1874) Dy
James, Louisa Ann to Daniel England 8-2-1847 (8-3-1847) G
James, M. C. to J. B. Lane 10-21-1860 Hn
James, M. L. to Jos. F. Moliter 3-5-1861 (3-7-1861) Sh
James, Margarett to Eli Jackson 2-22-1838 (2-27-1838) G
James, Maria A. to John L. Weed 4-19-1854 Sh
James, Maria Louisa to John W. A. Pettit 9-23-1849 Sh
James, Mariah to Jefferson Macklin 10-21-1851 Hr
James, Marinda to Thomas H. Baker 4-22-1861 (no return) Cr
James, Martha A. M. to Robert N. James 12-9-1850 G
James, Martha A. to Daniel T. White 4-30-1860 (5-1-1860) Sh
James, Martha A. to Zebadr Wilson 1-11-1858 We
James, Martha Ann to James R. Griffin 8-9-1848 (8-10-1848) Hr
James, Martha to Jesse Wiley 1-6-1841 Sh
James, Martha to Joel Pugh 8-24-1863 (8-25-1863) Dy
James, Mary C. to Robert B. James 8-19-1855 G
James, Mary Jane (Miss) to Jefferson Smith 7-26-1849 Sh
James, Mary Jane to Wm. M. Bell 2-25-1868 G
James, Mary L. to R. M. Winberry 1-3-1871 (1-5-1871) Dy
James, Mary Louisa to Thomas M. Daniel 8-28-1849 (9-6-1849) T
James, Mary P. to A. R. Wilson 7-1-1863 Cr
James, Mary to C. H. Williams 9-19-1860 G
James, Mary to James H. Mize 8-13-1857 We
James, Matilda F. to W. C. Anderson 8-4-1859 Sh
James, Mattie A. to John W. Wilson 10-22-1861 (no return) Hn
James, Mattie E. to W. B. Finley 12-29-1877 (12-30-1877) Dy
James, Minerva J. to David Thompson 8-16-1842 Hn
James, Mollie to Joel E. Light 12-12-1878 Dy
James, Nancy to James G. Beavers 4-27-1843 Sh
James, Nancy to Marion T. Shelbun? 7-10-1840 (no return) Hn
James, Prudence to Richard Fisher 11-7-1870 G
James, Rachel to J. W. Sudberry 3-19-1860 Hy
James, Rebecca B. to Samuel Lowry 12-27-1847 G
James, Rosanna to William H. Gibbs 2-27-1867 Be
James, Rosetta to James Scirratt 3-2-1862 Mn
James, Salina to Marcus Heath 7-22-1834 Sh

James, Sally to J. K. (Dr.) Huey 4-7-1869 Dy
James, Sarah Ann to Harmon J. Houser 8-5-1848 (8-7-1848) O
James, Sarah Ann to John Cole 1-3-1849 (1-4-1849) G
James, Sarah E. to John W. Price 5-9-1860 (5-15-1860) T
James, Sarah J. to Barnett A. Howard 8-14-1851 Hn
James, Susan to Abe Fields 3-31-1871 Hy
James, Susan to John Whitly 1-9-1869 G B
James, Susannah to William T. Pratt 12-15-1864 G
James, Sylvania to Henry H. Nichols 1-3-1834 Sh
James?, Manerva to Wm. A. J. Smith 12-28-1846 (12-31-1846) Hr
Jameson, Callie C. to James A. Winchell 9-3-1856 (9-4-1856) Sh
Jameson, Martha Ann to William Green Hill 12-7-1848 Hn
Jameson, Sarah Ann to Martin Flowers 7-26-1844 Sh
Jamess, Frances to W. C. Pugh 10-25-1860 G
Jamison, Elizabeth to Elisha Lamb 8-17-1847 Hn
Jamison, Jinnie to Peter Murry 6-24-1872 (no return) Cr B
Jamison, Juda E. to Henry Harris 7-9-1870 (no return) Cr
Jamison, Lethia to John Vaughn 11-12-1870 Hy
Jamison, M. E. to H. W. Benson 12-16-1873 (12-17-1873) T
Jamison, Martha Jane to James Kelso 8-11-1856 Hn
Jamison, Martha to Miles W. Sedberry 7-26-1858 Cr
Jamison, Mary E. to W. W. McBride 1-27-1857 (1-28-1857) T
Jamison, Mary to Thornton Parish 8-12-1870 (8-13-1870) T
Jamison, Missouri to Charles Clark 1-8-1870 (1-9-1870) Cr
Jamison, Nancy J. to Saml. H. Hood 12-22-1853 O
Jamison, Nancy to Benjamin Turner 2-26-1854 Hn
Jamson, T. S. to Wm. M. Nonnent 1-7-1849 (no return) F
Jane, Mary to Alexander McGregor 3-15-1849 Sh
Jane, Pate to James A. Powell 5-16-1866 Hy
Jane, Varnor to Joe Primble 3-21-1871 (no return) Hy
Janes, Angeline J. to Melville B. Alexander 12-21-1862 Hn
Janes, Ann to Alfred Tyler 12-24-1865 Hn
Janes, Ann to James Walker 10-3-1845 G
Janes, Henrietta J. to James B. Knott 6-15-1860 We
Janes, Josephine to W. W. Olive 4-23-1867 Hn
Janes, M. E. to James M. Reavis 1-25-1862 We
Janes, Mary to James M. Abney 3-1-1859 We
Janes, S. A. to J. R. Joyner 11-5-1860 (11-8-1860) Hr
Janes, Sarah Ann to A. M. Hamer 12-2-1854 (12-5-1854) Hr
Jansen, Emma M. to Charles J. Miller 12-3-1851 Hr
January, Emma to John Hassell 12-18-1860 G
January, Sallie A. to Thomas Sharp 12-8-1866 G
Jaque, Caroline to George S. Shroder (Schoder) 6-20-1853 Sh
Jarman, Elizabeth N. to Saml. J. Harrington 1-28-1846 (1-30-1846) Hr
Jarman, Mary A. to Joe T. Cannon 10-27-1843 Cr
Jarman, Mary D. to Albert D. Duncan 8-5-1831 (8-10?-1831) Hr
Jarman, Mary to Levi S. Woods 12-31-1853 (1-5-1854) G
Jarman, Philpina to Thomas M. Cuthbertwson 4-1-1824 (4-3-1824) Hr
Jarmon, Rosanna S. to Robert F. Jarmon 11-14-1845 (11-18-1845) Hr
Jarnagin, Martha L. to Amphias Smith 12-16-1844 (12-19-1844) Ma
Jarnigan, Jane to Paten House 12-10-1864 (12-11-1864) Sh
Jarnigan, Polly to Haliard King 11-25-1856 Hr
Jarratt, Ellen to Ollenson Henly 9-22-1878 Hy
Jarratt, Fanny M. to John E. Tyus 11-29-1865 Hy
Jarratt, Mary to Henry Warmath 11-3-1842 (11-5-1842) Ma
Jarrell, Syntha to James D. Merrell 2-22-1852 Cr
Jarret, Mary J. to Mark Livingston 2-17-1860 (2-18-1860) Cr
Jarrett, Ann to Clinton Sweet 12-27-1869 Hy
Jarrett, Dora to John A. Scott 10-7-1874 Hy
Jarrett, Eliza to Allen Robertson 7-30-1871 Hy
Jarrett, Ellen to Joe Cremus 4-6-1872 Hy
Jarrett, Ellen to Lawrence Tyus 12-24-1871 Hy
Jarrett, F. V. to B. S. Tyus 2-2-1872? Hy
Jarrett, Frances to Scott Read 1-17-1876 (no return) Hy
Jarrett, Kitty A. to William S. Mayfield 10-13-1843 (no return) F
Jarrett, Maggie E. to S. D. Whitten 9-24-1865 G
Jarrett, Malinda R. to James D. Pike 8-22-1872 Dy
Jarrett, Margaret to John O. Collins 1-24-1859 Cr
Jarrett, Martha to Charlie Grigg 7-5-1872 (no return) Hy
Jarrett, Mary to Anderson H. Merrett 6-10-1847 Cr
Jarrett, Mary to Casso Winfield 12-24-1872 Hy
Jarrett, Mary to Saml. Burke 11-8-1845 Hy
Jarrett, Mary to Wm. Tolley 9-27-1843 Cr
Jarrett, Nancy J. to Stephen A. Via 7-19-1871 (no return) Dy
Jarrett, Parilla to J. C. Merrett 7-30-1869 (8-1-1869) Cr
Jarrett, R. A. to T. J. Jones 7-22-1871 (7-23-1871) Cr
Jarrett, Rhoda to Matthew Hawkins 1-27-1885 (1-29-1885) L
Jarrett, Rosa to Jordan Whitelaw 1-1-1883 (no return) L
Jarrett, Sarah to Henry Knight 9-11-1844 (9-12-1844) Hr
Jarrett, Vina to William Maclin 11-21-1868 Hy
Jarrett?, Martha E. to Joseph B. Fowler 10-21-1861 (no return) Cr
Jarrolds, Minerva to John Sled 3-4-1855 Hn
Jarrott, Matilda to Robert A. Fields 11-9-1859 (no return) Hy
Jarry (Jenny), Eliza to Thomas M. Stroud 6-1-1850 Sh
Jarson?, Mildred A. to Wm. Ashurst 3-6-1873 (3-7-1873) T
Jarvis, Martha J. to W. W. Fonville 1-14-1859 G
Jayne, Mary E. to John Coats 6-21-1849 Ma

Jayne, Orva Ann to Geo. W. Talbot 6-25-1849 (6-27-1849) Ma
Jayro, Bettie to Bartlett Walker 5-6-1873 (5-7-1873) L B
Jayroe, Agnus G. to C. F. Sanford 5-11-1878 (no return) L
Jayroe, Frankie to T. C. McCallum 10-15-1880 (10-17-1880) L
Jayroe, Mary to Elias Clay 3-7-1868 (3-8-1868) L B
Jeames, Wena to Robert Moore 7-5-1861 Mn
Jeanes, Julia to Sihon Tatum 2-11-1862 Mn
Jeanes, S. E. to H. W. James 6-18-1863 Mn
Jeans, Allie to Boston Foster 8-11-1874 Hy
Jeans, Elizabeth to James T. Tomlinson 11-1-1855 (11-6-1855) O
Jeans, Malissa L. to Thomas R. Roberson 12-10-1865 Mn
Jeans, Mary to Robert B. Jones 3-11-1861 T
Jeffers, Elizabeth A. to Calvin Jackson 1-22-1863 Mn
Jeffers, Frances to Jeremiah Wright 10-2-1835 G
Jefferson, Amanda to King Wheeler 5-2-1868 (no return) F B
Jefferson, E. A. to John A. Carr 12-12-1877 Hy
Jefferson, Frances to D. S. Wise 6-30-1868 Hy
Jefferson, Jane to Martin Moore 1-18-1868 (no return) F B
Jefferson, Julia to William Benett 4-5-1870 Hy
Jefferson, Martha to John Daniel 1-2-1869 (no return) F B
Jefferson, Phebe Ann to Carter Smith 12-31-1866 (no return) F B
Jefferson, Phillis to Albert Hilliard 3-20-1869 (3-24-1869) F B
Jeffres, M. E. to F. H. Cox 11-4-1868 Hy
Jeffres, Mary A. to H. C. Milner 11-1-1854 We
Jeffreys, Amanda to Ned Studivant 3-26-1870 Hy
Jeffreys, Caroline to Scott Allen 3-11-1876 (no return) Hy
Jeffreys, Mattie to Richard Frierson 1-12-1881 L B
Jeffreys, Silla to Henry Hightower 12-28-1873 Hy
Jeffries, Annie to Jack Shaw 8-11-1877 Hy
Jeffries, Harriett to Wm. Lain 2-15-1870 (no return) Hy
Jeffries, Julia M. to W. O. Lackey 11-6-1879 L
Jeffries, Lavinia to Wm. P. Parks 3-31-1858 Sh
Jeffries, Mahala to Henry Kirkland 1-24-1870 (1-25-1870) F
Jeffries, Mary to Parminue Strans 8-1-1840 (8-4-1840) Ma
Jeffries, Permelia J. to Wm. A. Boren 12-12-1870 (12-13-1870) Ma
Jeffries, Roxana to J. W. Lankford 5-2-1877 Hy
Jeffryes, A. L. to P. E. Broocke 1-10-1871 Hy
Jeffrys, Blunett to W. W. Harmon 9-28-1865 G
Jeffrys, Sarah B. to William Y. Newbern 7-2-1840 (7-7-1840) Ma
Jehl, Johannah to Theodore Peterson 2-27-1861 (2-28-1861) Sh
Jelks, Alice to Erasmus F. Hicks 3-16-1858 (3-17-1858) Ma
Jelks, Caroline to Bill Anderson 2-21-1873 Hy
Jelks, Cinda to Moses Robertson 12-26-1868 (no return) Hy
Jelks, Louisa C. to John F. Sinclair 10-29-1849 (10-31-1849) Ma
Jelks, Matilda to Tom Jones 6-30-1870 Hy
Jelks, Tennessee to Geo. Nash 2-23-1880 (2-25-1880) Dy
Jemison, Mary A. to D. J. Hooper 8-13-1866 Be
Jemison, Mary to George Patten? 10-8-1855 (no return) Hn
Jenings, Hellena to William Donaldson 8-17-1842 G
Jenken, E. to J. M. Hailey 10-5-1865 G
Jenkins, Allice to L. S. Harris 7-29-1874 L
Jenkins, Amanda to E. F. Pool 10-1-1857 We
Jenkins, Arabella F. A. to William Elliott 10-1-1853 We
Jenkins, Ausena to Sterling Childers 10-24-1858 Hn
Jenkins, Caroline M. to Soloman P. F. Webb 12-16-1857 L
Jenkins, Caroline to J. W. Miller 12-14-1860 (no return) Hy
Jenkins, Cathrine to M. Winston 2-8-1852 We
Jenkins, Eliza P. to Thomas T. Snodgrass 3-27-1856 We
Jenkins, Eliza to Bradford Bridges 12-2-1849 Be
Jenkins, Eliza to Reddick Brown 2-18-1867 F B
Jenkins, Elizabeth to James Hicks 10-11-1852 (10-13-1852) Ma
Jenkins, Elizabeth to Thomas Kern 5-24-1841 (5-26-1841) T
Jenkins, F. S. to J. W. Glover 2-24-1853 Hn
Jenkins, Frances G. to W. D. Johnson 11-27-1878 L
Jenkins, Jane to Nathaniel Sanders 1-17-1866 L
Jenkins, Judy to William Turnbull 4-13-1866 (4-15-1866) F B
Jenkins, Julia L. to Rubinn Upchurch 1-22-1860 Hn
Jenkins, Justin T. to Willis Etheridge 10-24-1844 We
Jenkins, Laura to George W. Jones 2-21-1855 We
Jenkins, Lucy W. to William R. Palmer 12-4-1862 We
Jenkins, M. A. to H. J. Snodgrass 11-25-1869 (no return) Hn
Jenkins, M. A. to W. S. Saunders 8-1-1883 L
Jenkins, M. J. to W. B. Lacy 9-18-1867 (9-19-1867) Dy
Jenkins, Mariah to A. Berry 5-3-1854 We
Jenkins, Martha A. to Wm. S. Carson 4-17-1860 (4-22-1860) Hr
Jenkins, Martha C. to Newton Finley 2-17-1863 (no return) Cr
Jenkins, Martha J. to Thomas J. Mitchell 3-27-1856 We
Jenkins, Martha to John H. Lillard 5-11-1858 We
Jenkins, Martha to Leander W. Green 3-14-1857 Cr
Jenkins, Martha to M. C. McIlleavy 1-25-1856 Hn
Jenkins, Mary Ann to Jacob Boston 6-30-1870 (7-2-1870) Cr
Jenkins, Mary B. to G. H. Walker 12-3-1878 (no return) L
Jenkins, Mary H. to William Lamb 10-20-1853 Hn
Jenkins, Mary M. to William W. Ridgeway 11-18-1858 Hn
Jenkins, Mary to J. F. Morris 2-4-1875 L
Jenkins, Minerva to Jesse Gray 3-20-1832 Hr
Jenkins, Nancy E. to Patric Neenan 9-21-1861 Cr
Jenkins, Nancy E. to Patrick Newman 9-21-1861 Cr
Jenkins, Nancy to James Runolds 11-2-1837 (12-7-1837) G
Jenkins, Nancy to Wm. Chrisenberry 6-18-1849 Hn
Jenkins, Nettie A. to G. W. Thum 11-26-1873 L
Jenkins, Peggy Ann to John J. Smith 1-2-1849 Hn
Jenkins, S. A. E. to J. H. Hickman 12-28-1855 (no return) Hn
Jenkins, S. E. R. to W. W. Jenkins 2-10-1867 Cr
Jenkins, Sarah C. to Benj. Williams 3-23-1859 Cr
Jenkins, Sarah Elizabeth to Radford Booe 1-24-1857 Ma
Jenkins, Sarah G. to Joseph W. Barbee 1-7-1866 Hn
Jenkins, Sarah Jane to Wm. F. Cooper 1-28-1849 Hn
Jenkins, Sarah to John Koonce 9-17-1852 L
Jenkins, Susan to Edward Smothers 11-25-1842 Cr
Jenkins, Susan to G. W. Simpson 10-29-1876 Dy
Jenkins, Sylvester C. to Edward M. Ballard 4-22-1860 Hn
Jenkins, T. C. to K. O. Caplinger 1-19-1882 L
Jenkins, Tabitha to David Upchurch 6-1-1849 (no return) Hn
Jenkins, V. C. to M. L. Delashmut 10-14-1871 (10-19-1871) T
Jenkins, Virginia A. to Wm. Higgs 1-6-1846 (no return) We
Jenney?, Belle to C. F. Volkmar 12-9-1879 (12-9-1880?) L
Jennie, Bobo to Junias Plumer 12-12-1870 (no return) Hy
Jennie, Collier to Govan Powell 6-14-1876 (no return) Hy
Jennie, Duffer to W. F. Poston 11-6-1872 (no return) Hy
Jenning, F. J. to Lawson A. Clutts 9-18-1846 We
Jenning, Rhoda C. to A. Demerald 8-1-1851 (8-9-1851) L
Jennings, Anna to James Turner 1-25-1879 L
Jennings, Anne to Timothy McMahon 12-2-1861 (12-3-1861) Sh
Jennings, Annie to J. H. Mitchell 8-26-1874 L
Jennings, Catherine to Henry Tytus 6-13-1868 L B
Jennings, Elizabeth to George H. Lusk 9-19-1849 (9-20-1849) L
Jennings, Elizabeth to John Rodgers 3-13-1855 (3-16-1855) L
Jennings, Elizabeth to R. M. Wells 7-13-1880 L
Jennings, Fanny to John Blair 10-15-1875 (no return) Hy
Jennings, Lelia to John C. Lewis 12-21-1885 (12-29-1885) L
Jennings, Lucy S. to J. T. Fields 11-8-1876 Dy
Jennings, M. J. to H. A. Maness 6-24-1874 L
Jennings, Martha Ann to Isaac Newton 1-19-1863 Sh
Jennings, Martha to Wilie D. Manning 6-20-1859 (6-29-1859) L
Jennings, Mary D. to G. W. Colley 1-25-1869 L
Jennings, Mary E. to Emanuel Baker 8-24-1838 Sh
Jennings, Mary E. to Jacob B. Garner 10-28-1857 We
Jennings, Mary to W. J. Meadors 1-19-1886 (1-20-1886) L
Jennings, Millie to Sam Allen 12-14-1883 (maybe 1882?) L
Jennings, Nancy to Averett Smith 4-11-1846 (4-12-1846) L
Jennings, Priscilla to James S. Keltner 7-29-1844 (8-1-1844) L
Jennings, Rosella to Jefferson Keller 11-23-1876 (not certified) L
Jennings, S. A. to J. V. Meador 9-6-1880 (9-7-1880) L
Jennings, Sarah Ann to Stephen Smart 8-14-1843 (no return) We
Jennings, Sarah C. to J. M. Richardson 9-7-1864 (9-8-1864) L
Jennings, Sarah E. to William J. Overton 6-20-1861 (no return) Hy
Jennings, Sarah L. A. to James Ellis 9-30-1852 G
Jennings, Susan E. to Jesse Briley 1-18-1870 (no return) Hy
Jenno, Sarah E. to John H. Griffey 1-24-1861 Sh
Jeno (Jene), Martha to J. Robinson 1-27-1863 Sh
Jeno, Mary Elizabeth to James A. Robison 10-15-1861 Sh
Jeolson, Della to John Israel 5-7-1853 Cr
Jerk, Mary to Jacob Wikmiller 11-29-1864 Sh
Jerman, Eliza to John Wilkerson 1-27-1843 (1-30-1843) Ma
Jernagin, A. C. to R. T. Woolverton 5-11-1861 (5-22-1861) Hr
Jernagin, A. to John H. Morgan 3-27-1842 (3-31-1842) F
Jernagin, Amanda to Caleb Atkins 10-15-1866 Hn B
Jernagin, Amelia J. to David C. Booth 3-9-1839 (no return) F
Jernigan, Elizabeth J. to B. D. Finney 5-18-1846 (5-26-1846) F
Jernigan, Elizabeth K. to John H. Street 4-15-1861 (no return) Hn
Jernigan, Elizabeth to Braton Permenter 2-21-1849 (2-22-1849) G
Jernigin, Mary Ann to John Coates 9-8-1847 (9-19-1847) Hr
Jero___, Hannah to Joe Greaves 12-25-1867 (12-26-1867) L B
Jerrell, Missouri C. to John Smith 10-31-1844 W
Jerry (Jenny?), Lucinda J. to W. H. Bridgewater 1-23-1853 Sh
Jerry, Ann E. to Clarke Barber 1-18-1854 Sh
Jerry, Bettie to Henry Green 11-25-1869 Hy
Jerry, Margaret (Miss) to Leonidas Anderson 2-8-1858 Sh
Jerry, Martha E. to Clark Barber 2-18-1859 (3-17-1859) Sh
Jester, Callie J. to Robert Gates 10-29-1867 Ma
Jester, Maggie to Moses P. Williams 8-27-1873 (8-28-1873) L
Jester, Margarett to John Lowden 3-1-1841 Ma
Jester, Trifena to John M. Watt 9-1-1851 (9-2-1851) G
Jeter, Betty A. to Lenard R. Brasfield 9-2-1863 We
Jeter, Emma J. to P. D. Crutchfield 1-16-1873 Hy
Jeter, Lizie to A. H. Tatum 9-28-1875 Hy
Jeter, Lucinda to Sam Gregory 11-16-1869 (no return) Hy
Jeter, Margaret to George Neal 11-11-1870 (no return) Hy
Jeter, Martha to Isaac Armstrong 12-31-1869 Hy
Jeter, Mary E. to T. J. Shelton 8-12-1873 Hy
Jeter, Mary E. to William A. Gift 9-21-1848 Sh
Jeter, Mattie A. to C. T. Williams 1-6-1875 Hy
Jeter, Menerva to Hesekiah Vaulx 4-6-1872 Hy

Jeter, Minerva to Jerry Newsom 2-12-1878 (no return) Hy
Jeter, Sarah to Joseph Short 12-27-1877 Hy
Jett, Elizabeth A. to Finis E. Bryan 12-7-1868 Ma
Jett, Sarah to Daniel R. Whitley 1-5-1852 (1-6-1852) L
Jett?, Amanda to Andrew Macklin 10-23-1865 (10-29-1865) T
Jetton, Candace to Joe Lassiter 3-13-1869 G B
Jetton, Emely V. to Peter G. Fields 9-30-1845 G
Jetton, Emma to A. T. (Capt.) Gay 12-31-1867 G
Jetton, Fousanna W. to S. T. Hancock 9-27-1868 G
Jetton, Harriet to L. H. Ashley 7-29-1869 G
Jetton, Mary J. to Benjamin F. Everett 5-5-1852 (5-6-1852) G
Jetton, Mary J. to William Brotherton 7-4-1868 (7-5-1868) O
Jetton, Vilett C. to Griffin Wright 5-7-1846 G
Jetton, Winey to Alex Wade 6-16-1870 G
Jewell, Annie E. to Van B. Boddie 4-3-1861 Sh
Jiles, Fanny to H. H. Robbins 9-18-1874 Hy
Jiles, Leutitia to Richmond Vaughn 10-4-1873 T
Jimeson, Martha M. to David M. McKnight 9-4-1861 G
Jimmerson, A. J. to Wilie Potts 10-9-1850 (no return) Hn
Jimmerson, Martha B. to John N. Nix 8-30-1865 (8-31-1865) O
Jinkens, H. A. to J. R. Bibb 3-1-1871 (3-2-1871) L
Jinkens, Mattie to Isham Chambers 12-30-1872 (1-2-1873) O
Jinkins, Callie J. to Robert J. Hays 11-17-1862 We
Jinkins, Elizabeth C. to Hawood H. H. Bobbitt 2-20-1863 We
Jinkins, Margaret to Abner Gause 12-20-1873 (12-21-1873) L B
Job, Elizabeth C. to Henry W. Cowgill 6-11-1856 Sh
Job, Isabella L. to Mark Crawford 9-1-1857 Sh
Job, Sarah B. to Clemmon C. Chism 7-9-1856 Sh
Jobe, Catherine to William L. Brisendine 4-23-1844 Hn
Jobe, Elizabeth to James F. Alexander 6-17-1852 Hn
Jobe, Henrietta to Logan D. Brotherton 7-8-1835 Hr
Jobe, Malvina to William B. Hawkins 3-4-1858 Sh
Jobe, Mary P. to John B. Pillow 6-1-1841 Hn
Jobe, Mary to Thomas Blankenship 11-2-1857 Sh
Jobe, Polly to William Rosson 4-19-1826 Hr
Jobe, Susan to Joseph Harden 2-3-1845 Hn
Johns, Betty A. to E. B.(D?) W. Sowell 10-18-1865 G
Johns, Louisa (Mrs.) to Andrew Siegal 1-30-1852 (2-3-1852) Sh
Johns, Malvina A. to Jasper N. Argo 1-20-1870 G
Johns, Martha J. to Franklin J. Bruff 6-8-1869 G
Johns, S. to John(son?) M. Fox 2-3-1869 G
Johns, Sarah E. to Asville P. Cribbs 4-28-1863 Cr
Johns, Sarah E. to Asville P. Cribbs 4-28-1863 (no return) Cr
Johns, Tabitha E. to James f. Young 1-8-1863 G
Johns, Virginia F. to J. C. Harrison 12-20-1859 Sh
Johnson, A. E. to W. L. Shaw 12-24-1870 (12-25-1870) Dy
Johnson, A. M. to Abner W. Nobles 1-26-1875 (1-27-1875) L
Johnson, A. to P. M. Teel 11-13-1847 (11-18-1847) F
Johnson, Abigial? to Balsam Wynne 3-2-1867 Dy
Johnson, Abigil to Will H. Childress 7-17-1856 (7-20-1856) Hr
Johnson, Alpha T. to Dennis Cochran 10-19-1844 We
Johnson, Alphia to Andrew C. Elliott 10-18-1828 (10-19-1828) Hr
Johnson, Alsey Jane to Josiah L. Lacy 12-5-1843 Ma
Johnson, Amanda (Mrs.) to L. F. Jones 1-23-1867 G
Johnson, Amanda Ann to William Pullin 3-5-1868 T
Johnson, Amanda I. to William Spradlin 4-3-1876 (4-12-1876) Dy
Johnson, Amanda J. to A. J. Nelson 2-13-1856 (2-14-1856) Hr
Johnson, Amanda J. to Thomas J. Hill 3-21-1870 T
Johnson, Amanda to Alfred Black 10-7-1865 Mn
Johnson, Amanda to Anthony Cooper 9-21-1869 G B
Johnson, Amanda to Elijah H. Spencer 7-26-1851 (7-31-1851) Ma
Johnson, Amanda to J. H. Bishop 8-12-1869 F
Johnson, Anessa J. to James B. Gillespie 3-8-1866 G
Johnson, Angeline to Jerry Evans 8-19-1872 (8-5-1873) T
Johnson, Angeline to Leroy H. Williamson 1-5-1856 Cr
Johnson, Anlize to James C. Nowlin 12-22-1837 (12-24-1837) Hr
Johnson, Ann E. to Albert Buck 1-2-1878 Hy
Johnson, Ann E. to Wm. J. Spence 6-19-1866 Hy
Johnson, Ann Elizabeth to Noah Nelson 9-24-1850 (9-25-1850) Ma
Johnson, Ann to George Mann 4-2-1870 Hy
Johnson, Ann to Jackson Hargroves 8-2-1839 (9-2-1839) Hr
Johnson, Anna to Ben Bailey 10-20-1871 Hy
Johnson, Anna to Jesse A. Carter 9-19-1857 Hr
Johnson, Anna to Monroe Ware 11-21-1875 (5-3-1876) L B
Johnson, Anne to James Davis 3-22-1873 (3-23-1873) L B
Johnson, Annie to Jim Hemp 12-24-1874 T
Johnson, Annis to William H. Nobles 4-4-1844 Ma
Johnson, Anny to James Mills 8-30-1866 T
Johnson, Arabela to Alexander Rooks 9-1-1863 We
Johnson, Arminda D. to John B. Turner 4-7-1863 F
Johnson, Axcy to J. F. Dill 12-30-1855 Cr
Johnson, Balmy to Vines Baird 6-21-1866 (6-22-1866) O
Johnson, Barbara B. to James O. Dawson 1-9-1839 (1-11-1839) Hr
Johnson, Beckey to Charles Taylor 12-28-1869 T
Johnson, Benigna to Thomas McCary 9-19-1851 (9-21-1851) Hr
Johnson, Betsey to William Scott 5-18-1877 (no return) L
Johnson, Bettie to James E. Brooks 7-9-1878 (no return) Dy

Johnson, Betty A. to John Barnett 4-17-1862 (4-19-1862) O
Johnson, C. A. to Jacob M. Penick 5-21-1845 Hn
Johnson, C. A. to W. R. Patterson 12-23-1867 (no return) Dy
Johnson, Callie to Albert Wordlow 10-14-1875 Hy
Johnson, Camile Jane to William J. Owen 1-10-1859 (1-12-1859) L
Johnson, Candia to W. C. McIntyre 2-21-1855 (2-25-1855) Hr
Johnson, Carolina to George Winberry 6-21-1857 Be CC
Johnson, Caroline C. to Wiley H. Hilliard 10-30-1856 Cr
Johnson, Caroline M. to R. F. Reed 11-17-1840 Cr
Johnson, Caroline to Ben Bond 2-12-1870 Hy
Johnson, Caroline to Council B. Mayo 11-8-1843 Ma
Johnson, Caroline to George Winberry 6-21-1857 Be
Johnson, Caroline to Samuel Ray 9-22-1844 Hn
Johnson, Caroline to Thomas Ballerson 6-13-1861 (no return) L
Johnson, Caroline to W. A. Fuzzell 4-7-1864 Be
Johnson, Cassa to Major Standly 11-10-1835 (11-12-1835) Hr
Johnson, Catharine to Stephen J. Poitevent 2-13-1861 Sh
Johnson, Catherine to John Hanley 12-23-1856 (no return) We
Johnson, Catherine to Wesley Loil 12-7-1845 Sh
Johnson, Catherine to William B. Haltom 3-3-1853 Ma
Johnson, Celia to Elias G. B. Cook 10-26-1840 Ma
Johnson, Cely to Gideon Tucker 7-28-1832 G
Johnson, Cely to Uzzell Benson 6-16?-1833 Hr
Johnson, Charity to John M. Covington 12-17-1838 (12-20-1838) Hr
Johnson, Charity to John White 1-15-1874 Hy
Johnson, Charlotte to Robert Smith 9-11-1869 (no return) F B
Johnson, Clara to Geo. Washington Settle 1-7-1869 (no return) F B
Johnson, Clara to Henry McDowell 10-10-1868 (no return) F B
Johnson, Clarisa Ann to Rufus Goodman 12-19-1866 T
Johnson, Clarissa to Thomas Newsom 4-25-1837 Sh
Johnson, Cora to John Warren 1-11-1834 (1-16-1834) Hr
Johnson, Cynthia to J. W. Anthony 5-27-1830 Ma
Johnson, Dicy to Emanuel Johnson 3-31-1866 G
Johnson, Dirinda to Wm. M. Dodd 12-21-1856 Cr
Johnson, Done? to James Cradick 10-3-1869 G
Johnson, E. A. to John C. Kelly 4-30-1861 Be
Johnson, E. C. to Cyrus Sharp 5-27-1856 G
Johnson, E. C. to James A. Parker 4-25-1872 Dy
Johnson, E. P. to Daniel A. Young 2-18-1849 Hn
Johnson, E. T. to M. E. Lissenberry 2-1-1873 (no return) Cr
Johnson, Easter to Tom Grear 8-2-1867 (no return) F B
Johnson, Edmony to George Weaver 1-2-1868 Hy
Johnson, Edna M. to Jno. P. Burns 7-23-1868 (7-24-1868) F
Johnson, Edy to Nelson Allen 12-7-1872 (no return) Cr B
Johnson, Eliza A. to C. C. Williams 7-26-1853 Be
Johnson, Eliza A. to C. C. Williams 7-26-1853 Be CC
Johnson, Eliza D. to Green H. Moody 3-1-1848 (3-2-1848) F
Johnson, Eliza J. to William B. Manley 10-21-1850 Ma
Johnson, Eliza J. to William C. Livingston 5-8-1848 (5-9-1848) G
Johnson, Eliza to Daniel Egans 9-30-1870 (10-11-1870) L
Johnson, Eliza to Henry Winchester 3-7-1874 (3-11-1874) Dy
Johnson, Elizabeth C. to B. F. McCutcheon 10-25-1865 G
Johnson, Elizabeth C. to Henry L. Woodson 7-16-1854 (7-15?-1854) Hr
Johnson, Elizabeth C. to Samuel Neathery 3-21-1839 Sh
Johnson, Elizabeth E. to Neal Carrington 4-24-1852 Ma
Johnson, Elizabeth M. to William W. Hart 1-5-1857 (1-6-1857) Ma
Johnson, Elizabeth to A. J. Fields 2-11-1869 Be
Johnson, Elizabeth to Alexander Story 2-10-1843 Ma
Johnson, Elizabeth to Benj. Ward 11-27-1854 We
Johnson, Elizabeth to George Burton 1-21-1854 Cr
Johnson, Elizabeth to Harmon Jackson 12-28-1853 (12-29-1853) Hr
Johnson, Elizabeth to Henry Parris 9-15-1849 (9-27-1849) Hr
Johnson, Elizabeth to J. S. Covington 1-23-1853 Cr
Johnson, Elizabeth to James James (Johns?) 1-29-1853 L
Johnson, Elizabeth to James Williams 12-24-1849 Sh
Johnson, Elizabeth to John Liggate 3-22-1847 Sh
Johnson, Elizabeth to John Turner 12-20-1834 Hr
Johnson, Elizabeth to Mack Wills 1-10-1869 Hy
Johnson, Elizabeth to R. F. Buckelew 8-30-1851 (no return) F
Johnson, Elizabeth to Thomas Vinson 11-13-1848 (11-14-1848) G
Johnson, Elizabeth to Wesley Williams 11-19-1869 (11-21-1869) Dy
Johnson, Elizabeth to William Hogan 10-8-1866 (10-11-1866) Ma
Johnson, Elizabeth to William Wilson 3-7-1828 Sh
Johnson, Elizath? to Tisha Rice 12-2-1871 (no return) L
Johnson, Elizer to Allen Bobbitt 1-31-1867 G
Johnson, Ellen M. to James P. Chapman 11-3-1858 (11-4-1858) Sh
Johnson, Ellen to James Aiken 4-4-1872 Hy
Johnson, Elva to Jerry Buck 1-23-1872 (no return) Hy
Johnson, Elvira Catherine to Isham H. Brower 12-28-1855 (12-29-1855) Ma
Johnson, Emiline to Alexander Bond 7-16-1874 Hy
Johnson, Emiline to J. N. Thurmond 9-11-1873 Dy
Johnson, Emily to Dempsey Ursery 3-22-1852 (3-23-1852) Ma
Johnson, Emily to John Smith 2-5-1878 Dy
Johnson, Emily to Samuel Peeler 8-4-1857 Cr
Johnson, Emily to Winston Ellington 8-22-1868 (8-25-1868) Ma
Johnson, Emma H. to C. W. McRee 10-11-1869 (10-12-1869) F
Johnson, Emma to George Sherrill 12-25-1873 T

Johnson, F. J. to J. N. Robinson 12-17-1860 (no return) Hy
Johnson, Fannie to D. K. Page 8-5-1859 (no return) Cr
Johnson, Fannie to W. S. Glenn 10-19-1859 (10-20-1859) Sh
Johnson, Fanny to George Russell 3-6-1873 Hy
Johnson, Fanny to Horace Johnson 9-2-1874 Hy
Johnson, Fanny to W. H. Tucker 11-1-1859 Hy
Johnson, Flora to Thomas Allison 8-3-1871 L
Johnson, Florence I. to W. G. Anderson 7-27-1869 (7-29-1869) F
Johnson, Frances E. to Cornelias M. Arwood 1-16-1866 (1-17-1866) L
Johnson, Frances E. to Thomas L. Walpole 2-14-1861 L
Johnson, Frances to Berry Griggs 1-28-1864 L
Johnson, Frances to E. F. Fortune 11-17-1855 (11-6?-1855) Hr
Johnson, Frances to Joseph W. Oaks 11-20-1857 O
Johnson, Frances to William Huffman 9-4-1865 F
Johnson, Frances to Wm. Johnson 9-5-1846 Cr
Johnson, H. H. to W. S. Forsyth 6-11-1873 (6-15-1873) Dy
Johnson, H. M. to W. C. Nowell 11-30-1859 G
Johnson, H. S. to J. H. Morris 4-14-1859 We
Johnson, Hanna to Ruffin Jackson 12-?-1866 T
Johnson, Harriet A. to George H. McMahan 8-26-1863 We
Johnson, Harriet to James Byrn 5-23-1872 L B
Johnson, Harriet to Jas. M. Crowder 9-4-1849 (9-5-1849) F
Johnson, Harriet to Nelson Bond 12-11-1867 Hy
Johnson, Harriet to William Martin 12-5-1869 G B
Johnson, Harriett to James Lesley 2-15-1850 Cr
Johnson, Isabel to Lewis Taylor 12-21-1867 He
Johnson, Isabelle J. to W. E. Bivins 10-20-1868 Be
Johnson, J. E. to F. A. Slater 10-17-1874 (10-18-1874) Dy
Johnson, Jane C. to Anderson Stedham 4-12-1839 F
Johnson, Jane C. to Moses Hickerson 7-12-1838 Sh
Johnson, Jane to Caswell Hogans 8-3-1845 Ma
Johnson, Jane to Charlie Fitzpatrick 4-27-1885 L
Johnson, Jane to George F. Johnson 7-6-1844 (no return) F
Johnson, Jane to Jerry Skipper 12-4-1865 Hy
Johnson, Jemima to Frank Braden 2-28-1866 (no return) F B
Johnson, Jemima to George A. (of Miss.) Bagley 7-16-1861 Ma
Johnson, Jennie to Isaac Bell 12-24-1868 (12-28-1868) Cr
Johnson, Josephine to Moses Walker 9-12-1866 (9-27-1866) Dy
Johnson, Julia Ann to William Searcy 5-1-1869 (no return) Dy
Johnson, Julina to John R. Browning 11-20-1856 Be
Johnson, Kate to John Harvey 6-30-1863 Sh
Johnson, L. M. to R. L. Hart 5-10-1861 (no return) Cr
Johnson, L. V. to M. V. (Mo?) Bettis 11-21-1866 (no return) Dy
Johnson, Laura Ann to Sims Suggs 7-1-1839 Cr
Johnson, Laura J. to M. T. Turner 12-30-1859 (1-3-1860) Sh
Johnson, Leathia P. to John Kingston 2-4-1854 (2-5-1854) G
Johnson, Leona F. to Joseph W. Hudson 12-8-1868 Be
Johnson, Leonora to John P. Day 1-17-1870 (1-19-1870) Ma
Johnson, Lessie? to Ben Lyons 11-27-1867 T
Johnson, Lizzie to Jim Ware 1-3-1871 Hy
Johnson, Lotty to Henery Danal 3-23-1829 (2-9?-1829) Ma
Johnson, Louisa to Williamson King 1-9-1834 Sh
Johnson, Lucinda E. to James W. Ralph 8-5-1854 (8-27-1854) T
Johnson, Lucinda to John T. Stell 4-1-1861 (4-2-1861) Cr
Johnson, Lucinda to William Childress 8-6-1847 (8-8-1847) Hr
Johnson, Lucy A. to T. L. Slater 7-10-1868 (no return) L
Johnson, Lucy Ann to Lodwick Partin 6-10-1856 (6-11-1856) Sh
Johnson, Lucy F. to David C. Goodman 1-9-1858 (1-12-1858) G
Johnson, Lucy J. to M. A. Brinkley 2-23-1846 We
Johnson, Lucy T. D. to James L. Perry 9-12-1847 Sh
Johnson, Lucy to Daniel Smith 1-10-1850 We
Johnson, Lucy to James W. Camp 12-28-1854 Be
Johnson, Lucy to W. M. Barnes 2-28-1881 L
Johnson, Lue (Sue) to Allen Frost 1-25-1867 (no return) Hy
Johnson, Lydia A. to Matt D. Meriwether 11-14-1860 (11-15-1860) Ma
Johnson, Lydia A. to William W. Manley 6-15-1860 (6-17-1860) Ma
Johnson, M. A. to A. J. Estes 9-24-1870 (9-26-1870) O
Johnson, M. A. to H. Leslie 10-24-1844 Cr
Johnson, M. A. to James S. Massey 5-10-1860 Dy
Johnson, M. A. to M. B. Midgett 11-24-1860 (no return) Hy
Johnson, M. A. to W. W. Chapman 12-16-1878 (12-17-1879?) L
Johnson, M. E. to Robert Jamison 11-14-1866 (11-15-1866) Cr
Johnson, M. J. to F. M. Shaw 10-14-1868 G
Johnson, M. J. to J. Z. Ledsinger 12-2-1868 (no return) Dy
Johnson, M. J. to Thomas Orr 1-13-1870 Cr
Johnson, M. L. E. to S. J. Welch 8-18-1870 Dy
Johnson, M. S. to J. M. Smith 12-22-1885 L
Johnson, Madelena to John Hobbs 7-12-1843 (7-13-1843) Ma
Johnson, Maggie to Lewis Wilson 12-24-1875 (12-24-1874?) T
Johnson, Malinda to Boston Fielder 12-21-1868 (12-30-1868) Dy
Johnson, Manda to George Sims 7-4-1869 Hy
Johnson, Marcella to James Spence 3-9-1858 Be
Johnson, Marg to T. D. Moore 12-30-1862 Mn
Johnson, Margaret E. to James M. Johnson 10-6-1869 Ma
Johnson, Margaret J. to Wm. M. Johnson 1-4-1862 (1-5-1862) Hr
Johnson, Margaret to B. F. Rice 7-26-1854 Sh
Johnson, Margaret to Edward Sheels 4-12-1855 (4-1-1856?) Sh
Johnson, Margaret to George L. Bland 6-24-1848 Sh
Johnson, Margaret to John McCraw 9-21-1866 F
Johnson, Margaret to John McVay 11-18-1848 (no return) F
Johnson, Margaret to John Taylor 1-5-1870 T
Johnson, Margaret to W. Sulfrige 12-31-1872 (1-2-1873) T
Johnson, Margaret to Wm. A. Dacus 12-23-1845 Sh
Johnson, Margarett A. E. to Daniel E. McAlester 10-25-1847 (10-28-1847) G
Johnson, Margarett to Littleton Storey 3-5-1844 Ma
Johnson, Margory to John W. Palmer 8-12-1845 We
Johnson, Margrett to Bennett Highfield 12-29-1846 (12-31-1846) Hr
Johnson, Maria Jane to Jacob Musgrove 11-16-1878 Hy
Johnson, Maria to Robert Anderson 10-10-1879 (10-12-1879) L B
Johnson, Maria to Solomon Richards 11-21-1871 T
Johnson, Mariah to Lenson Outlaw 12-4-1871 (no return) Hy
Johnson, Marianna to Richard J. Fenner 3-23-1841 (3-24-1841) Ma
Johnson, Martha A. to Reuben Sewell 9-29-1841 Ma
Johnson, Martha A. to William J. Wray 8-23-1862 We
Johnson, Martha Ann to Olen West 11-1-1841 Ma
Johnson, Martha B. to A. R. Williams 5-13-1868 G
Johnson, Martha E to John J. Boon 7-10-1850 Ma
Johnson, Martha E. to William Nixon 5-3-1838 Hn
Johnson, Martha F. to Whitson H. Wilson 10-4-1858 (10-6-1858) Ma
Johnson, Martha J. to A. B. Lloyd 12-19-1868 (12-22-1868) F
Johnson, Martha J. to Abner J. Fletcher 6-17-1868 G
Johnson, Martha J. to Robert J. Williams 12-22-1852 Ma
Johnson, Martha J. to Visen? P. Wright 2-1-1848 (2-8-1848) F
Johnson, Martha J. to William L. Husky 7-12-1853 Sh
Johnson, Martha Jnae to Andrew J. McClish 12-27-1856 (12-28-1856) Ma
Johnson, Martha P. to John T. Anderson 7-15-1850 Ma
Johnson, Martha Sarah to John T. Cherry 1-28-1858 Ma
Johnson, Martha to Baltimore Downs 12-4-1867 (12-5-1867) F B
Johnson, Martha to Chas. Howell 9-25-1844 Sh
Johnson, Martha to Hiram N. Brown 1-27-1845 Hr
Johnson, Martha to James M. Conyers 10-2-1843 Hn
Johnson, Martha to Joseph Coock 10-1-1860 (no return) Hy
Johnson, Martha to Luke Williams 11-23-1870 (11-24-1870) Dy
Johnson, Martha to Thos. D. White 8-16-1849 Be
Johnson, Martha to Wade Hampton 1-29-1877 Dy
Johnson, Martha to William P. Lacy 1-10-1854 (1-12-1854) L
Johnson, Martha to Wilson Tolley 3-28-1840 (3-1?-1840) Ma
Johnson, Mary A. T. to T. F. Amos 12-2-1867 (12-5-1867) F
Johnson, Mary A. to Garrett W. Simmons 10-27-1848 (10-29-1848) F
Johnson, Mary A. to Hamilton Thornton 12-17-1856 (no return) F
Johnson, Mary A. to John B. Arnold 10-31-1849 (11-1-1849) G
Johnson, Mary A. to Moses C. Clark 8-13-1846 (8-14-1846) F
Johnson, Mary Ann to Jordan Gibson 2-18-1863 Sh
Johnson, Mary Ann to W. N. Farris 10-4-1838 Hr
Johnson, Mary Ann to Wiley W. Wiggins 3-10-1843 Sh
Johnson, Mary Ann to William Geo. W. Paschall 1-25-1849 Hn
Johnson, Mary Anne to John Land 11-12-1850 Sh
Johnson, Mary C. to James B. Harroe 11-25-1860 We
Johnson, Mary E. to Carrol Butler 2-2-1856 (2-5-1856) Hr
Johnson, Mary E. to John C. Ledbetter 11-27-1852 (11-28-1852) Ma
Johnson, Mary E. to John T. Davy 8-29-1870 G
Johnson, Mary F. to James Scott 6-23-1866 (no return) Cr
Johnson, Mary Frances to Joseph Allison 7-16-1839 Ma
Johnson, Mary H. to John McKinnie 12-2-1830 Sh
Johnson, Mary J. to James G. Webb 11-29-1857 We
Johnson, Mary J. to John W. Whitson 10-10-1850 (no return) L
Johnson, Mary J. to Robt. E. R. Greer 11-5-1867 (11-7-1867) F
Johnson, Mary Jane to Benjamin C. Miles 6-12-1877 Hy
Johnson, Mary Jane to John Bright 1-6-1859 Sh
Johnson, Mary Jane to Milton R. Morgan 11-17-1847 (11-18-1847) G
Johnson, Mary N. to George W. Ivie 2-11-1867 (2-13-1867) Dy
Johnson, Mary S. to C. (Dr.) Harris 8-23-1845 (8-25-1845) Ma
Johnson, Mary T. to Ira M. Hill 4-3-1849 Sh
Johnson, Mary W. to Elias Laster 11-1-1854 O
Johnson, Mary to Alscy Jordon 7-3-1841 (7-8-1841) Ma
Johnson, Mary to Andrew Hartgraves 7-14-1841 Sh
Johnson, Mary to Ben Alston 1-24-1870 T
Johnson, Mary to Elihu Prideman 9-25-1862 Mn
Johnson, Mary to Evans Read 1-4-1873 (1-6-1873) T
Johnson, Mary to Ewing Cameron 7-29-1874 O
Johnson, Mary to George W. Cox 6-23-1855 (6-26-1855) T
Johnson, Mary to George W. Patterson 8-16-1838 F
Johnson, Mary to H. W. Cotter, jr. 6-5-1867 (6-6-1867) Ma
Johnson, Mary to John Berry 2-15-1872 Hy
Johnson, Mary to John Garrash 3-14-1869 Be
Johnson, Mary to John Matheny 1-10-1856 We
Johnson, Mary to John Rogers 9-19-1861 Hy
Johnson, Mary to John Siler 6-18-1830 Ma
Johnson, Mary to Joseph W. Murphy 3-22-1860 Cr
Johnson, Mary to Kinchin Knoulen 6-10-1852 We
Johnson, Mary to Leroy F. Lockard 8-3-1846 (8-4-1846) L
Johnson, Mary to Lucas Woods 10-20-1855 (no return) Hn
Johnson, Mary to Robert Cruise 12-11-1855 We
Johnson, Mary to Thomas Skipper 7-4-1860 Dy

Johnson, Mary to Thos. Ezell 10-24-1855 Cr
Johnson, Mary to Wm. Thurston 9-30-1845 We
Johnson, Matilda to Alex M. King 12-14-1864 (12-15-1864) Sh
Johnson, Matilda to Solomon Johnson 12-28-1870 (no return) L
Johnson, Mattie A. to H. L. Carnal 10-20-1875 (10-21-1875) L
Johnson, Mattie to Joseph Brooks 10-28-1862 (no return) Dy
Johnson, Mattie to Rogers Smith 11-17-1877 Hy
Johnson, Melissa to B. D. (Rev.) Wikoff 5-30-1860 Sh
Johnson, Merilla H. to John R. Howell 6-3-1840 (6-4-1840) Hr
Johnson, Millie R. to C. G. House 10-3-1871 (no return) Hy
Johnson, Minerva to Jerry Morgan 4-16-1876 Hy
Johnson, Missouri A. to John H. Swindle 12-10-1868 G
Johnson, Mollie C. to Benjamin A. Howard 7-4-1860 Cr
Johnson, Mollie J. to J. H. Latham 5-27-1875 Hy
Johnson, Mollie J. to N. J. Mitchell 12-26-1855 (12-27-1855) L
Johnson, Mollie to T. W. Cox 11-4-1867 (11-5-1867) F
Johnson, Mollie to W. H. Gregory 10-6-1865 (no return) Cr
Johnson, Myra to Isiah Brown 12-28-1870 F B
Johnson, N. M. to T. J. Castellow 8-16-1865 (no return) Hy
Johnson, Nancy C. to John Coates 2-20-1839 Hr
Johnson, Nancy H. to Richard H. McNees 9-24-1828 (9-25-1828) Hr
Johnson, Nancy J. to Lenard Brown 11-8-1849 F
Johnson, Nancy J. to Robert E. Jones 8-8-1858 Cr
Johnson, Nancy L. to James Little 11-24-1857 (11-25-1857) Hr
Johnson, Nancy M. to W. R. B. Powell 10-23-1857 (11-5-1857) Hr
Johnson, Nancy T. to Thomas H. Bogle 7-31-1860 Hn
Johnson, Nancy to C. F. Maxey 2-13-1867 O
Johnson, Nancy to Crred B. Haskins 12-26-1848 (12-27-1848) Ma
Johnson, Nancy to Edward Weston 10-7-1867 G B
Johnson, Nancy to George Winston 1-15-1846 We
Johnson, Nancy to J. K. McIlister 3-29-1868 G
Johnson, Nancy to James Henry White 5-23-1866 Ma
Johnson, Nancy to John F. Robertson 7-31-1827 Hr
Johnson, Nancy to Milton Jones 12-26-1878 Hy
Johnson, Nancy to West Wilson 1-16-1873 Hy
Johnson, Nanie M. to W. L. Moultrie 3-30-1866 O
Johnson, Nannie to James E. Jeter 12-6-1869 (no return) Hy
Johnson, Nannie to William G. Foster 8-15-1859 (no return) We
Johnson, Narcissa to H. A. Honey 7-29-1845 Cr
Johnson, Narcissa to James L. Storey 5-15-1841 (5-19-1841) Ma
Johnson, Nola to Daniel Goode 6-11-1869 (no return) F B
Johnson, P. E. to David M. Steel 8-17-1845 We
Johnson, Parelee to Henry Lauderdale 11-12-1874 T
Johnson, Parlee to Marshall Starnes 5-27-1851 (5-28-1851) L
Johnson, Parmelia T. to James M. Douglas 6-14-1853 Hn
Johnson, Parmelia to Israel Stephens 6-23-1857 O
Johnson, Paulina E. to J. N. Appleberry 1-7-1857 (1-8-1857) Sh
Johnson, Pernicia to Ferlacky J. Johnston 3-14-1841 Hn
Johnson, Phillip to Ben Topp 2-21-1868 (2-22-1868) Dy
Johnson, Polly to Glanson Hudson 3-25-1866 Hy
Johnson, Polly to Turner Parker 9-27-1842 Cr
Johnson, Prissilla to Math Midgett 12-1-1871 Hy
Johnson, Rachel to Andrew J. Mann 1-31-1870 (no return) Hy
Johnson, Rebecca A. to John Pickard 10-6-1885 (10-8-1885) L
Johnson, Rebecca to Amos Elms 7-9-1840 (no return) F
Johnson, Rebecca to James H. Sheppard 10-15-1828 Hr
Johnson, Rebecca to John Simmons 4-30-1866 (5-2-1866) O
Johnson, Rebecca to Nathan Evans 12-23-1856 G
Johnson, Rendy to William Pender 2-2-1875 Hy
Johnson, Roxannah to James Box 10-7-1862 (10-8-1862) O
Johnson, Ruth to Henry Cockeram 7-30-1828 (4-6-1829) Hr
Johnson, S. A. M. to D. D. Dacus 10-30-1860 (11-2-1860) F
Johnson, S. A. to R. A. Moore 6-5-1851 Hn
Johnson, S. C. to E. D. McEwen 12-26-1872 Cr
Johnson, S. J. to G. H. Moody 9-20-1849 F
Johnson, S. J. to J. L. (Dr.) McGee 3-12-1868 G
Johnson, S. M. to J. W. Ballard 6-29-1868 (7-1-1868) T
Johnson, Sallie R. to R. T. Chambers 6-8-1878 (6-11-1878) Dy
Johnson, Sallie to J. R. McKinney 2-20-1867 (2-22-1867) Cr
Johnson, Sara to J. B. Dill 1-13-1857 Cr
Johnson, Sarah A. to John R. Sanders 11-15-1862 Hy
Johnson, Sarah A. to John W. Brown 9-7-1846 Ma
Johnson, Sarah Ann to James Dunnavant 7-29-1877 Hy
Johnson, Sarah Ann to Wm. J. Dearmore 10-4-1871 (10-5-1871) Ma
Johnson, Sarah C. to James M.? Brandon 12-28-1861 (1-6-1862) Cr
Johnson, Sarah C. to James W. Fussell 11-18-1857 Be
Johnson, Sarah C. to John sr. Eaton 9-13-1858 (9-14-1858) Hr
Johnson, Sarah C. to Middleton Maroney 11-25-1858 Sh
Johnson, Sarah E. to Emry Rooks 4-17-1867 G
Johnson, Sarah E. to James S. Bodkins 7-29-1869 G
Johnson, Sarah J. to Isaac L. Fletcher 4-1-1856 (4-2-1856) G
Johnson, Sarah J. to J. M. Branch 12-23-1872 (12-24-1872) Cr
Johnson, Sarah M. C. to Andrew Newsom 10-13-1851 (no return) F
Johnson, Sarah M. to G. G. Blair 12-10-1868 Hy
Johnson, Sarah M. to John Dugan 1-9-1851 (1-14-1851) G
Johnson, Sarah to A. Cook? 7-4-1842 F
Johnson, Sarah to Benjamin Turner 11-21-1831 Hr

Johnson, Sarah to Ed Mann 12-26-1868 Hy
Johnson, Sarah to Egbert Haywood 5-7-1828 (5-10-1828) Hr
Johnson, Sarah to George W. Childress 8-30-1853 (no return) L
Johnson, Sarah to Henry Burrow 3-1-1832 Sh
Johnson, Sarah to Isiah Hogan 12-20-1849 Ma
Johnson, Sarah to James L. Steel 1-21-1845 Cr
Johnson, Sarah to John F. Goodwin 11-22-1847 (11-24-1847) L
Johnson, Sarah to John Gann 8-13-1857 Sh
Johnson, Sarah to John W. Starnes 12-2-1867 (12-4-1867) T
Johnson, Sarah to Louis R. Clark 11-18-1851 Cr
Johnson, Sarah to Tom Parker 4-17-1869 (no return) Dy
Johnson, Sarah to William Loftin 12-8-1852 Ma
Johnson, Sarah to William Skipper 12-25-1860 Dy
Johnson, Sideous I. to James H. Nelson 11-1-1842 (11-3-1842) Ma
Johnson, Sinda to Sam Porter 1-7-1880 (1-13-1880) L B
Johnson, Sophia Caroline to John Kelley 11-5-1864 Sh
Johnson, Sue to J. B. Reames 12-11-1867 (12-12-1867) F
Johnson, Susan A. to James A. Fay 2-5-1859 We
Johnson, Susan B. to Allen Taylor 10-20-1847 (10-21-1847) G
Johnson, Susan J. to O. A. Jones 1-28-1868 (1-29-1868) Dy
Johnson, Susana Maria to John F. N. Sypes 11-6-1868 (11-8-1868) Ma
Johnson, Susanah R. to Dandridge M. Jordan 9-25-1852 (no return) F
Johnson, Susanah R. to John Allen 8-23-1852 (8-24-1852) Hr
Johnson, Susanna to James F. Williams 2-8-1858 (2-11-1858) Hr
Johnson, T. C. to P. T. Williams 11-14-1865 O
Johnson, Tabitha B. (Mrs.) to David Adams 9-12-1859 (9-13-1859) Sh
Johnson, Tempy S. to Leroy C. Gillaspie 10-29-1852 (10-30-1852) Ma
Johnson, Tennessee to Joe Davis 9-30-1871 (10-9-1871) Cr B
Johnson, Tenny to Wilson Kelton 6-22-___ (with 1870) G
Johnson, Tomantana to N. W. Williams 7-8-1845 (7-9-1846?) F
Johnson, Valenia to Elijah Starkey 9-5-1859 (9-6-1859) Hr
Johnson, Virginia C. to John F. Roberts 11-24-1869 G
Johnson, W. M. to R. W. Newton 7-29-1867 O
Johnson, Winerford to James McAlexander 8-21-1843 G
Johnson, Winney Edward to James Burks 2-2-1867 (2-3-1867) L B
Johnson, Winney to Calvin Sauls 10-4-1847 Ma
Johnson, Zula Belle to Wm. B. Tyus 3-29-1876 Hy
Johnson, Zurie to Henry Morris 12-28-1867 (1-3-1868) F B
Johnson, ___ to Emanuel Niblet 3-23-1873 Hy
Johnston, A. L. to L. L. Watson 9-24-1857 G
Johnston, A. to James H. Lawrence 6-14-1852 Hn
Johnston, Addie to Thomas D. Cobb 12-10-1867 L
Johnston, Angeline E. to Calvin L. Thompson 2-8-1870 (2-9-1870) Cr
Johnston, Ann C. to James M. White 10-2-1838 Ma
Johnston, Caroline E. G. to George Williams 9-7-1846 (no return) Hn
Johnston, E. M. to C. A. Smith 9-26-1879 L
Johnston, Eliza to Thos. Waller 11-15-1843 G
Johnston, Elizabeth Susannah to James Franklin Harper 4-3-1844 (4-4-1844) T
Johnston, Hannah to Osborn Rhodes 9-12-1867 (9-22-1867) T
Johnston, Hester A. to Benjamin Hart, jr. 11-17-1874 L
Johnston, Julia A. to R. W. Voss 12-26-1882 (12-27-1882) L
Johnston, L. W. to Wm. Grant 12-31-1866 Hy
Johnston, Laura to Buck Pierson 2-11-1880 L B
Johnston, Leah E. to William Smith 12-19-1852 Hn
Johnston, Luada to Sam Hamby 11-13-1870 G
Johnston, M. A. M. to Thomas W. Lumpkins 1-7-1861 (1-10-1861) Sh
Johnston, Margaret J. to Joseph F. Freeland 11-15-1870 (11-22-1870) F
Johnston, Mariah to Jacob Ross 6-19-1825 (7-19-1825) Hr
Johnston, Martha J. to Thomas H. Graves 2-16-1871 L
Johnston, Martha to Robin Fuel 10-20-1841 G
Johnston, Mary A. to William Greathouse 2-7-1850 Sh
Johnston, Mary Ann to J. M. Lard 5-2-1855 We
Johnston, Mary C. to John M. McDaniel 6-22-1864 G
Johnston, Mary E. to Fleming Franklin 2-3-1860 (no return) Hy
Johnston, Mary Elizabeth to Robert Evans 9-28-1867 Ma
Johnston, Mary to John H. Pounds 3-7-1859 (3-15-1859) G
Johnston, Mattie to W. S. Watson 7-8-1878 Hy
Johnston, Nancy H. to Benjamin D. Caple 4-20-1852 G
Johnston, Nancy to Andrew Terry 3-4-1847 O
Johnston, Nancy to Hiram Dawson 8-29-1829 (8-30-1829) G
Johnston, Sarah A. to William L. Slack 8-21-1843 (8-24-1843) Ma
Johnston, Sarah Jane to Bedford M. Estes 4-24-1854 (5-4-1854) Ma
Johnston, Sibly to Andrew P. Foster 2-17-1838 (2-21-1838) G
Johnston, Steve to Gabriel S. Tyler 3-18-1833 (3-19-1833) G
Johnston, Sue to J. M. Sappington 3-8-1870 G
Johnston, Susan T. to John G. Finnie 4-10-1849 Sh
Johnston, Tempie to Farrington B. Snipes 11-30-1868 (12-3-1868) Ma
Johnston, Winny to John Flemming 4-11-1849 (4-12-1849) F
Johnston?, M. A. to Jacob D. Watson 11-21-1847 Hn
Joice, Ann Eliza to Arthur F. Wooten 5-14-1842 (5-15-1842) T
Joice, Cordelia Ann to James Henry Bowers 1-12-1846 (not executed) T
Joice, Margaret to Jesse P. Sanders 9-1-1841 Sh
Joice, Susan to W. C. Hammond 6-5-1857 Sh
Joiner, Adelia to G. W. Parsons 10-18-1853 Sh
Joiner, Ann to William C. Loftin 9-1-1852 (9-2-1852) Sh
Joiner, Charity H. to Augustus Marshall 7-4-1860 Hn
Joiner, Elizabeth to William Capehart 11-28-1853 T

Joiner, Ester L. to D. Antoine Hess 10-26-1862 Mn
Joiner, F. A. to J. T. Rogers 5-14-1864 Cr
Joiner, Joanna to Henry Stewart 5-11-1867 (no return) F B
Joiner, Leddy to Miles Lasater 3-18-1844 (no return) Hn
Joiner, Malvina to James M. Lusk 1-12-1871 Ma
Joiner, Martha E. to E. P. Owenby 1-?-1867 (1-23-1867) Cr
Joiner, Martha to B. W. Brandon 11-11-1846 Cr
Joiner, Martha to Daniel Winsett 7-5-1852 Hn
Joiner, Mary Ann to William Chase 10-3-1839 Sh
Joiner, Nancy E. to Joel B. Robertson 7-21-1853 Hn
Joiner, Nancy to Jordan Fields 11-14-1872 (11-15-1872) T
Joiner, Nancy to William Williams 5-5-1841 (5-6-1841) G
Joiner, Pernetta to Jordan Payne 1-23-1835 Sh
Joinor, Susan to Samuel Lepperd 9-15-1842 G
Joleff, Virginia A. to William H. Hall 4-16-1847 G
Joliet, Nancy T. to W. H. Conley 3-1-1880 (3-14-1880) L
Jolley, Biga to Asa Greer 5-17-1854 (no return) We
Jolley, R. S. to Sterling H. Edmunds 12-28-1858 We
Jolly, Biga to Asa Greer 5-17-1854 We
Jolly, Emily C. to James Heathscott 9-29-1856 We
Jolly, Harriett Emily to Henry Graves 7-5-1840 Cr
Jolly, Martha G. to Robert Wright 9-21-1861 (no return) Cr
Jolly, Nancy to William Corder 4-25-1861 Cr
Jolly, Sarah Jane to J. S. Rochelle 3-27-1848 (3-29-1848) F
Jolly, Sirena to Jacob H. Black 3-17-1841 Cr
Jolnes, Jane to Wm. N. Edwards 8-24-1852 Sh
Jonagan, Susan to John Waller 9-2-1854 (9-3-1854) Hr
Jonakin, Sylvia to Peter Williams 5-19-1866 (8-11-1866) F B
Jones (Janes), Eliza to W. R. Fields 11-4-1860 We
Jones (Janes?), Coly Ann to Hiram G. Coker 11-20-1861 G
Jones, A. (Mrs.) to James McMillen 10-31-1871 O
Jones, A. E. to W. W. McDowell 3-28-1867 G
Jones, A. Fannie to George C. Holmes 11-26-1853 (11-27-1853) Sh
Jones, A. L. to James M. Butler 1-6-1858 Cr
Jones, Abba to J. S. Howe 6-22-1866 (6-24-1866) Dy
Jones, Ada to Robert Trew 8-26-1870 (8-29-1870) Dy
Jones, Adaline to Albert Baxter 4-1-1874 (no return) L
Jones, Adaline to B. J. Billsbury 6-19-1873 O
Jones, Addie to L. J. Wilkins 6-30-1863 Sh
Jones, Adella to Isaac N. Ivy 7-25-1882 (no return) L
Jones, Alabama to Wm. Wommack 3-27-1878 Hy
Jones, Alethia Munford to William Branch Booker 9-18-1852 (9-23-1852) T
Jones, Alice D. to H. E. Garth 4-25-1859 (4-26-1859) Sh
Jones, Alice to John Dumas 10-2-1873 (10-4-1873) Dy
Jones, Aly to Hugh D. Neilson 3-7-1833 G
Jones, Amanda M. to Thomas P. Morgan 11-2-1850 (11-3-1850) Ma
Jones, Amanda to David Armstrong 4-16-1873 (4-17-1873) Dy B
Jones, Amanda to Esquire Sangster 4-1-1869 Hr
Jones, Amanda to Jordon W. Richardson 11-27-1848 (11-28-1848) L
Jones, Amelia C. to R. E. Parnell 10-28-1868 (no return) Dy
Jones, Amelia to W. C. Chronister 10-17-1860 (10-8?-1860) Dy
Jones, Amy to Randel Gardner 12-9-1872 (no return) Hy
Jones, Aneliza T. to James A. Park 10-12-1858 (10-__-1858) O
Jones, Angeline to Ira Hill 12-17-1872 Hy
Jones, Angeline to Thos. B. Beavers 2-4-1858 G
Jones, Angeline to W. L. Geleun 7-1-1850 We
Jones, Angevona C. to James S. Cannon 10-5-1858 (10-6-1858) G
Jones, Ann E. to M. D. Jones 9-?-1860 (no return) Hy
Jones, Ann E. to Samuel P. Gregory 9-3-1851 (9-4-1851) Sh
Jones, Ann Eliza to John R. Boals 12-17-1860 (12-19-1860) Ma
Jones, Ann Eliza to Nathan Ross 6-10-1833 Sh
Jones, Ann Eliza to T. S. Tate 12-11-1860 (12-12-1860) Hr
Jones, Ann Eliza to W. A. Turner 5-14-1859 F
Jones, Ann J. to James N. Gardner 11-26-1856 Cr
Jones, Ann M. to Robert Fenner 7-23-1828 Ma
Jones, Ann Mariah to William L. Birdsong 12-17-1849 (12-20-1849) Hr
Jones, Ann S. to Samuel B. Harper 12-27-1827 (1-1-1828) Hr
Jones, Ann to Alfred Waldrop 7-19-1838 Hn
Jones, Ann to George S. Moore 2-3-1869 (2-4-1869) Cr
Jones, Ann to James Walker 10-3-1843 O
Jones, Ann to John Brand 1-4-1873 (1-5-1873) Cr
Jones, Anney to George D. Stone 1-6-1840 (1-8-1840) G
Jones, Annie to Shadrack Williams 10-18-1873 (10-19-1873) L
Jones, Arcady F. to Henry Bayley 6-12-1848 Ma
Jones, Arteny to Mit Baxter 2-17-1871 Dy
Jones, Astasia to F. W. Eison 6-13-1867 G
Jones, B. C. to W. W. Jacobs 3-9-1859 Sh
Jones, B. E. to L. B. Barham 9-16-1871 (9-17-1871) Cr
Jones, Becky to Simon Clay 12-26-1867 Hy
Jones, Beda A. to John D. Rogers 5-23-1865 (5-24-1865) Cr
Jones, Behethland C. to Richard Mason 10-7-1847 Sh
Jones, Bethany C. to Martin Morfield 4-27-1839 Hn
Jones, Betheland M. to M. M. Sanderlin 11-25-1849 Sh
Jones, Bettie E. to W. T. Walker 7-25-1877 Dy
Jones, Bettie G. to J. K. Easborn 9-26-1865 G
Jones, Bettie to Joseph Bacon 3-22-1875 (3-24-1875) Dy
Jones, Bobry to Manuel Johnson 4-1-1869 (no return) Hy

Jones, C. A. to A. H. McKee 12-11-1867 (no return) Dy
Jones, C. F. to William Whitlock 3-6-1874 (3-7-1874) Dy
Jones, C. to Martin Burrow 2-1-1866 G
Jones, Canda to Jesse Parks 5-17-1867 (5-18-1867) Dy
Jones, Caroline E. to Henry Barber 2-29-1868 Hy
Jones, Caroline L. to Benjamin A. Dunn 3-14-1843 Hn
Jones, Caroline R. to John H. Daniel (David?) 11-16-1853 Sh
Jones, Caroline to Albert Hicks 5-7-1864 Sh B
Jones, Caroline to Jacob M Davis 3-2-1866 (5-30-1866) T
Jones, Caroline to Munford S. Marsh 11-13-1829 (11-17-1829) Hr
Jones, Caroline to R. A. Howl? 10-1-1864 Hr
Jones, Caroline to R. B. White 1-28-1863 Be CC
Jones, Caroline to R. B. White 2-28-1863 Be
Jones, Cassie to L. T. Culp 12-19-1870 (12-22-1870) F
Jones, Catharine E. to William M. Craddock 11-1-1852 (11-3-1852) G
Jones, Catharine to D. C. Nixon 4-7-1864 Dy
Jones, Catharine to Henry Bell 5-25-1867 Dy
Jones, Catharine to James M. Richardson 4-4-1855 (4-10-1855) Hr
Jones, Catharine to Robert Ross 11-20-1872 Hy
Jones, Catherine to Benjamin Davis 9-1-1831 Hr
Jones, Catherine to Jas. M. Lassiter 7-?-1836 (7-28-1836) G
Jones, Catherine to Joseph Elam 10-6-1841 G
Jones, Catherine to Paul Umstead 1-30-1850 Cr
Jones, Catherine to Thomas Matthews 1-19-1866 (1-27-1866) F B
Jones, Celestia to James Phillips 11-9-1867 F B
Jones, Celyam to John Emery 6-5-1842 Hn
Jones, Chanie to John Read 12-23-1866 Hy
Jones, Charlete to Thos. L. Boswell 10-6-1837 G
Jones, Charlotte to E. C. Shilicutt 12-21-1846 O
Jones, Charlotte to singleton Britt 6-20-1876 (6-22-1876) Dy
Jones, Cherry to Anderson Steger 2-14-1870 (2-23-1870) F B
Jones, Christian S. to George W. Moore 2-2-1843 G
Jones, Christina M. to Jessee A. Sonthers 5-9-1849 G
Jones, Cinthia to Joel H. Stirman (Sturman) 4-9-1829 Sh
Jones, Clarissa to Robert Clear 1-13-1871 (no return) F B
Jones, Clemency Jane to James W. Jones 10-2-1851 Hr
Jones, Clotilda to John F. Crawford 6-21-1838 Ma
Jones, Cora to H. C. Anderson 1-1-1879 (1-8-1879) L B
Jones, Cornelia A. to John Snead 9-21-1854 Cr
Jones, Cornelia to J. P. Parsons 9-15-1878 Hy
Jones, Cyntha C. to John B. Jones 3-5-1850 Sh
Jones, Cynthia to Josiah Cather 12-25-1866 (12-26-1866) F B
Jones, D. to Stephen Johnson 2-16-1841 Cr
Jones, Darcus to Bennett Bush 8-8-1856 Be
Jones, Daruishia Belmont to William Van Pelt 7-22-1868 (7-17?-1868) Ma
Jones, Deffilue? to John Whiteman 12-23-1870 T
Jones, Delly Ann to John Wiley 9-14-1846 Sh
Jones, Delpha to James M. Mullens 5-28-1873 T
Jones, Dicie to Henry Anderson 2-2-1871 Cr B
Jones, Dicy to Andrew Parr 1-27-1869 (1-28-1869) L
Jones, Dinarza M. to John Williams 9-2-1862 Cr
Jones, Dorcas to Emery E. Williams 11-25-1834 Hr
Jones, Dorothy Ann to Samuel J. Rose 5-27-1847 (5-28-1847) T
Jones, E. A. to Thos. R. Bowers 11-18-1851 Cr
Jones, E. A. to William Culberhouse 9-12-1852 Hn
Jones, E. E. to Blair Pierson 2-18-1880 L
Jones, E. M. L. to T. H. B. Smith 5-16-1861 Mn
Jones, E. S. to Peas A. Smith 8-5-1858 Cr
Jones, E. to W. B. Jones 1-17-1868 G
Jones, E.L. to H. V. McArthur 2-25-1867 (2-27-1866?) Cr
Jones, Easter J. to J. R. Porter 12-6-1866 (12-5?-1866) Cr
Jones, Easter to Isaac Wood 9-27-1866 G
Jones, Eddie to E. R. Anthony 10-15-1885 L
Jones, Elender to James M. Gunter 4-7-1828 (4-13-1828) Hr
Jones, Elisabeth to James Wass? 8-22-1868 (8-23-1868) T
Jones, Eliza B. to Wyatt Hester 12-2-1823 (12-4-1823) Hr
Jones, Eliza Jane to William O. Fisher 12-30-1851 G
Jones, Eliza Jane to Wm. H. Arrington 8-1-1848 Cr
Jones, Eliza S. to Hiram Valentine 4-16-1851 Sh
Jones, Eliza V. to John B. Barnes 1-22-1848 (1-23-1848) Hr
Jones, Eliza to A. P. Womack 1-3-1842 (1-6-1842) F
Jones, Eliza to Author Tolls 2-28-1869 Be
Jones, Eliza to Edmond Rose 11-24-1866 T
Jones, Eliza to Elijah Oliver 7-28-1846 Sh
Jones, Eliza to George McCarty 2-8-1842 Sh
Jones, Eliza to Henry Enoch 7-18-1868 (7-19-1868) Dy
Jones, Eliza to John F. Aslin 1-4-1858 (1-7-1858) G
Jones, Eliza to Noel Spragins 1-30-1844 (2-1-1844) Ma
Jones, Eliza to Sidney Cooper 3-24-1835 Hr
Jones, Eliza to Simon Jones 12-26-1868 Hy
Jones, Eliza to Stephen Puryear 5-9-1885 (5-10-1885) L
Jones, Eliza to William Haywood 3-27-1836 Hr
Jones, Eliza to William Jones 3-20-1867 (no return) Hy
Jones, Elizabeth A. to Thomas H. Follis 12-21-1859 (12-22-1859) Ma
Jones, Elizabeth D. to Simpson Shaw 5-30-1837 (6-?-1837) G
Jones, Elizabeth E. to Henry Caskins 7-29-1844 Ma
Jones, Elizabeth H. to Jesse Waldran 12-13-1843 Sh

Jones, Elizabeth J. to John W. Hamilton 9-20-1852 (9-21-1852) O
Jones, Elizabeth J. to Thos. W. Jernigan 3-31-1853 G
Jones, Elizabeth L. to James L. Quin 9-23-1873 (9-25-1873) T
Jones, Elizabeth M. to James A. Carnes 10-28-1840 (10-29-1840) F
Jones, Elizabeth N. to William Roundtree 12-23-1846 (12-30-1846) L
Jones, Elizabeth S. to James R. Wiggins 6-27-1859 (6-30-1859) Hr
Jones, Elizabeth Susan to James W. Herring 7-10-1854 (7-12-1854) Sh
Jones, Elizabeth to B. H. Brooks 6-8-1856 Hn
Jones, Elizabeth to G. W. Tanksley 1-19-1863 Sh
Jones, Elizabeth to Hiram Erwin 2-8-1836 (or 2-6-1836) Sh
Jones, Elizabeth to Hughie Davis 10-7-1830 (10-14-1830) Hr
Jones, Elizabeth to Jacob Ormon 3-19-1838 F
Jones, Elizabeth to James Davis 2-19-1838 (2-28-1838) O
Jones, Elizabeth to James M. Browne 10-20-1859 We
Jones, Elizabeth to James M. Jones 9-10-1860 (9-13-1860) O
Jones, Elizabeth to Jarvis Jones 11-20-1851 O
Jones, Elizabeth to John Hassell 5-1-1855 G
Jones, Elizabeth to John Johnson 12-15-1826 (1-6-1827) Hr
Jones, Elizabeth to John Skinner 3-10-1825 Hr
Jones, Elizabeth to Joseph Hilliard 10-15-1873 (10-16-1873) O
Jones, Elizabeth to Josiah Hood 2-23-1860 O
Jones, Elizabeth to P. R. Roberts 10-18-1860 Sh
Jones, Elizabeth to W. H. Mathis 12-24-1860 G
Jones, Elizabeth to Will Henson 2-21-1835 Hr
Jones, Elizabeth to William Guinn 6-9-1860 (6-10-1860) O
Jones, Elizabeth to William H. Edmonds 11-5-1854 Hn
Jones, Elizabeth to Willy Allen 2-13-1841 Cr
Jones, Elizur to George Hogue 2-26-1847 (3-5-1847) O
Jones, Ella to Ike Morgan 12-30-1879 (12-31-1879) L B
Jones, Ella to J. H. Rockholt 12-21-1859 Sh
Jones, Ellen to Thomas Bond 1-17-1878 (no return) Hy
Jones, Ellie to Nathan Taylor 6-1-1877 Hy
Jones, Ellinor to Francis Williams 9-24-1836 (9-29-1836) O
Jones, Ellis to Jo Boyd 11-13-1879 (not executed) L B
Jones, Elmarine to Thomas W. Grimmer 5-19-1840 Hn
Jones, Elmira C. to David A. Allen 10-7-1849 Sh
Jones, Elmira to Wm. H. Davis 4-25-1866 (4-28-1866) F B
Jones, Elstuly to James R. Norwood 1-17-1856 Cr
Jones, Elvira B. to John W. McElyea 7-29?-1839 (7-10-1839) O
Jones, Elvira to Benjamin S. Janes 1-15-1859 We
Jones, Elvira to Green Robertson 1-27-1869 (1-28-1869) F B
Jones, Elya(Diya) Ann to Joseph D. Sauls 9-10-1856 (9-11-1856) Hr
Jones, Emelina C. to Joseph M. Dickson 1-5-1849 (1-8-1849) Ma
Jones, Emeline to Jas. A.? Craw 3-23-1864 (no return) Dy
Jones, Emeline to Wilkerson Harris 12-24-1866 (12-27-1866) F B
Jones, Emily B. to William K. Love 3-14-1840 (3-17-1840) Ma
Jones, Emily J. to Calvin C. Hundley 5-27-1861 (5-29-1861) Hr
Jones, Emily S. to John W. Thompson 12-9-1858 Cr
Jones, Emily W. to G. W. Goodloe 12-29-1852 (no return) F
Jones, Emily to Wiley Medlin 9-9-1868 (9-10-1868) Ma
Jones, Emma to E. J. Chaney 1-9-1878 (1-10-1878) L
Jones, Emma to Gregory Warner 3-29-1874 Hy
Jones, Emma to Henry Palmer 1-9-1873 Hy
Jones, Emma to Lewis M. Rogers 7-8-1878 Dy
Jones, Ester C. to John C. Merrett 2-26-1860 Cr
Jones, Esther to Hullam J. Reese 1-22-1846 Sh
Jones, Eva E. to Wm. A. Newsom 9-2-1864 Sh
Jones, Evelin to Aleck Scott 8-11-1866 (8-12-1866) F B
Jones, Exsey to F. M. Dunigan 12-17-1868 G
Jones, F. A. (Mrs.) to Walter Coleman 6-21-1864 Sh
Jones, F. C. to R. C. Bull 10-19-1852 Cr
Jones, F. to Robert E. Jeter 2-20-1850 We
Jones, Fannie to Arther Moise 1-27-1871 (no return) Hy
Jones, Fannie to J. C. Wilder 6-25-1872 (no return) Cr
Jones, Fanny to Ned Wiggins 11-22-1870 (no return) F
Jones, Fedelia to Joseph H. White 10-4-1857 We
Jones, Fender to Nelson Shaw 12-28-1868 (1-15-1869) F B
Jones, Flora A. to G. R. Nicholson 1-30-1868 Hy
Jones, Flora to John W. Bell 5-6-1869 F B
Jones, Frances A. (Mrs.) to John P. Samuels 11-12-1859 (11-13-1859) Sh
Jones, Frances C. to B. S. Simmons 12-13-1856 (no return) Hn
Jones, Frances E. to J. E. P. Addison 4-17-1878 (4-18-1878) L
Jones, Frances L. to Alfred L. Lunsford 12-20-1843 (12-21-1843) Ma
Jones, Frances to Ed Robinson 12-24-1870 (no return) F B
Jones, Frances to John Woods 3-25-1874 (3-26-1874) T
Jones, Frances to Joseph Hartley 12-28-1875 (no return) Hy
Jones, Frances to Peter Hainey 7-13-1862 We
Jones, Francis M. to A. M. Taylor 3-14-1865 (3-15-1865) L
Jones, Francis S. E. to Joseph W. Hooper 12-22-1852 Sh
Jones, Frankie to Armstead Grayson 7-4-1876 Dy
Jones, Georgia Ann to James Gwynn 7-13-1866 (7-28-1866) F B
Jones, Georgiana to Thos. P. Lockett 5-8-1854 Sh
Jones, Gertrude to Charley Lanier 11-8-1877 Hy
Jones, Gilla A. to R. P. Gooch 1-25-1854 Cr
Jones, H. (Mrs.) to W. F. Kizer 10-5-1870 Ma
Jones, H. A. to C. C. Betts 10-3-1862 G
Jones, H. M. to J. W. Brown 6-19-1855 (6-23-1856) Sh
Jones, H. M. to T. B. Harris 12-13-1859 (12-14-1859) F
Jones, Hannah to Neid? Parker 7-29-1876 Dy B
Jones, Hannah to Watkins Hines 12-26-1872 Hy
Jones, Hanner to Booker Reid 3-10-1874 T
Jones, Harriet A. to William Polsson 2-20-1862 We
Jones, Harriet Ann to Wilie Deming 10-18-1853 Hr
Jones, Harriet C. to James M. Smith 3-6-1855 Sh
Jones, Harriet J. to Wiley M. Parnell 10-24-1860 Cr
Jones, Harriet to Edmund Gilbert 12-20-1865 Hn
Jones, Harriet to George Washington 9-22-1870 F B
Jones, Harriet to James Strickland 8-26-1866 Hy
Jones, Harriet to Stephen Lewis Bailey 12-9-1885 (no return) L
Jones, Harriet to W. Brooks Ruffin 3-9?-1833 Hr
Jones, Harriett E. to Lenoir Bruton 11-16-1843 Ma
Jones, Harriett G. to Samuel G. Pegram 7-25-1836 (7-27-1836) Hr
Jones, Hellen to Lincefield Sexton 7-16-1844 (7-4?-1844) Ma
Jones, Hepsey Eliza to William Haygood Glisson 7-27-1852 O
Jones, Hester S. to William T. Grissom 2-17-1861 We
Jones, Huldy to Josiah S. Ford 12-18-1846 (12-20-1846) G
Jones, Ida to Fredrick Daniel 7-31-1855 (8-1-1855) Sh
Jones, Iredell to James Hutchins 4-2-1849 G
Jones, Isabella to J. B. Booker 6-3-1851 (6-4-1851) F
Jones, Isabella to P. H. Brooks 1-22-1857 We
Jones, Jacky Ann to John L. Tugwell 6-20-1861 Sh
Jones, Jane M. to Thomas Rawlings 1-29-1855 (2-1-1855) Ma
Jones, Jane to Allen Carroll 2-2-1826 (2-4-1826) Hr
Jones, Jane to David Gray 3-5-1849 (3-8-1849) O
Jones, Jane to George Hardy 3-16-1867 (3-19-1867) F B
Jones, Jane to Isaac Jones 10-7-1848 Hn
Jones, Jane to Jasper Bullington 12-24-1855 G
Jones, Jane to London Warren 3-22-1870 (4-9-1870) F B
Jones, Jane to Thomas C. Horne 12-15-1854 (12-20-1854) Sh
Jones, Jane to Thomas Lamberson 5-5-1847 Hn
Jones, Jane to Wade _____ 7-16-1858 Sh B
Jones, Janella? to Kinard Norman 7-1-1845 Hr
Jones, Janie to Jessie White 9-4-1871 Cr
Jones, Jenetta to Howard Morton 5-24-1875 Hy
Jones, Jennett to Jonas Watkins 11-16-1882 (11-18-1882) L
Jones, Jennie to Clark Brown 2-14-1884 L
Jones, Jennie to J. W. Hollomon 1-27-1874 (1-29-1874) O
Jones, Jennie to John W. Wiley 9-30-1871 (10-1-1871) T
Jones, Jenny to John Ashmore 12-3-1873 Hy
Jones, Josephine O. to Henry C. Pillow 7-1-1852 L
Jones, Josephine W. to A. B. Ballard 2-8-1860 Sh
Jones, Josephine to N.L. Lyles 4-7-1873 (4-10-1873) T
Jones, Julia A. to W. D. Robinson 10-8-1851 Cr
Jones, Julia Ann to Andrew J. Miller 12-29-1869 Hy
Jones, Julia to Robert Patterson 12-6-1866 F B
Jones, Julia to William F. Hall 12-21-1859 Sh
Jones, July to Jerry Ivens 7-31-1874 (8-1-1874) O
Jones, Julyie E. to J. A. King 12-31-1856 Cr
Jones, June to Larkin H. Ford 11-1-1843 Hn
Jones, Katharine to James Kennedy 3-5-1827 (3-8-1827) G
Jones, Katie A. to W. H. Biggs 7-25-1877 Dy
Jones, Katie to Louis Williams 9-4-1869 (10-7-1869) L B
Jones, Katie to Ruebin Baltimore 5-26-1866 (no return) Hy
Jones, Kidy to Crittenden Wagster 10-3-1838 O
Jones, L. A. to Milton Morris 3-6-1871 (no return) Cr
Jones, L. A. to Peter Koonce 4-20-1874 Hy
Jones, L. A. to W. F. Cowen 12-20-1871 T
Jones, L. E. to William R. Spoon 7-20-1878 (7-21-1878) Dy
Jones, L. F. to A. H. Collier 12-14-1865 O
Jones, L. J. to John Cox 1-22-1868 O
Jones, L. J. to Wiley B. Parnell 4-19-1873 (4-20-1873) Dy
Jones, Laney to Robt. Gargus 5-24-1846 We
Jones, Laura Ann (Mrs.) to Thos. C. Cole 1-8-1864 Sh
Jones, Laura E. to P. R. Mateer 9-17-1856 Sh
Jones, Laura to Anthony Clay 1-20-1876 L
Jones, Laura to R. J. Flanigan 8-26-1874 (8-27-1874) T
Jones, Laura to Wm. H. Taliaferro 2-6-1866 Hy
Jones, Laura to Wm. McAdoo 2-2-1866 (2-4-1866) Cr
Jones, Laviney to John M. Irvin 10-20-1853 Ma
Jones, Leander Caroline to Abram Hancock 3-19-1851 (3-20-1851) G
Jones, Lee to Joihn Baird 10-17-1868 G B
Jones, Leilia R. to Jason B. Sheffield 12-18-1871 (12-19-1871) O
Jones, Lelila to Finis E. Jones 6-25-1859 Hn
Jones, Leonah to Willis Eaton 2-4-1869 F B
Jones, Letta A. to Burton Winburn 7-7-1874 Hy
Jones, Linington to Watkins Moore 2-2-1843 G
Jones, Lizzie to Isaac Fisher 11-18-1874 Hy
Jones, Lizzie to Raphe Douglass 12-26-1879 Dy
Jones, Lola to T. S. Talley 6-20-1878 Dy
Jones, Louisa F. to Sylvester G. Parker 9-10-1851 (9-11-1851) Hr
Jones, Louisa to Marion Johnson 4-19-1866 O
Jones, Louisa to S. W. Lott 4-6-1875 (no return) Hy
Jones, Louisa to William A. Cowgill 6-25-1848 Sh

Jones, Louisa to William C. Wardlowe 9-1-1864 Mn
Jones, Louisiana L. to William K. Love 4-21-1836 G
Jones, Lucinda P. to Francis A. Follis 10-23-1860 (10-25-1860) Ma
Jones, Lucinda to Daniel Brown 12-29-1843 (12-31-1843) Hr
Jones, Lucinda to Thomas R. Hervey(Harvey?) 5-29-1848 (6-1-1848) Hr
Jones, Lucretia to Bud (Bird) Mullen 8-30-1823 Sh
Jones, Lucy Ann to Jesse B. Cobb 12-22-1847 (12-28-1847) Hr
Jones, Lucy Ann to M. B. Cook 1-24-1828 Ma
Jones, Lucy J. to C. M. Wheeler 10-9-1857 G
Jones, Lucy J. to O. M. Alsup 10-17-1844 Sh
Jones, Lucy to Henderson Morton 11-16-1867 G B
Jones, Lucy to Henry Shaw 12-4-1879 L B
Jones, Luella to Miles Rice 12-31-1868 F B
Jones, Lugenia to Thomas R. Milam 9-13-1850 Hn
Jones, Lutitia to Samuel Young 4-28-1855 (4-30-1855) Hr
Jones, Lyda to Louis Scurry 1-11-1866 T
Jones, Lydie to Charley Henry 3-9-1876 (no return) Hy
Jones, M. A. to Edward Nailling 2-27-1860 (2-29-1860) O
Jones, M. A. to J. W. Gaulden 12-20-1864 (12-21-1864) Dy
Jones, M. A. to L. B. Abbott 12-14-1866 (no return) Cr
Jones, M. A. to W. M. Wallace 12-20-1877 Hy
Jones, M. B. to C. B. Cole 6-9-1863 (6-10-1863) O
Jones, M. C. to T. A. Lawrence 9-13-1863 Hn
Jones, M. C. to W. T. Baird 2-4-1867 (2-12-1867) Cr
Jones, M. E. R. to W. L. Stricklin 1-26-1863 Mn
Jones, M. E. to F. M. Upchurch 1-21-1864 (no return) Hn
Jones, M. E. to W. H. Cowell 2-26-1872 Dy
Jones, M. F. to C. J. A. Brasfield 10-1-1855 (no return) We
Jones, M. J. to C. H. Smith 9-24-1869 Dy
Jones, M. J. to J. P. Bradberry 10-28-1866 G
Jones, M. L. J. to J. F. Allgee 1-1-1870 (1-2-1870) Cr
Jones, M. L. to Atwood Pierson 2-18-1880 L
Jones, M. O. to E. M. Widick 12-9-1868 Hy
Jones, M. P. to James R. Haralston 1-5-1858 Sh
Jones, M. T. to F. M. Cheek 10-13-1856 Hn
Jones, Maattie to James Williams 1-1-1873 (1-2-1873) T
Jones, Mabel to Lafayette Pitts 12-11-1867 (12-12-1867) Dy
Jones, Macy to J. T. Burnett 8-29-1865 Hy
Jones, Maggie to John Jordan 10-18-1870 (no return) F B
Jones, Malissa to William Isom 4-23-1874 (4-24-1874) L B
Jones, Manerva A. (Mrs.) to Moses Gillespie 3-18-1864 Sh
Jones, Manervie J. to Thomas H. Davis 9-8-1857 We
Jones, Margaret A. to Samuel S. Hurt 12-22-1863 (12-21?-1863) T
Jones, Margaret B. to James M. Clark 12-4-1848 Cr
Jones, Margaret C. to Hugh R. Cunningham 5-13-1851 Hn
Jones, Margaret E. to W. S. Lawson 7-19-1864 Sh
Jones, Margaret Elizabeth M to Robert Gillaspie 11-15-1851 Sh
Jones, Margaret to Charles Brooks 11-26-1883 (no return) L
Jones, Margaret to J. W. Argo 10-17-1859 Cr
Jones, Margaret to John Brown 2-20-1873 (no return) Hy
Jones, Margaret to John R. Matthews 12-19-1853 (12-22-1853) Sh
Jones, Margaret to Marshall Hunter 6-21-1867 (7-13-1867) F B
Jones, Margaret to Robert Dawson 1-12-1871 (no return) F B
Jones, Margarett A. to Aqula J. Goodloe 12-23-1843 (12-27-1843) G
Jones, Margarett Ann to Andrew J. Goodlow 8-17-1843 Ma
Jones, Margarett to I. T. C. Long 12-7-1866 O
Jones, Margarette to Allen Walker 7-29-1846 O
Jones, Margarette to Edwin Gay 7-19-1855 (11-11-1855) Hr
Jones, Margrett E. to James Henry White 2-8-1870 (2-9-1870) Dy
Jones, Maria to Roland McKinny 12-28-1853 Sh
Jones, Maria to Tom Morrow 1-7-1867 (1-10-1867) F B
Jones, Maria to Wm. McNabb 6-24-1845 Sh
Jones, Mariah to Nathan Martain 1-25-1873 (1-28-1873) T
Jones, Mariah to Sye Young 10-31-1868 (11-1-1868) F B
Jones, Marina Jane to William Self 2-12-1873 (2-13-1873) Dy
Jones, Maring to John Stephens 5-5-1841 (5-17-1841) Ma
Jones, Martha A. F. to John M. Davis 11-27-1824 Hr
Jones, Martha A. to E. D. Hudson 5-8-1877 (5-14-1877) Dy
Jones, Martha A. to J. G. Gambill 1-31-1867 Dy
Jones, Martha A. to Jesse Sutherland 5-6-1857 We
Jones, Martha A. to William A. Seawright 10-29-1862 Hn
Jones, Martha C. to Rascar R. Cole 12-29-1852 Sh
Jones, Martha C. to William Crow 1-29-1858 Sh
Jones, Martha E. to David A. Haynes 3-6-1851 Hn
Jones, Martha E. to J. W. Stricklin 4-23-1861 (4-24-1861) Hr
Jones, Martha F. to John W. Hill 12-6-1856 (12-7-1856) O
Jones, Martha G. to Robert S. Boyd 7-17-1861 (7-18-1861) Cr
Jones, Martha Helen to Elijah Snow 5-10-1862 (5-18-1862) Dy
Jones, Martha J. to A. J. Roach 11-23-1852 Sh
Jones, Martha J. to John W. Goodin 5-6-1859 Hn
Jones, Martha J. to William Grimes 2-6-1846 Ma
Jones, Martha Jane to George N. Hubbard 12-31-1862 (no return) Hy
Jones, Martha M. to James H. Winston 1-11-1843 (1-12-1843) Ma
Jones, Martha M. to W. A. Ryder 5-5-1860 O
Jones, Martha W. to Stuart McMullen 10-4-1869 (10-6-1869) F
Jones, Martha to A. J. Fletcher 7-28-1858 G
Jones, Martha to Allen Parr 12-8-1840 G

Jones, Martha to Buck McNeil 1-6-1866 (1-14-1866) F B
Jones, Martha to Frederick Bryant 7-27-1831 G
Jones, Martha to Henry McNeil 12-28-1865 (1-14-1866) F B
Jones, Martha to J. J. Elrod 8-4-1860 (no return) Hy
Jones, Martha to James Killbreath 1-13-1845 O
Jones, Martha to James Parnell 9-29-1869 (9-30-1869) Cr
Jones, Martha to James Harris 7-18-1868 Dy
Jones, Martha to John W. Abbott 12-7-1863 (12-18-1863) Cr
Jones, Martha to Joseph Hays 12-24-1840 L
Jones, Martha to Joseph Johnson 7-8-1872 T
Jones, Martha to Joseph Thomas 3-22-1877 Hy
Jones, Martha to S. N. J. Pope 7-19-1861 (no return) Cr
Jones, Martha to Sam Parks 6-8-1867 (6-9-1867) Dy
Jones, Martha to Wm. H. Smally 2-20-1850 Be
Jones, Marthy to Lewis Bass 5-8-1877 Hy
Jones, Mary (Mrs.) to John Butler 11-29-1862 (11-30-1862) Sh
Jones, Mary A. E. to James Cooper 4-5-1855 Hr
Jones, Mary A. to David W. Pound 7-23-1844 (7-25-1844) O
Jones, Mary A. to Ezekiel Sanderlin 5-1-1834 Sh
Jones, Mary A. to J. W. King 1-1-1873 (1-2-1873) Cr
Jones, Mary A. to John Zant 11-1-1853 Sh
Jones, Mary A. to Joseph Luker 3-20-1860 O
Jones, Mary A. to M. C. H. Stevens 1-11-1857 Hn
Jones, Mary A. to Wm. L. Montgomery 1-9-1845 Sh
Jones, Mary A. to Wm. Taylor 2-2-1847 Cr
Jones, Mary Abagail to Wm. H. C. McDurmit 4-27-1859 Ma
Jones, Mary Ann Eliza to Rufus W. Bagly (Bagby) 8-12-1850 Sh
Jones, Mary Ann M. to A. D. Lamkins 5-30-1864 Hn
Jones, Mary Ann to George Chipman 12-18-1852 Ma
Jones, Mary Ann to William H. Pate 5-26-1857 O
Jones, Mary Anna to W. Bond Dashill 9-28-1871 Ma
Jones, Mary C. to James A. Bower 1-12-1867 (1-15-1867) T
Jones, Mary C. to William B. Jones 11-3-1842 (11-10-1842) G
Jones, Mary C. to William Capps 2-18-1869 Cr
Jones, Mary D. to Danl. Harper 10-14-1825 Hr
Jones, Mary D. to Lorenzo D. Hamson 2-22-1866 G
Jones, Mary E. to Ben. P. Humphreys 4-23-1873 Hy
Jones, Mary E. to C. B. Heard 8-29-1859 (8-30-1859) G
Jones, Mary E. to G. W. Hayes 9-25-1871 (9-26-1871) O
Jones, Mary E. to George M. Fisher 2-4-1858 G
Jones, Mary E. to George W. Day 10-12-1848 (10-15-1848) Ma
Jones, Mary E. to J. S. Stricklin 12-25-1865 Hy
Jones, Mary E. to James O. Rainey 3-16-1852 Hn
Jones, Mary E. to James R. Davis 9-10-1850 Cr
Jones, Mary E. to John Harris 10-23-1856 O
Jones, Mary E. to Lewis Brown 2-9-1865 Mn
Jones, Mary E. to Lewis Grant 3-3-1858 Sh
Jones, Mary E. to Thomas N. Herly 3-12-1848 F
Jones, Mary E. to Thos. B. Creath 10-25-1849 Sh
Jones, Mary E. to Washington Strickling 1-21-1863 Mn
Jones, Mary Ellen to Chas. S. Taliaferro 6-15-1875 Hy
Jones, Mary F. L.(S) to John W. Baker 5-21-1835 Sh
Jones, Mary F. to A. L. Leftwick 3-4-1861 Sh
Jones, Mary F. to Jas. W. Edwards 1-17-1871 Cr
Jones, Mary F. to John H. Ragsdale 7-28-1852 (5?-30-1852) G
Jones, Mary F. to Thomas T. Harris 11-26-1856 Cr
Jones, Mary G. to Henry Waldron 1-3-1861 We
Jones, Mary H. to John J. Donnell 9-18-1866 (9-19-1866) Ma
Jones, Mary J. C. to T.? R. Wingo 2-18-1867 (no return) Cr
Jones, Mary J. to Felix G. Kinsey 2-11-1850 (2-15-1850) G
Jones, Mary J. to J. O. Alexander 2-29-1848 Hn
Jones, Mary J. to James Y. Reed 3-23-1861 Hr
Jones, Mary J. to Jas. M. Russell 9-1-1876 O
Jones, Mary J. to Thos. R. Pickens 11-5-1857 G
Jones, Mary Jane to Mose? Walker 7-23-1873 Dy
Jones, Mary Jane to Thomas R. Cocke 3-5-1840 F
Jones, Mary L. to D. S. Chaney 11-27-1872 (11-28-1872) L
Jones, Mary L. to William a. Bruce 12-20-1859 (12-22-1860?) We
Jones, Mary L. to Wm. L. Griffin 10-14-1868 (10-15-1868) F
Jones, Mary Pauline to Charles M. Cunningham 2-5-1848 (2-6-1848) O
Jones, Mary R. to Joseph M. Davis 5-11-1859 We
Jones, Mary T. S. to Thomas M. Ingram 10-30-1850 (11-14-1850) Hr
Jones, Mary W. to B. R. Lewis 6-10-1855 O
Jones, Mary to A. B. Tapscott 5-21-1866 G
Jones, Mary to Charles House 12-2-1870 (no return) Hy
Jones, Mary to E. A. Lawson 8-12-1867 O
Jones, Mary to George C. Sawyer 11-16-1857 Sh
Jones, Mary to George Cantrell 9-18-1856 Be
Jones, Mary to J. B. Wilson 9-25-1865 G
Jones, Mary to James A. Boyd 8-20-1850 Cr
Jones, Mary to James Martin 9-25-1869 (no return) F B
Jones, Mary to James T. Watkins 7-28-1858 (8-4-1858) O
Jones, Mary to James W. White 6-12-1882 L B
Jones, Mary to John Jones 12-28-1866 (12-29-1866) F B
Jones, Mary to John M. Edwards 12-13-1876 Hy
Jones, Mary to John Stubbs 7-6-1846 (7-14-1846) O
Jones, Mary to Joseph Wylie 3-19-1846 Sh

Jones, Mary to L. H. Malone 7-29-1851 F
Jones, Mary to M. R. Sikes 3-19-1855 Sh
Jones, Mary to Martin Johnson 6-15-1828 (6-19-1828) Hr
Jones, Mary to Patrick J. Lyons 11-26-1868 F
Jones, Mary to Peter F. Gates 9-27-1838 Hn
Jones, Mary to Thomas J. Waddley 7-30-1851 Hn
Jones, Mary to Thomas Pearce 9-9-1871 (9-10-1871) Ma
Jones, Mary to Tony Jones 5-26-1867 Hy
Jones, Mary to W. H. Watson 11-27-1871 (11-28-1871) Dy
Jones, Maryann C. to Eli Rayner 8-18-1841 (no return) F
Jones, Matilda to Adolphus Anderson 11-2-1866 (11-3-1866) F B
Jones, Matilda to Alfred Williams 12-29-1869 (12-30-1869) F B
Jones, Matilda to Ephran Fraizar 6-15-1865 T
Jones, Matilda to Ephriam Feazur 6-15-1867 (6-16-1867) T
Jones, Matilda to John Jones 2-5-1844 (2-8-1844) Ma
Jones, Mattie to W. H. Grammar 8-2-1882 L
Jones, May to Mack Bradford 6-22-1867 Hy
Jones, Maze to Guid Johnson 8-23-1877 O
Jones, Mildred A. to Perrey Holt 9-12-1842 (9-13-1842) G
Jones, Milinda to Lemuel W. Cruise 10-1-1833 Hr
Jones, Milly to Lee Cotten 7-2-1872 (7-13-1872) T
Jones, Milly to Richard Parks 2-1-1867 (2-2-1867) Dy
Jones, Minerva to C. H. Harris 12-2-1865 (12-3-1865) F B
Jones, Mirah L. to James Green 4-23-1849 (no return) Cr
Jones, Miss M. B. to Jas. W. Lemmon 2-5-1866 (2-8-1866) T
Jones, Missouri to Wm. Massey 11-11-1868 (11-14-1868) F B
Jones, Mollie to Billy Mitchell 12-15-1870 (12-30-1870) F B
Jones, Mollie to J. N. McFarlin 12-20-1866 G
Jones, Mollie to Jessie Palmer 6-22-1871 Cr
Jones, Mollie to M. Tansil 1-13-1874 Dy
Jones, Mollie to R. A. Newell 1-7-1867 (no return) Cr
Jones, Molly L. (Miss) to Wm. F. Allender 3-7-1864 (3-8-1864) Sh
Jones, Molly to Louis McKenzie 7-3-1878 (no return) Hy
Jones, N. A. to Josiah L. Rainey 6-29-1854 Hn
Jones, N. C. to J. H. Moore 7-12-1863 G
Jones, N. E. to M. B. Oliver 2-4-1867 G
Jones, Nancy A. to Henry C. Butler 3-26-1856 Cr
Jones, Nancy A. to Jno. T. Medlin 4-12-1871 (4-13-1871) Ma
Jones, Nancy A. to W. C. Todd 12-20-1866 G
Jones, Nancy Ann to Daniel L. Stockton 8-26-1833 (9-5-1833) Hr
Jones, Nancy Cobb to Gideon Taylor 6-24-1857 Hn
Jones, Nancy Emily to William Vanpelt 7-28-1866 (7-29-1866) Ma
Jones, Nancy Jane to David C. Howell 12-12-1851 (12-18-1851) Hr
Jones, Nancy Jane to Stephen B. Johnson 4-27-1847 (4-30-1847) T
Jones, Nancy M. to Albert B. S. Johnson 4-13-1848 (4-18-1848) Ma
Jones, Nancy to Alex Duke (not executed) Hy
Jones, Nancy to Augustus Williams 10-9-1860 Sh
Jones, Nancy to Benjamin Nolen 5-30-1850 Be
Jones, Nancy to David H. Crews 9-7-1842 Cr
Jones, Nancy to Ephram Moss 9-22-1864 (9-27-1864) O
Jones, Nancy to J. W. Deming 12-15-1845 (12-23-1845) Hr
Jones, Nancy to James Wells 6-5-1870 G B
Jones, Nancy to John Richardson 8-20-1868 (no return) Dy
Jones, Nancy to John t. Haily 12-23-1841 Hn
Jones, Nancy to Joseph P. Poe 10-?-1851 (no return) Hn
Jones, Nancy to Lewis Tucker 11-9-1868 (11-13-1868) F B
Jones, Nancy to Sam Smith 12-4-1869 (no return) F B
Jones, Nancy to Thomas Barnes 3-9-1843 (4-1-1843) G
Jones, Nancy to William Nicholas 10-4-1845 (10-9-1845) O
Jones, Nancy? to James Mills 12-7-1836 (12-8-1836) Hr
Jones, Nannie to Reuben Elkins 7-4-1868 (7-5-1868) O B
Jones, Nannie to W. H. McFarland 12-18-1869 G
Jones, Narcissey to Dick Morgan 10-16-1874 Hy
Jones, Nelly G. to Thomas Gufford 5-5-1844 Hn
Jones, Nicey to Henry Kellis 3-28-1867 (no return) L B
Jones, Octavia H.? to Joseph T. Phillips 12-18-1860 (12-19-1860) Ma
Jones, Octavia R. to Edwin Polk 7-29-1846 (7-30-1846) Hr
Jones, Oliva to Joseph Short 11-13-1834 Hr
Jones, P. A. to George Williams 6-3-1877 Hy
Jones, Pamely to James Barding 10-4-1840 Sh
Jones, Parmelia Ann to Hiram O. Cloys 9-15-1858 Hn
Jones, Patience to Hal Cocke 11-16-1869 (11-18-1869) F B
Jones, Patience to John Crowley 2-26-1848 Sh
Jones, Permelia to Charles Caldwell 6-21-1866 Hn B
Jones, Pernina S. to Tonneleuke P? B. Smith 5-21-1862 (5-24-1864?) Sh
Jones, Phoeba A. to Berry Prewitt 12-24-1867 (no return) F B
Jones, Polly Ann to Robert Waters 3-8-1854 Be
Jones, Polly E. to Nathaniel P. Jones 4-27-1839 Hn
Jones, Portia H. to Lewis Smith 3-3-1842 G
Jones, Presella L. to J. M. Gardner 3-4-1846 We
Jones, Priscilla to John Green 12-24-1878 (12-26-1878) L B
Jones, Priscilla to Nelson Harris 12-29-1870 F B
Jones, Prudence L. to George W. Fudge 4-7-1864 Sh
Jones, Prudence to Samuel J. Rose 8-21-1839 Sh
Jones, Prudence to Wm. Latham 7-3-1860 Sh
Jones, Queen to John Witt 12-30-1869 (1-1-1870) F B
Jones, Quixanna to Eli S. Metheny 8-31-1871 (9-3-1871) Cr

Jones, Rachel C. to P. A. Fisher 8-28-1866 G
Jones, Rachel to Esquire Welch 6-19-1877 Dy
Jones, Rachel to Morris Willis (Willy?) 1-19-1861 Sh
Jones, Rebecca C. to John Holland 12-1-1865 Be
Jones, Rebecca F. to Eli F. Evans 2-8-1870 (no return) Hy
Jones, Rebecca P. to Thos. Leach 5-12-1853 Sh
Jones, Rebecca to Charles Taliaferro 10-30-1862 Mn
Jones, Rebecca to David Hoedy (Hardy?) 1-1-1851 Sh
Jones, Rebecca to H. H. Benton 8-15-1866 (8-16-1866) Cr
Jones, Rebecca to Nickson Emmons 12-31-1862 Mn
Jones, Rebecca to R. S. Holman 3-9-1880 (3-17-1880) L
Jones, Rebecca to William T. Rountree 7-1-1852 L
Jones, Rhoda (Rebecca) to A. H. Adams 5-7-1829 Sh
Jones, Rosetta to Thomas H. Davis 1-11-1848 O
Jones, Rozy Ann to Robert Carter 9-5-1844 Hr
Jones, Rusia to Martin McLaughlin 3-22-1863 O
Jones, Ruth to Wm. M. Irwin 6-24-1837 (6-26-1837) G
Jones, S. E. to J. G. Meadows 10-10-1870 (no return) Dy
Jones, S. J. to J. F. Butcher 6-30-1874 O
Jones, S. J. to J. J. Gore 3-10-1863 (3-11-1863) O
Jones, S. J. to Jesse E. Rollins 9-6-1866 G
Jones, Sallie E. to G. R. Chamagne 1-31-1860 (2-1-1860) Sh
Jones, Sallie R. to George W. Moore 3-19-1868 Ma
Jones, Sallie to E. R. McClellan 3-7-1868 Hy
Jones, Sally A. to T. A. Meeke 5-7-1876 Hy
Jones, Sarah A. W. to Barzillai Hopper 5-24-1859 (5-25-1859) Hr
Jones, Sarah A. to Benjamin Rook 9-3-1866 (9-4-1866) F
Jones, Sarah A. to Crawford Jones 1-16-1855 (1-17-1855) G
Jones, Sarah A. to John J. Goodman 11-3-1859 G
Jones, Sarah Ann to Hayward Roberson 7-14-1867 Hy
Jones, Sarah Ann to James Ralston 10-27-1859 Sh
Jones, Sarah Ann to John W. Kirkland 1-1-1855 (1-4-1855) Hr
Jones, Sarah C. to Geo. L. Jones 1-16-1869 (1-17-1869) Ma
Jones, Sarah C. to J. P. Burrow 9-16-1846 Cr
Jones, Sarah C. to Nathaniel F. Barksdale 5-20-1852 G
Jones, Sarah C. to Willis Leyde 9-18-1865 (9-19-1865) O
Jones, Sarah E. F. to Nicholas Gooch 9-6-1865 Mn
Jones, Sarah E. to Jefferson Greer 6-30-1851 (7-3-1851) Sh
Jones, Sarah E. to W. H. Gresham 12-26-1860 Hn
Jones, Sarah F. to James M. Ray 8-1-1867 Hn
Jones, Sarah G. to Patrick H. Lewis 11-2-1850 Hn
Jones, Sarah Jane to John S. Munn 7-26-1849 Hr
Jones, Sarah M. to Blythe McCorkle 12-13-1855 Ma
Jones, Sarah M. to D. J. McBride 9-14-1854 Hn
Jones, Sarah M. to John T. Boston 9-17-1867 G
Jones, Sarah N. to W. N. Brasfield 2-2-1850 We
Jones, Sarah W. to Stephen D. Ross 2-16-1838 (2-23-1838) Ma
Jones, Sarah W. to Wm. H. (Dr.) Boyce 12-20-1836 Sh *
Jones, Sarah to A. W. Roberts 6-6-1865 (no return) Hy
Jones, Sarah to Calvin Cannady 6-13-1851 (6-18-1851) Sh
Jones, Sarah to David C. Russell 12-4-1852 (no return) F
Jones, Sarah to David Shepley 2-27-1878 (2-28-1878) Dy
Jones, Sarah to Elijah M. Arnold 9-9-1857 (9-10-1857) O
Jones, Sarah to G. W. Talley 8-9-1859 (8-10-1859) G
Jones, Sarah to Isaac B. Lowry 5-4-1863 Mn
Jones, Sarah to Jack Wheeler 3-29-1875 Hy
Jones, Sarah to John Fiveash 12-16-1845 Sh
Jones, Sarah to John Killough 10-12-1830 Hr
Jones, Sarah to Nasibet Petit 6-27-1840 (6-28-1840) G
Jones, Sarah to Poke Harrell 3-12-1872 (no return) Cr B
Jones, Sarah to Thomas Brooks 4-7-1867 Hy
Jones, Sarah to William Pankey 7-11-1832 (7-12-1832) O
Jones, Sellah to Charles Moody 4-14-1867 Hy
Jones, Sephronia W. to _____ G. Nichols 10-21-1857 Hn
Jones, Serilda Ann to George W. W. Crouch 5-7-1860 (5-8-1860) T
Jones, Sidney to Ned McFerrin 1-4-1868 (1-7-1868) F B
Jones, Sintha to James P. McElyea 7-16-1838 O
Jones, Siphronia to Wyatt G. Yow 12-23-1841 Hn
Jones, Sophia Ann to John Alexander 6-16-1866 (no return) F B
Jones, Sophia P. to John W. Mooring 1-15-1858 (1-18-1858) Ma
Jones, Sophronia Cathy to Alfred Britton Jones 7-13-1867 (7-14-1867) Ma
Jones, Susan (Mrs.) to Henry Newsom 7-6-1863 (7-7-1863) Sh
Jones, Susan A. to T. A. Johnson 11-13-1851 Hn
Jones, Susan Anna to J. B. Taylor 12-27-1876 (12-28-1876) Dy
Jones, Susan E. to James C. King 12-22-1866 (12-24-1866) Cr
Jones, Susan F. to W. H. Cole 1-7-1850 Hn
Jones, Susan Isabella to James M. Gilbert 8-9-1857 Hn
Jones, Susan J. to J. M. Stroud 7-24-1871 (7-26-1871) T
Jones, Susan M. to James McKnight 5-5-1841 (5-6-1841) F
Jones, Susan to Adam Dillinger 11-10-1859 We
Jones, Susan to Albert Smith 12-28-1854 Cr
Jones, Susan to Jack Harper 2-7-1870 T
Jones, Susan to Jackson Smith 10-17-1874 (10-20-1874) T
Jones, Susan to John S. Lawler 1-27-1838 Hn
Jones, Susan to Wm. Blankenship 12-4-1853 Cr
Jones, Susanah to Numan Haynes 10-10-1838 G
Jones, Susannah to John W. Edwards 4-3-1860 Hn

Brides

Jones, Susie to A. R. Biggs 11-30-1870 (12-1-1870) Dy
Jones, Susie to William Jones 12-10-1873 Hy
Jones, Sylvia to William C. Easterwood 1-10-1856 G
Jones, T. C. to I. S. Williams 9-9-1867 O
Jones, Tabby to Ed Hill 8-5-1874 (no return) Hy
Jones, Tabitha to Ezekial Atcheson 1-2-1844 Hn
Jones, Tabitha to William C. Handsbrough 10-17-1841 Hn
Jones, Tempa F. to Crawford Jones 10-23-1850 (10-24-1850) G
Jones, Tennessee to Andrew Washington 7-22-1874 Hy
Jones, Texanna to Marshall Holloway 1-23-1878 Hy
Jones, V. A. to W. A. Peery 1-31-1872 Dy
Jones, V. E. to Thos. E. Norvell 9-14-1864 Sh
Jones, Varna to Henry Clay 7-22-1871 (7-23-1871) Cr B
Jones, Virginia C. to J. W. Watson 5-14-1866 Hn
Jones, W. F. to J. J. Walls 2-23-1870? (2-23-1871) L
Jones, Willey to Henderson Baker 2-15-1841 (2-18-1841) G
Jones, Wilmoth G. to J. W. McMullen 8-24-1857 (8-25-1857) Sh
Jones, Winney Jane to Miles Kelly 5-2-1864 (no return) Hn
Jones, Winniford to Calvin Clayton 1-6-1842 Hr
Jones, lla to Addison Brown 4-26-1870 G
Jones?, Ester to Sam Dick 1-5-1869 T
Jonett, Susan to T. M. Travis 12-30-1872 (1-1-1873) Cr
Jonigan, Elizabeth to William Cannon 2-7-1845 (5-14-1845) G *
Joplin, Ann to Richard Pierce 8-9-1854 Hn
Joplin, Elizabeth to William Kennon 10-11-1859 Hn
Jopling, J. A. to W. F. Robertson 5-22-1883 (5-23-1883) L
Jordan, A. E. to J. F. Dunavant 7-26-1881 (7-27-1881) L
Jordan, Aggy to Isaac Caldwell 1-24-1867 (no return) L B
Jordan, Ailcy to John Voss 7-4-1877 (7-17-1877) L
Jordan, Alice to Dolph McDearmon 12-14-1881 (no return) L
Jordan, Amanda to Mark Vanderbilt 11-14-1854 (11-15-1854) L
Jordan, Analiza to Manly Roach 1-1-1852 Be
Jordan, Ann to George Lipe 4-25-1871 (4-27-1871) Cr
Jordan, Ann to Jacob Currin 2-15-1867 (no return) L B
Jordan, Ann to Joseph Williams 3-22-1833 G
Jordan, Barbra A. to B. H. Brewer 2-24-1853 Be
Jordan, Bettie to Joseph Gilliland 2-17-1869 (no return) L
Jordan, Bettie to Wiley M. Baird 9-2-1866 G
Jordan, Bittie to Prince Kent 9-16-1872 (9-21-1872) L
Jordan, CAthrine to Alexr. Moore 4-4-1870 (no return) L B
Jordan, Callie to Thomas Yancy 10-26-1867 G
Jordan, Celia to W. E. Hutchings 12-25-1863 G
Jordan, Chaney to Freeman Mebane 6-4-1869 (6-5-1869) F B
Jordan, Charlotte to Samuel Newhouse 12-29-1871 O
Jordan, Eliza C. to George W. Hurt 12-3-1866 (12-5-1866) L
Jordan, Elizabeth A. to Robert A. Burke 1-10-1859 (1-12-1859) L
Jordan, Emily S. to William E. Green 11-4-1845 (11-5-1845) F
Jordan, Emma to H. C. Scott 1-8-1878 (1-10-1878) Dy
Jordan, F. A. to A. J. Pettyjohn 9-13-1864 (9-14-1864) Cr
Jordan, Fannie R. to M. S. Martin 3-9-1869 (3-11-1869) Cr
Jordan, Fanny to Robert Field 9-17-1870 (no return) F B
Jordan, Frances to W. B. Trotter 1-13-1844 (1-16-1844) F
Jordan, I. M. H. to Edwin A. Graves 8-2-1864 (8-10-1864) L
Jordan, Jama to Alex Musgrove 8-3-1869 (8-5-1869) L B
Jordan, Jane to Boyd Bryant 1-18-1867 G
Jordan, Jennie to L. D. McReynolds 9-4-1869 (9-6-1869) L
Jordan, Josephine J. to John M. Rowe 10-1-1868 Cr
Jordan, Julia Ann to John J. Jacobs 12-12-1859 (12-15-1859) Hr
Jordan, July Ann to Silvestis Roberson 11-23-1870 (12-1-1870) Cr
Jordan, L. C. to A. W. Watson 1-15-1863 Be
Jordan, Laira A. T. to Thomas O. Livingston 2-2-1869 (2-3-1869) L
Jordan, Linda to Major Bates 12-10-1879 (no return) L
Jordan, Lotty to Henry Garmany 12-26-1866 G
Jordan, Lucinda to Henderson Campbell 7-20-1867 (no return) L B
Jordan, Lucindia to Tavner Lewis 1-3-1853 (1-5-1853) Hr
Jordan, Lucy to George Allen White 2-25-1875 L B
Jordan, M. E. to E. G. Harris 10-15-1879 (10-21-1879) Dy
Jordan, Maggie to Joe Johnston 9-25-1884 (no return) L
Jordan, Mahala A. to Jno. M. Ursery 1-13-1869 Ma
Jordan, Malinda to Moses Wilson 6-29-1867 (7-3-1867) F B
Jordan, Malinda to Wm. Collier 9-21-1869 (no return) F B
Jordan, Malissa to Thomas Green 6-12-1868 (no return) L B
Jordan, Margarett to Green Jordan 8-3-1869 G B
Jordan, Maria to Richard Phillips 10-21-1882 L
Jordan, Martha J. to Dewit C. Mitchell 12-3-1866 (12-5-1866) L
Jordan, Martha to Edward Gant 8-22-1868 (no return) F B
Jordan, Martha to Harper Bryant 8-16-1867 G B
Jordan, Martha to John A. Bolen 12-30-1859 (1-3-1860) G
Jordan, Mary A. to W. H. Mathis 6-8-1865 G
Jordan, Mary E. to William E. Green 10-9-1843 (10-11-1843) F
Jordan, Mary Emar to Willis T. Tucker 1-22-1868 Hy
Jordan, Mary J. to W. S. Butler 10-23-1856 Be
Jordan, Mary Jane to George Bowen 3-11-1840 (no return) F
Jordan, Mary P. to Hugh W. Lee 2-5-1868 (2-6-1868) L
Jordan, Mary R. to William C. Nixon 9-26-1865 L
Jordan, Mary to Israel Snead 11-17-1874 (11-18-1874) Dy
Jordan, Mary to Washington Fullen 6-6-1864 Sh

Jordan, Mazy to Jos. Cowell 1-14-1841 Be
Jordan, Melvina to James R. Wilson 8-15-1863 Mn
Jordan, Mira to Albert G. Love 6-24-1839 (7-3-1839) G
Jordan, Mollie to Felix Jones 10-12-1870 Hy
Jordan, Myrah to Dave Woodson 10-17-1868 G B
Jordan, Nannie to Joe Turner 12-26-1883 (12-27-1884?) L
Jordan, Paulina to Isaac N. Kelley 12-18-1848 (12-24-1848) T
Jordan, Queen to Paul Wright 12-30-1867 (no return) L B
Jordan, Rhoda to David Watson 2-2-1865 Be
Jordan, Sallie A. to Manroe Bell 9-12-1867 G
Jordan, Sallie to David Armour 3-29-1869 (4-1-1869) F B
Jordan, Sarah E. to W. S. Chapman 5-29-1861 G
Jordan, Sarah M. to J. T. Hill 1-13-1869 Be
Jordan, Sarah to Philip Jordan 1-22-1873 L
Jordan, Susan E. to B. R. L. Pierce 1-29-1857 Be
Jordan, Winifred to James Westbrook 8-27-1831 (9-1-1831) Ma
Jordan, Zerilda A. to John Simmons 1-18-1854 Sh
Jorden, Eliza to John M. Burke 12-20-1868 G B
Jorden, Elizabeth to dJohn Green 9-16-1838 (9-18-1838) Hr
Jorden, Jane to David A. Bradford 12-11-1861 (no return) L
Jorden, Lutisha to James Jones 1-3-1878 Hy
Jorden, M. to W. H. Cole 10-3-1837 Be
Jorden, S. Y. to E. D. Watson 10-17-1876 Hy
Jordian, Louisa E. to David Hurt 3-6-1845 G
Jordian, Martha to E. W. Hale 11-23-1839 (11-28-1839) G
Jordon, A. P. to William Spellings 3-22-1871 (3-23-1871) Cr
Jordon, C. A. to E. S. Mathis 9-4-1860 G
Jordon, Cherry to Arthur Currin 1-2-1871 (1-8-1871) L
Jordon, Jennie to W. H. Watson 8-2-1869 Hy
Jordon, Mary A. E. to Thos. H. Kelly 12-9-1847 Be
Jordon, Mary to Joseph Cowell 10-9-1847 Be
Jordon, Nancy M. to John G. Martin 3-29-1854 Cr
Jordon, Rebecca to James McFarland 8-22-1845 Be
Jordon, Susan M. to Irvin Finch 12-2-1843 (12-3-1843) Ma
Josalin, Lucinda to F. W. (or James) Elliett 4-25-1864 Sh
Joslin, Elizabeth (Mrs.) to E. F. Elliott 3-24-1864 Sh
Joslin, Harriett to Samuel B. Mixon 9-27-1832 L
Joslin, Lamanios to Thos. J. Wood 3-12-1857 G
Joslin, Martha E. to James Bain 4-18-1878 (4-21-1878) Dy
Joslin, Mary A. to Ely Evans 7-17-1833 (7-18-1833) G
Jostling, S. J. to T. N. Gill 3-12-1870 (3-13-1870) Dy
Jouett, Mary L. to Benjamin P. Gilbert 5-5-1846 (no return) Hn
Jourdan, Eliza E. to B. Vincent 6-25-1840 Cr
Jourdan, Eliza to Henry Jones 7-8-18__ (maybe 1870) G B
Jourdan, Elizabeth to Edmund Deshaze 6-19-1837 (6-20-1837) Hr
Jourdan, Mary to Ellen F. Bryan 12-31-1829 Hr
Jourdan, Ruth to G. W. Hale 8-30-1864 (9-1-1864) L
Jourden, Jane Maria to Whitson Macon 2-7-1849 (2-8-1849) Hr
Jourden, Mira to Richard B. Hutcherson 12-21-1835 (12-22-1835) G
Jourdon, Elizabeth to T. A. Green 12-30-1847 (no return) Cr
Jourdon, Susan J. to Wm. H. McClain 2-18-1860 Cr
Journagan, Jane to Jacob Hughey 8-28-1839 (8-29-1839) Hr
Joy, Ann to Gilbert Bass 2-15-1869 (3-8-1869) F B
Joy, Elizabeth J. to Thomas E. Moore 9-17-1846 Hr
Joy, Virginia F. to Leonidas Trousdale 12-21-1853 Hr
Joyce, Cordelia to Joseph McGowan 11-7-1854 T
Joyce, Elizabeth to Harbird K. Joyce 9-14-1853 Ma
Joyce, I. J. to R. A. Carlton 3-5-1861 G
Joyce, Maniza P. to John C. McCollum 9-9-1854 (9-14-1854) G
Joyce, Mary E. to Snowden H. Davis 10-21-1850 Ma
Joyce, Mary to A. J. Montgomery 2-5-1866 (2-8-1866) T
Joyce, Mary to Dennis Hendrick 4-12-1856 (4-13-1856) Sh
Joyce, Mary to William McDonald 6-20-1857 (6-21-1857) Sh
Joyce, Meniza to James M. Cunningham 7-24-1850 G
Joyce, Nancy to John F. Sinclear 9-11-1843 (9-13-1843) G
Joyce, Sarah E. to Nelson I. (Dr.) Hess, jr. 1-31-1865 G
Joyce, Winnaford to Joseph Cooper 7-23-1858 Sh
Joyes, Elizabeth to Jno. Brooks 1-10-1845 (1-12-1845) Hr
Joyner, Angeline to George Jeffreys 12-29-1875 (no return) Hy
Joyner, Anna E. to David A. Stewart 1-17-1877 Hy
Joyner, Catherine to George Carter 3-24-1862 (3-26-1862) O
Joyner, Cynthia G. to R. D. Casey 12-31-1857 (1-5-1858) Hr
Joyner, Eliza to Jef Clark 4-27-1871 Hy
Joyner, Elizabeth to G. H. Stevens 10-24-1856 T
Joyner, Evilina to D. R. Royster 11-15-1858 (11-16-1858) Sh
Joyner, H. F. to Peter P. Siler 6-27-1853 Hr
Joyner, Jane to J. M. Stephens 11-26-1874 (11-27-1874) T
Joyner, Laura to Henderson Cole 2-12-1876 (no return) Hy
Joyner, Margaret M. A. to Zachary Barker 2-21-1861 (2-16?-1861) Cr
Joyner, Maria to Joe Rayner 12-2-1875 (no return) Hy
Joyner, Martha G. to Albert G. Harvey 5-16-1848 Hr
Joyner, Mary C. to William L. Jones 12-7-1843 Hr
Joyner, Mary E. to J. W. King 11-19-1866 (11-20-1866) Cr
Joyner, Mary H. to Charles A. LeCoq 3-20-1861 Sh
Joyner, Mary J. to David W. Tyre 1-29-1860 Cr
Joyner, Priscilla to Ira V. Bradley 4-8-1851 (4-10-1851) O

Joyner, Sarah J. to Thos. G. Patrick 8-1-1844 (8-8-1844) Hr
Joyner, Sarah P. to Josiah Chambers 3-2-1863 (no return) Hy
Joyner, Susan to J. C. O'Bryan 2-15-1863 (2-16-1863) O
Joyner, Texanna to Nat Chilton 11-25-1875 (no return) Hy
Joyner, Winnie to Liss Light 5-6-1875 Dy
Judkins, Clarissa to Gardner Webb 4-25-1870 G
Judy, Shelton to Lossum Pullum 2-10-1876 (no return) Hy
Jukes, Susan to O. K. Vining 12-13-1854 Sh
Julia F., Smith to James H. Powell 8-25-1861 (no return) Hy
Julian, Martha Ann to Jno. Bettis 6-4-1864 (6-5-1864) T
Julian, S. A. to N. F. Crutchfield 12-6-1866 (no return) Hn
Julin, Margaret T. to Macon H. Freeman 10-18-1854 We
Julin, Martha A. to William M. Melton 9-23-1860 We
Julin, N. J. to John L. Pryor 10-29-1858 We
Junior, Thomas to Doxey Powers 11-21-1870 (no return) Hy
Jurance, Lew to George W. Parker 3-16-1844 Hn
Justice, Annie L. to Felix Perry 3-15-1842 Cr
Justice, El to Neely Moore 10-11-1855 Cr
Justice, Fannie to Nelson T. Davis 4-8-1872 (4-10-1872) Dy
Justice, Liza to Wm. H. McClure 11-23-1858 Cr
Justice, Louisa Ann to William A. McSwain 9-24-1852 (9-26-1852) Hr
Justice, Lucretia to Rufus S. Snow 11-27-1855 Hr
Justice, Martha A. to William A. Wolverton 1-17-1851 (1-23-1851) Hr
Justice, Mary J. to J. R. Sexton 9-17-1857 (9-24-1857) Hr
Justice, Molly E. to Lindsey Sanders, jr. 9-6-1865 Mn
Justice, Narcissa to Sanford M. Rowlett 9-19-1838 (no return) Hn
Justice, Sarah to James Capps 12-21-1839 Cr
Justine, Mary to Benjamine Woodard 12-7-1830 (12-9-1830) Ma
Justis, Bettie C. to W. A. Fuller 1-17-1877 Dy
Justis, Mollie J. to John T. Fuller 1-17-1877 Dy

Kahn, Sarah to Simon Kahn 1-8-1850 Sh
Kail, Nancy J. to E. W. Tyler 8-26-1870 Hy
Kain, Elizabeth to J. C. Orrell 12-10-1862 (12-11-1862) F
Kallis, E. P. to J. W. Riley 2-26-1868 G
Kana, Jane to Michael Dougherty 5-13-1863 Sh
Kane, Catherine to Timothy Downs 6-8-1863 Sh
Kane, Marie to James Burke 1-4-1848 (SB 1849?) Sh
Kane, Mary to Timothy Keough 9-6-1862 Sh
Kane, Susan E. to H. T. Blanton 8-18-1856 Hn
Kannaday, Kesiah to William Smith 1-12-1844 (2-17-1844) G
Karnes, Manirva to Jessee Sandford 2-24-1846 (2-25-1846) G
Karnes, Sarah to J. S. McClure 3-21-1867 G
Karney, Mary to Jeremiah Ryan 4-22-1860 G
Karns, Jane to William C. Edwards 4-3-1843 (5-3-1843) G
Karr, Eliza D. to W. C. Neely 10-31-1857 Sh
Karr, Jane to J. M. Laine 2-16-1846 (2-17-1846) F
Karr, Mary to Alfred Pool 9-15-1843 (9-17-1843) Ma
Karr, Sallie to Marshall Thomas 9-4-1868 (9-12-1868) F B
Kateman (Kattman), Catharine to John D. Herbers 10-7-1850 Sh
Kates, Rianna to Elijah Parish 12-18-1865 Cr
Kathey, Wrady to G. C. Hill 12-31-1855 (no return) Hn
Kathmund?, Elizabeth to Konrad Riden 12-6-1852 Sh
Katterman (Kattman), Elizabeth to John G. Herber 10-17-1849 Sh
Katzenback, Mary to W. E. Hendrick 12-24-1860 (12-25-1860) Sh
Kaufemann, Rica M. to Bernard J. John 4-21-1850 Sh
Kaufman, Sarah to J. Gaisman 3-8-1864 Sh
Kauzler, Cary to Julius Gother 12-26-1868 G
Kavanaugh, Martha A. to James D. Boswell 12-27-1877 Hy
Kay, Eliza to John Robb 12-1-1827 Ma
Kaywood, M. A. C. to H. J. Yancy 10-19-1859 F
Ke(e)llan, Mahala J. to Richard A. Hewatt 1-3-1854 (1-5-1854) O
Keaf, Joanah (Mrs.) to Patrick Woods 10-27-1864 (10-30-1864) Sh
Keahn, Jeanette to Moses Kaufman 10-14-1861 Sh
Kean, Bettie to Thos. R. Polk 2-27-1862 (3-12-1862) F
Kean, Delila to John Owens 2-16-1856 Sh
Kean, Johanna to Simon Downay 9-10-1856 Sh
Keane, Deborah to C. Cronin 3-5-1859 (3-6-1859) Sh
Keaney, Mary H. to D. J. Donavan 12-27-1869 (12-28-1869) Cr
Kearley, Chatarine to Orrin Lambert 3-13-1832 Hr
Kearley, Martha to Amon Y. Rook 1-15-1840 (1-22-1840) Hr
Kearney, Sarah to Robert H. Walton 1-8-1842 (1-9-1842) Hr
Kearns, Mary to J. M.(N?) Green 7-8-1863 Sh
Keas, Mary C. to Saml. D. Woods 1-2-1850 G
Keas, Nancy to William Easterwood 5-13-1852 (5-17-1852) G
Keath, Eveline to D. J. Hawks 12-5-1853 We
Keathley, A. J. to G. W. Keathley 1-10-1868 (could be 1-8) G
Keathley, An to W. F. Pate 4-25-1870 G
Keathley, Ann Eliza to Alexander Witherington 1-14-1859 (1-16-1859) Sh
Keathley, Arvazena to Presley L. Bottoms 7-25-1857 (7-26-1857) G
Keathley, Catharine to James Caraway 3-26-1843 (3-?-1843) O
Keathley, Elizabeth C. to William Warran 5-11-1839 (5-15-1839) G
Keathley, Essey to A. H. McNeeley 7-2-1839 (7-18-1839) O
Keathley, Eveline to R. W. Wilson 1-2-1864 (12-30-1864?) G
Keathley, Mallie to J. W. Gray 2-15-1870 G
Keathley, Margaret to James Martin 1-8-1861 G
Keathley, Mary Ann to Travis F. Graddy 2-21-1854 (2-23-1854) G

Keathley, Mary E. to John W. Holland 12-2-1869 G
Keathley, Mary to W. M. Pipkin 2-17-1857 Sh
Keathley, Nancy to James McNeeley 12-6-1841 (12-11-1841) O
Keathley, Sarah to Isaac F. Crain 9-9-1842 (10-1-1842) O
Keathley, Sina to Robert Warrin 9-11-1839 (9-12-1839) G
Keathley, Sophonia E. to Henry T. Wetherington 10-21-1851 (10-29-1851) G
Keathly, Charrity to David Flowers 1-31-1846 (2-1-1846) G
Keathly, Elizabeth to Jesse Carray 4-16-1838 (4-17-1838) G
Keathly, Louisa to A. B. Harget 1-1-1840 O
Keathly, Nancy to Wm. F. Dill 10-25-1860 Be
Keating, Jane N. to Elijah R. Bower 5-28-1845 (6-12-1845) G
Keating, Mary to Thomas H. Foster 4-30-1865 (no return) Hn
Keaton, Ann to Montgomery Allen 6-19-1869 G B
Keaton, Emily to B. F. Warpool 12-4-1865 (12-17-1865) Cr
Keaton, Mary C. to James A. Stewart 12-12-1849 Cr
Keaton, Mollie A. to J. W. Keaton 1-30-1873 (1-31-1873) Cr
Keaton, S. L. C. to S. C. Dowden 11-6-1869 (11-21-1869) Cr
Keaven, Mary to John M. Edgerly 10-16-1857 (10-18-1857) Sh
Kedd, Mary to Charles McNamee 1-27-1840 (no return) F
Kee, A. M. to Seth L. Mathews 10-29-1857 Cr
Kee, Cath to Sterling Adams 7-11-1839 Be
Kee, Catharine to James Greer 7-25-1839 Be
Kee, Clara A. to James Hicks 2-2-1865 Be
Kee, E. E. to James M. Hix 8-23-1866 (no return) Cr
Kee, Leona to James Black 12-16-1868 Be
Kee, Lilly to Joseph Jones 12-8-1868 (12-12-1868) F B
Kee, Louisa to Geo. W. Law 2-27-1873 Dy
Kee, Louisa to John M. Dunlap 7-29-1859 (8-2-1859) G
Kee, M. E. J. to John T. Blackwell 6-8-1872 (6-9-1872) Cr
Kee, Martha E. to W. A. Gardner 11-6-1858 Cr
Kee, Mary L. to W. C. Blair 10-11-1866 Cr
Kee, Mary to Isreal Sneed 11-5-1851 Cr
Kee, Sarah M. to A. W. Dill 10-25-1860 Be
Kee, Sookey to John Molin 8-8-1860 Be
Kee, Tensy E. to Walter C. Pugh 11-13-1860 (11-14-1860) Cr
Kee, Winnie to James Flake 12-19-1872 (no return) Cr
Keef, Bridget to Michiel Liddy 2-24-1853 Sh
Keef, Martha A. to Claibourn Sisco 2-24-1859 O
Keefe, Alice M. to B. S. Biglow 7-27-1857 Sh
Keefe, Ann to W. O'Brian 1-25-1853 Sh
Keefe, Bridget to William Crotty 4-24-1858 (4-25-1858) Sh
Keefe, Fannie V. to Allen Hoyle 12-18-1856 Sh
Keefe, Julia M. to G. M. Patterson 12-18-1856 (1-1-1857) Sh
Keel, Harriett A. M. to Jno. Henry Jones 12-28-1862 Sh
Keel, Louisa C. to W. J. Newell 4-30-1863 Sh
Keel, Louisa J. to David M. Sherman 1-12-1853 Hn
Keel, Marsilla to J. M. Watt 9-17-1860 (9-26-1860) Sh
Keel, Sarah A. to William Harvey 4-24-1863 G
Keeling, Catherine to Chesley King 1-1-1846 Cr
Keeling, Elizabeth to John Harris 8-29-1843 Cr
Keeling, Martha A. (Mrs.) to Walter Coleman 8-12-1852 Sh
Keeling, Sallie to Emerine Walker 1-6-1849 Cr
Keen, Anilee to Smith Pinson 8-29-1867 Hn
Keenan, Mrs. Nancy M. to James A. McGee 5-16-1860 T
Keenan, P. C. to H. N. Glosson 1-11-1868 G
Keener, Rica to Schyler Roberts 8-7-1849 Sh
Keener, Matilda to Geo. Washington 9-3-1866 (9-8-1866) F
Keer, Nancy J. to M. J. G. Pevahouse 6-24-1856 (6-25-1856) Hr
Keeser, Prudence to Elias M. Potter 5-16-1842 (5-18-1842) O
Keeth, Ceralda to James Wilson 12-13-1872 T
Keeth, Salina to J. W. Coleman 11-23-1854 (12-1-1854) G
Keeton, Susan A. to Charles B. Turner 1-7-1867 (1-8-1867) F
Kehoe, Mathia (Martha) to Francis M. Waldran 2-21-1845 Sh
Keilher, Mary to John Hackett 9-24-1864 Sh
Keim, Mary to Philipp Hask 5-20-1858 Sh
Keinman, Susan F. to David Eaves 9-1-1855 (9-2-1855) O
Keiroff, M. C. to James M. Klyce 4-24-1859 Hy
Keith, Gilly to P. A. Blakeley 8-2-1858 (8-3-1858) O
Keith, Gilly to P. A. Blakely 8-2-1856 (8-3-1856) O
Keith, Lydia to John H. Cooper 9-21-1857 (9-23-1857) O
Keith, Martha to Andrew F. Janes 5-15-1861 (5-16-1861) Hr
Keith, Mary Elizabeth to William Hufstutter 3-17-1857 (3-18-1857) O
Keith, Rachael to Wm. Davis 12-4-1867 O
Keith, Sarah Jane to Robert Williams 9-15-1852 (9-16-1852) O
Keithley, Louisa to A. B. Hargett 1-1-1849 O
Keithly, Elizabeth to G. B. Ham 1-2-1866 O
Kell, Nancy P. to Jimms P. Alexander 10-24-1871 (10-25-1871) Ma
Kellar, A. A. to John D. Roberson 11-27-1883 (11-28-1883) L
Kellar, Ada V. to G. W. Billings 11-29-1882 (11-30-1882) L
Kellar, Alice to Waddie Tatum 10-19-1882 L
Kellar, R. J.(I?) to A. B. White 11-30-1882 L
Keller, Alice to Isreal Parker 12-24-1875 (not executed) L
Keller, Ann to J. P. Bolton 12-26-1867 L
Keller, Bettie to Henry C. Rountree 1-19-1867 L B
Keller, Caroline to Andrew Smith 7-3-1876 (7-4-1876) L
Keller, Catherine to Thomas Willson 10-12-1874 (10-13-1874) L
Keller, Elizabeth to Joseph Maning 2-12-1871 Hy

Keller, Emma R. to Robert D. Roberson 12-22-1879 (12-24-1879) L
Keller, Eunice to John McGlothlin 11-2-1826 (11-4-1826) Hr
Keller, Francis H. to Joseph H. Wood 9-21-1875 L
Keller, Ida M. to Jo. S. Hale 2-2-1882 L
Keller, Joanna to John Frutay (Friday) 8-10-1861 (8-11-1861) Sh
Keller, Louisa to F. A. Mahler 10-10-1860 Sh
Keller, Mariah to Robert Cherry 2-21-1871 (2-22-1871) L
Keller, Mary A. E. to Jonathan (James?) P. Gillespie 8-25-1869 (9-1-1869) L
Keller, Mary Ann to Berthold (Capt.) Marshner 12-4-1862 Sh
Keller, Peggy to John Baker 4-21-1857 (4-22-1857) Sh
Keller, S. J. to Thomas P. Posey 2-27-1872 (2-28-1872) L
Keller, S. S. to J. W. Gant 12-23-1852 Sh
Keller, Susan to B. F. Baines 2-25-1874 (3-1-1874) T
Keller, Virginia H. to John T. Hallyburton 1-26-1858 (2-3-1858) L
Keller?, Sarah A. to Alexander Dunaway 12-24-1876 L
Kelless, Nancy to Morris Griffin 7-2-1872 (no return) L
Kelley, C. A. to A. A. Kelley 1-1-1874 T
Kelley, Christianna to John Gunter 9-16-1841 Hn
Kelley, D. A. to P. G. Kelley 12-14-1870 (12-15-1870) T
Kelley, Easter to George Beck 7-27-1833 Hr
Kelley, Elizabeth E. to James McClerkin 11-8-1856 (11-11-1856) T
Kelley, Frances G. to Benjamin F. Bennet 2-19-1846 Sh
Kelley, Lucinda to John Cummins 3-24-1851 (4-3-1851) T
Kelley, M. A. to L. T. Browder 11-27-1872 (11-29-1872) O
Kelley, M. A. to S. L. Jarrett 6-4-1873 Cr
Kelley, Mahala Jane to Robt. Mathews Wallis 3-11-1856 T
Kelley, Maria (Amanda?) T. to W. J. F. Dobbs 3-3-1873 Dy
Kelley, Martha Ann to Zachariah Ellison 11-3-1842 Sh
Kelley, Martha to Absolum H. Evans 6-30-1847 (7-1-1847) T
Kelley, Mary A. E. to T. L. Faulkner 10-7-1873 (10-9-1873) T
Kelley, Mary A. to W. H. Williams 7-4-1868 O
Kelley, Mary E. to John Pool 6-1-1848 Sh
Kelley, Nancy A. to William Buckley 4-30-1850 (no return) F
Kelley, Rosena to Martin Rohmer 5-24-1859 (5-25-1859) Sh
Kelley, Rutha J. to Thomas J. Watkins 10-28-1847 F
Kelley, Sarah Elenor to James M. Terry 9-20-1858 (9-21-1858) T
Kellin, ____ to Joseph Thompson no date (with Mar 1838) F
Kellison, Caroline J. to William H. Urbey 12-20-1861 We
Kellow, Emma to T. L. Plummer 12-13-1876 (12-14-1876) Dy
Kellow, Matilda J. to Newton C. Bancum 7-11-1861 G
Kellow, Matilda J. to Newton C. Baucum 7-11-1861 G
Kellow, S. A. E. to Willis W. Hall 9-30-1868 G
Kellow, S. E. to Wm. W. Moore 11-11-1874 (11-12-1874) Dy
Kelly, Alee to Johnathan Dausson 11-14-1832 (11-15-1832) G
Kelly, Ann to J. C. White 7-20-1872 (no return) Hy
Kelly, Annie R. to James H. Brogdon 5-23-1866 (5-24-1866) L
Kelly, Anny Elizabeth to Garland Snead 12-17-1850 We
Kelly, Arrilla to James C. Bradford 9-2-1868 (9-31-1868) T
Kelly, Betsey to Harvey Bond 3-6-1873 Hy
Kelly, Bridget to Patrick Riley 4-13-1860 Sh
Kelly, C. Belle to Jesse A. Williams 9-22-1866 (9-25-1866) F
Kelly, Caroline to Abram Meacham 1-4-1869 (1-10-1869) F B
Kelly, Catharine to A. Hurbert 6-18-1861 Sh
Kelly, Easther to Tho. Vernon 3-19-1837 (3-26?-1837) Hr
Kelly, Eliza to Cornelius Daly 7-13-1850 Sh
Kelly, Eliza to James Madden 3-5-1859 (3-6-1859) Sh
Kelly, Eliza to W. H. Eader 12-6-1860 Sh
Kelly, Elizabeth to Billy Williams 10-27-1869 (no return) F B
Kelly, Elizabeth to John Wilson 12-8-1840 Hn
Kelly, Ellen to Martin Gonnelly 7-14-1860 (7-15-1860) Sh
Kelly, Ellen to Patrick Conner 5-18-1857 Sh
Kelly, Elvira to Thomas Osborn 1-13-1835 Sh
Kelly, Frances to Jessee Reed 7-7-1856 (7-21-1856) G
Kelly, Hannah to Patrick Cusick 2-17-1862 Sh
Kelly, Harriet M. to Elsey Humphrey 12-12-1844 F
Kelly, Jane to John Williams 8-4-1867 Hn
Kelly, Jane to Thomas Palmore 3-5-1851 (3-6-1851) G
Kelly, Johanna to Thomas Godwin 8-29-1861 Sh
Kelly, Kate M. to John McSmith 1-1-1861 Sh
Kelly, L. A. O. to Henry Beasly 4-29-1865 (5-2-1865) F
Kelly, Lucy to Charles Chaney 1-3-1852 Cr
Kelly, M. E. to P. L. Summers 10-9-1862 Hn
Kelly, Malinda J. to John B. Baskins 12-16-1868 T
Kelly, Margaret J. to David T. Hodge 8-28-1848 (8-31-1848) Ma
Kelly, Margaret to Brian Sheahan (Sheny?) 6-15-1863 Sh
Kelly, Margaritta Maranda to James Brignadello 9-8-1860 (9-16-1860) Sh
Kelly, Martha A. to Wm. T. Agee 2-12-1857 G
Kelly, Martha Ann to James M. Ward 12-8-1841 T
Kelly, Martha C. to Willis A. Wilson 3-21-1868 T
Kelly, Martha J. to D. J. Conger 2-28-1860 Sh
Kelly, Martha J. to James Haley 10-2-1849 (no return) F
Kelly, Martha J. to Pitser R. Rainer 12-10-1850 (12-19-1850) Hr
Kelly, Martha to James E. McGehee 12-29-1841 G
Kelly, Mary A. to Hugh H. (Lt US Army) Smith 5-20-1864 Sh
Kelly, Mary A. to Matthew Wicker 5-15-1849 Hn
Kelly, Mary E. to C. C. Chaney 8-20-1862 G
Kelly, Mary E. to Wm. Power 11-?-1853 (no return) F
Kelly, Mary Jane to Daniel Richardson 10-29-1866 (no return) Hy
Kelly, Mary to James Moran 6-15-1863 Sh
Kelly, Mary to Joseph Mar 12-16-1858 Sh
Kelly, Mary to Nathan Jackson 6-28-1828 Ma
Kelly, Mary to Pat Riley 4-21-1860 (4-22-1869) Sh
Kelly, Mary to Peter Canahan 1-12-1863 Sh
Kelly, Mary to Thomas Dugan 7-16-1863 Sh
Kelly, Mary to William Baker 7-14-1853 (7-31-1853) G
Kelly, Minerva Victoria to W. (Dr.) Knight 11-7-1859 (11-17-1859) Sh
Kelly, Nancy to John W. West 12-17-1855 (12-20-1855) G
Kelly, Narsissa to David Umphery 1-24-1852 Cr
Kelly, Perlina J. to A. Smith 10-22-1856 G
Kelly, Racheal to Joseph Rhea 8-15-1835 (8-16-1835) Hr
Kelly, Rebeca to Steven Terry 1-3-1853 (1-25-1853) T
Kelly, S. J. to James E. Polston 12-20-1866 Dy
Kelly, Sallie to J. W. Saunders 11-8-1866 Be
Kelly, Sally to John Miller 2-18-1846 Ma
Kelly, Sarah Ann to W. T. Carmack 2-11-1856 (2-13-1856) Sh
Kelly, Sarah C. to Lemuel Williams 8-31-1867 (9-3-1867) T
Kelly, Sarah to Zephaniah Hines 2-10-1841 (2-11-1841) Hr
Kelly, Sophia to Duncan Taylor 1-12-1876 Hy
Kelly, Sophia to William P. Tate 2-7-1840 (7-30-1840) G
Kelly, Susan M. to S. A. McKnight 2-28-1865 (3-1-1865) Dy
Keloe, Eden to Jefferson Cagle 6-25-1866 (6-27-1866) O
Kelser, M. J. to T. A. Julian 10-20-1874 O
Kelsey, Elen C. to W. H. Langston 5-27-1850 Sh
Kelso, J. H. to J. D. Wilson 10-31-1865 Hn
Kelsoe, Eliza to John House 5-28-1861 (no return) Hy
Kelsoe, Katurah J. to Owen Slaughter 11-24-1862 (no return) Hn
Kelsoe, O. D. to D. L. Hines 11-22-1869 (no return) Hy
Keltner, A. P. to S. B. Johns 12-22-1873 (12-23-1873) L
Keltner, Anna to G. J. Underwood 11-19-1884 (11-20-1884) L
Keltner, Cordelia F. to Thomas A. Nicholas 3-14-1868 (3-16-1868) L
Keltner, E. S. to H. G. McCord 1-14-1885 L
Keltner, M. E. to J. A. Keltner 2-27-1886 (3-1-1886) L
Keltner, Mary Ann to P. H. Nicholas 4-10-1866 L
Keltner, Priscilla to James J. Osteen 7-31-1860 L
Keltner, Sarah E. to S. W. Austen 1-1-1863 L
Keltner, T. J. to J. S. Peryear 1-6-1872 L
Kelton, Catharine to Jesse Davison 11-18-1845 We
Kelton, Elizabeth M. to Jasper N. Hardy 1-4-1854 (1-5-1854) G
Kelton, Emily E. to William Laymon 7-9-1857 G
Kelton, Julia L. to James N. Hill 2-2-1854 G
Kelton, Lavina to A. C. Penn no date (with Jul 1841) G
Kelton, Mary A. to James T. Cock 1-29-1855 (1-30-1855) G
Kelton, Mary E. to F. P. Hill 1-16-1866 G
Kelton, Rosetta to Washington Swift 1-16-1870 G B
Kelton, Sarah C. to N. A. Dickey 12-5-1857 G
Kelts, Susan D. to Anthony DeVoto 10-31-1863 Sh
Kelzey, Rhoda A. to John G. Moore 4-11-1855 Hn
Kelzoe, Nany to Saml. J. Andrews 10-18-1845 G
Kemes, Ann to John F. Parker 3-28-1856 We
Kemp, Aly A. to Andrew J. Vallen 2-8-1859 We
Kemp, Ann to Henry Dunlap 12-24-1866 Hn B
Kemp, Elizabeth to Hiram Rumley 3-3-1841 Cr
Kemp, Elmira to Lemuel L. Ray 5-4-1834 Hr
Kemp, Emily to James W. Carter 11-13-1860 Hn
Kemp, Irena to David A. Neely 12-18-1844 Cr
Kemp, J. C. to K. M. Dodds 8-28-1861 Mn
Kemp, July Ann to Jeremiah Massey 7-5-1838 Sh
Kemp, Martha A. to Jefferson H. Womble 2-24-1862 We
Kemp, Martha to A. C. Jarried 4-17-1852 Cr
Kemp, Mary J. to D. W. Clouch 2-24-1862 Mn
Kemp, Mary to Augustus B. Fathey 12-9-1858 Hn
Kemp, Mary to Thomas J. Meadows 3-30-1859 We
Kemp, Matilda to Wiley Wilkerson 3-20-1866 (no return) F B
Kemp, Melinda to A. Brumage 12-12-1848 Cr
Kemp, Nancy to John Gillis 12-21-1843 Cr
Kemp, Olly to William Pitts 10-9-1873 L B
Kemp, Rosanna J. to S. D. Mann 10-30-1860 Hn
Kemp, Sarah to R. D. Baker 5-5-1863 (no return) We
Kemp, Tabitha L. to W. H. Carter 12-26-1863 (no return) Cr
Kemper, Sarah L. C. to Henry, jr. Stoddard 2-7-1859 (2-9-1859) Sh
Kenady, Eliza to Ivy S. Alfin 4-1-1841 (4-8-1841) G
Kenady, F. E. to W. T. McAlister 12-4-1868 Cr
Kenady, Mary to Charles W. Smith 4-10-1840 (4-12-1840) G
Kenady, May to William Martin 10-17-1861 Hn
Kenady, N. A. to Wm. C. Lewis 1-22-1846 We
Kenady, Rachell to John Cummings 3-15-1834 (3-16-1834) G
Kenady, Ruth Ann to James Holland 1-14-1865 (1-15-1865) Dy
Kencall, Margaret J. to J. N. M. Lynch 5-4-1853 L
Kendal, Sarah E. to W. G. Randle 1-29-1857 Hn
Kendall, Arkansas J. to Whitnel L. Cooper 6-16-1858 Hn
Kendall, Caroline to Moses Dyer 2-16-1847 Hn
Kendall, Celia Ann E. to John R. Rumley 1-18-1866 Hn
Kendall, Edith A. to James Stem 10-2-1853 Hn
Kendall, Eliza J. to V. C. Trevathan 3-5-1854 Hn

Kendall, Emeline E. to B. T. Howard 1-1-1853 Hn
Kendall, Isabella to O. P. Ashton 12-25-1867 Hn
Kendall, Jane to Charles Kendall 7-28-1867 Hn
Kendall, Judith to Martin Kendall 4-6-1867 Hn B
Kendall, Martha F. to John F. Kendall 8-31-1865 Hn
Kendall, Martha to Hiram C. Vinson 11-19-1844 F
Kendall, Martha to Leroy Olive 2-22-1860 Hn
Kendall, Mary E. to John A. Allen 11-17-1858 Hn
Kendall, Mary to C. D. Venable 2-1-1848 Hn
Kendall, Nancy O. to William H. Allen 12-14-1859 Hn
Kendall, Nancy to William Palmer 12-4-1845 Hn
Kendall, Sally to Jack Ridley 12-14-1867 Hn B
Kendall, Sarah A. to William A. Travathan 11-22-1854 Hn
Kendall, Sarah C. to Joseph McAbee 3-2-1866 (3-6-1866) O
Kendall, Sarah to B. L. Conyers 3-30-1848 Hn
Kendall, Sarah to Chas. D. Dixson 8-19-1839 (no return) Hn
Kendell, Elizabeth to Samuel Ealand 12-18-1856 Sh
Kendle?, Ruth to John R. Wandle? 7-11-1866 Hn
Kendrick, Ann to Benjamin Pippin 10-30-1861 T
Kendrick, Caroline to Harmon Gardner 1-18-1838 Hn
Kendrick, Catherine to Thomas N. Stephenson 3-15-1848 Ma
Kendrick, E. S. to James A. Dodds 12-15-1839 (12-18-1839) Ma
Kendrick, Fanny to William Pasmose 1-10-1843 (1-12-1843) Ma
Kendrick, Margaret to Jonathan Youngblood 2-1-1836 Hr
Kendrick, Mariah A. to William Bratton 6-28-1838 (no return) Hn
Kendrick, Martha to Felix G. Gibbs 1-10-1845 Ma
Kendrick, Mary C. to James S. Ramsey 4-4-1848 Hn
Kendrick, Matilda to James D. Gardner 3-17-1838 Hn
Kendrick, Sarah to Williamson H. Parham 12-23-1847 F
Keneda, Anjaline to Wm. C. Ridgeway 5-7-1846 (no return) We
Keneday, Emma to John Hill 6-4-1868 G
Kenedy, Elizabeth to Elisha Janes 6-17-1844 (no return) We
Kenedy, Fainy to Elias Crum 2-15-1831 T
Keneley, Alice A. to John Zimmerman 2-14-1870 (no return) L
Kenely, Jane R. M. to Edward H. White 3-31-1845 (no return) L
Kenfall, Louisa J. to Vincent B. Walker 12-12-1854 Hn
Kenley, Nancy to Samuel Sazer 12-29-1846 (1-5-1847) L
Kennady, Mary to Charles Shott 5-5-1851 (5-8-1851) Hr
Kennady, N. E. to R. C. Dickey 10-10-1872 Dy
Kennally, . H. to E. H. Duncan 9-20-1866 Hn
Kennan, F. A. to W. J. Prewett 9-15-1870 G
Kenneday, Lydia Ann to Henry M. Jones 8-30-1843 (9-2-1843) Hr
Kenneday?, Ellen F. to W. R. Neighbours 8-29-1877 L
Kennedy, A. S. to J.A. Foster 12-20-1866 G
Kennedy, Adelia P. to Mike Danaher 7-20-1866 (7-25-1866) F
Kennedy, Ann to Thomas Foley 10-22-1861 Sh
Kennedy, Bridget to David Roache 4-12-1856 (4-13-1856) Sh
Kennedy, Catherine to Patrick Meath 11-20-1845 Sh
Kennedy, E. to Barthly Foley 10-28-1863 Sh
Kennedy, Eliza to Isaac Hays 11-19-1832 (11-22-1832) Hr
Kennedy, Elizabeth to Patrick Lain 4-12-1846 Sh
Kennedy, Ellen to Dennis Quinlan 1-28-1854 (1-29-1854) Sh
Kennedy, Isabella to Anderson Lumkins 9-14-1850 (9-15-1850) Sh
Kennedy, Joana to Martin Fitzgerald 7-17-1852 (7-18-1852) Sh
Kennedy, Johanna to Thomas Gary 3-17-1863 Sh
Kennedy, Johanna to William Keith 10-20-1863 Sh
Kennedy, Lucy to Wesley C. Brown 10-28-1836 Hr
Kennedy, Manerva to J. S. Duncan 11-14-1869 G
Kennedy, Margaret to Joseph Mulcahy 2-13-1858 (2-14-1858) Sh
Kennedy, Martha A. to Thomas L. Killebrew 12-19-1865 Hn
Kennedy, Martha D. to Geo. S. Brasfield 9-29-1847 Sh
Kennedy, Martha to John H. Gauspobe 8-24-1847 Sh
Kennedy, Martha to William Vincent 1-1-1871 T
Kennedy, Mary (Mrs.) to Benjamin Babb 6-8-1859 (6-9-1859) Sh
Kennedy, Mary C. to John Parks 8-30-1854 Sh
Kennedy, Mary E. to J. R. McKinne 2-18-1856 (2-21-1856) Hr
Kennedy, Mary Jane (Mrs.) to Cesario Bias 6-22-1846 Sh
Kennedy, Mary M. (Mrs.) to Wm. Bridgwater 8-2-1854 Sh
Kennedy, Polly to Josiah L. Thedford 9-28-1828 (9-29-1828) G *
Kennedy, Priscilla to Jesse Davis 6-5-1828 (6-14?-1828) Hr
Kennedy, S. A. to S. S. Gleeson 11-5-1869 G
Kennedy, Sarah A. L. to Mathew S. Hawkins 2-7-1859 G
Kennedy, Sarah A. to Calvin S. Moon 3-26-1861 Hn
Kennedy, Sarah J. to Charles E. McWhirter 9-27-1854 (9-28-1854) G
Kennedy, Sarah Jane to A. Fike 3-16-1857 Sh
Kennelly, Ellen to M. McFeadden (McFadden) 1-17-1861 Sh
Kennelly, Mary R. to Thomas J. Hill 7-27-1839 (no return) L
Kennen, Matilda A. to Hillman Williams 9-22-1863 Sh
Kenney, Laura Ann to Wm. Cannon Flemming 4-13-1854 (4-15-1854) T
Kenney, Mary (Mrs.) to Daniel Sullivan 12-21-1863 (1-6-1864) Sh
Kenney, Virginia R. to Julian Bedford 8-4-1851 (8-5-1851) Sh
Kennie, Marion to A. C. Robinson 1-30-1860 Sh
Kennon (Kenmore?), Elizabeth to George E. Moore 9-1-1849 (9-5-1849) L
Kennon, Arabella to William J. Sykes 1-31-1848 Ma
Kennon, Eliza to William Kennon 12-17-1840 Hn
Kennon, Louisa A. E. to Allen K. Brandon 12-2-1869 Cr
Kennon, M. C. to O. B. Cromwell 4-20-1867 (4-21-1867) F

Kennon, Mary A. to Albert A. McAlexander 1-26-1859 (1-27-1859) G
Kennon, Mary H. to Henry L. Elcan 9-1-1865 (9-7-1865) T
Kennon, Mary T. to W. H. Hester 10-10-1856 We
Kennon, Nancy to John W. Adams 12-19-1868 (12-20-1868) Cr
Kennon, Rachel J. to Larkin A. Lewis 12-24-1849 Cr
Kennon, Sarah to Jesse Eskew 12-2-1850 (no return) Cr
Kennon, Susan to John B. Edminston 12-1-1842 Hn
Kensey, Elenora to J. A. Nance 1-26-1866 G
Kensey, Margarett A. to P. Ford 6-18-1858 (6-20-1858) G
Kensey, Nancy to James A. Carroll 3-21-1841 G
Kent, Celia A. to Fred L. Anthony 1-1-1877 (1-2-1877) Dy
Kent, Elizabeth J. to John T. Cain 6-13-1843 (no return) L
Kent, Fanny to Phil Pain 8-25-1870 T
Kent, Harriet Liller to Louis H. Silsby 4-28-1860 (4-29-1860) Dy
Kent, Judith Ann to Garrett Cooper 8-18-1849 (8-22-1849) T
Kent, M. A. to J. M. Poarch 2-29-1876 (3-1-1876) Dy
Kent, M. E. to B. P. Hobday 2-29-1876 (3-1-1876) Dy
Kent, Margaret S. to William E. Maddox 12-19-1848 Sh
Kent, Martha C. to Wm. H. Bradford 12-23-1845 (12-24-1845) L
Kent, Mary E. to S. R. Deardolph 10-6-1854 (no return) F
Kent, Sarah J. to Thomas H. Herndon 5-17-1865 F
Kent, Sarah K. to Peter R. Winningham 10-8-1842 (no return) L
Keoppen, Eliza to Wm. Wall (Mall) 6-24-1862 Sh
Kephart, Margaret to Robert Richey 12-25-1838 Sh
Kepler, Ottillie to Albert Schultz 12-22-1856 Sh
Kerbough, Mary E. to W. E. Sandlin 8-26-1879 (8-27-1879) L
Kerbrugh, A. M. to P. H. Stokes 9-1-1877 (9-13-1877) L
Kerbrugh, Christiana to Thomas Sorel 4-7-1877 (4-8-1877) L
Kerby, D. P. to Richard Carigton 3-27-1867 (3-28-1867) Cr
Kerby, Martha to Wm. C. Childress 12-18-1846 (12-19-1846) L
Kerby, Rebecca to Anthony Haywood Cazort 3-8-1848 (3-9-1848) Ma
Kerby, Sally to Leonard Lambert 2-5-1829 Hr
Kerby, Susan A. to G. A. Jones 11-22-1868 (12-10-1868) Cr
Kerby, Tennie W. to J. P. Davidson 10-18-1870 Hy
Kercey, Louiza to Aaron R. Stone 1-8-1846 Cr
Kerk (Kirk), Margaret to Jesse Barnet 9-10-1829 Sh
Kerksey, Emily to Silas Lassiter 1-1-1857 (1-5-1857) Ma
Kerley, Minerva to D. V. McKinney 10-30-1862 Sh
Kerley, Sarah J. to B. A. Johnson 10-9-1860 Dy
Kerly, Mary Ann to Wm. McGee 1-21-1833 Hr
Kerly, Polly Ann (Mrs.) to Enoch Brewer 12-28-1867 (1-2-1868) Cr
Kern, Sarah to Wm. T. Canmer 1-12-1854 Cr
Kernan, Alice (Mrs.) to John Kelly 7-28-1855 (8-5-1855) Sh
Kernay?, Giley to Larkin Hays 12-17-1829 Hr
Kernel, Eliza A. to Joshua Pool 3-22-1848 Cr
Kernell, Elizabeth A. to Edward C. Scott 5-27-1859 Sh
Kernodle, Julia A. to W. B. Simpson 8-11-1861 Mn
Kernodle, Roxannah to Andrew Malone 8-18-1862 Mn
Kernodle, S. A. V. to B. F. Patridge 1-5-1862 Mn
Kerr, Celia to William Long 6-16-1845 Ma
Kerr, Eliza A. to R. D. Anderson 12-13-1865 Mn
Kerr, Eliza G. to Gabriel M. Anderson 5-9-1849 Sh
Kerr, Elizabeth E. T. to Thomas R. Warren 9-19-1860 (9-20-1860) Hr
Kerr, Emily N. to James M. Patton 1-19-1848 F
Kerr, Esther V.? to Charles Lynn 7-18-1841 (6?-22-1841) F
Kerr, F. M. to W. G. Gray 1-21-1871 Cr
Kerr, Frances to John J. Welsh 10-27-1874 Hy
Kerr, Isabella D. to N. W. Coapland no dates (with Jun 1838) F
Kerr, Margaret to George M. Young 3-13-1850 Sh
Kerr, Margaret to Silas Marler 7-4-1842 Hr
Kerr, Maria to Horace Morton 12-28-1868 (1-3-1869) F B
Kerr, Martha to Willoughby Pugh 10-8-1840 Ma
Kerr, Mary A. to James Perry 12-11-1850 (no return) F
Kerr, Mary J. to Henry M. Pitman 6-30-1849 (no return) F
Kerr, Mary to Joseph Brooks 8-16-1865 Mn
Kerr, Msaggie W. to George T. Kinny 12-23-1873 (12-24-1873) T
Kerr, Nancy L. to Jo L. Graham 11-6-1860 (11-27-1860) Hr
Kerr, Susan to James A. Coppidge 3-12-1866 F
Kerr, Susan to Wm. A. Moore 7-28-1849 (7-29-1849) F
Kersey, Drusilla R. to John S. Mills 6-22-1858 O
Kersey, M. E. to F. M. Boon 11-27-1862 (11-28-1862) O
Kersey, M. L. to J. H. Sandling 7-22-1865 (7-23-1865) O
Kersey, Nancy to Albert Brown 12-22-1847 Sh
Kersey, Sophia Valzine to Nicholas Robinson 11-20-1870 G
Kershaw, Sarah A. to Wm. H. Rush 6-14-1871 (6-15-1871) Ma
Kerswell (Kernell?), Jane to James Davis 6-9-1853 Sh
Kesbitt, G. A. to F. M. Moore 3-24-1866 (3-29-1866) Cr
Keshan, Sarah to John Quinlan 11-14-1853 Sh
Kesterson, Kate to Robert Mertimer (Mortimer?) 4-10-1863 (4-12-1863) Sh
Kesterson, Kate to Robt. Mortimer 4-10-1863 Sh
Kesterson, Lucinda to Zachiriah Richardson 10-6-1832 (10-?-1832) Hr
Kesterson, Mary A. to Buchanan Abernathy 5-28-1849 Sh
Kesterson?, Rebecca to William Blackwood 1-11-1826 Hr
Ket, Sarah to Edward Barton 6-19-1843 Hn
Ketchum, Isadore to Jno. L. Webb 12-2-1868 F
Ketchum, Mary J. to Dudley Granberry 10-24-1868 (no return) F B
Ketchum, Mary J. to J. Perry 12-16-1850 (not endorsed) We

Keting, Lydia to Garland Sneed 6-21-1869 (6-22-1869) Cr
Keting, Mary to Richard Fennesy 1-22-1852 Sh
Ketler, Mary to M. W. Mason 11-19-1853 (11-20-1853) Sh
Ketton, Margrit to Wm. Wheeless 12-10-1846 We
Kevit, Louisa to John H. Reed 7-26-1836 G
Key, Almira N. to Elias D. Barnett 3-22-1848 (3-28-1848) Ma
Key, Amanda M. L. to Richard F. Gaines 6-9-1840 Sh
Key, Caroline to Thomas W. Ray 10-13-1858 Hn
Key, Charlotte J. to J. E. Hastings 11-2-1863 Hn
Key, E. J. to H. M. Corbin 9-28-1863 (10-15-1863) O
Key, Elizabeth M. to G. W. Pool 7-13-1836 Sh
Key, Elizabeth to Charles L. Summers 9-26-1838 Hn
Key, Elizabeth to Henry C. Cloyse 1-2-1846 Hn
Key, Elizabeth to Thomas Smith 3-7-1860 Be
Key, Elizabeth to W. J. Jones 1-23-1845 Hn
Key, Elizabeth to William M. Moody 1-25-1855 Hn
Key, Ida C. to John B. Brewer 9-16-1875 O
Key, Letty to Aaron Asbel 5-29-1850 F
Key, Lucinda to Abner Humphreys 3-28-1844 Hn
Key, M. E. to M. L. Dick 11-2-1863 Hn
Key, Malinda to Samuel Wilson 3-14-1854 Hn
Key, Maria A. R. (Mrs) to A. W. Pettus 8-9-1836 Sh
Key, Martha J. to Ryland Roberts 11-3-1849 Hn
Key, Mary E. to William H. Jones, sr. 9-15-1873 L
Key, Mary M. to William A. Via 11-5-1855 (11-7-1855) G
Key, Mary M. to William J. Brightwell 8-23-1858 G
Key, Mary to John Gentry 8-22-1865 (8-23-1865) Dy
Key, Mary to Leonedas McAdoo 12-3-1864 Cr
Key, Nancy C. to Bemin Pritchard 12-26-1869 Cr
Key, Nancy Parale to John G. Lawrence 11-14-1869 Cr
Key, Nancy to George N. Givens 1-19-1848 (no return) Hn
Key, Nancy to Hyram Trantham 8-15-1839 Hn
Key, Rebecca Elizabeth to James H. Ezell 12-28-1858 Ma
Key, Rebecca to William J. McGehee 1-21-1855 Hn
Key, Samuel to Robert Edmonds 10-2-1838 O
Key, Sarah Ann to William O. Key 12-23-1852 Hn
Key, Savanah to A. K. Newsom 8-12-1868 G
Key, Susan A. to James Johnson 3-27-1849 (4-12-1849) L
Keykendall, Nancy M. to James G. Boyd 7-16-1846 Cr
Keys, Eliza J. to Joseph W. Wyatt 4-18-1865 G
Keys, M. M. to James Ames 8-9-1858 G
Keys, Sarah E. to William B. Rogers 10-28-1858 G
Kibble, M. F. to S. R. Bailey 11-2-1875 (no return) Hy
Kicks, M. to Fielding Travis 10-29-1845 (no return) We
Kid, Molly to Edmond Willis 2-11-1869 G
Kidd, Elizabeth to Cirk (Kirk) Willson 6-23-1864 Sh
Kidd, Emeline to Jasper Black 7-12-1864 Sh
Kidd, Mary V. to W. R. Mitchell 1-26-1878 (1-28-1878) Dy
Kidwell?, M. A. to John B. Hammonds 12-19-1867 (12-20-1868?) G
Kiersey (Kinsey?), Martha to L. K. Norvill 9-1-1867 G
Kilberth, L.F. to T. Higdon 2-26-1863 Be
Kilbreah, Martha to Hutson Taylor 2-19-1868 Be
Kilbreath, Luisa J. to John P. Kirk 2-27-1863 Be
Kilby, Sarah to John Burton 12-4-1873 Hy
Kile, Margaret O. to John N. Harris 4-19-1870 (4-21-1870) Ma
Kile, Margarett A. to R. A. Williams 6-22-1856 Cr
Kiley, Elizabeth Ann to David F. Rider 6-20-1845 O
Kilgore, Lidia to Solomon G. Strothers 7-13-1830 Hr
Kilian, Lucinda to James Hamlin 2-23-1839 (3-17-1839) O
Killabrew, Mariah to George Moore 4-28-1866 Hn B
Killan, Fannie to Godfrey Donaldson 5-25-1872 (5-26-1872) Cr B
Killbreath, Matilda to Napoleon B. Pinckston 12-31-1869 (1-4-1870) Cr
Killebrew, Emmaline to Robert Kelso 1-6-1844 (no return) Hn
Killebrew, Martha M. to Samuel F. Spann 11-16-1848 Hn
Killebrew, N. J. to _____ 1-27-1848 Hn
Killebrew, Nancy J. to James G. Jones 1-21-1845 We
Killeen, Margaret M. to Morris Foley 4-13-1860 (4-15-1860) Sh
Killesinsky, Fredericka (Mrs.) to Charles Hoffman 6-18-1846 Sh
Killet, Miranda to John W. McElyea 2-20-1853 (2-24-1853) O
Killet, Sarah P. to George W. Lane 9-3-1863 Dy
Killet, Sarah to Thomas E. Hall 2-16-1871 Dy
Killfinin, Mary to Edward Keenen 8-13-1864 (8-14-1864) Sh
Killgore, M. A. to J. W. Killgore 1-25-1863 We
Killgore, Susan to Henry Hanes 2-26-1863 O
Killian, Emila to Leonard Mosier 10-21-1840 (5-27-1840) O
Killian, Mary Jane to Alexander Glover 4-28-1850 O
Killian, Mary to P. C. Kelly 5-19-1852 (5-20-1852) Sh
Killie, Nancy S. to Wilson King 1-5-1852 Cr
Killingsworth, Martha to William M. Gardner 3-24-1847 (3-?-1847) T
Killingsworth, Piety to Jesse Applewhite 4-10-1843 (4-12-1843) T
Killingsworth, Rebecca to Thomas C. Mitchell 1-11-1842 G
Killough, Angelian to D. C. Spain 9-21-1852 Cr
Killough, Mary R. to Thomas Rowland 6-6-1859 Cr
Killow, Martha A. to James W. Brown 11-6-1845 Cr
Killy, Elizabeth to Henry Richardson 2-20-1868 (2-25-1868) T
Kilmer, Manervia to Licurgus L. Mobly 7-8-1867 (7-10-1867) L
Kilpatrick, Cynthia C. to Christopher Glenn 12-4-1848 Ma

Kilpatrick, Hannah J. to William A. Glenn 1-21-1867 Ma
Kilpatrick, Harriet to James Cox 5-19-1855 Hr
Kilpatrick, Margaret A. to Henry A. Piffin 9-18-1866 Ma
Kilpatrick, Margaret J. to James Futhey 11-17-1869 (11-18-1869) T
Kilpatrick, Marth J. to James C. Nelson 3-22-1860 T
Kilpatrick, Mary to Sam Jones 9-14-1872 T
Kilpatrick, Rebecca to Medlin Stone 2-17-1869 (2-21-1869) Ma
Kilpatrick, Sarah to William Pentecost 12-29-1846 Ma
Kilpatrick, Tebitha H. to Richard B. Jarmon 12-19-1829 (12-24-1829) Hr
Kilzer, Aliry to John Estes 7-3-1865 G
Kilzer, Sarah Jane to Jno. A. Kilzer 7-26-1867 G
Kimball, Malvina to Asa A. Arnold 10-13-1859 Hn
Kimball, Margaret A. to Albert C. Wurzbach 5-15-1847 Sh
Kimball, Sarah J. to Edmond J. Orgain 2-5-1850 (2-7-1850) Ma
Kimbel, Elvira E. to James Glisson 9-18-1861 Hn
Kimble, Angeline W. to John A. Almond 8-30-1843 Hn
Kimble, Mary B. to Thomas Jones 9-21-1842 Sh
Kimble, Mary T. to Edward Lad 10-6-1866 (not executed) Ma
Kimbrel, Mattie E. to James F. Lillard 5-13-1876 (5-14-1876) Dy
Kimbrile, Eliza to Eli Locklear 6-12-1836 Sh
Kimbro, Mary A. to R. S. Biles 7-1-1866 G
Kimbro, Matilda A. to James A. Morrison 9-17-1853 G
Kimbro, Matilda M. to James A. Morrison 11-3-1853 G
Kimbro, Miss R. S. to A. Ravenall 1-7-1861 (1-8-1861) T
Kimbro, Nancy to Andrew Taylor 9-6-1869 T
Kimbro, Rebecca E. to James M. Halford 2-9-1847 G
Kimbro, Sally to R. E. McDaniel 6-9-1866 G
Kimbrough, Ann to Anderson B. Carr 7-24-1825 Sh
Kimbrough, Betsy to John Grooms 5-22-1830 Sh
Kimbrough, Cely to John Patterson 3-19-1835 Sh
Kimbrough, Emily Ann to Samuel H. Warren 11-7-1839 Sh
Kimbrough, Louisa to Charles Meux 1-24-1878 Hy
Kimbrough, Martha to Buckley Kimbrough 7-24-1825 Sh
Kimbrough, Martha to Green Scritchfield 9-1-1830 Sh
Kimbrough, Mary E. to W. F. Sigman 2-14-1838 Sh
Kimbrough, Mary to Warren Patterson 4-8-1836 Sh
Kimbrough, Nancy to David Aldridge 7-25-1841 Sh
Kimbrough, Narcissa to Peter Ammon 1-10-1833 Sh
Kimbrough, S. M. to G. W. Martin 11-19-1870 (no return) Hy
Kimbrough, Sarah to Bloomfield Boden 1-19-1838 (no return) Hn
Kimbrough, Sarah to Joseph Graham 11-4-1828 Sh
Kimey, Mary Margaret to William Justice 12-20-1856 (12-23-1856) T
Kinan?, Mary to Harrison Buck 3-17-1867 G
Kinard, Lydia Ann to William Hamlin 12-7-1846 Hr
Kincade, Jane to Robert D. Onley 12-23-1847 (no return) Hn
Kincaid, Ann E. to Willie B. Wadkins 4-14-1829 Ma
Kincaid, Delila Ann to Richard Ridgeway 1-5-1829 (1-8-1829) O
Kincaid, Ellen to Abram Bramlin 8-24-1871 O B
Kincaid, Jane to Thomas Stevens 1-31-1829 Ma
Kincaid, Maggie to Mansell Dover 7-6-1870 (7-14-1870) F
Kincaid, Nancy Amanda to David Patterson 9-30-1857 (10-1-1857) Ma
Kincaide, Lucinda E. to John Milling 5-11-1869 Ma
Kind, Mary to Green Moore 1-17-1855 Ma
Kindell, S. E. to M. S. Morrow 5-14-1863 (no return) We
Kindle, Cordie to Davie Davis 4-16-1873 (4-17-1873) T
Kindreck, Bettie to H. S. Pippins 9-6-1869 (9-7-1869) F
Kindred, Martha Sarah to George LaVoc 2-28-1856 G
Kindred, Mollie M. to A. B. Anderson 7-24-1866 Hn
Kindred, Nancy J. to Junior Burchett 1-27-1855 O
Kindrick, Nancy R. to George W. Henry 2-17-1855 (2-21-1855) Hr
Kindrick, Polly to Aaron Freeman 8-23-1853 (8-24-1853) Hr
Kine, Catharine to Martin Hay 6-24-1858 Sh
King, A. A. to John Brown 1-13-1854 (1-20-1854) Sh
King, A. C. to C. G. Johnson 7-2-1866 (7-3-1866) Dy
King, A. J. to J. W. Morris 9-23-1873 (9-24-1873) Dy
King, Agnes to Samuel Irvin 1-13-1844 (1-14-1844) F
King, Alice Z. to W. W. McCoy 9-13-1871 Dy
King, Amanda J. to J. D. Reynolds 3-30-1875 (4-1-1875) Dy
King, Ann E. to W. S. Scott 1-28-1874 (1-29-1874) Dy
King, Ann to Hiram B. Jones 1-31-1867 (2-1-1867) F
King, Ann to James M. Hart 7-28-1854 Ma *
King, Ann to John Cocke 3-22-1839 Sh
King, Annie to WM. Hollen 1-4-1878 (no return) Hy
King, Armasa to Thomas J. Collins 1-11-1841 (1-13-1841)] Hr
King, Arsena to William Oliver 10-21-1846 (10-22-1846) Hr
King, B. L. to James Pruett 3-8-1871 Cr
King, Bettie to J. F. Mills 9-29-1871 (10-3-1871) Dy
King, Bettie to Otey Scroggins 9-5-1868 (no return) L B
King, Biddy to William Scott 9-24-1846 (9-26-1846) G
King, Bridget to Barnett Kelly 11-26-1857 Sh
King, Bridget to Patrick Garvey 11-27-1861 (11-28-1861) Sh
King, C. W. to N. L. Joyner 7-6-1865 Cr
King, Cardilea A. to John C. Haywood 11-22-1866 (11-24-1866) Cr
King, Caroline E. to William B. Rigby 6-7-1854 (no return) Hn
King, Catharin to D. R. Adams 5-14-1866 (5-17-1866) Cr
King, Catharine to Jerimiah Harris 3-22-1836 Hr
King, Charity to Zachariah Goforth 6-2-1855 Be

King, Clay to N. W. K. Cotton 7-20-1878 Hy
King, Cytnha A. to Eli Blackburn Howell 12-2-1869 G
King, Delila to Carrol Anderson 7-20-1843 Sh
King, Dicey to Seaborn J. Stewart 1-14-1845 (1-19-1845) Ma
King, Dolly Ann to W. W. Ellis 11-8-1865 Be
King, Dora to W. T. Hunt 12-15-1869 Hy
King, E. A. to James F. Troy 8-25-1866 (8-26-1866) Dy
King, E. R. to D. C. Clark 5-16-1865 (no return) Hy
King, Eady to Samuel Duffey 10-22-1862 (10-23-1862) Ma
King, Elisa Ann to H. W. Crabb 11-29-1868 Be
King, Eliza J. to William A. Jones 12-23-1849 Sh
King, Eliza Jane to Robt. Glidewell 8-5-1845 (8-10-1845) Hr
King, Eliza to Isham Easley 11-16-1876 Hy
King, Eliza to Thos. J. Reynolds 10-26-1872 (10-27-1872) Dy
King, Eliza to Z. C. Nolen 2-9-1871 Hy
King, Elizabeth C. to Joseph G. Barding 7-15-1856 Sh
King, Elizabeth to E. C. Freeman 1-18-1854 Cr
King, Elizabeth to Harvy Leslee 12-30-1866 Be
King, Elizabeth to Isaac Hammon 11-2-1830 Hr
King, Elizabeth to James Lowry 4-5-1860 Hn
King, Elizbeth to Samuel Hollinsworth 7-23-1845 Hn
King, Ella to Paul Thompson 10-2-1878 Sh
King, Ellin to Joseph H. Yarbro 12-24-1845 (no return) F
King, Elvira to Howard Rowlin 7-28-1839 Cr
King, Emeline A. to W. L. Willis 11-5-1860 G
King, Emma to Z. C. jr. Nolen 1-29-1878 Hy
King, Eva A. to Robert I. Coles 8-6-1866 O
King, Everline to L. C. Robison 12-5-1871 (no return) Cr
King, F. M. to W. R. Massey 12-31-1865 G
King, Fannie to Dan Combs 3-4-1868 (1-1-1869) Cr
King, Fanny to Cary Thompson 5-2-1867 (5-5-1867) F B
King, Florence to William C. Dawson 7-22-1869 Hy
King, Frances to Richardson Harris 12-31-1868 (1-1-1869) Cr
King, Francis H. to John B. McLary 6-27-1829 F
King, Harriet C. to John C. Moore 4-22-1852 Cr
King, Harriet to Daniel Hicks 5-1-1871 Ma
King, Henrietta M. to W. L. Chambliss 5-23-1859 Sh
King, Isabella Clemintine to Dawson D. Newman 12-15-1843 (12-21-1843) Ma
King, Isabella to Bryant Carraway 1-9-1851 G
King, Jane to A. Lawrance 10-10-1854 Cr
King, Jane to Garland Taliaferro 9-4-1878 Hy
King, Jane to Solomon P. Wright 4-15-1841 O
King, Jane to William Robins 12-17-1840 F
King, Jennie to Ned Dupree 1-27-1874 Hy
King, Josephine to Thomas J. Cowgill 7-21-1853 Sh
King, Juantha B. to M. H. Adams 5-8-1863 Hn
King, Julia A. E. to Thomas A. Cock 5-14-1849 (5-15-1849) Ma
King, Julia to Wm. Mitchell 3-8-1877 Hy
King, Julian to D. A. Nash 5-25-1852 Sh
King, Julie E. to Z. B. Rose 1-2-1867 (no return) Cr
King, Keady to William A. Duffie 12-17-1846 (12-20-1846) Ma
King, L. D. to S. B. Gilkey 7-2-1863 (no return) Cr
King, L. E. to P. W. Starks 9-7-1855 We
King, L. V. to W. P. Cox 12-23-1873 (12-25-1873) O
King, Larcind E. to Arin Martin 7-6-1857 Cr
King, Lavenia to William S. Tyre 11-12-1846 Sh
King, Lenora to John F. Bell 12-24-1864 G
King, Lettie to John Jahuka 4-25-1859 Sh
King, Lillian C. to Seth L. Thornton 12-3-1867 (no return) Dy
King, Lillie to A. J. Crews 1-7-1869 G
King, Lou to Adam Estes 12-23-1869 (no return) L
King, Louisa M. to E. D. L. Tims 7-10-1861 Hr
King, Louisa to Robert Churchwell 4-3-1856 Sh
King, M. A. to S. L. Thornton 11-18-1874 (11-19-1874) Dy
King, M. C. to A. J. Crow 10-14-1872 Dy
King, M. C. to L. C. Kyle 2-6-1873 Cr
King, M. E. to M. R. Lewis 9-10-1875 (9-12-1875) Dy
King, M. E. to W. A. Hall 2-11-1867 (2-12-1867) Cr
King, M. F. to John W. Dickey 12-7-1857 (12-10-1857) Sh
King, M. J. to J. H. Smith 1-23-1860 Hy
King, M. J. to Saml. Rives 5-31-1866 O
King, M. J. to Stephen H. Dawson(Damson) 1-20-1845 Hr
King, M. J. to W. F. Holland 11-18-1867 (11-19-1867) Dy
King, Malissa Ann to M. G. Noen 4-12-1866 Hn
King, Margaret Ann to Benj. C. Long 5-28-1868 Ma
King, Margaret E. to A. W. Dumas 1-27-1869 T
King, Margaret to Elijah Kilzoe 2-20-1845 (2-23-1845) G
King, Margaret to John S. Duffey 2-12-1852 Ma
King, Margaret to Richd. Davenport 8-31-1867 (9-13-1867) Dy
King, Martha A. to F. L. Garner 10-19-1846 (no return) Cr
King, Martha Ann to Henry Winchester 12-24-1867 (12-25-1867) Dy
King, Martha Ann to Julius C. Harris 2-28-1859 (3-3-1859) Ma
King, Martha F. to Henry J. Ellis 8-27-1860 We
King, Martha J. to W. S. Walker 8-12-1869 (8-13-1869) Dy
King, Martha Jane to William N. Fussell 9-11-1866 (9-13-1866) Ma
King, Martha to Buster Turpin 9-10-1881 (no return) L B
King, Martha to Eli M. Bell 4-16-1845 Sh
King, Martha to John L. Brockman 12-27-1865 (12-28-1865) Dy
King, Martha to Solomon Smith 3-12-1848 Sh
King, Martha to Thomas Hankison? 6-29-1852 (7-1-1852) T
King, Mary A. C. to George T. Moore 12-4-1848 (no return) Hn
King, Mary A. M. to N. M. Ozment 2-1-1860 (2-2-1860) Hr
King, Mary A. to Isaac R. Burrow 12-23-1847 G
King, Mary A. to T. L. Tayler 6-18-1873 Cr
King, Mary Ann to Elias Boatwright 12-8-1868 (12-8-1869?) L
King, Mary Ann to Elijah Short 3-11-1843 (3-7?-1843) Hr
King, Mary Ann to Russell Conlee 8-15-1833 (8-16-1833) G
King, Mary Ann to William I. G. King 10-11-1838 Ma
King, Mary C. to Jeptha L. Fowlkes 5-30-1850 Sh
King, Mary E. to Samuel P. Reece 1-7-1861 (1-9-1861) Cr
King, Mary F. to Isaac Baker 8-1-1853 (8-2-1853) Hr
King, Mary F. to Jno. W. Walters 1-1-1869 (1-3-1869) Ma
King, Mary H. to Elwood Moore 9-25-1861 (9-29-1861) Cr
King, Mary L. to Alfred King 11-27-1839 (11-28-1839) Ma
King, Mary M. to Timothy S. Moody 9-2-1857 Hn
King, Mary to Abraham Holland 3-7-1874 (3-8-1874) L
King, Mary to Benjamin Gates 1-9-1841 Sh
King, Mary to David C. Keny 2-22-1858 We
King, Mary to E. C. Parker 3-12-1856 Sh
King, Mary to James Hassal 8-31-1840 Hr
King, Mary to James Y. Massey 2-13-1855 Cr
King, Mary to Nat Jordan 2-12-1873 Hy
King, Maryann to C. K. Thompson 12-16-1865 (12-18-1865) Cr
King, Matha to Frank Watkins 1-30-1873 Hy
King, Matilda Jane to Martin Edwards 8-12-1866 G
King, Mattie A. to R. B. Bledsoe 2-11-1869 G
King, Mattie J. to Richard L. Jones 11-15-1859 (11-17-1859) Sh
King, May Ann to Lafayette Moize 7-4-1850 (7-10-1850) Ma
King, Melinda to Robert D. Jackson 10-5-1835 Hr
King, Mervia to Elijah E. Cruise 11-1-1853 Cr
King, Mittie to Bedford Richerson 1-12-1870 Hy
King, Mollie to Daniel Moore 7-6-1872 (no return) Hy
King, N. C. to B. F. Ellender 9-15-1860 (9-16-1860) Cr
King, Nancy A. to James A. Rochell 12-11-1843 (no return) We
King, Nancy Angeline to J. V. Sheppard 5-13-1852 O
King, Nancy Ann to John A. Cole 1-3-1865 O
King, Nancy C. L.? to John Collins 8-2-1865 (8-4-1865) Cr
King, Nancy to Andrew Hoover 9-8-1843 O
King, Nancy to Daniel J. Mason 9-12-1852 Cr
King, Nancy to Isaac Esry 3-8-1851 (4-7-1851) O
King, Nancy to James L. Cannon 9-21-1852 O
King, Nancy to John H. Warmack 1-28-1853 Be
King, Nellie to John H. Maclin 3-19-1870 Hy
King, Paralee F. to William J. McFarland 10-29-1850 Ma
King, Polly Ann to Isaac S. Birdwell 1-1-1851 Be
King, Polly to Elijah Coffey 2-17-1825 Sh
King, Polly to Jesse Glidewell 11-7-1842 (11-8-1842) Hr
King, R. A. to T. H. Franklin 11-9-1869 (11-10-1869) Dy
King, Rax A. to Tom Scott 8-19-1869 Hy
King, Rebecca Jane to G. W. Tucker 1-22-1868 Be
King, Rebecca Jane to Sam'l. Craven 1-19-1853 (1-20-1853) O
King, Rebecca to John Jones 12-5-1865 Hn
King, Rebecca to William T. Lyon 1-1-1842 (1-3-1842) Ma
King, Roxie to Napoleon Jones 2-28-1878 Hy
King, S. D. to A. J. Morris 7-1-1878 (7-2-1878) Dy
King, S. E. to W. N. Baxter 7-7-1864 Sh
King, Sallie to Albert Overton 12-25-1874 Dy
King, Saluda J. to W. T. King 6-24-1869 Dy
King, Sarah Ann to Henry M. Mills 7-25-1849 Hr
King, Sarah Ann to William jr. Wilson 12-15-1848 (12-17-1848) Hr
King, Sarah E. to Robert W. Sims 10-10-1862 (10-23-1862) Ma
King, Sarah E. to Wiley Taylor 1-28-1867 G
King, Sarah F. to George W. Gibson 9-4-1862 Hn
King, Sarah O. to John W. Love 12-23-1862 Dy
King, Sarah to H. Leadford 5-11-1861 Mn
King, Sarah to Bray Hawkins 4-16-1840 Hr
King, Sarah to James S. Blakemore 3-22-1849 G
King, Sarah to Solomon Needham 4-28-1831 Sh
King, Sarah to Thos. F. Mosley 1-4-1870 Ma
King, Siney to Wm. Kent 10-12-1870 (no return) Hy
King, Sisley to Elis Cobb 12-16-1856 Cr
King, Sue F. to George J. Gear 11-27-1860 Sh
King, Susan E. to J. P. Laster 1-24-1863 (1-25-1863) Cr
King, Susan Jane to A. Wilson 8-28-1861 (8-29-1861) Sh
King, Susan T. to Tho. M. Broom 1-19-1865 (1-24-1865) F
King, Susan to H. Laster 6-23-1863 Cr
King, Susan to Joseph McFarlin 4-15-1861 (4-16-1861) Ma
King, Susan to Saml. Henson 10-17-1838 (10-18-1838) Hr
King, Susan to Samuel Carman 6-28-1847 O
King, T. J. to J. D.? Sugg 9-7-1866 (9-9-1866) Cr
King, Tabitha to W. L. Lard 5-3-1855 We
King, Tenness to N. M. Moore 12-3-1866 (11?-6-1866) Cr
King, Tina to Albert Waller 12-14-1853 (12-15-1853) Hr
King, Viny M. to John Whittington 10-30-1865 (10-31-1865) Dy

King, Winnie R. to John G. Blount 2-24-1869 Cr
Kingcade, Lucretia E. to Thomas M. Lemmond 4-23-1853 (4-26-1853) G
Kingm, Ann to Isaac Jackson 2-14-1864 O
Kingsbury, Alvira L. to James A. Meader 3-8-1855 (3-10-1855) Sh
Kingston, Elizabeth to Brinkley George 2-8-1846 We
Kingston, Martha to David Corbitt 12-19-1843 Sh
Kingston, Mary to James E. Corbitt 12-26-1841 Sh
Kingston, Nancy to Wm. Davis 7-23-1846 We
Kingston, Rosanna to John McCarver 12-26-1841 Sh
Kinley, V. A. to J. L. Humbles 12-18-1872 (12-19-1872) Dy
Kinman, Elizabeth to Lewis Dockins 1-31-1855 (1-29?-1855) O
Kinman, Maria Jane to Robert McCain 7-29-1847 O
Kinman, Mary Ann to Bennett Henderson 10-20-1855 (11-1-1855) O
Kinnaird, Polly to William M. Hansard 1-17-1833 Sh
Kinnard, M. A. to E. H. Bynum 3-7-1876 (3-9-1877) O
Kinnen, Catherine to Wm. Brown 4-26-1862 Sh
Kinney, E. C. to A. G. Street 5-7-1870 (5-9-1870) T
Kinney, Elvira to Dennis Slaughter 9-23-1851 (9-25-1851) T
Kinney, F. M. to W. E. Smith 12-10-1872 (12-11-1872) T
Kinney, Frances M. to William H. Davis 7-23-1857 T
Kinney, M. J. to J. C. Street 8-2?-1871 (8-3-1871) T
Kinney, P. A. to Jefferson Saunders 2-26-1886 (2-28-1886) L
Kinney, Parthenia to Thomas T. Hughlett 7-30-1856 O
Kinney, Sarah to Albert Munroe 12-28-1870 F B
Kinney, Susan to J. M. Terry 7-2-1874 T
Kinnie, E. C. to W. L. Milam 12-20-1870 Hy
Kinnon, Margaret A. to W. B. Hyde 12-29-1866 (12-30-1866) F
Kinny, J. E. to O. O. Wiseman 12-22-1873 (1-7-1874) T
Kinny, Martha Ann to Chesley G. House 11-26-1860 (no return) Hy
Kinsey, Celestia to P. W. Wilson 12-24-1874 O
Kinsey, Elizabeth to John F. Tuter 9-13-1842 (9-15-1842) G
Kinsey, Mary J. to Thos. G. Richee 1-26-1856 (1-29-1856) G
Kinsler, Elizabeth to Nickolas Kirth 7-19-1855 Sh
Kinsolving, Mary E. to James W. Hawkins 8-22-1857 Hn
Kinzler, Mary to Charles Kammerer 7-30-1857 Sh
Kirby, Alice R. to John F. McVey 6-13-1865 (6-14-1865) O
Kirby, Ann E. (Mrs.) to Henry C. Johnson 11-8-1869 Ma
Kirby, Carolina to Wm. Stewart 7-5-1846 Cr
Kirby, D. M. to Stephen Frost 3-29-1858 Hn
Kirby, Elizabeth I. to James M. McWhorter 1-14-1857 (1-17-1857) O
Kirby, Elizabeth W. to John Glover 1-5-1845 (1-8-1846) Ma
Kirby, Elizar to William Hunt 12-23-1869 Hy
Kirby, Elyna to S. P. Cloyd 1-21-1856 Cr
Kirby, Henretta J. to Sylvanus Taylor 10-12-1850 Ma *
Kirby, Julia Ann to J. J. Demery 7-6-1883 (7-8-1883) L
Kirby, Laura L. to Timothy J. Barnes 10-5-1869 (10-6-1869) Ma
Kirby, Lucinda to Henry Reynolds 9-17-1845 (9-19-1845) L
Kirby, Maria to James T. Jobe 3-14-1867 Hn
Kirby, Martha Jane to Albert B. Edwards 12-27-1876 Hy
Kirby, Martha to Galin Stokes 1-31-1844 Cr
Kirby, Martha to Owen J. Busick 9-25-1847 Ma
Kirby, Mary to George M. Bennett 4-15-1857 (4-16-1857) Ma
Kirby, Mary to Gilbert Cozart 1-1-1845 (1-3-1845) Ma
Kirby, Mattie E. to George W. Collins 12-14-1870 (12-15-1870) Ma
Kirby, Milia to Soloman Williams 7-21-1842 Cr
Kirby, Mollie W. to Wm. Isbell 3-4-1868 (3-5-1868) O
Kirby, Mollie to Andrew H. Bevill 12-13-1866 Ma
Kirby, Nancy E. to John L. Palmer 12-14-1850 Cr
Kirby, Nancy M. to A. J. Smith 10-18-1838 L
Kirby, Parthanan to Joseph Hordon? 9-22-1851 (no return) Cr
Kirby, Polly Ann to Ezekial Moore 3-1-1871 L
Kirby, R. T. to J. A. Herbert 11-17-1860 (no return) Hy
Kirby, Rebecca to John Elam 11-24-1866 (11-29-1866) Ma
Kirby, Sarah E. to S. R. Peebles 9-22-1859 (no return) Hy
Kirby, Sarah E. to William W. Wilson 1-26-1858 Hn
Kirby, Sarah J. to Matthew G. Scott 2-15-1855 Sh
Kirby, Susan A. to Lewis R. Peebles 12-5-1859 (no return) Hy
Kirk, Ann Eliza to Jackson D. C. Cobb 1-30-1861 Dy
Kirk, Anna (Amona?) S. to Calvin M. Fackler 1-10-1853 (1-12-1853) Sh
Kirk, Caroline to Isaac T. Sullivan 11-13-1866 (11-15-1866) O
Kirk, Catharine to Robert Knox 11-30-1823 (11-31?-1823) Hr
Kirk, Dorthy to Isaac N. Brewer 10-25-1845 (10-31-1865) Cr
Kirk, Eliza J. to George W. Jackson 4-27-1866 O
Kirk, Ellen J. to E. H. Green 9-6-1860 Dy
Kirk, Emiline to Perry Hamilton 12-30-1867 G B
Kirk, Emma C. to William J. Calloway 10-8-1867 Ma
Kirk, Emma E. to James A. Wheatley 11-17-1868 (11-18-1868) L
Kirk, Henrietta to James Crigler 11-22-1869 G B
Kirk, Louisa J. to Francis M. Bendall ?-?-1861? Mn
Kirk, Lucy to David Neasier 8-18-1853 Cr
Kirk, M. E. to T. M. Hobday 12-18-1876 (12-19-1876) Dy
Kirk, M. F. to John Straton 10-27-1863 O
Kirk, M. R. to S. R. Thompson 12-10-1873 T
Kirk, Martha to A. R. Neely 1-5-1853 Hr
Kirk, Martha V. to Danl. W. Heath 12-21-1864 (12-22-1864) Dy
Kirk, Martha to R. M. Barnes 8-13-1864 (8-16-1864) O
Kirk, Mary Jane to James G. Hamilton 7-22-1869 Cr

Kirk, Mary L. to Henry W. Baker 1-20-1863 (1-22-1863) Dy
Kirk, Mary Louisa to J. Calvin Jones 7-20-1858 (7-21-1858) Sh
Kirk, Matilda W. to Wicke H. Pace 10-26-1836 Hr
Kirk, Melissa H. to A. J. Heath 11-15-1869 (11-16-1869) Dy
Kirk, Milly to Harry J. Hatch 2-12-1861 (no return) Cr
Kirk, Sarah Ann D. to Henry M. Brock 6-22-1861 (6-30-1861) O
Kirk, Sarah F. C. to Dennis L. Adams 1-20-1845 Hn
Kirk, Sarah J. to Laten Nowell 9-7-1854 Be
Kirk, Susan E. to William A. Jones 1-24-1855 Sh
Kirk, Susan to A. L. Williams 11-18-1874 (no return) Dy
Kirk, Susan to Isaac Enochs 11-25-1851 (no return) Cr
Kirk, Susan to Thomas Cocoran 7-25-1840 Sh
Kirk, Telissa Ann to Geo. W. Wilkins 11-9-1854 (11-8?-1854) Hr
Kirk, Vilet to Daniel Darnall 12-27-1870 (12-29-1870) Cr B
Kirkby, Anna (Mrs.) to William Tourtello 7-1-1856 Sh
Kirkland, Amanda to H. A. Tyler 12-19-1866 Hn
Kirkland, Ann T. to George S. Jones 5-13-1868 (5-17-1868) Cr
Kirkland, Caroline to Horace Blalock 3-22-1870 (3-26-1870) F B
Kirkland, Fannie R. to J. M. Waggener 10-17-1850 Hn
Kirkland, Fannie R. to J. N. Waggener 12-17-1860 Sh
Kirkland, Fanny M. to William E. Jones 9-3-185 (9-6-1855) Hr
Kirkland, Jane to William R. Gilliam 10-7-1858 Hn
Kirkland, Mary M. to J. S. Henley 12-13-1866 Hn
Kirkland, Nancy to Wm. Abernathy 12-17-1850 Cr
Kirkland, Sarah S. to William M. Chrisenberry 10-7-1858 Hn
Kirkland, Tabitha J. to W. H. McFarland 7-10-1867 Hn
Kirkland, Tempy D. to James Ray 12-29-1862 (no return) Hn
Kirkland, Virginia to J. J. Cooper 12-22-1857 (1-7-1858) Hr
Kirkman, Martha A. to John A. Hon 11-27-1869 Hy
Kirkman, Rachael C. to Thomas Fleming 2-12-1859 (2-19-1858?) Hr
Kirkman, Serritha J. to J. W. B. Thomas 12-28-1865 Hy
Kirkpatrick, Catharine E. to A. L. Meigs 6-11-1855 (no return) F
Kirkpatrick, Cynthia J. to John W. McElwee 8-28-1847 Ma
Kirkpatrick, Mary H. to George T. Mahon 2-7-1848 (2-?-1848) Ma
Kirkpatrick, Pink to Governor Bird 4-9-1866 (no return) F B
Kirkpatrick, Rebecca J. to Joseph Wilks 12-6-1847 (12-7-1847) Ma
Kirkpatrick, Synthia Jane to Samuel R. N. Pendergrast 12-6-1843 Ma
Kirksey, E. J. to T. D. Howard 3-1-1879 (3-2-1879) L
Kirksey, M. E. to J. H. Curlin 10-6-1885 (10-7-1885) L
Kirksey, M. E. to W. B. Griffith 3-30-1880 (3-31-1880) L
Kirksey, Martha A. to Nathanial Dickson 8-24-1837 G
Kirksey, Martha Ann to James Pinckney Jones 7-13-1858 Ma
Kirksey, S. E. to J. R. Simmons 10-6-1885 (10-7-1885) L
Kirly, Elizabeth to J. W. Pendergrass 3-27-1872 Cr
Kirsey, Elizabeth to John A. Haley 2-14-1831 G
Kirsey, Elvira to Valdura Sanderlin 6-6-1862 Hy
Kirsey, Fanney to James Payne 2-6-1865 O
Kirtland, Blondina M. to James C. Calhoun 12-20-1858 (12-22-1858) Sh
Kirtland, Laura M. to A. J. Hays 6-18-1861 (6-20-1861) Sh
Kiser, Anne A. to James Parks 1-2-1845 Sh
Kissell, Lora to F. E. Hutcherson 7-7-1880 (no return) L
Kitchell, Ann to Michael Ryan 6-1-1853 Sh
Kitchen(s), Mary to Silas M. Hicks 1-9-1854 (1-10-1854) O
Kitchen, Ann to Michael McNamara 8-10-1848 Sh
Kitchen, Eliza to Elijah Brown 2-26-1855 (2-27-1855) T
Kitchen, Elizabeth to James A. Lewis 4-9-1850 (4-10-1850) O
Kitchen, Lucy C. to Pleasant Manasco 6-30-1860 (7-5-1860) T
Kitchen, Mary M. to James Manasco 6-30-1860 (7-7-1860) T
Kitchum, Ruth Ann to J. W. David 7-4-1870 (7-7-1870) T
Kittle, Polly to R. Belew 8-26-1838 Cr
Kittrell, Nancy M. to James A. Newsom 9-14-1854 (9-19-1854) Ma
Klein, B. to Joseph Beatus 9-7-1864 Sh
Klein, H. (Miss) to S. Schiffman 10-29-1864 Sh
Klinch, Carolina to Michael W. Kinney 2-10-1852 (2-14-1852) Sh
Klinck, Mary E. to G. W. Grader 11-11-1856 Sh
Kline, Victerine to V. D. Fuchs 9-4-1863 Sh
Klink, Frances J. to W. A. Smith 3-11-1859 (3-15-1859) Sh
Kluats, Susan to James A. Putman 5-19-1857 Hn
Kluigh, Sarah Jane to C. A. Allen 10-29-1856 (10-30-1856) T
Klutts, C. A. to Lawson A. Klutts 12-13-1861 (no return) Hn
Klutts, Eliza Ann to James H. Botts 9-?-1844 (no return) Hn
Klutts, Jane to John G. Price 2-17-1856 We
Klutts, Mary A. to William B. Boothe 8-2-1858 (no return) Hn
Klutts, Mary Ann to William Denning 1-2-1846 (no return) We
Klyce, A. D. to I. Steel 12-22-1868 Hy
Klyce, Bettie W. to James J. McKiel 7-20-1875 Hy
Klyce, Caroline to Wm. Tolbert 10-25-1868 Hy
Klyce, Dora to W. A. Nichols 12-28-1869 Hy
Klyce, Hattie to James Munford 9-18-1873 Hy
Klyce, Jane A. to W. M. Tatum 7-4-1866 Hy
Klyce, Kitty to Lewis Wood 12-25-1865 Hy
Klyce, Lizzie L. to Lamotte Stearns 1-22-1866 (1-23-1866) F
Klyce, M. F. to W. A. Nichols 11-23-1865 G
Klyce, Mollie to J. Blakemore 12-24-1861 (no return) Hy
Klyce, R. C. to J. H. Hampton 11-6-1871 (no return) Hy
Klyce, Sarah H. to J. B. G. Stevens 9-26-1870 Hy
Klyce, Sarah to H. S. Crichlow 11-22-1870 Hy

Knaff, Almira to Elijah Conley 8-18-1846 Sh
Knapp, Elizabeth Jane to Charles Jones 1-11-1844 Sh
Knapp, Lucy to Allen Nash 9-19-1837 Sh
Knapp, Susan A. to Perry W. Humphreys 12-18-1848 Sh
Kneeland, Martha J. to John Garrett 10-19-1867 (no return) Hy
Knewland, Louisa to Thos. Dickins 12-24-1867 (no return) Hy
Kney, Charlotte to George Thomas 8-19-1863 (8-20-1863) Sh
Kney, Louise to George Weinr (White) 12-15-1855 Sh
Knight, E. J. to Elmer Washburn 1-19-1860 Sh
Knight, Eliza to Willis Morris 12-29-1845 (1-1-1846) F
Knight, Elizabeth to L. T. Powers 1-15-1848 (1-17-1848) F
Knight, Elizabeth to Wm. Parrot 6-27-1858 T
Knight, Emily to W. G. Cross 4-6-1875? (4-8-1875) O
Knight, J. F. to H. A. Warren 1-23-1862 Mn
Knight, Jane to George C. Medlin 1-20-1852 (1-21-1852) Ma
Knight, Malenda to Jasper Richardson 3-8-1857 We
Knight, Maria J. to Samuel Collins 12-5-1850 Sh
Knight, Martha B. to J. L. Huffman 8-28-1861 (8-29-1861) O
Knight, Mary Ann to Joseph Winters 9-9-1850 (9-10-1850) F
Knight, Mary Ann to Will A. Stacy 10-3-1827 Hr
Knight, Mary C. to Wm. McDowell 9-16-1871 (9-17-1871) Dy
Knight, Mary E. to Ashley Midgett 5-6-1850 (5-8-1850) Ma
Knight, Mary E. to Elijah Knight 2-8-1863 Mn
Knight, Mattie to D. H. Reynolds 8-23-1873 (8-24-1873) Dy
Knight, Permelia to W. Holloway 8-22-1837 Be
Knight, Sally H. to William Hobbs 2-2-1835 G
Knight, Sarah A. to Jno. G. Williams 5-6-1858 (5-7-1858) Hr
Knight, Sarah J. to W. H. Moseley 5-5-1870 Dy
Knight, Sarah W. to John C. Gullespie 12-6-1866 O
Knoeppel, W. to Henry Lipperd 5-1-1855 Sh
Knoffle, Wilhemina to Henry Nolan 5-1-1860 (5-5-1860) Sh
Knott, Amanda to William McConnell 8-1-1844 Hn
Knott, Elizabeth to Martin B. Arnold 6-12-1845 G
Knott, Margaret J. to Milton S. Allen 11-9-1868 (no return) F
Knott, Nancy to W. R. Samuson? 12-18-1862 (no return) F
Knott, Polly to William Bain 12-25-1843 (12-28-1843) G
Knott, Sallie to Josiah W. Brown 8-20-1867 (8-22-1867) Ma
Knott, Sarah to William Hampton 2-15-1847 (2-16-1847) G
Knowles, Ann to Lewis Stell 4-22-1854 (4-23-1854) Sh
Knowles, Annie W. to Paul Gegg 12-23-1858 Sh
Knowles, Martha C. to J. W. Newnam 12-5-1877 (12-6-1877) Dy
Knowles, Mary E. to James G. Thomason 11-13-1878 Dy
Knowls, Elizabeth to John H. Kee 11-7-1867 Be
Knowls, Martha to John L. Short 11-7-1867 Be
Knox, Adaline to Archy Towns 12-4-1868 (12-17-1868) F B
Knox, Eliza C. to David A. Cherry 5-31-1854 (6?-1-1854) T
Knox, Elizabeth to William Randle (Randal) 2-2-1848 Sh
Knox, Emily to C. F. Dowlen (Dowell) 4-20-1861 Sh
Knox, Evaline to Frank Koser 8-27-1857 Sh
Knox, Harriet R. to Benjamin Wever (Weaver) 12-19-1863 (12-23-1863) Sh
Knox, Lucinda to Clarence Marshall 12-20-1870 (12-22-1870) F B
Knox, M. L. to D. R. Bondurant 7-9-1874 (7-10-1874) O
Knox, Margaret A. to Wm. M. Mitchell 1-27-1840 Cr
Knox, Mary B. to Kenneth Manning 2-13-1856 We
Knox, Mary D. to A. Webb 2-1-1850 (no return) F
Knox, Mary M. to David I. H. Templeton 2-7-1854 (2-10-1854) G
Knox, Mary to Gabriel Overall 7-22-1856 G
Knox, Sarah A. to B. W. Weaver 12-7-1860 (12-11-1860) Sh
Knox, Sarah B. to William Atchison, jr. 10-11-1848 G
Knox, Sarah V. to James B. Caldwell 1-18-1858 We
Knox, Shelley to J. T. Newsom 12-26-1872 T
Knox, Susan to John Ing 9-15-1855 (no return) F
Knox, Tempy to Liz Marshall 4-6-1871 (4-7-1871) F B
Knox, Thulina to L. R. Montgomery 1-21-1840 Sh
Knuckles, Frances to Jacob Fuqua 8-5-1872 Cr
Koch, Julia to Otto Haensel Zedwitz 6-29-1852 Sh
Koch, Mary to Geo. Holzleisber 3-4-1861 Sh
Koehler, Helena to Sebastian Brenner 9-15-1859 Sh
Koen (Cohen), Matilda A. to S. B. Arbuckle 11-24-1858 (11-30-1858) Sh
Koen, Elizabeth F. to W. A. Turner 9-18-1849 Sh
Koen, Elizabeth to Fenwick H. Berry 10-8-1841 Sh
Koen, Mary C. to William W. Hall 8-13-1861 (8-14-1861) Sh
Koen, Ollive to John R. Miles 10-8-1841 Sh
Koffman, Narcissa to Andrew M. McKalip 5-23-1854 (5-24-1854) Hr
Kohn, Catherine to W. W. Thomas 1-3-1863 Sh
Koler, Louisa to F. Henniger 6-10-1856 Sh
Kollinsworth, Elizabeth to James Haddon 1-25-1867 Ma
Koney, Lizette to Henry Kettman 11-14-1856 (11-16-1856) Sh
Koonce, Amanda to Taylor Neeley 11-26-1874 T
Koonce, Caroline to J. R. Chilcott 12-31-1844 L
Koonce, Caroline to Thomas Shaw 10-28-1868 (10-29-1868) L
Koonce, Darthula to P. H. Ramsey 11-24-1852 F
Koonce, Eliza M. to W. M. Burns 12-18-1859 (12-21-1859) T
Koonce, Fannie to Aaron Shaw 12-5-1877 Hy
Koonce, Joana P. to Sidney A. Moore 4-18-1861 (no return) Hy
Koonce, Juda to J. R. Graves 1-3-1877 L
Koonce, Julia N. P. to James H. Thompson 12-11-1850 F

Koonce, Margarette to Wm. T. Ball 1-26-1865 G
Koonce, Martha to John Jarman 2-18-1840 Sh
Koonce, Mary E. to Wm. W. Grimes 7-27-1870 (7-28-1870) L
Koonce, Matilda C. to Wm. J. Singleton 6-12-1860 Hy
Koonce, Nancy to H. M. Hays 12-9-1856 (12-10-1856) Sh
Koonce, Nealy to Bob Paine 11-18-1869 Hy
Koonce, R. Ann (Mrs.) to Joseph Crowder 12-19-1865 Hy
Koonce, S. J. to W. C. Hays 3-26-1856 (3-28-1856) Sh
Koonce, S. R. to J. W. Richardson 1-1-1874 L
Kowskie, Louisa Geneve to Fred Bosch 7-2-1864 Sh
Krafft, Clara F. to E. D. F. Morgan 3-2-1860 (3-3-1860) Sh
Krafft, Maria L. to Geo. H. Smith 4-16-1861 Sh
Krafft, Maria L. to Thomas James 3-4-1858 Sh
Kraft, Akafa to Romnald Kraft 4-24-1856 Sh
Kranche, Ida to Henry Bertschi 2-11-1860 Sh
Kreider, Mary to Lewis Ringwald 1-25-1859 Sh
Kreighton, Mariah J. A. to J. M. Thompson 3-25-1864 (4-6-1864) Sh
Kremer(Creamer), Nancy to William M. Ratten 4-1-1835 (4-5-1835) Hr
Krenkel, Caroline to F. H. Mulhaupt 11-2-1858 Sh
Krenkle, Philibene to A. Lewis Hooper 12-26-1856 Sh
Krouth, D. E. C. to W. K. Hodges 6-10-1860 (6-14-1860) F
Kulbeth, Mary to Tho. Evans Gray 9-16-1851 (9-17-1851) T
Kulbreath, Rosanna to Chas. Wm. Webb 12-19-1850 T
Kurby, Jane to James T. Wiggins 6-15-1832 Hr
Kurts, Lorina to Jas. Monroe Locke 1-2-1856 T
Kuykendall, Lucinda to William Berry 9-14-1854 Hn
Kuykendall, Nancy to John Crawford 3-9-1867 Hn
Kyle, Allice C. to J. A. Neely 2-6-1871 (2-8-1871) F
Kyle, Charatza to R. L. Kuykendall 2-10-1862 (2-11-1862) O
Kyle, Ellin to Dangerfreld? Carpenter 3-7-1835 (3-8-1835) Hr
Kyle, M. J. to J. R. Fuller 1-25-1871 (1-26-1871) Cr
Kyle, Margaret Ellen to John W. Hill 3-28-1867 Ma
Kyle, Mary Ann to E. Harper 1-14-1851 (no return) F
Kyle, Mary S. to James G. Perry 11-20-1851 Ma
Kyle, Mattie to Wm. J. Alexander 11-27-1865 (no return) F
Kyle, Pinkey to G. W. Butler 10-29-1867 Cr
Kyle, Sarah C. to Charles H. Brown 8-9-1854 Ma

L___, Elizabeth R. to Henry R. Clark 11-2-1865 G
LaBone, Sarah A. to Isaac W. Harris 6-2-1853 Sh
LaRouge, Celesta to Milton A. Mathess 4-13-1869 (no return) Hy
Lacewell, Judith to Alford Middleten 7-4-1858 We
Lacey, Eliza J. to Hugh G. Norton 7-4-1840 Hn
Lacey, Fannie to B. P. Wallace 1-15-1868 Hy
Lacey, Julia to Edward Bond 3-19-1867 (3-21-1867) F B
Lacey, Margarett to Lemuel Stone 1-23-1849 (1-24-1849) Ma
Lacey, Mary to Aaron Stanley 9-11-1833 (7?-23-1833) G
Lacey, Mattie to Smith Maclin 1-25-1871 T
Lack, Bethen to Robert Davis 2-16-1864 G
Lack, E. C. to Anthony Duke 12-11-1866 (no return) Dy
Lackey, Angeline to W. F. Wellington 12-19-1869 Hy
Lackey, Elizabeth to J. T. Miller 8-10-1871 Hy
Lackey, Elizabeth to Timothy Ellison 7-18-1839 Hr
Lackey, Evelyn A. to J. L. B. Barksdale 12-31-1867 L
Lackey, Lucy A. to Richard Henning 1-17-1861 (no return) L
Lackey, Margaret E. to William J. Stigler 12-28-1867 (no return) Hn
Lackey, Mary Ann to William Y. Carter 3-12-1859 Ma
Lackey, Mary E. to William P. Posey 1-20-1848 (1-20-1847?) L
Lackey, Mary to David Davis 6-14-1838 F
Lackey, Mary to William Bridges 10-20-1859 (no return) Hy
Lackey, Mary to William M. Ferrill 12-20-1876 (no return) Hy
Lackey, Matilda to Stephen Brooks 2-8-1840 (2-16-1840) Ma
Lackey, Permelia J. to William H. Guthrie 10-6-1853 Ma
Lackey, Violet G. to William M. Helm 2-4-1861 L
Lackie, Bettie to J. Polk Harston 11-28-1868 Ma
Lackie, Bettie to Thomas L. Carter 12-24-1867 (12-25-1867) Ma
Lackie, Elizabth. to Thos. Lackie 12-9-1849 (12-11-1849) F
Lacy, Allice to John Maclin 3-25-1874 (no return) Hy
Lacy, Delilah A. to W. N. Cook 11-22-1866 G
Lacy, Elizabeth A. to John R. Gaines 8-12-1861 (8-13-1861) L
Lacy, Elizabeth to Lewis L. Eddins 3-27-1832 Ma
Lacy, Emily to Samuel Hogg 4-17-1854 Hn
Lacy, Jane G. to Thomas James 11-1-1836 Hr
Lacy, Louizer to Thomas Cunningham 8-4-1868 G
Lacy, Lucretia L. to John J. Boon 3-28-1866 (3-29-1866) Ma
Lacy, Lucy to Henry Hastings 7-6-1867 T
Lacy, Margaret A. to G. W. Wilk 1-4-1866 (1-14-1866) Cr
Lacy, Margaret to John B. Johnson 2-1-1858 (2-2-1858) Ma
Lacy, Martha to Jim Bryant 8-31-1867 (9-7-1867) F B
Lacy, Mary A. to Eli Arnold 2-26-1862 Sh
Lacy, Mary E. to W. F. Pyland 1-19-1880 (1-20-1880) L
Lacy, Mary V. to William S. Midlebrooks 12-25-1849 Hr
Lacy, Mary to Joseph Brooks 7-21-1842 Hn
Lacy, Mary to Patrick Manahan 3-31-1857 Hn
Lacy, Mary to Wm. D. Jarrett 12-22-1871 (12-23-1871) Cr
Lacy, Nancy R. A. to Matt Rambo 10-16-1866 (10-20-1866) Dy
Lacy, Nancy to Butten Jones 8-13-1860 Dy

Lacy, Polly A. to William Jackson 1-6-1837 (1-10-1837) G
Lacy, Rebecca to Edward Wade 7-29-1829 Hr
Lacy, Susan E. to N. M. McKinney 2-6-1865 F
Ladd, Elisa to T. J. Briggs 2-19-1870 (2-24-1870) T
Ladd, Elizabeth to W. H. Hise 9-4-1874 (9-6-1874) T
Ladd, Mary to John Mauzy 8-21-1872 (8-25-1872) T
Ladd, Minerva A. to David B. Jones 10-27-1860 (10-28-1860) Hr
Ladd, Mollie M. to Thomas Goodman 3-24-1864 Sh
Lafavour, Elizabeth to William Coleman 3-5-1839 Hn
Lafers, Isabela to Thomas Martin 8-30-1854 We
Lafever, Josephine to ___ Windsor 11-4-1857 Hn
Lafloor, Mary to John Hilliard 9-16-1855 Cr
Lafloore, Ann E. to John T. Smith 12-11-1868 (12-13-1868) Cr
Laflor, Martha to Nimrod Burrow 2-16-1850 Cr
Lahal?, Nancy to B. B. Hand ?-4-1862 Be
Lahoff, Catharine to Hugh Hogan 1-7-1862 Sh
Lain, Hudah to George Whoohon? 12-2-1851 Be
Lain, Hulda to George Whooten 12-2-1851 Be CC
Lain, Lucy A. E. to R. B. Ramsey 2-17-1860 (2-19-1860) Sh
Lainer, Sophia J. to Jacob H. Hay 12-27-1854 G
Laird, Emma P. to N. W. Barber 10-4-1884 (10-5-1884) L
Laird, Mary to J. P. Hutcherson 4-14-1876 (4-16-1876) L
Laird, Parmelia C. to A. J. Oberst 1-8-1861 L
Laird, Virginia to Joseph F. Hobgood 11-23-1857 (11-24-1857) Sh
Laird, Wynaford to Allen? B. Jones 9-12-1853 (9-14-1853) L
Laismer (Larimer), Malinda E. to T. L. Rodgers 10-16-1849 Sh
Lake, Elizabeth to Joseph Terry 5-30-1885 (5-31-1885) L
Lake, Elvira to Jesse Thomas Faris 10-23-1848 (10-24-1848) T
Lake, Fannie to Thomas Hawkins 1-20-1875 (no return) Hy
Lake, Hannah J. to Lee Thornton 5-15-1869 L
Lake, Helen M. to Frank W. Royston 5-23-1849 Sh
Lake, Henrietta to Charles Bryant 6-2-1883 (6-3-1883) L
Lake, Julia to William Dewalt 12-30-1868 (12-31-1869) L B
Lake, Laura to A. A. Green 5-9-1860 (no return) Hy
Lake, Laura to Claiborne Green 9-18-1879 L
Lake, Malinda to Harrison Wright 4-3-1877 (4-4-1877) L B
Lake, Malissa to Frank Brooks 4-30-1883 (5-6-1883) L
Lake, Margarett Ann to John W. Scott 12-30-1851 (1-3-1852) Hr
Lake, Marion to D. C. Arbuckle 12-18-1852 (1-4-1853) Hr
Lake, Martha W. to George W. Harris 5-7-1836 Hr
Lake, Mary J. to N. H. Dunlap 1-20-1861 Hr
Lake, Mary Susan to Elisha B. Ray 1-27-1852 (1-28-1852) T
Lake, Mary to Joseph C. Williams 9-19-1840 Hr
Lake, Mary to Madison Barlow 11-6-1880 (11-7-1880) L
Lake, Mattie to Sad Colwell 3-25-1882 L
Lake, Mollie to Richard Ervin 1-3-1874 (1-4-1874) L B
Lake, Nicey to G. Wood 1-6-1883 (1-25-1883) L
Lake, Rena to Isaac Rhodes 12-10-1868 T
Lake, Rowena to Henry Watson 8-21-1879 L
Lake, Sarah Jane to John C. Spinks 12-26-1848 Hr
Lake, Susan to Dock Gentry 3-21-1874 (no return) L B
Lakey, Eliza to [John W. Summons(Summers?) 7-17-1838 Hr
Lakey, Nancy to A. J. Smith 5-23-1848 F
Lakey, Sarah to James H. Lakey 1-15-1851 F
Laks?, Cynthia C. to Windsor J. Spinks 10-31-1860 Hr
Lallier(Sallier?), L. J. to Joseph Hutchison 2-21-1857 (2-22-1857) Hr
Lally (Lolly?), Ann to John Dunn 12-8-1852 Sh
Lalon, Teressa to John Gallagher 2-10-1850 Sh
Lamar?, Isabella to Joseph A. McCommon 7-27-1835 Hr
Lamb, Amanda J. to John T. Douseford 2-17-1858 (2-18-1858) T
Lamb, Araminta E. to Lawson W. Kenady 8-1-1866 Sh
Lamb, Delila to Thomas R. Stigall 8-11-1858 Hn
Lamb, E. J. to T. J. Whitson 9-17-1861 (9-18-1861) T
Lamb, Eliza H. to Jesse I. Finely 1-1-1839 Sh
Lamb, Eliza M. to John Henry Deakins 9-19-1849 (9-20-1849) T
Lamb, Elizabeth to Harrison White 8-2-1848 Hn
Lamb, Elizabeth to James Fulcher 5-21-1858 Hn
Lamb, Elizabeth to John B. Finley 11-1-1845 Sh
Lamb, Elizabeth to John Bowen? Wiseman 12-12-1846 (12-24-1846) T
Lamb, Elizabeth to William R. Curtis 2-19-1868 (2-20-1868) L
Lamb, Erena to James Franklin Young 9-2-1844 (9-4-1844) T
Lamb, Isabella to Allen B. White 10-11-1853 Hn
Lamb, Louisa to Jesse P. Orr 6-2-1858 Hn
Lamb, M. J. to John Manor 12-26-1866 G
Lamb, Mahalah to Daniel W. Hering 12-6-1847 (12-22-1847) T
Lamb, Martha A. to Horace T. Blanton 7-4-1843 Hn
Lamb, Martha Ann to Nicholas Holly 6-9-1852 Hn
Lamb, Martha L. to N. H. Corley 6-23-1871 (6-27-1871) Dy
Lamb, Mary C. to W. A. Martin 9-5-1859 (9-6-1859) T
Lamb, Mary E. to J. J. Battson 8-27-1855 (no return) Hn
Lamb, Mary Frances to Edward Joseph Mariner 3-8-1850 (3-11-1850) T
Lamb, Mary to William Call 12-16-1858 Hn
Lamb, Nancy to Elijah Lamb 8-25-1847 Hn
Lamb, Paulina A. to Joel Currin Parish 2-18-1849 (2-22-1849) T
Lamb, Purnesa to John Lee 5-2-1833 Sh
Lamb, Sarah J. to Samuel T. McClain 3-15-1848 Hn
Lamb, Sarah to Jeptha Fowlkes 10-26-1852 Sh

Lamb, Sidney G. to Jeptha Fowlkes 6-11-1842 Sh
Lamb, Sidney G. to John C. T. Baker 11-11-1839 Sh
Lamb, Sophronia H. to Silas Moore 12-28-1861 Sh
Lambdin, L. P. to G. W. Prater 10-5-1845 (no return) Hn
Lambdin, Mary A. to John W. Brush 1-9-1861 Sh
Lambe, Mary E. to Jesse A. Jackson 12-24-1845 Hn
Lamber, Martha Jane to William G. Cox 4-25-1853 (5-5-1853) Hr
Lambert, Ann E. to W. E.? Rodgers 9-21-1864 (10-25-1864) T
Lambert, Anna to Lewis Acre 1-3-1839 (1-6-1839) Ma
Lambert, Delilah to William K. Steepleton 11-8-1850 Ma
Lambert, Eliza to Jerimiah Sullivan 1-17-1843 Ma
Lambert, Elizabeth to R. D. Swindle 3-30-1849 (4-1-1849) Hr
Lambert, Emily Ann to Eugene Campbell 10-27-1866 (10-30-1866) Ma
Lambert, Jane Catharine to Mathew G. Babb 2-5-1852 (2-8-1852) Hr
Lambert, Josephine to Orlando Carter 7-25-1859 (7-27-1859) Sh
Lambert, Julian to Andrew J. Estes 1-30-1850 (1-31-1850) Hr
Lambert, Mariah J. to A. E. Sweeton 10-24-1854 (10-25-1854) Hr
Lambert, Martha A. J. to Johnson McDaniel 12-22-1843 (no return) Hn
Lambert, Martha J. to Daniel R. Burn 12-31-1849 (12-16?-1849) Ma
Lambert, Martha J. to Reubin Estes 1-6-1846 (1-6-1846) Hr
Lambert, Nancy H. to W. B. W. Sweeton 1-18-1860 Hr
Lambert, Nancy to Archibald Mayfield 10-3-1859 Hr
Lambert, S. A. to A. C. Hendricks 9-21-1875 (9-30-1875) Dy
Lambert, Sarah to Geo. W. Gee 3-10-1852 (3-11-1852) Hr
Lambert, Sarah to T. M. Daniel 2-18-1853 (2-23-1853) Hr
Lambert, Sophia H. to Rob't McPherson 11-19-1867 O
Lambert, Stephanie to Edward Sebastian Isnarde 6-22-1861 Sh
Lamberth, Assennith to William H. Seddens 12-20-1853 Hr
Lambeth, Jane E. to Andrew Craig 3-17-1845 (3-18-1845) Hr
Lambeth, Litilia? to William Sasser 10-11-1850 (10-13-1850) Hr
Lammond, Sarah to D. L. Rigsby 12-5-1868 (12-7-1868) Cr
Lamn?, Elizabeth to P. N. Smotherman 7-9-1851 (no return) Hn
Lamons, Nancy to Robert Boles 3-3-1830 G
Lamphier-McLauphier?, Annie M. to George K. Duncan 3-1-1854 Sh
Lampkins, Analiza? to Willis W. Spann 2-23-1854 Hn
Lampkins, Genetta to S. D. Scott 11-29-1865 Hn
Lampkins, Jennie to William L. Berry 10-10-1861 Hn
Lampkins, Kizziah to William Roberts 10-16-1851 (10-16-1851) Hr
Lampley, Harriet to Abraham Neale 1-19-1857 Hn
Lampley, Lecy to William W. Lewis 5-5-1842 Hn
Lampricht, Lizzie to Andrew Renkert 1-30-1860 (2-2-1860) Sh
Lamsden, Margaret to Samuel Dameren 4-16-1854 We
Lancaster, Ann Eliza to Thomas Henderson 7-25-1848 Ma
Lancaster, E. H. to Robert E. Rhodes 4-8-1839 (4-9-1839) F
Lancaster, Elizabeth C. to Benjamin Totten 3-3-1847 (3-14-1847) O
Lancaster, Lyda A. to R. V. Haddley 7-27-1855 (7-30-1856) We
Lancaster, M. E. to John W. Yates 12-25-1866 O
Lancaster, Martha to Thos. P. Porteous 4-7-1863 Sh
Lancaster, Mary E. to Jas. T. Wells 6-12-1860 O
Lancaster, Mary to Joseph McKinney 2-5-1846 Hn
Lancaster, Pheriba to James Kelley 2-14-1856 Sh
Lancaster, S. J. to W. G. Bynum 3-6-1872 (3-7-1872) O
Lancaster, Sarah E. to Charles C. Owen 12-6-1855 (no return) F
Lancaster, Sue A. to Joel W. Smith 11-20-1877 (11-22-1877) O
Lance, Louisa to T. B. Burnett 12-10-1867 O
Lancer, Martha J. to John A. Weaver 10-15-1844 (no return) F
Land, Eliza to James L. Scott 7-5-1827 Hr
Land, M. W. to R. B. Neal 1-27-1868 (1-28-1868) F
Land, Martha to Asa J. Hardison 3-18-1858 Hr
Land, Mary Ann to Aaron Burt 1-27-1836 Sh
Land, Mary to T. R. David 7-14-1870 (7-17-1870) F
Land, Nancy A. to B. V. Odom 8-7-1860 (8-8-1860) O
Land, Sarah to Silas Wherry 7-22-1833 Sh
Land, Sophronia to J. S. Middleton 1-24-1883 (1-25-1883) L
Land, Susan O. to William A. Bennett 11-12-1861 Hr
Land, Susan to John D. Erwin 9-29-1847 (9-30-1847) T
Landers, Abagil to Thos. Barnett 8-6-1864 (8-7-1864) Sh
Landers, Emma to Bud Witt 8-18-1864 Sh
Landers, Mary to James Scott 6-14-1838 G
Landers, Mary to Levi Prewit 11-15-1851 Hn
Landford, Emily to Eldridge David 1-31-1872 (2-1-1872) Dy
Landin, Meriah E. to A. S. Davidson 5-5-1838 G
Landis, Lula to M. L. Harton 12-4-1877 Dy
Landregan, Catharine to Patrick O'Neil 2-5-1853 (2-7-1853) Sh
Landress, Mary to Thomas Nolan 7-26-1863 Sh
Landriss, Elizabeth (Mrs.) to John L. (D?) Goode 11-18-1864 Sh
Landrum, Catharine to L. P. Parker 7-15-1850 O
Landrum, Charlotte to Wm. Landrum 10-22-1844 We
Landrum, Harriett A. to Wm. M. Edwards 5-26-1866 O
Landrum, Ida to Marshall D. Majors 4-1-1878 (4-7-1878) L
Landrum, Lucy A. to Francis M. Turner 12-12-1859 (12-13-1860) We
Landrum, Mary A. to J. W. McConnell 6-21-1863 G
Landrum, Matilda to William Brown 8-5-1873 (8-15-1873) Dy
Landrum, Matilda J. to A. L. Butler 12-11-1883 L
Landrum, Mattie to W. W. Heughan 7-27-1877 (8-2-1877) Dy
Landrum, Minnie to T. J. Bacon 10-16-1883 (10-22-1883) L
Landrum, Nancy E. to Jessie W. Morris 11-5-1850 We

Landrum, S. E. to W. J. Colley 1-20-1879 (1-22-1879) L
Landrum, Sarah M. to John B. Wright 3-28-1877 (3-29-1877) Dy
Landrum, Susan E. to J. C. McConnell 10-16-1861 G
Landrum, Susan to Daniel Winn 6-26-1845 O
Landrum, Susan to Henry Landrum 6-28-1844 (no return) We
Landrum, Winnifred H. to Richard Wallace 11-14-1842 Sh
Lane, Ann S. to James Williams 12-26-1860 (12-27-1860) Hr
Lane, Ann to Thomas J. Thurman 11-20-1867 (no return) Hn
Lane, Bell (Mrs.) to Jefferson Malone ?-?-1863 (with Aug 1863) Cr
Lane, Caroline S. to William S. Hartsfield 1-5-1857 (1-6-1857) G
Lane, Caroline to Elias Gilford 11-25-1870 (no return) F B
Lane, Charity to George Patterson 11-27-1852 Ma
Lane, Delia to James P. Lucas 7-25-1885 (7-26-1885) L
Lane, E. A. to J. M. Robertson 12-24-1878 (12-26-1878) Dy
Lane, Eliza A. to W. W. Hunt 1-16-1861 G
Lane, Elizabeth E. to Phillip A. Wright 8-14-1843 (8-12?-1843) O
Lane, Elizabeth J. to Wm. Slade 6-27-1856 Sh
Lane, Emily to Wilson R. Wright 8-26-1847 O
Lane, Emily to Wilson Wright 8-26-1847 O
Lane, Eva J. to James H. May 9-3-1846 G
Lane, Gabriella Jane to Samuel H. Davis 9-3-1847 O
Lane, Harriet to Warney King 3-5-1874 Hy
Lane, Jennie to John Taylor 1-11-1872 Hy
Lane, Lavicia to E. B. Hugg 4-13-1869 (4-15-1869) F
Lane, Lucinda to Joseph Farris 6-30-1838 (7-3-1838) O
Lane, Lucy Ann E. to George T. Tarwater 12-3-1844 (12-5-1844) F
Lane, M. M. to John A. Wilson 12-13-1856 (12-18-1856) G
Lane, Martha J. to George P. Summers 11-7-1843 (11-8-1843) O
Lane, Martha J. to William O. Boykin 11-17-1852 Ma
Lane, Martha to Hiram Eady 5-29-1868 Dy
Lane, Mary A. to Wm. H. Morris 8-18-1849 Cr
Lane, Mary D. to Virgil H. Mayfield 7-3-1846 F
Lane, Mary E. to John A. Freeman 8-25-1866 (8-28-1866) T
Lane, Mary E. to John R. Jelks 1-18-1845 (1-22-1845) Ma
Lane, Mary to Daniel Taylor 11-27-1870 T
Lane, Mary to Jefferson M. Ridens 9-21-1862 Dy
Lane, Mary to W. C. Heskett 10-11-1867 (10-12-1867) O
Lane, Melissa C. to W. D. Sanders 5-12-1859 G
Lane, Mollie A. to Charles B. Allen 7-28-1864 G
Lane, Nancy B. to William H. Ellenton 9-22-1855 (10-4-1855) Ma
Lane, Nancy Jane to Louis Bender 6-15-1861 G
Lane, Nancy to Benjamin B. Dye 1-31-1843 (2-2-1843) F
Lane, Nancy to Jeremiah Ward 1-6-1840 (1-7-1840) O
Lane, Nannie to G. W. Dews 9-29-1867 Hy
Lane, Narsalyce? to Threlbut Wilkinson 3-14-1850 Sh
Lane, Polly to William D. Chamberling 9-5-1836 (9-8-1836) G
Lane, Prior A. J. to Franklin B. Tidwell 11-23-1842 (11-24-1842) Ma
Lane, R. Candace to J. B. Echols 1-19-1876 L
Lane, Sallie T. to John C. McLemore, jr. 6-24-1857 (6-25-1857) Sh
Lane, Sarah to Henry Thompson 3-1-1856 O
Lane, Sarah to John Tyler 1-16-1855 (1-17-1855) Sh
Lane, Sarah to _____ Thompson 3-1-1858 (3-6-1858) O
Lane, Susan to W. H. Davis 1-19-1871 T
Lane, Tabitha Ann to George Williamson 5-30-1828 Ma
Lane?, Fanny to John Johnson 7-17-1844 Cr
Laney, Caroline to Jonathan Gardner 10-5-1847 (10-30-1847) L
Laney, Catherine to John McClelland 3-6-1850 (3-7-1850) L
Laney, Elizabeth to Alfred W. Gray 4-12-1854 (4-19-1854) Hr
Laney, Mary Jane to Josiah Hall 4-22-1854 (4-23-1854) Hr
Laney, Sarah to Lorenzo D. Jones 1-13-1861 We
Laney, Victoria to Wm. M. Mallory 10-26-1870 (10-28-1870) Ma
Lang, Elvira to Richard Bell 4-4-1859 (4-7-1859) L
Langdon, Lutitia to C. K. Slaughter 11-24-1856 Sh
Lange, Nancy to William Dunagan 6-14-1863 G
Langenbacher, Rose to August Liabar 6-7-1855 Sh
Langford, Elizabeth to William S. Fowler 8-16-1852 Hn
Langford, Jane M. W. to Omer H. Stanley 12-22-1852 (12-23-1852) Ma
Langford, Martha E. to Armstead P. Pool 8-17-1848 Ma
Langford, May Ann to John Munn 5-20-1841 Ma
Langford, Mollie to Josephus Hart 7-13-1868 (no return) Hy
Langham, Mary M. to William Bathshears 7-5-1856 (7-11-1856) G
Langley, America E. to Elisha P. Shoemake 12-5-1862 We
Langley, Elizabeth to Noah Stuckey 5-9-1848 (5-11-1848) L
Langley, M. A. to B. F. Roberson 2-3-1880 (2-5-1880) L
Langlie, Mary to Johnathan Mann 3-28-1872 (no return) Cr
Langsford, Margaret to Henderson Turpin 9-18-1870 Hy
Langston, Elizabeth Jane to Nathaniel Pinnon 4-28-1854 (5-24-1854) O
Langston, Fannie to John Edney 12-22-1869 Hy
Langston, Jane to Silas Tettleton 10-14-1841 We
Langston, Margaret E. to Robert M. Brooks 9-6-1866 Ma
Langston, Martha Jane to Loveitt R. Muns 2-26-1845 Sh
Lanier, Amanda to Benjamine Whitis 2-5-1861 (2-20-1861) Dy
Lanier, Ann E. to John Boon 7-28-1874 T
Lanier, Ann Eliza to Malv. D. Fortenberry 4-11-1867 Hy
Lanier, Annie W. to W. A. Ellis 12-19-1865 (no return) Cr
Lanier, Bettie to Jno. R. (Dr.) Atkinson 12-6-1869 (12-8-1869) Ma
Lanier, C. to Francis Herron 10-15-1850 Cr

Lanier, Elizabeth M. to Robert F. Lanier 12-29-1846 Sh
Lanier, Frances to David Brewer 2-27-1861 (no return) Dy
Lanier, Jane to George McGaughey 2-21-1873 (4-21-1873) Dy
Lanier, Jennie to T. J. Alexander 9-2-1865 (9-3-1865) Cr
Lanier, Leanna to Albert Link 1-23-1873 Hy
Lanier, Lucinda to Ben Haskins 12-25-1877 (12-26-1877) Dy
Lanier, Lucy V. to James N. Parrish 12-9-1868 (12-16-1868) Ma
Lanier, Lucy to Tho. J. Potts 9-18-1865 (9-20-1865) F
Lanier, M. E. to Wm. R. Parham 2-20-1860 (2-22-1860) F
Lanier, Martha Jane to Alfred Moore 9-29-1842 L
Lanier, Mary E. to James Y. Lucas 12-25-1847 (no return) F
Lanier, Mary J. to Henry West 12-30-1873 Hy
Lanier, Mary to Abea Atkins 4-10-1848 (4-11-1848) F
Lanier, Missouri J. to Lemuel T. Lucas 11-6-1867 (no return) Dy
Lanier, Mollie J. to A. R. Waynick 10-13-1856 (10-30-1856) Ma
Lanier, Mollie to W. H. Smith 1-21-1875 Hy
Lanier, Polk to W. M. Johnson 1-1-1872 (no return) Dy
Lanier, Ritta to Richard Reddick 12-7-1868 (no return) Dy
Lanier, Sallie E. to Robt. G. Tucker 10-5-1868 (10-6-1868) F
Lanier, Sarah A. to Jas. M. Barber 3-5-1844 (3-6-1844) L
Lanier, Sarah A. to Newett N. May 11-3-1858 Ma
Lanier, Sarah L. to Wm. A. Hodge 10-17-1876 Dy
Lankford, Adelphi A. to Madison James 12-25-1869 (12-26-1869) Dy
Lankford, Cairo to Alex R. Russell 1-4-1859 (1-6-1859) L
Lankford, Caroline to William Gross 10-8-1857 Be
Lankford, Catherine to Thomas A. Arnold 5-26-1859 Hn
Lankford, Charity to James I. McDonald 3-2-1830 Ma
Lankford, Delphia M. to Calvin H. Harlan 1-24-1872 L
Lankford, Eliza J. to John M. James 4-15-1877 O
Lankford, Elizabeth P. to A. H. Hancock 10-6-1867 Hn
Lankford, Frances S. to S. C. Robbins 11-17-1877 (11-18-1877) Dy
Lankford, Francis C. to James R. Cothran 12-13-1864 (12-14-1864) L
Lankford, Gabella to James R. Heas 9-1-1841 Ma
Lankford, Hannah M. to George W. Byrn 10-8-1859 (10-9-1859) L
Lankford, Harriet to G. L. Rains 12-7-1869 (no return) L
Lankford, Harriet to Thad King 12-20-1877 Hy
Lankford, Julia to Humphrey Herrell 8-19-1871 Cr B
Lankford, L. M. to Jas. B. Watkins 12-6-1871 Hy
Lankford, Lou L. to Joseph Price 7-9-1879 L
Lankford, Louiza V. to George Arun 9-8-1857 Hn
Lankford, Lucy J. to R. W. Ramsey 10-16-1860 (10-15?-1860) Cr
Lankford, Margaret to Ross Sparks 1-18-1869 (1-21-1869) Cr
Lankford, Mary E. to James P. Bagby 12-11-1865 (12-14-1865) L
Lankford, Mary E. to Tignell Jones 3-8-1861 Hr
Lankford, Mary to Zack Berry 8-10-1867 G
Lankford, Minerva J. to E. P. M. C. Haley 6-8-1851 Hn
Lankford, Mollie F. to Ernest L. Taliaferro 2-9-1886 (2-11-1886) L
Lankford, Nancy Ann to William Carnall Jones 12-22-1847 (no return) L
Lankford, Perleva to Thos. J. Dunn 8-11-1842 L
Lankford, Sarah C. to J. A. Kenley 9-3-1878 (9-4-1878) Dy
Lankford, Sarah F. to William L. Patterson 3-10-1863 Hn
Lankford, Virginia E. to William D. Barfield 10-30-1852 (11-4-1852) L
Lanksley (Tanksley), Salina A. to Wm. Moore 1-19-1863 Sh
Lann, Nancy to Layfayette Baggett 2-23-1883 L
Lanney, Bridget to Patrick Hannon 1-27-1851 Sh
Lanningham, Catharine to Jefferson Brown 5-27-1873 Dy
Lanningham, Minerva to Charles Clay 7-2-1873 (7-3-1873) Dy
Lannom, Delilco to John Provine 1-9-1861 (no return) Hn
Lannom, Luizer to Jim Landis 2-9-1868 G B
Lannom, Nora to W. A. Thompson 5-1-1867 G
Lannom, Sue to W. H. Foster 9-10-1866 G
Lanny, Melissa to Thomas Carlesly 1-13-1855 (1-14-1855) L
Lanom, Catharine to Z. W. Branson 8-?-1862 G
Lanom, Elizabeth to John Burrow 11-6-1864 G
Lansden, Amanda to Elzey Dudley 7-17-1869 (no return) Cr
Lansdon, Alice to W. H. Roach 9-23-1867 (10-1-1867) Cr
Lansdon, Margaret L. to John R. Pearson 10-20-1840 F
Lanster, Susan to Young Gray 9-16-1847 Sh
Lanthrop, Mary Ann to James French 7-23-1845 F
Lany, M. A. to Frank M. Morgan 9-29-1868 Hy
Lany, Margaret C. to Geo. M. Leathers 7-24-1860 Hr
Lapley, Jane T. to W. J. Edwards 1-13-1867 Hy
Larance, M. J. to J. W. Eskew 11-15-1871 (11-16-1871) Cr
Laremore, T. A. to J. H. Shaf 7-27-1874 (7-29-1874) T
Larimore, A. R. to J. R. Johnston 1-8-1878 L
Larimore, Amanda to J. P. Keaton 2-25-1868 T
Larimore, Elsey to James A. Calhoon 9-17-1840 (10-15-1840) T
Larimore, Nancy to J. W. Barnet 2-11-1868 (3-3-1868) T
Larimore, W. P. to W. N. Myers 2-18-1873 (2-20-1873) T
Larisson, M. J. to J. Manly Jefferds 12-15-1859 (12-19-1859) Sh
Larkin, Elizer J. to J. U. Canada 12-23-1869 G
Larkin, Mary to John Burke 8-24-1842 Sh
Larrimore, H. to Joe Hall 12-17-1874 T
Larrimore, Hattie to James W. Dupree 10-24-1883 L
Larrison, Emma to Lee Wortham 2-4-1881 (not executed) L
Larrison, Emma to Nathan Rogers 12-16-1874 Hy
Larrison, Josephine to Joseph Jennings (Jinnans?) 2-13-1873 (2-22-1873) L B

Brides

Larrison, Sarah to Squire Bidden 11-10-1868 G B
Larrison, Tilda to W. J. Jones 12-16-1874 (12-17-1874) L B
Larson, Emma to Isaac Bradford 3-22-1884 (3-26-1884) L
Las?, Milly to Jos. R. Owen 1-23-1869 (1-24-1869) T
Lasater, Louisa M. to William J. Pool 2-28-1861 We
Lashlee, Catharine to James G. Ruff 1-23-1846 Be
Lashlee, Isabella to S. D. Ruff 4-12-1845 Be
Lashlee, Loucinda to Wm. Cockrell 10-17-1867 Be
Lashlee, Sarah to Saml. H. Akin 12-11-1849 Be
Lashlee, Temperance to J. M. Browning 1-13-1846 Be
Lashley, Elizabeth Jane to Thomas Colwell Shelby 3-4-1859 (3-10-1859) Sh
Lasiter, Altrecy to Henry F. O'Neal 2-25-1856 (no return) Hn
Lasiter, Ellen E. to Stephen P. Hicks 4-11-1850 (no return) Hn
Lasiter, Martha to James Perkins 9-29-1843 Hn
Lasiter, Martha to John M. Reynolds 8-29-1855 (no return) Hn
Lasiter, Mary J. to D. A. Bohanan 1-19-1858 Cr
Lasiter, N. J. to B. P. Dyer 10-25-1876 (10-26-1876) Dy
Lasiter, Nancy C. to Wm. McKehan 5-28-1860 (5-30-1860) Hr
Lasseter, Lucinda C. to James H. Galbreth 2-5-1866 (2-18-1866) T
Lassiter, Candes to Thos. Stanford 6-18-1840 Cr
Lassiter, Green H. to Sidney W. Blackwood 9-27-1857 Hn
Lassiter, Lucy A. to Boker C. Jarrall 4-3-1849 Ma
Lassiter, Lurana C. to R. T. Davis 1-10-1870 (no return) L
Lassiter, M. C. to C. C. Gentry 12-24-1866 G
Lassiter, Marthen to John V. Rogers 9-25-1853 Hn
Lassiter, Mary Ann to M. T. Cock 9-21-1852 (9-22-1852) Ma
Lassiter, Nancy to J. W. McCallister 6-18-1862 Mn
Laster, Columbia E. to John P. Hall 4-11-1877 (4-12-1877) Dy
Laster, Darcas to Elson C. Walker 2-18-1875 Hy
Laster, Harriet Jane to John D. Gray 11-24-1864 O
Laster, L. H. to J. J. Penick 10-19-1865 Hn
Laster, Marinaan to Joseph Ray 8-29-1871 (8-30-1871) Dy
Laster, Mary E. to J. L. Chrisman 10-31-1871 (11-3-1873?) Dy
Laster, Sarah to George W. Reynolds 2-21-1857 Hn
Lathain, Frances to William Sain 7-10-1838 (7-12-1838) G
Latham, Catherine T. to John B. Miller 10-24-1844 L
Latham, Elizabeth to Francis Wright 8-21-1853 (8-23-1853) Ma
Latham, Elizabeth to William P. Lacy 9-13-1858 Ma
Latham, Jane to A. P. Ewing 10-31-1881 (11-2-1881) L
Latham, Lucretia Paralee to Samuel Richardson 11-19-1855 Ma
Latham, M. E. to J. F. Beard 5-26-1885 (5-27-1885) L
Latham, Martha Ann to Wm. T. Herbert 3-11-1871 (3-15-1871) Ma
Latham, Mary Ann to William H. Wells 12-23-1850 (12-24-1850) Ma
Latham, Mary M. to Newton J. Cantwell 12-6-1855 We
Latham, Virginia H. to W. F. McCoy 10-19-1876 Dy
Latham, Virginia to Benjamin M. Smith 12-30-1861 (no return) We
Lathan, Sarah to James Gross 1-10-1855 (1-11-1855) T
Lathis, Barbery to James R. Brizendine 10-18-1860 Hn
Lathrick, Catherine to John L. Crews 2-4-1856 Ma
Latimer, Elizabeth to James Bedford 11-18-1854 (11-23-1854) O
Latimer, Harrett A. to J. H. Biddix 8-18-1864 O
Latimer, L. A. to L. W. Holford 11-23-1865 O
Latimer, Malvina to John Perry 9-12-1859 (9-14-1859) O
Latimer, Nancy E. to William Latimer 10-6-1855 (10-17-1855) O
Latimer, S. A. to J. B. Howell 11-27-1865 O
Laton, Mary E. to S. F. Robins 10-8-1862 Mn
Latta, Cynthia M. to Ebenezer Kilpatrick 1-13-1858 Sh
Latta, Lucy to J. G. Seat 10-18-1871 Dy
Latta, M. J. (Mrs.) to J. H. Verner 2-26-1866 G
Latta, Mary J. to Willis G. Reeves 11-6-1854 (11-8-1854) Hr
Latta?, Kate to T. C. Gordon 6-24-1879 (6-25-1879) Dy
Lattie, Elizabeth to Edmond W. Rains 11-15-1828 (11-18-1828) G
Lattie, Nancy to Moses B. Hawkins 7-29-1835 (8-2-1835) G
Lattimer, Margaret to Mark Mitchell 9-13-1853 Hn
Lattimore, Martha Ann to Thomas Broaden 1-12-1864 Be
Lattimore, Sarah A. to Jack Gammons 1-13-1868 Dy
Latty, Margaret to Henry Duffy 10-22-1839 (10-24-1839) G
Lauderdale, Betsy Ann to John Ford 4-14-1866 Y
Lauderdale, Clara H. to Josiah H. Lauderdale 4-4-1866 (4-4-1865?) T
Lauderdale, Eliza J. to James A. Hill 7-31-1867 (9-1-1867) T
Lauderdale, Lucy Jennie L. to William Carroll Doyle 7-25-1860 (no return) Dy
Lauderdale, Mary A. to John S. Reffington 11-18-1868 Dy
Lauderdale, Pecella to Hilary Cage 3-5-1869 T
Lauftmeister, Pauline to A. C. Schick 6-14-1859 (6-16-1860) Sh
Laughlan, Ann to Bryan Cullen 8-14-1852 (9-13-1852) Sh
Laughlan, Elizabeth to Thomas Deshaser 10-27-1851 O
Laughlan, Zelpha to Thomas Deshaser 4-26-1850 O
Laughlin, Clementine Elizabeth to James L. Young 7-14-1835 Hr
Laughlin, Margaret C. to William Downey 3-3-1837 (3-7-1837) O
Laughn, Martha Ann to Madison H. Chambers 12-8-1843 (no return) F
Laughorn, Eliza M. to Rufus E. Buffum 7-15-1846 F
Laughter, Cladus to Basel McVay 9-25-1847 F
Laughter, Martha to John S. Mayfield 6-16-1836 Y
Laughter, Sopha W. to William R. Driskill 10-24-1842 (12-15-1842) G
Laughter, Susan Jane to John H. Beard 4-29-1846 (4-6?-1846) F
Laughter, Susan Jane to Lemuel Langham 1-1-1846 (no return) F
Laughy, Virginia J. to Wm. B. (Rev.) Hill 10-30-1851 (no return) F

Laum (Launy, Lawry?), Matilda to Rufus Inman 12-21-1854 L
Laurance, Adaline to Alexander S. Wallace 4-26-1851 G
Lauren, M. A. to G. L. Fain 12-20-1855 Ma
Laurence, Anna M. to Joseph E. Moody 6-14-1849 (6-15-1849) F
Laurie, Isabelle to Lem Dawson 2-20-1866 Hn
Laurison, Alice to J. H. Smith 2-23-1886 (3-12-1886) L
Laurison, Sarah to Dick Nichols 1-30-1880 (2-1-1880) L B
Lavallett, Mary F. to Robert A. Marr 4-6-1850 Sh
Lavier, Martha B. to Henry W. Hall 5-15-1867 (5-16-1867) F
Lavin, Bridget to Michael Murphey 8-15-1861 Sh
Lavinia, Jones to J. B. Powell 12-23-1861 (no return) Hy
Lavis, Elizabeth J. to U. (Dr.) Alexander 1-27-1841 G
Law, A. L. to T. H. White 8-12-1856 Sh
Law, C. C. to Stephen M. Norris 2-3-1857 (2-16-1857) Sh
Law, Jane to Willis Stallings 11-19-1830 (11-24-1830) Ma
Law, Julia Gordon to William Henry Kerr 10-17-1859 (10-18-1859) Sh
Law, Virginia E. to Nathaniel M. Sneed 6-9-1856 (6-10-1856) Sh
Law?, Cyntha A. to H. S. Wilson 11-28-1844 Hn
Lawhorn, Angeline B. to Moses P. Crisp 9-18-1855 Hr
Lawhorn, Elizabeth (Mrs.) to N. A. Senter 12-19-1867 G
Lawhorn, F. E. to W. C. Williamson 1-20-1863 (1-21-1863) Dy
Lawhorn, M. A. to J. F. Stalkup 1-27-1870 (1-28-1870) Dy
Lawhorn, Mary Agnes to W. J. Wilson 3-17-1858 Hn
Lawhorn, Sarah E. to William Benson 10-19-1858 (10-26-1858) Hr
Lawhorn, Sarah G. to Thomas J. Gardner 5-4-1847 (5-?-1847) Hr
Lawler, Elizabeth to Edward Brennen (Brannen) 1-23-1864 Sh
Lawler, L. C. to John K. Thompson 4-6-1854 Sh
Lawler, Margaret to Thos. W. Bowie 8-30-1856 Sh
Lawler, Susan to Richard Tabner 5-1-1847 Sh
Lawrance, Elizabeth to R. K. Pinckley 10-13-1865 (10-15-1865) Cr
Lawrence, A. E. to S. F. Simmons 12-1-1869 G
Lawrence, Adeline H. to Dacton F. Collier 11-25-1859 (11-27-1860) We
Lawrence, Ann E. to Hiram D. Connell 8-21-1848 Sh
Lawrence, Ann Eliza B. to William R. Lacy 12-17-1867 (12-18-1867) Ma
Lawrence, Candis to William Crafton 9-5-1867 G
Lawrence, Elizabeth D. to Enoch Sanders 3-17-1839 Cr
Lawrence, Elizabeth H. to Calhoun W. Beadles 12-26-1859 (no return) We
Lawrence, Elizabeth to J. P. Brandon 12-12-1852 Hn
Lawrence, Emma to Willis Smith 8-2-1884 L
Lawrence, Exalina to David M. Quinley 2-12-1850 Ma
Lawrence, Frances C. to Wm. L. Radford 10-23-1855 Sh
Lawrence, Frances E. to Patrick E. Singleton 5-17-1855 (5-20-1855) G
Lawrence, Frances S. to John S. Williams 4-14-1846 Sh
Lawrence, Harriett A. to J. H. Banks 11-28-1867 Hn
Lawrence, Jane to Cader Piercy 7-19-1845 (7-20-1845) Ma
Lawrence, Jane to F. S. Simmons 3-17-1863 Hn
Lawrence, Katie M. to Ira O. Westbrook 11-15-1884 (11-16-1884) L
Lawrence, Louiza J. to James B. Dinkins 11-26-1846 Hn
Lawrence, Lydia to James Dawson 1-30-1856 Ma
Lawrence, Malissa to David C. Wallace 12-18-1856 Hn
Lawrence, Margaret to F. W. Ferguson 2-4-1837 Hr
Lawrence, Martha to Elisha T. Harbour 8-22-1868 (8-26-1868) Ma
Lawrence, Martha to James Dawson 4-12-1854 Ma
Lawrence, Martha to Sandy Alston 8-14-1868 G B
Lawrence, Mary A. to Anderson C. Farmer 1-4-1840 Hn
Lawrence, Mary E. to Jasper M. Jones 10-27-1850 Hn
Lawrence, Mary Tennessee to Charles Moore 12-25-1867 G B
Lawrence, Mary to Silas Pinkley 3-16-1843 Cr
Lawrence, Matilda to G. W. Butler 1-1-1856 We
Lawrence, Moniza to David T. Thurman 10-28-1858 Ma
Lawrence, Nancy L. to S. A. Green 7-1-1867 O
Lawrence, Parthenia E. to Ellis Davis 9-22-1870 G
Lawrence, Patsey to Alexander Thompson 3-21-1829 Ma
Lawrence, S. A. to J. W. Clemmens 9-16-1856 We
Lawrence, Sally M. to Jno. S. Lacy 12-1-1868 (12-2-1868) Ma
Lawrence, Sarah B. to Henry S. Peyton 12-27-1844 (no return) F
Lawrence, Sarah J. to Lemuel Brandon 1-22-1855 Hn
Lawrence, Sarah to William H. Dunn 11-10-1853 Sh
Lawrence, W. H. to G. N. Davidson 6-15-1870 O
Laws (Lane), Mary to Daniel Thomas 4-22-1849 Sh
Laws, Francis to William Collins 1-18-1878 Hy
Laws, M. A. to A. R. Tucker 2-13-1851 Cr
Laws, M. E. to J. M. Springer 11-13-1867 Cr
Laws, Mary to Samuel R. Wheeler 10-9-1843 We
Laws, Matilda Jane to Martin V. Dowdy 5-3-1859 (5-4-1859) Hr
Laws, Nancy P. to Lemuel M. Jelks 5-4-1850 (5-7-1850) Ma
Laws, Susan A. to Robert A. Pool 7-11-1850 Sh
Lawson, Adaline to George Board 6-19-1875 (6-20-1875) O
Lawson, America to John Williams 6-15-1882 (6-17-1882) L
Lawson, Clemintine to Benjamin F. Lackey 1-4-1854 (1-5-1854) Hr
Lawson, Ema? to Burrel Harris 2-4-1874 (2-14-1874) L B
Lawson, F. to Anderson Johnson 1-9-1851 Hn
Lawson, Harriet E. E. to Henry K. Brown 10-29-1857 O
Lawson, Louisa E. to Richard Stubblefield 8-20-1858 Hn
Lawson, Margrett to Saml. Damron 4-16-1854 We
Lawson, Mary B. to Cato Davis 2-13-1857 (2-18-1857) O
Lawson, Nancy C. to Wesly Holt 3-23-1858 We

Lawson, Nancy T. to Ephraim A. Lackey 5-13-1854 (5-14[18]-1854) Hr
Lawson, Rachel to Daniel Leath 9-18-1863 Mn
Lawson, Rebecca to John Wade 3-22-1875 O
Lawson, S. C. to G. R. Hicks 12-21-1864 O
Lawson, Susan Ann to Joseph H. Moorehead 5-26-1857 (5-28-1857) O
Lawson, Virginia to T. J. Estus 4-23-1875 L
Lawson, Volumnia W. to Samuel Landrum 2-21-1853 O
Lawthon, Sarah to Wash Anderson 3-13-1869 (3-14-1869) T
Lawton, A. L. to A. L. Roper 10-9-1870 G
Lax, Ann to Hiram D. Casey 5-21-1847 (5-23-1847) Hr
Lax, Delilah S. to Aaron J. Linville 1-5-1857 Hn
Lax, Rebecca to Bird Chumley 9-26-1848 Hn
Lax, Rebecca to Joseph Smith 8-24-1840 (no return) Hn
Lax, Sarah to William Gulledge 12-26-1842 (no return) Hn
Lax, Tabitha to David R. Compton 8-8-1853 (8-10-1853) Hr
Laxton, J. C. to William Bennett 7-19-1873 (7-20-1873) T
Laxton, Martha M. to William F. Privett 8-31-1843 Ma
Laxton?, Sarah E. to Thomas McMallen 1-26-1870 (1-27-1870)] T
Lay, Clotilda to James C. Griffin 6-25-1851 (no return) F
Lay, Elizabeth J. to James M. Johnson 8-28-1864 (9-4-1864) Cr
Lay, Elizabeth J. to James M. Johnson no date Cr
Lay, M. C. to J. V. Thornton 9-27-1859 (9-28-1859) F
Lay, Martha E. to David O. Owens 8-23-1854 (no return) F
Lay, Martha L. to J. C. Davis 8-16-1880 (8-17-1880) L
Lay, Mary (Mrs.) to Sandin Harriss 10-24-1882 (10-26-1882) L
Lay, Mary to Thos. S. Canada 4-8-1868 (no return) F
Lay, Mattie A. to J. E. Jeter 10-8-1866 Hy
Lay, S. E. to H. D. McLeod 12-11-1878 Hy
Laycock, E. J. to James S. Bates 12-5-1872 Cr
Laycock, L. F. to G. W. Kee 10-27-1872 Cr
Laycock, Nancy C. to Joseph C. C. Rhodes 1-5-1870 Cr
Laycock, Sarah E. to Sebrom Smothers 6-11-1870 (6-12-1870) Cr
Laycock, Winford to Wm. S. Mitchell 6-3-1846 Cr
Laycook, E. to Syrus Wilson 12-29-1851 Cr
Laycook, L. V. to J. B. Dill 2-13-1873 Cr
Laycook, Minnie C. to James D. Hill 2-4-1858 Cr
Laycook, R. A. to James H. Dilday 1-18-1855 Cr
Laycook, Sarah to Edwrd Harris 8-19-1840 (no return) Cr
Laycook, Sarah to James Forbess 8-7-1845 Cr
Layman (Sayman), Elizabeth to R. H. Adams 10-17-1866 G
Layne, Drucilla to William M. Kincaid 12-24-1829 Sh
Layne, J. to T. B. Glenn 11-15-1884 (11-16-1886?) L
Layne, Lucy to Wyatt Neal 11-14-1885 (12-13-1885)
Layne, Margart to Joseph Jester 4-15-1871 (4-30-1871) L
Layne, Mary to Albert Parker 3-10-1881 L B
Layne, Mary to Alexander Baker 7-9-1870 (7-10-1870) L
Lcy, Mary Jane to Henry J. Jackson 6-15-1861 (6-16-1861) Ma
LeCog (Secog), Eveline E. to P. H. Alexander 3-23-1849 Sh
LeRoy, Francis to W. V. Claridge 12-26-1863 (12-27-1863) Sh
Lea, Ada to Frank McCollaster 2-25-1871 Hy
Lea, Amanda to C. D. Lovelace 5-30-1850 We
Lea, Amanda to Nelson Lee 12-17-1872 Hy
Lea, Annie E. to William T. Myrick 4-3-1866 L
Lea, Annis to Wm. Williamson 11-10-1866 Hy
Lea, Charlotte to John? Johnson 9-8-1871 (9-12-1871) L
Lea, Charlotte to Paul Jones 7-8-1881 (7-24-1881) L
Lea, Clementina to Charles W. Gazzam 11-29-1827 Hr
Lea, Eliza J. to Thomas J. West 3-16-1846 (3-19-1846) G
Lea, Elizabeth F. to James Lowry 11-18-1846 We
Lea, Elizabeth Jaine to William Carooth 2-11-1852 L
Lea, Elizabeth to Archie Pierce 11-6-1872 (no return) L
Lea, Elizabeth to James Lowry 11-16-1846 We
Lea, Elizabeth to Rufus P. Neely 5-16-1829 (5-19-1829) Hr
Lea, Ellen to Frank Sturdevant 12-1-1878 Hy
Lea, Emma to Dalles Loving 12-27-1872 Hy
Lea, Emma to William Sangster 10-23-1880 (10-28-1880) L
Lea, Eveline to Harriss Larrison 6-29-1876 (6-30-1876) L
Lea, Fannie to Abraham Kenney (Kelley?) 5-24-1873 (5-29-1873) L B
Lea, Fanny to John Wright 2-15-1876 Hy
Lea, Frances A. to Alexander Howard 1-30-1838 (no return) L
Lea, Frances to Wm. B. James 11-30-1836 Sh
Lea, Georgiana H. to John M. Morrill 4-23-1855 Ma
Lea, Harriet to Joseph Smith 10-23-1839 (10-24-1839) Hr
Lea, Hester to William M. H. Newton 1-4-1824 Hr
Lea, I. G. to W. A. Glenn 12-23-1868 (no return) Hy
Lea, Jane to Brister Bond 11-9-1867 Hy
Lea, Julia to Julias Morgan 1-4-1871 (no return) L
Lea, Leanna to Austin Rayner 12-26-1870 (no return) Hy
Lea, Maria Jane to Wm. M. Stone 9-22-1867 Hy
Lea, Martha A. to Daniel West 5-28-1844 (6-15-1844) G
Lea, Mary E. to P. C. Broman 2-16-1868 Hy
Lea, Mary E. to William E. Barker 4-10-1848 (4-17-1848) G
Lea, Mary E. to William Pool 8-21-1849 (8-23-1849) Ma
Lea, Mary J. to Jno. Herring 3-24-1860 (no return) Hy
Lea, Mary L. to Calvin Graus 2-11-1859 Ma
Lea, Mary to Alexander Eison 1-7-1875 L B
Lea, Mary(Polly) to John Needham 1-31-1835 (2-?-1835) Hr

Lea, Matilda to Arsa Craig 12-16-1838 Cr
Lea, Matilda to Fedo Royster 2-12-1876 Hy
Lea, Ora to Jeramiah Porter 11-29-1874 (1-29-1875) L B
Lea, Rosana to Jesse Blalock 4-13-1833 (4-14-1833) Hr
Lea, Sarah L. to W. R. D. Howarton 10-26-1854 (10-29-1854) G
Lea, Susan to Rufus Roberts 2-22-1882 L
Lea, Swannanoa to Thomas F. Baynes 10-22-1873 Hy
Lea, Tissie to John Walker 12-28-1871 Hy
Lea, Zelphia J. to Jonathan S. Wiggs 8-21-1856 G
Leabnathy, Nancy A. to S. N. Brantly 8-12-1865 (no return) Hy
Leace, Rosana to John O. Drew 1-14-1852 Sh
Leach, Ann to Dennis Kirby 3-10-1850 Sh
Leach, Ardina to John jr. Briant 10-18-1870 (10-23-1870) Cr
Leach, Arminta H. to James Drummonds 1-4-1862 (1-5-1862) T
Leach, Charlotte Augustus to Francis Mellersh 6-4-1855 Sh
Leach, Eliza to A. J. Bowden 11-20-1853 T
Leach, Elizabeth Ann to W. F. Seymore 2-23-1863 (no return) Cr
Leach, Elizabeth ann to W. F. Seymore 2-23-1863 Cr
Leach, Elizabeth to Green B. Young 11-14-1849 T
Leach, Emily to Marcus Henry Hartsfield 12-29-1849 T
Leach, Harriet Ford to Hosea Carroll Brown 9-22-1852 T
Leach, Josephine to J. J. Cuningham 1-31-1871 (2-2-1871) Cr
Leach, L. J. to Mitt Anderson 3-8-1855 Cr
Leach, Louisa J. to A. T. Brooks 11-21-1850 Cr
Leach, M. A. to Charles H. Alston 11-6-1867 Dy
Leach, M. T. to Z. T. Browning 8-5-1872 (8-8-1872) Cr
Leach, Maggie G. to W. S. Firth 3-1-1870 (3-2-1870) F
Leach, Margaret J. to Allen Bell 12-26-1849 Cr
Leach, Martha E. to Benjamin C. McCollom 12-29-1868 (12-31-1868) Cr
Leach, Martha N. to James Keaton 12-29-1851 Cr
Leach, Mary A. to J. R. Jones 10-27-1866 (no return) Cr
Leach, Mary A. to James H. Brooks 1-13-1853 Cr
Leach, Mary F. to G. H. Brooks 12-1-1856 Cr
Leach, Mattie G. to L. H. Lockheart 10-27-1870 (no return) F
Leach, Nancy Ann to Benjamin F. Hartsfield 8-8-1855 T
Leach, Nancy to Thornton Rhodes 10-4-1851 (10-5-1851) T
Leach, Rachell to Wm. Browning 11-19-1857 Cr
Leach, S. E. to J. R. McAlexander 2-5-1866 (2-8-1866) Cr
Leach, S. E. to R. E. Mackecy 2-8-1856 Cr
Leachman, Mathaney J. to Joseph Dowdey 10-7-1845 O
Leacy, Powell to Geo. Powell 9-18-1871 Hy
Leadbetter, Eloner to Joshua Price 12-3-1838 Ma
Leaf, Biddy to Bob Robertson 2-4-1869 G B
Leak, Martha E. to John B. Mosely 11-5-1846 Sh
Leake, E. A. to Wm. Lancaster 6-6-1846 Sh
Leake, Frances C. to John N. Lewis 8-29-1833 Sh
Leake, Indiana H. to James Lenow 6-9-1842 Sh
Leake, Lucinda to William Robert Wilson 1-18-1856 Ma
Leake, Lucy Jane to Fred B. Fisk 5-25-1857 (5-27-1857) Sh
Leake, Lucy V. to Jno. B. Lancaster 7-22-1852 Sh
Leake, M. C. to Fletcher H. Tally 2-24-1858 Sh
Leake, Marcella J. to Thomas H. (A.) Rash 8-30-1837 Sh
Leake, Sarah S. to Saml. Mosby 7-20-1846 Sh
Leake, Sophia E. to Marcus E. Cochran 9-25-1849 Sh
Leamons, Nancy to Robert Boles 3-5-1831 G
Leander, Nancy T. to George W. Dunlap 11-19-1856 Cr
Leann, McCulle to Cary Pitts 1-5-1878 Hy
Leap, Barbara to G. N. Taylor 6-11-1863 O
Lear?, Lucretia to James A. L. Neely 4-1-1833 (4-14-1833) Hr
Learned, S. S. to H. S. Davis 2-4-1863 We
Learns, Mary L. to James A. Moore 10-19-1863 Sh
Leary, Kissiah E. to Thomas D. Greer 8-27-1838 Sh
Leary, Winopard to Joseph Spruce 6-8-1830 Ma
Leaser, Catharine to Gothilf Miller 3-18-1861 Sh
Leath, Alice to J. A. Griffin 5-1-1861 G
Leath, Augusta to Columbus Edwards 3-12-1868 G
Leath, Eliza to Bill Nunn 12-9-1869 G
Leath, Elizabeth M. to David Norris 8-31-1868 (9-2-1868) F
Leath, M. L. to Jefferson Smalwood 10-27-1861 Mn
Leath, Sallie A. to W. H. Brown 11-24-1870 G
Leath, T. C. to L. H. Jackson 1-11-1873 (1-12-1873) Dy
Leath, Vallie M. to P. M. Leath 7-12-1855 Sh
Leathers, Elizabeth to E. L. Nearin 2-21-1845 (2-23-1845) Hr
Leathers, Mary Ann to W. H. Pace 9-16-1835 Hr
Leathers, Sarah Jane to Benjamin W. Pirtle 9-16-1839 Hr
Leathus, Elizabeth to Lewis Lea 3-17-1874 (3-18-1874) L B
Leblance, Elvina to John P. Hoffman 11-20-1858 Sh
Ledbetter, Anna C. to Benjamin Patrick 9-5-1847 Sh
Ledbetter, Annie M. to Henry R. Hardy 11-12-1867 (11-13-1867) L
Ledbetter, Betsy Ann to John S. Burrow 12-21-1842 Ma
Ledbetter, E. V. to J. G. Haynes 5-4-1885 (5-5-1885) L
Ledbetter, F. E. to J. W. Acuff 5-31-1884 (6-1-1884) L
Ledbetter, Martha E. to John S. Chism 9-29-1855 (9-30-1855) L
Ledbetter, Martha F. to B. F. Boydston 12-28-1881 L
Ledbetter, Mary Ann to John H. Chapman 9-14-1863 (9-15-1863) L
Ledbetter, Mary Ann to Joseph F. Hargett 7-19-1862 (9-25-1862) L
Ledbetter, Mary Ann to Joseph F. Hargett 7-29-1862 (7-?-1862) L

Ledbetter, Mary E. to A. T. Bain 10-20-1870 G
Ledbetter, Mary E. to J. N. Meadows 2-22-1869 (2-29?-1869) L
Ledbetter, Mary E. to John P. Hogg 11-11-1865 (11-12-1865) L
Ledbetter, Mary G. to D. A. Robertson 9-19-1866 (9-20-1866) Dy
Ledbetter, Mary Jane to Joshua Keneday 3-19-1877 L
Ledbetter, Mary to John Lockard 7-15-1841 L
Ledbetter, Mattie J. to H. W. Johnson 1-3-1864 Sh
Ledbetter, Mattie J. to Henry W. Johnson 1-1-1864 (1-3-1864) Sh
Ledbetter, Minerva J. to A. L. Haynes 4-12-1879 (4-20-1879) L
Ledbetter, Nancy E. to James M. Lusk 4-29-1854 (4-31-1854) L
Ledbetter, Nancy M. to J. P. Belton 12-6-1882 (12-7-1882) L
Ledbetter, Nannie to J. M. Drummon 2-10-1870 Dy
Ledbetter, Rosa Lee to W. J. Prichard 2-13-1878 Dy
Ledbetter, Ruthy to Perry H. Brown no date (6-27-1852) L
Ledbetter, S. E. to W. G. Haynes 5-26-1873 (5-27-1873) L
Ledbetter, S. J. to Andrew Jackson Edwards 11-11-1878 (11-12-1878) L
Ledbetter, Sarah J. to James R. Ledbetter 5-30-1853 L
Ledbetter, Sarah Jane to James A. McIver 10-22-1853 (10-28-1853) L
Ledbetter, Sarah to Elijah G. Chism 5-18-1842 L
Ledsinger, A. O. to J. A. Fowlkes 6-3-1869 Dy
Ledsinger, Alice to Wyatt Smith 4-13-1871 (4-14-1871) Dy
Ledsinger, Catharine to James Newton Wynne 9-24-1869 (no return) Dy
Ledsinger, Cynthia A. to Tobe Wicks 12-27-1875 Dy
Ledsinger, Dora to Peyton Burkley 5-11-1878 (5-15-1878) Dy
Ledsinger, Eliza to James Stewart 12-28-1870 (12-29-1870) Dy
Ledsinger, Ellen to Jack Segraves? 12-27-1877 Dy
Ledsinger, Emma to Henry Haskins 9-24-1872 (9-26-1872) Dy
Ledsinger, Louisa M. to John M. Dunlap 1-3-1856 Cr
Ledsinger, Lucinda to Samuel Enochs 3-20-1873 Dy
Ledsinger, M. C. to J. P. Shaw 12-21-1869 Cr
Ledsinger, M. J. to G. W. Williams 10-7-1871 (10-8-1871) Cr
Ledsinger, Maggie E. to H. T. Grant 9-2-1873 Dy
Ledsinger, Mary to John Jordan 5-14-1878 (5-15-1878) Dy
Ledsinger, Penny to Charley Ruff 12-19-1867 Dy
Ledsinger, Phillis to Lee Davis 1-25-1877 (no return) Dy
Ledsinger, Ruth to John B. Collins 3-9-1843 Cr
Ledsinger, Z. F. to A. A. Fowlkes 4-4-1865 (4-6-1865) Dy
Lee, A. C. to G. S. Porter 3-12-1861 O
Lee, A. to George Petty 8-29-1867 G B
Lee, Adeline to John R. Webb 1-30-1866 Hn
Lee, Alice to J. W. Pearson 2-24-1886 (2-25-1886) L
Lee, Amanda Jane to D. R. Bradley 4-22-1866 Hn
Lee, Angelina R. to Lysander M. Campbell 6-15-1848 L
Lee, Ann to C. W. French 10-20-1862 (no return) Hn
Lee, Annie J. to W. N. Portis 5-12-1860 (5-16-1860) F
Lee, Annie to Allen Bostic 11-2-1867 (11-9-1867) L B
Lee, Caroline to Cullen French 1-2-1845 Hn
Lee, Catharine to Lewis Amis 11-11-1839 F
Lee, Cynthia to John M. Bigham 9-29-1865 (10-1-1865) Cr
Lee, Elizabeth J. to David Kendall 11-29-1849 Hn
Lee, Elizabeth to Dayerous Powell 7-3-1855 We
Lee, Elizabeth to John C. Bullington 2-11-1854 (2-16-1854) G
Lee, Elizabeth to John H. Williams 4-10-1845 L
Lee, Emma A. to John H. Martin 1-27-1885 (1-29-1885) L
Lee, Esther to G. Washington Smith 7-10-1841 (7-11-1841) Hr
Lee, Eugenia to Sidney Evans 12-11-1873 (no return) Hy
Lee, Eveline to Allen Green 9-13-1853 (9-16-1853) G
Lee, Frankie to Allen Rogers 10-30-1869 Hy
Lee, Georgia to Joe Lee 9-13-1880 (9-14-1880) L B
Lee, Hannah to Frank Rice 2-7-1877 Hy
Lee, Hardina to Montgomery Currin 2-2-1880 (2-4-1880) L
Lee, Harriet D. to Arthur McKinnie 3-23-1833 (3-26-1833) Hr
Lee, Harriet to Edmund Randle 1-4-1845 (no return) Hn
Lee, Huldah to J. H. Larkins 7-29-1885 (7-30-1885) L
Lee, Jane to Joseph Deberry 8-5-1868 (no return) Dy
Lee, Josie to Nathan Lee 3-28-1882 (3-29-1882) L
Lee, Judith F. to Wiley G. Day 1-25-1846 Sh
Lee, Kissie to Simon Jones 12-23-1879 (12-29-1879) L
Lee, Lizzie to John West 9-15-1880 L B
Lee, Louisa to Charles E. Butler 8-23-1852 (8-26-1852) G
Lee, Louisa to James A. Foutch 5-5-1846 Hn
Lee, Lucinda to Jefferson Irby 7-31-1843 (no return) Hn
Lee, Lucy to Madison Currin 2-17-1879 (2-20-1879) L
Lee, M. J. to E. E. Willis 10-8-1860 O
Lee, M. J. to J. A. R. Utley 11-24-1870 Cr
Lee, Malinda to F. A. Easterwood 8-26-1862 O
Lee, Malinda to Franklin Bennett 10-31-1843 F
Lee, Marcy C. to R. S. Brickum 10-6-1864 Mn
Lee, Margaret to G. W. Lacy 9-26-1878 (10-6-1878) L B
Lee, Margarett to William W. Williams 10-11-1850 O
Lee, Marinda to S. P. Hicks 10-25-1865 G
Lee, Martha L. to Joseph H. Dorand 4-7-1851 Sh
Lee, Martha to Gabriel Holmes 12-27-1838 Hn
Lee, Martha to Joseph Dick 9-26-1862 Hn
Lee, Martha to Noah Wimberley 5-13-1853 Hn
Lee, Mary A. to James Coffman 11-24-1840 Hn
Lee, Mary A. to John W. Benson 3-7-1844 We

Lee, Mary A. to R. C. Wallpool 8-7-1870 G
Lee, Mary Ann to James H. Hall 3-12-1842 (no return) Hn
Lee, Mary F. to Allen A. Barnes 12-11-1862 Hn
Lee, Mary J. to Richard J. Bevill 12-12-1867 (no return) Hn
Lee, Mary Jane to William Garrett 1-20-1883 (1-21-1883) L
Lee, Mary M. to Henderson Baucum 5-22-1842 Hn
Lee, Mary to Benj. L. Sanders 8-10-1836 Sh
Lee, Matilda to Henry F. James 9-30-1824 Sh
Lee, Matilda to Wm. H. McKisick 12-24-1867 F B
Lee, Mattie B. to Wm. N. Portis 11-1-1869 (11-3-1869) F
Lee, Melba? to D. T. Dover 12-5-1862 Mn
Lee, Middy M. to William Dortch 9-12-1848 Hn
Lee, Mollie to Lindsey Halliburton 1-6-1886 (no return) L
Lee, Nancy D. to Lander L. Wood 12-2-1856 (12-3-1856) G
Lee, Olive to Nathaniel Fields 8-14-1861 (8-15-1861) O
Lee, Parthenia to Robert Tate 9-29-1877 L
Lee, Pearcy Ann to Augustin P. Ford 8-9-1849 Hr
Lee, R. Ritter Clementine to Leander Wafer 2-13-1855 G
Lee, Rebecca J. to Pleasent Crissup 11-19-1862 Mn
Lee, Rebecca J. to Plesant Crisip 10-8-1862 Mn
Lee, Rebecca S. J. to Robert C. Miller 10-14-1853 (no return) Hn
Lee, Rebecca to Matthew Wiggs 4-9-1857 G
Lee, Rose to Washington Bond 12-13-1873 Hy
Lee, Sarah A. to H. G. Fox 3-11-1852 Sh
Lee, Sarah Ann to George B. Andrews 6-3-1848 Sh
Lee, Sarah Ann to Lewis Henpler (Henssler?) 8-8-1851 Sh
Lee, Sarah Ann to W. K. Davis 10-15-1857 (no return) Cr
Lee, Sarah L. to Madison Winchester 2-17-1858 Hn
Lee, Sarah Lucinda to J. T. Conner 2-8-1871 Ma
Lee, Sarah to Joseph Jenkins 1-2-1865 (no return) Hn
Lee, Sarah to Raney (Romeo?) Johnson 12-26-1885 (12-27-1885) L
Lee, Susan E. to John F. Pierson 1-29-1849 L
Lee, Susan to Wm. W. Easterwood 12-30-1844 (12-31-1844) Hr
Lee, Tenny to C. C. Bell 5-1-1870 G
Lee, Unicy to James W. Dickerson 2-11-1861 G
Lee, Vina to Frank Henderson 12-30-1869 Hy
Lee, Violet to William Brown 1-20-1870 (1-22-1870) F B
Lee, Wineford to Anthony Smith 5-25-1835 Hr
Leea?, Frances to Alfred Boyd 6-5-1833 (6-6-1833) Hr
Leech, Dora B. to Stephen Pierce 12-30-1869 (no return) Dy
Leech, E. V. to A. B. Campbell 6-13-1842 F
Leech, Emma to Anderson Bracker 11-16-1871 Hy
Leech, M. A. to T. K. Harvy 2-3-1866 (2-5-1866) Cr
Leech, Martha to G. N. Carter 3-14-1861 (no return) Cr
Leech, Nancy L. to William Edmonson 12-2-1833 Hr
Leefon, Margaret to Joseph McCain 3-25-1845 We
Leeman, Mary to Walter Jones 1-8-1870 G B
Leeper, Margaret E. to William P. McGowan 2-18-1841 Hn
Leeper, Mary to Nathaniel S. Hicks 2-24-1863 Hn
Leetch, Marian A. to Thomas V. Forisher 6-9-1864 Dy
Leete, Mariah J. E. to Enos A. Allen 5-9-1855 (5-11-1855) L
Leeton, Elizabeth to David Billingsly 12-31-1856 Hr
Lefever, Jane to C. Brown 1-31-1849 Hn
Lefever, Margaret Ann to Milton Taylor 8-25-1838 Hn
Lefever, Mary to Charles Spencer 4-2-1838 Hn
Lefever, Narcissa to John R. Story 1-9-1859 Hn
Lefever, Retha C. to Micajah Midgett 1-9-1844 Hn
Lefort, Pauline to Wm. T. Diemer 6-5-1849 Sh
Leftwick, S. E. to W. G. Stovall 2-8-1859 Sh
Legat, Tabitha A. to Robt. A. Rankin 10-10-1837 G
Legate, Charity K. to Wm. E. Myrick 10-9-1853 Be
Legate, Eliza Ann to William P. Cunningham 6-15-1841 (6-18-1841) O
Legate, Elizabeth to David Bird 1-5-1854 (1-12-1854) G
Legate, Jane to Charles M. Cunningham 7-6-1844 (7-10-1844) O
Legate, Louisa to David Myers 12-3-1855 O
Legate, Maniza to Isaac Pollard 11-24-1832 (11-28-1832) G
Legate, Mary F. to G. W. Fowler 1-10-1856 Be
Legate, P. A. to Chapel Heath 1-24-1864 Mn
Legett, Emeline to A. Hunt 3-14-1859 (3-15-1859) G
Legett, Mollie to J. S. Ellis 3-25-1872 L
Legget, Margaret to John Buchanan 12-11-1867 O
Legget, Ethreal to William R. Wallace 12-6-1849 Sh
Leggett, Lewisey to Geo. W. Knapp 5-18-1843 Sh
Leggett, Martha to Daniel G. Halliburton 1-18-1871 (1-19-1871) L
Leggett, Mary Ann to George Adams 2-3-1847 Sh
Leggett, Mary to Alexander Tweedle 2-20-1844 Sh
Leggett, Mary to John Murdaugh 2-12-1840 Hr
Leggett, Nancy J. to A. D. R. Swindle 9-13-1859 (9-14-1859) G
Leggett, Sarah to Robert Murdaugh 10-6-1840 Hr
Leggett, Susan to A. M. Smith 12-15-1868 (no return) Dy
Leggitt, Catherine to Joseph Ruffin 12-19-1849 Sh
Legon, Martha S. to F. M. Smeledge 9-1-1855 We
Legon, Mary A. to James N. Morris 12-12-1859 (no return) We
Leiden, Mary to Patrick Manley 2-26-1856 Sh
Leigh, Bell to A. C. Miller 4-24-1865 (5-25-1865) O
Leigh, Lowtica? to James C. Lurence 12-19-1867 Cr
Leigh, Lucy to John Bush 11-24-1861 Cr

Leigh, Marthy to Ben Sutton 4-6-1867 Hy
Leigh, Nancy C. to Thomas W. Stacy 8-23-1871 (8-24-1871) Cr
Leigh, Sarah A. Barbrey to Isarah Morris 11-3-1866 Cr
Leight, Mollie P. to Preston M. Tipton 2-6-1878 Dy
Leinhart, Caroline to Louis Leecray 11-15-1854 Sh
Leinkauf, Amalia to Herman Kaufman 2-23-1864 Sh
Leiper, Harriett to Richard S. Dobbins 1-14-1841 Hn
Leiper, Martha Jane to J. W. Burch 2-7-1856 Hn
Lemaster, Anna H. to R. S. Feild 10-28-1857 Sh
Lemaster, Margaret J. to H. L. Guion 10-20-1841 Sh
Leming, A. A. to Ephraim Parks 5-15-1861 Hr
Lemings, Martha S to Daniel D. Foster 12-17-1860 (12-27-1860) Hr
Lemmon, H. Ann to J. F. Bookout 12-31-1860 (1-1-1861) Dy
Lemmon, Sarah E. to J. J. Williams 12-20-1852 (no return) F
Lemmon, Sarah Irene to James Iredell Hall 12-26-1849 (12-27-1849) T
Lemmonds, Elizabeth to James J. House 10-5-1839 (10-15-1839) O
Lemmonds, Martha A. to John F. Neel 2-18-1843 (2-19-1843) O
Lemmons, Frances to Edward Smith 6-7-1867 (6-9-1867) Cr
Lemmons, Julia Ann (Mrs.) to Joseph S. Hamalton 11-1-1852 Sh
Lemmons, Julia N. to J. M. Johnson 2-14-1867 (no return) Cr
Lemmons, Lena to Wily Baker 12-17-1873 Dy
Lemmons, M. J. to William H. Henry 3-31-1860 (4-1-1860) Sh
Lemmons, Mary to Samuel R. Fuquea 12-6-1841 (12-9-1841) G
Lemmons, Mary to Thomas Neely 5-25-1843 Cr
Lemmons?, Martha to F. W. Dunkan 8-10-1862 Hn
Lemon, Amanda to Simpson Meredith 11-13-1867 Dy
Lemon, Mary to L. M. Pickerell 4-25-1844 Sh
Lemond, Mary S. L. J. to William Jackson 12-10-1857 (12-31-1857) Ma
Lemonds, Esther J. to William F. Guthrie 6-6-1858 Hn
Lemonds, Julina C. to Hubbard King 12-23-1852 Hn
Lemonds, Mary E. to Robert Brizendine 12-3-1856 Hn
Lemons, A. M. to T.J. Claxton 1-8-1866 F
Lemons, J. Ann to Benjamin R. Morgan 12-17-1857 Hn
Lemons, Judis A. to John M. Taylor 10-9-1848 (10-11-1848) F
Lemons, Louisa to W. C. White 2-13-1860 Cr
Lemons, Malinda to Thos. G. Harbor 8-23-1854 (8-24-1854) G
Lemons, Martha J. to W. H. Blythe 9-23-1865 O
Lemons, Mary J. to J. W. Lee 10-2-1865 (10-3-1865) Cr
Lemons, Mary Nancy to John Smith 1-3-1869 Cr
Lemons, Mary to Hugh Boyd 2-5-1855 (2-7-1855) Ma
Lemons, Mary to Wm. Tucker 5-23-1844 Cr
Lemons, Rose to Jack Dodson 5-10-1871 (no return) F B
Lemons, S. M. to Wm. Bowen 10-1-1867 (10-2-1867) Dy
Lemons, Sarah to Absalom Ellison 3-6-1839 Hn
Len (Lew? Low?), Catherine to S. M. Davidson 5-14-1859 (5-15-1859) Sh
Lenard, Thursa A. to William W. Duncan 8-23-1852 (8-26-1852) G
Lenea?, E. J. to B. D. Mills 10-7-1871 (10-9-1871) Cr
Lenier, Eliza to Fayett Williams 3-6-1867 Hy
Lenier, Jane to Mug Mann 1-8-1868 Hy
Lenier, Nancy E. to G. C. Coleman 1-21-1869 Hy
Lenimon, Martha M. to John Willson 9-20-1870 L
Lenn (Senn?), Terrace to John Lotter (Sotter?) 12-30-1854 Sh
Lennard, Lucy to James Beck 9-27-1836 Hr
Lennow, Indiana H. to Presley R. Peyton 1-31-1854 Sh
Lenord, S. P. to S. K. Duncan 10-7-1850 (10-15-1850) G
Lenow, Fannie to Wiley P. Taylor 1-12-1858 (1-13-1858) Sh
Lenox, Bettie to Hugh Deborn 7-17-1856 We
Lensdin, Ann C. to W. B. Bishop 11-14-1856 Cr
Lenshan, Ellen to Pat Mahoney 10-20-1864 Sh
Leonard, Ann Mariah to John F. Talafairo 2-24-1851 (2-26-1851) F
Leonard, Bridget to William Carter 7-1-1854 Sh
Leonard, Jeanette to John Hoffman 9-10-1869 G
Leonard, Julia M. to Simon Turner 6-28-1853 (no return) F
Leonard, Julia to Joseph Bryan 10-31-1856 (11-2-1856) Sh
Leonard, M. M. to Lewis H. Harget 12-24-1862 G
Leonard, Mahailey to G. M. Bradford 4-4-1851 Cr
Leonard, Margarett N. to M. M. Waller 9-30-1847 F
Leonard, Martha J. to Joseph F. Brown 10-25-1856 Sh
Leonard, Martha J. to Nuton A. Hamon 9-7-1852 F
Leonard, Martha J. to W. B. Pulliam 11-10-1856 Sh
Leonard, Mary to Martin Leary 5-30-1850 Sh
Leonard, Mary to Timothy Mangan 2-19-1849 Sh
Leonard, R. F. to A. F. Hall 1-9-1878 (1-10-1878) Dy
Leonard, Sarah W. to J. F. Eddleman 3-13-1866 G
Leonard, Wilhelmina to George Smalshwaite 7-3-1850 Sh
Leopard, Salvia to Joe Houston 2-28-1871 G
Leremore, Elizabeth N. to L. T. Bennett 4-25-1854 Sh
Leroy, Mary Ann to George W. Yeargin 12-30-1862 Dy
Leroy, Mary Ann to John Sawyer 6-26-1871 Dy
Lery, Babette to Abram Baker 10-17-1853 (10-18-1853) Sh
Lery, Fanny A. to Robertson P. Talley 4-8-1854 Cr
Leshlie, M. R. to Jerome Bevell 12-21-1872 (12-25-1872) Cr
Leslie, Catharine to Connor Flinn 9-19-1862 Sh
Leslie, Louisa to Francis Bennett 6-15-1852 Cr
Leslie, Margaret A. to Nelson Cox 4-4-1844 Cr
Leslie, Mary J. to Henry P. Smith 11-9-1872 (11-10-1872) Cr
Leslie, Sarah to Monroe King 11-12-1867 Be

Lesten, Sarah T. to Pleasant Sampson 1-5-1853 Cr
Lester, Elizabeth M. to William Fowler 6-22-1846 Hn
Lester, Harriet to Davy Richison 1-2-1868 (1-4-1868) F B
Lester, Juliand to Wm. C. Jordan 12-23-1839 (12-24-1839) F
Lester, Louiser C. to Wm. H. Justice 5-1-1866 (5-3-1866) Ma
Lester, Mary E. to William F. McKnight 4-15-1856 Ma
Lester, Mary to John S. Cates 11-6-1845 Hn
Lester, Rebecca Jane to John Vaughn 7-22-1837 (7-23-1837) Hr
Lester, Tranquilla E. to Marion S. Hargiss 5-30-1846 (6-10-1846) F
Let, Nancy to Solomon Collins 11-10-1848 Cr
Lete, S. P. to J. W. Hatcher 2-3-1869 G
Lethers, Martha to A. P. Vernon 6-29-1844 (7-4-1844) Hr
Letsinger, Mary E. to Wm. H. Jackson 11-13-1849 Cr
Lett, Eliza C. to Davidson B. Bobbett 2-2-1854 G
Lett, Elizabeth to John D. West 2-10-1871 (2-11-1871) Ma
Lett, Elizabeth to John J. Hicks 9-10-1856 G
Lett, Hannah to Wm. B. Dilday 3-23-1841 Cr
Lett, Janiah to John W. Lett 11-20-1848 Cr
Lett, M. M. to J. M. Wood 11-10-1869 G
Lett, Malinda to Stephen Dunkin 12-24-1866 (12-27-1866) Cr
Lett, Mary A. to Newton P. Berry 2-10-1862 (2-11-1862) Cr
Lett, Mary E. to Joseph N. Alexandner 7-11-1864 G
Lett, Nancy to Henry Freeman 1-2-1867 G
Lett, Nancy to John W. Lett 3-7-1854 Cr
Lett, Sarah P. to J. W. Ward 1-14-1869 G
Leuter, Lucinda to A. B. Hicks 11-6-1856 Cr
Leverett, Laura W. to S. T. Dougan 3-3-1871 (no return) F
Leverett, Sarah A. E. to F. P. Harris 8-7-1867 F
Levesque, Nancy to William Clampet 1-30-1839 (1-31-1839) F
Levett, Mary G. to Joseph Barbiere, jr. 10-30-1855 Sh
Levi, Josephine to Charles H. Rudy (Rodry?) 12-24-1860 Sh
Levi, Mary to M. Rothschild 3-26-1873 Hy
Levington, Elisa to Samuel J. B. Martin 9-23-1838 O
Levy (Luy-Sey?), Julia to Jacob Friend 10-8-1855 (10-8-1854?) Sh
Levy, Barbetta to Charles Schloss 9-13-1861 Sh
Levy, Easter to Sandy Davis 10-6-1867 G B
Levy, Emma C. to W. T. Anington 1-18-1860 G
Levy, Fanny A. to Pomfrett H. Warren 11-22-1870 F
Levy, Hannah to Carroll Douglass 8-23-1867 (9-7-1867) F B
Levy, Justine to Alexander Mayor 5-9-1860 Sh
Levy, Mary to Benjamin Gerson 10-11-1847 Sh
Levy, Mary to Dick Winfrey 7-13-1867 G
Levy, Mary to Jacob Louis 1-16-1861 Sh
Levy, Mina to M. L. Putzel 12-31-1861 Sh
Levy, Rachel to Ruffin O'Neil 11-10-1867 G B
Lewallian, Emily to Richard Davis 6-9-1842 Sh
Lewdermilk, Racheal to William Brown 1-21-1834 (1-23-1834) Hr
Lewellen, Elizabeth to Quincy J. Mathews 3-11-1862 Cr
Lewellen, Louiza Tennessee to William Smith 3-15-1870 (no return) L
Lewellen, Margaret to John Ballard 7-9-1866 (7-12-1866) T
Lewellen, Martha J. to John S. Silvers 5-11-1858 T
Lewis, Amanda J. to James I. Davis 9-25-1837 Sh
Lewis, Amanda to Richard Campbell 1-26-1869 G B
Lewis, Amelia Ann to William Richardson 10-8-1863 Mn
Lewis, Anjaline to James H. Barnes 10-14-1866 Be
Lewis, Ann H. to George W. Blair 7-3-1848 (7-6-1848) Hr
Lewis, Auze to Alexander Maney 12-21-1871 Hy
Lewis, C. P. to J. L. Baldridge 8-12-1860 We
Lewis, Caroline to Handy Peete 12-26-1878 Hy
Lewis, Caroline to Tom Balam 12-25-1869 (12-20?-1869) F B
Lewis, Carrie M. to William E. Lynn 12-2-1880 L
Lewis, Catherine (Mrs.) to Antonio J. Foster 11-20-1864 Sh
Lewis, Darthul to Thomas R. Harrisson 4-8-1830 (4-15-1830) G
Lewis, Dorthula P. to Henry G. Cole 8-17-1837 O
Lewis, Eliza D. to A. S. Day 11-9-1854 (no return) F
Lewis, Eliza J. to B. A. Galbreath 11-13-1861 Hn
Lewis, Elizabeth A. to Joseph A. Roberts 12-20-1859 We
Lewis, Elizabeth P. to William Harris 3-24-1867 Be
Lewis, Elizabeth to Alfred L. Henderson 1-24-1835 Sh
Lewis, Elizabeth to J. G. Perkins 2-8-1866 Hn
Lewis, Elizabeth to Jacob Phillips 12-26-1874 (no return) L B
Lewis, Elizabeth to John Thompson 11-23-1864 (11-24-1864) Sh
Lewis, Ellen to Olivar Thomas 1-27-1872 Hy
Lewis, Ellen to William Nolen 1-21-1873 (1-23-1873) L B
Lewis, Elvira to Jacob Turner 6-2-1865 (no return) Hn
Lewis, Emaline to N. M. Malone 1-4-1857 We
Lewis, Emily K. to Samuel L. Buster 11-15-1832 Sh
Lewis, Emily to R. G. Burrow 12-23-1844 Hr
Lewis, Emma J. M. E. to C. A. Black 7-2-1858 Hr
Lewis, Fannie to Henry Martin 10-28-1877 Hy
Lewis, Fanny to Abner Ross 4-28-1875 Hy
Lewis, Frances C. to Bennett Baley (Bagby) 10-4-1842 Sh
Lewis, Harriet to F. Russell 12-19-1872 O
Lewis, Jane to G. W. Ridgway 8-5-1845 We
Lewis, Jane to George Walker 12-22-1875 Hy
Lewis, Jennie to Eli Smith 11-14-1871 (11-15-1871) Ma

Lewis, Jennie to J. M. Currie 7-11-1885 (7-12-1885) L
Lewis, L. A. to J. M. McCrory 1-17-1880 (1-20-1880) L
Lewis, Lannie to Isaac J. Pearson 9-24-1870 (10-6-1870) F B
Lewis, Lidda to George Williams 2-18-1839 (2-25-1839) F
Lewis, Lizzie to J. M. Buckingham 3-23-1874 (3-24-1874) Dy
Lewis, Lucinda to G. A. Lewis 12-7-1871 Hy
Lewis, Lucy to J. H. Nelson 9-30-1879 (9-23?-1879) L B
Lewis, Lucy to Jerry Maynard 12-23-1874 Hy
Lewis, Lydia M. to John M. Alexander 9-28-1848 Hn
Lewis, M. A. D. to T. W. Branson 8-10-1865 G
Lewis, M. A. to R. W. Robinson 3-1-1859 (3-13-1859) Hr
Lewis, M. E. to T. T. Beaver 12-5-1871 Hy
Lewis, M. J. to L. L. Martin 8-5-1868 Cr
Lewis, Mahala to James Hester 12-25-1865 F B
Lewis, Malvena to Washington Shelby 10-7-1851 Be
Lewis, Manervy D. to Isaac M. Pipkins 12-13-1860 We
Lewis, Margaret B. to J. W. Doheny 3-27-1856 (4-9-1856) Sh
Lewis, Margaret to James W. Wallace 12-10-1865 Mn
Lewis, Maria L. to Bronson Bayliss 10-15-1849 Sh
Lewis, Maria Mary to William Evans 2-3-1846 (2-5-1846) F
Lewis, Martha Ann Tennessee to Edward L. M. Smith 7-18-1860 (7-19-1860) Ma
Lewis, Martha Ann to James G. Futrell 9-3-1866 (9-5-1866) Ma
Lewis, Martha Ann to Richard Hood 3-17-1851 (no return) F
Lewis, Martha J. to James Tedder 8-19-1866 Be
Lewis, Martha Rebecca Ann to John Woodson 8-26-1867 (8-28-1867) Ma
Lewis, Martha to Irvin Gibson 6-17-1840 G
Lewis, Martha to John Jacobs 12-9-1829 (12-10-1829) Hr
Lewis, Martha to Sam'l (Sammy) Allen 1-6-1868 G B
Lewis, Mary B. to John N. Walker 5-14-1870 (5-19-1870) Ma
Lewis, Mary B. to Peter Newbern 1-8-1885 L
Lewis, Mary B. to R. H. Crockett 4-8-1856 Sh
Lewis, Mary E. to Calvin C. Clement 7-10-1866 Ma
Lewis, Mary E. to Simon Hollaway 3-2-1873 Hy
Lewis, Mary E. to Wm. Jasper Alford 7-26-1859 Sh
Lewis, Mary Elizabeth to Gardner Lytle 11-12-1867 (11-13-1867) Ma
Lewis, Mary L. to J. M. Alexander 12-17-1839 (2-13-1840) L
Lewis, Mary V. to W. M. Edwin 10-26-1849 (10-30-1849) F
Lewis, Mary to Chas. E. Leonard 1-10-1851 (1-11-1851) Sh
Lewis, Mary to Franklin Reddick 9-11-1860 (no return) Hy
Lewis, Mary to Giles Marchbanks 10-11-1831 G
Lewis, Mary to John T. Wood 10-26-1857 Hn
Lewis, Mary to Peyton Smith 1-8-1879 (1-9-1879) L
Lewis, Mary to Theophilus Ellis 5-24-1848 Hn
Lewis, Mary to W. A. Swindle 7-20-1864 Be
Lewis, Mary to Wistley Duberry 10-15-1847 (10-17-1847) F
Lewis, N. J. to S. Williams 6-18-1858 G
Lewis, N. M. A. D. to B. M. Stubblefield 9-13-1867 G
Lewis, Nancy A. to Calvin Malone 1-8-1839 F
Lewis, Nancy C. to G. L. Johnson 11-27-1865 (11-28-1865) L
Lewis, Nancy F. to George W. Wood 7-25-1855 (no return) Hn
Lewis, Nancy to Andrew J. McFadden 7-11-1848 Hn
Lewis, Nancy to Charlie Cogchall 5-10-1883 L
Lewis, Nancy to Wm. Herrell 8-5-1857 (8-11-1857) Hr
Lewis, Olivia J. (Mrs.) to James R. Bourland 2-20-1871 (2-21-1871) Ma
Lewis, Penny to John Bolling 12-30-1866 Hy
Lewis, Polly to T. Hollandsworth 11-30-1840 Be
Lewis, R. J. H. to V. H. Kelley 1-4-1871 Cr
Lewis, R. J. to James W. Newton 11-9-1846 (no return) We
Lewis, R. J. to Jefferson Malone 5-26-1851 Hn
Lewis, Rachel to Daniel (David?) McGinsey 12-21-1872 (12-22-1872) L B
Lewis, Ritter to Lea Seat 12-29-1868 G B
Lewis, Sabina E. to J. H. McFadden 3-5-1850 Hn
Lewis, Sarah A. to James M. Carter 8-31-1860 O
Lewis, Sarah A. to Littleberry B. Arnold 3-9-1852 G
Lewis, Sarah F. to R. H. Crockett 11-10-1853 Sh
Lewis, Sarah J. to John A. Barton 12-23-1863 Hn
Lewis, Sarah J. to P. W. Cook 8-23-1848 Cr
Lewis, Sarah to George Washington 3-10-1868 (no return) F B
Lewis, Sarah to Lewis Baldwin 3-22-1845 (no return) Hn
Lewis, Sarah to Thomas Fletcher 11-27-1830 (12-2-1830) G
Lewis, Sibetta to T. J. Forsythe 11-11-1871 (no return) Hy
Lewis, Susan to Francis R. Clark 12-2-1869 Hy
Lewis, Susan M. to Dority Turner 10-23-1846 (10-27-1846) G
Lewis, Susan to H. C. Lewis 12-24-1871 Hy
Lewis, Susan to John Clark 4-6-1866 (no return) Hy
Lewis, Virginia to W. A. Moore 2-4-1878 (no return) Hy
Lewry, Charlotte to George Arun 1-11-1848 Hn
Leznik, Mary Ann to Marcus H. Stewart 12-19-1848 (12-21-1848) F
Lidda, Gilliam to Carter Powell 5-25-1871 Hy
Liddle, Elizabeth to Henry Webb 1-1-1846 (no return) We
Lieb (Lish), Elizabeth to Andrew Orsidy (Orsnly) 11-6-1849 Sh
Liedenstone, Hannah to Lorenze Netzel? 12-24-1845 Sh
Lienhardt, Joanna to Louis Gehe 4-16-1853 (4-17-1853) Sh
Lienhardt, Madaline to Philipp Weiler (Weiblen) 2-7-1850 Sh
Lierd, Nancy E. to John W. Lucus 6-16-1870 (6-26-1870) L
Lierd, Rody F. to Enoch P. Hutcherson 9-9-1871 (9-10-1871) L
Liffsy, Eliza to Shadrick Pearson 9-19-1864 (9-21-1864) Cr

Ligan, Louisa V. to James A. Baker 10-4-1849 Hn
Ligen, Martha J. to Zachariah Nash 9-17-1865 Hn
Ligen, Nancy to Enoch Baker 5-15-1864 Hn
Liggett, Mary A. to James Smith 5-10-1855 Hn
Liggett, Susannah to Peter K. Carley 1-26-1843 Hr
Light, A. R. to B. L. Tinkle 10-4-1870 G
Light, Anna to Joseph Sawyer 6-8-1870 Dy
Light, Artelia to Thomas Johnson 9-9-1875 Dy
Light, Chanie to Alfred Hollis 12-5-1878 (no return) Dy
Light, Dinkie to Lee Wells 10-26-1871 Dy
Light, Emma to Alex Harris 2-19-1880 (no return) Dy
Light, Emma to George Johnson 9-16-1870 Dy
Light, Emma to Wilson Lovelace 7-10-1880 (7-11-1880) Dy
Light, Helen to Jack Connell 5-4-1875 (5-5-1875) Dy
Light, Jane to John F. Connell 2-17-1871 (2-18-1871) Dy B
Light, L. J. to R. F. Tinkle 7-21-1864 G
Light, Margaret to Henry A. Robinson 4-5-1876 (4-6-1876) Dy
Light, Mary Ann to Henry Ray Walker 6-5-1866 Dy
Light, Mary E. to Thos. R. Moore 5-20-1869 Dy
Light, Mary to Jack Ferguson 6-27-1866 Dy
Light, Mollie to Charley Moore 12-25-1877 (12-27-1877) Dy
Light, Nancy to John Wesley Lock 7-29-1868 (7-30-1868) Dy
Light, Nannie to Austin Connell 10-6-1880 Dy
Light, Nielli to Callis Jordan 12-16-1874 (12-17-1874) Dy B
Light, Pettie to J. F. Johnston 1-27-1869 (1-28-1869) Dy
Light, S. A. to C. L. Claiborn 12-30-1872 (12-31-1872) Dy
Light, Sallie A. to P. L. Tipton 10-3-1874 (10-4-1874) Dy
Light, Scrappie E. to Parsha L. Fowlkes 11-12-1874 Dy
Light, Tennessee to Isaac Fowlkes 4-17-1877 Dy
Lightfoot, Caroline to Barby Broach 12-18-1844 (no return) Hn
Lightfoot, Mary Jane to Broadie H. Cozart 3-8-1838 (no return) Hn
Lightie, Martha A. to Wm. Hicks 3-12-1859 (3-18-1859) F
Lightle, Ellen to King Culberson 1-7-1868 (2-9-1868) F B
Lightle, Frances to William Arvinshire 7-15-1864 (7-17-1864) Cr
Lightner, Elzady to Thomas Mathews 8-2-1855 Be
Lightner, Sarah Jane to Moses McHughs 3-26-1845 Be
Ligon, A. A. to D. N. Rives 11-22-1877 Hy
Ligon, Ann Jane to Christopher Col. Sharp 9-6-1854 T
Ligon, C. E. to J. F. Hall 2-4-1873 (2-9-1873) T
Ligon, Harriet to Louis Sanford 4-17-1868 (4-18-1868) T
Ligon, Sue H. to M. Bell 5-16-1865 (5-17-1865) T
Lile, Candace to J. C. Gill 10-13-1847 (no return) F
Lile, H. A. C. to B. P. Griffin 10-5-1860 (10-18-1860) F
Lile, Mary F. to John Fly 11-29-1831 G
Lile, N. E. to William C. Coates 7-13-1846 Hr
Lile?, Martha Ann to James C. Mauldin 11-30-1842 (12-1-1842) Hr
Liles, Eliza to James M. Rodgers ?-?-1860 Cr
Liles, Eliza to James M. Rogers 8-27-1860 (9-7-1860) Cr
Liles, Elizabeth to Wm. T. Cagle 4-14-1860 (4-29-1860) Cr
Liles, Elizabeth to J. D. R. Green 4-16-1864 Cr
Liles, Elizabeth to T. H. H. Presson 12-?-1861 (12-15-1861) Cr
Liles, Emalina to Wm. Moore 10-7-1856 Cr
Liles, Frances to Alex McBride 2-20-1854 Cr
Liles, Lidda to N. W. Presson 11-29-1849 Cr
Liles, Maggie to James D. Martin 11-5-1856 Cr
Liles, Martha A. to James F. Rodgers 12-7-1854 Cr
Liles, Nancy P. to D. B. Robinson 11-4-1852 Cr
Liles, Nancy to Alexander McBride 11-21-1850 Cr
Liles, Sarah M. to John F. Phelps 11-25-1864 (11-26-1864) Cr
Liles, Susan to Marvell Butler 8-6-1860 Cr
Lillard, Lucinda D. to Richard Nuckolls 3-15-1855 Hr
Lillard, Sarah to Isaac W. Crawford 8-10-1846 (8-12-1846) Hr
Lilley, Mattie to Thomas Rich 9-8-1877 (9-9-1877) L
Lilley, Permelia J. to John A. Campbell 11-9-1852 (11-11-1852) O
Lillis, Nancy to Thomas Kane 6-23-1862 (6-24-1862) Sh
Lilly, Frances B. to Jesse P. Lowry 1-5-1838 (no return) Hn
Lilly, Martha to John C. McKamy 11-27-1863 (11-29-1863) O
Lilly, Mary R. to Edward J. Moody 12-1-1859 Hn
Lilly, Mary to Albert Marr 7-12-1882 L
Lilly, Sarah A. to Ashton Hawkins 9-15-1847 (no return) Hn
Lilly, U. R. to N.? P. Randle 8-5-1866 Hn
Liloe?, Emaline to Wm. Man 10-10-1857 Cr
Limberg, Mary to Theodore Pohl 10-30-1860 Sh
Limon?, Sarah O. to Geo. F. Wainwright 1-4-1847 (1-13-1847) F
Linch, Mary A. to E. W. Haywood 11-10-1871 Cr
Lincoln, Sarah E. to L. M. Force 6-11-1880 (6-13-1880) L
Linden, Mary J. to W. S. Underwood 3-15-1855 We
Linden, Sophia S. to R. E. Harling 10-17-1856 Cr
Linder, Jane to George W. Bats 3-26-1863 We
Linder, Martha E. to Henry Walker 8-31-1863 (no return) We
Linder, Mary C. to J. P. Linder 10-13-1877 (10-14-1877) O
Linder, Parale to George W. Smith 2-14-1872 T
Linderman, C. A. to Thomas Click 1-10-1880 (1-11-1880) L
Lindsay, Elizabeth to James W. Drummonds 2-15-1858 Cr
Lindsay, Lucindy to William Carter 3-25-1824 L
Lindsay, Mary E. to A. T. Ikard 1-1-1869 (1-5-1869) T
Lindsey, Betsey to Sanford B. Norris 9-8-1829 (9-10-1829) O

Lindsey, Caroline to John Collier 8-2-1852 Be
Lindsey, Delila to Jesse T. Lindsey 8-29-1843 (9-5-1843) F
Lindsey, Delilah to Joseph Abels 10-1-1846 (10-4-1846) F
Lindsey, Eliza Ann to Eli Outland 12-20-1853 Be
Lindsey, Elvira A. to Andrew J. Whitson 12-18-1866 L
Lindsey, Frances to Carter Anderson 1-2-1869 (1-5-1869) F B
Lindsey, Frances to George M. Slaughter 10-16-1854 Hn
Lindsey, Julia to John Golding 8-9-1859 L
Lindsey, Louisa Catharine to William Caraway 10-5-1866 Be
Lindsey, M. J. to Peter S. Nance 2-11-1849 Be
Lindsey, Martha J. to Daniel N. Carter 12-15-1852 Cr
Lindsey, Mary A. to Jas. A. Cole 1-20-1861 Be
Lindsey, Mary E. to C. A. Robins 4-13-1856 Be
Lindsey, Mary E. to John W. Jenkins 9-17-1872 (9-19-1872) T
Lindsey, Mary to A. B. A. Hamil 7-18-1867 L
Lindsey, Mary to Jackson French 8-25-1843 Cr
Lindsey, Matilda C. to Wm. B. Robins 4-27-1843 Be
Lindsey, Mollie to Andrew Wilkes 2-8-1871 (2-9-1871) F B
Lindsey, Nancy to B. Gross 3-25-1856 Be
Lindsey, Nelly to William Woodford 2-21-1866 Hn
Lindsey, Phebe to F. Campbell 11-18-1840 Be
Lindsey, Rackey to J. F. Gross 8-10-1865 Be
Lindsly, Mary Ann to William B. Harpole 1-2-1841 (1-7-1841) G
Lindsy, Richard (SB Rachel) to John J. Lowry 11-27-1845 Be
Lindy, C. Smiley A. to Haratio Butler 8-29-1856 Cr
Linebarger, Mary A. to F. S. Blalock 12-7-1868 (12-9-1868) F
Lineberry, Rebecca to Martin V. Lacefield 4-18-1861 Hr
Ling, Mary to Arther Harbert 10-12-1871 Hy
Linire (Lynne?), Mollie A. to Martin S. Hood 6-1-1874 L
Link, Ann to Wilson Taylor 2-18-1875 Hy
Link, Edmonia to John Wilson 3-28-1878 Hy
Link, Emily to Henry Smitheel 12-20-1877 Hy
Link, Watsie? Ann to Robert Cocke 9-15-1869 F B
Linkelake, Mary to Maurice Long 6-18-1859 Hy
Linkston, Margaret to Thos. Stewart 11-4-1863 Sh
Linley, Roena C. to Geo. W. Outlaw 3-10-1860 (no return) Hy
Linn, Louisa to Alfred E. Keller 11-7-1848 Sh
Linn, Martha to Reubin Hyde 11-8-1848 Sh
Linn, Mattie J. T. to L. L. Webster 7-13-1874 (7-15-1874) T
Linn, Sarah J. to James G. Hindman 2-1-1858 (2-2-1858) T
Linsdey, Sophronia L. to Samul S. Nelson 11-18-1848 (no return) F
Linsey, Arminta to John Stacey 11-6-1844 (11-?-1844) O
Linsey, Jane to John Wyatt 5-2-1843 Be CC
Linsey, Martha Ann to Allen K. Potts 10-26-1858 (no return) Hn
Linsey, Mattie E. to Charles H. Warren 12-22-1874 T
Linsey, Melissa Ann to Joel Lee? 11-15-1837 Hr
Linsey, Sarah Alingny? to Andrew Davis 7-23-1836 Hr
Linsey, Sarah to James L. Lyles 10-18-1837 (11-25-1837) O
Linson, Ann E. to J. M. Smith 9-1-1860 Hy
Linston, Fannie to Henry Nelson 12-20-1875 (no return) Hy
Linsy, Jane to John Wyatt 5-2-1843 Be
Linton, Margaret V. to W. F. Lamar 11-12-1870 (11-15-1870) Dy
Linton, Margaret to Archelus Keathly 1-1-1853 G
Linton, Margaret to Cyrus Dunn 11-12-1870 (11-15-1870) Dy
Linton, Martha D. to Thomas B. Carroll 11-1-1866 (11-8-1866) Ma
Linton, Mary M. to R.? M. Newto 12-19-1846 Hn
Linton, Sarah to John R. Walker 11-17-1848 G
Linton, Sarah to Moses Oliver 9-27-1854 (9-28-1854) G
Linville, Elizabeth to George Houston 6-11-1852 Cr
Linzy, Milly to Thomas Brewer 11-24-1870 (no return) Cr
Lions, Mary to George Vail 6-22-1852 (6-24-1852) G
Lipard, Eliza F. A. to R. B. Trusty 11-21-1859 (11-23-1859) O
Lipe, Lucinda F. to John H. Edwards 9-14-1871 Cr
Lipe, Lucinda to M. McMackin 12-27-1843 Cr
Lipe, M. F. to J. T. Hensler 9-1-1870 Cr
Lipe, M. J. to James M. Hodge 8-14-1863 Cr
Lipe, Martha J. to James H. Brooks 2-20-1850 Cr
Lipe, Martha J. to James M. Hodge no date (with Aug 1863) Cr
Lippard, Susan M. to C. H. Carroll 6-20-1866 O
Lippman, Maria to Ned? Barret 10-9-1868 (10-12-1868) T
Lipscomb, Margaret to Jessee Cross 6-6-1842 (no return) F
Lipscomb, Mary E. to R. S. Hudspeth 8-11-1870 G
Lipscomb, Sarah to Robert Boyd 12-10-1873 Hy
Liston, M. F. to F. M. Patterson 12-23-1868 Cr
Lite, Sarah L. to Wm. D. Fly 10-30-1838 (11-1-1838) G
Litle, America to Jacob H. Vaulx 3-21-1878 Hy
Litle, Georgiann to James K. P. Rogers 8-3-1869 Cr
Litrell, Nancy C. to William L. Hudson 7-11-1853 (7-13-1853) Hr
Litsinger, Margaret to Perry M. Hall 1-21-1847 Cr
Litsinger, Sarah to John W. Collins 3-9-1854 Cr
Litte, Mary Jane to Wm. J. Reynolds 2-5-1862 (no return) Dy
Little, Amanda to Branch H. Wordum 1-22-1855 Cr
Little, Amanda to David Phillips 7-3-1864 Cr
Little, Catherine to Thomas Franklin 9-30-1850 Hn
Little, Charlotty to Wm. R. White 10-12-1843 Cr
Little, Eliza Ann to Samuel P. Linton 10-10-1854 (10-12-1854) G
Little, Elizabeth A. to Thos. J. Walker 2-19-1859 Cr
Little, Elizabeth A. to William P. Scott 1-24-1852 G
Little, Elizabeth J. to Andrew J. Billings 4-16-1856 Hn
Little, Elizabeth to D. M. Pugh 1-2-1861 G
Little, Elizabeth to William Staton 9-10-1846 G
Little, Ellen to Christopher C. Presson 8-29-1852 Cr
Little, Emily to Pleasant B. Wells 1-14-1832 Hr
Little, Eugenia A. to M. L. Williams 11-10-1852 Sh
Little, Frances E. to Benj. Palmore 5-16-1863 (no return) Dy
Little, Howell A. to Abner L. Davidson 12-18-1862 G
Little, Jane to Elijah Jean 10-8-1850 (10-10-1850) Ma
Little, Jane to Elijah M. Bush 1-30-1839 (no return) Hn
Little, Julia A. to J. C. Margrave 1-7-1869 Hy
Little, Laura to Stephen Richardson 1-2-1871 (1-12-1871) F B
Little, M. A. to H. M. Pitner 11-4-1869 Hy
Little, Margaret A. to Joseph B. Stark 12-22-1868 (no return) F
Little, Margrett D. to William P. Jacob 5-27-1840 (6-25-1840) G
Little, Martha Ann to John Young 3-17-1854 G
Little, Martha F. to Thomas Lurry 2-17-1855 (2-27-1855) Sh
Little, Mary Ann to E. G. Duncan 6-14-1855 (6-15-1855) Hr
Little, Mary E. to Benjamin Boon 1-15-1850 G
Little, Mary E. to John W. Baker 7-3-1852 (7-8-1852) Ma
Little, Mary J. to Jacob S. Skiles 11-18-1858 Sh
Little, Mary O. to C. E. Williams 1-7-1840 Sh
Little, Mary Susan to J. M. Scott 2-2-1867 (2-4-1867) Cr
Little, Mary to John Putman 7-21-1842 Cr
Little, Mary to Thos. Stephen 9-17-1848 Cr
Little, Nancy D. to Nathen Ward 11-12-1846 Cr
Little, Nancy to Elisha M. Edgar 8-26-1840 Hn
Little, Nancy to James Merchant 6-26-1847 (no return) Hn
Little, Penelope A. to James B. Davis 12-18-1854 Sh
Little, Polly L. to Edwd. C. Leake 6-23-1857 Sh
Little, Sally to Boyd F. Bryant 3-9-1829 G
Little, Saphronia to Alfred Ray 11-25-1862 G
Little, Sarah A. to James E. Stephens 12-14-1853 (12-15-1853) Hr
Little, Sarah Ann to John Beazly 4-19-1863 Be
Little, Susan Lane to Henry Temp Reece 1-5-1865 (1-7-1865) Dy
Little, Susan to John Q. Stribbling 1-26-1853 (no return) Cr
Littlefield, Martha to John C. Newman 8-13-1846 Sh
Littlefield, Mary A. to Wm. Leverett 6-11-1851 (6-12-1851) Sh
Littleford, Harriet to William Thedford 10-18-1828 (10-19-1828) G
Littlejohn, Cathrine to Kit Brewer 3-1-1869 (3-5-1869) F B
Littlejohn, Martha to Mose Tappan 3-1-1869 (3-5-1869) F B
Littlejohn, Melvinia to William Richardson 1-4-1873 T
Littlejohn, Rebecca A. to Lafayett Erwin 2-27-1864 Mn
Littlepage, Lamira Ann to Thomas Clark 12-8-1866 (12-16-1866) Ma
Littleton, Eliza to George Evans 4-17-1840 O
Littleton, Hariett to William Cooper 4-15-1867 Hn B
Littleton, Jane L. to Thomas Taylor 2-23-1867 (no return) Hn B
Littleton, Jane to John Cooper 12-16-1865 (12-18-1865) O
Littleton, Martha to Henry Kirby 12-?-1861 (no return) L
Littleton, Martha to William Adkison 6-25-1859 (6-26-1859) L
Littleton, Odelia to Alexander H. McElyea 3-29-1854 (3-31-1854) O
Littleton, Parlee to G. R. Ennis 8-7-1862 (8-11-1862) O
Littleton, Sarah E. to James E. Calloway 9-26-1857 Hn
Littleton, Sarah to William W. Connell 8-6-1861 We
Littletown, Mary to George Pridogh 4-17-1845 Cr
Litton, Carni to R. Y. Kirkpatrick 7-31-1854 (no return) F
Litton, Elizabeth to William Adcock 4-25-1846 (4-28-1846) O
Litton, Julia Ann to Hugh R. Grissom 10-1-1856 O
Litton, Julia Ann to Hugh R. Guynn 10-1-1856 O
Litton, Mary Elizabeth to G. W. Guynn 9-15-1853 O
Litton, Mary to Samuel Mc. Johnston 4-23-1849 O
Litton, Rebecca J. to Mathew D. Allen 12-23-1868 (no return) L
Littrell?, Prudence to James Rose 9-27-1848 (9-28-1848) Hr
Littrull?, Thursday Matilda to Benjamin Haney 7-14-1849 (9-7-1849) Hr
Litus, Rachel to John Dickson 7-20-1867 T
Livermore, Mill Lilly to A. J. Vinson 10-6-1864 Sh
Lives?, Julits L. to D. J. Eskew 1-31-1857 (no return) Cr
Livingston, Adeline L. to Jasper N. Carlton 12-13-1859 (no return) Hy
Livingston, Carrie E. to W. C. McConnico 1-31-1877 Hy
Livingston, Cyntha Ann to D. D. Dewalt 9-4-1868 L
Livingston, Emma to Noah Bond 3-9-1871 Hy
Livingston, Louisa to H. S. Erman 9-3-1862 Sh
Livingston, Mary Luellen to Henry Fry 8-22-1874 (8-23-1874) T
Livingston, Mary to Moses Bond 3-26-1874 Hy
Livingston, Sarah to Nathan Rogers 9-8-1877 (no return) Hy
Livingstone, Josephine to George Statum 10-25-1877 Dy
Livington, Mary Angeline to Eli J. Freeman 8-24-1857 (8-25-1857) O
Llewellyn, F. E. to W. C. Rice 12-27-1879 (12-28-1879) L
Lloyd, Adaline A. to James W. Dupree 9-18-1871 L
Lloyd, Addie to W. H. Glenn 1-17-1883 L
Lloyd, Caroline to August Munroe Franklin 10-31-1868 (11-1-1868) L B
Lloyd, Charlotte to Spencer Miller 1-27-1883 (12?-26?-1883) L
Lloyd, D. A. to Wade H. Evans 4-13-1859 L
Lloyd, Dorritt to John S. Evans 12-3-1881 (12-7-1881) L
Lloyd, Elizabeth C. to Jonathan J. Nixon 6-17-1858 (6-18-1858) L
Lloyd, Georgia to Wm. P. McMullen 4-20-1868 (4-22-1868) F

Lloyd, Jesbella to Samuel Alston 3-7-1874 (3-8-1874) L B
Lloyd, Mary F. to John J. Alston 5-3-1859 (no return) L
Lloyd, Silvia to Ike Fisher 1-7-1878 L
Lloyd, Susan Ann to Ira Timmons 2-6-1878 L B
Lloyd, Ula to D. G. Thum 10-26-1885 (10-28-1885) L
Lloyd?, Artelia J. to Claudius B. Lloyd 12-2-1873 (12-?-1873) L
Lloyed, Susan M. to R. C. Drumwright 1-15-1872 (1-17-1872) L
Lloyed, Tobitha E. to Boardmon R. Cheek 2-10-1871 L
Lochridge, Matilda P. to James A. Medley 6-2-1851 (6-5-1851) F
Lock (Lack?), Malissa to Monroe Melton 8-24-1863 G
Lock (Lack?), Sophia to M. M. Melton 9-25-1865 G
Lock, Adeline E. to Andrew T. Brown 12-2-1850 (12-5-1850) Ma
Lock, E. E. to John Warren 10-8-1863 Mn
Lock, Elizabeth W. to Benjamin W. Clement 6-21-1843 (6-22-1843) G
Lock, Fatha to Franklin Thrasher 12-1-1825 Hr
Lock, Jane A. to W. H. McGee 9-7-1857 Cr
Lock, Julianna to Green Parrish 11-30-1825 Hr
Lock, L. A. to John Kurts 12-21-1858 T
Lock, Lenora C. to T. L. Giles 3-7-1853 (no return) F
Lock, Martha E. to John P. Simmons 9-30-1848 Ma
Lockard, Carrie E. to Edgar Harper 2-4-1885 (2-21-1885) L
Lockard, Charity E. to Robert J. Blackwell 12-10-1858 (12-16-1858) L
Lockard, Martha F. to William T. Mosley 2-21-1867 (no return) L
Lockard, Martha to Willis Fitzgerald 4-18-1876 L
Lockard, Mary A. W. to James H. Gargett 9-25-1862 (no return) L
Lockard, Mary Jamima to John W. Rainey 5-28-1868 L
Lockard, Mary to James W. Chism 4-16-1853 (4-17-1853) L
Lockard, Nancy C. to Moses B. Chism 9-16-1868 L
Lockard, Nancy to J. A. Fulkerson 2-22-1872 L
Lockard, Nancy to John Wood 9-16-1841 L
Lockard, Susan to James M. Alford 9-1-1876 L
Locke, Alice to Bascom Wright 7-28-1875 (no return) Dy
Locke, Ann C. to John M. Montgomery 1-15-1861 G
Locke, Emily Jane to John Holland 6-11-1844 T
Locke, Frances A. to William J. Jones 1-20-1852 Ma
Locke, Jane to D. M. B. Hashler 10-11-1854 (no return) F
Locke, Lutitia M. to John Woods 1-3-1842 (12?-23-1842) F
Locke, Maggie L. to Wm. B. Wilkinson 1-27-1859 (2-2-1859) F
Locke, Maggie to J. B. Kelly 2-16-1874 T
Locke?, Martha J. to Jimion S. Clements 6-22-1847 G
Locke, Martha L. to Benjamin Hart 5-12-1862 Sh
Locke, Mary A. to J. L. Turner 12-26-1853 (no return) F
Locke, Mary B. to James Hart 6-27-1850 Sh
Locke, Rebeca R. to John A. Poston 10-13-1864 Sh
Locke, Rebecca to Wm. Viers 1-6-1853 Sh
Locke, Sarah A. to Robert F. Brown 7-12-1855 Ma
Locke, Susan C. to W. W. Ferguson 12-21-1854 (12-23-1855?) Sh
Locke, Virginia C. to Wm. Pleasant Pewitt 4-25-1852 T
Locket, Nerva to John Somerville 2-16-1874 (2-25-1874) T
Lockett, Julia A. to Manuel Niblett 7-4-1867 Hy
Lockett, Mary L. to Bennett Sherman 11-6-1843 Sh
Lockey, Martha to Mose Lay 12-25-1871 Hy
Lockhart, Amanda F. to John L. Leach 2-19-1866 (2-21-1866) F
Lockhart, Elizabeth J. to John P. Baker 11-11-1866 Be
Lockhart, Elizabeth to Oliver Taylor 7-8-1839 Sh
Lockhart, Fannie A. to A. G. Leach 1-14-1868 (1-15-1868) F
Lockhart, Flora to Aaron Jones 4-25-1866 (no return) F B
Lockhart, Flora to Johnson Paine 1-28-1869 (1-30-1869) F B
Lockhart, Fredonia A. to Thomas B. Herren 10-28-1866 Be
Lockhart, Jane to James C. Massey 3-7-1861 L
Lockhart, Lucy to Ben Hamilton 2-21-1881 (2-24-1881) L
Lockhart, Lula to Horace Warden 10-5-1882 (no return) L
Lockhart, Nannie to Tecumseh Lanier 10-27-1874 Dy
Lockhart, Sally to Danel Jones 9-7-1867 (no return) Hy
Lockhart, Sarah E. to W. E. Morris 7-25-1864 Be
Lockheart, Elizabeth C. to Stephen J. Biggs 7-4-1836 (7-5-1836) O
Lockheart, Hipsy to Adam Munford 4-14-1871 (5-13-1871) L
Lockman, Margaret R. to B. C. Hicks 7-16-1861 Mn
Lockman, Milley A. to D. N. Lacefield 2-3-1863 Mn
Lockridge, L. L. to James F. Lanham 8-1-1861 We
Lockwood, Ada E. to J. L. Reister 12-7-1858 Sh
Locust, Amanda to Alfred Shaw 1-20-1872 Hy
Lodgings, Sarah Jane to F. M. McAlilly 7-27-1858 T
Lodgins, Louisa C. to James N. Malone 4-28-1865 (4-29-1865) Cr
Loeb, Josephina to Henry, sr. Baum 11-8-1884 (11-9-1884) L
Loeb, Sophia to Charles L. Gross 2-9-1864 Sh
Loffland, Rebecca F. to Linzey Wilson 4-26-1850 O
Lofland, Rebecca F. to Lindsay Wilson 4-26-1850 O
Lofte, Catherine I. to George F. Jones 10-14-1840 (10-15-1840) Ma
Loftin, Elizabeth to Pink Coonrod 3-17-1875 (no return) L
Loftin, Mary J. to B. Desha Hannan 2-8-1849 Sh
Loftin, Sarah T. to John Henning 3-3-1851 Sh
Lofton, Ophelia to Thomas Ross 1-3-1871 (1-15-1871) F B
Logan, Ann to William Jackson 4-22-1852 Sh
Logan, Elizabeth to Jerry Robinson 1-12-1872 (1-17-1872) T
Logan, Louisa to John Ingram 9-18-1873 T
Logan, Lucinda B. to Reynard Clack 7-1-1840 O

Logan, Margaret to James Barnes 1-6-1864 (1-7-1864) Sh
Logan, Marguerite to William H. Renick 3-19-1834 Sh
Logan, Mary E. to John P. Lusk 9-7-1864 Sh
Logan, Mary to John B. Clack 6-22-1838 (6-23-1838) O
Logan, Mary to T. S. Baker 10-24-1874 (10-25-1874) T
Logan, Nancy to Daniel Musley 8-30-1828 Ma
Logan, Sarah A. to A. J. Acree 4-19-1841 Sh
Logan, Sarah Ann to Silas Bailey 11-13-1869 (11-14-1869) F
Logan, Sarah B. to Thomas Christian 8-25-1841 (8-26-1841) Ma
Logan, Susan R. (Mrs.) to Wm. L. Sewart 12-23-1857 Sh
Logan, Susannah H. to Peter S. Clack 7-2-1839 O
Logan, Syntha to John S. White 5-31-1851 (6-1-1851) O
Loghlen, Margaret to Henry Dufferin 5-21-1864 (5-23-1864) Sh
Loghlen, Margaret to Henry Sufferin 5-21-1864 Sh
Logue, Phoeba to A. J. Bailey 1-11-1861 Sh
Logwood, Polly Walker to John A. Winston 10-18-1843 F
Lokey, Eliza J. to Jas. B. Smith 8-18-1859 Hr
Loller, Louisa to A. F. Reeves 5-2-1854 Sh
Loller, Martha to Levi Evans 9-15-1859 G
Lomax, Nancy J. to John B. Alexander 1-20-1859 We
Lonargan, Ellen to John Roach 11-1-1856 (11-3-1856) Sh
London (Landon?), Malvina Tennessee to G. W. Leake 7-20-1869 G
London, America to A. W. Bradley 2-1-1869 G
London, Elizabeth to Westley Hubert 1-31-1860 O
London, Eveline to Lemuel Leake 3-30-1849 (4-1-1849) Ma
London, Jane V. to Almus Grooms 1-24-1872 (1-25-1872) Cr
London, Mary A. to James H. Jones 2-6-1862 (2-11-1862) O
London, Mattie J. to J. Harvey Edmonston 6-20-1855 (6-21-1855) O
London, Nancy J. to N. S. Burrow 1-2-1860 (1-4-1860) G
London, Sarah N. to Parmenias Fifer 1-3-1860 Ma
Londu, Cynthia to Jesse Johnson 8-25-1846 (8-26-1846) Ma
Lone, Nancy to Wm. Cloar 10-6-1845 We
Loney, Lucrecia to Henry Lewis 1-20-1840 (12?-27-1840) F
Long, Amanda Jane to A. D. Lee 4-5-1865 Mn
Long, Amanda M. to Thomas J. Jones 3-16-1844 (6-24-1844) O
Long, Amanda S. E. to L. C. Woodard 2-18-1868 L
Long, Caroline D. to James Elrod 3-15-1855 Ma
Long, Caroline to Joseph Carnall 12-19-1849 (12-20-1849) L
Long, Caroline to T. L. Bridgeman 1-11-1850 Cr
Long, Cela to Jacob H. Short 5-8-1849 Hr
Long, Eliza P. to John P. Pryor 9-19-1845 Ma
Long, Elizabeth M. to William A. Burris 6-10-1861 (6-16-1861) O
Long, Elizabeth to Ebenezer Walker 10-27-1861 G
Long, Elizabeth to John Maupin 7-12-1843 O
Long, Elizabeth to Jonas Houser 1-5-1830 (2-4-1830) O
Long, Elizabeth to Robert Tate 7-25-1847 Cr
Long, Emer Eugenia to E. P. Strickland 6-23-1862 (no return) L
Long, Harriet Ann to John G. Mann 6-27-1860 (6-28-1860) Ma
Long, Harriet to Macal Beavers 1-14-1868 (1-16-1868) T
Long, L. T. to G. T. Bailey 11-15-1858 We
Long, Louvisa to James Smith 6-26-1883 (6-29-1883) L
Long, M. F. to T. J. Trosper 5-2-1864 Sh
Long, M. H. W. to Daniel A. Bridgeman 9-14-1850 Cr
Long, M. J. to S. M. Montgomery 3-8-1855 (no return) F
Long, Margaret (Mrs.) to John H. Davys 11-12-1864 Sh
Long, Margaret F. to James Conder 1-10-1854 Sh
Long, Margaret to H. W. Beaver 5-1-1862 T
Long, Margarett to Francis Carny 3-29-1864 (3-31-1864) Sh
Long, Margarett to Jonathan Whiteside 10-22-1846 O
Long, Maria to Isaac Mills 12-8-1827 Hr
Long, Martha to James Walker 6-30-1866 (7-1-1866) Cr
Long, Marthaann M. to Samuel M. Hudspeth 4-19-1840 (6-19-1840) F
Long, Mary A. to James M. Terrell 2-17-1863 We
Long, Mary E. to John H. Hill 6-16-1873 (no return) Hy
Long, Mary J. to Robert H. Chester 11-1-1853 Ma
Long, Mary to Samuel Park 1-29-1834 Hr
Long, Metilda to Everett Glisson 6-1-1858 G
Long, Minerva to Asa Estes 11-29-1827 Hr
Long, Nancy to Isaac H. McCoard 11-23-1846 (11-5?-1846) F
Long, Nancy to John T. Miller 4-20-1867 (4-19-1868?) L
Long, Nancy to Scarlet M. Glascock 3-7-1842 (3-10-1842) G
Long, Nancy to Thos. P. Newton 3-28-1865 O
Long, Parlee to J. A. Garner 12-1-1876 Hy
Long, Parlee to Peyton Gregory 12-24-1869 (no return) Cr
Long, Permelia to Saml. J. Marsh 6-20-1859 (6-21-1859) T
Long, Polly to Benajah Pate 10-22-1829 L
Long, Rebecca L. to Noah B. Houser 8-13-1840 O
Long, Rebecca to John Frank 1-22-1880 (1-25-1880) L
Long, Rhoda to Robt. H. Nichols 2-19-1870 (2-20-1870) Ma
Long, S. E. to J. M. Wilson 8-6-1863 G
Long, Salenia to Joe Denton 1-18-1873 (no return) Cr B
Long, Sarah G. to John D. Danbury 5-3-1855 Sh
Long, Sarah to Acan Mifflay 11-11-1865 Mn
Long, Sarah to Ambrose H. Crews 11-18-1874 (no return) Hn
Long, Sarah to Henry Kirby 1-22-1850 Cr
Long, Sarah to S. Wesley Wells 3-26-1849 O
Long, Susie to Robt. A. Treadwell 2-9-1869 Ma

Longbein, Amelia to Charles Erck 3-2-1858 Sh
Longbein, Therisee to Julius Gotchalk 7-14-1862 (7-15-1862) Sh
Longley, Crecy to Jno. C. Beard 7-26-1873 Hy
Longley, Elizabeth to John Smith 4-?-1844 (4-20-1844) O
Longley, Sarah Z. to B. H. Bobo 7-14-1838 (7-15-1838) O
Longly, Anna to Blackman H. Bird 7-28-1832 (8-2-1832) O
Longly, Elizabeth to William Stroud 3-10-1829 O
Longmyre, Leanna to Norwood Roper 8-14-1868 (8-16-1868) Cr
Longworth, Mary E. to George W. Walker 1-2-1861 (1-3-1861) Cr
Lonigan, Mary to Thomas Lonigan 6-16-1849 Sh
Lonsberry, Rebecca to Joseph Riley 8-24-1839 Hr
Looney, Bernetta to David W. Frazier 5-14-1857 Hn
Looney, C. A. to J. H. Claiborn 4-21-1865 (no return) Cr
Looney, Eliza to A. F. Brackin 4-15-1838 F
Looney, Harriett to William E. Curtis 2-19-1861 Hn
Looney, Jennie P. to John Boyle 9-17-1863 Sh
Looney, Julia to Cyrus P. Harris 7-8-1851 Hn
Looney, M. A. to S. A. Patterson 1-18-1865 (no return) Hn
Looney, Margarett to Thomas L. Biles 6-10-1846 Hn
Looney, Martha E. to Harris Diggs 10-30-1860 Hn
Looney, Mary D. to Will S. McCall 12-21-1854 Hn *
Looney, Mary P. to S. H. Steele 12-25-1866 (12-26-1866) L
Looney, Mary to Daniel McHugh 9-19-1859 Sh
Looney, Melissa D. to John D. Middlewest 12-21-1848 Hn
Looney, Phitney M. to David T. Whitnell 9-25-1843 Hn
Looney, Rachel to Samuel M. Carter 10-29-1850 Hn
Looney, Sarah J. to Green Cloar 1-31-1851 Hn
Looney, Susan T. to William W. McGehee 9-23-1854 Hn
Looper, Elizabeth to Isaac Hollinsworth 5-4-1848 Be
Lorance, Agnes to James H. Green 11-14-1866 (11-16-1866) Cr
Lorance, Ellen to Orange Chambliss 1-10-1873 (no return) Cr
Lorance, Hannah Jane to William Sadberry 9-26-1843 (10-5-1843) Hr
Lorance, Lavina C. to J. M. Cross 12-20-1869 (12-23-1869) Cr
Lorance, Margaret V. to W. C. Davidson 9-27-1860 G
Lorance, Martha J. to Simon M. E. Capps 10-2-1866 G
Lorance, Martha to Elijah Baley 9-5-1854 Cr
Lorance, Polly to William Dranna 5-29-1838 Hr
Lorance, Sophia to George W. Boaz 10-13-1866 (10-14-1866) Cr
Lorant, Nancy N. to Newton A. Ewing 12-15-1829 Hr
Lorate, Harriett to Isah Briant 1-1-1872 (no return) Cr B
Lorimore, Vicey to Henry Small 2-8-1871 T
Lorrence, Rebeca C. to Huy M. Farmer 11-2-1840 (no return) F
Lott, Catherine to Lewis Wilson 1-1-1873 Hy
Lott, Eveline to H.C. Read 4-27-1875 (no return) Hy
Lott, Isabella to A. Hamil 12-26-1882 L
Lottis, Harrett to Stephen F. Wetherford 11-22-1852 G
Lotty, Jane to John Wilson 2-22-1854 (3-7-1854) Sh
Louby, Margaret to Edward O'Donnell 7-14-1858 (7-15-1858) Sh
Louder, Elizabeth to E. B. Elinder 2-12-1851 Cr
Loughman, Catherine to Michael Burk 4-26-1851 (4-28-1851) Sh
Louis, Hanah to Osa Cambell 9-22-1870 G B
Louis, L. J. to L. M. Tosh 3-11-1868 Cr
Louis, M. E. to J. W. Kelly 1-2-1873 Cr
Louisa, Jones to Nuton Powell 1-4-1871 (no return) Hy
Louit, Clementine to Frank Menetree 5-27-1863 Sh
Louiville, Randa to Alf Harrison 7-1-1871 (no return) Hy
Louiza J., Bell to William Prescott 1-2-1861 (no return) Hy
Lourance, A. E. (Miss) to Isaac Anglemyer 4-28-1859 Sh
Lourance, Eliza M. to Zophar Lourance 4-15-1835 Hr
Loure, Paulina to George Staley 9-4-1851 Sh
Lourie, Jennie R. to Francis M. Crouch 10-2-1859 Hn
Louther, Catherine to W. D. Parkerson 5-8-1849 Hn
Louvet, Louisa Noeimi Esther to Emmanuel Trigallez 4-2-1859 Sh
Love, Ada B. to D. M. McKenzie 12-4-1869 (12-7-1869) Dy
Love, Ann to Alex Thomson 12-26-1866 Hy
Love, Ann to Rufus Wilson 12-31-1872 Hy
Love, Aura? to Joseph Campbell 1-30-1835 Hr
Love, Caroline to James Burton 10-1-1855 Ma
Love, E. M. to J. B. Wall 1-23-1866 (1-24-1866) F
Love, Fannie P. to William J. Webb 2-20-1861 Sh
Love, Frances to Tom Whitelaw 1-16-1870 Hy
Love, Hattie F. to Homer McKenzie 12-12-1870 (12-17-1870) Dy
Love, L. D. to Homer McKenzie 11-26-1877 Dy
Love, Larra to Bevely Sands 1-28-1872 Hy
Love, Lindy to Stephen Bullock 12-27-1866 Hn B
Love, Louisa F. to James R. Cody 10-24-1848 Hn
Love, M. A. (Mrs.) to John C. Williams 9-1-1864 Sh
Love, M. E. to J. M. Webb 12-20-1865 F
Love, Margaret to Wm. Stone 2-14-1834 (2-16-1834) Hr
Love, Martha J. to Robert T. Clark 2-22-1848 Hn
Love, Martha L. to W. J. Clendening 2-4-1867 (2-5-1867) Dy
Love, Mary E. to J. J. Cooke 7-17-1842 Hn
Love, Mary F. to Richard M. Whitfield 1-1-1855 Ma
Love, Mary Jane to Thomas Boyle 10-19-1841 (10-21-1841) Hr
Love, Mattie A. to N. P. Howard 5-6-1866 Hn
Love, Mattie E. to N. C. Howard 1-30-1865 (no return) Cr

Love, Paralee E. to John Mathis Brown 4-13-1858 Hn
Love, Rebecca A. to Wm. A. Bryant 1-1-1866 (1-4-1866) F
Love, S. E. to J. R. Wyatt 12-7-1867 G
Love, Sallie J. to George W. Cook 7-11-1856 Sh
Love, Sarah G. to J. W. Smith 11-19-1857 We
Love, Sarah Jane to Thomas C. Moore 7-12-1850 Cr
Love, Sarah to Herbert Edwards 1-12-1848 (1-13-1848) G
Love, Sarah to John Ritchey 4-23-1836 Hr
Loveall, Martha C. to W. L. Pinson 11-2-1870 (11-6-1870) Cr
Lovel, M. J. to S. O. Wilson 11-28-1872 O
Lovel, Nancy to John McW. Wilie 12-28-1843 Sh
Lovelace, Adaline M. to James R. Lovelace 9-5-1858 We
Lovelace, Alice to Joe Ruliford 12-31-1881 (1-1-1882) L B
Lovelace, Ann J. to John R. Nixon 6-6-1859 L
Lovelace, Ann to John Michael 11-17-1840 (no return) Hn
Lovelace, Anna M. to Wen. D. L. Duncan 9-26-1867 Dy
Lovelace, Caroline to William H. Newton 1-10-1871 Ma
Lovelace, Cassandra E. to Thomas W. Russell 5-24-1870 (no return) L
Lovelace, Claudia to J. W. Tinsley 3-21-1877 L
Lovelace, Cordelia M. to Francis M. Millem 8-21-1868 (9-?-1868) L
Lovelace, E. F. to S. C. Sorrell 7-29-1868 (no return) Dy
Lovelace, Emma to Abram Green 11-16-1868 (no return) L B
Lovelace, Eugenia V. to Francis E. Hudson 2-13-1856 (2-14-1856) Ma
Lovelace, F. A. to H. G. Putman 1-23-1870 (1-25-1871) Dy
Lovelace, Fannie S. to C. T. Nash 5-27-1867 (5-30-1867) Dy
Lovelace, Lucinda E. to James M. Campbell 7-8-1862 (no return) L
Lovelace, Mary W. to A.(N?) B. Strain 2-19-1866 (2-21-1866) L
Lovelace, Melvina F. to J. C. Lieper 1-8-1854 Hn
Lovelace, Rachel to Moses Thacker 12-21-1868 (no return) Dy
Lovelace, Sabetha W. to William C. Vantreese 6-8-1840 (6-10-1840) Ma
Lovelace, Sarah J. to Thomas M. Farmer 11-11-1857 We
Lovelace, Sarah to Henry Casey 12-25-1872 (12-26-1873?) L
Lovelace, Susan S. to Lawson P. Bedford 12-27-1860 L
Lovelace, Susan V. to Stephen M. Johnson 1-6-1859 Ma
Loveland, Annie to Wm. McMurrey 1-4-1864 Sh
Loveland, Mattie J. to William L. Dorsey 5-14-1861 Cr
Lovell, California to Sandford M. Bickerstaff 4-13-1869 (4-14-1869) Ma
Lovell, Elizabeth to William Carter 7-27-1831 Sh
Lovell, Martha E. to Henry Goodin 11-18-1857 Cr
Lovell, Mary Ann to Henry G. Coburn 8-30-1853 Sh
Lovell, Mary Rue to James Rue 5-1-1855 (5-3-1855) Sh
Lovell, Sarah to John Broachy 5-1-1858 (5-13-1858) Sh
Lovell, Susan to William E. Whitten 2-23-1850 (2-24-1850) Hr
Lovett, Chana to Abner S. Thomas 7-18-1850 (8-8-1850) G
Lovett, Jane to Eleazer P. Orr 8-6-1851 G
Lovett, L. B. to R. L. Jetton 9-2-1879 (9-10-1879) Dy
Lovett, M. A. to J. W. Wall 9-28-1868 (no return) Dy
Lovett, Nancy to A. B. Orr 10-14-1843 (10-15-1843) G
Lovett, Susan to J. L. Davis 10-1-1866 (10-10-1866) Dy
Lovewell, Jane to Colbert Mathews 2-2-1824 G
Lovill, Mary Jane to James M. Gately 11-9-1852 (12-22-1852) Ma
Lovin, Elizabeth to James R. Clark 6-24-1856 Sh
Lovin, Fanny to Isaac Miles 12-16-1866 G
Lovin, Fanny to Isaac Miller 12-16-1866 G
Lovin, Lavicy to William W. Holliday 12-9-1847 Ma
Lovin, Mary A. to Isaiah Stephens 4-26-1855 Sh
Lovin, Nancy to John Hutchinson 2-23-1851 (2-24-1851) O
Loving (Lowry), Molli to Enoch Daniel 12-10-1874 O
Loving, Alice C. to Ben F. Turner 11-5-1874 Hy
Loving, Caroline C. to R. W. Hargrove 10-15-1860 (10-16-1860) F
Loving, Caty to Robert Griffin 2-4-1867 (no return) F B
Loving, Elizabeth to Cullud Lane 1-6-1841 (2-16-1841) Ma
Loving, Ella to B. G. Ezzell 5-4-1872 (5-5-1872) Cr
Loving, Hannah to D. Witt 10-9-1883 L
Loving, Hannar to George Scott 9-20-1877 Hy
Loving, Hariet A. to Felix F. Porter 11-29-1859 Hn
Loving, Juliann to William Smith 4-14-1844 Hn
Loving, Juvel to Allen Hart 12-23-1866 Hy
Loving, Littie to Jeff Anderson 1-18-1869 Hy
Loving, Lucy A. to William H. Payne 3-3-1840 Hn
Loving, M. I. to T. H. Styers 11-25-1869 Hy
Loving, Margaret to Amos Hunter 12-27-1865 Hy
Loving, Mariah to John Brown 4-2-1855 (4-5-1855) Sh
Loving, Martha to Frank Shaw 12-13-1867 (no return) F B
Loving, Mary R. to John D. Vaughan 9-5-1866 Hy
Loving, Mary to Henry Gerrico 11-27-1867 O
Loving, Mary to L. C. Robison 4-22-1866 (no return) Cr
Loving, Mattie to W. C. McKendree 1-8-1866 (1-9-1866) F
Loving, Mollie E. to Astley C. Wright 10-29-1860 Hn
Loving, Mollie R. to J. Y. Boyd 1-29-1870 (no return) Hy
Loving, Mollie to Miles Winfield 10-30-1868 Hy
Loving, Nancy to John Webber 2-4-1837 Sh
Loving, Queen to Monroe Richmond 2-17-1883 (2-20-1883) L
Loving, Sallie P. to E. B. Davis 2-6-1860 (2-7-1860) F
Loving, Sarah Jane to J. H. Porteet 12-13-1862 (12-17-1862) Sh
Loving, Taldona to Albert Gary 2-1-1877 Hy
Lovit, Rebecca to W. J. Glassgow 10-10-1871 (10-12-1871) Dy

Lovitt, Sarah to William Munn 11-13-1839 Ma
Lovone, Sarah A. to John M. Gardner 1-18-1855 Cr
Low, Charity M. to James R. Pugh 1-20-1840 (1-24-1840) Hr
Low, Martha to James L. Dawson 2-18-1843 Hr
Low, Mary Jane to W. B. Holloway 12-25-1856 Sh
Low, S. A. to M. M. Thurmond 10-8-1860 (10-9-1860) Hr
Low, Sarah E. to Matthew McDowell 3-9-1852 (3-10-1852) Sh
Low, Sarah to Samuel Williams 5-29-1861 (5-30-1861) Hr
Low?, Mary Ann to George Damson? 5-19-1836 (5-22-1836) Hr
Lowall, Caroline to W. H. Elliner 10-22-1854 We
Lowden, Carilla E. to W. Evans 2-15-1867 G
Lowden, E. to James Evans 5-5-1869 G
Lowder, Lidda to Eli J. Lawrance 4-25-1844 Cr
Lowdermilk, Peggy to Benjamin Brown 10-6-1829 Hr
Lowe, Augusta to Frank Fealy 11-5-1861 (11-24-1861) Sh
Lowe, Cynthia A. to R. G. Patterson 4-11-1851 (4-15-1851) Hr
Lowe, Emeline to John Dogget 12-7-1872 Hy
Lowe, Felia to Johnson Bernard 8-7-1872 (1-16-1872?) T
Lowe, Frances M. to Francis M. Carroll 7-25-1838 (7-26-1838) Hr
Lowe, M. Amanda to Geo. D. Sollis 2-1-1879 Dy
Lowe, Marion M. to S. R. Hall 4-19-1856 (4-20-1856) Sh
Lowe, Martha J. to Meridith M. Thurman 5-17-1851 (5-20-1851) Hr
Lowe, Nancy to Dan Smith 12-7-1871 (12-9-1871) T
Lowe, Sarah A. to J. M. Bradley 5-25-1873 (5-21?-1873) Dy
Lowe, Sarah M. to E. N. Hunt 5-22-1857 (6-4-1857) Hr
Lowell, Sarah Ann to Thomas Smith 1-?-1862 (1-13-1862) Cr
Lowell, Sarah to Robert W. Gordon 1-7-1848 (1-20-1848) Ma
Lowery, Barsheeba to F. M. Brim 3-2-1856 We
Lowery, Elizabeth A. to Samuel R. Sipes 12-15-1859 (12-16-1859) Hr
Lowery, Elizabeth to Charles Carter 1-18-1845 Hn
Lowery, Ella to Henry Swanson 8-4-1871 Hy
Lowery, Ida to Robt. H. Ratliff 10-18-1875 (no return) Hy
Lowery, Louisa to Elliot Yarbrough 1-15-1843 Hn
Lowery, Lucy Jane to T. J. Ayers 9-28-1859 (10-2-1859) Hr
Lowery, Mariah P. to Kenneth P. Lowrey 2-4-1858 Hn
Lowery, Marietta H. to John Dowell 1-29-1858 Be
Lowery, Mary to Alexander Patterson 9-5-1862 Mn
Lowery, Mary to W. S. Simmons 12-12-1866 Hy
Lowery, P. A. to C. R. Dickinson 12-12-1867 (12-15-1867) F B
Lowery, Rebecca to Albert J. Williams 2-21-1850 Hn
Lowery, Rhody to S. B. Manns 10-5-1865 G
Lowery, Rosella to Newton Cox 6-16-1860 (6-24-1860) Cr
Lowery, Sally to Hiram Davis 7-5-1828 G
Lowery, Sarah A. L. to Erasmus J. Hutchins 7-7-1866 (7-8-1866) Cr
Lowery, Susan M. to James A. Williams 10-24-1854 Cr
Lowery, Susan R. to David McMackins 3-18-1863 (3-19-1863) Cr
Lowey?, Mary S. to John Reynolds 12-13-1866 G
Lowin?, Martha E. to Joel S. Tyson 11-4-1844 Hn
Lowrance, Elizabeth A. to Thos. M. Butler 1-22-1859 Cr
Lowrance, Fanny to Ned Lowrance 6-8-1870 G
Lowrance, M. E. to Henry Killion 2-14-1866 O
Lowrance, Maria Jane to William W. Beard 11-3-1855 (11-4-1855) Hr
Lowrance, Martha A. to James A. Williams 8-22-1869 G
Lowrance, Mary F. to Thos. A. Dickens 10-3-1855 (no return) Cr
Lowrance, Mary to James Skiles 5-26-1853 G
Lowrance, Sarah E. to John L. Edmondson 3-19-1867 G
Lowrence, Terry J. to C. G. Richardson 12-18-1851 Sh
Lowrence, V. A. to James A. Algee 9-3-1857 Cr
Lowrey, Elisabeth to M. S. Jay 1-21-1861 (2-17-1861) Sh
Lowrey, Sophia H. to J. J. Rawlings 11-2-1854 Sh
Lowrie, Bridget K. to John Behan 5-30-1862 Sh
Lowry, A. E. to Stephen W. Muzzall 6-24-1858 Hn
Lowry, A. E. to Wm. M. Webster 11-10-1878 Hy
Lowry, Eliza Ann to John Masey 10-16-1843 (no return) We
Lowry, Elizabeth to Washington Davis 2-6-1838 Hn
Lowry, Harriet to James Johnson 6-4-1864 (6-19-1864) L
Lowry, Jane E. to James Hockard 7-2-1850 We
Lowry, Lafronia A. to David J. Thomas 11-30-1858 Hn
Lowry, Louisa to Jordan Johnson 12-28-1869 G
Lowry, Lureta G. to Henry Smith 1-1-1846 Hn
Lowry, M. E. to J. A. Forem 1-11-1865 G
Lowry, Mahaly to Radford McFarland 2-3-1834 (2-4-1834) G
Lowry, Malinda to Nathan W. Ford 2-14-1853 (3-3-1853) G
Lowry, Malinda to William Dowell 12-30-1834 (1-1-1835) G
Lowry, Margarett to William Byars 1-13-1847 Hn
Lowry, Martha A. to Wm. Mitchell 10-15-1860 Hn
Lowry, Martha Ann to Green Wood 11-18-1844 (7-24-1845) F
Lowry, Mary F. to Alfred Sipes 2-6-1860 Hr
Lowry, Mary P. to George W. Atchison 6-23-1852 Hn
Lowry, Mary to Henry Underwood 8-30-1880 L B
Lowry, Nancy Ann Agnes E. to Greenbury Read 12-11-1846 (12-12-1846) L
Lowry, Nancy J. to Person K. Dorsett 12-28-1847 G
Lowry, Nancy to W. B. Dowell 9-6-1847 G
Lowry, Pemelia Lane to Isaac Dawson 5-1-1829 O
Lowry, Precilla to John A. Cox 9-3-1857 Hn
Lowry, Rebecca A. C. to Benjamin L. Hancock 7-28-1877 (7-29-1877) L
Lowry, S. E. to William Young 1-2-1856 (no return) Hn

Lowry, Sarah A. to H. D. Byars 5-25-1863 Hn
Lowry, Sarah to J. A. French 10-5-1865 Hn
Lowry, Sophia to William B. Thompson 5-22-1850 Sh
Lowry, Susan A. to P. W. Hudson 10-21-1860 Be
Lowry, Susan F. to Samuel R. Moody 9-2-1866 Hn
Lowry, Susan W. to Isaac Lowry 12-16-1841 Sh
Lowry, Susie to P. H. Barriet 12-4-1878 Hy
Lowry, Winnie J. B. to James R. Lowry 4-17-1859 Hn
Lowry, ____ to James R. Dossett 10-17-1854 G
Lowter, J. Mila to Samuel R. Hubbard 5-1-1861 G
Loyd, Caroline to Joseph Alison 1-3-1877 Hy
Loyd, Eliza to Daniel Holland 3-21-1848 Be
Loyd, Lavinia to Manson Lawrence 12-28-1867 G B
Loyd, M. A. to J. H. Hamby 5-24-1873 (5-25-1873) T
Loyd, M. C. to John Beasley 11-3-1856 Be
Loyd, M. L. to John Q. Jarrell 11-25-1869 G
Loyd, Martha to William Obrien 1-29-1867 (1-31-1867) T
Loyd, Melinda to George Spears 1-9-1838 Sh
Loyd, Sarah E. to W. J. Jones 12-31-1866 G
Loyed, A. T. to W. B. Sawyers 12-26-1876 (12-28-1876) O
Loyle, Louisa to Wesley Higgins 6-19-1860 Sh
Luallen, Mary Jane to Elsey Howard 8-29-1871 (8-30-1871) L
Luby, Margaret to Patrick Hoy (Houg) 4-23-1855 L
Lucado, Willy Ann to James E. McGowan 9-23-1850 (no return) F
Lucas, Amy to Ned Utley 1-4-1869 (1-8-1869) Cr
Lucas, Anna to Ransom Brown 9-28-1870 (no return) F B
Lucas, Irene to L. J. Stewart 11-18-1885 L
Lucas, Isadora to Albert Halliburton 12-18-1884 (12-19-1884) L
Lucas, Julia to Charley Jones 12-20-1872 Hy
Lucas, Lindy to Andrew Bradford 3-16-1874 L
Lucas, Lizzie W. to Henry M. Dilliard 1-20-1859 F
Lucas, Lorenda to James Stokes 12-6-1838 Cr
Lucas, Lucy to T. H. Milam 3-11-1885 (3-12-1885) L
Lucas, M. L. to John R. Griffin 9-3-1867 (no return) Dy
Lucas, Mariah to Henry McDowel 2-23-1867 (2-26-1867) F B
Lucas, Martha A. to R. T. Edgar 6-29-1865 Hn
Lucas, Martha to William Carroll 8-25-1855 (no return) F
Lucas, Mary C. to Thomas M. Edgar 6-27-1858 Hn
Lucas, Mary Elizabeth to Matthew Houston Ellis 6-25-1861 Sh
Lucas, Mary F. to J. B. Smith 4-8-1885 L
Lucas, Mattie J. to A. S. (Rev.) Johnson 12-13-1875 (no return) L
Lucas, Mattie to Drew Johnson 12-20-1872 Hy
Lucas, Parthena to Isaac Parrish 3-9-1876 (no return) Hy
Lucas, Provy to Archable W. Kirby 3-21-1844 Cr
Lucas, S. E. to J. G. Brantlen 2-28-1871 (2-29?-1871) Dy
Lucas, Sarah Young to Henry Stephen Murphery 3-14-1849 (3-15-1849) L
Lucas, Sarah to Wm. Kinney 3-22-1877 Hy
Luceford, Rebecca to W. K. Giddens 1-26-1872 (no return) Hy
Lucett, Julia to Patrick Kerby (Kelby) 5-12-1863 L
Lucey, Barsheba to Joseph Crocker 12-20-1842 (12-21-1842) L
Lucian?, Rhonda A. to John J. Brigg 2-7-1860 Cr
Luckado, Cardelia to William Edwards 8-21-1868 T
Luckado, Rebecca J. to Thos. A. Bostick 1-1-1850 (1-2-1850) F
Luckado, S. J. to J. S. Motley 12-17-1866 (12-19-1866) F
Lucken, Emily T. to J. Dix Mills 9-9-1858 (9-23-1858) Sh
Lucker, Sarah L. to John W. Grady 10-8-1862 G
Lucket, Jennie to C. G. Richardson 12-18-1851 Sh
Luckett, C. M. (Mrs.) to Thomas P. Alston 12-13-1872 (12-15-1872) L
Luckett, Elizabeth R. to Alexander M. Rafter 6-17-1854 (6-21-1854) Sh
Luckey, Allice to Dave Simmons 11-10-1867 G B
Luckey, Armenia B. to S. B. Dugger 2-17-1867 Hn
Luckey, Caroline to Stephen B. Goodrich 7-24-1858 (7-29-1858) Ma
Luckey, Mary to Joshua Rice 11-17-1868 G B
Luckey, Nancy P. to Robert Anderson 2-1-1863 Hn
Luckey, Sarah E. to Rufus K. Garrett 1-21-1851 (1-22-1851) F
Luckey, Victoria J. to John Nash 8-3-1863 (no return) Hn
Lucre, Mary A. to James H. Perdue 8-4-1866 O
Lucus, Elizabeth to Wm. Vinson 12-2-1840 Cr
Lucus, F. A. L. to E. M. Rice? 6-2-1850 We
Lucus, Lucy A. to Eli Bradford 2-21-1874 (2-22-1874) L
Lucus, Mary to Rice Grogan 9-9-1841 Cr
Lucus, Sarah C. to Perry Jas. Davis 6-24-1841 Cr
Lucy A., Mays to Ephraim Prescott 1-11-1870 (no return) Hy
Lucy, Green to Monroe Phillips 6-30-1877 Hy
Lucy, M. P. to L. B. Ray 12-26-1876 L
Lucy, Pelina to Sampson Gidcumb 7-14-1849 (7-15-1849) L
Lucy, Taylor to Horace Plummer 1-4-1875 (no return) Hy
Ludenback, Fredericka Rosa to Fred Emgel 3-8-1858 (3-10-1858) Sh
Ludwig, Elizabeth to B. Fritz 2-27-1852 Sh
Ludwig, Elizabeth to Joseph Rebman 2-16-1856 Sh
Luen, Eliza M. to J. W. Wilson 2-17-1858 We
Luggett, Amanda S. M. to Thompson C. Coates 12-17-1845 Hr
Luker, Charity to John W. Simpson 7-31-1856 O
Luker, Melenda to William Warner 6-1-1855 We
Lumbrick, Elizabeth to William Simmons 8-20-1861 Hn
Lumley, Bettie to J. B. Smith 7-27-1872 (8-1-1872) Dy
Lumley, Lucinda to J. M. Turner 1-31-1877 (2-1-1877) Dy

Lumley, Rebecca to J. H. Henry 1-1-1872 (1-4-1872) Dy
Lumley, Susannah to N. C. Pritchett 2-20-1879 Dy
Lummicons, Martha to John J. Bius? 6-24-1868 (6-25-1868) T
Lumpkin, Nancy Jane to T. T. Bennett 8-24-1858 (8-25-1858) Sh
Lumpkins, Narcissa to John W. Baker 10-31-1872 L
Lumsley, E. to John E. R. Carter 12-13-1844 (12-14-1844) F
Lunay, Mary to Walter Lawler 7-12-1856 (7-13-1856) Sh
Lunceford, M. E. to James Robbins 11-25-1870 (no return) Hy
Lundal, Susan E. G. to J. W. Jarrett 12-10-1838 (12-12-1838) F
Lundergin, Ellen to Thomas Hennessey 5-19-1860 (5-20-1860) Sh
Lundie, Mollie E. to Thomas J. Thomas 7-29-1866 Hy
Lundy (Lindy), Rebecca A. to Seth B. Turner 11-15-1850 Sh
Lundy, Cornelia L. to Geo. L. Parker 12-8-1855 Sh
Lundy, Ella to J. J. Coppedge 2-18-1874 (no return) Hy
Lundy, Martha W. to Jno. Grizzard 7-17-1848 Sh
Lundy, Mary E. to Bolin Peebles 2-19-1846 Sh
Lundy, Mildred W. to William Tillar 7-5-1845 Sh *
Lundy, S. Y. to L. J. Coffman 6-26-1862 (no return) Hy
Lundy, Susan H. to James J. Moore 8-3-1853 Sh
Lundy, Virginia A. to Edmond Irby 5-23-1853 Sh
Lune, Caroline to Moses Pamberger 6-5-1843 Sh
Lunford, Tennessee to Dabney Smith 1-14-1873 (1-16-1873) T
Lung, Crestine to F. Engell 3-6-1860 (3-7-1860) Sh
Lunge, Rosena to Chas. E. Wolf 8-19-1864 (9-1-1864) Sh
Lunsden, Margaret to Samuel Dameren 4-16-1854 We
Lunsford, A. N. C. Jane to J. W. Norris 3-24-1857 L
Lunsford, Alice to N. S. Tucker 3-24-1886 L
Lunsford, Amanda F. A. to J. L. Osteen 7-26-1855 L
Lunsford, Amanda F. to J. L. Osteen 3-19-1856 (no return) L
Lunsford, Amanda Jane to James C. Wharton 6-7-1842 (6-9-1842) T
Lunsford, Arenia to Thomas F. Nixon 5-30-1868 (no return) Dy
Lunsford, Celia A. to William R. Osteen 8-11-1852 (no return) L
Lunsford, Elizabeth to Hardy Osteen 8-12-1846 L
Lunsford, Mariah J. to Joseph Smith 10-29-1870 (10-30-1870) L
Lunsford, Mary Ann to H. N. Wheatley 8-3-1876 L
Lunsford, Mary C. to Arthur Totty 3-20-1855 L
Lunsford, Mary to Elliote H. Nixon 5-1-1837 Hr
Lunsford, Nancy E. to John C. Pope 4-19-1879 (4-20-1879) L
Lunsford, Rachael to Thomas Harrison 1-30-1850 (2-3-1850) L
Lunsford, Rachel M. to Scott Turner 12-25-1868 (no return) L
Lunsford, Sarah E. to James E. Meacham 11-27-1878 (11-28-1878) L
Lunsford, Sarah J. E. to Geo. Tho. Somers 8-5-1875 Hy
Lunsford, Sarah J. to J. S. Templeton 5-18-1861 (5-19-1861) L
Luny (Lurry), Elizabeth to W. M. Sanderlin 8-26-1841 Sh
Luny, Eliza Jane to G. W. A. Smith 4-4-1863 Mn
Luny, Lucy L. to B. F. Bland 1-4-1844 Sh
Luny, Sarah to David Wilson 8-31-1848 Sh
Lurry, Olive (Olvid) G. to William Lynch 12-23-1845 Sh
Lusk, Amanda L. to Henry D. Featherston 5-12-1862 (no return) Cr
Lusk, Ann to John W. Fitzgerald 6-19-1874 L
Lusk, L. H. to J. A. Lorance 1-11-1867 (1-16-1867) Cr
Lusk, Mary to W. Boydston 8-30-1838 L
Lusk, Nancy E. to Thomas W. Stanley 9-26-1859 L
Lusk, S. E. to W. N. Gracy 5-23-1881 (no return) L
Lusk, Sabra Ann to John H. Farmer 6-27-1862 (6-28-1862) L
Lusk, Talitha to Thos. Jennings 9-18-1849 (9-19-1849) L
Lusker, Mary J. to John H. Thomas 10-27-1854
Luster, Catherin to John Somerville 3-22-1869 (3-24-1869) T
Luster, Elizabeth to Thomas Hail 12-25-1832 (12-30-1832) G
Luster, Matilda to Robert Jones 8-12-1844 (8-13-1844) O
Luster, Susan E. to F. M. Robinson 12-29-1853 (12-29-1853) Ma
Lustre, Alcey to Thomas Pierce 1-12-1844 (1-14-1844) O
Luten, Jennie to James E. Gillespie 4-13-1869 (4-14-1869) L
Luten, M. E. to W. A. Dyer 12-29-1870 (1-1-1871) O
Luten, Nancy to Samuel Price 11-16-1867 L
Luter, Amy to George Greer 4-3-1869 (4-4-1869) Cr
Luter, Emily to James N. Duncan 10-18-1854 Cr
Luter, Martha A. to H. G. Jones 6-27-1864 Hn
Luter, Mary T. to J. H. Pinson 1-4-1859 Cr
Luter, Myra A. to George T. Poyner 3-15-1865 Hn
Luter, Permedie to S. S. Smith 12-2-1867 Hn
Luth, Sarah A. to Jourdan? P. Wend? 12-9-1846 Hn
Luther, Harriet A. to Modecai Holland 12-7-1842 Hn
Lutin, Sally H. to James W. Wilson 8-23-1852 (no return) L
Luton, Elizabeth Ann to John W. Jones? 3-14-1857 O
Luton, F. A. to M.K. Underwood 10-4-1884 (10-5-1884) L
Luton, Martha J. to W. E. Roberson 7-11-1868 (no return) L
Luton, Nancy C. to Allworth Sewell 8-18-1865 Mn
Lutrell, Elizabeth J. to James McCarter 12-15-1858 (12-26-1858) Hr
Luttrell, Lucinda to Thomas Bowers 12-28-1865 Hr
Luttrell, Mary Ann to Joseph Barber 7-28-1847 (7-29-1847) Hr
Luttrell, Matilda Ann to Frederick Shepherd 5-18-1844 (5-21-1844) Hr
Lutz, Caroline to Herman Langbein 12-2-1854 Sh
Ly_te, Elizabeth to J. B. Cavinor 8-5-1874 (8-9-1874) L
Lycen, M. E. to T. J. Simmons 8-31-1854 Be
Lyghtner, Ann to D. P. Caldwell 2-2-1859 O
Lygote, Marsher A. to Wm. A. Williams 11-20-1850 Cr

Lyle, Ann to Andrew J. Burford 11-17-1874 Hy
Lyle, Catherine to John Parks 1-13-1847 Sh
Lyle, Cordelia T. to Charles H. Welch 12-22-1868 (12-24-1868) T
Lyle, Sarah P. to Andrew J. Clark 4-15-1843 Hr
Lyles, Elizabeth to Demous Odom 3-1-1863 Mn
Lyles, Mary Martin to John B. Parsons 9-30-1853 (10-2-1853) T
Lyn, Ann Willis to Cornelius Yates 5-3-1870 T
Lynch, Catharine to John Madden 4-9-1858 Sh
Lynch, Elizabeth A. to Wm. P. Elmore 2-12-1853 Be
Lynch, Ellen to Jeremiah Lyones 8-25-1863 Sh
Lynch, Ellen to John Maiers 2-3-1863 Sh
Lynch, Jeheno to Patrick Barron 5-26-1858 (5-26-1858) Sh
Lynch, Kate to John Ohanlon 11-4-1869 Ma
Lynch, Laura to John McLeary 6-14-1864 G
Lynch, Lucretia to Allen Dillard 5-11-1831 (5-15-1831) Hr
Lynch, Mary Ann to John Honey 2-15-1847 (2-21-1847) F
Lynch, Mary E. to J. D. P. Turner 2-21-1869 Be
Lynch, Mary to Patrick Conner 4-21-1855 (4-22-1855) Sh
Lynch, Mary to William O. Herren 7-13-1862 Sh
Lynch, Mary to Wm. O'Herron 7-13-1862 Sh
Lynch, Milly Ann to Robert Foster 10-6-1866 Ma
Lynch, Missouri F. to William Motley 8-30-1851 (9-7-1851) G
Lynch, Nancy N. to Frederick Carpenter 2-11-1850 O
Lynch, Olive G. (Mrs.) to Robt. B. Shore 8-11-1853 Sh
Lynch, Rhoda Emeline to Robert Swift 6-3-1846 Be
Lynch, Sallie to B. N. D. Tannehill 11-4-1857 (11-5-1857) Hr
Lynch, Sarah Ann to Jesse W. Elmore 10-10-1844 Be
Lynch, Sarah to George W. Bledsoe 8-4-1835 G
Lyne, Elizabeth to Patrick Cosgrove 4-2-1853 Sh
Lynes, M. E. to Thos. W. Drummonds 7-8-1852 Cr
Lynn, Adaline to Alexander Morrison 3-16-1869 (3-6?-1869) T
Lynn, Agnes F. to B. F. Lackey 3-11-1880 L
Lynn, Charlotte O. to Robert Baker 1-29-1829 (1-30-1829) Ma
Lynn, Charlotte to W. M. Hunt 5-25-1853 Hn
Lynn, Elizabeth C. to James L. Neely 9-24-1857 (9-29-1857) Sh
Lynn, Elizabeth to Goolsberry Luvin (Loving?) 2-25-1839 Hn
Lynn, Eveleni to William Barnett 7-2-1828 (7-3-1828) Ma
Lynn, Frances to Garland Key 4-11-1839 Hn
Lynn, Jennie to S. T. Green 12-24-1872 O
Lynn, M. F. to A. B. White 9-19-1860 We
Lynn, Martha to Wade H. Turner 5-21-1828 O
Lynn, Mary Jane to Alison M. Watts 10-24-1854 (10-26-1854) Sh
Lynn, N. E. to R. M. McCallie 10-5-1868 (10-6-1868) T
Lynton, Mary to Thomas Patterson 12-31-1839 Hn
Lyon, Ann to Howell Olive 2-13-1839 Hn
Lyon, Eliza to Overall Sanderson 4-7-1831 G
Lyon, Elizabeth to James N. Watt 4-3-1841 (4-4-1841) G
Lyon, Elizabeth to Samuel McMinn 1-23-1843 (1-25-1843) G
Lyon, Jane to William P. Berry 2-16-1841 (no return) Hn
Lyon, Julia A. to John J. Cash 12-28-1859 Ma
Lyon, Lizzie C. to B. L. Rozell 2-26-1855 (2-27-1855) Ma
Lyon, Luize E. to William Sham 2-19-1831 (2-21-1831) G
Lyon, Mary H. to W. H. McClure 11-22-1860 Ma
Lyon, Nancy E. to Thomas J. Watt 9-4-1867 (9-5-1867) Ma
Lyon, Nancy L. to William Covington 12-7-1853 (12-8-1853) G
Lyon, Sarah A. to Thomas J. Watt 1-4-1854 (1-12-1854) Ma
Lyon, Sarah E. to Daniel Gauger 4-11-1843 G
Lyon, Sarah E. to Elias Heddin 8-3-1866 (8-7-1866) Dy
Lyon, Sarah J. to Lemuel K. Clifton 11-6-1845 Ma
Lyon, Sarah Jane to James N. Watt, jr. 3-16-1850 Ma
Lyon, Sarah to Robert Campbell 3-17-1828 Ma
Lyon, Susan to Edward Bannon 12-23-1873 T
Lyons, Bridget to John Connell 1-19-1861 (1-20-1861) Sh
Lyons, Louisa to Robert Denny 11-24-1836 (11-25-1836) Hr
Lyons, Margaret E. to William J. Oakes 4-11-1859 Ma
Lyons, Mariah to Richard Thompson 1-7-1847 G
Lyons, Martha E. to George Day 1-25-1854 G
Lyons, Mary L. to John Raye 6-27-1864 Sh
Lyons, May F. to Isaac Spencer 5-11-1874 Dy
Lyons, Nancy A. to John Lyon 5-6-1861 (5-9-1861) Dy
Lyons, Nancy to Edmond Sanders 12-13-1843 (12-14-1843) G
Lyons, R. I. to John Lyon 3-19-1866 (3-22-1866) O
Lyons, Susan to Edmund K. Flowers 2-7-1848 G
Lyons, Zerrah to Joshua P. Clark 4-17-1845 Cr
Lyson, Louisa E. to William Shane 2-18-1831 Ma
Lytaker, Elizabeth to Mosses Fite 8-27-1827 (9-6-1827) G
Lytle, E. A. to E. A. J. Rodgers 11-22-1851 Cr
Lytle, Milly M. to Moses Shannon 11-11-1839 (11-14-1839) Hr

M_y, Fanny T. to Thomas Chatman 7-7-1867 G
Mabane, Mary Jane to Dan A. Walker 2-20-1871 Hy
Mabene, Maria to Thomas Gray 5-4-1872 T
Maberry?, Elizabeth to Mark Elam 1-10-1855 (no return) F
Mabin, Malissa to Wiley Mabin 5-3-1867 (6-3-1867) F B
Mabin, Matilda to Mack Hudson 4-18-1867 (no return) F B
Mabins, M. J. to D. C. Absteen 12-24-1878 Hy
Mabon, Wiry? to Case Johnson 2-13-1870 (no return) Cr

Mabry, Lucindy F. to Jesse J. Williams 1-4-1848 Cr
Mabry, Sallie to James Chilton 3-2-1870 Hy
Mabson, Mary E. A. to Francis A. Duval 7-7-1857 Sh
Maburn, Nancy to Peter Vincent 1-3-1871 (1-14-1871) T
Mabury, Elizabeth to Willis R. Taylor 8-6-1850 Be
MacKey, Millie to Richard Williams 11-18-1864 Sh
Macafee, Jane to Charles Manasco 1-10-1866 T
Mace, Amanda Ann to Robert Warren 12-17-1840 (12-22-1840) Hr
Maceer, N. H. to Wm. F. Wigam 8-12-1862 Sh
Maceer, Nancy to Wm. F. Weigand 8-12-1862 Sh
Macey, Ellen to Alexander Parker 3-18-1857 Sh
Machaum(Michum), Frankey to Henry Dickson 7-4-1827 (7-5-1827) Hr
Mack, Ann to Edward Burke 4-28-1855 Sh
Mack, Josie to Joseph Williams 1-2-1873 Hy
Mack, Margaret to James Woods 6-4-1864 (6-6-1864) Sh
Mack, Mary (Mrs.) to Francis J. Neep 1-14-1864 Sh
Mack, Mary to James Daimod 4-16-1853 (4-24-1853) Sh
Macke?, M. M. to A. B. Griffin 8-7-1871 (8-8-1871) T
Mackey, Elizabeth to Wm. Best 9-24-1847 Sh
Mackey, Mary to Jeptha Chatham 12-4-1842 Sh
Mackey, Sarah Ann to Lemon Stocks 11-27-1840 Sh
Mackey, Sarah to Ebenzer Best 12-24-1835 Sh
Macklin, Ann to Henry Stokes 2-13-1869 G B
Macklin, Anna L. to Jack Fields 12-26-1868 (1-20-1870) T
Macklin, Emily J. to Jeff Jones 12-26-1878 Hy
Macklin, Indy to Richard Edwards 12-20-1867 T
Macklin, Lucy to Harry Robinson 8-24-1877 Hy
Macklin, Mary to George Roberts 12-19-1867 T
Macklin, Mary to James Gallagher 4-23-1867 (not executed) F
Macklin, Nancy E. to Alfred Moore 1-4-1867 G
Macklin, Sallie to Wedly Taylor 9-6-1866 T
Macklin, Sucky to Andrew Bland 2-4-1869 (no return) F B
Maclan, Roberta to George Jones 7-20-1867 (no return) Hy
Maclarby, L. J. to David North 12-25-1862 Mn
Maclin, Aggny? to Alfred Craig 12-14-1867 (12-21-1867) T
Maclin, Amy to J. H. Harrison 1-2-1878 Hy
Maclin, Ann to C. P. Lane 1-23-1874 (no return) Hy
Maclin, Anna to Thomas Hodge 3-20-1869 (no return) F B
Maclin, Ardell to Edward Sims 10-12-1874 (no return) L
Maclin, Bettie to Jerry Maclin 12-23-1866 (no return) F B
Maclin, Bettie to T. A. Walker 11-1-1865 Hy
Maclin, Betty to Wilk Harver 3-2-1874 (no return) Hy
Maclin, Cresy to Wm. E. Reed 7-17-1872 Hy
Maclin, Easter to William Maclin 2-27-1874 T
Maclin, Eliza S. to Wm. F. Brodnax 5-15-1865 T
Maclin, Elizabeth to Anderson Day 1-23-1877 (no return) Hy
Maclin, Elizabeth to John W. Cannon 5-17-1867 (no return) Hy
Maclin, Elizabeth to Nathan Fitzpatrick 11-12-1869 (11-13-1869) L
Maclin, Fannie N. to Charles Ware 12-27-1875 Hy
Maclin, Fanny to Mansfield Read 12-30-1865 (no return) Hy
Maclin, Fany to Peter Sanford 7-2-1867 Hy
Maclin, Frances to Wesley Jones 12-21-1869 T
Maclin, Frankie to Wm. Taylor 1-28-1870 T
Maclin, Gracey to James Jones 12-7-1874 T
Maclin, Hannah to Wm. Farrington 11-5-1869 Hy
Maclin, Harrit to George Reddick 12-31-1870 (1-2-1871) T
Maclin, Jane to Peter S. Johnson 1-15-1870 Hy
Maclin, Jennie to Ed Peete 12-26-1870 T
Maclin, Jenny to Claiburn Whitley 7-18-1868 T
Maclin, Josephine to Aaron McNight 2-9-1876 (no return) Hy
Maclin, Judy to Jeff Collier 12-26-1872 (no return) Hy
Maclin, Katy to J. A. Read 12-20-1873 Hy
Maclin, Katy to Solomon Jelks 7-4-1873 (no return) Hy
Maclin, Laura to Caldwell Taylor 12-28-1868 Hy
Maclin, Lily to Beverly Johnson 7-26-1867 (7-27-1867) T
Maclin, Louisa to George Maclin 4-8-1870 T
Maclin, Lucy to Tom Read 2-4-1872 Hy
Maclin, M. E. to Sam. B. Jones 4-2-1866 (no return) Hy
Maclin, M. L. to W. H. Foster 12-10-1872 (12-11-1872) L
Maclin, Mary E. to H. B. Ware 12-27-1874 Hy
Maclin, Mary F. to P. E. Northern 3-4-1874 (3-5-1874) T
Maclin, Mary Jane to John Dooler 3-22-1867 (no return) Hy
Maclin, Mary to John Junius Maclin 12-20-1878 Hy
Maclin, Mary to Kit Johnson 9-4-1879 (9-6-1879) L
Maclin, Mary to Levi Johnson 4-21-1872 Hy
Maclin, Mary to Nicholas Read 3-21-1870 Hy
Maclin, Mollie to Felix Burrow 4-17-1882 L
Maclin, Moriah to Samuel Jordan 11-5-1872 Hy
Maclin, Nannie to Hickman Ware 1-24-1876 Hy
Maclin, Priscilla to Mingo Buford 4-1-1870 (12-28-1870) F B
Maclin, Rachael to Booker Meux 12-30-1865 (no return) Hy
Maclin, Rachel to Joe Scott 12-1-1870 Hy
Maclin, Rebecca to Henry Lake 4-20-1871 L
Maclin, Rhode to David Whitley 6-16-1866 (6-17-1866) H
Maclin, Roxy to Albert McClish 12-26-1874 Hy
Maclin, Sallie to Henry Baynes 8-8-1869 Hy
Maclin, Sarah to Alfred Elcan 12-29-1876 Hy

Maclin, Sina to David Burrel? 12-23-1872 (12-26-1872) T
Maclin, Smith Ann to Levi Cannon 2-27-1867 T
Maclin, Sophia to Beverly Johnson 12-24-1869 (12-27-1869) T
Maclin, Temple to Levi Moss 11-16-1869 (no return) Hy
Macomb, M. S. to Thos. H. Webb 9-4-1867 (no return) Dy
Macon, Ann to George Wood 1-2-1866 Hy
Macon, Elizabeth to Johnathan Cox 10-31-1850 (11-7-1850) Hr
Macon, Hannah to Baptiste Maiar 8-21-1856 Sh
Macon, Jane to Christinberry Russell 11-14-1849 Ma
Macon, Joanna to Thomas Shaw 10-1-1869 (no return) F B
Macon, Julia A. to Thomas G. Boyed 9-17-1840 (9-24-1840) F
Macon, Louisa to James Sain 12-19-1843 (12-21-1843) Hr
Macon, Lucy K. to Sherwood Green 6-30-1837 (7-3-1837) Hr
Macon, Martha to William M. Crow 8-20-1865 Mn
Macon, Mary Jane to Nimrod Graham 8-17-1851 Hr
Macon, Mary to Hugh B. McCarty 4-4-1846 Hr
Macon, Wincy to James S. Jourdan 1-3-1848 (1-6-1848) Hr
Macourse, Charlotte to Isaac M. Gans 10-10-1859 Sh
Madary, Mary to John Crossno 10-16-1853 Be
Madden, C. J. to W. G. McCord 2-2-1865 Hn
Madden, Eliza to John OGuin 8-26-1857 Be
Madden, Emily F. to R. C. Benson 2-26-1859 (3-1-1859) Sh
Madden, Joanna to Michael Ryan 6-13-1853 Sh
Madden, Margaret E. to William W. Cummings 9-14-1857 Sh
Madden, Martha B. to Geo. W. Rushing 2-1-1853 Be
Madden, Mary A. to Thomas Lacy 12-23-1857 (12-28-1857) Sh
Madden, Mary C. to J. R. Greer 10-11-1857 Be
Madden, Mary to Edward Whalon 5-23-1857 (5-26-1857) Sh
Madden, Paralee to Lewis Pafford 5-26-1856 Be
Madden, Susan to F. M. Barton 11-17-1855 (11-18-1855) Sh
Madders, Labertha to Bennet Drake 1-5-1858 (1-6-1858) Ma
Maddind, Sarah C. to James M. McDonald 11-27-1844 (11-28-1844) Ma
Madding, Mary H. to Jacob A. Giltner 5-23-1849 Sh
Maddocks, Mary Ann to Moses Fletcher 10-12-1852 (10-14-1852) T
Maddon, Mary to Major H. Daughtrey 3-8-1846 Sh
Maddox, Ann to Robert Stevens 9-23-1860 (not endorsed) F
Maddox, Caroline to Henry Price 8-23-1867 (8-24-1867) F B
Maddox, Eliza Jane to Gains C. Dodds 5-24-1852 O
Maddox, Fannie to Abner S. Norman 11-14-1857 (11-15-1857) Sh
Maddox, Fannie to Stokely Stout 3-30-1861 (3-31-1861) Sh
Maddox, Mary Elizabeth to Wyatt Fussell 4-20-1842 (4-21-1842) Ma
Maddox, Mary S. to Hugh C. Henderson 4-28-1852 Ma
Maddox, Nancy to Robert H. Henderson 5-3-1855 Ma
Maddox, Rachel A. to Joel W. Altman 2-19-1849 (12-20-1849) Ma
Maddox, Rachel H. to W. H. Grider 1-21-1857 Sh
Maddox, Sarah Ann to Thomas Holt 10-4-1842 Hn
Maddox, Sophia C. to John M. Graves 4-3-1851 Sh
Maddra, Mollie to Hezekiah Strother 7-18-1873 (10-31-1873) Dy
Maddrey, Malinda to Stephen Sanders 1-4-1877 Dy
Maderis, Martha J. to T. S. Butler 2-1-1850 Cr
Madew (Maden?), Jerata Henderson to Socrates L. Murphy 10-7-1864 (11-24-1864) Sh
Madison, Araminta to Alex Wallace 8-1-1856 We
Madison, Elizabeth M. to Andrew J. Jester 9-16-1851 (9-17-1851) G
Madison, Sabra to John C. Shavour 3-17-1841 G
Madore, Ella to John Neel 12-28-1869 (no return) F B
Madry, Hetty (Mrs.) to Edward D. Hall 5-17-1828 Sh
Madry, Mary E. to Richard J. Hale (Hail) 8-5-1820 Sh
Madry, Mary to Andrew Smith 12-26-1867 Dy
Madry, Rebecca A. to John W. Tice 11-1-1855 Be
Madry, Salley A. to John B. Hale (Hail) 12-29-1829 Sh
Maelatesta, Natina to Frank Vaccaro 4-8-1859 (4-12-1859) Sh
Magary, Clarissa Ann to Marion Boone 12-25-1871 (12-27-1871) Dy
Magary, Lenora to Thomas Ledbetter 4-4-1872 (no return) Dy
Magby, Elisabeth to Moses N. Jones 3-7-1838 (3-11-1838) Hr
Magee, C. S. to William G. Gatevam 12-27-1852 We
Magee, Elizabeth J. to J. H. Raines 9-25-1863 Mn
Magee, Esther to Edward Lircher 5-24-1858 Sh
Magee, Lucinda Ann to Amos Whittington 10-4-1851 (10-29-1851) O
Magee, Martha to William Ford 12-7-1840 Hr
Magee, Mary to Chas. William Walker 12-27-1852 (12-28-1852) Sh
Magee, Rachel to Allen B. Laws 6-5-1852 Sh
Magehee, Eliza to A. Panesi 11-5-1856 Sh
Mager, Mary A. to W. N. Rains 6-6-1862 Mn
Mager, Nancy Ann to R. C. Lumpkins 3-21-1861 Mn
Magermus, L. to F. Faquin 6-11-1864 Sh
Magett, Mary E. to William H. Burnes 4-19-1847 (4-29-1847) F
Magevney, Mary A. to E. Miles Willett 9-28-1861 (10-1-1861) Sh
Maggard, Harriet to Jeff Williamson 1-20-1872 (1-21-1872) Dy
Maggard, Julia to Peter McDaniel 8-26-1869 (no return) Dy
Maggard, Martha to Jacob Foster 9-7-1870 (no return) Dy
Magill, Julina to Francis M. Barr 12-28-1847 Be
Maginis, Mary to James C. Chandler 11-22-1842 (11-23-1842) Ma
Magit, Emily L. to Rancelier Sann 6-19-1843 (6-21-1843) F
Magivney, Mary A. to G. A. Hanson 6-17-1856 Sh
Magivney, Sarah G. to D. H. Chapman 11-17-1864 Sh
Magness, Mary E. to Azariah L. Crenshaw 8-31-1846 (9-2-1846) F

Magrath, Bridget to John O'Brien 10-17-1855 Sh
Maguire, Alice C. to Washington Carson 4-18-1861 Sh
Maguire, Elizabeth to John McNamara 6-9-1852 (6-10-1852) Sh
Maguire, Mary to Patrick Cahill 6-9-1860 (6-10-1860) Sh
Maguire, Rosa to Thomas Kaine 8-14-1852 (8-15-1852) Sh
Maha (Malia?), Hannora to Patrick Cunningham 2-18-1862 Sh
Mahaffy, Louisa A. to John McGuirk 5-24-1853 (no return) F
Mahaffy, Sarah to George W. Treesse 8-13-1845 Sh
Mahan (Maha), Eveline to Benjamin B. Smith 4-9-1840 Sh
Mahan, Bridgett to Robert Cook 8-2-1853 Sh
Mahan, Harriet to A. J. Ellis 8-17-1866 (no return) Hy
Mahan, Kate Agnes to John Welsh 1-5-1864 Sh
Mahan, Mary A. W. to Robt. Reid 12-13-1853 Sh
Mahan, Mary to John Malorkney 5-22-1853 Sh
Mahan, Rebecca A. to Jo. Fletcher Smith 7-25-1867 (no return) Dy
Mahan, Rosa J. to Edward L. Curd 12-31-1838 Hn
Mahan, Serena Isibella to Joel H. Pursell 11-3-1862 (11-4-1862) Dy
Mahar, Catharine to John Taylor 2-3-1857 Sh
Mahar, Honora to James Scruggs 12-24-1850 Sh
Mahar, Manerva C. to P. M. Pate 1-7-1856 Sh
Mahar, Mary to Michael Madden 1-23-1856 Sh
Maher, Elizabeth to Michal Connell 5-7-1862 Sh
Maher, Joanna to John Rody 6-9-1854 Sh
Mahern(Mahan), Minerva to J.W. Crow 2-20-1832 (2-21-1832) Hr
Mahon, Angaline to Rupert Smith 5-10-1867 (5-11-1867) Dy
Mahon, Celemanda to Dennis Newter 10-31-1853 (11-1-1853) G
Mahon, Lucinda to Edward Curtis 1-25-1830 (2-4-1830) G
Mahon, Lucy to Thomas Boyd 9-1-1877 Hy
Mahon, Margaret to John Folan (Tolan?) 7-7-1860 (7-15-1860) Sh
Mahon, Mary Nany to Johnson Faulkland 2-14-1838 Ma
Mahony, Fanny to Daniel Moriarty 7-11-1857 (7-12-1857) Sh
Maier, Lina to Henry Rehkopt 4-5-1860 Sh
Maigue (Maguire?), Mary A. to Ephraim Abercrombie 3-9-1853 Sh
Mailey, Elizabeth Ann to Joshua M. Miller 7-28-1845 (8-1-1845) T
Mainard, Clarissa to John H. L. Harris 7-10-1839 (no return) Cr
Mainard, Eliza A. to Jephinah R. Duncan 9-26-1838 (no return) Cr
Mainard, Elizabeth to Henry Bevel 5-2-1858 Cr
Mainard, Mary J. to Noal W. Sanders 6-2-1860 Hy
Mainard, Polly to Jeremiah Gibson 7-23-1838 (no return) Cr
Mainer, Sarah to Joseph Sutton Rainer 3-22-1842 (10-?-1842) T
Mainor, Patiance D. to John Busby 10-31-1843 G
Mainor, Susannah to Henry Kenneday 8-12-1835 G
Mainor, Zella to John D. Davidson 9-20-1835 G
Mainord, Sarah A. to George A. Scarborough 5-2-1870 (5-5-1870) Ma
Major, Mary A. B. to P. D. Wedgewood 8-30-1856 (8-31-1856) Sh
Major, Narcissas S. to Jeremiah Moss 12-20-1860 We
Majors, Laura Bell to Wilson J. Jeffers 9-14-1863 Sh
Makeman, Kate to August (Orguse) Berg (Berry) 4-11-1861 Sh
Makey, Sally to James Munroe Phillips 12-23-1868 (12-24-1868) F B
Malaughney, Mary to William Griffin 7-7-1860 (7-8-1860) Sh
Malcar, Orpha J. to Cahl P. Owenby 12-13-1866 Cr
Malear, America to Samuel Fodge 7-19-1852 Hn
Malear, Nancy to Henry L. Bevil 7-26-1845 Hn
Malear, Rebecca to William G. Bevill 8-16-1844 Hn
Maleer, Frances to Joshua Duncan 4-1-1858 Hn
Maleer, Susan G. to T. G. Buchanan 1-28-1858 Hn
Malenay, Ellen to Dennis Toben 5-17-1862 Sh
Malery, Mary Martha to William R. Groves 7-1-1848 (7-2-1848) Hr
Malett, Nancy H. to J. V. Criggar 4-5-1863 O
Maley, Jane to S. R. Smith 6-20-1872 T
Maley, Julia Ann to Gideon G. McGee 8-23-1857 T
Maley, Larisa A. W. to E. B. Daniel 6-8-1858 T
Maley, Margaret F. to Robert H. Ralph 2-17-1870 (2-20-1870) T
Maley, Patiency to Tilman McGee 1-17-1867 T
Maley, Sarah E. to Alfred A. Myers 9-13-1855 T
Maley, Sarah to J. M. Daniels 1-31-1871 (2-2-1871) T
Maley, Virginia to Walter Napier 11-23-1872 (11-24-1872) T
Malin, Elizabeth L. to George M. Thornton 8-14-1855 Be
Malin, L. to John Luper 2-7?-1865 Be
Malin, Mary F. to Z. B. Howe 10-15-1869 Be
Malin, Nancy to John Smith 4-9-1854 Hn
Malin, Rebecca to Anthony M. Tittle 8-19-1841 Be
Malin, Susan A. to Michaels H. Wilkins 9-22-1859 Hn
Malissa, Vaulx to William Plummer 12-23-1878 Hy
Mallard, Tobitha Ana to Munrow Slaughter 4-21-1841 (4-25-1841) F
Mallay, D. Jane to John W. Bickers 8-7-1851 Hr
Mallery, G. A. to Warren Ross 11-13-1855 (no return) Hn
Mallery, Mary to William James 5-7-1844 (5-21-1844) Hr
Mallory, A. E. to Parish A. Gormon 9-6-1848 (9-12-1848) F
Mallory, A. T. to Benham H. (Dr.) Brown 2-22-1856 Sh
Mallory, Ann Mildred to Ashbey Reavis 12-21-1846 (12-24-1846) Hr
Mallory, Clemant A. to Isham N. Smith 11-23-1846 (11-26-1846) Hr
Mallory, Eliza C. to James P. Booker 2-29-1860 Sh
Mallory, L. A. to Wright Finch 12-21-1847 Hr
Mallory, M. L. to S. C. Meadows 12-22-1870 (no return) Dy
Mallory, Maria to Hiram Brumley 9-1-1857 (9-3-1857) Sh
Mallory, Mollie to J. M. Moore 1-6-1868 (1-8-1868) Dy

Mallory, Virginia to Andrew Percifull 9-25-1855 Ma
Malone, Amanda H. to John R. Cunningham 9-18-1855 Cr
Malone, Analiza to Rufus M. Deeds 3-12-1864 (3-13-1864) Sh
Malone, Ann Eliza to George Freeth 1-9-1863 (1-10-1863) F
Malone, Ann to Andrew Tate 12-24-1869 (no return) F B
Malone, Aramenta to Henry G. Jackson 11-19-1838 Sh
Malone, Bettie to Wm. G. Ray 11-15-1852 (11-18-1852) T
Malone, Caroline A. to James W. Boyd 2-6-1845 (2-8-1845) Ma
Malone, Carroline to John Dill 12-28-1841 (12-29-1841) G
Malone, Catharine to Asberry H. Parish 2-28-1867 (3-1-1867) F
Malone, Catherine (Mrs.) to A. H. Parish 2-18-1867 (no return) F
Malone, Catherine to William Maher 5-9-1846 Sh
Malone, Celia A. to Thomas R. Jones 1-19-1856 (no return) Hn
Malone, Cornelia D. to J. S. Vanhook 2-12-1862 Hn
Malone, Cynthia to Frances Newman 4-19-1849 Hn
Malone, Davie D. P. to Edward J. Carman 1-19-1866 Hy
Malone, E. G. to W. H. Mattice 7-19-1873 T
Malone, Edna E. to L. A. Scarbrough 3-21-1866 (3-22-1866) T
Malone, Eliza to Wilson Levi 1-11-1843 (no return) Hn
Malone, Georgianna to S. M. Brown 2-24-1858 (2-25-1858) Sh
Malone, Harriett to Wm. C. Roark 10-15-1845 Cr
Malone, J. C. to D. McGill 8-16-1860 Be
Malone, J. C. to John Payne 2-6-1866 Hy
Malone, Jane to James Mullin 7-1-1861 (7-7-1861) Cr
Malone, Judah to John L. Stafford 4-19-1837 (4-20-1837) Hr
Malone, Katie A. to John G. Scarbrough 4-1-1872 (4-2-1872) T
Malone, L. C. to John H. McClelland 8-14-1864 T
Malone, L. F. J. to F. D. Cassitt 12-10-1844 Hr
Malone, Leaner to John Williamson 2-23-1867 (2-28-1867) T
Malone, Lou Ann to Thomas A. Martin 12-4-1860 Hn
Malone, Louiza to John M. Nance 4-10-1867 Hn
Malone, Lucinda M. to William E. Winfield 11-10-1845 (11-12-1845) F
Malone, Lucy to Geo. W. Monroe 2-1-1855 Cr
Malone, M. B. to W. H. Murphey 1-17-1870 T
Malone, M. G. to David Orr 5-18-1855 We
Malone, M. P. to James M. McCarty 4-18-1848 Hn
Malone, Malinda to Edwin Anderson 1-13-1869 T
Malone, Malinda to Obadiah Lewis 10-23-1828 (10-23-1828) G
Malone, Manerva to Len Brooks 1-18-1868 Hy
Malone, Martha G. to James King 6-5-1851 Cr
Malone, Martha J. to Jesse McClure 11-28-1861 Hn
Malone, Mary A. to Samuel G. Johnston 1-22-1851 Hn
Malone, Mary A. to William Haislip 12-10-1847 (12-14-1847) G
Malone, Mary to Geor. C. Colter 1-4-1845 F
Malone, Mary to Geor. C. Colter 12-20-1844 (no return) F
Malone, Mildred E. to Charles E. Smith 9-20-1853 (9-22-1853) T
Malone, Nancy B. to J. L. Conn 2-24-1849 (2-25-1849) F
Malone, Nancy E. to John L. Munroe 1-7-1858? Hn
Malone, Nancy to Thomas Brannon 1-16-1862 Hn
Malone, Nancyann to A. Whitten 4-25-1842 F
Malone, Rose to Simon Maxwell 7-27-1872 Hy
Malone, Sarah Elizabeth to Jacob Roland 10-29-1874 (10-31-1874) T
Malone, Susa C. to Frederick S. Jackson 5-17-1841 (5-20-1841) F
Malone, Susan A. to T. W. Winn 10-23-1856 T
Malone, Susan E. to R. Phelps 1-27-1869 (1-30-1869) Cr
Malone, Ursley to John Estus 1-15-1845 Be
Malone, Virginia E. to Cleopas Paschal 10-18-1867 (no return) Hn
Maloney, Ann P. to Patrick Collins 11-9-1859 (11-10-1859) Sh
Maloney, Elizabeth J. to James T. Pardue 1-14-1856 (1-17-1856) O
Maloney, Margaret to John Otey 4-16-1858 Sh
Maloney, Mary to Jesse McIntosh 10-16-1850 O
Maloney, Nancy to J. C. Blackshar 3-1-1859 O
Maloney, Tennessee to Lewis H. Burton 8-24-1867 O
Malony, Napkin to Michael Carron 2-9-1864 Sh
Malory (Malany?), Margaret to David Dunn 9-18-1852 (9-20-1852) Sh
Malory, Sally to W. F. Harwell 3-17-1865 (3-21-1865) Dy
Malourney, Honarie to E. Holehen 10-11-1859 (10-16-1859) Sh
Maltbie, Catherine E. to John H. Temple 9-16-1847 Sh
Malugin, Susan to Edward Upton 1-17-1872 T
Maly, Louisa J. to Thomas Myers 8-17-1869 T
Man, Amelia to Charles Riner 10-4-1859 (10-5-1859) Sh
Man, Sarah L. to R. A. Kelton 10-7-1866 G
Manansco, Nancy to Wm. D. McNight 6-21-1844 Sh
Manard, Mary A. to James W. Stubblefield 9-8-1847 Cr
Manasco, Mary E. to John Wesley Stanus 9-6-1860 (9-13-1860) T
Manasco, Mary M. to H. C. Starnes 3-7-1865 (3-8-1865) T
Manasco, Mary to James W. Turnage 12-16-1868 (12-17-1868) T
Manasco, Matilda C. to W. H. Archer 2-8-1871 T
Manasco, Nancy Ann to James Tedwell 7-3-1867 (7-4-1867) T
Manasco, Nancy to Joseph M. Smith 12-30-1845 T
Manasco, Sarah to Solomon McBride 1-5-1834 Sh
Manaskco, Matilda to William A. Bennett 12-28-1848 Sh
Manaskie, Zena to John McNair 7-15-1847 Sh
Manaslk?, Mary to James W. Oumage? no date (with 1868) T
Manasses, Tennessee (Mrs.) to Asa Rossen 11-19-1862 Sh
Mance, Maggie to A. D. Currin 5-22-1880 (5-23-1880) L
Mandiville, Emily to Joset R. Robin 4-20-1852 Cr

Brides

Manees, Martha O. to Samel E. Cole 4-3-1850 (no return) F
Maner, Elizabeth to Richmond Davidson 12-25-1844 Cr
Manerd, Press to Pink Russell 3-27-1872 Hy
Manervia, Harbert to Merion Pucket 1-22-1872 Hy
Maness, G. A. to J. A. Klutts 5-1-1877 (no return) L
Maness, Mary to D. A. Klutts 10-30-1878 (10-31-1878) L
Maness, S. C. to R. C. Klutts 5-14-1879 L
Maness, Sarah to J. S. Yelverton 11-2-1865 Mn
Mangin, Bridget to Lawrence Harrison 4-14-1857 Sh
Mangin, Mary to Louis Donanhoner 4-5-1861 (4-7-1861) Sh
Mangrum, Elizabeth to Arthur Bland 5-8-1841 (5-9-1841) Ma
Mangrum, Hawkins to Alfred N. Weaver 11-12-1860 (11-13-1860) Ma
Mangrum, Hester to W. D. Foster 3-18-1863 O
Mangrum, Joanna to William West 7-17-1850 (7-18-1850) Hr
Mangrum, Lucy to William Bunton 8-10-1855 Hn
Mangrum, Mary A. E. to John H. Landrum 9-16-1859 We
Mangrum, Mary to William Brown 1-19-1867 (1-20-1867) Dy
Mangrum, Mollie L. to W. M. Barnes 3-8-1881 (no return) L
Mangrum, Nannie to Lucius Brown 11-18-1869 (11-21-1869) Dy
Mangrum, Rebecca to Oliver Francis 2-14-1842 (2-16-1842) F
Mangum, Rebecca to Reuben Higgs 11-6-1844 (11-10-1844) Hr
Manier, A. A. to H. L. Burton 2-4-1862 (2-10-1862) F
Manier, Armate to Moses F. Green no date (not married) Cr
Manies, Fanny to John S. Pearson 10-25-1855 Sh
Maning, Angeline to William R. Chipman 2-4-1867 (7-4-1867) L
Maniss, Josephine to William H. Suggs 1-18-1872 L
Manix, Betsy to Solomon Nunn 12-20-1878 Hy
Mankins, Mary to George Warren 5-2-1857 Hn
Mankins, Sarah to Samuel Moody 8-31-1857 Hn
Mankins, Susan B. to John A. Burnett 6-5-1859 Hn
Manle3y, Emily J. to F. J. W. McCord 8-13-1863 (8-23-1863) L
Manley, C. E. to John L. Taylor 11-17-1849 Cr
Manley, Charity to James Smith 12-26-1870 (12-28-1870) Dy
Manley, D. A. to Austin Russell 2-22-1844 Hn
Manley, Elizabeth to F. Taylor 1-31-1848 Cr
Manley, Emily J. to E. J. Pennington 6-5-1869 (6-6-1869) L
Manley, Emily J. to Henry H. Lunsford 10-10-1863 (no return) L
Manley, F. R. to A. W. Wynn 1-22-1852 Be CC
Manley, Frances A. to William Burnes 1-3-1877 L
Manley, Harriett O. to P. H. Duggins 1-24-1854 (no return) F
Manley, Julia to Jacob Carter 2-6-1867 Hn
Manley, Laura to Abner Taylor 3-30-1832 (3-31-1832) Hr
Manley, Louisa N. W. to John Carroll 12-30-1847 Ma
Manley, Lula to Joe Dark 10-29-1885 L
Manley, M. C. to W. A. Stone 10-17-1874 (no return) Dy
Manley, Martha E. to Robert B. Williams 7-19-1853 Ma
Manley, Martha J. to David G. Bratton 6-3-1871 (6-4-1871) L
Manley, Martha L. to Thomas Parrish 8-3-1847 (8-8-1847) F
Manley, Martha N. to Nathaniel Currier 1-18-1842 Hn
Manley, Mary F. to H. C. Durham 12-12-1865 (12-13-1865) F
Manley, Mary W. to Wm. B. Ramsey 2-25-1862 Be
Manley, Mary to Theof J. Manley 5-4-1847 F
Manley, Rachall to Lewis Elliott 1-8-1846 Sh
Manley, Sallie E. to William P. Covington 8-9-1860 Hn
Manley, Sarah J. to Pleasant R. Davis 9-18-1861 (9-19-1861) Ma
Manley, Sarah to Lewis G. Alford 11-29-1860 L
Manley, Sarah to Wesley Anderson 1-27-1858 Ma
Manley, Susan L. to Jas. Montgomery 11-5-1850 F
Manley, Winny to William Person 12-29-1871 L
Manly, Angeline to Benjamin Wynn 6-26-1847 Hn
Manly, F. R. to A. W. Wynn 1-22-1852 Be
Manly, Harriet to George Hudson 1-26-1869 (1-27-1869) Ma
Manly, Henrietta to Athelbert Alexander 8-23-1853 Sh
Manly, Rebecka Frances to Henry Martin Turnage 12-30-1857 (12-31-1857) T
Manly, Sarah A. to William E. Hill 2-14-1855 Hn
Manly, Sarah Jane to John Wynns 1-18-1849 Hn
Mann (Manson), Julia to Frank Settle 12-6-1850 Sh
Mann (Marr), Ann to John Leacy 5-15-1849 Sh
Mann, Adelade to Green Hunter 11-3-1868 (no return) Hy
Mann, Adeline to Nelson Tyus 10-11-1867 Hy
Mann, Alice to R. W. Young 10-2-1878 Hy
Mann, Ann Mariah to Stephen W. Cocke 4-2-1838 F
Mann, Anna to William Sawyer 7-9-1881 (7-10-1881) L
Mann, Annie to Simon Bowman 1-30-1869 Hy
Mann, Betty to Billy Wilson 7-20-1881 L B
Mann, Caroline E. to A. M. Wiswell 5-21-1857 Sh
Mann, Catherine A. to C. W. Jeter 11-14-1859 (no return) Hy
Mann, Charlotte to Joe Scott 9-15-1866 Hy
Mann, Cornelia to Andy Read 8-7-1869 Hy
Mann, Dicey L. to Thos. J. Mann 6-7-1862 Cr
Mann, Dora to Henry Partee 3-2-1870 (no return) Hy
Mann, Easter to Arch Henning 6-26-1875 L
Mann, Elizabeth A. to John W. Rodgers 2-16-1853 Cr
Mann, Elizabeth P. to William A. Nobles 12-11-1847 (12-14-1847) Ma
Mann, Ella to J. P. Barfield 2-13-1878 (2-14-1878) L
Mann, Emma B. to George W. Gordon 1-17-1876 (no return) Hy
Mann, Esper An T. to Joseph Mitchell 11-12-1870 (11-13-1870) Cr

Mann, Eva J. to W. D. Moore 4-28-1875 Hy
Mann, Fanny to Allen Lowry 7-9-1867 Hy
Mann, Febby to Randle Glenn 11-7-1874 (no return) Hy
Mann, Frances to Sam Holloway 12-24-1870 Hy
Mann, Harriet to Allen Brooks 7-17-1874 (no return) Hy
Mann, Hester to Jerry Scott 2-28-1870 Hy
Mann, Hester to John Bell Green 11-1-1884 L
Mann, Hester to Robert Anderson 12-24-1874 Hy
Mann, Julia to Jim Taylor 8-20-1870 Hy
Mann, Julie E. to C. G. Mann 5-19-1860 (5-20-1860) Cr
Mann, L. J. to J. C. Warmath 11-15-1876 L
Mann, Leana to Charles Harper 8-27-1881 L B
Mann, Lilly to Jerry Scott 3-18-1877 Hy
Mann, Lizzie C. to W. T. Wills 6-22-1869 Hy
Mann, Lizzie to George Hart 11-30-1876 Hy
Mann, Lou to Nat Livingston 9-25-1878 (9-25-1879?) L B
Mann, Louisa to Patee Mann 10-1-1871 Hy
Mann, Mandy to Calvin Buck 1-18-1876 (no return) Hy
Mann, Manerva to Albert Johnson 12-25-1868 Hy
Mann, Martha H. to Joel H. Estes 2-24-1862 (no return) Hy
Mann, Martha to O. P. T. Toombs 10-6-1870 (10-7-1870) O
Mann, Mary E. to Alexander Oliver 12-7-1866 G
Mann, Mary to Ben Wilson 9-19-1865 Hy
Mann, Mary to David Perkins 1-11-1883 L
Mann, Matilda to Charlie Trotman 5-12-1867 Hy
Mann, Miranda to John Bradford 12-29-1866 (no return) Hy
Mann, Moriah to Alx. Jones 5-4-1872 (no return) Hy
Mann, Nancy to Hugh Garmany 3-18-1861 G
Mann, Nancy to Robert Rogers 12-31-1877 Hy
Mann, Nora P. to A. C. Estes 11-6-1872 Hy
Mann, Phoebe to Jordan Best 9-16-1879 (9-24-1879) L B
Mann, Puss to Frank Jeffries 8-2-1878 (no return) Hy
Mann, Rebecca to T. C. Johnson 1-9-1867 G
Mann, Rose to Edmund Searcy 1-20-1881 L
Mann, Sarah to Charley Neloms 12-23-1875 (no return) Hy
Mann, Sarah to Frank Jones 1-5-1873 Hy
Mann, Sinda to James Swanson 12-20-1868 Hy
Mann, Zelin to Albert Savage 12-9-1877 Hy
Mann?, Martha to O. P. T. Toombs 10-6-1870 O
Mann?, Nora to Thomas Fisher 9-25-1869 (9-26-1869) L
Manness, Sarah to H. Lamb 4-12-1864 Sh
Mannet, Caroline to John Frank 4-25-1848 Sh
Mannigan, Mary to Patrick Kelly 1-19-1856 (1-20-1856) Sh
Manning, Addie to James Brown 7-16-1868 Dy
Manning, Ann to Jas. R. Bostick 8-5-1856 Sh
Manning, Cherry to George Jelks 5-8-1873 (no return) Hy
Manning, D. N. to E. T. Jones 5-10-1857 Cr
Manning, Docy J. to Frederick Thweatt 3-11-1840 Hn
Manning, Elizabeth to Edward W. Tatum 4-7-1851 (4-8-1851) F
Manning, Elizabeth to James H. McCain 1-7-1860 Sh
Manning, Emily to W. B. Nevill 12-20-1869 (12-23-1869) Cr
Manning, Fannie to David Whitlock 10-8-1869 Hy
Manning, Frances E. to Alexander Niseler 12-5-1858 Hn
Manning, Jane E. (Sarah) to Jno. P. Taylor 9-29-1847 Sh
Manning, Jane to J. W. Jones 4-10-1861 (4-11-1861) Dy
Manning, Julia A. to E. W. Crane 12-12-1884 L
Manning, Lucy to James Clever 9-6-1849 Cr
Manning, Maggie to N. Augustus Rose 11-16-1863 Sh
Manning, Martha A. to George Gatty 8-16-1853 (no return) Cr
Manning, Martha to O. Heath 8-17-1867 (8-18-1867) Dy
Manning, Martha to W. H. Stokes 8-5-1865 (8-6-1865) L
Manning, Mary to George, jr. Chipman 9-7-1862 L
Manning, Mary to John Maynor 9-21-1867 (no return) Hn
Manning, May Jane to Tillman Butts 3-1-1867 L
Manning, Nancy Tennessee to Thomas J. Chipman 9-27-1867 (9-19?-1867) L
Manning, Nancy to Frank Banks 12-23-1869 Hy
Manning, Nancy to H. R. Latham 12-13-1872 (12-14-1872) L
Manning, Nancy to Wiley D. Manning 2-14-1879 L
Manning, Nellie to Wm. H. Thayer 12-5-1863 (12-6-1863) Sh
Manning, Rachel to Washington Powell 1-22-1867 G
Manning, Texanna to Jefferson Brinkley 4-28-1868 (5-3-1868) Cr
Mannitt, C. A. to A. R. Wilson 10-22-1857 Cr
Mannon, Christian to Nathan Stagner 12-31-1861 Be
Mannon, Rebecca J. to Wiley C. Melton 2-24-1853 Be
Manoney, Bridget to Michael McIntyre 7-9-1860 Sh
Manor, Anne to William Grier 12-16-1863 G
Mansfield, Amanda to D. G. Haralson 6-2-1860 O
Mansfield, Armenia to Benj. Reddick 1-30-1866 (1-31-1866) Dy
Mansfield, Malvina to Phillip Smith 7-4-1867 Dy
Manson, Mary T. to Geo. M. Lloyd 2-13-1860 (2-15-1860) Hr
Manuel, Serrilda to E. W. Melton 8-2-1872 (8-3-1872) Cr
Manus, Louisa F. to George N. Brogdon 6-17-1868 (12-3-1868) Ma
Manwell, Margaret A. to John S. Mills 9-23-1860 We
Manx (Maux), Dora to Jacob Brust 11-16-1850 Hr
Maony?, T. A. to J. M. Cole 3-2-1865 Hn
Mara, Joana to Robert Scott 12-23-1854 Sh
Mara, Mary to Thomas Henesy (Hanasay) 8-8-1849 Sh

Maranan, Mary to Michael McGrath 1-10-1860 (1-11-1860) Sh
Marant, Nancy to Maltimore Reed 12-29-1868 Hy
Marberry, Amanda M. to Franklin W. Lee 5-19-1850 Hn
Marberry, Angeline to Henry Dowdy 5-3-1858 Hn
Marberry, Arcada to J. R. Medlin 3-29-1852 Hn
Marberry, Bethsheba to William Williams 4-7-1842 Hn
Marberry, Caroline to Jeshua McLane 10-10-1850 Hn
Marberry, Elizabeth to James Wharton 2-28-1849 Hn
Marberry, Emaline to William F. Green 7-18-1839 (no return) Hn
Marberry, Emaretta to Burel P. Wall 5-10-1861 Hn
Marberry, Frances A. to Jesse E. Wall 12-7-1858 Hn
Marberry, Jane to John F. Holladay 10-10-1846 Hn
Marberry, Margaret to John J. Hurt 10-5-1856 Hn
Marberry, Mary Ann to John J. Cole 1-17-1855 (no return) Hn
Marberry, Mary Jane to James B. Gutheridge 4-30-1846 Hn
Marberry, Mary to William A. Brown 7-13-1849 Hn
Marbry, Louisa to George Kirkendall 2-20-1867 Hn B
Marcey, Margaret to Wm. Stapleton 5-3-1854 (5-4-1854) Sh
March, Leminda Clementine to James J. Jacobs 7-10-1866 (7-12-1866) Ma
March, Rachael to Jacob A. Norton 6-28-1845 (7-1-1845) Ma
March, Victoria J. to J. N. Gibson 6-3-1868 F
Marchant, M. E. to F. C. Baker 9-18-1866 (9-19-1866) Dy
Marchant, Susn to W. T. Davis 10-15-1868 Dy
Marchbanks, Carolina to Nathn. Townsend 1-15-1846 Be
Marchbanks, Cary Ann to Kinchen G. Cole 11-15-1846 Be
Marchbanks, Eliza E. to J. J. Cole 7-17-1856 Be
Marchbanks, Eliza to Joseph Walker 10-14-1847 Be
Marchbanks, Elizabeth C. to A. B. Aden 9-10-1854 Be
Marchbanks, Frances to John W. Johnson 12-28-1863 Be
Marchbanks, Jane to Richard W. Roberts 8-29-1852 Be
Marchbanks, Mary Ann to Joseph J. Cole 8-25-1848 Be
Marchbanks, Maryann to John W. Sanders 8-29-1847 Be
Marchbanks, Sarah E. to William H. Key 4-19-1860 Be
Marcom, E. J. to D. W. Wateridge 11-28-1877 Hy
Marcom, Louisa J. to Dennis Clayton 11-30-1860 Be
Marcum, Emmaline to James M. Rogers 10-1-1855 (10-4-1855) G
Marcum, Fannie T. to William W. Olds 11-16-1876 (11-29-1876) Dy
Marcum, M. J. to Alcey Yates 12-28-1865 G
Marcum, Nancy to Paul S. Proctor 10-23-1850 (11-26-1850) G
Marcum, Rebecca to James M. Hammond 10-27-1848 (10-29-1848) F
Marcus, Jane to William W. Cantrell 8-8-1859 (no return) We
Marcy, Ellen to John Flynn 2-3-1854 (2-5-1854) Sh
Marell, Delilah E. to H. H. Keltner 2-9-1859 Sh
Maretto, Mary to Leon Berten 12-8-1862 Sh
Margall, Julia to John Davis 7-26-1873 (7-27-1873) Dy B
Margaret, Owen to William Potter 11-24-1875 (no return) Hy
Margaret, Yarbrough to James B. Pigue 2-11-1877 Hy
Margeram, J. F. to Wm. Ringwald 4-6-1864 Sh
Margrave, Susan Ellen to Freeman Patterson 9-22-1855 (9-23-1855) Ma
Margraves, G. I. to J. H. Bridger 7-10-1860 (no return) Hy
Margrove, Martha F. to John D. Baum 6-26-1865 (6-27-1865) F
Marial, Frances to James B. Laudaman 11-5-1850 (11-7-1850) F
Mariane, Rose to B. Rocco 9-1-1860 (9-3-1860) Sh
Mariner, Eliza Jane to Erasmus kSydenham Campbell 6-1-1844 (6-4-1844) T
Marion, Georgianna H. to Paris M. Dooley 12-11-1853 Sh
Maris, Emeline to Arthur Price 12-29-1866 F B
Maris, Maggie to John Posey 12-23-1885 (12-24-1885) L
Markham, Caroline W. to James L. Smithers 1-6-1852 (1-7-1852) Sh
Markham, Catharine M. to John F. Holt 3-1-1860 Sh
Markham, Elenor H. to Jesse M. Claiborn 5-4-1859 T
Markham, Elizabeth to John Caldwell 10-4-1851 T
Markham, Fannie P. to J. A. McMurry 11-28-1867 Hy
Markham, Jane to M. W. Weaver 11-13-1847 (11-14-1847) F
Markham, Martha A. to Aron T. Skinner 5-3-1863 Hn
Markham, Susan to James Burgess 9-8-1855 (9-10-1855) T
Markham, Veria to John Russell 4-21-1866 Hn
Markrum, Rebecca to John A. Bacchus 2-11-1855 Hn
Marks, Anna to D. C. Neal 6-26-1867 Ma
Marks, B. to A. Harris 12-18-1858 Hn
Marks, Julia to Benjamin E. Manuel 11-8-1846 Sh
Marks, Kate to William Bradley 3-8-1870 (3-9-1870) Ma
Marks, Mary A. to Jesse Ogle 11-10-1855 (11-19-1855) Sh
Marks, Mary A. to William Tait 1-31-1857 (2-1-1857) Sh
Marks, Mary Jane to Samuel Snowden 10-23-1856 (11-20-1856) Sh
Markus, L. C. to J. W. Brinkley 3-24-1874 (8-27-1874) O
Marlar, Bettie A. to H. C. Cocke 5-11-1867 (no return) F
Marlar, C. A. to Wm. W. Hooper 2-19-1845 Hr
Marlatt, Eliza R. to Americus Eastman 5-19-1859 Sh
Marlen, Ellin to R. F. Nallig 9-24-1857 We
Marler, M. to Isham Ritter 3-3-1845 Hr
Marler, Martha to Wm. W. Hooper 8-7-1843 Hr
Marler, Milly to Berry Spurlin 7-21-1837 Hr
Marley, Ann to Allen Moody 2-19-1840 O
Marley, Chaney to Taylor Tyus 12-13-1872 (12-19-1872) L
Marley, Dilly to Thomas Holt 7-31-1885 (8-1-1885) L
Marley, Nancy to John Patton 1-1-1868 (1-4-1868) L B
Marlow, Amanda C. to John Faulkner 9-25-1850 (9-26-1850) Ma

Marlow, Emelina to Madison Cozort 12-29-1847 (12-30-1847) Ma
Marlow, Julia Frances to Joshua M. Cozart 2-13-1858 (2-17-1858) Ma
Marlow, Mary Jane to James McMillan 2-26-1850 Ma
Marlow, Mary to Napolean B. Mills 12-25-1856 O
Maroney, Elizabeth to Haywood Williamson 1-3-1856 Ma
Maroney, Frances D. to Lunsford L. Kimball 12-28-1829 (12-29-1829) Hr
Maroney, Margaret to William Fox 12-13-1862 Sh
Maroney, Martha Ann to Andrew M. Eagan 9-2-1856 Ma
Marony, Ellen to Morris Dorney 5-21-1857 Sh
Maroonery, Ellen to Patrick Connell 11-20-1851 Sh
Marpin?, Susan P. to James M. Dowdy 12-19-1866 (no return) Hn
Marr (Mearr), E. F. to Charles Sutton 4-29-1861 Hy
Marr, A. I. to J. E. Glenn 10-29-1869 (no return) Hy
Marr, Angeline to David Tyus 4-30-1870 Hy
Marr, Caroline to Archie Brooks 12-28-1867 (no return) F B
Marr, Harriet H. to Richard H. Hatcher 4-4-1853 O
Marr, Margarett to T. B. Johnson 5-17-1866 Hy
Marr, Mary E. to Joseph S. Duvall 11-18-1873 Hy
Marr, Mary to Lonis Davis 12-23-1876 Hy
Marr, Matilda J. to Joseph B. Sutton 2-4-1860 Hy
Marr, Susan A. to Robert D. Watson 2-12-1849 O
Marr?, Ann to John Leary 5-1-1849 Sh
Marrick, Catharine to A. J. Turley 3-7-1856 Sh
Marrick, Fanny to Henry Kattman 2-10-1855 (2-17-1855) Sh
Marris, Julia to Frank Elgin 10-1-1870 (10-2-1870) Cr
Marrows, Frances to Sam Gooch 4-13-1873 Hy
Marrs, Annie to Fed Whitelaw 12-25-1871 Hy
Marrs, Laura Catherine to Wm. Joseph Orrell 12-17-1868 G
Marsh, Catharine to Wm. B. Ferrell 11-15-1851 (11-19-1851) Hr
Marsh, Daley to James M. Hart 5-31-1848 Hn
Marsh, Drusilla T. to John H. Johnson 12-17-1853 (12-20-1853) Ma
Marsh, Elizabeth S. to John I. Temples 3-24-1869 (3-28-1869) Ma
Marsh, Elizabeth to Coleman Toone 7-26-1852 Ma
Marsh, Fanny to James Willoughby 8-25-1857 Hr
Marsh, Hannah to John Mesham(Mesbow?) 12-5-1834 Hr
Marsh, Harriet to James Willoughby 12-17-1851 (12-16?-1851) Hr
Marsh, Louisa to William Smith 1-29-1856 (1-31-1856) Hr
Marsh, Margarett F. to John T. Morrow 9-9-1854 Hr
Marsh, Maria(Mana) to John J. Neely 7-1-1858 Hr
Marsh, Martha E. to W. T. Davidson 12-28-1869 (12-30-1869) T
Marsh, Mary E. to James F. Davis 10-23-1866 (10-24-1866) T
Marsh, Mary L. to Wm. R. Hunt 2-7-1871 (2-9-1871) F
Marsh, Mary to Granville Mathews 12-17-1840 (12-19-1840) Ma
Marsh, Missouri A. to Jonathan Snider 1-15-1849 (12-24-1848?) T
Marsh, Nancy A. to Thomas Evens 9-13-1848 (9-14-1848) Hr
Marsh, Nancy to James Smith 9-9-1851 Hr
Marsh, Nancy to Spencer Epps 1-4-1848 (1-5-1848) Ma
Marsh, Tappan to William T. Hudson 1-28-1840 (2-12-1840) F
Marshal, Demetria L. to S. D. Benge 12-16-1868 G
Marshal, Mary to Elias Gatlin 3-16-1866 Hy
Marshal, S. V. to John V. Carter 4-29-1868 O
Marshall, A. to Samuel Maclin 9-30-1871 (10-6-1871) T
Marshall, Adelaide to Martin R. Garrett 2-15-1849 M
Marshall, Amanda to Orange Harris 12-9-1868 (1-3-1869) F B
Marshall, Asenith M. to Andrew D. Weatherly 12-7-1858 (12-8-1858) Ma
Marshall, Carrie L. to John R. Faribee 12-24-1858 Sh
Marshall, Celia to John Vick 3-7-1859 Cr
Marshall, Clemagart to R. E. Grizzard 12-8-1869 G
Marshall, E. to G. A. Crawford 8-11-1868 G
Marshall, Eliza Jane to George Polk 7-25-1837 O
Marshall, Eliza P. to Thos. C. Crawford 2-9-1871 T
Marshall, Elizabeth to Charles Slig 4-14-1853 Sh
Marshall, Emeline to E. W. Champion 7-9-1868 F
Marshall, Emily C. to Jno. W. Smith 5-5-1864 O
Marshall, Eva to A. K. Graham 1-15-1866 (no return) F
Marshall, Frances to G. H Faulkner 7-7-1859 (no return) Hy
Marshall, Indianna to Joseph Smith 7-18-1874 (7-21-1874) L B
Marshall, Jane to David C. Stewart 8-13-1878 F
Marshall, Jane to John S. White 2-11-1847 (2-21-1847) O
Marshall, Jane to Stephen Mays 12-25-1868 G B
Marshall, Jane to Washington Stott 12-27-1871 Hy
Marshall, Josaphin to Andrew S. Hartis 10-31-1851 (no return) F
Marshall, Laura F. to Jas. R. Wallace 10-13-1868 (10-17-1868) F
Marshall, Leana to John Jefferson 1-28-1871 (no return) F B
Marshall, Louisa to Andrew Steim 7-3-1856 Sh
Marshall, Louisa to Randal Moorman 4-12-1869 F B
Marshall, Louisa to Samuel Knox 3-27-1869 F B
Marshall, Lucy to William Rodgers 1-13-1870 G B
Marshall, Lydia Frances to John W. Walker 12-13-1847 (12-?-1847) T
Marshall, Maggie to John Terry 9-29-1877 (10-4-1877) L
Marshall, Margaret E. to James B. Harper 2-26-1839 O
Marshall, Margaret V. to G. H. Worsham 5-21-1856 Sh
Marshall, Martha Ann Mariah to James A. Marshall 5-5-1836 (5-17-1836) O
Marshall, Martha L. to R. H. Murphey 9-30-1865 T
Marshall, Martha to Benj. (Joseph) Britt 7-31-1865 (no return) Hy
Marshall, Mary A. to Edward S. Ware 1-11-1868 Hy
Marshall, Mary A. to Josiah Maples 10-1-1853 (no return) F

Marshall, Nancy M. to Auston Rogers 3-17-1859 Cr
Marshall, Nancy T. to James F. Holloway 1-27-1859 Ma
Marshall, Pheby E. to S. A. Calhoun 11-22-1864 (11-23-1864) O
Marshall, Rebeca (Mrs.) to Norwood Scarlott 7-18-1860 Cr
Marshall, S. M. to S. M. Becton 12-26-1865 G
Marshall, Salina to Frank Johnson 12-30-1874 T
Marshall, Sarah Ann to Henry Parrish 8-2-1847 F
Marshall, Sarah E. to Thomas M. Price 3-5-1845 O
Marshall, Sarah E. to Thos. M. Price 3-3-1846 O
Marshall, Sarah Jane to Uriah Pinckney Yarbro 1-15-1853 (1-20-1853) T
Marshall, Sophia S. to Bob E. Jackson 3-17-1845 (no return) F
Marshall, Susan to John F. Williams 6-13-1842 (6-16-1842) Ma
Mart, Nellie P. to James A. Lyne 10-12-1871 Hy
Martain, Ruth C. to Samuel D. Wilson 1-29-1824 O
Martha A., Allen to D. c. Philips 8-29-1859 Hy
Martha Ann, Johnson to J. M. Powell 12-6-1865 Hy
Martha E., Day to S. C. Pool 2-25-1869 Hy
Martha, Clark to Colins Polk 1-25-1872 Hy
Martha, Plummer to Lovelace Plummer 9-28-1867 Hy
Marthy, Miller to Taylor Powell 10-10-1876 Hy
Martial, Sarah to Elijah Bowden 12-23-1853 Hn
Martin, A. C. to A. I. Jones 12-24-1859 We
Martin, A. H. to J. B. Wallace 2-3-1874 Hy
Martin, Ada B. to Rob Roy McGregor 6-10-1867 (7-6-1867) F
Martin, Amelia A. to John W. Kaler 11-26-1841 Hn
Martin, Anjalene to John Nicholas 4-30-1854 We
Martin, Ann to William Cain 1-30-1843 (2-1-1843) F
Martin, Ann to William Edwards 7-23-1866 G
Martin, Anna (Mrs.) to Jame Sweeny 4-11-1864 Sh
Martin, Anny to Henry H. Durrum 10-5-1826 Hr
Martin, Artilla to George Birdwell 6-10-1850 O
Martin, Barbary R. to Joel B. Sigmon 8-2-1847 G
Martin, Betty Ann E. to Sylvester Jones 12-19-1850 F
Martin, C. F. to John T. Brown 11-5-1858 O
Martin, C. to Wm. C. Moore 3-18-1841 Cr
Martin, Calidona B. to Addison Hinshaw 1-9-1844 F
Martin, Camilla to Henry Knott 2-6-1849 (2-7-1849) G
Martin, Caralin to John M. Davis 6-25-1859 We
Martin, Caroline to John Douglass 12-29-1866 (12-30-1866) F B
Martin, Caroline to John M. Dunn 5-10-1861 (no return) Hn
Martin, Charity to Andrew Jackson 3-21-1878 Dy
Martin, D. T. to Jeremiah Akin 4-11-1843 Be
Martin, Delia to Peter Callahan 2-16-1860 (2-17-1860) Sh
Martin, E. A. to John M. Dawson 1-10-1870 G
Martin, E. C. to W. L. Hope 11-4-1858 Hn
Martin, Eleanor to Dolphin Patterson 12-23-1831 Sh
Martin, Eliza A. to A. L. Kimble 9-8-1879 L
Martin, Eliza A. to James H. Allen 2-3-1868 (no return) Hy
Martin, Eliza H. to Nathan Williams 9-20-1841 Cr
Martin, Eliza J. to James Prewett 1-16-1844 Cr
Martin, Eliza to Gilbert Green 11-8-1839 Cr
Martin, Eliza to James Ridgeway 2-18-1840 Hn
Martin, Elizabeth A. to Thomas J. Amis 1-26-1860 O
Martin, Elizabeth A. to Anderson Liles 9-3-1851 Cr
Martin, Elizabeth A. to John W. Rowe 8-16-1855 Cr
Martin, Elizabeth E. to Elisha Paschall 9-28-1854 Hn
Martin, Elizabeth J. to Samuel Smith 3-30-1849 Hn
Martin, Elizabeth to G. E. Lancaster 2-25-1863 G
Martin, Elizabeth to J. W. Wright 12-25-1863 (12-27-1863) Sh
Martin, Elizabeth to James Maxwell 3-28-1848 Hn
Martin, Elizabeth to Stephen Boswell 9-17-1853 Be
Martin, Elizer to William Elam 3-16-1870 G B
Martin, Elvina to Samuel Paschall 8-17-1851 Hn
Martin, Emily to Jess L. Alexander 2-25-1863 Hn
Martin, Emma E. to Elijah F. Williams 2-2-1871 L
Martin, F. A. to Robert J. Blackwell 3-6-1877 (3-7-1877) L
Martin, F. W. to H. W. Collier 10-11-1859 We
Martin, Frances to John Wilson 3-16-1857 (no return) Hn
Martin, Frances to William A. Varner 4-19-1849 G
Martin, Georga Ann to William Edwards 4-17-1867 G
Martin, Gracia A. to Harry Moore 1-9-1867 G
Martin, Hanna? to J. M. Flemming 2-8-1870 T
Martin, Hannah M. to Francis L. Conner 2-10-1840 (2-13-1840) G
Martin, Harret M. to James Peterson 1-29-1850 (no return) F
Martin, Hattie (Mrs.) to W. A. Thomas 12-26-1870 Dy
Martin, J. A. to R. R. Pace 6-2-1860 O
Martin, Jane to Hiram Marsh 2-11-1839 (2-14-1839) Hr
Martin, Jane to Jones L. Soper 1-2-1841 (no return) F
Martin, Jane to Saml. F. McKinnie 2-28-1848 (3-2-1848) Hr
Martin, Jane to _____ Wiseman 1-26-1874 (1-28-1874) T
Martin, Josephine to C. Y. Gray 12-9-1863 O
Martin, Judith E. A. to John E. Hopkins 6-30-1838 Hr
Martin, Julia Ann to Louis Young 5-26-1862 (5-27-1862) O
Martin, Julia F. to Jas. M. Baird 6-7-1858 (6-8-1858) G
Martin, Kathrine to Yancy Moore 12-20-1850 Cr
Martin, L. E. to Samuel A. Robinson 2-2-1870 (2-13-1870) Cr
Martin, Larren T. to John T. Todd 12-16-1844 O

Martin, Louisa to John Fanon 1-5-1856 (1-10-1856) G
Martin, Louisa to William McGee 6-22-1833 (6-23-1833) Hr
Martin, Louisa to Wm. Johnson 4-25-1848 Cr
Martin, Louiza N. to Andrew J. Kirkland 7-2-1859 Hn
Martin, Lovey to Absolom D. Jenkins 8-31-1850 Sh
Martin, Lucinda J. to William E. Jenkins 8-21-1859 Hn
Martin, Lucinda to Henry Barnett 1-2-1877 (1-3-1877) Dy
Martin, Lucy to Solomon Cocke 2-18-1869 (2-20-1869) F B
Martin, Lucy to T. P. Harris 5-13-1863 (5-14-1863) F
Martin, Luiza to Joseph Newhouse 2-7-1853 (2-10-1853) O
Martin, M. C. to C. P. Daniel 9-27-1854 Hn
Martin, M. E. to S. W. Harper 12-19-1865 G
Martin, M. H. to W. C. Dickey 12-18-1866 O
Martin, Maranda to Moses Hunnell 10-8-1838 (10-18-1838) Hr
Martin, Margaret A. to Calvin S. Brown 9-9-1856 O
Martin, Margaret L. to Calvin S. Jones 12-7-1868 G
Martin, Margaret M. C. to Henry McGee 11-21-1846 (11-3?-1846) G
Martin, Margaret Y. to Wm. H. Herndon 2-20-1841 Hr
Martin, Margaret to Frederick Lafon 3-2-1843 Hn
Martin, Margarett A. to Pleasant Hinshaw 11-6-1841 (11-7-1841) F
Martin, Maria L. to James T. Harris 4-11-1856 Sh
Martin, Martha A. to A. M. Thompson 1-26-1875 Hy
Martin, Martha A. to L. C. Butts 2-15-1844 (2-25-1844) F
Martin, Martha C. to M. L. Crenshaw 12-13-1849 (no return) F
Martin, Martha M. to James A. Roberts 2-23-1857 (no return) Hn
Martin, Martha M. to James F. Martin 11-20-1866 (11-21-1866) Cr
Martin, Martha R. to Leonard Mathis 12-27-1864 G
Martin, Martha to Michael Diggs 5-30-1838 Cr
Martin, Mary A. to James M. Holt 1-25-1847 (1-28-1847) G
Martin, Mary A. to John Smith 12-1-1836 (12-8-1836) G
Martin, Mary Ann to Thomas A. Martin 10-26-1838 Cr
Martin, Mary Ann to Willis L. Somervell 1-11-1834 (1-16-1834) Hr
Martin, Mary E. to J. M. Stanly 7-23-1878 Hy
Martin, Mary E. to Marcus L. Davenport 12-24-1857 (no return) L
Martin, Mary E. to S. B. Pope 4-28-1860 (5-1-1860) G
Martin, Mary E. to W. A. Wilkerson 8-5-1867? Hy
Martin, Mary E. to Wm. L. Clayton 3-1-1853 (no return) F
Martin, Mary F. to James B. Black 11-27-1865 (no return) Hy
Martin, Mary F. to Samuel Jones 4-11-1860 Hn
Martin, Mary F. to Sidney M. Massengill 2-4-1864 Mn
Martin, Mary J. to John W. Bradley 4-2-1863 Hn
Martin, Mary S. to J. W. Pritchett 5-20-1869 Cr
Martin, Mary to B. H. Thompson 3-6-1851 (5-13-1851) Sh
Martin, Mary to Gus Braden 8-27-1869 F B
Martin, Mary to James Holt 4-9-1860 Sh
Martin, Mary to Paschal Graham 11-27-1844 Sh
Martin, Missouri to Samuel Blakemore 2-17-1872 (no return) Hy
Martin, Nancy E. to James F. Palmer 8-2-1856 Cr
Martin, Nancy L. to Asa French 8-5-1845 (no return) Cr
Martin, Nancy to A. M. French 10-26-1844 Cr
Martin, Nancy to Gilbert Cribbs 12-22-1824 (12-23-1824) G
Martin, Nancy to Greenberry Cunningham 5-12-1853 G
Martin, Nancy to James P. Lumbrick 8-9-1842 Hn
Martin, Nannie to J. B. Sappington 9-5-1869 G
Martin, Orpha L. (Mrs.) to Newton Munson 6-5-1845 Sh
Martin, Parmealia to William King 2-16-1830 Ma
Martin, Parthenia H. M. to Shelton D. Taylor 10-11-1846 T
Martin, Polly Ann to John Jones 10-26-1826 Hr
Martin, R. J. to Bryant Pope 2-23-1858 G
Martin, R. J. to P. J. Reeves 1-3-1863 (1-4-1863) F
Martin, Rosenia R. to Thomas J. Ray 11-21-1856 Hn
Martin, Sallie M. to L. C. Harwell 10-21-1872 (no return) Hy
Martin, Sarah Ann to H. M. Hatler 9-26-1849 Hn
Martin, Sarah E. to W. C. Taylor 3-5-1867 G
Martin, Sarah E. to William Simmons 9-17-1856 Hn
Martin, Sarah F. to William St. John 1-25-1875 (1-26-1875) L
Martin, Sarah Frances to Thomas J. Latham 8-23-1853 We
Martin, Sarah I. to John Lary 1-12-1875 (no return) Hy
Martin, Sarah J. to William H. Vandyke 10-14-1852 (no return) Hn
Martin, Sarah Jane to Robt. C. Gregory 12-9-1851 (no return) F
Martin, Sarah to G. W. Bradshaw 12-25-1863 (12-27-1863) Sh
Martin, Susan to Gideon Fox 2-8-1856 O
Martin, Szieber? C. T. to Wm. H. Green 1-21-1862 (no return) Cr
Martin, T. A. to Henry Crawford 2-28-1865 Hn
Martin, T. C. to M. T. House 11-2-1870 G
Martin, Texana V. to Joseph Crawford 1-8-1857 Sh
Martin, Tibitha to David Jones 1-5-1852 G
Martin, Tilla to Charles Utley 7-23-1870 G B
Martin, V. V. to B. F. Chambers 11-1-1871 (no return) Cr
Martin, Vashtine to John M. Holt 2-5-1864 G
Martina, Teresa to Giaconio Cupello 8-4-1859 (8-5-1859) Sh
Martindale, Peggy to Raiford Wright 3-28-1832 Hr
Marton, Isabella to James French 10-19-1856 Hn
Marton, Virginia E. to John W. Hunt 1-13-1842 (1-20-1842) F
Marvan, Rebecca to John Weaver 3-22-1856 (3-23-1856) G
Mary A., Calender to F. B. Ragland 9-5-1865 (no return) Hy
Mary Ann, Starns to G. H. Potts 4-3-1866 Hy

Mary C., Coleman to G. W. Powell 6-18-1874 (no return) Hy
Mary C., McNiel to John W. Powell 9-13-1866 Hy
Mary E., Cropno to A. J. Pipkin 6-28-1865 Hy
Mary E., McCool to Milton E. Ragland 4-19-1869 (no return) Hy
Mary J., Hughs to Alfred Philips 10-10-1866 Hy
Mary, Charles to James Pittner 7-26-1871 (no return) Hy
Mary, Gibson to Frank Tally 6-2-1864 Sh B
Mary, Harrison to Henry Prescott 11-29-1860 (no return) Hy
Mary, Nancy to William Brookshire 12-29-1841 (12-30-1841) Ma
Mary, Philips to K. S. Purvis 6-26-1877 (no return) Hy
Maschio, Mary to John Keneo 7-12-1860 (7-15-1860) Sh
Maschle, Magdaline to Morritz Holst 4-24-1861 Sh
Masco, Bridget to William Halleran 5-14-1860 (5-15-1860) Sh
Masebach, E. B. to R. C. McMahen 11-20-1871 (no return) Hy
Masey, Lucy E. to J. W. Crook 10-3-1853 Sh
Masey, Martha O. to James M. Lamb 4-21-1854 We
Mashburn, Hulda E. to John W. Lee 12-22-1846 (12-23-1846) Hr
Mashburn, Martha to John C. Reynolds 5-29-1847 Hr
Mashburn, Mary J. to Wm. Overton 9-30-1856 (10-2-1856) Hr
Mashburn, Mary Jane to William H. Hammons 2-26-1853 (2-27-1853) Hr
Mashburn, Mary to Prior Webb 10-10-1849 (10-11-1849) Hr
Mashburn, Nancy C. to P. H. Thompson 2-3-1858 (2-4-1858) Hr
Mashburn, Rachael to Thomas Sexton 7-4-1855 (7-24-1855) Hr
Mashburn, Sarah A. to Wm. T. Rainy? 9-4-1846 Hr
Mashburn, Sarah Ann to Sheppard Shelton 1-23-1849 (1-26-1849) Hr
Mashburn, Susan to William Rogers 1-9-1829 Hr
Mashburn, Vasty to Lewis Mashburn 2-6-1839 (2-7-1839) Hr
Mask, Catharine M. to W. F. Hancock 9-10-1855 (9-13-1855) Hr
Mask, Charlotte to Russel Alexander 12-30-1868 (12-31-1868) F B
Mask, Eliza to Nathaniel Cheairs 3-7-1853 (3-10-1853) Hr
Mask, Lina Ann to Grant Johnson 10-30-1868 (no return) F B
Mask, Martha to Thomas Chambers 10-23-1846 (10-28-1846) Hr
Mask, Mary A. to S. O. Myers 8-18-1852 Hr
Mask, Mary to Thomas H. Bayliss 4-8-1848 (4-13-1848) Hr
Mask, Sarah to John S.(L?) Roper 8-23-1838 Hr
Mask, Sarah to Thomas Hamer 11-10-1856 (11-19-1856) Hr
Mason, Abigail F. to William Ursery 8-3-1837 (8-3-1847?) Ma
Mason, Ann to Nathan Johnson 1-10-1857 (1-13-1856?) Ma
Mason, C. D. to D. A. Davis 10-25-1865 (10-26-1865) T
Mason, Eliza F. to James T. Devore 9-7-1866 (9-9-1866) Ma
Mason, Emma to Julius Davis 3-3-1883 L
Mason, Fannie to Frank Cubuss? 11-20-1875 (no return) Hy
Mason, Hanna to Frank Holloway 1-10-1872 (1-15-1872) T
Mason, Hariett to Thomas J. Callis 2-20-1861 G
Mason, Hariette to D. M. Thomas 10-11-1860 G
Mason, Harriet to Anderson Short 9-15-1875 Hy
Mason, Huldah to Archibald Buie 11-7-1839 Hn
Mason, Jane C. F. to Elisha Russell 1-9-1842 Cr
Mason, Jane R. to H. E. Bickers 7-25-1853 Hr
Mason, Judy to Nelson Wells 12-31-1868 (no return) F
Mason, M. J. to Thomas D. Sanders 1-15-1867 G
Mason, M. P. E. to Green Wortham 11-26-1860 (11-27-1860) Ma
Mason, M. P. to J. M. Hannah 2-14-1866 G
Mason, Margaret to George Spear 11-8-1829 Sh
Mason, Margaret to R. W. Wood 3-14-1870 (3-15-1870) Ma
Mason, Margaret to Turner Error 8-30-1867 (8-31-1867) F B
Mason, Margaret to William H. Piercy 3-7-1849 (3-8-1849) Ma
Mason, Maria E. to Nolen S. White 9-19-1871 (9-20-1871) Ma
Mason, Marietta to Thos. Nash Bland 5-10-1867 (5-11-1867) F B
Mason, Martha Ann to William Cleavis 6-1-1842 (6-9-1842) Ma
Mason, Martha F. to Adam C. Lawrence 4-22-1876 (4-23-1876) O
Mason, Mary J. to John T. Pounds 7-5-1859 (7-7-1859) Ma
Mason, Mary to John Mixon 7-3-1828 G
Mason, Mary to L. D. Matkins 1-21-1848 (no return) F
Mason, Mary to Nathan Hill 12-24-1869 F B
Mason, Mollie M. to P. F. Parker 10-17-1864 (10-18-1864) F
Mason, Olivia to Georg W. Bonner 2-6-1854 (2-7-1854) F
Mason, Rachael to Joshua J. Sanders 12-22-1840 (12-23-1840) Ma
Mason, Rebecca to Matthew M. Goodridge 2-12-1848 (2-17-1848) Ma
Mason, Sidney T.D.H.E. to John D. Cleaves 6-11-1852 (no return) F
Mason, Sue to Henry Mootry 4-8-1881 L B
Mason, T. E. to W. H. Barton 1-1-1856 (no return) Hn
Mason, Veria to Alexander Taylor 12-23-1874 T
Mason, Victoria to Barney Williams 9-9-1867 (9-12-1867) F B
Mass, Nancy to W. H. Thornton 11-28-1848 (11-6?-1848) F
Massee, Cary H. to Hudson W. Moss 6-22-1837 G
Massee, Sarah to Franklin Barrott 10-3-1839 G
Massengale, Eliza (Mrs.) to William Hutchinson 12-14-1861 (12-15-1861) O
Massengill, Frances M. to Newton Howe 12-26-1867 Be
Massengill, L. C. to William A. Alliston 8-26-1865 Mn
Massengill, Nannie D. to John B. Newton 4-7-1874 (7-3-1874) O
Massengill, Saluda C. to Thomas J. Smith 1-17-1868 Be
Masser, Jane to L. H. Pope 10-8-1840 Be
Massey, Adaline to Moses Rowland 1-23-1869 (1-27-1869) Cr
Massey, Caroline to Narcus R. Campbell 7-28-1852 Ma
Massey, Casander A. to Eli Gray 12-27-1849 Sh
Massey, Catherine to Collin Williams 1-10-1854 (1-11-1854) Ma

Massey, Cora I. to J. S. Lockhart 12-10-1873 (12-11-1873) Dy
Massey, Delina to Thomas M. Potts 2-4-1850 Hn
Massey, Dorcus to G. C. Percy 5-10-1855 Cr
Massey, E. J. to Jediah Roper 7-17-1848 Cr
Massey, Eliza Jane to Ezekiel Boyett 5-6-1848 (5-18-1848) Ma
Massey, Elizabeth A. to Abel C. Ray 12-21-1854 L
Massey, Elizabeth to Addison W. Bland 12-13-1848 Sh
Massey, Elizabeth to John Gage 9-28-1854 Sh
Massey, Elizabeth to Robt. Manny? 3-27-1859 Cr
Massey, Elizabeth to Sterling B. Haley 12-25-1832 G
Massey, Jane to John Brimingham 9-8-1852 Ma
Massey, Jane to L. C. Chandler 4-17-1852 Cr
Massey, Jennie to James H. Darden 12-9-1872 (12-12-1872) Dy
Massey, Jennie to Nathaniel E. Rice 4-3-1848 Cr
Massey, Katharine J. to Jessee J. Smith 9-7-1846 (9-6?-1846) G
Massey, Louisa A. to John W. Van Gilder 9-11-1849 Sh
Massey, Louisa to Benihar Bateman 4-30-1856 Sh
Massey, Louisa to Henry Hensley 11-5-1863 Sh
Massey, Lovina to E. A. Sowell 1-18-1858 Cr
Massey, Lucinda T. to H. G. Mustin 1-13-1859 (1-16-1859) Sh
Massey, Lucy E. to James H. Passmore 1-2-1855 Ma
Massey, M. A. to M. J. Anderson 10-27-1860 (10-28-1860) O
Massey, Martha A. to R. L. Milan 12-23-1848 Cr
Massey, Martha Ann to William M. Childress 3-30-1843 Sh
Massey, Martha to J. W. Thompson 3-25-1869 G
Massey, Martha to James Simmons 11-5-1846 Cr
Massey, Martha to John Stearns no date (with 1862) T
Massey, Martha to Thomas W. Pinson 10-24-1860 (10-25-1860) Cr
Massey, Mary Ann Eliza to William A. Byran 7-26-1844 Sh
Massey, Mary Ann to Charles G. Polk 12-27-1837 Sh
Massey, Mary E. to James H. Rhoads 11-30-1870 (12-1-1870) Cr
Massey, Mary Elizabeth to Wm. J. Rolings 1-10-1843 Sh
Massey, Mary Jane to B. A. Bright 3-15-1850 Be
Massey, Mary L. to Thomas L. Stanford 10-8-1865 (10-12-1865) Cr
Massey, Mary M. to Stephen Gibson 6-21-1857 Be
Massey, Mary to B. B. Simmonds 11-9-1863 (11-10-1863) Cr
Massey, Mary to John Crews 12-20-1839 Cr
Massey, Mary to Thomas A. Turner 10-10-1868 (10-11-1868) Cr
Massey, Melissa A. to W. H. (Wm. C.) Farr 9-7-1862 G
Massey, Minerva to S. W. Cowan 12-19-1837 Sh
Massey, Miranda to William Henry Adams 2-10-1859 (2-17-1859) Ma
Massey, Rebecca J. to James H. Morterson? 2-20-1843 (3-15-1843) T
Massey, Sarah E. to George W. Coghill 6-25-1847 (6-29-1847) F
Massey, Sarah U. to Warren A. Andrews 12-30-1841 Sh
Massey, Sarah to James Rice 4-17-1852 Cr
Massey, Sarah to John Hall 9-12-1857 Be
Massey, Sarah to Wm. Hartman 6-7-1857 Cr
Massey, Susan J. to J. E. Johnson 4-26-1859 We
Massey, Susan M. to Henry Lee 10-8-1849 Sh
Massters, Melvena to John R. Roach 8-12-1858 O
Massy, Levina to William C. Hogan 1-26-1842 (1-27-1842) F
Massy, Louisa N. to John Lyon 12-14-1853 Cr
Massy, Louisa to Samuel Curtis 6-19-1855 Be
Master, Manda M. to John M. Stephens 8-6-1860 (8-7-1860) O
Mastin (Martin?), Frances R. to C. W. Williams 12-17-1861 Sh
Mastisa, Mary to John W. Crockett 8-31-1833 G
Maston, Senith Elizabeth to John Manasco 4-22-1874 (4-23-1874) T
Matahis, Sina Adelina to Nelson Nusston 6-22-1854 G
Matcik, P. A. to John Dorsey 11-28-1870 Ma
Maten, Rosa N. to George W. Whitlock 6-29-1869 (7-1-1869) T
Mathena, S. E. to W. D. Harris 4-18-1867 O
Matheney, Araminta to John S. Taylor 10-10-1844 Hn
Matheney, Belle to J. H. Parmenter 2-19-1876 (2-20-1876) Dy
Mathenor, Tach to Milton R. Young 1-5-1869 (1-10-1869) O
Matheny, Alice to Abner Tom Scott 4-8-1879 Dy
Matheny, Amanda E. to William Griffith 5-20-1860 We
Matheny, E. C. to J. E. Everett 4-26-1867 (5-2-1868?) Cr
Matheny, Elizabeth J. to Elijah Lochart 8-9-1849 Be
Matheny, Louisanna to Isham Griffith 2-3-1862 We
Matheny, Lucretia to Andrew Hall 6-17-1851 (no return) Hn
Matheny, M. M. to D. J. Green 4-23-1869 (4-25-1869) Cr
Matheny, Manerva to William Logan 3-12-1861 (3-14-1861) Dy
Matheny, Martha A. to Isaac Hill 2-1-1863 Be
Matheny, Mary P. to J. W. Cox 1-24-1870 (1-27-1870) Cr
Matheny, Nancy Jane to Shepphard Landrum 4-20-1857 (4-27-1857) O
Matheny, Nancy M. to George W. Snider 12-20-1860 Hn
Matheny, P. A. to Hiram Glover 4-27-1844 (no return) Cr
Matheny, Palina to John N. Peebles 7-20-1861 (no return) Hn
Matheny, Perline to M. McConnell 3-23-1859 We
Matheny, Susan to William Prince 11-16-1860 (11-20-1861) We
Matherson, C. A. to L. W. Johnson 11-30-1875 (no return) Hy
Mathes, Julia A. to Scotland S. Crews 10-5-1846 Cr
Mathes, Mollie to Henry Raner 7-25-1885 (7-29-1885) L
Mathews, A. E. to R. A. Pierce 12-28-1869 (12-30-1869) O
Mathews, Agnis H. to Jacob Thedford 8-3-1866 G
Mathews, Ann S. to Robert Bullock 9-24-1839 F
Mathews, Claira to Nacie Tibbs 1-5-1871 Hy

Brides

Mathews, Edith to Allen Thompson 12-28-1872 T
Mathews, Elizabeth Ann to D. C. Dickey 9-29-1857 Be
Mathews, Elizabeth J. to James N. Haston 3-27-1856 Be
Mathews, Elizabeth L. to Will W. Wallace 1-4-1848 (1-6-1848) Hr
Mathews, Elizabeth to Richard Overton 12-18-1866 G
Mathews, Emeline to Ben Mathews 12-17-1874 T
Mathews, Fidelia E. to Miles F. Sloan 9-10-1866 (9-12-1866) Ma
Mathews, Georgiana to Robert K. McCarty 12-29-1860 Sh
Mathews, Henrietta to Henry Boynton 12-12-1876 Hy
Mathews, Isabella F. to Isaac Verhin 12-12-1850 O
Mathews, Kitty to Henry Lewis 2-5-1870 G B
Mathews, Louisa to Ezekiel Revel 3-5-1868 G
Mathews, Lydice to John W. Rhodes 10-10-1849 Cr
Mathews, M. A. to Chas. Swain 4-25-1851 (4-26-1851) Hr
Mathews, M. A. to George W. Simpson 7-29-1869 Hy
Mathews, M. H. to Henry R. Bond 7-12-1847 (7-15-1847) F
Mathews, Manerva to James Hallum 8-24-1845 Sh
Mathews, Margaret Ann to Jesse B. Curl 11-20-1843 (11-28-1843) F
Mathews, Margarette G. to Samuel M. Rig 9-9-1852 Cr
Mathews, Mariah to James M. Cole 6-1-1833 O
Mathews, Mariah to Jesse Dildia 12-29-1847 (1-4-1848) F
Mathews, Martha E. to Yett Dedmen 2-28-1858 Cr
Mathews, Mary A. E. to Thomas Barrom 2-28-1867 (3-5-1867) F
Mathews, Mary to Joseph L. Mewborn 11-16-1866 (11-20-1866) F
Mathews, Matty to Anderson Taylor 12-26-1868 (12-28-1868) F B
Mathews, Nancy to Elijah Jones 1-1-1855 (1-10-1855) O
Mathews, Nancy to Reubin Tennis 7-2-1831 (7-3-1831) Ma
Mathews, Nannie I. to George A. Jones 5-20-1869 G
Mathews, R. to W. N. Wilson 3-24-1865 O
Mathews, Rebecca J. to William F. McKnight 10-13-1828 (11-13-1828) G
Mathews, Rose to John Tucker 2-22-1868 Hy
Mathews, Sarah A. to Eli M. Burnes 11-10-1874 (no return) L
Mathews, Sarah to Arrim (Orrin?) Wright 7-23-1868 G B
Mathews, Sarah to John Richardson 11-21-1839 G
Mathews, Sarah to Roger Wilks 3-17-1869 Hy
Mathews, Seph W. to James H. Clark 3-14-1866 Sh
Mathews, Susan A. to Hugh M. Stewart 1-18-1847 Sh
Mathews, Susan E. to George Morrow 6-16-1862 (6-18-1862) O
Mathews, Susan J. to T. C. Lasseter 8-4-1864 Mn
Mathews, Susan to Jas. M. Swindle 12-17-1857 Hr
Mathews, Tennessee to James Sexton 9-4-1838 G
Mathews, Tizzina to Charles M. Wilson 8-26-1853 Cr
Mathews, Virginia to Thomas T.? Ramsey 7-29?-1858 (7-30-1858) Hr
Mathewson, Henrietta to Dick Johnson 12-23-1872 (12-27-1872) Cr B
Mathias, Mahala E. to John P. Laney? 8-18-1862 (8-20-1862) L
Mathias, Mahala to William Hill 4-10-1862 (no return) L
Mathies, F. to Peter Haurer 6-27-1859 Sh
Mathis, A. E. to John Brown 2-23-1867 G
Mathis, Alcey to Andrew Bell 2-21-1849 O
Mathis, Alcy to Andrew Bell 2-21-1849 O
Mathis, Alcy to Andrew D. Bell 2-21-1849 O
Mathis, Ann to Henry Royal 1-13-1870 G B
Mathis, C. A. to J. H. Pyland 9-29-1870 G
Mathis, D. J. to P. K. Dossett 10-20-1858 G
Mathis, Elizabeth J. to James G. Smotherman 12-13-1854 Hn
Mathis, Elizabeth to Benjamin Bond(Vaughan) 6-26-1834 Hr
Mathis, Elizabeth to L. F. Barham 1-28-1849 (no return) Hn
Mathis, Elizabeth to Sanford Tippitt 12-14-1866 (12-16-1866) Cr
Mathis, Elizabeth to T. W. Pender 5-10-1870 Hy
Mathis, Emma to David W. Turner 3-2-1870 (3-8-1870) Ma
Mathis, Emma to Clink Rhodes 12-25-1871 (12-26-1871) T
Mathis, Frances to William Crawford 12-29-1860 G
Mathis, Hanah to Jarrett Jamison 12-30-1869 G B
Mathis, Hannah to William Dunn 10-24-1859 Hr
Mathis, Harriet to Noah Adams 5-1-1873 Hy
Mathis, Ibernia to John Byrn 5-20-1876 L
Mathis, June to Robert Coalman? 5-7-1864 (no return) Hn
Mathis, L. A. to M. H. Parsley 2-3-1872 (no return) L
Mathis, Lucinda C. to James H. Smith 3-15-1859 (3-16-1859) G
Mathis, Lucinda E. to William Johnson 3-2-1859 (3-3-1859) G
Mathis, Lucretia F. to George M. Rust 1-9-1867 G
Mathis, M. A. to William B. Martin 1-26-1864 Hn
Mathis, M. C. to J. A. Estes 9-3-1860 G
Mathis, M. C. to S. A. Miller 1-24-1867 Cr
Mathis, M. E. to W. T. Estes 9-29-1856 G
Mathis, M. T. to William C. Shanklin 3-26-1856 G
Mathis, Mahala to Wm. McAdoo 8-6-1864 (no return) Cr
Mathis, Manerva A. to Isaac Crawford 3-9-1867 Hn B
Mathis, Margaret L. to James C. Anderson 8-3-1872 (8-4-1872) L
Mathis, Margaret to L. B. Revis 7-5-1873 (7-6-1873) L
Mathis, Margarett F. to William J. Barron 11-17-1856 G
Mathis, Mariah J. to Charles P. McLean 12-24-1840 G
Mathis, Mariah J. to John A. Guinn 4-14-1858 (no return) Hn
Mathis, Martha Ann to Charles Morris 10-26-1849 (10-28-1849) G
Mathis, Martha J. to Hamilton Alexander 9-16-1846 Hn
Mathis, Martha J. to J. W.? Watkins 11-28-1867 Hn
Mathis, Martha L. to Washington B. Carroll 1-1-1828 Hr

Mathis, Martha to John Newson 2-10-1845 Ma
Mathis, Martha to William Williams 9-24-1856 (no return) L
Mathis, Mary A. to G. W. Walker 9-8-1870 Hy
Mathis, Mary Ann to Ira Humphreys 10-14-1854 Hn
Mathis, Mary Ann to John H. Cole 12-17-1848 Be
Mathis, Mary Ann to William Laymon 3-9-1850 (3-10-1850) G
Mathis, Mary E. to George H. Price 10-22-1851 G
Mathis, Mary M. to Chasteen Ellington 9-17-1845 (9-18-1845) Ma
Mathis, Mary M. to John A. Smith 7-18-1849 Cr
Mathis, Mary P. to Pleasant G. Morgan 8-1-1866 (8-2-1866) Cr
Mathis, Mary to Ben Mathis 1-13-1870 G B
Mathis, Mary to Felix G. Morgan 10-15-1861 Cr
Mathis, Mary to J. E. Lykes 11-9-1877 (11-11-1877) O
Mathis, Mary to Joseph James 6-13-1866 G
Mathis, Melissa to George W. Barton 8-22-1852 Hn
Mathis, Miriah A. N. to Beverly E. Hillsman 9-2-1858 Cr
Mathis, N. M. to S. T. Tucker 7-20-1865 G
Mathis, Nancy C. to Thomas J. Irwin 2-5-1845 Hn
Mathis, Nancy Jane to John W. Watkins 5-16-1864 (no return) Hn
Mathis, Nancy M. to Elisha D. Smotherman 3-15-1860 Hn
Mathis, Nancy to John Steel 6-14-1860 Cr
Mathis, Patsy to Buck Williams 2-2-1867 G
Mathis, Permelia to John W. Marr 5-4-1858 G
Mathis, Rebecca T. to L. C. Covington 3-12-1857 We
Mathis, Rebecca to H. P. Alexander 1-3-1865 Hn
Mathis, Rebecca to Turner Woodall 7-13-1842 G
Mathis, Sallie to T. R.? Blow 2-?-1868 (2-6-1868) Cr
Mathis, Sarah J. to Thomas C. Woolard 2-6-1862 G
Mathis, Sarah M. to Finney Stewart 5-7-1861 Hn
Mathis, Sarah to Charles Graham 2-9-1860 Hn
Mathis, Susan M. to John B. Weaver 4-7-1855 (4-8-1855) G
Mathis, Susan to John A. Smith 12-9-1874 Hy
Mathis, Susana E. to Philip B. Carter 7-26-1837 (7-27-1837) G
Mathis, Syrena to S. H. Nelson 8-29-1867 G
Mathis, T. T. to John Y. Shepherd 4-26-1859 Cr
Mathis, Ursul M. to James F. Hickman 5-23-1866 (5-3?-1866) Cr
Mathis?, Prefom? to Charles Christopher Freeman 7-17-1843 (8-18-1843) T
Matlock, Ann to James J. Wilson 11-12-1852 Cr
Matlock, Elizabeth to D. J. Davis 4-19-1849 (no return) Cr
Matlock, Mary to Daniel N. McArthur 12-7-1858 Cr
Matlock, Melinda to John D. Billingly 3-8-1841 Cr
Matlock, S. A. E. to Geo. E. Rogers 2-14-1865 (2-16-1865) O
Matlock, Sarilda T. to James S. Walker 12-6-1846 Be
Matlock, Susan to Thomas Boone 11-24-1867 Be
Matmiller, Christine to Andrew Rinklin 5-9-1859 (5-10-1859) F
Matthew, Tabitha to Z. B. Rhodes 5-18-1843 Hn
Matthews, Alice to William H. Nelson 12-5-1867 (12-8-1867) Ma
Matthews, Amanda to John Holland 4-9-1861 Hr
Matthews, Bettie A. to J. H. Fisher 5-7-1866 (5-9-1866) F
Matthews, Cassander J. to William Lacy 1-7-1852 (no return) L
Matthews, Catherine E. to Benjamin W. Clement 12-21-1858 (12-22-1858) Ma
Matthews, E. M. to L. W. Griggs 8-22-1882 (8-23-1882) L
Matthews, Elizabeth C. to J. H. Foy 1-11-1854 (1-11-1855)? Sh
Matthews, Elizabeth J. to Robert C. Wyatt 3-13-1858 (3-18-1858) Ma
Matthews, Elizabeth to Pleasant Osbourn 2-7-1858 O
Matthews, Emma to W. M. Hall 2-3-1875 G
Matthews, F. B. to O. D. Brown 1-3-1868 (1-7-1868) O
Matthews, Harriett to Wes Jones 1-2-1868 (1-3-1868) F B
Matthews, Isabella to David Hull 12-5-1842 (12-13-1842) Hr
Matthews, Jane to Burril Souls 8-5-1829 (8-11-1829) Hr
Matthews, Jane to John Nelson 9-7-1840 (9-17-1840) Hr
Matthews, July A. to James B. Caton 10-2-1859 Cr
Matthews, K. E. to J. J. Porter 9-24-1866 G
Matthews, L. J. D. to J. E. Sparks 9-28-1859 F
Matthews, M. E. to Edgar Harper 12-16-1881 (no return) L
Matthews, Margaret E. to Robert Hunt 4-28-1857 (4-29-1857) Ma
Matthews, Martha Ann to William C. Stovall 10-30-1847 (11-4-1847) Ma
Matthews, Martha to John Darnell 7-13-1861 Hr
Matthews, Mary E. to Carren E. Boykin 4-17-1854 (4-18-1854) Ma
Matthews, Mary F. to Wm. M. Bigham 2-12-1857 Sh
Matthews, Mary to James Patterson 2-11-1856 (2-12-1856) O
Matthews, Mary to Reuben Bass 12-18-1837 Hr
Matthews, Mattie to Wm. M. Teahen 12-20-1870 (12-21-1870) Ma
Matthews, Milly to George A. Moalett 5-3-1857 O
Matthews, Nancy E. to John Bunyan Sloan 6-25-1869 (6-27-1869) Ma
Matthews, Nancy to Edmond? Covington 12-5-1854 (12-17-1855?) O
Matthews, Nancy to Hiram Light 4-2-1874 Dy
Matthews, Permia to John Brimmage 12-15-1858 Cr
Matthews, Sarah E. to P. B. Stewart 4-26-1847 Sh
Matthews, Sina to Thaddeus Wilson 11-26-1860 (11-27-1860) F
Matthews, Sue to Powhatton P. Bennett 12-16-1868 (12-19-1868) Ma
Matthews, Surany? to Stephen Jones 11-11-1836 (11-13-1836) Hr
Matthews, Tennie B. to Wm. J. Daley 2-28-1868 (no return) F
Matthews, Tommie to John H. McFerrin 1-24-1866 (1-31-1866) F
Matthews, Virginia P. to A. P. Cutler 2-28-1874 (3-1-1874) O
Matthewson, Mary to Robert Davis 11-9-1867 (no return) Hn
Matthis, Hannah to Sherwood Lowe 1-24-1831 Hr

Mattice?, S. E. to J. B. McDaniel 7-19-1873 (7-23-1873) T
Mattie E., Williams to James A. Poston 3-5-1873 Hy
Matty (O'Matty), Martha O. to Janus Lamb 4-21-1854 We
Mauldin, Eliza to Isaac Pursell 5-25-1867 Dy
Mauldin, Elizabeth to George Morphis 1-10-1842 (1-11-1842) Ma
Mauldin, Exes Jane to N. B. Hicks 2-29-1840 (3-12-1840) Hr
Mauldin, Mary W. to William T. Brown 2-24-1851 (2-27-1851) Hr
Maupin, E. J. to Samuel L. Harper 1-10-1848 O
Maupin, Frances J. to W. H. Grisham 12-19-1866 (no return) Hn
Maupin, Harriett J A. to John Hall 8-16-1860 Hn
Maupin, Martha J. to Comadore P. Park(s) 12-11-1854 (12-13-1854) O
Maupin, Mary Jane to Daniel Bracklin 10-17-1870 (10-22-1870) L
Maupin, Susan F. to James B. Harper 11-8-1849 O
Maurring?, Annie to A. P. Smith 12-1-1869 T
Maury, C. B. to J. B. Thomas 12-21-1865 F
Maury, Lucy J. to W. R. Baker 3-26-1855 (no return) F
Maury, M. E. to D. W. Collier 4-27-1865 F
Maury?, M. E. (Mrs.) to Thos. E. Fisher 9-1-1866 (9-2-1866) Dy
Maver, H. F. (Mrs.) to John Grigsby 5-2-1861 Sh
Mawns, Sally to Ase Brooks 1-19-1868 Hy
Max, Hariet L. to M. F. Hartfield 1-3-1870 (1-5-1870) T
Maxedon, Lucretia to W. A. Wilson 12-21-1865 Mn
Maxey, Betty A. to Robert N. Hill 9-10-1856 Ma
Maxey, Julia to Wm. Wilson 2-7-1871 Hy
Maxfield, Mary to John McDonald 2-14-1855 (2-15-1855) Sh
Maxfield, S. F. to E. C. Tull 5-5-1875 L
Maxville, Amanda to Henry Thurman 12-24-1868 G
Maxwell, Callie to G. P. Tinsley 5-7-1873 (5-8-1873) Dy
Maxwell, Cela A. to German W. Davis 4-16-1858 (4-18-1858) Hr
Maxwell, Elizabeth to James Rose 4-30-1832 (5-3-1832) Hr
Maxwell, Emily to John L. Key 2-8-1848 Hn
Maxwell, Gertrude R. to Nat Harper 12-28-1867 (1-8-1868) F
Maxwell, Gracy to Wash Matthews 1-2-1868 (1-3-1868) F B
Maxwell, H. to W. H. Forrest 7-9-1864 Sh
Maxwell, Jannett S. to Leonidas McKnight 2-7-1848 Sh
Maxwell, M. J. to J. R. King 7-30-1873 (7-31-1873) Cr
Maxwell, Martha J. to B. A. Ford 9-17-1850 Hn
Maxwell, Martha J. to James J. Williams 3-15-1854 Hn
Maxwell, Martha to John B. Tinker 4-23-1848 Be
Maxwell, Mary A. to Francis Baldridge 5-8-1854 (no return) We
Maxwell, Mary A. to Franklin Baldridge 5-4-1854 We
Maxwell, Mary A. to Phillip G. Austin 7-4-1860 We
Maxwell, Mary Eliza to James J. Maxwell 9-26-1867 (9-27-1867) T
Maxwell, Mary J. to H. L. Heflin 12-28-1867 (1-8-1868) F
Maxwell, Mary Jane to James C. Hays 5-4-1847 (no return) Hn
Maxwell, Mary to Wm. J. Oats 11-21-1844 F
Maxwell, Matilda A. to Tilman D. Corum 11-19-1847 (11-21-1847) Ma
Maxwell, Mollie to James Bringle 2-14-1872 T
Maxwell, Nancy A. to Charles Stewart 6-3-1841 Hn
Maxwell, Nancy J. to Danil W. Lowrance 9-29-1845 (10-11?-1845) Hr
Maxwell, Nancy to Jas. T. Winburn 9-22-1855 T
Maxwell, Parilee F. to Isaac Lassiter 12-7-1858 Hn
Maxwell, S. A. to W. M. Burk 2-29-1872 Cr
Maxwell, Sally to A. H,. Lorance 7-26-1848 (7-27-1848) Hr
Maxwell, Sarah to Thomas Musgrave 2-13-1828 Hr
Maxwell, T. S. to R. H. Richardson 1-23-1873 Hy
May, Amanda to Redden D. Shofner 12-6-1838 Cr
May, Anide to Joab Harrell(Howell) 1-11-1834 (1-13-1834) Hr
May, Clayrindy to Jordian W. Sadberry 2-16-1848 G
May, Cyntha to William A. Burnes 10-28-1837 (10-31-1837) Hr
May, Cynthia to A. M. Farrow 12-13-1862 (no return) Hy
May, Elise (Elize?) to A. R. Reinach 1-5-1858 Sh
May, Eliza H. to Wm. Johnson 9-1-1840 Cr
May, Elizabeth Nix to Jerome Carter 1-5-1844 Hn
May, Elizabeth to John Parmer 1-7-1841 Ma
May, Elizabeth to John R. Clark 2-13-1844 (2-15-1844) Ma
May, Elizabeth to Josephus Meeks 8-13-1838 (8-19-1838) Hr
May, Elizabeth to William I. Hutchison 5-25-1830 Ma
May, Ellen to Robert D. Hart 10-1-1862 (10-2-1862) Ma
May, Eveline to Frank Mason 12-24-1868 (12-27-1868) F B
May, Everett to James Fielder 2-28-1874 (3-1-1874) Dy
May, Fannie H. to Nathan I. Mainor 2-10-1868 (2-12-1868) Ma
May, Fannie W. to Wm. H. Hundly 5-23-1859 (5-24-1859) F
May, Frances to Peter Sexton 3-20-1843 (4-1-1843) G
May, Harriet D. to S. C. Benjamin 12-9-1857 (12-10-1857) Ma
May, Harriet L. to John Higdon 3-12-1868 Be
May, Harriett to Edward Cock 12-9-1858 Ma
May, Jennie to Marcus D. Smith 11-8-1864 Sh
May, Julia to James Kindrick 5-6-1844 (5-7-1844) Ma
May, Levina Ann to Jacob Anderson 4-28-1838 F
May, Louise to John Crunk 5-24-1826 Hr
May, Lucy to Bailey G. Rooks 9-24-1840 Ma
May, Mary C. to Doddridge Trader 8-2-1859 (8-3-1859) Ma
May, Mary E. to John H. Huffman 4-7-1841 Cr
May, Mary S. to Gideon J. Beuford 3-29-1852 (no return) F
May, Nancy M. to Wm. A. Rawlings 4-30-1849 (5-2-1849) F
May, Nancy to John J. Pearcy 11-25-1857 (2-5-1857?) Ma

May, Sarah C. to John A. Noe 11-14-1860 (no return) Hy
May, Sarah to Reuben Johnson 1-20-1846 (1-21-1846) Ma
May, Susannah to David McClendon 8-1-1827 (8-3-1827) Hr
May?, Lucy E. to William P. Dowdy 12-15-1846 (12-16-1846) F
Mayall, Julia to John Davis 7-26-1873 (no return) Dy B
Mayar, Cornelia A. to J. P. Shaw 12-24-1866 (12-26-1866) Cr
Mayberry, Caroline to Maston Randle 4-11-1865 (4-12-1865) Cr
Mayberry, Nancy to Rice King 7-4-1853 Be
Maye, Sarah to Johnathan Bough 8-25-1866 T
Mayer, T___ to Andrw J. Arnett 12-19-1844 Hn
Mayes (Meyer), Mildred L.(F?) to David Adams 10-7-1863 Sh
Mayes, Mary to Albert Thompson 1-21-1862 Hn
Mayes, Rachel J. to Edward H. Corbitt 5-22-1848 Sh
Mayes, Sallie to John Ward 9-9-1870 G
Mayes, Sarah V. to Edward Hobs 6-5-1862 Sh
Mayfield, Adaline to James Smith 4-7-1870 G
Mayfield, Amey P. to David Todd 8-19-1836 (8-20-1836) G
Mayfield, Ann E. to Ferney G. Driskell 2-16-1841 (3-1-1841) G
Mayfield, Cenith F. to John L. Connell 6-1-1857 (6-2-1857) G
Mayfield, Diannah to Nathan Gee 11-23-1853 (11-24-1853) Hr
Mayfield, Elizabeth Jane to William A. Reeves 8-26-1854 (8-27-1854) O
Mayfield, Emma H. to Silas M. Bobbett 8-23-1852 (8-24-1852) G
Mayfield, Hannah J. to F. M. Welch 5-3-1850 (5-9-1850) Hr
Mayfield, Harriet to Cisero Jelks 12-26-1871 Hy
Mayfield, Hulda E. to James G. Carter 1-12-1839 (1-15-1839) G
Mayfield, Jane T. to Alexander Clark 9-24-1850 (9-25-1850) G
Mayfield, Malinda E. to Stevin Oliver Babb 5-3-1858 (5-4-1858) Hr
Mayfield, Maranda S. to Samuel Hicks 9-15-1858 (9-16-1858) G
Mayfield, Mary Ann to William W. Moore 10-4-1864 G
Mayfield, Mary D. to John K. Wilburn 5-7-1866 (5-10-1866) F
Mayfield, Mary R. to John Robertson 2-5-1836 G
Mayfield, Mary to Jefferson Wilson 12-22-1832 G
Mayfield, Nancy Jane to J. W. Davis 12-12-1859 (12-13-1859) T
Mayfield, Nancy to Charles L. Thompson 1-27-1844 (1-30-1844) G
Mayfield, Nancy to T. P. Kirkman 12-21-1868 G
Mayfield, Parthena J. to Franklin Exum 12-26-1859 G
Mayfield, Polly to David Bowers 2-10-1844 (2-13-1844) G
Mayfield, Sallie A. to J. W. Tucker 9-26-1866 (9-27-1866) F
Mayfield, Sarah A. to John Tucker 8-14-1844 Sh
Mayfield, Sarah to John Sperling 1-31-1833 (2-5-1833) Hr
Mayfield, Sarah to Zechariah Barker 2-7-1865 Be
Mayfield, Sopha to Isaac Tharp 2-18-1847 G
Mayher, Johanna to Jeremiah Enwright 7-21-1860 (7-22-1860) Sh
Mayhew, Sarah C. to Eli Sweeten 8-17-1830 Sh
Maynard, Eliza Ann to Thomas Jennings 7-18-1883 L
Maynard, M. Jane to W. H. Pope 9-21-1870 (9-22-1870) Cr
Maynard, Malinda to Harvey M. Alexander 12-16-1869 (12-17-1869) Ma
Maynard, Mary F. to William R. Rooks 9-19-1863 (9-20-1862?) Ma
Maynard, Nancy to Elijah Graham 12-11-1854 We
Maynard, R. A. to T. J. Alexander 2-20-1855 We
Maynard, Sallie to James A. Fulkerson 9-27-1878 L
Maynard, Sarah Ann to G. B. Jennings 12-6-1865 (12-7-1865) L
Maynard, Sarah to Wm. M. Parker 2-25-1866 G
Maynard, Sinay to Charles Crewell 12-22-1869 G
Mayo, Bettie to Andy Jackson 7-3-1868 (7-4-1868) F B
Mayo, C. P. to James Marcus 11-13-1860 We
Mayo, Elizabeth to John Marcus 11-26-1845 We
Mayo, Harriet Ann to Edward G. Reddick 3-13-1846 (3-18-1846) F
Mayo, Jane Eliza to H. S. Taylor 9-18-1846 (no return) F
Mayo, Jane to William Pettus 12-30-1880 Dy
Mayo, Laura I. to William G. Cockrill 3-18-1867 (3-14?-1867) T
Mayo, Laura to Washington Johnson 12-30-1869 F B
Mayo, Manie to Joseph Curtice 6-30-1825 G
Mayo, Martha C. to John L. Gay 1-15-1844 We
Mayo, Martha S. to James N. Hart 11-22-1869 Ma
Mayo, Mary E. to Carns M. Swift 7-29-1844 F
Mayo, Mary to Benjamin C. Harison 1-23-1850 Sh
Mayo, Meter to Frank Toliver 12-28-1869 (1-1-1870) T
Mayo, Nancy J. to Freeman Morris 12-6-1850 (12-7-1850) F
Mayo, S. A. to George W. Bumpass 12-22-1868 (12-23-1868) F
Mayo, Sarah Jane to Jackson Smith 2-23-1858 Ma
Mayo, Sarah L. to Thos. J. Swift 2-1-1850 (2-5-1850) F
Mayo, Susanah to James T. Marcus 10-10-1850 (not endorsed) We
Mays (Hays?), Susan to Walter Morrell 10-12-1867 (no return) L B
Mays, Ann to Manuel Ashter 3-23-1867 Hy
Mays, Bell to John Robertson 3-23-1830 Ma
Mays, Drurie A. to Josiah B. Campbell 1-16-1867 L
Mays, E. M. E.? to William Gay 11-2-1865 G
Mays, Ella B. to Archibald J. Sneed 1-19-1869 (1-20-1869) Ma
Mays, Emily V. to Pleasant Henderson 1-30-1841 (2-3-1841) F
Mays, J. A. to W. T. Nicholson 5-23-1860 G
Mays, Jane to George McGee 1-23-1870 G B
Mays, Julia A. to Ruben S. Ingram 2-19-1850 G
Mays, Laura to James L. Sparks 11-3-1870 F
Mays, Lethe Jane to William H. Brent 4-30-1860 (5-1-1860) Dy
Mays, Letta (Mrs.) to William Mays 7-15-1866 G
Mays, Letty to William Redmond 6-27-1868 G B

Mays, Lilly to Hiram Partee 10-24-1854 (10-25-1854) G
Mays, Lilly to Logan McMurray 2-2-1870 G B
Mays, Louisa to Lewis James 1-22-1868 G B
Mays, Malinda to Alexander C. Shane 6-26-1861 Ma
Mays, Malinda to Harrison L. H. Stanley 3-7-1861 Ma
Mays, Margaret to Lee Ferguson 8-10-1874 G
Mays, Martha C. to Wiley B. Bondurant 7-21-1856 (7-23-1856) O
Mays, Martha J. to J. C. Clements 2-4-1862 Sh
Mays, Mary B. to James T. Eudaley 11-19-1862 Dy
Mays, Mary F. to Isaac N. Croom 5-19-1856 Ma
Mays, Mattie M. to William D. Wilkerson, jr. 4-3-1866 (4-4-1866) L
Mays, Mollie to Henry Nicholson 3-2-1867 G
Mays, Molly to Alfred O'Neal 1-1-1870 G B
Mays, Nancy Jane to Frederick Blake 4-21-1870 (4-24-1870) Ma
Mays, Nellie to William Femzer 12-7-1872 Dy
Mays, Rebecca J. to John J. Fielder 2-12-1835 (2-19-1385) G
Mays, Rebecca to Chapman Ingram 4-14-1866 G
Mays, Sallie to W. H. Johnson 12-31-1858 Sh
Mays, Sarah A. to James Swink 11-2-1852 (12-2-1852) Ma
Mays, Sarah W. to Wm. H. Henderson 5-8-1843 (no return) F
Mays, Susan to Samuel D. Spake 7-7-1846 (7-9-1846) G
Mays, Sylvia to Alex Williams 2-15-1877 Dy
McAda, Jane to Thomas Pearce 8-29-1830 Sh
McAdams, Frances A. to Joseph H. Ward 11-19-1856 We
McAdams, Margaret to William T. B. Davidson 7-12-1862 We
McAdams, Martha A. to James D. Barton 2-16-1861 (no return) We
McAdams, Susan to A. J. G. Tatum 12-26-1839 F
McAdoo, Adaline to Stephen McGraves 5-6-1866 G
McAdoo, Amanda J. to Daniel L. Atkins 10-10-1850 (no return) Hn
McAdoo, America J. to Quincy A. Harper 2-13-1866 Cr
McAdoo, Ann G. A. to Charles P. Byers 6-10-1851 Cr
McAdoo, C. T. to L. N. Drewrey 8-2-1871 (8-3-1871) Cr
McAdoo, Dathie to George Williams 11-5-1866 G
McAdoo, E. to Elisha? Fields 10-3-1850 Cr
McAdoo, Elizabeth E. to Simeon Ward 11-20-1844 Hn
McAdoo, Frances E. to Elijah Robinson 12-8-1858 (12-12-1858) Ma
McAdoo, Frances to Robt. Hailey 3-29-1870 G
McAdoo, Harriet to Wm. C. Peeples 10-26-1863 (no return) Cr
McAdoo, Julia A. to Samuel Boon 5-6-1870 G
McAdoo, Lavenia J. to Davie McCree 1-20-1858 Ma
McAdoo, Mary A. to John Cannie 3-18-1868 G
McAdoo, Phelora to Wm. B. Duncan 4-4-1854 Cr
McAdoo, Sharlett to John C. McClain 7-11-1839 Cr
McAdoo, T. C. to A. B. Hilliard 12-20-1854 Cr
McAfee, Elizabeth S. to William H. Nelson 11-22-1856 (12-1-1856) Ma
McAfee, Ruth C. to John Nelson, jr. 12-22-1845 Ma
McAfee, Sarah A. to Jesse Inman 8-16-1869 Ma
McAfee, Sarah E. to J. A. White 7-5-1869 (7-7-1869) Dy
McAfee, Sarah E. to James R. Wharton 11-26-1862 Mn
McAlelly, Elizabeth to Jobe Hicks 12-14-1833 (12-19-1833) G
McAlelly, Margarett to William C. Hicks 1-29-1846 G
McAlexander, Adaline to Ducan Killen 3-31-1844 Cr
McAlexander, Ann C. to Wm. E. Beard 4-20-1846 (4-26-1846) Hr
McAlexander, Eliza A. D. to John R. Holmes 7-2-1839 Cr
McAlexander, Eliza G. to John A. Garner 5-4-1850 (5-16-1850) Hr
McAlexander, Jennie to Thomas Fry 1-31-1871 Ma
McAlexander, Lucinda to James F. Hickman 11-29-1839 Cr
McAlexander, Mary E. to David A. McDonald 8-17-1852 Cr
McAlexander, Melinda N. to John W. Webber 11-19-1862 Sh
McAlfee, Mary Jane to Christopher L., jr. Johnson 3-31-1849 Ma
McAlfee, Minerva H. to Jarrett Hollinsworth 10-7-1848 Ma
McAlilley, M. R. to J. W. Harrison 2-26-1879 (2-29-1879) Dy
McAlilly, Sarah to James Vincent 6-16-1867 G
McAlister, Julia A. to David Baird 5-14-1861 G
McAlister, L. V. to John Douglas 4-15-1865 G
McAlister, Louisa to John Crockett 9-23-1846 (9-24-1846) O
McAlister, Lucindy to John Phillips 4-5-1852 Cr
McAlister, Martha J. to John F. Ford 11-6-1854 (11-13-1854) G
McAlister, Mary L. to A. C. Garrison 3-9-1852 O
McAlister, Mary to O. L. Chandler 1-28-1857 G
McAlister, Matilda to David Harper 7-20-1866 O
McAlister, Susan M. to G. W. Patton 7-5-1860 G
McAllila, Mary J. to Benjamin Yarbrough 3-5-1845 (3-6-1845) G
McAllister, Arabella to Alfred Z. Owens 1-19-1854 Cr
McAllister, Minerva to Wm. B. Rechard 9-26-1858 Cr
McAllister, P. to W. H. Miller 7-21-1868 G
McAllister, Sarah to John D. Lacy 9-1-1854 (9-3-1854) G
McAlpin, Lucinda to Z. Chambers 12-30-1862 Mn
McAmy, Manda C. to James W. Fields 11-2-1853 Cr
McAnally, Ann to Thomas Higgins 3-16-1852 (4-19-1852) Sh
McAnally, Bridget to Luke Calvey 1-18-1864 Sh
McAnally, Margaret to J. B. Palmo 1-15-1855 (1-16-1855) Sh
McAndless, Viney to Spencer Thompson 11-7-1837 O
McAnley, Mary A. to John M. Sanders 4-10-1867 Cr
McAnulty, Catherine to Michael Slaughter 7-24-1846 Sh
McAnulty, Dora to Thos. R. Bankhead 10-10-1868 (10-11-1868) F
McAnulty, Mary G. to John H. McClellan 5-29-1838 Hr

McAnulty, Nancy B. to Henry B. Misenheimer 3-2-1837 (3-7-1837) Hr
McArthur, M. J. to G. L. Jones 11-7-1852 Cr
McArthur, Mary A. to P. T. Butler 7-21-1862 (no return) Cr
McArver, Celia to Woodson Kinchey? 5-8-1828 Hr
McAskille, Mary to E. S. Thomas 2-26-1873 (2-27-1873) Cr
McAuley, Elizabeth L. to Turman C. Sanders 1-23-1859 Cr
McAuley, Indian to Wm. H. Gooch 2-10-1841 Cr
McAuley, J. J. to W. H. Bailey 7-24-1869 (7-25-1869) Cr
McAuley, Louisa J. to Wm. T. Jones 1-26-1857 Cr
McAuley, Louisa to Claborn Parish 7-18-1859 Cr
McAuley, M. E. to E. W. Autry 11-21-1868 (11-22-1868) Cr
McAuley, M. J. to James Lesslie 9-6-1871 (9-7-1871) Cr
McAulley, Mary C. to Henry L. Robertson 12-14-1865 Be
McAuly, Eliza to L. D. Rust 10-7-1850 Cr
McAuly, Margaret C. to Thomas Alsop 1-29-1852 Be
McAuly, Sarah J. to Wm. B. Benton 1-31-1856 Cr
McAutry, Roseanah to G. A. Guthrey 2-16-1863 (2-19-1863) O
McAvoy, Bridget to Cornelius Ryan 1-28-1856 Sh
McAvoy, H. to J. W. Hampton 9-30-1847 F
McBee, CAtherine to William Taggart 2-26-1827 Hr
McBee, Clarissa to Johnson W. Wortham 8-30-1837 Hr
McBee, Hannah to William Copeland 1-26-1825 (2-27-1825) Hr
McBee, Mary F. to A. S. Wrinkle 6-2-1867 Hn
McBee, Masie to W. B.(Green B.) Stokes 3-30-1827 (3-31-1827) Hr
McBlancett, Elizabeth A. to John Huggins 9-24-1845 Mn
McBomer, Allice to Thomas J. Tillman 8-5-1872 (8-7-1872) L
McBride, Amanda Minerva to Wm. Alen Lawrence? 3-12-1856 (3-13-1856) T
McBride, B. F. to Albert T. Jones 2-19-1854 Hn
McBride, Callie to Elijah Roberson 5-13-1885 (5-17-1885) L
McBride, Catherine to Ruffin Gough 4-19-1846 G
McBride, Crecy Ann to W. A. McBride 7-10-1884 L
McBride, E. F. to L. A. McBride 7-18-1854 Sh
McBride, Eliza to W. R. Crow 1-12-1870 (1-13-1870) Dy
McBride, Elizabeth to Joseph McClure 6-2-1829 G
McBride, Elizabeth to Joshua Coleman 11-24-1855 (11-26-1855) Hr
McBride, Elizabeth to Thomas Carnes 6-26-1835 (6-28-1835) Hr
McBride, Elizabeth to William Bottoms 6-26-1848 (7-6-1848) Hr
McBride, Hester R. to Thos. W. Williams 12-16-1842 (12-21-1842) G
McBride, Jane to George Medlin 1-17-1850 Cr
McBride, Louisa to Hugh Shott 2-1-1843 (2-3-1843) Hr
McBride, Louvina A. to Thomas Forbess 7-16-1866 (7-18-1866) T
McBride, Lucy F. to Wat Dotson 9-26-1867 Dy
McBride, Lydia J. to W. H. McRae 1-13-1869 Be
McBride, M. E. to L. J. Cockrell 2-10-1873 (2-11-1873) Cr
McBride, M. L. to R. M. Reed 12-9-1874 Dy
McBride, Margaret M. to Jacob F. Roberts 11-27-1849 Sh
McBride, Marth E. to James Stevens 4-3-1867 T
McBride, Martha E. to John H. Moore 3-16-1854 Cr
McBride, Martha J. to Robert A. Rice 1-?-1867 (1-16-1867) T
McBride, Mary Ann to John A. Carroll 9-3-1849 Sh
McBride, Mary E. to Mauris Julien Cherry 6-12-1863 Sh
McBride, Mary Eliz. to Peter Simpson Jackson 12-3-1855 (12-6-1855) T
McBride, Mary J. to Evander McNair 11-23-1860 (11-27-1860) T
McBride, Mary kSLusan to John Nelems 6-19-1847 (6-21-1847) Hr
McBride, Mary to Arthur Williams 12-21-1829 (12-24-1829) G
McBride, Mary to Littleberry Spain 7-28-1858 Hr
McBride, Mary to R. C. Allen 6-18-1856 G
McBride, Mary to Thomas E. Tansel 10-12-1871 Dy
McBride, Nancy Emily to A. M. Duncan 3-12-1856 (3-13-1856) T
McBride, Nancy J. to J. J. Laxton 2-2-1870 (2-3-1870) T
McBride, Nancy to John Q. Marshall 12-1-1852 T
McBride, Necy A. to Zachariah F. Denney 9-23-1867 O
McBride, Paula? to Sam Hughes 5-20-1874 T
McBride, Polly M. to John L. Wells 1-13-1831 Hr
McBride, Rachel L. to Robert M. Green 9-7-1867 T
McBride, Sarah E. to Stephen S. Thompson 5-25-1867 (5-27-1867) Dy
McBride, Sarah J. to John T. Roberts 3-15-1853 Sh
McBride, Sarah J. to Joseph Barrott 11-8-1843 Cr
McBride, Sina to A. Laremore 8-1-1872 (8-4-1872) T
McBroom, A. E. to Samuel W. Armstrong 2-13-1856 (2-14-1856) G
McBroom, Ella to John Sexton 2-10-1875 (no return) L
McBroom, Margaret Frances to Isaac Green 5-27-1869 (5-30-1869) L
McBroom, Meoma S. to James T. Taylor 8-7-1867 (no return) L
McBroom, Merica to Henry Blakely (Blakey) 7-23-1878 (7-24-1878) L
McBryde, Sarah (Mrs.) to James Scarbrough 4-13-1869 (4-14-1869) Ma
McCabe (McCake?), Josephine T. to James Bangs 7-29-1853 Sh
McCabe, Bridget to Michael Nash 11-12-1847 Sh
McCabe, Cintha to Perry Sutton 7-24-1859 Hy
McCabe, Indiana D. to George M. Hudnell 4-4-1855 Sh
McCabe, Margaret to Thomas Hogan 10-29-1846 Sh
McCabe, Mary M. to Moses E. Pratt 12-23-1867 (12-24-1867) Ma
McCade, Bridget to Thos. Quinn 5-24-1862 (5-25-1862) Sh
McCaig, Eliza Ann to Jno. W. Harris 12-16-1869 Ma
McCaig, Emily J. to James R. Denton 12-6-1862 Ma
McCaig, Julia F. to John W. Winston 5-28-1870 (5-31-1870) Ma
McCail, Margaret to Patrick Joyce 7-10-1863 Sh
McCain, Amanda to Belfast Strong 1-19-1869 (1-21-1869) T

McCain, Amanda to Tom White 8-1-1874 T
McCain, Caroline to Alfred Strong 12-2-1865 (12-7-1865) T
McCain, Eliza H. to A. J. Wilson 12-15-1857 T
McCain, Elizabeth to Benjamine Bennett 12-6-1872 (12-7-1872) Cr
McCain, Elizabeth to Henry Sulivan 12-12-1850 We
McCain, Elizabeth to Wm. A. Dunlop 3-14-1850 We
McCain, Lidia to Dennis Dorrity 12-1-1850 We
McCain, M. E. to J. W. Lynn 6-2-1869 (6-3-1869) T
McCain, M. J. to J. A. Moore 12-3-1866 (12-4-1866) T
McCain, Margaret E. to Alexander J. McQuiston 4-10-1845 T
McCain, Martha A. to John J. Faulkner 11-25-1867 (11-26-1867) T
McCain, Martha Jane to Jonathan Calvin Davis 9-13-1854 T
McCain, Mary (Mrs.) to Nat Mickens 5-23-1861 (5-28-1861) Ma
McCain, Mary C. to Joseph A. Dickson 9-15-1855 T
McCain, Polly to John Stephens 2-10-1848 (2-11-1848) Ma
McCaleb, Amanda to Josiah M. Alexander 11-23-1846 G
McCaleb, Mary Ann to Thomas Sawyers 8-15-1867 G
McCaleb, S. E. to John A. Rentfro 7-25-1848 G
McCaleb, Sarah E. to John C. Thompson 3-1-1853 (3-10-1853) G
McCalister, Emily to Miles Manly 10-19-1867 (10-20-1867) Dy
McCalister, Isabella E. to James T. Swindle 11-8-1842 (11-10-1842) G
McCalister, Lucenda E. to Wm. S. Hampton 3-14-1850 (no return) Cr
McCall, Abby to Abner Vincent 12-7-1868 (12-20-1869?) T
McCall, Ann to S. B. McLemore 4-5-1858 Sh
McCall, C. J. to L. F. Williams 11-16-1866 (11-21-1866) Cr
McCall, Mary to Elijah Foster 9-6-1838 Hn
McCall, Mary to William Whitley 5-26-1864 Mn
McCall, Maryann to G. W. Smith 1-15-1848 (1-17-1848) F
McCall, Matilda T. to Vollentine Bell 3-10-1841 (3-21-1841) G
McCall, Sallie A. to Alfred A. Langstaff 11-13-1871 (11-15-1871) T
McCall, Susan to Vernas? Sherrod 12-29-1866 T
McCalla, Charlotte Ann to John B. Gooch 1-11-1870 T
McCallester, Sarah S. to James W. Tucker 11-1-1841 G
McCalley, Jane E. to George W. Banner 12-30-1868 (1-2-1869) T
McCalley, Martha to L. J. Smith 9-19-1855 (no return) F
McCallister, Elizabeth to Stanly Rushing 1-9-1847 Ma
McCallister, Margaret R. to George L. Pratt 12-11-1848 (12-14-1848) G
McCallum, Mary L. to Geo. Seymore 2-4-1850 Cr
McCalop, Matilda to Henry Parker 12-20-1843 G
McCalvy, Roenna to Thos. M. Witherspoon 1-23-1838 G
McCamack, May J. to John Tuikler 12-17-1856 T
McCampbell, Mary E. to J. Y. McEntire 6-20-1866 Hn
McCampbell, Mary to Adam Vandyck 9-11-1866 Hn B
McCampbell, Sarah F. to Jasper Thomason 11-11-1857 Hn
McCampbell, Susan A. to Andrew R. Bryan 7-20-1859 Hn
McCamy, Margaret to W. D. Douch 11-30-1867 O
McCan, Elizabeth to Squire Wilson 3-16-1840 Hr
McCan, Gaberila A. to Anders Wilson 10-21-1845 (10-30-1845) Hr
McCane, Hettie to G. M. Savage 10-20-1870 G
McCane, Lucinda to H. W. Wright 11-16-1865 Cr
McCane, Martha to David ____ 1-2-1855 Hn
McCanla, Jane H. to William Paden 4-27-1840 T
McCann, D. A. to T. O. Barrett 5-28-1863 Mn
McCarey, Ellender to Benj. F. Trusty 1-1-1845 (1-2-1845) G
McCarey, Melinda to John Woodward 5-16-1825 O
McCargo, Sarah to Sanders Poole 6-10-1852 Sh
McCarley, Hariett to Washington Faris 12-16-1850 (12-18-1850) F
McCarley, Jane to Joseph McKnight 12-7-1839 (12-10-1839) F
McCarley, Martia to Rawlings Robertson 7-9-1846 F
McCarley, Mary to W. C. Reeves 12-21-1852 (no return) F
McCarley, Melinda to Abijah H. Boothe 2-2-1842 (2-3-1842) Hr
McCarmick, Mary E. to F. B. Russell 2-20-1868 Hy
McCarrol, Martha to Mathew Walt 1-12-1869 (1-28-1869) T
McCarroll, Eliza to W. C. Boswell 10-1-1864 (10-2-1864) T
McCarroll, Elizabeth to J. L. Williams 10-13-1842 Be
McCarroll, Elizabeth to J.L. Williams 10-13-1842 Be CC
McCarroll, Louisa to R. J. Wiseman 4-9-1853 Be
McCarroll, Louisa to R. J. Wiseman 4-9-1853 Be CC
McCarroll, Marietta to Saml. Wiseman 7-2-1848 Be
McCarroll, Nancy to Wm. L. Wilson 9-8-1854 (9-14-1854) T
McCarroll, Paralie F. to H. R. Reed 10-12-1853 Be
McCarroll, Sarah Ann to Robert Campbell 4-13-1847 Be
McCarroll, T. S. to J. H. Modlin 2-16-1875 (2-17-1875) Dy
McCartay, Martha to F. M. Coleman 6-9-1850 Hn
McCarter, Elizabeth J. to Robert L. Thompson 9-21-1835 (10-1-1835) Hr
McCarter, Harriet L. to T. E. Jones 1-13-1866 Cr
McCarter, Martha A. to John W. Childress 5-15-1859 (6-16-1859) Hr
McCarthy, Catharine F. to John Scott 7-21-1860 Sh
McCartney, Elizabeth to James M. White 9-17-1859 (9-22-1859) G
McCartney, Sarah J. to James S. Pratt 3-8-1858 (3-9-1858) G
McCartry, Mary to John R. Parker 10-11-1841 (no return) F
McCarty, Catharine to John Gleason 5-16-1858 Sh
McCarty, Catharine to Lowrence Kirby 3-17-1862 Sh
McCarty, Catharine to Michael Minehan 11-1-1855 (11-4-1855) Sh
McCarty, Francis J. (Mrs.) to Thos. J. Neel 6-12-1863 Sh
McCarty, Johanna to James Haley 11-27-1858 (11-28-1858) Sh
McCarty, Margaret to R. Donovan 4-23-1861 (4-24-1861) Sh
McCarty, Mary A. to Don Alonzo Spalding 8-3-1853 Sh
McCarty, Mary A. to James Ortry 12-2-1857 O
McCarty, Mary Ann to David Waher? 1-21-1849 Hn
McCarty, Mary to James Conway 9-16-1854 (9-17-1854) Sh
McCarve, Lucey to W. F. Shoemake 5-9-1874 L
McCarver, Amanda to R. J. E. Byrn 4-25-1874 (4-26-1874) L
McCarver, Lucindia to Isaac Ralph 1-6-1842 Hr
McCarver, Miranda to Thomas J. Tull 3-14-1854 Hr
McCarver, Nicey to William R. Groves 11-17-1858 Ma
McCarver, R. E. to G. W. Hansford 4-10-1856 (4-16-1856) Hr
McCarver, Susan to James Kelly 9-16-1846 Ma
McCarver, Susan to William West 5-2-1837 (5-7-1837) Hr
McCarver, Tabitha J. to John H. Tull 8-22-1859 Hr
McCaslin, Julia A. E. to Thomas J. Ford 10-30-1860 G
McCaslin, L. E. to A. P. Crocker 5-10-1864 G
McCaslin, Lucinda to Nathan Patrick 10-10-1859 (10-11-1859) G
McCaslin, Martha Ann to William S. Fowler 7-15-1850 (7-17-1850) G
McCaslin, Mary E. to John C. McKiney 12-17-1866 (12-18-1867?) Cr
McCaslin, Mary E. to Thomas J. Vickers 12-7-1867 (12-12-1867) Cr
McCaslin, Mary to J. H. McCollum 9-5-1867 G
McCaslin, Nancy to Joseph E. Matthews 5-15-1835 (5-19-1835) G
McCaslin, Nannie to Joseph Phillips 1-13-1870 G
McCaslin, Pheba to Baily Madison 5-6-1828 (5-22-1828) Ma
McCaslin, Susan E. to Young J. Hammons 1-15-1851 (1-16-1851) G
McCaslin, Susan J. to W. P. Ford 1-23-1861 G
McCauley, Eliza to George M. Beaver 1-22-1851 Cr
McCauley, Elizabeth M. to John Voss 12-12-1849 T
McCauley, Frances L. to C. H. Cogbill 10-30-1854 (no return) F
McCauley, Gertrude to Wm. Benj. Rust 6-29-1863 (6-30-1863) Sh
McCauley, Lucy A. to F. A. Massey 3?-13-1850 (no return) F
McCauley, Mary Hood to James Carroll Taylor 1-8-1845 (1-9-1845) T
McCauley, Mary Jane to James J. Thompson 12-?-1858 (12-9-1858) Ma
McCauley, Mary to Jonas? M. Smith 11-1-1848 F
McCauley, R. A. to T. E. Hanburg 2-12-1862 (2-16-1862) Sh
McCauly, Rachael A. to A. J. Cherry 12-17-1861 (no return) Hy
McCavley, Margaret to Beverly McGehee 12-29-1866 Hn B
McCaw, M. M. to D. B. Marshall 1-9-1868 O
McCearly], Sarah to Daniel Osment 12-26-1846 (12-27-1846) Hr
McCenley, Rebecca A. to Christian Ganthenheim 2-11-1853 Sh
McChord, Margaret to James Sellers 9-17-1855 Ma
McChristian, Emily to John M. Bucy 8-14-1843 (no return) Hn
McChristie, Lyde O. to John J. Bolding 1-3-1877 Hy
McCissick, Martha to James B. Love 9-24-1848 Hn
McClabahan, Susan to John McGevany 10-30-1838 (11-1-1838) Ma
McClain, Belle to H. E. Moffitt 7-1-1875 Hy
McClain, Charlotte to Will Eskridge 5-3-1857 We
McClain, Frances to J. W. Story 2-1-1866 Hn
McClain, J. A. to C. F. Meadow 3-31-1867 Hn
McClain, M. C. to John R. Kuykendall 9-13-1863 Hn
McClain, Martha to Ned Cocke 1-5-1871 F B
McClain, Mary A. to J. E. Kirkendall 12-8-1855 (no return) Hn
McClain, Mary A. to William Lowery 4-9-1857 We
McClain, Nancy R. to W. G. Spencer 5-26-1850 Hn
McClain, Nancy to James M. Jones 12-8-1857 Hn
McClain, Perlina to William Ward 8-5-1841 Hn
McClain, Sarah A. to John F. Hill 5-26-1859 Hn
McClain, Sarah Jane to J. H. Malone 8-30-1865 Hn
McClain, Virginia C. to Martin D. Lamb 1-12-1854 Hn
McClaland, Basora to George Wade 11-15-1854 (11-18-1854) Ma
McClame, Sallie Ann to H. M. Pritchard 8-12-1873 Cr
McClamick, Maggie D. to E. Z. Simmons 11-23-1870 T
McClanahan, Alsy M. to Stephen Scoggins 6-28-1836 (not executed?) Hr *
McClanahan, Jane to Robert McClelland 12-30-1868 G
McClanahan, Mary F. to Wm. F. Henry 12-9-1868 Ma
McClanahan, Mary M. to W. J. Morton 11-30-1865 Hy
McClanahan, Melissa W. to Clark Lewis 4-24-1831 Sh
McClane (McCana), Ann Eliza to Daniel W. Funk 5-16-1850 Sh
McClane, Lettie to Alfred Johnson 6-15-1867 (no return) F B
McClaney, F. M. to Francis M. Wilson 5-6-1863 Sh
McClannohan, L. R. to John T. Z. Marshall 11-26-1867 (11-28-1867) T
McClard, Julia A. to Madison Pope 4-6-1858 Sh
McClaran, Lucy E. to Geo. W. Sharp 3-25-1846 (3-26-1846) F
McClaran, Martha D. to A. V. B. Rolfe 12-12-1853 (no return) F
McClaren, Harriet F. to John D. Crossett 11-25-1868 (11-26-1868) F
McClaren, Mary to S. M. Davis 1-28-1853 (no return) F
McClaren, Nancy Jane to Zachariah Taylor Potts 6-26-1870 G
McClaron, Martha A. to A. M. Ward 2-16-1859 (2-17-1859) F
McClarran, E. A. to Wm. W. Nelson 1-28-1842 (2-10-1842) F
McClary, Sarah A. to F. J. H. McKinley 12-31-1851 (12-18?-1851) Hr
McClary, Ellen R. to Washington E. Hamilton 4-11-1838 Cr
McClary, Margarett to Joseph Hamilton 8-3-1830 G
McClary, Martha E. to James A. Hall 4-4-1843 Cr
McClary, Mary L. to Milton T. Tarvin 7-8-1836 (7-14-1836) G
McClary, Matilda to Donald McIver 3-14-1828 G
McClaskey, Martha to Thomas Walsh (Welsh) 1-20-1848 Sh
McClay, Abigail to Augustus W. King 12-4-1826 (12-5-1826) G
McCleary, Dicy to Willis Dickson 1-3-1867 G

McCleary, Mary A. to Isaac E. Clark 9-30-1830 Ma
McClellan, Belle J. to R. N. Davis 12-15-1859 G
McClellan, Bettie L. to R. M. Moore 2-2-1860 F
McClellan, Cate to Clem McCree 6-29-1867 G
McClellan, Eliza J. to George B. Hicks 10-9-1849 (10-10-1849) Ma
McClellan, M. C. to S. G. Sparks 5-16-1866 F
McClellan, Margaret E. to William L. Mays 2-5-1851 F
McClellan, Mary C. to Benjamin M. Hicks 10-26-1847 (10-28-1847) Ma
McClellan, Mary Coffy to David Alexr. Brunson 1-12-1846 (1-13-1846) T
McClellan, Penelope to Jesse Thomas 5-6-1828 Hr
McClellan, Permelia Jane to John Menasco? 3-8-1852 T
McClellan, Sarah A. to John A. Sheffield 2-3-1857 (2-19-1857) Hr
McClelland, Laura to Edward Deziel 12-20-1876 L
McClelland, Lida to Jno. J. W. Ingram 10-26-1868 (10-27-1868) Ma
McClelland, Mary Josephine to John G. McClelland 2-10-1867 (2-20-1867) L
McClelland, Nancy to John W. Hollamon 12-28-1838 L
McClelland, Sallie to Saml. Payne 2-17-1866 T
McClelland, Sarah J. to James K. P. Boydston 10-3-1866 L
McClelland, Susan to James Spencer Smith 2-9-1853 (2-15-1853) T
McClelland?, Mary to Henry Caldwell 8-23-1843 (8-24-1843) L
McClellen, Martha A. to James W. Tomlin 2-17-1852 Ma
McClemore, Sarah C. to Ezariah Pealer 7-5-1856 Cr
McClenahan, Nannie to Francis Thomas 1-14-1869 (1-20-1869) T
McClenahan, Sallie to S. W. Bedingfield 11-9-1874 (11-11-1874) T
McClennand, Agness to James M. McCommon 1-2-1846 (1-6-1846) Hr
McClerkin, Elizabeth to Alexander Hindman 3-26-1860 (3-29-1860) T
McClerkin, Martha H. to Robert P. Harper 5-17-1841 (5-18-1841) T
McClerkin, Mary E. to W. R. McLaughlin 3-7-1874 (3-18?-1874) T
McClerkin, Sarah Ann to Wm. H. Thompson 12-1-1873 T
McCleur, Mary to Joseph Bellue 5-29-1837 G
McCleur, Nancy to John W. Gately 7-3-1846 (7-7-1846) G
McClinsley, Louisa E. to David R.? Jackson 4-10-1848 (4-13-1848) F
McClintock, Mary E. to T. W. Layne 12-21-1881 (12-22-1881) L
McClintock, Rachel to Geo. Seymore 11-17-1863 (no return) Cr
McClish, Alice to John Crook 1-9-1886 (1-10-1886) L
McClish, Caroline to Jno. Alex Kirkpatrick 10-9-1848 Ma
McClish, Emma to Marion Stanford 1-30-1869 Hy
McClish, Judy to Jack Morland 6-4-1866 (no return) Hy
McClish, Layer to Henry Taylor 8-14-1877 Hy
McClish, Lillie to Robert Lucas 6-5-1884 L
McClish, Martha E. to Robert M. Neely 10-12-1859 Ma
McClish, Mary A. to John F. Lea 5-14-1855 (5-16-1855) Ma
McClish, Tiny to William Nance 3-1-1876 (no return) Hy
McClish, Vina to James Gallaway 1-17-1872 (no return) Hy
McClish, Vina to William Anthony 6-4-1866 (no return) Hy
McClohn, Tennessee to Wm. J. Smith 5-30-1858 Be
McClosky, Martha to J. A. Brown 4-6-1861 (5-2-1861) Sh
McCloud, Elizabeth to Joab Esery 5-11-1830 O
McCloud, Mary T. to Rufus Meek 7-25-1853 (7-26-1853) Sh
McCluer, H. A. to E. (C?) Marshall 4-6-1864 (4-7-1864) Sh
McCluer, Nancy to Ezekiel Hendrick 2-4-1830 Sh
McCluhen, Mary Jane to John A. Moore 11-31-1857 (12-1-1857) T
McClur, Jane to Owen West 10-12-1841 G
McClure, Annenter to John B. Delaney 1-20-1840 (no return) Cr
McClure, Caroline to R. A. Wynn 9-7-1845 Cr
McClure, Catharine Ann to John Watt 9-8-1848 G
McClure, Epsey to William McClure 2-16-1845 Hn
McClure, Ernestine to A. A. Raub 5-2-1864 Sh
McClure, Irene L. to Chas. Stout 5-10-1864 Sh
McClure, Isabella to James W. McCalla 5-19-1831 Sh
McClure, Jane to John Wilson 12-20-1831 Sh
McClure, Martha to Wm. Maxwell 3-17-1850 We
McClure, Mary E. H. to John N. Williamson 1-6-1868 (1-7-1868) Cr
McClure, Mary to James M. Balleu 6-5-1837 G
McClure, N. N.(Mrs.) to J. W. Jones 6-10-1866 G
McClure, Nancy to B. F. Pool 1-20-1856 Sh
McClure, Oney to Pleasant M. Marberry 5-25-1856 Hn
McClure, S. E. to P. T. Clark 11-26-1853 Sh
McClure, Sarah to W. J. L. Markham 11-12-1863 Hn
McClurkin, Nancy Jane to Augustus P. Moffatt 2-6-1850 T
McCluskey, Issabella to Michael Brandon 11-2-1864 (no return) Cr
McClusky, Emiline to Hardy Williamson 12-4-1867 (12-5-1867) Dy
McCollister, Elizabeth Jane to Josiah L. Claybrook 6-26-1849 (6-27-1849) G
McCollough, Mary Ann to Jacob J. R. Reeves 12-7-1855 Ma
McCollum, Ailsey to Henry Sims 8-26-1868 G B
McCollum, Amanda to L. L. Sanders 12-29-1863 Mn
McCollum, J. M. to J. F. Leach 1-?-1867 (1-15-1867) Cr
McCollum, L. B. to J. M. Roberts 8-10-1872 (8-13-1872) Cr
McCollum, L. F. to B. T. Frost 3-4-1872 (3-5-1872) Cr
McCollum, Lydia Bell to Middleton Bradford 11-26-1846 Sh
McCollum, M. A. to J. M. Farrier 2-10-1860 (2-12-1860) O
McCollum, M. A. to J. M. Farrior 2-10-1860 (2-11-1860) O
McCollum, Mahala to John H. Wright 11-10-1863 (11-12-1863) Cr
McCollum, Martha to G. T. Belew 5-25-1870 (5-26-1870) Cr
McCollum, Mary F. to James J. Johnson 3-3-1862 Mn
McCollum, Mary J. to J. M. Williamson 4-26-1866 Cr
McCollum, Nancy to Mark Spencer 3-9-1829 Ma
McCollum, Rebecca to John M. Johnson 5-24-1837 (5-?-1837) Sh
McCollum, Sarah A. to John C. Jones 5-12-1857 Cr
McCollum, Sarah to John A. Ward 7-5-1853 Cr
McColun, Sarah A. to Wm. T. Thrukill 10-13-1847 Cr
McCombs, Louisa Ellen to Thomas Wright 12-27-1864 Sh
McCombs, Mary A. to James H. Biggs 1-13-1859 G
McCombs, Mary J. to John S. Cothran 12-19-1853 (no return) F
McCombs, Rosa P. to J. R. Chamberlain 2-1-1877 Dy
McCombs, Sinay to Edwin P. Shipes 9-4-1854 (9-5-1854) Ma
McCommack, Mary to Arche English 9-23-1868 (9-24-1868) T
McCommon, Cynthia A. to T. J. Street 12-15-1860 (1-1-1861) Hr
McCommon, M. J. to J. C. Dixon 1-1-1861 Hr
McCommon, Martha C. to Nathan M. Mitchell 9-17-1842 (9-22-1842) Hr
McCommon, Mary Catherine L. to Nazerith Perry 11-10-1853 Hr
McCommon, Sarah Ann to George W. Thompson 1-1-1851 (1-2-1851) Hr
McCommon, Tabitha A. to J. F. Caldwell 2-20-1849 (2-22-1849) Hr
McCommons, Talibhta C. to William T. Rainey 10-17-1848 (10-19-1848) Hr
McCommun?, Elizabeth D. to B. B. Beard 12-16-1847 (12-23-1847) Hr
McConell?, Polly to Elijah Coffey 3-22-1847 Hr
McConico, Frances A. to Geo. Edward Davie 10-10-1877 Hy
McConnell, Bell to Albert Cooper 10-30-1872 (11-1-1872) T
McConnell, Elizabeth to John Krider 10-3-1851 (no return) F
McConnell, M. E. to D. G. Rose 10-12-1861 (no return) Hn
McConnell, Margaret J. to A. M. Kelly 12-18-1863 (no return) Hn
McConnell, Mary M. to Frank L. Barkley 11-19-1852 (11-22-1852) G
McConnell, Nancy to Ludwell Smith 3-16-1842 (no return) Hn
McConnell, Sarah D. to James W. Landrum 2-13-1861 G
McConnell, Sarah J. to Thomas J. Jones 11-1-1866 Hn
McConnell, Susan to Martin H. Adams 1-16-1854 Hn
McConnell, Susan to Martin H. Adams 1-24-1854 (no return) F
McCook (or Cook?), Lucy to Chris. Muller 10-22-1860 (10-23-1860) Sh
McCool, Annie E. to Samphord A. Miller 1-24-1878 Hy
McCool, Mattie E. to J. S. Ranlin 1-13-1869 (no return) Hy
McCool, Patsey to Moses Dancy 12-28-1871 Hy
McCool, Patsy to Harvey McCool 9-27-1869 Hy
McCord, Catherine E. to Josiah E. Campbell 6-22-1848 Sh
McCord, Elizabeth to James C. Butler 8-8-1843 Hn
McCord, Frances E. to Jacob Y. Hoofman 1-29-1852 Hn
McCord, Garzilla K. to James S. Stanfield 3-6-1853 Hn
McCord, Liddy to Miles Wilson 3-23-1839 Hr
McCord, Louisa E. to Wesley M. Hicks 8-27-1854 Hn
McCord, Louiza to Sameul H. Pealer 8-1-1843 Cr
McCord, Lydia A. to James O. Bond 5-24-1867 Hn
McCord, Mahala C. to William R. Hicks 4-3-1861 (no return) Hn
McCord, Margaret to E. A. Waters 12-2-1863 Hn
McCord, Martha H. to A. P. Arington 8-5-1873 (8-6-1873) Cr
McCord, Mary W. to Uriah Acres 2-29-1847 Hn
McCord, Nancy A. to Wm. R. Durrett 8-16-1870 Ma
McCord, Nancy C. to Chas. D. Hoofman 8-7-1851 Hn
McCord, Nancy C. to James J. Hedge 12-14-1848 Hn
McCord, R. E. to F. M. Stokes 8-18-1846 Cr
McCord, Rebecca to Amasa Gillet 1-9-1844 (1-11-1844) Hr
McCord, Walker to M. L. Wood 2-6-1883 L
McCord?, Elizabeth J. to Beverley F. Cate 9-30-1860 Hn
McCorkle, A. L. to E. P. Pope 11-5-1873 (11-6-1873) Dy
McCorkle, Catherine to John Merchant 12-20-1849 Hn
McCorkle, E. J. to J. L. Cawthon 2-19-1877 (2-21-1877) Dy
McCorkle, Elizabeth J. to Henry W. Reeves 12-19-1861 Dy
McCorkle, Ellen to Monk Smith 10-27-1875 (10-28-1875) Dy B
McCorkle, J. A. to J. B. Murrell 7-18-1858 Hn
McCorkle, M. C. to Joseph J. Mitchell 1-17-1848 Hn
McCorkle, M. L. to J. T. Gregory 5-24-1864 (5-25-1864) Dy
McCorkle, Margaret E. to John L. Lemonds 10-4-1865 Hn
McCorkle, Margaret E. to L. D. Canaday 6-30-1858 Hn
McCorkle, Mary Jane to Charles T. Strain 12-26-1860 (1-2-1860?) Ma
McCorkle, Matilda to William L. Dillahunty 1-1-1838 Hn
McCorkle, Nancy M. to Thomas H. Conway 8-9-1854 Hn
McCorkle, Rachel to James H. Oneal 5-16-1859 Ma
McCorkle, Susan L. to Robt. H. McNail 11-23-1869 G
McCormack, E. J. to J. J. Garret 12-17-1872 T
McCormack, H. A. to J. E. Shelton 12-22-1875 Dy
McCormick, Ann to Patrick Carney 2-1-1859 (2-3-1859) Sh
McCormick, Ann to Patrick Donnely 10-10-1854 Sh
McCormick, Celia F. to Henry Dale 8-13-1860 Sh
McCormick, Ellen to John McGuinn (McGrinn?) 10-21-1861 Sh
McCormick, Harriet N. to John S. Frierson 2-5-1855 (2-8-1855) T
McCormick, Julia Ann to A. W. Sidebottom 11-13-1867 (no return) Hn
McCormick, R. B. to Jas. L. McLintock 5-6-1867 T
McCorry, Mary P. to William F. Henderson 11-8-1847 Ma
McCowel, Anne Marie to Joseph J. T. Mason 11-23-1845 Hn
McCowel, Ann E. to Alfred H. Mays 11-7-1859 (11-8-1859) Ma
McCoy, B. M. to Charles Allen 12-27-1866 G
McCoy, Betsey to David McClanahan 7-28-1830 (7-28-1830) Hr
McCoy, Elizabeth to Flint Barnett 1-18-1859 O
McCoy, Frances M. to John H. Wood 6-18-1856 (6-19-1856) T
McCoy, Frances to Sebron Smothers 12-18-1868 (12-22-1868) Cr
McCoy, Frances to T. R. Newborn 7-23-1876 Hy

McCoy, Jane to O. D. Ward 3-5-1849 (3-14-1849) Ma
McCoy, Josephine A. to G. W. Stewart 11-23-1876 Hy
McCoy, Lavina to Lance Graves 1-18-1842 L
McCoy, Lou to T. J. Fitzhugh 2-28-1877 (2-29?-1877) Dy
McCoy, Louisa to Jno. G. Thomas 12-20-1875 Hy
McCoy, M. A. to J. H. Hamilton 11-13-1866 G
McCoy, Mahaley to James H. Mangrum 4-6-1858 (4-8-1858) G
McCoy, Martha Mary to Newton Henry Bond 2-9-1863 (2-10-1863) Sh
McCoy, Martha S. to Julus F. Smith 5-29-1862 Mn
McCoy, Martha to Wilie Markham 11-5-1849 (11-8-1849) G
McCoy, Mary Jane to Wright Briley 8-20-1877 Hy
McCoy, Mary Margaret to Craddock Vaughan 1-20-1846 (1-21-1846) T
McCoy, N. H. to W. D. Blankinship 3-12-1884 (3-13-1884) L
McCoy, Nancy E. to Samuel J. Cook 3-14-1859 (3-18-1859) G
McCoy, Pinckney A. to M. N. Gowan 1-2-1877 (1-4-1877) Dy
McCoy, R. C. to S. F. Frazier 12-19-1867 G
McCoy, Rebecca to John W. C. Mace 7-16-1850 (7-18-1850) Hr
McCoy, S. L. to J. M. Walker 12-19-1869 G
McCoy, Sarah E. to Joseph Boylan 1-18-1870 (no return) L
McCoy, Sarah Fina to G. W. Payne 3-22-1860 T
McCoy, Sarah V. to John Fitzhugh 10-20-1875 Dy
McCoy, Sarah to N. J. Stewart 9-4-1869 Hy
McCoy, Sophia to G. B. Davis 9-15-1859 Sh
McCoyen?, Jane M. to D. M. C. Miles 9-13-1828 Hr
McCracken, C. J. to J. J. Gray 11-2-1870 (11-4-1870) Dy
McCracken, M. E. to G. W. Mills 5-22-1869 (no return) Dy
McCracken, Madlena to William Atchison 6-8-1839 (no return) Hn
McCracken, Paula A. to James M. Gibson 3-24-1863 Cr
McCracken, Sarah A. to William H. Simms 8-10-1847 (8-11-1847) G
McCracken, Sarah to Oscar McCargo 1-22-1869 (1-28-1869) Cr
McCracken, Susan Jane to Wm. H. Spellings 10-28-1869 G
McCrackin, Eliza A. to John M. Cannon 12-26-1864 (12-27-1864) Cr
McCrackin, Ella to N. L. Bowman 4-24-1875 (4-28-1875) Dy
McCrackin, Fanlee A. to James M. Gibson 3-21-1863 (no return) Cr
McCrackin, Mattie to M. H. Higdon 2-14-1874 (2-18-1874) Dy
McCrackin, Polly to James M. Walls 9-11-1861 (no return) Dy
McCraey, Martha to Samuel C. Henderson 1-12-1856 (1-17-1856) G
McCraith, Alice to Byran Kiernam 3-2-1851 Sh
McCrare?, Mary to James L. Wright 9-1-1853 T
McCrary, Catharine to N. S. Hancock 8-23-1856 (8-28-1856) G
McCrary, Susan E. F. A. to Thomas D. Locke 11-29-1860 We
McCraw, Anne? to _____ Tycer 5-18-1863 T
McCraw, Bettie to Thomas H. Lamkin 4-1-1869 T
McCraw, Catharine to Braxton Melton 12-29-1869 (no return) F B
McCraw, Elizabeth to Thos. C. McCraw 10-26-1861 T
McCraw, Martha D. to John Craig 6-26-1866 (6-28-1866) T
McCraw, Mary A. to Mark Manual 11-12-1865 Mn
McCraw, Mary Elizabeth to Zachariah Tyre 2-9-1842 T
McCraw, Orlenia to Alfred H. Ralph 8-6-1855 (8-16-1855) T
McCraw, P. Ann to A. L. Forbiss 12-6-1859 (9-8-1859) T
McCraw, Patsey W. to Littleton W. Trobough 5-29-1844 T
McCraw, Penelope to Richard Turner Wright 11-18-1848 (11-20-1848) T
McCraw, Penelopee Ann to L. A. Forbiss 12-6-1859 T
McCrean, Almedia Ann to William H. Wheeler 9-26-1846 (10-4-1846) F
McCree, E. V. to William Taylor 12-1-1864 G
McCree, Ellen to John Wilkins 12-12-1866 G
McCree, Mitta A. to Baccus Carmack 11-8-1867 (11-10-1867) F B
McCreight, Harriet R. to Robert Miller 9-5-1848 (9-7-1848) T
McCreight, Mary Ann to Wm. James Strong 9-25-1850 (9-26-1850) T
McCreight, Mrs. M. A. to J. H. Blanchard 6-21-1846 T
McCrewry, Mary A. to Andrew J. Holliday 12-30-1857 Hr
McCrocker, Mary A. to Matthew C. Scoby 6-27-1839 Cr
McCrorry, M. C. to J. L. Perry 8-5-1866 Hn
McCrory, Anna R. to Alexander Ragan 9-3-1861 Ma
McCrory, Eleanor (Mrs.) to Richard Bess 4-30-1857 Ma
McCrory, Jane Milisse to Rufus P. Crawford 10-2-1848 (10-4-1848) Hr
McCrory, Martha to Crock Harris 2-22-1876 (2-24-1876) L
McCrory, Martha to Robert Galloway 8-7-1839 (8-8-1839) Hr
McCrory, Mary N. to Josh R. Woodson 2-2-1856 Hr
McCrory, Sarah L. to Jordan D. James 10-31-1859 (11-2-1859) Ma
McCrory, Susan J. to Claiborne Webb 2-4-1856 Ma
McCrory, Susan to Jessee H. Hicks 2-14-1861 (no return) Hy
McCue, Mary to Austin Daneri 8-11-1853 (8-21-1853) Sh
McCuiston, Elizabeth A. to James A. Moody 7-21-1860 Hn
McCuiston, Nancy to Joel Ethridge 2-1-1840 (no return) Hn
McCullaf, Sarah to Patrick Bourk 2-21-1862 (2-24-1862) Sh
McCullar, Mary to Lewis Seay 7-25-1863 Mn
McCuller, Nancy to Jo Brown 12-30-1873 T
McCuller, Sallie to Charley Anderson 2-1-1872 Hy
McCulley, Sarah to James Brinkley 3-1-1847 (3-3-1847) F
McCulloch, Adalaide to W. H. Marlow 11-20-1877 Dy
McCulloch, Charlott to Ben Thomas 8-24-1867 G B
McCulloch, Elizabeth to Thomas Murray 10-29-1862 (no return) Hy
McCulloch, J. E. to E. B. Cayce 4-23-1860 G
McCulloch, Lydia to Garland F. Green 7-16-1868 G B
McCulloch, Polly to John McCarty 9-22-1831 Sh
McCulloch, Sarah C. to Thomas J. Carter 11-12-1861 G
McCulloch, Susan to Merritt Reece 10-12-1867 G
McCulloch, Theodora to Jas. C. McDearman 12-4-1867 Hy
McCulloch, Frances O. L. to Charles Parish 8-29-1831 G
McCullock, Jennett to Peyton S. Hamilton 1-13-1849 (1-23-1849) Ma
McCullough, Ann to Thomas Friar? 1-28-1853 Hn
McCullough, Charlotte J. to John L. Duncan 2-18-1873 (2-20-1873) T
McCullough, Emily to William O. Travis 5-8-1866 Hn B
McCullough, Lucy to A. R. Pace 8-20-1875 (8-22-1875) Dy
McCullough, Mariah to Owen McCullough 5-21-1866 (no return) Hn B
McCullough, Martha D. to William H. Atkins 5-13-1866 Hn
McCullough, Mary A. T. to Edward R. Clement 8-10-1859 Ma
McCullough, Nancy Ann to W. H. Grigsby 11-16-1872 (11-19-1872) T
McCullough, Paralee to Caswell Teague 5-21-1866 (no return) Hn B
McCullough, R. J. to J. N. Reaves 10-18-1870 (10-19-1870) Cr
McCullough, Rebecca to William Tharpe 6-8-1867 (no return) Hn B
McCullough, Sarah to W. L. Teague 1-31-1861 Hn B?
McCullough, Susan Isabella to Lumbus Rushing 4-5-1856 (no return) Hn
McCullough, Susan L. to John M. Hobbs 8-18-1874 (8-20-1874) T
McCullough, T. J. to R. W. Bailey 12-1-1873 G
McCullum, Frances G. to Silas S. Clark 3-17-1841 Cr
McCully, Charity to Robt. McCally 2-24-1850 (3-5-1850) F
McCully, Lucy to George Matthews 9-4-1868 (no return) F B
McCully, M. C. to J. M. McCully 4-3-1860 (4-5-1860) F
McCully, M. E. to Wm. D. McLoid 11-23-1854 Cr
McCully, Mary E. to John Walis 1-3-1853 (no return) F
McCully, Salak? to Anderson Warren 4-20-1866 (no return) F B
McCully, Sarah E. to E. W. Harrison 9-18-1854 (no return) F
McCulough, Sarah to William Wilson 12-31-1857 T
McCure, Mary to Martin Dennie 8-11-1853 Sh
McCurley, Minerva to Monroe Richmond 1-5-1880 (1-6-1880) L
McCutchan, Martha to Caleb A. Robertson 9-17-1849 (9-19-1849) G
McCutchen, Bell to Anthony Perry 3-14-1868 Dy
McCutchen, Caroline to Jo B. McCorkle 12-20-1871 (12-21-1871) Dy
McCutchen, Georgia to John Barnes 3-7-1873 (3-25-1873) Dy
McCutchen, Laura A. to A. F. Dickson 11-26-1866 (no return) Dy
McCutchen, Margaret to R. F. Wigfall 7-23-1875 (7-24-1875) Dy
McCutchen, Mary J. to Jordan Kilzer 10-26-1860 G
McCutchen, Mary to J. S. Thompson 12-30-1868 (no return) Dy
McCutchen, N. C. to T. E. Blair 7-28-1873 (7-31-1873) Dy
McCutchen, Parlee to Ed Chamberlin 5-16-1872 Dy
McCutchen, S. A. to M. V. Akin 9-4-1871 (9-5-1871) Dy
McCutcheon, Mary F. to William A. Seawright 10-26-1852 (no return) Hn
McCutcheon, Nancy E. to John H. Bledsoe 12-11-1844 G
McCutchin, Martha to Jerry Mitchel 10-23-1872 (10-24-1872) Cr
McDade, Drucilla to William Morris 3-16-1840 (3-19-1840) F
McDade, Nancy to P. G. Womble 10-22-1844 (10-31-1844) F
McDaman, Judy Ann to David Campbell 3-8-1873 Hy
McDaman, Vina to George Campbell 7-11-1874 Hy
McDaniel, A. E. to Wm. Pettus 12-30-1871 (1-7-1872) O
McDaniel, Angeline to Geo. W. Moran 3-28-1860 (3-29-1860) Hr
McDaniel, Axie to J. P. Wall 12-22-1873 T
McDaniel, Derinda to Albe Roy Deena 12-10-1840 Sh
McDaniel, E. J. (Mrs.) to Benj. R. Calloway 1-25-1869 (1-27-1869) Ma
McDaniel, Elenor J. to Robert H. Carr 3-3-1853 G
McDaniel, Eliza A. to Daniel Folson 8-26-1869 (no return) Dy
McDaniel, Eliza A. to W. L. Herndon 4-16-1863 Be
McDaniel, Eliza J. to J. J. G. Cutler 10-26-1847 (11-9-1847) G
McDaniel, Elizabeth to J. W. Pitman 3-22-1846 We
McDaniel, Emily V. to Chas. Crenshaw 5-5-1825 Sh
McDaniel, Esther to S. M. Clement 1-30-1868 Be
McDaniel, Fannie to John A. Stamfield 6-3-1867 Hy
McDaniel, Fanny to Gideon Townsend 7-16-1846 Be
McDaniel, Jane to James Young 5-28-1840 Hn
McDaniel, Jane to John Bryant 9-16-1850 (9-17-1850) Hr
McDaniel, Jennie to Daniel Corbit 12-2-1861 (12-19-1861) Sh
McDaniel, Jennie to John H. Parker 12-6-1877 Hy
McDaniel, Julia to A. J. Heathcock 1-13-1878 Hy
McDaniel, Laura C. to David Mathis 2-8-1849 (no return) Hn
McDaniel, Louisa to Jesse Payne 2-25-1832 Sh
McDaniel, Lucy T. to John Ralston 8-29-1822 Sh
McDaniel, Lucy to George Desan 8-30-1821 Sh
McDaniel, Lura A. to Joseph J. Kinsey 5-26-1851 (5-27-1851) G
McDaniel, Lydia A. to John W. Smith 2-1-1848 Hn
McDaniel, M. M. E. to Wm. C. Baird 8-25-1873 (9-4-1873) T
McDaniel, Margaret A. to Canady Howell 10-26-1847 Sh
McDaniel, Margaret B. to Elias A. Goolsby 2-22-1845 (no return) We
McDaniel, Margaret to John McFadden 3-18-1841 Hn
McDaniel, Margarette to D. M. Pearce 3-17-1861 G
McDaniel, Martha A. to W. A. Harrell 2-8-1860 (2-16-1860) Sh
McDaniel, Martha A. to William Pettus 2-7-1845 (2-13-1845) G
McDaniel, Martha to J. D. Fry 9-4-1851 G
McDaniel, Martha to James McElroy 4-23-1846 Be
McDaniel, Martha to James Scott 2-12-1839 Hr
McDaniel, Mary A. to David A. Appleberry 4-5-1838 Sh
McDaniel, Mary E. to W. R. Stockdale 8-2-1863 Be
McDaniel, Mary J. to John L. Fly 9-25-1847 (12-3-1847) G
McDaniel, Mary to John Geoghegan 6-30-1856 (7-1-1856) Hr

McDaniel, Minerva to Rufus Smith 1-22-1880 (1-21?-1880) Dy
McDaniel, N. V. to N. K. Moore 12-25-1860 G
McDaniel, Nancy E. to John A. Gatlin 5-19-1855 (5-27-1855) Hr
McDaniel, Nancy L. to Russell Moore 10-16-1849 Sh
McDaniel, Nancy to Daniel McQuinig 12-17-1839 Be
McDaniel, Nancy to John Greer 6-10-1839 Be
McDaniel, P. to B. F. Acres 2-10-1842 Be
McDaniel, Penny A. to James W. Fithugh 1-11-1871 Hy
McDaniel, Rachael E. to Jas. A. McKnight 12-9-1858 G
McDaniel, Sally to Abraham McKirby 1-11-1830 (1-19-1830) G
McDaniel, Sarah A. to Norman Bond 9-26-1847 Sh
McDaniel, Sarah to John G. Harrell 12-5-1839 Sh
McDaniel, Susan A. to Elijah W. Penick 12-4-1845 Hn
McDaniel, V. A. to E. C. Nubbs 12-11-1860 Be
McDaniell, Margaret S. to Solomon Morris 3-7-1859 (no return) We
McDanile, Syrena to Leonard W. Hendley 12-10-1839 Hr
McDavid, Emma to R. R. Nash 10-11-1860 Dy
McDavid, Harriet to Thos. (Dr.) Nash 10-22-1868 Dy
McDavid, Lucy A. to William N. McKnight 1-16-1864 (1-17-1864) Dy
McDavid, Martha A. to Jos. S. Richardson 1-6-1864 (no return) Dy
McDavid, Mattie to W. W. Edwards 9-14-1870 Dy
McDavid, Rebecca A. to Wiley B. Tipton, jr. 10-9-1866 Dy
McDavitt, Rosella C. to Daniel, jr. Gober 3-27-1849 Sh
McDearman, Jane to Guy Thurmond 1-19-1878 L
McDearman, Mary A. to Berny Wakefield 11-6-1884 L
McDearman, Melvina to William H. Mason 3-9-1869 (3-14-1869) L
McDearman, Mollie E. to W. E. Burks 2-26-1872 (2-28-1872) L
McDearman, R. J. to J. F. Haskill 1-7-1869 (not executed) L
McDearmon, A. F. to Neil B. Rucker 3-13-1873 Dy
McDearmon, Jenny to Hannibal Fly 1-14-1869 G G
McDearmon, Lizzie to Charles Eison 3-11-1879 (3-12-1879) L B
McDearmon, M. (Mrs.) to R. W. Atkinson 11-11-1867 G
McDearmon, M. A. to W. J. Davidson 12-7-1852 Hn
McDearmon, Mary to George P. Pritchett 8-1-1847 Hn
McDearmon, Mary to Robert Thurmond 12-28-1871 L
McDearmon, Mary to Thomas Wright 3-5-1881 (3-9-1881) L
McDearmon, Mollie to Thomas Nelson 12-3-1885 L
McDearmon, P. A. to J. J. McGehee 1-2-1854 (no return) Hn
McDearmon, W. M. to J. P. Smith 12-19-1878 Dy
McDearmond, Frances Ida to Walter James Rogers 12-14-1866 (12-19-1866) L
McDearmont, Julia to Abraham B. Milton 6-24-1870 (6-26-1870) L
McDearmott, Mary to Thos. McCormick 5-1-1856 Sh
McDearon, Ellen to William Adams 12-28-1871 L B
McDermain, Judia to Alexander Alston 2-5-1869 (2-6-1869) L
McDermat, Ann to Patrick McLaughlin 7-28-1858 (5?-28-1858) Sh
McDermitt, Rila to James Rackley 11-24-1832 G
McDermot, Elizabeth to Pat McLaughlin 12-7-1860 Sh
McDermot, Mary to Roddy McDermot 6-9-1857 Sh
McDermott, Margarett to John Erskine 2-11-1861 Sh
McDier?, M. A. to H. W. McQuiston 2-26-1870 (3-1-1870) T
McDill, H. E. to R. W. McLaughlin 5-25-1871 (5-30-1871) T
McDill, Mary A. to Charles B. Simmonton 10-15-1866 (10-16-1866) T
McDogal, Parthema to James T. Williams 10-4-1857 We
McDon, Elmira to Hiram Dempsa 8-27-1868 Dy
McDonal, Lou T. to Joel T. Evans 12-9-1867 (12-10-1867) Ma
McDonald, Ann B. to Daniel Stephens 2-17-1848 Sh
McDonald, Annie to M. D. Fly 1-20-1869 G
McDonald, Catharine to Dennis Ryan 3-30-1861 (3-31-1861) Sh
McDonald, Catharine to Louis A. Nomandin 1-2-1860 Sh
McDonald, Catharine to Moore Stevens 12-24-1849 T
McDonald, Eliza to Samuel A. Baker 1-16-1845 O
McDonald, Elizabeth to Andrew J. Bottenberg 11-22-1864 Sh
McDonald, Elizabeth to James W. Johnson 3-8-1859 Sh
McDonald, Elizabeth to William Johnson 12-2-1852 Sh
McDonald, Emma C. (Mrs.) to Saml. D. McDonald 11-3-1869 Ma
McDonald, Irena to John C. McKoy 9-7-1852 (9-9-1852) Ma
McDonald, Jinnie to Joseph Carter 9-15-1869 (9-20-1869) Cr
McDonald, Johana to John Quisick 6-17-1855 Sh
McDonald, Judy to Byrd Smith 12-15-1861 L
McDonald, Kate to J. W. Graham 8-17-1863 Sh
McDonald, Lavinia to Alexander McDougald 3-3-1870 G
McDonald, M. Teresa to John W. Smith 1-8-1862 (1-16-1862) Sh
McDonald, Mary C. to Samuel B. Forrest 1-17-1852 Ma
McDonald, Mary E. to Jesse J. Brewer 7-19-1838 (7-20-1838) Hr
McDonald, Matilda to Alfred Hall 3-6-1849 (no return) Hn
McDonald, Mollie to Ezekiel Barham 12-8-1869 (12-9-1869) Cr
McDonald, Nancy to John F. Gatewood 11-3-1840 (11-15-1840) Hr
McDonald, Parthina to S. L. W. Jones 7-27-1859 Cr
McDonald, Rossa A. to J. K. P. Walker 7-17-1865 (7-19-1865) O
McDonald, S. J. C. to John J. Williams 7-5-1866 G
McDonald, S. J. to Robert G. Ezell 3-16-1858 Cr
McDonald, Sarah A. to Samuel A. Kelly 2-24-1857 Cr
McDonald, Sarah C. to B. W. Ragan 3-3-1857 G
McDonald, Sophona to John Reynolds 5-21-1861 (no return) L
McDonaugh, Mary A. to A. Urguhart 11-5-1859 Sh
McDonel, Nancy Jane to Thomas B. Madden 10-28-1863 Be
McDonnel, Kate to Thomas W. Green 8-13-1864 (8-15-1864) Sh

McDonnel, Melissa to J. W. Vetetoe 8-5-1861 Mn
McDonnell, Bridget to James Sullivan 11-1-1855 (11-4-1855) Sh
McDonnell, Hanorah to M. N. Krokroska 5-4-1864 Sh
McDonnell, Mary to James Castolow 7-30-1860 G
McDonough, Ann (Mrs.) to Thomas Joyce 11-19-1862 Sh
McDonough, Catherine to Michael Hanley 2-12-1850 Sh
McDonough, Eliza to Wm. H. Whistler 3-15-1851 (3-17-1851) Sh
McDonough, Kate? to P. T. Hughes 8-5-1860 Sh
McDormot, Ellin to Henry Ornsby 3-28-1864 Sh
McDougal, Kate to Bennett Downing 8-25-1869 Cr
McDougal, Mary A. to Richard J. Montgomery 2-18-1850 Cr
McDougal, Mary M. to David D. McCutchen 4-15-1858 G
McDougal, Susan to Samuel Wilson 3-15-1861 Sh
McDougald, Ann to John McLeod 8-20-1839 G
McDougald, Sarah to John R. Bledsoe 4-27-1843 G
McDouggle, Catharine to James McDonald 11-23-1869 (11-25-1869) T
McDougle, Fanny J. to Henry S. Jenkins 5-22-1859 We
McDougle, Margaret to Philemon Y. Bowers 7-2-1829 G
McDougle, Mary D. to Francis, jr. Bliss 7-5-1869 Hy
McDougold, Rebecca to William McLinn 12-18-1843 (12-21-1843) G
McDowd, Suckey A. to E. Arnold 8-5-1854 We
McDowel, Jane to Silas Car 4-14-1870 G B
McDowell, Amanda to Sidney Lynn 12-24-1866 (12-25-1866) F B
McDowell, Anna to Jos. McDowell 8-13-1866 (8-15-1866) F B
McDowell, C. F. H. to L. W. Blakemore 5-3-1854 G
McDowell, Catherine to Aaron Matthews 12-26-1870 (no return) F B
McDowell, Effie P. to James S. Matthews 11-17-1866 (11-20-1866) F
McDowell, Eveline L. to George B. Peters 7-29-1841 Hr
McDowell, Isabela Jane to Rufus S. Hardy 9-9-1847 Hr
McDowell, Jane to Joseph Thomas 2-28-1871 (9-22-1873) F B
McDowell, Juda to Henry Cleaves 1-6-1871 (1-16-1871) F B
McDowell, Lizzie H. to James T. Blair 2-26-1867 (2-28-1867) F
McDowell, Margaret L. B. to John Ashlin 7-25-1837 G
McDowell, Mary J. to W. T. Snowden 2-23-1860 G
McDowell, Mary to John Pope 11-7-1870 (11-14-1870) F
McDowell, Olly Ann to William F. Gill 10-10-1853 (10-12-1853) G
McDowell, R. A. to Horace Posey 11-10-1870 (1-4-1871) T
McDowell, T. B. to John T. Wood 2-7-1852 (2-8-1852) Hr
McDroit, Elener (Mrs.?) to Patrick McGrath 7-30-1864 Sh
McDunn, Adelia to William Frazier (Fracre) 3-5-1851 Sh
McDurtin, Elizabeth to Mortica Bailey 4-7-1846 (4-8-1846) G
McDurmit, Mollie to George A. Mayfield 3-22-1869 (3-24-1869) Ma
McDurmit, Nancy to Pinkny Baker 7-12-1842 (7-13-1842) G
McElever, Martha to Nashville Dolson 5-26-1843 Ma
McElmayee, Lucinda to James M. Hutcheson 9-14-1858 (9-16-1858) O
McElrey, Milley to Jonathan Nix 10-5-1844 (10-9-1844) O
McElroy, Angeline L. to Thomas N. Blackshear 12-11-1852 (1-5-1853) O
McElroy, Mary to Thos. Nolin 8-27-1842 V
McElroy, Sarah Ann to David M. Rogers 3-6-1845 Sh
McElroy, Winnie (Nannie) to Patrick King 3-4-1850 Sh
McElvain, Nancy to Isaac Stanley 7-16-1836 (7-17-1836) O
McElver, Eliza S. to Joseph Scott 2-18-1840 Ma
McElwain, Jane to Harry Yates 12-27-1869 F B
McElwain, Sutha to T. J. Hubbs 11-28-1839 Be
McElwee, Della to Isaac Johnson 12-22-1877 Hy
McElwee, Jane to William Sevier 10-29-1873 Hy
McElwee, Mary E. to Thomas A. Thorn 11-1-1871 Hy
McElwee, Sarah A. to James Jackson 11-19-1850 Ma
McElwee, Sophia to David Perkins 8-15-1872 (no return) Hy
McElyea, Eliza J(ackson) to Richard Watts 10-20-1850 Sh
McElyea, Louisa M. to Charles M. Cunningham 12-24-1855 (12-25-1855) O
McElyea, M. J. to S. C. Pile 9-21-1866 (9-23-1866) Dy
McElyea, Mary Ann to Edward E. Kendall 10-14-1858 O
McElyea, Mary to Duncan Roe 8-15-1839 Be
McElyea, Sarah L. to Morris Helms 8-22-1866 O
McElyen (McElzin), Elizabeth J. to W. C. Perry 5-11-1858 We
McEwen, Bridget to John C. Powers 9-18-1862 Sh
McEwen, Martha A. to William C. Noell 9-8-1840 (no return) Hn
McEwen, Mary E. J. to J. A. Pyland 9-6-1854 G
McEwen, Mary I. to Henry Dowling 10-9-1862 G
McEwen, Tennessee to Nathaniel G. Wood 9-10-1861 (9-16-1861) G
McEwings, Amanda T. to John H. Scates 1-26-1860 We
McFadden, Bettie to Joseph Warren 2-2-1868 G
McFadden, Bettie to Peter Menken 7-23-1874 (7-24-1874) T
McFadden, Callie H. to Jacob Silvertooth 2-14-1871 T
McFadden, Elizabeth to Daniel McCloud 8-1-1842 Hn
McFadden, Elizabeth to Willis A. Pillow 10-5-1854 (no return) Hn
McFadden, Emma to Thomas F. Hill 6-30-1869 G
McFadden, Hattie to Wm. Fuquah 10-13-1877 (10-15-1877) O B
McFadden, Jane to Malcolm McCloud 2-1-1854 Hn
McFadden, L. to M. T. Conyers 11-12-1850 Hn
McFadden, Laura to William M. Hall 11-31-1865 G
McFadden, Letitia L. to E.? H. Arnn 1-9-1863 Hn
McFadden, Lucinda to John (Joseph?) Russell 6-11-1867 G B
McFadden, Luella A. to C. J. Ozier 3-17-1860 F
McFadden, M. J. to T. L. Durrum 10-21-1862 F
McFadden, Manerva to Harrison Kirkland 2-18-1841 Hn

McFadden, Martha Jane to William A. Simpson 11-1-1849 Hn
McFadden, Mary E. to Archibald B. DeBruce 9-9-1866 Hn
McFadden, Mary J. to Wm. B. Collins 12-9-1849 Hn
McFadden, Mary to Harrison Kirkland 6-27-1854 Hn
McFadden, Miss Mollie to N. C. McFadden 1-29-1862 T
McFadden, Penelope to A. J. Stroud 6-7-1857 Hn
McFadden, Perlina to Joseph Thompson 3-2-1870 (3-17-1870) F B
McFadden, Pernicy to David Newman 2-28-1839 Hn
McFadden, S. A. to B. K. Boyd 4-11-1864 (4-12-1864) F
McFadden, Sarah E. to William H. McFarland 12-26-1863 Hn
McFadden, Sarah H. to William C. Neuman? 6-3-1866 Hn
McFadden, Sarah J. to George Jordan 7-29-1867 (8-7-1867) F
McFadden, Sarah to John H. Oates 9-24-1851 (no return) F
McFadden, Sarah to Joseph Carroll 8-30-1842 (no return) F
McFadden, Susan to Benjamin F. Pillow 6-23-1861 Hn
McFadden, Tabitha A. to John B. Walker 2-11-1856 Hn
McFadden, Winney to Beverly Shankle 11-19-1854 (no return) Hn
McFadden, Winny to John Elkins 11-21-1842 Hn
McFaddin, J. B. to H. W. Brown 12-31-1849 (1-1-1850) F
McFadin, Susan F. to Wesley A. Burnett 10-12-1858 T
McFall(McFarlin), Mary L. to Thomas Walker 11-14-1833 (11-27-1833) Hr
McFall, H. F. to James L. Bugg 11-20-1860 Sh
McFall, Mary Jane to Lucian N. Watson 8-26-1850 (8-29-1850) O
McFall, Mary Jane to Lusian N. Watson 8-26-1850 (8-29-1850) O
McFall, Nancy P. to J. H. Finger 10-29-1865 Mn
McFall, Sallie to N. G. Edwards 11-1-1871 O
McFarlan, Lydia V. to Griffin Eblin 5-12-1863 (no return) We
McFarlan, Rhosha to Andrew Dewberry 5-3-1859 Ma
McFarlan, Sarah A. to Charles M. Lemore 8-29-1849 Cr
McFarland (McFail?), Isbella to Tom Harris 2-14-1868 (no return) L
McFarland, Amanda to William H. Harris 12-7-1859 (12-8-1859) G
McFarland, Ann to Joseph W. Clark 7-24-1860 We
McFarland, Anna E. to D. M. Neblett 12-11-1868 (no return) Hy
McFarland, Betty to Thomas Nelson 1-3-1877 Hy
McFarland, Catie to Alfred Williamson 2-5-1869 (1?-14-1869) F B
McFarland, Chaney to Ben, sr. Bates 12-24-1878 (1-2-1879) L B
McFarland, Dicey to William J. Gowan 8-21-1851 G
McFarland, Ednie to Phillip H. Butler 7-27-1866 G
McFarland, Edny M. to J. H. Moore 4-20-1864 G
McFarland, Elizabeth to Charles C. Gentry 12-14-1863 Dy
McFarland, Elizabeth to Wiloly Gardner 12-1-1852 (12-2-1852) G
McFarland, Emily F. to William D. Yearging 2-3-1863 We
McFarland, Frances to James Maberry 2-25-1873 Hy
McFarland, Greeny to David Delph 1-23-1829 (1-24-1829) Ma
McFarland, Jane P. to H. H. Bethshares 9-24-1861 G
McFarland, Jane to Alfred W. Moore 5-23-1850 Cr
McFarland, Jennetta L. to John B. Knox 3-7-1848 (3-?-1848) T
McFarland, L. to J. W. Hall 12-9-1867 (11-12-1868?) G
McFarland, M. J. to J. T. King 3-24-1874 Dy
McFarland, Margaret J. to Aaron L. Norred 8-20-1857 Hn
McFarland, Mary A. to Charles W. Fultin 6-7-1848 (6-?-1848) T
McFarland, Mary E. to William London 2-7-1865 (no return) Hy
McFarland, Mary Jane to Thomas H. Hatch 10-20-1867 Hn
McFarland, Mary to A. P. Mays 12-22-1858 (12-23-1858) G
McFarland, Mary to Richard McGowan 11-21-1842 Ma
McFarland, Mattie to J. W. Johnson 4-16-1870 (no return) Hy
McFarland, Melisa to Jim Wordsworth 12-26-1871 Hy
McFarland, Nancy H. to John H. Long 2-3-1853 Hn
McFarland, Parmelia M. to John M. C. Hagood 3-17-1842 Hn
McFarland, Rebecca Ann to John Bryant 3-13-1869 G
McFarland, Rutha to William Taylor 3-13-1838 (3-22-1838) Ma
McFarland, Sarah Ann to Calvin Williams 4-8-1853 (4-10-1853) O
McFarland, Sarah G. to James P. Haygood 8-17-1847 Hn
McFarland, Sarah to James M. Woodard 12-19-1840 (12-14?-1840) Ma
McFarland, Susie (Mrs.) to Robt. H. Adams 8-22-1871 (8-22-1871) Ma
McFarland, Tabitha J. to James Griffin 3-7-1849 Hn
McFarland, Winnie E. to T. J. Graham 10-31-1874 Dy
McFarlane, Rebecca to James D. Wesson? 1-14-1844 (1-16-1844) T
McFarlen, Emaline M. to W. (Dr.) Taylor 2-9-1847 (2-11-1847) G
McFarlen, Jane to Wiley Bivens 2-24-1858 (2-25-1858) G
McFarlen, Martha L. to William J. Poindexter 2-15-1858 (2-17-1858) G
McFarlen, Mary Jane to R. M. Gowan 11-24-1854 (11-27-1854) G
McFarlin, Anne to J. W. McCoy 3-20-1879 Dy
McFarlin, E. F. to S. E. Johnson 12-27-1866 G
McFarlin, E. J. to L. P. Fitzhugh 10-8-1879 (10-9-1879) Dy
McFarlin, E. to J. Burket 12-3-1841 Be
McFarlin, Elizabeth to Ozy Borin 5-19-1870 (no return) Dy
McFarlin, Mary to John Nelson 2-14-1846 Ma
McFee, Mary to Thos. Irwin 11-12-1860 Sh
McFerin, Nancy Jane to John Applewhite 2-16-1841 (2-20-1841) T
McFerren, Ellen to John Ramsey 6-9-1869 T
McFerrin, Bitha to George Owens 2-15-1871 (no return) F B
McFerrin, Fannie to John Rumsey 9-11-1878 Hy
McFerrin, Louisa to Franklin Krits 9-3-1866 (no return) Hy
McFerrin, Mary L. to James C. Mewborn 11-2-1867 (11-7-1867) F
McFerrin, Mattie Lou to Joshua W. Mewborn 11-2-1867 (11-7-1867) F
McFerrin, Sallie W. to Timothy M. Cartwright 11-7-1870 (11-10-1870) F

McFerson, G. T. to J. W. Youree 9-29-1870 G
McFoslin, Eveline to William Poindexter 1-1-1855 (1-2-1855) G
McFoster, Lucy to J. H. Riddick 12-25-1860 Sh
McGarett, Sarah to David Little 1-28-1836 (2-2-1836) G
McGarg, Alice to A. M. Frost 12-16-1878 (12-18-1878) Dy
McGarg, Mariah to Wiley Paul 12-30-1878 (no return) Dy
McGarrity, B. M. to Ben Littlefield 6-11-1836 (6-?-1836) G
McGarrity, Elizabeth to Laurel Bryant 3-18-1837 (3-20-1837) G
McGarry, Bridget to Pat Shanly (Shanny) 1-7-1861 Sh
McGartary, Sarah A. to S. T. Demoss 12-26-1855 Cr
McGarth, Briget to Michael Archer (Archsed?) 8-24-1842 Sh
McGary, Sarah to Henry Wood 5-6-1876 (5-7-1876) Dy
McGary, Tennessee to Vincent Smith 12-27-1880 (12-29-1880) Dy
McGaugh, M. R. to R. F. Applegate 2-18-1861 (2-19-1861) O
McGaugh, Martha J. to John F. McMurry 9-22-1864 O
McGaughen, Victoria to Willis Swift 7-26-1873 (8-27-1873) Dy
McGaughey, Mary E. to William L. Rush 10-3-1866 L
McGaughey, Victoria to Thomas Mason 12-27-1876 (12-28-1876) Dy
McGaughey, Victoria to Willie Swift 7-26-1873 (no return) Dy
McGaughy, Harriet A. to Sabert L. Burks 10-20-1869 (10-21-1869) L
McGaughy, Laura to Thomas Hunt 3-19-1874 Dy
McGaughy, Myra to W. W. Walker 7-31-1867 Dy
McGavock, Lucinda E. to R. L. Hamil 4-17-1862 (no return) Hy
McGee, A. L. to J. H. Pearson 12-23-1874 (no return) Hy
McGee, Annie E. to Hardy Freeman 10-4-1866 G
McGee, Elda to Stephen Rains 11-2-1839 Ma
McGee, Elizabeth to John B. Harrison 10-27-1842 Hr
McGee, Jane to John E. Gardner 9-27-1838 F
McGee, Judy to Charley Perry 10-8-1852 Cr
McGee, L. T. to R. M. Dixon (Dickerson) 2-4-1873 Hy
McGee, Laura J. to Thomas J. L. King 9-16-1856 (9-17-1856) Sh
McGee, Margaret L. to G. W. Abney 10-29-1867 G
McGee, Martha to Daniel E. Jetton 7-9-1862 Hy
McGee, Martha to John Dickson 4-9-1867 G
McGee, Mary Ann (Mrs.) to G. R. Ellis 3-6-1868 G
McGee, Mary J. to Joseph Shelton 7-31-1854 (8-3-1854) Sh
McGee, Mary Jane to R. G. McGee 8-21-1839 (no return) F
McGee, Mattie to J. L. Wade 9-14-1865 G
McGee, Nancy C. to William N. Harrison 9-16-1846 Ma
McGee, Nancy to W. H. Willingham 9-22-1841 (9-27-1841) F
McGee, Sarah Ann to James Mitchel 2-8-1831 (2-10-1831) Hr
McGee, Sarah E. to M. W. Kerr 10-12-1869 G
McGee, Trangnella A. to Alfred P. Powell 4-1-1859 Ma
McGee, Virginia M. to J. F. Graves 12-15-1860 (12-23-1860) Sh
McGeehe, Mary E. to David Sanford 12-24-1855 (12-28-1855) G
McGeehe, Unica to Archells Thompson 8-6-1835 G
McGeer, Margaret A. (Mrs.) to Harrison Shockley 5-14-1864 (5-15-1864) Sh
McGehe(e), Caroline C. to Stephen G. Starke 2-12-1848 Sh
McGehe, Ruth F. to Stephen Nowlin 2-15-1842 Hr
McGehee, Catharine H. to John Siscoe 7-5-1842 (no return) F
McGehee, Eliza A. to John J. McGehee 5-28-1846 Hn
McGehee, Elizabeth A. to William H. Harri 6-27-1859 We
McGehee, Emily to T. C. Brann 11-5-1857 We
McGehee, Horpolacy? to Joseph B. Matthews 3-3-1843 Hr
McGehee, Isabell V. to B. F. Wallace 12-17-1857 Hn
McGehee, Jane to John T. Thompson 5-3-1838 (no return) F
McGehee, Karen M. F. to John M. Williams 8-27-1855 Hn
McGehee, Mary A. to D. C. Foster 1-8-1852 Hn
McGehee, Mary S. to Henry T. Morris 10-5-1854 Hn
McGehee, Parthenia to Cave Swor 2-15-1867 Hn B
McGehee, Polly Ann to William Gibbins 4-21-1842 Sh
McGehee, Rebecca to William E. Hays 3-7-1839 Hn
McGhe, Sarah to Anderson Eazel 9-6-1856 Sh
McGhee, Ann to William Toole 2-12-1861 Sh
McGhee, Martha M. to Daniel Irvin 7-7-1845 G
McGill, Angeline to John M. Shaw 2-22-1845 (2-25-1845) Hr
McGill, Eliza Ann to John S. Hubbs 9-9-1847 Be
McGill, Elizabeth P. to Joseph R. Ward 11-13-1856 Be
McGill, Elizabeth to W. J. Becton 1-10-1855 (1-11-1855) G
McGill, Emily to Charles Holmes 10-7-1830 Ma
McGill, Jane to T. Watson 6-16-1841 Be
McGill, Luisa to J. M. Brewer 2-24-1864 Be
McGill, Martha to William R. Hawkins 10-11-1855 Hn
McGill, Mary E. to Benjamin H. Green(Greer?) 9-17-1862 Be
McGill, Mary to Simpson Neber 6-3-1855 Be
McGill, Mattie to Andrew McNeal 11-1-1873 T
McGill, Nancy to F. M. Rushing 3-13-1844 Be
McGill, Rebecca A. to John Madra 6-11-1862 Be
McGill, Rebecca C. to J. M. Brewer 7-8-1866 Be
McGill, V. C. to John B. York 10-18-1870 (10-20-1870) Dy
McGinn, Laura A. to Charles Allison 12-3-1866 (12-4-1866) Dy
McGinnis, E. J. to Geo. B. Fuller 9-14-1863 (9-17-1863) Dy
McGinnis, Ellen K. to Thos. H. Phillips 10-5-1854 Sh
McGinnis, Fouzanna to Joh Ogles 4-7-1868 G
McGinnis, Julia Ann to David Jones 12-15-1866 (12-22-1866) Dy
McGinnis, Maggie J. to Wat B. Sampson 4-9-1861 Dy
McGinnis, Rebecca to Wm. Barham 11-30-1872 (12-1-1872) O

Brides

McGinnis, Sarah to Mebane Black 2-2-1871 (2-11-1871) F B
McGlathlen, Mary to Cain Mahoney 3-25-1860 We
McGlaughlin, Elizabeth to Geo. McClendon 12-22-1851 (12-23-1851) Hr
McGlauthron, Margaret to Mike Fitzpatrick 11-29-1877 (12-16-1877) L
McGlohn, Elizabeth to R. H. Smith 9-4-1860 Be
McGlohn, Margaret N. to T. J. Warmack 11-16-1854 Be
McGlohon, Mary to David Brigham 2-3-1846 Be
McGlothlin, Nancy E. to Wesley Dixon 10-12-1853 Ma
McGlown, Sarah to David Brewer 9-4-1844 Be
McGowan, Ann to James McGown (McGowern) 3-20-1856 Sh
McGowan, Elizabeth to William Tennant 10-25-1850 (10-27-1850) T
McGowan, Jane L. to William Maris 12-1-1841 (12-2-1841) Hr
McGowan, Louisa I. to Johnson O'Neal 2-25-1847 Sh
McGowan, Lucy to Henry Overton 11-19-1867 (11-23-1867) F B
McGowan, Margrie to W. M. Lockhart 6-19-1882 (no return) L
McGowan, Mary E. to J. T. Eubanks 12-20-1858 (12-24-1858) Hr
McGowan, Mary J. to Robert Payne 11-30-1857 Sh
McGowan, Sarah Ann to Samuel M. Hastings 1-17-1858 Hn
McGowan, Susan E. to James Houck 9-20-1858 (9-22-1858) Sh
McGowen, Ellen (Mrs.) to Samuel Jones 12-21-1863 Sh
McGowen, Manerva to Samuel W. Shores 11-24-1842 Sh
McGowen, Mollie to D. H. Shillman 12-13-1871 (12-14-1871) O
McGown, Susan to James P. Skillern 12-28-1841 Sh
McGowoan, Z. A. to Emerson O'Neal 2-11-1857 Sh
McGran, Rebecca to S. B. Farthing 9-1-1854 (9-2-1854) G
McGrath, Ann to James Crawford 5-20-1854 (5-21-1854) Sh
McGrath, Margarett to James Walsh 11-12-1862 Sh
McGrath, Mary Jane to Cornelius Ryan 6-16-1860 (6-17-1860) Sh
McGrath, Mary to Barney Reilley 5-21-1864 Sh
McGrath, Mary to Barney Riley 5-21-1864 (5-24-1864) Sh
McGrath, Mary to E. C. Brown 8-2-1862 Sh
McGrath, Mary to Peter Lewis 10-1-1853 (10-20-1853) Sh
McGraw, Bridget to Daniel Clifford 4-8-1861 Sh
McGraw, Mary (Mrs.) to Peter Montgomery 9-23-1863 Sh
McGraw, Sarah E. to Robt. Runnels 6-6-1865 G
McGraw, Sarah to John C. Langston 11-8-1841 Ma
McGraw, Sarah to John Reynolds 4-22-1844 Hn
McGree, Sarah J. to Thomas Bradford 10-2-1862 G
McGregor, Columbia W. to C. R. Harris 1-4-1865 T
McGregor, Elizabeth to J. W. Harris 7-15-1851 T
McGregor, K. F. to O. E. Martin 2-10-1874 T
McGregor, Mary Fannie to John L. Payne 2-6-1861 (2-7-1861) T
McGregor, Mary to James Wright 1-?-1871) (1-19-1871) T
McGregor, Mitty to Tyler Harris 1-3-1867 T
McGregor, Sarah to Thos. B. Kent 1-13-1866 T
McGregory, Caroline to Dick Alexandner 10-23-1869 G B
McGrew, Mary Jane to Richard Parke 12-1-1856 (12-2-1856) Sh
McGrigan, Alice to Michael McMullen 10-28-1846 Sh
McGrogan, Martha Burton to Wm. Henry Hill 2-8-1859 T
McGroom, Rebecca to William Anderson 6-22-1852 Ma
McGuice, Jerusha Ann Jane to Milton A. Coats 11-7-1857 (11-10-1857) T
McGuier, J. W. to Henry L. Harris 12-23-1874 T
McGuin, America F. to W. Wilkins 5-4-1859 T
McGuin, Sarah to M. A. Wormack 6-21-1869 Hy
McGuin, Susan to Landon B. Yarbrough 3-31-1846 (4-3-1846) T
McGuin? (McGuire?), Mary R. to Luther Johnson Craig 9-6-1871 L
McGuire, Ann E. to W. L. Peeler 12-19-1865 T
McGuire, Catharine to Thomas Keefe 5-12-1850 Sh
McGuire, Elizabeth to Albertis Chadwick 7-16-1858 (no return) Hn
McGuire, Emly to Alex. W. Fradle? 5-18-1854 T
McGuire, Martha to George D. Blair 2-9-1846 Ma
McGuire, Mary E. to James Harlow 9-16-1848 (9-18-1848) Hr
McGuire, Minerva Jane to Robert W. Smith 1-24-1852 (1-28-1852) T
McGuire, N. M. to J. E. Dobson 1-3-1865 T
McGuire, Rose to Patrick McCarthy 11-27-1858 Sh *
McGuire, Sarah E. to Wm. H. Griffith 10-20-1860 (10-21-1860) T
McGuire, Susan F. to John C. Flin 8-12-1856 (8-13-1856) Ma
McGusie, Eliza to John G. Mears 12-24-1856 (1-1-1857) T
McHala, Margaret (Mrs.) to Luke McDonnald 2-6-1864 (2-7-1864) Sh
McHala, Margaret (Mrs.) to Luke McDonnell 1-26-1864 Sh
McHenry, Elizabeth to Harvey Wyley 9-29-1841 (9-30-1841) F
McHenry, Jane Ann to Henry Bishup 1-17-1856 Be
McHood, N. M. to J. P. Peel 2-12-1872 (2-14-1872) Cr
McHugh, Mary E. to John H. Morrison 5-28-1862 Sh
McIlroy, Elizabeth to William Taylor 7-6-1824 (7-8-1824) Hr
McIlvain, Lydia A. to Edward Sossaman 8-26-1858 Sh
McIlwaine, Mary M. to W. L. Stegall 4-16-1872 T
McIlwaine, Sallie to H. J. Long 5-22-1871 (5-23-1871) T
McIlwaine, Tersa to R. L. Beaves 2-20-1873 T
McInteref, Shemima to William Graves 1-30-1849 F
McIntire, Ida F. to W. M. Brown 12-14-1878 (12-15-1879?) L
McIntire, Mariah to James Lee 3-14-1864 Sh
McIntire, Sarah E. to D. P. Masey 9-22-1861 Mn
McIntosh, Eliza to Henry G. Buckingham 10-18-1843 Sh
McIntosh, Emily to Henry Frazier? 3-24-1870 (3-30-1870) T
McIntosh, Josephine to J. W. Cribbs 10-9-1878 Dy
McIntosh, Laura J. to Robt. B. Hooks 12-12-1867 (12-15-1867) F

McIntosh, Laura J. to W. S. Turner 4-8-1867 Dy
McIntosh, Maggie A. to J. W. Cribbs 11-16-1875 (11-18-1875) Dy
McIntosh, Maggie to Sam Lea 1-7-1871 Hy
McIntosh, Margarett to J. R. Ross 1-2-1870 G
McIntosh, Mariah J. to William H. Walton 11-25-1869 T
McIntosh, Mary to Rollin J. Locke 11-30-1848 Ma
McIntosh, Samuella to Jacob F. Smith 10-24-1867 T
McIntyre, D. A. to R. Reynolds 1-3-1865 Mn
McIntyre, Flora M. to Robert A. Best 10-14-1884 (10-16-1884) L
McIntyre, Mary to George Evans 9-6-1841 T
McIntyre, Mary to George H. Rogers 2-20-1879 (2-23-1879) L
McIntyre, Rena to P. S. Spaugh 12-30-1879 (12-31-1879) L
McIree, Elizabeth to James Moore 12-21-1848 Sh
McIver, Anne M. to John G. Warner 9-11-1845 M
McIver, Betsy Ann to John R. Bowles 1-30-1856 (2-5-1856) Ma
McIver, Emily to James H. Hathaway 12-30-1862 (no return) Hy
McIver, Emily to William Walton 11-23-1836 Hr
McIver, Louisa A. to Nicholas L. Midyett 11-1-1856 (11-2-1856) Ma
McIver, Margaret to Josiah Ramage 9-9-1831 (9-15-1831) Hr
McIver, Martha to Lennard Piles 10-6-1827 (10-?-1827) Hr
McIver, Mary C. to John R. Reed 3-18-1841 (3-19-1841) Ma
McIver, Mary E. to L. N. Thompson 2-25-1874 L
McIver, Sarah Jane to John J. Thomas 12-8-1845 (12-9-1845) Ma
McKalip, Elmira to William G. Mager 10-19-1861 Mn
McKane, Eliza to Jacob Suliven 11-18-1860 We
McKane, Martha A. to David B. Walker 3-17-1868 (no return) Dy
McKangham, Mary to David Williams 9-27-1828 Hr
McKani, Bettie to W. H. Crane 10-19-1874 (no return) Dy
McKanna, Margreth to Francis B. Millard 8-6-1864 (8-7-1864) Sh
McKasey, Martha A. E. to Wm. D. Hilliard 5-28-1856 (no return) Cr
McKaughan, Frances C. to James Wade 5-13-1846 Hr
McKaughan, Nancy M. to John B. Boyte 7-6-1842 (7-7-1842) Hr
McKaughan?, Jane to William H. McBride 8-14-1829 Hr
McKaughn, Rebecca to Samuel Simpson 2-1-1833 Hr
McKaugn, Amanda A. to Thomas J. Billingsly 2-6-1849 (2-7-1849) Hr
McKay, Elizabeth to George McGuire 1-5-1836 Hr
McKay, Fanny to Henry T. McKay 1-3-1854 (1-4-1854) Sh
McKay, Jane C. to Jackson C. Rawlings 5-9-1849 Sh
McKay, Margaret to Edwin Gay 4-3-1829 Hr
McKearly, Rebecca to David Clinton 6-11-1833 (6-13-1833) Hr
McKeasy, Sarah Adaline to Silas W. McMullin 12-31-1845 F
McKee, Eleanor to Young Gray 12-23-1830 Sh
McKee, Elizabeth to A. L. Pace 8-10-1868 (8-11-1868) Dy
McKee, Frances A. to John Foster 1-6-1851 (1-7-1851) Hr
McKee, Harriet D. to Allen H. Smith 1-25-1870 (no return) F
McKee, Lidia S. to James L. Hailey 10-22-1865 Mn
McKee, Margarite to Henry Mitchell 12-26-1846 Sh
McKee, Martha to James Herron 1-12-1860 Sh
McKee, Mary Ann to Franklin Wood 10-10-1838 (10-15-1838) G
McKee, Mary Margaret to Martin Bizzle 1-26-1850 (1-27-1850) Hr
McKee, Mary T. to Isaac N. Haynes 8-20-1873 (8-21-1873) Dy
McKee, Mollie to John Green 1-2-1869 (1-3-1869) Dy
McKeehan, Nancy to Parkerson Hocker 5-7-1861 Sh
McKeen, ___ C. to R. N. Newell 6-17-1865 G
McKelley, Margaret A. to John W. Delph 3-25-1862 Dy
McKelly, L. D. to Peirce Smiddy 9-5-1857 (9-6-1857) Sh
McKelva, Nancy K. to Wm. N. Hammond 1-5-1852 (1-8-1852) G
McKelvey, Frances A. to William J. Hale 10-18-1856 (10-21-1856) G
McKelvey, Mary F. to Joseph D. Smith 5-30-1857 (5-31-1857) G
McKelvey, Susan J. to James M. Butler 9-20-1858 (9-22-1858) G
McKelvy, Amanda to N. N. Pounds 9-21-1862 G
McKelvy, Louiza to F. M. Glover 12-28-1858 (12-30-1858) G
McKelvy, Martha to Abraham Karnes 2-27-1843 (2-28-1843) G
McKelvy, Melinda A. to Joshua A. Hedgecock 11-10-1860 G
McKelvy, R. M. to James H. Smith 9-12-1867 G
McKelvy, Ruthy M. to William Buchanan 5-17-1859 G
McKelvy, Sarah J. to John W. McMinn 9-25-1866 G
McKencie, Mary S. to T. S. Tincher 8-3-1864 (8-4-1864) Sh
McKendree, Ann D. to Wm. H. Sledge 8-15-1850 (8-20-1850) F
McKendrick, Emily to Harrison Phillips 3-4-1828 G
McKenna, Margaret to Beverly A. Carter 12-22-1853 Sh
McKennan, Mary to Harrison Forrest 1-7-1870 (no return) Hy
McKennon, Mary E. to Wm. J. Robinson 9-3-1844 Cr
McKenny, E. A. to W. C. Grogan 11-14-1855 (no return) Hn
McKenny, Mary J. to J. C. Mills 5-6-1868 (5-7-1868) T
McKenon, Nancy A. to Felix Robertson David 1-25-1842 (1-26-1842) T
McKentosh, Nancy A. to John A. McKentosh 8-6-1842 (8-7-1842) G
McKenzie, Caroline to Thomas Kirk 9-7-1861 O
McKenzie, Catherine to Shavers Partee 5-5-1870 G B
McKenzie, Ida to John Kohnmann? 12-4-1878 G
McKenzie, Mary Jane to William H. Hord 1-23-1839 O
McKenzie, Mary to Ezekial Humphries 8-27-1837 Hr
McKenzie, Nancy Caroline to James P. Pierce 12-4-1867 Be
McKenzie, Nancy M. to Johna? Kindrick 12-18-1821 Mn
McKenzie, Nancy to B. F. Peeler 1-14-1869 Be
McKeown, Nancy to Richard McAllelly 4-10-1833 (4-11-1833) G
McKeown, Sarah to J. D. Rentfro 1-22-1857 G

McKerly, Mary Ann to T. A. Barnes 3-23-1833 Hr
McKevor, Julia to Thomas Geary 7-8-1855 Sh
McKey, Ellender to Thomas Burrows 7-9-1840 Sh
McKey, M. M. to W. M. Davidson 4-29-1865 G
McKezick, Mahaly to James Montgomery 12-17-1836 G
McKiney, Amanda J. to James H. Burns 11-28-1866 (12-2-1866) Cr
McKiney, Martha Ann to Joseph F. Artrup 3-9-1869 (3-10-1869) L
McKinley, E. R. to S. H. Childress 2-27-1878 (2-28-1878) L
McKinley, Isabella to Edward Ballinger 3-13-1858 (3-16-1858) L
McKinley, Louisa J. to Stephen A. Childress 12-26-1855 (12-27-1855) L
McKinley, Margaret S. to William G. Hogsett 8-22-1842 (8-24-1842) L
McKinley, Minda to Jerry Jones 10-29-1870 F B
McKinley, Sarah to Edward Ballinger 2-1-1843 (no return) L
McKinly, Mary A. C. to Josiah C. Bullington 11-8-1850 (11-14-1850) Hr
McKinne, Sarah J. to Hezekiah Cheshire 10-2-1854 (10-3-1854) Hr
McKinne, Zelphi A. E. to John McKee 12-12-1848 (12-16-1848) Hr
McKinnen, Elizabeth to Israel Watkins 6-6-1836 Hr
McKinnen, Sarah C. to Lewis A. McDonald 12-24-1870 (no return) Hy
McKinney (McKinna), Joanna to Peter T. Randel (Randle) 7-15-1849 Sh
McKinney, Amanda M. to James Tuft 5-10-1860 (5-13-1860) Sh
McKinney, Ann to Owen McPortland 4-4-1864 (4-5-1864) Sh
McKinney, Caroline to Robert Williamson 11-3-1858 Cr
McKinney, E. M. to Miles Williams 9-15-1863 Mn
McKinney, E. T. (Mrs.) to David McRee 11-11-1868 G
McKinney, Elizabeth to Elijah Hammett 8-2-1838 O
McKinney, Elizabeth to Stephens Matthews 3-9-1836 Sh
McKinney, Ellen to Geo. Sullivan 10-1-1854 Sh
McKinney, Frances E. to L. D. Cook 1-16-1865 (1-17-1865) Cr
McKinney, Frances to John Wayman 8-18-1841 T
McKinney, Hannah to Charles McSheyn 12-6-1866 Dy
McKinney, Harriet A. to H. T. Harper 1-24-1870 (1-26-1870) Cr
McKinney, Jane to Charles Adams 9-2-1830 O
McKinney, Kate R. to Wm. L. Neal 6-29-1866 (7-3-1866) F
McKinney, Laronia to Gilbreath Falls 2-8-1859 (2-9-1859) Sh
McKinney, Louisa to Wm. H. Hayley 1-28-1857 Cr
McKinney, M. R. to Albert G. Nevell 8-28-1854 (no return) F
McKinney, Margaret to C. G. Giles 3-28-1868 (3-29-1868) F
McKinney, Mary A. to James Forester 8-5-1835 (8-15-1835) G
McKinney, Mary to Morris Dougherty 6-9-1860 (6-11-1860) Sh
McKinney, Nancy to George Test (West) 2-5-1836 O
McKinney, Pressy Ann to John G. Merrill 2-7-1849 Hn
McKinney, Sarah J. to Allen jr. Johnson 9-20-1871 (9-21-1871) Cr
McKinney, Sarah to Jesse B. Ramsey 12-20-1847 Sh
McKinney, Sarah to John McDaniel 9-13-1832 Sh
McKinney, Sarah to John Nunnery 11-12-1842 Hr
McKinnie, Abacilla to Henry Carraway 3-14-1843 Hr
McKinnie, Ann to Wm. Halliburton 5-5-1877 (no return) Hy
McKinnie, Charlotte to Edmund Reaves 2-17-1838 Hr
McKinnie, Elizabeth C. to Thos. W. Hudson 5-7-1846 Hr
McKinnie, Elizabeth J. to James M. Mask 12-29-1851 (12-31-1852) Hr
McKinnie, Elizabeth Z. to Thomas Bowden 3-6-1843 (3-8-1843) Hr
McKinnie, Frances C. to James M. Field 8-11-1855 (8-12-1855) Hr
McKinnie, Francis E. to Andrew J. Norris 8-25-1871 (8-27-1871) L
McKinnie, Julia to Michial McKinnie 11-13-1832 (11-22-1832) Hr
McKinnie, Mary E. to McDaniel Webb 12-3-1849 (12-5-1849) Hr
McKinnie, Nanney to Wash D. Avent 11-17-1855 (11-19-1855) Hr
McKinnie, Sallie E. to T. L. McGee 4-10-1858 (4-22-1858) Hr
McKinnie, Susan N. to Eli Harris 7-22-1848 (7-27-1848) Hr
McKinnie, Susan to Joseph Sellars 3-3-1840 (3-4-1840) Hr
McKinnie, Susannah to William McKinnie 3-15-1826 (3-16-1826) Hr
McKinnon, A. B. to K. H. Parker 11-15-1877 Hy
McKinnon, Catharine to Tom J. Fergason 8-7-1860 (no return) Hy
McKinnon, Christian to Hubbard P. Scott 3-23-1843 (3-27-1843) L
McKinnon, Frances R. to Wm. H. Hathcock 9-3-1867 Hy
McKinnon, Louisa to James Betts 1-9-1866 Hy
McKinnon, Nancy C. to J. L. Betts 11-30-1869 Hy
McKinsey, Mary to Jefferson Jerman 2-3-1826 (2-7-1826) Hr
McKinsey, Rachel to David Gray 11-27-1839 (12-1-1839) Hr
McKinstrey, Margarett J. to Wm. S. Plaxter 1-13-1852 (no return) F
McKinza, Narcissa to Starling Nuckells 5-1-1832 (5-8?-1832) Hr
McKinza, W. A. T. to Joseph Young 3-21-1846 (3-22-1846) Hr
McKinzie, M. L. to H. C. Gant 10-11-1864 G
McKinzie, Narcissa C. to J. M. McClintock 8-11-1866 (no return) Cr
McKissick, Emma to David C. Pryor 11-2-1841 Sh
McKnatt, Martha E. to Samuel H. Trim 9-10-1872 T
McKnight, Catharine to Charles Marsh 12-22-1843 Ma
McKnight, Catherine B. to John Harton 6-8-1843 Ma
McKnight, Cynthia to Henry Howard 7-6-1854 Sh
McKnight, E. J. to A. C. Harrison 12-15-1875 (12-17-1875) Dy
McKnight, Eleathia J. to Josephus Perkins 1-24-1852 Ma
McKnight, Elizabeth to John Carter 1-3-1848 (1-6-1848) Ma
McKnight, Elizabeth to Peter West 3-2-1827 (3-4-1827) Hr
McKnight, Emeline to William T. Cox 2-23-1852 (7-24-1852) Sh
McKnight, Emily to W. D. Bloys 12-18-1849 (12-23-1849) O
McKnight, Emily to William D. Bloys 12-18-1849 (12-23-1849) O
McKnight, Harrell to Nathaniel M. Price 10-2-1843 (10-5-1843) Ma
McKnight, Jane Isabella to Samuel McLary 11-18-1834 (11-20-1834) G

McKnight, Louisa to W. O. Wilder 12-10-1869 (12-15-1869) F
McKnight, Lucy E. to Joseph E. Fortner 12-17-1850 Ma
McKnight, Margaret Jane to Henry F. Parker 9-10-1859 (9-11-1859) Ma
McKnight, Margarett W. (Mrs.) to Thomas J. Thedford 8-15-1844 G
McKnight, Margarette P. to J. J. Crawford 9-19-1844 (no return) F
McKnight, Mary E. to George T. Hurt 7-28-1874 Dy
McKnight, Mary E. to Samuel H. Sloan 5-28-1850 G
McKnight, Mary E. to William W. Garland 12-18-1854 (12-19-1854) Ma
McKnight, Mary Jane to Melvin McMurry 10-15-1865 Mn
McKnight, Mary L. to John T. Whitson 7-24-1879 Dy
McKnight, Mary Q. to James E. Newsom 8-29-1854 Ma
McKnight, Nancy Ann to Benj. F. Branch 10-13-1858 (10-14-1858) Ma
McKnight, Nancy E. to John D. Stone 2-6-1837 (2-7-1837) G
McKnight, Rosannah to Noah Parr 12-27-1880 (12-30-1880) Dy
McKnight, Sallie K. to Wm. A. McGill 3-9-1867 G
McKnight, Sarah E. to Sam Pierce 10-18-1871 (no return) Dy
McKnight, Sarah F. to Samuel J. Morrow 1-27-1852 Ma
McKnight, T. E. to Joseph McKnight 1-31-1854 G
McKnight, Zaby to William Blann 1-10-1832 (1-17-1832) G
McKorey, S. E. to D. J. Perry? 3-27-1867 Hn
McLain, Elizabeth to Amos Young 11-9-1868 (no return) F B
McLain, Elizabeth to Jordan Oatsfall 2-5-1844 Hr
McLain, Martha Ann to William R. Gadwell 1-20-1852 Hn
McLain, Nancy J. to James C. Puckett 1-6-1863 We
McLain, Nancy to Louis McQuistian 9-16-1865 T
McLaine, Margaretth to Jacob Chapman 1-16-1855 (1-18-1855) G
McLamore, Rebecca J. to William J. N. Wilbourn 11-17-1846 G
McLane, Elizabeth to Thomas Cary 3-22-1853 Cr
McLane, Margaret Ann to Thomas R. Monroe 8-20-1857 Hn
McLane, Mary to William D. Sled 12-16-1856 Hn
McLannahan, Lucky J. to Thomas S. Neal 10-16-1860 (no return) Hy
McLarty, Mary Jane to Richard Lake 12-19-1853 (12-22-1853) Hr
McLary, Frances H. to Jno. B. Smith 7-27-1858 Ma
McLaughlin, Rachel to Thomas McLaughlin 2-21-1824 (2-24-1824) Hr
McLaughlin, Uniun to Jonas Quimby 4-9-1848 Sh
McLaurin, Catharine to B. F. Kelton 1-25-1866 G
McLaurin, Mary E. to William S. Oakford 3-15-1848 G
McLean, Ann L. to Richard McAlilly 10-7-1856 (10-9-1856) G
McLean, Eliza Ann to John T. Hargrove 11-22-1848 Hn
McLean, Elizabeth to Alexander G. Downing 1-11-1831 Ma
McLean, Isabella C. to James D. McClellan 5-12-1832 Ma
McLean, Lyda to L. L. Morrison 10-18-1856 (no return) We
McLean, Marcia S. to Wm. Winston 7-24-1836 Sh
McLean, Maria L. to Joseph H. Mosby 11-31-1835 (SB 11-30?) Sh
McLean, S. J. to I. H. Turpin 9-16-1868 Hy
McLean, Sarah to Samuel Dennis (Dicus) 1-29-1848 Sh
McLean, Susan to J. M. Christenberry 8-4-1862 G
McLeary, Docia to John R. King 10-4-1827 G
McLeary, Eliza to Thomas Barnett 2-8-1843 Ma
McLeary, Elizabeth E. to Cyrus W. Weller(Miller?) 9-1-1840 (9-2-1840) T
McLeary, G. A. to J. A. Sullivan 2-18-1869 G
McLeary, J. A. to J. B. Davis 7-23-1863 G
McLeary, Martha to Joseph D. Sharp 2-19-1835 Sh
McLeary, Mary P. to Joseph L. Vaden 1-16-1867 G
McLeary, Susan to Martin Penn 5-20-1866 G
McLeland, Elizabeth to Samuel Mustin 11-1-1859 (11-2-1859) Sh
McLemore (McLane), Ellen J. to A. B. Shaw 2-1-1845 Sh
McLemore, Catherine D. to Thomas Gholson 9-16-1841 Sh
McLemore, Dora E. to John E. Boyd 5-12-1870 Ma *
McLemore, Dora to Joseph Haley 10-5-1869 (10-7-1869) Cr
McLemore, Elizabeth to Augustus C. Seavers 12-12-1855 (12-13-1855) G
McLemore, Elizabeth to Hudson Strayhorn 10-7-1871 (no return) Cr B
McLemore, Elizabeth to R. D. Fry 6-13-1860 (6-14-1860) Cr
McLemore, Lide to Samuel A. Johnson 11-16-1873 Hy
McLemore, Lucy B. to Samuel P. Bernard 3-24-1846 Sh
McLemore, Lucy to Jim Walker 1-18-1878 Hy
McLemore, Margaret B. to John W. Turner 2-10-1855 (2-13-1855) Ma
McLemore, Mary J. to James Cook 10-5-1869 (10-7-1869) Cr
McLemore, Mary L. to Daniel M. Briant 11-10-1866 (11-11-1866) Cr
McLemore, Mary N. to Samuel H. Blaydes 11-23-1852 (11-25-1852) Ma
McLemore, Mattie E. to Thomas B. Manning 4-13-1870 (4-24-1870) Cr
McLemore, Nannie D. to Thomas B. Cole 5-13-1856 (5-14-1856) Ma
McLemore, Sarah to Gus Rucker 8-9-1877 Hy
McLemore, Tilda to George Clay 7-28-1870 Hy
McLendon, Margaret to Alfred D. Philips 12-21-1853 (12-22-1853) Hr
McLennahan, H. J. to Lynn Boyaknir 1-20-1871 (1-22-1871) T
McLennan, Elizabeth to F. B. Adkins 3-7-1860 (3-8-1860) T
McLeod, Abigal to Joseph Smith 8-9-1845 Cr
McLeod, Alice to H. A. Grimes 12-25-1882 (12-26-1882) L
McLeod, Bettie C. to Hiram Johnson 8-14-1855 (8-15-1855) Ma
McLeod, Betty B. to Edwin Whitmore 12-18-1864 Hy
McLeod, E. C. to J. L. Nelson 11-6-1878 L
McLeod, Eliza Ann to John T. Anderson 12-21-1857 (no return) L
McLeod, Elizabeth to William Falkner 5-18-1869 (5-23-1869) L
McLeod, Francis A. to J. W. Lindsey 7-31-1867 L
McLeod, L. P. to G. W. Crowder 10-19-1881 L
McLeod, M. C. to Joseph A. Johnson 9-?-1857 Cr

McLeod, Mary C. to James Blare 2-22-1851 (no return) F
McLeod, Mary E. to George D. Chalk 12-23-1867 (12-25-1867) L
McLeod, N. C. to R. Jordan 8-11-1840 Be
McLeod, N. J. to J. F. Lamon 1-29-1877 L
McLeod, Norciss C. to R. P. Heathcock 9-28-1869 (9-29-1869) L
McLeod?, Loomy to William Burford 7-6-1844 (7-7-1844) F
McLeroy, Clarissa Jane to Silas Stroud 7-3-1848 (8-4-1848) O
McLeroy, Nancy L. to Thomas B. Hughes 7-14-1860 (no return) Hy
McLeroy, Rebecca to Joseph B. Love 12-12-1828 Ma
McLester, Susan J. to Franklin Adkins 10-22-1840 Hn
McLin, Amy L. to George Branch 8-19-1867 Hy
McLin, Amy L. to George Redrick 8-19-1867 Hy
McLin, Sarah J. to James Phillips 7-20-1863 G
McLin?, Charity to Wm. McFarlin 11-5-1850 Cr
McLinn, Frances to Laudin Davis 5-5-1871 T
McLioud, Elizabeth A. to James Prewett 11-10-1853 Cr
McLister, Cy to John Horton 4-25-1866 T
McLoad, Martha to George F. Hamilton 11-17-1853 (no return) F
McLorie, Catharine to William Field 7-11-1852 O
McLoughlin, Ellen to Patrick Flaharty 8-1-1851 Sh
McLour, Mary to David Cyrus 12-17-1851 (12-19-1851) G
McLure?, Julie A. to Jesse J. H. Jordeen? 4-2-1866 (no return) Cr
McLure, Gracy to Thomas Murray 2-11-1874 Hy
McMaccan, Margaret M. to William Moore 7-19-1862 (7-20-1862) L
McMacken, Maria J. to William White 9-21-1869 (9-23-1869) Cr
McMackens, Angeline to Allen Martin 12-25-1868 (12-27-1868) Cr
McMackens, Nancy Ann to John W. Jenkins 10-4-1869 (10-28-1869) Cr
McMackin, Elizabeth to F. H. Grissom 7-16-1873 (7-17-1873) Cr
McMackin, Josephine to W. B. Weddington 2-15-1871 Dy
McMackin, Leona J. to G. A. Leath 12-1-1874 (12-2-1874) Dy
McMackin, Lucinda to Andrew McMackin 10-9-1867 (10-10-1867) Cr
McMackin, Susan to Joshua Rodgers 12-27-1847 Cr
McMackins, Barbara to Tilley Weakes 2-8-1844 T
McMackins, Elizabeth F. to Robt. N. Rowland 11-25-1872 (11-26-1872) Cr
McMackins, Harriett A. to Wm. R. Nowell 8-17-1858 Cr
McMackins, Lucinda to Eli S. Moss 3-28-1870 (3-31-1870) Cr
McMackins, Mary M. to William A. French 9-12-1865 (9-14-1865) Cr
McMahan, Ann to Patrick Maloney 9-9-1848 Sh
McMahan, C. T. to J. W. Best 11-6-1872 Hy
McMahan, Catharine to James McNamara 11-5-1860 Sh
McMahan, Frances to David S. Manley 1-15-1862 (1-16-1862) Sh
McMahan, Joana to Patrick Lane 8-7-1854 Sh
McMahan, Martha J. to Green B. Curtis(Carter?) 1-11-1848 (1-12-1848) Hr
McMahan, Martha J. to William E. Boyd 4-9-1850 Sh
McMahan, Mary M. to Isiah Browning 5-15-1842 Sh
McMahan, Mary to John Conway 11-1-1860 Sh
McMahan, Mary to Patrick Carey 2-15-1854 Sh
McMahan, Rebecca to Acy Rains 1-15-1833 G
McMahan, Sarah to Wm. Smith 1-21-1842 Sh
McMahan, Susan to Thomas Cannon 1-8-1867 (no return) Hy
McMahan, Virginia to John W. Tucker 5-23-1855 We
McMahon, Elizabeth to S. C. Harpoll 1-6-1837 (3-1-1837) G
McMahon, Elizabeth to Solomon C. Harpole 1-6-1838 G
McMahon, Ellen to Dennis Quinlan 10-26-1861 (10-27-1861) Sh
McMahon, Joanna to Robt. Allen 3-3-1859 Sh
McMahon, Lizze to Jas. D. Martin 8-3-1864 Sh
McMahon, M. A. to Joseph W. Ross 1-5-1863 (no return) Hy
McMahon, M. C. to A. S. Simpson 10-1-1881 (10-5-1881) L
McMahon, Martha (Mrs.) to L. R. Harrison 12-6-1854 Ma
McMahon, Mary to Benjamin Wilkes 2-27-1834 Hr
McMahon, Mary to John McMahon 7-28-1857 Sh
McMahon, Mary to Matthew Cunningham 5-15-1860 Sh
McMahon, Mollie to J.(I.?) N. Stanley 5-28-1866 Hy
McMahon, Rachel to Benjamin Fuel 11-20-1828 (1-9-1829) G
McMahon, Sarah to William Cessna 2-28-1837 Sh
McManaman, Mary to James Mullera 8-26-1861 Sh
McManhon, Mary to James O'Brien (O'Bion) 8-20-1862 Sh
McMannus, Louisa J. to A. S. Larallette 12-31-1850 Sh
McManus (McManns?), Annie to Laurence Connor 7-6-1863 Sh
McManus, Catharine to Montravile G. Wilson 10-28-1854 Sh
McManus, Elizabeth A. to David H. Townsend 5-12-1844 Sh
McManus, Louisa J. to Albert T. Lavallette 12-31-1850 Sh
McMayhan, A. to John Heathscot 9-7-1856 We
McMelon, E. I. to T. W. Hall 8-25-1866 O
McMerter, Malissa A. to M. D. Wall 8-12-1866 Be
McMichael, M. M. J. to N. R. C. Barham 6-21-1863 We
McMicken, Delila to James H. Tilley 12-30-1861 (1-1-1862) Hr
McMigins, Francy to Armstead Green 12-26-1867 (12-28-1867) L B
McMillan, Adeline to John T. Rodgers 4-30-1866 (5-4-1866) Ma
McMillan, I. J. to W. L. Minton 8-18-1848 (8-23-1848) F
McMillan, Jane R. to Jerimiah E. Hendricks 7-9-1845 Sh
McMillan, Margaret L. to A. McLemore 1-20-1866 (no return) Hy
McMillan, Margaret to Sherrill Rowland 12-10-1846 Cr
McMillan, Mary Ann to Henry L. Guion 12-18-1838 Ma
McMillan, Mary to William Anderson 1-6-1837 (1-12-1837) Hr
McMillan, Nancy M. to Joshua McMillan 8-1-1839 (8-7-1839) Ma
McMillan, Phoebe to Benjamin Overton 9-24-1834 Sh

McMillan, Sarah to A. Trigg 7-14-1841 Sh
McMillen, Amanda P. to William G. Cockrill 7-1-1857 Ma
McMillen, Sallie A. to G. W. Perminter 12-31-1868 Hy
McMillen, Susie to William E. Chapman 12-20-1870 Dy
McMillin, Eland to John Childras 5-20-1830 (5-26-1830) G
McMillin, Jane to Green Boland 4-2-1830 (4-?-1830) G
McMillin, Nancy to Alexander Nelson 8-31-1856 Cr
McMillin, Sarah to Edward Cyle 4-16-1863 Sh
McMin, Sarah O. to Robert S. Bird 12-16-1867 (12-18-1867) T
McMinn, Elizabeth to Wiley W. West 8-9-1847 G
McMinn, Martha A. to William Goodman, jr. 2-17-1835 (2-19-1835) G
McMinn, Mary S. to Isaac B. Wallingford 9-12-1850 (9-13-1850) G
McMinn, Mary to J. A. Covington 8-11-1868 G
McMinn, N. M. to W. D. Bobbitt 10-23-1867 G
McMinn, Sarah to Willis Spear 1-18-1840 (1-30-1840) G
McMinns, Mary Jane to Tho. Jefferson Kelley 7-20-1850 T
McMins, Mary Jane to Thomas J. Kelly 12-3-1850 Sh
McMullen, Iva to James S. Boyd 5-7-1860 (5-10-1860) F
McMullen, Lucinda to C. M. McMullen 8-29-1853 (8-30-1853) Sh
McMullen, Lucy to Richard Chandler 1-31-1848 (2-1-1848) G
McMullen, Margaret to Marian Moore 1-22-1852 G
McMullen, Martha to J. F. Shelton 1-22-1857 (2-5-1857) Sh
McMullen, Mary Eliza to Willis Bishop 10-29-1840 Cr
McMullen, Mary L. to J. P. Woodson 10-13-1856 (10-15-1856) G
McMullen, Susam to J. B. Gragg 7-20-1857 (7-22-1857) Sh
McMullin, Anna E. to T. B. Lloyd 12-25-1865 (1-1-1866) F
McMullin, M. E. J. to J. W. Koonce 4-8-1874 (4-9-1874) T
McMullin, Margarett? J. to F. P. Tarply 9-24-1860 (9-25-1860) Cr
McMullins, Matilda J. to John W. Koonce 12-23-1867 T
McMullins, Sally to Jacob Ford 10-16-1839 (no return) Cr
McMurray, Emma G. to D. M. Carter 2-14-1862 (2-19-1862) Sh
McMurray, Kate to Emanuel M. Jones 3-17-1862 Sh
McMurray, Mary H. to Daniel M. Stewart 11-27-1866 Hy
McMurray, Molly to Jeff Brutus 2-8-1867 Sh
McMurry, Amanda J. to W. L. Richardson 4-11-1860 (no return) Hy
McMurry, Amanda to W. C. Day 1-15-1867 (1-16-1867) O
McMurry, Annie S. to R. M. Joyner 5-1-1870 Hy
McMurry, Callia M. to James T. Smith 2-3-1864 O
McMurry, Martha M. to William Mct. Old 6-18-1860 O
McMurry, Mary E. to Henry A. Applegate 10-31-1854 (11-1-1854) O
McMurry, Matilda to Alex Allen 3-8-1868 G B
McMurry, Mattie to M. C. King 10-13-1856 (10-15-1856) Sh
McMurry, Pataline to Vincent Johnson 2-20-1867 (no return) F
McMurry, Sarah to John J. Cameron 12-4-1866 (no return) Hy
McMurtry, Nancy to Isaiah Barnes 10-16-1851 Be
McNabb, Mary A. to Francis M. Gregory 8-25-1842 Sh
McNabb, Paramelia Frances to Henry Atkins 7-19-1856 (7-24-1856) Sh
McNail, Allis to Cobb McCorkle 6-27-1870 G B
McNail, Bettie to Will Smith 1-5-1880 (1-15-1880) Dy
McNail, Nancy J. to John Baxter 1-20-1853 G
McNaim, A. M. to W. A. Crowder 5-22-1871 (no return) Hy
McNaion, Eliza Jane to Turner M. Anderson 8-3-1869 Ma
McNair, Lavinia F. to John Fox 6-8-1869 G
McNair, Louiza to James A.(O?) Williams 4-28-1863 G
McNair, Martha to Robert L. Walker 4-24-1865 T
McNairy, Bridget to Daniel Conners 8-1-1862 (8-3-1862) Sh
McNairy, Ellen to Michl. Quinlin 4-30-1860 Sh
McNama, Margaret to Edward Foley (Haley?Holey?) 3-4-1851 Sh
McNamara, Ann to Jeremiah FitsJerrel 1-7-1873 (1-28-1873) Cr
McNamara, Bridget to John Norten 3-6-1859 Sh
McNamara, Ellen to Maurice Conway 10-20-1849 Sh
McNamara, Margaret to Thomas Hogan 2-25-1849 Sh
McNamara, Maria to Wm. Stephens 4-3-1853 (4-6-1853) Sh
McNamee, Ann to Thomas Boyd 12-30-1849 Sh
McNamee, C. J. to enj. Ward 3-20-1860 (3-21-1860) F
McNamee, Margaret to Michael McNamara 5-9-1859 (5-12-1859) Sh
McNamee, N. E. (Mrs.) to W. P. Lipscomb 2-15-1870 (3-2-1870) F
McNat, P. F. to J. H. Bird 11-8-1872 (11-12-1872) T
McNeal, Charity to Nelson Moore 10-14-1871 (no return) Hy
McNeal, Clora to Winchester Clark 9-20-1877 Hy
McNeal, Dicey to Captain Iverson 7-14-1866 (7-15-1866) F B
McNeal, Eliza to William Warmack 12-12-1854 Be
McNeal, Eliza to William Wygul 3-15-1864 Be
McNeal, Eliza to William Wygul 3-15-1864 Be CC
McNeal, Evelina S. to Erasmus Patton McDowell 4-23-1838 (4-24-1838) Hr
McNeal, Jane F. to David F. Brown 10-14-1829 (10-15-1829) Hr
McNeal, Mary Jane to Austin Miller 10-22-1849 (10-23-1849) Hr
McNeel, Flora J. to James C. Mathis 8-30-1860 G
McNeel, Rosanna to Andrew Johnson 7-3-1868 (7-4-1868) F B
McNeeley, Rachael to William Caton 10-20-1857 (10-25-1857) O
McNeely, Sarah to W. C. Norrid 8-11-1866 O
McNeely, Delila to John Flowers 9-4-1877 (9-5-1877) O
McNeely, Harriet Jane to Bethell Reeves 1-15-1844 O
McNeely, Jane to Henry Obrian 11-28-1856 O
McNeely, L. P. to A. T. McNeely 11-4?-1865 (11-3-1865) O
McNeely, Margaret to Joseph B. McNeely 1-6-1855 (1-10-1855) Sh
McNeely, Mary to William F. Neary 1-24-1861 (1-26-1861) O

McNeely, N. M. to L. W. Hargett 1-9-1866 O
McNeely, Nelly to John C. Floyd 12-29-1839 (1-2-1840) Hr
McNees, Mary A. to J. M. Crenshaw 2-9-1850 (2-10-1850) F
McNeese, Narcissus C. to William McCain 1-31-1853 (2-2-1853) Hr
McNeil, Ann to Stephen Taylor 1-6-1866 (no return) F B
McNeil, Arabella to Lewis Becket 1-1-1855 Sh
McNeil, Caroline to Horace McNeil 3-17-1866 (8-26-1866) F B
McNeil, E. to J. M. Reef 11-25-1847 Be
McNeil, Emma A. to E. T. Simons 6-6-1878 Hy
McNeil, Flora R. to John P. Caruthers 7-29-1861 Sh
McNeil, Jamima E. to Martin A. Green 12-3-1872 Dy
McNeil, Lila to John W. Pearce 10-24-1851 Be
McNeil, Linda to Jim Taylor 1-6-1866 (no return) F B
McNeil, Minerva to John Chandler 9-8-1877 (no return) Dy
McNeill, Angeline to William Trotter 9-4-1871 (9-7-1871) Cr B
McNeill, Anikee to Lindsey Cocke 2-7-1868 (no return) F B
McNeill, Irene? to W. B. Grizzard 1-19-1871 Cr
McNeill, Julia A. to Charles F. Hanna 8-10-1848 Cr
McNeill, Laura to Robert Polk 4-11-1867 (4-20-1867) F B
McNeill, Margaret E. to Joseph S. Hamlett 9-11-1854 (9-12-1854) Ma
McNeill, Mariah to Jeff Sullivan 8-10-1870 (8-11-1870) F B
McNeill, Martha to John Chersey 11-9-1867 (no return) F B
McNeill, Mary to Perry McKinney 8-5-1867 (8-10-1867) F B
McNeill, Octavia to Grandison Irwin 11-10-1868 (11-11-1868) F B
McNeill, Parlie to Dennis Grizzard 2-6-1872 Cr B
McNeill, Violet to Johnson Moore 5-25-1870 (5-28-1870) F B
McNerney, Mary to James Clifford 5-22-1856 (5-23-1856) Sh
McNerney, Mary to Patrick McMahon 7-25-1863 Sh
McNiel, L. to E. Reddick 10-10-1841 T
McNight, Hattie E. to G. H. Burrow 3-28-1870 G
McNight, Martha A. to A. V. Hyatt 4-27-1867 (4-28-1867) Cr
McNill, LeElla to Wm. H. Christie 9-13-1866 Hy
McNilly, Mollie to F. Hifield 6-17-1874 T
McNorton (Norton?), Maria to Michael Kelly 10-4-1853 Sh
McNutt, Cynthia to Thos. S. E. Joiner 10-21-1842 Sh
McNutt, Isabella W. to J. Curtis 9-29-1857 Hn
McNutt, Mary to Simeon Watkins 9-1-1840 Hn
McPherson, Adeline to G. R. Williams 8-17-1874 (8-19-1874) L
McPherson, Alba to William Pergreson 5-29-1845 Sh
McPherson, Ann Eliza to Jackson R. Henderson 4-30-1846 (no return) F
McPherson, E. P. to Lot Spurm 2-5-1868 G
McPherson, Mary M. to Thomas J. Hendrix 5-26-1877 L
McPherson, Sarah Eliza to Moses D. Cheeck 2-12-1844 Sh
McQLuiston, Martha to Robert B. Harper 9-9-1847 T
McQueen, Clarissa to Wesley Padgett 9-16-1856 Sh
McQueen, Sallie to Henry P. Nutter 9-24-1861 (10-8-1861) Sh
McQuinn, Louisa to Austin Cook 12-26-1857 Sh
McQuinn, Sophia A. to H. H. Lewis 9-24-1862 Hn
McQuisten, Elizabeth to James M. Wright 3-20-1841 (3-23-1841) T
McQuister, Eliza to Cornelius Bond 1-23-1866 T
McQuiston, E. W. to J. C. Castles 12-12-1870 (12-15-1870) T
McQuiston, Eliza A. to Andrew J. Wright 1-29-1868 (1-30-1868) T
McQuiston, Jennette to William D. Strain 12-17-1847 T
McQuiston, M. Bettie to J. Linsey Baird 12-6-1870 (12-8-1870) T
McQuiston, Margaret E. to R. P. Straing 11-22-1870 T
McQuiston, Margaret to Robert Simonton 9-4-1855 T
McQuiston, Martha to John Ready McDaniel 5-5-1851 T
McQuiston, Nancy Jane to William Baird 3-5-1844 T
McQuiston, Nancy to Henry Simonton 7-3-1871 (7-4-1871) T
McQuiston, Rachel to James Jordan 4-2-1866 (4-3-1866) T
McQuiston, Sarah Isabella to Saml. Dunn Dickson 10-9-1850 T
McQurry, Margaret to John Basford 5-5-1847 Be
McRae, E. J. to J. P. Byrn 11-14-1855 Be
McRae, Martha to C. M. Herrin 1-26-1869 Be
McRany?, Anna P. to E. A. Palmer 10-22-1856 Hn
McRea, Eliza to Duncan Hopper 12-11-1869 (12-12-1869) Cr
McRea, M. A. to J. C. Melton 12-12-1839 Be
McRed, Elizabeth to W. J. Greer 5-11-1843 Be
McRee, Cyntha A. to Henry A. McHenry 11-4-1852 G
McRee, Manda A. to Isaac C. Herin 7-20-1861 (7-21-1861) O
McRee, Mary Jane to Henry Smith 9-14-1854 O
McRee, Mattie D. to Galen E. Green 11-7-1864 (11-9-1864) Sh
McRee, Minerva to R. T. Burnett 12-14-1866 (12-16-1866) O
McRee, Sarah E. to Thomas Foster 7-5-1860 O
McRee, Sarah to Jabez Brown 8-22-1855 (8-23-1855) O
McRee, Sarah to S. M. Hicks 5-12-1864 O
McRight, Mary A. to A. S. Clark 12-29-1862 O
McRony, Matilda to Prince Lasslie 6-3-1876 O B
McSanland, Martha F. to James A. Coppedge 5-15-1864 (no return) Hy
McSpadden, Martha E. to Wm. F. Harris 7-16-1844 F
McSpadden, S. M. to Wm. Dickson 12-4-1852 (no return) Cr
McSwain, Elizabeth to John Cannon 12-3-1846 (no return) Hn
McSwain, Martha E. to Haywood Hern 3-43-1857 Cr
McSwain, Mary W. to P. C. Boyd 4-8-1852 Hn
McSwain, S. C. to H. S. Bradford 1-16-1856 (no return) Hn
McSwain, Sarah C. to Andrew J. Weldon 12-22-1852 Hn
McSwayne, Martha B. R. to Andrew M. M. Trawick 6-30-1867 Hn

McSwayne, Mary E. to W. J. C. Candler 8-30-1855 (no return) Hn
McTintrick, S. C. to W. J. McCollum 2-26-1859 Cr
McVan, Bridget to Thomas Delaney 5-1-1860 (5-2-1860) Sh
McVay, Mary Ellen to E. H. Covington 5-19-1864 Hn
McVay, Nancy to Patrick Boyte 8-3-1853 (8-4-1853) Hr
McVey, Cynthia to Nathan Francis 5-1-1848 Ma
McVey, Florida to John Lackey 11-22-1853 (11-23-1853) Hr
McVey, Mary Jane to Elias T. Butler 7-10-1848 (7-13-1848) Ma
McVey, Mary to Berry Kirby 8-24-1870 (8-25-1870) Cr
McWherter, Elizabeth A. to William S. Crews 12-7-1852 G
McWherter, Elizabeth J. to Joel W. Harrison 11-12-1844 G
McWherter, Jane to Allen S. Hord 3-5-1851 (3-6-1851) O
McWherter, Lucenda D. to John W. James 12-6-1837 G
McWherter, Margaret A. to Shadrack Wilson 6-8-1852 G
McWherter, Mary Jane to W. J. Philips 7-19-1852 We
McWherter, Mary to Henry Darnall 10-12-1831 O
McWherter, Nancy P. to John Turner 1-26-1858 We
McWherter, Ruth P. to Thomas G. Harte 11-11-1857 We
McWherter, Sarah E. to Benjamin W. Head 4-16-1861 We
McWherter, Virginia T. to J. D. Mitt 5-13-1858 We
McWhirter, Eliza to James Dowell 1-8-1857 G
McWhirter, Elizabeth (Mrs.) to J. A. Hardie 3-14-1869 G
McWhirter, Elizabeth A. L. to Carroll S. Parker 3-2-1843 G
McWhirter, Julia C. to Alexander Wells 12-18-1868 Ma
McWhirter, Paulina L. to James B. McWhirter 2-15-1832 Hr
McWhirter, Sentha L. N. to William R. Edmundson 3-11-1845 G
McWhorter, Rebecka to Lindsey K. Tinkle 2-23-1831 G
McWhorter, Rhoda Ann to George Patton 2-26-1831 (2-27-1831) G
McWilliams, Jane to Aulsey D. Roark 12-29-1845 (1-1-1846) Ma
McWilliams, Jane to John M. Fadly 10-17-1847 Sh
McWilliams, Margaret to Simon J. Burrow 1-6-1847 Cr
McWilliams, Mary to John McCue 12-8-1853 (12-18-1853) Sh
McWilliams, Nancy to Wm. R. Peebles 12-22-1842 Sh
McWilliams, Rebecca M. to James H. Medlin 10-9-1847 (10-13-1847) Ma
McWilliams, Sarah S. to George M. Hisaw no date Cr
Mc____, Martha Jane to John H. Farmer 11-27-1854 Be
Mcclish, Jane M. to James W. B. Thomas 3-13-1844 Ma
Mccoy, Ann to Samuel Spier 3-5-1861 G
Mccoy, Josephine to J. C. Dezern 8-5-1875 Hy
Mcgee, Sarah to Charles Denger (Denzer?) 5-8-1851 (5-9-1851) Sh
Mcguire, Ann to James Weaver 5-26-1838 F
Mcguire, L. L. to G. C. Miller 12-9-1879 (12-10-1879) L
Mcguire, Mrs. Harriett to John B. Walker 8-14-1858 (8-17-1858) Hr
Mcguire, Susan to Braddock Brooks 1-1-1867 (1-3-1867) F B
Mckinnon, Louisa to James Betts 1-1-1866 (no return) Hy
Mcquiston, Mary Ann to D. H. McQuiston 8-31-1870 T
Meacham, Caroline to William C. Neely 4-2-1852 (2-5-1852?) Ma
Meacham, Eliza J. to Thomas B. Harrison 4-6-1864 (4-7-1864) L
Meacham, Elizabeth to L. M. Mahan 9-13-1865 (9-14-1865) O
Meacham, M. A. (Mrs.) to D. T. Porter 2-3-1858 (2-4-1858) Sh
Meacham, M. J. to A. M. Fullen 10-31-1878 L
Meacham, Martha D. to John I. Taylor 2-19-1828 Ma
Meacham, Martha Jane to Willis G. Hogue 3-16-1854 O
Meacham, Mary C. to John F. Davidson 6-25-1861 O
Meacham, Mary Jane to E. B. Crockett 1-30-1850 O
Meacham, N. L. to J. W. Fullen 12-22-1875 L
Meacham, Nancy M. to Mashack Green 7-27-1861 (7-30-1861) O
Meacham, Nancy to Hays Stanley 6-2-1853 (7-2-1853) Ma
Meacham, Sarah E. to W. Green Byrn 10-6-1877 (no return) L
Meacham, Sarah to Thos. Morse 2-11-1841 Ma
Meacham, Wadie A. to T. L. Ruffin 9-3-1885 (9-5-1885) L
Meachum, Caroline to George R. Philips 7-19-1850 (7-25-1850) Hr
Mead, Helen to Charles H. Brackett 9-31?-1862 Sh
Mead, S. J. to A. S. Watson 1-31-1849 (2-1-1849) O
Meade, Elizabeth H. to John A. Lax 10-9-1859 Hn
Meade, Nancy H. to Alexander Butts 3-13-1855 (3-15-1855) O
Meadows, Alice to S. C. Miller 12-24-1879 (12-24-1880?) L
Meadows, Anjeletta to William S. S. Harris 7-3-1831 (7-4-1831) L
Meadows, Bettie to Campbell Wardlaw 9-22-1868 (9-26-1868) L
Meadows, Cassandra Ann to Joseph Hampton 1-5-1842 (no return) Cr
Meadows, Catharine to Green W. Parker 11-17-1852 O
Meadows, Cynthia to George W. Hail 11-9-1830 O
Meadows, Darinda to Frank Bicknell 3-23-1874 (3-25-1874) L
Meadows, Eliza to John Maynard 4-24-1861 L
Meadows, Eliza to William Hart 3-31-1841 Hn
Meadows, Elizabeth Ann to John W. Newsom 3-6-1855 (3-7-1855) Ma
Meadows, Eveline A. to Wm. R. Chisholm 3-2-1843 L
Meadows, Frances H. to James C. Acuff 11-1-1849 L
Meadows, Jane M. F. to Wm. W. Sharpe 12-15-1845 (12-17-1845) L
Meadows, Josephine S. to James L. Carter 10-1-1857 O
Meadows, Julia to W. M. Smith 6-1-1867 (no return) Dy
Meadows, Lydia B. to John B. Carter 1-23-1837 O
Meadows, M. E. to J. T. Quinn 11-29-1881 (no return) L
Meadows, M. I. to B. S. Steward 1-9-1873 L
Meadows, Malinda to James Stuckey 9-6-1847 (9-7-1847) L
Meadows, Manerva E. to James S. Kirkpatrick 4-11-1864 Dy
Meadows, Manurva C. to M. D. Webb 7-3-1865 (7-6-1865) L

Meadows, Martha Ann to Matthew M. Langley 4-12-1848 (no return) L
Meadows, Martha F. to Alfred Ledbetter 9-11-1860 L
Meadows, Mary A. to William D. Carson 3-4-1885 L
Meadows, Mary Ann to George W. Tanner 8-14-1838 (8-16-1838) O
Meadows, Mary Ann to Rolen Ledbetter 9-11-1860 L
Meadows, Mary F. to Richard R. Croom 4-21-1857 (4-29-1857) Ma
Meadows, Mary J. to James M. Jenkins 8-5-1862 (8-7-1862) L
Meadows, Mary M. to George W. Chism 6-4-1840 Hn
Meadows, Nancy E. to William R. Snider 12-16-1840 Hn
Meadows, Parthenia to William S. Hardin 5-7-1853 (5-10-1853) Ma
Meadows, Sarah J. to Sidney A. McCollum 4-27-1846 (2-11-1847) O
Meadows, Sarah to Elam Booth 1-11-1874 Hy
Meadows, Vandelia to A. J. Burkeen 12-21-1870 Dy
Meaghar (Menghar), Sarah to Thomas B. Huling 9-17-1828 Sh
Meagin, Mandy to James Palmer 12-12-1874 (no return) Hy
Mealy, Bridget to Patrick Connelly 10-25-1862 Sh
Means, Martha C. to George W. Jones 6-30-1853 Sh
Means, Prudence to Samuel C. Clowney 12-18-1835 Sh
Mear, M. to Martin Hofsi 11-3-1862 Sh
Mear, M. to Martin Hosse 6-?-? (after 1850) Sh
Mears, Lucinda to Andrew Montgomery 5-19-1849 (5-20-1849) T
Mears, Mary E. to T. M. Morrison 6-18-1861 (6-19-1861) T
Mears, N. W. to N. A. Sullivan 11-25-1871 (11-30-1871) T
Measler, Alpha to Wyatt Bird 4-22-1842 Hn
Measler, Amanda M. to James McElroy 8-14-1851 Hn
Measles, S. A. to W. H. Brumett 8-17-1881 (8-18-1881) L
Meaxey, Margaret to James V. Haskins 7-19-1865 Ma
Mebane, Amanda to Frank Hare 10-1-1870 (10-4-1870) F B
Mebane, Clara to King Freeman 12-24-1868 (12-25-1868) F B
Mebane, Cornelia to Allen Kirk 9-6-1866 (no return) F B
Mebane, Eliza E. to Charles Y. Gooch 10-31-1866 Cr
Mebane, Eliza to Burrel Ragland 12-29-1869 (12-9?-1869) F B
Mebane, Emeline to Ellet Hines 12-27-1870 (12-30-1870) F B
Mebane, Gracey to Henry Culpepper 12-28-1870 (12-29-1870) F B
Mebane, Hannah to William Franklin 12-27-1867 (no return) L
Mebane, Henrietta to William H. Smith 7-27-1870 (no return) F B
Mebane, Laura to James Foster 10-28-1868 (no return) F B
Mebane, Letha to Wiley Sutton 10-24-1868 L
Mebane, M. E. to T. T. Williams 10-26-1870 Cr
Mebane, Malvina to Daniel Rhodes 3-19-1866 (3-22-1866) F B
Mebane, Martha to Doremus N. Young 9-26-1865 Cr
Mebane, Mary F. to James Thompson 8-?-1859 Cr
Mebane, Mattie to Frank Levett 2-4-1870 (no return) F B
Mebane, S. F. to N.? B. Nesbitt 2-27-1867 Cr
Mebane, Tela to Levon H. Cox 6-30-1866 (7-15-1866) F B
Mebane, Vina to Elijah Sutton 12-12-1867 (12-15-1867) F B
Mebene, Elizabeth F. to W. S. Adams 4-23-1864 (4-24-1864) Cr
Mecham, Margarett to S. M. Howard 1-8-1867 (1-9-1867) O
Medanis, Margaret R. to Samuel Rumnell 8-19-1829 Ma
Medearis, Mary A. to T. A. Huffman 10-6-1861 Cr
Medearis, Sarah H. to Thomas B. Lourence 11-15-1834 (11-16-1834) G
Medearis, Susan H. to H. H. Butler 9-12-1860 (no return) Cr
Medford, Mary Ann to George W. Rogers 2-3-1840 (2-4-1840) Hr
Medkeff, Susan to John W. Guthery 2-22-1858 (no return) We
Medland, Elizur to Perry Birdsong 10-12-1848 O
Medley, Jane to Gideon Faray? 2-11-1867 (2-12-1867) Cr
Medley, Nancy to Edward Box 8-15-1845 (8-16-1845) O
Medlin, Agnes to William F. Young 7-31-1848 (8-1-1848) Ma
Medlin, Alice B. to W. J. Whitehead 10-11-1871 Hy
Medlin, Elizabeth to Willis W. Evans 3-19-1845 (3-23-1845) Ma
Medlin, Emeline to S. D. Palmer 11-17-1857 Cr
Medlin, Harriett to Mathew Williams 5-16-1840 (5-17-1840) Ma
Medlin, Lida to C. M. Finch 1-13-1876 (no return) Hy
Medlin, Lucy to William Phelps 3-9-1871 Ma
Medlin, Malvinia to B. G. Smith 12-2-1850 (12-1?-1850) G
Medlin, Martha S. to Thomas Pierce 1-4-1856 (1-6-1856) Ma
Medlin, Mary to J. Blackwell 12-29-1863 (no return) L
Medlin, Matilda J. to James B. Beard 1-29-1843 (no return) Hy
Medlin, Missouri E. to Meekins N. Jackson 8-2-1869 (8-8-1869) Ma
Medlin, Mollie E. to John A. Strayhorn 2-28-1866 Hy
Medlin, Phebe A. to Marshall Harris 12-26-1871 (no return) Hy
Medlin, Rebecca (Mrs.) to Nelson Davie 1-8-1862 (1-9-1862) Ma
Medlin, Rebecca to C. D. Edington 12-8-1840 Ma
Medlin, Siddy Ann M. to W. D. Williams 12-16-1859 (12-18-1859) Ma
Medlin, Susan C. to J. B. Smith 12-19-1851 Cr
Medling, Weltha to Benjamin Niel 5-11-1838 (5-17-1838) Ma
Medlock, Elvira to Lawrence O'Connar? 9-29-1861 Hn
Medlock, Isabella to John A. Hargroves 5-19-1845 (no return) Hn
Medlock, Lucinda A. to ___ McO'Conner 5-19-1867 Hn
Medlock, R. P. to N. C. Hampton 9-18-1846 Hn
Medly, Peggy to Benjamin Williams 9-4-1839 (9-1?-1839) Ma
Meehan, Margaret to James Greppin (Griffin?) 4-4-1861 Sh
Meek, Martha E. to A. S. Wiley 9-9-1859 Hr
Meek, Mary E. F. to Jefferson L. Meek 11-11-1862 G
Meek, Rebecca A. to James L. Randolph 6-30-1861 Mn
Meek, V. C. to Henry Mitchell 7-12-1863 Mn
Meeks(Merks?), Isabella to James Sanders 2-22-1838 Hr

Meeks, Margaret E. to William B. Cavenor 5-25-1853 (5-26-1853) Hr
Meeks, Martha E. to F. A. Johnson 12-11-1865 Mn
Meeks, Martha to James S. Gilman 4-10-1857 (4-16-1857) Hr
Meeks, Roena M. to W. H. Jenkins 5-2-1853 (5-10-1853) Hr
Meeler, Eveline to Ben Ellis 2-14-1874 (2-15-1874) T
Megee, D. T. P. to Joseph Spires 1-8-1861 Be
Megher, Anna to Cunelius Harigan 8-20-1864 (8-21-1864) Sh
Mehan, Margaret N. to Patrick Hickey 11-28-1859 Sh
Meier, Emelie M. C. to H. F. C. Fike 10-31-1869 (11-1-1860) Sh
Meier, Sophia to Herman Jowien 3-13-1861 Sh
Melear, Harriet to James B. Weddle 9-18-1861 Hn
Mellan, Marinda to Bernard Eisenschmidt 9-27-1842 Sh
Melley, Mary (Mrs.) to James N. Acres 6-6-1857 Ma
Mellish, Mary to William Roberts 2-17-1862 Sh
Melten (Mitten?), Charlotte T. to John D. Farmer 1-4-1856 (no return) We
Melton, Amanda J. to J. W. Brumager 1-3-1866 Be
Melton, America to John G. Moseley 12-25-1868 (12-26-1869?) L
Melton, Bashaby to Aga Hall 9-21-1841 Be
Melton, Centha Ann to Eli Howard 12-14-1838 (12-20-1838) G
Melton, Charity to Hyram Warrick 10-28-1847 Be
Melton, Charlotte L. to James Malin 11-21-1859 We
Melton, Crecy to Eltheldred Melton 11-21-1865 Be
Melton, Elizabeth to Joseph P. Braden 11-1-1843 (11-3-1843) F
Melton, Fanny to Beverly J. Crews 7-30-1870 (8-7-1870) Cr
Melton, Isabella to Asberry Whitley (Wheatley) 1-17-1867 Be
Melton, Julina to William Nash 3-7-1848 Be
Melton, Katharine to David Pafford 11-28-1846 Be
Melton, Lamyra to Hansel L. Wheatley 12-9-1866 Be
Melton, M. C. to D. V. Alexandner 2-28-1870 G
Melton, M. R. to J. H. Dillion 8-16-1866 Be
Melton, Malvina to C. B. Bush 10-27-1855 (no return) Hn
Melton, Marietta to J. W. Jones 12-22-1869 (no return) L
Melton, Martha Adaline to Robert W. Cooly 6-6-1852 Be
Melton, Martha J. to A. J. Hicks 10-27-1855 (no return) Hn
Melton, Martha J. to Wm. M. Pafford 8-31-1861 Be
Melton, Martha to Isaac G. Berry 3-11-1851 Be
Melton, Martha to John Farmer 12-8-1867 Be
Melton, Mary Ann to Alvy Melton 5-19-1853 Be
Melton, Mary Ann to Robert M. Graham 10-14-1846 Be
Melton, Mary to Thomas Childers 8-17-1848 Be
Melton, Nancy A. to R. M. Owen 3-14-1867 Hn
Melton, Nancy C. to John P. Wyatt 11-21-1851 Be
Melton, Narcessa J. to Wyly Walker 3-24-1839 Be
Melton, Patsy to J. G. Winchester 8-26-1842 Be
Melton, Patsy to J. P. Winchester 8-26-1842 Be CC
Melton, Pheby Jane to J. W. F. Berry 7-29-1850 Be
Melton, Pheby to David Y. Vester 2-1-1849 Be
Melton, Pheby to Jas. Sykes 11-7-1839 Be
Melton, Roxana to Pridgen Holland 5-5-1851 Be
Melton, S. E. to Thomas Reynolds 10-8-1868 G
Melton, Sarah Jane to Thos. Colier 7-19-1843 Be
Melton, Sarah Patience to John Pafford 11-30-1866 Be
Melton, Sintha to Etheldredge Melton 6-25-1839 Be
Melton, Susan Lucentia to James Gilroy 3-22-1865 Hn
Melton, Temperance to Jackson Farmer 2-18-1843 Be
Melugin, Annie E. to Simon dP. Driver 10-18-1869 (10-19-1869) T
Memmonds, M. J. to G. W. Swor 12-21-1865 Hn
Menafee, Mary Jane to Lewis Stevens 5-5-1871 (5-7-1871) T
Menascoe, Mary L. to David C. Booth 5-7-1866 (5-11-1866) T
Mendenall, Charlotte to Robert Morris 5-24-1841 Sh
Mendenall, P. J. to Truston Wilson 1-21-1847 Sh
Mendenall, Sarah A. to W. H. Axtell 12-10-1857 Sh
Mendermann, Dorothea to Wm. Ruschaupt 4-21-1862 Sh
Mendinall, Susan to Thomas J. Hunt 12-3-1834 Sh
Menees, Sarah E. to William M. Allen 10-21-1847 (10-23-1847) F
Menefee, Florence S. to Green W. Smitheal 10-27-1870 T
Menice?, Frances D. to Gilberth Fall 11-26-1839 F
Menley, Susan to James Williams 11-23-1833 Hr
Mentlow, May to Henry Green 10-13-1875 (no return) Hy
Menzies, Jane to Beng. Simmons 1-21-1869 Dy
Menzies, M. E. to H. Parks, jr. 2nd 10-27-1873 (10-28-1873) Dy
Menzies, Mariah to Wm. Horton 9-14-1868 (9-17-1868) Dy
Menzies, Sisler to Jerry Wyly 2-12-1867 Be
Merandy, Mary A. to J. H. Meeks 1-14-1868 Dy
Mercer, Dicy Ann to Isaac Anderson 4-26-1840 Cr
Mercer, Elizabeth to John C. Robison 1-13-1852 Hr
Mercer, Martha Ann to Lucus L. Bolton 8-28-1849 Sh
Mercer, Mary M. to John H. McGee 8-18-1856 (8-19-1856) Hr
Merchant, Mary A. (Mrs.) to George W. Muns 12-22-1863 Dy
Mercy, Ida to Allen Thompson 11-16-1877 Hy
Meredith, Ardis to Saml. B. Martin 2-17-1846 (no return) F
Meredith, Elizabeth to David C. Baucum 12-24-1865 Hn
Meredith, Leah to J. N. Harris 1-12-1869 G
Mereto, Ann to Geo. W. Messinger 1-9-1857 Sh
Mereweather, Sarah C. to Lilbourn A. Lewis 1-22-1866 (2-16-1866) O
Meria, Johanna to W. Clary (Cleary) 6-23-1845 Sh
Merick, Rhoda to Benjamin Brooks 2-3-1835 Hr

Meridith, Isabella S. to James H. Walker 4-20-1831 Ma
Meridith, Rebecca A. to Alexander T. Byrns 3-10-1831 Ma
Meritt, America to T. W. Hefley 12-30-1867 G B
Meritt, Lidy J. to J. S. Bullington 12-15-1870 Cr
Meritt, Minerva to Jacob M. Twigg 3-23-1850 (3-26-1850) G
Meritt, Rachel to Henry Bradford 12-30-1867 G B
Meriweather, Amy to John Jones 3-2-1867? (3-3-1867) F B
Meriweather, Elizabeth A. to Wellington Donaldson 2-6-1843 (2-11-1843) O
Meriweather, Elizabeth to Daniel Corbitt 6-1-1862 Sh
Meriweather, Jane R. to Ethelred E. Westbrook 5-23-1855 (6-24-1855) O
Meriweather, Marie to Richard S. Gough 9-1-1847 Sh
Meriweather, Parasade M. to Edmond Taylor 3-23-1843 (3-28-1843) Ma
Meriwether, Elizabeth to John Reaves 10-21-1841 Sh
Meriwether, Fannie to Gaither Tyson 12-11-1866 (12-12-1866) Ma
Meriwether, Jane Caroline to James A. Taylor 12-5-1839 Ma
Meriwether, Margarett to William B. Isler 9-22-1847 (10-21-1847) O
Meriwether, Martha B. to Geo. W. Thompson 12-22-1842 (1-3-1843) O
Meriwether, Sarah Elizabeth to George W. Trotter 4-28-1857 Ma
Merrell, Eliza Jane to Oliver R. Drover? 4-16-1845 Hn
Merrell, Louisa J. to George W. Jones 9-18-1856 Cr
Merrell, Martha to Martin V. McLure 12-14-1859 We
Merrell, Sallie to W. B. Mitchell 6-4-1857 Sh
Merrett, M. A. to G. M. Little 12-7-1872 (12-8-1872) Cr
Merrett, Martha to Alonzo McAdoo 1-13-1872 (no return) Cr
Merrewither, Elizabeth to Joe Scott 7-27-1872 Hy
Merrewither, Lucinda to J. Greenwood 3-25-1873 Hy
Merrick, A. F. to G. W. Adams 6-24-1866 G
Merrick, Frances E. to Peter A. Saunders 6-9-1867 Be
Merrick, Louisa to Henry Stagner 3-27-1851 Be
Merrick, M. to M. R. Jordan 5-15-1842 Be
Merrick, Mary E. to Thomas E. Prince 11-10-1850 Be
Merrick, R. L. to Patrick Kelly 2-27-1849 Be
Merrick, Sarah Ann to A. J. Nowell 10-17-1847 Be
Merrick, Susan to Eli Hatley 11-24-1839 Be
Merrill, A. J. to O. H. McCright 12-4-1860 Sh
Merrill, Frances M. to John G. Merrell 2-19-1863 Hn
Merrill, J. to G. W. Sargent 4-5-1871 (4-9-1871) T
Merrill, Lilly to Samuel Carpenter 2-7-1860 (2-9-1860) Sh
Merrill, Sarah J. to C. J. Culpepper 1-24-1865 Hn
Merrit, Catharine to N. H. Boswell 10-12-1865 (11-6-1865) T
Merrith, Mary E. to J. W. Richman 6-22-1859 Cr
Merritt, Dodeski Ann to W. McFarland 8-6-1869 G
Merritt, Elizabeth to John T. Coleman 2-2-1846 (2-3-1846) G
Merritt, Emeline to Wm. G. Bledsoe 9-18-1839 G
Merritt, J. C. to D. W. Gee 12-11-1866 Cr
Merritt, Juley A. to James W. Sampson 5-3-1843 Cr
Merritt, Mahala to Benjamin Fuell 10-2-1844 G
Merritt, Malinda to Robert C. Williams 9-23-1843 Cr
Merritt, Nancy to J. C. Merritt 4-28-1866 (4-29-1866) Cr
Merritt, Thevizah to Benj. C. Fewell 7-12-1841 (7-13-1841) G
Merriweather, Chany to Wm. Smith 1-9-1878 Hy
Merriwether, India to Green Walker 12-23-1872 Hy
Merriwether, Josephine to R. B. Donaldson 3-6-1860 (3-8-1860) O
Merriwether, Misouri to Philip Critendon 4-28-1871 Hy
Merriwether, R. R. to John P. Isler 12-7-1852 (12-21-1852) O
Merton, Kucy J. to Thomas B. Johnston 2-12-1846 Hn
Mescar, Margaret to Michael Griffin 1-28-1860 (1-30-1860) Sh
Meshly, Magdelina to Konrad Greminger 12-20-1854 (12-28-1854) Sh
Meshow?, Selina to Irvin Kennedy 6-26-1834 Hr
Messenger, Martha to John Douglass 4-9-1867 (4-13-1867) F B
Messenger, Mary to James Johnson 4-13-1871 (4-16-1871) F B
Messer, Barbary to Shadrich Cox 9-6-1849 Be
Messer, Elizabeth to John Brown 7-16-1873 (7-17-1873) Cr
Messer, Susan M. to Eli H. Butler 1-10-1839 F
Messick, Lydia A. F. to Hooper J. Powden 3-6-1851 (3-5?-1851) G
Messick, T. T. (Z? Z?) to Samuel Falwell 9-27-1859 (9-28-1859) Sh
Meter, F. E. to C. B. Denton 11-16-1875 (11-18-1875) L
Meter, M. M. to W. S. Vales 1-18-1876 (1-20-1876) L
Meter, Martha Jane to James M. Harden 2-20-1862 (2-21-1862) L
Meter, Mary E. to William F. McCoy 7-4-1861 L
Meter, Sarah E. to James J. Mangrum 8-19-1867 (8-20-1867) Dy
Metheny, Elmina to Samuel Baker 6-22-1853 Hn
Metheny, Mary E. to William H. Nichols 10-13-1853 Be
Meurhead, Nancy to Steel Bodkin 9-16-1835 G
Meux, Eliza to Fonzo Sweet 12-12-1872 Hy
Meux, Fannie to Lyttleton Harrison 8-17-1876 Hy
Mewbern, Anna L. to Wm. W. Newbern 6-20-1860 F
Mewborn, Georgia A. to H. J. Stanley 1-10-1871 (1-12-1871) F
Mews, Isabella to Samuel D. Kenneday 12-1-1840 Ma
Meyer, Caroline to Ezekiel Schwartz 12-15-1848 Sh
Meyer, Rosaline to W. H. Heidel 1-15-1855 (1-16-1855) Sh
Michael, Nancy to Elijah Ward 1-1-1838 Hn
Michaels, Amanda E. to W. L. Knight 12-26-1872 (no return) Dy
Michaels, Frances to T. J. Harris 6-4-1875 Dy
Michaels, M. to R. P. Powell 5-4-1872 (5-5-1872) Dy
Michan, S. A. to M. Okley 7-30-1854 We
Micheal, Nancy to Samuel B. Brown 7-31-1847 (8-4-1847) Ma

Michee, Olivia B. to Isaac Winston 10-11-1852 (no return) F
Michell, M. E. to Isaac W. Lowe 9-4-1872 (9-8-1872) Dy
Michell, Martha J. to Isaac Barker 11-19-1850 Cr
Michell, Winey F. to Wyly J. Robinson 9-29-1860 Be
Michels, Johane to Henry Henniger 1-13-1852 Sh
Michie, Irena E. to R. S. Houston 4-15-1863 Mn
Mickel, Rebecca to Luke Robinson 3-1-1858 (3-2-1858) Sh
Mickelberry, Elizabeth S. to Wm. B. Crenshaw 11-4-1845 Sh
Mickelberry, Martha to Robert T. Fortner 3-29-1851 (3-30-1851) T
Mickelberry, Sarah Ann Frances to Thomas J. Ross 3-28-1844 Sh
Mickelbury, Mary to R. L. Starks 1-7-1847 Sh
Mickleberry, Lucinda E. to William Weatherford 12-3-1835 Sh
Mickleberry, Mary S. to Wm. F. Harris 10-28-1823 Sh
Middlebrook, Caroline to John Sanders 10-19-1871 Hy
Middlebrooks, Maria to Louis Malone 12-27-1867 (12-28-1867) F B
Middleton, D. E. to John N. Reed 1-13-1858 (1-17-1858) G
Middleton, Martha E. to W. F. Elder 12-17-1883 (12-18-1883) L
Middleton, Martha to Robert Agnew 3-24-1846 (no return) Hn
Middleton, Obedience to Dennis Barnes 8-10-1865 Mn
Middleton, Sarah E. to Mason Fowler 11-30-1861 Mn
Middleton, Selina to Henry Bernard 9-18-1861 (9-19-1861) Sh
Middleton, Susan to Jno. T. May 9-17-1855 (9-19-1855) Sh
Middleton, Suta A. to Johnathan J. Haeslip 12-3-1855 (12-4-1855) G
Midgett, Anna to William Bond 3-24-1874 Hy
Midgett, Eleanor to David T. Moody 12-19-1848 (12-20-1848) Ma
Midgett, Lucy A. (Mrs.) to Eli Smith 9-27-1866 Hy
Midgett, Lucy to Allen Harden 9-30-1871 Hy
Midgett, Margarett E. to W. M. Midgett 12-27-1882 (12-28-1882) L
Midgett, Mary A. to John R. Duncan 12-21-1881 (12-22-1881) L
Midgett, Mary E. to James E. Stanley 10-9-1867 Hy
Midgett, Mary to Benjamin Dunn 8-10-1842 Hn
Midiant, Polly Ann to Jasper F. Lowrince 11-27-1839 Cr
Midleton, Nancy Jane to A. R. Gossett 4-18-1858 Be
Miers, Lucinda to William B. Hines 4-22-1850 Sh
Mifflin, Lou to James Colbert 6-4-1866 Dy
Mifflin, Mary to Archer Mosely 5-9-1874 (5-10-1874) Dy
Mige, Rebecca to L. M. Lee 11-6-1855 We
Mila, Elizabeth to Clark C. Deson 11-27-1844 (11-28-1844) T
Milam, E. C. to P. A. Walker 10-16-1866 (no return) Dy
Milam, Harriett to Jerry Nesbitt 2-3-1873 (2-6-1873) Cr B
Milam, Louisa to Thos. J. Pritchett 2-4-1863 (2-5-1863) Dy
Milam, M. S. to P. E. Gregson 5-4-1871 Dy
Milam, Margaret E. to Joseph Jones 11-19-1853 (no return) Hn
Milam, Nancy E. to W. S. Scott 4-8-1868 (4-9-1868) Dy
Milam, Rachael L. to James J. Carnal 1-26-1870 (1-27-1870) Cr
Milan, Lodusky to Levi Janes 7-22-1859 (no return) Hn
Milberry, R. S. Lee to W. D. Wimberley 9-5-1852 Hn
Milegan, Frances to Nathan W. Williford 2-16-1838 F
Milener, Sally Ann to George Taylor 2-8-1864 (2-11-1864) O
Miles, A. J. to S. H. Reeves 1-17-1868 (1-19-1868) O
Miles, Calley (Miss) to R. A. (Col.) Payne 9-27-1864 (9-28-1864) O
Miles, Cally to R. A. Payne 9-7-1864 O
Miles, Curlin to William H. Curlin 7-27-1842 Ma
Miles, Elizabeth Jane to Jacob Gruber 5-5-1846 Sh
Miles, Elizabeth to W. M. Pleasant 9-11-1858 We
Miles, Kate to Thos. McCowell 8-3-1864 Sh
Miles, Louisa Matilda to Henry Schmely 5-15-1871 Hy
Miles, M. M. to N. W. Alexander 6-19-1869 (no return) Hy
Miles, Margaret to James O. Conner 6-11-1848 Sh
Miles, Mary Elizabeth to James E. Tyson 10-27-1855 (11-1-1855) O
Miles, Nancy M. to William G. Bethel 8-26-1850 O
Miles, Parnesia? Ann to Patrick Dickson 12-29-1854 (12-31-1854) O
Miligan, Lucinda to Charlie Johnson 5-5-1884 (5-9-1884) L
Miligan, Rebecca to Joseph East 2-6-1838 F
Mill, D. R. (Mrs.) to Lilburn Young 1-18-1861 (1-20-1861) O
Millard, Leida to Jesse Jones 5-11-1874 Hy
Millen, Minerva to Green Berry Long 7-24-1843 (11-27-1843) Ma
Millen, Susannah to Larken Easteridge 12-27-1828 O
Miller (Milton), Charlotte to Samuel Moore 3-11-1838 Sh
Miller, Aanda to Ben Wooten 1-20-1869 T
Miller, Adaline to Richard Green 11-9-1872 T
Miller, Alice to Geo. Sandford 5-18-1878 (5-24-1878) Dy
Miller, Alva to A. W. Druse? 1-24-1871 (1-25-1871) T
Miller, Amanda to John R. Nash 11-14-1877 (11-15-1877) Dy
Miller, Amy to James Anderson 8-13-1870 (8-14-1870) F B
Miller, Ann M. to G. J. G. Thomason 2-21-1867 Hn
Miller, Ann to John Davis 9-29-1866 (no return) Hy
Miller, Anna to Eli Moore 2-26-1830 Ma
Miller, Anna to George W. Turnley 7-19-1853 (no return) F
Miller, Anna to John Collins 6-15-1874 Hy
Miller, Annie A. to John D. Thompson 2-21-1865 (2-22-1865) T
Miller, Annie E. to P. D. Fulkerson 8-29-1883 L
Miller, Annie J. to Robt. M. Baker 3-22-1854 (3-23-1854) Sh
Miller, Annie to Andrew Collins 5-21-1874 T
Miller, Annie to Horace Vaulx 12-19-1878 Hy
Miller, Annie to J. H. Ward 10-1-1877 (no return) Dy
Miller, Barbara to William H. Stephens 12-31-1838 (1-2-1839) Ma

Miller, Betsy J. to Charles Matthews 7-28-1856 Hr
Miller, Bettie to Jack Short 12-30-1869 Hy
Miller, Bettie to Sam Beard 3-10-1870 (no return) Hy
Miller, Caraline to John J. Ryker 2-10-1873 L
Miller, Caroline R. to Hugh B. Robinson 5-3-1855 G
Miller, Caroline to Anthony Tharpe 5-30-1844 Hn
Miller, Caroline to Henry M. Farrow 11-8-1868 Be
Miller, Caroline to John Coldwell 1-9-1873 Hy
Miller, Catharine to Howell Short 10-24-1842 Ma
Miller, Catharine to Thomas R. Smith 4-28-1853 Hr
Miller, Catherine to Jacob Myers 1-27-1846 Sh
Miller, Catty to Ben Short 10-13-1866 Hy
Miller, Charity to Robert McClellan 12-17-1874 Hy
Miller, Charlott to Jessey Bishop 4-10-1871 (no return) Hy
Miller, Delly to Samuel Wilkes 12-26-1872 Hy
Miller, Dicy to Elijah Cross 5-31-1838 F
Miller, Dinah to Peyton Miller 3-27-1874 Hy
Miller, Dora to Henry Phelps 4-20-1867 Hn
Miller, E. J. to J. N. Peebles 2-23-1856 (2-26-1856) G
Miller, E. to N. W. Puckett 10-16-1867 Hn
Miller, Easter to Stephen Mason 2-21-1871 (2-26-1871) F B
Miller, Eliza A. to William B. Simonton 12-18-1866 (12-19-1866) T
Miller, Eliza Jane to Robert P. McCraken 9-24-1851 (9-24-1851) G
Miller, Eliza M. to John F. Miller 10-26-1869 T
Miller, Eliza to John Baird 1-29-1868 T
Miller, Eliza to Michael Langan 10-20-1845 Sh
Miller, Eliza to Thomas Amos 1-14-1857 G
Miller, Eliza to Thos. C. Horne 10-5-1870 (10-10-1870) T
Miller, Elizabeth A. to James F. Holder 1-17-1867 G
Miller, Elizabeth to Benjamine F. Watts 10-8-1859 We
Miller, Elizabeth to Hiram Clyne 3-13-1843 Hr
Miller, Elizabeth to John H. Hunter 4-3-1844 Hn
Miller, Elizabeth to Thomas Fletcher 11-17-1835 (11-18-1835) G
Miller, Ellen to Rafe Right 8-10-1867 Hy
Miller, Emily to William H. Farley 9-22-1842 Hn
Miller, F. E. (Mrs.) to E. J. Golay 11-24-1857 Sh
Miller, Fanny to J. F. Wolff 4-10-1864 (4-13-1864) Sh
Miller, Frances A. E. to Joseph Pool 2-6-1861 L
Miller, H. A. H. to H. H. Phillips 1-15-1866 Dy
Miller, Hannah A. to William Elliott 1-23-1855 Sh
Miller, Harrett A. to Thomas Spencer 4-8-1852 G
Miller, Harriet N. to Wm. Badger 12-3-1851 (12-24-1851) Sh
Miller, Harriet to D. S. Johnson 9-8-1864 (9-9-1864) Sh
Miller, Helen to Eli Miller 1-4-1876 (no return) Hy
Miller, Indiana to William Clark 1-20-1866 Hy
Miller, Isabella Jane to Thomas Graham 3-2-1863 Sh
Miller, Isabella S. to Alex P. Waddell 6-6-1853 (no return) F
Miller, J. A. to T. J. Forbess 12-21-1870 (12-22-1870) T
Miller, J. W. to W. T. Harrison 1-4-1881 (no return) L
Miller, Jane E. to Richard G. Scott 5-5-1835 Sh
Miller, Jane E. to Robert Glass 3-29-1836 Sh
Miller, Jane to Isaac Anderson 1-28-1869 G B
Miller, Jane to J. G. Wilson 10-15-1876 Hy
Miller, Jane to Jackson Pinkston 8-26-1871 (8-29-1871) T
Miller, Jane to John Pool 1-29-1868 T
Miller, Jane to Peter Read 7-7-1866 T
Miller, Jane to Thomas E. Robbins 8-28-1882 L
Miller, Judith Elizabeth to J. N. Stagner 1-11-1863 Hn
Miller, Julia Ann to Isaac Stephens 1-7-1852 O
Miller, Julia to Joe Bowers 9-7-1867 F B
Miller, Julia to Robert C. Roberts 1-24-1861 Dy
Miller, Julian to John A. Hays 3-16-1842 (3-17-1842) G
Miller, Juliza F. A. to Smith Park 10-26-1841 G
Miller, Laura E. to James W. Porter 10-27-1870 G
Miller, Laura E. to Tristam B. Peck 11-24-1862 Mn
Miller, Laura to M. B. Simons 6-28-1862 Mn
Miller, Lavinia to John C. Riley 6-10-1876 (no return) Hy
Miller, Leah S. to Phillip C. Swayne 3-1-1854 Hn
Miller, Lottie A. to Solomon Reeves 5-7-1868 (5-15-1868) F B
Miller, Lou to Charley Alexander 11-12-1870 (11-17-1870) F B
Miller, Louisa (Mrs.) to James Dean 9-21-1863 Sh
Miller, Louisa A. A. to Thomas James 9-18-1855 (9-19-1855) Sh
Miller, Louisa to Andrew Rorburg 4-28-1859 Sh
Miller, Louisa to Thomas Crouch 4-9-1846 (no return) Hn
Miller, Louise to Thomas H. Drake 11-12-1844 Ma
Miller, Lucinda to Gilbert Wylie 2-13-1873 T
Miller, M. A. to W. M. Nichols 1-11-1865 (2-6-1865) T
Miller, M. C. to W. Jefferson Sing 5-3-1864 (5-5-1864) Sh
Miller, M. E. to E. S. Ellis 1-17-1872 (1-18-1872) T
Miller, M. E. to H. L. Jones 4-14-1865 Hn
Miller, M. E. to W. W. Spain 5-23-1860 Dy
Miller, M. L. to J. H. Hardison 8-29-1876 (8-31-1876) Dy
Miller, M. M. to J. T. Garrett 11-18-1877 Hy
Miller, M. to Anthony Ross 12-29-1869 (12-30-1869) T
Miller, Malsina to William Thurman 6-11-1849 (6-12-1849) Ma
Miller, Margaret to Benj. Tho. Adkins 10-2-1850 T
Miller, Margaret to Henry Smith 1-12-1846 (1-15-1846) T

Miller, Margaret to James Buttery? 12-16-1871 (12-17-1871) T
Miller, Margaret to John Hayne 8-3-1858 Sh
Miller, Margaret to Milton Elsten 2-15-1858 Ma
Miller, Margarett R. to Jesse R. Irwin 9-14-1844 (no return) F
Miller, Margarett to Robert Sellars 5-10-1832 G
Miller, Martha A. to John Simonton 5-18-1847 (5-21-1847) T
Miller, Martha Ann to Craton Mizell 8-23-1857 Hn
Miller, Martha P. to Archibald H. Harper 11-4-1871 Ma
Miller, Martha W. to James C. Holmes 2-11-1856 (2-13-1856) G
Miller, Martha to John Heathcot 3-1-1849 Hn
Miller, Martha to Wm. Cavenah 3-10-1852 Sh
Miller, Mary Ann E. M. to Masslon Whitten 11-11-1841 G
Miller, Mary C. to William F. Cannon 9-5-1873 L
Miller, Mary E. to A. D. Sessom 10-25-1855 (10-30-1855) Sh
Miller, Mary E. to Benjamin S. Harrison 4-28-1868 (4-30-1868) L
Miller, Mary E. to Jasper N. Smith 6-30-1855 (7-1-1855) Hr
Miller, Mary M. to William N. Eakin 9-17-1864 Sh
Miller, Mary W. to W. J. Simmons 2-25-1854 (no return) F
Miller, Mary to D. A. Merrill 12-29-1856 T
Miller, Mary to James M. Land 3-15-1872 (3-17-1872) L
Miller, Mary to Joseph Douglas 1-3-1878 Hy
Miller, Mary to Leonidas Bills 5-18-1857 Hr
Miller, Mary to Maurice Mitchell 9-5-1849 (9-9-1849) T
Miller, Mary to Nathaniel Stricklin 10-14-1840 (10-15-1840) Hr
Miller, Mary to Sherod S. Paul 6-19-1838 (6-21-1838) G
Miller, Mary to William W. Walters 10-20-1859 We
Miller, Matilda to Jacob Huffman 6-12-1836 O
Miller, Matilda to Joseph Tagg 2-29-1848 Sh
Miller, Matilda to Joshua Bowls 2-3-1870 Hy
Miller, Mattie E. to T. M. H. Mathis 12-14-1871 Hy
Miller, Millie to Rewbin Belerford 4-27-1873 Cr B
Miller, Milly to W. S. Blackshear 7-25-1854 Hn
Miller, Mina to Thomas Atkinson 6-22-1860 Sh
Miller, Minerva to Jack Tipton 6-22-1867 (6-23-1867) T
Miller, Mollie J. to J. W. Campbell 10-20-1871 (10-26-1871) T
Miller, Mollie to Bird Soward 2-7-1878 Dy
Miller, Nancy E. to John W. Wilie 7-31-1855 (8-2-1855) T
Miller, Nancy J. to William L. Gwaltney 6-14-1858 (6-17-1858) O
Miller, Nancy to J. T. Wolfe 4-4-1864 Sh
Miller, Nancy to James Anderson 5-6-1836 Sh
Miller, Nancy to James Barber 8-21-1861 L
Miller, Nancy to John M. Hewatt 5-30-1857 Sh
Miller, Nancy to Nicholas Perry 9-18-1849 (9-20-1849) Ma
Miller, Nancy to Richard Green 4-18-1874 T
Miller, Nancy to William F. Morgan 6-24-1872 L
Miller, Nancy to William Wallace 5-24-1864 Hn
Miller, Nancy to Wm. Bagwell 8-16-1840 Sh
Miller, P. (Mrs.) to Evin J. Smith 12-4-1866 O
Miller, P. F. to W. C. Colvitt no date (8-6-1873) Cr
Miller, Peggy to Anthony Taylor 12-28-1865 (no return) F
Miller, Polly C. to Ephraim Blair 4-12-1827 G
Miller, Polly C. to Ephraim Blair 4-12-1828 G
Miller, Pryam to Daniel W. Hogan 9-19-1866 O
Miller, R. V. C. to Albert C. Smith 12-27-1848 L
Miller, RAchel to Edward Radford Crouch 8-12-1844 (8-15-1844) T
Miller, Rachel to James L. McDougal 3-19-1846 Hn
Miller, Rebecca J. to Andrew W. Drew 3-25-1852 Sh
Miller, Rebecca to J. L. Moultrie 11-26-1863 (11-27-1863) O
Miller, Rebecca to John H. Dean 1-12-1857 (1-14-1857) G
Miller, Rilla Jane to Anderson Jones 3-30-1876 Dy
Miller, Roxanna to B. F. Cloys 2-13-1851 O
Miller, Rutelia to R. H. Daniel 1-22-1867 F
Miller, S. J. to J. E. Blankenship 8-29-1879 (8-31-1879) L
Miller, S. J. to T. J. Morphis 11-8-1863 Mn
Miller, S. to J. T. Chiles 1-16-1868 O
Miller, Sallie to Jack Culbreath 1-16-1872 Hy
Miller, Sally W. to Jas. W. (Rev.) Knott 5-27-1849 F
Miller, Sarah A. to G. F. Parish 9-17-1872 (9-19-1872) Cr
Miller, Sarah A. to Joseph H. Chipman 8-30-1873 (8-31-1873) L
Miller, Sarah C. to Henry Wagner 10-26-1851 Hn
Miller, Sarah E. to Abraham Miller 9-5-1857 (9-8-1857) O
Miller, Sarah Eliza to Isaac M. Jackson 5-25-1858 (5-26-1858) Ma
Miller, Sarah Jane to William C. Green 7-29-1863 Sh
Miller, Sarah Jane to William O. Davis 3-11-1869 Cr
Miller, Sarah R. to Wm. P. Bradley 4-18-1855 (5-1-1855) Sh
Miller, Sarah T. to William Sammons 8-19-1868 Hy
Miller, Sarah to Jackson Boon 7-3-1838 (7-4-1838) O
Miller, Sarah to Thomas L. Hauck 7-4-1863 (7-5-1863) O
Miller, Serena to Moses Lightfoot 10-25-1870 (no return) F B
Miller, Sidney to Charles Newsom 11-18-1870 Hy
Miller, Sophia H. to Wm. W. Wiggins 11-16-1859 Hr
Miller, Susan A. to George W. Turner 10-31-1854 (11-2-1854) T
Miller, Susan A. to J. W. Goldin 2-21-1856 (no return) Hn
Miller, Susan F. to Jackson F. Brothers 1-6-1879 (no return) Dy
Miller, Susan to Albert Smith 2-21-1873 (2-22-1873) T
Miller, Susanna C. to Jno. W. Penick 8-10-1859 F
Miller, Susie to Sherman Davis 12-26-1883 (12-28-1883) L

Miller, Tennessee to Jacob Heester 5-11-1861 Sh
Miller, Unicy? to Raiford C. Patterson 10-29-1842 (11-2-1842) Hr
Miller, V. Ann to Austin Peete 1-14-1873 T
Miller, Valery to Alexander Ragsdale 10-12-1843 Ma
Miller, Vick to J. J. Raney 3-26-1871 Hy
Miller, Virginia A. to Hankins E. Harendon 9-3-1839 F
Miller, W. A. to J. W. Hancock 1-2-1878 (no return) L
Miller, Willie to Lamuel F. Grayson 12-30-1868 (12-31-1868) Ma
Miller, Winnie to Jno. C. Best 12-21-1871 Hy
Millican, Ann Eliza to J. S. Brinkley 11-7-1867 Dy
Milligan, Fannie to Albert Smith 12-25-1884 (12-30-1885) L
Milliken, Elizabeth to John M. Fuller 10-24-1849 Hn
Milliken, Nancy Ann to John H. Poyner 9-15-1859 Hn
Milliken, Sarah J. to William K. Palmer 5-12-1853 Hn
Millikin, Elizabeth to Joseph Fowlk 12-6-1842 Sh
Millikin, Elizabeth to Thomas Sharp 10-8-1847 (10-10-1847) F
Millikin, Mollie E. to N. B. Price 6-9-1868 (6-10-1868) F
Milliner, J. A. to Robt. Conn 1-14-1868 (1-15-1868) O
Milliner, Sarah to John C. Brady 10-15-1864 O
Milliner, Settie to John C. Brady 2-15-1865 (2-16-1865) O
Millington, Kate to R. C. Blankenship 10-25-1860 Sh
Millone, Martha to Andrew J. Spruwell 5-17-1845 (5-23-1845) G
Mills (Miles), Nancy R. to John Marr 7-18-1846 O
Mills (Wills), Sarah F. to Jno. R. Wilson 8-9-1862 Hy
Mills, Abby to John M. Pennington 12-28-1831 (12-29-1831) Hr
Mills, Alice to Sandy Scott 2-5-1835 (2-6-1835) Hr
Mills, Amanda L. to Jesse Crouse 11-5-1847 (11-7-1847) Hr
Mills, Amanda to Daniel M. Allison 2-19-1870 (2-20-1870) Ma
Mills, Caroline S. to A. M. Adcock 5-13-1863 (5-14-1863) Cr
Mills, Caroline to John Bird 12-4-1842 Hn
Mills, Cyntha to James W. Chaddick 3-20-1837 (3-30-1837) Hr
Mills, Eliza J. to F. G. Ellis 12-1-1866 (12-2-1866) Dy
Mills, Eliza to John Horten 2-17-1858 We
Mills, Eliza to Simeon M. Jones 7-2-1848 Ma
Mills, Elizabeth Rebecca to Joseph Young 3-2-1854 O
Mills, Fanny G. to Robert Wiles 11-24-1851 O
Mills, Felicia to Jacob Anderson 11-14-1872 L B
Mills, Frances to Henry M. Savage 1-21-1858 (1-22-1858) Hr
Mills, Harrett to Newton C. Scott 7-7-1841 (7-8-1841) Hr
Mills, Harriet A. to Wm. A. Threadgill 11-28-1860 (no return) Cr
Mills, Harriett to Joseph Crouse 6-22-1843 Hr
Mills, Isabella A. to Robert M. Brown 10-19-1854 O
Mills, Jane to Hamilton Murley 2-4-1839 (2-7-1839) Hr
Mills, Jane to John Rogers 12-10-1845 Hr
Mills, Louisa to Lytle B. Roberts 2-8-1844 Hr
Mills, Lucy to John J. Taylor 11-16-1857 Ma
Mills, M. H. to J. C. Outlaw 12-29-1851 O
Mills, Malvina to James H. Norton 12-8-1856 (12-9-1856) Ma
Mills, Margarett Eveline to William C. Erven 2-6-1847 (2-7-1847) Hr
Mills, Martha A. to Jessee F. Dawson 1-18-1871 (1-19-1871) T
Mills, Martha J. to Banks M. Burrow 10-1-1867 (no return) Cr
Mills, Martha to John Dove 8-11-1863 (no return) Dy
Mills, Mary B. to Randolph Moore 11-15-1849 O
Mills, Mary E. to G. G. Cooper 7-27-1875 (7-29-1875) Dy
Mills, Mary E. to Saml. J. Mills 8-28-1865 T
Mills, Mary to James Hamilton 7-19-1845 (7-20-1845) Hr
Mills, Mary to Thomas Phillips 12-11-1860 O
Mills, Maryline to Amos Woodard 4-30-1861 Dy
Mills, Matilda M. to Elijah Draper 2-21-1857 (2-25-1857) L
Mills, Minerva to Thomas M. Norton 9-15-1860 (9-17-1860) Ma
Mills, Mollie A. to S. S. Hayley 12-5-1865 (12-14-1865) Cr
Mills, N. P. to James A. L. Crow 10-24-1866 (10-25-1866) Dy
Mills, Nancy A. to S. Burch 8-30-1870 Dy
Mills, Nancy H. to William A. Brown 9-8-1845 (9-9-1845) O
Mills, Nancy to John Harmon? 2-17-1857 O
Mills, Nannie to W. H. Read 12-20-1877 Dy
Mills, Polly to John Fletcher 5-17-1854 (5-21-1854) O
Mills, Polly to William G. Ingram 7-2-1848 Ma
Mills, Pollyann to James J. Brooks 10-14-1853 (10-15-1853) O
Mills, Rachel to John Roberts 5-17-1855 O
Mills, Rosa Ann Jane to W. D. Dawson 12-?-1869 (12-19-1869) T
Mills, Sarah to F. Fritz 11-15-1853 (11-18-1853) O
Mills, Sarah to John Ward 10-30-1848 (no return) F
Mills, Susan A. to W. D. Joynier 12-1-1868 Hy
Mills, Virginia to Richd. W. Whitehead 6-8-1836 Hr
Millsap, Elizabeth to William Brimm 6-8-1836 Hr
Milltenberger, Catharine to Charles Muller (Miller) 7-20-1860 Sh
Milner, Elizabeth P. to William Jones 6-15-1854 We
Milner, Lucinda C. to C. C. Oldham 12-17-1846 We
Milner, Miss to John E. Mosley 12-29-1849 We
Milner, Sophiah L. to Mason Ezzell 7-27-1854 We
Milon, L. E. to Peter Pearson 10-6-1866 (10-11-1866) Cr
Milsaps, Margaret to Joseph Dillard 10-20-1840 L
Milstead, Argen to James M. Edmunds 2-8-1855 Hn
Milstead, Elizabeth to Jesse B. Jackson 8-3-1856 Hn
Milstead, Mary to William Hart 12-25-1854 Hn
Milstead, Rebecca to James M. Edwards 11-23-1861 (no return) Hn

Milstead, Zepharum to James N. Hamilton 9-5-1862 Hn
Milsted, Ann E. to D. M. Inman 1-24-1860 Sh
Milton, Elizabeth N. to John C. Sale 11-22-1842 G
Milton, Lids M. to Ebin Rowland 8-6-1843 Cr
Milton, Mary Ann to Moses Slough 12-1-1851 Sh
Milton, Monan to Turner R. Gibbs 3-20-1844 (4-3-1844) G
Milton, Rebecca A. to Thos. Easter 8-11-1846 Cr
Milton, Sarah A. to J. G. Davis 10-27-1861 G
Milum, Mary Ann to T. A. Hollaway 1-4-1872 (no return) Cr
Milworth, Emily to George W. Heron 10-23-1862 (10-25-1862) O
Mims, Martha B. to Hugh L. Cook 12-17-1847 Sh
Mims, Mary to Benjamin West 7-4-1838 Sh
Mineard, Kissey to Jackson Hazle 11-24-1874 Hy
Minerva, Cotter to Harry Pike 2-16-1867 Hy
Mingea, Catharine to W. R. Comstock 9-9-1862 Sh
Minger, Anna to Wm. Henry Evans 2-3-1878 Hy
Mink, Jane to Charles Riley 1-22-1861 Sh
Minnis, Mary E. to John Harroldson 2-7-1849 Sh
Minor, Cordelia to Randell Jarrett 3-7-1874 Hy
Minor, Eliza to John Estes 7-15-1876 Hy
Minor, Harriett to Robert Jarrett 4-21-1871 Hy
Minor, Laura to Burton Bond 4-18-1878 Hy
Minor, Mima to Charley Murrell 4-25-1870 (7-17-1870) F B
Minor, Sallie to Jos. Cotherane 1-5-1866 (1-27-1866) T
Minster, H. M. to Gustavus Potter 12-9-1863 Sh
Minten, Anjalin to John Nicholas 4-3-1854 We
Minter, Elizabeth E. to Adolphus G. Dennis 4-20-1849 Hr
Minter, Hester A. to Wheetly Dennies 6-18-1855 (6-24-1855) Hr
Minter, Lydia Ann to B. A. Bangues 3-8-1844 (3-12-1844) Hr
Minter, Mary A. to Benjamin F. Williams 3-22-1842 Hr
Minter, Rebecca W. to Josiah S. White 4-20-1849 (4-24-1849) Hr
Minter, Sarah F. to E. R. Cage 1-20-1847 (1-21-1847) Hr
Minter, Sarah Jane to Timothy T. House 9-12-1853 Hr
Minton (Winton), Martha to Nathaniel Moore 9-18-1838 Sh
Minton, Dorthy to Joseph R. White 10-6-1862 Mn
Minton, Elizabeth A. to John G. Weaver 12-31-1865 Mn
Minton, Ellen to James M. Applegate 8-20-1838 (8-22-1838) O
Minton, Martha J. to Joseph S. Raynard 12-10-1833 (12-17-1833) Hr
Minton, Nancy Harper to Andrew W. Baldridge 1-20-1831 O
Minton, Perdilia (Permelia) to Ira B. Hitchcock 8-22-1847 Sh
Minton, S. J. to J. A. Strawn 3-31-1865 (4-1-1865) Dy
Minton, Susan C. to J. M. Hall 7-10-1861 (6-11-1861) Dy
Minton, Susan to M. M. Tilghman 11-29-1868 G
Mirack, Louisa to John H. Herod 4-2-1834 G
Miranda, Mary E. to Joseph C. Smith 2-18-1862 Sh
Mires, L. L. to Turner Barfoot 8-9-1842 Be
Mires, Mary Ann to John D. Hines 9-4-1844 Sh
Mirks, Easter to Charley Allen 3-2-1867 (no return) Hy
Mise, M. E. to C. J. Bryan 10-30-1858 Sh
Misers, Analizer to W. W. Davidson 3-15-1863 Be
Mishel (Miskel?), Hannah to John McNamara 7-30-1853 (7-31-1853) Sh
Miskelly, Jane to William Brandon 8-20-1838 (8-21-1838) L
Miskelly, Mary S. to Jobe P. Lawrens 3-1-1865 (3-2-1865) L
Misskelly, Eliza Ann to Josiah Baird 11-18-1856 (11-20-1856) L
Missouro, Matilda to Francis M. Lewis 12-22-1859 Sh
Mitchael, Nancy to P. E. Greer 7-3-1854 (7-4-1854) Hr
Mitchard, Dolly A. to N. E. Elks 9-18-1865 O
Mitchel, Adaline to G. W. Stover 12-26-1866 O
Mitchel, Annie to Thomas Miller 2-8-1877 (2-11-1877) L
Mitchel, Ary Ann to Turner Harris 6-11-1847 (6-17-1847) F
Mitchel, Ester Ann to Nelson Pearce 12-20-1849 We
Mitchel, F. R. Rebecca to John Wilson 4-15-1841 Sh
Mitchel, Lacy J. to F. P. Johnson 7-15-1844 (no return) We
Mitchel, Lucinda to Elcany Pafford 7-5-1857 Be
Mitchel, Lucy to Was. Adams 1-8-1840 Be
Mitchel, Margaret B. to Elias J. Bishop 10-12-1848 Sh
Mitchel, Margaret to William Vanwinkle 2-27-1843 Sh
Mitchel, Mary A. to W. D. Simmons 2-26-1858 Be
Mitchel, Mary E. to G. T. Penn 6-22-1864 G
Mitchel, Mary E. to John C. Smith 3-9-1857 G
Mitchel, R. H. (Mrs.) to C. B. Brame 8-20-1855 (no return) F
Mitchel, Sarah A. to Henry Brown 5-14-1828 G
Mitchel, Zady M. to Michael Flowers 12-27-1841 (12-28-1841) G
Mitchell, Adaline T. to Jesse Mydyett 10-24-1833 G
Mitchell, Adeline B. to Isaac Morrison 1-8-1849 T
Mitchell, Alice to George W. Walker 3-12-1870 (3-13-1870) Cr
Mitchell, Ama to Samuel Dunlap 3-27-1867 (no return) F B
Mitchell, Amanda E. to James R. Brooks 11-25-1839 O
Mitchell, Amarillas to Frederick G. Walbridge 6-29-1853 Sh
Mitchell, Ann A. to Robert H. Boon 11-1-1858 (11-4-1858) Ma
Mitchell, Ann E. to P. H. Hunter 9-2-1865 O
Mitchell, Ann to Able Stewart 12-26-1853 Hr
Mitchell, Ann to Andrew Darling 10-20-1861 (10-21-1861) We
Mitchell, Anna to William T. Senter 2-22-1870 G
Mitchell, Ansonetta M. to R. R. Minton 2-28-1869 G
Mitchell, Arabella E. to Henry B. Chiles 1-4-1851 (1-6-1851) F
Mitchell, Ardell to J. M. Cotton 8-14-1866 Cr

Mitchell, Arrena to John M. Jinkins 7-11-1861 We
Mitchell, Aurora to William D. Bloys 7-18-1844 O
Mitchell, Betsy to Harris Wiggins 12-31-1827 Hr
Mitchell, Bettie to J. M. Prichard 2-12-1878 (2-13-1878) L
Mitchell, C. M. to Jessee Jeter 12-2-1849 Hr
Mitchell, Camilea to Frank Hayes 11-18-1884 (11-19-1884) L
Mitchell, Catharine to Stephen Powers 5-19-1864 Sh
Mitchell, Catharine to Thomas Pearce 12-30-1847 Sh
Mitchell, Catherine T. to William N. Rutherford 4-3-1861 (4-4-1861) L
Mitchell, Clementine to John Robinson 7-7-1867 Be
Mitchell, Dora (Dona) to M. F. Blackburn 5-18-1874 O
Mitchell, E. J. to J. W. Baley 11-2-1856 We
Mitchell, E. J. to John W. Wilkes 3-13-1858 (3-17-1859?) Hr
Mitchell, E. J. to W. G. Bennett 9-8-1860 Sh
Mitchell, Eddie to George Dean 2-24-1886 (no return) L
Mitchell, Elisabeth J. to J. A. Wise 6-5-1854 Sh
Mitchell, Elizabeth E. to Thomas W. Jones 7-12-1848 (7-13-1848) G
Mitchell, Elizabeth Jane to Thomas S. Garrett 12-19-1848 (12-21-1848) Hr
Mitchell, Elizabeth P. to John W. Chrisp 12-23-1847 (12-25-1847) Ma
Mitchell, Elizabeth to A. B. Crenshaw 1-31-1861 G
Mitchell, Elizabeth to Hinson Lunnon 11-27-1843 Ma
Mitchell, Elizabeth to James McGill 5-16-1847 Be
Mitchell, Elizabeth to Littleton Ward 9-7-1831 (9-13-1831) G
Mitchell, Elizabeth to Washington Ivie 12-7-1846 (no return) F
Mitchell, Elizabeth to Willia G. Wright 2-8-1844 (2-27-1844) T
Mitchell, Ellen to John Connell 8-25-1864 Sh
Mitchell, Emily C. to Allen Williams 11-20-1843 Be
Mitchell, Emily C. to Allen Williams 11-20-1843 Be CC
Mitchell, Emily to Bob Sanderford 1-1-1867 G
Mitchell, Emoline to Marcus H. Cline 9-14-1839 (9-15-1839) Ma
Mitchell, Eveline to Henry Jones 12-28-1870 F B
Mitchell, Fanney to J. C. Harrell 3-16-1859 F
Mitchell, Fannie to Jacob Lee 12-28-1885 (12-29-1885) L
Mitchell, Fannie to Thomas Bates 12-27-1876 (12-29-1876) Dy
Mitchell, Fannie to Wm. Smith (Sith) 12-18-1872 Hy
Mitchell, Fenton to George Gibson 1-16-1843 Sh
Mitchell, Georgia Ann to William Moore 10-15-1868 (10-17-1868) F B
Mitchell, Hannah to Adam Smith 11-24-1834 Hr
Mitchell, Hannah to Frank Woodard 6-10-1877 O B
Mitchell, Hannah to James Moore 2-18-1869 F B
Mitchell, Harriet to Samuel Simpson 12-11-1838 (12-12-1838) Hr
Mitchell, Harriett to George Riddle 9-10-1849 O
Mitchell, Heloise V. to W. S. Henley 7-12-1878 (7-15-1878) L
Mitchell, Irene E. to A. D. Bennett 1-17-1841 Cr
Mitchell, Isonah to Ghos. C. Callhoon 12-20-1848 Cr
Mitchell, Jane to Spencer Bell 8-5-1869 (8-7-1869) F B
Mitchell, Jinnie to Sidney B. Nesbitt 9-12-1872 Cr B
Mitchell, Joann to Geo. Baucom 8-31-1872 (9-1-1872) Cr
Mitchell, Johnnie to R. M. Andrews 1-12-1886 (1-13-1886) L
Mitchell, Jollie? to Alfred Armstrong 8-29-1870 (no return) F B
Mitchell, Josephine to William Marlow 9-2-1853 (9-6-1853) O
Mitchell, Julia A. to E. B. Wilks 3-25-1869 Cr
Mitchell, Julia L. to William M. Tinnen 12-11-1858 (12-12-1858) T
Mitchell, Julian to Henderson Trusty 1-16-1830 G
Mitchell, June to Martin L. Hanis 12-16-1845 Hr
Mitchell, Kate E. to H. D. Stovall 1-8-1855 We
Mitchell, Laura to James T. Shankle 8-24-1869 (8-29-1869) T
Mitchell, Lizzie to Allen Copeland 10-12-1872 (no return) Dy
Mitchell, Lou Ellen to James Campbell 1-26-1877 (1-28-1877) Dy
Mitchell, Louisa G. to William Kerr 7-8-1837 (7-13-1837) Hr
Mitchell, Louisana to George Hill 12-28-1848 Ma
Mitchell, Louiza Jane to Major William Maclin 1-29-1868 (2-1-1868) L B
Mitchell, M. A. E. to Thomas J. Walton 7-2-1836 G
Mitchell, M. C. to James W. Victor 10-31-1864 Sh
Mitchell, M. E. to F. R. Prichard 8-25-1885 (8-26-1885) L
Mitchell, M. F. to J. N. Brewer 1-20-1872 (1-22-1872) Cr
Mitchell, M. J. to B. H.? Jones 1-1-1868 (1-2-1868) Cr
Mitchell, M. J. to John T. Kernan 8-20-1874 O
Mitchell, M. L. to Richard H. Briant 2-20-1861 (2-21-1861) Cr
Mitchell, M. L. to Richd. H. Briant 2-20-1861 (2-21-1861) Cr
Mitchell, M. O. to J. R. Fleming 2-5-1868 G
Mitchell, M. V. to D. A. Cropno 1-4-1869 (no return) Hy
Mitchell, Maggie to T. P. Martin 10-9-1874 (10-10-1874) T
Mitchell, Mainard to John G. Ballew 10-23-1860 (10-24-1860) Cr
Mitchell, Malissa L. to Allen C. Farrow 1-20-1867 Be
Mitchell, Mamaret? to John G. Belew 10-?-1860 (10-24-1860) Cr
Mitchell, Margaret to G. W. Alexander 10-14-1861 Sh
Mitchell, Margaret to Jacob Gordon 1-20-1870 T
Mitchell, Margarett to ____ Davenport 12-15-1838 (12-17-1838) Ma
Mitchell, Mariah to George Wilson 5-11-1864 (5-15-1864) O
Mitchell, Mariah to James Williams 9-10-1853 (9-23-1853) L
Mitchell, Marietta to G. N. Wade 11-17-1866 O
Mitchell, Martha J. to Abraham Newbill 9-2-1858 Cr
Mitchell, Martha to John Willett 4-4-1842 (4-7-1842) Ma
Mitchell, Martha to Samuel Freeman 1-6-1876 O B
Mitchell, Martha to Wm. E. Vaughn 2-7-1853 (2-17-1853) Sh
Mitchell, Mary (Mrs.) to Alonzo O. Green 3-15-1867 (3-17-1867) Ma

Mitchell, Mary A. to Thomas A. Mayberry 8-4-1849 Cr
Mitchell, Mary C. to Andrew Taylor 3-31-1846 (4-2-1846) F
Mitchell, Mary D. to J. H. Wilson 9-29-1872 T
Mitchell, Mary E. to Alonzo Dunavant 11-28-1853 (11-30-1853) L
Mitchell, Mary E. to Elisha Howard Verhine 10-21-1845 O
Mitchell, Mary E. to F. M. Mitchell 2-10-1867 Be
Mitchell, Mary June to T. R. Milam 8-23-1844 Hn
Mitchell, Mary L. to R. H. Crider 3-6-1869 (3-7-1869) Cr
Mitchell, Mary L. to William Barton 4-30-1847 F
Mitchell, Mary M. to Calvin Shofer 2-6-1854 (2-10-1854) Hr
Mitchell, Mary P. to r. C. Lea 12-6-1847 (12-23-1847) F
Mitchell, Mary c. to John F. Greenbery 1-4-1851 (1-6-1851) F
Mitchell, Mary to John Elgin 10-18-1844 F
Mitchell, Mary to Samul Shukle 10-11-1854 We
Mitchell, Mary to Wm. H. Stover 12-23-1862 O
Mitchell, Mattie J. to A. B. Conley 12-23-1868 G
Mitchell, May L. B. to Josiah W. King 12-12-1840 Ma
Mitchell, Mildred to Permanis Howard 1-1-1851 Hr
Mitchell, Millie to Jim Harris 11-1-1879 Dy
Mitchell, Milly to Isaac Griffin 1-20-1870 T
Mitchell, N. J. to James Cole 1-4-1848 Be
Mitchell, Nancy to John Smith 5-20-1846 G
Mitchell, Nancy to Luther Teel 12-2-1861 Sh
Mitchell, Nancy to Robert W. Sims 8-1-1853 (8-3-1853) Ma
Mitchell, Nancy to William Murrell 10-19-1829 Hr
Mitchell, Nannie to Coleman Hafford 11-5-1867 L
Mitchell, Narcissa E. to Leonard Dunavant 12-28-1852 L
Mitchell, P. W. to P. L. Hopper 3-20-1866 G
Mitchell, P. to N. Treanthan 7-30-1852 We
Mitchell, Pathanna to Pallen Fellosby 8-27-1850 We
Mitchell, Permelia to John Crudup 11-26-1858 (12-9-1858) O
Mitchell, Puss to Sam Evans 12-25-1868 (12-26-1868) F B
Mitchell, Rebacca to Lewis Powell 12-26-1866 (12-27-1866) Dy
Mitchell, Rhodie to John Bullock 1-11-1868 (1-21-1868) F B
Mitchell, Ridley J. to Geo. T. Hatch 1-16-1872 (no return) Cr
Mitchell, Rody to Johnson Rideout 12-9-1872 (12-13-1872) L B
Mitchell, S. A. to E. W. Boyett 12-22-1859 (12-25-1859) G
Mitchell, Sallie (Mrs.) to Richard Ray 1-17-1867 G
Mitchell, Sallie A. to John C. Hewlet 2-2-1866 (2-8-1866) F
Mitchell, Sallie to Houston Fitzgerald 1-22-1856 G
Mitchell, Sally to Will Hall 1-31-1855 Hn
Mitchell, Sarah A. to James R. Keating 11-26-1846 Cr
Mitchell, Sarah Ann to William H. Rogers 7-5-1836 Sh
Mitchell, Sarah Foster to J. D. Allain (Allen) 1-6-1844 Sh *
Mitchell, Sarah J. to J. W. Turner 12-9-1846 (no return) F
Mitchell, Sarah M. to Samuel L. Taylor 10-31-1860 T
Mitchell, Sarah V. to J. M. C. Liddle 1-1-1846 (no return) We
Mitchell, Sarah to George Canada 11-9-1844 (11-20-1844) G
Mitchell, Sarah to John Johnson 2-20-1856 Cr
Mitchell, Sariah Meriah to Stephen W. Hyott 11-1-1846 Be
Mitchell, Sophia T. to Zachariah M. Shackleford 11-10-1846 (11-12-1846) F
Mitchell, Sophronia E. to J. N. Cotton 3-29-1870 (no return) Cr
Mitchell, Sophronia E. to J. N. Cotton 7-25-1870 Cr
Mitchell, Spencer A. to Boyd Coggeshall 12-15-1878 Hy
Mitchell, Susan G. to Newton W. Warren 7-19-1853 (7-21-1853) G
Mitchell, Susan J. to C. E. Ragan 12-6-1865 G
Mitchell, Susan to Franklin H. Burton 12-7-1864 Be
Mitchell, Tempy to Henry Renfro 4-2-1867 G
Mitchell, Tennessee to David J. Montgomery 9-8-1842 Sh
Mitchell, Tennie E. to James W. Mathis 9-5-1867 T
Mitchell, V. L. to L. J. Foster 11-12-1874 (11-15-1874) O
Mitchell, Victoria to Andy Anderson 9-4-1865 (9-6-1865) F
Mitchiner, M. E. to P. D. Warlick 7-15-1867 (no return) Cr
Mitchner, Eugene to J. W. Stagner 3-2-1878 (3-23-1878) Dy
Mitchuer, H. to Tinzel Wade 1-20-1872 (1-21-1872) Dy
Mitchum, Elizah to R. E. Bumpass 11-18-1870 (11-22-1870) Cr
Mitchum, Emily to R. D. Caldwell 11-23-1857 Cr
Mitchum, Jane to Daniel Caldwell 2-21-1870 G B
Mitchum, M. to James Johns 5-10-1872 (5-12-1872) Cr B
Mitts, Hester Ann to John Russell 7-16-1831 (7-17-1831) G
Mitts, Polly to James Baker 1-8-1830 (1-14-1830) G
Mitts, Sarah A. to Alexander Fox 10-20-1853 (10-24-1853) G
Mitts, Sarah to Timothy Dowlen 1-13-1846 G
Mix?, Catherine to B. H. Lightfoot 11-23-1843 Hn
Mixon, Lenora to Benjamin F. Brockett 11-22-1849 Sh
Mixon, Sarah A. to William N. Edgar 11-29-1849 Hn
Mize (Musse), Bridgett to Balthasar Ingelass (Ingles) 2-28-1842 Sh
Mize, Lucinda to Samuel Soward 10-23-1837 Sh
Mize, S. H. to J. B. Dearmond 11-3-1859 Sh
Mizell, Emily to Wm. R. Pearce 3-19-1864 Be
Mizell, Mariah to James Williams 9-10-1853 (9-23-1853) L
Mizell, H. H. to P. O. Poter 2-20-1862 We
Mizell, L. S. to Jacob Turner 5-21-1873 (5-22-1873) Cr
Mizell, Martha to Joseph G. Sharp 11-16-1843 Ma
Mizell, Mary E. A. to Calvin Spivey 1-28-1847 Ma
Mizell, Mary W. to James M. Gray 1-2-1862 (no return) Hn
Mizell, Melica Ann to T. D. Shankle 1-6-1867 Hn
Mizell, Nancy to William Roberts 10-23-1853 Hn

Mizelle, Mary J. to Billups Barber 12-18-1856 (12-19-1856) We
Mizells, Mary to Green B. Clay 5-28-1851 (no return) L
Mizels, Margaret to T. R. Kennelly 3-10-1851 L
Mizzell, Perina J. to James A. McGill 10-16-1869 (10-20-1869) Cr
Mizzle, Mary A. to James F. Kirby 7-16-1853 (7-20-1853) L
Moanings, Elizabeth to William Brown 1-5-1870 (no return) F
Moberry, Levica A. to Benjamin F. Roberts 7-31-1857 We
Mobley, America Melissa to John W. Hopper 2-5-1868 G
Mobley, Annie W. to A. Eason 1-2-1872 Dy
Mobley, B. P. to L. C. Turner 8-25-1856 We
Mobley, Caroline to Jas. R. Brown 12-22-1855 G
Mobley, Delila to Willis L. A. Grady 2-23-1854 (3-13-1854) G
Mobley, Emily to W. K. Dial 1-17-1865 G
Mobley, Francis to John Cole 12-1-1826 G
Mobley, Malissie A. to Joseph W. Echols 11-8-1870 (11-9-1870) Dy
Mobley, Missouri to T. P. Hopper 8-30-1870 G
Mobley, Rachal to William K. Dial 12-30-1846 G
Mobly, Elizabeth to Ruben Pearce 5-13-1827 (5-16-1827) G
Mobly, Holy B. to Samuel D. Hughes 7-8-1867 (7-10-1867) L
Mobly, M. M. to B. M. Swann 10-8-1865 G
Mobly, M. M. to B. M. Swim 10-8-1865 G
Moffatt, Jane B. to Walter Brice 11-26-1858 O
Moffatt, Mariah to G. W. Harris 5-19-1866 O
Moffatt, Mary L. to James P. Weed 8-21-1847 (8-23-1847) O
Moffett, E. A. to A. D. Tillmon 11-9-1859 F
Moffett, Martha to Richard Oliver 8-14-1839 F
Moffit, Harriet to Cal Coward 12-30-1874 (12-31-1874) T
Moffit, Harriet to Jim Wells 9-5-1868 (9-6-1868) F B
Moffit, Martha to K.? Strong 11-15-1871 T
Moffitt, Cumfort to David Sparks 9-17-1827 Ma
Moffitt, Dolly H. to Eli Smith 12-12-1831 (12-15-1831) Hr
Moffitt, Mary to William Smith 10-29-1838 (10-30-1838) Hr
Moffitt, Sarah A. to Wesly C. Dodson 4-16-1853 (4-19-1853) Sh
Mofield, Elizabeth to Lewis Redden 9-20-1846 Hn
Mohon, Lizzy to Michael Mulligan 4-15-1861 Sh
Mohr, Margaret to Joseph Kensler 4-30-1858 Sh
Mohundro, Emily P. to Wm. C. May 7-24-1839] (7-28-1839) Hr
Mohundro, Nancy J. to J. C. Taylor 12-30-1865 Hn
Mohundrow(Omohundro), Mary A. to D. W. Jones 9-22-1867 Hn
Moldan, Elizabeth (Mrs.) to Joel Crenshaw 11-27-1836 Sh
Molena, Anna to Abram Jackson 8-6-1874 O
Moliter, Matilda A. to S. C. Garner 9-22-1858 (9-23-1858) Sh
Molitor, Cordelia L. to W. E. Wormell 7-23-1859 (7-26-1859) Sh
Molley, Dora to James Menley 7-9-1863 Sh
Mollie J., Williams to John H. Poston 12-6-1877 Hy
Mollie P., Bond to Geo. C. Porter 11-1-1870 Hy
Mollie, Johnson to F. S. Plummer 1-9-1871 (no return) Hy
Mollie, Somerville to Nelson Pewett 1-21-1871 (no return) Hy
Mollier, Bena to William Black 5-7-1862 Sh
Molloy, Sophia to Howell E. Jackson 5-31-1859 Sh *
Molloy?, Jane to George L. Campbell 7-24-1828 (7-29-1828) Hr
Monahan, Cecila to Morris Flanagan 4-23-1858 Sh
Moncreef, Druciller to Joseph Darby 11-7-1838 (11-15-1838) F
Moncreef, Lucinda to Dennis Speer 11-7-1838 (11-15-1838) F
Moncreeff, Jane to William Morris 11-5-1838 (11-7-1838) F
Moncreif, Martha A. to Phillip Webber 12-18-1849 (no return) F
Moncreif, Martha to Wm. Scisco 9-18-1847 (9-23-1847) F
Moncreif, Sarah to Wm. B. Ramsey 10-17-1854 (no return) F
Moncreiff, Ann to Joseph Darby 9-21-1844 (9-22-1844) F
Moncreiff, Permelia to Jno. W. Choat 9-19-1844 (9-20-1844) F
Moncrief, Agnes to Samuel Roseborough 1-13-1855 (1-14-1855) Sh
Moncrief, Elizabeth to John B. Randle 12-10-1853 (no return) F
Moncrief, Mary to B. O. Linton 1-9-1866 Hn
Moncrief, Mary to John Posten 7-10-1854 (no return) F
Mongomery, Hester to Geo. A. Petty 12-10-1870 (no return) Hy
Monheimer, Mina to Falk Morgenroth 2-15-1856 Sh
Monohan, Catherine to Thos. O'Donell 2-2-1863 Sh
Monom, Genevia to Clayton L. Bolling 7-1-1829 (7-2?-1829) Hr
Monroe, Elizabeth Jane to John M. Lowry 8-6-1840 Cr
Monroe, Jenney to Ike Hadley 12-4-1865 (12-9-1865) F B
Monroe, Lucinda to Wm. H. Lawrence no date (with 10-1867) Cr
Monroe, Margaret A. to Adam Atcheson 10-20-1839 Hn
Monroe, Martha J. to Geo. R. Green 5-27-1846 (no return) F
Monroe, Mary to J. L. Hancock 1-4-1881 L
Monroe, Mary to James Beranes? 12-6-1860 (11-6-1860?) O
Monroe, Rebeca to William Francisco 11-21-1861 (no return) Cr
Monroe, Rebecca to Wm. Monroe 7-22-1857 Cr
Monroe, Sarah Clementine to Thomas Morrison 3-6-1844 (3-7-1844) T
Monroe, Susan to John Fox 12-27-1866 Hn
Monroe, Susan to Van Malone 1-22-1865 Hn
Monroe?, Elizabeth to George W. Miller 3-9-1841 (3-10-1841) T
Monroney, Ellen to James Murray 1-21-1861 Sh
Montague, Amanda to Z. Wainwright 6-26-1870? Hy
Montague, Elvira W. to Zebulon P. Bowles 2-26-1845 Sh
Montague, Emaly Y. to John C. Brooks 8-8-1848 F
Montague, Frances to Moses J. Bradshaw 3-12-1844 (3-28-1844) F
Montague, Hester to Silas Babbs 9-25-1869 (6-15-1870) F B

Montague, Malissa A. to J. J. Blaydes 10-25-1865 Hy
Montague, Mary to Wm. Wallace 10-29-1867 (11-6-1867) F
Montague, Minerva L. to Samuel S. Brown 11-15-1848 Sh
Montague, Susan to John D. Tunadge 1-22-1844 (1-24-1844) F
Montcreath, Elizabeth to William Cassell 10-18-1852 (no return) F
Montcrief, Emily to David Lynch 10-30-1853 (no return) F
Montgomery, Adaliza to Philly Roberson 6-13-1850 Cr
Montgomery, Adelia to Granville Runnels 4-29-1871 (5-2-1871) T
Montgomery, Angile to Thomas Horn 12-25-1858 Cr
Montgomery, Ann Cornelia to Stephen L. Shelton 8-16-1869 (8-19-1869) Ma
Montgomery, Artemisia Ann to Lawrence Page 2-1-1851 (2-6-1851) T
Montgomery, Augusta to Lafayette McCrillis 12-27-1865 (12-28-1865) F
Montgomery, Caroline to Geo. Towns 12-24-1870 Hy
Montgomery, Caroline to S. H. Robinson 8-20-1854 Cr
Montgomery, Caroline to Wm. McNary 2-3-1870 (2-5-1870) F B
Montgomery, Catherine to Edward Tully 7-1-1849 Sh
Montgomery, Cynthia to Joseph A. Stafford 12-24-1834 (12-25-1834) Hr
Montgomery, E. B. to A. J. Swaim 7-21-1855 (7-22-1856) We
Montgomery, Elenora to Edmond Outland 10-10-1866 (10-11-1866) Ma
Montgomery, Eliza H. to S. H. Swaim 4-20-1858 We
Montgomery, Eliza J. to Syron? Parrish 12-10-1866 (12-13-1866) Cr
Montgomery, Eliza J. to Wm. C. Robertson 11-28-1838 G
Montgomery, Eliza to Priesty King 5-2-1844 Cr
Montgomery, Elizabeth E. to Wm. D. Fletcher 12-12-1870 Ma
Montgomery, Elizabeth to Anda M. C. Montgomery 9-9-1840 (9-10-1840) F
Montgomery, Elizabeth to Pleasant Robinson 12-21-1835 Hn
Montgomery, Ellen R. to Robert L. Lightforte 7-23-1851 (7-24-1851) Hr
Montgomery, Emma to Asa Buntin 4-28-1866 Ma
Montgomery, Eugenia to Green Thomas 12-22-1866 Be
Montgomery, Frances B. to Samuel J. Bell 1-16-1849 Ma
Montgomery, Frances to Amaziah Woodside 10-3-1860 (no return) Dy
Montgomery, Frances to John W. Davidson 10-18-1838 G
Montgomery, Isabella A. M. to Harmon Havercamp 2-5-1867 F
Montgomery, Isabella R. to Wiley B. Massey 2-10-1847 G
Montgomery, Jane to William A. Allen 9-1-1826 (9-7-1826) Hr
Montgomery, Louisa to Demos Gains? 9-29-1843 We
Montgomery, Louizer to Ralph Jones 6-1-1866 G
Montgomery, Lucy J. to Benj. J. Yearger 2-19-1849 Cr
Montgomery, M. J. to N. L. Robertson 12-2-1871 (12-3-1871) Dy
Montgomery, Mallasie to James Johnson 9-12-1839 Cr
Montgomery, Margaret E. to Jacob Miller 8-13-1844 Sh
Montgomery, Martha A. to Edward R. Jones 12-11-1844 G
Montgomery, Martha K. to Alexander M. Jones 1-26-1848 Ma
Montgomery, Martha to Levi Gifford 9-15-1864 Sh
Montgomery, Martha to Noah Stafford 6-23-1868 (7-2-1868) F
Montgomery, Martha to Thomas Hamilton 5-16-1857 (5-18-1857) T
Montgomery, Mary A. to James M. Sackett 8-8-1850 Sh
Montgomery, Mary E. to Joel Horn 12-23-1840 Cr
Montgomery, Mary E. to Wilson A. Burrow 9-20-1855 Cr
Montgomery, Mary Jane to Joseph Bell 12-28-1840 Ma
Montgomery, Mary M. to Henry Melton 7-17-1850 (7-18-1850) F
Montgomery, Mary N. to William Cozby 5-5-1866 T
Montgomery, Mary to John W. Adams 12-20-1846 Cr
Montgomery, Mary to Marcus Byles 8-26-1841 F
Montgomery, Matilda to John C. Simms 1-4-1841 G
Montgomery, Matilda to John Reid 11-14-1863 Sh
Montgomery, Mollie E. to W. J. Redd 1-19-1861 (1-24-1861) Hr
Montgomery, Nancy M. to T. S. Vaughan 9-7-1870 T
Montgomery, P. A. to D. W. Womble 10-20-1861 We
Montgomery, Pheeba A. to B. W. Farmer 10-23-1855 We
Montgomery, Polly to Louis Taylor 12-24-1867 T
Montgomery, Sallie J. to W. J. Crenshaw 12-3-1877 (12-4-1877) Dy
Montgomery, Sally to William Cromes 6-23-1830 (6-30-1830) G
Montgomery, Sarah E. to Joseph E. Miller 3-7-1866 (3-8-1866) Dy
Montgomery, Sarah E. to Nathan G. Hill 4-11-1855 G
Montgomery, Sarah J. to F. M. Davis 10-30-1859 We
Montgomery, Sarah to James Davis 12-6-1843 Sh
Montgomery, Sophia to Wm. A. Jones 6-18-1843 Cr
Montgomery, Victoria to V. S. Birdwell 1-8-1872 (1-10-1872) Cr
Montgomery, Zora to Elizah Piggue 7-14-1871 (7-15-1871) Cr
Montgomry, Sallie to Washington Downing 1-6-1869 (1-8-1869) T
Monton, Sarah to Elija Overton 4-4-1846 (4-5-1846) Hr
Montrose, S. B. to R. L. Hinton 8-22-1860 Dy
Mooberry, Mary A. J. to T. J. Charles 12-24-1855 (no return) F
Moodey, Mary L. C. to Thomas D. Franklin 5-3-1845 (5-7-1845) F
Moody, A. A. to M. H. Ingrim 2-28-1861 Sh
Moody, A. E. to George W. Baxter 6-11-1859 (no return) Hy
Moody, Amelia A. to William E. Tybass 4-5-1859 We
Moody, Ann C. to Reuben Davis 12-17-1870 (12-25-1870) Dy
Moody, C. C. to James W. Crafton 2-20-1856 G
Moody, Cassanda to Jacob Park 1-3-1866 (no return) F B
Moody, Dillie C. to James A. Lacey 1-24-1878 Hy
Moody, Ede to Alex Taylor 1-16-1868 Hy
Moody, Eliza to Solomon Jelks 10-26-1869 (no return) Dy
Moody, Elizabeth A. to Alexander P. Erwin 1-9-1858 Hn
Moody, Elizabeth M. to H. B. Satterfield 12-24-1867 O
Moody, Elizabeth to Elbert E. Davis 8-25-1854 Hn

Moody, Elizabeth to Elias Williams 1-19-1830 Sh
Moody, Elizabeth to Joel E. Bromagen? 1-31-1859 Hn
Moody, Emma to Zachary Wright 2-17-1867 G
Moody, Frances to James W. Steel 10-14-1857 Hn
Moody, Isabel to Benjamin Moss 3-28-1838 Hn
Moody, Julia A. to Lemuel A. Thomas 11-28-1867 Hy
Moody, L. M. to W. A. Wilkerson 11-10-1868 Hy
Moody, Lavinia C. to J. J. Guill 12-7-1865 Hn
Moody, Livinia to L. H. Milliken 7-5-1841 F
Moody, Lucy H. to A. J. Loving 4-25-1870 (no return) Hy
Moody, Lucy to Washington Lindsey 1-16-1868 Be
Moody, Lucy to Willis L. Williams 10-4-1840 Hn
Moody, M. J. to A. J. Donaldson 12-6-1868 G
Moody, Malinda to James R. Wilson 11-21-1856 Sh
Moody, Mannie to R. C. T. Bundy 9-18-1870 Hy
Moody, Margaret to John McCutcheon 5-20-1847 Hn
Moody, Margaret to Sam Barcklay 1-11-1866 Hy
Moody, Martha E. to John Dortch 8-26-1848 Hn
Moody, Martha R. to Matthew Richardson 10-27-1856 Hn
Moody, Martha to John P. Green 1-23-1857 Hn
Moody, Mary A. to Albert Morton 1-1-1868 (1-27-1868) F B
Moody, Mary A. to James M. Oliver 1-11-1855 Hn
Moody, Mary D. to James E. Wood 8-21-1852 (8-22-1852) G
Moody, Mary E. to S. H. C. Vaughan 11-24-1867 G
Moody, Mary E. to T. A. Erwin 5-6-1866 Hn
Moody, Mary Levinia to Leonard H. Millikin 7-5?-1841 Hr
Moody, Mary M. to James M. Williams 10-3-1859 (10-5-1859) O
Moody, Mary to George E. Higgenbottom 1-14-1834 Sh
Moody, Mary to Lemuel Sanderlin 12-24-1850 Ma
Moody, Maryline E. to D. W. Wooley 11-28-1874 (12-1-1874) Dy
Moody, Millie to Jessee Hill 12-5-1870 (12-8-1870) F B
Moody, Milly to Elijah Robbins 2-18-1828 G
Moody, Nancy A. to William Bucy 8-15-1852 Hn
Moody, Nancy to George Anderson 12-22-1866 (no return) F B
Moody, P. F. to J. J. Mills 8-19-1872 (8-21-1872) Dy
Moody, Rachel Ann to William C. Manley 1-21-1855 Hn
Moody, Sallie to Gilmore Capers 1-9-1873 Hy
Moody, Sarah M. to Vernon Rhodes 7-22-1845 (7-23-1845) F
Moody, Sarah to Ebenezer Warren 6-6-1833 Sh
Moody, Sarah to Peter Clayborn 5-4-1868 (no return) Hy
Moody, Susana to J. W. P. Boggs 11-11-1855 Hn
Moon(Moor), Elizabeth to Henry Jackson 8-2-1832 Hr
Moon(Moore), Frances M. to W. P. Anderson 12-26-1849 Hr
Moon(Moore), Mary Ann Eliza to Jas. H. Palmer 11-23-1844 (12-24-1844) Hr
Moon(Moore), Mary to Christopher Bullard 11-6-1844 (11-?-1844) Hr
Moon(Moore), Sarah to John Hardcastle 6-26-1830 Hr
Moon(Moore?), Frances to Wm. C. Johnson 6-1-1846 (6-11-1846) Hr
Moon(Moore?), Lucy to Wm. P. McKinnie 10-5-1846 (10-6-1846) Hr
Moon(Moore?), Margaret C. to Robert C. Hardwick 2-28-1850 (2-7?-1850) Hr
Moon, Elizabeth P. to James Gray 1-16-1835 Sh
Moon, Elizabeth to Z. M. Wells 5-27-1851 O
Moon, Frances to Jackson Cox 1-11-1868 Hy
Moon, Isabella to Thomas McClerry 12-4-1869 F B
Moon, Kezziah to Bennett Henderson 5-5-1843 Hn
Moon, Mary E. to M. H. Rison 2-16-1859 Hn
Moon, Mary to Benjamin Adams 9-10-1827 O
Moon, Milly to Caldwell Klutts 4-9-1843 Hn
Moon, N. J. to M. L. Reddick 10-8-1854 We
Moon, Nancy to A. S. Butler 10-24-1860 We
Moon, Nancy to B. W. Swindell 10-4-1838 Cr
Moon, Nancy to Joseph Craddock 11-16-1843 Hn
Moon, Parmelia to Thomas A. Childress 1-4-1849 Hn
Moone?, Nanny Jane to A. M. Weston 12-6-1855 Hn
Mooney, Elizabeth to D. S. Stroup 9-22-1867 Hn
Mooney, Elizabeth to John Trousdale 12-26-1842 (12-27-1842) Ma
Mooney, Louisianna to Christopher Hamlett 1-2-1867 (1-6-1867) Ma
Mooney, Lucy to William May 2-16-1871 Cr
Mooney, Margaret to Jeffrey Murray 5-11-1855 (5-13-1855) Sh
Mooney, Mary J. to Thomas W. Tate 12-3-1859 Hr
Mooney, Mary to James Collins 7-26-1851 (7-27-1851) Sh
Moor, Hanah M. to J. B. Walpole 1-11-1861 (1-13-1861) L
Moor, Harriet to Asbury Page 10-20-1867 Cr
Moor, Louisa to Henry Williamson 12-23-1841 Cr
Moor, Sarah Ann to Jessee J. Tharp 1-29-1851 (1-30-1851) F
Moor, Virginia L. to Henry Thompson 11-26-1853 G
Moorberry, Lucy to F. J. Charles 11-19-1863 G
Moore (Monroe-Munn), H. E. to J. T. Williams 1-16-1878 L
Moore, A. E. to H. W. Covington 12-26-1871 Hy
Moore, Adaline to Steven Box 11-25-1854 (11-30-1854) Hr
Moore, Adaline to William Conn 2-23-1839 Sh
Moore, Adaline to William J. Walker 11-4-1846 F
Moore, Adeline to Austin Miller 3-1-1873 Hy
Moore, Alice to Charles Allen 9-11-1866 Hy
Moore, Alice to Stephen Taylor 12-24-1872 Hy
Moore, Amanda M. to D. F. Cunningham 9-10-1862 G
Moore, Amanda M. to Jas. M. Hines 6-2-1861 Hy
Moore, Amanda to John Moore? 11-9-1869 Hy

Moore, Amanda to John S. Belotte 2-11-1853 Hr
Moore, Amy M. to Wyatt Lunsford 8-6-1846 L
Moore, Amy to Stephen Sanders 10-25-1853 (10-27-1853) Hr
Moore, Anabel to James A. Johnston 12-3-1879 (12-4-1879) L
Moore, Angeline M. to Christian Pohel 12-27-1865 Mn
Moore, Ann C. (Mrs.) to John Lowry 5-20-1868 (5-28-1868) L
Moore, Ann D. to William H. Ivy 7-22-1837 G
Moore, Ann L.(T?) to Joel Parker 3-18-1835 Hr
Moore, Ann to Andrew J. Green 2-2-1870 Hy
Moore, Ann to Chas. Bates 12-26-1870 Hy
Moore, Ann to Wm. Moore 2-1-1841 Cr
Moore, Anna E. to James S. Aden 1-10-1866 Hn
Moore, Anna E. to W. W. Ivie 8-1-1866 G
Moore, Anna R. to I. Y. Gibson 9-9-1851 Sh
Moore, Anna to Wm. Lindsey 1-20-1842 Cr
Moore, Araminta B. to Simpson Pinckley 3-9-1870 (3-10-1870) Cr
Moore, Arena to Dennis Glisson 10-22-1838 (no return) Hn
Moore, Arnilla to R. C. Murry 1-15-1865 Mn
Moore, Auzal Inza to William W. Dollar 12-15-1858 (12-16-1858) Ma
Moore, Bettie to Alfred Moize 12-16-1867 (12-19-1867) Ma
Moore, C. A. to Silas Matthews 9-19-1867 (no return) Dy
Moore, C. W. to E. R. Tilghman 8-5-1864 Sh
Moore, C. to James Murray 1-8-1844 (no return) Hn
Moore, Cairly W. to Thos. P. Walker 10-7-1856 Cr
Moore, Camilla T. to William Bone 11-2-1854 (11-24-1854) G
Moore, Candis M. to W. J. H. Nealey 1-2-1849 (no return) F
Moore, Canellis E. to B. J. Perry 11-21-1867 (11-22-1867) Cr
Moore, Caroline to Allen Whitehurst 2-29-1872 Hy
Moore, Caroline to J. P. Gordon 11-21-1869 Hy
Moore, Caroline to James Colbert 1-22-1833 Sh
Moore, Caroline to William Dickinson 3-11-1858 (3-12-1858) Ma
Moore, Catharine to Henry Cooper 2-11-1846 (2-12-1846) G
Moore, Catherine to Lure Rye 2-10-1847 Hn
Moore, Cathrine to Stephen Castleberry 1-8-1867 (1-16-1867) F B
Moore, Charity to John H. Johnson 5-16-1860 Hr
Moore, Clara Ann to A. J. King 12-9-1854 (12-6?-1854) Hr
Moore, Dacare to Aden Laughhon 6-21-1825 Hr
Moore, Deca J. to Sampson Blalock 8-4-1857 (no return) We
Moore, Delila to Robert N. Bradford 11-27-1866 Be
Moore, Delilah to David Younger 8-15-1863 Mn
Moore, Dicy to William H. Jernigan 10-10-1840 Hn
Moore, E. A. to J. W. Shoemake 5-24-1876 (5-25-1876) L
Moore, E. B. to J. J. Baker 8-24-1867 (8-25-1867) Dy
Moore, E. J. to A. H. Yancy 5-23-1860 (5-24-1860) F
Moore, E. W. to William Warner 9-14-1847 Sh
Moore, Easter to James Herron 3-12-1873 (3-13-1873) Cr B
Moore, Edwina to James A. Frost 1-12-1857 Cr
Moore, Eleanor to Minor B. Davidson 1-4-1842 T
Moore, Eley to H. Battle 8-2-1865 G
Moore, Elisa J. to Danl. Barry 5-29-1852 (5-30-1852) Sh
Moore, Eliza A. to J. M. Russom 12-25-1862 Mn
Moore, Eliza J. to Benton Williams 11-3-1863 O
Moore, Eliza J. to Danl. Barry 12-3-1851 Sh
Moore, Eliza to A. E. Carter 11-24-1855 Cr
Moore, Eliza to L. Dunning 9-7-1842 Hn
Moore, Elizabeth A. to Hirian A. Taylor 2-15-1853 Cr
Moore, Elizabeth A. to John W. Bishop 3-14-1844 L
Moore, Elizabeth C. (Mrs.) to Joseph J. Pardue 5-6-1861 (5-7-1861) Ma
Moore, Elizabeth F. to Columbus W. Thompson 1-17-1871 Dy
Moore, Elizabeth F. to Jerome P. Luker 2-25-1859 O
Moore, Elizabeth J. to Joseph W. Cooper 12-1-1842 G
Moore, Elizabeth M. to Elisha M. Paschal 9-10-1862 We
Moore, Elizabeth to Allen R. Gordon 11-3-1867 Hy
Moore, Elizabeth to B. T. Briley 10-4-1868 Hy
Moore, Elizabeth to Elex. Moore 9-3-1840 Cr
Moore, Elizabeth to George Burne 8-30-1856 (8-31-1856) Sh
Moore, Elizabeth to Harrison E. Cason 3-15-1858 (3-17-1858) O
Moore, Elizabeth to Henry H. Moore 12-17-1861 (no return) Hy
Moore, Elizabeth to James Manning 7-23-1850 Hr
Moore, Elizabeth to Mack Drummons 12-4-1843 (12-13-1843) T
Moore, Elizabeth to Michael Fields 11-28-1839 Hn
Moore, Elizabeth to Peter Perkins Smith 6-6-1845 (6-15-1845) T
Moore, Elizabeth to Robert McCullough 10-29-1851 (10-30-1851) T
Moore, Elizabeth to Solomon Saines 2-2-1870 (2-3-1870) F B
Moore, Ella B. to Henry Thompson 9-2-1874 L
Moore, Ella V. to William C. Coats 1-7-1867 (1-8-1866?) Ma
Moore, Ellen J. to T. T. Reader 1-9-1851 Cr
Moore, Ellen M. A. to Edward A. Bird 3-20-1861 Sh
Moore, Ellen to Archibald Marshall 10-13-1854 (11-1-1854) T
Moore, Ellen to James M. Farmer 9-7-1865 (no return) Hy
Moore, Elvira to Robt. McComb McEwin 11-15-1850 T
Moore, Elzira O. to Roberson Capel 3-19-1851 Sh
Moore, Em to Calvin Taylor 1-7-1868 Hy
Moore, Emaline to C. H. Wilson 11-3-1866 O
Moore, Emma to Lewis Z. T. Bolen 11-16-1870 (11-17-1870) Ma
Moore, Emmer to Sandy Williams 2-11-1869 Hy
Moore, Eugenia to Benj. Halcomb 6-8-1871 (no return) Hy

Moore, Eugenie P. to Jerry Manasco 2-27-1871 (3-1-1871) T
Moore, F. A. to D. D. Palmer 3-7-1866 G
Moore, Fanney to William D. Moss 1-19-1867 (no return) L B
Moore, Fannie C. to Jas. Dickey 5-12-1869 T
Moore, Fannie E. to W. R. Christain 11-20-1866 (11-23-1866) Cr
Moore, Filbis to Walton Warlick 1-5-1871 Cr B
Moore, Frances C. to Benj. J. Williams 1-7-1845 Be
Moore, Frances C. to Benjamin Williams 1-7-1845 Be CC
Moore, Frances D. to Robt. W. Benson 5-4-1859 (5-5-1859) Hr
Moore, Frances to John Smith 9-25-1861 Mn
Moore, Frances to Kirk Dickinson 7-16-1870 F B
Moore, Frances to Richard Hardin 4-29-1843 (4-30-1843) Ma
Moore, Frances to Robert J. Lewellen 9-4-1850 Ma
Moore, G. A. to John S. Steele 10-4-1869 (10-6-1869) Cr
Moore, H. C. to Jas. C. Edenton 11-21-1868 (11-24-1868) F
Moore, Hannah to George Gordan 10-16-1867 (10-19-1867) F B
Moore, Harrett to Tilghman Milton 12-2-1844 (12-3-1844) G
Moore, Harriet E. to William Bradford 10-2-1849 G
Moore, Harriet to Willis Klyce 8-28-1872 Hy
Moore, Harriett A. to David F. Ham 7-11-1840 (7-17-1840) Hr
Moore, Harriett to S. P. Woods 12-31-1868 (1-1-1869) Cr
Moore, Hattie C. to John A. Clark 4-10-1867 We
Moore, Helen V. to John R. Gammon 11-12-1866 (11-13-1866) Dy
Moore, Holtan to James B. Richards 9-18-1866 (9-20-1866) Ma
Moore, I. N. to A. J. Walters 2-19-1873 (2-20-1873) Cr
Moore, Isabella to Joseph King 6-26-1856 We
Moore, Isora E. to James Halcombe 12-11-1872 Hy
Moore, Jane to Frank Mulherin 4-6-1880 (no return) Dy
Moore, Jane to J. J. Downing 7-6-1867 (7-11-1867) Cr
Moore, Jane to Jas. A. McFarlen 12-21-1854 G
Moore, Jane to John J.? McCorkle 4-27-1840 (5-5-1840) T
Moore, Jane to W. Jones 12-15-1849 Sh
Moore, Jane to William Gaylor 1-10-1872 O
Moore, Jennett F. to Nevell Halcomb 6-8-1871 (no return) Hy
Moore, Josephine E. to Benjamin F. Guiteau 11-7-1864 (11-8-1864) Sh
Moore, Josephine S. to Wm. J. A. Bell 9-29-1842 Sh
Moore, Josephine to Banister Terrell 12-20-1856 Ma
Moore, Judith to John Townsend 5-2-1868 T
Moore, Julia A. to Joseph W. Moore 8-10-1852 Hn
Moore, Julia Ann to Arthur F. Finlay 5-16-1831 Sh
Moore, Julia C. to John McKey 4-4-1838 Sh
Moore, Julia F. C. to M. B. Barnes 11-5-1866 (11-12-1866) L
Moore, Julia to E. S. Prichard 1-25-1859 F
Moore, Julia to Wm. Boner 12-23-1858 (12-30-1858) T
Moore, Katherine to Calib Baker 12-31-1868 (1-1-1869) F B
Moore, L. E. to J. R. Brown 1-3-1866 Hn
Moore, L. V. to R. P. Wilkerson 9-11-1865 Mn
Moore, Laura to Handy Cleveland 6-21-1867 (6-22-1867) F B
Moore, Lavina to James Davis 11-18-1840 (11-19-1840) F
Moore, Leana to John Gross 5-30-1865 T
Moore, Leanah to Robert Cooper 11-18-1861 T
Moore, Leanna to Thomas Cowan? 5-5-1842 (5-12-1842) T
Moore, Lee to S. H. Henning 12-11-1880 (12-12-1881?) L B
Moore, Leer to George Jones 4-17-1871 T
Moore, Levina to Arthur Fuller 12-5-1836 (12-6-1836) G
Moore, Lilian J. to R. R. Cozort 11-14-1872 Hy
Moore, Lilly to Louis P. Estes 10-30-1875 (no return) Hy
Moore, Lizzie R. to A. E. Dupree 6-4-1880 (6-6-1880) L
Moore, Lizzie to Saml. Bradford 7-27-1878 (7-28-1878) L
Moore, Lizzie to Saml. Cunningham 7-9-1870 G B
Moore, Lou to Haywood Ruff 9-9-1880 (no return) Dy
Moore, Louisa M. to George W. Wells 12-19-1854 (12-20-1854) O
Moore, Louisa M. to John C. Harden 1-22-1846 Cr
Moore, Lucina to Hamblin L. Williams 1-12-1832 (1-17-1832) Hr
Moore, Lucinda to Archibald Breeding 11-15-1832 Hr
Moore, Lucinda to James F. Hamilton 4-15-1853 (4-21-1853) O
Moore, Lucinda to John Dyer 11-30-1840 Hn
Moore, Lucretia to Perry Wilson 9-5-1846 (9-6-1846) O
Moore, Lucy H. to John Tomlinson 9-3-1850 (9-12-1850) F
Moore, Lucy Jane to Henry Yancey 8-10-1870 (8-22-1870) F B
Moore, Lucy to Lucas King 12-21-1881 (no return) L B
Moore, Lue to Jno. W. (Dr.) Hayes 10-9-1872 Hy
Moore, Lyde L. to Jno. R. Jarrett 2-7-1872 Hy
Moore, M. A. E. to T. G. Turnage 7-9-1862 Sh
Moore, M. A. to Harvey Read 1-11-1869 Hy
Moore, M. A. to J. E. Dunaway 2-4-1865 (2-7-1865) L
Moore, M. A. to W. F. Soward 2-22-1882 (2-23-1882) L
Moore, M. C. to John Carmack 10-27-1860 (10-24?-1860) O
Moore, M. D. to J. M. Bragg 1-7-1873 (1-9-1873) T
Moore, M. E. (Mrs.) to T. J. Sanders 9-30-1875 (10-3-1875) Dy
Moore, M. E. to R. M. Vail 10-25-1871 (10-26-1871) L
Moore, M. E. to W. R. Jennings 1-15-1877 (1-16-1877) L
Moore, M. E. to Wilson H. Moody 6-6-1873 Hy
Moore, M. F. to Jasper N. Walker 12-2-1867 (12-3-1867) Ma
Moore, M. F. to M. H. Lake 12-20-1856 (12-23-1856) Hr
Moore, M. J. to J. T. Williams 10-1-1866 (no return) F
Moore, M. J. to S. M. Hart 3-11-1866 Hn

Moore, Maggie E. to H. A. Rainey 7-17-1872 Hy
Moore, Malicia to Henry Hooker 2-10-1841 Hn
Moore, Malinda to William H. Latham 10-31-1871 Ma
Moore, Malissa J. to Green Smith 1-28-1858 Cr
Moore, Malissa to Abel V. Underwood 12-2-1857 Hn
Moore, Malvina to William Redmon 10-11-1862 Mn
Moore, Maranda J. to George W. Sheridan 1-1-1860 Hn
Moore, Margaret A. to William S. McClelland 2-21-1872 (2-22-1872) L
Moore, Margaret C. to Jas. J. Porter 2-25-1873 (2-26-1873) Cr
Moore, Margaret Jane to John Cox Custer 12-3-1850 (12-8-1850) T
Moore, Margaret M. M. to James McGlothin 10-7-1860 (no return) L
Moore, Margaret to James Dickey 12-25-1861 T
Moore, Margaret to James Ray 7-25-1863 (no return) L
Moore, Margaret to Jonathan A. Nelson 8-17-1846 (8-18-1846) T
Moore, Margaret to Stephen Crawford 12-29-1868 F B
Moore, Margaret to W. Y. Cardwell 5-15-1863 Mn
Moore, Margaret to Wm. K. Bennett 2-24-1869 Hy
Moore, Margarett to Andrew Vinson 1-17-1872 (1-18-1872) Cr
Moore, Maria to William Ham 12-3-1850 (12-4-1850) Hr
Moore, Mariah Tucker to Mingo Johnson 1-19-1872 (1-20-1872) T
Moore, Mariah to George Crooms 1-24-1867 (1-25-1867) F B
Moore, Martha A. to Wm. A. Booth 4-2-1845 F
Moore, Martha C. to William H. Webb 12-21-1873 L
Moore, Martha E. to Jmaes A. Thurmon 3-19-1867 (3-21-1867) L
Moore, Martha F. to John M. Bradbury 3-16-1857 (3-18-1857) Ma
Moore, Martha J. to H. A. Traywick 1-1-1867 Cr
Moore, Martha J. to James M. Cook 12-29-1855 We
Moore, Martha L. to F. D. Cossett 6-7-1855 (no return) F
Moore, Martha M. to James Dinwiddie 6-21-1853 Cr
Moore, Martha M. to Overton Forbush 10-6-1834 (10-10-1834) Hr
Moore, Martha R. to John L. Ledbetter 11-21-1846 (11-22-1846) L
Moore, Martha to Ezekiel Faris 10-18-1841 Ma
Moore, Martha to Isaac Glasgow 1-11-1867 (1-19-1867) F B
Moore, Martha to Isaac Short 1-28-1840 Cr
Moore, Martha to James Hill 6-5-1863 Mn
Moore, Martha to John Harrison 7-6-1867 F B
Moore, Martha to John S. Baldridge 10-5-1846 (10-6-1846) G
Moore, Martha to T. H. West 2-15-1859 (no return) We
Moore, Martha to W. T. Rogerson 1-30-1867 G
Moore, Martha to Warren Adams 1-11-1849 (no return) F
Moore, Martha to William Roberson 8-27-1861 (8-30-1861) L
Moore, Mary A. to Henry T. Jones 2-6-1866 (2-8-1866) Cr
Moore, Mary A. to Jas. M. Brooks 11-17-1847 Hn
Moore, Mary A. to John Darnal 11-11-1857 (11-8?-1857) O
Moore, Mary A. to Lewis Sampson 11-6-1871 Hy
Moore, Mary A. to Nelson Finch 6-12-1845 Cr
Moore, Mary A. to W. W. Covington 11-20-1873 Hy
Moore, Mary A. to William Morton 2-7-1855 (2-8-1855) Sh
Moore, Mary America to Harry B. Christian 7-22-1839 (7-23-1839) Ma
Moore, Mary Ann to Frederick C. Ellinor 12-30-1838 Cr
Moore, Mary Ann to James M. Dickinson 7-16-1857 Hn
Moore, Mary Ann to John J. Collins 7-31-1838 Sh
Moore, Mary Ann to William Webster 12-21-1867 (12-22-1867) L
Moore, Mary C. to Jos. T. Sutherland 12-14-1871 Hy
Moore, Mary Caroline to William H. Robertson 5-5-1858 (5-8-1858) L
Moore, Mary D? to Jacob Long 5-1-1839 (5-2-1839) O
Moore, Mary E. to B. W. Sadler 12-26-1859 (12-29-1859) Hr
Moore, Mary E. to James A. Crook 1-4-1870 (no return) L
Moore, Mary E. to James Ticer 10-4-1859 (10-6-1859) Sh
Moore, Mary E. to Jas. J. Faulkner 10-7-1856 T
Moore, Mary E. to Martin Pierce 4-20-1867 (4-21-1867) Cr
Moore, Mary E. to Mathew Sanders 7-20-1866 Hy
Moore, Mary E. to W. R. Hamilton 7-21-1861 Mn
Moore, Mary E. to Wiley Bevans 11-5-1871 Cr
Moore, Mary E. to William G. Moore 12-21-1853 Hr
Moore, Mary E. to William Thompson 4-5-1864 Mn
Moore, Mary Frances to Rich French 8-21-1845 Cr
Moore, Mary J. to Alfred F. Davidson 6-20-1844 G
Moore, Mary J. to Clinton King 10-24-1871 (10-25-1871) Cr
Moore, Mary J. to George E. Allen 12-14-1877 (12-15-1877) L
Moore, Mary J. to L. Shoemake 7-14-1849 L
Moore, Mary Jane to Linsey Shoemaker 7-24-1820 Sh
Moore, Mary L. to James T. Persons 11-4-1851 (11-5-1851) Sh
Moore, Mary L. to John M. Dunlap 1-17-1854 (1-19-1854) G
Moore, Mary L. to John Pierce 5-8-1841 T
Moore, Mary L. to Melvil A. Moore 11-17-1869 (11-18-1869) T
Moore, Mary M. to Jesse K. Cox 9-14-1865 Hy
Moore, Mary Rena to George Hollandsworth 1-16-1868 Be
Moore, Mary to A. J. Murdock 11-20-1849 G
Moore, Mary to George W. Blackwell 7-30-1868 G B
Moore, Mary to Isah Webb 6-21-1837 (6-22-1837) G
Moore, Mary to J. W. Quinn 9-10-1860 (9-11-1860) Sh
Moore, Mary to John Setzer 9-27-1872 (9-29-1872) L
Moore, Mary to Milton P. Cross 3-1-1841 (3-3-1841) Hr
Moore, Mary to Robert R. McWilliams 2-29-1839 Ma
Moore, Mary to Robet M. Ellis 7-17-1880 (7-18-1880) L
Moore, Mary to Thos. Waters 1-30-1845 (no return) We

Moore, Mary to William Hoskins 8-5-1852 G
Moore, Matilda to Esekel P. Richmond 7-31-1848 (4?-3-1848) F
Moore, Matilda to Henry F. Atkins 2-23-1841 Hn
Moore, Mattie A. D. to Wm. A. Thompson 12-8-1870 Hy
Moore, Mattie A. to James M. Whittenton 1-6-1870 Ma
Moore, Mattie L. to Wm. F. Gordon 12-1-1869 Hy
Moore, Mildrid W. to William C. Stevens 8-22-1832 Sh
Moore, Milisa to Silas Needham 12-23-1866 G
Moore, Millie to Cilas Walpole 5-24-1876 L
Moore, Milly to T. S. Webb 10-16-1858 (10-17-1858) G
Moore, Minerva Ann to P. T. Jones 6-20-1851 (6-23-1851) Sh
Moore, Minnie L. to J. P. McCaul 12-1-1869 L
Moore, Missouri S. to Columbus Dortch 12-18-1860 Hn
Moore, Mollie A. to Marshall E. Smith 12-6-1866 Ma
Moore, Mollie E. to James W. Chambers 8-24-1871 (8-26-1871) L
Moore, Mollie F. to M. C. Hamilton 12-18-1876 (12-21-1876) Dy
Moore, Mollie H. to Hugh Delass 7-6-1868 (7-7-1868) Ma
Moore, Mollie to James K. Polk 12-27-1867 (12-26?-1867) Dy
Moore, Mollie to Tillman Washington 9-8-1867 G B
Moore, N. A. to J. R. Ozier 3-21-1871 Cr
Moore, N. E. H. to Wm. N. Davis 4-17-1864 (4-19-1864) O
Moore, Nancy A. to John M. Rowland 5-19-1847 G
Moore, Nancy A. to Jonathan Spencer 9-3-1860 (9-5-1860) T
Moore, Nancy A. to Jonathan Spencer 9-5-1860 T
Moore, Nancy A. to W. W. Higgins 11-15-1864 (11-16-1864) Sh
Moore, Nancy B. to J. M. Vincent 11-14-1868 G
Moore, Nancy C. to Samuel Tims 2-18-1845 (2-19-1845) T
Moore, Nancy Caroline to Robert M. Erwin 9-12-1867 (no return) L
Moore, Nancy Caroline to Thomas McClenden 6-6-1870 (6-7-1870) L
Moore, Nancy E. to Elijah Martin 2-25-1857 We
Moore, Nancy G. to G. W. L. Hazlewood 7-29-1862 (7-31-1862) O
Moore, Nancy J. to A. T. Martin 1-16-1845 Cr
Moore, Nancy J. to Joseph Daniel 9-19-1847 Cr
Moore, Nancy to Columbus Wright 2-24-1869 Cr
Moore, Nancy to John P. Sensing 4-24-1841 (no return) F
Moore, Nancy to Moses Dunlop 9-10-1846 We
Moore, Nancy to Wyatt Northcross 8-10-1867 G B
Moore, O. D. to James Kellow 8-8-1876 (8-9-1876) Dy
Moore, Parmelia A. to James P. Grier 3-19-1844 G
Moore, Patsey to Washington Hudson 7-8-1869 G B
Moore, Penni? to Wm. Brown 1-11-1871 (1-15-1871) T
Moore, Penny to John W. Johnson 9-21-1873 Hy
Moore, Priscilla to Mark Jackson 9-14-1841 (no return) Hn
Moore, R. M. to J. A. Humphrey 9-4-1860 (9-5-1860) F
Moore, Rachal to Albert Avery 12-17-1869 (12-18-1869) T
Moore, Rachel to Wat Taylor 11-12-1870 Hy
Moore, Rebecca to Bill Prier 2-12-1874 (2-13-1874) T
Moore, Rebecca to Ezekiel Haltom 12-10-1855 (12-18-1855) Ma
Moore, Rebecca to Robert M. Compton 11-26-1840 Ma
Moore, Rinday? to Anderson Sain (Sam?) 12-30-1866 G
Moore, Roda to John Hughs 3-30-1868 (no return) Hy
Moore, Rowana to Leander Griffin 7-12-1858 (no return) L
Moore, S. A. to R. H. Jetton 10-18-1871 Hy
Moore, S. A. to R. N. Read 9-22-1838 (no return) F
Moore, S. C. to A. B. Gibbons 2-13-1863 (no return) Cr
Moore, S. C. to G. W. Roberts 9-4-1855 (no return) Hn
Moore, S. E. to C. R. Featherston 9-30-1875 (no return) Dy
Moore, S. E. to J. R. McDaniel 12-24-1865 Hy
Moore, S. L. to T. H. Lovelady 9-28-1854 (no return) F
Moore, Sallie Ann to Wm. Holland 9-9-1857 (9-21-1857) T
Moore, Sallie to George Moore 6-19-1875 Hy
Moore, Sallie to S. J. Chester 11-21-1866 G
Moore, Sarah A. to B. F. Jones 9-21-1847 Cr
Moore, Sarah A. to David L. Rushing 10-17-1850 Be
Moore, Sarah A. to Thos. W. Tinkle 2-2-1861 (2-3-1861) Dy
Moore, Sarah A. to Wm. H. Garner 9-7-1865 L
Moore, Sarah E. to Cornelius M. Olive 11-18-1860 Hn
Moore, Sarah E. to Phillip E. Waddell 11-5-1846 G
Moore, Sarah Ellen to Noah David Salisbury 12-18-1883 (12-20-1883) L
Moore, Sarah G. to Beverly E. Albritton 11-24-1861 Hn
Moore, Sarah J. to Elihu Stout 5-11-1855 (5-13?-1855) Hr
Moore, Sarah Jane to James W. McKey 9-28-1857 (10-1-1857) Ma
Moore, Sarah L. to James L. Thurmond 7-21-1856 (7-22-1856) L
Moore, Sarah M. to Huel D. Culbreath 1-3-1868 (no return) F
Moore, Sarah to Peyton Walpole 2-19-1880 (no return) L
Moore, Sarah to Thomas R. Cordle 3-1-1855 Hr
Moore, Sarah to Thos. McGee 8-?-1842 (no return) F
Moore, Selena C. to J. H. Cook 9-21-1845 We
Moore, Sirena to John Cock 12-18-1844 (12-19-1844) G
Moore, Sue M. to W. H. Hayes 10-17-1872 Hy
Moore, Susan A. to Isaac S. Enochs 8-2-1854 Cr
Moore, Susan A. to William B. Kennon 9-14-1866 (no return) Cr
Moore, Susan E. to Edward M. Myrick 6-24-1844 Hr
Moore, Susan M. A. to David B. Porter 1-7-1843 Cr
Moore, Susan S. to Willie Ham 5-1-1844 (5-2-1844) Hr
Moore, Susan to Alexander Hayes 10-17-1855 Cr
Moore, Susan to David Patton 2-4-1863 (2-5-1863) L

Moore, Susan to Isaac Parker 12-15-1831 G
Moore, Susan to John Kelley 11-25-1876 (11-26-1876) L
Moore, Susan to Wm. R. Piper 12-2-1852 Cr
Moore, Sylvia L. to David M. Quinly 6-29-1846 Ma
Moore, Tabitha to Thomas Williams 12-2-1846 Hn
Moore, Tennie M. to John H. Walker 12-25-1848 Cr
Moore, Terese to J. B. Evans 3-15-1864 (3-17-1864) Sh
Moore, Texanna F. to Wm. A. Escue 12-28-1876 Hy
Moore, V. E. to J. E. Clifton 11-17-1875 L
Moore, V. E. to T. A. Smith 10-27-1877 (10-28-1877) L
Moore, Verginia to Neal S. Harwell 1-17-1871 (1-18-1871) Dy
Moore, Viney to William Pendleton 2-18-1869 (2-20-1869) F B
Moore, W. D. to O. J. Radford 8-2-1871 (8-22-1871) Dy
Moore, Winneford C. to James W. Harvard(Howard?) 2-3-1842 Hr
Moorefield, Elvira to West Harris 3-5-1860 (no return) Hn
Moorefield, Mary E. to James W. Carter 2-15-1852 Hn
Moorefield, Sarah A. to William H. Russell 7-15-1852 Hn
Mooreland, Louisa to Coleman Williams 8-14-1868 (no return) F
Moorer, Allice to John Hennissee 2-7-1872 (2-8-1872) L
Moorer, Ann E. to Bolling S. Fisher 11-29-1856 (no return) L
Moorer, Anna to William Norwood 3-8-1877 L B
Moorer, Bell to Reuben Blackwell 12-30-1885 (12-31-1885) L
Moorer, Ema to James Bailey 4-18-1873 Hy
Moorer, Harriet A. to B. C. Gause 12-25-1860 L
Moorer, Ida to Thomas Windrow 10-29-1880 (10-30-1880) L B
Moorer, Mary F. to B. D. Walker 5-11-1858 (5-12-1858) L
Moorer, Sarah to Robert Newton 9-22-1873 (9-5?-1873) L B
Moorer, Willie C. to Rob. B. Lipscomb 11-12-1883 (11-13-1883) L
Moores, Phoebe to William Foster 11-27-1856 O
Moores, Susan I. to Wade H. Pyles 6-23-1855 (6-24-1855) O
Mooring, Caroline to Jesse Gray 12-25-1847 Ma
Mooring, E. F. to Geo. T. Harrison 4-21-1866 (4-22-1866) Ma
Mooring, Eliza Jane to John W. Haley 4-1-1850 (4-4-1850) Ma
Mooring, Elizabeth to James S. Coates 11-9-1852 (11-11-1852) Ma
Mooring, Margaret C. to Robert C. Algee 12-27-1855 Ma
Mooring, Mary J. E. to Benjamin F. Fly 1-17-1846 (1-21-1846) Ma
Mooring, Sarah E. to Robert B. Shore 10-25-1848 Sh
Moorland, Rebecca to Job Bledsoe 4-30-1840 Sh
Moorman, Charity to Willis Asbury 1-28-1870 (2-5-1870) F B
Moorman, Eliza to John Golden 1-28-1869 (1-30-1869) F B
Mooton, Dosha W. to Joseph H. Farris 11-29-1842 O
Moplin, Mary J. to William J. Warran 8-2-1870 (not executed) L
Moppin, Henretta Ann to J. L. S. Latimer 1-1-1861 O
Morality, Mary to Lawrence Carney 8-25-1855 (8-26-1855) Sh
Moran, Agnes to B. D. Irvin 11-5-1856 We
Moran, Berdelia to John Walsh 8-9-1861 Sh
Moran, Cathrine to Alford Smith 5-27-1854 (5-28-1854) T
Moran, Margaret to John Denegan 6-1-1861 Sh
Moran, Martha H. to V. F. Scott 3-27-1856 We
Moran, Mary to John Manley 9-5-1863 Sh
Moran, Sarah L. C. to James L. Hill 11-14-1846 Sh
More, Nancy O. to D. S. Magee 10-24-1844 We
Morefield, Rebecca F. to John M. Arun 9-20-1858 Hn
Moreland, Mary (Mrs.) to Elijah Robertson 6-1-1858 (6-9-1858) Sh
Moreland, Mary to Elijah Roberson 6-1-1858 Sh
Moreland, Sarah to Guriah Thomas 2-28-1871 (4-3-1871) F B
Morents?, Angeline Jane to John Mailey? 4-5-1843 (4-6-1843) T
Morey, Amanda to Andrew J. Selby 1-27-1861 We
Morgan, Amanda to Alford Harris 10-11-1849 O
Morgan, Amanda to Alfred Thomas 10-11-1849 O
Morgan, Ann to Thomas Hannigan 2-21-1852 Sh
Morgan, Anna to Robert Allison 12-30-1878 (no return) L
Morgan, Anna to Robert Remson 1-17-1873 (1-19-1873) L B
Morgan, Annie to James Washington 12-28-1867 F B
Morgan, Asplie to A. A. Bennett 8-6-1840 Sh
Morgan, Betty to J. H. Maxwell 6-10-1880 L
Morgan, Caroline to H. J. Hoover 7-13-1864 Sh
Morgan, Carry to Jeff Gibson 2-22-1872 (no return) Hy
Morgan, Catherine to Alex Taylor 12-25-1878 Hy
Morgan, Catherine to Bryant T. Dawtry 5-22-1844 G
Morgan, Clara E. to William A. Gage 8-30-1864 (9-1-1864) Sh
Morgan, D. A. to T. E. Griffin 1-23-1878 (1-24-1878) Dy
Morgan, Docia (Doria?) A. to G. W. Masterson 5-5-1851 Sh
Morgan, E. C. to L. L. Ward 5-1-1861 Sh
Morgan, Elizabeth B. to Walter H. Caldwell 5-30-1843 O
Morgan, Elizabeth C. to Edward Vaughan 10-26-1854 We
Morgan, Elizabeth to Joseph W. Tary 8-20-1851 O
Morgan, Elizabeth to Joseph W. Taylor 8-20-1851 O
Morgan, Elizabeth to Joshua Sherrod 12-24-1866 (12-29-1866) T
Morgan, Elizabeth to Patterson Burnett (Burrett) 10-19-1855 We
Morgan, Elizabeth to Thos. L. Darnell 6-16-1844 G
Morgan, Ellen to James N. Hall 4-4-1860 Ma
Morgan, Emma to Amos Coleman 11-3-1876 Hy
Morgan, Emma to Newt Marshall 3-13-1871 (4-5-1871) F B
Morgan, Emma to Wesley Smith 8-28-1880 (8-29-1880) Dy
Morgan, Fannie to J. B. Kent 9-23-1865 T
Morgan, Frances Ann to Henry P. Turner 4-19-1848 Sh

Morgan, Frances to Elija Appelton 12-2-1847 Cr
Morgan, H. F. to Elijah Smith 3-2-1866 (3-4-1866) Dy
Morgan, Harriet to Wm. Tipton 8-11-1866 T
Morgan, Jane to Wm. Jackson 4-19-1848 Sh
Morgan, Jennie to Ben Green 10-25-1876 (no return) L B
Morgan, Jenny to Felix Daniel 1-24-1874 Hy
Morgan, Juby F. to Thomas S. Pegram 12-20-1862 (no return) Hn
Morgan, Julia Ann to Thomas T. Armstrong 4-18-1845 Sh
Morgan, Lelia to Bony Ray 1-8-1877 Hy
Morgan, Lou to James Turner Perry 12-17-1866 (12-20-1866) Ma
Morgan, Louisa J. to Theoophelus Sanders 11-23-1852 (11-24-1852) Sh
Morgan, Louisa to Charlie Burton 1-31-1876 L B
Morgan, Lu to Robert Eaton 11-23-1869 T
Morgan, Lucinda to Joshua C. Hatton no date Ma
Morgan, Lucy A. to James A. Oakly 7-30-1863 We
Morgan, Lucy N. to William Willie Dew 8-28-1846 O
Morgan, M. to N. Webb 11-29-1882 (no return) L
Morgan, Margaret to J. K. Everett 1-1-1867 (not executed?) Cr
Morgan, Martha A. to Henry Philips 1-4-1863 Hn
Morgan, Martha A. to Robert A. Mooreman 5-31-1838 Sh
Morgan, Martha E. to B. F. Barton 5-11-1864 Sh
Morgan, Martha E. to E. H. Word (Ward) 12-13-1848 Sh
Morgan, Martha F. to James Tucker 6-4-1851 G
Morgan, Martha to James C. Stewart 3-22-1866 G
Morgan, Martha to John Taylor 12-7-1872 (12-8-1872) L B
Morgan, Martha to Richard Key 3-20-1865 (3-22-1865) Cr
Morgan, Martha to William Johnson 4-28-1871 (no return) F B
Morgan, Mary A. P. to James Rhodes 6-26-1838 F
Morgan, Mary A. to W. W. Wages 1-16-1866 G
Morgan, Mary Ann to Burtis Innsford 9-23-1869 (9-24-1870?) Ma
Morgan, Mary Ann to Jno. Baysinger 11-10-1836 G
Morgan, Mary Ann to John M. Francis 6-19-1858 We
Morgan, Mary E. to D. L. Blakeley? 5-14-1851 (5-15-1851) F
Morgan, Mary E. to Tobias Anderson 11-6-1869 (11-9-1869) F B
Morgan, Mary Elizabeth to John B. Hendricks 10-20-1828 (10-25-1828) Hr
Morgan, Mary Ruth to Kinsey Harrison 11-1-1839 (11-7-1839) Ma
Morgan, Mary to Beverly Shankle 11-1-1861 (no return) Hn
Morgan, Mary to Thomas Moseley 11-7-1881 (11-10-1881) L B
Morgan, Mary to Thomas Ray 2-13-1847 (2-14-1847) G
Morgan, Matilda to Frank Swift 3-5-1878 Hy
Morgan, Menerva to Charles Morgan 6-21-1846 Cr
Morgan, N. E. to William Winchester 10-23-1862 Hn
Morgan, Nancy Jane to Elijah Turner 4-8-1867 (4-9-1867) Ma
Morgan, Nancy N. to T. Z. Harville 12-3-1867 O
Morgan, Nancy to John Roach 1-15-1828 (1-17-1828) G
Morgan, Nancy to William Burton 2-13-1851 (no return) F
Morgan, Pernelia C. to William Bell 4-1-1861 (4-3-1861) O
Morgan, Pheby to Wm. H. Rauson 11-10-1845 (no return) We
Morgan, Polly to Elisha Oglesby 12-8-1829 (12-10-1829) G
Morgan, Rose to Wyley Taylor 12-23-1873 (12-31-1873) L B
Morgan, Rosina to Dick Tipton 11-16-1865 T
Morgan, Sallie to William Clem 2-28-1882 L
Morgan, Sarah F. to I. G. Silverthorn 6-29-1863 (6-30-1863) O
Morgan, Sarah J. to George Owens 11-29-1871 (11-30-1871) Cr B
Morgan, Sarah P. C. to Joseph Soemrs 9-21-1854 Sh
Morgan, Sarah to Chas. Bulger 12-19-1846 Sh
Morgan, Vinetta to George Stevens 2-18-1877 Hy
Moriarty, Ellen to Dennis Lynch 4-21-1860 (4-22-1860) Sh
Moriarty, Hannora to Patrick Lee 2-22-1862 (2-23-1862) Sh
Morisay, Bridget to Martin Dolohay 4-12-1858 Sh
Morisay, Bridget to Michael Shae 11-1-1854 Sh
Morison, Amelia J. to John W. Griffin 12-30-1848 (12-31-1848) F
Morison, Mollie Ann to James W. Thompson 4-1-1878 (4-4-1878) L
Morley, Merandy G. to W. F. Nash 7-9-1868 (no return) Dy
Moroharty, Margaret to Michael McDonald 12-1-1855 Sh
Moroharty, Margaret to Michael McDonnell 12-1-1855 Sh
Morphis, A. E. to M. S. Howard 12-9-1841 Hn
Morphis, Amanda M. to James Crocker 6-20-1846 (6-21-1846) Hr
Morphis, Ann R. to A. F. Calhoun 4-10-1865 (4-13-1865) F
Morphis, Elizabeth to Charles McCoy 12-26-1838 (12-29-1838) Ma
Morphis, G. A. to Samuel H. Holmes 5-16-1844 Hn
Morphis, Mary Jane to Joseph Patterson 12-13-1845 Ma
Morphis, Milly Ann to William Manly 11-6-1841 (11-14-1841) Ma
Morphis, W. J. to James Penick 10-26-1865 Hn
Morphus, Eliza Jane to W. J. Brumley 8-27-1861 (8-29-1861) Hr
Morphus, Martha to Andrew J. Hodges 1-23-1839 G
Morrell, C. to ?. S. Vickers 1-1-1852 Cr
Morrell, Jane to H. S. Ward 2-20-1862 (2-21-1862) Sh
Morrell, Louis S. to Charles A. Bland 4-11-1846 (4-12-1846) Ma
Morrell, Mary to Hiram Farmer 5-18-1846 We
Morril, Eliza A. to R. M. Crow 2-10-1862 (2-12-1862) Hr
Morrill, Mary E. (Mrs.) to Willis W. Williams 2-25-1867 (2-27-1867) Ma
Morrion, Ellen C. to Charles H. Dorion, jr. 4-9-1857 Sh
Morris (Harris), Racheal A. to Osmund R. Brown 8-25-1857 O
Morris, A. C. to James W. Harris 2-16-1855 Cr
Morris, A. E. to R. S. Carney 3-5-1860 (no return) Hy

Morris, A. J. to E. H. Smith 9-30-1866 Hn
Morris, Ada L. to J. L. Yarbro 1-2-1883 (1-4-1883) L
Morris, Albina to C. J. Whitelsy 2-18-1840 Cr
Morris, Alliner to J. B. Wilson 3-24-1849 Cr
Morris, Amanda to Claiborne Vaulx 7-2-1870 Hy
Morris, Amandy to George L. Gardner 3-18-1866 G
Morris, Amelia Ann to John Hensley 4-8-1858 Ma
Morris, Amelia to Henry Snow 4-14-1860 (4-22-1860) F
Morris, Angeline to S. L. Johnson 11-28-1876 (11-29-1876) Dy
Morris, Angeline to William Mitchell 9-5-1868 (9-6-1868) Cr
Morris, Annie L. to Rob't S. Murphey 7-26-1877 O
Morris, Becky to Paul Robinson 8-5-1873 (no return) Hy
Morris, Birtie (Bettie?) to Watson Reynolds 6-24-1874 (no return) L
Morris, Catherine to Samuel A. Given, jr. 4-6-1846 (4-9-1846) L
Morris, Celia to Josiah Forester 7-7-1845 Be
Morris, Christiana E. to John H. Pounds 12-24-1866 (12-25-1866) Cr
Morris, Clarisa to James Lea 9-8-1828 (9-9-1828) Hr
Morris, Clorie to Frank Morris 12-30-1872 O
Morris, Delilah to William A. Aslin 6-21-1866 G
Morris, Dilly to Jackson Fox 10-27-1838 G
Morris, Dolly to Thomas King 4-29-1845 Be
Morris, E. J. to John N. Holt 5-5-1847 Sh
Morris, E. T. to Plesant R. Bessent 12-18-1867 (12-19-1867) Dy
Morris, Elbena to Byds Huggard 11-16-1857 We
Morris, Eliza A. to Alfred A. Sawyers 12-3-1865 Mn
Morris, Eliza to John S. Brotherton 6-13-1843 (6-15-1843) Hr
Morris, Elizabeth A. to Travis C. Brooks 7-5-1828 (7-8-1828) Ma
Morris, Elizabeth P. to Robert H. Thomas 10-14-1856 G
Morris, Elizabeth to Allen Dodd 12-21-1840 (no return) Cr
Morris, Elizabeth to J. E. Steel 3-8-1870 Hy
Morris, Elizabeth to James W. Worsham 6-12-1856 Hn
Morris, Elizabeth to Michael Willsford 9-19-1857 O
Morris, Elizabeth to William Riley 3-24-1858 Sh
Morris, Emiline to Benj. Watkins 7-29-1866 Hy
Morris, Frances L. to A. H. Spain 11-26-1869 (11-28-1869) Cr
Morris, Frances to Andrew J. Mills 8-27-1850 (8-29-1850) Hr
Morris, H. A. P. to G. W. Richardson 12-3-1874 L
Morris, Hanah to I. Thornton 12-28-1839 (12-30-1839) Ma
Morris, Harriet to Daniel Lane 6-8-1867 (no return) F B
Morris, Harriett to Thomas Stovall 5-24-1876 (5-25-1876) O
Morris, Hassie M. to Joshua E. Powell 1-5-1860 Hn
Morris, Holley to Samuel Oral 5-2-1842 Cr
Morris, J. E. (Mrs.) to Ivory Summers 1-11-1876 Hy
Morris, Jane to Mayfield Bell 11-28-1855 (12-3-1855) Hr
Morris, Jane to Oliver T. Morris 5-2-1854 (5-21-1854) G
Morris, Judy to Arther Bond 3-4-1875 Hy
Morris, Julia to Charles Wilson 12-24-1866 (12-27-1866) F B
Morris, Julia to Joseph M. Pankey 12-23-1863 (12-24-1863) O
Morris, Kate K. to Edwin K. Morris 8-4-1863 (no return) We
Morris, Kate to Peter Coghill 12-28-1871 O
Morris, Katharine S. to A. R. Tippett 2-16-1845 Be
Morris, Levina to Charley Coor 6-20-1843 (6-22-1843) Hr
Morris, Lotta to Andrew Swift 2-2-1870 (no return) F B
Morris, Lou L. to G. B. Davidson 12-17-1884 L
Morris, Louisa C. to A. W. Lindsey 1-15-1858 Be
Morris, Louisa to H. D. Brawner? 1-23-1869 (1-24-1869) Cr
Morris, Lu (Lee?) to H. C. Brown 10-28-1866 G
Morris, Lucinda to Isaiah Jones 1-28-1874 Hy
Morris, Lucinia J. to Andrew J. Pemberton 5-22-1856 Hn
Morris, Lucy Ann to Gus Gooden 11-5-1869 (11-6-1869) F B
Morris, Lucy F. to A. J. Hodge 10-9-1844 (10-13-1844) O
Morris, Lucy F. to Peter M. Mott 9-6-1849 L
Morris, Lucy J. to E. Marshall Joyner 2-27-1866 (3-1-1866) Cr
Morris, Lucy to John T. Simpson 9-19-1839 Sh
Morris, Luraney to Samuel A. Stow 5-24-1846 Sh
Morris, M. C. to A. A. Hall 6-30-1870 G
Morris, M. E. C. to W. G. White 10-15-1857 We
Morris, M. H. to James M. Gore 10-30-1866 (11-2-1865?) F
Morris, M. J. (Mrs.) to W. I. Myres 9-25-1866 O
Morris, M. J. to J. B. Alexander 2-3-1872 (2-4-1872) L
Morris, M. to Ruf. Davis 2-26-1872 O
Morris, Malinda J. to Thos. M. Williams 10-13-1857 We
Morris, Margarett to S. Y. Bigham 5-14-1860 (5-16-1860) Cr
Morris, Martha Ann to Davis Gillespie 6-17-1848 (no return) F
Morris, Martha Emiline to James Mathis 1-10-1850 L
Morris, Martha to Jim Douglass 12-20-1865 Hy
Morris, Martha to Robt. Williams 4-3-1868 (no return) F B
Morris, Martha to Spencer Scott 1-18-1877 Hy
Morris, Mary A. to J. R. Davis 10-29-1866 O
Morris, Mary A. to John J. Clark 4-29-1851 Cr
Morris, Mary A. to Thomas Aslin 2-6-1861 G
Morris, Mary C. to Isaac J. Carter 5-25-1844 F
Morris, Mary E. to G. W. Tatom 10-8-1867 (10-12-1867) F
Morris, Mary E. to Robert C. Thompson 1-8-1860 Hn
Morris, Mary F. to David C. Bradley 5-11-1856 Hn
Morris, Mary Jane to Hiram M. Jones 2-3-1845 (no return) F
Morris, Mary to Edward Fox 5-2-1837 (6-8-1837) G

Morris, Mary to John Williamson 7-20-1840 (7-23-1840) G
Morris, Mary to Lewis Johnson 2-10-1873 (2-13-1873) O
Morris, Mary to M. H. P. Weakley 12-24-1870 (3-15-1871) Dy
Morris, Mary to Robt. Lee 1-5-1866 (1-6-1866) F B
Morris, Mary to Wm. A. Sayles 2-14-1865 (2-15-1865) Cr
Morris, Mary to Zachariah Roberts 6-3-1855 O
Morris, Melinda to Charles Freeman 8-28-1843 (8-29-1843) Hr
Morris, Melissa A. to James D. Ray 9-29-1855 (9-30-1855) G
Morris, Minnie to E. Jouvenat 1-15-1862 Hr
Morris, Miriah M. to Benj. F. Duke 2-5-1871 Cr
Morris, Mollie to James Watkins 6-25-1875 Hy
Morris, N. A. to Green C. Pinckston 4-15-1872 (no return) Cr
Morris, Nancy J. to Thomas M. Hollyfield 3-29-1844 We
Morris, Nancy to David Hall 5-7-1860 (4?-8-1860) G
Morris, Nancy to Henry Malone 4-15-1838 Cr
Morris, Nancy to Thomas Reed 11-11-1850 We
Morris, Octavia to Isaac Shinault 12-18-1860 (12-19-1860) Hr
Morris, P. J. to Adsalom Arnold 5-9-1850 (no return) Hn
Morris, Penellop to Martin H. Johnson 11-28-1839 (no return) L
Morris, Persilla to P. H. Hatley 1-10-1869 Be
Morris, Priscilla to James H. Wisenor 12-19-1853 Sh
Morris, Rose to Henry Garmany? 9-14-1871 O
Morris, S. A. to Giles Coffman 12-24-1865 Hy
Morris, S. E. to W. H. Patton 7-20-1870 (no return) Hy
Morris, Saphronia J. to Z. N. Wilson 4-19-1863 G
Morris, Sarah A. to Isaac Garret 4-10-1867 Dy
Morris, Sarah A. to John W. Pool 6-1-1872 T
Morris, Sarah A. to Stephen A. Peeler 12-22-1866 (12-25-1866) F
Morris, Sarah Ann to B. N. Young 1-2-1850 We
Morris, Sarah Ann to Thomas C. Owen 12-9-1852 We
Morris, Sarah J. to Lewis J. Cherry 5-28-1856 G
Morris, Sarah to M. A. Jones 1-8-1850 F
Morris, Sidna A. to Willis J. Langford 2-28-1874 (3-1-1874) O
Morris, Susan Ann to William Fox 12-15-1846 (12-20-1846) G
Morris, Susan to Amos Anderson 5-9-1867 (no return) Hn B
Morris, Susan to R. A. Deleny 12-20-1860 (12-23-1860) Cr
Morris, Susan to Ruff & Ready Taylor 4-28-1866 Hy
Morris, Susan to Walter S. Fuqua 11-17-1868 (11-18-1868) Cr
Morris, Victoria to D.C. Cook 5-25-1873 Hy
Morris?, Harriett to James Barnes 3-16-1866 (no return) Cr
Morrisett, Catharine F. to G. A. Huffman 1-8-1872 (1-9-1872) T
Morrison, Ann M. to John Bartlett 8-19-1833 (8-20-1833) Hr
Morrison, Catharine to John Williams 7-7-1853 Sh
Morrison, Catharine to W. C. Sloss 1-1-1878 (4-4-1878) L
Morrison, Celia to James Brooks 8-8-1825 Sh
Morrison, Emerline to James Simmons 11-28-1868 (11-30-1868) T
Morrison, Harriet T. to James B. Shell 2-18-1854 Sh
Morrison, Julia E. to Joseph G. Delashmeit 7-1-1865 T
Morrison, L. C. to O. H. Lide 12-18-1849 Sh
Morrison, Laura to Needham Kilpatrick 6-3-1869 (6-4-1869) T
Morrison, Margaret C. to John F. Neel 10-18-1842 F
Morrison, Margaret to Patrick Myles 7-27-1862 (7-29-1862) Sh
Morrison, Margarett L. to David Williams 2-10-1849 Ma
Morrison, Martha E. to A. J. Biggers 2-11-1850 (2-12-1850) F
Morrison, Mary A. to Samuel W. Hudleston 9-3-1872 T
Morrison, Mary Ann to Edward Box 4-3-1847 O
Morrison, Mary M. to John M. McFadden 11-27-1844 (no return) F
Morrison, Mary to John McMullin 3-17-1857 (3-18-1857) Sh
Morrison, Matilda to A. Harris 1-4-1869 (1-8-1869) T
Morrison, Nancy Caroline to Jacob Wallace 1-19-1854 T
Morrison, Nancy to William Diffee 5-31-1864 Sh
Morrison, Nannie E. to W. T. Morgan 12-11-1874 T
Morrison, Ruthey to Joseph Box 2-22-1847 O
Morrison, S. C. to James J. Covey 11-21-1865 (11-26-1865) F
Morrison, Sarah (Mrs.) to James Clifford 10-21-1858 Sh
Morrison, Sarah E. to John R. Scott 2-19-1870 G
Morrison, Susanna to Henry Lynn 7-3-1869 T
Morrison?, Charlotte M. to H. P. Maxwell 3-19-1841 F
Morriss, Emeline to Zachariah Wiseman 5-4-1842 (no return) F
Morriss, Perlina C. to Daniel W. Frazier 12-1-1843 (11?-16-1843) F
Morriss, R. P. to S. Flutcher Harrell? (Howell?) 12-28-1872 (12-29-1872) L
Morriss, Sarah E. to James T. Gregory 8-3-1861 Sh
Morriss, Sarah F. to George Rushing 12-27-1862 Be
Morrissey, Margaret to Patrick Brody 1-16-1859 Sh
Morrow, Ann to David Griffith 11-9-1868 (11-13-1868) F B
Morrow, Ann to Thomas Polk(Pack) 12-18-1833 Hr
Morrow, B. H. to G. W. Mayfield 9-12-1853 (9-13-1853) Ma
Morrow, E. J. to W. T. Roach 7-8-1863 Mn
Morrow, Eliza to Lewis Taylor 3-27-1869 (4-1-1869) F B
Morrow, Elizabeth E. to John M. Meals 12-3-1846 (12-24-1846) Ma
Morrow, Elizabeth to John R. Orr 9-10-1857 (9-15-1857) O
Morrow, Ellen to Harrison Cherry 12-26-1868 (12-?-1868) L
Morrow, Elmira to Lewis M. Boyett 6-5-1852 O
Morrow, Emily to Jessee Boyd 1-19-1867 F B
Morrow, Emma F. to John A. Green 2-15-1857 Hn
Morrow, Frances G. to J. W. Morrow 11-26-1850 (11-27-1850) F
Morrow, Henrietta to George Thomas 5-10-1867 (5-20-1867) F B

Morrow, Indiana to David M. Parish 11-5-1866 (11-7-1866) L
Morrow, Jane to Aleck Boyd 3-28-1866 (3-31-1866) F B
Morrow, L. J. to W. H. Worel 10-17-1865 O
Morrow, Lavica Parker to Andrew Jackson Lewis 2-25-1859 (3-1-1859) Ma
Morrow, Malesa to Geo. W. Meals 9-26-1840 Cr
Morrow, Martha J. to Archy Y. Douglas 3-31-1845 (4-1-1845) Ma
Morrow, Mary Ann to James W. Carruthers 5-28-1846 Ma
Morrow, Mary E. to John C. Barnett(Bennett) 2-21-1832 (2-23-1832) Hr
Morrow, Mary to Joseph Jackson 1-13-1845 F
Morrow, Matilda to Nathan Grant 11-1-1838 Cr
Morrow, Millie Ann to George Morrow 8-20-1868 (8-27-1868) F B
Morrow, Nancy to Isaac Burns 1-3-1861 O
Morrow, P. R. to Henry A. Morgan 3-5-1868 G
Morrow, Rachel A. to Robert Allen 8-26-1870 (8-28-1870) F B
Morrow, Sarah E. to J. W. Mebane 7-24-1851 O
Morrow, Sarah H. to Daniel J. Meals 12-6-1843 (12-7-1843) Ma
Morrow, Sarah J. to Newton Morrow 12-22-1866 O
Morrow, Sintha to James W. Ray 8-16-1852 (8-17-1852) G
Morse, Hattie to Louis Botto 5-24-1864 Sh
Morten, Eliza to Joseph Malton 12-23-1862 (12-24-1862) Sh
Morten, Ella to Haywood Read 1-15-1874 Hy
Morten, Missouri E. to J. Robbins 1-20-1864 Sh
Morten, Sarah T. to Watkins H. Dodson 1-6-1844 (1-9-1844) G
Morton, Delphia R. to James W. Henderson 12-28-1859 Hn
Morton, E. F. to G. W. Tatum 12-23-1868 Hy
Morton, Eliza E. to J. F. Baxter 1-7-1870 (1-13-1870) F
Morton, Elizabeth to Edmund Jackson 4-4-1855 Hn
Morton, Emily to Matthew Nevill 10-27-1847 Sh
Morton, Jane H. to John A. Ward 1-2-1871 (1-5-1871) F
Morton, Kate to James Cohen 1-25-1864 (1-26-1864) Sh
Morton, M. L. O. to J. R. Mitchell 2-11-1877 Hy
Morton, M. M. to A. J. McCoy 1-4-1869 (1-5-1869) F
Morton, Margaret C. to Candour McKinny 11-20-1844 (no return) F
Morton, Martha H. to George O. Richmon 10-28-1839 (10-29-1839) G
Morton, Martha to N. R. Brent 12-21-1865 Mn
Morton, Martha to Thos. E. Tatum 5-31-1866 Hy
Morton, Mathia to James R. Nance 12-27-1841 Cr
Morton, Penicia A. to Henry M. Flatt 11-14-1862 Mn
Morton, Rebecca F. to W. R. Hastings 7-17-1861 Mn
Morton, Rhoda C. to Wm. C. McNeely 1-1-1869 (no return) F
Morton, Susan A. to Samuel D. Givens 5-5-1842 G
Morton, Susan Jane to E. G. Young 12-21-1869 Hy
Morton, Susan N. to Daniel McDougald 8-13-1835 G
Morton, Victoria to Solomon McDowell 1-6-1871 (no return) F B
Morton, Virginia to John M. Malone 12-10-1867 Hy
Mosby, Amanda to Tom Nowel 9-24-1868 (9-27-1868) F B
Mosby, Dicy to Anthony Price 2-15-1867 (2-16-1867) F B
Mosby, Lydia Ann to Britton Mosby 7-15-1870 (no return) F B
Mosby, Mary J. to William H. Wilson 5-18-1861 (5-19-1861) Sh
Mosby, Paralee to John McClellan 11-16-1867 (1-4-1868) F B
Mosby, Sarah to Stark Anerson? 8-16-1870 (9-4-1870) T
Moseley, Amanda R. to Thomas Thompson 12-24-1873 Dy
Moseley, Elizabeth A. to W. L. Fields 2-16-1857 (2-19-1857) L
Moseley, Ellen to James M. Adams 1-6-1876 Dy
Moseley, Ellen to James M. Adams 6?-6-1876? (with Apr 1876) Dy
Moseley, Mattie to Nelson Scott 2-5-1880 Dy
Moseley, Molly to Cyrus Mackey 12-26-1868 (12-29-1868) F B
Mosely, Catherine S. to John Marcum 11-17-1840 Sh
Mosely, Elizabeth A. to Joseph Penegar 12-17-1846 We
Mosely, Elizabeth E. to John F. Rogers 9-26-1836 G
Mosely, Harriet to Ike Alexandner 1-20-1868 G B
Mosely, M. F. to P. R. Champee 1-27-1877 (1-29-1877) L
Mosely, Margaret to Anderson Pearce 4-4-1869 G B
Mosely, Martha (Mrs.) to T. W. Montgomery 8-12-1866 G
Mosely, Mary to Nathan Jones 9-12-1869 G B
Mosely, Sarah F. to James M. Adams 11-7-1872 Dy
Moser, Lourana to Moses Holt 9-13-1869 Ma
Moser, Lucy A. to John H. Taylor 4-30-1859 (5-1-1859) O
Moser, Malinda to Elias J. Canady 11-19-1857 O
Moses (Masyl?), Lucy to Rush Bond 3-23-1875 Hy
Moses, Betsey to Tulley Eastridge 2-25-1828 O
Moses, Betsy to John Hannah 3-4-1871 (no return) Hy
Moses, Elin to Dock Winters 12-19-1877 Hy
Moses, Martha Ann to Richmond N. Shackleford 11-9-1854 Ma
Moses, Mary E. Perkins 1-23-1864 Be
Moses, Matilda to M. Gabriel 10-22-1863 Sh
Moses, Parthenia to Frank Campbell 5-22-1869 (no return) Hy
Mosgraves, Susannah to J. H. Woodard 3-12-1878 L
Mosier, Caroline to John Webster 3-28-1865 Mn
Mosier, Frances to W. S. Butler 11-26-1867 O
Mosier, Lear to J. R. Sipes 3-30-1864 Mn
Mosier, Malinda to John H. Moris 2-12-1876 O
Mosier, Mariah to Michael Bradburn 5-6-1854 (5-12-1854) L
Mosier, Martha Ann to John M. Glover 8-29-1854 (9-7-1854) O
Mosier, Mary A. to Charles M. Trout 12-23-1865 (12-24-1865) O
Mosier, Mary A. to Henry Guthry 1-16-1867 (1-17-1867) O
Mosier, Mary to B. C. Candee 5-4-1859 Sh

Mosier, Mary to John Mosier 8-4-1866 (8-5-18??) O
Mosier, Nina Ann to James Ledbetter 7-10-1842 Hn
Mosier, Parilee to Cleft Eastridge 8-21-1838 (8-23-1838) O
Mosier, Polly to Eli Bassham 10-27-1830 O
Mosier, S. A. to Jas. Henderson 4-17-1867 O
Mosley, A. J. to E. G. Mosley 7-27-1854 We
Mosley, Harriett E. to John M. Reeder 5-9-1850 Sh
Mosley, Jane to William Holder 8-6-1861 G
Mosley, Jennie to Henry Dilliard 12-27-1866 (1-2-1867) F B
Mosley, Judy to William T. Bonner 7-25-1843 F
Mosley, M. A. to John A. Tanner 11-21-1844 Sh
Mosley, Martha to H. Y. Jones 7-30-1868 G
Mosley, Mary A. E. to Daniel Clifton 2-12-1834 Sh
Mosley, Mary A. to H. J. Shanon 2-20-1855 We
Mosley, Mary A. to T. M. Bryan 8-18-1858 (8-20-1858) G
Mosley, Mary J. to William M. Davidson 10-13-1856 G
Mosley, Mary S. to W. C. Davidson 2-14-1860 G
Mosley, Sallie to Bernard Cox 12-27-1866 (1-12-1867) F B
Mosley, Sophia to Saml. T. Milner 12-27-1849 We
Mosley, Susan V. to S. F. Davidson 6-18-1863 G
Mosley, Susan to Alfred Hutchison 4-25-1861 (?-2_-1861) L
Mosly (Mosby), Mary E. to Albert M. Wood 10-2-1844 Sh
Mosly, Judith P. to Thomas W. Hunt 5-20-1841 G
Mosly, Minerva M. to George W. Grafford 11-26-1840 Ma
Moslyew, Viola to William Mitchell 12-28-1864 Be
Mosmon, Hariett R. to Eli Christopher 4-2-1844 Be
Moss, Almeda to Markens Williams 12-21-1842 Ma
Moss, America W. to William P. Youree 4-2-1838 F
Moss, Callie to G. W. Finch 10-19-1871 (10-22-1871) O
Moss, Camolia to Wm. Mizell 5-16-1850 Be
Moss, Desimony to James Boals 11-4-1829 (11-5-1829) G
Moss, Eliza to N. McNeill 8-23-1840 Be
Moss, Elizabeth to Henry Bard 10-26-1865 (10-29-1865) O
Moss, Elizabeth to William Boling 9-23-1826 G
Moss, Elizabeth to William Cain 12-2-1865 (no return) Cr
Moss, Elizabeth to William Kain 5-2-1866 (5-3-1866) Cr
Moss, Emma to Joseph Morgan 1-20-1872 (1-21-1872) Cr
Moss, Frances to George Heathscott 11-27-1856 We
Moss, Georgiana to A. F. Crews 7-28-1863 (no return) We
Moss, Jacsabena to William Pearce 1-24-1860 G
Moss, Joanna to D. J. Guthrie, jr. 11-21-1867 Hy
Moss, Lucy E. to P. A. Bourn 10-11-1870 (10-12-1870) T
Moss, Maggie to Samuel Stovall 12-27-1870 (12-28-1870) O
Moss, Martha Ann to Patrick H. Birdsong 12-20-1852 (12-21-1852) Hr
Moss, Mary J. to P. O. Hamer 1-18-1854 Hr
Moss, Mary S. to Charles S. Clemens 2-21-1860 We
Moss, Mary to C. W. Cooper 5-27-1855 Be
Moss, Mary to Reuben Doherty 12-28-1830 Ma
Moss, Mary to Richard Best 12-7-1853 (12-11-1853) G
Moss, Mattie to Ben Green 1-3-1873 (1-5-1873) L B
Moss, Melvina to Henry H. Hardy 10-21-1846 Hr
Moss, Nancy to Carroll Chambers 9-11-1845 We
Moss, Nancy to J. W. D. Haring 3-26-1850 (3-28-1850) F
Moss, Nancy to Matthew Wilhite 9-5-1833 Hr
Moss, Rachell to Peter Burrell 11-12-1873 T
Moss, Sarah to Benj. W. Perry 7-19-1827 G
Moss, Sarah to Elijah Quick 6-17-1837 (6-?-1837) G
Moss, Sarah to James Weatherford 7-21-1865 (7-26-1865) T
Moss?, Sophia? to J.? W.? Markham? 11-26-1862 T
Mote, M. T. to J. E. Crisp 1-20-1874 (1-21-1874) Dy
Moten, Letsey to George Hathorne 12-29-1865 (no return) Hy
Moten, Margaret J. to Julius S. Throgmorton 1-5-1842 Hn
Motheral, Ellinor E. to David Bright 12-13-1842 O
Motheral, Jane K. to John W. O'Neal 6-25-1840 O
Motheral, Martha Ann to Winfrey B. McConnell 5-17-1842 O
Motherel, Susan to Samuel D. Wilson 3-13-1860 O
Mothershed, Levinia to Simeon W. Bright 2-18-1853 Be
Mothershed, Lucy to Ruffin Cole 11-18-1852 Be
Motion, Malinda to Benj. Alexander 12-18-1872 (12-19-1872) Cr B
Motley, Elizabeth A. to J. A. Vaughan 11-13-1848 Sh
Motley, Emeline to Aaron Jackson 1-13-1842 G
Motley, Martha J. to Corsy O. D. Nevil 10-11-1861 (10-13-1861) L
Motley, Mary A. to Rufus Archie 1-29-1861 (1-30-1861) F
Motley, Mary Elizabeth to Henry Grinshaw Heyes 1-27-1862 Sh
Motley, R. R. to J. J. Koffman 10-6-1867 G
Motley?, Florence E. S. to J. C. Banden 8-21-1869 T
Motly, Elizabeth to Harris B. Pruitt 7-30-1845 (7-31-1845) G
Motly, Martha to Alston Bailey 12-2-1844 (12-26-1844) G
Moton, Harriett to Tilman Galamore 2-5-1842 Hn
Mott, M. S. to S. B. Ayers 12-13-1870 (12-21-1870) O
Mott, Willie Ann to Rob't P. Morris 7-3-1877 (7-4-1877) O
Motto, Eliza to Sebastian Kolb 11-13-1860 Sh
Moudy, Frances C. to John H. Jones 12-2-1845 (12-7-1845) G
Moudy, Rebecca C. to William R. Carroll 8-25-1846 (8-27-1846) G
Moulder, Sarah to Joseph Hudson 2-13-1830 Ma
Moule, Louisiana to Edward McFarland 5-10-1843 Sh
Moultrie, M. M. to B. W. Flemming 5-25-1867 O

Moultrie, Mary E. to William P. Stephens 11-19-1859 (11-20-1859) O
Moultrie, Rebecca Angeline to Robert C. Miller 10-1-1853 O
Mount, Caroline V. to W. E. Hedgecock 11-26-1868 G
Mount, Emily J. to W. H. Johns 4-1-1861 G
Mount, Lavenia to Marshall Thomas 3-3-1863 (no return) Cr
Mount, Levinia to D. M. Thomas 10-9-1862 (no return) Cr
Mount, Louisa R. D. to Jas. M. Akin 8-4-1870 G
Mount, Louisa to John N. (W.?) Hedgecock no date (with Jul 1864) G
Mount, Luvenia to George Cain no date (1860-1870) G
Mount, Mary F. to J. H. Hedgecock 9-29-1859 G
Mount, Mary to James Hampton 1-31-1867 G
Mount, Sarah F. to Wm. M. Baker 3-19-1862 G
Mounts, Angeline J. to Robert Evans Cloud 1-17-1843 (not executed) T
Mowdy, Amanda to Jas. H. Kirkwood 9-28-1843 We
Moxley, Emily C. to John A. Sturkie 4-9-1866 (4-10-1866) Ma
Moxley, Margaret to J. H. Brumley 6-5-1858 Sh
Moxley, Martha to Anderson Glover 4-10-1867 O
Moxley, Mary E. to James Hayley 1-23-1869 (1-24-1869) Ma
Mueller, Margaretha to Adolph Brassel 7-6-1861 Sh
Mugovan, Bridget to Dan Lanigan 4-4-1861 Sh
Muirhead, Mary to William Freeman 1-20-1831 G
Muirhead, Nannie to John L. Duncan 11-5-1877 (11-7-1877) Dy
Mulby, Ann to Edward Bruhl 10-29-1859 (11-1-1859) Hr
Muldan, Rody E. to Andrew Gossett 12-26-1831 Hr
Mulford, Lovina to Peter E. Tufts 1-25-1855 (1-27-1855) Sh
Mulherin, Amanda to Austin Connell 4-22-1872 (2-23-1872) Dy
Mulherin, Amanda to Bob Clark 6-13-1867 Dy
Mulherin, Sallie A. to James Brooks 12-27-1860 (no return) Hy
Mulherin, Tete to Alf? Smart 7-3-1877 Dy
Mulheron, Catherine to Daniel Dolan (Dola) 10-28-1845 Sh
Mulherren, Mandy to James Carnes 8-13-1868 (no return) Hy
Mulherrin, Margaret to W. J. Bronaugh 12-19-1860 (no return) Hy
Mulherrin, Texanna to Willis Chapman 12-22-1877 (no return) Hy
Mulholland, Helen J. to Joseph J. Powers 7-21-1862 (7-22-1862) Sh
Muligin, S. J. to J. S. Bashears 12-23-1874 T
Mullarney, Mary to Ed Whealan 2-12-1861 Sh
Mullen, Janie to Alexander McDonald 11-20-1878 Hy
Mullen, Mary to James Johnson 11-16-1842 (11-20-1842) Ma
Mullens, Emiline to David A. Young 1-1-1861 G
Mullens, Frances E. to George C. Millsted 5-3-1849 Hr
Mullens, Nancy to James W. Connell 12-21-1857 (12-22-1857) G
Muller, Mary F. to Henry Von Negler 12-24-1866 F
Mulliken, Matilda R. to Tho. Jeffreys Shelton, jr. 2-22-1864 F
Mullikin, Emeline to John J. Fleet 1-9-1847 Hr
Mullikin, Susan to William Maddox 12-11-1849 Hr
Mullin, Fannie to W. F. Covington 1-27-1872 Hy
Mullin, Jane to Thomas Higdon 11-7-1866 Cr
Mullin, Lou to Robt. Scarimon? 6-3-1867 (6-1?-1867) T
Mullin, Lucy Ann to James P. Arthur 2-16-1867 (2-17-1867) L
Mullin, M. W. to J.R. Carter 1-23-1878 Hy
Mullin, Perneta A. to A. J. Fields 12-4-1867 Cr
Mullinicks, Martha A. C. to John Allen Gossett 8-29-1852 Be
Mullinicks, Martha J. to Herman Cox 1-20-1858 Be
Mullinix, Eliza Ann Permelia to James M. Smith 9-23-1847 Be
Mullinix, Sarah J. P. to Franklin Smith 9-19-1844 Be
Mullins, Catharine to Patrick Welch 5-9-1853 (5-10-1853) Sh
Mullins, Elizabeth to James L. Russell 8-10-1829 (8-11-1829) Hr
Mullins, Elizabeth to Jas. Henry Braden 1-4-1870 (no return) Hy
Mullins, Ellen to Charly Eavans 6-30-1873 (no return) L
Mullins, H. E. J. to Alexander Young 10-29-1867 G
Mullins, Julia to Thomas Giles 12-31-1874 L
Mullins, Lou A. to E. P. Sutton 7-2-1866 (7-5-1866) L
Mullins, Lou A. to E. P. Sutton 7-2-1867? (7-5-1866) L
Mullins, Louisa to Albert P. Phillips 1-3-1853 (1-6-1853) G
Mullins, M. A. to G. W. Bouldin 4-13-1870 (4-14-1870) Cr
Mullins, Martha Ann to James C. Wise 7-4-1846 Hr
Mullins, Martha J. to S. B. Hailey 10-8-1863 We
Mullins, Mary R. to Robin Godwin 11-15-1859 Sh
Mullins, Mary J. to A. W. Thompson 10-16-1855 (no return) L
Mullins, Nancy to Thos. Scott 1-21-1856 (1-22-1856) G
Mullins, Permelia to James Barton 3-8-1859 Cr
Mullins, Sarah E. to James Carrele 4-8-1868 (4-12-1868) L
Mullins, Sarah Jane to Neil Thompson 9-11-1866 (9-13-1866) Ma
Mullins, Sarah to Willis Horn 7-7-1856 (7-13-1856) Hr
Mullins, Sinah M. to George W. Akin 8-21-1851 (8-22-1851) G
Mullins, Stacy to W. R. Michael 10-30-1854 (10-31-1854) L
Mullins, Susan to Abner Null 12-21-1846 (12-24-1846) Hr
Mullins, U. to Commodore Perry 4-9-1840 Hn
Mullins, U. to Perry (Commodore) McCrawley 4-9-1840 Hn
Mulvaney, Mattie A. to Thomas F. Sneed 9-25-1861 Sh
Mulvin, Mary Ann to Ferdenand Wilson 9-14-1863 Sh
Mumford, Ellen to John Donahay 1-9-1849 Sh
Munford, Ermine to Hugh Hall 5-29-1872 T
Munford, Sallie E. to Geo. D. Holmes 1-18-1866 T
Munn, Ann to James Carroll 3-13-1844 Sh
Munn, L. A. to J. E. Sanders 1-21-1872 Cr
Munn, Mary to John Eddins 12-13-1846 F

Munn, Nancy to Jonathan Armstrong 2-11-1844 Cr
Munn, Sarah Jane to Amos W. Barron 10-25-1859 (11-1-1859) Ma
Munn, Susan A. to B. F. Whitley 4-30-1861 (5-1-1861) Sh
Munn?, Elizabeth to John Spear 2-4-1845 Sh
Munns, Mary H. to T. B. Latour 7-4-1885 (7-5-1885) L
Munns, Mattie V. to James M. Robbins 12-13-1871 Hy
Munns?, S. E. to S. A. Denney 9-11-1876 (9-17-1876) Dy
Munrow?, Sarah A. to Andrew M Provine 4-24-1851 Hn
Munson, Myranda F. to William J. French 1-15-1852 Hn
Muray, Nancy J. to Jno. M. Daniel 11-21-1860 F
Muray, Sarah W. to A. C. McNeil 3-8-1854 Cr
Murchean, Rutha to Kinchin Freeman 6-11-1834 G
Murchison, Ann E. to Caleb Woods 8-5-1846 (8-13-1846) Ma
Murchison, Isabela to James F. Haddoway 4-23-1842 (4-24-1842) Ma
Murchison, Isabella M. to James W. Harris 11-16-1858 (11-18-1858) Ma
Murchison, Martha J. to John L. Walsh 2-16-1849 Ma
Murchison, Mary Jane to James C. Whaton 9-2-1841 (9-?-1841) Ma
Murchison, Sallie I. to John A. Givens 11-4-1871 (11-6-1871) Ma
Murdaugh, Elizabeth to Robert Cozby 8-5-1835 Hr
Murdaugh, Martha J. to William L. Knott 1-19-1858 Hr
Murdaugh, Mary to James A. Barham 11-2-1853 (11-3-1853) Hr
Murdough, Mary to William H. Redding 5-4-1863 (no return) Dy
Murdough, Rachael to Sydney S. Knott 1-10-1861 Hr
Murley, Malvina H. to Tho. M. Scott 11-28-1849 L
Murley, Mary to Jeremiah Hooper 12-18-1846 (12-20-1846) Hr
Murphey, A. F. (Mrs.) to W. R. Simpson 11-30-1872 (11-3?-1872) Dy
Murphey, Adelia (Mrs.) to Robert T. Hood 4-25-1859 L
Murphey, Bridget to Daniel Tolbert 7-3-1862 (7-6-1862) Sh
Murphey, Bridget to John Doty 5-15-1861 Sh
Murphey, Catharine to Paton Fox 3-5-1830 (3-18-1830) G
Murphey, Elizabeth F. to J. A. V. Goode 11-30-1853 (no return) F
Murphey, M. A. to James M. Perkins 10-27-1856 We
Murphey, Margaret to Dennis Canady 6-1-1864 Sh
Murphey, Mary A. to James T. Lutes 7-8-1864 (7-9-1864) Sh
Murphey, Mary A. to John R. Peeples 7-17-1866 O
Murphey, Mary E. to T. H. Harris 10-24-1874 (10-5?-1874) T
Murphey, Mary to Edward Gannon 6-7-1852 (1-5-1852) Sh
Murphey, Nancy to Berry Willson 12-20-1850 (no return) Hn
Murphey, O. E. to Jno. E. Harrison 8-13-1838 (no return) F
Murphey, S.B. to R. G. Goodman 11-18-1869 T
Murphey, Sarah A. to Joseph Harris 9-1-1869 (9-9-1869) T
Murphey, Sue to William Dyson 3-31-1873 (4-1-1873) T
Murphy, Ann to C. S. Abercromby 6-28-1858 (6-30-1858) Sh
Murphy, Bettie to C. H. Gregory 12-20-1882 L
Murphy, Betty C. to Howard K. Mullins 11-7-1855 O
Murphy, Catharine to Spencer Hull 5-19-1866 (8-11-1866) F B
Murphy, Clarinda to Robert Smith 2-1-1843 Sh
Murphy, E. G. to Thomas Forsyth 11-12-1863 Mn
Murphy, Eliza to A. P. Dies 10-17-1861 (10-18-1861) Sh
Murphy, Elizabeth C. to Oney S. Harvey 12-29-1847 (12-30-1847) Hr
Murphy, Elizabeth W. to J. F. Hull 3-2-1843 Hr
Murphy, Elizabeth to H. C. Griggs 9-9-1854 (9-13-1854) Hr
Murphy, Elizabeth to James A. Snipes 12-19-1853 (12-20-1853) L
Murphy, Elizabeth to M. Key 8-2-1859 Cr
Murphy, Elizabeth to Sterling B. Hogg 12-12-1831 G
Murphy, Elizabeth to William R. Wilson 3-19-1855 (no return) Hn
Murphy, Ella to Joles S. Appleberry 11-19-1884 L
Murphy, Ellen to H. B. Taylor 1-27-1867 G
Murphy, Ellen to James Mulcahy 6-13-1857 Sh
Murphy, Emily to John W. Smith 9-27-1849 Sh
Murphy, Emily to L. M. Busby 2-27-1856 Sh
Murphy, Esther to J. D. Paschal 6-12-1871 (1-12-1871?) O
Murphy, Eveline M. to Lerry Collins 1-8-1853 G
Murphy, Frances E. to Leroy Collins 12-24-1860 (12-25-1860) O
Murphy, Georga A. to P. J. Witt 12-4-1876 (12-6-1876) L
Murphy, Hager to Frank Bernard 2-6-1871 (3-5-1871) T
Murphy, Halley A. to Samuel M. Baxter 5-1-1855 We
Murphy, Harriett to Thomas E. Wilson 5-22-1858 (no return) Hn
Murphy, Honora to Morty Donaghue 1-26-1861 (1-27-1861) Sh
Murphy, Jane to James S. Marsh 1-12-1846 (1-25-1846) Hr
Murphy, Jane to Levin Phillips 3-8-1845 Be
Murphy, Jane to Sandy Rivers 12-24-1868 (not executed) F B
Murphy, Jane to Wm. Rowlett 6-28-1848 Sh
Murphy, Joanna F. to Priesley E. Parker 12-7-1853 Cr
Murphy, Joanna to Thos. Burk 5-20-1853 Sh
Murphy, Johanna to John Larkin 8-6-1859 (8-8-1859) Sh
Murphy, Julian to William Ohern 4-18-1857 (4-19-1857) Sh
Murphy, K. C. to Charles Chamberlane 3-5-1868 G
Murphy, Louisa J. to William M. Allman 9-28-1858 We
Murphy, Mahala to James Rodgers 12-23-1843 Sh
Murphy, Malinda to David Thomas 2-25-1828 G
Murphy, Manervia S. to Alfred A. Thomas 9-29-1841 G
Murphy, Margaret E. to W. F. Cooper 7-4-1870 (7-5-1870) Cr
Murphy, Margaret to Bryant Cannon 10-10-1843 (10-12-1843) Hr
Murphy, Margaret to _____ Addison Cooper 5-22-1843 T
Murphy, Margret to James M. Harvey 4-14-1845 Hr
Murphy, Martha H. to Levi M. Meals 1-31-1854 Cr

Murphy, Martha M. to Vachel W. Pullum 11-11-1848 (11-16-1848) Hr
Murphy, Martha to Clem Y. Souls? 8-5-1841 Hn
Murphy, Mary A. to George Pollock 6-28-1842 F
Murphy, Mary A. to James M. Johnson 4-26-1849 Cr
Murphy, Mary E. to Alfred H. Goodman 10-29-1866 T
Murphy, Mary E. to Leonidas F. Yancey 9-11-1865 (9-12-1865) F
Murphy, Mary to Francis Murphy 11-22-1862 Sh
Murphy, Mary to John Roark 2-14-1843 (2-15-1843) Hr
Murphy, Mary to Robert Ford 10-8-1836 Hr
Murphy, Mary to William Pendigrass 1-27-1866 (1-28-1866) Cr
Murphy, Minerva to James B. Fry 9-15-1857 (no return) Cr
Murphy, Nancy A. to Joseph C. Kirby 5-15-1862 (5-18-1862) Cr
Murphy, Nancy Ann to Joshua M. Miller 7-8-1847 T
Murphy, Nancy E. to John Donoven 6-15-1862 Mn
Murphy, Nancy to Isaac P. Richie 7-29-1834 (7-30-1834) Hr
Murphy, Nancy to James A. Edwards 5-30-1848 (6-1-1848) Hr
Murphy, Permelia W.(A?) to Thos. Randolph 10-7-1864 (10-11-1864) Sh
Murphy, Polly Ann to Stephen S. Gayler 12-14-1839 (12-19-1839) Hr
Murphy, Rachael to David W. Babb 1-27-1852 (1-29-1852) Hr
Murphy, Rachel to Edward L. Peters 6-30-1840 (7-2-1840) Hr
Murphy, Rachel to George Taylor 7-26-1856 (9-18-1856) Sh
Murphy, Rebecca to T. B. Williams 1-2-1850 Sh
Murphy, Rhody to James McWilliams 5-25-1847 (5-27-1840 Hr
Murphy, Sallie to Sidney Kincaid 10-1-1874 T
Murphy, Sarah T. to Greenville M. Bruff 6-8-1865 G
Murphy, Sarah to Jeremiah Lee 2-2-1841 (2-4-1841) Hr
Murphy, Sarah to John C. Warren 9-10-1828 (9-11-1828) Hr
Murphy, Sarah to R. A. Cook 12-23-1872 (12-24-1872) O
Murphy, Susan J. to F. P. Scruggs 7-19-1849 Sh
Murphy, Wilmouth to Hosea Belew 1-23-1839 Cr
Murrah, Mary E. to Charles R. Buchanan 12-23-1849 Sh
Murray, Agnes P. to A. A. Henderson 1-20-1841 Cr
Murray, Alice to Andrew Johnson 1-10-1877 (1-11-1877) Dy
Murray, Arrabella to Handy Kidd 12-31-1884 L
Murray, Catharine to John Moffat 5-22-1852 Sh
Murray, Eliza A. to J. N. Waters 6-13-1868 Dy
Murray, Eliza to Edward Connor 9-1-1860 (9-2-1860) Sh
Murray, Elizabeth to Jno. Beamish 3-27-1858 (4-4-1858) Sh
Murray, Elizabeth to Wm. A. Kerr 3-1-1861 Hr
Murray, Harriet to William M. Bowers 10-14-1844 (no return) Hn
Murray, Ida to Jerry Manney 4-1-1881 (4-2-1881) L B
Murray, Jane to W. B. Darden 12-25-1872 (12-26-1872) Dy
Murray, Josephine to Robert B. Graves 2-9-1870 (2-10-1870) Cr
Murray, Julia to Anthony Hart 5-8-1852 (5-9-1852) Sh
Murray, Lucy Ann to Samuel Little 3-30-1834 Sh
Murray, Margarett to Liberty H. McLaughlin 6-16-1862 (6-19-1862) Sh
Murray, Maria Jane to William Anderson 1-6-1879 (1-7-1879) L
Murray, Martha to Caleb Flack 3-11-1874 Dy
Murray, Mary A. to Jos. C. Moore 5-1-1853 Sh
Murray, Mary Ann to Daniel Creighton 6-26-1858 (6-27-1858) Sh
Murray, Mary to Wm. F. Nunn 10-25-1870 (10-26-1870) Dy
Murray, Minerva to Nathan Watson 5-15-1868 (10-25-1868) F B
Murray, Missouri to W. C. Blankenship 10-16-1879 Dy
Murray, Nicy to Andrew Carson 2-6-1840 Hn
Murray, P. C. to Wm. F. Black 1-26-1858 Hr
Murray, P. P. to J. K.(E?) Bradshaw 3-15-1862 Sh
Murray, Polly to J. D. Lane 8-6-1857 (8-20-1857) Hr
Murray, Rebecca J. to G. T. Hay 3-9-1874 (3-11-1874) Dy
Murray, Sarah J. to P. L. Blankenship 6-15-1872 (6-16-1872) Dy
Murray?, Aussale? N.? to Charles Boatman 2-16-1834 Hr
Murrell, Ann to Dallis Kyle 12-26-1870 (no return) F B
Murrell, Betty to John Jones 1-11-1870 (2-9-1870) F B
Murrell, Charlotte to George Wilson 1-22-1870 (1-29-1870) F B
Murrell, Dillah to Sumpter Williams 3-22-1869 (no return) F B
Murrell, Eliza E. to George N. Poston 2-15-1848 Sh
Murrell, Elizabeth to E. P. Skinner 11-18-1857 (11-19-1857) Hr
Murrell, Frances A. to G. D. Fee 8-8-1847 Sh
Murrell, Harriet to James Wilson 2-22-1868 (2-26-1868) F B
Murrell, Leander Jane to William P. Davis 3-12-1853 (3-15-1853) Ma
Murrell, Lou to Sam Allen 2-22-1868 (2-26-1868) F B
Murrell, Maria to Samuel Haynes 12-24-1878 (no return) Hy
Murrell, Mary A. to Andrew R. Pope 9-2-1865 (9-10-1865) F
Murrell, Mary Ann to Sam Mootre 4-29-1870 (5-1-1870) F B
Murrell, Mary Jane to Jesse C. Tucker 3-14-1850 Hr
Murrell, Mary to John Wilson 12-28-1870 (12-31-1870) F B
Murrell, Missouri E. to Benjamin T. Hardy 4-17-1853 (4-21-1853) Ma
Murrell, Permelia to Reuben Burrow 3-7-1842 (4-5-1842) F
Murrell, Sarah A. to Edmond A. Edmonson 3-20-1866 Ma
Murrell, Sarah A. to William T. Fausett 12-24-1850 Hr
Murren, Harriet to James C. Pewitt 12-23-1840 (12-24-1840) T
Murrill, Maria E. to Wm.R. Strange 2-9-1857 Sh
Murrin, L. P. to John Gacy 11-24-1867 T
Murrin, Mary Ann to Bryan Tillman 6-17-1865 T
Murry, Adalin to James Coffey(Coffer?) 3-2-1840 L
Murry, Ann to James Mohan 5-15-1861 (5-16-1861) Cr
Murry, Cilla to James Mull 5-4-1872 (no return) Cr B
Murry, Deborah to William H. Holliday 1-27-1838 Hn

Murry, Eliza A. (Mrs.) to John Cloyd 11-26-1855 (no return) F
Murry, Letha to A. Nash 7-19-1840 Be
Murry, M. W. to Asberry Freeman 12-7-1850 (1-7-1851) O
Murry, Margaret to Jerry Holt 1-31-1874 L B
Murry, Mary C. to Washington H. Wade 5-9-1841 (5-18-1841) T
Murry, Susan F. M. to Bradley Overton 10-22-1873 Hy
Murry, Vina to Emmerson Posey 3-5-1877 (3-7-1877) L B
Muse, Catharine to Obediah Cain 1-25-1847 Hr
Muse, Elizabeth to Benjamin F. Howard 1-31-1830 Ma
Muse, Elizabeth to Benjamine F. Howard 1-31-1831 Ma
Muse, Jane to Robert W. Brady 12-10-1855 (no return) Hn
Muse, Mary Jane D. to Jacob Hainline 12-26-1839 (1-16-1840) Hr
Muse, Nancy L. to B. O. Bryant 8-27-1870 (9-4-1870) Ma
Musgrave, E. M. to James A. Hudson 5-25-1859 (no return) Hy
Musgrave, Mariah to Edward Shurley 12-28-1872 Dy
Musgrave, Mehala to Joel Grantham 1-1-1829 Hr
Musgrave, Vina to Allen Lowry 3-13-1873 Hy
Musgrays, Vicy to Amos Moore 12-24-1868 Hy
Musick, Nancy to William Lockhart 10-23-1828 O
Muskel, Mary to Mike McDonald 7-14-1862 Hn
Muskeo (Muscheo?), A. to Frank Cuneo 8-13-1863 Sh
Musso, Mary to John A. Rousch 1-19-1864 Hn
Mustin, Frances Jane to William A. Roy (Leeroy) 12-30-1856 (1-1-1857) Sh
Mustin, Martha Caroline to James B. Dement 9-29-1852 (10-7-1852) Sh
Muston, Martha C. to Jonathan B. Smith 5-26-1858 (5-29-1858) Sh
Muze, Fredonia to G. G. McCole? 12-25-1856 Hn
Muzier?, Jane to Ed Fizer 4-5-1876 Dy
Muzzall, Julia Ann to Samuel Walters 8-31-1843 (no return) Hn
Muzzle?, Lucy to Samuel Walters 9-17-1860 Hn
Myares, Margaret E. to Henry C. Bagby 2-15-1862 We
Myers, Bettie A. to Alfred Page 7-24-1871 (7-26-1871) T
Myers, Catherine to Isaac Slippy 7-23-1850 Sh
Myers, Elizabeth ANn to Daniel Payne 9-3-1849 T
Myers, Elizabeth to Martin Simmons 9-16-1854 O
Myers, Elizabeth to Milam R. Bennett 12-3-1846 Cr
Myers, Emeline to R. C. Underwood 11-4-1842 Hn
Myers, Everline to William Page 7-5-1866 T
Myers, Johanna to John Sweeney 7-27-1857 Sh
Myers, L. A. to W. H. Francis 8-8-1866 (8-9-1866) T
Myers, L. P. to J. T. Buchanan 2-5-1867 (2-6-1867) O
Myers, M. F. to M. H. Hartsfield 9-29-1866 (9-30-1866) T
Myers, Margaret E. to George S. Cates 12-23-1873 T
Myers, Maria to Jeremiah Bowden 11-15-1853 T
Myers, Martha F. to F. W. Evritt no date (with 12-1861) T
Myers, Mary Ann to Wm. M. Miller 2-13-1856 Sh
Myers, Mary to John Cherry 4-1-1832 (4-5-1832) Hr
Myers, Mary to John Scott 9-1-1853 Hn
Myers, Mary to P. O. Donnell 11-8-1859 Sh
Myers, Mattie to A. C. Pitts 11-20-1883 L
Myers, Minerva Jane to Geo. Washington Walton 3-21-1849 T
Myers, Nancy C. to Moses F. Greene 1-19-1857 Hn
Myers, Nancyann to Phillip M. Seward 1-27-1840 (2-6-1840) F
Myers, Phebe C. to James Humphrey 10-11-1855 We
Myers, S. E. to J. H. Howard 5-10-1871 (5-11-1871) T
Myers, Sallie E. to William A. Fortner 12-17-1866 (12-16?-1866) T
Myers, Sophia to John Myers 10-28-1853 Sh
Myers, Susan P. to W. F. Coffman 7-18-1852 Hn
Myers, Susan to Marcus H. Hartsfield 11-30-1853 (12-1-1853) T
Myeyrs, Mary C. to Sam'l. Hamet 8-7-1858 (8-8-1858) O
Myirack, Matilda A. to James C. Tubberville 1-27-1862 (no return) We
Mylor, Julia R. (Mrs.) to James M. Wollard 5-21-1868 Ma
Myly, Henny to Joseph Warren 12-3-1865 Hn
Mynett, S. J. to John Robinson 9-22-1867 G
Mynor, Rurey to Leroy R. Dill 8-4-1843 G
Myrack, Sarah F. to George A. Doran 11-19-1856 We
Myres, Margarett to W. L. Underwood 11-5-1838 (11-6-1838) F
Myres, Mary J. to John Gills 7-21-1862 (7-25-1862) O
Myres, Susan R. to Russell Goforth 3-16-1859 T
Myrick, Dorcas to Wesley Myrick 10-7-1834 G
Myrick, Elvira to Micajah Mackleroy 10-7-1834 G
Myrick, Evaline G. to James H. Parker 1-7-1847 Hn
Myrick, Frances to Charles W. Turner 7-14-1851 (no return) Hn
Myrick, Harriet to Ripley S. Horn 10-10-1854 Hn
Myrick, Hixey to W. B. Hinchey 7-27-1842 Hn
Myrick, Jane to Hugh Harkins 2-3-1847 Hr
Myrick, Jane to R. L. Daniel 6-30-1860 (7-3-1860) Hr
Myrick, M. B. to Daniel Rhodes 7-10-1845 Hn
Myrick, Mary M. to Robert P. Derington 5-14-1851 Hn
Myrick, Nancy to Joseph Winsett 1-15-1852 Hn
Myrick, Phebe to David H. Rhodes 9-23-1860 Hn
Myrick, Polly to Thomas A. Snyder 7-20-1845 Hn
Myrick, Rhodiann to Isaac Crews 8-7-1856 Hn
Myrick, Sarah J. to John C. Boyd 11-30-1859 Hr
Myrick, Susan Ann to Carroll Snider 2-2-1867 (no return) Hn

Nabers, Louisiana to Edward D. Pride 7-16-1832 Sh
Nabers, Malinda to Jerimiah Highfield 11-10-1851 (11-11-1851) Hr
Nabers, Margaret to Efel D. Fortner 6-23-1838 (7-1-1838) Hr
Nabers, Nancy to James Ward 6-12-1830 (6-13-1830) Hr
Nabers, Sarah to Isaac J. Norton 7-11-1837 Hr
Nabors, H. E. to J. P. Kirkland 11-21-1864 (11-23-1864) Sh
Nabors, Jane to Nathaniel Guy 11-4-1871 (11-5-1871) Ma
Nabors, L.? A. to Joseph E. Lake 12-29-1845 Hr
Nabors, Martha A. to Calloway Caine 4-13-1841 Hr
Nabors, Mary Ann to Nathaniel Guy 4-10-1869 (4-15-1869) Ma
Nabors, Sarah R. to Lafayette Veal 3-31-1863 (4-2-1863) Sh
Nabrady, R. C. to John Hoppers 8-1-1843 Sh
Nagal, Christiana to Michael Nuss 5-23-1856 Sh
Nagle, Bridget to Fred Thomas 12-8-1862 Sh
Nagle, Mary to A. Mereto 12-27-1854 Sh
Naigle, Julia A. to Riley E. Wallace 3-17-1856 Sh
Nail, Elizabeth A. to E. N. Simmons 1-6-1840 Ma
Nail, Margarett to James W. Nanny 6-21-1840 (6-22-1840) Ma
Nail, Martha Jane to John Dennie 2-17-1855 (2-18-1855) L
Nail, Mary Ann to J. A. Hamilton 9-16-1837 (9-19-1837) Hr
Nail, Mary to George W. Simpson 4-8-1847 (4-9-1847) G
Nail, Mary to Jacob Fulbright 1-4-1830 (1-6-1830) Ma
Nail, Mary to Jacob Fulbright 1-4-1831 Ma
Nail, Nancy Jane to Jesse M. Allen 8-15-1868 G
Nail, Rebecca Jane to Gilliam Tharp 12-25-1847 (12-28-1847) F
Nail, Rebecca to John Pruett 2-7-1831 (2-9-1831) Hr
Naile, Ferriby (Lenity) to Jeremiah F. White 9-5-1835 Sh
Nailing, Mary L. to G. R. Newson 2-14-1855 O
Nailling, Lucy A. to George H. Raulston 7-4-1843 We
Nailling, S. L. to Benjamin T. St. John 5-12-1863 We
Nailon, Mary to John Woods 5-9-1857 (5-10-1857) Sh
Nailor, Margaret E. to William Rush 12-2-1850 (12-12-1850) Hr
Nailor, Rhoda Jane to Eliazer Burkhead 1-1-1856 (1-3-1856) Hr
Nairon, Elizabeth Ann to George B. C. Morris 10-13-1863 (no return) Hn
Nairon, Martha Ann to Ashley Askew 1-21-1846 Hn
Nall, Mary Ann to B. F. McCarty 4-17-1848 (4-18-1848) O
Nance, Adaline to Stephen Perry 10-11-1838 Hn
Nance, Angeline F. to John M. Nichols 9-1-1855 (no return) Hn
Nance, Ann E. to William D. March 6-11-1862 G
Nance, Elizabeth to James R. Hudson 8-9-1853 Be
Nance, Jane to Wm. Saulsburg 5-22-1879 Dy
Nance, Julia Ann to Wm. H. Greer 12-30-1849 Be
Nance, Julian to L. P. Wintz 11-29-1864 Hn
Nance, Lucinda J. to Robert B. Trimble 10-27-1851 G
Nance, Lucy to Calvin Thompson 8-4-1877 (8-26-1877) L
Nance, Malinda J. to John D. Paschall 10-9-1859 Hn
Nance, Martha A. to John H. Stoveall 4-8-1858 Hn
Nance, Martha J. to Wm. W. Deaton 9-20-1863 Be
Nance, Martha to James L. Freeman 2-27-1848 Hn
Nance, Mary A. to James P. Ince 10-22-1855 (10-23-1855) Ma
Nance, Mary Ann to Wm. J. Turner 1-9-1845 Be
Nance, Mary L. to Samuel J. Story 7-24-1866 Hn
Nance, Mary to Adogria? Wright 11-28-1864 Be
Nance, Mary to Alfred Paschall 4-?-1845 Hn
Nance, Mary to Anderson Wright 11-28-1864 Be CC
Nance, Mary to Eli Amick 8-30-1838 Hn
Nance, Mary to Jamerson Bledsoe 1-31-1843 Ma
Nance, Mary to Joseph Bohannon 12-18-1836 Hn
Nance, Nancy M. to Robert S. Bingham 5-4-1843 Hn
Nance, Sarah C. to Robert G. Foster 12-20-1857 Hn
Nance, Sarah to George Cabe 4-7-1859 Hn
Nance, Susan C. to Willis Atchison 7-10-1863 (no return) Hn
Nancy, Alderson to Wyatt Pewett 1-2-1869 Hy
Nancy, Cornelia F. to William P. Arnett 9-19-1860 Hn
Nanney, Mary to Joseph Gibson 11-11-1847 Hn
Nanney, Roda to James Barnhart 1-28-1858 Cr
Nannie M., Burford to John Gullett 3-4-1861 (no return) Hy
Nannie, Adaline to Nathaniel Brown 3-30-1869 Cr
Nannie, Catharine to John W. Crews 11-4-1865 (11-5-1865) Cr
Nanny, Barbara to James J. Edwards 9-27-1845 Ma
Nanny, Margaret to Ezekiel Case 7-14-1856 (7-15-1856) Ma
Nanny, Martha A. to William Vantrees 4-16-1850 (4-17-1850) Ma
Nanny, Martha E. to Charles T. Wyatt 7-27-1869 (7-28-1869) Ma
Nantz, Louisa C. to Emery A. Ferguson 6-17-1847 L
Napey, Matilda to Henry S. Bass 11-19-1827 Ma
Napier, Laura V. to John W. Gould 10-17-1853 Hr
Napier, Martha C. to Wilson N. Peacock 2-17-1846 (2-18-1846) Hr
Napier, Mary W. to John D. Perryman 6-3-1843 (6-4-1843) Hr
Nappier, Ellen D. to Christopher G. Joy 12-22-1842 Hr
Nappier, Louisa E. to John R. Craddock 6-5-1845 Hr
Naron, Malisa to W. C. Williams 5-4-1865 Hn
Narvin, Milly to Calvin William 1-23-1830 Ma
Nasbitt, Elvery to John Underwood 3-28-1867 G
Nash, Aby to David Alsop 12-14-1845 Be
Nash, Alice A. to F. M. Williamson 9-16-1868 Dy
Nash, Bridget (Mrs.) to Timothy Cunningham 6-25-1855 Sh
Nash, Cumiah to Stephen Walker 12-26-1865 Hy

Nash, Emeretta C. to William O. Boggs 2-19-1856 (no return) Hn
Nash, Emily to J. N. Nash 8-7-1865 (8-8-1865) Dy
Nash, Emma (Mrs.) to R. C. Coffman 12-3-1872 (12-5-1872) Dy
Nash, Fannie to William Sandford 12-26-1871 (12-27-1871) Dy
Nash, Fanny to Jenning? James 1-22-1867 (1-20?-1867) Dy
Nash, Hannah to Daniel Healy 4-7-1860 (4-14-1860) Sh
Nash, Hattie to L. H. Waters 4-10-1880 (4-18-1880) Dy
Nash, Julia to Shepard Mitchell 12-29-1875 (12-30-1875) Dy
Nash, Lucy M. to Jno. W. Taylor 3-30-1842 Sh
Nash, M. A. to Wm. M. Thurman 3-9-1866 (3-11-1866) Dy
Nash, M. F. to Geo. W. Wear 12-19-1872 (12-20-1872) O
Nash, Martha Jane to T. W. Redding 12-5-1877 (12-6-1877) Dy
Nash, Mary to Anthony Powers 1-7-1860 (1-8-1860) Sh
Nash, Mary to Daniel Ligtner 5-29-1850 Be
Nash, Mary to Isaac Slater 2-19-1867 (3-23-1867) Dy
Nash, Mary to James Patterson 10-24-1859 Sh
Nash, Miranda G. to W. N. Taylor 11-25-1878 (11-27-1878) Dy
Nash, Nancy H. to B. F. Scates 2-24-1874 O
Nash, Parthena to Danil Porter 11-30-1870 (12-3-1870) Dy
Nash, Rachel to Peter McGarg 3-2-1878 (3-7-1878) Dy
Nash, Sarah Ann to Sam'l. Watson 12-4-1856 (12-6-1856) O
Nash, Susan to Limus Porter 12-28-1872 (2-2-1873) Dy
Nat, Millie Jane to Harrison Brown 3-2-1878 (no return) Hy
Nave, Alvira T. to D. B. Norvell 10-24-1869 Hy
Nawl?, Martha J. to J. D. Mathis 3-10-1863 Hn
Nayce, Eliza to Augustus Young 12-26-1866 Hy
Nayce, Mary to Robert Carter 1-2-1867 (no return) Hy
Naylen, Laura to A. I. Hamilton 1-1-1867 (1-3-1867) O
Naylor, Amanda to John Yates 6-13-1870 O
Naylor, Bethany J. to T. J. Williams 6-29-1865 Mn
Naylor, Bethinia B. to Joberry King 10-26-1852 (10-27-1852) Hr
Naylor, S. C. to F. M. Clayton 12-1-1865 Mn
Naylor, Sarah J. to Thomas J. Thompson 9-9-1854 (9-13-1854) O
Ne____?, Camelus to G. W. Cotner 9-24-1855 (no return) Hn
Neagle, Ellen A. to James L. Williams 7-5-1859 Sh
Neal (Taylor), Bettie to Bartlet Jones 4-3-1869 Hy
Neal(e), Mary to Richard Ragan 10-25-1848 O
Neal, A. M. M. to A. J. Sheridan 9-30-1856 Hn
Neal, A. to J. F. Coleman 12-13-1866 G
Neal, Anner to King Watford 2-3-1877 Hy
Neal, Augustine to W. W. Cochran 12-27-1871 (12-28-1871) Dy
Neal, Caroline to William C. Anderson 10-19-1850 (10-20-1850) O
Neal, Cornelia A. to Edwin D. Dickinson 4-21-1841 F
Neal, E. A. to J. C. Tharp 7-13-1865 G
Neal, E. H. to J. J. Mann 11-3-1858 (11-9-1858) Sh
Neal, E. L. to W. M. Hunt 7-3-1867 G
Neal, E. O. to A. P. Gillam 1-19-1858 Hr
Neal, Eliza to Jesse C. North 5-27-1868 Dy
Neal, Eliza to Wm. Murphey 9-29-1839 (10-3-1839) F
Neal, Epps to Wm. E. Bryant 12-8-1873 (no return) Hy
Neal, Jemima to Benjamin Neal 5-22-1866 G
Neal, Josephine M. to Robert E. Mason 5-16-1854 (no return) F
Neal, K. C. to D. T. Jones 3-28-1867 Hn
Neal, Kate M. to T. J. Reid 1-15-1868 (1-22-1868) F
Neal, L. A. to E. T. Scott 12-23-1857 (12-25-1857) Sh
Neal, L. A. to Rewben J. Harrington 11-28-1876 (11-29-1876) Dy
Neal, L. F. to J. G. Doyle 10-16-1870 F
Neal, Lenore to Gabriel Holmes 10-12-1841 Hn
Neal, Levenia to G. W. Coleman 11-26-1865 G
Neal, Levenna to Monroe Hood 9-19-1861 O
Neal, Lidia C. to John D. Grigg 3-19-1860 Hn
Neal, Louisa to John F. Whitman 11-29-1862 Dy
Neal, Louisa to W. S. Bone 4-10-1867 G
Neal, Louisa to Walter Gibbs 2-27-1875 (2-28-1875) Dy
Neal, M. E. to John P. Baldridge 12-23-1866 Hy
Neal, Malinda A. to James S. Waldran 9-1-1853 Sh
Neal, Margarett E. to Jacob Hare 10-31-1853 (no return) F
Neal, Margarett to Thomas Foster 8-31-1854 St
Neal, Maria L. to T. W. Henley (Hurley?) 2-24-1855 Sh
Neal, Marthaann to Thomas S. Evans 1-30-1841 (2-18-1841) F
Neal, Mary E. to William L. Casey 1-11-1867 (1-15-1867) Ma
Neal, Mary to George W. Martin 12-14-1869 (no return) Hy
Neal, Mary to James Thomas 7-25-1872 Hy
Neal, Matilda to Samuel Dickson 12-23-1867 G
Neal, Nancy E. to John H. Shearman 10-3-1852 Hn
Neal, Naomi L. to J. D. Sinclair 9-26-1866 (9-27-1866) Dy
Neal, Oma to S. C. Johnson 3-20-1863 Be
Neal, Sallie A. to J. A. Wray 9-6-1862 (9-8-1862) F
Neal, Sarah F. to G. L. Cathey 1-18-1855 We
Neal, Sarah Jane to O. Price? 12-16-1852 Hn
Neal, Susan E. to William J. Canada 1-15-1873 (1-16-1873) Dy
Neal, Susan R. to Andrew J. Sheridan 11-4-1860 Hn
Neal, Victoria to James L. McDavid 1-29-1868 (no return) Dy
Neal, Vina to T. P. Jones 7-31-1866 Hy
Neal, Wallace L. to Jno. B. Reid 2-3-1859 (2-8-1859) F
Neal, Winnie to Samuel Legins 9-8-1870 G
Neally, Sally to John Whitfield 3-16-1841 (3-18-1841) F

Nealon, Margaret to Patrick Griffin 1-18-1862 (1-20-1862) Sh
Nealy, Eleanor E. to Nathan Johnson 5-23-1861 (6-2-1861) Hr
Nealy, Eliza J. to N. F. Harrison 2-10-1859 (2-16-1859) Sh
Nealy, Elvira to James Weathered 8-30-1837 Sh
Nearn, Martha to Wm. Jennings 10-22-1840 L
Nearns, Louisa Angelina to John F. Heiskell 6-28-1857 (6-29-1857) L
Nease, Elizabeth to John Grissom 9-9-1868 (9-17-1868) Cr
Neatherland, C. to James Kirk 1-20-1847 Cr
Neber, Sarah to James J. Turner 1-6-1852 Be
Neblett, M. A. to B. F. Thomas 12-2-1867 Hy
Neblett, Sue T. to T. K. Archibald 7-6-1870 (no return) F
Neckron, Martha C. to James Avery 1-29-1846 Hn
Nedrey, Elizabeth Ann to Solomon Watts 9-2-1839 (9-11-1839) O
Nedry, Elizabeth to James Glisson 6-25-1855 (6-28-1855) O
Nedry, Elzada to Asa S. Clark 12-30-1857 (12-31-1857) O
Nedry, Letty to Thomas H. Boyett 9-21-1850 (9-22-1850) O
Nedry, Margaret Ann to Richard W. Freeman 9-8-1855 (9-14-1855) O
Nedry, Mary E. to George W. Fentress 7-30-1857 O
Nedry, Mary L. to Richard J. Akin 6-3-1868 (6-4-1868) O
Nedry, Susan M. to Jeremiah Norrid 3-25-1839 O
Nedry, Susan Malinda? to James Matthews 2-9-1857 O
Neece, Edmonia T. to W. McReaves(Reaves?) 4-7-1859 (4-9-1859) Hr
Neece, Malinda to James P. Means 8-7-1848 (8-8-1848) Hr
Neece, Mary to Joel Hagler 2-1-1854 Hn
Needham, Elizabeth to Jethro Howell 8-17-1840 (8-18-1840) G
Needham, Epsa to Alexander B. Orr 7-12-1862 G
Needham, Josevine to Mack McCoy 6-30-1866 G
Needham, Martha E. to Elijah B. Tosper 12-30-1858 G
Needham, Martha to Charles A. Brown 12-21-1853 (12-22-1853) G
Needham, Mary Ann to A. F. Dunn 10-23-1870 G
Needham, Mary to R. F. Minton 1-13-1867 G
Needham, Mary to Timothy Bowers (Bonner?) 11-2-1853 (10?-3-1853) Sh
Needham, Matilda to Saml. F. Russell 6-18-1865 G
Needham, Nancy Ann to J. C. Tilghman 7-21-1864 G
Needham, Patsy to William Needham 4-17-1832 (4-19-1832) Hr
Needham, Rebecca to Saml. Couch 2-10-1842 Hr
Needham, S. to J. R. Carrol 11-18-1857 G
Needham, Sanai to John P. Simpson 6-15-1831 Ma
Needham, Sarah to Andrew Davis 8-15-1830 Sh
Needham, Susan to William R. Alexander 4-30-1830 Hr
Neeey, Jemima to George Williams 3-27-1847 (3-28-1847) O
Neel, Gracy to Lewis Kendrick 10-19-1867 (11-6-1867) F B
Neel, Isabla? to William Fitch 11-27-1874 T
Neel, L. A. to John D. Castles 10-19-1866 (10-23-1866) F
Neel, Lucinda to William Shaw 12-27-1870 (1-7-1871) F B
Neel, Mahaley to David Moore 10-12-1832 O
Neel, Margaret to E. A. Stewart 12-5-1860 F
Neel, Marietta C. to E. C. Douglass 12-1-1868 (12-3-1868) F
Neel, Martha to Henry Bell 11-1-1869 T
Neel, Mary to John J. Crouch 10-1-1847 F
Neel, Roxanna to Thomas Warren 2-27-1869 (3-28-1869) F B
Neeley, Jamie (Jennie?) to Thomas James 2-2-1876 (2-4-1876) L B
Neeley, Mary to Eton J. White 5-23-1844 (no return) We
Neeley, Mary to Maulden Reaves 11-12-1829 Ma
Neeley, Sarah E. to J. A. Hooks 12-18-1871 (12-21-1871) Dy
Neelly, Eighty Eveline to A. M. Callahan 3-1-1826 (3-7-1826) Hr
Neelly, Louisa to Carter C. Collier 3-4-1824 Hr
Neely (Nooby?), Mary L. to William W. Flinn 7-9-1855 (7-11-1855) Sh
Neely, Adaline to John L. Murray 8-28-1869 (8-29-1869) Cr
Neely, Adelia to James G. Bell 4-26-1831 Hr
Neely, C. C. to R. Rowell 3-11-1857 (3-12-1857) Sh
Neely, E. R. to W. H. Clark 1-16-1871 (no return) Cr
Neely, Easter to Base Fowlkes 12-12-1871 (12-13-1871) Dy
Neely, Eliza Jane to John Coates 2-26-1857 Ma
Neely, Elizabeth F. to A. G. Fumbanks 12-4-1866 Dy
Neely, Elizabeth to William Willis 6-9-1866 (6-10-1866) Ma
Neely, Farina J. to M. J. Migen 11-5-1856 Cr
Neely, Felicia to Robert Shorter 5-18-1854 St
Neely, Hannah A. to L. Paine 2-10-1859 (2-16-1859) Sh
Neely, Harriet to John A. Jarratt 5-7-1857 Hr
Neely, Jemima to George Williams 3-27-1847 (3-28-1847) O
Neely, L. A. to S. J. Montgomery 1-13-1869 Cr
Neely, Louisa to A. A. Coleman 7-6-1859 Hr
Neely, Lucinda M. to C. P. McGirnsey 12-8-1852 Sh
Neely, M. E. to James C. Grun? 10-14-1864 Cr
Neely, Margaret Ann to Floridore A. Keelen 7-15-1856 (7-16-1856) Ma
Neely, Margaret E. to Wm. M. Harrison 12-15-1847 Sh
Neely, Margaret S. to Nathan Johnson 11-30-1854 Hr
Neely, Margaret to Elihu C. Allison 9-11-1829 (9-17-1829) Hr
Neely, Margarett to G. N. Whitson 12-7-1864 G
Neely, Margery E. to John W. Jordan 10-7-1842 (12-12-1842) F
Neely, Mary A. to Edward Morgan 1-22-1860 Cr
Neely, Mary A. to S. W. Steele 8-4-1852 Sh
Neely, Mary Bell to James H. Unthank 7-24-1855 Hr
Neely, Mary C. to William W. Atwood 6-9-1829 (6-10-1829) Hr
Neely, Mary J. to Sanders Pool 4-6-1855 Sh
Neely, Mary L. to Albert B. Sorrell 4-21-1866 Dy

Neely, Mary M. to Isah Anderson 9-6-1848 Cr
Neely, Minnie to John T. Carthel 5-13-1857 Ma
Neely, N. T. to D. A. Freeman 9-2-1871 (9-3-1871) Dy
Neely, Nancy G. to Russell J. Crawford 11-5-1827 Hr
Neely, Nancy to Harrison B. Tosh 12-13-1831 Cr
Neely, Nancy to James Pool 1-1-1830 Hr
Neely, Roxanna S. to Benjamin Macklin 4-11-1853 (4-13-1853) Sh
Neely, S. A. to N. M. Muncrief 1-12-1864 Sh
Neely, S. J. to I. K. Smith 1-9-1867 O
Neely, Saletha to James M. Tosh 11-13-1845 Cr
Neely, Sarah E. to James M. Page 5-18-1860 (5-20-1860) L
Neely, Sarah I. to I. H. Smith 1-9-1867 (1-10-1867) O
Neely, Sarah to James C. Green 10-18-1860 Cr
Neely, Sarah to John M. King 8-14-1855 O
Neely, Virginia to G. W. Robertson 7-19-1865 (7-20-1865) Dy
Neely?, Sarah A. J. to Wm. C. Belieu 4-15-1846 (4-16-1846) Hr
Neesbit, Mary E. to A. B. Jones 11-23-1839 (11-27-1839) F
Neese, Mary A. to Samuel N. King 12-19-1860 Hn
Neese, Sarah J. to Jasper Hodge 12-27-1867 Hn
Neese?, Sarah to Riley Stubblefield 12-7-1851 Hn
Neff, Fredericka to H. Garagnon 11-19-1863 Sh
Neiching, Caroline to Ernest Rehkoff 3-8-1853 (3-9-1853) Sh
Neigbors?, Rebecca to Jesse L. Sellers 8-?-1867 (8-11?-1867) Cr
Neighbors, A. A. to W. F. Stewart 2-9-1856 Hr
Neighbors, Louisa J. to George T. Gullett 4-5-1866 L
Neighbours, Mary E. to Andrew Herring 7-4-1866 L
Neighbours, Nancy A. to Jas. E. Carden 12-18-1865 (12-19-1865) Cr
Neighbours, Sarah J. to John Z. Shaw 10-14-1862 Mn
Neighbours, V. A. to S. Mc. Rice 9-13-1872 (9-8?-1872) L
Neil, Elizabeth R. to William H. Smithern 2-4-1843 Ma
Neil, Levenia D. to R. L. Adams 2-13-1861 Sh
Neil, M. A. to G. T. Scott 5-26-1869 T
Neil, Mariah to Phil Ellington 2-16-1867 F B
Neil, Mildred N. to Wm. R. Pender 7-1-1867 Hy
Neiley, Mary C. to John C. Brown 1-8-1849 (1-10-1849) F
Neill, Elizabeth to George M. Brogden 10-18-1850 (10-20-1850) Hr
Neill, Evoline to William H. Smithern 1-9-1830 Ma
Neill, Frances A. to Wiley H. Grigg 10-5-1854 Hn
Neill, Harriet M. to William R. Neill 5-2-1866 Hn
Neill, Joanna to Philip Kelley 8-6-1855 (8-7-1855) Sh
Neill, Martha Ann to Christopher C. May 4-22-1852 (4-28-1852) Ma
Neill, Mary E. to Thomas H. Sheridan no date (1853-1867) Hn
Nelia, Curtis to Lewis Pinson 10-1-1876 Hy
Nell, Mary E. to Barney Rook 11-5-1865 Mn
Nellums, Lucinda to Matthew Yates 6-14-1852 Sh
Nellums, Penny Ann to Wm. Johnson 3-14-1839 F
Nelms, Elizabeth to Landon Chisty 10-4-1856 Sh
Nelms, Fannie to Howard McMorris 5-26-1877 O B
Nelms, Harriet to John J. Bumpass 9-29-1842 (10-11-1842) O
Nelms, Isabella to John T. Henry 6-21-1855 O
Nelms, Rebecca to Claibourn Sisco 10-5-1850 (10-8-1850) O
Nelson, A. M. to J. H. Williams 12-14-1877 (12-16-1877) Dy
Nelson, Adaline to Osco Polk 1-18-1868 F B
Nelson, Aggy to Lou J. Hutcheson 1-16-1868 (no return) L B
Nelson, Alice E. to C. F. Smith 3-1-1870 G
Nelson, Amanda to Littleton Maclin 12-14-1878 Hy
Nelson, Anna to David Dickey 3-23-1829 G
Nelson, Anna to Jno. Anderson 8-23-1870 G
Nelson, Annie to George French 9-15-1873 Hy
Nelson, Bettie to Boswell Washington 1-13-1876 Hy
Nelson, Bettie to Thomas Estes 2-17-1869 (2-18-1869) L
Nelson, Biner to Reubin Maclin 9-30-1871 (no return) Hy
Nelson, C. J. to J. M. C. Q. Wright 8-15-1856 (8-21-1856) G
Nelson, Callie to Wm. Cobbs 2-16-1867 F B
Nelson, Cheny to Davis Butler 1-16-1873 Hy
Nelson, Christina to Washington Johnston 1-12-1869 (1-19-1869) T
Nelson, Delia Ann to John Lanier 12-6-1873 T
Nelson, Dianna to Daniel Lake 3-2-1871 L
Nelson, Elisa to Charles Myers 2-4-1853 Sh
Nelson, Eliza J. to William T. Allen 12-30-1844 Ma
Nelson, Eliza to John Jones 12-27-1869 (no return) L
Nelson, Elizabeth A. to John B. Jackson 11-21-1855 Cr
Nelson, Elizabeth C. to David Simmons 10-3-1869 G
Nelson, Elizabeth J. to W. M. Allen 12-22-1858 T
Nelson, Elizabeth to John Trice 1-1-1842 Sh
Nelson, Elizabeth to Ben Franklin Bona 9-11-1838 Ma
Nelson, Elizabeth to Roy Chandler 3-17-1842 Cr
Nelson, Elizabeth to W. M. Allen 12-22-1858 T
Nelson, Ellen to Ned Gilbert 7-14-1867 Hy
Nelson, Elsworth to James A. Claxton 10-4-1865 (10-5-1865) F
Nelson, Emily to A. O. Edwards 4-27-1842 Sh
Nelson, Emily to B. F. Ray 4-1-1874 (4-5-1874) L
Nelson, Emily to W. J Beasley 1-26-1860 (no return) Hy
Nelson, Emma J. to Sterling Luton 2-25-1873 (2-26-1873) L
Nelson, Frances M. to Allen B. Avery 3-25-1845 Sh
Nelson, Frances to W. T. Allen 4-16-1853 Ma
Nelson, Geo. A. to Hampton Brooks 12-30-1871 Hy

Nelson, Hannah to Richard Nelson 1-6-1875 Hy
Nelson, Joanna? to A. C.? Cunningham 3-4-1867 (no return) L B
Nelson, Justianna to R. H. Mitchell 9-22-1861 Hr
Nelson, Katy to End Spears 7-28-1867 Hy
Nelson, L. M. to W. J. Suiter 11-1-1871 (11-2-1871) Cr
Nelson, L. V. to George W. Fraser 1-17-1860 (1-18-1860) Sh
Nelson, Laura T. to James Brett 6-5-1862 Sh
Nelson, Lou Ann to J. R. Caldwell 12-30-1866 Hn
Nelson, Louisa to Allen Trass? 1-26-1867 (2-18-1867) T
Nelson, Lucy Ann to Wm. Nelson 1-22-1870 (no return) Hy
Nelson, Lucy T. to Richard Wallace 10-15-1840 Sh
Nelson, Lucy to Jas. R. McCall 11-29-1871 Hy
Nelson, M. C. to G. A. McBride 1-4-1872 (no return) Cr
Nelson, M. E. to Wm. Nolen 12-8-1870 Hy
Nelson, Mahaley to Ewing Y. McNab 4-20-1839 Sh
Nelson, Malinda to David Evans 12-14-1839 (12-24-1839) F
Nelson, Maria L. to Thomas B. Winston 10-31-1853 Sh
Nelson, Martha J. to James M. Hill 11-13-1866 (11-16-1866) T
Nelson, Martha M. to John Moore 7-9-1845 Sh
Nelson, Martha to John H. Allen 12-10-1839 (12-12-1839) Ma
Nelson, Martha to Nathaniel Fuzzell 7-31-1841 Hn
Nelson, Mary A. to J. N. Hicks 2-7-1866 (2-8-1866) F
Nelson, Mary Ann to Levi Jinkins 5-19-1841 Sh
Nelson, Mary E. to Theron B. Barnett 4-15-1861 (4-18-1861) Ma
Nelson, Mary Elizabeth to Charles A. Hill 5-14-1839 (5-16-1839) Ma
Nelson, Mary Elizabeth to Charles W. Reeves 12-7-1869 Ma
Nelson, Mary F. to William A. Mann 8-10-1870 (8-11-1870) Cr
Nelson, Mary Frances to C. H. Jones 5-14-1867 Hy
Nelson, Mary Frances to John Harrison 8-27-1873 (8-28-1873) L
Nelson, Mary H. to Wm. G. Thompson 10-19-1857 (10-20-1857) Sh
Nelson, Mary Jane to John Nelson 8-20-1859 (8-21-1859) Sh
Nelson, Mary to Benjamin Lewis 11-2-1856 Ma
Nelson, Mary to Conway Conner 1-26-1883 (no return) L
Nelson, Mary to E. S. Wakefield 12-11-1865 (12-12-1865) L
Nelson, Mary to Middleton Smith 4-15-1875 L B
Nelson, Mattie Ann to G. W. Dewalt 4-1-1879 (4-4-1879) L
Nelson, Mattie to John Strain 12-20-1882 (12-21-1882) L
Nelson, Mildred A. to John R. Flippin 5-2-1871 Hy
Nelson, Mollie to Peter Johnson 12-24-1871 Hy
Nelson, Nancy J. to Henry Radford 10-8-1861 (no return) Hn
Nelson, Nancy to William Slaton 8-8-1859 (8-11-1859) Ma
Nelson, Narcissa H. to Joseph Clay 1-18-1854 L
Nelson, Nelly to James Young 11-20-1879 (no return) L
Nelson, Norvella to Thos. Young 3-24-1867 Hy
Nelson, Pamelia J. to John T. Robinson 9-14-1841 Sh
Nelson, Peggie to Lewis Middlebrook 12-21-1874 (no return) Hy
Nelson, Permelia J. to W. R. J. Carroll 7-6-1867 (no return) Cr
Nelson, Rebecca to Alexander Mullins 11-21-1870 (11-22-1870) Ma
Nelson, Rhoda Ann to Tomlin P. Allen 12-22-1840 (12-24-1840) Ma
Nelson, S. J. to W. S. Hall 12-19-1861 Hr
Nelson, Sallie E. to B. A. Powell 2-28-1866 (3-1-1866) F
Nelson, Sallie to Squire Mann 7-14-1867 Hy
Nelson, Sarah A. to N. G. Curtis 12-5-1855 (no return) F
Nelson, Sarah E. to George W. Pickler 7-16-1859 Cr
Nelson, Sarah J. to Raleigh Moore 9-22-1852 Ma
Nelson, Sarah L. to Jacob Allbright 10-1-1827 Hr
Nelson, Sarah W. to Jacob H. Butler 12-23-1858 Hr
Nelson, Sarah to Marcus P. Braswell 7-14-1846 Sh
Nelson, Sue to Perry Tanner 10-26-1872 Hy
Nelson, Susan H. to William Thompson 1-3-1839 Sh
Nelson, Susanna to Shofner Huffman 11-10-1847 Cr
Nelson, Willie to Prestin Austin 12-25-1869 Hy
Nelson, Winnie to James L. Dickey 11-23-1837 Sh
Nely, Mary E. L. to John Newton 1-21-1858 We
Nely, Rebecca A. to R. W. Galloway 12-19-1866 O
Nenan, Margaret to Thomas Connally 1-21-1864 Sh
Nerren, Sally to William Parker 3-26-1829 Ma
Nervell, Martha to John Crosland 9-8-1847 Cr
Nesbett, Myra L. to F. M. (Dr.) O'Daniel 8-31-1870 G
Nesbit, Martha R. to John W. Boals 5-22-1869 (5-23-1869) F
Nesbit, Selina? to Jehu? Murphy 12-10-1829 Hr
Nesbitt, Candis to Charles Jackson 1-28-1870 G B
Nesbitt, Eveline to David Shannon 2-15-1867 G
Nesbitt, Fanny (Mrs.) to W. T. Killow 12-4-1866 G
Nesbitt, Jane E. to John K. Pearce 1-22-1844 (1-23-1844) G
Nesbitt, Louisa C. to W. L. Daly 2-12-1863 G
Nesbitt, Martha A. to William C. Turner 3-13-1852 (3-15-1852) G
Nesbitt, Mary Frances to Geo. C. Cunningham 11-17-1868 G
Nesbitt, Tenie J. to Mark C. Henderson 12-29-1870 (12-30-1870) Ma
Nesitt, Mollie to William Mitchell 2-4-1869 G
Netherland, Matilda to Isaac Willoughby 8-26-1842 (no return) Hn
Netherly, Elizabeth to Jas. P. Priddy 11-19-1846 Sh
Nettles, Elizabeth to Alexander Shepherd 8-26-1841 F
Nettles, Frances to T. B. Davis 6-21-1860 G
Nettles, Martha A. to T. J. Ramsey 9-30-1856 G
Nettles, Martha L. to Waler Brice Morgan 7-8-1874 Hy
Nettles, Mary Jane to Henry Morgan 6-24-1867 (7-25-1867) Dy

Brides

Neuburger, Charlotte to Isaac Freiberg 2-1-1864 Sh
Neules, Nancy A. to G. W. Brunston 2-19-1872 (2-20-1872) Dy
Neutzel, Kate to George W. Farmer 12-24-1862 Sh
Nevels, Elizabeth to George Whitworth 5-15-1861 L
Nevels, Malinda J. to Reuben Taylor 3-22-1861 (3-27-1861) L
Nevels, Nancy Ann C. to George W. Mosley 3-27-1867? (4-4-1868?) L
Nevil, Sarah E. to William H. Swindle 11-24-1858 (11-25-1858) G
Nevill, Elizabeth to Thomas Barnes 8-20-1852 Ma
Nevill, Lydia C. to Joseph R. Davis 7-5-1865 G
Nevill, Mary A. to James C. Harris 3-17?-1857 (3-12-1857) O
Nevill, Mary Rebecca to Richard Henry Brewster 4-5-1854 (4-9-1854) Sh
Nevill, Mattie T. to R. J. Rhodes 4-9-1866 (4-15-1866) F
Nevill, Nancy J. to William J. Aitkin 11-21-1849 Sh
Nevill, Nancy to Walter Newman 2-1-1855 Sh
Neville, Amanda to Jno. Wesley Williams 7-18-1867 G
Neville, C. B. to J. M. Wright 8-23-1864 Hn
Neville, Caroline C. to Robert W. Brinson 3-22-1845 Ma
Neville, Cassanda H. to Henry Biggs 4-3-1854 (no return) F
Neville, Sarah to Robert Brinson 10-20-1853 Ma
Neville, Susan Jane to John Vincent King 1-31-1856 (2-7-1856) Ma
Neville, Weschina A. to Jacob Joyner 11-26-1861 (11-28-1861) Sh
Nevills, Claricy to Edmund Boykin 10-30-1869 F B
Nevills, Julia A. to John R. Hill 6-13-1850 Sh
Nevills, Permelia C. to J. A. Russell 8-27-1869 (8-29-1869) Cr
Nevills, Sarah J. to William W. S. Hill 10-31-1849 Sh
Nevis, Ann Maria to Beverly Franklin 5-26-1848 (no return) L
Nevis, Caroline to William Arrington 3-14-1847 Sh
Nevis, Julia Ann to John Brinson 2-10-1850 Ma
Nevis, Louiza to C. Conner 4-5-1858 (4-6-1858) G
Nevis, Margaret to Richard Freeman 5-6-1836 N
Nevis, Mary Eliza to Miles Arnold 7-11-1846 (7-12-1846) L
Nevis, Mary to Benjamin Walker 10-15-1851 (10-17-1851) G
Nevis, Sarah R. to William A. Cleaves 11-29-1843 L
New, Bettie to John Emerson 12-2-1871 (12-3-1871) L
New, Elizabeth to James Z. Gilbert 12-27-1838 Cr
New, Elza to William A. Thurmond 2-27-1866 (3-1-1866) L
New, Fanny to Robert Bigham 12-10-1868 (12-11-1868) Cr
New, Harriet to James Bates 3-7-1836 Hr
New, Katherine to Thomas King 9-22-1853 Cr
New, Louisa F. to Peter Thompson 1-1-1843 Cr
New, Lucrita to John Harris 8-15-1865 Mn
New, Mary to William J. Burrow 9-20-1854 (9-28-___) G
New, Ruth A. to Robert Bell 2-15-1851 G
New, Sally Ann to Lindsey Lea 3-12-1828 Hr
New, Sarah to Ezekial Moore 2-13-1869 (no return) L
New?, Mary Ann to Stephen Hightower 12-19-1836 Hr
Newall, Sallie J. to T. J. Ramsey 3-18-1862 F
Newbern, Anna to Wesley Yarnell 11-6-1862 (11-7-1862) Ma
Newbern, Henrietta to Josephus Cole 12-9-1877 Hy
Newbern, Julia E. to Moses S. Neely 10-25-1859 (10-30-1859) Ma
Newbern, Nancy to Simon Drake 8-7-1872 (no return) Hy
Newbern, Pauline A. to Cyrus C. Shipps 12-13-1858 (12-14-1858) Ma
Newberne, Almira to W. A. Cox 12-13-1877 Hy
Newberne, Emma M. to William Williams 7-9-1859 Sh
Newberry, Harriet Emeline to William Chitwood 1-11-1862 (1-12-1862) Sh
Newberry, Jane P. to Edward E. Crocker 7-10-1862 We
Newberry, Mary S. to William Gilliam 1-10-1860 (no return) We
Newbery, Mary A. to J. E. Almin 1-21-1855 We
Newbill, A. to J. R. McCrackin 12-15-1864 (no return) Cr
Newbill, Alice H. to H. C. Burns 12-19-1864 (no return) Cr
Newbill, Eliza to Anderson Jones 9-28-1869 (9-30-1869) Cr
Newbill, Elizabeth to William Jones 3-7-1866 (no return) Cr
Newbill, Harriett to Bowlen Clark 7-4-1870 (7-7-1870) Cr
Newbill, M. A. to J. M. Mitchum 2-9-1871 (no return) Cr
Newbill, M. A. to W. E. Landrum 12-3-1870 (12-6-1870) Cr
Newbill, Margaret to J. J. Bell 12-29-1857 Cr
Newbill, Nancy to Andrew Sayles 10-21-1848 Cr
Newbold, Caroline to Jacob Bechtold (Barthold) 2-28-1845 Sh
Newbold, Rosina to Jacob Alden 6-27-1848 Sh
Newborn, Anny to George Rose 2-11-1874 (no return) Hy
Newborn, Henrietta to Elisha Roach 11-19-1873 Hy
Newborn, Jane to Howel Read 3-13-1872 (no return) Hy
Newborn, Laura to Edward Read 2-23-1876 (no return) Hy
Newborn, Martha C. to Clinton Trotman 6-17-1866 Hy
Newborn, Martha to Booker Harbert 11-21-1873 Hy
Newborn, Matilda to Allen Lowry 2-25-1876 (no return) Hy
Newborne, Ellen to Isham Moore 3-12-1869 Hy
Newburn, Harriet to Joe Waddell 12-31-1865 Hy
Newburn, Priss to Calvin Duckworth 2-27-1877 Hy
Newby, Emma to Ed Thornton 3-2-1871 Hy
Newby, Louisa to Thomas Frisby 7-2-1857 Sh
Newby, M. A. to P. D. Crawford 10-10-1866 (10-11-1866) F
Newby, Mary K. to Charles W. Henry 1-5-1863 (no return) Hy
Newby, Milla to Jno. Williams 7-11-1868 (7-12-1868) F B
Newby, Susan B. to David M. Porter 1-24-1850 Sh
Newby, Susan to B. B. Horner 2-16-1850 (2-20-1850) F
Newby, Verda to Burrell Cogbell 2-11-1871 (no return) F B

Newcomb, Anna to J. A. Philmott 9-30-1864 Sh
Newel, Sudie to Jas. T. Amos 11-14-1871 (11-15-1871) Ma
Newell, Hannah to Jones Needham 2-3-1867 G
Newell, Jane to Lewis Perry 2-18-1843 (2-23-1843) G
Newell, Margrett to Everett Smith 9-17-1837 G
Newgent, Margaret to William Mulcahy 5-2-1857 (5-3-1857) Sh
Newhall, Cordelia M. E. to J. B. Beard 6-27-1857 (6-28-1857) Sh
Newhouse, Anna H. to H. B. Hoover 12-22-1835 (12-29-1835) G
Newhouse, Betsy to John Glenn 12-15-1869 G B
Newhouse, Dilsy to Sam McDougal 6-22-1868 G B
Newhouse, Eliza to Elijah C. Cain 4-30-1862 (5-1-1862) O
Newhouse, Elizabeth to Ephraim L. Collins 8-19-1861 O
Newhouse, Frances L. to John W. Allen 9-10-1863 G
Newhouse, Margaret to Jack Pettis 1-7-1867 G
Newhouse, Mary to Hardy Williams 12-30-1867 G B
Newhouse, Matilda to John Simmons 2-4-1858 (2-7-1858) O
Newhouse, Nancy to John A. Roe 1-10-1846 (1-15-1846) G
Newhouse, Prudance to David W. Hamilton 12-14-1846 (12-15-1846) G
Newhouse, Tabitha N. to Joseph W. Hill 12-29-1845 G
Newland, Eliza W. to Wm. C. Adams 5-4-1846 (5-5-1846) Hr
Newland, M. J. to H. B. Birdsong 12-27-1845 (12-31-1845) Hr
Newley, Margaret E. to William J. Hubbard 2-6-1877 L
Newmaier, Rosalie to R. Buck 1-31-1859 Sh
Newman, Alice to R. W. Howard 11-27-1878 (11-28-1880?) L
Newman, Amanda to David W. Eaton 10-9-1855 Hr
Newman, Caroline to Lewis Jansen 8-5-1853 (8-6-1853) O
Newman, Delinda to Jesse Hues 8-3-1872 (8-7-1872) L
Newman, Elizabeth Frances to Joseph Allen Green 3-4-1845 T
Newman, Elizabeth to Lewis Furguson 2-10-1843 Sh
Newman, Ellen Rose to John Ambrose Wheelock 9-19-1850 T
Newman, Gila Ann to William Pipkin 1-17-1855 (1-21-1855) Hr
Newman, Henrietta to John W. Kilgore 10-19-1844 (no return) We
Newman, Martha to George Dew 9-13-1876 L
Newman, Mary Ann to Richard Kennelly? 4-29-1856 (4-30-1856) L
Newman, Mary Fannin to James Rose 10-28-1856 (10-29-1856) T
Newman, Minerva to William Whitson no date (before 1851) Sh
Newman, Nancy J. to James Benson 10-2-1858 (10-7-1858) Hr
Newman, Narcissa to Wm. Johnson 12-20-1868 Be
Newman, Sarah J. to J. M. Quillen 9-15-1865 Be
Newman, Sophronia Jane to Joseph B. Nearn 11-10-1847 (no return) L
Newnan, Julia A. to Wm. P. Pinkstone 6-23-1865 (6-25-1865) Cr
Newnan?, Tamar to William Coulter 12-27-1869 (12-28-1869) Cr
Newport, Dorcas to C. B. Hodges 7-13-1848 Hn
Newport, Margaret L. to Willis H. Willis 5-9-1857 Hn
Newsom (Mewsom), Sarah to Thos. G. Davis 8-31-1840 Sh
Newsom, Alberter H. to Thomas D. Coffey 12-7-1870 Hy
Newsom, Amanda F. to William A. Phillips 1-26-1858 (1-27-1858) Ma
Newsom, Caroline to Simon Miller 8-26-1868 (no return) Hy
Newsom, Charlotte to Zack Lewis 12-10-1868 (12-11-1868) F B
Newsom, Eliza to Eli Ray 12-15-1866 (12-16-1866) Ma
Newsom, Elizabeth A. to Thomas B. Ramsey 10-10-1854 Hr
Newsom, Jane to David P. Jarrett 4-10-1839 (no return) F
Newsom, Lucinda to Moses J. Hardin 1-11-1858 (1-12-1858) Ma
Newsom, Lucy Ann to Lewis Short 1-18-1877 Hy
Newsom, Martha E. to Stephen B. Irvin 8-18-1860 (8-19-1860) Ma
Newsom, Mary A. to James B. Justice 1-12-1857 Ma
Newsom, Mary Ann to Austin Goodell 6-15-1855 (6-21-1855) Ma
Newsom, Mary E. to George W. Bonner 7-21-1865 T
Newsom, Mary M. to Hugh Montgomery 8-8-1839 F
Newsom, Mary to Alfred Carter 8-26-1868 F B
Newsom, Mary to Hezekiah Vance 10-23-1869 (10-29-1869) F B
Newsom, Melissa A. to George W. Humphrey 11-14-1859 (11-17-1859) Sh
Newsom, Narcissa F. to Christopher E. McEwen 5-26-1828 Ma
Newsom, Narcissa to Lemuel Stone 5-31-1854 Sh
Newsom, Penelope to J. S. Baird 9-24-1866 (9-25-1866) F
Newsom, Rachel (Mrs.) to Stephen Palmer 8-19-1857 Sh
Newsom, Sallie M. to Newitt Harris 10-24-1867 F
Newsom, Sarah C. to Moses T. Hardin 9-22-1846 Ma
Newsom, Susan C. to Thomas H. Smith 9-11-1862 (9-15-1862) Ma
Newsom, Tabby to Daniel Shaw 12-24-1877 Hy
Newsom, Tryphenia to Wm. Newsom 2-25-1868 (2-26-1868) F
Newsome, Cinthia to Tom Douglass 10-17-1878 Hy
Newson, Martha R. to Soloman C. May 11-20-1860 (11-21-1860) Sh
Newson, Mollie to James Shelley 3-13-1869 (3-15-1869) F B
Newson, Tennessee to Benjamin Hays 12-22-1847 Ma
Newton, Amanda M. to J. J. Hathaway 2-3-1871 (2-4-1871) L
Newton, E. S. to J. E. Richardson 1-26-1874 (1-27-1874) O
Newton, Elizabeth to J. P. Mathews 1-28-1846 (no return) We
Newton, Elizabeth to James S. Box 8-4-1845 (8-6-1845) O
Newton, Elizabeth to William Shepard 1-15-1844 Hn
Newton, F. M. to R. C. Jordan 1-15-1879 (1-16-1879) L
Newton, Fanny E. to Henry C. Bowers 8-22-1865 (8-23-1865) T
Newton, Georgia Ann to John B. Yancey 12-18-1868 (12-20-1868) T
Newton, Henrietta to Needham Pipkins 12-8-1834 Hy
Newton, Hester M. L. to Andrew Yarbro 1-17-1868 (2-6-1868) T
Newton, Jane to _____ ? Tharpe 1-13-1840 Hn
Newton, M. A. D. to W. W. Baswell 3-17-1860 (3-22-1860) F

Newton, Mahala A. to W. C. Frost 11-14-1855 We
Newton, Mary C. to William M. Hicks 6-26-1856 We
Newton, Mary L. to Richd. Appleberry 9-21-1846 (no return) F
Newton, Mary to Liston T. Cassian 10-26-1836 (10-27-1836) O
Newton, Nancy C. to James S. Patterson 9-5-1844 Hn
Newton, Nancy C. to William Gray 2-27-1854 We
Newton, Nancy J. to Gabriel A. Henderson 8-15-1855 (8-16-1855) Ma
Newton, Paralee to William B. Poynter 12-27-1848 (no return) Hn
Newton, Sallie to Green Gause 12-15-1874 (12-16-1874) L
Newton, Samantha A. to Thomas F. Hatch 8-1-1866 (8-2-1866) L
Newton, Sarah Jane to James H. Shaw 10-7-1848 (no return) Hn
Newton, Sarah to G. L. Bynum 1-6-1844 We
Newton, Sarah to Henry Walker 12-30-1848 O
Newton, Selah Ann to Silas Jenkins 4-29-1849 Hn
Newton, Susannah to Benjamin Hamblin 12-18-1831 (12-23-1831) Hr
Niceler, Elizabeth to Archa B. Chandler 6-22-1860 (no return) Cr
Nichelson, Mary to Ramsom Sullivan 3-4-1830 Ma
Nichol, Adeline to Littleberry Langford 2-1-1855 (2-4-1855) Ma
Nichol, Agnes to Henry Holladay 1-24-1849 Hn
Nicholas, Ann Jane to Zachriah Wright 12-8-1864 Sh
Nicholas, Catherine C. to John W. Orr 11-26-1851 Hn
Nicholas, Fanny to Moses M. Williams 7-29-1861 Sh
Nicholas, Omey to James A. Sharp 11-30-1841 (12-2-1841) O
Nicholas, Polly to Austin Perry 6-7-1847 (no return) Hn
Nicholas, Tabitha to John Gilliland 7-16-1841 (7-14?-1841) O
Nichold, Lucy E. H. to William H. Baldridge 8-26-1850 G
Nicholdson, Jane F. to G. W. Moore 10-6-1858 (10-7-1858) G
Nicholdson, Susanah to F. P. Maness 6-8-1872 (6-9-1872) L
Nicholls, Elizabeth to Thomas Richardson 10-30-1841 (10-31-1841) Hr
Nichols, Alice to E. S. Therman 10-14-1868 (10-15-1868) Dy
Nichols, Anne to Vaulentine Yates 6-21-1841 T
Nichols, Augustine to Luke Hatley 10-27-1863 Be
Nichols, Benvilla to James T. Ward 9-4-1839 Ma
Nichols, Bettie to A. W. Bigelow 11-4-1875 Dy
Nichols, Bettie to Walker Avery 7-27-1870 G
Nichols, Caroline to Jessee Lankford 5-16-1852 Be
Nichols, Cathorin to L. H. Carter 7-14-1873 Cr
Nichols, D. Dary to Burwell Bell 8-21-1855 Be
Nichols, Dolly A. to William D. Whitaker 9-7-1866 Hn
Nichols, Elizabeth to Davis Arnold 6-19-1837 (6-22-1837) O
Nichols, Elizabeth to Ezekiel Sale 11-14-1843 O
Nichols, Elizabeth to Harvey B. Holladay 9-28-1845 Hn
Nichols, Elizabeth to Jackson Bashen? 4-10-1862 (no return) Cr
Nichols, Elizabeth to John Duncan 2-22-1858 (3-1-1858) O
Nichols, Elizabeth to Jonathan Burleson 2-4-1833 (2-7-1833) Hr
Nichols, Ellen to James M. Carnal 6-28-1869 (6-29-1869) Cr
Nichols, Frances to Willis Ballard 11-7-1842 (11-8-1842) G
Nichols, Jane to C. J. Walton 5-3-1879 Dy
Nichols, Jennie to William D. Spain 7-12-1875 (7-13-1875) Dy
Nichols, Judith K. to James H. Campbell 7-22-1828 Ma
Nichols, Julia A. to G. P. Harrison 12-29-1869 Hy
Nichols, Lou to Marsh Tennant 3-4-1886 (3-6-1886) L
Nichols, Lucinda to Thomas D. Cody 8-3-1831 Hr
Nichols, Luraney to Turner F. Barber 2-18-1837 O
Nichols, Maggie to Jno. L. Martin 5-2-1866 Dy
Nichols, Martha to James H. Farr 9-19-1844 O
Nichols, Martha to Lawson H. Carter 2-6-1851 Cr
Nichols, Mary A. to James C. Shelby 12-20-1858 O
Nichols, Mary Ann to Ambrose H. Crews 9-12-1850 Hn
Nichols, Mary E. to John Thomas 10-15-1867 O
Nichols, Mary J. to John L. Barton 10-30-1867 (10-31-1867) Cr
Nichols, Mary June to Noah D. Hampton 5-20-1844 (no return) Hn
Nichols, Mary to David E. Young 10-22-1866 Be
Nichols, Mattie F. to John Davis 2-5-1864 Sh
Nichols, Melinda to Robert Vickery 5-24-1838 Sh
Nichols, Melinda to William S. Crocker 8-28-1855 G
Nichols, Nancy to Calvin Paschall 9-18-1858 Hn
Nichols, Nancy to Samuel Pettigrew 7-17-1826 (7-18-1826) Hr
Nichols, Rebecca E. to James A. Paschall 10-15-1867 (no return) Hn
Nichols, Rebecca to Wyly Hatley 3-8-1861 Be
Nichols, S. C. to W. E. Potter 10-8-1867 (10-9-1867) Dy
Nichols, Sally to G. B. Rayburn 11-4-1858 Be
Nichols, Sarah A. to Joseph Barham 5-4-1863 (5-7-1863) Cr
Nichols, Sarah A. to W. C. Witherspoon 12-22-1862 (12-30-1862) O
Nichols, Sarah Ann to John J. McAlexander 3-11-1847 Cr
Nichols, Susan F. to Davis J. Pugh 9-6-1867 (9-11-1867) Cr
Nichols, T. A. to J. Q. King 2-15-1866 G
Nichols, Tennessee to Jno. C. Metcalf 3-28-1855 (3-29-1855) Sh
Nichols, Viney to Ezekiel Garrison 3-6-1845 O
Nicholson, C. R. S. to Thos. H. Norvill 11-11-1868 Hy
Nicholson, Fanny to Jack Powell 12-23-1869 G B
Nicholson, Margaret to Joseph E. Winston 2-26-1848 (3-1-1848) Ma
Nicholson, Mary J. to E. G. Davis 8-26-1868 (no return) L
Nicholson, Mary to Nathaniel Nicholson 9-8-1827 (9-12-1827) Hr
Nicholson, Nancy to James Turner 1-12-1856 (1-13-1856) Ma
Nicholson, P. C. to A. A. Maynard 12-22-1885 (12-23-1885) L
Nicholson, Sallie A. to Franklin Gorin, jr. 1-19-1861 (1-21-1861) Sh

Nicholson, Sarah J. to Benjamin Davidson 1-10-1855 Sh
Nicholson, Tex to R. Y. Moses 11-18-1875 (no return) Hy
Nicholson, V. J. to A. J. Johnson 12-23-1865 (12-26-1865) F
Nickels, Matilda to Arvy Leonard 2-7-1853 Be
Nickelson, Susan A. to J. S. House 1-16-1868 Hy
Nickleson, Martha E. to Jno. L. Stuart 1-26-1871 Hy
Nickleson, Martha to Wesley Watkins 1-21-1870 Hy
Nickols, Mary Ann to Elbert Gay 11-19-1850 We
Nicks, Miriam to Henry Darr 5-28-1840 (5-31-1840) Ma
Nicks, Susan J. to C. R. Winn 10-21-1847 (no return) Hn
Nicolson, Emma A. to G. W. Pace 7-25-1867 Hy
Niece, Polly to L. H. Yates 12-4-1869 (12-5-1869) Dy
Niece, R. J. to P. W. Anthoney 2-18-1868 (no return) Dy
Niederegger, Rosalia to Samuel C. Clancy 1-18-1868 (1-19-1868) Cr
Niel, Almera to John R. Woodfolk 2-23-1842 (2-24-1842) Ma
Night, Martha B. to Alexander Clark 11-15-1866 Hy
Niland, Catharine to Thomas Greely 10-18-1859 Sh
Nimmo, Jane N. to Benjamin Landis 3-13-1850 G
Nimmo, Martha A. to Algernom S. Currey 4-20-1842 (4-21-1842) G
Nimmo, Mildred C. to William W. Peeples 6-16-1853 G
Nip, Martha to H. F. George 1-1-1861 O
Nipp, Elizabeth to Henry C. Dempsey 11-26-1861 O
Nipp, Francis A. to Thomas Madden 6-9-1860 (6-10-1860) O
Nipp, Mary J. to James A. West 9-25-1861 O
Nipp, Nancy I. to Martin C. Pruitt 7-20-1865 O
Nipp, Sarah Ann to William McRee 6-23-1857 O
Nipper, Cara to John Wesley McGhee 9-23-1856 Ma
Nipper, Sarah to James Griffin 7-13-1843 Ma
Nipper, Susan E. (Mrs.) to John Coats 1-12-1867 (1-13-1867) Ma
Nisler, Crissa to James Crossno 6-10-1845 Be
Nisler, Susan E. to Aaron H. Nisler 4-11-1867 Be
Nisser, Rosa Ann to Phillip Burrow 3-3-1842 Cr
Nix, Arilla to F. M. Barr 9-23-1846 (no return) Hn
Nix, Lydia Ann to August Browning 1-6-1853 (no return) Hn
Nix, Martha A. to James M. Shaw 1-27-1852 Ma
Nix, Martha J. to James Boaz 11-15-1865 Hn
Nix, Marza to John H. Crawford 2-13-1850 Hn
Nix, Pernicy to Alfred Berry 10-3-1839 Hn
Nix, Susan to Franklin Ray 9-21-1849 Hn
Nixon, Ada M. to W. A. Lloyd 12-12-1881 (12-14-1881) L
Nixon, Altetha E. to Robert Morriss 6-21-1841 (6-29-1841) Hr
Nixon, Amelia to Isham Coleman 5-1-1879 L
Nixon, America to A. D. Lunsford 5-23-1839 Hr
Nixon, Annie W. to S. W. Boyd 5-19-1869 (no return) Hy
Nixon, Belle to West White 8-4-1878 L
Nixon, C. J. to F. G. Ellis 3-2-1863 (3-4-1863) Dy
Nixon, Cornelia to JSames F. Ellis 5-12-1827 Hr
Nixon, Eliza A. to Boyd White 4-5-1860 Hn
Nixon, Elizabeth to Thomas _____ 9-27-1849 Hn
Nixon, Fannie to Robert Ferguson 12-20-1882 (no return) L
Nixon, Frances to John Green 12-4-1870 Hy
Nixon, G. B. to John G. Sawyers 1-21-1830 Sh
Nixon, Hannah to Robert Halliburton 12-24-1885 (12-28-1885) L
Nixon, Hannah to Welton Tinin 10-25-1885 (no return) L
Nixon, Henrietta to Thomas D. Overcast 1-19-1860 Hn
Nixon, Ida to J. D. Blankenship 1-14-1878 (1-15-1878) L
Nixon, L. D. to R. G. Browning 1-5-1886 (1-6-1886) L
Nixon, Lizzie to George D. Boyd 1-3-1882 (1-4-1882) L
Nixon, Louvinia to Wallace Lee 1-22-1884 L
Nixon, Lucinda to Frank Portis 12-13-1873 (12-14-1873) L
Nixon, Lula to J. Green Smith 12-26-1884 L
Nixon, Lydia to Seaborn J. Houghton 2-2-1885 (2-3-1885) L
Nixon, Margaret to Joel Foster 9-22-1829 Hr
Nixon, Martha Ann to Chrs. Ables 7-5-1860 (7-8-1860) L
Nixon, Martha to Wesley Broddie 12-23-1867 (12-26-1867) L B
Nixon, Mary C. to Thomas Lunsford 10-19-1847 (12-24-1847) Hr
Nixon, Mary E. to W. A. Halliburton 10-20-1868 (10-21-1868) L
Nixon, Mary Ella to William Piner 8-2-1883 L
Nixon, Mary J. to Benj. Hutchinson 10-18-1866 Hy
Nixon, Minnie to Wash Southall 8-11-1878 Hy
Nixon, Myra L. to Henry A. Lloyd 3-9-1860 (3-12-1860) L
Nixon, Nellie to Robt. Holloway 1-12-1869 (no return) Hy
Nixon, Permilla Ann to Wm. A. Neel 6-1-1847 O
Nixon, Rebecca to Dunkin Taylor 1-3-1869 Hy
Nixon, Rosa to Ellic Tucker 6-12-1867 Hy
Nixon, Sallie to Clarence E. Lloyd 10-31-1882 (11-2-1882) L
Nixon, Sallie C. to Benj. E. Haliburton 10-15-1861 (10-16-1861) L
Nixon, Sarah C. to Wm. A. Richardson 11-12-1876 Hy
Nixon, Selesta to Duncan E. Taylor 9-5-1856 L
Nixune, Fannie to Zelliver Bunch 2-15-1867 L B
Noah, M. A. to Green Bittix 7-31-1863 O
Noah, Mary J. to W. F. Pearce 1-17-1867 O
Nobels, M. A. to T. A. Peeble 9-16-1841 Be
Nobles, Alvina M. to William T. Stokes 9-11-1850 L
Nobles, Caroline M. to Andrew T. Brown 11-2-1846 Ma
Nobles, Eliza to John Carey 3-6-1843 (3-7-1843) G
Nobles, Emely J. to Robert J. Dodson 5-9-1846 (5-14-1846) G

Nobles, Emily to William Clifford 12-9-1847 Sh
Nobles, Hinna to William Sammons 4-10-1832 G
Nobles, Ida A. to George Bounds 2-28-1870 (3-2-1870) F
Nobles, Jamima to James B. Worden 1-4-1841 (1-7-1841) G
Nobles, Louisa to Lewis Alford 8-5-1852 L
Nobles, Lucinda to John Alford 6-27-1857 (6-28-1857) L
Nobles, Lucrecca to Reuben Whichard 12-13-1835 G
Nobles, Margaret A. to Reuben Lidrow 10-4-1849 G
Nobles, Margaret E. to Burtis Alford, jr. 8-4-1852 L
Nobles, Margarett S. to Richard Chradick 11-8-1849 (11-11-1849) G
Nobles, Martha H. C. to Bird Smith 2-24-1869 (2-25-1869) L
Nobles, Mary A. to Bryant Ringgold 12-28-1837 G
Nobles, Mary Ann to John E. Alexander 9-23-1847 G
Nobles, Mary Ann to Willis Randolph 4-20-1883 (4-23-1883) L
Nobles, Mary E. to Burtis Alford 10-11-1870 L
Nobles, Mary J. E. S. to Joseph Jordan 11-24-1857 L
Nobles, Nancy to Joseph Parker 2-24-1831 G
Nobles, Penelope to Obadiah Bullock 4-16-1840 Be
Nobles, Sarah E. to Robert H. Jackson 9-1-1867 G
Nobles, Sarah to Purcell C. Vaughn 1-10-1835 (1-13-1835) G
Noblin, Jane to John P. Boon 11-13-1843 (no return) We
Noel, Ann to William Mathis 10-16-1861 G
Noel, Bettie to Oscar Nunn 6-20-1869 Hy
Noel, Frances M. to J. E. (C.?) Hanks 10-6-1870 G
Noel, L. to Abram Nunn 12-27-1865 Hy
Noel, Laura to Jacob Hill 2-24-1869 (3-2-1869) Ma
Noel, Mary L. to Medley Harrison 3-2-1850 (no return) Hn
Noel, Mary L. to William M. Grant 2-11-1852 Sh
Noel, Sarah E. to Wm. M. King 5-15-1860 (no return) Hy
Noel, Sarah Jane to John W. Barron 9-8-1853 (9-11-1853) G
Noel, Theodotia to ___ Walters 3-26-1839 (no return) Hn
Noel, Virginia to Joseph Hamming 10-11-1840 (no return) Hn
Noell, M. E. to T. J. Briant 6-14-1866 Cr
Noell, Nancy to James R. Sinclair 2-15-1835 (no return) Hn
Nogent, Mary to Richard Sexten 11-15-1862 Sh
Noger, Josephine to Isaac Mayer (Meyer?) 10-29-1863 Sh
Nokes, Nancy E. to Daniel M. Craig 12-23-1848 (12-24-1848) F
Nolan, Julia to John Ellis 3-27-1857 Sh
Nolan, Margaret A. to G. W. Anthony 1-11-1883 (1-12-1883) L
Nolan, Margaret to James Timmons 8-29-1853 Sh
Nolan, Martha A. to Wm. Summers 10-11-1857 We
Nolan, Mary to Charles F. Howard 4-16-1863 Sh
Nolan, Mary to Charles Fagan 7-26-1863 (7-27-1863) Sh
Nolan, Mary to John P. O'Mahony 2-2-1862 (2-3-1862) Sh
Nolan, Missouri to W. H. Lea 12-5-1883 (12-6-1884) L
Nolan, Sarah to James Garrett 1-27-1843 Ma
Noland, Ellen to Peter Maloney 9-12-1859 Sh
Noland, Mary to John Gorman 10-26-1852 Sh
Noland, Pernecy to Zeddack Mulikin 2-23-1839 (2-28?-1839) Hr
Nolen, Ann to Henry Holloway 7-9-1878 (no return) Hy
Nolen, Anne to Henry Holaway 7-6-1878 (7-7-1878) L
Nolen, Claudia to W. W. Rutledge 6-4-1874 Hy
Nolen, L. A. to H. Adams 11-14-1841 Be
Nolen, Lizzbella to Frank Monroe 1-27-1876 L B
Nolen, Lula to James Skelly 4-10-1878 (4-11-1878) L
Nolen, Mary to John G. Stone 3-27-1838 (3-29-1838) Ma
Nolen, Mollie J. to Wm. C. Lea 12-29-1859 Hy
Nolen, Nancy S. to Azariah Moore 12-31-1860 (1-1-1861) O
Nolen, Sarah F. to Wm. W. Dupree 6-12-1861 Hy
Noles, Martha A. to John C. Womack 7-3-1859 O
Noles, Martha A. to John C. Wommack 7-3-1859 O
Noles, Susan C. to Franklin W. Hammond 12-21-1853 (12-22-1853) O
Nolin, Annie to James M. Bledsoe 3-6-1866 Hy
Nolin, Mary Ann to Henry S. Oliver 4-18-1847 Hn
Nolley, Indianna E. to J. P. Hughes 8-3-1854 (8-6-1854) Sh
Nolly, Eleanor A. to John R. Johnston 11-15-1865 (11-22-1865) F
Nolly, Virginia A. to Saml. W. Read 1-26-1853 Sh
Nolton, Martha P. to A. S. Bryant 8-31-1856 Cr
Noone, Sarah to Daniel Corley 1-6-1854 (1-7-1854) Sh
Nooner, H. B. to J. M. Cavender 1-31-1863 (12-24-1863?) We
Nooner, Nancy J. to James P. Cashion 11-9-1862 We
Norden, Mary F. to Joseph J. Jourden 1-9-1868 Be
Nordon, Christian to Wm. Haynes 3-28-1841 Cr
Nored, E.. to J. W. Darnell 5-12-1853 Hn
Nored, Harriet C. to John W. Wynn 7-17-1859 Hn
Nored, Julia M. to F. M. Wright 11-29-1860 Hn
Nored, Milly A. to James Jobe 3-19-1846 Hn
Norey, Lucy Ann to John G. Brown 1-5-1860 Sh
Norman, Delila to George Vaughan 1-15-1842 (1-16-1842) Hr
Norman, E. F. to J. B. Jones 12-4-1883 L
Norman, E. J. to R. H. Cole 11-28-1867 G
Norman, Elizabeth L. to Judson A. Culp 12-13-1850 (12-15-1850) F
Norman, H. E. to R. T. Coleman 12-1-1851 Cr
Norman, Jane to Miles Halmark 2-7-1839 (no return) Cr
Norman, Jinney to Bob Walker 1-9-1869 (no return) F B
Norman, Josephina to R. W. Carter 1-25-1860 Cr
Norman, Louisa to Nathan Boles 3-31-1845 (4-1-1845) F

Norman, Lucinda to William Simmons 5-2-1861 (5-12-1861) L
Norman, Malinda to Saml. Worrell 10-18-1867 (10-19-1867) F B
Norman, Margaret to Nelson Boals 5-12-1866 (no return) F B
Norman, Margarett to Wm. A. Coleman 1-13-1847 Cr
Norman, Martha C. to J. W. Measells 5-27-1867 (5-29-1867) L
Norman, Martha Jane to John Cannady 1-27-1870 (no return) Dy
Norman, Martha to James P. Fuqua 11-25-1853 Cr
Norman, Mary A. to W. B.? Hartman 10-1-1860 (10-2-1860) Cr
Norman, Mary Ann to Timothy m. Measles 5-27-1861 L
Norman, Mary E. to Jacob E. Carl 12-26-1853 (no return) F
Norman, Mary J. to George Wright 3-6-1855 Sh
Norman, Nancy E. to Joseph B. Mann 9-28-1852 L
Norman, S. J. to D. H. Jennings 7-26-1884 (7-29-1884) L
Norman, Sarah B. to Robert L. Wood 3-2-1835 Hr
Norman, Sarah to Aleck Farmer 6-28-1868 G B
Norman, Sarah to Thomas Volentine 10-28-1853 Hn
Norman, Sintha J. to Samuel Dewhit 10-8-1846 Cr
Norman, Susan to James E. Taliaferro 2-14-1868 G
Norman, Susan to Maddison Williams 5-16-1868 (no return) F B
Norment, Chincy to John Webster 7-3-1867 Dy
Norment, Elizabeth to R. A. Marsh 2-5-1844 (2-6-1844) Hr
Norment, Mary A. to Robert Elgin 3-19-1827 (3-21-1827) Hr
Noromore?, Lydia A. to Willis Richardson 2-15-1844 Hn
Norquist, Anna Ereka to John Landerstedet 9-6-1873 T
Norred, Elizabeth G. to John T. Hastings 12-12-1860 Hn
Norrid, Eunice to George Elam 12-17-1827 O
Norrid, Eunice to James Eastawood 2-29-1828 O
Norrid, Isabella to James Bramblett 8-31-1842 (9-1-1842) O
Norrid, Mary C. to C. P. Glover 2-5-1861 (2-6-1861) O
Norrid, Mary J. to Barnett O. Bryant 3-8-1867 O
Norrid, S. M. to C. R. Allen 8-4-1866 O
Norrington, Amanda C. to Enos Rainey 7-7-1865 (7-15-1865) Dy
Norris, Alesta? to James Wardlaw 9-18-1849 (9-22-1849) L
Norris, Ann E. to H. J. Tucker 3-26-1851 H
Norris, Clarissa to John M. Thompson 12-23-1847 (12-26-1847) Hr
Norris, Elizabeth A. to Wm. L. Eddins 6-12-1850 Sh
Norris, Ellen to Isaac Smith 12-5-1835 Hr
Norris, Emily to Robert Thompson 6-17-1835 (6-26-1835) Hr
Norris, Hannah to Elijah Bailey 1-12-1837 Hr
Norris, Harriet A. to Valerius F. Sanford 9-28-1859 (9-29-1859) Sh
Norris, Jane to J. S. Miller 4-3-1869 (4-4-1869) L
Norris, Jane to William H. Singleton 2-6-1868 L
Norris, Laura to C. C. McCarson 8-14-1867 (8-15-1867) F
Norris, M. E. to R. M. McEwen 10-6-1859 Sh
Norris, Margaret to Alexander Ramsey 10-26-1864 (10-27-1864) Sh
Norris, Margaret to James Kinnard 11-10-1841 Hr
Norris, Mary S. to B. Phelon 5-21-1855 Sh
Norris, Matilda to Martin Shell 2-24-1834 Hr
Norris, Naomi to J. K. Twyman 12-19-1881 L
Norris, S. J. to W. A. Ledbetter 9-19-1885 (9-20-1885) L
Norris, Sarah Jane to Hinton J. Pipkin 5-23-1840 (5-28-1840) Hr
Norris, Sarah to Levi Smith 1-22-1839 (1-25-1839) Hr
Norris, Tempy to William Walker 4-20-1836 Sh
Norris, Tennessee to Sam Alston 4-8-1885 L
Norris, Tennessee to Sam, jr. Alston 12-9-1884 L
Norris?, L. C. to J. P. Kesterson 12-29-1863 Hn
Norriss, Sarah C. to James C. Acuff 6-24-1853 (no return) L
Norrod, Elizabeth to Robert H. Kelton 8-6-1856 (8-13-1856) G
Norrow, Margaret to Benjamin Norrow 12-5-1842 (12-7-1842) Ma
North, E. J. (Mrs.) to N. L. Mays 6-27-1874 (6-28-1874) Dy
North, Mary W. to James Bates 5-8-1848 (5-9-1848) Hr
North, Rachel to Frederick W. Kean 7-8-1873 (not executed) L *
North, Susan to Senica S. C. Yapp 7-8-1873 (7-13-1873) L
North, Tamer J. to Thomas A. Younger 10-1-1860 (no return) Cr
Northcott, Emeline to Elijah Billingsley 2-21-1828 G
Northcross, Ettie to J. E. Davis 11-21-1860 G
Northcross, Kitty to William Greene 1-13-1870 G B
Northcross, Rachel to John Henry Taylor 12-27-1851 (1-1-1852) Hr
Northcross, S. M. to A. J. F. Day 5-8-1861 G
Northcut, Adeline to Nelson I. Hess 2-27-1830 (2-28-1830) G
Northcut, Artena to William W. Lynch 9-1-1852 G
Northcutt, Bitha Lavina to Daniel M. Wallice 6-14-1834 G
Northcutt, Martha to W. F. Neil 8-4-1867 G
Northem, A. M. to James B. Biggs 12-7-1863 G
Northern, Ester Ann to William Hudspeth 11-2-1846 Hn
Northern, Mary Ann to Thomas B. Parker 10-17-1856 O
Norton, Ann J. to Lemuel M. Crisp 1-1-1857 Hr
Norton, Anna to Peter McAnulty 6-14-1853 Sh
Norton, Betsy (Mrs.) to L. C. Mathis 3-4-1867 G
Norton, Caledonia J. to Willis H. Mathis 2-2-1860 G
Norton, E. to Daniel Merritt 2-2-1863 Sh
Norton, Elizabeth to Luke C. Mathes 12-19-1866 O
Norton, George Ann to Barney Burkes 2-18-1844 (12-24-1844) Ma
Norton, Indiana E. to Horace M. Keech 1-6-1862 Sh
Norton, Jane to John Causeby 3-3-1825 Hr
Norton, Julia A. to Harrel Brown 9-14-1853 Hn
Norton, Louiza to Pinkney Tilghman 1-15-1853 (1-18-1853) G

Norton, M. A. to W. H. Hewett 5-17-1858 (5-20-1858) Hr
Norton, Martha A. to J. A. Jones 8-24-1858 Hr
Norton, Martha J. to William Oliver 8-5-1844 (no return) Hn
Norton, Martha to De L. Carter 2-24-1859 (2-25-1859) Ma
Norton, Mary E. to Alex Williams 9-3-1867 Dy
Norton, Mary to George A. Harper 6-1-1861 Sh
Norton, Mary to James McBride 12-15-1845 (12-18-1845) Ma
Norton, Mollie J. to Wm. A. Whitmore 12-5-1860 Sh
Norton, Mourning to Addison Nanney 1-29-1852 Ma
Norton, Polly Ann to Solomon Doile 12-27-1847 (12-28-1847) Hr
Norton, Rachel to Benjamin M. Hillhouse 12-20-1833 Hr
Norton, Tennessee to J. M. Miles 8-27-1862 O
Norvel, M. A. to T. J. Evans 2-1-1866 Hy
Norvell, Amanda to John Johnson 8-21-1868 Hy
Norvell, Canely? M. to John J. Williams 3-27-1864 (3-27-1864) Cr
Norvell, Elizabeth Jane to Wm. Alexr. Winn 12-15-1857 (12-17-1857) Ma
Norvell, Inez to Edward M. Reading 2-18-1862 Sh
Norvell, J. P. to W. J. McFarland 12-18-1870 Hy
Norvell, Jane J. (Mrs.) to John S. Holland 2-21-1869 G
Norvell, Jane to W. W. Stephens 3-19-1874 Hy
Norvell, Louisa to George Meacham 9-1-1880 L
Norvell, Martha E. to Joseph Edwards 11-29-1843 Ma
Norvell, Mary Eliza to Porter B. King 6-23-1857 (6-24-1857) Ma
Norvell, Matilda to Henry Russel 1-7-1870 (1-8-1870) Cr
Norvell, Parnina H. to Francis Marion Craig 12-6-1859 Ma
Norvell, Susan A. to John E. Glass 11-2-1859 (11-3-1859) Ma
Norvell, Susan to Jackson Dinwiddie 8-4-1870 Cr
Norvell, Z. M. to J. W. Cates 1-18-1872 Hy
Norvill, Betsy to Thomas Thomason 8-1-1867 G
Norville, Elizabeth to David Horton 7-16-1870 Hy
Norville, Emily S. to R. A. Patterson 12-30-1867 G
Norville, Mary Elizabeth to Jesse D. Purcell 9-8-1846 O
Norville, S. A. M. to J. J. Lambert 1-4-1870 (no return) Hy
Norville, Sallie A. to William Eason 9-27-1869 Hy
Norwell, Manda E. to Wm. B. Hilliard 2-23-1854 Cr
Norwich, Ida to Allen McCutchen 7-8-1878 (8-1-1878) Dy
Norwood, B. J. to George J. Chapman 4-7-1854 (no return) L
Norwood, Elizabeth S. J. to John D. Hallmark 11-1-1850 Cr
Norwood, Lucinda to Robert Read 5-29-1827 Hr
Norwood, M. A. to W. S. Coleman 9-30-1858 Hr
Norwood, Martha H. to H. F. Abbott 10-8-1869 (10-10-1869) Cr
Norwood, Sallie E. to Eli C. Johnson 5-24-1870 (5-25-1870) Ma
Norwood, Sarah to John H. Bennett 11-29-1858 Cr
Notby, Mary to Joseph S. Mercer 8-13-1849 (no return) F
Notgrass, A. M. to B. F. Smith 11-24-1875 (11-25-1875) L
Notgrass, Ann to Robt. Kendrick 5-7-1846 (no return) F
Notgrass, Ann to Thomas T. Borun 11-11-1847 (no return) F
Notgrass, Mary E. to Jonathan P. Mitchell 3-4-1839 (3-13-1839) F
Notgrass, Susanah to Booker Boner 8-7-1851 (no return) F
Novacovich, M. to J. G. Rappner 11-9-1863 Sh
Nowel, Delila to John Smith 2-16-1839 Be
Nowel, Margaret to Andrew Curry 6-4-1832 Sh
Nowell, Chaney to Bill Adams 3-2-1867 Hy
Nowell, Elizabeth to Benjamin Harris 7-9-1858 (7-15-1858) Ma
Nowell, Ellen to Jesse L. Summers 9-12-1866 Be
Nowell, Fanny to Melancthou Goosby 11-23-1867 Hy
Nowell, Frances to Green Finch 8-29-1856 Cr
Nowell, Hester to Wm. Earp 10-24-1864 Be
Nowell, Luticia to James M. Pierce 2-21-1854 Be
Nowell, M. E. to M. H. Widener 9-30-1874 Hy
Nowell, M. W. to R. H. Stephen 5-10-1854 Cr
Nowell, Mariah to Jack Mann 11-25-1866 Hy
Nowell, Minerva to W. H. Witt 5-3-1865 G
Nowell, Nancy to Andrew C. Stuart 2-15-1855 Cr
Nowell, Nancy to Dorsey Davis 3-21-1843 Ma
Nowell, Nancy to James McCoy 1-5-1829 Ma
Nowell, S. M. to R. B. White 2-24-1869 Hy
Nowell, Sarah J. P. to John B. Walker 1-24-1867 Be
Nowlen, Elizabeth to James Davis 10-16-1862 O
Nowlen, Martha M. to J. C. Ayers 2-21-1858 We
Nowlin, Elizabeth to John Fobbs 6-19-1843 (no return) Hn
Nowlin, Lela to William Johnson 11-20-1846 We
Nowlin, Louisa W. to James C. Kelly 11-15-1846 (11-19-1846) F
Nowlin, Nancy H. to Thomas H. Dinwiddie 2-12-1846 Hn
Nubb (Nutt?), Mary Ann to James N. Morris 10-20-1854 (10-22-1854) Sh
Nuckles, Elizabeth to William H. Baldridge 12-28-1846 (12-29-1846) G
Nuckles, Mary Ann to Hugh S. Stone ?-14-1839 G
Nuckles, Sarah J. to A. S. Underwood 12-13-1843 (12-14-1843) G
Nuckolls, Emily to John Bradford 7-19-1849 Hr
Nuckolls, Jane to James Mullhall 12-28-1843 Hr
Nuckolls, Lucretia to N. B. Dorris 12-28-1857 Hr
Nuckolls, Narcissa C. to James M. Bradford 2-25-1860 (2-26-1860) Hr
Nuckolls, Olvizara? to Strong Crowley 6-24-1839 Hr
Nugent, Bridget to John Toomy 2-20-1860 Sh
Nugent, Mary to John Murphy 5-4-1853 (5-5-1853) Sh
Nugent, Norah to John Lawless 7-9-1844 Sh
Nuirhead, Susan to James Sandford 1-13-1877 (1-14-1877) Dy

Null, Elizabeth C. to H. M. Hanna 11-23-1843 Cr
Null, Jane to Elijah G. Duncan 1-5-1829 Hr
Null, Jane to Sampson Demoss 3-14-1842 (no return) Cr
Null, Louiza M. to Wm. P. Hill 2-24-1866 Cr
Null, Mary E. to George H. Rogers 10-13-1863 (no return) Cr
Null, Mary E. to H. B. Demoss 1-3-1855 (no return) Cr
Null, Melinda H. to James B. Bowles 9-30-1850 Cr
Null, Unis to Thomas Honey 12-31-1845 (no return) Cr
Nullers?, Francis to John E. Dyer 11-19-1863 O
Nunn, Alean to Asa Tweady 2-8-1869 Hy
Nunn, Amanda to Thos. H. Fuzzle 8-1-1861 Dy
Nunn, Bettie to Jessie Reddick 2-15-1868 Dy
Nunn, Bettie to Lea Green 8-17-1869 Hy
Nunn, Dinah to William Ware 11-27-1873 Hy
Nunn, Donie M. to Edward L. Cook 8-27-1878 (8-28-1878) Dy
Nunn, Eudora to Moses Wells 5-13-1877 Hy
Nunn, Jennie to Alexander Midgett 12-13-1868 Hy
Nunn, Mary A. to Stephen J. Jordan 10-17-1860 G
Nunn, Mary to John P. B. Fuell 1-30-1843 (2-2-1843) G
Nunn, Nancy to Fredrick Harrity 1-31-1878 (no return) Hy
Nunn, Sarah to Bud Brooks 1-1-1876 (no return) Hy
Nunn, Sarah to George S. Brassfield 2-11-1846 (2-12-1846) G
Nunnally, Mary to John Adams 12-24-1833 Hr
Nunnelly, Harriett to John L. Casey 11-23-1836 (11-24-1836) Hr
Nunnelly, Jane to John C. Armstrong 10-18-1837 (?-19-?) Hr
Nunnery, Elizabeth L. D. to Thomas Marchbanks 1-5-1864 Be
Nunnery, Marilda J. to Nathan Smith 1-8-1858 Be
Nusom, Ellen to Sam Perry 3-29-1867 (no return) Hy
Nusom, Maria to Robert Nelson 3-19-1873 Hy
Nutall, Celestia A. to J.E. Spencer 9-21-1859 Hr
Nutson, Margaret to Lacey Fisher 1-22-1870 (no return) F B
Nutt, Elizabeth to Rubin Ozier 5-21-1859 Cr
Nutt, Lydia to Robt A. Oliver 12-21-1843 Cr
Nutt, Martha to G. W. Simmons 12-21-1854 Cr
Nutt, Polly to Thomas Loyd 11-22-1837 Sh
Nutt, Rachel to Green Freeman 11-7-1839 Sh
Nutt, Sarah to Leonard Coker 7-11-1846 (7-12-1846) F
Nutt?, Mary Ann to Mathew Joyner 7-3-1837 (7-4-1837) Hr
Nuttall, Lucy C. to Henry C. Davis 6-30-1858 (7-1-1858) Ma

O'Banion, A. J. to A. Ross 8-4-1857 Sh
O'Brian, Catharine to Zebnia Shara 2-24-1851 (3-1-1851) Sh
O'Brien, Ann to Charles Staid 10-7-1861 Sh
O'Brien, Ellen to Charles E. Black 3-17-1855 Sh
O'Brien, Ellen to Richard Gallivan 1-13-1856 Sh
O'Brien, Johanna to Thomas Mahoney 9-15-1856 Sh
O'Brien, Leonora S. to D. B. Gally 6-11-1861 Hr
O'Brien, Mary E. to George B. Graham 1-30-1861 (1-3?-1861) Sh
O'Brien, Mary L. to James O'Conner 8-3-1864 Sh
O'Brien, Mary to John Ryan 1-9-1858 (1-10-1858) Sh
O'Brien, Susan L. to J. S. Moore 10-25-1859 Hr
O'Bryan, Mary to Mulucky? O'Conor 6-7-1871 (6-8-1871) T
O'Conner, Mary Ann to Danniel O'Conner 3-21-1853 O
O'Conner, Mary B. to Charles H. Gray 2-6-1869 Cr
O'Conner, Mary to Daniel O'Connell 2-2-1863 Sh
O'Conner, Susan to Henry Murphy 4-8-1868 Cr
O'Connors, Julia to John C. Creighton 10-11-1856 Sh
O'Daniel, Easter to Granville M. Bottom 12-21-1854 G
O'Daniel, Rachael to Martin L. Sloan 12-21-1854 G
O'Donner, Margaret to Henry Wilson 9-10-1863 (9-11-1863) Sh
O'Donner, Mary to Martin Donehue 4-?-1863 Sh
O'Donnon, Nora to Mike O'Hern (O'Herron) 2-4-1861 Sh
O'Gorman, Margaret to Patrick Lilly 9-1-1860 (9-2-1860) Sh
O'Hair, Ann to Thomas Shanaghan 7-4-1859 Sh
O'Hara, Mary to Hugh Gallagher 10-29-1855 Sh
O'Hara, Rose to John Gorman 1-18-1857 Sh
O'Hara, Rose to Michael O'Hara 12-24-1853 (12-28-1853) Sh
O'Harra, Catherine to John McQuillan 8-17-1862 Sh
O'Herron, Ellen to William O'Herron 2-11-1860 (not executed) Sh
O'Kelly, Cornelia to Jack Bland 8-10-1866 (8-11-1866) F B
O'Kelly, Susan to John W. Bobins 5-3-1847 (5-13-1847) F
O'Neal, Allie to Wm. Norwood 10-11-1845 Cr
O'Neil, Loretta to Thomas Whelan 2-8-1853 Sh
O'Neill, Pining B. to Jas. M. Younge 11-7-1865 (11-9-1865) Cr
O'Rian, Honora to Arnold Porter 9-11-1860 Sh
O'Sallee, Catharine to Socrates Puckett 8-29-1856 Hn
O'Steen, Addie to Jo H. Chipman 6-29-1881 L
O. A. L., Hill to A. M. Powell 9-23-1872 (no return) Hy
OKelly, N. B. to W. T. Wall 11-22-1864 (11-24-1864) F
O___s, Cassie E. to Hiram Marcum 12-25-1861 G
O'Brian, Elizabeth to William N. Willis 7-31-1866 Hn
O'Brian, Margaret to M. V. Corwin 4-20-1864 Sh
O'Brien, Ann to James Stanley 4-14-1860 (4-22-1860) Sh
O'Brien, Ellen to John Dinnie? 2-5-1853 (2-6-1853) Sh
O'Brien, Hannora to Richard Bunyon 5-20-1861 Sh
O'Brien, Johanna to Richard Payne 11-14-1857 (11-15-1857) Sh
O'Brien, Margaret to D. P. Goldsmith 4-7-1860 (4-16-1860) Sh

O'Brien, Mary to Michael Daly 7-12-1851 (7-20-1851) Sh
O'Brien, Mary to Michael St. John 9-20-1856 (9-21-1856) Sh
O'Brien, Mary to Patrick Summers 6-10-1856 (6-15-1856) Sh
O'Brien, Mary to Thomas Kelly 3-23-1854 Sh
O'Bryan, Anna to C. B. Galloway 1-4-1861 Sh
O'Bryan, Katherine to Moses Kramer 11-13-1843 Sh
O'Connel, Catherine to D. W. Turner 2-22-1864 Sh
O'Connell, Catherine to David Turner 2-9-1861 Sh
O'Connell, Margaret to Michael Cain 4-29-1861 Sh
O'Conner, Catherine to E. W. Turner 2-22-1864 Sh
O'Conner, Mary to Martin Hart 6-19-1849 Sh
O'Conner, Mary to Thomas Kelley 8-22-1870 (8-23-1870) Ma
O'Daniel, Adaline to Starling S. Bottoms 12-23-1860 G
O'Daniel, Martha J. to John Elrod 7-1-7-1862 G
O'Daniel, Martha to _____ 4-5-1849 Hn
O'Daniel, Millie to John Ideberger 5-20-1866 G
O'Daniel, Sarah A. to Jeremiah Keathley 12-25-1858 (12-26-1858) G
O'Dare, Bridget to John Dundon 2-17-1863 Sh
O'Day, Mary to Thos. Nairy 9-11-1863 Sh
O'Donald, Ellen to Edmond Pinder 11-3-1859 Sh
O'Donnell, Ellen to John Collins 2-25-1854 (2-27-1854) Sh
O'Donnell, Mary to Patrick Curn 4-27-1861 Sh
O'Haig, Ann to John Markey 3-29-1856 Sh
O'Hara, Ann to John Macky 3-29-1856 (3-30-1856) Sh
O'Hara, Bridget to Harrison Stump 11-20-1860 (11-24-1860) Sh
O'Harrell, Johanna to John Cartwell 8-28-1863 (8-30-1863) Sh
O'Hern, Bridget to John Henesee 7-5-1847 Sh
O'Larry, Catharine to J. H. Ivey 7-2-1864 (7-11-1864) Sh
O'Larry, Kate to Geo. W. Jackson 1-26-1864 Sh
O'Leary, Joanna to Wm. Green 3-17-1849 Sh
O'Malow, Bridget to John Cox 1-13-1861 Sh
O'Neal, Ellen to Alexander Burkes 11-1-1856 Sh
O'Neal, M. to Patrick Downs 5-16-1859 (5-18-1859) Sh
O'Neal, Mary M. to Andrew J. Jordan 7-31-1857 (8-2-1857) Ma
O'Neal, Mary to Michael Hally 6-18-1863 Sh
O'Neal, Matilda to John Norwood 9-16-1830 Ma
O'Neal, Narcissus E. to William Wilbourn 12-161852 O
O'Neal, Talitha C. to Isaac W. Ballard 11-7-1866 Ma
O'Neil, Amanda to Atlas H. Jones 12-14-1858 (12-16-1858) Ma
O'Neil, Bridget to D. Raffo 4-5-1856 (4-6-1856) Sh
O'Neill, Ellen to Patrick Kelly 6-9-1860 (6-10-1860) Sh
O'Neill, Margaret to John Kenna 10-25-1860 Sh
O'Neill, Mary J. to John G. Mathews 1-25-1854 Cr
O'Shee, Ellen to Edward Burns 1-3-1860 Sh
O'dannel, E. A. to W. P. Elrod 5-6-1870 G
Oakes, Margaret to George W. Dulin 11-8-1858 (11-14-1858) O
Oakes, Mary A. to John Johnston 11-29-1845 (1-10-1846) O
Oakes, Minerva to Robert S. Lyons 1-17-1842 Hr
Oakes, Susan Mariah to William Cherry 9-10-1853 (9-11-1853) O
Oakes, Tennessee to Josephus Norton 9-10-1853 (9-11-1853) O
Oakey, Mary A. to J. E. Doyle 2-4-1863 (2-10-1863) Sh
Oakley, Ann to Pinkney A. Wayatt 8-13-1863 (no return) We
Oakley, Elizabeth to Jonathan Matheny 3-6-1862 (no return) We
Oakley, L. H. to H. L. Churchman 7-31-1869 (8-1-1869) Dy
Oakley, M. E. to Charles Jehl 7-8-1861 Sh
Oakley, Martha A. to Wilson H. Neel 3-1-1852 (3-3-1852) Sh
Oakley, Mary Ann to James R. Rogin 2-22-1849 Sh
Oakley, R. P. to William Hunt 9-18-1878 (9-19-1878) Dy
Oakley, Rilly to Iverson Courts 7-9-1867 Hn B
Oakley, Sarah to Daniel Pounds 1-4-1860 We
Oakley, Vina to Elijah H. Grubb 1-29-1863 We
Oakly, Fereby H. to Jackson Ross 3-5-1840 Cr
Oakly, Gilly to William Thomas Walker 11-21-1867 Hn B
Oaks, America W. to Jesse V. Mullins 8-29-1860 (8-31-1860) T
Oaks, Mary A. to James M. Livingston 8-23-1851 (8-24-1851) O
Oar, Delila to John Johnston 10-25-1850 (10-27-1850) O
Oar, Susan to W. Caughorn 8-6-1841 Be
Oates, Elisa to W. G. Bradford 8-6-1848 Hr
Oates, Nancy C. to Wm. H. H. Williams 1-24-1871 (1-26-1871) F
Oates, Susan H. to R. E. Tatum 11-15-1852 (no return) F
Oats, H. A. E. to E. W. Tatum 12-27-1849 (no return) F
Oatsball(Oatsvall?), Sarah to G. Lewis 9-19-1843 Be
Obanion, Agness J. to N. H. Posten 12-8-1858 (12-9-1858) F
Obene, Jane to Joseph Denney 2-18-1862 Sh
Oberley, Paulina to J. T. Hampton 2-5-1842 (no return) F
Odam, Elizabeth to Daniel Neeves (Nevis) 1-18-1831 Sh
Odam, Elizabeth to H. C. McWhorter 10-18-1863 G
Odam, Sarah D. to John J. Rutherford 1-30-1844 Sh
Odell, Margaret T. to Alexander McGowan 5-7-1845 Sh
Odell, Martha J. to Benj. F. Ball 2-3-1848 Sh
Odem, Julia to Winslew Alexander 9-30-1858 We
Odle, Callie to J. R. Williams 8-22-1870 (8-28-1870) Dy
Odle, Elizabeth A. to Martin Cashion 3-24-1846 We
Odle, Elizabeth I. to Cader Sowell 2-27-1840 Ma
Odle, Margrett to Jacob F. Penn 5-21-1838 G
Odle, Mary to James Spencer 2-6-1828 (2-7-1828) Ma
Odle, Matilda to J. F. Penn 2-13-1867 G

Odle, Melissa C. to John Wm. Ross 10-30-1875 (10-31-1875) Dy
Odom, Elizabeth to F. M. Beck 6-3-1862 Be
Odom, Elvira Jane to Jessee Speaks 1-3-1854 Sh
Odom, Frances to James T. Nichols 6-4-1879 Dy
Odom, M. C. to L. Brickhouse 10-3-1861 G
Odom, Martha Jane to Wesley Cup 6-25-1857 T
Odom, Mary L. to Warren Patterson 7-12-1840 Sh
Odom, Mary to Adam Perkins 12-9-1861 (no return) We
Odom, Mary to Wm. Lea 11-14-1877 Hy
Odom, Mollie to J. S. Odom 8-25-1869 G
Odom, Nancy L. to J. M. Mays 8-14-1861 Dy
Odom, Rachael to Richard J. Cole 10-11-1846 Be
Odum, Ann to Adam Swayne 5-11-1867 (no return) Dy
Odum, Arrena to John Henson 10-21-1848 (10-22-1848) Hr
Odum, Frances E. to William Martin 3-21-1855 Hn
Odum, Sarah to Robert B. Brown 9-12-1865 Mn
Odum, Sarah to William Williams 7-12-1862 Hn
Odum, Tabitha A. to Ephraim McDaniel 1-20-1867 Hn
Oeder, Elizabeth to John Eisenmayer 5-9-1859 Sh
Officer, L. J. to H. C. Mattox 3-15-1862 Sh
Ogbourne (Oghowin), Sarah Ann Elizabeth to Joel Hall 5-20-1845 Sh
Ogin(Agin), Susan to John Lewis 8-25-1856 Hr
Ogles, Tennessee to G. C. Crawford 2-1-1870 G
Oglesby, Jame to Wm. C. Hale 3-16-1848 Sh
Oglesby, Mary E. to George H. Caldwell 11-20-1857 (11-24-1857) O
Oglesby, Matty to Lewis Needham 6-6-1829 G
Oglesby, Susannah to Erwin Smith 5-19-1832 G
Ohern, Mary to William Ohern 9-20-1857 Sh
Okelly, Matilda to Isaac Adkins 8-17-1867 F B
Okelly, Rebecca J. to Jackson Ashford 12-6-1870 (12-7-1870) F
Olahan, Nancy H. to John McEwin 2-15-1838 Ma
Olaver, Lucy J. to James C. Mathis 11-29-1847 (12-2-1847) G
Olaver, Rebecca to William F. Carr 8-9-1842 G
Old, Emaline E. to Thomas J. Brann 1-22-1863 We
Old, Martha A. to B. G. Hendrick 5-30-1842 (no return) F
Old, Mary A. to John McWherter 12-17-1860 We
Old, Mary E. to Shadrack Dickinson 1-24-1843 (1-25-1843) F
Old, Sallie Anna to Henry E. Hilliard 7-18-1860 F
Oldem, Martha to Jno. Dugan 6-10-1847 Sh
Oldham, Adelia to Adolphus Wilson 5-18-1878 Hy
Oldham, Amanda to Colonel Batchelor 1-8-1873 (no return) Hy
Oldham, Burtie to Tolbert Wilson 12-1-1869 Hy
Oldham, Caroline to George Glasscock 5-12-1836 Sh
Oldham, Delia to Ned Wardlaw 5-30-1877 L
Oldham, Edmonia to Haywood Harbert 2-6-1869 Hy
Oldham, Edmonia to Turner Outlaw 3-27-1870 Hy
Oldham, Eliza to Lewis Wilson 12-22-1877 Hy
Oldham, Eliza to Louis Wilson 8-9-1878 Hy
Oldham, Ellen to Oliver Link 12-25-1878 Hy
Oldham, Ellen to Shepard Harris 12-19-1883 (12-20-1883) L
Oldham, Jane to Frank Works 2-10-1872 (2-15-1872) Dy
Oldham, Laura E. to Alfred T. Read 7-24-1867 Hy
Oldham, Louisa C. to J. H. Owen 10-19-1880 L
Oldham, Louisa to Frank Johnson (not issued) Hy
Oldham, Louisa to John W. Fowler 9-12-1840 Sh
Oldham, Louiza to Frank Johnson 8-13-1868 (8-15-1868) L
Oldham, Lucinda to J. D. Wright 6-21-1874 Hy
Oldham, Lucinda to John W. Collins 3-1-1825 Sh
Oldham, Mariah to Jacob Hargrove 9-15-1866 Hy
Oldham, Mary Ann to Henry Jayroe 6-24-1882 L
Oldham, Mary Jane to David Brodie 12-25-1871 (12-26-1871) L
Oldham, Mary to Edward Lewis 7-22-1841 Sh
Oldham, Mary to Rueben Maclin 2-25-1884 (2-27-1884) L
Oldham, Mincy to John Carter 9-15-1885 L
Oldham, Nancy to Harry Shaw 1-31-1878 Hy
Oldham, Nancy to John Ford 3-29-1827 Sh
Oldham, Nancy to Richard Gay 11-28-1850 Sh
Oldham, Sarah Ann to Eli Anderson 12-19-1868 (12-20-1868) L
Olds, Anne? Ragan to Albert A. Davis 2-26-1842 Ma
Olds, Catherine P. to Jackson M. Clay 6-10-1868 (no return) L
Olds, Jamima to Joseph Green Clay 3-29-1873 (3-30-1873) L
Olds, Julia to James Belton 1-8-1862 (1-9-1862) Dy
Olds, Martha to Jo. Williams 2-10-1872 (2-19-1872) Dy
Olds, Mary F. to S. J. Bird 12-15-1873 (12-16-1873) Dy
Olds, N. J. to W. A. Tilman 9-28-1881 (9-29-1881) L
Olds, Nancy E. to John T. Voss 2-6-1866 L
Olds, Rebecca Alle to Charles Franklin Cates 7-27-1870 (7-28-1870) L
Olds, S. E. to J. A. Duncan 8-26-1880 L
Olds, Sarah F. to David Albrittain 12-15-1869 Dy
Olds, Sarah J. to John H. Thornton 12-2-1868 Dy
Olds, Susan M. to Columbus W. Cates 10-23-1877 L
Olfin, Mary I. to I. T. Iler 10-9-1866 O
Olgesby, Matty to Lewis Needham 6-6-1831 G
Olin, Marietta E. to John M. Hicks 5-14-1862 Sh
Oliphant, Georgia E. to B. F. Lane 6-4-1868 G
Oliphant, Margarett C. to Jno. C. A. Greer 6-5-1858 (6-8-1858) G
Oliphant, Martha A. to W. V. Hill 10-11-1858 (10-13-1858) G

Oliphant, Mary E. to James G. McGowan 10-16-1860 G
Oliphant, Nancy to Robert Bankhead 3-4-1846 (3-5-1846) F
Oliphant, Rebecca Ann to A. F. Ducast 2-2-1859 (2-3-1859) T
Oliphant, S. J. to M. E. Flowers 5-21-1865 G
Oliphant, S. L. to W. V. Hill 7-31-1862 G
Olipshaw, Rebecca to A. F. Dueast 2-22-1859 (2-3?-1859) T
Olivar, Jane to James A. Williams 8-27-1873 (8-28-1873) L
Olive, Almarinda to Harrison Fields 12-25-1860 Hn
Olive, Clara A. to M. T. Terry 12-21-1868 (12-22-1868) F
Olive, Eveline to W. T. Martin 10-5-1865 Hy
Olive, Frances K. to John E. Churchwell 3-12-1859 Hn
Olive, Helen to B. C. Powell 1-20-1848 Hn
Olive, Joy Catherine to Oliver C. Wagner 6-20-1850 (no return) Hn
Olive, Laurey F. to Miles F. Tyler 1-5-1864 Hn
Olive, Leanna to Geo. Alexander 10-13-1867 Hn B
Olive, Louisa to Caleb Ross 9-12-1839 Hn
Olive, M. E. to Wm. H. Vaughan 9-10-1872 (9-11-1872) Dy
Olive, Malissa to J. J. Jones 9-17-1866 (9-20-1866) O
Olive, Manda to John Abington 2-12-1874 O
Olive, Mary to Archibald Phelps 3-9-1852 Hn
Olive, Rebecca to M. D. Stephenson 12-5-1848 (no return) Hn
Oliver (Olum), Elizabeth to Levi Woton 3-18-1841 Sh
Oliver, Amanda M. to Joshua E. Brassfield 1-2-1854 Ma
Oliver, Ann to Patrick Fanner 12-29-1854 G
Oliver, Anna E. to Smith Lankford 9-10-1872 (9-11-1872) Cr
Oliver, Barbara A. to Milton Climer 12-22-1854 (12-25-1854) Ma
Oliver, Betsey to William Clark 2-26-1856 (no return) F
Oliver, Caroline to Elias Newman 3-13-1847 (3-16-1847) O
Oliver, Cordelia J. to Robert O'Neill 1-22-1839 Cr
Oliver, Eliza Ann to J. F. Forrester 12-21-1864 Sh
Oliver, Elizabeth G. to Littleberry G. Wilkerson 1-24-1844 (no return) F
Oliver, Elizabeth to Person Gates 1-8-1857 We
Oliver, Elizabeth to Wm. Arter 11-18-1838 F
Oliver, Flora to C. N. Roberts 8-29-1857 G
Oliver, Flora to Charles N. Roberts 9-11-1857 (9-10?-1857) Ma
Oliver, Frances to Robert Wesimen 9-23-1846 Cr
Oliver, Frances to Robt. Montgomery 11-4-1866 Hy
Oliver, Francis Lucinda to Albert Brassfield 3-2-1857 (3-5-1857) Ma
Oliver, H. H. to George W. Giffin 7-9-1861 (7-11-1861) O
Oliver, H. M. to J. M. Johnson 12-27-1871 (no return) Cr
Oliver, Ida B. to Edwin Whitmore, jr. ?-21-1864 Hy
Oliver, Joanna C. to Isaac B. Dawson 8-8-1861 We
Oliver, Lucinda D. to Jonathan Utley 5-23-1846 Ma
Oliver, M. C. to Newton Baker 8-11-1880 (8-12-1880) L
Oliver, M. W. to G. P. Chilcutt 1-18-1848 Hn
Oliver, Mahaley J. to George M. Martin 5-17-1848 Hn
Oliver, Malinda to D. T. Campbill 9-16-1857 We
Oliver, Margaret to Samuel Martin 4-20-1853 G
Oliver, Martha Jane to John W. Watkins 3-13-1850 Hn
Oliver, Martha S. to John Douglas(s) 8-18-1861 G
Oliver, Martha to John J. Hicks 4-27-1848 (no return) Cr
Oliver, Martha to Wiley Britt 9-9-1864 (9-11-1864) Cr
Oliver, Martha to Wily Britt 9-9-1864 Cr
Oliver, Mary Ann to C. Johnson 2-26-1839 Cr
Oliver, Mary B. to William H. Jones 6-6-1855 (no return) F
Oliver, Mary Cathrine to Wilson Wm. Coats 3-18-1854 (3-19-1854) T
Oliver, Mary E. to James Needham 3-5-1865 G
Oliver, Mary E. to Joshua Clarke 2-11-1858 Hn
Oliver, Mary Jane to Moses E. Pratt 9-9-1871 (9-10-1871) Ma
Oliver, Mary T. to Henry R. Johnson 10-13-1858 Cr
Oliver, Mary to George J. Burrow 7-13-1857 Cr
Oliver, Mary to John D. Nolen (Noles) 12-18-1847 O
Oliver, Mary to Oscar Dircks 9-9-1880 (9-12-1880) L
Oliver, Matilda (Mrs.) to Peyton S. Bell 8-4-1862 (8-10-1862) Ma
Oliver, Minerva to James Champion 11-11-1851 Hn
Oliver, N. L. to C. H. Ridley 3-7-1870 (3-9-1870) Cr
Oliver, Nancy C. to D. H. Hawson 11-15-1833 Sh
Oliver, Nancy to Chester T. Adams 10-30-1860 (11-1-1860) Ma
Oliver, Nancy to Thomas P. Able 11-2-1853 (11-3-1853) G
Oliver, Phoebe to John Payne? 4-11-1850 Hn
Oliver, Rhoda to Henry Miller 12-31-1854 Hn
Oliver, Rosanna to John Smith 2-2-1869 Hy
Oliver, Sallie to Allen Scott 12-20-1871 (12-21-1871) Dy
Oliver, Sally to William Adkins 11-26-1860 (11-27-1860) Ma
Oliver, Sarah Ann to John W. Hawthorn 2-15-1842 Sh
Oliver, Sarah Ann to Solomon Coats 5-28-1853 T
Oliver, Sarah C. to Jacob T. Mathis 7-10-1852 (7-12-1852) G
Oliver, Sarah E. to James H. Britt 10-?-1861 (10-20-1861) Cr
Oliver, Sarah E. to Marma D. Anderson 12-23-1850 Ma
Oliver, Sarah U. to James Henry Brock 4-18-1870 L
Oliver, Sarah to A. J. Haynes 10-19-1869 (10-20-1869) Cr
Oliver, Sarah to Jas. H. Demyers 1-12-1876 (1-13-1876) O
Oliver, Sarah to S. H. Wilson 1-5-1857 (no return) Hn
Oliver, Tennessee to J. E. Frost 11-11-1858 Hn
Oliver, Tennessee to Oliver Sturdivant 2-10-1868 G
Oliver, Victory to W. R. Henry 4-16-1865 Hn
Oliver, Virginia M. to Tarlton H. Graves 8-3-1858 (9-7-1858) Ma
Oliver?, Elizabeth to Edward Thompson 11-1-1866 Cr
Olmstead, Mary E. to Frank Swoboda 5-30-1885 (5-31-1885) L
Olmsted, Jessie M. to I.W. Cross 7-12-1849 Sh
Olsabrooks, Mary to Duncan Massey 5-12-1838 (5-17-1838) G
Omohundros, Harriet to James Olliver 12-26-1839 (12-31-1839) L
Oneal, A. to R. M. Ward 10-21-1867 (10-24-1867) Dy
Oneal, Charllotty to Athan Allen 12-9-1827 Ma
Oneal, Dionico M. to James M. Patterson 1-15-1848 (1-18-1848) G
Oneal, Elizabeth J. to James G. Jimerson 10-3-1861 Mn
Oneal, Lavina to Henry Patison 2-24-1838 (3-1-1838) G
Oneal, Love to Thomas C. Morgan 6-11-1842 G
Oneal, M. W. E. to W. H. Royster 7-27-1869 (no return) Dy
Oneal, Margaret to B. J. Nicks 1-16-1862 Mn
Oneal, Mary M. to G. W. Clayton 1-30-1863 Mn
Oneal, S. A. to W. D. Featherston 12-20-1865 (no return) Dy
Oniel, Martha Jane to Sydney Moore 12-14-1853 (12-15-1853) Ma
Onley, Permelia to John M. Daniel 5-14-1850 Sh
Only, J. P. to J. T. Olds 2-16-1878 (2-19-1878) Dy
Only, Leah to Wade Ashbrooks 1-21-1853 (1-22-1853) Sh
Onstead, M. S. F. to J. W. Owens 12-16-1861 Mn
Oppenheimer, Regina to Leon Helman 5-24-1858 Sh
Oquin, Eliza to Joshua Harding 2-7-1857 Sh
Ore, A. D. to J. C. Coleman 3-22-1873 (3-25-1873) T
Ore, Elizabeth F. to William H. Yager 3-18-1867 T
Ore, Elizaeth to George E. Luckey 9-3-1854 Hn
Orell, Robutte Ann to Beverly C. Nelson 7-27-1858 We
Orgain, Louisa S. to Thomas C. Barham 2-28-1848 (3-1-1848) Ma
Orgain, Mariah to Robt. Wolsey 12-15-1868 (12-19-1868) F B
Orgain, Martha E. to Thomas P. Hall 2-11-1840 Hn
Orgain, Martha to Ned Williamson 11-1-1867 F B
Organ, Arcada to Martin Tallley 4-27-1836 Sh
Orgelat, Elise to Victor Bataily 7-30-1864 Sh
Ormes, Sally to John Britingham 12-29-1829 G
Orms, Mariah to Barnet Furgarson 9-12-1841 (9-13-1841) G
Orms, Mary to William Riley 10-14-1841 G
Orms, S. J. to J. T. Flowers 4-6-1865 G
Ormsberry, Catherine to Wm. T. Thompson 9-21-1827 Sh
Orne, Haddie A. to D. Galbreath 7-7-1858 (7-8-1858) Sh
Ornell, Mary N. to Francis Parker 4-5-1860 We
Ornsby, Elisza to David Bell 8-21-1826 (8-23-1826) Hr
Orr, Alsey D. to Israel F. Outhouse 10-10-1843 We
Orr, Catharine to Jonathan McClure 6-9-1863 (no return) We
Orr, Elen to Alex Johnson 11-28-1865 (11-29-1865) Cr
Orr, Eliza to W. C. Grimes 4-22-1873 (4-23-1873) T
Orr, Elizabeth F. to J. T. Boyd 3-27-1867 G
Orr, Elizabeth to F. R. Billings 6-17-1847 Sh
Orr, Florence A. to Frank C. Whithorne 10-9-1866 Hn
Orr, Harriet N. to Luther McMullin 2-13-1854 Sh
Orr, Henry to Charles Lynn 1-4-1869 (1-5-1869) F
Orr, Lavinia to Authen J. Levto? 2-9-1869 T
Orr, Martha J. to John F. Starks 2-16-1854 Hn
Orr, Mary J. to J. R. Boughman 11-25-1844 We
Orr, Mary R. to James M. Wright 12-5-1865 Hn
Orr, Mary W. to John H. Moore 11-30-1840 (12-1-1840) Hr
Orr, Minerva to J. H. Scarce 9-2-1878 (9-5-1878) Dy
Orr, Minervy P. to Wm. Brady 10-27-1848 Cr
Orr, Nancy to Robt. Cannon 1-6-1848 Cr
Orr, Rebecca C. to William H. Barton 11-15-1865 Hn
Orr, Sophorina J. to Augustus R. Robbins 3-10-1869 Hy
Orr, Susan A. to James R. Bobbitt 1-19-1870 G
Orr, Susan A. to John Tanner 6-15-1854 (6-17-1854) O
Orr, Susan J. to Arthur Williams 2-19-1849 (2-20-1849) F
Orr, Susan to John B. Thompson 5-25-1870 (5-26-1870) T
Orrell, Mary to William Hobbs 10-4-1838 Hn
Orrell, Nancy J. to Calvin Bunn 8-17-1841 (no return) Hn
Orrell, Ruth to David Petty 3-21-1839 Hn
Orrell?, Martha C. to Green B. Johnson 8-26-1857 Hr
Orsborn, T. R. to F. M. Vance 9-26-1867 O
Orsbourn, Sarah to A. J. Caldwell 9-22-1866 (9-23-1866) O
Orsburn, Sarah A. to A. H. Caudle 3-7-1865 O
Orshin?, Juley Ann to Solomon McBride 5-20-1864 (3?-21-1864) T
Ortin, Lucy C. to Wright Kendrick 10-28-1863 Sh
Ortry, Elizabeth to S. T. McCarley 7-26-1857 O
Orvenshire, Margarett to S. R. Alien 4-10-1842 Cr
Orwell, Mary Ann to Isaac Lainn? 1-19-1847 T
Osberne, Carilile to G. W. Haily 11-29-1860 Be
Osborn, Dona to William Thompson 5-3-1871 T
Osborn, Elizabeth to John Prince ?-?-1837 Be
Osborn, Emma to Joseph L. McGee 5-16-1865 G
Osborn, Harriett E. to W. F. Lenoir 7-6-1858 (7-7-1858) Sh
Osborn, Jane J. to W. M. G. Huffman 10-8-1847 Cr
Osborne, Jane to John Bennett 12-13-1853 (12-15-1853) Sh
Osborne, Kate (Mrs.) to John Hunter 11-14-1864 Sh
Osborne, Martha to H. C. Massey 12-26-1853 Sh
Osborne, Mary to William Pace 11-18-1848 Be
Osborne, Rachel E. to L. D. Dilliard 11-19-1868 Dy
Osborne, Sally E. to John M. Grenade? 7-8-1863 We

Osborne, Sarah C. to Paschal Lamb 1-18-1837 Sh
Osborne, Susanna L. to Robert J. Morris 9-29-1849 (10-1-1849) T
Osboron, Susan J. to Joel H. Gilbert 3-4-1862 O
Osbourn, Sarah E. to John Francis McEwen 9-9-1878 (9-11-1878) L
Osbourne, Derinda A. to Eliphus Cunningham 11-11-1856 (12-1-1856) O
Osbourne, Eliza to Peter Dewalt 1-4-1886 L
Osbourne, Kizie to Ellar Searcy 10-29-1878 (11-1-1878) L B
Osburn, Caroline to James Smith 11-15-1877 Dy
Osburn, Lucinda to William Miller 12-26-1867 Hn B
Osburn, Nancy Ann to Jacob Shoults? 3-2-1858 Hn
Osburn, Nancy Jane to Salathiel Medaris 11-21-1851 (11-23-1851) O
Osburn, Sarah A. to J. N. Siddle 3-27-1853 (no return) Hn
Osburne, M. L. to Louis Burnett 6-2-1862 (6-5-1862) O
Osgood, Fannie C. to Franklin A. D. Myrick 10-28-1864 Sh
Osment, Rachael to Jesse King 9-28-1859 Hr
Ossman?, Melinda J. to Richard M. Phillips 12-28-1865 Hn
Ostean, N. M. to D. C. Johnson 8-30-1862 (9-3-1862) O
Osteen, Alice to Thomas E. Lockard 9-9-1878 (9-11-1878) L
Osteen, Cordelia J. to William Lunsford 9-11-1852 (9-12-1852) L
Osteen, Martha J. to Jeames Hall 1-22-1878 L
Osteen, Penecea A. to Wm. R. Cruse 3-5-1858 We
Osteen, Sarah E. to Wm. Mansfield 10-14-1858 We
Osteen, Sarah to Isaac Kelly 12-6-1846 We
Osteen, Sophronia E. to J. G. Keltner 10-14-1874 (10-15-1874) L
Ostuhhout, Lottie E. to C. B. Galloway 10-22-1861 (10-23-1861) Sh
Oswald, Catharine to John H. Robley 12-16-1858 Hr
Oswald, Jane M. to Luther Laird 11-19-1851 (11-20-1851) Sh
Oswald, Jane to George E. Townes? 4-22-1850 Sh
Otey, Frances E. to Thos. C. Anderson 7-19-1858 Sh
Otey, Mary F. to Daniel C. Govan 12-20-1853 Sh
Ott, Ellen to Isaac R. Hawkins 3-29-1843 Cr
Ott, Susan to Aulston Edwards 7-17-1850 O
Oughton, Burney to George Green 2-26-1880 (no return) L B
Oury, Alice to T. S. Coleman 1-2-1861 Hn
Oury, Mary Ann to T. E. Bagley 7-13-1852 Hn
Oury, Susan to C. D. Boaz 5-11-1858 Hn
Outerbridge, Chaney to Fed Bunch 6-15-1878 (no return) Hy
Outerbridge, Fanny to George Irons 8-16-1867 Hy
Outerbridge, Mary J. to E. G. Johnson 12-31-1851 (1-1-1852) L
Outhouse, Mary to Wm. L. Gentry 6-10-1858 We
Outland, Margaret A. to Wm. S. Wooten 12-15-1870 Ma
Outlaw, Almina T. to J. W. Williams 12-27-1848 O
Outlaw, E. T. to W. T. Cobb 1-25-1866 Hy
Outlaw, Elizabeth to Jno. R. Harris 5-8-1869 Hy
Outlaw, Elizabeth to Joseph Lavender 4-28-1852 (no return) F
Outlaw, Emily E. to Thomas W. Cash 6-26-1840 (8-27-1840) O
Outlaw, Julia Ann to Franklin White 10-1-1836 O
Outlaw, Martha A. to Frank Lewis 12-3-1870 (no return) Hy
Outlaw, Martha E. to M. R. T. Outlaw 9-24-1830 O
Outlaw, Martha to John Bond 5-31-1873 Hy
Outlaw, Martilda to Dave Read 12-9-1877 Hy
Outlaw, Mary to John W. Grissom 11-15-1869 (11-16-1869) F
Outlaw, Mattie to Martin Demorse 8-11-1870 L
Outlaw, Nancy to Sampson Gause 10-24-1878 (no return) L B
Outlaw, Polly to Nathan Nixon 12-10-1870 Hy
Outlaw, Rosenah C. to A. C. Jackson 4-29-1862 G
Outlaw, Sarah to George Herzog 9-10-1865 Mn
Outlin, Jane to Washington Green 8-8-1871 (no return) L B
Outterbridge, Mary Eunice to Robinson J. Cotten 12-6-1865 (12-14-1865) L
Overall, Amelia to G. W. Robinson 8-30-1865 G
Overall, Christina Jane to Archibald C. Levey 1-9-1840 G
Overall, Cornelia E. to A. A. Davidson 6-5-1860 (6-6-1860) G
Overall, Elizabeth J. to W. R. (Dr.) Hughes 11-15-1870 G
Overall, Elizabeth to Gary Gay 5-9-1831 (5-10-1831) Hr
Overall, Martha Ann to Henry Crenshaw 7-11-1869 G B
Overall, Mary C. to John W. Wyatt 3-2-1859 (3-3-1859) G
Overall, Mary L. to John S. Dickson 9-11-1862 G
Overall, Mattie M. to G. A. Timmons 8-16-1870 G
Overall, Paulina A. to L. C. Crenshaw 9-8-1869 G
Overall, S. A. (Mrs.) to R. P. Kimbro 2-7-1867 G
Overall, Sarah to Daniel Wyatt 12-31-1869 G B
Overbray, Martha A. to Morris G. Burton 7-29-1843 Hn
Overby, C. V. to F. J. Clois 10-31-1866 (no return) Hn
Overby, Martha E. to James N. Colly 8-25-1858 We
Overcast, Sarah J. to Samuel J. Gallimore 8-24-1861 Hn
Overcast, Tamsey Jane to John W. Anderson 8-1-1866 (no return) Hn
Overly, Sarah E. to O. H. Eldridge 10-13-1860 Hn
Overman, Utha to James U. Hobbs 2-26-1842 (2-28-1842) G
Overrocker, Sarah L. to Isaac P. Yates 1-13-1860 Sh
Overton, Abigale to J. F. Roach 10-23-1854 (10-26-1854) Hr
Overton, Agness to Jacob T. Pirtle 10-4-1852 (10-9-1852) Hr
Overton, Alice to R. T. Abernathy 3-20-1873 Hy
Overton, Amanda to Abram Lewis 12-17-1849 (1-20-1849) Hr
Overton, Amelia to William C. Smith 7-17-1851 Hr
Overton, Ann Elisa to Daniel Ingram 10-16-1878 Hy
Overton, Ann to Willie Humble 6-8-1840 Ma
Overton, Arkansas to Philip P. Phelps 9-23-1848 (9-28-1848) Hr

Overton, Caroline E. to Thomas W. Harris 1-21-1852 We
Overton, Elizabeth to John M. Lea 5-1-1845 Sh
Overton, Elizabeth to Martin Ogara 10-15-1868 G
Overton, Harriet to F. M. Ross 2-24-1862 F
Overton, Izora to Thomas Hamilton 4-30-1884 (5-6-1884) L
Overton, Louisa F. to Henry H. Walker 11-22-1866 Hy
Overton, Martha to Wm. Putman 11-24-1852 Cr
Overton, Rozana to Peter B. Ross 12-19-1849 (12-20-1849) F
Overton, Sarah Ellen to Daniel R. Chambliss 10-8-1849 (10-9-1849) Hr
Overton, Willis to Mary I. Clark 11-28-1842 Ma
Ovnall?, Susan America to David Cannon Slaughter 7-15-1850 (7-?-1850) T
Owen (Orren), Sarah to Andrew J. Polly 9-19-1854 (9-21-1854) O
Owen, Alice to R. W. Coltart 9-6-1865 (no return) Hy
Owen, Amanda R. to Sebastian P. Richmond 10-5-1833 O
Owen, Amanda to Edward Thomas 12-13-1877 Hy
Owen, Angeline to Andrew Humble 6-7-1873 (6-8-1873) Cr B
Owen, Ann H. to James Wilkins 7-19-1855 T
Owen, Annie M. to T. B. McEwen 7-25-1857 Sh
Owen, Barbie to Frank Mann 3-21-1868 (no return) Hy
Owen, Bettie to Eddie A. Tyson 2-7-1877 Hy
Owen, Cloie to Thos. H. Koen 3-5-1864 Sh
Owen, Delilah to Quintillian T. Whittenton 10-11-1862 Ma
Owen, Eleanor W. to Hiram H. Ralph 12-8-1846 (12-10-1846) T
Owen, Eliza Jane to _____ Norton 12-16-1851 Hn
Owen, Eliza to Henry Reeves 6-6-1868 L B
Owen, Elizabeth J. to S. J. Bingle 4-28-1860 (4-29-1860) T
Owen, Elizabeth to Eli Harris 12-13-1832 Hr
Owen, Elizabeth to Jefferson Warren 12-21-1831 (1-5-1832) Hr
Owen, Ella to Gus Roberson 3-20-1878 (3-21-1878) L
Owen, Ellen to Allen Martain 2-25-1869 T
Owen, Ellen to Jacob Jarrett 9-6-1873 Hy
Owen, Emiline to John Fisher 5-19-1869 (5-23-1869) L
Owen, Emily to Thomas Coleman 9-23-1871 T
Owen, Emma to Malcom Richardson 11-20-1867 Hy
Owen, Emmaline to Jack Jones 11-20-1870 Hy
Owen, Ezilda to Toney Borum 10-31-1869 Hy
Owen, Fony to Ed Coltart 6-3-1866 Hy
Owen, Frances to James W. B. Dannil 1-29-1868 T
Owen, Frances to Shadrack Webb 1-16-1850 Sh
Owen, Gertrude to Felix Mills 9-2-1867 (no return) L B
Owen, Hannah to Samuel Sloan 12-21-1841 Sh
Owen, Harriett to Robert Clark 12-19-1850 (no return) Hn
Owen, Henrietta to George W. Webb 6-11-1845 Sh
Owen, Holly to Henry Dorch 12-28-1868 (12-31-1868) T
Owen, J. F. to James P. Bagby 12-8-1855 (12-12-1855) Hr
Owen, Jane to Walker B. Wilson 6-8-1838 (6-11-1838) Hr
Owen, Jennette R. to William M. Cooke 5-22-1859 Hn
Owen, Kaziah T. to Joseph H. Cooper 3-15-1867 (3-16-1867) Ma
Owen, Levonia R. to B. W. Allen 12-15-1868 (12-16-1868) L
Owen, Louisa Adaline to Benjamin H. Ligon 11-22-1841 (11-26-1841) T
Owen, Lucy A. to Thos. C. Cogbill 10-18-1867 (10-30-1867) F
Owen, Lucy Ann to Mastin F. Bayn 5-9-1846 (5-14-1846) G
Owen, M. to G. D. Watkins 1-4-1872 Hy
Owen, Maggie B. to W. T. Stone 12-31-1867 Hy
Owen, Malinda to William Crews 11-18-1847 Hn
Owen, Manervy to Josiah Nolly 11-28-1848 (not executed) Sh
Owen, Margaret Jane to James J. Furgerson 10-10-1855 (10-11-1855) T
Owen, Margaret L. to William Raferty 12-4-1845 Hn
Owen, Margaret to Thomas Boyle 11-23-1847 (11-25-1847) Hr
Owen, Martha A. to Obadiath Cole 8-24-1866 O
Owen, Martha J. to James J. Furguson 1-15-1867 (1-22-1867) T
Owen, Martha L. to John H. Gant 10-8-1843 Sh
Owen, Martha to Charles Bates 9-6-1874 Hy
Owen, Martha to John Maclin 12-22-1871 Hy
Owen, Mary A. L. to Bazzell Gatewood 12-22-1858 We
Owen, Mary E. to M. T. Cooper 4-17-1856 Sh
Owen, Mary F. to R. Moses Green 11-25-1854 (no return) F
Owen, Mary to James P. Overall 1-22-1867 (1-23-1867) T
Owen, Mary to Jno. C. F. Hill 12-8-1837 Hr
Owen, Mary to Joseph Hopkins 12-21-1867 (no return) Hy
Owen, Mary to Robert Bell 8-10-1870 (8-11-1870) T
Owen, Mattie C. to Jessee M. King 10-31-1885 (11-1-1885) L
Owen, Melina to Thomas Gale 12-18-1867 (no return) Hy
Owen, Melissa to Peyton Smith 11-8-1851 (11-10-1851) L
Owen, Mollie to Malvin Howell 8-16-1868 Hy
Owen, Mollie to Patrick Bynum 3-26-1868 T
Owen, Mollie to Spead Smith 12-14-1868 (no return) L
Owen, Moriah to Allen Carlton 12-25-1871 Hy
Owen, Nancy to John Goforth 1-19-1867 T
Owen, Nancy to John Goforth 11-19-1867 (1-20-1867) T
Owen, Nancy to Young Gray 10-21-1851 (10-23-1851) T
Owen, Peggy to Smith Miller Feezor 6-18-1846 T
Owen, Polly Ann to Joseph M. Moss 2-11-1847 Hn
Owen, Priscilla to Clabourn Foster 10-8-1825 O
Owen, Rebecca to Saml. E. Stevenson 4-24-1866 (4-29-1866) T
Owen, Rhoda to Dempsey Bowden 1-10-1850 Hn
Owen, Rutha A. J. to Chas. D. Bostick 3-30-1848 (no return) Hn

Owen, Sallie E. W. to J. Hubbard Borum 6-15-1859 Hy
Owen, Sallie J. to R. Q. Scott 5-21-1867 G
Owen, Sallie W. to A. G. Smith 9-27-1870 (9-29-1870) F
Owen, Sallie to L. P. Jones 1-17-1861 F
Owen, Sally to Samuel Taylor 1-16-1877 Hy
Owen, Sarah E. to Jesse L. Summers 9-6-1857 (no return) L
Owen, Sarah J. to James F. West 11-4-1838 Sh
Owen, Sarah Jane to Andrew J. McClure 12-25-1857 Hn
Owen, Sarah M. to John Hawkins 5-14-1833 Sh
Owen, Sarah M. to William M. Calhoun 4-19-1857 (4-21-1857) O
Owen, Sarah to Sanford Randall 11-15-1878 (11-21-1878) L B
Owen, Siller to Eliga Taylor 2-21-1878 Hy
Owen, Sirena to Patrick M. Duffy 9-19-1844 Ma
Owen, Theodosia to B. C. Bettis 9-11-1871 (9-12-1871) Dy
Owen, Victoria to H. K. Manuel 3-15-1869 (3-16-1869) Cr
Owenby?, Martha L. to Hezekiah Coble 9-20-1866 (10-3-1866) Cr
Owens, Agatha to Thomas P. Hewlett 6-14-1824 O
Owens, Amanda to G. H. Wilson 2-15-1865 (2-20-1865) Cr
Owens, Arabella C. to Patrick Newson 9-19-1860 (9-20-1860) Cr
Owens, Arcena to Simeon Duffy 7-31-1845 Ma
Owens, Christine to Solomon Epley 7-23-1865 G
Owens, Clary to George Hartley 8-7-1845 (no return) We
Owens, Eliza to Thos. F. Warden 1-30-1860 (2-7-1860) G
Owens, Elizabeth to Henry S. Wilkins 10-18-1859 We
Owens, Emily to M. V. B. Thomas 7-17-1855 (7-19-1855) Sh
Owens, Isabella to James Heaggins 2-11-1871 (no return) F B
Owens, Jane to Jesse Shaw 10-20-1852 Cr
Owens, Julia to James Prichard 11-30-1840 Sh
Owens, Lean to John Waggoner 12-13-1864 Mn
Owens, Letitia to Simeon Duffy 12-12-1866 Ma
Owens, Lucinda to William P. Gillum 11-2-1827 G
Owens, Lucretia to William H. Diggs 4-19-1855 Hn
Owens, Malinda Jane to George Kilzer 8-8-1867 G
Owens, Martha J. to Daniel Frazier 11-20-1861 (no return) Hn
Owens, Mary A. to Henry Grimes 10-14-1860 G
Owens, Mary Ann to Geo. W. Cooke 5-28-1849 (no return) Hn
Owens, Mary Jane to John W. Crawford 1-17-1856 We
Owens, Mary to Isaac Russell 3-16-1875 L
Owens, Mary to Jacob Lowery 4-26-1830 (4-27-1830) Hr
Owens, Mary to Patrick Ahern 8-10-1847 Sh
Owens, Mary to Thomas Crutchfield 4-25-1863 Mn
Owens, Matilda Elizabeth to Allen Martin 9-15-1868 T
Owens, Nancy to Purley M. Booth 12-11-1839 Hn
Owens, Rebecca J. to Jesse L. Summers 8-2-1849 Hn
Owens, Rhoda A. to Josiah Hopkins 3-22-1859 (3-26-1859) O
Owens, S. W. to James T. Reynolds 6-1-1877 (6-2-1877) L
Owens, Sally to Person Capps 10-10-1855 We
Owens, Sarah to James Long 8-23-1843 (8-24-1843) L
Owens, Sarah to P. Greer 8-1-1848 L
Owens, Susan to William D. Thompson 10-16-1861 (no return) Hn
Owens, T. M. (Mrs.) to J. R. Collins 2-26-1885 (3-1-1885) L
Owens, Venina to M. P. Henry 11-15-1862 Mn
Owens, Winiford to Wm. B. Delaney 10-20-1847 Cr
Owens?, Luvenia to Sip Field 11-15-1869 (11-15-1869) T
Owensbey, Rebecca to M. Livingston 12-1-1863 (no return) Cr
Owensby, Betty to W. . Christenberry 9-2-1870 G
Ownbie, Amanda to STephen Cantrell 2-6-1851 Cr
Ownby, Harriet L. to Nathaniel Gibson 8-20-1857 Cr
Oxbury, Elizabeth to James McKarley 1-2-1835 Sh
Oxford, Catharine to William Harris 6-10-1852 Be
Oxford, Margaret E. to Moses Barnes 12-8-1850 Be
Ozburn?, Violett O. to John Cozby 11-30-1846 (12-1-1846) Hr
Ozier, Algenie? to Wilson Slaughter 12-21-1839 (12-26-1839) F
Ozier, E. A. to T. T. Cooper 7-12-1867 (no return) Cr
Ozier, Elizabeth to William T. Watlington 8-5-1847 Ma
Ozier, F. C. to E. N. Royall? 8-15-1867 Cr
Ozier, Julia to Jacob F. Gordon 1-13-1853 (no return) Cr
Ozier, Laury to Thomas McGill 3-4-1841 F
Ozier, Margaret A. to Matthew F. Latta 9-8-1852 Ma
Ozier, Marian to E. L. McAdoo 2-10-1846 (2-15-1846) Ma
Ozier, Mary A. to J. F. Garden 8-15-1859 (no return) F
Ozier, Mary M. to Wm. C. McCaskill 10-5-1854 (no return) F
Ozier, Mary to Sam Robertson 1-30-1869 (2-6-1869) F B
Ozier, Mary to W. M. Eitle 1-13-1869 F
Ozier, Mollie to Thomas Williams 1-7-1870 (1-10-1870) F B
Ozier, O. to R. N. Woods 2-27-1840 Cr
Ozier, Piny E. to Tho. Malone 12-16-1846 (12-17-1846) F
Ozier, S. A. J. to Wm. N. Hampton 6-1-1854 Cr
Ozment, Elizabeth S. to Alexander McCarley 12-28-1848 Hr
Ozment, Julia Anne to Samuel Daniel 4-2-1849 Sh
Ozment, Sarah to James P. Hollaway 4-20-1854 (4-24-1854) Hr

Pace, A. E. to F. T. Read 12-18-1871 (12-20-1871) T
Pace, Alvin A. to Isaac Lavell 8-21-1874 (9-8-1874) T
Pace, Eliza to Charles C. Freeman 1-16-1860 T
Pace, Elizabeth to Jefferson R. Bickers 12-22-1853 Hr
Pace, Elizabeth to Wm. Bennett 3-30-1871 Cr

Pace, Fanny to Wm. R. Anderson 9-12-1866 (9-13-1866) Ma
Pace, Jennie to J. T. Stockton 9-15-1874 (9-17-1874) Dy
Pace, Julia to Peter Franks 1-26-1864 Sh
Pace, Lizzie to W. L. Jones 9-19-1877 (9-20-1877) Dy
Pace, Louisa to John G. Baucom 12-8-1878 Hy
Pace, Martha C. to Richmond Herrin 10-4-1872 (10-6-1872) Dy
Pace, Martha E. to Elija Smith 12-19-1854 Ma
Pace, Martha L. (Mrs.) to W. Hockersmith 9-14-1866 G
Pace, Martha to James L. Glenn 6-18-1861 (6-23-1861) Hr
Pace, Mary A. N. to James A. Chandler 7-27-1860 Cr
Pace, Mary A. N. to James A. Chandler 7-?-1861 (7-7-1860?) Cr
Pace, Mary A. to Samuel Crockett 8-6-1866 G
Pace, Mary J. to John Offenshine 4-14-1869 (4-15-1869) Cr
Pace, Nancy Jane to James W. Harrell 8-20-1855 (8-21-1855) Hr
Pace, R. A. to A. J. Ellis 12-18-1876 (12-21-1876) Dy
Pace, Rachel to Philip Rushing 1-12-1846 Be
Pace, Saphronia H. to William H. Smith 10-8-1859 (10-9-1859) G
Pace, Sarah E. to William M. Busick 1-6-1858 G
Pachall, Susan A. to William J. Nanney 12-16-1860 We
Packard, S. H. to John Corbet 10-5-1858 T
Paddock, Rosalee to Hugh E. Masterson 12-30-1854 Sh
Paden, Isabelah to Adam R. Wylie 8-6-1838 F
Paden, Rachel to D. Smith 9-23-1871 (9-26-1871) T
Pafford, Elizabeth to A. H. Melton 9-14-1865 Be
Pafford, Elizabeth to James Arnold 3-17-1858 Be
Pafford, Isabel to Alfred G. Farrow 3-14-1847 Be
Pafford, Martha to Cooper Pafford 6-20-1852 Be
Pafford, Mary A. to W. R. Warrick 5-21-1868 Be
Pafford, Mary to John Werrick 11-28-1844 Be
Pafford, Nancy to Wm. Parker 11-10-1842 Be
Pafford, Polly to Lewis Holland 6-11-1839 Be
Pafford, Sarah to Mathew McKelvy 7-7-1850 Be
Pafford, Susanah to Americus Vick 3-23-1848 Be
Page, Clerda to Andrew J. Barham 11-29-1846 Cr
Page, Elizabeth to John Kimbro 2-28-1848 G
Page, Elizabeth to Robert Franklin 8-19-1828 G
Page, Fannie to John Roe 8-29-1874 (8-30-1874) T
Page, Jane to Hiram Pound 9-2-1828 (9-4-1828) O
Page, Josephine to James T. Smith 2-6-1868 G
Page, Lucy B. to William A. Lawson 11-6-1852 (11-10-1852) O
Page, Lucy to James H. Walker 2-7-1850 Hn
Page, Martha A. to John Q. Bradley 11-17-1869 T
Page, Martha to William R. Hicks 2-16-1854 L
Page, Mary C. to Archibald Grant 12-19-1864 (no return) Cr
Page, Mary C. to Elgin C. White 4-21-1838 (4-22-1838) G
Page, Mary E. to David S. Freeman 6-10-1847 Hn
Page, Mary E. to James R. Moore 9-18-1859 Hn
Page, Mary E. to Wade H. Frost 11-14-1854 (11-15-1854) O
Page, Mary to Andrew J. Livingston 1-25-1840 (1-29-1840) O
Page, Mattie to N. W. Sorrell 1-3-1872 Dy
Page, Nancy E. to Beverly B. Watson 3-4-1850 G
Page, Pinkey to Jack Scott 11-13-1875 (11-14-1875) L
Page, Rebecca A. to H. T. Burnam 7-22-1839 (7-25-1839) G
Page, Roseann to Josiah A. Eliff 12-24-1862 Mn
Page, Sarah Ann to William B. Walker 6-2-1838 F
Page, Sarah to E. P. Woods 4-14-1867 G
Page, Susanah to Thomas Starks 1-20-1858 We
Pahell, Nancy to Columbus Barnett 11-30-1868 Be
Pahol, Frances to John Ballowe 12-30-1866 Be
Pahol, Mary to E. N. Quillen 9-28-1865 Be
Pain, Lou to Phill Winrow 12-27-1877 L B
Pain, Marinda to John Kelly 2-22-1834 Hr
Pain, Martha to John Kathy 4-5-1855 Cr
Pain, Mary to David Duglass 5-30-1868 (5-31-1868) L B
Pain, Mary to Walter Allen 5-24-1848 Sh
Pain, Susan E. to A. J. Burten 2-14-1855 We
Paine, Eliza W. to Robt. Drysdale 7-30-1849 (8-2-1849) F
Paine, Eliza to T. E. Broyhill 9-24-1874 Hy
Paine, Harriet to John Webster 11-5-1869 F B
Paine, Laura to James P. Braden 11-10-1869 (11-11-1869) F
Paine, Lucinda to Isaac Reynolds 4-11-1874 (4-12-1874) Dy
Paine, Polly to Joseiah Hicks 5-16-1829 Sh
Paine, Rachal to David Jackson 11-15-1842 (11-17-1842) G
Painer, Anna to Edward (Edmund?) P. Green 6-20-1830 Sh
Paisley, M. J. to WM. A. Wilson 1-31-1854 (2-2-1854) Ma
Palma, Sarah G. to Wm. H. Waters 6-18-1855 (6-21-1855) Sh
Palmer, Amanda to Thomas Henning 11-10-1871 (11-12-1871) L
Palmer, Ann to Simon Carter 10-22-1870 (10-23-1870) F B
Palmer, Anna to Coleman Taylor 1-5-1869 Hy
Palmer, Annie to James David Pickler 2-12-1854 Cr
Palmer, Annie to John Etta 12-23-1874 Hy
Palmer, Betsy to Kelly Murrell 8-16-1873 (8-21-1873) Dy
Palmer, C. M. to H. F. Farnsworth 11-3-1843 Sh
Palmer, Carcilla M. to Pinkey R. Hayes 11-1-1859 Hn
Palmer, Caroline A. to William D. Smith 7-25-1868 (7-26-1868) T
Palmer, Caroline to Jackson Hall 1-3-1839 Cr
Palmer, Catherine to Isaac Williams 11-27-1843 Hn

Palmer, Catherine to W. M. Dennis 12-28-1847 Cr
Palmer, Chaney to John w. Sprout 10-18-1838 Hn
Palmer, Chaney to Sims Hunter 1-24-1867 (no return) Hy
Palmer, Charlotte to Samuel Crawford 12-27-1866 Hn B
Palmer, Cora to George McNeill 11-6-1867 Hn
Palmer, Elizabeth E. to David Fuqua 6-24-1844 (no return) Cr
Palmer, Elizabeth E. to William C. Adams 10-18-1853 Hn
Palmer, Elizabeth to Joseph A. Williams 2-3-1863 (2-4-1863) Cr
Palmer, Elizabeth to W. V. Roberts 2-14-1859 (2-15-1859) Sh
Palmer, Ellen to Calvin Pierson 1-9-1869 (1-10-1869) L
Palmer, Ellen to Washington Johnson 7-23-1868 (no return) Cr
Palmer, Ellen to Wilson White 7-2-1869 (7-4-1869) Cr
Palmer, Elsie to Robt. Grace 5-23-1877 (5-24-1877) Dy
Palmer, Emily to Newt Murphy 1-22-1876 (no return) Hy
Palmer, Fannie to John Bane 3-5-1859 Cr
Palmer, Hannah M. to Sidney J. Ceal 1-5-1854 Cr
Palmer, Harriett to Andy Tatum 12-26-1870 (12-29-1870) Dy
Palmer, Helen to Elisha Lay 4-17-1861 (4-18-1861) Sh
Palmer, Jennie H. to Hiram D. Glass 10-8-1872 L
Palmer, Lizie to Daniel E. Stockton 12-26-1859 Sh
Palmer, Lizzie to John McCulley 2-28-1883 L
Palmer, Louiza to John W. Myrick 3-18-1852 Hn
Palmer, Louverta to James Byrn 2-6-1869 (2-7-1869) L
Palmer, Lucy A. to Robert H. Oldham 1-24-1877 L
Palmer, Lucy to John H. Rigsby 11-26-1867 Hn
Palmer, Lutitia P. to George W. Bennett 12-19-1860 (12-20-1860) Cr
Palmer, M. A. E. to R. P. Farmer 11-24-1859 We
Palmer, M. B. G. to A. C. Tucker 12-7-1864 (12-8-1864) Cr
Palmer, M. J. to L. H. Hollingsworth 1-31-1877 (2-1-1877) Dy
Palmer, Malissa to Roland Gaulden 4-3-1878 (no return) Dy
Palmer, Margaret to Peter Baque 4-21-1855 (4-22-1855) Sh
Palmer, Martha A. to William Smith 8-7-1855 Hn
Palmer, Martha Ann to Joseph H. Fuqua 8-27-1840 Hn
Palmer, Martha D. to William S. Hightower 4-28-1866 (5-14-1866) Cr
Palmer, Martha F. to Joseph H. Wardlaw 1-23-1860 (no return) L
Palmer, Mary Ann to N. G. Brogdon 11-1-1854 Hn
Palmer, Mary Belle to W. D. F. Hafford 3-8-1859 F
Palmer, Mary E. to J. L. Horton 7-29-1871 Cr
Palmer, Mary J. to William Henderson Palmer 3-3-1849 (no return) Hn
Palmer, Mary M. to A. M. Cook 12-2-1850 Sh
Palmer, Mary to Henry Lamb 8-15-1866 Hn B
Palmer, Matilda C. to Will H. Palmer 10-30-1850 Hn
Palmer, Mattie to George W. Brown 10-5-1864 (10-7-1864) Cr
Palmer, N. C. to G. W. Wood 2-20-1869 (2-21-1869) Cr
Palmer, Nancy J. to G. W. Waldren 2-25-1875 Hy
Palmer, Nancy to Charley Edwards 10-14-1870 Hy
Palmer, Nancy to Harrison Brown 5-15-1879 L
Palmer, Orfrey M. to William C. Ross 12-8-1860 (12-9-1860) Cr
Palmer, Rutha to Elum F. Newell 12-29-1843 G
Palmer, S. H. L. to A. H. Smith 12-28-1870 Dy
Palmer, S. J. to B. F. Partee 5-1-1872 L
Palmer, Sallie to John Jones 12-24-1870 (no return) Hy
Palmer, Sally to Thomas H. Tayloe 10-25-1859 Hn
Palmer, Saphrona to Robert Barnhart 7-2-1866 (7-4-1866) Cr
Palmer, Sarah A. W. to R. L. Mitchell 12-25-1849 Sh
Palmer, Sarah to William Foust 12-20-1854 Hn
Palmer, Sarah? to Gova Cox 6-12-1855 Hn
Palmer, Susan D. to Edmund M. Davis 10-8-1853 Sh
Palmer, Susan Jane to William J. Brown 2-3-1847 (2-4-1847) F
Palmer, Tennessee to H. W. Tharpe 11-24-1852 Hn
Palmer, V. M. to Thomas M., jr. Scott 5-9-1876 L
Palmer, W. M. to W. H. Greer 9-3-1865 Hn
Palmer?, Mary Ann to West Harriss 11-25-1846 (11-26-1846) Hr
Palmon, Jottee to Whiten Bennett 7-17-1869 Hn
Palmor, Lucy Ann to Moses P. Martin 11-22-1848 F
Palmore, Charlott to Larkin L. Moore 11-17-1840 G
Palmore, Eliza to R. Harris 5-18-1871 (5-21-1871) Dy
Palmore, Elizabeth to William J. Flippin 12-13-1848 (12-21-1848) G
Palmore, M. E. to W. R. Little 2-22-1863 (no return) Hy
Palmore, Mary J. to Royal F. Brown 1-15-1847 (1-17-1847) F
Palmore, Nancy G. to Silas D. Witt 2-23-1861 (2-24-1861) Cr
Palmore, Nancy J. to William Rogerson 9-2-1859 Hy
Palston, Belgona to Riley William 1-11-1846 Hn
Palston, E. A. to Daniel McLean 12-17-1851 Cr
Pamphlett, Fanny to John L. Parker 5-6-1853 O
Pamplett, Nancy to Wiley Nix 2-3-1847 O
Pamplin, Mary F. to William Trace 7-11-1846 Sh
Pane, Catherine to Willy Lieuallen 10-12-1830 Ma
Pane, Emma to Emery Sweat 3-30-1868 (4-2-1868) F
Pane, Martha to Isaac Nash 9-22-1851 (no return) F
Pane, Nancy to Madison Burk 2-1-1852 Hn
Panesi, C. to A. Boggiano 2-23-1857 (2-24-1857) Sh
Pankey, Caroline to Jesse A. Thrasher 8-12-1858 Hr
Pankey, Caroline to W. G. Brown 12-11-1850 Hn
Pankey, Darcey? E. to Calvin Lee 9-3-1858 (9-5-1858) O
Pankey, Dorcias E. to Calvin Lee 9-5-1858 O
Pankey, Eliza C. to Elija Graham 2-27-1850 (2-28-1850) Hr

Pankey, Eliza to James Little 8-11-1852 (8-12-1852) Hr
Pankey, Elizabeth P. to B. C. P. Mathew 11-14-1838 (11-15-1838) O
Pankey, Emily S. to John Warren 1-29-1855 (1-30-1855) Hr
Pankey, Jane to Jehu H. Armstrong 1-13-1844 (1-17-1844) Hr
Pankey, Louisa to W. W. Hazlewood 3-15-1862 O
Pankey, M. J. to F. Lambeth 8-16-1856 (8-17-1856) Hr
Pankey, Margaret to J. N. B. Hobson 2-13-1860 Hr
Pankey, Martha to Ruffin Brown 7-22-1851 (7-24-1851) Hr
Pankey, Mary M. to John Cox 8-11-1852 (8-12-1852) Hr
Pankey, Nancy to James Yarbrough 3-10-1852 (3-11-1852) Hr
Pankey, Rebecca Ann to Washington D. Cheshier 8-31-1846 (9-1-1846) Hr
Pankey, Rebecca to James E. Smith 11-6-1848 (11-8-1848) Hr
Pankey, Sarah Ann to John Williams 5-26-1857 (5-27-1857) O
Panky, Frances to Osker Brown 12-27-1873 (12-30-1874?) O
Panky, May Ann Elizabeth to Enoch Sain 3-10-1847 (3-12-1847) Hr
Pannell, Eliza to Geo. Steele 5-16-1860 Hr
Pannell, N. A. to Wm. Lacewell 6-7-1875 O
Panst, Jane R. to Preston L. Childress 3-6-1841 (3-7-1841) Ma
Para, Pamela R. to B. P. Peery 12-17-1866 Dy
Paralee, Stamps to John W. Pipkin 12-21-1873 Hy
Parcham, Martha N. to Jno. M. Secrest 1-16-1846 F
Parchman, Eliza A. to William T. White 2-20-1841 (2-23-1841) F
Parchman, L. E. to Charles W. Slater 1-11-1843 (1-12-1843) F
Parden (Rarden?), Elizabeth (Mrs.) to Jere Old 11-18-1863 Sh
Pardue, Lenorah to John Jackson 5-30-1861 O
Pareson?, Jane to John Waters 12-6-1857 Be
Parham, Aregon to Henry Jones 8-22-1867 (no return) F B
Parham, Bedie A. to G. W. Norman 10-28-1859 We
Parham, Caroline to James N. Colthorp 9-24-1846 We
Parham, Emiline to James Dickerson 10-6-1853 We
Parham, Harriet C. to A. L. C. King 12-3-1844 We
Parham, Harriet to Geor. C. Gray 1-22-1845 F
Parham, Julia A. to ___ thas W. Dodson 8-11-1868 T
Parham, Lucinda to Henry Strange 6-7-1848 Cr
Parham, Lucy Ann to Wm. B. Morgan 12-27-1855 We
Parham, M. A. to J. N. Rodgers 4-15-1880 (4-16-1880) L
Parham, Mariah to Jake Read 1-17-1872 Hy
Parham, Mary to James Collins 5-11-1851 O
Parham, Nancy R. to E. D. King 1-20-1845 (no return) We
Parham, Susan M. to G. W. C. Killgore 5-4-1866 Hn
Parham, Unity A. to James M. Steele 11-21-1850 We
Parilee, Sarah to Ben Franklin 4-30-1866 Hy
Paris, Fanny to James Lucas 5-24-1877 Hy
Paris, Mary J. to G. P. Greaves 1-14-1879 L
Paris, Narcissa C. to Aron J. Gilliland 8-31-1853 (9-2-1853) G
Paris, Sarah to Joel Arnold 12-28-1848 G
Parish, Arminta to J. T. Rust 9-10-1870 (9-11-1870) Cr
Parish, Catharine to Wm. J. Gant 3-16-1870 F
Parish, Eliza J. to Thos. Riggs 5-29-1867 (5-30-1867) F
Parish, Elizabeth A. to S. W. Roberts 9-17-1861 (9-18-1861) Cr
Parish, Elizabeth to Henry Nichols 6-2-1850 Cr
Parish, Elizabeth to William Tyson 4-10-1857 Hn
Parish, Frances to Enos Lamb 2-5-1849 T
Parish, Jane H. to John M. Kelley 7-20-1867 O
Parish, Jane to Jacob Butler 2-8-1873 (2-9-1873) Cr B
Parish, Lizzie to Jones Baker 4-24-1867 (4-28-1867) F B
Parish, Louisa to J. W. Thomason 12-24-1869 (12-28-1869) Cr
Parish, Lucinda to Perley James 5-11-1846 T
Parish, Margaret to Chesley Dodd 10-7-1858 Cr
Parish, Martha J. to W. P. King 11-3-1868 (11-4-1868) Cr
Parish, Mary A. to E. T. Frances 12-9-1854 We
Parish, Parthena to William B. Jones 1-15-1846 O
Parish, Polly A. to John A. Miller 10-24-1858 Cr
Parish, Rena to Spencer Lynn 3-3-1870 (3-6-1870) L
Parish, Rianna to William Bateman 3-2-1871 (3-5-1871) Cr
Parish, Sallie to R. B. Meacham 5-22-1884 L
Parish, Sarah E. to John M. Gray 1-18-1849 Sh
Parish, Sarah F. to A. K. Abernathy 1-25-1865 Mn
Parish, Sarah F. to William Crews 12-15-1858 Cr
Parish, Winifred to John A. Autry 2-22-1844 Cr
Park, Ann E. to Washington S. Taylor 3-31-1853 Sh
Park, Eliza A. to Eben Rowland 3-13-1866 L
Park, Elizabeth to Edward C. Pollum 7-27-1850 O
Park, Elizabeth to John N. Park 11-21-1851 Cr
Park, H. J. to J. I. L. Gray 12-22-1863 (12-23-1863) O
Park, Jane C. to W. H. Caldwell 4-24-1861 (4-25-1861) O
Park, Jane R. to M. D. Deadrick 5-19-1857 Hr
Park, Jane to Alexander L. Hughes 4-2-1851 (4-3-1851) Hr
Park, Jane to Henry T. Chisum 10-26-1829 Hr
Park, M. C. to W. V. Carlock 9-25-1866 O
Park, M. Jennie to James H. Graves 7-20-1868 (7-21-1868) Ma
Park, Martha to J. May 12-26-1860 (12-27-1860) Hr
Park, Mary H. to Alfred Ratlieff 9-25-1866 O
Park, Mary L. to Wm. K. Poston 4-13-1843 Sh
Park, Rebecca to A. Coyle 8-21-1850 O
Park, Rebecca to Lewis M. Harris 1-5-1857 O
Park, Sarah M. to James H. Jewell 1-5-1850 (1-6-1850) Hr

Parkenson, Sarah M. to James A. Gee 1-11-1854 Cr
Parker, Alice to Emri Jones 1-25-1883 L
Parker, Amanda to Wm. F. Cooper 9-17-1862 (9-18-1862) Cr
Parker, Amelia E. to Granville T. Pillow 4-23-1850 Hn
Parker, Amy to W. C. Pafford 11-1-1840 Be
Parker, Angeline to E. D. Overton 11-14-1845 Sh
Parker, Annie Eliza to Charles Taylor 12-23-1873 (12-26-1873) T
Parker, Anny to Robert Briscoe 9-28-1873 Hy
Parker, Burtie to Richard Green 3-20-1873 Hy
Parker, Caroline to Elisha Dinning 12-4-1858 (no return) We
Parker, Caroline to Hudson Williams 11-2-1830 Ma
Parker, Catharine W. to Wm. C. Ervin 5-19-1841 Hr
Parker, Catharine to Daniel Barns 1-22-1844 (1-25-1844) G
Parker, Catherine to William Bryant 5-2-1867 Hn
Parker, Cicily D. to G. W. Culipher 12-14-1867 (no return) Hy
Parker, Clara A. to William Fountain 3-31-1859 (4-5-1859) Sh
Parker, D. E. to William L. Allen 11-6-1856 Hn
Parker, Deborah to James Taylor 11-15-1827 (11-18-1827) G
Parker, Deborah to Louis See 12-13-1831 G
Parker, Dona to Currie Tinnin 4-18-1877 L
Parker, Druciller A. to James A. Provow 11-6-1862 Hn
Parker, Edith A. to Henry McDaniel 11-26-1855 (no return) Hn
Parker, Eliza Ann to W. W. Sexton 8-15-1855 Hn
Parker, Eliza to Elisha Mitchell 9-29-1862 Mn
Parker, Eliza to Hector McNair 2-14-1852 (2-15-1852) T
Parker, Eliza to John Bedford 9-12-1862 (9-18-1862) F
Parker, Elizabeth C. to Charles B. Linn 12-24-1858 Hn
Parker, Elizabeth I. to Lafayette Weaver 9-11-1852 Hr
Parker, Elizabeth M. to M. D. Stout 10-24-1843 We
Parker, Elizabeth N. to Ruben Hammet 8-7-1837 O
Parker, Elizabeth S. to John D. Beattie 4-10-1856 Sh
Parker, Elizabeth to Alexander Campbell 12-26-1844 We
Parker, Elizabeth to Bryant Tettleton 12-30-1846 Ma
Parker, Elizabeth to James A. Rigsby 8-9-1854 Hr
Parker, Elizabeth to Luke M. Edwards 5-24-1833 G
Parker, Elizabeth to Zelmon Voss 4-29-1857 Ma
Parker, Elizabth to James Garner 11-15-1849 Be
Parker, Ella to John Mitchell 2-15-1872 Hy
Parker, Ellen to Tex Harris 9-29-1870 (10-1-1870) Dy
Parker, Emiline to J. Z. Leath 8-16-1872 (8-22-1872) Dy
Parker, Etta to Frank Washington 1-2-1873 Hy
Parker, Eudora to J. B. Tucker 4-1-1879 (4-2-1879) Dy
Parker, Eviline to John Pearson 1-25-1865 (1-26-1865) Cr
Parker, Fanny to George Borsh 12-14-1865 G
Parker, Frances C. to Robert N. Johnson 12-29-1873 (1-1-1874) L
Parker, Frances to Jerry Wilson 11-28-1867 G B
Parker, Frances to Wm. James Brown 11-13-1860 (11-15-1860) Hr
Parker, Harriet S. J. to Thomas B. Kirkland 10-23-1867 Hn
Parker, Harriett to William Throgmortin 1-14-1852 We
Parker, I. Etta to Henry C. Perry 9-5-1870 (9-7-1870) Dy
Parker, J. A. to Richard H. Hill 12-12-1853 Sh
Parker, J. J. to W. H. Blair 3-29-1870 G
Parker, Jane to David w. Bivins 2-2-1846 (2-6-1846) Ma
Parker, Jane to Richard Fields 8-28-1869 (no return) F B
Parker, Jane to Wm. H. Rosser 8-27-1841 Cr
Parker, Joanna to Joseph B. Terry 11-26-1856 Hr
Parker, Kitty to James Lewis 11-2-1878 (11-3-1878) L B
Parker, Kitty to John Hutchenson 5-30-1866 Hn B
Parker, L. E. A. (Mrs.) to Henry Roane 11-12-1850 (11-16-1850) G
Parker, L. E. to J. H. Harrison 7-28-1875 (7-29-1875) Dy
Parker, L. E. to J. M. Carnal 3-13-1867 (3-15-1867) Cr
Parker, Lettrice to Edward L. Peters 1-27-1827 (2-1-1827) Hr
Parker, Lila to Green Fitzpatrick 11-14-1868 (11-4?-1868) L
Parker, Lorena to John A. Murphy 2-12-1853 Cr
Parker, Lottsy to John Smith 2-21-1873 Hy
Parker, Louisa to Carroll Romly 11-6-1848 Be
Parker, Louisa to William Preston 3-19-1851 Hn
Parker, Lucy L. to William C. Hale 3-23-1843 (3-26-1843) O
Parker, Lucy to Eli Buchanan 6-30-1877 (7-1-1877) L
Parker, Lucy to Green Fowlkes 11-18-1870 Dy B
Parker, Lurane to Joseph Landrum 12-18-1855 (1-11-1856) O
Parker, Lurena to Thomas Nolen 1-31-1885 (no return) L
Parker, Luroney B. to Robert S. Reeves 1-18-1847 (1-21-1847) Ma
Parker, Lutitia to James Bowen 12-7-1872 O
Parker, M. A. to R. F. Honey 8-26-1859 (no return) Cr
Parker, M. E. to Thos. N. Adams 4-20-1856 Be
Parker, M. E. to With T. Oneal 1-7-1868 Ma
Parker, M. F. to B. H. Watson 9-26-1863 (9-27-1863) O
Parker, M. J. to Albert Johnson 12-25-1878 (12-26-1878) Dy
Parker, M. J. to J. L. Mitchell 10-1-1877 (10-2-1877) L
Parker, Malinda E. to John W. Dunlap 9-3-1850 Hn
Parker, Margaret Ann to Moses Meeker 11-21-1848 Sh
Parker, Margret to Elijah Holomon 2-17-1853 Be
Parker, Marilu? E. to Jas. H. Bass 4-3-1866 G
Parker, Martha A. V. to William M. McWhirter 7-17-1844 (7-18-1844) G
Parker, Martha A. to Thomas Outland 1-6-1858 (no return) Hn
Parker, Martha D. to W. F. Blakemore 6-7-1859 G

Parker, Martha E. to A. G. Moore 12-17-1856 We
Parker, Martha Jane to O. H. Allen 3-21-1867 Hn
Parker, Martha W. to Sterling B. Ford 3-29-1849 G
Parker, Martha to Conrad Kunkle 5-21-1857 Sh
Parker, Mary A. to R. M. Armstrong 3-14-1867 O
Parker, Mary Ann to Allen Cox 10-15-1858 (10-3?-1858) Hr
Parker, Mary Ann to Henry Travis 9-14-1848 (9-?-1848) T
Parker, Mary Ann to James M. Kelly 2-12-1853 Sh
Parker, Mary Ann to John Melton 1-10-1861 Be
Parker, Mary Ann to Wm. M. Maser 9-27-1855 T
Parker, Mary G. to Wm. H. Dilliard 12-6-1849 (no return) Cr
Parker, Mary J. to Pleasant H. Foster 8-2-1860 Hn
Parker, Mary Jane to Sidney J. Williams 12-6-1852 (12-7-1852) Sh
Parker, Mary M. to J. P. Dunlap 1-12-1865 Hn
Parker, Mary O. to V. A. Holt 3-4-1869 G
Parker, Mary S. to N. W. Rochell 12-8-1858 Cr
Parker, Mary W. to Reddick T. White 11-7-1867 Hy
Parker, Mary to David Stinson 12-28-1868 (12-29-1868) Dy
Parker, Mary to Horace Fuller 3-29-1884 (3-30-1886?) L
Parker, Mary to Isaac D. Maxwell 2-10-1842 L
Parker, Mary to James L. Brandon 12-17-1860 (no return) L
Parker, Mary to Jerry Edmonds 12-25-1874 T
Parker, Mary to John A. Dean 2-25-1848 (3-2-1848) Ma
Parker, Mary to John D. Thomas 1-31-1849 O
Parker, Mary to M. G. Campbell 12-25-1867 O
Parker, Mary to Patrick Tully 5-17-1861 Sh
Parker, Mary to Philip N. Smith 4-28-1842 Hr
Parker, Mary to Samuel Walker 8-17-1842 Sh
Parker, Mary to Thomas G. Graham 2-8-1838 Hr
Parker, Mary to Washington Ingram 12-13-1869 (12-26-18689) F B
Parker, Massa to George W. Taylor 9-10-1828 (9-12-1828) Hr
Parker, Matilda A. to J. R. Duncan 9-1-1860 Hn
Parker, Matilda J. to Elisha Russell 7-14-1853 Cr
Parker, Mollie F. to Antony S. Cook 12-21-1868 G
Parker, Mollie to John Hardin 2-12-1869 (no return) Dy
Parker, Mollie to W. B. (Dr.) York 1-14-1867 (1-15-1867) Dy
Parker, Nancy E. to John Miller 4-22-1866 Hn
Parker, Nancy Jane to Wm. M. Cuff 1-26-1865 Be
Parker, Nancy to George A. Bolin 6-23-1856 (6-24-1856) Ma
Parker, Nancy to Jacob Finley 11-14-1826 Hr
Parker, Nancy to John Baker 12-7-1846 We
Parker, Nancy to John T. White 11-6-1844 We
Parker, Nannie to Silas Roach 12-25-1873 Hy
Parker, Obedience to Richard Finley 11-24-1836 Hr
Parker, Olivia C. to James Fish Hr
Parker, Parthena to Isaac Menzies 10-24-1872 (9?-24-1872) Dy
Parker, Parthena to James Harris 3-5-1874 Dy
Parker, Pheracia to John Wry 1-25-1841 (no return) Hn
Parker, Phinity to Arthur Bowen 11-21-1848 Sh
Parker, Rebecca J. to John W. Watson 12-18-1860 Cr
Parker, Rebecca to John C. Richards 12-12-1838 Sh
Parker, Rebecca to Ralph Petty 7-3-1859 Hn
Parker, Rebecca to Samuel Conner 1-30-1829 Ma
Parker, Rebeccah to Amos C. Reynolds 1-16-1838 Hr
Parker, Rosusey Fine to Matthew Crowly 12-16-1843 (12-17-1843) Hr
Parker, S. A. to W. S. Luton 12-11-1876 (12-12-1876) O
Parker, S. E. to W. L. Carnall 1-23-1873 Cr
Parker, Sally to Alen Betts 12-15-1829 G
Parker, Sarah Ann to William Wilson 8-18-1845 Sh
Parker, Sarah E. to R. T. Ponder 10-19-1872 (10-24-1872) Dy
Parker, Sarah E. to W. S. Ellis 5-4-1853 Hr
Parker, Sarah J. to John W. Atkinson 4-8-1852 Hn
Parker, Sarah Jane to Aquilla Mullican 5-17-1853 Hr
Parker, Sarah L. to Samuel S. Johnson 7-3-1854 Ma
Parker, Sarah to Gillum Harris 9-2-1834 Hy
Parker, Sarah to Jo. Wilson 5-10-1883 (no return) L
Parker, Sarah to W. T. Piercy 11-5-1868 Dy
Parker, Sarah to William F. Roberts 8-10-1862 We
Parker, Sue to Alfred Currie 11-15-1871 Hy
Parker, Susan E. to Robert F. Brown 10-18-1865 (10-25-1865) Dy
Parker, Susan H. to Eli P. Jenkins 11-29-1859 Ma
Parker, Susan R. to Samuel R. Markham 5-1-1867 Hy
Parker, Susan V. to James R. Walsh 12-19-1876 (12-20-1876) L
Parker, Susan to Adam Douglas 6-14-1873 (6-15-1873) T
Parker, Susan to Hezekiah C. Thompson 7-3-1852 (7-8-1852) G
Parker, Susan to Thomas Glass 3-18-1842 Hn
Parker, Syntha A. to D. H. Blankenship 7-4-1865 G
Parker, Violett to Levi Gunn 9-19-1867 G
Parker, Willie Ann to W. F. Ross 1-21-1861 (1-23-1861) Hr
Parker, Zabra to John Conner 2-23-1831 Ma
Parkes, Catherine to William Willis 12-19-1849 Sh
Parkes, Jane to Eli Cox 10-1-1832 (10-?-1832) Hr
Parkes, Martha to William Reatherford 6-27-1863 (6-28-1863) O
Parkes, Susan to H. K. Northway 10-14-1852 (no return) F
Parkes, Susan to Alexander Byars 9-29-1858 We
Parkes, Tennessee to John Clack 6-27-1863 (6-28-1863) O
Parkinson, Mary Elizabeth to William Crosby 4-15-1839 Ma

Parks, Adeline to Smith Hamilton 5-30-1860 (5-31-1860) G
Parks, Ann to Isaac Hunt 12-24-1867 (12-26-1867) F B
Parks, Biney to Robert Gately 2-1-1859 F
Parks, Drusilla to Henry Watson 9-26-1884 L
Parks, Eliza Ann to Billington Taylor 8-12-1861 We
Parks, Eliza to Amos Foster 9-30-1826 (10-3?-1826) Hr
Parks, Elizabeth Ann to H. S. Newsom 1-6-1862 (1-7-1862) Sh
Parks, Elizabeth to Obediah Carlton 12-8-1857 We
Parks, Elizabeth to Oswill C. Walker 12-18-1849 Be
Parks, Elizabeth to Samuel Reed 8-6-1831 G
Parks, Ella to Frank McKindry 12-20-1870 (no return) F B
Parks, Emeline to G. M. Cravins 11-26-1857 We
Parks, Fannie to George Jackson 12-5-1874 Hy
Parks, Fanny to John Griffin 9-15-1841 Cr
Parks, Harriet to Bob Estes 1-27-1875 L B
Parks, Jane to William P. Johnson 11-24-1857 (11-26-1857) Hr
Parks, L. C. to sM. Thompson 12-10-1872 (12-11-1872) Dy
Parks, Lutie A. to A. B. Tigrett 5-14-1873 (5-15-1873) Dy
Parks, Maggie F. to Richard S. Smith 7-25-1874 L
Parks, Mahala to W. S. Knox 3-17-1866 (3-18-1866) F
Parks, Malissa to George Willis 12-23-1847 Sh
Parks, Mariah to William Jackson 11-16-1872 (11-18-1872) Dy
Parks, Martha F. to Chas. P. Brown 2-4-1864 Sh
Parks, Martha J. to Lewis Baird 4-12-1871 (no return) Dy
Parks, Mary A. to Thos. W. Gemwell 4-1-1845 Sh
Parks, Mary Ann to John F. Moore 9-13-1855 (9-15-1855) Hr
Parks, Mary C. to P. D. Job 3-12-1858 (3-16-1858) Hr
Parks, Mary C. to R. H. Oliver 7-23-1855 Sh
Parks, Mary M. to D. F. McIntosh 12-2-1865 G
Parks, Mary to Sam Parks 11-20-1877 (11-23-1877) Dy
Parks, Mary to Wm. H. Lynn 9-16-1858 We
Parks, Matilda to John Halliburton 9-26-1869 G B
Parks, Mollie I. to Walter Scott Draper 11-24-1870 Dy
Parks, N. A. to W. S. Hamilton 2-20-1867 G
Parks, Nancy Ann M. to John F. Burney 7-9-1851 (7-13-1851) G
Parks, Nancy E. to J. W. Phillips 3-23-1861 We
Parks, P. P. to W. D. McMasters 11-4-1861 Sh
Parks, Parena V. to J. N. Wyatt 12-13-1864 (no return) Dy
Parks, Rosanna to James M. Ptts 10-8-1859 Sh
Parks, Sarah to Clark S. Butler 1-19-1848 Cr
Parks, Sophrina E. to John W. Hodge 4-29-1846 Cr
Parks, Susan to J. Tubbs 1-3-1860 Be
Parlow, Martha J. to George W. Upton 7-1-1867 (7-17-1867) Ma
Parmele, Millie to Amos Munford 9-4-1862 Sh
Parmer, Christian to W. H. Monroe 2-28-1850 We
Parmer, Elisabeth to Buck Sutton 1-12-1878 Hy
Parmer, Margaret to Cullen Benson 2-7-1839 Hr
Parmer, Mary Jane to Andrew Jackson 4-15-1852 We
Parmer, May to John Butler 11-5-1838 Ma
Parmer, P. to Levy Higgs 6-10-1852 We
Parnashia, Mary to Jas. Bogino (Bojianno) 3-28-1864 Sh
Parnell (Pannell), M. E. to Calvin Atkinson 4-25-1876 (4-28-1876) O
Parnell, Lucy A. to Wm. Hugely 2-19-1866 (2-20-1866) F
Parnell, Margaret to William Boyd 12-13-1862 (12-16-1862) Dy
Parnell, Martha A. to Levi Cothran 4-3-1861 (4-4-1861) Dy
Parnell, Martha J. to Percy Keelin 6-9-1853 Cr
Parnell, Mattie V to B. L. Ellsberry 10-31-1870 (no return) Cr
Parnell, Virginia A. to Lycurgus Robertson 12-25-1857 Sh
Parr, Alice T. to Nathan Lee 11-22-1884 (3-6-1885) L
Parr, Almedia C. V. to Wiley P. Sugg 12-8-1855 L
Parr, Augusta to Thomas Franklin 7-21-1877 (7-22-1877) L B
Parr, Belle to Robert Pitts 6-12-1880 (6-13-1880) L B
Parr, Cordelia to John W. Halliburton 12-22-1884 (12-24-1884) L
Parr, Dolly J. to Andrew J. Altum 12-8-1838 (12-13-1838) O
Parr, Dolly to Andrew J. Cross 7-19-1840 Sh
Parr, Edwina? to John Soward 2-24-1876 (no return) Dy
Parr, Elen to David Gray 8-17-1866 O
Parr, Emma R. to John J. Bailey 6-18-1851 F
Parr, Emma to John McCoy 3-28-1883 L
Parr, Fannie to Henry Tytus 3-7-1883 (3-15-1883) L
Parr, Frances A. to John W. Vaughn 12-21-1843 Sh
Parr, Frances E. to Charles K. Jones 2-19-1850 (2-20-1850) L
Parr, Henrietter to Lewis Jones 1-11-1874 L B
Parr, Lou to Sandy Maggard 1-12-1878 Dy
Parr, Lucy to Sylar Pierson 4-5-1870 (5-1-1870) L
Parr, Martha to D. D. Vaden 7-29-1856 G
Parr, Mary Ellen to Henry H. Cherry 4-28-1877 (not executed) L
Parr, Mary to J. W. Diggs 2-12-1878 (2-13-1878) Dy
Parr, Mary to Nick Braden 4-1-1880 L B
Parr, Mary to William Pickard 2-28-1848 (2-29-1848) O
Parr, Matilda F. to James Eison 12-29-1874 L
Parr, Matilda T. to William H. Wright 5-9-1848 (5-10-1848) L
Parr, Mitt to Allen Eison 2-13-1879 L B
Parr, Mittie to George McNairy 3-11-1878 (not executed) L
Parr, Rainer to George Dunlap 10-14-1878 (10-16-1878) L B
Parr, Rebecca to Hamilton Savage 2-17-1857 (2-18-1857) Hr
Parr, Sarah to Jasper Sumerow 8-2-1872 (8-3-1872) L B

Parris, Alpha Jane to Andrew Thomas King 3-7-1852 (3-9-1852) Hr
Parris, Jane to James M. Burnett 11-26-1853 (11-27-1853) G
Parris, Susan V. to William Gibson 2-28-1861 (3-7-1861) Hr
Parrish, A. M. to James Matthews 7-14-1840 (7-16-1840) Ma
Parrish, A. W. to Francis M. Roberts 1-30-1861 We
Parrish, Alsa J. to William H. Bryant 12-30-1846 Ma
Parrish, B. J. to J. A. Brooks 1-26-1859 Ma
Parrish, Bettie to Wm. Gardner 11-12-1867 (11-13-1867) Dy
Parrish, Caroline to James Buckley 2-13-1857 We
Parrish, E. E. to Jas. R. Erbridge 12-9-1852 We
Parrish, Elizabeth to Marion Armstrong 9-19-1853 G
Parrish, Emelin to Shim Cook 2-19-1867 (2-21-1867) Ma
Parrish, Emily J. to Benj. F. Farmer 11-6-1865 Dy
Parrish, Janettie A. to A. A. Kellow 12-27-1876 Dy
Parrish, Jo Ann E. to B. W. M. Warner 10-28-1844 (no return) F
Parrish, Katie Ida to Hartwell P. Tucker 2-17-1857 Sh
Parrish, Lucinda to Murry Saunders 7-15-1867 (7-16-1867) Dy
Parrish, Margaret J. to Joseph H. Davie 2-22-1859 We
Parrish, Martha K. to W. A. Colley 6-6-1865 Hn
Parrish, Martha R. to W. A. Davidson 6-23-1868 O
Parrish, Martha to Alfred Hill 9-7-1870 (9-18-1870) F B
Parrish, Martha to William W. Kirby 10-30-1855 O
Parrish, Mary Ann to Henry Nichold 5-7-1851 (5-8-1851) G
Parrish, Mary Elizabeth to William E. Stewart 9-21-1860 (9-23-1860) Ma
Parrish, Mattie J. to William C. Shelton 12-17-1867 (12-19-1867) Ma
Parrish, Mildred A. to Benj. A. Mosley 10-7-1867 (10-16-1867) T
Parrish, Miss to W. B. Abbington 9-30-1850 We
Parrish, Nancy S. to Jesse A. Shanklin 12-30-1857 We
Parrish, Parthena to William Cates 11-18-1839 Hr
Parrish, S. N. to W. A. Davis 2-1-1866 G
Parrish, Salina to M. D. Hodge 12-31-1872 (1-1-1873) Dy
Parrish, Sarah to T. P. Stewart 2-5-1868? (1-6-1868) O
Parrish, Susan to John Hix 9-25-1850 G
Parrott, E. F. (Mrs.) to J. A. Blackburn 2-9-1869 (no return) Dy
Parrott, Elmina to John L. Chappell 12-18-1838 Ma
Parrott, P. E. to J. W. McKinstry 11-16-1869 (11-17-1869) F
Parrott, Sallie to W. C. Cruchfield 10-30-1867 (no return) Hy
Parrow, Elizabeth Ann to Nathan P. Robeson 11-14-1851 Be
Parsley, Jessee to J. E. Burks 12-5-1883 L
Parsley, Nancy S. T. to S. P. Andrews 12-13-1870 Dy
Parsley, Nora to J. E. Burks 2-16-1886 L
Parson, Caty to Thomas J. Hampton 12-23-1841 Cr
Parson, Louisa to Amos Roach 9-25-1849 Cr
Parson, Mary F. to Charles H. Williams 2-16-1860 Hn
Parson, Nancy to J. C. Butler 9-24-1868 G
Parsons, Ann to Wm. Edwin Barnes 11-27-1855 Sh
Parsons, Chloe L. to Hubbard R. Sweet 5-1-1863 Sh
Parsons, Elizabeth to John A. Young 4-10-1866 Cr
Parsons, Elizabeth to Wm. J. Brimley 2-23-1857 (3-8-1857) T
Parsons, Fannie E. to J. R. Stone 12-20-1870 (12-21-1870) L
Parsons, Indiana to Joseph O. Freeman 5-14-1859 (5-16-1859) T
Parsons, Lowina A. to Thos. Parsons 2-15-1857 Cr
Parsons, Lucinda to William Hicks 6-9-1859 Hn
Parsons, Mariah to James Whiteker 2-27-1864 Hn
Parsons, Mary to John W. King 11-5-1869 (11-9-1869) Cr
Parsons, Mary to Saml. Jones 9-8-1857 T
Parsons, Matilda M. to Jesse Palmer 4-15-1843 (4-16-1843) T
Parsons, Sarah F. to James S. Whitehorn 11-27-1869 (11-28-1869) Cr
Parsons, Sarah Jane to Joseph C. Sellers 5-25-1850 Cr
Parsons, Sarah ?. to W. H. Harris 11-8-1869 (11-9-1869) Cr
Partee, Ada to Robert Coachman 7-8-1880 L B
Partee, Ann to Thomas Nelson 1-22-1878 Hy
Partee, Drucilla F. to Algernon S. Oldham 7-9-1856 (no return) L
Partee, Jane to Alford Patterson 4-19-1882 (4-27-1882) L B
Partee, Laura E. to Robert H. Oldham 1-8-1851 L
Partee, Mary J. to Henry Dickson 6-14-1869 (no return) Hy
Partee, Mary to Ed Jones 11-16-1882 L
Partee, Mary to Spencer Fuller 10-9-1878 (10-10-1878) L B
Partee, Narcissa H. to John J. Nelson 9-26-1849 L
Partee, Sarah C. to Pressley Glass 12-20-1848 L
Parteet, Cerilla J. to W. J. Weaver 2-18-1869 (no return) Dy
Parten, Pernethia E. to W.A. McCuan 10-4-1867 (no return) Hn
Parten, Susan L. to John H. Hensley 5-12-1858 G
Parting, Amy to Zachariah McLune 1-5-1859 We
Partlow, Mary Ann to Lucien Mayo 12-21-1859 (12-22-1859) T
Partlow, Mary E. to William L. White 9-9-1839 (no return) F
Partlow, Nancy J. to Lucian Maye 5-31-1866 T
Partlow, Uminie to James Williams 9-11-1873 T
Partridge, Jane to Ickabad Flowers 12-21-1833 Hr
Partridge, Nancy(Ann) to Bailey Mayfield 8-1-1833 (8-7-1833) Hr
Pascal, Racheal to NiNicholass Fortune 4-30-1834 Hn
Pascal, Rebecca to Andrew Dorron 12-10-1840 Hn
Pascal, Savana T. E. to John T. Jones 1-19-1874 (1-21-1874) L
Paschal, Crissa to Samuel W. Wilson 3-12-1863 Hn
Paschal, Elizabeth to John Shaull 8-13-1844 (8-14-1844) F
Paschal, Hettie to R. H. Osborne 8-3-1881 L
Paschal, Jane to _____ Paschal 10-22-1845 Hn

Paschal, M. A. to J. T. Harpole 6-23-1872 (9-26-1872) O
Paschal, Margaret to Aquila Paschal 4-20-1842 Hn
Paschal, Martha A. to Thompson H. Higgs 7-17-1862 (no return) We
Paschal, Mary J. to Soloman Holden 12-10-1869 (12-12-1869) L
Paschal, Rebecca to Hugh McKelvy 1-3-1860 Hn
Paschal, Sarah to E. E. Rinks 11-6-1864 Mn
Paschal, Sarah to Geo. W. David 12-9-1845 (12-10-1845) F
Paschal, Sela B. to Charles B. Nanney 12-3-1862 We
Paschall, Atila to James M. Boyd 11-7-1846 Hn
Paschall, Cincinattia to Alfred H. Peeples 9-16-1860 We
Paschall, Dolly to Thomas Mooney 1-25-1839 Hn
Paschall, Dyanna to Richard Mason 3-12-1862 We
Paschall, Frances to James Barton 1-10-1849 Hn
Paschall, Jane D. to C. P. Orr 12-31-1844 Hn
Paschall, Lucy to John B. McGehee 2-26-1845 Hn
Paschall, Martha J. to James C. Turner 8-6-1861 We
Paschall, Mary A. to Thos. D. Courts 5-17-1846 Hn
Paschall, Mary E. to Peter B. Pirtle 9-21-1858 We
Paschall, Mary F. to J. A. Sheridan 1-25-1866 Hn
Paschall, N. J. to E. D. McGehee 2-5-1867 Hn
Paschall, Rebecca M. to J. R. Nicholas 11-1-1860 We
Paschall, Sarah Jan to J. P. Orr 9-27-1866 Hn
Paschall, Sarah to Lewis? Doran 12-12-1844 Hn
Paschall, Susan to Robert Wilson 5-17-1846 Hn
Paschell, Emily to Ezekeal Pope 11-12-1857 (no return) We
Pass (Parr), Missiniah G. to Schuylar H. Roberts 5-11-1841 Sh
Paste, Louisiana to Wm. Lemons (Clemons) 5-11-1864 Sh
Pasteur, G. A. to J. R. Simpson 2-19-1866 (2-20-1866) Cr
Patatersen, Elizabeth (Mrs.) to E. B. McNab 11-2-1864 Sh
Pate, A. M. to Jefferson Moore 12-26-1868 (no return) Dy
Pate, Ann to Walter S. Fuqua 5-20-1863 Cr
Pate, Ann to Walter S. Fuqua 5-20-1863 (no return) Cr
Pate, Ashley? W. to David W. Henry 7-29-1861 (no return) Cr
Pate, C. L. to Israel Muldrow 11-19-1877 (11-20-1877) O B
Pate, Caroline to C. J. Evert 12-28-1855 (no return) Cr
Pate, Catherine to Richard Dudley 7-18-1872 Cr B
Pate, Dicy to Miles L. Davidson 1-30-1840 G
Pate, E. B. to T. W. Pate 8-2-1876 O
Pate, Edny to Cullin Benson 7-1-1835 Hr
Pate, Elizabeth to Henry Pryor 10-21-1829 (10-22-1829) O
Pate, Elizabeth to James B. Benson 11-30-1836 H
Pate, Elizabeth to Richd. Simmons 12-11-1870 (12-15-1870) Cr B
Pate, Elizabeth to Weston Kealthley 11-14-1853 G
Pate, Ella F. to J. D. B. Tipton 8-15-1874 (8-16-1874) Dy
Pate, Hannah to E. S. Wakefield 7-20-1881 (no return) L
Pate, Lorenza to Matthew Young 2-13-1830 (2-14-1830) O
Pate, Louisa to William Burk 3-26-1859 (no return) We
Pate, M. E. to W. B. Brewer 11-24-1875 Dy
Pate, M. J. to H. H. Browder 4-25-1863 (4-26-1863) Dy
Pate, M. J. to Jo Green Ferguson 11-30-1870 (nor return) Dy
Pate, M. J. to Smith C. Kerby 5-5-1860 O
Pate, Margarete D. L to W. W. Hughlett 3-10-1862 (no return) We
Pate, Martha Ann to T. H. Marshall 2-23-1869 G
Pate, Martha E. to Archelus B. Branch 4-17-1850 (4-21-1850) G
Pate, Martha J. to J. W. Connell 10-27-1868 G
Pate, Martha to Henry Long 9-8-1838 (9-11-1838) G
Pate, Martha to P. T. Walton 5-23-1865 (no return) Cr
Pate, Mary H. to Melton A. Killough 2-16-1841 Cr
Pate, Mary J. to Geo. J. Parish 1-27-1859 We
Pate, Mary to A. L. Thomas 10-3-1849 Hn
Pate, Mary to James Cannon 12-12-1846 (12-13-1846) G
Pate, Nancy to A. B. Alphine 9-27-1863 G
Pate, Olive to Crawford Michell 1-22-1867 (1-24-1867) Dy
Pate, Penelope to Robert Melton 7-20-1840 (8-30-1840) G
Pate, S. V. to J. K. Pate 2-27-1873 (3-2-1873) Dy
Pate, Sallie F. to A. P. McCallister 10-20-1869 (10-21-1869) Dy
Pate, Sallie to Bryant Fitzhugh 11-18-1867 Dy
Pate, Sarah to Abraham Enleo 7-12-1836 (1-12-1836?) O
Pate, Sarah to Edward S. Ham 3-16-1867 Cr
Pate, Sary Ann to Wm. Crutchfield 12-15-1858 We
Pate, Susan A. E. to James W. Reynolds 7-23-1857 L
Pate, Susan E. to Hayden Ellis 2-6-1856 We
Pate, Sythia to John E. M. Mayfield 11-10-1836 Hr
Pate, Tennessee to John W. Rushing 9-25-1865 (9-28-1865) Cr
Pate, Victoria to Peter Merriwether 10-30-1878 L B
Pate, Virginia W. to Thos. B. Sellers 12-21-1870 (12-24-1870) O
Pate, Z. S. to William T. Hunter 11-18-1872 (11-19-1872) Dy
Pateet, Maria to Abraham Madison Stout 10-24-1849 Sh
Paten, Martha A. to Saml. McNaire? 5-3-1867 T
Paterick (Patrick), Elizabeth to William Randle 9-27-1843 Sh
Paterick (Patrick), Sarah Ann to George Randal (Randle) 1-8-1845 Sh
Paterson, Juliann to Mathew G. Bagg 10-7-1854 (10-9-1854) Hr
Paterson, Mary to Henry Price 4-10-1869 (4-11-1869) L
Pates (Dates?), Cama to Bill Johnston 11-11-1876 (11-12-1876) L
Pates, Catherine to Joseph Dible 7-19-1877 Hy
Patey, Jane to Harvey W. Connell 11-30-1864 Hn
Paton, Martha E. to C. B. Calhoun 11-4-1863 (no return) Hn
Paton, T. P. to David Bradley 6-10-1859 Cr
Patrick, Annie C. to Page H. Patrick 1-23-1861 (1-24-1861) Dy
Patrick, Barbia R. to Caleb R. Clements 7-15-1856 G
Patrick, Celeste C. to John A. Hudson 11-6-1854 (11-7-1854) Sh
Patrick, Currilla A. to Charles A. Hayward 4-10-1862 Sh
Patrick, Cynthia A. to Stephen B. Maner 1-1-1858 (1-10-1858) G
Patrick, Eliza Jane to Jason Greer 9-12-1851 (9-14-1851) G
Patrick, Fredonia O. to Martin T. Armstrong 12-15-1857 Sh
Patrick, Harriet A. to James H. Rogers 11-24-1855 (11-28-1855) Sh
Patrick, Hollan to William Bailey 6-3-1839 (6-13-1839) L
Patrick, L. A. to C. W. Rodgers 12-8-1875 (12-9-1875) Dy
Patrick, Louisa C. to Kenneth Garrett 8-1-1853 (8-2-1853) Sh
Patrick, Mary A. to J. L. Lewis 6-29-1869 G
Patrick, Mary C. to Anthony M. Clement 11-1-1852 G
Patrick, Mary E. to John H. Jones 1-13-1851 (1-14-1851) Sh
Patrick, Mary to William Williams 4-2-1873 (4-3-1873) Dy
Patrick, Nancy E. to J. B. Aslin 9-9-1852 G
Patrick, Nancy to Thompson White 5-20-1863 G
Patrick, Olive P. to William Ramsey 1-16-1830 (1-17-1830) Hr
Patrick, S. C. (Mrs.) to Jesse Bazemore 4-6-1864 Sh
Patrick, Sallie to Robert Miller 12-22-1869 F B
Patrick, Sarah to P. L. Arnold 12-31-1846 Sh
Patrick, Sarah to Thomas Riden 7-2-1839 Ma
Patrick, Susan to H. W. Guy 6-8-1881 (6-10-1881) L
Patridge, Louisa A. to William Pipkins 1-16-1863 Mn
Patridge, Martha to Calvin Jackson 3-23-1852 Hr
Patridge, Susan to Joseph Hendly 2-24-1839 Hr
Patsy, Miller to Sam Pewett 11-26-1870 (no return) Hy
Patten, L. E. to R. F. Elder 1-1-1866 (1-7-1866) Cr
Patten, Malinda to Abraham Branch 12-17-1867 G B
Patten, Mary A. to S. D. Redus 2-20-1858 Sh
Patten, O. J. to T. W. Hendron 2-5-1867 Hy
Patten, Sally to J. M. Delany 12-6-1865 Cr
Patten, Sarah E. A. to Wilson F. Mathews 7-7-1846 We
Patterson, A. J. to J. W. Diggs 9-22-1852 Hn
Patterson, Alsey to Jim Delap 8-11-1866 (8-12-1866) F B
Patterson, Amanda to John Scales 2-26-1872 (2-27-1872) Cr
Patterson, Amanda to John Scates 3-4-1870 (no return) Cr
Patterson, Ann H. to Jas. H. Smith 7-5-1858 G
Patterson, Artemesia to James C. Bowden 2-26-1855 (no return) Hn
Patterson, Betsey to John W. Odam 8-7-1821 Sh
Patterson, C. G. to William Cass 12-31-1860 (1-1-1861) Sh
Patterson, C. L. to Thomas B. Veasey 1-29-1848 Hn
Patterson, C. P. to J. T. Morgan 10-30-1869 (11-3-1869) T
Patterson, Callie to Natan Partee 12-23-1882 (12-26-1882) L
Patterson, Caroline to Alexander Russell 7-6-1865 Mn
Patterson, Caroline to Jack Kile 12-31-1869 (1-1-1870) Cr
Patterson, Caroline to William Hughes 12-28-1840 Ma
Patterson, Cathanne to John Hooper 2-10-1858 Hn
Patterson, Celia A. to William H. Highfill 9-11-1852 (9-19-1852) Hr
Patterson, Celia to Jim Payne 12-18-1875 (no return) Hy
Patterson, Charlotte to John sr. Henson 3-28-1859 (3-29-1859) Hr
Patterson, Desdamonia to Samuel G. Turner 6-19-1863 G
Patterson, E. A. to E. W. Penick 9-15-1853 Hn
Patterson, E. B. to W. J. Mays 10-1-1855 (10-2-1855) G
Patterson, Ela to Calvin Henderson 9-18-1842 Ma
Patterson, Eliza J. to Isaac Harlin 5-25-1863 (5-27-1863) Cr
Patterson, Eliza Jane to Isaac Harlin 5-25-1863 Cr
Patterson, Eliza Jane to Wallace Rivers 1-19-1871 F B
Patterson, Eliza to Adam Fowler 11-25-1865 (4-14-1866) Cr
Patterson, Elizabeth A. to Columbus W. Caleb 1-12-1852 G
Patterson, Elizabeth to H. W. Fowler 10-5-1854 We
Patterson, Elizabeth to J. C. Looney 1-7-1864 Hn
Patterson, Elizabeth to S. S. Mathis 10-18-1861 G
Patterson, Elizabeth to William T. Coker 5-9-1860 (no return) Hy
Patterson, Emily to John M. Crockett 7-15-1859 (7-17-1859) G
Patterson, Emma A. to John M. Dickson 12-18-1866 (12-20-1866) Cr
Patterson, Frances to Thomas Clark 8-19-1845 Ma
Patterson, Francis to James B. James 5-5-1862 (5-10-1862) Sh
Patterson, Hellen to Harvy Mitchum 6-1-1866 (6-7-1866) Cr
Patterson, Henrietta to Harry Wirt 12-27-1867 (12-31-1867) F B
Patterson, Hester A. to Abner A. Evins 2-15-1848 G
Patterson, Isabella to William Robinson 6-10-1844 Sh
Patterson, Jane to Jack Adams 12-51867 G B
Patterson, Jane to James P. Alexander 2-20-1829 G
Patterson, Jarette to B. F. Short 11-12-1862 G
Patterson, Jessie M. D. to Gideon M. Bransford 11-8-1875 (11-11-1875) O
Patterson, Julia A. to Clemuel Carroll 8-21-1864 Mn
Patterson, Julia E. to Sidney C. Russell 12-16-1867 F
Patterson, Julia G. to James Brown 8-31-1860 Sh
Patterson, Julia to R. A. Brown 3-22-1877 (3-23-1877) L
Patterson, Julia to Wm. O'Brien 2-22-1861 Sh
Patterson, Lavinia to Willis Bell 1-27-1876 Dy
Patterson, Lexanah to N. W. Pigue 12-27-1855 G
Patterson, Louisa F. to Henry J. F. Davidson 7-26-1860 We
Patterson, Louisa to Ben Franklin Bosheers 8-14-1869 (3?-15-1869) Ma
Patterson, Louisa to D. H. McLure 7-7-1852 Cr

Brides

Patterson, Lucinda to James Turner 7-23-1862 G
Patterson, Lucinda to John Culee? 2-12-1867 (2-13-1867) Cr
Patterson, Lucinda to William P. Howlett 10-1-1866 (10-2-1866) Ma
Patterson, M. A. to D. C. David 6-22-1858 Sh
Patterson, Malinda to Levy Young 2-18-1832 (2-21-1832) Ma
Patterson, Malvina E. to F. M. Hooper 1-21-1861 (1-22-1861) Hr
Patterson, Margaret C. to Ezra I. Arnold 3-23-1848 G
Patterson, Margaret to Newton Mayfield 1-24-1852 G
Patterson, Margaret to Thomas Daniel 2-14-1876 Dy
Patterson, Margaret to Vinson M. L. Taylor 9-17-1844 (9-19-1844) G
Patterson, Margarett H. to Wiley W. Thomas 7-16-1849 (7-17-1849) Ma
Patterson, Margarett to Levi J. Turner 4-9-1855 (4-10-1855) G
Patterson, Marina to Stephen Outerbridge 8-19-1845 Ma
Patterson, Marion to Thomas Henderson 11-2-1852 Ma
Patterson, Martha Ann to Dick Rivers 2-12-1870 (2-13-1870) F B
Patterson, Martha C. to Samuel H. Wiley 1-12-1860 Hn
Patterson, Martha E. to Samuel Williamson 12-15-1859 O
Patterson, Martha S. to Jabez Bingham 10-1-1855 Ma
Patterson, Martha to Alfred Flowers 12-26-1845 (12-28-1845) G
Patterson, Martha to J. W. Wilson 5-10-1879 (5-11-1879) L
Patterson, Martha to Sancho Clay 9-21-1868 Cr
Patterson, Mary (Mrs.) to J. V. Smith 12-18-1852 (no return) F
Patterson, Mary (Mrs.) to Reuben Daniels 5-30-1864 (6-4-1864) Sh
Patterson, Mary A. to Edward V. Corbitt 1-16-1852 (1-29-1852) Sh
Patterson, Mary A. to S. P. Phillips 1-23-1850 F
Patterson, Mary Ann to John Denning 11-30-1842 Hn
Patterson, Mary Ann to Silas M. Kemp 10-14-1844 (no return) We
Patterson, Mary E. A. to Wellington Scearce 2-15-1860 O
Patterson, Mary E. to Thomas J. Boon 10-21-1862 G
Patterson, Mary J. to C. R. Mount 5-29-1861 (could be Apr) G
Patterson, Mary J. to H. W. Mooring 10-11-1841 Cr
Patterson, Mary J. to Samuel Kellow 12-26-1867 G
Patterson, Mary Jane to Ezekiel F. Voss 12-28-1847 (12-30-1847) L
Patterson, Rosy to David Thomas 3-2-1867 Hy
Patterson, Mary to Hiram Hammon 10-4-1828 O
Patterson, Mary to James Turner 12-5-1842 (12-8-1842) G
Patterson, Mary to Jas. S. McWherter 12-20-1845 (12-21-1845) G
Patterson, Mary to John Crockett 10-15-1833 (10-17-1833) G
Patterson, Mary to William Patterson 12-29-1845 (1-7-1846) G
Patterson, Mary to William Taylor 3-7-1846 (3-11-1846) G
Patterson, Maryana to William Freeman 1-17-1870 (1-18-1870) T
Patterson, Matilda to Malachi Holloman 8-5-1857 Ma
Patterson, Milly to I. C. Thornton 11-23-1858 We
Patterson, Minerva to George Dortch 8-16-1867 (8-18-1867) F B
Patterson, Molba? to Gip Jones 2-28-1871 (3-2-1871) Cr
Patterson, Mollie to Orange Whittaker 1-17-1876 (no return) Dy
Patterson, Mooney to Andrew Walker 9-9-1869 (9-11-1869) T
Patterson, N. M. to J. A. Torrey 2-2-1858 Sh
Patterson, Nacy C. to Pleasant McBride 12-5-1854 Cr
Patterson, Nancy J. to Henry McClanahan 2-2-1869 (2-7-1869) F B
Patterson, Nancy J. to James C. Cope 2-21-1861 (no return) Hn
Patterson, Nancy M. to Montreal Newsom 6-4-1857 Sh
Patterson, Nancy to Freeman Cross 6-19-1837 (6-20-1837) G
Patterson, Nancy to Louis Matheny 8-17-1861 (8-31-1861) Dy
Patterson, Nancy to Soloman Nevill 10-12-1840 Cr
Patterson, Nancy to W. F. Arnold 10-30-1867 G
Patterson, Naomi to Thomas Carlton 2-23-1853 (2-24-1853) G
Patterson, Octave S. to James Graham 7-17-1855 Sh
Patterson, Parilee to Milton Hart 11-19-1860 Cr
Patterson, Parilee to Milton J. Hart 11-19-1860 (11-20-1860) Cr
Patterson, Permelia to Thomas Overton 10-5-1869 Ma
Patterson, Phila to R. A. Browder 11-27-1871 (11-29-1871) O
Patterson, Rebecca to Andy Hall 10-20-1858 G B
Patterson, Rosietta to Archile Rivers 9-24-1870 F B
Patterson, Sarah A. to Jack Gammons 3-13-1868 (1?-14-1868) Dy
Patterson, Sarah to C. W. Greer 1-13-1874 (1-18-1874) Dy
Patterson, Sarah to James P. Reed 3-7-1831 (3-?-1831) G
Patterson, Sarah to John M. Wells 9-27-1845 (9-28-1845) G
Patterson, Sarah to John Pitts 9-3-1855 (9-4-1855) G
Patterson, Sarah to William Hood 11-26-1848 L
Patterson, Susan C. to Eldridge J. Gallion 3-10-1863 Hn
Patterson, Susan C. to F. M. Griffin 2-12-1859 (2-15-1859) G
Patterson, Susan M. to Andrew J. Webber 1-1-1851 G
Patterson, Susan to Nathaniel Henderson 11-1-1859 (11-2-1859) Ma
Patterson, Susan to Thos. E. Clark 4-26-1851 (4-30-1851) Sh
Patterson, Tabitha to Hampton Smith 3-11-1861 (3-15-1861) G
Patterson, Telia to Alfred Reives 9-7-1872 Cr B
Patterson, Temperance A. to George C. Ayers 11-25-1868 Ma
Patterson, Texan to E. C. Butler 5-15-1866 G
Patterson, Tilia to John Hart 8-31-1870 (no return) Cr
Patterson, Vicey to Edward Covington 5-18-1859 Ma
Patteson, Ann H. to Phillip Mitchell 9-17-1867 (9-25-1867) F B
Pattillo, Jennie to Henry Fraser 1-2-1867 F B
Pattillo, Mary E. to Amariah Rodgers 10-9-1844 Sh
Pattilo, Amanda to Wm. F. Crook 6-25-1849 (no return) F
Pattilo, Paulina C. to Augustus Pearce 1-9-1851 Sh
Pattison, Annie E. to W. B. Mitchell 1-6-1859 Sh

Pattison, Mary to Herman Harrison 10-4-1828 (9-18-1828?) O
Pattison, Mary to Plase Ezzell 5-19-1873 (5-29-1873) Cr B
Patton, Armelia to William L. Hall 12-11-1847 (12-23-1847) F
Patton, Bettie to Cornelius Shaw 1-25-1883 L
Patton, Eliza F. to R. B. Shepard 3-16-1857 G
Patton, Elizabeth O. to James M. Neel 11-22-1841 (11-23-1841) F
Patton, Emaly V. to James Tucker 1-23-1848 (1-27-1848) G
Patton, Fanny to James Waddington 1-28-1875 (1-29-1875) O
Patton, Frances to W. G. Day 12-7-1853 (no return) F
Patton, H. J. to M. S. Rhodes 12-11-1847 (12-23-1847) F
Patton, Isabell S. A. to Samuel M. Crabtree 12-6-1843 Cr
Patton, Jane A. to Thos. A. Flippin 2-27-1852 We
Patton, Liddie to Robt. Holmes 4-15-1863 G
Patton, Louisa to Francis M. Glover 5-7-1854 (no return) Cr
Patton, M. E. to W. P. Wilkins 10-12-1869 (10-13-1869) Cr
Patton, M. H. to A. H. Patton 11-27-1845 Cr
Patton, Maggie to Polk Malone 11-7-1872 (no return) Hy
Patton, Margaret C. to E. G. Coleman 10-12-1847 F
Patton, Margaret to James N. Patton 5-9-1861 (no return) Hy
Patton, Martha Ann to Thomas Dodson 10-21-1844 (10-23-1844) F
Patton, Martha W. to Mathew M. Taylor 8-6-1856 (8-7-1856) G
Patton, Mary J. to J. R. Campbell 1-9-1858 Cr
Patton, Mary J. to Thomas A. Overton 1-7-1858 Cr
Patton, Mary Jane to Jerimiah W. Robertson 2-11-1854 (2-19-1854) Hr
Patton, Mary Jane to Zacheus Wilson 8-30-1848 Hn
Patton, Mary to Josiah Hodges 7-10-1839 Ma
Patton, Mary to S. C. Wright 2-27-1857 Cr
Patton, Mellissa to Andrew J. Haynes 1-26-1852 (no return) Cr
Patton, Mollie E. to Stephen P. Townes 5-4-1864 G
Patton, Mollie to Fed Green 10-8-1872 (10-10-1872) L
Patton, Pairlee to Washington C. Enochs 10-9-1856 Cr
Patton, R. E. to M. V. Davidson 10-24-1866 Dy
Patton, Rosa E. to G. E. Trimble 12-19-1866 Hy
Patton, Rosy to A. G. Love 11-22-1870 (11-24-1870) Cr
Patton, Sallie E. to M. W. Matthews 11-3-1883 (11-4-1883) L
Patton, Sarah A. to Richard Webb 9-1-1864 G
Patton, Sophronia to R. L. Shaw 10-7-1865 (10-10-1865) F
Patton, Tommie to Calvin L. Barringer 12-24-1862 (no return) F
Patton, Willie E. to J. W. Zellner 11-3-1866 (11-6-1866) F
Paty, Louisa to Augustus Guevokowsky 4-7-1857 Sh
Paul, Elizabeth to John S. Causey 11-22-1853 Hn
Paul, Lizzie to Wm. Harris 2-19-1876 (4-15-1876) Dy
Paulock, Ann to George E. Harrison 4-7-1847 (4-14-1847) O
Paulson, Laura J. to R. M. Haden 6-23-1869 (6-24-1869) F
Pavatt, Lennia C. to C. K. Wyly ?-?-1839 Be CC
Pavid, Rosaline to H. D. Stallings 5-21-1854 Sh
Paxton, Eliza M. to James Oldham 4-21-1853 Sh
Paxton, Fanny to Tapley Oldham 1-20-1853 Sh
Paxton, N. J. to J. Jessen 10-22-1859 (10-25-1859) Sh
Payen (Payne?), Marth_ to Joseph Balderson 9-12-1838 (9-13-1838) L
Payne, Adelia P. to Ezekiel B. Owen 9-29-1832 Sh
Payne, Ann to Moses Adkins 1-7-1874 (1-8-1874) T
Payne, Appe to John L. Bukley 2-4-1851 (2-5-1851) L
Payne, Christiana to Thomas S. Carney 6-6-1858 We
Payne, Cloah to James Gorley 8-9-1844 (8-11-1844) O
Payne, E. E. to A. J. Payne 2-12-1877 Hy
Payne, Eliza to Samuel McCracken 11-12-1849 Cr
Payne, Elizabeth F. to T. H. Walton 6-23-1862 (no return) Dy
Payne, Georgeanna to James Blaydes 12-25-1873 T
Payne, H. T. to Humphrey Cobb 11-26-1828 (no return) Sh
Payne, Harriett to W. M. Parker 1-4-1838 Sh
Payne, J. A. to David A. Gardner 2-15-1870 (2-16-1870) Dy
Payne, Jane E. to William Cobb 12-17-1829 Sh
Payne, Jonnah to James B. Bird 7-24-1851 G
Payne, Josephine to Thomas Moore 5-30-1859 Sh
Payne, Julia Ann to John Ragan 12-2-1852 (12-9-1852) O
Payne, Laura A. to John F. Miller 4-11-1871 (4-12-1871) T
Payne, Lizzie to Wm. Carney 6-18-1878 (no return) Hy
Payne, Lucinda to Madison Wade 6-17-1869 G B
Payne, M. E. to Andrew Burkin 4-3-1867 G
Payne, M. F. to J. J. Norment 11-5-1869 (no return) Hy
Payne, Maggie to Daniel Hayden 9-21-1869 (9-24-1869) T
Payne, Malinda E. to James E. Bloyde 4-33-1866 T
Payne, Manerva to Calup Wyatt 1-11-1872 Hy
Payne, Martha P. to Fred. R. Smith 10-2-1852 (no return) L
Payne, Martha to Simon Adams 12-26-1871 Hy
Payne, Mary (Mrs.) to John G. Hawthorn 6-24-1841 Sh
Payne, Mary to Ben N. Eskridge 9-19-1858 We
Payne, Mary to George W. Redding 12-16-1869 (12-23-1869) F
Payne, Mary to J. R. Manasco 9-24-1861 (9-27-1861) T
Payne, Mary to John Conner 9-26-1848 L
Payne, Mary to R. F. Compton 11-25-1851 Sh
Payne, Matilda to Burrell Patterson 8-16-1869 G
Payne, Nancy C. to Thomas Kersey 12-29-1844 Sh
Payne, Nancy C. to William H. Fowler 12-26-1846 (12-27-1847?) F
Payne, Nancy C. to Wm. E. M. Graham 8-16-1843 Hr
Payne, Perneacy to Alex H. Scates 9-28-1842 Cr

Payne, Rachel S.? to James F. Dickson 11-22-1865 (11-23-1865) T
Payne, Rachel to Peter Walker 8-12-1874 Hy
Payne, Rebecca Anne to James W. Brown 2-3-1848 Sh
Payne, Rebecca to James H. D. Parrish 8-3-1860 We
Payne, Rebecca to Scott Smith 12-3-1872 (12-4-1872) T
Payne, Rose to John Evans 12-21-1867 (12-26-1867) T
Payne, S. L. to S. P. Green 7-21-1862 (no return) Hy
Payne, Sally to Samuel Parker 4-12-1838 Sh
Payne, Sarah to Green Morris 11-26-1870 Hy
Payne, Susan to J. H. Shelton 10-12-1867 (10-13-1867) Dy
Payole, Paulien to Silvain Davis 6-16-1864 Sh
Payton, Sarah B. to Elisha W. Harris 11-19-1846 (11-24-1846) F
Pea?, Sarah to Joseph Jordan 1-8-1879 (1-9-1879) L
Peace (Pearce), Eleanora to Paul C. Key (Kay) 7-13-1846 Sh
Peacock, Emily to Anderson Cates 8-5-1848 (8-13-1848) O
Peacock, Fannie to Nelson Motley 3-4-1875 (3-5-1875) Dy
Peacock, Lucy Ann to Wm. J. Graham 8-7-1851 O
Peacock, Maria B. to Wm. P. Fisher 4-17-1839 Sh
Peacock, Mary Ann to John B. Vickery 2-27-1861 Hn
Peacock, Nancy to Thomas Kirkland 11-29-1847 Hn
Peacock, Octavy to Henry Townsend 11-3-1880 (11-4-1880) Dy
Peacock, Percinda to Steven M. Thompson 6-4-1859 Cr
Peacock, Sarah to John J. Sawyers 9-27-1867 (9-28-1867) T
Peacock, Sarah to Thomas F. Bruce 1-28-1846 (2-12-1846) O
Peak, Catharine (Miss) to Thos. Alexander 1-28-1858 Sh
Peak, F. H. to R. H. Herndon 12-24-1854 (no return) F
Peak, Frances M. to R., jr. Glenn 10-29-1846 Sh
Peak, Malinda to Allen G. Stewart 4-5-1869 G
Peak, Martha to John Sorrels 2-21-1856 Sh
Peak, Mary J. to S. M. Norwood 5-7-1857 Sh
Peak, Susanna to John D. Waldrop 10-18-1842 Hn
Peake, Charity to William Meroney 11-9-1830 Ma
Peake, Henrietta to Martin Conner 9-21-1877 Hy
Peake, Martha E. to J. R. Montgomery 11-14-1844 Sh
Peal, Martha to Joseph Harrison 10-1-1845 (10-2-1845) G
Peal, Martha to William Davis 4-21-1860 (4-22-1860) O
Peal, Sallie to W. N. Howell 3-29-1876 (no return) Hy
Peal, Sarah Ann E. to John C. Bailey 2-3-1862 (no return) Dy
Peal, Sarah to Joel Furgarson 1-1-1845 (1-2-1845) G
Peal, Winaford to Thomas Furgarson 11-17-1845 (11-20-1845) G
Pealey, Patsey to Hulypus Kirk 1-23-1842 Hy
Pearce, Adaline to William J. Baldridge 10-7-1870 G
Pearce, Amanda to Rightmon Jordon 7-30-1843 Be
Pearce, Ann E. to R. L. Veazey 11-29-1862 Hn
Pearce, Caralin to Barton Luster 3-3-1868 (3-4-1868) T
Pearce, Caroline to Jonathan Davis 4-18-1859 G
Pearce, Catharine to G. W. Billings 1-18-1855 Hn
Pearce, Dulla to John Crafton 8-14-1871 (8-17-1871) Cr
Pearce, E. Jane to W. L. McKenzie 11-26-1848 Be
Pearce, E. to Andy Jackson 5-3-1870 G B
Pearce, E. to D. N. Nisler 5-1-1840 Be
Pearce, Eliza to Crockett Ethridge 12-26-1852 Hn
Pearce, Elizabeth to John O. Henderson 6-30-1850 (6-6?-1850) G
Pearce, Elizabeth to Samuel Crowell 5-13-1852 (5-18-1852) Ma
Pearce, Esperann to E. J. Looney 12-28-1844 We
Pearce, F. A. B. to T. D. Foresyth 1-15-1873 Cr
Pearce, Frances to Elias Johnson 12-25-1860 (12-2?-1860) L
Pearce, Harriet E. to W. B. Gibbs 10-5-1854 We
Pearce, I. E. to Hezekiah Butler 6-12-1859 Cr
Pearce, Letha A. to O. L. Morris 4-6-1860 (4-8-1860) G
Pearce, Louiza to Josiah Powel 8-30-1864 G
Pearce, Lucy to John M. Gill 5-10-1845 Sh
Pearce, M. A. to Andy Hamett 4-17-1872 (no return) Cr B
Pearce, M. C. to R. H. Sims 1-2-1859 We
Pearce, Martha A. to Ebenezer Vaughn 3-29-1856 (no return) Hn
Pearce, Martha to Isac Wyatt 1-11-1840 (no return) Hn
Pearce, Martha to Lewis White 2-5-1852 Be CC
Pearce, Martha to Luder(Leeder?) White 2-5-1852 Be
Pearce, Mary Jane to F. W. Hastings 12-28-1856 Hn
Pearce, Mary M. to Wm. J. Rodgers 12-4-1865 (12-6-1865) F
Pearce, Mollie E. (Mrs.) to W. T. (Rev.) Bolling 4-14-1870 G
Pearce, Nancy S. to James D. Spears 9-23-1862 G
Pearce, Nancy to W. J. Hall 4-16-1868 G
Pearce, Pietty to William Priddy 3-4-1847 Sh
Pearce, R. A. to K. L. Ward 2-3-1841 Be
Pearce, Rebecca A. to William D. Johnson 3-27-1864 G
Pearce, Roena H. to James N. Forrest 2-23-1851 Be
Pearce, Sarah Ann to James Nunnery 7-20-1847 Be
Pearce, Sarah E. to Geo. W. Jameson 7-27-1842 Sh
Pearce, Sarah M. to William A. Edwards 2-26-1861 We
Pearce, Sarah to Benjamin F. Brock 10-27-1846 We
Pearce, Sarah to John A. Newbill 12-8-1869 (12-9-1869) Cr
Pearce, Sarena to John Hornsbury 4-14-1862 (no return) Hn
Pearce, Su H. (Mrs.) to Gideon Lewis Cain 4-1-1868 G
Pearce, Vena to Monroe Jones 12-28-1869 (no return) Dy
Pearcy, Harriet to Dempsey Nowell 7-1-1828 Ma
Pearcy, Julia A. to Wm. M. Meals 7-22-1865 (7-25-1866?) Cr

Pearcy, Rosa A. to J. J. Nickols 9-28-1880 (9-29-1880) L
Pearcy, Sarah C. to James B. Booth 7-5-1870 Hy
Pearl, Margret L. to Wm. Walker Willias 5-14-1871 Hy
Pearman, M. A. F. to A. T. Crossett 2-17-1866 (2-20-1866) Cr
Pearman, M. A. to J. B. Crossett 1-8-1864 (no return) Cr
Pearman, Mary Jane to Walter C. Crewes 10-24-1860 (no return) Cr
Pearman, Susan A. to D.? Marshall 1-5-1863 (1-7-1863) Cr
Pearman, Susan A. to M. D. Marshall 1-5-1863 (no return) Cr
Pearmon, M. A. to J. B. Crossett 1-8-1864 (no return) Cr
Pearse, Nancy J. to William F. Winsett 11-11-1866 Hn
Pearson, Bettie to Abe Smith 7-4-1868 (7-10-1868) F B
Pearson, C. E. to J. L. Surratt 11-8-1864 Mn
Pearson, Caroline to Ceasar Chilton 2-28-1883 L
Pearson, Clarrisa to Martin Smith 3-30-1867 (4-14-1867) L B
Pearson, Effarilla to Jery Murphey 5-25-1872 (5-26-1872) Cr B
Pearson, Elizabeth to J. F. Brown 7-24-1854 (no return) F
Pearson, Elizabeth to John Bachelor, jr. 9-2-1865 (9-5-1865) L
Pearson, Elizabeth to Kelly Sanders 3-12-1844 (no return) F
Pearson, Fredonia to Peter Britt 5-29-1871 (5-30-1871) Cr
Pearson, Mary E. to George W. Duncan 11-22-1852 (11-25-1852) Ma
Pearson, Mary T. to Edward T. Transau 12-7-1855 (12-13-1854?) Ma
Pearson, Mary V. to James A. Pearson 12-18-1860 (no return) L
Pearson, Mary W. to Robt. T. Pickens 3-14-1870 (3-15-1870) F
Pearson, Mary to Thomas F. Berry 3-10-1870 Ma
Pearson, Molly A. to Thos. Macbeth 4-15-1864 (4-17-1864) Sh
Pearson, Nancy to Wm. Thomas 12-20-1831 (12-22-1831) Hr
Pearson, R. B. to R. T. Manning 10-28-1868 Hy
Pearson, Sallie A. to Henry Yarbrough 11-10-1858 Ma
Pearson, Sue to John G. Woolfolk 11-3-1868 (11-5-1868) Ma
Pearson, Susan S. to Jas. L. W. Brown 8-9-1854 (8-16-1854) G
Pearson, Tryphena to William W. Turner 11-1-1845 (no return) F
Pearyear, Nancy to Soloman King 6-16-1870 (11-20-1870) L
Peate, Sarah to Adifears Mann 1-16-1869 Hy
Peay, Emily J. to Thomas J. Duncan 4-17-1858 (no return) Hn
Peay, Mary G. to Henry H. Smith 11-17-1853 Hn
Peck, Elizabeth to Thomas Raines 10-29-1851 (10-30-1851) Hr
Peckins, Easter R. to Thomas C. Rogers 8-7-1862 (8-17-1862) O
Peden, Amanda to Charles L. Cate 4-30-1844 Hn
Peden, Calpurnia C. to William Rogers 2-13-1851 Hn
Peden, Parilee A. to John J. Mitchell 1-5-1860 Hn
Peebles, Angeline to Abram Jones 12-25-1867 Hy
Peebles, Ann to Babe Jarrett 5-4-1870 Hy
Peebles, Catharine to Arter Bailey 11-4-1869 (11-9-1869) F B
Peebles, Chany to Bently Cal 4-22-1867 F B
Peebles, Frances to Charles Anderson 12-29-1866 Hy
Peebles, Ida to Samuel A. Bishop 10-15-1873 Hy
Peebles, Martha to James M. Capps 4-14-1864 Be
Peebles, Mary to G. M. Ashley 11-15-1860 Be
Peebles, Mary to Willis Taylor 12-31-1873 Hy
Peebles, Queen to M. Currie 12-18-1878 Hy
Peebles, Siller to Lemuel Wade 7-20-1868 Hy
Peebles, Susanna to John H. Allen 3-1-1876 (no return) Hy
Peel, Arminta to Saml. M. Watt 12-28-1859 (12-29-1859) Sh
Peel, Clarissy to Thomas F. Cate 11-16-1841 (no return) Hn
Peel, Elizabeth to Henry Kincey 12-17-1860 G
Peel, Ester to John T. Deets 8-13-1840 Hn
Peel, Julia to W. J. Follis 10-31-1871 Dy
Peel, Katherine to J. D. Robertson 11-3-1852 Hn
Peel, Louiza to Edward Thedford 11-4-1850 (11-6-1850) G
Peel, Lucinda E. to Daniel M. Bland 12-1-1853 (12-8-1853) Sh
Peel, M. to W. B. Carroll 12-29-1869 G
Peel, Martha to George Blackwood 2-13-1860 Sh
Peel, Mary E. to Peter H. Kinsey 3-19-1850 (3-27-1850) G
Peel, Mary E. to Wm. L. Hays 8-11-1867 Hy
Peel, Mary F. to A. Patrum 1-17-1862 Hn
Peel, Mary F. to William A. Bottoms 1-29-1870 (no return) L
Peel, Rachael to Bryant Caraway 8-23-1852 (8-26-1852) G
Peeler, Anne to George W. Dunn 10-4-1859 Hn
Peeler, Joycy to Joseph Webb 9-20-1854 Hr
Peeler, Martha to George Coats 1-23-1866 T
Peeler, N. E. to Wm. D. Childress 8-1-1861 Be
Peeler, Sarah E. to E.B. Whitley 12-31-1866 (1-1-1867) T
Peeples, Ann to Daniel Cate 1-13-1867 Hn B
Peeples, Emily J. to J. L. Fields 10-4-1854 We
Peeples, Hariet G. to C. T. Edwards 1-16-1856 We
Peeples, J. J. to B. A. L. Rogers 10-29-1856 We
Peeples, Liddie Ann to Peter Muzzall 1-8-1867 Hn
Peeples, Margaret C. to Charles W. Turner 1-24-1860 Hn
Peeples, Nancy E. to Ransom H. Jones 1-28-1858 Hn
Peerson, Mary to Willis Johnston 1-18-1868 (1-19-1868) L B
Peery, Ann to Arcabald Peery 5-5-1844 We
Peery, Donie to J. Buck Finley 1-13-1874 Dy
Peery, Martha A. to Henry Thomas 3-23-1858 (no return) We
Peery, Missy to Prince Powell 8-23-1869 (no return) Dy
Peery, Mollie to M. Sherwood 6-12-1869 (6-13-1869) Dy
Peery, N. J. to E. P. Mays 1-24-1878 Dy
Peery, T. A. to E. P. Tevilla 11-10-1868 Dy

Peet, Harriett to Orange Jones 12-23-1878 Hy
Peete, Ann to Ferry Peete 12-23-1865 (12-25-1865) T
Peete, Minerva to Richard Cooper 2-21-1867 (2-23-1867) T
Peete, Rhody Ann to Lenard Clement 6-1-1866 (6-2-1866) T
Peete, Sallie to Richard E. Bullington 12-27-1869 T
Peete, Susan to Robert Green 3-22-1869 (3-?-1869) T
Peevey, Susan to J. M. Jones 2-4-1861 (2-5-1861) L
Pegram, Martha E. to B. P. Wheeler 5-1-1855 We
Pegram, S. F. to B. A. Crawford 10-29-1857 We
Pegran, Martha T. to Munford Wilson 6-8-1835 Hr
Peirce, Annie C. A. (Mrs.) to J. H. D. Evans 9-24-1870 (9-25-1870) Ma
Peker, Annette to John Umback 3-28-1861 (4-7-1861) Sh
Peler, M. B. P. to James M. Williams 11-10-1870 Cr
Pell, Ella to T. Lee Wells 2-26-1879 Dy
Pell, Martha to David Connell 11-25-1875 Dy
Pemberton, Harriett to John P. Webb 11-12-1862 G
Pemberton, Jane to Reuben McVey 6-6-1844 (6-11-1844) Ma
Pemberton, Lucy A. to James N. Rust 9-29-1853 G
Pemberton, Nancy J. to William M. Senter 12-5-1857 (12-6-1857) G
Pendegraft, Sarah to Micheal Solan 4-14-1855 (4-23-1855) Sh
Pender, Eliza to Julius Stevens 3-12-1870 Hy
Pender, Ellen to D. W. Stokeley 3-22-1880 (3-18?-1880) L
Pender, Harriet to Matt Mann 9-13-1866 Hy
Pender, Judy to Andrew Mathews 12-14-1875 (no return) Hy
Pender, Julia to Abram Gracy 11-21-1878 Hy
Pender, Julia to Tom Rivers 3-1-1871 Hy
Pender, Mary G. to John Mathews 3-11-1863 (no return) Hy
Pender, Mattie to Ovid Walker 2-9-1874 Hy
Pender, N. J. to C. C. Speed 3-24-1862 Hy
Pender, Nancy to Albert Fuller 1-6-1875 (no return) Hy
Pender, Nancy to Sam Wharton 2-26-1871 Hy
Pender, Naomi to Turner Ivey 7-31-1872 Hy
Pender, Winny to Joe Ervin 4-7-1875 Hy
Pender, Winny to Thos. Jones 9-3-1867 (no return) Hy
Pendergass, Ellen to Patrick Cusack 4-16-1860 Sh
Pendergrass, Elizabeth to Joseph R. Jones 6-29-1839 (7-10-1839) O
Pendergrass, Frances Eleanor to James K. Schooley 1-1-1850 T
Pendergrass, Martha to Ruben Pearcy 1-26-1859 Cr
Pendergrass, Nancy to Beverly Cannon 6-22-1840 (6-23-1840) G
Pendergrast, Lucinda to James Eason 6-11-1856 Ma
Pendleton, Abbey to Lycurgus Scott 1-29-1838 (1-30-1838) Hr
Pendleton, Eliza A. to Mark B. Sappington 12-21-1832 Sh
Pendleton, Eliza to David Lovel (Lorel?) 2-9-1852 (2-12-1852) Sh
Pendleton, Margaret to Benjamin E. Leland 12-5-1850 Sh
Pendleton, Mariah P. to J. W. Parr 4-1-1865 (4-2-1865) L
Pendygrass, J. E. to S. H. Butler 9-28-1871 Cr
Penhouse, Catharine to John P. Crump 8-19-1846 Sh
Penick, Birda to Jasper Moore 12-20-1869 (no return) L
Penick, Charlotte to Frances Carter Powers 3-25-1875 (3-28-1875) L
Penick, E. J. to Eli Compton 2-18-1867 (2-19-1867) Cr
Penick, Fanny to Moses Hagler 12-27-1866 Hn B
Penick, Mary A. to Samuel S. Fields 12-15-1859 Hn
Penick, Mary J. to Robert S. Collins no date (1838-1852) Hn
Penick, Mary to Marion Johnson 7-21-1869 Be
Penick, Rachael J. to Matthew Bell 12-23-1840 Hn
Penick, Sarah A. to Marion Wood 12-18-1866 (12-19-1866) Cr
Penn, Amanda E. to James H. Hays 2-27-1844 Ma
Penn, Bell to Eaton Bond, jr. 12-9-1867 Ma
Penn, F. O. to G. C. Cartwright 9-19-1865 G
Penn, Huleah? to William Diggers 6-13-1851 (6-15-1851) Sh
Penn, Levenia L. to E. S. Campbell 12-7-1864 G
Penn, M. A. to J. A. Nowlin 11-3-1868 G
Penn, M. A. to M. A. Gober 11-24-1865 (11-29-1865) F
Penn, Maria W. to E. W. Mallory 12-2-1858 Sh
Penn, Martha J. to B. F. Harris 1-24-1859 G
Penn, Mary B. to J. N. Brown 10-11-1848 Sh
Penn, Mary P. to Harrison Conlee 1-2-1858 G
Penn, Mary R. to William H. Harvey 11-15-1849 G
Penn, Mary to Asa Woodward 12-10-1831 (12-11-1831) Ma
Penn, S. E. to C. W. Martin 11-16-1865 G
Penn, Sarah E. to Benjamin F. Harris 3-20-1844 G
Penn, Tennessee S.(L?) to D. A. Richmond 12-6-1860 G
Pennel, Ellen M. to Bird L. Mathews 6-3-1861 (6-5-1861) T
Pennel, M. E. to W. D. Cash 1-21-1874 (1-24-1874) T
Pennel, Mary Jane to H. Sullivan 10-23-1856 (11-3-1856) T
Pennel, S. E. to G. B. Cash 12-7-1868 (12-9-1868) T
Pennell, Massey Lavinia to Joseph B. James 5-18-1849 (not executed) T
Pennell, Massey Lavinia to Walter Archer Coleman 10-30-1849 (11-2-1849) T
Pennelton, Julia to Daniel Millane 9-21-1862 Sh
Penney, Martha A. to Zachariah Biggs 11-23-1837 G
Pennie, Amanda L. to W. H. Mathis 12-4-1872 (12-8-1872) L
Pennington, Amelia to T. J. Chipman 11-24-1880 L
Pennington, Annie E. to E. W. Fight 12-23-1865 L
Pennington, E. E. to K. B. Davidson 10-13-1875 L
Pennington, Eliza J. to James J. Baker 7-21-1856 (8-4-1856) G
Pennington, L. A. to J. T. Roberson 9-15-1879 L
Pennington, Lucinda L. to William H. Garrett 5-28-1870 (no return) L

Pennington, Margaret to David Conner 5-27-1861 Sh
Pennington, Martha P. to R. P. Crihfield 2-12-1872 L
Pennington, Mary E. to James F. Carson 12-16-1879 (no return) L
Pennington, Mary E. to William Walston 2-12-1845 G
Pennington, Mary F. to William Michum 10-21-1874 (10-22-1874) L
Pennington, Mary to P(arse) A(lphonse) Misskelly 7-22-1867 (no return) L
Pennington, Nancy Ann to John James 6-22-1878 (6-23-1878) Dy
Pennington, Plura A. to M. F. Hendron 12-22-1885 (no return) L
Pennington, S.(L.?) C. to W. R. Simmons 12-18-1867 G
Pennington, Sarah L. to James H. Screws 1-8-1867 G
Pennington, Susan to James A. Rambo 4-25-1861 Dy
Penny, Caroline to C. H. Hailey 5-18-1870 Ma
Penny, M. J. to D. J. Grady 1-25-1866 G
Penny, Sarah A. to W. J. Grady 1-25-1866 G
Penny, Sarah B. to C. T. Archer 2-20-1869 (2-24-1869) T
Penny, Susan to Ruffin Moore 9-23-1868 G B
Penson, M. E. to Mathew M. Lawton? 1?-30-1868 T
Pentecost, Elizabeth to L. W. Reddick 4-5-1859 (no return) We
Pentecost, Martha Ann to John W. Jenkins 2-13-1845 We
Pentecost, Mary A. to John R. Maddox 5-4-1855 We
Pentecost, Mary E. to Robt. W. Taylor 6-22-1866 Ma
Pentecost, Nancy to J. W. Brown 7-14-1846 We
Pentecost, Nannie C. to Jason L. Wood 1-4-1870 Ma
Pentecost, Rebecca to William M. Jones 12-23-1856 (12-25-1856) O
Pentecost, Sarah to Peter Bryant 11-24-1863 (11-25-1863) O
Pentecost, Susan to Kinchen Killebrew 9-9-1862 We
Pentegrass, Lucinda to Silas Avery 6-18-1845 (6-23-1845) G
Peonse, Wilhelmina to Jno. Schmidt 1-15-1852 Sh
Peoples, C. A. to R. H. Watkins 6-18-1850 Hy
Peoples, Elizabeth Ann to Edward W. Nevill 12-22-1840 Cr
Peoples, Elizabeth to W. G. Tate 9-20-1872 (9-29-1872) Dy
Peoples, Harriet to Alge Jamison 12-13-1871 (no return) Cr
Peoples, M. J. to J. P. King 11-8-1859 (11-9-1859) G
Peoples, Martha E. to Thomas L. King 12-11-1860 G
Peoples, Martha to Robert A. Rainey 8-23-1838 Cr
Peoples, Mary A. to Robert D. Reed 7-31-1855 (no return) Hn
Peplow, Sarah H. to A. G. Parks 5-29-1858 Sh
Pepper, Selva A. to William Younger 9-18-1855 We
Peppers, Elizabeth to S. F. Bittick 5-17-1866 O
Percell, Sinther to David Pickler 3-12-1840 Cr
Percifull, F. E. to D. C. Garrett 1-25-1874 Hy
Percival, Willie E. to J. W. Anthony 1-3-1883 (1-4-1883) L
Percy, Martha Ann to William R. Baker 12-13-1843 (12-15-1843) Ma
Perdice, J. J. to Wm. Chandler 8-7-1851 Cr
Peres, Sarah to Lewis Lyons 12-1-1862 Sh
Perkins, A. C. to J. A. Barham 2-9-1843 Be
Perkins, A.? J. to Henry H. Reynolds 1-25-1862 (no return) Hn
Perkins, Betsy to Robert Williams 11-8-1867 Hy
Perkins, Caroline to James R. Williams 10-10-1849 Be
Perkins, Catherine to T. J. Koonce 12-26-1866 (12-27-1866) L
Perkins, Dicy to Henry Read 3-15-1876 (no return) Hy
Perkins, Dilsy to Tom Hamilton 9-17-1870 (no return) Hy
Perkins, E. J. to N. J. Dunlap 2-3-1872 (2-5-1872) Cr
Perkins, Eliza to John Ed. Jefferson Williams 1-21-1886 L
Perkins, Elizabeth to Solm. O. Graves 9-9-1853 (no return) F
Perkins, Felias to Wm. Patterson 7-14-1867 Hy
Perkins, Frances to Henry Edney 10-8-1873 Hy
Perkins, Harriett to W. H. Pope 2-28-1866 (3-1-1866) Cr
Perkins, Julia to Warren Dupree 12-26-1866 Hy
Perkins, Kitty L. to T. M. Milam 12-20-1865 (12-27-1865) F
Perkins, Louisa to William H. Crihfield 11-16-1866 (11-23-1866) L
Perkins, Lucy to John N. Daniel 12-28-1858 Hn
Perkins, Lydia Ann to Alfred W. Howard 11-21-1856 (11-23-1856) O
Perkins, Lydia to S. V. Aden 6-4-1844 Be
Perkins, M. J. to O. A. Horn 2-17-1866 (no return) Hn
Perkins, Margaret to Abram A. S. Jones 10-27-1858 (10-1858) O
Perkins, Martha to Marion Smith 12-7-1866 (12-16-1866) F
Perkins, Mary B. to Hugh J. Douglass 9-7-1843 (9-8-1843) F
Perkins, Mary E. to Benj. L. D. Byler 1-14-1861 (1-15-1861) L
Perkins, Mary E. to George W. Gallimore 8-15-1870 (8-16-1870) Cr
Perkins, Mary E. to P. T. Hudson 5-9-1866 F
Perkins, Mary J. to N. H. Previtt 3-?-1852 (no return) F
Perkins, Mary R. to Petser Medlin 11-3-1853 Ma *
Perkins, Mary T. to James Fentress 8-24-1859 Hr
Perkins, Mary to W. D. Dunnavant 5-30-1869 Hy
Perkins, Milly to Gillis Cole 7-28-1867 Hy
Perkins, Mollie to W. G. Turner 1-17-1877 (1-18-1877) L
Perkins, Molly to William S. Johnson 7-17-1868 (no return) Cr
Perkins, Nancy to John Harper 8-4-1840 Cr
Perkins, Nancy to John W. McElyea 6-22-1855 (6-24-1855) O
Perkins, Nikolas Ann to George A. Brinkley 3-26-1844 Hr
Perkins, P. P. to John T. Akins 3-24-1858 Cr
Perkins, Paulina to Dudley Dunn 6-22-1833 Sh
Perkins, Rebecca F. to James A. Pipkin 2-24-1868 L
Perkins, Rebecca S. to Alfred Rushing 3-19-1851 Be
Perkins, Reny to Andrew Taylor 10-31-1871 (no return) Cr B
Perkins, S. E. to R. E. Smith 4-24-1860 (5-1-1860) F

Perkins, Sarah to E. E. B. Brown 12-24-1866 (1-1-1867) Cr
Perkins, Sarah to John Brackin 8-9-1853 Cr
Perkins, Susan J. to Henry S. Garrett 8-2-1867 (8-4-1867) L
Perkinson, Ann Branch to John W. Hudson 9-27-1841 (9-28-1841) T
Perkinson, Eliz. Anderson to Edmund Booker 6-29-1846 (7-2-1846) T
Perkinson, Mary to John L. Stanley 8-2-1827 Sh
Permator, Mary H. to Benjamin Emison 11-20-1854 (11-22-1854) Ma
Permenter, Elizabeth to E. H. Faulkner 9-1-1860 (no return) Hy
Permenter, Mary E. to G. W. Boling 3-15-1866 Hy
Permenter, Mary E. to James W. Moss 12-11-1865 (no return) Hy
Permenter, Sallie to James M. Wray 12-15-1868 Hy
Permenter, Sarah E. to J. N. Clark 12-7-1871 Hy
Perminter, N. E. to Ray McLaughlin 7-16-1877 Hy
Perminter, Unicy to Stephen Rains 7-6-1841 (no return) Hn
Perrett, Eliza to William Webb 9-27-1860 Cr
Perritt, Caroline J. to Elmore Neely 9-13-1857 Cr
Perritt?, Mary to J. M. Reynolds 5-15-1869 (5-16-1869) Cr
Perry, Adaline to Benjamin S. Brooks 5-23-1850 Ma
Perry, Agnis to Samuel Blunt 7-29-1877 Hy
Perry, Amanda to Lee Walker 4-3-1873 Hy
Perry, Ann Eliza F. O. to John C. M. Garland 9-5-1854 Ma
Perry, Anna E. to J. C. Cole 5-26-1857 (5-27-1857) Sh
Perry, Callie to Wm. Greaves 2-21-1878 Hy
Perry, Catharine T. to John W. Lee 3-5-1855 (3-7-1855) Hr
Perry, Celicia to John T. Coleman 7-30-1855 (7-31-1855) Ma
Perry, Cely to Joseph Davis 7-4-1870 G B
Perry, Dilsey to Armsted Green 12-16-1875 Hy
Perry, E. L. to F. E. Mahon 12-3-1864 (12-13-1864) Dy
Perry, E. W. to Chamberlin H. Anderson 2-7-1845 (2-9-1845) Hr
Perry, Edney to James King 12-13-1874 Hy
Perry, Eliza Jane to Reubin S. Scott 5-20-1850 (5-23-1850) Hr
Perry, Eliza to William T. Deloach 9-9-1850 Ma
Perry, Elizabeth to H. H. Williams 12-30-1867 (12-31-1867) F
Perry, Elizabeth to Jessee Gordan 11-9-1870 Dy
Perry, Elizabeth to Richard B. B. Randolph 1-4-1842 Hr
Perry, Elizabeth to Richard B. B. Randolph 5-6-1844 (5-30-1844) Hr
Perry, Elizabeth to William P. Hopper 1-4-1845 Ma
Perry, Frances to Moses Walker 10-19-1870 Hy
Perry, Frances to W. H. Howell 9-3-1869 (9-5-1869) Dy
Perry, Francis A. to William N. Coleburn 8-14-1854 (8-15-1854) Ma
Perry, George to Hugh House? 6-1-1869 (6-2-1869) T
Perry, Harriett to Andrew Rodgers 7-20-1847 Cr
Perry, Helen M. to Gale H. Kyle 7-25-1843 Ma
Perry, Hesperan A. to James P. Hudson 7-8-1867 Ma
Perry, Hester to Eli Stevans 3-26-1878 Hy
Perry, Hester to Thomas G. Good 4-28-1850 Hn
Perry, Jackey Ann to Elias Moore 2-4-1850 (2-5-1850) Hr
Perry, Josephine to Ned Manning 7-11-1865 (7-17-1865) Dy
Perry, Julia to Joseph Nunn 12-28-1867 (no return) Dy
Perry, Kate to Isaac Newsom 1-25-1872 Hy
Perry, Kezirah to Elijah W. Graves 7-7-1845 Hr
Perry, L. A. to Thomas O. Nicholas 12-26-1849 Hn
Perry, Lavinia to Richard Kelly 1-31-1859 Hn
Perry, Lou to S. A. McAlwee 6-27-1878 (no return) Hy
Perry, Loutisia to Alexander Currie 1-4-1877 (no return) Hy
Perry, Lucinda to Cato Walker 1-2-1871 (1-5-1871) F B
Perry, Lucretia to Joshua Baker 5-11-1839 Hy
Perry, Lucy Ann to Samuel Orr 1-24-1857 Hn
Perry, M. A. to J.M. Maness 7-9-1873 L
Perry, M. B. to A. C. Bowers 2-8-1866 Hn
Perry, M. L. to J. M. Baulch 11-11-1871 (11-16-1871) Dy
Perry, M. P. to J. R. McNeill 12-16-1862 (12-24-1862) F
Perry, Margaret to George Singleton 12-30-1867 (1-1-1867?) L
Perry, Martha A. to James T. Etherage 1-25-1851 (no return) Hn
Perry, Martha J. to John W. Gailey 9-25-1862 We
Perry, Martha J. to J. Henry? Thomas 3-25-1858 We
Perry, Martha to Jacob Ing 2-17-1844 Ma
Perry, Martha to Richard Gallimore 2-27-1850 (no return) Hn
Perry, Martha to Thomas J. Henry 3-25-1858 We
Perry, Mary Ann to Edward M. Hall 9-3-1857 Hn
Perry, Mary E. D. to Charles E. Carnatzan 9-9-1857 (9-10-1857) Ma
Perry, Mary E. to Simon McNeill 12-9-1867 (12-16-1867) F
Perry, Mary J. to J. H. Nunn 10-16-1871 (10-17-1871) Dy
Perry, Mary J. to John M. Jones 10-19-1844 Cr
Perry, Mary Jane to Isaac Pettyjohn 2-13-1845 We
Perry, Mary to J. Etherage 1-31-1846 (no return) Hn
Perry, Mattie J. to David M. Hampton 12-19-1866 (12-20-1866) Ma
Perry, Maudy to Chas. D. Carroll 6-2-1869 Ma
Perry, Mollie H. to Gillam J. Moore 11-15-1871 Ma
Perry, Mozella to Jno. B. Tucker 10-1-1866 (10-10-1866) Dy
Perry, Nancy J. to J. M. Trousdale 12-2-1867 (no return) Hn
Perry, Nancy to Billy Suesberry 11-25-1871 Hy
Perry, Nancy to J. W. Kirk 10-29-1859 (11-2-1859) O
Perry, Nancy to W. H. Glisson 12-30-1867 (no return) Hn
Perry, Patina C. to James M. Webb 1-14-1848 (1-18-1848) F
Perry, Prudence N. to William S. Perry 1-19-1848 (1-20-1848) Hr
Perry, Rachel to John Brown 12-28-1874 Hy

Perry, Rebecca to J. W. Glover 7-8-1868 (7-9-1868) F
Perry, Renie to William Brown 5-27-1871 (6-1-1871) Dy
Perry, S. E. to Wesley Parker 3-8-1862 G
Perry, Sarah A. to Wm. L. Rutherford 11-28-1866 (11-29-1866) Ma
Perry, Sarah to Bartlett Rhodes 3-25-1850 Hn
Perry, Susan E. to John H. Throgmorton 9-15-1867 Hn
Perry, T. A. to J. B. Lilly 8-7-1870 Hy
Person (Pirson), Mary W. to Saml. A. Michum 2-2-1854 (2-8-1854) Sh
Person, Amona to Phil Thompson 1-30-1873 (1-31-1873) L
Person, Ann E. to James A. Mason 5-15-1871 (5-16-1871) Ma
Person, Elizabeth to Joseph C. Fisher 10-2-1849 Sh
Person, Hibernia A. to Gilbreth Neill 12-8-1869 Ma
Person, Lavinia A. to Wade H. Bolton 12-19-1836 Sh
Person, Louisa to Gabriel I. Slaughter 5-4-1842 Sh
Person, Lucinda H. to Francis L. Roulhac 4-10-1844 Sh
Person, M. C. to Saml. James Armour 1-17-1855 Sh
Person, Martha A. to Hershall S. Porter 6-14-1853 Sh
Person, Martha Ann to Nelson Avant 1-23-1872 (1-28-1872) T
Person, Martha E. to Thomas D. Tomlinson 8-27-1866 (8-28-1866) Ma
Person, Mary T. G. to John P. E. Bolton 6-9-1841 Sh
Person, Mary to William M. Tidwell 6-17-1841 Ma
Person, Matilda W. to William B. Hill 1-19-1843 Sh
Person, Nancy to Charles Hill 5-17-1848 Sh
Person, Sallie E. to W. J. Donaldson 1-24-1849 Sh
Person, Sarah Ann to Samuel A. Young 10-12-1852 Sh
Person, Susan A. to Constantine Paine 7-8-1856 (7-10-1856) Sh
Person, Tabitha E. to John McNeil 6-16-1835 Sh
Persons, Anna T. to James M. Towns 4-5-1865 (no return) Cr
Persons, Medora Alice to John E. Gwinn 1-6-1868 (1-8-1868) Cr
Persons, Susan to Martin Fisk 3-30-1834 Sh
Perteat, Elizabeth to Zachariah Biggs 10-31-1840 (11-1-1840) G
Perutes?, Mary Ann to James F. Jackson 7-12-1848 (no return) Hn
Pervis, Jennie E. to S. T. Terrill 6-16-1866 Hy
Pervis, Virginia to Calvin Laster 6-25-1866 (no return) Hy
Peryear, Julia to George Anderson 1-6-1873 (1-9-1873) L
Peter, Adaline to Ephran Williams 11-27-1856 Cr
Peter, Emeline to Calvin W. Duncan 11-12-1866 Hn
Peter, Nancy to Adam Boyd? 12-1-1865 (12-3-1865) T
Peters, Ann Maria to Alfred N. Clayton 9-10-1846 (10-16-1846) Hr
Peters, Anne to Isaac Greer 10-30-1867 G B
Peters, Harriet A. to Wesley S. Acree 1-4-1870 (1-6-1870) Ma
Peters, Mahala to Arter (Arthur?) Overton 10-31-1844 Sh
Peters, Margaret to Bernard Sorbet 7-8-1856 Sh
Peters, Mary Cass to John W. Weaver 9-30-1835 Sh
Peterson, Catherine to Burress Blackwood 3-23-1841 Sh
Peterson, Elizabeth to B. F. Ellis 1-27-1863 L
Peterson, Floranna to William Gilson 7-4-1837 Sh
Peterson, Harriet to John W. Robertson 1-26-1864 (1-29-1864) Dy
Peterson, Hattie to John Walker 11-14-1878 Hy
Peterson, Jemima to Benjamin Parker 7-13-1842 Sh
Peterson, Louisa to John Logan 3-7-1833 Sh
Peterson, Pheby to J. W. Robertson 8-26-1861 (8-27-1861) Dy
Peterson, Sarah Ann to Robert M. Ellis 3-26-1862 (no return) Hy
Peterson, Sarah L. to John D. Legett 10-23-1871 (no return) L
Pethel, Mary to Willis Rasberry 1-3-1867 Be
Pethel, Priscilla A. to Wm. Bush 9-8-1856 Be
Petigrue, Virginia W. to Jonathan B. Griffin 12-30-1852 Hr
Petis, Mary Ann to Moses A. House 2-17-1834 G
Petit, Lizzie E. to James Gunter 5-18-1872 (5-22-1872) T
Petree, Mary Ann to Joseph F. O'Neal 4-16-1853 O
Petree, Sarah E. to Wesley M. Guinn 2-17-1867 Hn
Petree, Sarah Eliza to W. M. Guinn 9-23-1864 (no return) Hn
Pettard, Elizabeth to Wesley Moore 10-21-1846 Cr
Pettey, Rebecca D. to George S. Wright 2-26-1861 T
Pettie, Laura B. to Wm. B. Robinson 3-8-1870 (3-10-1870) T
Pettie, Winnie to Esquer Tyus 2-21-1872 Hy
Pettigrew, Eliza to John E. Davis 3-14-1868 (3-15-1868) Ma
Pettigrew, Emeline to Peter Waggoner 4-13-1845 Be
Pettigrew, Louisanna to Lafayette Smith 3-5-1866 (3-6-1866) Ma
Pettijohn, Margery to Bassel Deal 11-22-1845 O
Pettis, Tillah to Haywood Chaffin 1-2-1869 F B
Pettit, E. V. to A. B. Pulliam 6-4-1862 F
Pettit, Florida C. to J. Q. A. Thompson 9-19-1860 (9-20-1860) Ma
Pettit, Julia A. to Aratus T. Cornelius 2-17-1862 (2-18-1862) Sh
Pettit, Sarah to Andrew Nash 12-17-1870 (12-18-1870) F B
Pettus, Becky to Lewis Bowers 12-27-1869 (12-23?-1869) F B
Pettus, Carroline to Lemual W. Hollan 1-11-1841 (1-14-1841) G
Pettus, Dorrah to Carroll Patton 1-21-1871 O
Pettus, Elizabeth to Henry M. Pierce 12-12-1851 (12-16-1851) G
Pettus, Emily to Samuel F. Bone 5-11-1855 (5-13-1855) G
Pettus, Hannah Jane to Thomas B. Fenner 7-22-1853 (7-26-1853) Ma
Pettus, Lavinia A. to Travis B. Canon 1-19-1860 (no return) Hy
Pettus, Mary E. to John McDonald 11-10-1857 Ma
Pettus, Mary F. to L. R. Coleman 1-18-1866 Hy
Pettus, Rebecca W. to John D. Wright 9-9-1835 (9-22-1835) G
Pettus, Rebecca to Thomas Giles 12-7-1876 L B
Pettus, Willie to A. G. Kimbrough 4-12-1876 Hy

Petty (Perry?), Mary An to James R. Parker 12-18-1848 F
Petty, Adeline E. to John E. Jarvis 1-5-1864 G
Petty, Carolin to William T. Hunt 7-1-1844 (no return) F
Petty, Clementine S. to Henry Arnold 12-20-1858 (12-22-1858) G
Petty, E. J. (Mrs.) to T. C. Grady 2-8-1864 Sh
Petty, Elizabeth M. to N. Bryan 11-26-1853 (11-27-1853) T
Petty, Elizabeth to Peter R. B. Ballard 2-10-1850 Sh
Petty, Elizabeth to William D. Ferguson 4-19-1858 Sh
Petty, J. A. to S. A. Tinkle 6-1-1874 (no return) Dy
Petty, Kisiah to T. Whitehead 2-20-1840 Be
Petty, Kisiah to T. Whitehead 2-20-1840 Be CC
Petty, Lucy C. to James Aspy 11-4-1846 Cr
Petty, Margaret E. to Francis M. Ray 10-31-1867 Hn
Petty, Martha J. to Fantry Roberts 12-12-1867 Cr
Petty, Martha L. to Richard Bryns 11-24-1844 Cr
Petty, Martha to B. Myers 12-26-1849 Hn
Petty, Mary to Thomas H. Hopkins 8-19-1855 Cr
Petty, Mary to W. F. Hale 4-21-1863 Mn
Petty, Mrs. Mary A. to James E.? Nicholson 10-21-1874 T
Petty, Orlina Jane to Robert Lowry 12-29-1855 (1-5-1856) T
Petty, P. J. to H. G. Haynes 2-7-1856 (no return) Hn
Petty, Rutha A. to Israel E. Mainard 8-7-1866 Cr
Petty, S. E. to Bennett Crawford 3-9-1851 Cr
Petty, Sarah C. to John J. Eliott 9-1-1840 (9-2-1840) F
Petty, Sarah E. to Archabald Sutton 7-9-1864 Mn
Petty, Sarah J. to James M. Bowden 8-10-1854 Hn
Petty, Sarah to John Russell 9-12-1843 Be
Petty, Susan A. R. to Ivey B. Mathis 12-9-1846 Cr
Petty, Vina A. to J. L. Snowden 11-14-1867 Cr
Petty, W. S. to S. H. Davis 4-7-1860 (4-9-1860) O
Pettyjohn, Easter C. to Willis G. Williams 9-5-1850 Hn
Pettyjohn, Mary to George G. Burns 9-12-1852 Hn
Pettyjohn, N. P. to J. T. Berryhill 2-20-1869 (2-21-1869) Cr
Pettyjohn, Sarah M. to Abram W. Roberson 3-5-1857 Hn
Pettyjohn, Sarah to Benjamin C. Branch 1-18-1845 G
Pettyjohn, Sarah to John Liston 4-18-1842 (no return) Hn
Pety, Sarah R. to Hiram Fain 4-5-1842 F
Peveyhouse, Martha to Richard Henley 2-13-1865 (no return) L
Peviard?, A. H. to E. H. Amis 6-26-1869 (6-27-1869) F
Pew, Catherine Manerva to John Pew 11-21-1850 Hr
Pewett, Hattie to Alx. Capell 3-6-1870 Hy
Pewett, Jane to Woodson Parr 12-23-1867 (no return) L B
Pewett, Julia Ann to Fed Davis 5-2-1867 (no return) F B
Pewett, Melinda to Stephen Roberson 3-23-1867 Hy
Pewett, Mittie to Matt Douglass 9-2-1866 Hy
Pewett, Nancy to Zilmon Voss 2-8-1855 L
Pewett, Sallie to John E. Douglas 2-28-1860 (no return) Hy
Pewett, Tennie to A. D. Hutchison 12-19-1868 Hy
Pewett, W. Martha to John C. Pennington 12-24-1868 (12-25-1868) L
Pewitt, Ann E. to John Scallions 8-29-1874 (8-30-1874) L
Pewitt, Ann Eliza to Green Smith 2-15-1865 T
Peyton, Emily to George Y. Smith 12-10-1846 Sh
Peyton, Mary Jane to John Wells 6-6-1857 (6-7-1857) Ma
Pfisterer, Mary Ann to W. F. Berthold 10-30-1858 Sh
Pfleuger, Sarah A. to A. J. Wimberley 1-31-1867 Hn
Pfleuger?, Nancy E. to John C. Miller 1-27-1858 Hn
Phaland, Eliza to S. B. Miller 4-4-1849 G
Phallis, Jarucia Ann to William Lewis Cash 11-3-1853 G
Pharr, Jane M. to William L. Dewoody 8-27-1851 Sh
Pharr, Josephine T. to Andrew Stewart 9-16-1857 Sh
Pharr, Margaret B. to Wm. F. (Dr.) Walsh 11-5-1851 Sh
Pharr, Susan to Stanton Parr 12-19-1868 (no return) L B
Phearce, Emma to Albert Barnard 10-3-1870 G B
Phelan, Amanda to Daniel Blackburn 5-29-1865 G
Phelan, Elendar A. to Joshua Gaza 5-5-1842 G
Phelan, Mahala to John H. Parker 1-22-1855 G
Phelan, Sarah A. to Calaway Mathews 10-21-1850 (10-?-1850) G
Phelan, Sarah E. to Henry H. Skiles 10-27-1858 (10-28-1858) G
Phelan, Sarah to Jones Glascock 1-24-1844 G
Phelan?, M. C. to J. W. Cobb 12-13-1858 Sh
Phelps, Arkansas to P. M. Rainer 8-7-1858 (8-8-1858) Hr
Phelps, E. Parilee to Nelson Parham 2-2-1867 Hn B
Phelps, Elizabeth to Sherwood L. Liles 7-3-1866 (12-27-1866) Cr
Phelps, Elizabeth to William W. Baker 1-8-1851 Hn
Phelps, Ellen to Lawrence Alston 3-28-1874 T
Phelps, Hanna R. to Moses M. Rigsby 8-12-1862 (no return) Cr
Phelps, Judith to Fetus Baker 11-8-1842 (11-9-1842) Ma
Phelps, Julia to Henry Parsons 10-10-1857 Cr
Phelps, Lucisa N. to John Morison? 8-12-1856 (8-14-1856) T
Phelps, Martha to Michael Manning 5-20-1861 (no return) Hn
Phelps, Mary Ann to John J. Steel 4-22-1847 Hn
Phelps, Mary to Maj. W. Witherington 5-26-1853 (6-26-1853) G
Phelps, May T. to Allen K. Jones 12-23-1854 (12-26-1854) Ma
Phelps, Neadis Isis to Milton Hunt 9-27-1847 (9-30-1847) T
Phelps, Piety J. to R. D. Thomason 2-8-1859 Hn
Phelps, S. A. to M. A. McClain 11-10-1884 Hn
Phelps, Sarah E. to N. J. Rogers 5-15-1873 Cr

Phelps, Sarah I. to E. D. Lasiter 9-2-1858 We
Phelps, Sarah to William M. Owens 12-21-1856 Hn
Phelps, Susan M. to Ily D. Turnage 10-26-1847 (11-10-1847) T
Phelps, Susan to W. R. Crouch 2-1-1863
Phelps, Viann W. to James Wofford 9-11-1856 Hn
Phelts, Elizabeth J. to Thomas J. Atkins 9-28-1861 (no return) We
Phifer, Ann Elizabeth to Uriah Phifer 6-11-1850 Be
Phifer, Katherine to Daniel B. Herndon 3-19-1844 Be
Phifer, Martha J. to William J. Bratton 6-27-1852 Ma
Phifer, P. E. to Thomas Hatley 12-25-1867 Be
Phifer, Sarah J. to T. Stround 12-26-1860 Be
Phifer, Sarah to John Davis 12-25-1853 Be
Phifer, Susan to J. Evans 9-20-1864 Be
Philipis, L. E. to James E. Crockett 8-13-1847 O
Philips, Eliza Ann to W. B. Jackson 5-23-1869 Hy
Philips, Elizabeth to Able C. Turner 1-21-1851 (1-26-1851) O
Philips, Elizabeth to Benjamin Brown 1-4-1838 Sh
Philips, Elizabeth to Samuel Malone 12-12-1835 (12-17-1835) G
Philips, Jane to James Jarnigan 10-21-1851 Hr
Philips, Jennie to Benjamin M. Revel 7-10-1863 G
Philips, Louisa to Duke Payne 10-19-1871 (no return) Hy
Philips, Louiza to D. Connell 1-4-1858 (1-7-1858) G
Philips, Manerva A. to Amos C. Roark 10-11-1858 (10-12-1858) Sh
Philips, Margaret to John M. Johnson 8-27-1849 (8-29-1849) Hr
Philips, Martha A. to J. E. Douglass 3-9-1868 (no return) Hy
Philips, Martha A. to James Farherne (Farberne?) 9-20-1863 Sh
Philips, Mary A. (Mrs.) to Cedric B. Randall 11-27-1864 Sh
Philips, Mary C. to Geo. M. Pate 10-6-1862 (no return) Hy
Philips, Mary N. to Alfred C. Rucker 11-4-1854 (11-8-1854) T
Philips, Mary to Allen Bass 6-9-1867 Hy
Philips, Mary to James N. Mitchell 12-16-1862 Hn
Philips, Nancy A. to Green Williams 1-1-1839 (1-3-1839) G
Philips, Nancy E. to Ishmael N. Hardaway 1-12-1853 Sh
Philips, Prudillar to Arden Saunders 8-31-1859 Hn
Philips, R. J. to Joab E. Hays 1-6-1852 O
Philips, S. E. to Robert B. Bailey 3-15-1843 (3-18-1843) F
Philips, Sarah Ann to A. F. Mitchell 12-18-1844 (12-19-1844) Hr
Philips, Sarah to E. B. Speck 12-12-1864 Sh
Philliips, Margaret to J. S. Darling 1-27-1855 O
Phillip, J. E. to John Simpson 12-15-1851 Cr
Phillips, A. M. to R. S. Stith 2-14-1854 (no return) F
Phillips, Adeline to Willis Dowdy 3-13-1869 (3-27-1869) F B
Phillips, Ann to Frank Johnson 2-22-1867 (2-24-1867) F B
Phillips, Caroline to Whitson Pool 11-21-1848 G
Phillips, Catheran to Jasper Moore 3-1-1867 (3-16-1867) T
Phillips, Celina to Thos. C. Taylor 2-25-1841 G
Phillips, Dolly to Major Watkins 10-17-1868 (10-31-1868) F B
Phillips, E. J. to Hiram Beaver ?-?-1860 Cr
Phillips, E. S. to J. W. Mason 10-16-1855 (10-17-1855) Sh
Phillips, Eliza A. M. to Anderson McGill 3-11-1841 Cr
Phillips, Eliza A. to Will M. Watkins 9-27-1860 Dy
Phillips, Eliza to William D. Moss 9-14-1882 L
Phillips, Elizabeth C. to D. H. Bently 12-27-1852 (no return) F
Phillips, Elizabeth to George W. Smith 2-11-1852 Hn
Phillips, Elizabeth to John Nix 1-1-1861 O
Phillips, Elizabeth to Thos. Belew 2-13-1844 Cr
Phillips, Ellen to M. W. Outlaw 1-22-1885 (1-23-1885) L
Phillips, Flavia to John V. Ryan 3-30-1871 (4-4-1871) T
Phillips, Hannah M. to Wm. H. Gaddy 1-29-1861 Hr
Phillips, Harriet to J. T. Morris 3-27-1860 O
Phillips, Isabella to F. Barnhart 3-20-1852 Cr
Phillips, Jane to John H. Miller 2-26-1842 (3-1-1842) G
Phillips, Jane to Warrin Pierce 12-24-1869 (12-27-1869) O
Phillips, Jincy to William Robbins 8-21-1838 (8-23-1838) O
Phillips, Julia A. F. to W. B. Savage 9-22-1860 (9-23-1860) Hr
Phillips, Julia A. to W. W. Graves 12-25-1850 F
Phillips, Leah to Felix D. Lane 8-11-1847 F
Phillips, Lemess? to Solimon Vincent 12-25-1867 T
Phillips, Leuize to Edward G. Bowden 11-11-1846 Hn
Phillips, Lousanna to John Kelly 3-11-1854 (3-12-1854) T
Phillips, Lucinda E. to Mark Grady 1-28-1861 (no return) We
Phillips, M. E. to G. W. Dunn 4-10-1864 Hn
Phillips, M. N. to G. S. Flemmings 12-7-1864 (not endorsed) F
Phillips, M. P. to John P. Phillips 12-31-1866 F
Phillips, Manda to B. S. Pritchard 2-16-1860 Cr
Phillips, Manerva J. to Richd. Robers 2-20-1870 Hy
Phillips, Maria to Warner Harrol 11-9-1833 Sh
Phillips, Marry J. to R. A. Wesbrook 12-4-1854 (no return) F
Phillips, Martha Jane to Andrew J. Bridges 8-11-1840 Cr
Phillips, Martha Jane to John Cooper 8-1-1849 Hn
Phillips, Martha M. to Hollis F. Newman 7-25-1854 (no return) L
Phillips, Martha M. to James Fairbourn 4-2-1863 Sh
Phillips, Martha S. to C. C. Akin 9-1-1842 Sh
Phillips, Martha T. to Sidney H. Tomlinson 4-8-1848 (4-15-1848) G
Phillips, Martha to Robert Culp 1-12-1866 (1-15-1866) F B
Phillips, Martha to Samuel Allen 1-17-1868 G
Phillips, Mary A. H. to Thomas Shelton 11-30-1874 (12-2-1874) Dy

Phillips, Mary Ann to John W. Bailey 4-21-1842 Sh
Phillips, Mary C. to C. W. Webb 10-30-1858 Cr
Phillips, Mary E. to Geo. M. Carricker 9-16-1857 Hr
Phillips, Mary E. to W. D. Buckley 3-20-1869 (3-23-1869) F
Phillips, Mary E. to William M. Smith 9-29-1869 (12-3-1869) F
Phillips, Mary F. to J. W. Bowelen 1-2-1867 Cr
Phillips, Mary H. to F. H. Chrisman 7-10-1848 L
Phillips, Mary J. to McCord Delaney 6-20-1859 Cr
Phillips, Mary K. to Charles C. Walton 7-30-1879 (7-31-1879) Dy
Phillips, Mary to Archeball Simmons 8-24-1842 Cr
Phillips, Mary to C. C. Faulkner 10-23-1874 (no return) Hy
Phillips, Mary to Claiborn A. Freeman 2-3-1845 (4-2-1845) G
Phillips, Mary to E. V. Lowrey ?-?-1862? Mn
Phillips, Mary to James M. Taylor 2-2-1849 O
Phillips, Mary to John Conyers 4-14-1853 Cr
Phillips, Matilda to Franklin Wright 3-6-1857 (3-12-1857) O
Phillips, Melissa to Thomas J. Gibson 12-22-1851 (no return) Cr
Phillips, Nancy P. to J. M. Combs 11-13-1863 (no return) Hn
Phillips, Nancy to James T. Collins 9-30-1850 Cr
Phillips, Nannie to William Marsh Folwell 11-22-1854 Sh
Phillips, Neely to Wm. Percell 12-29-1844 Cr
Phillips, Nettie to Peter J. Allen 9-8-1866 (9-9-1866) Ma
Phillips, Phetama to James P. Gray 1-31-1843 (2-7-1843) Hr
Phillips, Polina A. A. to Henry Hamilton 11-26-1859 We
Phillips, Polly to John Henson 12-19-1856 Hr
Phillips, Polly to John Sanders 4-2-1826 Sh
Phillips, Provie E. to John H. Guill 6-3-1868 (6-4-1868) Dy
Phillips, S. F. to F. M. Estes 10-13-1875 Dy
Phillips, S. F. to R. A. Hale 7-14-1858 We
Phillips, Sallie A. to W. C. Armstrong 10-21-1868 (10-22-1868) F
Phillips, Sarah I. to Thos. J. Tosh 12-26-1854 Cr
Phillips, Sarah to H. L. Bray 10-13-1859 Hr
Phillips, Sarah to W. H. Riley 9-8-1859 Hr
Phillips, Sidney to Allen Brogdon 9-29-1847 G
Phillips, Sophona M. to Edwin C. Buck 11-7-1850 Sh
Phillips, Susan A. to Benjamin B. Baggett 7-27-1843 Sh
Phillips, Susan E. to John Thomas Rose 2-14-1854 T
Phillips, Susan H. to John L. Bellew 2-9-1862 (no return) Cr
Phillips, Susan Jane to William J. Rooker 1-3-1860 (1-5-1860) Ma
Phillips, U. J. to R. J. Bell 11-27-1868 (11-29-1868) Cr
Phillips, Unity to John W. Montgomery 8-23-1843 We
Phillips, Virginia F. to Richard B Lyon 10-10-1849 (10-11-1849) G
Phillips, Zelpha A. D. to Francis M. Sellers 12-14-1847 Cr
Phillips, Zetha A. to Wm. P. Springer no date (1838-1859) Cr
Phillips, Zilphana Jane to Richard A. Cole 10-23-1844 Be
Phillys, Sarah to Williamson Rowlin 1-23-1840 Cr
Philpot, Harriett to Henry P. Mitchell 12-21-1848 Sh
Philpot, Mary to James Thompson 6-1-1833 (6-4-1833) Hr
Philpott, Emily to James A. Heaslet 5-3-1827 Hr
Philpott, Mary A. (Mrs.) to John Blackwell 1-18-1843 (no return) F
Philpott, Mary to John Blackwell 11-2-1829 Hr
Philps, Wilmoth C. to Harrison Simpson 12-11-1860 Cr
Phin, Louiza A. to Charles Linn 10-21-1858 Hn
Phipps, Jane to Joseph Cooper 11-20-1865 (11-31?-1866?) Cr
Phipps, Mary S. to Joseph L. Crawford (Cranford) 1-9-1840 Sh
Phipps, Nancy to John A. Argo 4-1-1841 Cr
Phipps, Narcissa A. to James S. Reece 5-7-1867 (no return) Cr
Phoebus, Sophia to W. B. Means 10-28-1847 Sh
Piber, Susan E. to V. B. Dodge 9-1-1846 O
Pibus, Prudy to Sina Jeffers 12-25-1873 Hy
Pickard, Ardelia to Thomas Pickard 1-9-1872 (1-14-1872) L
Pickard, Catharine to James M. King 2-5-1844 (2-6-1844) O
Pickard, E. C. to W. J. Faires 4-28-1857 T
Pickard, Ellen M. to C. V. Akin 1-26-1885 (1-29-1885) L
Pickard, Irena R. to Henry M. Loveene? 7-2-1872 (7-4-1872) T
Pickard, M. T. to J. H. Croach 11-16-1867 O
Pickard, Mahala to W. H. Wooten 9-24-1861 T
Pickard, Margaret to Washington Singleton 2-28-1872 (3-9-1872) T
Pickard, Mary J. to J. D. Easley 2-13-1860 (2-14-1860) T
Pickard, Ruth to Thomas G. Churchwell 3-12-1842 (3-13-1842) O
Pickard, Sarah to George Morrow 8-19-1856 O
Pickens, Ann to Thomas Crutchfield 10-21-1849 Hn
Pickens, Elisabeth J. (Mrs.) to L. A. Bly 9-14-1864 Sh
Pickens, Eliza to Martin Pearce 8-14-1869 (8-15-1869) Ma
Pickens, Elizabeth H. to J. H. Evans 10-9-1862 Mn
Pickens, Leeann E. to James B. Key 5-14-1856 Hr
Pickens, M. C. to W. C. Baldwin 1-31-1842 (2-6-1842) F
Pickens, Martha to Abraham Lawrence 2-17-1837 Hr
Pickens, Mary A. to T. H. Foote 11-23-1869 (11-25-1869) F
Pickens, S. A. to B. Finch no date (1864 or 65?) F
Pickens, S. S. to Wm. B. Cooper 8-28-1870 Cr
Picket, Ellen to Henry Burris 8-2-1851 (no return) F
Picket, Susan to Edward White 4-12-1871 (4-13-1871) L
Pickett, Alice to Sam Tipton 12-14-1881 (12-26-1881) L B
Pickett, Caroline to Russell Owen 12-21-1871 Hy
Pickett, Catharine E. to Andrew C. Russell 3-16-1853 Sh
Pickett, Eliza to William Hampton 10-21-1865 (no return) Cr

Pickett, Emily to George Boyd 12-1-1874 (no return) Hy
Pickett, Fanny A. to Thomas Y. Haynes 12-21-1869 (12-22-1869) Cr
Pickett, Jane to York Estis 12-22-1870 Hy
Pickett, Lucy A. to William Mathews 10-28-1877 L
Pickett, M. A. to James Lockhart 2-7-1859 (6-20-1859) Hr
Pickett, Margaret to Patrick Sullivan 7-6-1852 Sh
Pickett, Mary L. to Albernon S. Vigus 10-13-1859 Sh
Pickett, Mary to Ed D. Jenkins 9-23-1844 (9-26-1844) F
Pickett, Sallie E. to Thos. A. Anthony, jr. 12-19-1877 Hy
Pickins, Eliza J. to James L. Crawford 2-6-1867 (2-7-1867) F
Pickins, Margaret E. to Francis M. Griffin 12-24-1847 (12-28-1847) F
Pickins, Mary to William McClain 12-4-1839 (12-5-1839) Hr
Pickins, Nancy O. to Benjamin F. Meliam 10-13-1851 (no return) F
Pickins, Susan A. to H. S. Rogers 11-20-1867 (11-26-1867) F
Pickins, Uphemia to L. J. Utley 4-27-1870 Hy
Pickler, Any (Mrs.) to Latent Pearce 8-20-1860 (8-24-1860) Cr
Pickler, Martha J. to Henry H. Harrison 9-27-1863 Be
Pickler, Mary J. to J. W. Allen 7-30-1863 Cr
Pickler, Nanc S. to John N. Freelin 12-7-1867 (12-15-1867) Cr
Pickler, Nancy E. to Henry E. Wynn 8-21-1863 Be
Pickler, Sarah A. to N. David Presson 3-8-1860 Cr
Pickler, Sarah E. to W. M. Williams 1-14-1858 Cr
Pickler, Sarah to David Pinson ?-?-1860 Cr
Pickler, Susan J. to W. B. Bradberry 1-27-1864 (1-31-1864) Cr
Pickler, Syntha to Lewberry Hill 8-25-1844 Be
Pickler, T. P. to George W. Freeland 8-27-1869 (8-29-1869) Cr
Pickles, Mary J. to J. W. Allen 12-5-1863 Cr
Picot, Elizabeth to F. E. Stainback 2-15-1854 Sh
Pierce, Amanda to S. H. P. Lester 6-14-1875 (no return) Dy
Pierce, Angelina to Peter Sales 1-10-1878 Dy
Pierce, Ann Elizabeth to Wm. Mothershed 6-15-1856 Be
Pierce, Anna to E. L. Perkins 12-21-1854 (12-23-1854) Sh
Pierce, Arena W. to Isaac W. Pierce 1-5-1856 Be
Pierce, Catharine to John Reynolds 9-7-1857 O
Pierce, Della to James Dunn 7-26-1871 (7-28-1871) Ma
Pierce, Dollie to Wm. Howell 5-24-1869 Dy
Pierce, Elila to W.C. Barns 11-29-1865 Be
Pierce, Eliza Priscilla to William Boydston 9-18-1862 (9-22-1862) L
Pierce, Eliza to G. F. Hults 8-22-1855 (8-23-1855) Sh
Pierce, Elizabeth to John Delf 12-30-1872 Dy
Pierce, Elizabeth to Malden Y. Goad 2-22-1841 (3-14-1841) Ma
Pierce, Elizabeth to Robert Cooper 2-28-1865 Hn
Pierce, Ellen to Geo. (Capt.) Sprague 6-13-1863 (6-14-1863) Sh
Pierce, F. E. to W. W. Jordan 12-4-1871 Dy
Pierce, Fannie to Douglass Caldwell 12-15-1857 Sh
Pierce, Frances E. to Henry Boon 3-19-1862 Dy
Pierce, Henrietta to Washington Nelson 5-21-1885 L
Pierce, Isabella to John Craig 5-3-1869 G
Pierce, Isabella to Louis Southern 12-?-1865 (12-30-1865) Dy
Pierce, Jane to R. A. Grayham 10-13-1859 (no return) Cr
Pierce, Joanna to Ephraim Dority 12-13-1871 Dy
Pierce, Julina to J. B. Moor 1-11-1857 Be
Pierce, Kissiah to David C. Matheney 3-5-1846 Hn
Pierce, Lacy J. to W. A. Quillin 7-22-1855 Be
Pierce, Louisa to James H. Matheney 11-7-1844 Hn
Pierce, Lucritia to William Amos 5-23-1875 L B
Pierce, M. E. to J. J. Lane 10-15-1868 G
Pierce, Manerva to Redmond Richards 10-9-1850 (10-10-1850) Ma
Pierce, Margaret to Roland Gaulden 3-4-1876 (4-12-1876) Dy B
Pierce, Margaret to Willie Wood 4-4-1858 Hn
Pierce, Marry E. to John J. Henslee 3-6-1868 (no return) Cr
Pierce, Martha A. to Charles H. Bethany 7-8-1861 Be
Pierce, Martha A. to Liberty Walker 9-18-1852? (9-18-1851) Sh
Pierce, Mary C. to Daniel Nichols 2-2-1849 Cr
Pierce, Mary D. to Aaron Wadkins 8-15-1861 Be
Pierce, Mary D. to James B. Driskell 9-16-1848 (no return) Cr
Pierce, Mary E. to William F. Vaughn 4-2-1867 Hn
Pierce, Mary Jane to B. A. Powell 10-24-1867 Dy
Pierce, Mary P. to John T. Howell 8-19-1867 Dy
Pierce, Mary to Benjamin Marbry 1-11-1868 Be
Pierce, Mary to Dudley Alexander 5-5-1858 Ma
Pierce, Mary to J. T. McGlohon 7-9-1863 Be
Pierce, Mary to Malcomb McKenzie 12-24-1854 Be
Pierce, Mary to Marcus S. Rascoe 9-17-1858 Hn
Pierce, Missouri to J. M. Gold 7-24-1872 Dy
Pierce, Mollie to A. A. Steward 12-23-1875 L
Pierce, Mollie to Billy Fitzpatrick 4-30-1883 (not used) L
Pierce, Mollie to D. A. Shaw 1-16-1872 Dy
Pierce, Nancy E. to J. B. Lindsey 11-12-1857 Be
Pierce, Nancy M. to Calvin Carelton 1-9-1861 (1-10-1861) F
Pierce, Nancy to Nathan Williams 3-25-1857 Be
Pierce, Nancy to Nathan Williams 3-25-1857 Be CC
Pierce, Nancy to Robt. E. Quinan 10-2-1861 Sh
Pierce, Narcissa D. to Thos. P. Evens 9-16-1848 (no return) Cr
Pierce, Paralee to Robert Wells 10-7-1868 L
Pierce, Paulina S. to Thomas J. Morse? 9-23-1838 Hn
Pierce, Phillip to Charley Foulkes 10-30-1880 (10-31-1880) Dy

Pierce, Rachel to R. Carter 1-14-1865 Be
Pierce, Rachel to Whitmill P. Adams 11-16-1853 Ma
Pierce, Roda to Rupert Jones 10-14-1870 Dy
Pierce, Ruth to Jacob McCon 4-15-1873 (4-16-1873) Dy B
Pierce, Sallie R. to George A. Simpson 10-16-1861 Hn
Pierce, Sallie to M. R. Hendricks 3-23-1874 (3-24-1874) Dy
Pierce, Sarah Ann (Mrs.) to C. A. Willcher 12-3-1864 (12-4-1864) Sh
Pierce, Sarah to James Askew 3-15-1846 Hn
Pierce, Sarah to William Bettis 8-1-1833 Sh
Pierce, Susan to D. R. Fields 9-14-1865 Dy
Pierce, Susan to Zachariah Quinn 5-9-1867 Dy
Pierce, Susannah to Philip Delph 8-2-1879 (8-3-1879) Dy
Pierce, Tabitha to William Harrell 10-20-1846 (10-29-1846) Ma
Pierce, Theatus to William Throgmorton 12-29-1841 Hn
Piercey, Nancy L. to Barzilla Hopper 4-22-1844 Ma
Piercifull, Mary to Shadrich Baker 1-14-1850 (1-17-1849?) Ma
Piercy, Catherine to Abner W. Mason 1-9-1850 Ma
Piercy, Ellen to P. G. Marsh 7-17-1861 (7-18-1861) Sh
Piercy, Henrietta to Elijah Young 6-13-1884 (no return) L
Piercy, Jane to Elisha Lawrence 12-26-1848 Ma
Piercy, Lucinda to John Goad 8-17-1838 Ma
Piercy, Nancy C. to Elias Langford 3-6-1850 (3-8-1850) Ma
Piercy, Nancy D. to Wm. N. Massey 1-27-1856 Cr
Piercy, Sarah to Burrell Jones 12-26-1853 Ma
Piercy, Susan A. to John O. Glover 3-7-1850 (3-8-1850) Ma
Piercy, Telitha to James Canaven 12-17-1856 (12-18-1856) Ma
Pierson, Ada F. to C. S. McKinney 2-20-1872 L
Pierson, Clarisa to Henry Williams 9-16-1873 (9-17-1873) L B
Pierson, Ella to Thomas J. Sawyers 1-1-1872 (1-4-1872) L B
Pierson, Emma to Arnold Allen 11-12-1868 (no return) L B
Pierson, Hannah to Pinkney Collinsworth 1-24-1868 (no return) L B
Pierson, Lizzie to James Johnson 8-13-1879 (8-15-1879) L B
Pierson, Lucy to William Lanier 9-5-1870 (9-22-1870) L
Pierson, Milly to Henry Wright 12-25-1873 L B
Pig, Dilly A. to Joseph Darnell 3-5-1851 O
Pigel, Silvia to Robert Hudgen 12-26-1872 Cr B
Pigg, Dilly A. to Joseph Darnall 3-5-1847 O
Pigg, Emily C. to William C. Stennett 12-11-1848 (12-18-1848) O
Pigues, Elizabeth to Lewis Flowers 12-19-1868 G B
Pikston, Sarah to W. P. Radford 12-22-1857 Be
Pilcher, Catherine to John Winters 4-22-1839 Sh
Pile, Lucinda to Henry Moore 6-25-1869 T
Piles, Catharine to Jackson Ealom 7-24-1854 Sh
Piles, Hester to Samuel Deason 11-1-1834 Hr
Piles, Maria Jane to Stephen L. Pipkins 2-20-1861 Hr
Piles, Mary Ann to Pleasant Lusby (Lisby) 3-17-1845 Sh
Piles, Sally to Jesse Pipkin 1-4-1828 (1-6-1828) Hr
Piles, Sarah to Augustus Thebold 11-14-1860 (11-15-1860) Hr
Pilkington, Ann Eliza to James Osburn Hint? 12-9-1851 (12-10-1851) T
Pilkinton, Elizabeth A. to George Jackson 7-14-1861 We
Pillow, Josie to P. M. Sawyer 10-6-1876 (10-10-1876) L
Pillow, Julia A. to Benjamin Jobe 12-23-1863 (no return) Hn
Pillow, Julia N. to Benjamin N. Jobe 11-24-1863 Hn
Pillow, Lutetia to Monroe Dollison 6-29-1882 L
Pillow, Narcissa to Calvin S. Hooper 1-19-1859 (1-20-1859) L
Pillow, Rebecca to John L. Curbey? 5-25-1863 (no return) Hn
Pillow, Sarah E. to Cyrus Crihfield 4-15-1861 (4-17-1861) L
Pillow, Tennesee to David Tatum 12-24-1872 (12-26-1872) L B
Pillows, Luenida to Thompson Moore 12-20-1866 G
Pilly?, Louisa to Haskin Tyus 1-26-1875 L
Pinchback, Mary Ann to James T. Sutton 4-18-1848 (4-19-1848) F
Pinckley, M.J. to Wm. C. Chambers 2-2-1871 Cr
Pinckley, N. C. to James W. Belew 11-9-1870 (11-10-1870) Cr
Pindergast, Catharine to David O'Brien 9-21-1857 Hr
Pingleton, Elizabeth to Neil Smith 5-20-1861 (5-26-1861) Hr
Pingleton, Sary E. to Elisha Scates 11-25-1858 We
Pinington, Martha A. to Howel Vick 1-6-1846 G
Pinion, Martha A. to David Gage 12-24-1844 G
Pinkard, Henrietta to G. G. Bell 12-30-1854 (12-31-1854) Sh
Pinkerten, Nancy M. to William F. Smith 5-31-1859 We
Pinket, Margarett to Samuel Maurach? 11-2-1840 F
Pinkett, Mary Ann to Franklin Flemming 12-21-1831 Sh
Pinkins, Caleder to Henry Myers 2-18-1875 Hy
Pinkley, Savanah to John C. Holloway 4-1-1841 Cr
Pinkston, Deliah to Jacob Smothers 10-14-1848 Cr
Pinkston, Elizabeth to G. W. Winberry 6-17-1861 Be
Pinkston, Elizabeth to Thos. Norwood 1-2-1866 Cr
Pinkston, Emanuel to Charley Cooper 6-25-1840 Cr
Pinkston, Emily M. to Jabez T. Boyd 8-25-1868 (8-26-1868) Cr
Pinkston, Eviline to Pinkney H. Melton 6-22-1861 Be
Pinkston, Harriet to Jesse Smothers 4-5-1846 Cr
Pinkston, Jane to William Turner 6-1-1861 (no return) Dy
Pinkston, Lidia to Elijah W. Melton 11-26-1864 Be
Pinkston, Lucinda to H. Brackin 7-7-1841 Cr
Pinkston, Lydia to Granville Trout 2-12-1857 Cr
Pinkston, Lydia to John Billings 1-10-1849 Cr
Pinkston, Manda C. to James G. Boyd 2-24-1853 Cr

Pinkston, Manda L. to Wm. J. Orily 2-18-1863 Be
Pinkston, Martha to Green Smothers 10-22-1845 Cr
Pinkston, Martha to John Hutchison 12-1-1871 (no return) Cr
Pinkston, Mary A. to Wm. C. Newman 8-6-1861 (8-9-1861) Cr
Pinkston, Mary C. to Henry P. Simmons 4-13-1853 Cr
Pinkston, Mary E. to H. F. Nelms 3-5-1870 (3-6-1870) T
Pinkston, Melissa F. to Edmond Finch 10-25-1869 (10-28-1869) Cr
Pinkston, Rhody J. to J. T. Espy 7-24-1865 Dy
Pinkston, Sarah C. to Granvill M. Trout 11-18-1864 Be
Pinkston, Syntha to James H. Short 7-23-1851 Be
Pinner?, Jane to Alfred Young 12-7-1852 T
Pinnon, Martha E. to W. H. H. Murray 11-23-1876 Dy
Pinon, Mary Ann to Light N. Parker 1-31-1856 O
Pinon, Mary C. to T. J. Roney 12-20-1867 O
Pinson (Pierson?), Virginia to Ezekiel Williams 4-24-1869 (4-29-1869) L B
Pinson, Ann E. to E. Jackson 10-24-1867 Hn
Pinson, Caroline to George W. Humble 12-22-1853 Cr
Pinson, Eliza Elin to P. B. Johnson 11-7-1874 (11-8-1874) T
Pinson, Elizabeth to Richard Phillips 12-27-1850 Cr
Pinson, Ellen to Daniel P. Rodgers no date (1838-1859) Cr
Pinson, Estella Ann to Wm. Campbell Norton 9-7-1852 T
Pinson, Gafa P. to John P. Sutton 2-5-1855 Cr
Pinson, Laura to James H. Hunley 10-25-1872 T
Pinson, Lou to Abram Green 8-24-1883 (8-30-1883) L
Pinson, Louisa L. to Sherwood Fors 6-28-1846 Cr
Pinson, Martha J. to Samuel V. Fields 11-28-1865 (no return) Cr
Pinson, Martha to B. H. Nesbett 1-6-1852 Cr
Pinson, Mary J. to B. H. Nesbett 9-27-1848 Cr
Pinson, Mary J. to Thomas R. Green 5-15-1857 Cr
Pinson, Mary to James R. Bonds 10-17-1841 Cr
Pinson, Matilda D. to Newton H. Martin 2-20-1865 (2-25-1865) Cr
Pinson, Nancy to J. A. Thomas 1-10-1870 T
Pinson, Nancy to J. A. Thomas 1-10-1870 (1-13-1870) T
Pinson, P. C. to J. R. Massey 2-25-1870 (2-28-1870) Cr
Pinson, R. A. to David Malone 11-21-1850 Cr
Pinson, Rebecca to Byrd McKinney 1-16-1859 Hn
Pinson, Sealeana L. to Aaron Lipe 8-25-1841 Cr
Pinyan, Ellen to Ben T. Walker 11-3-1877 (11-4-1877) Dy
Piolate, Caroline to Henry Fletcher 8-8-1843 G
Piper, Lucinda to Henry Davis 5-28-1844 Sh
Piper, Mary A. to Wm. Keating 2-18-1850 Cr
Pipes, Isabela to James H. Scholding 6-13-1876 (6-14-1876) L
Pipins, Lucinda to John Nichols 3-25-1857 Be
Pipkin, Ann Eliza to Robert Brown 11-23-1857 Hr
Pipkin, Jane C. to William Todd 1-12-1858 (1-14-1858) Ma
Pipkin, Luan to Thomas Harrell 5-15-1848 (5-18-1848) Ma
Pipkin, M. A. to John G. Thum 1-10-1878 L
Pipkin, Mary A. H. to Allen M. Thompson 9-17-1855 (9-18-1855) Hr
Pipkin, Mary Jane to James Owen Wence 9-20-1847 Sh
Pipkin, Minerva M. to James M. Piles 4-3-1861 (4-4-1861) Hr
Pipkin, Sarah M. to Wm. Croom 3-3-1863 Sh
Pipkins, Ellen to S. M. Roy 12-13-1876 L
Pipkins, Jane to Philip Smith 1-2-1845 We
Pipkins, Kissiah H. to John H. Brown 12-28-1853 (12-29-1853) Hr
Pipkins, Mattie P. to George W. Wood 9-10-1879 L
Pipkins, Nancy A. to Isaac Stafford 7-19-1855 We
Pipkins, Nancy H. to W. H. Pipkins 3-13-1869 (no return) L
Pipkins, Nancy to Robert Price 11-22-1862 Mn
Pipkins, O. A. to E. J. Crihfield 2-12-1884 (2-14-1884) L
Pipkins, Rebecca to Elijah Billingsley 2-25-1828 (2-26-1828) G
Pipkins, Talitha to Wm. Henson 6-2-1856 Hr
Pippens, Caroline to Wm. M. Horton 2-12-1867 Be
Pippin, Frances to David T. Thurman 1-30-1854 Ma
Pippin, Margaret to Louis Jones 3-15-1871 (3-20-1871) F
Pippin, Susan to James Lindley 7-30-1866 (7-31-1866) F
Pirtle, Ann to Joe Walker 12-31-1866 (1-1-1867) F B
Pirtle, Elizabeth to Richard Lamb 1-7-1828 (1-8-1828) Hr
Pirtle, Malinda to Joseph D. Hackney 11-15-1852 Hr
Pirtle, Martha to Wiley A. Carrington 4-30-1859 (5-2-1859) Hr
Pirtle, Mary Ann to Isaac B. Hubbard 1-3-1849 Hr
Pirtle, Mary Ann to Thomas L. Carter 9-10-1859 Hr
Pirtle, Mary Ann to William Black 2-6-1854 (2-12-1854) Hr
Pirtle, Mary to Thomas Smith 8-6-1827 (8-7-1827) Hr
Pirtle, Nancy to Danl. W. Brown 7-30-1859 Hr
Pirtle, Rebecca to Benjamin A. Harriss 12-27-1837 (12-28-1837) Hr
Pitchard, Margaret to Isaac Lowe 3-10-1843 (3-12-1843) L
Pitchford, Lively to Boldin Finch 5-23-1829 Hr
Pitman, Amanda E. to John R. Woodson 10-7-1848 F
Pitman, Mary Ann to Samuel Park 1-29-1848 (1-31-1848) Hr
Pitner, M. A. to Charley Miller 7-27-1869 Hy
Pitt, Easther F. to Gilbert McKenzie 2-10-1846 Be
Pitt, Martha J. to Alsey McDaniel 10-17-1844 Be
Pitt, Mary to William H. Winn 3-1-1865 (3-3-1865) T
Pittma, Elizabeth to Benj. A. Yeargain 10-25-1853 (10-26-1853) G
Pittman (Pellman?), Talithia to W. E. Cook 3-2-1877 (3-4-1877) L
Pittman, Catherine to J. T. Neal 3-28-1866 Hy
Pittman, Elizabeth to Thomas Ford 8-16-1858 Sh

Pittman, Jincy Ann to Laborne Haislip 12-9-1871 (12-10-1871) L
Pittman, Leuvenia M. to L. G. H. Pittman 11-16-1847 (11-18-1847) G
Pittman, Margaret M. to William Hutcheson 6-18-1867 (6-19-1867) L
Pittman, Mary A. to Charles M. Johnson 1-24-1853 (1-27-1853) G
Pittman, Mary P. to Thomas J. Turner 12-5-1860 (12-6-1860) L
Pittman, N. S. to M. L. Anderson 1-17-1878 L
Pittman, Nannie to Dave Mebane 2-20-1871 (2-21-1871) F
Pittman, Winniford to Asberry Steward 12-5-1878 L
Pittmon?, Wineford to Thomas L. Koonce 3-26-1873 L
Pitts, Ada to Charles Young 3-13-1884 L
Pitts, Caldonia to T. W. Watson 12-13-1871 (12-14-1871) L
Pitts, Dinah to Al Young 1-13-1880 (1-14-1880) L
Pitts, Elizabeth F. to George C. Webb 11-12-1857 (no return) L
Pitts, Elizabeth to William Wasson 7-28-1844 Sh
Pitts, Emily E. to Robert A. Williams 10-25-1876 (no return) L
Pitts, F. A. to R. H. Revis 11-28-1876 (11-29-1876) L
Pitts, Franky to John Roundtree 7-13-1872 (7-14-1872) L
Pitts, Henrietta M. to James A. Glenn 11-18-1852 L
Pitts, Jennie to B. Frank Langley 12-17-1874 L
Pitts, Kessandria to Peter Winn 3-7-1840 (3-27-1840) O
Pitts, Linda to Ziba Anderson 12-24-1877 (12-25-1877) L B
Pitts, Louisiana to A. B. F. Chambers 12-20-1842 (12-23-1842) L
Pitts, Lucenda C. to Thomas V. Barnes 9-28-1861 (9-30-1861) L
Pitts, Lucinda to Henry P. Barefield 3-28-1849 (3-29-1849) L
Pitts, Lucy Ellen to William Salisbury 3-26-1856 (3-27-1856) L
Pitts, Margaret to Nelson Young 1-11-1883 L
Pitts, Martha A. to Isaac Cunningham 6-23-1866 (6-24-1866) L
Pitts, Martha E. to R. F. Viar 8-22-1866 (8-23-1866) Dy
Pitts, Martha G. to A. J. McCorkle 7-21-1856 (7-24-1856) G
Pitts, Mary A. to W. E. Curtis 7-30-1869 (no return) Dy
Pitts, Mary E. to Andrew J. Nunn 12-10-1860 (no return) L
Pitts, Mary to John A. Johnson 1-25-1849 Cr
Pitts, Mary to Thomas Cotham 2-21-1869 (no return) Dy
Pitts, Millie to Cooper Moore, jr. 9-5-1867 G B
Pitts, Rody to Charles Inns 12-17-1870 Hy
Pitts, Rosa to Jim Green 3-3-1868 (3-?-1868) L B
Pitts, Sarah F. to David Ford 12-4-1846 L
Pitts, Sarah H. to David Ford 2-20-1846 (no return) L
Pitts, V. A. to J. J. Hamilton 1-22-1879 (1-23-1879) Dy
Plant, Elizabeth A. to Joshua V. Smith 6-14-1841 (6-15-1841) F
Plant, Malinda to George M. Smith 1-11-1843 (1-12-1843) F
Plant, Mary J. to W. T. Abbington 12-3-1866 (12-4-1866) F
Plant, Permelia H. to Felix Owens 1-12-1839 (1-15-1839) F
Plant, Sarah to Green W. Bobbitt 12-15-1845 (12-16-1845) F
Plant, Sarah to Moses McCarty 8-31-1831 Hr
Plant, Susan E. to W. C. Pearce 11-30-1866 (12-5-1866) F
Platt, Amelia to Horace Bigelow 4-6-1869 Hy
Platt, Berthie to Meier Newman 5-18-1864 Sh
Platt, Elizabeth to Duke Baker 2-11-1863 Dy
Pleasant, A. E. to I. W. Powel 3-20-1866 (3-22-1866) O
Pleasant, Emily B. to William Kenan Hill 6-12-1855 Sh
Pleasant, M. A. to T. L. Anthony 10-29-1849 (11-4-1849) F
Pleasants, Lucy W. to N. J. Cocke 10-14-1845 (10-15-1845) F
Pleasants, Millie to James H. Meacham 2-22-1837 O
Pleasants, Paulina M. to William Ragsdale 10-18-1847 (10-20-1847) F
Pleasants, Sarah J. to Nathanl. Blain 4-9-1842 (4-14-1842) F
Pled;ge, Sarah E. to D. R. Carter 11-26-1855 (11-27-1855) Hr
Pledge, Mary E. to Jas. M. Peers 3-28-1855 (4-2-1855) Hr
Pledge, Melora S. to Robert A. Burrow 7-25-1852 (9-8-1852) Hr
Plot, Sallie to John Carrol 1-13-1862 Sh
Plott, Sallie J. to Samuel A. H. Haines 3-18-1862 (3-20-1862) Sh
Pluckrose, Mary L. to James Penney 3-2-1863 Sh
Plumer, Adeline to George W. Read 5-19-1874 Hy
Plumley, Mary E. to John W. Bucham 5-30-1872 T
Plummer, Ann R. to Oscar F. Prescott 7-25-1844 Sh
Plummer, Annie E. to W. R. Johnson 1-21-1869 F
Plummer, Catherine to Thos. Walker 6-18-1853 Sh
Plummer, Ella to Swail Douglass 1-10-1876 (no return) Hy
Plummer, Harriet to Ben Douglas 3-13-1878 Hy
Plummer, Jennie to J. W. White 7-25-1871 (7-13?-1871) Cr
Plummer, Looky to Wm. Maclin 12-20-1871 T
Plummer, Mary A. to Wm. C. Noble 2-2-1864 Sh
Plummer, Mary to Wm. O. Noble 10-5-1864 (10-6-1864) Sh
Plummer, Sarah D. to Alfred S. Jones 11-28-1855 Sh
Plunk, Girldine to James A. Young 2-15-1864 Mn
Plunk, Lucy to A. R. Sewell 2-27-1862 Mn
Plunk, Melisa to Daniel Malone 8-5-1862 Mn
Plunk, Nancy E. to Franklyn Brack 1-17-1863 Mn
Plunk, Narcissa to Harrison Malone 5-7-1861 Mn
Plunkett, Catharine to Andrew Brady 6-13-1853 Sh
Plunkett, Jane to James Rice 2-4-1856 Sh
Podge, Martha to Thomas Mikel 2-6-1849 Hn
Podge, Penesa to Joseph McMichael 4-9-1851 Hn
Poe, A. M. to W. F. Thompson 1-10-1864 Be
Poe, Eliza H. to N. S. Hermon 10-16-1853 Hn
Poe, Eliza to William H. Palmer 2-5-1845 (no return) Hn
Poe, Elizabeth to James J. Bowden 10-12-1848 Hn

Poe, Jane to John Davis 2-7-1850 Be
Poe, Lucy Ann to Alvin Jordon 9-14-1845 Be
Poe, Martha C. to Alexander McIver 12-8-1830 Ma
Poe, Rachael to James H. Bridges 9-22-1846 Be
Poe, Sarah Jane to John P. Daugherty 4-20-1853 Hn
Poe, Texanna to E. M. Lake 10-2-1875 (10-7-1875) L
Poff, Frances to J. W. Henderson 2-20-1867 (2-21-1867) T
Poff, Lucinda to Yancy Weaver 1-15-1874 Hy
Poindexter, America C. to James V. McFarlin 7-5-1859 (7-7-1859) Ma
Poindexter, Angeline to Henry McFarland 5-11-1868 (5-16-1868) F B
Poindexter, Betsy to Tom Jordan 1-4-1869 F B
Poindexter, Catharine to Richard Rives 9-25-1869 F B
Poindexter, Elmira to Joseph Wilson 12-20-1869 (12-30-1869) F B
Poindexter, Elvira to John Boyd 12-26-1867 (12-27-1867) F B
Poindexter, Emily J. to William Johnson 3-20-1869 F B
Poindexter, Evalin to S. M. Hayley 3-21-1871 (no return) Cr
Poindexter, Fannie to George J. Whittle 5-1-1867 (5-11-1867) F B
Poiner, Cordelia L. to Green? L. Irwin 12-18-1844 Hr
Poiner, Elizabeth to B. H. Bodwell 10-25-1847 Hn
Poiner, Mary S. to Henry Holly 9-10-1838 (9-11-1838) Hr
Poiner, Perlina to John H. Bowden 10-29-1845 (no return) Hn
Poiner, S. F. to B. F. Elicker 1-25-1866 Hn
Pointer, Martha M. J. to Stephen B. Jones 1-20-1862 We
Pointer, Polly to John Nance 7-23-1862 (no return) Hn
Poke, Dollie to Tobias Dickson 3-1-1868 Hy
Poke, Margaret to Hal Anderson 12-28-1869 (1-1-1870) F B
Pole, Emily (Mrs.) to Denning Presley 2-8-1868 Ma
Poleston, Caroline to Henry Abbet 8-28-1865 Be
Polk, Ann to John C. McNeill 5-10-1859 (6-15-1859) Hr
Polk, Benigna to William H. Woods 7-12-1834 Hr
Polk, Catherine W. to J. M. Crockett 1-14-1837 (1-17-1837) O
Polk, Clarissa to Andrew Taylor 6-7-1824 (6-11-1824) Hr
Polk, Dilly to C. P. James 9-17-1869 (no return) F
Polk, Dollie to Robert Greaves 1-9-1878 (no return) Hy
Polk, Eliza to Calumbus Hogan 12-1-1869 (12-2-1869) T
Polk, Eliza to William jr. Nuckolls 9-5-1850 Hr
Polk, Elizabeth to Alfred Neal 9-16-1829 (10-3-1829) Hr
Polk, Emily to James L. Person 11-23-1858 (11-24-1858) Sh
Polk, Emma O. to R. M. Bouchette 12-31-1842 (1-3?-1843) F
Polk, Eugenia to Alexander G. Neilson 7-18-1827 Hr
Polk, Harriet to Thomas Jackson 10-17-1874 (10-28-1874) T
Polk, Henrieta E. to A. H. Avery 4-10-1848 (4-12-1848) F
Polk, Henrietta B. to H. M. Lynn no date (with 5-1860) Sh
Polk, Henrietta B. to J. L. Bolton 1-28-1861 (1-30-1861) Sh
Polk, Jane G. to John Smoot 5-3-1842 Hr
Polk, Louisa to T. J. Chambers 9-27-1858 (9-28-1858) Sh
Polk, Lucy N. to William N. Lennard 4-18-1827 Hr
Polk, Martha H. to Robert D. Durrett 11-8-1841 F
Polk, Mary A. to Geo. Davis 11-19-1842 (11-17?-1842) F
Polk, Mary E. to Douglass R. Hunt 4-3-1846 (4-8-1846) F
Polk, Mary Jane to B. S. Brown 1-29-1857 Sh
Polk, Mary Jane to J. M. Redus 10-22-1859 (10-25-1859) Sh
Polk, Mary to Jacob Garrett 9-12-1829 (10-3-1829) Hr
Polk, Mary to Nathaniel Rodgers 2-23-1843 Hr
Polk, Mary to Wardlaw Howard 12-29-1834 Hr
Polk, Mattie E. to Samhl. H. Thomas 2-8-1871 (no return) F
Polk, Nancy (Mrs.) to John L. Phillips 8-11-1882 (8-12-1882) L
Polk, Rachel to Prit Drane? 12-3-1868 (12-4-1868) T
Polk, Sarah to Caleb S. Knott 9-5-1863 Sh
Polk, Sarah to M. Doyle 12-16-1851 Sh
Polk, V. G. to P. H. Bowen 3-9-1864 F
Pollard, Elizabeth to Francis Perry 12-3-1827 (12-6-1827) G
Pollard, Mahaly C. to Cullen Andrews 9-25-1856 G
Pollard, Martha Elizabeth to Izeral Crain Watson 9-20-1870 L
Pollard, Mary L. to J. P. C. Meacham 12-16-1874 L
Pollard, Meinga? to Robert Joyce 11-16-1839 Cr
Pollard, N. J. to R. A. Braden 2-3-1879 (2-4-1879) L
Pollard, Rebecca to Mark Forest 1-24-1829 (1-31-1829) G
Pollard, Sarah Ann to Simeon Cudd 1-11-1849 G
Pollard, Susan to Thomas W. McCollam 12-29-1851 (1-8-1852) G
Pollerd, Blanch to Charney Hilliard 2-4-1871 (2-12-1871) F B
Pollock, Amanda to J. C. Jacobi 1-9-1855 (1-11-1855) Sh
Pollock, Eliza Jane to Alexander Settle 7-30-1870 (8-5-1870) Ma
Pollock, Elizabeth to Thomas Marlow 8-14-1852 (8-19-1852) O
Pollock, F. to Daniel Lacewell 9-21-1850
Pollock, Martha A. to Geo. W. Bryant 7-24-1865 (7-25-1865) F
Pollock, Martha J. to D. M. Pogue 6-17-1865 (6-18-1865) L
Pollock, Martha to William Davis 10-2-1855 O
Pollock, Mary A. to J. L. Taylor 4-12-1851 O
Pollock, Melinda Jane to Edward T. Shelton 3-11-1848 (3-16-1848) O
Pollock, Nancy E. to Winfield Scott 12-28-1858 (1-6-1859) O
Pollock, R. P. to D. W. Eaton 11-5-1869 F
Pollock, Samanthy to Charles Edmonds 12-13-1869 (12-16-1869) F
Polly, Elizabeth A. to John C. McKamey 4-9-1859 (4-14-1859) O
Polly, Rebecca to William Williams 2-13-1858 (2-14-1858) O
Polly, Short to Austin Powell 11-21-1868 Hy
Polsgrove, Amanda to James Asbell 4-29-1857 O

Polsgrove, Cynthia Ann to John Morrow 4-9-1857 O
Polsgrove, Elizabeth to William G. McElyea 8-17-1856 (8-18-1856) O
Polsgrove, Virginia H. to William J. Grayham 7-25-1858 O
Polston, Dumbilla to J. M. Rodgers 8-14-1876 (8-15-1876) Dy
Polston, Martha J. to J. B. Bateman 6-22-1869 (6-23-1869) Cr
Pond, Nancy to Nelson Mitchell 2-3-1840 (2-6-1840) F
Pondell, Nancy to J. H. Key 2-21-1860 Cr
Ponder, Caroline to McCamy W. Osburn 5-5-1846 Be
Ponder, Exery to Britton Tully 1-28-1846 Cr
Pooch, Nancy to Wm. M. Tipton 12-25-1866 Dy
Pool, Amanda to Joseph A. Clayton 6-22-1847 Sh
Pool, Ann to John Smith 9-26-1870 T
Pool, Bammer to George Maburn 9-7-1871 (9-9-1871) T
Pool, Caroline to E. H. Root 12-25-1843 Sh
Pool, Elizabeth to Isaac Glass 9-11-1848 (9-14-1848) Hr
Pool, Emily E. to R. W. Stroud 10-29-1854 Hn
Pool, Hester to John T. Key 12-29-1834 Sh
Pool, Levina to Moses Cowan 6-13-1844 F
Pool, M. E. C. to Jesse Boon 12-12-1865 (12-15-1865) F
Pool, M. E. to L. W. Trobough 5-21-1862? T
Pool, M. to Henry Row 4-16-1868 (no return) F B
Pool, Martha A. to E. Mis? Kelly 12-27-1865 Dy
Pool, Martha A. to E. Miskelly 12-27-1865 (12-30-1865) Dy
Pool, Martha A. to Thomas Carlton 10-28-1852 We
Pool, Mary A. to Lafayette Schroeder 1-2-1853 Hn
Pool, Mary J. to John G. Pool 1-21-1861 (1-23-1861) Sh
Pool, Matilda to John T. Heady 10-3-1850 Sh
Pool, Nancy Ann to Granberry Daniel 8-16-1842 Ma
Pool, Rosanna to Jesse Red 12-30-1869 (no return) F B
Pool, Sarah to Washington Read 11-28-1828 (11-30-1828) Hr
Pool, Suentia to F. M. Settles 1-28-1844 Hn
Pool, Tebitha D. to John Vantresse 12-25-1840 Hr
Poole, Elizabeth E. to W. L. Allison 9-4-1865 (9-7-1865) O
Poole, Elizabeth to Samuel Washington 3-22-1830 Hn
Poole, Fanny to Nathan Petty 1-29-1859 (1-31-1859) Sh
Poole, Louisa to Van Forrester 5-3-1852 (5-6-1852) Sh
Poole, Rachel to John Hensley 1-23-1858 F
Poor, America J. to H. L. Gwyn 2-4-1865 (2-6-1865) F
Poor, Cornelia to Joe Holleman 12-26-1866 (12-27-1866) F B
Poor, Sarah A. to J. J. Lowry 7-17-1860 (7-19-1860) T
Poor, Thomis? to Lewis Walker 4-3-1830 Ma
Poore, M. F. to William Neal 12-22-1856 (no return) F
Poore, Polly to George Freeman 7-9-1846 (no return) Hn
Poors, Margaret to Henry Johnson 2-12-1852 Sh
Pope, Arabella to John T. Moore 12-28-1867 Ma
Pope, B. F. to J. F. Brown 4-9-1866 (no return) Cr
Pope, Caledonia to Henry F. James 1-?-1864 (1-15-1864) Sh
Pope, Calta E. J. to Samuel S. Cochran 1-15-1862 We
Pope, Cornelia W. to A. T. Gossett 1-14-1871 (1-17-1871) F
Pope, D. E. to J. H. Pierce 1-19-1876 (no return) Dy
Pope, D. L. to H. C. Hart 2-15-1876 Dy
Pope, Darthula to Richard H. Byrns? 1-19-1869 (1-24-1869) Cr
Pope, Delany to Samuel Tittle 11-13-1838 Be
Pope, E. C. to Eli Cox 3-9-1852 We
Pope, Eliza to Archabald Canady 1-14-1842 (1-20-1842) G
Pope, Eliza to W. T. Reycroft 6-8-1870 (10-5-1870) Dy
Pope, Frances N. to Robert J. Strayhorn 1-26-1859 (1-27-1859) Ma
Pope, Harriett J. to Charles Cowell 11-19-1840 Be
Pope, J. to Edward Barnes (Baines?) 4-4-1853 (4-16-1853) L
Pope, Jane B. to Edwin T. Taliaferro 5-27-1845 G
Pope, Judith M. to Fredrick Ingate 7-3-1855 (7-4-1855) Sh
Pope, Judith M. to Wynham Robertson 9-22-1847 Sh
Pope, K. C. to Benj. F. Tucker 10-13-1857 (9?-18-1857) Hr
Pope, Katie G. to Daniel Russell 2-16-1876 Hy
Pope, Laura A. to M. T. Kernan 5-28-1872 (no return) Cr
Pope, Louisa E. to Willie B. Miller 5-19-1845 Sh
Pope, M. E. to T. F. Ray 1-7-1869 Dy
Pope, Margaret A. to J. H. Pipkins 7-16-1870 (7-17-1870) F
Pope, Maria P. to St. Clair M. Morgan 5-4-1854 Sh
Pope, Mariah L. to Neil McLeod 9-10-1844 L
Pope, Martha A. to G. L. Short 10-8-1857 G
Pope, Martha to Samuel Simmons 9-7-1878 (9-17-1878) Dy
Pope, Martha to Thos. Johnston 4-9-1839 (4-11-1839) G
Pope, Mary E. to O. E. Lanier 10-28-1867 (10-29-1867) Dy
Pope, Mary to James Crews 11-5-1849 (11-8-1849) G
Pope, Narcissa C. to James S. Boyd 2-26-1851 L
Pope, Narcissa to Presley T. Beard 3-2-1857 G
Pope, P. to William Crews 1-19-1857 G
Pope, Peney to John Wolard 10-30-1839 (10-31-1839) G
Pope, Percy to James Alexander 6-8-1854 G
Pope, Sarah to James Brewer 2-12-1876 (2-10?-1876) Dy
Pope, Sentha J. to David Hisaw 9-2-1844 G
Popkins, Nancy to Nathaniel Newbill 7-26-1866 (no return) Cr
Porch, Louisa C. to Benjamin F. Taylor 4-18-1861 (no return) We
Porch, Mary A. to L. L. Wright 5-18-1859 (5-22-1859) Hr
Porter, A. to J. W. Cooper 9-2-1847 Hn
Porter, Alice to Luke Nash 10-8-1877 (10-9-1877) Dy

Porter, Amand to Ed White 2-21-1873 (2-23-1873) Cr
Porter, Anna M. to John M. Clark 10-11-1853 Hn
Porter, Bettie W. to E. H. Porter 10-3-1861 Sh
Porter, C. E. to E. C. Trimble 10-28-1850 Hn
Porter, Camilla to Charles G. Jones 10-9-1865 (10-11-1865) F
Porter, Caroline to John Chub 7-3-1858 Sh B
Porter, Caroline to M. L. Dickerson 8-10-1859 (no return) Hy
Porter, Cary to David Williams 5-14-1850 Sh
Porter, Catharine S. to William R. Gardner 11-26-1866 (12-2-1866) Cr
Porter, Darcus to Archibal Pope 3-19-1856 (3-20-1856) G
Porter, Diana W. to Israel M. L. Barker 11-27-1860 Hn
Porter, E. F. to A. T. Burns 12-16-1872 (12-19-1872) Cr
Porter, E. P. to J. D. C. Atkins 11-23-1847 Hn
Porter, Eliza Jane to Quince Tomlinson 1-1-1872 (1-3-1872) L B
Porter, Eliza to Cullen Strickland 6-6-1849 (6-7-1849) Hr
Porter, Elizabeth to Lemuel Powell 3-25-1851 (3-27-1851) Hr
Porter, Ellen to W. N. Woodfin 2-12-1856 Hn
Porter, Eva L. to Eugene T. Harris 2-6-1866 Hn
Porter, Fannie to Marcus Bowen 12-28-1872 (12-30-1872) Dy
Porter, Fanny E. to Z. S. A. Mitchell 3-27-1867 G
Porter, Flora to Jonathan J. Downing 12-14-1840 Cr
Porter, Frances E. to T. D. G. McClellan 8-29-1848 F
Porter, Frances to Letas Beckett 5-30-1871 (6-1-1871) Dy
Porter, Geraldine to Dixon G. Fowler 10-20-1859 Hn
Porter, Glora to Luke Johnson 2-18-1882 (2-21-1882) L
Porter, Harriet to Dempsie Mabin 4-28-1868 (no return) F B
Porter, Huldah to Uriah Walker 12-12-1876 (12-13-1876) Dy
Porter, Isabella to Joel Parr 9-8-1840 Sh
Porter, Italie G. to J. W. Rhea 4-12-1860 Sh
Porter, J. A. to W. D. Jones 11-6-1861 Cr
Porter, Julia Ann to Dennis Jackson 7-2-1869 (no return) F B
Porter, Louisa to Allen Swift 2-5-1870 G B
Porter, M. A. to T. J. Vanderville 10-18-1858 (10-19-1858) Sh
Porter, M. C. to Thomas R. Tharpe 6-9-1851 Hn
Porter, M. T. to J. H. Spain 2-19-1873 Cr
Porter, Mahala to John Bowden 9-16-1865 Hn
Porter, Mahulda to Louis Hill 5-19-1880 (5-20-1880) Dy
Porter, Malinda to James A. Thomas 11-29-1841 (11-30-1841) G
Porter, Margaret A. to John M. Paine 11-1-1869 F B
Porter, Margaret to Frank McCutchen 12-3-1873 (12-4-1873) Dy
Porter, Martha L. to George W. Hawk 9-21-1853 Cr
Porter, Martha to Perry Porter 2-14-1870 (2-15-1870) Cr
Porter, Mary A. E. to John C. W. Nunn 9-4-1854 (9-5-1854) G
Porter, Mary A. to William E. Cullum 7-20-1848 (no return) F
Porter, Mary B. to F. A. Henry 1-8-1883 L
Porter, Mary C. to James H. Wood 10-23-1876 (10-24-1876) Dy
Porter, Mary C. to John T. Swayne 4-29-1851 Sh
Porter, Mary D. to J. B. Wilkes 1-21-1868 G
Porter, Mary D. to William G. Hurt 5-12-1860 Hn
Porter, Mary E. to H. H. Richardson 1-30-1844 L
Porter, Mary E. to Marcus Jones 11-27-1848 Sh
Porter, Mary P. to Francis M. Lucus 7-1-1872 (no return) L
Porter, Mary to J. W. Emerson 12-21-1871 Hy
Porter, Mary to Pleasant Fitzgerald 10-25-1866 Hn
Porter, Matilda to John Flowers 12-6-1856 (12-7-1856) G
Porter, Matilda to Robert P. Crockett 10-16-1841 (10-21-1841) G
Porter, Nancy A. D. to W. G. Weaver 12-26-1869 G
Porter, Nancy C. (Mrs.) to John Ward 1-12-1864 (1-13-1864) Sh
Porter, Nancy L. to H. W. (W. H.) Wilson 1-4-1865 G
Porter, Nancy P. to Solomon Human 12-17-1833 G
Porter, Nancy to George W. Lovitt 11-22-1852 (11-23-1852) G
Porter, Nancy to James Christian 7-16-1870 (5?-11?-1870) F B
Porter, Nancy to John A. Bailey 7-4-1853 G
Porter, Persia M. to John C. Hawkins 5-27-1863 Cr
Porter, Rebecca T. to H. C. Hale 10-14-1864 (10-16-1864) Cr
Porter, Rebecca W. to Flemming G. Dawson 10-31-1843 Hn
Porter, Rebecca to Marion Owls 2-19-1866 (no return) Hn
Porter, Rosetta to Owen Travis 11-24-1867 Hn B
Porter, S. B. to L. W. Howard 1-18-1882 (1-19-1882) L
Porter, Sallie W. to J. M. Gilbert 12-28-1858 Hn
Porter, Sarah A. to Nathaniel H. Graves 8-1-1859 G
Porter, Sarah A. to Wm. Smith 3-6-1853 Cr
Porter, Sarah J. to William T. Haskell 2-7-1838 Hn
Porter, Sarah Jane to S. W. Flowers 5-25-1864 G
Porter, Sarah M. to Henry L. Flowers 2-14-1865 G
Porter, Sarah to Green M. Howell 1-5-1856? (1-5-1857) G
Porter, Susan Ann to John Jackson 4-6-1867 (4-14-1867) F B
Porter, Susan J. S. to James D. Woods 12-16-1857 Hn
Porter, Susan Jane to Manuel Porter 5-21-1866 (no return) Hn
Porter, Susan M. to Abner Hopton 1-20-1847 Sh
Porter, Susan M. to Christopher S. Cooper 3-30-1850 (3-31-1850) G
Porter, Susan to Samel Scott 12-24-1872 (12-30-1872) Dy
Porter, Virginia W. to R. H. Deener 2-27-1869 (2-28-1869) F
Porterfield, E. J. to W. E. Burrow 3-2-1871 Cr
Porterfield, Elizabeth to James McMackin 12-17-1843 Cr
Porterfield, Nancy to C. W. Ramsey 3-13-1861 (3-14-1861) Sh
Portice, Mary F. to James E. Akin 12-25-1847 (12-30-1847) Hr

Portis, Equilla to Eli Chapman 3-1-1850 (3-3-1850) Hr
Portis, Julet A. to Wm. Utley 11-17-1848 Cr
Portis, Martha A. to B. H. Cullum 11-?-1853 (no return) F
Portis, Mary A. to James Caudle 9-18-1840 Hn
Portis, Sarah A. to Clinton D. Portis 10-20-1849 G
Posey, B. O. to A. M. Buckhannan 12-4-1849 (12-5-1849) L
Posey, Frances Caroline to William R. Boyd 6-1-1843 L
Posey, Jane H. to Harry Spurling (Sparling?) 5-1-1854 Sh
Posey, Martha to March Coggschall 9-4-1885 (9-5-1885) L
Posey, Mary J. T. to James A. Jeffries 1-21-1867 L
Posey, Mary to Harvey W. Brown 1-28-1854 (no return) F
Posey, Medora Va. to Richard M. S. Martin 6-16-1870 L
Posey, Milley W. to John R. Hazzard (Haggard?) 12-1-1858 L
Posey, Sarah A. S. to Jno. H. Boyd 6-1-1843 L
Postin, Rachel A. to J. W. Caldwell 10-17-1871 (no return) Hy
Poston, Mary P. to James A. Paine 7-11-1856 Hr
Poston, Mattie to Clay. Montgomery 1-8-1874 Hy
Poston, Nancy C. to Jacob Burnett 1-8-1867 (1-9-1867) Dy
Poston, Nancy Caroline to Marion Duffee 11-11-1865 (no return) Dy
Poston, Sophronia E. to J. C. Folts 12-23-1844 Hr
Poteet, Savannah E. to A. F. Ray 6-22-1877 (6-24-1877) Dy
Pots, Emerine to B. F. Wagoner 4-20-1864 We
Pots, Emma to B. F. Wayne 6-20-1854 We
Potter, Amanda M. to Thos. H. Johnson 12-21-1867 (12-22-1867) Dy
Potter, Catharine to George W. Bennett 12-18-1862 (no return) Hy
Potter, Delia L. to Thomas C. English 2-15-1853 (3-1-1853) Sh
Potter, Frances to Sam Hill 3-24-1866 Hy
Potter, M. J. to E. P. Carter 11-18-1864 G
Potter, Mary Ann to Newton J. Bevill 3-16-1858 Hn
Potter, Sallie to Eli Newburn 12-21-1871 (no return) Hy
Potter, Sarah to Shedrach Rice 3-19-1870 (3-24-1870) L B
Potter, Viney to Isaac King 10-25-1865 Hy
Pottow(Pillow?), Iola to J. E. Soward 5-1-1880 (5-4-1880) L
Potts, Adeline to George W. Patterson 9-2-1877 (9-23-1877) L
Potts, Angeline to Martin Lindsey 10-16-1858 G
Potts, Annie to Jackson Downing 6-12-1870 Hy
Potts, Drucilla to Wilson Stem 2-5-1845 (no return) Hn
Potts, Elizabeth M. to Thomas Lamb 7-21-1847 Hn
Potts, Evalina to Richard Y. Williford 1-1-1854 Hn
Potts, Helen P. to James H. Price 12-15-1868 (12-16-1868) Ma
Potts, Louisa E. to Zachariah M. Conyers 11-7-1857 Hn
Potts, Louisa to W. S. Menden(h)all 5-9-1864 (5-12-1864) Sh
Potts, Martha to Harmon Simmons 1-29-1844 Hn
Potts, Martha to Joseph Lamb 4-20-1841 Hn
Potts, Mary J. to W. R. Pearce 10-13-1860 (10-16-1860) Sh
Potts, Mary to Zibia H. William 1-7-1839 (no return) Hn
Potts, Mattie to George W. Baker 9-28-1873 Hy
Potts, Nannie J. to Geo. D. Blair 10-14-1868 Hy
Potts, Sarah E. to William F. Brooks 11-14-1850 Sh
Potts, Sarah Jane to John W. Alexander 12-18-1860 Hn
Potts, Susan Ann to Geo. W. Wilson 11-9-1857 (11-12-1857) Sh
Potts, Susan to James Peek 5-1-1835 Hr
Potts, Tennessee to C. Comsay 4-30-1865 Hn
Pound, Martha to P. E. Holmes 2-6-1837 (2-9-1837) G
Pounds, Elizabeth C. to John F. Ward 1-26-1860 (no return) We
Pounds, Elizabeth R. to William Harrison 8-1-1842 (8-3-1842) G
Pounds, Elizabeth to Thomas D. Jones 8-14-1865 G
Pounds, Emily A. to Franklin D. Bryant 1-12-1870 G
Pounds, Julia to Wiley A. Waldrop 1-3-1846 (1-8-1846) G
Pounds, Louiza M. to W. L. Sanders 1-4-1858 (1-5-   ) G
Pounds, Lucy Jane to John Wesley Waldrop, jr. 6-9-1867 G
Pounds, Mary C. to J. L. Sanders 2-9-1862 G
Pounds, Mary J. to James A. Dodd 3-25-1869 Dy
Pounds, Mary to Arthur Smith 11-10-1849 O
Pounds, Melissa Elizabeth to Henry Bennet Jones 6-8-1866 Ma
Pounds, Nancy J. to Jessee A. Patrick 1-8-1852 G
Pounds, S. E. to T. G. Conley 3-10-1867 G
Pounds, Sarah to John R. Thedford 3-12-1851 G
Powe, Margaret L. to James Bray 2-17-1853 Hn
Powel, Lizzy to John Whitley 1-4-1868 Hy
Powel, Mary E. to William Barnhart 8-19-1871 (8-21-1871) Cr
Powel, Mary to Abner Thorgmorten 10-10-1846 (no return) We
Powel, Nancy to Bennet Woodward 10-25-1862 (10-26-1862) Ma
Powell, A. E. to H. F. (T.?) Fullerton 6-3-1868 G
Powell, Alice to Wm. H. Ammons(Powell?) 7-28-1847 (7-29-1847) Hr
Powell, Amanda to John R. Crawford 1-12-1850 (1-24-1850) Hr
Powell, Amanda to John Sanders 6-25-1848 Sh
Powell, Amanda to Peter Pillow 10-2-1871 Dy
Powell, Ann to Willis Ward 12-2-1869 (no return) Dy
Powell, Anna to J. S. Thomas 9-11-1867 L
Powell, Anna to John Herron 6-4-1874 (no return) Hy
Powell, Ara to Jos. Epperson 12-17-1868 Hy
Powell, Artimissa to John W. Shelton 11-2-1852 Ma
Powell, Bertha to David Asher 5-23-1864 Sh
Powell, Binga H. to J. W. Keeble 9-10-1855 (no return) F
Powell, Caroline to Willis A. Hogue 10-11-1849 O
Powell, Catharine F. to Robert W. Cozzart 12-2-1859 (12-8-1859) G

Powell, Charity to Thomas R. Hawkins 12-4-1844 Sh
Powell, Charley M. to Robert S. Phillips 11-20-1855 (no return) F
Powell, Cretia to Samuel Love 11-25-1866 Hn
Powell, Dina to Richd. Anderson 8-30-1871 (no return) Hy
Powell, E. C. to G. M. Milliken 2-8-1849 Hn
Powell, Eliza to Jesse Gunter 12-30-1846 Hn
Powell, Elvina to A. H. Beaton 2-7-1860 Be
Powell, Emma to George W. Powell 11-23-1878 (11-27-1878) L
Powell, Emma to Thos.H. Estes 10-20-1869 Hy
Powell, F. A. (Mrs.) to T. C. Coppedge 6-4-1866 (no return) Hy
Powell, F. A. to J. P. Gregory 10-27-1875 (no return) Hy
Powell, Fanny to William H. Poe 11-4-1879 L
Powell, Frances A. to John McAfee 2-1-1859 G
Powell, G. A. J. to Allen Hill 5-6-1861 (5-9-1861) Sh
Powell, G. A. to J. V. Robertson 3-15-1866 Hn
Powell, Henrietta to Henry Mitchell 10-19-1877 (10-21-1877) Dy B
Powell, Isabella to Benj. Jones 12-24-1868 Hy
Powell, Isabella to Calvin Reddick 12-22-1868 (no return) Hy
Powell, Isabella to Isaac Dodson 3-6-1878 Hy
Powell, Jane to Edward J. Gorton? 12-15-1840 (no return) Cr
Powell, Jane to Phillip King 12-10-1878 (12-11-1878) Dy
Powell, Jennett to Burl Hines 10-1-1866 (no return) Hy
Powell, Katie to Zachariah Douglas 3-23-1877 Hy
Powell, Laura to Seaton B. Burks 4-29-1854 (5-2-1854) L
Powell, Lavinia A. to W. R. Bradford 12-12-1866 (12-19-1866) L
Powell, Lenora to Saml. B. Bradshaw 9-15-1863 (no return) Dy
Powell, Leusi to James H. Brint 3-16-1850 (3-19-1850) Hr
Powell, Louisa to Jas. B. Wells 3-24-1842 Sh
Powell, Lucy to J. S. Branson 4-3-1866 G
Powell, Lucy to William Pearcy 9-4-1836 Sh
Powell, Lydia to Judithan C. Shelton 12-21-1859 (12-22-1859) Ma
Powell, M. E. to J. J. Richardson 12-9-1874 Hy
Powell, Mahala to L. R. McNatt 11-24-1862 Mn
Powell, Maria J. to Eleazar Gaugh 8-2-1856 (8-3-1856) Hr
Powell, Maria to John Howling 11-29-1877 Hy
Powell, Mariah to Sam Deberry 12-18-1874 (no return) Hy
Powell, Martha H. to Thomas W. Branson 1-3-1863 G
Powell, Martha J. to George C. Street 9-2-1852 Hn
Powell, Martha V. to Henry H. Perry 5-25-1860 (no return) Hy
Powell, Martha W. to Prescott Hall 11-21-1849 Hn
Powell, Martha to Delaney Whitehurst 2-28-1868 Hy
Powell, Mary A. to Alman Case 8-6-1860 O
Powell, Mary Ann E. to D. F. Gadd 12-9-1857 Hr
Powell, Mary Ann to William Caldwell 5-13-1869 (5-16-1869) L
Powell, Mary Anne to Daniel P. Alexander 4-1-1847 Hn
Powell, Mary Eliza to Marshal Winters 2-29-1872 Hy
Powell, Mary F. to Porter Lanier 12-17-1867 Ma
Powell, Mary M. to John A. McNeill 2-6-1871 (no return) Hy
Powell, Mary Rose to Geo. W. Davis 10-26-1841 Sh
Powell, Mary W. to John Baxter 5-1-1845 Hn
Powell, Mary to John Birdwell 6-25-1858 Be
Powell, Matilda to Henderson Stanback 1-4-1871 (1-11-1871) F
Powell, Mattie J. to J. T. Lillard 4-8-1876 (no return) Hy
Powell, Mattie to John Austin 12-4-1878 Hy
Powell, Mexico to Isaac Dorch 7-20-1854 Be
Powell, Nancy J. to Thomas J. Ingraham 11-5-1855 (11-14-1855) G
Powell, Nancy to Henry Wolfe 1-2-1862 Mn
Powell, Nancy to J. G. Bowman 1-5-1870 Dy
Powell, Nelley A. to Isaac Copland 12-23-1867 (12-31-1868?) T
Powell, Octave B. to John G. Coffey 11-2-1865 (11-8-1865) L
Powell, Olivia Eliz. Jane to Hamon (Harmon?) Bostic (Bolster) 6-8-1843 Sh
Powell, Rebecca F. to Robert Phillips 1-7-1842 (no return) Hn
Powell, Rosena to Peter Gillum 11-4-1875 (no return) Hy
Powell, S. J. to H. T. Haste 5-25-1865 L
Powell, Susan A. to John G. Johnson 11-21-1862 (11-22-1862) L
Powell, Susan N. to John Kelley 2-6-1871 (2-7-1871) L
Powell, Susan to John Baldwin 11-8-1871 (no return) Hy
Powell, Susan to Thomas A. Howard 7-16-1850 Hn
Powell, Tennessee to W. H. Sherrard 11-15-1865 Hy
Powell?, Amanda L. to Jones J. Williams 12-21-1841 (12-27-1842?) T
Power, Henrietta Christmas to James Faulk 10-28-1843 (11-2-1843) T
Power, Sarah Christmas to William Culbreath 4-23-1849 (4-26-1849) T
Powers, Alice to Patrick Culligan 7-14-1862 Sh
Powers, Catharine to Joseph Baker 6-13-1860 Sh
Powers, Eliza to H. B. Baker 10-5-1856 We
Powers, Elizabeth to W. G. Clark 2-3-1851 Sh
Powers, Ellen to Patrick Regan 2-22-1851 Sh
Powers, Esther Ann Margaret to Samuel H. Curtis 8-2-1853 (8-3-1853) L
Powers, Hannah A. to Wm. Carter 11-10-1849 Cr
Powers, Jennie A. to Charles R. Felts 11-4-1862 We
Powers, Joanna to William F. Hill 12-19-1870 L
Powers, Julia to Michael Coddy 1-24-1863 Sh
Powers, Julia to R. J. Turrantine 11-4-1857 Sh
Powers, Lucinda to Howard Baker 1-13-1860 Be
Powers, Lucinda to J. P. Smyth 12-9-1858 We
Powers, M. E. to Calvin Jones 3-8-1870 Dy
Powers, M. to C. C. Bledsoe 1-10-1867 G

Powers, M. to George W. Rowlett 10-10-1852 Hn
Powers, Martha J. to Richard C. Bertow 3-23-1848 Hn
Powers, Martha to Robt. H. Beith (Birth) 1-10-1856 Sh
Powers, Mary (May?) to J. L. Birnbaum 2-15-1859 (2-16-1859) Sh
Powers, Mary A. to G. W. Hooper 12-8-1858 We
Powers, Mary E. to James Bradford 6-30-1842 Hn
Powers, Mary to Anthony Nash 12-3-1860 Hn
Powers, Mary to Drew Williams 7-13-1843 We
Powers, Mary to John Beal 9-4-1830 Sh
Powers, Maylissa G. C. to Elijah B. Bowles 12-30-1850 Hn
Powers, Nancy J. to James Baker 3-12-1856 We
Powers, Nancy to Limpulas Gardner 12-25-1850 We
Powers, Pamela to Seaborn? J. Wiley 6-16-1853 (6-17-1853) Sh
Powers, Paralee to John W. Curby 8-8-1876 (8-9-1876) Dy
Powers, Rachel E. to William H. Finley 6-13-1848 Hn
Powers, Sutecall M. to J. H. Parham 2-6-1858 (no return) We
Powley, Elizabeth to Henry Eckert 6-28-1862 (6-29-1862) Sh
Poyner, Angeline D. to Isaiah Mathis 10-15-1850 Hn
Poyner, Ann Eliza to E. E. Hamilton 1-7-1858 Hn
Poyner, Ann R. to Sanford M. Darnell 11-18-1851 Hn
Poyner, Elizabeth to David B. Pipkins 4-15-1848 (4-16-1848) Hr
Poyner, Ellen C. to John W. Maxwell 10-25-1850 Hn
Poyner, Frances to Johns Brantly 6-20-1840 (6-27-1840) Hr
Poyner, Jula Ann to Buckhanan James 12-20-1845 (12-23-1845) Hr
Poyner, Margaret to Meredith McKelvin 8-15-1850 Hn
Poyner, Nancy C. to Thadeus C. S. Tart 6-7-1859 Hn
Poyner, Nancy to E. R. Rison 7-25-1849 Hn
Poyner, Rachel to William Henry 3-13-1855 Hn
Poyner, Tennessee to E. E. Hamilton 5-9-1844 Hn
Poynter, Rutha G. to Truman W. Stephens 12-18-1848 (no return) Hn
Pracht, A. O. to T. W. Pope 12-5-1877 Hy
Prader, Sarah to Thomas L. Duncan 3-4-1852 Sh
Prather, Eliza to C. C. Taliaferro 8-31-1854 Hn
Prather, Mollie J. to Nathan B. Peoples 3-28-1861 Hn
Prato, Louisa to Louis Young 9-17-1868 (no return) Dy
Pratt, Arreanna to Thos. S. McAllester 11-22-1852 (11-23-1852) G
Pratt, Elizabeth R. to Thomas M. Darnell 11-16-1861 Mn
Pratt, Harriet J. to J. C. Stanly 4-16-1847 F
Pratt, Jane to Henry Ward 1-6-1867 G
Pratt, Louiza to Jonathan Hudson 2-2-1863 Hn
Pratt, Martha J. to Reason I. James 6-9-1861 G
Pratt, Mary Elizabeth to J. C. Murdough 11-23-1867 G
Pratt, Mary to Andy Hutson 2-12-1862 Hn
Pratt, Mary to Jim Belew 3-13-1869 G
Pratt, Nancy to James M. Hammonds 9-1-1852 Hn
Pratt, Sarah to Smith Cantwell 12-19-1850 Cr
Preast, Sarah A. to Chester M. Rogers 10-6-1861 We
Preer, Sarah to Josiah Leggett 10-13-1857 Sh
Preist, Harrett T. to Jerry G. Noell 4-23-1856 Cr
Prendergrast, Cynthia J. to John W. McElwee 8-31-1847 Ma
Prendergrast, Mary Ann to Frederick Chipman 4-19-1852 (4-20-1853) Ma
Prentiss, Charlotte to John Grant 1-10-1863 Sh
Prescott, Elizabeth to Thomas S. Condrey 8-10-1867 (8-11-1867) L
Prescott, M. J. to J. E. Young 7-21-1885 L
Prescott, Margarett to William T. Huline 3-27-1838 (3-29-1838) L
Prescott, Mary Jane to Gardiner B. Locke 7-10-1836 Sh
Prescott, Sarah A. to Thos. L. Warner 1-4-1851 (1-7-1851) L
Presgrove, Frances E. to Hiram Purdee 11-17-1863 (no return) Dy
Presley, Arabella to Hartwell Patiller 1-27-1868 Ma
Presnell, Geraldine P. to Benjamin Kendall 7-4-1857 Hn
Presnell?, I. F. to H. H. Barnes 12-16-1854 (12-24-1854) O
Preson, Elizabeth to Calvin Spivey 1-6-1842 Ma
Presson, Angeline to David L. Little 12-12-1852 Be
Presson, Charlotte Jane to A. L. Wiseman 10-23-1847 Be
Presson, Cindy R. to Marcellius Cain 1-27-1843 Be
Presson, Drucilla to William Smith 12-20-1855 Be
Presson, Eda to Wm. F. Presson 1-31-1844 Be
Presson, Elizabeth A. to Miles W. Little 2-15-1867 Be
Presson, Frances E. to Allen D. Crossno 7-16-1851 Be
Presson, Llisa J. to Thomas A. Mysell (Mizell) 6-28-1863 Be
Presson, Louisa to W. D. Durden 6-10-1868 Be
Presson, Lucinda E. P. to H. T. Presson 12-18-1860 Be
Presson, Lucinda to Thomas H. Presson 11-30-1867 Be
Presson, M. M. to Levin Rushing 7-2-1845 Be
Presson, Mahaly to John Toomar Presson 8-7-1866 Be
Presson, Malinda L. to Jas. H. Presson 6-28-1868 Be
Presson, Maranda to C. T. Craig 6-5-1862 Be
Presson, Martha E. to Andrew Gilbreath 6-29-1860 Be
Presson, Martha J. to Wm. T. Stigal 5-17-1863 Be
Presson, Martha T. to Robert Harper 5-16-1858 Be
Presson, Mary Ann to William Warrick 3-27-1851 Be
Presson, Mary E. to H. G. Durden 7-9-1868 Be
Presson, Mary to Dav? Watson 9-29-1840 Be
Presson, Matilda to Wm. H. Presson 3-22-1847 Be
Presson, Nancy A. to Jasper N. McKelvy 11-14-1867 Be
Presson, Nancy Jane to James H. Bridges 8-26-1851 Be
Presson, Nancy to Josiah McDaniel 8-21-1853 Be

Presson, Patience C. to John B. Presson 7-11-1861 Be
Presson, Penelope C. to John G. Holland 1-4-1854 Be
Presson, Phebee Jane to Jacob Bond 4-29-1855 Be
Presson, Polly Ann to John Wiseman 1-26-1854 Be
Presson, Polly Ann to John Wiseman 1-26-1854 Be CC
Presson, Polly to J. Presson 6-5-1842 Be
Presson, Sarah to Allen D. Crossno 8-19-1847 Be
Presson, Sarah to John Helms 2-20-1848 Be
Presson, Sinter Ann to William Bond 11-7-1855 Be
Presson, Susan A. to R. H. Craig 4-26-1868 Be
Presson, Susan F. to Charles Craig 12-13-1849 Be
Presson, Tabitha C. to Abel Rushing 4-3-1850 Be
Presson, Talisha C to James Watson 12-12-1851 Be
Preston, Amanda to Henry Hurst 1-11-1850 Hr
Preston, Dionitia A. to Lawson T. Barnett 1-5-1847 (no return) F
Preston, Joanna A. to John H. Gordon 12-19-1861 Ma
Preston, Julia to John R. Woolfolk 2-18-1861 (6-18-1861) Ma
Preston, Sarah J. to J. W. Darden 1-7-1855 (no return) F
Prewett, A. M. to J. L. Jenkins 12-24-1860 Hr
Prewett, Louisa Lavinia to Joseph Lewis Gardner 2-1-1846 T
Prewett, Mary A. to Dudley Evans 4-16-1845 Cr
Prewett, Mary A. to Willis Hutchison 3-17-1861 Be
Prewett, Mary E. to John K. Gordon 1-1-1861 Hr
Prewett, Mary F. to J.C. Stinson 9-26-1860 (10-24-1860) Hr
Prewett, Mary Jane to L. L.(F.?) Oliver 2-24-1870 G
Prewett, Matilda to James G. D. Martin 11-8-1849 Cr
Prewett, Nancy to Walter Mills 12-25-1849 Cr
Prewett, Sabella to B. A. Clifft 2-19-1859 (2-22-1859) Hr
Prewett, Susan to James M. Fleet 6-14-1843 Hr
Prewitt, E. J. to H. H. Hursh 1-23-1862 (1-28-1862) Hr
Prewitt, Eliza Jane to Thomas Williamson 11-16-1850 (11-28-1850) Hr
Prewitt, Elizabeth R. to W. R. Bateman 6-25-1870 (6-26-1870) Cr
Prewitt, Elizabeth to Hardeman Bishop 11-20-1855 (11-22-1855) Hr
Prewitt, Elizabeth to John P. Taggart 4-3-1848 (4-4-1848) Hr
Prewitt, Elizabeth to Wm. Simmons 12-23-1852 T
Prewitt, Jane to Benjamin L. Norton 10-6-1841 (10-7-1841) Ma
Prewitt, Lucy to Jordan Douglass 12-27-1867 (1-5-1868) F B
Prewitt, Malinda C. to John H. Clark 4-12-1860 Ma
Prewitt, Mariah W. to Milton W. Prewitt 8-9-1847 (8-12-1847) Hr
Prewitt, Marietta H. to James E. Hogshead 11-3-1841 Ma
Prewitt, Mary Elizabeth to John R. Wormath 10-23-1874 (10-24-1874) T
Prewitt, Nancy E. to William R. Tagart 7-10-1852 (7-13-1852) Hr
Prewitt, Sarah A. to L. Tanner 4-9-1856 (4-23-1856) Hr
Prewitt, Sarah J. to Robert C. Dean 3-8-1849 Sh
Prewitt, Sarah to J. H. Johnson 1-4-1849 Hr
Prewitt, Sarah to Nathan Vick 1-5-1843 Ma
Preyer, Matilda to Stephen Crockett 12-29-1869 (12-30-1869) L
Price (Brice?), Deanna to Thomas J. Byrn 2-1-1860 L
Price, A. C. to J. G. Arnold 10-15-1870 (10-16-1870) Cr
Price, Adaline to Johnun? Carroll 12-30-1839 (no return) F
Price, Amanda C. to James M. Felts 3-11-1862 Cr
Price, Amanda to Benjamin Weston 10-8-1846 Sh
Price, Annie J. to James D. Stewart 3-9-1869 G
Price, Betsy to Jesse Guest 2-14-1879 (3-3-1879) L B
Price, Caroline to Albert Henning 3-25-1876 L
Price, Catherine to Elijah Gibson 2-15-1843 Sh
Price, Clarrissa E. to William A. Ross 7-19-1848 (7-23-1848) G
Price, Darthula V. to Geo. N. Morrow 3-23-1856 (4-1-1856) Hr
Price, Drusilla to S. T. Bowan 12-25-1856 Hn
Price, E. J. to J. W. Brown 3-12-1874 L
Price, Eliza Ann to Levi Stone 8-16-1845 (8-17-1845) G
Price, Eliza to William Privett 3-16-1855 (no return) L
Price, Elizabeth A. to Edmund F. Duke 5-18-1849 (5-20-1849) Hr
Price, Elizabeth H. to William D. Bogg 1-23-1853 (2-8-1853) O
Price, Elizabeth to A. G. Hornesby 2-29-1860 (3-1-1860) Hr
Price, Elizabeth to Emanuel Davis 11-23-1848 G
Price, Elizabeth to Henry Brewer 10-31-1839 (11-1-1839) Hr
Price, Elizabeth to J. S. Moore 9-11-1855 We
Price, Elizabeth to J. W. Brundridge 7-3-1855 (no return) We
Price, Elizabeth to Joseph N. Phelps 12-15-1870 (no return) Cr
Price, Elizabeth to Reuben C. Dickins 3-20-1852 (3-25-1852) G
Price, Elizabeth to S. Adams 11-15-1867 (no return) Hn
Price, Elizabeth to Thomas Oliver 4-21-1859 We
Price, Ellen to James M. Brann 11-16-1854 We
Price, Esther to Robert Lowery 10-15-1828 Ma
Price, Fannie to Anthony Bordeaux 8-4-1869 (no return) F B
Price, Jane to John C. Allen 3-21-1844 (3-23-1844) F
Price, L. E. to T. J. Walker 1-14-1867 (1-20-1867) Dy
Price, L. K. to W. T. Bennett 6-25-1865 G
Price, Lanty to James White 8-6-1863 We
Price, Louisa to J. C. Bostian 10-5-1859 (10-6-1859) Hr
Price, Louisa to John Branstudd 2-18-1863 Mn
Price, Louisa to John Isaiah W. Pettie 1-22-1853 Cr
Price, Louisa to Stephen J. Price 10-17-1857 L
Price, Lucille W. to Orris Harris 8-30-1858 Hr
Price, Lucinda to Lewis Thompkins 12-7-1872 (12-29-1872) L B
Price, Lucra to J. D. Thogmodden 2-19-1867 (3-22-1867) Dy

Price, Luncinda to Abraham Jenkins 11-9-1840 (11-12-1840) F
Price, Malissa to Thomas W.(M?) Wallace 2-24-1840 (2-25-1840) Hr
Price, Margaret to John Hawks 2-28-1857 We
Price, Martha Ann to Alez Beasley 4-20-1852 We
Price, Martha Jane to A. W. C. Lea 7-16-1847 L
Price, Martha Jane to M. N. Langley 5-23-1846 (no return) L
Price, Martha to Daniel Perry 2-5-1845 Cr
Price, Martha to J. N. Brann 12-17-1850 We
Price, Mary A. E. to Robert Ervin 2-5-1848 (2-10-1840) G
Price, Mary A. to Simon P. Tanner 4-23-1851 Sh
Price, Mary A. to W. H. Baker 5-21-1864 (no return) L
Price, Mary Ann to Elisha R. Hunt 10-11-1842 (10-13-1842) Ma
Price, Mary Ann to Harry (Henry) M. Farmer 4-27-1871 F
Price, Mary Ann to Wm. H. Baker 5-21-1864 (5-22-1864) L
Price, Mary C. to Wm. L. Penson 1-2-1844 Cr
Price, Mary E. to Geo. Palmer 5-19-1864 Sh
Price, Mary E. to George D. Brooks 12-1-1866 (no return) Hn
Price, Mary E. to Jermiah T. Rust 12-22-1859 We
Price, Mary Jane to Samuel H. Jackson 11-6-1850 O
Price, Mary S. to John Hudson 9-4-1845 Hr
Price, Mary S. to P. G. Elder 3-16-1862 Mn
Price, Mary V. to Thomas L. Dupree 12-12-1876 (12-13-1876) L
Price, Mary to Michael Carney 1-2-1868 O
Price, Mary to Wm. L. White 3-1-1848 (3-2-1848) O
Price, Mollie Jane to Nathan Daughety 8-3-1867 (no return) F
Price, Mollie to George McDonald 1-19-1871 Cr B
Price, Mollie to J. A. Atkins 3-23-1869 (no return) Dy
Price, Mot to Reuben Brooks 4-30-1872 (5-1-1872) O
Price, Nancy M. to Archie R. Coleman 10-29-1866 (no return) Hy
Price, Paralee to Thomas Woods 2-21-1867 Be
Price, Rachel to Thomas Reid 3-9-1834 Sh
Price, Rebeca to A. Arrington 7-3-1865 (7-6-1865) Cr
Price, Rebecca to Joseph Davidson 6-15-1853 Be
Price, S. A. (Mrs.) to W. B. Rall 5-1-1855 (5-2-1855) Sh
Price, S. A. to Wm. Bloyce 10-3-1862 (10-5-1862) O
Price, Sarah to A. H. Adams 9-13-1866 Hn
Price, Sarah to Daniel Stamps 7-10-1860 L
Price, Sarah to John Jones 7-26-1844 (7-28-1844) O
Price, Sarah to Robert Joyner 12-28-1868 (12-3-1869?) T
Price, Sarah to William Lea 5-16-1863 Mn
Price, Sophronia to James M. Fullerton 9-8-1870 Ma
Price, Susan A. to Crockett Young 1-15-1859 We
Price, Susan E. to B. F. Magee 9-1-1852 (no return) F
Price, Susan to Rutherfer D. Sooter 10-4-1838 Cr
Price, Susannah to Jackson Brazeal 4-10-1836 (4-12-1836) Hr
Prichard, Alice to Green Fizer 2-24-1875 (2-26-1875) Dy B
Prichard, Almedia to Wm. A. Boon 1-17-1877 (1-18-1877) Dy
Prichard, Bettie to Hilliard Smith 12-22-1874 (12-23-1874) Dy
Prichard, D. J. to J. W. Norsworthy 12-18-1878 (12-19-1878) Dy
Prichard, Elizabeth to Shad Parsons 8-27-1845 Cr
Prichard, Fannie to Haf Haskins 8-16-1873 (8-17-1873) Dy
Prichard, Finetta to B. H. Mitchell 10-19-1876 Dy
Prichard, Kisann to W. J. Holland 2-1-1865 (2-2-1865) Dy
Prichard, M. M. to James W. Kent 2-5-1879 (2-6-1879) Dy
Prichard, Mary Ann to Dennis McCain 8-21-1869 (8-22-1869) Cr
Prichard, Mary F. to L. C. Hafford 9-14-1876 Dy
Prichard, Mary M. to James House 4-16-1867 (no return) Dy
Prichard, Mary to W. H. Leach 1-14-1852 (1-15-1852) Sh
Prichard, Mollie to Elmore Maddrey 12-12-1877 (12-13-1877) Dy
Prichard, Sarah A. to G. W. Prichard 9-7-1868 (no return) Dy
Prichard, Sarah A. to Joseph D. Keath 11-13-1874 (11-14-1874) Dy
Prichett, Meriah to E. W. Pope 1-10-1842 Cr
Priddy, Ellen M. to Nicholas P. Bond 9-11-1861 Sh
Pride, Esther to John Stratton 1-21-1850 (1-22-1850) O
Pride, L(e)acy to Uriah Stratton 1-2-1849 O
Pride, Leacy to Uriah Stratton 1-2-1849 O
Pride, M. A. to W. H. Khyle 10-2-1867 O
Pride, Malisa to Joseph Hooker 9-29-1864 Sh
Pride, Nancy to James Stratton 2-5-1857 O
Pridgeon, Nancy to Hansel Williams 11-?-1844 Hn
Pridy, Martha A. to Geo. T. Lane 7-14-1851 Sh
Priest, Anna E. to F. G. Williams 10-19-1871 (no return) Cr
Priest, Caroline to Joe Hawkins 12-30-1871 (no return) Cr B
Priest, Cathrine M. to Isaac J. Bullock 11-27-1841 Cr
Priest, Elen to Thomas D. Vauters 1-18-1865 Cr
Priest, Frances to Richard Marcus 12-13-1855 We
Priest, Harriet to Thomas Priest 7-9-1860 (7-10-1860) Ma
Priest, Lucindy to Wm. Jobes 5-25-1848 Cr
Priest, Susan to John B. Pirtle 5-6-1850 (5-8-1850) Hr
Priest, V. R. to J. D. Mayo 11-23-1854 We
Priest?, E. A. to James Pirtle 5-5-1847 Hr
Prigg, Elizabeth to A. M. Strickland 7-23-1849 Cr
Prim, Mary to Joseph Shade 3-16-1863 Hy
Prim, Mary to Madison Floyd 2-17-1846 Hn
Prince, Armanda to William Lewis 8-17-1854 Be
Prince, Catherine to Lewis Kim 3-15-1858 Sh
Prince, Cynthia P. to Anderson Fry 6-1-1870 (6-9-1870) T

Prince, Elizabeth to John A. Martin 1-28-1843 Cr
Prince, Elizabeth to John W. Brundridge 7-4-1855 We
Prince, Emma E. to W. D. Baker 12-10-1864 (12-14-1864) Cr
Prince, Fannie to Berry Carter 12-14-1872 (12-19-1872) Cr B
Prince, Jane W. to Green Broach 5-10-1844 Cr
Prince, Jane to Elias Gunter 2-11-1856 We
Prince, Lilly Ann to A. J. Massey 2-3-1871 T
Prince, Lucy A. to Adolphus Briant 11-19-1868 Cr
Prince, Martha Ann to Charles Marshall 2-10-1857 Hn
Prince, Martha Ann to G. W. Simmons 1-17-1864 Be
Prince, Martha C. to Jas. H. Reed 4-22-1865 Be
Prince, Martha E. to J. B. Englihs 11-27-1858 T
Prince, Martha G. to George W. Neal 9-8-1852 Be
Prince, Mary to Henry Lewis 6-7-1846 Be
Prince, Nancy to John Harris 11-25-1853 Be
Prince, Nancy to W. A. Rolland 11-9-1848 Hn
Prince, Paulina to L. Ludi 10-3-1856 Sh
Prince, Prudence to Thomas Barnes 6-29-1852 Hn
Prince, Sarah E. to Morgan H. Prince 9-5-1855 (no return) Hn
Prince, Sarah E. to Nathan S. Petty 12-2-1850 Sh
Prince, Susan E. to A. G. Hawkins 11-10-1869 (11-11-1869) Cr
Prince, Zilpha Ann to John S. Prince 10-13-1860 (no return) Hn
Prist, Ablone to John H. Cantrell 1-24-1859 T
Pritchard, Cordelia E. to James A. Burton 6-19-1871 (no return) Cr
Pritchard, Eliza C. to Joseph W. Grogan 1-12-1869 (1-13-1869) Cr
Pritchard, Elizabeth E. to Elias Burns 3-15-1841 T
Pritchard, Elizabeth to Thomas G. Roper 7-15-1868 (7-16-1868) Cr
Pritchard, Elizabeth to Thos. Morgan 11-11-1848 Cr
Pritchard, Emarline to Stephen Kelly 7-23-1846 Cr
Pritchard, Jane to Henry Cook 1-1-1839 Cr
Pritchard, M. J. to D. H. Williams 1-28-1868 (1-30-1868) Cr
Pritchard, Martha J. to Wade U. Poole 8-17-1852 Cr
Pritchard, Mary E. to David M. Buckett 2-6-1853 Cr
Pritchard, Mary M. to Josiah Anderson 2-?-1862 (no return) Cr
Pritchard, Mary M. to W. B. Hale 2-14-1861 G
Pritchard, Mourning E. to William Phillips 9-11-1860 Cr
Pritchard, Susan E. to Thomas L. Kee 8-12-1868 (8-13-1868) Cr
Pritchet, Ivy Ann to Braxton Carter 8-6-1845 Sh
Pritchet, Virginia L. to Abel C. Miller 1-13-1859 Hn
Pritchett, Clarissa to Marcus L. Dickinson, jr. 6-3-1856 Sh
Pritchett, Jane to James Medom? 2-17-1849 Hn
Pritchett, Maria to William S. Looney 12-20-1853 Hn
Pritchett, Martha J. to Levin Dillen 5-16-1857 Sh
Pritchett, Martha to John Clarke 3-30-1852 Sh
Pritchett, Sarah Jane to Albert Hampton 4-16-1870 (4-17-1870) Dy
Privett, E. A. to J. D. Appleberry 12-23-1863 (12-29-1863) F
Privett, Elizabeth to Thomas Price 3-15-1855 (3-16-1855) L
Privett, Martha E. to Jno. Walker 10-14-1868 (10-21-1868) F
Privett, Mary Ann to J. R. Blackbern 10-29-1862 (10-30-1862) Dy
Privett, Nancy to J. T. North 8-18-1877 (8-19-1877) Dy
Privett, Willie Jane to John Childress 8-29-1869 G
Privett, Winnie to J. C. Taylor 12-21-1870 Hy
Privette, Matilda J. to R. G. Appleberry 1-13-1865 (1-18-1865) F
Probusaugh?, Mary E. to G. C. Crider 10-2-1871 (10-?-1871) T
Prock, Parile to T. E. Marchbanks 3-1-1863 Be
Procton, Mary to J. W. Rigsbee 2-16-1873 Hy
Proctor, Fannie to George O. Carter 11-30-1876 Hy
Proctor, Frances to Allen Coakley 8-3-1867 G B
Proctor, Louisa V. to W. A. Davis 11-22-1873 (11-27-1873) T
Proctor, M. E. to W. S. Erwood 1-8-1872 (1-9-1872) T
Proctor, Martha to Anthony Trigg 1-16-1869 G B
Proctor, Nettie to Phillip Jones 11-18-1870 G B
Proctor, Sarah H. to Gaston Jarrett 1-13-1876 (no return) Hy
Propst, Mary Ann to Peter Mormoner 7-10-1852 We
Province, B. A. to S. A. Dinwiddie 8-29-1871 (8-31-1871) Cr
Province, Eliza A. to James Bobbitt 2-19-1845 Cr
Province, Mary J. to John W. H. Martin 10-16-1866 (no return) Hn
Province, Mary P. to John Bobbitt 12-10-1845 Cr
Provine, Elizabeth to J. V. Rison 12-6-1853 Hn
Provine, Elizabeth to Ludwell Smith 1-1-1858 Hn
Provine, Harrie A. to William R. Barton 11-4-1850 (11-6-1850) Ma
Provine, Maryann to E. R. Alexander 12-15-1841 (no return) F
Provine, S. T. to W. C. Diggs 1-6-1853 Hn
Provine, Sarah to Harry Porter 5-28-1866 Hn
Provow, Mary to Thomas J. Moody 10-24-1849 Hn
Provow, Susan A. to W. G. Ward 12-20-1866 Hn
Pruden, Elizabeth to John Powell 10-4-1847 (10-5-1847) Ma
Pruden, Martha to W. C. Ross 11-4-1864 (11-6-1864) Sh
Pruett, Catharine A. to Jasper N. Cole 11-15-1865 (11-19-1865) Cr
Pruett, Eliza J. to W. T. Haywood 12-7-1865 (12-10-1865) Cr
Pruit, Mary S. to Julius Keston 8-24-1854 Sh
Pruit, Mary V. to Wm. D. Dilda 10-20-1864 Cr
Pruitt, Cynthia to L. P. Lanier 1-1-1868 (1-2-1868) Dy
Pruitt, Elizabeth W. to John P. Gill 9-15-1848 G
Pruitt, Hannah to Andrew J. Pounds 7-2-1855 (7-5-1855) G
Pruitt, Lucy D. to George W. Gill 6-17-1844 G
Pruitt, Martha to Harrod P. Welch 12-22-1829 G

Pruitt, Mary V. to W. D. Dilda 10-20-1863 (10-25-1863) Cr
Pruitt, Mary V. to William D. Dilday 10-20-1863 (no return) Cr
Pruitt, Mary to Elijah Kilzar 10-31-1841 (not executed) G
Pryer, Manervy to Wesley Simmons 1-11-1870 (1-12-1870) F B
Pryer, Martha A. to John J. Hurt 2-3-1845 (no return) Hn
Pryer, N. J. to C. J. Chapman 6-18-1868 O
Pryer, Sarah to William W. Huddleston 3-1-1863 (no return) Hn
Pryor, Amelia Caroline to George Rufus Wynne 11-15-1852 (11-17-1852) Sh
Pryor, B. P. to B. B. Tyson 12-23-1867 O
Pryor, Barbara E. to William F. Ragan 2-15-1854 (2-16-1854) O
Pryor, Elizabeth to Charles J. F. Hurt 1-17-1854 Hn
Pryor, Fannie to Anderson C. Bettis 11-26-1856 Sh
Pryor, Julia to Francis Tod 10-8-1851 Sh
Pryor, Louisa to John W. Wicker 4-13-1852 O
Pryor, Lucy A. M. to Thomas B. Caraway 1-5-1856 (no return) We
Pryor, Lucy A. M. to Thomas B. Caraway 1-6-1856 We
Pryor, Martha E. to James H. Alexander 9-14-1837 Hr
Pryor, Martha to Solomon Jones 5-11-1871 (5-14-1871) L
Pryor, Mary J. to E. W. Jones 5-14-1857 Hn
Pryor, Mary to H. Carroll Long 3-4-1852 We
Pryor, Mary to William M. Nelms 4-3-1854 O
Pryor, Sarah C. to J. B. Rainey 4-9-1857 Hn
Pryor, Sarah to William Hatfield 9-9-1870 (9-11-1870) L
Pucker, Susan A. to Samuel Williams 8-19-1867 (8-20-1867) Cr
Pucket, Mary C. to Thomas J. Irwin 4-23-1841 F
Pucket, Mary to Thomas Murray 5-7-1860 Sh
Puckett, Amanda to James Simmons 2-8-1855 O
Puckett, Caroline to Henry Martin 8-17-1866 Hn
Puckett, E. A. (Mrs.) to J. W. C. Davidson 2-3-1869 G
Puckett, F. G. to H. B. Toombes 2-21-1857 (3-1-1857) Hr
Puckett, Jo Ann to James W. Cresap 11-10-1857 (11-19-1857) O
Puckett, Lizzie to James F. Scott 12-10-1868 Ma
Puckett, Lucy A. E. to John W. Martin 12-4-1856 Hn
Puckett, Lula E. to C. P. Walker 10-18-1866 Hn
Puckett, Mary E. to A. J. Willowby 10-28-1866 Hn
Puckett, Mary M. to John J. Shinault 9-19-1861 (9-21-1861) Hr
Puckett, Mary to Robert J. Ballew 11-1-1836 Sh
Puckett, Nancy to J. H. Emerson 9-24-1845 We
Puckett, Rachael to James Tipton 9-20-1832 G
Puckett, Rebecca to John Evans 4-1-1841 G
Puckett, Sarah Ann to Samuel Fowler 11-2-1851 Hn
Puckett, Sarah D. to Iverson W. Page 8-12-1841 Hn
Puckett, Susan V. to W. C. Martin 11-30-1863 (no return) Hn
Puckett, Tennessee to Lewis Hagler 12-13-1866 Hn B
Puckett, Vilet to Martin B. Key 2-8-1853 (2-10-1853) Ma
Puett, Elizabeth T. to Alexander Warren 6-7-1858 (6-8-1858) O
Puett, ____ to Solomon Jones 1-21-1868 Hy
Pugh, Amanda E. to W. T. McLeary 9-14-1854 (10-3-1854) Hr
Pugh, Fannie J. to T. B. Berry 5-6-1871 (5-7-1871) Dy
Pugh, Georgia to B. B. Greaves 5-9-1875 L
Pugh, Kittie D. to John W. Hicks 11-15-1874 Hy
Pugh, Louisa to N. J. Michell 12-2-1869 (12-5-1869) Dy
Pugh, Martha to Edward Dixon 7-21-1841 (7-22-1841) Hr
Pugh, Mary E. to Leopold Buhse? 8-22-1874 (8-26-1874) T
Pugh, Mary E. to Littleton O. Gooch 3-16-1869 (3-17-1869) Cr
Pugh, Mary to Anderson Braden 5-18-1867 (no return) L B
Pugh, Mollie to C. G. Johnson 2-2-1875 Dy
Pugh, Nancy T. to N. C. Joiner 11-5-1867 Cr
Pugh, Neety Jane to John A. Pipkin 1-16-1848 Hr
Pugh, Racheal to Worley Linvell 3-23-1829 Hr
Pugh, Sarah to Bill Britton 3-11-1876 (no return) Hy
Pugh, Sarah to Edward Dickson 11-30-1842 (12-1-1842) Hr
Pugh, Venus to Joe Spivey 1-2-1874 Hy
Pulla(Pully), Martha to Samuel W. Ridge 7-17-1829 Hr
Pullam, Alsa to Persan Ussery 2-7-1840 Hr
Pullam, Ann to Leonard Malone 8-18-1849 (9-1-1849) Hr
Pullam, Elizabeth to R. W. Moore 4-3-1863 O
Pullen, Elizabeth G. to John Smith 1-31-1826 G
Pullen, Laura L. to R. G. McLewain 11-18-1858 (11-23-1858) T
Pullen, M. J. (Mrs.) to Amos Hays 8-25-1868 O
Pullen, Mary to W. P. Lipscomb 2-4-1868 (2-26-1868) F
Pulley, Martha W. to Richard H. Dennis 9-1-1869 Hn
Pulley, Nancy A. to William H. Jones 8-2-1856 (8-7-1856) Sh
Pulliam, A. E. to C. M. Waller 2-7-1859 F
Pulliam, Almira to John Michie 4-9-1866 (no return) F B
Pulliam, Ann to Charles Session 9-4-1868 (9-5-1868) F B
Pulliam, Ann to Peter McCarley 6-11-1868 (6-13-1868) F B
Pulliam, Jane to Geo. W. Beasley 9-29-1859 Hr
Pulliam, Judy to Archibald Wiggins 2-7-1871 (2-15-1871) F B
Pulliam, Louisa to Jack Jones 4-14-1866 (4-22-1866) F B
Pulliam, Mary V. to William Sheeks 7-12-1842 O
Pulliam, Mary V. to William Sheeks 7-12-1842 (7-19-1842) O
Pulliam, Mary to Jim Walker 12-24-1867 (12-25-1867) F B
Pulliam, Rachel C. to Joseph A. Hill 6-6-1859 (6-7-1859) F
Pulliam, Rosanna to John T. Middleton 6-14-1858 Hr
Pulliam, Sallie A. to R. L. Walker 12-4-1866 (12-29-1866) F
Pulliam, Sarah E. to Stephen A. Norton 12-8-1847 Sh

Pullim, Everline to Giles Smith 10-27-1866 (10-28-1866) T
Pullim, July to Noah Stevenson 12-16-1865 T
Pullims, Julia to Noah Stevenson 12-16-1865 (12-26-1865) T
Pullin, Mary A. to J. J. McDow 10-30-1865 (11-1-1865) T
Pullman, Eliza to Joseph Pippin 11-5-1838 (11-?-1839?) F
Pullman, Laura to James Ware 5-17-1877 Hy
Pullum, Caroline to John W. Shinault 1-13-1840 (1-14-1840) Hr
Pullum, Sarah E. to Reuben M. May 2-15-1854 Ma
Pully, Betsy to Samuel Shipman 11-21-1828 (11-23-1828) Hr
Pully, Mary to John Wynn 9-15-1846 Be
Pully, Susanah to Benjamin Newhouse 8-10-1829 (8-13-1829) Hr
Punch, Elizabeth J. to A. D. S. Foster 4-26-1856 (4-27-1856) Hr
Punch, Elizabeth to W. W. Taylor 4-6-1848 Hr
Punch?, Martha Jane to Philip S. Winn 1-11-1843 T
Purcell, Margaret to Ben Maybern 5-21-1885 L
Purcell, Susan to John I. Hall 4-9-1845 Hn
Purcill, Mary to John Dillon 5-5-1863 Sh
Purdle, Priscilla to Jack Jones 11-13-1875 (no return) Dy
Purdy, Frances A. to Joseph Barker 6-23-1866 (6-28-1866) Dy
Purdy, Lizzie to G. M. Graves 12-16-1865 Cr
Purdy, Mary E. to R. L. Crafton 6-18-1866 (6-22-1866) Dy
Purgson (Penguson), Delphy to Hyram Morrison 7-10-1831 Sh
Purham, Louisa to Ed Thornton 12-29-1880 (12-30-1880) L B
Purkins, Dilcy to Amos Mann 1-14-1872 Hy
Purkins, Harriett A. to Geo. W. Keese 7-26-1847 Sh
Purkins, L. A. to Wm. Oliver 3-9-1872 Hy
Purkins, Nannie to John Williams 12-26-1868 Hy
Purnell, A. E. to W. H. Loud(Land) 12-14-1858 (12-16-1858) Hr
Purnell, Elvicy D. to William R. Bucy 5-11-1840 Hn
Pursell, Emily to S. H. Chitwood 4-16-1867 (no return) Dy
Pursell, Mary to Richard C. Wimberly 9-28-1842 Sh
Purser, A. C. to Jas. A. Cathey 1-1-1874 O
Purser, Ann to James Griffith 2-6-1854 Sh
Purser, Winney to Wm. Phillips 8-9-1838 Sh
Purslay, Elnora to William D. Newlett? 11-8-1865 (11-11-1865) Cr
Pursley, Jennie to J. H. C. Berry 11-29-1863 O
Pursley, M. to Thos. Adelbert 5-1-1869 O B
Pursley, Mary A. to John M. Henry 12-13-1859 (12-18-1859) O
Pursley, Mary to Larry Glynne 11-20-1861 (11-29-1861) Sh
Pursley, Silva J. to Freeland Caldwell 7-20-1875 O
Pursley, Susan to William S. Jordan 11-9-1863 O
Purson (Pierson?), Julia to Scott Jones 12-25-1873 L B
Purtle(Pirtle?), Louisa Jane to John G. Chisum 6-3-1839 (6-6-1839) Hr
Purvace, Elizabeth to Samuel Reaves 1-6-1830 (1-7-1830) O
Purvis, Ann Elizabeth to James Hooper Cotton 4-2-1853 (4-4-1853) T
Purvis, Lucinda to A. M. Muzzall 11-23-1842 Hn
Purvis, Lucy to J. F. Varner 11-8-1870 Hy
Purvis, Martha to Washington Brack 3-28-1839 Hn
Purvis, Sarah J. to Charles P. Briant 12-31-1868 Cr
Purvise, Alice to Aaron Winters 4-10-1827 O
Puryear, Julia to Wm. Mahone 2-14-1868 (2-15-1868) L B
Puryear, Linda to Hardy Sawyer 5-19-1883 (5-20-1883) L
Puryear, Lucy to J. P. Baxter 3-20-1880 (3-21-1880) L
Puryear, Mary to Nathan Branch 3-4-1886 L
Push, T. E. to Morgan G. French 3-24-1849 Hn
Putman, E. J. to J. C. Burrow 11-30-1854 Cr
Putman, Harriet to Jiles Bryant 2-28-1847 Cr
Putman, M. S. to W. B. Dean 8-5-1870 (8-7-1870) T
Putman, Mary M. (Mrs.) to Jesse McCollum 7-3-1860 (7-5-1860) Cr
Putman, Mary M. to Jessy McCollum 7-3-1860 (7-5-1860) Cr
Putman, Mary to Elridge Haynes 9-8-1842 Cr
Putman, Mary to Jabreal Chandler 8-7-1854 Cr
Putman, Sarah to Thomas N. Howell 10-10-1859 (no return) Cr
Putnam, Mary Ann Elizabeth to Thomas R. Williams 12-11-1857 (12-12-1857) O
Putnam, Melissa to W. C. M. Johnson 11-27-1854 Sh
Putnam, Nancy to Mathew A. Glass 12-22-1831 G
Pybas, ____ E. to R. D. Harwood, jr. 6-3-1861 G
Pybass, America to Matthew D. Caton 9-1-1868 G
Pyland, Callie to D. L. Long 10-14-1882 (10-15-1882) L
Pyland, Electy C. to William Garrett 12-30-1854 (12-31-1854) G
Pyland, Mary E. to G. M. Anderson 12-13-1872 (12-15-1872) L
Pyland, Mary F. to J. W. Ford 8-28-1866 G
Pyland, Nannie D. to H. C. Clark 11-20-1883 (11-21-1883) L
Pyland, S. G. to J. E. Dance 9-6-1870 Hy
Pyland, Tempa N. to Jackson Cleek 3-23-1868 Dy
Pyland?, Malissa F. to Charles L. Martin 1-14-1865 L
Pyle, Jennie to William Ingalls 12-8-1864 Sh
Pyle, Mary A. to Henry S. Keatley 10-18-1854 Sh
Pyle, Pheraby B. to Mark Langston 4-4-1854 Sh
Pyles, Adeline to Mathew Cullison? 10-26-1867 (11-4-1867) T
Pyles, Mary Louisa to Sion W. Boon 4-17-1856 (4-8?-1856) Ma
Pyles, Virginia A. to Robt. M. Sharp 10-24-1866 (10-25-1866) Ma
Pyron, Martha M. to Thos. D. Baggett 2-21-1853 (no return) F
Pyron, Willie Ann to B. G. Baber 6-4-1862 Sh
Quamby, Emma to Squire Shires 4-18-1859 Sh
Quarles, Catherine to Hardin G. Forister 7-3-1835 Sh

Quarles, Malissa Jane to David G. Willis 7-18-1860 (7-19-1860) O
Questa, Mary to John B. Vaccaro 4-2-1861 (4-7-1861) Sh
Quick, Nancy to A. M. McCaleb 1-13-1861 G
Quillen, Chlorina H. to George Moor-? 4-19-1864 Be
Quillen, Clorina to E. T. Evans 10-27-1868 Be
Quillin, Mary E. to Edward F. Evans 11-4-1856 Be
Quilling (Quillen), Georgiann to B. N. Holland 10-23-1866 Be
Quimblay, Caroline to William Warmath 10-7-1828 Ma
Quimby, Fanny to G. W. Hughes 7-24-1876 (no return) Hy
Quimby, M. A. to J. S. Herendon 11-24-1878 Hy
Quimby, Sarah to Geo. Washington Stewart 7-4-1822 Sh
Quimmly?, Mary to William Shadrach Starling 7-20-1846 (7-30-1846) T
Quin, Susan J. to W. E. Spear 10-30-1856 (no return) We
Quinaly, Patsey Safroney to Relix Grundy Hallum 10-22-1846 (10-26-1846) T
Quinby, Nancy J. to David Goss 7-12-1859 Hy
Quinby, Sarah E. to Warren Wyatt 12-13-1870 Hy
Quindlin, Bridget to William Cummins 4-24-1855 (4-27-1855) Sh
Quinichet, Judith A. to John F. Hamlin 5-17-1839 Sh
Quinlan, Catherine to Peter Holt 7-21-1862 Sh
Quinlan, Margaret to John McMahon 10-28-1861 Sh
Quinley, Elizabeth J. to William Dawson 2-12-1849 Ma
Quinley, L. E. to J. N. Williams 4-7-1876 Hy
Quinley, Nancy E. to Jackson Dawson 10-30-1841 (11-3-1841) Ma
Quinley, Rebecca to Wilson Moore 1-22-1849 (2-3-1849) Ma
Quinly, Martha C. to Samuel Watt 12-18-1841 (12-19-1841) Ma
Quinn, Alethia M. to A. D. Bryant 10-15-1866 (no return) Cr
Quinn, Ann to Wm. Stevenson 10-1-1859 (10-2-1859) Sh
Quinn, Bridget (Mrs.) to D. Y. Desmond 11-3-1863 Sh
Quinn, Bridgett to Patrick Moroney 7-14-1845 Sh
Quinn, Elizabeth to L. M. Stafford 8-3-1840 Sh
Quinn, Elvira (Mrs.) to John W. Elliott 1-28-1864 Sh
Quinn, F. M. to John H. Green 1-19-1869 (1-22-1869) Cr
Quinn, Jane to James Fisher 8-5-1847 Cr
Quinn, M. A. E. to M. R. Considine 12-2-1858 (12-3-1858) G
Quinn, M. C. to Robert Dougherty 8-3-1840 Cr
Quinn, M. F. to J. W. Hedgecock 7-2-1866 (no return) Cr
Quinn, Maria to Henry Lenaghan 7-3-1852 (7-5-1852) Sh
Quinn, Martha A. to Thomas Skipper 4-1-1846 (4-2-1846) G
Quinn, Martha to H. S. Flippin 1-6-1866 (no return) Cr
Quinn, Mary L. to T. G. Harris 1-7-1850 Cr
Quinn, Mary to Dormick Marksman 5-16-1860 (5-17-1860) Sh
Quinn, Mary to John Randal 7-15-1847 Sh
Quinn, Nancy E. to Aaron Bellew 5-22-1858 Cr
Quinn, Nettie to J. L. Colwell 1-30-1878 (1-31-1878) L
Quinn, Rosanna to Christopher Barton 4-29-1858 Sh
Quinn, Sarah to H. Harvey 1-2-1843 (no return) Cr
Quinn, V. A. to W. H. Holmes 9-8-1871 (9-9-1871) Cr
Quirk, Bridget to Beverly Kible (Kibbe?) 11-3-1854 Sh
Quisenberry, Frances M. to Archibald Gibson 6-5-1838 (no return) Hn
Quisenberry, Martha E. to William Hamilton 1-21-1858 (no return) Hn

R---, Sarah J. to Joseph C. Black 12-17-1867 G
R____?, Enia to Alfred Harris 10-14-1859 (no return) Cr
Rachel, Sarah Ann to Wm. Davis 10-7-1850 (no return) F
Rachels, Margaret to Robert Orrell 1-27-1856 We
Rachels, Mary to Benjn. Davis 8-27-1850 (8-29-1850) F
Rachels, Mary to John Glover 3-4-1834 Sh
Radditt, Harriett to Hugh McCaddan 12-30-1832 Sh
Raden, Ellen to Pattie Brody 5-21-1864 (5-24-1864) Sh
Rader, Mary B. to Leander M. Richardson 10-17-1846 G
Radford, A. J. to J. G. Arnold 11-4-1874 (no return) Dy
Radford, Caroline to Alex Mitchell 1-25-1869 (no return) Dy
Radford, Elizabeth to Thomas Bevill 9-15-1853 Hn
Radford, Ellinor to Ezra Childers 4-1-1841 Hn
Radford, Henenretta to George W. Seaton 8-26-1844 (8-27-1844) F
Radford, Lovey to Thomas Williams 8-19-1849 Hn
Radford, M. J. to J. P. Bell 5-16-1867 Dy
Radford, M. J. to W. C. Dickey 10-25-1879 (10-26-1879) Dy
Radford, Margaret to Stephen H. Snow 8-19-1850 (8-22-1850) F
Radford, Mariah P. to Robert J. Bond 7-24-1861 Be
Radford, Marion to Melzer Shepherd? 1-15-1851 (1-16-1851) F
Radford, Mary Jane to Thomas J. Rumbly 11-5-1857 Be
Radford, Mary to Charles I. Nelson 12-17-1844 Be
Radford, Nancy C. to James A. Walker? 2-20-1859 Be
Radford, Rebecca to Beverly Melton 10-8-1864 Be
Raff, Ada to V. H. Swift 11-2-1863 Sh
Rafferty, Annie to George Jones 9-24-1860 Sh
Raffity, Sarah A. to William F. Hall 4-9-1840 (no return) Hn
Raffo, Precilla to Frederick Steele 7-15-1861 Sh
Ragan, Bridget to John Coleman (Callenan?) 4-28-1860 (4-29-1860) Sh
Ragan, Elizabeth T. to J. B. G. Babb 1-3-1866 G
Ragan, Elizabeth to Patrick Gill 10-17-1859 Sh
Ragan, Ellen to Michael Lyons 11-12-1861 Sh
Ragan, Elmina F. to Joshua J. Taylor 3-11-1868 G
Ragan, Emiline J. to Alfred P. Yancy 9-10-1859 (9-15-1859) G
Ragan, Gella to Ben Scott 2-1-1869 G B
Ragan, Jemima to Lott Breeding 11-21-1833 Hr

Ragan, Leah? to Enoch King 3-14-1837 (3-15-1837) Hr
Ragan, Lucindia to Isaac Shinault 12-16-1833 (12-17-1833) Hr
Ragan, Lucy to Anthony Sanderford 12-29-1866 G
Ragan, Margaret M. to Benjamin F. Koen 10-7-1839 F
Ragan, Margarett A. to Robert R. Grady 5-31-1855 (6-9-1855) G
Ragan, Martha W. to John W. Webb 12-21-1836 G
Ragan, Martha W. to Samuel Webster 2-6-1827 Hr
Ragan, Mary C. to A. G. Stalens 12-5-1859 G
Ragan, Mary C. to James R. Bland 10-26-1860 (10-27-1860) Hr
Ragan, Mary W. to E. H. Toms 11-8-1870 G
Ragan, Mary to Patrick Flynn 4-13-1861 (4-14-1861) Sh
Ragder, Absgullah H. to Wm. C. Brewer 11-24-1851 G
Raggin, Moody F. to Edward T. Pollard 10-3-1871 (10-4-1871) Ma
Ragland, Alice to Richard Crawford 1-17-1878 Hy
Ragland, Eliza to Sandy Smith 2-11-1868 Hy
Ragland, Ella E. to Samuel H. Chester 6-18-1878 (no return) Hy
Ragland, Fanny to John B. Norman 10-31-1865 (11-1-1865) Cr
Ragland, Josephine to Jack Truesdale 12-4-1866 (no return) F B
Ragland, Laura M. to Daniel B. Anderson 12-5-1842 Sh
Ragland, Lila to Nathan H. Grogan 5-21-1869 Cr
Ragland, Martha to Oliver Robinson 2-17-1866 F B
Ragland, Mary E. to L. _levin C. Rembert 7-6-1853 Sh
Ragland, Maseriah to Robt. Wood 3-4-1871 Hy
Ragland, S. V. to C. D. Dunlap 7-6-1853 Sh
Ragland, Sara to George McFarland 11-27-1865 (12-30-1865) F B
Ragland, Sarah to Lewis Edwards 3-9-1868 (3-21-1868) F B
Ragsdale, Elizabeth to A. J. Howell 5-6-1861 We
Ragsdale, Elizabeth to Travis Lyell 2-25-1855 Hn
Ragsdale, Louisa to John Davis 4-15-1854 (4-18-1854) G
Ragsdale, M. A. to Frank Collier 12-4-1873 (1-1-1874) O
Ragsdale, Martha to Gilbert Nichols 11-14-1853 (11-15-1853) O
Ragsdale, Mary to Thomas K. Edmonds 5-9-1867 G
Ragsdale, Melinda to William Harrison 2-18-1832 (1-23-1832) Ma
Ragsdale, Nancy Ann to Henry Wilson 10-27-1830 Ma
Ragsdale, Susan F. to F. W. Blankenship 1-3-1869 G
Raiford, Bettie to Sam E. Hammond 11-8-1864 Sh
Raiford, Evalina A. to John J. Steger 6-9-1848 (6-11-1848) F
Raiford, Jane to James S. Soap 1-25-1840 (no return) F
Rainbo, Jane to T. H. Waggoner 11-14-1855 (no return) We
Rainer, Catharine to Edward Coodey 5-28-1829 Hr
Rainer, Frances to Jasper Jones 8-29-1867 (9-23-1867) F B
Rainer, Louisa W. to Geo. E. McDaniel 4-24-1861 (4-25-1861) Hr
Rainer, Mary Matilda to Albert G. Parrott 10-4-1849 (10-18-1849) Hr
Rainer, Rosella to Frank Ketchum 10-28-1868 (no return) F B
Rainer, Susan Ann to Henry Wellions 3-13-1843 (3-13?-1843) Hr
Raines, Ann to C. McCulloch 12-28-1866 G
Raines, Elizabeth to Joseph J. Lloyd 10-20-1845 Ma
Raines, Frances E. to William H. Dunaway 9-1-1866 (9-6-1866) Ma
Raines, Fredonia to William Bunn 2-3-1883 (2-4-1883) L
Raines, Julia E. to Zack, jr. Biggs 11-21-1865 G
Raines, M. R. to W. F. McBroom 12-7-1867 G
Raines, Malinda to Joseph F. Hazelwood 6-6-1849 (6-7-1849) G
Raines, Margaret E. to William W. Newman 12-8-1857 (12-10-1857) Ma
Raines, Margaret to R. J. Davidson 2-19-1884 (2-20-1884) L
Raines, Martha A. to Elijah Stigall 5-25-1858 (5-27-1858) G
Raines, Martha L. to Thomas J. Freeman 7-28-1852 G
Raines, Martha to Freeman Patterson 11-30-1850 (12-3-1850) Ma
Raines, Mary J. to John A. Sterling 12-23-1866 Hn
Raines, Mary to George F. Sloan 11-21-1860 (11-22-1860) Ma
Raines, Matilda to Thomas G. Gaskins 7-16-1858 (7-18-1858) Ma
Raines, Mima to Robt. Allen 5-4-1866 G
Raines, R. C. to F. P. Lowerence 3-8-1858 G
Raines, Ruth A. to John N. Bell 8-25-1859 G
Raines, Sally A. to Jerome B. Hyde 4-24-1860 (4-26-1860) Ma
Raines, Temperance to John Masman? 4-28-1853 H
Raines, Ursula P. to Blackmon G. Hays 11-30-1859 Ma
Rainey, A. J. to William L. Coffman 12-20-1870 (12-21-1870) L
Rainey, Anne to Bob Robinson 2-25-1869 G B
Rainey, Becky to Mitchell Lucas 12-22-1877 (12-23-1877) L
Rainey, Cornelia F. to Wm. Robinson 1-8-1861 Sh
Rainey, Delia to R. E. Trimble 2-28-1885 (3-5-1885) L
Rainey, E. C. to Wm. B. Richardson 8-9-1864 (8-12-1864) Cr
Rainey, Eliza Ann to Josiah H. D. Thompson 10-8-1855 (10-16-1855) Hr
Rainey, Emily to Wilie Voss 7-27-1858 (7-28-1858) L
Rainey, Fannie to J. P. Sturgin 7-6-1859 Sh
Rainey, Jane to Garland Scott 7-12-1868 G B
Rainey, L. C. to H. M. Taylor 2-4-1875 Dy
Rainey, M. F. to W. G. Welch 10-29-1870 (10-30-1870) Dy
Rainey, Mary E. to John W. Wiggin 8-15-1843 (no return) Hn
Rainey, Mary Francis to Harrison Simmons 1-15-1868 Ma
Rainey, Nancey J. to Charles H. Ward 12-18-1866 L
Rainey, Nancy to Daniel Guthrie 1-17-1848 (1-18-1848) Hr
Rainey, Rebecca to Levin Savage 8-4-1829 Hr
Rainey, Susan N. to Saml. Irvin 10-2-1837 (10-12-1837) Hr
Rainor, Rachel to Tom Benson 1-18-1868 Hy
Rains, Amanda to J. C. Rains 3-4-1863 Mn
Rains, Anne M. to H. H. Word 9-23-1841 G

Rains, Delila to Thomas Gaskins 1-16-1833 (12-16-1833) G
Rains, Delila to Thos. Gaskins 11-16-1832 G
Rains, Fanny to Aleck Mackey 11-30-1870 (12-1-1870) F
Rains, Lucinda J. to George M. Bevill 8-9-1855 (no return) Hn
Rains, Lucindy to G. H. Pearson 11-5-1840 Hn
Rains, Martha Ann to Fredrick Waggoner 1-8-1863 Mn
Rains, Mary to Hartwell Stigall 10-24-1853 Hn
Rains, Mary to James Jackson 9-14-1850 Sh
Rains, Mary to William S. Dougherty 6-23-1830 G
Rains, Nancy to Allen C. James 7-29-1850 (8-1-1850) G
Rains, R. J. to W. J. Hulsey 1-8-1862 Mn
Rains, Susan to Bradley Medlin 10-14-1840 Ma
Rainy, Sarah C. to H. G. Adams 3-1-1858 Hr
Rake, Hanah to Ben Williams 1-27-1866 Hy
Rakob, Caroline to Frederick Simpson 1-23-1855 Sh
Ralls, Margaret to Jesse Cook 12-26-1832 O
Ralls, Rebecca Ann to John L. Stafford 7-27-1848 O
Ralls, Sarah Ann J. P. to John Whittaker 5-10-1866 Hn
Ralls, Sarah to Columbus Goar 12-21-1854 We
Ralph, America J. to M.W. Taylor 4-16-1857 T
Ralph, Cathrine to Albert Goodman 4-11-1872 T
Ralph, Eliza to Peter P. Wood 4-12-1849 T
Ralph, Elizabeth to James K. Farmer 7-30-1841 (8-3-1841) T
Ralph, Jane to William Werter Angus 7-16-1849 (7-17-1849) T
Ralph, Jetty F. to James H. Owen 4-16-1857 T
Ralph, Margaret to David Adams 9-30-1873 (10-1-1873) T
Ralph, Martha Ann to Forney W. Redding 8-2-1851 (no return) F
Ralph, Mary A. to Wm. O. Wiseman 8-14-1852 T
Ralph, Mary Ann to Henry Beavers 12-19-1846 (12-25-1846) T
Ralph, Mildred J. to Michael Beaver 4-21-1853 T
Ralph, Nancy Jane to Henry Windiss 4-21-1847 (4-22-1847) T
Ralston, Bettie C. to L. K. Gillespie 2-12-1867 G
Ralston, Eliza to E. W. Brooks 11-8-1858 Sh
Ramage, Margaret to James Y. Rook 2-27-1828 Hr
Ramey, Ann to Wilie Holt 8-14-1839 Hn
Ramey, Fanny A. to Tandy P. Mills 11-5-1851 (11-6-1851) O
Ramey, Martha Jane to W. N. Rutland 5-6-1852 (5-12-1852) Sh
Ramey, Nancy to Caleb Tait 7-30-1846 O
Ramey, Parthenia to A. T. Taylor 5-10-1868 G
Ramispuger, R. to E. H. Hall 3-14-1850 Sh
Ramsay, Caphronia to R. B. Overall 10-19-1870 G
Ramsay, Catherine to Austin Martin 12-18-1838 Hn
Ramsay, M. to John Price? 3-3-1846 Hn
Ramsay, Martha A. to E. D. Overall 9-22-1863 G
Ramsay, Tabitha to John Goodin 4-5-1852 Hn
Ramsay, Vicy to Hugh B. Snider 8-15-1840 Hn
Ramsey, A. A. to J. W. Phillips 11-9-1865 G
Ramsey, A. to W. B. Eaves 3-17-1866 Hn
Ramsey, America J. to John Lynch 12-24-1855 (1-20-1856) Sh
Ramsey, Arbella to Elisha Eschew 10-5-1863 G
Ramsey, C. A. to L. W. Turner 1-23-1866 G
Ramsey, Caroline to James R. Ramage 11-2-1864 (11-3-1864) Sh
Ramsey, Cynthia to Robert Nutt 12-25-1831 Sh
Ramsey, Eliza Jane to Hugh Boyd 6-1-1859 Hn
Ramsey, Elizabeth E. to Rosell Needham 10-26-1836 Hr
Ramsey, Elizabeth F. to P. B. Myers 11-21-1864 (11-22-1864) Sh
Ramsey, Elizabeth to Alfred Hall 9-27-1862 O
Ramsey, Elizabeth to W. M. A. McFarlin 8-30-1859 Cr
Ramsey, Elizabeth to William B. Eaves 10-20-1859 Hn
Ramsey, Frances C. to John Snow 11-17-1840 Sh
Ramsey, Harriet to Robert Harris 8-9-1869 G B
Ramsey, L. P. to R. H. Nettles 12-16-1866 G
Ramsey, Loucy to Thomas F. Collins 12-27-1866 (no return) Cr
Ramsey, M. A. to T. F. Tate 11-23-1872 (11-26-1872) O
Ramsey, M. F. to L. W. Turner 8-19-1863 G
Ramsey, M. T. to T. J. Latimer 3-4-1868 G
Ramsey, Mahuldy to William T. Land 7-25-1827 (7-26-1827) Hr
Ramsey, Margaret to James W. Fields 6-18-1838 Hr
Ramsey, Martha A. to John S. Jones 7-31-1849 Sh
Ramsey, Martha to Calvin Tucker 2-17-1845 (2-20-1845) T
Ramsey, Mary A. to James H. Wheeler 10-24-1842 (10-27-1842) F
Ramsey, Mary Alice to James H. Robinson 2-20-1868 G
Ramsey, Mary E. to T. J. Buchanan 3-5-1867 O
Ramsey, Mary M. to B. B. Cannaday 10-31-1857 Sh
Ramsey, Mary W. to John A. Doherty 6-20-1867 Be
Ramsey, Mary to Sherred Jones 11-12-1846 Sh
Ramsey, Nancy E. to John T. Holcomb 3-28-1854 Hn
Ramsey, Nancy to S. E. Hogan 9-21-1843 F
Ramsey, Salome to John W. Grant 1-17-1842 Sh
Ramsey, Sarah A. to Washington E. Jones 7-18-1854 (7-19-1854) G
Ramsey, Sarah F. to William Elder 7-23-1834 G
Ramsey, Sarah to Philip I.? Kearney 1-6-1829 Hr
Ramsey, Susan N. to Christopher H. Plant 11-17-1845 (12-2-1845) F
Ramsy, Catharine L. to D. J. Newbern 11-18-1850 (11-19-1850) Hr
Ramsy, Hanah to John Murchison 8-3-1829 (8-9-1829) Hr
Rand, Maggie to Michael Mahon 11-5-1867 Hy
Randal, Lucy F. to Bernard G. Gordon 12-18-1839 Cr

Randal, Martha to Wm. Jones 1-8-1869 (1-16-1869) F B
Randall, Amanda M. to Thomas E. Jones 9-30-1861 (10-1-1861) Cr
Randall, Eliza M. to James E. Roberson 5-17-1853 Sh
Randall, Sarah to W. T. Randle 1-6-1862 (1-16-1862) Sh
Randle, E. to I. N. Manly 10-18-1838 (no return) Hn
Randle, Elizabeth R. to Thomas P. Jernigan 4-4-1846 Hn
Randle, Harriett C. to John M. Bopford 12-22-1859 Hn
Randle, Lucy to Hyman Taylor 2-13-1839 Hn
Randle, M. C. to J. B. Pearson 3-4-1868 G
Randle, Patience to Abraham McNeill 1-20-1871 (1-22-1871) Cr B
Randle, S. P. to J. B. Liggon 8-31-1847 Hn
Randle, Susan F. to Joseph B. Manley 6-23-1847 (no return) Hn
Randle, Susan to Polk Skinner 6-16-1870 G B
Randle, Tabitha E. to Spencer Walters 2-1-1842 Hn
Randle, Temperance to John Upshaw 8-23-1842 Hn
Randol, Lucy to Thomas C. McNeal 2-21-1861 G
Randol, Mary E. to J. H. B. Hollerman 3-19-1874 L
Randol, Mollie to John W. Powell 9-27-1862 G
Randolf, Catherine to William R. Gibbens 8-19-1863 Sh
Randolph, Altimira to L. H. Johnson 8-17-1838 (8-19-1838) Ma
Randolph, Angeline to John O. Dillender 2-24-1864 Dy
Randolph, Della to Isaac Brown 1-2-1871 Hy
Randolph, Dilly A. to Shep Johnston 4-21-1884 (4-22-1884) L
Randolph, Elizabeth A. to Joseph R. Bradshaw 7-2-1861 Mn
Randolph, Elizabeth to Theopulus Shaw 6-5-1850 (6-6-1850) Hr
Randolph, Josephine to Thos. Newman 5-10-1856 (5-11-1856) Sh
Randolph, Julia to James Shoemake 10-11-1860 Dy
Randolph, Mary E. to Bennett G. Hall 1-20-1845 (1-21-1845) G
Randolph, Mary to Jefferson McCann 4-5-1873 (4-11-1873) T
Randolph, S. (Mrs.) to J. G. Moore 11-28-1854 Sh
Randolph, Sarah to Joseph Hawkins 6-27-1847 Sh
Randolph, Spanzy? Jane to George Perry 1-15-1849 G
Raney, Martha R. to John Wesley Newman 1-19-1874 (1-20-1874) L
Raney, Mary Ann to John C. Dunn 5-29-1856 Sh
Raney, Nancy to H. M. Hill 5-28-1864 (no return) Cr
Raney, R. C. to G. W. Rucise? 2-8-1854 Cr
Raney, Samella E. to Thomas R. Chambers 8-8-1876 (8-10-1876) L
Rankin, Angeline to A. J. Minton 6-23-1863 Mn
Rankin, Eliza H. to Calvin Williams 2-13-1835 Hr
Rankin, Elizabeth to Garner D. Campbell 11-11-1850 (11-14-1850) Hr
Rankin, Emily A. to John M. Harpole 7-15-1851 (7-16-1851) O
Rankin, Emily F. to Hendley Stone 9-7-1843 (9-14-1843) Hr
Rankin, Jamsey to J. F. Holder 8-12-1862 (8-18-1862) Sh
Rankin, Levina to Robert M. Jobe 1-12-1845 Hn
Rankin, M. J. to E. T. Arnold 2-6-1858 We
Rankin, Mary Ann C. to Thurene E. Reynolds 12-14-1840 Hr
Rankin, Mary Anne to James M. Smith 10-2-1856 Hn
Rankin, Mary to John M. Park 12-16-1848 (12-21-1848) Hr
Rankin, Mary to Thos. W. Stitt 7-6-1843 (no return) We
Rankin, Nancy (Jane) to Sample A. Fortner 1-9-1858 (2-11-1858) Hr
Rankin, Sarah M. to James W. Cowgill 12-13-1853 (12-14-1853) Sh
Rankins, Elizabeth J. to William O. Davidson 11-9-1843 G
Rankins, Mary to Thos. W. Still 7-6-1843 We
Rankins, T. S. to William Terry 11-30-1852 Hn
Rankstead, Sarah to James Furguson 5-18-1844 Sh
Raoch, Nancy E. to Amos Martin 11-18-1839 Cr
Raper, Nancy C. to Stephen C. Ball 11-28-1859 (11-29-1859) F
Raphaelsky, Elizabeth to M. Isaacs 9-20-1862 Sh
Rappenchen, Teresa to Lewis Hoag 2-28-1855 Sh
Rasberry, Rebecca to Andrew Jackson 7-22-1841 (7-29-1841) Ma
Rasberry, Tibatha to Dickson Jackson 11-5-1836 Ma
Rasberry, Tobitha to Dickson Jackson 5-13-1843 (5-14-1843) Ma
Rasbury, E. E. J. to R. P. Brown 5-24-1863 Mn
Rasbury, Lacy to David Beesley 11-4-1839 Be
Rasbury, Susanah to F. M. Seward 7-5-1853 Be
Rasco, Nancy J. to Calven S. Brown 9-16-1860 We
Rash, Marrilla I. to Matthew Woodson 4-18-1839 Sh
Rash, Nancy A. to L. B. McGee 12-3-1863 O
Rasons, May Ann to Alfred Combs 9-24-1838 (9-25-1838) Ma
Raspberry, Ann to Benjamin K. Bowden 10-21-1857 Hn
Raspberry, Rebecca to Jessee Jones 1-27-1830 Ma
Rateree, Mary Scott to J. M. Burson? 6-2-1851 (no return) Hn
Rateree, S. M. to J. D. Rowlett 1-14-1866 Hn
Rates, Mary Ann to Thomas L. Hicks 6-7-1860 Be
Ratliff, Jnnu? to John P. Johnson 5-7-1845 (5-14-1845) Hr
Rauling, Olivia A. to N. F. Lemaster 10-21-1857 Sh
Rauls, Malinda E. to S. H. Johnson 7-28-1868 (7-30-1868) Dy
Rausher, Catharine to John Romer 4-11-1857 (4-13-1857) Sh
Raut, Silar to July Shepard 4-11-1876 (4-14-1876) L
Raven, Ellen to Patrick Brody 5-21-1864 (5-22-1864) Sh
Rawles, Alcenia A. to G. G. B. Patton 1-9-1861 (no return) Dy
Rawles, M. J. to J. W. Marchant 2-9-1876 Dy
Rawles, Mary C. to Wm. J. Shaw 2-13-1867 Hy
Rawling (Bowling), Nancy J. (I?) to S. V. Hardin 8-29-1831 Sh
Rawlings, Annis to John Powell 12-17-1869 (no return) F B
Rawlings, Caroline R. to James Floyd 12-21-1865 (12-24-1865) F
Rawlings, Dilsa to Chas. Parks 9-13-1867 (no return) F B

Rawlings, Eliza to William Trigg 10-27-1827 Ma
Rawlings, Emily to William Todd 11-27-1832 Hr
Rawlings, Lizzie to Archy Dowdy 2-14-1868 (2-21-1868) F B
Rawlings, Lucinda to Wash Fitchugh 1-8-1867 (1-12-1867) F B
Rawlings, Malinda (Mrs.) to Thomas R. B. Lawrence 4-14-1885 (no return) L
Rawlings, Mattie to Lewis Davis 12-23-1874 Hy
Rawlings, Ruth W. to J. T. Quigley 10-3-1861 Sh
Rawlinigs, Eliza C. to A. J. White 4-4-1864 (4-5-1864) Sh
Rawlins, Sarah E. to Edmund Taylor 9-26-1878 Hy
Rawls, C. F. to A. A. Rawls 2-5-1878 Hy
Rawls, George Henrietta to John M. Frazier 12-5-1864 (12-12-1864) Sh
Rawls, J. C. to R. G. Herring 4-1-1868 Hy
Rawls, Martha Jane to Louis? M. Roberts 4-3-1848 (no return) F
Rawls, Rebecca H. to John H. Jones 3-7-1860 (no return) Hy
Ray, Adaline to A. D. Crouch 7-28-1859 Hn
Ray, Alice C. to J. R. Robertson 8-28-1849 Hn
Ray, Alsey Carlene to Nathan Holley 6-9-1852 Hn
Ray, Amanda E. to P. H. Kirkland 9-30-1866 Hn
Ray, Amanda to William E. Corley 5-5-1855 Hn
Ray, Angeline to James R. Hill 10-17-1867 (no return) Hn
Ray, Angeline to Jno. A. Hood 3-10-1860 (3-13-1860) F
Ray, Ann to John C. Proctor 2-20-1864 Mn
Ray, Ann to Oren D. Bevett 3-30-1863 Mn
Ray, Anne to John G. Parker 7-25-1850 Hr
Ray, Areadna to Andrew H. Farrington 7-15-1845 F
Ray, Betheny to Oscar Lytle 1-5-1869 (no return) L
Ray, Betsey to Madison Alexander 12-16-1865 Hn
Ray, Bettie to P. C. Thompson 11-2-1863 T
Ray, C. A. to W. R. Coody 11-14-1853 (no return) F
Ray, Caledonia to A. Miller 6-20-1885 L
Ray, Catharine to James W. Stafford 8-26-1862 (no return) We
Ray, Debbie Angeline to Robert Rogers 6-28-1868 G
Ray, E. F. to J. E. White 12-19-1864 G
Ray, Eliza Ann to Sam'l. M. Shaw 3-16-1855 (3-18-1855) O
Ray, Eliza to Right M. Grooms 3-12-1852 We
Ray, Elizabeth C. to William W. Sleight 11-16-1862 Hn
Ray, Elizabeth to Harrison White 11-27-1839 Hn
Ray, Elizabeth to Isaac M. Bledsoe 4-7-1859 G
Ray, Elizabeth to John Burns 3-29-1869 (no return) Dy
Ray, Elizabeth to John Stricklin 1-27-1857 Hr
Ray, Elizabeth to Saml. S. Caldwell 1-1-1856 (1-3-1856) Hr
Ray, Ellen E. to Pitser M. Crawford 2-6-1860 (2-9-1860) Hr
Ray, Emily C. to Benjamin F. Brown 11-14-1846 (11-15-1846) Ma
Ray, Eugenia C. to B. F. Ridgway 9-20-1862 (no return) Hn
Ray, Fannie W. to Thomas L. Harris 10-19-1859 (10-26-1859) Hr
Ray, Fannie to Jack Mix 5-21-1875 Hy
Ray, Frances to S. T. Lunsford 5-18-1869 (no return) Dy
Ray, Gilly to John H. McCutchan 12-24-1856 G
Ray, Harriet to Stroder Starnes 7-16-1864 L
Ray, Jane E. to William J. Yeates 11-27-1850 (11-28-1850) G
Ray, Jane to William Landrum 6-27-1844 We
Ray, Joella to J. R. D. Jennings 6-9-1877 (6-14-1877) L
Ray, Josephine to D. C. Booth 8-25-1882 (8-27-1882) L
Ray, Laura A. to G. W. Rously 10-30-1875 Hy
Ray, Lotta to Edward Robins 1-16-1843 G
Ray, Louisa to D. P. Robertson 5-10-1848 Hn
Ray, Louiza to J. J. Adams 12-16-1866 Hn
Ray, Lucinda to W. M. Stalls 12-13-1860 Hn
Ray, M. S. to H. R. Carpenter 5-11-1878 (5-13-1878) Dy
Ray, M. S. to R. E. Doyle 11-25-1876 (11-26-1876) L
Ray, M. T. to E. S. Rinks 12-14-1862 Mn
Ray, Maggie to Kitchen Boggs 12-7-1869 (12-8-1869) F
Ray, Malinda to John P. Matthews 2-27-1867 G
Ray, Malvina? to George W. Whitson 9-8-1853 L
Ray, Margaret to Thomas Howell 11-22-1859 (11-25-1859) Ma
Ray, Martha A. to William H. Nelson 3-5-1859 (3-9-1859) G
Ray, Martha M. to Robert W. Cole 10-11-1842 Hn
Ray, Martha to John T. Parker 10-29-1856 (10-30-1856) Hr
Ray, Martitia to Livra? Williams 2-28-1868 (3-1-1868) Cr
Ray, Mary (Mrs.) to James Huff 6-17-1861 O
Ray, Mary A. to W. B. Hicks 12-30-1857 Hr
Ray, Mary A. to William P. Cook 1-27-1864 Mn
Ray, Mary Ann to James A. Taylor 7-29-1854 O
Ray, Mary Ellen to William H. Hutchinson 5-3-1856 (5-4-1856) O
Ray, Mary Frances to John Leroy Hutchison 2-24-1853 T
Ray, Mary to A. B. Sasenson(Sarrenson?) 6-21-1860 (2-22-1860) Sh
Ray, Mary to George Williamson 9-23-1865 (9-24-1865) Dy
Ray, Mary to Jasper Hizer 2-23-1857 (2-26-1857) Hr
Ray, Mary to John W. Morrow 5-24-1853 (6-1-1853) G
Ray, Maticia? J. to John Moser 8-13-1859 (1-29-1860) O
Ray, Matilda Ann to John Ryan 4-5-1879 (4-6-1879) L
Ray, Nancy E. to James E. Martin 2-1-1877 Hy
Ray, Nancy to Saml. W. Hutcherson 12-7-1873 (12-31-1873) T
Ray, Polly to M. D. Holder 9-11-1847 (9-14-1847) G
Ray, Riller to Asa Kingkade 10-12-1867 (10-30-1867) T
Ray, Ruth to Joseph L. Rosson 2-24-1851 Hr
Ray, S. C. to H. C. Aspray 1-15-1872 (no return) Dy
Ray, Sallie to P. W. Cooper 11-20-1875 (11-24-1875) Dy
Ray, Sarah Ann to William H. Smith 6-2-1849 (6-6-1849) O
Ray, Sarah Ann to William P. Miller 2-12-1858 (no return) Hn
Ray, Sarah Jane to John L. Autrey 4-11-1857 (4-12-1857) O
Ray, Sarah to Hugh Rodgers 2-6-1835 Sh
Ray, Sarah to Leander Acuff 7-10-1875 (7-12-1875) L
Ray, Sudie to Morris Hallum 8-26-1879 (8-28-1879) Dy
Ray, Susan E. to George R. Basinger 10-14-1868 G
Ray, Susan to Elijah Morrow 7-23-1853 (7-24-1853) G
Ray, Susan to Nathaniel S. Moore 2-3-1858 (2-4-1858) L
Ray, Susan to T. C. Smith 10-17-1868 (10-21-1868) Cr
Ray, Tabitha to Caswell Miflin 1-21-1847 G
Ray, Virginia to James Lamb 12-5-1854 (no return) Hn
Ray, Zedie to Nelson Heathcock 1-8-1871 Hy
Ray?, Sarah A. to J. R.? Mitchell 12-6-1860 Cr
Ray?, Susan C. to James E. Polston 6-26-1860 Dy
Raybern, Harriet F. to Wallace Evans 8-6-1864 (no return) Dy
Raybourn, Fanny to Thomas Myers 12-11-1856 Be
Raybourn, Pheraby to John L. Myers 4-25-1858 Be
Rayburn, Emanda to J. S. Reynolds 5-14-1869 Be
Rayden, Marabeth to Hilliard Fort 2-19-1857 Cr
Raydon, Martha to Tim Hinnon 1-8-1878 (1-10-1878) L
Rayger, Mary E. to Ed Ashley 6-26-1882 (6-27-1882) L
Raylor, Rachael to Henry Alison 10-14-1865 (no return) Hy
Raymon, Ann to Archabald Dougherty 12-29-1853 Sh
Rayn, Susan T. to Francis Loving 11-28-1839 (no return) F
Rayner, Annie to Andrew Jackson 1-5-1869 Hy
Rayner, Feby A. to Jemy Taylor 3-21-1868 Hy
Rayner, Mary to John Williams 9-8-1827 (9-13-1827) Hr
Rayner, Minnie to H. C. Sangster 5-31-1859 Hy
Rayner, Susan L. to Enoch L. Daniel 2-20-1850 Sh
Rayner, Tidy to Dave Mann 1-30-1869 Hy
Rayner, Will to Thomas Johnson 11-11-1874 (no return) Hy
Rayner, Kesiah to Benedict Yeary 11-1-1827 (11-2-1827) Hr
Raynor, Selia to James Vaughan 8-1-1868 (8-2-1868) L
Raynor, Sylva to Jim, jr. Cook 3-23-1867 Hy
Raynr, Sue P. to John B. Fitzpatrick 11-14-1867 Hy
Re(a)dman, Frances to William Nash 11-8-1834 O
Rea, Susan H. to Albert G. Stewart 1-2-1840 Sh
Rea, Susan J. to Lovett Morris 4-25-1866 (4-29-1866) F
Reace? (Page?), V(irginia) to John W. Darbey 12-9-1863 Sh
Reach, Mary E. to William Sinclair 1-10-1859 (1-22-1859) G
Reach, Susan to Zelman Smith 6-2-1846 Cr
Read, Adalin to Harrison Gaines 1-15-1872 (1-18-1872) T
Read, Agness to Ed Haywood 4-9-1869 (no return) Hy
Read, Alice to Goin Roberts 7-15-1879 (7-16-1879) L
Read, Ama L. to Charles L. Wood 4-5-1856 (4-6-1856) Ma
Read, Ann to Joe Brantly 4-8-1876 (no return) Hy
Read, Anna B. to James W. Peebles 11-24-1869 Hy
Read, Anna to Robert Carpender 8-1-1877 Hy
Read, Annie to William Watkins 12-12-1876 Hy
Read, Becky to Jas. A. Whitelaw 2-14-1878 Hy
Read, Caroline to Henry Ivey 10-31-1871 Hy
Read, Dorothy A. to Henry C. Taylor 2-16-1864 (no return) Cr
Read, Eliza A. to William K. Bennett 3-1-1849 (3-5-1849) Ma
Read, Elizabeth M. to William T. Erwin 11-25-1869 T
Read, Elizabeth to Henry Baker 8-3-1858 (8-12-1858) Ma
Read, Ellen to Nelson Jarrett 1-13-1866 Hy
Read, Ema to J. E. Jones 3-4-1874 Hy
Read, Emily E. to Daniel Shofner 8-4-1845 Cr
Read, Emma to Thomas Adams 12-28-1866 Hy
Read, Hannah to Dick Whitelaw 1-17-1872 Hy
Read, Harriet to Jim Blydes 1-6-1870 Hy
Read, Jane to Frank Sheppard 12-6-1866 Hy
Read, Jane to Pleasant Guardner 8-31-1838 (no return) F
Read, Jennie Lewis to P. B. Anderson 9-23-1874 Hy
Read, Julia Ann to Mitchell Holoway 11-11-1869 Hy
Read, Julia to Charles King 7-28-1866 (no return) Hy
Read, Laura E. (Mrs.) to S. B. Shelton 12-18-1875 (12-19-1875) L
Read, Lina to Bob Watkins 3-31-1872 Hy
Read, Lou to Wm. M. Scott 3-18-1875 Hy
Read, Louisa H. to James S. Maclin 8-3-1864 (no return) Hy
Read, Lucy to Gourius Marrow 3-12-1871 Hy
Read, Lucy to Olison Henly 1-22-1876 (no return) Hy
Read, Lucy to Rufus Cooper 10-1-1869 Hy
Read, Lyde to Ben H. Wear 5-2-1869 Hy
Read, Margret to Bob Wilson 2-21-1870 Hy
Read, Marhea to Jim Holloway 1-20-1870 (no return) Hy
Read, Martha T. to Clinton King 12-23-1841 Cr
Read, Mary Ann to Wm. E. Nation 3-22-1843 (no return) F
Read, Mary E. to Tom Tucker 4-12-1872 Hy
Read, Mary F. A. to J. A. Edmonson 10-20-1870 G
Read, Mary Irene to H. M. Clarke 12-23-1839 (12-25-1839) Ma
Read, Mary Jane to Robt. W. Haywood 4-4-1861 (no return) Hy
Read, Mary L. to Moses D. Mitchell 5-2-1869 Hy
Read, Mary to Douglass Read 12-15-1869 (no return) Hy
Read, Mary to Henry B. Glimp 2-4-1865 G

Read, Mary to Manuel Davy 9-16-1865 (no return) Hy
Read, Mary to William Gibson 5-8-1871 T
Read, Mary to William W. Winford 12-30-1868 T
Read, Miledge to William Miller 2-5-1874 Hy
Read, Missouri to Henry Reynolds 10-18-1841 L
Read, Mollie L. to D. B. Raworth 3-16-1870 Hy
Read, Mollie to Wm. Nixon 12-24-1878 Hy
Read, Moriah to Taylor Tapscott 1-24-1878 Hy
Read, N. J. to John T. Read 12-30-1869 T
Read, Nancy to Berry Johnson 6-10-1834 (6-12-1834) Hr
Read, Nancy to Daniel Taylor 9-10-1857 Ma
Read, Nancy to Scott Read 9-8-1866 Hy
Read, Nancy to Willis Drake 12-28-1869 (no return) Hy
Read, Nannie to G. W. Mills 1-9-1877 (1-10-1877) Dy
Read, Phebe to John Turner 5-28-1870 Hy
Read, Polly to Oliver Morris 2-27-1875 Hy
Read, Rhoda to Hiram Seaton 12-10-1840 Hr
Read, S. A. to W. E. Moore 11-30-1868 G
Read, S. T. to Kenneth Rayner 12-24-1867 Hy
Read, Sallie L. to G. B. Baskerville 11-16-1869 Hy
Read, Sarah E. to Jonathan Coleman 11-14-1853 (11-16-1853) O
Read, Sarah E. to Will P. Bond, jr. 12-18-1866 Hy
Read, Sarah Jane to Thomas H. Cargal 11-8-1851 (no return) F
Read, Sarah to F. Arnold 7-20-1854 We
Read, Sarah to G. F. Enochs 9-28-1848 (no return) Cr
Read, Sarah to Royal Read 11-25-1865 (no return) Hy
Read, Sue T. to Asa O. Mann 5-7-1878 Hy
Read, Susan to Batt Hill 12-15-1867 Hy
Read, Susan to James Johnson 12-7-1841 Cr
Read, Susan to John H. Beechum 7-12-1859 Cr
Read, Winny to G. V. Enochs 12-28-1869 (12-30-1869) Cr
Reader, Amanda to Wm. G. Leach 1-19-1856 Cr
Reader, Amandy J. to Wm. L. Lacey 8-14-1845 Cr
Reader, Mily A. to W. T. J. Melton 12-27-1867 (12-28-1867) Cr
Reader, N. A. to J. K. Turlington 2-16-1858 We
Ready, Isabella C. to F. A. Breakenridge 6-1-1841 Sh
Reagan, Ciely to Moses Foren 4-27-1824 (4-29-1824) Hr
Reagan, Cynthia to William Baker 5-8-1828 (5-11-1828) Hr
Reagan, Elizabeth to Mathew L. Punch 10-11-1838 (10-12-1838) Hr
Reagan, Jane to Edwin Crawford 2-24-1824 (2-26-1824) Hr
Reagan, Martha B. to John Price 8-1-1853 (8-15-1853) Hr
Reagan, Martha J to lHiram G. Hinson 9-28-1846 (9-30-1846) Hr
Reagan, Mary to Richard Hatley 1-5-1825 (1-9-1825) Hr
Reagan, Nancy C. to John D. Smith 12-1-1854 (12-3-1854) Hr
Reagan, Sarah J. to James B. Young 11-4-1858 Hr
Reager, M. J. to Wm. H. Crocker 10-11-1860 G
Real, Mary to Denis Lucey 1-20-1855 (1-21-1855) Sh
Real, Mary to Edmond Barry 8-11-1857 (8-18-1857) Sh
Reames, S. J. to J. S. Amis 11-14-1865 (11-16-1865) F
Reams, Delila C. to John Wilson 6-18-1864 Sh
Reams, Elizabeth to D. C. Morris 4-2-1859 (4-3-1859) F
Reams, Lucinda to James Halliwell 8-18-1857 (8-19-1857) Sh
Reams, M. J. to A. M. Hood 2-3-1864 (not endorsed) F
Reams, Malinda to Frank Walton 12-24-1868 F B
Reams, Mary A. to John D. Hull 12-14-1868 Be
Reans, Amanda to Jonah Forester 1-7-1858 We
Reasens?, C. A. to E. L. Johnson 7-15-1846 Hr
Reasin, Catharine to John Kreher 1-28-1860 (1-30-1860) Sh
Reason, Mary to John Powell 7-19-1847 (7-27-1847) Hr
Reasons, E. A. to J. W. Loyd 11-2-1865 G
Reasons, Edney to James Lewis 8-31-1841 G
Reasons, Elizabeth B. to William S. Cherry 8-30-1851 (8-31-1851) G
Reasons, Jane to Thomas N. Sims 8-31-1857 G
Reasons, Lavina to Calvin B. Reasons 2-2-1848 G
Reasons, Lizzie to J. W. Whitehorn 7-9-1872 (7-15-1872) Dy
Reasons, Martha J. to John A. Harpole 6-10-1866 G
Reasons, Sarah to Moody Young 7-22-1852 (7-23-1852) G
Reatherford, Bettie J. to John W. Shelton 1-30-1861 T
Reatherford, Georgia Ann to W. R. M. Logan 12-28-1859 T
Reaves, Eliza C. to Anderson Faris 7-29-1840 (7-30?-1840) Hr
Reaves, Eliza to Richard North 5-28-1840 Cr
Reaves, Elizabeth C. to John McKinnie 3-8-1841 (3-11-1841) Hr
Reaves, Elizabeth to Harvey Hawkins 1-20-1831 Sh
Reaves, Elizabeth to J. J. Porter 1-17-1871 (1-18-1871) Cr
Reaves, Elizabeth to James Griffe 7-10-1855 Cr
Reaves, Frances A. to William Gaither 12-12-1844 Sh
Reaves, H. J. to T. J. Vaden 5-21-1881 (no return) L
Reaves, Jone? to Moses Johnson 1-4-1871 T
Reaves, Juda A. to Franklin A. Butram 5-25-1863 O
Reaves, Juda to Marshal Skiles 2-28-1873 Hy
Reaves, Kitty to Jonathan Jones 10-13-1844 Cr
Reaves, Leah to William C. Miles 12-24-1829 O
Reaves, M. C. to John W. Riley 1-16-1860 O
Reaves, M. T. to J. W. Morris 4-14-1879 (4-18-1879) Dy
Reaves, Martha I. to Andrew Blair 11-7-1855 Cr
Reaves, Millea to Benjamin Thomas 2-1-1877 Hy
Reaves, Nancy to John Jenkins 7-26-1846 Sh

Reaves, Purlie F. to John Russell 1-19-1871 Hy
Reaves, Sallie to Robt. Mathis 12-25-1873 Hy
Reaves, Sophronia A. to B. B. Rutherford 9-3-1861 Hr
Reaves, Susan to Norman W. Jones 7-25-1848 Sh
Reavis, Elizabeth to Samuel M. Thomas 11-6-1849 Ma
Reavis, F. A. to J. Y. Blankenship 1-21-1882 (1-24-1882) L
Reavis, Mary Ann to Dempsey C. Neal 11-13-1856 Ma
Reay, Elizabeth J. to John H. Whitworth 2-18-1852 (2-19-1852) Sh
Rebsamen, Paulina to Franz H. Finne 6-23-1858 Sh
Rece, Mary Ann to J. H. Beavers 6-27-1863 (7-5-1863) Cr
Redd, Catharine E. to David W. Sumner 6-7-1841 (not endorsed) F
Redd, Mary Jane to William W. Farley 4-17-1851 (4-20-1851) Hr
Redden, Bridget to Michael Drummon 8-18-1857 Sh
Redden, Catherine to Thomas Barnes 4-4-1857 (4-5-1857) O
Redden, Lexey to John C. Ward 2-24-1841 Hn
Redden, Martha I. to Sidney I. Thompson 3-12-1842 Ma
Redden, Mary to Patrick Howard 10-6-1857 Sh
Redden, Paralee A. to William Finley 12-31-1869 (1-5-1870) Cr
Redden, Tabitha to Bartlett Simmons 1-12-1844 Hn
Reddett, Matilda to Amos S. Person 12-15-1847 Sh
Reddick, Amanda to Francis Reddick 3-9-1864 Dy
Reddick, Arcenia to Alexander Clinard 4-5-1860 (4-6-1860) Ma
Reddick, Asena to Aron Hudson 9-19-1847 Hn
Reddick, Bettie to Peter Taylor 3-2-1866 (3-3-1866) F B
Reddick, Caroline to Rice Neal 12-23-1865 (12-25-1865) F B
Reddick, Casandra to Charles Jones 10-13-1866 (no return) F B
Reddick, Disey E. to J. W. Pyland 8-13-1860 (8-17-1860) Dy
Reddick, Edy to Sandy Askew 1-15-1869 (no return) F B
Reddick, Eliza to William Click 4-13-1847 Be
Reddick, Elizar J. to John P. Johnson 1-4-1860 We
Reddick, Jane to Sterling Alsop 11-7-1848 Be
Reddick, Julian to Joab Tue 9-20-1840 Be
Reddick, Lucy A. to G. T. Eason 12-2-1871 (no return) Hy
Reddick, Luvena to Bob Green 2-1-1870 (no return) Hy
Reddick, Mahala to Monroe Eddins 9-8-1866 F B
Reddick, Mary to Isaac Goolsby 1-20-1862 Be
Reddick, Mary to J. C. White 6-18-1855 We
Reddick, Mary to Wesley Childress 1-25-1867 Be
Reddick, Sallie E. to John R. Wilkinson 3-7-1871 Ma
Reddick, Sallie E. to T. S. Neal 2-22-1869 (2-24-1869) F
Reddick, Sarah E. to John N. Scates 9-29-1856 (no return) We
Reddick, Sarah E. to John T. Burks 7-17-1869 (7-19-1869) Cr
Reddick, Tempe to Howlbert? Williams 9-1-1866 (no return) F
Reddin, Emay K. to Cooper B. Jones 5-27-1847 G
Reddin, Mary J. C. to W. H. H. Morris 7-18-1867 (7-17?-1867) Dy
Reddin, Mary L. to George M. Rosamon 10-22-1866 (10-24-1866) Ma
Redding, Jane to Irvin E. Carson 8-29-1846 (no return) Hn
Redding, Levina to Boland Dodd 10-28-1841 Ma
Redding, Lydia F. to Henry Jackson 7-16-1856 (7-17-1856) Ma
Redding, Martha Ann to Henry Staggs 12-23-1863 (no return) Dy
Redding, Martha Ann to J. L. Gray 11-22-1865 (11-23-1865) Dy
Redding, N. L. to Thomas J. Dew 10-22-1872 Dy
Redding, Sarah S. to Newton R. Prichard 1-1-1866 Dy
Reddit, Martha M. to Elijah Collins Hughes 10-11-1859 Sh
Reddit, Sarah E. to Willis C. Winberry 12-22-1858 Sh
Reddit, Syntha C. to Burrel B. Neville 5-24-1853 Sh
Redditt, Addie to Jerry Lewis 9-11-1880 (9-12-1880) Dy
Redditt, Eliza M. to Warner L. Buckly 10-13-1834 Sh
Redditt, Evelina G. to Warner (Warren?) L. Buckleys 11-14-1839 Sh
Redditt, Jane Catherine to Henry B. Stewart 12-1-1848 Sh
Redditt, Louisa to Shadrach Shivers 9-24-1844 Sh
Redditt, Martha to Edward H. Wortham 5-17-1849 Sh
Redditt, Synthia to Paschal Buckly 5-3-1836 Sh
Reddyn, Ellen (Mrs.) to Peter Harty 2-10-1864 (2-9?-1864) Sh
Redeck, Athy to Bob Rucker 9-11-1868 Hy
Redeck, Sarah to Henry Pafford 9-23-1851 Be
Rededenton, Ann to Thomas Heniley 6-5-1858 Sh
Reden, Arbelia to William Vaughn 1-2-1849 Hn
Reden, Delora to Wm. F. Elender 10-8-1850 Hn
Reden, Elviva M. to Abram H. Harpole 10-19-1860 (10-21-1860) Ma
Redford, A. Isabella to John A. Holt 11-7-1860 (11-8-1860) Sh
Redford, Josephine to W. R. Gunnis 3-6-1861 Sh
Redford, Julia A. to W. M. Shelton 7-7-1852 Sh
Redford, Lucy to Josiah Nolly 2-15-1849 Sh
Redford, Sarah to William Sullivan 12-23-1860 Hn
Redick, Eliza L. to William T. Cox 3-13-1849 G
Redick, Emma to Charles Pratt 9-24-1880 (9-25-1880) L B
Redick, Maria M. to Isaac C. Nunn 12-20-1866 (no return) Dy
Redin, Mary to C. W. Lee 1-21-1847 Hn
Reding, E. A. to James R. Bridges 12-23-1844 Cr
Reditt, Martha A. to Marcus P. Braswell 7-20-1842 Sh
Redley, Silla to Porter McCutchen 2-4-1867 Dy
Redman, Eliza to John Crawley 5-22-1853 Sh
Redman, Elizabeth to Dawson Sanderford 4-11-1868 G B
Redman, Emma to C. H. Reed 2-16-1864 Sh
Redmon, Martha A. to J. H. Moore 10-9-1864 Mn
Redmon, Nancy to James Anderson 5-18-1825 O

Redmond, Cyntha to Winifred Wright 3-18-1845 Cr
Redson (Reason?), C. L. to S. A. Wilson 1-4-1861 G
Redus, D. F. to J. L. Ayers 4-16-1850 F
Redwin, Mary A. to David B. Price 1-25-1849 Sh
Redwine, Maria to Thomas C. Shelly 6-14-1856 Ma
Redy, Sarah to James Donovan 3-1-1862 Sh
Reebner, Louisa to Jacob Strehl 6-18-1851 (6-19-1851) Sh
Reece, Adaline to James Ingram 4-4-1873 (4-5-1873) T
Reece, Bettie to James Rudd 2-26-1873 (2-27-1873) T
Reece, Eliza J. to Robert Pankey 10-14-1859 O
Reece, Eliza J. to Robert Panky 10-14-1860 O
Reece, Elizabeth A. to N. Williams 1-9-1871 (1-11-1871) Dy
Reece, Frances to William Beard 1-23-1861 (no return) Hy
Reece, Mary E. to Wm. P. Stricklin 12-6-1851 (12-11-1851) Hr
Reece, Mary to J. S. Simpson 5-15-1872 O
Reece, Mary to Matthew Hum 11-11-1858 We
Reece, Mattie to B. W. Overton 12-16-1867 (12-17-1867) F
Reece, Norah J. to J. R. McHood 9-5-1872 Cr
Reecks?, P. to F. Elks 3-22-1860 Hr
Reed (Reece), Elizabeth to James Smith 1-26-1830 G
Reed, Allice to F. N. Ayers 9-28-1864 O
Reed, Ann E. to D. M. Lankford 1-14-1847 Cr
Reed, Ann Laura to J. Shelby Reed 2-12-1859 Sh
Reed, Ann W. to Enoch Rumley 8-18-1850 Cr
Reed, Callie to Henry King 7-17-1873 Hy
Reed, Caroline to William King 12-14-1860 (12-19-1860) Cr
Reed, Clarissa to Thomas J. Waller 1-1-1847 (1-7-1847) F
Reed, E. P. to J. M. James 4-11-1871 (4-12-1871) Dy
Reed, Eliza A. to G. H. Winfield 5-17-1866 Hy
Reed, Elizabeth H. to Hugh A. Fullerton 3-13-1837 (3-16-1837) G
Reed, Elizabeth M. to William H. Carson 1-2-1845 Hn
Reed, Elizabeth to A. G. Hill 11-23-1847 Cr
Reed, Elizabeth to Bassell Norrid 1-27-1842 O
Reed, Elizabeth to G. V. Enochs 9-11-1865 (9-12-1865) Cr
Reed, Elizabeth to Thomas Crosbie 5-12-1862 Sh
Reed, Elizabeth to Thomas Crosby 5-12-1862 Sh
Reed, Eveline to William R. Smith 6-19-1857 (6-23-1857) G
Reed, Feeby to John Bond no date (not issued) Hy
Reed, Hannah Adeline to Stephen H. Russell(Russell) 9-8-1827 Hr
Reed, Harriet to Walter Eastep 6-10-1862 Sh
Reed, Harriett to Bonaparte Thompson 1-22-1870 F B
Reed, Irene to George Butler 10-12-1866 T
Reed, Julia A. to J. C. Mitchell 7-13-1866 G
Reed, Laura to Thomas Allen 9-12-1867 (9-13-1867) O
Reed, Lucinda to William Stubblefield 5-14-1867 G
Reed, Lucindia to Thos. Williams 10-12-1830 Hr
Reed, Lucy to Cadda W. Youngblood 1-30-1844 Hn
Reed, Lucy to E. M. Waller 1-21-1851 (no return) F
Reed, M. A. E. to John H. Lowrance 11-15-1863 Dy
Reed, M. to W. A. Wallace 3-9-1863 (3-25-1863) Dy
Reed, Maranda to Thomas Snider 6-13-1854 Hn
Reed, Margaret to A. J. Roycroft 9-21-1841 G
Reed, Margaret to Matthew Black 1-30-1828 (2-3-1828) Hr
Reed, Margaret to William Dickinson 4-4-1829 Ma
Reed, Margarett A. to William A. Wyatt 10-3-1855 (10-4-1855) G
Reed, Martha A. to Benjamin Hirlson 10-26-1863 O
Reed, Martha M. to J. M. Bready 9-27-1854 Hn
Reed, Martha to C. L. Reed 9-11-1866 (9-19-1866) T
Reed, Martha to Silas Douglas 1-6-1870 F
Reed, Martha to Tony Donald(son?) 11-30-1867 G B
Reed, Mary (Mrs.?) to Alexander Gray 2-10-1864 (2-11-1864) Sh
Reed, Mary A. to Isaac C. Mitchell 1-5-1847 (1-7-1847) G
Reed, Mary Ann to Allen Fox 11-23-1848 G
Reed, Mary Ann to J. M. Hays 5-19-1859 Sh
Reed, Mary J. to James Johnson 6-12-1867 (6-13-1867) Cr
Reed, Mary J. to Thomas F. Bell 10-3-1869 G
Reed, Mary M. C. to Samuel L. Lorance 1-30-1840 (2-2-1840) G
Reed, Mary M. to Thomas H. Cheek 4-6-1859 Sh
Reed, Mary to Moses Joiner 6-9-1841 Cr
Reed, Mary to Theodrick Minton 12-16-1848 G
Reed, Mary to W. M. Hoskins 1-17-1874 (1-18-1874) Dy
Reed, Matilda Jane to Elbert Allen Young 2-1-1868 G
Reed, Matilda to Henry Strong 12-19-1866 T
Reed, Melvina to Frederick Burton 12-28-1868 (12-29-1868) F B
Reed, Milla to James Brown 9-25-1868 F B
Reed, N. M. to L. H. Akin 3-6-1861 G
Reed, Nancy A. to Robert L. Wilson 1-17-1841 (1-18-1841) Ma
Reed, Nancy J. to A. J. Fullerton 9-22-1868 Dy
Reed, Nancy M. to Thomas A. Akin 10-25-1855 G
Reed, Peggy to John Turner 7-8-1833 (7-9-1833) Hr
Reed, Permelia to Wm. R. Anderson 9-21-1839 Hr
Reed, Priscilla to H. C. Cunliff 11-28-1860 (11-29-1860) F
Reed, Rachael E. to William R. Kimbro 7-16-1858 (7-17-1858) T
Reed, Rachel to Valcian C. G. Wright 2-24-1829 G
Reed, Rebecca to Francis Perry 1-24-1848 (1-25-1848) G
Reed, Rebecca to John Wallice 1-7-1862 G
Reed, Sallie Ann to H. B. Pomeroy 1-21-1879 (1-22-1879) Dy
Reed, Sarah A. to Samuel Ingram 8-28-1860 G
Reed, Sarah J. to James N. McDaniel 1-16-1854 (1-17-1854) G
Reed, Sarah Jane to W. J. Davis 11-27-1866 (11-28-1866) Dy
Reed, Sarah to Jacob Hicks 9-2-1852 G
Reed, Sarah to John Mann 12-26-1865 (no return) Hy
Reed, Sarah to John Perry 12-9-1857 G
Reed, Tennessee to David C. Fox 3-16-1869 G
Reed, Violett to Levett Cathey 8-30-1866 G B
Reeder, Mollie to John Williams 12-29-1874 (12-30-1874) L
Reeder, Sarah to Alonzo Herrick 12-23-1868 (12-24-1868) F
Reedon, Mahala to Samuel Reedon 1-9-1862 Hr
Rees, M. E. to William R. Williams 7-27-1863 (7-28-1863) Cr
Rees, Martha E. to William R. Williams 7-27-1863 Cr
Reese, Ardinia? to John C. Blackburn 4-28-1841 (5-4-1841) T
Reese, Blanche to John Dill 7-13-1845 (no return) L
Reese, Eliza to Charles E. Copeland 11-23-1841 (no return) F
Reese, Evelina to James M. Miller 12-24-1844 (no return) F
Reese, Louisa to Allen Little 7-6-1847 Ma
Reese, Sarah to George g. Lane 10-12-1832 Hr
Reese, Sarah to L. H. Evans 9-1-1874 (9-2-1874) Dy
Reeth?, Margaret to Henry L. Williams 3-12-1859 (3-24-1859) O
Reevely, Mary Ann to William M. Weatherly 12-15-1856 Ma
Reevely, Mary Jane to Thomas D. Wright 11-13-1855 Ma
Reeves, Adaline to Nathan Shaddinger 9-5-1867 F
Reeves, Adeline to George G. Perkins 10-8-1845 (10-9-1845) Ma
Reeves, Agnes to William P. Brown 11-2-1847 (11-3-1847) O
Reeves, Ann T. to Thos. G. Taylor 12-14-1854 O
Reeves, Ann to Ewing Merrill 8-2-1843 (no return) Hn
Reeves, Ann to James C. Bradford 7-24-1855 Ma
Reeves, Caroline to Alexander 9-15-1859 O
Reeves, Caroline to Steven Estes 1-5-1867 (no return) Hy
Reeves, Catherine to Richard T. McKnight 12-31-1844 (1-2-1845) Ma
Reeves, E. A. to John L. McDonald 10-20-1856 (10-22-1856) G
Reeves, E. C. to Hugh Jacobs 10-8-1862 O
Reeves, E. J. to A. P. Brooks 6-15-1846 Sh
Reeves, E. J. to J. H. Sanders 3-6-1870 O
Reeves, E. M. to Jas. A. Buchanan 2-7-1865 (2-9-1865) O
Reeves, Emeline to Calvell Wilson 1-12-1838 (12-13-1838) Ma
Reeves, F. O. to S. A. Elam 8-18-1859 G
Reeves, Frances A. E. to Wm. C. Baker 8-9-1869 (8-12-1869) Ma
Reeves, Frances A. to Andrew J. Studvant 9-7-1852 (no return) F
Reeves, Frances to Plummer Evans 1-21-1869 F B
Reeves, H. T. to James H. Clayton 10-24-1855 (no return) F
Reeves, Isabella J. to John T. R. Legate 2-25-1842 (2-28-1842) O
Reeves, J. M. to J. F. Burkhart 8-29-1860 (9-4-1860) T
Reeves, Jane L. to Thomas J. Brown 9-29-1852 (9-30-1852) O
Reeves, Jane to B. G. Estridge 5-6-1848 O
Reeves, Jane to B. G. Estridge 5-6-1848 (5-7-1848) O
Reeves, Jane to Claton Rogers 2-9-1848 Be
Reeves, L. V. to W. J. Jackson 7-7-1865 O
Reeves, Leah to Columbus Cunningham 5-19-1855 (5-24-1855) O
Reeves, Letta to John Nedry 3-5-1838 O
Reeves, Louisa to George W. Smith 7-19-1855 Be
Reeves, Louisanna E. to Robert M. McKnight 4-13-1839 Ma
Reeves, Lourena (Mrs.) to James Thornton 5-17-1867 (5-19-1867) Ma
Reeves, Lucenda to John Duncan 4-3-1839 (4-4-1839) Ma
Reeves, Lucinda to Charles Sims 12-5-1868 G B
Reeves, Lyddia to Nat Howard 12-25-1869 (12-31-1869) F B
Reeves, M. A. to Virgil E. Rush 10-1-1879 L
Reeves, M.F. to J. A. Wilson 10-19-1870 (10-20-1870) F
Reeves, Maggie to L. G. Danner 7-30-1869 G
Reeves, Mariah T. D. to David H. Parker 5-24-1853 Ma
Reeves, Martha A. to John M. Harrison? 2-28-1853 (3-1-1853) O
Reeves, Mary A. to Naman Littleton 4-11-1860 (4-12-1860) O
Reeves, Mary C. to Josiah Gleason 12-14-1850 O
Reeves, Mary C. to W. C. Threadgill 7-18-1848 (8-1-1848) O
Reeves, Mary E. to W. B. West 12-14-1871 (12-16-1871) O
Reeves, Mary F. to T. W. Crowder 12-16-1865 F
Reeves, Mary P. to Wilson S. Easterwood 4-14-1858 G
Reeves, Mary S. to D. S. Reeves 9-12-1867 O
Reeves, Mary to R. D. Jones 2-28-1856 (3-5-1856) Hr
Reeves, Musadora to L. L. Boyd 1-27-1866 (1-30-1866) F
Reeves, N. L. to D. C. King 7-16-1867 G
Reeves, Nancy Ann to William W. Wynn 11-25-1853 (12-4-1853) O
Reeves, Nancy E. to William W. McNeeley 2-24-1843 (3-2-1843) O
Reeves, Nancy Witt to Joshua Darden 11-23-1865 (11-28-1865) F
Reeves, Nancy to David Baley 12-27-1871 Hy
Reeves, Nancy to Thomas Boyett 1-17-1838 (1-21-1838) O
Reeves, Polly to Stark Fleetwood 7-21-1824 Sh
Reeves, Rebecca M. to Otis L. Story 3-5-1841 (3-1?-1841) Ma
Reeves, Rebecca to Wesley Harris 3-11-1869 F
Reeves, Rose to Jordan McNeill 11-9-1867 (no return) F B
Reeves, Sarah A. to Wm. W. Tanner 7-19-1856 (7-22-1856) O
Reeves, Sarah E. to A. F. Coleman 10-29-1861 G
Reeves, Sarah G. to John W. Blankinship 12-30-1850 (1-1-1851) G
Reeves, Sarah S. to Martin Simmons 12-6-1861 (12-19-1861) O
Reeves, Sarah to Lawson Taylor 8-13-1870 T

Reeves, Susan to Thomas Murtaugh 2-9-1869 (2-11-1869) Ma
Reeves, Turzey J. to John M. Brown 12-2-1844 (12-3-1844) O
Reeves, Victoria to Alexander Adams 1-17-1867 Be
Reevze, Mary T. to Elijah D. Shipman 1-11-1865 (6-1-2-1865) O
Regan, Kitty to George Hess 12-31-1868 G
Regenn, L. F. to Geo. W. Bennett 12-1-1857 G
Regoult, Mary to Joseph Jonah Batiste Magalon 7-25-1848 Sh
Rehkoff, Caroline to Joseph Grieshaber 3-1-1853 (3-2-1853) Sh
Reibert, Caroline R. to Robert Hungerazo? 3-25-1863 Sh
Reich, Elizar to Robert Collilns 2-26-1859 (2-27-1859) O
Reid, Belle to Arch Jordan 2-23-1869 G
Reid, Charlotte Caonia to THomsa L. Kincaid 9-2-1856 (9-3-1856) Ma
Reid, Cresa to William Swift 4-20-1867 (no return) F B
Reid, Docia A. to James A. Ray 6-7-1867 O
Reid, Eliza to John Blackmon 9-21-1842 (9-22-1842) Ma
Reid, Elizabeth T. to M. A. Simmons 1-1-1851 Sh
Reid, Elizur to Robert Collins 2-26-1859 (2-27-1859) O
Reid, Ellen to Charles Bovett 11-28-1843 Sh
Reid, Lenora Dee to Joseph H. Abington 5-14-1861 Sh
Reid, M. A. to John T. Powers 5-4-1858 Sh
Reid, Martha Ann to John B. Thompson 12-24-1861 T
Reid, Mary C. to John P. Smith 9-11-1845 Sh
Reid, Mary to Thos. M Greer 1-1-1846 Ma
Reid, Mary to Wade W. Lyon 11-2-1869 Ma
Reid, Peggie to Andrew Fulks 3-8-1869 (no return) F
Reid, Rachel to Alexander Wells 9-30-1841 Sh
Reid, S. J. to R. A. Mickleberry 1-7-1857 (1-8-1857) Sh
Reid, Sally to Dennis Bryan 11-6-1851 Sh
Reid, Sophronia to Jesse Duncan 2-2-1850 (2-13-1850) Ma
Reid, Susan R. to R. H. Gennett 3-15-1851 Sh
Reid, Susan to John Stark 11-24-1858 (11-26-1858) Sh
Reider, Kate A. to A. W. Blair 5-22-1870 G
Reily, Mary to Martin Runnels 3-20-1859 Sh
Reiney, Eda to William Latimer 8-30-1870 G
Reiney, Emilie to John R. Dailey 10-23-1862 Sh
Reinhardt, Amanda to Rowland Horsley 12-1-1835 Sh
Reinhardt, Eugenia L. to Benjamin N. Sawtelle 7-5-1855 Sh
Reinhardt, Harriett to Jas. Rich Wray 1-5-1846 Sh
Reinhardt, Margaret to Daniel L. Miller 3-28-1848 Sh
Reinhardt, Mary Ann Elizabeth to Samuel Carr 6-18-1844 Sh
Reinhardt, Mary E. to Alexander Shaw 2-5-1856 Sh
Reinhardt, Rebecca to Charles Allen 1-26-1848 Sh
Reis, Margaret (Mrs.) to F. Wesche 10-26-1864 Sh
Reives, Rosetta to Johnson Lockett 7-1-1867 (no return) Hy
Rembert, Harrett M. to Jacob N. Moon 2-26-1844 Sh
Rembert, Louisa R. to Jno. Pollard Trezevant 12-2-1841 Sh
Renfro, Charity to Eli C. Harris 6-30-1853 (no return) Cr
Renfro, E. C. to Thomas O. Travis 10-12-1861 (no return) Hn
Renfro, Emily E. to W. L. Davidson 8-9-1866 G
Renfro, Mahala to James Snowden 4-16-1855 (no return) F
Renfro, Melissa C. to Wm. A. Odle 11-1-1869 Dy
Renfro, Susan R. to James P. Melton 12-5-1866 Hn
Renfro, Susan to John Galbreath 1-11-1860 Hn
Renfroe, Ann to Thomas J. Curlin 2-4-1858 Sh
Renfroe, Emily to John W. Bishop 2-4-1862 L
Renfrow, Maria to Thomas A. Loving 11-8-1873 Hy
Renfrow, Mary A. to John Newmon 7-2-1872 (7-4-1872) L
Renfrow, Ruth E. to W. A. Shelton 7-13-1861 (7-14-1861) O
Renick (Reynick), Phebe to Young Thomas Logan 2-28-1835 Sh
Renn (Penn?), Mary J. to James T. Mitchell 11-23-1866 G
Rennalds, Josephine to A. G. Slagle 10-4-1870 Hy
Rennick, Racheal to John D. Carroll 1-28-1828 Hr
Rennolds, Emily to Thomas Whitelaw 3-28-1853 (3-29-1853) Sh
Reno, Nancy J. to James M. Crawford 2-4-1851 (2-6-1851) Sh
Renolds, Jane E. to Archibald Craft 11-19-1838 Hr
Renshaw, Emma to Joseph Potts 1-31-1839 Hn
Renshaw, Sarah E. to Hasting P. Howard 3-11-1859 Hn
Rentfro, Elizabeth to Thos. Yarbery 4-22-1841 G
Rentfro, Emaly to Joseph Weatherspoon 12-16-1843 (12-21-1843) G
Rentfro, Mary A. E. to Calvin M. Harrison 7-15-1846 (7-16-1846) G
Rentfro, N. A. to William M. Davis 8-25-1859 G
Rentfrow, Nancy to M. N. Howard 6-7-1877 L
Reosier, Ellen to James D. Carrigan 1-16-1877 (1-17-1877) L
Replogle, Margaret E. (Mrs.) to John D. Pipkins 8-22-1870 G
Replogle, Nancy Ann to Willie T. Harns 2-18-1845 Ma
Replogle, Susan to Micajah Keith 5-19-1832 Ma
Reprogle, Rebecca to John W. Yopp 8-6-1855 Hr
Resiner, Sarah to Melton Coleman 11-8-1832 Sh
Rest, Sarah to Joseph Strehl 1-22-1851 (1-23-1851) Sh
Revel (Reid), Martha to A. C. Robinson 5-13-1849 Sh
Revel, C. S. to Wm. S. May 8-29-1864 (9-1-1864) Cr
Revel, Eliza to Henry E. Sills 12-17-1855 Sh
Revel, Esshia C. to Edward Wallace 1-16-1834 O
Revel, Mary to Martin Robinson 9-24-1846 Sh
Revel, R. E. to W. F. Simpson 11-8-1866 (11-9-1866) Cr
Revel, Sophia J. to Isaac M. Gunter 11-12-1862 G
Revell, Lucy A. to David E. Mayo 2-16-1868 Hy

Revell, Margaret A. to D. T. P. Hally 8-1-1856 (8-5-1856) Sh
Revell, Mary to Neal McKinnon 8-19-1859 (no return) Hy
Revelle, M. J. to J. F. Kail 1-14-1873 Hy
Revelle, N. J. to R. E. Kail 12-21-1872 (no return) Hy
Revelle, S. R. to T. H. Pittman 12-26-1872 Hy
Revely, Margaret to George Bishop 1-17-1853 (1-18-1853) Ma
Revely, Martha E. to Boyce E. Sherman 10-15-1857 (10-18-1857) Ma
Revely, Martha E. to Henry Butler 2-12-1845 Ma
Revely, Martha E. to Martin S. George 11-30-1857 (12-3-1857) Ma
Revely, Susan E. to William J. Sipes 12-24-1862 (12-25-1862) Ma
Reviere, Willie to Joseph New 3-23-1880 L
Revil, Nancy to Thomas J. Bryant 12-3-1857 Cr
Reville, C. Helen to John W. Watson 6-21-1861 Sh
Reville, Martha E. to J. W. Henderson 12-28-1865 Hy
Reycroft, Martha A. to Alfred Brewer 2-27-1878 Dy
Reynolds, Amanda King to J. R. Eatherly 1-27-1879 (1-29-1879) Dy
Reynolds, Amanda M. to John B. Cox 5-23-1843 (5-25-1843) Hr
Reynolds, Ann M. to Laban J. Garrison 10-8-1857 (10-15-1857) L
Reynolds, Ardelia to A. H. Hooper 8-27-1873 (8-28-1873) L
Reynolds, Bettie to Henderson Hays 4-24-1884 L
Reynolds, Clementine to John F. Paschall 12-8-1852 Hn
Reynolds, Eliza C. to J. M. Miller 7-12-1879 (no return) L
Reynolds, Eliza to Thomas Stiles 12-16-1852 Hn
Reynolds, Elizabeth Ann V. to James M. Reynolds 2-18-1864 Cr
Reynolds, Elizabeth J. to John J. Williamson 4-4-1857 (no return) Hn
Reynolds, Elizabeth ann V. to James M. Reynolds 2-18-1864 (no return) Cr
Reynolds, Elizabeth to Nathaniel Scott 11-15-1835 (11-19-1835) Hr
Reynolds, Frances E. to Burrell Wall 5-27-1862 (no return) Hn
Reynolds, Frances to David Howell 12-29-1884 (12-30-1884) L
Reynolds, H. B. to J. M. Childress 11-7-1881 (no return) L
Reynolds, Ibby to John P. Nooner 11-15-1832
Reynolds, Isabella to Granville Halliman 8-2-1854 Hn
Reynolds, Jane to W. M. Hall 8-1-1871 (8-2-1871) Dy
Reynolds, Jane to William Adams 7-31-1850 (no return) L
Reynolds, L. D. E. to James L. Thurmond 8-25-1877 (8-29-1877) L
Reynolds, Letty Ann to Henry Kerby 3-19-1846 L
Reynolds, Lina to William C. Garrett 4-3-1844 (5-17-1844) Ma
Reynolds, Lucinda to G. G. Harold 2-12-1869 (no return) Dy
Reynolds, Lucinda to Robert McKinney 9-30-1828 Sh
Reynolds, Lucy Ann to George W. Cole 5-14-1846 Sh
Reynolds, Malinda C. to Edward Underwood 12-23-1868 L
Reynolds, Margrett M. to Daniel Sinclair 3-22-1847 (3-25-1847) Hr
Reynolds, Martha Ann to Solomon Hoofman 1-10-1849 Hn
Reynolds, Martha E. to Jesse Baker 12-4-1869 (12-5-1869) Dy
Reynolds, Martha J. to Garland Lively 1-29-1866 (no return) Dy
Reynolds, Martha J. to Wm. Luskey 11-26-1856 Cr
Reynolds, Martha Jane to Jonathan McKinney 1-25-1851 (2-2-1851) L
Reynolds, Martha to Pleasant Hill 6-1-1833 (6-4-1833) G
Reynolds, Mary A. to George T. Culverhouse 1-3-1861 Hn
Reynolds, Mary Ann E. to James G. Bucke 12-26-1854 (12-31-1854) Hr
Reynolds, Mary J. to Wiley D. Manning 2-1-1862 (2-2-1862) L
Reynolds, Mary L. to James H. Saterfield 7-19-1836 (7-20-1836) Hr
Reynolds, Mary to Josephus S. Perry 10-11-1859 (10-12-1859) G
Reynolds, Minirva to Jesse S. Byrd 11-21-1860 T
Reynolds, Nancy R. to John R. Rogers 8-9-1853 Be
Reynolds, Nancy to Thomas Floyd 2-29-1840 (3-4-1840) Hr
Reynolds, Peggy A. to Joseph Craig 7-8-1862 (7-10-1862) O
Reynolds, Polly to James Glidell 9-23-1856 Hr
Reynolds, R. E. to W. O. Christie 10-16-1877 Dy
Reynolds, R. M. to Thomas McKennee 2-2-1852 (2-8-1852) L
Reynolds, Rachel to A. B. Neely 12-31-1840 L
Reynolds, Rebecca to Jacob Spencer 1-18-1870 (1-16?-1870) Dy
Reynolds, Rebecca to Thomas W. Walker 3-29-1858 Hr
Reynolds, Roda G. to William C. Elzey 10-24-1867 L
Reynolds, Roxey S. V. to Bennet S. Griffith 2-16-1870 Hy
Reynolds, Sallie to A. A. McGraw 12-31-1872 Dy
Reynolds, Sally to William W. Warters 2-13-1844 Be
Reynolds, Sarah A. to Joseph Jones 11-8-1858 Hn
Reynolds, Sarah E. to J. F. Carter 8-24-1868 (8-27-1868) L
Reynolds, Sarah E. to W. B. Aaron 4-23-1863 Hn
Reynolds, Sarah J. to Benj. F. Dunham 11-26-1862 (11-27-1862) L
Reynolds, Sarah M. to Andrew Lidy 8-1-1831 (8-2-1831) Hr
Reynolds, Sarah to Giles Henson 3-29-1845 Hn
Reynolds, Tabitha to Henry Saunders 5-2-1858 (5-8-1858) L
Rezer, Mary M. to Willem Sctarz 5-29-1851 (6-3-1851) Sh
Rhay, Parthena A. to Robert M. Abernathy 3-11-1874 (3-12-1874) L
Rhea, E. L. to John Rhea 12-22-1840 F
Rhea, Ella to H. Cary 5-1-1866 F
Rhea, Ester (Easter) to Joseph Nale 2-19-1831 Sh
Rhea, Isabell to King Levy 12-29-1868 (1-16-1869) F B
Rhea, Lucinda to S. A. Miller 8-28-1849 F
Rhea, Margarett J. to Nicholas Long 7-12-1848 F
Rhea, Mehala to William Davidson 7-20-1834 Sh
Rhea, Susan A. to Miles D. Webb 6-4-1844 (no return) L
Rhelahan, Mary to Michael Leary 5-21-1860 Sh
Rhine, Mary to William House 11-5-1869 (11-11-1869) F B
Rhoades, Lucy V. to C. L. Jackson 8-9-1869 (no return) Hy

Rhoads, Eliza to Jonathan Hampton 1-4-1853 Hn
Rhoads, Elland to James Myrick 10-6-1840 Hn
Rhodes, A. J. to R. L. Vawton 11-15-1869 (no return) Cr
Rhodes, A. K. to James H. M. Hall 4-22-1838 F
Rhodes, Adaline to Henry Perminter 9-20-1867 (9-22-1867) Cr
Rhodes, Alice A. to Elam F. Thomas 9-3-1844 T
Rhodes, Amanda? S.? to Allen Harvell 11-28-1867 T
Rhodes, Antoinette to Jean (John) Leveque 7-16-1853 (7-20-1853) Sh
Rhodes, Bettie to John Fowler 3-13-1873 T
Rhodes, Charlotte to William S. Garner 9-10-1835 Sh
Rhodes, Charlotte to William Sasser 1-15-1842 (1-16-1842) Hr
Rhodes, Cornelia to Jackson Lea 8-6-1868 (no return) Hy
Rhodes, Eliza J. to Stephen Durden 6-19-1867 (no return) Hn
Rhodes, Emily to Madison Nelms 9-14-1853 (9-15-1853) Hr
Rhodes, Emily to Robert Gentry 9-29-1851 (9-30-1851) Hr
Rhodes, Eviline to Chas. A. Coor 8-10-1854 (8-11-1854) Hr
Rhodes, Eviline to Wilson King 5-11-1865 (5-14-1865) Cr
Rhodes, Fannie to Alfred Martin 9-5-1868 (9-6-1868) F B
Rhodes, Fannie to Lee Miller 1-9-1873 T
Rhodes, Frances D. to John Staritt 5-16-1865 T
Rhodes, Frances E.? to John Garrett 5-16-1865 (5-17-1865) T
Rhodes, Frances P. to A. J. Vawter 1-2-1866 (no return) Cr
Rhodes, Georgia A. to J. B. Cole 9-25-1867 T
Rhodes, Harriet to Henry Clark 12-20-1869 (12-22-1869) Cr
Rhodes, J. C. to W. B. Harvey 3-31-1869 (no return) F
Rhodes, Jack Ann to George Washington 8-6-1870 (8-7-1870) T
Rhodes, Leah F. to George Locke 6-10-1868 (6-11-1868) Ma
Rhodes, Lue E. to L. M. Russell 1-2-1866 Hy
Rhodes, M. E. to O. E. Hamilton 10-26-1868 (10-29-1868) T
Rhodes, Malinda to Sylis J. Jones 3-24-1859 Cr
Rhodes, Martha J. to Robert Snider 5-18-1867 (no return) Hn
Rhodes, Mary A. E. to Wm. W. Greenway 9-5-1850 F
Rhodes, Mary E. to Yancy E. Wilks 12-16-1869 Cr
Rhodes, Mary J. to D. H. Smith 2-6-1869 (2-7-1869) T
Rhodes, Mary to Washington Maclin 1-19-1868 (1-20-1868) T
Rhodes, Matilda to J. M. Humphrys 4-14-1857 (4-20-1857) Sh
Rhodes, Millie to Turner Worlds 1-20-1872 Hy
Rhodes, Nancy E. to John W. Louds 1-18-1842 Cr
Rhodes, Nancy to Henry McClanahan 3-31-1871 (4-1-1871) T
Rhodes, Narcissa to Thomas E. Toller 9-6-1845 (9-14-1845) Hr
Rhodes, Perlina to Nathaniel M. Overall 11-25-1845 (11-27-1845) O
Rhodes, Rhoda M. to N. T. Bansfield(Bunsfield) 12-7-1858 (12-9-1858) Hr
Rhodes, Sarah A. to R. C. Garrett 5-1-1848 (5-3-1848) F
Rhods, Rosesetty to John Griffith 11-23-1858 We
Rial, Margerett to James Shoal 7-22-1866 Be
Rial, Martha to Jesse Foust 6-27-1838 Hn
Rial, Mary to Catlet Corley 6-25-1840 Hn
Rian?, Cathorin to Owen Carroll 2-11-1851 Sh
Rice, A. S. C. to Thomas M. Blackwell 3-1-1842 (no return) L
Rice, Ann Eliza to George Holmes 7-27-1847 (7-?-1847) T
Rice, Ann to George Aninston 12-26-1878 L
Rice, Aurelia J. to Tandy W. Erwin 12-12-1860 Sh
Rice, Betsey to John Cunningham 10-25-1882 L
Rice, Burdie to John Drake 2-13-1872 (no return) Hy
Rice, Caroline to Clayburn Edwards 2-16-1869 (2-17-1869) L
Rice, Caroline to Robert Rice 3-19-1873 (3-20-1873) L B
Rice, Cary to Saml. Richardson 5-2-1846 (5-3-1846) F
Rice, Celia Ann to John Graham 11-18-1876 Hy
Rice, Celia Ann to Spencer P. Daniel 12-31-1845 (1-8-1846) F
Rice, Charity to Wm. Locust 2-11-1870 (no return) Hy
Rice, Eliza G. to Hugh T. Hanks 3-17-1865 (3-18-1865) T
Rice, Elizabeth to Elisha M. Bradford 4-3-1882 (4-15-1882) L
Rice, Ellen to William Hurdle 12-13-1882 (12-14-1882) L
Rice, Emma to Henry Jackson 4-28-1871 Hy
Rice, Fanny to Mark Bowen 10-13-1866 (10-14-1866) Dy
Rice, Hallie to William Witherspoon, jr. 3-29-1868 (4-2-1868) Ma
Rice, Hannah to Richard Parker 8-12-1882 L
Rice, Hariet L. to S. R. Smith 2-27-1866 (2-28-1866) T
Rice, Harriet to Charles Ward 2-21-1872 (2-23-1872) Dy
Rice, Harriet to Robt. Coachman 6-28-1867 T
Rice, Jane to Lee Anderson 3-12-1874 Hy
Rice, Jennie to Wm. H. Buchanan 12-19-1878 Hy
Rice, Joe May to Lawrence E. Talbot 2-16-1871 Ma
Rice, Julia to J. V. Shelton 1-10-1866 G
Rice, Kerron R. to John N. Lewis 3-16-1846 (no return) F
Rice, Lany to London Shepard 12-15-1869 (no return) L
Rice, Laura to Charles Brown 8-14-1871 (8-27-1871) L B
Rice, Laura to Walter Bond 2-8-1884 (2-10-1884) L
Rice, Lilly to Thos. J. Blackwell 12-16-1879 (12-18-1879) L
Rice, Louisa to David Walker 8-24-1876 L B
Rice, Lucy to Thomas Flourney 8-9-1860 Sh
Rice, Lue to Jordon Jones 12-23-1870 (no return) Hy
Rice, Margaret to William McBride 2-7-1847 T
Rice, Maria to Patrick Bannon 12-1-1850 Sh
Rice, Martha A. A. to Wm. D. Walton 4-16-1856 T
Rice, Martha E. to Benjamin Coleman 2-8-1858 (2-10-1858) L
Rice, Martha to T.J. Barton 11-23-1872 (11-26-1872) Cr

Rice, Martha to William W. Huddleston 2-20-1838 Hn
Rice, Mary A. to Alfred W. Owen 10-30-1865 (11-2-1865) T
Rice, Mary A. to G. H. Yarbrough 11-23-1876 Hy
Rice, Mary Susan to Peter Green 12-24-1885 L
Rice, Mary to C. F. Schnerring 11-6-1862 Sh
Rice, Mary to J. M. King 4-7-1881 (no return) L
Rice, Mary to John Stevens 11-6-1866 T
Rice, Mary to Wash Williams 4-4-1876 Hy
Rice, Mattie L. to F. B. Gause 11-12-1867 (11-15-1868?) L
Rice, Mattie to Lewis Williams 4-9-1875 (4-21-1875) L
Rice, Millie to J. R. Rice 7-22-1882 (7-23-1882) L
Rice, Mollie L. to Hiram Mann 11-2-1857 (11-4-1857) L
Rice, Mona Agnes to John Madison Butler 7-17-1843 (7-19-1843) T
Rice, Nancy C. to James C. Cook 8-29-1861 (no return) Hy
Rice, Nancy J. to A. E. Mills 7-26-1851 O
Rice, Nancy to Humphrey D. McElyea 2-25-1847 O
Rice, Narissa C. to John B. Vancleave 5-23-1858 Hn
Rice, Nicie to Green Crews 8-28-1871 (8-31-1871) Cr
Rice, Nora to F. A. Johnson 4-4-1885 (4-8-1885) L
Rice, Parthena to Harris Akers 1-20-1872 (1-23-1872) Cr
Rice, Patty to Richard Neely 10-7-1882 L
Rice, Permelia to Henry D. Bradford 12-30-1874 (no return) L B
Rice, R. H. to J. H. Flowers 11-13-1860 T
Rice, Rebecca J. to R. P. Raines 8-1-1867 Hn
Rice, Rebecca to John B. Hinchey 7-24-1849 Hn
Rice, Roberta to G. D. Rudd 12-6-1880 (12-7-1880) L
Rice, Sally to John Walker 3-30-1843 Hn
Rice, Sarah C. to W. J. Osborn 3-18-1863 (no return) Hy
Rice, Sarah to Robert Hagler 12-17-1868 (12-18-1868) Cr
Rice, Sela to Peter Rice 1-14-1868 Hy
Rice, Sue to Richard Rice 11-5-1874 L B
Rice, Susan M. to Thomas A. Anthony 6-21-1853 (6-22-1853) L
Rice, Susan to Arch Leonard 6-5-1883 L
Rice, Susan to Fanteleroy Pass 2-25-1845 Sh
Rice, Tannie to Rowe B. Simmons 2-5-1867 Hn
Rice, Vickie to Primus Currie 7-12-1868 Hy
Rice?, Harriet Anderson to John Walter Morehead 7-12-1843 (7-18-1843) T
Rich, Frances to J. A. Harper 9-3-1850 (no return) F
Rich, Julia L. to Henry C. Gwynn 6-25-1866 (6-28-1866) F
Rich, Lucy H. to W. A. Harper 11-11-1853 (no return) F
Rich, Rosa I. to C. A. Bringle 1-2-1871 (1-5-1871) T
Rich, Susan Isabelle to George Borsh 4-8-1869 G
Richard, Bedy to William Emison 12-27-1850 (1-2-1851) Ma
Richard, Isabell to James Townsend 2-9-1867 T
Richard, Nancy A. to J. D. Parker 11-30-1876 Dy
Richards, Bettie M. to J. W. Pittman 3-2-1864 Sh
Richards, Easter to John Harris 6-27-1866 T
Richards, Eliza C. to Wm. H. Bridges 10-20-1857 Sh
Richards, Elizabeth to Cullen W. Jackson 1-30-1856 (1-31-1856) Ma
Richards, Elizabeth to F. H. Richards 2-23-1857 Sh
Richards, Elizabeth to Samuel Neal 4-13-1841 T
Richards, L. R. to P. G. Kenneth 1-4-1858 Sh
Richards, M. E. to W. J. Whitehead 11-8-1876 Hy
Richards, Martha C. to John F. Cromwell 11-24-1857 Sh
Richards, Martha J. to W. D. McDaniel 4-14-1862 Mn
Richards, Mary Ann to Williford Williams 1-8-1862 (1-9-1862) Ma
Richards, Mary J. to R. B. Parker 12-27-1871 (12-28-1871) Dy
Richards, Mary Jane to C. R. Crooke 7-20-1858 We
Richards, Mary R. to A. D. Gibson 11-21-1860 Sh
Richards, Mary to Newton Ellington 10-9-1866 (10-11-1866) Ma
Richards, Rebecca to W. B. Rogers 1-21-1869 G
Richards, Rebecca to Thomas Pierce 12-27-1853 (12-29-1853) Ma
Richardso, Martha to Thomas Ray 3-29-1863 Hn
Richardson, Ailsey to Henry Bradford 5-20-1834 Sh
Richardson, Amanda to Logan Clark 3-2-1869 (3-3-1869) T
Richardson, America to Williams Adams 11-28-1868 (11-29-1868) L
Richardson, Ann E. to James Robertson 9-29-1869 (9-30-1869) Dy
Richardson, Bettie to George Halfacre 12-4-1876 L
Richardson, Bettie to William Thomas 4-10-1869 (4-11-1869) L
Richardson, Celia to J. B. Wallace 12-8-1856 Hr
Richardson, Clary Ann to Andrew J. Patterson 1-5-1833 G
Richardson, Clary to William Dover 1-17-1859 (1-19-1859) G
Richardson, Cora to James Oldham 2-4-1874 G
Richardson, E. to J. C. Wright 1-10-1867 G
Richardson, Elizabeth to Banks M. Burrow 10-11-1832 (10-12-1832) G
Richardson, Elizabeth to Nathaniel Taylor 11-27-1843 (11-30-1843) G
Richardson, Ella to James Hill 2-3-1870 T
Richardson, Emma to Lewis Rice 8-3-1875 (no return) Hy
Richardson, Emma to William W. Wheeler 2-1-1871 L
Richardson, Fanny to Buck Sangster 4-14-1867 Hy
Richardson, Florence to J. L. Pankey 5-19-1867 G
Richardson, Frances R. to George W. Lockard 12-16-1856 L
Richardson, Frances to J. V. Trafford 6-11-1870 (6-12-1870) Dy
Richardson, Frances to Thomas J. Alford 12-29-1845 (12-30-1845) G
Richardson, Frances to Walton H. Vaughn 9-10-1832 (9-15-1832) Hr
Richardson, Gatsy to Calvin H. Step 1-22-1853 Be
Richardson, Hannah to G. W. Anderson 10-22-1877 Hy

Richardson, Harriet to Henry Williams 12-28-1868 (12-30-1868) T
Richardson, Jane to Cyrus A. Allen 2-27-1849 T
Richardson, Jane to Thomas W. Skiles 12-20-1858 T
Richardson, Juley A. to O. Conlee 5-29-1837 (6-1-1837) G
Richardson, July A. to Orvill Conlee 5-29-1839 G
Richardson, Letty to Allen Betts 7-2-1867 G
Richardson, Lizzie to Joseph Allison 7-4-1872 L
Richardson, Lizzie to Robert Gordon 5-8-1872 T
Richardson, Long to Madison Sanders 1-9-1870 G B
Richardson, Lucinda to Oliver C. May 4-4-1836 (4-5-1836) Hr
Richardson, Lucy D. to Saml. D. Speake 10-27-1841 G
Richardson, Lucy J. to Jno. C. Anderson 10-3-1859 Hr
Richardson, Lydia to Thomas D. Mackey 1-9-1867 G
Richardson, Malinda to Nathan McMullen 5-7-1827 (5-15-1827) G
Richardson, M. E. to John Hammons 8-8-1853 G
Richardson, Margaret E. to John Hammons 8-8-1853 G
Richardson, Martha A. to James Gibson 12-22-1847 (12-23-1847) G
Richardson, Martha Jane C. to James McLillie 8-7-1871 (8-8-1871) T
Richardson, Martha to Clark Brown 1-3-1871 (1-5-1871) T
Richardson, Mary A. to Richd. H. McGaughey 9-1-1845 (no return) L
Richardson, Mary C. to James W. Marsh 7-30-1847 (8-1-1847) Ma
Richardson, Mary E. to Joseph R. Matthews 3-4-1867 Hy
Richardson, Mary E. to William F. Watkins 4-30-1878 Hy
Richardson, Mary F. to Joseph O.(C.) Stephens 6-21-1858 (6-23-1858) Hr
Richardson, Mary J. to William R. Rooks 1-21-1853 (1-23-1853) G
Richardson, Mary to Aaron Hutcheson 8-31-1869 T
Richardson, Mary to Benjamin H. Hubbard 1-30-1834 G
Richardson, Mary to Lacy Allen 3-1-1857 Be
Richardson, Mary to Milton Bessent 10-2-1867 G
Richardson, Mary to Robt. H. Burrow 5-1-1873 (no return) Cr B
Richardson, Mollie to Milton Boon 3-25-1868 (3-31-1868) Ma
Richardson, Nancy A. to S. T. C. Gibbons 12-15-1869 (12-16-1869) Cr
Richardson, Nancy to Robert A. McMurry 11-3-1860 (no return) Hy
Richardson, Nancy to Wash Bailey 1-25-1871 (1-26-1871) F B
Richardson, Nancy to William Garner 6-2-1835 Hr
Richardson, Prudence to William Williamson 9-8-1856 (9-10-1856) Hr
Richardson, R. A. to Jno. K. Carper 11-18-1869 Hy
Richardson, R. C. to M. H. Williams 12-25-1866 Hy
Richardson, Rebecca G. to James M. Brewer 10-3-1835 (10-7-1835) G
Richardson, Rebecca to Dock Wood 12-18-1866 (1-20-1867) Dy
Richardson, Rebecca to James A. Lackey 3-10-1842 L
Richardson, Rebecca to Saml. D. Spate 9-26-1839 G
Richardson, S. . to L. M. Franchey 4-29-1876 L
Richardson, Sallie L. to G. C. Jeffries 10-4-1877 Hy
Richardson, Saloda to Alexander H. Mobley 12-23-1852 G
Richardson, Sarah Ann Eliz. to Henry James Mailey 5-16-1843 (5-18-1843) T
Richardson, Sarah J. to Charles W. Tidwell 3-26-1868 Cr
Richardson, Selva to William Slaydon 1-2-1868 G B
Richardson, Susan A. to Alfred Ferrell 1-5-1843 G
Richardson, Susan D. to Charles Davenport 12-17-1873 (12-18-1873) Dy
Richardson, T. E. to R. R. Clark 5-3-1868 Hy
Richardson, Tamer to John H. Tims 7-31-1861 (8-1-1861) Hr
Richardson, Verginia L. to Jos. H. Smither 10-10-1870 (10-11-1870) Dy
Richardson, Wincey C. to Wm. C. C. Comer 11-14-1860 (11-15-1860) Hr
Richardt, Henrietta to C. W. Wirwa 9-21-1868 (9-22-1868) F
Richars?, Caroline to Thomas J. McCaslin 12-18-1866 (12-19-1866) Cr
Richarson, Martha E. to Samuel J. Matthews 12-7-1868 (12-8-1868) Ma
Richarson, Mary Ann to Daniel Friel 4-2-1870 (9-29-1872?) T
Richer, Mary Jane to Matthew Pitts 2-18-1861 G
Richer, Nancy C. to H. A. McHenry 10-15-1856 G
Richerson, Millley R. to Calvin Huston 7-2-1873 T
Richerson, Tamey to Dudley Diggs 1-13-1857 Ma
Richetts, Eliza Ann to William F. Jones 9-15-1858 Ma
Richey, A. C. to J. B. Walls 1-30-1869 F
Richey, Elizabeth to Andrew J. Webb 2-18-1838 F
Richey, Susan J. to A. J. Davis 1-6-1869 (1-7-1869) F
Richie, E. F. to S. R. Robertson 10-23-1856 (no return) We
Richie, Elizabeth J. to Curtise C. Smith 10-7-1862 We
Richie, Harriett to James H. Groom 12-17-1855 We
Richie, Regina M. to Alenn Walker 10-16-1850 We
Richie, S. C. to Thomas E. Young 12-22-1877 (12-23-1877) Dy
Richie, Sarah to Thomas Lowery 12-14-1853 (no return) F
Richland, Louisa to LaFayette Bryant 4-22-1858 Sh
Richley, Mary to John Turner 5-7-1862 Sh
Richmond, Margaret to John Davis 7-3-1867 (7-4-1867) Dy
Richmond, Susan to Carville Smith 6-2-1868 G
Richter (Richten), Emelline (Emelie) to Frederick Peters 11-29-1849 Sh
Rickets, Elizabeth to Edward C. Townsend 9-1-1855 (9-2-1855) Sh
Ricketts, A. E. to J. D. Cocke 12-27-1864 (12-29-1864) F
Rickman, Eliza to Samuel I. Garrett 2-7-1842 (2-8-1842) Ma
Rickman, Eugenia to J. J. Jones 1-26-1874 (1-28-1874) O
Rickman, Mary to William J. Hart 12-3-1866 (no return) Hn
Rickoff (Riekoff), Caroline to W. M. Miller 5-31-1854 Sh
Ricks, Eliza A. to Manley Dupree 12-17-1867 (12-18-1867) L
Ricks, Lou to Antney Read 12-2-1871 Hy
Ricks, M. L. to J. P. Drake 5-17-1875 Hy
Ricks, Mary A. to William Oswell 5-22-1845 Hr
Ricks, Olivia to Danl. M. Guin 9-13-1832 Hr

Ricks, V. A. to T. H. Stanfield 8-21-1865 Hy
Riddick, Barbery to Wesley Childress 10-2-1856 Be
Riddick, Manervy to Timothy Pafford 9-15-1853 Be
Riddle, Charlotte to Haden Johnston 4-24-1850 (no return) F
Riddle, Elizabeth A. to William M. Griggs 1-31-1849 (2-1-1849) Hr
Riddle, Elizabeth Ann to Nathan W. Tuttle 2-2-1826 Hr
Riddle, Elleanor G. to E.A. Randolph 10-3-1854 Hr
Riddle, Jennet to Talafaro B. Chaffin 12-27-1831 (12-29-1831) Hr
Riddle, Lydia to James Blackly 12-8-1866 O
Riddle, Martha S. to James L. White 9-19-1866 O
Riddle, Martha to Samuel M. McElyea 12-29-1856 (12-30-1856) O
Riddle, Mary E. to Daniel B. Sain 1-13-1838 (1-14(16)-1838) Hr
Riddle, Nancy to John C. Whitaker 1-14-1833 (1-15-1833) Hr
Ridens, Dicey to W. H. Simmons 6-17-1869 Dy
Ridens, M. M. to D. B. Neal 10-5-1871 Dy
Rideout, E. J. to Wm. S. Stallings 12-25-1860 (not executed) F
Rideout, Eliza J. to James H. Hammond 1-17-1861 (1-20-1861) F
Rideout, Liza F. to S. C. King 6-16-1857 (6-17-1857) Sh
Rideout, Martha G. to Sterling L. Wesson 9-22-1855 Sh
Rider, Catharine to Almeron Smith 12-9-1864 Sh
Rider, Martha to Rolin Miller 10-14-1846 (10-15-1846) Ma
Rider, Sarah R. to James R. White 12-22-1840 (12-24-1840) Ma
Ridge, Lucinda to David Liddleton 12-29-1843 We
Ridge, Martha to Giles McGee 12-17-1861 Sh
Ridgeway, Ann to William Kelton 8-26-1844 (no return) We
Ridgeway, Anna to Walter Surratt 7-22-1829 (7-23-1829) O
Ridgeway, Elizabeth to James W. Bransford 2-29-1852 Hn
Ridgeway, Ellen to Simon Fowler? 12-28-1868 (12-29-1868) O
Ridgeway, Louisa Anna to Samuel C. Ridgeway 2-11-1840 Hn
Ridgeway, Mary Ann to S. F. Ridgeway 12-19-1866 (no return) Hn
Ridgeway, Nancy to J. M. Pate 2-27-1870 O
Ridgeway, Offa to Willis A. Fiser 1-3-1841 Hn
Ridgeway, Rachael E. to Willis Witherington 2-26-1856 (2-27-1856) G
Ridgeway, Sarah to William Paschal 10-10-1839 Hn
Ridgway, Sarah to William Edmondson 11-8-1827 O
Ridley, Adelia C. to T. J. Oliver 10-17-1866 (10-18-1866) Cr
Ridley, America to Amos Brown 2-9-1878 (no return) L B
Ridley, Ann E. to Charles Hamlin 1-1-1860 Hn
Ridley, Dinkey to Anthony King 8-8-1879 (8-14-1879) L B
Ridley, Ema to James Parker 3-9-1876 L B
Ridley, Frances to Louis Tyus 9-1-1876 (no return) L
Ridley, Margaret to J. J. Suter 12-28-1854 Sh
Ridley, Matilda to Edom Keys 6-14-1868 Cr
Ridley, Rose to Bill Smith 12-21-1878 (12-22-1878) L
Ridley, Sallie to W. M. Carson 1-14-1862 (no return) Cr
Ridout, Bettie to H. A. Butts 12-4-1875 (no return) Hy
Ridout, Mary C. to G. W. Alford 5-19-1861 Sh
Rie, M. A. W. to J. W. Conley 8-15-1882 (no return) L
Rieley, Mary to Hudson Martin 10-14-1864 (10-15-1864) Sh
Riely (rylett), Margaret to A. Daneri 8-17-1855 (8-19-1855) Sh
Rieper, Babette to Joseph Goodman 7-23-1863 Sh
Rieser, Mary to Ernest Levi 12-9-1856 Sh
Rieves, Lou to Henry Harris 8-15-1867 (8-17-1867) F B
Rieves, Mary to James Roberson 8-26-1840 Cr
Rieves, Mary to James Roberson 8-26-1840 (no return) Cr
Rigger, Elizabeth to Elijah Wyatt 12-9-1846 Sh
Riggins, Louisa Jane to Joseph H. Scarbrough 9-21-1856 Hr
Riggs, Ann to Calvin F. Oliver 10-18-1860 We
Riggs, Eliza to John W. Downey 2-20-1860 F
Riggs, Francis J. to John C. Ellison 3-19-1864 O
Riggs, Harriet to John Doherty 6-22-1854 Cr
Riggs, Latitia to W. C. Rossom 10-17-1861 (10-11?-1861) Cr
Riggs, Louisa J. to Elijah F. Warren 8-12-1854 (8-17-1854) Hr
Riggs, M. J. to James M. Goad 7-22-1856 (7-23-1856) Hr
Riggs, Mary Ann to William N. Moore 10-16-1850 (10-22-1850) Hr
Riggs, Mary C. to William Malone 12-8-1862 F
Riggs, Mary to Edward Roach 11-10-1830 Hr
Riggs, Sarah J. to R. F. Bostick 4-24-1861 We
Right (Wright?), Rena to R. E. Jordan 5-18-1876 (6-4-1876) L
Right, Cate to Charles Carter 4-16-1870 G B
Right, L. W. to A. S. Sutton 12-11-1871 Hy
Rightsdale, Mandy to James Johnson 12-16-1867 F B
Rigney, Kate to Thomas Kirwan 1-22-1861 (1-31-1861) Sh
Rigney, Mary to Patrick Sullivan 2-21-1857 (2-22-1857) Sh
Rigsbee, Gilly A. to A. C. Penn 3-10-1858 (3-11-1858) G
Rigsbey, Mildred to Alex. M. Clinton 2-6-1877 Hy
Rigsby, Caroline to R. H. Coats 12-9-1858 We
Rigsby, Eliza H. to Daniel B. Crider 5-26-1838 (5-27-1838) G
Rigsby, Galaney to Alexander Williams 10-18-1847 (10-19-1847) T
Rigsby, Hester Ann Hamilton to Henry Jackson Dacus 1-20-1852 (1-22-1852) T
Rigsby, Ponta to Wiley A. I. Hampton 1-29-1856 Cr
Rigsby, Rebecca M. to John E. Halford 3-1-1841 (3-9-1841) G
Rigsly, Sarah to Madison Conlee 12-9-1839 (12-11-1839) G
Riker, Caroline to Thomas Ashmore 8-30-1878 (9-1-1878) L
Riley (McKelroy?), Catharine to Dennis McKelvey 7-17-1858 Sh
Riley, A. Elizabeth to A. C. Long 8-18-1862 Sh

Riley, Amanda E. to Elbert Welty 7-3-1861 (7-4-1861) Hr
Riley, Angaline to Grant Z. Harrison 5-13-1847 G
Riley, Bridget to Patrick Collins 8-26-1861 Sh
Riley, Catharine to Michael Halpin 5-2-1857 (5-3-1857) Sh
Riley, Centha to Edwin H. Crocker 12-5-1842 (12-6-1842) G
Riley, Deletha to William Sheparson 3-3-1856 (3-6-1856) L
Riley, E. V. to G. A. Dunn 12-14-1874 (12-15-1874) T
Riley, Elizabeth to Martin V. Ray 9-20-1866 O
Riley, Francis E. to Quinton C. King 3-27-1861 We
Riley, Harriet to David Reed 11-15-1853 O
Riley, Jane (Mrs.) to J. B. Caudell 10-2-1867 O
Riley, Jane to Alexander Bennett 11-12-1857 Cr
Riley, June to Henry G. Rainy 6-23-1846 (6-25-1846) Hr
Riley, M. C. to M. G. Furgerson 7-25-1864 (7-27-1864) L
Riley, Margaret E. to J. P. Grogan 10-29-1849 (no return) Cr
Riley, Margarette A. to George Levy Cooper 3-11-1865 G
Riley, Mary E. to H. I. Clampit 2-13-1849 Sh
Riley, Mary J. to John Lilly 5-8-1860 (5-10-1860) Sh
Riley, Mary to Andy Hession 7-28-1855 Sh
Riley, Mary to Henry Fazzi 7-26-1862 Sh
Riley, Rilla Ann to Dick Dumas 8-14-1867 Hn
Riley, S. J. A. to W. F. B. C. Key 2-21-1855 (2-?-1855) Sh
Riley, Sarah E. to J. H. Rimmer 1-10-1864 Mn
Riley, Sarah E. to Samuel Clampit 1-16-1854 (1-18-1854) Sh
Riley, Susn A. to Duke Crocker 11-6-1867 (no return) Hn
Rily, Susan to D. Furgerson 5-7-1866 O
Rimpson(Simpson?), Molly to Andrew Jackson 7-5-1879 (7-10-1879) L
Rimspah, Rachel to Johannes (John) Aselmeyer 11-6-1861 (11-7-1861) Sh
Rinds, Sarah J. to Hiram S. Neely 8-7-1856 O
Rine, Maria to William Lunsford 1-12-1837 (1-22-1837) Hr
Rine, Mary to Patrick Melone 11-8-1862 Sh
Rinehart, Eula Virginia to J. F. French 2-5-1863 Hn
Riner, A. J. to James S. Caldwell 11-17-1861 Sh
Ring, Angeline to A. F. Clark 2-22-1861 (2-24-1861) O
Ring, Mary H. to Wm. B. Jones? 9-30-1864 O
Ringer, Narsissa to A. McVay 10-20-1864 Sh
Ringgold, Elizabeth to William Grice 11-30-1843 G
Ringold, Arsenia to E. Grist 8-1-1866 G
Ringold, Gemima to Nehemiah Biggs 7-8-1842 G
Rinkle, Martha to Riley Odom 4-5-1864 Mn
Rint, M. J. to J. A. Hargett 1-9-1866 O
Riplett, Mary Jane to A. Twedle 7-10-1863 Sh
Ripley, Dora to C. W. Ware 12-7-1864 Sh
Ripley, Willie B. to Thomas S. King 9-11-1877 (9-12-1877) Dy
Riplogle, Dosha to James Ferrell 6-21-1851 (7-24-1851) Hr
Rippins, Mary Elizabeth to Charles W. Keller 3-12-1863 Sh
Riprogle, Mary to Richard Rogers 10-19-1858 Hr
Risin, P. E. to John O. Smyth 7-22-1863 We
Risley, Mary Ann to Edward Fisher 12-7-1855 Sh
Rison, Tibetha B. to John Q. A. Cannon 1-15-1846 Cr
Ritch?, Nancy to John A. Hampton 6-25-1864 Hn
Ritchey, Lucy K. to James B. Gilliam 1-18-1870 (1-20-1870) F
Ritchie, Louisa to Robert S. Dongan 2-28-1839 Hr
Ritchie, Lucinda to Jackson Bell 1-29-1853 Sh
Ritchie, Lucy Ann to Joseph W. Guter 9-2-1860 We
Ritchie, Mary Jane to Samuel Maynard 7-21-1869 (7-22-1869) Cr
Ritchie, Mary to Wm. F. McClain 4-8-1835 Hr
Ritchie, Tabitha to John Evans 6-26-1847 F
Rittenberry, Jane to Samuel Riddle 7-2-1858 (9-5-1858) O
Rittenberry, Mary E. to Frederick W. Jones 2-1-1849 O
Rittenberry, Mary Jane to Frederick W. Jones 2-1-1849 (2-26-1849) O
Rittenburg, Lucy to Samuel Riddle 3-4-1861 (5-21-1861) O
River, Ella C. to J. R. Parchman 1-8-1883 (1-9-1883) L
Rivers, Elizabeth D. to Saml. W. Morgan 3-13-1832 Sh
Rivers, Emeline C. to William B. Grove 12-22-1831 (12-23-1831) Hr
Rivers, Jane to Dick Rivers 2-19-1870 F B
Rivers, Mariah to Dick Johnson 2-9-1867 (2-10-1867) F B
Rivers, Mary A to Charles C. Churchill 7-8-1857 (7-15-1857) T
Rivers, Mary E. to G. P. Rogers 7-11-1870 (7-14-1870) F
Rivers, Mary Lucette to Edwin Dickinson, sr. 12-27-1870 F B
Rivers, Mat to Anderson Boyle 1-12-1869 (1-17-1869) F B
Rivers, Nancy to John Walton 12-26-1870 (1-2-1871) F B
Rivers, Perlina to Andrew Anderson 11-18-1869 (11-21-1869) F B
Rivers, R. E. to S. P. Wilson 12-13-1864 O
Rivers, Sallie to Thos. J. Johnson 6-12-1867 F
Rivers, Sarah Lucy to Robert W. Shelton 1-24-1829 Hr
Rivers, Sarah to Wm. Wilkerson 12-22-1869 F B
Rivers, Sophia to Dick Tatum 1-1-1870 F B
Rives, A. R. to A. D. Bright 10-18-1867 (10-24-1867) F
Rives, Anna W. to John M. Schwar 9-21-1868 (9-30-1868) F
Rives, Bettie J. to L. L. Thomas 11-1-1877 Hy
Rives, Jenny to Ike Nolly 1-15-1870 (1-19-1870) F B
Rives, Lucy Ann Tennessee to Imri S. Pitts 11-12-1872 (no return) L
Rives, M. E. to R. W. Pitman 10-29-1866 (10-31-1866) F
Rives, Maranda to Ned McElwain 2-19-1870 (2-20-1870) F B
Rives, Mary to Wilson Allen 2-3-1841 (2-4-1841) F
Rives, Sallie J. to Leonidas C. Chaffin 12-20-1869 (12-21-1869) F

Rives, Sally A. to W. M. Rives 9-17-1838 F
Rives?, Martha C. to John M. Rainey 7-22-1873 (7-23-1873) Dy
Rix, Robertia to Erasmus Cannon 1-25-1872 Hy
Rizzi, Mary to Luzaro Badinelli 6-30-1857 Sh
Rlayner, Ann to Robert Smith 3-8-1867 (3-9-1867) T
Ro(w)land, Catharine to Byrd Short 6-23-1854 O
Roach, A. M. to Samuel L. Irwin 5-24-1855 Sh
Roach, Abigail to Thos. C. Oakley 4-7-1852 Sh
Roach, Angeline to Allen W. Pervis 5-19-1842 Cr
Roach, Anney to Jerrimiah H. Dill 2-28-1841 G
Roach, Cora A. to W. M. Shephard 4-26-1872 (no return) Cr
Roach, E. N. L. to Fin Wilson 1-5-1857 Cr
Roach, Elizabeth E. to Isaac Woodell 4-9-1859 Hr
Roach, Elizabeth J. to Thos. L. Gulledge 10-14-1845 (no return) Cr
Roach, Elizabeth W. to John Chandler 5-4-1843 Cr
Roach, Elizabeth to Reubin Leathers 7-28-1852 Hr
Roach, Esther to Edward McCarty 12-11-1832 Sh
Roach, Georgia Ann to Wm. Lecorner 4-1-1874 (4-2-1874) O
Roach, Harriet Tennessee to William J. Gordon 11-2-1860 (11-5-1860) Ma
Roach, Isabella J. to James A. Winsett 11-18-1845 (11-19-1845) F
Roach, Lenora M. to D. S. Ezzell 12-31-1872 (1-1-1873) Cr
Roach, Lorindo to James C. Williams 9-26-1832 (10-14-1832) G
Roach, Lucinda to Samuel Roberts 3-15-1852 (3-22-1852) T
Roach, M. J. to F. F. Harvey 1-5-1857 (no return) Cr
Roach, Malinda C. to Matthew Hewlin 3-29-1851 O
Roach, Margaret A. to Charles L. Simmons 2-15-1844 Sh
Roach, Martha A. to John C. Davis 1-27-1847 (1-28-1847) G
Roach, Mary J. to A. Reid 11-20-1838 F
Roach, Mary S. to Geo. W. Rushen 8-12-1840 Cr
Roach, Mary to John Craig 3-15-1864 (3-16-1864) Cr
Roach, Mary to Zedekiah Stone 12-26-1854 (12-27-1854) Sh
Roach, May to John Craig 3-15-1865 (no return) Cr
Roach, Miamma A. to George W. Fowler 2-5-1855 We
Roach, Missouri A. to Wm. R. Newson 7-5-1859 Cr
Roach, Nancy Jane to James M. Stone 3-7-1866 Ma
Roach, Rebecka to James Connell 7-25-1826 (6-26-1826) G
Roach, S. A. to H. B. Thomas 10-31-1867 (11-5-1867) Cr
Roach, Sarah E. to John W. Howard 12-11-1855 Cr
Roach, Sarah Jane to James W. Mathis 6-19-1869 Ma
Roach, Sarah L. to Samuel L. Irwin 4-29-1847 F
Roach, Susan to A. Cox 11-12-1855 Sh
Roach, Tisha to Henry Alexander 5-3-1869 (no return) Cr
Roachell, Charlott to Albert R. Flippin 9-19-1849 (no return) Cr
Roachell, Lavinia Susan to Hansford A. Fields 1-17-1849 (1-24-1849) G
Roachell, Nancy B. to Allen B. White 3-12-1838 Cr
Road, Rebecca to William Cruse 8-2-1833 (8-7-1833) Hr
Roads, C. C. to W. J. Dublin 11-22-1854 We
Roads, Matilda to James Williams 10-1-1845 (no return) We
Roads, Nancy to John Wiggans 4-10-1854 We
Roan, Christina E. to John B. Pullin 10-30-1865 (10-31-1865) T
Roan, M. R. to F. T. Billing 11-25-1868 (11-26-1868) T
Roan, Zetton A. to Wesley H. Allmore 1-17-1854 Cr
Roane, Emily B. to Malcolm H. Goodrich 2-11-1852 (2-12-1852) Ma
Roane, Henrietta to Andrew J. Whitley 8-25-1851 T
Roane, S. J. to R. F. Williams 1-1-1872 (1-4-1872) T
Roaney, Candas M. to Albert Finley 2-3-1864 (no return) Cr
Roark, Amanda to Elisha Haulton 6-25-1850 (6-28-1850) Hr
Roark, Elizabeth J. to Abner T. Scott 1-8-1870 (1-9-1870) Cr
Roark, Ester A. to J. E. Gross 11-16-1854 Cr
Roark, Lucinda to P. Whitworth 9-5-1850 Sh
Roark, Mary Jane to Allen Nealey 12-2-1844 T
Roark, Phoebe to Philip Henry 5-26-1850 Sh
Roark, Rebecca F. to Thomas D. Hudson 2-9-1854 (2-21-1854) Hr
Roark, Sally to William Kirk 4-21-1850 Sh
Roark, Sarah to B. W. Brandon 12-14-1850 Cr
Roark, Sarah to Geo. G. Burkhead 12-30-1847 Hr
Roark, Winny to Robert Simpson 3-5-1849 Cr
Roarke, Elizabeth to Archibald Kirk 6-12-1851 (6-14-1851) Sh
Robb, Elizabeth D. to Johnson Williams 8-27-1833 G
Robb, Martha A. F. to Henry Kelly 12-21-1852 G
Robb, Martha Jane to Hugh Y. Bone 4-25-1839 G
Robb, Mary Ann to James B. Harris 4-22-1835 Hr
Robb, Mary J. to Ripley Brady 4-11-1855 (4-12-1855) G
Robbins, Harriett B. to Robert M. Galloway 11-29-1843 Sh
Robbins, Louiza A. to Asberry Webb 9-12-1860 Dy
Robbins, Lucy to Hubbard Cozart 7-23-1866 (7-24-1866) Ma
Robbins, M. to Stephen Higgs 1-2-1856 (no return) Hn
Robbins, Martha to John Doyl 5-7-1867 Hy
Robbins, Martha to S. T. Elrod 9-15-1877 Hy
Robbins, Mary A. to Charles S. Hatcher 9-6-1838 Sh
Robbins, Mary Caroline (Mrs.) to Elliot Robbins 12-28-1858 Sh
Robbins, Mary M. to G. W. Thompson 10-22-1871 Hy
Robbins, Mary to Henry Caton 1-11-1868 G
Robbins, Milley to Thomas Moon 10-28-1851 O
Robbins, Pennie to William Collier 1-7-1872 Hy
Robbins, S. A. S. J. to Larkan Bramblett 6-15-1850 (6-19-1850) O
Robbins, S. B. to Mortimer Stephens 1-30-1878 (no return) Dy

Robbins, S. E. to W. J. Seaton 2-8-1872 Hy
Robbins, S. J. to W. H. Jones 10-10-1878 Hy
Robbins, Sarah Jane to W. F. Chilcut 3-11-1865 (no return) Hn
Robbins, Susan A. to Henry Brown 8-20-1879 (8-21-1879) Dy
Robbs?, Sallie to Ben Morgan 7-17-1871 T
Roberds, Narcissa to Samuel Autry 1-14-1851 Cr
Roberson, A. J. to J. R. Worrell 1-1-1866 Hy
Roberson, A. J. to J. R. Worrell 1-2-1866 Hy
Roberson, Alice to R. G. Montgomery 1-4-1866 Hy
Roberson, Ancy to Jesse J. Capps 7-29-1862 We
Roberson, Ann to W. P. King 12-16-1872 (12-17-1872) Cr
Roberson, B. A. to J. W. Wood 5-5-1873 (5-7-1873) L
Roberson, B. J. (Mrs.) to R. H. Carroll 10-21-1863 Sh
Roberson, Caroline to Mack Grimes 9-9-1877 Hy
Roberson, Catherine to S. B. Lane 11-25-1867 (11-26-1867) L
Roberson, Chany to Gilbert Jelts 7-21-1867 Hy
Roberson, Clarisa to Hardy Furgerson 11-17-1870 Hy
Roberson, E. M. to S. D. Jenkins 11-26-1873 L
Roberson, Elizabeth to E. G. Rankins 11-11-1856 (11-26-1856) G
Roberson, Elizabeth to John B. Walpole 7-31-1839 (no return) L
Roberson, Eugenia to John M. Burkett 10-13-1869 (10-14-1869) Ma
Roberson, Hariett to H. Gray 1-30-1851 F
Roberson, Hettie to Jerry Smith 12-5-1872 Hy
Roberson, Jane C. to John C. Ford no date (with 1861) T
Roberson, Jane to Charles Johnson 12-23-1865 Mn
Roberson, Jane to James Pewit 2-24-1877 (2-25-1877) L
Roberson, Josephine to David Ingram 8-30-1882 (8-31-1882) L B
Roberson, Julia F. to William J. Edwards 9-24-1879 (9-25-1879) L
Roberson, Lizzie to Wm. Whitelaw 1-6-1867 Hy
Roberson, Lucy J. to Josiah Allen 11-3-1842 G
Roberson, M. A. to Pleasant Fullen 1-13-1864 L
Roberson, Margaret to Thomas Rains 10-7-1859 Hn
Roberson, Martha A. to John P. Lashlee 12-26-1864 Be
Roberson, Martha J. to James S. Loveless 12-15-1856 (12-16-1856) G
Roberson, Martha R. to John F. Peel 7-6-1854 Hn
Roberson, Martha to Benj. Franklin Dodd 3-16-1869 L
Roberson, Mary E. to J. H. Tatum 12-28-1865 Hy
Roberson, Mary E. to Jeremiah Sewell 2-27-1862 Mn
Roberson, Mary to Churchwell B. Ducker 11-7-1860 (11-8-1860) Ma
Roberson, Mary to Lee Claxton 7-21-1880 L
Roberson, Mary to Solomon Kellar 2-20-1873 Hy
Roberson, Melisa to David Sidney Moore 1-2-1866 L
Roberson, Missouri to Dennis Barrington 12-28-1867 (1-1-1868) F B
Roberson, Mollie to A. J. Pitts 10-27-1883 (10-28-1883) L
Roberson, N. E. to J. W. Wood 6-2-1877 (6-3-1877) L
Roberson, Nancy to John Miller 1-23-1840 F
Roberson, Parthenial to Stephan Dougless 1-25-1868 (no return) Hy
Roberson, Pernissa R. A. to Thomas Black 11-6-1865 (11-7-1865) Dy
Roberson, Rebecca to Mathew Thomas 9-30-1843 L
Roberson, S. J. to Isaac N. Dozier 9-23-1856 G
Roberson, Sarah A. to Franklin J. Terrill 5-16-1850 G
Roberson, Sarah A. to John Richmond 9-28-1870 (no return) Hy
Roberson, Sarah E. to Harbert H. Haynes 4-21-1843 Ma
Roberson, Sarah J. to J. C. Gilliland 8-30-1862 G
Roberson, Sarah to A. J. England 6-13-1867 Be
Roberson, Summerfield to Joseph G. Payne 4-19-1859 L
Roberson, Susan to Houston Rowsey 12-4-1884 L
Roberson, Susana to James Oxford 5-?-1861 Be
Roberson, T. J. to J. J. Bateman 4-4-1867 Cr
Roberson, Tennessee to Wes McDearman 12-11-1884 (12-12-1884) L
Roberson, Tennessee to Wm. P. Woodard 12-24-1866 (12-25-1866) Ma
Roberson, Tildy to Green Clark 7-5-1877 Hy
Roberson, Tina Bet to John Gregory Johnson 1-20-1877 (not certified) L
Roberson, Virginia A. to John L. Bivins 2-6-1875 G
Robert, Eliza Ann to Cullen Preswood 2-28-1863 (3-1-1863) Sh
Roberts, A. E. to J. M. Kirk 9-16-1869 Cr
Roberts, Abegale C. to Edward Summers 5-12-1857 We
Roberts, Adaline to Eli McCorkle 12-27-1847 (12-28-1847) Ma
Roberts, Alethea to James Oliver 11-5-1850 Hr
Roberts, Altamyra to Thomas Waller 8-9-1842 (8-11-1842) Hr
Roberts, Amanda to William King 10-27-1879 Dy
Roberts, Belle J. to Marvila Lowe 2-25-1878 (2-27-1878) Dy
Roberts, Bettie C. to J. C. Anderson 5-17-1861 (5-22-1861) Sh
Roberts, Bettie to Alfred Neese 12-19-1860 Hn
Roberts, Caledonia to Thomas E. Loyd 1-13-1857 We
Roberts, Caroline to Burrell W. Wynn 5-20-1846 Be
Roberts, Caroline to John Nealy 4-24-1870 G
Roberts, Caroline to Willie S. Harris 4-17-1841 Ma
Roberts, Clancy D. to William R. Darby 1-12-1841 F
Roberts, Clarissa to Thomas Pebles 10-5-1850 Hr
Roberts, Cyntha Ann to C. F. Philips 11-3-1853 Be
Roberts, Della to Thomas Carray 6-1-1867 (no return) Cr
Roberts, E. G. to John V. Willoughby 8-23-1855 (no return) Hn
Roberts, Eliza H. M. to Silas P. Ligon 2-14-1852 Sh
Roberts, Eliza Jane to Samuel jr. Vails 3-28-1844 Hr
Roberts, Eliza to Henry P. Thomas 4-10-1841 (4-15-1841) Hr
Roberts, Elizabeth C. to Edward D. Hammons 10-7-1870 (10-9-1870) F

Roberts, Elizabeth C. to Stephen B. Jones 9-9-1839 Hr
Roberts, Elizabeth J. to William E. Lee 12-27-1865 O
Roberts, Elizabeth to E. J. Head 8-21-1845 We
Roberts, Elizabeth to Harvy M. Gossett 9-15-1841 Hr
Roberts, Elizabeth to Henderson Sparkman 12-25-1854 (12-27-1854) G
Roberts, Elizabeth to Magnis Tate 11-12-1848 Hr
Roberts, Elizabeth to Saml. R. Graham 10-22-1866 (10-23-1866) Cr
Roberts, Elizabeth to William W. Owen 11-28-1850 Sh
Roberts, Elizabeth to Wm. Green 2-27-1849 (no return) Cr
Roberts, Emiline J. to Washington Riley 12-23-1854 (12-24-1854) G
Roberts, Emily J. to John Bateman 11-15-1848 F
Roberts, Emily S. to W. M. Knight 11-16-1847 (11-17-1847) F
Roberts, Emily S. to W. M. Night 11-16-1847 (11-17-1847) F
Roberts, Eugenia P. to T. I. Band (Bard?) 8-15-1858 We
Roberts, F. M. to T. O. Tucker 1-11-1860 We
Roberts, Fannie V.? to G. B. Barker 12-1-1870 Hy
Roberts, Frances to W. F. Chilcut 1-1-1856 (no return) Hn
Roberts, Francis A. to A. S. Lyles 2-3-1866 (2-4-1866) O
Roberts, Gabella Ann to Jordan Jamison 1-13-1870 T
Roberts, Hannah M. to Henry P. Wimberley 7-24-1860 Hn
Roberts, Hannah to George W. Fowler 11-19-1854 Hn
Roberts, Hannah to Henry W. Langly 11-27-1867 Hn
Roberts, Harriet A. to John N. Roberts 5-19-1871 (5-21-1871) Cr
Roberts, Harriett R. to William Rowlette 6-5-1847 Sh
Roberts, Henrietta to Richard Golding 11-4-1872 L
Roberts, Isabella to Harvey A. Roberts 4-3-1855 Ma
Roberts, Isabella to Martin Van Buren 12-27-1870 (12-29-1870) F B
Roberts, J. L. (Mrs.) to F. T. Scott 2-16-1861 (2-20-1861) Sh
Roberts, Jane to John Cherry 12-17-1849 (1-8-1849?) G
Roberts, Janie F. to James D. Darbey 1-28-1839 (1-29-1839) F
Roberts, Judeth to John S. Welch 7-29-1846 We
Roberts, Judy F. to Ellison T. Potts 9-19-1857 (9-20-1857) Ma
Roberts, Laurah J. to James L. Laird 9-22-1860 (9-3?-1860) O
Roberts, Letty to Jesse Carley 8-17-1849 (8-19-1849) Hr
Roberts, Louisa to L. D. Williams 1-8-1865 Cr
Roberts, Lucy D. to James W. Knight 1-6-1861 We
Roberts, M. D. to A. P. Cantrell 9-21-1854 We
Roberts, M. J. (Mrs.) to W. C. Roberts 2-4-1863 Sh
Roberts, M. L. to J. W. jr. Drummon 6-2-1873 (6-4-1873) T
Roberts, Madeleine L. to Wm. E. Bayley 2-16-1863 Sh
Roberts, Mahala to George Lewellen 8-1-1861 Y
Roberts, Malinda J. to George W. Redditt 11-6-1866 (11-8-1866) T
Roberts, Manurva to Wm. Jones 8-13-1839 (8-22-1839) G
Roberts, Margaret C. D. to William S. Cannon 5-26-1860 We
Roberts, Margaret Jane to Thomas C. Dickins 1-14-1854 (1-17-1854) G
Roberts, Margaret to George Stagner 2-8-1848 G
Roberts, Margarett to George Hollowell 10-23-1864 (10-26-1866?) Cr
Roberts, Martha A. to A. D. Cockron 5-21-1857 Cr
Roberts, Martha A. to Jas. M. Phillips 6-4-1859 (6-5-1859) Hr
Roberts, Martha A. to John D. Whitlocke 7-31-1864 G
Roberts, Martha A. to Saml. E. Gaither 3-31-1871 (4-4-1871) F
Roberts, Martha J. to Robert W. Crisenberry 1-5-1862 Hn
Roberts, Martha Jane to Albert Ambrose Kelley 10-27-1855 (10-29-1855) T
Roberts, Martha Jane to Wm. J. Taylor 5-12-1850 We
Roberts, Martha L. to J. H. Roberts 9-7-1865 G
Roberts, Martha to Charles Root 9-27-1831 Sh
Roberts, Martha to W. J. Peterson 2-21-1877 (2-22-1877) L
Roberts, Mary (Mrs.) to J. R. Smith 3-29-1879 (3-30-1879) Dy
Roberts, Mary A. to D. C. Turner 12-21-1854 We
Roberts, Mary Ann to William Daniel Rice 7-26-1847 (7-?-1847) T
Roberts, Mary C. to Lewis Wimberley 4-20-1851 Ma
Roberts, Mary E. to William A. Jackson 1-18-1863 Hn
Roberts, Mary F. to J. Sid Smith 3-17-1874 (3-19-1874) L
Roberts, Mary L. to Wm. L. Moore 1-29-1850 Cr
Roberts, Mary to C. Swiney 1-11-1870 (1-12-1870) F
Roberts, Mary to George Morphis 1-6-1849 Ma
Roberts, Mary to James L. Kincannon 4-13-1861 (4-15-1861) Sh
Roberts, Mary to Thomas Michal 1-13-1852 We
Roberts, Millie to Hiram Davis 11-2-1876 Hy
Roberts, Mollie to J. R. Biggs 12-16-1864 (maybe 1863) G
Roberts, Nancy M. to William B. Chains 2-12-1852 We
Roberts, Nancy to Austin A. King 5-12-1828 (5-13-1828) G
Roberts, Nancy to George Chisam 12-4-1869 G
Roberts, Nannie to G. W. Taylor 2-11-1868 G
Roberts, Naomi to Thomas D. Roberts 12-21-1837 Sh
Roberts, Narcissa to L. W. Travis 7-17-1855 (no return) We
Roberts, Narcissa S. to Saml. N. (Dr.) Page 3-7-1869 G
Roberts, Narcissa to Thomas P. Williams 9-25-1861 (no return) Cr
Roberts, Permenda A. to John M. Smith 1-6-1849 Cr
Roberts, Permilia to John Swindle 7-26-1836 Hr
Roberts, Rebecca to Larkin Tims 6-10-1843 (6-11-1843) Ma
Roberts, Rebeccah to John Williams 8-21-1866 Cr
Roberts, Rhodia to Thomas H. Wilson 10-14-1856 Hn
Roberts, Rosalind A. to William F. Pace 11-19-1854 Be
Roberts, Sarah Ann to Finis Ewing Sheridan 10-3-1866 Hn
Roberts, Sarah C. to Thomas Jenkins 12-6-1841 (12-15-1841) Hr
Roberts, Sarah Eliz. to Perley? James 10-25-1852 (10-31-1852) T

Roberts, Sarah G. to M. C. Moore 1-8-1853 Hn
Roberts, Sarah H. to Isaac Rowland 11-17-1847 Cr
Roberts, Sarah to Alexander Bell 9-16-1871 T
Roberts, Sarah to Thomas I. Little 5-22-1860 We
Roberts, Susan A. to Charles M. Whealor 12-7-1852 We
Roberts, Susan A. to Wesley B. Bevill 10-9-1856 Ma
Roberts, Susan to Henry C. Gwynn 12-18-1865 (12-20-1865) F
Roberts, Susan to Solaman Richardson 7-18-1874 (7-22-1874) T
Roberts, Susan to T. M. Ladd 9-7-1845 We
Roberts, Sutilia C. to Jos. J. Brown 11-16-1858 (11-17-1858) G
Roberts, Zillah Syrena to Joseph Newton Walker 7-6-1866 (7-8-1866) Ma
Robertson, Alice to Green Montgomery 12-30-1865 (no return) Dy
Robertson, Amanda M. F. to Jesse H. Alsobrook 6-23-1835 Sh
Robertson, Amanda to George Langster 3-9-1856 (4-9-1856) Hr
Robertson, Ann to W. M. Taylor 1-1-1867 Hn
Robertson, Artemicia to James D. James 1-12-1840 Hn
Robertson, Asenath Bell to Edward F. Apperson 6-24-1880 (no return) L
Robertson, Catharine to James Cunningham 11-29-1837 (11-30-1837) G
Robertson, Catherine to William Champion 11-25-1826 Hr
Robertson, Cornelia to J. W. Childress 12-5-1882 (12-6-1882) L
Robertson, D. to James McHood 1-1-1866 Cr
Robertson, Dibby E. to Jessee Flowers 11-19-1839 (11-29-1839) G
Robertson, Edna F. to Jeremiah Bull 7-12-1851 (no return) F
Robertson, Eliza J. to Haywood Hampton 1-4-1862 (1-5-1862) Cr
Robertson, Elizabeth to Irvin Hicks 2-22-1878 (2-23-1878) Dy
Robertson, Elizabeth to James A. Hope 8-19-1852 (8-22-1852) O
Robertson, Elizabeth to John F. Dodd 8-2-1862 (8-3-1862) Dy
Robertson, Elizabeth to Willis Stafford 12-22-1868 F
Robertson, Emily E. to Aquilla H. Carouth 5-23-1850 Hr
Robertson, Emily to J. F. Williams 1-2-1869 O
Robertson, Emma H. to R. K. Neel 11-25-1865 (11-29-1865) F
Robertson, Eugenie C. to H. C. Churchman 12-16-1872 (12-17-1872) Dy
Robertson, F. J. to W. H. Frank 5-30-1859 F
Robertson, Frances E. to James H. Gurley 7-29-1848 (8-1-1848) Hr
Robertson, Frances I? to W. W. McCarley 3-12-1859 (3-15-1859) Hr
Robertson, Frances N. to Frederick Christian 10-13-1827 Sh
Robertson, Frances to Benjamin Sutton 2-10-1845 (2-13-1845) Hr
Robertson, Frances to Curtis Moore 2-10-1845 (2-13-1845) Hr
Robertson, Hannah to Nathanial Williams 2-8-1842 (2-10-1842) G
Robertson, Harriet M. to Robert Kingkaid 1-1-1866 (no return) Dy
Robertson, Harriet to Alexander A. Lacky 3-9-1830 (3-25-1830) Ma
Robertson, Harriet to Caleb Ross 3-3-1862 (3-4-1862) Dy
Robertson, Henretta to Scott Lee 12-24-1874 Hy
Robertson, Henrietta to Irvin Hicks 8-25-1877 (no return) Dy
Robertson, Hester V. to Stephen Alley 3-1-1842 Sh
Robertson, J. J. to J. D. Green 12-23-1862 (12-30-1862) F
Robertson, Jane to Henry Smith 4-8-1861 (no return) Dy
Robertson, Julia Ann Eliza to Thomas J. Caldwell 5-12-1835 Sh
Robertson, L. J. to J. N. Cooper 7-27-1874 (7-29-1874) T
Robertson, Lou to Albert Overton 12-28-1872 (12-31-1872) Dy
Robertson, Louisa to Eli B. Holmes 11-8-1857 Be
Robertson, Lucinda A. to Joshua Joyner 7-28-1842 Cr
Robertson, Lucinda to James Jordon 1-20-1846 Hr
Robertson, Lucinda to Pinkney Stafford 2-14-1867 (2-15-1867) F
Robertson, M. E. to John T. Hicks 12-28-1859 Hr
Robertson, Malbily J. to Thomas M. Moore 7-26-1856 Cr
Robertson, Malissa J. to W. L. Nesbitt 2-13-1841 G
Robertson, Marenah to Thomas Acklin 11-9-1870 (11-10-1870) Dy
Robertson, Margaret A. to Hayne J. Klinck 8-11-1856 (8-14-1856) Sh
Robertson, Margaret Ann to John D. McClanahan 10-17-1840 (10-22-1840) T
Robertson, Margaret to John Jones 9-6-1867 Dy
Robertson, Mariah to Joseph Ivans 7-1-1829 Sh
Robertson, Martha A. to Moses Sanders 3-11-1866 Hy
Robertson, Martha Adeline to Addison H. Douglass 2-2-1842 Hr
Robertson, Martha An to James A. King 3-6-1848 (3-16-1848) F
Robertson, Martha C. to William M. Graves 3-7-1877 (no return) L
Robertson, Martha to Abe Bogard 7-18-1869 G B
Robertson, Martha to Ephraim Powers 10-7-1840 Dy
Robertson, Mary Ann H. to David R. Corkburn 3-12-1853 G
Robertson, Mary E. to James Henry Coker 1-16-1871 (1-17-1871) Dy
Robertson, Mary E. to James R. Keeble 11-23-1862 Hy
Robertson, Mary E. to John Pool 5-12-1870 F
Robertson, Mary F. to George H. Hiflin 11-28-1854 (no return) F
Robertson, Mary L. to R. S. (Dr.) Bright 1-24-1867 G
Robertson, Mary O. to Ridley Clifton 4-30-1860 T
Robertson, Mary to Billy Hall 4-1-1867 (4-3-1867) T
Robertson, Mary to R. W. Maloan 10-28-1857 We
Robertson, Mary to Thomas Edwards 11-26-1835 G
Robertson, Minerva to Lafayette Tanner 4-7-1854 (4-13-1854) Hr
Robertson, Mollie to Berry Gant 2-6-1883 (2-7-1883) L
Robertson, Moriah to Smith Nowell 3-2-1867 Hy
Robertson, N. E. to J. S. Miller 10-20-1869 Hy
Robertson, N. P. to E. F. Stayton 3-1-1873 (3-3-1873) Cr
Robertson, Nancy R. to Vinson R. Allen 1-29-1839 (1-31-1839) G
Robertson, Nancy to John P. Osburn 4-13-1854 Hn
Robertson, Nancy to John W. Spicers 1-14-1856 (no return) We
Robertson, Nancy to Saunders Utley 1-14-1834 G
Robertson, Neomi to William Jones 4-19-1838 (4-26-1838) Hr
Robertson, Polly to John Keith 11-11-1837 G
Robertson, Rebecca to Ransom Odam 11-11-1830 (11-15-1830) Ma
Robertson, Rhoda A. to James S. Wood 9-1-1852 G
Robertson, S. A. to P. S. Simons 3-21-1859 Sh
Robertson, S. C. to J. W. Easterwood 3-2-1863 (3-3-1863) O
Robertson, Sallie L. to J. E. Purvis 9-1-1885 (9-2-1885) L
Robertson, Sarah A. L. to John Head 1-6-1842 Sh
Robertson, Sarah Ann (Mrs.) to Edmond Johnson 7-13-1868 G B
Robertson, Sarah Eliza to Andrew Jackson Gamble 1-6-1852 (1-7-1852) Hr
Robertson, Sarah J. to H. Y. Fields 7-11-1859 Cr
Robertson, Sarah to William Hickman 5-14-1850 G
Robertson, Sarah to William, jr. Collier 3-10-1831 (3-13-1831) Ma
Robertson, Shelley to Marshal Herring 15-18-1858 T
Robertson, Susan A. to Thos. J. Teague 12-23-1857 Sh
Robertson, Susan to Benj. Hilderbrand 3-28-1833 Sh
Robertson, Susan to H. Bowers 11-9-1882 (no return) L
Robertson, Susan to Wilson Barrett 6-4-1840 G
Robertson, Tranquilla to Henry Kirkpatrick 8-22-1843 Ma
Robertson, Trilucia to John M. Durham 1-23-1845 F
Robertson, V. A. to N. T. Skelton 9-21-1864 Sh
Robertson, Virginia to J. H. Burkett 10-6-1870 (no return) Dy
Robertson, Vina E. to W. B. Brooks 2-9-1874 (2-11-1874) Dy
Robertson, Z. A. to B. T. Cowell 7-10-1879 (no return) Dy
Robertson, Zilpha to Geo. F. Banks 4-5-1868 Hy
Robeson, Emeline C. to Wm. Montgomery 1-28-1864 (2-1-1864) Cr
Robeson, Emeline C. to Wm. Montgomery 1-29-1864 (no return) Cr
Robeson, Lidia J. to William N. Hammett 11-16-1865 Cr
Robeson, Louisa to M. M. Morris 3-31-1865 (4-6-1865) Cr
Robey, E. M. to J. F. Wilson 1-11-1870 O
Robey, Mary to J. G. French 10-20-1868 Cr
Robinett, Margaret E. to G. W. Minton 5-29-1858 Sh
Robinett, Susan L. to James S. Watt 4-19-1853 (4-21-1853) Sh
Robins, Alsey J. to Sidney W. Goodin 4-12-1857 Hn
Robins, Caroline N. to A. J. Matlock 10-8-1850 Sh
Robins, Catherine to William D. Adkinson 6-28-1830 O
Robins, Elizabeth to George Robertson 8-5-1845 Be
Robins, Elizabeth to Charles Waldow 7-5-1856 (7-6-1856) O
Robins, Lucinda A. to Robert B. McAdoo 9-13-1860 Hn
Robins, Martha A. to Sydney Scott 5-15-1849 Sh
Robins, Matildy F. to John S. Abernathy 1-9-1843 Sh
Robins, Nancy A. to E. G. Stamps 7-20-1875 (7-21-1875) L
Robins, Nancy Messiniah to W. W. Morgan 7-5-1856 (7-6-1856) O
Robins, Nancy to R. J. Jackson 11-14-1878 Hy
Robins, Rebecca to Jacob G. Vincent 8-24-1843 We
Robins, Sallie to Beverly Young 5-27-1861 Hy
Robins, Sarah H. to Joseph W. Chilcut 8-31-1859 (no return) Hn
Robins, Tempy to Isaac Rown 6-5-1845 Be
Robins, Tennessee H. to C. G. Galloway 10-8-1850 Sh
Robinson, A. E. to B. W. Pewbeck 1-7-1857 Cr
Robinson, Ada to W. H. Edwards 2-10-1863 Sh
Robinson, Aggy to Allen Faulk 5-7-1869 T
Robinson, Aggy to Allin Faulk 5-7-1868 T
Robinson, Amanda to William Leathers 6-21-1844 Ma
Robinson, Amy to Sam Adkins 2-14-1867 T
Robinson, Ann L. to Joel T. Evans 11-6-1856 G
Robinson, Ann M. to John Jackson 1-29-1842 (2-3-1842) Ma
Robinson, Annie E. to James Buford Mitchell 1-13-1880 (1-14-1880) L
Robinson, Bettie to John H. Matthews 12-29-1869 Ma *
Robinson, C. J. to James Shoemate 12-3-1864 Hy
Robinson, Caroline to Andrew C. Satterfield 4-2-1838 (no return) F
Robinson, Catharine to Henry Hooker 10-5-1853 G
Robinson, Catherine to Ellis Mathis 9-11-1867 G B
Robinson, Cathrine to T. L. Harris 2-1-1850 Cr
Robinson, Cleopatra to Harvy S. Clark 9-16-1854 (10-19-1854) Hr
Robinson, Dicy Ann to Robt. E. Prewett 10-31-1868 (11-3-1868) Ma
Robinson, E. J. to J. A. Zellner 2-26-1872 (2-27-1872) Cr
Robinson, Eliza A. to John C. Lanier 10-6-1853 Ha
Robinson, Eliza C. to Lemuel Montague Dixson 7-24-1851 Sh
Robinson, Eliza E. to John A. Holland 5-27-1861 G
Robinson, Eliza F. to James B. Turnage 12-3-1866 (12-4-1866) T
Robinson, Eliza to Mills Eason 2-12-1863 (no return) Hy
Robinson, Eliza to Samuel L. Norwood 3-27-1867 Ma
Robinson, Elizabeth R. E. A. to Samuel Bell 11-26-1846 Sh
Robinson, Elizabeth to Alexander Stark 1-21-1861 Sh
Robinson, Elizabeth to Alfred Nunn 12-23-1867 (12-26-1868?) G B
Robinson, Elizabeth to H. O. Easum(Eastham?) 3-29-1848 Hr
Robinson, Elizabeth to Thomas King 2-4-1851 Cr
Robinson, Elizabeth to William C. McCarlin 2-10-1862 Ma
Robinson, Elizabeth to Wm. T. Tillman 12-11-1865 Hy
Robinson, Elly Jane to John C. Hardin 1-2-1858 Hr
Robinson, Frances V. to L. G. Bryant 9-25-1860 Sh
Robinson, Georgeanna to J. W. Elmore 11-27-1850 (11-28-1850) Hr
Robinson, Grace Jane to William H. Caldwell 1-21-1858 O
Robinson, H. M. to William Anthony 7-1-1865 (no return) Hy
Robinson, Hepsy Ann to Dennis McFarlin 8-5-1852 Ma
Robinson, I. Rosgarell to D. W. C. Churchland 1-5-1857 Cr

Robinson, Isabella to Edward Cadwallader 9-2-1852 Sh
Robinson, Jane D. to John B. Hogue 3-26-1840 O
Robinson, Jane to Winfield Williams 12-11-1847 (12-22-1847) Ma
Robinson, Jennie A. to Ben H. Atkinson 3-29-1859 (3-30-1859) Sh
Robinson, Jennie A. to M. C. Butler 2-3-1885 L
Robinson, Jettie to Wm. Patson 3-8-1853 Cr
Robinson, Julia A. to Wm. A. Brown 1-11-1855 Cr
Robinson, Kizar to James Ware 6-13-1844 Cr
Robinson, Laura A. to Calvin Angel 2-12-1866 (2-1?-1866) T
Robinson, Litha to James Brown 1-13-1869 G B
Robinson, Loty to Overton Pyles 2-19-1833 (2-?-1833) Hr
Robinson, Lovicy Ann to Adam M. Darnell 9-29-1842 Cr
Robinson, Lucy Jane to William W. Pirtle 5-14-1850 (5-16-1850) Hr
Robinson, M. L. to Jas. H. Burnett 8-15-1864 O
Robinson, Malinda to Henry W. Shelton 1-5-1858 Ma
Robinson, Margaret E. to E. F. Pierson 7-30-1863 Sh
Robinson, Margaret M. to Joseph Gilliland 2-7-1848 Ma
Robinson, Margaret to Amos McCane 12-25-1860 (12-27-1860) Cr
Robinson, Margaret to J. W. Stubilfield 6-5-1856 We
Robinson, Martha A. to Lander D. Algee 9-14-1846 Cr
Robinson, Martha Ann to N. M. Morris 1-22-1864 Cr
Robinson, Martha Ann to N. M. Morris 1-22-1864 (no return) Cr
Robinson, Martha C. to Jas. L. Vaughan 8-16-1851 Sh
Robinson, Martha C. to Nathaniel M. Hale 2-2-1865 G
Robinson, Martha J. to Jacob W. Nowell 6-27-1860 (no return) Hy
Robinson, Martha to D. W. C. Cunningham 1-5-1856 Cr
Robinson, Mary A. to Johnathan Mobley 10-26-1846 (10-28-1846) G
Robinson, Mary A. to Jonaathan Ball 9-20-1843 (no return) L
Robinson, Mary A. to Thomas B. Thompson 2-2-1853 Ma
Robinson, Mary Ann to Henry Banks Meacham 12-11-1854 (12-?-1854) Sh
Robinson, Mary E. to Ezekiel Z. Alexander 7-20-1846 (7-24-1846) Hr
Robinson, Mary E. to James R. West 5-31-1862 G
Robinson, Mary E. to Jesse W. Swink 2-14-1843 Cr
Robinson, Mary J. to J. B. Glover 8-28-1853 Cr
Robinson, Mary J. to John Eskew 7-26-1856 Cr
Robinson, Mary L. to James McHood 12-2-1843 Cr
Robinson, Mary N. to George Cornell 12-25-1848 Sh
Robinson, Mary Virginia to Henry K. Hilderbrand 5-19-1869 Ma
Robinson, Mary to Bryant Cowell 5-20-1848 (5-21-1848) L
Robinson, Mary to Jeremiah Janagin 12-28-1847 Cr
Robinson, Mary to Jesse Towns 11-19-1840 Sh
Robinson, Mary to John M. Thompson 1-20-1843 Cr
Robinson, Mary to L. D. Furgerson 12-31-1867 G
Robinson, Mary to Thomas Jefferson Allen 1-17-1843 (not executed) T
Robinson, Mary to W. S. Fields 3-10-1873 (3-28-1873) L
Robinson, Mary to Willis L. Reeves 9-19-1846 (9-24-1846) G
Robinson, Mary to Wm. Edwards 11-2-1858 Cr
Robinson, Mary to Wm. F. Cunningham 10-1-1860 (10-2-1860) Cr
Robinson, Maryann to George W. Tiller 10-19-1839 (5-13-1840?) F
Robinson, Matilda to Samuel Lee 8-1-1858 Hn
Robinson, Mattie A. to Henry C. Burnett 1-8-1866 G
Robinson, Mollie A. to W. D. Ramsey 3-13-1867 G
Robinson, Mollie M. to John Young Dysart 11-15-1869 (11-16-1869) Ma
Robinson, Molly to Tony Etheridge 3-21-1874 Hy
Robinson, Nancy Ann to Abner B. Mercer 4-12-1850 (4-16-1850) Hr
Robinson, Nancy Ann to Pleasant W. Cook 8-4-1848 Cr
Robinson, Nancy E. to J. L. Jeanes 6-2-1865 Mn
Robinson, Nancy H. to F. G. Goodman 12-17-1862 (11-26-1861?) G
Robinson, Nancy to B. F. Johnson 10-18-1859 (no return) Hy
Robinson, Nancy to James Hart 1-20-1839 (2-7-1839) O
Robinson, Nancy to William R. Rogers 5-7-1828 Hr
Robinson, Narcissa to Saml. M. Woods? 1-13-1844 (1-18-1844) T
Robinson, R. A. to David S. Moore 11-22-1854 (11-23-1854) Hr
Robinson, Rebecca L. to Joseph A. Mercer 2-20-1860 (2-23-1860) Hr
Robinson, Rebecca to James G. Montgomery 9-16-1841 Ma
Robinson, Rebecca to Ned Barton 1-23-1870 G B
Robinson, Sallie A. to James C. Whitson 9-14-1868 (9-15-1868) L
Robinson, Sallie to Thomas McQuiston 12-19-1870 (12-24-1871?) T
Robinson, Sally to Samuel McAily 12-28-1866 G
Robinson, Sally to ____ Hedgepeth 11-18-1852 G
Robinson, Sarah A. E. to William Allison 8-20-1848 Ma
Robinson, Sarah A. to Wm. H. Joyner 9-26-1848 Cr
Robinson, Sarah E. to Joseph J. D. Biggott 11-29-1865 G
Robinson, Sarah to Elick Subject 9-22-1877 Hy
Robinson, Sarah to James A. Walton (Walter?) 12-29-1846 (12-30-1846) L
Robinson, Sarah to Jesse Osborn 7-14-1836 Sh
Robinson, Sarah to John Chisum 12-29-1834 Hr
Robinson, Sarah to Joseph J. Fellows 2-6-1847 (not executed) T
Robinson, Sarah to Pryor L. Vernon 9-27-1852 Hr
Robinson, Sarah to William Legate 4-7-1827 Hr
Robinson, Sophia to R. B. Love 11-17-1851 Cr
Robinson, Susan A. to Valentine S. Vann 1-3-1855 (1-4-1855) Ma
Robinson, Victoria to Emanuel Jackson Martin 9-10-1870 G
Robinson, ary to Lewis W. Miller 5-13-1844 (5-17-1844) T
Robinus, Mary to George B. Woods 4-24-1849 Cr
Robirson?, Sallie to G. W. Ringer 5-2-1885 (5-3-1885) L
Robison, America P. to William T. Boyd 4-29-1870 (5-1-1870) Cr
Robison, Eliza to Henry Williamson 5-3-1870 (no return) Cr
Robison, Frances E. to Robert F. Knight 5-25-1869 Cr
Robison, H. J. to J. G. Roe 12-20-1866 G
Robison, Mary A. to G. W. Parker 1-13-1868 (1-14-1868) Cr
Robison, Mary E. to John Martin 2-2-1869 G
Robison, Mary F. to Ebenezer Starnes 9-22-1848 (no return) L
Robison, Nancy C. to William W. Price 12-8-1841 (12-9-1841) Ma
Robison, Nellie to Henry Joseph 5-29-1867 T
Robison, Sarah to Archey McNiel 3-2-1872 Hy
Robley, Mary to James M. McKnight 1-18-1845 Ma
Robson, Caroline to James Litteral 10-27-1843 Hr
Robson, Crotia Ann to Neel Barter? 6-4-1829 Hr
Roche, Mary to Michael Roche 1-21-1858 Sh
Rocheld, Martha J. to William F. Forrester 10-23-1844 (10-24-1844) Ma
Rochell, E. F. to Edward C. Dougherty 1-23-1841 (no return) Cr
Rochell, Hellen to J. H. D. Corlan 4-30-1840 Cr
Rochell, Leatha to William Rummage 4-13-1846 Cr
Rochell, Mary Jane to N. J. Sorrell 10-9-1861 Hy
Rochell, Nancy to John Forester 6-26-1840 (no return) Cr
Rochell, Nancy to M. S. Berry 11-21-1868 (11-22-1868) Cr
Rochell, Pherobe to Charles Enquehart? 12-28-1848 Hn
Rochell, Sarah to Wilson Barns 10-31-1862 (no return) Cr
Rochella, Mercina to James King 11-15-1847 Hn
Rochester, Adaline (Mrs.) to H. B. Robinson 2-18-1864 Sh B
Rock, Barbara to John Raggio 2-7-1859 Sh
Rockwell, W. (Mrs.) to John A. Washburn 5-3-1838 Sh
Roddy, Vilett B. to James Scott 12-8-1832 (12-10-1832) G
Rodey, Nancy to Joseph Robbins 1-9-1832 (1-12-1832) G
Rodger, Catharine to Elisha Morris 6-28-1848 (6-29-1848) F
Rodger, Martha T. to John D. Glakin? no date (with 1867) T
Rodgers, Abiger C. to James E. Jones 2-2-1853 F
Rodgers, Amanda to E. G. Randle 3-9-1843 Cr
Rodgers, Ann P. to G. W. Ammons 8-22-1851 (no return) F
Rodgers, Bettie to W. L. Irbey 9-26-1866 T
Rodgers, C. L. to J. R. Polston 10-31-1878 (no return) Dy
Rodgers, C. M. to J. W. Ridout 9-5-1864 (9-7-1864) Sh
Rodgers, Catherine to Nick Combs 12-17-1837 (12-20-1837) O
Rodgers, E. A. to Wm. N. McCord 9-19-1854 Cr
Rodgers, E. J. to Thomas W. Lankford 1-24-1851 Cr
Rodgers, E. W. to Wm. M. Tate 12-18-1856 Cr
Rodgers, E. Y.? to J. R. Rodgers no date (with Aug 1866) Cr
Rodgers, Earnestine to T. J. Henderson 12-23-1870 (12-25-1870) Dy
Rodgers, Eliza E. to James S. Waldran 8-29-1850 Cr
Rodgers, Elizabeth S. to J. M. Farrow 3-21-1853 Sh
Rodgers, Elizabeth W. to Richard T. Payne 5-1-1854 (5-6-1854) T
Rodgers, Elizabeth to Anderson Gibson 7-30-1841 (8-3-1841) G
Rodgers, Elizabeth to Obed Nicholson 9-30-1852 Cr
Rodgers, Elizabeth to Samuel A. Allen 12-23-1840 Hn
Rodgers, Emily to J. F. Young 12-28-1866 (1-2-1867) F
Rodgers, Emma (Emily?) F. to W. W. Hodge 1-21-1858 Sh
Rodgers, Francis to James Snell 5-4-1853 Sh
Rodgers, Hester Ann to James L. Little 2-18-1852 Cr
Rodgers, Hetta to John Webb 4-26-1870 F
Rodgers, Julia to M. P. Shepherd 3-4-1862 (3-5-1862) Sh
Rodgers, Kate to N. O. Rhodes 12-7-1864 Sh
Rodgers, Kattie (Mrs.) to B. Semirello 10-8-1863 Sh
Rodgers, Lydia to David Cox 1-16-1850 Cr
Rodgers, M. E. to James E. Jones 12-19-1855 Cr
Rodgers, M. to Joseph Garibalde 11-7-1857 (11-8-1857) Sh
Rodgers, Margaret E. to Benjm. H. Wheeler 11-18-1853 (11-19-1853) Sh
Rodgers, Margaret to James Roberts 3-3-1858 G
Rodgers, Margot to Bawdy Parish 1-6-1841 Cr
Rodgers, Martha F. to John D. Flanigan 3-13-1867 T
Rodgers, Martha to Zachriah Richard Berry 9-6-1858 (9-16-1858) G
Rodgers, Mary Ann F. to H. I. Easterwood 12-6-1849 G
Rodgers, Mary E. to Alfred Allen 11-7-1850 Cr
Rodgers, Mary E. to Caleb T. Harris 2-3-1869 (2-24-1869) F
Rodgers, Mary E. to J. P. Stewart 3-27-1842 Sh
Rodgers, Mary E. to John W. Tiller 8-6-1860 (8-16-1860) F
Rodgers, Mary E. to William B. Hamner 2-21-1854 (2-23-1854) Sh
Rodgers, Mary to Charles Harris 7-17-1856 Hn
Rodgers, Mary to Charles McCarty 7-15-1853 Sh
Rodgers, Mary to Wm. Y. Mills 8-16-1841 (8-17-1841) Hr
Rodgers, Minter Lee to David McMackin 2-10-1846 Cr
Rodgers, N. A. to G. D. Moore 1-23-1867 Cr
Rodgers, Nancy A. to Lawrence Kerniham 7-29-1868 (no return) F B
Rodgers, Nancy to Jesse Harvey 11-10-1866 (11-20-1866) Cr
Rodgers, Nancy to John A. Wilson 1-3-1853 (no return) F
Rodgers, Nancy to Loverance J. D. Perse 6-29-1843 Cr
Rodgers, Nancy to Smith Fields 8-20-1856 Cr
Rodgers, Nanney to Moses Myrick 5-24-1842 Hn
Rodgers, Nannie C. to Robt. C. Barnhart 12-20-1855 Cr
Rodgers, Narcissa to Elisha Rowe 12-22-1840 Cr
Rodgers, Pelina L. to Samuel F. Harrison 11-26-1853 (11-29-1853) Sh
Rodgers, Rebecca E. to Wilie B. Morris 5-12-1851 (5-14-1851) Cr
Rodgers, Rhoda M. to Henry F. Clark 4-30-1870 (5-1-1870) Ma
Rodgers, S. E. to J. A. Wright 12-24-1850 Cr

Rodgers, Sallie L. to Richard Locke 10-18-1866 G
Rodgers, Sally to William P. Merygin? 10-16-1866 (no return) Dy
Rodgers, Sarah A. to James R. Hodge 12-16-1853 Cr
Rodgers, Sarah A. to Wilson Loyd 2-16-1859 (2-22-1859) Sh
Rodgers, Susan to James C. Wallis 8-16-1858 Cr
Rodgers, Virginia F. to David E. Lourence 8-12-1857 Sh
Rodner, Fanny to Geo. C. Sperbeck 5-17-1864 (5-19-1864) Sh
Rodner, Jennie to Henry Clark 9-26-1864 (9-27-1864) Sh
Rodner, Maria C. to Adolph Bernard 10-6-1860 (10-7-1860) Sh
Rodny, Jane to William Asher 3-15-1857 Hn
Rodrey, Lucy Ann to R. B. Rives 1-18-1855 Sh
Rody, Nancy to Joseph Robins 1-9-1831 G
Roe, A. E. to J. H. Coates 7-21-1871 (7-26-1871) T
Roe, A. L. to R. H. Baird 2-7-1866 G
Roe, Caroline to John E. Robinson 10-11-1869 (10-14-1869) Ma
Roe, Cynthia C. to Newton W. King 10-15-1868 (10-18-1868) T
Roe, Elizabeth to Jas. Abner Billings 11-21-1855 11-21-1855 T
Roe, Juli to Thomas Hanna 1-3-1870 G B
Roe, Lucy Ann to J. C. N. Glass 11-11-1858 T
Roe, M. A. E. to William R. Bryant 1-13-1859 G
Roe, Margaret E. to William Shaw 12-18-1855 (12-19-1855) G
Roe, Martha F. M. to Francis M. Newhouse 1-13-1858 (1-14-1858) G
Roe, Martha to Jno. W. Young 8-4-1874 (8-12-1874) T
Roe, Mary M. to J. B. Coates 11-18-1871 (11-21-1871) T
Roe, Mary to F. H. Bilberry 3-7-1848 Cr
Roe, Maryann to James C. Foster 1-25-1843 (2-2-1843) F
Roe, Matilda J. to D. L. Glass 8-31-1859 (9-1-1859) T
Roe, Prudence to G. P. Crews 6-3-1861 G
Roe, Sarah J. to A. H. Rust 9-11-1855 (9-12-1855) G
Roe, Sarah J. to J. W. Baird 9-19-1866 G
Roe, Sarah J. to James W. Crafton 4-3-1854 G
Roe, Sarah M. to Thos. Wood 12-11-1865 (12-13-1865) T
Roe, Sharlott to Spinia? Billings 9-3-1856 T
Roe, Sue to H. M. Fly 3-3-1870 G
Roeana T., Dodd to J. S. Preesler 12-23-1877 Hy
Roffe, Emily C. to Jesse Glasgoe 8-30-1846 (no return) We
Roffe, Sarah to W. H. Grimes 2-23-1860 We
Roffe, T. C. to H. G. Hester 2-22-1863 We
Roffner?, Eliza to Wm. T. Vanpelt 9-27-1844 F
Rogan, Ann to Michael McNamara 7-30-1843 Sh
Roger, Mary J. to George R. Brasfield 10-6-1848 (10-17-1848) Ma
Rogers (Royers?), Mary Jane to Mareau? J. Tucker 1-3-1866 (no return) L
Rogers, Agnes to Thomas Walker 5-9-1850 We
Rogers, Amanda J. to A. J. Mizell 11-28-1867 (1-6-1868) Cr
Rogers, Amanda to Frank Pillow 9-12-1878 Dy
Rogers, Amea? E. to William Roberts 1-2-1862 (no return) Cr
Rogers, Ann L. to William D. Waller 2-27-1862 Ma
Rogers, Ann to F. W. Deats 11-24-1840 (no return) Hn
Rogers, Ann to William B. Foster 5-1-1835 (5-14-1835) Hr
Rogers, Anna E. to William Roberts 1-1-1862 (1-2-1862) Cr
Rogers, Anna to William Roberts 12-31-1861 (1-1-1862) Cr
Rogers, Annie to Henry Hunter 12-26-1868 Hy
Rogers, Arilia D. to Samson Vanderpool 5-26-1842 (5-29-1842) F
Rogers, Bethuenia P. to Wm. M. Justice 12-25-1861 (1-1-1862) Hr
Rogers, Betsy Ann to Abraham Harmon 3-8-1828 O
Rogers, Betsy(Elizabeth) to Scion Grantham 9-29-1838 (10-3-1838) Hr
Rogers, Bettie to Anthony Lake 12-24-1878 (no return) Hy
Rogers, C. to C. Hilliard 9-11-1850 Cr
Rogers, Caroline to Henry Owens 4-29-1867 Hy
Rogers, Carrie F. to Bernard P. Dickinson 1-28-1869 (no return) F
Rogers, Catherine to Samuel G. Orr 3-11-1859 Hn
Rogers, Celia A. to J. H. Thorpe 8-6-1860 Hr
Rogers, Clara to James Church 4-2-1864 Sh
Rogers, D. A. to C. A. Bridges 4-1-1858 (no return) Cr
Rogers, Dora to Alfred Whitmore 10-27-1873 Hy
Rogers, Drucilla to Thos. J. Frazier 9-10-1850 We
Rogers, E. C. to Robert A. Prater 5-5-1847 O
Rogers, Edith E. to John H. Deberry 11-27-1867 (11-28-1867) Ma
Rogers, Edmonia to Lewis Taylor 11-14-1878 Hy
Rogers, Edmony to Sandy Tucker 1-7-1875 Hy
Rogers, Eliz. to Richard Wallace 3-3-1829 Ma
Rogers, Eliza M. to William Denney 7-12-1847 (7-18-1847) F
Rogers, Eliza to Charles Haynes 7-25-1838 (no return) Cr
Rogers, Eliza to W. B. Foster 5-1-1851 Hr
Rogers, Elizabeth A. C. to Tom H. Etheridge 12-25-1843 We
Rogers, Elizabeth H. to Isaac N. McCommon 6-19-1838 Hr
Rogers, Elizabeth J. to Jacob M. Webb 11-23-1843 Hr
Rogers, Elizabeth M. to William Cheak 1-30-1846 Hr
Rogers, Elizabeth W. to John P. Weir 5-5-1842 Ma
Rogers, Elizabeth to D. W. Harrison 2-23-1856 (2-24-1856) G
Rogers, Elizabeth to Hamilton F. Forbes 6-15-1843 Hn
Rogers, Elizabeth to James T. Hodges 12-26-1848 (1-4-1849) Hr
Rogers, Elizabeth to John H. McNeal 9-21-1850 Ma
Rogers, Elizabeth to Samuel Stone 8-3-1863 (no return) Cr
Rogers, Elizabeth to Thomas Davis 10-14-1826 (11-20-1826) Hr
Rogers, Ella S. to B. G. McCleskey 6-27-1866 Hy
Rogers, Ellen to Dallas Loving 12-28-1869 Hy
Rogers, Ellen to Tom Gill 8-27-1876 Hy
Rogers, Em C. to W. H. Landrum 3-6-1862 G
Rogers, Emma to Isaac Graves 12-22-1870 Hy
Rogers, F. E. (Miss) to Wm. H. Allen 1-21-1862 Sh
Rogers, Fanny E. to Richard H. Fenner 8-29-1853 (8-30-1853) Ma
Rogers, Frances A. to Levi Lowrance 10-7-1847 Sh
Rogers, Frances to Joel A. Butler 1-1-1868 (1-5-1868) Cr
Rogers, Frances to Mansil Webb 1-25-1853 (1-27-1853) Hr
Rogers, Harriet to Jack Rogers 12-27-1865 Hy
Rogers, Harriett W. to Peter H. Burnett 8-13-1828 (8-20-1828) Hr
Rogers, Harriett to Gus Lavines 1-10-1878 Hy
Rogers, Isabella to James H. Crutchfield 9-21-1848 Cr
Rogers, Jane S. to Jacob Loudermilk 10-23-1838 Hr
Rogers, Jane to Andrew Udaley 12-23-1841 G
Rogers, Jane to Archibald Gibson 11-13-1844 Hy
Rogers, Jane to Jackson Turner 6-20-1858 We
Rogers, Jane to Peter Stokely 7-7-1867 Hy
Rogers, Jane to Stephen Walker 9-26-1852 Be
Rogers, Judiath S. to John Massey 4-22-1871 (4-26-1871) Cr
Rogers, Julia A. to Wm. Barnhart 1-17-1850 Cr
Rogers, Kitty to Wyatt Henderson 11-1-1867 (11-2-1867) F B
Rogers, Laretha to Leander Pearce 10-14-1846 G
Rogers, Leona F. to George D. Brooks 9-5-1867 Hn
Rogers, Lezinka to Wm. F. Capell 5-25-1876 Hy
Rogers, Louisanna C. to Geo. W. Duke 12-10-1849 Sh
Rogers, Louvinia to John H. Stokes 11-29-1871 Hy
Rogers, Lucinda to Solomon Boulin 6-11-1825 O
Rogers, Lucy kA. to A. F. Phillips 11-18-1871 T
Rogers, Lucy to Alx. Steavans 2-8-1878 Hy
Rogers, Lucy to E. B. Pendleton 10-12-1869 Dy
Rogers, Lydia M. to Smith C. Belote 7-15-1844 F
Rogers, M. C.? to A. T. M. Woolen 4-2-1860 (4-10-1860) Cr
Rogers, M. E. to J. A. Burket 1-23-1878 (1-24-1878) Dy
Rogers, M. E. to N. E. McDearmon 1-15-1872 (1-16-1872) Dy
Rogers, M. H. to E. F. Jordan 11-13-1840 Be
Rogers, M. J. to F. J. Key 2-20-1868 G
Rogers, M. M. to J. W. Cox 3-23-1868 G
Rogers, Mahaly to James Perry 8-23-1849 Hn
Rogers, Mailha J. to Joseph Hamilton 10-26-1848 Cr
Rogers, Malissa M. to John C. Taylor 10-3-1855 (no return) Hn
Rogers, Margaret C. to George Richardson 9-4-1873 (9-14-1873) T
Rogers, Margaret S. to Henry Johnson 3-16-1876 (no return) Hy
Rogers, Margaret to Saml. McCracken 7-25-1868 (7-28-1868) Cr
Rogers, Martha A. to Jas. W. Bonds 9-5-1857 Hr
Rogers, Martha E. to Brainard Bardwell 1-11-1845 Sh
Rogers, Martha F. to Jonas B. Snider 7-11-1858 Hn
Rogers, Martha J. to Alexander Manuel 4-21-1864 (4-23-1864) Cr
Rogers, Martha L. J. to H. P. Guy 1-4-1865 F
Rogers, Martha L. J. to W. B. T. Rogers 9-30-1857 Sh
Rogers, Martha M. to Robert B. Payne 8-15-1859 Cr
Rogers, Martha to A. H. McNeely 7-21-1853 O
Rogers, Martha to Alexander Rogers 3-13-1875 Hy
Rogers, Martha to T. M. Holiday 1-24-1871 (1-25-1871) F
Rogers, Martha to Z. T. Gaston 10-29-1866 (10-30-1866) Ma
Rogers, Mary A. to Wm. P. Martin 12-15-1860 (not endorsed) Cr
Rogers, Mary Ann to Jarman Hudson 12-17-1842 (12-20-1842) Hr
Rogers, Mary Ann to Philip K. Lester 12-1-1855 (12-2-1855) Sh
Rogers, Mary B. to B. L. Armstrong 10-4-1847 Sh
Rogers, Mary E. to David C. Simons 5-9-1868 (5-10-1868) Dy
Rogers, Mary E. to G. W. Malear 1-20-1866 (3-4-1866) Cr
Rogers, Mary E. to J. B. Harriss 10-12-1857 (11-8-1857) Hr
Rogers, Mary E. to Jesse T. Ammons 10-28-1848 (10-29-1848) Hr
Rogers, Mary Elizabeth to Peter Baker 7-21-1852 Sh
Rogers, Mary J. to R. H. (Dr.) Harvey 6-16-1869 F
Rogers, Mary J. to W. C. Call 2-13-1860 O
Rogers, Mary Jane to Henry Willbanks 12-25-1862 Hn
Rogers, Mary Jane to W. G. Hooker 1-7-1855 Sh
Rogers, Mary to Berry Lee 10-7-1845 (10-9-1845) F
Rogers, Mary to Elhennan McGraw 10-31-1844 Hy
Rogers, Mary to Elisha Williams 2-15-1844 (no return) F
Rogers, Mary to Thomas G. Horne 8-24-1837 Sh
Rogers, Mary to Thomas Malone 5-2-1858 Sh
Rogers, Mary to W. Suffield 12-21-1841 (12-25-1841) F
Rogers, Matilda to John Arnold 12-19-1854 Hn
Rogers, Mattie to Henry Jones 12-4-1873 (no return) Hy
Rogers, Mildred C. to Job H. Goodlett 10-28-1856 (10-29-1856) Ma
Rogers, Minnie to Allen Ware 10-30-1873 Hy
Rogers, Minnie to Robt. Wilson 9-30-1873 Hy
Rogers, Mintie S. to A. R. Carnes 3-5-1862 (3-6-1862) Cr
Rogers, Mollie to Harvey Shields 10-16-1870 Hy
Rogers, N. P. to J. I. Crawford 8-4-1861 O
Rogers, Nancy E. to F. M. Bilbrey 1-17-1865 Cr
Rogers, Nancy E. to Isaac L. Cardwell 3-12-1844 Hn
Rogers, Nancy R. to Wm. F. Garner 6-10-1861 (not endorsed) Cr
Rogers, Nancy to Henry Stanley 8-24-1878 (8-25-1878) Dy
Rogers, Nancy to Thomas Ferrill 10-7-1853 Hr
Rogers, Nancy to William H. Wells 6-18-1827 Hr

Rogers, Nannie E. to William A. Blackwell 1-11-1859 (1-12-1859) L
Rogers, Nannie to Fayett Allen 8-12-1874 Hy
Rogers, Olivia J. to John T. Lewis 7-27-1857 (7-29-1857) Ma
Rogers, Oney to Samuel Ray 11-27-1833 (11-29-1833) Hr
Rogers, Parisade to John Campbell 12-24-1869 (no return) F B
Rogers, Patience to A. R. Stokely 5-18-1875 Hy
Rogers, Peggy to Thomas B. Dyke 1-26-1838 (1-8?-1838) Hr
Rogers, Perlina C. to William S. Arnold 3-2-1854 Hn
Rogers, Polly(Mary) to Robert Thompson 11-24-1834 Hr
Rogers, Rebecca to Belfield S. Shearin 11-24-1854 Hr
Rogers, Rebecca to Gidion Rocksey 7-22-1841 Ma
Rogers, Rilley to S. W. Autery 12-21-1863 (12-23-1863) Cr
Rogers, S. E. W. to T. B. McKey 9-18-1861 (9?-29-1861) Hr
Rogers, Sallie J. to George McCrary 2-15-1866 G
Rogers, Sally Ann to Clark Arnold 2-3-1853 Hn
Rogers, Sally to Joseph Cox 12-19-1837 (12-21-1837) Hr
Rogers, Sarah Ann to Calvin J. Holley 10-9-1830 (10-10-1830) Hr
Rogers, Sarah C. to Joseph J. Henson 2-22-1851 (3-5-1851) Hr
Rogers, Sarah Jane to Christopher Hensley 11-4-1864 Sh
Rogers, Sarah Jane to James Thomason 11-17-1847 G
Rogers, Sarah M. to Glenn O. Burnett 1-4-1830 (2-1-1830) Hr
Rogers, Sarah P. to Henry N. Moore 11-14-1868 L
Rogers, Sarah S. E. to J. A. Welch 7-30-1850 (not endorsed) We
Rogers, Sarah to Henry Dickson 5-28-1869 G B
Rogers, Sarah to J. W. Rose 12-17-1856 (12-18-1856) Hr
Rogers, Sarah to Richard Sanders 7-18-1840 (no return) Hn
Rogers, Sarah to Thomas S. Wells 8-18-1830 Hr
Rogers, Sarah to WM. J. Anderson 3-9-1854 Cr
Rogers, Senie F. to James Paschall 11-16-1859 We
Rogers, Sopha to James Smith 11-24-1841 Sh
Rogers, Sophia A. to Joseph W. Moxley 11-10-1868 (11-11-1868) Ma
Rogers, Susan E. F. A. to William H. McCrary 2-24-1857 We
Rogers, Susan E. to George W. Hacket 11-8-1845 (11-18-1845) F
Rogers, Susannah to John Terry 1-15-1838 (1-16-1838) Hr
Rogers, Tennessee C. to Benjamin J. F. Owen 12-27-1861 (12-29-1861) Sh
Rogers, Winna R. to J. A. Wright 8-22-1864 (8-25-1864) Cr
Rogers, Winney M. to J. W. Boyd 7-12-1864 Hn
Rogerse, R. V. to Thos. Allen 12-30-1856 (1-1-1857) Sh
Rogin, Nancy to W. L. Gooch 10-18-1869 (10-20-1869) Cr
Rohern, Alice to Thomas Mulcaley 6-9-1860 (6-10-1860) Sh
Roil, Janie Ann to Henry Culbreath 3-31-1870 (4-1-1870) T
Roland, Lurana to Light Parker 8-17-1849 (8-22-1849) O
Roland, Martha F. to Augustus Verhine 8-28-1866 (8-29-1866) O
Roland, Mary to David Looney 7-1-1845 Sh
Roland, S. A. to J. W. B. Cox 12-25-1867 O
Roland, Sarah to Wesley K. Bomer 10-24-1854 Hn
Roland, Virginia to William C. Holloway 11-17-1858 (12-1-1858) Ma
Rolands, Lucy to Alexander Phillips 1-13-1867 Cr
Rolen, Emeline to William Landrum 8-12-1858 (8-13-1858) O
Rolin, Martha to James Finley 5-12-1863 O
Rollan, Harriet R. to Westley Rhodes 12-27-1855 Hr
Rollens, Elizabeth A. to James J. Thompson 7-13-1863 (no return) Cr
Rollings, Mary Elizabeth to James M. Alexander 3-15-1855 Ma
Rollins, Ellen H. to James D. Carlton? 2-8-1871 (2-9-1871) Cr
Rollins, Emily D. to J. H. Davis 2-28-1870 (2-29?-1870) Cr
Rollins, Manerva F. to Richd. T. Partete 9-24-1861 (9-29-1861) Cr
Rollins, Marassela C. to John Baxter 8-5-1865 (8-6-1865) Cr
Rollins, Mary Ann to William T. Griffin 12-21-1866 (12-23-1866) Ma
Rollins, Mary E. to Cyrus Smith 8-5-1865 (8-6-1865) Cr
Rollins, Mary E. to James Adams 9-20-1854 (12-21-1854) Ma
Rollins, Mattie to W. F. Moseley 5-7-1884 (5-10-1884) L
Rollins, Nancy R. to Edward H. Goodrich 6-2-1866 (6-3-1866) Ma
Rollins, Rebecca to Hugh Roberson 7-21-1838 Cr
Rollins, Tennessee to W. T. Holland 12-29-1879 (1-1-1880) L
Rolls, Mary J. H. to William T. Blakemore 12-13-1834 G
Rolong, Margaret G. to James J. Rankin 1-2-1856 Hr
Rolph, Octavo to William Miller 10-1-1870 (10-2-1870) L
Rolyere? (Rogers?), Margier B. to Thos. G. Clark 10-8-1838 (10-9-1838) F
Romans, Minnie to Charles Moore 6-13-1885 (6-14-1885) L
Rome, M. M. to Wm. M. Pearce 1-4-1862 Cr
Rome, Z. A. to Allen Rumley 1-8-1852 Cr
Romine, Sarah E. to Harvey F. Clifford 7-30-1874 (7-31-1874) L
Ron?, Edny to Robert Box 7-31-1830 (8-10-1830) Hr
Rone, Eliza E. to Joseph A. W. Mathis 2-14-1848 G
Rone, Josephine to Hugh A. Thompson 11-21-1862 (12-3-1862) Ma
Rone, Martha A. to William J. Seehorn 4-28-1860 (4-29-1860) Ma
Rone, Menerva to Harvey D. Oneal 12-9-1868 (12-13-1868) Ma
Roney, A. G. to A. H. Gibson 11-1-1879 (11-5-1879) Dy
Roney, Catherine to Phillip Hamilton 11-28-1836 (11-29-1836) O
Roney, Harrett M. to W. G. Traylor 8-2-1853 Cr
Roney, L. S. to G. E. Autrey 2-8-1848 (2-10-1848) O
Roney, M. A. to John W. Waldrum 3-2-1860 (3-8-1860) O
Roney, M. Y. to D. D. May 2-13-1851 Cr
Roney, Melinda to William D. Boothe 9-5-1855 (9-6-1855) O
Roney, N. A. to J. C. Buchanan 8-6-1872 (no return) Cr
Roney, Nancy to Caleb Tate 7-30-1847 O
Roney, Rosannah M. to William G. Autrey 1-27-1858 (1-28-1858) O

Rony, Everlina to Andrew A. Carr 9-12-1838 (9-14-1838) G
Rooers?, Malvina to Thomas J. Blakemore 11-15-1858 We
Rook, Amy to Paul May 1-2-1827 (1-4-1827) G
Rook, Axalina to Thomas Pearcy 7-30-1830 (7-31-1830) Ma
Rook, Elinder to Van S. Bell 7-2-1833 (7-10-1833) Hr
Rook, Pamillia Ann to Thomas Parker 8-12-1846 (8-16-1846) Hr
Rook, Polly to Abram Cox 10-24-1830 (11-3-1830) Hr
Rook, Tempe to Hezekiah Highfield 9-17-1829 Hr
Rooker, Nancy to Peter S. Reeves 11-12-1835 G
Rooks (Brook), Nancy to Doctor F. Whitley 8-27-1846 Sh
Rooks, E. S. to W. J. Powell 11-22-1866 (11-25-1866) Dy
Rooks, Emily B. to Charles Nelson 9-9-1869 Ma
Rooks, Jennie to W. P. Jefferies 1-17-1872 Hy
Rooks, Julia R. to Ansolem Stobaugh 8-31-1870 (9-1-1870) Ma
Rooks, Lucinda to John Blankenship 1-5-1859 (1-6-1859) G
Rooks, Margarette T. to William M. Meek 8-21-1861 G
Rooks, Martha A. to James M. Stephenson 3-16-1866 (3-18-1866) Ma
Rooks, Martha A. to James Sarrell 11-18-1851 (11-21-1851) Sh
Rooks, Martha J. to D. H. Stokes 8-23-1868 Hy
Rooks, Mary A. to Norfleet Fairless 11-26-1840 Ma
Rooks, Nancy to Anderson J. Barns 1-26-1842 (1-?-1842) T
Rooks, Nancy to Asbury Early 11-16-1869 (no return) Dy
Rooks, R. R. to W. V. Hill 11-4-1868 Hy
Root, Martha (Mrs.) to Marshall M. Wise 4-17-1837 Sh
Rop (Ross?), Ceznshin P. to Albert H. Johnson 12-12-1858 We
Roper, Amanda to Levi Swift 12-5-1869 G B
Roper, C. H. to James R. Oliver 9-4-1865 O
Roper, Edney to Collin Gardner 6-29-1872 O
Roper, Elizer to Harvey Donegan 12-26-1866 G
Roper, Ellen to George Roberson 10-12-1866 O
Roper, Mariah M. to M. C. Cloys 6-27-1858 O
Roper, Mary Ann to H. C. Cox 10-24-1866 (10-25-1866) Cr
Roper, Mary E. to W. P. Ripley 2-24-1872 (2-25-1872) Dy
Roper, Nancy to Sharod Cox 10-12-1840 Cr
Roper, R. A. to James P. Ball 9-30-1863? 10-1-1859 O
Roper, Sarah E. to J. B. Bradshaw 3-16-1878 (3-17-1878) Dy
Roper, Sarah M. to E. W. Gage 8-28-1859 O
Rorrell, Jane to John A. Soung 5-8-1847 (5-28-1847) F
Rosamon, Sarah N. to Wm. A. G. Avery 9-3-1866 (9-9-1866) Ma
Rosan, Mary to Samuel L. Stevens 8-18-1840 (no return) F
Rose (Rorex?), Martha L. to John C. Davis 6-9-1855 Sh
Rose, A. E. to G. K. Ballard 6-1-1883 (6-3-1883) L
Rose, Adeline to J. F. M. Coley 1-8-1852 (1-11-1852) Sh
Rose, Amanda to George P. Collinsworth 9-6-1873 T
Rose, Amanda to Robert E. Whitley 1-6-1869 T
Rose, Amanda to Sandy Bledsoe 12-20-1867 (12-27-1867) T
Rose, Amelia to Anthony Jones 7-29-1873 (8-14-1873) T
Rose, Catharine to Parham Adams 5-29-1855 (5-31-1855) Sh
Rose, Catherine to Wesley Woolfirk 4-4-1873 (4-8-1873) T
Rose, Delaney to Harison McGee 12-12-1848 Cr
Rose, E. A. R. to John Donely 6-29-1870 T
Rose, Edney to Henry Currin 10-20-1872 Hy
Rose, Eliza to H. A. Rogers 12-7-1858 Sh
Rose, Elizabeth C. M. to C. C. McDaniel 5-18-1859 (5-19-1859) Hr
Rose, Ellen Conway to Richard James Jones 1-7-1850 (1-10-1850) T
Rose, Ellen to Thomas Adkins 5-13-1846 (5-14-1846) Hr
Rose, Ema J. to Jos. E. Dickinson 11-24-1873 Hy
Rose, Emaline to Leonard Stringer 3-26-1849 Hn
Rose, Jane to Albert Smith 1-18-1869 (1-19-1869) T
Rose, Jerutia to William W. Thompson 8-12-1837 (8-17-1837) Hr
Rose, Julia A. to J. W. Fisher 4-16-1878 Hy
Rose, M. L. to A. A. Pinckley 7-12-1872 (no return) Cr
Rose, Maria L. to Erasmus T. Rose 3-27-1845 Sh
Rose, Martha to John L. Tully 9-12-1839 Cr
Rose, Martha to William F. Winstad 12-20-1860 We
Rose, Martha to _____ 10-?-1851 Hn
Rose, Mary A. to James T. Southall 10-15-1859 Hy
Rose, Mary Ann to James Stewart 6-29-1867 (7-1-1867) Ma
Rose, Mary Ann to Wm. Adams 5-28-1859 O
Rose, Mary E. to Frederick Baxter 7-31-1845 Sh
Rose, Mary Eliza to John J. Philips 6-23-1857 (6-24-1857) T
Rose, Mary Jane (Mrs.) to James W. Alexander 10-7-1841 Sh
Rose, Mary L. to Joseph Etherly 4-15-1868 (4-18-1868) T
Rose, Mary M. to B. F. Bullington 3-31-1855 (4-?-1855) Hr
Rose, Mary to James McGee 12-9-1854 Hr
Rose, Mary to Lamuel Britt 7-22-1839 (7-25-1839) Hr
Rose, Melinda to John McDonald 6-5-1849 Sh
Rose, N. C. to M. L. Stokes 1-3-1881 (1-4-1881) L
Rose, Nancy A. J. to Bryant Davis 12-24-1855 (12-26-1855) Hr
Rose, Nancy Ann to James H. Rhodes 5-23-1844 (6-2-1844) Hr
Rose, Nancy J. to Haywood Stevens 12-17-1851 (12-18-1851) T
Rose, Nancy to Jefferson Holland 1-26-1847 (1-27-1847) G
Rose, Patti W. to John Green Hall 12-21-1871 T
Rose, Rebecca E. to John Morefield 7-9-1870 (7-10-1870) F
Rose, Rutha to James K. Reader 2-1-1849 (no return) Cr
Rose, Sallie to Ed Dickson 3-21-1872 T
Rose, Sally M. to T. G. Thompson 11-1-1841 (11-6-1841) Hr

Rose, Sarah Ann to John James Philips 7-25-1849 (8-1-1849) T
Rose, Sarah E. to W. L. Harsten (Hasting) 3-4-1871 (no return) Hy
Rose, Sarah K. to W. W. Castor 1-21-1861 (1-24-1861) Hr
Rose, Sarah to John M. Porter 2-15-1848 Hr
Rose, Susan P. to Arthur K. Taylor 1-12-1856 (1-13-1856) Sh
Rose, Susannah to William Porter 5-19-1841 (5-20-1841) Hr
Rose, Tennessee to Jack Williams 1-4-1878 Hy
Roseman, Mary Jane to Chesterfield Warmoth 1-10-1859 (1-11-1859) Ma
Roseman, Nancy to William J. Bell 9-19-1855 (9-20-1855) Ma
Roseman, Rutha L. to James M. Warren 12-9-1862 Ma
Roseman, Sarah E. to Carroll Jackson 10-27-1858 (10-28-1858) G
Rosemond, Margarett E. to William J. Henderson 12-17-1850 Ma
Rosen, Adaline to W. A. Porter 3-20-1867 G
Rosenbum, Tennessee M. to William H. Germon 12-12-1853 Ma
Rosenthal, Caroline to Morris Jaretsky 9-16-1869 Ma
Rosewater, Jane to Eliot Flagg 1-14-1860 Hy
Roshel?, Ann Elizabeth to Thomas Moore 10-31-1859 (11-1-1859) Hr
Roson, Sarah E. to Lemuel B. Smith 1-15-1861 O
Ross, Adeline to Thomas W. Coley 1-20-1850 Hn
Ross, Alice to Steaphan Hammons 3-1-1878 Hy
Ross, Amanda to George H. Todd 4-13-1852 (4-15-1852) Ma
Ross, Amanda to George Williamson 1-7-1869 F B
Ross, Aney to Elijah Melton 8-17-1843 Cr
Ross, Ann to Mansfield Manifee 9-1-1869 (no return) F B
Ross, Annie to Jesse Caraway 8-15-1866 G
Ross, Arabella to Wm. Black 4-19-1851 F
Ross, Arminta to James W. Moss 2-5-1845 Hn
Ross, Artula to M. M. Holt 9-21-1862 G
Ross, Betsy to William Hillsman 11-29-1869 (no return) Cr
Ross, Betty to Wody Driver 5-13-1871 (5-15-1871) T
Ross, C. A. to William Foster 1-2-1870 G
Ross, Caroline to Henry Teagner 12-26-1867 F B
Ross, Catherine to James B. Ferrell 12-23-1850 (12-26-1850) Ma
Ross, Cathrine to Thos. J. Stewart 1-22-1842 Cr
Ross, Celia to William Blaydes 1-19-1871 F B
Ross, City to Haywood Tucker 1-15-1852 Hn
Ross, Cynthia C. to Charles Grimmet 8-27-1860 (8-28-1860) Hr
Ross, E. P. to R. P. Scarbro 12-3-1866 (12-5-1866) Cr
Ross, Eliza C. to Wm. J. Driggers 11-23-1854 Ma
Ross, Elizabeth to Ephraim Carter 7-16-1842 Hn
Ross, Elizabeth to James Henderson 5-14-1861 (5-15-1861) O
Ross, Elizabeth to John W. Elkins 2-6-1855 Hn
Ross, Elizabeth to Joseph M. Cooper 3-6-1844 Cr
Ross, Elizabeth to M. V. Sewell 1-28-1864 Mn
Ross, Elizabeth to Solsly Farthing 9-25-1843 (9-26-1843) G
Ross, Elizas J. to Willis W. Manning 11-1-1860 We
Ross, Emily C. to Jas. M. Edwards 2-26-1852 We
Ross, Emily E. to C. C. Cadwell 7-10-1849 Sh
Ross, Emma to J. W. Shelton 2-3-1875 Hy
Ross, Emma to William Hardison 3-5-1871 Hy
Ross, F. A. to E. M. Cole 12-2-1856 (12-3-1856) Sh
Ross, Helen to James W. Daniel 8-5-1850 (8-8-1850) Ma
Ross, Henrietta to Rev. G. W. Jackson 1-16-1872 Hy
Ross, Jane to James Chilcut 2-22-1851 (no return) Hn
Ross, Jane to Jesse Crenshaw 2-24-1845 We
Ross, Louisa to A. Hunsucker 3-11-1869 (3-23-1869) F
Ross, Lucindy to Edward Stewart 11-16-1843 Cr
Ross, Lucy E. to Drewry Sanders 2-11-1846 Cr
Ross, Lydia A. to Clem S. Cole 12-17-1867 (12-19-1867) F B
Ross, M. J. to Jacob L. Kinsley 12-7-1864 O
Ross, M. J. to W. D. Lacy 1-26-1884 (1-27-1884) L
Ross, Maggie to James Smith 12-21-1876 (12-24-1876) Dy
Ross, Margrett K. to Thomas Hickman 3-9-1847 (4-8-1847) Hr
Ross, Mariah to J. A. Covington 5-1-1869 (no return) We
Ross, Mariah to Willis Oldham 9-5-1869 Hy
Ross, Martha A. to Tilson Murphy 6-24-1870 (6-25-1870) Cr
Ross, Martha Ann to Sehern Payne 1-27-1845 (no return) We
Ross, Martha J. to J. R. Young 10-9-1860 Be CC
Ross, Martha J. to Jesse W. Palmer 11-14-1867 (11-17-1867) Cr
Ross, Martha J. to William H. Bratton 2-8-1853 (2-10-1853) Ma
Ross, Martha W. to T. P. Slater 7-3-1851 (7-15-1851) Sh
Ross, Martha to Elbert Gay 10-20-1838 (no return) Hn
Ross, Martha to Granville Bonds 2-3-1857 Be
Ross, Martha to James W. Phelps 1-13-1886 (1-17-1886) L
Ross, Martha to John L. Henry 11-5-1840 Ma
Ross, Martha to John Morgan 1-8-1839 Sh
Ross, Marthy J. to J. R. Young 10-9-1860 Be
Ross, Mary Ann T. to William W. Edmonds 12-22-1836 (12-23-1836) O
Ross, Mary Ann to Jessee Christopher 8-29-1860 Be
Ross, Mary Ann to Thomas Smith 3-2-1836 (3-3-1836) G
Ross, Mary Ann to Thomas Taylor 10-13-1856 Sh
Ross, Mary Ann to William T. Hubbs 2-20-1851 O
Ross, Mary J. to Buckner Harwell 10-2-1867 (10-3-1867) F
Ross, Mary J. to Daniel Henson 10-19-1860 Hr
Ross, Mary Jane to Jas. Carlington 12-23-1846 Ma
Ross, Mary Jane to Nathan Sulivan 10-8-1840 Sh
Ross, Mary Matilda to Enoch Eskue? 7-29-1841 Hr

Ross, Mary R. to Caswell Smith 12-29-1863 Mn
Ross, Mary to Alfred Wenbury 9-1-1842 Cr
Ross, Mary to Jackson Bailey 11-9-1867 G B
Ross, Mary to Joseph B. Holt 10-24-1862 G
Ross, Mary to Joshua Hudson 1-12-1842 (1-19-1842) Hr
Ross, Mary to William M. Lumbrick 10-22-1858 Hn
Ross, N. A. to William Vest 7-29-1870 (8-4-1870) F
Ross, Nancy (Mrs.) to Robert N. Newsom 2-16-1867 (2-17-1867) Ma
Ross, Nancy E. to John J. Hansel 3-8-1860 Be
Ross, Nancy Eveline to James Shilcut? 12-22-1864 (no return) Hn
Ross, Nancy H. to T. H. Plemons 10-14-1852 Hn
Ross, Nancy Jane to P. G. Tucker 11-9-1846 We
Ross, Nancy Jane to Paschal G. Tucker 11-9-1846 (11-19-1846) We
Ross, Nancy to Andrew Jackson Bond 6-29-1850 Cr
Ross, Nancy to David Kirby 10-29-1846 Cr
Ross, Nancy to Joseph Sikes 3-3-1849 F
Ross, P. A. to Samuel Ross 8-13-1861 We
Ross, Parthenah S. to A. G. Booker 4-8-1853 Be
Ross, Phereby G. to W. B. Crenshaw 1-13-1853 (1-26-1853) Sh
Ross, Phidy to John Pinkston 2-21-1841 Cr
Ross, Rachael to John K. Walker 10-20-1849 (10-21-1849) O
Ross, Rachel to James Winbury 3-22-1849 Be
Ross, Roda to Samuel Henry 4-12-1830 (4-13-1830) G
Ross, Sallie to Alfred Cobb 3-2-1867 (not endorsed) F B
Ross, Sarah C. to Nicholson G. Dixon 8-5-1858 Ma
Ross, Sarah E. to John W. Notgrass 3-22-1852 (no return) F
Ross, Sarah to Benj. O'Neil 4-20-1845 F
Ross, Sarah to Isaac Harris 3-19-1839 (no return) Cr
Ross, Sarah to Jesse Harris 10-14-1843 (no return) Hn
Ross, Sarah to Wm. C. Bird 8-31-1858 Cr
Ross, Susan Frances to Robert H. Franklin 12-8-1853 O
Ross, T. A. to C. A. Hallies 7-7-1858 We
Ross, Vickey T. to J. J. Herman 5-25-1861 O
Ross, Willie to Jesse Wright 11-21-1872 (11-22-1872) T
Rossel, Nancy to Thomas Murphy 7-26-1863 Be
Rosser(Roper), Mary P. to Nathan Roberts 10-20-1831 Hr
Rosser, Maggie to J. R. Pearce 12-3-1866 (12-5-1866) F
Rosser, Maria to Durell Griffin 11-3-1870 (11-8-1870) F
Rossin, Cynthia A. to James McAdams 8-18-1853 Sh
Rossin?, Debby to Littleberry Spain 9-30-1850 Hr
Rosson, Amanda J. to S. W. Atkinson 10-31-1871 (11-2-1871) O
Rosson, Eliza A. to A. J. Carson 3-4-1856 (3-6-1856) Hr
Rosson, Elizabeth to John Null 3-22-1845 (3-23-1845) Hr
Rosson, Margret to Thomas Higgs 12-30-1845 Hr
Rosson, Mary to Allen Ayres 8-21-1830 (8-22-1830) Hr
Rosson, Mary to J. M. Barnes 7-8-1860 G
Rosson, Metilda to L. P. Clark 11-15-1860 G
Rosson, Phoebe N. to John J. Teadford 2-14-1850 (2-19-1850) Hr
Rosson, Susan Caroline to Moses Ray 11-17-1836 Hr
Rosson, Susan to Thomas L. Duncan 6-6-1854 (12-5-1854) Hr
Roswell(Boswell?), Harriet M. to William Douglas 4-25-1853 Be
Roth, Mary to Charles Foster 6-15-1860 Sh
Roth, Sarah to Thomas Terril 4-30-1867 Hy
Rothemer, Margaret E. to William Charles Milten 10-23-1863 Sh
Rothemer, Margaret E. to Wm. Chas. Newton 10-23-1863 Sh
Rothgarber, Dora to Soloman Marks 4-20-1860 Sh
Rothgerber, Maria to Isaac D. Bloomingdale 2-10-1859 Sh
Rothrock, Margaret D. to W. J. Fields 5-6-1864 (5-7-1864) Cr
Rothrock, Susan A. to Lycurgus McCracken 11-10-1863 Cr
Roton, Mary Ann to Michael Wesley Hoke 10-21-1851 T
Roton, Sarah A. to R. F. Mayer 10-23-1862 Mn
Rouch, ____ to Rufus Perkins 2-10-1860 Hr
Roulet, M. A. to R. D. Bowden 5-20-1856 We
Roulker?, Eleanor H. to R. G. Goodman 8-7-1866 T
Roundtree, Elizabeth A. to James Howell 7-10-1833 (7-14-1833) Hr
Roundtree, Elizabeth to Wm. E. M. Spedder 9-17-1851 Cr
Roundtree, Elvira L. to William A. Bridgemon 11-18-1834 G
Roundtree, Evalina M. to Burrell Gossett 1-28-1840 G
Rourke, Bridget (Mrs.) to George Cooper 11-30-1864 Sh
Rousan, Clara to Robt. P. Sullivan 5-29-1867 (5-30-1867) T
Rouse, M. J. to E. M. Barnett 3-15-1863 G
Route, Mary H. to J. M. Boswell 2-7-1857 (2-8-1857) Hr
Routen, Elizabeth to W. D. Baldridge 5-14-1855 (5-15-1855) G
Routon, Elizabeth to Harry Little 2-10-1860 Be
Routon, Mary P. to William S. Sutherlin 11-12-1853 Hn
Routon, Perneta H. to Felix B. Hagler 1-19-1841 Hn
Rovers, Bridget to Michael McLeughlin 8-15-1863 Sh
Row, M. C. to W. M. Frinch 2-10-1865 (3-12-1865) Cr
Row, Rebecca to Willis W. Willeford 9-26-1839 Hn
Rowden, Elizabeth to Jesse Davis 11-17-1866 (11-18-1866) Dy
Rowder, Lucy to Pryus Patton 2-23-1867 (3-11-1867) F B
Rowe, Amanda M. to A. A. Dugger 12-7-1854 Hn
Rowe, Catherine to Robert C. Peak 1-29-1846 Hn
Rowe, Corian to Robert Rodgers 11-8-1839 Cr
Rowe, Elizabeth M. to B. Z. Haywood 1-21-1868 (1-28-1868) Cr
Rowe, Elizabeth to Burrett A. Peak 1-27-1847 Hn
Rowe, Elizabeth to James A. Simpson 2-28-1854 Hn

Rowe, L. A. to W. M. Carr 2-28-1860 (3-3-1860) Sh
Rowe, L. J. to Isaac F. Marbry 9-5-1867 Be
Rowe, Louiza F. to John W. McGehee 2-27-1851 Hn
Rowe, Mahala to John Rodgers 1-10-1841 Cr
Rowe, Maria L. to Peter Francisco 1-24-1861 Be
Rowe, Martha M. to John M. Balylock 2-5-1867 Be
Rowe, Mary Jane to Alexander Harman 12-6-1843 Hn
Rowe, Mary S. to Ferrell Pruett 12-6-1870 (12-8-1870) Cr
Rowe, Nancy A. to James C. Bilbry 4-17-1871 (4-20-1871) Cr
Rowe, Nancy C. to Robert M. Pruett 10-2-1865 (10-8-1865) Cr
Rowe, Nancy E. to William M. Rowe 11-28-1871 Cr
Rowe, Sarah to W. T. Higdon 5-27-1867 (5-29-1867) Cr
Rowe, Susan Mahaly to R. W. Myzell 4-14-1867 Be
Rowe, Susan to E. J. Cunningham 8-4-1847 Be
Rowe, Susana E. to John J. Martin 10-12-1858 Cr
Rowen, Catherine to M. E. Doyle 4-30-1854 Sh
Rowlan, Adaline to John Fletcher 1-11-1859 Cr
Rowland, Anne E. to J. T. Boswell 3-20-1861 (no return) Cr
Rowland, Caren Elizabeth to Henry F. Asbury 3-28-1857 (3-29-1857) O
Rowland, E. E. C. (Mrs.) to Van Ward 10-1-1848 Sh
Rowland, Elizabeth to J. M. Grooms 2-19-1866 Cr
Rowland, Ella to Levi Butler 8-24-1870 Cr
Rowland, Ennis to W. H. Lowrey 12-31-1872 (1-1-1873) Cr
Rowland, Josephine to John Cooper 1-11-1872 Cr
Rowland, L. J. to John B. Benton 12-30-1852 Cr
Rowland, Lucy J. to Thos. P. Williamson 9-21-1866 Hy
Rowland, M. F. (Mrs.) to Lagrand P. Phillips 8-25-1860 (8-26-1860) Cr
Rowland, Malissa Jane to E. B. Wilborn 8-14-1868 (8-16-1868) Cr
Rowland, Margaret C. to J. C. Barnhart 4-?-1867 (4-21-1867) Cr
Rowland, Margaret to J. M. Pickler 12-29-1866 (12-31-1867?) Cr
Rowland, Martha to David J. Rodgers 1-11-1855 Cr
Rowland, Mary A. to E. Washington Palmer 3-17-1863 Hn
Rowland, Mary A. to Joe T. Hern 6-20-1843 Cr
Rowland, Mary J. to E. W. Penick 11-11-1858 Cr
Rowland, Nancy to James H. Porterfield 10-31-1843 Cr
Rowland, Nancy to T. B. Rowland 1-24-1867 Cr
Rowland, Polly A. to John C. Hern 1-21-1847 Cr
Rowland, Sarah E. to G. N. Dillon 2-3-1868 (2-5-1868) Cr
Rowland, Sarah H. to J. W. Groom 12-1-1860 (12-2-1860) Cr
Rowland, Sarah H. to James W. Grooms 2-22-1870 Cr
Rowland, Sarah P. to Benjamin Boswell 12-12-1860 Cr
Rowland, Sarrah E. to James Moore 10-6-1870 Cr
Rowland, Susan to S. A. Kimberlin 10-26-1875 (10-27-1875) O
Rowland, Synthia A. to Phineous Gray 1-28-1870 (2-1-1870) Cr
Rowlet, M. A. to R. T. Elliott 4-20-1856 We
Rowlett, Mary M. to J. R. Rateree 11-29-1866 Hn
Rowlett, Tilda to Henry Nolly 7-19-1867 (7-20-1867) F B
Rowly, Amanday to Robert Mangrum 11-16-1867 (no return) Dy
Rowntree, Nancy to Otha C. Pollard 12-24-1845 (12-25-1845) G
Rowsey, Elizabeth C. (Mrs.) to William N. Stoe 12-30-1868 (12-31-1868) Ma
Rowson, Sarah Francis to James Hubbard 11-6-1873 L B
Rox?, Lucy C. to Dausey Sanders 2-11-1846 Cr
Roy, Beulah to J. F. Pipkin 11-21-1881 (11-23-1881) L
Roy, Eliza to Lemuel Crain 12-31-1855 (1-1-1856) Sh
Roy, Elizabeth to John McCoy 9-24-1855 (9-31?-1855) Sh
Roy, Francis Elizabeth to John Clark Withington 4-10-1870 (4-13-1870) L
Roy, Mary E. to B. S. Jones 11-29-1871 (12-3-1871) O
Royal, Eliza W. to Finis E. Wirt 1-27-1833 Cr
Royall, Nannie to W. A. McCall 10-?-1867 (10-29-1867) Cr
Roycroft, Samarimus (Sue) to R. A. McKee 1-8-1867 (1-10-1867) Dy
Royer, B. A. to John Pickard 10-13-1874 (10-22-1874) L
Royester, Jane to Samuel Donelson 12-23-1841 Sh
Royester, Mary E. to John W. Nelson 5-26-1842 Sh
Royester, Mary to Shepard Boyd 12-14-1873 Hy
Royester, Sarah C. to Alexander Donelson 9-30-1841 Sh
Royster, Ann B. to James Clark 1-31-1856 Sh
Royster, Bettie S. to Jonathan Joyner 4-19-1851 (5-6-1851) Sh
Royster, Mary H. to Wm. H. Chambers 11-28-1849 Sh
Rual?, Ana Liza to Thomas Little 12-26-1861 Cr
Rualdo, Mary to William Forester 12-31-1830 (1-10-1831) G
Ruce?, Nancy L. to G. W. Wright 1-31-1870 (2-10-1870) Cr
Rucker, A. R. to J. M. Chambers 12-18-1872 (12-19-1872) Dy
Rucker, Adline to E. E. Work 12-25-1867 Hy
Rucker, Alvira S. to S. H. McDearman 12-17-1870 (12-22-1870) Dy
Rucker, Catharine to James B. Blakemore 5-30-1839 G
Rucker, Cinthia W. to WilliamH. Counsel 1-10-1832 Hr
Rucker, Cynthia W. to William G. Stute 10-31-1842 (11-4-1842) Ma
Rucker, Elizabeth to A. G. Macon 12-22-1863 (12-23-1864?) L
Rucker, Ellen to Phill Elder 3-29-1875 (no return) Hy
Rucker, Elnora to Thomas Caldwell 12-28-1872 (1-2-1873) L
Rucker, Emiline to Jerry Jetton 6-30-1866 (no return) Hy
Rucker, Hester Ann to William S. Kelton 6-1-1859 G
Rucker, Jane to Howard Eison 9-3-1873 (no return) L B
Rucker, Janie to Howard Eison 9-3-1873 (9-4-1873) L
Rucker, Lucinda to Douglass Ruffian 3-1-1883 L
Rucker, Lucy to Moses White 3-4-1877 Hy
Rucker, M. V. to C. S. Chambers 12-20-1876 (12-21-1876) Dy

Rucker, Mary E. D. to James W.(M?) Spight 12-31-1840 Hr
Rucker, Mat to Samuel Carter 11-25-1870 Hy
Rucker, Mollie to William King 11-21-1875 (no return) L
Rucker, Mona to Charles Pierson 12-26-1867 (no return) L B
Rucker, Olivia to Cyrus Davis 4-8-1844 (4-9-1844) Hr
Rucker, S. A. to J. M. McDearmon 12-22-1874 (12-23-1874) Dy
Rucker, Susan J. M. to John Henry Pyland 11-27-1867 L
Rucker, Victora to John S. Winstad 11-18-1860 We
Rucker, W. Mosella to James M. Brooks 7-31-1860 (no return) Hy
Rudd, Anne E. to James H. Spain 4-9-1860 Hy
Rudd, Laura to Henry Burton 1-4-1870 (no return) Hy
Rudd, Lidia to William A. Brown 11-18-1861 (no return) Hy
Rudd, Morning E. to Jeremiah E. Underwood 10-10-1852 We
Rudd, S. P. to Asa A. Brown 2-10-1862 (no return) Hy
Rudd, Samanthy P. to Ulis Samuel 7-13-1867 Hy
Rudd, Sarah P. to Chancy Malone 6-10-1852 Hn
Ruddell, Catharine F. to David Wylie 9-16-1856 Sh
Rudder, Famie to J. W. Harper 10-16-1878 Dy
Rudder, Marian to Stephen McCann 10-29-1874 Dy
Rudder, Rosaline to W. H. Rowark 12-4-1867 Dy
Ruddle, Elizabeth to Charles R. Gordon 4-11-1855 (4-12-1855) Hr
Ruddle, Margaret M. to Henry W. Duncan 1-2-1849 (1-3-1849) Hr
Ruddle, Mary E. to George G. Thompson 12-14-1870 Ma
Ruddle, Sarah M. to William Needham 9-10-1836 Hr
Rudisill, Amanda F. to Jno. M. Shelby 4-11-1833 Sh
Rudisill, Harriet L. to Wm. T. Morehead 12-24-1857 Sh
Rudisill, Margaret A. to J. M. Alexander 2-22-1848 Sh
Rudisill, Margaret to David Muncrief 3-15-1858 (3-24-1858) Sh
Rudisill, Susan A. to Charles A. LeCoq 9-15-1852 Sh
Rudolph, Mary to John A. Carithers 8-22-1831 Hr
Ruff, A. C. to J. T. Laflore 8-17-1859 Cr
Ruff, Amanda to David McMackin 12-24-1866 Cr
Ruff, Caroline to Fillmore Tipton 2-28-1877 Dy
Ruff, Clarkie to T. J. Rial 12-29-1868 (12-30-1868) Cr
Ruff, Elizabeth to Thos. Finley 12-16-1846 (no return) Cr
Ruff, Jackie E. to George M. Drew 9-12-1846 (no return) Cr
Ruff, Julia to Newnham Reynolds 3-9-1859 Hr
Ruff, Lucenda to Andrew McMahan 5-4-1840 Ma
Ruff, Mariah to William Tipton 10-31-1874 Dy
Ruff, Martha J. to Levi D. Williams 8-4-1852 Cr
Ruff, Mary to Wm. O'Connor 7-16-1859 Sh
Ruff, Sarah to Daniel Harris 2-5-1842 Ma
Ruffian, Charity to Charles Buckner 1-24-1883 (no return) L
Ruffin, Agnes C. to David S. Bass 8-9-1866 (8-12-1866) F
Ruffin, Basina to James D. Ruffin 7-8-1834 (7-17-1834) Hr
Ruffin, Callie to Ned Read 12-3-1874 L B
Ruffin, Eliza A. to Henry L. Pettus 9-25-1851 Hr
Ruffin, Lucy Ann to Charles W. Hunt 9-2-1834 Hr
Ruffin, Lucy E. to Lemuel H. Whitfield 4-14-1854 (4-15-1854) Sh
Ruffin, Maria A. to Edwin H. Price 4-27-1836 (4-29-1836) Hr
Ruffin, Martha to Geor. W. Wilson 12-15-1842 Ma
Ruffin, Mary L. to Obediah Gravett 12-22-1856 (12-24-1856) Hr
Ruffin, Roena R. to E. B. Turner 9-21-1867 (9-25-1867) F
Ruffin, Sarah to Oliver Mulherrin 2-28-1876 L
Rugg, Lavinia to Wm. C. Riley 2-12-1855 (2-14-1855) Sh
Rule, Mary to Richard Landragan 11-21-1859 Sh
Ruleman, Emarilla J. to William Carr 12-23-1848 Sh
Rumage, Sarah L. to P. B. Caps 9-13-1870 Cr
Rumbley, Martha Jane to Reuben D. Bridges 10-26-1851 Be
Rumbley, Rilley Ann to William Kendall 7-15-1847 Hn
Rumbly, Belinda to John T. Easley 4-29-1838 (no return) Hn
Rumbly, Mary to Jackson Smily 10-20-1866 Hn
Rumbly, Nancy to John F. Kendall 4-29-1855 Hn
Rumeley, Martha to W. G. Nugent 9-10-1860 (9-15-1860) O
Rumgk?, B. to John Daiz 9-4-1855 Sh
Rumley, A. to Wilie Smothers 7-20-1843 Cr
Rumley, Caroline to Granville Barnes 2-23-1860 Cr
Rumley, Caron H. to James Upchurch 4-3-1842 Hn
Rumley, Emma to Henry Abbott 2-2-1860 Cr
Rumley, Malvina to Elijah Al---ty? 7?-7-1864 Be
Rumley, Minerva to James C. Moore 1-25-1846 Cr
Rumley, Nancy to F. M. Rhodes 5-24-1843 Cr
Rumley, Nancy to J. F. McFarland 1-6-1872 Dy
Rumley, Nancy to Sal W. Haynes 11-14-1872 Cr
Rumley, Permelia to William Sherwood 12-14-1871 (5-23-1871?) Cr
Rumley, Rebecca to Thomas Mullin 2-23-1861 (2-24-1861) O
Rumley, SarahJ. to Riley N. Merrett 3-23-1847 Cr
Rumly, Nancy to Wilson B. Rhodes 11-16-1861 (11-11?-1861) Cr
Rumney, Francis to A. L. Crockett 10-26-1850 Cr
Runalds, Elenor M. to John D. Crank 2-3-1844 (2-7-1844) G
Runalds, Elizabeth to Walter Thedford 11-3-1845 (11-6-1845) G
Runalds, Mahaly to Berry Cantrel 3-20-1841 (3-28-1841) G
Runalds, Mary to Lemuel Nance 10-7-1845 (10-11-1845) G
Runck, Elizabeth to Henry Tschudi 11-25-1859 (11-27-1859) Sh
Rundell, Mary to Absalom A. Hooper 6-10-1845 Sh
Runkle, Hepsebeth to Robert T. Cross 1-19-1837 Sh
Runkle, Lucinda A. to John L. Parham 10-17-1832 Sh

Runnells, Fanny to Jacob Nance 10-31-1878 Hy
Runnells, Martha to W. G. Newgent 10-10-1860 O
Runnells, Mary to William Yarbrough 4-27-1862 G
Runnels, Milly C. to Wm. C. Berry 4-3-1844 Cr
Ruschhaupt, Minnie to Theodore Ostmann 4-4-1860 (4-9-1860) Sh
Ruse, R. C. to W. M. Taylor 10-7-1862 (10-12-1862) Cr
Rush (Rust?), Lucinda to William B. Jenkins (Jennings?) 9-23-1854 (9-24-1854) L
Rush, Barbara to Peter Hartz 11-27-1861 Sh
Rush, Bolinda F. to Lon O. Thompson 7-5-1870 (7-13-1870) L
Rush, Martha to George Johnson 5-18-1853 L
Rush, Mary J. to John T. Halliburton 8-2-1875 (8-3-1875) L
Rush, Mary to Arthnald Cannon 2-12-1852 Sh
Rush, Mildred M. to W. H. Mullikin 12-16-1868 L
Rush, Sarah E. to J. K. P. Bowie 1-9-1867 L
Rushen, Kisie H. to W. B. Houseman 8-28-1869 (9-1-1869) L
Rushen, Matilda to Silas Hughes 11-17-1852 (no return) F
Rushin, Mahaley to William Haily 7-26-1841 (7-29-1841) G
Rushin, Nancy to James Cary 2-5-1851 (2-6-1851) O
Rushin, Sarah E. to Thomas C. Brown 12-3-1860 (12-9-1860) Cr
Rushing, America J. to James C. Lindsey 9-3-1860 Be
Rushing, B. D. Caroline to Joseph A. Greer 7-3-1854 Be
Rushing, D. to J. McGill 9-22-1841 Be
Rushing, Eliza G. C. to John A. Nober 7-18-1850 Be
Rushing, Eliza P. to William H. Ward 10-14-1860 Hn
Rushing, Elizabeth to Madison Rockliff 7-12-1863 Mn
Rushing, Harriet to Alexandria McAuley 2-25-1869 Be
Rushing, Jemima to James A. Greer 8-5-1847 Be
Rushing, Jemima to Obadiah Waters 1-1-1845 Be
Rushing, Jemima to William Cottingham 11-2-1843 Be
Rushing, Katharine to Ellis T. Presson 3-14-1850 Be
Rushing, L. to T. P. Dorris 3-10-1842 Be
Rushing, Lively to Benjamin McGhee 8-22-1846 Ma
Rushing, Malinda to G. W. Edington 12-2-1856 Be
Rushing, Manervy Jane to Mack Watson 12-15-1867 Be
Rushing, Martha B. to John Bush 5-2-1858 Be
Rushing, Mary Ann to Calvin Rushing 11-15-1847 Be
Rushing, Mary C. to James Neabor 2-17-1852 Be
Rushing, Mary to William Brummet 12-15-1867 Be
Rushing, Minerva to James Robertson 10-27-1841 (10-28-1841) Ma
Rushing, Nancy A. to Newton C. Elmore 12-20-1866 Be
Rushing, Nancy Ann to William Perritt 9-2-1849 Be
Rushing, Nancy D. to W. L. Greer 3-1-1860 Be
Rushing, Olly to J. K. Nance 3-28-1841 Be
Rushing, Par to A. T. Corbitt 4-11-1839 Be
Rushing, Rebecca to Harrison Williams 5-30-1866 Be
Rushing, Salina to Spencer Bomer 1-17-1839 Be
Rushing, Sarah A. to Elias B. Boyd 9-18-1855 (no return) Hn
Rushing, Sarah A. to James M. Holdsbrooks 6-28-1853 Be
Rushing, Sarah Ann to William Armor 3-9-1845 Be
Rushing, Sophiah to W. C. Rushing 1-19-1853 Be
Rusk, Mary A. to Charles Gore 4-5-1838 Hn
Russ, C. A. to J. R. Hall no date (with Mar 1866) Cr
Russ, Emaline to Mack R. Cook 12-13-1831 G
Russ, Fredica to A. N. Correll 3-24-1864 Sh
Russ, S. J. to T. H. Midgett 11-24-1869 (no return) Hy
Russel, Mary E. to W. H. H. Massey 9-26-1870 (9-28-1870) Cr
Russell, Adaline to John Bowers 10-28-1853 (no return) Hn
Russell, Aley M. to W. A. Kendrick 12-28-1859 Ma
Russell, Alsey to Winfrey A. Lester 8-7-1841 (8-8-1841) O
Russell, Ann A. to John J. Bucknor 8-31-1850 (no return) Hn
Russell, Ann Eliza to Hamilton Black 3-29-1854 (3-30-1854) Hr
Russell, Ann to Adam Perkins 10-4-1862 Hn
Russell, Bridget to Hugh McCann 6-8-1861 (6-9-1861) Sh
Russell, Canvass B. to Francis M. Barron 9-28-1858 G
Russell, Caro to E. R. Crandel 2-22-1873 (2-25-1873) L
Russell, Dallia to Tilford Stone 2-5-1839 Cr
Russell, Delila Jane to Alexander Givens 9-2-1850 Hn
Russell, Delphia Ann to Nehemiah M. Almond 10-20-1858 Hn
Russell, Dely C. to William A. Swain 12-25-1865 Mn
Russell, Elizabeth A. to David C. Sauls 1-22-1867 (1-23-1867) L
Russell, Elizabeth H. to John M. Prewett 11-30-1859 Ma
Russell, Elizabeth to James Kendrick 3-12-1856 Ma
Russell, Emaline to Pinkney J. Petty 10-18-1857 Cr
Russell, Fanny to Henry Markham 2-21-1864 Hn
Russell, Jane P. to James W. Patterson 11-13-1845 Hn
Russell, Jane to Edmond Smith 3-6-1841 Cr
Russell, Julia to James Kane 3-2-1864 Sh
Russell, Letia to A. J. Davis 5-14-1884 L
Russell, Louisa A. to John M. Morgan 2-8-1858 O
Russell, Louisa to H. H. Martin 2-1-1844 Cr
Russell, Lucy to Manuel Haymes 5-19-1866 (no return) Hn
Russell, M. M. to P. D. Watson 1-13-1869 G
Russell, Maegret? to Anderson Lynch 12-6-1868 Be
Russell, Malinda C. to Goodwin Green 7-16-1846 (7-28-1846) Ma
Russell, Malinda to Pinckney Bell 7-18-1866 O
Russell, Margaret A. to Wilbourn Russell 12-24-1846 Cr
Russell, Margarett C. to James A. Marks 6-19-1845 Ma
Russell, Martha A. to Benjamin Kendall 2-5-1854 Hn
Russell, Martha E. to J. W. Gunter 8-20-1862 (no return) Cr
Russell, Martha to H. G. Hays 10-3-1854 Hn
Russell, Martha to William Stutham 5-30-1849 (5-31-1845) T
Russell, Mary A. to Andrew J. Allen 1-25-1870 Ma
Russell, Mary Ann to Campbell Kitchens 7-3-1861 (7-10-1861) O
Russell, Mary Easter to Jenkins Rice 3-24-1875 (4-2-1875) L B
Russell, Mary Jane to Volney S. Alston 9-1-1860 (no return) L
Russell, Mona J. to David M. Chapples 9-7-1850 Cr
Russell, Nancy Elizabeth to James E. Davis 12-12-1859 Ma
Russell, Nancy M. to A. McKey 8-14-1857 Cr
Russell, Nancy to David Mathews 1-18-1856 Be
Russell, Nancy to Emanuel Spainham 6-27-1847 O
Russell, Nancy to Henry Crichfield 2-5-1852 (2-15-1852) L
Russell, Paralee to Allen Price 8-14-1861 Be
Russell, Pearl F. to Elizah C. Shaw 8-23-1873 (8-24-1873) T
Russell, Rosanna to James Crawford 10-3-1854 Cr
Russell, Rosey to Francis Gideon 12-30-1839 O
Russell, S. E. to W. W. Wall 5-1-1868 G
Russell, Sabra to Henry Callis 4-4-1860 (4-5-1860) O
Russell, Sarah A. to Eullen M. Miller 2-28-1849 Cr
Russell, Sarah A. to James W. Brown 7-23-1850 (7-26-1850) O
Russell, Sarah E. to Reuben M. May 3-14-1855 (3-15-1855) Ma
Russell, Sarah J. to William M. Barr 9-12-1859 (9-13-1859) Ma
Russell, Sarah P. to Samuel B. Allen 7-30-1839 (no return) Hn
Russell, Sarah to Right Price 9-1-1860 Be
Russell, Sue to Jessy Rhoads 3-24-1872 Hy
Russell, Susan P. to Robert D. Orr 7-21-1852 Cr
Russell, Teresa to C. T. Hughes 3-13-1851 Hn
Russey, Mary J. to John E. G. Davis 8-13-1840 Hr
Russian, Marilda Jane to Thos. Grooms 9-5-1867 Cr
Russom, Ann to Robert Rush 12-13-1865 Mn
Russom, Louisa A. to Drue F. Bassham 9-10-1865 Mn
Russom, Rebecca E. to Joseph Hicks 3-1-1863 Mn
Russom, S. J. to J. M. Smith 3-10-1880 (3-11-1880) L
Rust (Rash), Margaret M. to James T. Blackford-Blackwell 6-8-1848 Sh
Rust, A. S. to Robert H. Hall 4-18-1864 (4-20-1864) Cr
Rust, Deliar A. to Isaac Shoffner 9-5-1871 (9-6-1871) Cr B
Rust, Dorothy A. to John B. McAuley 8-20-1838 Cr
Rust, Elizabeth A. to Anderson Evans 1-6-1861 We
Rust, Ellender to Wellington H. Bledsoe 1-19-1843 G
Rust, Elmasand to R. W. Ridings 12-7-1856 Cr
Rust, Evaline to William B. Lomax 7-11-1859 We
Rust, Jamiah to John A. Hollowell 1-12-1852 (no return) Cr
Rust, Jestin to William Robertson 12-9-1827 G
Rust, L. A. to James Haywood 4-28-1844 Cr
Rust, L. F. to W. A. Peery 4-11-1855 We
Rust, Louisa J. to A. H. Chesap 3-1-1855 G
Rust, Margaret to Cyrus Gastin 12-31-1867 G B
Rust, Martha J. to A. I. J. Mathis 1-10-1855 G
Rust, Martha to John Boyd 2-18-1841 Cr
Rust, Mary Elizabeth to James E. Langford 10-11-1848 (10-18-1848) G
Rust, Mary H. to Wesley S. King 12-10-1850 Sh
Rust, Nannie M. to John T. Rowlett 7-31-1870 G
Rust, Narcisa to John Reed 10-1-1857 We
Rust, Puty to Wm. Robinson 1-7-1855 Cr
Rust, Randy J. to L. F. McMackins 12-23-1869 (12-29-1869) Cr
Rust, Rowann to E. W. Haywood 3-24-1869 Cr
Rust, S. J. to S. T. Johnson 5-31-1867 (6-2-1867) Cr
Rust, Sallie Ophelia Polk to S. B. Williams 7-30-1868 G
Rust, Sarah B. to William H. Bridges 10-18-1831 (10-20-1831) G
Rust, Sarah to Henry Warell 11-8-1856 Cr
Rutchmann, Rosalia to Hermann Schattlin 2-3-1860 Sh
Ruth, Elizabeth to James R. Brown 11-15-1862 Mn
Ruth, Fredonia M. to D. M. C. Stuckey 4-10-1867 (4-11-1867) L
Ruth, Naomi F. to William N. Leak 1-26-1878 (1-30-1878) L
Rutherford, Albina to Wm. R. Rosingbun 10-21-1847 Cr
Rutherford, Betty to W. H. Young 10-5-1876 Hy
Rutherford, Casandra to George Gray 1-10-1833 Hr
Rutherford, D. P. to Lucian N. Bruce 3-2-1857 (3-3-1857) Sh
Rutherford, Elizabeth to Daniel H. Hoffman 6-30-1847 Sh
Rutherford, Linn to Nelson Taylor 11-20-1869 Hy
Rutherford, Louisa A. C. to George I. Walden 12-29-1830 (1-2-1831) Hr
Rutherford, Louisa to James Madison Leach 7-17-1849 T
Rutherford, Lucinda to Washington Hudson 8-19-1836 (9-16-1836) Hr
Rutherford, Mary E. to William C. Wright 5-3-1848 L
Rutherford, Mollie to John Dodd 11-9-1871 Ma
Rutherford, Nancy C. to William B. Ragan 9-3-1847 (9-5-1847) Hr
Rutherford, Nancy to J. H. Alston 12-25-1869 Hy
Rutherford, Rebecca to Tunce Thomas 12-11-1869 Hy
Rutherford, Sallie B. to Saml. R. Shelton 5-4-1857 (5-5-1857) T
Rutherford, Sarah Ann to John T. Gooch 3-2-1865 Mn
Rutherford, Sarah to William A. Shilling 3-2-1836 (3-10-1836) Hr
Rutherford, Sophia J. to Jesse Biggs 7-18-1867 Ma
Rutherford, Teula to John Brown 12-18-1873 Hy
Rutland, Marina F. to William Goyer 8-19-1852 Sh

Rutledge, Angeline to Finis Capps 12-25-1868 G
Rutledge, Ann E. to William R. Tyson 11-13-1845 (11-16-1845) G
Rutledge, Emely J. to William C. Roberts 9-29-1849 (10-4-1849) G
Rutledge, Harrett to Arch Jones 12-15-1876 Hy
Rutledge, Jane to William H. Davis 12-6-1848 Sh
Rutledge, Leah to Gillum Wiles 4-4-1840 Sh
Rutledge, Lucy to Thomas Brooks 12-1-1845 Sh
Rutledge, Malinda to Daniel Luker 10-27-1856 (10-29-1856) O
Rutledge, Mary A. to Jeremiah A. Tilman 7-24-1851 G
Rutledge, Mary E. to William Henry 12-25-1856 (12-20?-1856) Ma
Rutledge, Mary F. to Jno. H. Garnett 12-15-1868 F
Rutledge, Mary to Andrew B. Howell 11-28-1840 Sh
Rutledge, Melinda to Daniel Luker 10-27-1854 (10-29-1854) O
Rutledge, Nancy to John R. Branon 7-29-1841 (8-11-1841) O
Rutlidge, Angeline to George A. Adkins 10-19-1843 G
Rutlidge, H. A. to J. A. Spencer 8-19-1866 G
Ruttlemager, Lisetta to Peter Lavrenz 2-28-1855 (3-1-1855) Sh
Ryals, Sarah to Peter Foust 10-21-1840 Hn
Ryan, Alice to Charles Turner 9-15-1855 (9-16-1855) Sh
Ryan, Alice to John Whelen 1-17-1860 Sh
Ryan, Amelia Vanclaire? to Jas. Henry Claiborn 10-26-1852 T
Ryan, Ann to Martin McKinney 1-25-1862 (1-28-1862) Sh
Ryan, Anna to Jermiah McCormick 10-18-1868 Sh
Ryan, Betsy to Richard Whaling 11-26-1846 Sh
Ryan, Bridget to John Sullivan 1-6-1862 Sh
Ryan, Bridget to Patrick Mannix 11-7-1858 Sh
Ryan, Bridget to Tobias Butler 1-21-1856 Sh
Ryan, Bridget to Patrick Lyons 9-11-1859 Sh
Ryan, Catharine to Michael Casey 7-11-1857 (7-12-1857) Sh
Ryan, Eliza to William Gilliam 11-23-1878 Hy
Ryan, Elizabeth to Patrick Meade 10-8-1854 Sh
Ryan, Ellen to Daniel Quinlen 6-2-1855 (6-3-1855) Sh
Ryan, Ellen to John Reardon 4-4-1853 Sh
Ryan, Ellen to Martin Callahan 10-16-1852 (10-17-1852) Sh
Ryan, Harriet to John P. Hanson 9-29-1860 Sh
Ryan, Joana to Thos. Moloughbury 10-18-1851 (10-19-1851) Sh
Ryan, Joannah to Thomas E. Barker 8-31-1855 (9-1-1855) Sh
Ryan, Johanna to Eugene Conway 4-23-1848 Sh
Ryan, Julia A. to Edwin S. Emerson 4-7-1851 Sh
Ryan, Mary E. to Alsey Rowland 10-19-1858 (no return) Hn
Ryan, Mary to Feldman Fisher 9-5-1860 Sh
Ryan, Mary to Martin FitzGerald 7-17-1854 Sh
Ryan, Mary to Michael Tyrell 6-11-1853 (6-12-1853) Sh
Ryan, Winneford to Cornelius Driskell 9-18-1858 (9-19-1858) Sh
Ryland, Malissa to C. L. Martin 1-14-1865 L
Rynder, Elizabeth to Samuel Hays 6-8-1857 (6-9-1857) O
Ryne (Ryan?), Hannora to Richard Fanasy 5-20-1852 Sh
Ryne, Catharine to Wm. Locket (no date) Hy
Ryne, Sarah Ann to Raleigh Smith 6-16-1847 (6-17-1847) L
Ryon, Amanda to W. L. Wilson 4-17-1874 L
Ryster, Elizabeth to James Pugh 12-5-1853 (12-8-1853) G

Sacer(Sasser), Emily to Solomon Granthan 9-8-1838 (9-9-1838) Hr
Sadbury, Lucentia to Jack Sims 2-10-1868 G
Saddler, Maggie to David E. Haynie 1-10-1871 (1-11-1871) T
Saddler, Margaret to Marien Rhodes 12-21-1858 We
Sadler, Martha A. to Robt. S. Clemens 7-16-1860 Dy
Sadler, Charlotte to John White 5-6-1871 (5-7-1871) F B
Sadler, Emily to Frank Gaise 4-4-1867 (4-6-1867) T
Sadler, Mary G. to John L. Haynie 12-19-1872 T
Sadler, Mary to Aaron Pullin 11-26-1865 (11-6?-1865) T
Sadler, P. A. to Henry Palmer 3-23-1867 (3-30-1867) T
Sadler, S. A. to B. R. Herndon 11-24-1849 Hr
Sadler, Sarah A. to Thomas J. Fowler 11-13-1856 We
Sadler, Sarah Ann to James Campbell 12-22-1859 Hr
Saffarrans, Caroline V. to H. J. Price 1-16-1860 Sh
Safferrans, Mary E. to James F. Schobel 12-30-1852 Sh
Saggs?, Lucinda to James P. Harrison 11-23-1860 Hn
Saichern?, Martha to Calvin Fowlkes 10-9-1876 Dy
Sain, Elizabeth A. to Alpha Bailey 1-9-1855 (1-11-1855) Hr
Sain, Frances to William May 9-30-1852 L
Sain, Hester to Cornelius McDaniel 12-9-1848 (12-14-1848) Hr
Sain, Mary to Benjamin A. Bailey 10-26-1844 (10-29-1844) G
Sain, Nancy to Eliphalet Brown 1-6-1834 (1-9-1834) Hr
Saine?, Harriett to G. W. Strother 11-26-1867 (no return) Hn
Sainford, Cynthia to John Karnes 7-21-1851 (7-23-1851) G
Saint John, Martha L. to J.(T?) F. Crihfield 8-23-1864 (8-25-1864) L
Saint John, Parmelia C. to William H. Crihfield 2-11-1859 (2-16-1859) L
Saint, Margaret to Richard Grooms 3-5-1863 Sh
Saint, Mary F. to John W. Smith 5-31-1860 Sh
Sale, Dorithey to Francis M. Livingston 3-20-1848 (3-?-1848) G
Sale, Mary Lucinda to Alford W. Harris 2-24-1846 (no return) F
Sale, Virginia S. to Orville Yearger 10-9-1848 (no return) F
Salemon, Mary S. to William Mosley 8-26-1845 (9-11-1845) G
Sales, Cyntha P. to William Lane 8-13-1841 (8-26-1841) G
Sales, Julia A. S. to John S. Loving 4-25-1849 Sh
Sales, Mary D. to Jacob Miller 3-26-1860 Sh

Sales, Susannah to Moses Dunlap 11-8-1879 (11-9-1879) L B
Salisberry, Sarah L. to T. N. Evans 9-28-1868 (10-1-1868) L
Salisbury, Catherine to H. N. Mount 10-18-1866 Dy
Salisbury, Mary A. to Jesse S. Robinson 2-20-1867 Dy
Salisbury, Mary Ann to John Nugent 3-20-1848 (3-21-1848) L
Salisbury, Rebecca to W. G. Voss 2-22-1881 (2-23-1881) L
Salisbury, S. E. to J. C. Farmer 11-6-1876 (11-8-1876) Dy
Salisbury, Sarah to David Ford 1-5-1858 (1-6-1858) L
Sallee, Martha A. to William O. Howard 8-30-1854 Hn
Sallie A., Brezel to R. F. Pittman 1-23-1867 Hy
Sallie, Elizabeth J. to Wm. C. Herndon 12-28-1867 (1-1-1868) Ma
Salliers, Mattie J. to W. M. Hurley 8-15-1874 (8-16-1874) T
Salmon, Elizabeth J. to James A. Douglass 10-26-1841 (10-27-1841) F
Salmon, Martha to T. M. Vaughn 12-20-1865 Hn
Salmon, Nancy B. to Paschall Boyd 5-8-1865 (no return) Hn
Salmon, Nancy T. to James H. Roberson 12-1-1847 F
Salmon, Sarah C. to John B. Grubbs 12-17-1857 Hn
Salmons, Martha to John Lucus 2-28-1841 Cr
Salsberry, Frances to Wells W. Hall 1-27-1865 (1-28-1865) Dy
Salsberry, Rachael C. to Henry C. Nale 7-29-1865 (8-?-1865) L
Samford, Mary C. to John P. Blackwell 3-24-1856 (no return) Hn
Samford, Sarah C. to Martin W. B. Volentine 12-24-1860 Hn
Sammon, Mary to Patrick Phelan 10-7-1854 (10-8-1854) Sh
Sammon, Nancy M. to George M. Polsgrove 11-24-1855 (11-27-1855) O
Sammons, Ann to Thomas Kenney 4-11-1840 Hr
Sammons, Betsey to Edmund Britt 5-20-1829 (5-24-1829) G
Sammons, Julia to Benjamin F. Underwood 4-5-1854 O
Sammons, Margaret to John S. Watson 3-18-1863 O
Sammons, Martha to Martin Moore 3-6-1841 (3-11-1841) Hr
Sammons, Martha to William E. Tilliman 12-23-1852 G
Sammons, Mary F. to J. D. Carrne 2-5-1863 O
Sammons, Milley to John Darnald 4-29-1843 (5-1-1843) G
Sammons, Nancy D. to George M. Polsgrove 7-10-1849 O
Sammons, Nancy N. to Robert M. Thompson 1-10-1866 O
Sammons, Sue A. to J. A. Sammons 8-15-1872 Hy
Sammons?, A. F. to H.B. Coleman 2-20-1867 G
Sample, Delila E. to Leroy P. Magee 9-16-1851 (10-7-1851) O
Sample, Fanny H. to James Lewis 5-10-1842 (5-12-1842) F
Sample, Lucinda to William Thomas 3-9-1857 (3-12-1857) Sh
Sample, Nancy to Richard A. Abnathy 3-8-1873 (3-9-1873) T
Sample, Ruth J. to Roland K. Campbell 1-18-1853 (2-7-1853) O
Sample, S. C. to T. C. Powell 5-1-1854 (5-3-1854) O
Sample, Susan A. to Yarnall Reece 7-3-1849 (7-4-1849) O
Sampson, Bettie to T. T. Morgan 1-3-1872 (no return) Cr
Sampson, Eliza J. to Wm. Marshall 8-6-1844 Cr
Sampson, J. P. to R. S. Walker 11-7-1861 Cr
Sampson, Lou P. to Joseph H. Wardlaw 9-5-1866 L
Sampson, Sarah B. to Samuel B. Carson 3-12-1868 Dy
Sampson, Sarah to W. B. Rhoads 10-27-1870 L
Sampson, Tennessee F. to Cornelius Parent 4-28-1862 (5-1-1862) O
Sampson, Virginia to Jno. W. Wicker 8-15-1864 (8-16-1864) O
Samse, Augusta to George Vogts 9-18-1856 N
Samuel, Elizabeth G. to Jefferson Clark 11-24-1841 Ma
Samuels, Emma Francis to Joseph Price 5-4-1874 (5-5-1874) L
Samuels, Mary E. (Mrs.) to J. Q. Cannon 6-30-1860 (7-1-1860) Sh
Samuels, Sylva to Edwin Chambers 10-10-1868 T
Sandage, Catherine to Peter Peterson 6-1-1846 Sh
Sandeford, Bell to William Isla 10-25-1866 G
Sandeford, Drucilla to Danl. C. Treadwell 12-2-1830 Sh
Sandeford, M. R. E. to J. H. McDowell 11-2-1865 O
Sanderford, Drucilla E. to Joel C. Massey 8-30-1849 Sh
Sanderford, Martha to W. Wilson Yandell 2-25-1852 (2-26-1852) G
Sanderford, Mary T. to Calvin W. Bland 11-12-1851 (11-13-1851) Sh
Sanderford, Pricella N. to Nathaniel J. Hockaday 9-7-1847 G
Sanderford, Sarah Ann to William Williams 9-4-1849 (9-5-1849) G
Sanderford, Sarah T. to Robert N. Bond 1-14-1829 Sh
Sanderford, Virginia F. to Albert J. Webb 10-2-1847 (10-3-1847) G
Sanderlin, Elizabeth to Hinchie (Kinchie) Seward 12-13-1850 Sh
Sanderlin, Elizabeth to John M. McBride 7-19-1852 Sh
Sanderlin, Lavinia to William Johnson 1-13-1851 (1-15-1851) Sh
Sanderlin, Louine to Patrick McQuin 10-8-1855 Sh
Sanderlin, Mary Adaline to Wm. Muncrief 1-15-1858 (1-17-1858) Sh
Sanderlin, Nancy to Jessee K. Williams 9-15-1842 Sh
Sanderlin, Sarah E. to H. M. Blake 1-21-1856 Sh
Sanderlin, Tennessee to Henry R. Biggs 1-1-1855 (1-4-1855) Sh
Sanderman? Bucy, Julia to James D. Cleaves 5-11-1852 (no return) F
Sanders, Abedian to Edward Ozwell(Oswald) 10-15-1856 Hr
Sanders, Adaline to Thomas Allen 11-21-1870 (11-23-1870) Ma
Sanders, Afferilla to Amos D. L. Rhine 9-22-1854 L
Sanders, Amanda to John Dennis 5-21-1868 L
Sanders, Amanda to Thos. A. J. Cassels 6-7-1851 G
Sanders, Amanda to William C. Johnson 12-9-1842 Ma
Sanders, Ann to Haywood Mathews 9-30-1865 O
Sanders, Anna to Allen McDowell 10-6-1869 F B
Sanders, Bettie to Watson Bond, jr. 2-4-1874 Hy
Sanders, Caroline to David Kinkead 3-27-1868 (3-29-1868) L
Sanders, Catharine to Francis Hester 6-16-1856 (6-19-1856) Sh

Sanders, Catherine to George Thomason 9-28-1867 O
Sanders, D. L. to A. M. Sanders 2-19-1863 Mn
Sanders, Deliah to Isaac Hibbs 12-27-1843 We
Sanders, E. F. to Saml. S. Owen 5-22-1860 (5-23-1860) Sh
Sanders, Eliza Jane to David J. Baker 2-3-1848 Be
Sanders, Eliza M. to James F. Johnson 6-19-1839 Ma
Sanders, Elizebeth to B. A. Farmer 7-31-1870 G
Sanders, Elizabeth J. to E. D. M. Perkins 3-31-1863 Mn
Sanders, Elizabeth L. to Matthias Ward, jr. 5-25-1836 Sh
Sanders, Elizabeth to Charles Bradberry 2-9-1843 F
Sanders, Elizabeth to David Moore 6-20-1868 (6-25-1868) L
Sanders, Elizabeth to Jno. H. McGraw 8-12-1845 Hr
Sanders, Elizabeth to Joseph H. Asbridges 12-17-1852 Cr
Sanders, Elizabeth to L. S. Hailey 12-22-1847 (no return) F
Sanders, Emaline to Richard Davis 1-8-1870 (1-9-1870) T
Sanders, Emily to Charles Hill 12-17-1869 (no return) F B
Sanders, F. A. E. to J. A. McCraw 12-7-1870 (12-8-1870) T
Sanders, Florence E. to J. S. King 11-20-1873 Hy
Sanders, Georgeanna to John W. Moore 8-20-1873 Hy
Sanders, Hannah C. to James Radford 12-9-1858 (1-15-1859) O
Sanders, Harriet to Sidon Harris 11-28-1866 Hy
Sanders, Ida to Thos. L. Robertson 10-28-1863 Sh
Sanders, Isabella to Wiley Smothers 3-24-1859 Cr
Sanders, Isabella to William Gibson 7-21-1841 (7-22-1841) F
Sanders, Jane E. to B. F. Norris 5-8-1861 L
Sanders, Jane to daniel Williams 1-19-1870 (no return) F B
Sanders, Josephine to Andrew Brown 6-24-1867 G
Sanders, Josephine to Polk Howard 12-22-1876 (1-24-1877) Dy
Sanders, Julia E. to J. W. Daniel 1-13-1873 (no return) Hy
Sanders, Julia to Peter Rogers 8-9-1875 (no return) Hy
Sanders, L. J. to Joseph Fennell 9-17-1872? Hy
Sanders, Linda to M. Bradford 2-3-1875 (no return) Hy
Sanders, Louisa (Mrs.) to J. W. Waldrop 3-1-1865 G
Sanders, Louisa J. to James M. Roberts 8-2-1858 (8-3-1858) O
Sanders, Louisa T. to James Pool 1-28-1867 F
Sanders, Lucinda to Wesley N. Higgens 12-24-1848 Sh
Sanders, Lucinda to Wm. Robertson Acuff 12-3-1859 L
Sanders, Lucy A. to John M. Richey 1-6-1856 (1-9-1859) F
Sanders, Lucy A. to Samuel McKinney 8-15-1854 (no return) F
Sanders, Luisa E. to James I. Oliver 9-18-1869 (no return) Hy
Sanders, M. J. to A. R. Dunavant 3-24-1861 G
Sanders, M. J. to J. C. Adams 4-15-1859 (4-20-1859) F
Sanders, Mahulda to Elisha Mathis 8-22-1853 G
Sanders, Malinda C. to B. J. Baker 10-11-1849 Be
Sanders, Malisa to Robert C. Moore 10-31-1848 Ma
Sanders, Mariah P. to Charles B. Jester 8-5-1845 G
Sanders, Martha A. to John W. Best 8-8-1849 Sh
Sanders, Martha A. to W. I. Sanders 2-4-1867 O
Sanders, Martha B. to L. A. Childress 4-15-1865 (5-28-1865) T
Sanders, Martha B. to Timothy Gleason 3-5-1849 (3-13-1849) G
Sanders, Martha C. to Jeremiah Stephens 10-2-1855 (10-3-1855) O
Sanders, Martha E. to Levi Pettigrew 1-2-1862 Mn
Sanders, Martha H. P. to James Y. Hix 11-10-1856 (11-11-1856) G
Sanders, Martha J. (Mrs.) to Benjamin J. Williams 3-17-1847 G
Sanders, Martha J. to Levie J. Ward 7-30-1862 We
Sanders, Martha to Alexander Hale 7-22-1831 (7-?-1831) Hr
Sanders, Martha to Asberry Fletcher 4-6-1866 (4-10-1866) F B
Sanders, Martha to Ransom T. Worrell 5-14-1862 Hy
Sanders, Mary A. L. to M. C. Oakley 11-21-1859 (11-23-1859) G
Sanders, Mary Ann to John Bolin 8-31-1840 Hr
Sanders, Mary Ann to T. T. (F. F.)? (Dr.) Church 9-10-1853 (9-11-1853) O
Sanders, Mary Ann to William A. Webb 4-9-1841 (4-13-1841) Ma
Sanders, Mary E. to Henry F. Birdsong 3-19-1866 Ma
Sanders, Mary E. to Wm. T. Manning 3-19-1856 Sh
Sanders, Mary Jane to Ebenezer Best 7-7-1858 L
Sanders, Mary M. to Robert H. Lake 9-8-1828 Ma
Sanders, Mary to Hiram H. Stone 3-3-1827 Ma
Sanders, Mary to James Kilbreath 3-1-1855 Be
Sanders, Mary to Jas. Boon 3-18-1872 Hy
Sanders, Mary to John Warren 2-3-1844 Hn
Sanders, Mary to Solomon Morphis 11-21-1846 Ma
Sanders, Mary to Thomas J. Roberson 6-8-1882 (no return) L
Sanders, Minerva to Levi Adkinson 1-2-1856 (1-6-1856) O
Sanders, Miranda to Isaac Danner 5-12-1866 G
Sanders, Nancy C. to Thomas J. Cupples 6-19-1868 (7-5-1868) Ma
Sanders, Nancy S. to Jessee R. Chapman 5-8-1873 (5-14-1873) T
Sanders, Nancy W. to Samuel M. Stewart 1-1-1851 Sh
Sanders, Nancy to Henry Reynolds 9-27-1849 L
Sanders, Nancy to Jonathan J. Young 8-17-1843 Hr
Sanders, Nannie to Wm. H. Easly 11-25-1877 Hy
Sanders, Ortry to Reubin Palmer 12-12-1867 F B
Sanders, P. M. to J. W. Phelps 8-6-1873 Hy
Sanders, Partheny to J. B. Maxwell 2-22-1852 We
Sanders, Polly to Littleton Caple 1-8-1840 (1-9-1840) F
Sanders, Rachel (Mrs.) to A. A. Sanders 10-16-1864 Sh
Sanders, Rachel to Needham Raiford 8-13-1841 Hr
Sanders, Rebecca to Henry Lockard 11-5-1881 L

Sanders, Rusiah A. to V. R. Neal ?-?-1862? Mn
Sanders, Sarah J. to John W. Stout 7-31-1851 Cr
Sanders, Sarah to T. W. Vaughan 4-15-1865 (5-24-1865) T
Sanders, Selina C. to W. A. Archer 12-7-1859 G
Sanders, Sophia S. to William Russell 2-17-1855 (2-20-1855) O
Sanders, T. E. to William Kirk 10-18-1875 Dy
Sanders, Tibitha to Joseph Young 9-7-1847 Sh
Sanders, V. A. to K. M. Shepherd 12-24-1862 Mn
Sanders, Vick to Edmond Carney 9-1-1874 Hy
Sanders?, Ida to Thos. L. Robinson 10-28-1863 (10-29-1863) Sh
Sanderson, A. M. to W. J. Ruleman 9-8-1863 Sh
Sanderson, Elizabeth to John Gay 12-23-1839 Sh
Sanderson, Elizabeth to W. H. Cotton 4-5-1871 (4-11-1871) Dy
Sanderson, Jerusha A. G. to Stephen Hanson 10-14-1839 Sh
Sanderson, Lucinda to James Monroe Manning 2-3-1871 (2-5-1871) L
Sanderson, Martha Ann to James P. G. Garrett 1-3-1867 Ma
Sanderson, Martha Ann to W. M. Sulivine 3-22-1852 We
Sanderson, Nancy A. to C. J. Dowdy 3-1-1863 O
Sandford, Jennie (Mrs.) to W. E. Mitchum 12-13-1866 G
Sandford, Mary T. to Archibald O. Corum 12-11-1849 O
Sandford, Polly to William Connell 10-16-1834 (10-23-1834) G
Sandford, Sarah P. to Noah C. Smith 5-20-1850 (5-21-1850) G
Sandiford, Joanna R. to George L. Douglas 8-31-1835 Sh
Sandiford, Martha T. to Henry L. Moran 12-6-1836 Sh
Sandiford, Susan P. to Sylvester Bond 3-5-1839 Sh
Sandlin, Jennie to Marion Newten 3-3-1871 (no return) Hy
Sandlin, Mary Elizabeth to Joab Phillips 11-24-1857 O
Sandlin, Sallie to A. N. Wright 10-20-1874 (10-22-1874) Dy
Sandsberry, S. E. to A. D. Shaw 2-11-1874 L
Sane, M. to R. Wilson 12-14-1856 We
Sane, Nancy Jane to Josiah Cooper 5-3-1854 G
Sane?, Letta to Allen Wilkins 7-14-1870 G
Saners, Lucy A. to Wm. M. Burkett 1-25-1870 (1-26-1870) Ma
Sanford, Eliza J. to John S. Smithson 2-24-1853 Ma
Sanford, Eudora E. to William Hethcock 9-14-1858 (9-16-1858) G
Sanford, Fannie S. to James R. Alexander 12-8-1858 T
Sanford, Frances to Ed Davis 7-5-1881 L B
Sanford, Isabella P. to Samuel C. Bowman 5-18-1856 Hn
Sanford, Lucinda to William Taylor 7-7-1857 G
Sanford, Lureny to Wm. O. Lovelace 12-26-1853 (1-11-1854) Ma
Sanford, Lyra to F. M. Woodard 9-18-1866 O
Sanford, M. A. to W. C. Person 3-8-1876 L
Sanford, Maria to William Morrow 1-3-1879 L B
Sanford?, Mary A. to N. W. Lambeth 7-10-1865 (7-12-1865) F
Sanford, Mary E. to Henry C. Chiles 6-20-1861 O
Sanford, Mary Jane to John Uriah Green 4-7-1853 T
Sanford, Mary L. to Archibald O. Corum 12-11-1849 O
Sanford, Mary to G. W. Simmons 10-26-1865 O
Sanford, Mary to Shirley Fisher 2-14-1874 (2-15-1874) T
Sanford, Nancy to Joshua Weaver 8-28-1830 Ma
Sanford, Priscilla to George Goodram Townsend 11-10-1842 T
Sanford, Rosa L. to William C. Stevens 12-23-1871 (no return) L
Sanford, S. E. to C. D. Jones 8-18-1869 (8-19-1869) Dy
Sanford, Sarah Ann to Marcus C. Green 3-23-1848 T
Sanford, Sarah to Joseph A. Hardage 2-10-1846 Ma
Sanford, Susanah C. to James Hicks 8-15-1832 (8-16-1832) G
Sanford, 'Amanda? to Thomas? Hall 1-20-1869 (1-21-1869) T
Sanford, kSina to Thos. Aldridge 1-11-1866 (1-13-1866) T
Sangster, Anna E. to R. W. Sevier 2-23-1878 Hy
Sangster, Mary Jane to Calvin George 3-14-1872 Hy
Sangster, Mary to Albert Ervin 6-13-1867 Hy
Sangster, Mary to Stephen Odell 12-23-1865 Hy
Sangster, Sharlett to Frank King 1-2-1872 Hy
Sangueneth, May to Joseph Botto 6-10-1847 Sh
Sanling, Anabell to J. L. Haviall 7-10-1865 (7-11-1865) O
Sannoner, Maria B. (Mrs.) to Charles K. Hall 8-3-1864 Sh
Sansberry, Mary E. E. to John L. Morris 1-29-1873 L
Sanson, Ann Eliza to Saml. Winstead 12-12-1850 We
Santiford, Mary T. to James M. Massey 9-11-1838 Sh
Sappington, Cherry (Chessy?) to John Sammons 5-19-1866 G
Sappington, Elizabeth M. to Albert G. Yancy 8-10-1854 G
Sappington, Lucy H. to Walter D. Dabney 11-19-1829 Sh
Sappington, M. E. (Mrs.) to John W. Harris 11-10-1869 G
Sarah Ann, Pittman to James Poland 5-23-1867 (no return) Hy
Sarah E., Jordan to Alexander Philips 1-18-1866 Hy
Sarah E., Rogers to David Pike 12-26-1877 Hy
Sarah J., Fielder to Harrison Phillips 12-5-1872 (no return) Hy
Sarah J., Harrell to H. P. Pipkins 8-30-1870 Hy
Sarah J., Rutledge to Adison L. Rainey 9-16-1859 (no return) Hy
Sargeant, Emeline to Jacob Baughman 10-8-1857 Hy
Sargent, Elizabeth to A. N. Moore 6-7-1879 (no return) Dy
Sargent, Ellen to Green Bond 12-27-1872 Hy
Sargent, Mary Ann to David L. Smith 2-22-1848 F
Sarett, Atilla to A. Bruce 11-12-1840 Be
Sarrett, Mahaly to Gilford Sanders 1-5-1851 Be
Sarrett, Mary L. to H. G. Hollingsworth 11-21-1849 Be
Sarrett, Sarah to Edmond Durden 3-2-1856 Be

Brides

Sarrett, Susan Ann to W. L. Sarrett 4-25-1847 Be
Sartor, Mary B. to Woodson J. Sanders 1-2-1846 (1-5-1846) G
Sartor, Sarah Ann to Henry Hale 1-26-1853 G
Sassems, Nancy to George M. Kirk 8-9-1826 (8-10-1826) Hr
Sasser, Betsy A. to Ransom Stephens 11-26-1849 (12-3-1849) Hr
Sasser, Bettie to Isaac Cranbury 3-7-1868 (3-8-1871?) T
Sasser, Elizabeth to John Wamble 1-5-1852 (1-8-1852) Hr
Sasser, Mary Z. to Hillery H. Stanly 2-2-1847 Hr
Sasser, Milly to Calvin Rice 9-4-1867 L
Sasser, Sarah J. to Jas. M. Martin 2-16-1853 (no return) F
Satterfield, C. A. to William Donnan 2-28-1859 Hr
Satterfield, Caroline to Henry L. Thues 2-12-1859 (2-13-1859) Ma
Satterfield, Susan R. to C. T. Wood 6-27-1856 (6-28-1856) Sh
Saul, Elizabeth to Berry Futrell 7-25-1853 (7-28-1853) Hr
Sauls, Amanda to John C. Russell 1-13-1857 (1-14-1857) Hr
Sauls, Belison to Sidney Johnson 2-19-1852 (no return) Hn
Sauls, Eliza H. to Richard N. Williams 12-24-1844 F
Sauls, Frances to W. P. Busey? 11-5-1865 Hn
Sauls, Nancy to Gilbert Carter 2-?-1851 Cr
Saulsberry, L(ucy) E(mma) to W. J. McMackin 8-19-1873 (8-21-1873) L
Saunders(Launders?), Martha to John Goodwin 3-22-1828 Hr
Saunders, Abba to A. Fenel 7-7-1883 (7-8-1883) L
Saunders, Alfarnia to John C. McClelland 1-7-1847 L
Saunders, Amy to Jonah Robertson 8-25-1830 Sh
Saunders, Ann Eliza to Robert Richardson 8-8-1868 (8-9-1868) Dy
Saunders, Annie to G. H. Shirley 1-22-1861 (1-29-1861) Sh
Saunders, Antonia to Wm. S. McMahan 12-20-1855 Sh
Saunders, Betsey to Hiram Morrison 5-20-1825 Sh
Saunders, E. C. to A. C. Somerville 10-27-1875 (10-28-1875) L
Saunders, E. V. to John F. Parks 12-27-1859 Hr
Saunders, Elizabeth to Wyat Smith 3-22-1846 (no return) L
Saunders, F. C. to B. A. England 12-2-1859 (12-6-1859) F
Saunders, Florinda to W. W. Thomas 2-13-1861 Be
Saunders, Gyaura? to Geo. W. Pate 10-28-1874 F
Saunders, Julian to B. F. Kerby 4-11-1876 (4-23-1876) L
Saunders, L. C. to Samel J. Kellow 10-29-1874 Dy
Saunders, Letty to Thomas Brown 2-28-1834 Sh
Saunders, Luzene to James Harrison 10-27-1858 Hn
Saunders, M. C. to J. A. Baker 12-24-1846 Be
Saunders, Margaret to W. N. Wilson 4-25-1878 (4-28-1878) L
Saunders, Mary R. to W. N. Ditto 10-9-1866 (10-11-1866) Dy
Saunders, Mary to Wm. Allison 7-16-1843 Hr
Saunders, Mollie to William Wright 12-18-1872 T
Saunders, Nancy to ___ Langham (Langhorn 4-2-1829 Sh
Saunders, Nannie B. to Isaac Jones 5-11-1861 (5-12-1861) Sh
Saunders, Polly to Thomas N. Saunders 6-23-1857 Hr
Saunders, Rebeca to Gideon Brogdon 7-6-1883 (7-8-1883) L
Saunders, Rebecca F. to S. G. Rambo 2-24-1863 (2-26-1863) Dy
Saunders, Rhoda to Monroe Thomas 11-16-1866 G
Saunders, Sarah to Tom Cotton 2-10-1872 (2-11-1872) T
Saunders, Tabita to George B. Thompson 3-10-1831 (3-11-1831) Hr
Savage, Amanda to John Bohanon 11-18-1852 Hr
Savage, Caroline to Ab Covington 8-3-1876 Hy
Savage, Cynthia Ann to John C. Tims 9-23-1830 Hr
Savage, Elizabeth to John Turner 12-20-1860 Hr
Savage, Elizabeth to Wm. S. Liggett 12-18-1841 (12-26-1841) Hr
Savage, Jane to James Casey 8-4-1829 Hr
Savage, Martha to John Hinson 4-16-1849 Ma
Savage, Mary E. to James B. Hale 10-18-1851 (10-30-1851) Hr
Savage, Mary to Peter Hunnel 1-21-1836 Hr
Savage, Mattie to Henry Kirkpatrick 8-30-1875 (9-?-1875) L
Savage, Mattie to W. H. Prichard 12-18-1878 (12-24-1878) Dy
Savage, Mollie to J. T. Meadows 12-18-1883 (12-19-1883) L
Savage, Nancy to Moses B. Faris 10-26-1842 (10-28-1842) Hr
Savage, Paulina to W. P. Atkins 2-1-1886 (2-9-1886) L
Savage, Polly Ann to John Carley 9-26-1840 (9-27-1840) Hr
Savage, Sarah Jane to Jesse King 7-5-1841 (7-6-1841) Hr
Savage, Satira to W. D. Hankins 6-1-1861 (6-2-1861) Hr
Saveley, Rebecca to John L. Roberts 11-11-1858 Hr
Savington, Mary Jane to B. Wooston 12-20-1879 (no return) L B
Sawen, Saluda to James R. Miles 11-23-1858 We
Sawrie, Elizabeth to L. H. Dunaway 2-28-1866 (3-6-1866) Dy
Sawrie, Martha H. to James M. Collingsworth 11-20-1855 (11-22-1855) Ma
Sawyer, Adeline to Phillip Delph 9-18-1866 Dy
Sawyer, Agnis to Joe Murrell 3-30-1867 F B
Sawyer, Ann Rebecca Frances to Josiah B. Campbell 9-18-1857 (9-23-1857) L
Sawyer, Catherine to Haulditch Hipp 10-5-1859 (no return) L
Sawyer, Catherine to Wm. Foust 10-23-1867 (no return) Dy
Sawyer, Elizabeth to Benjamin Deason 9-21-1842 (9-22-1842) L
Sawyer, Elizabeth to John L. Thurmond 2-4-1867 (no return) L
Sawyer, Ella to George Pearce 11-23-1878 (11-23-1879) L B
Sawyer, Fanny to R. M. Johnson Benton 12-22-1869 (no return) Dy
Sawyer, Hannah to Daniel Foust 4-16-1872 Dy
Sawyer, Harriet to C. J. Fumbanks 2-1-1879 (2-2-1879) Dy
Sawyer, Idella to C. A. Rooks 2-17-1877 (2-18-1877) L
Sawyer, Lucinda to James King 7-29-1880 Dy
Sawyer, Manerva to Sandy Newbern 8-19-1874 L B

Sawyer, Marissa to W. H. Gooch 12-20-1869 Dy
Sawyer, Martha C. to W. G. M. Cole 2-16-1871 Dy
Sawyer, Mary Bell to Lewis Roberson 4-7-1870 L
Sawyer, Mary to Henry Colridge 2-28-1868 (no return) L B
Sawyer, Mary to John H. Kelly 10-15-1859 Sh
Sawyer, Puss to Phillip Bowling 12-25-1871 (12-27-1871) Dy
Sawyer, R. J. to E. G. Cribbs 11-18-1869 (11-19-1869) Dy
Sawyer, Rachel M. to R. B. Sharp 11-30-1866 (12-3-1866) L
Sawyer, Sarah E. to John W. Wright 11-30-1852 (12-2-1852) L
Sawyer, Sarah H. to J. M> Ferrell 12-15-1870 Dy
Sawyer, Susan to B. S. Greenlaw 2-9-1831 Sh
Sawyer, Susan to Jasper Newton Schrimsher 5-10-1862 Sh
Sawyer, Tennessee to Jimmie Rollins 8-1-1870 Dy
Sawyer?, Malinda to John Owen 12-26-1868 (12-27-1868) T
Sawyers, A. E. to Richard Brinkley 2-16-1842 (2-17-1842) F
Sawyers, Ann M. to Neill McCloud 1-15-1827 Sh
Sawyers, Elizabeth to Homer Osten 7-27-1834 Sh
Sawyers, Feribe to Asaph Green 1-2-1826 Sh
Sawyers, M. J. to George W. Shelton 10-13-1873 T
Sawyers, Mary J. M. to John Price 9-20-1827 Sh
Sawyers, Sallie to August Wakefield 4-17-1869 (4-18-1869) T
Sawyers, Susan A. to Andrew Smith 7-13-1872 (no return) Dy
Sawyers, virginia to George Sherrod 2-28-1866 (3-1-1866) F
Saxton, M. M. to J. W. T. Berry 3-1-1868 G
Saxton, Mary F. to Thomas Hapgood 4-20-1867 Ma
Sayers, C. H. to G. F. Sherrod 7-2-1868 (7-8-1868) F
Sayers, Elizabeth to William Greear 7-26-1855 We
Sayers, Josephine to Robert Murrell 2-12-1870 (no return) F B
Sayers, Lilie C. to H. R. Sherrod 4-5-1869 (4-15-1869) F
Sayles, Elizabeth to Elijah Hardin 5-5-1852 Be
Sayles, Elizabeth to Uriah Phifer 7-23-1846 Be
Sayles, F. J. to C. Wilder 1-11-1867 Cr
Sayles, Nancy to R. A. Hadbeck 2-1-1859 (no return) Cr
Scaggs, Mirina to George W. Peterson 12-1-1836 Sh
Scags, Jane (Mrs.) to L. P. Osborn 10-6-1864 (10-11-1864) Sh
Scale, L. A. to William A. Rives 11-17-1851 (no return) F
Scales, Aloda Ann to William Alderson 12-18-1833 O
Scales, Caledonia M. to H. F. Hamner 12-23-1834 Sh
Scales, Carie L. to W. H. January 5-14-1867 G
Scales, Elizabeth to John H. Jones 1-8-1846 Sh
Scales, Jane C. to Andrew Drummond 4-10-1845 Sh
Scales, Margaret to J.B. Parsons 3-13-1872 T
Scales, Sarah J. to Andrew J. Curtis 1-25-1870 T
Scales, Sarah to John Williams 12-24-1868 (12-25-1868) Cr
Scales, Susie T. to Jas. J. Coker 5-2-1870 (5-3-1870) Dy
Scales, Tabby to Ben Tatum 12-17-1873 Hy
Scalion, Elizabeth to Tho. Cunningham 1-8-1846 F
Scalions, Sarah Ann to Isaac Green Dodd 4-30-1870 (no return) Dy
Scallarn, Elizabeth to Pennell Kell 12-23-1829 (12-24-1829) G
Scalling, Maggie to John Herring 12-16-1863 Sh
Scallion, Lavina to William Gentry 1-9-1836 (1-10-1836) G
Scallions, Chartally to Wm. H. Taler 7-29-1841 F
Scallions, Fannie to T. W. Davis 12-25-1871 (12-26-1871) L
Scallions, Josephine to A. F. Gadis(Galdis-Galdy) 12-23-1876 (12-24-1876) L
Scallions, Louisa to P. G. Voss 10-8-1873 (10-9-1873) L
Scallions, Martha to Henry Evans 8-16-1867 (9-18-1867) Dy
Scally, Kate to John Johnson 4-20-1864 (4-23-1864) Sh
Scanerlin, Margaret to Thomas Walsh 5-10-1862 (5-11-1862) Sh
Scarborough, Amanda J. to Jordan A. Houston 11-14-1859 (11-15-1859) Ma
Scarborough, Caroline to J. A. Underwood 12-25-1838 (12-27-1838) O
Scarborough, Caroline to James E. Owens 11-17-1856 Hn
Scarborough, Martha C. to Timothy J. Acre 4-25-1844 We
Scarborough, Martha J. to Henry Watson 12-4-1860 We
Scarborough, Mary to A. M. Hudson 3-26-1846 We
Scarborough, A. J. to C. L. Barnard 9-28-1852 (no return) F
Scarbrough, H. M. to Alex Rousenbun 2-5-1845 Cr
Scarbrough, Harriet to Spencer Whitelow 10-27-1866 Hy
Scarbrough, Holly to Hugh McEwen 7-25-1843 Cr
Scarbrough, Sarah E. to S. E. Smith 2-4-1865 F
Scarlett, Mary E. to N. J. Peel 1-12-1871 (1-13-1871) Cr
Scates, Elizabeth S. W. to John M. Dickson 12-21-1843 Cr
Scates, Ellen to J. H. Hall 2-8-1855 We
Scates, J. E. to A. J. Garrison 12-12-1859 (12-13-1859) O
Scates, Judician Ann to James Moore 12-14-1845 Cr
Scates, Lavinia R. to C. H. Ferrell 4-7-1864 G
Scates, Marsha to Nelson Mitchum 12-5-1870 Cr
Scates, Martha E. to T. F. Caraway 5-3-1857 Cr
Scates, Polly A. to H. H. Blackwell 12-30-1866 (maybe 1870) G
Scates, Virginia to W. P. Richards 9-24-1873 (9-25-1873) O
Scearce, Katharine to James W. Bransford 3-12-1858 O
Schabel, Mary C. to James (Jno.) W. Moore 1-12-1867 (no return) Hy
Schad, Margeret to William Funke 2-3-1851 Sh
Schafer, Lena to Joseph Sternberger 5-31-1876 Hy
Schafner (Chofner), Catharine to John N. Miller 10-1-1855 (10-2-1855) Sh
Scheen, Martha Ann to Thomas Tims 9-11-1858 (9-12-1858) T
Schelli, Minna to John Seiber 5-12-1857 Sh
Scherer, Catharine to Mathias Keim 1-6-1860 (1-7-1860) Sh

Schindler, Clara to George F. Abel 10-28-1845 Sh
Schlatter, Mary to Henry Winkelman 8-31-1857 (9-1-1857) Sh
Schlosser, Christiana to Emil Wolff 12-26-1853 Sh
Schmidt, Elizabeth to A. Charles Schick 6-20-1860 (6-21-1860) Sh
Schneider, Catharine to Charles Arnold 8-23-1851 Sh
Schobert, Lisette to George Schade 10-31-1857 Sh
Schoesser, Christine to Wm. Remlen 2-4-1861 Sh
Schoolcraft?, Ella to J. A. Humes 12-31-1870 (1-1-1871) Dy
Schooley, Ellen F. to W. B. Russell 3-4-1869 (3-7-1869) T
Schottlin, Anna to John Geugel 9-12-1856 Sh
Schrader, Mary to B. H. Hengholt 5-20-1862 Sh
Schraeder, Mary to Adolph Miller 1-5-1858 (1-9-1858) Sh
Schrigs?, Louiza to William Elder 7-6-1861 (7-9-1861) T
Schroeder, Margaret to Emanuel Weiss 10-23-1849 Sh
Schuffisser, Susan to Fredrick Guthery (Gutlege) 1-21-1850 Sh
Schuhmann, Ernstine to D. Zweifel 1-25-1858 (1-26-1858) Sh
Schuldheis, Josephine to Frederick Ries 11-21-1862 (11-22-1862) Sh
Schully, Lizzie to Martin R. Wells 2-20-1861 Sh
Schultz, Elizabeth to Washington Quinton 12-1-1840 Hn
Schultz, Margaret to R. D. Imes 3-29-1850 Sh
Schums, Hannah to Joe Williams 12-26-1878 Hy
Schutt, Maria to Landon H. Smith 2-21-1851 (2-22-1851) Sh
Schwartz, Elizabeth to Edward Siebenman 1-14-1851 Sh
Schwartz, Fanny to Louis Ottenheimer 10-15-1853 (10-18-1853) Sh
Schweizer, Maria to J. H. Rohwer 12-3-1860 Sh
Scipper, Martha to Alexander Turner 12-9-1842 (12-10-1842) G
Scirratt, Emily to W. E. Scott 9-12-1861 Mn
Scmutz?, Rose to John P. Hoffman 7-9-1853 Sh
Scobey, Isabel to Sevraves Jones 1-29-1873 (1-30-1873) Dy
Scobey, M. A. to J. A. Smith 12-11-1878 (12-19-1878) Dy
Scobey, M. A. to J. S. Stockton 12-2-1878 (12-5-1878) Dy
Scobey, M. A. to M. A. Lightfoot 11-4-1875 (no return) Dy
Scobey, Parthena to L. C. Scobey 11-22-1871 (11-24-1871) Dy
Scobey, S. S. to B. F. Pace 11-1-1879 (11-4-1879) Dy
Scobey, Sophia E. to Jesse A. Green 8-1-1877 Dy
Scoby, Jane to Wm. Barker 1-7-1858 Cr
Scoby, Lucy E. to Saml. E. Huguley 12-13-1864 (12-14-1864) Dy
Scoby, M. E. to W. J. Scott 10-25-1860 Cr
Scoby, Martha J. to S. H. Moore 12-11-1865 (12-13-1865) Dy
Scoby, Mary to John H. Barlow 2-1-1864 (2-11-1864) Cr
Scoby, Mary to John H. Barlow 2-1-1864 (no return) Cr
Scoby, Melissa to W. W. Haynes 11-19-1866 (no return) Dy
Scoby, Nancy E. to E. M. Elsberry 9-7-1846 Cr
Scoby, P. A. to W. W. Haynes 12-30-1869 (no return) Dy
Scoby, T. A. to Jo. D. Pace 9-7-1869 (9-8-1869) Dy
Scoggins, Juda E. to John R. Harty 8-16-1855 Hr
Scoggins, Martha A. P. to Wm. D. Lucas 7-12-1851 (7-13-1851) Sh
Scoggins, Nancy E. to Thomas J. Mitchell 12-16-1858 (12-17-1858) Hr
Scoot, Harret? to John Y. McGuire 10-13-1845 (10-14-1845) Hr
Scot (Scat?), G. D. to L. R. Heslip 11-16-1860 G
Scot, Mollie to Thomas Warren 2-4-1885 (2-5-1885) L
Scot, Sarah to Allen Williams 3-13-1858 (3-14-1858) T
Scott, A. E. to Chas. E. McQuirter 2-10-1867 G
Scott, A. R. to A. B. Campbell 11-8-1857 Sh
Scott, Adra to Jas. H. Moore 6-18-1859 (6-19-1859) O
Scott, Allison E. to Wm. G. Adams 1-18-1839 Sh
Scott, Alsey to Lewis Smith 9-3-1854 Cr
Scott, Amanda L. to Noah Damon? 11-14-1849 (11-15-1849) Hr
Scott, Amanda to Charles Needham 10-30-1861 (no return) Hn
Scott, Amanda to Needham Charles 10-30-1861 (no return) Hn
Scott, Amanda to Priest Stanton 3-20-1873 Hy
Scott, Amelia J. to Wm. H. Neel 2-23-1856 (2-28-1856) Sh
Scott, Ann M. to Z. L. McLester 2-15-1859 Hn
Scott, Ann to Adam Lockhart 5-25-1861 (5-26-1861) Hr
Scott, Ann to Milton Gourdlock 9-4-1869 F B
Scott, Ann to William J. Acree 8-14-1859 We
Scott, B. A. to Shelton Long 10-8-___ (with 1870) G
Scott, Bettie A. to Elijah Falker 2-13-1872 G
Scott, Biddy (Mrs.) to Benjamin F. Bond 10-20-1858 (10-21-1858) Ma
Scott, Bridget to Charles Linahan 10-25-1856 (10-26-1856) Sh
Scott, C. R. to T. J. McMillen 9-10-1859 (10-10-1859) Hr
Scott, Carrie to Thomas C. Park (12-8-1857) Hr
Scott, Catharine E. to Wm. H. Leach 12-10-1860 T
Scott, Catharine R. to F. A. Enochs 8-30-1869 (9-16-1869) T
Scott, City to John Britten 11-8-1871? Hy
Scott, Cora to B. C. Gause 9-28-1869 Hy
Scott, E. C. to E. B. Nugent 11-28-1865 Hy
Scott, Eighty to James Farris 5-15-1848 Hr
Scott, Eliza (Mrs.) to B. L. Stewart 8-30-1869 (9-2-1869) L
Scott, Eliza K. to S. R. Starks 8-26-1847 Sh
Scott, Eliza to Andrew Brown 3-7-1872 T
Scott, Eliza to James W. Culpepper 2-11-1863 Hn
Scott, Elizabeth A. to William T. Mathis 7-12-1848 (7-16-1848) G
Scott, Elizabeth G. J. to Elisha Scott 7-12-1852 (7-29-1852) G
Scott, Elizabeth to Governor Belew 11-13-1850 (11-14-1850) G
Scott, Elizabeth to Samuel Grooms 2-11-1854 Hn
Scott, Elizabeth to Will Lockhart 12-23-1837 Hr

Scott, Elvira to Allen Stewart 7-18-1869 Hy
Scott, Emily to John Wesley Lloyd 12-23-1881 (12-24-1881) L
Scott, Emma E. to T. E. Voss 12-28-1880 (12-29-1880) L
Scott, Etha Jane to Richard H. Allen 12-4-1846 (12-6-1846) O
Scott, Evaline to R. H. Tosh 12-11-1870 (12-13-1870) Cr
Scott, Fanny E. to R. H. Clark 7-14-1868 G
Scott, Frances to B. F. Hurley 12-8-1863 Wn
Scott, Frances to Bailey Gause 2-28-1874 (no return) Hy
Scott, Frances to J. G. Tosh 3-1-1866 Cr
Scott, Hannah to Samuel E. Hays 2-6-1835 Hr *
Scott, Hannah to Samuel E. Hays 2-6-1836 (2-11-1836) Hr
Scott, Harriet H. to Richard W. Green 5-8-1839 (5-15-1839) F
Scott, Jane (Mrs.) to Joseph A. Owen 2-3-1857 (2-4-1857) Sh
Scott, Jane to A. A. Berryhill 12-16-1849 Cr
Scott, Jane to Henry Halliburton 2-14-1874 L B
Scott, Jennie H. to John W. Kirkpatrick 12-15-1879 L
Scott, Jennie to Tom Dallas 9-29-1877 (no return) L B
Scott, Jinnie to Alex Haughey 12-23-1874 Hy
Scott, Joanna L. to Joseph M. Proctor 10-26-1868 F
Scott, Joanna to George Oldham no dates (not executed) Hy
Scott, Julia Ann to Sterling Carlton 1-3-1867 (1-6-1867) F B
Scott, Julia to Sterling Boment 9-2-1870 G B
Scott, Kate to Thomas Seymore 1-1-1862 Sh
Scott, L. A. to D. P. Jenkins 1-21-1861 (1-24-1861) Cr
Scott, L. J. to Richard Tredway 9-21-1869 (1-1-1870) T
Scott, Levina to James Pettit 8-15-1844 G
Scott, Liney(Siney) to John Freeman 4-4-1831 (4-14-1831) Hr
Scott, Lirzah to Robt. A. H. McCorkle 12-1-1828 (12-4-1828) G
Scott, Louisa to John W. Sellers 9-27-1839 Cr
Scott, Lucinda to Joseph R. Edwards 1-2-1833 O
Scott, Lucy to T. J. Tyas 4-18-1878 L B
Scott, Lussella to Wm. R. Sellers 6-16-1858 Cr
Scott, Luticia to Robert Lynn 3-17-1852 Sh
Scott, M. A. to T. J. Oliver 1-8-1861 G
Scott, Maggie A. to J. G. King 10-22-1866 (10-4?-1866) F
Scott, Mahala to John Rector 1-18-1875 (1-19-1875) L
Scott, Malvina sims to J. J. H. Lee 12-2-1847 Sh
Scott, Malvina to John Williams 7-7-1866 (no return) F B
Scott, Margaret Ann to P. B. Land 5-11-1848 Sh
Scott, Margaret to Asa Nix 11-28-1863 Sh
Scott, Margaret to Philip B. Lane 7-10-1846 Sh
Scott, Margarette to Lebanon D. Mathis 4-18-1841 G
Scott, Martha (Mrs.) to Henry White 10-30-1850 Sh
Scott, Martha J. to Hugh M. Brooks 1-16-1856 Sh
Scott, Martha L. to J. C. Thompson 7-13-1857 O
Scott, Mary A. to Anderson McKinney 3-28-1854 Cr
Scott, Mary A. to Granvill H. Butler 2-6-1872 Cr
Scott, Mary A. to Henry P. Raney (Roney-Ramy?) 6-2-1852 L
Scott, Mary E. to G. W. Earnhart 11-13-1867 (11-14-1867) F
Scott, Mary E. to William C. Dyall 3-26-1864 Sh
Scott, Mary E. to Wm. G. Parker 6-14-1861 Hr
Scott, Mary J. to John Belote 12-10-1858 (12-14-1858) Sh
Scott, Mary Jane to John Swailes 2-18-1851 (2-20-1851) Sh
Scott, Mary L. to Thomas Summers 3-19-1865 Be
Scott, Mary to John Ballew 3-2-1863 Cr
Scott, Mary to John Ballew 3-2-1863 (no return) Cr
Scott, Mary to John Thompson 3-6-1872 (3-10-1872) O
Scott, Mary to John Waller 10-11-1849 Hr
Scott, Mary to William Dunlap 4-23-1866 G
Scott, Matilda to Jason Springer 11-12-1853 Cr
Scott, Matilda to W. T. Bennett 6-15-1856 Cr
Scott, Melissa J. to W. R. Acuff 7-25-1882 (8-1-1882) L
Scott, Mildred E. to Washington Wallingford 10-9-1859 Hn
Scott, Minnie to George Tucker 7-1-1867 (7-6-1867) T
Scott, Minnie to William Green 2-20-1871 L B
Scott, Mollie to George Prestidge 7-21-1870 G
Scott, Mollie to Thomas Lawrence 8-9-1870 G B
Scott, Nancy to Elisha Bevill 6-15-1853 Hn
Scott, Nancy to S. H. Straughn 4-24-1861 Sh
Scott, Nellie to Amos Roach 3-15-1842 Cr
Scott, Nelly to H. L. Parker 1-14-1874 (no return) Hy
Scott, Norah to Thomas Bates 12-23-1873 (12-24-1873) L B
Scott, Ophelia Ann to Samuel Tozier 7-18-1861 Sh
Scott, Paralee R. to George P. Boyd 2-1-1857 We
Scott, Patsy to John Cleveland 10-27-1873 (no return) Hy
Scott, Rachal to Henry Mutton? 10-17-1876 Hy
Scott, Rachel to Jeff Wardlaw 12-27-1879 (12-28-1879) L B
Scott, Rebecca H. to Samuel White 6-28-1842 (6-29-1842) Hr
Scott, Rebecca to Samuel P. Ingram 11-6-1841 (11-12-1841) Hr
Scott, Reubecca to Isham House 1-25-1844 We
Scott, Rutha to Wm. W. Pharris 9-1-1861 O
Scott, S. R. to Thomas Kirkpatrick 3-7-1871 L
Scott, Sallie to Ira Moore 5-24-1859 Sh
Scott, Sally to Thomas Morris 8-12-1839 Cr
Scott, Sarah E. to John V. Morton 4-27-1853 G
Scott, Sarah E. to William H. Terry 12-16-1852 Ma
Scott, Sarah L. to John A. Rodgers 4-21-1858 (4-22-1858) G

Scott, Sarah T. to Joseph B. James 9-6-1849 Sh
Scott, Sarah to Hardy Sellers 1-2-1840 Cr
Scott, Sarah to James Osbourn 9-7-1856 O
Scott, Seragh Jane to H. H. Falls 10-27-1852 (10-28-1852) Hr
Scott, Susan E. to J. W. McDowell 9-12-1853 Cr
Scott, Susan Jane to James W. Britton 9-21-1854 (9-23-1854) O
Scott, Susan Jane to Wm. M. Springer 9-18-1847 Cr
Scott, Susan to Enoch Gaskins 12-10-1867 (12-24-1867) Ma
Scott, Susan to George Currie 11-3-1866 Hy
Scott, T. C. to J. L. Trimble 2-26-1873 (2-27-1873) Dy
Scott, Vernelia to A. J. Langum 12-21-1844 (no return) F
Scott, Virginia M. to T. M. Downing 9-10-1850 (9-11-1850) F
Scott, Virginia T. to R. C. Wright 6-7-1850 Sh
Scott, Virginia to D. P. Carney 11-4-1867 (11-5-1867) F
Scrape, Eliza E. to Richard McGee 2-19-1846 G
Scrape, Susan M. to Samuel W. Hatchett 10-21-1852 G
Scripson?, Abigal to John McPherson 2-8-1834 Hr
Scritchfield, Sinia to Wm. Lovill 6-2-1848 Sh
Scrobrough, Mary J. to G. L. Smith 8-4-1866 (8-5-1866) Cr
Scroggins, Ella to Phillip Rogers 10-14-1880 Dy
Scroggins, Matilda to Nash Jones 7-24-1875 (7-25-1875) Dy B
Scrogin, M. A. L. P. to A. H. LeCoq 5-14-1857 Sh
Scrope, S. E. to W. C. McGee 4-25-1861 G
Scruggs, Amanda M. to Loyd Ford 11-22-1837 Sh
Scruggs, Ann Eliza to David Woodward 10-20-1840 Sh
Scruggs, Clara Anne to George W. Myrick 4-14-1844 Sh
Scruggs, Elizabeth M. to Wm. Boggan 4-16-1841 Sh
Scruggs, Linton B. to James Ford 11-11-1836 Sh
Scruggs, Lucy A. to R. C. Smith 11-28-1867 Hn
Scruggs, M. P. to J. B. Utley 5-30-1873 (no return) Cr
Scruggs, Maria (Mrs.) to George W. Truehart 12-5-1850 Sh
Scruggs, Martha B. to G. W. Chandler 11-29-1869 G
Scruggs, Mary W. to James M. Key 7-14-1836 Sh
Scruggs, Mary to Martin Noble 3-12-1840 Sh
Scruggs, Mary to Middleton Black 1-2-1849 Sh
Scruggs, Mollie E. to W. H. Horton 2-2-1860 Sh
Scurlock, Kate L. to William D. Clark 5-24-1869 Ma
Sea, Eliza to L. M. Watson 10-9-1864 Mn
Seaborn, Selina to Nathan Peeples 9-13-1867 (9-15-1867) Ma
Seahorn, Rebecca L. to John F. Fouth 3-30-1867 Ma
Seaier, Margaret A. to F. T. Keisacker 3-1-1853 Sh
Seals, M. A. to H. M. Thomason 8-14-1869 (no return) Dy
Searcey, Angeline to E. Amix 11-7-1874 (11-8-1874) L
Searcey, Clara to H. W. Dudley 8-10-1875 Dy
Searcey, Elizabeth E. to John W. Smith 12-4-1866 (12-5-1866) T
Searcey, Nancy Jane to Wylie Stevens 6-3-1855 T
Searcy, A. A. to a. J. M. Amick 3-16-1875 (3-17-1875) Dy
Searcy, Ann Eliza to Moody Passmore 1-2-1854 Ma
Searcy, Malissa to W. A. Ray 8-14-1861 Hn
Searcy, Mary D. to B. F. Mitchel 5-19-1866 (5-25-1866) T
Searcy, Mary Frances to J. A. Turner 9-13-1868 G
Searcy, Nancy I. to Franklin Worel 3-4-1867 O
Sears, Jennie A. to J. S. Rogers 12-11-1868 (no return) Hy
Sears, Lucy Ann to William F. Provow 10-25-1850 Hn
Sears, Martha to Creed F. Greer 8-8-1866 Hn
Seat (Seah?), Mattie F. to John S. Grider 12-27-1860 Sh
Seat, A. R. (Mrs.) to T. H. Marshall 11-2-1867 (not executed) G
Seat, Amanda R. to William A. Johnston 1-5-1859 G
Seat, Angeline J. L. to James H. Dyson 9-29-1834 (10-10-1834) G
Seat, Elizabeth to William Fulgham 3-13-1828 G
Seat, Idortha S. A. to Thos. W. Jordian 3-8-1841 (3-11-1841) G
Seat, Mary Jane to A. J. Williams 9-29-1840 (10-1-1840) G
Seat, Paralee to Peyton Cooper 11-22-1868 G B
Seate(Scott?), Elizabeth to George Pervis 6-29-1838 Hr
Seaton, Ally M. to Joseph Burleson 10-8-1827 (11-1-1827) Hr
Seaton, Elizabeth V. to David Williams 9-26-1834 Hr
Seaton, Margaret to S. W. Mathis 4-23-1861 Hn
Seaton, Minerva Jane to Aaron Burleson 8-21-1838 (8-23-1838) Hr
Seaton, Sarah G. to A. G. Barrett 4-13-1832 (4-16-1832) Hr
Seats, Susan to Lawrence Butler 11-15-1860 (11-18-1860) Ma
Seavey, Cordilia to Edward Canfield Sterling 9-7-1850 Sh
Seawell, L. A. (Mrs.) to Silas Wood 10-13-1845 Sh
Seawright, America A. to Eli A. Brundidge 8-3-1865 Hn
Seawright, F. E. to T. P. Snow 2-17-1864 (no return) Hn
Seawright, Margaret to William McFadden 3-23-1854 (no return) Hn
Seawright, Nancy to Jasper N. Burnett 4-3-1851 Hn
Seawright, Sidney M. to James E. Diggs 8-8-1860 Hn
Seay, Ida R. to Nelson I. Hess, jr. 11-16-1867 (11-20-1867) Ma
Seay, Lucinda to Nathan Usrey 4-9-1846 Sh
Seay, Lucy to William Harvey 5-8-1828 Sh
Seay, Malissa A. to Thomas H. Parton 7-7-1867 Hn
Seay, Martha Jane to Robt. J. Murphy 11-6-1852 (11-7-1852) T
Seay, Rebecca to John Mann 2-6-1851 Sh
Sebastian, Martha Ann to Kimbro Hornsby 4-6-1833 Hr
Sebastin, Hetta Eliza to Headly Polk 6-3-1845 Hr
Sedberry, Catharine to Burrie T. Williams 2-28-1856 Cr
Sedberry, Mary A. to Legvi Taylor 8-17-1854 Cr

Sedberry, Mary C. to James J. Hale 6-23-1855 Cr
Sedberry, Susan to John C. Taylor 8-6-1854 Cr
Sedberry, Una to C. Butler 10-14-1855 Cr
Sedbury, S. B. to W. H. Perkins 10-4-1869 G
See, E. J. to James Fowler 2-22-1853 Hn
Seebis (Seckis), Celina to Emanuel Levy 7-22-1850 Sh
Seigler, Catherine to Hugh McClellan 8-6-1839 Sh
Seigler, Charity A. to William J. Whitehead 1-13-1848 Sh
Seitz, Clarrissa to F. Beurer 4-10-1858 Sh
Selby, Adamie (Mrs.) to B. Richmond 5-21-1851 (6-9-1851) Sh
Seldon, Mahala W. to Daniel V. Corbitt 2-24-1853 Sh
Seles?, Rebecca to Daniel Mathews 3-6-1856 Cr
Self, Deller M. to Levi T. Heath 4-6-1863 (4-8-1863) Dy
Self, Elizabeth to J. C. Park 2-1-1847 Be
Self, M. E. to J. B. Linton 7-13-1874 Hy
Self, M. to Anthony Brinkley 10-10-1847 Cr
Self, Mary Elizabeth to Robert J. Norman 12-12-1849 G
Self, Mary S. to J. A. McClish 9-30-1871 (no return) Hy
Self, Mary to Willoughby Self 4-2-1833 G
Self, Milly A. to William S. Brambalow 10-18-1849 G
Self, N. J. to N. W. McCoy 12-23-1875 Dy
Sellars, Elizabeth to Ruben W. Biggs 3-2-1830 (3-22-1830) G
Sellars, Kisiah to Thomas M. Watson 6-29-1835 (7-2-1835) G
Sellars, Matilda Cela Ann to Samuel Dunlap 9-14-1848 G
Sellars, Nancy E. to H. T. Springer 12-7-1871 (no return) Cr
Sellars, Nancy to Andrew Blair 10-8-1831 (10-9-1831) G
Sellars, Nancy to Andrew Blair 10-8-1835 G
Sellers, Clementine to R. B. Springer 12-9-1865 (12-19-1865) Cr
Sellers, Elizabeth Ann to Thos. K. Brown 2-3-1847 (2-4-1847) Hr
Sellers, Elizabeth to Burell Sellers 4-30-1840 Sh
Sellers, Henrietta L. to James Townsend 6-3-1871 (6-11-1871) Cr
Sellers, Henrietta to Parsons Vincent, jr. 3-28-1838 Cr
Sellers, Henrietta to William Simpson 1-29-1861 Cr
Sellers, Isabel L. to R. H. Davis 12-11-1868 (12-15-1868) Cr
Sellers, Kerah H. to Thomas A. Thompson 7-29-1834 (7-31-1834) Hr
Sellers, Kezier? to William McKey 10-18-1847 (10-19-1847) Hr
Sellers, Kizza to Charles Forrester 10-23-1839 G
Sellers, Malinda to Sollomon W. Harpole 12-27-1842 O
Sellers, Martha E. to Nick G. Joyner 2-7-1866 (2-8-1866) Cr
Sellers, Nancy E. to Charles H. Tidrow 6-10-1851 (6-11-1851) G
Sellers, Nancy to Elisha Easterwood 12-27-1837 G
Sellers, Polly to Anson Brown 12-30-1835 (12-31-1835) Hr
Sellers, Sarah C. to John B. Walker 4-5-1844 (no return) F
Sellers, Zilpha to John W. P. Wilson 10-4-1838 Cr
Sellers?, Mariah to James Alford 3-31-1847 (4-1-1847) Hr
Selph, Ann M. to William R. Sparkman 8-30-1847 (9-1-1847) G
Selph, Elizabeth to David Gray 2-17-1855 (2-18-1855) O
Selph, Louisa E. to W. H. Davis 12-13-1849 L
Selvidge, Martha E. to James B. Patterson 8-30-1865 G
Selvidge, Mary F. to W. N. Pate 10-9-1867 G
Semons, Margaret to Henry Harrison 9-1-1870 G
Semons, Nancy Ann to Frunler Parker 10-14-1848 (10-15-1848) G
Semore, S. I. to James H. Drigers 1-18-1843 (no return) Cr
Semore, Silva to William McDanniel 7-6-1878 (no return) Hy
Seniago, Rosa to M. Lavezzo 4-16-1860 (4-22-1860) Sh
Senn, F. to F. Bachele 6-2-1855 (6-7-1855) Sh
Senn, Mary to Peter Steinbrecker 10-2-1858 Sh
Senonah, Merinda to James B. Taylor 7-30-1832 Sh
Sensemon, Malinda to Hazael Hewit 12-22-1849 (12-25-1849) Ma
Senter (Smith?), Julia to James Dawson 10-13-1866 G
Senter, Amanda E. to John W. Rust 3-29-1863 G
Senter, Eliza C. to William N. Adair 1-1-1855 (1-4-1855) G
Senter, Elizabeth to Daniel Bancroft 8-22-1840 (8-23-1840) Ma
Senter, Emma to Moses Mitchell 2-4-1863 G
Senter, Fannie to Wm. D. Thompson 12-11-1866 (12-12-1866) Ma
Senter, Frances to Micajah Fly 9-15-1846 (9-17-1846) G
Senter, Martha A. to Robert D. Boon 10-20-1856 Ma
Senter, Martha J. to D. H. Woldridge 1-24-1860 (1-25-1860) G
Senter, Martha Jane to William H. Rust 9-6-1849 G
Senter, Mary Jane to Samuel G. Turner 12-6-1852 (12-7-1852) Ma
Senter, Mary M. to A. L. Fulghum 12-9-1867 (12-10-1868?) G
Senter, Mattie E. to J. T. Hill 12-22-1868 G
Senter, Nannie M. to S. M. Raney 12-8-1869 G
Senter, Rebecca F. to J. H. Fields 9-8-1861 G
Seratt, Polly to Thomas Geylard 8-1-1828 (8-3-1828) G
Serconas, W. C. to J. H. Ethridge 10-8-1864 Cr
Sergant, Martha Ann to John Vincen 4-20-1873 Hy
Sergant, Susan to George Mitchell 1-26-1874 Hy
Serratt, Elizabeth M. to John N. Bell 5-14-1840 G
Serratt, Elizabeth to Alex C. Ridgway 6-17-1837 (6-18-1837) G
Serratt, Elizabeth to Alex C. Ridgway 6-17-1839 G
Sesselman, Ursulina to Louis Willheit 11-3-1859 Sh
Sessem, S. E. to J. L. Brown 10-15-1861 Sh
Setten, Mollie to James Akin 11-11-1876 (11-12-1876) L
Setters, Louise E. to Wm. H. Gwin 12-18-1854 Cr
Settle, Mary to William B. Cole 3-5-1840 Hn
Settle, Mary to Wm. W. Anderson 3-16-1866 (no return) F

Settle, Susan E. to D. M. Padin 7-19-1849 F
Settles, Mary to Vincent Horn 3-7-1843 Be
Settles, Nancy C. to Hosea Springer 11-8-1865 (11-8-1865) Cr
Seven, Elizabeth to Thomas R. Curlin 5-19-185? (with 1851) O
Severe, Betheny to Alfred Gleason 7-22-1828 Ma
Severe, Elizabeth to Leander C. Holt 10-14-1830 Ma
Sevier, Annie E. to Norris J. Wiggin 1-19-1864 Sh
Sevier, Elizabeth to James Wilson 10-13-1841 Ma
Sevier, Jane L. to James A. Dickson 1-29-1849 Cr
Sevier, M. C. to T. M. Potter 10-18-1870 Hy
Sevier, Martha to Thomas P. Parn (Parm-Parir) 10-15-1850 We
Sevier, Mary to Stynax Jones 8-28-1873 Hy
Sevier, Sarah E. to Richd. Aiken 12-13-1851 (no return) F
Sevier, Sarah J. to E. H. Clay 4-10-1860 (no return) Hy
Sevier, Sarah to Reubin Walker 2-21-1872 Hy
Sevier?, Matilda to James Walls 10-24-1866 Dy
Seviere, Susie to Aden Whitson 1-5-1874 (1-8-1874) L
Sewall, Mary M. to Henry Goad 12-23-1841 Ma
Seward, Emily W. to J. B. Thomas 3-23-1858 (3-26-1858) Sh
Seward, Jenny to John Davis 8-17-1870 G B
Seward, Julian to J. A. House 11-15-1838 F
Seward, Leona J. to Albert Smith 7-9-1869 G B
Seward, Loucretia to Dempsey M. Sanderlin 8-22-1848 Sh
Seward, Martha Ellen to G. W. Bragg 4-11-1869 G
Seward, Mary to Daniel W. Canada 1-13-1852 (1-27-1852) Sh
Seward, Susan E. to W. W. Sanderlin 12-24-1850 Sh
Sewel, Judy A. to Dewey H. Hankins 11-7-1846 Hn
Sewell, Adeline to Thomas Lyon 6-20-1870 (7-3-1870) Ma
Sewell, Caroline to John Terry 12-13-1865 Mn
Sewell, Elizabeth C. to Milton A. Henderson 11-9-1854 Ma
Sewell, Martha Parthenia to Lewis C. Cox 11-16-1867 (11-27-1867) Ma
Sewell, Mary A. to George W. Sipes 4-25-1861 Mn
Sewell, Nancy Ann to Enoch R. Walker 11-18-1868 (11-19-1868) Ma
Sewell, Nancy to Henry Smith 9-11-1865 Mn
Sewell, Narcissa to Thomas Warren 7-27-1862 Mn
Sewell, Rachel to Franklin Lambert 11-15-1855 Ma
Sewell, Reuben to Martha A. Johnson 9-29-1841 Ma
Sexton, Catharine to John Gunn 11-24-1855 (11-26-1855) Sh
Sexton, Eliza C. to Eli Rainer 1-18-1854 (1-19-1854) Hr
Sexton, Eliza Jane to Christopher C. Butler 3-8-1851 G
Sexton, Elizabeth to Coleby Randle 5-6-1851 Hn
Sexton, Elizabeth to Jessee T. Goff 4-11-1848 Hr
Sexton, Emily to David Rhodes 3-11-1841 Cr
Sexton, Geraldine H. Ann to George W. Gunn 3-2-1857 Hn
Sexton, Hannah L. to George J. Gardner 11-4-1856 (11-6-1856) L
Sexton, Jane to Francis McLain 7-25-1866 (8-20-1866) T
Sexton, Jerusha A. to Saml. J. Doyle 1-7-1860 (1-10-1860) Hr
Sexton, M. A. to J. W. Hood 11-17-1860 (11-18-1860) Hr
Sexton, M. J. to David C. Simons 3-5-1857 O
Sexton, Malinda to Mansel Cooper 4-25-1844 (5-28-1844) T
Sexton, Margaret to Richard B. McDougal 3-11-1858 We
Sexton, Martha E. to E. A. Butler 10-12-1850 (10-13-1850) G
Sexton, Martha E. to Gilbert A. West 9-2-1848 (9-10-1848) G
Sexton, Mary A. to Joseph Beleau (Belew) 2-18-1850 Sh
Sexton, Mary E. to John Higdon 5-19-1847 Cr
Sexton, Mary to William Patterson 3-13-1839 (3-14-1839) G
Sexton, Melinda to Josiah Davis 4-23-1838 (no return) Hn
Sexton, Nancy C. to Thos. W. Noel 2-26-1859 (2-27-1859) G
Sexton, Nancy to John Blakely 9-20-1863 G
Sexton, Nannie to G. K. Ballard 4-27-1885 (4-29-1885) L
Sexton, Sarah Ann to E. C. Butler 9-14-1848 G
Sexton, Sarah E. to Samuel J. Hill 12-28-1862 G
Sexton, Sarah E. to William D. Summers 8-8-1854 Hn
Sexton, Sarah J. to William H. Bells 1-3-1849 (1-4-1849) G
Sexton, Sarah to Nathan Ramsay 2-10-1859 Hn
Sexton, Tennessee to Johnithan Dawson 6-10-1847 (6-15-1847) G
Sexton, Winnie to R. H. Cunningham 2-26-1882 (2-28-1882) L
Seymore, Caroline to H. W. Walker 2-7-1861 G
Seymore, Elizabeth to Wm. H. Hill 8-23-1847 Cr
Seymore, Mary to M. H. Travis 12-16-1866 G
Seymore, Nancy to Josiah A. Hill 2-13-1845 (no return) Cr
Seymore, Nannie to G. G. Walker 12-21-1868 (12-22-1868) Cr
Seymore, Ritter to Adam Brown 2-22-1869 (2-28-1869) Cr
Seymour, Ella to Wm. Braswell 7-19-1866 (7-21-1866) F B
Seymour, Isabella to B. P. Garrison 4-4-1864 F
Seymour, Kate to William Weston 2-3-1863 Sh
Seymour, M. J. to J. N. Wall 4-27-1853 F
Shabel, Ann C. to Theodore Betts 5-15-1849 Sh
Shackelford, Liza to Ned Wiggins 5-18-1866 (no return) F B
Shackelford, Lucinda to Henry Clay Cole 5-14-1866 (no return) F B
Shackelton, Jane to John F. Cole 4-3-1866 (no return) Dy
Shackleford, Celia to John Mathews 3-23-1867 (no return) F B
Shackleford, Emily to Adam Heaslett 11-15-1867 (no return) F B
Shackleford, Harriett to Alexander Crawford 4-8-1828 Hn
Shackleford, Mary A. M. E. to William C. Morton 11-13-1856 Hn
Shackleton, Amanda to Jonathan Nichols 4-28-1866 (no return) Dy
Shackleton, E. S. to James T. Green 6-26-1875 (6-27-1875) Dy
Shackleton, M. E. to J. D. Crawford 1-19-1876 Dy
Shackleton, Martha to Alfred T. Nichols 4-26-1870 (4-27-1870) Dy
Shackleton, Mary A. to J. W. H. Oakley 10-24-1871 (10-25-1871) Dy
Shad, Mattie to Hiram Richardson 12-15-1869 (12-16-1869) Cr
Shad, Rachel to Nelson Caldwell 5-10-1870 (5-14-1870) Cr
Shade, Mollie to William Adams 1-11-1871 Hy
Shadwick, Mary Ann to James H. Ramsey 3-5-1848 Hn
Shadwick, Mary to P. McShane 11-7-1868 (11-8-1868) Cr
Shadwick, Sarah to Edmund Spain 12-18-1845 Hn
Shafner, A. P. to R. H. Billoate 9-1-1858 Cr
Shafter, Sarah C. to Levi Couch 12-1-1849 (no return) F
Shahon, Lizzie to J. S. Moore ?-?-1867 (4-28-1867) Dy
Shain, Ann to J. A. Gilliland 10-26-1865 G
Shain, E. M. to Silas B. Honey 9-28-1843 Sh
Shain, Margarette to Samuel Hicks 1-5-1856 (1-8-1856) G
Shaine, Mary to James Coker 3-22-1844 (3-23-1844) F
Shaller, Maria C. to Henry Frick 10-10-1842 Sh
Shanahan, Mary A. to Alpheus W. Reeves 4-22-1852 Sh
Shanahan, Mary to Tim Ryan 9-5-1851 (9-7-1851) Sh
Shane, Eliza W. to P. H. Jackson 1-3-1859 (1-4-1859) G
Shane, Elizabeth to Benjamin M. Adair 2-14-1833 G
Shane, Elvira A. to E. M. Witt 11-24-1860 G
Shane, Hannah to Edmond Moore 3-22-1867 G
Shane, Julia Ann Jane to Greenwood Booth 8-29-1849 (8-30-1849) G
Shane, M. L. to James G. McKelvey 8-30-1860 G
Shane, Martha E. to J. F. Butler 9-18-1840 G
Shane, Martha to Daniel Stephison 11-7-1831 G
Shane, Mary E. to James P. Arnold 1-5-1852 (1-6-1852) G
Shane, Mary to Henry Shaw 3-18-1867 G
Shane, Nancy A. to John Umsted 6-2-1858 (12-7-1858) G
Shane, Nancy E. to Caleb H. Covington 12-16-1850 (12-17-1850) G
Shane, Nancy to David Holt 4-13-1846 (4-16-1846) G
Shane, Sarah J. to Alexander M. House 12-17-1855 (12-20-1855) G
Shankle, Amanda to William H. Billings 7-17-1868 (7-19-1868) T
Shankle, Bettie to J. W. Reynolds 9-26-1878 (9-27-1878) Dy
Shankle, Eliza P. to John Steel 11-15-1848 Cr
Shankle, Ellen to G. L. Huffman 11-20-1871 (11-21-1871) T
Shankle, Fannie to Am? Downing 1-17-1867 T
Shankle, Franky Jane to William Joseph Roe 8-17-1867 (8-18-1867) T
Shankle, Laura L. to Isaac S. Lee 6-29-1880 L
Shankle, Margaret J. to George W. Whitworth 10-17-1858 Hn
Shankle, Margaret to John Puckett 12-20-1858 (no return) Hn
Shankle, Mary E. to William White 3-3-1869 Cr
Shankle, Nancy to Munro Kelley 8-12-1873 T
Shankle, Sarah to Isaac Wimberley 11-8-1838 Hn
Shankle, V. L. to James G. Riley 1-1-1866 T
Shanklin, L. M. to V. C. Parrish 7-16-1857 We
Shanklin, Mary J. to Colman Brann 10-22-1857 We
Shanklin, Mary to Thomas List 3-3-1830 O
Shanklin, S. A. to John Y. Parrish 12-23-1861 (no return) We
Shanks, Cassandra P. to M. B. Frierson 9-28-1848 Sh
Shanks, Ellen H. to Thomas H. Allen 6-30-1847 Sh
Shannon, Caroline to Valdura Sandlin 12-17-1859 Hy
Shannon, Joanna to James Henry 10-18-1859 Sh
Shannon, Mary to Marcus Wright 8-27-1840 Sh
Shannors, Mary to Geo. Berdsell 6-7-1864 Sh
Shapard, Sally to Nick Ware 7-5-1873 Hy
Shar, Eleaner J. (Mrs.) to Calvin D. Hart 1-17-1863 (1-18-1863) Sh
Sharber, Fannie P. to W. N. Porter 8-1-1870 Dy
Sharkman, E. C. to J. P. Armstrong 12-23-1866 G
Sharp, Adaline L. to David T. Holloway 7-24-1855 T
Sharp, Ann Jane to James M. Barrett 4-3-1861 T
Sharp, Annie to G. A. Debow 10-6-1860 Sh
Sharp, Armedia A. to Charles J. Maxwell 9-21-1852 (no return) F
Sharp, Caroline S. to John P. Henry 2-18-1858 Sh
Sharp, Caroline to Daniel Robinson 1-15-1868 G B
Sharp, Catharine Lavina to Reese McCommon 3-24-1848 (3-28-1848) Hr
Sharp, Catharine to Pleasant Davis Benson 1-11-1850 (1-16-1850) T
Sharp, E. C. to John B. Arnold 12-2-1869 G
Sharp, Eliza B. to B. F. Hazlewood 7-4-1860 G
Sharp, Elizabeth to J. W. Hays 9-26-1870 (9-27-1870) T
Sharp, Elizabeth to John Smithey 1-9-1825 Hr
Sharp, Elizabeth to William M. Coates 7-24-1848 G
Sharp, Fannie to J. M. McFadden 11-4-1863 (11-5-1863) F
Sharp, Isabella to L. M. Caldwell 5-20-1868 G
Sharp, Jamima to Martin Cartmell 10-25-1827 Ma
Sharp, Jamima C. to Charles Hogsett 3-18-1846 Ma
Sharp, Louisa J. to William J. Thomas 12-21-1858 Ma
Sharp, Margaret A. to James W. Caruthers 12-15-1856 (12-16-1856) Ma
Sharp, Margaret J. to John J. Hall 3-15-1841 (3-18-1841) T
Sharp, Margarette E. to Henry V. Replogle 1-13-1857 (1-14-1857) G
Sharp, Martha A. to T. A. Sharp 2-24-1864 G
Sharp, Mary E. to Thos. G. Hurey 8-9-1853 Cr
Sharp, Mary J. to W. A. Smith 12-10-1866 (12-12-1866) Ma
Sharp, Mary M. to John H. Leopard (Leopan) 12-18-1843 We
Sharp, Mary to Edward Hughes 8-13-1861 L
Sharp, Mary to John P. Henry 5-10-1842 (5-11-1842) G

Sharp, Mary to N. H. Blanton 8-31-1866 G
Sharp, Mary to Sterling S. Roane 4-28-1841 (4-27?-1841) T
Sharp, Mattie to Thomas Hooks 4-11-1869 Hy
Sharp, Minerva to Brently Butler 3-6-1855 Cr
Sharp, N. Jane to James H. Thomas 11-3-1868 (11-4-1868) Ma
Sharp, Nancy E. to C. T. Lipard 7-2-1850 (7-7-1850) O
Sharp, Nancy to C. T. Lipart 7-2-1850 (7-7-1850) O
Sharp, Naoma to Walker Guthrey 7-26-1848 O
Sharp, P. P. to W. F. Kerr 12-18-1867 G
Sharp, Virgina A. (Mrs.) to John H. Thomas 1-26-1869 Ma
Sharp, Wenney A. to Henry Hardy 1-15-1867 G
Sharpe, Charlotte to Lewis Lowder 1-25-1839 Cr
Sharpe, Eliana M. to W. H. Rowsey 1-23-1851 Hr
Sharrock, Fannie to Ransom E. Hopper 11-1-1866 Ma
Shaughnessy, Mary to Thomas Gannon 6-26-1860 Sh
Shauners, Mary to George Bridgett 6-7-1864 Sh
Shaver, Eliza to Amos Roberts 8-26-1868 Cr
Shaver, Martha to John J. Morgan 11-8-1855 Cr
Shaver, Nancy to W. H. Caudle 1-11-1867 (1-17-1867) Cr
Shaver, Rachel P. to Albert Morgan 12-31-1856 Cr
Shavers, Emily to Stephen Clement 1-22-1867 G
Shaw, Agness E. to William Coward 6-7-1845 (6-12-1845) Hr
Shaw, Alice to Jim King 1-15-1874 Hy
Shaw, Alice to Turner Curry 3-21-1875 Hy
Shaw, Allice to Stephen King 1-19-1876 (no return) Hy
Shaw, Amanda E. to Christopher D. Allen 7-22-1868 G
Shaw, Ancie to J. C. Fly 12-20-1865 Hy
Shaw, Annie L. to Thomas H. Brightwell 1-14-1869 F
Shaw, Annie to Elias Armstrong 12-25-1848 Cr
Shaw, Annie to Jim Read 4-18-1869 Hy
Shaw, Arner to Lewis Nelson 3-19-1870 Hy
Shaw, Becky to Cornelius Franklin 12-25-1867 F B
Shaw, Bettie J. to Ed Dickinson, jr. 12-17-1868 F
Shaw, Catherine to Hannibal Macklin 5-3-1869 G B
Shaw, Centha to Major Bledsoe 12-22-1837 G
Shaw, Chaney to Joshua Morrow 4-28-1871 (5-1-1871) F
Shaw, Charlotte to Peter Thornton 12-26-1876 Hy
Shaw, Cinthia to Silas Daniel 1-15-1874 Hy
Shaw, Clarecy A. to Joseph T. Baldwin 11-14-1851 (no return) F
Shaw, Cora E. to R. T. Coleman 10-25-1876 Hy
Shaw, Cordelia A. to F. M. Burford 10-22-1849 (10-25-1849) Hr
Shaw, Eleanor to James V. Patton 3-15-1832 Sh
Shaw, Eliza J. to Edmund B. Perry 1-2-1869 (1-6-1869) F
Shaw, Eliza J. to William Blake 1-8-1852 (no return) F
Shaw, Eliza N. to C. C. Glover 4-29-1854 (no return) F
Shaw, Eliza to D. H. Chews 9-15-1853 Cr
Shaw, Eliza to Joseph Fowler 2-25-1869 (2-26-1869) F B
Shaw, Elizabeth to William C. Lax 6-22-1848 Hn
Shaw, Ella to James Jones 12-12-1878 Hy
Shaw, Ellen to B. G. Alison 6-4-1862 (no return) Hy
Shaw, Ellen to Lewis C. Winters no date (Spring 1852) L
Shaw, Emeline T. to Creed Woodson 12-20-1847 F
Shaw, Emily to W. B. Hay 2-22-1875 (no return) Hy
Shaw, Emma W. to Perry G. Carter 11-9-1843 (11-14-1843) Ma
Shaw, Fannie M. to John N. Smith 9-20-1854 (9-19?-1854) Ma
Shaw, Fannie to Jacob Musgraves 12-28-1873 Hy
Shaw, Fannie to Tom Taylor 1-20-1874 Hy
Shaw, Fanny to Edward Selby 10-9-1869 (10-20-1869) F B
Shaw, Frances M. to John S. Biles 6-23-1845 (6-24-1845) F
Shaw, Hannah to Henry Walker 2-16-1847 (3-14-1847) G
Shaw, Harriet to Richmond Barbee 10-9-1869 Hy
Shaw, Isabell Jane to John G. Drake 2-13-1867 Hy
Shaw, Jane E. to Richard Dillon 2-20-1867 T
Shaw, Jane to Isaac Lawhorn 1-3-1872 (no return) Cr
Shaw, Jincy to Peter Harper 1-20-1877 Hy
Shaw, Laura to Ferd. Wood 5-8-1871 (5-9-1871) Ma
Shaw, Lavanda to D. M. Edmundson 9-15-1832 (9-18-1832) Hr
Shaw, Lemiza to Robert S. Kirkman 12-30-1844 (1-2-1845) G
Shaw, Lizzie to Silas Bond 12-14-1876 Hy
Shaw, Lizzie to Zack Anthony 3-24-1876 (no return) Hy
Shaw, Lou to George Holman 5-2-1878 (no return) Hy
Shaw, Lucy to John Collins 5-22-1883 L
Shaw, Lucy to Wallace Mann 1-28-1874 Hy
Shaw, M. L. to Phillip McElmurry 6-22-1870 (6-23-1870) Dy
Shaw, M. Precilla to J. Coleman Tharp 7-30-1856 G
Shaw, Mahala C. to R. G. Saunders 2-18-1842 F
Shaw, Mahala to Tho. Wright 9-4-1845 F
Shaw, Malina to R. S. McComack 11-29-1841 (12-9-1841) F
Shaw, Malisha to Frances M. Cleaver 12-25-1848 Cr
Shaw, Maranda J. to James W. Gardner 8-12-1846 G
Shaw, Margaret J. to Augustus C. Fasmyre 12-19-1848 Ma
Shaw, Margaret N. to J. S. Wright 1-29-1869 (1-30-1869) T
Shaw, Margaret to John Bennett 5-8-1840 (5-12-1840) T
Shaw, Mariah to Sam Cross 8-9-1866 (no return) F B
Shaw, Martha J. L. to H. W. Bloodworth 2-1-1848 Sh
Shaw, Martha Jane to Edward B. Baw 1-15-1844 (1-18-1844) F
Shaw, Martha to Austin Southall 1-2-1873 Hy

Shaw, Martha to Daniel E. Shaw 11-24-1865 (11-?-1865) T
Shaw, Martha to Nathan Morgan 12-8-1853 Cr
Shaw, Mary S. to J. G. Wilbourn 12-18-1867 F
Shaw, Mary to Clark Jarrett 1-3-1885 (1-8-1885) L
Shaw, Mary to Omma Mann 2-26-1868 (no return) Hy
Shaw, Matilda to Bob Clark 1-1-1869 (no return) Hy
Shaw, Menerva to Augustus C. Carter 2-12-1846 Cr
Shaw, Minty K. to William Cabainess 8-5-1850 Hn
Shaw, Mollie to Rufus C. Taylor 5-7-1869 (no return) F
Shaw, Moria to Golden Curtis 11-3-1877 Hy
Shaw, Moriah to Aaron Taylor 12-19-1872 Hy
Shaw, Nancy A. N. to Allen N. Massey 1-23-1867 Ma
Shaw, Nancy to George Wilkins 4-28-1857 (4-29-1857) T
Shaw, Nellie to Austin Harris 10-25-1870 (10-30-1870) F B
Shaw, R. L. to T. S. Anthony 11-3-1874 Hy
Shaw, R. to IJ. P. Lynn 1-9-1871 (1-10-1871) T
Shaw, Rebecca to E. White 2-22-1861 (no return) Cr
Shaw, S. Rhoeba S. to David B. Owen 1-6-1868 (1-7-1868) Ma
Shaw, S. Urilda to Wise A. Cooper 9-5-1866 G
Shaw, Sabry to Ananias Austin 2-16-1869 Hy
Shaw, Sallie to Burgis Merrill 1-20-1864 (1-7?-1864) T
Shaw, Sallie to John Stewart 1-2-1866 Hy
Shaw, Sallie to W. J. Wade 12-21-1871 Hy
Shaw, Sarah E. to John W. Wooley 12-6-1858 Ma
Shaw, Sarah F. to F. W. Appleberry 1-19-1859 (1-26-1859) Sh
Shaw, Sarah J. to Robt. W. Fenton 2-20-1867 (2-21-1867) T
Shaw, Sarah J. to Robt. W. Fenton 2-26-1867 (2-27-1867) T
Shaw, Sarah M. to Samuel P. Clark 9-3-1874 Hy
Shaw, Sarah to Wm. D. Davis 2-20-1856 Cr
Shaw, Scilla to Robert Dixon 2-4-1867 Hy
Shaw, Susan to John Cameron 4-3-1869 Hy
Shaw, Susan to Wm. Smith 11-24-1853 Cr
Shaw, Valeria to Robt. N. Christian 7-28-1866 (8-?-1866) F
Shaw, Violet to Monroe Morgan 12-5-1878 Hy
Shaw?, Caroline to S. A. Hunter 9-22-1877 (9-23-1877) L
Shawn, Julia to J. P. Cochran 1-14-1857 We
Shay, Joanna to Lackey Brandon 12-23-1868 (12-24-1868) Cr
Shay, Mary A. to James Bradley 10-22-1860 Sh
Shea, Joanna to Thomas Nugent 6-7-1855 Sh
Shea, Mary to Joseph Taylor 6-29-1857 (6-27?-1857) Sh
Shea, Mary to Michail Boylan 2-12-1861 Sh
Shea, Mary to Patrick Carmady 11-15-1851 Sh
Shea, Mary to Patrick Sullivan 10-2-1851 Sh
Sheals, Lucy to George Walker 2-22-1872 L B
Shearer, Minerva to S. W. Ledbetter 7-25-1850 L
Shearin, Lucy W. to John W. Justice 12-23-1858 Hr
Shearin, Mary L. to L. B. Bell 9-28-1865 Hy
Shearman, Mahala to Robert Griggs 2-6-1866 L
Shearman, Mary E. to Charles Craig 8-28-1856 (no return) L
Shearman, Nancy E. to William H. Mathis 12-16-1865 (12-17-1865) L
Shearon, Arabella to Albert Sharon 8-8-1851 (8-10-1851) Hr
Shearon, Elizabeth to Samuel Dunlap 10-30-1848 (10-31-1848) L
Shearon, Jane to Arthur Carroll 2-13-1850 (2-14-1850) O
Shearon, M. A. to L. W. Smith 12-25-1867 O
Sheay, Mary to John Dorney 4-14-1856 Sh
Sheckels?, Sarah Ann to Jos. John Carter 12-27-1842 (12-28-1842) Hr
Sheehan, Ellen P. to James Cunningham 4-29-1862 (4-30-1862) Sh
Sheehan, Johanna to James O'Brien 7-11-1859 Sh
Sheehy, Mary to John Shehan 7-8-1862 (7-9-1862) Sh
Sheeley, Maria to James Mullen 5-15-1863 Sh
Sheen, Clarisa to Edmund Stowes 12-26-1867 Sh
Sheen, Mary to Charles J. Jackson 7-16-1860 Sh
Sheets, Louisa to John C. Wilson 7-3-1828 O
Sheets, Mary Ann to Edward J. W. Peters 3-11-1854 (3-12-1854) Hr
Sheets, Nancy A. to Calvin Bowles 5-30-1854 (6-1-1854) Hr
Sheets, Sarah to T. Bray 1-15-1857 Hr
Shefard?, Flomida to J. R. Bugg 12-27-1858 O
Sheffield, Mary E. to B. R. Harvey 1-13-1845 Sh
Sheffield, Mary L. to James R. Sharp 3-12-1850 T
Shehan, Ann (Mrs.) to John Ren 7-2-1864 (7-6-1864) Sh
Shehan, Eliza to Martin Karting 6-2-1860 (6-4-1860) Sh
Shehan, Hannah to John? (Thos.?) Blackmore 6-27-1864 Sh
Shehan, Hannah to Thomas Conboy 4-25-1863 Sh
Shehan, Honora to David Leen 4-5-1856 (4-6-1856) Sh
Shehee, Hannah to John Norton 7-4-1863 Sh
Shelby, Jane E. to Joshua Crain 7-29-1847 Sh
Shelby, Louisa to George W. White 7-11-1836 Hr
Shelby, Malinda to Alfred Kelly 2-16-1835 Hr
Shelby, Mary Hays to John C. McGehee 7-4-1848 Sh
Shelby, Mary Isabella to John Joseph McFarland 1-5-1847 Sh
Shelby, Mary J. to John C. Ferrell 11-8-1858 (11-11-1858) G
Shelby, Nancy A. to Wm. M. Wilson 12-14-1845 Sh
Shelby, Nancy S. to W. F. Bodkin 3-19-1867 G
Shelby, Nancy to Tennessee Agnew 8-26-1865 O
Shelby, Olive V. (Mrs.) to Francis M. Tubbs 11-19-1870 (11-20-1870) Ma
Shelby, Rachel C. to Brinkley B. Barker 9-5-1840 (9-6-1840) O
Shell, Aletha J. to D. B. Archer 1-28-1867 (no return) Hn

Shell, Elizabeth R. to Edward Travis 10-23-1847 (no return) Hn
Shell, Hanah to Abraham Whitney 10-11-1862 Sh
Shell, S. A. to N. C. Powell 9-27-1863 Hn
Shelley, Adline to John Park 1-16-1855 Cr
Shelley, Nancy to James Parke 2-27-1840 Cr
Shelly (Shelby?), Mollie Ann to W. B. Williamson 3-26-1860 (3-27-1860) Sh
Shelly, Ellen to Alexander Shawl 10-3-1865 U
Shelly, Martha C. to Riley Gatlin 4-26-1835 (4-29-1835) Hr
Shelly, Martha J. to Jacob Pittman 10-30-1845 Ma
Shelly, Mary Ann to William Reeves 9-18-1843 Ma
Shelton, Ann Frances to Aaron W. Harkins 2-4-1856 Ma
Shelton, C. M. to Richard A. Stroud 4-15-1851 O
Shelton, Cleary to J. W. Williams 4-25-1850 (4-27-1850) O
Shelton, Cleary to W. Williams 4-2-1850 (4-7-1850) O
Shelton, E. E. to J. M. Moseley 8-5-1874 (no return) Dy
Shelton, Eliza (Mrs.) to John E. Lewis 11-21-1864 Sh
Shelton, Eliza J. to John B. Morphis 11-26-1855 (11-28-1855) Hr
Shelton, Eliza to William Lea 7-18-1866 Hy
Shelton, Elizabeth J. to John C. Willingham 10-28-1844 (no return) We
Shelton, Elizabeth M. to M. D. Pate 12-16-1869 Dy
Shelton, Elizabeth W. to Henry Newton 5-22-1852 Ma
Shelton, Elizabeth to James T. Harper 12-7-1868 (12-10-1868) Ma
Shelton, Ella to C. C. Poindexter 11-15-1873 (11-18-1873) T
Shelton, Ellen to Frieland Perry 7-28-1869 G B
Shelton, Frances M. to G. W. Slaughter 10-3-1861 Hn
Shelton, H. M. to Ezell Marks 1-16-1849 Hn
Shelton, Hannah to Sampson Moore 12-20-1866 Hy
Shelton, Harriett to George Tucker 1-8-1869 (1-9-1869) F B
Shelton, Indiania to John Wood 7-27-1868 T
Shelton, Isabella to John B. Moore 11-18-1847 T
Shelton, Izena to Henry Hines 8-24-1872 (no return) L B
Shelton, Judy to Ephreham Hawk 12-16-1871 (12-17-1871) T
Shelton, Lethe to Manin Tackett 5-17-1858 (5-18-1858) Hr
Shelton, Leticia to Issac A. Epperson 6-6-1843 Sh
Shelton, Lillie to Lewis Wood 10-31-1873 Hy
Shelton, Lilly to Frank Trimble 1-6-1870 F
Shelton, M. A. to J. F. Hunter 10-28-1875 Dy
Shelton, M. M. to J. A. Walker 10-16-1869 (10-17-1869) Dy
Shelton, M. R. to J. C. Fly 6-30-1869 G
Shelton, Mahala to Charner B. Colvin 12-21-1876 (12-25-1876) Dy
Shelton, Mahala to John H. Moss 1-27-1863 (1-29-1863) Dy
Shelton, Martha J. to James Langley 4-2-1860 (4-5-1860) L
Shelton, Martha W. to William D. Umstard 1-4-1847 G
Shelton, Mary Ann to Alex C. McDonald 4-26-1852 Sh
Shelton, Mary Ann to Christopher Rives 7-12-1838 F
Shelton, Mary C. to Isaac Howitt 12-19-1854 We
Shelton, Mary to Dave Archbell 12-26-1868 (12-28-1868) F B
Shelton, Mary to Fagan Westbrooks 3-6-1867 O
Shelton, Mary to James Warmack 11-28-1873 (12-11-1873) Dy
Shelton, Mary to W. A. Steven 9-18-1869 (9-19-1869) T
Shelton, Mary to W. A. Stevens 9-18-1869 T
Shelton, Mattie to Charles Bailey 12-23-1869 (no return) F B
Shelton, Melisa V. to Bartlett L. Dupree 2-17-1869 (2-18-1869) L
Shelton, Mildred E. to Stephen M. Powell 11-7-1859 (11-8-1859) Ma
Shelton, Minerva to J.(I?) P. Campbell 1-8-1845 Sh
Shelton, Nancy C. to Wm. N. Chapman 4-24-1845 We
Shelton, Peep to Ed Woodfork 1-5-1870 (no return) F B
Shelton, S. A. B. to B. P. Payne 8-17-1866 Dy
Shelton, S. E. (Mrs.) to Jeptha Box 12-10-1865 (12-18-1865) G
Shelton, S. E. to D. L. Neighbors 3-25-1874 (3-25-1875?) L
Shelton, S. E. to G. W. Walker 3-5-1879 (3-6-1879) Dy
Shelton, Sally N. to Hiram C. Trout 3-13-1854 (3-14-1854) G
Shelton, Sarah B. to John C. Pailey 3-24-1866 (3-26-1866) Ma
Shelton, Sarah E. to David C. Green 11-1-1858 (11-3-1858) Sh
Shelton, Susan C. to S. H. Moor 12-30-1878 (1-1-1879) Dy
Shelton, Teressa (?) to John R. Phillips 1-6-1850 Sh
Shelton?, Mary M. to John A. Vincent 2-14-1843 T
Shenault, Emma to S. W. Faulk 10-19-1872 (10-24-1872) T
Shenault, M. J. to S. S. Littlejohn 12-18-1865 Mn
Shenon, Mary A. to J. Y. West 1-8-1874 Hy
Sheoril, Morning to William Noble 5-11-1866 Hy
Shepard, Bella to Drury (Fayette Co.) Carter 8-19-1848 (8-21-1848) Ma
Shepard, Elizabeth to Rufus Hill 12-16-1870 (12-17-1870) T
Shepard, Elvina to John Joyner 5-29-1850 Hn
Shepard, Emmer to Isaac Eaton 4-10-1871 T
Shepard, Mollie J. to Henry Monroe 6-18-1869 (6-20-1869) F
Shepard, Nancy to Daniel McAlister 1-18-1850 O
Shepard, Sallie E. to Thomas J. Morris 4-?-1871 (5-1-1871) T
Shephard, Amy to Andrew Jackson 3-13-1869 (3-15-1869) F
Shephard, Mary A. to Jno. L. T. Sneed 8-26-1848 (8-27-1848) Hr
Shephard, Noah to Emanuel Alexander 7-21-1869 (7-29-1869) F B
Shepherd, Elizabeth A. to Thos Turner 3-4-1843 Hr
Shepherd, Elizabeth B. to William Roark 12-27-1832 Hr
Shepherd, Jane to M. P. Hill 11-14-1854 Sh
Shepherd, Lucy to Lewis Beal 7-4-1866 O
Shepherd, M. C. to W. A. Dozier 2-19-1867 G
Shepherd, Martha A. to Wm. Langston 11-28-1849 (11-29-1849) L

Shepherd, Martha Ann to Jesse D. Strayhorn 3-10-1873 T
Shepherd, Milly to Peter Adams 1-5-1867 G
Shepherd, Molly to Jacob Algea 2-14-1870 (2-15-1870) Cr
Shepherd, N. J. to D. N. Shilling 6-19-1840 Be
Shepherd, Nancy A. to Samuel F. Martin 10-15-1840 Cr
Shepherd, Nancy E. to James Styles 9-10-1839 (no return) Hn
Shepherd, Nancy E. to William Ballard 10-26-1846 (10-27-1846) F
Shepherd, Nancy to Daniel McAlister 1-18-1850 O
Shepherd, Octavia to Lum? Tho. Moore 12-19-1855 (12-20-1855) T
Shepherd, Opelia to Joseph Johnson 2-14-1872 (2-15-1872) O
Shepherd, S. M. to J. B. Hendricks 3-7-1866 Hn
Shepherd, Sarah E. to Robert Y. Moore 1-27-1855 Cr
Shepherd, Virenna to James Massey 12-17-1868 (12-18-1868) Cr
Shepherd, _____ to R. N. Hardy 7-19-1852 Cr
Sheppard, Elizabeth to T. W. Miller 7-16-1859 (7-17-1859) Sh
Sheppard, ElizabethS. to R. H. D. Ewell 11-2-1843 Hr
Sheppard, Ellen to Jacob Gerlinger 10-21-1862 Sh
Sheppard, Florence to J. R. Bugg 12-27-1858 O
Sheppard, Mary to G. B. Wharton 12-16-1847 Hn
Sheppard, Susan to Richard Perry 12-17-1879 (12-18-1879) L B
Shepperd, Cela to Wm. Dixon 12-21-1875 (no return) Hy
Shepperd, Dilsey to George Bradford 1-11-1876 (no return) Hy
Shepperd, Mary Ann to Milton J. Hamer 11-7-1838 (11-8-1838) Hr
Shepperd, Susan to Ephraim Smith 1-29-1876 Hy
Sheppeson, Emma to W. D. Sykes 10-11-1882 L
Sherell, Elizabeth F. to Jas. Marcum 3-30-1858 G
Sherfield, Mallissa C. to Wm. A. Browne 11-29-1844 (11-30-1844) F
Sherfield, Ruth to A. T. Butler 3-28-1870 (3-30-1870) Cr
Sherfield, Sarah F. to Halcum Jackson 8-16-1856 (8-14?-1856) O
Sheridan, Emily to A. J. Neill 12-8-1865 Hn
Sheridan, Margaret E. to John W. McMichael 11-19-1854 Hn
Sheridan, Martha J. E. to James W. A. Oliver 3-28-1866 Hn
Sheridan, Mary C. to Joseph w. Reynolds 5-8-1849 Hn
Sheridan, Mary to Alston G. Rice 4-18-1860 Sh
Sherill, Martha to Wm. Hall 10-14-1865 (2?-14-1865) T
Sherl, Elizabeth to William S. Temple 11-27-1854 (11-30-1854) Ma *
Sherley, Mittie to Nash Palmer 11-26-1874 Hy
Sherly], Sarah to Daniel Olds 9-11-1824 Hr
Sherman, Delithia to Ephraim Fletcher 1-17-1866 Hy
Sherman, Elizabeth to Loftin McKimon 3-4-1850 Ma
Sherman, Frances A. to Henry H. Hankins 9-23-1843 (9-28-1843) Ma
Sherman, Laura E. to C. M. Taliaferro 2-4-1875 Hy
Sherman, Louisa J. to David M. Sherman 8-23-1854 (no return) Hn
Sherman, Lucy to Henry B. Tensly 3-13-1872 Hy
Sherman, Mary R. to William A. Christian 1-15-1859 (1-20-1859) Ma
Sherman, Morning to William Henry Gray 10-6-1869 Hy
Sherman, Narcissa C. to William W. Womble 3-9-1848 Ma
Sherman, Sarah to William Paulett 2-15-1864 Hn
Shermaster, N. to J. F. Duncan 1-8-1862 Sh
Shern, Frances to Arther Barns 12-18-1838 (12-20-1838) G
Sherod, Mary to Moses Bishop 5-18-1841 Cr
Sherod, Mary to William Edwards 11-7-1859 (no return) Hy
Sherrel, Hetty to Marcus J. Pennington 9-4-1834 Sh
Sherrell, Harriett to James Phillips 8-6-1853 (no return) F
Sherrell, Leah to Andrew Adams 3-17-1866 (3-25-1866) T
Sherrell, Martha A. to M. A. Fields 7-13-1872 (no return) Cr
Sherrid, Celia to Moses Smith 8-4-1866 T
Sherril, Laura] to Geo. W. Hall 12-29-1865 (1-3-1866) T
Sherril, Martha to Wm. Hall 10-14-1865 T
Sherrill, Anna E. to John A. Cary 12-22-1874 (12-23-1874) T
Sherrill, Elizabeth M. to Joseph Forsyth 11-13-1866 (11-15-1866) T
Sherrill, Elizabeth to Theodore Geist 9-3-1858 Sh
Sherrill, Flora to Leroy Smith 10-6-1870 T
Sherrill, Harriet to Furgus Alston 1-7-1874 T
Sherrill, Hulda to John P. Gist 5-7-1840 Cr
Sherrill, Isa L. to J. G. Adams 12-4-1873 T
Sherrill, Lavinia F. to John S. Temple 9-15-1856 Ma
Sherrill, Lizzie to Alex Johnson 6-19-1869 (6-20-1869) T
Sherrill, Mary A. E. to James Balton 8-25-1859 Cr
Sherrill, Siller to Alex Stitt 7-20-1872 T
Sherrin, Cynthia to William Rogers 4-20-1851 (6-2-1851) O
Sherrod, Caroline V. to John W. Durant 11-2-1844 T
Sherrod, Catharin to Moreau P. Estes 11-27-1874 T
Sherrod, Eliza Rufina to Joseph D. Whitley 12-16-1854 T
Sherrod, Eliza to Calvin Bond 12-24-1866 (no return) F B
Sherrod, Emma C. to Peyton J. Smith 12-7-1870 (12-11-1870) F
Sherrod, Frances Ann to Jonas C. Shelton 12-26-1866 (12-28-1866) F B
Sherrod, Louisa to Peter Bond 12-6-1873 Hy
Sherrod, M. E. to W. S. Payne 12-24-1877 (12-25-1877) Dy
Sherrod, Martha Ann to Adam Dabney Clements 5-3-1847 (5-6-1847) T
Sherrod, Mary S. to John C. Jacobs 5-9-1859 (5-10-1859) F
Sherrod, Nia to Jno. G. Sherrod 12-26-1865 (12-29-1865) T
Sherrod, Pheby to Minn Walker 3-6-1872 L
Sherrod, Susan to James Sumner 11-14-1866 Hy
Sherrod, Tempa to Noah Bond 2-10-1866 (2-15-1866) T
Sherron, Elizabeth to Nathan Barron 12-17-1835 G
Sherron, Lucretia to Constant Thedford 10-2-1843 (10-12-1843) G

Sherron, Martha J. to W. D. West 8-14-1872 Hy
Sherron, Nancy to James M. Pounds 2-2-1846 (2-4-1846) G
Sherron, Temperance A. to Willie Clift 11-30-1854 Hr
Sherry, Mary A. to Jas. W. McCracken 5-12-1853 Sh
Sherwood, Anna B. to Henry D. Franklin 12-8-1869 (12-9-1869) Ma
Sherwood, Henrietta to J. D. Pace 11-29-1871 Dy
Sheth, Sarah M. Handy to George W. Shaw 9-21-1860 (9-27-1860) O
Shetter, Narcissa to Samuel H. Winford 8-4-1842 Sh
Shettie, Astalyssa to James Smith 1-10-1841 Sh
Shettlesworth, F. C. to John Sorrels 9-23-1847 Sh
Shettleworth, Cornelia to Jno. A. Arnold 1-8-1885 L
Shickles, Nancy to Levi Mullekin 12-29-1846 Hr
Shidecker, Louisa to Frederick Rosenthal 1-16-1863 Sh
Shields, Ann to James Mahn 9-8-1852 Sh
Shields, Jane to Benjamin Reeves 12-27-1869 (12-30-1869) F B
Shields, Livinia to Aaron Camp 12-1-1867 Hy
Shikle, Mary (Mrs.) to Thomas N. Pate 12-5-1870 O
Shilcutt, Nancy to Haywood Lea 12-26-1871 Hy
Shilling, Amanda to Joseph Baker 12-31-1840 Be
Shilling, Delila to Wm. C. Barne 9-22-1848 Be
Shinalt, Mary to Henry Snow 12-11-1844 (12-12-1844) F
Shinault, Casandra to Wm. R. Winn 11-24-1841 F
Shinault, Hannah to Henry Webster 12-6-1827 Hr
Shinault, Mary A to W. E. Ballard 2-22-1866 F
Shinault, Mary E. to R. M. Lax 12-26-1854 (12-28-1854) Hr
Shinault, Mary to Lennard Malam 12-28-1839 (12-29-1839) Hr
Shinault, O. E. to J. M. Ritchie 12-1-1866 (12-4-1866) F
Shinault, Rosanna to Erasmus R. Cothran 1-10-1838 (1-11-1838) Hr
Shinault, Rosanna to Zachariah Davis 5-22-1824 Hr
Shinault, Sallie to W. L. Wily 2-1-1860 F
Shinel, Hetty to Francis C. Keyor? 9-21-1841 (no return) F
Shinn, Martha Jane to John A. Baker 5-31-1848 (6-8-1848) Hr
Shinn, Rebecca C. to F. M. Mays 9-24-1851 (no return) F
Shinn, Sarah to Minas Sparks 1-27-1851 F
Shinness, Nellie S. to Samuel Sweeney 12-24-1862 Sh
Shipan, Mary A. to Lewis Cardinal 7-26-1853 Sh
Shipard, Susan to Cyrus Walker 12-31-1872 (1-1-1873) L
Shipley, Jane to Robert T. Steeley 12-15-1841 (no return) Hn
Shipley, Mary Ann to Thomas J. Chilcutt 9-3-1854 Hn
Shipman, Alsy to N. O. J. Brewer 7-1-1847 Cr
Shipman, Belinda to William B. Garrison 12-2-1826 (12-7-1826) Hr
Shipman, Charlott to E. H. Derryberry 8-?-1860 (8-14-1860) Cr
Shipman, Elizabeth C. to John F. McCalab 2-24-1848 G
Shipman, Elizabeth to Uriah Costello 11-15-1826 (11-16-1826) Hr
Shipman, Jennie to J. M. Proctor 7-28-1869 G
Shipman, M. P. (Mrs.) to E. K. Manning 12-14-1872 (12-15-1872) Dy
Shipman, M.A. to E. W. Derybery 1-8-1868 (1-9-1868) Cr
Shipman, Marinda to James Caton 11-10-1846 G
Shipman, Martha P. to James T. Davis 7-19-1868 G
Shipman, Menerva to John Harley 1-5-1829 (1-8-1829) Hr
Shipman, Nancy P. to John W. Baley 12-20-1842 G
Shipman, Nancy to Nathaniel M. Smith 7-6-1851 Cr
Shipman, Sarah to James Caborne 4-25-1826 Hr
Shipman, Sarah to Thomas W. McNeely 3-31-1860 (4-1-1860) O
Shirley, Anna to J. A. Lipscomb 12-29-1868 (12-31-1868) F
Shirley, Eliza to Alex Sikes 5-29-1869 Hy
Shirley, India to Jack Hart 8-18-1867 Hy
Shirley, Mary A. to Edward H. Blome 7-17-1870 Hy
Shirley, Mary J. to Ed Long 9-8-1870 (no return) Hy
Shirley, Mary to Moses Barnes 8-29-1853 Be
Shirley, Mat to Sneed Waddel 12-10-1878 Hy
Shirly, Liza to Moses Taylor 12-27-1867 Hy
Shirman, Susan M. to William Braden 8-3-1846 (8-4-1846) L
Shirrin, M. J. to J. M. Rodgers 10-12-1877 O
Shirt (Short?), D. A. to John G. Sherwood 9-1-1864 Sh
Shism, Pruble to G. M. Shaw 12-19-1883 (12-20-1883) L
Shivers, A. C. to R. I. P. Shivers 9-19-1842 Sh
Shivers, Emma F. to James M. Spears 12-31-1869 (1-2-1870) Ma
Shivers, Jona to Sam Blakemon 2-20-1869 Hy
Shivers, Josee A. to Frank Ridley 11-24-1869 Hy
Shivers, Margaret A. to William Jackson 12-18-1849 Sh
Shivers, Mary Paralee to Benj. Franklin Forsyth 8-22-1871 (8-23-1871) Ma
Shivers, P. C. to Jesse Shivers 10-26-1843 Sh
Shivers, Parmelia to Tillman Gregory 9-24-1838 Sh
Shivers, R. A. to J. B. Shivers 3-23-1875 O
Shleihan, Ottelaan to Joseph App 6-14-1854 (6-15-1854) Sh
Shnieder, Elionie to Charles Kawinkel 12-3-1852 Sh
Shoaf, Christinea to J.E. Davis 11-25-1874 T
Shoemake, Angey E. to Edward A. Tucker 1-11-1863 We
Shoemake, Anna to B. F. Chipman 7-17-1879 L
Shoemake, Eliza J. to Thomas E. Meacham 9-14-1854 L
Shoemake, Elizabeth to Bowling Adcock 9-26-1860 Dy
Shoemake, Lucinda to Zebulon Martin 12-23-1850 (12-24-1850) L
Shoemake, M. L. to O. G. Lunsford 2-13-1880 (2-16-1880) L
Shoemake, Martha E. to William Henry Cox 6-24-1873 L
Shoemake, Mary E. to Alexander Cox 3-29-1875 L
Shoemaker, Elmira to C. A. Spinks 10-6-1875 (10-11-1875) L

Shoemaker, Frances to Thomas Wilson 2-20-1869 (2-25-1869) L
Shoemaker, Margaret F. to W. S. Hawley 2-9-1871 (2-24-1871) F
Shoemaker, Martha J. to S. Ellis 1-25-1871 (1-26-1871) F
Shoemaker, Mary to Jacob McCain 12-14-1844 Ma
Shoemaker, Polly to Moses Johnson 3-17-1829 Ma
Shoemaker, Sarah E. to Stephenas Gardner 9-4-1862 (9-11-1862) L
Shoemaker, Susanna to Charles Hall 11-17-1869 G
Shoemate, A. C. to W. C. Ditto 12-15-1869 Hy
Shoemate, Martha E. to Abram Cooper 4-16-1867 (no return) Hy
Shoenman, Anna to John George Wachter 1-18-1856 (1-19-1856) Sh
Shoeterick?, Elizabeth to John Sayles 3-16-1866 (3-23-1866) Cr
Shoffner, Eveline to Beverly Townes 8-1-1868 (8-3-1868) Cr
Shoffner, Mary Ann to Andrew Nesbitt 2-19-1870 (2-20-1870) Cr
Shoffner, S. E. to P. T. Kirk 8-13-1866 (8-14-1866) Dy
Shofner, Dosha to Cain Shofner 10-9-1869 (10-10-1869) Cr
Shofner, E. A. to W. E. Earley 4-9-1873 (4-10-1873) Dy
Shofner, Eliza to Isaac Pinson 11-7-1864 (11-8-1864) Cr
Shofner, Elizabeth M. to R. D. Bell 1-10-1866 Cr
Shofner, Fannie to J. D. Pace 10-30-1867 Dy
Shofner, Lettie to Levin Palmer 12-20-1869 (1-10-1870) Cr
Shofner, M. Ella to E. A. Thomas 2-17-1873 (2-19-1873) Cr
Shofner, Mary A. to Nelson Watson 1-6-1842 Cr
Shofner, Mary Ann to Marion Edwards 3-16-1864 Cr
Shofner, Maryann to Marion Edwards 3-16-1864 (no return) Cr
Shofner, Metisla to Nelson Walton 4-28-1846 Cr
Shofner, Sarah to Andrew Jackson 2-25-1870 (2-26-1870) Cr
Shoop, Jane to P. G. Cockran 1-9-1851 (1-11-1851) Sh
Shopher, Nancy J. A. to Giles Scroggins 1-19-1858 (1-20-1858) Hr
Shore, Elizabeth to Joe Cross 12-20-1867 (12-22-1867) F B
Shore, Fannie F. to W. J. Morris 11-30-1859 (12-4-1859) F
Shore, Frances A. to John E. Lester 12-2-1843 (12-3-1843) Hr
Shore, Julia T. to James Maneer (Manees) 4-8-1850 Sh
Shore, Nancy C. to Samuel Asberry 4-17-1858 (4-18-1858) O
Shore, Sallie A. V. to Harrison Herron 10-7-1867 (10-17-1867) F
Shore, Sarah A. O. to James D. Carter 5-28-1846 (6-10-1846) F
Shores, Adaline E. to Rancey Pleasant 3-16-1852 O
Shores, Lucinda to Anthony Houser 11-27-1858 (12-1-1858) O
Shores, S. C. to W. A. Powell 1-24-1868 O
Shores, Sarah to Owen Boon 3-12-1845 Be
Short (Sharp?), S. A. to P. C. Hill 9-1-1866 G
Short, Alice to Wash. Williams 10-13-1874 Hy
Short, Ann to Edward Norton 9-27-1833 Hr
Short, Bet to James Cole 8-13-1868 (no return) Hy
Short, C. A. to Joseph H. Harrison 9-23-1847 Sh
Short, Charlotte to Edward H. Stewart 10-25-1849 (11-17-1849) Hr
Short, Delelah to Wm. B. Jones 4-25-1846 (4-30-1846) Hr
Short, Delila to Robert P. Edmundston 1-7-1839 (1-13-1839) G
Short, Elizabeth L. to Jordon B. Boone 1-8-1844 (1-11-1844) Ma
Short, Elizabeth to Joseph Cloud 2-24-1836 Hr
Short, Elizabeth to Robert Trosper 8-19-1841 (8-22-1841) G
Short, Elizer A. to W. M. Cates 2-25-1869 G
Short, Fanny N. to Wm. Smith 4-2-1858 (no return) We
Short, Henrietta to Rufus Hill 1-12-1876 (no return) Hy
Short, Liley to H. G. Coker 8-19-1869 G
Short, Lucinda to Benjamin Bumpass 3-30-1829 (4-5-1829) Hr
Short, Lydia to Barnett Riddle 1-28-1864 O
Short, Maggie to G. G. Russell 9-29-1860 (9-30-1860) Sh
Short, Martha to Geo. Kilbreath 2-5-1839 Be
Short, Mary E. to Wm. M. Grimes 7-9-1862 G
Short, Mary M. to J. C. Bird 12-11-1856 We
Short, Mary to Thomas H. Peak 8-16-1843 Hn
Short, Matilda to William D.? Peak 2-7-1844 Hn
Short, Nancy to Peter Miller 8-28-1867 (no return) Hy
Short, Nancy to Peyton Miller 3-22-1873 Hy
Short, Nellie to Henry Thomas 12-23-1869 Hy
Short, R. G. to F. T. Seymore 11-12-1868 Hy
Short, Sallie to Jerry Williams 12-24-1868 Hy
Short, Sarah F. to William F. McCaleb 1-30-1865 G
Short, Sarah J. to M. E. Mosley 1-18-1858 G
Short, Sarah J. to William R. Harrison 1-19-1858 G
Short, Sarah Jane to Francis M. Forrest 9-25-1851 Be
Short, Sarah Jane to John Nobles 9-4-1853 Be
Short, Sarah to John Cole 1-7-1841 Be
Short, Sarah to Wm. Ross 4-11-1867 Hy
Short, Sophia to William Norton 9-25-1832 Hr
Short, Susan to Ansil A. Short 5-24-1849 Be
Short, Virginia to Joseph Harder 1-22-1838 Hn
Shorter, A. E. to C. L. Pickens 3-4-1858 Sh
Shorter, Josephine E. to James R. Burks 12-7-1857 Sh
Shotwell, Jonah A. to Z. T. Ridgeway 11-8-1871 O
Shotwell, Phebe to Isaac J. Hunt 12-21-1848 Hn
Shoulders, C. J. to Thaddius T. T. Bilbro 11-26-1853 Sh
Shoulong, Belle to John Rice 9-30-1881 (10-13-1881) L
Shous?, Nelly to Micajah Manard 1-30-1853 Sh
Show, Annie to C. C. Welbourn 1-5-1860 F
Shrieger, Hannah to Lewis Gennette 6-13-1859 (6-19-1859) Sh
Shroat, Mary M. to Andrew J. Nichols 5-19-1858 Hn

Shrote, America to Luyton C. Hawes 10-6-1851 Hn
Shubell, Sallie to J. W. Williams 2-17-1869 Hy
Shuck, M. E. to W. R. Acuff 4-2-1877 (4-3-1877) L
Shuck, Martha Ann to Wilson Cage 1-11-1855 (1-11-1856?) O
Shuford, Eliza Jane to George W. Ashford 11-29-1856 (12-2-1856) Ma
Shuford, Susan A. to James E. Woodard 3-17-1868 (3-18-1868) Cr
Shuford, Susan A. to William W. Nichols 10-16-1862 (10-22-1862) Ma
Shull, Rachel to Andrew J. Moore 6-8-1836 Hr
Shull, Sarah A. to W. E. Shelton 8-9-1863 Mn
Shultz, Delila M. to Harvey C. Starnes 6-1-1867 (6-2-1867) T
Shumaker, R. A. to W. H. Applewhite 6-22-1870 (6-23-1870) Dy
Shuman, Sopha to Christopher Kohl (Cole?) 4-9-1863 Sh
Shumate, Ann to B. M. Rutledge 12-29-1857 G
Shumate, H. V. to Joshua C. Lee 12-1-1853 Ma
Shumate, Mary Ann (Mrs.) to John J. Holloway 3-11-1868 G
Shumate, Mary E. to T. L. Traylor 9-10-1875 Hy
Shumate, Mary Jane to John L. Cock 2-26-1857 Ma
Shuran, Amanda to Asberry Cooper 3-30-1873 Hy
Shute, Lorenia to Lemuel W. Rust 3-20-1830 Ma
Shutts (Shults), Charlotte I. to David Cummings 11-13-1850 Sh
Shutts, Rebecca to Thomas Kemp 8-14-1861 Mn
Shutts, Susan E. to John V. Hutcherson 7-11-1861 Mn
Shweitzer, Kate to Henry Kuttenberg 7-8-1863 Sh
Sibley, Elizabeth to William Goode 9-25-1855 Sh
Sibley, Nannie to Samuel D. McClure 9-19-1861 Sh
Sidle, M. J. (Mrs.) to Robert L. Smith 9-27-1853 Sh
Sigler, Martha E. to Samuel Hammontree 11-13-1858 (11-16-1858) Sh
Sigler, Mary to John Bolton 1-6-1842 Sh
Sigler, Sarah J. to Robert H. Gift 12-22-1858 (12-23-1858) Sh
Sigman, Amedia A. to Tandy M. Branson 2-3-1852 G
Sigmor, Nancy A. to John A. Carr 12-17-1851 (12-18-1851) G
Signaigo, Mary to John B. Zanone 9-12-1857 (9-13-1857) Sh
Sigrary?, Amanda to Green Fowlkes 2-14-1880 (2-16-1880) Dy
Sikes, Mary Ann to Joseph Toney 6-2-1848 Sh
Siler, A. M. (Mrs.) to James C. Wright 12-15-1858 Sh
Siler, M. T. to W. P. Brown 8-2-1873 (8-3-1873) T
Siler, Mary A. to Thomas Sommerville 4-26-1838 Hr
Siler, Mary Ann to James C. Lake 11-25-1857 (11-26-1857) T
Siler, Mary to James R. Sharp 11-10-1858 T
Siler, Nancy to Cirus Wright 3-1-1867 (3-2-1867) T
Sills, Frances R. to J. G. Dorris 2-14-1861 Hr
Silsby, Alice to John H. Thomas 12-28-1872 Dy
Silsby, Hellen to James Donald 1-12-1871 Dy
Silsby, Mary to Henry Ward 12-20-1865 (12-24-1865) Dy
Silsby, Millie to Wm. Smith 6-14-1876 (6-15-1876) Dy
Silver, Bridget to Michael Smith 6-11-1857 Sh
Silvers, Ellen to Daniel Coughlin 6-18-1862 (6-19-1862) Sh
Silvertooth, Elizabeth to Richard H. McCord 7-24-1853 (no return) L
Sim (Linn?), Frances to James Steelman 5-6-1850 Sh
Simerson, M. E. to W. H. Rogers 10-23-1866 (10-25-1866) F
Simeton?, Margaret A. to R. T. Wilson 2-24-1866 T
Simister, Mary A. to Joseph Gaunt 6-6-1854 Sh
Simm, Martha Louise to Alfred E. Keller 11-7-1848 Sh
Simmonds, Adeline M. to Philip E. Gee 9-14-1866 (no return) Hn
Simmonds, Nancy to John Arnold 11-27-1848 Be
Simmons, Alice to Lou Jones 12-26-1870 F B
Simmons, Alla to E. Moffatt 11-9-1864 Hn
Simmons, Amanda to James H. Davis 9-1-1870 (9-24-1870) Ma
Simmons, America J. to William R. Sheridan 7-18-1847 Hn
Simmons, C. D. to S. G. Chrisp 4-30-1868 G
Simmons, Caroline L. to Robert S. Thompson 11-10-1868 G
Simmons, Caroline to L. B. Hammons 3-2-1854 (no return) F
Simmons, Clarissa to Henry A. Shipman 1-2-1861 G
Simmons, Dee A. to Ben May 4-27-1857 Sh
Simmons, E. A. to F. M. Adams 12-29-1855 (no return) Hn
Simmons, E. C. to Edward Arbuckle 2-24-1848 Hn
Simmons, E. J. to W. A. Bryan 4-26-1853 (no return) F
Simmons, E. T. to James A. Dixon 3-11-1871 Hy
Simmons, Edney Ann to William Dozer 7-3-1838 (7-12-1838) G
Simmons, Eliza E. to W. A. Elam 4-7-1853 G
Simmons, Eliza H. to John N. Wright 11-20-1854 Be
Simmons, Eliza H. to John N. Wright 11-20-1854 Be CC
Simmons, Eliza J. to Jas. Edwards 12-18-1843 Hr
Simmons, Eliza to G. B. New 5-1-1830 (5-2-1830) Hr
Simmons, Elizabeth to Henry Rice 11-27-1868 (no return) Hy
Simmons, Elizabeth to Joseph Cheatham 1-11-1856 (1-12-1856) O
Simmons, Elizabeth to Thos. G. Wingo 11-17-1847 Cr
Simmons, Ellen to Ben Sommerville 10-18-1870 T
Simmons, Emely M. to Peter A. Crook 9-17-1853 (no return) F
Simmons, Emila to James M. Rogers 5-21-1843 (no return) F
Simmons, Esserline to John Francisco Antonio 5-16-1867 Hn
Simmons, Frances to David Simmons 10-12-1850 Cr
Simmons, Hannah O. (Mrs.) to Benj. H. Blume 3-20-1867 Ma
Simmons, Heisey H. to Stephen Sanders 4-18-1838 Hr
Simmons, Jane H. to W. B. Bass 11-20-1869 G
Simmons, Jane to W. D. Spivy 10-22-1857 (10-26-1857) Hr
Simmons, Jesse C. to J. D. Dickey 9-19-1865 (9-20-1865) O

Simmons, L. to Malcum Clark 11-27-1867 G
Simmons, Laura E. to M. W. Eudaily 6-30-1869 (no return) Dy
Simmons, Laura J. to Nelson Kennady 9-18-1839 Hn
Simmons, Louisa to Leroy Collins 12-23-1861 (12-25-1861) O
Simmons, Louisa to Wm. Massey 11-15-1857 Cr
Simmons, Lucinda to Thos. Hicks 7-3-1856 Cr
Simmons, Lucy to Alonzo R. Roberson 12-17-1876 Hy
Simmons, M. E. to Rob't Q. Kennady 3-5-1867 O
Simmons, M. J. to W. E. H. Hill 12-12-1870 (12-15-1870) T
Simmons, M. W. to C. S. Craig 10-14-1866 Hn
Simmons, Margaret A. to Thomas C. Thompson 1-1-1861 (1-3-1861) Hr
Simmons, Marina W. to Richard B. Trotter 10-5-1837 Sh
Simmons, Martha Ann to Benjamin Newhouse 3-31-1856 O
Simmons, Martha J. to Hiram Wiles 7-2-1853 (7-4-1853) Sh
Simmons, Martha J. to John W. Browder 9-3-1853 (9-5-1853) Ma
Simmons, Martha J. to Thomas Carroll 6-16-1867 Hn
Simmons, Martha W. to W. H. White 3-5-1866 (3-28-1866) O
Simmons, Mary Ann to Anderson Miller 12-28-1868 F B
Simmons, Mary Ann to Henry Andrews 8-27-1850 Be
Simmons, Mary Ann to Tom J. Pewett 10-27-1861 (10-29-1861) T
Simmons, Mary Eliza to Alexander White 2-22-1847 (2-23-1847) Hr
Simmons, Mary F. to Edward L. Sanford 12-23-1857 Ma
Simmons, Mary J. to William H. Nolly 10-13-1868 (10-14-1868) F
Simmons, Mary Josephine to Nathan Wilson 1-9-1867 Be
Simmons, Mary to James Lee 2-8-1842 F
Simmons, Mary to John Newhouse 9-10-1861 O
Simmons, Mary to John Newhouse 9-11-1861 O
Simmons, Mary to R. C. Pierce 11-6-1848 (no return) Cr
Simmons, Mary to Robert Hollingsworth 4-3-1859 Hn
Simmons, Mary to Wm. B. Barton 3-15-1851 O
Simmons, Matilda J. to Wiley Slaughter 12-16-1850 (12-23-1850) F
Simmons, Matilda to John F. Watts 12-5-1861 (no return) We
Simmons, N. L. to H. G. Duffer 1-26-1871 (1-29-1871) Cr
Simmons, Nancy A. to Robert T. Manual 9-23-1860 We
Simmons, Nancy to Abram Spears 9-8-1841 Sh
Simmons, Nancy to E. T. Walker 4-9-1861 G
Simmons, Nancy to Elias Forte 10-13-1825 (10-15-1825) Hr
Simmons, Necia to Wm. W. Cargel 12-28-1843 Cr
Simmons, Octavia to S. B. Maupin 3-30-1870 G
Simmons, Paralee to John W. Mays 1-23-1869 (1-25-1869) Ma
Simmons, Penelope to Edward Jeffreys 4-8-1835 (4-13-1835) G
Simmons, Percilla to Jesse Harriss 9-20-1856 (10-1[7]-1856) Hr
Simmons, Polly Ann to John Gibson 2-3-1862 (2-6-1862) Dy
Simmons, Polly to John Conish 7-2-1870 F B
Simmons, Priscilla S. to George A. Lipscomb 12-25-1854 (no return) F
Simmons, Rhoda to Cezar Johnson 2-8-1871 Hy
Simmons, Sarah Eliz. to Jno. W. High 9-11-1850 F
Simmons, Sarah G. to J. W. Cannon 1-11-1855 (1-16-1855) G
Simmons, Sarah M. to James M. Baxter 12-27-1855 We
Simmons, Sarah P. to Isaac Albritten 7-25-1852 Hn
Simmons, Sarah T. to James R. Mooney 10-12-1868 (no return) Hn
Simmons, Sarah to G. A. Isham 1-8-1870 (1-13-1870) F
Simmons, Sophia W. to Joshua? C. Lundy 8-4-1845 (8-5-1845) F
Simmons, Surania A. to Bayliss H. Upchurch 10-6-1859 Hn
Simmons, Susan to W. A. Blake 12-7-1865 G
Simmons, T. S. to D. C. Bradley 12-30-1863 Hn
Simmons, Tempe to Dock Forrest 2-22-1866 (no return) F B
Simmons, Winneford to William R. White 10-29-1863 G
Simms, Allice E. to Saml. E. Champion 3-4-1868 (3-5-1868) F
Simms, Amanda to Charles A. Tinsley 3-17-1868 (no return) Dy
Simms, Eliza to Zack Moore 8-22-1877 (8-23-1877) L
Simms, Francis to Robert Bates 1-24-1877 (1-29-1877) L B
Simms, G. A. to Jas. M. Culbreath 3-25-1868 (3-26-1868) F
Simms, Henrietta to James Moore 1-29-1866 (2-4-1866) F
Simms, Jemima S. to A. M. McCorkle 11-3-1852 F
Simms, Laura J. to J. L. Tilman 3-1-1884 (3-2-1884) L
Simms, Leah to Edmond Snow 2-10-1831 Sh
Simms, Lizzie to W. M. Smith 3-3-1873 Dy
Simms, Lydia to John Evans 8-15-1869 G
Simms, M. J. to J. M. Hill 3-27-1875 (3-28-1875) L
Simms, Martha E. to Wm. Gatewood 8-1-1858 Hr
Simms, Mattie O. to B. H. Lucas 10-2-1865 (10-3-1865) F
Simms, Sarah to Ellison Childress 7-13-1829 Hr
Simon?, Louisa A. to ____ Crofford 6-19-1864 (6-21-1864) T
Simons, Amanda to George Clifford 7-21-1862 Mn
Simons, M. S. to James L. McDowell 12-1-1852 Cr
Simons, Maggie to W. E. Trout 12-31-1878 (1-1-1879) Dy
Simons, Martha A. to James A. Webber 5-3-1875 (5-4-1875) Dy
Simons, Martha E. C. to J. E. Patillo 9-11-1850 (9-11-1850) F
Simons, Martha to Enoch Muirhead 4-21-1831 G
Simons, Racheal to Joseph Thomas 8-10-1867 Hy
Simons, S. J. to J. M. Ripley 1-24-1876 (1-26-1876) Dy
Simons, Susan to John Wheatley 9-24-1866 (9-27-18??) O
Simonton, Leticia to Wm. Ross? McCain 2-13-1856 T
Simonton, M. E. to J. C. Moffet 9-20-1870 T
Simonton, Margaret A. to Miles M. Hammond 5-9-1853 Ma
Simonton, Margret to E. P. Lucado 6-28-1856 (7-11-1856) T

Simonton, Martha Jane to Albert Gallatin McCuin 7-25-1850 T
Simonton, Sallie to C. F. Strong 9-25-1860 (9-26-1860) T
Simore, Susan to G. W. White 4-7-1852 Cr
Simpkin, Sarah Ann to John Foster 5-5-1830 (5-6-1830) Hr
Simpkins, Louisa to Ben Mitchell 5-13-1870 (5-15-1870) F B
Simpson, A. M. (Mrs.) to T. B. Worrell 3-1-1853 (no return) F
Simpson, Amanda C. to George W. Sutton 10-26-1853 (11-12-1853) Hr
Simpson, C. E. to David Sanders 9-30-1858 Hr
Simpson, Catharine to John S. Hunt 1-16-1849 (1-17-1849) Hr
Simpson, Eliza C. to E. J. Kiger 12-24-1874 Dy
Simpson, Elizabeth F. to L. W. Gaines 8-31-1875 (9-1-1875) L
Simpson, Elizabeth to Henry Murray 3-25-1857 Sh
Simpson, Elizabeth to John M. Childress 1-12-1871 Dy
Simpson, Elizabeth to John R. Brown 1-10-1842 (1-11-1842) O
Simpson, Elizabeth to William Bennett 5-8-1875 (no return) Hy
Simpson, F. J. to Job Stricklin 10-2-1861 (10-3-1861) Hr
Simpson, Frances to F. M. Waters 1-1-1870 (1-3-1870) Dy
Simpson, Frances to Marshall Seddens 11-24-1828 Hr
Simpson, Fredonia to W. V. Anderson 12-28-1852 (12-30-1852) Sh
Simpson, Gracy to John W. Climer 11-27-1843 Ma
Simpson, Harriet E. to John Townly 9-16-1865 (no return) Hn
Simpson, Harriet to William Cole 8-31-1858 Hr
Simpson, Irena to Robert Harriss 11-10-1877 (11-11-1877) L B
Simpson, J. A. to D. M. Loving 2-28-1868 (no return) Dy
Simpson, Jacky C. to John W. Medanis 11-9-1842 Cr
Simpson, Jane M. to John M. White 8-4-1846 Ma
Simpson, Jane to Lorenzo D. Mathis 7-18-1868 (7-19-1868) Ma
Simpson, Jane to Needham Ingram 12-18-1830 (12-23-1830) Hr
Simpson, Keziah E. to Robert D. Freeland 10-23-1867 (no return) Hn
Simpson, Louisa M. to John D. Sweat 12-23-1870 (no return) Hn
Simpson, Louisa to Daniel W. Word 8-22-1844 G
Simpson, Louisa to Stephen Jenne 10-11-1856 O
Simpson, Louisa to William Kelton 3-17-1859 We
Simpson, M. E. to V. M. Burton 12-15-1864 Hn
Simpson, M. F. to A. C. Braden 2-26-1878 (2-27-1878) L
Simpson, Mahala to William H. Smith 1-12-1850 (1-14-1850) G
Simpson, Margery J. to Wm. V. Anderson 8-5-1854 (8-30-1854) Sh
Simpson, Martha (Mrs.) to Daniel Holder 5-9-1843 G
Simpson, Martha A. to Walker Turnage 3-27-1844 (3-28-1844) T
Simpson, Martha Ann to Jesse Simpson 7-31-1872 (8-1-1872) T
Simpson, Martha S. to Hugh M. Lynn 4-9-1862 T
Simpson, Martha to Jonathan Mills 12-28-1878 (12-29-1878) Dy
Simpson, Martha to L. B. Roberts 2-16-1845 Hn
Simpson, Martha to Thomas Williams 3-29-1855 Hn
Simpson, Mary G. to John Wright 7-31-1872 (8-1-1872) T
Simpson, Mary J. to Albert Watson 11-20-1868 (11-22-1868) Dy
Simpson, Matilda to Jeremiah Evans 11-27-1852 (11-30-1852) L
Simpson, Misa (Miza?) to John J. Willis 7-7-1839 (7-8-1839) L
Simpson, N. A. to H. G. Gaines 1-3-1881 (1-4-1881) L
Simpson, N. D. to H. H. Bate 11-24-1873 (11-25-1873) T
Simpson, Nancy Ann to James M. Stewart 2-8-1864 (2-11-1864) O
Simpson?, Nancy I. to W. D. Ward 12-22-1853 Hr
Simpson, Nancy J. to Thomas Williams 12-23-1845 (no return) Hn
Simpson, Nancy to John T. Dowell 3-13-1843 (3-15-1843) T
Simpson, Octevy to Williama Chiles 1-30-1860 (1-31-1860) O
Simpson, Penny to Charles Alexander 2-12-1876 (no return) Hy
Simpson, Polly Ann to S. Stevens 9-29-1856 T
Simpson, Rebecca to A. S. Hord 7-8-1861 O
Simpson, Rebecca to Abraham Thompson 8-18-1855 O
Simpson, Sarah A. to Francis M. Rhodes 12-28-1853 O
Simpson, Sarah A. to James H.? Carrington 3-28-1860 (no return) We
Simpson, Sarah J. to Benjamin F. Mead 8-16-1847 (8-17-1847) O
Simpson, Sarah to John B. Davis 10-12-1846 (10-15-1846) T
Simpson?, Susan to S. C. Knight 2-20-1855 (2-21-1855) Hr
Simpson?, Caroline to Anderson Jones 12-23-1876 (12-26-1876) L
Sims, Alabama S. to Thomas H. Ward 11-30-1859 We
Sims, Ana to T. J. Ivy 12-30-1876 (1-1-1877) L
Sims, Bashiba to Shelton Littrell 12-29-1849 (12-30-1849) Hr
Sims, Caroline to Edmund Patterson 12-15-1884 (12-16-1884) L
Sims, Catharine to Martin Holliday 8-8-1859 (8-9-1859) Hr
Sims, Docia M. to Daniel Glisson 2-18-1851 (2-20-1851) G
Sims, Dovy to Jerry Johnson 8-24-1871 Hy
Sims, Eliza Ann to W. C. Thomason 5-17-1868 G
Sims, Elizabeth C. to G. W. Tatum 8-31-1850 (9-3-1850) G
Sims, Elizabeth J. to Allen Flowers 11-23-1853 (11-24-1853) G
Sims, Elizabeth to G. W. Sims 6-29-1856 We
Sims, Elsie Manna to Moses Trigg 12-31-1873 T
Sims, Emily F. to Elijah R. Reavis 1-22-1862 We
Sims, Fannie R. to Benj. J. Allen 11-6-1855 (no return) F
Sims, Jane to Jesse Glidwell 8-7-1841 (8-8-1841) Ma
Sims, Jane to Thomas Glidwell 11-4-1840 Ma
Sims, Josephine to Riley Thornton 9-27-1870 Hy
Sims, Lotty to Aleck Harris 7-9-1868 G B
Sims, M. J. to E. H. Lanon 2-5-1868 Hy
Sims, Maggie J. to Wm. J. Thompson 12-10-1870 (12-11-1870) Ma
Sims, Margaret C. to N. L. Hale 3-21-1858 We
Sims, Mary Jane to Harry Clay 1-16-1877 (1-22-1877) L B
Sims, Polly A. to George Kirk 10-23-1871 Dy
Sims, Polly Eliza to Giles O'Daniel 8-15-1855 G
Sims, Sarah E. to John Kelsoe 1-1-1868 Hn
Sims, Sarah R. to Frances M. Cleaver 10-5-1854 Hn
Sims, Virginia M. to William J. G. Birdsong 7-26-1862 (7-30-1862) Ma
Sinclair, Eliza to Henry Stevens 3-8-1870 (no return) Dy
Sinclair, Harriet to Harry Buchanan 12-30-1869 G B
Sinclair, Jane to Johnson Hicks 1-21-1868 G B
Sinclair, Lucreatia R. to Isaac L. Jetton 10-27-1853 G
Sinclair, M. Alice to J. L. Daniel 11-25-1869 (11-30-1869) Dy
Sinclair, M. L. to H. S. Brodie 2-7-1872 L
Sinclair, Margaret F. to William P. Smith 7-25-1854 O
Sinclair, Nannie B. to J. F. Osborn 10-1-1867 (no return) Dy
Sinclair, Narcissa C. to Charlie E. Butler, jr. 11-7-1876 (11-8-1876) L
Sinclair, Parale F. to R. G. Thomas 5-8-1875 L
Sinclair, Sarah to William Fenex 1-25-1843 Hn
Sinclair, V. L. to F. S. Chapman 3-8-1876 L
Sinclear, Elizabeth to John F. Phillips 9-9-1845 G
Singletary, C. C. to M. D. Anderson 5-18-1863 (no return) Dy
Singleterry, M. J. to T. F. Simpson 9-16-1868 (9-26-1868) Dy
Singleton, A. F. to W. M. Bradley 10-23-1866 (10-24-1866) Dy
Singleton, Ann E. to J. A. Webb 11-15-1854 L
Singleton, Caroline (mrs.) to William Mann 7-19-1873 (7-20-1873) Dy
Singleton, Caroline to Josiah Bateman 9-23-1867 (no return) Cr
Singleton, Elizabeth to John Holmes 9-3-1832 (9-20-1832) G
Singleton, Ellen to H. H. McClure 5-17-1867 (5-18-1867) Dy
Singleton, Emeline to M. W. Johnson 11-12-1869 (11-18-1869) Cr
Singleton, Jane to Jas. M. Pickens 1-24-1853 (no return) F
Singleton, Jane to Josiah Williams 9-2-1880 L
Singleton, Jane to Ransom Hamilton 7-29-1870 (no return) Dy
Singleton, M. M. to T. I. Grant 4-22-1866 (4-22-1865?) O
Singleton, Martha to William Cate 12-15-1852 Hn
Singleton, Mary J. to John A. Little 10-10-1839 Hn
Singleton, Mary to James Carroll 1-25-1834 G
Singleton, Mattie to D. Brock 3-29-1875 Dy
Singleton, May J. to Benj. H. Castelaw 10-22-1855 L
Singleton, Nancy H. to Isaac J. Ledbetter 12-22-1862 L
Singleton, Sarah to J. W. Richardson 1-8-1856 (1-9-1856) L
Singleton, Sarah to Joseph McCoy 1-28-1832 (1-29-1832) Hr
Singleton, Susannah H. to Pinkney A. Musgrave 9-6-1867 (9-8-1867) L
Sinkler, Elizabeth to Samuel E. Agnew 2-23-1853 (2-24-1853) O
Sinkler, Margaret Jane to Nicholas F. Inman 1-2-1857 O
Sinkler, Mary Ann to John Miller 9-27-1847 (9-28-1847) O
Sinkler, Minerva to Archibald C. Garrison 2-18-1858 O
Sinthicum, Mollie A. to J. H. Clay 12-24-1870 (no return) Hy
Sinthycorn, Roxey to J. A. Clay 9-22-1869 Hy
Sipes, Elizabeth to Thomas Cupples 2-?-1848 (3-1-1848) Ma
Sipes, Mary C. to Daniel Osben 12-26-1853 (12-27-1853) Ma
Sires?, Thursday to Samuel Watt 9-28-1861 G
Sisco, B. to L. G. Turner 1-6-1863 O
Sisco, Elizabeth F. to Calvin S. Floyd 10-16-1850 (10-17-1850) F
Sisco, Mary to George N. Allen 11-24-1845 (no return) F
Sisco, Sarah Jane to David C. Pollock 1-4-1858 (1-7-1858) O
Siser?, Margaret to Lawrence Stephens 12-4-1854 (12-15-1854) T
Sisk, Susannah to John Dobson 3-22-1853 Sh
Siske, Persilla C. to Luke Seay Mathis 8-2-1864 G
Sissil, Jane to Isaac S. Peterson 12-19-1885 (12-22-1885) L
Sistrunk, F. A. to William Bates 1-13-1882 (1-17-1882) L
Sistrunk, Rejoiner to T. L. Ashmore 1-7-1869 (1-12-1869) L
Sitler, Emily W. to William Plant 6-20-1843 (no return) F
Sitner, Harriet to John George Boyd 3-19-1872 T
Siver, Roxey to William Burdell 12-14-1864 Sh
Skaggs, Mary Ann to Robert M. Dillard 5-13-1847 Hn
Skallings, M. J. to J. C. Cook 1-26-1880 (1-29-1880) L
Skeggs, Alamerana to Washington Kelley 8-16-1842 Sh
Skeggs, M. V. to J. F. Lamb 7-17-1866 Hy
Skeggs, Rosina B. to J. W. Brewer 11-21-1866 (11-22-1866) F
Skelly (Kelly?), Mary to J. M. Rice 2-24-1859 Sh
Skelly, Catharine to Alexander Tynsen 4-26-1858 (4-27-1858) Sh
Skelly, Martha to Reid Blackwood 7-7-1856 Sh
Skelton, Ella V. to R. W. Wells 11-3-1860 Hy
Skepper, Sarah F. to John Goodrich 12-27-1864 (no return) Dy
Skiles, E. L. to Luther Barrett 2-24-1869 L
Skiles, Jane C. to Rufus Blackburn 12-15-1853 G
Skiles, Laura to Sam Jones 2-15-1872 Hy
Skiles, Margaret E. to Benjamin S. Cowan 12-15-1853 G
Skiles, Melissa I. to J. G. Hays 12-30-1869 L
Skiles, Ruthy B. to William Butler 3-10-1857 (3-11-1857) G
Skillen, ____ to Joshua Thompson no dates (with May 1838) F
Skillern, Ida to J. Hicks 9-3-1871 G
Skillern, Rebecca J. to Samuel H. Mulherin 8-2-1860 Ma
Skinner, Cynthia to Sylvester Woods 1-13-1848 Hn
Skinner, Elizabeth to Calvin B. Hull 3-22-1842 Hn
Skinner, Flora Ann to Alexander Slaughter 11-28-1869 G B
Skinner, Frances to David Tusley 6-22-1867 G B
Skinner, Louisa to Archabald Campbell 12-24-1847 (12-30-1847) Hr
Skipper, Easter to Bob Pulliam 12-31-1867 (1-4-1868) F B

Skipper, Ella to Green North 10-7-1867 Dy
Skipper, Harrett to William C. Guinn 5-16-1846 (5-17-1846) G
Skipper, Julian to Christian J. Barger 6-30-1860 (7-1-1860) Dy
Skipper, Lizzie to King Bird 12-24-1869 (12-29-1869) F B
Skipper, Martha to Robert Baker 7-13-1858 (7-27-1858) L
Skipper, Martha to S. H. Newland 2-20-1850 (no return) L
Skipper, Nancy Ann to Henry Clay Hix 10-31-1864 G
Skipper, Nancy J. to Millington Copeling 10-11-1860 G
Skipper, Sallie to Sion Turner 3-19-1870 G
Skipwith, E. C. to L. J. Wilson 2-27-1860 (2-28-1860) Sh
Skur, Elisabeth A. to Melvin Tarble 9-24-1864 (9-25-1864) Sh
Skyles, Ann S. to William G. Butler 9-27-1848 (9-28-1848) G
Skyles, Nancy J. to W. A. McLean 3-29-1866 G
Slacey (Stacey?), S. E. to J. G. Colwell 9-11-1876 (9-12-1876) L
Slack, Liza to Henry Smith 2-24-1872 O
Slade, Helen to Thos. H. Kean (Keon) 7-21-1846 Sh
Slager, Rosa to Augustus Ginzburger 6-11-1864 Sh
Slanty, Jane to Jackson Sutton 1-17-1857 Cr
Slass, V. T. to Plesant Manasco 11-2-1868 (11-4-1868) T
Slate, Amanda (Mrs.) to Alexander Bradley 1-12-1864 Sh
Slate, Caroline to William Redditt 12-24-1845 Sh
Slate, Loucretia Jane to John H. Winbury 10-30-1850 Sh
Slate, S. D. to N. B. Scott 12-14-1853 Sh
Slater, Harriet A. to James H. Curtis 9-25-1862 (9-26-1862) L
Slater, Martha to Wm. B. Shearman 1-14-1863 L
Slater, Penney L. to Reuben Taylor 7-26-1864 L
Slaton (Staton?), Fanny to T. Stone 1-17-1867 G
Slaton, Elizar O. to Marion Cobb no date (8-22-1869) Cr
Slaton, Mary A. E. to James H. Rogers 10-1-1855 (10-4-1855) G
Slaton, Tobitha L. to R. J. Carlton 10-20-1856 (10-21-1856) G
Slattery, Ellen to Nicholas Magrave 5-12-1855 Sh
Slaughter, Ailvice? to Wm. S. Jones 12-31-1839 F
Slaughter, Laura L. to W. W. McClarty 4-7-1868 (4-12-1868) F
Slaughter, Lucy A. to James R. Fallin 1-18-1871 T
Slaughter, M. A. to G.? J. Green 10-22-1866 (10-25-1866) F
Slaughter, M. A. to J. R. McCarty 1-29-18686 (2-1-1866) F
Slaughter, M. F. to R. E. McCheven 12-3-1866 (12-5-1866) F
Slaughter, Martha to Benjamin F. Boon 2-27-1844 Sh
Slaughter, Mary C. to John C. Garland 4-21-1868 T
Slaughter, Mary F. to Wm. Booth 2-12-1868 F
Slaughter, O. J. to J. M. Black 1-29-1866 (2-1-1866) F
Slaughter, Polly to James Alsup 10-24-1829 Hr
Slaughter, Sarah Jane to James L. Schrimsher 6-1-1868 (6-20-1868) L
Slaughter, Susan Eliz. to James Jefferson Culbreath 1-20-1851 (1-23-1851) T
Slauson, Grissey to Wilson Luckado 6-20-1853 (no return) F
Slaydon, Affey A. to Isaac James 6-29-1858 G
Slayton, Elizabeth to R. S. Hudspeth 12-25-1867 (12-26-1867) Dy
Slayton, Letty M. to William H. Cail 6-21-1855 G
Slayton, Martha A. to Richard Crichfield 1-21-1868 Dy
Slayton, Mary E. to Jesse Bailey 9-26-1868 (9-27-1868) Dy
Slayton, Sarah to Alfred Childers 12-23-1867 Dy
Slayton, Sarah to T. E. Lewellyn 3-6-1876 (3-8-1876) Dy
Sled, Lydia C. to William Jarrell 3-2-1854 Hn
Sledge, Appless P. to James H. McNeill 4-17-1855 Sh
Sledge, M. E. to S. S. Robertson 8-15-1855 Ma
Sledman, Matilda to John C. Baley 12-4-1827 Ma
Slew, Mary to Patrick Crowe 9-8-1860 (9-9-1860) Sh
Sley, Mary Ann to H. J. Harrison 8-5-1856 Sh
Slider, Sarah to John L. Guy 11-15-1865 O
Sloan, Anna to J. H. Alford 12-14-1870 (12-15-1870) F
Sloan, Deborah M. to John L. Pool 10-11-1839 (10-17-1839) F
Sloan, Elizabeth C. to William P. York 9-22-1850 Sh
Sloan, Elizabeth H. to Johnson Isbell 12-24-1834 (12-26-1834) G
Sloan, Ellen to W. F. Snow 6-28-1860 G
Sloan, Frances to Robert R. Sloan 1-5-1836 (1-6-1836) G
Sloan, Helen to Wm. C. Priest 7-2-1860 (7-4-1860) Hr
Sloan, Kissiah C. to Martin B. Jones 2-25-1841 (2-26-1841) G
Sloan, Malissa C. to Henry T. McFarland 7-21-1854 (7-23-1854) G
Sloan, Mary to Thomas J. Allison 1-5-1857 (1-6-1857) O
Sloan, Mollie A. to John S. Armstrong 2-18-1864 G
Sloan, Nancy E. to John A. Steel 7-10-1856 (7-21-1856) G
Sloan, Sallie to Robert Alexander 1-23-1860 G
Sloan, Temperance to Jesse Wolfe 6-29-1850 (6-30-1850) Hr
Sloane, Martha A. to S. A. Boyett 5-13-1869 F
Slocum, Harriett to Alfred Crowell 6-14-1849 Ma
Slone, Martha J. to James H. Warner 10-29-1839 (11-7-1839) F
Sloss, Amanda to Wm. C. Reynolds 1-13-1857 (1-22-1857) T
Sloss, Katie to A. M. Tate 4-20-1881 (4-25-1881) L
Sloss, Rebecca A. to Jessee Lockett 3-4-1861 (3-17-1861) T
Slough, Hetty to Jacob W. Meisenhimmer 12-25-1835 Sh
Slow, P. E. to Jno. B. Steel 9-27-1859 (9-28-1859) F
Sluter, Angeline to Levine Regas (Ragan) 4-24-1863 Sh
Small, A. A. E. to E. M. Cole 2-21-1860 (2-29-1860) F
Small, Elizabeth J. to Jacob Joyner 3-13-1851 Hn
Small, Lucy L. to Chas. L. Powers 1-28-1857 Sh
Small, Pleasan to Milus Alexander 2-28-1867 T
Small, Rebecca A. to S. P. Moore 11-14-1866 (11-15-1866) Ma

Smaller, Mary Ann to Rodolphus Spangle 8-17-1861 (8-20-1861) Sh
Smalley, E. T. to J. T. Zarber 4-10-1842 Be CC
Smalley, Mary to Hardin Joyce 4-16-1838 (4-19-1838?) Hr
Smallwood, Frances W. to Hamden McClanahan 6-5-1860 Hn
Smally, Caroline to Alfred Mabury 10-21-1847 Be
Smally, Elizabeth M. to Joseph W. Halford 12-19-1840 (12-23-1840) G
Smally, Elizabeth to B. Bell 1-2-1856 Be
Smally, Jane Elizabeth to J. C. Tilton 2-2-1848 (2-3-1848) Hr
Smally, Martha Jane to Allen J. Tucker 11-7-1859 Sh
Smalman, Mary A. D. to Jehu Graham 6-26-1851 F
Smart, Charlotte to L. M. Lee 3-5-1863 Hn
Smart, Emaline to A. J. Wright 12-1-1855 (no return) We
Smart, Martha E. to W. J. Funderbunk 4-13-1869 (4-15-1869) Ma
Smart, Nancy A. to Samule D. Golden 2-21-1860 We
Smart, Sarah to J. M. Arnett 12-18-1858 (12-22-1858) Hr
Smawley, E. J. to T. J. Yarber 4-8-1842 Be
Smawley, M. A. to T. Jones 4-10-1842 Be
Smelage, Harriet to Elcaner Parish 6-10-1844 We
Smiley, E. J. to L. M. Lee 3-5-1863 Hn
Smiley, Eliza to Benjin F. Miller 7-27-1844 Sh
Smiley, Rebecca to S. B. Sprowl 12-31-1867 Hn
Smiley?, Elizabeth to Henry Russell 1-8-1857 Hn
Smith, A. J. to G. F. Smith 12-17-1843 Hr
Smith, Ada M. to W. H. Lucy 6-28-1883 L
Smith, Adaline to Eatley Readen 8-?-1859 Cr
Smith, Adaline to Elisha Uptigrove 6-24-1860 Be
Smith, Adaline to William McVey 6-12-1867 (6-25-1867) F
Smith, Addie to James C. Ray 12-21-1870 (12-22-1870) Ma
Smith, Adeline to Parris Walker 1-11-1871 (no return) L
Smith, Agness W. to D. S. Boxley 11-23-1835 Hr
Smith, Ajesty to Calvin Norris 4-18-1839 Hr
Smith, Albertine to Thomas Kinney 5-25-1846 T
Smith, Allace to Joshua Small 5-12-1873 T
Smith, Allice to Ephm. Smith 1-2-1868 T
Smith, Almira P. to E. J. Williams 11-24-1858 (11-28-1858) Sh
Smith, Ama to George Moore 12-25-1872 (12-26-1872) Cr B
Smith, Amanda E. to J. D. Evans 1-18-1870 (no return) Hy
Smith, Amanda Jane to Mark Vanderbilt 10-23-1845 T
Smith, Amanda to Andrew Bishop 1-27-1869 Dy
Smith, Amanda to Edmond Swain 8-28-1868 (8-29-1868) T
Smith, Amanda to J. K. P. Ellis 3-20-1866 G
Smith, Amanda to Jeff Goforth 8-5-1879 (8-7-1879) Dy
Smith, Amanda to John Chilton 1-10-1878 Hy
Smith, Amanda to John W. Taylor 9-28-1863 Hn
Smith, Amanda? to Geo. Golston 12-15-1866 (12-16-1866) T
Smith, Amelia to Wm. J. Sturdivant 9-4-1855 (9-5-1855) Hr
Smith, Angaline to John M. Harris 10-25-1872 (10-27-1872) T
Smith, Angelina to Wm. A. Swindle 11-10-1850 Be
Smith, Ann A. to A. Perry 1-8-1873 (1-9-1873) L
Smith, Ann B. to John B. Lacy 12-15-1853 (12-16-1853) Hr
Smith, Ann Eliza to Flem Dunevant 12-16-1876 (12-21-1876) Dy
Smith, Ann Jane to Hamilton McClanahan 11-5-1829 Hr
Smith, Ann L. to Frank Milton 12-27-1865 T
Smith, Ann M. to John F. Denning 8-13-1863 We
Smith, Ann to Benj. F. Ray 5-26-1860 (no return) L
Smith, Ann to Bob Macklin 5-13-1869 T
Smith, Ann to James Goodwin 6-20-1870 T
Smith, Ann to Jefferson Pierce 8-27-1868 Dy
Smith, Ann to Jesse Williamson 12-11-1869 (12-12-1869) Cr
Smith, Ann to Jim Price 5-4-1867 G B
Smith, Ann to John Bowlen 5-2-1859 Sh
Smith, Ann to Robert Townsend 5-11-1867 Be
Smith, Anna C. to Wm. Hendren (Henden) 6-1-1840 Sh
Smith, Anne E. to L. T. Coalman 11-24-1871 Hy
Smith, Anner to Isham Goodwin 11-28-1868 T
Smith, Annie to Andrew Johnson 7-12-1873 (7-13-1873) Dy
Smith, Annie to H. L. Guon 4-14-1857 Sh
Smith, Anny to Washington Elam 7-29-1867 G B
Smith, Araminta A. to Jno. Sterling 8-4-1846 Sh
Smith, Artemissa J. to William B. Wilson 9-18-1865 Cr
Smith, Artie Caroline to Isaac Volentine Williams 11-20-1855 Ma
Smith, Barbara to Joe Kaughman 1-22-1880 (1-25-1880) L
Smith, Barbara to William Beck 4-25-1860 Sh
Smith, Bashly to Rich D. Wagster 9-11-1845 We
Smith, Berthy A. to Richard Powers 9-?-1844 (no return) Hn
Smith, Betsy P. to James H. Tisdale 1-16-1832 (1-17-1832) Hr
Smith, Bettie to Joseph Marshall 10-12-1847 T
Smith, Bettie to R. S. Fain 1-17-1872 Dy
Smith, C. A. to W. M. Moore 10-11-1882 L
Smith, C. C. to H. B. Turner 12-16-1867 (12-19-1867) F
Smith, Calodonia to Jacob Spivey 1-30-1851 Sh
Smith, Carlotta to William R. Corcy 10-14-1863 Hn
Smith, Carolina L. to Thomas R. Polk 12-15-1841 F
Smith, Caroline E. to Samuel Beavers 7-11-1852 Hn
Smith, Caroline N. to William A. Anderson 9-30-1856 Hn
Smith, Caroline to F. N. Cudd 8-24-1870 G
Smith, Caroline to George Fitze 3-15-1873 T

Brides

Smith, Caroline to Henry Welch 2-15-1836 (2-18-1836) G
Smith, Caroline to W. A. Pitts 10-23-1860 Dy
Smith, Caroline to Wiley M. Hicks 12-24-1866 (12-25-1866) Dy
Smith, Carra to Neal Bond 1-1-1866 (no return) Hy
Smith, Carrie to Toney Moore 3-26-1874 (3-28-1874) Dy
Smith, Catharine A. to Daniel K. Cockrahane 5-17-1843 (5-18-1843) F
Smith, Catharine H. to William Wilkins 7-14-1852 (7-15-1852) T
Smith, Catharine to John Wilson 12-28-1868 (12-31-1868) T
Smith, Catharine to Wm. C. Love 7-3-1838 G
Smith, Catherine C. to Riley Phillips 2-16-1860 Cr
Smith, Catherine E. to Chas. G. Smith 1-13-1870 T
Smith, Catherine E. to Gaml.? C. Dickey 4-3-1871 (4-20-1871) T
Smith, Catistia J. to C. P. Smith 6-13-1863 Mn
Smith, Celia C. to F. Adams 11-15-1844 Sh
Smith, Celia to G. A. Allen 4-20-1847 Be
Smith, Chainey to Butler Williams 9-12-1871 (9-16-1871) T
Smith, Charity to J. H. Whitelaw 1-4-1876 Hy
Smith, Charlott D. to C. W. Edwards 10-21-1856 G
Smith, Cheslina? to Samuel Stewart 7-13-1861 (7-18-1861) L
Smith, Christiana to William B. Carter 7-28-1839 Sh
Smith, Christianna G. to John Dawson 12-19-1838 (12-20-1838) Hr
Smith, Claway? to George Gibson 4-29-1868 T
Smith, Cordelia C. to W. F. Bridges 5-25-1865 (5-30-1865) Cr
Smith, Cordelia to M. Logan Anderson 3-25-1870 (3-30-1870) F
Smith, Cornelia A. to Wm. B. Langly 3-12?-1842 (no return) F
Smith, Cynthia to Jesse Marlar 8-15-1846 (no return) F
Smith, D. E. to M. B. Dyer 4-26-1859 (4-28-1859) F
Smith, D. to James Bromly 11-26-1850 Cr
Smith, Darcus to Frank McLemore 12-12-1870 (12-15-1870) T
Smith, Darcus to J. W. Saunderson 5-4-1872 (5-5-1872) Dy
Smith, Deborah to Wm. O. Rice 11-15-1860 (11-16-1860) Sh
Smith, Delia Ann to George Smith 7-1-1868 (7-19-1868) T
Smith, Delia to Wm. Trout no date (c. Sep 1866) T
Smith, Dephy to Charles Adams 1-1-1838 (1-6?-1838) Hr
Smith, Di to Sam Hopkins 2-4-1868 Hy
Smith, Dicy to Martin Briant 1-28-1836 (2-5-1836) G
Smith, Dis Ann to P. W. Smith 2-28-1865 Be
Smith, Donna to Spencer Goodman 3-29-1871 (4-4-1871) T
Smith, Dortha A(labama) to Benj. F. Williams 12-12-1865 (12-13-1865) Dy
Smith, Dovey to Gideon W. Mainard 8-21-1837 (8-31-1837) G
Smith, Drusilla to Bob Harris 12-15-1871 T
Smith, E. A. to W. H. Farris 2-3-1868 (2-5-1868) F
Smith, E. F. to J. S. Hall 12-7-1868 (12-8-1868) Dy
Smith, E. P. to Sidney Smith 6-11-1831 Hr
Smith, Eda to John Dill 7-5-1836 (7-7-1836) G
Smith, Elisabeth to James V. Haskins 11-30-1857 (12-10-1857) Hr
Smith, Eliza (Mrs.) to James Wilkinson 11-13-1864 Sh
Smith, Eliza Clewellyn to Cowell? Culbreath 8-3-1841 (8-5-1841) T
Smith, Eliza J. to C. W. Flanakin 1-23-1858 (2-4-1858) T
Smith, Eliza J. to Wm. B. Moore 3-4-1838 Cr
Smith, Eliza Jane to B. B. Buchanan 1-25-1847 Sh
Smith, Eliza T. to Jack Smith 1-4-1869 T
Smith, Eliza to Andrw J. Bowling 9-17-1851 (9-18-1851) G
Smith, Eliza to Felix Fletcher 11-19-1869 (no return) F B
Smith, Eliza to Hesikiah Strother 10-4-1880 (10-17-1880) Dy
Smith, Eliza to John Burrus 8-5-1856 (8-6-1856) G
Smith, Eliza to Joseph M. Busick 9-15-1858 (9-16-1858) O
Smith, Eliza to William Nolen 11-29-1875 L B
Smith, Eliza to Wm. W. Fogg 12-23-1847 Sh
Smith, Elizabet Ellen to Robert G. Jamison 10-21-1869 T
Smith, Elizabeth (Mrs.) to Charles Hampton 11-3-1866 G
Smith, Elizabeth A. to Charles Philip Edwards 9-11-1859 Sh
Smith, Elizabeth A. to D. D. Maxwell 2-1-1842 Cr
Smith, Elizabeth A. to Edward L. Provow 12-18-1858 Hn
Smith, Elizabeth A. to Harrison Baker 4-19-1838 Hn
Smith, Elizabeth A. to M. Fly 5-6-1847 Cr
Smith, Elizabeth A. to R. R. Gwyn 12-19-1842 F
Smith, Elizabeth A. to W. M. Waddle 2-8-1868 Cr
Smith, Elizabeth B. to Andrew J. Newsom 10-21-1865 (no return) F
Smith, Elizabeth C. to Marcus L. Anderson 3-7-1867 Be
Smith, Elizabeth C. to William R. Powell 11-21-1849 Hn
Smith, Elizabeth E. to Jon S. Vanhook 4-26-1851 Hn
Smith, Elizabeth Jane to William Hatley 2-8-1844 Be
Smith, Elizabeth R. to John C. Ward 4-3-1859 Hn
Smith, Elizabeth to A. T. Butler 3-11-1846 Cr
Smith, Elizabeth to Alexander Rhodes 8-19-1869 T
Smith, Elizabeth to Benjamin Edwards 10-6-1827 G
Smith, Elizabeth to Benjamin Edwards 10-6-1828 (10-14-1828) G
Smith, Elizabeth to Calvin Lewis 11-17-1844 Be
Smith, Elizabeth to Geo. Robinson 2-28-1844 Cr
Smith, Elizabeth to Henry Graves 4-23-1864 Be
Smith, Elizabeth to Henry Whitlaw 4-28-1849 (4-29-1849) Ma
Smith, Elizabeth to Henry Willson 10-3-1863 Sh
Smith, Elizabeth to J. H. Rosson 5-1-1860 Sh
Smith, Elizabeth to Jeremiah Hollady 6-5-1847 (6-13-1847) Hr
Smith, Elizabeth to Jess Sturtivant 7-10-1841 (7-14-1841) Ma
Smith, Elizabeth to Jesse Bowden 2-19-1847 (no return) F

Smith, Elizabeth to John B. Stacey 3-17-1852 O
Smith, Elizabeth to John French 8-3-1839 (8-4-1839) O
Smith, Elizabeth to John N. Nailing 10-15-1845 We
Smith, Elizabeth to John Pettijohn 2-1-1845 (2-2-1845) O
Smith, Elizabeth to Lemuel Poyner 11-14-1840 (11-15-1840) Hr
Smith, Elizabeth to Lucius H. Alderson 11-11-1853 Hn
Smith, Elizabeth to Pall Barner 10-30-1870 G
Smith, Elizabeth to Robert Pope 5-16-1834 G
Smith, Elizabeth to Sidney Hall 4-4-1870 (4-10-1870) T
Smith, Elizabeth to Stephen R. Smith 8-4-1856 (8-7-1856) O
Smith, Elizabeth to Thomas Young 9-10-1849 Hr
Smith, Elizabeth to W. D. Cole 4-30-1863 Be
Smith, Elizabeth to William H. Chappell 12-15-1855 (no return) Hn
Smith, Elizabeth to Willis Wood 6-23-1846 Ma
Smith, Elizabeth to Wm. Stephenson 7-5-1840 Cr
Smith, Elizah to J. W. S. Long 8-29-1838 (8-30-1838) F
Smith, Elizer to Wm. G. Crockett 10-26-1841 Cr
Smith, Ella V. to H. P. (Dr.) Cotton 10-3-1870 (10-5-1870) Ma
Smith, Ella? to Bill Woods 10-4-1873 T
Smith, Ellen C. to James McCorkle 6-28-1861 (6-30-1861) O
Smith, Ellen to Asa Margan 10-28-1865 T
Smith, Ellen to Benjamin F. James 9-24-1852 (9-28-1852) G
Smith, Ellen to Daniel T. Hooey 7-9-1869 (7-11-1869) F
Smith, Ellen to Ferdinand Alexander 12-17-1879 L
Smith, Ellen to Henry T. Sumerow 12-20-1853 (12-21-1853) L
Smith, Ellen to John Hudson 11-27-1830 (12-2-1831) Hr
Smith, Ellen to Manuel Bolton 1-4-1868 G B
Smith, Ellen to Wm. Hatfield 12-17-1847 Sh
Smith, Elmira to Wm. Sanders 12-21-1844 (12-22-1844) F
Smith, Elvira to George H. Sumerow 11-21-1854 (11-23-1854) L
Smith, Elvora to Ed Williamson 11-27-1868 Cr
Smith, Emaline to W. Hill 10-16-1873 T B
Smith, Emeline to Enoch Anderson 5-6-1847 Be
Smith, Emeline to Henry Jones 11-26-1869 T
Smith, Emeline to Thomas Kinney 9-26-1855 T
Smith, Emeline to W. H. D. Dickens 1-12-1868 (1-2-1868) T
Smith, Emeline to William Burrow 12-12-1848 (12-13-1848) Ma
Smith, Emeline to Wm. C. Anderson 8-8-1837 Sh
Smith, Emeritter to James D. Leigh 3-13-1867 (3-14-1867) Cr
Smith, Emerline to Clay Yarbro 12-25-1866 T
Smith, Emiline to Ivy Cole 11-3-1866 (11-4-1866) O
Smith, Emily to Jacob Taylor 9-16-1876 Hy
Smith, Emily to James L. Haggard 1-16-1839 (no return) Cr
Smith, Emily to Jessee Robinson 12-8-1876 Hy
Smith, Emily to Silas McCullough 8-19-1871 T
Smith, Emily to Wm. C. Ryan 1-11-1851 (1-15-1851) L
Smith, Emma to F. M. Adams 11-26-1865 Hn
Smith, Eoma to T. A. Tanner 1-7-1854 G
Smith, Euphemia to Robt. F. McClennin 2-10-1859 Sh
Smith, Evaline H. to John T. Douglass 1-21-1842 T
Smith, Evaline to James Brady 1-8-1876 (no return) L
Smith, Evaline to Johnathan Lowry 7-9-1844 Hn
Smith, Evaline to W. W. Mullins 3-30-1864 Be
Smith, Evaline to Wesley Clark 12-30-1846 Sh
Smith, Evaline to Wm. Ray Whitlock 2-5-1849 (2-8-1849) T
Smith, Eve to John Fred Delless 12-26-1871 L
Smith, F. A. to G. W. F. Crunch 4-27-1852 (no return) F
Smith, F. C. to J. D. Coleman 2-22-1864 O
Smith, F. E. to James A. McCaskill 12-19-1856 (no return) F
Smith, F. P. to E. A. McMackins 1-5-1872 (1-7-1872) Cr
Smith, Fanie (Mrs.) to Alse Garrett 9-12-1866 (9-13-1866) Dy
Smith, Fannie to Green Anderson 12-22-1869 T
Smith, Fannie to Henry Percell 11-28-1868 (no return) L
Smith, Fannie to Levi Shepherd 4-10-1873 (4-11-1873) Dy
Smith, Fannie to Peter Rucker 12-10-1873 (12-14-1873) L B
Smith, Fannie to Richard Woodson 2-12-1874 Dy
Smith, Fanny to George W. Reeves 12-19-1842 (12-22-1842) O
Smith, Fanny to John W. Whitford 12-8-1872 Hy
Smith, Fany to John Scott 6-19-1869 T
Smith, Fielder to James Cockron 2-12-1839 Cr
Smith, Frances A. to George M. Roseman 1-30-1860 (no return) Hy
Smith, Frances A. to Philemon T. Burford 3-4-1842 (no return) F
Smith, Frances B. to Albert W. Posey 4-20-1859 L
Smith, Frances C. to L. Y. Blakley 12-21-1865 Mn
Smith, Frances J. to Willie Coor 5-2-1836 (5-5-1836) Hr
Smith, Frances to Andy Hall 6-6-1873 (6-14-1873) T
Smith, Frances to Asa Bradshaw 2-28-1871 (3-3-1871) Dy
Smith, Frances to Charley Alison 12-15-1872 Hy
Smith, Frances to James McClelland 9-22-1859 T
Smith, Frances to James Parier 3-15-1874 Hy
Smith, Frances to Layton Choat 12-22-1860 Sh
Smith, Frances to Miles Floyd 11-30-1865 Dy
Smith, Frances to Wm. Spence 2-22-1878 (2-23-1878) Dy
Smith, Gatsy H. to M. C.? Newberry 7-20-1842 F
Smith, Genny to Harry Green 10-9-1868 Hy
Smith, Gletha to James Vincent 1-27-1842 (1-28-1842) G
Smith, Gracy to Peter Barnes 6-12-1867 Hy

Smith, H. A. to C. S. Fowler 1-10-1856 We
Smith, H. R. to A. B. Christian 6-24-1868 (6-25-1868) Cr
Smith, H. T. to S. S. Collins 7-19-1855 Cr
Smith, Hannah to Alexander Smith 5-10-1852 T
Smith, Hannah to Wade Gaines 4-16-1874 (4-23-1874) T
Smith, Harriet J. to J. M. Witherington 1-27-1866 (1-28-1866) T
Smith, Harriet Jo to Benj. F. Smith 5-20-1868 (5-24-1868) Cr
Smith, Harriet to Columbus Jenkins 11-11-1873 (11-12-1873) T
Smith, Harriet to Cyrus W. Hutchison 12-16-1849 T
Smith, Harriet to George C. Barfield 1-30-1829 Ma
Smith, Harriett R. to Thomas R. Porter 9-27-1858 Cr
Smith, Harriett R. to Wm. W. Moore 7-8-1854 Cr
Smith, Harriett to Jacob Pioneer 3-16-1836 Sh
Smith, Harriett to Madison Walker 12-28-1871 Hy
Smith, Hellen to J. W. Myers 4-2-1874 T
Smith, Henrietta to Nathaniel Wortham 4-29-1852 T
Smith, I. J. to J. K. McClerkin 3-28-1871 (3-29-1871) T
Smith, Idotha to Jerome B. Cooley 2-25-1846 O
Smith, Isabella F. to John H. Barret 12-14-1870 F
Smith, Isabella to Dan Simmons 3-17-1875 (3-18-1875) Dy
Smith, Isabella to Whit F. Alston 2-10-1873 (2-12-1873) T
Smith, Jane A. to William A. Smith 8-10-1848 F
Smith, Jane M. to Thomas M. Williams 5-25-1861 T
Smith, Jane R. to James Owen 11-5-1838 (no return) F
Smith, Jane T. (Mrs.) to Thos. P. Clement (Weakley Co) 3-16-1870 Ma
Smith, Jane to A. McGee 12-5-1860 (12-6-1861) We
Smith, Jane to A. P. Utterback 10-15-1857 Hn
Smith, Jane to C. H. (Dr.) Nelson 8-29-1860 Sh
Smith, Jane to James Stevenson 1-6-1855 Ma
Smith, Jane to Joshua Cooley 6-29-1860 (6-30-1860) O
Smith, Jane to Nathan James 6-30-1869 G B
Smith, Jane to Ned Smith 11-18-1870 Hy
Smith, Jane to Robt. Looney 9-11-1844 (no return) We
Smith, Jane to S. W. Moore 4-22-1854 (4-27-1854) Sh
Smith, Jane to William G. Stephens 11-23-1832 (11-24-1832) G
Smith, Jane to Wm. Hemphill 12-20-1871 T
Smith, Jemima J. to John A. Cheatham 4-12-1860 Hn
Smith, Jennie to G. A. Glover 4-9-1872 (4-10-1872) O
Smith, Jennie to George Tyree 2-24-1868 G B
Smith, Jennie to Marshall Currin 2-12-1874 (no return) Hy
Smith, Jennie to Newton Clements 6-21-1872 Hy
Smith, Jennie to Samuel Henderson 2-22-1883 (3-10-1883) L
Smith, Joanna to William Byars 12-26-1871 Hy
Smith, Joella to James Dorsey 1-14-1869 Dy
Smith, Josephine to Matthew Dumas 2-16-1874 Dy
Smith, Josie to J. I. Fenn 2-7-1872 Dy
Smith, Judie to Peter Rodgers 9-27-1871 Hy
Smith, Julia Ann to James Hall 1-29-1871 (no return) Dy
Smith, Julia C. to H. W. Beaver 10-29-1873 (11-3-1873) T
Smith, Julia D. to Joseph H. Wardlaw 7-10-1850 L
Smith, Julia P. to George A. Coon 12-9-1874 Dy
Smith, Julia to George Alston 11-29-1866 (11-30-1866) T
Smith, Julia to Henry Alexander 1-24-1878 Hy
Smith, Jullia (Mrs.) to F. A. Parker 5-13-1869 (5-16-1869) F
Smith, Jullia A. to J. W. Renfrow 10-10-1865 G
Smith, Kate (Mrs.) to N. B. Murphy 6-19-1869 (6-22-1869) L
Smith, Kate M. to Jessee Tucker 10-24-1857 (10-25-1857) G
Smith, Kate to Preston L. Smith 6-5-1867 (6-6-1867) L
Smith, Kezir? to William Campbell 1-30-1866 (1-31-1866) T
Smith, Kissiah to William Runalds 4-21-1847 (4-22-1847) G
Smith, L. C. J. to R. J. Hall 2-26-1881 (3-3-1881) L
Smith, L. C. to H. C. Dozier 8-31-1866 G
Smith, L. E. to J. T. Pace 7-22-1873 (7-24-1873) Dy
Smith, L. J. to J. H. L. Cathey 7-27-1871 (7-30-1871) O
Smith, L. M. T. to F. M. Nelson 11-22-1877 (11-25-1877) Dy
Smith, L. M. to John Boughner (Beughner?) 7-28-1864 Sh
Smith, L. P. to F. M. Brownlow 6-2-1860 (6-7-1860) F
Smith, L. Virginia to John H. French 1-11-1853 (1-12-1853) Sh
Smith, Laura E. to Needham Stevens 12-15-1874 (12-16-1874) T
Smith, Laura to Benjamin Herron 3-23-1869 (3-24-1869) Cr
Smith, Laura to Louis Gray 12-10-1870 T
Smith, Lavenia to W. C. Barcroft 10-19-1875 (no return) Hy
Smith, Lavicy to Will W. Rhodes 4-4-1839 (4-10-1839) Hr
Smith, Lean to Horace Spickernagle 12-31-1853 (1-1-1854) Sh
Smith, Lee Ann to Claudius Velasques 7-30-1850 Sh
Smith, Leer to Andrew J. Ross 9-14-1837 (9-21-1837) G
Smith, Leir to William Young 11-11-1826 G
Smith, Lenora to William W. Femister 1-14-1864 Sh
Smith, Lettie to Geo. Sams 1-7-1873 Hy
Smith, Letty to William Akins 11-6-1839 Cr
Smith, Levicy C. to Peter Culp 10-20-1867 Hy
Smith, Levina to Thomas Baker 12-22-1829 (1-26-1830) G
Smith, Lizzie to Andrew Runstetter 4-9-1860 Sh
Smith, Lizzie to Jordon Hart 5-28-1870 T
Smith, Louisa Ann to Andrew Jackson Douglass 12-21-1846 T
Smith, Louisa F. to John B. (R.?) Elmore 3-13-1861 (3-14-1861) Sh
Smith, Louisa to Thomas R. Wheatley 12-23-1871 (12-24-1871) L
Smith, Louisa to William Clarke 1-24-1863 (1-26-1863) Sh
Smith, Louisianna C. to John C. Pace 2-25-1847 (3-?-1847) T
Smith, Louiza to L. G. Parham 5-27-1871 (6-7-1871) Cr
Smith, Lucinda C. to John J. Sherrod 5-13-1857 T
Smith, Lucinda to Cord Norman 7-15-1857 (7-19-1857) L
Smith, Lucinda to Ira Beliles 6-6-1835 Hr
Smith, Lucinda to Jno. Prior 10-21-1846 We
Smith, Lucinda to John L. Pryor 10-19-1846 We
Smith, Lucinda to Monroe Vinson 2-15-1871 L
Smith, Lucretia Jane to Thomas J. Hill 4-16-1869 (4-18-1869) T
Smith, Lucy A. to John H. Bell 10-9-1866 Ma
Smith, Lucy A. to Newell T. Strayhorn 1-3-1844 Ma
Smith, Lucy A. to Robt. L. Doak 1-20-1862 (no return) Dy
Smith, Lucy Ann to John A. Pearce 2-5-1870 (2-10-1870) F
Smith, Lucy C. to Isaac C. Mathis 11-4-1856 (11-5-1856) O
Smith, Lucy Ellen to Saml. P. C. Johnson 2-5-1844 T
Smith, Lucy G. to John Y. Rust 2-25-1846 Cr
Smith, Lucy Jane to James M. Woodard 8-3-1869 (no return) Cr
Smith, Lucy R. to David D. Blair 6-18-1838 (6-21-1838) G
Smith, Lucy T. to J. M. Neal 10-5-1869 Hy
Smith, Lucy to Alex Tipton 6-3-1879 Dy
Smith, Lucy to James Fowlkes 12-1-1870 Dy B
Smith, Lucy to Josiah Moore 6-10-1831 G
Smith, Lucy to Minor Wood 1-20-1869 Dy
Smith, Lucy to Silas McMurry 10-22-1870 (10-23-1870) O
Smith, Luriraney to Eli Stanley 4-6-1828 Ma
Smith, Lutita to Kinan Branch 9-7-1869 Hy
Smith, Lyda to Asa Perry 2-2-1843 (2-4-1843) G
Smith, Lydia M. to Nathl. W. Staples 10-2-1852 (10-21-1852) Sh
Smith, M. A. to J. W. Beard 12-23-1863 Hn
Smith, M. C. to C. W. Waddall 8-21-1838 F
Smith, M. C. to L. W. Barnes 10-8-1865 Mn
Smith, M. E. to A. Blackburn 8-1-1870 (8-5-1870) O
Smith, M. E. to F. E. Scobey 12-11-1878 (12-12-1878) Dy
Smith, M. E. to James F. Sudberry 11-25-1873 (no return) Dy
Smith, M. E. to John F. Newsom 8-6-1860 Hr
Smith, M. F. to J. S. Thompson 8-12-1867 (8-13-1867) Dy
Smith, M. F. to J. W. Echols 12-26-1876 (12-27-1876) Dy
Smith, M. F. to W. J. Jenkins 5-24-1880 (5-25-1880) L
Smith, M. J. to D. G. Griffin 9-14-1860 (no return) Hy
Smith, M. J. to J. H. Tipton 4-12-1871 (no return) Dy
Smith, M. J. to J. P. Troy 9-14-1863 (9-15-1863) Dy
Smith, M. J. to J. W. Payne 2-20-1871 (3-7-1871) T
Smith, M. J. to James T. Elliss 4-25-1865 (-26-1865) O
Smith, M. J. to Phillip J. Neely 12-19-1859 (12-22-1859) Hr
Smith, M. S. to S. W. Jones 5-12-1866 Hn
Smith, M. S. to T. B. Johnson 11-9-1847 Cr
Smith, Maggie to James Harper 12-29-1870 Hy
Smith, Malinda R. I. to John L. Ogles 6-19-1852 (6-20-1852) G
Smith, Malinda to George Howerd 8-17-1872 T
Smith, Manda H. to James R. Davis 3-22-1855 G
Smith, Margaret A. V. to Simon Cruse 12-24-1878 Hy
Smith, Margaret Ann to Elijah Robert Himey 8-20-1857 T
Smith, Margaret Ann to Isaac N. Little 2-20-1862 Hn
Smith, Margaret Ann to Wm. Franklin Archer 12-5-1849 T
Smith, Margaret E. to Benjamin K. Harper 1-31-1838 (2-1-1838) O
Smith, Margaret J. to Robert C. Johnston 1-30-1842 Hn
Smith, Margaret to Frederick Lodvig 9-29-1851 Sh
Smith, Margaret to J. G. Toombs 1-3-1866 (SB 1867) G
Smith, Margaret to William Vaughn 2-10-1859 Hn
Smith, Margaret to Wm. C. Sessom 10-25-1855 Sh
Smith, Maria to Charles Winn 2-23-1866 (2-24-1866) T
Smith, Mariah F. to Everett G. Miles 1-13-1846 O
Smith, Mariah J. to Wm. H. Harrison 4-3-1868 (4-4-1868) T
Smith, Mariah to Andrew Johnson 2-5-1876 (no return) Hy
Smith, Marry (Amey?) to Jordan Burrow 5-19-1871 (5-20-1871) Cr
Smith, Martha A. (Mrs.) to Vinis Turner 7-14-1873 (7-15-1873) L
Smith, Martha A. B. to Thomas B. Bronaugh 5-17-1879 (5-23-1879) L
Smith, Martha A. F. to Walter M. Murphy 1-10-1844 (1-11-1844) Hr
Smith, Martha A. to G. W. Williams 2-27-1868 G
Smith, Martha A. to H. B. Holcomb 10-3-1867 Hn
Smith, Martha A. to J. M. Daniel 12-1-1864 Sh
Smith, Martha A. to John F. Parker 4-4-1860 (no return) We
Smith, Martha Ann Frances to James T____ 12-10-1842 (12-15-1842) T
Smith, Martha Ann to John W. McElyea 1-23-1850 Sh
Smith, Martha Ann to Plesat (Pleasant) W. Mullinix 8-18-1847 Be
Smith, Martha Ann to William Simmons 12-10-1839 Ma
Smith, Martha C. to Solomon C. Sparks 3-23-1841 Hr
Smith, Martha E. to Geo. Brimen 12-28-1878 (no return) Dy
Smith, Martha E. to Wm. T. Firth 11-15-1859 (12-13-1859) F
Smith, Martha G. to James M. Hollin 1-30-1856 Cr
Smith, Martha H. to C. G. Griffith 12-13-1858 (12-15-1858) T
Smith, Martha J. to George G. Brooks 11-27-1862 (no return) Hy
Smith, Martha J. to Green C. Rogers 7-31-1866 (8-2-1866) Cr
Smith, Martha J. to James M. Hollowell 1-30-1866 Cr
Smith, Martha J. to Jno. B. Caroway 1-14-1868 (1-16-1868) F
Smith, Martha J. to Nathaniel Warren 10-27-1851 (10-29-1851) Sh

Smith, Martha J. to Samuel L. Chilton 2-16-1870 Cr
Smith, Martha J. to Victor Clampet 10-17-1854 (no return) F
Smith, Martha J. to W. A. Finch 11-12-1849 (11-14-1849) Hr
Smith, Martha J. to W. B. Morrow 7-17-1855 (7-19-1855) Hr
Smith, Martha J. to W. S. Bell 2-22-1859 Hr
Smith, Martha J. to William Walker 5-30-1840 (no return) Hn
Smith, Martha Jane to James Moses 4-23-1853 (4-25-1853) O
Smith, Martha Jane to Spencer A. Spicer 12-16-1852 Be
Smith, Martha M. to E. Anderson 1-17-1861 Sh
Smith, Martha S. to Moses Vaughan 11-20-1865 (11-22-1865) T
Smith, Martha T. to William S. Wright 6-26-1863 (7-2-1863) Dy
Smith, Martha W. to Charles J.? Fisher 12-3-1868 (12-9-1868) T
Smith, Martha W. to James W. Manning no date (with Oct 1852) F
Smith, Martha to Africa Shaw 9-26-1871 Hy
Smith, Martha to Harrison Malone 11-8-1872 T
Smith, Martha to Jacob Honeycut 12-7-1859 (12-8-1859) O
Smith, Martha to James H. Norton 6-21-1866 (6-22-1866) Ma
Smith, Martha to James McAlexander 2-23-1852 (2-24-1852) Ma
Smith, Martha to Joshua Harris 2-10-1845 Cr
Smith, Martha to Lauson Autney 1-15-1870 Hy
Smith, Martha to P. W. Lunsford 4-3-1878 (4-7-1878) L
Smith, Martha to Richard Dawson 9-15-1842 (9-16-1842) Ma
Smith, Martha to Richard R. Cole 5-1-1838 Cr
Smith, Martha to Samuel Craig 9-20-1862 (9-21-1862) Ma
Smith, Martha to William Housden 11-12-1851 Hn
Smith, Martha to Zachariah Dement 12-3-1857 O
Smith, Mary A. E. to Samuel Singer 2-3-1859 Ma
Smith, Mary A. to B. W. Johnson 9-31?-1854 Cr
Smith, Mary A. to James H. Hastings 10-12-1853 Hn
Smith, Mary A. to Jerrod J. Ethridge 10-1-1847 (10-3-1847) G
Smith, Mary A. to John B. Warren 2-9-1858 Cr
Smith, Mary A. to John C. Neal 1-14-1847 (no return) Hn
Smith, Mary A. to Robert Wren 8-1-1865 (no return) Cr
Smith, Mary A. to W. A. J. Walker 9-7-1870 (no return) Dy
Smith, Mary A. to Wm. J. Meadow 7-25-1864 (7-26-1864) O
Smith, Mary Ann to George Snyder 11-18-1857 Sh
Smith, Mary Ann to Isaac Harrison 7-8-1854 (7-9-1854) Sh
Smith, Mary Ann to James Aslin 12-24-1853 G
Smith, Mary Ann to John W. Arbuckle 10-7-1852 (10-10-1852) G
Smith, Mary Ann to Joseph D. Glasgoe 10-14-1845 (no return) We
Smith, Mary Ann to Levi Gordon 10-19-1858 Cr
Smith, Mary Ann to Wesley Byars 11-14-1877 Hy
Smith, Mary Ann to West W. Wiggins 6-1-1839 (6-5-1839) Hr
Smith, Mary C. to Anthony Graham 2-2-1870 (2-3-1870) Ma
Smith, Mary C. to Geo. Wilson 2-2-1846 (2-5-1846) Hr
Smith, Mary C. to James T. Hopkins 4-5-1860 (no return) Hy
Smith, Mary C. to John Brassell 10-24-1871 T
Smith, Mary C. to Thomas Peacock 12-17-1840 Sh
Smith, Mary D. to Nathaniel C. Carpenter 10-29-1849 (11-1-1849) Ma
Smith, Mary E. to Absolum T. J. Humphreys 10-7-1844 (10-24-1844) T
Smith, Mary E. to Allen G. Gooch 4-27-1852 (4-28-1852) Ma
Smith, Mary E. to B. W. McAdams 4-6-1869 F
Smith, Mary E. to G. L. Kinney 12-16-1873 (12-17-1873) T
Smith, Mary E. to Henry A. Ridley 9-15-1853 (no return) F
Smith, Mary E. to Isaac R. Shelton 5-8-1855 (5-20-1855) Sh
Smith, Mary E. to Isaac Winfield 10-9-1872 T
Smith, Mary E. to J. A. Arwood 8-19-1882 L
Smith, Mary E. to John P. Samuels 8-30-1855 Sh
Smith, Mary E. to Robert Clark 12-19-1863 (12-21-1863) Sh
Smith, Mary E. to Stephen Franklin 11-1-1864 (10?-1-1864) Sh B
Smith, Mary E. to W. D. Woodson 12-18-1850 Be
Smith, Mary F. to A. D. Wells 1-16-1867 L
Smith, Mary F. to E. R. Barcus 6-28-1852 Sh
Smith, Mary F. to Samuel A. Hogue 3-22-1851 (3-27-1851) Hr
Smith, Mary G. to Charles Love 9-22-1839 Sh
Smith, Mary I. to W. H. Cole 9-8-1866 O
Smith, Mary J. to Columbus Blasingame 4-14-1874 T
Smith, Mary J. to John T. Steele 5-29-1867 (5-30-1867) Cr
Smith, Mary J. to Marion J. Philips 10-4-1855 (10-5-1855) G
Smith, Mary J. to W. A. Thurmond 6-6-1884 (6-15-1884) L
Smith, Mary J. to Wm. H. Allison 1-13-1876 (no return) Hy
Smith, Mary James to Samuel Duncan 12-27-1855 Hr
Smith, Mary Jane to Elisha Hardester 6-18-1839 (no return) Cr
Smith, Mary Jane to G. W. Jones 6-10-1861 (6-11-1861) T
Smith, Mary Jane to George W. Lunsford 1-9-1867 (no return) L
Smith, Mary Jane to James D. Davis 12-14-1834 Sh
Smith, Mary Jane to Porter Black 9-28-1865 Mn
Smith, Mary Jane to Sherwood R. Davis 4-2-1870 (4-3-1870) Ma
Smith, Mary L. to George A. Woodson 8-4-1851 Hr
Smith, Mary L. to John P. Taylor 6-2-1858 V
Smith, Mary Louisa to Alexander McDaniel 2-8-1835 (2-12-1835) Hr
Smith, Mary M. to Isaac W. Bliss 8-5-1850 Sh
Smith, Mary M. to J. H. Hollenbeck 12-1-1857 (12-7-1857) Sh
Smith, Mary P. to W. P. Harwell 1-1-1878 Hy
Smith, Mary S. to S. D. Anderson 12-5-1861 Mn
Smith, Mary T. to Nazareth J. Bentley 9-19-1867 (9-20-1867) L
Smith, Mary T. to Samuel Y. Giffin 2-13-1838 O

Smith, Mary W. to B. F. Hamm 9-5-1861 Mn
Smith, Mary to A. B. Bledsoe 7-4-1858 Cr
Smith, Mary to Alex Connell 5-27-1871 (5-28-1871) Dy
Smith, Mary to B. F. Miller 11-12-1867 O
Smith, Mary to Bob Fitzgerald 1-1-1868 G B
Smith, Mary to Daniel Wynn 10-8-1845 (no return) Hn
Smith, Mary to E. B. Best 8-31-1882 (9-3-1882) L
Smith, Mary to E. Best 4-5-1882 (9-3-1882) L
Smith, Mary to Eugene Magerney 5-31-1840 Sh
Smith, Mary to F. M. Wimberley 12-2-1866 Hn
Smith, Mary to Henry Brown 12-30-1871 T
Smith, Mary to Henry C. Clarke 5-25-1854 Sh
Smith, Mary to Hosea Barker 3-21-1841 Sh
Smith, Mary to Ivason Booser 9-28-1871 T
Smith, Mary to J. B. Parsons 6-9-1866 (6-10-1866) T
Smith, Mary to James M. Neal 9-28-1838 (9-30-1838) F
Smith, Mary to James Welch 6-26-1845 Sh
Smith, Mary to James Wright 5-4-1861 Sh
Smith, Mary to John Bauden 4-14-1842 Sh
Smith, Mary to John Lewis 9-30-1855 Be
Smith, Mary to John Rose 12-30-1851 (1-1-1852) Sh
Smith, Mary to Joseph Kirby 12-14-1871 (12-15-1871) Cr
Smith, Mary to Joseph R. Hamilton 6-20-1838 Sh
Smith, Mary to Joseph Springer 10-24-1866 G
Smith, Mary to Kelley Goodman 11-3-1866 (11-4-1866) T
Smith, Mary to Martin Kennedy 8-8-1853 Sh
Smith, Mary to N. C. Corley 8-27-1867 G
Smith, Mary to Thomas Wells 2-17-1866 (2-18-1866) Dy
Smith, Mary to Washington Ligon 1-17-1874 (1-4?-1874) T
Smith, Mary to William Dwyer 2-24-1859 (2-25-1859) Sh
Smith, Mary to William Jackson 2-6-1867 F B
Smith, Matilda Ann to Aden Johnson 10-1-1842 (10-6-1842) F
Smith, Matilda C. to Joseph Turner 10-11-1841 (10-21-1841) F
Smith, Matilda M. to J. C. Bolem 4-16-1868 Be
Smith, Matilda to Charles Frazier 8-21-1869 (8-23-1869) T
Smith, Matilda to Hardin Smith 7-18-1883 (7-26-1883) L
Smith, Matilda to R. F. Roberts 9-8-1842 Sh
Smith, Mattie A. to Edward Matthews 4-13-1859 (4-14-1859) Ma
Smith, Mattie E. to John C. Howell 12-24-1877 L
Smith, Mattie G. to T.R. Wheatley 10-16-1869 (10-17-1869) L
Smith, Mattie to Ananias Bond 3-5-1873 (no return) Hy
Smith, Mattie to Annias Bond 3-15-1873 T
Smith, Mattie to Charles Carter 4-11-1871 (4-15-1871) F B
Smith, Mattie to Charley Parris 10-24-1885 (10-25-1885) L
Smith, Mattie to Chas. Brodenaux 1-22-1875 Hy
Smith, Mattie to Columbus Jenkins 11-21-1884 (11-30-1884) L
Smith, Mein? to Henry Johnson 11-30-1878 (12-1-1878) Dy
Smith, Mildred to John Smith 12-29-1868 (12-31-1868) T
Smith, Milla to Nelson Roberts 11-18-1868 F B
Smith, Minerva to Antelpes? Bond 5-5-1871 (5-7-1871) T
Smith, Minerva to John Smith 3-23-1862 G
Smith, Minnie E. to E. McDaniel 2-26-1874 T
Smith, Minnoy? to William McIntosh 7-29-1865 T
Smith, Miss ___ to Jacob McCoy 4-2-1874 Dy
Smith, Miss to B. F. Talliaferro 2-24-1846 (no return) We
Smith, Mitty to Henry Wilson 12-22-1875 Hy
Smith, Molinda to Harmon Chapman 11-7-1843 We
Smith, Mollie E. to N. S. Moore 12-14-1880 L
Smith, Mollie to George Smith 8-8-1878 Dy
Smith, Mollie to Harry Ferrell 7-7-1868 G B
Smith, Mollie to Sandy Taylor 7-25-1872 Hy
Smith, Molly to Thomas Tucker 4-18-1876 Hy
Smith, Moslie J. to Milton Brown 8-1-1866 G
Smith, Namie to J. A. Owen 12-4-1866 T
Smith, Nancy A.? to James S. Clark 2-6-1869 (2-10-1869) T
Smith, Nancy C. to Hider A. D. Sample 8-24-1862 (8-25-1862) O
Smith, Nancy E. to J. T. Jarrett 7-30-1857 Cr
Smith, Nancy Eliz. Ellen to Alfred Moore 1-23-1849 (1-30-1849) Hr '
Smith, Nancy H. to George W. Harris 10-19-1839 Ma
Smith, Nancy J. to Alfred Roten 5-18-1861 Mn
Smith, Nancy J. to Edwin B. Flemming 1-8-1851 Sh
Smith, Nancy J. to P. W. Gorden 1-1-1866 Cr
Smith, Nancy Jane to J. B. Hardeman 6-30-1863 Mn
Smith, Nancy M. to William G. Wicker 3-17-1866 (3-18-1866) O
Smith, Nancy O. (C.?) to Nicholas L. Midgett 7-19-1868 G
Smith, Nancy S. to Fred Marion Miller 11-4-1850 (11-6-1850) T
Smith, Nancy S. to James K. Hill 5-12-1840 (5-13-1840) Hr
Smith, Nancy W. to Jame J. Clements 3-6-1871 (3-16-1871) T
Smith, Nancy to Beverly Anderson 1-6-1844 Ma
Smith, Nancy to Gideon Perry 4-5-1857 We
Smith, Nancy to Henry Y. Billings 8-1-1855 T
Smith, Nancy to Jno. M. Carroll 1-1-1838 (1-2-1838) G
Smith, Nancy to John Watson 1-29-1868 Be
Smith, Nancy to Joseph Byrn 10-24-1874 (4-4-1875) L
Smith, Nancy to K. David Howel 7-22-1853 Sh
Smith, Nancy to Lawson Quinn 4-12-1861 (no return) Cr
Smith, Nancy to M. W. Hood 2-24-1877 (2-25-1877) Dy

Smith, Nancy to Nick Moore 10-28-1880 Dy
Smith, Nancy to R. H. Parkison 1-20-1858 Be
Smith, Nancy to Robert B. Cheatham 7-2-1857 Hn
Smith, Nancy to Saml. Robert Smith 1-13-1844 (1-14-1844) T
Smith, Nancy to Taylor Fowlkes 8-14-1868 (8-16-1868) Dy
Smith, Nancy to Thos. Stewart 12-8?-1846 Cr
Smith, Nancy to William G. Moore 9-3-1832 G
Smith, Nannie to R. L. King 3-27-1878 Hy
Smith, Nany to James Perminter 2-19-1846 G
Smith, Narcisas to Ricahrd I. Benson 10-23-1849 G
Smith, Nicy B. to George Shepperd 11-14-1830 Ma
Smith, O. J. to Washington Scalhurst? 11-19-1852 (no return) F
Smith, O. to William Hetawer 4-29-1867 (4-13?-1867) T
Smith, Obedience J. A. J. to John T. Colvitt 12-2-1867 G
Smith, Ovilla to J. L. Gillespie 9-6-1880 (9-8-1880) L
Smith, P. A. to John Mitchell 10-27-1863 (10-28-1863) L
Smith, P. T. to J. A. Stanley 1-14-1880 (1-15-1880) L
Smith, Pamelia Jane to Charles Dennis 4-17-1854 (4-18-1854) Hr
Smith, Paralee to Coley Blakemore 8-1-1868 G B
Smith, Patience A. to David Watson 1-13-1868 Be
Smith, Patsey to John Ronalds 3-17-1838 (3-20-1838) G
Smith, Pattie to Scott Wisdom 6-17-1870 (6-18-1870) Ma
Smith, Peggy to Zachius Ezell no date (with Dec 1837) O
Smith, Penelolpe to Thos. Eskridge 4-7-1849 F
Smith, Penelope C. to George W. Dandrige 1-1-1856 Sh
Smith, Permiley F. to John W. Hedge 4-4-1856 Cr
Smith, Phoebe R. to James G. Thomas 11-15-1868 G
Smith, Polly L. to Dolphus Brown 9-23-1867 T
Smith, Polly to Benjamin Rook 12-16-1829 (12-17-1829) Hr
Smith, Polly to David H. Smith 2-4-1841 H
Smith, Polly to Haden McCormack 2-16-1831 G
Smith, Polly to Samuel Webb 8-25-1828 G
Smith, Polly to Samuel Webb 8-28-1827 (8-30-1827) G
Smith, R. L. to Isa. Stoker 1-25-1845 We
Smith, R. L. to W. H. L. Todd 11-19-1866 O
Smith, Rachael C. to John S. Dement 12-22-1853 (12-23-1853) G
Smith, Rachael to Thos. Ross 9-12-1835 (9-20-1835) G
Smith, Rachel to James Mann 6-21-1867 G B
Smith, Rainor to Austin Coleman 12-24-1867 G B
Smith, Rebecca Burton to Duncan Roberts 12-1-1856 Cr
Smith, Rebecca E. to A. J. Wheatley 11-25-1871 (10?-29-1871) L
Smith, Rebecca M. to Edmond Allen 12-30-1838 F
Smith, Rebecca S. to Smith Leach 6-13-1854 Cr
Smith, Rebecca to George M. D. Lawrance 1-23-1844 G
Smith, Rebecca to J. F. Smith 1-3-1867 Dy
Smith, Rebecca to Manuel? Frosh 3-2-1878 (3-3-1878) Dy
Smith, Rebecca to Melvin Ross 8-23-1834 (8-25-1834) G
Smith, Rosa E. to L. G. Allison 1-30-1883 L
Smith, Rosa Jane to Jessee Aldridge 6-30-1850 Sh
Smith, Rosana to J. A. T. McAfee 9-14-1864 (9-15-1864) T
Smith, Rozanah to Franklin Singly 5-12-1859 G
Smith, Ruena to Daniel P. Dickey 8-29-1845 Ma
Smith, Ruth J. to Sidney Busbee 2-11-1862 Hn
Smith, S. E. to I. N. Williamson 10-6-1868 G
Smith, S. E. to J. S. Renshaw 10-12-1871 L
Smith, S. E. to W. H. Carver 10-2-1871 O
Smith, S. L. to L. C. Glimp 3-24-1881 (3-25-1881) L
Smith, S. T. to J. F. Black 8-4-1876 (8-5-1876) Dy
Smith, S. V. to N. B. Tarrant 1-4-1870 (1-5-1870) Dy
Smith, S. to Jacob Hicks 1-31-1861 Be
Smith, Sabina J. to J. G. Hawks 10-5-1858 We
Smith, Safroney to Landon Bradford Yarbrough 6-2-1853 T
Smith, Safronia E. to Azariah Jennings 7-30-1856 L
Smith, Sallie A. to Joseph Banker 11-15-1872 (11-17-1872) Dy
Smith, Sallie P. to Jas. W. Wiggins 1-14-1871 (1-15-1871) F
Smith, Sallie to Charles Barman? 7-8-1867 (7-9-1867) T
Smith, Sallie to Smart Rice 3-22-1871 L
Smith, Sally M. to Robert Reddick 1-17-1838 Sh
Smith, Sally to Willoughby Rogers 1-4-1837 Hr
Smith, Samuella to Charles A. Yarbro 3-10-1869 T
Smith, Sarah A. to Mark Hardy 8-22-1868 (8-23-1868) Ma
Smith, Sarah A. to Thomas G. Hill 2-7-1848 (2-8-1848) Hr
Smith, Sarah A. to Z. T. Akin 10-7-1863 (no return) Dy
Smith, Sarah Angelina to John A. Parker 8-18-1847 (8-19-1847) L
Smith, Sarah Ann to John R. Dunn 8-6-1854 Hn
Smith, Sarah Ann to Joseph A. King 2-1-1845 We
Smith, Sarah B. to John R. Moore 8-16-1859 Cr
Smith, Sarah B. to William Smith 9-10-1868 G
Smith, Sarah C. to Royal Jennings 11-20-1856 L
Smith, Sarah E. to Bailey L. Wooten 11-8-1855 Sh
Smith, Sarah E. to Wm. M. Cole 12-11-1868 Be
Smith, Sarah F. to Chas. F. Griffin 12-27-1871 (1-25-1872) T
Smith, Sarah F. to Thomas A. Wood 1-3-1874 (1-4-1874) T
Smith, Sarah F. to William A. Grant 7-14-1862 Mn
Smith, Sarah J. to Alfred Goforth 4-27-1858 (5-12-1858) L
Smith, Sarah J. to James D. Cousins 12-9-1869 (no return) L
Smith, Sarah Jane to James S. Reed 1-21-1850 G

Smith, Sarah Jane to James S. Reed 7-16-1850 G
Smith, Sarah Jane to James Smith 4-8-1852 Hn
Smith, Sarah L. to Thomas J. Ridley 6-9-1852 (no return) F
Smith, Sarah M. to Andrew P. B. R. Butram 10-27-1849 G
Smith, Sarah M. to John R. Horseley 9-10-1855 (9-11-1855) Sh
Smith, Sarah O. to A. J. Hogg 10-25-1864 Be
Smith, Sarah V. to John M. Pratt 10-24-1854 (10-26-1854) G
Smith, Sarah W. to Cary Parr 10-4-1838 Sh
Smith, Sarah to B. F. Lock 3-1-1860 T
Smith, Sarah to Ben F. Locke 3-1-1860 (3-3-1860) T
Smith, Sarah to Casper M. Smith 2-27-1844 T
Smith, Sarah to Charles Crenshaw 5-6-1836 Sh
Smith, Sarah to Henry Haley 12-27-1872 T
Smith, Sarah to Henry Ledbetter 9-9-1873 (9-10-1873) L
Smith, Sarah to Henry Stevens 1-30-1866 Hn
Smith, Sarah to John H. Davis 1-16-1851 Sh
Smith, Sarah to John McDaw 9-1-1867 (9-12-1867) T
Smith, Sarah to John Voss 8-22-1853 L
Smith, Sarah to Lemuel Day 9-12-1871 (9-13-1871) Dy
Smith, Sarah to Overton Upchurch 1-13-1850 Hn
Smith, Sarah to Robert Thurmond 12-22-1885 (12-24-1885) L
Smith, Sarah to Sampson Hisaw 4-10-1845 (no return) Cr
Smith, Sarah to Thomas G. Brechieno 6-14-1851 Cr
Smith, Sarah to Thomas Jenkins 1-28-1857 Hn
Smith, Sarah to Thopson Bruff 3-12-1836 G
Smith, Sarah to Wm. H. Hays 11-22-1851 Hn
Smith, Sarah to Wm. Akins 12-7-1852 Cr
Smith, Sarah to Wm. M. Bartlett 5-18-1859 (5-19-1859) Sh
Smith, Selah Ann M. to John H. Connell 3-14-1864 (no return) Cr
Smith, Selahann M. to John H. Connell 3-14-1864 (no return) Cr
Smith, Sophia to Andrew Jackson 10-12-1870 Dy
Smith, Sue to B. W. Parkman 7-9-1874 O
Smith, Sue to Harck Taylor 7-17-1874 Hy
Smith, Susan C. to John Davidson 7-26-1853 G
Smith, Susan C. to Julius C. Harris 11-18-1852 Ma
Smith, Susan Giles to Jessee Strange 11-17-1842 T
Smith, Susan Jane to Zach Dozey 8-5-1879 (8-7-1879) Dy
Smith, Susan W. to C. C. Carr 5-26-1866 (5-29-1866) T
Smith, Susan to A. G. Oliver 7-23-1840 Hn
Smith, Susan to Azariah Moore 9-7-1869 G
Smith, Susan to Cyrus P. Robinett 12-20-1853 (12-22-1853) Sh
Smith, Susan to Edward Thomas 3-31-1870 T
Smith, Susan to F. H. Lockett 6-2-1847 (no return) F
Smith, Susan to George Russel 8-20-1869 (8-22-1869) F B
Smith, Susan to James Lewis 4-16-1873 (4-17-1873) L B
Smith, Susan to James S. McIntosh 9-14-1867 (9-15-1867) T
Smith, Susan to John H. Smith 12-22-1858 (12-23-1858) T
Smith, Susan to Joseph Baird 2-25-1871 (2-26-1871) Dy
Smith, Susan to Lewis Harden 10-30-1873 Hy
Smith, Susan to S. A. Hart 7-31-1855 (no return) F
Smith, Susan to William Smith 1-15-1868 T
Smith, Susan to Wm. C. Johnson 7-24-1845 Cr
Smith, Sylva to Sandy Smith 9-6-1869 (9-7-1869) T
Smith, T. A. to James R. Black 12-3-1872 L
Smith, T. E. to Brigus Longworth 10-28-1866 G
Smith, Tabitha E. to F. M. Akin 7-14-1868 G
Smith, Tebitha Emaline to Robert Sevier Williams 2-13-1854 (2-15-1854) T
Smith, Tempa to John Moses 8-12-1869 (no return) Hy
Smith, Tennessee to Bedford Smith 11-7-1878 Dy
Smith, Tennessee to Robert Parker 12-17-1879 (no return) Dy
Smith, Tyresee to James R. Reader 12-1-1856 Cr
Smith, Ugenia to D. A. Stratten 2-3-1864 L
Smith, V. J. to S. L. Tilman 12-17-1879 (12-18-1879) L
Smith, Valensa to Henry Elliott 7-1-1840 Hn
Smith, Victoria E. to W. H. Carruth 11-23-1869 Hy
Smith, Victoria to W. F. Gilliland 2-19-1865 G
Smith, Viney to A. J. Fullen 5-12-1838 (5-17-1838) L
Smith, Virginia E. to George W. Smith 10-30-1867 T
Smith, Virginia to Albert Kimbrough 5-1-1843 Hr
Smith, Winney to Enoch Owens 11-20-1864 Mn
Smith, Winnie to John Johnson 3-1-1871 (3-2-1871) T
Smith, Winnie to John Stevens 9-17-1866 T
Smithdorch, James? to James G. Ritchy 1-15-1841 Ma
Smitheal, Narcissa Caroline to William Hamelton 9-11-1867 T
Smithee, Nancy C. to Alfred A. Shelton 11-25-1858 Sh
Smither, Mary E. (Miss) to W. J. Ashford 6-2-1858 Sh
Smither, Roberta to D. D. Worden 11-21-1864 Sh
Smithey, Martha F. to G. B. Lampkins 10-6-1863 Hn
Smithson, E. S. to W. G. Brooks 12-31-1866 (no return) F
Smithson, Ruth to John P. Rose 5-2-1868 Hn
Smithwich, Elizabeth to William P. Lacy 7-19-1853 (7-21-1853) Ma
Smithwick, Betty B. to J. M. Johnson 1-24-1881 (1-25-1881) L
Smithwick, Fannie A. to Jefferson G. Fields 9-16-1863 (9-17-1863) Sh
Smithwick, Mary Ann to Gaston G. B. Freeman 7-6-1843 (7-7-1843) Ma
Smithwick, Mmary to John McFarlen 11-25-1843 Ma
Smithwick, Prudence to N. L. Doer? 8-20-1860 (8-22-1860) Dy
Smithwick, Sarah C. to Tilmon Murphy 10-6-1845 Hr

Smitoe, Alfred Sarah to William R. Pay 9-16-1839 Ma
Smoot, Harriett to James T. Shelly 1-25-1844 Cr
Smoot, M. A. to R. D. Carr 10-14-1866 (no return) Cr
Smoot, Narcissa P. to Joseph F. Evans 11-23-1853 Cr
Smoot, Sarah to Clinton Gipson 2-21-1864 Hn
Smort, Marget to Saml. W. Rust 6-16-1842 Cr
Smotherman, Edy C. to Samuel W. Alexander 4-2-1849 Hn
Smotherman, Elvira to John B. Atkins 9-9-1845 Hn
Smotherman, Nancy N.? to J. M. Murrell 10-3-1867 Hn
Smothers, C. E. to C. J. Tidwell 1-1-1870 Hy
Smothers, Caroline to John P. Barnes 11-15-1868 Be
Smothers, Fanny to Henry Webb 10-23-1853 Be
Smothers, Fanny to Henry Webb 10-23-1853 Be CC
Smothers, Hulda to Bryant Dees 3-9-1843 Cr
Smothers, Lydia to Levi W. Forest 1-10-1854 Be
Smothers, M. A. to J. H. Pittman 9-21-1865 Hy
Smothers, Martha to Bery Blakeny 3-9-1861 (3-10-1861) Cr
Smothers, Mary Jane to Quincy H. Lewis 5-8-1867 (no return) Hy
Smothers, Mary to Malcolm Henry 2-8-1846 Cr
Smothers, Nancy C. to Green B. Pinkston 5-20-1857 Cr
Smotherson?, Virginia C. to J. W. Rubotton 8-25-1854 (no return) F
Smullin, Marey E. to Thomas Perry 12-3-1864 (12-5-1864) O
Smyth, Elizabeth J. to David L. Campbell 11-21-1844 Hn
Smyth, Malenda to A. D. Smyth 1-7-1858 We
Smyth, Nancy J. to J. G. Alkins 6-8-1854 We
Snead, Antoinette H. to Joseph Bond 2-22-1848 Sh
Snead, Janie to W. T. McCall 5-20-1872 (no return) Cr
Snead, S. A. to J. F. Baker 1-6-1873 (1-7-1873) Cr
Snead, Virginia W. to John Hallum 11-26-1853 Sh
Sneathen, Elizabeth J. to Wm. Howell 6-14-1843 O
Sneed, A. M. to J. J. Williams 9-14-1851 (no return) F
Sneed, Amza N. to William R. Williams 2-5-1860 Hn
Sneed, Ann M. (Mrs.) to Joseph B. Littlejohn 1-9-1843 (1-10-1843) F
Sneed, Ann to Thomas Romine 9-8-1843 (no return) F
Sneed, Caledonia to Giles Wiley 11-22-1867 (11-24-1867) F B
Sneed, Catharine to Thomas Brand 7-15-1845 We
Sneed, Elizabeth to A. J. Sneed 1-11-1871 (1-12-1871) Cr
Sneed, Elizabeth to Benjamin Bell 12-29-1860 (12-31-1860) Hr
Sneed, Elizabeth to John Henry Smith 1-22-1866 Hn
Sneed, Elizer to John Durham 4-9-1840 Sh
Sneed, Ellen to W. H. H. Thompson 1-19-1871 (1-20-1871) Cr
Sneed, Frances to Richard Wilson 3-4-1870 Cr
Sneed, L. M. E. to R. Watkins 7-20-1838 F
Sneed, Lottie to Wilson Allen 2-1-1871 (no return) F B
Sneed, Lucinda F. to Robt. Bayley 1-10-1872 (1-11-1872) T
Sneed, M. to J. Sneed 12-25-1865 (no return) Hn
Sneed, Mary Jane to Samuel M. Williamson 9-29-1841 (10-4-1841) F
Sneed, Mary to John H. Hall 1-4-1854 Cr
Sneed, Richard Jane to Hinton Hall 1-20-1842 Sh
Sneed, Tabitha to Preston Dinwiddie 12-25-1865 (no return) Hn
Sneider, Magdalenor to Charles Schuck 3-9-1858 Sh
Snell, Elizabeth C. to Alexander Sacket 2-19-1852 (2-20-1852) Sh
Snell, Ellen to Irvin Davis 1-11-1860 Sh
Snell, H. C. to M. D. L. Pate 7-21-1874 (7-22-1874) Dy
Snell, Isabella to Amon Smith 11-17-1852 Sh
Snell, M. F. to M. A. Flowers 9-29-1870 G
Snelling, Julia A. to B. R. Stafford 12-19-1856 (no return) F
Snellings, Arbelier F. to J. T. Scott 8-6-1869 (8-8-1869) F
Snellings, Malisa to George Steed 1-2-1869 G B
Snellings, Sarah J. to John E. Pankey 8-20-1869 (8-21-1869) F
Snider, Agga to Carter Estridge 9-6-1837 (9-7-1837) O
Snider, Alabama S. to Jesse T. Glover 3-17-1867 Hn
Snider, Asena to George Sparks 12-10-1845 Hn
Snider, C. to John Sumption 2-13-1861 Sh
Snider, Christena to John Killien 8-1-1839 (8-4-1839) O
Snider, Christiana E. to John L. Lancaster 10-30-1855 (10-31-1855) Ma
Snider, Edy to John E. Grainger 2-7-1841 Hn
Snider, Elizabeth to Mikel Emery 7-17-1847 (no return) Hn
Snider, Elizabeth to Thomas Warren 11-25-1841 (11-28-1841) O
Snider, Elizabeth to Wyly Shores 3-26-1845 Be
Snider, Isabella to Solomon Christopher 7-18-1850 Hn
Snider, Jane to James A. Whitmore 7-24-1856 T
Snider, Jane to Matthew Council 9-4-1847 Hn
Snider, L. to Green L. Baker 3-15-1849 Hn
Snider, Lauretta J. to Eli Christopher 5-31-1849 Be
Snider, Louisa J. to James R. Graves 7-31-1856 Ma
Snider, Lourana E. to Lewis G. Metheney 2-1-1863 Hn
Snider, M. A. to J. H. Wagster 12-1-1868 G
Snider, Martha J. to Elisha Arnold 2-26-1857 We
Snider, N. to W. M. Hicklin 10-4-1866 Hn
Snider, Nancy to James Akers 10-29-1865 Be
Snider, Pernicy H. to J. C. Melton 12-11-1866 Hn
Snider, Rebecca to John T. Neel 12-5-1839 (12-12-1839) O
Snider, Rebecca to Squire Markham 4-5-1840 O
Snider, Susan to B. J. Hampton 11-14-1854 Hn
Snider, Susan to Uriah Snider 12-1-1838 O
Snidere, Lucinda to Elijah Arnold 8-12-1862 We

Snidy?(Sniedy?), Aggy to Hugh Wilson 6-5-1828 Hr
Snipes, Mary to William H. House 4-17-1845 Hn
Snoddy, Celia Ann to Zack Lea 1-14-1870 G B
Snodgrass, Eliza J. to W. C. Bennett 10-18-1855 We
Snodgrass, Frances C. to William R. Bryant 8-3-1861 (8-5-1861) Ma
Snodgrass, M. A. to R. C. Haskins 10-26-1862 Hn
Snodgrass, Nancy M. to Laban Carter 9-3-1861 Hn
Snodgrass, Sallie to Gilbert T. Christian 4-9-1866 Ma
Snores, Emma to William J. Cooper 2-25-1884 L
Snow, Anna to Richmond Treadway 12-27-1877 (no return) L B
Snow, Anna to Richmond Treadway 4-2-1879 L B
Snow, Caroline to Halewell Shelton 12-31-1850 We
Snow, Elizabeth to Caswell Shore (Thore) 4-17-1837 O
Snow, Elizabeth to H. L. Harwell 12-21-1875 (12-22-1875) Dy
Snow, Elizabeth to Thos. M. Newberry 7-13-1857 We
Snow, Frances Jane to W. H. Freeman 10-8-1850 Sh
Snow, Harriet to Thomas Jordon 4-9-1870 (4-23-1870) L
Snow, Isabella S. to V. M. Benham 7-27-1867 Dy
Snow, Jane to James W. Allen 4-20-1844 (4-23-1844) O
Snow, Lucinda to A. S. Pasco Elliott 12-19-1844 F
Snow, Margarett to H. H. Milbern 4-12-1865 (4-14-1865) O
Snow, Martha Ann to Hilliard Shelton 1-19-1850 We
Snow, Mary Molly Ann to John S. Doskins 2-1-1847 O
Snow, Mary C. to Wiley G. Bramblett 12-9-1844 (12-10-1844) O
Snow, Mary J. to Robert Pearce 4-8-1849 Hn
Snow, Mary M. to Ira S. Robson 11-12-1870 (11-13-1870) F
Snow, Matilda C. to Benjamin T. Landrum 6-18-1852 (6-20-1852) O
Snow, Matilda to William L. Landrum 6-25-1849 O
Snow, Nancy to Andrew Pollock 3-15-1847 O
Snow, Permilia to W. T. Davis 9-27-1865 (9-28-1865) F
Snow, Sarah to Albert Jones 8-13-1860 (no return) Dy
Snow, Sarah to Jesse Nix 7-21-1847 O
Snow, Sarah to N. W. Hartwell 4-4-1844 Sh
Snowden, Claresy A. to George N. Ayers 1-23-1845 Cr
Snowden, Cornelia A. to Richard F. Butts 1-1-1855 Ma
Snowden, Eliza A. to J. P. Wayman 12-13-1854 (12-14-1854) Sh
Snowden, Mary Ann to John Anderson 6-18-1846 Ma
Snowden, Mary to John L. Welch 1-1-1859 (1-4-1859) Sh
Snowden, Nancy to Dupay Pierre 9-7-1859 Sh
Snowden, Ritter K. to W. S. B. Lacy 4-4-1866 (4-5-1866) Cr
Snyder, A. L. J. to Jeremia Woods 10-8-1857 Sh
Snyder, Eliza to Francis A. Roe 9-17-1849 Sh
Snyder, Gertrude to Frederick Horlacker 6-7-1852 (6-8-1852) Sh
Snyder, Margaret to William Jericho 10-24-1860 (10-25-1860) Sh
Soap, Huldah A. to S. B. Whitson 10-31-1845 (no return) F
Soap, Sarah T. to Johnson G. Ford 12-19-1842 (no return) F
Soape, N. E. to Bernard E. Skinner 6-13-1845 (no return) F
Sober, M. L. to Richard M. Leon 8-29-1850 We
Sockette, Malinda E. to J. E. Rudolph 8-13-1856 Hn
Sofge, C. M. to C. F. Humingway 10-25-1858 (11-25-1858) Sh
Solan, Winford to V. R. Crawford 4-30-1863 Sh
Solari, Maria to John Casoretti 5-18-1860 (5-29-1860) Sh
Solles, Mary to John Reason 8-10-1842 (8-11-1842) G
Sollis, Sina to Adam Sollis 2-3-1843 (2-4-1843) G
Soloman, Caroline to R. R. Crawford 4-22-1867 Hy
Solomon, Amelia to Isaac Peritz 7-5-1853 (7-6-1853) Sh
Solomon, Lizzie to Christopher Sherwin 5-11-1861 (5-12-1861) Sh
Solomon, Martha A. to James T. Yarbrough 1-25-1844 (1-31-1844) F
Solomon, Martha to Thos. H. Wilson 2-13-1861 (2-14-1861) T
Solomon, Mary E. to J. C. Mills 9-2-1872 (9-6-1872) T
Solon, Maria to Alexander Wallace 3-18-1857 Sh
Solon, Mary to Edwd. Mulcahy 10-13-1850 Sh
Solon, Mary to Richard Lundergan 4-19-1856 (4-20-1856) Sh
Som, Lenora to John Baum 3-25-1859 (3-26-1859) Sh
Someral, Lue to George Smith 10-12-1873 Hy
Somerow, E. R. to W. F. Sumerow 10-28-1874 L
Somerow, Mary E. to James C. Alsobrook 9-12-1849 L
Somerow, Milly to Allen Pillow 1-7-1868 (no return) L B
Somers, Ann to John A. Gilcust 9-4-1860 We
Somers, Calidonia to Robert Dunevant 2-28-1875 Hy
Somers, Elizabeth J. to William I. McLure 11-25-1860 We
Somers, Ellen to R. J. McKissick 10-6-1858 (10-7-1858) Hr
Somers, Jane to William A. Stigall 1-29-1852 Sh
Somers, Martha Ann to Jas. H. Bugg 11-18-1872 O
Somers, Martha to W. B. Foster 8-31-1860 (9-2-1860) Hr
Somers, Mary J. to Jesse W. Thomas 12-3-1845 (12-4-1845) Ma
Somers, Matilda to John Pitman 9-13-1872 O
Somers, Theresa A. to M. S. Lampkins 10-31-1861 (no return) Hn
Somervel, Rosa C. to James Knox Gibson 11-20-1866 (no return) Hy
Somervell, Emma to Jacob Hurt 12-8-1866 (12-9-1866) T
Somervell, Hannah to Jack Robinson 12-8-1866 (12-9-1866) T
Somervill, Catherine T. to T. W. Green 10-26-1869 (10-27-1869) T
Somervill, Eliza to Bill Robertson 12-16-1865 (12-25-1865) T
Somervill, Grace to Saml. Rhodes 9-30-1869 T
Somervill, Gussie M. to W. M. Tarvoaler 10-27-1859 (11-17-1859) T
Somervill, Kysiah to Boston Coats 7-2-1866 T
Somervill, M. B. to A. C. Somervill 10-10-1859 (10-11-1859) T

Somervill, Margaret to William Jackson 12-29-1866 (12-31-1867?) T
Somervill, Mary Hillen to Thos. W. Roane 11-13-1858 (11-17-1858) T
Somervill, Renetta to Gilbert Vaughan 3-24-1869 T
Somerville, Agnes to Edmond Maclin 9-23-1871 Hy
Somerville, Annie E. to J. N. Harris 1-18-1869 T
Somerville, Eleanor H. to Willia Macon 12-25-1843 T
Somerville, Ellin G. to John M. Somerville 8-3-1868 (8-4-1868) T
Somerville, Fannie M. to R. J. Black 4-12-1869 (4-14-1869) T
Somerville, Kate Aubry to S. P. Green 10-13-1869 (10-20-1869) T
Somerville, Lizzie to Lorenzo Dowell 12-25-1871 T
Somerville, Mary T. to Frank J. Whitley 4-5-1874 (4-13-1874) T
Somerville, Mary to Nelson Sanford 3-30-1867 (3-31-1867) T
Somerville, Tempe J. to Henry J. Livingston 11-28-1872 Hy
Sommerauer, M. A. to F. Geo. Sterbler 2-1-1860 Sh
Sommers, Catharine B. to D. M. Hilliard 10-19-1859 We
Sommers, Martha to Thomas M. Adams 9-18-1862 We
Sommers, Sarah F. to Elijah J. Julin 8-5-1860 We
Sommervill, Ann F. to Geo. Ardmore? Taylor 11-16-1852 T
Sommervill, Mary to W. F. Sommerville 12-28-1865 (12-30-1865) T
Sope, Lethia to John Pope 12-15-1842 (no return) F
Sorrel, Susan to Marian Collins 6-14-1867 (6-18-1867) L
Sorrell, Fannie to Wm. D. Tarkington 4-3-1878 (4-4-1878) Dy
Sorrell, Frances to Lewis Battle 8-11-1860 (8-16-1860) Ma
Sorrell, Helen to Isiah Lea 12-27-1862 (1-3-1863) Dy
Sorrell, Hellen to Chas. Clay 10-6-1864 (no return) Dy
Sorrell, Margaret E. to William H. Buns 7-2_-1866 (7-24-1866) L
Sorrell, Mary to W. C. Eason 1-1-1873 Dy
Sorrell, P. A. to T. G. Neely 2-20-1866 Dy
Sorrell, S. M. to W. A. Flowers 3-19-1867 Dy
Sorrells, Caroline to W. Belinger 11-29-1842 Sh
Sorrels, Nancy J. to James W. Childress 7-25-1868 (7-26-1868) L
Soults, Ann E. to John S. Peek 11-27-1862 Sh
Southall, Lee G. to Wilie A. Glover 12-5-1863 (12-13-1863) F
Southall, Manerva to Jefrey Owen 2-19-1876 (no return) Hy
Southall, Mary to James Croom 10-19-1850 Ma
Southerel, Harriet A. to J. W. Porter 8-29-1868 (8-30-1868) Cr
Southerland, Malinda to H. B. Walker 2-9-1842 (2-10-1842) F
Southerland, Martha J. to Thomas B. Walters 3-27-1855 We
Southerland, Peggy to Allen Minor 1-3-1849 (no return) F
Southerland, Sarah A. to John R. Bryant 8-18-1853 Cr
Southerland, Sarah P. to William J. Conner 6-5-1838 Hn
Southerlin, Sarah A. to Newton J. Blackwood 2-15-1859 Hn
Southern, Lucy A. to John Bookout 6-28-1878 (no return) Hy
Southern, Martha J. to James B. Crook 7-?-1844 F
Southern, Martha to Albert Fowlkes 12-28-1866 Dy
Southern, Susan to James H. Cooper 6-28-1870 Dy
Souward, Carolina to James Ivy 12-28-1842 Sh
Soward, Addie to Parry Eison 4-3-1879 (4-4-1879) L B
Soward, Denkey to Cale Rucker 1-15-1885 L
Soward, Dixie to Allen Arnold 1-15-1885 L
Soward, Ellen to Andrew Currin 9-1-1885 (no return) L
Soward, Josephine to Julian Parr 12-23-1875 L
Soward, Lewella G. to J. S. Sharp 12-14-1868 (12-15-1868) L
Soward, Lue to Byrd Isham 12-16-1885 (12-17-1885) L
Soward, Mary M. to Isaac L. Parker 9-8-1860 (9-10-1860) L
Soward, Savanah to Nathan Alsobrook 12-20-1883 L
Soward, Susan Ann to M. M. Faulkner 11-2-1854 (11-8-1854) L
Soward, Susan C. to Simmonds D. Alsobrook 1-28-1859 (2-2-1859) L
Soward, Susanah to Anderson McGuire 12-22-1868 L
Soward, Viginia to M. L. Nearn 11-23-1866 (11-26-1866) L
Sowell, Eliza to William Stedham 12-14-1848 (no return) F
Sowell, Mary to Habon Kirby 1-3-1849 Ma
Sowell, Nancy to Boswell Deel 9-26-1860 (5-21-1861) O
Sowerson, Nannie to Lewis Thurmond 9-28-1876 L B
Sp_ill, Aimy to Prince Tomberlin 10-20-1869 G B
Spadder, J. M. to W. B. Weddington 8-15-1857 Cr
Spain, D. M. A. to A. W. M. Martin 8-7-1871 Cr
Spain, Eliza to F. M. Logue 12-15-1869 (12-22-1869) Cr
Spain, Elizabeth F. to William J. Northcut 7-16-1868 Cr
Spain, Emily to L. C. Benns 12-6-1871 (12-7-1871) Dy
Spain, Fannie L. to W. H. Price 1-18-1870 O
Spain, Harriet to W. J. Linsey 11-22-1871 (no return) Cr
Spain, Helen to L. C. Bemis? 12-6-1873 (12-7-1873) Dy
Spain, Jane to James B. Southerland 10-29-1860 (no return) Dy
Spain, Lizzie to J. B. Thompson 2-25-1878 (2-27-1878) Dy
Spain, M.L. to W. B. Montgomery 2-8-1873 (2-9-1873) Cr
Spain, Margaret E. to Powell S. Taylor 7-18-1867 Dy
Spain, Mary Ann to B. W. Williams 3-9-1848 Hn
Spain, Mary E. to James F. Wilkinson 3-19-1878 (3-25-1878) Dy
Spain, Nancy E. to D. G. Porter 12-10-1868 (12-11-1868) Cr
Spain, Sallie E. to John B. Young 11-6-1866 (11-8-1866) F
Spain, Sarah F. to J. M. Shaver 12-25-1874 (12-27-1874) O
Spain, Sarah to Ammon Coleman 10-20-1828 Sh
Spaine, Mollie to M. L. Fagan 10-28-1867 Hn
Spalding, Margaret to Francis Littan 3-20-1869 (3-21-1869) L
Spalding, Racheal to Jeramiah Needham 10-23-1827 Hr
Span, Mahala to George W. Hubbard 3-31-1863 (no return) We

Span, Sarah A. to Elijah McClure 3-18-1855 We
Spann, Elizabeth to James Roberson 11-6-1864 Hn
Spann, Nancy W. to Samuel Paschall 11-14-1839 Hn
Sparkes, Sally P. to Thomas Jones 7-7-1853 (no return) F
Sparkman, Ann Maria to James Y. Barker 7-5-1854 O
Sparkman, Elizabeth (Mrs.) to E. W. Hutchins 3-13-1867 G
Sparkman, Elizabeth to Jonathan McF. Branch 12-22-1856 Sh
Sparkman, Hatta to Green Currie 12-13-1877 Hy
Sparkman, Julia A. to John T. Wilson 7-13-1867 (7-14-1867) Dy
Sparkman, M. A. to Ben Barker 12-23-1868 G
Sparkman, Patsey to Edwin Mathis 12-13-1830 (12-14-1830) G
Sparkman, Sarah to Davy Cox 12-19-1867 (no return) Hy
Sparks, Amanda M. to Edward O. Davis 3-20-1851 Sh
Sparks, Ann to G. W. Orr 11-23-1857 Sh
Sparks, Ann to M. S. Dinwiddie 11-2-1863 (11-5-1863) Cr
Sparks, Betty to James Price 9-16-1869 (9-18-1869) Cr
Sparks, E. A. to D. S. Birkhead 8-17-1861 (8-19-1861) Hr
Sparks, Elizabeth C. to Thos. J. Carson 11-22-1854 Cr
Sparks, Etseta to Ezekeil Thomas 1-19-1853 Cr
Sparks, Frances to Julius Ridley 12-31-1868 (1-7-1869) Cr
Sparks, Margarett to Steward Carson 11-21-1872 Cr B
Sparks, Martha to John Tison 12-24-1846 Cr
Sparks, Mary Ann to Ambrose Harmon 11-12-1839 Cr
Sparks, Mattie to J. T. Grundy 7-26-1871 Cr B
Sparks, Nancy L. to Wm. Melier 11-10-1846 Cr
Sparks, Nelly to Samuel Baucum 3-8-1870 Cr
Sparks, Sallie E. to R. T. Fowler 2-4-1867 (2-14-1867) Cr
Sparks, Sallie to Henry Knox 12-11-1878 Hy
Sparks, Sarah to Samuel Tyson 1-8-1845 Cr
Sparks, Susan to Wm. Patterson 10-7-1857 Hr
Sparks, Wilmath P. to Ambrose B. Mitchell 8-18-1858 Cr
Spate, Lemony to G. W. Lowry 3-22-1865 Hn
Spead, Sarah Ann to Wm. Coal 6-6-1846 (no return) We
Spear, Mary E. to Wilsen Kelly 1-18-1860 We
Spear, Spicy to Joseph Spear 7-2-1851 Sh
Speares, Elizabeth to Nathaniel Rutledge 8-23-1843 (8-24-1843) F
Spears, Caroline to Edwin York 12-5-1834 G
Spears, Martha L. to James P. Grooms 1-11-1863 We
Spears, Mary J. to Zachariah Dement 5-11-1862 G
Spears, Miss Sarah to George Davis 1-12-1852 (1-14-1852) Hr
Spears, R. C. to Jesse Keal 12-20-1866 G
Spears, Rebecca to J. W. Powell 9-22-1862 G
Spears, Sallie to John H. Pickler 7-11-1871 (no return) Cr
Spears, Sarah to Hiram Irwin 11-30-1837 Sh
Spearse, Mary E. to William N. Brasfield 10-7-1846 We
Spearse, Mary E. to Wm. N. Brasfield 10-8-1846 We
Speckernagle, C. G. to Wm. P. Bowers 2-8-1858 (2-9-1858) Sh
Speckernagle, Sue A. (Mrs.) to B. Howcott 10-31-1860 Sh
Speed, Lizzie A. to William A. Graham 8-29-1862 (no return) Hy
Speed, V. C. (Mrs.) to James E. Polston 5-9-1883 (5-17-1883) L
Speer, Janetta to William L. Crow 5-26-1854 Sh
Speer, Sarah to Wm. N. Jones 5-29-1837 (5-30-1837) G
Speer, Tobitha to John M. Taylor 8-16-1838 F
Speers, Alice to Claborn Calhoun 8-11-1876 (8-12-1876) O
Speh, Mary Ann to John H. McMillan 10-9-1871 (10-10-1871) Ma
Speight, Malinda A. to Frank Saxon 4-4-1875 Hy
Speight, Malisa P. to James R. Ray 2-1-1877 Hy
Speight, Martha A. N. to Adison W. Sheridan 2-5-1861 Hn
Speight, Mary Ann to James M. Sheridan 12-19-1857 Hn
Speight, Salie E. to J. F. P. McMurry 2-1-1877 Hy
Speller, Tomasia to George Taylor 7-5-1877 Hy
Spellings, A. T. (F?) to L. B. Keel 8-11-1870 G
Spellings, E. T. to Robert D. Shoffner 9-20-1869 (9-23-1869) Cr
Spellings, Lavina to Thomas Staton 1-21-1836 (1-22-1836) G
Spellings, Lucretia to B. J. Taylor 1-11-1869 G
Spellings, Martha A. to A. M. Bennett 12-31-1872 (no return) Cr
Spellings, Martha to Wm. P. Chambers 10-13-1847 Cr
Spellings, Mary F. to Nathaniel E. Edwards 10-6-1865 (10-8-1865) Cr
Spellings, Verna to Robert Owens 1-8-1857 Cr
Spence, Anna E. to John P. McLeod 5-1-1878 Hy
Spence, Clary to William Tipton 5-8-1879 (5-9-1879) Dy
Spence, E. E. to A. M. Frazier 12-27-1866 Be
Spence, Fanny A. to James H. Bray 8-14-1869 Ma
Spence, Hager to Wilson Nance 2-11-1876 L
Spence, Jane to James Thurston 4-30-1851 Hn
Spence, Margaret to Jack Anderson 6-2-1866 Dy
Spence, Mary to Alex Tipton 5-30-1866 (6-2-1866) Dy
Spence, Melinda to Edmund Bridges 8-11-1831 Ma
Spence, Mollie to Richard Smith 3-16-1878 Dy
Spence, N. to M. Hellums 7-12-1862 (no return) Hn
Spence, Palmira to Robt. H. Ferguson 10-7-1863 Dy
Spence, Rebecca E. to Robert L. Taylor 11-18-1879 (11-19-1879) L
Spence, Rebecca to Stephen Paschall 6-19-1838 Hn
Spence, Samtha O. to B. F. Burks 8-4-1885 (8-5-1885) L
Spence, Sarah A. to A. L. Tancel 6-18-1868 Dy
Spence, Sarah to E. N. Quillin 11-14-1867 Be
Spence, Sophiah to Joseph Wood 8-7-1845 We

Spence, Susan to Randle Light 8-11-1866 Dy
Spence, Tennessee to Robert Rodgers 1-1-1880 Dy
Spence, Tennessee to Samuel Barnett 8-11-1866 Dy
Spencer, Amanda M. to James G. Phalen 10-7-1842 G
Spencer, Amanda to Charley Jenkins 9-28-1871 Hy
Spencer, Anna to Wm. Snow 10-22-1849 (10-24-1849) F
Spencer, C. S. to J. A. Sweat 3-31-1861 Mn
Spencer, Elizabeth to William J. Spencer 6-27-1826 G
Spencer, Emeline to Isaac Wiseman 9-25-1866 T
Spencer, Emily J. to Jas. R. Taylor 10-19-1858 G
Spencer, Harrit to Meredith H. Neal 12-4-1845 F
Spencer, Jamima to Bartlett Gooden 7-20-1847 (7-27-1847) G
Spencer, Jane to Andrew J. Hardage 7-24-1839 Ma
Spencer, Lidy E. to Thos. J. McMaster 1-12-1869 Ma
Spencer, Linthia to Richard Stewart 9-11-1867 O
Spencer, Lucy Ann to Arch Reed 8-29-1873 (8-30-1873) L B
Spencer, Lucy to Wm. H. Marriot 12-12-1860 Sh
Spencer, Malissa Jane to William F. Clark 8-16-1866 Hn
Spencer, Margaret to Harrison D. Scott 3-6-1845 Cr
Spencer, Mary Ann to Henry Jane 6-15-1840 Ma
Spencer, Mary J. to Jas. C. Canady 2-24-1859 G
Spencer, Mary W. (Mrs.) to Creed P. Halley 7-18-1839 F
Spencer, Mary to Frederick Klenk 1-3-1853 Ma
Spencer, Mary to Winifred Fowler 11-6-1844 Hn
Spencer, Mary to Wm. H. Phelan 10-16-1850 G
Spencer, Minerva to James L. Brogdon 3-20-1839 Ma
Spencer, Molly to Albert Robinson 8-28-1876 (no return) Hy
Spencer, Parthena to Thomas Morison 7-12-1838 Sh
Spencer, Sarah to William Scott 8-9-1862 G
Spencer, Susan Jane to Joel B. Vaughn 2-11-1858 G
Spencer, Susan to John Hobbs 1-9-1850 (1-10-1850) G
Spenser, Elizabeth M. to Thomas Gaither 1-20-1839 (1-21-1839) O
Spenser, Sarah E. to T. N. Bell 10-3-1865 Hn
Spenser, Sarah E. to W. T. Taylor 2-5-1854 Hn
Speres, Elizabeth to James Bodkins 4-23-1833 (4-24-1833) G
Sperling, Sally to John Kohoe 3-4-1845 Sh
Sperling, Sarah to Jesse Henson 3-7-1827 (3-14-1827) Hr
Sperry, Sarah to Joshua Miller 3-26-1849 Sh
Sphere, Louana to Owen Smith 9-7-1833 (10-8-1833) G
Spicer, Eliza C. to R. M. Giles 10-17-1848 Sh
Spicer, Pacena to James M. Spicer 1-31-1846 Be
Spicer, Sarah E. to John T. Williams 6-18-1848 Be
Spickernagle, Isabella to John Houston 1-29-1846 Sh
Spier, Ann E. to Rufus McShared 6-27-1862 G
Spike, Lucy to Sam Drake 8-19-1868 (no return) F B
Spikes, T. A. to J. E. Stovall 12-17-1873 O
Spiller, Emma to Thomas Gay 11-22-1884 (11-23-1884) L
Spiller, Sallie to James Doolin 12-23-1869 (12-29-1869) F B
Spillers, Mary to Joseph Hartley 10-8-1881 (10-9-1881) L
Spillings, Rebeca A. to Thomas E. Enboe? 9-6-1865 (9-8-1865) Cr
Spilman, Julia to John Casey 2-1-1864 (2-2-1864) Sh
Spinger, M. E. to R. B. Huston 8-6-1877 L
Spinster, Elizabeth to Wm. J. Thomison 12-10-1840 Cr
Spinster, Susan to Alfred Harris 1-7-1840 Cr
Spires, Mary J. to C. Moore 1-12-1860 Be
Spires, Mary to Geo. W. Rushing 11-19-1846 Be
Spitler, Ruth R. to James A. Adkins 2-13-1839 Sh
Spiven, Hegal to Wm. B. Alphin 1-12-1871 Hy
Spivery, Elizabeth to Edward Danderage 1-3-1870 (no return) Hy
Spivey, Anna to Green Hunter 12-28-1871 Hy
Spivey, Emaline to John M. McCall 8-30-1843 (8-31-1843) F
Spivey, Emaline to Samuel Waller 8-11-1848 Sh
Spivey, Gatsy Ann to Thomas C. Olds 9-22-1847 L
Spivey, Jane to Levi Garrison 8-12-1871 Hy
Spivey, Louisa to John W. Guthridge 12-25-1834 Sh
Spivey, M. to Phillip McNutty 4-13-1863 Mn
Spivey, Martha Jane to Joseph Woodard 2-12-1863 L
Spivey, Mary Jane to James J. De la Hay 3-17-1841 Sh
Spivey, Mattie to Thomas, jr. Ingram 5-29-1871 (5-31-1871) Ma
Spivey, Merry to Edmond Tucker 5-30-1871 Hy
Spivey, Millie to Peter Davis 12-23-1871 Hy
Spivey, Nancy to Richard Crihfield 9-11-1855 L
Spivey, Nannie to Osbourne Roberts 12-1-1881 L B
Spivey, Naomi to James Allen 2-14-1878 (no return) Hy
Spivey, Rebecca to Isaac Sanders 2-7-1848 (2-10-1848) L
Spivey, Rebecca to James M. Graham 7-15-1881 (no return) L B
Spivy, Mary to Billy Patterson 10-23-1874 Hy
Spoon, Emily to Manuel Butler 8-19-1841 Cr
Spoon, Lucy to A. B. Canada 12-20-1875 (12-21-1875) Dy
Spoon, Sarah A. to W. G. Palmer 1-14-1870 (1-16-1870) Cr
Spoon, Tiressa to James Forbes 9-9-1876 (9-15-1876) Dy
Spooner, Mary H. to Francis A. Duval 5-3-1853 (5-5-1853) Sh
Spradlin, Addie to Jas. H. Vinson 10-3-1871 O
Spradlin, M. S. to H. H. Hogan 9-29-1876 (9-30-1876) O
Spratt, Mary T. to William D. Brigance 3-14-1842 Ma
Spratt, Nancy C. to E. H. Smith 11-25-1830 Ma
Spring, Elizabeth to John H. Albritton 3-31-1852 Ma

Spring?, Alsse to Jesse Moore 11-26-1858 Cr
Springer, Burnetta to Scott Pinckley 3-29-1869 (3-31-1869) Cr
Springer, Frances to Wm. B. F. Lunday 5-9-1847 Cr
Springer, Martha to Allen Mayo 7-25-1865 G
Springer, Mary Ann to John Richards 3-18-1863 Mn
Springer, Susan E. to M. R. Browning 1-21-1868 (no return) Cr
Springer, Triona L. to Andrew Stewart 12-5-1865 (12-6-1865) Cr
Springer, Triona L. to Andrew Stewart? 12-5-1865 (12-6-1865) Cr
Springfield, Charity to James F. Ingram 6-29-1850 (6-30-1850) Hr
Springfield, Charity to Thomas I. Neely 1-29-1840 Ma
Springfield, Elizabeth to J. B. Carrington 6-21-1861 (6-22-1861) Hr
Springfield, Jenny to Gardner Porter 12-1-1869 (no return) F B
Springfield, Judy to Nathan Degraffenreid 12-25-1866 (12-27-1866) F B
Springfield, Julia to James Henderson 11-12-1875 (no return) Hy
Springfield, Julia to John Center 3-19-1874 Hy
Springfield, Lucy to Wm. Patterson 11-11-1869 F B
Springfield, Marion to Albert Ross 10-31-1877 Hy
Springfield, Mary E. to James M. Creps (Cress?) 11-14-1871 Ma
Springfield, Nellie to Tennessee Hunt 12-31-1868 (1-2-1869) F B
Springfield, Siddy J. to E. S. Duncan 9-5-1859 (9-6-1859) Hr
Springfield, Susan to Wm. Jones 1-23-1869 (no return) F B
Springfield, Temperance to Anderson S. Skillern 1-25-1847 Ma
Sproul, Esther to Richard Seawright 12-21-1853 (no return) Hn
Sprouse, Nancy to John Dove 9-14-1830 Ma
Sprout, Chany to George McQurter 2-5-1853 Hn
Sprows, Mary to Preston Sullivan 4-3-1841 (5-5-1841) Ma
Spry, Laura to W. A. Fulkerson 2-20-1877 L
Spurier, Hellen M. to Nathaniel Moore 7-4-1859 (7-5-1859) G
Spuriers, Isamiah to J. M. Bradshaw 8-13-1870 G
Spurlin, Penny to William Fellow 6-3-1831 (6-12-1831) Hr
Spurlin, Rebecca H. to Absolom C. Spurlin 12-19-1847 Sh
Spurling, Frances to Randle Hamilton 12-11-1833 Hr
Spurling, Mary to Bird Bazel 6-22-1827 (6-24-1827) Hr
Spurlock, Eliza J. to G. W. Griffin 12-21-1852 (no return) F
Spurlock, Mary to Washington Parrot 12-17-1846 Ma
Spurriers, Hellen to J. G. Richards 2-11-1879 Dy
Squalls, Ella to Lewis Wyatt 3-7-1872 Hy
Squiers, Martha to Thomas White 9-5-1872 T
Squires, Ann to Israel Morris 7-4-1841 Sh
Squires, Martha to Thomas White 9-5-1872 (9-13-1872) T
Sraynie?, Addie to Jas. L. Stitt 9-12-1860 (9-13-1860) T
Srogent (Scogin), Margaret to Augustus Long 12-4-1849 Sh
St. Clair, Catharine M. to Horace Head 3-6-1855 O
St. Clair, Ida C. to Henry Hanswait 10-8-1864 Sh
St. Clair, Sarah to Michael Gafford 8-4-1838 Sh
St. John, Mary E. to Elias J. Crihfield 10-21-1861 L
St. John, Sarah to T. J. Killick 11-8-1884 (11-9-1884) L
St. Leger, Margaret to Edwin Baldwin 8-6-1845 Sh
Staap (Stoop?), Katharine to Joseph Walter 11-4-1862 Sh
Stabough, Jane to Josiah Brook 5-20-1830 (5-25-1830) Hr
Stacey, Jane to John Maupin 9-27-1852 (9-29-1852) O
Stackerd, Sarah J. to W. J. Kirkpatrick 5-10-1854 (no return) F
Stackhouse, Lucinda to Peter Scott 5-15-1846 Sh
Stackhouse, Mary to John Russell 1-20-1843 Sh
Stacup, Anna to Henry Hunter 11-7-1830 G
Stacy, Eliza Ann to John Warington 9-20-1847 (9-23-1847) F
Stacy, Hulda to Willie Horn 3-16-1843 Cr
Stacy, Irine to James T. Sherrell 6-7-1838 Cr
Stacy, Louisa to James Roley 2-10-1848 Cr
Stacy, Mary E. to Wm. H. Allen 4-3-1845 Cr
Stacy, Mary T. R. Johnston 7-8-1851 O
Stacy, Susan to Earby Benson 9-25-1852 (no return) F
Stafford, Alice to Edward Burk 4-5-1850 Sh
Stafford, Alice to Timothy Burk 11-31-1848 Sh
Stafford, Ann E. to G. W. Boling 1-14-1854 (no return) F
Stafford, Bettie to John S. Reid 9-28-1869 G
Stafford, Candas to Wm. H. Stephens 11-20-1867 (11-21-1867) F
Stafford, Cornelia A. to J. M. Adams 2-7-1866 F
Stafford, Eliza to Pomp Newman 5-6-1867 (5-30-1867) T
Stafford, Elizabeth to Mosses Case 5-7-1863 We
Stafford, Emley to Stephen Hern 8-5-1844 (8-8-1844) F
Stafford, H. A. to J. B. Stafford 6-22-1867 (6-23-1867) F
Stafford, Harriet (Mrs.) to John E. Pattillo 2-12-1870 (2-13-1870) F
Stafford, Jennetta to Moses Jones 1-2-1869 (1-3-1869) Cr
Stafford, Lidda to H. G. Glover 6-25-1846 (no return) Cr
Stafford, Lucinder (Mrs.) to Lovel E. Cropper 12-30-1864 Sh
Stafford, Lucyan to Joel Rushing 2-19-1846 Be
Stafford, Margaret to William Johnson 8-1-1870 (8-2-1870) F
Stafford, Martha B. to John K. Earl 10-7-1863 (10-8-1863) F
Stafford, Mary E. to Andrew J. Whitby 12-21-1868 (12-24-1868) F
Stafford, Mary F. to J. P. Stafford 10-6-1862 (10-7-1862) F
Stafford, Mary M. to Wm. H. Stevens 11-1-1862 (not endorsed) F
Stafford, Mary Thomas to Daniel W. Paremore 8-8-1871 T
Stafford, Mary to R. C. Pulliam 8-20-1847 O
Stafford, Nancy to Stephen Cannon 3-16-1866 (3-21-1866) F
Stafford, Peggy to Jeremiah Webb 10-31-1838 (11-3-1838) G
Stafford, Rebecca H. (N.) to Richard Flora 3-1-1854 O

Stafford, S. B. to J. L. Wagener 10-23-1866 (10-30-1866) F
Stafford, Sarah Ann to James Robertson 5-31-1838 Hr
Staggs, Clem to G. A. Smith 4-20-1876 Dy
Staggs, Eliza C. to Giles F. Moody 10-2-1867 (no return) Dy
Staggs, Joseph Isabella to R. D. Stull 1-30-1877 Dy
Staggs, Josephine to Alexander Beretto 2-25-1854 (2-26-1854) Sh
Staggs, Rhoda Nice Caroline to Thomas J. Goforth 6-6-1868 (6-7-1868) L
Staggs, Sallie to John Roper 10-10-1863 (11-3-1863) Dy
Stagner, Caroline to Isaac Gore 7-3-1839 Hn
Stagner, Delila to John Wyatt 12-5-1854 Be
Stagner, Delila to John Wyatt 12-5-1854 Be CC
Stagner, Eliza J. to James Shadrick 12-24-1849 Hn
Stagner, Josephine to John Miller 2-17-1865 (no return) Hn
Stagner, Malinda to Samuel Hardeman 8-27-1857 Be
Stagner, Martha to Thomas Watkins 7-14-1851 Hn
Stagner, Mary Ann to John H. Cooper 9-23-1846 Be
Stagner, Susan to Elbert Miller 8-23-1857 Hn
Stailey, Eliza A. to R. L. Henley 5-1-1858 Sh
Stailey, Lida A. to R. S. Lawrence 3-17-1859 Sh
Stailey, Margaret Theessa to W. H. McCarty 5-31-1861 Sh
Stainback, Allice M. to Wm. M. Ingram 10-21-1867 (10-24-1867) F
Stainback, Lucy E. to Levin H. Coe 12-20-1866 F
Stainback, Maria to David Green 11-27-1866 (12-2-1866) F B
Stainback, Sarah to Benjamin O'Hannen (O'Harver) 7-26-1847 Sh
Stainbuck, Amanda to David Green 2-28-1878 (no return) Hy
Stake, America to James Coffman 11-17-1874 (11-18-1874) T
Stalcup, Anna to Henry W. Hunter 11-7-1831 G
Stalcup, Harriet A. to W. M. Ballentine 12-6-1867 (no return) Dy
Stalcup, Margaret to J. F. Andrews 6-22-1872 (6-21?-1872) Dy
Stalcupple, Dollie to Charles Thomas Stokes 9-15-1879 L
Stalkup, A. R. to S. R. Williams 10-17-1878 (10-18-1878) Dy
Stall, N. C. to J. R. Tucker 9-25-1856 Sh
Stallcup, Mary Ann to William A. Bailey 7-21-1863 (no return) Dy
Stallcup, Millie to R. W. Dickey 11-23-1871 Dy
Stalling, L. F. to J. K. P. Reddick 12-19-1866 (12-20-1866) Dy
Stallings, Ann to W. B. Nash 1-7-1867 (no return) Dy
Stallings, Clementina to Aaron C. Basford 7-1-1843 (7-2-1843) L
Stallings, Harriet to M. V. B. Reddick 10-26-1860 (10-27-1860) Dy
Stallings, Jane to William Howell 9-6-1864 (9-7-1864) Sh
Stallings, Lucinda to Joseph Denton 4-2-1849 F
Stallings, M. E. to W. M. Dean 3-6-1878 (3-7-1878) Dy
Stallings, Melissa to Joseph Harris 7-11-1869 G B
Stallings, Paris to Peter Byassee 4-8-1871 (4-9-1871) Dy
Stallings, Sarah to Alexander Dickson 11-7-1828 Ma
Stallins, L. C. to W. H. Ferrell 3-1-1866 G
Stallins, Nancy to Calvin Mackado 5-16-1871 T
Stalls, Catharine to William Morrison 5-16-1850 Sh
Stalls?, Martha J. to John N. Manning 1-3-1851 Hn
Stamper, Alice L. to T.(S?) K. Blankinship 11-1-1883 L
Stamper, M. A. to W. H. Stamper 7-23-1879 (7-24-1879) L
Stamper, Mary A. to Burgess Bolling 5-5-1851 (no return) F
Stamps, Delia A. to Jesse Riley 11-2-1859 (11-3-1859) Sh
Stamps, E. E. to W. T. Deloach 11-23-1880 (11-26-1880) L
Stamps, Elizabeth to Alexander Hughs 9-18-1855 (9-20-1855) G
Stamps, L. A. to J. H. Copher 10-4-1868 Hy
Stamps, Mary to William Thornton 12-25-1867 (no return) Hn B
Stamps, Sarah Ann to B. F. Hughes 2-9-1876 (no return) Hy
Stamps, Sarah J. to J. W. McIntyre 6-28-1879 (6-29-1879) L
Stamps, Virginia to J. F. Hughes 1-9-1877 Hy
Stamps?, Theay to John Brumbelow 8-28-1834 Hr
Stan, Sarah to Tucker Hutchens 12-12-1839 (12-22-1839) G
Stanback, Eliza (Mrs.) to Chas. L. Bernard 11-26-1857 Sh
Standback, Rebecca to Clement Belotte 7-23-1855 (8-16-1855) Hr
Stander, Susanna to C. Oldenberge 6-22-1859 Sh
Standfield, J. B. to R. J. Woods 7-27-1871 Cr
Standley, Emaline to Benjamin Parker 6-7-1851 (6-8-1851) O
Standley, Louisa M. to James T. Hall 1-20-1861 G
Standley, Manda to Samuel Brightwell 11-10-1855 (11-11-1855) G
Standley, Martha A. D. to John M. Eddins 12-22-1841 (12-23-1841) F
Standley, Mary Elizabeth to Isaac Bason 12-26-1840 (12-29-1840) F
Standlin?, Mary Frances to Benjamin Franklin F. Crihfield 6-29-1857 (7-10-1857) L
Standly, Polly to Mastin Prewitt 2-26-1838 (2-27-1838) Hr
Stanfield, C. A. to R. D. Williamson 11-19-1865 Hy
Stanfield, Jerleen to Wm. J. Berryhill 8-?-1863 (no return) Cr
Stanfield, Jerlien to W. J. Berryhill 8-9-1863 Cr
Stanfield, Mary E. to James P. Hastings 2-13-1850 Hn
Stanfield, Zenovia C. to J. D. Jones 6-10-1871 (no return) Hy
Stanford, Ann to Stephen Hillsman 12-20-1871 (12-21-1871) Cr
Stanford, Demetius to Williard Driggs 4-18-1839 Cr
Stanford, Julia to W. A. Harper 4-28-1849 (no return) Cr
Stanford, Louisa to Jobe Hill 8-28-1869 (9-1-1869) Cr B
Stanford, M. J. to Harvest Olive 4-12-1858 Cr
Stanford, Mary M. to Calvin J. Morgan 7-3-1853 Cr
Stanford, Mary to James Lemons 3-20-1842 Cr
Stanley, A. E. to Blak Crittendon 11-14-1874 O
Stanley, A. N. to L. C. Davis 2-8-1871 (4-9-1871) O

Stanley, Catharine to Aeneas McCallister 6-6-1856 Sh
Stanley, D. to Jno. H. Martin 9-12-1870 (no return) Hy
Stanley, Elizabeth to B. F. Stanley 8-24-1867 O
Stanley, Elizabeth to Finas Lytaker 3-3-1834 (3-6-1834) G
Stanley, Elizabeth to James Davis 4-12-1858 (4-14-1858) O
Stanley, Elizabeth to John W. Clay 1-21-1861 (1-22-1861) L
Stanley, Frances E. to D. R. Dupree 1-24-1861 (no return) Hy
Stanley, H. A. to J. F. Stanley 8-24-1867 O
Stanley, Idea to Thos. Gale 9-9-1867 (no return) Hy
Stanley, Julia Ann to John Green 5-20-1857 (5-24-1857) O
Stanley, Levina to James L. Atcherson 10-26-1827 Sh
Stanley, Louisa to W. H. Goodman 10-16-1880 (10-25-1880) L
Stanley, Lucy C. J. to Burwell S. Moseley 2-16-1846 (2-19-1846) F
Stanley, Lucy to G. W. Smith 5-22-1861 O
Stanley, M. T. to Edward Collins 12-25-1867 O
Stanley, Malvina to Wyatt Walker 12-23-1854 (12-24-1854) O
Stanley, Mariah to Joe D. Shaw 9-5-1831 G
Stanley, Martha E. to Martin McCool 2-5-1844 (2-7-1844) T
Stanley, Martha to Silas Turner 12-17-1866 Hy
Stanley, Mary A. to C. R. Thomas 12-24-1860 Hy
Stanley, Mary A. to Ulysess S. Perkins 1-15-1850 Cr
Stanley, Mollie L. to O. C. Stanley 11-26-1870 Hy
Stanley, Nancy C. to John P. Cook 10-17-1867 Hy
Stanley, Rebecca A. to Joel Winn 12-14-1854 Cr
Stanley, Sally to Anthony Lewis 9-21-1824 Sh
Stanley, Sarah A. (Mrs.) to Joseph A. Brooks 8-1-1860 (8-2-1860) Ma
Stanley, Sarah to Jo. Saunders 2-8-1869 (no return) Dy
Stanley, Sarah to John Jones 12-27-1864 (12-29-1864) O
Stanly, Clarissa M. to John W. Clift 4-5-1832 Sh
Stanly, Fannie to George S. Jones 12-19-1867 (no return) Cr
Stanly, Nancy E. to James M. Read 7-12-1878 (no return) Hy
Stanly, Rebecca C. to John W. Furgerson 8-19-1856 (8-20-1856) Ma
Stanly, Sarah to M. C. Turner 10-12-1859 O
Stanly, Sullie to W. M. Lovell 2-24-1868 Hy
Stanly, Susan E. to W. H. Pickins 9-29-1849 (9-30-1849) F
Stanly, Susan to Ansell Batchelor 8-19-1874 Hy
Stansberry, Ellen to J. S. Evans 9-18-1855 (no return) F
Stanton, Ann M. to Benj. F. Taylor 11-4-1847 Sh
Stanton, Eve to Edward Stanton 12-24-1867 Hy
Stanton, Jane P. to Sam'l L. Gookin 9-25-1845 Sh
Stanton, Jane to Henry Howell 3-30-1878 (no return) Hy
Stanton, Julian to Neverson Brown 5-19-1877 Hy
Stanton, Rachel to Edwin O. Perrin 4-4-1850 Sh
Stanton, Virginia to Wm. Tyus 3-18-1877 Hy
Staples, Julia to O. F. Hunsaker 7-10-1860 Sh
Staples, Louiza to W. L. Sawyer 1-8-1862 (1-9-1862) Sh
Staples, Lusey Ann to G. W. Stone 10-22-1860 (10-25-1860) L
Stapleton, Ann to Wm. Mahoney 8-17-1861 (8-18-1861) Sh
Stapleton, Mary to John Hannagin 8-23-1851 (8-24-1851) Sh
Stark, Jane to John S. Potter 4-7-1852 (4-8-1852) Sh
Starkey, Annie to Jerry T. Glidewell 12-24-1867 (12-25-1867) Ma
Starkey, Eliza J. to John A. Roach 8-13-1867 (8-16-1867) Ma
Starkey, Minerva I. to Thomas P. Harding 12-4-1850 Hy
Starkey, Nancy to Edwin Corbit 7-3-1849 Sh
Starkey, Tennessee to W. D. Smith 7-2-1851 Sh
Starks, Maggie M. to R. H. M. Cockrell 12-24-1858 Sh
Starks, Mary to Haywood Branch 8-28-1845 Sh
Starks, Mary to John Johnson 1-2-1872 Hy
Starks, Melinda to Richard Adams 4-26-1867 (no return) Hy
Starks, Phillie to Jack Jones 11-18-1878 Hy
Starky, Nancy to Hugh Middleton 2-29-1828 Hr
Starling, Elizabeth to Nathanl. Harris 7-23-1850 (no return) F
Starling, Elizabeth to Nathl. Harris? 7-25-1850 (no return) F
Starnes, Amanda to R. G. Ensley 10-23-1869 (10-24-1869) T
Starnes, Amanda to William Nobles 1-27-1853 L
Starnes, Lavinia to James Knight 12-1-1852 L
Starnes, Lodicia C. to J. F. Bryan? 9-19-1863 Be
Starnes, Maria Amanda to David Davenport 4-25-1849 (4-26-1849) T
Starnes, Martha to William H. Selfridge 10-2-1849 (10-3-1849) T
Starnes, Mary Catharine to Hiram Malachi Yount 3-12-1851 (3-13-1851) T
Starnes, Nancy to Raymond B. Harmes 9-29-1846 Sh
Starnes, Rebecca to Alexander Dacus 8-15-1850 (8-18-1850) T
Starnes, Sarah E. to James Ewart 6-30-1857 T
Starns, Harriet to Irvin Jones 11-7-1877 (11-8-1877) L
Starns, Nelly to David Smith 12-28-1826 Sh
Starr, Agnes A. to Wm. E. Patton 1-27-1840 (1-28-1840) F
Starr, Malinda to Zachariah Reese 10-13-1841 (10-15-1841) T
Starrert, Ruth to Smith Parks 5-1-1866 O
Starrett, Demaris to Thos. N. Vestal 1-1-1845 (1-2-1845) F
Starrett, Mary M. to Thomas J. Terrill 3-23-1842 (3-24-1842) O
Starrett, O. B. to C. P. McDaniel 1-30-1875 (1-20?-1875) O
Starrett, P. J. to L. P. Hadley 3-11-1859 O
Starrett, S. E. (Mrs.) to Noah Green 3-13-1873 Dy
State (Slate?), Harriet L. to Joel Sawyer 7-5-1853 Sh
Staten, Mariah to James Belew 11-19-1867 G
Staten, Rosanah to John Simmons 4-6-1856 Hn
Staten?, Mary E. to Lewis C. Edgar 9-17-1863? Hn

Staten?, Sally A. to George Washington 1-13-1843 Hr
Statham, Evaline to John Jackson 3-11-1865 (3-13-1865) O
Statham, Lucinda to William Gill 4-6-1853 (4-6-1857?) O
Stations, Lusinda to William A. Bennett 7-22-1848 (no return) F
Statler, Fannie to Robert E. Smith 1-27-1858 Hr
Staton, E. M. to William Diggins 2-27-1866 G
Staton, Elizabeth to Malachi Gregory 7-28-1842 Sh
Staton, Nancy (Mrs.) to Charles B. Robley 3-31-1870 Ma
Staton, Nancy to Magilba Rogers 12-8-1832 G
Staton, Sally to Fair M. Little 10-13-1829 (10-22-1829) G
Staton, Sarah A. to Thomas W. Lowry 4-28-1858 Hn
Statum, Levina to Wiley S. Carter 8-4-1845 (8-5-1845) G
Statum, Luandy to William Gills 4-6-1848 O
Statzle, Mary to Nickolas Wegmann 4-26-1856 Sh
Steadham, Jane C. to John C. Lightle 12-20-1864 (12-22-1864) F
Steadham, Ripsey to Wm. H. C. Johnson 12-17-1838 (12-20-1838) F
Steadman, Mary E. to Hughs Pipkins 9-25-1855 (10-10-1855) Ma
Steagall, Martha to Robt. B. McMahan 5-13-1846 (5-17-1846) Hr
Steager, Priscilla to Jesse Nevil 11-15-1869 (11-18-1869) F B
Steale (Steate), Angelina to Charles F. King 4-13-1841 Sh
Steaphenson, A. J. to Wm. C. Miles 2-14-1865 O
Stedham, Elizabeth to Judel? (J. W.?) Parchman 10-6-1838 (10-8-1838) F
Stedham, Jane to Aretny Mathews 4-2-1849 (5-3-1849) F
Stedham, Martha to A. L. Pickins 12-21-1842 (12-22-1842) F
Stedman, Cynthia to Ben Williams 11-16-1870 (11-18-1870) Dy
Stedvent, Martha S. to Samuel L. Caldwell 11-4-1851 Cr
Stedwell, Collie H. to J. W. Penn 5-16-1860 (5-17-1860) G
Steel (Stell), Martha E. to J. P. Barnhill 8-20-1848 Sh
Steel, E. to John Siddle 12-29-1840 (12-31-1840) F
Steel, Elizabeth to Jasper Guill 11-19-1857 Hn
Steel, Elizabeth to John A. Powers 10-2-1858 We
Steel, Elizabeth to Solomon Todd 7-23-1862 Hy
Steel, Elizabeth to Thos. H. Philips 7-29-1843 We
Steel, Frances to Jas. C. Davis 5-22-1870 Hy
Steel, Jane E. to Francis E. Davis 5-10-1842 (no return) F
Steel, Linda Ann Eliza to W. G. Carver 3-5-1870 (3-9-1870) Cr
Steel, Lucy Ann E. to Richard C. Burton 8-11-1857 Hn
Steel, M. A. to H. C. Crdier 12-26-1871 (no return) Cr
Steel, Margaret R. to Henry D. Brantly 3-27-1866 Hy
Steel, Margarett A. to J. J. Walker 10-30-1865 G
Steel, Margarette to George Roberson 4-11-1861 G
Steel, Mary V. to B. F. C. Brooks 3-8-1858 Hr
Steel, Mary to David B. Carnes 10-7-1828 (10-9-1828) Hr
Steel, Mollie to William Bogles 3-1-1868 G B
Steel, Ruthy to Thomas Hamilton 11-29-1828 (12-4-1828) Hr
Steele, Bulah to S. J. Pierce 1-26-1882 L
Steele, Elizabeth to M. S. Williams 9-25-1860 Hn
Steele, Elizabeth to Theodore Lackie 12-27-1836 (12-28-1836) Hr
Steele, Emma J. to W. C. Cobb 12-12-1877 Hy
Steele, Jennie to G. A. Lusk 11-30-1881 L
Steele, Jinnie to Carroll Humble 6-20-1868 (6-21-1868) Cr
Steele, Margaret J. to Wm. Lafayette Henderson 8-31-1864 Sh
Steele, Martha L. to James B. Arnold 11-5-1867 (11-7-1867) Cr
Steele, Mary E. to John Rawlstone 12-9-1860 We
Steele, Mary J. to Asa C. Ratteree 12-27-1860 Hn
Steele, Melvina to G. W. Kile 12-6-1869 Cr
Steele, Miss Fannie to Wm. H. Wall 11-28-1864 (11-29-1864) T
Steele, Pena to Crocket Wainwright 12-27-1866 Hy
Steele, Prudence E. to Robert W. Carnes 11-10-1842 Hr
Steele, Rebecca A. to Moses C. Oliver 5-20-1866 Hn
Steele, Sarah A. to Harry McGuiver? 10-29-1869 (11-13-1869) T
Steele, Sarah H. to Elijah N. Moody 9-19-1860 Hn
Steele, Sophronia J. to Elhanon S. Chandler 1-12-1853 L
Steeley, Ann C. to Elijah Young 1-21-1847 (no return) Hn
Steeley, Hulda Ann to J. W. Steel 6-6-1865 Hn
Steeley, Mary Ann to Joseph Henderson 6-19-1841 (no return) Hn
Steelman, Elizabeth J. to Alison T. Steelman 10-10-1848 Sh
Steelman, Julia A. to John H. Hankins 11-28-1860 Sh
Steelman, Louisa to John Sanders 7-26-1880 L
Steelman, Melinda to John C. Kirkendall 2-16-1832 Sh
Steelman, Sarah to James Morris 11-19-1855 (11-20-1855) Sh
Steely, Ann to James Baker 2-24-1846 (no return) Hn
Steely, Eliza A. to Thomas J. Freeland 12-18-1853 (no return) Hn
Steely, Malinda Jane to Eli Walker 7-9-1857 Hn
Steen, Mary J. to S. A. Ferrell 2-18-1865 (no return) Dy
Steen, Sarah F. to James M. Yates 3-29-1866 (no return) Dy
Stegall, Eliza J. to Jas. H. Harbson 7-1-1850 (7-9-1850) F
Stegall, Harriet Ann to James R. Waldrup 12-7-1867 (12-10-1867) Ma
Stegall, L. E. to C. M. Alexander 3-6-1862 Mn
Stegall, Margaret to William Pierce 9-9-1862 Dy
Stegall, Martha to Jas. H. Curtis 1-7-1846 Sh
Stegall, Martha to John Taylor 2-2-1864 (2-3-1864) Dy
Stegall, Mary A. S. to Jacob Serat 12-18-1861 Mn
Stegall, Mary to John Dickson 2-13-1845 Cr
Stegar, Frances I. to Joseph E. Douglass 2-15-1838 F
Steger, Fannie C. to R. L. Knox 1-29-1866 (1-31-1866) F
Steger, Judy to Oliver Parks 1-29-1870 (2-22-1870) F B

Stein, Annie to John H. Steele 11-20-1882 (no return) L
Stein, Mary Ann to Henry Steele 10-19-1882 (no return) L
Steinberg, Otelia to Anderson Boschwitz 3-11-1864 Sh
Steiner, Elizabeth to J. E. Hartung 11-20-1854 Sh
Steinhammer, Mary M. to Jos. Koller 12-31-1860 (1-1-1861) Sh
Stell, Mary F. to John S. Turner 11-14-1861 Sh
Stell, Sarah J. to John McSmith 3-4-1853 Sh
Stellar, Susannah to Charles Yearbory 4-15-1833 (4-17-1833) G
Stellman, Harriet Jane to William B. Houston 10-4-1842 Sh
Step, Abcesla? to A. P. Crocker 11-17-1870 Hn
Step, Malinda to William Roswell(Boswell?) 11-1-1852 Be
Step, Sarah F. to W. R. Barbee 1-14-1857 (1-15-1857) Sh
Stephen, Elizabeth to Philip Wehrum 2-10-1858 Sh
Stephen, Emily to John P. Alexander 2-19-1848 (no return) Hn
Stephens(on), Nancy J. to John G. Bettis 1-25-1859 (1-27-1859) O
Stephens, A. E. to J. P. Bradford 8-19-1866 G
Stephens, Abitha to William Alexander 9-19-1846 Hn
Stephens, Ammana F. to Levi Stunten 5-12-1857 We
Stephens, Ann to Stephen Pollard 2-24-1828 G
Stephens, Anna to B. H. Sullivan 2-23-1876 Dy
Stephens, Argeanta Rebecca to Robert Ferguson 8-2-1848 Ma
Stephens, Bethena to William H. Maxwell 8-25-1825 Hr
Stephens, Bridget to John Casey 5-16-1864 Sh
Stephens, Bunavista to William Burk 8-24-1870 G
Stephens, Caroline to Ephraim Moss 8-29-1862 (8-31-1862) O
Stephens, Caroline to William Franklin 10-28-1847 Hn
Stephens, Creacy to R. Henry 8-3-1869 G
Stephens, E. S. to Joshua Nixen 1-23-1856 (no return) Hn
Stephens, Eliza to N. W. McGhee 7-31-1843 Sh
Stephens, Elizabeth A. to Hugh Tyler 8-20-1846 Hn
Stephens, Elizabeth B. to L. M. Campbell 9-8-1842 Hn
Stephens, Elizabeth to Angelo Sturla 8-11-1849 Sh
Stephens, Elizabeth to Asa Bishop 5-23-1850 Hr
Stephens, Elizabeth to Robert H. Brown 10-29-1855 (11-1-1855) G
Stephens, Fanny M. to J. J. Neely 5-11-1848 Hr
Stephens, Henrietta to H. T. Blanton 6-7-1864 Hn
Stephens, Jane M. to Amos Black 10-26-1857 Ma
Stephens, Jane to George Weatherly 9-22-1866 (9-30-1866) T
Stephens, Joan to Greenberry Barton 12-20-1855 Hn
Stephens, Leamma to Elisha Cook 9-25-1859 O
Stephens, Malinda R. to Lee Cunningham 10-22-1868 G
Stephens, Margaret to T. J. Hill 6-1-1862 Mn
Stephens, Martha Jane to Henry Johnson 9-20-1853 (9-21-1853) G
Stephens, Martha P. to N. O. Gill 10-13-1870 G
Stephens, Martha to Saml. Nelms 6-12-1838 (6-26-1838) Hr
Stephens, Mary A. to Almus F. Baldridge 9-21-1856 We
Stephens, Mary Ann to H. J. Cole 5-16-1864 (no return) Hn
Stephens, Mary E. to Edmund Cooper 10-22-1844 Hr
Stephens, Mary E. to J. B. Tyler 6-29-1864 (6-30-1864) O
Stephens, Mary J. to J. S. Clark 11-14-1859 (no return) Hy
Stephens, Mary Jane to Alexander H. Claridge 8-21-1854 Ma
Stephens, Mary Jane to J. W. Womble 1-4-1841 (1-7-1841) F
Stephens, Mary to J. D. Chandler 8-11-1856 Cr
Stephens, Mary to Jas. D. Cousins 3-26-1858 (4-3-1858) G
Stephens, Milly to John Edmonson 10-16-1839 L
Stephens, Nancy to Henry Parr 4-4-1877 (4-3?-1877) L B
Stephens, Nancy to ____ Johnson 4-4-1877 (not executed) L
Stephens, Olive to John Shell 10-23-1845 (no return) Hn
Stephens, Parthenia to Eli B. Spencer 7-22-1830 Sh
Stephens, Permella to Charley Allen 2-7-1871 (2-9-1871) F B
Stephens, Rachel to B. B. Conway 4-19-1849 Hn
Stephens, Sarah E. to D. L. Chaffin 1-30-1851 (1-31-1851) F
Stephens, Sarah M. to William F. McGuire 4-7-1858 T
Stephens, Zellah to John Cook 8-27-1865 G
Stephenson, A. C. to R. S. McClintock 12-8-1862 Mn
Stephenson, Charity to Robert Black 7-10-1843 (9-26-1843) O
Stephenson, Eliza J. to Nathan McKeehan 6-25-1859 (6-26-1859) Sh
Stephenson, Eliza Jane to William Hodges 12-13-1841 Hr
Stephenson, Elizabeth to Lewis Williams 12-15-1842 Sh
Stephenson, Emily to Payton Parker 6-17-1844 Hr
Stephenson, Emma to Ephraim Frazier 2-1-1868 (2-2-1868) Dy
Stephenson, J. A. to Jno. P. Thompson 12-24-1863 (12-25-1863) O
Stephenson, Louisa B. to Wm. G. Stephenson 12-30-1861 Sh
Stephenson, Martha Jane to T. H. Sinclair 7-13-1847 O
Stephenson, Martha R. to Benj. J. Edwards 10-28-1854 (10-29-1854) Hr
Stephenson, Mary Ann to B. D. Franklin 9-22-1844 We
Stephenson, Mary Elizabeth to Amos A. Edwards 8-5-1850 (8-6-1850) Hr
Stephenson, Mary J. to J. C. Wilkins 2-22-1871 (2-25-1871) T
Stephenson, Mary to Ishmal Bailey 5-24-1847 Cr
Stephenson, Matilda L. to Joshua D. Wright 1-10-1844 Hr
Stephenson, Nancy A. to Franklin Longly 8-29-1851 (9-1-1851) O
Stephenson, Rebecca to Lenke H. Gullett 10-9-1847 (10-14-1847) O
Stephenson, Sarah Ann to Calvin Philly 12-25-1838 Hr
Stepherson, Malinda to William L. Dunlap 4-28-1869 (5-4-1869) L
Stephins, Mary L. to Sanford T. Creed 3-20-1848 (3-24-1848) O
Stepp, Tamer to John Duglas 10-19-1843 Be
Sterling, Susan to Anderson Lucas 4-17-1850 (4-18-1850) F

Stern (Starnes), Eliza to Samuel Watt 8-19-1847 Sh
Sterritt (Stenett), Sussanah S. to William M. Smith 1-22-1853 (1-23-1853) O
Stetson, Antoinette L. to Arthur Matt. (Capt.) Sherman 6-1-1863 Sh *
Steuler, Angeline to Louie Ragan 4-24-1863 (4-26-1863) Sh
Stevens, Alice to Green Turnage 8-23-1872 (8-25-1872) Dy
Stevens, Amanda to David Brogden 1-14-1868 Hy
Stevens, Amanda to Matthew Routy 12-1-1866 Dy
Stevens, Callie to Daniel Morgan 1-20-1878 Hy
Stevens, Caroline to Alfred McCall 10-16-1869 T
Stevens, D. to James H. Stevens 3-2-1859 Hn
Stevens, Drusilla to John Rains 5-9-1836 Sh
Stevens, Eliza J. to Hiram F. Cummins 3-19-1844 Hn
Stevens, Eliza to Thomas J. Oates 6-8-1846 T
Stevens, Elizabeth Winney to William Henry Harrison 11-22-1845 T
Stevens, Elizabeth to A. D. Taylor 12-25-1860 (no return) Hn
Stevens, Elizabeth to W. H. Mason 2-25-1870 (2-27-1870) T
Stevens, Elizabeth to W. R. Evans 12-27-1865 (12-28-1865) T
Stevens, Ella N. to John M. Pierce 4-29-1876 (4-30-1876) Dy
Stevens, Ellen B. to Ben F. Edwards 12-18-1872 Hy
Stevens, Evaline to David Combs 3-2-1869 T
Stevens, F. E. to J. D. Davis 1-15-1866 (1-16-1866) F
Stevens, Fannie to Geo. E. Scott 4-28-1874 Dy
Stevens, Fannie to Zach Watkins 10-11-1876 (10-12-1876) Dy
Stevens, Frances to Lewis Stevens 1-19-1844 (1-24-1844) F
Stevens, Georgia A. to J. M. Brackin 4-10-1878 Dy
Stevens, Georgia to Frank W. Luscumbe 9-10-1872 Dy
Stevens, Kate to WM. Kerr 4-6-1869 (no return) Dy
Stevens, L. to James Lewis 11-16-1864 (11-17-1864) T
Stevens, Louiza to Haywood Cannon 10-29-1856 T
Stevens, Lucy to John C. Norvell 2-10-1871 (no return) Hy
Stevens, Mamie to Jo. E. Sharp 11-6-1878 (11-7-1878) Dy
Stevens, Martha Ann to Joel Stevens 8-18-1852 (8-19-1852) T
Stevens, Mary Ann to Robert A. Foster 10-19-1843 Hn
Stevens, Mary L. to M. M. Marshall 2-24-1879 Dy
Stevens, Mary to Alexander Sears 7-31-1869 T
Stevens, Mildrid C. to Alfred Broomly 12-23-1868 (12-24-1868) T
Stevens, Nancy to Jacob M. Brodnax 12-7-1874 T
Stevens, Nancy to Jonas Murphey 11-1-1871 (11-2-1871) Dy
Stevens, Olive E. to L. D. L. Paschall 1-21-1866 (no return) Hn
Stevens, Pheriby to M. C. Young 9-28-1853 (9-29-1853) Hr
Stevens, Rachel J. to Samuel McClish 6-9-1862 (no return) Hn
Stevens, Sarah Ann to Pitser Miller 12-19-1834 (12-21-1834) Hr
Stevens, Sarah to Nathan McCoy 5-8-1880 (5-9-1880) Dy
Stevens, Susan Ann to John J. E. Bryant 8-1-1853 (8-3-1853) T
Stevens, Susan Ann to Robert Searcy 8-3-1851 (8-10-1851) T
Stevens, Susan E. to William B. Thompson 11-7-1849 (11-8-1849) Hr
Stevens, Susanah to James Home 9-25-1857 T
Stevens, Viney to John Sharp 9-15-1866 (9-22-1866) T
Stevens, Zosco Z. to John Bradley 1-1-1829 Sh
Stevenson, Eliza H. to Oliver G. Gurley 2-28-1856 Sh
Stevenson, Jane to Green Smith 11-13-1852 Cr
Stevenson, Margaret A. to James E. Billington 2-24-1864 Hn
Stevenson, Margaret E. to John J. Templeton 3-12-1866 (3-14-1866) T
Stevenson, Nancy Issabella to Jerimiah Burton 12-10-1850 (12-13-1850) Hr
Stevenson, Nancy J. to T. P. Chronister 1-7-1868 Dy
Stevenson, Nancy to George McCam 11-4-1870 T
Stevenson, Ozella to J. F. Pierce 3-2-1875 Dy
Stevenson, R. J. to Thomas Wylie 1-19-1857 (1-22-1857) Sh
Stevenson, Sarah J. E. to Atlas M. Hogan 8-1-1866 Ma
Steveson, Martha to E. W. Hill 9-5-1870 (9-7-1870) T
Steviss?, Susan to Jas. R. Shepard 9-13-1871 T
Steward, Callie to Turner Moore 12-24-1868 (no return) Hy
Steward, Cintha R. to P. J. Fullen 10-12-1871 L
Steward, Cynthia E. to Montgomery Anderson 8-8-1849 (8-16-1849) Ma
Steward, Easter to Isham McFarland 12-18-1870 Hy
Steward, Juntha J. to Joseph Turpin 12-5-1860 (12-26-1860) Dy
Steward, M. H. to J. L. Vaughan 12-15-1856 (12-17-1856) Hr
Steward, Martha D. to Nelson C. Jordan 2-26-1859 (3-1-1859) Ma
Steward, Mollie to William Keith 11-27-1869 Ma
Steward, Mrs. Hulda to Wesley Laster 1-2-1854 Hr
Steward, N. S. to W. R. Mills 11-1-1859 (11-3-1859) Hr
Steward, Nancy E. to William L. Brent 12-9-1849 Hn
Steward, Polly to Thomas W. Grubbs 7-17-1838 Sh
Steward, R. O. to H. B. Akin 1-18-1875 (1-20-1875) L
Steward, Sarah T. to Thos. J. Farris 12-23-1856 (12-25-1856) Hr
Steward, Sarah to Alsy Morphis 2-13-1835 Hr
Steward, Tabith to Wilie Sanders 5-26-1870 L
Stewart, A. L. to Jno. S. McMahen 11-10-1860 (no return) Hy
Stewart, Alberta H. to N. R. Hilliard 8-30-1859 (no return) Hy
Stewart, Allice B. to A. R. Tatum 12-20-1869 (12-23-1869) F
Stewart, Amanda I. to Wm. G. Mullen 11-2-1866 O
Stewart, Amanda to John C. Black 2-6-1854 Ma
Stewart, Angeline Frances to Anderson Bailey 1-7-1867 (1-8-1867) Ma
Stewart, Bettie J. to J. L. Hampton 2-26-1869 (no return) Dy
Stewart, C. C. to J. C. Batey 1-2-1871 (1-5-1871) T
Stewart, C. V. to T. M. Melugin 12-11-1862 F
Stewart, Caroline C. to Andrew J. Williams 12-17-1846 F

Stewart, Caroline to Silas Shaw 8-12-1871 Hy
Stewart, Caroline to Turner Earl 9-9-1870 (no return) F B
Stewart, Catharine to John P. Hampton 8-23-1869 (8-26-1869) F
Stewart, Catharine to William Bond 10-11-1852 Sh
Stewart, Cermanthia Ann to Charles R. Jennings 6-10-1869 (6-16-1869) L
Stewart, E. (Mrs.) to H. Smith 4-24-1860 Sh
Stewart, E. J. to R. W. Priest 12-9-1852 Sh
Stewart, Edy Ann to Wm. Marchbanks 1-30-1853 Be
Stewart, Elisabeth to John D. Braden 11-23-1848 (11-30?-1848) F
Stewart, Eliza J. to James A. Faucett 6-2-1858 (6-6-1858) Ma
Stewart, Eliza to Joel Herring 1-22-1856 (1-2_-1856) Sh
Stewart, Elizabeth C. to Zachariah Lockett 2-2-1846 Hr
Stewart, Elizabeth to Claiborne Johnson 10-8-1834 Sh
Stewart, Elizabeth to J. H. Johnson 6-17-1878 Dy
Stewart, Elizabeth to John Finley 2-12-1845 Cr
Stewart, Elizabeth to John S. Futrell 11-25-1841 Hn
Stewart, Ella Green to G. N. Shoemake 7-2-1881 (7-3-1881) L
Stewart, Elmena L. to William H. Jackson 7-25-1838 (7-26-1838) Ma
Stewart, Fanny to Thomas Montague 2-26-1870 (2-27-1870) F B
Stewart, Fedelia to Jefferson Messick 6-26-1831 Sh
Stewart, Hannah to Henry Peebles 12-11-1878 Hy
Stewart, Henrietta to Saml. Henry Hughes 7-15-1850 (7-16-1850) T
Stewart, Irena to Thomas Baird 5-11-1859 (5-12-1859) G
Stewart, Jane to John Golden 12-27-1845 Ma
Stewart, Jane to John L. Marchbanks 4-8-1852 Be
Stewart, Julia A. E. to Joseph Cromm 10-13-1856 (10-15-1856) Ma
Stewart, Julia A. to John J. Collins 3-3-1866 (3-8-1866) Ma
Stewart, Katie to Balam Boylan 2-18-1871 (no return) F B
Stewart, L. A. to D. T. Jones 8-11-1869 (8-13-1869) F
Stewart, Lavinia E. to D. H. Selph 12-21-1852 Mn
Stewart, Letty to Albert Simmons 12-24-1873 (12-25-1873) Dy
Stewart, Lorina to J. W. Finley 10-6-1857 (no return) Cr
Stewart, Louisa A. to John B. Carson 7-9-1857 (no return) L
Stewart, Louisa to John B. McKnight 8-10-1842 Sh
Stewart, Louisa to Thomas J. Morris 2-26-1862 (2-27-1862) Cr
Stewart, Lucy E. to William Clark 9-26-1861 Mn
Stewart, Lula to I. H. Johns 1-10-1885 (1-11-1885) L
Stewart, M. A. to John A. Gordon 2-15-1872 Hy
Stewart, M. E. to F. M. Hughes 1-30-1863 Sh
Stewart, M. J. to J. L. Morris 1-8-1879 L
Stewart, M. J. to J. T. Bridges 12-11-1872 Cr
Stewart, M. L. to T. N. Sampson 11-21-1857 Cr
Stewart, M. to Joseph McCarty 4-18-1830 Sh
Stewart, Maggie to Joe Boyd 10-22-1871 Hy
Stewart, Mahala L. to William J. Taylor 7-18-1870 (7-21-1870) Ma
Stewart, Margaret E. to John W. Barker 7-17-1858 Cr
Stewart, Margarett T. to Samuel S. Liston 5-27-1856 Cr
Stewart, Maria to William R. Moore 12-22-1847 (12-23-1847) Ma
Stewart, Mariah to Thomas W. Dunn 11-26-1855 (no return) Hn
Stewart, Marilda to John L. Casey 8-8-1844 Hr
Stewart, Martha Ann to Lewis S. Smotherman 12-24-1857 Hn
Stewart, Martha E. (Mrs.) to Jess Box 3-11-1870 (3-13-1870) Ma
Stewart, Martha Jane to Atlas H. Jones 10-11-1855 Ma
Stewart, Martha to J. C. Stevenson 8-12-1863 F
Stewart, Martha to William D. Peterson 12-20-1842 (12-22-1842) Ma
Stewart, Mary (Mrs.) to John Allan 1-21-1863 (1-22-1863) Sh
Stewart, Mary A. to Solomon Johnson 1-12-1847 (1-13-1847) Ma
Stewart, Mary Ann to Robert N. Parks 1-31-1842 (2-2-1842) Hr
Stewart, Mary Ann to Thomas J. Patterson 2-16-1867 Hn
Stewart, Mary C. to Wm. F. Allen 11-24-1842 Sh
Stewart, Mary E. to James J. Culbreth 1-22-1844 (1-?-1844) T
Stewart, Mary Jane to John Mathis 10-26-1841 Hn
Stewart, Mary L. to James L. Feuqua 10-22-1861 G
Stewart, Mary M. to Thomas Dickens 6-2-1830 Ma
Stewart, Mary V. to W. L. Tharpe 11-1-1866 Hn
Stewart, Mary to Enoch Tysen 12-23-1870 Hy
Stewart, Mary to William Scruggs 10-23-1845 Sh
Stewart, Mary to Wm. J. Bryant 12-20-1846 Cr
Stewart, Matilda to W. Moore 11-25-1852 Sh
Stewart, Matta to John Ledsinger 12-31-1872 (1-1-1873) Dy
Stewart, Mattie E. to John M. Knight 6-10-1869 (no return) L
Stewart, Mattie M. to R. N. Parks 2-13-1860 (2-16-1860) F
Stewart, Melvina A. to J. D. R. Fain 8-8-1860 G
Stewart, N. W. to J. R. Green 8-6-1861 Mn
Stewart, Nancy E. to Andrew M. Magee 10-16-1866 O
Stewart, Nancy E. to B. F. Wimberley 4-27-1868 Dy
Stewart, Nancy to James Hanna 4-9-1842 Hr
Stewart, Nancy to John Patterson 3-15-1874 Hy
Stewart, Nancy to Nathan W. Steadman 12-19-1855 Ma
Stewart, Nancy to W. J. Atkins 7-15-1860 Hn
Stewart, Nancy to William Brannon 2-10-1864 (no return) Hn
Stewart, Narcissa M. to John M. Morton 2-6-1841 F
Stewart, P. C. to H. A. Chambless 1-18-1870 Cr
Stewart, Parthenia to John B. Morris 5-4-1854 Ma
Stewart, R. E. to W. B. Glisson 1-22-1861 Sh
Stewart, Rebecca A. to J. W. Thompson 12-29-1869 (12-30-1869) L
Stewart, Rebecca E. to John N. Barger 12-1-1860 (12-4-1861) We

Stewart, Rose to Harrison Brown 6-9-1868 (6-10-1868) F B
Stewart, S. A. to T. M. Butler 11-25-1868 G
Stewart, S. M. to C. Mundinger 7-26-1864 (7-28-1864) Sh
Stewart, Sarah A. to Isaac Futrell 2-4-1839 (2-5-1839) Hr
Stewart, Sarah E. to E. B. Britt 12-2-1859 (12-15-1859) Sh
Stewart, Sarah E. to John R. Murphy 9-14-1868 (9-20-1868) Cr
Stewart, Sarah J. to William P. Hamilton 11-1-1858 (11-3-1858) Ma
Stewart, Sarah to Thos. C. D. Howell 6-15-1835 G
Stewart, Sarah to William R. Littleton 12-6-1860 Hn
Stewart, Snophia to Samuel Green 3-15-1877 Hy
Stewart, Susan A. to Saml. Jones 9-9-1867 (not endorsed) F
Stewart, Susan E. to Wm. N. Fortune 5-15-1861 Hr
Stewart, Thurza Ann to Benjamin Talley 2-28-1841 Ma
Stewart, Vick to Sam Boyd 10-15-1871 Hy
Stewart, Viney to Mik Foust 3-5-1868 Dy
Stewart, Virginia to James Arnold 10-6-1845 T
Stickley, Irene E. to Henry E. Hezekieh 4-17-1849 Sh
Stickney, Emmer to J. W. Bryan 12-7-1868 Hy
Stidam, Sarah F. to James Price 12-14-1868 (12-16-1868) F
Stidham, Mary J. to W. A. King 1-13-1868 (1-14-1868) F
Stidham, Mary to G. W. S. Johnson 1-8-1845 (1-9-1845) F
Stidham, Milla to Moses Gardner 9-13-1867 (no return) F B
Stienbow, Hannah to Henry Harris 12-13-1873 (no return) Hy
Stier, Elizabeth to Isaac Croom 7-22-1840 (8-13-1840) Ma
Stiers, F. J. to E. O. Webb 7-19-1865 Be
Stigall, Jane to Daniel F. McElyea 9-17-1861 Be
Stigall, Louina to J. A. Presson 6-26-1853 Be
Stigall, Martha E. to Will A. Freeland 11-11-1853 Hn
Stigall, Mary J. T. to Reuben Bedwell 6-29-1858 Hn
Stigall, Nancy E. to Joshua Roper 6-19-1844 (6-20-1844) F
Stiger, Carolina E. to Wm. Pearson 3-13-1841 (no return) F
Stiger, Ellen to L. M. New 8-18-1859 Sh
Stiggall, Nancy G. to T. H. B. Roberson 12-30-1857 (12-31-1857) G
Stiles, Elizabeth to S. W. Alexander 2-18-1852 Hn
Still, Tucy to Hally? McCullough 12-28-1871 T
Still?, Cynthia to William Wilson 11-17-1829 (11-25-1829) Hr
Stiller, Catharine to David Watson 7-5-1834 G
Stiller, Sarah to Alex Foren 7-5-1834 G
Stillman, Mary Ann to Rufus King
Stilsy, Virginia to Robert B. King 4-28-1857 Cr
Stilwell, Hannah R. to L. Hughs 12-10-1868 G
Stinnett, F. R. to Andrew Parks 4-13-1875 (4-15-1875) Dy
Stinson, Eliza J. to Albert? S. Norman 10-29-1845 (10-30-1845) Hr
Stinson, Louisa J. to Amanuel Lefevre 1-27-1850 Hn
Stinson, Mary J. to Thomas Medlock 7-30-1838 Hr
Stinson, Mary to Miles Philley 6-4-1838 Hr
Stinson, Sarah E. to Claiborn Smith 2-7-1843 Hr
Stith, Cornelia E. to Stephen H. Steele 4-28-1858 (no return) L
Stith, Francis F. to M. F. DeGraffenried 4-15-1861 (4-16-1861) Sh
Stith, M. L. to Oscar R. Robbins 10-11-1869 (10-12-1869) Dy
Stitt, A. E. to R. S. Hall 11-10-1858 (11-11-1858) T
Stitt, Mary to Thomas Rice 9-26-1873 (10-6-1873) T
Stitt, Mollie to Lafayett Whitis 12-22-1869 (12-23-1869) T
Stitt, Nancy to Anderson Wellingham 3-19-1869 (4-11-1869) T
Stockard, Frances E. to Wm. I. Whitsett 10-25-1843 Cr
Stockard, H. F. to Frances Cooley 10-23-1856 We
Stockard, H. J. to M. J. Duke 10-17-1859 We
Stockard, Louizer R. to G. W. Wood 12-20-1860 G
Stockard, Mary A. R. to John C. Todd 11-6-1861 G
Stockard, Mary C. to James L. Jackson 12-5-1861 G
Stockdale, Elizabeth to Edward J. Blunt 1-15-1868 Be
Stockdale, Martha Ann to Joseph H. Legate 5-8-1853 Be
Stockdale, Mary Ann to D. F. Cheatham 2-21-1856 Be
Stockdale, Mary Caroline to G. W. Cagle 4-5-1866 Be
Stockdale, Nancy J. to H. R. Pierce 12-10-1857 Be
Stocker, Nancy to Moses Avenshire 2-1-1844 Cr
Stockette, Malinda E. to J. E. Rudolph 8-13-1856 Hn
Stockinger, Eliza D. to Nathan F. Plumer 10-26-1846 (11-5-1846) F
Stockinger, M. A. to D. G. Hineman 2-9-1859 F
Stockinger, Margaret to David Fausett 4-27-1862 (4-30-1862) F
Stockley, Emaline to David Williams 11-10-1870 (12-14-1870) T
Stockley, Jane to William Mitchell 5-27-1872 (6-14-1872) T
Stocks, Almira to Caswell Stocks 5-30-1842 Sh
Stocks, E. to William H. Gregg 10-28-1854 (10-29-1854) Sh
Stocks, Eliza to James M. Newson 1-21-1834 Sh
Stocks, Margaret to John H. Evetts 4-18-1837 Sh
Stocks, Sarah Ann to James J. Wilkins 2-28-1863 Sh
Stocks, Sarah Ann to James Y. Wilkins 2-28-1863 (3-1-1863) Sh
Stockton, Eliza to William Cole 6-17-1835 Hr
Stockton, M. O. to A. D. Keith 9-14-1854 Hr
Stockton, Maria A. to S. W. Muncrief 2-13-1851 (2-19-1851) Sh
Stockton, Pheby to Calvin Campbell 11-3-1848 (11-9-1848) Hr
Stoddard, Mary V. to Caswell Miller 11-11-1831 G
Stoddard, Pheobe to Thos. Maguire 4-19-1853 (5-1-1853) Sh
Stoddert, Mary Jane to William Caruthers 6-6-1859 (6-7-1859) Ma
Stoemer, Louisa to Wm. Tegethoff 9-1-1860 Sh
Stoffle, Jane to John Wynitt? 1-14-1846 Hn
Stoffle, S. to William Burd 3-30-1845 Hn
Stofle, Elizabeth to James Pool 6-9-1859 Hn
Stogdale(Stockdale), Emiline to Thomas A. Rolls 8-18-1860 Be
Stokeland, Mary E. to Forrest Jones 1-29-1883 L
Stokeley, Fannie to Sims Colter 3-2-1870 Hy
Stokeley, Mariah to Jorden Grant 2-22-1872 (no return) Hy
Stokeley, Mary to Taylor Nelson 11-6-1871 Hy
Stokely, Alice to Hilliard Barnes 3-7-1881 (3-18-1881) L B
Stokely, Gus to Lee McCulloch 12-28-1885 (12-29-1885) L
Stokely, Izora to Henry W. Moore 10-2-1873 Hy
Stokely, Janey to Asbury Barnes 2-4-1881 (2-26-1881) L B
Stokely, Jenny to Ben Berlen 2-10-1876 (no return) Hy
Stokely, Lizzie to Church Jones 2-10-1876 (no return) Hy
Stokely, Rose to Ben Stokely 12-13-1869 Hy
Stokely, Texana to A. Duprees 12-22-1868 (no return) Hy
Stoker, Elizabeth E. to F. C. Ross 1-21-1858 We
Stoker, Elizabeth to John Smith 3-5-1851 Cr
Stoker, Florida Ann to James R. Hodge 7-4-1872 (no return) Cr
Stoker, Mary S. M. to William P. Matthews 10-22-1854 O
Stoker, Nancy S. to James N. Mathews 3-24-1850 O
Stoker, Nancy to Melten Brann 11-3-1857 We
Stoker, Polly to Grasty Mansfield 2-7-1839 O
Stoker, Sarah C. to W. J. Tucker 12-21-1854 We
Stokes, A. to William H. Bushart 5-23-1852 Hn
Stokes, Ann M. to Thos. Coley 3-31-1841 (4-1-1841) G
Stokes, Annie to William Mayo 2-26-1860 We
Stokes, California to Pinkney Wyatt 12-28-1866 (12-29-1866) Cr
Stokes, Catharine Murphy to Willia Anthony Crouch 4-12-1845 (4-15-1845) T
Stokes, Delph to Wm. Little 9-28-1854 Cr
Stokes, Delphia Ann to John P. Tapley 2-13-1860 Hy
Stokes, E. J. to E. J. Pullen 11-10-1853 Hn
Stokes, Elizabeth to Sampson Rogers 11-7-1853 (11-15-1853) T
Stokes, Emily A. to James E. Crouch 1-14-1846 (2-24-1846) T
Stokes, Frances to Thos. J. Baugh 7-26-1854 (1-?-1854) T
Stokes, Gatsey to Elias Avenshire 12-12-1848 Cr
Stokes, Jenny to Benjamin Cobb 5-25-1841 (5-27-1841) T
Stokes, Josephine to J. R. Starnes 7-20-1853 (7-21-1853) T
Stokes, Lucy to Drewery Edwards 9-30-1841 Cr
Stokes, M. A. (Mrs.) to G. W. Wilson 7-23-1885 L
Stokes, M. E. to J. M. Stevens 2-26-1872 T
Stokes, M. W. to R. G. Blankenship 10-5-1850 (no return) L
Stokes, Malvina to L. A. Robertson 12-22-1862 (12-23-1862) Dy
Stokes, Martha to James Hodge 5-14-1843 Cr
Stokes, Mary E. to R. A. Olds 1-25-1878 (1-28-1878) L
Stokes, Mary to J. Jones 1-17-1859 Sh
Stokes, Matilda S. to James R. Henderson 11-18-1869 Hy
Stokes, Minty Ann to B. F. Gilliland 1-1-1868 (no return) L
Stokes, Nancy to Giles Bland 7-27-1871 (no return) Hy
Stokes, Neely D. to Miles D. Edwards 4-1-1852 Cr
Stokes, Sally to John McCord 2-5-1846 Cr
Stokes, Sarah H. to Meredith Holmes 5-25-1838 F
Stokes, Susan S. to J. W. Phillips 10-7-1852 Cr
Stokes, Susanna J. to Pleasant Wortham 10-5-1845 Sh
Stokley, Sarah to Jack Whitton 3-28-1878 Hy
Stoll, Elizabeth to Fredrick Heckle 11-1-1859 (11-2-1859) Sh
Stoll, Magdelina to Conrad Bollinger 3-23-1859 Sh
Stone, A. A. to Z. R. White 11-7-1866 (no return) Cr
Stone, Agnes A. to John S. Rochell 11-29-1854 Ma
Stone, Cyntha C. to Jas. A. Williamson 4-21-1863 (no return) Cr
Stone, Dennis to W. L. Wright 10-16-1865 (10-18-1865) Dy
Stone, E. F. to Isaac M. Holmes 11-30-1867 G
Stone, Eliza to John Blair 9-19-1845 Ma
Stone, Eliza to W. A. Patterson 9-30-1841 Cr
Stone, Eliza to Wm. R. Long 1-22-1839 Cr
Stone, Elizabeth Ann to Plivin Cardwell 1-20-1839 Cr
Stone, Elizabeth H. to George W. Wallingsford 1-23-1841 (1-24-1841) G
Stone, Elizabeth S. to James M. Rogers 2-26-1838 (3-13-1838) Hr
Stone, Elizabeth to Anderson Dale 1-9-1830 Hr
Stone, Elizabeth to Anderson Parker 6-13-1838 Cr
Stone, Elizabeth to James F. Haynes 2-21-1865 (no return) L
Stone, Elizer to Moss (Moses?) Robbins 3-15-1869 G B
Stone, Emiline to Thomas E. Boaz 11-19-1872 Dy
Stone, Emiline to Henry Smith 6-25-1867 Hy
Stone, Fanny to S. L. Gaines 10-4-1882 (10-5-1882) L
Stone, Fereby to James F. Fowler 2-7-1839 Cr
Stone, Frances P. to Thomas C. Alcebrook 12-22-1857 (no return) L
Stone, Frances to William Humble 5-25-1841 (5-26-1841) Ma
Stone, Jane to Henry Hardester 11-25-1833 (11-27-1833) G
Stone, Jane to Joseph F. McEwen 10-27-1867 G
Stone, Jane to Saml. Snellgroves 2-16-1856 (2-17-1856) Hr
Stone, Jane to Walker Jones 1-1-1845 (1-3-1845) O
Stone, Jane to William Newland 2-1-1845 (2-6-1845) Hr
Stone, Julina to William A. Baw 1-13-1852 (no return) F
Stone, Jurncia to John Jones 10-25-1847 (11-15-1847) O
Stone, Laura A. to Nat Tipton 11-21-1850 T
Stone, Louis A. to James V. Tupell 10-3-1844 Ma
Stone, Louisa J. to W. R. Bateman 1-12-1885 (1-14-1885) L

Stone, Lucinda F. to Sterling Farley 7-7-1847 F
Stone, Lucy to Alexander G. Little 3-22-1853 G
Stone, Lucy to Thomas Zellers 4-29-1826 O
Stone, Manerva Ann to William Farley 10-4-1848 (no return) F
Stone, Margaret C. to Caleb D. Bryant 4-10-1854 (4-18-1854) Ma
Stone, Margaret to Michael Burk 8-11-1859 Cr
Stone, Margaret to William Hurt 3-25-1840 Cr
Stone, Martha C. to George C. Harley 12-8-1845 G
Stone, Martha C. to Wm. H. Claxton 2-21-1859 (2-23-1859) G
Stone, Martha D. to John R. Cherry 4-10-1849 F
Stone, Martha Hill to Edwin James Morgan 8-10-1852 (8-11-1852) T
Stone, Martha J. to Daniel P. Cribbs 12-23-1845 Cr
Stone, Martha to E. M. Pannell 5-16-1860 Hr
Stone, Martha to H. H. Holt 1-22-1860 We
Stone, Mary A. M. to W. M. McEwen 11-6-1867 G
Stone, Mary A. R. to James M. Terry 11-26-1841 (12-7-1841) G
Stone, Mary A. to Horrace C. Knolton 8-15-1848 (8-17-1848) Hr
Stone, Mary A. to William Vantress 4-22-1848 (4-26-1848) Ma
Stone, Mary Ann to J. R. Doyle 1-18-1860 (1-20-1860) Hr
Stone, Mary C. to Washington L. Row 12-7-1842 (12-20?-1842) F
Stone, Mary E. to Frances Buirckman 8-18-1865 (8-19-1865) O
Stone, Mary J. to William W. Norman 5-16-1860 (5-20-1860) L
Stone, Mary W. to Alexander Ross 1-16-1849 (1-18-1849) G
Stone, Mary to George H. Guthrie 1-16-1844 Cr
Stone, Mary to Marian Emerson 7-4-1867 (7-7-1867) Ma
Stone, Millisy W. to Wiert F. Still 8-5-1839 (no return) L
Stone, Nancy to Samuel Stone 12-21-1843 Cr
Stone, Nancy to William R. Herron 3-14-1844 Be
Stone, Narcissa M. (Mrs.) to Benjamin F. Gates 5-4-1859 Ma
Stone, Ophelia to Saml. Craig 4-3-1871 Ma
Stone, Permelia Olen to Charles H. Mullins 12-19-1868 (12-20-1868) L
Stone, Rebecca to John Ferguson 11-23-1849 Sh
Stone, S. F. to A. E. McAdoo 11-17-1859 (11-20-1859) G
Stone, Sarah A. Vanosten to Allen H. Rowe 12-3-1860 (12-5-1860) Sh
Stone, Sarah Ann to Merlin Perry 12-5-1854 Ma
Stone, Sarah Ann to Watt Cash 6-29-1850 (7-1-1850) Ma
Stone, Susan K. to Wm. T. C. Cribbs 9-12-1843 Cr
Stone, Susan to James West 11-3-1851 (11-12-1851) Sh
Stone, Syntha J. to Thos. Akins 3-1-1847 Cr
Stone, Tennie to J. T. C. Palmer 11-17-1876 (12-19-1876) Dy
Stone?, Zelphia to Alfred Stone 12-6-1838 G
Stony, Ellen Elizabeth to S. M. Plant 7-19-1851 (no return) F
Storeer, Martha to J. R. Wright 6-15-1861 (6-16-1861) O
Story, Lucy to Samuel Lamar 2-25-1826 (2-26-1826) O
Story, Manessa to Robert C. Merton 10-13-1855 (no return) Hn
Story, Siryna E. to George W. Willson 10-26-1863 Hn
Stott, Lucy to Harm. Meriweather 8-10-1866 Hy
Stott, Martha to Henry Warren 1-29-1873 Hy
Stott, Mattie S. to John M. Stott 5-10-1874 Hy
Stott, Peggy to Ely Peters 1-1-1867 Hy
Stout, Caroline to S. G. Drewry 12-14-1843 (no return) We
Stout, Emily to J. C. Connel 2-12-1855 (no return) We
Stout, Martha A. to Daniel G. Gailey 12-23-1862 We
Stout, Mary P. to John A. Austin 5-25-1866 (5-27-1866) Ma
Stout, Mary to John P. Rose 8-12-1854 (8-13-1854) Hr
Stout, S. C. to James Roberson 7-10-1858 We
Stovall, Angeline to Henry Gray 7-14-1872 (7-15-1872) O
Stovall, Bettie to Joseph M. Gregory 4-18-1854 Sh
Stovall, Emily to Jesse Walker 7-4-1853 (7-7-1853) O
Stovall, I. F. to H. C. Clements 10-11-1865 O
Stovall, Lucinda R. to John Harper 9-28-1843 O
Stovall, Luetta Jane to John W. Walker 4-6-1857 (4-8-1857) O
Stovall, Mary J. to James Clement 12-9-1865 (12-13-1865) O
Stovall, Mary to Thomas Harris 12-6-1842 (12-7-1842) F
Stovall, S. J. to George W. Durham 10-25-1858 (10-31-1858) Sh
Stovall, Willey Ann to James W. Farris 2-11-1862 (2-11?-1862) O
Stoveall, Mary to Nathan Adams 10-5-1843 (no return) We
Stover, Syntha Ann to Adam Huffstutter 3-15-1859 (3-17-1859) O
Stow, Septima J. to Wm. H. Brann 9-25-1855 We
Straden (Staden), Sarah to John H. White 3-11-1844 Sh
Strader (Shader), Margaret to Jackson White 12-25-1842 Sh
Strahorn, L. J. to Franklin Perry 12-23-1867 (no return) Dy
Strain, Diana to Warren Hunter 1-6-1870 (no return) L
Strain, Elizabeth to Hardy Harrington 7-28-1840 Ma
Strain, Elizabeth to William J. Billips 11-10-1849 (11-15-1849) G
Strain, Flora to Jasper Miller 7-24-1877 (7-25-1877) L
Strain, Frances J. to Cardy Warrel 7-3-1852 Ma
Strain, Jane to John J> Faulkner 11-8-1871 (11-9-1871) T
Strain, Jane to Samuel Sainford 1-19-1847 (1-20-1847) G
Strain, Louisa to John W. Barfield 12-24-1857 (no return) L
Strain, M. C. to Samuel L. Bibb 7-14-1870 (7-17-1870) L
Strain, Martha to William W. Wilson 3-28-1829 Ma
Strain, Mary Ann to Samuel G. Tatum 9-14-1854 L
Strain, Rose to Nelson Barnett 12-9-1869 (no return) L
Straine, Elizabeth to S. D. Prichard 12-5-1864 (12-7-1864) Dy
Stram, Sarah J. to Wm. M. Steward 12-14-1850 (12-17-1850) F
Strang, Rebecca to Wm. Leigs 12-18-1860 (12-19-1860) Sh

Strange, Amanda J. to Janus M. Stricklen 3-10-1868 Dy
Strange, Anne Belle to James Clement 10-29-1874 T
Strange, Charity to Thos. Green 2-18-1873 (3-25-1873) T
Strange, E. to Angus McKay 1-14-1864 Sh
Strange, L. J. to E. F. Vernon 9-11-1878 (9-16-1878) L
Strange, Lucy V. to James T. Smithwick 11-25-1847 Sh
Strange, Mary A. to Clavin C. Cleaves 11-7-1844 Sh
Strange, Mary Henry to W. W. Murray 1-4-1869 Cr
Strange, Sallie W. to John H. Taylor 3-20-1855 Sh
Strassler, Emma to Edward Rudin 1-15-1861 Sh
Straten, Margaret to Dave Proctor 12-26-1867 G B
Straton, Mary A. to Henry Walker 1-6-1869 G B
Stratton, Augusta to Benjamin F. Fleming 11-2-1853 Sh
Stratton, Henrietta F. to Job H. Goodlett 6-15-1848 Sh
Stratton, Margaret M. to C. W. Alexander 7-3-1858 (7-5-1858) Sh
Stratton, Martha J. to Jno. W. Waldrum 2-19-1867 O
Stratton, Virginia C. (Mrs.) to Lucius L. Weatherly 5-4-1869 (5-6-1869) Ma
Strauchn, Mary A. E. to Henry C. Murchison 5-31-1871 (no return) Hy
Straus, Lizatte to Maier Pump 5-21-1859 (5-22-1859) Sh
Strauss, Caroline to J. H. Lehman 9-18-1856 Sh
Strauss, Rosa to Marx Bloom 5-12-1854 Sh
Strauther, Susan to Briant Flowers 8-4-1836 (8-14-1836) G
Strawbridge, Jane to James A. Etharage 12-26-1844 Hn
Strawn, Julia to Joseph D. Haynes 11-20-1860 (11-21-1860) Dy
Strawn, Mary to William Addison Kirk 10-24-1848 (11-1-1848) T
Strawn, Stacy S. to W. T. Pace 12-29-1865 (12-30-1865) Dy
Stray, Mary Jane to John W. Robinson 1-7-1869 G B
Stray, Sarah Ann to Coleman Roberson 4-20-1850 (4-21-1850) G
Strayhorn, Ann to William Pope 8-20-1838 (8-25-1838) Ma
Strayhorn, Deliah to Abriham Moore 3-10-1873 (3-13-1873) Cr B
Strayhorn, Emolen to M. H. Null 10-7-1853 Cr
Strayhorn, Esther to Hardy Herron 1-19-1869 (1-21-1869) Cr
Strayhorn, Julia Ann to M. Drennon 12-17-1861 (12-22-1861) T
Strayhorn, Julia to Richard Elem 7-26-1872 (no return) Cr
Strayhorn, Louisa to Joseph Malow 7-25-1854 Sh
Strayhorn, N. J. to S. M. Hart 2-29-1872 Hy
Strayhorn, Orabella to Oswill Newby 12-18-1841 (12-22-1841) Ma
Strayhorn, Sarah Jane to Thaddeus D. Cooper 10-12-1859 Ma
Strayhorn, Silvey to Toney Nesbitt 2-27-1869 Cr
Street, Bettie to S. T. Johnson 5-30-1879 (no return) Dy
Street, Bridget to George B. Pate 8-24-1845 L
Street, Charlotte M. to A. A. Yarbro 3-20-1872 (3-21-1872) T
Street, Martha Ann to Asa Cox 12-2-1841 Hn
Street, Mary to Wesley Wilson 12-29-1866 Hy
Street, Sallie E. to Jas. J. Martin 9-14-1864 Sh
Street, Sarah to James Walker 4-12-1849 Hn
Strengths, Mary S. to Daniel N. Fowler 8-1-1877 Hy
Stribbling, M. A. H. to W. I. Ezell 5-27-1858 Cr
Stribbling, Sarah to Andrew Dickson 1-9-1870 G B
Striblin, Parlee to Add Cuningham 1-14-1873 Cr
Stribling, Elizabeth to J. H. Cload 1-5-1853 Cr
Stribling, Mary Elizabeth to Thadeus Pope 12-13-1853 Ma
Stribling, Mary J. to James S. Barker 3-22-1857 Cr
Stribling, Nancy A. to Nathaniel Benton 9-12-1848 (9-13-1848) Ma
Stribling, Nancy J. to M. L. Bullington 12-19-1871 (no return) Cr
Strickland, C. V. to James M. Vaughn 1-2-1878 (1-4-1878) L
Strickland, Candis to Dick Baker 4-4-1868 F B
Strickland, Dixie E. to Hammond E. Price 10-13-1884 (10-16-1884) L
Strickland, Ellen to Anderson Teague 8-25-1866 (8-26-1866) F B
Strickland, Fanny to William H. Carson 4-4-1855 Sh
Strickland, L. A. to John B. Griffin 12-27-1870 (12-28-1870) L
Strickland, L. H. to M. (Dr.) Bell 4-23-1859 (not endorsed) Sh
Strickland, Laura to Cain Neville 9-7-1867 F B
Strickland, Lola M. to J. B. Hart 12-16-1885 L
Strickland, Lucretia J. to B. H. Whittaker 1-18-1871 F
Strickland, Lucy A. to Wm. C. Forbess 11-10-1852 Cr
Strickland, Lucy J. to Jno. W. Whitaker 12-15-1868 (12-16-1868) F
Strickland, Malinda to Henry C. Mitchel 4-20-1843 Be
Strickland, Malisa E. to Samuel W. Montgomery 1-7-1848 (1-9-1848) Hr
Strickland, Martha J. to Thomas Ferguson 10-26-1853 (10-27-1853) L
Strickland, Mary to Benjamin Rogers 4-23-1851 Hr
Strickland, Mary to Wm. Shannon 12-9-1877 Hy
Strickland, Matilda to Thomas Nelson 5-3-1866 (no return) Hy
Strickland, Menerva A. to George M. Ferguson 10-24-1861 L
Strickland, Nancy E. to J. P. Cole 6-26-1870 G
Strickland, Rachel A. to Briggs Barker 7-1-1852 Be
Strickland, S. J. to John Allen 3-17-1869 Be
Strickland, Sally to W. C. Lournigan 10-14-1862 Be
Strickland, Susan to James C. Martin 2-27-1869 (2-28-1869) F B
Strickland, Susana to Bill Phillips 4-20-1868 F B
Stricklin, A. C. to C. W. McCommon 10-6-1860 (10-11-1860) Hr
Stricklin, Catherine to Willington Keefe 3-20-1868 Ma
Stricklin, Dosia to Hamilton J. Sanders 8-4-1869 Hy
Stricklin, Eliza to Joseph D. Allen 2-26-1844 Sh
Stricklin, Liza to Armstead Grayson 4-2-1867 Dy
Stricklin, Margaret C. to William H. Wilson 1-13-1846 (no return) L
Stricklin, Melissa A. to O. H. P. Johnson 7-7-1857 (7-8-1857) Hr

Stricklin, Nancy to Alex Wayson 1-15-1878 Dy
Stricklin, Nancy to John Douvall 5-12-1868 Hy
Stricklin, Sophia E. to William R.? Humphreys 3-2-1852 (3-3-1852) L
Striclin, Mariah O. to W. S. Warren 2-19-1869 (no return) Dy
Strictlin, Drucilla to Joe Bowling 12-12-1870 (no return) Hy
String, Jane E. to Jno. D. Banks 12-13-1864 (12-14-1864) T
String, Margaret E. to John Adkinson no date (with 1862) T
String, Nancy (Mrs.) to Francis Baugh 3-18-1863 Sh
Stringer, Elizabeth to Andrew Lunamand 4-10-1858 (4-11-1858) Sh
Stringer, Susana to W. O. Carroll 8-22-1862 (9-3-1862) Sh
Stringfellow, Martha to Levy S. Thomas 7-30-1864 Sh
Stringlin, Elizabeth to Chas. Rainer 2-6-1854 Sh
Stroh, Catharina to Charles Saander 10-8-1861 Sh
Strong, Catharine D. to John W. Reach 2-2-1857 (2-3-1857) G
Strong, Eliza to Lewis Caroway 1-27-1872 (2-6-1872) T
Strong, Elizabeth to Hosia Parker 9-7-1847 G
Strong, Elizabeth to L. McCain 9-23-1865 T
Strong, Frances to H. O. Banks 4-25-1871 (4-26-1871) T
Strong, George A. to Wallace Kitchen 3-27-1869 (3-30-1869) T
Strong, Jane to M. L. Benge 1-1-1840 Sh
Strong, Laura V. to William Felts 10-31-1854 (11-2-1854) G
Strong, Lotty to Archibald M. Simonton? 2-19-1842 (3-3-1842) T
Strong, Louisa Elmira to Ro. M. Banks 1-10-1853 (1-12-1853) T
Strong, M. A. to W. M. Belew 1-31-1867 G
Strong, M. E. A. to Thomas B. McGee 12-19-1877 Hy
Strong, Maggie to John T. Taylor 11-25-1874 Hy
Strong, Margaret E. to John Atkison 3-18-1862 (3-20-1862) T
Strong, Martha L. to David Moffett 10-23-1867 (10-24-1867) T
Strong, Mary A. to John McLoughland 12-8-1860 (12-12-1860) T
Strong, Mary Ann to John C. Carter 12-21-1836 T
Strong, Milley to Richard Adams 9-30-1865 (10-28-1865) T
Strong, Nannie L. B. to J. W. Wells 10-21-1872 L
Strong, Rebecca to Joseph McNeely 1-7-1841 Sh
Strong, Sarah E. to John S. Harrel 4-1-1861 (4-9-1861) Sh
Strong, Sarah J. to John G. Mathews 12-23-1850 T
Strong, Sarah T. to Jerry T. Taylor 1-2-1878 Hy
Strong, Sarah to Joseph B. Patrick 8-28-1845 Sh
Strother, Catharine to E. N. Pierce 6-26-1855 (6-27-1855) G
Strother, E. J. to W. E. Tinkle 12-25-1866 G
Strother, Eliza E. to C. Nicholas 10-21-1871 (10-22-1871) Dy
Strother, Elizabeth to Lewis H. Taylor 1-8-1840 Sh
Strother, Elvira to William E. Roberts 12-24-1869 (no return) Dy
Strother, Eron to Jared House 12-27-1848 Sh
Strother, July to Johnathan Henry 4-15-1836 (4-17-1836) G
Strother, Mary Helen to Hosea Buck 7-17-1850 Sh
Strothers, Hannah to John Clifton 12-23-1841 (12-30-1841) Hr
Stroud, Biddey to Benjamin Haley 12-18-1839 (12-19-1839) O
Stroud, Clara J. to Adam Hufstutter 12-22-1851 (12-23-1851) O
Stroud, Elizabeth to John Chamberlin 4-7-1833 Sh
Stroud, Elizabeth to Lewis Moody 4-26-1855 (no return) Hn
Stroud, Elizabeth to Silas Longly 6-5-1830 (6-14-1830) O
Stroud, Elizabeth to William Box 4-18-1836 O
Stroud, Isa to James Herald 12-29-1833 O
Stroud, J. C. to L. D. Allen 1-2-1859 Hn
Stroud, Lucina P. to Henry Wimberley 11-16-1847 Hn
Stroud, M. S. to S. B. Shaffin 3-29-1869 (3-31-1869) Cr
Stroud, Margaret J. to William T. Shelton 3-22-1843 (3-23-1843) O
Stroud, Martha H. to John W. Akin 11-21-1870 (11-23-1870) T
Stroud, Martha J. to John J. Sullivan 6-30-1857 (no return) Hn
Stroud, Mary A. to James W. Stroud 11-27-1857 Hn
Stroud, Matilda to Stephen Vaughn 7-11-1857 Hn *
Stroud, N. J. to A. J. Fisher 10-7-1874 (10-8-1874) T
Stroud, Sarah E. to John C. Terry 12-4-1853 Hn
Stroud?, Tabitha Geraldine to R. R. Brooks 1-1-1867 Hn
Strouse, C. A. to J. W. Jackson 12-12-1865 (12-16-1865) Cr
Strouse, Sarah (Mrs.) to Thomas E. Fisher 10-21-1873 (10-22-1873) L
Strout?, Emma to Geo. Arnold 9-22-1851 Sh
Struther, Frances to Lewis Lee 12-31-1869 Hy
Struthers, Eliza B. to John B. Alston 12-12-1866 Hy
Stuard, Nancy to Elijah Wilbourn 11-29-1843 (11-30-1843) G
Stuart, Elizabeth to Jesse W. Beavers 12-26-1852 Hn
Stuart, Elizabeth to John Laymon 11-24-1836 G
Stuart, Emily to J. N. Patterson 10-3-1861 (no return) Hn
Stuart, Frances A. to William H. Adkins 2-12-1842 (2-17-1842) Hr
Stuart, Venie to William Lee 1-9-1873 Hy
Stubblefield, Eliza to Samuel L. Stout 8-16-1861 We
Stubblefield, Lucinda to Z. B. Scates 9-1-1861 We
Stubblefield, Margarett E. to Z. T. Gibson 11-9-1867 G
Stubblefield, Martha H. to John G. Forrest 9-25-1865 (no return) Hn
Stubblefield, Mary A. to Wm. G. Porter 2-5-1850 We
Stubblefield, Nancy J. to Alexander Stubblefield 11-12-1844 We
Stubbs, Ellen to Silas Carr 3-10-1885 (3-15-1885) L
Stubbs, Martha G. to B. F. Gibson 11-15-1863 (no return) Cr
Stubbs, Mourning to John Stubbs 11-4-1856 (11-5-1856) O
Stubbs, Rachel R. to John T. Bowls 8-9-1831 Ma
Stubbs, S. C. to M. A. Crawford 1-6-1868 (1-9-1868) Cr
Stubbs, Susan L. to Joseph G. Milam 9-3-1870 (no return) Cr

Stubelfield, Martha B. to J. D. Hanley 3-30-1857 We
Stublefield, Minerva to A. P. Lovens 9-22-1867 Hn
Stucken, Martha J. to James Warren 11-22-1860 Dy
Stuckey, Cora C. to Wilson W. Alford 6-23-1854 L
Stuckey, Elizabeth to William Deason 3-16-1848 L
Stuckey, Mary E. to William Sawyer 11-23-1854 L
Stuckey, Melinda to David Barry (Burney?) 5-4-1853 L
Stuckey, Sarah to Robert Jackson 6-10-1864 (12-23-1864) L
Stuckey, Syrenie E. to A. R. (or R. A.) Jenkins 10-6-1869 L
Stuckley (Starkey), Mary (May) to David L. Ridgeway 3-27-1849 Sh
Studard, Catherine to Thos. Rhoades 1-27-1872 Hy
Studivan, Nannie to Henry Robertson 3-2-1870 (3-7-1870) F B
Stull, Mollie to John Roberts 5-20-1876 (5-21-1876) L
Stull, P. (Mrs.) to A. Fleming 9-16-1866 G
Stults, Mary E. to G. M. Bradford 9-17-1855 G
Stults, N. E. to G. F. Jones 1-25-1876 (1-26-1876) Dy
Stumphf, Ignata to Conrad Schmidt 8-15-1855 (8-16-1855) Sh
Stunston, A. E. to M. A. Stevenson 5-6-1863 (no return) We
Sturdevant, Ann to Reuben S. Marlow 1-30-1870
Sturdevant, L. F. to S. B. Lovelace 12-21-1881 (12-22-1881) L
Sturdevant, Lucinda R. to Thomas D. Day 3-4-1868 Ma
Sturdevant, Martila to William Bradford 2-18-1868 (2-20-1868) Ma
Sturdivan, Eliza to Wesley Sangster 4-4-1872 Hy
Sturdivant, Catherine to Feereby Wilkins 12-9-1850 (12-11-1850) Ma
Sturdivant, D. E. to E. G. Butler 2-9-1865 G
Sturdivant, Elizabeth to William G. L. Harrell 1-16-1850 (1-17-1850) Ma
Sturdivant, Fanny to Washington Webb 11-28-1868 G B
Sturdivant, Frances to Stephen Hart 7-28-1847 Hn
Sturdivant, Margaret A. to Benjamin W. McFadden 9-23-1866 Hn
Sturdivant, Mary M. to Robert B. Smith 3-28-1836 Hn
Sturdivant, Silvey to Scipio Peebles 4-7-1866 (no return) Hy
Sturges, Apalipa (Assalissa?) to Marcus Waddell 1-22-1853 (1-24-1853) Sh
Sturges, Sarah Louisa to Thos. Starling 4-6-1859 (4-7-1859) Sh
Styers, Ann E. to C. Autry 1-16-1873 L
Styers, Mary E. to L. M. Lovelace 3-6-1865 L
Styles, Elizabeth Jane to Benjamin Wilson 1-25-1862 O
Styles, Jane to William Dorin 9-6-1841 Hn
Subber, Margaret to Simon W. Kephart 4-5-1831 Sh
Subtle, Phebi to Wm. H. Shields 3-4-1846 (no return) We
Suckett, Elizabeth to John Egan 1-6-1855 (no return) F
Sudberry, F. E. to James Saulsbury 12-30-1871 Dy
Sudberry, Jane to King Green 1-1-1878 Dy
Sudberry, Nancy to Henry Ranser 1-3-1866 (1-20-1867) Dy
Sudberry, Tabitha to John Barr 1-3-1871 (1-4-1871) Dy
Sudbury, N. E. to S. J. Yates 11-14-1866 Dy
Suddeth, R. A. to C. J. Conner 12-24-1855 (12-25-1855) Sh
Sugg, Nancy E. to J. W. King 12-3-1868 (12-6-1868) Cr
Sugg, Sallie E. to Orvid Gibson 2-19-1870? (3-16-1869?) L
Sugget, Virginia C. to Sam H. Smith 8-20-1855 (no return) F
Suggett, Frances C. to Wm. W. Todd 8-26-1865 F
Suggett?, Mary E. to Daniel I. Wells 11-24-1836 Hr
Suggs, Anna to Peter McFadden 11-24-1877 L
Suggs, Caroline to Thomas King 2-20-1864 (2-22-1864) Cr
Suggs, Clara to James Walker 6-2-1881 (no return) L B
Suggs, Clara to Lafayett King 12-2-1881 (12-15-1881) L B
Suggs, Clery? A. to Janes Kee 11-10-1860 (11-17-1860) Cr
Suggs, Frances to Morris Griffin 12-20-1882 (no return) L
Suggs, Harriat to Jo Winters 12-30-1875 (12-31-1875) L B
Suggs, Harriett S. to John W. Ledbetter 1-3-1844 Sh
Suggs, Julian to Benj. F. Haltom 12-15-1855 (12-19-1855) Hr
Suggs, Lucinda to James A. Hatch 4-5-1861 (no return) Cr
Suggs, M. L. to Daniel Haynie 3-15-1852 Sh
Suggs, Mary A. to J. W. Horn 1-11-1867 (1-13-1867) Cr
Suggs, Mary C. to _____ Thomson 1-30-1844 Sh
Suggs, Mattie to Cesa Lea 1-30-1869 Hy
Suggs, Nancy to William J. Blair 2-6-1856 (2-7-1856) Hr
Suggs, Winnie C. to Granvil L. Hatch 4-7-1873 (4-9-1873) Cr
Sugs, Eveline to J. C. King 2-20-1866 (2-25-1866) Cr
Suiter, Elizabeth to Jesse Willbanks 11-29-1862 (no return) Hn
Sulfrick, Martha to David Loovell 3-3-1859 (3-9-1859) T
Sulivan, Elizabeth to Wm. McCain 11-11-1846 We
Sulivan, Elizabeth to Wm. N. McCain 11-18-1846 We
Sulivan, Ella to P. C. Tipton 2-10-1875 Hy
Sulivan, Jane to John Harris 7-10-1854 (7-18-1854) Hr
Sulivan, Loiza to J. M. Morris 3-11-1866 Hy
Sulivan, Lucenda to Hal Taylor 7-12-1868 Hy
Sulivan, Lucinda to Benjamin Winford 10-5-1843 Sh
Sulivan, Mollie to John Willoughby 7-23-1874 Hy
Sulivan, P. A. to M. C. Ross 9-22-1863 (11-16-1863) Dy
Sulivant, Lucretia W. to Zacariah C. Alvis 8-26-1841 Sh
Sulivant, Rutha An to L. A. Buchanon 2-3-1848 (2-7-1848) F
Sullenger, Sarah to John Bass 4-15-1826 (4-20-1826) Hr
Sullens, Susan to Thomas W. Glover 7-27-1841 Hn
Sullins, Elizabeth to James Taylor 1-18-1850 Be
Sullivan, Ann to Wesley Rowlin 1-23-1840 Cr
Sullivan, Bridget to Ptrick Twohig 11-12-1861 Sh
Sullivan, Caroline to John Thomas Caldwell 12-29-1868 G B

Sullivan, Charlotte to Henry Black 12-30-1870 (no return) Hy
Sullivan, Charlotty to John Wilkerson 1-19-1853 Cr
Sullivan, D. P. (Mrs.) to John D. Andrews 8-30-1864 Sh
Sullivan, Dicy A. to James L. Burdick 5-10-1861 (5-14-1861) T
Sullivan, Elizabeth A. to Jesse M. Johnson 8-6-1860 (8-8-1860) Sh
Sullivan, Elizabeth to Jessee Morris 12-30-1869 Hy
Sullivan, Ellen to J. S. Lovelace 12-20-1869 G
Sullivan, Ellen to Micheal? Grady 12-2-1862 Sh
Sullivan, Frances A. to W. C. Slaughter 11-18-1867 (11-19-1867) F
Sullivan, Jane to A. G. McPherson 3-3-1861 Be
Sullivan, Judith to John Shehan 8-7-1854 Sh
Sullivan, Julia to Peter Sullivan 8-7-1858 (8-8-1858) Sh
Sullivan, Katty to Richard McDonald 10-17-1868 F B
Sullivan, L. F. to E. Ammons 12-9-1854 (no return) F
Sullivan, Louisa to Jas. W. McAnaly 7-21-1857 (7-22-1857) Hr
Sullivan, Lula to James Williams 1-7-1880 (1-8-1880) L
Sullivan, Lydia to Isaac Kee 3-30-1844 F
Sullivan, Margaret J. to Thomas W. Boyd 3-21-1861 Sh
Sullivan, Margaret T. to Zachariah Wyatt 5-20-1869 (no return) Cr
Sullivan, Margaret to Nash Carroll 10-28-1854 Sh
Sullivan, Mary Ann to John McDonald 7-8-1852 Hr
Sullivan, Mary C. to R. D. Davis 12-18-1875 Hn
Sullivan, Mary J. to J. H. Rose 10-28-1869 (10-31-1869) F
Sullivan, Mary J. to William Wright 6-28-1871 (7-2-1871) T
Sullivan, Mary R. to Saml. M. Yarbro 12-26-1870 (12-29-1870) T
Sullivan, Mary to Chas. H. Sigrest 11-21-1859 Sh
Sullivan, Mary to Edward Coltyn 4-5-1856 (4-6-1856) Sh
Sullivan, Mary to Jerry Gallavin 6-30-1860 (7-4-1860) Sh
Sullivan, Mary to John Radford 2-25-1855 Hn
Sullivan, Mattie P. to J. F. Benton 12-22-1874 (12-23-1874) T
Sullivan, Mollie to Henry Outlaw 12-27-1884 (12-28-1884) L
Sullivan, Namie? to W. C. Davis 3-12-1866 (3-15-1866) T
Sullivan, Nancy E. to David McDonald 12-24-1866 (12-26-1866) F
Sullivan, Nancy E. to W. B. Greer 12-2-1866 Hn
Sullivan, Nancy Wade to Benjamin C. Bailey 12-8-1845 (12-10-1845) T
Sullivan, Nancy to Gabriel McCraw 6-29-1841 T
Sullivan, Nancy to John Sellars 2-2-1850 Hn
Sullivan, Polly to Jesse M. Morris 4-6-1850 (4-7-1850) F
Sullivan, Rebecca M. to Enoch Sevier 1-5-1846 (1-6-1846) F
Sullivan, S. to A. C. Sullivan 11-9-1839 Ma
Sullivan, Sallie to Peter D. 3-7-1850 Cr
Sullivan, Sarah A. R. to F. M. McClanahan 5-1-1860 Sh
Sullivan, Sarah D. to William H. Shelton 10-13-1835 Sh
Sullivan, Sarah E. to Blunt Harvey 3-4-1868 (3-10-1868) F
Sullivan, Sarah to Samuel Black 4-16-1850 Cr
Sullivan, Sullie E. to T. L. Harper 12-27-1869 Hy
Sullivan, Susan Ann to David Fletcher Moore 9-17-1844 (9-19-1844) T
Sullivan, Temperance to W. H. Hobson 4-27-1840 (5-2-1850) F
Sullivan, Tennessee to James Gallagher 1-4-1870 (1-6-1869?) F
Sullivant, Nancy to John W. Slater 2-24-1845 (no return) F
Sultsman, Eva to Phillip Weener (Werner?) 2-4-1861 Sh
Sulzmann, Susanna to Anton Smith 6-7-1859 (6-8-1859) Sh
Sumer, Eliza A. to William H. Harel 10-16-1861 Hn
Sumerow, Ann to Nelson Taylor 1-25-1869 (2-17-1869) L
Sumerow, C. L. to Chas. F. Herring 10-27-1875 Dy
Sumerow, Cherry to Gilbert Wincheste 12-29-1871 L
Sumerow, Ema T. to Samuel A. Anthony 11-2-1874 L
Sumerow, Hester Ann to Cas Browning 1-29-1878 (no return) L B
Sumerow, Lula to Joseph Crockett 1-3-1880 (1-6-1880) L
Sumerow, Martha A. to Benjamin M. Hall 12-5-1860 (no return) L
Sumerow, Martha E. to John Rucker 3-16-1857 (no return) L
Sumerow, Minnie to Robert Alsabrook 1-20-1886 (1-24-1886) L
Sumerow, Nancy E. to Isaac J. Winston 9-18-1873 L
Sumerow, Pennie to Richard Parr 12-23-1871 (12-26-1871) L B
Sumerow, Sarah E. to Jesse M. Sumerow 10-3-1854 (10-5-1854) L
Sumers, A. E. to J. W. Sumers 3-31-1874 (4-3-1874) O
Sumers, Nancy M. to Josephus Vaughn 12-23-1856 We
Sumervill, Tinah to Charles Somervill 12-27-1867 T
Summerow, Maggie to C. B. Lawrence 12-23-1884 (12-24-1885?) L
Summers (Inman?), Rebecca to Moses B. Moultrie 5-24-1847 (5-25-1847) O
Summers, Ann P. to James N. P. Smith 1-23-1868 Be
Summers, Anna to Benjamin B. Wilkes 3-17-1877 Hy
Summers, Annie to M. D. Wells 12-9-1884 L
Summers, E. M. to D. L. Green 12-22-1873 Dy
Summers, Eathea M. B. to Ren Pruit 9-17-1849 G
Summers, Eliza A. to Edward A. Mullins 12-10-1849 Ma
Summers, Isadora to Anthony Chrisman 5-1-1868 G B
Summers, Jane to Charles Tinsley 10-10-1854 G
Summers, Josie to James Hollingshead 7-16-1875 (no return) Hy
Summers, Louisa to R. M. Coker 9-6-1880 L
Summers, M. A. F. to C. F. Sinklar 11-29-1866 (11-29-18??) O
Summers, M. A. T. to C. F. Sinklar 11-29-1866 O
Summers, Margret N. to G. P. Swindle 8-19-1868 Be
Summers, Mary to Charles Myers 9-19-1867 G
Summers, Minerva J. to John Sayles 12-18-1856 Cr
Summers, Rachael to Hickerson L. Doyle 8-13-1841 (8-18-1841) Ma
Summers, Raussa to James L. Cashon 2-13-1839 (2-21-1839) O
Summers, Sarah A. to L. P. Owens 3-16-1858 We
Summers, Sarah F. to W. P. Mitchel 7-?-1862) Be
Summersett, Sarah F. to James R. Latimer 5-12-1862 (5-15-1862) O
Summonds?, Eliza A. to Levy Swenny 9-25-1855 (no return) Hn
Summons, Eliza to Spincer Bradford 2-14-1842 G
Sumner, Alice to Tom Johnson 1-12-1871 (no return) F B
Sumner, Frances to James Boman 4-24-1860 (4-25-1860) Ma
Sumner, Laura to Peter Beard 2-22-1871 Hy
Sumner, Martha A. to Jesse Redd 3-8-1859 (3-13-1859) F
Sumner, Penelope to Wm. C. Jenkins 12-21-1840 F
Sumner, Sallie to Thomas Hollinghead 1-21-1875 Hy
Sumner, Sarah to John Bryant 3-5-1849 (3-11-1849) F
Sumrow, Madorah E. to W. E. Hearring 7-15-1876 (7-16-1876) L
Sundheim, Louisa to John Fink 5-19-1856 Sh
Suplee, Margaret to George C. Bolles 9-23-1858 (8?-26-1858) Sh
Supples, Margaret to Michael O'Hare 4-20-1840 Sh
Suralle, W. M. to Arch Carr 7-16-1862 (7-17-1862) Sh
Surber, Rebeca to J. H. Watson 12-20-1867 (12-22-1867) Cr
Surcene?, Jane to James Deson 5-18-1852 Hn
Surcey, J. E. to J. H. Dyer 7-18-1865 (7-19-1865) L
Surpit, M. L. to Wm. J. Devenport 2-13-1849 (2-14-1849) F
Surratt, E. to W. D. Murray 3-28-1861 Mn
Surratt, E. P. to J. M. Dodd 10-13-1864 Mn
Surratt, Mariah to Nathan Freeman 6-4-1864 Mn
Susan, Bowers to George Phillips 1-17-1875 Hy
Susana J., Holloway to J. D. Rice 11-3-1873 (no return) Hy
Sutherland, Ditha to Joe Morgan 9-12-1867 F
Sutherland, Mary to John Gibson 12-22-1858 Cr
Sutherland, Sadie T. (Mrs.) to Frank M. Sinclair 10-16-1867 L
Sutherland, Selena C. (Mrs.) to Moses Lynch 12-31-1839 F
Sutherland, Susan J. to W. J. Devenport 3-28-1870 (3-29-1870) F
Sutherlin, Parmelia to Oscar Little 1-29-1857 Cr
Suton, Becky to Munroe Parmer 2-18-1867 Hy
Sutten, Alice to John Currie 5-25-1872 (no return) Hy
Suttle, Martha D. to Robt. C. Buford 11-27-1848 (no return) F
Suttlemire, Elmira to Francis M. Edgington 6-1-1864 Sh
Suttles, A. F. to Isaiah Pain 12-16-1839 Be
Suttles, Mary to Jackson Wilkerson 3-28-1859 Hr
Sutton, Alice to James Parchman 2-21-1877 Hy
Sutton, Almeda G. to J. M. Walton 11-3-1850 Hn
Sutton, Anna Bell to James P. Robinson 12-30-1868 (1-19-1869) Ma
Sutton, Anna L. to Abner L. Rodgers 9-1-1851 (9-2-1851) L
Sutton, Bettie P. to J. A. Bradford 12-17-1878 (12-18-1878) L
Sutton, Bettie to Isac Shilcut 1-31-1878 Hy
Sutton, Eva to Simon Campbell 3-7-1873 (3-8-1873) L B
Sutton, Hugh Elgria to B. B. Edwards 10-24-1860 (no return) We
Sutton, Judith A. to W. C. Sutton 12-4-1878 Hy
Sutton, Judith C. to Jonathan A. Campbell 2-9-1853 L
Sutton, Lizzie to Jacob Etter 12-18-1872 Hy
Sutton, Lucinda to W. P. Perkins 3-12-1863 Mn
Sutton, M. J. to R. J. Graves 10-23-1865 (no return) Hy
Sutton, M. V. to W. A. Walker 5-16-1859 We
Sutton, Mariah to Lewis Maclin 9-11-1869 Hy
Sutton, Mary to W. F. McCabe 11-24-1859 Hy
Sutton, Mollie to Simon Fleming 12-25-1869 Hy
Sutton, N. H. to J. S. Sutton 8-15-1868 Hy
Sutton, Nelly to John Everton 2-1-1863 Mn
Sutton, Rebecca to Samuel Kinnard 12-10-1873 (no return) Hy
Sutton, Sally to Joseph Johnson 1-3-1868 (no return) Hy
Swades, Dicy to William J. Chapman 8-22-1842 Hn
Swaim, Mary E. to William J. Faust 3-5-1863 We
Swain, Martha to Josiah Billberry 1-1-1866 (1-10-1866) Cr
Swain, Sallie to George W. Jones 9-21-1871 Dy
Swain, Susanna to J. N. Johnson 11-7-1861 Mn
Swan, Archebia Ann to Francis A. Fogg 12-17-1839 (12-20-1839) Ma
Swan, Catherine to George W. Birch 12-13-1858 (12-16-1858) Ma
Swan, Darcas S. to J. T. Palmer 10-31-1839 (11-6-1839) F
Swan, Mary Jane to Samuel C. Lynch 1-7-1846 Hy
Swan, Milly to Bob Price 10-27-1854 (1-2-1855) Sh
Swan, Nancy C. to Harvey W. Grunade 12-10-1830 (12-15-1830) Ma
Swan, Sarah to William S. Cody 12-8-1853 (12-13-1853) G
Swand (Sword), Eliza to Jesse H. Whaley 12-31-1842 Sh
Swann, Darcus (Mrs.) to R. Staggs 4-3-1871 (4-9-1871) Dy
Swanner, Amanda to John Travis 12-12-1877 Dy
Swanner, Ann to John C. Davis 6-25-1879 (6-28-1879) Dy
Swanner, Bell to J. L. Pugh 12-11-1877 (12-12-1877) Dy
Swanner, Efarilla to George W. Willis 12-23-1863 (no return) Dy
Swanner, Paralee to Wm. E. Lumly 4-9-1872 (no return) Hy
Swanson, Mary H. to Joseph Pheland Ward 9-17-1840 Sh
Swanson, Mary Jane to R. A. Pruden 7-31-1855 Sh
Swarigen?, Lucie to Sidney Broach 9-12-1867 Cr
Swarringer?, Sarah to Wm. H. Sparks 10-?-1859 Cr
Swayne, Angeline N. to William M. Chappel 7-20-1848 Hn
Swayne, Bettie T. to A. L. Elcan 11-3-1869 (11-4-1869) T
Swayne, Ellen to Elijah Hannah 1-6-1871 Cr B
Swayne, J. A. to J. W. Davis 1-9-1879 Dy
Swayne, Nannie to Mitchel Sparks 12-23-1872 (12-24-1872) Cr B

Brides

Swayne, Virinda C. to Phillip Myers 9-7-1862 (9-8-1862) Cr
Sweaney, W. C. to J. H. Etheridge 10-8-1863 Cr
Sweaney, W. C. to J. H. Etheridge 10-8-1863 (no return) Cr
Sweany, Caroline E. to N. T. Newbill 6-23-1866 (no return) Cr
Sweargim, Earline to Ned Bledsoe 7-23-1868 (7-29-1868) Cr
Swearingain, Lovenna S. to James H. Bostick 3-31-1831 Sh
Swearingen, Elizabeth H. to William W. Jones 2-5-1850 Sh
Sweat, Clementine to J. P. Lamb 12-14-1843 (no return) Hn
Sweat, Eliza to Henry Henning 10-19-1877 (10-?-1877) L
Sweat, Martha J. to J. L. Turner 12-14-1863 (no return) Hn
Sweat, Mary A. to John Milstead 7-17-1844 Hn
Sweat, Mary to John Thurgood 9-20-1869 Hy
Sweat, Nancy to Beverly Shankle 1-1-1860 Hn
Sweat, Nancy to Riley Shankle 1-27-1850 Hn
Sweat, Nancy to Sullavan Cyer ?-?-1861? Mn
Sweatt, Nancy J. to Daniel G. Morton 11-20-1856 Hn
Sweatt, Sarah to James M. Hamilton 8-15-1853 Hn
Sweeney, Catharine to Martin Glancey 10-13-1851 (10-17-1851) Sh
Sweeney, Julia to James McGraw 11-16-1845 Sh
Sweeney, Mary to Geo. A. Allen 8-18-1850 Sh
Sweeney, Mary to Peter Owen 1-5-1867 (1-6-1867) T
Sweeney, Matilda to John McGrath 4-23-1861 Sh
Sweeny, Alice to Patrick Brown 7-23-1861 Sh
Sweeny, Anne to Adolphus Britton 11-30-1852 (12-2-1852) Ma
Sweeny, Mary Louisa to Samuel W. McKnight 4-10-1856 Ma
Sweeny, Mary to Jerry Brosnahier 8-29-1859 Sh
Sweeny, Sarah to Adolpha Britten 8-26-1841 Ma
Sweet, America to J. R. Roberts 10-26-1869 Hy
Sweet, Bettie to T. J. (Dr.) Walker 3-4-1868 Hy
Sweet, Cathern to Bob Currie 12-29-1871 (no return) Hy
Sweet, Eliza to Wily Taylor 4-14-1866 Hy
Sweet, Ella to T. S. Chamblin 5-3-1870 Hy
Sweet, Fanny to Cornelius Wilson 3-16-1876 Hy
Sweet, Jenny to Filemore Sutton 2-19-1876 Hy
Sweet, Maggie to Henry Owen 6-12-1872 (no return) Hy
Sweeton, Mahala to Michael Griffin 4-19-1860 Hr
Sweeton, Malinda to John R. Clark 4-13-1832 (4-15-1832) Hr
Sweeton, Nancy to P. N. Estes 10-3-1861 Hr
Sweeton, Permelia Jane to Jackson Bohanon 8-4-1841 Hr
Sweeton, Synthia to Ellis Harlin(Hardin?) 8-14-1826 (8-15-1826) Hr
Swen?, Harriet to Lewis Pemberton 1-8-1846 Hn
Sweney, Frances Jane to George W. Gorin? 4-19-1842 (5-2-1842) T
Sweney, Rebecca to James F. Sloan 12-29-1869 (1-6-1870) Cr
Swift, Adrienne to J. S. Hawkes 11-21-1878 Dy
Swift, Ally C. to W. R. Webber 11-16-1867 (no return) F
Swift, Amelia to Sam Haskins 4-30-1874 (5-1-1874) Dy
Swift, Barbara A. M. to Alexander Fef   ? 5-4-1843 Hn
Swift, Corsicana? to G. M. Parkinson 12-8-1863 (no return) Cr
Swift, Eliza C. to Arther B. Jones 12-14-1852 (no return) F
Swift, Frances B. to John F. Drewry 9-10-1845 Hn
Swift, Frances to John Fraser 2-21-1867 (no return) F B
Swift, India M. to Henry D. Green 12-21-1859 (12-22-1859) F
Swift, Juliett to William Doughty 2-13-1838 (no return) Hn
Swift, Lucinda to Alson Y. Johnson 7-19-1846 Be
Swift, M. to A. Taylor 8-20-1841 Be
Swift, Mahaley to Jesse Webb 8-10-1848 (no return) Hn
Swift, Marietta to Leland Trout 12-10-1866 (no return) F
Swift, Martha A. to John A. Cole 3-13-1843 (3-22-1843) F
Swift, Mary A. to P. W. Groves 11-13-1863 (11-18-1863) Dy
Swift, Mary J. to William Lee 2-12-1864 (no return) Hn
Swift, Minerva to Peter McDaniel 4-2-1874 Dy
Swift, Nancy A. to William Edwards 7-29-1870 (8-1-1870) Dy
Swift, Virginia to William A. Fair 1-7-1847 Hn
Swift, Winney Ann to Ephraim Reed 1-7-1869 (2-4-1869) F B
Swim?, Susan to James Price 12-2-1866 Hn
Swindell, Margarette J. to Edward D. Browning 9-28-1862 G
Swindell, Susan A. to Caswell C. Patterson 10-10-1861 G
Swindle, Catherine E. to Wm. D. Robertson 1-6-1848 Be
Swindle, E. E. to Elijah Bryant 9-28-1865 G
Swindle, Elizabeth to Nathan Daley 10-15-1846 G
Swindle, Emily Adaline to Josiah D. Miller 9-14-1853 (9-15-1853) Hr
Swindle, Louisa C. to J. J. Butler 4-25-1861 Be
Swindle, M. E. to John M. Robeson 8-23-1855 Be
Swindle, Margarette to Calvin Clever 5-15-1855 (5-16-1855) G
Swindle, Martha to George Lindsey 12-10-1865 Hn
Swindle, Martha to John T. Jones 4-13-1836 Hr
Swindle, Mary to Abraham Gossett 4-25-1856 Be
Swindle, Rachael to James Caruth 9-1-1868 G
Swindle, Roena C. to Nehemiah Nunnery 7-30-1850 Be
Swindle, Sarah Ann to Andrew J. Meador 8-25-1866 Hr
Swindle, Sarah L. to Josiah C. Abernathy 5-26-1866 (5-7?-1866) Cr
Swindle, Sarah to John C. Hinnant 1-20-1850 Be
Swiney, Jane to Senior Worashum 12-28-1854 Cr
Swiney, Jane to Thomas Crews 10-25-1838 Cr
Swiney, Louisa to Hugh McCusker 2-18-1861 Sh
Swinford, Omy to Christopher Brandon 3-13-1831 Sh
Swink, Lavinia to Alexander C. Murrell 9-9-1871 (9-13-1871) Ma

Swink, Mariah G. to John Evans 7-16-1839 Ma
Swink, Martha E. to J. W. Owens 11-21-1867 G
Swink, Mary C. to Thomas J. Butler 1-19-1869 (1-21-1869) Ma
Swink, Mary E. to John C. McWhorter 1-22-1865 G
Swink, Mary S. to Elijah (Memphis TN) Price 4-17-1853 Ma
Swink, Sarah E. to John B. Scarborough 7-30-1856 Ma
Swink, Sophia E. to Thomas J. Nesbitt 4-20-1870 (4-21-1870) Ma
Swinney, Caroline to E. N. Williams 1-18-1859 Cr
Swinney, Charlotte to R. a. Vickers 1-8-1858 Cr
Swinney, E. F. to Wm. W. Spain 9-13-1855 Cr
Swinney, Eliza A. to W. G. Hicks 10-8-1857 Hn
Swinney, Elizabeth T. to M. W. Roney 7-18-1854 Cr
Swinney, Fannie to D. L. Biggs 2-9-1843 Cr
Swinney, Leweellen to Em. A. Swinney 2-13-1842 Cr
Swinney, Mahaley to Hiram V. Gray 10-24-1840 Hn
Swinney, Martha N. to Benjamin C. Settle 10-18-1848 Hn
Swinney, Martha to T. H. French 1-17-1872 (no return) Cr
Swinney, Mary J. to Allen J. Crocker 6-10-1854 Cr
Swinney, Mary to Michael Liston 6-17-1856 Sh
Swinney, Mattie L. to L. M. Walton 1-1-1866 (1-4-1866) Cr
Swinney, Sallie to William French 8-10-1871 Cr
Swinney, Tenney C. to W. M. Harrell 7-27-1872 (7-28-1872) Cr
Switzer, Christena to John Howan 10-25-1862 Sh
Swor, Alabama to J. N. Adams 2-14-1867 Hn
Swor, Caroline to Abram Simmonds 11-2-1865 Hn
Swor, D. P. to G. W. Lewis 1-15-1845 Hn
Swor, Elizabeth to Joseph F. Wilson 3-30-1843 Hn
Swor, Jane to John B. Crissenberry 10-4-1838 (no return) Hn
Swor, Mahala to Gabriel W. Hanly 6-27-1843 Hn
Swor, Margaret ann to John T. Parks 5-25-1863 Hn
Swor, Martha to A. R. Finley 10-12-1841 (no return) Hn
Swor, Mary E. to Merida Wilson 11-27-1855 Hn
Swor, Mary to John S. Ray 1-8-1846 Hn
Swor, Matilda A. to William J. King 1-22-1861 Hn
Swor, Nancy J. to William Bridges 11-13-1839 Hn
Swor, Rebecca A. to Anthony Jackson 9-29-1853 Hn
Swor, Rilla A. to Robertson Throgmorton 6-10-1841 Hn
Swor, Sarah to Isaac A. Wilkerson 12-5-1848 Hn
Swor, Tennessee A. to H. Wilson 10-12-1865 Hn
Syfert, Emma M. to Thomas S. Jukes 2-16-1863 Sh
Sykes, Callie A. to Simeon B. Rushing 12-28-1870 (12-29-1870) Ma
Sykes, Elvira G. to Allen P. Vick 10-27-1869 (10-28-1869) Ma
Sykes, Emeline to B. S. Browning 12-4-1845 Be
Sykes, M. G. to Wm. R. Perkins 11-30-1847 Be
Sykes, Martha to John D. Elam 12-8-1845 Ma
Sykes, Mary E. to John H. Hester 12-28-1869 Ma
Sykes, Omy to C. Key 8-30-1841 Be
Sykes, Paralee to Bethel Holland 9-27-1857 Be
Sykes, Pevy to Dennis Mercer 7-5-1843 Be
Sykes, Sarah J. (Mrs.) to Danl. J. (Gibson Co) Birmingham 8-19-1869 Ma
Sykes, Sarah to F. A. Cuff 12-23-1845 Be
Syler, Martha A. to Charles Staton 3-12-1845 Hn
Syles, Mary Ann to Jerome B. Brandon 9-1-1847 (9-2-1847) L
Sylvester, Malvina to John Ligon Ralph 9-24-1851 T
Sylvester, Martha Ann Minerva to William Holford 12-22-1840 (12-24-1840) Hr
Sypert, Mary L. to Horace H. Curtiss 8-31-1853 Ma

Taber, Lucinda to James Plank 10-9-1833 Hr
Tabscott, Neely to Collins Combs 9-30-1873 Hy
Tacker, Naomi E. to Lawson M. Reynolds 8-14-1861 Mn
Tacket, E. J. to Jno. Edwin Baxter 11-13-1872 T
Tackett, Mary Ann to James Crawford 2-20-1861 (2-21-1861) Hr
Tadlock, Mary E. to Robert F. Ricks 12-12-1864 (12-13-1864) L
Taggart, Elizabeth to Benjamin Owens 11-3-1830 Hr
Taggart, Mary Jane to Robert Pirtle 3-13-1830 (3-17-1830) Hr
Tague, Nancy A. to C. N. Kay 2-8-1872 Dy
Tailor, Malesey D. to Rubin H. Beasley 12-5-1855 We
Tailor, Martha M. to Samuel G. Williams 9-17-1846 We
Talbot, Jane M. to Silas F. Field 4-24-1854 (4-25-1854) Ma
Talbot, Kate to Louis Desobry 7-23-1859 (7-24-1859) Sh
Talbot, Ruth to H. B. Martin 3-25-1862 Sh
Talbott, Jane to Henry E. Wellborn 12-5-1853 F
Taliafero, Sarah T. to John T. Duke 7-22-1860 G
Taliaferro, Annie to Peter Richardson 1-3-1869 Hy
Taliaferro, Corie to Dred Jones 1-20-1870 (no return) Hy
Taliaferro, Elizabeth W. to John Stewart 6-16-1835 G
Taliaferro, Ella to Jerry Stewart 5-7-1874 Hy
Taliaferro, Elmonia to Nelson Sangster 4-29-1876 Hy
Taliaferro, Fannie L. to Philip Yancey 11-13-1866 Hy
Taliaferro, Gracie to Thomas Fleming 1-17-1878 Hy
Taliaferro, Harriet to Abin Foust 1-1-1867 Hy
Taliaferro, Helen to Anthony Joyner 2-1-1877 Hy
Taliaferro, Helen to William Burrows 8-22-1867 Hy
Taliaferro, Jane to Henry Sumner 1-1-1870 Hy
Taliaferro, Julia to Joe Williams 5-1-1872 Hy
Taliaferro, Julius to Aaron Taylor 7-20-1867 Hy
Taliaferro, Kate to Steven Taylor 1-10-1869 Hy

Taliaferro, Kitty to Charles Loving 2-16-1866 Hy
Taliaferro, M. A. to J. M. Carnell 7-24-1880 (7-25-1880) L
Taliaferro, M. A. to S. H. Mathews 11-25-1868 Hy
Taliaferro, M. L. to W. A. Dillard 4-1-1879 (4-2-1879) L
Taliaferro, Martha A. to N. D. Collins 1-15-1865 G
Taliaferro, Mattie to J. E. Sutton 2-7-1885 (2-8-1885) L
Taliaferro, Nancy to Archer Wiggins 4-6-1866 Hy
Taliaferro, Sallie to Jessee Smith 2-8-1871 Hy
Taliaferro, Sophia L. to Horace G. Jordan 9-28-1866 Hy
Taliaferro, Victoria G. to Robert H. Green 4-23-1866 Ma
Taliaferro, Virginia C. to John H. Glass 12-18-1850 G
Talleferro, Bettie to W. S. Jarrett 12-24-1878 Hy
Talley, Amanda to Scott Overton 12-21-1874 (12-30-1874) Dy B
Talley, Arrianna Pernett to Milton Jackson Ballard 4-5-1848 T
Talley, Eliza to William Searcy 7-24-1875 (7-25-1875) Dy B
Talley, Elizabeth to James W. Wright 5-14-1861 Dy
Talley, Emily Mildred to Joseph Elder 7-2-1849 (7-5-1849) T
Talley, Julia to Millard Southern 4-6-1878 (4-7-1878) Dy
Talley, Mariah to George Peacock 3-24-1870 (no return) Dy
Talley, Martha to John Jones 4-13-1831 (4-14-1831) O
Talley, Martha to William Massey 3-21-1861 G
Talley, Mattie to Nelson Shaw 1-27-1880 (no return) Dy
Talley, Prudie to C. A. Rose 11-19-1860 (11-20-1860) Sh
Talley, T. S. to Osborne Strong 12-27-1876 Dy
Talls (Falls?), Sallie J. to W. J. Stafford 1-25-1868 (no return) F
Tally, E. E. to W. W. Davidson 8-15-1861 (8-20-1861) Sh
Tally, Eliza M. to Isaac Taylor 5-19-1852 O
Tally, Elizabeth to James Pyron 5-5-1825 O
Tally, Fannie E. to S. A. Simmons 7-21-1870 (7-24-1870) Ma
Tally, Lety to Cokely P. Williams 2-17-1831 Hr
Tally, Martha V. to Frank T. Rice 11-6-1865 (11-9-1865) L
Tally, Mary F. to Willis Thomson 12-18-1860 (12-20-1860) Sh
Tally, Mary to John Evins 7-27-1844 (7-29-1844) G *
Tally, Mattie (Mollie?) P. to Newton Currie 8-6-1866 (8-8-1866) L
Tally, Nancy C. W. to Phillip T. Burford 5-19-1838 O
Tally, Sarah E. to Chas. W. Fallon 10-6-1840 T
Tally, Urilda C. to John W. Rose 4-25-1867 T
Talty, Catherine (Miss) to Francis St. Clair 4-21-1864 Sh
Tam?, Frances Jane to Neapolheo? D. Byrd 12-24-1846 (12-30-1846) T
Tamey?, Louise to Edward Davis no date (with 12-1874) T
Taner, Nancy to Abner D. Thomas 6-19-1834 G
Tangany, Ellen to Edward Leehy 10-24-1859 Sh
Tangnay, Eliza to Patrick Maroney 10-22-1859 (10-23-1859) Sh
Tannehill, Mary J. to J. L. Morphys 6-27-1855 (7-5-1855) Hr
Tanner, Ann (Mrs.) to Austin Mann 10-22-1867 L
Tanner, Ann to Austin Mann 10-19-1867 (no return) Hy
Tanner, Caroline to Orrange Richards 10-29-1867 (10-30-1867) F B
Tanner, Catherine to James E. Hopper 1-30-1841 Ma
Tanner, Charlotte to Benjamin Halfacre 11-20-1884 L
Tanner, Eliza R. to Jarratt Ross 12-13-1866 O
Tanner, Elizabeth T. to A. W. Meek 12-27-1849 Sh
Tanner, Elizabeth to B. G. East 10-29-1861 Mn
Tanner, Elizabeth to James H. Pardue 3-26-1856 (3-27-1856) O
Tanner, Ellen to Matthew Parker 3-31-1861 Sh
Tanner, Emma A. to Robert Mann 11-1-1871 Hy
Tanner, Evelina to Alexander Dudley 2-28-1854 (3-1-1854) Ma
Tanner, Jane to Bill Williams 11-3-1867 Hy
Tanner, Jessie B. to S. H. Embrey 10-24-1874 (no return) Hy
Tanner, Julia A. R. to Charles V. Hart 3-30-1861 (3-31-1861) Sh
Tanner, Lockey to Charles Nix 4-22-1836 O
Tanner, Martha J. to John H. Carpenter 11-11-1846 O
Tanner, Martha Jane to John H. Carpenter 11-11-1840 O
Tanner, Mary A. to F. H. Stewart 4-7-1852 Sh
Tanner, Mary Ann to A. A. McElyea 11-12-1860 (11-18-1860) O
Tanner, Mary T. to Jas. H. Cobbs 4-11-1850 F
Tanner, Rosanna to Noel K. Johnson 2-14-1848 Ma
Tanner, S. J. to William I. Garnell 2-29-1849 O
Tanner, Sarah Jane to William S. Gamel 2-27-1849 (3-1-1849) O
Tanner, Sarah to James Hewit 3-1-1858 Sh
Tanner, Susan Elizabeth to James Autrey 5-13-1856 O
Tanner, Vilet to Allen Barker 6-20-1842 (6-21-1842) O
Tanner?, Susan to Saml. B. Robinson 5-23-1860 (5-24-1860) Sh
Tansel, Louisa to John Terry 12-15-1863 (12-20-1863) O
Tansel, Pocahontas to James W. Edwards 3-12-1866 Dy
Tansil, E. P. to J. M. Durham 5-14-1855 (no return) We
Tansil, Emely to Caleb E. Baxter 12-25-1843 We
Tansil, Emily J. to Stephen Japan 9-19-1862 O
Tansil, Nancy (Mrs.) to William T. Layne 12-16-1874 (12-25-1874) L
Tansill, Josie J. to J. F. Percival 12-27-1881 (12-28-1881) L
Tappan, Mariah to Matthew Brewer 3-1-1871 (3-2-1871) F B
Tappscott, Lucy to Charley Maclin 2-27-1873 (3-1-1873) L B
Tapscott, Amanda C. to James D. Sherman 4-15-1866 Hy
Tapscott, Emma to Mat Parker 1-12-1872 (no return) Hy
Tapscott, Sina to Aaron Alexander 12-30-1868 Hy
Tarbish, Margaret A. to Wm. M. M. Drappin 5-13-1856 (5-14-1856) T
Tarbutton, Hanna H. to Arthur A. Jackson 3-31-1845 (4-1-1845) Ma
Tarbutton, Martha to John Betty 11-25-1830 (11-30-1830) Ma

Tarkington, J. T. to Wilson A. Bunnell 7-31-1863 Dy
Tarkington, Mary E. to Pleasant Tipton 11-3-1868 Dy
Tarleton, Marian to Sylvester Robbins 3-5-1879 (3-6-1879) Dy
Tarley, Sallie F. to M. C. Scott 10-31-1867 (no return) F
Tarpley, Nancy E. to L. P. Cooper 3-1-1867 Hy
Tarpley, P. Rebecca to R. L. Dalton 1-29-1862 Sh
Tarpley, S. C. to Benjamin F. Folger 1-1-1858 Sh
Tarply, Sarah V. to George R. Rutter 7-10-1861 Sh
Tarply, Susan C. to N. C. Giles 11-7-1860 Cr
Tarr, Ann to Thomas Neild 9-17-1859 Sh
Tarrant, L. A. to J. W. King 7-9-1878 (7-10-1878) Dy
Tarrant, L. A. to M. L. King 7-18-1876 (no return) Dy
Tarrant, M. F. to D. E. Fuller 9-8-1869 (9-9-1869) Dy
Tarry, Lucey to Riland Day 4-15-1867 (4-27-1867) T
Tarry, Lutia to Lewis Williamson 3-21-1866 T
Tarry?, P. A. to Newton Johnson 9-8-1849 (no return) F
Tart, Emaly H. to James H. Callicott 10-14-1846 Hn
Tart, N. V. to R. W. Williams 11-2-1864 (no return) Hn
Tarver, Elizabeth to David J. Merriwether 10-31-1849 Ma
Tarver, Fannie L. to Buren B. Waddell 6-9-1857 Ma
Tarver, Mary W. to Linsey P. Rucker 11-15-1836 Hr
Tarver, Wilnoth C. (Mrs.) to Willie B. Dickinson 8-2-1871 (8-3-1871) Ma
Tarwater, Sarah C. to James W. Barger 1-3-1856 We
Tate, Adaline to J. L. Cochrill 1-30-1877 (1-31-1877) Dy
Tate, Alice B. to S. B. Suratt 12-21-1857 (12-22-1857) Sh
Tate, Amanda J. to G. L. Barker 4-29-1871 (4-30-1871) T
Tate, Betsy to Henry Alexander 7-19-1867 (no return) F B
Tate, Catharine to Joshua Hazlewood 5-27-1826 (6-7?-1826) Hr
Tate, E. A. to James H. Ozier 11-25-1862 Cr
Tate, Elizabeth to J. F. Ballard 3-24-1855 Sh
Tate, Elizabeth to John Underhill 1-15-1862 Sh
Tate, H. W. to James Weaver 6-24-1841 Sh
Tate, Jamima J. to Stephen J. Bobbitt 2-16-1863 G
Tate, Julia to Carter Morgan 4-5-1867 (no return) F B
Tate, Kissey L. to Amos Smith 3-11-1844 We
Tate, Laura Jane to Henry L. Buckley 8-16-1831 Sh
Tate, Louisa M. to Greenbury Williams 8-26-1849 Be
Tate, Louiza C. to James R. Jones 7-1-1850 (7-4-1850) G
Tate, Lucinda to Henry Morgan 8-17-1883 O
Tate, Manerva to William C. McKilvy 12-10-1842 (1-22-1842?) G
Tate, Margarett V. to William Johnson 5-25-1848 (5-31-1848) F
Tate, Maridna J. to Lewis Campbell 10-19-1860 (9?-19-1860) O
Tate, Martha S. to Henry Owen 3-27-1856 Sh
Tate, Mary Ann to William Hazlewood 5-29-1827 Hr
Tate, Mary E. to W. C. Nowel 1-15-1866 (1-17-1866) T
Tate, Mary M. to L. M. Morgan 2-13-1867 O
Tate, Narcisa L. to William B. Greenlaw 8-1-1838 Sh
Tate, Parisett to James H. Davis 1-8-1861 Cr
Tate, Rachal A. to Thomas B. Jones 9-22-1846 (10-10-1846) G
Tate, Sarah E. to E. A. Weatherford 12-11-1866 T
Tate, Sarah H. to Hinkly Hollowell 12-27-1855 Cr
Tate, Sarah R. to John W. Langford 12-17-1849 (12-18-1849) G
Tate, Sarah to C. C. McMahan 1-31-1857 (2-1-1857) Sh
Tate, Sarah to George Luster 12-25-1865 Mn
Tate, Susan F. to Wm. A. Neely 2-3-1862 (2-9-1862) O
Tate, Susan to Turner J. Fuller 7-1-1841 Ma
Tate, W. L. to J. W. Mullen 8-2-1854 (8-3-1854) Hr
Tates, Malissy to Batie Jones 3-28-1878 L
Tatom, Levina to William Reason 7-7-1838 (7-9-1838) G
Tatom, Rachael to Henry Thompson 12-6-1870 (12-21-1871) F B
Tatom, Ruth to Giles Dennis 6-1-1868 (no return) F B
Tatum (Graham), Martha (Emily) to Thomas J. Simpson 9-22-1861 Mn
Tatum, Adaline to Grant Powel 9-7-1870 (no return) L
Tatum, Ann B. to G. W. Webb 8-12-1868 (8-20-1868) Dy
Tatum, Bita to Synan Merriwether 1-11-1873 (no return) L
Tatum, Cordelia to John Stevens 12-25-1866 (12-26-1866) F
Tatum, Cynthia to S. G. Booth 10-18-1866 G
Tatum, Elizabeth J. to Samuel C. Brooks 3-23-1843 (3-24-1843) F
Tatum, Elizabeth to Henry Howell 4-21-1851 (5-1-1851) G
Tatum, Elizabeth to John McBarrett 5-14-1861 Mn
Tatum, Emma L. to H. O. Norman 4-13-1860 (4-15-1860) F
Tatum, Isabella to Hammon Avery 3-3-1869 G B
Tatum, Lucanda E. to David C. Evans 10-27-1850 (10-31-1850) G
Tatum, Lucinda to W. C. Thetford 12-8-1869 G
Tatum, Lucretia C. to Jasper W. Craig 8-8-1850 G
Tatum, Lurana to Thomas Rice 6-8-1867 (6-9-1867) L B
Tatum, M. A. to S. A. Chitwood 8-29-1866 (no return) Dy
Tatum, M. M. to Thomas Neise 11-15-1862 Mn
Tatum, Martha E. to Joseph Trailer 9-25-1861 Hy
Tatum, Martha to Thomas Farley 10-6-1843 (10-10-1843) F
Tatum, Mary E. to Wm. C. Linebarger 11-21-1865 (11-22-1865) F
Tatum, Mary M. to Thomas Carr 12-3-1853 (12-4?-1853) Ma
Tatum, Mary to John W. Baker 1-31-1842 (2-2-1842) F
Tatum, Mary to Willis Dickinson 12-26-1868 F B
Tatum, Rachel to Hamp Billeps 12-14-1869 (no return) F B
Tatum, Rebeca to Joseph J. Farley 11-20-1840 (11-26-1840) F
Tatum, Rebecca to George Golin 8-27-1869 (no return) F B

Tatum, Rosett to Harry Robinson 3-30-1867 G B
Tatum, Tennessee to W. B. Williams 7-14-1849 (no return) F
Tauman, Leticia E. to Randolph J. Monroe 7-15-1848 Sh
Tauner, Mary E. to Charles V. Hart 3-27-1858 Sh
Taurman, Jane E. to James W. Gillespie 1-11-1845 Sh
Taylaor, Sarah F. to Thomas F. Short 11-2-1853 Hr
Tayler, Caroline to Wesley Green 12-30-1871 Hy
Tayler, Isabella to Edward Forsythe 7-13-1865 G
Tayler, Martha to John H. Briges 2-16-1864 (no return) Cr
Tayler, Mary to B. B. Jamerson 4-15-1861 (4-17-1861) Cr
Taylo, Nancy E. to Christopher Robertson 11-1-1854 (11-2-1854) Hr
Taylor, A. M. to J. S. Rodgers 11-23-1869 (11-24-1869) Dy
Taylor, A. S. to Francis P. Hynds 11-14-1861 We
Taylor, Adaline to C. K. Jameson 2-24-1863 (no return) Cr
Taylor, Adaline to C. K. Jamison 2-24-1863 (no return) Cr
Taylor, Adelia to Allen Taylor 7-4-1866 O
Taylor, Adeline to Ro. Taylor Johnson 12-29-1875 (no return) Hy
Taylor, Adley to A. W. Sweatt 9-15-1866 Hn
Taylor, Agnes C. to J. R. Walpole 3-29-1865 (no return) L
Taylor, Agnes to Robin Read 9-8-1867 Hy
Taylor, Agnus C. to John R. Walpole 3-29-1865 (3-30-1865) L
Taylor, Alice to Alfred B. Gayford 8-25-1854 Sh
Taylor, Amanda to J. D. King 1-5-1856 (1-6-1856) G
Taylor, Amanda to Thomas Byrd 6-23-1857 (6-25-1857) O
Taylor, Amanda to W. E. Goode 11-16-1873 Hy
Taylor, Amelia to Lewis Taylor 12-30-1870 Hy
Taylor, Ann Jane to Robert Douglass 12-22-1866 (12-26-1866) F B
Taylor, Ann M. to Charles P. King 11-14-1855 (11-15-1855) Sh
Taylor, Ann to Henry Moore 11-4-1866 Hy
Taylor, Ann to Henry Read 12-16-1866 Hy
Taylor, Ann to Jack Taylor 12-12-1872 Hy
Taylor, Ann to Michael Maha 1-11-1858 (1-20-1858) Sh
Taylor, Ann to Wilkins Smithin 12-22-1868 T
Taylor, Anna to Toby Laurison 9-8-1877 (9-12-1877) L B
Taylor, Annie to Frank Lea 7-15-1871 Hy
Taylor, Annie to Tom Gill 12-1-1873 Hy
Taylor, Annis to William C. Patterson 10-17-1854 G
Taylor, Anny to Lea Bradford 7-21-1867 Hy
Taylor, Apphia A. to John Chester 10-24-1848 Ma
Taylor, B. A. to J. W. James 9-25-1857 (no return) We
Taylor, Barberry to William C. Norrid 7-29-1850 O
Taylor, Barberry to William C. Norrid 8-12-1850 Hn
Taylor, Bertie to Sanford Bradford 12-29-1871 Hy
Taylor, Bet to Billy Jones 2-1-1868 Hy
Taylor, Bethe to R. T. Williams 12-25-1861 (no return) Cr
Taylor, Betsy Ann to Austin Galloway 10-26-1875 (no return) Hy
Taylor, Betsy M. to Stephen Bradford 2-25-1871 (no return) Hy
Taylor, Betsy to Thomas Harrell 11-19-1838 Ma
Taylor, Bettie to Sam Adkins 4-6-1867 (4-7-1867) F B
Taylor, Bettie to William Johnson 5-20-1869 T
Taylor, Burtie to Wash Wilson 12-24-1874 Hy
Taylor, C. V. to A. S. Wilkins 3-24-1863 G
Taylor, Camdis D. to Alexander Carroll Wood 4-10-1854 (4-12-1854) T
Taylor, Caroline to Jiles Hicks 10-20-1875 (no return) Hy
Taylor, Caroline to Milton Jett 8-16-1867 Hy
Taylor, Cath to Jerry Smith 1-1-1868 Hy
Taylor, Catharine T. to John T. Wood 2-5-1869 Cr
Taylor, Catharine to Jessee Stafford 10-17-1851 (no return) F
Taylor, Catharine to John W. Swain 11-8-1841 Sh
Taylor, Catharine to Ludwig Schneider 2-11-1856 Sh
Taylor, Catharine to Richard W. Baird 9-13-1845 O
Taylor, Catherine A. to Thomas A. Wilson 1-1-1873 Hy
Taylor, Catherine to Henry Williams 3-5-1870 Hy
Taylor, Celister to Dave McElwe 8-24-1877 Hy
Taylor, Charity to John W. Rice 12-31-1859 (no return) Hy
Taylor, Charlotte to Bennett Burn 11-15-1844 (11-19-1844) Ma
Taylor, Charlotte to Caleb Jacobs 12-24-1866 (12-25-1866) T
Taylor, Chatherine to Henry Towns 3-6-1871 T
Taylor, Clara to Wiley Taylor 5-19-1867 Hy
Taylor, Clementine to William Williams 12-30-1845 (12-31-1845) G
Taylor, Cornelia to Charles Wainwright 4-23-1866 (4-28-1866) F B
Taylor, Cressy to David Archer 12-26-1866 (12-28-1866) F B
Taylor, D. A. to J. H. Bethewen 1-9-1873 (1-12-1873) Cr
Taylor, Delina to John Rosson 12-7-1853 (12-8-1853) Hr
Taylor, Demarias to John B. Wilson 10-9-1869 (no return) L
Taylor, Demeris to L. J. Lunsford 5-1-1869 (5-2-1869) L
Taylor, Dolly to Kircus Wood 1-5-1868 Hy
Taylor, Dora to Stephen Wiles 1-6-1871 Hy
Taylor, Duencia to Ned Evins 4-28-1870 (5-20-1870) L
Taylor, Duley to William Alston 5-6-1867 T
Taylor, E. A. to John A. Claiborne 12-18-1866 Hy
Taylor, E. Julia to Wm. M. Smith 9-22-1853 (no return) F
Taylor, E. N. to A. H. Thompson 12-24-1851 Cr
Taylor, Easter Jane to Fred Augustus Mill 7-24-1867 (7-25-1867) T
Taylor, Edie Lewis to Sidney Taylor 12-15-1875 Hy
Taylor, Edmonia to Squire Farmer 6-22-1875 (no return) Hy
Taylor, Ela to Scott Morris 1-1-1874 Hy

Taylor, Elenor C. to William McCombs 1-5-1865 G
Taylor, Eliza Ann to Robert Webb 8-26-1854 (8-26-1854) Hr
Taylor, Eliza C. to J. W. Benton 2-18-1859 (2-20-1859) Sh
Taylor, Eliza Jane to Richard R. Dashiell 1-10-1850 (1-15-1850) Ma
Taylor, Eliza to George Nettle 12-22-1877 Hy
Taylor, Eliza to George W. Jarvis 3-20-1855 (3-29-1855) O
Taylor, Eliza to Joseph Bennett 3-24-1856 (3-25-1856) Sh
Taylor, Elizabeth A. to John E. Dunlap 10-16-1858 (no return) We
Taylor, Elizabeth E. to John R. Hicks 12-19-1854 (12-21-1854) Ma
Taylor, Elizabeth G. to Henry R. Bevils 12-22-1832 Hr
Taylor, Elizabeth M. to J. M. Phelan 12-21-1865 G
Taylor, Elizabeth P. to Samuel D. Jackson no date (1838-1852) Hn
Taylor, Elizabeth to B. P. Boyd 9-10-1867 Hy
Taylor, Elizabeth to Daniel Peters 5-17-1868 G
Taylor, Elizabeth to George Reed 12-31-1853 G
Taylor, Elizabeth to Henry Dunlap 12-17-1866 (12-20-1866) Ma
Taylor, Elizabeth to James Wiley 2-8-1836 Hr
Taylor, Elizabeth to John Wesley Sanders 3-25-1841 Hr
Taylor, Elizabeth to Sam'l Inman 7-3-1852 (7-8-1852) Sh
Taylor, Elizabeth to Samuel W. Phillips 12-13-1832 Sh
Taylor, Elizabeth to Valentine Bunch 9-28-1857 O
Taylor, Elizabeth to William B. Guy 11-8-1851 (11-13-1851) O
Taylor, Ellen H. to J. M. Webb 11-17-1865 (11-20-1865) F
Taylor, Ellen to Jack Dewitt 12-26-1870 (12-27-1870) F B
Taylor, Ellen to John Upchurch 1-20-1866 (1-21-1866) T
Taylor, Ellen to Wm. McCallum 10-3-1863 G
Taylor, Elvina to Joseph B. White 8-3-1868 Ma
Taylor, Emily Caroline to William Everett 1-14-1851 (1-16-1851) O
Taylor, Emily S. to John W. Dale 8-10-1856 Hn
Taylor, Emily to Ewing Willoughby 1-13-1836 Hr
Taylor, Emily to Wesley Smith 9-16-1863 G
Taylor, Emma to Clayburn Parker 12-5-1868 (no return) Hy
Taylor, Emma to Jas. A. Wilder 10-8-1877 Hy
Taylor, Emma to Michael Burrell 12-30-1868 (12-31-1868) F B
Taylor, Emma to Nathan Yancy 1-5-1871 Hy
Taylor, Emma to Richd. Taylor 12-12-1872 Hy
Taylor, Emmer to Isaac Sweet 12-28-1876 Hy
Taylor, Esther to Lovelace Boyd 8-24-1878 L
Taylor, Ettie to Charles Dowen 1-10-1878 Hy
Taylor, Eudora to Paul Macklin 6-21-1867 T
Taylor, Fannie to A. R. Swindle 2-6-1873 Dy
Taylor, Fannie to Charlie Taylor 8-16-1877 Hy
Taylor, Fannie to Charlie Thomas 4-5-1871 Hy
Taylor, Fannie to Frank Lewis 3-15-1873 L
Taylor, Fannie to Jesse W, jr. Page 11-12-1856 Sh
Taylor, Fannie to Jim Taylor 4-18-1868 (no return) F B
Taylor, Fannie to Partain Haywood 5-25-1846 (no return) Cr
Taylor, Fannie to Perry Sherron 6-9-1878 Hy
Taylor, Fanny to James M Easley 2-27-1877 Hy
Taylor, Fanny to James Taylor 2-11-1869 T
Taylor, Fanny to Thos. F. Cupp 1-20-1869 Hy
Taylor, Frances A. to James Allan Taylor 2-6-1843 (2-8-1843) T
Taylor, Frances E. to John H. Hay 9-13-1867 (no return) Dy
Taylor, Francis Ann to William A. F. Barry 5-27-1841 Sh
Taylor, Francis J. (Mrs.) to Jacob W. Welch 4-15-1862 (4-27-1862) Ma
Taylor, Francis to H. M. Short 11-14-1860 (11-4-1861) We
Taylor, Frankey to Wm. Jones 9-20-1867 (9-21-1867) F B
Taylor, Frankie to Phillip F. Butler 12-23-1852 Cr
Taylor, Georgia N. to Richard Dogwood 9-27-1848 (no return) Cr
Taylor, Georgianna to James H. Mann 10-11-1865 Hy
Taylor, Georgianna to Sam Midgett 6-12-1875 (no return) Hy
Taylor, Goodlow to Patrick McLin 9-5-1867 (no return) Hy
Taylor, H. A. to B. M. Bradford 10-3-1872 Hy
Taylor, H. A. to Richard Mann 12-10-1867 Hy
Taylor, H. I. to R. R. Pace 7-25-1865 O
Taylor, H. R. E. to John G. Martin 5-23-1859 (5-25-1859) F
Taylor, Hamar to George Bean 1-1-1872 (1-7-1872) T
Taylor, Hannah to Claiborne Weaver 11-1-1875 Hy
Taylor, Hannah to Daniel Moody 12-24-1865 Hy
Taylor, Hardenia A. to H. G. Ballard 5-3-1847 (5-4-1847) F
Taylor, Harriet to Alfred Cherry 12-2-1873 (no return) Hy
Taylor, Harriet to Sam Smith 9-6-1870 (9-21-1870) F B
Taylor, Harriet to William Dunlap 10-20-1856 Ma
Taylor, Harriett to Armstead Crowley 1-17-1871 (no return) Hy
Taylor, Harriett to Hume H. Darby 12-7-1838 Cr
Taylor, Harriett to Jeff Gains 2-17-1872 Hy
Taylor, Hattie to W. A. Taylor 10-11-1877 Hy
Taylor, Hellen to J. Baylam? 2-26-1869 T
Taylor, Henrietta to Calvin Deberry 12-27-1877 Hy
Taylor, Henrietta to Milton Jett 5-26-1866 (6-2-1871?) T
Taylor, Hester Ann to Ras.? Terry 4-7-1866 (4-29-1866) T
Taylor, Hrrett to Adison Wiley 11-20-1849 Cr
Taylor, Ida to Robert Hill 12-27-1877 Hy
Taylor, Irene to Alfred Battle 12-11-1867 Hy
Taylor, Isabella to William B. Gleason 12-16-1850 O
Taylor, Isau? to Jackson Walton 12-15-1874 T
Taylor, Jane A. to Wm. P. Douglas 3-5-1856 (3-6-1856) O

Taylor, Jane Eleanor to Edwin Robert Peete 10-21-1851 (10-22-1851) T
Taylor, Jane Lavinia to William H. Moss 12-16-1852 O
Taylor, Jane M. to John C. Reid 4-19-1845 Sh
Taylor, Jane to Willis Jones 9-?-1863 O
Taylor, Jarusha Jane (Mrs) to James D. Stewart 11-3-1867 Cr
Taylor, Jennie V. to John R. Bond 2-7-1872 Hy
Taylor, Jennie to Robt. Taylor 8-22-1872 Hy
Taylor, Jennie to Wm. Winn 1-17-1866 (1-20-1866) T
Taylor, Jenny to Ransom Lewis 4-4-1868 (4-5-1868) F B
Taylor, Joanna to Claiborn Parker 11-26-1873 Hy
Taylor, Josey to George Anderson 6-19-1869 G B
Taylor, Judith to David Woodard 8-8-1864 (8-10-1864) T
Taylor, Judy to Noah Vaughan 12-26-1867 G B
Taylor, Julia A. D. to William Griffin 6-4-1853 (6-7-1853) O
Taylor, Julia Ann M. to Tinsley Chowning 5-11-1839 (6-12-1839) Hr
Taylor, Julia to F. B. Winston 11-24-1868 Hy
Taylor, Julia to George Taylor 11-5-1867 Hy
Taylor, Julia to L. B. Hawkins 3-5-1860 (no return) Hy
Taylor, Julia to William Robertson 4-21-1870 (no return) Hy
Taylor, Jurasha to Joseph Sharp 3-6-1839 (3-7-1839) G
Taylor, Kittie E. to John Taylor 1-29-1874 Hy
Taylor, L. A. to J. A. Smith 8-29-1862 (8-30-1862) O
Taylor, L. F. to Wm. D. Sellers 5-24-1873 (5-25-1873) Cr
Taylor, L. J. (Mrs.) to Wm. L. Nooner 11-18-1869 (11-21-1869) Ma
Taylor, Laura A. to A. O. Dunefee 9-30-1874 O
Taylor, Laura C. to J. W. C. Scharmahoran 1-1-1859 (1-7-1859) Ma
Taylor, Laura R. to Wm. B. Wiggs 6-3-1861 Sh
Taylor, Laura T. to Charles R. Davis 3-24-1856 Sh
Taylor, Laura to Augustus C. Reid 3-1-1869 (3-3-1869) Ma
Taylor, Laura to Richmond Matthews 12-24-1868 (12-28-1868) F B
Taylor, Laura to Ruffin Jackson 11-11-1871 T
Taylor, Levinia to Sam Taylor 1-25-1868 T
Taylor, Lillie to A. F. Yancy 5-29-1875 Hy
Taylor, Lindie (Ludie) to Henderson Taylor 2-19-1870 Hy
Taylor, Lindy to Jack Allen 2-3-1867 Hy
Taylor, Linie to Joseph H. Fulton 11-4-1874 Hy
Taylor, Liser to John Carter 1-8-1868 (no return) Hy
Taylor, Liza Jane to Joel Hudson 9-17-1867 Hn
Taylor, Lizy to Wm. Nickson 3-10-1869 Hy
Taylor, Lizzie L. to Alex C. Caldwell 8-20-1868 Ma
Taylor, Lizzie to David Mann 2-2-1872 (no return) Hy
Taylor, Lizzie to James Lanier 3-13-1873 Hy
Taylor, Lou to Davy Ross 12-23-1867 (12-27-1867) F B
Taylor, Lou to R. H. Halliburton 8-31-1870 (9-1-1870) Dy
Taylor, Louisa E. to F. T. McCarver 12-18-1866 O
Taylor, Louisa H. to P. J. G. V. Coleman 9-10-1838 (no return) Hn
Taylor, Louisa K. to James J. Webb 8-23-1867 (8-25-1867) Cr
Taylor, Louisa to Bill Lanier 3-2-1866 (no return) Hy
Taylor, Louisa to Elisha Paschall 9-22-1856 Hn
Taylor, Lucinda M. to James M. Rose 8-1-1871 (8-2-1871) Ma
Taylor, Lucinda to Benjamin McCalester 9-2-1848 Cr
Taylor, Lucinda to Ellis Taylor 6-30-1871 Hy
Taylor, Lucinda to Frank Tatum 3-31-1866 (4-1-1866) F B
Taylor, Lucinda to Richard Williams 11-8-1877 Hy
Taylor, Lucretia to David Madding 12-20-1869 (12-28-1869) F B
Taylor, Lucretia to Joseph Click 8-15-1855 Be
Taylor, Lucy A. to Jackson Granberry 1-18-1868 (1-26-1868) F B
Taylor, Lucy Ann to James H. Grace 11-17-1852 (11-18-1852) G
Taylor, Lucy Ann to John G. Hargis 6-24-1840 (6-25-1840) Ma
Taylor, Lucy E. to W. A. Lee 10-15-1859 (10-16-1859) G
Taylor, Lucy Hunt to Franklin C. Heard 12-15-1874 Hy
Taylor, Lucy Jane to Loyd Robertson 12-28-1868 T
Taylor, Lucy to Bill Anderson 4-5-1871 (4-6-1871) F B
Taylor, Lucy to Elijah Overton 2-19-1838 Hr
Taylor, Lucy to John Jett 10-17-1871 Hy
Taylor, Louusia to John Young 2-26-1872 L B
Taylor, Lutish to Nowell Taylor 1-9-1869 T
Taylor, Lydia A. to Jack Taylor 2-19-1868 Hy
Taylor, Lydia J. to John W. Fransisco 11-24-1857 Cr
Taylor, Lydia to John Scoggins 3-20-1837 (3-22-1837) Hr
Taylor, Lydia to Simpson S. Ryan 5-7-1867 G
Taylor, Lydia to Stuart Clark 12-22-1827 (12-23-1827) O
Taylor, Lydia to Stuart Clarke 12-22-1827 O
Taylor, M. C. to W. H. Burgess 12-14-1876 Dy
Taylor, M. C. to William Watt 12-29-1865 O
Taylor, M. E. A. to James L. Burton 8-1-1871 (8-2-1871) Ma
Taylor, M. L. to W. E. Hilliard 3-6-1872 (3-7-1872) Cr
Taylor, M. M. to S. H. Ball 1-5-1876 Dy
Taylor, M. N. to John D. Furgerson 4-25-1865 G
Taylor, Mandy to Giles Bailey 2-3-1867 Hy
Taylor, Manerva L. to Charles Rogers 1-30-1878 Hy
Taylor, Manervy to John McNeely 10-29-1844 O
Taylor, Margaret (Mrs.) to David B. Dickson 8-25-1845 (8-26-1845) G
Taylor, Margaret E. C. to James N. Taylor 10-16-1866 (10-18-1866) Dy
Taylor, Margaret J. to J. S. Norvill 12-7-1867 (12-11-186_) G
Taylor, Margaret V. to Thomas A. Hamberlin 3-17-1864 Sh
Taylor, Margaret to James Walpole 12-22-1865 (12-24-1865) L

Taylor, Margaret to Jim James 7-4-1868 T
Taylor, Margaret to John Whitelaw 1-13-1866 Hy
Taylor, Maria Jane to Willis Haywood 8-26-1866 Hy
Taylor, Maria L. to John C. Carpenter 12-23-1857 (12-24-1857) Ma
Taylor, Mariah to Alfred Canady 8-25-1845 (8-28-1845) O
Taylor, Mariah to George Smith 9-11-1868 (9-26-1868) F B
Taylor, Martha A. to Alvin E. Taylor 1-2-1860 (1-3-1860) F
Taylor, Martha A. to Andrew A. Porter 10-17-1846 (10-22-1846) F
Taylor, Martha A. to Andrew Friemmer 4-21-1866 (4-26-1866) Ma
Taylor, Martha A. to E. E. Smith 9-29-1861 G
Taylor, Martha A. to John McCoy 5-5-1870 (5-8-1870) Ma
Taylor, Martha A. to John S. Wilcox 9-18-1859 Hn
Taylor, Martha A. to Lewis D. Fortner 12-16-1854 (no return) F
Taylor, Martha Ann to Jeremiah Stephens 11-27-1856 (11-28-1856) O
Taylor, Martha B. to J. M. B. Putnam 9-13-1867 G
Taylor, Martha E. to Levi Ozier 11-5-1870 (11-6-1870) Cr
Taylor, Martha E. to T. T. Young 8-2-1856 (8-4-1856) L
Taylor, Martha E. to Thomas G. Walpole 1-12-1871 Hy
Taylor, Martha E. to William P. Abbott 6-3-1855 Hn
Taylor, Martha H. to Edward Braden 11-7-1871 T
Taylor, Martha J. to James A. Gales 1-8-1863 We
Taylor, Martha J. to James A. Reed 12-20-1854 (12-24-1854) Sh
Taylor, Martha Jane to Anderson Heiskell 2-6-1878 Hy
Taylor, Martha Jane to David N. Rutledge 12-26-1851 G
Taylor, Martha L. to J. W. C. Smith 1-19-1861 Hr
Taylor, Martha S. to D. W. Mitchell 3-15-1869 (3-9?-1869) L
Taylor, Martha to Alex Mathall 2-14-1872 Hy
Taylor, Martha to Drury B. Williams 8-31-1852 (9-5-1852) Ma
Taylor, Martha to Jim Jones 6-20-1868 Hy
Taylor, Martha to John H. Bridges 2-16-1864 (no return) Cr
Taylor, Martha to John R. Thadwick 12-23-1849 G
Taylor, Martha to John Spencer 1-22-1831 (1-23-1831) Ma
Taylor, Marthy Jane to Martin Jacocks 1-18-1877 Hy
Taylor, Mary A. S. to Jon C. Volentine 4-18-1848 Hn
Taylor, Mary A. to J. R. Rust 2-24-1856 Cr
Taylor, Mary A. to Samuel Jamison 11-17-1853 Cr
Taylor, Mary A. to Wm. J. Nichols 11-13-1846 Cr
Taylor, Mary Ann to Andrew Guthrie 4-12-1843 Ma
Taylor, Mary Ann to Billey Bullock 2-27-1868 T
Taylor, Mary Ann to Edward Philpott 4-25-1829 Hr
Taylor, Mary Ann to Henry A. Rives 11-22-1838 F
Taylor, Mary Ann to James C. Mote 9-12-1845 Ma
Taylor, Mary Ann to James G. Mahaffy 3-26-1838 Ma
Taylor, Mary Ann to James Rutledge 8-11-1851 (8-13-1851) G
Taylor, Mary Ann to Robert S. Kendall 9-1-1859 O
Taylor, Mary Ann to William Bostic 12-20-1843 Hn
Taylor, Mary Ann to William C. Jernigan 8-16-1849 (8-19-1849) Hr
Taylor, Mary C. to B. W. Lauderdale 3-13-1860 Sh
Taylor, Mary C. to Baxter J. Williams 9-23-1841 (9-30-1841) Ma
Taylor, Mary C. to John G. Bell 11-10-1856 Ma
Taylor, Mary D. to I. B. Gibson 9-28-1865 O
Taylor, Mary E. C. to Joseph H. Sharp 12-22-1858 (12-26-1858) G
Taylor, Mary E. to James McVey 6-29-1867 Hn
Taylor, Mary E. to John C. Green 7-15-1850 Cr
Taylor, Mary E. to Joseph E. Fortner 10-12-1853 (10-13-1853) L
Taylor, Mary E. to Robt. H. French 12-16-1867 (12-17-1867) Ma
Taylor, Mary E. to Thomas L. Taylor 8-29-1867 G
Taylor, Mary F. to Benj. F. Morris 5-1-1848 Sh
Taylor, Mary F. to Elijah E. Hornbeak 4-2-1863 (no return) We
Taylor, Mary F. to J. G. Chambers 8-3-1859 F
Taylor, Mary J. to Isaac Bradford 12-30-1875 Hy
Taylor, Mary J. to Jessee Tiner 3-8-1859 G
Taylor, Mary J. to Jonathon Winford 11-20-1843 Sh
Taylor, Mary J. to Sugars McLemore 7-28-1862 (no return) Cr
Taylor, Mary Jane to Ashly G. Willoughby 7-3-1841 (7-5-1841) Hr
Taylor, Mary Jane to Granville H. Hogan 7-23-1845 (7-24-1845) F
Taylor, Mary Jane to H. L. Cannon 10-8-1850 G
Taylor, Mary L. to Ad Green 12-29-1875 (no return) Hy
Taylor, Mary L. to Andrew J. Douglas 12-17-1866 T
Taylor, Mary L. to J. W. Williamson 3-5-1860 (3-7-1860) F
Taylor, Mary Lucy to Phillips Peete 6-5-1867 (6-8-1867) T
Taylor, Mary M. to Robert F. Allison 1-3-1871 (1-5-1871) F
Taylor, Mary S. to Charles L. Read 7-20-1852 (no return) F
Taylor, Mary S. to Frank Myers 11-13-1868 (11-15-1868) F
Taylor, Mary S. to Washington Currie 9-6-1853 (9-13-1853) Ma
Taylor, Mary to Guin (Given) Gambley 9-3-1844 We
Taylor, Mary to J. A. Estis 12-22-1868 T
Taylor, Mary to J. Jackson 5-16-1872 (7-24-1872) T
Taylor, Mary to J. T. Morriss 8-27-1864 Mn
Taylor, Mary to James Cannon 12-22-1840 G
Taylor, Mary to June Moore 1-27-1877 Hy
Taylor, Mary to Osborn Henry 3-8-1845 Hn
Taylor, Mary to Preston Brooks 12-19-1873 Hy
Taylor, Mary to R. B. Jamerson 4-15-1861 (4-17-1861) Cr
Taylor, Mary to Richman Saunders 1-7-1872 T
Taylor, Mary to Robert Greer 3-8-1859 Sh
Taylor, Mary to Samuel Hannis 4-10-1824 (4-11-1824) Hr

Taylor, Mary to Thomas Humphrey 12-25-1869 (12-26-1869) F B
Taylor, Mary to Willis Rhodes 8-30-1870 T
Taylor, Matheny to William Newton 8-4-1834 O
Taylor, Matilda C. to John G. Taylor 3-17-1864 G
Taylor, Matilda to Ervin Stephens 11-28-1862 (12-4-1862) O
Taylor, Mattie J. to Edward G. Sewell 11-30-1859 Sh
Taylor, Mattie to James A. Taylor 12-28-1875 Hy
Taylor, Mattie to Richard White 3-27-1875 Hy
Taylor, Mila Melissa to Alexander L. Davidson 2-11-1836 O
Taylor, Mildred to J. B. Bradford 4-3-1873 Hy
Taylor, Millie to George Washington 2-26-1870 Hy
Taylor, Milly to Edward H. Spain 7-24-1844 Be
Taylor, Missouri E. to Thomas S. Valentine 12-23-1860 Hn
Taylor, Mollie Bet. to William F. Brodnax 12-24-1862 (12-25-1862) T
Taylor, Mollie R. to Lawriston Hardwicke 2-1-1871 (2-2-1871) Ma
Taylor, Mollie to Jordan Malone 3-11-1880 (no return) L
Taylor, Moria to Nelson Capell 11-22-1877 Hy
Taylor, Moriah to George Washington 2-23-1871 Hy
Taylor, N. E. to John H. Thomas 10-26-1857 (10-27-1857) Ma
Taylor, N. J. to S. H. Walker 12-24-1865 Hn
Taylor, N. M. to J. D. Stewart 6-8-1861 (6-11-1861) Sh
Taylor, Nancy A. to George Lovless 6-20-1853 (6-22-1853) L
Taylor, Nancy A. to W. V. McLaughlin 5-29-1864 Mn
Taylor, Nancy Angeline to William Shackleford 3-5-1868 G
Taylor, Nancy Ann to Terry Yeats 2-18-1837 (2-20-1837) Hr
Taylor, Nancy C. to J. R. Thompson 1-11-1841 (no return) Hn
Taylor, Nancy C. to R. C. A. Thomason 2-13-1861 (2-16-1861) Cr
Taylor, Nancy E. to Calvin C. Roycroft 11-30-1846 (12-2-1846) F
Taylor, Nancy E. to J. C. Hedgepith 3-27-1855 We
Taylor, Nancy G. to Phillip Weaver 11-15-1841 Ma
Taylor, Nancy H. to William W. Walker 6-22-1848 (no return) F
Taylor, Nancy J. to Isaac Williams 1-16-1867 G
Taylor, Nancy J. to John L. Culvert 2-20-1859 We
Taylor, Nancy J. to William T. Sills 8-16-1856 (8-17-1856) Hr
Taylor, Nancy Jane to Albert Stobaugh 2-10-1857 Ma
Taylor, Nancy S. to Henry A. Barry 5-17-1841 Sh
Taylor, Nancy S. to James W. Hicks 10-17-1860 (10-18-1860) Ma
Taylor, Nancy to Alfred Loyd 12-25-1838 Sh
Taylor, Nancy to Archibald Bennett 7-25-1839 F
Taylor, Nancy to Charles Holland 8-24-1832 Hr
Taylor, Nancy to Emmet Fleming 9-28-1872 (no return) Hy
Taylor, Nancy to Gray B. Barker 1-7-1851 (1-8-1851) G
Taylor, Nancy to J. C. Haughton 1-19-1831 O
Taylor, Nancy to John Sangster 9-12-1867 Hy
Taylor, Nancy to Nathaniel Taylor 1-2-1866 T
Taylor, Nancy to W. M. Brandon 4-17-1867 (4-18-1867) L
Taylor, Nannie C. to Joseph Haenar 4-2-1862 Sh
Taylor, Nannie to Joseph Sweat 3-29-1886 (4-22-1886) L
Taylor, Nelly B. to John N. Porte 12-31-1855 (1-1-1855?) G
Taylor, Noel to Ben Johnson 1-1-1876 (no return) Hy
Taylor, Norah to Sam Taylor 3-19-1874 Hy
Taylor, Octavia to H. D. Harris 5-21-1868 Hy
Taylor, Olivia A. to J. D. Rowe 4-9-1864 (no return) Hn
Taylor, P. F. to David Miller 9-2-1856 (no return) We
Taylor, P. J. to J. P. Bludworth 7-6-1869 Be
Taylor, Pamiel? to Alex Nelson 4-28-1866 T
Taylor, Parthena Ann to George Butler 3-13-1856 T
Taylor, Parthena to S. Dacus 2-15-1852 We
Taylor, Pernina A. to Francis M. Wallace 1-21-1858 Hn
Taylor, Phebe to Nelson Taylor 12-25-1866 Hy
Taylor, Philis to Albert Taylor 5-6-1867 T
Taylor, Phoebe Ann to Peter Green 1-20-1876 (no return) Hy
Taylor, Poke to Jim Loving 11-15-1870 (no return) Hy
Taylor, Polly to Henry Mudings 5-2-1867 Hy
Taylor, Polly to Jno. A. Cunningham 9-10-1861 (no return) Dy
Taylor, Polly to William Hill 5-18-1866 (5-19-1866) F B
Taylor, Prescilla to Wm. W. Jones 9-19-1870 (9-22-1870) Ma
Taylor, Puss to John Keer 3-4-1868 (3-7-1868) F B
Taylor, R. E. to T. H. Cooper 10-14-1868 Cr
Taylor, R. E. to W. D. Castello 11-27-1884 L
Taylor, R. G. to Thomas Sharp 12-23-1866 G
Taylor, R. I. to John Smith 1-28-1877 Hy
Taylor, R. J. to J. A. Laster 1-9-1869 (no return) Dy
Taylor, Rachel B. to John S. McKaughan 1-21-1848 (1-23-1848) Hr
Taylor, Rachel Elizabeth to James Crayton Ridings 8-18-1867 G
Taylor, Rachel to George Covington 12-25-1877 Hy
Taylor, Rebeca to John Glasco 1-15-1855 We
Taylor, Rebecca Ann to John Price 3-30-1854 Ma
Taylor, Rebecca to Joe Compton 12-8-1884 (12-9-1884) L
Taylor, Rebeckha to Hugh M. Bigham 2-19-1831 G
Taylor, Roberta to R. V. Mann 12-20-1865 Hy
Taylor, Rosa to Thomas Bond 2-19-1868 Hy
Taylor, Rose to David Shaw 3-22-1876 Hy
Taylor, Roxanna to Robert Sutton 7-10-1869 Hy
Taylor, Sallie H. to Richard T. jr. Brodnax 1-18-1867 (1-23-1867) T
Taylor, Sallie P. to Wm. L. Williamson 3-5-1860 (3-7-1860) F
Taylor, Sallie to Caldwell Taylor 2-20-1866 T

Taylor, Sally to Jim Jones 11-19-1875 (no return) Hy
Taylor, Sarah A. to N. Leap 11-1-1873 (11-2-1873) O
Taylor, Sarah A. to Saml. H. Wheeler 10-13-1854 (10-14-1854) G
Taylor, Sarah Ann to J. W. Ballentine 9-26-1865 G
Taylor, Sarah Ann to Thomas W. Pulty 11-28-1847 Be
Taylor, Sarah E. to C. W. Preston 12-19-1849 (12-22-1849) F
Taylor, Sarah E. to Granderson Chilton 7-3-1878 (no return) Hy
Taylor, Sarah E. to Holloway Morris 9-2-1854 (9-3-1854) Sh
Taylor, Sarah Elizabeth to Wm. H. Criswell 1-18-1868 G
Taylor, Sarah F. to James F. Bennett 8-4-1856 G
Taylor, Sarah Frances to Calvin Chobell 12-6-1867 G
Taylor, Sarah Frances to F. G. Cossitt 8-29-1861 (8-30-1861) Hr
Taylor, Sarah H. to Frederick N. Muehler 1-20-1844 T
Taylor, Sarah H. to Wm. L. Gooch 12-10-1844 Cr
Taylor, Sarah J. to Fayette Taylor 12-26-1874 Hy
Taylor, Sarah J. to W. J. Stallcupp 4-10-1869 Dy
Taylor, Sarah J. to W. P. Wilson 3-10-1855 (no return) F
Taylor, Sarah Jane to Madison Bradford 1-12-1867 Hy
Taylor, Sarah Jane to Richard Sherrod 6-9-1856 Ma
Taylor, Sarah Jane to Samuel P. Caldwell 5-29-1855 (5-30-1855) Ma
Taylor, Sarah Jane to William P. Wilson 12-27-1854 Ma
Taylor, Sarah Jane to William P. Wilson 3-12-1855 Sh
Taylor, Sarah L. to William D. Childress 11-22-1850 (12-2-1850) G
Taylor, Sarah M. A. to Jerry S. Stubenfield 12-17-1857 Hn
Taylor, Sarah M. to R. B. Alexander 3-29-1838 F
Taylor, Sarah O. to Wm. M. Scott 12-21-1844 (12-29-1844) F
Taylor, Sarah to A. B. Oliver 8-13-1854 Hn
Taylor, Sarah to Edmund Taylor 10-3-1878 Hy
Taylor, Sarah to Fayette Taylor 12-31-1875 Hy
Taylor, Sarah to John Harris 9-19-1877 Hy
Taylor, Sarah to John Wilson 7-24-1869 (7-25-1869) F B
Taylor, Sarah to Pat Claiborn 10-20-1865 Hy
Taylor, Sarah to Robert F. Johnson 6-13-1864 (no return) Hy
Taylor, Sarah to Washington Howell 8-18-1877 Hy
Taylor, Sarah to Willis Mann 9-10-1842 (9-11-1842) Ma
Taylor, Sarah to Wm. H. Snoden 6-17-1844 (6-26-1844) F
Taylor, Selena B. to Peter Kendall 8-17-1857 Sh
Taylor, Sophia to Henry Shields 4-3-1872 Hy
Taylor, Sophronia to James Cronan 10-11-1853 (10-13-1853) O
Taylor, Sophronia to Peter Campbell 1-30-1882 (2-2-1882) L
Taylor, Sue M. to Andrew J. Hall 5-16-1866 Ma
Taylor, Sue M. to Ben J. Sanford 10-29-1873 (10-30-1873) T
Taylor, Susan A. to Benjamin F. Newton 12-23-1862 We
Taylor, Susan A. to Sipio Tumer 12-20-1872 (12-26-1872) T
Taylor, Susan C. to Nathan S. Kirby 3-27-1848 Sh
Taylor, Susan Jane to John N. Whaley 1-17-1842 (1-20-1842) Hr
Taylor, Susan M. to E. T. Buffaloe 1-9-1862 (no return) Hy
Taylor, Susan M. to Timothy S. Pepper 12-10-1872 L
Taylor, Susan to Calvin Jones 8-15-1860 (8-16-1860) Cr
Taylor, Susan to Hans Capell 1-18-1843 Ma
Taylor, Susan to J. W. Allison 5-8-1866 G
Taylor, Susan to Jas. W. Crow 3-17-1851 O
Taylor, Susan to Taylor Boyd 9-18-1878 L B
Taylor, Susan to W. J. Mcdurmott 7-13-1869 (no return) Hy
Taylor, Susan to William Miller 2-25-1871 (no return) F B
Taylor, Tamar to Jesse Jacocks 2-24-1875 Hy
Taylor, Tempy to Wm. King 10-17-1877 Hy
Taylor, Tena to Paul Edwards 6-17-1871 (no return) Hy
Taylor, Tibitha to John S. Gibson 10-14-1848 (no return) Cr
Taylor, Veniann to Isaac Bowers 5-19-1868 F B
Taylor, Vergun to Albert Maclin 12-24-1869 T
Taylor, Victoria to Ned Cook 8-1-1868 T
Taylor, Victorine to Honore Castagnere 10-9-1854 Sh
Taylor, Vina to Edmond Link 1-25-1873 Hy
Taylor, Violet J. to Andrew M. Hart 6-12-1843 (6-13-1843) Ma
Taylor, Virginia Triplett to Richard B. Somervill 3-13-1847 (3-16-1847) T
Taylor, Virginia to Coleman Mann 3-25-1877 Hy
Taylor, Virginia to William Robinson 12-8-1845 (12-17-1845) T
Taylor, Winney to Hamilton Arnold 1-28-1865 O
Taylor, Winny to Thos. Hollomon 4-5-1843 Be
Taylor, Zelvey E. to Whitley A. Haywood 11-1-1866 Cr
Taylor, Zilpha H. to Sawnee B. Lawrence 10-22-1868 Ma
Taylor, 'Bettie to Harvey Maclin 1-14-1868 T
Teagart, Susan M. to Thomas I. Neely 7-31-1838 (8-4-1838) Ma
Teage?, Catharine to Robertson Hood 10-10-1848 F
Teague, Catharine to James M. Walton 11-24-1847 (11-25-1847) Hr
Teague, Dorothy H. to John Ellison 2-20-1843 (2-21-1843) Hr
Teague, Elizabeth C. to Moses S. Allen 4-17-1856 Ma
Teague, Elizabeth to John J. Walton 12-27-1838 Hr
Teague, Emily to Milton H. Knox 12-30-1843 (no return) F
Teague, Eveline to Daniel Jones 1-1-1867 F B
Teague, Jennetta to Harry Pepper 12-17-1867 G
Teague, Louisa to Henry D. Dunbar 12-4-1860 (12-6-1860) Sh
Teague, Mary A. to Jas. C. Love 12-24-1855 Hr
Teague, Minerva to William M. Price 7-17-1846 (7-23-1846) F
Teague, Oregon N. to Wm. S. McLemore 12-21-1861 (12-24-1861) Hr
Teague, Peninah to James Alexander 12-25-1856 Ma

Teague, Rhoda to Isaiah Flin 12-31-1828 Hr
Teague, Sarah E. to Jesse Russell, jr. 4-22-1868 Ma
Teague, Sarah to Lusnford Whitaker 7-8-1835 Hr
Teague, Sarahann to Jerome B. Gressom 7-16-1844 (no return) F
Teal (O'Teal?), Sallie O. to G. W. Cone 12-13-1858 (12-15-1858) Sh
Teal, Martha A. to John L. Rodgers 11-22-1850 Sh
Teams, L. A. to James Davis 12-9-1865 (12-10-1865) F
Teams, Virginia to S. L. Farmer 1-28-1864 Sh
Teat, Neettie to T. H. Cook 6-13-1874 (6-14-1874) Dy
Teater, C. B. to G. B. Godsey 11-22-1867 O
Teater, Elizabeth to Pearson M. Park 10-17-1857 (10-20-1857) O
Teater, Margaret M. to Robt. H. Thomas 7-27-1878 (7-28-1878) Dy
Tedder, Anna M. to Wesley Hatley 3-14-1850 Be
Tedder, Elizabeth Ann to Jackson Hatley 3-27-1845 Be
Tedder, Martha to Andrew J. Smith 8-6-1846 Be
Tedder, Mary to William Lupo 11-21-1865 Be
Tedder, Nancy to Cullen Luper 2-28-1853 Be
Tedford, Mary A. C. to Admiral G. Roach 10-21-1868 (10-22-1868) Ma
Tedford, Matilda to Andrew J. Carson 2-28-1854 Hr
Tedford, Militha to Thomas J. Tipler 1-22-1842 (2-3-1842) Hr
Tedford, Polly to Willie Davis 8-14-1830 (8-16-1830) Hr
Tedford, Sophronia O. to A. C. Nelms 11-20-1843 (11-22-1843) Hr
Tedington, Susan to John Ursery (Ussery?) 9-25-8170 G
Tedleton, Susan to Martin McConnel 3-7-1859 O
Teel, Elizabeth E. to Clement N. Rodgers 2-6-1850 Sh
Tefft, Mary to Charles Schmidt 7-20-1857 Sh
Teimans, Louise to Henrich Sievert 11-14-1864 Sh
Telford, M. S. to W. H. Hood 3-3-1862 (3-5-1862) Dy
Teller, Margarett E. to John A. Bryan 9-12-1854 (no return) F
Temmens, Ann F. to M. D. L. McGuire 10-28-1860 We
Temple, Fannie to H. W. Long 3-2-1871 Hy
Temple, Margaret W. to Robert W. Towns 11-27-1854 (11-30-1854) Ma
Temple, Martha M. to Thomsa J. Wrenn 5-10-1847 (5-13-1847) G
Temple, Mary A. to Benj. A. Cannon 2-6-1860 (no return) Hn
Temple, Mary E. to Samuel Johnson 3-15-1855 Ma
Temple, Mary E. to W. Holmes 5-22-1849 Sh
Temple, Mary F. to John F. Thomas 1-6-1862 We
Temple, Mary to William H. Little 7-12-1847 Ma
Temple, Nancy H. to Joseph Lovelace 5-26-1857 (no return) L
Temple, Nannie to Thomas J. Pearson 2-20-1869 (2-24-1869) Ma
Temple, Sarah Ann to Sam Thompson 3-26-1868 (no return) F B
Temple, Sarah E. to John A. Dial 3-3-1855 (no return) L
Temple, Susan E. to Claborn Hetherington 2-23-1850 O
Temple, Susan M. to John F. Sherrill 10-12-1850 Ma
Temple, Susan to Henry Warren 12-24-1869 (2-26-1870) F B
Temple, Susan to James W. Strong 1-28-1858 We
Temple, Therina to Henry H. Winders 1-16-1840 Sh
Temples, Amanda J. to Pearson Gwinn 6-8-1863 Mn
Templeton, Eliza F. to John J. Glenn 3-19-1860 We
Templeton, Elizabeth to Benjamin Sturdivant 1-4-1848 Ma
Templeton, F. J. to H. M. Dickey 12-8-1869 (12-10-1869) Dy
Templeton, M. C. to J. C. Holt 4-3-1865 (4-5-1865) Dy
Templeton, Maggie E. to Henry J.W. Mayo 2-24-1868 (2-26-1868) T
Templeton, Mary A. to James H. McClain 1-5-1858 We
Templeton, Nancy to James M. C. Frazier 8-18-1863 (no return) We
Templeton, Sallie to B. P. Autrey 6-12-1885 (no return) L
Templeton, Susan C. to Geo. C. Patrick 7-29-1856 (7-31-1856) Sh
Templey, Mary Ann to William Ables 2-10-1869 L
Tenant, Julia Ann to Jerry Rogers 1-29-1875 Hy
Tenant, Mary to Joseph H. Walker 4-12-1850 T
Tenfel, Gertnie to F. G. Muller 10-20-1858 We
Tenfel, Verena to George Gibbs 7-23-1858 Sh
Tening, Sarah J. to Nat Wardlaw 9-17-1885 L
Tennant, Jane W. to James S. Smith 8-5-1857 T
Tennant, Margaret to Jefferson Elam 1-21-1852 (1-25-1852) T
Tennant, Mary to John McCullough 4-8-1851 (4-9-1851) T
Tennant, Purlina M to Smith M. Feezor 3-5-1849 (3-8-1849) T
Tennie, Bullock to Isham Pewett 1-19-1869 Hy
Tenz (Terry?), Josephine to Bonifaz Mohler 8-23-1859 Sh
Teppett, Faney G. to Flover Shelton 5-3-1852 We
Ternas, Ellen C. to David Goss 9-6-1873 (9-11-1873) T
Teroging, Susan J. to Richard Murray 1-25-1839 Hn
Terrell, Elizabeth to William J. Davis 3-20-1841 Ma
Terrell, Emily to William H. Ross 12-28-1849 Hn
Terrell, Judith to Elzey Rutledge 4-6-1824 G
Terrell, Julia to J. H. Sanders 12-1-1872 Hy
Terrell, Lewis? to Ira Johnson 8-24-1839 Hn
Terrell, Mary to H. W. Wright 5-9-1831 (5-10-1831) G
Terrell, Mary to Robert Orey 6-28-1863 Hn
Terrell, Nancy to Wm. Newbery 10-6-1845 (no return) We
Terrell, Paralee to W. L. May 8-22-1878 Hy
Terrell, Rebecca J. to E. G. Richardson 8-1-1863 (8-2-1863) O
Terrell, Sarah Ann E. to William J. Davis 9-1-1841 (9-2-1841) Ma
Terrell, Unity M. to James Summers 12-12-1844 We
Terrence, Mary E. to Henry E. Wade 12-19-1854 (no return) F
Terrence, Sarah J. to Richard T. Wade 12-19-1853 (no return) F
Terril, Mary Cedona to Robert Rankin 7-3-1844 G

Terrill, Beadi A. to B. A. Rogers 4-25-1859 We
Terrill, E. J. to Thomas Williams 11-23-1869 G
Terrill, Frances S. to Joseph B. Stanley 2-26-1852 (3-9-1852) G
Terrill, Martha J. to Robert K. White 1-4-1874 Hy
Terrill, Mary E. to L. S. Mayo 12-27-1850 (12-28-1850) F
Terrill, Sarah to John Beasley 9-4-1862 (no return) Hy
Terrill, Sarah to John Owens 11-30-1882 (12-1-1882) L
Terrill, Susan C. to Guy S. Jones 1-6-1838 (1-9-1838) O
Terry, A. M. to H. D. Foust 1-22-1852 Hn
Terry, C. P. to Wm. E. Warner 5-8-1863 (5-10-1863) Cr
Terry, C. R. to Wm. E. Warner 5-8-1863 (no return) Cr
Terry, C. to Homer Laws 2-4-1873 (2-10-1873) O
Terry, Caroline to Acuff Cox 3-28-1867 Hn
Terry, E. V. to T. C. McKinney 6-27-1868 (7-1-1868) Cr
Terry, Eleanor to James G. Jenkins 8-9-1830 Hr
Terry, Eliza R. to James P. Weick 11-3-1853 (no return) Hn
Terry, Elizabeth to Vincent Cooksey 9-28-1842 (9-29-1842) Hr
Terry, Elizabeth to William Henley 10-6-1853 (10-7-1853) Hr
Terry, Emily M. to Edwin Pittman 9-4-1864 G
Terry, F. E. to D. M. Barkdale 10-27-1856 (no return) We
Terry, Frances E. to David M. Barksdale 10-27-1856 We
Terry, Jane to H. Pope 3-17-1852 Cr
Terry, Mary A. to J. F. Edwards 11-30-1843 (no return) Hn
Terry, Mary E. to Stephen B. Davis 5-16-1866 G
Terry, Marya M. to William Smith 1-23-1851 O
Terry, Millard A. to J. N. Hansbrough 12-14-1857 Cr
Terry, Molly to Thomas M. Patton 12-18-1866 (no return) Cr
Terry, Nancy A. to John C. Williams 10-5-1849 Hr
Terry, Nancy to Elvin A. Goolsby 7-2-1839 Hn
Terry, Sarah C. to J. W. Lambkin? 3-26-1850 Hn
Terry, Sarah J. to John W. Shepard 6-24-1871 O
Terry, Susan to Isaac R. Phillips 9-29-1844 Sh
Terry, Susan? to Hiram Ammon 11-1-1832 Hr
Test, E. S. (Mrs.) to Thos. T. Ashby 2-15-1860 (2-16-1860) Sh
Test?, Mary to Wm. Jones 9-8-1850 We
Teter, M. J. to W. H. Chumley 11-27-1865 (11-28-1865) O
Tevilla, M. to M. F. Campbell 1-11-1871 Dy
Th?, L. to J. B. Bridges 1-2-1842 Be
Th____ton, Johnella to George West 11-13-1874 (11-27-1874) L
Thacker, Barthema to Samuel Crabtree 7-6-1844 (no return) F
Thacker, Eliza to Tandy Key 12-4-1830 Sh
Thacker, Ellen to John D. Lacy 3-12-1870 Hy
Thacker, Ellen to John P. Hutchinson 8-5-1867 (8-6-1867) T
Thacker, Fannie to C. E. Perrygo 4-10-1869 Hy
Thacker, H. E. to M. H. Goodloe 9-5-1870 (no return) Dy
Thacker, M. E. F. to R. J. M. Byrn 3-27-1862 (no return) Dy
Tharp, Margaret to Geo. Saddler 1-23-1869 (no return) F B
Tharp, Margaret to Thomas Cofield 3-9-1870 (no return) F B
Tharp, Pamela to Wm. May 12-19-1841 Sh
Tharp, Sarah Jane to Thos. W. Shore 3-12-1842 (3-15-1842) F
Tharp, Susan to Nelson Wall 8-3-1847 (8-11-1847) F
Tharpe, Dorcas to Edward Tharpe 12-25-1866 Hn B
Tharpe, Elizabeth to Charles Teague 11-17-1866 Hn B
Tharpe, Elizabeth to David Mann 12-23-1856 Hn
Tharpe, Ella E. to Will W. Porter 10-24-1864 Hn
Tharpe, Eveline to Mark Tharpe 5-21-1866 Hn B
Tharpe, Jane B. to James T. Dunlap 10-25-1838 (no return) Hn
Tharpe, Jimicy to Moses Barfield 5-18-1866 (no return) Hn B
Tharpe, Mary E. to B. B. Carr 3-22-1876 (no return) Dy
Tharpe, Mollie E. to S. H. Fizer 2-4-1867? (no return) Hn
Thasee, Ellen L. to John Hunter 11-9-1843 Ma
Thayer, Catherine to John Schanaber (Schualer) 1-22-1846 Sh
Theadford, Ophelia to William Ward 9-28-1860 (10-20-1860) O
Thedford, Delitha to James Hill 1-13-1857 G
Thedford, Elizabeth R. to William W. Connell 12-27-1843 (12-28-1843) G
Thedford, Elvira to Thos. J. N. K. H. Thedford 2-10-1846 (2-12-1846) G
Thedford, Gemina to John C. Birdsong 11-23-1841 Ma
Thedford, Hannah to Josias Thedford 12-27-1859 G
Thedford, Honey to Joseph Pecks 12-25-1832 G
Thedford, Margaret to Jacob Flowers 5-21-1836 (5-?-1836) G
Thedford, Martha R. to William T. Carroll 10-23-1852 (10-28-1852) G
Thedford, Mary to James Arnold 4-6-1836 G
Thedford, Mary to Samuel M. Dunn 9-19-1879 (9-30-1879) Dy
Thedford, Mrs. to G. W. Harper 7-22-1874 (no return) Dy
Thedford, Nancy to Alfred B. Harris 12-6-1843 (12-7-1843) G
Thedford, Sally to Abner C. Roach 10-24-1827 G
Thedford, Sarah F. to David W. Nevill 10-20-1871 (10-22-1871) Ma
Thedford, Sarah M. to Spencer M. A. G. W. Harris 2-28-1842 G
Thedford, Susan to William Williams 4-28-1846 (5-29-1846) G
Theodocia, Cole to W. S. Powell 11-24-1873 (no return) Hy
Theraby (Pheraby), Elizabeth to Lewis Clark 6-14-1864 Sh
Theridge, Elizabeth to Belfield W. Prior 12-21-1848 Sh
Thetford, Alvira to J. W. Demoss 12-27-1860 G
Thetford, E. P. to W. A. Williams 10-11-1877 (no return) Dy
Thetford, Elizabeth to James G. Hall 2-8-1834 (2-16-1834) G
Thetford, Fannie B. to Henry H. Hollinsworth 5-13-1876 (5-14-1876) Dy
Thetford, Harriet L. to James L. Daugherty 6-23-1859 (6-26-1859) O

Thetford, Honey to Preston Holt 8-23-1833 (8-25-1833) G
Thetford, L. R. J. to J. D. Askridge 8-10-1875 (8-11-1875) Dy
Thetford, Lenora J. to Solomon S. Hall 3-25-1868 (no return) Dy
Thetford, Louisa to Thomas Herndon 4-20-1853 G
Thetford, Margaret to James Daniel 8-16-1875 (8-18-1875) Dy
Thetford, Mary T. to G. W. Robinson 1-27-1870 G
Thetford, Mary to Zack Hudson 3-16-1863 G
Thetford, Nancy J. to Ephraim N. Brown 2-24-1861 G
Thetford, Nancy to Hillorry Flowers 4-4-1835 (4-5-1835) G
Thetford, Nancy to John W. Cantrel 10-15-1862 G
Thetford, Sallie to F. H. Hudson 2-23-1869 G
Thetford, Sarah M. to Andrew J. White 11-9-1852 (11-11-1852) G
Thetford, Sarah to W. H. Crocker 5-8-1862 G
Thetford, Susan Ann to Josiah Runnells 6-16-1867 G
Thetford, T. J. to Robert Rutledge 1-27-1858 (1-28-1858) G
Theus, Elizabeth Lager to James G. Womack 12-24-1844 Ma
Thevis, Georgeanna to Sam Cooper 9-21-1876 Hy
Thogmortin, Manda to Robert Barlow 12-24-1867 (1-16-1868) Cr
Thogmorton?, Lucy Jane to Wm. M. Holland 2-22-1858 Be
Thom, Dolloy to Samuel Harris 8-16-1838 Ma
Thom, Julia A. to B. F. Wood 3-17-1863 G
Thom, Martha to Isaac Hasteto 3-3-1842 Ma
Thom, Martha to R. J. Huckaby 12-23-1869 G
Thom, Mary to James M. Cobb 10-23-1842 (10-25-1842) Ma
Thom, Theresa to James Bursh 4-13-1840 (4-1-1840) Ma
Thomas, A. ?. to I. M. C. Goodloe 1-1-1855 G
Thomas, A. M. to J. F. McMurry 12-2-1869 Hy
Thomas, A. M. to W. S. Gardner 7-20-1843 Cr
Thomas, Alabama T. to Wm. R. Danforth 10-14-1858 (no return) Cr
Thomas, Alabama to James Coleman 12-24-1867 (1-5-1868) Cr
Thomas, Allezarah A. to Samuel M. Davidson 12-2-1852 G
Thomas, Altaquory to Richard L. Pate 3-10-1840 Cr
Thomas, Amanda J. to William Howard 1-10-1872 (no return) Cr
Thomas, America J. to Milton H. Johnson 8-30-1834 (9-2-1834) G
Thomas, America to Isaiah Hunter 2-4-1869 Cr
Thomas, Angeline to William Coward 1-7-1874 (1-8-1874) T B
Thomas, Ann M. to George D. Chalk no date (not executed) Hy
Thomas, Ann to Cipio Peebles 12-23-1867 (no return) Hy
Thomas, Arabella to James R. Thompson 12-30-1868 (12-31-1868) Cr
Thomas, B. A. to R. C. Stone 12-31-1866 (1-3-1867) F
Thomas, Barbara to D. B. Y. (Rev.) McCord 2-5-1846 Hn
Thomas, Becy S. to J. R. Notgrass 12-21-1871 Hy
Thomas, Brunetta to Washington L. Noell 9-29-1840 Cr
Thomas, C. C. to B. P. Dance 10-16-1866 Hy
Thomas, C. E. to J. V. King 2-19-1861 (3-5-1861) O
Thomas, C. M. to Jonathan Pritchard 5-4-1867 (5-8-1867) Cr
Thomas, C. S. to Robert R. James 10-19-1874 (10-21-1874) T
Thomas, Carolin to James M. Beson 12-22-1869 (12-25-1869) T
Thomas, Caroline C. to James H. Boon 12-11-1850 (12-12-1850) G
Thomas, Caroline S. to Thomas Shelton 2-5-1840 (2-7-1840) F
Thomas, Caroline to George Washington Sherrill 12-26-1866 (12-27-1866) T
Thomas, Caroline to James F. Thomas 10-28-1861 Sh
Thomas, Caroline to Jerome Griffin 8-22-1835 (8-23-1835) G
Thomas, Caroline to R. E. McAdoo 9-22-1849 Cr
Thomas, Caroline to W. R. Cannady 10-7-1864 (10-18-1864) Sh
Thomas, Catherine to Wm. T. Sherman 12-19-1869 Hy
Thomas, Clementina to T. Kummisink 3-1-1859 Sh
Thomas, Clementine to Oswald Williams 3-20-1860 (3-22-1860) Sh
Thomas, E. A. to John L. King 1-6-1842 Hn
Thomas, E. H. to W. H. Ward 4-8-1861 (4-9-1861) O
Thomas, E. J. to N. D. Greer (Grier?) 2-1-1866 G
Thomas, E. P. to John Christian 3-5-1838 Ma
Thomas, E. to W. H. Traywick 10-20-1852 Cr
Thomas, Edie to William Dunlap 12-30-1869 G B
Thomas, Elisa to John Isom 9-3-1828 Hr
Thomas, Eliza W. to Sam H. Mulherrin 12-5-1865 Hy
Thomas, Eliza to James D. Arnold 12-17-1849 (12-17-1850?) Ma
Thomas, Elizabeth A. to Silas M. Josslyn 9-10-1833 (9-19-1833) Hr
Thomas, Elizabeth F. to Pleasant G. Wright 12-8-1857 Cr
Thomas, Elizabeth Jane to Robert Kenahan (Kernehan) 12-19-1844 Sh
Thomas, Elizabeth S. to Aaron Freeman 1-18-1853 H
Thomas, Elizabeth to Augustus Hatcher 1-11-1868 (1-12-1868) F B
Thomas, Elizabeth to Cove Cooper 11-3-1839 Hn
Thomas, Elizabeth to Dennis Wright 1-18-1879 (1-22-1879) L
Thomas, Elizabeth to E. D. Hammonds 9-24-1859 Hr
Thomas, Elizabeth to Elisha Saunders 9-2-1846 L
Thomas, Elizabeth to Garret L. Mathis 9-19-1838 Hn
Thomas, Elizabeth to William Shaw 1-17-1863 (1-22-1863) Dy
Thomas, Ellendor L. to John J. McKnight 2-21-1837 G
Thomas, Elmira J. to Horace Wilson 9-29-1857 (10-1-1857) G
Thomas, Elvira to Tom Johnson 6-8-1867 Hy
Thomas, Emeline to Thomas L. Jones 1-10-1854 G
Thomas, Emily to J. D. Castellow 6-15-1869 Hy
Thomas, Eulah H. to Richard H. Rives 11-15-1873 (11-18-1873) T
Thomas, F. A. to Thos. Hemly 12-23-1851 (no return) F
Thomas, F. G. to John Fonville 1-8-1863 (1-12-1863) Dy
Thomas, Fannie to Burril Boyd 12-22-1866 T

Thomas, Flora to Franklin Taylor 12-21-1868 (12-25-1868) F B
Thomas, Frances R. to Robert Billingsly 12-8-1846 Ma
Thomas, Frances to William Butler 11-14-1868 Hy
Thomas, Francis to Nathan Crockett 9-30-1845 (no return) We
Thomas, Georgian to Luther Turner 4-10-1858 (4-11-1858) Ma
Thomas, Guentiller to D. R. Kirk 10-8-1851 Be
Thomas, H. E. to B. D. Shafnor 8-22-1849 (no return) F
Thomas, Harriet R. to James W. King 8-11-1853 Sh
Thomas, Harriett E. to Lewis Wahl 3-7-1861 G
Thomas, Harriett V. to Joseph B. Harper 10-16-1864 G
Thomas, Isabel J. to John Smithwick 5-9-1860 Hy
Thomas, Jane to Alonza White 6-22-1848 Ma
Thomas, Jane to B. F. Jonstone 9-8-1877 O
Thomas, Jane to William T. Johnson 1-8-1852 Ma
Thomas, Joysy W. to John Joslyn 11-15-1833 (11-21-1833) Hr
Thomas, Judd D. to Andrew J. Utley 9-10-1850 Be
Thomas, Julia A. to Wm. J. Hicks 9-28-1858 (no return) L
Thomas, Julia to William M. Bevil 10-23-1851 Hn
Thomas, Kesia to William Reed 3-15-1843 (3-16-1843) G
Thomas, L. J. to T. J. Wilks 11-19-1870 Hy
Thomas, Liza Jane to James Comer 8-5-1867 (8-9-1867) F B
Thomas, Lizzie D. to J. B. Faulk 10-23-1867 O
Thomas, Louisa to G. A. Wolfe 3-16-1859 (3-21-1859) Sh
Thomas, Louisa to George Bethshares 3-19-1870 Ma
Thomas, Lousinia to Thos. W. Coleman 1-29-1846 Cr
Thomas, Lucinda to Thomas D. Hammons 12-19-1837 Hr
Thomas, Lucy Ann to John L. Davis 12-2-1844 (12-20-1844) F
Thomas, Lucy to David L. R. Littleton 1-15-1857 We
Thomas, Lucy to Napolian William 8-1-1867 (8-2-1867) T
Thomas, Lydia R. to Wm. B. Drake 7-1-1871 (7-2-1871) Ma
Thomas, M. A. to I. W. Murray 3-12-1867 Hy
Thomas, M. A. to J. C. Drennon 9-28-1869 Hy
Thomas, M. J. to W. H. Wilkes 4-20-1868 G
Thomas, M. to M. McCray 10-26-1869 (10-28-1869) F
Thomas, Mahala to Francis N. Arnold 9-29-1858 Ma
Thomas, Malinda E. to Columbus W. Roberts 7-19-1860 Hn
Thomas, Malissa to William Steele 2-19-1869 G B
Thomas, Margaret J. to J. M. Canady 11-5-1863 Sh
Thomas, Margaret to Scott Henderson 10-29-1874 L
Thomas, Margarett Ann to Abner D. Thomas 2-12-1845 (no return) F
Thomas, Marinda to Thos. G. Underwood 8-16-1848 Sh
Thomas, Martha A. to J. F. Roach 6-7-1858 Hr
Thomas, Martha A. to Marcus Barrott 3-19-1844 G *
Thomas, Martha A. to William Previtt 7-14-1855 (7-16-1855) L
Thomas, Martha C. to R. W. Hall 1-10-1843 Hn
Thomas, Martha E. to George M. Fisher 12-14-1837 G
Thomas, Martha K. to W. T. Goldsby 10-22-1851 Sh
Thomas, Martha L. to William L. McCracken 10-22-1861 Cr
Thomas, Martha M. to Nathe. C. Bailey 12-26-1870 (12-27-1870) Ma
Thomas, Martha R. to R. N. Nesbitt 1-3-1855 (no return) F
Thomas, Martha to John Bushart 4-30-1845 Hn
Thomas, Martha to John Prescott 3-10-1845 (3-18-1845) L
Thomas, Martha to T. S. Carson 8-15-1839 Be
Thomas, Mary A. to Lemuel Love 2-26-1840 (2-27-1840) G
Thomas, Mary A. to Lewis H. Woodard 9-4-1855 (no return) L
Thomas, Mary A. to Louis Capell 10-14-1868 Hy
Thomas, Mary A. to Malcomb McCollum 12-8-1839 Sh
Thomas, Mary A. to P. H. Cantrell 12-10-1846 We
Thomas, Mary Adeline to Jefferson Saunders 9-17-1846 L
Thomas, Mary Ann to Jas. M. Irven 1-31-1850 Ma
Thomas, Mary Ann to Reuben Bomar 3-28-1844 Hn
Thomas, Mary C. to Harvell M. Ward 3-14-1850 O
Thomas, Mary C. to Wm. Polk 7-23-1839 (7-30-1839) F
Thomas, Mary E. to James W. Clark 1-2-1866 (1-3-1867?) Ma
Thomas, Mary Jane to A. L. Clair 11-11-1852 G
Thomas, Mary Jane to William H. Holmes 9-14-1841 G
Thomas, Mary M. to Richard T. Hagler 12-13-1859 We
Thomas, Mary to Burrell Bell 7-10-1852 Be
Thomas, Mary to Enoch McAdoo 9-9-1857 Cr
Thomas, Mary to John M. Wilkes 4-21-1858 G
Thomas, Mary to Will Parker 5-7-1836 Hy
Thomas, Mary to William R. Chandler 7-21-1857 (7-2?-1857) Ma
Thomas, Mary to Willis Walker 1-20-1876 Hy
Thomas, Matilda J. to Cradock R. Parham 3-27-1849 O
Thomas, Mattie to William Thomas 10-24-1870 F B
Thomas, Milinda to C. G. Cribbs 11-15-1864 Sh
Thomas, Mollie E. to W. F. Strength 3-12-1878 Hy
Thomas, Mollie to George Taliaferro 1-18-1878 Hy
Thomas, Mollie to William Wallace 4-19-1874 Hy
Thomas, Molly to William G. Teague 10-14-1831 Hr
Thomas, Monah to Daniel Hassell 1-23-1856 (1-24-1856) G
Thomas, N. A. to D. L. Dickey 2-13-1861 G
Thomas, Nancy E. to Eli W. Ing 3-18-1853 (2?-20-1853) G
Thomas, Nancy E. to J. W. Snow 9-28-1859 (9-29-1859) Hr
Thomas, Nancy E. to W. E. Bowen 1-17-1872 O
Thomas, Nancy M. to Stokeley Stroud 2-8-1856 Sh
Thomas, Nancy to Benjamin Alsup 12-25-1833 Hr

Thomas, Nancy to John Farzin 7-25-1840 Hn
Thomas, Nancy to Samuel King 10-20-1861 Hn
Thomas, Narcissa to Robt. Collier 11-28-1878 Hy
Thomas, P. A. to S. W. Conner 11-24-1864 G
Thomas, P. A. to S. W. Cormer 11-24-1864 G
Thomas, P. M. to John M. Maynard 4-28-1855 (5-1-1855) Ma
Thomas, Rachael M. to William H. Terell 1-29-1849 G
Thomas, Rachal L. to John S. Fullerton l7-24-1838 (7-26-1838) G
Thomas, Rachel to Nathan Johnson 7-29-1850 (7-30-1850) Ma
Thomas, Rebecca C. to Henry Valentine 10-2-1846 We
Thomas, Rebecca T. to Joseph R. Parker 2-13-1860 F
Thomas, Ronanah C. D. to W. A. McLain 3-1-1855 G
Thomas, Sallie to Thomas E. Glass 5-3-1871 Hy
Thomas, Sarah A. to Owen H. Edwards 12-19-1859 (12-20-1859) O
Thomas, Sarah A. to William Vaden 5-16-1855 We
Thomas, Sarah E. to Silas W. Edwards 12-3-1857 Ma
Thomas, Sarah J. to R. H. Solmon 2-10-1867 Hn
Thomas, Sarah Jane to Andrew J. Williams 9-26-1860 (10-2-1860) Ma
Thomas, Sarah L. to John B. Cochran 7-19-1844 (no return) We
Thomas, Sarah L. to William L. Thomas 1-15-1868 G
Thomas, Sarah to Alfred Hutchison 4-2-1849 L
Thomas, Sarah to Asberry Lampley 4-20-1851 Hn
Thomas, Sarah to Bill Williams 12-24-1877 (12-25-1877) L B
Thomas, Sarah to Washington Noell 8-21-1838 Cr
Thomas, Sarah to William McBride 9-23-1829 (9-24-1829) G
Thomas, Susan A. to William A. Pullen 2-20-1868 T
Thomas, Susan C. to A. L. Bond 2-9-1869 Be
Thomas, Susan C. to N. L. Look 2-19-1862 Sh
Thomas, Susan J. to G. L. Elder 5-14-1863 Mn
Thomas, Susan M. to Josiah Home 10-16-1848 (10-18-1848) T
Thomas, Susan to F. E. Becton 7-16-1859 (7-17-1859) G
Thomas, Susan to George Currie (not executed) Hy
Thomas, Susan to Powell Bowling 1-16-1861 G
Thomas, Susan to T. S. Feeman 2-12-1850 G
Thomas, Susan to Willis H. Lane 6-29-1841 G
Thomas, Susan to Wm. J. Bryant 12-20-1870 (12-22-1870) Cr
Thomas, Tabitha J. to Joseph M. Bledsoe 12-29-1868 (12-31-1868) Ma
Thomas, Theresa to Benjamin Nearn 10-3-1843 (10-8-1843) L
Thomas, Tobitha A. to W. G. Black 2-20-1860 G
Thomas, Tobitha to William Langston 6-18-1825 (6-19-1825) Hr
Thomas, Z. A. to James H. Griffin 1-6-1851 (no return) F
Thomas?, Caroline M. H. to Samuel B. Mayberry 1-20-1842 Cr
Thomasin?, M. S. to John Bragg 1-1-1856 (no return) Hn
Thomason, Amanda to H. D. Sexton 9-13-1866 G
Thomason, Ann I. to Benjamin Phillips 3-11-1858 O
Thomason, E. Ann to N. Nunnery 9-6-1847 Be
Thomason, Elmira J. to W. F. Tyson 4-2-1867 Hn
Thomason, Elvyra to Simion Morris 12-20-1845 (12-23-1845) F
Thomason, Hannah to James M. Swindle 1-29-1863 Be
Thomason, Hannah to Stephen Walker 7-22-1850 Be
Thomason, Jenkins to Henry Joyner 2-8-1850 (no return) Hn
Thomason, M. E. to W. S. McCain 10-20-1867 Hn
Thomason, Margaret E. to John Hedge 3-11-1857 Cr
Thomason, Martha A. to David Gardner 4-8-1840 G
Thomason, Mary A. to William Crawley 1-4-1844 Hn
Thomason, Mary H. to J. M. Roberts 8-23-1864 (8-24-1864) Cr
Thomason, Mary to Samuel Swearengin 7-29-1846 Cr
Thomason, Mildred to Benjamin Williams 12-5-1839 Sh
Thomason, Nancy to Dennis Howe 2-18-1868 Be
Thomason, R. E. C. to Madison F. Herndon 4-22-1854 G
Thomason, Rachele to Zebadee Howe 1-23-1848 Be
Thomason, S. C. to Benj. Phillips 5-17-1860 G
Thomasson, Elizabeth C. to James Biggs 12-16-1847 G
Thomerson, Elizabeth to James Bevard 10-26-1844 Cr
Thompson, A. M. to D. M. (SB F. M.) Capps 1-10-1864 Be
Thompson, Abigale L. to John S. Craft 12-18-1833 Sh
Thompson, Adda to George Young 2-13-1871 (no return) L
Thompson, Alice to Joe Warren 3-25-1885 (3-26-1885) L
Thompson, Almeter to W. B. Simmons 1-20-1852 (no return) F
Thompson, Amanda to Richard P. Gibson 8-17-1867 (no return) Dy
Thompson, America A. to Isham N. Smith 10-29-1838 Hr
Thompson, America to James H. Forest 1-15-1851 (no return) Cr
Thompson, America to John M. Meadows 11-26-1861 We
Thompson, Ann B. to Job A. Lewis 3-14-1842 Sh
Thompson, Ann E. to D. M. Barwell 10-8-1860 (10-24-1860) F
Thompson, Annie to Isaac Anderson 1-14-1869 Hy
Thompson, B. L. to L. F. Deshony 10-28-1872 (10-29-1872) Cr
Thompson, Barbara E. to George N. Allbright 12-14-1865 (no return) Hy
Thompson, Betsy to James K. Slone 2-14-1843 Sh
Thompson, Bettie to Samuel McPherson 12-15-1875 L
Thompson, C. A. to H. G. D. Collins 11-19-1870 (no return) Hy
Thompson, Caroline to J. Taylor 12-3-1874 T
Thompson, Caroline to Joseph T. Eckles 12-13-1841 Sh
Thompson, Catharine A. to Daniel W. Wright 6-28-1860 Sh
Thompson, Charity T. to Stewart Flinter 5-31-1832 (6-3-1832) G
Thompson, Chester A. to P. B. Coppage 3-1-1870 G
Thompson, Christina to James H. Nelson 10-31-1859 (11-1-1859) Ma

Thompson, Cora to W. H. Bickers 7-25-1882 (7-26-1882) L
Thompson, Cyntha to Fountain McGehee 1-13-1839 (1-24-1839) F
Thompson, Cyntha to Pateric Morris 12-25-1849 O
Thompson, Cynthia to Fountain McGehee 1-13-1839 (no return) F
Thompson, Cynthia to Francis M. Pyles 9-7-1854 Ma
Thompson, Cynthia to Robertson Murrell 1-21-1867 (1-22-1867) F B
Thompson, Dolly to Thomas Higdon 3-14-1839 Be
Thompson, Dorcus Melissa to Wm. Thos. Ford 1-28-1851 T
Thompson, E. A. C. to John S. R. Cowan 2-8-1869 (2-10-1869) F
Thompson, E. F. to J. W. Miller 7-21-1874 (no return) L
Thompson, E. P. to Wm. D. Davis 8-13-1863 O
Thompson, E. V. to John W. Luttrell 1-20-1857 (1-22-1857) Hr
Thompson, Edie to William Littleton 12-29-1870 (no return) F B
Thompson, Edmny? to Lewis Ware 11-3-1868 (10?-5-1868) L
Thompson, Eliza Ann to Thos. B. Willoughby 6-15-1854 (6-29-1854) Hr
Thompson, Eliza to Nathan C. Smith 5-17-1871 (5-18-1871) Dy B
Thompson, Eliza to Sam Mayfield 12-29-1870 Hy
Thompson, Elizabeth A. to H. B. Ramsey 11-7-1846 Sh
Thompson, Elizabeth C. to Gordan W. Stone 6-19-1839 L
Thompson, Elizabeth H. to E. P. Hollis 9-6-1859 We
Thompson, Elizabeth H. to William T. High 12-28-1853 (12-29-1853) Sh
Thompson, Elizabeth J. to B. B. Lamb 11-22-1865 (no return) Hn
Thompson, Elizabeth J. to James A. Nance 4-11-1850 Hn
Thompson, Elizabeth J. to Martha? Ashlock 4-19-1859 Hn
Thompson, Elizabeth J. to William B. Moore 3-29-1832 (4-1-1832) G
Thompson, Elizabeth to Charles Burrus 3-16-1835 (3-19-1835) Hr
Thompson, Elizabeth to Edward Fonville 5-6-1848 (5-9-1848) O
Thompson, Elizabeth to Jerramiah P. Woodard 9-29-1836 (10-2-1836) G
Thompson, Elizabeth to Maxwell Cooke 9-26-1837 (9-28-1837) O
Thompson, Elizabeth to Peter Tyus 10-12-1869 Hy
Thompson, Elizabeth to Randolph Mayfield 11-6-1843 Hr
Thompson, Elizabeth to W. H. Donald 10-1-1866 O
Thompson, Elizabeth to William Elliott 9-12-1850 (9-17-1850) Sh
Thompson, Elizabeth to William Williams 7-19-1841 (7-20-1841) L
Thompson, Ella H. to A. E. Clemmons 10-24-1877 (no return) L
Thompson, Emily F. to Y. H. Warren 3-3-1858 Cr
Thompson, Emily to Samuel Ledbetter 12-13-1843 Sh
Thompson, Eveline to James Thompson 2-15-1869 (2-17-1869) O
Thompson, Fannie C. to Jacob Shew 7-27-1870 (7-28-1870) Ma
Thompson, Flora to Alexander Harden 1-28-1841 Hn
Thompson, Frances E. to John A. Garner 6-29-1852 Hr
Thompson, Frances to John Abbott 2-3-1852 Be
Thompson, G. A. to Phillip P. Brooks 4-11-1883 (4-12-1883) L
Thompson, G. L. to T. F. Hudgens 8-26-1879 (8-27-1879) L
Thompson, H. M. to P. McIrby 11-3-1858 (11-4-1858) Sh
Thompson, H. M. to Saml. J. Estridge 6-14-1852 We
Thompson, Harriet to A. B. Hill 1-23-1865 (1-24-1865) T
Thompson, Harriet to Benj. F. L. Clarke 2-13-1847 Hr
Thompson, Harriet to John Baker 6-1-1867 (no return) L B
Thompson, Harriett to J. C. Pearce 12-18-1866 (12-20-1866) Cr
Thompson, Hattie to Jordan Jarrett 1-25-1877 Hy
Thompson, Henrietta to A. M. F. Carpenter 2-27-1861 (3-13-1861) O
Thompson, Henrietta to Cato Persons 2-6-1866 Hn
Thompson, Holly S. to Milton C. Young 1-2-1854 (2-1-1854) Hr
Thompson, Isabella to Calvin Z. Jarrell 1-12-1858 Be
Thompson, Isabella to Robert Bickers 11-1-1847 (11-18-1847) Ma
Thompson, Jane to Lovelace Coleman 10-10-1877 Hy
Thompson, Jane to William Clark 6-30-1866 (no return) F B
Thompson, Jane to William Myrick 5-24-1842 (5-31-1842) Hr
Thompson, Jemimah (Samanth?)J. to George W. Kennon 9-1-1849 (9-5-1849) L
Thompson, Joana to Robert Taylor 3-14-1870 (3-17-1870) L
Thompson, Julia A. to John A. Anderson 12-13-1870 (12-17-1870) F B
Thompson, Julia Ann to Washington G. Robb 12-11-1833 (12-12-1833) Hr
Thompson, Julia M. to Francis Wylie 12-12-1854 (12-13-1854) T
Thompson, L. J. to G. B. Osteen 3-28-1883 L
Thompson, L. J. to P. P. Hutchison 1-26-1870 G
Thompson, L. P. to Cuthbert H. Jones 1-3-1849 Hn
Thompson, Laura A. to Samuel J. Eskridge 2-26-1862 We
Thompson, Laura W. to Wm. E. Miller 12-9-1856 (12-17-1856) Sh
Thompson, Lavina to Joseph Kelley 6-13-1833 G
Thompson, Lennie to Saml. Will Adkins 12-29-1870 T
Thompson, Levinia E. to John B. Patton 2-22-1842 (2-23-1842) G
Thompson, Lillie (Mrs.) to W. H. Jackson 2-7-1864 Sh
Thompson, Louisa Augusta to James Willis Gidcomb 7-14-1870 L
Thompson, Louisa E. to H. B. Baker 3-5-1852 L
Thompson, Louisa E. to _____ 2-5-1849 Hn
Thompson, Louisa F.? to Lowranza D. Simpson 9-14-1840 (no return) Hn
Thompson, Louisa to James J. Gossett 12-10-1858 Be
Thompson, Louisa to Wm. Estes 1-21-1870 (no return) Hy
Thompson, Lucinda to G. E. Spence 10-1-1867 (no return) Dy
Thompson, Lucinda to Robert Couch 12-24-1872 Dy
Thompson, Lucinda to T. H. Aiken 10-29-1868 (no return) Dy
Thompson, Lucinda to William Henning 2-26-1879 L
Thompson, Lucy H. to Hugh Flippo 7-27-1867 O
Thompson, Lucy T. to John J. Dowdy 11-10-1853 Hr
Thompson, Lucy to Lee Dewalt 12-18-1878 L

Thompson, Lue to James B. Shelton 10-30-1867 (10-31-1867) T
Thompson, Lydia to Baseley Jackson 8-27-1849 (8-28-1849) Ma
Thompson, M. E. (Mrs.) to John L. Keltner 11-7-1883 (11-8-1883) L
Thompson, M. E. to J. A. Moore 1-14-1868 (1-15-1868) Dy
Thompson, M. E. to Oscar F. Collins 3-20-1867 (3-28-1867) Ma
Thompson, M. J. to John H. Smith 11-1-1865 Hy
Thompson, M. P. to J. M. Porter 10-17-1859 (10-18-1859) G
Thompson, M. to James H. Goodrich 7-6-1870 Dy
Thompson, M? A. to A. J. Warran 1-22-1884 L
Thompson, Maggie to D. W. Conley 12-30-1875 (1-1-1876) L
Thompson, Malinda F. to Marion J. Holly 12-9-1869 Ma
Thompson, Margaret C. to Christopher A. Simonton 2-5-1848 (2-10-1848) T
Thompson, Margaret E. to John J. Barnett 4-6-1867 (4-9-1867) Ma
Thompson, Margaret Jane to Hemphill Smith 11-13-1867 T
Thompson, Margaret to Eli Paschel 2-3-1831 Hr
Thompson, Margaret to J. W. Thomas 2-27-1865 F
Thompson, Margaret to John L. Grove 1-2-1860 (1-24-1860) Hr
Thompson, Margarett to Benjamin Frierson 12-24-1870 (no return) F B
Thompson, Margarett to George H. Hall 9-13-1834 Hr
Thompson, Maria L. to Avery Hunt 7-4-1844 Ma
Thompson, Maria L. to Green C. Lundsford 1-8-1866 (1-16-1866) L
Thompson, Maria O. to George H. Martin 2-3-1868 (no return) Hy
Thompson, Maria to Lewis Cowan 9-18-1872 T
Thompson, Mariah to Jett Williams 3-16-1875 Hy
Thompson, Marsha to Jordan Wordlow 12-28-1871 Hy
Thompson, Martha A. R. to Jarret Thompson 5-15-1865 Dy
Thompson, Martha A. T. to McKelva Bean 3-14-1842 G
Thompson, Martha A. to Hiram Wiles 6-28-1849 Sh
Thompson, Martha Ann to William M. Smith 2-21-1866 L
Thompson, Martha E. to John A. Sain (Sam?) 5-9-1865 G
Thompson, Martha G. to W. C. Johnson 6-1-1867 (6-2-1867) F
Thompson, Martha to James Shelly 2-6-1854 Sh
Thompson, Martha to Jas. T. Simmons 10-7-1851 (no return) F
Thompson, Martha to John Currie 12-30-1866 Hy
Thompson, Martha to Raymond A. Blankenship 7-17-1855 Ma
Thompson, Mary A. to Nathan Holloway 9-24-1861 Hr
Thompson, Mary A. to Wm. Crain 6-20-1843 Sh
Thompson, Mary A. to Wyatt Hickman 2-16-1838 (2-20-1838) Hr
Thompson, Mary Ann E. to R. C. Ray 3-28-1866 Hn
Thompson, Mary Ann to Andrew H. Clark 11-4-1871 (11-6-1871) Ma
Thompson, Mary Ann to Hugh D. Moore 6-20-1844 F
Thompson, Mary Ann to Nathan Michals 12-8-1840 Cr
Thompson, Mary Ann to Thomas Hines 11-17-1846 (11-19-1846) Hr
Thompson, Mary B. to Ellison P. Fuller 9-6-1843 (9-7-1843) L
Thompson, Mary C. F. to A. J. Thompson 12-19-1871 (no return) Cr
Thompson, Mary C. to George W. Styers 12-23-1885 L
Thompson, Mary C. to Mark A. Hatley 2-14-1867 Be
Thompson, Mary C. to Peter D. Ennis 2-8-1871 (2-9-1871) T
Thompson, Mary E. to J. S. Ward 1-27-1868 Dy
Thompson, Mary E. to James V. Fortune 8-4-1856 (8-7-1856) Hr
Thompson, Mary E. to Thomas Searcy 12-30-1872 (1-1-1873) L B
Thompson, Mary E. to W. C. Carter 5-7-1849 O
Thompson, Mary F. to J. A. Samuels 12-4-1874 (12-9-1874) L
Thompson, Mary F. to W. R. Lucas 12-14-1859 Sh
Thompson, Mary J. (P.) to Allen J. Greenwood 2-14-1850 O
Thompson, Mary J. to Wm. K. Childress 11-18-1849 Sh
Thompson, Mary Jane to Richard T. Graves 10-30-1845 Hn
Thompson, Mary P. to T. P. Stephens 12-20-1866 Hn
Thompson, Mary R. to Samuel H. Caldwell 12-24-1860 Hn
Thompson, P. R. to Henry Stags 10-22-1865 O
Thompson, Mary to J. W. Jarrett 2-20-1872 (2-21-1871?) L
Thompson, Mary to John Percifal 11-11-1856 Ma
Thompson, Mary to Johnathan Baley 2-5-1845 G
Thompson, Mary to Jordan Johnson 10-25-1883 L
Thompson, Mary to Lawrence A. Campbell 4-26-1869 (4-27-1869) F
Thompson, Mary to Robert C. Flemming 4-3-1838 Cr
Thompson, Mary to Taylor Malone 2-28-1870 (3-2-1870) F
Thompson, Mary to Thomas Allen 1-7-1869 F B
Thompson, Mary to William Crank 11-28-1853 (12-1-1853) G
Thompson, Matilda to Jas. B. Harris 7-29-1847 Sh
Thompson, Mattie W. to James, jr. Hannah 11-10-1857 Sh
Thompson, May F. to Sam Redditt 12-21-1848 Sh
Thompson, Melinda A. to Banyan Payne 6-15-1835 Sh
Thompson, Middey to A. Pierce 2-25-1856 (no return) Hn
Thompson, Milissa Jane to Jesse McIntosh 8-10-1841 (9-22-1841) O
Thompson, Mindie? to W. O. Childress 6-13-1879 (6-15-1879) Dy
Thompson, Minta to John Woodfin 4-4-1868 F B
Thompson, Mira Jane to James C. Goforth 4-20-1860 L
Thompson, Mollie D. to Frank M. Taylor 11-24-1868 (11-26-1868) F
Thompson, Molly to John Robinson 11-7-1864 Sh
Thompson, N. E. to C. J. Simonton 7-24-1865 (7-25-1865) T
Thompson, Nancy A. to H.K. Frederick 9-22-1860 (9-23-1860) Hr
Thompson, Nancy M. to Blackman H. Bird 6-17-1843 O
Thompson, Nancy to D. F. Yancy 8-27-1865 Hy
Thompson, Nancy to Dennis Young 1-19-1870 Hy
Thompson, Nancy to James Brigance 4-10-1859 Hy
Thompson, Nancy to James C. Merrick 4-17-1839 (4-21-1839) F

Thompson, Nancy to James Huffman 11-12-1857 T
Thompson, Nannie J. to A. J. Ivy 1-21-1867 (1-24-1867) F
Thompson, Pamelia A. to William A. Wood 9-14-1843 L
Thompson, Patsey to James Madison 2-1-1867 (2-16-1867) F B
Thompson, Pauline (Mrs.) to Wilie Carlisle 1-12-1864 Sh
Thompson, Penina to John Horn 2-27-1853 Be
Thompson, Penny to Samuel Craft 10-30-1833 Sh
Thompson, Phoeby to Samuel Herrin 9-26-1866 (no return) Dy
Thompson, Priscilla to James L. Gossett 3-29-1829 Hr
Thompson, Rebecca A. to Stephen Jones 4-27-1855 (5-7-1855) Sh
Thompson, Rebecca J. to Thomas H. Ary 11-12-1856 Hn
Thompson, Rebecca W. to John Reaves 1-13-1869 Be
Thompson, Rebecca to James Trigg 11-17-1840 Sh
Thompson, Rebecca to Jarrett Nelson 12-21-1846 Ma
Thompson, Rebecca to Josh Donaldson 7-12-1849 Sh
Thompson, Rebecca to William Horton 12-24-1834 (12-26-1834) Hr
Thompson, Rhoda C. to Andrew A. Beasley 10-25-1855 Be
Thompson, S. A. to J. Darnall 2-15-1867 Hn
Thompson, S. E. to John W. Burnett 2-9-1871 Hy
Thompson, S. to Dave Boyd 7-16-1859 Cr
Thompson, Sal A. to M. E. Stone 4-11-1839 L
Thompson, Sallie to David Cox 11-16-1876 Hy
Thompson, Sally T. to John A. Williams 11-21-1853 Sh
Thompson, Sarah Ann E. to Tho. McCarter 3-4-1857 (3-5-1857) Hr
Thompson, Sarah C. to William W. Hammonds 1-2-1850 Ma
Thompson, Sarah D. to Charles G. Brown 10-19-1869 (10-21-1869) Cr
Thompson, Sarah E. to A. W. Rinehart 3-24-1877 (no return) Hy
Thompson, Sarah E. to Danl. Roads 4-6-1863 (4-8-1863) Dy
Thompson, Sarah J. to John H. Graves 11-8-1867 (11-10-1867) Ma
Thompson, Sarah J. to John J. Smithwick 12-20-1855 We
Thompson, Sarah J. to Miles B. Janes 9-24-1846 Hn
Thompson, Sarah to D. J. Ball 7-14-1864 G
Thompson, Sarah to Elias Davis 3-15-1840 Be
Thompson, Sarah to Jno. W. McKizzick 12-14-1850 Hr
Thompson, Sarah to John Rose 7-15-1835 (7-23-1835) Hr
Thompson, Sarah to William J. Marshall 5-31-1847 (4?-?-1847) T
Thompson, Sarilla to John C. Harris 10-17-1827 (10-18-1827) Hr
Thompson, Susan E. to William K. Holmes 11-13-1845 Ma
Thompson, Susan H. to Alfred Wesson 3-27-1847 Sh
Thompson, Susan H. to Zack M. Richa 4-14-1852 (no return) We
Thompson, Susan R. to Lemuel L. Cherry 1-8-1859 (1-13-1859) Ma
Thompson, Susan to George W. Cole 12-3-1849 Sh
Thompson, Susan to Lewis A. Bickers 11-1-1848 Ma
Thompson, Susan to M. C. McAvoy 6-30-1867 G
Thompson, Susannah M. to William Husbands 4-16-1847 (4-22-1847) G
Thompson, T. A. to Edwin W. Martin 7-3-1857 Cr
Thompson, T. B. to J. N. Meadow 1-1-1878 (1-2-1878) L
Thompson, Tabitha A. to Paul M. Halliburton 10-28-1857 L
Thompson, Tabitha V. to J. N. Samuels 12-18-1876 (12-21-1876) L
Thompson, Tennessee to Caswell P. Hall 2-17-1849 (2-22-1849) G
Thompson, Tilda to Henry Palmer 1-3-1868 (1-11-1868) F B
Thompson, Virginia to Andrew Blackwell 8-6-1875 (8-12-1875) L
Thomson, Cornelia A. to V. A. Rodgers 11-25-1857 Cr
Thomson, Elizabeth D. to Geo. W. McCommon 2-9-1853 (2-10-1853) Hr
Thomson, M. M. to A. W. Anderson 12-20-1859 (12-21-1859) Sh
Thomson, Margrett to Jefferson McClelland 11-15-1859 (11-22-1859) Sh
Thomson, Mary E. to William Joyner 11-12-1844 Sh
Thomson, Sarah Ann to Henry C. Massey 11-14-1842 Sh
Thonton, Hallie to Henderson Laycook 11-8-1853 Cr
Thopson, P. R. to H. N. Swayne 10-14-1865 O
Thorn (Thom?), Maggie to Samuel Little 2-15-1859 (2-16-1859) Sh
Thorn, Julia A. M. to Thomas S. Baird 10-17-1867 G
Thorn, Nancy C. to Lafayette McHaney 10-2-1860 G
Thorn, Perimila to Porter Davis 2-2-1859 Cr
Thorn, Sarah E. to John H. Jones 7-5-1866 Cr
Thornley, Mollie J. to C. R. Lewis 12-27-1882 (12-28-1882) L
Thornsbrough, Mary A. to James T. Lawsen 1-20-1858 We
Thornton, Bettie to Wash Thurman 8-26-1869 (8-28-1869) F B
Thornton, E. to W. H. Dickson 7-16-1855 Sh
Thornton, Eliza to William Stagner 8-24-1853 Be
Thornton, Feriby to Daniel Crayne 3-12-1842 (3-20-1842) O
Thornton, Florence L. to B. F. House 7-18-1876 Hy
Thornton, H. S. to B. C. Stuart 12-22-1869 Hy
Thornton, Henrietta to Francis Marley 11-27-1860 (no return) L
Thornton, Henrietta to Wm. R. McGlothlin 1-6-1862 Hr
Thornton, L. to George Williamson 7-21-1866 (7-22-1866) F
Thornton, Lavinia A. to Josiah R. Carroll 6-11-1853 (6-26-1853) G
Thornton, Lucinda to Zeb Pulliam 1-22-1866 (2-28-1866) F B
Thornton, M. E. to J. G. Porter 2-12-1866 G
Thornton, Martha to Aaron Dallas 12-21-1871 (no return) L
Thornton, Mary to Eleanor Williams 12-21-1845 We
Thornton, Millie to Daniel Estes 12-15-1877 Hy
Thornton, Mina to Campbell Pulliam 12-18-1865 (12-26-1865) F B
Thornton, Nancy to Silas Reynolds 7-22-1831 Sh
Thornton, Nancy to William Taylor 9-1-1866 Hy
Thornton, Nellie to Merrick Fitzpatrick 12-15-1885 (12-17-1885) L
Thornton, Polly to Henry Borum 8-2-1879 (8-3-1879) L B

Thornton, Prudie to A. L. Barker 9-24-1867 (no return) Hn
Thornton, R. to S. M. Kemp 4-8-1857 We
Thornton, Rebecca A. L. to William F. Sparks 10-19-1853 Hn
Thornton, Rebecca A. to Albert Utley 10-2-1853 Be
Thornton, Sallie F. to A. H. Thornton 5-2-1866 (5-3-1866) F
Thornton, Sarah Ann to Peterson Mosley 9-11-1838 F
Thornton, Sarah to Henry Looton(Tuoton?) 3-19-1858 (3-21-1858) Hr
Thornton, Susan S. to James B. Thorton (Horton?) 5-8-1854 (no return) L
Thornton, Susan to Richard Harris 1-30-1877 (1-31-1877) Dy
Thornton, Thirza to James M. Winsten 8-28-1861 We
Thornton?, Lucy to William J. Anderson 5-26-1857 Be
Thornton?, Martha E. to Abraham W. Berry 5-20-1849 F
Thorp, Mary L. to Saml. A. Wells 9-16-1857 (9-20-1857) Sh
Thorp, Rebecca Jane to James P. O'Kelley 9-25-1843 (10-3-1843) F
Thorp, Rose to William Perry 3-3-1875 (no return) Hy
Thorpe, Virginia to J. M. Farley 12-29-1870 (no return) F
Thorton, Louisa to George Wilson 2-14-1875 Hy
Thrailkill, Nancy to John W. Boney 2-12-1842 (2-13-1842) Hr
Thrailkill, Nancy to Perry Brown 4-18-1848 (4-20-1848) Hr
Thraneer?, Mahala to Johram Bradford 5-23-1863 (5-24-1863) O
Thrasher, Rachel M. C. to Martin Hensly 1-22-1846 (1-23-1846) Hr
Threadgill, Harriet E. to George W. Haley 9-20-1867 (no return) Cr
Threadgill, Sarah F. to W. W. Mills 11-18-1865 (no return) Cr
Thredgill, Martha A. to W. T. Oliver 12-2-1867 (12-4-1867) Cr
Threldkel, Sarah M. to R. M. Alexander 11-11-1867 O
Threlkill, Caroline to Franklyn Ingle 11-7-1862 Mn
Threlkill, Luce to John W. Smith 10-10-1862 Mn
Thrift, Eliza S.? to John C. Marler 1-1-1841 (1-5-1841) F
Thrift, Mary Ann to David Humphrey 11-21-1842 Hr
Throgmartin, Mary E. to Joseph Bowls 10-23-1861 (no return) We
Throgmartin, Nancy to Wm. Onsman 9-6-1865 (9-7-1865) O
Throgmorten, Sallie to M. B. Briggs 7-21-1867 Be
Throgmorton, Edy to Hawkins H. Callehan 10-2-1839 Hn
Throgmorton, Jane to Richard Gallimore 1-15-1855 Hn
Throgmorton, M. J. to F. M. Jackson (no date) (with 1866) O
Throgmorton, Margaret to J. W. Gallemore 1-28-1864 Hn
Throgmorton, Margaret to James W. Throgmorton 9-4-1848 (no return) Hn
Throgmorton, Mariah P. to Thomas W. W. Henley 11-6-1844 Hn
Throgmorton, Mary E. to A. L. Redden 4-7-1862 (no return) Hn
Throgmorton, Mary F. to Wm. T. Pierce 1-24-1867 Be
Throgmorton, Mary J. to J. W. Barnwell 1-12-1848 Hn
Throgmorton, Mary to John H. Richey 1-28-1838 (no return) Hn
Throgmorton, Mary to Larkin J. Gallimore 10-22-1846 Hn
Throgmorton, Pameta to William Latta 11-6-1842 Hn
Thum, Eliza J. to Ira G. Barfield 1-20-1851 (1-22-1851) L
Thum, Ella to H. J. Barfield 10-30-1877 (10-31-1877) L
Thum, Mary E. to Peter L. Lankford 12-11-1865 (12-13-1865) L
Thum, Sallie A. to Willie E. Alston 2-19-1861 (no return) L
Thum, Susan E. to Rufus P. Jacobs 3-5-1866 (3-7-1866) L
Thurman, Elizabeth to James S. Alestock 7-26-1837 Hr *
Thurman, Elmena to H. H. L. Brogden 12-14-1857 We
Thurman, F. E. to John L. Farmer 12-5-1872 Hy
Thurman, Lucy to W. F. Beard 3-12-1863 Mn
Thurman, Nancy to Vann Miller 4-20-1854 Ma
Thurman, Octavia L. to B. R. Reynolds 9-21-1882 (9-24-1882) L
Thurman, PatienceAmanda to Ben Sharp 12-30-1870 Hy
Thurmon, S. M. to A. Canada 8-20-1868 (8-23-1868) Dy
Thurmond, Amanda J. to George W. Chambers 11-4-1874 L
Thurmond, Amelia L.(S?) to Jessee D. Franklin 1-25-1849 (1-30-1849) Hr
Thurmond, Ann L. to Benj. Porter 3-30-1843 L
Thurmond, Caroline M. to R. H. Carroll 3-21-1836 (3-24-1836) Hr
Thurmond, E. F. to Hosea Boren 3-20-1878 Dy
Thurmond, F. C. to Daniel J. Meter 8-12-1874 (8-13-1874) L
Thurmond, Fannie to J. D. Glisson 12-23-1876 (1-4-1877) Dy
Thurmond, Frances A. to R. F. Chambers 5-4-1868 (5-13-1868) L
Thurmond, Hasentine to Jackson Stricklan 2-18-1871 (2-19-1871) Dy
Thurmond?, Luiza F. to David A. Moore 5-15-1863 (5-16-1863) L
Thurmond, M. E. to C. M. Franklin 10-22-1859 (10-27-1859) Hr
Thurmond, Martha to Geo. Lee 12-17-1873 Hy
Thurmond, Mary Bell to Calvin Thompson 6-19-1884 L
Thurmond, Mary O. J. to Titus Hoalms 10-18-1862 (no return) Hn
Thurmond, Nancy A. to P. W. Hart 9-11-1873 Dy
Thurmond, Roberta (Mrs.) to Jethro King 4-30-1879 Dy
Thurmond, Sarah C. to John S. Crawford 5-27-1863 (5-28-1863) L
Thurmond, Sarah Caroline to David Ford 7-4-1859 (7-6-1859) L
Thurmond, Sarah L. to N. P. Long 1-26-1866 (1-27-1866) L
Thurmond, Sarah to Daniel Hunt 3-21-1833 (3-26-1833) Hr
Thurston, Elizabeth to Zera Summers 9-30-1863 Hn
Thurston, Margarett to Daniel Watt 4-14-1867 G B
Thurston, Mary G. to Archibald Phillips 11-11-1844 Hn
Thurston, W. M. (Mrs.) to Wm. Wray 6-2-1850 Sh
Tibbadore, Elizabeth to John McCabe 9-26-1885 (10-11-1885) L
Tibbs, Eliza to Lewis Rapoleand 1-10-1876 (no return) Hy
Tibbs, Harriett to Henry Lake 10-6-1876 Hy
Tibbs, Milly to Cornelius Flemming 12-22-1875 (no return) Hy
Tibbs, Neely to Richd. Martin 12-28-1871 Hy
Tibbs, Polly to James Frazier 12-25-1870 Hy

Tice, Mary E. to James F. Greer 2-18-1869 Be
Tickell, Eliza to Edward More 5-30?-1840 (5-5-1840) O
Ticon, Elisabeth to L. Flerms? 7-7-1856 T
Tidwell, D. F. to W. G. Hancock 6-27-1863 O
Tidwell, Eliza J. to Wm. H. Rains 8-1-1848 (no return) F
Tidwell, Lucinda to David Booth 11-30-1865 Mn
Tidwell, Margaret E. to J. R. Williams 2-14-1857 We
Tidwell, Mary E. to Thomas J. Landrum 4-21-1859 O
Tidwell, Mary F. to William Tidwell 12-11-1861 Mn
Tidwell, Mary to John B. Lowry 2-21-1835 (4-27-1835) G
Tidwell, Nancy A. to Phillip G. Scott 11-11-1862 O
Tidwell, Sarah A. to Miners L. Thompson 4-29-1844 (5-7-1844) Ma
Tidwell, Sarah C. to Andrew Myers 6-6-1850 Sh
Tidwell, Susan A. to James E. Landrum 4-232-1859 (4-24-1859) O
Tieran, Cyrian to Bertrand Ibos 1-8-1855 Hn
Tiernan, Celia to Frank Doyle 11-15-1864 Sh
Tiger?, Catherine to Atheriah Gayler 12-3-1834 Hr
Tigert, Mary C. to Washington M. Burrow 8-18-1844 Ma
Tigret, Mary J. to Barnabas Edward 11-9-1853 G
Tigrett, Sarah M. to Hugh B. Robinson 12-19-1838 Ma
Tilden, Lavinia E. (Mrs) to James H. Pye 7-4-1850 Sh
Tildon (Gildon?), Mary to John Winbush 1-5-1884 (1-6-1884) L
Tiles, Elizabeth to T. H. W. Presson 12-13-1861 (12-15-1861) Cr
Tilghman, Adaline to Joseph H. Cortney 6-30-1864 G
Tilghman, C. T. to W. A. White 2-11-1867 G
Tilghman, Cynthia E. to William F. Reed 3-14-1866 G
Tilghman, Elizabeth E. to Washington Needham 1-14-1847 G
Tilghman, Jane to William B. Campbell 11-26-1846 Sh
Tilghman, Mary J. to James A. Clarke 6-18-1856 Hn
Tilghman, Mirna to Franklin Needham 10-13-1846 (10-5?-1846) G
Tilghman, S. J. to J. F. Garrison 2-18-1867 G
Tiller, Lavinia F. to James D. Bryant 1-27-1852 (no return) F
Tiller, R. J. to John F. Able 10-19-1867 (10-23-1867) F
Tilley, Elizabeth C. to R. A. Sims 3-4-1855 We
Tilley, Nancy E. M. to Nathan Petty 10-22-1860 T
Tillman, Caroline to Wm. Cannon 6-11-1861 (6-13-1861) Hr
Tillman, Eliza E. to Gilbert P. Campbell 5-16-1861 We
Tillman, Eliza to John J. Bray 12-2-1854 (no return) We
Tillman, Elizabeth to John Calvin Brown 1-3-1852 (1-11-1852) Hr
Tillman, Lucy A. to Thomas H. Byler 3-16-1869 (no return) L
Tillman, Mahala to Joe Wolfe 3-20-1871 Hy
Tillman, Margarette to J. W. Needham 1-1-1861 G
Tillman, N. R. to J.W. McCord 5-5-1877 (5-9-1877) L
Tillman, Rebecca B. to B. F. Pennington 1-11-1853 (no return) F
Tillman?, Jane A. to James E. Mullin 10-13-1858 Cr
Tilly, Frances N. to William N. Throgmorton 1-12-1859 Hn
Tilman, Addie to R. C. Bradford 2-12-1884 (2-14-1884) L
Tilman, Annie to Thomas Mills 3-27-1880 (3-28-1880) L
Tilman, Emma to Edward Gorene 12-25-1867 G B
Tilman, Emma to Edward Greene 12-25-1867 G B
Tilman, Frances to Wm. Hughes 10-23-1873 T
Tilman, Nancy T.(G?) (Mrs.) to J. M. Clay 2-27-1884 (2-28-1884) L
Tilman, Sarah C. to Alen R. Luck 11-26-1849 (12-5-1849) F
Tilman, Sarah Jane to Charlie Edwards 9-15-1879 L
Tilman, Sarah P. to William D. Butler 10-13-1868 (no return) L
Tilmon, Nancy Ann to Bryant Foster 12-2-1841 Hr
Tilmon, Nancy C. to Henry Bizzell 4-20-1857 Hr
Tilmon, Nancy to J. P. Wright 3-5-1867 (3-10-1867) Cr
Tilor, Jane to Evander Wallis 8-8-1845 We
Tilson, Mary Jane to Isaac T. Humphrey 6-28-1845 Sh
Timberman, Mary J. to Alex'r R. Pool 7-1-1852 O
Timberson, Elizabeth to Richard Carter 7-9-1840 Cr
Timens, Susana to Wm. Glidewell 11-6-1861 (11-7-1861) T
Timmes?, D. A. to W. M. Vail 12-19-1878 Dy
Timmins, Eliza J. to D. W. Reid 12-20-1858 (12-21-1858) Sh
Timmonds, Margaret to John H. Wood 6-5-1862 (6-8-1862) Sh
Timmons, Elizabeth to J. Spitznagel 12-30-1858 Sh
Timmons, M. E. to John E. Moore 10-24-1866 (no return) Hy
Timmons, Nancy M. to Augustus S. Tindell 12-27-1848 L
Timms, Ellen to Silas Johnson 12-21-1864 (12-22-1864) T
Timms, Josephine to James Wilkins 4-21-1868 (4-23-1869?) T
Timms, Leeana to James A. Nolen 12-17-1853 (12-18-1853) Ma
Timms, Lydia A. to C. E. Lee 8-27-1874 T
Timms, Mary Ann to Timothy Glidwell 8-18-1853 Hr
Timms, Mary T. to M. C. Timms 12-28-1871 (12-29-1870?) T
Timms, Mary to Robert Edward 2-15-1830 Ma
Timms, Matilda to Vinson Timms 7-23-1849 Ma
Timms, N. J. to J. W. Daniel 12-15-1874 Dy
Timms, Nancy to Wm. Starnes 7-9-1860 (7-12-1860) T
Timms, Phoebe to John G. Houseman 2-27-1838 Hn
Timms, S. F. to C. C. Byrd 8-11-1874 (8-13-1874) T
Timms?, Sarah Ann to Francis Marion Pennell 1-1-1851 (1-4-1851) T
Tims, Ann to Peter A. Collins 1-18-1842 Hr
Tims, Catherine A. to L. A. Barker 6-3-1871 T
Tims, Irena E. L. to Nathaniel Tims 2-15-1871 T
Tims, Lucinda to thomas Davidson 11-2-1847 (11-3-1847) T
Tims, Lydia to Joel Hammers 8-31-1846 (9-3-1846) Hr

Tims, Matilda to William Starkey 2-11-1829 Ma
Tims, Mattie to Thomas Emmett 7-22-1877 Hy
Tims, Missouri Angeline to Robert Smith 5-2-1857 (5-1?-1857) Ma
Tims, Missouri Ann to George W. Tims 2-27-1856 (2-28-1856) Ma
Tims, Nancy to John Hammers 5-22-1867 T
Tims, Sarah E. to James N. Jackson 2-15-1848 Hr
Tims, Sarah to John Edwards 7-8-1839 (7-10-1839) Ma
Tims, Sarah to William Glidewell 12-17-1840 Ma
Tims, Susan to Nash Glidewell 8-22-1838 (8-23-1838) Ma
Tinbee, Pamelia to Bowlin Watts 4-12-1854 We
Tincle, Catherine to Robert Jackson 1-14-1837 (1-15-1837) G
Tincle, Salley to David B. Dixon 12-8-1824 (12-9-1824) G
Tiner, Jane to H. B. Bradford 8-12-1864 G
Tiner, Martha to R. B. Flowers 8-19-1866 G
Tiner, Nancy E. (Mrs.) to John Lary 5-1-1863 (5-5-1863) O
Tinker, Martha to Joseph R. Matthews 2-9-1868 Be
Tinkle, A. H. to Joab Branson 1-21-1862 G
Tinkle, Cemantha L. to W. H. Wreen 2-28-1860 (3-1-1860) G
Tinkle, Elizabeth to James S. Reager 9-21-1869 G
Tinkle, Letta C. to James M. Kenady 9-5-1855 G
Tinkle, Mary to C. S. Hutchens 11-6-1855 (11-6-1855) G
Tinkle, Sallie E. to W. E. Barker 1-23-1869 G
Tinkle, Sarah M. to P. Jones 4-13-1854 G
Tinkle, Susan M. to Latima Brickhouse 5-10-1854 (5-11-1854) G
Tinley, Rosa to Richard Sneed 5-19-1846 Be
Tinnan, Malina to Saml. D. Mitchell 9-5-1855 (9-8-1855) T
Tinnen, Elizabeth Jane to Nathaniel C. Hoffler 12-12-1853 (12-13-1853) T
Tinnen, Isabel to William Stanford 5-18-1867 (5-19-1867) T
Tinsley, Emma to George Bell 9-7-1872 T
Tinsley, Mary to John C. Byram 10-28-1855 (10-31-1855) Sh
Tinsley, May to F. C. Espey 1-20-1875 (1-22-1875) Dy
Tinsley, Sarah A. to Christopher Jackson 2-20-1867 (2-21-1867) Ma
Tipit, Siss to Napolean B. Chalk 7-6-1862 We
Tipler, Elizabeth to David Reaves 12-28-1840 (12-31-1840) Hr
Tipler, Mary Jane to Nathan M. Burnes 7-31-1846 (8-4-1846) Hr
Tippet, L. to R. Odle 12-12-1842 Be
Tippet, Sarah E. to Parke Smith 12-23-1862 Mn
Tippett, Mary A. to Robert C. Nall 8-25-1859 Sh
Tippett, Rhoda A. to Samuel Robinson 1-6-1861 Be
Tippett, S. A. to G. W. Pratt 1-22-1863 Be
Tipping, Ann M. to Wm. Mitchell 7-25-1864 (7-27-1864) Sh
Tipping, Mary E. to Thos. H. Boswell 11-11-1864 (11-12-1864) Sh
Tipton, A. C. to C. Doherty 10-15-1868 Dy
Tipton, Abigail to William Harris 3-25-1850 O
Tipton, Agnes V. to V. G. Wynn 12-20-1865 Dy
Tipton, Ann D. to James R. Sanford 2-9-1859 T
Tipton, Caroline to Charles Bomar 9-17-1850 Hn
Tipton, Cenus? to Bowlin Adams 12-15-1870 Dy B
Tipton, E. R. to A. W. Tarkington 1-5-1867 (1-7-1867) Dy
Tipton, Elizabeth B. to Nathan P. Thomas 3-30-1846 O
Tipton, Fannie to Edward Fizer 7-23-1874 (no return) Dy
Tipton, Fannie to Louis Barnett 1-3-1877 (1-4-1877) Dy
Tipton, Frankie to Guy Bynan 11-4-1872 (11-5-1872) T
Tipton, Indy to Ephraim Morgan 1-11-1866 T
Tipton, L. J. to Thos. S. Lauderdale 1-30-1861 T
Tipton, Lavenia to James Atkins 2-14-1872 (2-4?-1872) Dy
Tipton, Loutesia to George Gray 1-23-1877 Hy
Tipton, Lucretia to B. Brewer 10-30-1849 (11-2-1849) F
Tipton, M. J. to Jas. G. Raulstone 8-8-1864 O
Tipton, Margaret to Pierce Moore 2-25-1871 (2-26-1871) Dy
Tipton, Martha A. to Stephen M. Corbet 7-27?-1864 7-13-1864 O
Tipton, Martha to Thomas M. Gamble 11-23-1849 (11-29-1849) O
Tipton, Mary Ann E. to Isaac Dillard 3-26-1832 Ma
Tipton, Mary E. to Robt. Selvidge 6-14-1868 G
Tipton, Mary to Amos Jay Matthews 10-29-1846 (11-?-1846) T
Tipton, Mattie E. to H. T. Tipton 2-20-1866 Dy
Tipton, Queen to John W. Lauderdale 11-3-1870 Dy
Tipton, Rozelle to Saml. W. Sanford 12-2-1874 Dy
Tipton, Sallie to Albert Morgan 7-26-1866 T
Tipton, Seraphina C. to LaFayette Hill 11-15-1855 T
Tirill, Susan to Benj. Ezell 2-2-1858 Cr
Tisdale, Arpy? to Wm. H. Crews 2-7-1855 (2-8-1855) Hr
Tisdale, Elizabeth A. F. to Isaac T. Crews 11-5-1853 (11-7-1853) Hr
Tisdale, Elizabeth to David Lofland 4-7-1824 Hr
Tisdale, Ellen T. to Richard S. Biggs 10-17-1874 (10-18-1874) Dy
Tisdale, M. A. to Martin Pierce 12-5-1871 (no return) Dy
Tisdale, Mary Jane to John Crews 12-31-1849 (1-10-1850) Hr
Tisdale, Matilda to Andrew Jackson 12-27-1845 (9?-30-1845) Hr
Tison, Jerldean to J. M. Pemberton 11-11-1864 (no return) Hn
Titcomb, Betsy to Heyborrow? Thompson 5-19-1866 (no return) F B
Tittle, Mar. to W. C. Anderson 5-31-1839 Be
Tittle, Mary to M. Harrison 4-13-1847 Be
Tittleton, Maria to Zebina C. Ewing 3-18-1850 (3-?-1850) Ma
Tittsworth, M. A. to L. C. Madox 7-25-1860 O
Titus, Eliza to Jack Davidson 5-7-1857 Sh B
Titus, Elizabeth to Isaac Jinkens 5-4-1843 Sh
Titus, Mary E. to James H. Edmondson 2-9-1853 Sh

Titus, Matilda to Charlie Sims 9-14-1881 (9-15-1881) L B
Titus, Sarah to James Matthews 10-8-1866 T
Tivool?, Synthia to Alexander Gaines 9-4-1872 T
Toben, Bridget to William Keefe 11-25-1855 Sh
Toben, Katharine to William Crummey 2-8-1858 Sh
Tobin, Sarah to Christopher Lawler 10-10-1860 Sh
Toby, Elizabeth to Gilbert Measles 2-12-1835 Sh
Todd, Adline to J. D. M. Glisson 11-26-1865 Hn
Todd, Amanda to George N. Wilson 8-5-1868 Cr
Todd, Annie to William A. Trotter 4-29-1861 (5-2-1861) Dy
Todd, Arminta J. to George W. Tucker 10-1-1857 Hn
Todd, Caroline to Williams Chapman 3-26-1850 Ma
Todd, E. F. (Mrs.) to W. T. Thomas 10-19-1869 Cr
Todd, Elizabeth to Adam Huntsman 6-13-1829 (6-14-1829) Ma
Todd, Frizzy A. to James H. Lawrence 12-8-1846 (12-9-1846) Ma
Todd, Grizzy Ann R. to John E. King 5-23-1861 Hn
Todd, Icey to Anderson Byars 7-20-1860 (no return) Hn
Todd, J. H. to J. S. Oliver 12-15-1867 Hn
Todd, Jane S. to John S. Watkins 11-8-1843 (11-9-1843) Ma
Todd, Jane to J. C. Kenady 1-13-1846 We
Todd, L. J. to J. L. Todd 3-3-1866 (3-4-1866) F
Todd, Lucy Ann to David G. High 3-1-1859 Hn
Todd, M. A. to J. R. Clemmons 12-29-1875 Dy
Todd, M. Amanda to A. Horton 11-26-1874 Dy
Todd, Margaret J. to Gastin Hailey 12-14-1859 (12-15-1859) Hr
Todd, Mariah to William Daws 12-16-1840 (12-17-1840) Ma
Todd, Martha to Abraham Adams 10-22-1840 Hn
Todd, Martha to Newton Henley 1-11-1872 Cr
Todd, Mary Ann to Thos. J. Lovelace 10-9-1843 We
Todd, Mary E. to Milton B. Ownby 12-30-1858 Hn
Todd, Mary J. to David G. High 11-18-1855 We
Todd, Mary to Joe Shaw 5-28-1884 (5-31-1884) L
Todd, Mary to Wiliam G. Humphrey 2-1-1844 Ma
Todd, Missouri to Joseph C. Pinner 4-20-1870 Dy
Todd, Nancy M. to Nicholas D. Harding 12-18-1866 (12-20-1866) Ma
Todd, Nancy to A. J. Cantrell 9-18-1866 Hn
Todd, Nancy to G. R. Gooch 7-26-1865 (7-27-1865) Dy
Todd, Patience E. to James W. Matheney 3-28-1858 Hn
Todd, Sabrina to M. G. West 9-1-1874 (no return) L
Todd, Sallie H. to Newton C. Perkins 11-13-1861 Sh
Todd, Sarah A. to R. B. Griggs 1-27-1867 G
Todd, Sarah H. to Oscar S. Stephenson 2-12-1845 (no return) Hn
Todd, Sarah to William M. Boon 11-19-1866 (11-22-1866) Ma
Todd, Sarah to William Oliver 4-4-1846 (4-5-1846) Ma
Toddy, Mary C. E. to Amos Latham 12-2-1861 L
Toddy, Mary Louisa to Wm. Jefferson Donelsen? 11-13-1855 (11-15-1855) T
Tolbert, Elizabeth to James Pinson 12-24-1855 Cr
Tolbert, Margarett to Evans Jordon 4-27-1847 Be
Tolbert, Rebecca to John Noel 4-26-1845 (4-27-1845) F
Tolbert, Rosanah H. to James McHenry Campbell 11-30-1864 (12-2-1864) L
Toleson, Arabella to Elisha Crews 6-20-1844 Cr
Toleson, Clady L. to Joseph Eses 12-10-1845 Cr
Toller, Clarissa A. to Josiah Ammons 3-8-1842 (3-16-1842) Hr
Toller, Winneford to Blaney Harper 1-7-1832 G
Tomblinson, Ellen J. to W. L. Burnett 12-20-1852 (no return) F
Tomblinson, Mary to Wm. Akins 5-16-1871 (5-17-1871) Cr
Tombs, J. A. to J. F. Baird 3-8-1860 O
Tombs, Mary to Ara T. Little 1-25-1859 Cr
Tombs, Susan E. to Henry D. Winsett 7-8-1860 Hn
Tombs, Virginia to Green Boden 5-6-1865 (no return) Hn
Tomkins, Rachal M. to J. E. Raybourn (Rayborn) 10-16-1844 (no return) We
Tomlin, Ella to Robert S. Lindsey 10-24-1866 Ma
Tomlin, L. C. to L. C. Crenshaw 5-16-1867 F
Tomlin, Lyde to Jno. T. Botts 12-1-1868 Ma
Tomlin, Margaret C. to John B. Hayley 6-23-1860 (6-27-1860) Ma
Tomlin, Mary Lou to James M. Houston 2-16-1870 Ma
Tomlin, Nancy E. to James T. Hayley 11-6-1856 Ma
Tomlin, Sarah E. to Jos. T. Mann 4-22-1850 Ma
Tomlinson, C. A. to H. P. Guy 8-9-1854 (no return) F
Tomlinson, Caroline to James Flaherty 8-31-1846 (9-1-1846) Ma
Tomlinson, Catharine E. to T. G. Benchbark 7-8-1852 (no return) F
Tomlinson, E. J. to J. H. C. Potter 1-10-1882 (1-11-1883) L
Tomlinson, E. J. to John Guy 7-3-1849 (7-11-1849) F
Tomlinson, M. E. to W. H. Marony 11-16-1876 (11-20-1876) O
Tomlinson, Margaret M.J. (Mrs.) to S. T. Boaz 11-13-1867 (11-14-1867) Cr
Tomlinson, Martha F. to George M. Ferguson 12-24-1867 G
Tomlinson, N. T. to F. J. Thurmond 11-27-1876 (11-28-1876) L
Tomlinson, W. M. to W. J. McGee 12-2-1855 Be
Tompkins, Eliza to N. M. Medlin 11-16-1859 Cr
Tompkins, Mary J. to Samuel B. M. Linny 5-13-1839 Cr
Tompkins, Mary to Henry T. Bain 1-25-1852 Be
Tompkins, Matelada to T. G. Medlen 10-26-1857 (no return) We
Tompkins, Nancy to P. W. Rowlett 1-5-1844 Sh
Tompkins, Susanna to Thomas B. Martin 3-29-1829 Sh
Toney, Susan Frances to James Houston 8-16-1843 Sh
Toof, Fannie E. to T. B. Reynolds 5-25-1857 Sh
Tooke, Ann to C. Leaveque 7-3-1847 Sh

Tool, Ann to Shed Richardson 9-5-1871 T
Toola, Ellen to John Nowlan 5-27-1850 Sh
Tooley, Mary Jane to Isaac P. L. Harris 3-5-1857 O
Toombs, Cinderella E. S. to James M. Sinkler 7-25-1856 O
Toombs, Mary J. to L. W. Pipkins 6-6-1869 G
Toombs, P. to W. F. Rawles 8-27-1872 Dy
Toomey, Catherine to Richard Hickey 11-24-1845 Sh
Tooms, Lucy Ann to Frank M. Walters 12-7-1857 (12-10-1867?) Ma
Tooms, T. S. to B. W. Battle 4-20-1865 G
Toon, Caroline H. to W. H. Bossett (Bopett?) 2-14-1854 Sh
Toone, Adeline to Wesly Stone 8-30-1844 Ma
Toone, Elizabeth R. to James W. Price 4-28-1852 (4-29-1852) Hr
Toone, Mary A. V. to Thomas P. Marsh 12-26-1842 (12-29-1842) Ma
Toone, Mary A. to David Thron 6-8-1857 Hr
Toone, Nannie to Luke Carrington 12-10-1858 (1-11-1859) Hr
Toone, Rebecca J. to Robert J. Pirtle 12-20-1848 (12-21-1848) Hr
Toone, Sarah E. to Isaac W. Pirtle 11-12-1844 (11-14-1844) Hr
Toones, Elizabeth F. to John W. Baker 9-16-1867 (9-18-1867) Ma
Toons, Eliza A. to Robert R. Black 5-10-1855 Hr
Top, Harriett to Sidney Allen 8-3-1870 (no return) Hy
Topp, Catharine Elizabeth to Wm. B. Ross 5-25-1861 Sh
Topp, Matilda to John Simpson 6-1-1867 (6-10-1867) Dy
Tops, Caroline to Tom Ford 8-30-1870 (no return) Hy
Torbet, Lucretia to John Martin 3-6-1842 Hn
Torian, Sarah A. to M. J. Johnson 1-7-1861 (1-8-1861) Sh
Torrance, Julia Ann to James Welborn Teague 12-18-1860 (12-19-1860) F
Torrence, Malinda to G. Graves 9-22-1849 (11-27-1849) F
Torrence, Nancy to Robert Flemming 2-21-1859 (2-23-1859) F
Torrey, Francis G. to Chas. J. Turnbull 2-23-1856 (2-24-1856) Sh
Torry, Molly P. to C. A. Beehn 8-12-1861 (8-13-1861) Sh
Tosh, Emeritta to William A. Williams 12-11-1865 (12-12-1865) Cr
Tosh, Maranda to Wm. A. Terrill 11-16-1873 Hy
Tosh, Margaret to A. W. Rowark 2-9-1859 Cr
Tosh, Margaret to George R. Phillips 11-10-1853 Cr
Tosh, Marizila to P. S. Hamilton 12-6-1858 Cr
Tosh, Mary J. to M. W. Wilson 8-14-1844 (no return) Cr
Tosh, Nancy to John Z. Kelly 1-10-1866 Cr
Tosh, Tabatha to John W. Sellers 1-25-1853 Cr
Tosh, Z. L. to J. M. Kelly 12-19-1872 Cr
Toten, Margarett to Washington Scallion 10-12-1836 (10-13-1836) G
Totten, Callie E. to Baker C. Springfield 11-23-1869 (11-24-1869) Ma
Totten, Elizabeth C. to David A. Golden 12-11-1847 (12-13-1847) O
Totten, Judith M. to Collins L. Bradley 6-4-1834 O
Totten, Matilda to Milichi Watts 11-13-1830 O
Totten, Sallie C. to Nicholas Lewis Allen 3-6-1830 O
Totty, Cynthia to Robert Carter 10-21-1844 Hn
Totty, N. Catharine to Wm. H. Fuller 7-9-1855 (7-19-1855) T
Tourant, M. to Chas. Edmonds Vioujas (Virugus?) 12-1-1859 Sh
Towell?, Mattie V. to R. H. Harrison 5-5-1856 T
Towery, Hariet J. to W. C. Hutchins 4-4-1868 (4-6-1868) Cr
Towls, Lucey A. to E.H. Freear 4-29-1853 (no return) F
Townes, Amanda M. to W. J. Kerr 12-17-1867 (12-19-1867) Cr
Townes, Belle to Henry Williams 9-18-1878 (9-25-1878) L B
Townes, Judy to Abe Winrow 9-5-1878 (9-6-1878) L B
Townes, Mary to J. Dennis Moore 5-4-1866 (5-6-1866) Cr
Towns, E. C. to J. C. Trainer 3-7-1871 (3-8-1871) Cr
Towns, Isabella to A. W. King 8-29-1851 (no return) Hn
Towns, M. E. (Mrs.) to Jack G. Jackson 12-1-1868 G
Towns, Mollie E. to C. C. Harris 12-25-1865 (no return) Cr
Towns, Susan to Elisha T. Uzzell 1-31-1834 Sh
Towns, Virginia C. to P. M. Wallick 10-14-1867 (10-16-1867) Cr
Towns, W. F. to W. G. Richardson 11-26-1872 (11-27-1872) Cr
Townsel, M. A. to W. W. Stoker 2-8-1867 Cr
Townsell, Mary to Green Adams 8-20-1845 Be
Townsend, Amanda to George W. Towsend 4-8-1864 (4-9-1864) Cr
Townsend, Caroline Elizabeth to William Goodrum 7-12-1849 T
Townsend, Emeline S. to Jos. C. Hindman 2-2-1870 T
Townsend, Frances E. to Oliver B. Farris 12-29-1865 (12-31-1865) T
Townsend, Jane to Rubin A. Embrey 3-7-1835 Hr
Townsend, Louisa to Robt. Thompson Foster 12-1-1851 (12-4-1851) T
Townsend, Lucetta P. to P. E. Tisdale 10-10-1857 (10-15-1857) T
Townsend, Lucy A. to John S. McNeal 11-23-1857 (11-26-1857) T
Townsend, Luisa to H. A. Lemaire 7-9-1863 Be
Townsend, Maria Ketuna to Peter Townsend 2-6-1850 (2-7-1850) T
Townsend, Martha to Balis Forrest 11-21-1844 Be
Townsend, Mary Ann to John A. Jones 8-5-1840 (8-9-1840) Hr
Townsend, Mary E. to Charles J. Allen 6-23-1835 Hr
Townsend, Mary Jane to Daniel Mordecai Rhodes 8-11-1846 (8-?-1846) T
Townsend, Minerva to John Fennell 5-21-1870 (5-22-1870) Ma
Townsend, Miss Mary Ann to Adam Rode 5-20-1874 T
Townsend, Nancy E. to George W. W. Townsend 8-2-1865 T
Townsend, Nancy to Pleasant Job 5-17-1832 Sh
Townsend, Polly to John C. Manuell 12-18-1827 Hr
Townsend, R. to N. Pearce 11-25-1841 Be
Townsend, Rice to Samuel Green 6-15-1872 (no return) L
Townsend, Sarah ANn to James Cicero Rhodes 7-23-1844 (7-?-1844) T
Townsend, Sarah E. to Anderson J. Anderson 7-12-1869 (7-13-1869) T

Townsend, Sarah E. to Andrew J. Anderson 7-12-1867 T
Townsend, Susan Ann to Benjamin Forest 3-17-1851 Be
Townsend, Susanna W. to Aaron S. Bell 2-11-1851 (2-13-1851) T
Townson, Mary A. to Young Shoot 3-3-1847 Cr
Townzel, Molly Catherine to Charles Thos. Wilkins 5-20-1870 (5-22-1870) Ma
Townzen, Polly Ann to Jesse Taylor 11-2-1853 Be
Towsend, Elizabeth to Wm. B. Spoon 1-2-1866 (1-5-1866) Cr
Trabucco, Gerolima to Carlo Lagomargino 4-10-1858 (4-11-1858) Sh
Traftor, Elizabeth to John H. Robinson 12-25-1849 (12-27-1849) G
Trail, Nancy Jane to John A. Wilson 1-8-1861 Hy
Trail, Sallie N. to J. D. Shoemate 6-21-1871 Hy
Trainer, Sarah A. to Adolphus B. Wilson 2-22-1869 (2-24-1869) F
Transon, Fannie to Light Forrest 2-2-1877 Hy
Transon, Laura to Green Senter 12-8-1869 G
Transou, C. J. to Victor M. Harris 7-6-1858 (7-7-1858) Ma
Trantham, M. E. to H. L. Edwards 10-23-1875 (10-24-1875) O
Trantham, Maria to Elihu Withers 3-15-1838 Hn
Trantham, Melissa to West Wilkins 5-19-1840 T
Trantham, Nancy W. to Samuel Newberry 9-25-1844 (no return) We
Trantham, Tabitha C. to Westley Owen 9-27-1848 Hn
Tranthan, Isabella P. to Francis E. Bennett 3-3-1858 (3-4-1858) Sh
Tranthum, Nancy to Isaiah Paliner? 5-31-1838 Hn
Trap, Synthia to John Lucas 6-23-1850 Sh
Trapp, Julia E. to Sam B. Carver 5-15-1860 (5-16-1860) Sh
Traub, Mary A. V. to James Kimble 5-24-1838 Sh
Travis, Amandia A. to William H. Butler 8-21-1862 Be
Travis, Ann to Ute S. Halliburton 7-23-1855 G
Travis, Annis to George Patterson 5-17-1866 Hn B
Travis, Caroline to James A. Craig 8-14-1860 Hn
Travis, Caroline to John A. Burton 12-30-1843 (no return) Hn
Travis, Debu to Henry Patterson 5-20-1866 Hn B
Travis, Elizabeth to Patrick O'Keeffe 11-27-1859 Sh
Travis, Harriet C. to Jessie James 10-8-1847 Hn
Travis, Louisa Joice to James A. Quinn 5-29-1847 Cr
Travis, Lucy E. to R. S. Harris 8-30-1854 We
Travis, Margaret to James Loveing 7-17-1836 O
Travis, Martha A. to Cezar Porter 5-15-1866 Hn B
Travis, Martha to I. G. Harris 7-6-1843 Hn
Travis, Mary G. to John Crutchfield 12-31-1840 Hn
Travis, Mary Jane to Gloster Worsham 5-20-1866 Hn
Travis, Rachel to Job Dorris 12-16-1866 Hn B
Travis, S. E. to T. D. McKinzie 10-20-1868 (10-22-1868) Cr
Travis, Sarah Millington to Wesley Warren 8-6-1839 (no return) Hn
Travis, Sarah to John S. McDearmon 4-2-1854 Hn
Travis, Susan E. to John Reece 1-26-1867 (1-30-1867) Cr
Trawick, Harriett to G. M. Robinson 11-20-1851 Cr
Trawick, Martha Ann to John R. Read 10-28-1845 Cr
Trayler, Pamelia to George Jamison? 10-20-1855 (10-25-1855) T
Traylor, Ann to W. W. Galbreath 5-6-1867 (5-7-1867) T
Traylor, Caraline to Charles A. Combes 1-26-1848 (1-27-1848) F
Traylor, Margaret A. to Peter A. Avant 2-19-1855 (2-21-1855) Hr
Traylor, Mary to W. P. Brown 12-21-1871 Hy
Traylor, Sarah L. to James M. Curlin 4-10-1861 T
Traylor, Tilda to H. C. Adkins 7-30-1870 (7-31-1870) Cr
Trayner, Margarett to Harmon Simpson 1-8-1833 (1-9-1833) G
Traynor, Lucinda to Wm. Pritchett 6-7-1838 G
Traywick, Cheesa J. to Izer Lanbinck 11-10-1852 Cr
Traywick, Jane to Samuel Neal 5-18-1869 (5-20-1869) Cr
Traywick, Manerva C. to Sidney A. Johnson 9-26-1866 (10-4-1866) Cr
Traywick, S. F. to J. N. Warbritton 2-5-1870 (2-6-1870) Cr
Treadaway, Caroline to Willis Davis 10-24-1874 (10-25-1874) T
Treadaway, M. M. to W. Riley Peel 2-22-1873 (2-25-1873) Dy
Treadwell, Emily to Marion E. Hudson 12-7-1842 Sh
Trease, Elizabeth to S. A. Larrell 2-21-1863 Mn
Tredwell, Drucilla R. to Stephen English 1-9-1841 Sh
Treese, Ann to W. L. Glenn 7-26-1859 (7-28-1859) Hr
Treese, Issabella to Thomas Kerr 10-17-1854 (10-18-1854) Hr
Trent, Emily to Wesley Baxter 7-6-1867 (7-7-1867) F B
Trent, Jennie to Henry Stainback 7-13-1866 (not executed) F B
Trent, Louisa C. to James A. Anderson 5-24-1852 (no return) F
Trent, Maggie to W. C. (Rev.) Gray 5-11-1863 (5-20-1863) F
Trent, S. J. to Edward Wilkerson 12-31-1849 Hn
Trent, Tabby to Dandrage Farris 12-1-1868 (12-27-1868) F B
Trentham, Nancy to Richard Martin 10-30-1872 (10-31-1872) T
Trenton, Eliza A. to F. Berners 4-24-1861 Hn
Treumen, Mulinda to Samuel Blackley 1-28-1837 (2-2-1837) G
Trevathan, Adaline to William B. Winsett 5-5-1859 Hn
Trevathan, K. A. to W. W. Cleaver 4-5-1854 (no return) Hn
Trevathan, Mary to S. M. Hobby 6-16-1867 Hn
Trezavent, Virginia L. to William Harrison 8-16-1870 Ma
Trezevant, Anna F. to Geo. P. C. Rumbough 5-17-1859 (5-18-1859) Sh
Trezevant, Elizabeth C. to George Keim 4-24-1856 Sh *
Trezevant, Ora C. to Rich'd H., jr. Parham 2-2-1858 (2-3-1858) Sh
Trezevant, Rachael to M. C. Young 5-8-1861 (5-9-1861) Sh
Trezevant, Susie to Walton Watkins 10-17-1871 (10-18-1871) Ma
Trezvant, Lucyann to James T. Fuller 7-25-1848 (no return) F
Tribbe, Victoria to Gerard Marcela 1-6-1863 Sh

Trice, Augusta B. to Henry J. Price 6-2-1859 Sh
Trice, Augusta to Randal M. Irwin 11-16-1854 Sh
Trice, Flora to George Young 12-17-1870 Hy
Trice, Louisa R. to James L. Dickey 11-20-1850 Sh
Trice, Mary F. to A. R. Coleman 8-1-1853 Cr
Trice, Sarah (Mrs.) to A. Baxter 11-17-1846 Sh
Trice, Susan (Mrs.) to John R. Murchison 10-4-1869 (10-5-1869) Ma
Trice, Z. M. to Joseph C. Hancock 11-13-1844 We
Trigg, Caroline to Frank Sexton 9-18-1871 (9-25-1871) T
Trigg, Catharine J. to Frank Williams 7-31-1854 Sh
Trigg, Charlett to Daniel Pews 7-2-1872 (7-13-1872) T
Trigg, Claricy to Phill Smith 7-2-1872 (9-30-1872) T
Trigg, Elizabeth R. to Edward Irby 4-1-1859 (4-5-1859) Sh
Trigg, Famy to Matt Archey 7-2-1872 (7-13-1872) T
Trigg, Lizzie J. to Henry C. Walker 3-22-1852 Sh
Trigg, Lucy Jane to Charles A. Stockley 5-13-1846 Sh
Trigg, Mary F. to George Floyd 1-31-1855 We
Trigg, Phebe to Aaron Kelly 11-27-1872 (12-16-1873?) T
Trigg, Rachael C. to John O. McGehee 2-14-1850 Sh
Trigg, Sarah (Mrs.) to C. S. Palmore 3-3-1858 (3-10-1858) Sh
Triggs, Julia A. to John Ciger 4-5-1856 We
Trim (Grim), Susan Elizabeth to Marion Pitts 2-13-1858 O
Trim, Louisa to R. M. Prater 9-12-1868 (9-15-1868) T
Trimble (Tamble?), Leila G. to J. Bell Ferguson 11-30-1882 L
Trimble, Alice J. to Thomas J. Tilman 1-19-1882 L
Trimble, Emmaline to John W. Summer 2-21-1843 (no return) Hn
Trimble, Julia E. to Wesley Evans 5-17-1861 O
Trimble, M. E. to L. D. Wallace 2-28-1869 Hy
Trimble, Mary to Atlas Cook ?-13-1852 We
Trimble, Mollie to D. B. Tanner 12-6-1869 Hy
Trimble, Pamelia to Bowlen Watt 4-12-1854 We
Trimm?, Mary to G. W. Redden 9-?-1874 (9-22-1874) T
Trip, Amanda to Horace Williamson 2-10-1866 (2-17-1866) F B
Trip, Mary Jane to Lewis Miller 12-25-1867 (12-28-1867) F B
Trip?, Virginia to Chas. H. Hicks 12-27-1870 Hy
Tripp, Amelia to James Beasley 2-23-1867 (3-4-1867) F B
Tripp, C. S. to J. P. Hilliard 3-24-1866 (1-1?-1866) F
Tripp, Emily A. to Howel T. Pollard 9-14-1844 Sh
Tripp, Salina to John Milton 3-10-1857 Sh
Trobaugh, Elizabeth to M. A. Slone 12-22-1874 (12-23-1874) T
Trobough, D. R. to J. G. McBride 2-22-1869 (2-27-1869) T
Trobough, D. W. to D. L. McBride 6-16-1866 (6-20-1866) T
Trobough, Elizabeth J. to Jacob Sullivan 12-21-1842 (12-23-1842) T
Trobough, Elizabeth to Albert Adkins 4-14-1866 T
Trobough, Jiffy R. to J. C. Goforth 1-3-1866 (1-1?-1866) T
Trobough, Martha P. to Wm. N. Edwards 8-20-1861 (8-22-1861) Sh
Trobough, Mary E. to N. M. Lindsey 2-28-1862 T
Trobough, Nancy to Newman Bland 12-9-1865 T
Trobough, Nancy to Willis Morrow? 10-8-1873 T
Trosdale, L. A. to Ned Crenshaw 9-8-1874 T
Trosper, Jane to Scarlet M. Glascock 9-15-1838 (9-16-1838) G
Trosper, Mary A. to Thompson Edmundson 9-14-1857 G
Trosper, Mulindy to John Edmundson 8-25-1838 (8-30-1838) G
Trotman, Junior to Geo. Macafee 1-3-1869 Hy
Trotter, Caroline to John H. Boult 12-9-1839 (12-19-1839) F
Trotter, Cornelia F. to James S. Evans 1-28-1851 (1-29-1851) F
Trotter, Elizabeth J. to Thomas L. Organ 10-1-1844 (10-9-1844) F
Trotter, Frances E. to Zachary Shaw 3-20-1855 (no return) F
Trotter, Manervy Ann to Presley D. Boyed 10-28-1852 (no return) F
Trotter, Martha A. to C. B. Mayo 4-1-1878 (4-9-1850) F
Trotter, Mary Eliza to C. W. Richardson 2-17-1845 (no return) F
Trotter, Mary V. to J. T. Z. Hilliard 9-24-1860 (9-25-1860) F
Trotter, Matilda P. to Richard Vaughan 1-8-1840 (1-10-1840) F
Trotter, Mildred E. to Samuel J. Hawkins 5-15-1855 Sh
Trought, Martha J. to Robert P. Jones 12-24-1849 Cr
Trousdale, Ann to Samuel Gladney 3-13-1829 Ma
Trousdale, Candis to Henry Seymour 12-29-1868 F B
Trousdale, Emily to Caswell Edwards 1-7-1867 F B
Trousdale, Florenza A. to S. A. Haywood 11-3-1866 (no return) Hn
Trousdale, Lucy Ann to John Landis 2-28-1850 Hn
Trousdale, Mailsey Jane to Wm. Montgomery no date (with 11-1874) T
Trousdale, Martha to John Cave 2-24-1855 Hy
Trousdale, Mary E. to William D. Landis 4-24-1856 Hn
Trousdale, Viola to R. S. Callaway 9-13-1841 (no return) Hn
Trout, Amanda C. to John R. Cock 4-12-1867 G
Trout, Elizabeth to Jefferson Robertson 12-28-1840 (12-31-1841) G
Trout, Elizabeth to John McSharp 1-9-1846 (1-12-1846) G
Trout, J. A. to W. G. Hearn 6-5-1873 Dy
Trout, Jane to John B. McRee 8-13-1863 G
Trout, Mollie E. to Samuel Lewis 8-6-1862 G
Trout, Nancy J. to James H. Fields 10-31-1842 G
Trout, Polly to J. H. Smith 10-4-1871 (no return) Dy
Trout, Sarah A. to Henry F. Reed 12-19-1846 (1-6-1847) G
Trout, T. A. to B. D. Simms 2-1-1865 G
Trowbridge, Elisabeth M. to Joseph B. Parks 5-22-1852 (5-23-1852) Sh
Troxer, Winnie M. to William Terrill 3-12-1874 Hy
Troy, M. to J. R. Whittenton 8-26-1869 (8-27-1869) Dy

Truehart, Elizabeth O. to Edward Burnly 2-5-1851 Sh
Truehart, Maria Louisa to Robert H. McKay 4-10-1857 (4-13-1857) Sh
Truel, Lucinda to David Wright 4-7-1870 Hy
Truett(Pruett), Elizabeth to John Reed 3-18-1828 Hr
Truit, Eliza to James Lynn 1-26-1859 Sh
Truitt, Agnes to Wesley H. Lauderdale 3-26-1869 (4-4-1869) T
Trule (Trub?), Mary to Benjamin Dolle (Dobb?) 7-26-1855 Sh
Trulove, Mary to James Rucker 12-23-1873 Hy
Truman, Catharine E. to John C. Hartsfield 10-3-1853 (10-4-1853) G
Trumball, Annie Z. to B. E. Hammar 10-29-1860 (10-30-1860) Sh
Trump, Elizabeth to John Brown 6-23-1826 Sh
Trumpy, Sophie Louise to Moreau Brewer 12-24-1857 Sh
Truob, Barbara to Melchior Pfyfer 5-30-1868 (6-5-1869?) Ma
Trusdale, Martha Ann to Mansfield Rhodes 11-6-1869 (11-7-1869) T
Trusdale, Sina Ann to Moses Weathers 12-30-1873 (12-3?-1873) T
Trusdile, Mary to Danil Branch 11-4-1871 (11-5-1872?) T
Trusty, Ann to Josiah Singleton 5-19-1853 O
Trusty, Tabitha to John W. NIcholson 1-29-1845 Sh
Tubbs, Adeline to Thomas V. Lee 8-22-1854 Sh
Tubbs, Elizabeth to Marion McGill 12-28-1853 Be
Tubbs, Malinda to Joseph Naremore 1-31-1867 Be
Tubbs, Martha to Augustin Brunche 12-2-1849 Sh
Tubbs, Mary to Geo. W. Parks 6-8-1854 Be
Tubbs, Rhoda Jane to Nathan F. Hartley 4-1-1857 Sh
Tubbs, Susan to George Hicks 12-25-1866 Be
Tuberville, Martha A. to James A. Fowler 12-22-1858 We
Tuberville, Mira to Alexander Stewart 5-12-1827 (5-15-1827) Hr
Tuck, Elizabeth to Thomas W. Parker 10-21-1858 We
Tuck, Martha Ann to E. H. Rawls 10-23-1860 We
Tuck, S. E. to Benjamin D. Hynds 1-15-1862 We
Tucker, A. J. to L. P. Pickard 12-16-1865 (12-20-___) O
Tucker, Addie A. to M. Rhea 12-14-1870 F
Tucker, Alice G. to William B. Edwards 1-28-1867 Ma
Tucker, Alice to George Harris 7-15-1878 Hy
Tucker, Allice A. to Thomas P. Edings 10-15-1859 (10-18-1859) T
Tucker, Amanda E. to M. Shoemake 6-13-1850 (6-23-1850) L
Tucker, Ann E. to David E. Palmer 1-27-1852 (no return) F
Tucker, Ann Jane to Bird Wolverton 10-27-1835 Hr
Tucker, Annie to Jacob I. Taylor 9-12-1873 Hy
Tucker, Becca to Allen Mann 10-28-1874 Hy
Tucker, Bettie to Chesley Burch 12-14-1873 Hy
Tucker, Caroline to John B. Lissey 5-3-1860 Cr
Tucker, Catherine to Charley Mitchel 12-24-1868 (12-26-1868) F B
Tucker, Clara to Wm. Poindexter 8-10-1866 (8-12-1866) F B
Tucker, Cornelia A. to B. S. Mathis 11-8-1866 Hn
Tucker, Cornelia A. to W. M. Brizendine 12-30-1865 (no return) Hn
Tucker, Dollie to Willis Smith 10-19-1870 (10-10?-1870) Dy B
Tucker, E. C. to J. B. Trout 3-25-1867 (2?-28-1867) Dy
Tucker, E. M. to J. S. Curtis 9-3-1860 (no return) Hy
Tucker, E. R. to J. L. Banks 9-18-1872 Dy
Tucker, Eliz. Murphy to Henry M. Turnage 10-14-1850 (10-16-1850) T
Tucker, Eliza to Doc Price 12-29-1870 (no return) Dy
Tucker, Elizabeth A. to J. H. Fuqua 12-13-1869 (12-15-1869) Cr
Tucker, Elizabeth O. to Jas. A. Harris 12-15-1866 (12-6?-1866) T
Tucker, Elizabeth W. to Joseph J. Wright 3-8-1831 Sh
Tucker, Elizabeth to C. L. Culpepper 1-31-1856 Hn
Tucker, Elizabeth to Irvin Dorset 4-28-1865 G
Tucker, Elizabeth to Willis S. Pruett 12-18-1851 Sh
Tucker, Ella (Mrs.) to John Webb 12-24-1866 (12-25-1866) Dy
Tucker, Ella to John Dunn 4-25-1878 Hy
Tucker, Ester to James McGowen 7-30-1831 Sh
Tucker, F. B. to J. L. Baynes 6-23-1859 (6-30-1859) Sh
Tucker, F. L. to W. H. Cook 10-12-1865 Hy
Tucker, Fanny to Moses Forest 12-4-1868 (no return) Hy
Tucker, Frances E. to Joseph S. Tucker 8-23-1869 (8-24-1869) T
Tucker, Frances M. to John G. Mears 6-18-1860 (6-29-1860) T
Tucker, Frances V. to W. F. Bowers 11-24-1856 (11-25-1856) T
Tucker, Frances to Robert J. Johnson 12-29-1852 L
Tucker, Harriet F. to W. E. McDearmen 7-13-1869 (7-15-1869) L
Tucker, Harriet to Harry Grimm 1-3-1872 (1-4-1872) Dy
Tucker, Harriet to James R. Fulkerson 7-30-1852 (8-5-1852) L
Tucker, Helen to Cannon Smith Wooton 9-28-1843 T
Tucker, Hulen H. to William A. Tucker 12-20-1867 (12-23-1867) T
Tucker, Jennie to Isaac A. Harris 12-24-1873 (12-25-1873) Dy
Tucker, Judy to Ned Dearmore 2-8-1877 Dy
Tucker, K. J. (Mrs.) to G. S. Sims 11-22-1860 (11-25-1860) Sh
Tucker, Laura to Alex Beaumont 8-11-1870 Dy
Tucker, Laura to Geo. Bradshaw 11-25-1875 Dy
Tucker, Lina to Isiah Boylan 4-8-1871 (no return) F B
Tucker, Lucinda to George Kenny 1-11-1834 (1-13-1834) Hr
Tucker, Lucy A. to Alfred M. Harper 11-5-1867 (no return) Dy
Tucker, Lucy Ann to George W. Little 11-?l-1844 (no return) Hn
Tucker, Lucy E. to Dossey Harrell 12-22-1862 (12-23-1862) Dy
Tucker, Lucy to Major F. Cook 4-28-1880 T
Tucker, Lucy to William Bell 11-7-1878 (no return) Dy
Tucker, M. A. to A. B. (Dr.) Haskins 5-19-1873 (no return) Dy
Tucker, M. A. to J. L. Sims 12-25-1869 G

Tucker, M. B. to B. Caraway 1-8-1866 G
Tucker, Margarette L. to Lewis Penny 2-11-1856 (2-13-1856) G
Tucker, Mariah C. to Robert Strain 1-27-1859 L
Tucker, Martha (Mrs.) to E. R. Midgett 10-19-1867 (no return) Hy
Tucker, Martha F. to John F. Ray 8-5-1862 (8-19-1862) Dy
Tucker, Martha J. to George J. Malone 10-8-1859 (no return) Hn
Tucker, Martha T. to W. H. Sims 5-19-1864 G
Tucker, Martha to E. O. Shelton 10-8-1849 (10-17-1849) F
Tucker, Martha to James O. Golden 1-9-1859 Hn
Tucker, Martha to Waddy S. Tatum 3-9-1844 (3-13-1844) L
Tucker, Mary A. to Jasper T. Stokes 12-20-1853 Cr
Tucker, Mary Ann to Robt. R. Bogguss 9-6-1875 (9-9-1875) Dy
Tucker, Mary B. to Frank H. Williams 5-24-1856 Sh
Tucker, Mary E. to Wiley Durden 11-14-1870 (11-15-1870) F
Tucker, Mary E. to Y. B. Turner 11-19-1866 (11-20-1866) T
Tucker, Mary F. to Robert Bogle 2-21-1844 (2-22-1844) G
Tucker, Mary F. to Wm. H. Bullington 8-8-1858 Cr
Tucker, Mary J. to Enoch Needham 1-31-1861 G
Tucker, Mary L. to John H. Thurmond 6-21-1847 (no return) L
Tucker, Mary to Ephram Klutt 11-27-1850 (no return) Hn
Tucker, Mary to Isaac A. Ing 6-8-1866 G
Tucker, Mary to Wm. A. Rodgers 7-8-1841 Cr
Tucker, Mat to Geo. Poindexter 1-1-1868 (1-2-1868) F B
Tucker, Mira to Hugh Debow 12-25-1861 (12-26-1862?) O
Tucker, Mirah J. to John D. Hafford 11-17-1868 L
Tucker, Mollie J. to James P. Tucker 9-4-1862 Hy
Tucker, N. C. to J. F. Halfacre 1-2-1883 (1-3-1883) L
Tucker, Nancy E. to J. R. Ross 1-24-1856 Hn
Tucker, Nancy Jane to Henry J. Mailey 1-23-1851 T
Tucker, Nannie to George Rogers 8-7-1874 (8-12-1874) Dy
Tucker, Nerva to Adam Brown 7-13-1867 (8-3-1867) F B
Tucker, Noon? to Peter Connell 8-9-1877 Dy
Tucker, P. A. to W. A. Matheny 9-29-1868 (10-1-1868) Cr
Tucker, Polly A. to Joshua Macklin 12-24-1870 (no return) F B
Tucker, R. M. to Sam'l W. McMurry 4-16-1872 (4-18-1872) O
Tucker, Rose to Horace Peete 4-13-1872 Hy
Tucker, Rose to John Cabness 3-17-1869 (no return) F B
Tucker, S. E. D. to W. T. Lee 8-7-1870 G
Tucker, S. E. to R. a. Bailey 6-20-1868 G
Tucker, Sallie Ann to Jessie Tucker 4-10-1869 (4-11-1869) F B
Tucker, Sally Anna to Phillip Young 12-24-1866 (no return) F B
Tucker, Sally to Henry Ashley 2-18-1869 (2-21-1869) F B
Tucker, Sarah A. to Daniel Collins 8-23-1865 (8-28-1865) O
Tucker, Sarah J. to Samuel Morrow 10-1-1860 (10-10-1860) Dy
Tucker, Sarah O. to M. D. Ozier 10-2-1855 (10-4-1855) Ma
Tucker, Sarah to Absalom Warson (Watson) 5-10-1849 Sh
Tucker, Sarah to Dred Brown 12-22-1876 Hy
Tucker, Sarah to Granville Taylor 12-25-1877 (12-27-1877) Dy
Tucker, Sarah to Green Faby 5-8-1831 Sh
Tucker, Susan to S. M. Scott 3-5-1862 Hn
Tucker, Susan to V. Caraway 2-8-1866 G
Tucker, Virginia to William H. Cooper 4-30-1860 (no return) We
Tucker, Zenobia? to Dave Baxter 2-1-1877 Dy
Tucker?, Virginia to J. F. Bratton 1-4-1870 (1-5-1870) L
Tuckniss, Jennie R. to A. T. Hilliard 12-1-1866 (12-2-1866) F
Tudor, Celia to Harmon Cocke 12-28-1829 (12-31-1829) Hr
Tuel, Polly to Daniel Sparks 9-17-1827 Ma
Tuff, Amanda (Mrs.) to Thos. Moore 3-3-1864 (3-6-1864) Sh
Tuggall, Margaret A. to Samuel S. Brannon? 9-4-1846 Hn
Tuggall, Margaret to Samuel S. Brannon 5-26-1846 (no return) Hn
Tuggle, Arnetta to Henry Jones 3-13-1874 Hy
Tuggle, M. J. P. to Eli Northern 12-3-1846 Hn
Tuggle, Maria J. to Joel Mann 4-19-1860 (no return) Hy
Tuggle, Maria to Berny Moore 10-6-1866 (no return) Hy
Tuggle, Mony to Jim Perkins 8-8-1867 Hy
Tuggle, Polly Ann to Stephen Dennis 12-8-1842 Hn
Tugwell, Harriet to Baily Jarrett 4-3-1869 Hy
Tugwell, Nancy P. to Robert Traylor 6-25-1864 Hy
Tuley, A. E. to J. H. Pierce 1-29-1861 (2-1-1861) O
Tull(Taber?), Elizabeth Martin to Robt. Kyle 12-16-1835 Hr
Tull, A. K. to William Kennedy 12-22-1879 (12-24-1880?) L
Tull, Elizabeth to Craven L. Taylor 11-7-1854 Hr
Tull, J. A. to E. Cantwell 2-26-1881 (no return) L
Tull, Maaranda A. to William Kennedy 3-16-1875 (3-18-1875) L
Tull, Mahala to John M. King 1-16-1874 (1-19-1874) L
Tull, Parthenia Adaline to James Duncan 4-8-1879 L
Tulley, Mary Jane to Isaac P. L. Morris 3-5-1857 O
Tully, Mary E. to Jeramiath Veltilla 3-11-1839 Cr
Tumage, Jane to Alfred Richard 1-14-1871 T
Tumage, Malvina to Rufus Henderson 3-16-1871 (3-19-1871) Dy
Tumbough, Charity to P. M. Tipton 8-3-1843 F
Tune, Jane to Joseph R. Edwards 9-17-1849 (9-19-1849) O
Tune, Mary to Joseph A. Swindle 3-15-1837 (3-16-1837) Hr
Tuning?(Luning?), Julia Ann to Wyatte Harlon 9-19-1850 Hr
Tunstull, Fanny to Daniel Mathis 1-11-1868 Hy
Turbeville, Elinord to James Moore 9-28-1857 Hn
Turbeville, Elsa to Austin Greene 12-26-1867 Hn B

Turbeville, Henrietta S. to John D. Turbeville 12-25-1867 Hn
Turbeville, Lucinda to C. F. Turbeville 2-12-1851 Hn
Turbeville, M. E. to Benjamin Lewis 1-28-1856 (no return) Hn
Turbeville, Martha A. to Isaiah A. Pryor 5-23-1855 Hn
Turbeville, Mary E. to George W. Wright 8-28-1854 (no return) Hn
Turbeville, Nancy Jane to Thomas L. Darnell 9-3-1857 Hn
Turbeville, Oliver B. to Thomas P. Hare 1-10-1848 (1-13-1848) F
Turbeville, Susan R. to Isaac C. Stow 10-24-1861 We
Turbin, Donia to Mack Hazel 12-4-1880 (12-5-1880) L B
Turk, Sarah E. to Javan H. Maddox 4-21-1852 O
Turk, Sary E. to H. Maddox Javan 4-21-1852 O
Turley, Irene to James Cobourn 2-24-1857 (2-25-1857) Ma
Turley, L. A. to E. Arnold 1-25-1859 (2-21-1859) Sh
Turley, Mary E. to Thomas W. Harris 3-24-1842 Ma
Turlington, Eliza to Anderson B. Harris 12-4-1845 Sh
Turlington, Ellen G. to Jonathan Ready 8-4-1853 Sh
Turlington, Mary L. to C. D. Madding 6-1-1845 Sh
Turnage, Adeline to Frank Seward 2-17-1869 (2-21-1869) F B
Turnage, Ann to Amos Grimm 4-7-1877 (4-9-1877) Dy
Turnage, Bettie to Ephran P. Fletcher 5-27-1867 (6-2-1867) T
Turnage, Christinna to Thomas C. Lane 3-4-1852 (3-8-1852) Ma
Turnage, Dinkie to Umphrey Law 4-16-1872 (4-18-1872) Dy
Turnage, E. M. to J. S. Bowles 3-21-1871 (3-23-1872?) T
Turnage, Elizabeth W. to George W. Rogers 1-11-1841 (1-12-1841) T
Turnage, Henrietta to Mark Grizzard 3-10-1873 (3-13-1873) T
Turnage, Julia Catharine to James N. Smith 4-17-1850 T
Turnage, Lee R. to Archibald Henderson Taylor 6-30-1858 Sh
Turnage, Margaret C. to William Delashmet 12-1-1840 (12-2-1840) T
Turnage, Margaret to John Boyd 8-13-1873 (8-14-1873) T
Turnage, Mary Amanda to Albert Gallatin Lanton 12-16-1843 (12-22-1843) T
Turnage, Miss L. G. to M. L. Delashmit 12-16-1874 (12-17-1874) T
Turnage, N. W. to J. D. Smith 1-7-1861 (1-10-1861) T
Turnage, Narcissa to John A. Cathey 11-19-1835 Sh
Turnage, S. to Henry Thomas 12-24-1873 (12-27-1873) T
Turnage, Sarah P. to Solomon R. Forbess 1-26-1870 (1-27-1870) T
Turnage, Verlinske B. to George W. Delashmet 12-7-1867 (12-10-1867) T
Turnbow, Alletha T. to G. W. Tatum 9-28-1852 (no return) F
Turnbow, Sarah Jane to Bennett Sanders 5-24-1863 Hn
Turnbull, Mary to Wm. H. Ladd 5-16-1855 Sh
Turner, A. Jane to Henry Standback 4-30-1868 G B
Turner, Adaline S. to Hudson C. Graves 2-22-1844 (2-26-1844) Ma
Turner, Adaline to David Leak 11-2-1869 O
Turner, Adaline to Isaiah Carter 12-23-1846 (no return) We
Turner, Alice to A. S. Thompson 1-31-1886 L
Turner, Alice to Gentry Springfield 8-1-1883 (8-2-1883) L
Turner, Amanda S. to Alfred Deets 9-15-1846 Hn
Turner, America I. to Lemuel D. Bright 1-19-1860 We
Turner, Angeline to William Martin 12-25-1855 We
Turner, Ann H. to Henry T. Burnam 6-3-1841 (6-9-1841) G
Turner, Ann to Joseph Thuman 12-9-1830 Ma
Turner, Anna to John Baker 12-22-1869 (no return) L
Turner, Annie to William Waddy 12-23-1871 (12-24-1871) Dy
Turner, B. P. to Richard Daughirda 8-29-1861 We
Turner, Becca to Stephen Graves 12-30-1874 (no return) L B
Turner, Berlinda to John B. Hogg 3-28-1839 G
Turner, Bettie Ann to E. B. Lewis 11-7-1867 (no return) Hn
Turner, Bettie to Nathan Thomas 8-6-1867 (no return) L B
Turner, Callie to Charles Jones 10-21-1874 T
Turner, Catherine to Jonah Hyde 1-6-1870 G B
Turner, Cherry to Rush Barnes 6-12-1878 Hy
Turner, Clarissa to John Watkins 11-24-1840 Hn
Turner, Cornelia C. to John D. Elliott 9-9-1856 (9-10-1856) Sh
Turner, D. T. to H. C. Tomlinson 6-14-1865 (6-15-1865) F
Turner, Delila to Jonathan Laney 5-23-1828 Ma
Turner, Dicey to John Higgins 8-28-1869 Hy
Turner, E. A. to W. L. E. North 8-6-1869 (no return) Hy
Turner, E. C. to L. H. Malone 10-4-1867 (10-6-1867) Cr
Turner, E. E. to Robert Anderson 1-31-1865 Be
Turner, E. H. to H. E. Newsom 4-18-1861 Mn
Turner, E. W. to J. W. Averett 8-14-1873 O
Turner, Easter to Thomas Lee 12-30-1873 (12-3?-1873) T
Turner, Edy to William J. Hill 2-27-1843 Hr
Turner, Elenor M. to Travis E. Hall 9-27-1850 G
Turner, Eliza J. to Wm. L. Forrest 5-10-1845 (no return) Cr
Turner, Eliza Jane to J. W. Thomason 9-15-1862 (no return) Hn
Turner, Eliza to J. T. Miller (Minton?) 8-24-1869 L
Turner, Elizabeth J. to John C. Robinson 12-23-1848 (12-26-1848) Hr
Turner, Elizabeth W. to James Y. McGuire 8-11-1845 (8-12-1845) Hr
Turner, Elizabeth to D. C. Askew 1-7-1860 Be
Turner, Elizabeth to George T. Blincon (Blucon) 9-1-1836 Sh
Turner, Elizabeth to Isaac R. Harris 6-18-1850 Hr
Turner, Elizabeth to James McCulloch 6-7-1849 Hn
Turner, Elizabeth to Vanburen Coldwell 9-10-1870 Hy
Turner, Ella Lee to E. L. Ruth 11-12-1879 L
Turner, Ella to Ransom Morris 1-20-1873 Hy
Turner, Ellen to Philip Winrow 2-7-1874 (no return) L B
Turner, Emeline to Wm. H. H. Kearney 3-20-1866 (3-22-1866) Ma

Turner, Emly to Henry C. Travis 2-4-1860 We
Turner, Estell to Thos. A. Ewell 2-9-1870 (2-10-1870) F B
Turner, Eveline to Tillman Duncan 7-27-1874 T
Turner, Fannie C. to James S. Maley 12-31-1866 (1-1-1867) T
Turner, Fanny to Charles Brown (Bronn?) 6-9-1869 (6-10-1869) L B
Turner, Fanny to William Smith 2-17-1869 (2-20-1869) F B
Turner, Frances to Samuel R. Brooks 10-13-1852 Hr
Turner, Francis S. to William Tilton 1-22-1861 Sh
Turner, H. A. to W. F. Foulks 1-15-1874 O
Turner, Harriet N. to Armstead H. Fisher 12-12-1857 (12-15-1857) L
Turner, Harriet to Jack Johnson 12-26-1867 Hy
Turner, Harriet to John Hester 3-3-1842 (no return) Hn
Turner, Hester Ann to Harrison L. Fitzpatrick 12-12-1871 (12-13-1871) L
Turner, Jane M. to John T. Lindsey 12-18-1836 Sh
Turner, Jane to Andrew Jackson Pewit 11-11-1856 (11-4?-1856) L
Turner, Jane to W. H. Davis 12-29-1868 G B
Turner, Jennie E. to Flavius J. Penn 9-4-1864 G
Turner, Julia to York Seward 9-20-1868 G B
Turner, Katie to L. L. Rice 2-28-1885 (3-1-1885) L
Turner, Laura A. to W. T. Drumwright 12-9-1874 L
Turner, Lizzie to George Thompson 10-15-1883 (10-20-1883) L
Turner, Lou to William Hughes 12-21-1868 (12-23-1868) L
Turner, Loucinda A. to John Morris 6-21-1854 We
Turner, Louisa to Daniel Webster 12-25-1869 (12-31-1869) F B
Turner, Louisa to James Hutchinson 12-15-1856 (12-16-1856) O
Turner, Lovey A. to M. A. Hall 1-25-1869 (no return) Dy
Turner, Lucretia to Cicero Beaty 2-25-1861 Hr
Turner, Luisa G. to Matthew Ward 6-19-1842 Hn
Turner, Lydia J. to William B. Binyon 2-21-1843 G
Turner, M. E. to D. W. Draper 1-12-1870 G
Turner, M. E. to R. A. Presson 10-9-1871 (no return) Cr
Turner, M. J. E. to J. C. Baker 2-1-1881 L
Turner, M. J. to Geo. H. Cary 10-29-1863 O
Turner, M. J. to W. D. Stewart 12-30-1879 (12-31-1879) L
Turner, M. S. to W. C. Gammon 12-28-1867 O
Turner, M. Z. to A. M. Dupree 12-31-1879 (1-1-1880) L
Turner, Margaret E. to John W. Summers 10-1-1870 (10-6-1870) F
Turner, Margaret E. to M. A. Robbins 1-5-1876 Dy
Turner, Margaret J. to Charles F. Miller 5-6-1873 L
Turner, Margaret Jane to James A. Eadleman 3-17-1870 G
Turner, Margarett E. to Marcus Clay 1-18-1859 (1-20-1859) G
Turner, Margarett to E. A. Freeman 12-20-1855 We
Turner, Margarett to G. W. Yarbrough 5-13-1873 (5-14-1873) Cr
Turner, Mariah to Berry Sims 1-31-1872 (no return) L
Turner, Marian to Gambrill Cox 9-13-1830 (9-16-1830) Ma
Turner, Martha E. to B. R. Cole 12-30-1866 Be
Turner, Martha L.? to James L. Childress 12-16-1867 (12-18-1867) Cr
Turner, Martha to Charles Weaver 11-26-1860 Hy
Turner, Martha to E. P. Strickland 5-24-1854 (no return) L
Turner, Martha to J. W. Barker 3-11-1860 Be
Turner, Martha to Peter Curtin 12-23-1880 L
Turner, Martha to Tom Purty 2-8-1868 L B
Turner, Martha to William Demoss 8-12-1875 (8-13-1875) L
Turner, Martha to William Hunt 3-26-1850 (3-28-1850) G
Turner, Mary A. to Ollen Boyte 12-12-1848 (12-21-1848) Hr
Turner, Mary Ann to Lodwick(Ridwick) Moore 10-18-1848 (10-19-1848) Hr
Turner, Mary E. to A. H. Taylor 11-26-1861 G
Turner, Mary E. to John Chandler 4-9-1866 (4-12-1866) Cr
Turner, Mary E. to John W. Barham 12-20-1865 Hy
Turner, Mary E. to John W. Bonds 1-2-1860 (1-3-1860) Sh
Turner, Mary J. to Major Ferrell 1-24-1843 G
Turner, Mary Jane to C. H. Wright 8-30-1860 (9-4-1860) Cr
Turner, Mary Jane to William J. Miller 3-9-1852 (no return) F
Turner, Mary Jane to William L. Graves 12-27-1854 (12-28-1854) Ma
Turner, Mary to Beal Short 1-30-1872 Hy
Turner, Mary to F. M. Groghan 7-4-1874 (7-5-1874) L
Turner, Mary to J. J. Owens 11-11-1876 (11-14-1876) Dy
Turner, Mary to James Newman 7-18-1849 Sh
Turner, Mary to John B. Travis 8-4-1842 Cr
Turner, Mary to Robert Holland 11-6-1867 T
Turner, Matilda J. to Joseph White 11-11-1851 Sh
Turner, Mattie S. to Chas. S. Taliaferro 3-16-1870 Hy
Turner, Mattie T. to J. K. P. Wyatt 11-1-1865 G
Turner, Missouri S. to Rodwier? J. Boyers 5-19-1843 (5-21-1843) F
Turner, Mollie E. to W. T. Werner 6-22-1871 Hy
Turner, Mollie V. to Phillip Cole 2-1-1868 Ma
Turner, Nancy E. to Thomas I. Farris 11-9-1866 (11-10-1866) O
Turner, Nancy to Cains Campbell 12-16-1828 Ma
Turner, Nancy to Richard Mitchell 11-20-1846 (no return) Hn
Turner, Nancy to Samuel Cruse 2-9-1857 We
Turner, Nannie E. to James L. Hickox 11-6-1867 Hy
Turner, Patience to Wiley R. Lake 2-2-1859 Hn
Turner, Patsy A. to H. Banks 8-18-1869 G
Turner, Penny to Pat Burford 12-29-1875 (no return) Hy
Turner, Piggy to Harry Clay 1-31-1872 (no return) L B
Turner, Rebecca J. to James W. Cooper 11-18-1860 Hn
Turner, Rebecca to Willis Cage 1-2-1881? (1-4-1882) L B
Turner, Rhoda to John B. Travis 9-27-1840 Cr
Turner, Roda A. P. to Jesse Morris 12-3-1855 We
Turner, S. C. to E. B. Stewart 10-12-1878 (no return) L
Turner, S. V. to J. D. Pate 10-8-1867 (10-10-1867) Cr
Turner, Sallie B. to B. D. Burch 5-12-1860 T
Turner, Sallie to A. J. Cooper, sr. 6-20-1869 G
Turner, Sallie to Allen Thompson 1-3-1872 L
Turner, Sarah A. to E. W. Kirkland 3-24-1867 G
Turner, Sarah Ann to W. J. Yarbrough 12-18-1865 (12-20-1866?) Cr
Turner, Sarah C. to Andrew Hart 4-16-1860 Dy
Turner, Sarah Jane to Wm. J. Todd 3-14-1846 We
Turner, Sarah to Robt. Allison 11-5-1861 Sh
Turner, Sharlott E. to James F. Kellebrew 2-21-1858 We
Turner, Sisan? to Nathan Winbush 1-5-1884 (1-6-1884) L
Turner, Susan S. to Samuel J. Wilson 12-26-1864 (12-29-1864) Sh
Turner, Susan to Ben Tatum 8-29-1873 Hy
Turner, Susan to George Fullen 12-27-1877 L
Turner, Susan to John Bennett 3-25-1873 (3-27-1873) O
Turner, Susan to Zack Harris 6-20-1869 G B
Turner, Z. T. to S. D. Verhines 1-28-1873 (1-29-1873) O
Turner?, Rebecca Ann to Jefferso Jameson 12-13-1862 (no return) Hn
Turney, J. E. M. to R. W. Mitchell 2-10-1875 (2-19-1875) Dy
Turnham (Turnbow), Elizabeth to James S. Moore 6-21-1831 (7-23-1831) O
Turnham, Emeline to John Moore 7-13-1859 O
Turnham, Martha C. to Joel Moore 11-4-1844 (11-7-1844) O
Turnipseed, Clara to David Sanderford 2-10-1870 G B
Turnley, Emeline to Ned Jones 1-11-1868 F B
Turnley, Kittie to James Taylor 5-18-1867 F B
Turnley, Leathy to Alfred Pearson 11-19-1867 F B
Turnley, Viola to W. W. Sorrell 10-23-1877 (10-24-1877) Dy
Turpin, Caron Ann to J. J. Fielder 9-1-1838 (9-4-1838) G
Turpin, Jackan to Ichabold M. Lucas 1-18-1845 (no return) L
Turpin, Jane to Sam Borum 4-16-1885 (4-16-1886?) L
Turpin, Mary A. to D. A. Bruce 2-6-1861 Be
Turpin, Mary Jane to William C. Brandford 3-24-1853 Hn
Turpin, Mary to Isaac J. Doughty 8-15-1839 Hn
Turpin, Willie to William Henderson 3-1-1876 (no return) Hy
Turrentine, M. E. to J. W. Trout 12-20-1866 (12-23-1866) Dy
Turrentine, Mary I. to Wm. L. Hendricks 9-16-1869 G
Tutor (Lutor), Mary J. to Thomas A. Atkerson 10-16-1844 We
Tuttle, Elizabeth to Moses L. Bolin 12-5-1866 Hn
Tuttle, Frances to John T. Vanhook 7-22-1849 Hn
Tuttle, Rebecca to Eli Murphy 7-4-1826 (7-5-1826) Hr
Twain, Mary C. to H. McAdams 12-1-1856 Cr
Tweedle, Sophronia to Peyton Hall 12-29-1874 (12-28?-1874) T
Tweedy, Martha A. to Thomas Miller 1-14-1826 (1-16-1826) Ma
Tweety, Louisa to Solomon Nunn 1-4-1871 (no return) Hy
Twiford, Elizabeth to Benjamin W. Hill 8-7-1850 Sh
Twigg, Fannie A. to Richard M. Bullock 1-10-1860 (no return) We
Twigg, Mary I. to James Caldwell 9-21-1859 We
Twigg, Rebecca to Allen Dunagan 5-15-1847 (5-16-1847) G
Twilla, Margaret Ann to John B. McIntosh 1-24-1878 Dy
Twilla, Victoria to Sid Anderson 7-16-1870 (7-17-1870) Dy
Twisdale, A. E. to Henry Holoway 12-26-1859 (12-28-1859) T
Twisdale, Ann Eliza to Henry Halaway 12-26-1859 T
Twisdale, Fannie to C. Malone 1-3-1870 T
Twisdale, Martha Ann to John Calvin Settle 6-22-1850 (6-25-1850) T
Twiss, Nancy C. to Charles Bard 11-19-1857 We
Twyford, Ann to John H. Rea 11-14-1843 Sh
Twyford, Catherine to Martin Shelton 12-25-1849 Sh
Twyford, Martha J. to G. B. Dane 5-5-1853 Sh
Twyford, Nancy Ellen to Isaac W. Keller 12-4-1856 (3-18-1857) Sh
Twyman, Mima to H. H. Walker 2-11-1873 T
Tyas, Elvira to Alfonzo Colwell 4-22-1878 (no return) L B
Tyas, Emma to Alexander Fullen 12-25-1876 (by 1-1-1877) L
Tyas, Lou to L. Nelson 12-24-1883 (12-26-1883) L
Tyas, Mollie to George Peebles 1-21-1884 (1-23-1884) L
Tyler, America W. to H. Gurley 5-28-1840 O
Tyler, Ann E. to James H. Weaks 4-11-1851 G
Tyler, Granada to David J. Williford 1-5-1870 (1-6-1870) Ma
Tyler, Helen W. to V. D. Clarke 10-26-1848 O
Tyler, Julia C. to Silvester Bailey 3-28-1833 Hr
Tyler, M. C. to D. P. W. Alexandner 12-19-1866 G
Tyler, Mary A. to Hiram Kail 1-17-1866 Hy
Tyler, Mary Jane to George W. Jones 12-7-1852 (12-9-1852) G
Tyler, Mary W. to Robert A. Lewis 1-22-1855 (1-23-1855) O
Tyler, Perney E. to John M. Bolls 7-28-1857 (7-30-1857) G
Tyler, Sarah Ann to William LaBone 12-2-1844 Sh
Tyler, Sarah J. to Elgie Wilkerson 11-8-1877 Hy
Tyler, Susan to C. C. Sims 7-23-1861 G
Tylor, Helen W. to Obediah Clark 10-26-1848 O
Tylor, Martha A. to Guy S. Miles 4-12-1840 O
Tyner, Julia Ann to Wynn Shelton 11-7-1850 Ma
Tyner, Sarah Ann to Joseph Douglas 12-20-1863 Be
Tyner, Sarah Jane to W. Camp 2-21-1861 Be
Tyner, Sarah R. to William H. Watson 2-4-1843 (2-10-1843) Ma
Tyner, Susan A. to D. W. Alexander 12-25-1874 (12-27-1874) O

Tynes, Elnore A. to Samuel J. House 1-9-1871 (1-10-1871) Cr
Tyree, N. C. to R. E. Cooper 12-24-1860 G
Tyree, Susan to John Warfield 7-8-18__ (probably 1870) G B
Tyree?, Mary Louisa to Jas. W. Trobough 10-24-1856 (10-25-1855?) T
Tyrer, Lavince R. to A. J. Brake 11-2-1859 (11-3-1859) O
Tyrus, Sarah M. to John Smith 12-14-1836 Sh *
Tysen, Margaret (Mrs.) to James Allen Taylor 9-14-1869 (9-16-1869) Ma
Tyser, Mary E. to I. H. Harelson 2-24-1872 (2-25-1872) O
Tyson, Caroline to Samuel Hutton 4-4-1850 Sh
Tyson, E. A. to Needham H. T. 1-8-1859 (1-9-1859) G
Tyson, Eliza Ann to John Fly 4-23-1830 Ma
Tyson, Elizabeth to Constantine Terrell 12-11-1872 Hy
Tyson, Ellen to W. R. Johnson 9-15-1860 (9-20-1860) Sh
Tyson, Exeline to Woodward Howell 11-3-1840 O
Tyson, Frances to William Lankston 10-25-1872 O
Tyson, H. J. to J. W. Dodd 10-4-1869 G
Tyson, Hannah to Wilson Stewart 1-12-1871 Hy
Tyson, Laura to Solmon Daniel 12-3-1871 Hy
Tyson, Lucinda to John L. Key 3-18-1862 Hn
Tyson, Lydia Ann to John R. Alston 3-8-1831 Ma
Tyson, Lydia to Robert C. Tilghman 10-31-1851 G
Tyson, M. A. to W. B. Tilghman 3-28-1866 G
Tyson, Mahala to A. J. Tilghman 10-21-1845 (10-29-1845) G
Tyson, Margaret to Charles Curry 3-19-1873 Hy
Tyson, Margarett to Wm. N. Mitchell 12-5-1837 G
Tyson, Mariah to Thomas J. Valentine 7-3-1857 (no return) Hn
Tyson, Mary A. to Henderson Conlee 3-7-1828 (3-13-1828) G
Tyson, Mary A. to James? H. Beard 12-14-1848 Hn
Tyson, Mary E. to William F. Floyd 1-16-1854 G
Tyson, Mary J. to Leroy C. Gillispie 10-28-1845 (11-1-1845) Ma
Tyson, Mary to James Read 3-15-1877 Hy
Tyson, Matilda to James Wilson 2-6-1851 (2-9-1851) G
Tyson, Nancy to Peter Scott 12-26-1853 Hn
Tyson, S. to A. N. Reed 11-23-1850 O
Tyson, Sarah to Charles W. Cate 12-16-1845 (12-10?-1845) Ma
Tyson, Virginia A. to Samuel S. Cowsert 1-25-1856 (1-27-1856) O
Tyus, Adaline to Sam Thomas 10-5-1871 Hy
Tyus, Bet to John Jarrett 2-5-1868 Hy
Tyus, Caroline to George Turner 6-12-1875 Hy
Tyus, Cherry to William Gause 3-27-1874 (no return) Hy
Tyus, Cina to Charlie Williams 12-10-1878 Hy
Tyus, Clarissa to Matt Smith 8-12-1875 Hy
Tyus, Eliza J. to B. D. McClaren 10-20-1847 Sh
Tyus, Eliza to Geo. Turner 7-25-1872 Hy
Tyus, Eliza to Wm. Lee 12-12-1877 Hy
Tyus, Em Eliza to John Cunningham 11-24-1875 (no return) Hy
Tyus, Flora A. to Sive Graves 3-10-1870 Hy
Tyus, Harriet to Abe Burch 12-23-1878 Hy
Tyus, Henrietta to Matt Hawkins 2-19-1878 (no return) Hy
Tyus, Henryetta to Sandy Green 11-6-1875 (no return) Hy
Tyus, Lucy to Dick Moris 3-9-1872 Hy
Tyus, M. L. (Mrs.) to John Furgerson 1-28-1873 Hy
Tyus, Martha to Joseph Flowers 1-26-1875 Hy
Tyus, Mary Ann to James Blackwell 7-21-1862 (7-22-1862) L
Tyus, Mary E. to Buford Yancy 12-26-1870 Hy
Tyus, Mary G. to William H. Kimble 11-30-1842 Sh
Tyus, Mary to Fillmore Fergason 2-14-1878 Hy
Tyus, Mattie H. to William H. Klyce 10-15-1863 (no return) Hy
Tyus, Rebeca to Wyatt Turner 12-16-1869 Hy
Tyus, Salina to George Palmer 4-10-1869 (no return) Hy
Tyus, Sue (Lue) to George Page 4-4-1868 (no return) Hy
Tyus, Virginia to Henry Tyus 12-6-1873 Hy

Ulcer (Alcey), Lovely to Samuel Martin 7-13-1843 Sh
Ullman, Emma to William Hartlage 9-3-1864 Sh
Ulmo, Cornelia to R. W. Havens 11-24-1858 Sh
Umhold, Henriette Sophia to Chas. Alte 8-2-1861 Sh
Umphrey, Elizabeth to H. A. Robinson 9-28-1855 Cr
Umphrey, Martha to Elien Ligh 11-26-1856 Cr
Umphries, Sophia to Robert Taylor 3-2-1865 (3-8-1865) L
Umpstead, Augustina to John D. Montgomery 4-12-1849 Cr
Umpstead, Melony? to J. E. Hampton 3-11-1856 Cr
Umstard, Mary A. to William E. Jackson 8-12-1846 G
Umstard, Winaford to William M. Bratton 5-6-1848 (5-9-1848) G
Umstead, Arminta to John Parrish 8-7-1845 Cr
Umstead, Lucinda to George W. Lee 6-1-1846 (6-3-1846) G
Umstead, Mary to Samuel Parrish 9-5-1848 Cr
Umstead, Partenia J. to John M. Holt 11-1-1848 (11-2-1848) G
Umstead, Rebecka to Samuel Shane 12-5-1831 G
Umsted, B. J. to J. L. Harder 10-5-1858 G
Umsted, Malvina to Peter Shelton 1-21-1869 G B
Umsted, Mollie P. to E. J. Witt 9-18-1869 G
Umsted, R. A. to J. E. Simpson 4-22-1868 G
Umsted, Susan to D. C. Harris 11-20-1854 (11-21-1854) G
Underhill, Mrs. to Wm. E. Jones 12-16-1859 Sh
Underwood, Amanda E. to William D. Temus 7-4-1860 We
Underwood, Amy M. to Robert M. Kirk 10-14-1858 (no return) Hn
Underwood, Cynthia to Thomas S. Estill 8-22-1824 Sh
Underwood, Eleanora to W. H. Fitch, jr. 10-3-1857 (10-6-1857) Sh
Underwood, Eliza J. to Henry D. Harper 11-28-1842 G
Underwood, Eliza J. to Richardson Brewster 7-16-1856 (7-17-1856) Sh
Underwood, Elizabeth to J. B. Myers 1-17-1854 Hn
Underwood, Emily to Thomas Crafton 5-23-1868 G B
Underwood, Fredonia to William M. James 10-29-1851 Sh
Underwood, Julia Ann to David N. Underwood 5-2-1863 Hn
Underwood, Louisa to G. B. Norman 4-14-1857 (no return) We
Underwood, Lucy Jane to Samuel Cloud 5-13-1858 Ma
Underwood, Martha A. to Josiah L. Wade 10-6-1853 (10-7-1853) G
Underwood, Martha to Robert L. Yancey 10-21-1861 (10-22-1861) Sh
Underwood, Mary C. to James C. McCraig 9-6-1853 (9-?-1853) G
Underwood, Mary E. to Lemuel Watson 9-26-1863 (10-?-1863) O
Underwood, Mary Jane to Joshua R. Petty 2-20-1850 Hn
Underwood, Mary to Joseph Holloman 9-14-1848 G
Underwood, Melinda to Madison Head 3-13-1833 Sh
Underwood, Minerva J. to Samuel J. Page 5-22-1858 We
Underwood, Penelope to James Moore 9-4-1856 We
Underwood, Sarah A. to Milton C. Jones 6-19-1865 Hn
Underwood, Sarah E. to George H. Lucus 2-1-1876 L
Underwood, Sarah to George W. Fisher 5-5-1855 Cr
Underwood, Susan E. to W. H. H. Hawkins 3-6-1861 O
Underwood, Valenta to Boyd Bailey 4-1-1892 Sh
Underwood, sr., Polly (Mrs.) to William J. Newbern 5-2-1844 G
Uninger, Rosina to John Leck 9-29-1854 Sh
Unninger, Caroline to John Ringwold 8-9-1858 Sh
Upchurch, Abarilla to L. L. Hendricks 11-1-1859 Hn
Upchurch, Adaline to Henry Jones 7-14-1872 (7-15-1872) T
Upchurch, America to Thomas Y. Willeford 12-30-1846 Hn
Upchurch, Angeline to George T. Diggs 1-10-1861 Hn
Upchurch, Ariel to A. C. Wright 8-30-1863 Hn
Upchurch, Barbara J. to George R. Grisham 3-16-1848 (no return) Hn
Upchurch, Catherine to Peter Snider 5-6-1847 Hn
Upchurch, Elia E. to Thomas J. Wynns 2-29-1848 Hn
Upchurch, Elizabeth C. to Joseph A. Dacus 7-25-1866 (7-26-1866) T
Upchurch, Elizabeth to James R. Meaks 1-4-1848 Hn
Upchurch, Elizabeth to Simeon Hunt 5-25-1856 Hn
Upchurch, Frances J. to John S. Gamlin 6-10-1865 Hn
Upchurch, Hariet to Westley Simmons 10-20-1858 Hn
Upchurch, Jeanette to Thomas L. Darnell 3-5-1848 Hn
Upchurch, L. A. to A. M. Owen 1-15-1862 T
Upchurch, Lucy A. to Richard Norred 2-4-1848 Hn
Upchurch, M. to John A. McCloud 8-10-1862 Hn
Upchurch, Mahala to James James 6-2-1851 Hn
Upchurch, Martha to Samuel Hewitt 5-2-1828 (5-4-1828) O
Upchurch, Mary J. to Jourden Aycock 10-13-1846 Hn
Upchurch, Maryland to Isaac S. Roberts 6-18-1857 Hn
Upchurch, Mrs. Sarah to Thos. B. Walk 1-5-1865 Hn
Upchurch, Nancy C. to Hewitt Weaks 5-5-1853 Hn
Upchurch, Nancy C. to John F. Lee 1-1-1852 Hn
Upchurch, Nancy to James Ables Whittaker 6-24-1856 Hn
Upchurch, Polly to Thomas F. Lilly 12-4-1845 Hn
Upchurch, S. J. to Vincent P. Kelley 12-30-1858 T
Upchurch, Sarah Ann to Daniel Frazier 9-2-1838 Hn
Upchurch, Sarah Ann to S. E. Emery 12-28-1864 Hn
Upchurch, Sarah J. to Vincent P. Kelley 12-30-1858 T
Upchurch, Sarah to George W. Jackson 11-1-1854 Hn
Upchurch, Susan to James Bradford 11-6-1849 Hn
Uprchurch, Keran H. to W. R. Weeks 9-15-1859 Hn
Upshaw, Ann E. to A. H. Adams 12-3-1847 F
Upshaw, H. R. W. to J. B. Ragland 4-28-1860 (5-1-1860) Sh
Upshaw, Manivesy E. to Oliver P. Stout 1-2-1843 Hn
Upshaw, Mary V. M. to Carson R. Dalton 1-21-1857 Sh
Upshaw, Sarah M. to W. P. Hughes 3-2-1861 (3-4-1861) O
Upstead, Rebecca to Andrew B. Hampton 12-30-1855 Cr
Uptegrove, M. A. to John M. Smith 7-24-1865 Be
Uptengrow, Hanna C. to Elija Pinkston 10-24-1855 Cr
Uptergrove, Jane to Wm. S. Butler 8-30-1854 Cr
Uptergrove, Susan to Andrew Robinson 3-13-1853 Cr
Upton, Ann C. to John N. Peebles 5-12-1853 Hn
Upton, Bettie S. to R. A. Newbill 8-26-1868 (no return) Cr
Upton, Eveline to Bushrod Hicks 6-7-1843 Hn
Upton, Mary Ann to Josiah Teague 10-19-1852 (10-20-1852) Hr
Upton, Mary J to John Q. Miller 5-12-1860 (5-13-1860) O
Upton, Mary to Thos. G. N. Smith 12-7-1854 Ma
Upton, Matilda to Shevarts Hurst 10-31-1842 (10-4?-1842) Ma
Urbey(Irby), Mary to J. S. Smith 4-20-1865 Be
Urbey, Mary E. to George W. Cheatham 11-15-1860 (no return) We
Urbey, Nancy C. to Carroll C. Simmons 11-1-1860 (no return) We
Uric, Ellen to August Riebert 12-31-1855 Sh
Ursery, Elizabeth to Joseph Teddleton 8-9-1867 (8-10-1867) Ma
Ursery, Jane to Alsey Jordon 11-20-1845 (11-27-1845) Ma
Ursery, Sarah A. to Thomas G. May 10-31-1855 (11-1-1855) Ma
Ursery, Susan M. to William B. Johnson 8-2-1855 (8-9-1855) Ma
Ury, Lucinda to Anthony Dailey 7-27-1866 O
Usery, Lucy to James C. Bradford 10-5-1844 Ma

Usery, Mary E. to John W. Usery 9-24-1870 (9-27-1870) Ma
Usery, Mary Elizabeth to Washington Bryant 4-30-1854 Hr
Usery, Sarah to William Johnson 1-13-1848 Ma
Usher, Ann to John jr. Lax 2-26-1849 (2-27-1849) Hr
Usher, Eliza J. to Darius Robinson 1-17-1843 Hr
Usher, Nancy C. to Cannon Smith 12-22-1848 (12-20?-1848) Hr
Usher, Rebecca A. to Geo. L. Whitmore 11-10-1845 (11-12-1845) Hr
Usher, Sarah to David Gordon 3-21-1827 G
Usher, Sarah to Thomas H. Hancock 2-9-1848 (2-10-1848) Hr
Ussery, Elizabeth to J. M> Reeves 12-17-1860 (12-19-1860) Hr
Ussery, Martha A. to Wm. T. Lee 11-16-1860 Hr
Ussery, Matilda F. to John H. Webster 7-15-1861 (7-18-1861) Hr
Ussery, Sarah J. to Wm. A. Cardwell 1-12-1857 Hr
Utley, A. J. to T. G. Tittle 3-20-1842 Be
Utley, E. E. to John W. Green 6-9-1868 G
Utley, Elizabeth E. to D. A. Gossett 1-7-1869 Be
Utley, Jane to Silas Hawkins 2-14-1868 G B
Utley, Louisa S. to Felix F. Reaves 7-16-1846 Be
Utley, M. C. to A. Marchbanks 12-21-1842 Be
Utley, M. C. to T. H. R. Jett 12-7-1844 Be
Utley, Martha to W. S. Cooper 5-22-1865 (no return) Cr
Utley, Nancy A. to Robert M. Moore 12-13-1849 Cr
Utley, Sarah C. to Joseph Summers 8-25-1862 Be
Utley, Sue to Andrew Taylor 9-14-1870 (9-15-1870) Ma
Utley, Syntha to W. C. Campbell? 11-22-1848 Be
Utley, T. A. to F. M. Utley 2-5-1867 Hy
Utley, Viola to T. A. Corbitt 2-17-1858 Be
Utley?, Martha to B. A. Denny 10-15-1866 (10-17-1866) Cr
Uty, Phredonia A. to C. H. Thompson 3-26-1854 Be
Vaden, Adalin to Gideon Goodrich 10-18-1855 We
Vaden, Angelina M. to William R. Jett 5-26-1847 Sh
Vaden, Dorithy Frances to Alexander Mobley 2-1-1849 G
Vaden, Ellen to Oliver Belew 1-16-1869 G
Vaden, Hannah W. to Thomas J. Hailey 10-28-1858 G
Vaden, Henritta A. to John E. Gleason 7-14-1859 G
Vaden, Martha Jane to A. T. Robertson 10-27-1845 (11-2-1845) Hr
Vaden, Martha S. to Albert W. Bledsoe 10-31-1843 G
Vaden, Mary Jane to Samuel A. Jones 11-5-1853 G
Vaden, Mary M. to Samuel J. Dunn 12-22-1837 Sh
Vaden, Virginia H. to Joseph K. Waddy 9-20-1851 (9-24-1851) Sh
Vagts, Augusta (Mrs.) to Cristean Hug 12-3-1864 (12-4-1864) Ma
Vaiden, Matilda E. to George E. Moore 1-2-1872 (1-3-1871?) L
Vail, Elosie? to John Pew 7-28-1869 (7-30-1869) Dy
Vail, Emma to Joseph W. Duffey 7-?-1871 (7-28-1871) Ma
Vail, Harriet R. to Nathaniel W. Warren 4-2-1864 (4-4-1864) Dy
Vail, Jane to John Robinson 1-22-1848 (1-23-1848) Ma
Vail, Nancy to Lafayette Daniel 8-3-1847 Hn
Vail, Sarah C. to E. H. Sandlin 3-3-1870 Dy
Vails, Amanda M. to Wm. F. Roberts 12-12-1839 Hr
Vails, Ann J. C. to Augustus Astin 4-26-1854 (4-27-1854) Sh
Vails, Arrena to Gabriel Dillard 12-26-1837 Hr
Vails, Elizabeth to Robert Campbell 2-27-1847 Hr
Vails, Louisa to Wm. H. Owens 12-29-1842 (12-30-1842) Hr
Vails, Lucinda to Will Carvan 1-1-1853 (1-2-1853) Hr
Vails, M. E. to M. L. Grugett 12-16-1874 Dy
Vails, Mary Ann to Jackson Bohanan 7-23-1848 Hr
Vale, Martha W. to J. Pewett 5-23-1860 (5-24-1860) L
Vale, Sarah Jane Elizabeth to O. L. Thurmond 3-2-1868 (3-10-1868) L
Valenten, Amanda to N. Futerell 1-14-1858 We
Valentine, Charity to William Burton 3-23-1854 Ma
Valentine, D. T. to E. A. Y. Cester 8-9-1865 Hn
Valentine, Letta J. to Sherrod J. Burton 11-30-1858 Hn
Valentine, Margaret to William Ford 7-14-1852 We
Valentine, Maria M. to J. H. Taylor 2-1-1867 Hn
Valentine, Martha Ann to Saml. H. Weatherly 11-13-1866 Ma
Valentine, Martha J. to Jess J. Johnson 12-8-1859 We
Valentine, Mary E. to T. F. M. Janes 3-18-1858 Hn
Valentine, Mary F. to J. P. Fisher 1-16-1867 Hn
Valentine, Mary to George K. Crutchfield 1-25-1845 (no return) We
Valentine, Sarah Frances to John Thomas Connor 12-22-1856 (12-23-1856) Ma
Vales, Ann to William Hood 4-22-1858 Sh
Valley, Kate to Solaman Howard 3-20-1867 (3-21-1867) T
Valliant, Martha B. to Peter King 2-19-1855 (2-20-1855) O
Valliant, Matilda to Robert T. Carver 12-10-1855 (12-12-1855) O
Valliant, Nancy to J. H. King 4-4-1859 (4-7-1859) O
Van Campen, Ellen to Joseph Frothschild 9-18-1866 (9-20-1866) F
Van Demark, Sophia to Anton Freadarich Heuer 2-14-1851 Sh
Van Eaton, N. B. to D. C. Franklin 10-20-1879 (10-21-1879) Dy
Van Maning, Elizabeth to Christopher C. Beaton 12-26-1865 Be
Van Pelt, Catherine to Isaac Z. Gibson 6-10-1846 Sh
Van Pelt, M. H. to Thomas B. Mynatt 12-10-1846 Sh
Van Pelt, Susan A. to Fountain P. Young 12-9-1862 (12-11-1862) Ma
Van Wagnen?, Annie to J. S. Chiles 5-13-1858 Sh
VanBuren, Caroline to W. T. Bond 2-18-1861 (no return) Hy
VanBuren, Martha A. to D. H. Smith 7-25-1861 Hy
VanBuren, Mary to R. W. Rice 10-9-1862 (no return) Hy
VanPelt, Helen D. to M. A. Smith 10-12-1864 (10-13-1864) Sh

Vanalsin, Sarah to Elmore Meek 12-19-1846 Sh
Vanatta, Mary to James Cary 1-4-1849 O
Vanatta, Mary to William Cary 1-4-1849 (1-13-1849) O
Vanbiber, Ellen to William W. Rush 12-25-1857 (12-27-1857) L
Vanbunn, Chena to Alex Stokley 11-6-1871 Hy
Vanburen, Julian to Anthony Smith 3-14-1877 Hy
Vancamp, Louisa to Charles Moore 1-26-1860 Ma
Vance, Jane to William Joyner 12-30-1861 (1-1-1862) Sh
Vance, Margaret to Levi P. Duncan 6-8-1841 (6-9-1841) O
Vance, Mary to T. P. C. Russell 7-27-1837 O
Vance, Raciel to Charles Maclin 7-21-1877 (7-27-1877) L B
Vance, Rhoda to Murdoch M. Murchison 11-7-1852 Ma
Vancleave, Elizabeth to Alfred W. Stem 11-27-1850 Hn
Vancleave, Elizabeth to W. D. Myrack 3-22-1867 (3-24-1867) Cr
Vancleave, Harriet to J. H. Richardson 7-22-1846 Hn
Vancleave, Mary Ann to _____ G. Holden 12-18-1851 Hn
Vancleave, Nancy C. to I. Cole _____ 12-22-1859 Hn
Vancleave, Sallie A. to James B. Clendenin 10-30-1862 Hn
Vancleave, Sarah J. to W. R. Clement 12-23-1866 Hn
Vancleave?, M. L. to J. M. Breedlove 3-1-1866 Hn
Vancleive, Sallie to Bevily Bates 3-8-1872 (3-10-1872) Cr
Vandegrift, Edna F. to Jessee Scott 10-30-1861 (10-31-1861) Hr
Vandergrifft, Martha Ann to John Scott 7-25-1861 (7-15?-1861) Hr
Vanderver, Margaret to P. R. Mitchell 1-4-1873 (1-5-1873) T
Vandike, A. E. to J. R. Lyon 3-5-1868 Hy
Vandouser, Mary to William A. Bruce 11-25-1862 Ma
Vandyck, Lizzie to Henry Curley? 8-25-1865 (no return) Hn
Vandyck, Mary E. to C. B. Crutchfield 10-13-1852 Hn
Vandygraff, Jane to Thomas Byrum 3-13-1869 (no return) L
Vandygriff, Mary E. to Carrol Climer 1-22-1853 (1-30-1853) Hr
Vanhog, Sally to Hinson Landon 11-11-1861 G
Vanhook, Jena to D. F. Cox 9-25-1864 Hn
Vanhook, Margaret to James McWilliams 1-2-1832 Sh
Vanhook, Melissa to John Lewis 9-19-1853 Hn
Vanhook, Susan M. to C. C. Maydwell 4-23-1861 Sh
Vanhook, Winney P. to John W. Hicks 2-23-1865 Hn
Vanhorn, A. E. to Benj. C. Dennis 7-14-1856 (7-17-1856) Sh
Vanhorn, Harriet to John Wehrum (Warham?) 2-19-1861 Sh
Vann, Balsora to Samuel C. McClellan 1-14-1829 Ma
Vann, Bolsoa to Osias Wade 7-30-1855 Ma
Vann, Mary to Justin L. Edwards 3-14-1832 Ma
Vann, Nancy to William Haly 1-27-1845 Hn
Vann, Rutha Ann to John M. Smith 10-15-1858 Ma
Vann, Susan A. (Mrs.) to Horace H. Hutchings 6-22-1858 Ma
Vanog, Nancy to Absolum W. Nobles 12-2-1846 K
Vanpelt, Cora A. to J. K. Morris 10-25-1869 (11-26-1869) F
Vanpelt, Lydia to David Haney 10-1-1869 (10-2-1869) F B
Vanpelt, Nancy E. to Thomas J. Lindsey 12-21-1859 (no return) Hy
Vanpelt, Sarah Jane to Henry A. Thomas 2-7-1850 (2-8-1850) Ma
Vantreese, Rhoda to William Dickerson 11-19-1864 (11-20-1864) Ma
Vantrence, Jane to James Alford 3-9-1841 Ma
Vantrice, Catharine to James Read 11-24-1828 (11-27-1828) Ma
Vantrice, Sarah to Richard M. Davis 12-20-1842 (12-29-1842) Ma
Vantrip, Mary Ann to John Lovett 11-17-1847 (11-18-1847) O
Vanzandt, Mary Ann to William Osgen 12-26-1842 (12-27-1842) Ma
Vardeman, Matilda C. to J. H. Styers 11-28-1869 Hy
Varnal, Sarah to Solomon Bass 1-1-1839 Sh
Varnell, Louisa A. to William Ellis 7-17-1842 Sh
Varner, Cassa A. to Edmund J. Glascock 1-11-1853 G
Varner, Elizabeth to D. H. Fairless 12-28-1865 G
Varner, Manervia to Essex Rutherford 1-24-1878 Hy
Varner, Rebecca to David Haist 8-10-1843 G
Varvell, Elizabeth to B. W. Sandlin 1-27-1861 (1-29-1861) O
Vasser, Catherine to David Owen 12-27-1842 Sh
Vasser, Sarah S. to Wm. T. M. Davis 3-20-1844 Sh
Vassor (Vapor?), Juliana to John King 9-23-1840 (9-24-1840) L
Vauen?, Mariah Jane to James W. Osborn 1-3-1865 (no return) Hn
Vaughm, Jerleen to Benj. F. Mayo 7-9-1863 We
Vaugan, Nancy I. to John Welch 12-27-1852 (12-28-1852) Hr
Vaugh, Mary M. to David Chandler 10-23-1850 Cr
Vaughan, Amandy to William Davis 1-8-1862 G
Vaughan, Ann to Edward G. Allen 12-14-1844 (12-19-1844) T
Vaughan, Anna to Jiff Crews 3-7-1870 G B
Vaughan, Clara A. to Geo. W. Jackson 1-7-1847 (1-14-1847) F
Vaughan, Claricy J. to James Young 1-13-1857 T
Vaughan, Edna to Tom Dance 2-1-1868 G B
Vaughan, Elizabeth to Jas. M. Runnell 8-16-1848 Sh
Vaughan, Emeline to W. R. Gardner 6-11-1861 (6-13-1861) Cr
Vaughan, Fannie E. to L. E. Davies 11-27-1860 (11-28-1860) Sh
Vaughan, Frances R. to James T. Calhoun 1-14-1854 (1-17-1854) Sh
Vaughan, Hellen to M. P. Enochs 9-22-1874 Dy
Vaughan, Lavinia to Charles Perry 1-31-1850 Hn
Vaughan, Lucy B. to Joseph L. Glover 9-26-1843 Sh
Vaughan, Lucy E. to B. H. Hawkins 2-4-1840 Sh
Vaughan, Luesa to Alfred M. Edwards 12-1-1859 We
Vaughan, M. C. to J. N. Roe 10-30-1860 G
Vaughan, Maria C. to Lemmel D. Harrell 10-10-1844 Sh

Vaughan, Martha J. to W. R. Jone 11-20-1867 G
Vaughan, Martha U. to L. H. Pyron 11-6-1861 Sh
Vaughan, Martha to John Stinnett 11-2-1854 Sh
Vaughan, Martha to Joseph Howard 2-22-1868 (2-23-1868) L
Vaughan, Mary E. to Samuel McK. Wilson 6-11-1855 (6-12-1855) Sh
Vaughan, Mary E. to William Jones 4-24-1860 (no return) We
Vaughan, Mary J. to Thomas C. Howard 4-28-1852 T
Vaughan, Mary J. to W. H. Jobes 10-17-1874 (10-18-1874) Dy
Vaughan, Mary L. to W. D. Peterson 6-16-1856 (6-17-1856) Sh
Vaughan, Mary to Albert Bugg 9-30-1866 (SB 1870?) G
Vaughan, Mary to Archer Lampkin 6-4-1870 T
Vaughan, Mary to Collumbus Howard 1-29-1869 (2-8-1869) L
Vaughan, Nancy R. to Hiram Scott 4-8-1831 Hr
Vaughan, Norciss to Jessee Griffeth 11-11-1868 (11-12-1868) L
Vaughan, Paralee to Giles McDougald 9-22-1869 G B
Vaughan, Rebecca to Carlton Allen 4-3-1843 (4-4-1843) T
Vaughan, Sallie L. to John Dunavan 3-29-1870 (no return) Hy
Vaughan, Sarah J. to William F. Jewett 9-1-1842 Hn
Vaughan, Sarah M. to Matha Adkinson 12-10-1850 We
Vaughan, Sarah to James L. Hawkins 12-21-1837 Sh
Vaughan, Susan A. to Hammet Roberts 1-23-1867 G
Vaughan, Susan to James Armstrong 3-20-1871 Dy
Vaughan, Susan to John D. G. Wynn 10-2-1853 G
Vaughan, Susanah J. to John P. Ferrell 5-4-1864 G
Vaughan, Sylla J. to John Curtis 12-15-1853 Hn
Vaughn, A. J. to J. M. Perry 12-23-1857 We
Vaughn, A. S. to D. S. Allen 9-1-1842 Hn
Vaughn, Almira J. to William S. Willowford 12-17-1859 (no return) Hn
Vaughn, Amanda to Harry Cherry 1-17-1870 Hy
Vaughn, Amy C. to John Brown 7-3-1862 Mn
Vaughn, Ann Marie to William Bond 9-16-1831 Sh
Vaughn, Ann to Asa Hutcheson 11-16-1843 We
Vaughn, Becky D. to Henry P. Oliver 6-3-1858 We
Vaughn, Catherine to Joseph Scott 12-18-1878 Hy
Vaughn, Elizabeth A. to E. M. Downing 6-10-1868 T
Vaughn, Elizabeth to George P. Muyrhead 7-12-1837 G
Vaughn, Elizabeth to Thos. W. Cariven 1-18-1842 Cr
Vaughn, Elizabeth to William Forren 11-16-1843 G
Vaughn, Ella C. to James Thomas Moore 7-11-1874 (7-12-1874) L
Vaughn, Emily to John Will Banks 12-27-1864 (no return) Hn
Vaughn, F. L. to Thos. Robinson 2-2-1852 Cr
Vaughn, Hannah A. to T. M. D. Crowder 8-11-1861 Hn
Vaughn, Harriet to William Carroll 9-3-1860 (9-5-1860) O
Vaughn, Huldey R. to William Key 12-21-1844 (12-22-1844) O
Vaughn, Jane M. to Joseph F. Cloud 1-22-1832 Hr
Vaughn, Jane to Varner Giles 7-14-1867 Hn
Vaughn, Jerusha to Thomas Willson 4-25-1843 (4-27-1843) F
Vaughn, Julia A. to Sam D. Savely 12-8-1867 Hy
Vaughn, Kate to Henry Allison 9-21-1867 (9-21-1867) T
Vaughn, Lanah to John H. Jones 12-7-1857 Hn
Vaughn, Lucy to James H. Thomason 11-20-1851 Hn
Vaughn, M. A. to R. P. Sanders 10-13-1858 G
Vaughn, Maria to Robert Hays 8-4-1876 Hy
Vaughn, Martha H. to John M. Manning 2-17-1844 (2-18-1844) O
Vaughn, Martha to Wm. Duncan 10-31-1845 (no return) Cr
Vaughn, Martha to Wm. Marrs 5-9-1846 (5-10-1846) Hr
Vaughn, Mary E. to William Mobly 10-2-1852 O
Vaughn, Mary Jane to J. B. Chaffin 11-30-1838 (no return) F
Vaughn, Mary to John Donaldson 2-7-1844 (2-8-1844) G
Vaughn, Matilda P. to M. High 1-11-1851 (1-16-1851) F
Vaughn, Minerva to William M. Gallimore 9-30-1851 Hn
Vaughn, Nancy M. to Daniel Sepune 12-20-1841 G
Vaughn, Nancy M. to John K. Norton 12-14-1859 Hn
Vaughn, Rachel to Edward Mulholland 6-2-1864 Sh
Vaughn, Sarah H. to Wm. J. Evans 5-15-1851 Sh
Vaughn, Sarah J. to Joseph N. Whitehorn 1-30-1856 Cr
Vaughn, Susan A. to T. J. Ford 2-17-1858 G
Vaught, Elizabeth to Josiah Thornton 8-27-1833 (9-3-1833) Hr
Vaught, Mary (Mrs.) to Guilford Browning 1-16-1868 G
Vaught, Mary to James Mitchell 9-12-1835 Hr
Vaught, Sarah Ann to James W. Bledsoe 10-9-1838 Sh
Vaught, Sarah to Samuel Harvey 8-1-1844 (8-20-1844) Hr
Vaughter, M. A. to G. L. Roper 5-18-1868 (5-19-1868) Cr
Vaughter, M. E. to W. H. Algee 6-28-1867 Cr
Vault, Sarha L. (Mrs.) to John G. Granger 10-14-1867 (10-15-1867) Ma
Vaulx, Callie to Jordan Hill 12-22-1866 (no return) Hy
Vaulx, Catherine G. to Lewis B. Shapard 7-24-1860 Ma
Vaulx, Eva to Washington Currie 5-30-1878 Hy
Vaulx, Eveline to William Thomison 5-29-1875 Hy
Vaulx, Harriet to John Smith 6-10-1868 Hy
Vaulx, Harritt to Mike Read 5-16-1869 Hy
Vaulx, Isen to Rush Short 9-6-1876 Hy
Vaulx, Liley to Isaac Holloway 5-31-1869 Hy
Vaulx, Mary Eliza to Alexander C. Robertson 11-11-1852 Hy
Vaulx, Matilda E. to Charles N. Gibbs 6-5-1850 Ma
Vaulx, Sallie E. to W. A. Caldwell 1-13-1873 (no return) Hy
Vawter, Mary Jane to John D. Leach 12-11-1852 Cr

Vawter, Sarah E. to Richard Q. Mullin 10-11-1855 Cr
Vawter, Susan A. to Silas R. Wyatt 1-13-1866 (1-15-1866) Cr
Vawters, Mary S. to S. J. Love 1-4-1859 Cr
Veazey, Adeline to West Moody 5-20-1866 Hn B
Veazey, Jackah to James Morphis 2-22-1838 Hn
Veazey, Jane L. to Allison E. Carter 12-15-1841 Hn
Veazey, Mary F. to James C. Patterson 9-5-1846 Hn
Veazey, Mollie E. to W. H. Allen 12-28-1865 Hn
Veazey, S. E. to J. C. Bessent 6-16-1869 G
Veazey, Samantha B. to Henry N. Alexander 8-7-1867 Hn
Venable, Caroline to William Capaman 8-29-1868 G B
Venable, Elvina to John Edwards 1-3-1848 Hn
Venable, Lizzie to W. T. Wells 2-10-1875 Hy
Venable, Mary E. to John W. Trevathan 4-2-1858 Hn
Venable, Sarah F. to James M. Roberson 3-31-1859 Hn
Veneer, Susan to Dick Richardson 5-9-1874 T
Ventreese, Frances to Marcus S. Bledsoe 3-15-1856 Ma
Veragut, Johanna to Olloise Truthman 5-21-1862 Sh
Verhine, Ann B. to E. C. Curlin 1-12-1866 O
Verhine, Eleanor J. to George W. Hogan 1-27-1856 (1-29-1856) O
Verhine?, M. E. to W. A. Edwards 11-24-1842 (10?-29-1842) O
Verible, Mary Ann to James Martin 1-23-1828 Ma
Vermilion, Martha A. to Ezekiel Pope 9-27-1861 We
Vermillion, Nancy E. to David R. Riche 10-13-1861 We
Vernatta, Lucinda to Richard L. Adams 7-15-1848 O
Vernon, Ellen A. to James A. Sumners 2-23-1852 (2-24-1852) Hr
Vernon, Hellen E. to Edward Robinson 2-9-1850 (2-19-1850) Hr
Vernon, Julia to Garland Anderson 10-17-1854 Hr
Vernon, M. E. to J. W. McIntyre 8-21-1870 (no return) L
Vernon, Martha A. to W. J. Hutcherson 11-22-1875 (no return) L
Vernon, Mary (Mrs.) to William Jones 10-12-1867 G B
Vernon, Mary Jane to J. B. Erman 5-1-1879 (5-4-1879) L
Vernon, Nancy H. to Daniel Tinkle 4-14-1858 (4-15-1858) G
Vernon, Nancy J. to A. J. Rogers 3-6-1869 (3-9-1869) L
Vernon, Nancy to James Robinson 3-26-1860 Hr
Verser, Ann to W. A. Chaney 12-5-1857 (12-6-1857) T
Verser, Lizzie C. to Young F. Marley 5-19-1857 (5-20-1857) Ma
Verser, Lucy A. to John Connor 12-1-1856 (12-17-1856) Ma
Verser, Margarett to William H. Cleaves 3-8-1843 Ma
Vertun?, A. to Gabril Granbury 12-28-1869 (12-30-1869) T
Vesey, Manerva to Joseph N. David (Dawe-Daniel) 11-5-1853 (11-6-1853) Sh
Vester, Isabella to David Herndon 9-3-1850 Be
Vester, Mary Jane to William Berry 2-8-1854 Be
Vester, Nancy to Richard Lewis 4-2-1863 Mn
Vester, Penelope to James Pafford 6-12-1843 Be
Vester, Phebee to J. B. French 9-10-1854 Be
Vester, Rosey Ann to Albert Berry 12-27-1855 Be
Vester, T. A. to J. R. Lewis 5-22-1861 Mn
Vetetoe, Amanda to John L. Cantrel 8-31-1862 Mn
Vevely, Jane D. to Benj. F. Mills 8-8-1866 (8-16-1866) Ma
Via, Barbara F. to H. C. Hodge 1-22-1878 (1-24-1878) Dy
Via, Martha J. to S. G. Stewart 6-8-1864 G
Via, Polly to R. L. Shaw 12-10-1874 Dy
Via, Sarah N. to William Irvine 3-27-1865 G
Viah?, Mary F. to J. B. M. Stevenson 1-3-1866 (no return) Dy
Viar, Melissa E. to Thomas Viar 11-16-1865 (no return) Dy
Vice, Angeline to James A. Vancleave 12-23-1866 Hn
Vick, Amanda D. to William L. Anderson 4-29-1848 Ma
Vick, J. L. to R. J. Church 12-18-1867 G
Vick, Martha D. to R. H. Goodman 11-14-1866 G
Vick, Milly to Samuel R. Fuqua 2-26-1853 G
Vick, N. H. to G. W. Powell 11-14-1866 G
Vick, Nannie to Geo. W. Church 9-5-1870 (9-11-1870) Dy
Vick, Octavia A. to James A. Dusmuke 11-16-1854 Ma
Vick, Sarah S. (Mrs.) to Joel Rushing 2-2-1858 (2-3-1858) Ma
Vick, Sarah T. to John W. Sykes 8-28-1866 Ma
Vickers, Andromedia to Z. H. Berry 12-24-1872 Cr
Vickers, Centha to James J. Etheridge 8-24-1837 G
Vickers, Jane to James S. Glass 4-29-1843 (5-4-1843) Hr
Vickers, Mary A. to A. Gibson 6-17-1854 We
Vickers, Mary Y. to A. N. Vickers 6-25-1857 Cr
Vickers, P. A. to A. B. Churchwell 1-11-1849 Cr
Vickers, Polley to James McAlister 11-5-1828 Sh
Vickers, Sallie H. (Mrs.) to H. M. Carr 9-3-1863 Sh
Vickers, Sarah to Eli Ray 8-13-1856 G
Vickery, Elizabeth to John W. Moon ?-8-1845 Hn
Vickery, Mary A. to S. B. Bruce 1-7-1853 Hn
Vickery, Parle to Darmond Millsaps 7-29-1841 L
Vickery, Roanna to Reuben McClure 10-28-1849 Hn
Vickory, Elizabeth to George Milsap 5-29-1839 L
Victory?, Charlotte to Jesse Trantham 7-22-1849 Hn
Vier, Rebecca to Gedion Goodrich 1-24-1846 (1-27-1846) G
Vlckery, Elizabeth to Jesse McClure 4-25-1850 Hn
Villner, Mary to S. Lewis 2-28-1863 Hn
Vincent, Amelia to James Wilson 5-21-1832 Hr
Vincent, Catharine to Joseph Levy 5-18-1859 (5-19-1859) Sh
Vincent, Catharine to Nathaniel Mingea 4-6-1858 Sh

Vincent, D. to Alvin Rowland 10-12-1846 (no return) Cr
Vincent, E. C. to J. G. Wells 2-9-1842 (2-10-1842) F
Vincent, E. C. to Jno. P. A. Hays 12-17-1846 We
Vincent, Elizabeth to Redman Anderson 7-30-1832 (8-3-1832) Hr
Vincent, Elizabeth to Wm. O'Neal 5-17-1845 Cr
Vincent, Emiline to William Oldham 1-10-1855 We
Vincent, Emily to John Tarbutten 12-5-1855 (12-13-1855) O
Vincent, Fannie to Azariah L. Kimbro 12-22-1864 Sh
Vincent, Harriet to Josephus Moss 11-18-1843 (no return) We
Vincent, Leona to George H. Woods 5-1-1843 Cr
Vincent, Letha (Lettie) to Andrew (Anderson) Scott 9-4-1849 (9-1?-1849) O
Vincent, M. K. to John H. Kindred 12-17-1857 We
Vincent, Manervia A. to Reuben Ross 11-7-1860 We
Vincent, Margarett A. to Adam Clark 11-25-1863 G
Vincent, Mary E. to M. T. Harris 2-9-1858 We
Vincent, Mary J. to Wm. K.? Williamson 7-9-1861 (7-10-1861) Cr
Vincent, Mary Jane to James Byers 5-15-1851 T
Vincent, Mary to James Penn 2-25-1828 (2-28-1828) Ma
Vincent, Mary to Nathaniel Ragan 2-9-1842 (2-10-1842) Hr
Vincent, Nancy A. to S. J. B. Martin 12-2-1846 (12-9-1846) O
Vincent, Nancy to Stephen Harbert 7-20-1840 (7-23-1840) Ma
Vincent, Nannie to James A. Hood 7-26-1884 (7-27-1884) L
Vincent, Naomi to Patrick Kearns 3-26-1856 Sh
Vincent, Polly Evalene to John Griffin 6-24-1851 O
Vincent, S. to Harbert Overby 11-17-1846 (no return) We
Vincent, Salina to Jas. M. Berryhill 12-8-1841 Sh
Vincent, Sarah A. to Edward Davie 1-14-1869 (1-21-1869) Ma *
Vincent, Sarah B. to Joe H. Spain 12-29-1845 Cr
Vincent, Sarah K. to Willis V. Taylor 1-14-1840 Hr
Vine, Cally to Joseph Rice 12-?-1878 Hy
Vines, Malvina to William Briley 4-1-1872 Hy
Vines, Mary A. to John J. Christian 12-23-1848 Sh
Vining, Susan E. (Mrs.) to B. P. Tucker 10-31-1859 Sh
Vinney, Saphona to William H. Mann 4-10-1851 (4-11-1851) G
Vinson (Viner), Letha to Andrew Scott 9-4-1849 (9-1?-1849) O
Vinson, Alice to W. H. Hampton 12-25-1872 Dy
Vinson, Caroline to William Chisum 1-3-1848 Ma
Vinson, Eliza Jane to Benjamin Freezer 1-24-1862 (no return) Hn
Vinson, Eliza to Frank Fowlkes 11-27-1875 Dy
Vinson, Elizabeth H. to L. H. Ware 1-20-1846 Ma
Vinson, Elizabeth R. to Jos. Harriman 9-17-1859 (9-18-1859) Hr
Vinson, Elizabeth to A. L. Monroe 2-17-1869 (2-18-1869) O
Vinson, Elizabeth to Jesse B. Branch 10-6-1842 Ma
Vinson, L. to Stephen Chambers 9-21-1841 Cr
Vinson, Louisa E. to John R. Robinson 1-24-1843 Cr
Vinson, Manerva F. to Thomas T. Gatland 12-8-1866 (no return) Cr
Vinson, Marilane to James A. Barker 1-23-1863 Be
Vinson, Martha A. B. to William Crawford 11-3-1853 Hr
Vinson, Martha to James B. Mills 1-24-1856 (1-26-1856) Hr
Vinson, Martha to John C. Wallace 4-15-1855 Hn
Vinson, Martha to Robt. Moore 2-19-1872 (2-20-1872) Cr
Vinson, Mary to Philip Northern 12-4-1841 Ma
Vinson, Nancy A. to James Henderson 8-14-1855 (8-16-1855) Ma
Vinson, Nancy L. to W. W. Wade 9-27-1865 (9-28-1865) O
Vinson, Nancy to Charles J. Burnett 2-24-1841 (2-26-1841) Hr
Vinson, Nancy to James Wilson 4-23-1872 (4-24-1872) Dy
Vinson, Susan to Manuel Parker 12-25-1869 (no return) Cr
Vinsor, Prisslor to Wm. M. Branch 8-9-1857 Cr
Vinton, Mira to James Pugh 3-22-1861 (3-23-1861) Sh
Viots, Thysby to Normal Sarlett 11-11-1851 Cr
Vire, Narcissa to Joseph Harrison 5-15-1866 (5-16-1866) Dy
Vivier, Clara F. to Charles B. Dickinson, jr. 10-15-1861 Sh
Voges, Johona to Fredrick Schuttkies 9-5-1861 Sh
Volentine, Emeline to Samuel Burton 6-5-1855 Ma
Volentine, Mary E. to William T. Taylor 4-28-1844 Hn
Volentine, Mary J. to James Weatherly 11-7-1860 Ma
Volentine, Mary J. to Joseph F. Connor 12-12-1868 Ma
Volentine, Nancy J. to Obadiah Crouch 11-4-1860 Ma
Volentine, Susan to Rubin Pirce 4-15-1839 (4-17-1839) G
Vollmer, Josephine to Henry G. Hampe 5-28-1860 (5-29-1860) Sh
Volmer, Louisa to John Hendy 12-10-1864 (11-11-1864) Sh
Voncleave?, E. A. to William A. Carroll 1-20-1852 Hn
Voorheis, Charlotte to G. S. Miles 4-21-1855 (5-1-1855) O
Vorwerk, Rebecca to Jacob Berkle (Ruckle?) 3-29-1860 Sh
Voss, Janie to J. F. Hendren 10-31-1882 (11-1-1882) L
Voss, M. J. to A. R. Gibson 12-18-1883 (12-19-1883) L
Voss, M. L. to J. W. W. Voss 11-3-1883 (11-4-1883) L
Voss, Malinda to Ransom Tenning 8-4-1878 Hy
Voss, Mallie to J. V. Savage 5-25-1882 (no return) L
Voss, Mary Ann to William T. Tilman 9-17-1850 L
Voss, S. E. to G. W. Pennington 12-2-1874 (12-5-1875) L
Voss, Sarah C. to Thomas M. Johnson 12-23-1862 (no return) L
Voss, Sarah E. to R. J. Hooker 3-9-1863 (3-10-1863) L
Voss, Susan to Washington Pewett 9-7-1859 L
Votter, Fannie to James Wells 2-23-1878 Hy
Vowel, A. W. to S. J. Lanier 4-12-1858 (no return) We
Vowel, Nellie to John W. Chalk 5-28-1872 (6-9-1872) L

Vowell, Alice to James Rogers 3-3-1886 L
Vowell, Frances to Soloman J. Lenien 6-25-1854 We
Vowell, H. C. to Rufus W. Montgomery 2-26-1863 (no return) We
Vowell, Nancy E. to G. W. Dameron 12-19-1855 We

Wacasen, Caroline to Frederick Henrich (Henry) 1-23-1842 Sh
Wacker, Sarah Jane to John Motley 10-21-1839 (no return) F
Wadd, Clarissa to Jerry Stewart 6-10-1866 Hn B
Waddell, Clementine C. to Wm. T. Ashcraft 12-27-1852 (12-28-1852) Sh
Waddell, Lucy to John Cole 1-24-1829 Ma
Waddell, Mary A. to Michael Manning 4-15-1858 Hn
Waddell, Mary Ann to John M. Sanders 9-11-1856 Ma
Waddell, Mary to William Harbut 12-30-1829 (12-31-1829) Ma
Waddell, Rebecca to Alfred A. Barding 12-30-1851 Sh
Waddington, Helena to Edwin A. Goldsby 2-3-1847 Hn
Waddle, E. J. to W. E. Hale 12-2-1866 G
Waddle, Frances B. to James K. Pinkney 3-2-1845 Cr
Waddle, Judy Ann to David Cameron 1-6-1877 Hy
Waddle, Lidia to W. R. Towell 12-23-1839 (1-7-1840) Ma
Waddle, Martha Jane to William H. Sanders 12-12-1840 (12-14-1840) Ma
Waddle, Mary Jane to Richard r. Townes 10-18-1838 Sh
Waddle, Moriah S. to Samuel Smith 10-24-1844 Cr
Waddle, Ruth L. to Isaac L. Davis 12-26-1847 Sh
Waddle, Susan A. to Samuel M. Hutchinson 2-14-1850 Sh
Waddleton, Elizabeth to Patrick Sauls 1-30-1843 (2-2-1843) Ma
Waddy, Alice E. to W. B. McGowan 9-5-1867 Hn
Waddy, Elizabeth K. to Coleman Bird 3-4-1827 (5-6-1827) O
Waddy, Juddath D. to Marion Waddy 12-3-1860 O
Waddy, Judith D. to Nathaniel P. Ramsey 4-26-1863 G
Waddy, M. R. to R. L. West 2-26-1863 G
Waddy, Martha H. to Bradford Edwards 7-14-1855 (7-15-1855) G
Waddy, Sarah K. to Jon A. Duncan 12-26-1860 G
Wade, A. E. to W. B. House 7-26-1854 G
Wade, Alice C. to W. G. Sappington 9-28-1859 G
Wade, America C. to Wm. M. Harrison 9-27-1852 G
Wade, Anabella to Harrison Hicks 12-2-1850 Hn
Wade, Beckey to Adrian Hood 7-10-1868 (no return) F B
Wade, Betty to Tom Nelson 6-13-1868 G B
Wade, Charlotte to Charles Williford 12-27-1868 G B
Wade, Christina to William Brown 12-28-1867 G
Wade, E. F. to M. L. Chambers 10-24-1859 (10-26-1859) F
Wade, E. M. to J. T. Holbrook ?-?-1861? Mn
Wade, Elanor to Alexander McDougald 8-8-1834 G
Wade, Eliza to Washington Lillard 11-6-1873 Dy
Wade, Elizabeth O. to Enoch G. Ivey 8-15-1844 G
Wade, Elizabeth to John Mansfield 5-5-1845 Hn
Wade, Ellen to C. P. Wily 1-23-1867 O
Wade, Emily A. to William H. Thurston 9-8-1855 Hn
Wade, Ethelenda to Edward F. Bumpass 10-10-1849 Hn
Wade, Euphobia to James Ellis 11-16-1847 Hn
Wade, Fannie A. to B. B. Buckley 12-17-1874 (12-20-1874) O
Wade, Frances A. (Mrs.) to Josiah F. Penn 11-7-1850 G
Wade, Frances A. to James T. Wade 12-24-1840 G
Wade, H. S. to C. B. Crutchfield 6-12-1855 Hn
Wade, I. E. to J. B. Edmondson 2-27-1866 G
Wade, Ida A. to Henry C. Chrisp 12-15-1869 G
Wade, J. D. to D. D. Brizendine 1-7-1866 Hn
Wade, John P. to R. D. Jones 9-20-1854 G
Wade, Julia to Abraham Salter 12-24-1865 Mn
Wade, July to Richard Welch 6-17-1843 (6-18-1843) G
Wade, Katie to Willis Caruthers 7-14-1875 O
Wade, L. A. to W. A. Banks 4-15-1868 G
Wade, L. L. to James M. Watson 11-24-1868 (11-26-1868) T
Wade, Liza to York Londa 7-13-1867 F B
Wade, Louiza to Napolian B. Key 10-24-1872 O
Wade, Lucinda to James C. Ray 2-2-1842 Hn
Wade, Lucinda to John Deener 1-7-1869 (no return) F B
Wade, M. C. to B. L. Partee 12-21-1853 G
Wade, M. C. to J. W. S. Sappington 4-14-1858 G
Wade, Maggie E. to William E. Turner 1-3-1866 T
Wade, Mandy to Jesse B. Curl 2-20-1847 (3-10-1847) F
Wade, Manerva C. to J. L. Grigg 1-26-1858 G
Wade, Margaret J. P. to Alexander Timms 12-17-1873 (12-23-1873) T
Wade, Mary A. to W. B. Williams 3-30-1858 G
Wade, Mary Ann to W. H. Hale 11-21-1848 Hn
Wade, Mary C. to Seith Harrison 12-4-1856 G
Wade, Mary E. to Robert D. Ivey 11-19-1861 G
Wade, Mary J. to John L. Brown 12-5-1853 Hn
Wade, Mary to Abner G. Lane 3-3-1853 G
Wade, Mary to Henry C. Bert? 10-26-1844 (10-31-1844) F
Wade, Mary to W. A. Arnold 5-26-1868 Be
Wade, Mattie to Henry Tr___? 11-22-1873 (11-23-1873) O
Wade, Met to John O'Daniel 4-28-1869 G B
Wade, Peggy to A. R. Hicks 12-25-1873 T
Wade, Precilla L. to James M. Dodd 11-5-1846 G
Wade, R. C. to Jas. G. Blakemore 3-8-1860 G
Wade, Ruth to Luke H. Gullett 1-7-1854 (1-8-1854) O

Wade, Sallie Ann to R. E. Hughes 12-18-1868 (12-20-1868) F
Wade, Sally to George Ozier 1-25-1871 (1-26-1871) F B
Wade, Sarah E. to Edward G. Bartlett 10-27-1856 (10-29-1856) Sh
Wade, Sarah J. to F. H. Underwood 10-1-1867 Hn
Wade, Tempy to Jas. Owen 1-2-1874 O
Wadkins, Amanda to George Williams 8-24-1862 (no return) Hn
Wadkins, Mary J. to A. H. Webb 12-19-1853 (12-22-1853) L
Wadkins, Nancy R. to W. H. Bilbrey 12-29-1870 Cr
Wadley, Mary Jane to William W. Layn 3-10-1856 (3-16-1856) Ma
Wadley, Paralee to William W. Baily 8-18-1855 (8-19-1855) Ma
Wadlington, Euphania to John F. Price 1-19-1870 Ma
Wadner, Ellen to Thos. Fitzgerald 11-27-1869 Hy
Wadrill, Martha Ann to John M. Taylor 10-11-1858 Cr
Wafford, Cerilda to Nathan Wright 5-13-1847 Hn
Wafford, L. C. to John A. McCommon 8-5-1857 (8-6-1857) Hr
Wages?, M. L. to C. C. Cannon 3-13-1873 T
Waggener, Annalizar to James H. Fleming 3-4-1860 We
Waggener, Elizabeth to Henderson Parrish 12-3-1857 We
Waggoner, Amanda M. to Francis M. Whitworth 3-16-1854 Ma
Waggoner, Elvirah F. to Thomas P. Derham 12-24-1845 (no return) We
Waggoner, Lizzie to Jessee Patten 10-12-1867 (10-13-1867) T
Waggoner, Lula to J. B. Philips 1-12-1867 Be
Waggoner, Martha to Josiah Hodges 5-2-1844 Ma
Waggoner, Mary G. to Wm. J. Sykes 11-20-1866 Ma
Wagner, Catharine to William Benjes (Burgis) 4-22-1850 Sh
Wagner, Sina to John Smith 1-15-1874 T
Wagnon, Lockey Ann to John F. Womack 3-7-1843 Sh
Wagnon, Rebecca to E. P. Womack 12-2-1842 Sh
Wagoner, Lucy to Robert M. Roach 11-27-1866 Hn
Wagoner, Paralee to John F. Johnson 5-13-1862 (5-14-1862) Ma
Wagsted, Deevy to Moses Nichol 5-25-1860 (no return) Dy
Wagster, A. P. to J. C. Lasater 12-2-1858 We
Wagster, Josephine to William S. Robinson 10-8-1867 (10-10-1867) Ma
Wagster, Martha J. to Franklin Nance 2-23-1854 Hn
Wagster, Martha to Hanson Cravans 12-27-1845 We
Wagster, Mary E. to James P. Owens 7-13-1866 G
Wagster, Nannie J. to James G. Dudley 7-26-1854 (no return) Cr
Wagster, Pantha to James C. Coley 1-6-1864 G
Wagster, Pantha to James C. Corley 1-6-1864 G
Wagster, S. M. to Organ Buckley 12-3-1867 O
Wagster, Sarah M. to John B. Carlton 10-28-1858 We
Wagster, T. L. to D. J. Morris 1-21-1865 (1-23-1865) O
Waid, A. to Bill Wright 4-9-1870 G
Wails, Susan to John Burns 7-15-1864 Sh
Wainright, Mollie J. to J. H. Adams 12-14-1871 (no return) Hy
Wainscot, Sarah J. to James Julin 5-28-1855 We
Wainscott, Ann to Wyatt Shankle 2-9-1843 Hn
Wainscott, Rebecca Ann to J. P. Lee 10-23-1864 Hn
Wainwright, Cornelia to Matthews Crawford 12-29-1868 F B
Wainwright, Elizabeth to Henry Ware 9-7-1867 Hy
Wainwright, M. A. to R. G. Cates 7-12-1866 Hy
Wainwright, Sarah (Mrs.) to Wm. Mavis 7-17-1855 (no return) F
Wair, Georgiana to Jas. M. Walton 7-15-1858 Sh
Waisler, Mary to John Bar 2-5-1857 Sh
Waits, Eliza E. to John J. Gant 12-22-1875 (12-23-1875) Dy
Wakefield, J. L. to L. M. Burkhead 1-11-1877 L
Wakefield, M. T. to J. A. Webb 12-16-1885 L
Wakefield, Martha J.(H?) to William W.(H?) Holland 12-16-1851 (12-18-1851) L
Wakefield, Matilda E. to A. H. Crook 10-24-1871 (10-25-1871) L
Wakefield, Matilda to James B. Hutcherson 9-15-1841 (9-16-1841) L
Wakefield, S. L. to Mc. W. Haynes 10-15-1877 (10-18-1877) L
Wakefield, T. T. to E. J. Drake 8-17-1875 L
Wakelan, Harriett to Adam Todd 4-6-1867 (no return) Hn B
Wakeland, Paralee to J. J. Blake 5-22-1867 Hn
Walace, Huldah to William A. Caudle 11-18-1853 O
Walden, Maria to Calvin Musgrave 7-21-1830 (7-29-1830) Hr
Walden, Mary to Washington Adams 2-18-1832 Hr
Walden, Permelia E. to Francis M. Cook 8-8-1872 Hy
Walden, Roenna M. E. to James L. Todd 8-2-1848 Ma
Walder, Catharine to Conrad Maiar 9-27-1858 Sh
Waldran, Eliza Jane to Robert P. Ware 5-13-1850 Sh
Waldran, Elizabeth to James Johnson 7-17-1854 Sh
Waldran, Margaret to Z. A. Rudisill 8-10-1840 Sh
Waldran, Mary M. to John A. Marshall 5-6-1844 Sh
Waldran, S. Almeda to Elbert A. White 2-6-1849 Sh
Waldran, Sally A. to Wm. H. Stratton 5-4-1859 (5-5-1859) Sh
Waldrip, Malissa to William S. Williams 1-18-1836 (1-19-1836) G
Waldron, Jane H. to Wm. F. Hayne 4-13-1844 Sh
Waldron, Mary to John Beazley 4-14-1840 Sh
Waldron, Tabitha Elizabeth to Lane Nichols 8-23-1868 G
Waldrop, Charlotta J. to Elisha Moore 3-25-1857 G
Waldrop, Delila to William M. Darnold 2-19-1848 (2-21-1848) G
Waldrop, Eliza Jane to James A. Baker 8-27-1843 Hn
Waldrop, Elizabeth to A. M. Davidson 10-17-1856 (10-18-1856) G
Waldrop, Gabrella to Rayland R. Walls 3-13-1851 G
Waldrop, Louisa J. to Hiram C. May 7-19-1858 (7-27-1858) Hr

Waldrop, Louisa to Benj. F. Arnold 3-30-1848 G
Waldrop, Margaret to Charles W. Wilson 10-8-1839 Hn
Waldrop, Martha A. to Enoch D. Waldrop 7-12-1846 G
Waldrop, Pamelia to Christopher Cress 10-7-1838 Hn
Waldrop, Permelia M. to Stephen B. Orr 11-11-1849 Hn
Waldrope, Ester E. to Josiah Vick 1-3-1851 (1-9-1851) G
Waldrope, Isilla to A. G. Tilman 2-16-1854 G
Waldroup, Martha A. to Isham Thomas 11-15-1861 We
Waldrup, H. C. to Holland Y. James 1-23-1847 (no return) Hn
Waldrup, Isbele to James Cooksey 6-15-1832 Hr
Waldrup, Lucinda to W.I. Lamb 8-13-1858 We
Wales, Fanny (Mrs.) to Robert Adams 1-26-1864 Sh
Wales, Martha J. to Jefferson Burton 5-27-1854 (5-28-1854) G
Wales, Mary E. to Henry W. Cowgill 4-19-1862 (4-20-1862) Sh
Waley, Eleanor to Cornelius Van Campber 6-28-1848 Sh
Walk, Alcy to William Lauderdale 5-24-1867 (5-26-1867) T
Walk, Alice to Joseph M. Yarbro 1-2-1867 T
Walk, Amanda to John Loyd 10-19-1869 T
Walk, F. M. to Jno. M. Shelton 11-27-1873 T
Walk, Jane to Richmond Cotherum 12-7-1869 (12-8-1869) T
Walk, Lucy A. to Jas. S. McIntosh 7-21-1866 T
Walk, Miss Lucy to James S. McIntosh 4-9-1862 T
Walk, Nancy to Henry Tornton 8-18-1870 (8-19-1870) T
Walk, Sarah to Howard Houlsouser 12-29-1858 (12-28?-1858) T
Walk, Susan Ann to Charles W. Archer 6-20-1855 T
Walker, A. C. A. to A. J. Pierce 1-6-1864 Dy
Walker, A. G. to J. T. Meneece 4-18-1872 O
Walker, Ada to Simon Crawford 7-16-1870 (no return) F B
Walker, Adaline S. to Henry V. C. Wynne 2-27-1851 G
Walker, Adaline to Charles King 8-15-1884 L
Walker, Adaline to George Homan 8-1-1867 (8-9-1867) T
Walker, Addie to Thomas C. Ferrill 1-11-1866 Dy
Walker, Alice to Dallas Mahon 1-28-1868 (2-10-1868) Dy
Walker, Amanda C. to Licurgas W. Williams 4-19-1855 (4-22-1855) G
Walker, Amanda M. to Joseph W. O'Brian 3-16-1847 (4-19-1847) F
Walker, Amanda to Lee Green 2-12-1870 (2-25-1870) F B
Walker, Amanda to William Grammer 8-2-1861 (8-4-1861) Sh
Walker, Analiza to William Devinney 8-28-1842 Sh
Walker, Angeline to A. Cartwright 1-19-1869 (2-5-1869) F B
Walker, Ann J. to J. E. Brown 12-28-1857 Cr
Walker, Ann to Abe Fleming 10-25-1873 Hy
Walker, Ann to Ed McLean 9-5-1884 (9-6-1884) L
Walker, Ann to Edmund Shankle 10-8-1838 (no return) Hn
Walker, Ann to Jacob F. Eitel 1-12-1843 Sh
Walker, Ann to Thomas Moorer 12-29-1870 (no return) L
Walker, Anna L. to A. E. Parris 7-2-1863 (7-3-1863) O
Walker, Anna to Isham Conner 3-17-1850 We
Walker, Anna to Walker Hines 10-5-1871 Hy
Walker, Anna to Wesley Sutton 1-9-1878 Hy
Walker, Annis to Riley Williams 4-13-1873 Hy
Walker, Arabella C. to W. W. Simmons 10-23-1861 (no return) Dy
Walker, Artelia E. to Samuel Whorton 9-14-1852 (no return) F
Walker, Ava to Mat Harrison 12-29-1868 G B
Walker, Barbary to P. M. Tipton 11-16-1865 Dy
Walker, Belle to C. M. Anthony 12-23-1879 (12-24-1880) L
Walker, Bettie to Daniel Smith 11-13-1869 Hy
Walker, Betty to Danl. Rawlins 12-31-1872 Hy
Walker, Bora to Alex Fry 5-4-1880 (no return) L
Walker, C. A. to W. R. Kee 8-10-1862 Be
Walker, Callie to Jno. C. Claybrook 12-11-1869 (no return) Hy
Walker, Caroline A. to Benjamin F. Dill 4-1-1841 Sh
Walker, Caroline to John Kessler 1-2-1862 Sh
Walker, Catharine H. to James, jr. Correy 1-29-1857 Sh
Walker, Catherine to Hudson Scott 4-3-1876 (no return) L B
Walker, Charita to Dennis Smith 1-18-1871 (1-19-1871) Dy B
Walker, Charity to Caswell Shaw 3-3-1866 (3-5-1866) F B
Walker, Charity to James Parker 11-19-1873 Hy
Walker, Charlotte to J. C. Stone 1-4-1875 Hy
Walker, Charlotte to Nimrod Estes 6-1-1841 (1-3-1842) Ma
Walker, Cinthy to Tim Rollings 7-5-1877 Hy
Walker, Clarrissa to Wilson Newsom 1-2-1878 Hy
Walker, Clary to Charles Cuningham 12-29-1871 (11-30-1871) Cr B
Walker, Crecy to Nelson Taylor 7-28-1866 Hy
Walker, Cynthia M. to Eli Shankle 1-20-1857 Hn
Walker, Daffne to Dee Caruthers 1-17-1868 F B
Walker, Delia to David Woods 12-6-1879 (12-8-1879) Dy
Walker, Dolly Ann to John J. Henderson 9-9-1860 Hn
Walker, Dora to A. White 3-18-1861 Cr
Walker, E. H. to J. W. Buchanan 4-9-1857 Hn
Walker, E. J. to Chas. Thos. Oldham 3-18-1842 T
Walker, E. M. to W. A. Milam 10-17-1866 G
Walker, Eliza Ann to John Field 4-18-1863 (4-19-1863) Sh
Walker, Eliza E. to Henson Howard 7-30-1838 G
Walker, Eliza J. to William (Willis) C. Simpson 4-8-1848 (4-9-1848) O
Walker, Eliza Jane to Killis McDonald Smith 6-13-1853 (6-14-1853) Hr
Walker, Eliza to Dave Foster 12-16-1876 (12-24-1876) Dy
Walker, Eliza to George Holiday 11-19-1873 Hy

Walker, Eliza to George Williamson 3-30-1867 (4-7-1867) F B
Walker, Eliza to John C. Goodrich 7-11-1848 Sh
Walker, Elizabet J. to John B. Walker 3-4-1852 T
Walker, Elizabeth (Mrs.) to George Hardee 5-23-1868 (5-24-1868) Ma
Walker, Elizabeth A. to Achilles Plunkett 12-1-1836 Sh
Walker, Elizabeth A. to James L. Harvy 11-14-1842 (11-15-1842) F
Walker, Elizabeth Ann to Charles S. Rush 3-12-1844 Sh
Walker, Elizabeth C. to William F. England 12-20-1848 Hn
Walker, Elizabeth M. to Andrew J. Hays 4-17-1855 (4-18-1855) Sh
Walker, Elizabeth to B. R. Blake 12-31-1850 Cr
Walker, Elizabeth to Enoch Walker 12-23-1834 G
Walker, Elizabeth to H. D. Bantau 3-22-1851 (3-23-1851) O
Walker, Elizabeth to J. N. Prewett 12-8-1871 (no return) Cr
Walker, Elizabeth to J. P. Blackman 6-27-1866 (6-28-1866) O
Walker, Elizabeth to James Jones 3-8-1856 (3-9-1856) G
Walker, Elizabeth to John Dooley 1-7-1841 Sh
Walker, Elizabeth to Michael Kelly 6-2-1863 Sh
Walker, Elizabeth to Wm. A. Lowland 12-21-1863 (12-22-1863) Sh
Walker, Elizabeth to Wm. C. Waller 12-29-1858 Sh
Walker, Elizar to Warren Billingsby 10-7-1860 We
Walker, Ellen to Richard T. Johnson 10-8-1849 Sh
Walker, Elsia to Edwin Taliaferro 12-23-1869 Hy
Walker, Elve (Elsie?) A. to David Williams 2-7-1842 *(no return)* L
Walker, Emeline to L. H. Jackson 7-21-1856 G
Walker, Emily R. to Charles D. Walker 3-3-1847 (3-4-1847) T
Walker, Emily to Albert Neal 3-20-1871 (no return) F B
Walker, Emily to Henderson Hines 12-30-1875 (no return) Hy
Walker, Fanny to James Maberry 2-9-1867 (2-16-1867) F B
Walker, Flora to Lovelace Boyd 4-8-1876 (no return) Hy
Walker, Frances A. to Wm. Thomas 2-17-1842 Sh
Walker, Georgeann to Levi Kitchem 1-19-1844 F
Walker, Gracy to Richd. Boyd 1-18-1876 (no return) Hy
Walker, H. A. to B. C. Walker 2-1-1862 Hy
Walker, Hannah A. to Benjamin F. Wimberley 3-26-1858 Hn
Walker, Hannah M. to Thomas J. Taylor 1-7-1868 (1-8-1868) L
Walker, Hannah W. to Robt. Nicholson 3-30-1854 Sh
Walker, Hannah to Saml. S. McElwee 1-27-1855 Ma
Walker, Harret to W. E. Simpson 8-17-1875 (8-19-1875) O
Walker, Harriet (Mrs.) to A. B. Walker 11-15-1865 Hy
Walker, Harriet E. to John W. Callicott 10-9-1851 Hn
Walker, Harriett to Wash Anderson 5-26-1872 Hy
Walker, Helen to Champ Hubbard 10-4-1869 (no return) F B
Walker, Helen to Elijah Lovelace 12-16-1884 (12-17-1884) L
Walker, Helen to John S. Rice 8-5-1856 Be
Walker, Henretta to Martin Conner 12-31-1874 Hy
Walker, Hester to David Jett 1-30-1872 (no return) L B
Walker, Hester to John Baker 10-19-1868 (10-30-1868) F B
Walker, Idella to G. W. Reynolds 3-6-1876 (3-8-1876) Dy
Walker, Irene E. to Thomas R. Duncan 4-24-1861 Sh
Walker, Isabella to David Lewis 12-3-1859 Sh
Walker, Jane F. to D. M. Jones 11-8-1866 Hn
Walker, Jane L. to George W. Billings 11-6-1847 (11-18-1847) T
Walker, Jane to Alexa McCullough 11-29-1851 (11-30-1851) Sh
Walker, Jane to Elisha Collins 1-7-1863 (1-11-1863) Sh
Walker, Jane to Green Poe 8-6-1844 Be
Walker, Jane to James Walker 10-2-1844 (10-15-1844) G
Walker, Jane to John Kirkpatrick 7-30-1849 (8-14-1849) T
Walker, Jane to Parnemus Fifer 2-20-1844 (2-21-1844) G
Walker, Jennie to Henry Taliaferro 12-27-1874 Hy
Walker, Jennie to James Duggins 4-30-1870 G
Walker, Jerusah D. to John A. Smith 10-25-1859 (10-28-1859) T
Walker, Joanna to Parker Johnson 1-3-1880 (1-4-1880) L
Walker, Josephine O. to Hugh L. White 6-30-1867 Be
Walker, Judia to Saml. Admas? 3-17-1866 T
Walker, Katie to July Shepherd 12-4-1872 (12-5-1872) L B
Walker, Kisa to Polk Howard 1-26-1870 (no return) Dy
Walker, L. A. to W. H. Butler 9-28-1869 G
Walker, Laura to G. W. Willis 2-13-1884 (no return) L
Walker, Lavinia to Charley Easley 2-9-1867 Hy
Walker, Lillie to R. G. Anthony 10-26-1882 L
Walker, Liuisa? to Volentine Walker 11-1-1870 (11-2-1870) Ma
Walker, Louisa J. to W. S. Sugg 1-18-1864 (1-20-1864) L
Walker, Louisa to L. Black 8-14-1854 (no return) F
Walker, Lucinda to Robert Harden 2-3-1857 Be
Walker, Lucy Ann to James B. Walker 7-13-1852 Be
Walker, Lucy to Antny Turner 1-28-1870 (1-30-1870) F B
Walker, Lucy to Crocket Mann 1-31-1872 Hy
Walker, Lucy to George Carnes 4-28-1866 (5-13-1866) F
Walker, Luizer C. to George I. Cook 2-9-1868 G
Walker, Lusinda to Henry Brandon 3-23-1867 (3-24-1867) T
Walker, Luzinda to Thomas J. Slocum 7-23-1857 (7-27-1857) Ma
Walker, M. A. to A. C. Walker 8-3-1869 (8-4-1869) Dy
Walker, M. C. to H. H. Mitchell 12-12-1860 (12-13-1860) F
Walker, M. E. to G. E. Chandler 11-13-1874 (11-15-1874) O
Walker, M. E. to John W. Massey 3-1-1879 (3-5-1879) Dy
Walker, M. J. to A. J. Little 5-14-1864 (no return) Cr
Walker, M. J. to John T. Cates 1-4-1870 G

Walker, M. L. (Mrs.) to Daniel S. Tucker 2-19-1872 (2-20-1872) Dy
Walker, M. to John W. Towson 2-2-1865 (2-6-1865) Cr
Walker, Malinda J. to Thomas Arnold 3-3-1838 (3-4-1838) L
Walker, Malinda to B. F. Doomis 10-16-1855 (no return) Hn
Walker, Malinda to Jim Rhodes 1-14-1870 G B
Walker, Manerva J. to Joseph J. J. Hale 8-15-1849 (8-16-1849) G
Walker, Margaret E. to Harvey P. Smith 10-6-1842 Hr
Walker, Margaret to Bryant White 3-24-1870 (no return) Dy
Walker, Margaret to Dave Coldwell 10-5-1872 (10-6-1872) T
Walker, Maria B. to John A. Sannoner 10-31-1853 (11-2-1853) Sh
Walker, Maria to Mitchel Sullivant 1-18-1866 Hy
Walker, Mariah to Charles Beasley 12-12-1868 (12-13-1868) F B
Walker, Martha A. C. to Leonard Baker 1-10-1872 (1-11-1872) Dy
Walker, Martha A. to Alexander Campbell 9-6-1856 (9-7-1856) Hr
Walker, Martha Agnes to Charles Webster Hoffler 8-7-1849 T
Walker, Martha Ann to William N. Dillard 8-22-1837 (8-24-1837) G
Walker, Martha Ann to Wm. H. Rogers 3-4-1853 Sh
Walker, Martha J. to Elias Halliburton 4-2-1875 (no return) Hy
Walker, Martha M. to James A. Joodard 3-13-1861 T
Walker, Martha P. to S. R. Haleman 4-13-1854 Hn
Walker, Martha to John Williams 9-6-1879 (9-7-1879) L B
Walker, Martha to Joseph England 1-21-1828 G
Walker, Martha to Peter Strain 12-25-1866 T
Walker, Martha to Rachael Cooper 10-16-1839 Be
Walker, Martha to Robert A. Hill 1-10-1848 L
Walker, Martha to Rufus Crocker 3-11-1848 (3-16-1848) G
Walker, Martha to T. B. Anderson 12-18-1867 (no return) Hy
Walker, Martha to Wm. Turner 5-12-1869 (no return) Dy
Walker, Mary A. (Mrs.) to James Dillon 1-15-1868 G
Walker, Mary A. to Wm. H. Polsgrove 11-23-1871 O
Walker, Mary A. to William F. Jackson 6-22-1853 (6-23-1853) G
Walker, Mary Ann to A. W. Caldwell 11-2-1868 (no return) F
Walker, Mary Ann to John G. Adams 6-17-1849 Sh
Walker, Mary B. to W. B. Smith 2-6-1861 (2-7-1861) Dy
Walker, Mary C. to R. R. Ridley 9-10-1851 *(no return)* F
Walker, Mary Catharine to R. W. Floyed 4-13-1852 (no return) F
Walker, Mary E. to David C. Phelan 11-18-1863 G
Walker, Mary E. to Felix Hornsby 12-1-1863 Sh
Walker, Mary F. to James W. King 1-15-1857 (1-18-1857) Ma
Walker, Mary J. to James N. Rust 9-5-1860 G
Walker, Mary J. to John Crab 3-29-1873 (3-30-1873) Cr
Walker, Mary J. to John D. Graves 10-18-1853 Hn
Walker, Mary J. to John Quinn 3-12-1861 Be
Walker, Mary Jane to George Washington Manasker 12-19-1848
   (12-7?-1848) T
Walker, Mary Jane to William J. (Dr.) Drake 5-3-1859 Ma
Walker, Mary L. to John H. Lindsey 12-26-1877 Hy
Walker, Mary M. to Asa A. Atkins 12-14-1874 (12-15-1874) Dy
Walker, Mary R. E. to J. M. Young 9-4-1876 (9-6-1876) Dy
Walker, Mary to Ephraim Brown 5-31-1835 Hy
Walker, Mary to F. Whiten 12-13-1855 Hn
Walker, Mary to J. S. Chamberlain 11-22-1877 Dy
Walker, Mary to Jessee Grayham 5-5-1873 (7-4-1873) T
Walker, Mary to John Macklin 11-12-1874 Hy
Walker, Mary to Russell Moore 3-20-1854 (3-21-1854) T
Walker, Mary to Thomas N. Jackson 2-16-1841 Hn
Walker, Mary to W. H. Macon 9-28-1871 Dy
Walker, Mary to Wm. Delashmet 2-14-1855 (2-15-1855) T
Walker, Mary to Wm. Standley 1-28-1849 (2-1-1849) O
Walker, Matilda J. to Archibald Warren 6-8-1858 Sh
Walker, Matilda to Wm. Y. Fuqua 7-25-1840 (no return) Cr
Walker, Mily A. to Isaak K. McCaddams 11-19-1856 We
Walker, Minerva to Eli Jones 3-14-1856 (3-18-1856) G
Walker, Miss to Providence Williams 2-5-1838 (no return) F
Walker, Mollie to Allen Hay 5-23-1878 Hy
Walker, Mrs. Salina to Albert Roane 7-19-1867 (7-21-1867) T
Walker, N. C. to W. T. Ward 11-26-1873 T
Walker, Nancy E. to A. L. Ray 11-5-1860 (11-6-1860) Dy
Walker, Nancy M. to John N. Chambliss 6-4-1852 (6-6-1852) Hr
Walker, Nancy M. to William M. McFerren 11-20-1852 (no return) F
Walker, Nancy to Breten Long 2-14-1850 We
Walker, Nancy to Frank Dickerson 4-16-1872 Hy
Walker, Nancy to George W. Ford 7-18-1829 Sh
Walker, Nancy to James Drummons 1-15-1842 (1-16-1842) T
Walker, Nancy to James Pearson 3-28-1869 G B
Walker, Nancy to Wesley V.? Ross 9-16-1838 Hn
Walker, Nannie F. to J. W. Bullin 1-27-1873 O
Walker, Narcissa J. to William Masters 3-26-1863 O
Walker, Neely Ellender to William Walker 8-8-1846 (8-9-1846) Ma
Walker, Nella to Richard Smith 1-18-1866 G
Walker, Otey to Valintine Walker 1-18-1850 (1-20-1850) Ma
Walker, Patience to Charley Devinney 8-4-1841 Sh
Walker, Patsy to Jerry Goodman 7-16-1878 (no return) Hy
Walker, Paulina S. to Jesse R. Haynie 8-13-1850 Hy
Walker, Polly to John Long 3-8-1865 (3-10-1865) Cr
Walker, Polly to William England 2-28-1827 G
Walker, Pricilla S. to David Adams 9-19-1855 (no return) F

Brides

Walker, R. F. to Thomas Holeman, jr. 1-9-1860 (1-10-1860) Sh
Walker, Rachael to Thomas Newsom 5-30-1844 Sh
Walker, Rachel to Isaac Thomas 12-27-1876 Dy
Walker, Rachel to Lewis Gurley 12-14-1851 (12-24-1851) O
Walker, Rebecca J. to James H. King 7-21-1849 (7-25-1849) G
Walker, Rebecca to Theo. Arnold 8-27-1839 (9-4-1839) Ma
Walker, Rhoda to William Wilsons 12-21-1853 (12-22-1853) Sh
Walker, Rosannah S. to Robert J. Caldwell 9-26-1860 Hn
Walker, Rose to Isham Williams 8-29-1874 Hy
Walker, Roxanna to T. W. Scott 8-11-1853 (no return) F
Walker, Rutha to James H. McDowell 4-1-1834 (4-3-1834) G
Walker, S. E. to John E. Wood 8-3-1874 (8-6-1874) T
Walker, S. J. to Thomas W. Palmer 2-15-1861 We
Walker, S. M. to F. M. Davis 3-22-1866 G
Walker, Sallie J. to S. D. Reeves 11-12-1866 G
Walker, Sarah A. to William R. Haywood 9-1-1852 G
Walker, Sarah Ann to E. J. Davis 1-9-1862 Sh
Walker, Sarah E. to Beverly Bomar 10-20-1840 Cr
Walker, Sarah Elizabeth to Henry Harrison 1-2-1842 (1-3-1842) T
Walker, Sarah F. to G. W. Billings 12-11-1865 (12-19-1865) T
Walker, Sarah H. to William Moore 7-4-1838 (7-5-1838) O
Walker, Sarah M. to E. C. Robards 4-16-1867 Ma
Walker, Sarah P. to Fielding A. Lucas 9-15-1841 Sh
Walker, Sarah T. to B. S. Fant 4-25-1849 Sh
Walker, Sarah to Benjam. Timms 8-31-1869 (9-1-1869) T
Walker, Sarah to David H. Stewart 7-3-1845 Sh
Walker, Sarah to Henry C. Clarke 3-21-1870 Hy
Walker, Sarah to Henry Foster 12-11-1880 (12-17-1880) Dy
Walker, Sarah to James P. Scarbrough 12-17-1860 (no return) Hn
Walker, Sarah to R. H. Milner 11-26-1840 O
Walker, Siney to David Arnold 8-10-1841 G
Walker, Sophronia to Thomas B. Ferrell 4-14-1859 O
Walker, Susan M. to William Smith 1-5-1860 (no return) F
Walker, Susan to E. H. Crocker 12-26-1836 (1-5-1837) G
Walker, Susan to James Hallums 3-29-1861 Sh
Walker, Susan to James R. Weaks 1-15-1867 Hn
Walker, Susan to Lafayette Tharp 6-5-1863 Sh
Walker, Susan to Robert Mann 7-29-1844 (7-31-1844) Ma
Walker, Tabitha W. to V. L. Rose 1-14-1852 Hn
Walker, Uginia to Luther Hessey 1-7-1868 Hy
Walker, V. A. to C. M. Stewart 2-13-1860 Sh
Walker, V. C. to H. H. Mitchell 12-30-1866 (1-3-1866) F
Walker, Vanleer S. to Marian F. Parker 1-11-1854 (1-12-1854) G
Walker, Zelpha A. to Hugh Cravesn 10-7-1867 O
Walker, Zilpha C. to Alfred Gurley 3-1-1857 O
Wall, Adelia to A. G. Gilbert 6-23-1861 Hn
Wall, Ann E. to Elvin Haynes 3-15-1867 Hn B
Wall, Elizabeth A. to John S. Herndon 11-5-1862 (11-6-1862) F
Wall, Fannie to Ral Moore 12-1-1871 Hy
Wall, Jane to W. L. Alexander 3-8-1866 O
Wall, Louiza E. to Isiah Huffman 8-23-1849 Cr
Wall, Louiza E. to Jeremiah Frazure 11-13-1851 (no return) F
Wall, M. A. to James A. Seymour 11-7-1854 (no return) F
Wall, Margaret B. to James S. Barger 8-28-1855 Cr
Wall, Margaret M. to William C. Allen 12-23-1847 F
Wall, Margaret R. to Wm. T. Humphreys 11-2-1850 (no return) F
Wall, Margarett A. to James M. Gilliam 1-16-1843 (1-17-1843) F
Wall, Martha J. to A. G. Holt 10-28-1847 (no return) F
Wall, Martha J. to John D. Brandon 4-27-1853 Cr
Wall, MarthaH. to Jacob W. McCord 12-20-1860 Hn
Wall, Mary E. to Wyatt B. Watkins 8-23-1853 (no return) F
Wall, Mary L. to A. C. Holmes 5-1-1873 Cr
Wall, Mollie E. to Wm. J. Harper 12-31-1870 (no return) Hy
Wall, Nancy A. to Andrew J. Coleman 3-8-1842 Hn
Wall, Sarah A. to J. B. Crawford 4-21-1859 (4-20?-1859) F
Wall, Sarah E. to F. E. Alexander 4-4-1864 (no return) Hn
Wall, Sinia E. to William H. Hester 4-3-1841 (4-5-1841) F
Wall, Susan C. to Green D. Dillahunty 11-20-1839 Hn
Wall, Tempy to J. P. O'Kelly 8-18-1859 (8-21-1859) F
Wallace, Anna to Alex Whitehead 11-13-1879 (12-27-1879) L B
Wallace, Araminta to Barney Mack 10-27-1860 Cr
Wallace, Baker to George Morgan 11-11-1882 (11-16-1882) L
Wallace, Catherine to Henery Shea (Shaer) 10-7-1862 Sh
Wallace, Catherine to Henery Shoer 10-7-1862 Sh
Wallace, Cathrine to John McGraw 8-22-1847 Cr
Wallace, Dona to Lea Guthrie 3-5-1864 Sh
Wallace, Eliza Catharine to Wm. Thomas Byrd 8-28-1867 (8-29-1867) Ma
Wallace, Eliza to A. D. Denning 10-7-1866 Hn
Wallace, Eliza to William A. Brand 11-20-1850 We
Wallace, Elizabeth J. to J. (Dr.) Bobbett 12-31-1845 (1-1-1845) G
Wallace, Elizabeth to George Parrish 11-3-1863 Cr
Wallace, Elizabeth to John Mayberry 11-15-1866 (11-18-1866) T
Wallace, Elizabeth to W. T. Kidd 12-31-1878 (1-1-1879) Dy
Wallace, Ella to Jeff Mayben 2-14-1878 (2-17-1878) L
Wallace, Emily E. to Jas. E. Cobb 12-25-1873 Hy
Wallace, Esther A. to Albert S. Miller 4-15-1840 Sh
Wallace, Etna to John A. Ellis 11-28-1850 Sh

Page 303

Wallace, Frances A. to Marion D. Jones 2-23-1863 (no return) Hy
Wallace, Frankie J. to Thomas R. Loflin 5-28-1866 G
Wallace, H. E. to John R. Fite 5-27-1863 Dy
Wallace, Harriet G. to John A. Ellis 9-8-1855 (9-10-1855) Sh
Wallace, Harriet to Esquer Jeter 12-1-1872 Hy
Wallace, Jane to James Todd 1-6-1861 Hn
Wallace, Jane to John J. Jones 10-27-1861 (no return) Hy
Wallace, Leathy R. to James Peebles 11-9-1848 (no return) Hn
Wallace, Lucinda E. to Walter Richards 10-7-1845 Sh
Wallace, M. E. to J. A. Hogue 1-3-1861 (1-4-1861) Hr
Wallace, Margarett to George W. Carroll 12-21-1870 (12-22-1870) F
Wallace, Martha B. to William T. Dickins 2-26-1845 (2-27-1845) G
Wallace, Martha to George Parish 2-14-1844 Cr
Wallace, Mary E. (Mrs.) to Saml. G. Martin 12-2-1861 (12-5-1861) Sh
Wallace, Mary E. to John R. Fite 10-23-1852 (10-24-1852) G
Wallace, Mary H. to James H. Owens 11-15-1855 (no return) Hn
Wallace, Mary M. to Henry W. Pemberton 3-21-1853 (3-22-1853) G
Wallace, Mary to Michael Cusick 3-4-1863 Sh
Wallace, Mary to Wm. H. McCool 11-29-1876 Hy
Wallace, Mayville to William Prock 8-12-1861 (8-13-1861) Dy
Wallace, Nancy J. to G. S. Milam 3-15-1865 Dy
Wallace, Nancy to H. T. Willingham 11-8-1847 (11-9-1847) F
Wallace, Olivia to William O'Neal 12-31-1878 (1-2-1879) L B
Wallace, Polly to John Young 2-8-1845 (2-9-1845) G
Wallace, Rachael to Jeremiah S. Crain 2-5-1829 Ma
Wallace, Rebecca C. to Thomas Todd 9-15-1857 Hn
Wallace, Rebecca to Frank G. Sampson 2-6-1868 Dy
Wallace, Sarah Jane to E. R. McCain 6-30-1846 (no return) We
Wallace, Sarah to Geo. W. Bill 7-10-1850 (no return) F
Wallace, Sarah to Green Reynold 3-13-1850 G
Wallace, Sarah to Leander D. Lawrence 12-13-1845 (12-15-1845) G
Wallace, Sarah to Patrick Mulloy 2-21-1850 Sh
Wallace, Sintha A. to Jonathan Reed 10-23-1860 Hn
Wallace, Susana to J. A. Wallace 3-25-1873 (3-27-1873) Dy
Wallace, Tennessee M. to J. J. Sherley 11-5-1865 Mn
Wallace, Teressa to Lemiel Taylor 9-8-1830 Ma
Wallace, Virginia to Robert F. Willcox (Nilcex) 7-21-1863 (7-22-1863) Sh
Wallacle, Margarett (Miss) to James D. Alborn 4-15-1864 Sh
Wallae, Adaline to Mose Fowlkes 9-4-1876 Dy
Wallan, L. Evaline to R. T. Golden 8-22-1866 (8-23-1866) Dy
Wallden, Demaras to Silas L. Rachels 8-25-1859 We
Waller, Aletha F. to Madison Linton 10-10-1855 Hn
Waller, Anna Reid to John J. Bolton 11-10-1874 (11-11-1874) T
Waller, Billy to Jas. Abington 12-12-1851 (no return) F
Waller, Catharine to C. Crenshaw 2-18-1874 T B
Waller, Catharine to S.(L) B. Roberts 10-4-1850 Hr
Waller, Eliza to Jessee B. Morgan 1-17-1850 G
Waller, Elizabeth M. to P. T. Glover 1-2-1867 O
Waller, Elmira B. to James R. Olive 11-14-1854 (11-15-1854) Sh
Waller, Emma to John Talley 11-21-1874 T
Waller, Lucinda to Irwin Parrott 3-4-1846 (3-5-1846) F
Waller, Lucy Janie to James W. Thompson 2-9-1839 (2-12-1839) F
Waller, M. N. to N. P. Ferrell 11-2-1854 (no return) F
Waller, Malinda to Willis Walton 12-11-1860 F
Waller, Margaret E. (Mrs.) to J. Parrott 12-11-1854 (no return) F
Waller, Martha E. to Absolum C. Ralph 7-28-1852 (no return) F
Waller, Martha F. to Edward G. Waller 2-7-1845 (2-18-1845) F
Waller, Mary J. to Joshua C. Hinchey 12-1-1850 F
Waller, Nancy E. to D. M. Stokes 11-22-1853 Hn
Waller, S. A. to T. B. Carter 2-28-1866 (3-1-1866) Cr
Waller, Sarah to Erwin Estes 9-9-1861 Hr
Waller, Susan A. to L. G. Waller 4-27-1846 (5-3-1846) F
Waller, Virginia to Isaac Gordon 4-25-1875 Hy
Wallice, Annitha to Harris Bradford 8-20-1859 G
Wallice, Arenia to J. B. George 4-28-1860 Cr
Wallice, Burline to James Ball 12-2-1863 G
Wallice, Clarisa Ann to John Baker 6-5-1869 (no return) L
Wallice, Eliza to Stephen Wallice 9-20-1862 G
Wallice, Jane to John Reynolds 12-2-1859 (12-3-1859) G
Wallice, M. A. to D. H. Leonard 10-5-1863 G
Wallice, Nancy to Jas. A. Jack 2-10-1857 G
Wallice, Penny to Thomas Reynolds 3-7-1861 G
Wallice, S. A. to Jonathan Wallice 1-13-1857 G
Wallice, S. to Hiran Wallis 3-12-1852 Cr
Wallice, Sarah J. to Nathaniel Williams 4-5-1856 (4-6-1856) G
Wallice, Sarah to James Perry 6-24-1862 (6-25-1862) G
Wallingford, Matilda to William McMinn 2-29-1844 G
Wallingsford, Martha B. to Henry Gately 3-7-1836 G
Wallingsford, Mary Ann H. to Green Jacobs 10-21-1834 (10-23-1834) G
Wallis, Ba y C. to Henry Aldridge 4-16-1869 G
Wallis, Belinda to Alexander Rogers 1-29-1828 (2-2-1828) Ma
Wallis, Elizabeth to Rob't A. Flippo 7-17-1867 (7-25-1867) O
Wallis, Frances to N. G. Jackson 12-24-1855 G
Wallis, Franky to M. R. Caudle 11-8-1859 (11-10-1859) O
Wallis, Jane to Lewis Petty 10-30-1855 Cr
Wallis, Jane to Solomon Riley 6-21-1855 O
Wallis, L. E. to I. M. Bell 1-23-1867 O

Brides

Wallis, M. J. to J. H. Baskins 7-13-1864 (7-14-1864) T
Wallis, M. J. to William L. Amos 12-2-1867 (12-5-1867) Ma
Wallis, Martha A. to LaFayette Wiles 12-12-1855 (12-13-1855) Sh
Wallis, Mary E. to Charles S. Moore 5-26-1867 G
Wallis, Mary to John Henry Cox 9-24-1870 (9-28-1870) L
Wallis, Mary to Spencer Wilson 10-1-1866 (10-5-1866) T
Wallis, Minerva to John Bulling 12-13-1865 G
Wallons, Ann to George W. Nichols 5-26-1853 Sh
Walls, Almedy to H. D. Noel 17-18-1865 G
Walls, Amanda J. to Nonod Hicks 4-24-1855 (4-26-1855) G
Walls, Drusilla C. to Allen C. Johnson 9-2-1857 Hn
Walls, Edney to John McCullough 7-14-1853 G
Walls, Elizabeth to Fonzey Jones 9-16-1850 (9-17-1850) G
Walls, Elizabeth to L. T. Williams 8-13-1872 (8-15-1872) Cr
Walls, Ella to Ethelbert L. Pierce 11-21-1872 Dy
Walls, Harriet A. to Jack Thomas Champion 3-10-1849 (3-13-1849) Hr
Walls, Harriet A. to L. P. Ray 12-25-1865 G
Walls, Jane to Henry Washington 12-28-1868 (1-18-1869) F B
Walls, Jennie to H. L. Crate 3-14-1872 Hy
Walls, Louisa to Charles H. Nelson 10-14-1856 Ma
Walls, Margaret to Isaac D. Gore 3-24-1859 G
Walls, Mary Ann to J. W. Williamson 4-21-1868 Be
Walls, Mulinda to Elisha Belch 1-6-1844 (2-3-1844) G
Walls, Sallie B. to R. M. Harper 1-22-1878 Hy
Walls, Selah to John Swink 11-23-1865 G
Walls, Sidney to Alex F. Hayes 11-18-1852 Hn
Walls, Susan G. to Jacob Blessing 9-8-1856 (9-11-1856) G
Walls, Vicia to W. T. Hargrove 8-11-1866 O
Walpole, Amanda J. to George W. Chambers 1-22-1869 (2-1-1869) L
Walpole, Fannie to Erasmus? Thurmond 1-1-1884 L
Walpole, Lula to William Duncan 7-26-1880 L
Walpole, M. F. to J. T. Younger 7-21-1864 (7-25-1864) Cr
Walpole, Mary to William A. Johnson 8-31-1839 (no return) L
Walpole, Mary(Nancy) to Thomas J. Bryant 12-29-1856 (1-1-1857) Hr
Walpole, Sarah C. to Wm. J. Voss 3-18-1861 (3-19-1861) L
Walpole, Sarah Caroline to Josias M. Chambers 12-29-1845 (1-1-1846) L
Walpole, Sarah E. to Erasmus Thurmond 9-13-1879 (no return) L
Walser, Ernestine to P. H. Heinrich 11-15-1859 (11-16-1859) Sh
Walsh, Dinebia to Frank B. Hamilton 11-18-1869 Ma
Walsh, Georgia Ann to Charles Wilson 8-26-1874 O B
Walsh, Italia A. to Joseph H. Cash 5-12-1859 L
Walsh, Mary F. to A. Hamilton Burkhead 1-28-1869 Ma
Walsh, Mary to Charles Looney 11-23-1861 (11-24-1861) Sh
Walsh, Mary to S. C. Jones 10-11-1864 Mn
Walsh, Sarah A. to Council B. Mayo 2-1-1870 Ma
Walsin, Fanni A. to S. McDavid 10-1-1867 (10-2-1867) Dy
Walston, Isabel to Amasa Hodges 10-24-1850 Sh
Walston, Lucy Jane to Henry M. Sexton 7-4-1866 (7-5-1866) Ma
Walter, Anner to Henry Gray 2-6-1877 Hy
Walter, Filo Mina to Urs. Gunti 1-31-1860 Sh
Walter, Lovey F. to Joseph J. McGuire 6-20-1858 Cr
Walter, Lucinda to Joseph K. Sloane 1-15-1852 (1-19-1852) Sh
Walter, M. C. to A. L. Brantley 8-13-1885 (not endorsed) L
Walter, Martha S. to E. J. Jackson 12-3-1868 Cr
Walters, Bettie to John P. Irion 1-21-1864 Hn
Walters, E. J. to E. A. Comer 9-20-1863 Hn
Walters, Elizabeth to James Geurin 12-24-1867 Hn
Walters, Emily to William R. Haynes 8-25-1848 Hn
Walters, J. N. to J. W. Smith 12-2-1869 Cr
Walters, Joana to Samuel Johnson 1-9-1857 We
Walters, Martha Ann to Wm. Martin Longmire no date Ma
Walters, Martha to John D. Crider 9-5-1850 Cr
Walters, Sarah Ann to Robert Rushing 10-17-1839 Hn
Walther, Sarah A. to John Cunningham 12-27-1846 Hn
Walton, Amanda A. to William H. Dillahinty 12-17-1866 (12-18-1866) T
Walton, America to Willis Stafford 8-16-1866 (no return) F B
Walton, Becka to Needham Smith 4-14-1874 (4-15-1874) T
Walton, Bettie to Solaman Haynes 12-11-1866 (12-13-1866) T
Walton, Eliza to James Askew 10-20-1842 Cr
Walton, Hattie M. to Edward B. Trezevant 7-6-1858 Sh
Walton, Jemimia to Marion Reynolds 7-31-1854 (8-2-1854) L
Walton, Jennie to Adam Devenport 10-24-1864 Sh
Walton, Louiza to John Patterson 9-12-1851 (no return) Hn
Walton, Lucy to Thomas Walton 1-9-1867 (1-17-1867) F B
Walton, M. A. to John L. Jones 7-21-1864 (7-23-1864) Cr
Walton, M. A. to W. T. Fields 12-22-1869 O
Walton, M. J. to J. H. Wyatt 1-8-1867 G
Walton, Martha to W. E. Mitchell 9-21-1864 O
Walton, Mary Ann to Ambrose B. Mitchell 11-16-1843 (no return) Hn
Walton, Mary E. to William S. Innman 9-28-1847 L
Walton, Mary G. to J. W. Morroe 12-2-1873 (12-3-1870?) O
Walton, Mary J. to Jefferson K. Bradley 6-30-1847 O
Walton, Mary M. to John W. Rose 4-21-1858 T
Walton, Mary to James Wyse 4-26-1869 Hy
Walton, Minerva A. to George G. Dunn 9-3-1856 G
Walton, Minerva to Jerre Ford 1-20-1870 T
Walton, S. V. to R. A. Williams 11-13-1867 Hn

Walton, Sarah E. to J. C. Kinney 2-20-1873 T
Walton, Sarah F. to Richard B. Owen 12-18-1867 T
Walton, Sarah to I. M. Caldwell 12-21-1866 (12-25-1866) O
Walton, Sarah to M. L. Davis 1-19-1854 (no return) F
Waltrop, Elizabeth A. to Harrison Holt 7-14-1842 (7-17-1842) G
Wamack, Indiana S. to Charles Crenshaw 10-29-1855 (10-30-1855) Sh
Wamble, Mahaly F. to Moses P. Walters 1-28-1863 Mn
Wandell, Mary E. to James L. Maginnis 1-29-1862 (1-30-1862) Sh
Wanger, Mary to Andrew Smith 6-9-1860 (6-11-1860) Sh
Want, Martha A. to Andrew J. Sumpter 8-20-1858 (8-23-1858) Sh
Want, S. A. (Mrs.) to J. W. Wilkerson 11-3-1863 Sh
Want?, Mamie J. to J. Cas Tipton 6-5-1870 Dy
Wap (Wass?), Hannah to James F. Baugh (Baughman) 5-21-1859 (5-22-1859) Sh
Warbane, Ellen to Richard Bason 7-15-1851 Sh
Warbrittan, Mary F. to Samuel S. Hane 10-7-1865 (10-8-1865) Cr
Warbritton, Elizabeth to Nathen Kirk 12-4-1850 Cr
Warbritton, Emma C. to James R. McArnally 3-11-1867 (3-13-1867) Cr
Warbritton, Mary Jane to Nathan Kirk 1-24-1870 (1-29-1870) Cr
Warburton, M. S. to Lodwick Partin 6-9-1855 Sh
Ward (Wood?), Elizer to Tom Jenkins 7-24-1866 G
Ward (Word?), Cintha A. to Eli Tilghman 3-3-1862 G
Ward (Word?), E. H. to E. M. Chandler 9-30-1868 G
Ward (Word?), Julia to A. Marshall 1-2-1866 G
Ward (Word?), Lanorea L. to M. L. Trellien 9-6-1865 G
Ward (Word?), N. A. to W. B. Taylor 5-8-1866 G
Ward, Amanda A. M. to Daniel S. Cleaver 3-20-1864 Hn
Ward, Ann E. to Archibald I. T. White 1-25-1859 (1-26-1859) O
Ward, Ann E. to James H. Humphreys 10-6-1857 (10-7-1857) Sh
Ward, Ann to W. R. Hunt 8-28-1843 (no return) Hn
Ward, Asenith to John E. Davis 10-12-1868 (10-14-1868) Dy
Ward, Barbary A. to Thos. F. Babbett 5-16-1860 F
Ward, C. N. to J. N. Peebles 3-15-1859 We
Ward, Callie D. to C. W. Cates 2-9-1885 (2-10-1885) L
Ward, Caroline H. to Simeon P. Witt 2-23-1853 (2-24-1853) Sh
Ward, Caroline to Charles Rutledge 12-27-1841 (12-28-1841) O
Ward, Catherine to Robert G. Espy 11-18-1846 (11-19-1846) L
Ward, Celia to Ben Jenkins 3-25-1880 L B
Ward, Charity C. to William H. Gamel 5-16-1855 L
Ward, Cynthia P. to R. R. Hodges 5-24-1862 (no return) Hy
Ward, D. M. to E. R. Fuller 8-26-1862 Mn
Ward, Dicy to Theophilus J. Ward 1-20-1853 Be
Ward, Drucilla to Robert H. Elmore 2-25-1863 Cr
Ward, Drucilla to Robert H. Elmore 2-25-1863 (2-27-1863) Cr
Ward, Eliza E. to Benjamin J. Brewerr 12-26-1867 Be
Ward, Eliza Jane to Aaron C. Bassford 9-25-1856 Hn
Ward, Elizabeth E. to Henry Lane 4-7-1846 O
Ward, Elizabeth J. to A. F. Gibbs 1-8-1850 Hn
Ward, Elizabeth J. to Ashly R. Crawford 2-26-1848 (3-2-1848) Hr
Ward, Elizabeth S. to Wylie B. Edington 2-23-1852 Be
Ward, Elizabeth T. to John W.. Vaughn 1-10-1861 Hn
Ward, Elizabeth W. to Wm. J. Stephenson 4-1-1839 Cr
Ward, Elizabeth to Elias H. Hooker 12-21-1845 (no return) Cr
Ward, Elizabeth to F. A. Kemp 8-23-1846 We
Ward, Elizabeth to John Bond 1-11-1843 Be
Ward, Elizabeth to John Nance 10-25-1845 Hn
Ward, Elizabeth to Josiah Busby 9-20-1846 We
Ward, Elizabeth to Major Thompson 2-6-1834 Sh
Ward, Elizabeth to R. R. Hodges 10-14-1867 G
Ward, Elizabeth to Thomas Trainer 1-3-1833 (1-4-1833) G
Ward, Elizabeth to William Carter 5-7-1829 Sh
Ward, Emma D. to James E. Moore 4-6-1866 Hy
Ward, Etta to B. F. O'Daniel 3-31-1874 (4-1-1874) O
Ward, Eveline to William Ward 7-15-1852 Be
Ward, F. A. to Wm. D. Lancaster 11-25-1864 O
Ward, Hannar A. to Lewis W. Reddick 10-6-1862 We
Ward, J. R. to M. B. Flippin 4-7-1866 (4-8-1866) Cr
Ward, Jane to John A. Wilson 10-13-1842 Hn
Ward, Jane to Wm. Mesley 9-12-1858 We
Ward, Jemima C. to F. P. Dorris 11-29-1863 Hn
Ward, Josephine to H. H. Tinkle 1-11-1869 L
Ward, Josephine to F. M. Allen 8-2-1873 (8-3-1873) O
Ward, Julia Ann to William C. Stephens 3-9-1853 G
Ward, June to James Hays 8-6-1859 Hn
Ward, L. C. to T. M. Patterson 1-4-1870 (1-5-1870) Dy
Ward, Laura to T. D. Montgomery 10-7-1866 (10-30-1866) G
Ward, Leila to Anderson Herrington 1-14-1882 L B
Ward, Lucinda A. to Wm. Murry 6-22-1843 We
Ward, Lucinda to W. B. Edington 3-24-1862 Be
Ward, Lucretia to James N. Barr 3-14-1838 (no return) Hn
Ward, Lucy Ann to Samuel M. Fry 12-23-1848 (12-26-1848) Ma
Ward, Lucy to Henry Jones 3-2-1842 Hn
Ward, Lucy to John Henning 2-13-1878 L B
Ward, Luisa C. to James R. Keath 10-17-1846 (9?-18-1846) G
Ward, Luiza to Richard Shelton 12-27-1871 (12-28-1871) T
Ward, M. E. to James P. McKnight 1-6-1863 (1-14-1863) O
Ward, M. E. to M. A. Avrett 11-6-1868 (11-8-1868) Dy

Ward, M. F. to W. H. Key 6-28-1865 (no return) Hn
Ward, M. H. to Robert H. Pollock 7-17-1850 O
Ward, M. J. to T. R. Akin 12-9-1874 (12-10-1874) Dy
Ward, M. L. to T. P. Reynolds 9-6-1865 G
Ward, M. P. to R. W. Wagster 8-20-1877 (8-21-1877) L
Ward, Maranda F. to John K. Quin 9-9-1853 (9-13-1853) L
Ward, Margaret E. to Thomas E. Parham 12-7-1852 Hn
Ward, Margaret Jane to A. F. McGehee 11-27-1854 (11-28-1854) Hr
Ward, Margaret O. to Cornelius Ringly 5-8-1851 Sh
Ward, Martha A. to James Cole 12-2-1860 We
Ward, Martha A. to Richard B. Jones 6-17-1866 G
Ward, Martha Ann to Wm. F. Crawford 5-10-1845 (5-22-1845) Hr
Ward, Martha H. to Benajah S. Taylor 9-21-1854 Sh
Ward, Martha J. to Augustus B. Goodin 10-3-1848 (10-5-1848) Ma
Ward, Martha J. to James Blackburn 5-15-1845 G
Ward, Martha J. to Thos. A. Ward 2-2-1860 Be
Ward, Martha R. to Daniel B. Jack 1-21-1871 (1-24-1871) F
Ward, Martha to David McGinnis 8-29-1860 (8-31-1860) O
Ward, Martha to George Tatum 2-12-1878 L
Ward, Martha to Hartwell H. Brooks 12-22-1846 (no return) Hn
Ward, Martha to James Jones 9-2-1870 (9-6-1870) Dy
Ward, Martha to James Moore 1-8-1861 Hn
Ward, Martha to John Holion 9-6-1839 (no return) Cr
Ward, Mary Ann to James Lashley 8-17-1840 F
Ward, Mary Ann to T. S. Edington 6-26-1862 Be
Ward, Mary C. to David D. Murphee 9-23-1867 Cr
Ward, Mary C. to William J. McKelvie 10-5-1861 Be
Ward, Mary E. to Alfred T. Harget 10-5-1857 (10-13-1857) O
Ward, Mary E. to Nathan F. Fulks 1-31-1846 (1-31-1846) O
Ward, Mary F. to H. C. Johnson 1-6-1858 We
Ward, Mary J. C. to Andrew H. Kerr 3-3-1846 Sh
Ward, Mary J. to Stephen W. Lowry 8-25-1856 (8-26-1856) G
Ward, Mary Jane to John Richardson 6-26-1867 (no return) Dy
Ward, Mary Jane to John jr. McGill 9-17-1848 Be
Ward, Mary W. to Dempsey M. Sanderlin 3-30-1842 Sh
Ward, Mary to Aaron Lanier 9-26-1866 (no return) Dy
Ward, Mary to John Cunningham 12-27-1869 (12-28-1869) F B
Ward, Mary to John K. Palmer 10-11-1843 Hn
Ward, Mary to John Kelley 6-11-1862 (no return) Hn
Ward, Mary to John W. Bratton 7-3-1834 G
Ward, Mary to Lewis Robinson 10-21-1848 G
Ward, Matilda to James Evans 1-6-1869 Dy
Ward, Melitia to Henry Mayfield 12-23-1866 G
Ward, Mildred to Spencer G. Barton 12-23-1841 G
Ward, Mollie to Amos Bumpass 6-18-1870 (6-19-1870) Dy
Ward, Mosella to Anderson Yates 1-21-1866 G
Ward, Nancy C. to Asberry M. Webb 7-9-1853 G
Ward, Nancy C. to Hartwell Mosley 12-15-1858 G
Ward, Nancy C. to William H. Robertson 1-31-1858 Hn
Ward, Nancy G. to Josiah Russell 2-8-1845 We
Ward, Nancy M. to William Blackburn 1-2-1845 G
Ward, Nancy S. to Thomas S. Nance 5-26-1859 Hn
Ward, Nancy to J. W. Kitcham 12-16-1854 (no return) We
Ward, Nancy to Michael King 9-6-1828 Ma
Ward, Nancy to William Brady 2-22-1858 (2-24-1858) O
Ward, Nancy to Willis R. Harman 10-12-1862 We
Ward, Partheny to Burrel F. Ward 12-26-1866 Be
Ward, Permelia C. to William E. Reynolds 9-9-1853 (9-13-1853) L
Ward, Pernica to M. L. Mayo 5-3-1855 (no return) We
Ward, Polly to George Welch 1-6-1844 (1-7-1844) Hr
Ward, Polly to Morris Goad 3-25-1830 Ma
Ward, Priscilla to Moses H. Williams 5-27-1838 (5-30-1838) Hr
Ward, Rebecca A. to J. W. Ward 11-29-1860 Be
Ward, Rebecca E. to Samuel M. West 1-23-1862 L
Ward, Rena to Henry Rhodes 11-13-1868 (11-16-1868) F B
Ward, Rhoda E. to George Tatum 8-6-1857 (no return) L
Ward, Rhoda to Julius Jones 9-28-1843 Hn
Ward, S. D. to T. F. Bobbitt 1-6-1871 (1-10-1871) F
Ward, S. E. to B. F. Evans 1-4-1868 O
Ward, S. P. to M. D. Swaim 8-28-1852 We
Ward, Sada to J. R. Oliver 11-5-1872 (11-6-1872) O
Ward, Sallie P. to C. A. Goodlow 5-14-1868 (5-16-1868) Dy
Ward, Sarah A. to Ervin Pepper 3-24-1844 Cr
Ward, Sarah A. to Henry W. Hastings 1-3-1855 Hn
Ward, Sarah A. to Westley G. Philips 11-18-1863 Hn
Ward, Sarah An to James A. Todd 9-3-1844 (9-4-1846) F
Ward, Sarah Ann to James Greer 7-11-1852 Be
Ward, Sarah B. to John T. Cain 10-15-1852 We
Ward, Sarah H. to Jacob Mobly 1-12-1860 Hy
Ward, Sarah N. to William A. G. Toombs 12-19-1855 G
Ward, Sarah to Edward Ward 10-18-1839 Sh
Ward, Sarah to John B.? Bailey 9-24-1864 (no return) Dy
Ward, Sarah to Nathaniel Parham 12-11-1846 (no return) Hn
Ward, Sarah to Thomas Huskey 6-15-1835 Sh
Ward, Sarah to Thomas R. Farabough 12-16-1846 Hn
Ward, Sarah to Wm. Ketchum 8-2-1846 We
Ward, Sarrah to Robert Kennedy 7-12-1865 G
Ward, Sophia M. to A. N. Hogue 8-17-1859 O
Ward, Surmanthilus E. to Jefferson Marcum 9-21-1850 (9-22-1850) G
Ward, Susan to Aaron White 11-30-1878 (12-1-1878) Dy
Ward, Susan to Jesse N. (W.?) Ward 4-3-1867 G
Ward, Susan to T. B. Branden 8-29-1860 We
Ward, Susan to William Martin 12-7-1847 Hn
Ward, T. C. to N. W. Rochell 1-18-1841 Cr
Ward, T. C. to Thomas S. Nance 8-13-1864 (no return) Hn
Ward, Virginia to J. H. Jones 8-20-1877 (8-21-1877) L
Ward, W. E. to M. C. Lawrence 1-18-1865 Hn
Ward, Zely A. to Joseph D. Felts 1-6-1862 (no return) We
Warden, Barbery to John A. Wesson 7-19-1849 F
Wardford, Mary E. to Danl. Moore 2-16-1876 (no return) Hy
Wardlaw, Alsie to Lewis Beard 2-14-1878 L
Wardlaw, Angeline to Theodore Gammen? 2-2-1867 L B
Wardlaw, Chany to Daniel Conner 1-26-1867 L B
Wardlaw, Charity A. (Mrs.) to Thomas J. Sawyer 8-16-1883 (no return) L
Wardlaw, Easter to Willis Robertson 4-1-1885 (4-2-1885) L
Wardlaw, Eddie to W. K. Lackey 12-8-1881 L
Wardlaw, Ellen to Green Parks 10-4-1871? (no return) L B
Wardlaw, Ema to Ruff Thompson 12-3-1874 L B
Wardlaw, Holly to Hugh Leeper 8-3-1843 L
Wardlaw, Jane to William Baxter 12-18-1855 (12-19-1855) L
Wardlaw, M. E. to John W. Clark 11-24-1869 L
Wardlaw, Mahala to Bass Pugh 5-2-1885 L
Wardlaw, Manda to Dick Pierce 4-14-1883 L
Wardlaw, Margaret to James J. Brooks 12-21-1859 L
Wardlaw, Martha H. to Alpha J. Folets? 6-24-1857 L
Wardlaw, Mary Ann to A. Benton 2-27-1839 (3-7-1839) L
Wardlaw, Mary Ann to David G. Thum 12-20-1853 (maybe 12-21) L
Wardlaw, Mary F. to Jesse M. Meacham 10-3-1855 (10-4-1855) L
Wardlaw, Mary to Author Scott 11-18-1882 (11-20-1882) L
Wardlaw, Mollie to Harrison Estes 9-26-1885 (9-30-1885) L
Wardlaw, Pamelia to John C. Hale 1-27-1847 (1-28-1847) L
Wardlaw, Peggie to Sam Clark 8-20-1885 (8-23-1885) L
Wardlaw, Rowena to John E. Gray 9-7-1856 (9-18-1856) L
Wardlow, Elizabeth to Thomas M. Powell 12-24-1861 Mn
Wardlow, Mary to Edward (Capt.) Pendergrast 7-25-1862 Ma
Wardlowe, Lucinda to Troy B. Erwin 12-14-1862 Mn
Wards, Kate E. to Alexander W. Kircheval 10-24-1863 (10-25-1863) Sh
Ware, Adelaid to W. B. Hargrove 1-15-1867 Hy
Ware, Adline to Robert Hoyle 2-25-1869 (no return) Hy
Ware, Amanda (Mrs.) to Wm. J. Link 12-12-1866 Hy
Ware, Angeline to Jack Foster 4-27-1866 (no return) Hy
Ware, Ann T. J. to Starkey B. Hare 8-15-1846 (8-18-1846) F
Ware, Anna to Clark Steavins 12-26-1877 Hy
Ware, C. Catharine to Robert F. York 12-23-1854 (12-24-1854) Sh
Ware, C. M. to J. D. Crafton 6-3-1862 (no return) Hy
Ware, Caroline to David Evans 9-22-1866 Hy
Ware, Dilsey to Thomas Alexander 11-25-1874 Hy
Ware, Edy to John Nelson 10-20-1866 Hy
Ware, Elizabeth T. to David T. Martin 1-21-1850 Cr
Ware, Elizabeth to Jefferson Marshall 9-3-1844 Sh
Ware, Ellen to Nic Harris 7-11-1878 (no return) Hy
Ware, Emiline to Cornelius Owen 9-29-1876 Hy
Ware, Emma to Cezar Fowler 1-18-1875 Hy
Ware, Harrett to John Rosson 10-31-1871 O
Ware, Harriet to Lewis Boyd 1-4-1871 (no return) Hy
Ware, Harriett to John Turner 4-14-1877 Hy
Ware, Huldah to James W. Douglass 8-3-1846 Sh
Ware, Isabella to Hugh Lamb 2-21-1874 Hy
Ware, Jennie D. to Andrew J. Gibson 1-22-1867 (no return) Hy
Ware, Jennie to Sam Alexander 8-17-1872 Hy
Ware, Kate to Winston Coleman 4-24-1873 (no return) Hy
Ware, Lucy C. to Whitmill Crain 11-11-1847 Sh
Ware, Lucy G. to David Hare 3-26-1840 Sh
Ware, Maggie A. to W. H. Adams 2-5-1874 (no return) Hy
Ware, Martha to Dock Rutherford 12-18-1867 Hy
Ware, Martha to George Munly 12-7-1876 Hy
Ware, Mary B. to John A. Hare 12-20-1839 Sh
Ware, Mary E. to Thos. C. Topp 1-15-1855 Sh
Ware, Mary N. to L. J. Lett 8-26-1868 Hy
Ware, Mary to Joe Connell 12-27-1866 (no return) Hy
Ware, Missouri to James L. McDaniel 12-8-1835 Sh
Ware, Nancy T. to W. A. Edwards 1-24-1854 Cr
Ware, Nancy to Robert Davis 10-1-1870 (no return) Hy
Ware, Sarah Ann to James A. Todd 9-3-1846 (no return) F
Ware, Sarah to Joseph W. Slater 10-15-1844 Sh
Ware, Solona to Adam Ware 12-21-1870 Hy
Ware, Susan A. to J. P. Pace 2-15-1866 (no return) Cr
Ware, Susan R. to James P. Moses 12-20-1865 Hy
Wareham, Ann to Mathias (Metellus) Marshall 5-18-1863 (5-19-1863) Sh
Warfield, Harriet G. to N. D. Bell 11-10-1857 Sh
Warford, Duann W. to Thos. J. Ready 9-18-1855 (no return) F
Warford, M. F. to W. T. Lee 5-14-1873 (5-15-1873) O
Warford, Martha to Wm. Neal 1-25-1858 Hr
Warford, Nancy to Sam Phillips 1-31-1870 (2-1-1870) F B

Warford, Ruan J. to Russell P. Crawford 5-7-1858 (5-11-1858) Hr
Warick, Martha to Wyatt Arnold] 2-21-1847 Be
Warlick, Cynthia J. to William G. Smith 1-18-1848 Ma
Warlick, Emma C. to Joseph E. McDonald 10-3-1859 (10-6-1859) Ma
Warlick, Harriet to James Boon 11-19-1869 G B
Warlick, Laura to Theophilus Bond 4-1-1852 Ma
Warmack, Elizabeth F. to Hubbard L. Lindsey 3-16-1864 Be
Warmack, Mary to Thos. Green 4-1-1877 Hy
Warmack, Milly Jane to H. L. Brooks 12-13-1866 Be
Warmack, Mollie to Becton Eckford 12-12-1866 T
Warmack, Sarah Ann (Mrs.) to Solomon Crosby 9-1-1860 (9-4-1860) Sh
Warmack, Sarah J. to Robert B. Hindricks 3-24-1858 Hn
Warmath, Annie to W. W. Eckford 12-12-1865 T
Warmick, Jane to Josiah Mathis 5-28-1839 Hn
Warmick, Martha to Moses G. Thompson 7-6-1839 (no return) Hn
Warmick, Mary E. to John C. Provine 10-25-1866 Hn
Warmick, Nancy E. to Andy Martin 7-28?-1840 Hn
Warmock, Candis to Henry C. Boswell 7-14-1844 Be
Warmoth, Sarah A. to William R. Lewis 3-17-1852 (3-18-1852) Ma
Warner, H. A. to Isaac S. Parker 10-29-1850 Sh
Warner, Martha A. to Robt. J. Koonce 9-17-1851 (9-30-1851) Sh
Warner, Mary S. to Wm. A. Brevard 12-23-1858 Sh
Warner, Sophia B. to Richard P. Marr 5-13-1846 We
Warnick, Burchis to William T. Eddins 1-23-1854 (1-24-1854) Sh
Warpole, Martha to Amos Faulkner 12-21-1863 (no return) Dy
Warpool, Mattie to Moses Sanders 3-18-1872 Hy
Warpooll, Ellen to John H. McCollum 1-?-1867 (1-16-1867) Cr
Warr, Angerona to James F. Humphrey 8-16-1852 Hr
Warr, Clary to George Washington 9-11-1869 (9-26-1869) F B
Warr, Lizzie Ann to Calvin Culpepper 7-2-1870 (no return) F
Warr, Louisa T. to George W. Minter 2-13-1849 (2-14-1849) Hr
Warrack, Anna to Henry Boys 7-17-1839 Be
Warran, Rosanna to Henry Nickolson 9-26-1868 (no return) F B
Warre, S. M. to James Chambers 10-12-1868 (12-13-1868) Dy
Warrell, Millie to James Park 2-12-1860 Cr
Warren, Adaline to Ananias Shepard 3-7-1872 (3-11-1872) O
Warren, Ailsy to Isaac M. Hubbard 6-1-1849 (6-3-1849) Hr
Warren, Ailsy to John J. Tedford 12-5-1859 (12-15-1859) Hr
Warren, Aletha J. to W. M. Milner 12-29-1859 O
Warren, Amanda A. to William Wood 11-1-1842 Hn
Warren, Amanda to Alec. Bowlin 8-30-1862 (9-1-1862) Dy
Warren, Amanda to Joseph Brown 12-24-1870 (12-25-1870) F B
Warren, Anna to Andrew Pearce 12-25-1868 (no return) F B
Warren, Anna to James M. Murray 12-22-1870 F
Warren, Bettie to Henry Johnson 12-24-1869 (no return) F B
Warren, C. F. to Saml. Miller 8-9-1852 Cr
Warren, Caroline to Perry Warren 12-3-1866 (12-8-1866) F B
Warren, Carroline to Thos. Flowers 2-24-1860 (2-26-1860) G
Warren, Catharine J. to James Mathis 2-17-1851 (2-22-1851) G
Warren, Charity M. to Joseph L. Locke 12-5-1832 Sh
Warren, Eliza to Abraham Bayles 11-25-1826 (or 11-26?) Sh
Warren, Elizabeth Jane to Nehemiah Smith 11-23-1840 (12-23-1840) O
Warren, Elizabeth P. to Adam Finch 12-30-1856 We
Warren, Elizabeth to Jesse A. Brown 6-30-1839 Hn
Warren, Elizabeth to Jno. L. Wood 1-3-1848 (1-4-1848) Hr
Warren, Elizabeth to Moses Brock 10-14-1854 (10-15-1854) Sh
Warren, Elizabeth to W. J. Griffin 11-7-1866 (no return) Dy
Warren, Emmer C. to George W. Cordts 1-15-1878 Hy
Warren, Frances E. to William Clark 9-25-1867 (no return) Cr
Warren, Hannah to Lewis Henning 8-5-1839 (no return) Hn
Warren, Harriet S. to John D. Lankford 6-8-1848 (6-11-1848) L
Warren, I. T. to T. L. Phillips 8-26-1865 O
Warren, Jane to Henry Holliday 8-8-1838 Hn
Warren, Lina C. to W. H. McKnight 1-13-1868 G
Warren, Lydia C. to Young Ashley 4-18-1844 (no return) We
Warren, M. E. to D. J. Hansbrough 11-5-1867 (11-7-1867) O
Warren, M. F. to A. J. Connell 10-5-1868 (no return) F
Warren, Madona Ann to John R. New 11-26-1864 (11-27-1864) Sh
Warren, Manerva to Jerry Rowlett 5-29-1875 O
Warren, Margratt to Thomas Hamack 4-26-1838 (4-28-1838) G
Warren, Mariah (Mrs.) to J. R. Cerley 12-28-1872 (12-31-1872) Dy
Warren, Martha J. to Nathan L. Davis 10-7-1869 Dy
Warren, Mary Ann to Adgion M. Vamer 11-26-1864 (11-27-1864) Sh
Warren, Mary C. to P. C. Pinkerton 10-16-1859 We
Warren, Mary to Green Wirt 1-2-1866 (no return) F B
Warren, Mary to J. L. Stokes 4-24-1883 (4-27-1883) L
Warren, Melia to Jacob Rice 3-2-1867 G
Warren, Mira to Ed Gant 3-1-1871 (3-3-1871) F B
Warren, Mollie to LeGrand Ross 12-18-1866 (12-19-1866) F B
Warren, N. A. to C. B. Buch 11-1-1866 G
Warren, Nancy Ann to M. M. Palmore 7-25-1871 (no return) Dy
Warren, Nancy B. to Calvin Rushing 3-8-1852 (no return) Hn
Warren, Nancy E. to D. G. Hines 12-24-1855 (1-2-1856) G
Warren, Nancy J. to Washington Bond 5-5-1836 Sh
Warren, Nancy to R. W. Sumrow 1-7-1867 Dy
Warren, Nancy to Thomas Williams 1-21-1870 (2-19-1870) F B
Warren, Nancy to William Ridgeway 11-8-1827 O

Warren, Narsissa J. to Thomas B. Yancy 4-13-1871 F
Warren, Perry? to Ben Jamin Oakley 8-12-1867 (no return) Dy
Warren, Pink to John Thomas 9-7-1867 (no return) F B
Warren, R. P. to M. W. Smart 7-15-1879 (7-17-1879) Dy
Warren, Rosa to Joe Harrison 12-27-1865 (12-30-1865) F B
Warren, S. C. to James Kendall 10-29-1844 Hn
Warren, S. C. to S. M. McLeary 1-8-1867 G
Warren, Sallie C. to William A. Jetton 11-23-1874 (11-24-1874) Dy
Warren, Sally to Thomas Beard 7-10-1830 Hr
Warren, Sarah Ann to David C. Galard 9-4-1850 (9-5-1850) G
Warren, Sarah to James Farrell 8-4-1866 (no return) F
Warren, Sarah to Washington Smith 11-18-1841 (11-22-1841) O
Warren, Sarah to William Higgenbottom 11-9-1836 Sh
Warren, Susan C. to Jess Akers 1-2-1844 Cr
Warren, Susan L. to John F. Collins 12-26-1844 Hn
Warren, Susanah to J. T. Wood 6-6-1851 (6-7-1851) Hr
Warren, Susie A. to Nathaniel C. Oneal 9-22-1879 (no return) Dy
Warren, Turah to Edmund Young 1-17-1839 Hn
Warren, Virginia to Thomas W. Love 12-16-1858 Hn
Warren, Zilpha to William Greenly 10-12-1834 (10-15-1834) Hr
Warren, Zylpha to G. W. Dozier 2-18-1873 (2-19-1873) Dy
Warrick, Catharine to Samuel H. Davidson 12-1-1851 Be
Warrick, Catharine to Wm. Gossett 12-24-1863 Be
Warrick, Eliza to James Davis 5-8-1851 Be
Warrick, Elizabeth to R. B. Rushing 3-31-1848 Be
Warrick, M. J. to W. D. Markham 8-14-1848 Be
Warrick, Perlina M. to Joseph N. B. Collins 7-28-1857 Be
Warrick, Sally to John Phifer 1-13-1848 Be
Warrin, Martha to Arther Smith 5-7-1838 (5-8-1838) G
Warrington, Mary E. to W. E. Folks 7-8-1852 Sh
Warthwait?, Catherine to Thomas Busic 7-20-1872 (7-21-1872) T
Warton, Harriet to Hunter Cap (Cass?) 1-3-1874 (1-4-1874) L B
Wasden, Elizabeth to J. D. Jackson 8-6-1864 Sh
Wash, Elizabeth G. to H. B. Baty 12-18-1838 (12-20-1838) F
Wash, Nancy to John C. Levister 12-25-1862 We
Washama, Martha to Houston Barnes 11-17-1858 O
Washbourne, Lucinda to John P. Page 11-26-1846 Hn
Washburn, Percilla to John H. Cain 10-18-1829 Hr
Washburn, Rebecca B. to C. P. Roane 5-26-1857 (5-27-1857) Sh
Washington, Bettie to Johnson Browery 4-24-1873 Hy
Washington, Emily P. to G. W. Baldwin 4-30-1849 (5-2-1849) Hr
Washington, Frances to Harrison Graham 1-2-1871 (1-4-1871) F
Washington, Leathy to Geo. Johnson 12-12-1872 Hy
Washington, Mary to Shover Thornton 5-15-1884 (5-13?-1884) L
Washington, Mollie to John Connelly 11-6-1875 L
Washington, Rebeca M. to Peter M. Dupree 11-21-1840 (11-25-1840) F
Washum, Emily J. to J. E. Rose 9-1-1867 Hn
Wassen, Sarah A. to LeeRoy Vest 2-14-1856 Sh
Wassey, S. A. to W. T. King 10-17-1871 (10-19-1871) Cr
Wasson, Anna to Micajah Mason 3-25-1841 We
Wat, Jane to John Rose 4-18-1853 (4-21-1853) Sh
Wat, Wilmouth J. to Cyrus E. Mathis 10-30-1844 Ma
Waterage, Martha J. to G. D. Williams 12-15-1868 G
Wateredge, Mary B. to W. B. Simpson 5-15-1878 Hy
Wateridge, Mollie E. to G. W. Castellowk 11-25-1866 Hy
Wateridge, Sarah N. to S. B. Forrest 11-21-1869 Hy
Waters, Catharine to Daniel McMahon 9-7-1861 (9-9-1861) Sh
Waters, Delia C. to John Donelson 1-13-1849 (2-13-1849) Ma
Waters, Margaret S.? to G. P. Atkins 12-13-1871 T
Waters, Mary Ann to Ephraim Powers 8-7-1876 (8-9-1876) Dy
Waters, Mary C. to Hugh N. Anderson 1-30-1845 Ma
Waters, Mary V. to T. E. Freeman 11-7-1866 Cr
Waters, Sarah to Matthew Presson 8-27-1865 Be
Waters, Sarah to Wm. Underwood 12-14-1877 (12-20-1877) Dy
Watkins, Agnes to Cullen Roberson 12-23-1857 Hn
Watkins, Amanda to Gus House 12-27-1877 Hy
Watkins, Amanda to William Strickland 5-8-1875 (5-9-1875) Dy
Watkins, Amy to Booker Cunningham 6-7-1838 (no return) Hn
Watkins, Amy to Wm. Moore 10-30-1868 (10-31-1868) F B
Watkins, Angell to Felix Baum 4-7-1849 Sh
Watkins, Ann R. to J. J. Williams 10-30-1865 (10-31-1865) F
Watkins, Anna to Peter Taylor 11-8-1875 Hy
Watkins, Annie to William Tucker 2-26-1873 L
Watkins, Betsy to John Ragland 12-28-1865 (12-30-1865) F B
Watkins, Caroline to Sam Maclin 6-8-1872 (6-9-1872) L B
Watkins, Catharine T. to E. M. Leake 3-20-1844 (no return) F
Watkins, Della to Allen James 12-15-1868 G
Watkins, Dirzean to Wm. Austin 3-22-1877 Hy
Watkins, Eliza Ann to W. J. Nunnery 3-22-1853 (3-24-1853) Sh
Watkins, Elizabeth I. to P. Shivers 2-3-1840 (2-6-1840) Ma
Watkins, Elnory E. to Jonathan T. Bryan 3-23-1844 (3-28-1844) F
Watkins, Emily P. to R. W. Henley 11-12-1870 (no return) Hy
Watkins, Evaline to Sampson Jones 1-14-1869 Hy
Watkins, Fannie T. to John A. Hunt 5-15-1860 Sh
Watkins, Fannie to George W. York 4-18-1870 (no return) Dy
Watkins, Frances J. to J. G. Crossett 1-18-1854 (no return) F
Watkins, George Ann to Joe Adams 10-29-1874 Hy

Brides

Watkins, Harriet C. to N. L. Lawrence 5-31-1855 Sh
Watkins, Hattie A. to C. W. Fackler 1-15-1859 Hr
Watkins, Hepzhibad to John P. Lane 12-17-1844 (12-19-1844) Ma
Watkins, J. C. to W. L. Waggoner 12-24-1873 Hy
Watkins, Jane E. to Wm. C. Viser 6-25-1844 (no return) F
Watkins, Lizzie to Steven Gause 12-26-1867 Hy
Watkins, Lizzie to Stewart Burnett 4-25-1875 (no return) Hy
Watkins, Louisa to T. S. Heyward, jr. 4-17-1860 Sh
Watkins, Lucy A. to Scott Henley 2-1-1871 Hy
Watkins, Lucy M. to Benedict S. Robey 3-3-1867 Hn
Watkins, Lucy R. to Isham B. Harris 9-15-1859 Hn
Watkins, Margarett to Robert M. Bondurant 7-2-1847 (no return) F
Watkins, Martha A. to David K. May 9-12-1855 Sh
Watkins, Martha A. to John C. Throgmorton 2-22-1862 Hn
Watkins, Martha A. to K. D. May 9-10-1855 Sh
Watkins, Martha to Hiram Winston 4-18-1873 Hy
Watkins, Martha to J. M. Williams 7-8-1848 Cr
Watkins, Martha to Philip J. Kelch 8-20-1859 (no return) L
Watkins, Mary Ann to Alfred M. Grainger 7-26-1854 Hn
Watkins, Mary J. to Saml. M. Neel 11-28-1866 F
Watkins, Milly to Henry Allen 9-25-1869 (no return) F B
Watkins, Mrs. to John Pittman 4-15-1851 Sh
Watkins, N. J. to T. J. Cook 11-5-1867 (no return) F
Watkins, Nancy to Anderson Edwards 8-9-1860 (no return) Cr
Watkins, Nannie J. to Jesse R. Phillips 12-2-1869 (12-7-1869) Ma
Watkins, Nannie J. to John W. Willoughby 6-27-1867 Ma
Watkins, Nanny to James Covington 11-17-1846 Hn
Watkins, Parmelia to George W. Slaughter 4-7-1844 Hn
Watkins, Ripey to Crawley Smith 1-18-1867 Hy
Watkins, Sarah A. E. to James R. Carrigan 4-7-1857 (4-8-1857) L
Watkins, Sarah A. to Daniel Johnson 2-11-1871 (2-16-1871) F B
Watkins, Sarah J. to John Peacock 2-1-1851 Sh
Watkins, Sarah T. to Samuel A. Grable 3-28-1862 (4-4-1862) F
Watkins, Tabitha L. to Robert H. Cox 10-19-1866 (10-21-1866) Ma
Wats, Elizabeth A. to David McDonald 10-6-1853 Cr
Watson, Agnes to Daniel Baker 12-17-1868 (12-25-1868) F B
Watson, Ann to John Riddle 10-25-1853 O
Watson, Beady to Wm. McGill 8-8-1860 Be
Watson, Caroline to Alfred Coop 10-27-1845 (10-29-1845) L
Watson, E. J. to S. L. Forsythe 2-24-1855 (2-25-1855) Sh
Watson, E. to T. Cottingham 6-10-1841 Be
Watson, Eleanor to Alfred B. Gooch 5-19-1841 Ma
Watson, Eliza to Charles Box 12-22-1861 Be
Watson, Eliza to David L. Perkins 12-20-1852 (no return) F
Watson, Elizabeth to Ezikeal Pollard 12-29-1871 L
Watson, Elizabeth to George Swift 10-17-1848 Sh
Watson, Elizabeth to J. M. C. Robertson 8-1-1832 (8-2-1832) Hr
Watson, Elizabeth to James Neal 7-31-1855 (8-3-1855) O
Watson, Elizabeth to Samuel C. Leggatte 12-28-1833 G
Watson, Elizabeth to T. W. Spann 9-12-1861 G
Watson, Ellen to J. W. Phelan 10-27-1875 Dy
Watson, Ellen to John Hethcock 9-15-1863 G
Watson, Ellen to Spencer Demunbrie 12-7-1848 Sh
Watson, Frances to James R. Westbrook 8-31-1853 Hr
Watson, Frances to Jessee Tyner 12-22-1841 (12-23-1841) G
Watson, Georgia Ann to John B. Darnel 8-2-1850 O
Watson, Georgiana to Jack Cravens 12-8-1869 G B
Watson, Harriet M. to John L. Moultrie 12-16-1854 (12-17-1854) O
Watson, Ida to Finis Bowers 12-26-1870 (no return) F B
Watson, Jane to William M. Graves 12-3-1838 Ma
Watson, Jerusha to Alex Bowlin 10-13-1847 Hn
Watson, Julia to Thomas A. Crews 3-14-1855 (3-15-1855) Ma
Watson, L. J. to J. R. Griffin 9-3-1872 (9-5-1872) Dy
Watson, L. Melinda to Stephen Dyer 10-5-1848 Ma
Watson, L. P. to J. A. Ford 2-3-1873 (2-5-1873) T
Watson, Libby Ellen to Charles Morland 5-18-1867 (5-21-1867) L
Watson, Lucretia W. to John P. Brooks 9-20-1845 (9-25-1845) Ma
Watson, Lucy to Herris Wright 12-23-1873 (12-24-1873) L B
Watson, M. J. to C. C. Reed 11-25-1875 O
Watson, M. M. B. to Josiah Kettle 5-14-1846 L
Watson, Margaret Ann to Richard Joyce 1-31-1863 Sh
Watson, Margaret C. to Washington T. Exum 12-11-1854 (12-13-1854) Ma
Watson, Martha E. to W. P. Higgins 1-12-1868 Hy
Watson, Martha J. to Newton P. Watkins 2-6-1869 (no return) Dy
Watson, Martha Jane to Benj. J. Barker 8-10-1843 Be
Watson, Martha to John W. Forbess 11-11-1856 Cr
Watson, Martha to George H. Moxley 7-16-1832 O
Watson, Martha to J. W. Rodgers 7-22-1879 Dy
Watson, Martha to Thomas T. Deaton 12-7-1867 Be
Watson, Martha to William Oliver 4-3-1862 G
Watson, Mary A. to T. J. Sumner 11-28-1867 Hy
Watson, Mary Ann to Benjamin F. Moore 2-9-1869 (2-11-1869) F
Watson, Mary Ann to David McGill 4-9-1844 Be
Watson, Mary C. to D. B. Crocker 2-25-1869 Hy
Watson, Mary E. to Burwell Blackman 9-8-1846 (9-10-1846) Ma
Watson, Mary E. to J. M. Todd 4-5-1864 Hn
Watson, Mary E. to Jas. D. Hight 12-23-1858 G

Watson, Mary Jane to John T. Oakley 4-13-1864 Sh
Watson, Mary Jane to Mark Tyler 5-12-1879 Dy
Watson, Mary Jane to Olliver C. Grayham 5-22-1859 O
Watson, Mary Jane to Thomas Moriarty 12-27-1866 Be
Watson, Mary Jane to William G. Singleton 7-17-1856 O
Watson, Mary to Franklin Priest 2-18-1847 Cr
Watson, Mary to James Buris 10-16-1875 (no return) Hy
Watson, Mary to James Goforth 9-8-1882 L
Watson, Mary to John Wheeler 7-25-1843 Sh
Watson, Mary to Sanford White 7-16-1857 O
Watson, Minerva (Mrs.) to John F. West 3-31-1870 (4-3-1870) L
Watson, Nancy E. to Robert C. Brown 9-1-1869 L
Watson, Nancy S. to Marion Cook 10-16-1861 (no return) We
Watson, Nancy to Daniel R. Allison 6-29-1843 Ma
Watson, Nancy to Wm. Whitlock 1-19-1867 (1-21-1867) Dy
Watson, Pheby E. to William Blasingame 1-10-1876 (1-11-1876) L
Watson, Prutie to William Robertson 12-23-1869 Hy
Watson, Rebecca to John P. Hilliard 3-5-1863 We
Watson, Rosa to Johnston Stokeley 12-27-1883 L
Watson, Russie P. to Samuel Olive 2-20-1860 Hn
Watson, Ruth to Thomas McFadden 11-10-1838 F
Watson, Ruthy to Richard Ellington 12-19-1835 (12-22-1835) G
Watson, S. A. to J. B. Young 11-22-1860 G
Watson, S. E. to Wm. H. Killong 10-8-1856 Cr
Watson, S. H. to Samuel A. Thompson 5-14-1846 L
Watson, Sarah C. to William Burton 8-23-1848 F
Watson, Sarah E. to Jno. M. McFadden 1-8-1846 F
Watson, Sarah J. to Alexander H. Cathey 2-9-1853 Ma
Watson, Sarah Jane to J. R. Rayner 4-9-1863 Sh
Watson, Sarah M. to Thomas J. Seals 3-10-1856 O
Watson, Sarah to Thomas King 12-16-1857 Be
Watson, Sarah to William Maxley 7-13-1835 (8-6-1835) G
Watson, Susan Ann to John H. Simison 11-9-1847 F
Watson, Susan to Jacob Barquty 7-29-1847 Sh
Watson, Tabitha A. to Michael Cary 8-6-1843 Cr
Watson, Tabitha to C.? M. Hutchins 1-22-1868 Cr
Watson, Tennessee to John S. Rook 10-2-1861 Dy
Watson, Versia to Powell Holcomb 1-19-1881 L
Watson, Vianna C. to Daniel Henderson 10-31-1859 Sh
Watson, Virginia E. to Wm. D. Lowrance 1-5-1870 G
Watson, Willie L. to J. W. Acuff 1-19-1884 (1-20-1884) L
Watson, Winnie W. to John A. Autry 9-19-1847 Cr
Watt, Elizabeth to W. W. Moore 11-6-1854 (11-?-1854) G
Watt, J. Emly to James Cash 8-24-1850 G
Watt, Jane to Irvin Nichols 2-2-1830 Ma
Watt, Louisa F. to Miles J. Sloan 11-14-1861 (11-17-1861) Ma
Watt, Mariah S. to Wiley Taylor 11-15-1849 (11-18-1849) G
Watt, Mary M. to Nicholas Nivell 2-2-1842 (2-3-1842) Ma
Watt, Nancy N. to James McClure 9-22-1846 Ma
Watt, Paralee to Alexander Kimble 2-8-1850 Ma
Watt, Parmelia T. to Shephard B. Hicks 8-15-1848 (8-20-1848) Ma
Watt, Piety to Allen Smith 7-9-1846 Sh
Watt, Rebecca J. to R. L. Hailey 10-21-1860 G
Watt, Rebecca to John M. Lovell 5-26-1852 G
Watt, Susan L. to L. B. Stovall 3-19-1860 Sh
Watt, Susan to Samuel Farmer 9-14-1846 Ma
Watt, Trythana to John S. Holland 2-16-1869 G
Watten, Harriett to Heck Taylor 10-5-1871 Hy
Watter, Emerlin to Sandy Alsten 1-10-1867 T
Watters, Eliza H. to James A. Gober 8-6-1845 (8-7-1845) F
Watterson?, Margaret to Anderson Wilson 2-1-1870 (no return) F B
Wattes, Meboly to Benj. Wattes 5-6-1852 Cr
Watts, Clemsa to Kentiance G. Tally 11-18-1842 G
Watts, Delilah to Cullen J. Boyett 2-12-1846 G
Watts, Elizabeth to Robert Brown 7-4-1848 Sh
Watts, Emarine to Stephen Mitchell 1-27-1855 O
Watts, Fannie to G. W. Bogel 12-25-1877 (12-27-1877) O
Watts, Fanny M. to Samuel Taylor 1-22-1849 (1-25-1849) G
Watts, Frances E. to John R. Crouch 1-8-1843 Ma
Watts, Francis to William Dickson 12-31-1845 We
Watts, Fransis? Jane to Joseph T. Harelson 6-7-1828 Ma
Watts, Isabella to Daniel B. Fields 11-3-1857 G
Watts, J. D. to N. H. McFadden 11-27-1873 T
Watts, Martha J. to James M. West 12-22-1862 (1-14-1863) O
Watts, Mary W. to William M. Allen 12-2-1847 (12-14-1848?) F
Watts, Matilda C. to David Golden 12-31-1845 We
Watts, Nancy to Vinson Watts 9-28-1841 O
Watts, Virginia A. P. to J. H. Watts 1-22-1862 G
Wauller?, Mary to Jonathan J. Russell 8-23-1853 Cr
Waxter, Emily to Cornelius Bulger 6-20-1861 (6-21-1861) Hr
Wayman (Wagnore), Julia A. to F. M. Arnold 10-24-1849 Sh
Waynesberg, Mary to S. L. Bryant 10-13-1859 Sh
Waynesburg, Virginia J. to John Wm. Hinchee (Hinchen?) 8-20-1853 (8-21-1853) Sh
Wayson, Margaret to W. F. McBride 4-2-1877 (4-3-1877) Dy
Wayson, Mary E. to William Cate 11-30-1872 (12-4-1872) Dy
Weakes, F. M. to N. C. Morris 5-7-1861 Be

Weakes, Martha J. to H. Stigall 11-16-1854 Hn
Weakley, Ella A. to John F. Doyle 9-17-1861 (9-18-1861) Dy
Weakley, M. A. to B. N. Fryer 11-28-1864 (11-29-1864) Dy
Weakley, Mariah to Thomas Bowlin 10-29-1866 (maybe 1870) G
Weakley, Mary K. to W. L. Watkins 2-14-1866 Dy
Weakly, Isabella T. to Martin L. Sloan 3-9-1868 (3-10-1868) Dy
Weakly, Jane to Allen Finley 12-7-1865 Dy
Weaks, Eliza A. to D. L. Russell 4-14-1842 Hn
Weaks, Elizabeth to Benjamin F. Vantreese 9-29-1852 Ma
Weaks, Elizabeth to Jesse Indman 10-19-1854 Hn
Weaks, Malisa to William Manor 12-12-1868 (12-17-1868) L
Weaks, Margaret to Eli Forehand 2-17-1829 Ma
Weaks, Sarah to Joseph Brannon 8-4-1859 Hn
Weams, Harriet to Albert Covington 2-20-1873 Hy
Wear, Lea to Wm. Wilson 3-30-1866 O
Wear, Mary Ann to Jethro Howell 2-28-1871 (3-1-1871) O
Wearthemier, Cecelia to Isaac Ehrman 2-25-1863 Sh
Weatherall, Adeline to A. J. Stevenson 12-18-1860 Sh
Weatherall, Martha J. to Wesley H. Brown 5-22-1854 Sh
Weatherford, Ada to J. H. Osborne 11-7-1833 Hr
Weatherford, Elizabeth to Allen Rasberry 10-18-1847 (10-19-1847) G
Weatherford, Ellen L. to James A. Williams 9-20-1859 T
Weatherford, Lucy E. to John L. Pollard 11-18-1867 (11-19-1867) T
Weatherford, M. C. to H. J. Hansbro 2-4-1861 (2-7-1861) Cr
Weatherford, Mary H. to Wm. R. Tate 11-18-1867 (12-19-1867) T
Weatherford, Nancy J. to William G. Baker 12-27-1847 (12-28-1847) G
Weatherford, Sarah E. to Elihu Morse 12-13-1865 (12-14-1865) T
Weatherfor, Mary A. to George Warner 9-15-1867 Hn
Weatherington, Harriet to William Beauty 1-19-1860 T
Weatherington, L. F. to C. A. Smith 2-24-1879 (2-27-1879) Dy
Weatherington, M. F. to H. J. Pace 12-9-1874 (12-10-1874) Dy
Weatherlan, Abigail to John W. Nichloas 5-3-1860 We
Weatherly, Elizabeth J. to William N. Robins 12-1-1858 Hn
Weatherly, Elizabeth C. to George W. Day 10-28-1856 (10-30-1856) Ma
Weatherly, Margaret to John R. Paisley 9-17-1857 (9-29-1857) Ma
Weatherly, Sarah Catherine to Greenville A. J. Baker 5-21-1866 (no return) Hn
Weathers, Elizabeth Ann to David H. Jones 1-15-1867 Ma
Weathers, Jane E. to James C. Crider 2-13-1845 Cr
Weathers, Madaline to Jesse Spencer 3-27-1844 Hn
Weathers, Malissa J. to James B. Valentine 3-8-1842 Hn
Weathers, Narcissa to William J. Derryberry 7-19-1869 Ma
Weathers, Sopherina H. to Wilborn H. Graves 7-18-1854 Cr
Weatherspoon, Susan to John D. Robbins 11-2-1829 (11-3-1829) G
Weathington, Ann to Anthony Bledsoe 2-26-1857 T
Weathington, L. P. to James Murrin 2-11-1860 T
Weaver, Cyrena Jane to James G. Mays 6-24-1859 (6-28-1859) Ma
Weaver, Delila to Frederick Shofer 11-4-1825 (11-6-1825) Hr
Weaver, Elizabeth to Charles McGann 11-30-1870 Hy
Weaver, Emma Be.. to J. A. Hood 11-1-1877 Hy
Weaver, Frances H. to Andrew Patrick 12-29-1862 (12-30-1862) Ma
Weaver, Frances to I. A. Dodge 12-22-1866 O
Weaver, Harriet M. to John C. Sheets 5-20-1860 Hy
Weaver, Hester A. to Sidney Porter 7-31-1870 G
Weaver, Jane to Napoleon King 7-26-1854 (7-27-1854) Sh
Weaver, Lena to J. H. Haralson 12-20-1877 Hy
Weaver, Lucinda to John J. Mason 12-1-1833 Sh
Weaver, Lucy L. to Wm. L. Weever 11-14-1863 (11-15-1863) Sh
Weaver, M. L. to I. B. Martin 12-17-1868 Hy
Weaver, Martha to B. F. Kerr 2-25-1863 Mn
Weaver, Martha to Charles Adkins 7-26-1852 (7-27-1852) T
Weaver, Martha to James Peel 11-27-1828 Ma
Weaver, Martha to James R. Ledbetter 11-3-1841 Ma
Weaver, Mary C. to John H. Albrecht 10-13-1858 Sh
Weaver, Mary C. to Wilson Cooper 9-12-1853 (9-15-1853) Ma
Weaver, Mary E. J. to John A. Fry 5-?-1863 Mn
Weaver, Mary to Robed Obar 1-12-1832 Ma
Weaver, Mary to W. H. Willoughby 2-24-1860 (2-26-1860) Sh
Weaver, N. A. to K. J. Watson 9-12-1849 (9-13-1849) F
Weaver, Nancy G. to Archibald S. Rogers 2-20-1849 (2-22-1849) Ma
Weaver, O. J. to Jno. Domyer 10-9-1882 (10-10-1882) L
Weaver, Peggy to Joseph Rummage 12-29-1825 Hr
Weaver, Pemetea C. to Alexander Ray 6-22-1854 G
Weaver, Rebecca T. to James A. Plemons 8-20-1854 Hn
Weaver, Renis (Romia) to Samuel Norris 8-26-1854 (8-27-1854) Sh
Weaver, S. F. to J. T. Hunter 11-9-1876 Hy
Weaver, Sarah to Nathan Rachels 8-19-1852 T
Weaver, Serpeta P. to Jno. L. Brown 6-28-1841 Sh
Weaver, Sophia A. to W. B. McKee (McRee) 10-10-1850 Sh
Weaver, Susan M. to James D. Mathis 1-3-1862 G
Weaver, Susan to Berry Stubbs 3-9-1866 L
Weaver?, Clarinda A. to Ag? D. Hunter 10-19-1841 (10-21-1841) T
Weaver?, Nancy to Alfred Robinson 7-23-1831 Hr
Webb (West?), Sarah E. to G. W. Hutcherson 10-12-1871 (10-13-1871) L
Webb, A. D. to G. W. Yancy 10-15-1857 Cr
Webb, A. L. M. to John Braden 8-27-1846 L
Webb, Alpha to Montgomery Anderson 1-10-1844 Ma
Webb, Amanda E. to J. C. C. Cotton 11-6-1862 G

Webb, Amanda E. to Solomon G. Meadows 11-17-1852 L
Webb, America to Saml. A. Perry 10-5-1846 (no return) F
Webb, Ann to Nat. McLemore 7-16-1867 G
Webb, Barthinia S. to James E. Whyte 7-22-1847 Ma
Webb, Callie to Ambrose L. Evans 12-10-1867 L
Webb, Callie to W. G. Herron 1-15-1868 (1-16-1868) F
Webb, Caroline E. to James Mitchum 12-1-1857 Cr
Webb, Caroline to Daniel Burrow 2-13-1871 (2-16-1871) Cr
Webb, Caroline to Silas Lassiter 9-8-1860 (9-9-1860) Ma
Webb, Caroline to William Avetts 6-28-1846 Sh
Webb, Carolyn to W. A. Moore 10-15-1857 O
Webb, Charity to James McDummet 3-16-1836 G
Webb, Drusilla to W. R. Thompson 1-18-1881 L
Webb, E. A. to John Perry 1-31-1850 F
Webb, E. B. to W. T. Andrews 12-13-1876 (no return) L
Webb, Easter to Alexander Dennis 10-14-1871 T
Webb, Eliza Jane to John Oliver 11-26-1853 Hr
Webb, Elizabeth A. to Thomas H. Lee 9-16-1853 Ma
Webb, Elizabeth to Benjamin Rodery (Roding) 1-17-1844 (no return) We
Webb, Elizabeth to George W. Foren 2-9-1850 (2-13-1850) G
Webb, Elizabeth to Lewis Hill 12-13-1843 Sh
Webb, Elizabeth to N. R. Stewart 12-29-1855 (no return) F
Webb, Elizabeth to William Smith 9-24-1846 Hr
Webb, Elizar J. to William V. Brann 8-18-1859 (8-21-1860) We
Webb, Ellen to C. C. Daniels 1-23-1867 (1-24-1867) F
Webb, Emeline to Benjamin Parker 9-8-1870 (9-11-1870) L
Webb, Emely to Jas. H. Sheron 12-7-1838 (12-11-1838) G
Webb, Emily to James Manasco 6-21-1859 (6-23-1859) T
Webb, Emily to Robt. Allen 12-20-1848 F
Webb, Fannie G. to Henry T. Forbes 9-12-1855 (no return) F
Webb, Fanny H. to George L. Smith 11-8-1853 Ma
Webb, Fanny to J. M. Tomery 5-17-1861 (5-23-1861) Sh
Webb, Frances A. to Daniel Justice 2-16-1856 (2-17-1856) Hr
Webb, Frances E. to David A. Burleson 1-4-1868 (1-5-1868) L
Webb, Frances E. to Henry Crider 1-31-1850 Cr
Webb, Frances to Green Berry Rogers 5-21-1834 Sh
Webb, Gina to George D. McWherter 3-4-1863 We
Webb, Harriet E. to James L. Heckon? 12-20-1858 Hr
Webb, Hester to Davy Fields 6-15-1867 (6-18-1867) T
Webb, Isabella F. to H. A. Brann 11-5-1858 We
Webb, Jane to Burrel Anderson 12-24-1869 (12-25-1869) T
Webb, Jane to Hugh Wilson 10-8-1844 (10-10-1844) O
Webb, Jane to Jesse Davis 4-9-1856 Cr
Webb, Joella to Dennis F. Sawyer 8-15-1872 (8-16-1872) Dy
Webb, Lavinia to Columbus Sullens 1-31-1864 Be
Webb, Lee Ann to John A. Rigsly 4-2-1841 (4-6-1841) G
Webb, Levenia to Judge Sharp 5-5-1866 G
Webb, Lou to Willis Gauldin 1-21-1870 (1-31-1870) Dy
Webb, Louisa A. to Pleasant Via 11-14-1876 Dy
Webb, Louisa to John H. McLain 1-5-1860 (no return) We
Webb, Louisa to William Wilson 12-2-1830 Sh
Webb, Louiza to James A. W. Hess 12-8-1831 G
Webb, Lowrana? to Benj. Franklin Pace 1-26-1856 (1-29-1856) T
Webb, Lucinda J. to Henry C. Balinger 11-21-1865 (no return) Cr
Webb, Lucinda to A. T. Booker 1-21-1845 (no return) F
Webb, Lucinda to Isaiah Burton 10-16-1843 Hn
Webb, Lucinda to James R. Harris 8-13-1854 Hn
Webb, Lucinda to William Williams 12-12-1868 G B
Webb, Lucinda to Wm. Jas. Roberts 4-11-1855 T
Webb, Lucretia A. to J. B. Hinsen 11-17-1840 G
Webb, M. M. to J. W. Dodson 8-12-1860 Be
Webb, M. V. to James Braden 5-13-1847 L
Webb, Mahalia to Isaac Laymon 11-22-1842 G
Webb, Malissa to Charles J. Shaw 1-19-1848 (1-20-1848) F
Webb, Malissa to Herman Dempsey 11-2-1850 We
Webb, Manie G. to Hamilton Parks, jr. 10-5-1878 (10-7-1878) Dy
Webb, Margaret to T. J. Ethridge 12-13-1866 Hn
Webb, Martha A. to William P. Sandrs 3-16-1846 (3-17-1846) G
Webb, Martha M. to Franklin Conley 12-30-1869 Cr
Webb, Martha S. to William M. Kerns 11-17-1856 (11-18-1856) G
Webb, Martha to J. T. Muzzall 11-7-1854 Hn
Webb, Martha to John Bennett 6-28-1871 Dy
Webb, Mary A. to G. F. Robertson 11-11-1855 We
Webb, Mary Ann to E. W. Newborn 3-23-1869 F
Webb, Mary Ann to William C. Mashburn 11-30-1849 (12-5-1849) Hr
Webb, Mary B. to Geo. Rummage 2-5-1853 Cr
Webb, Mary C. to Henry Cantey 12-6-1861 Sh
Webb, Mary C. to Lycurgus Thompson 5-28-1856 Sh
Webb, Mary E. to Christopher Cooper 1-12-1860 (1-13-1860) G
Webb, Mary Elizabeth to Nathan H. Whitlow 11-1-1854 Ma
Webb, Mary F. to Henry J. Elliott 2-5-1868 Ma
Webb, Mary F. to W. R. Burney 11-5-1877 (11-6-1877) L
Webb, Mary Jane to D. C. Parker 11-27-1860 (11-28-1860) Hr
Webb, Mary Jane to Janes Valentine 9-8-1853 (9-11-1853) Ma
Webb, Mary to Clark Bryant 6-15-1867 (6-20-1867) F B
Webb, Mary to David Weaks 10-27-1837 Sh
Webb, Mary to H. S. Brandon 10-17-1866 Cr

Webb, Mary to John Hayes 11-6-1833 Sh
Webb, Mary to John Leird 2-13-1869 (2-14-1869) L
Webb, Mary to R. H. Duffy 4-15-1863 G
Webb, Mary to R. W. Lynch 6-3-1854 (no return) F
Webb, May to John Clifton 9-28-1858 (10-7-1858) Hr
Webb, Miranda to Samuel J. Wilkins 8-3-1843 G
Webb, Nancy C. to Harbert H. Edwards 11-10-1853 (11-13-1853) Hr
Webb, Nancy C. to Samuel McKane 10-9-1865 G
Webb, Nancy Jane Catherine to James Francis Hull 8-12-1868 G
Webb, Nancy M. to Needham J. Powell 11-24-1849 (11-27-1849) Hr
Webb, Nancy to John N. Bennett 1-19-1856 Cr
Webb, O. A. to P. J. Carlton 12-26-1869 G
Webb, Parale M. E. to John D. Foster 12-22-1852 L
Webb, Rachel to Alfred F. Harris 1-5-1850 (no return) Cr
Webb, Rebecca to James W. Keaton 12-14-1859 (12-24-1859) Ma
Webb, S. E. to B. F. Thompson 12-20-1871 (no return) Cr
Webb, S. E. to B. S. Morris 12-4-1879 L
Webb, S. E. to L. M. jr. Jones 1-7-1873 (no return) Cr
Webb, Sallie to Cit L. Bell 3-8-1871 Ma
Webb, Sallie to James M. Guy 2-8-1870 G
Webb, Sarah A. M. to Benjamin Citchins 10-18-1864 O
Webb, Sarah A. to John A. Williams 12-22-1858 Hn
Webb, Sarah A. to John B. Bettis 12-17-1848 Sh
Webb, Sarah Ann to G. B. Payne 12-4-1869 (12-22-1869) F
Webb, Sarah R. to Rufus W. Webb 2-13-1856 G
Webb, Sarah to E. J. Swift 3-12-1859 Cr
Webb, Sarah to Frank Carroll 7-17-1866 (7-26-1866) F
Webb, Sarah to Hyram Barnett 2-10-1832 (2-14-1832) Hr
Webb, Sophia C. to Mason Moss 7-3-1858 (7-4-1858) T
Webb, Susan to B. R. Nolen 11-4-1850 (11-6-1850) O
Webb, Susan to W. G. Webb 12-12-1860 (12-13-1860) Cr
Webb, Sutelda E. to William D. Scott 4-30-1849 (4-1?-1849) G
Webb, Tabathy to Stephen M. McWherter 11-9-1852 We
Webb, Virginia Ida to James A. Crook 2-21-1876 (2-24-1876) L
Webb, Wethly to Norman Webb 12-7-1843 Ma
Webb?, Susan to W. Z.? Wiles? no date (with 12-1860) Cr
Webber, Louisa A. to J. C. Baker 4-2-1855 M
Webber, M. L. to F. B. Crenshaw 7-11-1859 (7-13-1859) F
Webber, Mary A. to Henry N. Davis 5-5-1857 Sh
Webber, Mary B. to James W. Dupuy 9-26-1849 Sh
Webber, Mary E. to A. M. Hamner 11-2-1854 Sh
Webber, S. F. to D. A. Harrell 3-7-1855 (3-14-1855) Sh
Webber, Sarah Jane to Starke Dupuy 7-6-1846 Sh
Webber, Susan F. to Edwin Anthony 12-11-1850 Sh
Weber, Frances to Nathan Branson 4-29-1839 Sh
Weble, Rosanna to M. B. Vurrant Morgan 5-28-1860 Hn
Webster, Anna to Hillman Crockett 2-22-1883 (2-24-1883) L
Webster, Emeline to T. H. Russell 8-1-1836 (8-23-1836) Hr
Webster, Emiline to Daniel Walton 1-20-1872 (2-1-1872) Dy
Webster, Emiline to James F. Gates 12-15-1846 Hr
Webster, Flora to Levi T. Shorter 3-31-1868 (no return) Dy
Webster, Jane C. to Jesse B. Shearin 2-16-1857 (2-18-1857) Hr
Webster, Lucinda to Charles Reagan 6-16-1827 Hr
Webster, Margaret N. to S. M. High 10-9-1854 (10-10-1854) Sh
Webster, Martha J. to James M. Gardner 5-13-1869 (5-17-1869) F
Webster, Martha to James Bankhead 2-5-1845 (2-6-1845) F
Webster, Mary E. to D. C. Cuningham 3-12-1857 We
Webster, Mary V. to David C. White 1-8-1848 (1-13-1848) F
Webster, Mary to Jonas C. Rudisill 10-17-1844 Sh
Webster, Matilda J. to Miles C. Cunningham 3-9-1854 Hn
Webster, Penelope G. to George W. Thompson 12-20-1849 Sh
Webster, Sarah R. to Jno. P. Wheeler 7-29-1849 Hr
Webster, Sarah to S. Jones 10-16-1851 Hn
Webster, Tempe to Josiah Taylor 2-27-1832 (3-1-1832) Hr
Wechtenhausen, Evelin to Peter Hein 5-8-1845 Sh
Weckesser, Eliza to John Wind 10-21-1856 Sh
Weddie, Martha to Andrew Pearson 1-13-1872 Hy
Weddington, Callie to Glasgow Thompson 3-20-1861 G
Weddington, Dorcas to Jim Sherman 2-7-1868 G B
Weddington, Elvira S. to William B. Powell 8-24-1852 Hn
Weddington, Mary to Taylor Gadlin 2-7-1868 G B
Weddle, Maggie M. to George W. Rooks 7-19-1867 G
Weddle, Mary to Joseph Ivey 2-3-1877 Hy
Wedington, Eliza J. to James M. B. Roach 7-14-1853 Cr
Wedington, Emeline to William E. Batsel 3-20-1854 O
Wedington, Mary E. to John E. Evans 3-31-1851 O
Weed, Amanda to Benj. B. Jaines 9-26-1853 Sh
Weed, Anthior to Wm. M. Jones 9-13-1846 Sh
Weed, Martha A. to Wm. W. Innes 8-9-1843 Sh
Weedin, Melisa Ann to L. B. King 6-18-1844 Hr
Weeks, Nancy E. to Elisha M. Edgar 12-27-1864 Hn
Weeks, Nancy to Wilson R. Walker 1-5-1850 (no return) Hn
Weeks, S. J. to E. J. Foster 12-17-1860 Sh
Weever, Lucy L. to Wm. L. Weaver 11-14-1863 Sh
Weever, Randa to John E. Anderson 6-21-1870 Dy
Wegman, Mary to John Werkmeister 9-30-1854 Sh
Wehman, Elizabeth to Chas. Duvall 6-28-1875 O

Weibel, Sarah to James Boro 7-26-1851 Sh
Weints, Henrietta to John B. Soemrs 2-1-1854 Sh
Weir, Ann B. to Donald D. Weir 2-14-1842 (2-15-1842) Ma
Weir, Margaret E. to William Scoggins 4-5-1859 (4-6-1859) Hr
Weir, Margaret to David D. Weir 8-10-1830 Ma
Weisener, Therissa to Frederick Pfemfert? 11-10-1859 Sh
Weiskopf, Rose to Jacob Greenberg 8-7-1862 Sh
Weisler, Mary to Hermann Walter 3-10-1863 Sh
Weithington, Fanny to A. J. Lancaster 7-3-1867 Hy
Welborne, Sarah to James Upton 12-1-1864 O
Welch, Aley A. H. to John Campbell 8-24-1837 G
Welch, Amelia to Wily Thom 11-26-1838 (11-29-1838) Ma
Welch, Attie F. to John Hadden 12-17-1868 G
Welch, Catharine to Michael Doyle 1-13-1859 (1-14-1859) Sh
Welch, Cornelia to J. S. Hannah 12-19-1865 Mn
Welch, Elizabeth to John W. Marrs 12-17-1842 (12-18-1842) Hr
Welch, Elizabeth to Wm. C. Page 10-8-1832 (10-9-1832) G
Welch, Ellen to Martin Rodgers 1-12-1858 Sh
Welch, Ellen to Stephen Leonard 2-4-1854 (2-6-1854) Sh
Welch, Harriet H. to James Castles 9-2-1828 (9-4-1828) G
Welch, Hattie to John W. Vaughan 12-11-1860 Sh
Welch, Indiana to W. P. Landrum 12-3-1856 W
Welch, Isabella S. to L. M. Pery 1-3-1861 (no return) We
Welch, Jane F. to William Gardner 5-23-1844 G
Welch, Johanna to Patrick Connell 5-12-1859 Sh
Welch, Julia to Matthew Underwood 12-4-1862 G
Welch, Louizer to William Hutcher 9-22-1867 G
Welch, Luizer to William Jarrett Robertson 7-12-18__ (probably 1865) G
Welch, Margaret to Jeremiah Brown 8-12-1857 Sh
Welch, Martha to Stephen Scoggins 2-6-1837 (2-7-1837) Hr
Welch, Mary A. to Jno. W. Roads 4-3-1844 We
Welch, Mary A. to John W. Roach 3-29-1844 (no return) We
Welch, Mary M. to O. C. Frazier 11-24-1872 Hy
Welch, Mary to Gustave Lubbren 3-6-1860 Sh
Welch, Mary to John Grogan 11-22-1856 (11-23-1856) Sh
Welch, Mary to Major Bledsoe 8-26-1847 G
Welch, Marzell to Thomas N. Paine 2-1-1843 G
Welch, Nancy to Hearvy Nettles 9-9-1834 (9-10-1834) G
Welch, Nancy to Stephen Herriman 1-25-1851 (1-26-1851) Hr
Welch, Parlee to Monroe Rogers 8-13-1872 O
Welch, Phebe J. to Calvin Paget 5-16-1849 Sh
Welch, Polly to Jessee Reagan 12-20-1838 Hr
Welch, Polly to John McFarlen 8-18-1843 G
Welch, S. M. to L. D. Leird 9-10-1871 L
Welch, Sarah A. to John D. Savage 6-20-1872 (6-21-1872) L
Welch, Sarah Jane to B. G. Valentine 9-7-1856 Hn
Welden, Elden to John Montgomery 1-9-1843 Sh
Weldon, Emily to James House 12-23-1866 Hn B
Weldon, Mississippi E. to J. T. Worshum 11-16-1846 (no return) We
Weldon, Nancy to J. N. Moody 8-22-1862 (no return) Hn
Wellar, Virginia to John W. Dyer 1-29-1849 (1-30-1849) F
Wellborn, Virginia O. to Oliver Oates 3-22-1855 Sh
Wellehan, Margaret to Andrew Sullivan 4-14-1863 Sh
Weller, Elizabeth E. to Benj. Haskins Ligon 12-30-1846 (12-31-1846) T
Weller, Mary Ann to Richd. Brinkley 12-26-1848 (no return) F
Weller, Mary S. to James Allen McLeary? 7-17-1855 (7-18-1855) T
Weller, Sarah A. to Saml. D. McLeary 10-11-1841 (10-?-1841) T
Wellingstone, Kate (Mrs.) to Armin (Dr.) Szerinzi 9-14-1863 Sh
Wellington, Avie to James Hillman 2-12-1870 (no return) Hy
Wellins, Polly to Joel Rainer 9-27-1837 Hr
Wellman, Ruthey to Alvin Warren 12-24-1834 (12-28-1834) Hr
Wellon, Alice to C. F. Kirckner 7-19-1854 Sh
Wells(Wills?), Minerva to Gary Gay 1-29-1850 (1-31-1850) Hr
Wells, A. E. to N. E. Sutton 8-5-1878 L
Wells, Addie M. to Levi Walker 2-14-1876 Hy
Wells, Alice to Thomas Mattress 7-16-1881 (7-17-1881) L
Wells, Arbella to J. W. Carter 3-11-1846 Hn
Wells, Caroline to Thomas L. Rodgers 2-21-1867 Be
Wells, Catherine to Robert Barton 7-3-1851 Hn
Wells, Dora to Granville Tharp 12-14-1870 F B
Wells, Elizabeth to Auren Blackwell 1-24-1871 (1-25-1871) L
Wells, Elizabeth to Jno. Adams 1-4-1838 (1-5-1838) Hr
Wells, Elizabeth to T. L. Robertson 6-16-1859 Hy
Wells, Elizabeth to Wesley Jones 12-31-1873 T
Wells, Eller to Wm. H. Coker 12-11-1867 Hy
Wells, Harriet E. to J. W. Temple 12-17-1862 (12-28-1862) F
Wells, Harriet to J. H. McCrary 4-13-1867 G
Wells, Lissa to John Keltner 1-21-1871 (no return) Hy
Wells, Lucinda to Thomas Smith 3-27-1843 Hn
Wells, M. A. to W. L. Savage 3-31-1874 (no return) L
Wells, Margaret V. to John H. Dill 8-8-1866 (8-3?-1866) L
Wells, Margarett A. L. to Johns R. Neely 10-29-1845 (10-31-1845) Ma
Wells, Mariah to Dallis Lucus 1-19-1876 (1-20-1876) L B
Wells, Martha J. to James A. Millsted 10-10-1872 (10-13-1872) L
Wells, Martha J. to S. S. Goodner 2-10-1864 (2-11-1864) Sh
Wells, Martha M. to Jas. (Jos.) H. McCommon 3-9-1858 (3-10-1858) Hr
Wells, Martha P. to John Burton 6-28-1839 (6-29-1839) F

Wells, Mary C. to W. R. Chism 8-14-1869 (8-15-1869) L
Wells, Mary E. to James Nicely 5-11-1864 O
Wells, Mary Jane to John Payne 5-29-1858 (5-30-1858) O
Wells, Mary to Henry Hays 10-25-1860 Sh
Wells, Mary to Peter Johnson 1-12-1874 T
Wells, Mary to W. H. Osborne 6-17-1879 (6-18-1879) L
Wells, Missouri A. to Robert W. Grizard 1-1-1866 Hy
Wells, Mollie F. to Aaron T. Sanders 1-18-1870 (1-19-1870) F
Wells, Mollie R. J. to Isaac A. Williams 12-25-1866 (12-28-1866) F
Wells, Nancy to Wm. H. Porter 4-2-1858 (4-4-1858) Sh
Wells, Nannie E. to Lacy L. Brown 11-28-1866 Ma
Wells, Rosina to W. F. Harwell 11-15-1865 (11-21-1865) F
Wells, Sarah A. to Moses Sheron 4-14-1865 O
Wells, Sarah F. to Norborne E. Sutton 9-9-1867 (9-11-1867) L
Wells, Sarah M. to John Kenney 5-21-1857 Hr
Wells, Sarah to Rolla Poindexter 12-12-1854 (no return) F
Wells, Sophia Ann to Mike Lucas 4-5-1869 (4-6-1869) F
Wells, Sue to R. W. Kirby 1-8-1868 Hy
Wells, Susan to James H. Jones 1-1-1850 Hr
Wells, Susana to John Wilson 9-20-1873 (9-21-1873) L
Wells, T. E. to J. B. Patterson 7-2-1881 (7-3-1881) L
Welsh, Elizabeth to George W. Fink 2-28-1849 Sh
Welsh, Ellen to John Weiser 12-7-1857 Sh
Welsh, Hanorah to James Obrien 7-9-1862 (7-12-1862) Sh
Welsh, Hester to John C. Wilson 6-14-1864 Sh
Welsh, Jane to Murphy G. Holt 12-28-1843 (1-4-1844) Ma
Welsh, Martha to J. W. Mustin 1-8-1852 Sh
Welsh, Mary to Patrick Cunningham 11-25-1856 Sh
Welsh, Sarah to Martin Dunn 3-13-1849 Sh
Wemby, Fanny Q. to Jerry Price 2-18-1867 Hn
Wendell, Margaret to Martin Eykes 9-18-1861 Sh
Wenderoth, Henrietta to W. H. Weller 10-30-1861 Sh
Wenderoth, Margaret to Jacob Steinkuhl 7-3-1849 Sh
Wenderoth, Mary to Thomas F. Kirk 8-21-1852 (8-22-1852) Sh
Wenstram?, Jane E. to Francis Trice 10-22-1855 (10-23-1855) T
Wersham, Mary Ann to A. B. Hall 3-27-1885 (no return) L
Weseney, Sarah Ann to George D. McDonald 8-11-1851 G
Weshl (West?), Lucy A. to Isaac Lucas 4-10-1867 (4-11-1867) L
Wess, Emaline to Albert Kinion 3-1-1863 Mn
Wessen, Amand J. to John C. Murray 12-19-1860 (12-20-1860) Dy
Wessen, Isabella J. to J. J. Wood 9-13-1864 (10-18-1864) Sh
Wessen, Margaret to Wm. L. Burks 3-20-1862 Sh
Wesson, Caroline to Andy Cox 11-4-1845 Sh
Wesson, Cary Ann to Benjamin Wesson 1-5-1841 Sh
Wesson, Elizabeth P. to John J. Woods 2-24-1853 Sh
Wesson, F. E. to J. W. Oslin 12-20-1871 (12-21-1871) Dy
Wesson, Frances A. to Freeman A. Carroll 9-8-1848 Sh
Wesson, Joice to Zedikiah Anderson 10-22-1857 Sh
Wesson, Lucy Ann to James Carlisle 7-4-1848 Sh
Wesson, Lucy M. to F. A. Lock 3-12-1853 (no return) F
Wesson, Margaret to Hartwell T. Williams 7-19-1852 Sh
Wesson, Margaret to John Edwards 1-14-1847 Sh
Wesson, Martha D. to J. J. Wood 1-22-1857 Sh
Wesson, Mary Ann to George W. Wesson 2-11-1851 (2-14-1851) F
Wesson, Mary E. to John E. Vernon 9-22-1871 (9-25-1871) Dy
Wesson, Mary to John C. Walker 1-15-1846 Sh
Wesson, Mary to John C. Walker 7-11-1838 Sh
Wesson, Mildred to J. S. Meredith 7-19-1871 (7-25-1871) Dy
Wesson, Minta to Thomas McGill 1-15-1856 Be
Wesson, Nancy H. to Joseph H. Fry 8-31-1853 (9-1-1853) G
Wesson, Sarah G. to Ezekial Hubbard 12-19-1838 Sh
Wesson, Susan A. to James A. Bryant 10-1-1863 Sh
Wesson, Susan H. to S. W. Ledbetter 5-19-1848 Sh
West, Alafare? to Hugh W. Hood 12-24-1861 O
West, Ann M. to James Roper 5-25-1848 Hr
West, Ardenia to Sydney Conley 9-18-1860 Sh
West, Bettie to William Dodson 10-10-1871 (10-11-1871) Ma
West, Cattie to Charles McFarland 9-30-1875 (10-17-1875) L B
West, Corddia C. to Jesse F. Gardner 9-10-1868 G
West, Cynthia to William A. Jones 8-21-1838 Sh
West, E. R. to J. R. Rush 12-22-1880 L
West, E. W. to J. W. McKinstry 2-24-1860 Sh
West, Elizabeth J. to W. P. Merrell 4-6-1863 We
West, Elizabeth M. to Thos. R. Crosbey 11-28-1854 (11-29-1854) G
West, Elizabeth T. to Granville V. Mounce 9-19-1865 (10-12-1865) L
West, Elizabeth to James Arnold 8-3-1855 (8-5-1855) G
West, Elizabeth to James Graham 1-6-1876 L B
West, Elizabeth to Peter C. Gilmore 11-14-1829 Sh
West, Elizabeth to William Henderson 3-6-1845 G
West, Ellen F. to Peyton C. Smith 12-11-1855 (no return) L
West, Georgie B. to B. B. Covington 12-22-1880 L
West, Harriett A. to William Owen 2-12-1829 Sh
West, Jane B. to William C. Moore 12-31-1838 Sh
West, Jane to Andrew S. Gatlin 10-2-1836 Hr
West, Jennett to Joshua Baker 11-3-1855 (11-6-1855) G
West, Josie H. to R. G. Newton 2-26-1878 (2-27-1878) L
West, Julia A. to James Turner 10-9-1850 G

West, Lizzie to James P. Kincaid 3-3-1874 (3-4-1874) T
West, Louisa Elmira to Thomas F. Boyett 12-8-1852 (12-9-1852) O
West, Lucretia Ann to J. W. Buchanan 2-20-1862 O
West, Lucy Anna to Theopolus Hathaway 11-7-1853 Sh
West, Lucy J. to B. F. Paskell 3-12-1863 Hn
West, M. O. T. to J. F. Tilman 6-10-1879 (6-11-1879) Dy
West, Manerva M. to Joseph P. Boyett 6-30-1849 (7-12-1849) G
West, Margaret E. to James M. Koonce 7-22-1868 (7-26-1868) L
West, Martha E. to James A. Price 1-17-1854 (1-18-1854) G
West, Martha Jane to Thos. S. Arnold 7-4-1861 Sh
West, Martha to Samuel Outlaw 10-18-1877 Hy
West, Mary A. to J. P. West 2-13-1878 L
West, Mary Ann to Abraham E. Norrid 8-18-1846 (8-25-1846) G
West, Mary E. to J. H. Barnwell 10-9-1865 G
West, Mary E. to James E. Boyett 2-13-1860 (2-16-1860) O
West, Mary E. to Josiah Stagner 6-15-1856 Hn
West, Mary E. to WilliamH. Fewell 2-8-1844 (2-9-1844) Hr
West, Mary J. to A. J. Webber 6-8-1862 G
West, Mary J. to W. H. Barrow 1-21-1869 G
West, Mary V. to James H. Brockwell 9-4-185? with 1858 O
West, Mary to Daniel Lathrop 6-22-1864 Sh
West, Mary to John Etheridge 6-1-1841 (6-3-1841) G
West, Matilda J. to John Hopper 11-6-1851 Sh
West, Nancy E. to James M. Roberson 10-19-1863 G
West, Nancy Jane to W. M. Huggins 12-24-1856 Hn
West, Nancy M. to P. W. Turnham 7-15-1851 O
West, Nancy to W. J. Lorance 12-24-1863 G
West, Nanie to Nelson Davis 9-10-1876 Hy
West, Nannie E. to Charles R. Ganden 3-30-1860 Sh
West, Nettia to L. N. Irwin 2-1-1866 G
West, Percilla to Buck Williams 6-8-1867 (6-11-1867) T
West, Prudence to William S. Barrett 10-7-1854 (10-12-1854) O
West, Rebecca to Blunt H. Owen 2-11-1830 Sh
West, Rosa to Jas. K. Johnson 1-8-1867 (no return) F
West, Sallie Ann to L. W. Pipkin, jr. 10-21-1865 G
West, Sallie to William Wheelons 11-21-1872 L
West, Sarah Ann to L. W. Pipkin, sr. 11-2-1865 G
West, Sarah J. to A. R. Vick 10-21-1859 F
West, Sarah J. to Jessee Price 9-9-1844 (9-12-1844) G
West, Sarah Jane to James F. Tarrentine 10-1-1857 O
West, Sarah Jane to James Kim 1-30-1864 Sh
West, Sarah M. to Alexander Eason 5-11-1857 (5-20-1857) L
West, Seleta to Elias W. May 7-24-1838 Ma
West, Susan E. to J. W. House 1-7-1869 G
West, Susan V. to Joseph A. Whitington 12-23-1869 (no return) L
West?, Harriet to Peter McFadden 3-8-1867 (no return) L B
Westbrook, Ann E. to John J. Ross 7-3-1838 O
Westbrook, Cyntha to Henry Campbell 3-17-1875 L B
Westbrook, Della to James A. Paul 9-13-1866 L
Westbrook, E. T. (Miss) to Valentine B. Sevier 6-24-1857 (6-25-1857) Sh
Westbrook, Eliza to Loveitte R. Muns 1-2-1848 Sh
Westbrook, Harriet A. to Samuel I. Maxey 4-4-1860 We
Westbrook, Laura to Jordan Coleman 1-14-1873 Hy
Westbrook, Levinia to John Davis 12-29-1846 (12-31-1846) F
Westbrook, Lula to Silas Gause 10-28-1880 L B
Westbrook, Mary A. to W. H. Mitchell 2-4-1878 (1?-6-1878) L
Westbrook, Mary Ann to Osborn Gatewood 2-15-1848 Sh
Westbrook, Mary Jane to James M. Savage 7-21-1858 (7-24-1858) Hr
Westbrook, Mary to Bevley Taylor 3-9-1870 (no return) L
Westbrook, Nancy to Joseph Casey 7-16-1850 (7-21-1850) Hr
Westbrook, Pearcy to William Monroe 11-8-1852 Hr
Westbrook, S. V. to R. A. Williford 4-25-1864 (4-26-1864) Sh
Westbrook, T. J. to A. J. Pierce 12-11-1869 (12-12-1869) Dy
Westbrooks, Anjaline to J. D. Hawks 12-30-1857 We
Westbrooks, Mariah to J. A. Brigance 8-4-1863 (no return) We
Westbrooks, Tempy to Leander McKnight 12-13-1879 (no return) L
Westen, Mary J. to Benjamin F. Gates 12-22-1859 We
Wester, Amanda W. to A. W. Davis 9-8-1852 Sh
Wester, Catharine to Isaac Sumner 5-24-1853 Be
Westerbrook, Margaret E. to Daniel C. Johns 11-26-1840 Ma
Westerman, Eliza E. to Jesse A. Dennistion 5-9-1856 (5-10-1856) O
Western, Alice E. to Hiram Vickers 5-29-1872 Hy
Western, Laura E. to Joseph G. Vickers 5-29-1872 Hy
Westmoreland, Clarissa L. to Moses B. Swindle 9-11-1868 (9-12-1868) Cr
Westmoreland, Luan to John Morgan 10-17-1870 (10-18-1870) L
Westmoreland, Lucy to Ephraim Evans 2-1-1871 (2-6-1871) F B
Westmoreland, Mary to Franklin Townson 1-6-1872 (1-7-1872) O B
Weston, F. D. to C. A. Foster 12-4-1838 (1-22-1839) F
Weston, Fannie to Bailey Gause 1-20-1881 (no return) L B
Weston, Lucretia to Roberson Lewis 9-2-1855 Hn
Weston, Parthenia to George Roberts 10-25-1852 Hn
Wethen, Elizabeth to Lewis V. Read 11-27-1867 (11-28-1867) Dy
Wetherington, Cornelia to Wilson Byrnes 8-17-1867 (8-18-1867) T
Wetherley, Martha to Wm. Kelly 2-9-1846 L
Wetherly, M. F. to William Stoker 7-23-1865 (7-28-1865) O
Wetherly, Margaret to T. Solomon M. McCord 1-3-1861 Hn
Wethers, Georgiana to H. L. Ricketts 6-5-1880 (6-6-1880) L

Wethers, Lyde to James S. Smith 1-19-1870 (1-20-1870) Ma
Wetherspoon, M. J. to J. B. Sullivan 2-19-1864 G
Wethford, Sarah to William Read 10-4-1848 (no return) L
Wethington, Mary A. to William Edward 10-5-1852 (10-6-1852) G
Wethington, Mary to W. P. Davis 9-27-1869 (9-28-1869) Dy
Wetli, Amelia L. to Augustus Keaner 2-3-1849 Sh
Wetter, Josephine to Jacob Lacroix 11-4-1861 (1-9-1862) Sh
Wetz, Roser to Fred Smith (Smidtz) 3-8-1858 (3-10-1858) Sh
Wetzel, Genevieve to Charles Lienhardt 2-7-1850 Sh
Wever, Annie M. to E. G. Chambers (Chalmers) 7-3-1860 Sh
Whalan, Mary to Pat;rcik McLaughlin 10-25-1842 Sh
Whalen, Anne Maria to Thos. Callens 5-5-1862 Sh
Whalen, Kate (Mrs.) to Patrick Burke 9-27-1863 Sh
Whaler, Sarah to A. W. Miller 10-4-1864 Sh
Whaley, E. B. to Charles Wood 6-21-1858 (6-22-1858) Sh
Whalin, Anne Maria to Thos. Collans 5-5-1862 Sh
Whalin, Joanna to John Dulin 9-17-1852 (9-18-1852) Sh
Whaling, Mary to James Welch 6-30-1845 Sh
Whalings, Julia to Wm. Mahan (Maher) 7-17-1850 Sh
Whalon, Mary to Richard Jones 6-3-1869 (no return) Hy
Wham?, Nancy Jane to David Hemphill McQuerter 5-6-1853 T
Whartin, Lizzie to Allen Bond 12-31-1869 (no return) Hy
Wharton, Caroline R. to John A. McCain 4-20-1847 Hn
Wharton, Harriet M. to James F. Thompson 3-24-1841 Hn
Wharton, Martha M. to John W. Love 8-3-1831 Ma
Wharton, Mattie to James D. Reid 11-6-1866 (11-8-1866) Ma
Wharton, Mollie to Edward D. Graves 12-31-1879 (1-1-1880) L B
Wharton, Nancy to John Kimbel 8-12-1836 Sh
Wharton, Sallie B. to Wm. W. Butler 11-8-1877 Hy
Whealan, Elizabeth to Lewis Neumyer 10-24-1859 Sh
Wheatley, Amanda to John K. Balch 9-15-1830 Sh
Wheatley, Elizabeth to W. H. Hamilton 7-30-1867 Be
Wheatley, Frances M. to James R. Clay 5-16-1866 L
Wheatley, Jane E. to John C. Weaver 9-19-1860 (9-20-1860) Sh
Wheatley, Kate S. (Miss) to D. D. Saunders 3-14-1860 Sh
Wheatley, Kate to John D. James 5-18-1863 (5-21-1863) Sh
Wheatley, Martha to B. R. Stone 2-22-1858 (2-24-1858) L
Wheatley, Martha to James Berry 3-1-1860 Be
Wheatley, Mary Ann to M. S. Parker 5-22-1863 Be
Wheatley, Nannie to W. D. New 11-20-1880 (11-21-1880) L
Wheatley, Narciss to John F. Lumpkins 9-13-1869 L
Wheatley, Susan C. to Miles Carey 10-11-1839 Sh
Wheatly, Dulcena to Isaac Hooper 6-2-1856 Be
Wheatly, Milly to James R. Miller 11-25-1863 O
Wheatly, Sarah to Harrell Nobles 9-15-1853 Be
Wheeler, A. E. J. to Thomas Morris 6-13-1858 We
Wheeler, Amanda to Wiley Puckett 7-6-1847 O
Wheeler, Aurelia A. to Wm. W. Hubbard 6-29-1850 We
Wheeler, Emily to Silas C. Crockett 12-11-1852 (12-14-1852) O
Wheeler, Harriet to B. Barns 1-21-1866 G
Wheeler, L. L. to J. R. Roach 12-10-1862 (12-4?-1862) O
Wheeler, M. A. to M. G. Reasons 11-17-1877 (11-21-1877) Dy
Wheeler, M. E. to G. B. Granberry 3-21-1862 Sh
Wheeler, M. J. to J. P. Taylor 11-21-1857 G
Wheeler, Margaret to M. C. Reasons 2-9-1878 Dy
Wheeler, Mariah to Samuel Peeples 8-8-1861 We
Wheeler, Missouri P. to Edward Talbot 9-26-1870 (9-27-1870) Ma
Wheeler, Nancy to John Bland 7-7-1836 Sh
Wheeler, Nannie to John W. Harton 7-31-1869 (8-1-1869) Dy
Wheeler, Nellie to James (Junus?) Bond 4-4-1885 (4-9-1885) L
Wheeler, S. J. to M. F. Gambell 12-23-1874 (12-24-1874) O
Wheeler, Sarah A. to F. H. Thompson 8-14-1860 (no return) Dy
Wheeler, Sarah J. to Charles C. Winstead 1-11-1855 We
Wheeler, Susan A. to William Connell 9-26-1867 G
Wheeler, Susan to Harbert Joyce 4-14-1845 Ma
Wheeler, Tonser to Wm. P. Hutchins 11-3-1866 (11-4-1866) F
Wheeless, M. F. to J. B. Lee 12-24-1881 (no return) L
Wheeless, Mahala to Andrew Fry 11-13-1879 L
Wheelin (Wheeler), Maria to John M. McColley 4-3-1837 Sh
Wheler, Mollie to Ambros Henderson 3-25-1871 (no return) Hy
Wheller, Mary C. to S. G. Stoodley 9-20-1860 Sh
Wherry, Dolly to Sain A. Tansil 5-7-1875 Dy
Wherry, Dorcus to Edwin Herring 12-23-1834 Sh
Wherry, E. A. to T. N. Lynne 1-16-1860 (1-18-1860) Sh
Wherry, M. A. to A. J. Grugett? 1-15-1874 Dy
Wherry, M. E. to J. L. Calton 9-26-1874 (9-27-1874) Dy
Wherry, Margarete to Elihu T. Land 7-2-1833 Sh
Wherry, Martha E. to E. W. Moore 1-13-1853 (1-18-1853) G
Whibby (Whitby?), Ida to Jackson Green 2-28-1880 (3-3-1880) L
Whichard, Penelope to Thompson Hunt 2-18-1856 (2-21-1856) G
Whicker, Margaret to William Reed 5-30-1870 G
Whicker, Martha A. to D. A. Richmond 10-15-1867 G
Whiley, Louisa to Jacob Dickson 3-13-1868 (3-15-1868) Ma
Whillis, Susan to Anderson Hawkins 6-30-1844 Cr
Whippell, M. Ann to J. P. Cox 4-21-1870 (4-24-1870) O
Whippell, N. M. to C. A. Ragan (Logan) 3-19-1868 (3-21-1868) O
Whipple, Ann Eliza to George A. Felts 1-26-1857 (1-29-1857) O

Whipple, Sarah E. to Isaac W. Caldwell 12-27-1838 O
Whipple, Sarah L. to Albert A. Barnard 1-6-1864 Sh
Whirl, Winnie to Frank Turpin 7-8-1876 Hy
Whirley, Martha Jane to N. M. Lumley 12-12-1864 Sh *
Whit, Amanda to J. B. Hicks 3-6-1861 Mn
Whit, Harriet to John Pennington 12-13-1862 (12-14-1862) Dy
Whitaker, Amanda to John A. Bowers 1-24-1831 Hr
Whitaker, America to Jackville R. Easter 6-27-1833 (6-30-1833) Hr
Whitaker, Dorthey E. to Albert A. Hall 11-6-1826 (11-14-1826) Hr
Whitaker, Eliza to Allen Mayfield 1-28-1870 Hy
Whitaker, Henrietta to Hiram Mann 7-10-1869 (no return) Hy
Whitaker, Jane T. to R. G. Wedington 1-4-1858 (1-5-1858) G
Whitaker, M. L. to W. H. Norvell 6-19-1869 Hy
Whitaker, Martha to Nicholas Greener 2-22-1862 (2-23-1862) Ma
Whitaker, Martha to William R. Jacobs 12-17-1849 (12-20-1849) Hr
Whitaker, Mary M. to Phillip Catnar 11-14-1848 (11-16-1848) F
Whitaker, Mary P. to G. R. Grisham 2-16-1867 Hn
Whitaker, Melissa to Richard H. Marshall 11-11-1856 (11-12-1856) O
Whitaker, Nannie to E. D. Peebles 4-27-1859 (4-28-1859) F
Whitaker, R. to John Garcelon 5-25-1859 (5-29-1859) Sh
Whitaker, Sarah F. to C. J. Mauldin 9-13-1859 (no return) Hy
Whitaker, Sarah to John Lambert 12-17-1862 Mn
Whitamore(Whitaman?), Sarah to Meshack Price 4-9-1857 L
Whitamore, Mary E. to Miles D. Webb 4-24-1854 (4-25-1854) L
Whitby (Whitley), Cynthia to Douglass Chapman 12-3-1846 Sh
Whitby, Ellen to John D. Hibbitt 1-21-1862 Sh
Whitby, Jeannette to Joseph F. Rasbury 3-31-1886 (4-4-1886) L
Whitby, Lucinda to James McKee 11-17-1848 (11-24-1848) Hr
Whitby, Nancy L. to Perryman Bryant 7-29-1841 Sh
Whitby, Parmenta (Mrs.) to Charles J. H. Ness 9-30-1856 (10-1-1856) Sh
Whitchard, Margarett R. to W. L. Ward 3-15-1866 G
Whitchard, Mary to Thomas Dunlap 8-28-1856 G
White, A. G. to J. P. King 12-18-1878 Dy
White, A. P. to J.M. Reed 2-26-1867 G
White, Agethy to John H. Cobb 12-25-1873 Hy
White, Alice to W. H. Applewhite 12-25-1874 (no return) Dy
White, Amanda to Andrew V. Boden 12-1-1866 (no return) Hn
White, Ann C. (Mrs.) to Benj. H.? Legon 5-11-1855 (no return) F
White, Ann to S. F. McNutt 1-5-1848 (1-11-1848) Hr
White, Ann to William Ligon 3-15-1867 (3-17-1867) F B
White, Annie C. to John D. Wilhelm 8-28-1866 (8-30-1866) Ma
White, Annie E. (Miss) to Jas. W. Anderson 8-22-1864 Sh
White, Annie to J. M. Jackson 4-29-1868 (no return) Dy
White, Arbella to W. P. Dickson 10-13-1870 F B
White, Armanda M. to John B. Hester 4-16-1835 Sh
White, Augusta to Alexander Erskine 12-12-1861 Sh
White, Bhethsheba? to J. A. Cox 12-17-1872 (12-19-1872) Cr
White, C. A. to J. P. A. Cobb 6-21-1862 Mn
White, Caldonia to J. H. Carvin 2-24-1874 Hy
White, Callie V. to C. C. Anderson 12-20-1882 (12-21-1882) L
White, Candis to Alex Helm 11-8-1884 L
White, Caroline to Jack Blackwell 6-22-1868 (6-25-1868) T
White, Caroline to John Bell 9-9-1849 Cr
White, Caroline to William R. Dodd 10-30-1861 Dy
White, Carrie to James Turner 4-20-1876 (4-21-1876) L B
White, Casamie to W. M. Malcomb 3-4-1866 Hn
White, Catharine to Geo. F. Blackburn 6-23-1858 Sh
White, Catharine to H. Griffin 10-9-1860 Sh
White, Catharine(Elisabeth) to Ira Atkinson 7-11-1859 Hr
White, Celia to James G. Williams 7-29-1855 Hn
White, Colistia A. to Wm. A. Jernigans 6-14-1845 Sh
White, Corina B. to Tyra H. Tanner 1-18-1854 (1-19-1854) O
White, Cortin L. to Thomas Thurman 3-12-1863 Mn
White, Delia to James C. Gooch 2-22-1869 (2-28-1869) Ma
White, Drucilla to Edward A. McMillan 7-28-1841 T
White, E. A. to James C. Bell 12-21-1853 Cr
White, E. J. to Andrew Percifull 12-4-1879 L
White, E. J. to Sam Anthony 8-30-1877 (no return) L
White, E. L. to S. P. Draper 9-16-1866 L
White, Eliza to B. Milam 1-7-1879 (no return) Dy
White, Eliza to J. C. Hubbs 10-6-1853 Be
White, Eliza to James Macklin 12-27-1877 Hy
White, Eliza to John Dillaney 6-24-1868 L
White, Eliza to Redmond Jefferson 4-18-1872 (4-22-1872) Dy
White, Eliza to Wallace Newman 10-30-1844 Ma
White, Eliza to William Green Newman 8-13-1870 (8-14-1870) L
White, Elizabeth (Mrs.) to John G. Powel 12-9-1863 Sh
White, Elizabeth C. to John B. Hester 6-24-1854 Sh
White, Elizabeth E. to J. Ezzell 7-17-1860 (no return) Cr
White, Elizabeth E. to Samuel Crowley 4-23-1851 (4-24-1851) Hr
White, Elizabeth I. to Henry B, Misenheimer 10-25-1838 Sh
White, Elizabeth to Archabald O. Corum 2-19-1839 O
White, Elizabeth to George W. Stricklin 9-30-1843 (no return) F
White, Elizabeth to James B. Irvin 12-14-1835 (12-15-1835) Hr
White, Elizabeth to Joseph A. King 1-24-1850 We
White, Elizabeth to S. A. Cobb 12-24-1864 (no return) Hy
White, Elizabeth to Valentine Walker 3-14-1853 (3-15-1853) Hr

Brides

White, Ellen Ann to Martin Harvey Kurts? 9-24-1853 (9-28-1853) T
White, Ellen S. to J. W. Travis 11-27-1866 Hn
White, Ellen to Billy Jones 4-6-1872 Hy
White, Ellen to Michael Murry 11-12-1856 Sh
White, Emily L. to Lewis E. Mills 2-2-1859 (2-3-1859) G
White, Emily to Cezar Chilton 7-23-1870 Hy
White, Eugenia A. to Wm. E. Cochron 12-19-1871 (no return) Hy
White, F. E. to M. P. G. Cochran 10-26-1870 Hy
White, F. J. to James R. Green 12-6-1875 (12-7-1875) Dy
White, Fannie to Lewis Washington 5-17-1877 Dy
White, Flora to William H. Hunt 3-17-1857 G
White, Florella to D. C. Walker 2-5-1856 Be
White, Frances A. to John H. Terry 5-29-1837 G
White, Frances E. to Henry F. Sowell 12-30-1869 Ma
White, Frances J. to Frank H. Dougan 12-19-1877 (no return) Hy
White, Frances to William Irion 1-7-1851 (1-16-1851) Hr
White, Harriet M. to Robert T. Webb 10-31-1860 (11-1-1860) Ma
White, Hester Ann to James Cruise 3-2-1844 (3-6-1844) Hr
White, Jane Mariah to William Gague 11-3-1849 (11-4-1849) G
White, Jane S. to McFarlen Oakley 5-19-1858 (5-20-1858) G
White, Jane to J. M. Montgomery 11-3-1834 (11-4-1834) Hr
White, Jane to Lewis O. Harmon 6-11-1868 O
White, Jennie A. to James J. Smith 11-6-1876 (no return) Dy
White, Joanna to Newborn Taylor 12-22-1866 Hy
White, Josey to John Wells 4-19-1873 (4-20-1873) T
White, Josie to Wilson Clinton 2-17-1876 (no return) Hy
White, June to Volantine C. Brandon 8-7-1844 Hn
White, Kate to S. T. Costen 2-16-1861 (2-18-1861) Sh
White, L. A. to E. H. Chaffin 2-9-1854 (no return) F
White, L. F. to W. C. Lemons 4-4-1872 G
White, Lanith to G. B. Frazier 11-13-1855 (no return) F
White, Laura A. to James White 7-19-1876 Hy
White, Laura W. to James T. Leath 12-2-1862 Sh
White, Laura to H. A. Farnsworth 10-7-1856 O
White, Laura to Peter Read 11-28-1872 (no return) L B
White, Leathy to Reuben Beasley 12-3-1870 (12-29-1870) F B
White, Levy to Caswell J. Moore 3-2-1846 (3-8-1846) G
White, Lizzie to W. A. J. Chamberlin 2-4-1862 Sh
White, Louisa E. to Wm. Connell 7-15-1841 Sh
White, Louisa to James A. Aley 10-1-1876 Hy
White, Louisa to Wm. M. Revis 12-12-1850 We
White, Louisiana C. to Wm. P. Blackstone 1-25-1849 Sh *
White, Lucinda to Harrison Walker 1-11-1868 O
White, Lucinda to Peter Glass 1-8-1874 Hy
White, Lucretia B. to John C. Caldwell 4-15-1844 (4-16-1844) O
White, Lucy to Charlie Young 10-21-1870 (1-22-1871) Dy
White, Lucy to Jim Reagan 5-25-1877 (5-27-1877) Dy
White, M. A. to J. J. Johnson 12-2-1868 (12-3-1868) Dy
White, M. A. to J. M. Armstrong 11-10-1862 G
White, M. E. to J. N. Mathew 12-4-1862 (12-5-1862) O
White, M. E. to J. S. Waller 8-1-1870 (8-5-1870) T
White, M. E. to R. A. Webb 12-8-1865 Hy
White, M. J. C. to J. H. Parker 12-20-1862 (12-21-1862) Sh
White, M. L. to C. G. Merriman 8-21-1855 (8-22-1855) Sh
White, M. to John D. G. Wynn 9-16-1841 Cr
White, Mahaily to Richard Washam 5-20-1866 Hn B
White, Malinda (Mrs.) to Martin Dodson 12-12-1872 (no return) L
White, Malinda to Solomon Hines 7-23-1836 (7-28-1836) G
White, Manda to Charles Wheeler 2-2-1839 Be
White, Manda to Charles Wheeler 2-2-1839 Be CC
White, Manerva to William Hunt 6-21-1869 Cr
White, Manirva to James A. Flippin 10-24-1846 (10-28-1846) G
White, Margaret C. to Geo. B. Tinsley 11-17-1850 (11-20-1850) G
White, Margaret E. to David B. Johnson 1-2-1855 Sh
White, Margaret Jane G. to George S. Scarbrough 11-10-1840 (11-12-1840) Hr
White, Margaret M. to Zachariah J. Doyle 11-11-1868 (11-12-1868) T
White, Margaret S. to N.? Alexander 11-20-1867 (no return) Hn
White, Margaret to Ben Jones 1-11-1871 T
White, Margaret to Berry White 9-3-1859 Cr
White, Margaret to Elisha G. Malone 6-24-1858 (6-27-1858) O
White, Margaret to J. C. Davis 11-17-1874 Hy
White, Margaret to Sylvester Gilbert 5-2-1863 Sh
White, Margaret to Timothy Berry 11-8-1859 Sh
White, Margarett to Frank Irvine 2-26-1866 (no return) Cr
White, Margarett to Richarad H. Crider 7-25-1854 Cr
White, Margarette to William Burnett 12-12-1861 G
White, Mariah E. to Isaac N. Farris 1-9-1854 O
White, Mariah to Tom Newborn 12-27-1870 Hy
White, Marie to Martin Van Buren 8-12?-1868 T
White, Martha C. to L. L. Davis 3-4-1854 Sh
White, Martha Jane to King W. Ward 4-15-1851 (5-1-1851) Hr
White, Martha M. to Jesse S. Burford 5-9-1842 Hr
White, Martha M. to Robert McKenna 11-9-1861 Sh
White, Martha N. to Jno. W. Measle 7-9-1873 Hy
White, Martha P. to Marion J. Stephens 11-19-1855 (11-21-1855) G
White, Martha R. to John Carter 11-14-1865 (11-15-1865) Cr
White, Martha to David McCloud 1-31-1870 (no return) Cr

White, Martha to Sterling G. Spain 11-24-1847 Cr
White, Mary A. to George H. Hawson 2-11-1869 Ma
White, Mary A. to J. J. W. Northern 10-23-1859 We
White, Mary Ann to Edmond J. Booker? 8-3-1842 (8-4-1842) T
White, Mary Ann to Michael Healy 2-4-1856 Sh
White, Mary Ann to Raleigh Hammers 7-4-1859 (7-5-1859) Ma
White, Mary Ann to William P. Simpson 12-11-1858 (12-13-1858) T
White, Mary Ann to Zachariah Smith 9-5-1831 (9-11-1831) G
White, Mary C. to E. M. Ricks 6-19-1872 (no return) Hy
White, Mary C. to Henry Hifiley 10-14-1847 Cr
White, Mary C. to W. M. Reed 1-1-1851 Sh
White, Mary E. J. to Samuel Neely 1-2-1841 (1-7-1841) G
White, Mary Elizabeth to Anail Watson 7-1-1854 (7-2-1854) Ma
White, Mary Jane to Harrison G. Folts 6-7-1841 Hr
White, Mary Jane to Phillip R. Jones 9-22-1841 (10-5-1841) Hr
White, Mary L. to Augustus W. Walk 8-?-1866 (8-30-1866) T
White, Mary L. to Edwin Campbell 8-6-1860 (8-7-1860) Sh
White, Mary L. to Robert J. Lewis 8-12-1857 O
White, Mary M. to Leander B. Page 10-2-1851 (10-3-1851) O
White, Mary S. to James Adams 11-29-1848 Sh
White, Mary W. to Jeremiah Holliday 8-28-1827 (8-31-1827) Hr
White, Mary to A. H. Lemmons 2-11-1867 (2-12-1867) Cr
White, Mary to Benj. Franklin 3-19-1851 (no return) Cr
White, Mary to Calvin Roberts 12-29-1866 (12-31-1866) F B
White, Mary to Claiborne Adams 1-24-1853 Sh
White, Mary to Hardy Bloodworth 12-7-1848 Cr
White, Mary to Henry Carr 2-25-1838 Sh
White, Mary to John Edwards 4-2-1874 Hy
White, Mary to Thos. M. Williams 2-16-1845 Cr
White, Mary to Willis Carpenter 3-13-1883 L
White, Maryann to J. S. Peacock 1-26-1841 Be
White, Matilda to William Sparks 10-7-1874 Hy
White, Mattie W. to C. P. Moore 11-30-1874 O
White, Mattie to Anthony Holliman 12-26-1877 Hy
White, Mattie to Julian B. Campbell 12-22-1880 (12-23-1880) L
White, Minnie L. to H. A. Tripp 7-10-1864 Sh
White, N. A. C. to William B. Hardison 3-18-1851 (3-19-1851) Hr
White, N. E. to W. J. Ragens 10-5-1868 (10-8-1868) T
White, N. L. to S. P. Taylor 9-20-1866 G
White, N. S. to H. C. Lemons 12-7-1871 (no return) Cr
White, N. V. to Lafayett Grissom 10-29-1856 G
White, Nancy A. to H. N. Johnson 10-15-1866 (no return) Dy
White, Nancy B. to John W. King 7-9-1846 We
White, Nancy E. to B. A. White 2-6-1860 Hy
White, Nancy E. to Charles R. Belote 8-31-1854 Ma
White, Nancy E. to G. W. Bonds 4-1-1868 O
White, Nancy F. to H. M. Conley 3-5-1861 Be
White, Nancy F. to John F. Hicks 10-22-1846 We
White, Nancy J. to James H. Bringle 11-11-1868 (11-12-1868) T
White, Nancy J. to Jno. F. Hicks 10-19-1846 We
White, Nancy to J. S. Swindle 12-14-1857 Be
White, Nancy to Joe Jordan 3-17-1869 (3-18-1869) L
White, Nancy to John McLaughlin 10-11-1854 (10-12-1854) T
White, Nancy to Tho. Williams, sr. 8-5-1844 We
White, Nannie M. to W. B. Sapp 12-2-1884 L
White, Nicey to Glouster White 3-31-1867 Hy
White, Nina C. to John C. Goodwin 12-13-1854 (12-14-1854) Sh
White, Olive (Mrs.) to M. G. Phelps 8-5-1867 G
White, Paralee to W. W. Fedrick 5-5-1863 (5-6-1863) Dy
White, Patience E. to C. H. Stockard 4-4-1867 G
White, Patience to Charles H. Ross 8-11-1839 G
White, Patience to Riland Walls 2-26-1845 We
White, Pricilla A. to W. T. Elmore 7-16-1862 (no return) Hy
White, Rebbecca to Diocles S. Stafford 1-10-1853 Cr
White, Rebecca J. to L. N. Donnell 3-7-1838 Hn
White, Rizpah E. to William R. Gough 10-28-1844 O
White, Rosa to Stephen Demsey 7-24-1866 G
White, S. S. to G. T. Culley 3-10-1867 G
White, Sallie J. to Robt. W. Norment 11-25-1867 (11-28-1867) F
White, Sarah Ann to Robert F. Lea 12-24-1850 G
White, Sarah C. to Ralph Williams 5-28-1844 Hn
White, Sarah C. to Robert Marbury 12-6-1866 Hy
White, Sarah C. to Sam A. Fuller 10-21-1859 We
White, Sarah C. to Sam Long 8-21-1861 T
White, Sarah E. to E. C. Wallace 5-8-1877 (5-9-1877) L
White, Sarah E. to John H. Arnold 2-23-1853 (2?-1-1853) G
White, Sarah E. to Sampson Blaloch 11-10-1851 G
White, Sarah E. to William Flora 4-28-1859 Sh
White, Sarah Elizabeth to Elisha J. Crawford 8-7-1866 Ma
White, Sarah F. to David H. Jones 1-16-1863 (no return) Dy
White, Sarah F. to W. H. Stockard 9-18-1860 G
White, Sarah J. to C. Forrest 12-23-1866 Hn
White, Sarah J. to G. T. Morris 3-14-1866 G
White, Sarah J. to James Wyatt 12-17-1849 Cr
White, Sarah J. to Justin H. Edwards 11-19-1860 (no return) Hy
White, Sarah Jane to Robert Jackson 10-21-1866 Hy
White, Sarah M. to Michael Leonard 8-26-1836 Sh

White, Sarah S. to James M. Woods 6-18-1836 (6-19-1836) G
White, Sarah to Jesse Maddox 10-30-1848 Sh
White, Sarah to Thos. Wallace 8-3-1847 Cr
White, Sarah to William Swindle 5-22-1856 Be
White, Sarrah J. to J. A. Vaughan 6-28-1866 G
White, Sophronia A. to Edmond Tucker 4-10-1874 L B
White, Susan A. to James W. McBride 9-12-1860 We
White, Susan A. to John Bell 7-21-1862 (no return) Hy
White, Susan to John Hicks 8-16-1855 Be
White, Susan to Washington Green 3-17-1884 (3-22-1884) L
White, Susan to Wm. Hunt 2-6-1869 (no return) Hy
White, T. A. to W. M. J. Boaz 3-2-1859 Cr
White, Tabetha to Wallace W. Boughton 4-11-1863 Mn
White, Tabitha to W. E. Davis 4-16-1864 (4-17-1864) Sh
White, Theodocia to William King 10-1-1846 (10-15-1846) O
White, Theodosia (Theodora) to Wyatt Clarke 1-23-1843 Sh
White, Vetury to John D. Smith 12-8-1850 Be
Whitehad, Mary E. to V. B. Sevier 7-10-1862 Hy
Whitehead, Betty to William Cunningham 11-7-1848 Sh
Whitehead, Charity to Samuel A. Poston 1-11-1855 Sh
Whitehead, Elizabeth Jane to William Clark 1-29-1839 F
Whitehead, Ibby to Richard Moore 7-15-1865 (no return) Hy
Whitehead, J. A. R. to J. C. Davison 9-25-1848 (9-28-1848) F
Whitehead, Judy? to W. P. Morris? 11-23-1849 F
Whitehead, Liza to Billy Bowers 6-24-1869 Hy
Whitehead, Lizzie to Jessee Howard 4-28-1869 Hy
Whitehead, Lucy A. to James A. Moody 1-24-1866 Hy
Whitehead, Lucy J. to W. J. Wallace 3-30-1875 Hy
Whitehead, M. to John Jordan 12-11-1847 (12-16-1847) F
Whitehead, Mary E. to William Higdon 2-28-1861 Be
Whitehead, Mary to J. D. Williams 1-16-1860 (1-17-1860) O
Whitehead, R. F. to Thomas J. Smith 9-6-1853 (no return) F
Whitehead, Susan to William Bagwell 2-14-1863 (2-16-1863) O
Whitehead, Temperance to William Teague 12-6-1845 (12-11-1845) F
Whitehead, Tennessee to D. A. Nunn 6-20-1871 Hy
Whitehorn, Jacky to John Rone 3-24-1856 Cr
Whitehorn, Jane to V. A. Davis 3-14-1837 Hr
Whitehorn, Martha to James M. Ezell 11-7-1847 (no return) Cr
Whitehorn, Martha to James McGill 11-1-1847 Cr
Whitehorn, Paralle to Alfred Devine 8-19-1868 (8-21-1868) Cr
Whitehorn, Rebecca to Thos. W. Stacy 7-31-1845 Cr
Whitehorn, Sarah Emily to Thomas Sanders 4-18-1842 (4-22-1842) Hr
Whitehurst, A. M. to Joseph King 1-8-1874 Hy
Whitehurst, Emma O. to David A. Matherson 3-13-1878 Hy
Whitehurst, J. A. to W. P. Thompson 12-23-1857 (12-24-1857) Sh
Whitehurst, M. C. to J. M. Capps 12-18-1868 G
Whitehurst, Susan to Wash. McCarnel 10-11-1867 Hy
Whitelaw, Alice to Solomon Coleman 12-26-1874 Hy
Whitelaw, Ann to Buck Mann 12-28-1865 (no return) Hy
Whitelaw, Berter to Turner Shaw 3-17-1876 Hy
Whitelaw, Bertha to Thomas Sangster 11-28-1877 Hy
Whitelaw, Bettie to Turner Shaw 11-28-1878 Hy
Whitelaw, Bittie to James P. Whitelaw 2-17-1869 Hy
Whitelaw, C. H. to W. L. Whitelaw 2-17-1869 Hy
Whitelaw, Callie to Tom Sanders 6-2-1870 Hy
Whitelaw, Edmonia to Frank Hogie 7-7-1866 Hy
Whitelaw, Eliza to Robert Read 8-4-1878 Hy
Whitelaw, Ellen to H. F. Jones 2-18-1869 Hy
Whitelaw, Ellen to Jerry Wiley 4-27-1871 Hy
Whitelaw, Frances to O. King 12-28-1875 (no return) Hy
Whitelaw, Hannah to David Whitelaw 10-30-1878 Hy
Whitelaw, Julia A. to B. W. Alison 1-6-1875 Hy
Whitelaw, Julia P. to Lewis Taylor 12-16-1875 Hy
Whitelaw, Lear to Albert Hawkins 12-23-1877 (no return) Hy
Whitelaw, Lizzie to Aaron Loving 5-13-1876 Hy
Whitelaw, Lucy to Shedrick Burten 9-9-1871 (no return) Hy
Whitelaw, Lue to Jack Rudd 3-8-1873 Hy
Whitelaw, Mary E. to Henry Banie 6-29-1872 Hy
Whitelaw, Mary to H. C. Nolen 11-11-1863 (no return) Hy
Whitelaw, Mollie to James Read 9-20-1872 Hy
Whitelaw, Moria to Wm. Whitelaw 11-15-1876 Hy
Whitelaw, Nannie to Lysander Houk 5-6-1860 (no return) Hy
Whitelaw, Patsey to Richd. Clark 11-30-1872 Hy
Whitelaw, Rosa to Jas. Weatherspoon 1-19-1878 Hy
Whitelaw, S. A. to Andrew Loving 1-28-1869 Hy
Whitelow, Eliza to Frank Rhoades 3-21-1868 (no return) Hy
Whiten, Ople--- to J. M. Blackburn 9-20-1860 G
Whitenton, Mary F. to John I. Brown 11-16-1869 Ma
Whitesell, Elizabeth to A. T. Glover 8-5-1859 (no return) We
Whitesell, Mary to Henry Jenkins 12-29-1843 (no return) We
Whiteside, Axelina to Everett G. Piercy 7-28-1847 (7-29-1847) Ma
Whiteside, Margaret E. to John L. Guy 8-26-1840 (8-27-1840) O
Whiteside, Margaret M. to J. C. Faulk 8-27-1840 (8-27-____) O
Whiteside, Margaret to John L. Guy 8-26-1840 (8-27-1840) O
Whiteside, Mary E. to H. Butler 7-23-1845 Cr
Whiteside, Sally A. to John McDade 9-24-1859 We
Whitesides, Elizabeth C. to George H. Long 9-1-1842 O

Whitesides, Eudora to William H. Cox 10-23-1866 Ma
Whitesides, Margaret to Asa L. Trott 10-30-1828 Sh
Whitesides, Margaret to Moses Thomas 1-6-1844 (1-7-1844) L
Whitesides, Sarah E. to A. J. Nelms 11-10-1863 (11-12-1863) O
Whitess, Martha to Stephen Wilson 9-11-1837 Hr
Whitethorne, Ruth V. F. to Columbus Robins 8-3-1857 (8-4-1857) O
Whitfield, Eliza to William Clayton 1-19-1854 Hn
Whitfield, Elizabeth to William P. Wimberley 3-12-1850 Hn
Whitfield, Lucy A. to William Walker 6-15-1848 Hn
Whitfield, Malvina to Alexander McKinney 7-9-1846 Sh
Whitfield, Martha J. to Henry James 5-26-1862 Sh
Whitfield, Mary A. N. to Alexander G. Criddie 10-?-1843 Hn
Whitfield, Mary to Isham Dalton 7-8-1856 O
Whitfield, Mary to S. E. Rosson 9-22-1837 Hr
Whitfield, N. E. L. to Z. H. Curlin 9-21-1859 Sh
Whitfield, Nancy ann to Charles B. Whitson 2-13-1855 (no return) F
Whitfield, Sarah L. to L. Farmer 12-21-1860 (12-24-1860) Sh
Whitfield, Sarah to Henry Smith 4-6-1878 Hy
Whitford, Sarah Jane to James M. Marsh 12-20-1859 Hr
Whitford, Sarah to George W. Tate 8-13-1836 Hr
Whitington, Emeline to James B. Wilson 8-22-1843 (8-23-1843) Ma
Whitker, Amanda to James Sherman 2-13-1867 (2-14-1867) L
Whitley, Ann E. to John S. Peete 10-21-1844 T
Whitley, Artimisa F. to Jordon Butler 3-2-1869 (3-10-1869) Cr
Whitley, Betsy to J. N. Reed 3-22-1868 G
Whitley, Bettie to John W. Williams 3-29-1861 (3-31-1861) Sh
Whitley, Callie to J. W. Arnett 5-13-1873 (5-14-1873) Dy
Whitley, Elizabeth to Stephen D. Aydlott 10-1-1851 (10-8-1851) Sh
Whitley, Frances to Harrison Brickum 3-14-1861 Mn
Whitley, Jane to James Nicholson 1-5-1837 Hr
Whitley, Judia to Addison Corrington 7-10-1831 (8-9-1831) G
Whitley, K. to Isaac Shaw 12-22-1870 T
Whitley, Laura F. to James L. Wooten 12-17-1855 Sh
Whitley, Lucratis to Thomas Fletcher 3-19-1835 G
Whitley, M. A. to James L. Cooper 5-21-1867 (5-23-1867) T
Whitley, Martha Jane to Wm. N. Smith 10-26-1869 G
Whitley, Mary to J. W. Boyett 2-12-1861 G
Whitley, Milly to R. F. Lumpkins 5-2-1867 G
Whitley, Nancy E. to Enoch Flowers 12-30-1853 (1-1-1854) Sh
Whitley, Nancy to Wylie Cobb 6-25-1856 O
Whitley, Patsey to James Foster 11-15-1870 T
Whitley, Pina to Thomas Curby 11-22-1838 O
Whitley, Polly to Henry Thompson 8-31-1866 T
Whitley, Sallie M. to Joseph Peete 10-3-1864 (10-5-1864) T
Whitley, Susan to Martin Y. Taylor 2-21-1849 (2-22-1849) G
Whitley, W. S. to W. J. McCall 11-1-1873 (11-7-1873) T
Whitlock, Amanda J. to Robert Guthrie 10-4-1845 Hn
Whitlock, Catherine to Alexander Spine 4-29-1830 Hr
Whitlock, Eliz. Ann to George Croghan Pinkston 3-19-1850 T
Whitlock, Eliza to Josiah Goforth 1-7-1850 (1-16-1850) T
Whitlock, Harriet C. to John Bevill 10-21-1850 Hn
Whitlock, M. M. to A. S. Polsgrove 9-28-1865 O
Whitlock, Mary C. to Granderson Sharp 2-4-1868 (2-5-1868) T
Whitlock, Susan to John T. Brown 4-16-1857 T
Whitlocke, Mariah D. to L. F. Bonfels 7-26-1842 (7-27-1842) G
Whitlow, Emanda E. to George S. Williamson 2-11-1871 Ma
Whitlow, Mary E. to William Bell 4-8-1843 (5-11-1843) G
Whitlow, Nancy S. to Jacob E. Vanhook 11-19-1844 Ma
Whitlow, Phinela to James R. Cole 2-17-1842 Ma
Whitly, E. J. to T. H. Ward 11-22-1864 (11-23-1864) Sh
Whitly, Miranna to Z. A. Carr 10-4-1847 Sh
Whitly, Patience to Dempsy Hunt 11-18-1865 (12-10-1865) T
Whitly, Susanna to Jesse Whitly (Whitby) 6-15-1841 Sh
Whitman, Jane to Alexander Jones 11-30-1843 T
Whitman, Lucy A. to William N. Miller 2-7-1859 (2-8-1859) Sh
Whitmon, Amandy P. to Hamilton Mask 12-13-1847 (12-14-1847) Hr
Whitmore, Alice to Monroe Roberson 5-13-1885 (no return) L
Whitmore, Alice to Polk Taylor 12-30-1885 (12-31-1885) L
Whitmore, Eliza A. L. to Edward Ragsdale 8-20-1855 (no return) F
Whitmore, Eliza B. to James T. Pugh 8-21-1835 (8-27-1835) Hr
Whitmore, Harriet to Wm. Faulkner 7-2-1867 Hy
Whitmore, Lizzie A. to Jerry Bracken 1-1-1868 (2-3-1868) F B
Whitmore, Lucy to Patrick Thornton 7-26-1867 (7-27-1867) F B
Whitmore, Martha V. to Houston Mitchell 11-30-1853 Hr
Whitmore, Mary E. to Peter A. Vaughn 12-18-1848 (1-2-1849) F
Whitmore, Sally P. to Newel W. Harris 10-4-1852 (no return) F
Whitmore, Susan P. to W. H. (Dr.) Tharp 11-22-1852 (no return) F
Whitmore, Virginia to J. M. A. Scales 9-16-1854 (no return) F
Whitney, Jane to Matthew Bronte 8-2-1842 L
Whitney, Martha C. to Benj. F. Powers 10-7-1850 (10-6?-1850) F
Whitney, Sarah to William A. Pinkard 6-20-1855 (6-21-1855) Sh
Whitney, Virginia to John Triller? 4-22-1853 (no return) F
Whitsen, Nancy M. to James N. Lewis 2-17-1859 We
Whitsett, Elizabeth to Willie W. Whittsett 11-28-1832 Sh
Whitsett, Margaret to J. L. Sweeny 5-3-1831 Sh
Whitsitt, Mary Eliza to Felix G. Dooley 5-16-1837 Sh
Whitson, Edney C. to Berry Griggs 3-2-1859 (3-3-1859) L

Whitson, Eliza Jane to Robert F. Wood 12-23-1869 (no return) Dy
Whitson, Eliza to Obediah McGuire 88-7-1846 (8-13-1846) T
Whitson, Elizabeth to Kenneth B. Anderson 11-7-1844 L
Whitson, Elvira to Chas. Parks 12-26-1867 G B
Whitson, Jane to William Henry Meacham 7-30-1857 (no return) L
Whitson, Judy Ann to Frank Smith 1-17-1877 Dy
Whitson, L. M. L. to L. D. Bland 8-24-1865 G
Whitson, Maggie E. to A. J. Gannon 9-24-1868 G
Whitson, Mariah to John Dunevant 12-12-1871 (12-13-1871 Dy
Whitson, Martha to John Thomas Williams 6-?-1854 (6-14-1854) L
Whitson, Mary A. to Huston Craig 8-16-1869 L
Whitson, Mary Ann to John Billings 8-29-1850 L
Whitson, Mary J. to Henry T. Pitts 9-24-1857 L
Whitson, May E. to Edmund C. Goodwin 9-28-1848 (no return) Hn
Whitson, Millie to Craig Perry 1-17-1877 Dy
Whitson, Molonia A. V. to Levi E. Pedigo 12-23-1867 (12-24-1868) L
Whitson, Sallie F. to B. F. Ellis 2-17-1886 L
Whitson, Susanah to Robert H. Owen 2-16-1859 T
Whitson, Susanah to Robert H. Owen 7-16-1859 T
Whitt, Ellen to Owen Ligon 12-27-1866 F B
Whitt, M. F. to J. H. Burnham 12-21-1870 (12-22-1870) Dy
Whitt, Soprona R. to J. W. Williams 5-8-1869 (no return) Dy
Whittaker, Charlotte to William Davis 9-13-1872 O
Whittaker, Drucilla to Robert C. Nall 9-8-1857 O
Whittaker, Sarah E. to F. J. Izard 5-2-1854 (no return) F
Whittamore-Whittaman, Martha to David B. Anderson (Andrews?) 11-23-1853 (11-24-1853) L
Whitteker, Elizabeth to Gilbert Lane 7-16-1853 (7-17-1853) O
Whitteman, Emily to A. J. Boling 12-6-1865 (12-10-1865) Dy
Whittemore, Emily to A. J. Boling 12-6-1865 (12-10-1865) Dy
Whitten, A. E. to John Holcomb 12-17-1874 Hy
Whitten, Carrie to James M. Gilbert 5-18-1869 Cr
Whitten, Elizabeth to Bryant? B_____ 6-17-1852 Hn
Whitten, G. A. to T. V. Fooshee 6-24-1868 G
Whitten, Harriet to William Hicks 12-29-1873 T
Whitten, Mary Jane to Edward A. Anderson 11-9-1846 (11-12-1846) F
Whitten, Mary W. to W. G. Hurn 8-22-1865 G
Whitten, Narcissa to Hezekiah Sinclair 12-26-1838 Hn
Whittenberger, Nannie E. to John W. Burton 2-24-1862 G
Whittenton, Elzira to E. Johnson 8-2-1869 (12-28-1869) Dy
Whittenton, H. D. to Z. T. Gleaves 12-20-1871 (12-21-1871) Dy
Whittenton, M. E. to M. J. Rankin 1-30-1867 (2-3-1867) Dy
Whittenton, Martha to Sam Johnson 6-3-1869 (no return) Dy
Whitthorn, Ann to Nelson Wells 12-27-1869 F B
Whitthorne, Annie to John W. Wright 12-26-1870 (1-5-1871) F
Whittington, Eliza to Tom Johnson 2-19-1868 (no return) Dy
Whittington, Frances Ann to Christopher C. Harris 2-10-1848 (2-14-1848) Ma
Whittington, Laney to Barney King 9-29-1856 (10-16-1856) Ma
Whittington, Mary Jane to Joseph M. Dalton 10-13-1842 Ma
Whittington, Mary to Meredith Johnson 1-16-1848 Be
Whittington, Sally to W. R. George 3-7-1864 (3-10-1864) O
Whitton, Rebecca Ann to Sam Dishough 8-10-1844 (8-13-1844) F
Whitworh, Ann Elizabeth to Rounsville Williams 12-28-1859 (12-29-1859) Ma
Whitworth, Ann to Henry Petty 8-21-18682 Dy
Whitworth, Ann to Thomas Ownby 1-19-1848 Cr
Whitworth, Elizabeth C. to R. S. Harris 3-21-1855 We
Whitworth, Elizabeth J. to James R. Eckles 4-20-1859 (4-21-1859) Sh
Whitworth, Elizabeth to J. B. Mosley 1-19-1865 (1-21-1865) L
Whitworth, Louisa to Richard Hargis 12-23-1857 Ma
Whitworth, M. J. to James H. Rudolph 9-3-1846 Hn
Whitworth, Margaret C. to George Waggoner 4-26-1861 Ma
Whitworth, Mary (Lucy?) A. to Jefferson C. Ferguson 2-4-1852 (2-5-1852) Sh
Whitworth, Mary G. to Joseph Warner 9-4-1856 (noncomeatibus) Ma
Whitworth, Mary G. to Stephen B. Waggoner 12-23-1856 Ma
Whitworth, Mary M. to John C. Pearce 8-11-1861 We
Whitworth, Mattie to Henry Hill 12-14-1870 (12-15-1870) T
Whitworth, Sarah to William Poplen 10-11-1841 Hn
Whitworthy, Eleanor to John P. Lanery (Lavery?) 12-23-1849 (12-24-1849) L
Whyte, M. D. C. to Benjamin W. Evans 3-19-1839 (3-21-1839) F
Whyte, Phereby to R. B. Stover 9-8-1866 (9-10-1866) F
Wiatt, Mary G. to Josiah F. Ayers 8-8-1846 Sh
Wicker, Clarinda to Samuel Hunter 2-28-1850 Hn
Wicker, E. A. to G. W. Jemison 3-21-1866 O
Wicker, Eliza to John Hood 12-13-1865 O
Wicker, Isabella to James K. Jimerson? 4-28-1857 O
Wicker, Mary Ann to John Wright 5-3-1856 (5-7-1856) O
Wicker, Nancy D. to John Pryer 12-24-1852 O
Wicker, Nancy to Monroe Shearman 1-19-1855 Hn
Wicker, Rachel to L. C. Vaught 12-1-1858 (12-2-1858) O
Wicker, Rebecca J. to Robert Crockett 7-16-1851 O
Wicker, Sarah to Edward M. Slider? 7-23-1855 (7-26-1855) O
Wickersham, Nannie to J. F. Bandy 12-23-1875 (no return) L
Wickham, Almira J. to Thos. J. Rawlings 6-29-1848 Sh
Wickham, Elizabeth (Miss) to Wm.L. Allen 7-24-1856 Sh
Wickham, Rebecca E. to James E. Martin 6-3-1839 Sh
Wickham, Sarah E. to John O. Greenlaw 6-5-1839 Sh
Wickham, Susan to E. B. Harrel 10-22-1846 Sh

Wicks, Ann E. to R. H. Alexander 3-29-1852 (3-30-1852) G
Widner, Catherine to James M. Gardner 1-27-1877 (no return) Hy
Widner, M. C. to R. F. Miller 3-1-1870 (no return) Hy
Wiebel, Christian to Jack Sanguinetti 1-18-1855 (1-20-1855) Sh
Wiett, Matilda to James Lewellen 2-2-1866 O
Wigg, Susan L. to Laurence McCafflin 5-5-1870 Ma
Wiggington, Nancy ann to Jonathan Mills 12-7-1864 Sh
Wiggins, Annie E. to Thomas J. Warr 11-21-1865 (no return) F
Wiggins, Emely to Hardin Jones 7-18-1838 Ma
Wiggins, Hannah T. to Thomas G. Mullins 9-10-1862 (9-11-1862) Ma
Wiggins, Jane to William Philips 8-23-1856 Hr
Wiggins, M. J. T. to John R. Dodson 5-21-1878 (5-23-1878) Dy
Wiggins, Mariah to John Gilbert 1-9-1871 Cr B
Wiggins, Narcisa to Thos. Gilbert 1-9-1871 Cr B
Wiggins, R. E. to H. B. Waller 12-14-1869 (no return) F
Wiggins, Sophia H. to Samuel D. Lambert 2-9-1864 O
Wiggle, Amie to John P. Perkins 8-9-1865 Mn
Wigglesworth, Edmonia to Baker Mebane 12-29-1870 (no return) F B
Wiggs, Caroline to Loi R. Wiggs 10-1-1840 Ma
Wiggs, Martha E. to William D. Harper 2-13-1845 (2-27-1845) Ma
Wiggs, Mary I. to Ryland Chandler 5-17-1838 Ma
Wiggs, Nancy R. to Calvin Flowers 11-3-1864 G
Wiggs, Sarah E. to George T. Shelton 12-20-1859 Ma
Wiggs, Susan S. to Alexander Howell 8-3-1854 Ma
Wilbanks, Elisabeth Nancy to Miles Wade Kerr 4-22-1865 T
Wilbanks, Lydia T. to James W. Morris 2-6-1856 We
Wilbanks, Martha A. to William Jones 12-28-1860 (1-1-1861) Hr
Wilbanks, Mary A. to J. S. Wilbanks 5-11-1860 (5-20-1860) Hr
Wilbanks, S. S. to David Lee 10-31-1861 (no return) We
Wilborn, Catharine to Jonas B. Meadows 5-11-1848 O
Wilborn, Elizabeth to David Smith 12-4-1845 Cr
Wilborn, Jincy to John Renfroe 3-11-1845 Cr
Wilborn, Mary to William Cobb 2-13-1849 O
Wilborn, Mary to William Cobb(s) 2-13-1849 (2-21-1849) O
Wilborn, Nannie to John Calhoon Davis 1-5-1854 (no return) F
Wilborn, Narcissa to William Erwin 10-15-1831 (10-18-1831) G
Wilborne, J. P. to Meshack Franklin 4-26-1866 (5-2-1866) F
Wilbosern, Sidonia to Joseph Bair 5-22-1860 Dy
Wilbourn, M. D. to J. C. Word 2-4-1864 (2-10-1864) F
Wilbourn, Tennessee to George T. White 10-19-1853 O
Wilbourn, Virginia W. to Thomas K. Williams 11-1-1855 (11-3-1855) O
Wilbourne, Narcissa to William Ervin 12-16-1833 (12-17-1833) G
Wilburn, Diana to P.L. Nance 10-12-1865 Hn
Wilburn, Frances to John W. Harris 1-12-1854 Sh
Wilburn, Parthenia to A. M. Hall 3-28-1866 Hn
Wilburn, Sarah E. to Sampson Lane 9-7-1854 (no return) F
Wilcocks, Susan to Ross Preston 4-16-1877 (9-12-1877) O B
Wilcox, Eliza Jane to A. S Thompson 8-12-1849 Hn
Wilcox, Elizabeth (Mrs.) to T. L. Beard 11-12-1855 (11-13-1855) Sh
Wilcox, Mary S. to W. C. Bowers 12-8-1846 We
Wilcox, Mary to John Lowry 2-1-1824 Sh
Wilcox, Mary to John W. Beatty 12-10-1863 O
Wilcox, N. J. to J. M. White 11-9-1870 (11-10-1870) Cr
Wilcox, Nancy L. to James C. Byler 6-6-1859 (6-9-1859) L
Wilcox, Susan to William L. D. Thacker 8-14-1831 Sh
Wild, Josephine G. to Henry Buehl 2-8-1861 (2-9-1861) Sh
Wildan, Matilda to John Hynes 10-20-1859 (no return) Cr
Wildar, Susan to Richard A. Edwards 8-11-1842 L
Wildberger, Alice to Lewis Vaccaro 8-29-1855 Sh
Wildberger, Rosenia to Joseph Cuneo 9-3-1860 Sh
Wilden, Mary A. M. to Wm. H. Lesenberry 12-24-1847 Cr
Wilder, Eliza to Frank Wissmer 6-6-1860 (6-9-1860) Sh
Wilder, Frances A. to A. H. Patterson 10-3-1864 (no return) Cr
Wilder, Julia to E. F. Harper 1-5-1861 Sh
Wilder, Martha J. to Elijah A. Scates 11-20-1849 Cr
Wilder, Rachel to Charly Morris 8-19-1868 (no return) Hy
Wilder, Sarah E. to Lafayette Scates 11-6-1850 Cr
Wildon, Emaline to Sammie S. Watson 7-14-1853 Cr
Wilds, Elizabeth to W. J. Rogers 1-15-1866 (1-18-1866) F
Wildt, Theresa to Joseph Oishei 4-22-1858 Sh
Wildur, Mary to William K. Thweatt 10-25-1842 (10-27-1842) G
Wiles, Adaline R. to John H. Trainer 1-23-1867 (1-24-1867) F
Wiles, Hararet M. to William T. Cameroans 11-19-1859 Sh
Wiles, Mary Elizabeth to Christopher Owen 10-6-1855 (10-24-1855) Sh
Wiles, Mary M. to William H. McGee 5-21-1855 G
Wiles, Mollie to W. S. Graham 5-16-1873 (no return) Cr
Wiles, Sary A. to John Dominger 4-9-1849 O
Wiley, Ann Vastine to H. D. Myrick 12-24-1865 (no return) Hn
Wiley, Ann to Dock Musgraves 11-23-1872 Hy
Wiley, Aramissa to E. H. Smith 2-17-1868 (2-19-1868) Cr
Wiley, Cynthia A. to Edward V. Baker 10-9-1849 Sh
Wiley, Eliza to John Bowers 8-14-1867 (no return) Hn
Wiley, Elizabeth J. to J. P. Love 3-22-1855 (no return) F
Wiley, Elizabeth J. to Wm. C. Duncan 7-17-1861 (7-18-1861) Hr
Wiley, Ellen to Green Holley 10-22-1872 Hy
Wiley, Fannie to Melvin Whitby 10-12-1864 Sh
Wiley, Jane to Henry Baily 12-24-1872 T

Wiley, July Ann to Wm. Smith 10-1-1849 (10-2-1849) F
Wiley, M. E. to A. R. Lankford 10-2-1865 Hn
Wiley, N. E. to P. H. Wilson 12-17-1872 T
Wiley, Rebecca A. to Peter Baker 12-24-1845 Sh
Wiley, Sallie to Haywood Collier 12-5-1873 Hy
Wiley, Sarah E. to Henry J. Koonce 1-30-1855 (1-31-1855) Sh
Wilgerson, Victoria J. to Samuel R. Luckey 2-16-1856 (no return) Hn
Wilhelm, Josephine to John W. White 9-8-1866 (9-9-1866) Ma
Wilhelm, Margaret to Joseph Richardson 2-8-1862 Mn
Wilhington, Harriett to William M. Pipkin 2-1-1859 (2-3-1859) G
Wilie, Mary J. to Berry L. Spring 12-18-1860 (12-19-1860) Ma
Wilie, Mary W. to Jas. B. Cunningham 9-7-1869 (9-9-1869) Ma
Wilie, Matildy to William G. Bradford 1-24-1829 Hr
Wilie, Susan A. B. to James H. Buntin 2-8-1870 Ma
Wilingham, Jennie to Elias Anthony 1-20-1877 Hy
Wilker, Mahaly J. to W. H. White 7-28-1857 Sh
Wilkerson, Amanda to Ike Tucker 12-26-1866 Hy
Wilkerson, Ann to Charles Wilkerson 11-18-1866 Hy
Wilkerson, Cornelia to J. W. McMullin 12-23-1858 Cr
Wilkerson, Eliza to Lemon Gay 1-2-1834 Hr
Wilkerson, Harriott to William J. C. Spellings 12-20-1843 G
Wilkerson, Lucie A. C. to James W. Nelson 10-22-1866 L
Wilkerson, M. J. to G. L. Alexander 1-19-1869 (no return) Hy
Wilkerson, Mary Jane to Wm. F. Corbitt 1-23-1847 Sh
Wilkerson, Mary to Elijah Gwyn 12-28-1868 (12-5?-1868) F B
Wilkerson, Missouri A. J. C. to Jos. D. Parham 3-26-1851 (no return) F
Wilkerson, Mrs. S. B. to C. W. Henry 11-28-1851 (12-10-1851) Hr
Wilkerson, Nancy M. to W. H. Bashears 2-26-1862 Mn
Wilkerson, Pollie to E. Shepard (Sherman) 12-25-1869 Hy
Wilkerson, Rebecca J. to Jason Prince 12-22-1863 Hr
Wilkerson, Sarah A. to P. D. Bryant 4-22-1863 (no return) Hn
Wilkerson, Susan to N. Gwynn 8-10-1866 (8-12-1866) F B
Wilkerson, Susanna to Almeron Dickerson 5-24-1829 Hr
Wilkerson?, Nancy to Joseph Cheairs 11-7-1842 (no return) F
Wilkes, A. E. J. to Perry C. Wilkes 11-12-1856 (11-13-1856) Hr
Wilkes, A. E. to G. F. Miller 1-30-1867 Hy
Wilkes, E. B. to H. M. Dickey 9-24-1878 Hy
Wilkes, Elizabeth A. to Daniel A. Ross 10-14-1860 (10-15-1860) Hr
Wilkes, Elizabeth A. to John House 10-15-1860 Hr
Wilkes, Elizabeth to Hardy Saunders 7-6-1836 (8-7-1836) Hr
Wilkes, Emily to Pleasant Batts 1-26-1871 (1-28-1871) F B
Wilkes, Fannie to Wat Vaughter 5-7-1874 Hy
Wilkes, Henrietta C. to H. A. Sammons 11-11-1859 (11-7?-1859) Hr
Wilkes, Juliann to Ezekiel Owens 10-11-1847 (10-12-1847) Hr
Wilkes, Martha F. to Wilie Sammons 10-4-1850 (10-10-1850) Hr
Wilkes, Martha J. to L. G. Baker 10-6-1847 Sh
Wilkes, Martha N. C. to James W. Bond 1-16-1856 (1-22-1856) Ma
Wilkes, Martha to Robert Marshall, jr. 11-12-1857 Sh
Wilkes, Mary D. to John E. Pearson 11-7-1852 (11-10-1852) Ma
Wilkes, Mary J. to Abner J. Fletcher 12-10-1849 (12-12-1849) G
Wilkes, Mary M. to John H. Sammons 10-16-1854 (10-26-1854) Hr
Wilkes, Rose to Solomon Fields 7-4-1868 G B
Wilkeson, Mary to John Brown 3-15-1836 Hr
Wilkins, Achsa G. to John D. Armour 11-1-1849 Sh
Wilkins, Addie J. to J. J. (Dr.) Chrisp 5-8-1867 G
Wilkins, Ann E. to Jesse S. Lenox 9-29-1854 (10-4-1854) O
Wilkins, Ann Eliza to John Holden 12-11-1841 F
Wilkins, Bettie C. to Benjamin F. Peeples 4-2-1867 Hn
Wilkins, C. C. to J. H. Cribbs 11-11-1868 Dy
Wilkins, Catherine E. to Young Bradford 4-3-1860 (4-5-1860) Ma
Wilkins, Charlotte E. to Henry Matlock 12-31-1855 (1-1-1855?) Ma
Wilkins, Elizabeth A. to Francis S. Lacey 7-9-1862 Dy
Wilkins, Ellen to Noel M. Pressley 5-29-1861 (5-30-1861) O
Wilkins, Emeline to James N. Higgins 8-2-1839 (8-4-1839) G
Wilkins, Evaline to Henry Dumas 1-10-1867 Hn B
Wilkins, Fannie to Elza Offill 11-17-1874 O
Wilkins, Fannie to Frank Burton 12-2-1875 Dy
Wilkins, Fanny to Jacob Haste 1-8-1867 G
Wilkins, Harrett J. to Robert P. Caldwell 5-15-1851 (5-19-1851) G
Wilkins, Henrietta O. to Benjamin Houston 10-27-1845 (10-29-1845) F
Wilkins, Henrietta to Phil Jones 1-29-1871 (no return) Hy
Wilkins, Jane to G. W. Jackson 6-10-1876 (6-11-1876) L
Wilkins, Josephine to A. P. Powell 1-14-1874 (no return) Dy
Wilkins, Josephine to John F. Hammers 1-24-1871 T
Wilkins, M. F. to D. P. Ferrill 2-22-1866 Dy
Wilkins, M. P. to John H. Mason 12-25-1853 Sh
Wilkins, Margarett to William Baker 7-28-1846 Ma
Wilkins, Mary A. to Wesley F. Jones 10-28-1847 G
Wilkins, Mary Ann to D. L. Dalton 8-23-1849 (8-28-1849) Hr
Wilkins, Mary Ann to James H. Bryant 4-9-1852 (4-16-1852) Ma
Wilkins, Mary Catharine to Robt. Alex Williams 2-18-1861 (2-19-1861) T
Wilkins, Mary J. to John Thompson 11-10-1843 (no return) F
Wilkins, Mary L. to Christopher C. Crane 11-3-1860 (11-4-1860) Cr
Wilkins, Mary R. to Thomas Collins 9-29-1867 Be
Wilkins, Mary to Henry Fletcher 7-17-1834 G
Wilkins, Mary to Robt. Harrison 3-17-1867 G B
Wilkins, Nancy (Mrs.) to Solomon D. Ford 11-30-1860 Ma
Wilkins, Nancy Jane to John E. Harrison 5-17-1853 (5-?-1853) T
Wilkins, Nettie to Robert Fennell 1-7-1875 Hy
Wilkins, Rebecca to John G. Johnson 2-23-1852 (2-24-1852) Hr
Wilkins, S. A. to W. H. McGuffin 9-4-1860 G
Wilkins, S. R. to F. J. Jones 2-13-1856 (no return) Hn
Wilkins, Sarah A. E. to Brinkley Matlock 12-20-1866 G
Wilkins, Sarah L. to John S. McCulloch 10-28-1847 G
Wilkins, Sarah S. to Joshua J. Griffin 11-13-1851 G
Wilkins, Sarah to Andrew Kilpatrick 8-16-1842 (8-18-1842) Ma
Wilkins, Sarah to Robert Lessley Dicus? 6-21-1853 T
Wilkins, Susan C. to J. S. Camerhorn 6-3-1868 G
Wilkinson, Clara Eliza to George Wilson 12-11-1830 (12-12-1830) O
Wilkinson, Clarissa F. to B. H. Cooper 1-3-1861 (1-7-1861) Hr
Wilkinson, Elisa Virginia to James B. Edwards 10-29-1827 (10-30-1827) Hr
Wilkinson, Elizabeth to L. W. Foster 12-28-1852 Hr
Wilkinson, Hannah D. to J. C. Nash 6-10-1863 O
Wilkinson, Jane to Simon Beal 12-25-1843 Ma
Wilkinson, Joycy Ann to Matthew D. Garrett 3-6-1843 Hr
Wilkinson, L. J. to J. T. W. Milam 7-15-1862 (no return) Hy
Wilkinson, Lucinda to William Ballard 3-31-1863 O
Wilkinson, Margaret E. to D. F. Taylor 6-2-1879 Dy
Wilkinson, Martha H. to Thomas B. Gilliam 9-16-1857 (10-17-1857) Sh
Wilkinson, Mary A. to Jas. F. Batt 10-14-1846 Sh
Wilkinson, Mary E. to Hiram Edmonson 11-15-1857 O
Wilkinson, Mary to W. L. Bailey 1-4-1832 (1-5-1831?) Hr
Wilkinson, Nancy A. to J. C. McKean 11-3-1830 Hr
Wilkinson, Nancy E. to Marcus Rickman 8-21-1841 (8-23-1841) Ma
Wilkinson, Parilee to Lewis Moore 12-20-1853 (12-21-1853) Hr
Wilkinson, S. E. D. to J. Cozart 10-2-1871 (10-3-1871) Dy
Wilkinson, Willie to Wm. E. Franklin 2-7-1871 (2-8-1871) F
Wilkison, Adaline to R. L. Short 10-15-1849 (11-25-1849) Hr
Wilks (Whitker), Eliza to M. Crosson (Crossor?) 4-20-1854 Sh
Wilks, A. L. to B. A. Compton 12-5-1877 Hy
Wilks, A. R. F. to C. A. Forbess 3-25-1858 Cr
Wilks, Barbrey B. to Nelson P. Smith 2-11-1846 Cr
Wilks, Eliza Jane to William W. Stanley 2-14-1854 G
Wilks, Eliza to Archibald B. House 11-21-1840 Hr
Wilks, Eliza to Solomon Wilson 2-23-1878 Hy
Wilks, Elizabeth to George W. Crockett 4-15-1839 (4-16-1839) G
Wilks, Frances M. to William M. Halford 10-1-1842 (10-2-1842) G
Wilks, Heneretta C. to Charles Griffey 10-18-1849 G
Wilks, Manerva to Baker Dandridge 8-26-1865 F
Wilks, Milly? E. to John S. Laycock 12-27-1866 Cr
Wilks, Naoma T. to J. W. Sammons 12-3-1858 (12-9-1858) Hr
Wilks, Narcissa Jane to William Hamilton 7-27-1835 Hr
Wilks, Susan to John Johnson 3-3-1849 Cr
Willaford, Lucy to William Etherage 10-14-1849 Hn
Willams, Sarah to Tom Palmer 1-7-1867 (no return) Hy
Willard, Amanda (Mrs.) to J. W. Love 7-5-1869 G
Willard, J. A. A. S. to James M. Powell 5-24-1851 (5-28-1851) L
Willard, Mary H. to Sugars T. Evans 12-20-1848 (12-28-1848) L
Willbanks, M. A. to Philoman W. Smith 2-21-1861 We
Willborn, Gincy to Joseph Webb 12-25-1867 G
Willeford, Nancy E. to W. T. Betty 4-25-1868 G
Willett, Hannah S. to Peter G. Foster 3-16-1853 Hn
Willett, Mary Adaline to William C. Simmons 11-23-1841 Hn
Willett, Mary E. (Mrs.) to Rufus N. Binkley 2-18-1869 Ma
Willett, Mary J. to Saml. R. Richards 9-15-1858 Sh
Willett, Sarah M. to Robert W. Foster 3-24-1845 Hn
Willey, Mary to William H. Tisdale 3-21-1825 (3-24-1825) Hr
Willheight, Ann to William Holley 4-20-1833 M
Willhellmis, Nancy Jane to James B. Breck? 3-20-1873 T
Willialms, Susan F. to James W. Morrow 5-4-1858 (5-13-1858) O
William, Dilly to Moses Medlin 8-14-1867 (3-10-1870) Ma
William, Emily E. to Jas. C. Cunningham 2-14-1861 (no return) Hy
William, Harriet to Wm. McMackin 2-26-1843 Cr
William, Sophia to J. M. Cartwell 11-6-1860 G
Williamls, Leon to James Dickson 6-17-1859 (6-18-1859) O
Williamls, Sarah E. to Hiram Dickenson 4-13-1863 (4-14-1863) O
Williams, A. A. to N. L. Kemp 6-18-1863 Mn
Williams, A. B. to F. A. C. McGehee 8-27-1855 Hn
Williams, A. E. to J. A. Hart 8-10-1875 L
Williams, A. P. to Elvis B. Whitehorn 8-10-1867 (8-11-1867) Cr
Williams, A.? to J. C. Merrett 4-4-1849 Cr
Williams, Abigail A. to Jackson Scruggs 4-12-1843 Sh
Williams, Abigail to James Hartsfield 3-12-1849 T
Williams, Adaline to O. R. Rust 3-6-1844 Cr
Williams, Adeline to Riley Elliott 2-27-1845 (no return) We
Williams, Aleatha J. to Minus Dickson 10-24-1849 (no return) Cr
Williams, Alevia W. to James H. Young 6-16-1857 (6-21-1857) Ma
Williams, Alice to Moak? Ealver? 12-27-1869 T
Williams, Allice to Thomas Holoman 12-18-1878 Hy
Williams, Almira to Albert M. Odel 9-17-1866 (no return) Dy
Williams, Almira to John W. Williams 1-15-1852 O
Williams, Amanda Jane to A. M. Overall 11-15-1869 (11-16-1869) T
Williams, Amanda Jane to Nathaniel Britt 8-26-1857 (8-27-1857) Ma
Williams, Amanda Katharine to Daniel Tinkle 10-11-1828 G

Williams, Amanda Paralee to William L. Douglas 11-8-1855 O
Williams, Amanda to David Green 12-21-1866 (12-22-1866) Dy
Williams, Amanda to John Bray Knox 8-8-1851 (8-17-1851) T
Williams, Amanda to Munroe Mitchell 12-27-1870 (12-28-1870) F B
Williams, Amanda to W. J. Rogers 5-11-1865 (5-12-1865) T
Williams, Amanda to William Teague 8-27-1846 Ma
Williams, Amdy to W. A. Collier 8-6-1844 Cr
Williams, America C. to Henry I. Ward 10-12-1852 (10-14-1852) G
Williams, America to Daniel Walker 1-16-1869 G B
Williams, America to Elijah Tilson? 6-23-1863 L
Williams, Anabeck to Reuben T. Crockett 3-1-1845 (3-2-1845) O
Williams, Angeline to W. J. Berry 12-21-1868 (12-23-1868) T
Williams, Ann B. to David Dunning 6-11-1847 Hn
Williams, Ann E. to Peter Hewett 2-24-1862 Sh
Williams, Ann E. to William H. Devereux 11-18-1852 (no return) F
Williams, Ann Henry to Charles A. Clements 12-21-1847 (not executed) T
Williams, Ann T. to Nimrod Ford 8-28-1830 Sh
Williams, Ann Z. to Martin Shaw 8-3-1846 Ma
Williams, Ann to Elisha Walkers 1-1-1866 (1-2-1866) O
Williams, Ann to Ezekiel P. McNeal 1-22-1835 Hr
Williams, Ann to Joseph Taylor 1-5-1841 L
Williams, Ann to Robert McAba 2-29-1852 We
Williams, Ann to Thos. Welch 4-?-1866 (4-19-1866) O
Williams, Anna E. to B. B. Bunch 10-14-1866 Hn
Williams, Anna Lee to Willis Peeler 3-13-1874 (3-4?-1874) T
Williams, Annie C. to H. S. Randle 1-19-1869 G
Williams, Annie L. to John Sangster 12-7-1885 (12-10-1885) L
Williams, Annie to George Braden 8-9-1867 (8-10-1867) F B
Williams, Annie to H. T. Spraggins 1-25-1879 (1-26-1879) Dy
Williams, Annie to Nelson Sherrell 12-11-1871 (12-14-1871) L
Williams, Arley to Reuben Winston 5-19-1883 (no return) L
Williams, Armento to Wm. Hilliard 9-27-1849 Cr
Williams, Artemissia to Thomas L. Clark 9-8-1863 (no return) L
Williams, Arvey Egenia? to William Bradley 12-15-1873 (12-17-1873) L
Williams, Azalee H. to R. J. Moore 10-25-1868 G
Williams, B. B. (Mrs.) to R. E. Bogle 5-13-1871 (5-14-1871) Dy
Williams, Babe to Frank Coonrod 2-22-1882 (2-23-1882) L
Williams, Bell to George Millard 11-12-1873 (11-13-1873) Dy
Williams, Belle to J. W. McFarlin 3-20-1879 Dy
Williams, Belle to James Pickett 12-25-1878 L B
Williams, Betsy to James Chase 2-7-1825 Sh
Williams, Betsy to William Wilson 6-6-1831 Sh
Williams, Bettie E. to Charles Williams 8-9-1880 (8-15-1880) L
Williams, Bettie to W. H. Taylor 2-22-1882 (2-23-1882) L
Williams, C. B. to W. C. Burks 11-28-1882 L
Williams, C. C. to B. C. Ford 5-29-1862 Sh
Williams, C. M. to James McFarland 1-15-1857 O
Williams, C. S. to G. L. Brandon 11-6-1872 Dy
Williams, C. to G. W. Fly 9-6-1865 G
Williams, Callie to James Smith 1-8-1874 Dy
Williams, Carolina A. to Samuel S. Sykes 4-10-1848 Ma
Williams, Caroline A. to Wm. Darnell 2-3-1848 Cr
Williams, Caroline to Robt. C. Barnhart 1-22-1872 (no return) Cr
Williams, Caroline to Westley Bomar 1-2-1867 Hn B
Williams, Caroline to Wm. R. Redditt 1-28-1862 Sh
Williams, Cassanna to Jessee A. Arwood 2-14-1878 L
Williams, Catharine to Fredrick Taflor 9-6-1859 Sh
Williams, Catharine to Hal Boyd 1-13-1859 (1-17-1859) Hr
Williams, Catharine to Joel M. Pugh 1-22-1879 (1-23-1879) Dy
Williams, Catharine to Millard Murrell 3-1-1870 (9-?-1870) F B
Williams, Catherine J. to John Mitchell 9-1-1859 (no return) L
Williams, Catherine to Edward David 2-19-1837 Sh
Williams, Caty to Benjamin Wallace 1-2-1862 Mn
Williams, Chaney to Wilson Overton 12-31-1872 Hy
Williams, Charity to Anthony Dickens 12-23-1872 T
Williams, Ciddy Ann to Elisha Jackson 11-30-1859 (12-8-1859) Ma
Williams, Clara J. to S. Perry Moore 7-2-1864 (7-3-1864) Sh
Williams, Claricy to John Henry Glassgo 8-18-1884 (no return) L
Williams, Clarissa to Henry Finch 1-29-1838 (no return) Hn
Williams, Clarkey Ann to Alex P. Rector 5-21-1870 (5-22-1870) Ma
Williams, Clary A. to Benj. Lancaster 12-19-1868 Hy
Williams, Cornelia A. to M. M. Faulkner 12-26-1867 L
Williams, Cyntha A. to James B. Crawford 6-7-1852 Hr
Williams, Cynthia Ann to Josiah Smith 8-29-1850 Hn
Williams, D. M. to Thomas Dewhitt 12-31-1866 (1-1-1867) Cr
Williams, Delila to Jacob Head 2-6-1846 Hn
Williams, Delila to John W. Metheney 4-21-1858 Hn
Williams, Della to Walter A. Wilson 5-28-1881 L
Williams, Delphi to Jesse M. Allen 3-5-1845 (3-12-1845) G
Williams, E. A. to Doctr. G. T. Steele 9-4-1851 (no return) F
Williams, E. B. to A. T. Jamison 3-13-1869 (3-14-1869) Cr
Williams, E. D. to A. C. Price 12-28-1845 We
Williams, E. K. to Solomon W. Vanhook 1-25-1871 Ma
Williams, Easter to Joihn F. Tan ? 2-26-1839 Hn
Williams, Edmonia to Haywood Drake 9-24-1874 Hy
Williams, Edney J. to James J. Brownlow 7-13-1840 (no return) F
Williams, Ela Ann to Edmond Kelley 7-5-1838 F

Williams, Elena to Masias J. Moore 9-9-1834 (9-10-1834) Hr
Williams, Eliza (Mrs.) to Dupont Nicklas 5-1-1863 Sh
Williams, Eliza (Mrs.) to Richard Hood 1-6-1858 (1-7-1858) Sh
Williams, Eliza A. to Richard S. Nance 5-10-1863 Be
Williams, Eliza Anne to Asbury Warren 7-23-1847 (8-4?-1847) Hr
Williams, Eliza F. to John W. P. Nevil 8-19-1869 G
Williams, Eliza J. to Allen Lane 6-18-1868 Be
Williams, Eliza J. to B. F. Johns 3-3-1863 G
Williams, Eliza J. to Daniel Rice 4-25-1877 (4-26-1877) L B
Williams, Eliza M. to William C. Dawson 11-27-1854 Sh
Williams, Eliza V. to John T. Martin 2-14-1870 (2-18-1870) L
Williams, Eliza to Alexander Bratton 8-18-1860 (8-19-1860) Cr
Williams, Eliza to Andrew Phillip 8-31-1837 Sh
Williams, Eliza to Barnett Cobb 12-29-1871 O
Williams, Eliza to Ben Davie 2-17-1866 Hy
Williams, Eliza to Carter Smith 5-22-1872 (5-29-1872) O
Williams, Eliza to Henry M. Ballard 7-16-1861 (8-17-1861) T
Williams, Eliza to Henry S. Peach 3-21-1863 (3-29-1863) Sh
Williams, Eliza to Jeff Coleman 12-10-1870 (no return) Hy
Williams, Eliza to Marion Thompson 7-15-1856 (7-16-1856) O
Williams, Eliza to R. D. Rhodes 2-11-1847 Cr
Williams, Eliza to William Edwards 12-16-1834 Sh
Williams, Elizabet M. to George F. Monroe 12-24-1873 (1-5-1874) T
Williams, Elizabeth Ann to Edward Thomas Harris 1-6-1849 (1-7-1849) T
Williams, Elizabeth Ann to Robert N. McClellan 11-20-1842 (12-1-1842) Ma
Williams, Elizabeth Ann to Wm. C. Pew 10-8-1838 (10-14-1838) Hr
Williams, Elizabeth F. to James E. Hays 7-14-1866 G
Williams, Elizabeth M. to Francis V. Pegram 10-11-1863 We
Williams, Elizabeth M. to James N. Gray 3-7-1857 (3-12-1857) Sh
Williams, Elizabeth M. to Thomas C. Mason 12-30-1839 Hn
Williams, Elizabeth to A. F. Routon 7-11-1847 Be
Williams, Elizabeth to Albert Garthur 10-15-1839 Hn
Williams, Elizabeth to Andrew McGowan 8-4-1866 (8-7-1866) T
Williams, Elizabeth to B. V. Mop? 12-7-1858 We
Williams, Elizabeth to Benjamin Barham 5-24-1848 (5-25-1848) O
Williams, Elizabeth to F. D. Nelms (Helms) 5-28-1841 (5-27?-1841) O
Williams, Elizabeth to Farris Hall 1-16-1874 L
Williams, Elizabeth to Gibson Whittington 8-20-1840 Ma
Williams, Elizabeth to H. T. Bradford 7-15-1845 Hn
Williams, Elizabeth to Harrison Clark 1-30-1841 (2-14-1841) Hr
Williams, Elizabeth to I. P. Robertson 1-20-1866 O
Williams, Elizabeth to J. G. Lane 5-8-1841 O
Williams, Elizabeth to James Burns 11-1-1879 (11-2-1879) Dy
Williams, Elizabeth to James Davis 3-4-1828 O
Williams, Elizabeth to John Ellington 5-17-1838 (5-18-1838) Ma
Williams, Elizabeth to John G. Dillian 12-18-1856 Be
Williams, Elizabeth to John Hicks 6-4-1867 Hy
Williams, Elizabeth to John Silvertooth 11-14-1850 L
Williams, Elizabeth to John Wesley Stewart 7-18-1867 G
Williams, Elizabeth to Levin B. Moone 12-13-1828 (12-18-1828) Hr
Williams, Elizabeth to Lewis Hollir 5-5-1859 (no return) Hy
Williams, Elizabeth to Martain Hall 10-8-1870 T
Williams, Elizabeth to Michael Emery 4-29-1855 Hn
Williams, Elizabeth to Peter Ford 1-3-1852 (1-7-1852) Ma
Williams, Elizabeth to Reuben Daughby 9-9-1839 Ma
Williams, Elizabeth to T. O. Bredon 4-17-1855 L
Williams, Elizabeth to W. H. Hill 12-27-1845 (12-28-1845) F
Williams, Elizabeth to Washington Johnson 4-17-1856 L
Williams, Elizabeth to Willis Hicks 8-15-1855 Cr
Williams, Elizabeth to Wm. Batton 7-28-1842 T
Williams, Elizabeth to Wm. L. Heath 1-1-1860 (no return) Hy
Williams, Elizabeth to Yimri? Richardson 5-26-1848 (5-22?-1848) Hr
Williams, Ellen L. to Eli Martin 4-27-1878 (no return) L
Williams, Ellen to Alexander Duke 12-4-1869 (12-5-1869) Cr
Williams, Ellen to Alonzo Short 12-10-1874 Hy
Williams, Eller to Henry Williams 8-31-1875 (9-3-1875) L B
Williams, Elmyra to C. C. Fowler 3-9-1881 L
Williams, Elvira A. to W. Henderson 2-3-1842 Sh
Williams, Elvira to Prince Townsend 12-30-1885 L
Williams, Emiline to Sandy Smith 7-5-1877 Dy
Williams, Emily F. to James M. Mathews 12-16-1865 (12-18-1865) Dy
Williams, Emily to Claude Williams 1-23-1866 (no return) F B
Williams, Emily to Isaac Tappan 1-4-1867 F B
Williams, Emily to Joseph John Byran? 4-24-1850 (4-25-1850) L
Williams, Emily to Sam Shivers 12-22-1869 Hy
Williams, Emma J. to Wm. C. Elliot 12-17-1870 (12-22-1870) F
Williams, Emma to Cecil Fleming 1-29-1870 (1-31-1870) Ma
Williams, Emmer to Alexander Williams 12-27-1870 (12-28-1870) T
Williams, Eugenia to William Rogers 1-30-1867 L
Williams, F. A. to A. J. Williams 10-12-1863 (10-13-1863) O
Williams, F. A. to R. S. Coleman 11-7-1855 Hn
Williams, F. E. to M. J. C. O'Malley 3-7-1870 (3-8-1870) Cr
Williams, F. to W. F. Morton 5-9-1849 Hn
Williams, Fannie A. to Thomas D. Thompson 1-16-1865 (1-17-1865) L
Williams, Fannie to Henry Ross 5-8-1869 (no return) F B
Williams, Fanny to Major Gilliland 9-23-1869 (no return) L B
Williams, Feriby F. to Ezekiel B. W. Hobbs 10-16-1848 (10-17-1848) Ma

Williams, Fidelia E. to Nathaniel Perry 12-31-1868 Ma
Williams, Frances A. to David C. Williams 1-12-1848 Hn
Williams, Frances A. to James R. Jenkins 11-13-1866 L
Williams, Frances A. to Richard H. McCord 1-11-1854 (1-12-1854) Hr
Williams, Frances E. P. to George H. Vasser? 1-13-1851 Sh
Williams, Frances E. to Willie A. Morgan 4-26-1850 Hn
Williams, Frances Jane to John G. Jones 2-21-1843 Sh
Williams, Frances to Garnet Parker 10-4-1854 Sh
Williams, Franky to Morris Strong 1-1-1868 (1-2-1868) Dy
Williams, Fredonia W. to Robert W. Burk 1-16-1872 (1-17-1872) L
Williams, Funtrey? to B. D. Hatch 8-?-1861 (no return) Cr
Williams, G. M. to W. F. Etheridge 1-4-1866 Hn
Williams, H. L. to H. C. Falwell 3-21-1859 Sh
Williams, Hannah E. to William H. Crofford 5-19-1845 (5-20-1845) Hr
Williams, Hannah to Hamsen Buck 12-20-1871 (no return) Hy
Williams, Hannah to Perry Rankin 5-25-1872 Hy
Williams, Harriet A. to A. J. Outlaw 12-28-1859 (no return) Hy
Williams, Harriet to James Light 12-16-1875 Dy
Williams, Harriett to C. A. Williamson 1-15-1861 G
Williams, Harriett to Nathan Watkins 11-6-1877 Hy
Williams, Henrietta Zetta to William Johnson 10-17-1881 (10-20-1881) L B
Williams, Henrietta to John E. Ohara 12-3-1861 (12-5-1861) Ma
Williams, Hetta to Jack Connell 12-2-1869 (no return) Dy
Williams, Huldy to William Smith 12-4-1830 Ma
Williams, Ioda B. to L. P. Jones 1-11-1864 (1-13-1864) Sh
Williams, Isabell M. to W. S. Blake 9-15-1840 Hn
Williams, Isabella M. to W. S. Blakemore 9-15-1840 Hn
Williams, J. E. to E. J. Pearsall 5-14-1850 (5-16-1850) F
Williams, J. L. to E. C. Eaphland 5-12-1850 (5-16-1850) O
Williams, Jane C. to William Hutcherson 2-26-1855 (3-1-1855) L
Williams, Jane H. to R. W. Williams 7-20-1856 Hn
Williams, Jane to A. M. Perkins 10-3-1866 (10-4-1866) Dy
Williams, Jane to Elisha Jackson 4-17-1872 (4-18-1872) Dy
Williams, Jane to Joseph Deberry 11-25-1876 Hy
Williams, Jane to Saml. Allen 12-28-1870 T
Williams, Jane to Thomas Vantreese 1-31-1855 (2-1-1855) Ma
Williams, Jane to W. H. Harrison 10-14-1862 Dy
Williams, Jane to W. W. W. Dickson 4-1-1852 We
Williams, Jane to William Moore 9-12-1853 (9-22-1853) O
Williams, Jane to Wm. H. White 4-9-1870 Hy
Williams, Jennie to Austin Mann 2-4-1880 (2-5-1880) L
Williams, Jennie to John A. Vican 6-6-1879 (6-15-1879) Dy
Williams, Jennie to Wm. L. Harris 5-7-1870 Ma
Williams, Jennie to belton Brown 9-17-1868 (9?-19-1868) F
Williams, Joanna to Douglass Griffin 5-23-1867 Hy
Williams, Joe to J. H. Souther 4-5-1875 (4-6-1875) L
Williams, Jose to Ed Shuffy 2-9-1877 Hy
Williams, Julia A. J. E. to James C. Smith 2-14-1856 (2-18-1856) G
Williams, Julia A. to George W. Holliday 8-6-1847 (8-15-1847) F
Williams, Julia Ann to James Beard 10-3-1867 G B
Williams, Julia Ann to William Russell 2-17-1870 Cr
Williams, Julia M. to A. L. Dupuy 10-14-1856 (11-18-1856) Sh
Williams, Kate (Mrs.) to Jesse Mark 6-25-1870 (6-26-1870) Ma
Williams, Katy to Jas. W. Trigg 2-20-1869 (3-1-1869) T
Williams, Kisiah to John W. Norman 1-12-1875 (1-13-1875) L
Williams, Kittie to John Naill 11-30-1870 (no return) Hy
Williams, Kitty to Andy McKinley 1-17-1871 F B
Williams, L. A. to E. D. B. Rives 12-27-1854 (no return) F
Williams, L. B. to Wm. P. S. Fielder 9-13-1838 G
Williams, L. E. to G. B. Edmonson 3-3-1874 O
Williams, L. I. to W. F. Miller 5-4-1867 O
Williams, Laura J. to George A. Stovall 4-7-1859 Sh
Williams, Laura L. to Colen M. Patterson 11-26-1868 Ma
Williams, Laura to Nelson Blair 2-22-1883 (no return) L
Williams, Laury Ann to William Goodwin 7-26-1831 Ma
Williams, Lena Jane to Joseph N. Hayse 8-10-1870 L
Williams, Letitia to Richard G. Scott 10-12-1836 Sh
Williams, Licetta A. to J. L. Barnett 2-14-1851 O
Williams, Lidia to D. C. Perkins 2-4-1841 Be
Williams, Liller to Lane Warren 8-4-1870 (8-7-1870) T
Williams, Lizzie to Ben Sherrod 8-31-1867 (no return) F B
Williams, Lizzie to John Highams 6-21-1860 Sh
Williams, Louisa H. to James Hope 10-24-1860 Sh
Williams, Louisa to Andrew Caplinger 12-1-1858 (no return) L
Williams, Louisa to B. C. Morgan 2-27-1853 Be
Williams, Louisa to Charles Burns 1-10-1861 Hr
Williams, Louisa to Daniel McMilan 1-16-1858 Cr
Williams, Louisa to Elisha Jackson 1-20-1846 (1-28-1846) Ma
Williams, Louisa to H. C. McCord 1-31-1851 Cr
Williams, Louisa to Henry Clayton 1-14-1869 (1-16-1869) F B
Williams, Louisa to Robt. Carson 8-3-1871 (no return) Hy
Williams, Lucinda to Epps Walker 10-30-1869 F B
Williams, Lucinda to J. E. Totty 2-9-1861 Be
Williams, Lucinda to John Hudgens 11-30-1848 Hn
Williams, Lucindy Ann to Wm. Johnson 11-11-1845 Cr
Williams, Lucindy J. to Edward Combs 1-31-1843 Cr
Williams, Lucretia E. to A. F. Smith 7-18-1869 G

Williams, Lucy A. to O. B. Strong 2-10-1864 G
Williams, Lucy Ann to Addison Kerr 4-11-1850 Sh
Williams, Lucy Ann to Wesley Brewer (Bisner) 3-22-1848 Sh
Williams, Lucy E. to William J. Pitts 9-3-1866 (9-4-1866) L
Williams, Lucy J. to A. C. Etheridge 10-15-1867 Hn
Williams, Lucy S. to Edward R. Harris 5-14-1861 Sh
Williams, Lucy to Eton Davis 9-6-1855 Hn
Williams, Lucy to John Ridout 12-26-1837 Sh
Williams, Lucy to Mack Jordan 4-24-1869 (4-29-1869) F B
Williams, Lucy to Ray Alston 2-3-1867 Hy
Williams, Lucy to Willis Cason 3-12-1883 (3-16-1883) L
Williams, Lukky to Bedford Jackson 12-27-1869 T
Williams, Luretta to E. M. Lowery 4-4-1839 Hn
Williams, Lydia to John Granberry 12-25-1866 (12-27-1866) F B
Williams, M. A. to B. G. Pate 7-15-1866 G
Williams, M. A. to J. A. Jackson 5-1-1866 (5-3-1866) O
Williams, M. A. to J. N. Snowden 8-23-1860 Sh
Williams, M. A. to S. H. Russell 9-24-1863 Mn
Williams, M. C. to D. F. Wood 2-4-1880 L
Williams, M. E. W. to B. F. Veazey 12-31-1869 G
Williams, M. E. to J. P. Sowers 8-1-1871 Dy
Williams, M. E. to J. W. Ragan 9-11-1863 G
Williams, M. J. to Z. N. Williams 2-1-1866 G
Williams, M. M. to J. T. Hopper 5-22-1871 (no return) Cr
Williams, M. M. to T. M. Howard 1-19-1878 (1-20-1878) L
Williams, M. O. to William P. Caldwell 12-11-1851 Hn
Williams, M. W. to J. D. Taylor 1-6-1862 (1-8-1862) F
Williams, M. to J. W. Payne 1-26-1863 Sh
Williams, M. to J. W. Poyner 1-26-1863 (1-28-1863) Sh
Williams, Maggie E. to Levin Lake 10-28-1864 (10-29-1864) F
Williams, Mahala to James Hill 1-14-1879 (1-16-1879) Dy
Williams, Mahulda A. to Basey D. Kemp 3-17-1869 Cr
Williams, Malinda to George A. Ore 1-5-1846 (no return) Hn
Williams, Malinda to John Guffey 12-28-1835 Sh
Williams, Malinda to John Jones 1-12-1837 Hr
Williams, Manerva Ann to Patrick Lavell 12-12-1859 (12-13-1859) T
Williams, Maranda C. to H. H. Tharpe 2-23-1863 Hn
Williams, Margaret A. to Henry F. Stigall 9-10-1865 Be
Williams, Margaret J. to R. J. Davidson 3-5-1867 (3-6-1867) L
Williams, Margaret to Alexander Cassan 10-12-1867 T
Williams, Margaret to B. F. Grant 4-29-1874 Hy
Williams, Margaret to F. C. Whitfield 2-3-1867 Hn
Williams, Margaret to James A. K. M. Everett 11-13-1860 Hr
Williams, Margaret to John Smith 10-23-1869 (10-24-1869) F
Williams, Margaret to John Vicary 1-11-1851 Sh
Williams, Margaret to March Morris 1-2-1868 (1-5-1868) F B
Williams, Margaret to T. N. Aslin 1-28-1866 G
Williams, Margarett E. to John F. Ford 10-13-1828 Hr
Williams, Maria to Henry Powell 1-22-1841 Sh
Williams, Maria to Wm. Brown 4-20-1854 Sh
Williams, Mariah to Albert Harrison 2-13-1869 G B
Williams, Mariah to Alfred Porter 6-9-1866 (10-13-1866) G
Williams, Mariah to Dempsy Horn 4-21-1871 (no return) Hy
Williams, Mariah to Hugh Montgomery 12-6-1843 (12-7-1843) Ma
Williams, Marry to Alvert Gibson 6-19-1873 Cr
Williams, Marth M. to Henry Lee 10-11-1854 (no return) F
Williams, Marth to Henry H. Haywood 11-14-1866 (11-18-1866) Cr
Williams, Martha A. to Isaac O. Sawyers 5-9-1848 (5-10-1848) F
Williams, Martha A. to John R. Westbrook 9-3-1850 Hr
Williams, Martha A. to Levi Evans 7-14-1858 G
Williams, Martha A. to Samuel H. Bennett 10-29-1868 Cr
Williams, Martha A. to Thomas A. Whicker 3-28-1863 G
Williams, Martha Ann to Isaac S. Roberts 2-4-1863 Hn
Williams, Martha Ann to Thomas C. Jordian 10-16-1839 (10-17-1839) G
Williams, Martha C. to David W. Johnson 2-14-1859 (2-15-1859) Ma
Williams, Martha E. to David M. Billings 1-13-1866 T
Williams, Martha E. to Gideon Brogden 7-5-1859 (no return) L
Williams, Martha E. to Thos. A. Carter 12-24-1855 Cr
Williams, Martha E. to Wesley C. Carter 10-28-1857 O
Williams, Martha E. to William R. Palmer 5-2-1861 (no return) We
Williams, Martha Elizabeth to Benjamin M. Williams 3-21-1843 Sh
Williams, Martha H. to John R. McGaughey 12-21-1870 (12-22-1870) L
Williams, Martha H. to S. C. Harpole 11-12-1860 G
Williams, Martha Ione to W. B. Richardson 10-1-1842 (10-6-1842) Ma
Williams, Martha J. to Thos. H. Tiller 11-7-1868 (11-9-1868) F
Williams, Martha J. to W. H. Morris 7-1-1862 G
Williams, Martha Jane to H. Harris 7-30-1851 (no return) F
Williams, Martha Jane to William H. Odam 12-16-1848 (12-20-1848) T
Williams, Martha P. to Augustus Kelly 7-20-1846 (7-23-1846) F
Williams, Martha S. to John Rideout 11-29-1852 Sh
Williams, Martha to Burrel Short 10-3-1848 Be
Williams, Martha to Henry Hall 3-25-1870 (no return) Dy
Williams, Martha to J. N. Mitchell 7-27-1861 Sh
Williams, Martha to Matthew G. Bobbitt 12-14-1846 (12-15-1846) Ma
Williams, Martha to Nickolas Mason 12-24-1868 (12-26-1868) F B
Williams, Martha to O. B. Parker 10-5-1840 (10-6-1840) F
Williams, Martha to Richard A. Brown 8-2-1854 G

Williams, Martha to Steven Tucker 1-18-1875 Hy
Williams, Martha to Thos. J. Strong 11-11-1870 (11-16-1870) F
Williams, Martha to William Vaughan 8-13-1834 Sh
Williams, Mary A. to Daniel S. Lacy 4-14-1858 (4-15-1858) Ma
Williams, Mary A. to Geo. W. Ballard 3-12-1850 Be
Williams, Mary A. to J. F. Gregory 3-20-1868 G
Williams, Mary A. to James A. Smith 2-19-1849 Cr
Williams, Mary Ann to Jackson Hill 5-30-1848 Sh
Williams, Mary Ann to Nathaniel Croft 1-5-1860 Hn
Williams, Mary Ann to Wm. A. Vantreese 12-8-1866 (12-20-1866) Ma
Williams, Mary C. to John S. Sandsberry 12-24-1855 L
Williams, Mary C. to Thomas Brown 10-3-1865 Mn
Williams, Mary C. to Thomas D. Hampton 12-23-1861 (12-25-1861) O
Williams, Mary E. to A. P. Sells 6-23-1871 Hy
Williams, Mary E. to Henry King 10-12-1864 (10-14-1864) L
Williams, Mary E. to James M. Joiner 9-17-1860 (9-18-1860) Cr
Williams, Mary E. to T. J. Webb 9-9-1873 Hy
Williams, Mary E. to William B. Wallace 3-28-1848 Ma
Williams, Mary F. to J. E. Hardican 8-17-1869 (no return) Dy
Williams, Mary F. to Nat Wesson 12-24-1867 (no return) Dy
Williams, Mary F. to Samuel O. Ballard 3-25-1841 F
Williams, Mary H. to E. M. Witt 12-20-1865 G
Williams, Mary J. to John H. Ayers ?-?-1861? Mn
Williams, Mary J. to Richard Heathscott 7-25-1856 We
Williams, Mary J. to T. M. Nance 2-11-1875 Hy
Williams, Mary Jane to Everett Wallace 7-28-1857 (7-30-1857) Ma
Williams, Mary Jane to J. N. Allen 12-28-1859 (12-29-1859) Sh
Williams, Mary Jane to Jacob Stone 5-30-1842 F
Williams, Mary Jane to Wm. C. Brown 1-31-1863 (2-4-1863) L
Williams, Mary K. to J. Marshall Woodward 2-23-1857 Sh
Williams, Mary L. to Nathan M. Peoples 2-12-1851 (no return) F
Williams, Mary M. to Thos. Liftey 10-17-1853 Cr
Williams, Mary Margaret to Jesse Byrd 6-14-1855 T
Williams, Mary O. to Robert Williams 10-4-1858 (10-6-1858) Sh
Williams, Mary P. to Green B. Cox 2-6-1845 Cr
Williams, Mary P. to S. C. Childers 8-11-1863 We
Williams, Mary S. to George W. Woods 10-28-1882 (10-29-1882) L
Williams, Mary S. to Nathan M. Peoples 11-19-1850 (license lost) F
Williams, Mary V. to James Marsden 5-23-1842 (5-24-1842) F
Williams, Mary W. to B. F. Wilson 3-10-1848 Sh
Williams, Mary W. to George C. Lemonds 10-16-1867 Hn
Williams, Mary to Albert C. Williams 8-17-1866 Hy
Williams, Mary to Amos Boyd 2-6-1861 (2-8-1861) Hr
Williams, Mary to David H. Bentley 12-16-1834 Sh
Williams, Mary to Elija G. Eaphland 10-9-1849 O
Williams, Mary to Enos Norvell 10-3-1855 (10-4-1855) G
Williams, Mary to F. Danchower 10-13-1866 O
Williams, Mary to Felix Johnson 6-26-1861 Ma
Williams, Mary to Frazier Gray 10-17-1839 Hn
Williams, Mary to G. R. Schrimsher 6-2-1858 (6-6-1858) Hr
Williams, Mary to Gabriel Wall 11-20-1869 G B
Williams, Mary to George McCollum 1-2-1866 G
Williams, Mary to Harmon Bishop 10-9-1834 Hr
Williams, Mary to Henry Guy 7-5-1870 (7-17-1870) F
Williams, Mary to Ishmael Hamilton 9-11-1838 (9-13-1838) O
Williams, Mary to J. A. Gardner 12-1-1882 (12-3-1882) L
Williams, Mary to J. A. Johnson 1-13-1873 (1-16-1873) T
Williams, Mary to James C. Bradford 12-9-1844 G
Williams, Mary to James Gerfee? 12-1-1840 Cr
Williams, Mary to James Oliver 12-9-1866 G
Williams, Mary to Jas. Trumen 12-31-1851 (1-1-1852) Sh
Williams, Mary to Jeff Porter 5-3-1870 (no return) F B
Williams, Mary to John B. Stevens 3-22-1850 T
Williams, Mary to John Taylor 1-3-1876 Hy
Williams, Mary to R. Brinnin 2-1-1865 O
Williams, Mary to Robert Tucker 12-25-1868 (12-26-1868) F B
Williams, Mary to Roland Stringer 1-23-1849 Hn
Williams, Mary to Samuel B. Scott 12-17-1845 (12-19-1845) T
Williams, Mary to V. Dozier 3-1-1854 (no return) F
Williams, Mary to W. R. Harvell 9-7-1874 (9-9-1874) T
Williams, Mary to William Little 4-7-1866 (4-15-1866) Cr
Williams, Mary to William Shaw 5-8-1871 (5-11-1871) T
Williams, Mary to Wm. Hellons 3-9-1867 O
Williams, Mary to Wm. Smith 4-1-1844 Hr
Williams, Mary? A. to _____ Trobough 4-18-1863 (4-21-1863) T
Williams, Maryann to Smith C. Belote 7-10-1848 (no return) F
Williams, Masa to Thomas C. Bass 9-10-1832 Sh
Williams, Matilda to Henry Dowland 1-16-1832 (2-4-1832) G
Williams, Matilda to Jameson Upchurch 10-9-1862 Be
Williams, Matilda to W. D. Spicer 4-7-1855 Hy
Williams, Mattie J. to J. B. Nixon 11-17-1881 L
Williams, Mattie L. to George W. Martin 5-23-1878 Hy
Williams, Mattie to J. W. Wesley 12-25-1874 (no return) Dy
Williams, Mattie to W. M. Smith 12-16-1865 G
Williams, May to Manuel Hagler 1-22-1867 Hn B
Williams, Melinda P. to Fielding G. Bray 9-11-1855 We
Williams, Melinda P. to Wesley P. Mount 6-9-1860 (6-17-1860) G

Williams, Millie to Aaron Dewitt 6-28-1884 L
Williams, Millie to Charles Rutherford 11-13-1873 T
Williams, Minerva to Ruben K. Stephens 11-2-1870 (11-3-1870) Ma
Williams, Minerva to William Ship(p) 1-5-1832 Sh
Williams, Mira E. to Griffin L. Roper 7-11-1853 (8-7-1853) G
Williams, Missouri A. B. to James J. Williams 6-22-1857 T
Williams, Missouri J. to A. F. Haynes 8-27-1868 (no return) L
Williams, Missouri to Alexander Barron 5-2-1831 Ma
Williams, Mollie M. to Saml. O. Lemons 9-18-1871 (9-21-1871) T
Williams, Mollie to Ed Moody 8-20-1877 (8-30-1877) L B
Williams, Mollie to F. L. Sutton 12-29-1868 L
Williams, Mollie to James Johnson 12-28-1878 (no return) L B
Williams, Mollie to Robert Gaines 9-6-1879 L
Williams, Molly to Benjamin Mullin 3-22-1873 Hy
Williams, Murphy M. to R. S. J. Terry 11-1-1859 (11-2-1859) Sh
Williams, N. E. to E. F. Talley 2-18-1880 L
Williams, Nancy A. to H. C. Petty 12-26-1865 (12-27-1865) Cr
Williams, Nancy A. to James M. Wheeler 10-19-1863 G
Williams, Nancy C. to Albert A. Carter 10-12-1856 Cr
Williams, Nancy C. to Epperson W. Harper 8-25-1832 (8-30-1832) G
Williams, Nancy C. to G. W. Hern 12-3-1851 (no return) Cr
Williams, Nancy C. to Harvy T. Little 1-12-1867 (1-13-1867) Cr
Williams, Nancy H. to Joseph Bond 2-21-1843 Hn
Williams, Nancy J. to Lafayette Baxter 9-1-1870 Hy
Williams, Nancy J. to Nelson Hunter 2-13-1868 (no return) F B
Williams, Nancy J. to Robert C. Harris 9-28-1857 (9-23?-1857) O
Williams, Nancy W. to James M. Harper 3-17-1858 G
Williams, Nancy to Caswell Worrel 1-2-1866 (no return) Dy
Williams, Nancy to Charles Hubbard? 11-18-1856 O
Williams, Nancy to Cornelius Owen 12-29-1869 Hy
Williams, Nancy to Everett Carey 11-11-1841 (11-12-1841) Ma
Williams, Nancy to Henry Radford 9-22-1847 Hn
Williams, Nancy to Jackson Dunning 1-11-1838 (1-18-1838) G
Williams, Nancy to John Bird 8-16-1859 Hy
Williams, Nancy to John Whitson 12-10-1867 (12-11-1867) L
Williams, Nancy to P. L. Dowdy 4-7-1842 (4-13-1842) F
Williams, Nancy to Peter M. Connel 3-19-1845 (3-25-1845) G
Williams, Nancy to Richard Moses 4-4-1873 Hy
Williams, Nancy to Robert Read 10-4-1855 We
Williams, Nancy to Tom McAdams 2-19-1867 (2-10-1867) T
Williams, Nancy to Vincent L. Pendergrast 11-13-1866 (11-14-1866) Ma
Williams, Nancy to William B. Pryor 6-19-1860 Hy
Williams, Nancy to William Richars 8-15-1842 Ma
Williams, Nancy to William T. King 4-10-1861 Dy
Williams, Nancy to Wm. Johnston 6-9-1866 (6-12-1866) T
Williams, Nancy to Zepheniah Collins 4-9-1850 Be
Williams, Nannie E. to Frank B. Winfree 2-28-1871 Ma
Williams, Nannie J. to Ed A. Garland 10-19-1859 Sh
Williams, Narcissa to George B. Peters 5-9-1839 Hr
Williams, Narcissa to W. T. Penington 3-24-1871 Hy
Williams, Oney to Erastus J. Kyle 7-17-1839 Cr
Williams, P. L. to R. B. Reynolds 5-14-1870 (5-15-1870) Cr
Williams, Panthaer W. to Thomas J. Blair 2-12-1855 (2-13-1855) G
Williams, Parmelia to James F. Randolph 10-8-1859 Ma
Williams, Parthena to Martinn Jones 9-22-1866 O
Williams, Parthina to Jesse Hicks 1-9-1867 (1-10-1867) Dy
Williams, Patsy Elizabeth to John P. Callahan 5-28-1849 (6-7-1849) L
Williams, Penina to John W. Luster 8-3-1853 O
Williams, Peninah to Allen Bryant 4-15-1850 (4-18-1850) Ma
Williams, Pennelope to James Jackson 7-12-1860 We
Williams, Pernetta E. to Josiah S. Robertson 9-28-1867 (9-29-1867) Ma
Williams, Pheriba to J. Q. Shaw 7-13-1841 (7-14-1841) F
Williams, Phillis to Ned Oldham 12-26-1866 (12-28-1866) F B
Williams, Polly to Albert Ross 11-4-1869 (no return) F B
Williams, Polly to D. C. Flemming 10-13-1844 Be
Williams, Polly to William Thedford 10-13-1837 (10-15-1837) G
Williams, R. Caroline to David Hoad 7-2-1859 (7-3-1859) Ma
Williams, R. M. F. to Samuel N. Gammons 2-17-1858 (no return) Hn
Williams, R. to T. Caswell 1-20-1842 Be
Williams, Rachel to Luke Thomas 12-16-1870 (12-28-1870) Cr B
Williams, Rebecca C. to Benjamin M. Robinson 9-8-1856 O
Williams, Rebecca J. to Lewis C. Jamison 1-29-1867 G
Williams, Rebecca J. to William N. Belotte 10-31-1854 (11-2-1854) Hr
Williams, Rebecca L. to Thomas Wakefield 7-14-1849 (7-19-1849) L
Williams, Rebecca O. to Samel M. Kerr 12-21-1850 (12-25-1850) F
Williams, Rebecca to A. M. Wright 1-2-1866 D
Williams, Rebecca to Ephram Bradford 3-27-1834 (7-4-1834) O
Williams, Rebecca to John Henry Mitchell 9-22-1871 (9-24-1871) L
Williams, Rebecca to Josiah Aldridge 1-12-1843 Hn
Williams, Rhodie to Charles Cole 1-7-1877 Hy
Williams, Rhody to Daniel Sawyer 5-12-1866 (5-16-1866) Dy
Williams, Rispha to William Martindale 5-19-1830 (5-21-1830) Hr
Williams, Roanna to J. G. Smithwick 5-24-1850 (5-26-1850) F
Williams, Rodey A. to R. Lashley 3-12-1867 Hy
Williams, Rosa Ann to William J. McKenna 10-11-1848 (10-12-1848) Ma
Williams, Rosa to George Mitchell 8-9-1871 (8-10-1871) T
Williams, Rowena Eliza to Barham Perry 8-27-1869 (9-1-1869) Ma

Williams, Rowena to Wm. R. Ellington 9-21-1869 (9-29-1869) Ma
Williams, Roxanna F. to R. G. Moore 2-9-1864 (3-10-1864) Cr
Williams, Roxanna F. to R. G. Moore 2-9-1864 (no return) Cr
Williams, S. A. to James P. Ethridge 4-26-1873 (4-27-1873) Dy
Williams, S. E. to S. G. Templeton 8-21-1865 (8-22-1865) Dy
Williams, S. F. to Robert W. Wood 3-1-1871 L
Williams, S. Frances to H. S. Milum 10-28-1861 Sh
Williams, S. J. to H. T. Kersey 11-4-1860 O
Williams, S. J. to S. R. Borden 8-21-1861 Hn
Williams, S. M. to E. J. Webb 8-13-1879 (8-14-1879) L
Williams, Sallie M. to Henry H. Swink 5-23-1871 Ma
Williams, Sallie to Frank McCraw 1-17-1874 (1-18-1874) T
Williams, Sallie to H. C. Pearce 11-15-1870 G
Williams, Sallie to Rye Hayns 1-2-1871 Cr B
Williams, Sally A. to J. S. Sansberry 4-7-1874 L
Williams, Sally Ann to William Hardy 2-1-1847 (2-4-1847) Hr
Williams, Sally to Frank Goodloe 2-9-1870 G
Williams, Samantha to John Inglish 4-19-1863 Mn
Williams, Sanna? to Joe Williams 9-21-1867 (9-22-1867) F B
Williams, Saphronia to H. Fodge 2-4-1865 (no return) Hn
Williams, Sarah A. to Daniel E. Warren 4-6-1853 Hr
Williams, Sarah A. to James H. Lee 3-2-1846 (no return) Hn
Williams, Sarah A. to N. W. Wrenn 11-23-1859 (11-24-1859) G
Williams, Sarah A. to Thomas H. Turner 12-23-1863 G
Williams, Sarah A. to W. R. Langley 3-7-1866 G
Williams, Sarah Ann Elizabeth to Felix Josiah Hall 12-13-1856 (12-14-1856) Ma
Williams, Sarah Ann to Peter Bradford 1-22-1867 Hn
Williams, Sarah C. to Andrew O. Garrett 12-14-1859 We
Williams, Sarah C. to L. G. Giles 11-12-1872 Cr
Williams, Sarah E. to John R. Prichard 12-24-1864 (12-25-1864) Dy
Williams, Sarah E. to William James 3-13-1843 Hr
Williams, Sarah F. to Chas. A. Baucom 8-21-1870 Hy
Williams, Sarah J. to James Byrum 2-9-1858 (2-10-1858) L
Williams, Sarah Jane to A. G. Lambeth 3-11-1850 (3-21-1850) Hr
Williams, Sarah Jane to A. Manning 2-14-1852 (no return) F
Williams, Sarah Jane to James Sneed 2-28-1866 Hn
Williams, Sarah L. to James A. Smith 12-17-1868 (no return) L
Williams, Sarah L. to John Sanford 5-19-1867 G
Williams, Sarah O. to John C. Williams 11-5-1868 T
Williams, Sarah O. to S. W. Overton 2-25-1855 We
Williams, Sarah W. to John T. Wilson 10-6-1852 Sh
Williams, Sarah to Brinkley Carnell 8-1-1859 Cr
Williams, Sarah to Ephaim McInturf 2-12-1874 Hy
Williams, Sarah to Ezekiel Wakefield 8-13-1846 L
Williams, Sarah to Henderson Conlee 12-30-1835 Hr
Williams, Sarah to James Snow 1-18-1861 (1-20-1861) O
Williams, Sarah to James Thedford 3-12-1862 G
Williams, Sarah to John Millikin 2-20-1854 (no return) L
Williams, Sarah to Joseph Gunham 11-7-1857 (11-8-1857) O
Williams, Sarah to Joseph Turnham 11-7-1857 (11-8-1857) O
Williams, Sarah to N. A. Crocker 5-11-1868 G
Williams, Sarah to N. K. Shiron 10-10-1863 (10-11-1863) O
Williams, Sarah to Silas Harroldson 9-28-1829 Sh
Williams, Sarah to T. R. Crampley 8-24-1874 (8-25-1874) Dy
Williams, Sarah to William Thompson 11-26-1843 Be
Williams, Sarah to Wyatt Petty 9-15-1838 Hn
Williams, Sarahann M. to J. F. Rogers 6-16-1871 (6-18-1871) Cr
Williams, Scelia A. to John A. Sheton 4-22-1865 (no return) Dy
Williams, Seney to James J. Lane 10-1-1840 O
Williams, Silphia to Fleming Haile(Hails?) 5-25-1829 (5-1?-1829?) Hr
Williams, Sinith Ann to Henry McKinney 6-5-1873 Hy
Williams, Sopha to Spencer Pigue 7-5-1868 G B
Williams, Sophronia to B. B. Rankin 12-31-1860 Ma
Williams, Sophy to Lewis Taylor 10-13-1867 Hy
Williams, Stacey Ann to J. W. McBroom 7-23-1883 L
Williams, Susan (Mrs.) to Thomas J. Cobel 9-7-1867 (9-10-1867) Ma
Williams, Susan A. to H. A. Simmons 4-11-1860 Hn
Williams, Susan A. to N. Barker 6-5-1853 Be
Williams, Susan An to John Pouge? 12-22-1849 (12-23-1849) F
Williams, Susan C. to Wilie J. Tomlinson 6-1-1858 Hn
Williams, Susan E. to Henry C. Clack 1-1-1867 O
Williams, Susan E. to John Lee 6-1-1867 (6-3-1867) Dy
Williams, Susan E. to R. M. Vaughan 1-7-1856 Sh
Williams, Susan F. to James D. Jackson 1-19-1860 G
Williams, Susan J. to A. H. Webb 9-18-1850 L
Williams, Susan M. to John W. C. Hendron 2-1-1841 (2-3-1841) Ma
Williams, Susan M. to Z. M. Tate 10-31-1839 Sh
Williams, Susan to Abraham Eaton 1-18-1847 (no return) F
Williams, Susan to Bernard Riley 8-13-1846 L
Williams, Susan to Brandon Palmer 1-2-1867 (no return) Hy
Williams, Susan to Isaac Hudson 12-30-1868 (12-31-1868) F B
Williams, Susan to Thomas Sale 12-19-1870 (12-25-1870) T
Williams, Susan to Wm. Dodson 11-23-1854 cr
Williams, Susan to _____ Theure (Theurer) 7-21-1846 Sh
Williams, Susana R. to James Claybrook 6-7-1865 G
Williams, Susanah C. to John D. Scott 7-1-1828 (7-3-1828) G
Williams, Susanah E. to James M. Godby 9-14-1852 (no return) F

Williams, Susie E. to J. D. Montgomery 11-15-1869 (11-18-1869) F
Williams, Sylvia to Maxy H. Walker 12-23-1875 Hy
Williams, Syntha Ann to George Walker 7-10-1865 G
Williams, Tabisha to Moses Ballenger 2-10-1845 Be
Williams, Tabitha A. to A. C. Edwards 11-8-1871 Cr
Williams, Tempa to Jesse Green 3-1-1839 Cr
Williams, Tempe to Smedley Lynch 3-21-1855 Sh
Williams, Temperance H. to Calvin M. Hervey 12-14-1841 Hr
Williams, Tempy R. to James M. Duke 1-28-1854 (no return) F
Williams, Tennessee Ann to Brown Belote 8-28-1846 (no return) F
Williams, Tennessee Ann to Henry W. Yarbrough 2-14-1846 (no return) F
Williams, Tennessee to Henry Whitmore 12-11-1884 L
Williams, Tennessee to R. W. Jones 1-22-1866 (1-25-1866) Cr
Williams, Tissy to Wm. Churchwell 8-29-1844 Cr
Williams, V. C. to H. J. Williams 6-7-1879 (6-8-1879) L
Williams, V. V. to J. H. Hudson 9-9-1856 L
Williams, Venia to Albert Robertson 10-5-1878 (10-6-1878) L
Williams, Victoria A. to John D. McKnight 3-9-1867 (3-14-1867) T
Williams, Virginia to D. B. Gully 1-6-1858 Be
Williams, Virginia to Wm. Dickinson 12-27-1865 (12-28-1865) F B
Williams, Wincy Jane to Everett Williams 10-13-1866 G
Williams, Zarina to Beverly R. McKinnie 3-24-1839 (3-28-1839) Hr
Williams, Zebu H. to David G. Willis 10-5-1846 Hn
Williams, Zilphia to George Grif (Griss?) 12-29-1840 L
Williams, Zylphia J. to A. M. Williams 6-24-1873 Dy
Williamson, Adaline to Jesse Wood 10-19-1867 (10-20-1867) F B
Williamson, Addie to B. Ezell 9-21-1870 (9-22-1870) Cr
Williamson, Ader to Ben Roberson 11-25-1869 Hy
Williamson, Alice to Geo. W. Troutman 9-20-1860 Hn
Williamson, Amanda to S. H. M. W. Edney 12-24-1853 Sh
Williamson, Amanda to S. W. Edney 1-7-1854 Sh
Williamson, Anna M. to C. W. Cherry 7-17-1849 (7-18-1849) F
Williamson, Annette to John Hall 6-23-1866 F B
Williamson, Annie C. to R. S. Parham 2-23-1853 (no return) F
Williamson, Burda to Henry Tilson 4-1-1871 (4-2-1871) F B
Williamson, Callie to Geo. E. Campbell 10-18-1871 Ma
Williamson, Caroline E. to Clement P. Fitz 9-3-1849 (10-3-1849) Ma
Williamson, Caroline to Fielding C. Gardner 5-21-1839 (5-25-1839) F
Williamson, Caroline to S. M. Richards 2-24-1873 (no return) Dy
Williamson, Carrie C. to E. A. Benson 2-17-1862 (2-19-1862) Sh
Williamson, Catharine to James Q. Neill 1-3-1855 Sh
Williamson, Cinthey to John Mills 10-14-1847 Cr
Williamson, Clementine C. to Wm. McMillin 2-2-1869 Ma
Williamson, Cordelia to Thos. W. Jones 5-29-1866 F
Williamson, Cornelia to Henry Cocke 1-23-1869 F B
Williamson, E. G. to G. B. Wilson 10-17-1867 O
Williamson, E. M. to W. R. Birmingham 6-6-1866 (6-7-1866) O
Williamson, E. T. to W. Willis 12-11-1860 Sh
Williamson, Easter to Lamb Wilkerson 3-12-1870 T
Williamson, Eliza to William D. Wilson 9-3-1842 (9-4-1842) Ma
Williamson, Eliza to Willis Williamson 5-25-1867 F B
Williamson, Elizabeth J. to B. F. Simes 5-31-1855 We
Williamson, Elizabeth J. to G. W. Williamson 9-7-1864 (no return) Cr
Williamson, Elizabeth to Jesse J. Curlin 11-3-1852 (11-7-1852) O
Williamson, Elizabeth to Joseph Y. Diskill 9-28-1837 G
Williamson, Elizabeth to Saml. Rhodes 10-27-1866 (12-1-1866) T
Williamson, Elly to John Hamilton 3-11-1842 Cr
Williamson, Fannie to Henry Smith 1-12-1871 Hy
Williamson, Fannie to Hilliard Revis 1-11-1868 (1-12-1868) F B
Williamson, Fannie to John A. Metcalf 3-3-1858 (3-7-1858) Ma
Williamson, Fathy to Robert Macklin 1-29-1866 T
Williamson, Frances to Chas. Turner 4-17-1866 T
Williamson, Frances to buck Williamson 1-13-1866 (1-14-1866) F B
Williamson, H. J. to John T. Ragland 2-14-1861 Cr
Williamson, H. L. to D. J. Meriwether 4-2-1860 (4-4-1860) F
Williamson, Hannah to Elisha Altom 4-16-1849 (4-6?-1849) Ma
Williamson, Harriet to Tap Barbour 9-27-1870 G
Williamson, Jane to Bob Rhodes 1-15-1868 (1-16-1868) F B
Williamson, Jane to James Duke 2-28-1870 G
Williamson, Juda to Henry Wood 1-20-1874 T
Williamson, Julia A. to R. D. Lindsey 10-29-1861 (no return) We
Williamson, Julia to George Henderson 12-27-1869 F B
Williamson, Julia to Wiley Rivers 1-24-1871 (2-2-1871) F B
Williamson, L. J. to F. C. Moore 2-11-1879 (2-12-1879) Dy
Williamson, Laura to Tom Prince 8-3-1867 (no return) F B
Williamson, Lenora J. to Franklin B. Gallin 2-16-1853 (no return) Cr
Williamson, Lenora to W. H. Ragland 4-27-1870 (4-28-1870) Cr
Williamson, Louisa M. G. to Elijah Brooks 1-13-1836 Sh
Williamson, Louisa P. to Monroe E. Terry 11-18-1868 G
Williamson, Louisa to Isaac Allen 1-16-1871 (1-19-1871) F B
Williamson, Louisa to Joe Matthews 9-5-1868 (9-6-1868) F B
Williamson, Lucinda to E. M. Tomiss 10-12-1850 We
Williamson, Lucinda to Jesse Edwards 7-1-1840 Sh
Williamson, Lucy B. to F. B. Veach 12-30-1858 We
Williamson, Lucy L. to John B. Fields 1-3-1868 (1-9-1868) F
Williamson, Lydia A. to Jim Shaw 2-8-1870 (2-10-1870) F B
Williamson, M. A. to J. Q. Murrell 8-30-1859 (8-31-1859) F

Williamson, M. D. to J. W. Carter 1-14-1867 (no return) Cr
Williamson, M. J. to R. E. Guthrie 9-9-1851 Cr
Williamson, Mag to Lewis Jones 4-24-1867 (no return) F B
Williamson, Mahaly to Billam? Field 12-4-1830 Hr
Williamson, Malinda F. to Robert F. Haun 5-24-1870 G
Williamson, Margaret E. to C. L. Roach 12-18-1863 Hn
Williamson, Margaret J. to J. M. Johnson 1-10-1849 (1-11-1849) F
Williamson, Mariah to John Mickum 9-18-1847 Ma
Williamson, Martha G. to Robert N. (W.) Allen 9-14-1837 Sh
Williamson, Martha J. to James S. Moffett 5-14-1860 O
Williamson, Martha W. to J. F. Allen 10-29-1862 G
Williamson, Martha to Jacob Pegees 4-18-1867 F B
Williamson, Martha to James L. Penn 6-4-1851 F
Williamson, Martha to Miles Warr 5-5-1871 (5-6-1871) F B
Williamson, Mary A. to P. G. Johnson 10-5-1862 G
Williamson, Mary Ann to William Griffin 2-12-1844 Sh
Williamson, Mary C. to Robert C. Gilkey 1-27-1852 Cr
Williamson, Mary E. to Flournoy T. Simmons? 12-12-1866 (12-13-1866) Dy
Williamson, Mary E. to Jno. W. Sykes 1-10-1871 (1-11-1871) Ma
Williamson, Mary E. to William J. Robinson 4-30-1850 (5-1-1850) Ma
Williamson, Mary I. to Floridore A. Keelen 4-8-1871 Ma
Williamson, Mary J. (Mrs.) to George Wood 6-8-1853 (no return) F
Williamson, Mary J. to Thos. J. Frazier 5-28-1867 Dy
Williamson, Matilda to Cater Williamson 3-19-1866 F B
Williamson, Mattie to William C. Hutson 1-9-1877 (1-10-1877) Dy
Williamson, May E. to Mac McCay Mitchell 10-26-1867 (10-29-1867) F B
Williamson, Melissa A. to Robert J. Ruffin 4-24-1856 Ma
Williamson, Minerva to Fil Chester 5-11-1868 (no return) F B
Williamson, Mollie to B. A. Bessent 12-7-1877 (12-8-1877) Dy
Williamson, Nancy (sen.) to Robert C. Neely 9-14-1858 Ma
Williamson, Nancy P. to A. J. Anderson 7-4-1853 (no return) F
Williamson, Nancy to Wesley Dickinson 3-16-1867 F B
Williamson, Patsey to Alexander Taylor 2-27-1817 T
Williamson, Pattie to Edward Childress 9-4-1879 (9-7-1879) Dy
Williamson, Penny to Peter Thompson 2-13-1867 (2-15-1867) T
Williamson, Priscilla A. to W. E. Stainback 4-25-1865 (4-26-1865) F
Williamson, Priscilla B. to R. S. Parham 11-25-1854 (no return) F
Williamson, Prudence (Mrs.) to John A. Mills 12-12-1876 (12-14-1876) Dy
Williamson, Rebecca C. to Henry Rosser 8-15-1870 Ma
Williamson, Roberta F. to James M. Howard 2-4-1845 Sh
Williamson, S. A. to B. A. Jones 1-7-1867 (no return) Cr
Williamson, S. P. to J. E. Wilson 9-14-1874 (9-17-1874) T
Williamson, Sallie T. to J. L. Granberry 10-9-1865 (10-12-1865) F
Williamson, Sallie to D. P. Steele 2-1-1875 Hy
Williamson, Sarah A. to John W. Tiner 11-24-1859 Ma
Williamson, Sarah F. to David Reid 10-3-1849 (10-10-1849) Ma
Williamson, Sarah to Simon Rhodes 1-15-1868 (1-16-1868) F B
Williamson, Susan G. to Thomas F. Lee 7-10-1855 (7-11-1855) Sh
Williamson, Susan to Lott Pagie 3-29-1871 F B
Williamson, Susan to Wesley Laws 9-23-1856 Cr
Williamson, Tempe J. to W. R. Simpson 12-16-1874 Dy
Williamson, Tempy to Fayette Jones 12-25-1866 (12-29-1866) F B
Williamson, Vic to Monroe Thompson 12-25-1867 F B
Williamson, Willie Ann to Peter Price 2-4-1871 (no return) F B
Williamson, Winnie to Charles N. Johnson 9-24-1867 (9-26-1867) Ma
Willie, Anna J. to James P. Lamb 12-12-1859 Hn
Willie, Elizabeth to James J. Barnett 3-22-1834 (3-27-1834) Hr
Willie, Sallie to C. E. Perrago 7-31-1870 Hy
Williford, E. M. to Fielden Stephens 8-30-1840 Hn
Williford, Elizabeth to George McCarter (McCarty) 9-1-1837 Sh
Williford, M. J. to T. J. Wood 9-13-1865 G
Willin, Sarah (Miss) to John W. Armstrong 1-7-1858 Sh
Willingham, Anna to Hiram Farmer 1-9-1844 We
Willingham, Eliza A. to James A. Overton 7-4-1843 We
Willingham, Ellen J. to David W. Manning 12-19-1860 We
Willingham, Lucy to Bill Williamson 3-2-1871 Hy
Willingham, Nancy T. to Francis C. Folkner 11-10-1855 (no return) F
Willingham, Nancy to Isaac Hall 9-21-1864 Sh
Willingham, Nancy to W. T. Wiggens 9-14-1861 Sh
Willis, Ann G. to William C. Anderson 8-7-1847 Hn
Willis, Ann J. to James P. English 10-?-1863 O
Willis, Anna to Wm. Gilliland 8-8-1845 Be
Willis, Annie to A. B. Coffee 2-11-1859 (2-12-1859) Sh
Willis, Carey to R. A. Willson 12-13-1864 (no return) Hn
Willis, Carrie to Adriance Stern (Storm?) 11-2-1859 (11-3-1859) Sh
Willis, Clory Ann to James G. Maloney 8-12-1852 Sh
Willis, Elizabeth C. to Frank A. W. Burton 10-31-1844 Ma
Willis, Elizabeth H. to Francis M. Shaw 7-31-1856 G
Willis, Evelina to Samuel B. Crawford 12-11-1845 Hn
Willis, Frances to Charles Miller 11-17-1866 G
Willis, Jane to Granderson Woods 3-8-1842 Hn
Willis, Jane to James B. Wood 5-13-1828 Ma
Willis, Kate B. to E.B. Bumpass 5-8-1859 Hy
Willis, Lucinda M. to Richard N. Lusk 12-2-1872 (12-3-1872) L
Willis, M. C. to W. C. Walker 12-18-1866 G
Willis, Margaret to Nathan Stamps 7-17-1867 (8-10-1867) Dy
Willis, Marian to Dvid Howell? 8-17-1861 (no return) Dy
Willis, Martha to Battle Robertson 9-29-1830 Ma
Willis, Mary A. to Thomas W. Bell 12-5-1848 (not executed?) Sh
Willis, Mary Ann to A. Wilson 12-28-1865 Hn
Willis, Mary Ann to Ward Walker 7-2-1868 G
Willis, Mary J. to James Dill 3-27-1874 (11-29-1874) T
Willis, Mary V. to Wm. A. Steele 9-2-1866 Be
Willis, Missouri E. to John Oldham 9-27-1856 (9-28-1856) Sh
Willis, Mitty to Daniel Glisson 1-3-1867 Hn
Willis, Nancy A. to J. W. T. Hilliard 9-16-1854 (no return) F
Willis, Nancy to Joseph Branch 1-7-1864 (no return) Cr
Willis, Nancy to William Hoard 10-15-1827 Ma
Willis, Patsey to Ed Straton 12-23-1868 (12-24-1869?) G B
Willis, Rebeca to Boyed Williams 2-13-1839 (2-14-1839) F
Willis, S. to Ransom Thompson 8-19-1854 G
Willis, Sarah F to Jas. P. Smith 3-12-1868 (no return) F B
Willis, Susan J. to Henry Buell 3-16-1860 Sh
Willis, Susan J. to James Bell 9-26-1850 G
Willis, Susan to Austin Calhoun 11-30-1867 Hn B
Willis, Susan to Gabriel Jackson 11-20-1841 (11-23-1841) F
Willis, U. D. to H. C. Walker 5-25-1864 G
Willis, Virginia A. to E. B. Lewis 5-27-1861 Sh
Willitt, Lucy to C. L. Powers 10-1-1861 Sh
Willouby, Evelina to Elihue G. Graham 8-24-1850 (8-25-1850) Hr
Willoughby, C. A. M. to D. T. Smith 10-4-1857 Hr
Willoughby, Elizabeth J. to Silas M. W. Marsh 11-8-1842 Hr
Willoughby, Elizabeth L. to Joshua J. Yarbrough 3-9-1859 (3-10-1859) Hr
Willoughby, Jackey Ann to M. G. Scott 9-10-1857 Hr
Willoughby, Mamena? to Andrew H. Burkhead 11-28-1844 Hr
Willoughby, Margaret to Thomas Harris 12-3-1835 Hr
Willoughby, Martha to Thomas Walker 3-1-1841 Hr
Willoughby, Nancy to Thomas O. Burkett(Burkhead) 2-7-1839 (2-8-1839) Hr
Willoughby, Polly to George Winston 2-25-1858 We
Willoughby, Sarah to Jesse F. S. Adams 12-22-1859 (12-25-1859) Sh
Wills, Addie to John Lattimer 11-8-1876 Hy
Wills, Ann E. to E. L. Wills 1-12-1848 Be
Wills, Annie M. to E. B. Greaves 4-11-1861 Hy
Wills, Artelia J. to Thomas J. Graves 1-28-1840 (1-30-1840) F
Wills, Caroline to Andrew Link 12-26-1866 Hy
Wills, Frances to Briggs Gantling 1-12-1839 (1-15-1839) F
Wills, Jane to C. Morgan 8-27-1844 We
Wills, Lizzie to Tom Ewing 12-23-1866 (12-29-1865?) F B
Wills, Mahaly to Nicles Taylor 2-4-1868 Hy
Wills, Mary C. to Albert M. Carlton 1-4-1871 Hy
Wills, Mary E. to L. Thompson 11-25-1852 Hn
Wills, Millie to Clayborn Clemens 10-29-1871 Hy
Wills, Nancy A. to _____ Garvins 3-24-1850 Sh
Wills, Polly to Jim Shaw 3-28-1872 Hy
Wills, Sallie to Peter Read 12-17-1865 Hy
Willsen, Amanda M. to Charles A. Parratt 12-12-1858 We
Willson, Amanda A. to William E. Henry 4-18-1848 Hn
Willson, Betsey to George Tyler 1-2-1869 F B
Willson, Frances E. to Samuel G. Orr 11-17-1845 Hn
Willson, Jane to James Henderson 4-21-1870 (4-23-1870) T
Willson, Louisa to James S. Mathew 11-18-1862 We
Willson, Louiza J. to Robert P. Woods 12-31-1861 (1-5-1862) Cr
Willson, Lucinda A. to Jake Thompson 10-11-1867 (no return) L B
Willson, M. E. to S. S. Crass 6-11-1865 Hn
Willson, Marg. to George Merrell 12-18-1863 We
Willson, Martha J. to Dickson M. Johnston 10-3-1847 Hn
Willson, Mary A. R. to Benjamin Clark 8-21-1851 Hn
Willson, Mary A. to Aaron G. Allmon 2-10-1862 We
Willson, Mary F. to James Warren 3-15-1859 (no return) We
Willson, Mary Jane to Jess G. Noel 5-19-1850 Hn
Willson, Mary S. to James M. Westbrook 8-30-1860 We
Willson, Mary to James King 10-23-1862 (no return) We
Willson, Sarah A. to James H. Melton 3-16-1853 (no return) F
Willson, Sarah C. to William H. Woodrough 12-15-1860 (no return) We
Willson, Sarah M. to Benjamin F. Ashlock 3-11-1851 Hn
Willson, Sarah to John Holoman 3-29-1865 Be
Willson, Sarah to Nicholas L. Lankford 11-29-1831 G
Willson, Susan E. to Lewis G. Parriatt 10-5-1861 (no return) We
Wilman, Anna to Maurice Block 5-17-1848 G
Wilmoth, Margaret A. to W. J. Simmons 12-23-1855 We
Wilon, Margaret E. to William J. Simmons 9-24-1861 (9-25-1861) O
Wiloughby, Amanda to Hamilton Savage 9-3-1849 (9-6-1849) Hr
Wilson, A. E. to A. G. Butler 12-5-1857 Cr
Wilson, A. L. to J. L. Matheny 4-12-1863 Be
Wilson, A. to _____ 1-4-1855 Hn
Wilson, Adaline to Jacob Flowers 1-10-1867 G
Wilson, Adelaide to Rufus Smith 9-23-1857 Sh
Wilson, Agnes to Caroline Covington 9-16-1869 (9-18-1869) Cr
Wilson, Agnes to Thomas Jones 4-27-1866 Hy
Wilson, Allis to G. F. Thomerson 2-12-1866 O
Wilson, Amanda T. to James R. Burrow 2-?-1845 Ma
Wilson, Amanda to G. W. Rapp 5-9-1859 Sh
Wilson, Amanda to Governor Weaver 10-14-1874 T
Wilson, Amanda to Wm. A. Null 3-20-1845 Cr

Wilson, Amelia C. to Samuel Ray 12-19-1860 (12-10?-1861?) Hr
Wilson, America J. to James H. Burnett 6-19-1865 (6-27-1865) O
Wilson, Ann to John G. Adams 1-9-1830 Sh
Wilson, Ann to William Gray 8-22-1853 (8-23-1853) G
Wilson, Anna to Thomas Hunt 6-15-1866 Be
Wilson, Annie to J. C. Callis 10-2-1863 Sh
Wilson, Annie to John Oglesby 11-4-1867 (11-5-1867) T
Wilson, Annis to John W. Lawrence 12-14-1841 (12-21-1841) F
Wilson, Ardenia to Amos Reaves 12-26-1873 (12-27-1873) L
Wilson, Banna E. to Bryant Word 2-3-1843 (2-5-1843) G
Wilson, Belle to Samuel Towns 1-27-1875 Hy
Wilson, Belvadora to Thomas Kelsall 5-24-1859 (5-25-1859) Sh
Wilson, Caroline to D. A. Buchannon 12-7-1864 (12-8-1864) Cr
Wilson, Caroline to D. A. Buckannan 12-7-1864 Cr
Wilson, Caroline to Eli Ayres 10-13-1829 (10-15-1829) Hr
Wilson, Caroline to Henry Estes (not executed) Hy
Wilson, Caroline to N. M. Bittick 11-4-1865 (11-5-1865) O
Wilson, Caroline to Ralph Owen 12-22-1865 Sh
Wilson, Catherine J. to Charles T. Reed 7-31-1842 Hn
Wilson, Catherine to Andrew McFarland 11-28-1829 (11-29-1829) O
Wilson, Catherine to Will Hardy 12-15-1880 (12-16-1880) L B
Wilson, Charley M. to S. T. Swearingen? 10-16-1849 (no return) Hn
Wilson, Charlotte to Nelson Huddleston 10-8-1849 (10-10-1849) Hr
Wilson, Clora R. (Mrs.) to W. J. Richardson 9-6-1864 Sh
Wilson, Columbia to Harrison Willie 1-29-1836 Sh
Wilson, Cyntha to Isaac Furguson 2-1-1844 Hn
Wilson, D. Ann to Daniel Holland 11-7-1850 Be
Wilson, D. C. to J. C. N. Greer 4-20-1867 G
Wilson, D. G. to William Hurt 12-6-1855 Hn
Wilson, D. N. to Stephen Tucker 3-13-1867 (3-14-1868?) G
Wilson, Delia to Wm. A. Manning 2-26-1856 Sh
Wilson, Delila to Philip Deaton 3-2-1836 (3-6-1836) Hr
Wilson, Delphina E. to James L. Cooper 12-7-1861 Ma
Wilson, Dicy Jane to John W. Crockett 1-12-1854 G
Wilson, Dolly to Thomas Hampton 3-29-1848 (3-31-1848) G
Wilson, E. J. to H. J. Wiles 3-24-1866 F
Wilson, E. P. to G. W. Sims 1-16-1856 (1-17-1856) G
Wilson, E. S. to William Cates 8-29-1871 (8-30-1871) T
Wilson, Effey J. to Jesse M. Scott 4-16-1832 O
Wilson, Eliza M. to Lindsey J. Leach 8-19-1841 Cr
Wilson, Eliza P. to Wm. B. Billingsly 5-19-1851 G
Wilson, Elizabeth A. to W. P. Orsburn 3-12-1861 O
Wilson, Elizabeth Ann to Joel J. Green 5-1-1867 (5-2-1867) L
Wilson, Elizabeth P. to James T. Paschall 1-10-1866 G
Wilson, Elizabeth W. to Ruebin W. Oliver 2-3-1836 Hr
Wilson, Elizabeth to Anderson Edwards 4-22-1841 Ma
Wilson, Elizabeth to Eli Beard 3-5-1867 O
Wilson, Elizabeth to James R. McKee 5-10-1838 O
Wilson, Elizabeth to John Bennett 9-13-1848 Hr
Wilson, Elizabeth to John M. Carroll 9-6-1852 (9-7-1852) G
Wilson, Elizabeth to John Sullivan 1-9-1855 (1-11-1855) T
Wilson, Elizabeth to Lewis B. Rond 2-12-1846 Sh
Wilson, Elizabeth to M. Neighbor 11-28-1864 Be
Wilson, Elizabeth to Nathaniel K. Sherron 2-13-1844 G
Wilson, Elizabeth to P. B. Wilson 6-14-1852 Hn
Wilson, Elizabeth to Stephen Witherington 5-16-1861 G
Wilson, Elizabeth to W. H. Tosh 1-22-1852 Cr
Wilson, Ella to Dan Boyd 1-1-1871 Hy
Wilson, Ellen to Nicholas Morton 4-3-1851 Sh
Wilson, Elphady C. to Willis S. Barton 9-19-1856 (9-23-1856) G
Wilson, Elvira A. to John A. Johnson 1-28-1863 (no return) Dy
Wilson, Elvira to James B. Hays 12-22-1858 Hn
Wilson, Elvira to John H. Paul 11-29-1853 (no return) Hn
Wilson, Emaly to Larkin Bennett 11-9-1857 Hn
Wilson, Emely to John E. Dyer 7-24-1861 (7-25-1861) O
Wilson, Emily to Wm. J. Kelly 1-19-1850 Cr
Wilson, Emina to Barney Alexander 12-7-1874? T
Wilson, Emma L. to H. M. Houston 7-9-1868 T
Wilson, Emma to Joseph Burnett 12-29-1877 Hy
Wilson, Fanny to Jerry Mitchel 2-1-1867 (2-16-1867) F B
Wilson, Feraby to Edward McCormack 5-26-1867 Be
Wilson, Flora to Edmond Gayl 11-28-1869 Hy
Wilson, Florence to Lewis Taylor 3-7-1869 Hy
Wilson, Frances C. to G. W. Oliver 8-17-1865 Mn
Wilson, Frances J. to Travis C. Coleman 10-4-1854 Hn
Wilson, Frances P. to G. W. Edwards 10-15-1866 (10-16-1866) Cr
Wilson, Frances P. to R. C. Moutrie 11-16-1866 O
Wilson, Frances to David Paschall 8-23-1846 Hn
Wilson, Frances to David Wilson 2-4-1857 Cr
Wilson, Francis Elizabeth to James S. Hipp 9-10-1872 (9-11-1872) L
Wilson, H. D. to W. D. New 3-15-1863 Mn
Wilson, H. E. to J. T. Crumb 1-18-1871 (1-19-1871) Cr
Wilson, Hannah W. to Christopher T. Clark 9-2-1851 Hr
Wilson, Harriet to David Thompson 5-4-1866 (5-6-1866) F
Wilson, Harriett B. to Luther Penney 11-10-1839 Sh
Wilson, Henrietta to John Rodgers 10-9-1884 (10-11-1884) L
Wilson, Ibby to John Carter 4-10-1840 (4-12-1840) F
Wilson, Isabella to Jonathan Medford 4-20-1871 F
Wilson, J. A. to A. A. McKnight 2-25-1856 (2-28-1856) G
Wilson, J. F. to J. H. Acuff 2-17-1877 (2-19-1877) L
Wilson, Jane D. to C. M. Orr 11-2-1866 (no return) Hn
Wilson, Jane M. to William Costler 11-26-1843 (12-3-1843) G
Wilson, Jane to Haywood Smith 6-24-1861 (6-25-1861) Hr
Wilson, Jane to John T.(F?) Simpson 11-21-1837 Sh
Wilson, Jane to Napoleon King 7-22-1857 Sh
Wilson, Jane to Reuben Stafford 10-5-1867 Hy
Wilson, Jane to Robert Fletcher 12-5-1855 Sh
Wilson, Jennet to William Kidd 1-2-1866 (1-10-1866) T
Wilson, Jennie to John Anderson 10-10-1872 Hy
Wilson, Jerusha to George W. Paschal 10-1-1839 (no return) Hn
Wilson, Josephine to R. K. Harvey 4-11-1857 (no return) We
Wilson, Julia A. to Joseph Humphrey 8-19-1859 (no return) Cr
Wilson, Julia A. to Joseph W. Exum 9-18-1867 (9-19-1867) Ma
Wilson, Julia to Jesse Taylor 2-20-1872 Hy
Wilson, Kate to Charles May 6-13-1859 Sh
Wilson, Laura Ann to Stephen Baker 7-5-1866 (7-6-1866) F B
Wilson, Laura to Peter Cochran 6-11-1868 (6-12-1868) O B
Wilson, Lavinia J. to William Y. Newbern 3-16-1840 Hr
Wilson, Leanor E. to B. P. Orr 12-5?-1859 Hn
Wilson, Lindia to George W. Rollins 3-21-1873 (3-23-1873) L
Wilson, Livinia Jane to Robert A. Franklin 6-29-1842 Hr
Wilson, Louisa P. to William H. McGehee 8-20-1849 Hn
Wilson, Louisa W. to S. J. Herron 2-28-1869 G
Wilson, Louisa to Jefferson Russom 2-12-1863 Mn
Wilson, Lucinda to William H. Edwards 1-28-1846 Ma
Wilson, Lucresa to Robert Landran 4-28-1831 G
Wilson, Lucy A. to James W. Fowler 12-12-1855 We
Wilson, Lucy B. to M. H. Smith 3-7-1859 (3-9-1859) Hr
Wilson, Lucy to Bartley Moon 12-12-1867 G B
Wilson, Lucy to Read Pearson 8-31-1878 Hy
Wilson, Lydia to James H. Smith 6-26-1845 Sh *
Wilson, Lydia to Wm. Curley 9-27-1840 Cr
Wilson, M. Callie to Jno. F. Fanville 2-22-1869 Ma
Wilson, M. J. (Mrs.) to H. C. Beckman 12-20-1864 Sh
Wilson, M. J. to R. B. F. Carter 12-10-1868 Cr
Wilson, M. R. to M. E. Hearing 1-7-1864 Sh
Wilson, M. to R. Fields 1-28-1864 G
Wilson, Malic K. to E. M. Cearnall 6-27-1869 Be
Wilson, Malinda to Allen Hill 1-25-1840 Ma
Wilson, Malinda to Andrew Saunders 7-1-1858 Hn
Wilson, Malinda to P. T. M. Fouler 4-1-1846 We
Wilson, Malissa to Richard H. Ridgeway 3-28-1851 (4-1-1851) G
Wilson, Malvina to H. C. Gooden 12-20-1855 (no return) Hn
Wilson, Mareno to Mack Johnson 2-12-1868 (2-15-1868) F B
Wilson, Margaret (Mrs.) to S. C. Barnett 6-25-1859 (6-26-1859) Sh
Wilson, Margaret C. to Murray A. Brandon 2-2-1869 Cr
Wilson, Margaret E. to James A. Moore 5-14-1864 (5-16-1864) T
Wilson, Margaret E. to William P. Thompson 3-14-1853 (3-15-1853) G
Wilson, Margaret F. to J. M. Dodd 3-4-1864 Sh
Wilson, Margaret L. to John Steele 1-6-1845 (1-9-1845) T
Wilson, Margaret M. to Isaac Verhine 12-12-1853 (12-15-1853) O
Wilson, Margaret to E. H. Stroud 12-26-1883 (12-27-1883) L
Wilson, Margaret to R. R. Evans 2-13-1861 (2-15-1861) Sh
Wilson, Margaret to William H. Howard 2-2-1842 (2-4-1842) L
Wilson, Margaret to William Wood 12-23-1870 T
Wilson, Margarett to Ben Ballard 1-21-1867 G
Wilson, Maria J. to Jas. P. Walker 1-13-1842 (no return) L
Wilson, Mariah to Howel Evans 1-4-1876 (no return) Hy
Wilson, Mariah to Thomas Turner 6-12-1878 (6-13-1878) Dy
Wilson, Martha A. D. to James J. Baker 12-14-1847 (3-26-1848) Ma
Wilson, Martha A. to Peter R. Nance 2-24-1846 Hn
Wilson, Martha E. to R. C. Simonton 9-5-1859 T
Wilson, Martha Jane to Wm. S. Moffatt 4-16-1856 (4-17-1856) T
Wilson, Martha to Allen W. Bond 2-2-1826 Sh
Wilson, Martha to Anderson Adams 9-21-1870 (9-22-1870) T
Wilson, Martha to E. L. Hatchel 9-6-1871 (9-12-1871) T
Wilson, Martha to E. Paschall 3-13-1867 Hn
Wilson, Martha to Henry Cline 8-13-1862 Mn
Wilson, Martha to Leon Sherwood 3-17-1862 Sh
Wilson, Martha to Thomas L. Ross 2-1-1849 (2-4-1849) Hr
Wilson, Martha to W. H. Ryle 8-30-1859 Cr
Wilson, Mary A. to F. M. Cody 1-14-1860 (1-17-1860) F
Wilson, Mary A. to James M. Harrison (Hanna?) 10-29-1848 L
Wilson, Mary A. to Thomas S. Nance 10-19-1854 Hn
Wilson, Mary A. to William H. Rogers 7-25-1840 (7-30-1840) G
Wilson, Mary A. to William S. Brown 8-27-1846 (no return) F
Wilson, Mary Ann to Thomas Holland 11-23-1852 (no return) F
Wilson, Mary C. to Benjamin W. King 7-5-1861 (7-6-1861) O
Wilson, Mary C. to Henry W. Wynkoop 6-3-1862 Ma
Wilson, Mary C. to Robert M. May 3-31-1866 Ma
Wilson, Mary E. R. to Wm. J. Keen 11-9-1848 Sh
Wilson, Mary E. to A. V. Clark 12-4-1866 Hn
Wilson, Mary E. to Elmore C. Hopper 7-18-1855 (7-19-1855) G
Wilson, Mary E. to James J. Kinney 10-27-1862 (no return) Hy

Wilson, Mary F. to Marshall B. Keathly 11-25-1854 G
Wilson, Mary J. to G. W. Turk 2-13-1856 (2-14-1856) Sh
Wilson, Mary J. to Isaac Kendall ?-24-1844 (2-29-1844) F
Wilson, Mary Jane to J. C. Sims 1-31-1865 (no return) Dy
Wilson, Mary M. to R. A. Cannon 11-6-1856 Hn
Wilson, Mary M. to Robert Jones 11-20-1852 (11-25-1852) Ma
Wilson, Mary P. to John O'Conner 4-22-1845 Cr
Wilson, Mary T. to Abram M. West 7-19-1856 (7-22-1856) O
Wilson, Mary to Abram Jones 12-28-1865 Hy
Wilson, Mary to Alfred M. Bedford 10-23-1847 O
Wilson, Mary to Benjamin F. Bibb 2-21-1851 Hr
Wilson, Mary to Grandison Oldham 12-28-1871 Hy
Wilson, Mary to Isaiah Wilson 12-12-1855 Hn
Wilson, Mary to J. A. Childress 8-20-1856 Be
Wilson, Mary to James Holton 5-7-1841 (5-8-1841) T
Wilson, Mary to James Lyer? 1-18-1836 Hr
Wilson, Mary to Richmond(Richard) L. Barringer 12-26-1853 (12-27-1853) O
Wilson, Mary to Simeon Richardson 5-8-1874 T
Wilson, Mary to Solomon Waggener(Wagner) 4-14-1834 Hr
Wilson, Mary to William Porter 12-7-1856 Hr
Wilson, Matilda C. to Doctor H. Ward 10-9-1863 G
Wilson, Matilda Jane to John Smith 1-20-1844 F
Wilson, Mattie L. to John A. Johnston 7-25-1866 L
Wilson, Mattie to B. C. Nolen 10-18-1870 (no return) Hy
Wilson, Mattie to J. B. Howell 9-17-1873 Hy
Wilson, Mattie to Martin Bell 8-19-1867 (8-24-1867) F B
Wilson, May C. to Jesse B. Franklin 11-10-1845 Hr
Wilson, Melvina C. to William Pugh 9-6-1858 (9-8-1858) G
Wilson, Minerva to Serel Evans 8-31-1833 (?-19-183-) Hr
Wilson, Minnie (Mrs.) to Capt. Milo Thielemann 11-24-1862 Sh
Wilson, Miria L. to William A. Compton 1-5-1853 Ma
Wilson, Mrs. Elizabeth to Geo. W. Whitfield 9-7-1850 (9-10-1850) Hr
Wilson, Myema to Jerry Morgan 11-5-1877 Hy
Wilson, N. C. to D. W. Harston 12-29-1860 Ma
Wilson, Nancy A. to Parish G. Nevils 5-5-1850 Sh
Wilson, Nancy M. to Greenberry Dyal? 6-13-1836 Hr
Wilson, Nancy P. to J. H. Gwaltney 6-19-1858 (6-20-1858) O
Wilson, Nancy to James L. Hatcher 5-15-1852 O
Wilson, Nancy to James L. Hatcher no date (with Oct 1837) O
Wilson, Nancy to John A. Ross 2-3-1843 (2-4-1843) Hr
Wilson, Nancy to John B. Allen 1-27-1832 O
Wilson, Nancy to John P. Erwin 12-24-1866 (12-25-1866) T
Wilson, Nancy to M. Newsom 5-3-1860 Sh
Wilson, Nancy to Milton James 5-11-1861 (5-12-1861) O
Wilson, Nancy to Noah Dickson 12-16-1847 Ma
Wilson, Naomy E. to Simeon W. Cate 1-19-1858 Hn
Wilson, Narcissa E. to James Demoss 3-18-1847 Cr
Wilson, Olive S. to Silas M. Potter 4-15-1869 (no return) L
Wilson, Perlina to York Fleetwood 5-6-1871 (no return) Hy
Wilson, Phebe A. to Ninian F. Steel 8-27-1846 (no return) F
Wilson, Phoebe Ann to Patrick Binson 12-27-1861 Sh
Wilson, Pink to Major Sowell 12-24-1866 G
Wilson, R. D. to C. N. Clark 4-12-18847 O
Wilson, R. E. to R. Z. McDaniel 1-4-1869 (1-5-1869) Dy
Wilson, Rebecca Emeline to Cleyton D. Sanders 6-4-1856 (6-5-1856) O
Wilson, Rebecca J. to Burwell Alsup 8-10-1857 Be
Wilson, Rebecca to John D. Summers 5-14-1853 (no return) Hn
Wilson, Rhody to Simon H. Minton 12-25-1831 Sh
Wilson, Rosalie A. to John E. Boykin 11-6-1855 (11-7-1855) Ma
Wilson, Ruth to Essex Williams 10-20-1871 T
Wilson, S. A. to William Stults 12-1-1857 G
Wilson, S. C. to J. Collins 3-4-1866 G
Wilson, S. E. (Mrs.?) to John Graham 10-27-1863 Sh
Wilson, S. E. to A. Hobson 12-13-1881 (12-14-1881) L
Wilson, S. H. to C. W. Park 2-4-1867 O
Wilson, S. J. to J. M. Roberson 10-3-1852 Hn
Wilson, S. L. O. to L. P. Allen 1-12-1861 Cr
Wilson, Sallie (Mrs.) to David Laughlin 3-23-1863 (3-25-1863) Sh
Wilson, Sallie M. to Hukbald? D. Hunt 12-21-1848 F
Wilson, Saluda A. to J. J. A. Roach 11-15-1858 (11-24-1858) G
Wilson, Sarah A. to Emmet T. Morgan 7-27-1858 (8-10-1858) Ma
Wilson, Sarah Ann to Benjamin F. Transee 10-4-1847 Ma
Wilson, Sarah Ann to Frazor Titus 8-21-1843 Sh
Wilson, Sarah Ann to William H. Young 12-6-1836 Sh
Wilson, Sarah C. to Hamner King 9-6-1858 (9-8-1858) Ma
Wilson, Sarah E. to James G. Algee 12-31-1840 Cr
Wilson, Sarah E. to James H. Robinson 1-24-1848 (1-25-1848) Hr
Wilson, Sarah E. to Josiah A. Morrow 7-8-1847 T
Wilson, Sarah J. to Pinkney Brown 12-1-1852 (12-4-1852) Sh
Wilson, Sarah Jane to Alfred Wilson 4-4-1861 Be
Wilson, Sarah Jane to Alfred Wilson 4-4-1861 Be CC
Wilson, Sarah Jane to Joseph House 11-22-1838 Cr
Wilson, Sarah Jane to William D. Elder 1-28-1857 (1-29-1857) O
Wilson, Sarah R. to J. Eugene Talbot 11-27-1849 Sh
Wilson, Sarah to Henry Hatch 9-21-1858 (9-23-1858) Hr
Wilson, Sarah to I. S. Mitchell 5-14-1829 Sh
Wilson, Sarah to James Thomas 11-22-1852 (11-23-1852) Hr
Wilson, Sarah to John Cody 11-17-1853 Cr
Wilson, Sarah to John H. Brimmage 4-10-1850 Cr
Wilson, Sarah to Mat Alston 1-16-1871 T
Wilson, Sarah to Samuel Allen 12-13-1832 O
Wilson, Sarah to William H. McQuiston 9-26-1855 T
Wilson, Sarah to William Lee 10-26-1860 (10-28-1860) Hr
Wilson, Silvia to Andrew Walker 1-4-1873 (1-9-1873) Cr B
Wilson, Sophia to Thomas M. Harper 6-9-1857 (6-10-1857) Sh
Wilson, Sophronia to J. M. Chisholm 12-15-1884 (12-17-1884) L
Wilson, Sritha Ann to Ira Bell 9-15-1860 (9-16-1860) L
Wilson, Susan A. to Caleb D. (L.) Allen 12-17-1863 G
Wilson, Susan B. to M. C. Cheek 12-25-1849 Hn
Wilson, Susan E. to Daniel I. Harrelson 5-4-___ (5-6-1855) O
Wilson, Susan J. to H. W. Greer 7-30-1856 (7-31-1856) G
Wilson, Susan to George A. Lunsford 2-19-1861 Ma
Wilson, Susan to James M. Sanders 4-5-1842 Sh
Wilson, Susan to Jorden Henderson 11-9-1866 T
Wilson, T. J. D. to William Riley Short 10-5-1868 G
Wilson, Virginia E. to Wm. A. Price 2-1-1848 Sh
Wilson, Viva to Lee Bradford 12-17-1870 (no return) Hy
Wilson, W. P. to W. A. Thurmond 8-28-1877 (8-29-1877) L
Wilson, Wm. A. to M. J. Paisley 2-2-1854 Ma
Wilson, Zelpha to W. A. Dill 12-22-1857 We
Wilsonn, Martha A. to Benjamin F. Price 11-17-1847 Sh
Wilt, Miram C. to Ruben W. Ross 11-8-1857 We
Wily, Fannie to Ridman Pascal 5-6-1872 O
Wimberley, Anna to Joseph W. Cook 1-19-1867 Hn
Wimberley, Jane to Levi D. Frazier 3-14-1848 Hn
Wimberley, Martha to William Wainscott 2-27-1843 Hn
Wimberley, Mary A. M. to James A. Cannon 9-8-1865 (no return) Hn
Wimberley, Mary E. to Alexander C. Shaw 2-14-1860 Hn
Wimberley, Mary M. to Robert A. Owens 2-24-1859 Hn
Wimberley, Sarah Jane to Isaiah M. Mathis 2-3-1847 Hn
Wimberley, Sarah to Robert W. Williams 2-9-1858 Hn
Wimberley, Sarah to Wilson Shankle 1-17-1839 Hn
Wimberley, Winny to William Beck 3-4-1858 Hn
Wimberly, Catherine to Gilbert Thompson 10-22-1838 Hn
Wimberly, Catherine to William A. Chrisenberry 11-16-1865 Hn
Wimberly, Elizabeth to William Whitfield 11-7-1850 Hn
Wimberly, Emily to ___ Pennick 5-28-1843 Hn
Wimberly, S. A. to ___ Hastings 11-19-1866 Hn
Wimberly, Sarah to James Meredith 2-1-1866 Hn
Wimbush, Martha to John H. Routon 2-19-1855 Hn
Wimbush, Sarah A. to Philip Routon 7-22-1858 Hn
Wimpy, M. M. to J. H. Woodard 7-11-1868 Hy
Winberg, Elizabeth to Abrom Hay 10-14-1866 (no return) Cr
Winberry, Jamima to W. R. Prewet 10-11-1871 (10-12-1871) Dy
Winberry, Martha to Iram Chadwick 9-17-1870 (9-18-1870) Dy
Winberry, Mary Jane to George H. Webb 10-21-1855 Be
Winberry, Mary Jane to George H. Webb 10-21-1855 Be CC
Winborn, Eliza to Fountain E. Hancock 2-28-1885 (3-1-1885) L
Winborn, M. L. to Jas. A. Webb 1-20-1868 (1-21-1868) F
Winbourn, N. A. to T. B. Clark 1-17-1872 Hy
Winbourne, Mary F. to J. R. Harris 12-15-1869 F
Winburn, Amanda J. to W. J. F. Dobbs 11-4-1869 Dy
Winburn, Sarah E. to H. B. Smith 10-13-1866 Hy
Winbush, Henrietta to Beverly Graham 12-24-1883 (12-27-1883) L
Winbush, Nillie to Russell Webb 12-13-1875 (12-19-1875) L B
Winchester, Ann Eliza to Jim Gray 10-17-1877 (10-20-1877) Dy
Winchester, Frances C. W. to William Vance, jr. 10-4-1846 Sh
Winchester, Laura to Jno. Nelson 8-15-1844 Sh
Winchester, Lissidia to Charles H. Organ 3-22-1860 Sh
Winchester, S. A. to J. W. Petree 1-16-1866 Hn
Winchester, Valeria to Robert E. Richards 8-15-1856 (8-16-1856) Sh
Wind (Wine?), Barabara to Philip Maurer 11-22-1860 Sh
Wind, E. C. to J. W. Odell 8-6-1875 (no return) L
Winder, Harriet to John S. Hollin 5-11-1866 (5-12-1866) F B
Winders, Elizabeth Ann to David Holabaugh 12-9-1841 Sh
Winders, Sarah to George Fletcher 3-7-1849 Sh
Windham, Martha to John Tilmon 10-13-1842 (10-17-1842) T
Windiote, Rebecca to Frederick J. Attwood 4-17-1854 (4-18-1854) Sh
Windle, Nettie to C. R. Martin 11-2-1863 Sh
Windows, Neoma N. to John Parks 1-14-1841 Sh
Windrow, Mary H. to Howell T. Jordan 12-15-1857 (no return) L
Windsor, Jane to James Cole 7-3-1853 Hn
Winfield, Easter to Tom Walker 1-12-1871 Hy
Winfield, Elenora L. to Michael Doble 1-29-1870 Ma
Winfield, Lucy to H. Walter Lewis 8-9-1870 (8-10-1870) F
Winfield, Lucyann E. to Sampson H. Sane 11-28-1838 (no return) F
Winfield, Margaret to Sam Peete 12-10-1874 Hy
Winfield, Marry F. to G. W. Robertson 2-10-1845 F
Winfield, Nisha A. to J. J. Bounds 7-18-1865 F
Winford, Alice to Paul Clements 8-31-1866 (9-13-1866) T
Winford, Elizabeth to J. L. Stone 12-18-1860 (12-20-1860) Sh
Winford, Elizabeth to Reding Corbett 7-31-1841 Sh
Winford, Jane to Thomas R. Gibson 11-22-1840 Sh
Winford, Louisa to Andrew Smith 4-27-1870 T

Winford, Nancy A. to Neal B. Sparks 3-23-1846 Sh
Winford, P. J. to M. L. Sory 5-11-1857 (5-12-1857) Sh
Winford, Pearcey to Wm. C. Powell 1-1-1861 (no return) Hy
Winford, R. C. to Richard A. Blalock 12-10-1870 (12-14-1870) T
Winford, S. V. to Andrew Winford 7-25-1865? (7-26-1866) T
Winford, Sarah to Wm. R. Johnson 2-14-1833 Sh
Winfred, Mary J. to R. E. Harris 12-8-1869 (12-9-1869) Dy
Winfred, Sarah to Robert Pickel 12-22-1840 Sh
Winfrey, Lelia to William Matthews 10-27-1865 (10-28-1865) F B
Winfrey, Priscilla to William Langley 12-30-1868 (12-31-1868) F B
Winfrey, S. P. to Geo. A. Moxey 9-18-1866 (9-19-1866) Ma
Winfrey, Sarah A. to Benj. Watkins 1-23-1851 (no return) F
Winfrey, Sarah Jane to George W. Mathews 11-6-1843 Sh
Winfreys, M. to James Rash 2-29-1864 O
Wingate, Ellenor B. to Calvin A. Vandike 8-4-1859 Hy
Wingate, Mary Frances to Columbus A. Yancy 8-23-1862 Hy
Wingerman, Elizabeth to William Buskamp 5-31-1856 (6-3-1856) Sh
Winget, S. E. to D. H. Taylor 10-12-1865 Hy
Wingo, A. V. to W. A.(H?) Ward 12-23-1868 G
Wingo, Arabella E. to T. J. Featherstone 12-10-1869 G
Wingo, Eliza to Foster Meadows 12-24-1870 (12-27-1870) Cr
Wingo, Elizabeth to Martin Gilbert 1-4-1871 (1-5-1871) Cr
Wingo, Emily S. to D. B. Davenport 3-27-1861 G
Wingo, Harriet to Isham Everett 4-28-1870 (5-1-1871?) Cr
Wingo, Jenny to Armstead Dammond? 2-1-1870 (2-2-1870) Cr
Wingo, M. E. A. to D. (Rev.) Liles 10-6-1855 Cr
Wingo, Nancy H. to J. L. Spence 3-28-1871 O
Wingo, Nancy to Tillmon Gillon? 10-7-1850 (no return) Cr
Wingo, Sallie E. to R. L. Holt 8-29-1871 (9-3-1871) Cr
Winiford, Margaret to Thomas J. Anderson 12-21-1842 Sh
Winingham, Lizzie to John Sears 12-23-1876 Hy
Winkle, Caroline to James Vaughan 9-10-1843 Cr
Winkle, Katharine to George Greer 12-16-1848 Hn
Winn (Norrod), Sarah P. to James S. Capps 8-28-1868 Cr
Winn, Agnis to Seaton Hudspeth 10-17-1848 (10-19-1848) F
Winn, Agnis to Seten Hudspeth 10-17-1848 F
Winn, Celia to Frank Glenn 4-20-1876 L B
Winn, Elizabaeth to John W. Conway 11-4-1841 F
Winn, Iva Ann to Joseph Dearing 6-24-1856 T
Winn, Jane C. to Charles A. Bowers 12-23-1847 Sh
Winn, M. E. to F. A. Williams 8-10-1867 (8-11-1867) Cr
Winn, Manda C. to P. W. C. Foster 2-21-1858 Cr
Winn, Mariah to James Devaughn 11-1-1873 (11-5-1873) T
Winn, Mary Ann J. to John W. Bond 1-26-1838 Sh
Winn, Mary J. to Elijah Sanders 6-30-1846 (7-1-1846) G
Winn, Mary T. to G. W. Shelby 10-13-1849 (10-16-1849) O
Winn, Mary to Lawrence Tyus 4-16-1883 (no return) L
Winn, Mary to Pelly Hill 12-24-1873 (12-25-1873) T
Winn, Miss M. E. to H. H. Wiseman 12-27-1860 T
Winn, Rhoda to Wm. Gatewood 10-17-1866 (10-20-1866) T
Winn, Sarah Jane to Elias O. Yarbre? 10-25-1855 T
Winn, Sarah to George Roberts 8-25-1845 O
Winn?, Amand to Edmond Stevens 1-27-1873 (1-28-1873) T
Winningham, F. A. to H. D. Whitehurst 3-4-1868 Hy
Winningham, Susan to John Smith 5-30-1861 Mn
Winns, Margaret to Luther R. Venable 3-14-1838 (no return) Hn
Winns, Martha to George Stockdale 5-20-1866 Hn B
Winrow, Fannie to Edward Bryant 5-25-1867 L B
Winrow, Lucy to Jones Green 3-24-1874 (3-26-1874) L B
Winrow, Mollie to Thomas Greaves 10-20-1876 (no return) L
Winscott, Nelly to Isaiah Simpson 1-29-1866 Hn
Winser, Rebecca to J. W. Wilson 5-13-1858 Hn
Winsett, Amanda to Michael Kelly 2-25-1857 Hn
Winsett, Caroline to Thomas Barbee 12-4-1838 Hn
Winsett, Jane to Isaiah Holmes 12-26-1851 Hn
Winsett, Joe to Wm. A. Bell 10-19-1865 (10-22-1865) F
Winsett, Malinda to Wilson Bruce 10-17-1839 Hn
Winsett, Martha J. to John H. Palmer 8-25-1860 (no return) Hn
Winsett, Nancy H. to John B. Guinn 1-12-1859 Hn
Winsett, Nancy M. to Lawrence G. Hastings 11-23-1860 Hn
Winsett, Nancy to Philip Bruce 6-15-1843 Hn
Winsett, Nancy to Robert Jackson 11-8-1860 Sh
Winsett, Sallie E. to M. M. Cox 1-10-1867 Hn
Winsett, Sarah to J. R. Lassiter 6-26-1866 (no return) Hn
Winslow, Lenora (Mrs.) to Thomas Fesmire 10-6-1869 (10-14-1869) Ma
Winstead, Almira to E. H. Bowling 4-19-1844 (no return) We
Winstead, E. J. to S. C. Bowlin 7-10-1856 We
Winstead, Elizabeth to Andrew J. Rea 12-10-1850 We
Winstead, Mary A. to Andrew Byars 12-23-1857 We
Winstead, Susan M. to Hilman Walker 10-27-1856 We
Winston, Ann E. to Robert I. Bryan 12-17-1867 (12-19-1867) Ma
Winston, Arabella W. to J. H. Johnson 8-10-1862 We
Winston, Catherine P. to J. I. Hillis 9-17-1856 We
Winston, Dilcey to James Henderson 9-15-1873 (9-16-1873) L
Winston, Elizabeth C. to David C. Ralston 10-24-1849 Sh
Winston, Emily A. to John W. Mayo 2-2-1842 F
Winston, Gilly C. to J. M. Gooldsby 1-8-1857 We

Winston, Mary E. to Whitson A. Harris 1-24-1848 (1-28-1848) F
Winston, Mary to Mac MacNiel 5-9-1877 (5-10-1877) L
Winston, Mollie to Thomas Reed 2-10-1867 G
Winston, Nannie S. to R. N. Irvine 4-20-1853 We
Winston, P. C. to W. V. Sims 4-5-1855 We
Winston, Permelia to Ira Harris 5-5-1874 (5-6-1874) T
Winston, Sarah F. to William W. Weatherly 12-15-1858 (12-5?-1858) Ma
Winston, Sarah to Ira Adams 11-4-1865 (11-14-1865) T
Winston, Victoria to J. G. Sneed 11-26-1862 (11-27-1862) F
Winston, Victoria to J. G. Sneed 11-26-1862 (not endorsed) F
Winston, Virginia to Elias Tomlinson 3-4-1856 (3-5-1856) O
Winston?, Angelin to William Smith 7-9-1869 F
Winter, Martha to W. A. Allen 5-31-1862 (no return) We
Winter, Mary E. to Otho Williams 11-4-1857 Sh
Wintercast, Catharine to John B. Morris 12-24-1860 (12-25-1860) Sh
Winters, C. A. to Marion Beasley 10-4-1852 We
Winters, Caroline to Grant Farmon 5-25-1832 Sh
Winters, Frances A. to L. G. Rasbury 11-7-1862 Dy
Winters, Frances L. to Henry Holley 1-28-1848 Sh
Winters, L. J. to H. L. McCarroll 1-30-1875 (2-3-1875) Dy
Winters, M. A. to G. V. Underwood 3-16-1871 (3-17-1871) O
Winters, M. A. to J. H. Modlin 2-16-1875 (2-17-1875) Dy
Winters, Mary J. to Orange Lowry 5-28-1858 Hn
Winters, Mary to Joel S. Enlow 4-23-1825 O
Winters, Mary to T.? Roach 1-21-1862 Cr
Winters, Matilda Louisa to George W. Fentriss 12-13-1827 O
Winters, Sarah to Ben Johnson 12-23-1875 (no return) Hy
Winters, Susan to William L. Francis 11-29-1861 We
Wintiser, Jennie to Donaldson Powers 2-20-1879 L
Wire(Wise?), Jane to Larkin T. Smyth 11-2-1825 Hr
Wirt, Catharine to Willis M. Green 3-15-1838 F
Wirt, Catharine to Wm. J. Cannon 11-9-1854 (no return) F
Wirt, Frances to Peter Jordan 2-20-1869 (3-21-1869) F B
Wirt, Levice to Wm. H. Montgomery 4-7-1831 Sh
Wirt, Mary to Ed Warren 12-26-1866 F B
Wisdom, Hettie to P. H. Tapps 10-9-1865 Mn
Wisdom, Martha M. to Robert K. Bradshaw 11-5-1850 Hr
Wise, Agnes to Jake Bond 12-27-1877 Hy
Wise, Emma to Peter Shaw 1-10-1878 Hy
Wise, Emmeline to N. A. Fields 8-28-1879 (8-29-1879) L
Wise, Julia F. to Thos. W. Hart 3-30-1868 (no return) Hy
Wise, M. C. to J. W. Banister 8-18-1869 Hy
Wise, Mollie to L. Robertson 12-30-1882 (12-31-1883) L
Wise, Rachel to James Duckworth 2-9-1876 (2-10-1876) Dy
Wise, Rebecca to George Groves 6-5-1844 Hn
Wise, Sarah Ann to William H. Greer 7-2-1850 Ma
Wiseman, Amand L. to Henry K. Farmer 9-21-1867 (9-24-1867) T
Wiseman, Angeline to Lemuel Thompson 2-24-1850 Be
Wiseman, Dora to William S. 5-30-1874 (no return) Dy
Wiseman, Elanor to Jacob Smith 8-17-1841 T
Wiseman, Elender to Milton Wiseman 3-3-1850 Be
Wiseman, Elizabeth to Columbus Curd 11-1-1864 Hn
Wiseman, Elizabeth to John M. Patrick 12-24-1866 Hn
Wiseman, Frances to Thos. H. Tillman 1-1-1862 T
Wiseman, J. A. to J. Wiseman 4-5-1841 Be
Wiseman, J. S. to J. Wiseman 4-5-1841 Be CC
Wiseman, Julia Ann L. to James O. Mailey 3-27-1853 T
Wiseman, M. E. to Wm. A. Kinney 2-29-1860 T
Wiseman, Madaline to George Gilbreath 8-8-1852 Be
Wiseman, Margaret to Geo. Tillman 2-27-1871 (2-28-1871) T
Wiseman, Martha to Allen Herrin 8-7-1855 Be
Wiseman, Mary A. (Mrs.) to George W. Chappel 2-22-1870 Ma
Wiseman, Mary E. to Franklin Wiseman 11-4-1852 Be
Wiseman, Mary E. to George Nobles 7-18-1866 (7-19-1866) T
Wiseman, Mary E. to Wm. A. Kinney 2-29-1860 T
Wiseman, Mary S. to William A. Kiney 2-29-1860 T
Wiseman, Matilda Elizabeth to Alfred B. Owen 3-15-1849 T
Wiseman, Matilda to Noah Brown 12-26-1865 (12-28-1865) T
Wiseman, May E. to Franklin Wiseman 11-4-1852 Be CC
Wiseman, Miry to John Reynolds 3-31-1861 Be
Wiseman, Miry to Newton Kurr 7-22-1869 Be
Wiseman, Nancy A. to G. W. McDaniel 7-5-1863 Be
Wiseman, Permelia Jane to Benjamin Thompson 10-31-1844 Be
Wiseman, Rebecca to William Bond 4-6-1856 Be
Wiseman, Sallie to L. L. Warr 9-9-1868 T
Wiseman, Sallie to William Brown 1-7-1874 (1-10-1874) T
Wiseman, Sarah to J. Hicks 1-8-1839 Be
Wiseman, Sarah to J. W. Best 2-5-1868 T
Wiseman, Sarah to Wiley Stevens 3-18-1865 (3-21-1865) T
Wiseman, Sarah to Wm. P. Presson 12-15-1850 Be
Wiseman?, Frances Jane to John Carr Myers 2-25-1858 T
Wisenor, Eliza to W. B. Burns 9-8-1854 G
Wisner, Nancy to Micheal White 8-20-1842 Sh
Wissen, Caroline L. to Joseph J.? Talley 4-22-1840 (4-23-1840) T
Wissling, Katherina to Gottlieb Schveizer 3-8-1862 Sh
Wisson, Elizabeth H. to J. W. Sanders 1-31-1853 (no return) F
Wit, Mary Jane to John W. Sile 10-14-1843 (10-19-1843) G

Withare (Withers), Catherine M. to Fred Miller 5-27-1847 Sh
Witherford, Mary A. D. to William G. Baker 8-30-1854 G
Witherington, Ann L. to Patrick Stewart 1-13-1859 G
Witherington, Ann to N. M. Travis 1-4-1854 G
Witherington, E. to Lewis Herring 8-15-1844 Sh
Witherington, Julia to Sterling Elrod 6-3-1869 G B
Witherington, Louisa Jane to Thomas D. Wood 7-1-1842 T
Witherington, Martha to John Billings 12-5-1846 (12-6-1846) T
Witherington, Mary to Aaron Bledsoe 9-11-1854 T
Witherlington, Elizabeth to Harmon Reddin 12-28-1839 Ma
Withers, Lydia C. to Ransom Burns Hicks 10-8-1861 (10-9-1861) Ma
Witherson, Eliza to David Pewett 12-21-1875 (no return) Hy
Witherspoon, Lucinda to Jordan Greenwood 3-25-1873 Hy
Witherspoon, Mary to Wm. T. Miers 6-30-1844 G
Witherspoon, Nancy J. to James Ford 10-7-1866 Hn
Witherspoon, P. J. to J. S. Cowan 2-27-1868 Hy
Witherspoon, Sarah A. to T. M. Robertson 9-29-1842 Hn
Witherspoonn, Martha H. to R. D. Trabue 1-12-1860 Sh
Withington, Sarah Ann to Wm. Porter Burgitt 12-17-1855 (12-20-1855) T
Witman, Magdaline to Hewer Senn (Lenn?) 11-18-1854 Sh
Witt, Bettie to George Chipman 8-23-1862 (8-24-1862) L
Witt, Drucilla B. to Saml. E. Champion 1-12-1871 F
Witt, Eliza Ann to Alexander Cook 12-24-1840 (12-26-1840) G
Witt, Kitty to Tom Lewis 2-1-1868 (2-2-1868) F B
Witt, Louisa to Joseph Clark 2-17-1848 Hn
Witt, Martha L. to J. J. Brewster 4-8-1855 Sh
Witt, Martha to Henry Cheaney 8-19-1865 (no return) Hy
Witt, Mary to Aleck Parker 6-7-1877 L
Witt, Mary to Charles Lowe 12-24-1874 (12-27-1874) L B
Witt, Mary to Solomon Green 3-2-1872 (not executed) L B
Witt, Rebecca E. to William S. Eldridg 12-24-1856 (12-25-1856) G
Witt, Susan Jane to A. J. Warren 9-26-1874 Hy
Wittenborough, Sarah A. to James Jourdan 5-12-1842 Hn
Wittig, Catharine to John Kappel 1-31-1853 Sh
Wittman, Margaretha to Louis Eppinger 4-25-1861 Ma
Wittman, Matilda to Edward Iffland 6-29-1869 (7-1-1869) Ma
Wlkinson, Melissa P. to James Vaughan 11-9-1860 (11-11-1860) Hr
Woddy, Elizabeth A. to William B. Boyett 10-8-1858 (10-14-1858) G
Woerne, Salomea to Peter Weirich 9-6-1864 Sh
Wofford, Elizabeth F. to Robert M. Cravens 2-3-1843 (no return) Hn
Wofford, M. M. to James L. Cravens 10-16-1860 Hn
Wofford, Mollie to J. W. Waldron 1-1-1877 (1-4-1877) Dy
Woldram, Elenida to Lihue Taylor 7-29-1839 (8-1-1839) F
Wolen, Lousella to David Hindman 2-26-1870 T
Wolf, Barbrier to John Searcy 7-7-1856 Sh
Wolf, Caroline to H. Kaufman 10-30-1854 (10-31-1854) Sh
Wolf, Louisa (Mrs.) to John Rose 4-11-1860 (4-17-1860) Sh
Wolf, Mollie R. to D. A. Clark 10-26-1858 Sh
Wolf, Sarah Jane to Matthew Caraway 5-4-1864 Sh
Wolf, Sarah to A. G. Phillips 2-15-1857 Cr
Wolfe, Annie T. to J. W. VanWagener 10-29-1855 Sh
Wolfe, Babethe to Elias Leowenstein 1-20-1864 Sh
Wolfe, Laney to Conrad Asmear (Azamire?) 3-2-1855 (3-4-1855) Sh
Wolff, Cordelia to R. H. Rawls 2-11-1869 Cr
Wolff, Sarah to T. Folz 8-29-1856 Sh
Wollard, Martha to Calvin Flowers 3-21-1859 (3-22-1859) G
Wollard, Penina to Bryant Andrews 10-15-1850 G
Wollard, Penny E. to Wm. R. Wallis 1-17-1840 G
Wollard, Rebecca A. to Alexander K. Miller 12-20-1837 Sh
Wollerford, Frances to Wm. Bragg 9-30-1850 (no return) F
Wolton, Martha A. to James M. White 11-4-1852 Sh
Wolverton, Deliah to Robert W. Moore 2-25-1864 Mn
Wolverton, Elizabeth to Allen Hanks 1-23-1833 (1-24-1833) Hr
Wolverton, Lucinda P. to James C. Peck 12-3-1864 (12-4-1864) Sh
Wolverton, Mary to George A. Shelton 10-27-1835 Hr
Womac, Eliza E. to Andrew B. Hurley 6-6-1848 (6-8-1848) F
Womack, Fady J. to Shelby A. Bettis 2-12-1850 Be
Womack, Mariah A. to Francis W. Campbell 12-19-1859 (12-20-1859) Ma
Womack, Mary to Enoch King 6-12-1841 Hr
Womack, Rebecca to James L. Cozby 2-21-1839 (2-25-1839) Hr
Womack, Sarah A. to Robt. D. Anderson 3-10-1868 (3-20-1868) Ma
Womack, Talitha to Andrew J. Robertson 4-7-1839 Be
Womble, Delila Jane to R. T. Mann 10-18-1875 (no return) Hy
Womble, Josephine to John McDade 10-22-1844 F
Womble, Lucinda to Reubin West 11-24-1872 Hy
Womble, Mary E. to Emmor Weaver 9-6-1867 Hy
Womble, Mary S. to John Baker 2-1-1860 We
Wommack, Mary Ann to W. D. Smith 5-24-1855 We
Wood, A. E. to Montezuma Jones 10-11-1849 Hr
Wood, A. J. to S. Scofield 11-2-1856 We
Wood, Alice B. to E. G. Rowe 3-29-1869 (3-30-1869) Cr
Wood, Alvira to John W. Barrett 5-17-1863 G
Wood, Amanda C. to Saml. Roe 1-4-1869 (1-5-1869) T
Wood, Amanda to George Steward 1-1-1878 Dy
Wood, Amanda to Joseph Maxwell 11-28-1861 T
Wood, Amanda to Luther Borden 10-24-1861 Sh

Wood, Amanda to Polk Rodgers 12-27-1871 Dy
Wood, America J. to Jas. Henry Tillman 1-8-1872 (1-11-1872) T
Wood, Amy C. to W. R. Crawford 12-20-1859 (12-21-1859) Hr
Wood, Amy to Robt. Shepard 11-4-1865 (11-6-1865) T
Wood, Angeline to John T. Brown 12-18-1841 (12-19-1841) Hr
Wood, Ann E. to Seaton B. Burks 12-21-1843 (no return) L
Wood, Ann to Andrew Robinson 9-7-1866 (9-16-1866) T
Wood, Bettie D. to C. A. (Dr.) Chapman 12-17-1866 (12-18-1866) Ma
Wood, C. A. to J. P. Thurmond 2-15-1865 Dy
Wood, Caroline to Benjamin Williams 1-13-1847 (1-14-1847) Hr
Wood, Caroline to Charles Bomer 12-9-1858 Hn
Wood, Catharine to James Harper 12-1-1857 (12-12-1857) Sh
Wood, Catherine to Thos. H. Williamson 4-25-1844 Sh
Wood, Cordelia to Robert Elam 3-29-1858 (4-1-1858) T
Wood, Cornelia P. to Thomas Black 10-18-1842 Sh
Wood, E. T. (Mrs.) to James F. Terry 6-1-1861 (6-3-1861) Sh
Wood, Eddie to J. R. Burks 11-21-1885 (11-24-1885) L
Wood, Eliza to Alfred Thomas 10-2-1873 Hy
Wood, Eliza to James H. Palmer 1-27-1859 Hn
Wood, Eliza to John Murphy 8-11-1847 L
Wood, Eliza to Talbert Thompson 3-6-1871 (3-8-1871) T
Wood, Eliza to William Jolly 12-23-1841 Sh
Wood, Elizabeth F. to B. S. Johnson 4-19-1846 Sh
Wood, Elizabeth H. to Haywood F. Harris 7-31-1848 (no return) Cr
Wood, Elizabeth J. to E. A. G. Hall 1-15-1873 (1-16-1873) Cr
Wood, Elizabeth to Harvey Lacy 12-11-1849 Hn
Wood, Elizabeth to John H. Lett 10-12-1852 G
Wood, Elizabeth to John Oliver 9-24-1838 Ma
Wood, Ella to Orlando P. Foster 4-11-1860 (no return) Hn
Wood, Emma A. to P. B. Tatum 4-24-1866 Dy
Wood, Emma to James E. Williams 11-12-1878 (11-13-1878) L
Wood, Emma to James Thomas 7-29-1877 Hy
Wood, Evaline to Wm. C. Gowen 1-14-1839 (no return) Cr
Wood, Fannie A. to David Dewalt 4-1-1885 (4-2-1885) L
Wood, Fannie to W. A. Neil 2-14-1861 Sh
Wood, Felicia Ann to Henry Chipman 2-10-1872 (2-12-1872) L
Wood, Florida E. to Thomas W. Walker 8-23-1858 (8-25-1858) Ma
Wood, Frances J. to Cornelius Smith 7-30-1860 (7-31-1860) Sh
Wood, Hettie to Gid Rogers 5-3-1874 Hy
Wood, J. A. to J. R. Gaskins 5-15-1858 Cr
Wood, Jane L. to Jonathan Buckner 1-21-1846 (1-28-1846) L
Wood, Jane M. to Paul T. Jones 2-26-1849 (3-1-1849) Hr
Wood, Jane to John T. Lashlee 1-23-1850 Be
Wood, Judah to Patrick Wood 5-24-1866 Hy
Wood, Kate to Wm. McG. Wayman 11-22-1860 Sh
Wood, Laura H. to Robt. H. Shepperd 12-29-1858 (12-30-1858) Hr
Wood, Lavicey Ann to Anderson Mailey 3-16-1848 T
Wood, Lizzie to William Hall 10-13-1882 (10-16-1882) L
Wood, Lou E. to J. C. Dupree 11-15-1881 L
Wood, Luciller to Moses Hay 12-10-1870 (12-11-1870) T
Wood, Lucinda to Henry Hipp 12-7-1867 L B
Wood, Lucy Ann to James Hayse 11-20-1856 Hn
Wood, Lucy Ann to John Mainard 4-23-1854 Hn
Wood, Lucy C. to Wilson T. Bills 12-2-1857 Hr
Wood, Lucy to John Maggard 12-29-1875 (1-2-1876) Dy
Wood, M. A. V. to Albert Travis 12-24-1851 Sh
Wood, M. E. E. to A. H. P. Keller 9-22-1875 L
Wood, Mandy to Egbert Taylor 12-25-1874 Hy
Wood, Margaret J. to J. H. Hill 3-12-1866 G
Wood, Margaret to George Manual 10-18-1872 (10-19-1872) T
Wood, Maria C. to Thomas A. Parran 11-2-1848 Hr
Wood, Maria to Gilford Ashe 12-30-1874 Hy
Wood, Martha Ann to James Prince 10-23-1845 Be
Wood, Martha H. to W. H. Wood 4-21-1853 G
Wood, Martha to Enoch F. Snowden 11-26-1847 Sh
Wood, Martha to F. M. Swinney 1-29-1852 Hn
Wood, Martha to H. H. Torrence 9-12-1869 Sh
Wood, Martha to Joshua Estes 3-25-1843 (3-26-1843) Hr
Wood, Martha to Theophilus Rogers 1-18-1836 Sh
Wood, Martha to William H. Ligon 9-12-1842 (9-20-1842) T
Wood, Mary A. to James S. Pringle 4-4-1868 (4-5-1868) L
Wood, Mary Ann to Isaac Wesson 1-24-1856 Sh
Wood, Mary Ann to W. A. Walker 2-1-1855 Be
Wood, Mary E. to Henry J. Hyde 1-9-1872 L
Wood, Mary F. to Jordan C. Wood 12-16-1868 G
Wood, Mary G. to M. J. Hark 11-8-1877 Dy
Wood, Mary J. to Robt. L. Harris 1-18-1873 (1-19-1873) Cr
Wood, Mary Jane to Henry B. Ligon 1-4-1848 (1-5-1848) T
Wood, Mary L. to Martin Key 4-3-1842 Cr
Wood, Mary M. to J. W. E. Moore 12-8-1874 Hy
Wood, Mary M. to Napoleon Hill 7-7-1858 (7-8-1858) Hr
Wood, Mary to Benj. F. Boydston 8-28-1843 (8-30-1843) L
Wood, Mary to Elijah Comer 10-25-1837 Hr
Wood, Mary to Joel Watters 3-4-1841 Hn
Wood, Mary to John Anderson 1-27-1867 (no return) Dy
Wood, Melissa Ann to Robert Weatherly 11-13-1866 Ma
Wood, Mollie to John C. Rogers 10-16-1873 Hy

Wood, Nancy A. to John Nobles 11-25-1857 Be
Wood, Nancy E. to Henry A. Hampton 7-17-1869 (7-18-1869) Cr
Wood, Nancy E. to W. O. Hobson 4-18-1874 (4-19-1874) Dy
Wood, Nancy R. L. to James M. Lewis 11-9-1843 Cr
Wood, Nancy to W. N. Griffin 10-16-1864 (no return) Hn
Wood, Nancy to Wilson Ferrell 11-11-1847 Sh
Wood, Narcissa to Joseph M. Massey 4-13-1869 G
Wood, Patsy to Yancy Henderson 2-26-1870 (no return) Dy
Wood, R. E. to J. B. Meacham 2-16-1886 L
Wood, Rachel to George Thompson 1-18-1869 (1-20-1869) L
Wood, Rachel to Isuah? Thompson 11-18-1871 (no return) L
Wood, Rhoda to Major Estes 10-23-1845 Hr
Wood, Rosa to John Voss, jr. 5-12-1877 Hy
Wood, Ruth to P. P. Paschell 8-16-1855 We
Wood, S. M. to J. F. Kirkland 10-26-1869 Hy
Wood, Sarah A. to R. S. Carter 10-14-1862 (10-16-1862) Cr
Wood, Sarah B. to George W. Wilkerson 10-20-1843 Hr
Wood, Sarah C. to Nathan F. (J) Alsbrook 11-1-1846 Sh
Wood, Sarah J. to William T. Landers 12-17-1869 (12-19-1869) Ma
Wood, Sarah S. to Edward Campbell 2-3-1848 Hn
Wood, Sarah to Samuel Spence 12-22-1845 (no return) We
Wood, Sarah to Thomas Waddle 11-30-1847 Sh
Wood, Sary E. to Clark Stone 5-4-1840 G
Wood, Susan A. to W. S. Trout 11-20-1866 (no return) Dy
Wood, Susan to A. H. Kimbrough 1-19-1865 Be
Wood, Susan to Albert Simmons 8-5-1841 O
Wood, Susan to Benjamin Neal 11-21-1846 (11-23-1846) Ma
Wood, Susan to Majer Gregory 7-29-1871 (no return) Hy
Wood, Tabitha A. to J. M. Graves 9-16-1874 L
Wood, Theny P. to James G. Pertle 10-23-1845 We
Wood, Tibatha to Dimeon Ferril 1-28-1841 Sh
Wood?, Laura to Andrew Strong 10-26-1869 T
Woodall, Adaline to Stephen A. Smith 7-24-1844 Hn
Woodall, Elizabeth J. to George Q. Holmes 12-29-1842 Cr
Woodall, P. D. to Edward Langham 11-26-1868 Hy
Woodard, Catherine to Melton Studdard 10-8-1840 Cr
Woodard, Celea A. to John M. Jordan 1-1-1853 (1-2-1853) G
Woodard, Eliza to John H. Brough 1-16-1836 Hr
Woodard, Jane to J. H. Baird 5-31-1864 (6-1-1864) O
Woodard, June Asha to W. M. Bell 4-23-1849 Cr
Woodard, M. A. to J. T. Burrow 8-13-1856 Cr
Woodard, Margaret E. to Wm. M. Motley 3-10-1867 G
Woodard, Martha to Benjamin Bickers 8-15-1840 (8-17-1840) F
Woodard, Mary E. to Alford T. Bibb 9-17-1857 (no return) L
Woodard, Mary L. to John K. Dunning 8-28-1864 (no return) Cr
Woodard, Mary Louisa to Thos. W. Robinson 10-20-1853 G
Woodard, Mary M. to Edwin Fish 2-21-1850 Cr
Woodard, Mary to Has. Chamberlin 1-3-1842 Ma
Woodard, Mary to Zach. Burch 11-22-1844 Cr
Woodard, Matilda A. to Henry Saunders 11-15-1880 (11-19-1880) L
Woodard, N. F. to A. L. Ryan 10-27-1877 (10-28-1877) L
Woodard, Sallie to Major Howell 7-28-1853 L
Woodard, Winniford A. to James R. Bryant 10-13-1849 Cr
Woodard, Zelpha to Aaron W. Woodard 3-12-1838 (5-20-1838) Ma
Wooddard, Julianna to Calvin J. Hardy 11-24-1830 Ma
Woode, Sarah Ann to Charles Henry Nicholas 6-18-1870 (6-19-1870) L
Wooden, Eliza to Green Crisp 11-11-1864 Mn
Wooden, Martha E. to W. H. Zornes (Zanes?) 9-9-1863 G
Wooden, Mary J. to Benj. R. Belote 12-28-1856 Hr
Wooden, Selia to Perry Hill 11-16-1875 (11-18-1875) L
Woodfin, Elizabeth F. to John M. Batt 9-19-1840 (9-24-1840) F
Woodfin, Mary T. to Thomas A. Osborn 2-17-1853 Hr
Woodfin, Sarah T. to Wm. H. Hardy 9-18-1877 O
Woodfolk, Allia G. to Thomas F. Lane 11-11-1871 (11-12-1871) Ma
Woodfolk, Lucy to Gabe McCully 12-24-1870 (no return) F B
Woodfolk, Mary to Tom Shelton 12-27-1867 (no return) F B
Woodley, Catharin to Wesley Eldridge 7-1-1869 T
Woodruff, Ann E. to William B. Ingram 1-3-1854 G
Woodruff, Annie to John Wilson 1-22-1881 L
Woodruff, Elizabeth to J. J. McDonald 12-4-1860 O
Woodrum, Eliza E. to Henry C. Vaden 11-6-1862 G
Woods, Amanda R. to Jesse A. Brown 5-12-1857 Hn
Woods, Ann J. to Stephen J. Lester 2-7-1838 F
Woods, Anna to Anthony Bassmore 8-11-1877 (no return) Hy
Woods, Armanda Jane to Matthew S. Bryant 10-4-1847 (9-6-1848) Ma
Woods, Bridget to Patrick Donolon (Donalson) 7-25-1857 (7-26-1857) Sh
Woods, C. C. to Wm. E. Briseman 6-21-1859 (6-22-1859) T
Woods, Charity C. to L. W. Jones 10-1-1850 Cr
Woods, Cordia to William Dreums? 5-10-1873 T
Woods, Delilah to Richard C. McNeeley 11-6-1865 O
Woods, Delizar to George N. Bell 12-20-1855 G
Woods, Elizabeth J. to A. F. Betts 10-14-1854 (10-19-1854) G
Woods, Elizabeth W. to William Floyd (Flora) 8-6-1845 Sh
Woods, Elizabeth to Abraham Patton 11-6-1826 G
Woods, Elizabeth to Jesse D. Carr 5-23-1843 Sh
Woods, Ella to Adam Higbee 12-25-1868 (12-26-1868) F B
Woods, Ellen to Hail Gossett 5-7-1870 (5-8-1870) Cr

Woods, Ellinor to Dempsey Saunders 2-14-1843 Hn
Woods, Emily to P. Atkerson 5-16-1843 Cr
Woods, Hariet to A. Scarbrough 1-1-1850 (no return) Hn
Woods, Huldy to C. H. Lunsford 3-20-1869 (3-29-1869) L
Woods, Indiana to George W. Barr 3-12-1865 Be
Woods, Jane to Patrick Kelly 9-30-1859 (10-2-1859) Sh
Woods, Kittie to George Franklin 12-26-1871 Hy
Woods, Louisa Jane to J. F. Alexander 12-28-1864 (no return) Hn
Woods, Lucinda to Barnett Ferguson 9-21-1826 G
Woods, M. E. to S. P. Lawson 12-12-1866 O
Woods, M. W. to P. M. Cooper 6-30-1880 (7-1-1880) L
Woods, Malinda to Mose Dancy 5-22-1873 Hy
Woods, Margaret Ann to Joseph S. McAnulty 11-17-1842 (11-18-1842) Hr
Woods, Martha D. to Thomas J. Taliaferro 5-2-1866 Hn
Woods, Martha E. (Mrs.) to R. M. Hurt 4-24-1860 Cr
Woods, Martha to Jeromiah P. Wood 5-27-1868 (5-28-1868) Ma
Woods, Martha to Matthew Edwards 10-24-1850 Sh
Woods, Martha to Peter Sexton 9-12-1839 G
Woods, Mary A. to Andrew D. Woods 2-14-1870 (2-15-1870) Ma
Woods, Mary A. to Vinson Parsons 7-10-1855 Cr
Woods, Mary A. to Wm. T. Harris 11-8-1854 Cr
Woods, Mary Ann to Drury Johnson 12-13-1851 (12-14-1851) Ma
Woods, Mary Catharine to Wilford F. Hampton 7-30-1860 (10-1-1860) O
Woods, Mary F. to C. A. S. Richardson 12-21-1857 (12-24-1857) Sh
Woods, Mary J. to J. H. Bruce 9-24-1868 Be
Woods, Mary J. to James Young 1-4-1869 (no return) L B
Woods, Mary M. to John McKenzie 12-28-1865 Mn
Woods, Mary M. to R. G. Aycock 12-12-1854 G
Woods, Mary to Walter Shinault 6-19-1849 (6-27-1849) Hr
Woods, Mary to Wm. Har 5-12-1865 (6-1-1865) Cr
Woods, Mary to Wm. Hurt 5-12-1865 (no return) Cr
Woods, Masouri to David Hart 9-3-1846 We
Woods, Mattie to Edward Ellis 4-17-1872 (4-18-1872) Dy
Woods, Mollie to Boss Fowlks 9-25-1879 Dy
Woods, Nancy E. to T. F. McNeeley 8-5-1866 G
Woods, Nancy to Anderson Smith 1-30-1869 G B
Woods, Nancy to James E. Hughes 11-22-1865 G
Woods, Nancy to Leroy F. Lockard 9-11-1839 (9-13-1839) L
Woods, Nancy to Miles Mathews 1-16-1871 (1-19-1871) Dy B
Woods, Narcissus to Joseph H. Webster 1-17-1851 (1-19-1851) T
Woods, Nora to John Dewitt? 8-30-1877 (crossed out) Dy
Woods, Nora to John Smith 8-30-1877 (no return) Dy
Woods, Sallie to Phil Lea 11-19-1881 L B
Woods, Sally to Zachariah D. Childers 4-24-1842 Hn
Woods, Sarah Ann to Wm. C. Peoples 11-26-1839 Cr
Woods, Sarah Jane to S. A. Greer 9-16-1868 (9-17-1868) Dy
Woods, Sarah to Henry C. Lee 7-27-1851 Hn
Woods, Sarah to John C. Cocrum 2-23-1867 (3-11-1867) T
Woods, Sarah to William A. James 1-17-1866 Hn
Woods, Scyntha to Newt Coats 1-15-1866 T
Woods, Silly to Virgin Disen 11-26-1871 Hy
Woods, Sophia W. to Thomas G. Jones 1-15-1838 (1-18-1838) G
Woods, Susan Ann to J. W. Whichard 3-25-1879 (3-28-1879) Dy
Woods, Susan Y. to T. A. Duke 7-15-1868 Cr
Woodsen, Fanny to R. B. Ing 12-2-1866 G
Woodson (Hutcherson), Martha to Thomas Williams 7-19-1868 G B
Woodson, Amanda E. to William R. Pearce 6-1-1859 (6-2-1859) G
Woodson, Amanda to Squire Jeter 8-19-1870 (no return) Hy
Woodson, Catherine to George Adams 3-14-1876 (no return) Hy
Woodson, Dilila P. to F. G. Goodman 12-15-1836 (12-28-1836) G
Woodson, E. V. to F. N. Copeland 7-15-1842 Hn
Woodson, Emeline to Jerry Gillem 9-25-1878 (no return) Hy
Woodson, Isabella to John A. Gatlin 9-17-1854 Hr
Woodson, Lucy E. M. J. to Joshua Hardin 6-15-1848 Sh
Woodson, M. A. to J. F. Bodkins 3-28-1868 G
Woodson, M. A. to W. H. Lee 4-14-1878 Hy
Woodson, Margaret to John Clarke 12-31-1869 Hy
Woodson, Mariella to Geo. B. Guernant 10-27-1852 (10-28-1852) Sh
Woodson, Martha Jane to Miles H. Travis 4-28-1849 (4-29-1849) G
Woodson, Mary J. to R. W. Peacock 8-4-1852 G
Woodson, Mary to Rufus Pettus 12-23-1876 Dy
Woodson, Menervia to Steven Cruchfield 12-31-1869 Hy
Woodson, Nancy J. to T. P. Dalton 1-5-1860 Sh
Woodson, Nannie R. (Miss) to Wm. H. Sawyer 12-15-1864 Sh
Woodson, Sallie P. to W. W. Bondurant 11-8-1869 (11-9-1869) F
Woodson, Sarah R. to Miles H. Travis 4-2-1853 (4-3-1853) G
Woodson, Susan A. to James A. McAlister 9-25-1870 G
Woodson, Susan E. G. to Hugh Bodkins 11-21-1867 G
Woodson, Virginia to Joseph J. Weatherly 1-31-1839 Hn
Woodson, Wilmoth B. to William D. Hyer 5-7-1840 Hn
Woodward, Elizabeth to Elisha Robertson 5-24-1860 Hr
Woodward, Elizabeth to Robert W. Eckold 10-19-1847 Sh
Woodward, Mary to John W. West 8-14-1867 G
Woodward, Sarah E. to G. W. Fletcher 3-23-1855 (no return) Cr
Woodward, Victoria to F. G. Capers 3-16-1858 Sh
Woodward, Virginia to James S. Lamphier 7-15-1845 Sh
Woolard, Elizabeth to Henry Howell 3-25-1863 G

Woolard, M. E. to L. P. Duncan 6-21-1862 O
Woolberton, Mary A. to Saml. W. Rogers 9-29-1860 Hr
Wooldridge, Francis to William Porch 12-6-1859 (no return) We
Wooldridge, Harriet C. to Jas. G. Simpson 3-6-1861 (3-7-1861) Sh
Wooldridge, Mollie H. to T. J. Latham 3-6-1861 (3-7-1861) Sh
Wooley, Christain A. to John T. Smith 7-19-1858 (7-21-1858) Ma
Wooley, Eliz. Ann to David B. Cheairs 11-30-1841 (12-1-1841) Hr
Woolfkill, Susan A. (Mrs.) to John Ing 11-17-1863 Sh
Woolfolk, Artie to J. L. Williams 12-6-1870 (12-7-1870) Ma
Woolfolk, Ellen to Thos. B. Utley 11-3-1868 (11-4-1868) Ma
Woolfolk, Mildred A. to William A. W. Davie 4-5-1869 (4-7-1869) Ma
Woollard, Sarah (Mrs.) to Benj. Marion Spencer 7-6-1869 Ma
Woollen, L. L. to W. C. O'Neill 10-25-1870 (10-26-1870) Cr
Woolley, Mary Jane to Jno. W. Hollis 8-15-1868 (8-16-1868) F
Woollum, Elvira T. to William Minson 5-24-1847 (no return) F
Woolly, Harriet to Allen Dorman 12-5-1846 F
Woolsey, Martha C. to Thos. F. Peyton 7-23-1851 (7-24-1851) Sh
Wooten, Amanda to T. F. Sweat 4-28-1858 Sh
Wooten, Athey to Burrell Warf 1-3-1850 T
Wooten, Lidia A. to Home? Dedrick 12-24-1866 (12-27-1866) T
Wooten, Lola to G. B. Sale 11-16-1869 (11-17-1869) T
Wooten, Martha to Alexander Hannah 1-22-1846 Cr
Wooten, Mary F. to Jacob A. Sullivan 9-7-1869 (9-8-1869) T
Wooten, Mary to Anthony B. Coward 12-14-1841 (12-15-1841) T
Wooten, Matilda to James Brooks 3-16-1861 T
Wooten, N. A. to Richard Pullin 2-4-1867 (2-15-1867) T
Wooton, Harriet L. to Charles Howell Adkins 9-11-1853 (9-13-1853) T
Wootten, Louisa Jane to James R. Ellis 3-9-1853 O
Wootten, Marthaan to Saml. B. Burge 10-20-1839 (10-24-1839) F
Wootten, Mary H. to Henry H. Skiles 8-30-1856 G
Word (Ward?), Sally to Valse Fly 2-28-1869 G B
Word, A. U. M. S. to Moses B. Hawkins 10-16-1844 G
Word, Betty N. to T. J. Flippin 2-24-1864 (2-25-1864) F
Word, Emma V. to J. V. Jones 12-11-1867 (no return) F
Word, Harriett to Ruffin Yates 2-27-1839 (2-28-1839) G
Word, Lemory to Edmund Green 9-25-1845 G
Word, Louisa to Tom McCulley 12-25-1866 (no return) F B
Word, Martha to Cornelius Word 1-13-1870 G B
Word, Mary A. E. to Elisha Bilch 2-9-1841 G
Word, Mary A. to John Fleltcher 9-26-1859 (9-27-1859) O
Word, Mary J. to Thos. Hargett 7-5-1867 (no return) Hy
Word, Minerva to J. L. Cleere 10-3-1854 (no return) F
Word, Nancy to Thos. B. Crider 1-19-1843 G
Word, Penelope to Hugh Cooper 3-22-1843 (3-23-1843) G
Word, Sarah to Isaack Alexander 9-11-1838 G
Word, Sarah to John S. Burtus 7-27-1853 (no return) F
Word, Sarah to Washington Walker 12-23-1871 (12-26-1871) Dy
Word, Sarah to William Freeman 7-30-1840 G
Word, Susan to Robert Wilson 6-21-1883 (6-29-1883) L
Word, Symantha C. to William L. Lawrence 3-9-1859 G
Wordlow, Mattie J. to W. H. Holloway 12-26-1871 (no return) Hy
Worel, N. F. to N. N. Garrison 9-15-1867 O
Worel, _____ to W. G. Garrison ?-?-1867 (with 9-1867) O
Worf, Atha to Jackson Bowls (Rowls) 2-16-1853 Sh
Work, Martha E. to W. A. Griffith 11-17-1867 Hy
Workman, Ann E. to Thomas Huggan 11-12-1854 We
Workman, Catharine to Joseph Bynum 6-26-1854 We
Workman, Eliza J. to James Piercey 4-22-1863 We
Workman, Jane to James Palmer 2-16-1855 (no return) We
Workman, Silviann to Geo. F. Pepper 6-3-1851 Sh
Worl, Mary to Thos. P. Snowden 12-24-1838 Ma
Worland, Elizabeth to W. S. Bruce 1-27-1848 Sh
Worlds, Polly Ann to William Pinon 2-17-1852 (2-18-1852) O
Worlds?, Polley to J. W. Polston 12-22-1866 (12-23-1866) Cr
Worley, Clara A. to Marmaduke Y. Harston 12-30-1845 (1-1-1846) Ma
Worley, Frances to Alfred King 3-28-1829 Ma
Worley, Margarett to John W. Williams 1-6-1851 F
Worly, Sarah to P. M. Wood 1-28-1867 (1-30-1867) O
Wormack, Sarah W. to Joseph Smith 2-25-1834 Sh
Wormack, Sarah to John S. Wyatt 4-15-1859 Hy
Wormack, Sarah to Rufus Sandford 3-10-1872 Hy
Wormelay, Catherine to D. George A. Smith 4-19-1849 Sh
Wormick, Susanna to E. Richardson 11-29-1866 T
Wormik, Sallie to James C. Rice 1-5-1872 (1-10-1872) T
Wormster, Prudence to W. G. Culver 4-25-1850 Sh
Wornick, Eliza O. to James Murphy 7-26-1872 (no return) Hy
Worrell, Eliza J. to J. M. Martin 12-26-1863 (1-17-1864) F
Worrell, Elizabeth to Halsted Butts 11-18-1850 (11-20-1850) Ma
Worrell, Emily to James Parks 10-12-1859 Cr
Worrell, H. C. to Jno. S. Renfroe 12-22-1868 (12-23-1868) F
Worrell, M. B. to R. T. Cobb 11-9-1870 (11-10-1870) F
Worrell, Margaret to James M. Martin 9-16-1854 (9-21-1854) Hr
Worrell, Mary B. to Tobias Grider 1-5?-1839 F
Worrell, Mary J. to J. C. Hill 5-14-1870 (5-15-1870) Cr
Worrell, Mary J. to James T. Thompson 2-31-1852 Ma
Worrell, Rebecca C. to B. H. Grider 1-28-1845 F
Worrell, Sallie A. to G. B. Hawkins 1-17-1866 F

Worrels, Mary to John E. Mosely 9-30-1869 (no return) Dy
Worsham, Amanda to Robert T. Key 3-25-1869 Cr
Worsham, Lavenia to Andrew Johnson 12-28-1869 (12-9?-1869) F B
Worsham, Lucy to J. J. Newsom 7-12-1860 Sh
Worsham, Mary Anne to John M. Weston 10-2-1862 Hn
Worship (Bishop?), E. A. to LaFayette Holland 12-21-1878 (12-24-1878) Dy
Wortham, A. W. to John W. Hunter 6-6-1860 Sh
Wortham, Ellen to Jack Dyson 8-28-1869 T
Wortham, F. D. to A. M. Neal 2-13-1873 Hy
Wortham, Georgiana to Peter Rucker 1-20-1879 (1-29-1879) L B
Wortham, Harriet to M. G. Fraser 2-20-1867 F
Wortham, Hursay to James S. Baker 3-26-1845 (4-1-1845) G
Wortham, Indiana to Spencer Cannon 1-10-1870 T
Wortham, Margaret E. to J. J. Edwards 1-13-1858 (1-14-1858) Sh
Wortham, Mary E. to Jackson L. Aydelotte 12-24-1851 G
Wortham, Mary H. to Emmitt E. Smith 9-13-1873 Hy
Wortham, Mary to Billy Dyer 8-9-1869 T
Wortham, Mary to Joseph Y. Gray 8-19-1840 (9-22-1840) F
Wortham, Nancy W. to Wesley G. Barker 12-13-1851 (12-14-1851) G
Worthan, Estelia to John G. Henry 2-18-1840 (2-20-1840) F
Worthen, Maryan to George Dougan 11-27-1843 F
Worthington, Wealthy to Henry A. Paschal 3-9-1839 Hn
Worthy, R. M. to William Hicks 3-20-1870 F
Worthy, Sarah A. to Anderson Burr 2-7-1854 Sh
Wrather, J. M. to M. H. Johnson 11-6-1864 G
Wray, Catherine to John P. Rodgers 6-11-1862 Sh
Wray, Centha to Tillman Johnson 7-8-1856 (no return) We
Wray, Emily E. to Samuel P. Alexander 12-23-1862 We
Wray, Frances to Andrew Jones 7-9-1870 F B
Wray, Lizzie C. to J. W. Karr 1-3-1853 (no return) F
Wray, Lizzie to Henry Richardson 3-11-1871 (3-14-1871) F B
Wray, M. A. to Wm. F. Scates 2-28-1858 Cr
Wray, M. E. to H. R. Parnell 12-19-1868 (12-20-1868) Cr
Wray, Martha C. to James C. Whyte 10-24-1840 (10-25?-1840) F
Wray, Martha to Matt Hood 12-27-1867 (12-31-1867) F B
Wray, Mary G. to James H. Murray 1-21-1846 F
Wray, Susey H. to John A. Wilson 8-3-1869 Hy
Wray, Virginia A. to J. Y. Boyd 1-1-1851 F
Wren, Abigale E. to Zachariah Greer 12-20-1851 (12-23-1851) G
Wren, Lucinda to Green B. Fields 1-2-1851 Cr
Wren, Martha A. to Thomas Fagan 12-15-1868 G
Wren, Martha Ann to J. C. Marteen 8-22-1865 Hn
Wren, Mary Emeline to John E. Ward 9-1-1869 G
Wren, S. A. to F. W. Turner 6-27-1870 (6-29-1870) Cr
Wren, Sarah A. P. to James M. Provine 10-15-1846 Sh
Wrenn, Margarett to Henry F. Cowen 7-21-1847 (7-22-1847) G
Wrenn, Mary Ann to William G. Haltom 2-19-1839 Ma
Wrenn, Sarah E. to Henry H. Brown 5-23-1842 (5-26-1842) Ma
Wrenn, Syntha A. to H. L. Hammond 6-29-1866 G
Wrens, Emily to Benjamin Arrington 11-19-1857 Hn
Wright, Ada to Daniel Chaney 12-20-1871 (12-21-1871) L B
Wright, Addie E. to George W. Hurt 12-14-1877 (12-16-1877) L
Wright, Agnes to Wm. White 7-21-1877 Hy
Wright, Almira to Erasmus Graham 3-9-1847 (not exec.) O
Wright, Alvira to Charles Bailey 5-13-1845 (5-14-1845) O
Wright, Amanda to C. T. Jones 1-7-1855 Cr
Wright, Amanda to Reuben Taylor 10-10-1868 (10-11-1868) L B
Wright, Amanda to Richard N. Lester 2-20-1839 Cr
Wright, Amanda to T. H. Brinkly 1-7-1868 (1-8-1868) Dy
Wright, Angeline C. to James A. Wright 12-5-1850 Hn
Wright, Angeline to Charles Ford 2-13-1867 Dy
Wright, Ann F. to James H. Gibson 7-15-1850 (7-23-1850) G
Wright, Anne E. to J. W. Hood 9-9-1868 G
Wright, Bettie P. to A. F. Tillery 12-21-1866 (12-23-1866) L
Wright, Bettie to Saml. Low 1-1-1868 (no return) F B
Wright, Caledonia to Alex Jordan 9-19-1885 (9-20-1885) L B
Wright, Camilla to Richardson Whitbey 12-15-1827 Sh
Wright, Candis to Gray Rodick 1-20-1840 (1-22-1840) Ma
Wright, Caroline to J. W. McCoy 2-1-1862 (2-2-1862) Sh
Wright, Catherine to John Moore 11-12-1869 T
Wright, Celia to Harry Edwards 8-4-1870 (8-11-1870) F B
Wright, Charlott to Alexander McCord 12-2-1857 (12-3-1857) L
Wright, Clementine to H. L. Lassiter 2-28-1857 (3-5-1857) Hr
Wright, Cynthia Jane to Aganza? Benton Brooks 11-27-1848 (11-30-1848) T
Wright, Docia to Joseph Maberry 9-26-1847 O
Wright, Drucilla to William Arnold 11-11-1870 (no return) L
Wright, E. E. to Columbus L. Nolen 3-9-1874 Dy
Wright, E. M. to W. R. Turney 12-11-1866 O
Wright, Easter to Jarrett Bell 10-15-1845 (10-16-1845) O
Wright, Edline to James M. Henderson 9-19-1838 Ma
Wright, Elisabeth to Robt. H. Drappin 7-17-1856 T
Wright, Eliza Anne to James B. Murry 6-16-1842 Sh
Wright, Eliza to James McCain 3-16-1864 Sh
Wright, Eliza to N. J. H. Parr 1-25-1865 G
Wright, Elizabeth A. to Prichard Cowser? 3-25-1843 T
Wright, Elizabeth A. to S. K. Drummonds 2-22-1871 (2-23-1871) T
Wright, Elizabeth to Hiram Piles 12-30-1833 (1-3?-1834) Hr

Wright, Elizabeth to James E. Turbeville 2-10-1859 Hn
Wright, Elizabeth to John Crews 10-31-1832 (11-1-1832) Hr
Wright, Elizabeth to Lewis Swinny 12-25-1852 (no return) F
Wright, Elizabeth to Reuben McWhorter 12-13-1832 O
Wright, Elizabeth to Samuel Green 3-13-1859 Hn
Wright, Elizath. A. to William H. Yancy 12-21-1867 (12-22-1867) T
Wright, Ellen to Shade Bostick 12-27-1882 (12-28-1882) L
Wright, Elmira to James Cary 12-8-1849 (12-12-1849) O
Wright, Emily M. to Robt. B. Dixon 9-?-1850 Cr
Wright, Emma to John Whaling (Whiting?) 4-6-1869 (4-9-1869) L
Wright, Etta to John G. Owen 1-7-1877 Hy
Wright, Fanny C. to J. T. Latimer 10-17-1867 Be
Wright, Fanny to Aaron Ford 2-14-1880 (2-18-1880) L
Wright, Frances to Green S. McNabb 5-27-1854 Hn
Wright, Francis to Green Campbell 12-20-1875 L B
Wright, George Anna to Thomas Morrow 4-15-1869 F B
Wright, Hannah to John White 7-27-1877 (no return) L B
Wright, Harinah J. to Francis M. Stoker 10-12-1856 Cr
Wright, Harriett to Sim Barham 8-5-1873 (8-6-1873) Cr B
Wright, Hassie A. to Ed. G. Anderson 12-30-1879 (1-1-1880) L
Wright, Henrietta to Peter Lightfoot 11-29-1864 Sh B
Wright, Hester to John Greenberry 10-7-1867 (no return) F B
Wright, Hettie to Alf Nelson 2-3-1881 L B
Wright, Indiana to Jesse M. Soward 1-23-1850 L
Wright, Irene O. to J. D. Wall 12-20-1866 O
Wright, Jane to David Davis 11-30-1867 G B
Wright, Jane to Henry Wipper 3-21-1849 Sh
Wright, Jennie T. to Saml. S. Craig 3-13-1862 T
Wright, Jennie to James W. Whitten 6-16-1874 (no return) Dy
Wright, Jessie L. (Mrs.) to Wm. N. Walker 6-20-1863 (6-28-1863) Sh
Wright, Jobie A. to Benjamin A. Williams 6-26-1861 (6-27-1861) Cr
Wright, Julia Ann to James W. Smith 11-30-1844 (no return) F
Wright, Julia Ann to Lee Pickard 8-20-1849 O
Wright, Julia Ann to Lee Pickard 8-28-1847 O
Wright, Julia Ann to Thos. Gingry 1-27-1867 (no return) L B
Wright, Julia ann to Andrew J. Gillespie 2-12-1844 (2-13-1844) F
Wright, Juliana to Saml. Hamerick 3-13-1847 (3-16-1847) F
Wright, L. J. to P. L. Dozier 7-30-1864 O
Wright, L. M. to John W. Dickerson 6-25-1855 (7-4-1855) G
Wright, Laura to John J. Rayder 4-14-1863 G
Wright, Lavicey to Almon Cayce 9-24-1855 (10-4-1855) O
Wright, Lavinia to George McNairy 8-8-1879 (8-10-1879) L B
Wright, Leana to Nathan Hares 1-4-1854 Sh
Wright, Leander to Thomas Kirk 1-13-1855 Sh
Wright, Leonia W. to Charles A. Hurt 2-27-1884 L
Wright, Lola to J. M. Klyce 12-22-1884 (12-23-1884) L
Wright, Louisa C. to John H. Hudson 1-31-1848 (2-3-1848) Ma
Wright, Louisa to John C. Lewis 1-1-1846 Hn
Wright, Lucinda to Jordan Weathers 2-23-1874 T
Wright, Lucy Ann to Edwin H. Hinton 1-26-1842 (1-27-1842) L
Wright, M. A. to J. S. Johnson 12-28-1864 O
Wright, M. N. to R. N. Enocks 12-17-1872 Cr
Wright, Maggie to John H. Blackwell 1-19-1873 Hy
Wright, Margaret A. to Joseph Elliot 9-2-1849 Sh
Wright, Margaret J. to Richard H. Browning 3-18-1861 (3-20-1861) L
Wright, Margaret to David H. McQuistin 4-8-1843 (4-11-1843) T
Wright, Margaret to Lawson Lane 1-26-1870 T
Wright, Margaret to Patrick Doyle 3-15-1859 Sh
Wright, Margarette to A. B. Flowers 7-30-1862 G
Wright, Margret J. to John H. Brooks 1-28-1858 Sh
Wright, Martha A. to Harry S. Physick 1-19-1863 Sh
Wright, Martha A. to John P. Doherty 9-15-1853 Cr
Wright, Martha A. to Robert C. Moore 1-21-1847 Hn
Wright, Martha D. to William R. Wicker 5-22-1861 Sh
Wright, Martha P. to Isaac M. Miller 7-25-1855 (7-26-1855) T
Wright, Martha T. to Jackson Montgomery 10-6-1838 (10-8-1838) F
Wright, Martha to Calvin Adkinson 6-13-1868 (6-14-1868) O
Wright, Martha to David Morse 5-28-1857 Hn
Wright, Martha to Lytle Newton 1-7-1858 Ma
Wright, Martha to Samuel Young 1-18-1877 L B
Wright, Mary A. E. to Leoma Flowers 10-5-1842 (10-6-1842) G
Wright, Mary A. E. to William C. Nored 2-28-1856 (no return) Hn
Wright, Mary A. H. to Ezekiel Smith Williams 1-29-1855 (1-31-1855) T
Wright, Mary E. to David A. Williams 12-16-1845 (12-17-1845) L
Wright, Mary E. to James C. Hastings 2-26-1863 Hn
Wright, Mary E. to P. N. Brewer 10-25-1855 Be
Wright, Mary E. to Wm. G. Vaugh 3-28-1855 Cr
Wright, Mary Elizabeth to Franklin H. Edwards 12-7-1853 O
Wright, Mary F. to F. T. Hafford 6-18-1864 (6-19-1864) L
Wright, Mary J. to J. E. Blankenship 11-28-1871 (12-20-1871) Dy
Wright, Mary Jane to J. B. D. Speer 2-4-1857 (2-5-1857) Sh
Wright, Mary Jane to Stephen S. Howard 12-9-1863 (no return) Dy
Wright, Mary S. to Wm. P. Fletcher 1-26-1843 Cr
Wright, Mary to George Williamson 2-20-1869 (no return) F B
Wright, Mary to Isaac S. Hill 6-10-1867 (6-11-1867) T
Wright, Mary to Leroy Hall 6-21-1876 Hy
Wright, Matilda J. to William Orterbridge 12-19-1873 (12-20-1873) L B

Wright, Matilda to Monroe Bumphass 2-16-1874 (2-24-1874) T
Wright, Matilda to Samuel Stailey 8-16-1850 Sh
Wright, Mattie A. to J. B. Christian 11-6-1866 G
Wright, Milla (Mrs.) to A. Wilber (Milber?) 1-1-1863 Sh
Wright, Mollie L. to S. A. Heddin 10-5-1869 (no return) Dy
Wright, N. J. R. to A. M. Mayfield 3-13-1857 Sh
Wright, Nancy A. to Isaac M. Malone 8-31-1858 Cr
Wright, Nancy A. to Jas. A. Marshall 1-9-1860 (1-10-1860) O
Wright, Nancy Ann to John Thompson 10-11-1853 (10-13-1853) G
Wright, Nancy Ann to Wm. Turfim 2-17-1863 (2-18-1863) Dy
Wright, Nancy C. to Samuel K. Horning? 9-21-1842 T
Wright, Nancy J. to John Bonds 1-13-1852 Cr
Wright, Nancy M. to Banyan Tayne? 7-22-1841 T
Wright, Nancy to Coleman Wicker 1-2-1841 Hn
Wright, Nancy to Elisha Diggs 6-28-1848 Hn
Wright, Nellie A. to C. G. Alexander 12-5-1865 Hn
Wright, Permelia A. to J. O. C. Watkins 9-22-1856 (no return) L
Wright, Precilla to Thomas Burris 3-5-1825 (3-6-1825) Hr
Wright, Puss to John Allen 3-19-1870 (4-16-1870) F B
Wright, R. F. to Jno. A. Burrow 10-3-1860 G
Wright, Rebecca Ann to James C. Pickett 11-28-1864 Sh
Wright, Rebecca to F. W. Schmidt 7-8-1861 Sh
Wright, Rebecca to J. M. Lauderdale 5-4-1869 Dy
Wright, Rebecca to James C. Parnell 4-12-1873 (4-13-1873) Dy
Wright, Rebecca to W. T. Trusty 2-7-1872 (no return) Dy
Wright, Rebecca to Wm. H. Vandergrift 3-14-1861 Sh
Wright, Ruth M. to Abner M. Wall 1-23-1840 (1-25-1840) O
Wright, Rutha C. to William C. Cunningham 9-12-1844 G
Wright, Sallie to Anderson Campbell 8-17-1881 (8-18-1881) L
Wright, Sarah A. to John Potts 12-24-1850 (no return) Hn
Wright, Sarah A. to Samuel Howard 12-29-1868 (12-30-1868) F B
Wright, Sarah E. to John H. D. _____ 7-4-1858 Hn
Wright, Sarah J. to A. H. Kirk 10-3-1867 Dy
Wright, Sarah J. to William H. Holaman 11-20-1843 (11-26-1843) G
Wright, Sarah J. to William H. Holamon 11-20-1843 G
Wright, Sarah to B. Turbeville 5-19-1852 Hn
Wright, Sarah to David I. May 1-15-1843 Cr
Wright, Sarah to Edward Wright 2-20-1875 (2-21-1875) L
Wright, Sarah to Henry Larrison 10-20-1885 (10-21-1885) L
Wright, Sarah to James H. Somerow 11-26-1849 (11-28-1849) L
Wright, Sarah to John M. Sharp 9-1-1849 (9-2-1849) O
Wright, Sarah to John White 6-9-1833 Hn
Wright, Sarah to Vance Huffman 3-26-1857 (3-27-1857) Hr
Wright, Sarah to Wm. S. Tyer 3-11-1857 Sh
Wright, Senia to Henry Evans 2-25-1868 (no return) Dy
Wright, Susan A. to Henry Floyd 12-23-1854 (12-24-1854) Sh
Wright, Susan L. to John A. Floyd 10-12-1861 (10-20-1861) Dy
Wright, T. C. to Wyatt Nicholson 12-3-1847 (12-15-1847) F
Wright, T. J. to J. F. Clendenin 12-20-1865 Hn
Wright, Tennessee to J. M. Gleaves 12-21-1876 Dy
Wright, Theodocia M. to Joseph M. Davis 12-19-1839 O
Wright, Valiria M. to Lucion B. Gilchrist 1-26-1848 G
Wright, Virginia A. to Thomas J. Holcomb 1-22-1862 G
Wright, Virginia to Henry Darnel 9-4-1834 O
Wright, W. S. to M. Beram 3-9-1847 (3-14-1847) O
Wright, Winney to John Cooper 8-28-1833 Hr
Wright, Zada P. to William G. Crank 12-17-1846 (12-19-1846) L
Wrightout, Ann to Manuel Brown 9-25-1875 (no return) Hy
Wrightsell, Dean? to James M. Morris 3-24-1842 F
Wrightsell, Sarah to William H. Parkes 11-9-1841 (11-11-1841) F
Wrigs, A. W. to Samuel B. Gibson 11-2-1841 Sh
Wrinkle, Nancy J. to J. W. Beck 12-8-1865 Mn
Wunderlich, Margrett to Fredrick Hoffman 10-11-1862 Sh
Wyant, Ann to N. S. Bruce 12-31-1851 (1-1-1852) Sh
Wyant, Margaret to Samuel C. Mount 6-23-1852 Sh
Wyant, Oran to Joel Akin 12-5-1842 Sh
Wyatt, Adaline to George McCutcheon 10-10-1869 G B
Wyatt, Agness to H. M. Crisap 11-13-1873 O
Wyatt, Amanda to Green Prichard 11-29-1877 Dy
Wyatt, Ann to Thomas Wilson 3-4-1869 Be
Wyatt, Bettie A. to Gabriel Ehrhard 12-15-1871 (no return) L
Wyatt, Dorcas to John Mitchell 9-12-1858 We
Wyatt, Elizabeth H. to Jacob T. Grier 1-26-1842 (1-27-1842) G
Wyatt, Elizabeth to Columbus C. Huzza 10-14-1858 O
Wyatt, Ellen to John Overall 10-6-1870 G
Wyatt, Emily to George McCulloch 12-30-1868 G B
Wyatt, Fannie to Alex Jones 1-2-1872 Hy
Wyatt, Frances J. to C. H. Crossno 10-22-1863 Be
Wyatt, Jane to Allen Moody 4-26-1843 O
Wyatt, Joanna to Martin Fowlks 8-28-1879 Dy
Wyatt, L. O. to H. A. Dunlap 11-1-1871 Hy
Wyatt, Laura to Jerry Prichard 4-2-1877 (4-5-1877) Dy
Wyatt, Lecia to James Bobbett 2-7-1854 G
Wyatt, Lucinda to Wm. A. Stagner 12-22-1853 Be
Wyatt, Lucy A. to Robert M. Anderson 8-18-1849 Sh
Wyatt, Lydie A. to Felix H. Brackens 7-16-1869 (7-17-1869) Cr
Wyatt, M. E. to W. W. Pride 12-21-1867 O

Wyatt, Margaret A. to Francis M. Stoker 10-31-1857 Cr
Wyatt, Margaret to Abram Fowler 12-25-1856 Sh
Wyatt, Margaret to Jack Moore 4-6-1880 (4-8-1880) Dy
Wyatt, Margaret to Robt. Jackson 8-27-1839 Be
Wyatt, Martha W. to Lewis C. Crenshaw 10-13-1852 (10-14-1852) G
Wyatt, Mary E. to Samuel Ferrell 9-17-1851 G
Wyatt, Mary to Lorenza D. Cash 4-4-1843 (4-6-1843) Ma
Wyatt, Matilda to Henderson Hay 11-15-1877 Hy
Wyatt, Nancy to Henry McNail 8-1-1869 G B
Wyatt, Nancy to John Bailey 12-29-1868 G B
Wyatt, S. A. R. to L. F. Bogle 1-31-1862 G
Wyatt, S. C. to R. H. White 11-28-1870 (11-30-1870) Cr
Wyatt, Susan to Henry Barns 4-19-1838 Cr
Wyblood (Hyblood), Temperance to Wiley Harding 9-12-1837 Sh
Wycoff, Lydia to Daniel Muntz 1-7-1825 Hr
Wyett, Becky to Tom Wynne 12-24-1867 (12-26-1867) Dy
Wyett, Mary to John J. Morris 2-16-1853 Cr
Wyett, Mary to W. C. Dorris 9-27-1858 (9-28-1858) O
Wyett, Mary to Wm. H. Dickie 9-14-1856 Cr
Wygal, Elizabeth C. to J. H. Hudson 3-11-1868 Be
Wygul, Mary M. to W. H. Hudson 12-27-1864 Be
Wyles, Margarett to James Wilson 8-21-1833 (8-22-1833) O
Wyley, Terrissa M. to Wiley F. Blackard 12-22-1855 (12-24-1855) Ma
Wylie, M. J. to W. M. Patric 7-30-1861 G
Wylie, Martha to Wm. A. Clark 9-28-1868 F
Wylie, Mary E. to Abner J. Hanner 1-3-1857 T
Wylie, Mary Isabella to Elbert S. Maloney 9-24-1855 (10-8-1855) O
Wyly, Ader to James P. Thomason 12-17-1867 Be
Wyly, Artimissa to F. P. Saunders 1-6-1845 Be
Wyly, Camilee to Sanmartin Barnett 5-31-1850 Be
Wyly, Cinda to Ambrose Clark 2-26-1867 Be
Wyly, Eliza to Geo. W. Reaves 10-7-1847 Be
Wyly, Joly to Oliver Tolls 2-28-1869 Be
Wyly, Lua to Horace Lashlee 9-15-1867 Be
Wyly, Martha to Henry Spearman 2-25-1867 Be
Wymmer, Elizabeth to Ham Caney 4-24-1860 Sh
Wynn, C. C. to George W. Jackson 8-3-1853 Hn
Wynn, Elizabeth to Isaac L. Shelly 2-20-1847 O
Wynn, Elizabeth to Josiah Bone 8-18-1849 (8-21-1849) O
Wynn, Elizabeth to Will Boyd 12-22-1841 Hn
Wynn, Elizabeth to William J. Jackson 3-1-1849 Hn
Wynn, Elizabeth to Willis H. Lane 9-3-1847 O
Wynn, Frances E. to T. T., jr. Goldsby 12-12-1849 Sh
Wynn, Isabella to Lewis C. Parish 6-5-1848 (6-11-1848) O
Wynn, Jane to Thomas Stewart 9-25-1827 Ma
Wynn, Jemima to Wiliston Parker 9-3-1847 O
Wynn, June to Thomas Jackson 11-14-1850 Hn
Wynn, Lizzie C. to Otis H. Holeman 9-15-1857 Sh
Wynn, M. to George W. Chilcutt 7-8-1847 Hn
Wynn, Martha Ann to John S. Lilley 2-9-1855 (2-13-1855) O
Wynn, Martha C. to William Edwards 7-21-1846 (7-23-1846) G
Wynn, Martha to James Kendall 10-1-1856 Hn
Wynn, Nancy Su. Mah. Eliz. to Jacob Casey 9-8-1867 Be
Wynn, Polly to William Williams 3-7-1855 (3-8-1855) O
Wynn, Roxalina to D_____ Lindsey 1-25-1857 Be
Wynn, S. E. to Joseph N. Travis 10-28-1863 Hn
Wynn, Sally to James Nored 1-24-1867 Hn
Wynn, Susan to William Henly 5-27-1847 O
Wynne, Angaline to Sam Pierce 3-30-1867 (4-1-1867) Dy
Wynne, Angeline to Edmond Enochs 8-19-1870 (no return) Dy
Wynne, Angeline to Pharaoh Starks 12-23-1879 Dy
Wynne, Anna to W. H. Douglas 11-20-1861 Sh
Wynne, Bettie to John Turner 8-21-1878 (8-28-1878) Dy
Wynne, Clarissa to Allen Johnson 1-4-1873 (no return) Dy
Wynne, Ella to Amos Grimm 1-3-1874 Dy
Wynne, Emaline to John T. Whitson 4-4-1861 Dy
Wynne, Frances to Miller McKennie 5-20-1876 Dy
Wynne, Frances to Thomas Powell 1-8-1880 Dy
Wynne, Harriet J. to Jno. A. (Dr.) Williams 3-27-1877 (no return) Dy
Wynne, Henrietta to William Galloway 7-14-1864 Sh
Wynne, Jane M. to Samuel Henshaw 7-20-1857 (7-21-1857) Sh
Wynne, Jane to Jeff Wynne 12-26-1867 (no return) Dy
Wynne, L. M. to P. J. Flack 12-17-1872 Dy
Wynne, Louella to George Sinclair 2-11-1874 (2-12-1874) Dy
Wynne, Louisa to Jo Hicks 3-2-1867 Dy
Wynne, Lutitia to Charley Ruff 10-13-1866 (no return) Dy
Wynne, Missouri A. to John B. Downing 12-23-1857 (12-24-1857) Sh
Wynne, Nancy to Thomas Box 2-21-1866 O
Wynne, Pricilla P. to J. M. Bond 11-28-1853 (11-29-1853) Sh
Wynne, Rebecca W. to Stith L. Wynne 12-23-1851 Sh
Wynne, Susan to Bob Clark 1-2-1879 Dy
Wynne, Tabitha G. to Wm. A. Cathron 2-20-1840 Sh
Wynns, Adaline to Richard B. Sturdivant 10-14-1846 Hn
Wynns, Martha Ann to John F. Upchurch 2-14-1855 Hn
Wyrick, Amanda to James Johnson 12-4-1875 Dy
Wyse, Alice to Sam Dean 1-13-1871 (no return) Hy
Wyse, E. J. (Mrs.) to E. White 1-26-1870 Hy

Wyson, Frances to William C. Scrape 10-24-1844 G
Wytt, Caroline to John C. Turner 2-10-1839 Cr
Wzant, Hattie to Joseph Tagg 11-1-1858 (11-17-1858) Sh
Yancey, Alice to William Rutledge 12-9-1885 (12-12-1885) L
Yancey, Amanda W. to J. J. Clark 11-19-1855 (11-22-1855) G
Yancey, Belle Emma to Hiram Parker 12-18-1868 F B
Yancey, Catharine G. to George A. Lipscomb 9-4-1847 (no return) F
Yancey, Catherine to John Wiley 8-17-1866 (no return) F B
Yancey, Charlotte to Harris Chaffin 12-28-1868 F B
Yancey, Elvie G. to A. W. Howell 10-1-1878 (10-2-1878) Dy
Yancey, Harriet to John Moon 4-20-1866 G
Yancey, Isabella R. to Geo. R. Witt 9-1-1846 F
Yancey, Jane to Mills Elam 5-16-1870 G B
Yancey, Lissa to Joe Yancey 12-18-1868 (1-9-1869) F B
Yancey, Lizzie J. to Wm. H. Allen 5-14-1866 (5-15-1866) F
Yancey, Martha C. to Newton C. Patton 6-23-1848 G
Yancey, Martha to Burrell Wise 12-27-1831 (12-25?-1831) Hr
Yancey, P. T. to W. F. Chambliss 11-27-1866 F
Yancey, Sue to Anthony Wills 12-24-1867 Hy
Yancey, Susan M. to Joel A. Light 9-21-1852 (9-26-1852) G
Yancy, Analiza to Thomas S. Black 3-6-1852 (no return) F
Yancy, Ann to John Higgins 1-25-1873 Hy
Yancy, Betsy to Green Jordan 1-31-1870 G B
Yancy, Bettie to Z. W. Heath 1-26-1869 (1-27-1869) F
Yancy, E. L. to E. E. Jordan 10-1-1879 (10-2-1879) L
Yancy, Elizabeth F. to George W. Sanders 8-11-1843 Sh
Yancy, Elizabeth W. to James S. Wood 2-12-1849 (2-13-1849) G
Yancy, Elvira J. to William A. Pledge 10-27-1849 (11-1-1849) F
Yancy, Fannie to Lafayett Leechman 10-22-1871 Hy
Yancy, L. D. to J. B. Moore 2-5-1868 (1?-11-1868) Cr
Yancy, Louisa E. V. to Thomas M. Broom 3-20-1860 (3-22-1860) F
Yancy, M. E. to W. S. Moore 10-29-1868 G
Yancy, Margaret to Daniel Lemons 11-5-1860 (no return) Hy
Yancy, Martha to Bob Hafford 12-19-1878 Hy
Yancy, Mary A. to George R. Witt 2-10-1841 (2-11-1841) F
Yancy, Mary M. to J. A. Stanfield 12-12-1881 (12-15-1881) L
Yancy, Matilda to Charles Woodson 4-20-1870 G
Yancy, Mattie V. to Jno. H. Gates 12-2-1867 (12-6-1867) F
Yancy, Mollie to Joe Bond 12-2-1871 Hy
Yancy, Mollie to Lee Bradford 12-5-1878 Hy
Yancy, Nancy to B. M. Williamson 12-13-1860 Hy
Yancy, Queen to Henry Keel 1-8-1876 (no return) Hy
Yancy, Sally to Dock Washington 8-22-1868 Hy
Yancy, Sarah A. to Walker Taliaferro 3-28-1843 G
Yancy, Sarah to James Henry 3-10-1846 Sh
Yancy, Susan to Bennet Ragan 4-17-1838 (4-19-1838) G
Yandell, Mariah to Chas. B. Talley 10-3-1869 G B
Yandell, N. E. to A. G. McCarmond 6-16-1870 G
Yanike, Augusta to John P. Albert 7-28-1855 Sh
Yant, M. A. to Franklin Brownlow 8-17-1876 (8-20-1876) O
Yarber, J. to W. Bell 1-12-1842 Be
Yarborough, Marthaann to Thos. Williams 12-24-1839 (no return) F
Yarbory, Nancy to Minor M. Winn 3-15-1846 G
Yarbro, Amanda to Coleman Hall 10-15-1873 (10-16-1873) T
Yarbro, Amanda to Gobe Wilson 8-11-1874 (8-12-1874) T
Yarbro, Ann Liza to Frank Fortune 11-21-1867 T
Yarbro, Ann to Henry Millen 11-19-1868 T
Yarbro, Anna to F. F. Davis 7-15-1874 T
Yarbro, Anna to Wm. Wright 5-7-1873 T
Yarbro, Caroline to Lippman jr. Howsar 8-27-1867 (8-29-1867) T
Yarbro, Charletta to Saml. Strong 12-11-1867 T
Yarbro, Charlotte to Zack Williams 4-18-1873 (4-13?-1873) T
Yarbro, Elizabeth to S. H. Brown 6-5-1856 T
Yarbro, Freesave? to Granderson Bledsoe 3-10-1873 (3-11-1873) T
Yarbro, Louisa to Washington Goodram 11-20-1867 (11-21-1867) T
Yarbro, M. B. to G. T. Smith 11-19-1872 (11-20-1872) T
Yarbro, M. J. to W. A. Max 8-19-1868 (8-26-1868) T
Yarbro, Mary E. to James L. Ayers 5-12-1858 T
Yarbro, Mary to George W. Walton 6-8-1870 (6-9-1870) T
Yarbro, Mary to Isaac Payne 4-17-1869 (6-9-1869) T
Yarbro, Sophronia to James K. Kinney 1-24-1861 T
Yarbro, Susan to Lymas Lauderdale 12-18-1872 T
Yarbroh, Harriet E. to Jas. M> Smith 2-7-1864 T
Yarbroh, Mary to Pompey Calhoun 9-29-1866 (10-29-1866) T
Yarbroh, R. V. to John W. Morton 3-21-1865 (3-22-1865) T
Yarbroh, R. V. to John W. Moton 3-21-1865 T
Yarbroh, Sallie J. to James W. Upchurch 2-18-1861 T
Yarbrok, Catharine to Robert W. Warmouth 2-3-1858 (2-4-1858) T
Yarbrough, Arlesa to Samuel H. Justice 3-16-1853 (3-17-1853) Hr
Yarbrough, Arlesia to Nathan Parlow 8-15-1870 (8-18-1870) Ma
Yarbrough, Elizabeth J. to Edward Willoughby 6-15-1854 (6-22-1854) Hr
Yarbrough, Elizabeth M. J. to James W. Thompson 12-28-1850 (1-2-1851) G
Yarbrough, Elizabeth M. to David H. Pipkin 9-28-1853 (9-29-1853) Hr
Yarbrough, Elizabeth to James Taylor 5-23-1848 Be
Yarbrough, Elizabeth to Joel S. Raines 8-27-1832 Hr
Yarbrough, Ellen to William Clayton 2-3-1871 F B

Yarbrough, Eurilda to Lafayette Young 11-22-1860 Hn
Yarbrough, Hessie to Jas. L. Butler 2-27-1868 G
Yarbrough, Jane to George R. Rains 1-5-1836 Hr
Yarbrough, Lissa to Jesse Scroggins 3-6-1835 (3-11-1835) Hr
Yarbrough, Martha Mahalda to James R. Butts 8-23-1870 (8-25-1870) Ma
Yarbrough, Martha to Bradford Baggett 1-11-1882 L
Yarbrough, Martha to William Wiley 10-1-1853 (10-3-1853) Sh
Yarbrough, Mary E. to Augustus W. Smith 9-29-1845 (10-2-1845) T
Yarbrough, Mary to Jacob Atcheson 1-5-1840 (no return) Hn
Yarbrough, Mary to Nathan Baxter 8-31-1850 Cr
Yarbrough, Meranda to Marcellas Knott 3-17-1860 Hr
Yarbrough, Parella to Regis Jarvis 1-5-1836 Hr
Yarbrough, Rebecca A. to James Davis 2-11-1852 G
Yarbrough, Rebecca A. to James M. Armstrong 3-15-1849 G
Yarbrough, Ruthy Jane to Littleberry S. Swaggart 1-17-1842 (no return) F
Yarbrough, Sallie to Simon A. Collins 9-12-1870 Ma
Yarbrough, Temperance to David Kizer 2-9-1848 Cr
Yarbrough, Tempie A. to Paul T. Harris 11-12-1866 (11-15-1866) Ma
Yarbrough, Wincy to Elijah Lowery 7-18-1839 Hn
Yarbroy?, Betsy to Jarvis Sweeton 2-2-1836 Hr
Yarington, Sallie to Eli A. Moody 12-10-1870 (12-11-1870) Dy
Yates, Arcisa to T. E. Crider 9-11-1860 G
Yates, C. M. I. to R. A. Medards 9-24-1860 (10-2-1861?) G
Yates, Donie to J. R. Jackson 10-3-1870 (no return) Dy
Yates, Elizabeth A. to John W. Pritchett 1-6-1859 Hn
Yates, Elizabeth to Henry Cook 10-19-1849 (11-8-1849) G
Yates, Elizabeth to William H. Brooks 10-13-1846 Hn
Yates, Emily to John Tedder 1-13-1864 Be
Yates, G. A. to Junius Tomlinson 2-5-1868 F
Yates, Jestina to Daniel E. Jetton 7-22-1841 G
Yates, Lavenia V. to Samuel A. Winstead 12-20-1861 (not endorsed) We
Yates, Louisa B. to David C. Green 11-14-1866 (11-15-1866) O
Yates, Mahala to Isaac Canaday 12-22-1847 (12-23-1847) G
Yates, Martha to Braxter Carter 12-29-1856 (12-30-1856) Sh
Yates, Mary Adaline to Charly Bell 11-17-1852 Be
Yates, Mary Jane to James Powers 2-23-1859 Hn
Yates, Mary to Samuel J. Crider 2-28-1835 (2-29?-1835) G
Yates, Mary to William H. Compton 5-21-1860 (no return) Hn
Yates, Monian to Julian Tarver 12-17-1867 (12-18-1867) Ma
Yates, Nancy to Abner Allen 1-4-1864 (1-5-1864) O
Yates, Partilla to James Canada 1-10-1849 (1-11-1849) G
Yates, S. A. J. to W. L.(S.?) Reagan 10-2-1860 G
Yates, Sally to Frederick W. Deater 3-14-1839 (no return) Hn
Yates, Sarah to James Thompson 2-22-1845 (2-23-1845) G
Yates, Sarah to Thos. E. Edwards 9-26-1852 Hn
Yates, Sarrah A. to J. A. Peel 3-19-1866 G
Yates, Sobina to John W. Moore 10-29-1835 (10-29-1835) G
Yates, Washington Ann to William R. Marchbanks 10-3-1854 Be
Yeargain, Nancy A. to Benj. F. Brock 12-31-1852 (1-2-1853) G
Yeargain, Sarah M. to Henry C. Pittman 12-8-1852 (12-9-1852) G
Yeargan, Emeline to John R. Reynolds 7-31-1870 G
Yearger, Mary to Jacob Katzenmeier 5-31-1847 Be
Yearwod, Katie to J. P. Jones 5-1-1869 (5-4-1869) Dy
Yearwood, Amanda A. to Leomiao Caseldine 2-12-1863 Mn
Yearwood, Mary E. to J. M. Douglass 12-19-1867 Hy
Yeary, Anny to John Campbell 7-10-1828 (4-6-1829) Hr
Yeary?, Cassandria to Leroy Montgomery 1-30-1827 Hr
Yeates, Caroline to Simpson L. Marler 3-4-1841 F
Yeates, Elizabeth to Benjamin L. Coleman 11-14-1853 (11-17-1853) O
Yeates, Frances M. to James G. Tinsley 8-7-1852 (8-12-1852) G
Yeates, Jenette to A. Layfett Briles 1-3-1859 (1-4-1859) Sh
Yeates, Joanah to Clemments Moody 9-13-1849 Be
Yeates, Parolle to Andrew Bell 10-21-1852 G
Yeates, Salitha E. to David Thompson 8-2-1849 Be
Yeats, Mary Semantha to Henry J. Dowland 11-21-1870 G
Yelverton, Dicy to Sanford Norman 10-20-1868 (no return) Hy
Yelverton, Nannie J. to Charles B. Lovelace 11-14-1877 Hy
Yelvington, Margaret to B. F. Marbury 9-20-1868 Hy
Yerger, Mary M. to Arthur Rucks 10-27-1851 (10-28-1851) Sh
Yergon, Amalia to M. D. Blay 7-1-1840 Cr
Yerout, Margarett to Clark L. Stone 2-15-1842 Ma
Yewing(Ewing), Melinda to Robert Jones 4-2-1827 (4-5-1827) Hr
Yoakum, Ellen to Edward E. Black 11-17-1840 Sh
Yoiung, Sarah S. to Lewis Pemberton 11-6-1849 Hn
Yokum, Mary C. to G. W. Yopp 12-2-1859 Hn
Yong, Louvinia to Henry Ward 9-22-1869 (9-23-1869) L B
Yonger, Mary A. to G. W. Nowlin 1-5-1867 (no return) Cr
Yopp, Martha Jane to Dugan Park 10-26-1858 (11-3-1858) Hr
Yopp, Mary C. to Saml. B. Rogers 2-4-1861 (2-7-1861) Hr
York, Eliza Jane to John T. Buchanan 8-22-1866 (8-26-1866) Ma
York, Elizabeth to Callin Hays 12-25-1847 (12-28-1847) Ma
York, Elizabeth to Henry P. Thompson 12-14-1841 Sh
York, Elizabeth to William Cribbs 10-1-1830 G
York, Loset M. to Thomas Black 2-21-1843 Ma
York, Mahilda G. to Robert P. Dunnway 12-28-1847 (12-30-1847) Ma
York, Martha Ann to Edgar Harper 10-29-1872 (10-30-1872) L
York, Martha to Mathew Quinn 1-2-1841 G

York, Mary C. E. to Ephraim J. Lee 6-1-1858 Ma
York, Mary E. to John Lowrey 2-27-1875 (2-28-1875) L
York, Mary Jane to Isaac C. Stephen 10-29-1839 Ma
York, Mary to F. M. Stroud 2-25-1864 (2-30-1864) Sh
York, Mary to Robert Hutchins 8-6-1868 Cr
York, Nancy Ann to Silas Johnson 12-21-1852 (12-25-1852) Sh
York, Nancy J. to J. P. Irby 1-16-1871 (no return) F
York, Rhody to Robert Smith 5-9-1855 (12-9-1855) L
You, Nancy to Thomas H. Kellow 1-20-1875 (1-21-1875) Dy
Youchman, Permelia J. to Daniel St. John 8-15-1838 (8-16-1838) O
Young, Abigail to Jacob Sulivan 9-1-1850 Hr
Young, Adaline to Thomas Stephens 8-2-1861 We
Young, Adeline to John Redditt 1-9-1839 Sh
Young, Ailsey to Wesley Eison 1-8-1880 L
Young, Alice to George Johnson 11-12-1874 L B
Young, Amanda A. to Jonathan A. Robinson 11-13-1845 Cr
Young, Amanda to B. Harris 1-29-1886 (1-31-1886) L
Young, Amanda to Henry C. Davis 8-20-1860 We
Young, Amanda to Wash Conner 12-26-1866 (12-27-1866) F B
Young, Amelia to Henry Merriwether 5-2-1868 Hy
Young, Amelia to William Faxon 1-2-1874 Hy
Young, Ann A. to David T. Butler 6-18-1852 (6-23-1852) Hr
Young, Ann to Charles Harris 1-22-1870 (2-13-1870) Cr
Young, Annie Sophia (Miss) to Wm. R. Armstrong 3-14-1858 Sh
Young, Annie to Jo Mitchell 11-23-1878 (11-24-1878) L
Young, Annie to Saml. Brooks 1-23-1860 Sh
Young, Arcada to George C. Nicholson 10-23-1835 Sh
Young, Bethena to H. C. Buckhanon 9-10-1846 We
Young, Caldona to Moses Whitelaw 12-13-1876 (12-14-1876) Hr
Young, Caldonia to John Nelson 2-5-1866 Hy
Young, Callie to Soloman Bailey 12-27-1877 Hy
Young, Catharine P. to Saml. Tate 3-10-1852 We
Young, Catharine to Jefferson Lacewell 12-24-1858 (12-26-1858) O
Young, Catharine to John Marx 11-21-1859 Sh
Young, Celia Ann (Mrs.) to Patrick Miles 6-9-1868 G
Young, Clarissa to Charles W. Williams 12-16-1835 (12-17-1835) G
Young, Clarissa to Charles W. Williams 12-16-1836 G
Young, D. E. to H. D. C. Baker 9-9-1867 (9-11-1867) T
Young, Deena to William Lowery 11-26-1856 We
Young, Delor? to Lawson Eison 1-22-1874 L
Young, Drucinda E. to Richard S. Pitts 12-18-1855 Ma
Young, E. C. to John W. Harris 4-3-1871 (5-2-1871) F
Young, E. R. to David A. Nunn 9-29-1873 (9-30-1873) L
Young, Elisabeth M. to William W. Greenway 5-2-1848 F
Young, Elisabeth to Lemuel Jones 8-6-1846 We
Young, Eliza to Edmond Parr 12-23-1867 (12-26-1868?) L B
Young, Eliza to Jno. T. Fowler 2-28-1871 Ma
Young, Eliza to Norah Center 7-27-1873 Hy
Young, Elizabeth J. to William P. Best 1-21-1847 Sh
Young, Elizabeth V. to David E. Haymes 12-23-1864 Hn
Young, Elizabeth to A. J. Dunn 10-7-1853 (10-9-1853) Hr
Young, Elizabeth to Eli Cox 4-19-1847 (4-20-1840 Hr
Young, Elizabeth to George Jones 4-11-1840 Ma
Young, Elizabeth to Isom Shoate 9-29-1856 G
Young, Elizabeth to M. Midyitt 11-30-1854 We
Young, Elizabeth to Mumphred H. Cole 4-24-1840 (5-5-1840) F
Young, Elizabeth to William S. Futrell 8-29-1849 Hn
Young, Ella to John Graham 7-4-1874 (no return) Hy
Young, Ellen D. to William F. Talley 2-28-1857 (3-18-1857) L
Young, Ellen to Alfred Currin 10-31-1866 F B
Young, Ellen to Anderson Edward 2-18-1868 T
Young, Ellen to Soleman Green 1-27-1873 (1-28-1873) L
Young, Emily to J. C. Cooper 4-1-1856 G
Young, Emma to Chas. G. Mason 1-22-1866 (1-24-1866) F
Young, Emma to Henry Davis 1-4-1873 Hy
Young, Ferdy A. to Paul Mullins 9-12-1859 (9-14-1859) G
Young, Frances A. to L. D. Suttle 12-29-1856 (12-30-1856) L
Young, Fredonia to James W. Smith 10-27-1835 Sh
Young, Genetha Ann to Wm. M. Cates 8-19-1846 We
Young, Harriet to Benj. F. Young 9-13-1849 (9-12?-1849) G
Young, Harriet to Joseph Jorden 10-29-1867 (10-30-1867) T
Young, Harriett to Allen Mitchel 2-1-1878 Hy
Young, Helen to George Williams 6-23-1866 Hy
Young, Jane to Charles E. Fetherston 12-4-1852 G
Young, Jane to Dolphin Wilson 10-30-1875 L
Young, Jane to Geo. Chambers 11-30-1872 (12-1-1872) T
Young, Jane to Hardy Dean 2-11-1843 (2-14-1843) Ma
Young, Jane to James G. Humphreys 5-6-1861 Hn
Young, Jane to John Exum 4-15-1840 (4-16-1840) F
Young, Jane to Lewis Ehrlick 11-14-1859 Sh
Young, Jane to Robert B. Neil 6-29-1861 Sh
Young, Jemimah Ann to Jno. G. Whitson 7-9-1846 (no return) F
Young, Julia A. F. to Archibald McMillan 10-23-1856 (10-26-1856) Ma
Young, Julia C. to John W. Jackson 1-12-1867 (1-13-1867) T
Young, Julia M. to Oliver R. Miller 12-31-1856 Sh
Young, Julia to Henry Morris 12-23-1838 Hn
Young, Julia to William M. Crawford 3-13-1866 Hn

Young, L. D. to J. T. Crawford 12-20-1869 (12-22-1869) Cr
Young, L. Ida to James A. Anthony 12-18-1878 L
Young, L. M. to J. R. Harding 9-12-1865 Hn
Young, Laura to M. M. Warren 5-19-1883 (5-24-1883) L
Young, Lizzie (Mrs.) to S. B. Hailey 12-2-1869 G
Young, Louensia to Allen Eison 1-16-1871 (1-17-1871) L
Young, Louisa to James Hancock 10-18-1855 Hn
Young, Lucinda to John H. Patterson 1-20-1860 Cr
Young, Lucinda to Matt W. Flowers 4-16-1842 (4-17-1842) G
Young, Lucy A. to Robert E. Jeter 12-12-1856 We
Young, Lucy H. to Edwin H. Cobbs 12-15-1845 (no return) F
Young, Lucy to Marcus Bledsoe 3-20-1850 (3-21-1850) Ma
Young, M. A. to S. J. Chaney 12-12-1850 Hn
Young, M. J. to John H. Goad 12-17-1874 T
Young, Maca to Jordan Greer 8-24-1870 Hy
Young, Malinda to Thomas Landrum 3-1-1850 (3-3-1850) O
Young, Margaret J. to Huston L. Vowell 10-9-1862 We
Young, Margaret S. to Wm. W. Ware 10-3-1854 (10-4-1854) Sh
Young, Margaret to Henry Hicks 7-29-1844 Sh
Young, Margaret to John J. Brasfield 8-17-1850 (8-22-1850) Ma
Young, Margaret to Thomas Green 10-18-1869 (no return) Dy
Young, Marina to John Collins 5-31-1879 (6-8-1879) L
Young, Martha A. A. to John G. Gentry 3-7-1861 Dy
Young, Martha Ann to Billy Barlow Scott 6-8-1870 (6-9-1870) L
Young, Martha Ann to Luby? Demar 12-20-1873 T
Young, Martha C. to Wm. Reed 6-24-1858 We
Young, Martha E. to John Mannien 8-30-1871 (no return) Hy
Young, Martha J. to Chas. W. Carter 1-27-1862 (1-28-1862) Ma
Young, Martha J. to James D. Frensley 10-8-1851 Hn
Young, Martha L. to Francis A. Bond 12-3-1850 Ma
Young, Martha T. to Jepther Cooper 10-28-1852 Cr
Young, Martha to James Gallagher 8-6-1862 Sh
Young, Martha to James Hudgens 12-8-1840 Hn
Young, Martha to Lafayett Ryan 1-27-1874 (1-27-1875?) L
Young, Mary A. to Edmund Snow 3-10-1844 Sh
Young, Mary A. to G. B. Carter 1-18-1864 (1-19-1864) Sh
Young, Mary A. to W. W. Miller 10-26-1844 Sh
Young, Mary Ann to Burtis Lunsford 5-27-1843 (6-8-1843) Ma
Young, Mary Ann to G. Y. Swindell 2-6-1866 Hn
Young, Mary Ann to James Alexander 6-5-1867 Be
Young, Mary E. to Lewis L. Cox 11-10-1869 (11-11-1869) Ma
Young, Mary E. to William King 11-9-1855 Sh
Young, Mary F. to Thomas Ward 11-8-1865 Hn
Young, Mary J. to Felix G. Grable 5-12-1848 Hn
Young, Mary J. to H. P. Baldridge 11-13-1856 We
Young, Mary Jane to Winston Ellington 6-6-1859 (6-8-1859) Ma
Young, Mary R. to A. M. Mainard 6-9-1868 O
Young, Mary to Calvin Haskins 12-22-1866 (12-24-1866) F B
Young, Mary to Edward Cooper 12-27-1873 Cr
Young, Mary to J. T. Smart 5-19-1861 We
Young, Mary to William Beasley 7-19-1870
Young, Mathena to J. B. McClelland 7-14-1846 Hn
Young, Matilda to B. F. Burrows 3-2-1866 (no return) F
Young, Matilda to Fred L. Warner 8-6-1859 (8-7-1859) Sh
Young, Mattie Ella to John Mason 10-23-1880 (10-24-1880) L
Young, Millie A. to Benjamin R. Parks 4-17-1880 (4-26-1880) L
Young, Moriah to Henry Briley 4-20-1872 Hy
Young, Nancy E. to Thomas A. Rowe 2-23-1853 Hn
Young, Nancy M. to S. T. Brooks 1-9-1862 Mn
Young, Nancy P. to W. F. Dorris 12-4-1851 Hr
Young, Nancy to Ellis Low 2-7-1831 Ma
Young, Nancy to W. I. Collins 2-3-1867 G
Young, Nonnanda A. to David G. Walker 11-4-1849 Sh
Young, Nora A. to David C. Clark 11-22-1877 (11-25-1877) Dy
Young, Oney to A. J. Hollinger 4-22-1863 Sh
Young, P. A. F. to J. B. Murphy 12-31-1859 (1-4-1860) F
Young, Parmelia Frances to James L. Vaughan 9-6-1854 (9-7-1854) Sh
Young, Peggy to Davy Pillow 7-7-1877 (7-8-1877) L
Young, Portia Ann E. to Jacob W. Johns 8-19-1868 G
Young, R. E. to John G. Key 11-10-1868 (11-12-1868) Ma
Young, Rebecca E. to John M. Ross 1-30-1863 Mn
Young, Rebecca to Patrick Nooning 12-20-1865 Mn
Young, Renzie to Peyton Barnett 12-26-1843 O
Young, Rhoda to John C. Stockton 8-3-1826 Hr
Young, Rosa to Lit Henning 1-15-1879 (no return) L
Young, S. to Thomas A. Crawford 10-18-1852 Hn
Young, Sallie Bell to John Henning 12-23-1885 (12-24-1885) L
Young, Sallie to Sam Dixen 2-17-1872 Hy
Young, Sally to John Pickler 7-4-1867 Be
Young, Sally to William Odom 10-16-1862 Be
Young, Sarah A. C. to James Scoggins 6-30-1855 (7-4-1855) Hr
Young, Sarah A. to Noah Rushing 2-27-1853 Hn
Young, Sarah Ann to J. R. Walker 10-22-1850 F
Young, Sarah Ann to Jones K. Orr 5-15-1835 (5-21-1835) Hr
Young, Sarah J. W. to Wade H. Davis 12-17-1866 (12-27-1866) L
Young, Sarah Jane to Richard Joiner 10-30-1848 (11-21-1848) O
Young, Sarah S. to Washington G. Vandal 11-25-1846 Sh
Young, Sarah to Jackson Turner 9-27-1854 Be
Young, Sarah to Peter Gilbert 11-30-1878 Hy
Young, Sarah to Tom Brown 8-31-1867 (9-7-1867) F B
Young, Sarah to William Jones 12-29-1825 G
Young, Sophia A. to J. A. Jones 11-5-1867 (no return) Hn
Young, Susan C. to W. A. Smith 8-10-1862 Mn
Young, Susan E. to John S. Haltom 9-24-1853 (10-6-1853) Ma
Young, Susan J. to P. C. Witt 3-18-1872 Hy
Young, Susan to William Henry Evens 2-11-1851 (2-13-1851) Hr
Young, Urilsa to Thomas Childers 3-6-1866 Hn
Young, Virginia Ann to Albert Parker 11-12-1870 (11-22-1870) L
Young, Winnie to John Lewis Jones 11-20-1883 (11-21-1883) L
Youngblood, Elizabeth to Benjamin Brown 1-20-1831 (1-22-1831) Ma
Youngblood, Jula Ann to Stanhope? McCommons 12-29-1846 (12-31-1846) Hr
Youngblood, Mary E. to John E. Haynes 1-11-1845 (1-12-1845) L
Younger, Caroline to Ralph Morgan 12-16-1868 (12-17-1868) Cr
Younger, Centhia Jane to George Gresham 2-18-1863 Hn
Younger, Dollie to R. C. Gelby 8-13-1866 (no return) Cr
Younger, Elizabeth to Robert Sayles 6-20-1849 Cr
Younger, Kate to E. J. Coleman 11-14-1865 (11-15-1865) Cr
Younger, L. A. to L. S. Howard 7-8-1867 (7-10-1867) Cr
Younger, L. E. to J. C. Roach 5-20-1872 (5-21-1872) Cr
Younger, Martha E. to Miles W. Needham 1-22-1863 Mn
Younger, Mary Ann to Wm. M. Younger 2-20-1839 Cr
Younger, Mary J. to Benjamin Watts 10-16-1860 (10-6?-1860) Cr
Younger, Mattie to J. A. Oneil 2-28-1871 Cr
Younger, Nancy M. E. to John N. Viar 10-24-1860 (10-25-1860) Cr
Younger, Rebecca to Raysdon Laymond 9-20-1848 Cr
Younger, Susan C. to D. S. Crittenden 1-22-1861 We
Younger, Vina to Spencer Jones 1-31-1871 (2-2-1871) Cr
Yount, Mary to Alexander Murphey 1-12-1874 (1-13-1874) T
Yount, Sarah A. E. to Peter L. Feezor 7-27-1854 T
Youth, Elizabeth to Robert Phillips 12-15-1864 O
Yow, Amanda to C. B. R. White 10-20-1874 (10-21-1874) Dy
Yow, Eliza Ann to William Nance 11-18-1846 Hn
Yow, Leonie to A. C. Sorrell 9-12-1870 (9-13-1870) Dy
Yow, Susan to N. E. Story 9-28-1864 Hn
Yow, Tennessee to Rufus C. Hill 12-3-1865 Hn
Yowe, M. R. to J. H. Sorrell 12-22-1870 Dy
Yowell, Mary M. to Bennett S. Aden 7-12-1865 Hn
Yunt, Eliza to Sterling Pinner 12-31-1847 (1-7-1848) T

Zachry, Martha to John L. Williams 2-9-1858 G
Zamples, Ruth to Sterling Burrow 2-6-1834 Hr
Zane, Elizabeth to J. Hugh Whitehead 7-12-1868 G
Zaracor, Martha to Elijah Hood 5-12-1866 O
Zarecor, Nannie S. to T. R. Roper 10-20-1869 G
Zarecor?, Jennie to M. H. Dickey 9-29-1875 (no return) Dy
Zaricor, Allice A. to Thomas H. Holloman 11-7-1866 O
Zarman, Frances to John Cathy 12-27-1848 Sh
Zeller, M. A. to J. B. Laine 10-9-1859 Sh
Zellner, Helen M. to Pliney B. Londrith 6-21-1859 (6-23-1859) F
Zellner, L. J. to J. F. Pickins 11-15-1852 (no return) F
Zerico, Fanny J. to John M. Davis 1-26-1859 G
Zerrico, Amanda M. to William Loving 12-27-1842 (12-28-1842) G
Zimmerman, Caroline to F. Schulthus 7-2-1857 Sh
Zimmerman, Feede to J. Shilling 10-5-1864 Sh
Zimmermann, Caroline to John Schmeller 11-19-1858 T
Zimmermann, Elizabeth to F. Sommehalder 3-4-1858 (3-8-1858) Sh
Zouk, Malam to Henry Vesperman 7-20-1863 Sh

BIBLIOGRAPHY

BOOKS

Carroll County Historical Society, Carroll County, Tennessee Marriages 1838-1859, McKenzie, TN (no date)

Davis, Bettie B., Lauderdale County, Tennessee Marriages 1838-1867, Memphis, TN, 1983

____, Shelby County, Tennessee Marriage Bonds & Licenses 1850-1865, Memphis, TN, 1983

Fischer, Marjorie Hood, Haywood County, Tennessee Marriage Records, 1859-1878, Vista, CA, 1987

Gary, Grace Dietzel and Carolyn West Stricklin, Obion County, Tennessee Marriage Records 1824-1877, Union City, TN, 1978

Gossum, Mary Louise and Emily B. Walker, Gibson County, Tennessee Marriage Records Volume A, June, 1860 - November, 1870, South Fulton, TN, 1984

Inman, W. O., Henry County, Tennessee Marriages 1838-1852, Paris, TN, 1974

____, Henry County, Tennessee Marriages 1853-1867, Paris, TN, 1974

Lydia Russell Bean Chapter, NSDAR, Benton County, Tennessee Marriages 1832-1857, Knoxville, TN 1962

Sistler, Byron and Barbara, Carroll County, TN Marriages 1860-1873, Nashville, TN, 1988

____, Dyer County, TN Marriages 1860-1879, Nashville, TN, 1989

____, Fayette County, TN Marriages 1838-1871, Nashville, TN, 1989

____, Hardeman County, TN Marriages 1823-1861, Nashville, TN, 1986

____, Madison County, TN Marriages 1838-1871, Nashville, TN, 1983

____, Tipton County, TN Marriages 1840-1874, Nashville, TN, 1987

Smith, Jonathan K. T., Genealogical Gleanings in Benton County, Tennessee, Memphis, TN, 1974

Tennessee Genealogical Society, Shelby County, Tennessee Marriage Records 1819-1850, Memphis, TN, 1957

Weakley County Genealogical Society, Weakley County, Tennessee Marriage Records 1843-1863, Martin, TN, 1980

Whitley, Edythe Rucker, Marriages of Gibson County, Tennessee 1824-1860, Baltimore, MD, 1982

PERIODICALS

Brown, Albert, "McNairy County, Tennessee Marriages 1861-1865", Ansearchin' News, Vol. 34, p. 147 and Vol. 35, p. 33, published Memphis, TN

Mitchell, Mary Ann and Charlotte Thornton, "Madison County, Tennessee, Loose Marriage Bonds 1823-1832", Family Findings, Vol. 1, pp. 9, 39, published Jackson, TN.

www.ingramcontent.com/pod-product-compliance
Lightning Source LLC
Chambersburg PA
CBHW081149290426
44108CB00018B/2490